HISTORY
OF THE WORLD
MAP BY MAP

FOREWORD BY
PETER SNOW

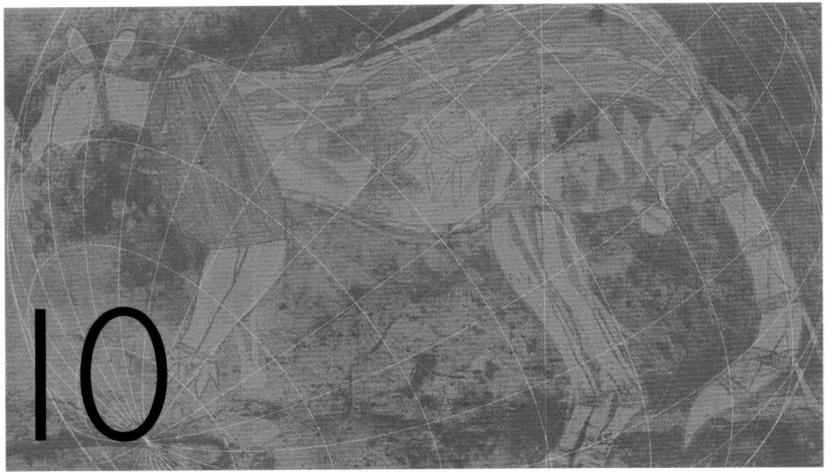

CONTENTS

DK | Penguin Random House

DK LONDON

Lead Senior Editor Rob Houston
Senior Editors Peter Frances, Janet Mohun
Editors Suhel Ahmed, Polly Boyd, Claire Gell, Martyn Page, Tia Sarkar, Kaiya Shang, Kate Taylor
US Editors Kayla Dugger, Jennette ElNaggar
Project Management Briony Corbett
Managing Editor Angeles Gavira Guerrero
Associate Publisher Liz Wheeler
Publishing Director Jonathan Metcalf

Cartographers Simon Mumford, Ed Merritt, Martin Darlison, Helen Stirling

Senior Art Editors Duncan Turner, Ina Stradins
Project Art Editors Steve Woosnam-Savage, Francis Wong
Designer Ala Uddin
Jacket Design Development Manager Sophia MTT
Jacket Designer Surabhi Wadhwa
Producer (Pre-production) Jacqueline Street-Elkayam
Producer Jude Crozier
Managing Art Editor Michael Duffy
Art Director Karen Self
Design Director Phil Ormerod

DK INDIA

Senior Editor Dharini Ganesh
Editor Priyanjali Narain
Assistant Editors Aashirwad Jain, Shambhavi Thatte
Picture Researcher Deepak Negi
Picture Research Manager Taiyaba Khatoon
Jackets Editorial Coordinator Priyanka Sharma
Managing Editor Rohan Sinha
Managing Jackets Editor Saloni Singh
Pre-production Manager Balwant Singh
Senior Cartographer Subhashree Bharati
Cartographer Reetu Pandey
Cartography Manager Suresh Kumar

Senior Art Editor Vaibhav Rastogi
Project Art Editor Sanjay Chauhan, Pooja Pipil
Art Editors Anjali Sachar, Sonali Sharma, Sonakshi Singh
Assistant Art Editor Mridushmita Bose
Managing Art Editor Sudakshina Basu
Jacket Designer Suhita Dharamjit
Senior DTP Designers Harish Aggarwal, Vishal Bhatia
DTP Designers Ashok Kumar, Nityanand Kumar
Production Manager Pankaj Sharma

COBALT ID

Designer Darren Bland
Art Director Paul Reid
Editorial Director Marek Walisiewicz

HISTORY
OF THE WORLD
MAP BY MAP

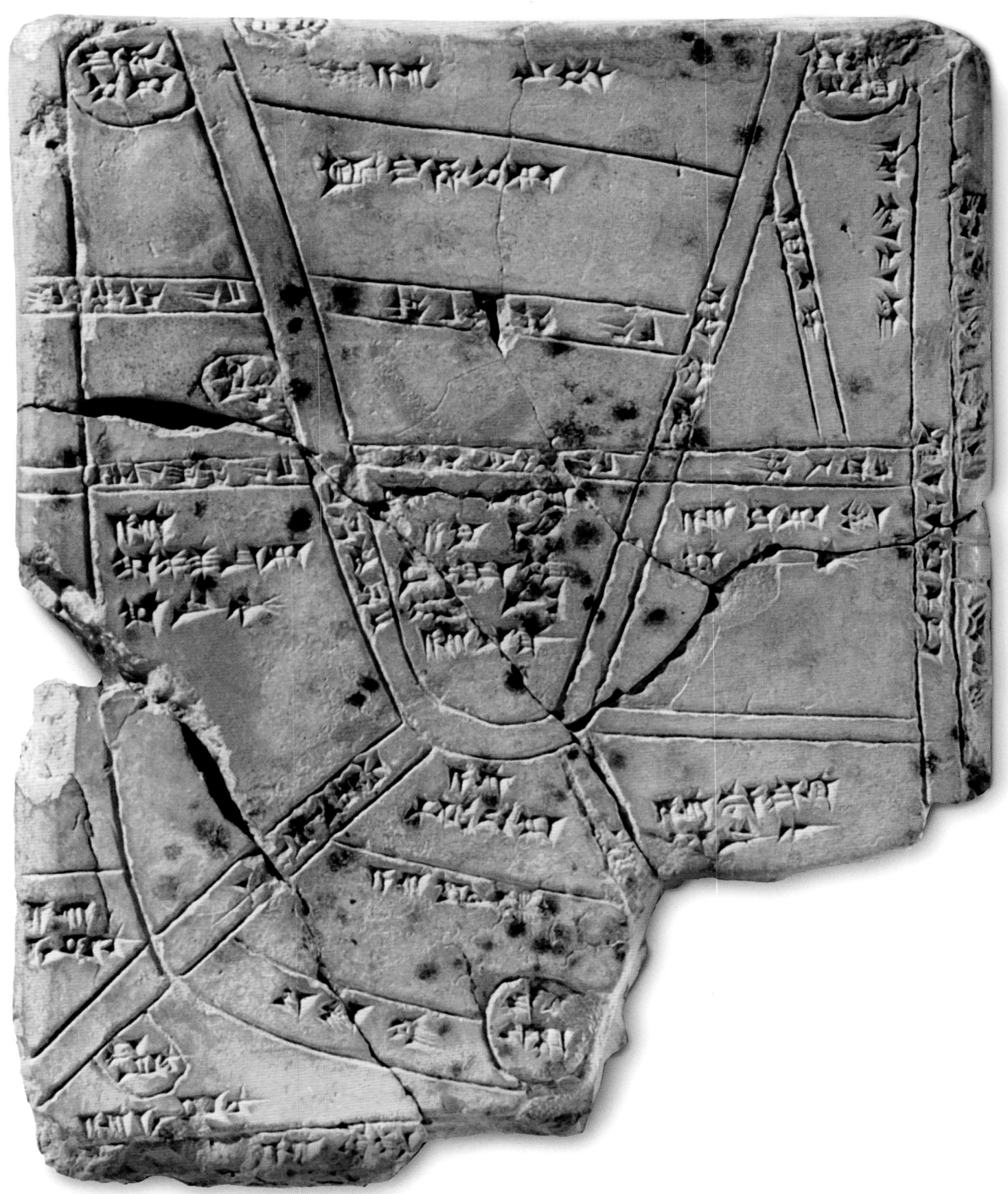

MIDDLE AGES   500–1450 CE

THE EARLY MODERN WORLD   1450–1700

First American Edition, 2018
Published in the United States by DK Publishing
1745 Broadway, 20th Floor, New York, NY 10019

Copyright © 2018 Dorling Kindersley Limited
DK, a Division of Penguin Random House LLC
22 23 24 25 14 13 12 11
001–278615–Oct/2018

A catalog record for this book is available from the Library of Congress.
ISBN 978-1-4654-7585-5

DK books are available at special discounts when purchased
in bulk for sales promotions, premiums, fund-raising, or
educational use. For details, contact: DK Publishing Special Markets,
1745 Broadway, 20th Floor, New York, NY 10019
SpecialSales@dk.com

Printed and bound in United Arab Emirates

For the curious
www.dk.com

186

REVOLUTION AND INDUSTRY 1700–1850

228

PROGRESS AND EMPIRE 1850–1914

CONTRIBUTORS

PREHISTORY
David Summers, Derek Harvey

THE ANCIENT WORLD
Peter Chrisp, Jeremy Harwood, Phil Wilkinson

THE MIDDLE AGES, THE EARLY MODERN WORLD
Philip Parker

REVOLUTION AND INDUSTRY
Joel Levy

PROGRESS AND EMPIRE
Kay Celtel

THE MODERN WORLD
Simon Adams, R. G. Grant, Sally Regan

CONSULTANTS

PREHISTORY
Dr. Rebecca Wragg-Sykes Palaeolithic archaeologist and author, chercheur bénévole PACEA laboratory, Université de Bordeaux

THE ANCIENT WORLD
Prof. Neville Morley Professor of Classics and Ancient History, University of Exeter

Prof. Karen Radner Alexander von Humboldt Professor of the Ancient History of the Near and Middle East, University of Munich

THE MIDDLE AGES
Dr. Roger Collins Honorary Fellow in the School of History, Classics and Archaeology, University of Edinburgh

THE EARLY MODERN WORLD, REVOLUTION AND INDUSTRY
Dr. Glyn Redford FRHistS, Honorary Fellow, *The Historical Association*

PROGRESS AND EMPIRE, THE MODERN WORLD
Prof. Richard Overy FBA, FRHistS, Professor of History, University of Exeter

CHINA, KOREA, AND JAPAN
Jennifer Bond Researcher, SOAS, University of London

INDIA
Prof. David Arnold Professor of Asian and Global History, Warwick University

PRECOLUMBIAN AMERICAS
Dr. Elizabeth Baquedano Honorary Senior Lecturer, Institute of Archaeology, University College London

270

THE MODERN WORLD   1914–PRESENT

Smithsonian

Established in 1846, the Smithsonian is the world's largest museum and research complex, dedicated to public education, national service, and scholarship in the arts, sciences, and history. It includes 19 museums and galleries and the National Zoological Park. The total number of artifacts, works of art, and specimens in the Smithsonian's collection is estimated at 156 million.

FOREWORD

This book tells the story of life on Earth in more meticulous detail and with more arresting pictures than I've ever seen before. I believe that in this digital age, maps are more important than ever. People are losing sight of the need for them in a world where our knowledge is reduced to the distance between two zip codes. For me, a journey—certainly the contemplation of a journey—is a voyage across a map. But this beautiful book offers the added dimension of a state-of-the-art journey through time. These maps display the story of the world in delightfully accessible form. They demonstrate in a spectacular way how there is no substitute for the printed page, for the entrancing spread of color across paper that we can touch and

feel. The maps are large; the colors are bold. Text boxes spring out from places whose history matters. Clear and easily readable graphics reveal the ups and downs of empires, cultures, wars and other events both human and natural that have shaped our world from the beginning.

To me, history without maps would be unintelligible. A country's history is shaped by its geography—by its mountains and valleys, its rivers, its climate, its access to the sea, and its raw materials and harvests just as much as it is shaped by its population, its industry, its relations with its neighbors and its takeover by invaders from abroad. This book is more than a historical atlas: it describes the

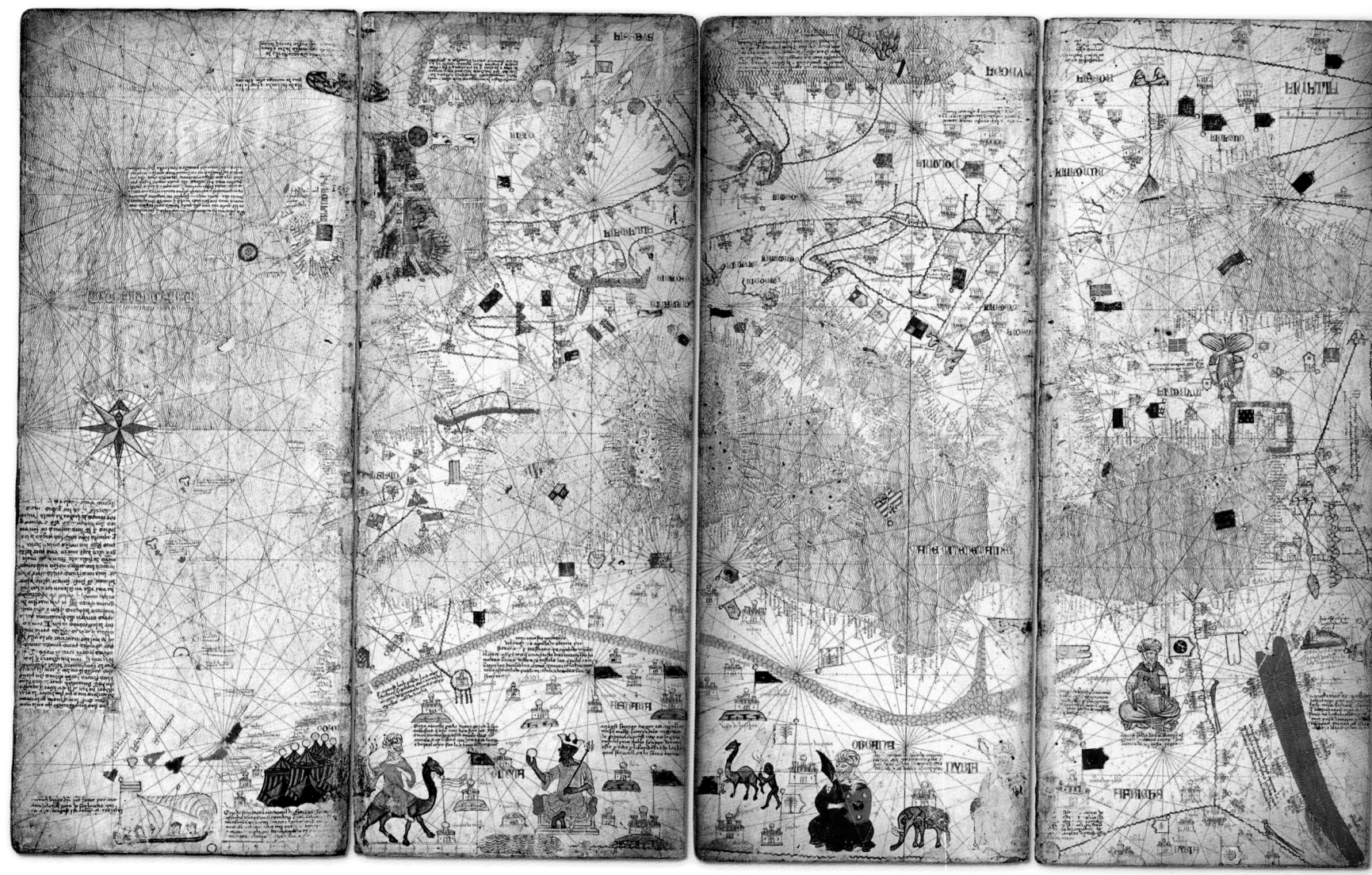

geography of history but adds revealing pictures as well. For me, the history of World War I is admirably summed up by the map that describes the buildup to it on pages 268–269 and the following maps and accounts of the fighting, including the telling picture of the trenches.

I've been using maps to tell stories all my life as a television journalist and historian. The stories of the European Union and the collapse of communism were my constant companions when recounting the events of the last half century. That part of recent history only makes sense if it is also described by maps like those on pages 320–321 and 336–337. I have spent many hours as a journalist

making maps with graphics artists at the BBC and ITN to illustrate the story of wars in the Middle East and Vietnam. Far better ones are now displayed for us in this book on pages 328–29 and 332–33. No historian can do justice to the story of the rise and fall of the great empires like that of the French Emperor Napoleon without maps like those on pages 208–211.

For its depth of learning and its variety of ways of giving us a picture of the history of our planet, this magnificent account—map by map—is second to none.

PETER SNOW British broadcaster and historian

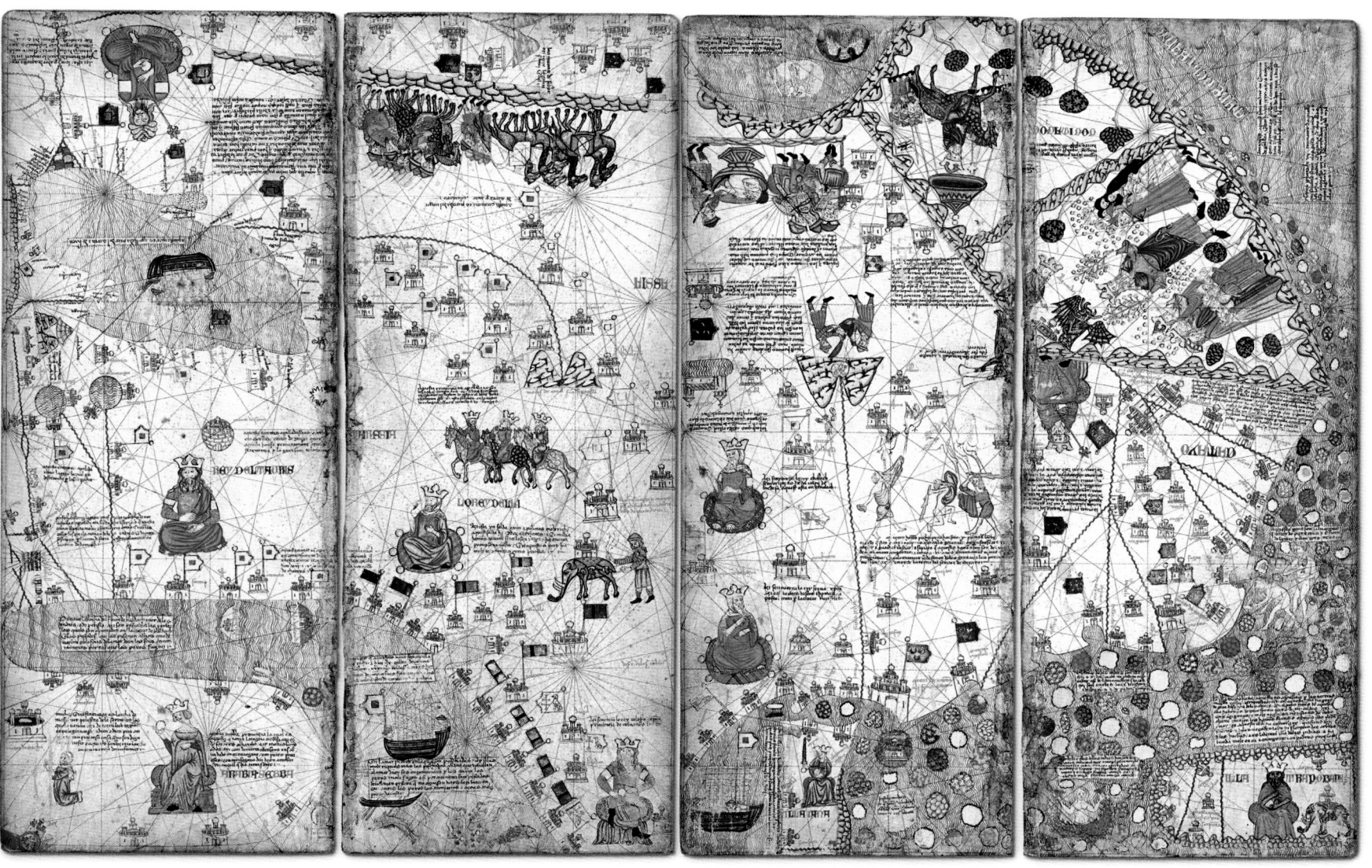

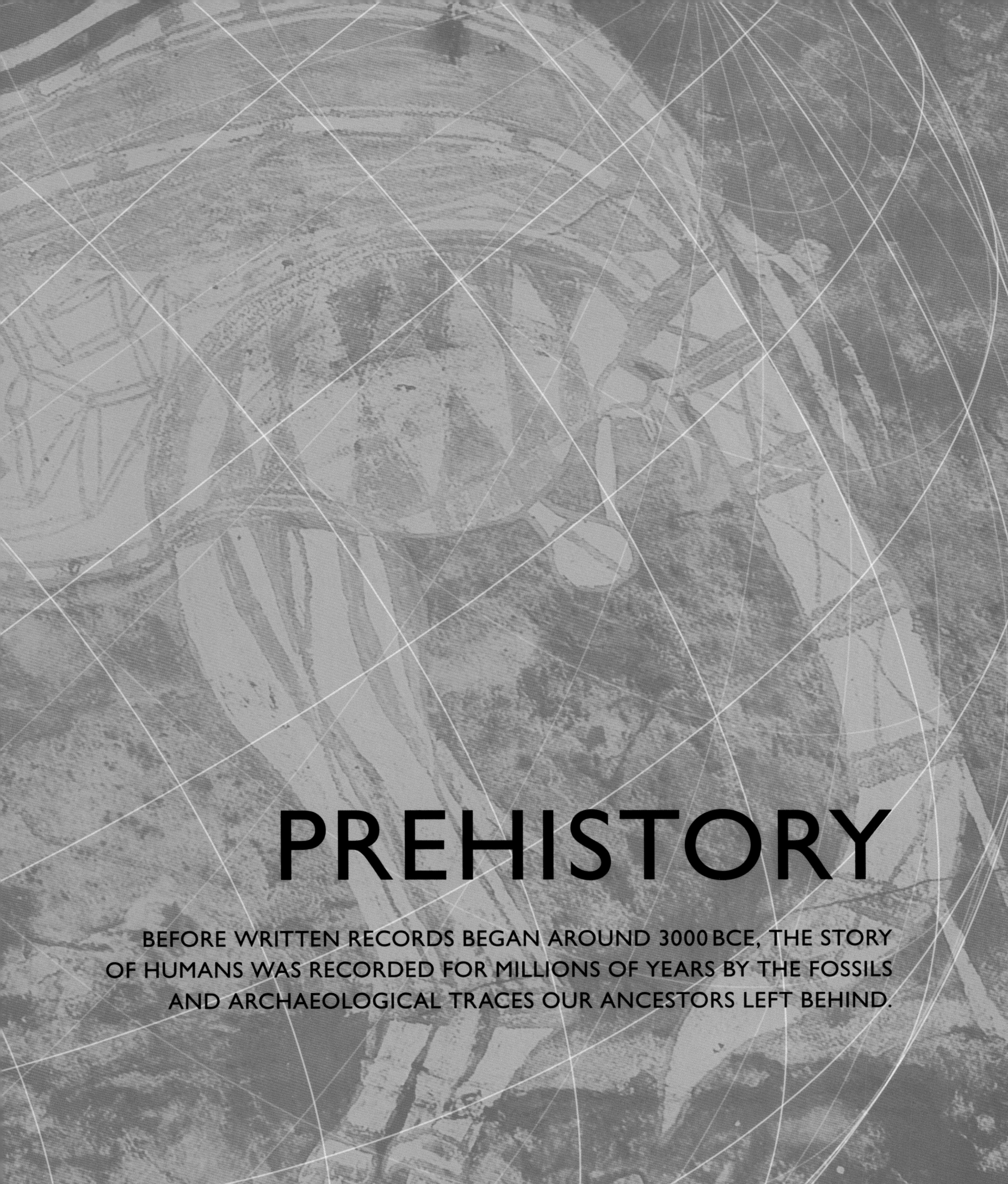

PREHISTORY

BEFORE WRITTEN RECORDS BEGAN AROUND 3000 BCE, THE STORY
OF HUMANS WAS RECORDED FOR MILLIONS OF YEARS BY THE FOSSILS
AND ARCHAEOLOGICAL TRACES OUR ANCESTORS LEFT BEHIND.

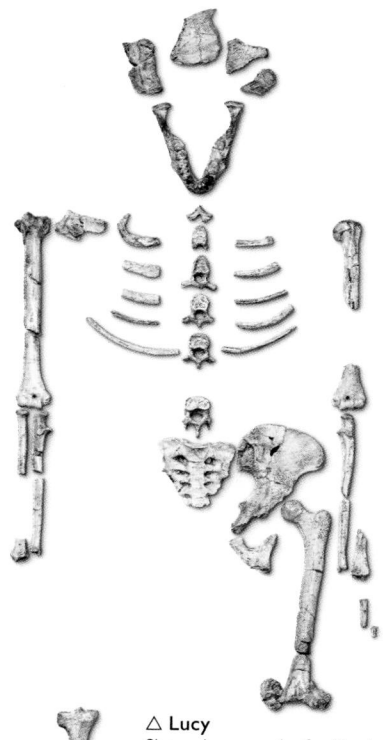

△ Lucy
Shown here are the fossilized remains of the apelike Lucy—a member of the genus *Australopithecus* from east Africa from over 3 MYA. The fossil is sufficiently complete to suggest that Lucy walked upright on two legs.

FROM APES TO FARMERS

The history of humankind is rooted in a part of the animal kingdom that includes monkeys, apes, and other primates. It took millions of years of evolution—over countless generations—for apelike ancestors to become modern *Homo sapiens*.

Scientific evidence links all humans to apes. Specifically, chimpanzees are our closest nonhuman relatives, and DNA—the ultimate bloodline indicator—suggests that we separated from a common ancestor some 6.5 million years ago (MYA). Indeed, humans are apes—albeit in an upright, naked form.

Monkeys, apes, and humans are primates that have a large brain, grasping digits, forward-facing eyes, and nails instead of claws. Fossilized remains of animals that lived in the distant past provide tantalizing evidence of just how apes became modern humans. Skeletons turn into fossils when they become mineralized into rock—a process that usually takes at least 10,000 years. Fossilized remains are usually fragmentary, but an expertise in anatomy helps scientists use the fossil record to reconstruct extinct species. Fossils can also be dated so scientists can build up a chronology of evolutionary change. For example, African fossils of a primate called *Proconsul*, dated to 21–14 MYA, resembled a monkey. But it lacked a tail—a feature more typical of apes—suggesting that *Proconsul* could have been the earliest known member of the ape family.

Hominids and hominins
Modern great apes (gorillas, orangutans, and chimpanzees), humans, and their prehistoric relatives are united in a biological family called hominids. As well

> *"We can see the focus, the center of evolution, for modern humans in Africa."*
>
> CHRIS STRINGER, BRITISH ANTHROPOLOGIST

as lacking a tail, they have bigger brains than their monkey ancestors. This meant that many prehistoric hominids doubtless used tools to forage for food—just as chimpanzees do today. Great apes also became bigger than monkeys, and many spent more time on the ground. One group evolved to walk on two legs, which freed grasping hands for other tasks.

This group—called hominins—includes humans and their immediate ancestors and dates back at least 6.2–6.0 million years to the species *Orrorin tugenensis*—a very early bipedal hominin found in Kenya.

The first humans
Not all hominins were direct ancestors of living people, but at least one branch of the genus *Australopithecus* might have been. Belonging to the genus *Homo*, the first humans were fully bipedal, with arched feet that no longer had opposable grasping toes and an S-shaped spine centered above a wide pelvis. Such adaptations helped them run quickly on open ground. The earliest species—*Homo habilis*, from 2.4 MYA—may have

△ Flint and stone
For nearly 2 million years, human technology was represented by stone flake tools and hand axes. These were made by hitting flint or other workable rock with stone to produce sharp cutting edges.

THE RISE OF MODERN HUMANS
Even before the emergence of modern humans (*Homo sapiens*) almost 300,000 YA, hominins had developed the traits that would make them a dominating force on the planet. From just under 1 MYA, hominins were controlling fire—for cooking, and later to help with manufacturing processes. But with *Homo sapiens* came a more complex culture. Archaeological evidence indicates that these modern humans dispersed widely from their center of origin in Africa before 200,000 YA.

185,000 YA *Homo sapiens* migrates from Africa and into Asia 1.5 million years after the first hominins first left the African continent

135,000–100,000 YA Seashells perforated and used as ornamental beads in Middle East and North Africa are first jewelry—and earliest evidence of drilling

DISPERSAL

CULTURE

TECHNOLOGY

180,000 YA | 160,000 YA | 140,000 YA | 120,000 YA

165,000 YA Earliest evidence of pigment use at Pinnacle Point, South Africa, for painting or as part of a tool handle

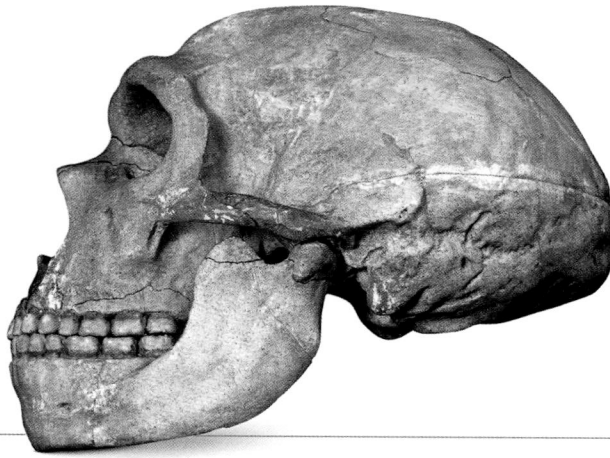

◁ **Close cousins**
Neanderthals—the closest extinct human species to modern humans, *Homo sapiens*—had larger skulls with more prominent eyebrows. *Homo sapiens* and Neanderthals were sufficiently similar to interbreed where they coexisted.

remained in Africa, but we know that later other *Homo* species dispersed widely across Eurasia.

The rise of *Homo sapiens*

Only one species of human—*Homo sapiens*—came to dominate the world after emerging from Africa about a quarter of a million years ago. Remarkably, brain capacity doubled between *Homo habilis* and *Homo sapiens*. Bigger brainpower meant that humans could skillfully manipulate the environment and resources around them—ultimately leading to the emergence of complex cultures and technologies.

For much of its time, *Homo sapiens* coexisted with other human species. In Ice-Age Eurasia, chunky-bodied Neanderthals (*Homo neanderthalensis*) successfully lived in a range of environmental conditions, developing their own advanced cultures. But the world's climate became especially unsuitable, and only *Homo sapiens* prevailed. They spread farther—reaching Australia by 65,000 YA and South America possibly by 18,500 YA. Evidently, *Homo sapiens* had the social structures to succeed in ways that their competitors could not. The first modern humans were efficient hunter-gatherers, inventing new technologies that helped them

acquire more food and travel farther. This meant that they thrived in many different places, from the frozen Arctic to the hot tropics. Then, within the last 20,000 years, all around the world, modern humans began to abandon their nomadic ways in favor of fixed settlements, turning their skills to farming the land, supporting bigger societies, and—ultimately—planting the seeds of civilization itself.

△ **Early artists**
These depictions of Ice Age animals on the walls of the Lascaux Caves in southern France are about 17,000 years old. Similar paintings nearby show that prehistoric humans had developed a degree of creative expression as early as 30,000 years ago.

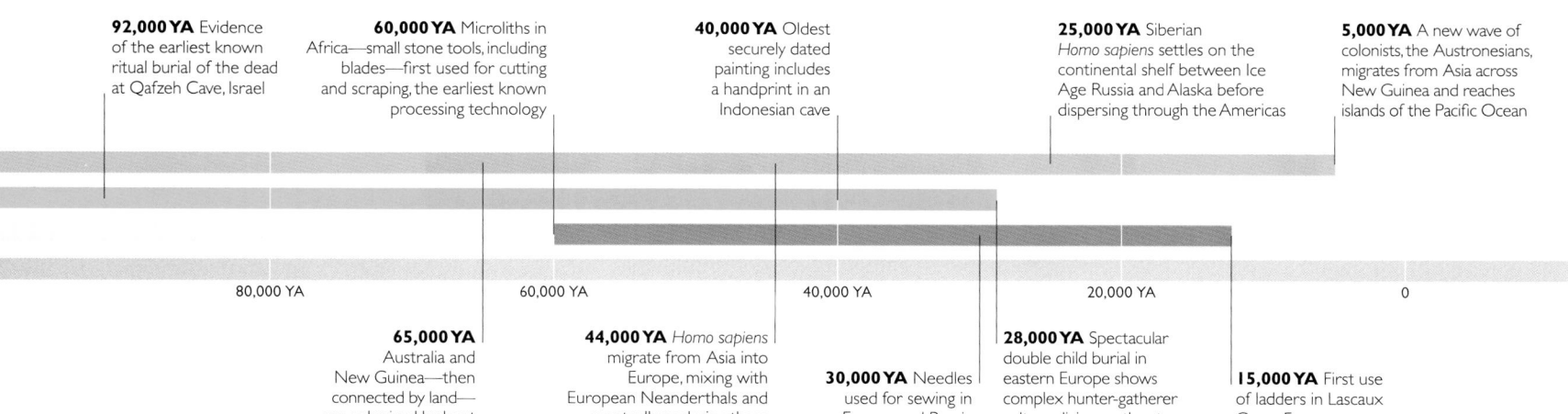

92,000 YA Evidence of the earliest known ritual burial of the dead at Qafzeh Cave, Israel

60,000 YA Microliths in Africa—small stone tools, including blades—first used for cutting and scraping, the earliest known processing technology

40,000 YA Oldest securely dated painting includes a handprint in an Indonesian cave

25,000 YA Siberian *Homo sapiens* settles on the continental shelf between Ice Age Russia and Alaska before dispersing through the Americas

5,000 YA A new wave of colonists, the Austronesians, migrates from Asia across New Guinea and reaches islands of the Pacific Ocean

80,000 YA   60,000 YA   40,000 YA   20,000 YA   0

65,000 YA Australia and New Guinea—then connected by land—are colonized by boat

44,000 YA *Homo sapiens* migrate from Asia into Europe, mixing with European Neanderthals and eventually replacing them

30,000 YA Needles used for sewing in Europe and Russia

28,000 YA Spectacular double child burial in eastern Europe shows complex hunter-gatherer cultures living on the steppes

15,000 YA First use of ladders in Lascaux Caves, France

THE FIRST HUMANS

The human story began in Africa 7 or 6 million years ago. Through the fossil record of this vast continent, we can draw a complex family tree of human relatives of which our species, *Homo sapiens*, is the last to survive.

We have fossil evidence for the existence of about 20 different species of African "hominin"—members of the human lineage that diverged from that of chimpanzees 7–10 million years ago. Each has been assigned to a biological group or "genus," but the relationships between the groups and species are still debated. Only certain hominins were the ancestors of modern humans; others, such as the *Paranthropus* species, may represent evolutionary dead ends.

Human evolution was not an inevitable, linear progression from apes. Some of our ancestors developed adaptations—in different combinations—that would ultimately mark out modern humans. Perhaps most notably, a larger brain enabled complex thought and behavior, including the development of stone-tool technologies, while walking on two legs became the main form of locomotion.

The earliest fossils assigned to our species—dated to around 300,000 years ago—were found in Morocco, but other early specimens have been found widely dispersed across Africa. This has led scientists to believe that the evolution of modern humans probably happened on a continental scale.

> *"I think Africa was the cradle, the crucible that created us as* Homo sapiens.*"*
>
> PALEOANTHROPOLOGIST DONALD JOHANSON, 2006

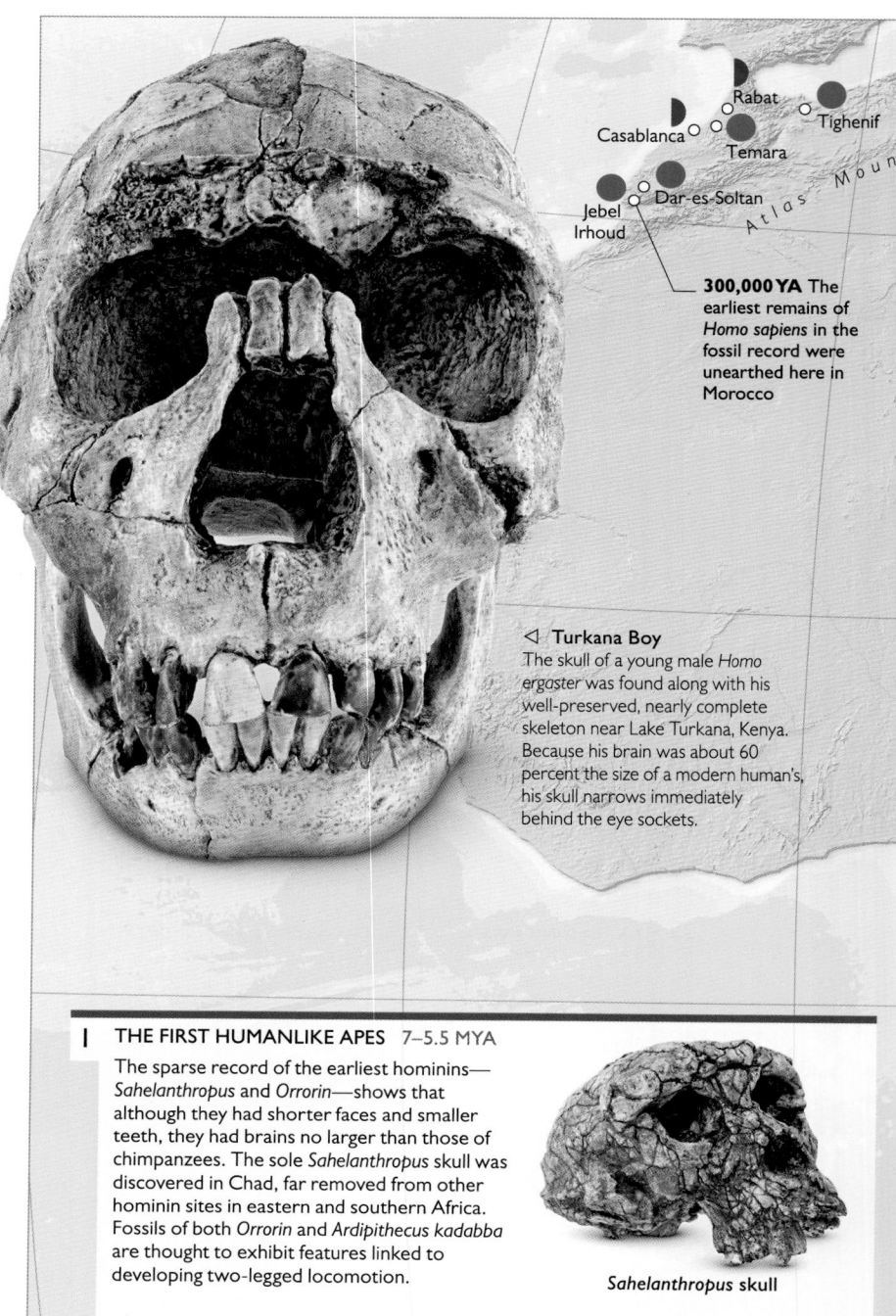

300,000 YA The earliest remains of *Homo sapiens* in the fossil record were unearthed here in Morocco

◁ **Turkana Boy**
The skull of a young male *Homo ergaster* was found along with his well-preserved, nearly complete skeleton near Lake Turkana, Kenya. Because his brain was about 60 percent the size of a modern human's, his skull narrows immediately behind the eye sockets.

I | THE FIRST HUMANLIKE APES 7–5.5 MYA

The sparse record of the earliest hominins— *Sahelanthropus* and *Orrorin*—shows that although they had shorter faces and smaller teeth, they had brains no larger than those of chimpanzees. The sole *Sahelanthropus* skull was discovered in Chad, far removed from other hominin sites in eastern and southern Africa. Fossils of both *Orrorin* and *Ardipithecus kadabba* are thought to exhibit features linked to developing two-legged locomotion.

Sahelanthropus skull

▲ *Sahelanthropus*   ▼ *Orrorin*   ■ *Ardipithecus*

EARLY HOMININ MIGRATION

Archaeological evidence from Asia and Europe suggests that by about 2 million years ago, hominins had begun to leave Africa for the first time—long before *Homo sapiens* began to disperse (see pp.16–17). Experts once assumed that the migration corresponded with the appearance of *Homo ergaster*, but older species might have been the pioneers—a 1.7-million-year-old fossil found in Dmanisi, Georgia, resembles the earlier *Homo habilis*. The earliest known hominin fossils from Southeast Asia are of *Homo erectus*—an Asian variant of *Homo ergaster*, found on the island of Java and dating to 1.8 million years ago. Stone tools from the Nihewan Basin, China, date to 1.6 million years ago. Two sites in Spain's Sierra de Atapuerca show that hominins had reached western Europe by 1.2 million years ago.

KEY

→ Likely route   ○ Sites of fossil finds

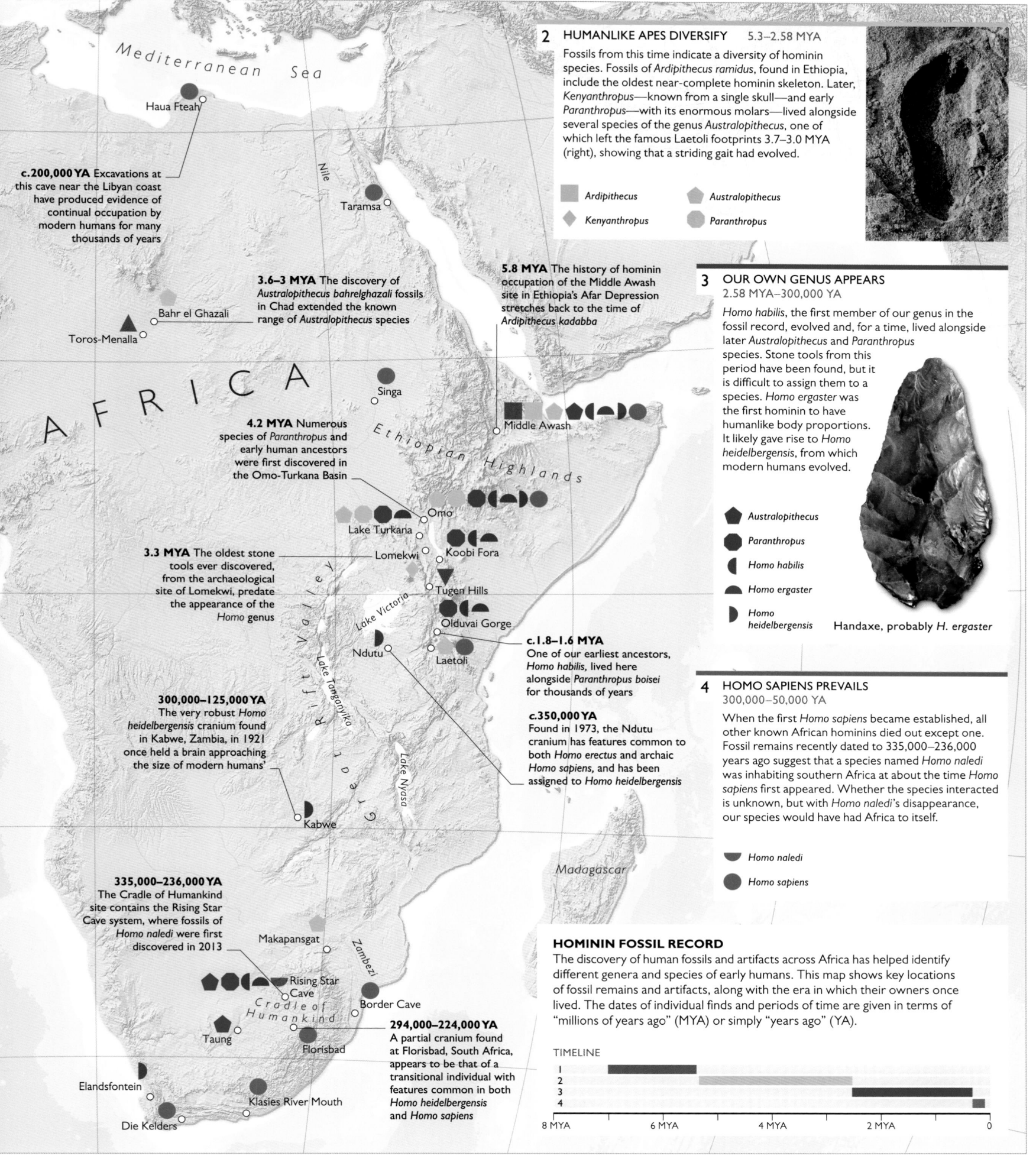

2 HUMANLIKE APES DIVERSIFY 5.3–2.58 MYA

Fossils from this time indicate a diversity of hominin species. Fossils of *Ardipithecus ramidus*, found in Ethiopia, include the oldest near-complete hominin skeleton. Later, *Kenyanthropus*—known from a single skull—and early *Paranthropus*—with its enormous molars—lived alongside several species of the genus *Australopithecus*, one of which left the famous Laetoli footprints 3.7–3.0 MYA (right), showing that a striding gait had evolved.

■ *Ardipithecus*   ⬠ *Australopithecus*

◆ *Kenyanthropus*   ⬡ *Paranthropus*

c.200,000 YA Excavations at this cave near the Libyan coast have produced evidence of continual occupation by modern humans for many thousands of years

3.6–3 MYA The discovery of *Australopithecus bahrelghazali* fossils in Chad extended the known range of *Australopithecus* species

5.8 MYA The history of hominin occupation of the Middle Awash site in Ethiopia's Afar Depression stretches back to the time of *Ardipithecus kadabba*

3 OUR OWN GENUS APPEARS
2.58 MYA–300,000 YA

Homo habilis, the first member of our genus in the fossil record, evolved and, for a time, lived alongside later *Australopithecus* and *Paranthropus* species. Stone tools from this period have been found, but it is difficult to assign them to a species. *Homo ergaster* was the first hominin to have humanlike body proportions. It likely gave rise to *Homo heidelbergensis*, from which modern humans evolved.

⬠ *Australopithecus*

⬡ *Paranthropus*

◖ *Homo habilis*

◗ *Homo ergaster*

◖ *Homo heidelbergensis*

Handaxe, probably *H. ergaster*

4.2 MYA Numerous species of *Paranthropus* and early human ancestors were first discovered in the Omo-Turkana Basin

3.3 MYA The oldest stone tools ever discovered, from the archaeological site of Lomekwi, predate the appearance of the *Homo* genus

c.1.8–1.6 MYA One of our earliest ancestors, *Homo habilis*, lived here alongside *Paranthropus boisei* for thousands of years

c.350,000 YA Found in 1973, the Ndutu cranium has features common to both *Homo erectus* and archaic *Homo sapiens*, and has been assigned to *Homo heidelbergensis*

300,000–125,000 YA The very robust *Homo heidelbergensis* cranium found in Kabwe, Zambia, in 1921 once held a brain approaching the size of modern humans'

4 HOMO SAPIENS PREVAILS
300,000–50,000 YA

When the first *Homo sapiens* became established, all other known African hominins died out except one. Fossil remains recently dated to 335,000–236,000 years ago suggest that a species named *Homo naledi* was inhabiting southern Africa at about the time *Homo sapiens* first appeared. Whether the species interacted is unknown, but with *Homo naledi*'s disappearance, our species would have had Africa to itself.

◗ *Homo naledi*

● *Homo sapiens*

335,000–236,000 YA The Cradle of Humankind site contains the Rising Star Cave system, where fossils of *Homo naledi* were first discovered in 2013

294,000–224,000 YA A partial cranium found at Florisbad, South Africa, appears to be that of a transitional individual with features common in both *Homo heidelbergensis* and *Homo sapiens*

HOMININ FOSSIL RECORD

The discovery of human fossils and artifacts across Africa has helped identify different genera and species of early humans. This map shows key locations of fossil remains and artifacts, along with the era in which their owners once lived. The dates of individual finds and periods of time are given in terms of "millions of years ago" (MYA) or simply "years ago" (YA).

TIMELINE

1
2
3
4

8 MYA   6 MYA   4 MYA   2 MYA   0

Map labels: Mediterranean Sea, Nile, Haua Fteah, Taramsa, Bahr el Ghazali, Toros-Menalla, AFRICA, Singa, Middle Awash, Ethiopian Highlands, Omo, Lake Turkana, Lomekwi, Koobi Fora, Tugen Hills, Lake Victoria, Olduvai Gorge, Great Rift Valley, Ndutu, Laetoli, Lake Tanganyika, Lake Nyasa, Kabwe, Zambezi, Madagascar, Makapansgat, Rising Star Cave, Border Cave, Cradle of Humankind, Taung, Florisbad, Elandsfontein, Klasies River Mouth, Die Kelders

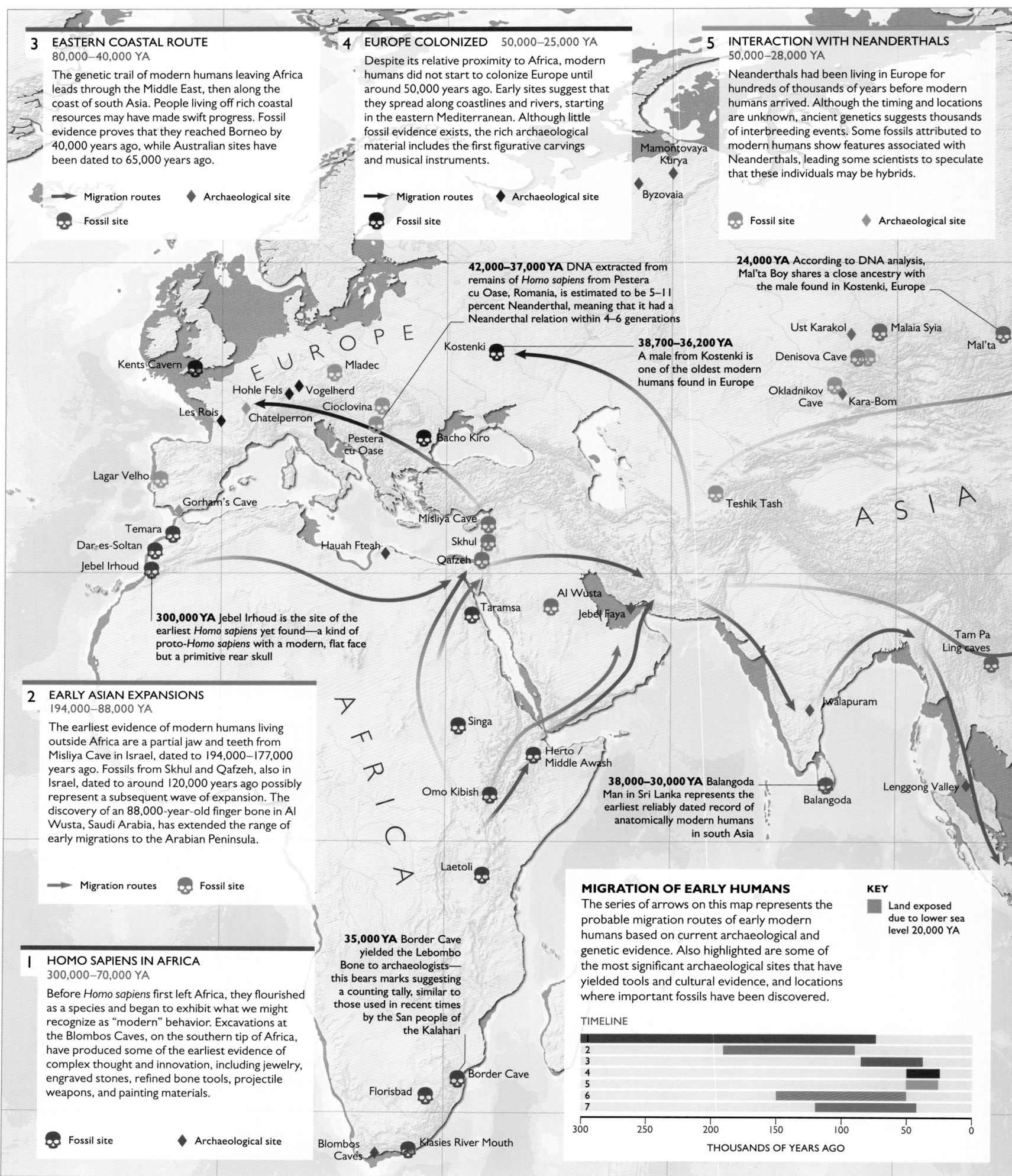

3 EASTERN COASTAL ROUTE
80,000–40,000 YA

The genetic trail of modern humans leaving Africa leads through the Middle East, then along the coast of south Asia. People living off rich coastal resources may have made swift progress. Fossil evidence proves that they reached Borneo by 40,000 years ago, while Australian sites have been dated to 65,000 years ago.

→ Migration routes ◆ Archaeological site
💀 Fossil site

4 EUROPE COLONIZED 50,000–25,000 YA

Despite its relative proximity to Africa, modern humans did not start to colonize Europe until around 50,000 years ago. Early sites suggest that they spread along coastlines and rivers, starting in the eastern Mediterranean. Although little fossil evidence exists, the rich archaeological material includes the first figurative carvings and musical instruments.

→ Migration routes ◆ Archaeological site
💀 Fossil site

5 INTERACTION WITH NEANDERTHALS
50,000–28,000 YA

Neanderthals had been living in Europe for hundreds of thousands of years before modern humans arrived. Although the timing and locations are unknown, ancient genetics suggests thousands of interbreeding events. Some fossils attributed to modern humans show features associated with Neanderthals, leading some scientists to speculate that these individuals may be hybrids.

💀 Fossil site ◆ Archaeological site

42,000–37,000 YA DNA extracted from remains of *Homo sapiens* from Pestera cu Oase, Romania, is estimated to be 5–11 percent Neanderthal, meaning that it had a Neanderthal relation within 4–6 generations

38,700–36,200 YA A male from Kostenki is one of the oldest modern humans found in Europe

24,000 YA According to DNA analysis, Mal'ta Boy shares a close ancestry with the male found in Kostenki, Europe

300,000 YA Jebel Irhoud is the site of the earliest *Homo sapiens* yet found—a kind of proto-*Homo sapiens* with a modern, flat face but a primitive rear skull

2 EARLY ASIAN EXPANSIONS
194,000–88,000 YA

The earliest evidence of modern humans living outside Africa are a partial jaw and teeth from Misliya Cave in Israel, dated to 194,000–177,000 years ago. Fossils from Skhul and Qafzeh, also in Israel, dated to around 120,000 years ago possibly represent a subsequent wave of expansion. The discovery of an 88,000-year-old finger bone in Al Wusta, Saudi Arabia, has extended the range of early migrations to the Arabian Peninsula.

→ Migration routes 💀 Fossil site

38,000–30,000 YA Balangoda Man in Sri Lanka represents the earliest reliably dated record of anatomically modern humans in south Asia

1 HOMO SAPIENS IN AFRICA
300,000–70,000 YA

Before *Homo sapiens* first left Africa, they flourished as a species and began to exhibit what we might recognize as "modern" behavior. Excavations at the Blombos Caves, on the southern tip of Africa, have produced some of the earliest evidence of complex thought and innovation, including jewelry, engraved stones, refined bone tools, projectile weapons, and painting materials.

💀 Fossil site ◆ Archaeological site

35,000 YA Border Cave yielded the Lebombo Bone to archaeologists— this bears marks suggesting a counting tally, similar to those used in recent times by the San people of the Kalahari

MIGRATION OF EARLY HUMANS

The series of arrows on this map represents the probable migration routes of early modern humans based on current archaeological and genetic evidence. Also highlighted are some of the most significant archaeological sites that have yielded tools and cultural evidence, and locations where important fossils have been discovered.

KEY

▨ Land exposed due to lower sea level 20,000 YA

TIMELINE

Map labels: Mamontovaya Kurya, Byzovaia, Kents Cavern, Mladec, Hohle Fels, Vogelherd, Les Rois, Cioclovina, Chatelperron, Kostenki, Ust Karakol, Malaia Syia, Mal'ta, Denisova Cave, Okladnikov Cave, Kara-Bom, Pestera cu Oase, Bacho Kiro, Lagar Velho, Gorham's Cave, Teshik Tash, Temara, Dar-es-Soltan, Jebel Irhoud, Hauah Fteah, Misliya Cave, Skhul, Qafzeh, Al Wusta, Jebel Faya, Tam Pa Ling caves, Taramsa, Iwalapuram, Singa, Herto / Middle Awash, Balangoda, Lenggong Valley, Omo Kibish, Laetoli, Border Cave, Florisbad, Blombos Caves, Klasies River Mouth

Timeline axis: 300, 250, 200, 150, 100, 50, 0 — THOUSANDS OF YEARS AGO

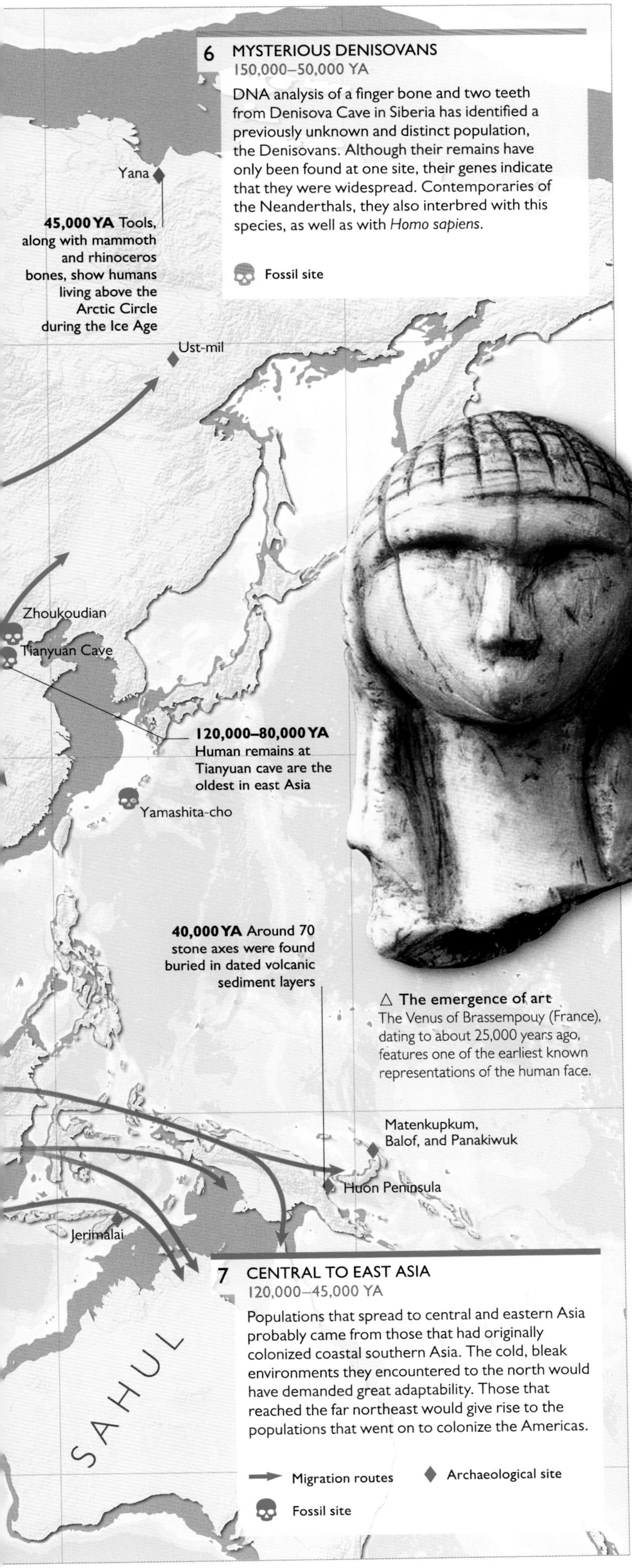

6 MYSTERIOUS DENISOVANS
150,000–50,000 YA

DNA analysis of a finger bone and two teeth from Denisova Cave in Siberia has identified a previously unknown and distinct population, the Denisovans. Although their remains have only been found at one site, their genes indicate that they were widespread. Contemporaries of the Neanderthals, they also interbred with this species, as well as with *Homo sapiens*.

💀 Fossil site

Yana

45,000 YA Tools, along with mammoth and rhinoceros bones, show humans living above the Arctic Circle during the Ice Age

Ust-mil

Zhoukoudian

Tianyuan Cave

120,000–80,000 YA Human remains at Tianyuan cave are the oldest in east Asia

Yamashita-cho

40,000 YA Around 70 stone axes were found buried in dated volcanic sediment layers

△ **The emergence of art**
The Venus of Brassempouy (France), dating to about 25,000 years ago, features one of the earliest known representations of the human face.

Matenkupkum, Balof, and Panakiwuk

Huon Peninsula

Jerimalai

SAHUL

7 CENTRAL TO EAST ASIA
120,000–45,000 YA

Populations that spread to central and eastern Asia probably came from those that had originally colonized coastal southern Asia. The cold, bleak environments they encountered to the north would have demanded great adaptability. Those that reached the far northeast would give rise to the populations that went on to colonize the Americas.

→ Migration routes   ◆ Archaeological site

💀 Fossil site

OUT OF AFRICA

The modern human, *Homo sapiens*, is a truly global species, inhabiting every continent. Our colonization of the planet started before 177,000 years ago, when groups began dispersing from their African homeland. By 40,000 years ago, our species lived in northern Europe and central and east Asia, and had crossed the sea to Australia.

Ancient hominins had moved from Africa into Asia and Europe well over a million years before our species first appeared (see p.14). But the details of how *Homo sapiens* relates to these earlier species are still emerging gradually with every fossil and archaeological discovery from the period. Genetic and archaeological evidence now overwhelmingly favors the Recent African Origin model, also known as the "Out-of-Africa" theory, which proposes that *Homo sapiens* evolved in Africa and later spread across the Old World, replacing all other hominin species.

Homo sapiens first left Africa some time after 200,000 years ago, and some groups appear to have reached east Asia by at least 80,000 years ago and perhaps as early as 120,000 years ago. Either via the Horn of Africa or the Sinai Peninsula, the first migrants traveled east along Asia's southern coastline and either north into China or eastward across Southeast Asia. Subsequent groups headed through central and eastern Asia and finally northwest into Europe.

As they moved into new territories, *Homo sapiens*' progress may have been hindered, particularly in Europe, by their encounters with other hominins, including Neanderthals and Denisovans. Little is yet known of the Denisovans, but the Neanderthal was the first fossil hominin discovered and is now known from thousands of specimens. Evidence of interaction with both species lives on in our genes.

"I, too, am convinced that our ancestors came from Africa."

KENYAN PALEOANTHROPOLOGIST RICHARD LEAKEY, 2005

THE STORY IN OUR GENES
EVIDENCE IN HUMAN DNA

By comparing the genetic makeup of living people from all over the world, scientists are able to analyze the evolutionary relationships between different populations. This has enabled them to confirm our African origins and describe how and when our species spread around the world. Genetic material (DNA) has also been extracted from the fossils of some extinct species. Analysis of the DNA of Neanderthals and Denisovans has revealed that they both interbred with *Homo sapiens* and contributed some of their genes to modern human populations.

The Vedda people of Sri Lanka
DNA analysis has been used to show that these are the earliest native inhabitants of Sri Lanka.

THE FIRST AUSTRALIANS

More than 60,000 years ago, hardy, resourceful people arrived in Australia after crossing the seas from Asia. They became Aboriginal Australians and went on to establish a unique way of life with a distinct culture.

During the last ice age, Australia, New Guinea, and Tasmania were joined in a single landmass (see p.17), which was colonized by a seafaring people who crossed the seas from Asia on bamboo vessels. These people were the first Australians. Their journey through the continent followed coastlines and river valleys. Archaeological evidence suggests that by 30,000 years ago, they had spread far and wide, from Tasmania in the south to the Swan River in the west and northward into New Guinea.

△ **Ancient art**
Discovered in western Australia in 1891, the ancient Bradshaw rock paintings show human figures engaged in display or hunting.

Indigenous Australians

Australia's indigenous peoples were seminomadic; instead of developing agricultural societies, they moved with the seasons. They lived in small family groups but were connected through extensive social networks. Already adept at hunting and gathering, they developed new technologies such as boomerangs, fish traps, and stone axes shaped by grinding. Over time, the groups became culturally diverse. In the far north, people of the Torres Strait—between Australia and New Guinea—became distinct from the Australian Aborigines. Aboriginal life became centered on relationships between people and the natural world, or "Country," which included animals, plants, and rocks. These links, which have lasted into modern life, are formalized in the "Dreaming": oral histories of creation combined with moral codes, some of which are reflected in art.

THE COLONIZATION OF AUSTRALIA

The earliest known archaeological sites in Australia are 65,000 years old—a date that conforms with genetic evidence for the origins of indigenous Australians. Fossils of humans and their animal prey, as well as artifacts from the time, indicate that populations were centered around coastlines and the Murray–Darling river basins.

Madjedbebe Rock Shelter
65,000 YA

Nawarla Gabarnmung
45,000 YA

AUSTRALIA

Upper Swan River
40,000 YA

Willandra Lakes
40,000 YA

Devil's Lair
48,000–43,000 YA

Penrith
50,000–40,000 YA

Tasmania
30,000 YA

KEY

◆ Archaeological site pre-30,000 YA

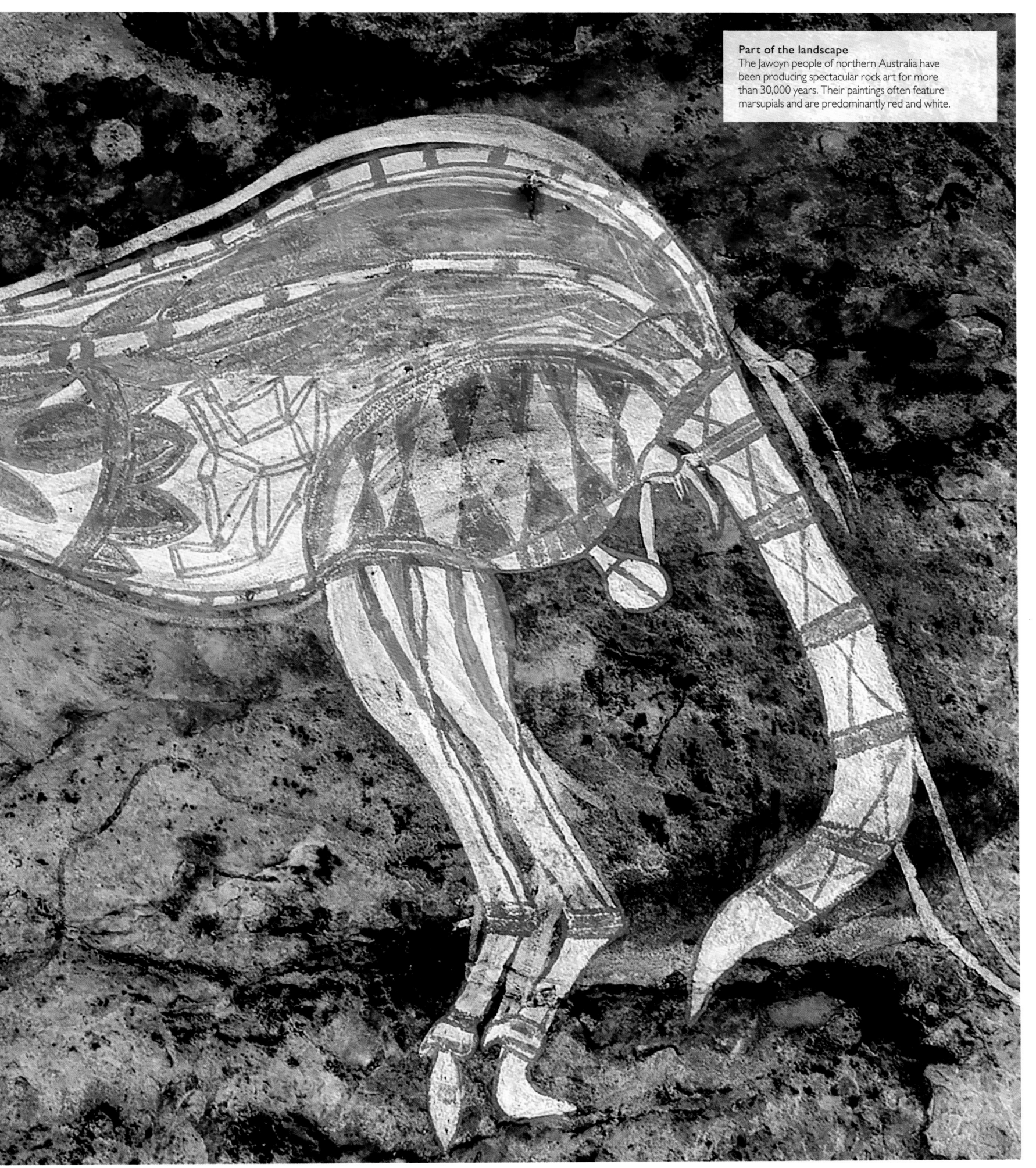

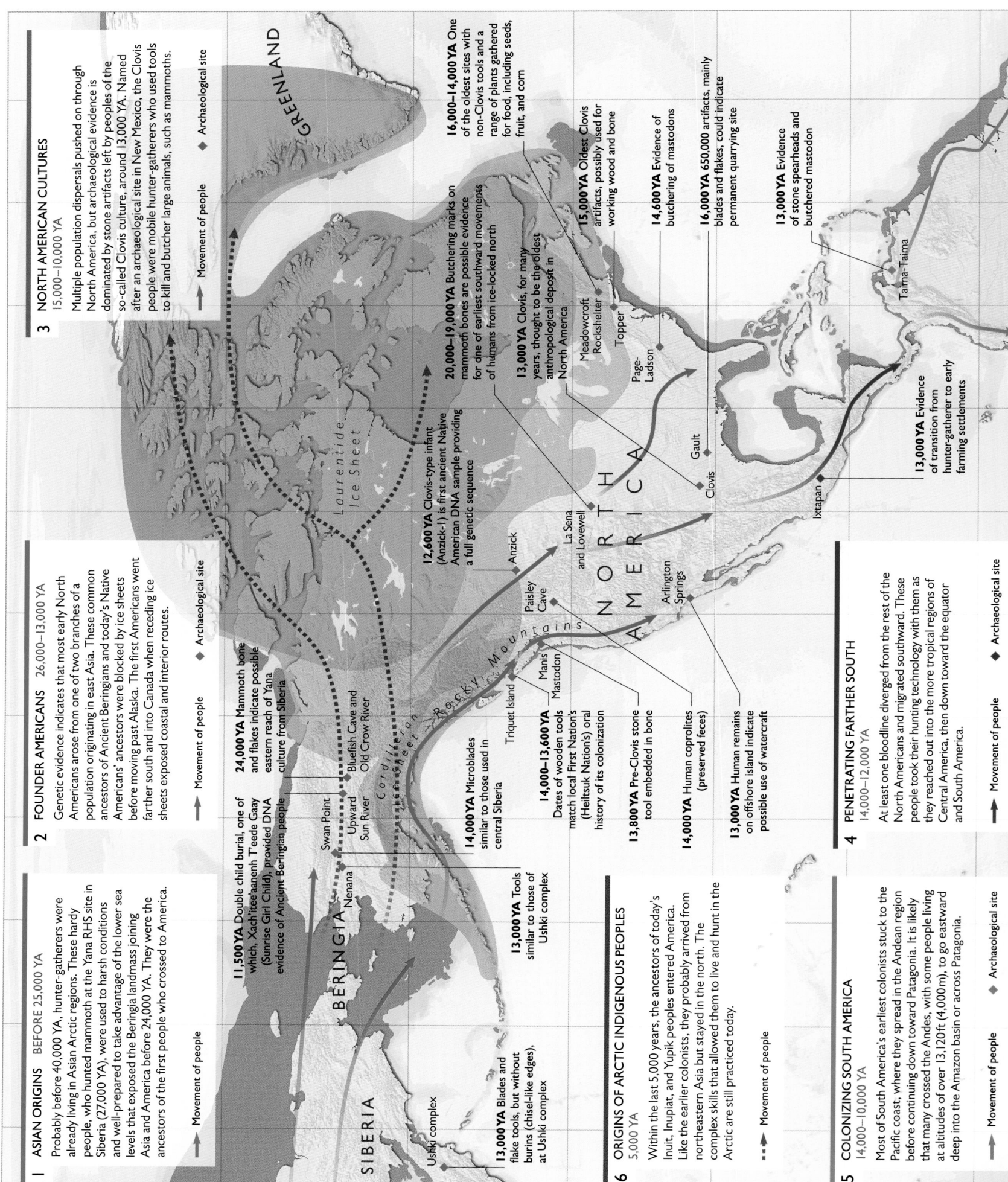

1 ASIAN ORIGINS BEFORE 25,000 YA

Probably before 40,000 YA, hunter-gatherers were already living in Asian Arctic regions. These hardy people, who hunted mammoth at the Yana RHS site in Siberia (27,000 YA), were used to harsh conditions and well-prepared to take advantage of the lower sea levels that exposed the Beringia landmass joining Asia and America before 24,000 YA. They were the ancestors of the first people who crossed to America.

→ Movement of people

13,000 YA Blades and flake tools, but without burins (chisel-like edges), at Ushki complex

2 FOUNDER AMERICANS 26,000–13,000 YA

Genetic evidence indicates that most early North Americans arose from one of two branches of a population originating in east Asia. These common ancestors of Ancient Beringians and today's Native Americans' ancestors were blocked by ice sheets before moving past Alaska. The first Americans went farther south and into Canada when receding ice sheets exposed coastal and interior routes.

→ Movement of people   ◆ Archaeological site

24,000 YA Mammoth bone and flakes indicate possible eastern reach of Yana culture from Siberia

11,500 YA Double child burial, one of which, Xach'itee'aanenh T'eede Gaay (Sunrise Girl Child), provided DNA evidence of Ancient Beringian people

13,000 YA Tools similar to those of Ushki complex

3 NORTH AMERICAN CULTURES 15,000–10,000 YA

Multiple population dispersals pushed on through North America, but archaeological evidence is dominated by stone artifacts left by peoples of the so-called Clovis culture, around 13,000 YA. Named after an archaeological site in New Mexico, the Clovis people were mobile hunter-gatherers who used tools to kill and butcher large animals, such as mammoths.

→ Movement of people   ◆ Archaeological site

16,000–14,000 YA One of the oldest sites with non-Clovis tools and a range of plants gathered for food, including seeds, fruit, and corn

20,000–19,000 YA Butchering marks on mammoth bones are possible evidence for one of earliest southward movements of humans from ice-locked north

13,000 YA Clovis, for many years, thought to be the oldest anthropological deposit in North America

12,600 YA Clovis-type infant (Anzick-1) is first ancient Native American DNA sample providing a full genetic sequence

15,000 YA Oldest Clovis artifacts, possibly used for working wood and bone

14,600 YA Evidence of butchering of mastodons

16,000 YA 650,000 artifacts, mainly blades and flakes, could indicate permanent quarrying site

13,000 YA Evidence of stone spearheads and butchered mastodon

6 ORIGINS OF ARCTIC INDIGENOUS PEOPLES 5,000 YA

Within the last 5,000 years, the ancestors of today's Inuit, Inupiat, and Yupik peoples entered America. Like the earlier colonists, they probably arrived from northeastern Asia but stayed in the north. The complex skills that allowed them to live and hunt in the Arctic are still practiced today.

→ Movement of people   ◆ Archaeological site

14,000 YA Microblades similar to those used in central Siberia

14,000–13,600 YA Dates of wooden tools match local First Nation's (Heiltsuk Nation's) oral history of its colonization

13,800 YA Pre-Clovis stone tool embedded in bone

14,000 YA Human coprolites (preserved feces)

13,000 YA Human remains on offshore island indicate possible use of watercraft

5 COLONIZING SOUTH AMERICA 14,000–10,000 YA

Most of South America's earliest colonists stuck to the Pacific coast, where they spread in the Andean region before continuing down toward Patagonia. It is likely that many crossed the Andes, with some people living at altitudes of over 13,120ft (4,000m), to go eastward deep into the Amazon basin or across Patagonia.

→ Movement of people   ◆ Archaeological site

4 PENETRATING FARTHER SOUTH 14,000–12,000 YA

At least one bloodline diverged from the rest of the North Americans and migrated southward. These people took their hunting technology with them as they reached out into the more tropical regions of Central America, then down toward the equator and South America.

→ Movement of people

13,000 YA Evidence of transition from hunter-gatherer to early farming settlements

Map labels

SIBERIA

Ushki complex

BERINGIA

Nenana

Swan Point

Upward Sun River

Bluefish Cave and Old Crow River

GREENLAND

Laurentide Ice Sheet

Cordilleran Ice Sheet

Rocky Mountains

NORTH AMERICA

SOUTH AMERICA

OCEAN

Anzick

La Sena and Lovewell

Meadowcroft Rockshelter

Topper

Page-Ladson

Gault

Clovis

Arlington Springs

Paisley Cave

Manis

Mastodon

Triquet Island

Ixtapan

Taima-Taima

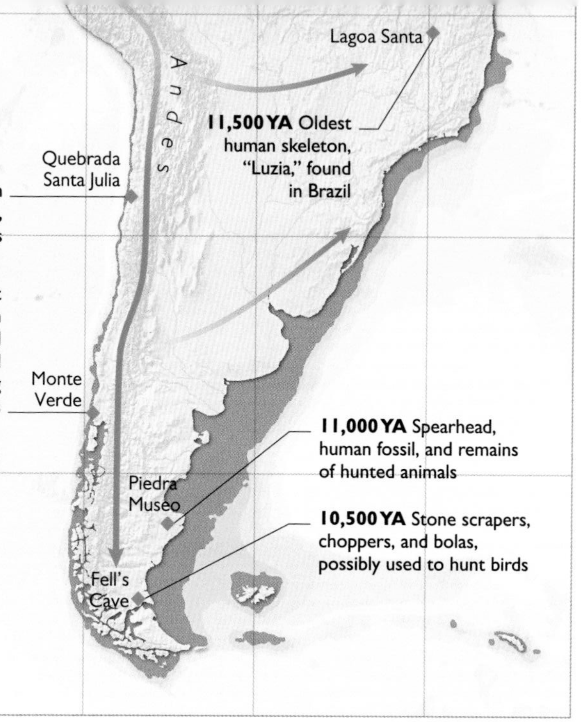

COLONIZING A NEW WORLD

Genetic studies and archaeological evidence from sites in Siberia, North America, and South America show that humans moved over a land bridge joining America to Asia at least 30,000–20,000 years ago (YA). As the land emerged from an ice age, these people then spread through the entire continent, possibly reaching along the coasts of southern South America by 18,000 YA.

KEY

Extent of ice sheet 24,000 YA	Land exposed by lower sea level at height of Ice Age
Extent of ice sheet 15,000–12,500 YA	

TIMELINE

1,500 YA Oldest human skeleton, "Luzia," found in Brazil — Lagoa Santa

11,000 YA Spearhead, human fossil, and remains of hunted animals

10,500 YA Stone scrapers, choppers, and bolas, possibly used to hunt birds — Piedra Museo

13,100 YA Human habitation with living floor, hearth, and horses

18,500–14,500 YA Oldest human habitation in South America, possibly a coastal culture; unusually good preservation including hearths, hide, and plants — Monte Verde

Quebrada Santa Julia

Fell's Cave

Andes

PACIFIC

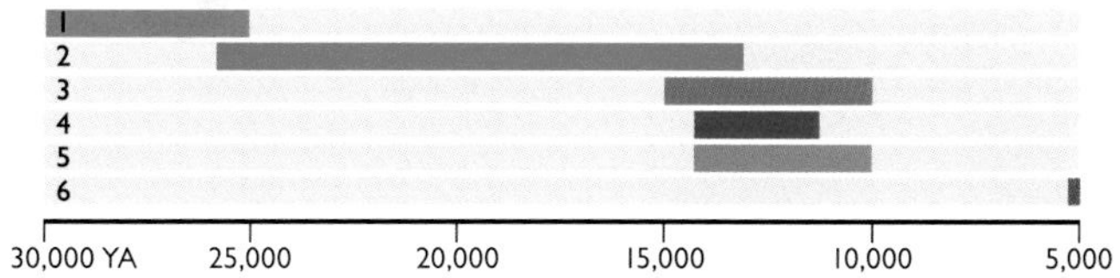

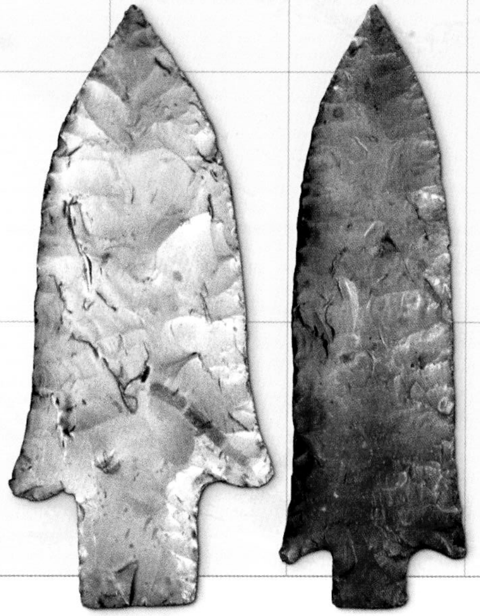

◁ **Clovis spearheads**
Bifacially worked (chipped into shape on each side) flint points were characteristic products of Clovis technology across North America.

PEOPLING THE AMERICAS

By the time Columbus set foot in the Americas in 1492, the continents had been peopled for thousands of years. The real discoverers of these new worlds had come from Siberia. They conquered ice and snow and trekked enormous distances to colonize a landmass of prairieland, desert, rainforest, and mountains.

Some 24,000 years ago, the world was locked in an ice age, when an Arctic ice sheet covered much of the northern world. With so much water frozen in glaciers, ocean levels were low enough to expose a connection of land, known as Beringia, between Asia and North America. This meant that people could walk across from one continent to the other, until their way became blocked as ice sheets closed in on them. There, America's founding peoples were isolated for thousands of years, until warmer times melted the ice and opened up corridors to the south, possibly as early as 20,000 YA.

DNA evidence from archaeological sites and the DNA of Native Americans alive today shows that two distinct populations split from the founding group that had entered the new lands across Beringia.

Only one of these went on to settle the Americas—the ancestors of Native Americans. The other population—known as the Ancient Beringians—may have been isolated on or outside Beringia until after the glacial melt, as evidence of their DNA is distinct from that of any past or present Native Americans. Genetics show that between 17,500 and 14,600 YA, the group that had entered America branched again into two new lineages, northern and southern. People who continued farther followed routes along the Pacific coast and far into the interior. Some became separated over vast distances but remained genetically similar, suggesting that they moved rapidly. Within a few thousand years, they had established themselves in Central America, and just centuries after that had entered Patagonia.

"They made prehistory, those latter-day Asians who, by jumping continents, became the first Americans. Theirs was a colonization the likes and scale of which … would never be repeated."

DAVID J. MELTZER, *FIRST PEOPLES IN A NEW WORLD: COLONIZING ICE AGE AMERICA,* 2009

THE CLOVIS
STONE AGE HUNTERS

The hunter-gatherer Clovis people were once viewed as the first Americans, but archaeological sites predating the Clovis period show this is not the case. However, the Clovis became a widespread influence. They used bifacial stone points and blades to hunt many of North America's large mammals, such as bison, mammoths, and sabertooth cats. In addition to the changing climate and habitats of these species, hunters were possibly one of the main factors that led to their extinction.

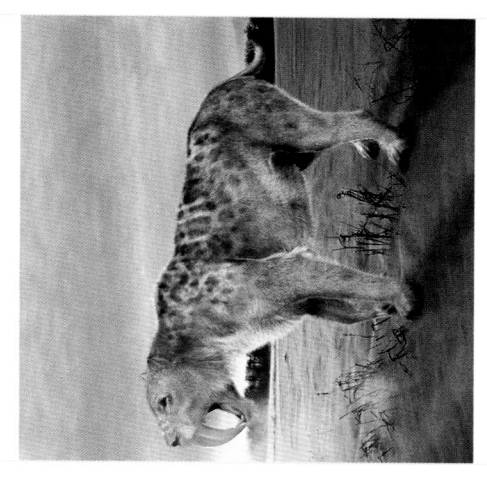

Extinct sabertooth cat

THE FIRST FARMERS

Working the land to grow food was an entirely new way of life for prehistoric humans. It turned them from nomads into farmers—and created settlements with permanent buildings, larger societies, and the potential to develop more elaborate technology and culture.

△ **Innovative tools**
Wooden tools called adzes had blades made from stone that were sufficiently strong to fell trees, open up land for pasture, or dig hard ground.

The earliest humans mostly lived in small nomadic bands and went wherever food was plentiful. They tracked the migrations of large animals as they hunted for meat, just as they followed the seasonal bounties of fruit and seeds. They built—and rebuilt—simple camps, carrying a few lightweight belongings with them.

This hunter-gatherer existence supported humans through the last ice age, but about 12,000 years ago, a rise in Earth's temperature opened up a world of alternative possibilities. One species of human—*Homo sapiens*—successfully emerged into this warmer world. By this time, these modern humans had spread far beyond their African ancestral home into Asia, Australasia, and America. And independently, all over the world, they had begun creating permanent farming settlements.

Settling down

Permanent camps with stronger houses made sense in places where the land was especially fertile—such as on floodplains of rivers. Settlers could support more hungry mouths by hunting, fishing, and gathering plant food around a local foraging ground that was rich in resources. This was just a small step from farming, as

▷ **Early farming villages**
This settlement at Mehrgarh in modern Pakistan dates from 7000 BCE. It had mud-brick houses and granaries to store surplus cultivated cereal grain.

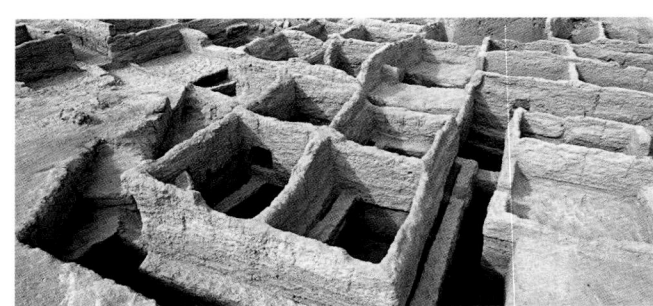

it was more convenient to nurture or transplant food plants closer to home or plant their seeds and tubers (some recent evidence suggests people had started to do this as early as 23,000 years ago)—while the most amenable wild animals were confined to pens. These first farms produced more food to feed more people, so settlements could grow bigger and even produce a surplus to help with leaner times. Valuable food stores—defended from competing camps—became another reason to stay in one place.

Domestication

By about 10,000 BCE, agriculture had emerged in Eurasia, New Guinea, and America, with farmers relying on local plants and animals as favored sources of food. They learned that some species were more useful than others, and so these became staple parts of their diets.

In the fertile floodplains of Mesopotamia (modern Iraq), local wild wheat and barley became the cereal grains of choice, while goats and sheep provided meat. East Asia's main cereal grain was rice, and in Central America, farmers cultivated corn. In all cases, the first farmers selected the most manageable and high-yielding plants and animals. Over time and generations, their choices would change the traits of wild species, as crops and livestock passed on their characteristics to form the domesticated varieties we use today. With

SETTLED LIVING

As modern humans dispersed around the world, they relied on local plants and animals for sustenance. Nomadic societies gave way to settled communities as people planted the first crops or corralled the first livestock. Domestication of wild species began from about 12,000 years ago. The first farmers used the most edible species that were easiest to harvest, growing their food in abundance, providing enough to support larger populations, and ultimately outcompeting hunter-gatherers.

11,000–9000 BCE Wheat and barley are grown in southwest Asia to produce non-shattering seed heads that are easier to harvest—the first domesticated cereal grains

10,000 BCE Lentils, peas, and chickpeas in the Middle East provide an additional source of protein—improving the dietary balance along the Fertile Crescent

CROPS

ANIMALS

| 11,000 BCE | 10,000 BCE | 9000 BCE | 8000 BCE |

10,000 BCE In southwest Asia, local animals—including sheep, goats, pigs, and cattle—are domesticated and will become globally important livestock

10,000–5000 BCE Corn domesticated in Central America becomes the staple cereal grain in the Americas, while squash plants are selectively bred to reduce bitterness of their taste

◁ **Working the land**
A wooden model, from 2000 BCE, of a man plowing the land with oxen, depicts the earliest kind of scratch plow, which cut a furrow through hard ground ready for sowing seeds.

domestication, settlements became increasingly reliant on the limited kinds of plants and animals that provided the bulk of their food. As a result, although food was plentiful, it sometimes lacked dietary balance. More time was needed to work the land, and livestock could be lost during droughts. People's health was often poor, as crowded settlements encouraged the spread of infectious disease among humans, as well as their livestock.

Ultimately, agriculture's success, or otherwise, was a trade-off between these risks and benefits. In some parts of the world—such as the Australian interior—conditions favored more traditional nomadic lifestyles, and here humans largely remained hunter-gatherers. As farmers gained a better understanding of the needs of their crops and livestock, they developed ways of overcoming risks and increasing productivity. They learned how to use animal dung as fertilizer or to irrigate the land by diverting rivers—curtailing effects of seasonal drought. In Egypt, for example, the waters of the Nile were used for large-scale irrigation of farmland, helping to lengthen growing seasons.

Over time, food productivity became material wealth: more food not only fed more people but facilitated trade, too. At the same time, larger settlements could support people with different skills, such as craftsmen and merchants. It meant that the agricultural revolution would have far-reaching consequences for the history of humankind—including the emergence of industrial towns and cities.

> "Farming was the precondition for the development of ... civilizations in Egypt, Mesopotamia, the Indus Valley, China, the Americas, and Africa."
>
> GRAEME BARKER, BRITISH ARCHAEOLOGIST, FROM *AGRICULTURAL REVOLUTION IN PREHISTORY*, 2006

△ **Feral ancestor**
The Armenian mouflon from south-western Asia is the possible ancestor of the domesticated sheep, which was one of the earliest animal species to be tamed, at around 10,000 BCE.

7000 BCE Rice plants grown in the fertile Yangtze River valley in China are bred to provide larger, more nutritious grains

5000 BCE Potato plants are grown in Peru and northern Argentina—the ancestors of potatoes used as a staple today

4000 BCE Pearl millet is grown in the Sahel regions and—along with sorghum—becomes one of the staple cereal grains of Africa

3000 BCE Dromedary camels are domesticated in Africa and Arabia—and used for transportation or for their meat and milk

2000 BCE Turkeys are domesticated in Mexico and used for meat and their feathers, and later have ceremonial significance

| 6000 BCE | 5000 BCE | 4000 BCE | 3000 BCE | 2000 BCE |

7000 BCE Cattle domesticated in northern Africa, predating the emergence of most crops on the African continent

5500 BCE Horses are domesticated in central Asia

5000 BCE Llamas, alpacas, and guinea pigs are domesticated in South America; llamas are used for meat, wool, and as beasts of burden

4000 BCE Chickens are used as food and for cock-fighting in southern Asia, although genetic evidence suggests a much earlier origin as a domesticated bird, possibly before 10000 BCE

ORIGINS OF AGRICULTURE

When hunter-gatherers abandoned their nomadic life and became the first farmers, they were doing more than feeding their families. They were kick-starting an agricultural revolution that would have enormous implications for the future of humanity.

Evidence for agriculture's origins comes from archaeology and from DNA of crops or livestock and their wild counterparts. No one knows exactly why people started to work the land. Perhaps they transplanted wild crops closer to home for convenience or saw the potential of germinating seeds. Whatever happened, as climates warmed in the wake of the Ice Age and populations swelled, people around the world—entirely independently—became tied to farming. It brought a stable source of nourishment and sometimes, when yields were good, a surplus to sustain people through leaner times. Tending crops or corralling livestock demanded that communities stayed in one place long enough to reap the harvest. Other reasons for staying in one location would have been that the new farming tools were too heavy to carry from place to place and any food surplus had to be stored. While agrarian settlements grew to become the seeds of civilization, their communities spread, taking their skills, plants, and livestock with them.

"… Almost all of us are farmers or else are fed by farmers."

JARED DIAMOND, FROM *GUNS, GERMS, AND STEEL*, 1997

DOMESTICATION REVOLUTION
WILD SPECIES TO CROPS AND LIVESTOCK

The crops and livestock that humankind uses today descended from wild species that had rather different characteristics. Farmers chose to breed from individuals that served them best, such as by selecting ones that provided better yields or were more easily managed. This so-called artificial selection, applied over many generations and sometimes across centuries, gave rise to domesticated forms of plants and animals.

Teosinte (original wild plant)

Produce of artificial selection
Bigger cobs of domesticated corn (left) are descended from wild corn (right).

Modern corn cob

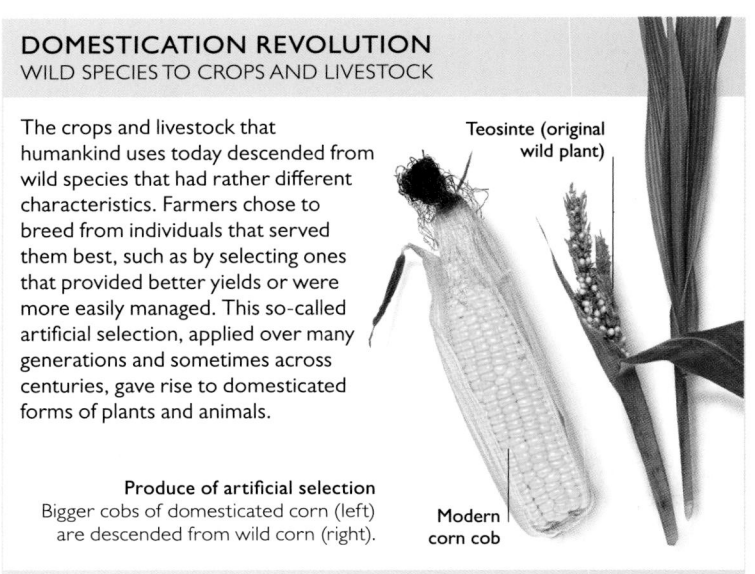

5 DIFFERENT KINDS OF CROPS AND LIVESTOCK: AMERICA 10,000–2000 BCE

Across the Old World, similar kinds of crops and livestock were being used in separate centers of agriculture. But the early colonizers of the Americas found entirely new plants, such as squashes and corn. The variety of these plants increased as people from different regions exchanged their produce. The only large animals suitable for domestication in the Americas, llamas and alpacas, were both found in the Andes.

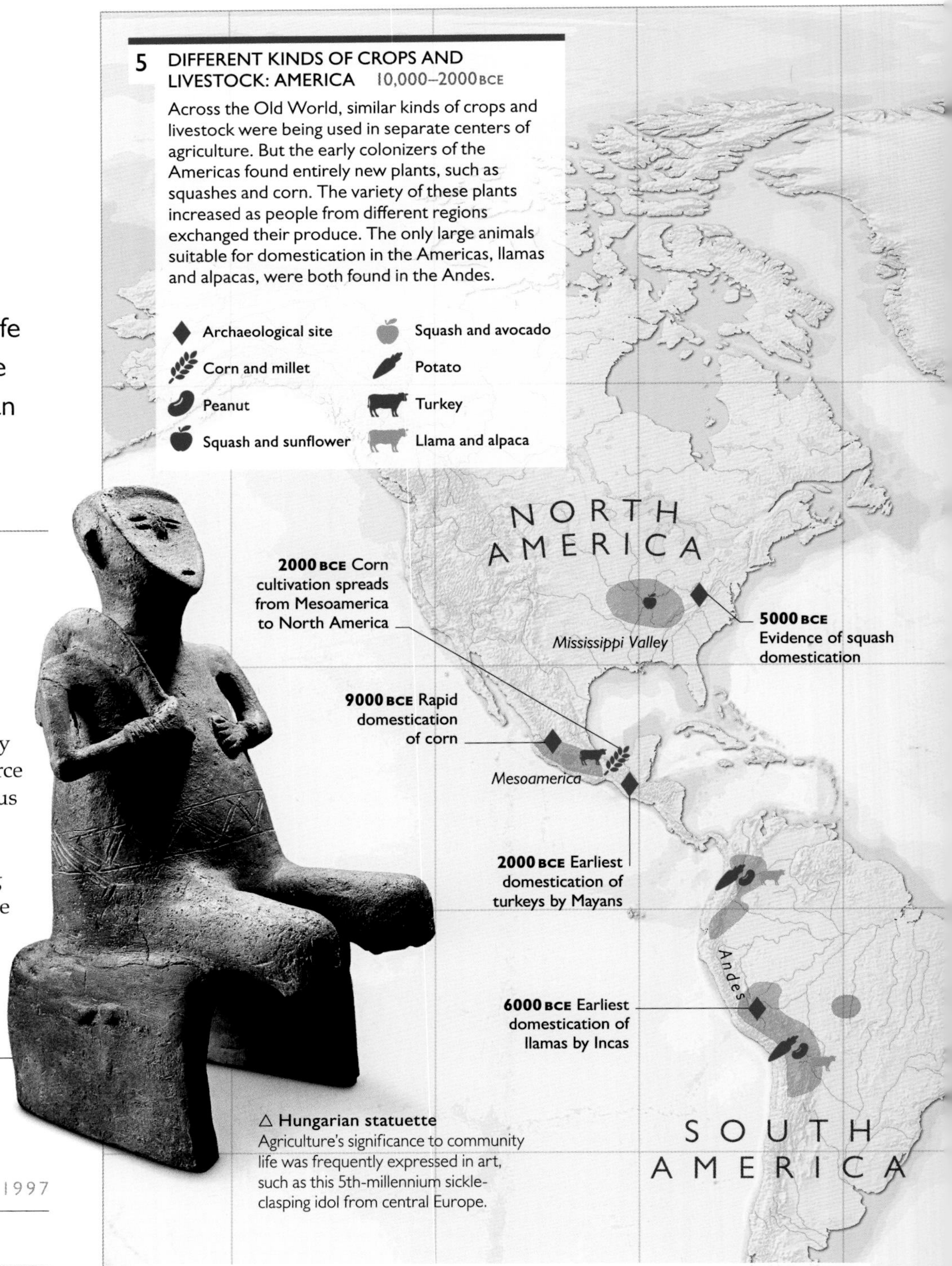

- ◆ Archaeological site
- Corn and millet
- Peanut
- Squash and sunflower
- Squash and avocado
- Potato
- Turkey
- Llama and alpaca

NORTH AMERICA

2000 BCE Corn cultivation spreads from Mesoamerica to North America

Mississippi Valley

5000 BCE Evidence of squash domestication

9000 BCE Rapid domestication of corn

Mesoamerica

2000 BCE Earliest domestication of turkeys by Mayans

6000 BCE Earliest domestication of llamas by Incas

Andes

SOUTH AMERICA

△ **Hungarian statuette**
Agriculture's significance to community life was frequently expressed in art, such as this 5th-millennium sickle-clasping idol from central Europe.

ADVENT OF AGRICULTURE

Agriculture arose independently in different parts of the world before diffusing into adjacent regions. Each area developed its own specific crops, dependent on the region's climate, and some produce went on to become globally important as communities expanded across the world.

KEY
- Main independent centers of domestication
- Secondary centers
- Cereal grains
- Legumes
- Fruits and vegetables
- Livestock
- Tubers and roots

SIZE KEY
- Globally important produce
- Mainly regional produce

TIMELINE

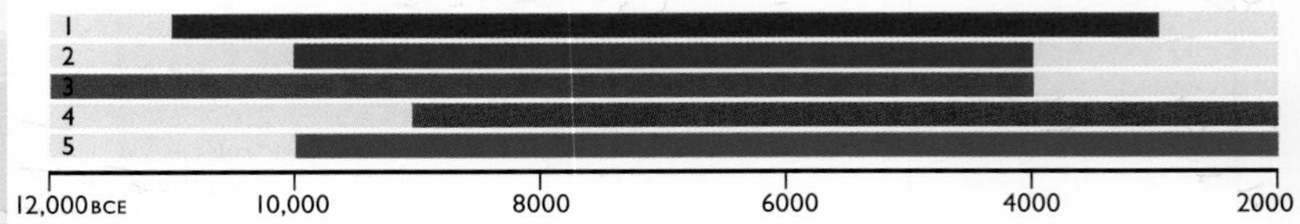

12,000 BCE — 10,000 — 8000 — 6000 — 4000 — 2000

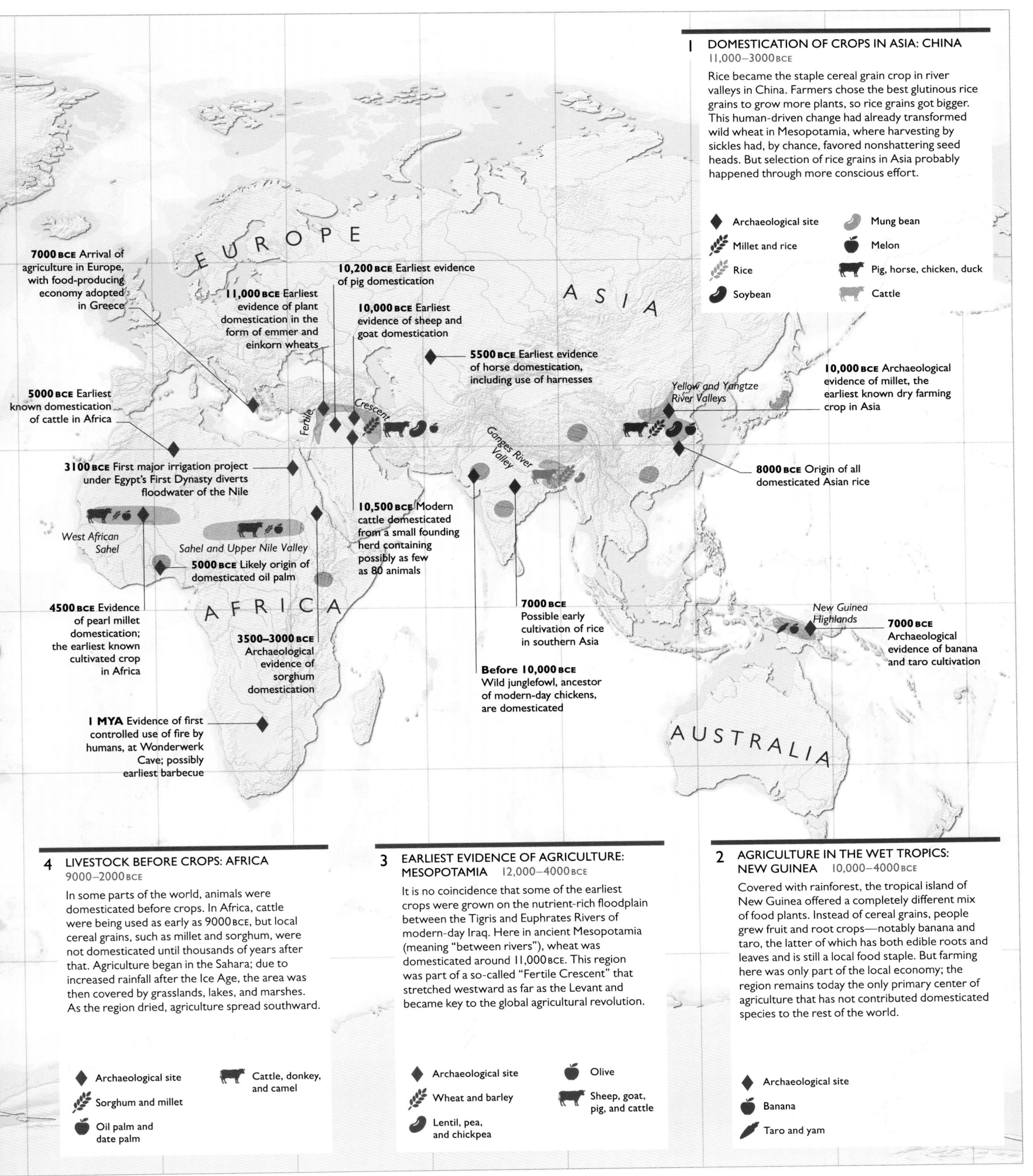

1 DOMESTICATION OF CROPS IN ASIA: CHINA
11,000–3000 BCE

Rice became the staple cereal grain crop in river valleys in China. Farmers chose the best glutinous rice grains to grow more plants, so rice grains got bigger. This human-driven change had already transformed wild wheat in Mesopotamia, where harvesting by sickles had, by chance, favored nonshattering seed heads. But selection of rice grains in Asia probably happened through more conscious effort.

- ◆ Archaeological site
- Millet and rice
- Rice
- Soybean
- Mung bean
- Melon
- Pig, horse, chicken, duck
- Cattle

7000 BCE Arrival of agriculture in Europe, with food-producing economy adopted in Greece

11,000 BCE Earliest evidence of plant domestication in the form of emmer and einkorn wheats

10,200 BCE Earliest evidence of pig domestication

10,000 BCE Earliest evidence of sheep and goat domestication

5500 BCE Earliest evidence of horse domestication, including use of harnesses

10,000 BCE Archaeological evidence of millet, the earliest known dry farming crop in Asia

Yellow and Yangtze River Valleys

5000 BCE Earliest known domestication of cattle in Africa

Fertile Crescent

Ganges River Valley

8000 BCE Origin of all domesticated Asian rice

3100 BCE First major irrigation project under Egypt's First Dynasty diverts floodwater of the Nile

10,500 BCE Modern cattle domesticated from a small founding herd containing possibly as few as 80 animals

West African Sahel

Sahel and Upper Nile Valley

5000 BCE Likely origin of domesticated oil palm

4500 BCE Evidence of pearl millet domestication; the earliest known cultivated crop in Africa

3500–3000 BCE Archaeological evidence of sorghum domestication

7000 BCE Possible early cultivation of rice in southern Asia

New Guinea Highlands

7000 BCE Archaeological evidence of banana and taro cultivation

Before 10,000 BCE Wild junglefowl, ancestor of modern-day chickens, are domesticated

1 MYA Evidence of first controlled use of fire by humans, at Wonderwerk Cave; possibly earliest barbecue

4 LIVESTOCK BEFORE CROPS: AFRICA
9000–2000 BCE

In some parts of the world, animals were domesticated before crops. In Africa, cattle were being used as early as 9000 BCE, but local cereal grains, such as millet and sorghum, were not domesticated until thousands of years after that. Agriculture began in the Sahara; due to increased rainfall after the Ice Age, the area was then covered by grasslands, lakes, and marshes. As the region dried, agriculture spread southward.

- ◆ Archaeological site
- Sorghum and millet
- Oil palm and date palm
- Cattle, donkey, and camel

3 EARLIEST EVIDENCE OF AGRICULTURE: MESOPOTAMIA
12,000–4000 BCE

It is no coincidence that some of the earliest crops were grown on the nutrient-rich floodplain between the Tigris and Euphrates Rivers of modern-day Iraq. Here in ancient Mesopotamia (meaning "between rivers"), wheat was domesticated around 11,000 BCE. This region was part of a so-called "Fertile Crescent" that stretched westward as far as the Levant and became key to the global agricultural revolution.

- ◆ Archaeological site
- Wheat and barley
- Lentil, pea, and chickpea
- Olive
- Sheep, goat, pig, and cattle

2 AGRICULTURE IN THE WET TROPICS: NEW GUINEA
10,000–4000 BCE

Covered with rainforest, the tropical island of New Guinea offered a completely different mix of food plants. Instead of cereal grains, people grew fruit and root crops—notably banana and taro, the latter of which has both edible roots and leaves and is still a local food staple. But farming here was only part of the local economy; the region remains today the only primary center of agriculture that has not contributed domesticated species to the rest of the world.

- ◆ Archaeological site
- Banana
- Taro and yam

VILLAGES TO TOWNS

As nomadic hunter-gatherers began farming, for the first time in history human populations became anchored to fixed points on a map of civilization. Settlements grew in size and complexity; the first villages became the first towns.

Just as agriculture turned humans into a more sedentary species, so the settlements they made drove the attributes of modern human society: material accumulation, industry, and trade. This happened in places around the world, but nowhere is the evidence for it clearer than in southwest Asia. Here, the first farmers produced enough food on fertile soils to support denser populations. Although life was labor-intensive, and there was a greater risk of disease from overcrowding and malnutrition, there were benefits of living together in one place over a long period. People could concentrate on producing a surplus and perfect skills to make their lives easier. Clay was baked into bricks for making stronger houses or fashioned into large storage vessels. As towns grew, they were sometimes fortified with surrounding walls. Shells from the Mediterranean showed wide trade links developing, while copper gradually supplanted flint for better tools. As society itself divided into craftspeople, merchants, and their leaders, these first local industries brought material wealth that formed the basis of the first exchange economies.

"… it made sense for men to band together … for … management of the environment."

J.M. ROBERTS, FROM *HISTORY OF THE WORLD*, 1990

POTTERY IN THE STONE AGE
HARNESSING THE POTENTIAL OF CLAY

Fired clay had been used to make figurines and pots before 20,000 YA. It later became important in constructing dwellings. Wet clay was used to reinforce brushwood walls. Solid bricks gave protection from the elements and enemies, while creative clay technology was used to fashion more decorative pots.

Halaf vase
Mesopotamian pottery was decorated with geometric designs as early as 6000 BCE.

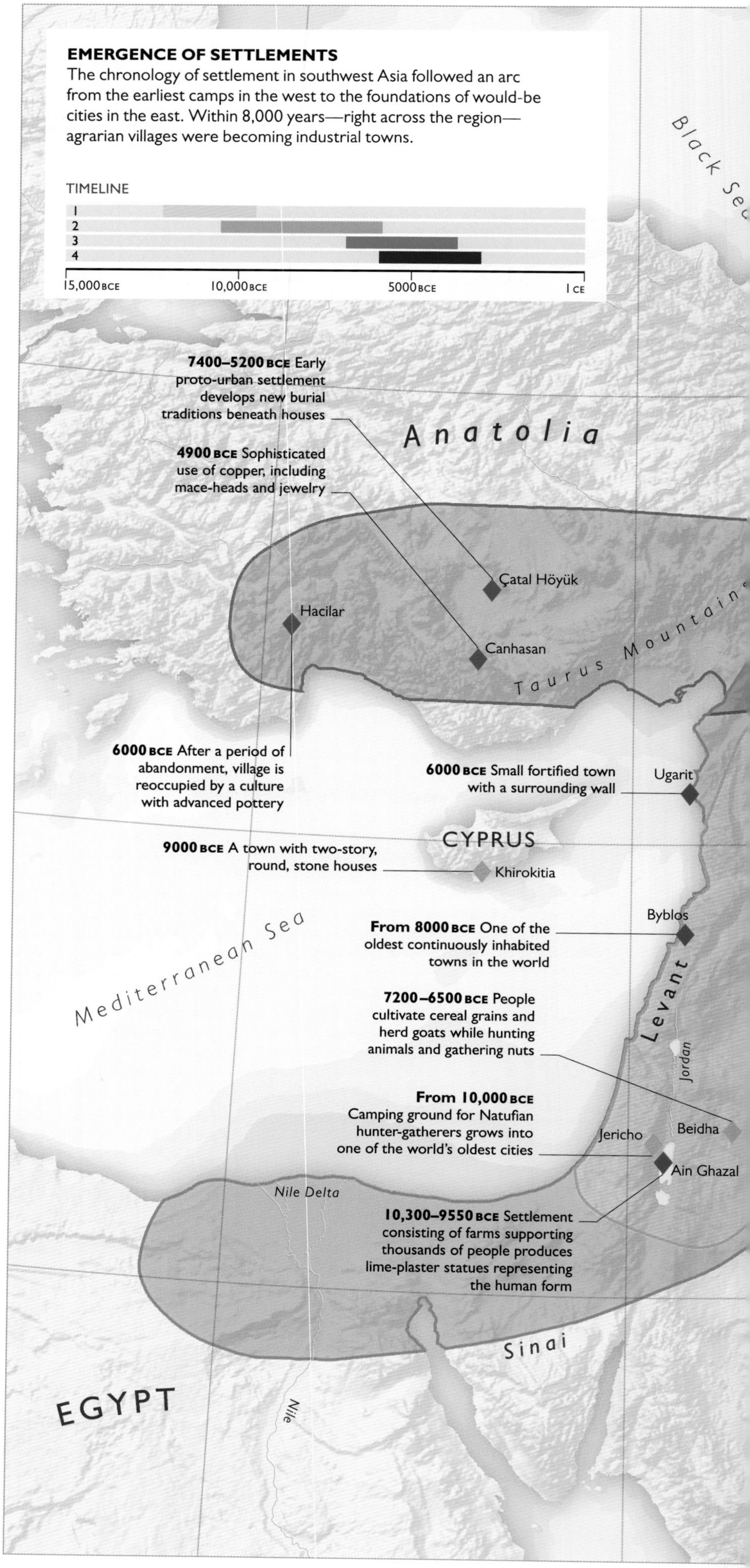

EMERGENCE OF SETTLEMENTS

The chronology of settlement in southwest Asia followed an arc from the earliest camps in the west to the foundations of would-be cities in the east. Within 8,000 years—right across the region—agrarian villages were becoming industrial towns.

TIMELINE

1
2
3
4

15,000 BCE   10,000 BCE   5000 BCE   1 CE

Black Sea

Anatolia

7400–5200 BCE Early proto-urban settlement develops new burial traditions beneath houses

4900 BCE Sophisticated use of copper, including mace-heads and jewelry

Çatal Höyük

Hacilar

Canhasan

Taurus Mountains

6000 BCE After a period of abandonment, village is reoccupied by a culture with advanced pottery

6000 BCE Small fortified town with a surrounding wall

Ugarit

CYPRUS

9000 BCE A town with two-story, round, stone houses

Khirokitia

Byblos

From 8000 BCE One of the oldest continuously inhabited towns in the world

7200–6500 BCE People cultivate cereal grains and herd goats while hunting animals and gathering nuts

Mediterranean Sea

Levant

Jordan

From 10,000 BCE Camping ground for Natufian hunter-gatherers grows into one of the world's oldest cities

Jericho

Beidha

Ain Ghazal

Nile Delta

10,300–9550 BCE Settlement consisting of farms supporting thousands of people produces lime-plaster statues representing the human form

Sinai

EGYPT

Nile

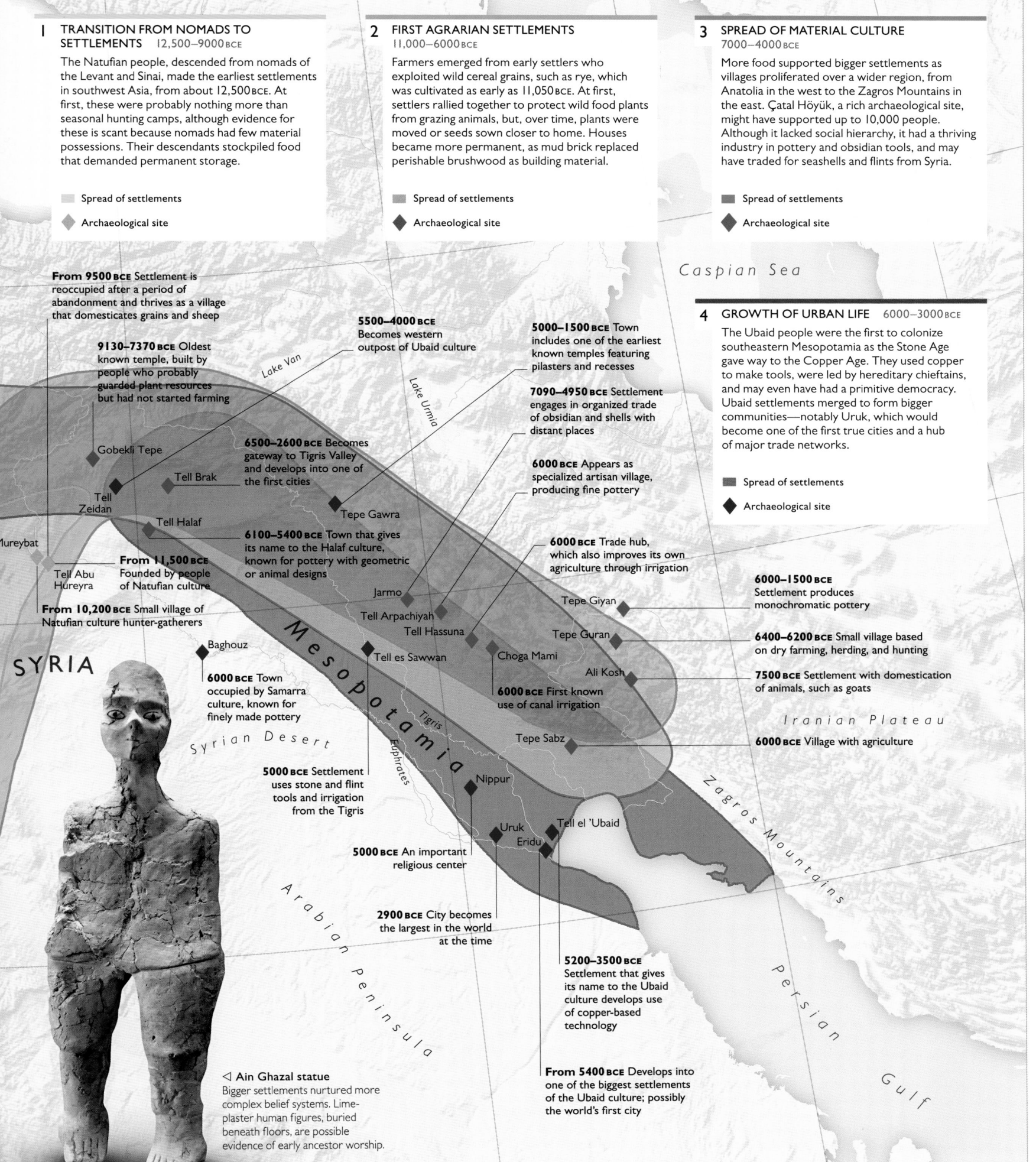

1 TRANSITION FROM NOMADS TO SETTLEMENTS 12,500–9000 BCE

The Natufian people, descended from nomads of the Levant and Sinai, made the earliest settlements in southwest Asia, from about 12,500 BCE. At first, these were probably nothing more than seasonal hunting camps, although evidence for these is scant because nomads had few material possessions. Their descendants stockpiled food that demanded permanent storage.

- Spread of settlements
- Archaeological site

2 FIRST AGRARIAN SETTLEMENTS 11,000–6000 BCE

Farmers emerged from early settlers who exploited wild cereal grains, such as rye, which was cultivated as early as 11,050 BCE. At first, settlers rallied together to protect wild food plants from grazing animals, but, over time, plants were moved or seeds sown closer to home. Houses became more permanent, as mud brick replaced perishable brushwood as building material.

- Spread of settlements
- Archaeological site

3 SPREAD OF MATERIAL CULTURE 7000–4000 BCE

More food supported bigger settlements as villages proliferated over a wider region, from Anatolia in the west to the Zagros Mountains in the east. Çatal Höyük, a rich archaeological site, might have supported up to 10,000 people. Although it lacked social hierarchy, it had a thriving industry in pottery and obsidian tools, and may have traded for seashells and flints from Syria.

- Spread of settlements
- Archaeological site

4 GROWTH OF URBAN LIFE 6000–3000 BCE

The Ubaid people were the first to colonize southeastern Mesopotamia as the Stone Age gave way to the Copper Age. They used copper to make tools, were led by hereditary chieftains, and may even have had a primitive democracy. Ubaid settlements merged to form bigger communities—notably Uruk, which would become one of the first true cities and a hub of major trade networks.

- Spread of settlements
- Archaeological site

◁ **Ain Ghazal statue**
Bigger settlements nurtured more complex belief systems. Lime-plaster human figures, buried beneath floors, are possible evidence of early ancestor worship.

THE
ANCIENT
WORLD

ANCIENT HISTORY STRETCHES FROM WHEN THE FIRST CITIES
DEVELOPED AROUND 3000 BCE TO THE FALL OF POWERS SUCH AS
THE ROMAN EMPIRE AND HAN CHINA IN THE FIRST CENTURIES CE.

THE FIRST CIVILIZATIONS

Fertile soil, warm climate, and an ample supply of water, along with agriculture and a stone-working technology, allowed the first urban civilizations to develop. The earliest is thought to have flourished in Mesopotamia (modern-day Iraq) around 3500 BCE.

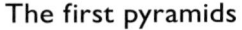

△ **Ram in the thicket**
A fine example of Sumerian craftsmanship, this elaborately crafted statuette of a wild goat searching for food comes from the city-state of Ur in ancient Mesopotamia.

Of all the factors that helped civilizations grow, water was perhaps the most important. The earliest known civilization was born in Sumer, in southern Mesopotamia, in the fertile region between the rivers Tigris and Euphrates. The Sumerians were drawn to the area they settled in because of the abundance of fresh water the rivers provided.

A thriving trading center of the Sumerian civilization, Uruk is generally considered to be the world's first city. It boasted 6 miles of defensive walls and a population that numbered between 40,000 and 80,000 at the height of its glory in 2800 BCE. Other Sumerian city-states that contributed significantly to the civilization included Eridu, Ur, Nippur, Lagash, and Kish. Probably the most important Sumerian invention was the wheel, followed by the development of cuneiform writing.

The first pyramids

Just as the Sumerians depended on the rivers Tigris and Euphrates, the Egyptian civilization could not have come into existence without the Nile. The water from the Nile flooded the plains for 6 months annually, leaving behind a nutrient-rich layer of thick, black silt. This meant that the early Egyptians could cultivate crops, including grains, and fruit and vegetables.

> *"This is the wall of Uruk, which no city on Earth can equal."*
>
> EPIC OF GILGAMESH, c. 2000 BCE

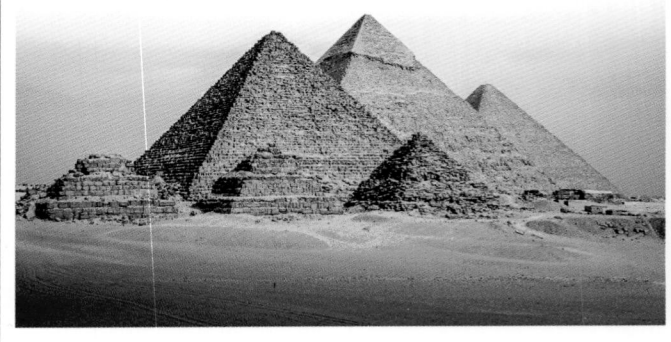

△ **Architectural wonder**
Giza's pyramids were the tombs of three Old Kingdom pharaohs. From left to right, the three large pyramids seen here are the tombs of Menkaure, Khafre, and Khufu.

Around 3400 BCE, two Egyptian kingdoms flourished—Upper Egypt in the Nile Valley and Lower Egypt to the north. Some 300 years later, King Narmer unified the two kingdoms, establishing Memphis as the capital of united Egypt. It was near Memphis, at Saqqara, that the Egyptians built their first pyramid around 2611 BCE. The step pyramid was designed by Imhotep—one of King Djoser's most trusted advisors—as a tomb to house the corpse of his royal master. More than 130 pyramids followed. The most significant of these was the Great Pyramid, constructed at Giza for Khufu, who reigned from 2589 to 2566 BCE. Two more pyramids were erected on the same site for the pharaohs Khafre and Menkaure, Khufu's successors. Although completely unrelated, pyramid-shaped

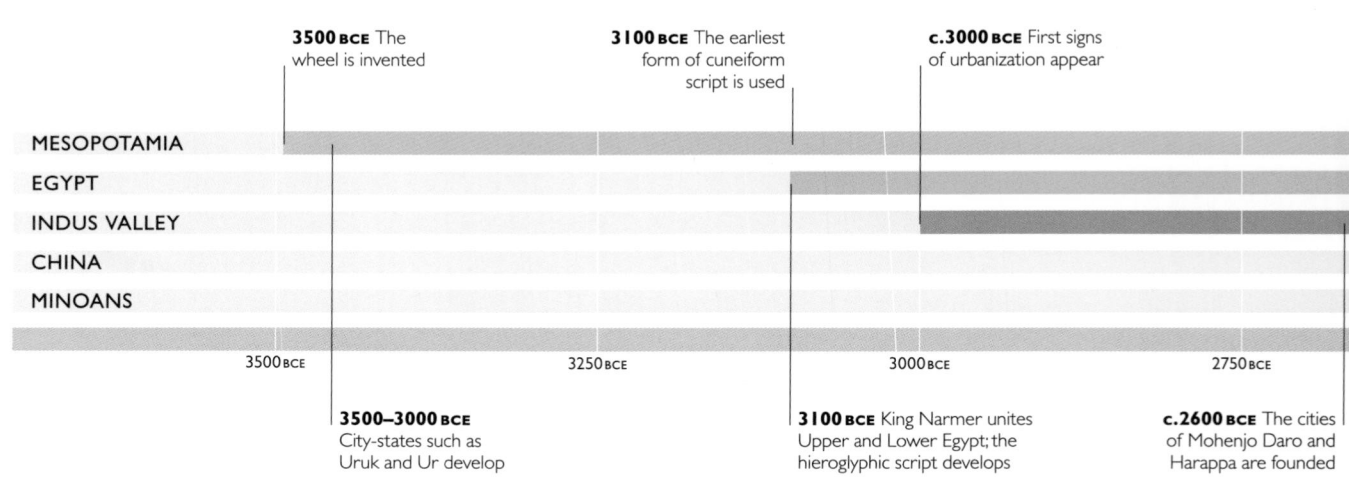

ANCIENT CIVILIZATIONS

City-based civilization is thought to have originated in Mesopotamia (the area between the rivers Euphrates and Tigris), followed by Egypt's Nile Valley. Civilizations grew independently in the fertile basins of the Yellow River in China and the Indus Valley in today's Pakistan and India. In each case, a great river created the conditions for intensive, efficient agriculture. Early cities also grew in Peru, for reasons not yet fully understood. In Europe, the Minoans built highly developed urban settlements centered on grand palaces.

3500 BCE The wheel is invented

3100 BCE The earliest form of cuneiform script is used

c.3000 BCE First signs of urbanization appear

MESOPOTAMIA

EGYPT

INDUS VALLEY

CHINA

MINOANS

3500 BCE   3250 BCE   3000 BCE   2750 BCE

3500–3000 BCE City-states such as Uruk and Ur develop

3100 BCE King Narmer unites Upper and Lower Egypt; the hieroglyphic script develops

c.2600 BCE The cities of Mohenjo Daro and Harappa are founded

▷ **Ritual vessel**
This Chinese bronze food bowl, or *gui*, was probably made between 1300 and 1050 BCE. It was used in Shang religious rituals.

structures were also constructed in what is now Peru by the Norte Chico civilization, builders of the first cities in Americas, sometime before 3000 BCE.

Civilizations of the east

Rivers played an equally important part in the development of civilizations in the Indus Valley (in the northwestern part of south Asia) and northern China. The Indus Valley people are known today as Harappans after Harappa—one of their greatest cities, along with Mohenjo Daro. The Harappans prospered from 3300 to 1900 BCE. Until recently, the Harappans were thought to have been overrun by Aryan invaders from the north, but a more modern theory suggests that tectonic shifts that affected the rivers on which they relied were the cause of the Indus Valley collapse. Yet another theory suggests that the drying up of local rivers led to the culture's decline.

A Chinese civilization flourished along the Huang He, or Yellow River, in the north. As with the Egyptian and Harappan civilizations, here, too, seasonal floods enriched the soil. This encouraged the development of farming, while the river itself provided a useful trade route. By 2000 BCE, bronze-working, silk-weaving, and pottery were being practiced.

The mysterious Minoans

Around the same time that the Chinese civilization was developing, another influential civilization was emerging on the Mediterranean island of Crete. Its people are known as the Minoans, so named by the British archaeologist Sir Arthur Evans to honor Minos, a legendary ruler who may or may not have existed. The Minoans were a great maritime trading power, exporting timber, pottery, and textiles. Trade brought wealth, and they built many palaces—Knossos being the most impressive. The Minoan civilization declined in the late 15th century BCE. Some historians attribute this to a volcanic explosion on the island of Thera (modern-day Santorini), while others argue that it was the result of an invasion by the Mycenaeans from mainland Greece.

▽ **Artistic expression**
This colorful fresco, depicting a Minoan funeral ritual honoring a dead nobleman, decorates a sarcophagus dating from the 14th century BCE.

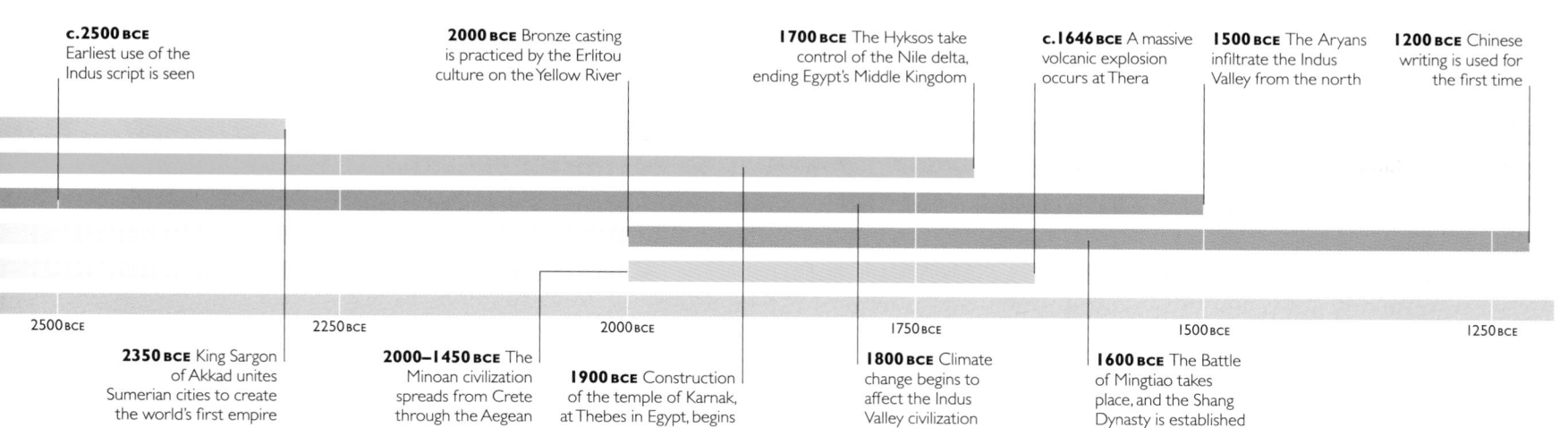

c.2500 BCE Earliest use of the Indus script is seen

2000 BCE Bronze casting is practiced by the Erlitou culture on the Yellow River

1700 BCE The Hyksos take control of the Nile delta, ending Egypt's Middle Kingdom

c.1646 BCE A massive volcanic explosion occurs at Thera

1500 BCE The Aryans infiltrate the Indus Valley from the north

1200 BCE Chinese writing is used for the first time

| 2500 BCE | 2250 BCE | 2000 BCE | 1750 BCE | 1500 BCE | 1250 BCE |

2350 BCE King Sargon of Akkad unites Sumerian cities to create the world's first empire

2000–1450 BCE The Minoan civilization spreads from Crete through the Aegean

1900 BCE Construction of the temple of Karnak, at Thebes in Egypt, begins

1800 BCE Climate change begins to affect the Indus Valley civilization

1600 BCE The Battle of Mingtiao takes place, and the Shang Dynasty is established

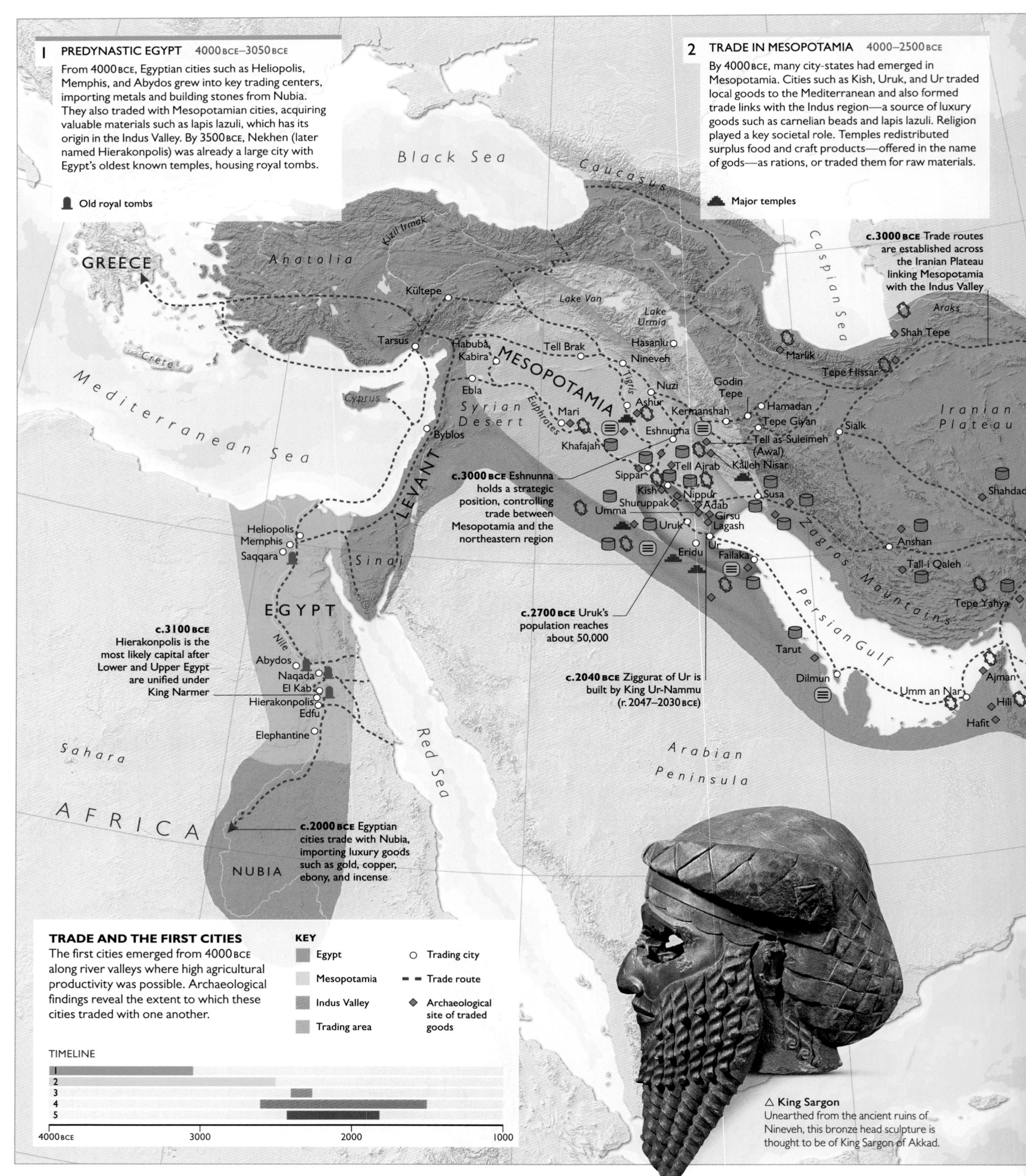

1 PREDYNASTIC EGYPT 4000 BCE–3050 BCE

From 4000 BCE, Egyptian cities such as Heliopolis, Memphis, and Abydos grew into key trading centers, importing metals and building stones from Nubia. They also traded with Mesopotamian cities, acquiring valuable materials such as lapis lazuli, which has its origin in the Indus Valley. By 3500 BCE, Nekhen (later named Hierakonpolis) was already a large city with Egypt's oldest known temples, housing royal tombs.

🪦 Old royal tombs

2 TRADE IN MESOPOTAMIA 4000–2500 BCE

By 4000 BCE, many city-states had emerged in Mesopotamia. Cities such as Kish, Uruk, and Ur traded local goods to the Mediterranean and also formed trade links with the Indus region—a source of luxury goods such as carnelian beads and lapis lazuli. Religion played a key societal role. Temples redistributed surplus food and craft products—offered in the name of gods—as rations, or traded them for raw materials.

🛕 Major temples

c.3000 BCE Trade routes are established across the Iranian Plateau linking Mesopotamia with the Indus Valley

c.3000 BCE Eshnunna holds a strategic position, controlling trade between Mesopotamia and the northeastern region

c.2700 BCE Uruk's population reaches about 50,000

c.2040 BCE Ziggurat of Ur is built by King Ur-Nammu (r. 2047–2030 BCE)

c.3100 BCE Hierakonpolis is the most likely capital after Lower and Upper Egypt are unified under King Narmer

c.2000 BCE Egyptian cities trade with Nubia, importing luxury goods such as gold, copper, ebony, and incense

TRADE AND THE FIRST CITIES

The first cities emerged from 4000 BCE along river valleys where high agricultural productivity was possible. Archaeological findings reveal the extent to which these cities traded with one another.

KEY

- Egypt
- Mesopotamia
- Indus Valley
- Trading area
- ○ Trading city
- - - Trade route
- ◆ Archaeological site of traded goods

TIMELINE

1
2
3
4
5

4000 BCE — 3000 — 2000 — 1000

△ **King Sargon**
Unearthed from the ancient ruins of Nineveh, this bronze head sculpture is thought to be of King Sargon of Akkad.

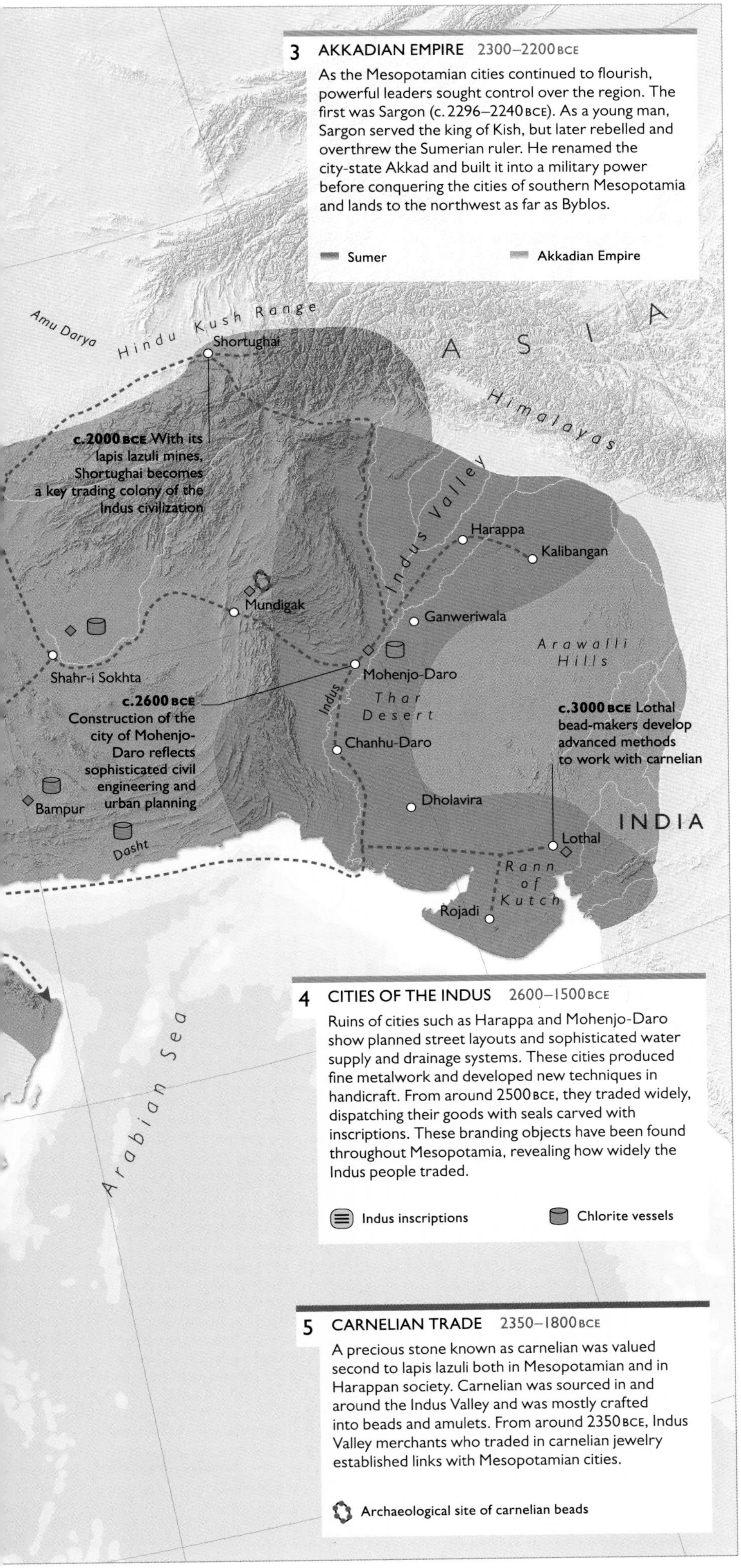

3 AKKADIAN EMPIRE 2300–2200 BCE

As the Mesopotamian cities continued to flourish, powerful leaders sought control over the region. The first was Sargon (c. 2296–2240 BCE). As a young man, Sargon served the king of Kish, but later rebelled and overthrew the Sumerian ruler. He renamed the city-state Akkad and built it into a military power before conquering the cities of southern Mesopotamia and lands to the northwest as far as Byblos.

■ Sumer   ■ Akkadian Empire

c. 2000 BCE With its lapis lazuli mines, Shortughai becomes a key trading colony of the Indus civilization

c. 2600 BCE Construction of the city of Mohenjo-Daro reflects sophisticated civil engineering and urban planning

c. 3000 BCE Lothal bead-makers develop advanced methods to work with carnelian

4 CITIES OF THE INDUS 2600–1500 BCE

Ruins of cities such as Harappa and Mohenjo-Daro show planned street layouts and sophisticated water supply and drainage systems. These cities produced fine metalwork and developed new techniques in handicraft. From around 2500 BCE, they traded widely, dispatching their goods with seals carved with inscriptions. These branding objects have been found throughout Mesopotamia, revealing how widely the Indus people traded.

▤ Indus inscriptions   ⬖ Chlorite vessels

5 CARNELIAN TRADE 2350–1800 BCE

A precious stone known as carnelian was valued second to lapis lazuli both in Mesopotamian and in Harappan society. Carnelian was sourced in and around the Indus Valley and was mostly crafted into beads and amulets. From around 2350 BCE, Indus Valley merchants who traded in carnelian jewelry established links with Mesopotamian cities.

⬡ Archaeological site of carnelian beads

THE FIRST CITIES

The first known cities developed along fertile river plains in Mesopotamia (modern Iraq), Egypt, and the Indus Valley. They became thriving trading centers with an organized social structure, and flourished in the fields of art, craft, and architecture.

By 3000 BCE, agricultural advances led to food surpluses in some parts of the world, namely the river valleys of the Nile in Egypt, the Indus, and the Tigris and Euphrates in Mesopotamia, allowing the communities living in these regions to branch out into a range of craftwork—from metalworking to masonry. This gave rise to the first markets, which channeled wealth into these sites, and in doing

> *"The Mesopotamians viewed their city-states as earthly copies of a divine model and order."*
>
> J. SPIELVOGEL, FROM *WESTERN CIVILIZATION* VOL. 1, 2014

so formed the nucleus of the world's first cities. These urban centers mostly grew on the riverbanks, in close proximity to fertile farmland and sources of clay for brick-making. The rivers served as vital routes for transporting raw material such as timber, precious stones, and metals into the cities. Trade goods also moved over land, in particular across the Levant and the Iranian Plateau, linking the cities of all three regions. Most notably, carnelian beads and seals (branding marks on documents accompanying goods) from the Indus Valley have been found widely in Mesopotamia. Many Mesopotamian cities grew into powerful city-states, some of which eventually became the capitals of some of the earliest known empires.

STANDARD OF UR
MESOPOTAMIAN ARTIFACT, 2600–2400 BCE

Excavated from the royal tombs of Ur in the 1920s, the Standard of Ur is a tapered box decorated with scenes. The original purpose of the artifact remains a mystery, but the images on the two side panels, dubbed the "War Side" and the "Peace Side," form a narrative that offers a vivid insight into the different aspects of life in the ancient city. The scenes also include the earliest known image of wheels used for transportation.

EGYPT OF THE PHARAOHS

Egypt was among the most enduring civilizations in the ancient world. With its succession of powerful rulers, unique religion and art, and trading networks, the culture exerted its influence in the Nile Valley and beyond for more than 3,000 years.

From c. 2700 to 1085 BCE, Egypt's kings, or pharaohs, ruled the Nile Valley for three long, separate periods, named by historians the Old, Middle, and New Kingdoms.

Egypt's ancient civilization grew along the banks of the River Nile, which was the main artery for travel and trade. The river was also rich in fish and flooded annually, covering the banks with fertile mud, making for a highly productive agricultural region. While Egypt's pharaohs ruled over this riverside zone, their influence spread much farther afield, mainly through land and sea trading expeditions, which became more widespread in the Middle and New Kingdom eras. The Egyptians developed their own system of writing, and the pharaohs bolstered their wealth by employing scribes to record goods traded and to ensure taxes were collected.

The Egyptian people worshipped multiple gods and also regarded the pharaohs as deities, which lent spiritual weight to the ruling power. The strength of the pharaohs' authority is evident in the impressive burial sites built during the ancient era, including the pyramids of the Old Kingdom and the colossal temples and tombs of the later kingdoms.

> *"The All-Lord himself made me great. He gave to me the land while I was in the egg."*
>
> RAMESSES II, PHARAOH OF THE NEW KINGDOM, 1279–1213 BCE

REGION UNDER EGYPTIAN CONTROL

The maps show the boundaries of the Old, Middle, and New Kingdoms of Ancient Egypt and include the trade routes that linked the sites of oases, cities, the great temples, forts, and pyramids.

KEY

🌴🌴 Oasis

TIMELINE

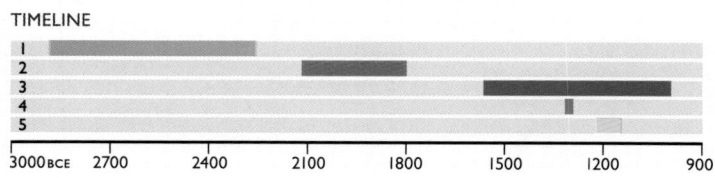

| 3000 BCE | 2700 | 2400 | 2100 | 1800 | 1500 | 1200 | 900 |

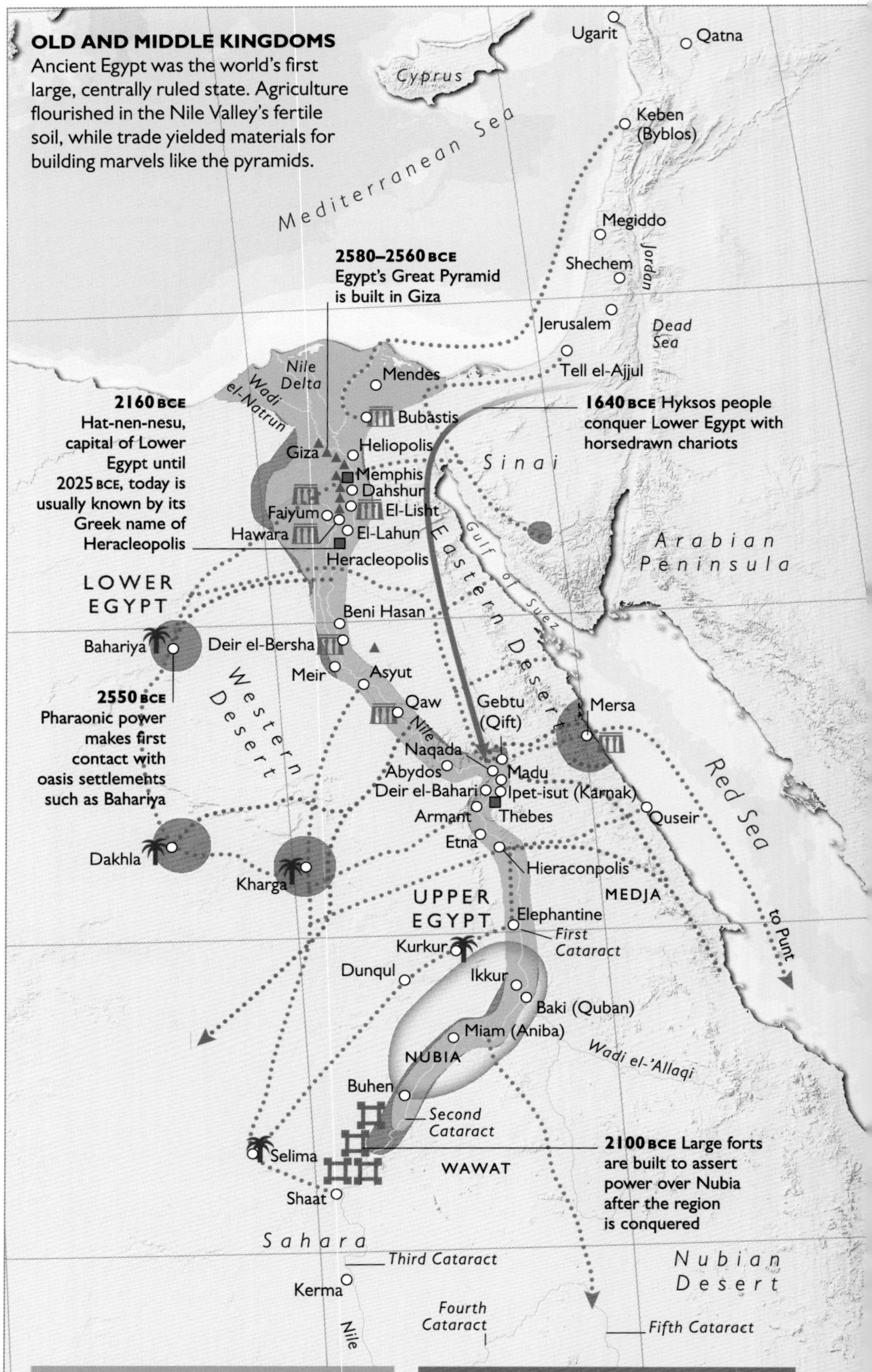

OLD AND MIDDLE KINGDOMS

Ancient Egypt was the world's first large, centrally ruled state. Agriculture flourished in the Nile Valley's fertile soil, while trade yielded materials for building marvels like the pyramids.

2580–2560 BCE Egypt's Great Pyramid is built in Giza

2160 BCE Hat-nen-nesu, capital of Lower Egypt until 2025 BCE, today is usually known by its Greek name of Heracleopolis

1640 BCE Hyksos people conquer Lower Egypt with horsedrawn chariots

2550 BCE Pharaonic power makes first contact with oasis settlements such as Bahariya

2100 BCE Large forts are built to assert power over Nubia after the region is conquered

Mediterranean Sea

Cyprus • Ugarit • Qatna

Keben (Byblos)

Megiddo

Shechem

Jerusalem

Dead Sea

Tell el-Ajjul

Nile Delta • Mendes

Bubastis

Heliopolis

Giza

Memphis • Dahshur

Faiyum • El-Lisht

Hawara • El-Lahun

Heracleopolis

Sinai

Arabian Peninsula

LOWER EGYPT

Bahariya • Deir el-Bersha

Beni Hasan

Meir • Asyut

Western Desert

Qaw

Naqada • Gebtu (Qift) • Mersa

Abydos • Madu

Deir el-Bahari • Ipet-isut (Karnak)

Armant • Thebes

Dakhla

Kharga

Etna

Hieraconpolis • Quseir

UPPER EGYPT

Elephantine — *First Cataract*

Kurkur

Dunqul • Ikkur

Baki (Quban)

Miam (Aniba)

MEDJA

Wadi el-'Allaqi

Buhen

Second Cataract

Selima

WAWAT

Shaat

Sahara

Third Cataract

Kerma

Fourth Cataract

Fifth Cataract

Nubian Desert

Nile

Gulf of Suez

Eastern Desert

Red Sea

to Punt

NUBIA

1 OLD KINGDOM 2700–2180 BCE

By 2700 BCE, a succession of rulers had centralized their power in Egypt and governed from the capital, Memphis. The grand pyramids built during this era were symbolic of their power. The valley prospered as merchants traveled into the Western Desert and along the Red Sea coast to ply their trade. However, in 2180 BCE, a period of low flood and the ensuing famine resulted in Egypt splitting into two realms—Upper and Lower Egypt.

Region of control	Kingdom capital
▲ Pyramid	••• Trade routes

2 MIDDLE KINGDOM 2040–1786 BCE

By 2040 BCE, the rulers of Thebes had grown increasingly powerful and become rulers of all of Egypt. Their domain was slightly larger than that of the Old Kingdom, and their merchants traveled farther to establish new trade links. In 1640 BCE, pharaonic rule ended (for just over a century) when the Hyksos people, from the Levant, conquered Lower Egypt.

Additional region of control	🏛 Temple
→ Hyksos invasion	⌸ Fort
•••→ Trade routes	Nubian chiefdoms

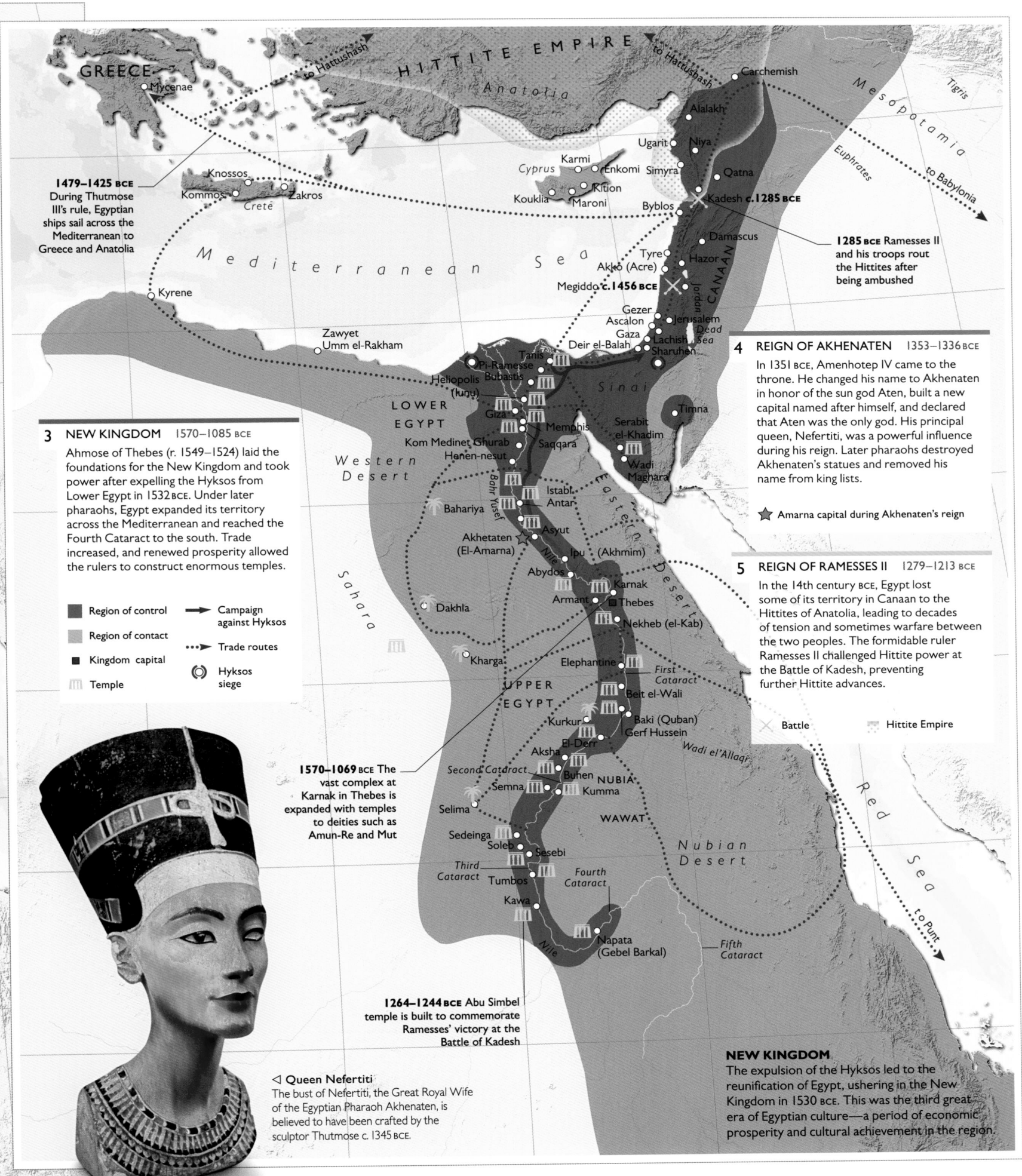

1479–1425 BCE During Thutmose III's rule, Egyptian ships sail across the Mediterranean to Greece and Anatolia

1285 BCE Ramesses II and his troops rout the Hittites after being ambushed

4 REIGN OF AKHENATEN 1353–1336 BCE

In 1351 BCE, Amenhotep IV came to the throne. He changed his name to Akhenaten in honor of the sun god Aten, built a new capital named after himself, and declared that Aten was the only god. His principal queen, Nefertiti, was a powerful influence during his reign. Later pharaohs destroyed Akhenaten's statues and removed his name from king lists.

⭐ Amarna capital during Akhenaten's reign

3 NEW KINGDOM 1570–1085 BCE

Ahmose of Thebes (r. 1549–1524) laid the foundations for the New Kingdom and took power after expelling the Hyksos from Lower Egypt in 1532 BCE. Under later pharaohs, Egypt expanded its territory across the Mediterranean and reached the Fourth Cataract to the south. Trade increased, and renewed prosperity allowed the rulers to construct enormous temples.

- ■ Region of control
- ▨ Region of contact
- ■ Kingdom capital
- ▥ Temple
- → Campaign against Hyksos
- ···▶ Trade routes
- ◎ Hyksos siege

5 REIGN OF RAMESSES II 1279–1213 BCE

In the 14th century BCE, Egypt lost some of its territory in Canaan to the Hittites of Anatolia, leading to decades of tension and sometimes warfare between the two peoples. The formidable ruler Ramesses II challenged Hittite power at the Battle of Kadesh, preventing further Hittite advances.

✕ Battle ▨ Hittite Empire

1570–1069 BCE The vast complex at Karnak in Thebes is expanded with temples to deities such as Amun-Re and Mut

1264–1244 BCE Abu Simbel temple is built to commemorate Ramesses' victory at the Battle of Kadesh

◁ **Queen Nefertiti**
The bust of Nefertiti, the Great Royal Wife of the Egyptian Pharaoh Akhenaten, is believed to have been crafted by the sculptor Thutmose c. 1345 BCE.

NEW KINGDOM
The expulsion of the Hyksos led to the reunification of Egypt, ushering in the New Kingdom in 1530 BCE. This was the third great era of Egyptian culture—a period of economic prosperity and cultural achievement in the region.

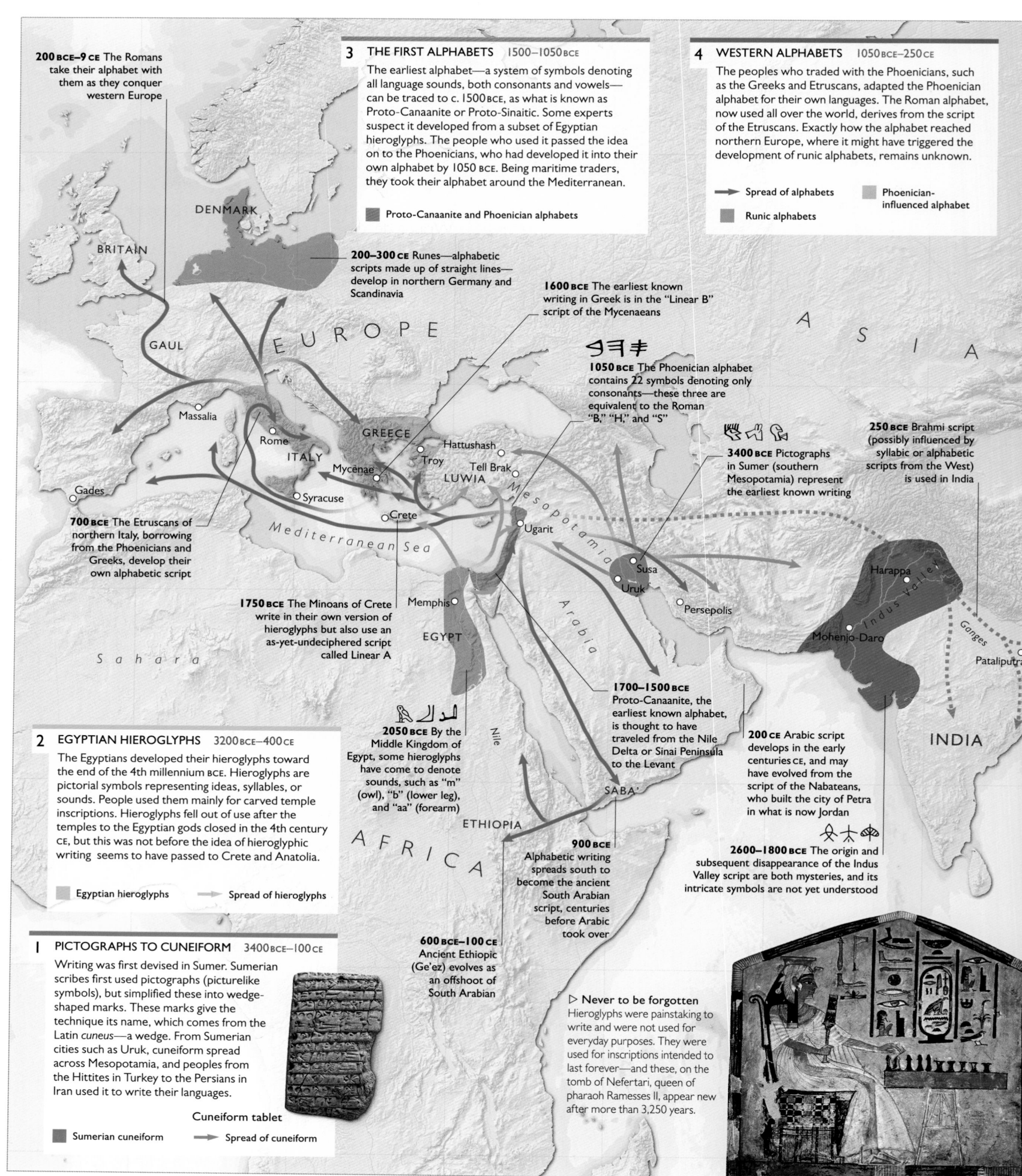

200 BCE–9 CE The Romans take their alphabet with them as they conquer western Europe

3 THE FIRST ALPHABETS 1500–1050 BCE

The earliest alphabet—a system of symbols denoting all language sounds, both consonants and vowels—can be traced to c. 1500 BCE, as what is known as Proto-Canaanite or Proto-Sinaitic. Some experts suspect it developed from a subset of Egyptian hieroglyphs. The people who used it passed the idea on to the Phoenicians, who had developed it into their own alphabet by 1050 BCE. Being maritime traders, they took their alphabet around the Mediterranean.

■ Proto-Canaanite and Phoenician alphabets

4 WESTERN ALPHABETS 1050 BCE–250 CE

The peoples who traded with the Phoenicians, such as the Greeks and Etruscans, adapted the Phoenician alphabet for their own languages. The Roman alphabet, now used all over the world, derives from the script of the Etruscans. Exactly how the alphabet reached northern Europe, where it might have triggered the development of runic alphabets, remains unknown.

→ Spread of alphabets

■ Runic alphabets

■ Phoenician-influenced alphabet

200–300 CE Runes—alphabetic scripts made up of straight lines—develop in northern Germany and Scandinavia

1600 BCE The earliest known writing in Greek is in the "Linear B" script of the Mycenaeans

1050 BCE The Phoenician alphabet contains 22 symbols denoting only consonants—these three are equivalent to the Roman "B," "H," and "S"

3400 BCE Pictographs in Sumer (southern Mesopotamia) represent the earliest known writing

250 BCE Brahmi script (possibly influenced by syllabic or alphabetic scripts from the West) is used in India

700 BCE The Etruscans of northern Italy, borrowing from the Phoenicians and Greeks, develop their own alphabetic script

1750 BCE The Minoans of Crete write in their own version of hieroglyphs but also use an as-yet-undeciphered script called Linear A

1700–1500 BCE Proto-Canaanite, the earliest known alphabet, is thought to have traveled from the Nile Delta or Sinai Peninsula to the Levant

200 CE Arabic script develops in the early centuries CE, and may have evolved from the script of the Nabateans, who built the city of Petra in what is now Jordan

2600–1800 BCE The origin and subsequent disappearance of the Indus Valley script are both mysteries, and its intricate symbols are not yet understood

2 EGYPTIAN HIEROGLYPHS 3200 BCE–400 CE

The Egyptians developed their hieroglyphs toward the end of the 4th millennium BCE. Hieroglyphs are pictorial symbols representing ideas, syllables, or sounds. People used them mainly for carved temple inscriptions. Hieroglyphs fell out of use after the temples to the Egyptian gods closed in the 4th century CE, but this was not before the idea of hieroglyphic writing seems to have passed to Crete and Anatolia.

■ Egyptian hieroglyphs

→ Spread of hieroglyphs

2050 BCE By the Middle Kingdom of Egypt, some hieroglyphs have come to denote sounds, such as "m" (owl), "b" (lower leg), and "aa" (forearm)

900 BCE Alphabetic writing spreads south to become the ancient South Arabian script, centuries before Arabic took over

600 BCE–100 CE Ancient Ethiopic (Ge'ez) evolves as an offshoot of South Arabian

1 PICTOGRAPHS TO CUNEIFORM 3400 BCE–100 CE

Writing was first devised in Sumer. Sumerian scribes first used pictographs (picturelike symbols), but simplified these into wedge-shaped marks. These marks give the technique its name, which comes from the Latin *cuneus*—a wedge. From Sumerian cities such as Uruk, cuneiform spread across Mesopotamia, and peoples from the Hittites in Turkey to the Persians in Iran used it to write their languages.

Cuneiform tablet

■ Sumerian cuneiform

→ Spread of cuneiform

▷ **Never to be forgotten**
Hieroglyphs were painstaking to write and were not used for everyday purposes. They were used for inscriptions intended to last forever—and these, on the tomb of Nefertari, queen of pharaoh Ramesses II, appear new after more than 3,250 years.

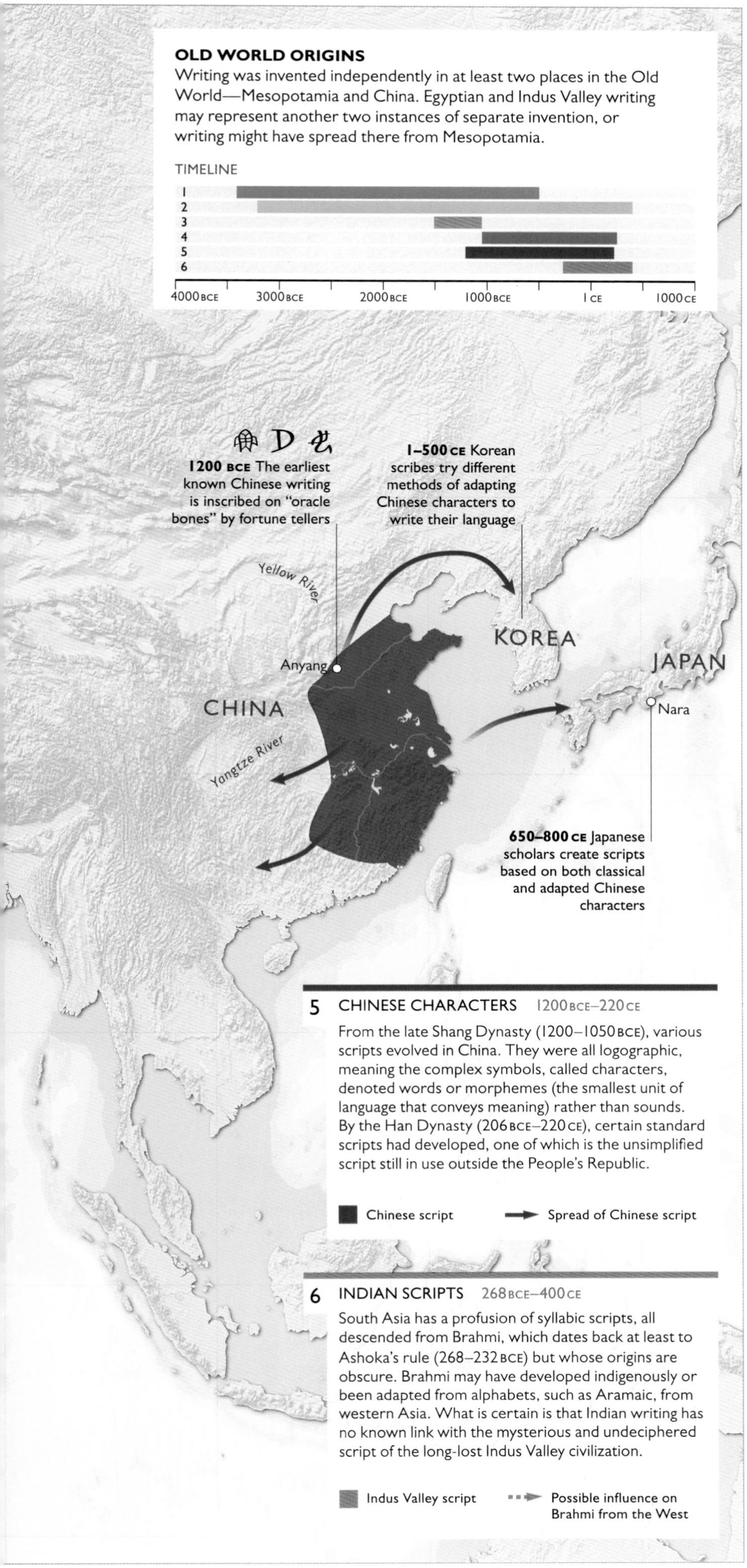

OLD WORLD ORIGINS

Writing was invented independently in at least two places in the Old World—Mesopotamia and China. Egyptian and Indus Valley writing may represent another two instances of separate invention, or writing might have spread there from Mesopotamia.

TIMELINE

4000 BCE 3000 BCE 2000 BCE 1000 BCE 1 CE 1000 CE

1200 BCE The earliest known Chinese writing is inscribed on "oracle bones" by fortune tellers

1–500 CE Korean scribes try different methods of adapting Chinese characters to write their language

Yellow River

KOREA

Anyang

JAPAN

CHINA

Nara

Yangtze River

650–800 CE Japanese scholars create scripts based on both classical and adapted Chinese characters

5 CHINESE CHARACTERS 1200 BCE–220 CE

From the late Shang Dynasty (1200–1050 BCE), various scripts evolved in China. They were all logographic, meaning the complex symbols, called characters, denoted words or morphemes (the smallest unit of language that conveys meaning) rather than sounds. By the Han Dynasty (206 BCE–220 CE), certain standard scripts had developed, one of which is the unsimplified script still in use outside the People's Republic.

■ Chinese script   → Spread of Chinese script

6 INDIAN SCRIPTS 268 BCE–400 CE

South Asia has a profusion of syllabic scripts, all descended from Brahmi, which dates back at least to Ashoka's rule (268–232 BCE) but whose origins are obscure. Brahmi may have developed indigenously or been adapted from alphabets, such as Aramaic, from western Asia. What is certain is that Indian writing has no known link with the mysterious and undeciphered script of the long-lost Indus Valley civilization.

▨ Indus Valley script   ▪▪▶ Possible influence on Brahmi from the West

THE FIRST WRITING

Writing developed first in c. 3400 BCE in western Asia, but also independently in China, Mesoamerica, and possibly the Indus Valley. From the start, symbols represented spoken language in different ways—either as words and ideas, the language's sounds, or a mixture of both.

By the 4th millennium BCE, cities had developed in Egypt, China, the Indus Valley, and Mesopotamia. The societies that built these cities traded on a large scale and had complex, organized religions. Both of these developments encouraged literacy—for writing accounts and goods traded or for recording calendars and sacred lore.

The earliest writing—in Mesopotamia—began as pictures scratched on damp clay tablets that were then baked in the sun to create a permanent document. Slowly, these evolved into "cuneiform" symbols made of wedges. Many surviving cuneiform tablets list goods or contain tax records, although there are also religious and literary works written with the technique. Around the same time, the Egyptians developed their hieroglyphs and later, the Chinese evolved their written characters, both of which were used for religious purposes initially. Alphabetic scripts, which originated in Sinai or the Levant, caught on widely as the Phoenicians disseminated their version. Alphabets needed only 20–30 symbols, as opposed to the hundreds used in syllabic scripts or the thousands in Chinese.

"Do not answer back against your father."

FROM THE SUMERIAN *INSTRUCTIONS OF SHURUPPAK*—PERHAPS THE WORLD'S EARLIEST SURVIVING LITERATURE, c. 2600 BCE

MESOAMERICAN SCRIPTS
WRITING OF THE OLMECS, ZAPOTECS, AND MAYA

Civilizations in Mesoamerica invented their own writing systems, but they did not spread beyond the region. Inscriptions date back to the mysterious Cascajal Block, possibly carved by Olmecs around 800 BCE. The Zapotecs used a pictographic script from at least 400 BCE and were followed by the Maya, whose intricate symbols, or glyphs (right), combined logograms (denoting ideas) and syllabic script. Maya glyphs came into use c. 300 BCE and remained current until the Spanish conquest (see pp.152–153).

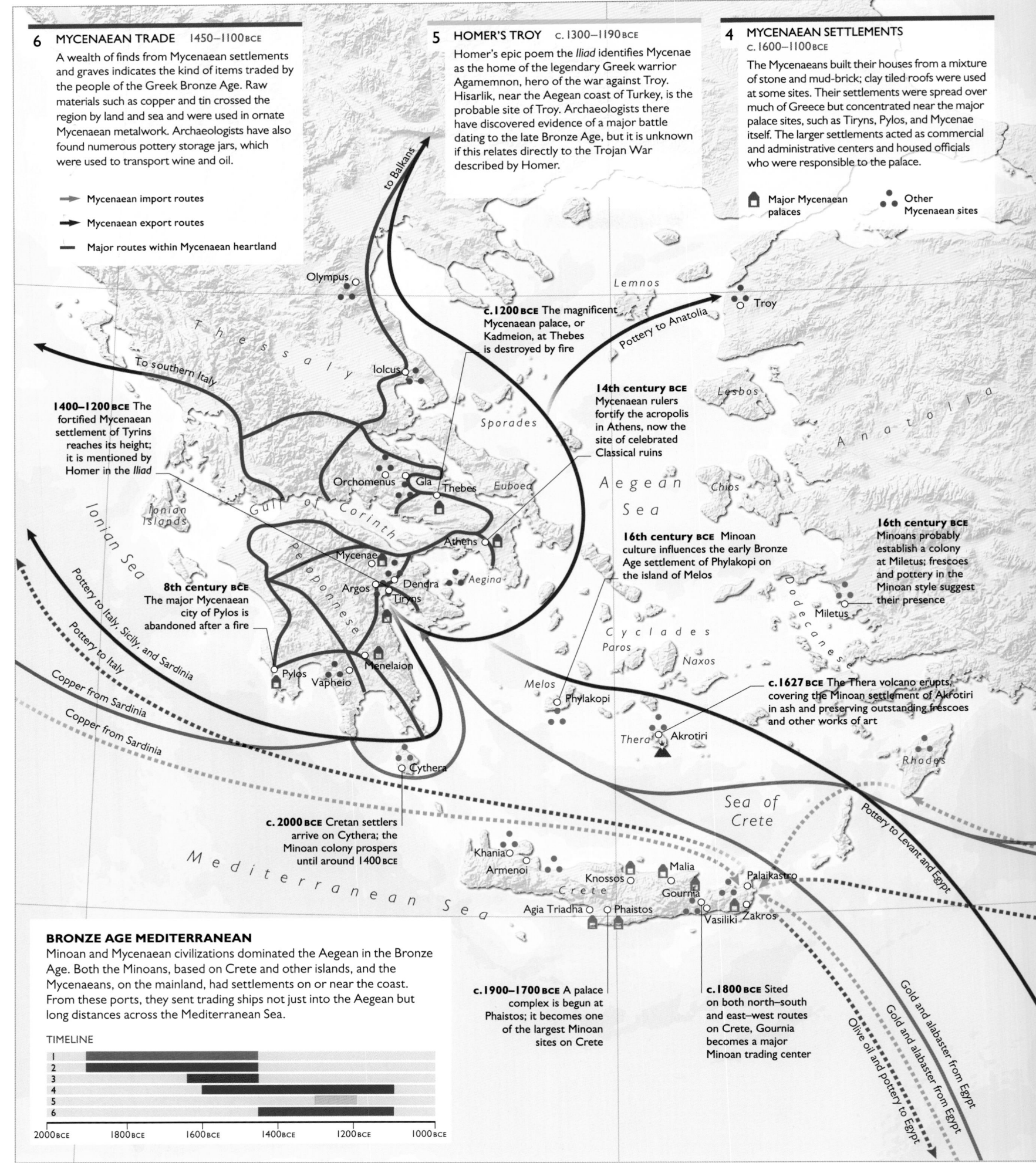

6 MYCENAEAN TRADE 1450–1100 BCE

A wealth of finds from Mycenaean settlements and graves indicates the kind of items traded by the people of the Greek Bronze Age. Raw materials such as copper and tin crossed the region by land and sea and were used in ornate Mycenaean metalwork. Archaeologists have also found numerous pottery storage jars, which were used to transport wine and oil.

→ Mycenaean import routes

→ Mycenaean export routes

— Major routes within Mycenaean heartland

5 HOMER'S TROY c. 1300–1190 BCE

Homer's epic poem the *Iliad* identifies Mycenae as the home of the legendary Greek warrior Agamemnon, hero of the war against Troy. Hisarlik, near the Aegean coast of Turkey, is the probable site of Troy. Archaeologists there have discovered evidence of a major battle dating to the late Bronze Age, but it is unknown if this relates directly to the Trojan War described by Homer.

4 MYCENAEAN SETTLEMENTS c. 1600–1100 BCE

The Mycenaeans built their houses from a mixture of stone and mud-brick; clay tiled roofs were used at some sites. Their settlements were spread over much of Greece but concentrated near the major palace sites, such as Tiryns, Pylos, and Mycenae itself. The larger settlements acted as commercial and administrative centers and housed officials who were responsible to the palace.

🏠 Major Mycenaean palaces   ● Other Mycenaean sites

c. 1200 BCE The magnificent Mycenaean palace, or Kadmeion, at Thebes is destroyed by fire

14th century BCE Mycenaean rulers fortify the acropolis in Athens, now the site of celebrated Classical ruins

1400–1200 BCE The fortified Mycenaean settlement of Tyrins reaches its height; it is mentioned by Homer in the *Iliad*

16th century BCE Minoan culture influences the early Bronze Age settlement of Phylakopi on the island of Melos

16th century BCE Minoans probably establish a colony at Miletus; frescoes and pottery in the Minoan style suggest their presence

8th century BCE The major Mycenaean city of Pylos is abandoned after a fire

c. 1627 BCE The Thera volcano erupts, covering the Minoan settlement of Akrotiri in ash and preserving outstanding frescoes and other works of art

c. 2000 BCE Cretan settlers arrive on Cythera; the Minoan colony prospers until around 1400 BCE

c. 1900–1700 BCE A palace complex is begun at Phaistos; it becomes one of the largest Minoan sites on Crete

c. 1800 BCE Sited on both north–south and east–west routes on Crete, Gournia becomes a major Minoan trading center

To southern Italy

Pottery to Italy, Sicily, and Sardinia

Pottery to Italy

Copper from Sardinia

Copper from Sardinia

Pottery to Anatolia

Pottery to Levant and Egypt

Gold and alabaster from Egypt

Gold and alabaster from Egypt

Olive oil and pottery to Egypt

to Balkans

Thessaly · *Sporades* · *Euboea* · *Aegean Sea* · *Lesbos* · *Chios* · *Anatolia* · *Ionian Islands* · *Ionian Sea* · *Peloponnese* · *Gulf of Corinth* · *Cyclades* · *Dodecanese* · *Sea of Crete* · *Mediterranean Sea* · *Crete*

Olympus · Iolcus · Orchomenus · Gla · Thebes · Athens · Mycenae · Argos · Dendra · Tiryns · Aegina · Pylos · Vapheio · Menelaion · Cythera · Melos · Phylakopi · Thera · Akrotiri · Rhodes · Miletus · Paros · Naxos · Lemnos · Troy · Khania · Armenoi · Knossos · Malia · Agia Triadha · Phaistos · Gournia · Vasiliki · Zakros · Palaikastro

BRONZE AGE MEDITERRANEAN

Minoan and Mycenaean civilizations dominated the Aegean in the Bronze Age. Both the Minoans, based on Crete and other islands, and the Mycenaeans, on the mainland, had settlements on or near the coast. From these ports, they sent trading ships not just into the Aegean but long distances across the Mediterranean Sea.

TIMELINE

1					
2					
3					
4					
5					
6					

2000 BCE — 1800 BCE — 1600 BCE — 1400 BCE — 1200 BCE — 1000 BCE

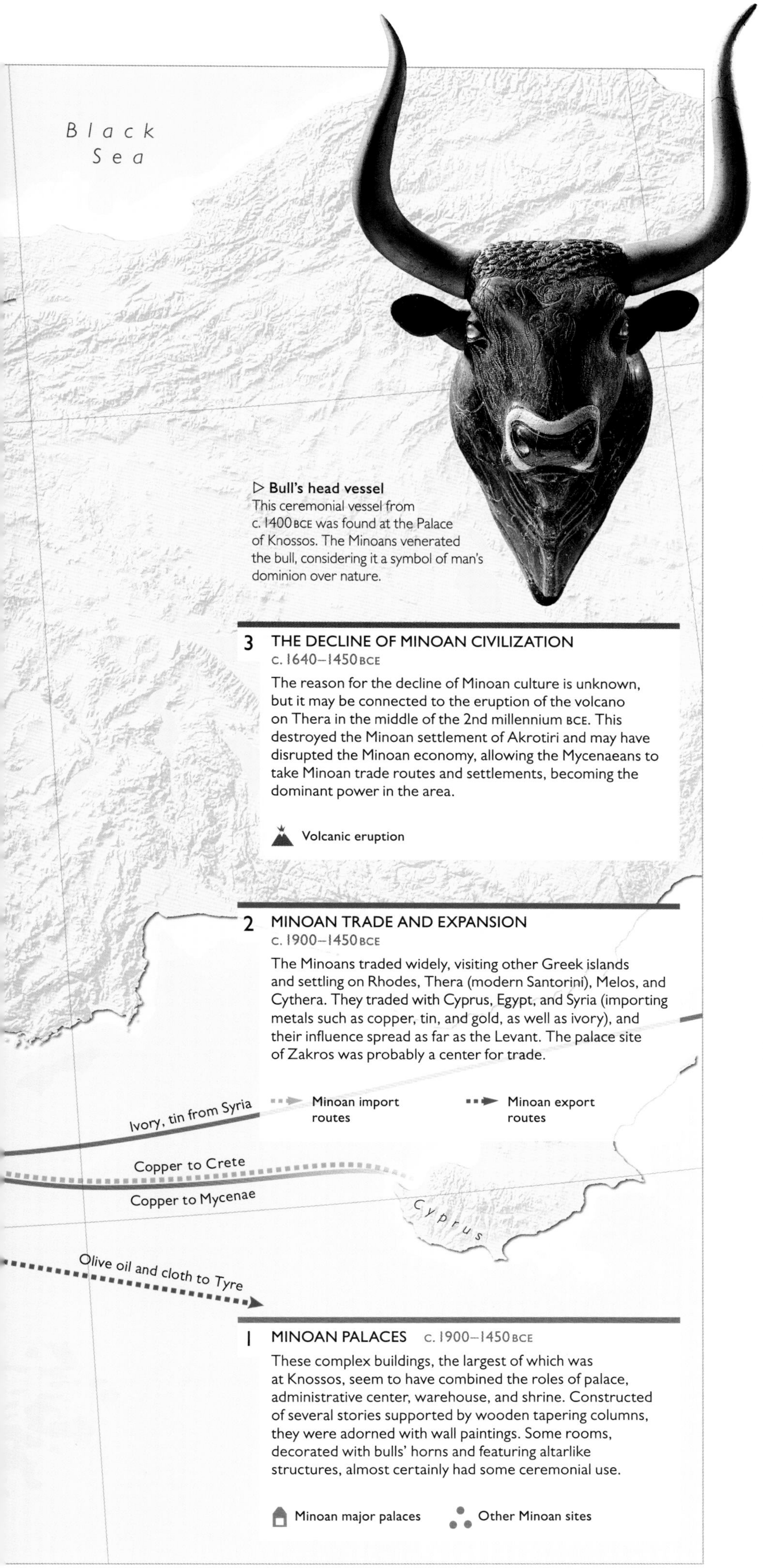

MINOANS AND MYCENAEANS

During the Bronze Age, first the Minoan and then the Mycenaean cultures dominated Greece and the Aegean. These peoples developed a range of skills—such as metalworking, architecture, and literacy—that laid the foundations for the later Classical civilization of Greece.

The Minoan culture—considered by some to be the first European civilization—flourished on Crete in the 2nd millennium BCE. Many mysteries still surround the Minoans; scholars have been unable to decipher their writing, so do not know their exact dates, or even what they called themselves—the word "Minoan" is a modern term of convenience. But they are known to have been highly influential in trading across the Mediterranean, leaving inscriptions at several places on the Greek mainland, as well as on some islands in the Aegean. Minoan civilization was centered on several large, elegantly decorated Cretan palaces that were not fortified, suggesting they were a peaceful people.

From the mid-15th century BCE, the Mycenaeans—based on mainland Greece—became the dominant power. They were a trading people, exchanging goods with mainland Italy, Sicily, and Sardinia. They also wielded military power, as seen by their fortified palaces, and impressive weaponry and armor. Their script, known as Linear B (probably derived from Cretan Linear A) has been deciphered and was used to write an early form of Greek.

The Mycenaeans created several independent states in mainland Greece with settlements on many of the islands. Each state centered on a palace, and most were capable of major engineering projects, such as stone fortifications, harbors, dams, and roads. Disputes between the states may have contributed to the decline of the Mycenaean civilization after about 1100 BCE.

Black Sea

▷ **Bull's head vessel**
This ceremonial vessel from c. 1400 BCE was found at the Palace of Knossos. The Minoans venerated the bull, considering it a symbol of man's dominion over nature.

3 THE DECLINE OF MINOAN CIVILIZATION
c. 1640–1450 BCE

The reason for the decline of Minoan culture is unknown, but it may be connected to the eruption of the volcano on Thera in the middle of the 2nd millennium BCE. This destroyed the Minoan settlement of Akrotiri and may have disrupted the Minoan economy, allowing the Mycenaeans to take Minoan trade routes and settlements, becoming the dominant power in the area.

🌋 Volcanic eruption

2 MINOAN TRADE AND EXPANSION
c. 1900–1450 BCE

The Minoans traded widely, visiting other Greek islands and settling on Rhodes, Thera (modern Santorini), Melos, and Cythera. They traded with Cyprus, Egypt, and Syria (importing metals such as copper, tin, and gold, as well as ivory), and their influence spread as far as the Levant. The palace site of Zakros was probably a center for trade.

Ivory, tin from Syria

Copper to Crete

Copper to Mycenae

Cyprus

Olive oil and cloth to Tyre

┄┄➤ Minoan import routes   ┅┅➤ Minoan export routes

1 MINOAN PALACES   c. 1900–1450 BCE

These complex buildings, the largest of which was at Knossos, seem to have combined the roles of palace, administrative center, warehouse, and shrine. Constructed of several stories supported by wooden tapering columns, they were adorned with wall paintings. Some rooms, decorated with bulls' horns and featuring altarlike structures, almost certainly had some ceremonial use.

🏠 Minoan major palaces   ⁝ Other Minoan sites

KNOSSOS
EUROPE'S OLDEST CITY

At its height, Minoan Knossos was a large city of 10,000–100,000 people. At its heart was the palace complex, which had 1,300 rooms covering some 6 acres (2.4 hectares). As well as large, beautifully decorated residential or ceremonial rooms, there were many rooms set aside for storage. These rooms contained hundreds of large jars for oil, grain, or other foods. Grain mills also formed part of the palace complex.

Fresco fragment
The walls of the palace at Knossos were decorated with images of animals, mythological creatures, and people.

BRONZE AGE CHINA

Chinese culture began to take on its distinctive form in the Bronze Age, from about 1600 BCE onward, with the development of writing during the Shang Dynasty and its successor, the Zhou. Politically, China was still a collection of separate states, with one or more of the states taking a leading role at different times.

Most historians date the Bronze Age in China to c. 2000–c. 770 BCE, although the widespread use of bronze continued for centuries. The period coincides with the beginnings of literacy in China and with the rule of two influential dynasties, the Shang (c. 1600–1027 BCE) and the Zhou (1046–256 BCE).

The Shang controlled much of northern China, creating a feudal system with a core state and a number of vassal states. Its rulers cemented their power using rituals such as ancestor worship and divination using "oracle bones" (bones incised with written messages). The Shang moved their capital city several times, the last and largest being at Anyang, where archaeologists have uncovered a royal tomb containing bronze artifacts and oracle bones. They extended their influence through trade with northern and central Chinese neighbors, and with people of the steppes to the west.

Around the 11th century BCE, Ji Chang of the Zhou—a people from the Shang's western border—led a rebellion, and the Shang were conquered. The Zhou developed systems of coinage, and writing evolved into something closer to the modern Chinese script. Two of the most influential philosophers of all time, Confucius and Laozi, were active under the Zhou Dynasty.

SHANG CHINA

Before the Shang, the Yellow River valley was occupied by sophisticated cultures for centuries. The region became the Shang's heartland, where they made vassals of a number of local states.

KEY

● Shang city ••• Trade route ⇨ Main Shang campaign

TIMELINE

1
2
3
4

2200 BCE | 2000 | 1800 | 1600 | 1400 | 1200 | 1000

◁ **Shang bronze work**
This owl-shaped vessel exemplifies the exquisite patterns with which Shang metalworkers decorated their products; these included tableware, such as food and drinking vessels.

Yellow River

2nd millennium BCE
A western trade route links China with central Asia; it is a forerunner of the Silk Road between eastern and western Asia

BEFORE THE SHANG c. 2070–1600 BCE

A series of neolithic cultures predate the Shang in China—archaeologists have, for example, revealed the remains of the Longshan culture in the Yellow River valley and the Yueshi culture in the Shandong region. Other sites, such as Erlitou with its impressive buildings, tombs, and paved roads, point to more sophisticated cultures, such as the Xia Dynasty (who are thought to have existed from 2070 BCE).

★ Possible Xia capital ▬ Yueshi culture, c. 1900–1500 BCE
▬ Longshan culture, c. 3000–2000 BCE

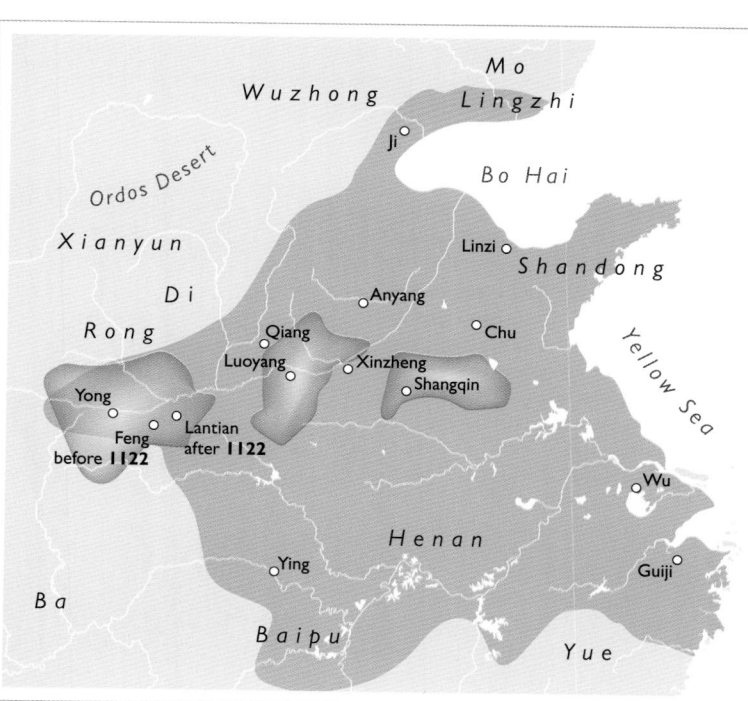

Mo
Wuzhong
Lingzhi
Ji
Bo Hai
Ordos Desert
Xianyun
Linzi
Shandong
Di
Anyang
Rong
Qiang
Chu
Luoyang
Xinzheng
Yong
Shangqin
Feng before 1122
Lantian after 1122
Yellow Sea
Ba
Ying
Wu
Henan
Guiji
Baipu
Yue

ZHOU CHINA

Zhou began as a vassal state in the far west of the Shang Empire. Toward the end of the Shang period, the Zhou challenged their overlords, moving eastward and establishing strongholds along the Yellow River before removing the Shang rulers by 1046 BCE. By 1000 BCE, their influence was felt across most of China, including the Shang's neighboring peoples, the Baipu, and encompassed the whole area to which urban civilization had spread.

KEY

▬ Distribution of urban civilization by c. 1000 BCE

▬ Zhou strongholds

○ Zhou capitals

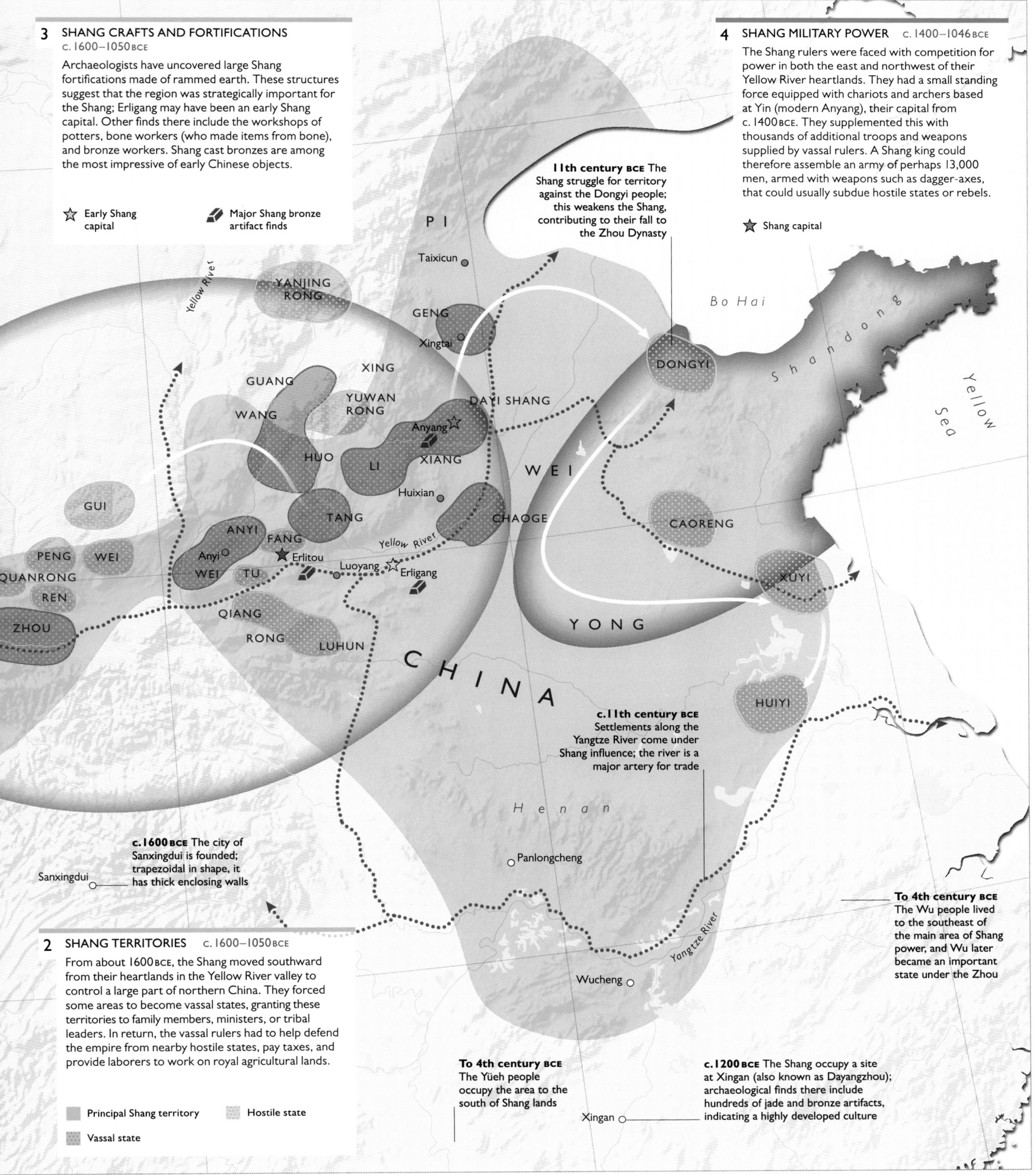

3 SHANG CRAFTS AND FORTIFICATIONS
c. 1600–1050 BCE

Archaeologists have uncovered large Shang fortifications made of rammed earth. These structures suggest that the region was strategically important for the Shang; Erligang may have been an early Shang capital. Other finds there include the workshops of potters, bone workers (who made items from bone), and bronze workers. Shang cast bronzes are among the most impressive of early Chinese objects.

☆ Early Shang capital

🔶 Major Shang bronze artifact finds

4 SHANG MILITARY POWER c. 1400–1046 BCE

The Shang rulers were faced with competition for power in both the east and northwest of their Yellow River heartlands. They had a small standing force equipped with chariots and archers based at Yin (modern Anyang), their capital from c. 1400 BCE. They supplemented this with thousands of additional troops and weapons supplied by vassal rulers. A Shang king could therefore assemble an army of perhaps 13,000 men, armed with weapons such as dagger-axes, that could usually subdue hostile states or rebels.

⬡ Shang capital

11th century BCE The Shang struggle for territory against the Dongyi people; this weakens the Shang, contributing to their fall to the Zhou Dynasty

c. 11th century BCE
Settlements along the Yangtze River come under Shang influence; the river is a major artery for trade

c. 1600 BCE The city of Sanxingdui is founded; trapezoidal in shape, it has thick enclosing walls

2 SHANG TERRITORIES c. 1600–1050 BCE

From about 1600 BCE, the Shang moved southward from their heartlands in the Yellow River valley to control a large part of northern China. They forced some areas to become vassal states, granting these territories to family members, ministers, or tribal leaders. In return, the vassal rulers had to help defend the empire from nearby hostile states, pay taxes, and provide laborers to work on royal agricultural lands.

▦ Principal Shang territory

▦ Vassal state

▦ Hostile state

To 4th century BCE
The Yüeh people occupy the area to the south of Shang lands

c. 1200 BCE The Shang occupy a site at Xingan (also known as Dayangzhou); archaeological finds there include hundreds of jade and bronze artifacts, indicating a highly developed culture

To 4th century BCE
The Wu people lived to the southeast of the main area of Shang power, and Wu later became an important state under the Zhou

BRONZE AGE COLLAPSE

Between 1225 and 1175 BCE, several Bronze Age societies of the eastern Mediterranean collapsed. Citadels across the region were sacked by unknown enemies, and the Hittite Empire and Mycenaean kingdoms were destroyed.

△ **Last writing**
This fire-blackened tablet is one of the last documents of the Mycenaean civilization. It is written in an early Greek script called Linear B.

The first victim was the Hittite Empire, whose capital, Hattusa, was sacked around 1200 BCE. Meanwhile, in Greece, the Mycenaeans, fearing attack from the sea, were fortifying their palaces. Despite all preparations, the palaces were destroyed by fire. Egypt was also attacked, by a coalition from the Aegean they referred to as the "Sea Peoples." Pharaoh Ramesses III describes defeating the invaders in the 1170s. Driven out of Egypt, the Sea Peoples went on to conquer and settle the coast of the Levant.

The cause of the collapse remains unclear. It is unlikely that the Sea Peoples were solely responsible. There is evidence that climate change was the underlying cause of a cascade of disintegration. The period was exceptionally dry, and drought could have led to famine, weakening the palace economies and making them vulnerable to attack. Other factors that might have contributed to the collapse include earthquakes and internal rebellions. As cities fell, their populations were displaced and began to migrate, in turn unsettling other kingdoms. After the collapse, trade in bronze, which had previously been conducted on a large scale, was disrupted, and people turned increasingly to iron.

THE FALL OF BRONZE AGE CITIES

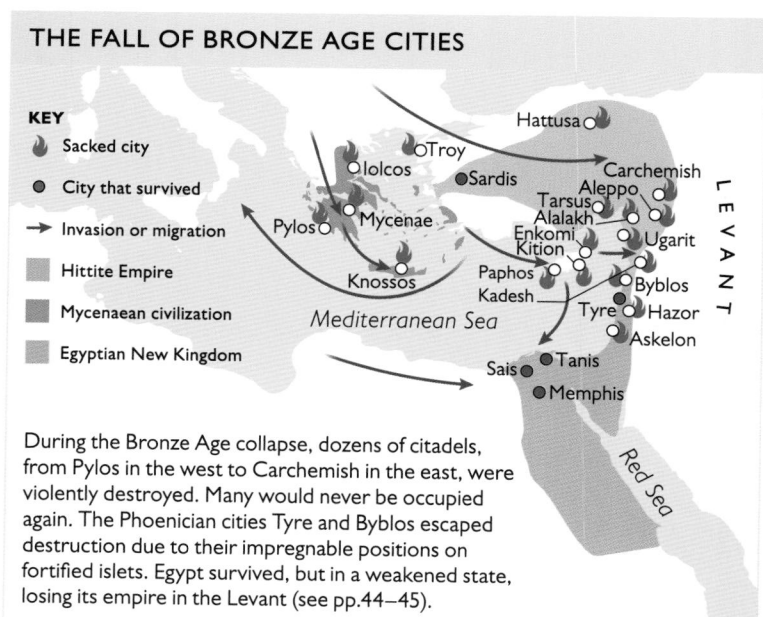

KEY
- 🔥 Sacked city
- ● City that survived
- → Invasion or migration
- Hittite Empire
- Mycenaean civilization
- Egyptian New Kingdom

Hattusa
Troy
Iolcos
Sardis
Carchemish
Aleppo
Tarsus
Alalakh
Pylos
Mycenae
Enkomi
Kition
Ugarit
Knossos
Paphos
Kadesh
Byblos
Tyre
Hazor
Askelon
Sais
Tanis
Memphis
Mediterranean Sea
LEVANT
Red Sea

During the Bronze Age collapse, dozens of citadels, from Pylos in the west to Carchemish in the east, were violently destroyed. Many would never be occupied again. The Phoenician cities Tyre and Byblos escaped destruction due to their impregnable positions on fortified islets. Egypt survived, but in a weakened state, losing its empire in the Levant (see pp.44–45).

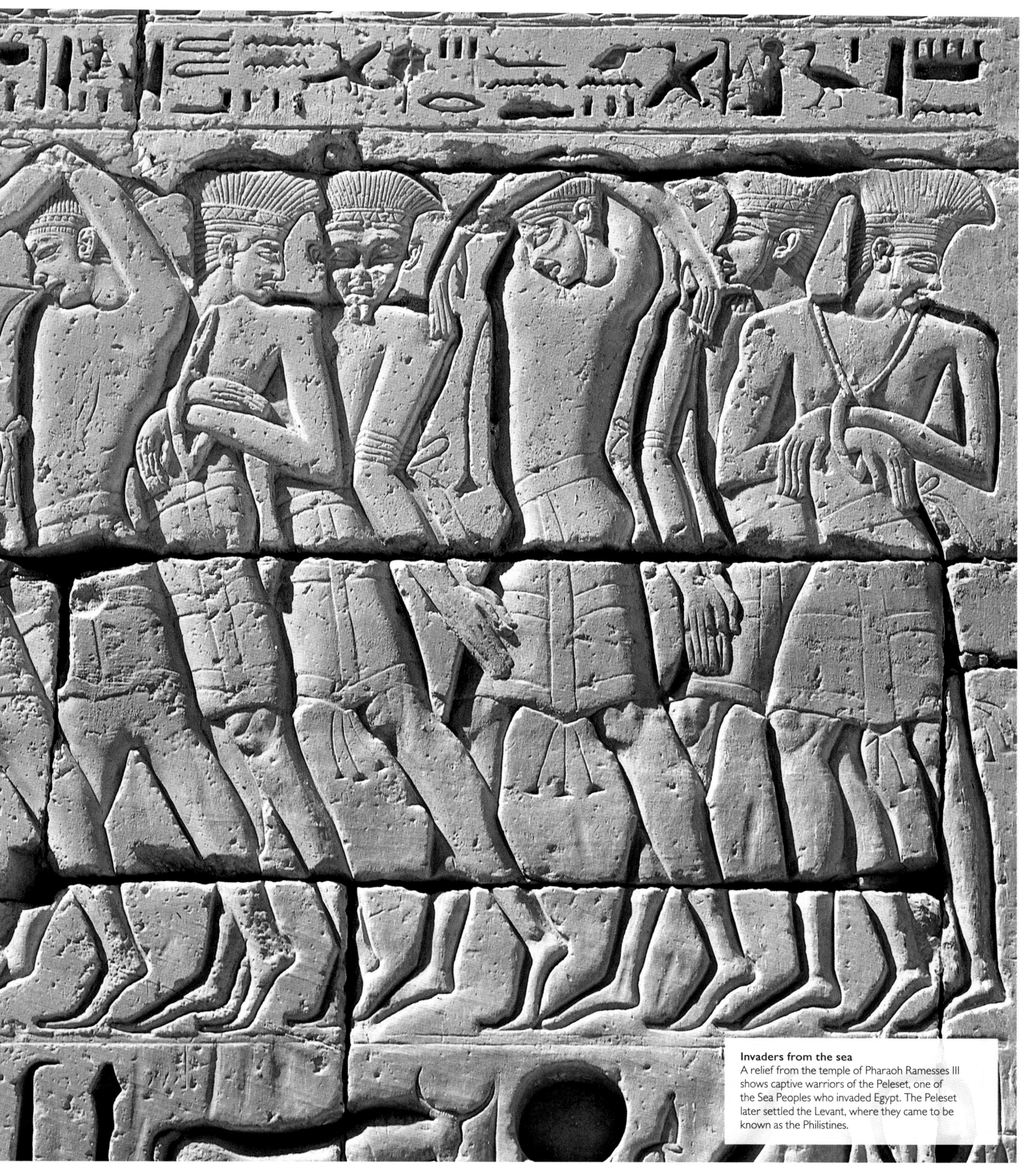

Invaders from the sea
A relief from the temple of Pharaoh Ramesses III shows captive warriors of the Peleset, one of the Sea Peoples who invaded Egypt. The Peleset later settled the Levant, where they came to be known as the Philistines.

THE ANCIENT LEVANT

The Levant is the fertile land to the east of the Mediterranean, called Canaan in the Hebrew Bible. It was dominated by powerful neighbors, but the resistance to Rome of one group of its people—the Jews—resulted in their expulsion, accelerating their diaspora across Asia and Europe.

The Levant was fought over by the great powers of the Bronze Age (see pp.42–43), including Egypt, the Hittites, and the old Assyrian state. It was full of rich and important cities such as Megiddo and Jericho when the biblical kingdom of Israel came into existence in around 1020 BCE. However, the region had been in decline for centuries, and its powerful neighbors were weak. On the coast, ports grew into city-states that became known as "Phoenician" in the Greek world (see pp.54–57). Phoenicians went on to form a network of trading colonies that eventually controlled most of the Mediterranean. Settlers on the coast to the south of the Phoenicians became known as Philistines. Meanwhile, Israel split into two kingdoms named Israel and Judah and spent centuries under the domination of first Assyria, then Babylon, then Persia.

By the time of the New Testament of the Bible, the former Hebrew kingdoms had become the Roman vassal state of Judea, and the teachings of Jesus Christ were spreading through the Roman Empire (see pp.86–87). Rebellions against Rome, including the Great Jewish Revolt (66–74 CE) and the Bar Kokhba Revolt (132–135 CE) then led to the destruction of Jerusalem, the dispersion of the Jewish people (now named Jews after Judah), and the merging of Judea with its neighbors to make a new Roman province called Syria Palaestina, after the Philistines.

MASADA
LAST BASTION OF JEWISH REVOLT

Herod the Great built a fortified palace at this spectacular mountaintop fortress in the desert, and it was here that the Zealots of the Great Jewish Revolt took their last stand against the Romans. After the Roman armies laid siege to Masada for 6 months, Jewish historians record that they built a siege ramp and set fire to the inner defensive walls. The 900 Jews inside reportedly killed themselves to avoid slavery.

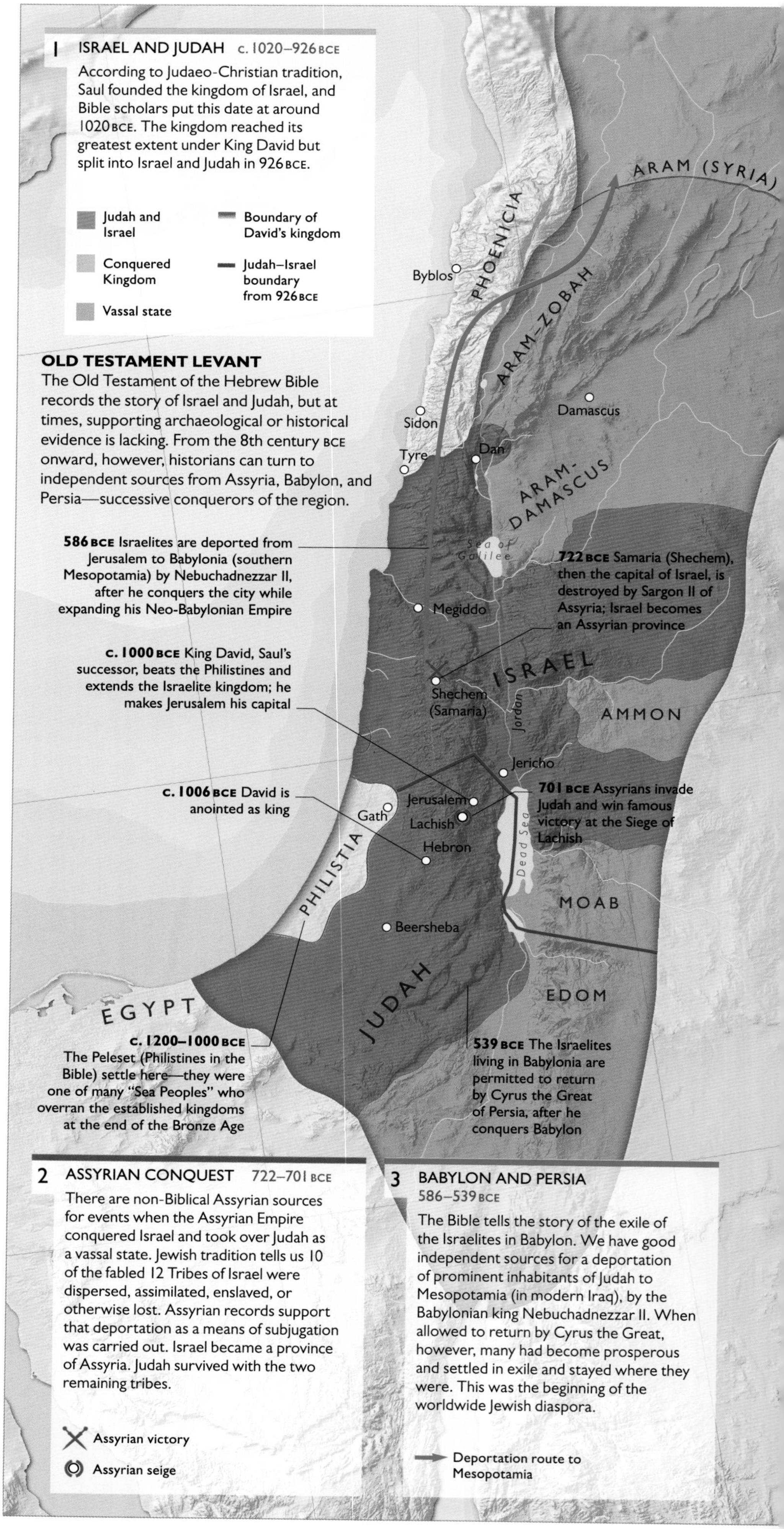
1 ISRAEL AND JUDAH c. 1020–926 BCE
According to Judaeo-Christian tradition, Saul founded the kingdom of Israel, and Bible scholars put this date at around 1020 BCE. The kingdom reached its greatest extent under King David but split into Israel and Judah in 926 BCE.
Judah and Israel
Conquered Kingdom
Vassal state
Boundary of David's kingdom
Judah–Israel boundary from 926 BCE
OLD TESTAMENT LEVANT
The Old Testament of the Hebrew Bible records the story of Israel and Judah, but at times, supporting archaeological or historical evidence is lacking. From the 8th century BCE onward, however, historians can turn to independent sources from Assyria, Babylon, and Persia—successive conquerors of the region.
586 BCE Israelites are deported from Jerusalem to Babylonia (southern Mesopotamia) by Nebuchadnezzar II, after he conquers the city while expanding his Neo-Babylonian Empire
c. 1000 BCE King David, Saul's successor, beats the Philistines and extends the Israelite kingdom; he makes Jerusalem his capital
c. 1006 BCE David is anointed as king
c. 1200–1000 BCE The Peleset (Philistines in the Bible) settle here—they were one of many "Sea Peoples" who overran the established kingdoms at the end of the Bronze Age
722 BCE Samaria (Shechem), then the capital of Israel, is destroyed by Sargon II of Assyria; Israel becomes an Assyrian province
701 BCE Assyrians invade Judah and win famous victory at the Siege of Lachish
539 BCE The Israelites living in Babylonia are permitted to return by Cyrus the Great of Persia, after he conquers Babylon
ARAM (SYRIA)
PHOENICIA
ARAM-ZOBAH
ARAM-DAMASCUS
Byblos
Sidon
Tyre
Dan
Damascus
Sea of Galilee
Megiddo
ISRAEL
Shechem (Samaria)
Jordan
AMMON
Jericho
Jerusalem
Gath
Lachish
Hebron
Dead Sea
PHILISTIA
MOAB
Beersheba
EGYPT
JUDAH
EDOM
2 ASSYRIAN CONQUEST 722–701 BCE
There are non-Biblical Assyrian sources for events when the Assyrian Empire conquered Israel and took over Judah as a vassal state. Jewish tradition tells us 10 of the fabled 12 Tribes of Israel were dispersed, assimilated, enslaved, or otherwise lost. Assyrian records support that deportation as a means of subjugation was carried out. Israel became a province of Assyria. Judah survived with the two remaining tribes.
Assyrian victory
Assyrian seige
3 BABYLON AND PERSIA 586–539 BCE
The Bible tells the story of the exile of the Israelites in Babylon. We have good independent sources for a deportation of prominent inhabitants of Judah to Mesopotamia (in modern Iraq), by the Babylonian king Nebuchadnezzar II. When allowed to return by Cyrus the Great, however, many had become prosperous and settled in exile and stayed where they were. This was the beginning of the worldwide Jewish diaspora.
Deportation route to Mesopotamia

ROMAN RULE AND REVOLT

In the time of the biblical New Testament, the central parts of Israel and Judah had become the Roman province of Judea. Revolts against Rome by the people—now known as Jews—resulted in their expulsion and resettlement in Egypt, Babylonia, and throughout the Roman Empire.

△ **Message on a coin**
This sestertius of Emperor Vespasian shows one Jew sitting and another Jew with his hands tied, reminding all Judean citizens who carried it of their subservience to Rome.

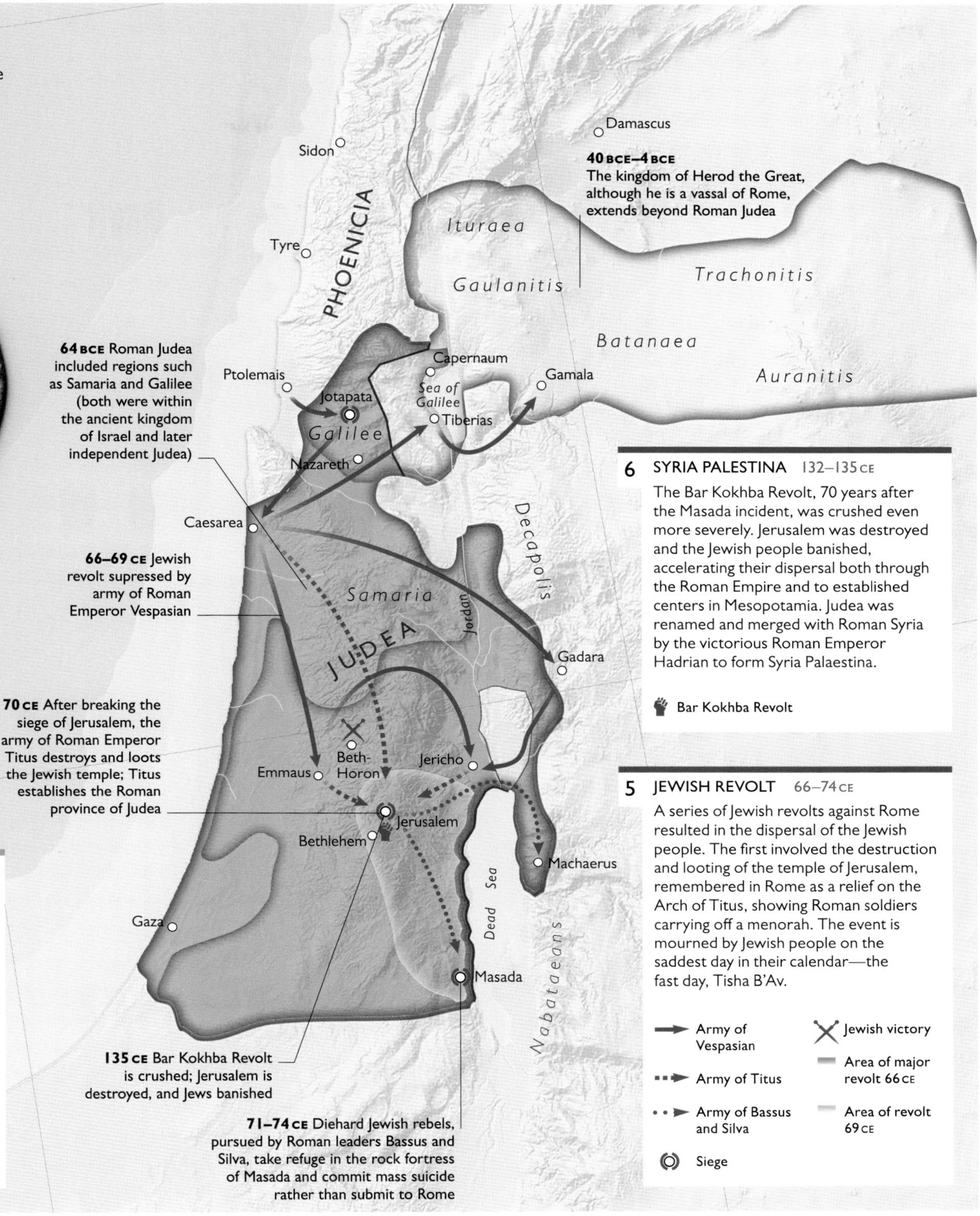

64 BCE Roman Judea included regions such as Samaria and Galilee (both were within the ancient kingdom of Israel and later independent Judea)

66–69 CE Jewish revolt supressed by army of Roman Emperor Vespasian

70 CE After breaking the siege of Jerusalem, the army of Roman Emperor Titus destroys and loots the Jewish temple; Titus establishes the Roman province of Judea

40 BCE–4 BCE The kingdom of Herod the Great, although he is a vassal of Rome, extends beyond Roman Judea

4 ROMAN RULE 63 BCE–66 CE

Judea was conquered by Rome. Until then, it was a kingdom that won its independence from the Hellenistic (Greek) Seleucid Empire, set up by Alexander the Great, which crumbled in 110 BCE. The Romans set up Judea as a client state. Herod the Great assumed the throne as Rome's vassal in 40 BCE and proceeded to extend his kingdom.

— Frontier of Roman Empire and client states

— Kingdom of Herod

▨ Roman province of Judea

135 CE Bar Kokhba Revolt is crushed; Jerusalem is destroyed, and Jews banished

71–74 CE Diehard Jewish rebels, pursued by Roman leaders Bassus and Silva, take refuge in the rock fortress of Masada and commit mass suicide rather than submit to Rome

6 SYRIA PALESTINA 132–135 CE

The Bar Kokhba Revolt, 70 years after the Masada incident, was crushed even more severely. Jerusalem was destroyed and the Jewish people banished, accelerating their dispersal both through the Roman Empire and to established centers in Mesopotamia. Judea was renamed and merged with Roman Syria by the victorious Roman Emperor Hadrian to form Syria Palaestina.

✊ Bar Kokhba Revolt

5 JEWISH REVOLT 66–74 CE

A series of Jewish revolts against Rome resulted in the dispersal of the Jewish people. The first involved the destruction and looting of the temple of Jerusalem, remembered in Rome as a relief on the Arch of Titus, showing Roman soldiers carrying off a menorah. The event is mourned by Jewish people on the saddest day in their calendar—the fast day, Tisha B'Av.

→ Army of Vespasian
⋯▶ Army of Titus
∙∙▶ Army of Bassus and Silva
◎ Siege

✕ Jewish victory
▬ Area of major revolt 66 CE
▬ Area of revolt 69 CE

Map labels: Damascus, Sidon, Tyre, PHOENICIA, Ituraea, Gaulanitis, Trachonitis, Batanaea, Auranitis, Ptolemais, Capernaum, Gamala, Jotapata, Sea of Galilee, Tiberias, Galilee, Nazareth, Caesarea, Decapolis, Samaria, JUDEA, Jordan, Gadara, Emmaus, Beth-Horon, Jericho, Jerusalem, Bethlehem, Machaerus, Gaza, Dead Sea, Masada, Nabataeans

---

THE LEVANT

The narrow strip of land beside the eastern Mediterranean features in the Old Testament and the New Testament of the Hebrew Bible but also in the records of powerful neighbors, such as Egyptians, Assyrians, Persians, and Romans.

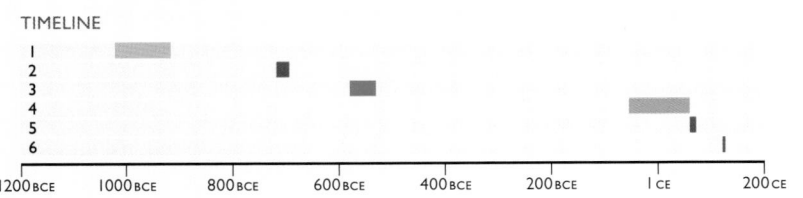

TIMELINE
1 2 3 4 5 6

1200 BCE   1000 BCE   800 BCE   600 BCE   400 BCE   200 BCE   1 CE   200 CE

"I protest openly that I do not go over to the Romans as a deserter of the Jews, but as a minister from thee."

FLAVIUS JOSEPHUS, JEWISH-ROMAN HISTORIAN, IN *THE JEWISH WAR*

THE IRON AGE

When Bronze Age people learned how to smelt iron, they sparked off a technological revolution. Exactly where and why they first turned from bronze to iron is a mystery. The most likely explanation is that when supplies of tin and copper, the two constituents of bronze, ran short, necessity became the mother of invention.

Until recently, archaeological evidence suggested that ironworking first started in central Anatolia, Turkey, some time between 2000 and 1300 BCE, with the Hittites—an ancient Anatolian people—being credited with pioneering the new technology of iron smelting (heating iron ore to extract the metal). It was believed that the Hittites began to forge iron artifacts as early as the 18th century BCE and

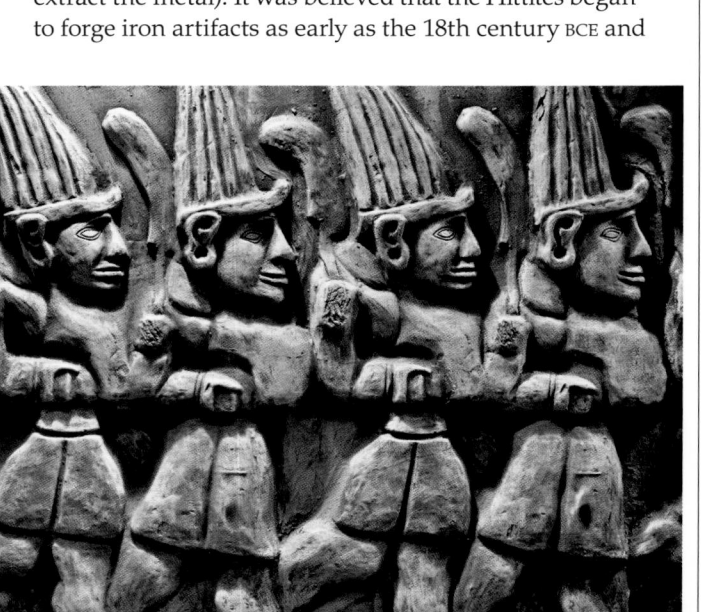

▽ **Ruling the underworld**
A relief cut into the rocks of a temple in Hattusa—the ancient capital of the Hittites, in modern Turkey—depicts 12 deities of the underworld. The Hittites worshipped more than 1,000 deities.

▷ **Signs of iron in Europe**
Dating from 750–450 BCE, this iron dagger was found in one of the thousand graves discovered at Hallstatt (modern Austria), the hub of central Europe's first Iron Age culture.

that their iron weapons—including swords, battleaxes, spear points, and arrowheads—gave them a massive military advantage over their neighbors. Following the collapse of their empire, their knowledge spread through the Middle East and from there to Greece and the Aegean region, eventually reaching central and western Europe. Modern archaeological research, however, has challenged this picture. It is now thought that Indian metalsmiths may have discovered how to forge iron at roughly the same time as the Hittites, or even earlier.

Early ironsmiths

Archaeological excavations of megalithic burial sites in Uttar Pradesh in northern India and Malabar in the south have uncovered iron artifacts dating from 2012 BCE and 1882 BCE. Other excavations in the Ganges valley have uncovered iron artifacts dating from around the same time that the Hittites were forging their first iron implements, while iron daggers found at sites in Hyderabad in southern India are thought to date from 2400–2000 BCE. In Europe, ironworking began with the Greeks, possibly as early as 1050 BCE. A few hundred years later, the Celts (the collective name for a variety of tribes in

THE BEGINNINGS OF THE IRON AGE

The Iron Age began almost 4,000 years ago, starting independently in central Anatolia (in modern Turkey) and India. Later, the knowledge of iron smelting and forging spread into central Europe via Greece and then through the rest of the continent. Iron, which was more widely available than the tin and copper needed to make bronze, replaced bronze for use in almost all utilitarian objects, from weapons to plows to utensils.

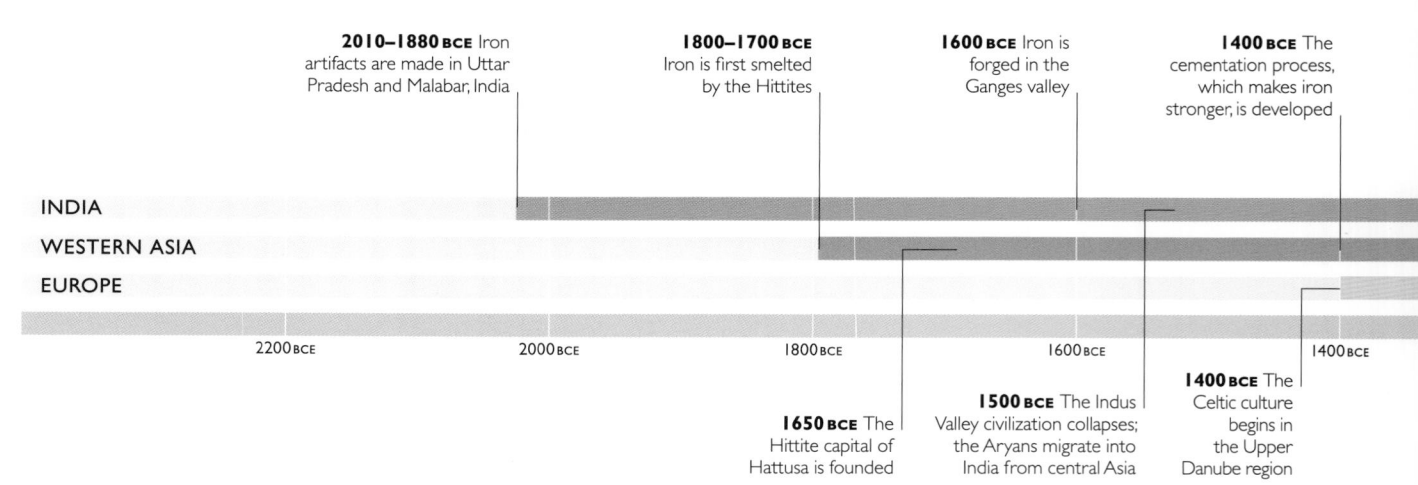

2010–1880 BCE Iron artifacts are made in Uttar Pradesh and Malabar, India

1800–1700 BCE Iron is first smelted by the Hittites

1600 BCE Iron is forged in the Ganges valley

1400 BCE The cementation process, which makes iron stronger, is developed

INDIA
WESTERN ASIA
EUROPE

2200 BCE   2000 BCE   1800 BCE   1600 BCE   1400 BCE

1650 BCE The Hittite capital of Hattusa is founded

1500 BCE The Indus Valley civilization collapses; the Aryans migrate into India from central Asia

1400 BCE The Celtic culture begins in the Upper Danube region

◁ **The versatile Celts**
The Celts were skilled at working various metals, not just iron. Discovered in a peat bog near Gundestrup, Denmark, in 1891, this cauldron was made from silver between the 2nd and 1st centuries BCE.

Europe) became masters of the craft.

The oldest archaeological evidence demonstrating their skill at forging iron and other metals comes from Hallstatt, near Salzburg in Austria. Tomb excavations there, which started as early as the mid-19th century, uncovered a rich treasury of grave goods, including iron swords dating from around 700 BCE. Why the culture centered around Hallstatt collapsed is uncertain.

The Hallstatt culture was replaced by the La Tène culture, which appeared in the mid-5th century BCE. Excavations have revealed more than 2,500 iron swords with decorated scabbards, as well as other metalwork items. The La Tène culture was artistically prolific. Its influence spread through much of western Europe as the Celtic tribes expanded out of their original homelands.

Worldwide usage

In Africa, knowledge of iron smelting seems to have developed at much the same time as it was spreading through western Europe. Some historians put this down to the Phoenicians, who carried their knowledge of iron

> "[The Celts] are quick of mind and with good natural ability for learning."
>
> DIDORUS SICULUS, GREEK HISTORIAN

smelting to their north African colonies, notably Carthage. The majority view now is that it was more likely a local development. Whatever the truth, there is no disputing the fact that African iron-making was extremely varied, with many distinct local technologies evolving over the centuries.

There is clear evidence of iron smelting in Ethiopia, the region of the Great Lakes, Tanzania, Ghana, Mali, and central Nigeria around the Niger and Benue Rivers, where the Nok culture emerged. In some respects, African metalsmiths were ahead of Europe. In east Africa, for instance, they were producing steel as early as 500 BCE.

From bronze to iron

Wherever and whenever the transition from the Bronze Age to the Iron Age happened, it brought with it significant changes to everyday life, from the way ancient peoples cultivated their crops to how they fought their wars. Some civilizations, however, missed out on the Iron Age altogether. In Central and South America, for example, various civilizations, most notably the Incas, were skillful metalworkers in gold, silver, copper, and bronze, but they simply never made the transition to iron.

▽ **Traditional metalworking**
Iron has been smelted and forged in Africa for three millennia. This 19th-century engraving shows small-scale ironworking near Lake Mobutu in east Africa.

ASSYRIA AND BABYLONIA

The Iron Age in the Middle East was an age of empire. The Assyrians, based in what is now northern Iraq, created the blueprint for a new type of extensive state that employed direct and indirect rule to place a range of peoples and territories under the control of one sovereign.

After 1200 BCE, in the aftermath of the migrations at the end of the late Bronze Age (see pp.42–43), small-scale local states replaced large regional powers such as the Hittite state and the New Kingdom of Egypt. The kingdom of Assyria, protected by the Tigris River and the Taurus and Zagros Mountains, survived the upheaval despite losing peripheral territories to Aramaean clans. From 900 BCE, it started to grow again at the expense of these smaller neighbors.

Besides incorporating territories and putting them under eunuch governors loyal only to the king, the Assyrian Empire greatly favored indirect rule. From the eastern Mediterranean to what is now Iran, client rulers swore sacred oaths to accept the sovereignty of the god Ashur and his human representative, the Assyrian king, in return for local power. The empire was held together by these bonds of mutual obligation and by an innovative relay postal system—for the first time, information traveled much faster than if carried by a single messenger. The succeeding Babylonian Empire adopted much of this blueprint but replaced Ashur with its own god, Marduk, and dispensed with eunuch governors.

> *"The god Ashur is king, and Ashurbanipal is [his] representative, the creation of his hands."*
>
> CORONATION HYMN OF ASHURBANIPAL OF ASSYRIA

BABYLONIAN LAW
JUSTICE CARVED IN STONE

King Hammurabi of Babylon (r.1792–1750 BCE) compiled a set of 282 rulings, which were recorded on stone steles set up in temples across his realm. These laws were to "prevent the strong oppressing the weak" and specified fines and punishments to suit specific social contexts. More than 1,000 years later, in the days of the Assyrian and Babylonian Empires, Hammurabi was still revered as a model ruler.

Stele of Hammurabi
The king receives authority, symbolized by a measuring tape and a ruler, from the god Shamash, the patron of justice.

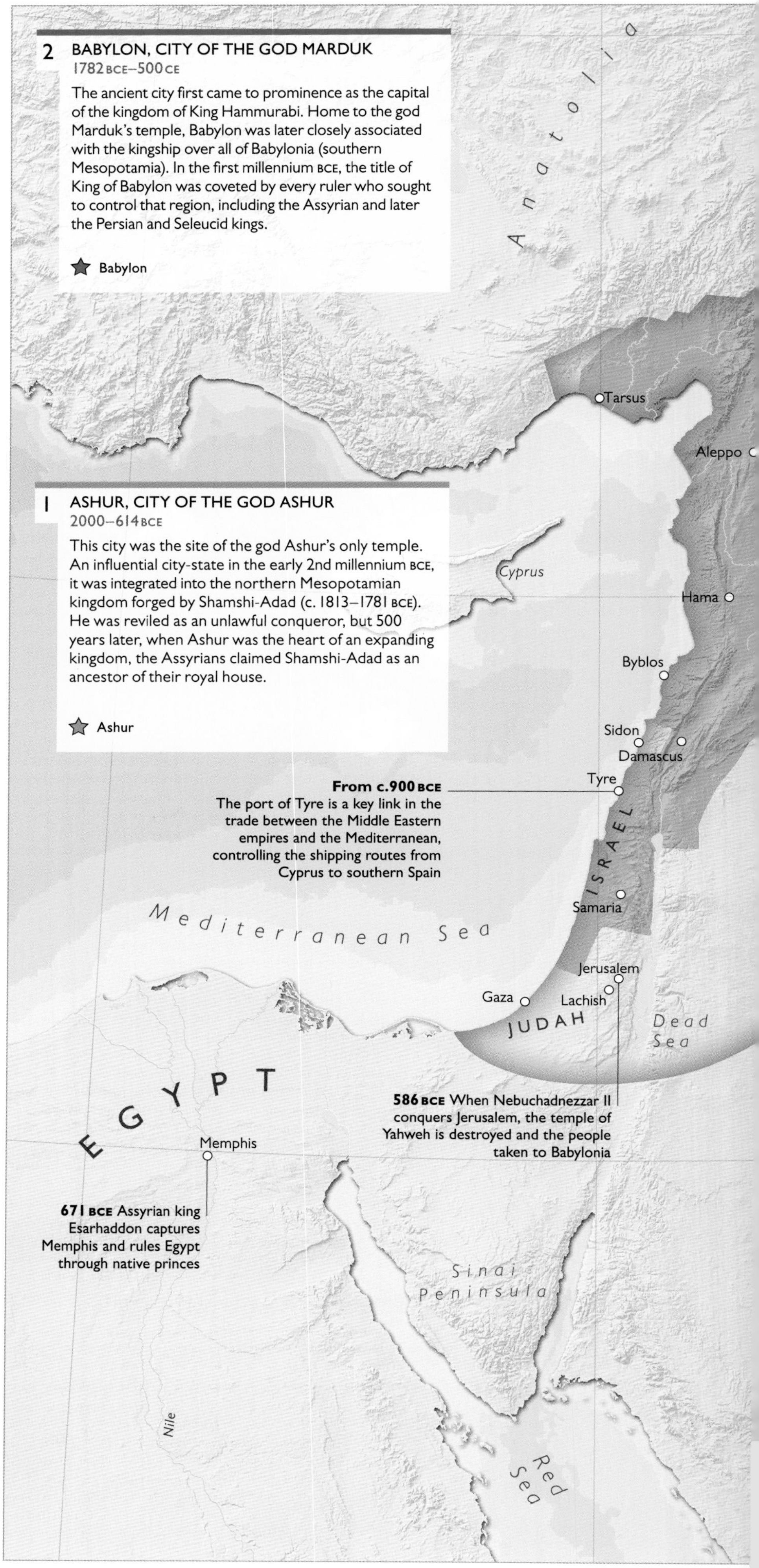

2 BABYLON, CITY OF THE GOD MARDUK
1782 BCE–500 CE

The ancient city first came to prominence as the capital of the kingdom of King Hammurabi. Home to the god Marduk's temple, Babylon was later closely associated with the kingship over all of Babylonia (southern Mesopotamia). In the first millennium BCE, the title of King of Babylon was coveted by every ruler who sought to control that region, including the Assyrian and later the Persian and Seleucid kings.

⭐ Babylon

1 ASHUR, CITY OF THE GOD ASHUR
2000–614 BCE

This city was the site of the god Ashur's only temple. An influential city-state in the early 2nd millennium BCE, it was integrated into the northern Mesopotamian kingdom forged by Shamshi-Adad (c. 1813–1781 BCE). He was reviled as an unlawful conqueror, but 500 years later, when Ashur was the heart of an expanding kingdom, the Assyrians claimed Shamshi-Adad as an ancestor of their royal house.

⭐ Ashur

From c.900 BCE
The port of Tyre is a key link in the trade between the Middle Eastern empires and the Mediterranean, controlling the shipping routes from Cyprus to southern Spain

586 BCE When Nebuchadnezzar II conquers Jerusalem, the temple of Yahweh is destroyed and the people taken to Babylon

671 BCE Assyrian king Esarhaddon captures Memphis and rules Egypt through native princes

Anatolia
Tarsus
Aleppo
Cyprus
Hama
Byblos
Sidon
Damascus
Tyre
ISRAEL
Samaria
Mediterranean Sea
Jerusalem
Gaza
Lachish
JUDAH
Dead Sea
EGYPT
Memphis
Sinai Peninsula
Nile
Red Sea

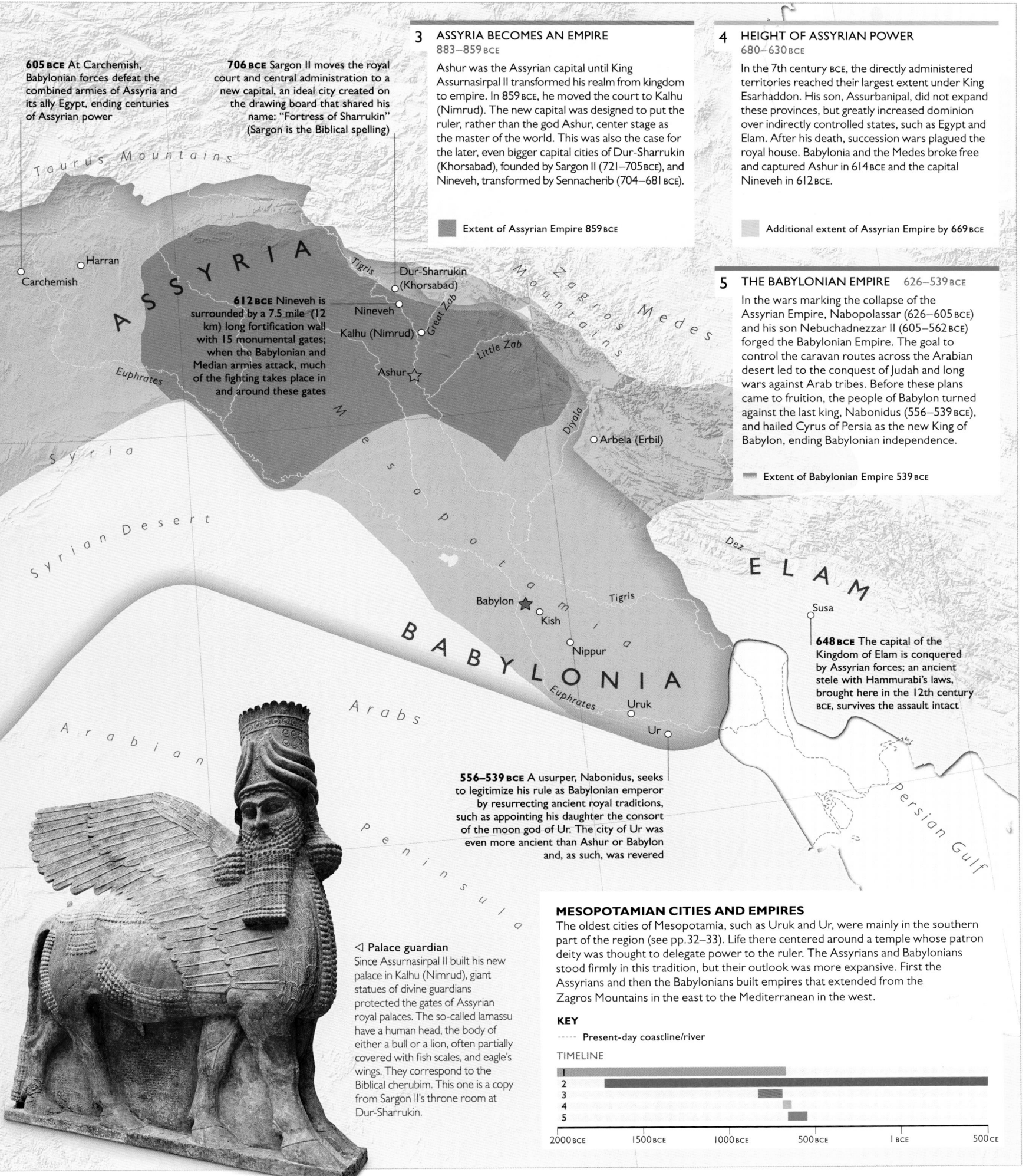

605 BCE At Carchemish, Babylonian forces defeat the combined armies of Assyria and its ally Egypt, ending centuries of Assyrian power

706 BCE Sargon II moves the royal court and central administration to a new capital, an ideal city created on the drawing board that shared his name: "Fortress of Sharrukin" (Sargon is the Biblical spelling)

3 ASSYRIA BECOMES AN EMPIRE
883–859 BCE

Ashur was the Assyrian capital until King Assurnasirpal II transformed his realm from kingdom to empire. In 859 BCE, he moved the court to Kalhu (Nimrud). The new capital was designed to put the ruler, rather than the god Ashur, center stage as the master of the world. This was also the case for the later, even bigger capital cities of Dur-Sharrukin (Khorsabad), founded by Sargon II (721–705 BCE), and Nineveh, transformed by Sennacherib (704–681 BCE).

☐ Extent of Assyrian Empire 859 BCE

4 HEIGHT OF ASSYRIAN POWER
680–630 BCE

In the 7th century BCE, the directly administered territories reached their largest extent under King Esarhaddon. His son, Assurbanipal, did not expand these provinces, but greatly increased dominion over indirectly controlled states, such as Egypt and Elam. After his death, succession wars plagued the royal house. Babylonia and the Medes broke free and captured Ashur in 614 BCE and the capital Nineveh in 612 BCE.

☐ Additional extent of Assyrian Empire by 669 BCE

5 THE BABYLONIAN EMPIRE   626–539 BCE

In the wars marking the collapse of the Assyrian Empire, Nabopolassar (626–605 BCE) and his son Nebuchadnezzar II (605–562 BCE) forged the Babylonian Empire. The goal to control the caravan routes across the Arabian desert led to the conquest of Judah and long wars against Arab tribes. Before these plans came to fruition, the people of Babylon turned against the last king, Nabonidus (556–539 BCE), and hailed Cyrus of Persia as the new King of Babylon, ending Babylonian independence.

☐ Extent of Babylonian Empire 539 BCE

612 BCE Nineveh is surrounded by a 7.5 mile (12 km) long fortification wall with 15 monumental gates; when the Babylonian and Median armies attack, much of the fighting takes place in and around these gates

648 BCE The capital of the Kingdom of Elam is conquered by Assyrian forces; an ancient stele with Hammurabi's laws, brought here in the 12th century BCE, survives the assault intact

556–539 BCE A usurper, Nabonidus, seeks to legitimize his rule as Babylonian emperor by resurrecting ancient royal traditions, such as appointing his daughter the consort of the moon god of Ur. The city of Ur was even more ancient than Ashur or Babylon and, as such, was revered

◁ **Palace guardian**
Since Assurnasirpal II built his new palace in Kalhu (Nimrud), giant statues of divine guardians protected the gates of Assyrian royal palaces. The so-called lamassu have a human head, the body of either a bull or a lion, often partially covered with fish scales, and eagle's wings. They correspond to the Biblical cherubim. This one is a copy from Sargon II's throne room at Dur-Sharrukin.

MESOPOTAMIAN CITIES AND EMPIRES

The oldest cities of Mesopotamia, such as Uruk and Ur, were mainly in the southern part of the region (see pp.32–33). Life there centered around a temple whose patron deity was thought to delegate power to the ruler. The Assyrians and Babylonians stood firmly in this tradition, but their outlook was more expansive. First the Assyrians and then the Babylonians built empires that extended from the Zagros Mountains in the east to the Mediterranean in the west.

KEY

----- Present-day coastline/river

TIMELINE

1					
2					
3					
4					
5					
2000 BCE	1500 BCE	1000 BCE	500 BCE	1 BCE	500 CE

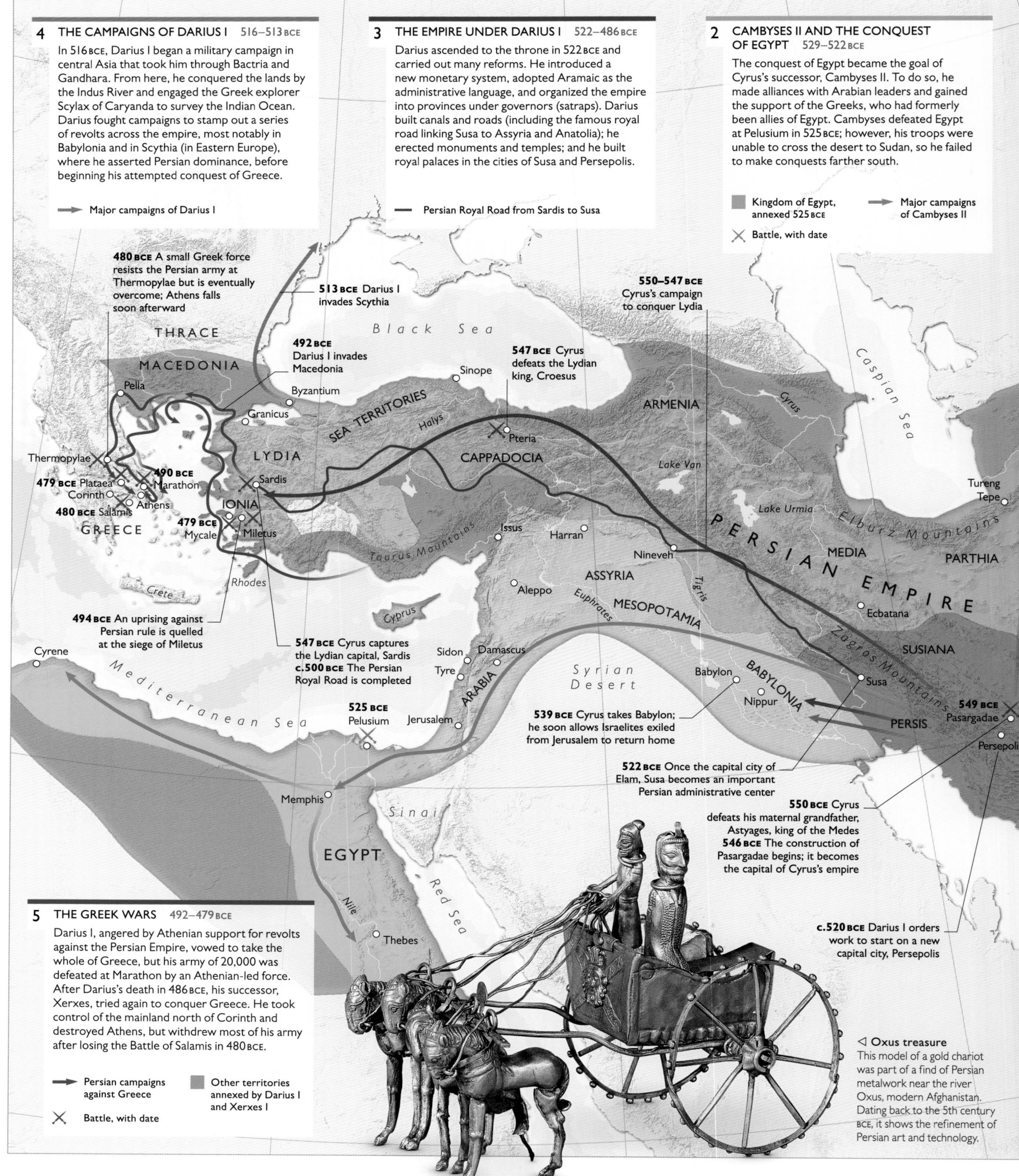

4 THE CAMPAIGNS OF DARIUS I 516–513 BCE

In 516 BCE, Darius I began a military campaign in central Asia that took him through Bactria and Gandhara. From here, he conquered the lands by the Indus River and engaged the Greek explorer Scylax of Caryanda to survey the Indian Ocean. Darius fought campaigns to stamp out a series of revolts across the empire, most notably in Babylonia and in Scythia (in Eastern Europe), where he asserted Persian dominance, before beginning his attempted conquest of Greece.

→ Major campaigns of Darius I

3 THE EMPIRE UNDER DARIUS I 522–486 BCE

Darius ascended to the throne in 522 BCE and carried out many reforms. He introduced a new monetary system, adopted Aramaic as the administrative language, and organized the empire into provinces under governors (satraps). Darius built canals and roads (including the famous royal road linking Susa to Assyria and Anatolia); he erected monuments and temples; and he built royal palaces in the cities of Susa and Persepolis.

— Persian Royal Road from Sardis to Susa

2 CAMBYSES II AND THE CONQUEST OF EGYPT 529–522 BCE

The conquest of Egypt became the goal of Cyrus's successor, Cambyses II. To do so, he made alliances with Arabian leaders and gained the support of the Greeks, who had formerly been allies of Egypt. Cambyses defeated Egypt at Pelusium in 525 BCE; however, his troops were unable to cross the desert to Sudan, so he failed to make conquests farther south.

■ Kingdom of Egypt, annexed 525 BCE
→ Major campaigns of Cambyses II
✕ Battle, with date

480 BCE A small Greek force resists the Persian army at Thermopylae but is eventually overcome; Athens falls soon afterward

513 BCE Darius I invades Scythia

492 BCE Darius I invades Macedonia

550–547 BCE Cyrus's campaign to conquer Lydia

547 BCE Cyrus defeats the Lydian king, Croesus

THRACE

Black Sea

MACEDONIA

Pella

Byzantium

Sinope

ARMENIA

Caspian Sea

Granicus

SEA TERRITORIES

Halys

Pteria

Cyrus

LYDIA

CAPPADOCIA

Lake Van

Thermopylae ✕

Sardis

Lake Urmia

Elburz Mountains

Tureng Tepe

479 BCE Plataea
Corinth
490 BCE Marathon
Athens

IONIA

479 BCE Mycale

Miletus

Taurus Mountains

Issus

Harran

Nineveh

PERSIAN EMPIRE

MEDIA

PARTHIA

480 BCE Salamis

GREECE

Rhodes

Crete

Cyprus

ASSYRIA

Aleppo

Euphrates

MESOPOTAMIA

Tigris

Ecbatana

Zagros Mountains

SUSIANA

494 BCE An uprising against Persian rule is quelled at the siege of Miletus

Cyrene

Mediterranean Sea

547 BCE Cyrus captures the Lydian capital, Sardis
c.500 BCE The Persian Royal Road is completed

Sidon
Tyre

Damascus

ARABIA

Syrian Desert

Babylon

Nippur

BABYLONIA

Susa

PERSIS

549 BCE Pasargadae ✕

Persepolis

525 BCE Pelusium ✕

Jerusalem

539 BCE Cyrus takes Babylon; he soon allows Israelites exiled from Jerusalem to return home

522 BCE Once the capital city of Elam, Susa becomes an important Persian administrative center

550 BCE Cyrus defeats his maternal grandfather, Astyages, king of the Medes
546 BCE The construction of Pasargadae begins; it becomes the capital of Cyrus's empire

Memphis

Sinai

Red Sea

EGYPT

Nile

Thebes

c.520 BCE Darius I orders work to start on a new capital city, Persepolis

5 THE GREEK WARS 492–479 BCE

Darius I, angered by Athenian support for revolts against the Persian Empire, vowed to take the whole of Greece, but his army of 20,000 was defeated at Marathon by an Athenian-led force. After Darius's death in 486 BCE, his successor, Xerxes, tried again to conquer Greece. He took control of the mainland north of Corinth and destroyed Athens, but withdrew most of his army after losing the Battle of Salamis in 480 BCE.

→ Persian campaigns against Greece
■ Other territories annexed by Darius I and Xerxes I
✕ Battle, with date

◁ **Oxus treasure**
This model of a gold chariot was part of a find of Persian metalwork near the river Oxus, modern Afghanistan. Dating back to the 5th century BCE, it shows the refinement of Persian art and technology.

THE EXPANSION OF PERSIAN TERRITORY

Cyrus conquered a huge swathe of western and central Asia, from Anatolia to what is now Afghanistan. His successors added gains in Egypt and Greece and ruled distant satrapies, such as Sogdiana, via governors known as satraps.

KEY

▬ Persian Empire at greatest extent

TIMELINE

	600 BCE	550	500	450	400
1					
2					
3					
4					
5					

Oxus (Amu Darya)

CHORASMIA

SOGDIANA

c.530 BCE Cyrus is defeated against the Massagetae and killed

516 BCE Darius I reaches Gandhara at the northern reaches of the Indus River

○ Balkh

○ Merv

545–540 BCE Cyrus pushes into central Asia

GANDHARA

BACTRIA

○ Herat

SATTAGYDIA

ARIA

○ Kandahar

INDIA

○ Nad-i Ali

Iranian Plateau

ARACHOSIA

Indus

515 BCE Darius I conquers the Indus Valley region

SAGARTIA

○ Bampur

GEDROSIA

○ Hormuz

MAKRAN

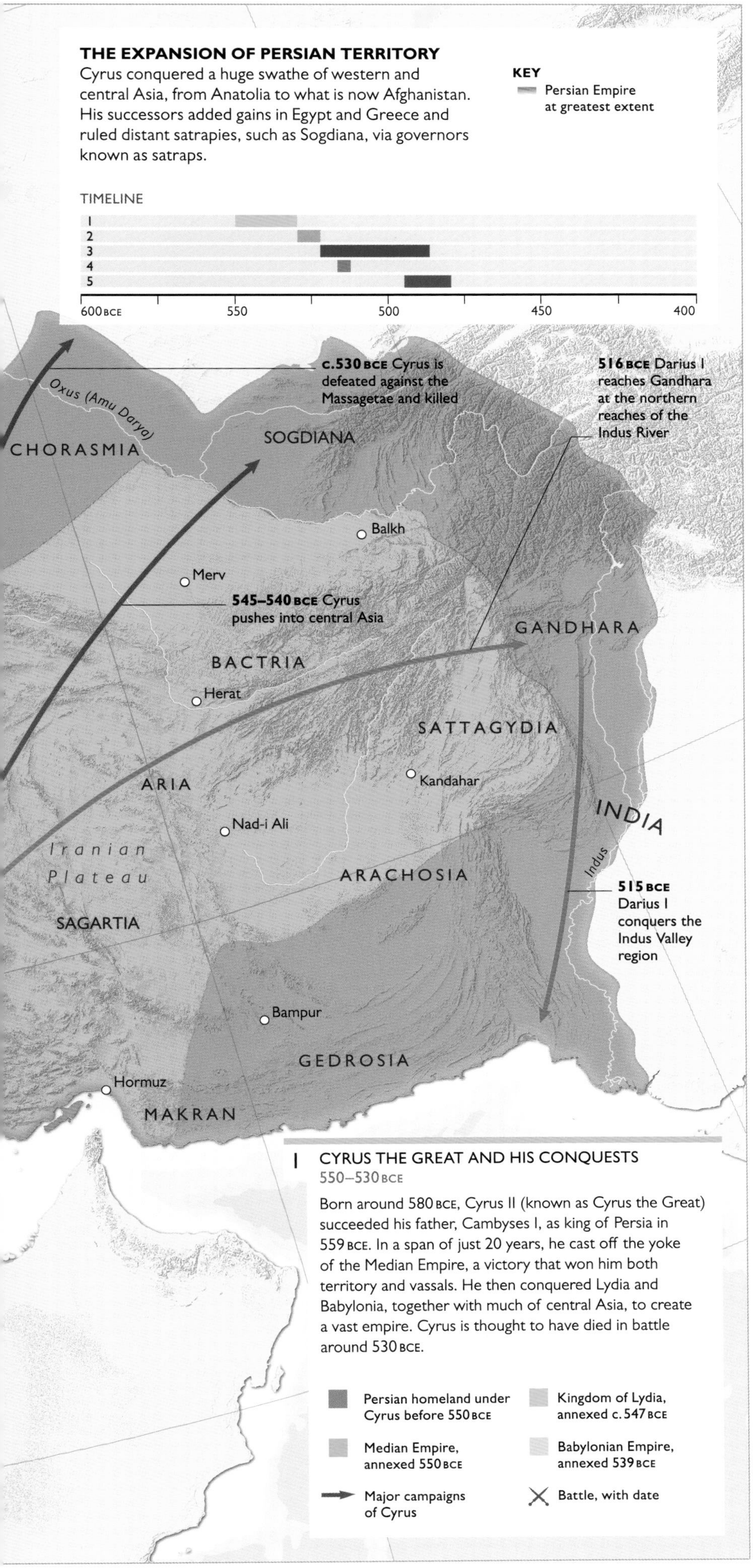

1 CYRUS THE GREAT AND HIS CONQUESTS
550–530 BCE

Born around 580 BCE, Cyrus II (known as Cyrus the Great) succeeded his father, Cambyses I, as king of Persia in 559 BCE. In a span of just 20 years, he cast off the yoke of the Median Empire, a victory that won him both territory and vassals. He then conquered Lydia and Babylonia, together with much of central Asia, to create a vast empire. Cyrus is thought to have died in battle around 530 BCE.

■ Persian homeland under Cyrus before 550 BCE

■ Median Empire, annexed 550 BCE

→ Major campaigns of Cyrus

■ Kingdom of Lydia, annexed c.547 BCE

■ Babylonian Empire, annexed 539 BCE

✕ Battle, with date

RISE OF THE PERSIAN EMPIRE

The Persian Empire was enormous, stretching from Europe to India, and lasted from the military victories of its founder, Cyrus the Great, in the mid-6th century BCE until it was conquered by Alexander the Great some 200 years later.

In 612 BCE, the Assyrian city of Nineveh was destroyed by an alliance of the Assyrians' former subject peoples, including the Babylonians and Medes. The Medes and Persians were Indo-European peoples originally from central Asia, who occupied respectively the area southwest of the Caspian Sea and lands north of the Persian Gulf. To start, the Medes were the dominant power, but c.550 BCE, the Persians—under a series of dynamic kings—began a series of conquests that created the largest empire the world had seen to date.

> *"Brevity is the soul of command. Too much talk suggests desperation on the part of the leader."*
>
> ATTRIBUTED TO CYRUS IN *CYROPEDIA*, c. 370 BCE

The Persians were tolerant conquerors—Cyrus the Great respected the beliefs and customs of the people he ruled and famously freed the Israelites who had been taken captive in Babylon. The Persians invested in organization, appointing local governors known as satraps to rule each province, and built roads and canals to enable troops and traders to move with ease. This organization, and their ability to deploy their armies quickly, enabled them to maintain their vast territories. The Persian Empire was still a major power when it was conquered by Alexander the Great in the 4th century BCE.

PASARGADAE
THE FIRST PERSIAN CAPITAL

Around 546 BCE, Cyrus the Great began to build the first Persian dynastic capital at Pasargadae, near the modern city of Shiraz. Its royal remains—which include the palace, audience hall, gatehouse, and the tomb of Cyrus himself—are some of the most impressive of the Persian Empire and show the influence of the peoples that Cyrus conquered. Later, Cambyses II founded another capital at Susa, and Darius built a third at Persepolis.

Protective winged spirit
This 5th-century BCE relief decorated a door in the ancient city of Pasargadae.

FIRST CITIES IN THE AMERICAS

The first city-based cultures in the Americas emerged from around 3500 BCE in coastal Peru, predating the first cities in southern Mexico and North America by about two millennia. All early American urban cultures built grand sites of worship and engaged extensively in trade.

CARAL
THE AMERICAS' FIRST URBAN CIVILIZATION

A substantial city by 2600 BCE, Caral was part of Peru's Norte Chico civilization. Other Norte Chico cities may be even older. Like many later pre-Columbian cities, Caral featured monumental architecture, such as platform mounds and plazas. These remains of a sunken plaza in Caral, 130 ft (40 m) across, were discovered in the late 1990s. The plaza is thought to have been used for communal acts of worship.

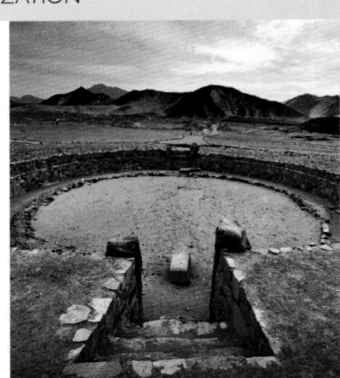

From around 5000 BCE, agricultural practices started replacing the hunter-gatherer lifestyle in the Americas, giving rise to the first settlements.

The Norte Chico culture in the Supe Valley region of coastal Peru emerged as the earliest known urban civilization on the continent, around 4000 BCE. The civilization included more than 30 large settlements, and it established its first major city around 3500 BCE. It thrived for more than 2,000 years. Early civilizations in other regions of

the Americas include the Olmecs of southern Mexico and the Adena and Hopewell Mound Builder cultures of the upper Mississippi and Ohio valleys.

Unique cultures evolved in all these ancient communities, each defined by its arts, crafts, and religious practices, though they all built large-scale earthworks—platforms, pyramids, or mounds—mainly for ceremonial purposes. The towns and cities also traded, using rivers and other routes along coastal plains to transport goods.

EARLY CIVILIZATIONS IN AMERICA
From about 1500 BCE, farming cultures flourished in central America, and the Olmecs built their first cities. In North America, the Adena culture was among the first Mound Builders to emerge from about 1000 BCE, followed 800 years later by the Hopewells.

KEY
◆ Major urban centers

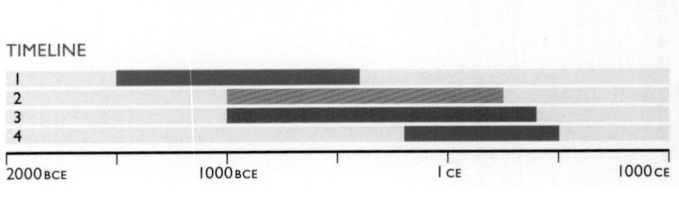

MESOAMERICA'S ANCIENT CULTURES
By 1000 BCE, much of Mesoamerica was inhabited by farming communities, which grew into cities through trading in essential and exotic goods.

2 EARLY MAYA 1000 BCE–250 CE
From 1000 BCE, the Maya began forming complex urban settlements with an elite class and entrenched religious practices. These settlements also featured ceremonial sites in the form of plazas and earthen mounds. Maya artwork during this period drew influence from the Olmecs.

▬ Area of influence to 1000 BCE ◆ Preclassic sites
▬ Additional area of influence 800 BCE

1 OLMECS 1500 BCE–400 BCE
The Olmecs are known for their monumental earth platforms and mounds, fine jade artifacts, and giant head sculptures. Archaeological evidence suggests that the Olmecs created the first writing system and calendar in Mesoamerica. From their heartland in San Lorenzo, they traded widely into western Mexico and established trade relations with many Maya sites along the southern coast.

▬ Area of influence → Trade route
◆ Olmec sculpture site ◆ Olmec settlement

1000–700 BCE Ceramics produced in Tlatilco bear an Olmec influence

300 BCE Preclassic Maya construct among the earliest giant pyramid temples, bearing large stucco masks depicting the deities of Maya mythology

1200–900 BCE San Lorenzo is a major center for Olmec culture

300 BCE Monte Albán is among the fastest-growing cities in Mesoamerica, with a population of more than 5,000

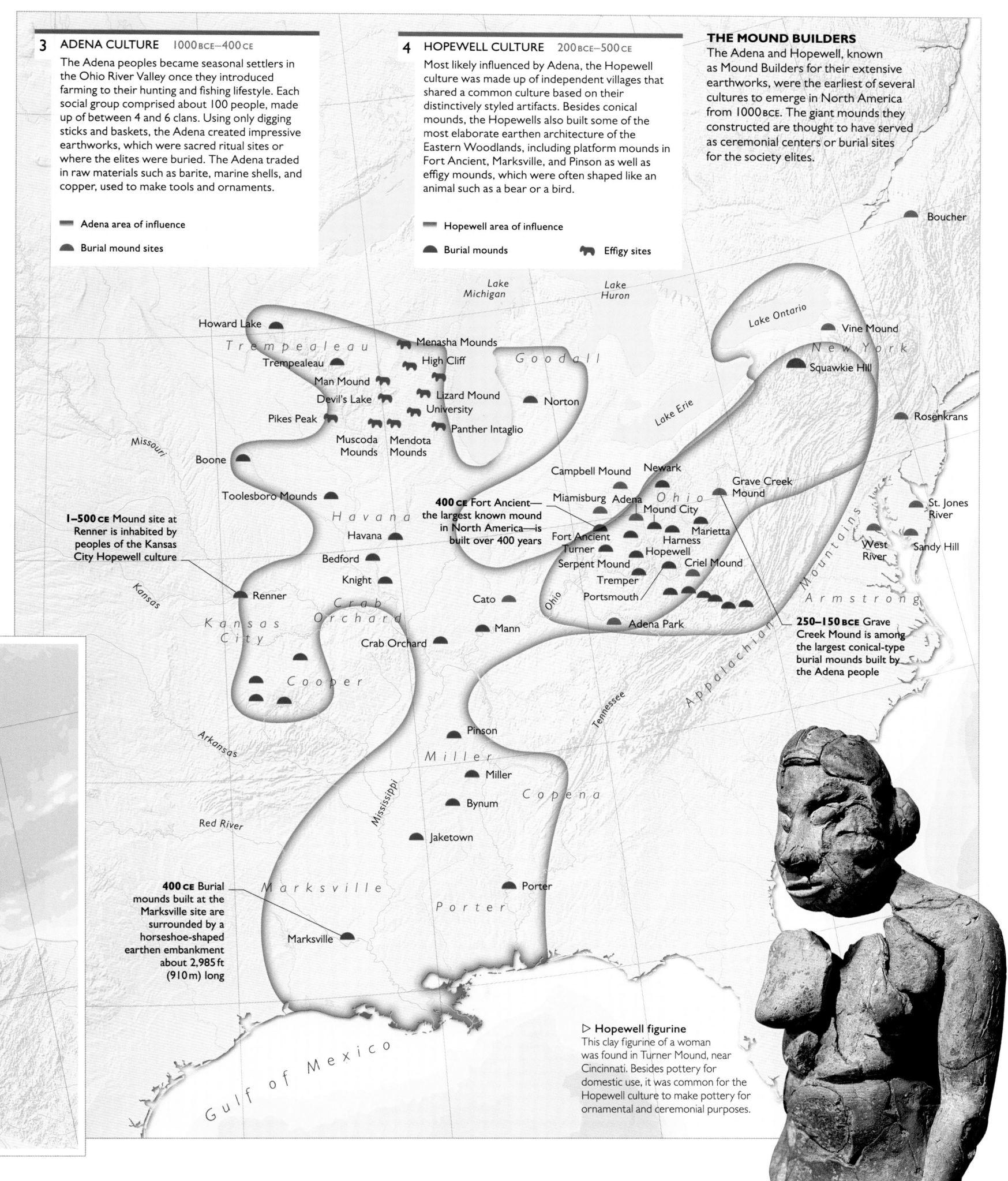

3 ADENA CULTURE 1000 BCE–400 CE

The Adena peoples became seasonal settlers in the Ohio River Valley once they introduced farming to their hunting and fishing lifestyle. Each social group comprised about 100 people, made up of between 4 and 6 clans. Using only digging sticks and baskets, the Adena created impressive earthworks, which were sacred ritual sites or where the elites were buried. The Adena traded in raw materials such as barite, marine shells, and copper, used to make tools and ornaments.

- ▬ Adena area of influence
- ◗ Burial mound sites

4 HOPEWELL CULTURE 200 BCE–500 CE

Most likely influenced by Adena, the Hopewell culture was made up of independent villages that shared a common culture based on their distinctively styled artifacts. Besides conical mounds, the Hopewells also built some of the most elaborate earthen architecture of the Eastern Woodlands, including platform mounds in Fort Ancient, Marksville, and Pinson as well as effigy mounds, which were often shaped like an animal such as a bear or a bird.

- ▬ Hopewell area of influence
- ◗ Burial mounds
- 🐾 Effigy sites

THE MOUND BUILDERS

The Adena and Hopewell, known as Mound Builders for their extensive earthworks, were the earliest of several cultures to emerge in North America from 1000 BCE. The giant mounds they constructed are thought to have served as ceremonial centers or burial sites for the society elites.

Boucher

Lake Michigan
Lake Huron
Lake Ontario
Lake Erie

Howard Lake
Trempealeau
Menasha Mounds
High Cliff
Goodall
Vine Mound
New York
Squawkie Hill
Trempealeau
Man Mound
Devil's Lake
Lizard Mound
University
Norton
Pikes Peak
Panther Intaglio
Rosenkrans
Muscoda Mounds
Mendota Mounds
Boone
Campbell Mound
Newark
Grave Creek Mound
St. Jones River
Toolesboro Mounds
Havana
Miamisburg Adena
Ohio
Mound City
Marietta
West River
Sandy Hill

400 CE Fort Ancient—the largest known mound in North America—is built over 400 years

Fort Ancient
Harness
Turner
Hopewell
Serpent Mound
Criel Mound
Tremper
Portsmouth

1–500 CE Mound site at Renner is inhabited by peoples of the Kansas City Hopewell culture

Havana
Bedford
Knight
Renner
Crab Orchard
Cato
Kansas City
Mann
Adena Park

250–150 BCE Grave Creek Mound is among the largest conical-type burial mounds built by the Adena people

Armstrong
Appalachian Mountains

Crab Orchard
Cooper

Arkansas
Pinson
Miller
Miller
Copena
Bynum
Jaketown

400 CE Burial mounds built at the Marksville site are surrounded by a horseshoe-shaped earthen embankment about 2,985 ft (910 m) long

Marksville
Porter
Porter

Missouri
Kansas
Red River
Mississippi
Tennessee
Ohio

Gulf of Mexico

▷ **Hopewell figurine**
This clay figurine of a woman was found in Turner Mound, near Cincinnati. Besides pottery for domestic use, it was common for the Hopewell culture to make pottery for ornamental and ceremonial purposes.

THE PHOENICIANS

In the 1st millennium BCE, the Phoenicians were the leading seafaring merchants of the Mediterranean. Expert craftworkers, they specialized in luxury goods, including carved ivory, metalwork, and textiles.

△ **Phoenician warship**
This Phoenician warship is a bireme, propelled by two rows of oars. Although the bireme was later improved by the ancient Greeks, it may have been invented by the Phoenicians. A row of shields protects the upper deck.

The Phoenicians lived in port cities in what is now Lebanon. Among these, the most significant were Byblos, Tyre, and Sidon, each ruled by a king. It was the Greeks who named these people "Phoenicians" after their most expensive product, a nonfading purple (*phoinix* in Greek) dye derived from the murex sea snail.

The mountains of Lebanon were covered in cedar forests, which supplied the Phoenicians with long, straight timber. They used the cedar to build their ships and also exported it to Egypt, Greece, and Mesopotamia, which were all short on good timber. Their cities were also centers of craft production, producing purple textiles, glassware, engraved bronze bowls, and wooden furniture decorated with ivory panels. The craftworkers were influenced by Egyptian art, which the Phoenicians spread across the eastern Mediterranean and Mesopotamia. Alongside their own products, they traded in tin and silver from Spain, copper from Cyprus, Arabian incense, African ivory, Egyptian papyrus, Indian spices, and silk from Persian merchants.

Colonies and exploration

From the 10th century BCE, the Phoenicians founded colonies, as trading stations, across the Mediterranean. One such colony, Carthage (in North Africa), later became the center of a great empire. Searching for new markets, the Phoenicians became the greatest navigators of the ancient world. Beyond the Mediterranean, they explored the Atlantic coast of Europe and, around 600 BCE, circumnavigated the whole of Africa. Their lasting legacy is their alphabet, which had just 22 letters. Adapted by the Greeks, the Phoenician alphabet formed the basis of all western writing systems.

▷ **Cultural influences**
This Phoenician ivory carving shows a human-headed winged animal, Mesopotamian in origin, wearing an Egyptian royal headdress.

Cedar for the royalty
Assyrian kings imported cedar from Lebanon to build their palaces. A frieze from the palace of King Sargon II (722–705 BCE) shows Phoenicians bringing cedar logs, towing them alongside their ships.

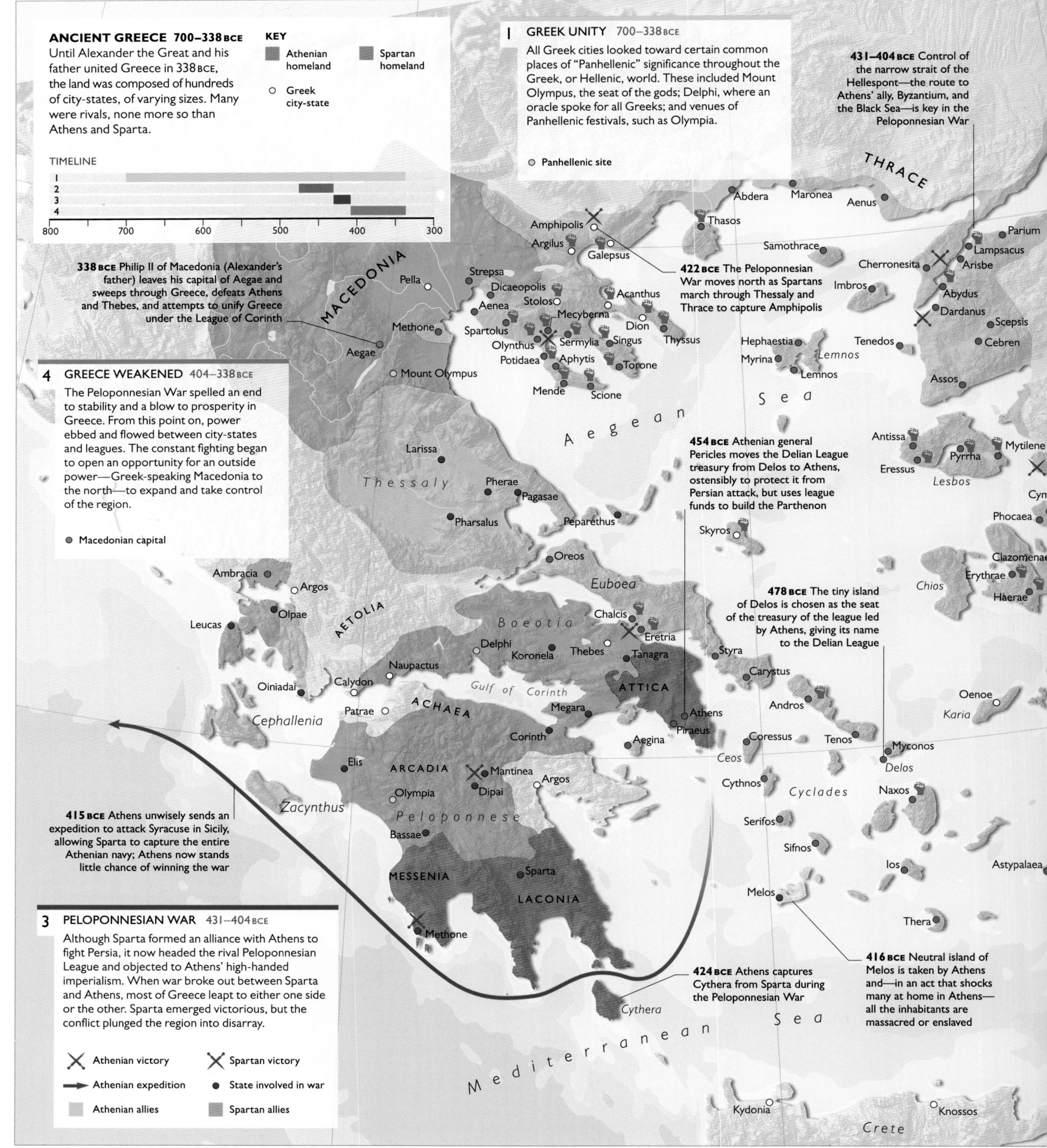

ANCIENT GREECE 700–338 BCE

Until Alexander the Great and his father united Greece in 338 BCE, the land was composed of hundreds of city-states, of varying sizes. Many were rivals, none more so than Athens and Sparta.

KEY

- ▮ Athenian homeland
- ▮ Spartan homeland
- ○ Greek city-state

TIMELINE

1					
2					
3					
4					

800   700   600   500   400   300

1 GREEK UNITY 700–338 BCE

All Greek cities looked toward certain common places of "Panhellenic" significance throughout the Greek, or Hellenic, world. These included Mount Olympus, the seat of the gods; Delphi, where an oracle spoke for all Greeks; and venues of Panhellenic festivals, such as Olympia.

- ○ Panhellenic site

431–404 BCE Control of the narrow strait of the Hellespont—the route to Athens' ally, Byzantium, and the Black Sea—is key in the Peloponnesian War

338 BCE Philip II of Macedonia (Alexander's father) leaves his capital of Aegae and sweeps through Greece, defeats Athens and Thebes, and attempts to unify Greece under the League of Corinth

422 BCE The Peloponnesian War moves north as Spartans march through Thessaly and Thrace to capture Amphipolis

454 BCE Athenian general Pericles moves the Delian League treasury from Delos to Athens, ostensibly to protect it from Persian attack, but uses league funds to build the Parthenon

478 BCE The tiny island of Delos is chosen as the seat of the treasury of the league led by Athens, giving its name to the Delian League

4 GREECE WEAKENED 404–338 BCE

The Peloponnesian War spelled an end to stability and a blow to prosperity in Greece. From this point on, power ebbed and flowed between city-states and leagues. The constant fighting began to open an opportunity for an outside power—Greek-speaking Macedonia to the north—to expand and take control of the region.

- ● Macedonian capital

415 BCE Athens unwisely sends an expedition to attack Syracuse in Sicily, allowing Sparta to capture the entire Athenian navy; Athens now stands little chance of winning the war

3 PELOPONNESIAN WAR 431–404 BCE

Although Sparta formed an alliance with Athens to fight Persia, it now headed the rival Peloponnesian League and objected to Athens' high-handed imperialism. When war broke out between Sparta and Athens, most of Greece leapt to either one side or the other. Sparta emerged victorious, but the conflict plunged the region into disarray.

- ✕ Athenian victory
- ✕ Spartan victory
- → Athenian expedition
- ● State involved in war
- ▮ Athenian allies
- ▮ Spartan allies

424 BCE Athens captures Cythera from Sparta during the Peloponnesian War

416 BCE Neutral island of Melos is taken by Athens and—in an act that shocks many at home in Athens—all the inhabitants are massacred or enslaved

THRACE

Abdera · Maronea · Aenus · Thasos · Samothrace · Parium · Lampsacus · Arisbe · Cherronesita · Imbros · Abydus · Dardanus · Scepsis · Cebren · Assos · Tenedos

Amphipolis · Argilus · Galepsus · Strepsa · Dicaeopolis · Stolos · Acanthus · Aenea · Mecyberna · Spartolus · Dion · Singus · Thyssus · Olynthus · Sermylia · Potidaea · Aphytis · Torone · Mende · Scione · Methone

MACEDONIA · Pella · Aegae

Mount Olympus

Hephaestia · Myrina · Lemnos · Lemnos

Antissa · Mytilene · Pyrrha · Eressus · Lesbos

Cym... · Phocaea · Clazomenae · Erythrae · Haerae · Chios

A e g e a n   S e a

Larissa · Thessaly · Pherae · Pagasae · Pharsalus · Peparethus · Skyros

Ambracia · Argos · Olpae · AETOLIA · Leucas

Oreos · Euboea · Chalcis · Eretria · Styra · Carystus · Andros · Oenoe · Karia

Boeotia · Delphi · Koronela · Thebes · Tanagra · ATTICA · Athens · Piraeus · Aegina · Coressus · Tenos · Myconos · Delos

Naupactus · Gulf of Corinth · Megara · Corinth · Ceos · Cythnos · Cyclades · Naxos

Oiniadai · Calydon · Patrae · ACHAEA · Serifos

Cephallenia · Elis · ARCADIA · Mantinea · Argos · Olympia · Dipai · Sifnos · Ios · Astypalaea

Zacynthus · Peloponnese · Bassae · Melos · Thera

MESSENIA · Sparta · LACONIA · Methone

Cythera · S e a

M e d i t e r r a n e a n   S e a

Kydonia · Knossos · Crete

Byzantium
Chalcedon
Astacus
Selymbria
Perinthus

*Sea of
Marmara*

oconnesus

Cyzicus

Phrygia

2 DELIAN LEAGUE 478–431 BCE

In the wake of the Persian Wars (492–480 BCE),
many Greek cities formed a league of cooperation,
whose leaders met annually on the tiny, central
island of Delos. Athens emerged as the leader of
this league but became ever more heavy-handed
in its leadership, sparking innumerable revolts,
which it crushed ruthlessly.

● States within   🖐 States in revolt
  Delian League   against Athens

P E R S I A N
E M P I R E

ysia

Anatolia

Magnesia   Sardis

Lydia

478–470 BCE Ephesus and the
other cities of Ionia join the
Delian League to protect
themselves from Persia,
swelling league numbers
to around 200 cities

Colophon
Ephesus
Ionia
Pygela
Priene   Latmus
Myus
Miletus   Pedasa
Iasus   Mylasa
Cindye   Hydissus   Idyma
Madnases   Syangela   Cyllandioi
Termera   Halicarnassus   Calynda
Calydnioi   Telandria
Cos   Telmessus

Caria

Cnidus
Nisyros   Ialysus
              Bricindarioi
Camirus
              Lindus

Dodecanese

Rhodes

Carpathos

THE GREEK CITY-STATES

In a seminal period for Western civilization, the Greek
people spread through the Mediterranean, exporting their
culture as they went. But they were never unified politically.
Leagues of independent city-states became close-knit only
when faced with a common threat.

The cornerstone of Greek civilization
was the *polis*, or city-state. These self-
governing communities, frequently
isolated by Greece's rugged terrain,
were based on walled cities with
outlying villages and farmland. Despite
being fiercely independent, these
hundreds of city-states, scattered
around the Mediterranean, had
language, religion, and many cultural
practices in common. Even remote
colonies strove to express their
identity with the building of
temples and theaters and the

◁ **Bust of Pericles**
The so-called "first citizen of Athens," Pericles
led Athens during the Peloponnesian War.
Although a strong proponent of democracy
at home, he made many enemies abroad.

output of fine ceramics. The Greek
world was also more or less united at
times in loose confederations, never
more so than when the need arose to
repulse the invading Persian Empire
(see pp.58–59). The major alliance that
arose in the aftermath of the Persian
Wars, the Delian League, became
dominated by Athens—to the
annoyance not only of many other
league members but also of other
leagues—principally that headed by
Sparta. Athens' ruthless leadership of
what had effectively become its empire
sucked it into conflict with Sparta at
a time when they were both great
nations. By the end of the war, they
were weakened and depleted, leaving
a power vacuum for others to fill.

*"The strong exact what they can, and the weak
suffer what they must."*

THUCYDIDES, HISTORY OF THE PELOPONNESIAN WAR, 400 BCE

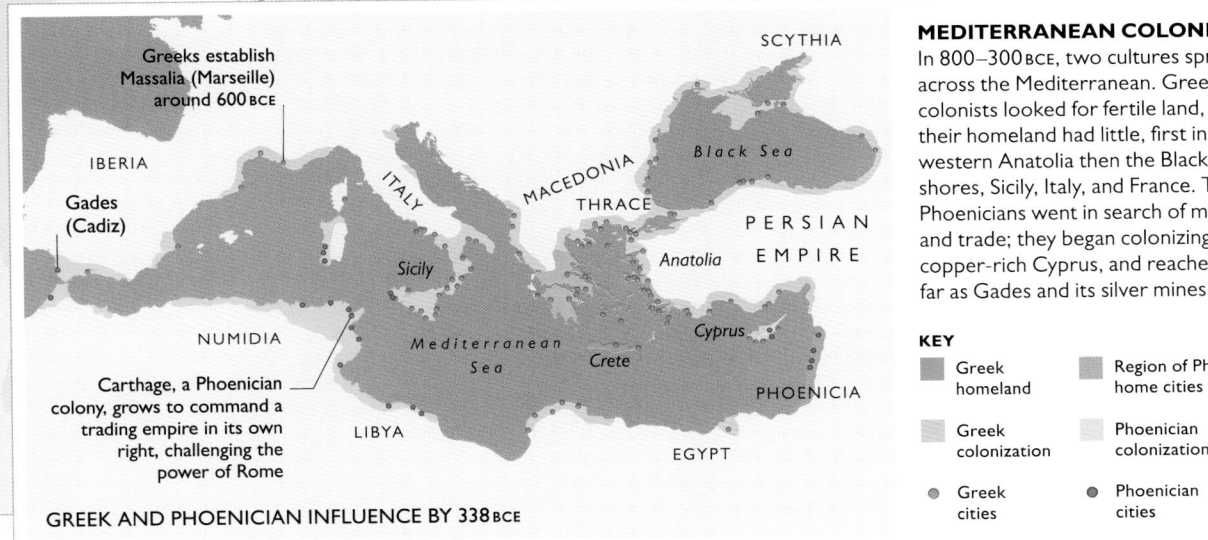

Greeks establish
Massalia (Marseille)
around 600 BCE

SCYTHIA

IBERIA

ITALY

MACEDONIA

Black Sea

THRACE

Gades
(Cadiz)

Sicily

Anatolia

P E R S I A N
E M P I R E

NUMIDIA

*Mediterranean
Sea*

Crete

Cyprus

Carthage, a Phoenician
colony, grows to command a
trading empire in its own
right, challenging the
power of Rome

LIBYA

EGYPT

PHOENICIA

GREEK AND PHOENICIAN INFLUENCE BY 338 BCE

MEDITERRANEAN COLONISTS

In 800–300 BCE, two cultures spread
across the Mediterranean. Greek
colonists looked for fertile land, since
their homeland had little, first in
western Anatolia then the Black Sea
shores, Sicily, Italy, and France. The
Phoenicians went in search of metals
and trade; they began colonizing
copper-rich Cyprus, and reached as
far as Gades and its silver mines.

KEY

■ Greek
  homeland

■ Greek
  colonization

● Greek
  cities

■ Region of Phoenician
  home cities

■ Phoenician
  colonization

● Phoenician
  cities

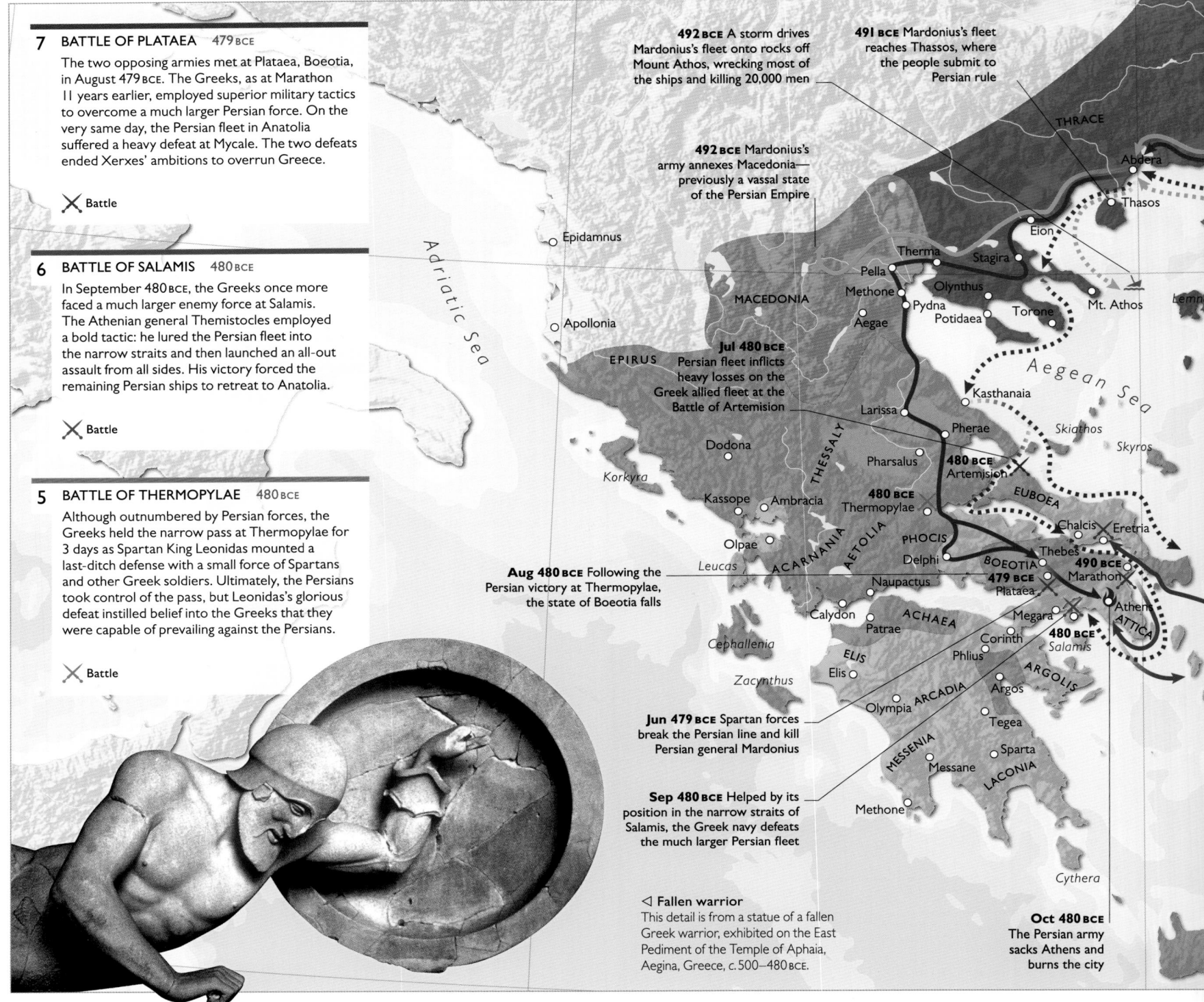

7 BATTLE OF PLATAEA 479 BCE

The two opposing armies met at Plataea, Boeotia, in August 479 BCE. The Greeks, as at Marathon 11 years earlier, employed superior military tactics to overcome a much larger Persian force. On the very same day, the Persian fleet in Anatolia suffered a heavy defeat at Mycale. The two defeats ended Xerxes' ambitions to overrun Greece.

✕ Battle

6 BATTLE OF SALAMIS 480 BCE

In September 480 BCE, the Greeks once more faced a much larger enemy force at Salamis. The Athenian general Themistocles employed a bold tactic: he lured the Persian fleet into the narrow straits and then launched an all-out assault from all sides. His victory forced the remaining Persian ships to retreat to Anatolia.

✕ Battle

5 BATTLE OF THERMOPYLAE 480 BCE

Although outnumbered by Persian forces, the Greeks held the narrow pass at Thermopylae for 3 days as Spartan King Leonidas mounted a last-ditch defense with a small force of Spartans and other Greek soldiers. Ultimately, the Persians took control of the pass, but Leonidas's glorious defeat instilled belief into the Greeks that they were capable of prevailing against the Persians.

✕ Battle

492 BCE A storm drives Mardonius's fleet onto rocks off Mount Athos, wrecking most of the ships and killing 20,000 men

491 BCE Mardonius's fleet reaches Thassos, where the people submit to Persian rule

492 BCE Mardonius's army annexes Macedonia—previously a vassal state of the Persian Empire

Jul 480 BCE Persian fleet inflicts heavy losses on the Greek allied fleet at the Battle of Artemision

Aug 480 BCE Following the Persian victory at Thermopylae, the state of Boeotia falls

Jun 479 BCE Spartan forces break the Persian line and kill Persian general Mardonius

Sep 480 BCE Helped by its position in the narrow straits of Salamis, the Greek navy defeats the much larger Persian fleet

◁ **Fallen warrior**
This detail is from a statue of a fallen Greek warrior, exhibited on the East Pediment of the Temple of Aphaia, Aegina, Greece, c. 500–480 BCE.

Oct 480 BCE The Persian army sacks Athens and burns the city

GREECE AND PERSIA AT WAR

Following a series of revolts in its western provinces, the vast Persian Empire pushed westward in 492 BCE in an attempt to conquer the Greek city-states and colonies around the Aegean Sea. This led to a destructive series of wars in which their superior military tactics and some timely good fortune helped the Greeks halt the much larger Persian forces.

By about 550 BCE, the Persian Empire had expanded westward, moving into Anatolia, where its armies had defeated the powerful king of Lydia, Croesus, and conquered numerous Ionian cities, which until then had been colonies of Greece. In 499 BCE, however, the Ionian Greeks in the city of Miletus rebelled against Persian rule, triggering uprisings not only in Ionia but also in cities across the Persian western frontier.

The Persian military response precipitated the first wave of hostilities, in which the Persian forces took 5 years to crush the Ionian rebellion, finally recapturing Miletus in 494 BCE. Then, in retaliation for the support the Greek city-states of Athens and Eretria had given to the Ionian cities during their revolt, Persia's King Darius (r. 522–486 BCE) launched a military invasion of Greece in 492 BCE. The attack was two-pronged: a land and naval campaign directed at Thrace and Macedonia, headed by the Persian general Mardonius,

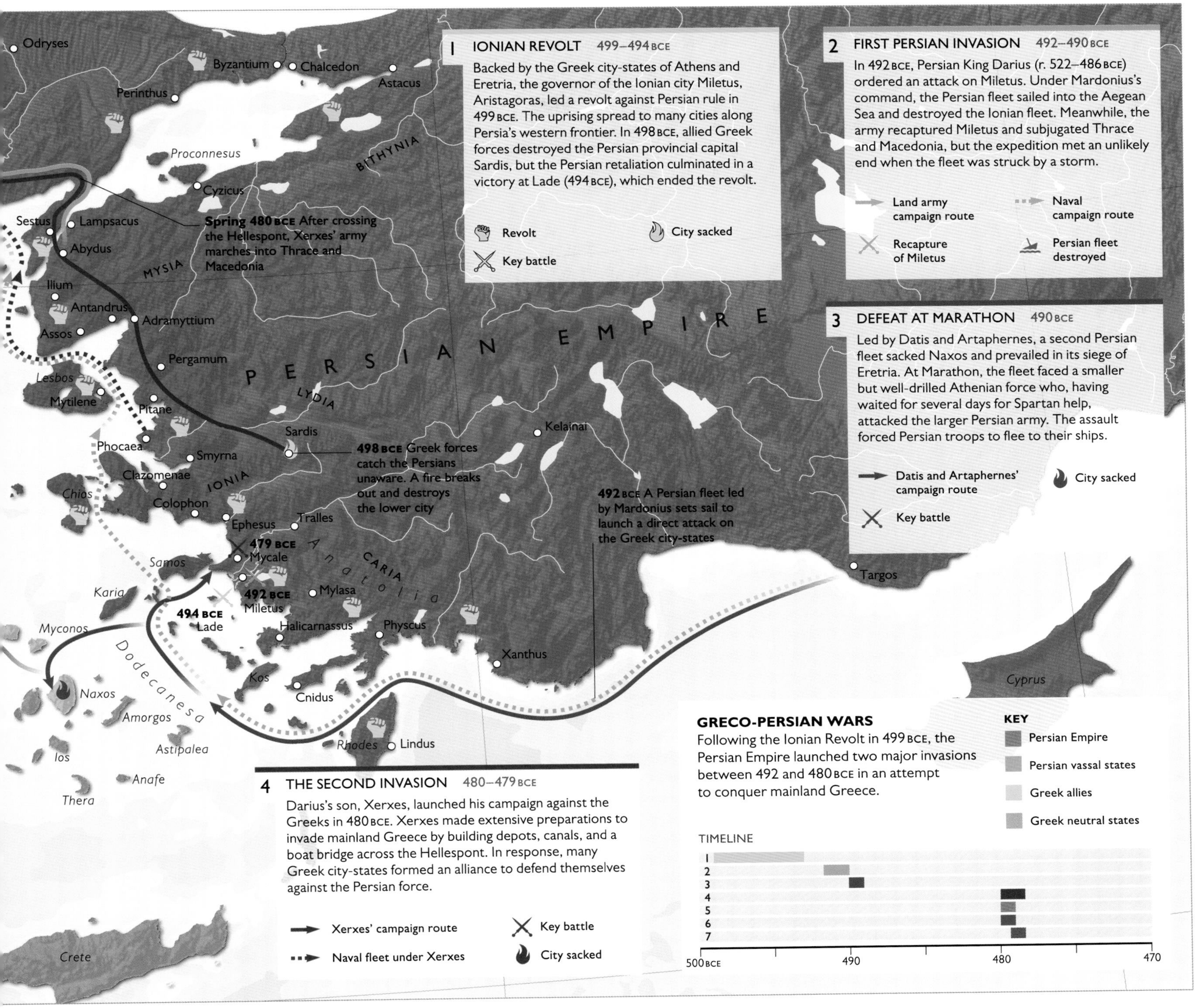

Odryses

Byzantium ○ Chalcedon

Perinthus   Astacus

Proconnesus

BITHYNIA

Cyzicus

Sestus ○ Lampsacus

Spring 480 BCE After crossing the Hellespont, Xerxes' army marches into Thrace and Macedonia

Abydus

MYSIA

Ilium

Antandrus ○ Adramyttium

Assos

Pergamum

Lesbos

Mytilene ○ Pitane

Phocaea

Smyrna   Sardis

Clazomenae

IONIA

Chios   Colophon

Ephesus ○ Tralles

498 BCE Greek forces catch the Persians unaware. A fire breaks out and destroys the lower city

LYDIA

Kelainai

Anatolia

Samos

479 BCE Mycale

CARIA

Karia

492 BCE Mylasa

494 BCE Miletus

Lade   Halicarnassus   Physcus

Myconos

Dodecanesa

Kos   Cnidus

492 BCE A Persian fleet led by Mardonius sets sail to launch a direct attack on the Greek city-states

Xanthus

Naxos

Amorgos

Astipalea

Ios

Rhodes ○ Lindus

Targos

Cyprus

Anafe

Thera

Crete

PERSIAN EMPIRE

1 IONIAN REVOLT   499–494 BCE

Backed by the Greek city-states of Athens and Eretria, the governor of the Ionian city Miletus, Aristagoras, led a revolt against Persian rule in 499 BCE. The uprising spread to many cities along Persia's western frontier. In 498 BCE, allied Greek forces destroyed the Persian provincial capital Sardis, but the Persian retaliation culminated in a victory at Lade (494 BCE), which ended the revolt.

✊ Revolt   🔥 City sacked

⚔ Key battle

2 FIRST PERSIAN INVASION   492–490 BCE

In 492 BCE, Persian King Darius (r. 522–486 BCE) ordered an attack on Miletus. Under Mardonius's command, the Persian fleet sailed into the Aegean Sea and destroyed the Ionian fleet. Meanwhile, the army recaptured Miletus and subjugated Thrace and Macedonia, but the expedition met an unlikely end when the fleet was struck by a storm.

→ Land army campaign route   ⇢ Naval campaign route

✕ Recapture of Miletus   ⚓ Persian fleet destroyed

3 DEFEAT AT MARATHON   490 BCE

Led by Datis and Artaphernes, a second Persian fleet sacked Naxos and prevailed in its siege of Eretria. At Marathon, the fleet faced a smaller but well-drilled Athenian force who, having waited for several days for Spartan help, attacked the larger Persian army. The assault forced Persian troops to flee to their ships.

→ Datis and Artaphernes' campaign route   🔥 City sacked

✕ Key battle

4 THE SECOND INVASION   480–479 BCE

Darius's son, Xerxes, launched his campaign against the Greeks in 480 BCE. Xerxes made extensive preparations to invade mainland Greece by building depots, canals, and a boat bridge across the Hellespont. In response, many Greek city-states formed an alliance to defend themselves against the Persian force.

→ Xerxes' campaign route   ✕ Key battle

⇢ Naval fleet under Xerxes   🔥 City sacked

GRECO-PERSIAN WARS

Following the Ionian Revolt in 499 BCE, the Persian Empire launched two major invasions between 492 and 480 BCE in an attempt to conquer mainland Greece.

KEY

▬ Persian Empire

▬ Persian vassal states

▬ Greek allies

▬ Greek neutral states

TIMELINE

```
      1
      2
      3
      4
      5
      6
      7
500BCE            490            480            470
```

and a second led by Datis and Artaphernes. The missions brought many Greek cities under Persian control and also turned Macedonia into a client kingdom. But, the Persian armies were eventually forced to withdraw, as a storm wrecked Mardonius's fleet off the coast of Mount Athos. The second Persian army suffered a loss against the smaller but more tactically astute Athenian army at the Battle of Marathon in 490 BCE.

Ten years later, Xerxes I (r. 486–465 BCE), Darius's son and successor, restarted hostilities against Athens, having spent several years planning his campaign. Once more, the Persian forces outnumbered their Greek counterparts, in part because Athens could not always persuade other Greek states (in particular, the militaristic city of Sparta) to join them in battle. Nevertheless, the Persians were unable to exploit this advantage, and the Greek city-states ensured their independence with victories at Salamis and Plataea.

DARIUS I
550–486 BCE

Darius I was the third Persian king of the Achaemenid Empire, during whose reign the empire reached its peak. His administrative skill combined with his strong and intelligent leadership earned him the title of Darius the Great. He also built the magnificent city of Persepolis and left behind inscriptions telling the story of his successes.

Great King Darius
The king sits on his throne in a bas-relief exhibited in Persepolis, c. 500 BCE.

ALEXANDER THE GREAT

The young king of Macedonia, Alexander III, ascended to the throne in 336 BCE following his father's death, inheriting a highly efficient army. Within 10 years, he conquered the vast Persian Empire, creating a realm that stretched from Greece to the River Indus. Although the empire fell soon after his death, it left a lasting cultural mark throughout the region.

On his succession to the Macedonian throne in 359 BCE, King Philip II (r. 359–336 BCE) transformed his army into the world's most effective fighting machine—based on the heavy infantry phalanx armed with long pikes. During his reign, his armies mounted efficient sieges to gain control of Thessaly, Illyria, and Thrace, and asserted control over the Greek mainland despite Greek hostility. However, just as Philip was preparing to invade Persia in 336 BCE, he was assassinated by one of his bodyguards.

Alexander becomes king

Philip's 21-year-old son, Alexander III, immediately claimed the throne and wielded his military force to suppress the revolts that had erupted in Greece and the Balkans following Philip's death. Thereafter, Alexander set out to realize his late father's ambitions, leading an army of 30,000 soldiers and a 5,000-strong cavalry on a masterfully drilled military campaign to conquer the Persian Empire. Alexander swept through the Persian territories of Anatolia, Syria, and Egypt without losing a single battle. He then marched east to the Persian homeland, waging a tireless campaign, and by 327 BCE

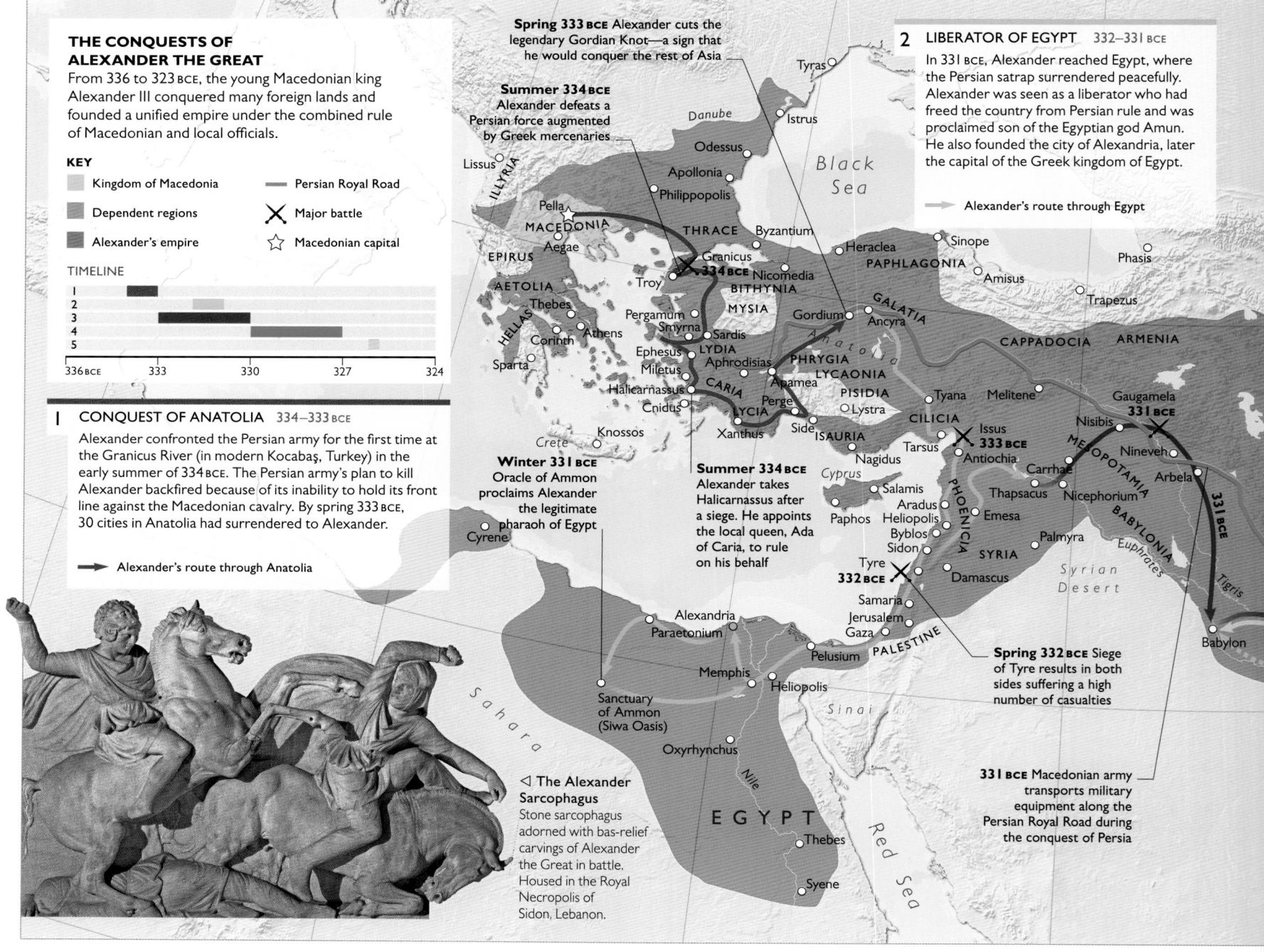

THE CONQUESTS OF ALEXANDER THE GREAT
From 336 to 323 BCE, the young Macedonian king Alexander III conquered many foreign lands and founded a unified empire under the combined rule of Macedonian and local officials.

KEY

- Kingdom of Macedonia
- Dependent regions
- Alexander's empire
- Persian Royal Road
- ✕ Major battle
- ☆ Macedonian capital

TIMELINE
1
2
3
4
5
336 BCE   333   330   327   324

1 CONQUEST OF ANATOLIA 334–333 BCE
Alexander confronted the Persian army for the first time at the Granicus River (in modern Kocabaş, Turkey) in the early summer of 334 BCE. The Persian army's plan to kill Alexander backfired because of its inability to hold its front line against the Macedonian cavalry. By spring 333 BCE, 30 cities in Anatolia had surrendered to Alexander.

➤ Alexander's route through Anatolia

Spring 333 BCE Alexander cuts the legendary Gordian Knot—a sign that he would conquer the rest of Asia

Summer 334 BCE Alexander defeats a Persian force augmented by Greek mercenaries

Winter 331 BCE Oracle of Ammon proclaims Alexander the legitimate pharaoh of Egypt

Summer 334 BCE Alexander takes Halicarnassus after a siege. He appoints the local queen, Ada of Caria, to rule on his behalf

2 LIBERATOR OF EGYPT 332–331 BCE
In 331 BCE, Alexander reached Egypt, where the Persian satrap surrendered peacefully. Alexander was seen as a liberator who had freed the country from Persian rule and was proclaimed son of the Egyptian god Amun. He also founded the city of Alexandria, later the capital of the Greek kingdom of Egypt.

➤ Alexander's route through Egypt

Spring 332 BCE Siege of Tyre results in both sides suffering a high number of casualties

331 BCE Macedonian army transports military equipment along the Persian Royal Road during the conquest of Persia

◁ **The Alexander Sarcophagus**
Stone sarcophagus adorned with bas-relief carvings of Alexander the Great in battle. Housed in the Royal Necropolis of Sidon, Lebanon.

crushed the Achaemenid Dynasty—rulers of the first Persian Empire. Alexander forged an empire that stretched from Greece to the River Indus and introduced Greek culture to the vast realm. In addition, he was an astute diplomat and encouraged the mixing of cultures, adopting Persian customs in an attempt to unify his empire and establish trade routes between Asia and Europe.

Alexander set his sights on invading India next, but his weary troops refused to fight on, forcing their king to lead them home. Alexander survived a perilous journey across the Makran desert, but in 323 BCE—at the age of 32—he died in Babylon of a fever, exhaustion, or possibly from being poisoned. A tussle for power ensued after his death and led to the breakup of his vast empire.

"... the end and object of conquest is to avoid doing the same thing as the conquered."

ALEXANDER III, FROM *LIVES* BY PLUTARCH, c. 100 CE

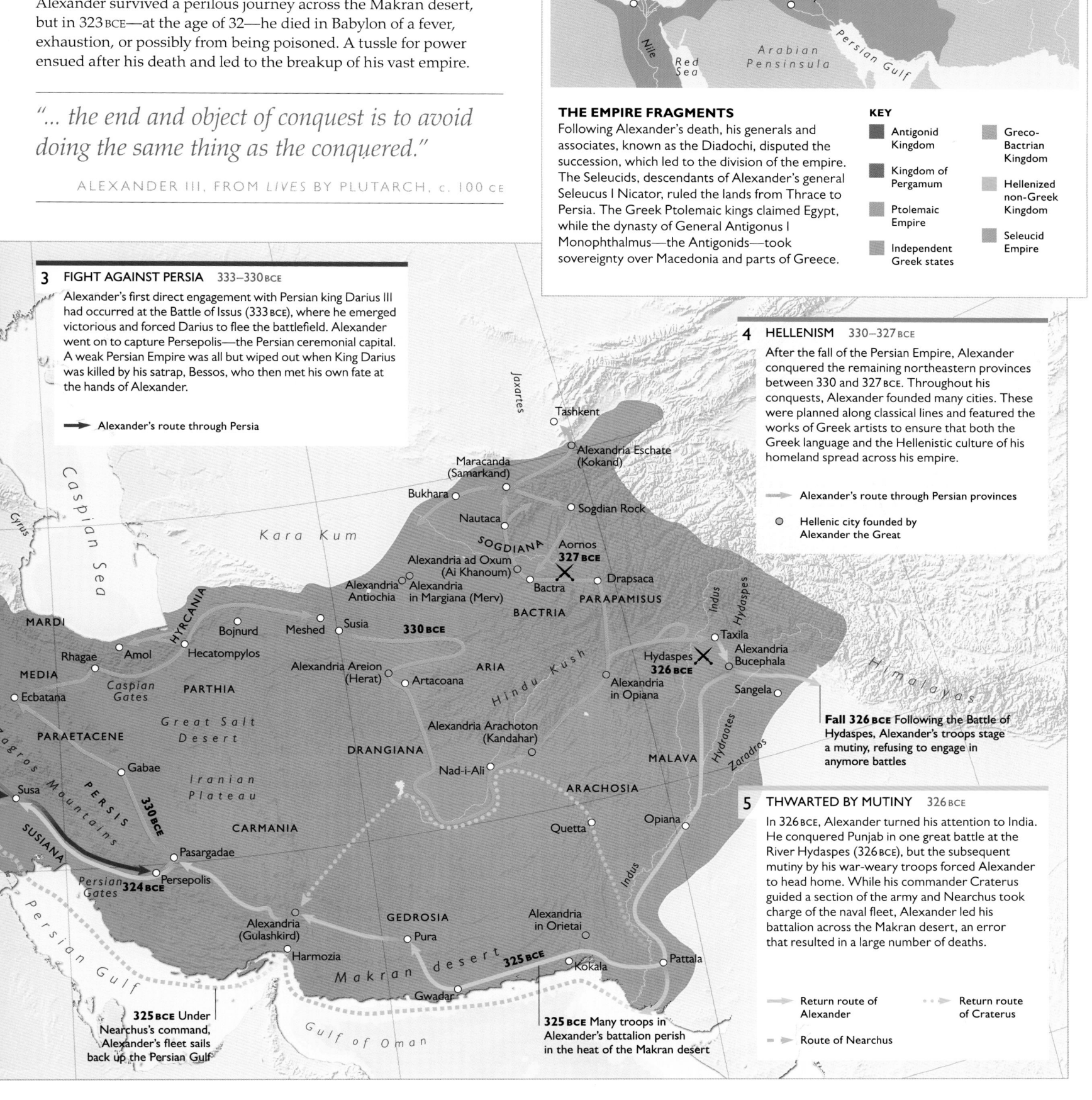

THE EMPIRE FRAGMENTS
Following Alexander's death, his generals and associates, known as the Diadochi, disputed the succession, which led to the division of the empire. The Seleucids, descendants of Alexander's general Seleucus I Nicator, ruled the lands from Thrace to Persia. The Greek Ptolemaic kings claimed Egypt, while the dynasty of General Antigonus I Monophthalmus—the Antigonids—took sovereignty over Macedonia and parts of Greece.

KEY
- Antigonid Kingdom
- Kingdom of Pergamum
- Ptolemaic Empire
- Independent Greek states
- Greco-Bactrian Kingdom
- Hellenized non-Greek Kingdom
- Seleucid Empire

3 FIGHT AGAINST PERSIA 333–330 BCE
Alexander's first direct engagement with Persian king Darius III had occurred at the Battle of Issus (333 BCE), where he emerged victorious and forced Darius to flee the battlefield. Alexander went on to capture Persepolis—the Persian ceremonial capital. A weak Persian Empire was all but wiped out when King Darius was killed by his satrap, Bessos, who then met his own fate at the hands of Alexander.

→ Alexander's route through Persia

4 HELLENISM 330–327 BCE
After the fall of the Persian Empire, Alexander conquered the remaining northeastern provinces between 330 and 327 BCE. Throughout his conquests, Alexander founded many cities. These were planned along classical lines and featured the works of Greek artists to ensure that both the Greek language and the Hellenistic culture of his homeland spread across his empire.

→ Alexander's route through Persian provinces

○ Hellenic city founded by Alexander the Great

Fall 326 BCE Following the Battle of Hydaspes, Alexander's troops stage a mutiny, refusing to engage in anymore battles

5 THWARTED BY MUTINY 326 BCE
In 326 BCE, Alexander turned his attention to India. He conquered Punjab in one great battle at the River Hydaspes (326 BCE), but the subsequent mutiny by his war-weary troops forced Alexander to head home. While his commander Craterus guided a section of the army and Nearchus took charge of the naval fleet, Alexander led his battalion across the Makran desert, an error that resulted in a large number of deaths.

→ Return route of Alexander
⋯→ Return route of Craterus
→ Route of Nearchus

325 BCE Under Nearchus's command, Alexander's fleet sails back up the Persian Gulf

325 BCE Many troops in Alexander's battalion perish in the heat of the Makran desert

THE CLASSICAL AGE

Conventionally, the term "classical civilization" has been used to define the two different but related cultures that developed in the Mediterranean world from about 800 BCE to 400 CE. The first of these emerged in and around Greece, and the second rose in Rome, from where it spread across the entire European world.

△ **Iconic design**
This bronze helmet from the 6th century BCE was first worn by soldiers of the city-state Corinth but later gained popularity throughout Greece.

The immense contribution of Greece to western civilization is universally recognized. Although Athens has traditionally been given the greatest credit for this advance, modern historians believe that there is far more to the story.

Rise of the city-states

It was during the Archaic Period (800–479 BCE) of Greek history that the seeds of Greek civilization were sown. It was an age of experimentation and intellectual ferment. City-states such as Athens, Sparta, Corinth, Argos, Eleusis, Thebes, Miletus, and Syracuse emerged. The population expanded, and by classical times, it is estimated that there were more than 1,000 communities scattered across the Greek world.

Art and architecture flourished, and cities along the coast of Anatolia (modern-day Turkey) became important centers of early philosophical and other intellectual developments. The great plays of Sophocles, Euripides, Aeschylus, and Aristophanes were first staged at the Theater of Dionysus Eleutherus on the southern slopes of Athens' Acropolis. Herodotus and Thucydides were the first great historians. Socrates, Plato, and Aristotle revolutionized philosophy, all three founding their own philosophical schools. Other notable figures of the time included the statesmen Solon and Pericles, the generals

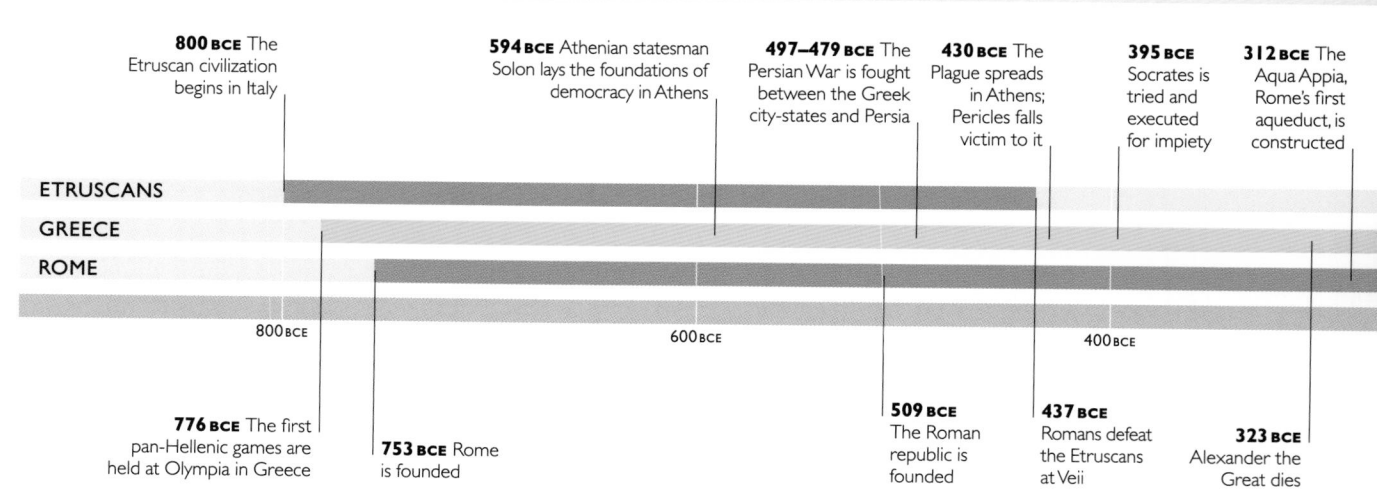

△ **Greek art**
The Greeks used vases for storage and at occasions such as weddings. The painting on this vase, which dates from 530 BCE, depicts the hero Hercules.

Alcibiades and Themistocles, the poets Pindar and Sappho, the sculptor Phidias, and the physician Hippocrates—the father of modern medicine.

Success in war cemented these achievements. The defeat of the invading Persians at the town of Marathon in 490 BCE and at the island of Salamis 10 years later are regarded as pivotal moments in world history. Had the Persians emerged victorious, it is likely that the Greek achievements, which form the building blocks on which modern Western civilization is founded, would have been stifled at birth.

Spread of Greek influence

Greek city-states lost most of their power following the conquest of Greece by Philip II of Macedon in 338 BCE; however, Greek culture did not come to an end. Rather, it was spread across the eastern Mediterranean and far into Asia by the Macedonians. While the vast empire created by Alexander the Great (the son of Philip II) did not survive his death in 323 BCE—his generals divided it among themselves—what survived was the notion of "Greekness," which permeated every aspect of daily life. Almost everyone in the former empire spoke a form of colloquial Greek. The rulers encouraged the growth of learning in the empire. In Egypt, under the Macedonian general Ptolemy I, the university at Alexandria became home to the mathematicians Euclid, Eratosthenes,

POWERFUL CIVILIZATIONS

Various civilizations rose and fell in the Mediterranean region during the so-called Classical period of world history. However, the Greek and Roman civilizations emerged as the most dynamic during this era. The Etruscan civilization is also included in this timeline because of its close links with the early days of Rome. The city of Rome itself has a long history but played a relatively minor part until the Romans expanded their influence in the 3rd century BCE.

800 BCE The Etruscan civilization begins in Italy

594 BCE Athenian statesman Solon lays the foundations of democracy in Athens

497–479 BCE The Persian War is fought between the Greek city-states and Persia

430 BCE The Plague spreads in Athens; Pericles falls victim to it

395 BCE Socrates is tried and executed for impiety

312 BCE The Aqua Appia, Rome's first aqueduct, is constructed

ETRUSCANS

GREECE

ROME

800 BCE

600 BCE

400 BCE

776 BCE The first pan-Hellenic games are held at Olympia in Greece

753 BCE Rome is founded

509 BCE The Roman republic is founded

437 BCE Romans defeat the Etruscans at Veii

323 BCE Alexander the Great dies

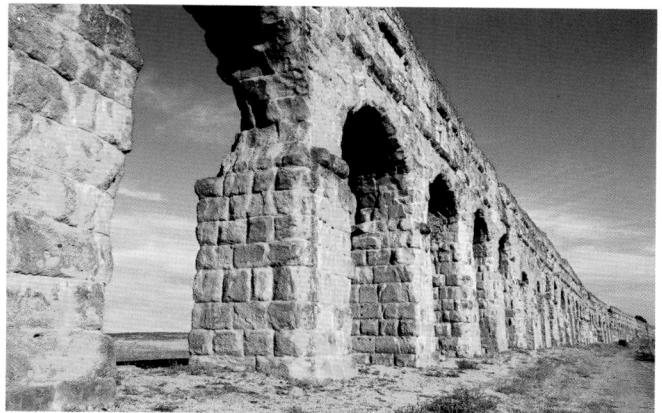

◁ **Public works**
The Aqua Appia was the first aqueduct built to supply Rome with drinking water. It dropped only 33 ft (10 m) in height along its length of 10 miles (16 km). Commissioned in 312 BCE, it was an early sign of the skill and ambition of Roman infrastructure projects.

and Archimedes, along with the inventors Heron and Ktesibios. The great library there came to be a wonder of the ancient Mediterranean world.

Rise and fall of Rome

Rome arose from a small trading settlement on the banks of the River Tiber. Initially, it came under the influence of the powerful Etruscan civilization to its north. The last Etruscan king, Lucius Tarquinius Superbus, was driven out by the Romans in 509 BCE, after which Rome became a republic, ruled by a senate and two consuls, elected annually.

It was war that made the republic great. Its increasing dominance in Italy brought it into conflict with its Mediterranean rival city Carthage. The defeat of the Carthaginians ensured Roman dominance of the western Mediterranean. The successful wars that the Romans fought against the Macedonians and others in the east gave Rome control over the entire Mediterranean region.

In the 1st century BCE, Rome was still a republic, with powerful senators such as Julius Caesar. Whether he would have made himself emperor had he not been assassinated must remain speculation. It was Octavian, his adopted great-nephew, who, after a bitter civil war, became Rome's first emperor in 31 BCE, taking the title Imperator Caesar Augustus.

In the 3rd century CE, the empire went through a period of crisis due to pressure on its frontiers and as a result of political instability, and it was divided into a western and an eastern half. Emperor Diocletian restored stability, partly by appointing colleagues to share his authority. Some later emperors, notably Constantine, ruled alone. It was he who legalized Christianity and founded Constantinople to rival Rome as the imperial capital. Following him, the eastern and western halves of the empire increasingly went their separate ways.

"Freedom is the sure possession of those alone who have the courage to defend it."

PERICLES, ATHENIAN STATESMAN, 495–429 BCE

◁ **Romanized Greek art**
Roman artists were influenced by their Greek counterparts. This marble statue of a discus-thrower is a Roman version of a Greek original that was lost. The Greek statue was cast in bronze in the 5th century BCE by the sculptor Myron.

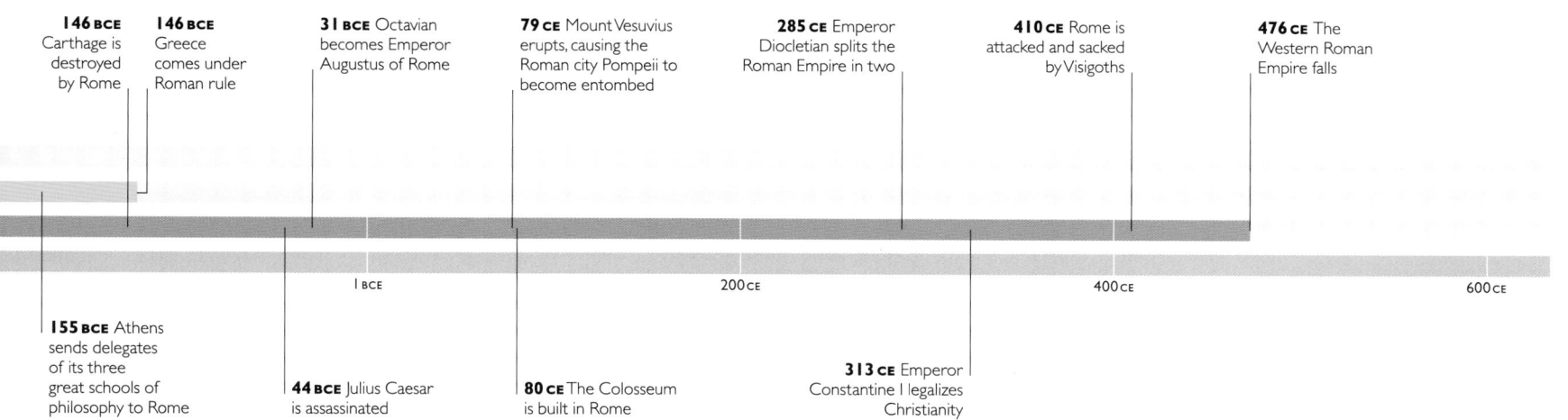

146 BCE Carthage is destroyed by Rome

146 BCE Greece comes under Roman rule

31 BCE Octavian becomes Emperor Augustus of Rome

79 CE Mount Vesuvius erupts, causing the Roman city Pompeii to become entombed

285 CE Emperor Diocletian splits the Roman Empire in two

410 CE Rome is attacked and sacked by Visigoths

476 CE The Western Roman Empire falls

I BCE

200 CE

400 CE

600 CE

155 BCE Athens sends delegates of its three great schools of philosophy to Rome

44 BCE Julius Caesar is assassinated

80 CE The Colosseum is built in Rome

313 CE Emperor Constantine I legalizes Christianity

THE PEOPLES OF ITALY IN 500 BCE

Before Rome's expansion, Italy's most influential people were the Etruscans. A number of independent Italic-speaking peoples, such as the Aequi, occupied compact territories in central Italy.

1 THE ETRUSCANS c. 700–270 BCE

From around 700 BCE, the Etruscan civilization developed in three centers: the heartland of Etruria (modern Tuscany, Lazio, and Umbria), the valley of the Padus (Po) River, and in Campania to the south. The Etruscans became one of the most influential civilizations in the Mediterranean until their eventual displacement by the professional armies of Rome and their absorption into the Roman administration.

▨ Etruscan heartlands

8th century BCE onward The Carthaginians hold many coastal areas of Sardinia and encourage cereal grain farming inland

2 THE ETRUSCAN LEAGUES c. 700–400 BCE

To consolidate their power and strengthen their trading links, individual Etruscan cities formed alliances, or leagues. There were small alliances among the Etruscans of the Padus Valley and Campania, but the largest of them was the Etruscan League in Etruria. Twelve city-states belonged to the league, and they met annually, probably at their sacred sanctuary in Volsinii, to elect a leader.

○ City of the Etruscan League

3 MAGNA GRAECIA c. 700–250 BCE

Much of southern Italy was occupied by Italic-speaking peoples, such as the Sabini and the Samnites, but there were also Greek colonies in the south and in Sicily. The Greek presence was so strong that the Romans called the area Magna Graecia ("greater Greece"). Greek cities such as Naples and Syracuse were very powerful and brought Greek culture—including the Greek alphabet—to Italy. The Romans took over the area in the 3rd century BCE.

▨ Greeks

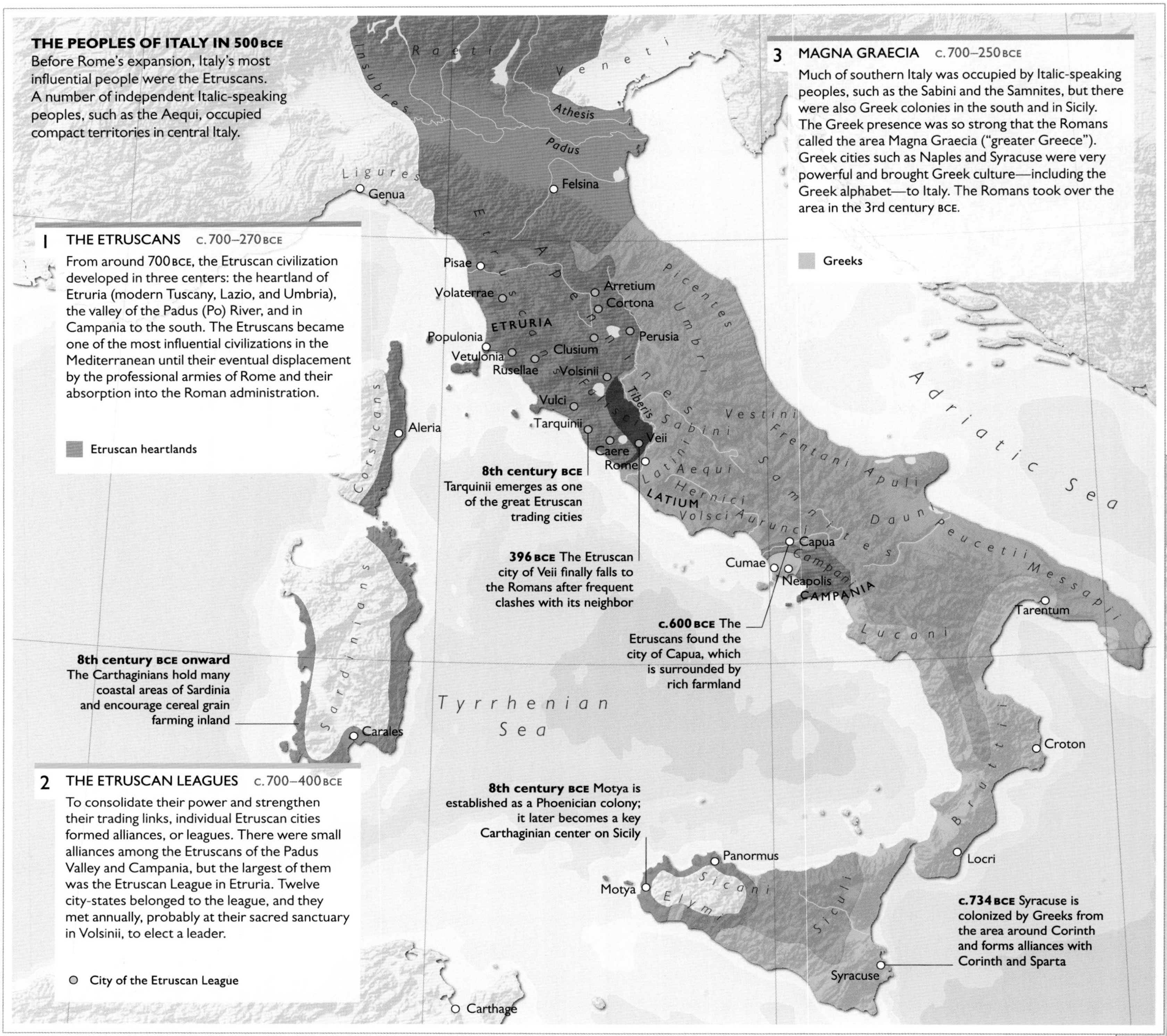

8th century BCE Tarquinii emerges as one of the great Etruscan trading cities

396 BCE The Etruscan city of Veii finally falls to the Romans after frequent clashes with its neighbor

c. 600 BCE The Etruscans found the city of Capua, which is surrounded by rich farmland

8th century BCE Motya is established as a Phoenician colony; it later becomes a key Carthaginian center on Sicily

c. 734 BCE Syracuse is colonized by Greeks from the area around Corinth and forms alliances with Corinth and Sparta

ETRUSCAN ART
TOMB DECORATIONS

The Etruscans developed art in various forms, including realist figurative sculpture in bronze and terracotta, engraved gems, vase paintings, and frescoes (right). Much of this art was strongly influenced by the Greeks. Most of the best surviving examples of frescoes and terracotta sculptures are from tombs, especially those found in Tarquinia, Italy.

SHIFTING POWER IN ITALY, 500–200 BCE

In 500 BCE, the Italian peninsula was home to many different tribes, as well as colonies founded by the Carthaginians of north Africa and the Greeks. By the end of the 2nd century BCE, Rome was the dominant presence in Italy and was continuing to expand.

KEY

▨ Italic-speaking peoples

▨ Italic-speaking peoples and Etruscans

▨ Carthaginians

TIMELINE

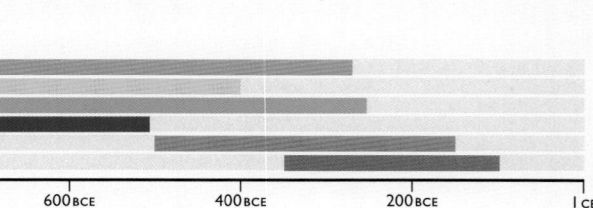

ETRUSCANS AND THE RISE OF ROME

By about 800 BCE, the dominant people in northern Italy were the Etruscans—people who lived in city-states and spoke a unique, non-Indo-European language. One of the cities they ruled was Rome, which began to grow into a major power from 500 BCE, annexing its neighbors and founding colonies throughout Italy.

The Etruscan civilization most probably grew out of an interaction between migrants from the eastern Mediterranean and the Villanovans, iron-age people who lived between the Padus (Po) River valley and the site of Rome.

The Etruscans flourished in this part of northern Italy, which they called Etruria, and in the area of Campania, around modern Naples. They built cities, developed distinctive styles of art—especially mural painting and sculpture—and formed trading alliances.

Rome was originally a settlement in Latium. Central Italy was home to a number of Italic peoples—the Umbri, Sabini, and others—who spoke Indo-European languages. Up until 509 BCE, Rome was ruled by kings of Etruscan origin. Rome then became a republic, governed by two annually elected magistrates, known as consuls. The Roman Republic expanded its territory, first into Latium, then into Etruria and the south. It did this through military victories over the Sabini and Aequi peoples of central Italy and by defeating Veii, an Etruscan city northwest of Rome. The Romans consolidated their position by founding colonies that gave them dominance over much of Italy. By the early 3rd century BCE, Rome had nearly 300,000 citizens, distributed across the Italian peninsula. Roman culture was influenced by its contact with both the Etruscans and the Greeks.

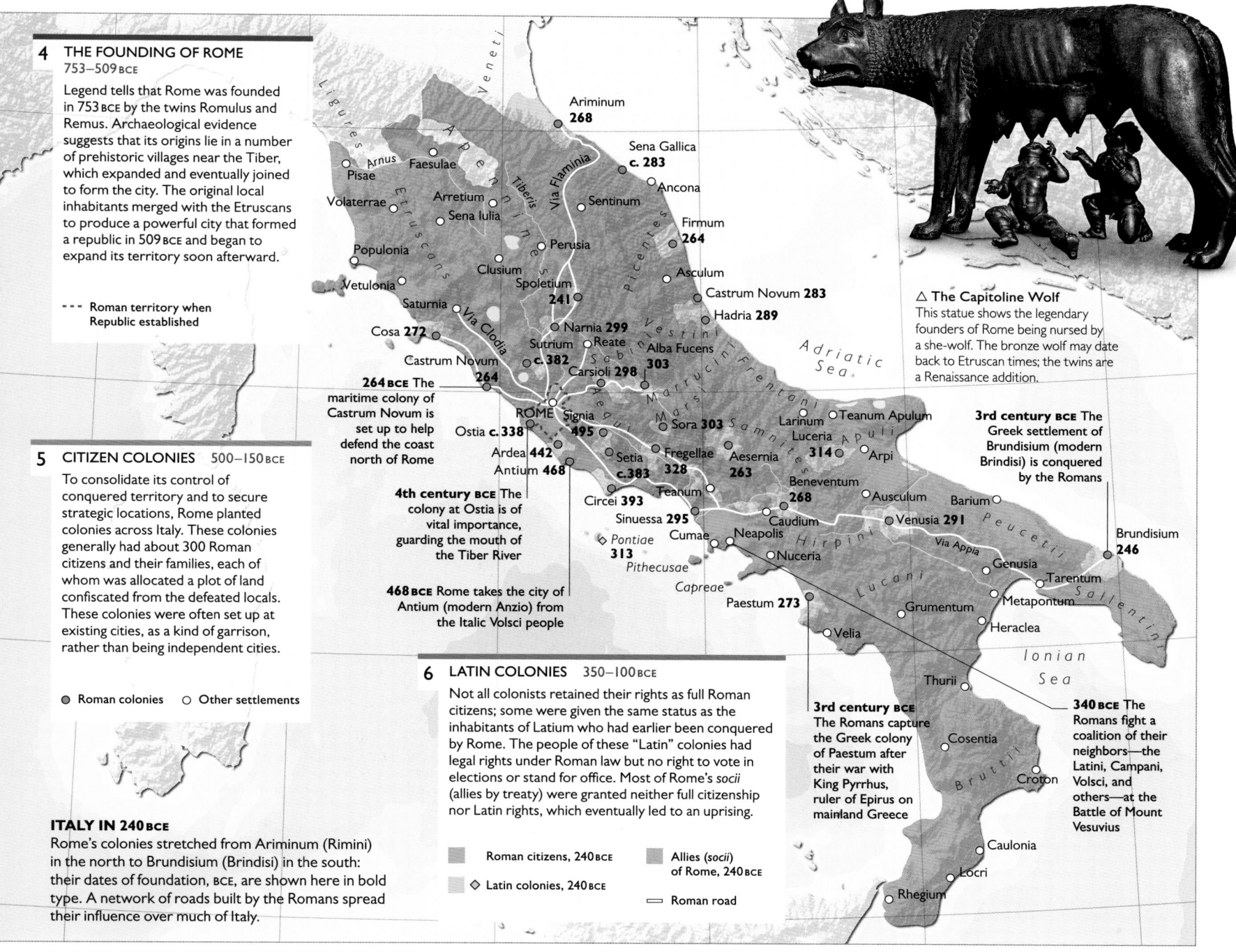

4 THE FOUNDING OF ROME
753–509 BCE

Legend tells that Rome was founded in 753 BCE by the twins Romulus and Remus. Archaeological evidence suggests that its origins lie in a number of prehistoric villages near the Tiber, which expanded and eventually joined to form the city. The original local inhabitants merged with the Etruscans to produce a powerful city that formed a republic in 509 BCE and began to expand its territory soon afterward.

- - - Roman territory when Republic established

5 CITIZEN COLONIES   500–150 BCE

To consolidate its control of conquered territory and to secure strategic locations, Rome planted colonies across Italy. These colonies generally had about 300 Roman citizens and their families, each of whom was allocated a plot of land confiscated from the defeated locals. These colonies were often set up at existing cities, as a kind of garrison, rather than being independent cities.

● Roman colonies   ○ Other settlements

ITALY IN 240 BCE
Rome's colonies stretched from Ariminum (Rimini) in the north to Brundisium (Brindisi) in the south: their dates of foundation, BCE, are shown here in bold type. A network of roads built by the Romans spread their influence over much of Italy.

264 BCE The maritime colony of Castrum Novum is set up to help defend the coast north of Rome

4th century BCE The colony at Ostia is of vital importance, guarding the mouth of the Tiber River

468 BCE Rome takes the city of Antium (modern Anzio) from the Italic Volsci people

6 LATIN COLONIES   350–100 BCE

Not all colonists retained their rights as full Roman citizens; some were given the same status as the inhabitants of Latium who had earlier been conquered by Rome. The people of these "Latin" colonies had legal rights under Roman law but no right to vote in elections or stand for office. Most of Rome's socii (allies by treaty) were granted neither full citizenship nor Latin rights, which eventually led to an uprising.

- Roman citizens, 240 BCE
- ◇ Latin colonies, 240 BCE
- Allies (socii) of Rome, 240 BCE
- ═ Roman road

△ **The Capitoline Wolf**
This statue shows the legendary founders of Rome being nursed by a she-wolf. The bronze wolf may date back to Etruscan times; the twins are a Renaissance addition.

3rd century BCE The Greek settlement of Brundisium (modern Brindisi) is conquered by the Romans

3rd century BCE The Romans capture the Greek colony of Paestum after their war with King Pyrrhus, ruler of Epirus on mainland Greece

340 BCE The Romans fight a coalition of their neighbors—the Latini, Campani, Volsci, and others—at the Battle of Mount Vesuvius

Map labels:

Ariminum 268, Sena Gallica c. 283, Ancona, Sentinum, Faesulae, Arnus, Pisae, Volaterrae, Arretium, Sena Iulia, Populonia, Clusium, Perusia, Firmum 264, Vetulonia, Spoletium 241, Asculum, Saturnia, Castrum Novum 283, Hadria 289, Cosa 272, Narnia 299, Sutrium c. 382, Reate, Alba Fucens 303, Castrum Novum 264, Carsioli 298, ROME, Signia 495, Sora 303, Larinum, Teanum Apulum, Ostia c. 338, Ardea 442, Setia c. 383, Fregellae 328, Aesernia 263, Luceria 314, Arpi, Antium 468, Circei 393, Teanum, Beneventum 268, Ausculum, Barium, Sinuessa 295, Caudium, Venusia 291, Pontiae 313, Cumae, Neapolis, Nuceria, Genusia, Tarentum, Pithecusae, Capreae, Metapontum, Paestum 273, Grumentum, Heraclea, Velia, Thurii, Cosentia, Croton, Caulonia, Locri, Rhegium

Region labels: Veneti, Ligures, Apennines, Tiberis, Via Flaminia, Etruscans, Picentes, Vestini, Sabini, Marrucini, Frentani, Adriatic Sea, Marsi, Aequi, Samnites, Apuli, Hirpini, Via Appia, Peucetii, Lucani, Sallentini, Bruttii, Ionian Sea

ROME BUILDS ITS POWER BASE

As the Roman Republic expanded in the 3rd century BCE, it came into conflict with the well-established Carthaginian civilization. Rome's victory in the three ensuing Punic Wars gave it hegemony over the western Mediterranean, and further Roman victories in Greece pushed Roman power eastward as well.

In the early 3rd century BCE, Rome's power was confined mainly to its colonies in Italy. In 264 BCE, it began to expand its influence, first and foremost by fighting a series of wars with Carthage, then the most powerful city in the western Mediterranean.

Carthage had been founded by the seafaring Phoenician civilization (*Punicus* in Latin, hence Punic Wars), which had thrived in the eastern Mediterranean from around 1500 BCE. Carthage was not a formal empire but the preeminent city in a league of cities that defended one another and maintained trading networks. Located on the coast of what is modern Tunisia,

it built up formidable sea power, with a fleet of around 350 ships by the year 256 BCE. To defeat Carthage and its allies, Rome not only had to fight skilled Carthaginian generals in land battles but had to build and equip its own navy. Roman victories against Carthage brought it many provinces: Sicilia (Sicily), Corsica, and Sardinia after the first Punic War (264–241 BCE); two Spanish provinces after the second (218–201 BCE); and the province of Africa (northern Tunisia), on the site of Carthage itself, in the third (149–146 BCE). Further victories in Greece gave Rome the dominant position in the Mediterranean that it would hold until the 5th century CE.

> "I have come not to make war on the Italians, but to aid the Italians against Rome."
>
> HANNIBAL AT THE BATTLE OF LACUS TRASIMENUS, 217 BCE

THE ROMANS IN GREECE
Greece was disrupted by political tensions because the most powerful cities, such as Corinth and Athens, wanted independence from the main powers in the region—the Macedonians and the Seleucid Empire of Persia. This gave Rome the chance to move into the area. After a number of military victories, beginning with the Battle of Corinth in 146 BCE, Rome was to gain many Greek cities and later set up provinces, which they called Macedonia, Achaia, and Epirus.

Masio Scampa
Heraclea Lyncestis
Apollonia
MACEDONIA
EPIRUS
Nicopolis
Patras
Corinth
Athens
ACHAIA

ROMAN PROVINCES IN GREECE c. 100 BCE

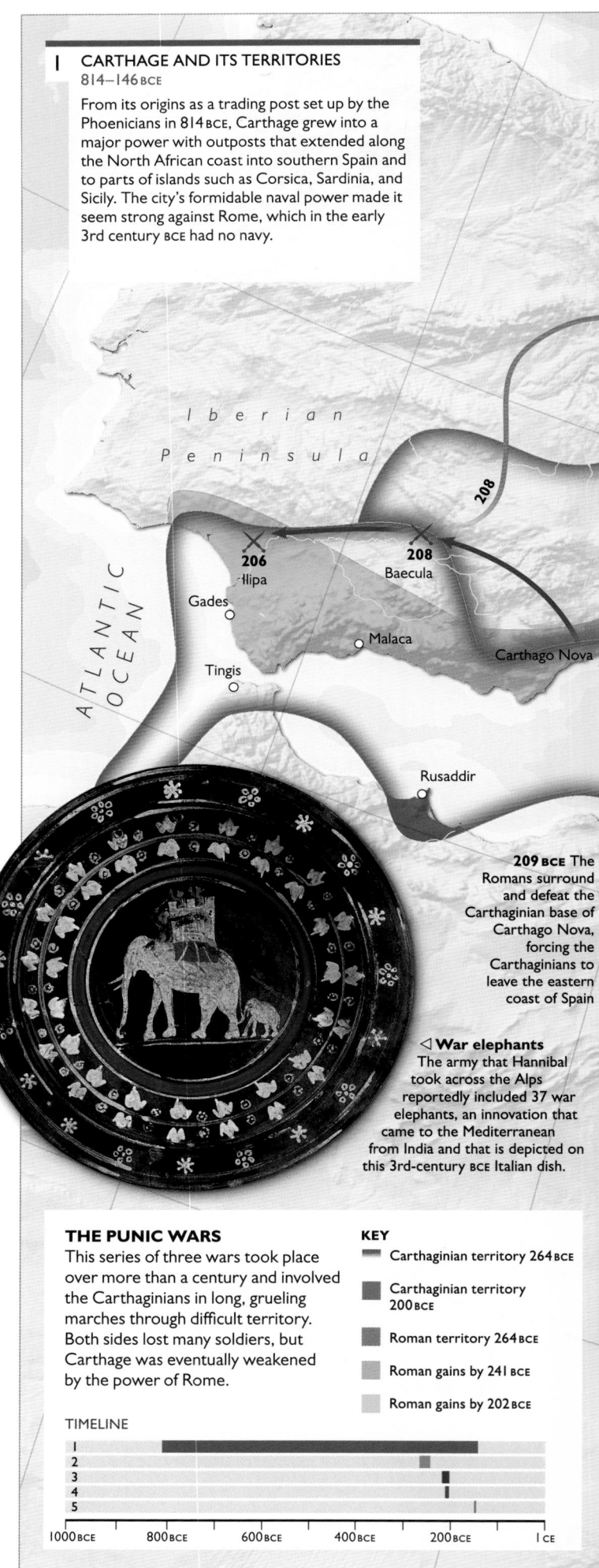

CARTHAGE AND ITS TERRITORIES
814–146 BCE
From its origins as a trading post set up by the Phoenicians in 814 BCE, Carthage grew into a major power with outposts that extended along the North African coast into southern Spain and to parts of islands such as Corsica, Sardinia, and Sicily. The city's formidable naval power made it seem strong against Rome, which in the early 3rd century BCE had no navy.

Iberian Peninsula
208
206 Ilipa
208 Baecula
Gades
Malaca
Tingis
Carthago Nova
ATLANTIC OCEAN
Rusaddir

209 BCE The Romans surround and defeat the Carthaginian base of Carthago Nova, forcing the Carthaginians to leave the eastern coast of Spain

◁ **War elephants**
The army that Hannibal took across the Alps reportedly included 37 war elephants, an innovation that came to the Mediterranean from India and that is depicted on this 3rd-century BCE Italian dish.

THE PUNIC WARS
This series of three wars took place over more than a century and involved the Carthaginians in long, grueling marches through difficult territory. Both sides lost many soldiers, but Carthage was eventually weakened by the power of Rome.

KEY
- Carthaginian territory 264 BCE
- Carthaginian territory 200 BCE
- Roman territory 264 BCE
- Roman gains by 241 BCE
- Roman gains by 202 BCE

TIMELINE
1 2 3 4 5
1000 BCE | 800 BCE | 600 BCE | 400 BCE | 200 BCE | 1 CE

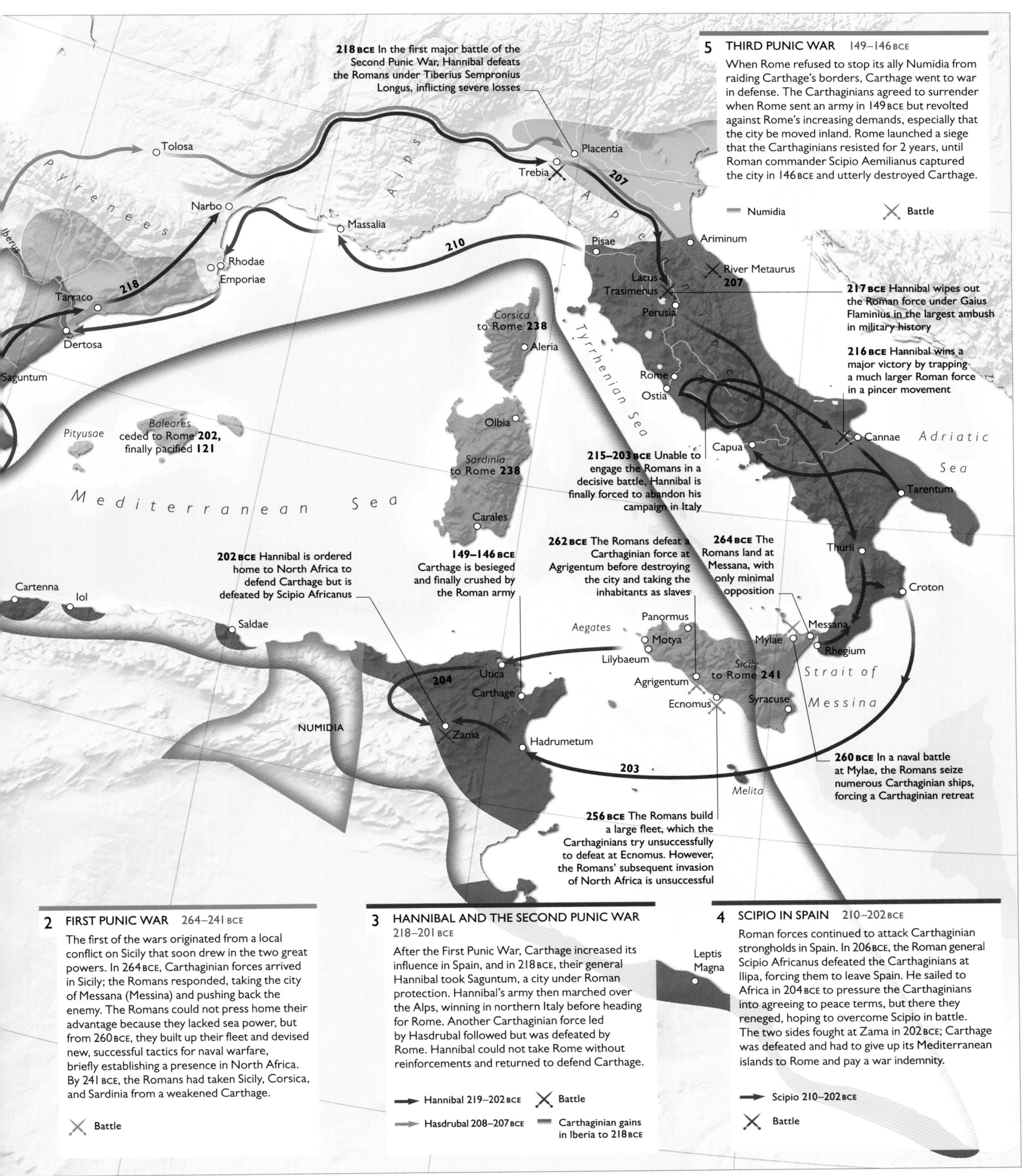

218 BCE In the first major battle of the Second Punic War, Hannibal defeats the Romans under Tiberius Sempronius Longus, inflicting severe losses

5 THIRD PUNIC WAR 149–146 BCE

When Rome refused to stop its ally Numidia from raiding Carthage's borders, Carthage went to war in defense. The Carthaginians agreed to surrender when Rome sent an army in 149 BCE but revolted against Rome's increasing demands, especially that the city be moved inland. Rome launched a siege that the Carthaginians resisted for 2 years, until Roman commander Scipio Aemilianus captured the city in 146 BCE and utterly destroyed Carthage.

—— Numidia ✕ Battle

217 BCE Hannibal wipes out the Roman force under Gaius Flaminius in the largest ambush in military history

216 BCE Hannibal wins a major victory by trapping a much larger Roman force in a pincer movement

Corsica to Rome **238**

Baleares ceded to Rome **202,** finally pacified **121**

Sardinia to Rome **238**

215–203 BCE Unable to engage the Romans in a decisive battle, Hannibal is finally forced to abandon his campaign in Italy

264 BCE The Romans land at Messana, with only minimal opposition

202 BCE Hannibal is ordered home to North Africa to defend Carthage but is defeated by Scipio Africanus

149–146 BCE Carthage is besieged and finally crushed by the Roman army

262 BCE The Romans defeat a Carthaginian force at Agrigentum before destroying the city and taking the inhabitants as slaves

Sicily to Rome **241**

260 BCE In a naval battle at Mylae, the Romans seize numerous Carthaginian ships, forcing a Carthaginian retreat

256 BCE The Romans build a large fleet, which the Carthaginians try unsuccessfully to defeat at Ecnomus. However, the Romans' subsequent invasion of North Africa is unsuccessful

2 FIRST PUNIC WAR 264–241 BCE

The first of the wars originated from a local conflict on Sicily that soon drew in the two great powers. In 264 BCE, Carthaginian forces arrived in Sicily; the Romans responded, taking the city of Messana (Messina) and pushing back the enemy. The Romans could not press home their advantage because they lacked sea power, but from 260 BCE, they built up their fleet and devised new, successful tactics for naval warfare, briefly establishing a presence in North Africa. By 241 BCE, the Romans had taken Sicily, Corsica, and Sardinia from a weakened Carthage.

✕ Battle

3 HANNIBAL AND THE SECOND PUNIC WAR 218–201 BCE

After the First Punic War, Carthage increased its influence in Spain, and in 218 BCE, their general Hannibal took Saguntum, a city under Roman protection. Hannibal's army then marched over the Alps, winning in northern Italy before heading for Rome. Another Carthaginian force led by Hasdrubal followed but was defeated by Rome. Hannibal could not take Rome without reinforcements and returned to defend Carthage.

→ Hannibal 219–202 BCE ✕ Battle
→ Hasdrubal 208–207 BCE ▬ Carthaginian gains in Iberia to 218 BCE

4 SCIPIO IN SPAIN 210–202 BCE

Roman forces continued to attack Carthaginian strongholds in Spain. In 206 BCE, the Roman general Scipio Africanus defeated the Carthaginians at Ilipa, forcing them to leave Spain. He sailed to Africa in 204 BCE to pressure the Carthaginians into agreeing to peace terms, but there they reneged, hoping to overcome Scipio in battle. The two sides fought at Zama in 202 BCE; Carthage was defeated and had to give up its Mediterranean islands to Rome and pay a war indemnity.

→ Scipio 210–202 BCE
✕ Battle

c.142 CE The Romans extend the northern frontier to the Antonine Wall before withdrawing later back to Hadrian's Wall

9 CE Rome loses territory south of the Elbe after a defeat by Germanic tribes

3 THE CONQUEST OF BRITAIN 55 BCE–c.50 CE

Julius Caesar unsuccessfully attempted to invade Britain in the 50s BCE, but the country was conquered from 43 CE onward under the emperor Claudius. The Romans took the southeast easily after a major battle but encountered resistance elsewhere, especially in Wales and the north, so the country took decades to bring under imperial control. During the 2nd century, the Romans established a northern border by building Hadrian's Wall.

▬ Roman Britain

Antonine Wall c.145 CE

Hadrian's Wall c.125 CE

121 BCE Gallia Narbonensis (Languedoc and Provence) becomes the first Roman colony in France

1st and 2nd centuries CE The Romans gradually absorb Spain into the empire, assimilating local tribes and putting down rebellions

58 BCE Julius Caesar reaches the River Rhine; the river becomes the Roman Empire's northern frontier

2 NORTH AFRICA 33 BCE–44 CE

In 33 BCE, the Berber kingdom of Mauretania became a Roman client kingdom. It was later annexed by Rome, and from 44 CE, was ruled directly as the provinces of Mauretania Caesariensis and Mauretania Tingitana. Farther east, Octavian defeated his rival Mark Antony and his lover Queen Cleopatra VII of Egypt, creating the province of Aegyptus in 30 BCE. North Africa became a valued supplier of corn, marble, slaves, and other goods to Rome.

▬ Roman provinces in North Africa

49–44 BCE The city of Carthage, destroyed during the Punic Wars, is rebuilt by the Romans: it becomes an important "granary" of the empire

31 BCE Octavian defeats Mark Antony and Cleopatra at the Battle of Actium, giving Rome control of Egypt

27 BCE The ancient Greek city of Ephesus is made capital of the province of Asia by Augustus

1 THE CONQUEST OF GAUL 58–50 BCE

The Romans had annexed the southern parts of Gallia (Gaul) in 121 BCE, but the whole territory (the extent of modern France and Belgium) was conquered between 58 and 50 BCE by Julius Caesar. As well as opening up sources of raw materials, including lead and silver, this conquest allowed Rome to take advantage of the River Rhine as a line of communication. It also won Julius Caesar popularity and his army's loyalty.

▬ Roman Gaul

80 BCE The city of Alexandria formally passes into Roman hands; it remains an important center for shipping grain across the Mediterranean

◁ **The Arch of Trajan**
This relief shows the Emperor Trajan being greeted by Roman citizens. It is part of the decorative scheme on an arch built in his honor in 114–117 CE in Benevento, southern Italy.

THE ROMAN EMPIRE UNDER HADRIAN

By the time of the emperor Hadrian (r. 117–138 CE), the Roman Empire had reached a size that would last until the late 3rd century. Organized into provinces, such as Cappadocia, its frontiers stretched from Spain to Syria.

KEY

- ▬ Extent of Roman Empire c. 120 CE
- ⌗ Legion headquarters
- ⚓ Major naval base
- ⊙ Provincial capital
- — Major road
- ⌅ Fortified frontier

TIMELINE

```
    100 BCE        1 CE        100 CE       200 CE
1   ▬
2        ▬▬▬▬▬
3      ▬▬▬▬▬▬▬▬▬▬
4                        ▬▬▬
5                           ▬▬▬▬▬▬
```

4 TRAJAN'S CONQUESTS 98–117 CE

The emperor Trajan (r. 98–117 CE) sought to expand the empire, especially in the east, with conquests in Dacia and Nabataea (which became the province Arabia). Trajan then restored a client king in Armenia, who had been deposed by the Parthians. In 113 CE, he sacked Ctesiphon, the capital of the Parthian Empire (territory previously ruled by the Persians and Seleucids), bringing Mesopotamia under Roman control.

▬ Territories conquered by Trajan

17 CE Cappadocia becomes a Roman province under Emperor Tiberius

1st century CE The city of Antioch is rebuilt by the Romans, who see it as an eastern capital

68 BCE The Roman leader Pompey besieges Jerusalem, defeating the Jews and making Judea into a client kingdom

Map labels: Sarmatians, Bosporan Kingdom, Black Sea, Bithynia et Pontus, Sinope, Trapezus, Armenia, Caucasus, Caspian Sea, Zela, Satala, Galatia, Cappadocia, Melitene, Caesarea, Lycia, Cilicia, Samosata, Cyrrhus, Parthian Empire, Assyria, Mesopotamia, Tigris, Euphrates, Tarsus, Seleucia, Antioch, Syria, Laodicea, Salamis, Raphanaea, Cyprus, Tripolis, Dura Europos, Ctesiphon, Damascus, Tyrus, Caparcotna, Caesarea Maritima, Bostra, Jerusalem (Aelia Capitolina), Judaea, Arabia, Petra, Memphis, Aegyptus, Red Sea, Nile

5 THE ROMAN–PARTHIAN WARS 113–197 CE

Trajan annexed parts of the Parthian Empire in 113 CE both to defend Rome's client kingdom Armenia and to consolidate the eastern frontier. Trajan's successor, Hadrian, reversed this move and set the boundary of the empire back at the Euphrates. The Parthians, however, again tried to take Armenia, prompting a Roman counter-attack in 161 CE. The Romans sacked the capital Ctesiphon again in 197 CE.

▬ Parthian Empire

ROMAN EMPIRE AT ITS HEIGHT

Rome's territories expanded steadily during the period of the Republic. By the time of the accession of the first emperor, Augustus, in 27 BCE, Rome controlled all of the Mediterranean. By 120 CE, the empire's borders were settled, and it entered the period of its greatest stability.

The Roman Republic grew by military conquest and by establishing client kingdoms that accepted Roman domination in return for stability and good trading relations. The first emperor, Augustus, adopted a policy of not expanding Roman boundaries, which was followed by many later emperors, with exceptions such as Trajan, who added substantial but short-lived provinces in the east.

Guarding this huge empire was the job of an army of some 300,000 men, mostly based in camps along the empire's boundaries. The Roman navy protected shipping on the Mediterranean that carried the trade on which the city depended—everything from raw materials and slaves to foods such as grain and olive oil. Relations with the provinces were usually harmonious: the Roman way of life proved very attractive, helped to stimulate further trade, and encouraged people of conquered territories to become "Romanized" and accept imperial rule. The resulting balance of military power and economic prosperity kept the area relatively stable and peaceful in the first 200 years of the empire.

> *"You cheer my heart, who build as if Rome would be eternal."*
>
> AUGUSTUS CAESAR

FROM REPUBLIC TO EMPIRE
POWER STRUGGLES IN ROME

When Julius Caesar seized power as a dictator in 49 BCE, it set Rome on a path from republic to empire. After Julius Caesar's assassination in 44 BCE, Mark Antony, Lepidus, and Octavian ruled the Republic as a triumvirate, but they vied for power, and a series of disputes and civil wars ensued. Octavian ousted Lepidus in a political maneuver and then defeated Antony in battle, becoming the first emperor, under the name Augustus Caesar, in 27 BCE.

Bust of Julius Caesar
Julius Caesar was a powerful military leader and politician. His actions helped bring about the end of the Republic.

THE ROOTS OF INDIAN HISTORY

In the 2nd millennium BCE, after the decline of the Indus Valley civilization, a people calling themselves *Arya* (noble ones) migrated from the Iranian plateau into northwest India. They spoke Sanskrit, an Indo-European language.

What is known of this time in the Indian subcontinent comes mostly from the Indo-Aryans' sacred texts—the four *Vedas* (from the Sanskrit word for knowledge)—composed and passed on orally. Mostly liturgical texts, used while offering sacrifices to deities such as Indra, the god of war, the Vedas also provide evidence of social structures.

△ **Delicate pottery**
From 1000 to 600 BCE, distinctive painted grayware pottery, decorated with simple lines or geometric designs, spread across northern India. It was so thin and delicate that it must have been a luxury or ritual item.

This period is called the Vedic Age. The early *Rig Veda*, composed from 1500 BCE onward, shows the Indo-Aryans as nomadic pastoralists—chariot-riding tribal warriors raiding each other for cattle. From around 1100 BCE, they moved east to the Ganges plain, where they became settled farmers.

Many villages appeared, where people grew rice, wheat, and barley. Later, several large towns, fortified with ditches and embankments, developed. Marking the beginning of India's caste system, social classes appeared: the priestly *brahmins*, who composed and memorized the *Vedas*; the *kshatriyas*, or noble warriors; the *vaishyas*, or traders; and the *shudras*, or servants. The society changed from a tribal system, where assemblies of chieftains chose a king, or *raja*, to hereditary kingship. New kings received their legitimacy from sacrificial rituals overseen by the *brahmins*, which imbued each new king with divine power.

THE FIRST INDIAN KINGDOMS

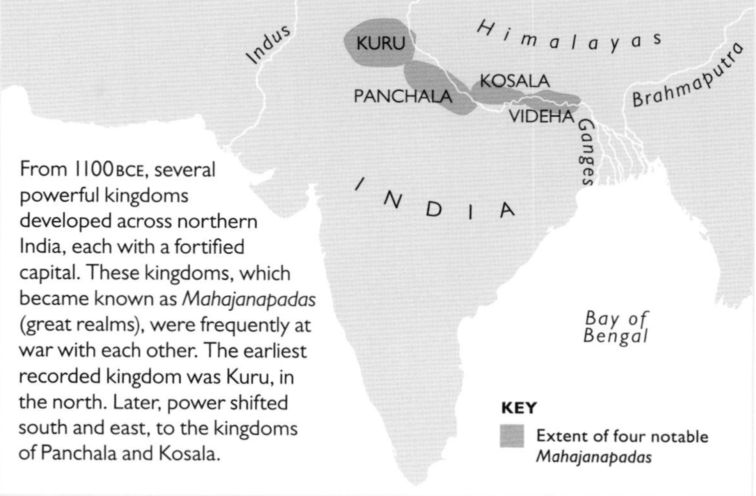

From 1100 BCE, several powerful kingdoms developed across northern India, each with a fortified capital. These kingdoms, which became known as *Mahajanapadas* (great realms), were frequently at war with each other. The earliest recorded kingdom was Kuru, in the north. Later, power shifted south and east, to the kingdoms of Panchala and Kosala.

KURU
PANCHALA
KOSALA
VIDEHA
Indus
Himalayas
Brahmaputra
Ganges
INDIA
Bay of Bengal

KEY
Extent of four notable *Mahajanapadas*

Epic war
A war for the throne of Kuru is the subject of the later Hindu epic, the *Mahabharata*. This scene shows the warrior Karna (center) using a magical weapon to kill Ghatotkacha, who is half-human and half-demon.

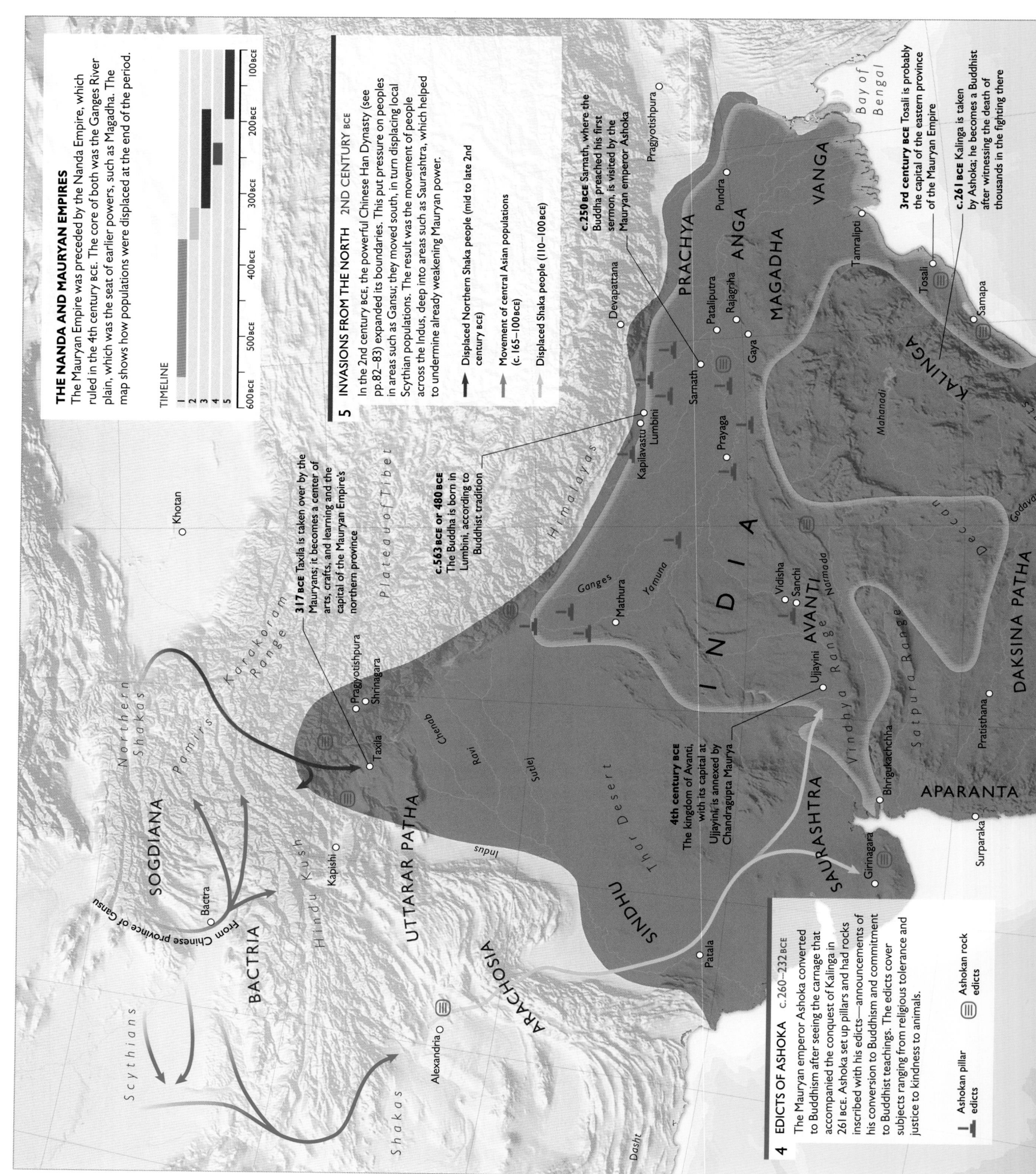

THE NANDA AND MAURYAN EMPIRES

The Mauryan Empire was preceded by the Nanda Empire, which ruled in the 4th century BCE. The core of both was the Ganges River plain, which was the seat of earlier powers, such as Magadha. The map shows how populations were displaced at the end of the period.

TIMELINE

1
2
3
4
5

600 BCE   500 BCE   400 BCE   300 BCE   200 BCE   100 BCE

5 INVASIONS FROM THE NORTH 2ND CENTURY BCE

In the 2nd century BCE, the powerful Chinese Han Dynasty (see pp.82–83) expanded its boundaries. This put pressure on peoples in areas such as Gansu; they moved south, in turn displacing local Scythian populations. The result was the movement of people across the Indus, deep into areas such as Saurashtra, which helped to undermine already weakening Mauryan power.

→ Displaced Northern Shaka people (mid to late 2nd century BCE)

→ Movement of central Asian populations (c. 165–100 BCE)

→ Displaced Shaka people (110–100 BCE)

317 BCE Taxila is taken over by the Mauryans; it becomes a center of arts, crafts, and learning and the capital of the Mauryan Empire's northern province

c.563 BCE or 480 BCE The Buddha is born in Lumbini, according to Buddhist tradition

c.250 BCE Sarnath, where the Buddha preached his first sermon, is visited by the Mauryan emperor Ashoka

3rd century BCE Tosali is probably the capital of the eastern province of the Mauryan Empire

c.261 BCE Kalinga is taken by Ashoka; he becomes a Buddhist after witnessing the death of thousands in the fighting there

4th century BCE The kingdom of Avanti, with its capital at Ujjayini is annexed by Chandragupta Maurya

4 EDICTS OF ASHOKA c.260–232 BCE

The Mauryan emperor Ashoka converted to Buddhism after seeing the carnage that accompanied the conquest of Kalinga in 261 BCE. Ashoka set up pillars and had rocks inscribed with his edicts—announcements of his conversion to Buddhism and commitment to Buddhist teachings. The edicts cover subjects ranging from religious tolerance and justice to kindness to animals.

⊥ Ashokan pillar edicts

▥ Ashokan rock edicts

Map labels

Khotan

Northern Shakas

SOGDIANA

Bactra

From Chinese province of Gansu

BACTRA

Scythians

Shakas

Kapishi

Hindu Kush

Alexandria

ARACHOSIA

Dasht

Patala

SINDHU

SAURASHTRA

Girinagara

Bhrigukachchha

APARANTA

Surparaka

Pratisthana

DAKSINA PATHA

Satpura Range

Vindhya Range

Narmada

Godavari

Deccan

UTTARAR PATHA

Pragjyotishpura
Shrinagara
Taxila

Karakoram Range

Pamirs

Plateau of Tibet

Chenab
Ravi
Sutlej
Indus

Thar Desert

Mathura

Vidisha
Sanchi
Ujjayini
AVANTI

INDIA

Ganges
Yamuna

Kapilavastu
Lumbini

Himalayas

Devapattana

Sarnath
Prayaga

Pataliputra
Rajagriha
Gaya

MAGADHA

PRACHYA

ANGA

VANGA

Pundra

Pragjyotishpura

Bay of Bengal

Tamralipti

Mahanadi

Tosali

Samapa

KALINGA

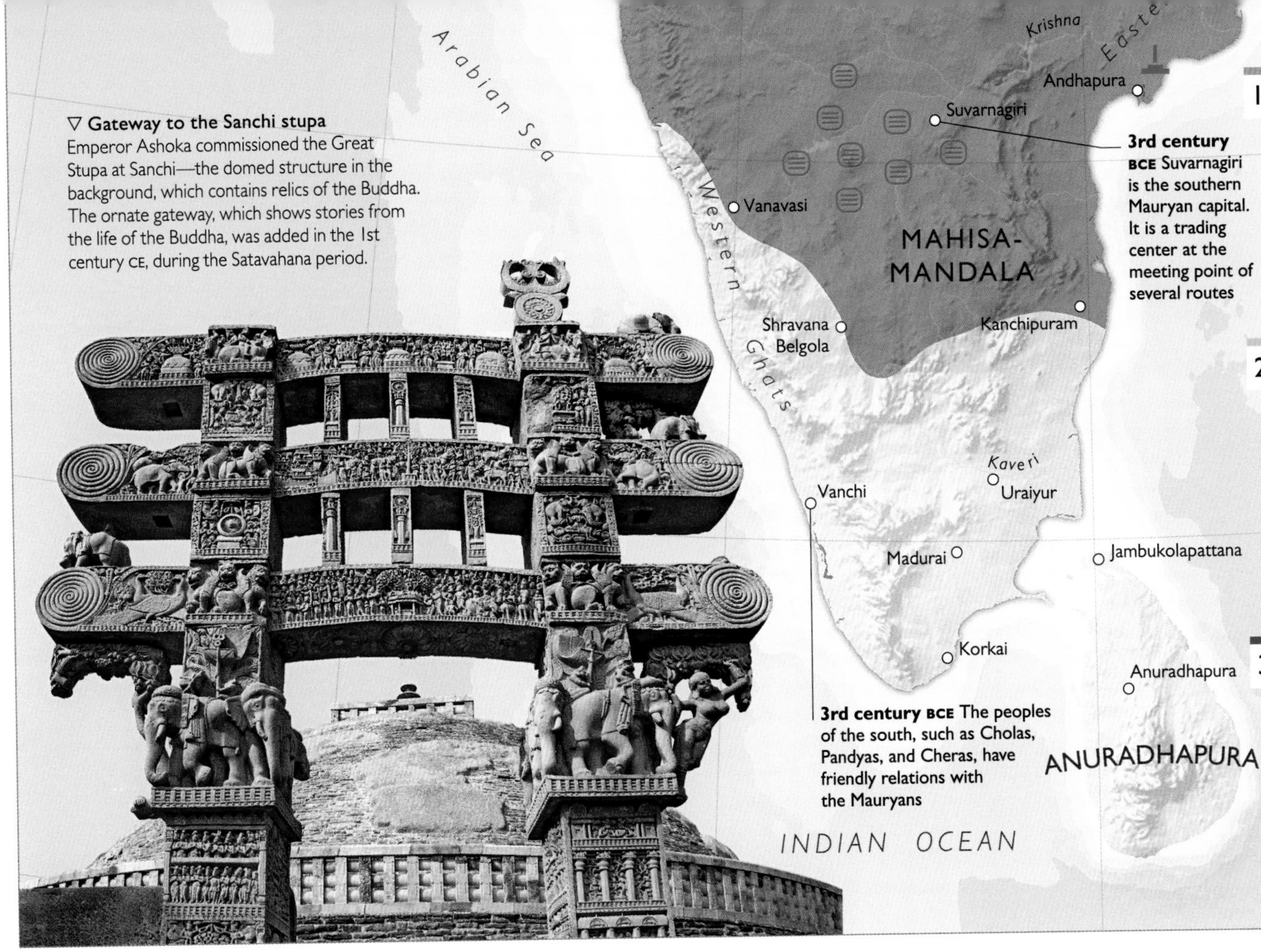

MAURYAN INDIA

India's largest ancient empire was founded by Chandragupta Maurya in c. 321 BCE. The Mauryan emperors—particularly the great Ashoka—worked to unite India for the first time, to increase prosperity through agriculture and trade, and to promote nonviolence through Jainism and, especially, through the Buddhist faith.

India was a patchwork of independent states until the 6th century BCE, when one state, Magadha, began to take over its neighbors, creating an empire on the plain of the Ganges River. Magadha formed the basis of a larger empire that emerged under the Nanda Dynasty in the mid-4th century. However, India's great Mauryan Empire came into being when Chandragupta Maurya filled a vacuum in the northwest caused by the death of Alexander the Great. He formed an army, marched on Magadha, defeated its king, and was made emperor. At the end of his life, he converted to Jainism, encouraging social awareness and nonviolence.

The Mauryans came to rule all of India except the far southern tip. They maintained power using a system of provincial governors and a well-organized civil service. Traders were taxed, and the government collected tolls from roads and river crossings. Ashoka, who ruled as emperor c. 268–232 BCE, eventually renounced war and became a committed Buddhist, building and repairing stupas, sponsoring Buddhist missionaries, and passing laws in line with the compassionate tenets of the faith. Mauryan rule lasted until the 180s BCE, when the last emperor was assassinated.

ASHOKA PILLARS
ANNOUNCEMENTS OF BUDDHIST FAITH

Twenty pillars inscribed with Ashoka's edicts still survive, including one (below) at Sarnath near Varanasi. Most of the inscriptions are written in the Brahmi script, a form of writing that became widespread during the Mauryan period and was used throughout India. Dozens of later south Asian scripts derive from Brahmi, including Devanagari, often used to write the Sanskrit language.

1 MAGADHA   c. 558–365 BCE

The state of Magadha in northeastern India became dominant during the time of the Buddha, who spent much of his life there. Magadha expanded under its ruler Bimbisara (c. 558–491 BCE), who took over the state of Anga to the east of his homeland and bolstered his power with marriage alliances, so preparing the way for later rulers of Magadha to extend their territories.

2 NANDA EMPIRE   c. 365–321 BCE

Nanda, the first northern Indian empire, began in Magadha and expanded westward in the 4th century BCE. It was governed by a network of ministers, and trade was eased by a standardized system of weights and measures. The Nanda rulers imposed their power with a vast army. They were famous for their great wealth, and their capital at Pataliputra was especially lavish.

  Maximum extent of Nanda Empire 321 BCE

3 MAURYAN EMPIRE   c. 321–185 BCE

In 321 BCE, Chandragupta Maurya conquered the Nanda Empire, gaining support from Nanda factions who resented their rulers' wealth. He extended his empire westward into the edges of the area previously occupied by Alexander the Great; Chandragupta's son and successor, Bindusara, later added territory in southern India. The empire was the largest India had seen, and lasted until 181 BCE.

  Maximum extent of Mauryan Empire 185 BCE

▽ **Gateway to the Sanchi stupa**
Emperor Ashoka commissioned the Great Stupa at Sanchi—the domed structure in the background, which contains relics of the Buddha. The ornate gateway, which shows stories from the life of the Buddha, was added in the 1st century CE, during the Satavahana period.

3rd century BCE Suvarnagiri is the southern Mauryan capital. It is a trading center at the meeting point of several routes

3rd century BCE The peoples of the south, such as Cholas, Pandyas, and Cheras, have friendly relations with the Mauryans

Andhapura

Suvarnagiri

MAHISA-MANDALA

Kanchipuram

Kaveri
Uraiyur

Jambukolapattana

Madurai

Korkai

Vanchi

ANURADHAPURA

Anuradhapura

INDIAN OCEAN

Krishna

Eastern

Western Ghats

Vanavasi

Shravana Belgola

Arabian Sea

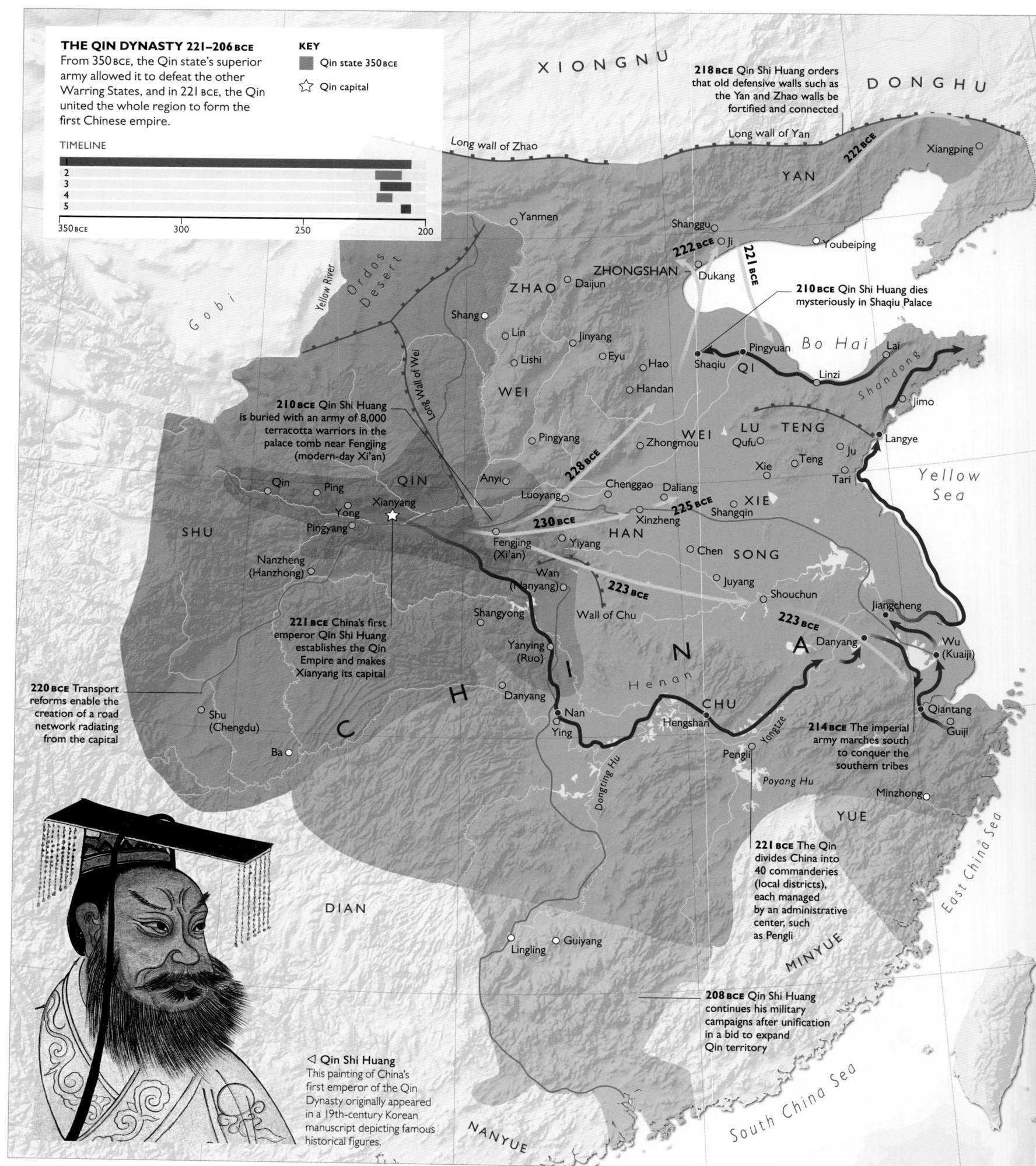

THE QIN DYNASTY 221–206 BCE
From 350 BCE, the Qin state's superior army allowed it to defeat the other Warring States, and in 221 BCE, the Qin united the whole region to form the first Chinese empire.

KEY
Qin state 350 BCE
☆ Qin capital

TIMELINE

1			
2			
3			
4			
5			

350 BCE   300   250   200

XIONGNU

DONGHU

218 BCE Qin Shi Huang orders that old defensive walls such as the Yan and Zhao walls be fortified and connected

Long wall of Zhao

Long wall of Yan

222 BCE

Xiangping

YAN

Yanmen

Shanggu

ZHONGSHAN

222 BCE Ji

221 BCE

Youbeiping

ZHAO

Daijun

Dukang

210 BCE Qin Shi Huang dies mysteriously in Shaqiu Palace

Shang

Bo Hai

Lin

Jinyang

Lai

Lishi

Eyu

Pingyuan

Qi

WEI

Hao

Shaqiu

Linzi

Shandong

Handan

Jimo

210 BCE Qin Shi Huang is buried with an army of 8,000 terracotta warriors in the palace tomb near Fengjing (modern-day Xi'an)

Pingyang

WEI

LU

TENG

Yellow Sea

Zhongmou

Qufu

Anyi

Luoyang

228 BCE

Chenggao

Daliang

Xie

Ju

Teng

Tari

Langye

Qin

Ping

Xianyang

225 BCE

XIE

Yong

230 BCE

Xinzheng

Shangqin

Pingyang

Fengjing

Yiyang

HAN

SONG

SHU

(Xi'an)

Chen

Nanzhong
(Hanzhong)

Wan
(Nanyang)

223 BCE

Juyang

Shouchun

Jiangcheng

221 BCE China's first emperor Qin Shi Huang establishes the Qin Empire and makes Xianyang its capital

Shangyong

223 BCE

Danyang

Wu
(Kuaiji)

Yanying
(Ruo)

Wall of Chu

C H I N A

Henan

220 BCE Transport reforms enable the creation of a road network radiating from the capital

Danyang

Nan

Qiantang

Shu
(Chengdu)

Ying

CHU

Hengshan

Guiji

Ba

Dongting Hu

Yangtze

Pengli

214 BCE The imperial army marches south to conquer the southern tribes

Poyang Hu

Minzhong

DIAN

YUE

East China Sea

221 BCE The Qin divides China into 40 commanderies (local districts), each managed by an administrative center, such as Pengli

Lingling

Guiyang

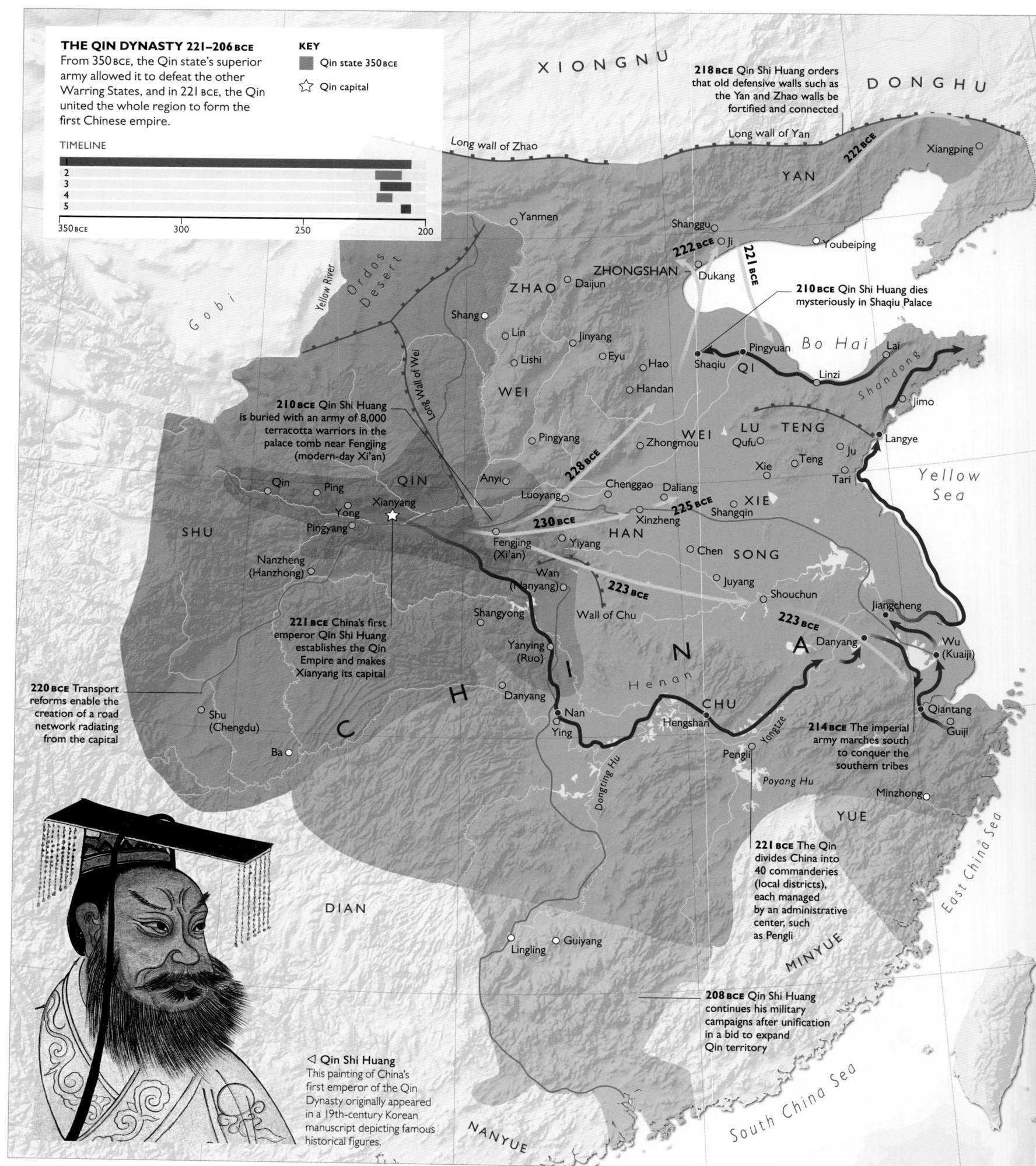

◁ Qin Shi Huang
This painting of China's first emperor of the Qin Dynasty originally appeared in a 19th-century Korean manuscript depicting famous historical figures.

MINYUE

208 BCE Qin Shi Huang continues his military campaigns after unification in a bid to expand Qin territory

NANYUE

South China Sea

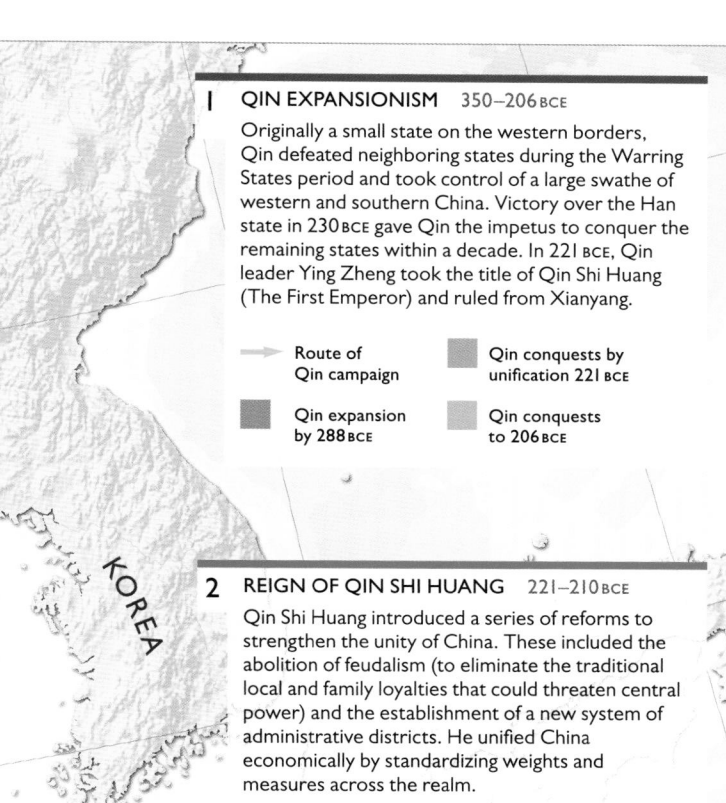

KOREA

1 QIN EXPANSIONISM 350–206 BCE

Originally a small state on the western borders, Qin defeated neighboring states during the Warring States period and took control of a large swathe of western and southern China. Victory over the Han state in 230 BCE gave Qin the impetus to conquer the remaining states within a decade. In 221 BCE, Qin leader Ying Zheng took the title of Qin Shi Huang (The First Emperor) and ruled from Xianyang.

→ Route of Qin campaign

■ Qin expansion by 288 BCE

■ Qin conquests by unification 221 BCE

■ Qin conquests to 206 BCE

2 REIGN OF QIN SHI HUANG 221–210 BCE

Qin Shi Huang introduced a series of reforms to strengthen the unity of China. These included the abolition of feudalism (to eliminate the traditional local and family loyalties that could threaten central power) and the establishment of a new system of administrative districts. He unified China economically by standardizing weights and measures across the realm.

◉ Administrative center

3 FORTIFYING DEFENSIVE WALLS 218–206 BCE

Faced with the threat of attacks from nomadic people in the north and west, Qin Shi Huang mobilized a labor force numbering thousands to construct a unified fortification out of the defensive walls, built by several Chinese rulers during the Warring States period. The Great Wall would become the Qin Dynasty's most famous legacy.

⊔⊔ Early sections of the Great Wall

4 QIN TRANSPORT NETWORKS 220–214 BCE

Another major construction to begin during Qin Shi Huang's reign was a complex road system to allow easier travel between cities and encourage trade nationwide. The emperor also ordered the construction of a major canal linking the Xiang and the Li Jiang Rivers to ferry supplies to the army.

— Imperial roads

5 THE FALL OF QIN 210–206 BCE

In 210 BCE, Qin Shi Huang died while on a tour of eastern China. The people were told that he was making the trip to inspect the empire, but it was in fact a quest to find an elixir of immortality. Civil disorder erupted following the emperor's death and ended with the Qin Dynasty collapsing in 206 BCE.

➤ Qin Shi Huang's tour

● Town visited during Qin Shi Huang's tour

CHINA'S FIRST EMPEROR

After a period in which numerous Chinese states fought for supremacy, it was the Qin state that eventually triumphed and unified China in 221 BCE. The Qin emperor, Qin Shi Huang, established a strict and highly centralized form of rule—a system that would become the model for China's future governance.

Between the 11th and 8th centuries BCE, China was made up of a mosaic of city-states loyal to the Zhou Dynasty, which employed a form of feudalism to rule the land. However, following the Warring States period (475–221 BCE), in which the Qin state triumphed over the Zhou Dynasty and six other rival states, the Qin leader, Ying Zheng, unified China under his leadership.

As the Qin's first emperor, Ying Zheng took the name Qin Shi Huang and replaced the old kinship-based government with an efficient bureaucratic system. He proved a formidable ruler with a clear vision for the realm, establishing a ruthless penal code to enforce his despotic rule. He actively suppressed philosophies—by the burning of books—that he felt either criticized or challenged his authority. His untimely death in 210 BCE, however, preceded the swift decline and end of his dynasty in 206 BCE. Although the Qin Empire lasted only 15 years, it had set up institutions that paved the way for Liu Bang to form the more enduring Han Dynasty (see pp.82–83).

> *"I am Emperor, my descendants will be numerous ... my line will not end."*
>
> EMPEROR QIN SHI HUANG

THE WARRING STATES PERIOD

China was a patchwork of states, each ruled by high-ranking nobles who swore allegiance to the Zhou kings. But as the Zhou's authority waned, the stronger states saw their opportunity and fought one another to gain control of China. In what historians call the Warring States period (475–221 BCE), six major states—Chu, Han, Yan, Qi, Qin, and Zhao—fought one another for dominance over the region.

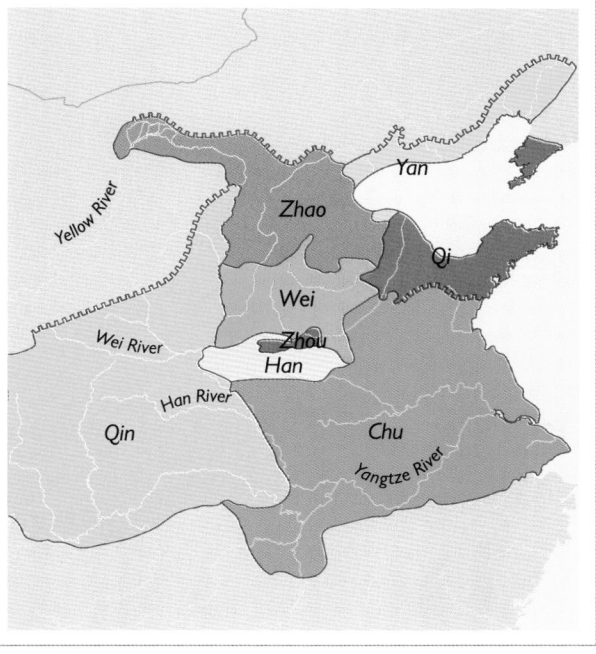

KEY

— State boundary

ᴖᴖ Wall

■ Imperial state

TERRACOTTA ARMY

In 1974, farmers digging wells in Xi'an, China, unearthed the first of four vast pits containing an army of terracotta figures. About 7,000 life-size warriors, 150 cavalry horses, 130 chariots, and 520 chariot horses were found.

△ **Warrior's face**
The warriors' heads were made in molds, with features such as facial hair added by hand modeling. No two faces are the same.

The army had been buried in 210 BCE to protect Qin Shi Huang, the First Emperor of China (see pp.74–75), who lies in his tomb under a vast artificial mountain. According to Sima Qian, a historian from the early Han Dynasty (see pp.82–83), the tomb was built by 700,000 men and held a model of China, with its palaces. The tomb has still not been excavated, partly because of the archaeological challenge it presents but also because of the awe in which the First Emperor is still held by the Chinese.

Ruling from the afterlife

The First Emperor had planned to continue ruling from his tomb for eternity, so he was buried with everything he might need. He was accompanied by terracotta civil servants and entertainers—acrobats, wrestlers, and musicians. The army was there to protect him in the afterlife from the vengeful ghosts of all the men he had killed while on Earth. Nearby pits held suits of armor made of stone plates, as well as 40,000 bronze weapons whose blades remained razor sharp. They had been plated with chromium oxide to protect them from corrosion, a technique only reinvented in the 20th century.

Before the First Emperor, there had been no tradition of life-size, realistic statues in China. A theory suggests a Greek inspiration, but the style of the terracotta army remained distinctively Chinese.

▽ **Eternal transportation**
This half life-size scale model of a chariot pulled by horses is made of bronze. It provided the emperor transportation for tours of his kingdom in the afterlife.

Standing guard
For more than 2,000 years, the terracotta warriors have been standing at attention in massed ranks. They face east, with the tomb they are protecting directly behind them.

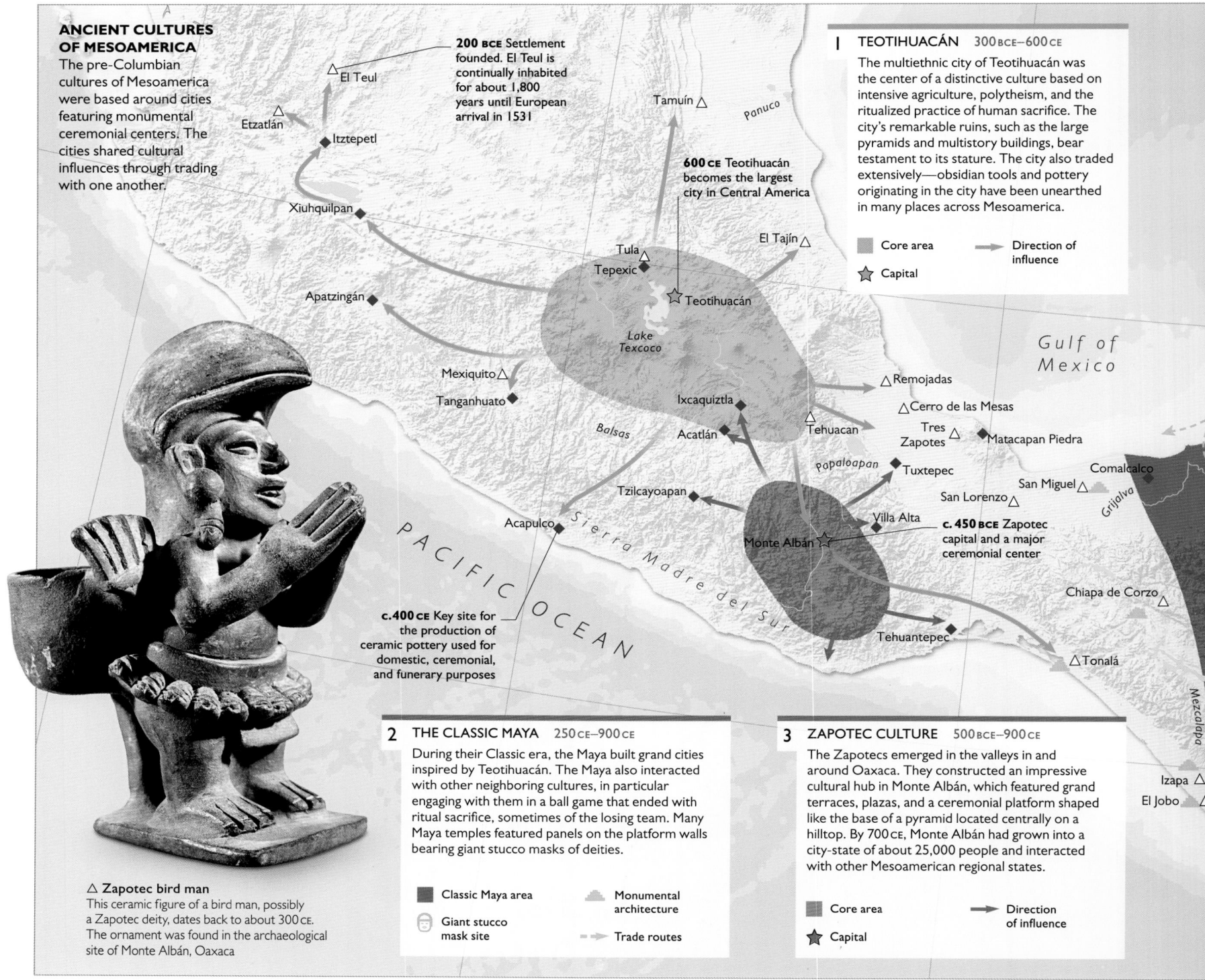

ANCIENT CULTURES OF MESOAMERICA
The pre-Columbian cultures of Mesoamerica were based around cities featuring monumental ceremonial centers. The cities shared cultural influences through trading with one another.

200 BCE Settlement founded. El Teul is continually inhabited for about 1,800 years until European arrival in 1531

600 CE Teotihuacán becomes the largest city in Central America

1 TEOTIHUACÁN 300 BCE–600 CE
The multiethnic city of Teotihuacán was the center of a distinctive culture based on intensive agriculture, polytheism, and the ritualized practice of human sacrifice. The city's remarkable ruins, such as the large pyramids and multistory buildings, bear testament to its stature. The city also traded extensively—obsidian tools and pottery originating in the city have been unearthed in many places across Mesoamerica.

Core area • Direction of influence
Capital

c.400 CE Key site for the production of ceramic pottery used for domestic, ceremonial, and funerary purposes

c.450 BCE Zapotec capital and a major ceremonial center

△ **Zapotec bird man**
This ceramic figure of a bird man, possibly a Zapotec deity, dates back to about 300 CE. The ornament was found in the archaeological site of Monte Albán, Oaxaca

2 THE CLASSIC MAYA 250 CE–900 CE
During their Classic era, the Maya built grand cities inspired by Teotihuacán. The Maya also interacted with other neighboring cultures, in particular engaging with them in a ball game that ended with ritual sacrifice, sometimes of the losing team. Many Maya temples featured panels on the platform walls bearing giant stucco masks of deities.

Classic Maya area • Monumental architecture
Giant stucco mask site • Trade routes

3 ZAPOTEC CULTURE 500 BCE–900 CE
The Zapotecs emerged in the valleys in and around Oaxaca. They constructed an impressive cultural hub in Monte Albán, which featured grand terraces, plazas, and a ceremonial platform shaped like the base of a pyramid located centrally on a hilltop. By 700 CE, Monte Albán had grown into a city-state of about 25,000 people and interacted with other Mesoamerican regional states.

Core area • Direction of influence
Capital

ANCIENT AMERICAN CIVILIZATIONS

In the period 250–900 CE, increased agricultural productivity in Mesoamerica, led to the rise of the great cities of Teotihuacán and Monte Albán. The cities influenced the Maya city-states to the east, ushering in a time of prosperity known as the Classic Maya period. Meanwhile, the mastery of irrigation techniques allowed a succession of empires to rule the Andean region of South America.

Teotihuacán and Monte Albán (the Zapotec capital) were Mesoamerica's two most powerful trading centers in the early Classic era. Teotihuacán traded with the first Classic Maya cities to form in the highlands, and its influence reached other similar independent Maya states that were emerging in the Yucatan Peninsula at this time. The Maya culture would reach its high point during the Classic period, evident in the architecture, the widespread use of written inscriptions, and the complex Maya calendar.

All three cultures based their cities around ceremonial zones, often with pyramidal temples that served as sites of rituals, including human sacrifice. They also built recreational ball courts and sculpted stelae to glorify their rulers.

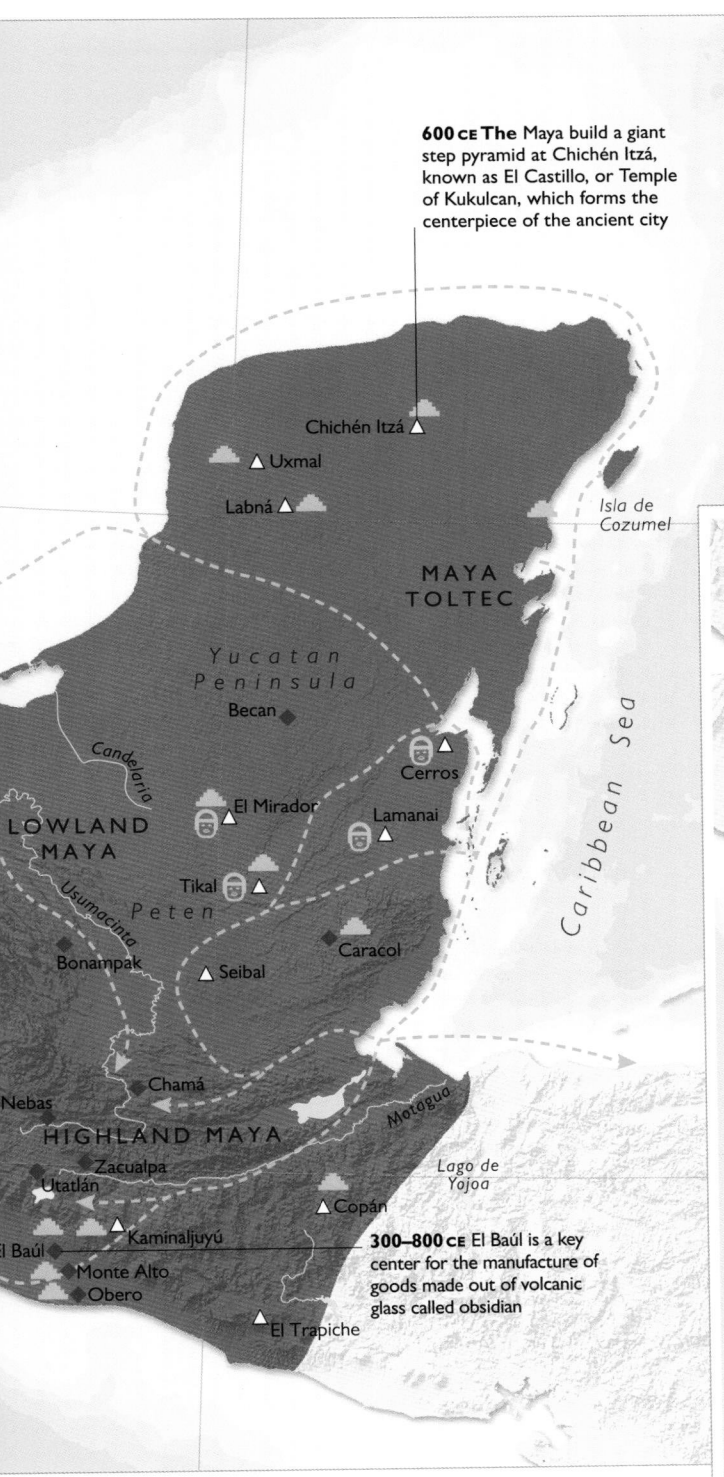

600 CE The Maya build a giant step pyramid at Chichén Itzá, known as El Castillo, or Temple of Kukulcan, which forms the centerpiece of the ancient city

300–800 CE El Baúl is a key center for the manufacture of goods made out of volcanic glass called obsidian

PRE-COLUMBIAN AMERICA

The ancient cultures of Central America were made up of large city-states, which traded with one another. The civilizations on the Andean coast of South America, meanwhile, built large empires through conquests.

KEY

▼ Irrigated river valley
△ Major settlements
◆ Other archaeological sites

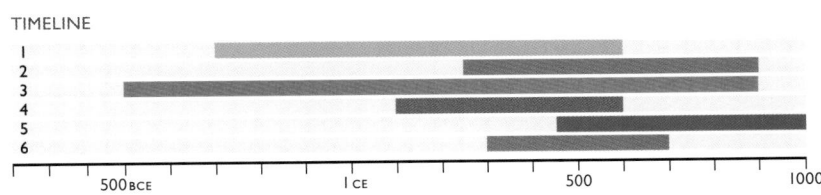

TIMELINE

EMPIRES OF THE ANDEAN COAST

Between 100 and 1000 CE, a succession of cultures— starting with the Moche— mastered irrigation techniques, which formed the foundation of the empires they built along the Andean coast.

c.100 CE Moche people build the Huaca del Sol—an adobe brick temple—in the coastal desert of the Moche Valley of what is now Peru

4 MOCHE SOCIETY 100–600 CE

The Moche people channeled streams flowing down from the Andes into an extensive system of irrigation canals, enabling them to grow corn (maize), beans, and other crops. Iconography on Moche artifacts sheds light on the society's customs and includes depictions of processions and rituals. The culture collapsed in about 600 CE, possibly at least partly due to environmental factors, such as prolonged droughts.

— Moche society ★ Capital

5 HUARI EMPIRE 450–1000 CE

The Huari culture flourished from about 600 CE. It was among the first politically centralized civilizations in the New World that expanded as a result of its economic and military might. The empire constructed a major road network, which allowed its rulers to govern the realm from the capital Huari.

— Huari roads ▨ Huari Empire

c.300–700 CE City of Tiahuanaco builds an extensive empire and, by 700, rules over more than 3 million subjects

600–800 CE City of Pachacamac is thought to have served as a key administrative center for the Huari Empire

6 TIAHUANACO 300–700 CE

By 500 CE, the city of Tiahuanaco had a population of about 40,000. The city center contained a complex of temples, courtyards, terraces, and statues. The site is best known for its monumental gateways, built with a giant single block of stone as the lintel and carved with cosmic and religious imagery. The rulers must have wielded power over a large workforce for the construction of the city's grand palaces and sophisticated rainwater drainage systems.

■ Core area
▨ Area of influence

In northern Peru, the agriculture-based Moche civilization emerged from about 100 CE. Most probably, the Moche started as a group of autonomous states that came together through sharing a common culture. However, around 600 CE, the Moche civilization collapsed—possibly as a result of climate change—and was superseded by the Tiahuanaco and Huari cultures. These latter civilizations expanded more widely along the northern coast of the Andes. Among the most impressive achievements of the Huari Empire was its construction of a network of roads linking the provincial cities to the capital Huari. The Huari drew inspiration from Tiahuanaco-Huari mythology to develop a new art style, which influenced the regional architecture and pottery.

c.400 As the Picts move south, Irish Celts settle in the northern parts of the British Isles and become Scots

1 VISIGOTHS 378–418 CE
The Visigoths (western Goths) defeated the Romans at Adrianopolis (Edirne) in 378 before moving west. Led by their king Alaric, they reached Rome in 410 and sacked the city. By 418, they had settled in southern Gaul, allowed to stay by Rome in return for service as mercenaries. This agreement did not last, and the Visigoths established their own capital at Tolosa (Toulouse).

⇨ Visigoths   ▪▪▶ Goths

2 THE HUNS 370–440 CE
The Huns arrived in what is now southern Russia from central Asia in the 370s. From here, they moved west, conquering the territory of the Alans and overwhelming the eastern Goths. Under their powerful leader Attila, they established a large eastern European empire, centered on what is now Hungary, near the borders of both the eastern and western Roman Empires.

→ Hun migration to Hungary

c.441 Germanic peoples from northern Europe begin to settle in Britain
c.457 Britons flee Kent after an Anglo-Saxon victory at Aylesford

456 The Visigoths begin to expand their kingdom in southern Gaul. They conquer most of Iberia by c. 500

414 Athaulf, leader of the Visigoths, marries Galla Placidia, daughter of the late Roman Emperor Theodosius, at Narbo

453 Attila dies, and the Huns' empire disintegrates

452 The Huns sack Aquileia, opening a way into northern Italy for Attila

492–493 The Visigoths under Theoderic besiege Ravenna, the western Roman capital

376 Thousands of Goths move into Roman territory in Dacia and Lower Moesia

410 The Visigoth king Alaric dies; the Visigoths abandon their plan to invade Africa

428–429 The Vandals cross the Strait of Gibraltar into North Africa; the kingdom they establish lasts until the 6th century

430 The Vandals take the city of Hippo; St. Augustine, church father and bishop of the city, dies during the siege

396–397 Athens and Corinth are among the cities ravaged by the Visigoths

378 A force of Goths, Alans, and others defeats the army of the Eastern Roman Empire

ATLANTIC OCEAN
SCOTLAND
Picts
Scots
Irish Celts
IRELAND
BRITAIN
North Sea
Baltic Sea
Angles
Saxons
Franks
GERMANY
Vistula
Thames
Londinium 457
Rhine pre-357
Scheldt 486
Sueves pre-406
Vandals pre-406
Carpathian Mountains
Seine
Meuse
Lutetia
GAUL
451 Catalaunian Fields ✕
Borbetomagus
Danube 451
406–407 Alans
KINGDOM OF THE VISIGOTHS c.418
Saône
443
A l p s
Mediolanum
Verona
Ticinum
Aquileia
Patavium
PANNONIA
EMPIRE OF THE HUNS c.420
DACIA
Goths pre-376
Tisza
420
Rhône
418
414
409
Narbo
Tolosa
Alans, Vandals, Sueves
Po
Genua
Ravenna
489
Visigoths from 382
LOWER MOESIA
441
Danube
Ostrogoths from 450
Douro
Sueves
Alans
Tagus
456
Toletum
IBERIA
Tarraco
WESTERN ROMAN EMPIRE (From 395)
410
455
Rome
ITALY
Adriatic Sea
THRACE
Adrianopolis 378 ✕
Philippopolis
Constantinople
Corsica
Balearic Islands
Sardinia
Neapolis
395
EASTERN
Strait of Gibraltar
429
Corduba (Córdoba)
Malaca
Carthago Nova
Panormus
Sicily
GREECE
Thermopylae
Corinth
Athens
Ephesus
Vandals
439
Hippo
Carthage
Crete
MAURETANIA
NUMIDIA
Atlas Mountains
Mediterranean Sea
AFRICA
Leptis Magna
c.456

7 FRANKISH EXPANSION 357–550 CE
The Frankish tribes who lived along the empire's border on the Rhine sometimes cooperated with their Roman neighbors and sometimes raided their lands. In 357, their large domain was recognized by the empire, and when Roman power collapsed in the 5th century, the Franks, united under the Merovingian Dynasty, conquered most of Gaul.

→ Franks

6 OSTROGOTHS 453–493 CE
The Ostrogoths (eastern Goths) were one of the peoples subjugated by the Huns in the 4th century. They settled in the Roman province of Pannonia, and after the death of Attila in 453, moved westward and then to northern Italy. From there, under their great leader Theoderic, they extended their power across Italy in the 480s and 490s.

→ Ostrogoths

5 THE CAMPAIGNS OF ATTILA 440–453 CE
Led by Attila, the Huns devastated the Balkans and Thrace, attacked Greece, and extracted tribute from the Eastern Roman emperor. They then invaded Gaul, where they were defeated by the Romans at the Battle of the Catalaunian Fields in 451. The Huns moved into Italy, sacking numerous cities, before the Roman Empire sued for peace and Attila finally left Italy.

→ Campaigns of Attila

3 THE GREAT MIGRATION 406 CE

In the winter of 406, a vast group of nomadic peoples—Alans, Vandals, and Sueves—migrated westward and crossed the Rhine into Roman territory. From here, they moved through Gaul and into the Iberian Peninsula, where the Alans and Sueves settled. The Vandals moved on farther, crossing the Strait of Gibraltar into North Africa in 429.

⤑ Alans, Vandals, and Sueves ⟶ Alans

c.370 The Huns make their first appearance in the west, having arrived from central Asia

Volga

Huns
pre-**376**

370 After reaching the Volga across the steppes, the Huns start their rapid movement westward

Don

Alans
pre-**376**

▷ **Visigothic brooch**
This bronze and garnet brooch, found in southwest Spain, dates from the 6th century. The eagle shape was adapted by the Visigoths from the Roman imperial insignia.

Black Sea

ROMAN EMPIRE
(From 395)

ASIA MINOR

○ Antioch

SYRIA

Cyprus

4 MIGRATIONS TO BRITAIN c. 400–460 CE

By the early 5th century, Rome had withdrawn its troops from Britain in order to fight invaders elsewhere. In 410, Emperor Honorius instructed the cities of Britain to "look to your own defenses," marking the end of Roman rule in the province. Abandoned by Rome, Britain was invaded and settled by Picts, Irish Celts, and Angles and Saxons from northern Europe.

⟶ Irish   ⟶ Picts   ⟶ Angles and Saxons

MIGRATIONS OF PEOPLES 300–500 CE

The 4th and 5th centuries saw long-distance population movements across western Asia and Europe. These changes weakened the power of the Roman Empire, destroyed major cities such as Rome, and paved the way for the western empire's disintegration at the end of the 5th century.

KEY

▆ Extent of Roman Empire c. 390   ✕ Major battle

TIMELINE

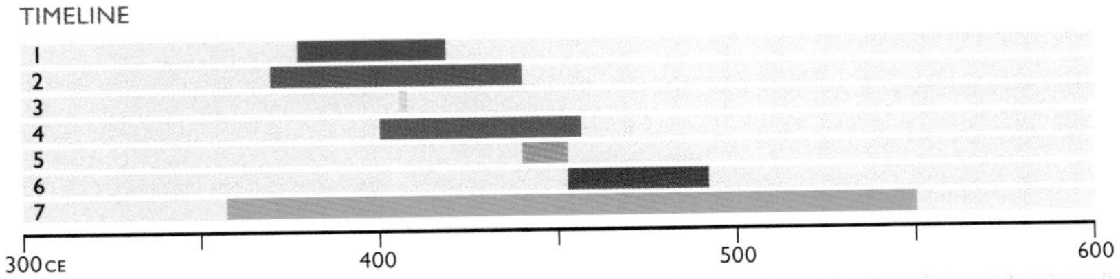

1
2
3
4
5
6
7

300 CE   400   500   600

AGE OF MIGRATIONS

The decline of the Roman Empire was accelerated in the 4th and 5th centuries by invasions of nomadic peoples from the east. This caused a cascade of movement, with new peoples settling in Europe and North Africa and changing the balance of power.

From the late 4th century onward, a series of peoples moved into lands previously governed by the Romans. Many of these newcomers, such as the Alans and the Huns, originated in central Asia, but others, such as the Franks, were people from near the empire's borders. The invaders came for different reasons. The nomadic Huns came to plunder, moving quickly across the landscape and taking whatever they could. Others, facing problems such as famine or displacement due to invasion at home, were desperate to find somewhere new to settle. For example, the Visigoths (western Goths), who had previously been settled in the Danubian Plain near the Black Sea, made agreements with Rome, gaining land in return for supplying mercenaries to the empire's armies.

By the time the invasions began, Roman power was already in decline. There were many reasons for this—famine, unemployment, inflation, and corruption all played their part. So did the empire's size, which made it hard to govern and led to its division into eastern and western halves in 285 CE. The invasions weakened it further, and the leaders of the mercenary forces were well placed to take over parts of the empire in the 5th century after Rome itself fell.

> *"Attila was a man born into the world to shake the nations, the scourge of all lands."*
>
> JORDANES, GOTHIC HISTORIAN, c. 551

THE DIVIDED EMPIRE
EASTERN AND WESTERN REALMS

Troubled by enemies to the north and east, and riven by internal strife, Diocletian decided that the empire was too large to rule as one realm. He split it in two in 285, ruling the eastern part himself, with the west governed by Maximian. There were subsequent periods of unification, but the east–west administration system survived for centuries, until the western empire was dissolved in 480.

3rd-century bust of Emperor Diocletian

HAN DYNASTY

Rebel leader Liu Bang reunified China in 206 BCE and founded the Han Empire. He instated a highly effective centralized government based on the system introduced by Qin Shi Huang's former Qin Empire. At the height of the Han's 400-year rule, China was the dominant cultural, political, and economic force in Asia.

The Han era (206 BCE–220 CE) is considered a golden age in Chinese history, during which the realm flourished in the areas of commerce, technology, arts, and politics. Through its conquests, the dynasty also brought a huge swathe of central Asia under its rule, creating an empire that at its height was comparable in size and wealth to its Roman counterpart. To consolidate its power, the Han fortified the Great Wall and set up military garrisons to protect its outposts. These measures allowed the empire to open the Silk Road—a major trade artery—in 130 BCE (see pp.102–103) and establish

lucrative commercial links with the wider world, exporting luxury goods such as silk and lacquerwork. Under the Han, technology advanced, the coinage was standardized, Chinese calligraphy evolved into an art, and technological innovations culminated in the invention of cast iron tools, silk-weaving looms, and paper. However, despite the Han's military achievements, the steppe peoples, in particular the Xiongnu, remained a constant threat. In tandem with peasant rebellions in the 2nd century, they played a pivotal role in eroding the empire's authority and bringing about its eventual downfall.

> "Where will I find brave men to guard the four corners of my land?"
>
> EMPEROR GAOZU, FROM *SONG OF THE GREAT WIND*, 195 BCE

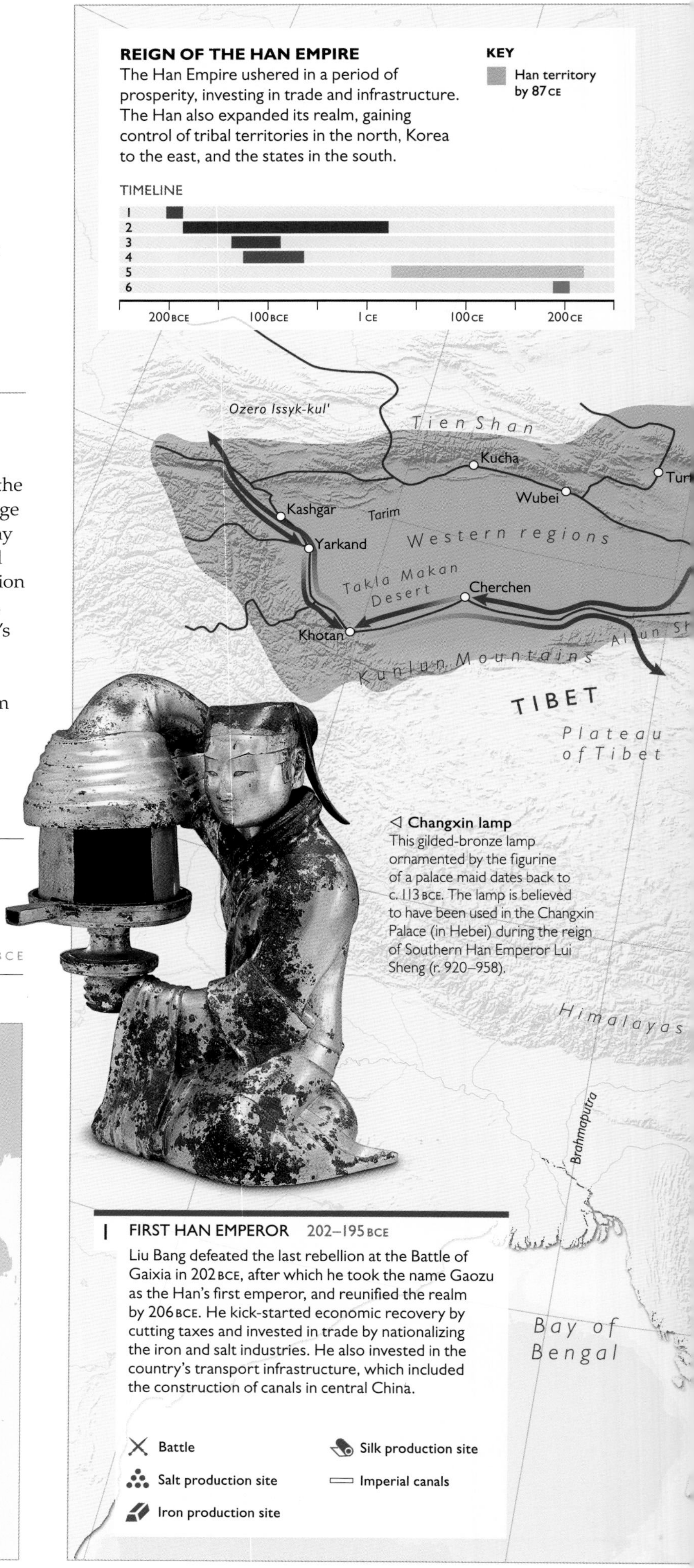

REIGN OF THE HAN EMPIRE

The Han Empire ushered in a period of prosperity, investing in trade and infrastructure. The Han also expanded its realm, gaining control of tribal territories in the north, Korea to the east, and the states in the south.

KEY
- Han territory by 87 CE

TIMELINE

1
2
3
4
5
6

200 BCE — 100 BCE — 1 CE — 100 CE — 200 CE

◁ **Changxin lamp**
This gilded-bronze lamp ornamented by the figurine of a palace maid dates back to c. 113 BCE. The lamp is believed to have been used in the Changxin Palace (in Hebei) during the reign of Southern Han Emperor Lui Sheng (r. 920–958).

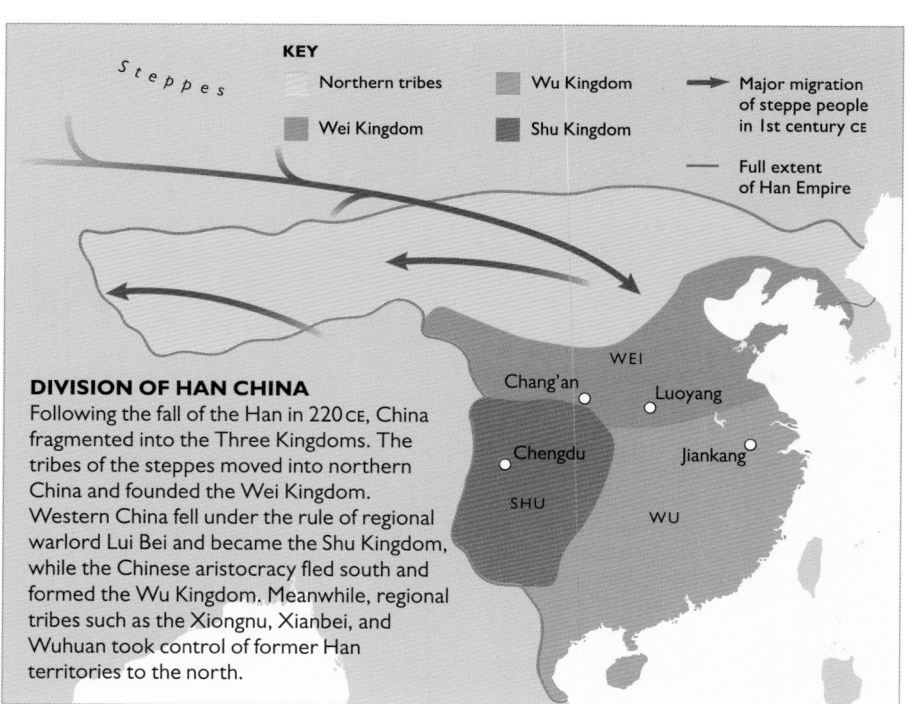

DIVISION OF HAN CHINA

Following the fall of the Han in 220 CE, China fragmented into the Three Kingdoms. The tribes of the steppes moved into northern China and founded the Wei Kingdom. Western China fell under the rule of regional warlord Lui Bei and became the Shu Kingdom, while the Chinese aristocracy fled south and formed the Wu Kingdom. Meanwhile, regional tribes such as the Xiongnu, Xianbei, and Wuhuan took control of former Han territories to the north.

KEY
- Northern tribes
- Wei Kingdom
- Wu Kingdom
- Shu Kingdom
- → Major migration of steppe people in 1st century CE
- — Full extent of Han Empire

FIRST HAN EMPEROR 202–195 BCE

Liu Bang defeated the last rebellion at the Battle of Gaixia in 202 BCE, after which he took the name Gaozu as the Han's first emperor, and reunified the realm by 206 BCE. He kick-started economic recovery by cutting taxes and invested in trade by nationalizing the iron and salt industries. He also invested in the country's transport infrastructure, which included the construction of canals in central China.

- ✕ Battle
- ⚒ Iron production site
- ⛏ Salt production site
- 🐛 Silk production site
- 🛶 Imperial canals

6 THE YELLOW TURBAN REBELLION 184–205 CE

The Han resumed its military activity against the northern tribes. The cost of war in tandem with a drought in 184 CE inflicted poverty and famine upon the realm. Large-scale peasant revolts ensued throughout eastern and central China and led to the rise of the Yellow Turbans—a rebel movement founded on a Taoist sect. The rebellion lasted 20 years and eroded Han authority.

▬▬ Rebellion areas   ⟶ Rebellion march into the capital

5 THE LATER HAN 25–220 CE

In 9 CE, former palace official Wang Mang usurped the throne and proclaimed the Xin Dynasty. Wang Mang's reign proved unpopular and prompted peasant rebels to besiege the capital in 23 CE. Thereafter, power returned to the Han lineage, and Luoyang was named the new imperial capital. By forming alliances with the various northern tribes, the later Han gained control of territories to the north and west.

☆ Imperial capital   ▨ Territories added by later Han (25–200 CE)

4 EXTENDING THE GREAT WALL 133–57 BCE

Despite the Han's military successes, tribes such as the Xiongnu, Xianbei, and Wuhuan remained a constant threat, which prompted the government to extend the Great Wall right across China's northern border. The extension not only provided a defense against northern tribes but also allowed the Han to open a safe passage westward and establish profitable trade links with the outside world, giving rise to the famous Silk Road (see pp.102–103).

▰▰▰ Han Great Wall

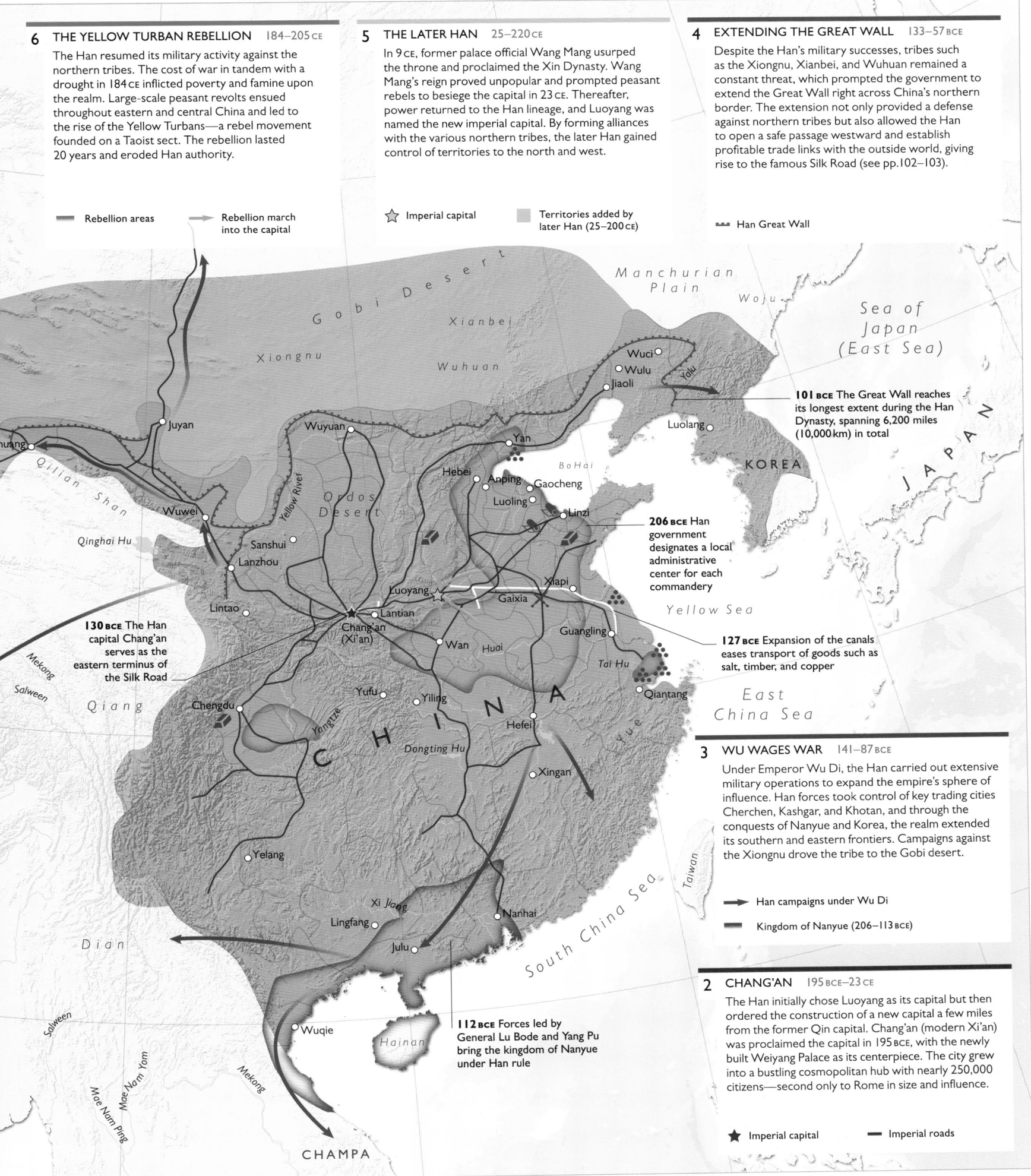

101 BCE The Great Wall reaches its longest extent during the Han Dynasty, spanning 6,200 miles (10,000 km) in total

206 BCE Han government designates a local administrative center for each commandery

130 BCE The Han capital Chang'an serves as the eastern terminus of the Silk Road

127 BCE Expansion of the canals eases transport of goods such as salt, timber, and copper

112 BCE Forces led by General Lu Bode and Yang Pu bring the kingdom of Nanyue under Han rule

3 WU WAGES WAR 141–87 BCE

Under Emperor Wu Di, the Han carried out extensive military operations to expand the empire's sphere of influence. Han forces took control of key trading cities Cherchen, Kashgar, and Khotan, and through the conquests of Nanyue and Korea, the realm extended its southern and eastern frontiers. Campaigns against the Xiongnu drove the tribe to the Gobi desert.

⟶ Han campaigns under Wu Di

▬▬ Kingdom of Nanyue (206–113 BCE)

2 CHANG'AN 195 BCE–23 CE

The Han initially chose Luoyang as its capital but then ordered the construction of a new capital a few miles from the former Qin capital. Chang'an (modern Xi'an) was proclaimed the capital in 195 BCE, with the newly built Weiyang Palace as its centerpiece. The city grew into a bustling cosmopolitan hub with nearly 250,000 citizens—second only to Rome in size and influence.

★ Imperial capital   ▬▬ Imperial roads

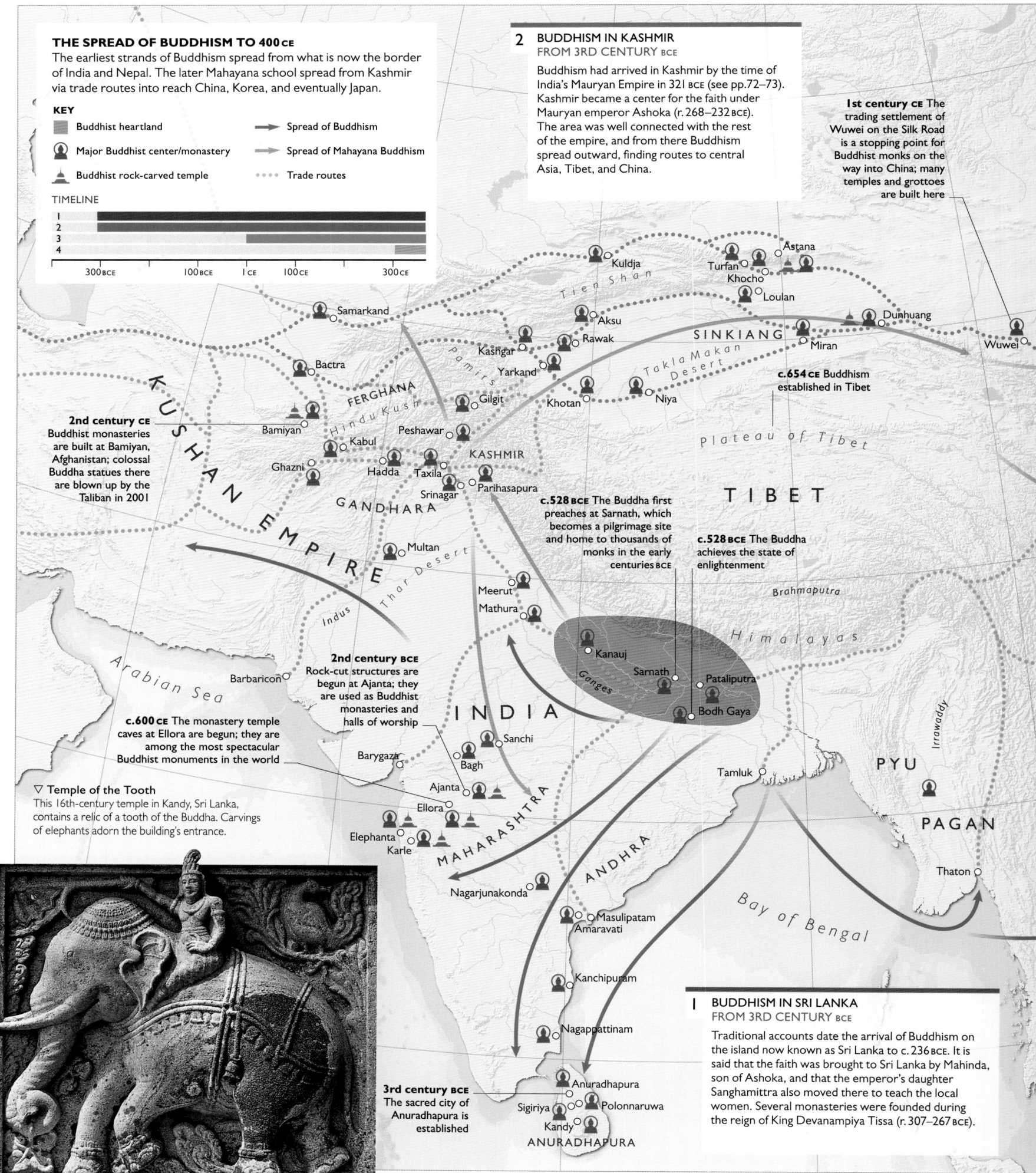

THE SPREAD OF BUDDHISM TO 400 CE

The earliest strands of Buddhism spread from what is now the border of India and Nepal. The later Mahayana school spread from Kashmir via trade routes into reach China, Korea, and eventually Japan.

KEY

- ▨ Buddhist heartland
- 🏛 Major Buddhist center/monastery
- 🛕 Buddhist rock-carved temple
- ➡ Spread of Buddhism
- ➡ Spread of Mahayana Buddhism
- ⋯ Trade routes

TIMELINE

1					
2					
3					
4					

300 BCE — 100 BCE — 1 CE — 100 CE — 300 CE

2 BUDDHISM IN KASHMIR
FROM 3RD CENTURY BCE

Buddhism had arrived in Kashmir by the time of India's Mauryan Empire in 321 BCE (see pp.72–73). Kashmir became a center for the faith under Mauryan emperor Ashoka (r. 268–232 BCE). The area was well connected with the rest of the empire, and from there Buddhism spread outward, finding routes to central Asia, Tibet, and China.

1st century CE The trading settlement of Wuwei on the Silk Road is a stopping point for Buddhist monks on the way into China; many temples and grottoes are built here

2nd century CE Buddhist monasteries are built at Bamiyan, Afghanistan; colossal Buddha statues there are blown up by the Taliban in 2001

c.654 CE Buddhism established in Tibet

c.528 BCE The Buddha first preaches at Sarnath, which becomes a pilgrimage site and home to thousands of monks in the early centuries BCE

c.528 BCE The Buddha achieves the state of enlightenment

2nd century BCE Rock-cut structures are begun at Ajanta; they are used as Buddhist monasteries and halls of worship

c.600 CE The monastery temple caves at Ellora are begun; they are among the most spectacular Buddhist monuments in the world

▽ **Temple of the Tooth**
This 16th-century temple in Kandy, Sri Lanka, contains a relic of a tooth of the Buddha. Carvings of elephants adorn the building's entrance.

3rd century BCE The sacred city of Anuradhapura is established

1 BUDDHISM IN SRI LANKA
FROM 3RD CENTURY BCE

Traditional accounts date the arrival of Buddhism on the island now known as Sri Lanka to c. 236 BCE. It is said that the faith was brought to Sri Lanka by Mahinda, son of Ashoka, and that the emperor's daughter Sanghamittra also moved there to teach the local women. Several monasteries were founded during the reign of King Devanampiya Tissa (r. 307–267 BCE).

5th–6th centuries CE Buddhist sculptors adorn the Yungang Grottoes near Datong with figures of Bodhisattvas—people who have achieved enlightenment

c.550 CE Buddhism introduced to Japan

372 CE Buddhism is established in Korea when a missionary sent by the Chinese emperor Fu Jian arrives in the country

713–803 CE The Leshan Giant Buddha, at 233 ft (71 m) in height, is built near the city of Chengdu

(map labels) Gobi Desert · Datong · Peking · Hejian · Wuyi · Gaoyang · Ye · Luoyang · Tianshui · Chang'an · Nanyang · Xinye · Xiangyang · Jiangling · Chengdu · Wuchang · Changsha · Kaifeng · Linhuai · Jiankang · Wuxing · Fuzhou · Guangzhou (Canton) · Pyongyang · Kaesong · KOREA · Yellow Sea · East China Sea · CHINA · Formosa · Hainan · NANZHAO · Cattigara · Mekong · South China Sea · Yangtze

---

THE SPREAD OF BUDDHISM

From its origins in northern India and Nepal, Buddhism spread through Asia from the 5th century BCE to the 3rd century CE. It won the support of powerful figures, such as the Mauryan emperor Ashoka, which ensured that it took root across the continent.

Buddhism is based on the teachings of Siddhartha Gautama, known as the Buddha (the enlightened one). The Buddha is said to have been born in Lumbini, but his life dates are widely disputed (he may have died in 420–380 BCE). He did not write his teachings down, so initially his ideas were spread by word of mouth, and there were disagreements between his disciples over the exact meaning of his teachings. This led to a number of different early "schools" of Buddhism that spread around India, and across the sea to Sri Lanka and Myanmar, in the centuries after the Buddha died.

One of the earliest schools, which still survives today, is Theravada Buddhism, which emphasizes the individual route to enlightenment. It developed in Sri Lanka, where its sacred writings, the Pali Canon, were compiled in the 1st century BCE. From here, Theravada spread to what is now Myanmar, Cambodia, Laos, and Thailand. The other major branch of Buddhism, Mahayana Buddhism, stressed the importance of helping others to reach enlightenment. It became especially strong in Kashmir and spread across India in the 3rd century BCE. By the 1st century CE, the faith had been adopted by the Kushan emperor Kanishka in central Asia and was being carried along the Silk Road to China.

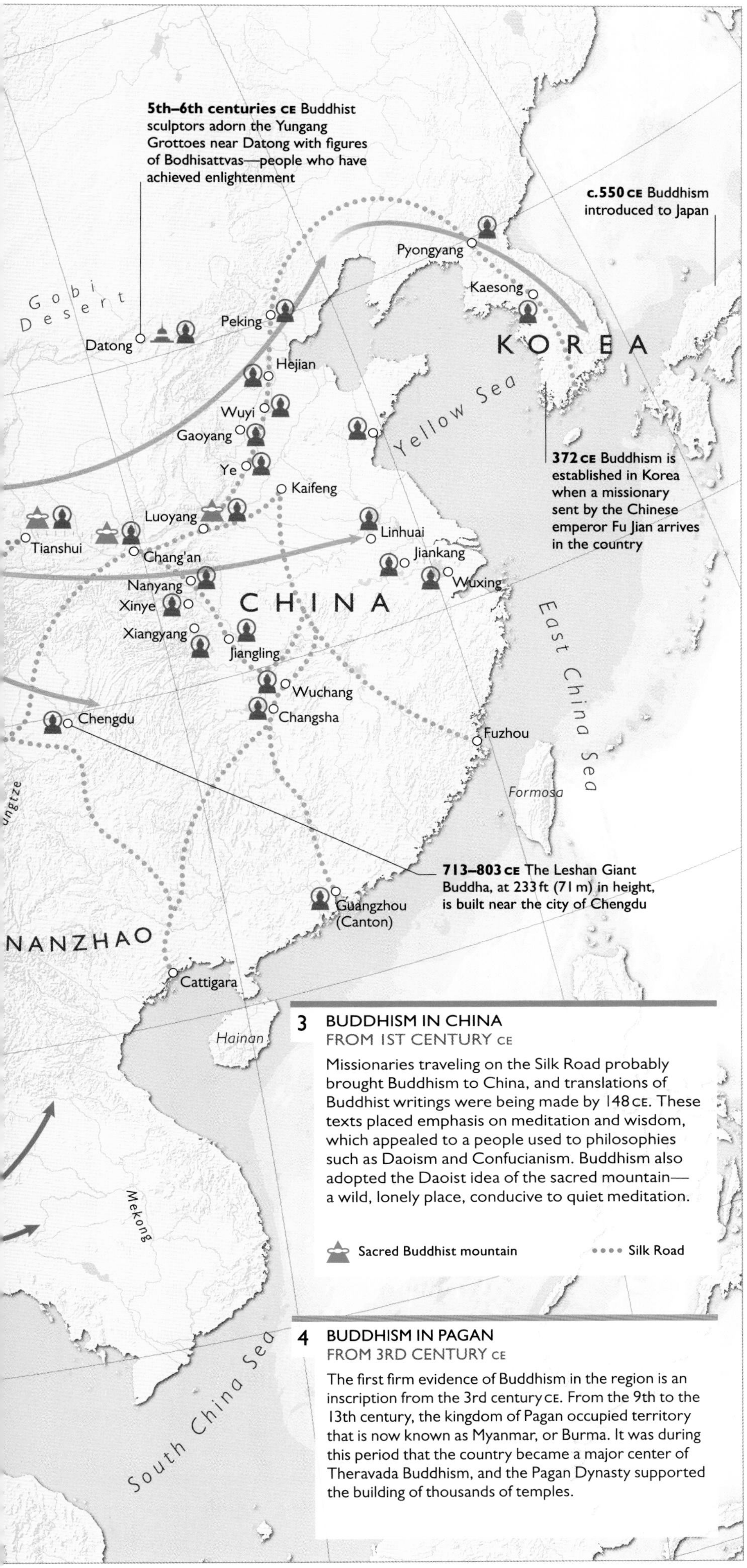

---

3 BUDDHISM IN CHINA
FROM 1ST CENTURY CE

Missionaries traveling on the Silk Road probably brought Buddhism to China, and translations of Buddhist writings were being made by 148 CE. These texts placed emphasis on meditation and wisdom, which appealed to a people used to philosophies such as Daoism and Confucianism. Buddhism also adopted the Daoist idea of the sacred mountain—a wild, lonely place, conducive to quiet meditation.

▲ Sacred Buddhist mountain   ···· Silk Road

---

4 BUDDHISM IN PAGAN
FROM 3RD CENTURY CE

The first firm evidence of Buddhism in the region is an inscription from the 3rd century CE. From the 9th to the 13th century, the kingdom of Pagan occupied territory that is now known as Myanmar, or Burma. It was during this period that the country became a major center of Theravada Buddhism, and the Pagan Dynasty supported the building of thousands of temples.

THE ORIGINS OF BUDDHISM
The Buddha traveled mainly in the plain of the Ganges River. He preached to all classes of society that, while life involves suffering, this suffering can be overcome by following the path he described.

KEY
◆ Places visited by the Buddha

···· Major routes

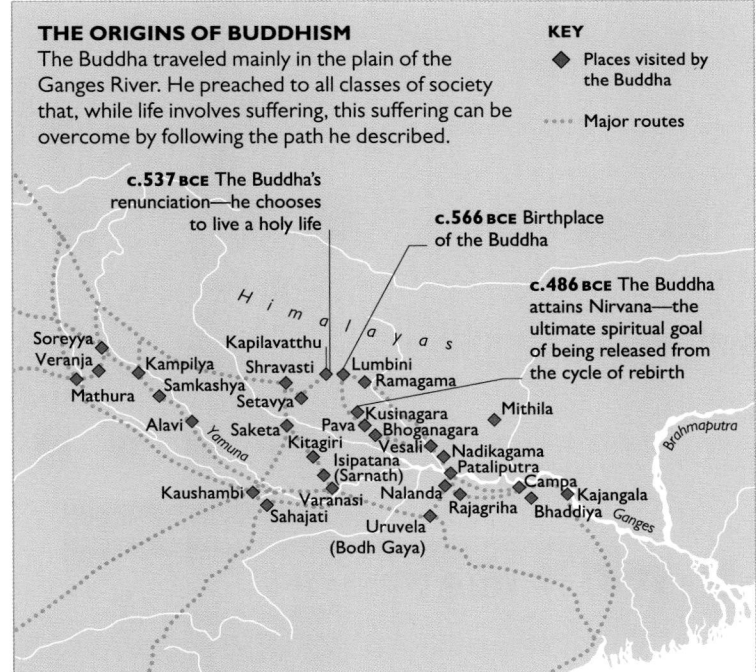

c.537 BCE The Buddha's renunciation—he chooses to live a holy life

c.566 BCE Birthplace of the Buddha

c.486 BCE The Buddha attains Nirvana—the ultimate spiritual goal of being released from the cycle of rebirth

(map labels) Himalayas · Soreyya · Veranja · Mathura · Kampilya · Shravasti · Samkashya · Setavya · Kapilavatthu · Lumbini · Ramagama · Mithila · Alavi · Saketa · Kitagiri · Pava · Kusinagara · Bhoganagara · Vesali · Nadikagama · Isipatana (Sarnath) · Pataliputra · Campa · Kaushambi · Varanasi · Nalanda · Kajangala · Sahajati · Uruvela (Bodh Gaya) · Rajagriha · Bhaddiya · Yamuna · Ganges · Brahmaputra

THE RISE OF CHRISTIANITY

Christianity spread across the Roman Empire and some neighboring areas in the first centuries CE. Its adherents were persecuted until the early 4th century, when the religion gained official recognition, having gradually found more favor among the elite.

Most notable among the missionaries who spread the Christian message in the 1st century CE were Peter, who according to tradition founded the church at Rome, and Paul, a Jewish convert who made a series of missionary journeys in Asia Minor, Greece, the Aegean, and Italy. They initially addressed Jewish communities but soon won a wider audience. Christian ideas appealed to the poor, but also shared concerns with classical philosophy. Some pagan scholars attacked it, but others recognized its moral value, and by the 2nd century CE, Christian writers were offering a robust intellectual defense.

The excellent communications and administrative framework of the empire gave the Christian faith arteries along which it spread and a template for church organization. By the end of the 1st century, there were churches all over the eastern Mediterranean and in Rome, and the following century saw churches founded across the whole Mediterranean and beyond. Some emperors saw Christianity as a threat and persecuted believers, but Constantine gave the religion official approval in 313 CE, rooting it strongly in the empire.

> *"We multiply whenever we are mown down by you; the blood of Christians is seed."*
>
> TERTULLIAN (THEOLOGIAN) FROM *APOLOGETICUS*, 197 CE

THE EARLY CHURCH IN ROME
WORSHIP IN THE SEAT OF EMPIRE

The Saints Paul and Peter probably arrived in Rome around 50 CE and were martyred, most likely under the emperor Nero, in c. 64 CE. There were bishops in Rome by the late 1st century but, at that time, a church was often a room in a private home, since Christians were widely persecuted. By the early 4th century, their faith was more widely accepted, and more churches were built.

Catacombs of Rome
Christians favored burial over cremation. They decorated the city catacombs where they placed their dead with frescoes.

---

457 CE According to tradition, St. Patrick founds his main church at Armagh

3rd century CE There are some Christians in Britain in the Roman period, especially from the 3rd century onward

177 CE Reports of persecution at Lugdunum (Lyon) are the first evidence of Christian beliefs in Roman Gaul

1st century CE Christianity probably reaches Spain; there are churches in cities such as Toletum (Toledo) by the late Roman period

2nd century CE There are Christians in Carthage; the city is home to the influential Latin theologian Tertullian

Map labels: Armagh, Eburacum, Segontium, Deva, North Sea, BRITAIN, Londinium, GERMANY, ATLANTIC OCEAN, Colonia Agrippina, Rotomagus, Augusta Treverorum, Castra Regina, Argentoratum, GAUL, Rhine, NORICUM, Turoni, Vesontio, RAETIA, Alps, Bituricae, Aquileia, Vienna, Lugdunum, Mediolanum, Burdigala, Rhône, Ravenna, Ariminum, Mutina, Arelate, ITALY, Pyrenees, Narbo, Rome, Corsica, Ostia, Bracara, HISPANIA, Tarraco, Toletum, Sardinia, Carales, Sicily, Emerita Augusta, Balearic Islands, Mediterranean Sea, Corduba (Córdoba), Hispalis, Carthago Nova, Carthage, Gades, MAURETANIA, Lambaesis, Volubilis

---

ORIGINS IN PALESTINE   c. 30–50 CE

According to the Acts of the Apostles (the fifth book of the New Testament), Jesus's persecuted followers dispersed from Palestine to set up Christian communities at such centers as Antioch. The faith seems to have spread slowly in the eastern Mediterranean until the work of missionaries, such as St. Paul, took it farther afield.

THE SPREAD OF THE FAITH

Christianity spread quickly, with churches founded across the Roman Empire from the 1st century onward. From the 4th century, the diversity of the religion caused the emperor concern, so he convened councils of church leaders to resolve disagreements on points of doctrine.

KEY
- Roman Empire 250 CE
- Christian areas outside Roman Empire

TIMELINE
1
2
3
4
5
6
7

1 CE   100   200   300   400   500   600

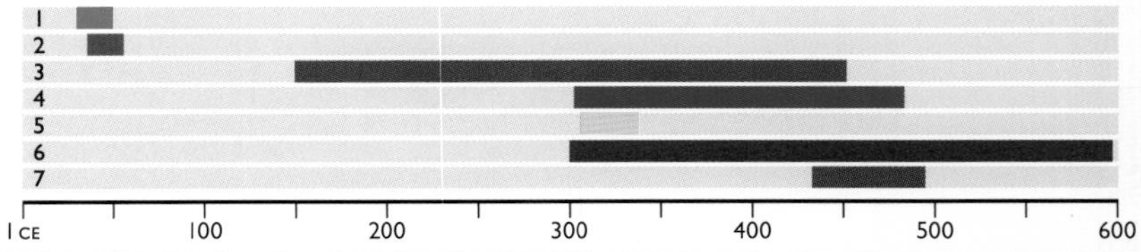

7 IRELAND 430–492 CE

St. Patrick, a Romano-British missionary, is said to have been the first person to bring Christianity to Ireland, probably in the early 5th century; according to tradition, he became the first bishop of Armagh. There were certainly Christians in Ireland by 430 CE, because in this year the pope in Rome sent Paulinus to preach to the people there "believing in Christ."

6 CHURCH ORGANIZATION c. 300–600 CE

The early church was organized in a similar way to the Roman Empire, with its leaders based in main cities. Patriarchs were the most senior bishops, followed by archbishops. Five patriarchs claimed primacy, but it was the bishopric of Rome that gradually established authority over the churches in the western empire, although it never gained authority in the east.

✠ Christian Patriarchate by 600 CE

✠ Christian Archbishopric by 600 CE

⚓ Other Christian churches by 600 CE

5 CONSTANTINE 306–337 CE

In the early 4th century, the emperor Constantine converted to Christianity. In the Edict of Milan (313 CE), he gave the religion legal status, and in 325, he convened the Council of Nicaea, a meeting of church leaders to agree on key theological issues, such as the divinity of Jesus and the calculation of the date of Easter. This and later councils united the Roman Empire's churches, but also led to schisms that formed branches such as the Oriental Orthodox church.

◯ Church council

c. 50 CE Paul visits Thessalonica and preaches at one of the city's synagogues

325 CE The Council of Nicaea repudiates Arianism, a heresy that was gaining a substantial following, and produces the Nicene Creed

c. 70 CE Antioch becomes a major Christian center; it is here that adherents are first called Christians

c. 50 CE Paul visits Corinth for the first time; he returns to the city in 58 CE

c. 52–54 CE Paul lives in Ephesus; the port becomes a center for missionary activity

c. 60 CE Titus, one of Paul's many converts, becomes the first bishop of Crete

4 ARMENIA 301–484 CE

In 301, Armenia became the first country (it was outside the Roman Empire) to adopt Christianity as its state religion. In 428 CE, the Sassanid Persians took over eastern Armenia and tried to impose Zoroastrianism, which provoked rebellion. The Armenians waged a guerrilla war against this oppression, and eventually, in 484 CE, the Persians agreed to a treaty granting them religious freedom.

▷ Constantine the Great
This marble head formed part of a 40-ft- (12-m-) high statue of the emperor, made around 315 CE. Constantine awarded Christians new rights and became a patron of the faith.

2 ST. PAUL AND THE EARLY CHRISTIAN CHURCHES c. 35–55 CE

St. Paul's four missionary journeys took him as far afield as Asia Minor, Greece, Rome, and possibly Spain. He founded churches as he went and encouraged his followers to start even more. Among the most famous of these 1st-century foundations were the Seven Churches of Asia Minor, mentioned in the Bible's Book of Revelation.

3 THE COPTIC CHURCH c. 150–451 CE

A fragment of St. John's Gospel written in the Coptic language found in Upper Egypt shows that Christianity had arrived in the region by the mid 2nd century. Coptic theological views gradually diverged from those of other churches. This came to a head at the Council of Chalcedon in 451 CE, when the Copts split away from the other Christian churches.

c. 340 CE King Ezana of Aksum (Ethiopia) is converted to Christianity by a Syrian Christian named Frumentius, called Abba Salama in Ethiopian literature

ST. PAUL'S JOURNEYS

→ First
→ Second
→ Third
→ Fourth
△ The Seven Churches of Asia Minor

MIDDLE
AGES

IN MEDIEVAL TIMES, 500–1450 CE, THE CHRISTIAN CHURCH KEPT THE
STATUS QUO IN EUROPE, WHILE PARTS OF ASIA AND THE AMERICAS
REACHED NEW CULTURAL AND TECHNOLOGICAL HEIGHTS.

THE MIDDLE AGES

The Roman Empire's collapse by the 5th century was followed by a millennium in which Europe became an economic and political backwater, eclipsed by a technologically advanced China and by a powerful Islamic empire.

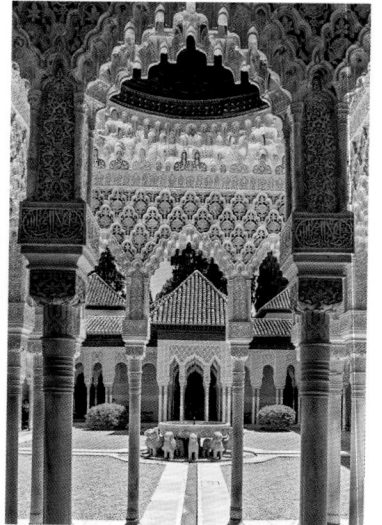

△ **Golden mask**
This "Mask of the Winged Eyes" from the Sicán culture, at its height in coastal northern Peru around 900–1100, demonstrates pre-Inca mastery of gold working.

By the 6th century, large empires that had dominated the classical world fell to attacks by neighboring peoples. In western Europe, the invaders had begun to build their own states, which retained elements of Roman law and administration but with the infusion of a Christian culture. A form of government known as vassalage developed, in which nobles held lands from their sovereigns in exchange for military service, while the lower orders held theirs in return for their labor, a system known as feudalism. None of the Germanic successors to Rome succeeded in uniting its former territories. The empire of the Carolingian ruler Charlemagne (r. 768–814) came closest, but it fell apart after his death. Islamic armies from North Africa overwhelmed Visigothic Spain in 711.

In Central America, the Maya city-states had collapsed by 900. In the same region, the Aztec Empire emerged in the 14th century, paralleled in South America with the rapid growth of the Inca state in the mid-15th century. In India, Hun invaders had destroyed the Gupta Empire by 606. Stability was only partially restored in the early 13th century by a sultanate based in Delhi.

Islam and the Crusades

Islam first appeared in Arabia in the early 7th century and spread rapidly, creating a vast empire that extended from Spain to central Asia. Its rulers—the Umayyad and, later, the Abbasid caliphs—presided over a prosperous and culturally vibrant realm, but the difficulties of ruling such a vast area proved impossible to overcome. By the 10th century, it had begun to break apart into competing emirates and rival caliphates. Into this fragmented sphere arrived the first European military expedition outside the continent for centuries.

△ **Moorish marvel**
The ornate Court of the Lions, built c. 1370 by the Nasrid Sultan Muhammad V at the Alhambra palace in Granada, is typical of the sophistication of late Islamic Spain.

Europe in the Middle Ages

The Crusades were campaigns to gain control of the holy city of Jerusalem from the Muslims. The Crusaders succeeded in establishing Christian-controlled states in Palestine between 1096 and 1291, but fell to a series of resurgent Islamic powers, including the Mamluks in Egypt and the Seljuk Turks.

The Papacy, which had inspired the crusaders, remained a potent political as well as spiritual force in Europe, and engaged in a long struggle for recognition of its primacy over secular rulers. This led it into a conflict with the Holy Roman Emperors—the German-based rivals to their claim (see pp.116–119).

Europe had been buffeted by further invasions: by the Vikings, who preyed on northwestern Europe's coastlines for two centuries from around 800; by the

TURBULENT TIMES

The early Middle Ages—from the 6th to the 10th centuries—was a time of turbulence, as the collapse of the major civilizations of the classical world was followed by the emergence of new powers, such as the Franks in western Europe, the Islamic empire in the Middle East, and the Tang Dynasty in China. The 13th and 14th centuries saw renewed instability, as the Mongols created a vast Eurasian empire and a plague pandemic killed an estimated 25 million people in Europe.

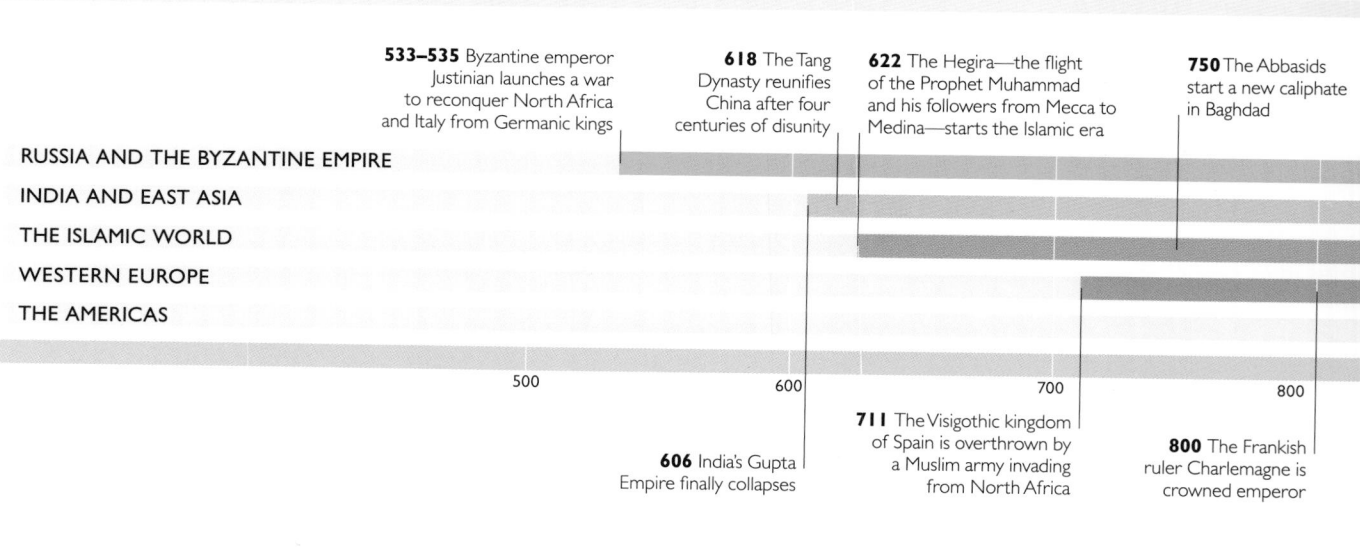

533–535 Byzantine emperor Justinian launches a war to reconquer North Africa and Italy from Germanic kings

618 The Tang Dynasty reunifies China after four centuries of disunity

622 The Hegira—the flight of the Prophet Muhammad and his followers from Mecca to Medina—starts the Islamic era

750 The Abbasids start a new caliphate in Baghdad

RUSSIA AND THE BYZANTINE EMPIRE

INDIA AND EAST ASIA

THE ISLAMIC WORLD

WESTERN EUROPE

THE AMERICAS

500   600   700   800

711 The Visigothic kingdom of Spain is overthrown by a Muslim army invading from North Africa

606 India's Gupta Empire finally collapses

800 The Frankish ruler Charlemagne is crowned emperor

◁ **The dance of death**
The 15th-century frieze *Danse Macabre* by German artist Bernt Notke shows the heightened European preoccupation with mortality at the time of the Black Death, when death seemed to strike the rich and poor indiscriminately.

Magyars, who established themselves on the Hungarian plain around 900; and by the Mongols, able horseback archers, who descended on eastern Europe in the 1240s.

Rise of the Mongols

The Mongols also conquered China, which had been united by the Sui Dynasty in 589 and then prospered under the Tang Dynasty from 618 and the Song Dynasty from 960.

At the eastern end of the Silk Road, which transmitted wealth and new ideas between east Asia and the Middle East, China pioneered the use of gunpowder, printing, and the marine compass but never succeeded in taming the Mongols, who also attacked Southeast Asia, destroying the kingdom of Pagan in modern Myanmar and threatening the Cambodian state of Angkor. Their armies tried to invade Japan, too, but were twice driven back by storms. Japan continued to be ruled by the shoguns—dynasties of military strongmen backed by clans of samurai warriors whose military ethos dominated the state.

European revival

Despite a global pandemic of plague and Mongol intrusion on its eastern fringe, Europe survived and prospered. The plague, or Black Death, killed more than one-third of the continent's population. However, it also improved the lot of the peasantry, whose labor was now a scarcer commodity, thus undermining the roots of feudalism.

New ideas now began to emerge in Europe. In Italy, a revived interest in classical art and ideas gave birth to the rich cultural movement of the Renaissance (see pp.160–161).

Italian merchants pioneered methods of banking, and the maritime empires of Venice and Genoa spread across the eastern Mediterranean. By 1450, Europe's ambitions and horizons were beginning to expand again.

▽ **Mongols defeated**
This 19th-century engraving by Japanese artist Kuniyoshi Utagawa shows the Japanese monk Nichiren summoning storms that destroyed Mongol fleets in 1274 and 1281.

"And believing it to be the end of the world, no one wept for the dead, for all expected to die."

CHRONICLER AGNOLO DI TURA ON THE BLACK DEATH IN ITALY, 1348

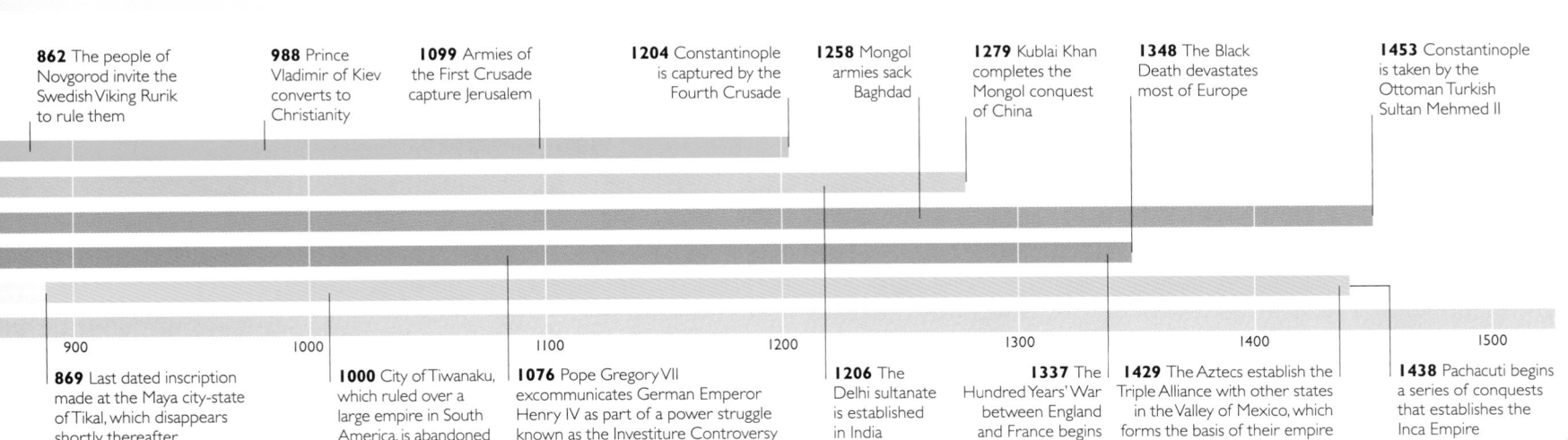

862 The people of Novgorod invite the Swedish Viking Rurik to rule them

988 Prince Vladimir of Kiev converts to Christianity

1099 Armies of the First Crusade capture Jerusalem

1204 Constantinople is captured by the Fourth Crusade

1258 Mongol armies sack Baghdad

1279 Kublai Khan completes the Mongol conquest of China

1348 The Black Death devastates most of Europe

1453 Constantinople is taken by the Ottoman Turkish Sultan Mehmed II

900   1000   1100   1200   1300   1400   1500

869 Last dated inscription made at the Maya city-state of Tikal, which disappears shortly thereafter

1000 City of Tiwanaku, which ruled over a large empire in South America, is abandoned

1076 Pope Gregory VII excommunicates German Emperor Henry IV as part of a power struggle known as the Investiture Controversy

1206 The Delhi sultanate is established in India

1337 The Hundred Years' War between England and France begins

1429 The Aztecs establish the Triple Alliance with other states in the Valley of Mexico, which forms the basis of their empire

1438 Pachacuti begins a series of conquests that establishes the Inca Empire

THE BYZANTINE EMPIRE

In 330, Roman Emperor Constantine moved the capital from Rome to the former Greek colony of Byzantium, which later became Constantinople. In 395, the Empire split in two, and in 476 the western half collapsed. The Eastern Roman Empire, however, endured for another 1,000 years, helped by the might of Constantinople.

After the last western Roman emperor was deposed in 476, the Eastern Roman Empire (called Byzantine by historians) continued as the sole entity of Roman sovereignty—though predominantly Greek-speaking (unlike its fallen Latin-speaking western counterpart).

By 554, Emperor Justinian I (r. 527–565) had reconquered large parts of the western Mediterranean coast, including Rome itself, which the empire held for two more centuries. To mark his achievements, Justinian ordered the construction of the church of Hagia Sophia, which would later become the center of the Eastern Orthodox Church while also inspiring a new wave of architecture, in particular across the Islamic world. However, in the 7th century, Byzantium lost North Africa and its Middle Eastern territories to the

rising power of Islam, and much of the Balkans fell to invaders led by the Slavs. Although the Byzantine Empire rallied under the Macedonian Dynasty (867–1056), regaining lost territory, its split from the Church of Rome (1054) and the resulting threat it posed to the Pope's authority led the Venetians to divert the army of the Fourth Crusade to the sacking of the Byzantine capital instead, permanently weakening the empire.

Nevertheless. throughout much of its 1,000-year existence, the Byzantine Empire buffered Europe from newly emerging forces to the east, and its thriving capital exerted great influence upon the fields of art, literature, science, and philosophy—both as an intellectual hub and as custodian of Ancient Greek texts, thereby helping to shape modern European civilization.

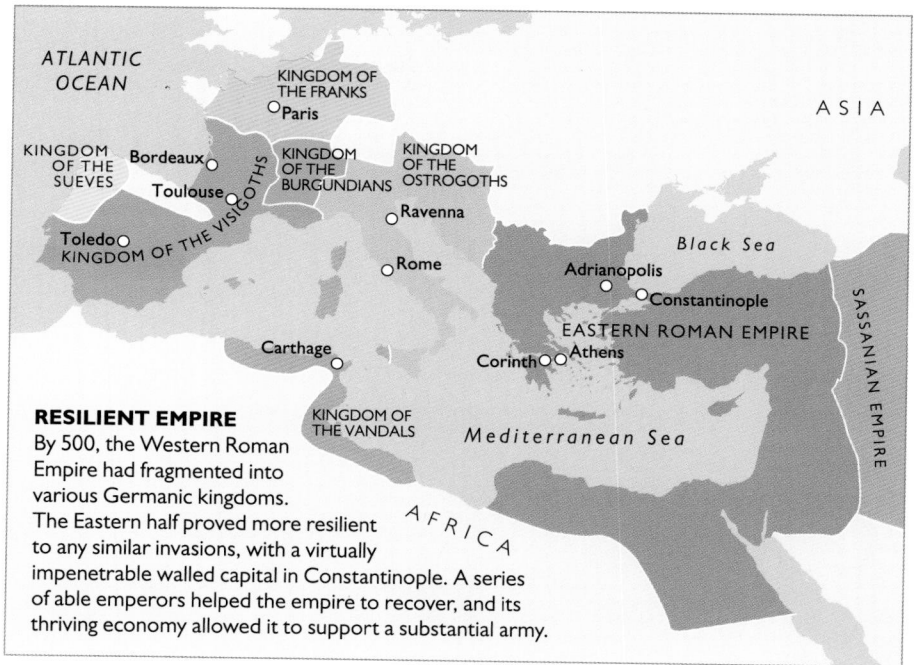

RESILIENT EMPIRE
By 500, the Western Roman Empire had fragmented into various Germanic kingdoms. The Eastern half proved more resilient to any similar invasions, with a virtually impenetrable walled capital in Constantinople. A series of able emperors helped the empire to recover, and its thriving economy allowed it to support a substantial army.

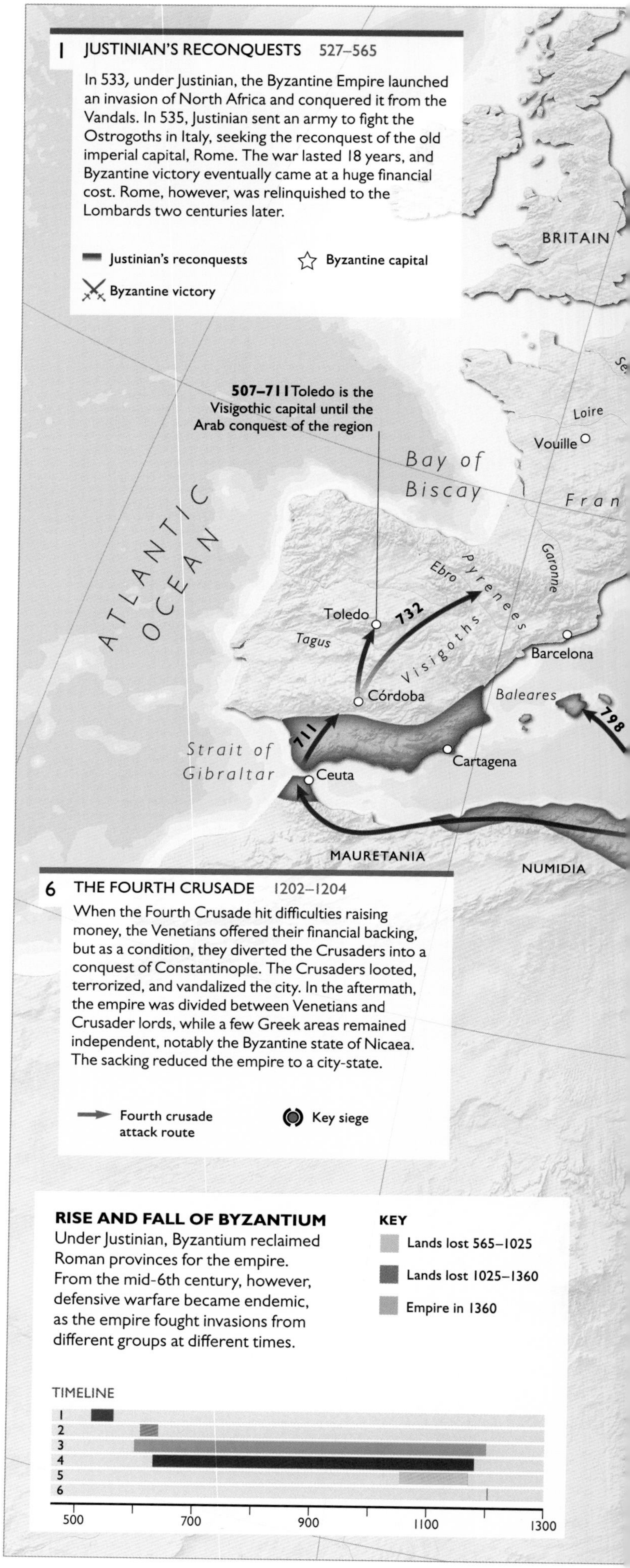

---

1 JUSTINIAN'S RECONQUESTS 527–565

In 533, under Justinian, the Byzantine Empire launched an invasion of North Africa and conquered it from the Vandals. In 535, Justinian sent an army to fight the Ostrogoths in Italy, seeking the reconquest of the old imperial capital, Rome. The war lasted 18 years, and Byzantine victory eventually came at a huge financial cost. Rome, however, was relinquished to the Lombards two centuries later.

━━ Justinian's reconquests   ☆ Byzantine capital

✗ Byzantine victory

507–711 Toledo is the Visigothic capital until the Arab conquest of the region

6 THE FOURTH CRUSADE 1202–1204

When the Fourth Crusade hit difficulties raising money, the Venetians offered their financial backing, but as a condition, they diverted the Crusaders into a conquest of Constantinople. The Crusaders looted, terrorized, and vandalized the city. In the aftermath, the empire was divided between Venetians and Crusader lords, while a few Greek areas remained independent, notably the Byzantine state of Nicaea. The sacking reduced the empire to a city-state.

→ Fourth crusade attack route   ◎ Key siege

RISE AND FALL OF BYZANTIUM
Under Justinian, Byzantium reclaimed Roman provinces for the empire. From the mid-6th century, however, defensive warfare became endemic, as the empire fought invasions from different groups at different times.

KEY
▨ Lands lost 565–1025
▨ Lands lost 1025–1360
▨ Empire in 1360

TIMELINE

500   700   900   1100   1300

2 DEFENDING AGAINST PERSIA 610–641

Byzantine emperor Heraclius (r. 610–641) came to power in the midst of an invasion of the empire by the Sassanid Persians. The Sassanids had already seized control of Egypt and the Levant and attempted a siege of Constantinople. In 627, Heraclius launched a counterattack into the Persian capital, Ctesiphon, and surrounded the city, eventually forcing a peace deal that subdued the Sassanid threat.

→ Persian invasions   ⇢ Heraclius's counterinvasion
★ Persian capital

3 NOMADIC RAIDS 600–1200

In the 10th century, seminomadic peoples, such as the Slavs, Avars, and Bulgars, invaded the Balkans—the region between the Greek Peloponnese and the Danube River. In 1014, Byzantine emperor Basil II (r. 976–1025) destroyed the Bulgarian Kingdom and annexed the territory—a feat for which he earned the nickname "Bulgar-Slayer." However, revolts against Byzantine rule in 1185 led to a loss of the Balkans and undermined the Byzantine Empire.

→ Nomadic raids   ✗ Byzantine victory

4 ISLAMIC INVASION 629–1180

Under the leadership of the first caliphs, Arab Muslim armies invaded both Sassanid Persia and the Byzantine Empire. At the Battle of Yarmuk in 636, the Byzantine army suffered a huge loss. In the aftermath, first Syria and Palestine and then Egypt were conquered by Arab armies and fell under the influence of Islam. Under the rule of the Macedonian Dynasty (867–1056), the Byzantine Empire managed to recapture territories lost to Muslim conquests in the 7th century.

→ Muslim invasions   ✗ Byzantine defeat

5 BYZANTINE–SELJUK WARS 1048–1071

The Seljuk Turks, a group of warriors on horseback from central Asia, invaded the Byzantine Empire in the 11th century. During the Battle of Manzikert (1071), the Byzantine Emperor Romanus Diogenes was taken prisoner. The Seljuk threat to Constantinople forced Byzantium to send a distress call to Rome, which triggered the First Crusade (see pp. 106–107).

✗ Byzantine defeat
→ Seljuk Turks invasion

Seljuk cavalry armed for battle

▷ **Emperor Justinian**
This mosaic depicting Byzantine emperor Justinian is on the wall of the Basilica of San Vitale in Ravenna. It was completed in 547 after Justinian had reconquered the old imperial capital.

1202 Army of the Fourth Crusade pillages the port of Zara

1014 Basil II defeats Bulgars and annexes Bulgarian Kingdom

1091 Byzantine Empire loses most of Anatolia to Seljuk Turk invasion

552–553 Battle of Mons Lactarius

533 Battle of Ad Decimum. Byzantine victory in Carthage leads to the collapse of the Vandal Kingdom

1071 Manzikert

627 Byzantine troops march into the Persian capital to counter the Sassanid invasion

636 Battle of Yarmuk

THE ASCENT OF ISLAM

Beginning with a series of revelations received by the prophet Muhammad around 610 CE, the new faith of Islam rapidly gained followers in Arabia. Within a century, armies fighting under its banner had conquered a vast swathe of territory from Persia to Spain.

Muhammad was born around 570 into an influential merchant family in Mecca. From the age of 40, he experienced a series of divine revelations, and from around 613, he began to preach that there was only one God, Allah. His condemnation of polytheism and idol worship was unpopular, and he was forced to flee to the town of Yathrib (Medina). His message of monotheism began to attract followers, and he soon built up an army that captured Mecca.

Under Muhammad's successors, known as caliphs, Muslim forces defeated the Byzantine and Persian Empires, which had been severely weakened by a war between them that lasted from 602 to 628. The Byzantine Empire lost Syria, Palestine (including the holy city of Jerusalem), and Egypt to the Muslims, but the Sassanian Persian Empire was conquered in its entirety, bringing the fledgling Islamic state new provinces from Iraq to the borders of India.

The Umayyad caliphs, a dynasty that ruled the Islamic empire from 661 from their capital at Damascus, established a complex administration that made use of the experience of Greek-speaking officials in the former Byzantine provinces. They encouraged the integration into the empire of peoples beyond Arabia; and as ever more people converted to the faith, Islamic armies pushed westward, conquering the remainder of North Africa and much of Spain by 711. Briefly, in the mid-8th century, all this territory was united under the authority of a single ruler, guided by a faith whose tenets had by now found written form in a sacred book, the Qur'an.

THE DIVISION OF ISLAM 634–661 CE
SUNNI AND SHIA

The question of who should hold political and religious authority within Islam after the death of Muhammad proved incredibly divisive. Many felt the succession should pass through the family of Ali, the son-in-law of Muhammad, and these formed the Shia (the party of Ali), while others, who rejected this view and adhered to the Umayyads in Damascus and their successors, became the Sunni. This division in Islam has persisted until the present day.

Calligraphic succession
In this 18th-century Turkish artwork, the red writing indicates Allah; the central name in blue is Ali, first Imam of the Shia; the green writing gives the name of the prophet Muhammad.

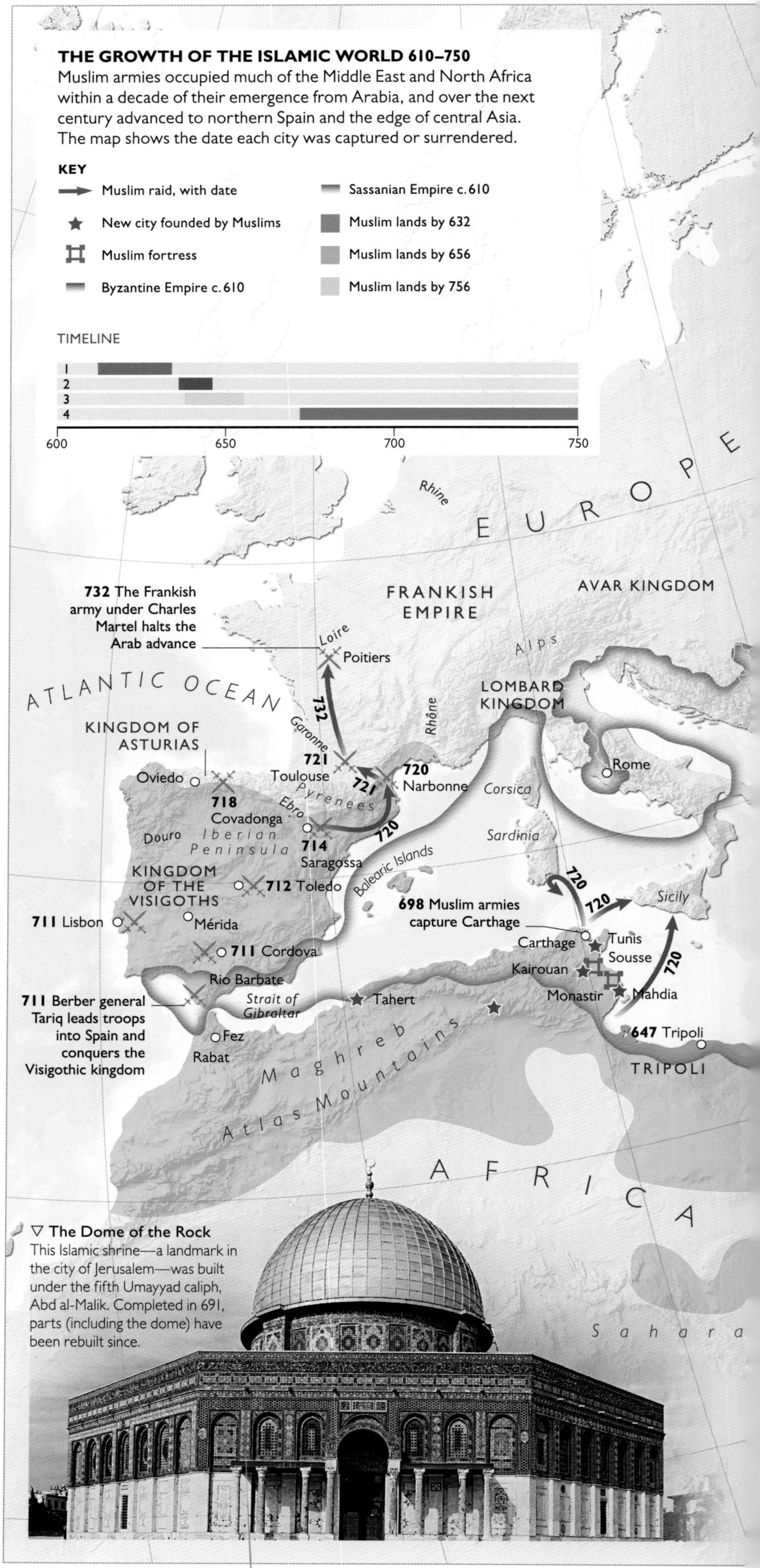

THE GROWTH OF THE ISLAMIC WORLD 610–750
Muslim armies occupied much of the Middle East and North Africa within a decade of their emergence from Arabia, and over the next century advanced to northern Spain and the edge of central Asia. The map shows the date each city was captured or surrendered.

KEY

→ Muslim raid, with date
★ New city founded by Muslims
⛫ Muslim fortress
▬ Byzantine Empire c. 610
▬ Sassanian Empire c. 610
■ Muslim lands by 632
■ Muslim lands by 656
■ Muslim lands by 756

TIMELINE

1
2
3
4

600   650   700   750

732 The Frankish army under Charles Martel halts the Arab advance

EUROPE
FRANKISH EMPIRE
AVAR KINGDOM
LOMBARD KINGDOM
Rome
ATLANTIC OCEAN
KINGDOM OF ASTURIAS
Oviedo
718 Covadonga
721 Toulouse
721
720 Narbonne
Corsica
Sardinia
Balearic Islands
714 Saragossa
712 Toledo
Ebro
Douro
Iberian Peninsula
KINGDOM OF THE VISIGOTHS
711 Lisbon
Mérida
711 Cordova
Rio Barbate
Strait of Gibraltar
711 Berber general Tariq leads troops into Spain and conquers the Visigothic kingdom
Fez
Rabat
Tahert
Maghreb
Atlas Mountains
698 Muslim armies capture Carthage
Carthage
Tunis
Sousse
Kairouan
Monastir
Mahdia
647 Tripoli
TRIPOLI
AFRICA
Sahara
Rhine
Loire
Garonne
Rhône
Alps
Pyrenees
Sicily
Poitiers

▽ The Dome of the Rock
This Islamic shrine—a landmark in the city of Jerusalem—was built under the fifth Umayyad caliph, Abd al-Malik. Completed in 691, parts (including the dome) have been rebuilt since.

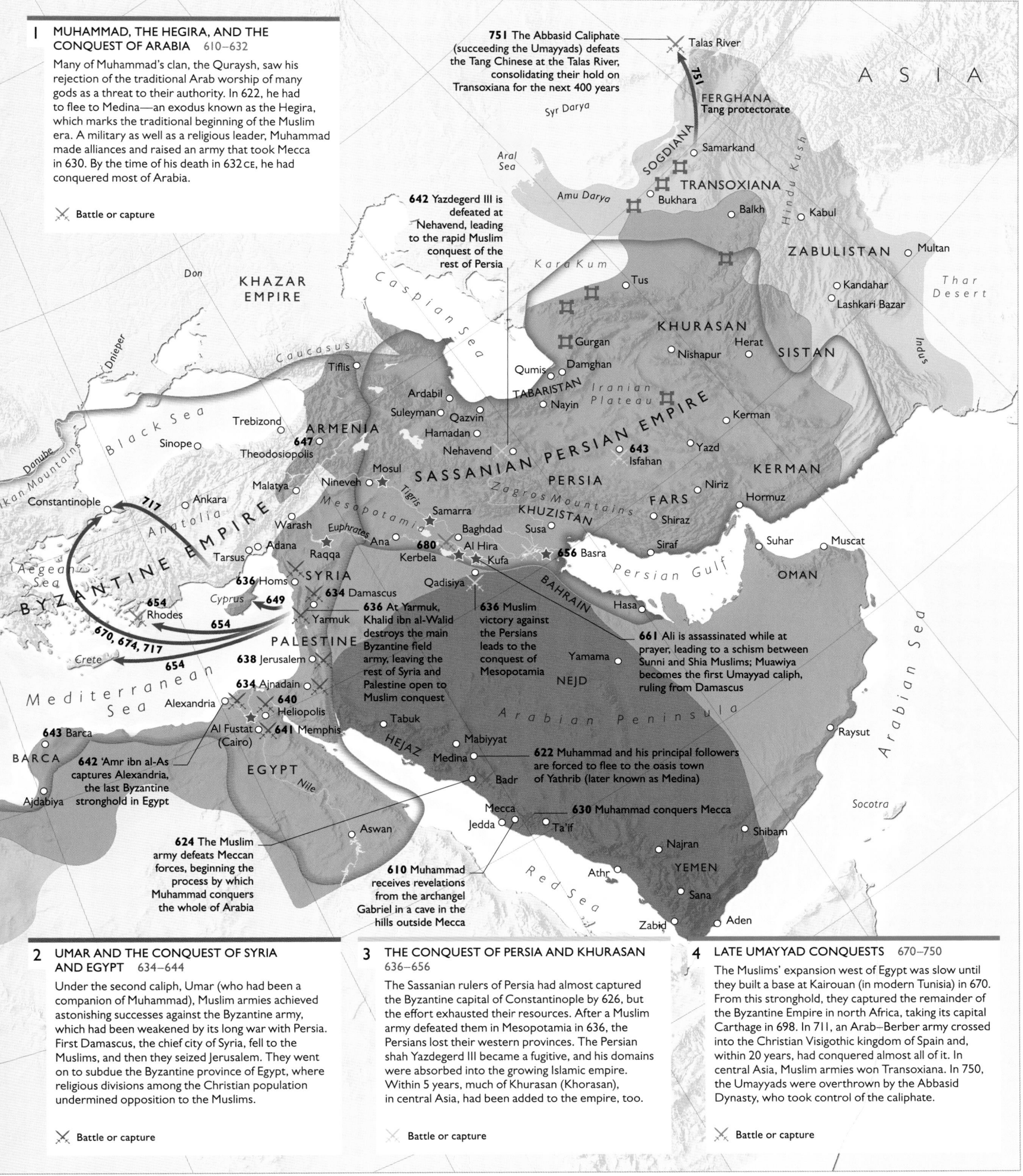

1 MUHAMMAD, THE HEGIRA, AND THE CONQUEST OF ARABIA 610–632

Many of Muhammad's clan, the Quraysh, saw his rejection of the traditional Arab worship of many gods as a threat to their authority. In 622, he had to flee to Medina—an exodus known as the Hegira, which marks the traditional beginning of the Muslim era. A military as well as a religious leader, Muhammad made alliances and raised an army that took Mecca in 630. By the time of his death in 632 CE, he had conquered most of Arabia.

✕ Battle or capture

751 The Abbasid Caliphate (succeeding the Umayyads) defeats the Tang Chinese at the Talas River, consolidating their hold on Transoxiana for the next 400 years

642 Yazdegerd III is defeated at Nehavend, leading to the rapid Muslim conquest of the rest of Persia

636 At Yarmuk, Khalid ibn al-Walid destroys the main Byzantine field army, leaving the rest of Syria and Palestine open to Muslim conquest

636 Muslim victory against the Persians leads to the conquest of Mesopotamia

661 Ali is assassinated while at prayer, leading to a schism between Sunni and Shia Muslims; Muawiya becomes the first Umayyad caliph, ruling from Damascus

643 Barca

642 'Amr ibn al-As captures Alexandria, the last Byzantine stronghold in Egypt

624 The Muslim army defeats Meccan forces, beginning the process by which Muhammad conquers the whole of Arabia

610 Muhammad receives revelations from the archangel Gabriel in a cave in the hills outside Mecca

622 Muhammad and his principal followers are forced to flee to the oasis town of Yathrib (later known as Medina)

630 Muhammad conquers Mecca

2 UMAR AND THE CONQUEST OF SYRIA AND EGYPT 634–644

Under the second caliph, Umar (who had been a companion of Muhammad), Muslim armies achieved astonishing successes against the Byzantine army, which had been weakened by its long war with Persia. First Damascus, the chief city of Syria, fell to the Muslims, and then they seized Jerusalem. They went on to subdue the Byzantine province of Egypt, where religious divisions among the Christian population undermined opposition to the Muslims.

✕ Battle or capture

3 THE CONQUEST OF PERSIA AND KHURASAN 636–656

The Sassanian rulers of Persia had almost captured the Byzantine capital of Constantinople by 626, but the effort exhausted their resources. After a Muslim army defeated them in Mesopotamia in 636, the Persians lost their western provinces. The Persian shah Yazdegerd III became a fugitive, and his domains were absorbed into the growing Islamic empire. Within 5 years, much of Khurasan (Khorasan), in central Asia, had been added to the empire, too.

✕ Battle or capture

4 LATE UMAYYAD CONQUESTS 670–750

The Muslims' expansion west of Egypt was slow until they built a base at Kairouan (in modern Tunisia) in 670. From this stronghold, they captured the remainder of the Byzantine Empire in north Africa, taking its capital Carthage in 698. In 711, an Arab–Berber army crossed into the Christian Visigothic kingdom of Spain and, within 20 years, had conquered almost all of it. In central Asia, Muslim armies won Transoxiana. In 750, the Umayyads were overthrown by the Abbasid Dynasty, who took control of the caliphate.

✕ Battle or capture

THE RULE OF THE CALIPHS

The Umayyads, who had ruled over the Islamic world from 661, fell in 749–750. Their empire was inherited by a new dynasty, the Abbasids, but its integrity was soon challenged as local rulers broke away, leaving the Abbasids with control over little more than Baghdad.

The Umayyad Caliphate (see pp.94–95) collapsed after a brief civil war in 749–750, which was partly caused by their discrimination against non-Arab Muslims. The Abbasids, a dynasty descended from the uncle of Muhammad, rose to power and—from its base in Baghdad—was able to restore stability. However, controlling the vast Muslim empire eventually proved an impossible task. A series of civil wars between 809 and 833 weakened the caliphate, and numerous local dynasties broke away: Spain had already been lost to a branch of the Umayyads in 756 and Ifriqiya (the area around Tunisia) became independent under the Aghlabids from 800. In Egypt, the Tulunids threw off central control in 868, and the Fatimids later grew strong there. The Buwayhids firmly established themselves in Iran from 926, and the Ghaznavids occupied eastern territories from about 977.

As the new dynasties emerged, Abbasid rule withered away until the caliph was a mere cypher, ruling a small sliver of land in Mesopotamia. Even this was swept away by a Mongol invasion in 1258, which sacked Baghdad and put an end to the caliphate.

"Don't be satisfied with stories. How things have gone with others. Unfold your own myth."

RUMI, 13TH-CENTURY ISLAMIC SCHOLAR AND POET

THE GOLDEN AGE OF ISLAM

SCIENCE AND CULTURE UNDER THE ABBASIDS

Scholars of all types congregated in the Abbasid capital of Baghdad. Accessible from both Europe and Asia, the city became a place to exchange ideas, many of which had reemerged from the translation of classical works by Arab scholars. Abbasid caliphs, including Harun al-Rashid and his son al-Ma'mun, directly encouraged learning and scholarship in Baghdad by establishing a House of Wisdom.

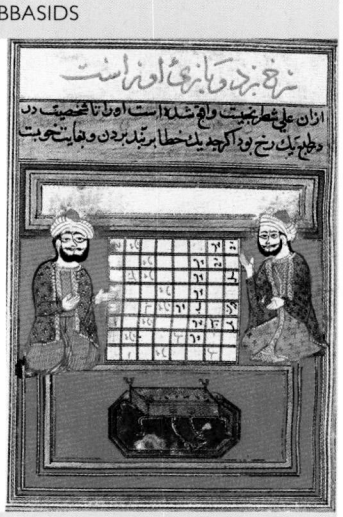

Games of the Golden Age
Having reached Baghdad from India via Persia, chess became popular in the Muslim world, as shown in this 9th-century illustration.

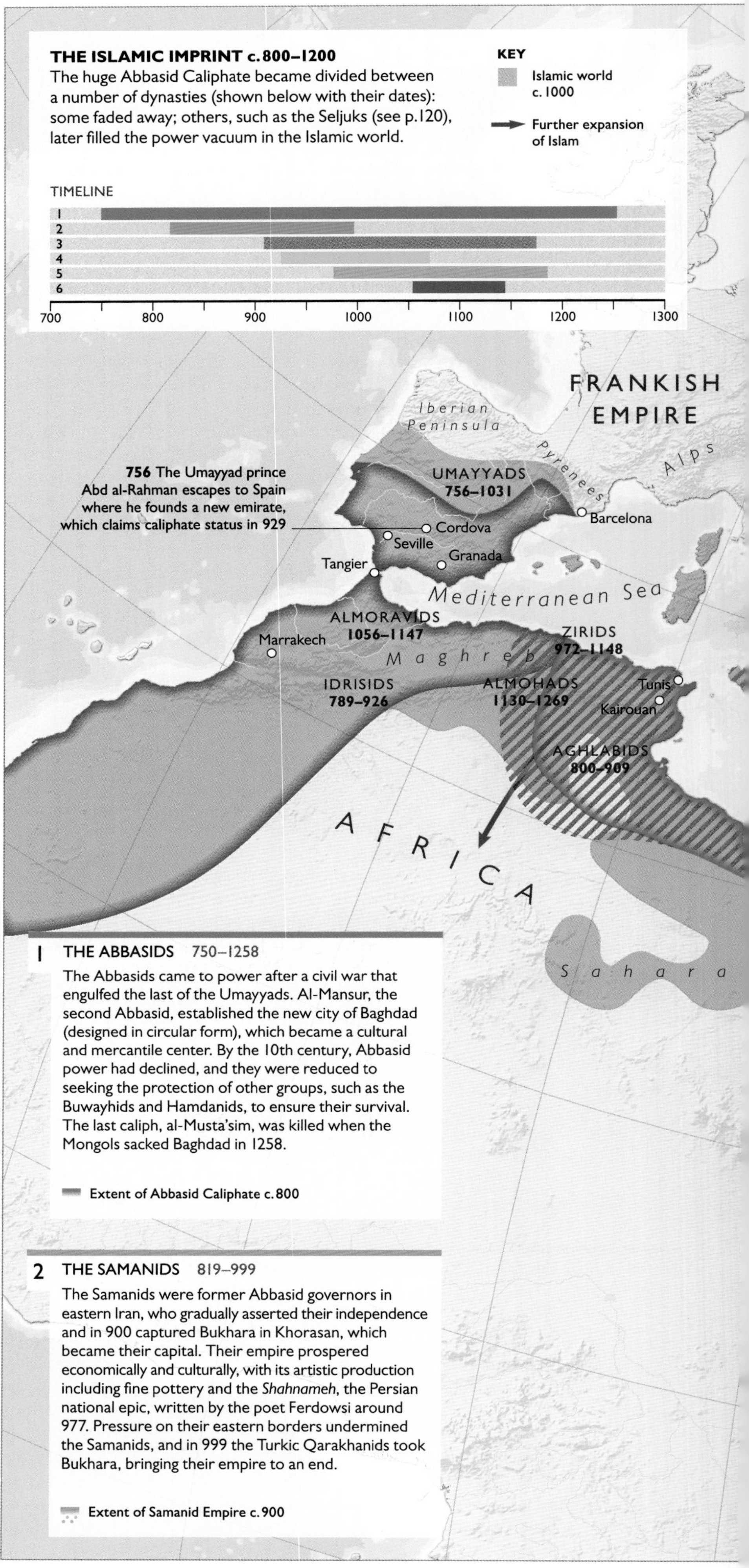
THE ISLAMIC IMPRINT c.800–1200
The huge Abbasid Caliphate became divided between a number of dynasties (shown below with their dates): some faded away; others, such as the Seljuks (see p.120), later filled the power vacuum in the Islamic world.
KEY
Islamic world c.1000
Further expansion of Islam
TIMELINE
1
2
3
4
5
6
700
800
900
1000
1100
1200
1300
FRANKISH EMPIRE
Iberian Peninsula
Pyrenees
Alps
UMAYYADS 756–1031
756 The Umayyad prince Abd al-Rahman escapes to Spain where he founds a new emirate, which claims caliphate status in 929
Barcelona
Cordova
Seville
Granada
Tangier
Mediterranean Sea
ALMORAVIDS 1056–1147
Marrakech
Maghreb
ZIRIDS 972–1148
IDRISIDS 789–926
ALMOHADS 1130–1269
Tunis
Kairouan
AGHLABIDS 800–909
AFRICA
Sahara

1 THE ABBASIDS 750–1258

The Abbasids came to power after a civil war that engulfed the last of the Umayyads. Al-Mansur, the second Abbasid, established the new city of Baghdad (designed in circular form), which became a cultural and mercantile center. By the 10th century, Abbasid power had declined, and they were reduced to seeking the protection of other groups, such as the Buwayhids and Hamdanids, to ensure their survival. The last caliph, al-Musta'sim, was killed when the Mongols sacked Baghdad in 1258.

Extent of Abbasid Caliphate c.800

2 THE SAMANIDS 819–999

The Samanids were former Abbasid governors in eastern Iran, who gradually asserted their independence and in 900 captured Bukhara in Khorasan, which became their capital. Their empire prospered economically and culturally, with its artistic production including fine pottery and the *Shahnameh*, the Persian national epic, written by the poet Ferdowsi around 977. Pressure on their eastern borders undermined the Samanids, and in 999 the Turkic Qarakhanids took Bukhara, bringing their empire to an end.

Extent of Samanid Empire c.900

6 THE ALMORAVIDS 1056–1147

A confederation of Berber tribes, the Almoravids were at the center of an 11th-century religious revival aimed at purifying Islam. They combined religious fervor with conquest, taking Morocco and founding the city of Marrakech in 1062. Asked by the Islamic kingdoms in Spain to help them resist Christian reconquest (see pp.122–123), the Almoravids crossed into Iberia, where they came to dominate in the south under their leader Yusuf Ibn Tashfin. By 1145, however, they were being forced out of Spain and challenged in north Africa by another revivalist movement, the Almohads, who captured Marrakech in 1147.

▬ Almoravid territory c.1100

5 THE GHAZNAVIDS 977–1186

The Ghaznavids, a dynasty of Turkic origin, established themselves in Ghazni, in Khorasan, from 977, and gradually expanded until they took over the western portion of the former Samanid Empire by 1005. They then conquered the eastern portion of the Buwayhid Empire before a disastrous defeat by the Seljuks at Dandanaqan in 1040 reduced them to a small area of eastern Khorasan, where they ruled until 1186.

▬ Ghaznavid territory c.1028

✕ Battle

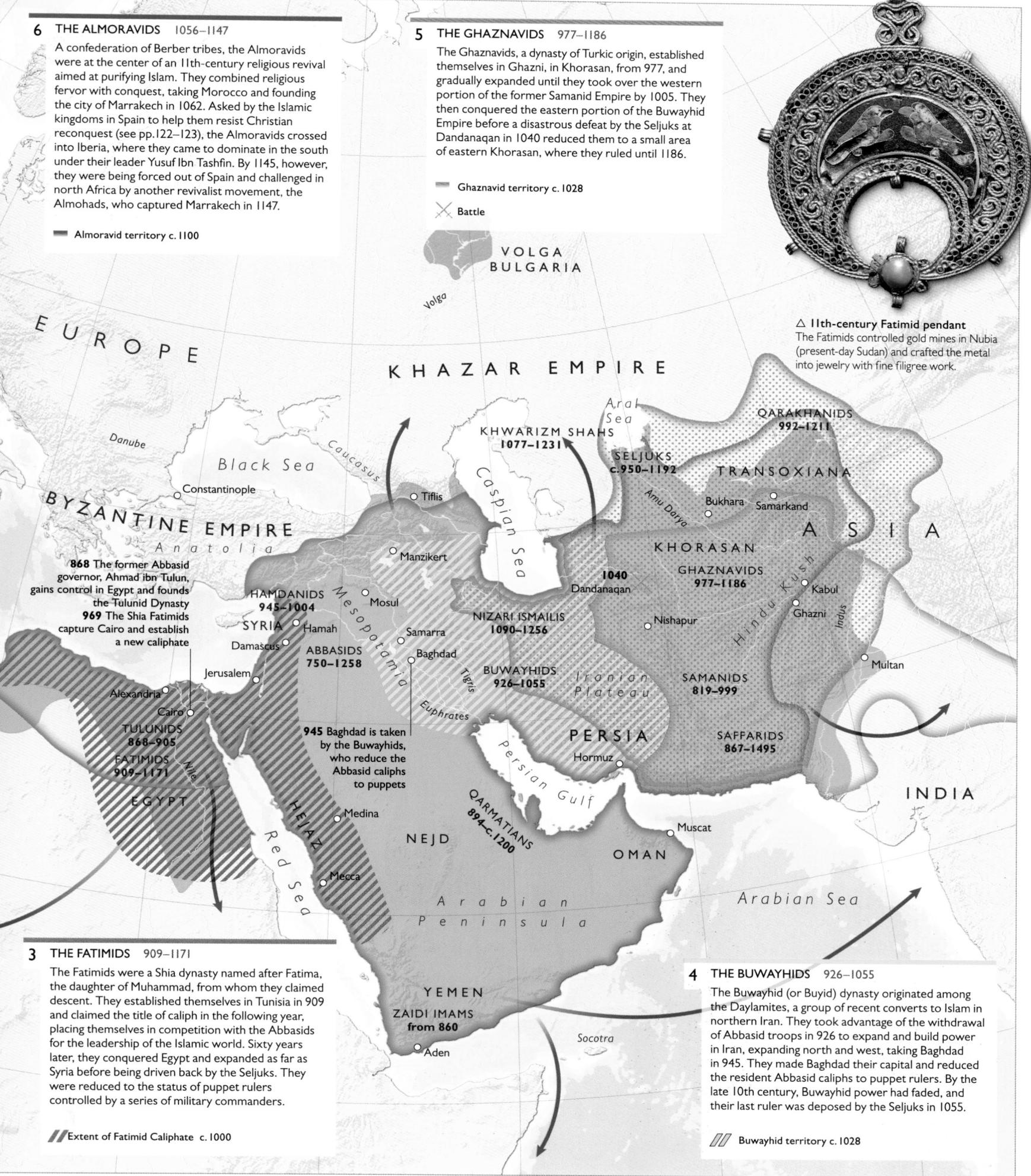

△ 11th-century Fatimid pendant
The Fatimids controlled gold mines in Nubia (present-day Sudan) and crafted the metal into jewelry with fine filigree work.

868 The former Abbasid governor, Ahmad ibn Tulun, gains control in Egypt and founds the Tulunid Dynasty
969 The Shia Fatimids capture Cairo and establish a new caliphate

945 Baghdad is taken by the Buwayhids, who reduce the Abbasid caliphs to puppets

3 THE FATIMIDS 909–1171

The Fatimids were a Shia dynasty named after Fatima, the daughter of Muhammad, from whom they claimed descent. They established themselves in Tunisia in 909 and claimed the title of caliph in the following year, placing themselves in competition with the Abbasids for the leadership of the Islamic world. Sixty years later, they conquered Egypt and expanded as far as Syria before being driven back by the Seljuks. They were reduced to the status of puppet rulers controlled by a series of military commanders.

▨ Extent of Fatimid Caliphate c.1000

4 THE BUWAYHIDS 926–1055

The Buwayhid (or Buyid) dynasty originated among the Daylamites, a group of recent converts to Islam in northern Iran. They took advantage of the withdrawal of Abbasid troops in 926 to expand and build power in Iran, expanding north and west, taking Baghdad in 945. They made Baghdad their capital and reduced the resident Abbasid caliphs to puppet rulers. By the late 10th century, Buwayhid power had faded, and their last ruler was deposed by the Seljuks in 1055.

▨ Buwayhid territory c.1028

THE VIKINGS

At the end of the 8th century CE, the Vikings, a warrior-people from Scandinavia, burst forth from their homelands and for the next two centuries spread across Europe and the Atlantic as raiders, traders, and settlers.

Scandinavia in the 8th century was divided into small territories ruled by warlords. Instability grew as these chiefs fought to unite regions and a growing population put pressure on resources. Attracted by the wealth of trading centers and monasteries in northwest Europe, young men took up raiding and became known as Vikings. What followed was an amazing expansion enabled by fast and maneuverable Viking longships, used for raiding, and sturdier ocean-going knorrs, used for longer trading voyages. Vikings from Norway and Denmark exploited

> "They overran the entire kingdom and destroyed all the monasteries to which they came."
>
> ANGLO-SAXON CHRONICLE, 869

weaknesses in France, Britain, and Ireland to strike their victims unaware, seizing plunder and exacting tribute. In the 9th century, the Vikings in these areas turned from raids to conquest, carving out territories that in some cases they ruled for centuries. Their search for land also took them across unexplored waters to Iceland, Greenland, and finally the coast of North America around 1000.

In the East, Swedish Vikings, in the role of traders, penetrated the navigable rivers of what is now Russia and Ukraine to dominate trade with Constantinople and the Arabs and to exact tribute from Slavic tribes. These Varangians (as the eastern Vikings were called) founded Kievan Rus', the first Russian state.

LEIF ERIKSON
VIKING EXPLORER

Son of Erik the Red—founder of Viking Greenland—Leif Erikson is the star of sagas telling of the exploration of the lands we now know as North America. Other than the archaeological site of L'Anse aux Meadows in Newfoundland, it is difficult to know exactly where Vikings such as Erikson and his crew went, but they must have reached forested lands south of the tundra-clad Labrador Coast (which they knew as Markland) since they were desperate for timber.

Commemoration
A modern monument in Iceland recognizes Erikson, the first European known to have reached the Americas.

---

4 VOYAGES TO VINLAND c. 1000–1400

Greenland was colonized from Iceland in 986 by Erik the Red, a fugitive fleeing a sentence of outlawry. It was a marginal land, where a few thousand Vikings lived by hunting seals and walruses and raising cattle, but it was the base for exploring North America in search of timber, which was in short supply in Greenland. They named the most distant land they reached "Vinland."

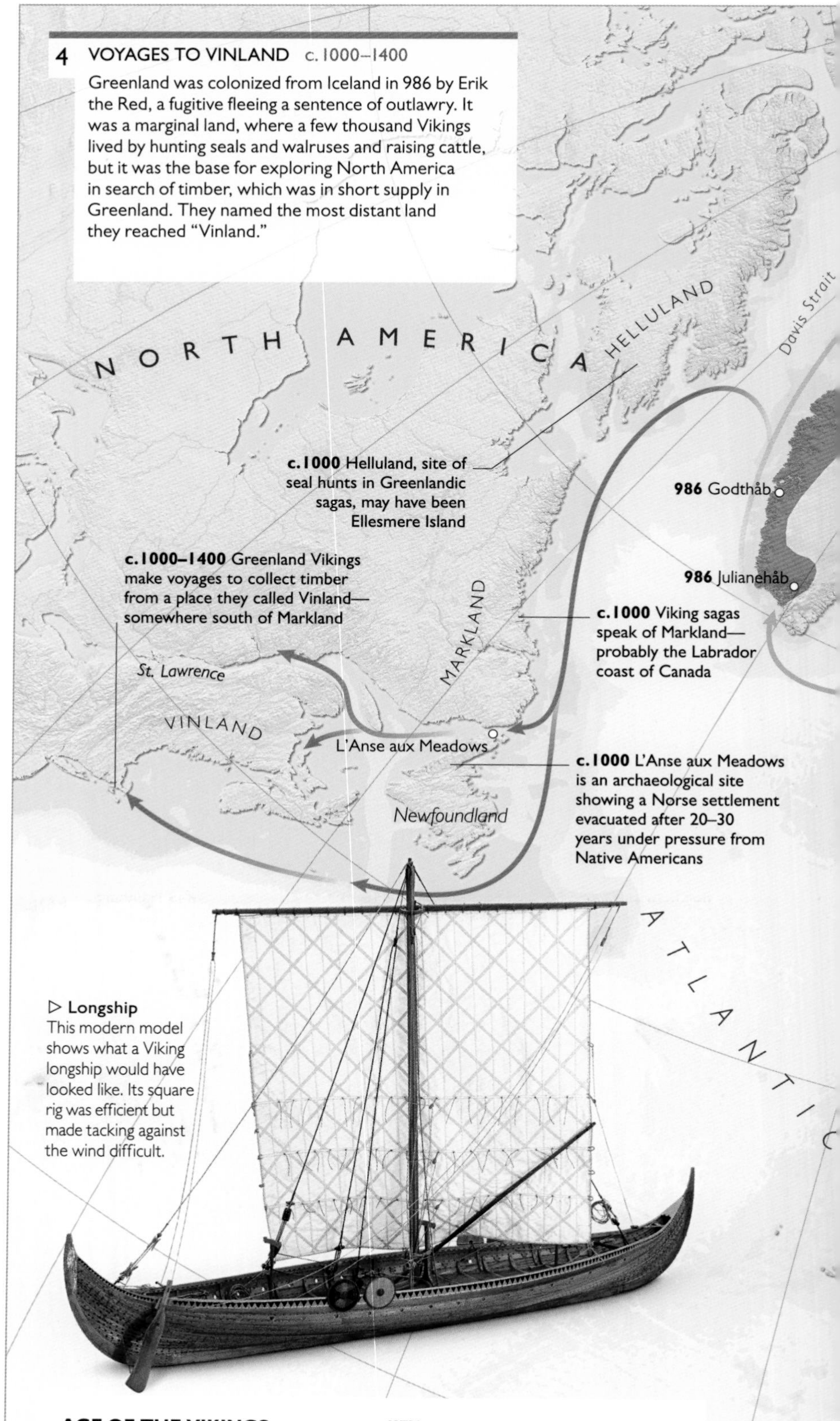

NORTH AMERICA

HELLULAND

Davis Strait

c.1000 Helluland, site of seal hunts in Greenlandic sagas, may have been Ellesmere Island

986 Godthåb

986 Julianehåb

c.1000–1400 Greenland Vikings make voyages to collect timber from a place they called Vinland—somewhere south of Markland

MARKLAND

c.1000 Viking sagas speak of Markland—probably the Labrador coast of Canada

St. Lawrence

VINLAND

L'Anse aux Meadows

Newfoundland

c.1000 L'Anse aux Meadows is an archaeological site showing a Norse settlement evacuated after 20–30 years under pressure from Native Americans

ATLANTIC

▷ **Longship**
This modern model shows what a Viking longship would have looked like. Its square rig was efficient but made tacking against the wind difficult.

AGE OF THE VIKINGS
European history from 790–1060 was dominated by the Vikings. Although their raids petered out by 1100, territories they established lived on into the 15th century.

KEY

■ Sweden	••• National borders
■ Norway	— Holy Roman Empire border
■ Denmark	→ Viking voyage, colored according to region

TIMELINE

	700	900	1100	1300	1500
1					
2					
3					
4					
5					
6					

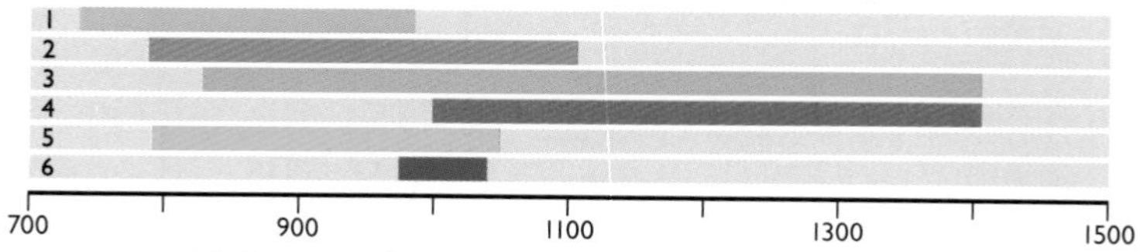

3 THE NORTH ATLANTIC 825–1408

The Vikings were explorers, crossing oceans in search of lands to settle. From the north coast of Scotland, it was a short hop to the Faroes, which were settled around 800. Viking ships ranged westward, sighting Iceland in the 830s and settling it in the 870s. There, they established a republic with the world's oldest parliament, the Althing—independent until the 1240s.

■ North Atlantic settlements

2 THE BRITISH ISLES 793–1103

The first Viking raids on Britain were in the 790s. The early targets were unarmed monasteries, which the Vikings knew would be full of treasure. The raids became larger in scale, and in 865, the arrival of the Danish "Great Heathen Army" led to the conquest of most of the Anglo-Saxon kingdoms of England.

■ British and Irish settlements

1 THE SWEDES AND KIEVAN RUS' 750–988

Swedish Vikings pushed east, raiding and settling in lands now called Russia, Belarus, and Ukraine. Sometimes known as Varangians, this people's other name, Rus, gave Russia its modern name. The Rus founded the first state in Russia—a confederation of Slavic peoples named Kievan Rus' after one of the cities they established—Kiev.

■ Area of Varangian (Viking) influence

GREENLAND

875 Norwegian Vikings take control of the northern British islands and establish the Earldom of Orkney; it is ceded to Scotland in 1468

873 Reykjavik ICELAND c. 860

c. 860

c. 800 Faroe Islands

793 Vikings make their first overseas raid, on the rich monastery on Lindisfarne Island in the kingdom of Northumberland

Shetland Islands

Orkney Islands

Lewis

SCOTLAND

793 Lindisfarne

866–954 Jorvik (York) is capital of the Danelaw—a Viking kingdom in northern England

IRISH KINGDOMS **866** York

841 Dublin

DANELAW

836 Limerick ENGLAND

London

WELSH PRINCIPALITIES

860–902 Vikings occupy the fortified port they built in Dublin

911 Frankish king Charles the Simple grants lands in Normandy to the Vikings

NORMANDY

841 Rouen

BRITTANY

843 Nantes

842 Noirmoutier

857 Vikings push into southwest France and ally with Frankish ruler of Aquitaine Pippin II

844

FRANCE

LEÓN

CASTILE NAVARRE

844 Lisbon

CALIPHATE OF CORDOVA

844 Seville

Trondheim

NORWAY

Kaupang (Skiringssal)

Sigtuna

Birka

SWEDEN

Paviken

DENMARK

Ringsted Lund

Ribe

Hedeby

Jomsborg (Wolin)

845 Hamburg

834 Dorestad

HOLY ROMAN EMPIRE

Baltic Sea

North Sea

 Truso

POLAND

BOHEMIA-MORAVIA

845 Vikings sack Paris and exact tribute from the Franks

845 Paris

BURGUNDY

Pisa

CROATIA

VENETIAN REPUBLIC

Rome

PAPAL STATES

859–862

Sardinia

859 Balearic Islands

Tunis

Sicily

HUNGARY

BULGARIA

750 First Viking settlement outside Scandinavia, Staraya Ladoga, is founded

VOLGA BULGARIA

Bulgar

750 Staraya Ladoga (Aldeigjuborg)

Novgorod (Holmgard)

Gnezdovo

862 Rurik the Viking founds the city of Novgorod, meaning "new town"

KIEVAN RUS'

988 Grand Prince Vladimir of Kiev converts to Christianity

882 Kiev (Könugard)

950 Viking raids extend down river Volga, eventually reaching Arab-ruled Azerbaijan

Volga

KIEVAN RUS'

Sarkel

Itil

Caspian Sea

839 Constantinople (Miklagard)

Black Sea

BYZANTINE EMPIRE

Mediterranean Sea

907 Viking–Byzantine trade treaty helps Vikings to exchange furs—acquired as tribute from the Slavic peoples of the Kievan Rus'—for gold in the markets of Constantinople

OCEAN

1053 Norman knights, acting as mercenaries supported by the pope, the Lombards, and the Byzantine emperor, take over Sicily

5 VIKINGS BECOME NORMANS 799–1066

The first Viking raids in France were in 799 against a monastery on the northwest coast. At first, the strong rule of the Frankish king Charlemagne held the Vikings at bay, but when he died in 814, the raids increased. In 911, a Viking warlord, Rollo, agreed to stop raids in return for a grant of land in Normandy. The settlers became French-speaking Normans, losing their Viking identity. Normans would go on to conquer England and Sicily.

■ Norman settlements

6 VARANGIAN GUARD 988–1050

The Rus founded small principalities and began to raid farther afield, attacking Constantinople, the capital of the Byzantine Empire, several times. In 988, Vladimir, the prince of Kiev, became a Christian, and relations with Byzantium improved; he even provided a contingent, known as the Varangians, to become the Byzantine emperor's bodyguard—employed in recognition of their fighting qualities. By the mid-11th century, the Viking raids in the area had ceased.

THE NORMANS

Originally a band of Viking raiders, the Normans acquired land in northern France, where they established a duchy. They then spread more widely, and by the mid-11th century had conquered England, Sicily, and much of southern Italy.

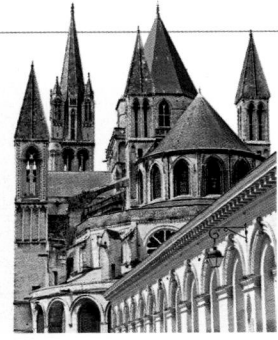

Norman abbey
With its arcaded Romanesque nave, the Saint-Etienne Abbey in Caen, France, is a fine example of Norman architecture.

In 911, as marauding Viking armies overwhelmed northern France, the Frankish king Charles the Simple made a pact with a group of Norwegian Vikings led by Rollo. In exchange for land, Rollo agreed to keep other Vikings away. He only partly held to his agreement, slowly expanding his holdings in what became known as Normandy (the land of the Northmen). By the time he bequeathed Normandy to his son William Longsword in 927, a mixed culture had emerged: part-French, part-Scandinavian, and increasingly Christianized. In 1066, William the Conqueror, the great-great-great grandson of Rollo, invaded England to assert a claim to its throne. His success marked the beginning of an Anglo-Norman Dynasty whose descendants still rule.

Setting down roots

Elsewhere, ambitious Normans took military service with feuding local autocratic rulers in southern Italy from the early 11th century. Later, led by ruthless warriors such as the de Haubevilles and Robert and Roger Guiscard, they carved out their own fiefdom in southern Italy. In 1060, Roger Guiscard invaded Sicily, conquering much of it within a decade and establishing a kingdom where a hybrid Arab-Norman culture flourished until its conquest by the German Hohenstaufens in 1194.

THE NORMAN CONQUEST

After William the Conqueror won at Hastings in 1066, he consolidated his rule over England, awarding land to his followers. Upon his death, Normandy and England were divided between his sons Robert Curthose and William Rufus. After Robert's defeat by William's successor, Henry I of England, at Tinchebrai in 1106, England and Normandy were reunified.

KEY
→ Invasion route ■ Normandy
✕ Battle

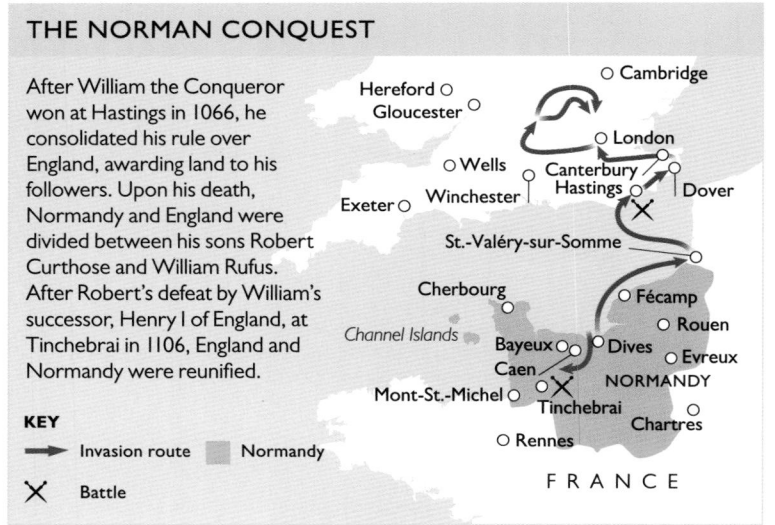

Tapestry of war
In this scene from the Bayeux Tapestry, woven to commemorate the Norman victory over the English at Hastings in 1066, William the Conqueror (right) removes his helmet to show his followers that the rumor that he had been killed was false.

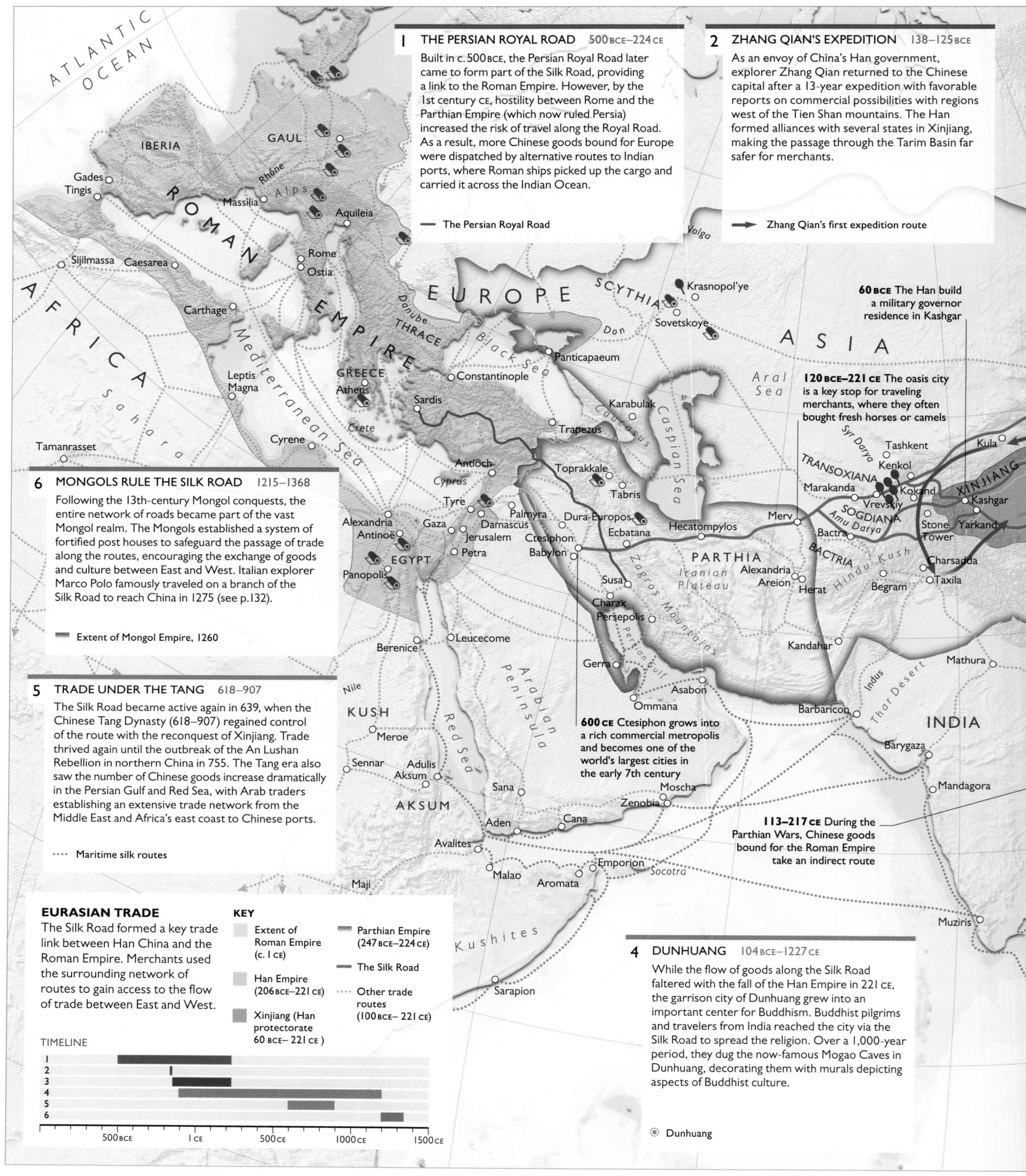

1 THE PERSIAN ROYAL ROAD 500 BCE–224 CE

Built in c. 500 BCE, the Persian Royal Road later came to form part of the Silk Road, providing a link to the Roman Empire. However, by the 1st century CE, hostility between Rome and the Parthian Empire (which now ruled Persia) increased the risk of travel along the Royal Road. As a result, more Chinese goods bound for Europe were dispatched by alternative routes to Indian ports, where Roman ships picked up the cargo and carried it across the Indian Ocean.

— The Persian Royal Road

2 ZHANG QIAN'S EXPEDITION 138–125 BCE

As an envoy of China's Han government, explorer Zhang Qian returned to the Chinese capital after a 13-year expedition with favorable reports on commercial possibilities with regions west of the Tien Shan mountains. The Han formed alliances with several states in Xinjiang, making the passage through the Tarim Basin far safer for merchants.

→ Zhang Qian's first expedition route

60 BCE The Han build a military governor residence in Kashgar

120 BCE–221 CE The oasis city is a key stop for traveling merchants, where they often bought fresh horses or camels

6 MONGOLS RULE THE SILK ROAD 1215–1368

Following the 13th-century Mongol conquests, the entire network of roads became part of the vast Mongol realm. The Mongols established a system of fortified post houses to safeguard the passage of trade along the routes, encouraging the exchange of goods and culture between East and West. Italian explorer Marco Polo famously traveled on a branch of the Silk Road to reach China in 1275 (see p.132).

— Extent of Mongol Empire, 1260

5 TRADE UNDER THE TANG 618–907

The Silk Road became active again in 639, when the Chinese Tang Dynasty (618–907) regained control of the route with the reconquest of Xinjiang. Trade thrived again until the outbreak of the An Lushan Rebellion in northern China in 755. The Tang era also saw the number of Chinese goods increase dramatically in the Persian Gulf and Red Sea, with Arab traders establishing an extensive trade network from the Middle East and Africa's east coast to Chinese ports.

···· Maritime silk routes

600 CE Ctesiphon grows into a rich commercial metropolis and becomes one of the world's largest cities in the early 7th century

113–217 CE During the Parthian Wars, Chinese goods bound for the Roman Empire take an indirect route

EURASIAN TRADE

The Silk Road formed a key trade link between Han China and the Roman Empire. Merchants used the surrounding network of routes to gain access to the flow of trade between East and West.

KEY

▨ Extent of Roman Empire (c. 1 CE)

▨ Han Empire (206 BCE–221 CE)

▨ Xinjiang (Han protectorate 60 BCE– 221 CE)

— Parthian Empire (247 BCE–224 CE)

— The Silk Road

···· Other trade routes (100 BCE– 221 CE)

4 DUNHUANG 104 BCE–1227 CE

While the flow of goods along the Silk Road faltered with the fall of the Han Empire in 221 CE, the garrison city of Dunhuang grew into an important center for Buddhism. Buddhist pilgrims and travelers from India reached the city via the Silk Road to spread the religion. Over a 1,000-year period, they dug the now-famous Mogao Caves in Dunhuang, decorating them with murals depicting aspects of Buddhist culture.

⊚ Dunhuang

TIMELINE

500 BCE   1 CE   500 CE   1000 CE   1500 CE

THE SILK ROAD

The extension of Han control in China in the 2nd century BCE made communication with the rest of the world easier and safer. The network of roads linking East and West operated for 1,500 years and became famous for the luxurious Chinese silk that traveled along them.

The origin of the Silk Road can be traced back to the Han Empire's conquest of the Tarim Basin around 120 BCE, when its armies banished various tribal groups from the region. This allowed the empire to open a safe passage for trade that stretched from the Chinese capital Chang'an (Xi'an) to a wealth of cities in central Asia and beyond.

The Han engaged in vibrant trading with India, Persia, and the Roman Empire, where Chinese silk was highly coveted by the ruling class. Besides the luxury goods that traveled along the route, including silk, spices, precious stones, and ornaments, the Silk Road was also a conduit for the dissemination of religion, philosophy, technology, language, science, and even disease.

Trade along the route faltered following the collapse of the Han in 221 CE but revived in the Tang era (618–907) when China partially recovered its central Asian provinces. Trade fell again in the 8th century after the Tibetans and Uighurs took control of Xinjiang, but 500 years later the route experienced a major resurgence following the Mongol conquests (see pp.130–131). The importance of the Silk Road fell again after the Mongol Empire's decline in the 14th century, and in the 16th century it was replaced by maritime trading routes.

> *"The Seres (Chinese) are famous for the woollen substance obtained from their forests."*
>
> PLINY THE ELDER, FROM *NATURALIS HISTORIA*, 79 CE

Map annotations

△ Marco Polo's expedition to China
This illustration from the *Catalan Atlas*, 1375, depicts the caravan of Italian explorer Marco Polo traveling to China along the Silk Road in 1275.

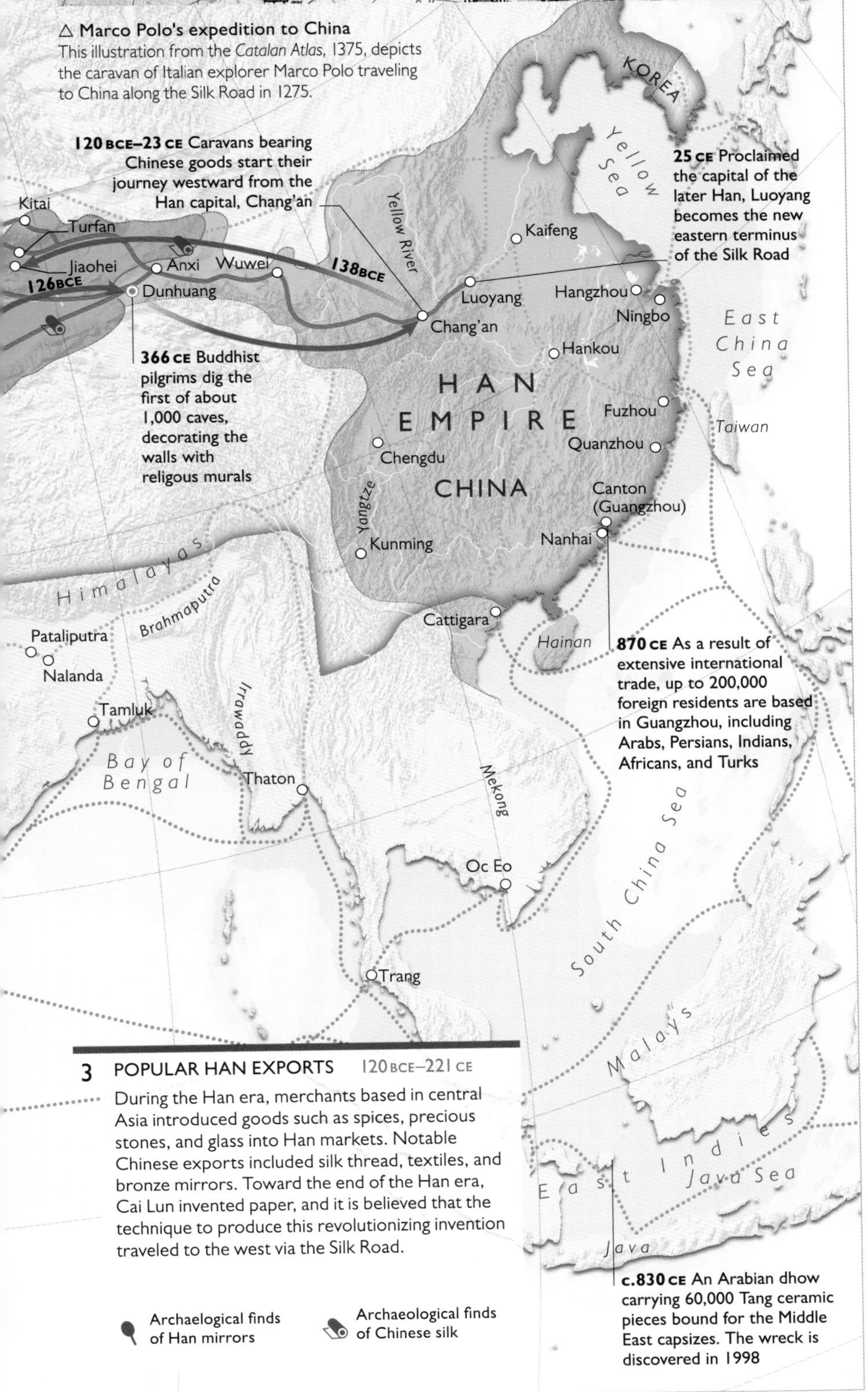

120 BCE–23 CE Caravans bearing Chinese goods start their journey westward from the Han capital, Chang'an

25 CE Proclaimed the capital of the later Han, Luoyang becomes the new eastern terminus of the Silk Road

366 CE Buddhist pilgrims dig the first of about 1,000 caves, decorating the walls with religous murals

870 CE As a result of extensive international trade, up to 200,000 foreign residents are based in Guangzhou, including Arabs, Persians, Indians, Africans, and Turks

c.830 CE An Arabian dhow carrying 60,000 Tang ceramic pieces bound for the Middle East capsizes. The wreck is discovered in 1998

3 POPULAR HAN EXPORTS   120 BCE–221 CE
During the Han era, merchants based in central Asia introduced goods such as spices, precious stones, and glass into Han markets. Notable Chinese exports included silk thread, textiles, and bronze mirrors. Toward the end of the Han era, Cai Lun invented paper, and it is believed that the technique to produce this revolutionizing invention traveled to the west via the Silk Road.

● Archaeological finds of Han mirrors
◆ Archaeological finds of Chinese silk

Map labels: KOREA, Yellow Sea, Yellow River, Kitai, Turfan, Jiaohei, Anxi, Wuwei, Dunhuang, 126BCE, 138BCE, Kaifeng, Luoyang, Hangzhou, Ningbo, Chang'an, Hankou, East China Sea, HAN EMPIRE, Fuzhou, Quanzhou, Taiwan, Chengdu, CHINA, Canton (Guangzhou), Kunming, Nanhai, Yangtze, Himalayas, Brahmaputra, Cattigara, Hainan, Pataliputra, Nalanda, Tamluk, Irrawaddy, Bay of Bengal, Thaton, Mekong, Oc Eo, South China Sea, Trang, Malays, East Indies, Java Sea, Java

CHINESE SILK
UNIQUE CHINESE EXPORT

Once China introduced silk to the West in the 1st century BCE, the material became popular among elites in the Roman Empire. The silk-making process was unknown in the West until around 550 CE, when Byzantine Emperor Justinian I persuaded two monks to smuggle silkworms from China inside their bamboo canes.

Silk-making in China
This is a section of a larger 12th-century silk painting that depicts court ladies preparing silk.

12TH-CENTURY RENAISSANCE IN EUROPE

The 12th century saw the establishment of universities and of new monastic orders and the translation of important scientific manuscripts from Arabic into European languages.

KEY

——— Frontiers 1200

TIMELINE

1
2
3
4
5

700 · 800 · 900 · 1000 · 1100 · 1200 · 1300 · 1400

1 CHARLEMAGNE'S RENAISSANCE 800–814

The crowning of Charlemagne as "Emperor of the Romans" in 800 brought about a sense that the Roman Empire had been revived in western Europe. Literature, arts, writing, architecture, and scriptural studies flourished under his rule. The cultural gains of Charlemagne's court dissipated soon after his death in 814 and the passage of the imperial title to a series of German nobles.

▬ Extent of Charlemagne's empire, 814

2 THE CISTERCIANS AND THE NEW MONASTICISM 1098–1153

The Cistercians emerged as the old monastic orders came to be seen as wealthy, self-serving, and distant from their original spiritual missions. Founded in 1098, the Cistercians spread under the influence of St. Bernard of Clairvaux and had over 300 monasteries throughout Europe by his death in 1153. With a rigorous observance of the Rule of St. Benedict, the Cistercians became noted for their piety and offered "the surest road to heaven."

✝ Major Cistercian house with date of foundation

1130s A school of translators established by Archbishop Raymond translates many Arabic and Hebrew works

1078 Anselm is elected as Abbot of Bec, which becomes an important theological school

1160s Student numbers at Oxford University grow; it gains a royal charter in 1248

1209 Students fleeing unrest in Oxford help to establish Cambridge University

1088 Bologna, an important center for legal studies, becomes the first university in Europe

10th century onward The medical school at Salerno acts as conduit for Arabic medical works

Labels on map

SCOTLAND
IRELAND
WALES
ENGLAND
NORWAY
SWEDEN
DENMARK
North Sea
Baltic Sea
KINGDOM OF GERMANY
POLAND
FRANCE
Alps
KINGDOM OF ITALY
VENETIAN REPUBLIC
SERBIA
PAPAL STATES
KINGDOM OF SICILY
LEÓN
NAVARRE
PORTUGAL
CASTILE
ARAGON
Pyrenees
ALMOHAD EMPIRE
ATLANTIC OCEAN
Mediterranean Sea
Balearic Islands
Corsica
Sardinia
Sicily

1140 Newbattle
1142 Melrose
1142 Mellifont
1150 Jervaulx
1132 Rievaulx
1132 Fountains
1147 Kirkstall
1143 Alvastra
Lübeck
Oxford
c.1209 Cambridge
early 12th century London
1128 Waverley
Canterbury
1143 Wagrowiec
1132 Camp
Cologne
Bec
Rheims
c.1200
Chartres
Paris
c.1250 Angers
Meung
c.1236 Orléans
Tours
1115 Clairvaux
1114 Pontigny
1115 Morimond
1127
1124 Lützel
Ebrach
1135 Eberbach
1098 Cîteaux
1112 La Ferté
1137 Heiligenkreuz
1348 Prague
1142 Czikador
1332 Cahors
1229 Toulouse
1339 Grenoble
1303 Avignon
Milan
1204 Vicenza
1222 Padua (law)
Venice
1142 Czikador
Béziers
Narbonne
Montpellier (medicine) 12th century
Marseille
1248 Piacenza
Genoa
1088 Bologna (law)
Pisa
1215 Arezzo
1246 Siena
1308 Perugia
Rome
c.1140
1245
1224 Naples
Salerno (medicine) since 9th century
León
1132 Moreruela
Pamplona
1308 Coimbra
1148 Alcobaça
1218 Salamanca
Segovia
Tarazona
1300 Lérida
1290 Lisbon
Toledo
Barcelona
1254 Seville
Cordova
Palermo
Rhine
Elbe

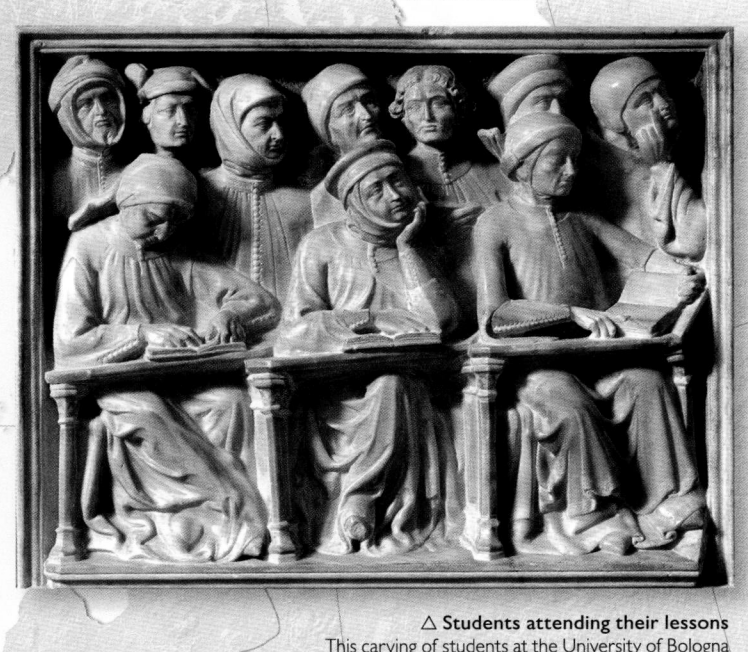

△ **Students attending their lessons**
This carving of students at the University of Bologna dates from around 1412 and adorns the tomb of the great teacher and legal thinker Bartolomeo da Saliceto.

5 DEVELOPMENTS IN LITERATURE AND SONG 1100–1200

The 12th century saw an upsurge in literature in the vernacular (local languages), many of them epic poems such as the German sagas the *Nibelungenlied* and Wolfram von Eschenbach's *Parzival*. In southern France troubadours, traveling performer-poets, spread *chansons de geste* ("songs of deeds," tales of romance, heroic deeds, and courtly love), such as the *Chanson de Roland*, which recounted episodes from Charlemagne's campaigns against the Muslims in northern Spain in the 770s.

1149
Jedrzejów

4 INFLUENCE OF ARAB SCHOLARSHIP 1085–1300

Many scientific and philosophical works by Greek scholars had survived only in the Islamic world, often translated into Arabic and added to by Muslim writers. In the 12th century, these filtered into Europe, through areas such as Sicily and parts of Spain such as Toledo that had recently been conquered from Muslim powers. Manuscripts of many works by Aristotle, Ptolemy, and Euclid were then translated into Latin and helped fuel the 12th-century revival in scholarship.

 Center of contact with Arab scholarship

▪ Muslim lands reconquered by Christians 1030–1200

▪ Muslim lands reconquered by Christians 1200–1300

3 THE NEW UNIVERSITIES 1088–1348

In the 12th century, scholars such as Abelard (at Paris) and Anselm of Aosta (at Bec) taught classes in theology and logic that attracted large numbers of students. Their schools developed into *studia generalia*, or universities, which offered a wider range of courses. Bologna University was among the first of these institutions.

 University with date of foundation

🏛 Other important theological school

MEDIEVAL RENAISSANCE

The 12th century saw the intellectual, spiritual, and cultural life of Europe undergo a renewal. This encompassed the revival of monasteries, the foundation of schools and universities, the development of new architectural forms, and the acquisition of knowledge through translations from Greek and Arabic manuscripts.

After the fall of the Roman Empire in the West in the 5th century, much classical knowledge was lost, and most remaining manuscripts were confined to monasteries. Although there were local cultural revivals in France under Charlemagne (r. 768–814), in England under Alfred the Great (r. 871–899), and in Germany under Otto I (r. 962–973), they did not long survive the deaths of their royal patrons. However, in the late 11th century, a new movement began, in part stimulated by a desire for a return to purer forms of religious observance and in part by the needs of increasingly complex royal bureaucracies. New monastic movements, such as the Cistercians, gave impetus to a revival of spirituality, and schools grew up around cathedrals and abbeys that welcomed lay students and clergy alike. They taught a curriculum that focused on logic, grammar, and rhetoric but also encouraged debate and academic disputation. The largest centers, such as Paris and Bologna, attracted students from all over western Europe and developed into universities. Scholars there enjoyed access to works that had been unknown in Europe since the fall of Rome, as well as original Arabic works and translations of classical authors that came via the former Islamic territories in Sicily and Spain.

> *"By doubting we come to examine, and by examining we reach the truth."*
>
> PETER ABELARD, FRENCH THEOLOGIAN, 1079–1142

GOTHIC ARCHITECTURE
A NEW LANGUAGE OF CONSTRUCTION

In the early 12th century, a new architectural style replaced the solid masses and round arches typical of the previous Romanesque tradition. Known as Gothic, its pointed arches, ribbed buttresses, and soaring vaults allowed for higher ceilings and the penetration of more light into buildings (with windows often glazed in decorative stained glass). The style became the predominant one for large churches and cathedrals in western Europe for the next 300 years.

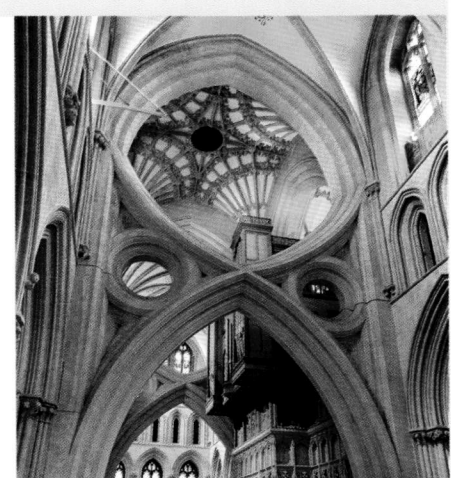

Wells Cathedral
This 12th-century English cathedral is one of the earliest examples of architecture that is wholly Gothic in style.

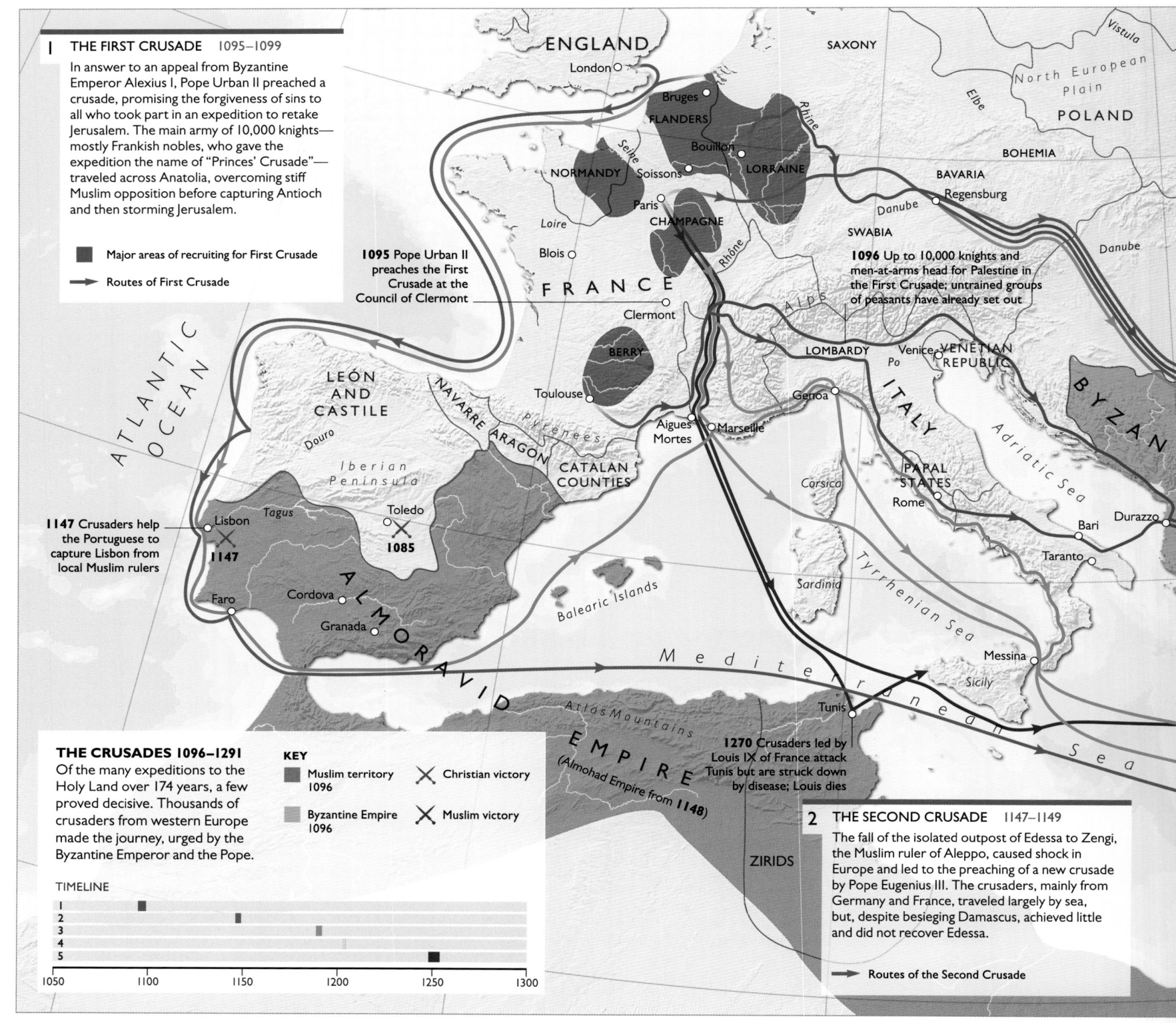

1 THE FIRST CRUSADE 1095–1099

In answer to an appeal from Byzantine Emperor Alexius I, Pope Urban II preached a crusade, promising the forgiveness of sins to all who took part in an expedition to retake Jerusalem. The main army of 10,000 knights—mostly Frankish nobles, who gave the expedition the name of "Princes' Crusade"—traveled across Anatolia, overcoming stiff Muslim opposition before capturing Antioch and then storming Jerusalem.

■ Major areas of recruiting for First Crusade

→ Routes of First Crusade

1095 Pope Urban II preaches the First Crusade at the Council of Clermont

1096 Up to 10,000 knights and men-at-arms head for Palestine in the First Crusade; untrained groups of peasants have already set out

1147 Crusaders help the Portuguese to capture Lisbon from local Muslim rulers

1085

1147

1270 Crusaders led by Louis IX of France attack Tunis but are struck down by disease; Louis dies

THE CRUSADES 1096–1291

Of the many expeditions to the Holy Land over 174 years, a few proved decisive. Thousands of crusaders from western Europe made the journey, urged by the Byzantine Emperor and the Pope.

KEY

■ Muslim territory 1096
■ Byzantine Empire 1096
✕ Christian victory
✕ Muslim victory

TIMELINE

1
2
3
4
5

1050 1100 1150 1200 1250 1300

2 THE SECOND CRUSADE 1147–1149

The fall of the isolated outpost of Edessa to Zengi, the Muslim ruler of Aleppo, caused shock in Europe and led to the preaching of a new crusade by Pope Eugenius III. The crusaders, mainly from Germany and France, traveled largely by sea, but, despite besieging Damascus, achieved little and did not recover Edessa.

→ Routes of the Second Crusade

THE CRUSADES

Beginning in 1095, a series of military expeditions set out from Christian Europe to capture Jerusalem and the Holy Land, which had been part of the Islamic Caliphate since the mid-7th century. These Crusades established states in the area, but once Muslim rulers had overcome their previous disunity, they expelled the crusaders, capturing their last important stronghold in 1291.

Jerusalem fell into Muslim hands in 639, when the Caliphate took the provinces of the Byzantine Empire in Palestine and Syria. In the 11th century, a new Muslim group—the Seljuk Turks—gained more Byzantine territory and threatened the rights of Christian pilgrims to visit Jerusalem. In response to an appeal from the Byzantine emperor, the Pope called for a crusade—an armed expedition—to liberate the Holy City. Thousands of knights responded and marched to Palestine, where they captured many Muslim-controlled cities, including Jerusalem itself. The crusaders established states in Palestine, but their numbers were few, and Muslim counterattacks resulted in the fall of Edessa in 1144, a disaster that sparked the Second Crusade. The Third Crusade was inspired by the loss of

3 THE THIRD CRUSADE 1189–1192

In 1187, Saladin, the Muslim ruler of Egypt, captured Jerusalem, prompting the calling of a further crusade. A crusader army led by King Richard the Lionheart of England and King Philip Augustus of France succeeded in checking Saladin's advance and took the important cities of Jaffa and Acre, but was unable to recover Jerusalem—which had been the goal of the expedition.

→ Routes of Third Crusade

4 THE FOURTH CRUSADE 1202–1204

Called by Pope Innocent III, the crusade originally set out to reconquer Jerusalem, but its army was diverted by Alexios Angelos, an exiled Byzantine prince who promised the crusaders a great reward if they helped him recover his throne. Instead, the crusaders sacked Constantinople (the capital of the Christian-controlled Byzantine Empire), divided the empire among their leaders, and never reached Jerusalem.

☆ Capital of Byzantine Empire

5 THE SEVENTH CRUSADE 1248–1254

Led by King Louis IX of France, the crusade set out to destroy the Ayyubid Dynasty in Egypt and Syria, then recapture Jerusalem (which the Muslims had retaken in 1244). Louis captured Damietta in 1249, but the crusade became bogged down in a siege of Mansurah, in which many crusaders died. Louis was captured and was ransomed, the price of his return being Damietta, leaving the crusade a total failure.

→ Routes of the Seventh Crusade

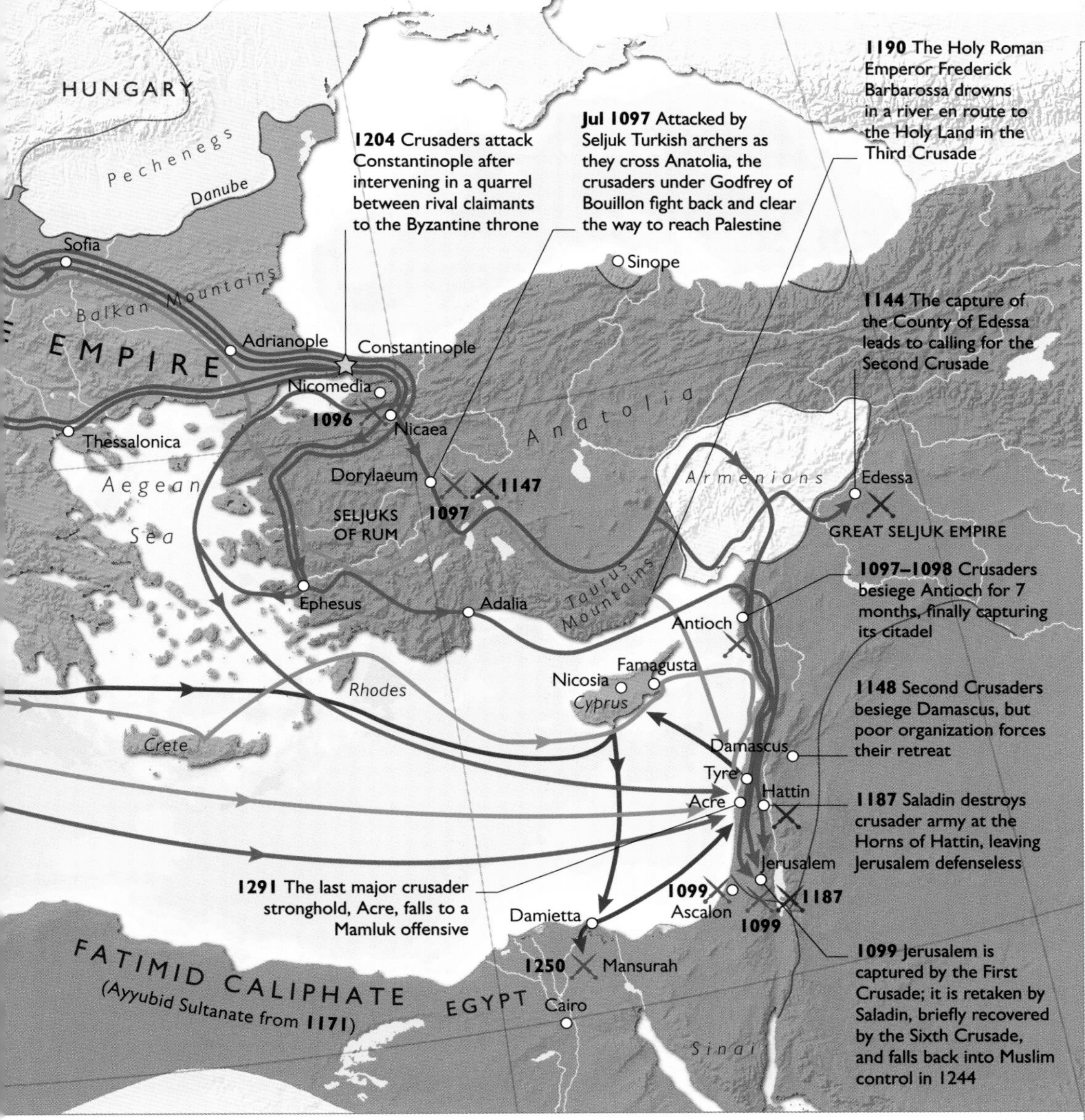

1190 The Holy Roman Emperor Frederick Barbarossa drowns in a river en route to the Holy Land in the Third Crusade

1204 Crusaders attack Constantinople after intervening in a quarrel between rival claimants to the Byzantine throne

Jul 1097 Attacked by Seljuk Turkish archers as they cross Anatolia, the crusaders under Godfrey of Bouillon fight back and clear the way to reach Palestine

1144 The capture of the County of Edessa leads to calling for the Second Crusade

HUNGARY

Pechenegs

Danube

Sofia

Balkan Mountains

EMPIRE

Adrianople

Thessalonica

Constantinople

Nicomedia

1096

Nicaea

Dorylaeum

1147

1097

SELJUKS OF RUM

Ephesus

Adalia

Aegean Sea

Rhodes

Crete

Sinope

Anatolia

Armenians

Taurus Mountains

Antioch

Edessa

GREAT SELJUK EMPIRE

1097–1098 Crusaders besiege Antioch for 7 months, finally capturing its citadel

1148 Second Crusaders besiege Damascus, but poor organization forces their retreat

1187 Saladin destroys crusader army at the Horns of Hattin, leaving Jerusalem defenseless

Nicosia

Famagusta

Cyprus

Damascus

Tyre

Acre

Hattin

Jerusalem

1099

Ascalon

1187

1099

1291 The last major crusader stronghold, Acre, falls to a Mamluk offensive

Damietta

1250

Mansurah

FATIMID CALIPHATE
(Ayyubid Sultanate from 1171)

EGYPT

Cairo

Sinai

1099 Jerusalem is captured by the First Crusade; it is retaken by Saladin, briefly recovered by the Sixth Crusade, and falls back into Muslim control in 1244

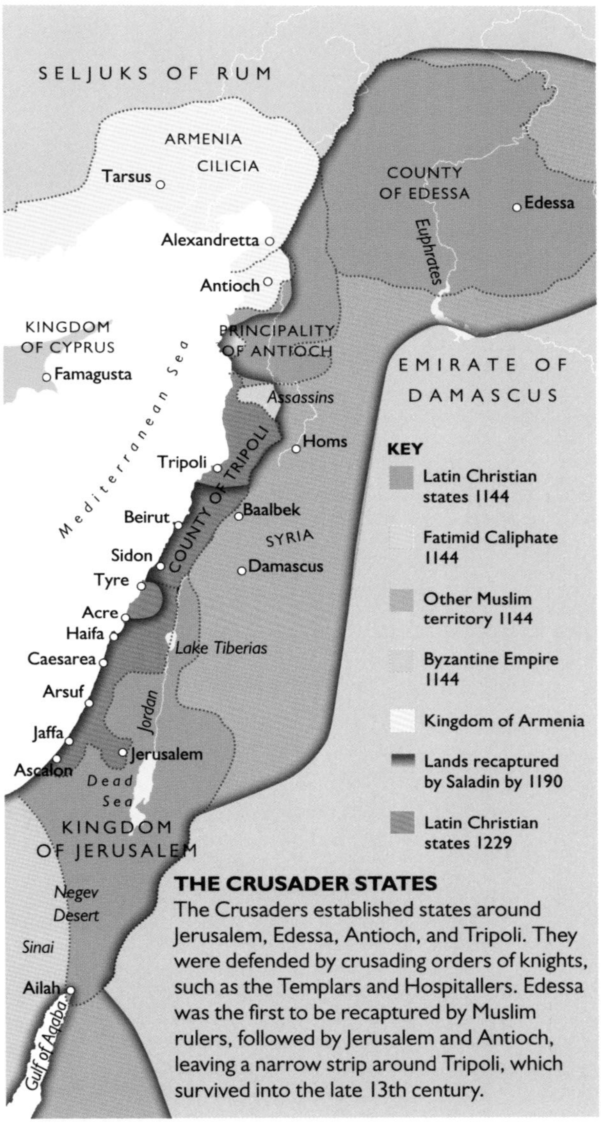

THE CRUSADER STATES

SELJUKS OF RUM

ARMENIA CILICIA

Tarsus

Alexandretta

Antioch

KINGDOM OF CYPRUS

Famagusta

COUNTY OF EDESSA

Edessa

Euphrates

PRINCIPALITY OF ANTIOCH

Assassins

EMIRATE OF DAMASCUS

Tripoli

Homs

Mediterranean Sea

Beirut

Sidon

Tyre

Acre

Haifa

Caesarea

Arsuf

Jaffa

Ascalon

Baalbek

SYRIA

Damascus

COUNTY OF TRIPOLI

Lake Tiberias

Jordan

Jerusalem

Dead Sea

KINGDOM OF JERUSALEM

Negev Desert

Sinai

Ailah

Gulf of Aqaba

KEY

- ▪ Latin Christian states 1144
- Fatimid Caliphate 1144
- Other Muslim territory 1144
- Byzantine Empire 1144
- Kingdom of Armenia
- Lands recaptured by Saladin by 1190
- Latin Christian states 1229

The Crusaders established states around Jerusalem, Edessa, Antioch, and Tripoli. They were defended by crusading orders of knights, such as the Templars and Hospitallers. Edessa was the first to be recaptured by Muslim rulers, followed by Jerusalem and Antioch, leaving a narrow strip around Tripoli, which survived into the late 13th century.

Jerusalem to Saladin in 1187; while it halted the Muslim advance, it did not recover the Holy City. With no coherent strategy to secure the crusader states, several subsequent crusades were launched to address immediate crises. Jerusalem was eventually recovered in 1229 in the Sixth Crusade, but later expeditions were largely ineffective and aimed at Muslim-controlled regions outside Palestine, such as Egypt in 1249 and Tunis in 1270. The area under crusader control gradually shrank until campaigns by the Ayyubids and Mamluks retook the last of the Crusader castles, ending with the fall of Acre.

▷ **The departure for the Second Crusade**
This 12th-century fresco from a Templar chapel in southwest France shows knights leaving for the Holy Land. Most would be away for years in Palestine, and some would settle there.

THE INHERITORS OF ROME

The Western Roman Empire's fall was followed by the rise of several kingdoms of Germanic invaders in former Roman provinces. While the level of continuity with Roman life varied, within 200 years, some of their systems harked back, at least in part, to Rome.

△ **Roman elite**
This late 4th-century ivory diptych portrays the Roman general Stilicho and his wife and son. Regent for Emperor Honorius, the part-Vandal Stilicho was one of the Western Empire's most powerful men.

Pressure grew on the Roman frontiers along the Rhine and the Danube Rivers from the 3rd century, as Germanic invaders migrated westward. In 406, helped partly by problems within the empire, large numbers of Vandals, Alans, and Sueves flooded across the Rhine and fanned out through Gaul and Spain. As the empire's grip on these provinces contracted, its ability to raise taxes to support the army diminished, accelerating the process by which the newcomers had to be accommodated rather than expelled. Other encroachments followed. After some reshaping of the invading ethnic groups, the Western Roman Empire was left with a presence of Visigoths, Ostrogoths, Burgundians, and Franks. The Roman hold on the western provinces had slipped away, not as a result of a single defeat, but through simple lack of resources to defend them.

New kingdoms

By 418, a Visigothic kingdom had been established at Toulouse, which expanded to include much of southwestern France and Spain. This displaced the Vandals, who, in

▷ **Fortune for the church**
This jeweled cross is part of a cache of votive objects donated by the Visigothic kings of Spain to a church in the 7th century. After the conversion of King Reccared to Catholicism in 589, the Church became a key player in the consolidation of royal power in Spain.

429, crossed over into North Africa, where they founded their own kingdom (see pp.92–93). Northern France fell out of imperial control in the mid-5th century, as Frankish tribes pushed westward, and finally, in 476, Italy succumbed to an advance led by Odovacer, who was, in turn, supplanted by Ostrogoths under Theoderic the Great in 493. The Roman province of Britain, which had broken away from the empire in 411, suffered complete political collapse as Angles and Saxons mounted invasions across the North Sea.

Europe after Rome

The disappearance of the security that the Roman Empire had guaranteed had profound consequences. Trade declined, the economy collapsed in many areas, and long-distance communication became more difficult. Urban settlements contracted, disappearing almost entirely in England. Even Rome, which once had a population of more than half a million, shrank to only around 30,000 inhabitants by the 7th century. The new rulers adopted some elements of Roman life. As chieftains of war-bands, they were ill-equipped to rule large, static populations and, in Italy in particular, many of the former senatorial elite took service with their new masters. Statesmen such as Cassiodorus served under Theoderic and attempted to reconcile Ostrogoths and Romans. Gaul retained a centralized administration with tax-levying powers,

THE NEW ORDER

The early 5th century saw Germanic invaders breach the Rhine frontier of the Roman Empire. This was followed by a rapid collapse of imperial control over its western provinces. The Franks established a kingdom in northern France and expanded through the south and east, while the Visigoths overran Spain and the Vandals occupied Roman North Africa. In these areas, the new Germanic rulers gradually established administrations. England, however, remained divided among smaller kingdoms.

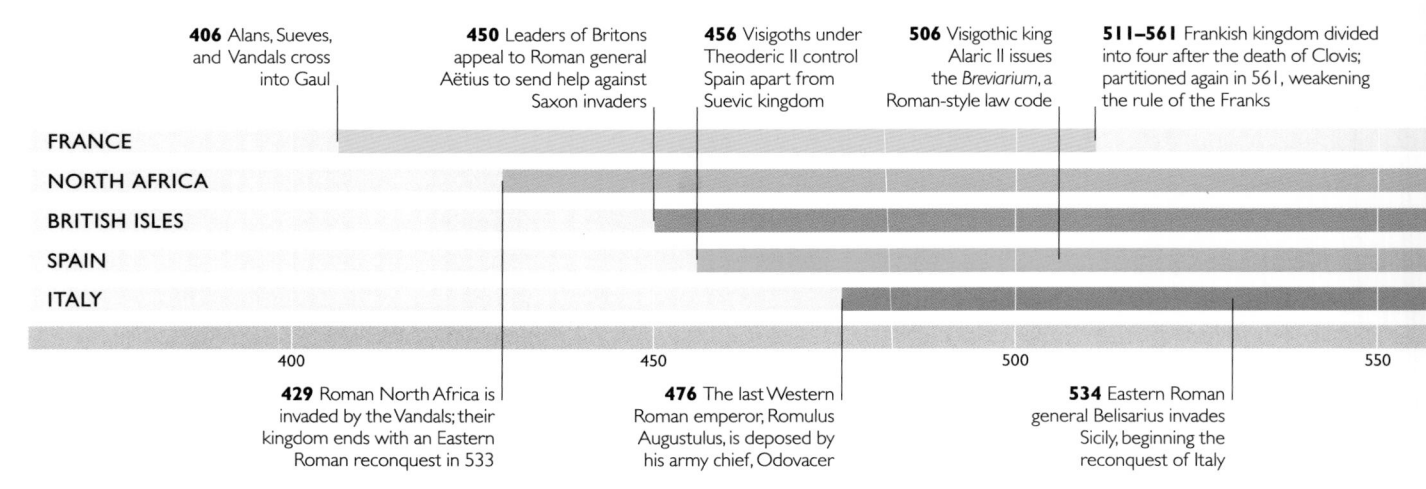

406 Alans, Sueves, and Vandals cross into Gaul

450 Leaders of Britons appeal to Roman general Aëtius to send help against Saxon invaders

456 Visigoths under Theoderic II control Spain apart from Suevic kingdom

506 Visigothic king Alaric II issues the *Breviarium*, a Roman-style law code

511–561 Frankish kingdom divided into four after the death of Clovis; partitioned again in 561, weakening the rule of the Franks

FRANCE
NORTH AFRICA
BRITISH ISLES
SPAIN
ITALY

400   450   500   550

429 Roman North Africa is invaded by the Vandals; their kingdom ends with an Eastern Roman reconquest in 533

476 The last Western Roman emperor, Romulus Augustulus, is deposed by his army chief, Odovacer

534 Eastern Roman general Belisarius invades Sicily, beginning the reconquest of Italy

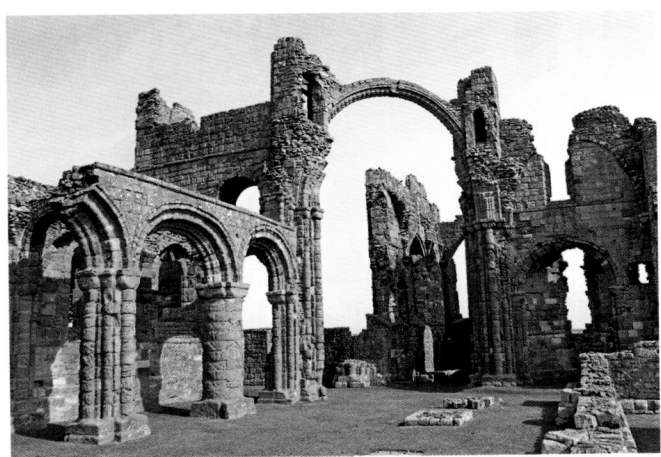

◁ Holy ruins
These are the remains of the 12th-century Benedictine priory on Lindisfarne Island, off the northeast coast of Northumbria, England. It was built on the site of an earlier abbey destroyed by the first Viking raid on England in 793.

▷ Anglo-Saxon helmet
This reconstruction of a helmet found in an early 7th-century ship burial at Sutton Hoo, East Anglia, England, shows the great skill of Anglo-Saxon metalworkers.

while in Spain, the Visigoths combined the interests of Romans and Goths, issuing law codes that legislated differently for the two groups. In Britain, however, the prolonged military struggle between the invading Anglo-Saxons and indigenous Britons meant that not even fragments of the old Roman administration survived.

In 533–534, the emperor of the surviving Eastern Roman (Byzantine) Empire, Justinian, launched a military campaign to recover Rome's western provinces and destroyed the Vandal kingdom of North Africa. His campaign in Italy led to a 20-year war that ended with the fall of the Ostrogothic kingdom in 553. It also left the peninsula ravaged, unable to yield any taxes and ripe for a new invasion by the Lombards, who conquered much of the peninsula in 568–572, confining the Byzantines to a series of scattered enclaves.

Recovery and consolidation

Elsewhere, however, despite several civil wars, the 7th century saw a process of consolidation. In England, larger kingdoms emerged, most notably Northumbria in the north, Mercia and East Anglia in central England, and Wessex and Kent in the south. All of these converted to Christianity in the century following a mission in 597 sent by Pope Gregory I and led by one of his monks, Augustine. Lombard Italy stabilized after the invasion period, when Lombard king Agilulf (r. 590–616) made peace with the Franks following a series of invasions. In 643, King Rothari issued a law code setting down the customary law of the Lombards in written form for the first time.

By 700, Visigothic Spain, Frankish Gaul, and Lombard Italy had achieved relative stability. There, and in still-fragmented Anglo-Saxon England, the persistence of Latin as a means of formal written communication and the spread of the Christian Church provided living reminders of continuity with the late Roman world. If the invaders who settled in the Roman Empire discarded some of what they found there, they also inherited much from their Roman predecessors.

> "This King Rothari collected … the laws of the Lombards … and he directed this code to be called the Edict."
>
> PAUL THE DEACON, FROM *HISTORY OF THE LOMBARDS*, c. 790

568 Lombard invasion of Italy begins

664 Dispute between Celtic Christians in Anglo-Saxon kingdoms and those from Rome settled by Synod of Whitby

698 Muslim Arab army captures Carthage

600

650

700

750

800

597 Sent by Pope Gregory I to convert the English, Augustine arrives in Canterbury

633 Penda of Mercia defeats and kills King Edwin of Northumbria to begin a 160-year Mercian supremacy among the English kingdoms

711 Arab Muslim army crosses from North Africa and conquers the Visigothic Kingdom

774 Lombard kingdom comes to an end after invasion by Frankish-Carolingian ruler Charlemagne

THE HUNDRED YEARS' WAR

A conflict between the kings of England and of France over the English rulers' claim to the French throne began in 1337 and lasted for 116 years. While at times the English managed to conquer large parts of France, by the end of the conflict in 1453, they retained only the port town of Calais.

Edward III of England had a claim to the French throne through his mother, the sister of Charles IV of France. When Charles died without an heir, Edward laid claim to the French throne against his rival, Philip. This, combined with Edward's earlier refusal to pay homage to the French monarch for land he held, led to war. The conflict fell into three phases. In the initial phase (1337–1360) under Edward III, the English won significant victories. This phase came to an end with the Treaty of Brétigny, which left England with enlarged holdings in France. In the second phase

(1369–1389), the English initially made large gains but were pushed back. This phase ended in a truce, with England retaining only Calais and small areas around Brest, Bordeaux, and Bayonne. In the early 1400s, France was in a state of virtual civil war between supporters of the Duke of Burgundy and the Armagnacs. Taking advantage of this disruption, Henry V of England resumed war with France in 1415. At first, English forces took huge areas. However, inspired by Joan of Arc, the French fought back, and by the end of the war, England held only Calais.

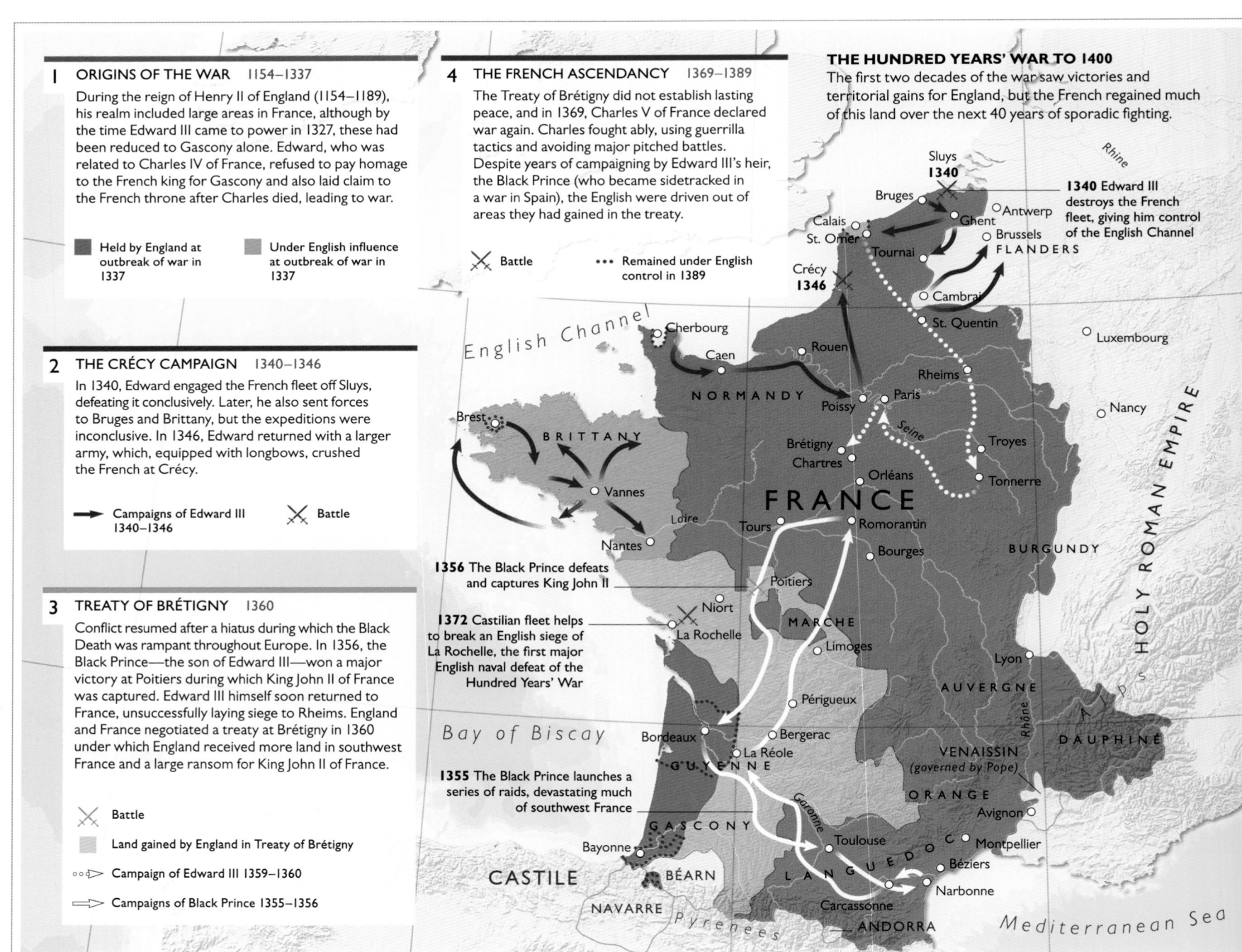

1 ORIGINS OF THE WAR 1154–1337
During the reign of Henry II of England (1154–1189), his realm included large areas in France, although by the time Edward III came to power in 1327, these had been reduced to Gascony alone. Edward, who was related to Charles IV of France, refused to pay homage to the French king for Gascony and also laid claim to the French throne after Charles died, leading to war.

- ■ Held by England at outbreak of war in 1337
- ■ Under English influence at outbreak of war in 1337

2 THE CRÉCY CAMPAIGN 1340–1346
In 1340, Edward engaged the French fleet off Sluys, defeating it conclusively. Later, he also sent forces to Bruges and Brittany, but the expeditions were inconclusive. In 1346, Edward returned with a larger army, which, equipped with longbows, crushed the French at Crécy.

- → Campaigns of Edward III 1340–1346
- ✗ Battle

3 TREATY OF BRÉTIGNY 1360
Conflict resumed after a hiatus during which the Black Death was rampant throughout Europe. In 1356, the Black Prince—the son of Edward III—won a major victory at Poitiers during which King John II of France was captured. Edward III himself soon returned to France, unsuccessfully laying siege to Rheims. England and France negotiated a treaty at Brétigny in 1360 under which England received more land in southwest France and a large ransom for King John II of France.

- ✗ Battle
- ■ Land gained by England in Treaty of Brétigny
- ∘∘∘▷ Campaign of Edward III 1359–1360
- ▷ Campaigns of Black Prince 1355–1356

4 THE FRENCH ASCENDANCY 1369–1389
The Treaty of Brétigny did not establish lasting peace, and in 1369, Charles V of France declared war again. Charles fought ably, using guerrilla tactics and avoiding major pitched battles. Despite years of campaigning by Edward III's heir, the Black Prince (who became sidetracked in a war in Spain), the English were driven out of areas they had gained in the treaty.

- ✗ Battle
- ••• Remained under English control in 1389

THE HUNDRED YEARS' WAR TO 1400
The first two decades of the war saw victories and territorial gains for England, but the French regained much of this land over the next 40 years of sporadic fighting.

1340 Edward III destroys the French fleet, giving him control of the English Channel

1356 The Black Prince defeats and captures King John II

1372 Castilian fleet helps to break an English siege of La Rochelle, the first major English naval defeat of the Hundred Years' War

1355 The Black Prince launches a series of raids, devastating much of southwest France

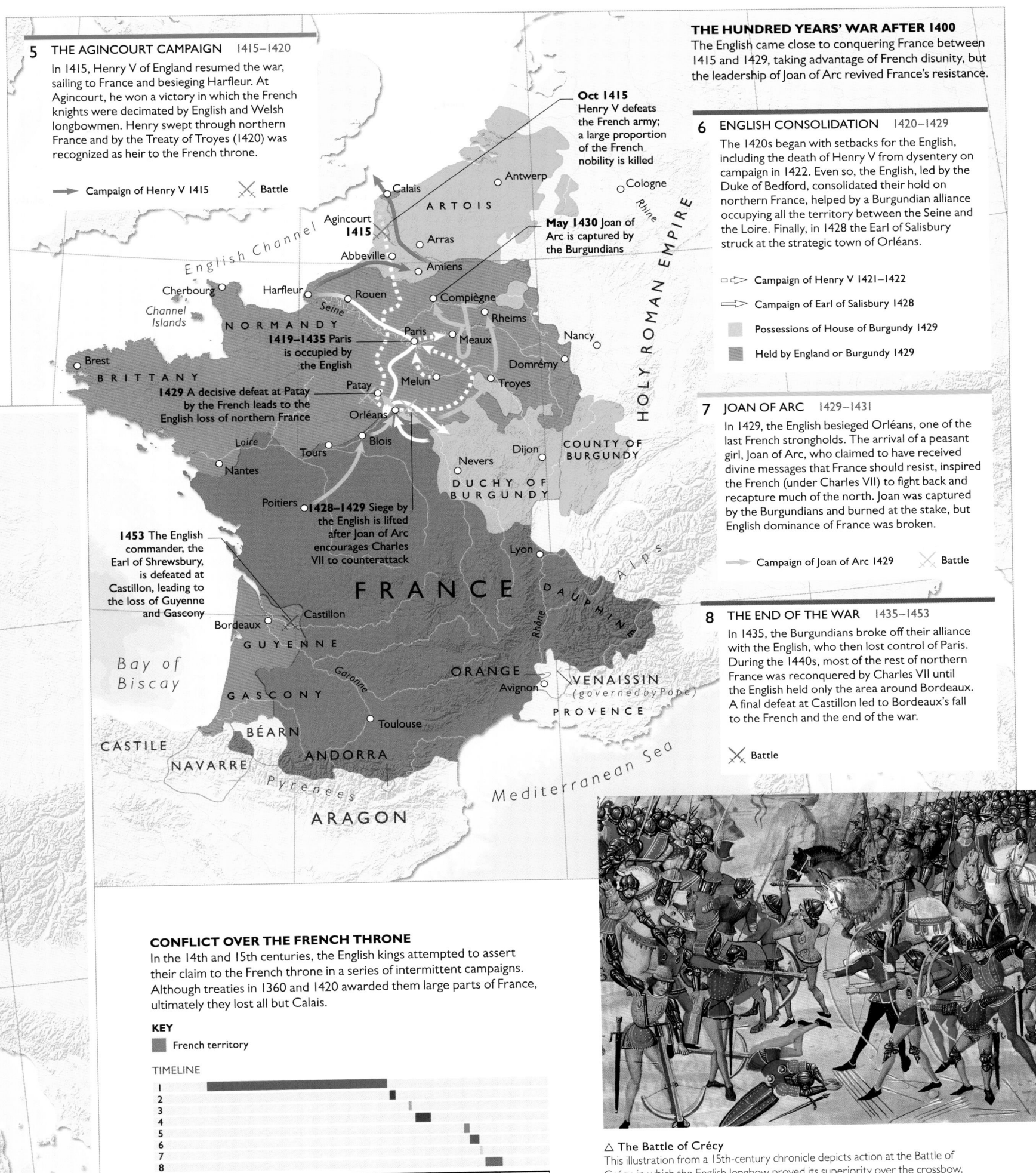

5 THE AGINCOURT CAMPAIGN 1415–1420

In 1415, Henry V of England resumed the war, sailing to France and besieging Harfleur. At Agincourt, he won a victory in which the French knights were decimated by English and Welsh longbowmen. Henry swept through northern France and by the Treaty of Troyes (1420) was recognized as heir to the French throne.

→ Campaign of Henry V 1415   ✕ Battle

Oct 1415 Henry V defeats the French army; a large proportion of the French nobility is killed

May 1430 Joan of Arc is captured by the Burgundians

1419–1435 Paris is occupied by the English

1429 A decisive defeat at Patay by the French leads to the English loss of northern France

1453 The English commander, the Earl of Shrewsbury, is defeated at Castillon, leading to the loss of Guyenne and Gascony

1428–1429 Siege by the English is lifted after Joan of Arc encourages Charles VII to counterattack

THE HUNDRED YEARS' WAR AFTER 1400

The English came close to conquering France between 1415 and 1429, taking advantage of French disunity, but the leadership of Joan of Arc revived France's resistance.

6 ENGLISH CONSOLIDATION 1420–1429

The 1420s began with setbacks for the English, including the death of Henry V from dysentery on campaign in 1422. Even so, the English, led by the Duke of Bedford, consolidated their hold on northern France, helped by a Burgundian alliance occupying all the territory between the Seine and the Loire. Finally, in 1428 the Earl of Salisbury struck at the strategic town of Orléans.

▭⇨ Campaign of Henry V 1421–1422

⇨ Campaign of Earl of Salisbury 1428

▮ Possessions of House of Burgundy 1429

▨ Held by England or Burgundy 1429

7 JOAN OF ARC 1429–1431

In 1429, the English besieged Orléans, one of the last French strongholds. The arrival of a peasant girl, Joan of Arc, who claimed to have received divine messages that France should resist, inspired the French (under Charles VII) to fight back and recapture much of the north. Joan was captured by the Burgundians and burned at the stake, but English dominance of France was broken.

→ Campaign of Joan of Arc 1429   ✕ Battle

8 THE END OF THE WAR 1435–1453

In 1435, the Burgundians broke off their alliance with the English, who then lost control of Paris. During the 1440s, most of the rest of northern France was reconquered by Charles VII until the English held only the area around Bordeaux. A final defeat at Castillon led to Bordeaux's fall to the French and the end of the war.

✕ Battle

CONFLICT OVER THE FRENCH THRONE

In the 14th and 15th centuries, the English kings attempted to assert their claim to the French throne in a series of intermittent campaigns. Although treaties in 1360 and 1420 awarded them large parts of France, ultimately they lost all but Calais.

KEY

▮ French territory

TIMELINE

1
2
3
4
5
6
7
8

1100   1200   1300   1400   1500

△ **The Battle of Crécy**

This illustration from a 15th-century chronicle depicts action at the Battle of Crécy, in which the English longbow proved its superiority over the crossbow, which was slower to load and had a shorter range.

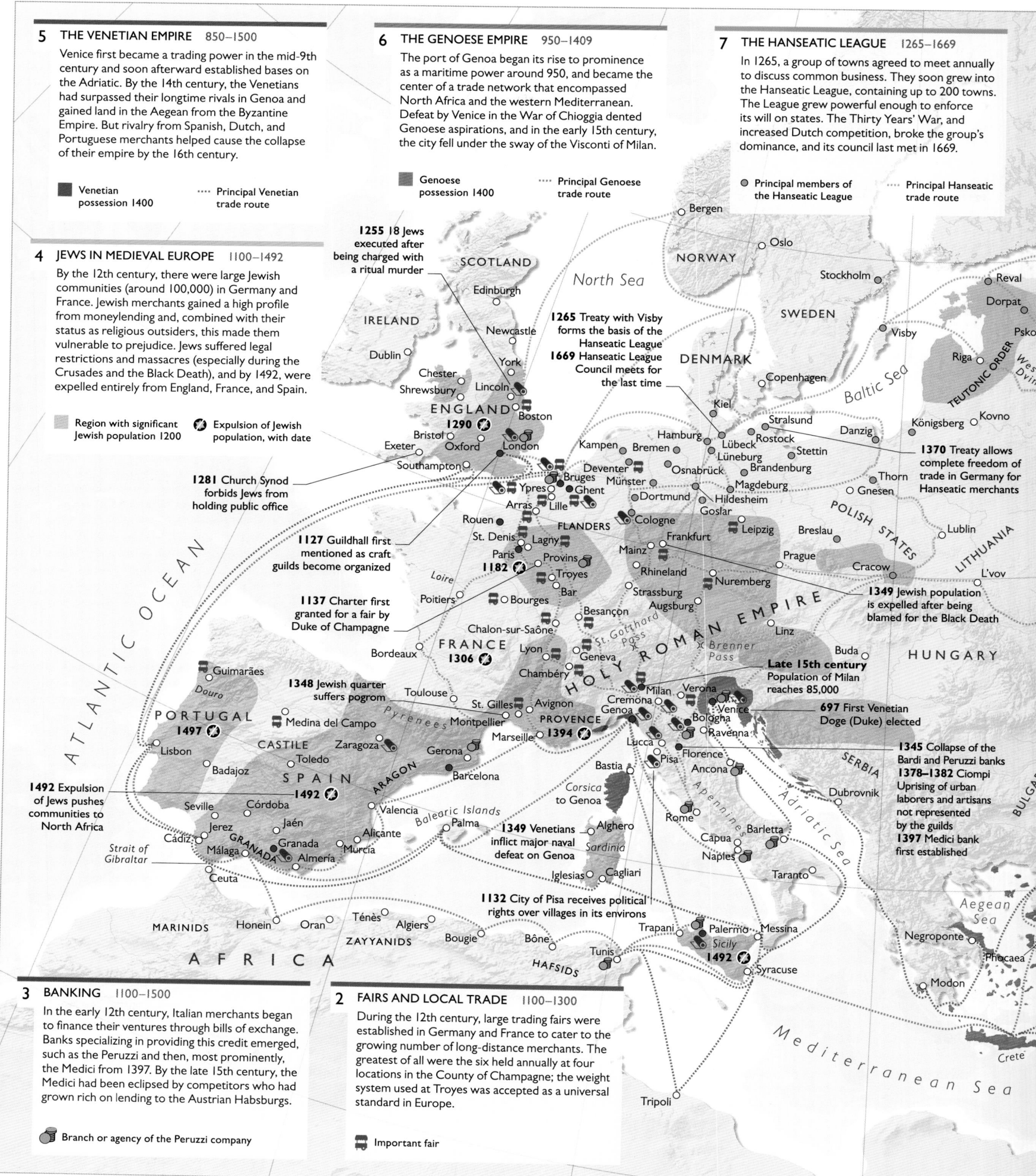

5 THE VENETIAN EMPIRE 850–1500

Venice first became a trading power in the mid-9th century and soon afterward established bases on the Adriatic. By the 14th century, the Venetians had surpassed their longtime rivals in Genoa and gained land in the Aegean from the Byzantine Empire. But rivalry from Spanish, Dutch, and Portuguese merchants helped cause the collapse of their empire by the 16th century.

■ Venetian possession 1400
⋯ Principal Venetian trade route

6 THE GENOESE EMPIRE 950–1409

The port of Genoa began its rise to prominence as a maritime power around 950, and became the center of a trade network that encompassed North Africa and the western Mediterranean. Defeat by Venice in the War of Chioggia dented Genoese aspirations, and in the early 15th century, the city fell under the sway of the Visconti of Milan.

■ Genoese possession 1400
⋯ Principal Genoese trade route

7 THE HANSEATIC LEAGUE 1265–1669

In 1265, a group of towns agreed to meet annually to discuss common business. They soon grew into the Hanseatic League, containing up to 200 towns. The League grew powerful enough to enforce its will on states. The Thirty Years' War, and increased Dutch competition, broke the group's dominance, and its council last met in 1669.

● Principal members of the Hanseatic League
⋯ Principal Hanseatic trade route

4 JEWS IN MEDIEVAL EUROPE 1100–1492

By the 12th century, there were large Jewish communities (around 100,000) in Germany and France. Jewish merchants gained a high profile from moneylending and, combined with their status as religious outsiders, this made them vulnerable to prejudice. Jews suffered legal restrictions and massacres (especially during the Crusades and the Black Death), and by 1492, were expelled entirely from England, France, and Spain.

■ Region with significant Jewish population 1200
✡ Expulsion of Jewish population, with date

1255 18 Jews executed after being charged with a ritual murder

1265 Treaty with Visby forms the basis of the Hanseatic League
1669 Hanseatic League Council meets for the last time

1281 Church Synod forbids Jews from holding public office

1127 Guildhall first mentioned as craft guilds become organized

1137 Charter first granted for a fair by Duke of Champagne

1290

1182 ✡

1306 ✡

1348 Jewish quarter suffers pogrom

1497 ✡

1492 Expulsion of Jews pushes communities to North Africa

1492 ✡

1370 Treaty allows complete freedom of trade in Germany for Hanseatic merchants

1349 Jewish population is expelled after being blamed for the Black Death

Late 15th century Population of Milan reaches 85,000

697 First Venetian Doge (Duke) elected

1345 Collapse of the Bardi and Peruzzi banks
1378–1382 Ciompi Uprising of urban laborers and artisans not represented by the guilds
1397 Medici bank first established

1349 Venetians inflict major naval defeat on Genoa

1132 City of Pisa receives political rights over villages in its environs

1492 ✡

3 BANKING 1100–1500

In the early 12th century, Italian merchants began to finance their ventures through bills of exchange. Banks specializing in providing this credit emerged, such as the Peruzzi and then, most prominently, the Medici from 1397. By the late 15th century, the Medici had been eclipsed by competitors who had grown rich on lending to the Austrian Habsburgs.

🪙 Branch or agency of the Peruzzi company

2 FAIRS AND LOCAL TRADE 1100–1300

During the 12th century, large trading fairs were established in Germany and France to cater to the growing number of long-distance merchants. The greatest of all were the six held annually at four locations in the County of Champagne; the weight system used at Troyes was accepted as a universal standard in Europe.

🚚 Important fair

Map labels:
Bergen, Oslo, Stockholm, Reval, Dorpat, Pskov, Visby, Riga, Kovno, Königsberg, Danzig, Thorn, Gnesen, Lublin, L'vov, Copenhagen, Kiel, Stralsund, Rostock, Stettin, Brandenburg, Magdeburg, Breslau, Prague, Cracow, Hamburg, Bremen, Lübeck, Lüneburg, Osnabrück, Hildesheim, Goslar, Leipzig, Frankfurt, Nuremberg, Kampen, Deventer, Münster, Dortmund, Cologne, Mainz, Rhineland, Strassburg, Augsburg, Besançon, Linz, Buda, Bruges, Ghent, Ypres, Arras, Lille, Rouen, St. Denis, Lagny, Paris, Provins, Troyes, Bar, Bourges, Poitiers, Chalon-sur-Saône, Lyon, Geneva, Chambéry, St. Gotthard Pass, Brenner Pass, Milan, Verona, Cremona, Genoa, Bologna, Venice, Ravenna, Lucca, Pisa, Florence, Ancona, Rome, Capua, Naples, Taranto, Barletta, Dubrovnik, Bergen, Scotland, Edinburgh, Ireland, Dublin, Newcastle, York, Chester, Shrewsbury, Lincoln, Boston, England, Bristol, Exeter, Oxford, London, Southampton, Flanders, France, Bordeaux, Guimarães, Douro, Portugal, Lisbon, Badajoz, Castile, Toledo, Medina del Campo, Zaragoza, Gerona, Barcelona, Aragon, Spain, Seville, Córdoba, Jaén, Granada, Valencia, Palma, Alicante, Murcia, Almería, Málaga, Jerez, Cádiz, Ceuta, Granada, Strait of Gibraltar, Toulouse, St. Gilles, Montpellier, Avignon, Provence, Marseille, Bastia, Corsica, Sardinia, Cagliari, Iglesias, Alghero, Balearic Islands, Honein, Oran, Ténès, Algiers, Bougie, Bône, Tunis, Trapani, Palermo, Messina, Sicily, Syracuse, Negroponte, Phocaea, Modon, Crete, Tripoli, Marinids, Zayyanids, Hafsids, Africa, North Sea, Norway, Sweden, Denmark, Baltic Sea, Teutonic Order, West Dvina, Polish States, Lithuania, Holy Roman Empire, Hungary, Serbia, Bulgaria, Apennines, Adriatic Sea, Aegean Sea, Mediterranean Sea, Atlantic Ocean, Pyrenees, Loire

1255 18 Jews executed after being charged with a ritual murder

1281 Church Synod forbids Jews from holding public office

TRADE IN EUROPE

New industries emerged in Europe from the early 12th century, and a web of trading routes expanded. Towns and their populations grew rapidly, and new techniques such as banking were developed by companies like the Peruzzi.

KEY

···· Main overland route

🧶 Major textile town

○ Other trading center

TIMELINE

	800	1000	1200	1400	1600	1800
1						
2						
3						
4						
5						
6						
7						

1 THE GROWTH OF TOWNS 1100–1358

Rapid economic development meant that by 1300, Milan, Genoa, Naples, Florence, and Palermo had over 100,000 inhabitants and Paris perhaps 200,000. Many towns developed governments or merchant guilds. But increasingly, crowded towns bred political unrest, disease, and intolerance. Urban populations became restive, with major uprisings in Flanders in 1348–1359 and Paris in 1358.

● Town with population over 50,000

Novgorod

RUSSIAN PRINCIPALITIES

Moscow

Vitebsk Smolensk

Mogilev

Kiev

KHANATE OF THE GOLDEN HORDE

Dnieper

to New Sarai

Tana

New Sarai, at present-day Kolobovkan in Russia, is one of the largest cities of the medieval world

Moncastro

Kaffa

Black Sea

Trebizond

TREBIZOND

Anatolia

1182 Venetian merchants massacred during a riot due to their domination of the city's maritime trade

to Tabriz

Constantinople

BYZANTINE EMPIRE

RUM

SELJUK STATES

Ephesus

Taurus Mountains

LITTLE ARMENIA

IL-KHANATE

to Baghdad

Aleppo

Antioch

Rhodes

Famagusta

Cyprus

Beirut

Acre

Jerusalem

1218–1219 Genoese fleet besieges Damietta as part of the Fifth Crusade

Damietta

Alexandria

Nile

MAMLUKS

Cairo

1492 Many Jews expelled from Spain settle in North Africa and the eastern Mediterranean

MEDIEVAL EUROPEAN TRADE

From the 12th century, Europe experienced a period of economic and population growth. Guilds and town councils threatened royal monopolies of power, and merchants pioneered new methods of banking. Yet not all shared the fruits of this prosperity, and Jewish communities suffered increasing persecutions.

Europe saw a renewed flourishing of urban life in the 12th century. New towns were built under royal patronage in England and France, and others expanded significantly in size. Fairs sprang up, where merchants traveled from across the continent to acquire goods and hawk their wares. Cities became more important, too, as many places acquired their own councils that were not always amenable to royal persuasion, while in Italy a network of independent city-states developed. The area became a fertile ground for innovation in finance, including the establishment of the first investment banks. The wealth generated by their merchants enabled Genoa and Venice to establish maritime empires in the Mediterranean and become international powers in their own right. Similarly, in northern Europe, the Hanseatic League—a federation of trading cities—developed after 1265 and dominated trade in the Baltic and North Seas for two centuries. Jewish communities, however, were expelled from much of western and southern Europe. They had previously played a central role in providing moneylending services, but by 1500, main centers of Jewish life on the continent had shifted to eastern Europe, Italy, and the lands under Muslim control.

△ **Jewish wedding ring**
This ornate ring comes from Colmar, in northeastern France, which had a thriving Jewish community by the 13th century.

CLOTH TRADE
THE FIRST GREAT EUROPEAN INDUSTRY

Cloth was the first commodity in medieval Europe whose production grew into a great industry. The main centers were in Flanders, England, and Italy, which all had access to important sources of wool. The spinning, weaving, fulling (cleansing the cloth and making it thicker), and dyeing processes provided employment to large numbers of artisans and incomes for merchants. Guilds, associations of artisans and merchants, were established in major cities, and merchants used their wealth to endow lavish cloth halls—where cloth was sold.

Textile workers dyeing cloth

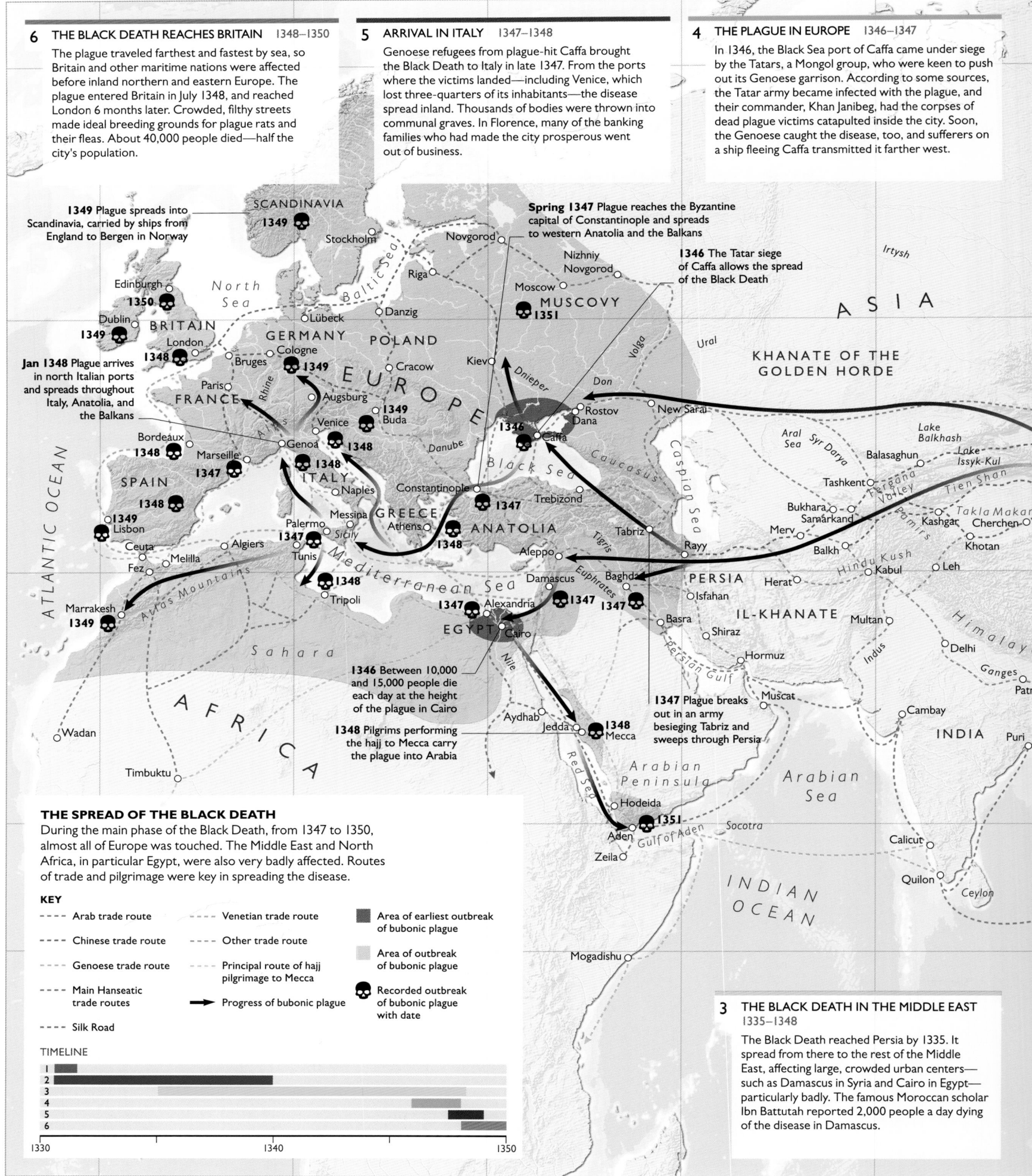

6 THE BLACK DEATH REACHES BRITAIN 1348–1350

The plague traveled farthest and fastest by sea, so Britain and other maritime nations were affected before inland northern and eastern Europe. The plague entered Britain in July 1348, and reached London 6 months later. Crowded, filthy streets made ideal breeding grounds for plague rats and their fleas. About 40,000 people died—half the city's population.

5 ARRIVAL IN ITALY 1347–1348

Genoese refugees from plague-hit Caffa brought the Black Death to Italy in late 1347. From the ports where the victims landed—including Venice, which lost three-quarters of its inhabitants—the disease spread inland. Thousands of bodies were thrown into communal graves. In Florence, many of the banking families who had made the city prosperous went out of business.

4 THE PLAGUE IN EUROPE 1346–1347

In 1346, the Black Sea port of Caffa came under siege by the Tatars, a Mongol group, who were keen to push out its Genoese garrison. According to some sources, the Tatar army became infected with the plague, and their commander, Khan Janibeg, had the corpses of dead plague victims catapulted inside the city. Soon, the Genoese caught the disease, too, and sufferers on a ship fleeing Caffa transmitted it farther west.

THE SPREAD OF THE BLACK DEATH

During the main phase of the Black Death, from 1347 to 1350, almost all of Europe was touched. The Middle East and North Africa, in particular Egypt, were also very badly affected. Routes of trade and pilgrimage were key in spreading the disease.

3 THE BLACK DEATH IN THE MIDDLE EAST 1335–1348

The Black Death reached Persia by 1335. It spread from there to the rest of the Middle East, affecting large, crowded urban centers—such as Damascus in Syria and Cairo in Egypt—particularly badly. The famous Moroccan scholar Ibn Battutah reported 2,000 people a day dying of the disease in Damascus.

THE BLACK DEATH

In 1347, a new disease entered Europe from China and central Asia. The bubonic plague, or Black Death (after the black spots it caused on the skin), spread rapidly, and, with no cure available, killed around 150 million people—roughly one-third of the world's population.

The Black Death was transmitted through the bite of infected rat fleas, so it spread quickly in the crowded, unsanitary conditions of medieval towns. It moved along trade routes once it reached Italy in 1347, and over time developed into more virulent forms. Doctors prescribed sweet-smelling posies, complex brews of herbs and spices, and the fumigation of rooms, only the last of which—by killing the fleas—had the slightest effect in stopping the epidemic's course. Those who tried to flee simply spread the disease to new areas.

The disease caused terror and an outpouring of mysticism, and also had profound social consequences. There was a huge rise in crime—the murder rate in England doubled—as people broke faith with traditional values. Peasants, now scarce in number, could demand better conditions and pay from their feudal masters.

By the end of 1350, the Black Death had mainly run its course, but there were many recurrences; even today, there are occasional cases all over the world.

> *"They sickened by the thousands daily, and died unattended and without help."*
>
> GIOVANNI BOCACCIO, FROM THE *DECAMERON*, 1348–1353

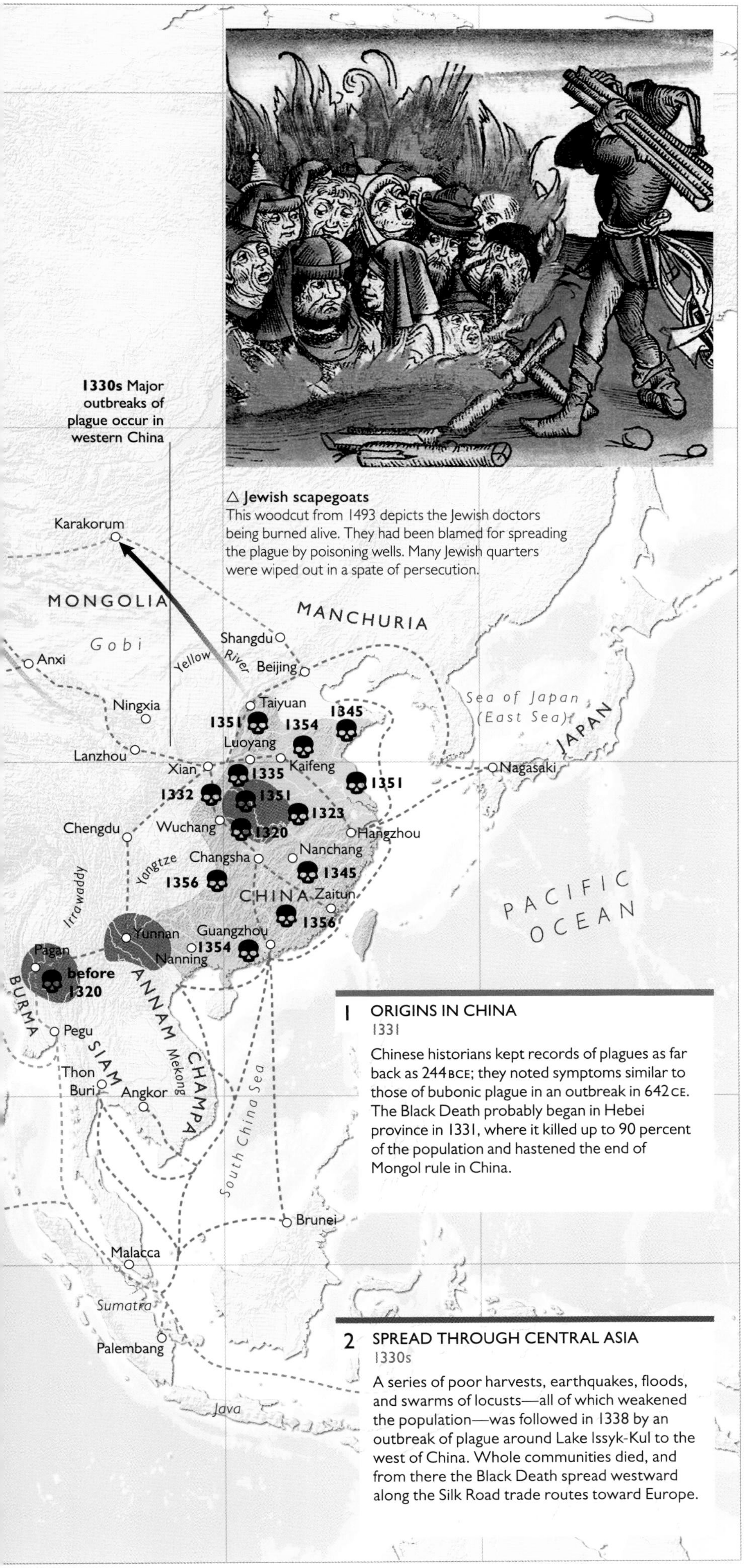

△ Jewish scapegoats
This woodcut from 1493 depicts the Jewish doctors being burned alive. They had been blamed for spreading the plague by poisoning wells. Many Jewish quarters were wiped out in a spate of persecution.

1330s Major outbreaks of plague occur in western China

1 ORIGINS IN CHINA
1331

Chinese historians kept records of plagues as far back as 244 BCE; they noted symptoms similar to those of bubonic plague in an outbreak in 642 CE. The Black Death probably began in Hebei province in 1331, where it killed up to 90 percent of the population and hastened the end of Mongol rule in China.

2 SPREAD THROUGH CENTRAL ASIA
1330s

A series of poor harvests, earthquakes, floods, and swarms of locusts—all of which weakened the population—was followed in 1338 by an outbreak of plague around Lake Issyk-Kul to the west of China. Whole communities died, and from there the Black Death spread westward along the Silk Road trade routes toward Europe.

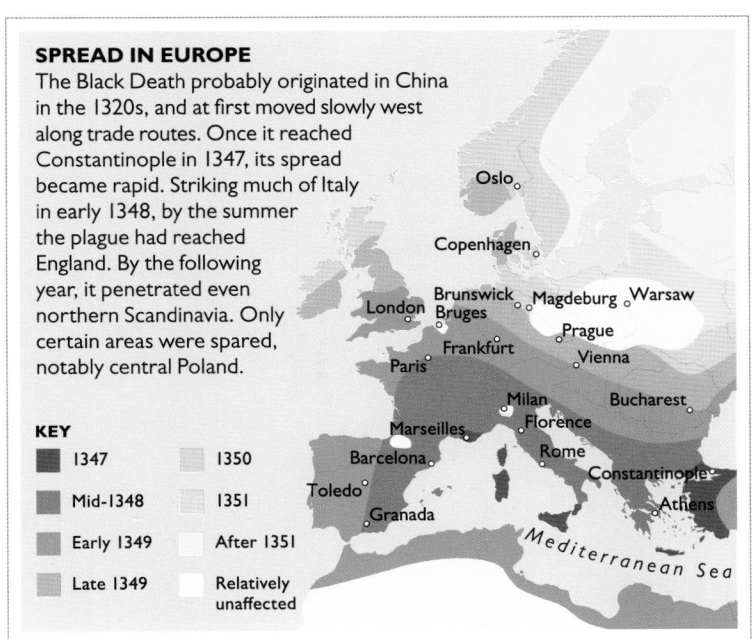

SPREAD IN EUROPE
The Black Death probably originated in China in the 1320s, and at first moved slowly west along trade routes. Once it reached Constantinople in 1347, its spread became rapid. Striking much of Italy in early 1348, by the summer the plague had reached England. By the following year, it penetrated even northern Scandinavia. Only certain areas were spared, notably central Poland.

KEY

■ 1347	1350
■ Mid-1348	1351
■ Early 1349	After 1351
■ Late 1349	Relatively unaffected

Coronation and excommunication
This painting shows Pope Innocent III both conferring the imperial crown on Frederick II (on the right) and removing it from Otto IV (on the left). It demonstrates the power of a pope to make and unmake emperors.

THE EMPEROR AND THE POPE

During the 11th and 12th centuries, relations between popes and rulers of the Holy Roman Empire were fraught with tensions, as both laid claim to supreme authority within the empire. It was only when imperial authority declined within Germany that the struggle between them finally subsided.

From the 10th century—with the empire extending across what is now Germany, the Czech Republic, and parts of France—there was a tussle for power between popes and emperors. While popes maintained that ultimate authority should rest with them as heads of the Church, emperors vigorously defended their position as supreme secular rulers. The struggle, known as the Investiture Controversy, focused on the monarch's right to invest bishops, who in turn had to pay homage to the emperor for their lands. Pope Gregory VII refused to accept this, and excommunicated Emperor Henry IV twice, first in 1076 and again in 1080. The Investiture Controversy was resolved in 1122 through a compromise whereby bishops in the empire could have a dual investiture, once by the Emperor for their lands and once by the Pope for their spiritual position.

△ **Crowning glory**
The ornamental crown seen here was used for the coronation of Holy Roman Emperors from the late 10th century.

Shift in the seat of power

Popes continued to interfere in imperial succession until 1356, when a document known as the Golden Bull decreed that emperors would be chosen by a college of electors—three bishops and four (later six) German princes. This gave German princes more power in their territories. Also, the shift of the power base of the Habsburg emperors toward Austria and Spain in the 15th and 16th centuries, the rise of specifically German imperial institutions such as the Imperial Diet, and the weakening of the Catholic Church in Germany after the Reformation (see pp.166–167) meant that by the 17th century, the Papal–Imperial rivalry had become largely irrelevant.

◁ **Divine coronation**
This 11th-century miniature depicts Christ crowning Emperor Henry II. The idea that an emperor's power was bestowed by God undermined claims of papal authority.

THE HOLY ROMAN EMPIRE

The crowning of the Frankish ruler Charlemagne as emperor in 800 marked the birth of an institution that came to be called the Holy Roman Empire. Although it survived for over a millennium, the empire's territorial core contracted until it became largely German and a sometimes chaotic mosaic of multiple and overlapping jurisdictions.

When Pope Leo III offered a new imperial title to Charlemagne, the ruler of the Franks, it was partly through nostalgia for the lost stability of the Roman Empire and a desire for protection. Having conquered much of northwest Europe since his accession in 768, he seemed an appropriate successor to the Caesars of old. However, the disintegration of the Frankish Empire into civil war after Charlemagne's death in 814 meant that imperial power was often short-lived. Sometimes there was no recognized emperor, until the Ottonian family acquired the title "Emperor of the Romans" in 962—an event most now regard as the true beginning of the empire. Thereafter, the empire became mainly a German affair, passing through the hands of successive dynasties: the Ottonians, Salians, Hohenstaufen, Luxembourg, and Habsburgs. Imperial lands were ceded to local princes and towns while the emperor was in Italy or on crusade

or when he was preoccupied with campaigning. This caused a general weakening of imperial control. Stronger emperors, such as Henry IV, tried to assert imperial authority, clashing with the Papacy over the right to appoint bishops. But his humiliation in being excommunicated and forced to make penance in 1077 demonstrated the limit of the imperial writ.

The empire briefly reached a new apogee under Frederick II in the early 13th century, when Sicily came into the imperial orbit. But a long domination by the Habsburgs from 1438, who also had lands outside the Holy Roman Empire to rule, contributed to a further withering of imperial power. The settlement at the end of the Thirty Years' War (see pp.168–169) in 1648 gave the German states almost complete independence, and the forced abdication of the last emperor, the Habsburg Francis II, in 1806 ended a defunct institution.

ORIGINS OF THE EMPIRE

Charlemagne's coronation in 800 was the first occasion a ruler was crowned "Emperor of the Romans." After his death in 814, civil wars and partitions in 843 and 870 led to the emergence of Frankish-controlled kingdoms based in France, Italy, and Germany. The last of these became the core of the Holy Roman Empire.

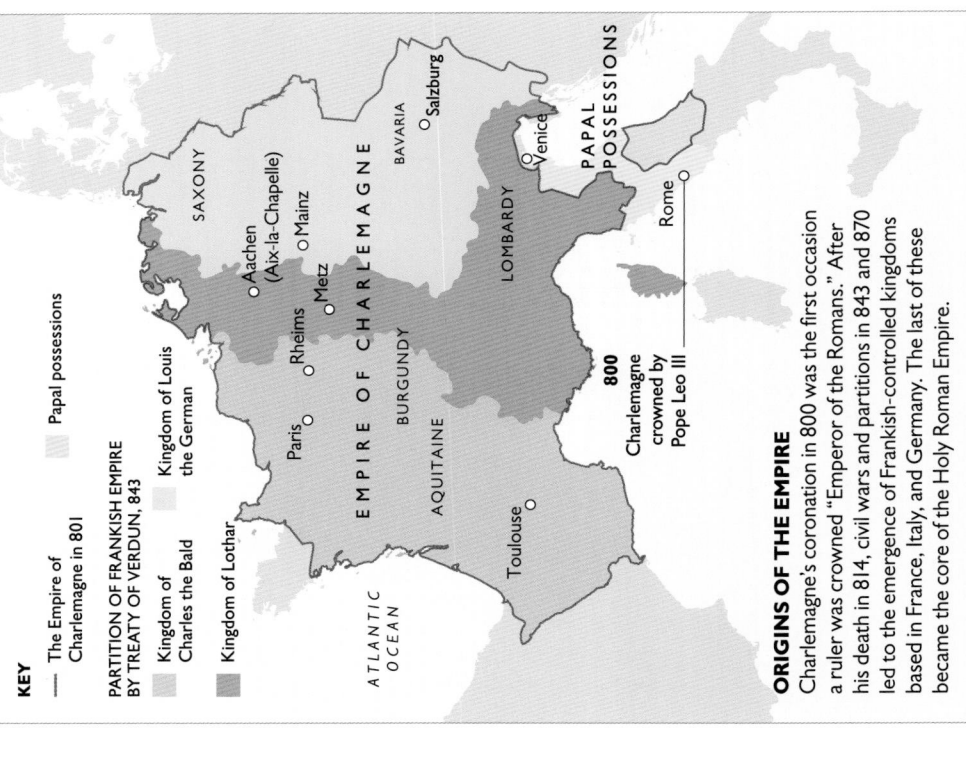

KEY

— The Empire of Charlemagne in 801

▨ Papal possessions

PARTITION OF FRANKISH EMPIRE BY TREATY OF VERDUN, 843

▢ Kingdom of Charles the Bald

▢ Kingdom of Louis the German

▨ Kingdom of Lothar

800
Charlemagne crowned by Pope Leo III

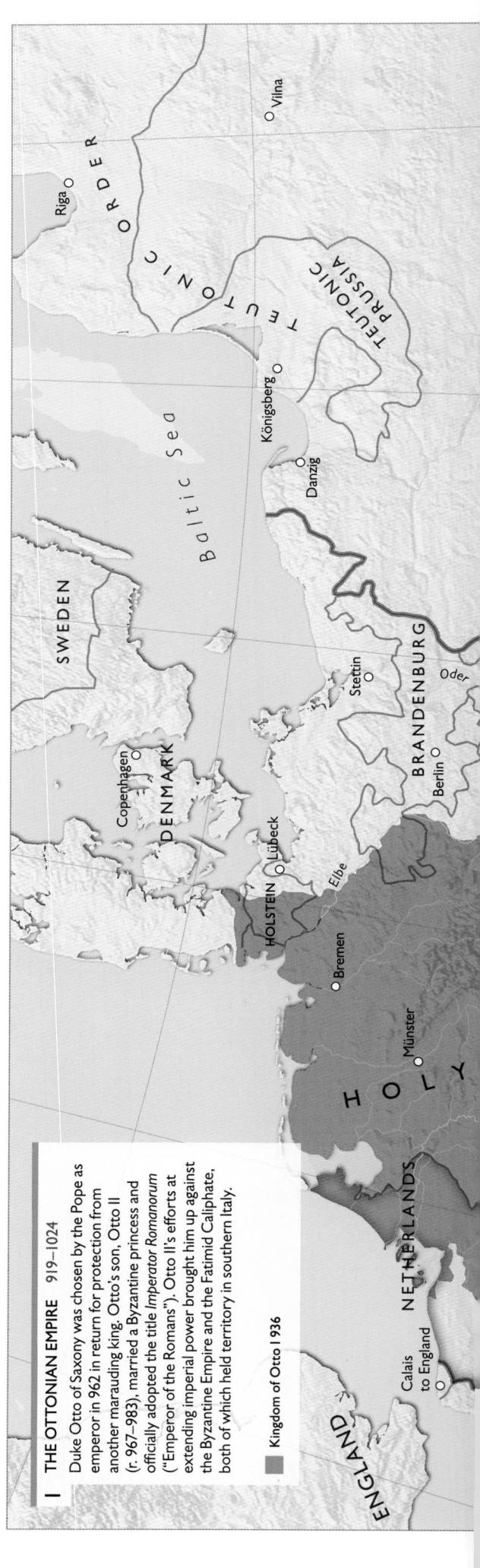

1 THE OTTONIAN EMPIRE 919–1024

Duke Otto of Saxony was chosen by the Pope as emperor in 962 in return for protection from another marauding king. Otto's son, Otto II (r. 967–983), married a Byzantine princess and officially adopted the title *Imperator Romanorum* ("Emperor of the Romans"). Otto II's efforts at extending imperial power brought him up against the Byzantine Empire and the Fatimid Caliphate, both of which held territory in southern Italy.

▨ Kingdom of Otto I 936

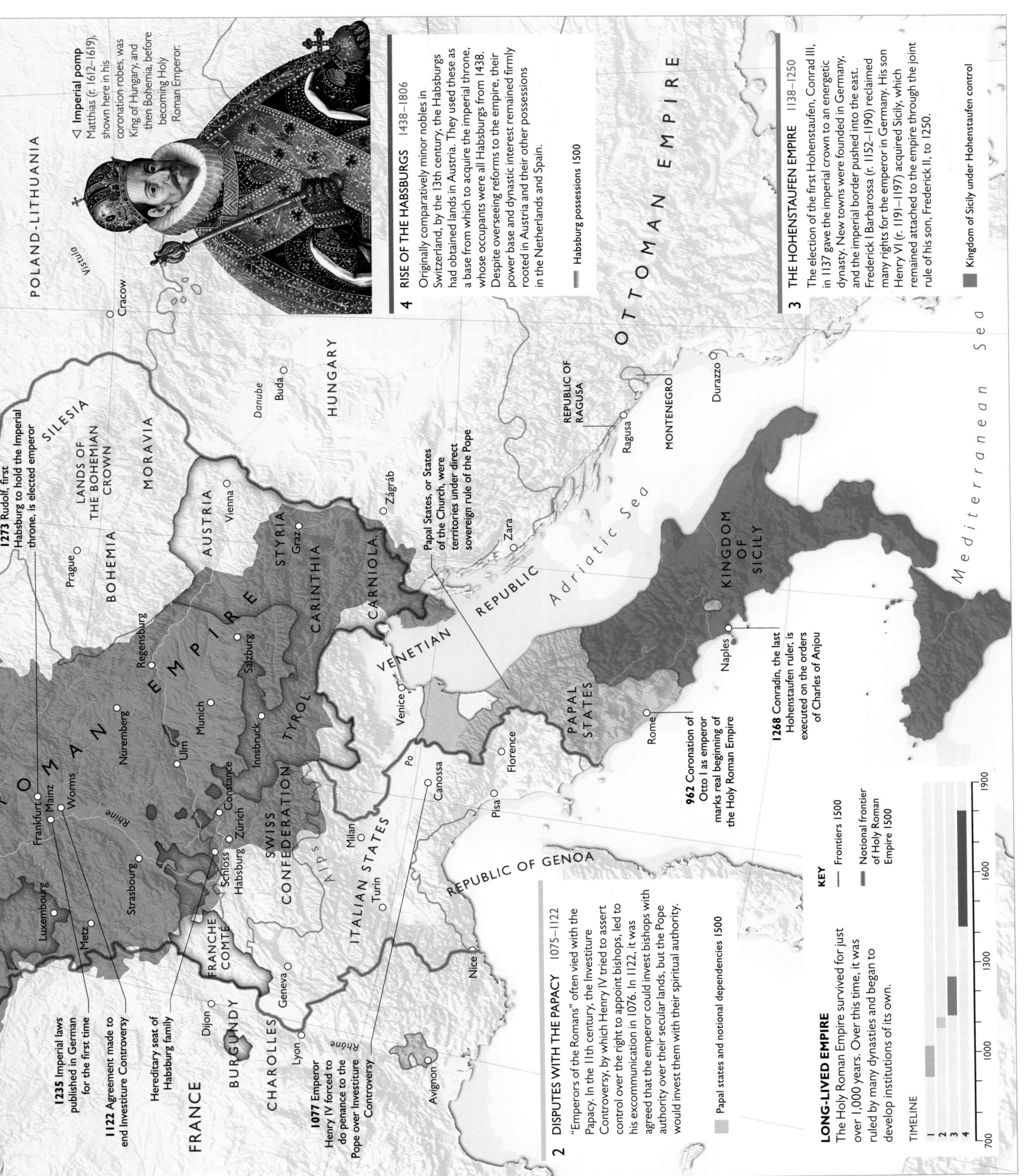

◁ **Imperial pomp**
Matthias (r. 1612–1619), shown here in his coronation robes, was King of Hungary, and then Bohemia, before becoming Holy Roman Emperor.

4 RISE OF THE HABSBURGS 1438–1806

Originally comparatively minor nobles in Switzerland, by the 13th century, the Habsburgs had obtained lands in Austria. They used these as a base from which to acquire the imperial throne, whose occupants were all Habsburgs from 1438. Despite overseeing reforms to the empire, their power base and dynastic interest remained firmly rooted in Austria and their other possessions in the Netherlands and Spain.

▬ Habsburg possessions 1500

3 THE HOHENSTAUFEN EMPIRE 1138–1250

The election of the first Hohenstaufen, Conrad III, in 1137 gave the imperial crown to an energetic dynasty. New towns were founded in Germany, and the imperial border pushed into the east. Frederick I Barbarossa (r. 1152–1190) reclaimed many rights for the emperor in Germany. His son Henry VI (r. 1191–1197) acquired Sicily, which remained attached to the empire through the joint rule of his son, Frederick II, to 1250.

▬ Kingdom of Sicily under Hohenstaufen control

POLAND–LITHUANIA

Vistula

Cracow

SILESIA

LANDS OF THE BOHEMIAN CROWN

MORAVIA

BOHEMIA

Prague

Danube

Buda

HUNGARY

AUSTRIA

Vienna

Zágráb

STYRIA

Graz

CARINTHIA

CARNIOLA

1273 Rudolf, first Habsburg to hold the Imperial throne, is elected emperor

R O M A N   E M P I R E

Regensburg

Salzburg

Innsbruck

TYROL

Zara

Ragusa

MONTENEGRO

REPUBLIC OF RAGUSA

Durazzo

Papal States, or States of the Church, were territories under direct sovereign rule of the Pope

VENETIAN REPUBLIC

Venice

Adriatic Sea

O T T O M A N   E M P I R E

Nuremberg

Munich

Ulm

FRANKFURT

Frankfurt

Mainz

Worms

1235 Imperial laws published in German for the first time

1122 Agreement made to end Investiture Controversy

Hereditary seat of Habsburg family

Strasbourg

Metz

Luxembourg

FRANCE

Rhine

Schloss Habsburg

Constance

Zürich

SWISS CONFEDERATION

Alps

Milan

Po

Turin

ITALIAN STATES

Florence

Pisa

Canossa

PAPAL STATES

Rome

Naples

KINGDOM OF SICILY

Mediterranean Sea

962 Coronation of Otto I as emperor marks real beginning of the Holy Roman Empire

1268 Conradin, the last Hohenstaufen ruler, is executed on the orders of Charles of Anjou

Dijon

BURGUNDY

CHAROLLES

Geneva

Lyon

Rhône

Avignon

Nice

REPUBLIC OF GENOA

FRANCHE COMTÉ

1077 Emperor Henry IV forced to do penance to the Pope over Investiture Controversy

2 DISPUTES WITH THE PAPACY 1075–1122

"Emperors of the Romans" often vied with the Papacy. In the 11th century, the Investiture Controversy, by which Henry IV tried to assert control over the right to appoint bishops, led to his excommunication in 1076. In 1122, it was agreed that the emperor could invest bishops with authority over their secular lands, but the Pope would invest them with their spiritual authority.

▬ Papal states and notional dependencies 1500

LONG-LIVED EMPIRE

The Holy Roman Empire survived for just over 1,000 years. Over this time, it was ruled by many dynasties and began to develop institutions of its own.

KEY

— Frontiers 1500

▬ Notional frontier of Holy Roman Empire 1500

TIMELINE

700 1000 1300 1600 1900

1
2
3
4

RISE OF THE OTTOMANS

In the late 13th century, the Ottoman Turks were one of several emirates fighting on the borders of the Byzantine Empire. By 1500, they had conquered much of Anatolia and parts of the Balkans and had taken Constantinople. Their sultanate stretched from Hungary to Mesopotamia.

As the Byzantine Empire weakened in the 11th century, new Muslim groups surged into Anatolia, principal among them the Seljuk Turks. Within a century, they, too, had fragmented, leaving a large number of small, competing Islamic states. In the 1290s, one of them—the Ottomans—took advantage of their position right against the Byzantine border to expand and attract warriors eager for glory.

By the 1350s, Ottoman armies had crossed into Europe; they soon occupied most of what was left of Byzantine territory, defeating Serbia, Bulgaria, and Hungary, the main Christian principalities of the Balkans. In 1402, the Ottomans suffered a defeat by the Mongols, but they soon recovered and, in 1453, Sultan Mehmed II seized the prize of Constantinople, the Byzantine capital. From there, the Ottoman sultans ruled and, over the next two centuries, continued to expand their domain into a huge multinational empire. Eventually, however, the Ottoman expansion was brought to an end by the Safavids in Persia and the Habsburgs in Europe (see pp.172–173).

RISE OF THE OTTOMAN EMPIRE

From their origins as a small emirate in northwest Anatolia around 1300, the Ottomans rose rapidly, conquering most of the Byzantine Empire's possessions in Asia by 1400. Within 60 years, they had captured Constantinople and overrun most of the Balkans.

KEY
- Holy Roman Empire c. 1480
- Frontiers in 1481
- Siege, with date

TIMELINE

1200 — 1300 — 1400 — 1500

◁ **Mehmed II**
This Turkish miniature from around 1585 shows the great sultan, who conquered Constantinople and extended the Ottoman Empire.

THE SELJUKS

Even before the Ottoman expansion, Byzantine control over Anatolia had been weakened by the Seljuks, a Turkic people who had migrated west from central Asia. They defeated the Byzantines at Manzikert in 1071, after which they overran most of Anatolia and established the Sultanate of Rum, which survived until 1308.

KEY
- Byzantine frontier in Asia c. 1025
- Byzantine Empire 1095
- Seljuk Empire c. 1095
- Byzantine territory overrun by Seljuks by 1095
- Other Muslim dynasty
- Battle

3 OTTOMANS IN THE BALKANS 1354–1389

In 1354, the Ottomans crossed over to Gallipoli, establishing a foothold in Europe. Under Murad I, they occupied much of Thrace, making Edirne (Adrianople) their new capital. The defeat of Serbia at the Battle of Kosovo (1389) marked the beginning of Ottoman supremacy in the Balkans.

- Conquests of Murad I 1362–1389
- Battle
- Ottomans enter Europe 1354
- Ottoman capital 1369

2 THE CONQUEST OF ANATOLIA 1326–1402

Under Orhan, the Ottomans conquered most of the remaining Byzantine cities in northwest Anatolia, leaving only isolated outposts. Anatolia was later unified under Ottoman control by Orhan's grandson (the son of Murad I), Bayezid I, who conquered the beyliks in the southwest soon after he became sultan in 1389.

- Conquests of Orhan 1326–1362
- Conquests of Bayezid I 1389–1402

4 MONGOL THREAT 1400–1405

In 1400–1401, the Mongol prince Timur, angered by Bayezid I's demands for tribute from one of his vassals, invaded the Ottoman Empire. At Ankara in 1402, Timur crushed the Ottomans, causing many of the former beyliks of Anatolia to break away from Ottoman rule. Only Timur's death in 1405 saved the Ottomans from further losses.

△△ Ottoman eastern frontier following Timur's invasion 1402

⚔ Battle

5 THE SIEGE OF CONSTANTINOPLE 1451–1453

By the time Mehmed II became Ottoman sultan in 1451, the Byzantine Empire consisted of little more than the city of Constantinople. Mehmed throttled the city's supply lines and laid siege to it in April 1453. The Byzantine emperor Constantine XI resisted for nearly 8 weeks before the Ottomans finally took the city. The Byzantine Empire was at an end, and the Ottoman Empire had a new capital.

★ Ottoman capital 1453

6 CONQUESTS OF MEHMED II 1460–1481

Having captured Constantinople, Mehmed II dealt with the remaining fragments of the Byzantine Empire, capturing Morea in 1460 and the breakaway Empire of Trebizond in 1461. The defeat of Bosnia in 1463 and the reduction of Wallachia and Moldavia to vassal status meant that resistance to Ottoman rule in the Balkans was confined to a few scattered fortresses and the Venetian possessions in Greece and along the Adriatic coast.

Vassal of Ottoman Empire by 1481
Further Ottoman conquest by 1481
Under Venetian control c. 1460

1 THE ORIGINS OF THE OTTOMAN EMPIRE 1280–1326

After the collapse of the Seljuk Empire, western Anatolia was divided into a number of competing states, known as beyliks. One of them, based around the small town of Söğüt, began to expand in the 1280s under Osman. His son, Orhan, captured the important Byzantine town of Bursa in 1326 and made it his capital. From here, he conquered much of the rest of Anatolia and sent the first Ottoman army into Europe.

Ottoman territory 1326
★ Ottoman capital 1326
Anatolian beyliks c. 1300

THE RECONQUISTA

Islamic armies overran the Iberian peninsula in the early 8th century. Christian rulers slowly reversed this process in the Reconquista ("reconquest"), which culminated with the fall of Granada in 1492 and the expulsion of most of Spain's Muslim population.

The Visigothic kingdom of Spain rapidly fell to an Islamic army that crossed from Muslim-held North Africa in 711, and by 718, only a small area in the remote Asturian mountains remained unconquered. The subsequent reconquest of the Muslim-ruled parts of Spain and Portugal (al-Andalus) by Christian states took nearly eight centuries. First, the far northeast was recaptured by the armies of the Frankish ruler Charlemagne, rather than by the comparatively weak Spanish Christian kingdoms. Gradually, though, Castile and Leon in the west and Navarre and Aragon in the east gathered strength and pushed southward.

The emergence of crusading ideology from the late 11th century accelerated the Reconquista, as Christian armies were now infused with the sense of fighting a religiously justified war. The political fragmentation of the Umayyad Caliphate also weakened the Muslim hold on central Spain, leading to the loss of the strategic city of Toledo in 1085. An influx of new groups from North Africa—first the Almoravids and then the Almohads—reunited al-Andalus, but a crushing defeat by Alfonso VIII of Castile in 1212 reduced the Muslim-held area to Granada. By then, a much shorter process of reconquest had taken place in Portugal.

Granada survived as an Islamic emirate until 1492, when Ferdinand II of Aragon and Isabella of Castile sent an army to besiege the town. Its fall, after a brief resistance, marked the end of Islamic Spain and the completion of the Reconquista.

THE INQUISITION
THE FIGHT AGAINST HERESY IN SPAIN

For centuries, Muslims, Jews, and Christians coexisted in Spain, but by the late 14th century, a desire for religious unity grew in the country. Jews and Muslims were forcibly converted to Christianity, and the converts became targets for persecution. In 1478, Pope Sixtus IV authorized the establishment of the Inquisition, which led to public tests of faith and execution of "heretics." The accused were dressed up and paraded in an Auto da fe ceremony (right) while their guilt and punishment were decided.

1 ORIGINS OF THE RECONQUISTA 711–900

In 711, an Arab-Berber army led by Tariq ibn Ziyad was sent by the Umayyad caliph into Spain, where it defeated Roderick, the Visigothic king. Within 5 years, Muslim forces had conquered all but the northern fringes of Spain. Their advance was halted around 718, when Asturian chieftain Pelayo defeated a Muslim army at Covadonga. Gradually, the Asturian kingdom consolidated as the nucleus of Christian resistance.

Limit of Umayyad Caliphate 732

2 CHRISTIAN ADVANCES 1030–1080

By the early 11th century, the ruling Umayyad Caliphate had broken down into dozens of small emirates (or taifas). The taifas were less able to resist Christian advances, particularly those of the kingdoms of Léon and Castile in the west and Aragon in the east. Many taifas were forced to pay tribute to the Christian kingdoms.

3 THE ALMORAVIDS 1086–1165

In 1085, Alfonso VI of Léon-Castile captured Toledo, the old capital of Visigothic Spain, leaving Islamic Spain vulnerable to Christian advances. In desperation, the rulers of the taifas appealed to Yusuf, the emir of the Almoravids, a strict Islamic sect from North Africa. He defeated Alfonso at Sagrajas and swept through central and eastern Spain, undoing many recent Christian advances.

→ Almoravid campaigns 1086–1115
▬ Frontier of Almoravid Empire 1115

4 THE ALMOHADS 1165–1228

In 1165, an African Muslim group, the Almohads, entered Spain and renewed Islamic opposition to Christian encroachments. In 1195, they won a stunning victory against Alfonso VIII of Castile at Alarcos, opening up southern Spain to Almohad dominance. In 1212, Alfonso struck back, destroying the Almohad army at Las Navas de Tolosa and weakening the Muslims' military capacity.

▬ Frontier of Almohad Empire 1180

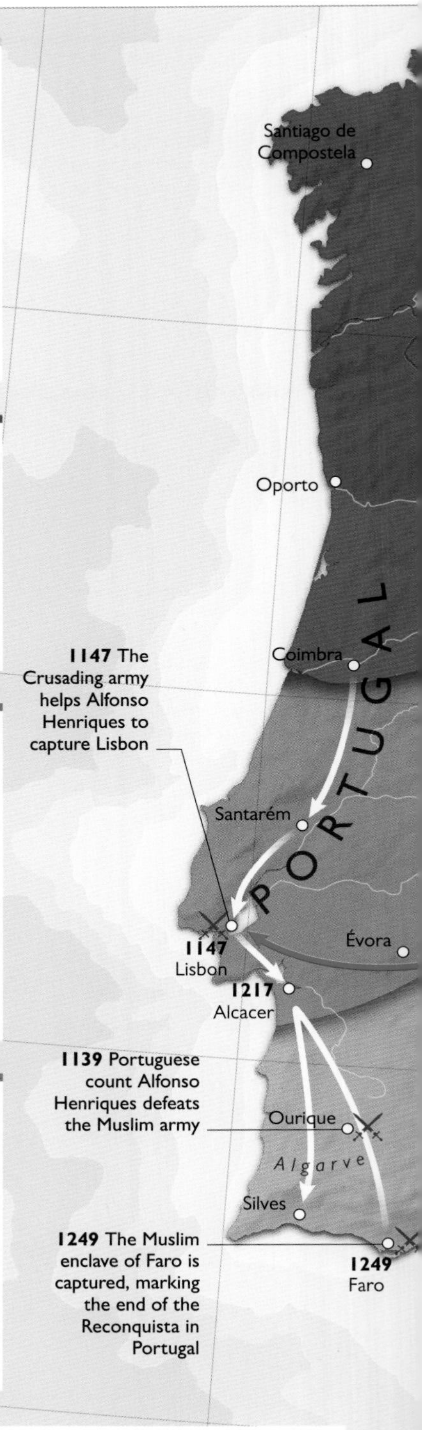

Santiago de Compostela

Oporto

PORTUGAL

Coimbra

1147 The Crusading army helps Alfonso Henriques to capture Lisbon

Santarém

1147 Lisbon

Évora

1217 Alcacer

1139 Portuguese count Alfonso Henriques defeats the Muslim army

Ourique

Algarve

Silves

1249 The Muslim enclave of Faro is captured, marking the end of the Reconquista in Portugal

1249 Faro

THE RECONQUEST OF SPAIN

The Reconquista, by which the Christian kingdoms of Spain reconquered the Iberian Peninsula, took over 700 years to complete. Progress was slowest when the Muslims united around movements such as the Almoravids and Almohads.

KEY

✕ Muslim victory with date
✕ Christian victory with date

EXTENSION OF CHRISTIAN CONTROL

By 1030
By 1115
By 1180
By 1280
By 1492
— Frontiers 1493

TIMELINE

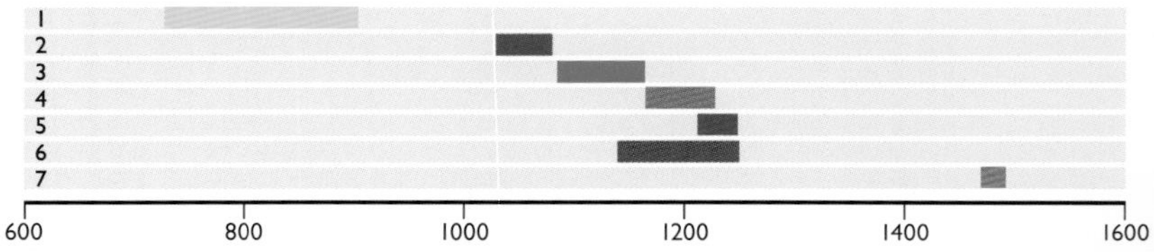

1
2
3
4
5
6
7

600   800   1000   1200   1400   1600

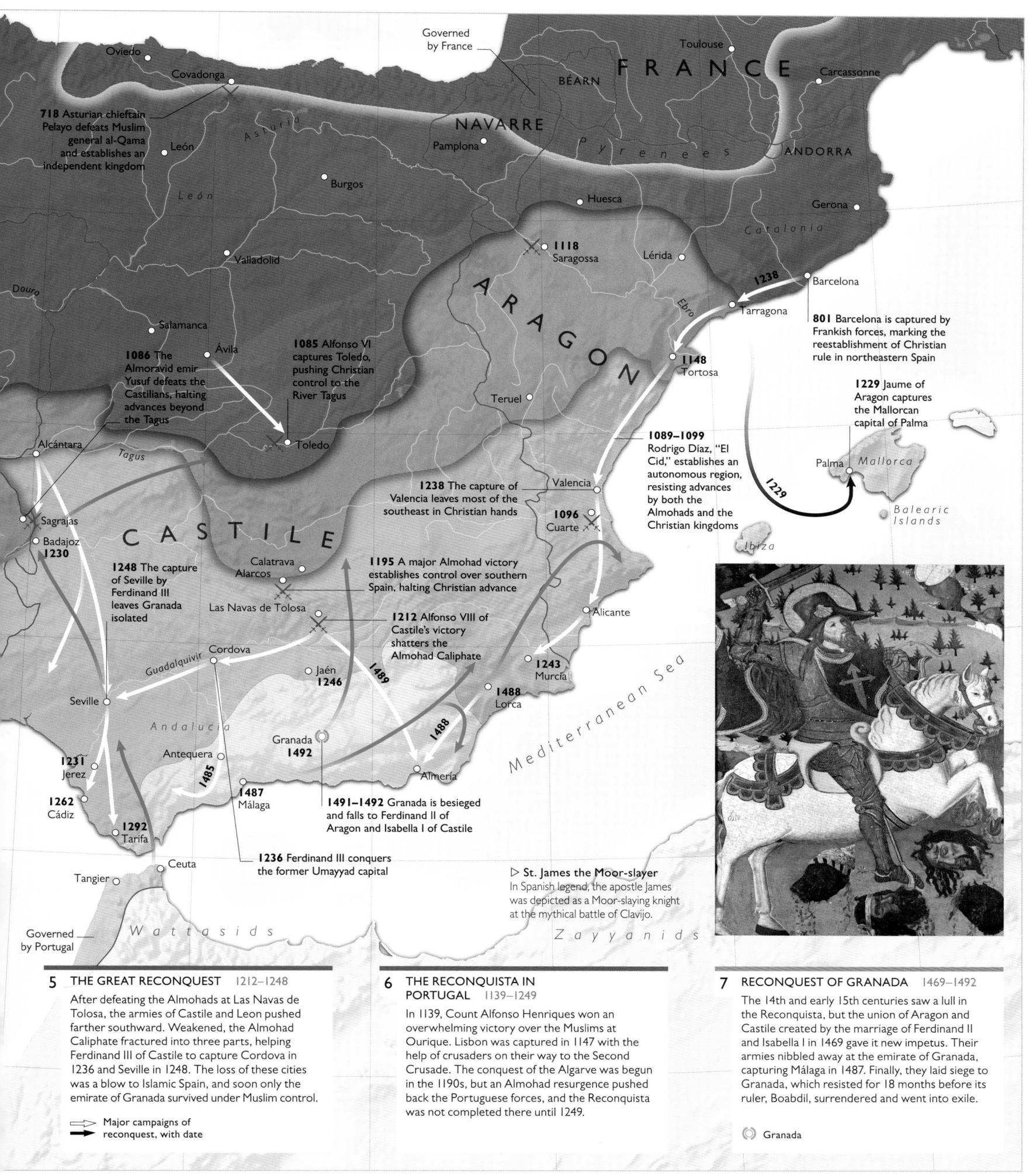

718 Asturian chieftain Pelayo defeats Muslim general al-Qama and establishes an independent kingdom

Governed by France

801 Barcelona is captured by Frankish forces, marking the reestablishment of Christian rule in northeastern Spain

1086 The Almoravid emir Yusuf defeats the Castilians, halting advances beyond the Tagus

1085 Alfonso VI captures Toledo, pushing Christian control to the River Tagus

1118 Saragossa

1238 Tarragona

1148 Tortosa

1229 Jaume of Aragon captures the Mallorcan capital of Palma

1089–1099 Rodrigo Díaz, "El Cid," establishes an autonomous region, resisting advances by both the Almohads and the Christian kingdoms

1238 The capture of Valencia leaves most of the southeast in Christian hands

1096 Cuarte

1248 The capture of Seville by Ferdinand III leaves Granada isolated

1195 A major Almohad victory establishes control over southern Spain, halting Christian advance

1212 Alfonso VIII of Castile's victory shatters the Almohad Caliphate

Las Navas de Tolosa

Calatrava
Alarcos

Cordova

1243 Murcia

1488 Lorca

Jaén **1246**

Granada **1492**

Antequera

1231 Jerez

1262 Cádiz

1292 Tarifa

Almería

1487 Málaga

1491–1492 Granada is besieged and falls to Ferdinand II of Aragon and Isabella I of Castile

1236 Ferdinand III conquers the former Umayyad capital

Badajoz **1230**
Sagrajas
Alcántara

Ceuta

Tangier

Governed by Portugal

Wattasids

Zayyanids

▷ **St. James the Moor-slayer**
In Spanish legend, the apostle James was depicted as a Moor-slaying knight at the mythical battle of Clavijo.

FRANCE
Toulouse
Carcassonne
BÉARN
NAVARRE
ANDORRA
Pyrenees
Oviedo
Covadonga
León
Burgos
Pamplona
Huesca
Gerona
Catalonia
Valladolid
Salamanca
Ávila
Lérida
Barcelona
Ebro
ARAGON
Teruel
Valencia
Toledo
Tagus
CASTILE
Guadalquivir
Seville
Andalucía
Alicante
Palma
Mallorca
Balearic Islands
Ibiza
Mediterranean Sea
Douro
Asturias
León

---

5 THE GREAT RECONQUEST 1212–1248

After defeating the Almohads at Las Navas de Tolosa, the armies of Castile and Leon pushed farther southward. Weakened, the Almohad Caliphate fractured into three parts, helping Ferdinand III of Castile to capture Cordova in 1236 and Seville in 1248. The loss of these cities was a blow to Islamic Spain, and soon only the emirate of Granada survived under Muslim control.

→ Major campaigns of reconquest, with date

6 THE RECONQUISTA IN PORTUGAL 1139–1249

In 1139, Count Alfonso Henriques won an overwhelming victory over the Muslims at Ourique. Lisbon was captured in 1147 with the help of crusaders on their way to the Second Crusade. The conquest of the Algarve was begun in the 1190s, but an Almohad resurgence pushed back the Portuguese forces, and the Reconquista was not completed there until 1249.

7 RECONQUEST OF GRANADA 1469–1492

The 14th and early 15th centuries saw a lull in the Reconquista, but the union of Aragon and Castile created by the marriage of Ferdinand II and Isabella I in 1469 gave it new impetus. Their armies nibbled away at the emirate of Granada, capturing Málaga in 1487. Finally, they laid siege to Granada, which resisted for 18 months before its ruler, Boabdil, surrendered and went into exile.

◎ Granada

MEDIEVAL EAST ASIA

China was the dominant power in east Asia in the 6th–15th centuries. Its form of government was imitated widely in the region, from Japan to Korea and Vietnam. However, just like the other states of the period, China, too, suffered long periods of disunity and conquest by foreign powers.

In China, the division that followed the collapse of the Han Dynasty in 220 ended only when the Sui Dynasty captured Nanjing, the capital of six successive Southern dynasties, in 589. The Sui, and their successors the Tang, intervened repeatedly in neighboring states, and Chinese rule expanded deep into central Asia. Although economically strong, Tang rule was undermined by fighting among factions, a defeat at the hands of an Arab army in 751, and a major revolt 4 years later. A weakened Tang Dynasty limped on until 907, when China fell apart again, to be restored in 960 by the Song, whose rule saw a period of economic and technological progress. However, by 1127, the Jurchen, a nomadic group from the north, had reduced the Song to a southern kingdom based in Nanjing. This in turn fell in 1251–1279 to the Mongols, whose leader

◁ **Off to work**
A merchant rides a camel in this Tang-era terracotta figurine. Bactrian camels—hardy species capable of carrying heavy loads—were ideal for the Silk Road trade through central Asia.

▷ **Symbol of peace**
This 11th-century wooden statue from Japan shows a seated Buddha. The hand gesture symbolizes peace and the protection of believers from fear. Buddhism was the state religion during the Nara period.

Genghis Khan established the Yuan, the first non-Chinese dynasty to rule China. In time, Mongol rule weakened, and in 1368, the rebel general Zhu Yuanzhang captured Beijing, declaring himself the first emperor of the Ming Dynasty.

Japan and Korea

A centralized Japanese state emerged during the Nara period (710–794), with a Chinese-style bureaucracy, a system of provinces, and the dominance of Buddhism. In 794, the imperial court moved to Heian (modern-day Kyoto) to reduce the influence of Buddhist monks, but over time, powerful aristocratic families such as the Minamoto and Taira took real power away from the emperor. Rivalry between them led to the Genpei War in 1180–1185, ending with the defeat of the Taira and the establishment of a Minamoto military government, or shogunate, at Kamakura. The emperors became symbolic leaders—although Emperor Go-Daigo did spark a revolt in 1331, in an attempt to assert imperial power. The shoguns, first the Kamakura and then the Muromachi, became the real rulers. By the mid-15th century, however, the shogunate in turn lost power to the daimyo, local warlords, as Japan fragmented into a series of warring statelets.

POWER SHIFTS IN EAST ASIA

The medieval period saw the process of state formation in Southeast Asia and Japan, both of which were strongly influenced by Chinese models of government and by Buddhism. In China itself, a period of disunity was followed by the reestablishment of strong central control under the Tang and Song Dynasties. India, in contrast, fragmented after the collapse of the Gupta Empire in the 6th century, and many separate dynasties ruled the north and south of the subcontinent.

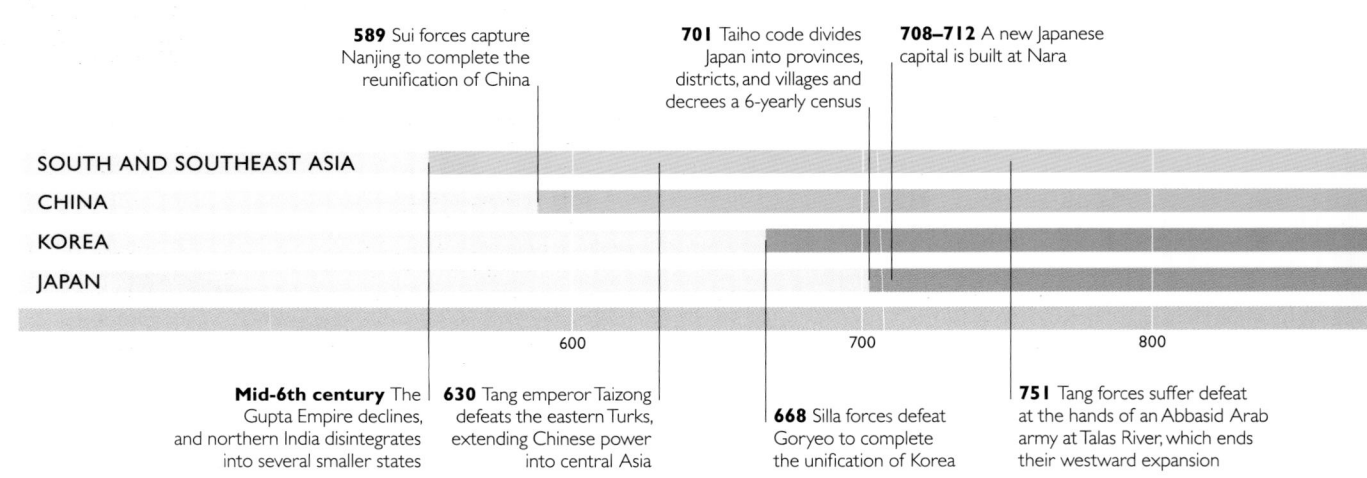

589 Sui forces capture Nanjing to complete the reunification of China

701 Taiho code divides Japan into provinces, districts, and villages and decrees a 6-yearly census

708–712 A new Japanese capital is built at Nara

SOUTH AND SOUTHEAST ASIA
CHINA
KOREA
JAPAN

600　　700　　800

Mid-6th century The Gupta Empire declines, and northern India disintegrates into several smaller states

630 Tang emperor Taizong defeats the eastern Turks, extending Chinese power into central Asia

668 Silla forces defeat Goryeo to complete the unification of Korea

751 Tang forces suffer defeat at the hands of an Abbasid Arab army at Talas River, which ends their westward expansion

◁ **Heavenly dancers**
This intricate carving from the 12th-century Angkor Wat temple complex in Cambodia depicts four *apsaras*, or heavenly dancers, who provided entertainment to gods and granted favors to humans in the heaven of the Hindu god Indra.

After the departure of Chinese administrators in 313, the Korean peninsula was divided between three warring states: Goryeo, Silla, and Paekche. China tried to reconquer Korea, but Silla exploited Chinese attacks on the other two states to reunite Korea under its rule in 668. Unified Silla installed a Chinese-style bureaucracy but collapsed amid a wave of revolts around 900. In 935, Wang Kon founded the Goryeo Dynasty, reuniting Korea, but Mongol invasions from 1231 reduced Korea to a vassal (subordinate) state, until King Kongmin reasserted its independence in 1356. Chinese pressure continued until, in 1388, Yi Song-gye defeated the Ming and established the Choson Dynasty, which ruled Korea until 1910.

Kingdoms of Southeast Asia
The period from the 9th to the 11th centuries saw a series of strong territorial states being established in Southeast Asia. The Pagan kingdom under Anawrahta united most of what is now Myanmar, while the Angkor kingdom (in today's Cambodia) under Suryavarman II reached the height of its power. In 1181, the Angkor Empire under Jayavarman VII defeated the Champa Empire, which had ruled southern

> *"Baekje [Paekche] is at full moon, Silla is at half moon."*
>
> PROPHECY PREDICTING THE RISE OF SILLA, 669

Cambodia since the 7th century and had also sacked Angkor in 1177. However, the Southeast Asian kingdoms suffered under Mongol attacks, which weakened Pagan and nearly defeated the Vietnamese kingdom of Dai Viet. By the late 15th century, the great medieval kingdoms were crumbling: the Champa capital Vijaya was captured by Dai Viet, and Angkor was sacked by the Thai kingdom of Ayutthaya.

Smaller states had risen in northern India after the fall of the Gupta Empire in the mid-6th century. These were united by Harsha Vardhen of the Pushyabhuti Dynasty, but his kingdom fell apart after his murder in 647. It was only after the invasion of Muhammad of Ghur in 1192 and the founding of the Delhi Sultanate in 1206 that northern India was reunited once more. The south of India developed separately; the Chola Empire expanded in the 10th–11th centuries, occupying northern Sri Lanka and ports along the Malay peninsula, but it collapsed in the 12th century. The kingdom of Vijayanagara, founded in 1336, dominated southern India until its conquest by the Mughals in the 17th century.

▽ **Divine architecture**
The 10th-century Mukteshwar Temple in Odisha, southern India, forms part of a larger complex of temples there. Dedicated to the Hindu god Shiva, it was built under the Somavanshi Dynasty, which ruled parts of southeastern India between the 9th and 12th centuries.

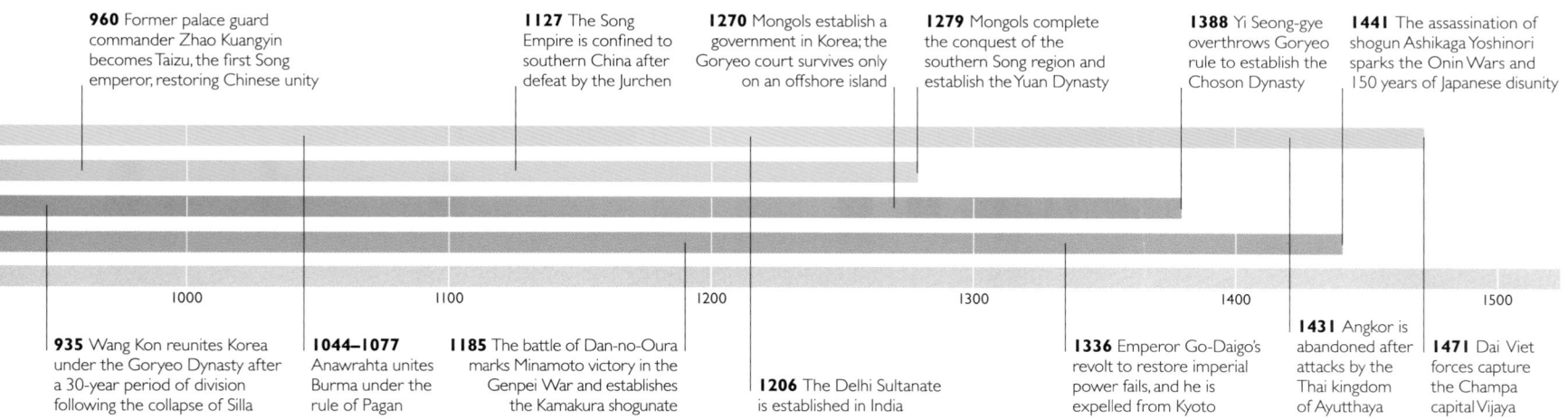

960 Former palace guard commander Zhao Kuangyin becomes Taizu, the first Song emperor, restoring Chinese unity

1127 The Song Empire is confined to southern China after defeat by the Jurchen

1270 Mongols establish a government in Korea; the Goryeo court survives only on an offshore island

1279 Mongols complete the conquest of the southern Song region and establish the Yuan Dynasty

1388 Yi Seong-gye overthrows Goryeo rule to establish the Choson Dynasty

1441 The assassination of shogun Ashikaga Yoshinori sparks the Onin Wars and 150 years of Japanese disunity

1000   1100   1200   1300   1400   1500

935 Wang Kon reunites Korea under the Goryeo Dynasty after a 30-year period of division following the collapse of Silla

1044–1077 Anawrahta unites Burma under the rule of Pagan

1185 The battle of Dan-no-Oura marks Minamoto victory in the Genpei War and establishes the Kamakura shogunate

1206 The Delhi Sultanate is established in India

1336 Emperor Go-Daigo's revolt to restore imperial power fails, and he is expelled from Kyoto

1431 Angkor is abandoned after attacks by the Thai kingdom of Ayutthaya

1471 Dai Viet forces capture the Champa capital Vijaya

TANG AND SONG CHINA

After a long period of disunity following the fall of the Han Dynasty, China was reunited under the Sui and then the Tang and Song Dynasties. China prospered, and Chinese power prevailed across central Asia before the Song were finally conquered by the Mongols.

Following the end of the Han Dynasty in 220 CE, China broke apart. The Sui Dynasty (581–618) reunified China, but after a rebellion in 618, Li Yuan took the throne. He and his son, Li Shimin, established the Tang Dynasty, enacting reforms that brought order to the provinces of China. In 639, Li Shimin (by now Emperor Taizong) sent armies into Turkestan, establishing Tang control over a string of strategic trading settlements, such as Dunhuang.

In 755, the dynasty was weakened by a revolt led by general An Lushan; although imperial forces regained control, a series of weak rulers later led to the Tang's collapse in 907. A dozen rival kingdoms vied for power until the Song Dynasty subdued the others and established rule over the whole country by 960. In this resurgent China, trade guilds emerged, paper money was adopted on a large scale, and inventions such as gunpowder and the magnetic compass came into widespread use. By the early 12th century, the dynasty had begun to weaken; nomadic Jurchen tribes conquered the north of China, confining the Song to the south of their former territory.

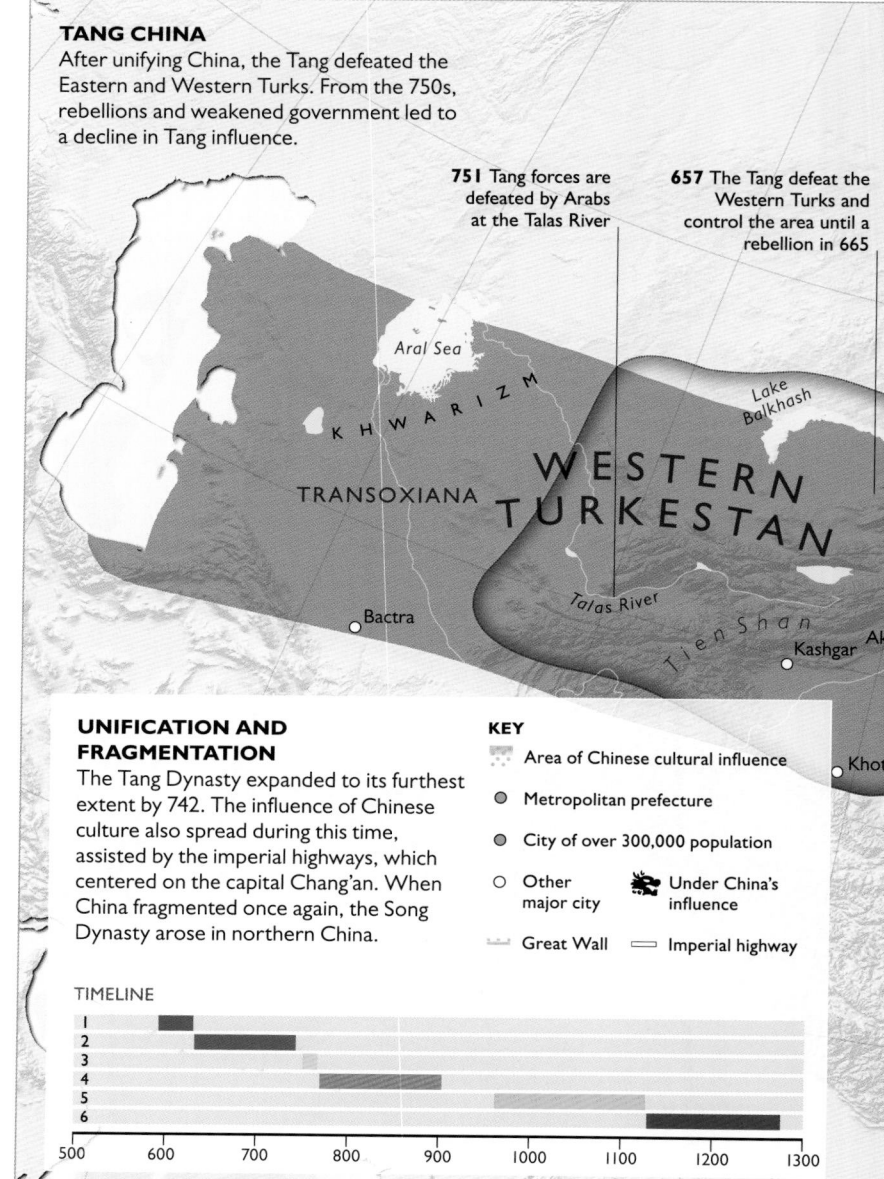

TANG CHINA

After unifying China, the Tang defeated the Eastern and Western Turks. From the 750s, rebellions and weakened government led to a decline in Tang influence.

751 Tang forces are defeated by Arabs at the Talas River

657 The Tang defeat the Western Turks and control the area until a rebellion in 665

UNIFICATION AND FRAGMENTATION

The Tang Dynasty expanded to its furthest extent by 742. The influence of Chinese culture also spread during this time, assisted by the imperial highways, which centered on the capital Chang'an. When China fragmented once again, the Song Dynasty arose in northern China.

KEY

- ▨ Area of Chinese cultural influence
- ● Metropolitan prefecture
- ● City of over 300,000 population
- ○ Other major city
- 🐉 Under China's influence
- ⊏⊐ Great Wall
- ⊏⊐ Imperial highway

TIMELINE

500 — 600 — 700 — 800 — 900 — 1000 — 1100 — 1200 — 1300

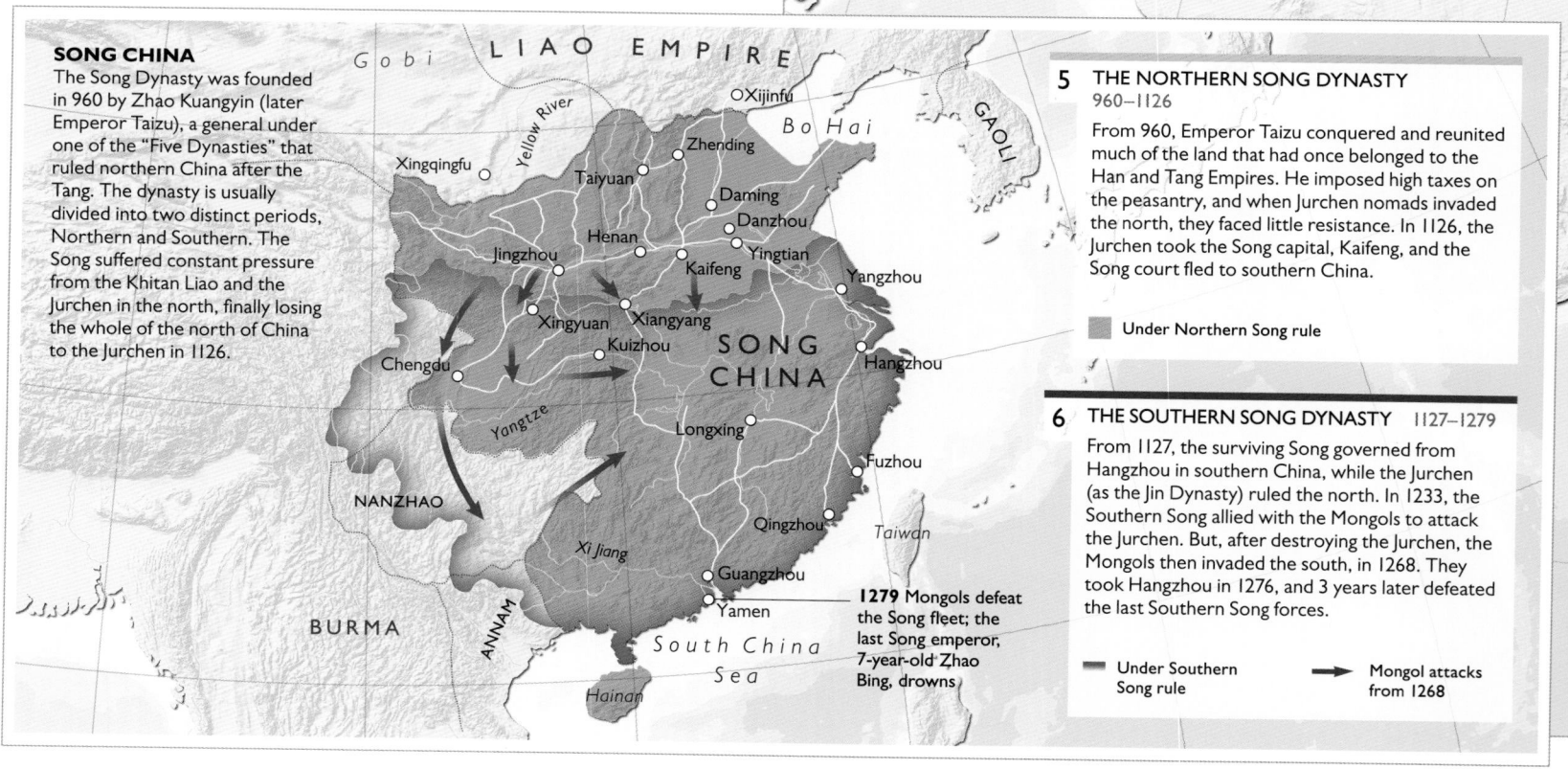

SONG CHINA

The Song Dynasty was founded in 960 by Zhao Kuangyin (later Emperor Taizu), a general under one of the "Five Dynasties" that ruled northern China after the Tang. The dynasty is usually divided into two distinct periods, Northern and Southern. The Song suffered constant pressure from the Khitan Liao and the Jurchen in the north, finally losing the whole of the north of China to the Jurchen in 1126.

1279 Mongols defeat the Song fleet; the last Song emperor, 7-year-old Zhao Bing, drowns

5 THE NORTHERN SONG DYNASTY
960–1126

From 960, Emperor Taizu conquered and reunited much of the land that had once belonged to the Han and Tang Empires. He imposed high taxes on the peasantry, and when Jurchen nomads invaded the north, they faced little resistance. In 1126, the Jurchen took the Song capital, Kaifeng, and the Song court fled to southern China.

■ Under Northern Song rule

6 THE SOUTHERN SONG DYNASTY   1127–1279

From 1127, the surviving Song governed from Hangzhou in southern China, while the Jurchen (as the Jin Dynasty) ruled the north. In 1233, the Southern Song allied with the Mongols to attack the Jurchen. But, after destroying the Jurchen, the Mongols then invaded the south, in 1268. They took Hangzhou in 1276, and 3 years later defeated the last Southern Song forces.

■ Under Southern Song rule   ➝ Mongol attacks from 1268

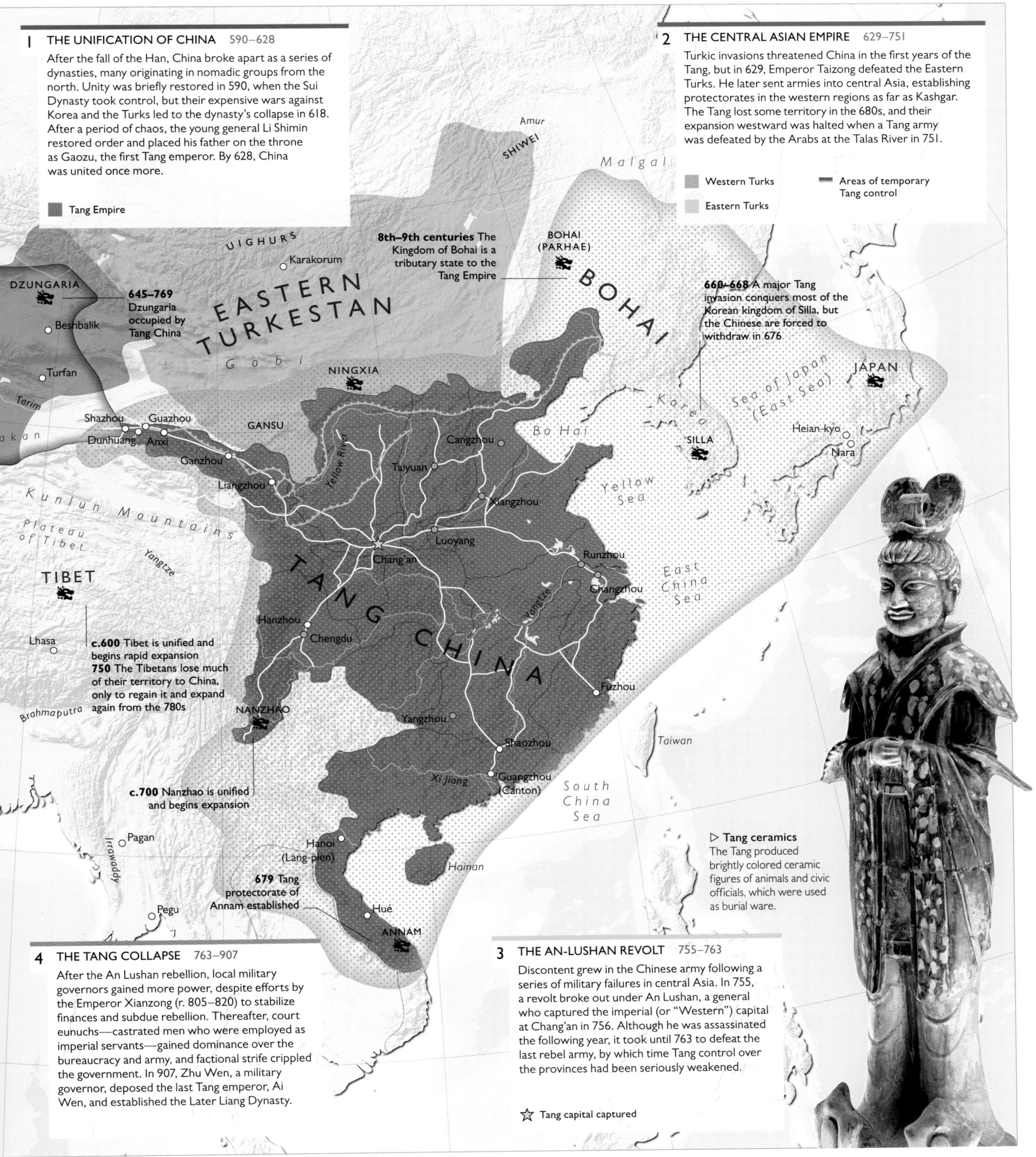

1 THE UNIFICATION OF CHINA 590–628

After the fall of the Han, China broke apart as a series of dynasties, many originating in nomadic groups from the north. Unity was briefly restored in 590, when the Sui Dynasty took control, but their expensive wars against Korea and the Turks led to the dynasty's collapse in 618. After a period of chaos, the young general Li Shimin restored order and placed his father on the throne as Gaozu, the first Tang emperor. By 628, China was united once more.

■ Tang Empire

2 THE CENTRAL ASIAN EMPIRE 629–751

Turkic invasions threatened China in the first years of the Tang, but in 629, Emperor Taizong defeated the Eastern Turks. He later sent armies into central Asia, establishing protectorates in the western regions as far as Kashgar. The Tang lost some territory in the 680s, and their expansion westward was halted when a Tang army was defeated by the Arabs at the Talas River in 751.

■ Western Turks
■ Eastern Turks
— Areas of temporary Tang control

8th–9th centuries The Kingdom of Bohai is a tributary state to the Tang Empire

645–769 Dzungaria occupied by Tang China

660–668 A major Tang invasion conquers most of the Korean kingdom of Silla, but the Chinese are forced to withdraw in 676

c.600 Tibet is unified and begins rapid expansion **750** The Tibetans lose much of their territory to China, only to regain it and expand again from the 780s

c.700 Nanzhao is unified and begins expansion

679 Tang protectorate of Annam established

▷ **Tang ceramics**
The Tang produced brightly colored ceramic figures of animals and civic officials, which were used as burial ware.

4 THE TANG COLLAPSE 763–907

After the An Lushan rebellion, local military governors gained more power, despite efforts by the Emperor Xianzong (r. 805–820) to stabilize finances and subdue rebellion. Thereafter, court eunuchs—castrated men who were employed as imperial servants—gained dominance over the bureaucracy and army, and factional strife crippled the government. In 907, Zhu Wen, a military governor, deposed the last Tang emperor, Ai Wen, and established the Later Liang Dynasty.

3 THE AN-LUSHAN REVOLT 755–763

Discontent grew in the Chinese army following a series of military failures in central Asia. In 755, a revolt broke out under An Lushan, a general who captured the imperial (or "Western") capital at Chang'an in 756. Although he was assassinated the following year, it took until 763 to defeat the last rebel army, by which time Tang control over the provinces had been seriously weakened.

☆ Tang capital captured

MEDIEVAL KOREA AND JAPAN

Korea and Japan both began developing a centralized bureaucratic monarchy in the 8th century, drawing strong influence from the Tang Dynasty of neighboring China. In addition, the cultural landscapes of both states were largely shaped by the arrival of Buddhism from China in the 4th century.

In the mid-7th century, the Korean state of Silla enlisted the military support of Tang China to defeat the rival kingdom of Koguryo and Paekche to unify the country under its leadership. After ruling for almost three centuries, Silla disintegrated in the ensuing chaos following the fall of China's Tang Dynasty in 906. Thereafter, the Goryeo state (founded in 901 by former Koguryo leaders) reunified Korea in 936 and presided over a period of economic and cultural

prosperity. However, a series of Mongol attacks from 1231 eventually resulted in Goryeo's fall and, from 1270, it became a vassal state of the Mongol Yuan Empire for the next 80 years.

In Japan, the introduction of Buddhism in 538 coincided with the fall of Yamato rule, as powerful clans and regional kingdoms fought for power. The Taiku Reforms of 646 paved the way for Japan to unify under a centralized government based on the Chinese model.

The emperors of the Nara period slowly lost power, first to the Fujiwara family in the 10th and 11th centuries, and then to the samurai, who supported a military dictatorship called the shogun. The powerful Kamakura shogunate thwarted two Mongol invasions, but it was eventually toppled by a rival clan, and thereafter power ebbed to the local daimyo, or domain lords, leading to a century-long civil war (see pp.180–181).

" … my armor and helmet were my pillow; my bow and arrows were my trade … "

YOSHITSUNE MINAMOTO, MINAMOTO GENERAL, c.1189

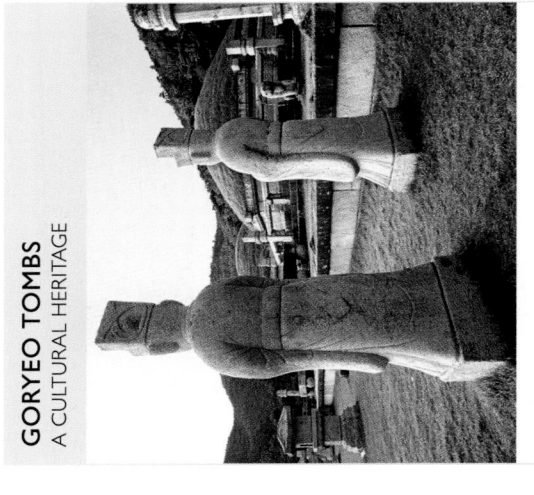

GORYEO TOMBS
A CULTURAL HERITAGE

The best-known remains of the Korean Goryeo kingdom are the tombs of its society's elites. Built of stone and covered by stone or earthen mounds, these tombs are customarily adorned with wall paintings. In the complex of tombs around Gaegyeong (modern Kaesong), the Goryeo capital, among the most famous is the Hyonjongrung Royal Tomb of King Kongmin. The twin mounds contain the remains of the monarch and his wife—the Mongolian princess Noguk.

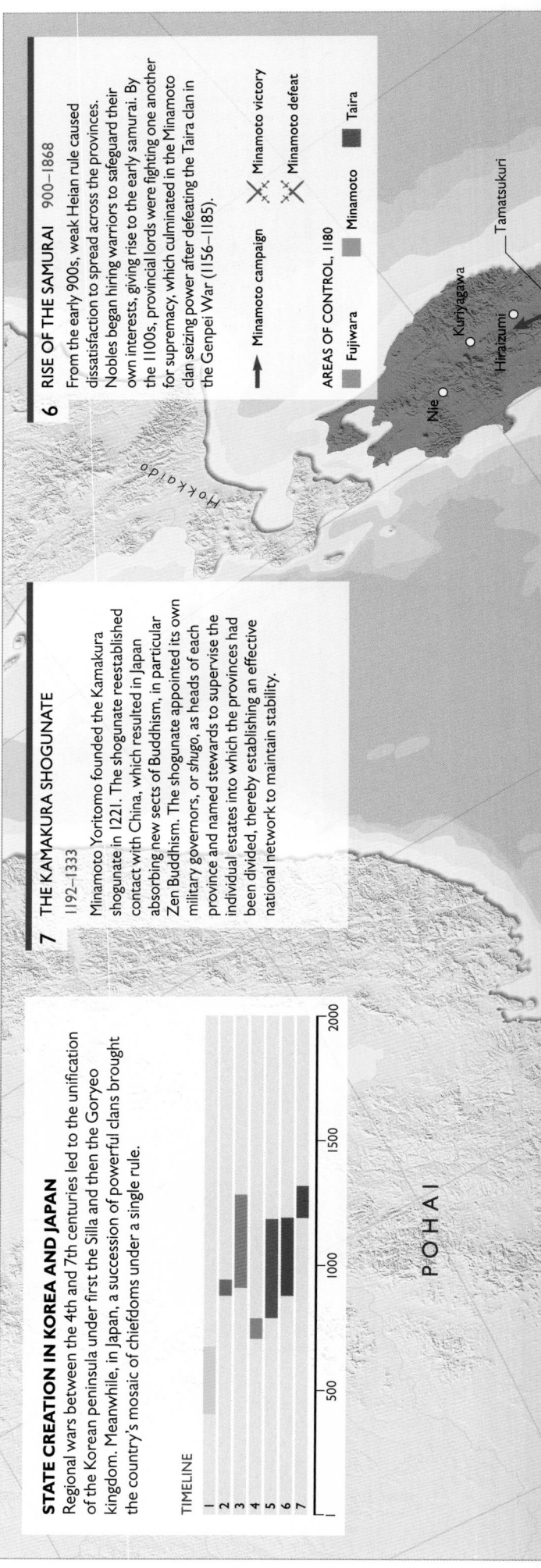

STATE CREATION IN KOREA AND JAPAN
Regional wars between the 4th and 7th centuries led to the unification of the Korean peninsula under first the Silla and then the Goryeo kingdom. Meanwhile, in Japan, a succession of powerful clans brought the country's mosaic of chiefdoms under a single rule.

TIMELINE

1
2
3
4
5
6
7

500   1000   1500   2000

6   RISE OF THE SAMURAI   900–1868

From the early 900s, weak Heian rule caused dissatisfaction to spread across the provinces. Nobles began hiring warriors to safeguard their own interests, giving rise to the early samurai. By the 1100s, provincial lords were fighting one another for supremacy, which culminated in the Minamoto clan seizing power after defeating the Taira clan in the Genpei War (1156–1185).

→ Minamoto campaign
✕✕ Minamoto victory
✕✕ Minamoto defeat

AREAS OF CONTROL, 1180
■ Fujiwara   ■ Minamoto   ■ Taira

7   THE KAMAKURA SHOGUNATE
1192–1333

Minamoto Yoritomo founded the Kamakura shogunate in 1221. The shogunate reestablished contact with China, which resulted in Japan absorbing new sects of Buddhism, in particular Zen Buddhism. The shogunate appointed its own military governors, or *shugo*, as heads of each province and named stewards to supervise the individual estates into which the provinces had been divided, thereby establishing an effective national network to maintain stability.

Hokkaido

Nie
Kuriyagawa
Hiraizumi
Tamatsukuri

POHAI

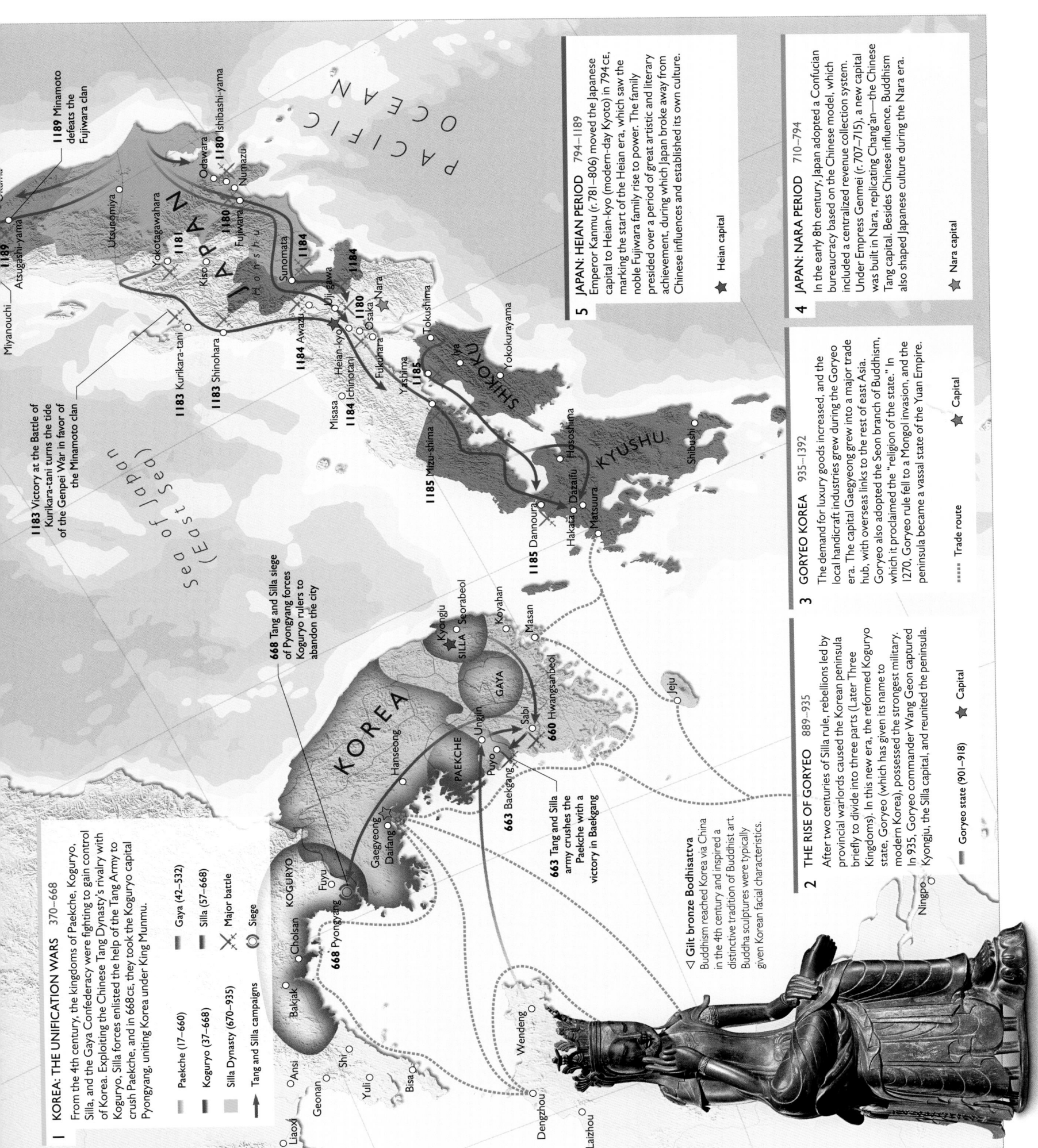

PACIFIC OCEAN

1189 Minamoto defeats the Fujiwara clan

Atsugashi-yama

1189

Miyanouchi

Utsunomiya

Yokotagawahara

Odawara

1180 Ishibashi-yama

Nunazu

1181

1180

1180 Fujiwara

1184

Kiso

Awazu

1184 Awazu

Sunomata

Ungawa

1184

1184 Ichinotani

Osaka

Nara

Heian-kyo

Fukuhara

Misasa

1184 Ichinotani

1183 Victory at the Battle of Kurikara-tani turns the tide of the Genpei War in favor of the Minamoto clan

1183 Kurikara-tani

1183 Shinohara

H o n s h u

Tokushima

Iya

Yashima

1185

Yokokurayama

SHIKOKU

Mizu-shima

Hososhima

KYUSHU

Shibushi

Hakata Dazaifu

Matsuura

1185 Dannoura

Sea of Japan (East Sea)

668 Tang and Silla siege of Pyongyang forces Koguryo rulers to abandon the city

Kyongju

Seorabeol

SILLA

Koyahan

GAYA

Masan

Hwangsanbeol

660

Sabi

Ungjin

Puyo

663 Baekgang

PAEKCHE

Hanseong

Gaegyeong

Daifang

KOGURYO

Fuyu

668 Pyongyang

Cholsan

Bakjak

Ansi

Shi

Yuli

Bisa

Geonan

Wendeng

Liaox

Dengzhou

Laizhou

Ningpo

Jeju

663 Tang and Silla army crushes the Paekche with a victory in Baekgang

---

1 KOREA: THE UNIFICATION WARS 370–668

From the 4th century, the kingdoms of Paekche, Koguryo, Silla, and the Gaya Confederacy were fighting to gain control of Korea. Exploiting the Chinese Tang Dynasty's rivalry with Koguryo, Silla forces enlisted the help of the Tang Army to crush Paekche, and in 668 ce, they took the Koguryo capital Pyongyang, uniting Korea under King Munmu.

- Paekche (17–660)
- Koguryo (37–668)
- Silla Dynasty (670–935)
- Gaya (42–532)
- Silla (57–668)
- ✕ Major battle
- ⊚ Siege
- → Tang and Silla campaigns

2 THE RISE OF GORYEO 889–935

After two centuries of Silla rule, rebellions led by provincial warlords caused the Korean peninsula briefly to divide into three parts (Later Three Kingdoms). In this new era, the reformed Koguryo state, Goryeo (which has given its name to modern Korea), possessed the strongest military. In 935, Goryeo commander Wang Geon captured Kyonglju, the Silla capital, and reunited the peninsula.

○ Capital

3 GORYEO KOREA 935–1392

The demand for luxury goods increased, and the local handicraft industries grew during the Goryeo era. The capital Gaegyeong grew into a major trade hub, with overseas links to the rest of east Asia. Goryeo also adopted the Seon branch of Buddhism, which it proclaimed the "religion of the state." In 1270, Goryeo fell to a Mongol invasion, and the peninsula became a vassal state of the Yuan Empire.

- ▨ Goryeo state (901–918)
- ─ Goryeo state
- ⋯⋯ Trade route
- ★ Capital

4 JAPAN: NARA PERIOD 710–794

In the early 8th century, Japan adopted a Confucian bureaucracy based on the Chinese model, which included a centralized revenue collection system. Under Empress Genmei (r. 707–715), a new capital was built in Nara, replicating Chang'an—the Chinese Tang capital. Besides Chinese influence, Buddhism also shaped Japanese culture during the Nara era.

★ Nara capital

5 JAPAN: HEIAN PERIOD 794–1189

Emperor Kanmu (r. 781–806) moved the Japanese capital to Heian-kyo (modern-day Kyoto) in 794 ce, marking the start of the Heian era, which saw the noble Fujiwara family rise to power. The family presided over a period of great artistic and literary achievement, during which Japan broke away from Chinese influences and established its own culture.

★ Heian capital

△ **Gilt bronze Bodhisattva**
Buddhism reached Korea via China in the 4th century and inspired a distinctive tradition of Buddhist art. Buddha sculptures were typically given Korean facial characteristics.

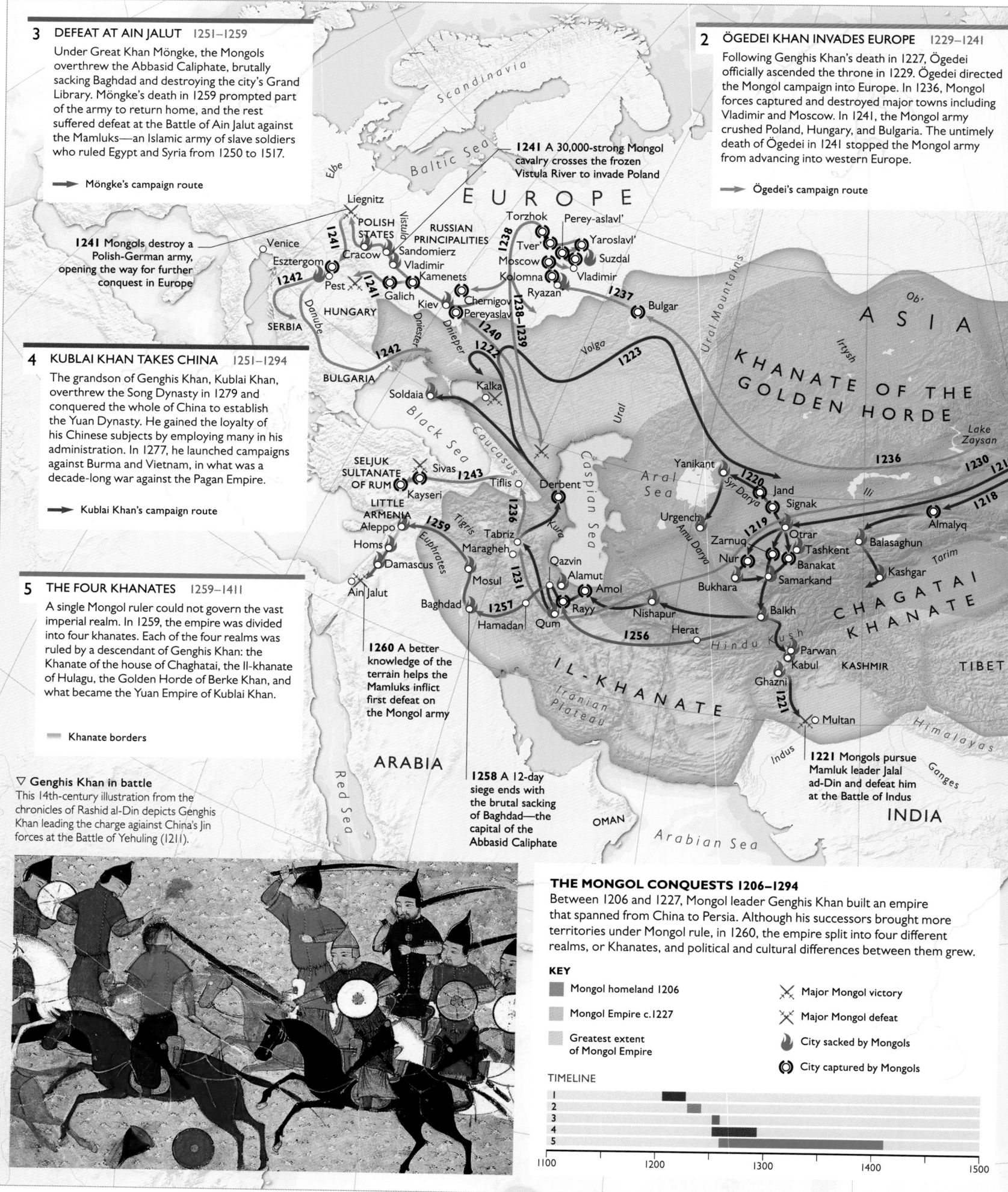

3 DEFEAT AT AIN JALUT 1251–1259

Under Great Khan Möngke, the Mongols overthrew the Abbasid Caliphate, brutally sacking Baghdad and destroying the city's Grand Library. Möngke's death in 1259 prompted part of the army to return home, and the rest suffered defeat at the Battle of Ain Jalut against the Mamluks—an Islamic army of slave soldiers who ruled Egypt and Syria from 1250 to 1517.

→ Möngke's campaign route

2 ÖGEDEI KHAN INVADES EUROPE 1229–1241

Following Genghis Khan's death in 1227, Ögedei officially ascended the throne in 1229. Ögedei directed the Mongol campaign into Europe. In 1236, Mongol forces captured and destroyed major towns including Vladimir and Moscow. In 1241, the Mongol army crushed Poland, Hungary, and Bulgaria. The untimely death of Ögedei in 1241 stopped the Mongol army from advancing into western Europe.

→ Ögedei's campaign route

1241 A 30,000-strong Mongol cavalry crosses the frozen Vistula River to invade Poland

1241 Mongols destroy a Polish-German army, opening the way for further conquest in Europe

4 KUBLAI KHAN TAKES CHINA 1251–1294

The grandson of Genghis Khan, Kublai Khan, overthrew the Song Dynasty in 1279 and conquered the whole of China to establish the Yuan Dynasty. He gained the loyalty of his Chinese subjects by employing many in his administration. In 1277, he launched campaigns against Burma and Vietnam, in what was a decade-long war against the Pagan Empire.

→ Kublai Khan's campaign route

5 THE FOUR KHANATES 1259–1411

A single Mongol ruler could not govern the vast imperial realm. In 1259, the empire was divided into four khanates. Each of the four realms was ruled by a descendant of Genghis Khan: the Khanate of the house of Chaghatai, the Il-khanate of Hulagu, the Golden Horde of Berke Khan, and what became the Yuan Empire of Kublai Khan.

▬ Khanate borders

1260 A better knowledge of the terrain helps the Mamluks inflict first defeat on the Mongol army

1258 A 12-day siege ends with the brutal sacking of Baghdad—the capital of the Abbasid Caliphate

▽ **Genghis Khan in battle**
This 14th-century illustration from the chronicles of Rashid al-Din depicts Genghis Khan leading the charge agiainst China's Jin forces at the Battle of Yehuling (1211).

1221 Mongols pursue Mamluk leader Jalal ad-Din and defeat him at the Battle of Indus

THE MONGOL CONQUESTS 1206–1294

Between 1206 and 1227, Mongol leader Genghis Khan built an empire that spanned from China to Persia. Although his successors brought more territories under Mongol rule, in 1260, the empire split into four different realms, or Khanates, and political and cultural differences between them grew.

KEY

▬ Mongol homeland 1206	✕ Major Mongol victory
▬ Mongol Empire c.1227	✕ Major Mongol defeat
▬ Greatest extent of Mongol Empire	🔥 City sacked by Mongols
	⟳ City captured by Mongols

TIMELINE

1
2
3
4
5

1100 1200 1300 1400 1500

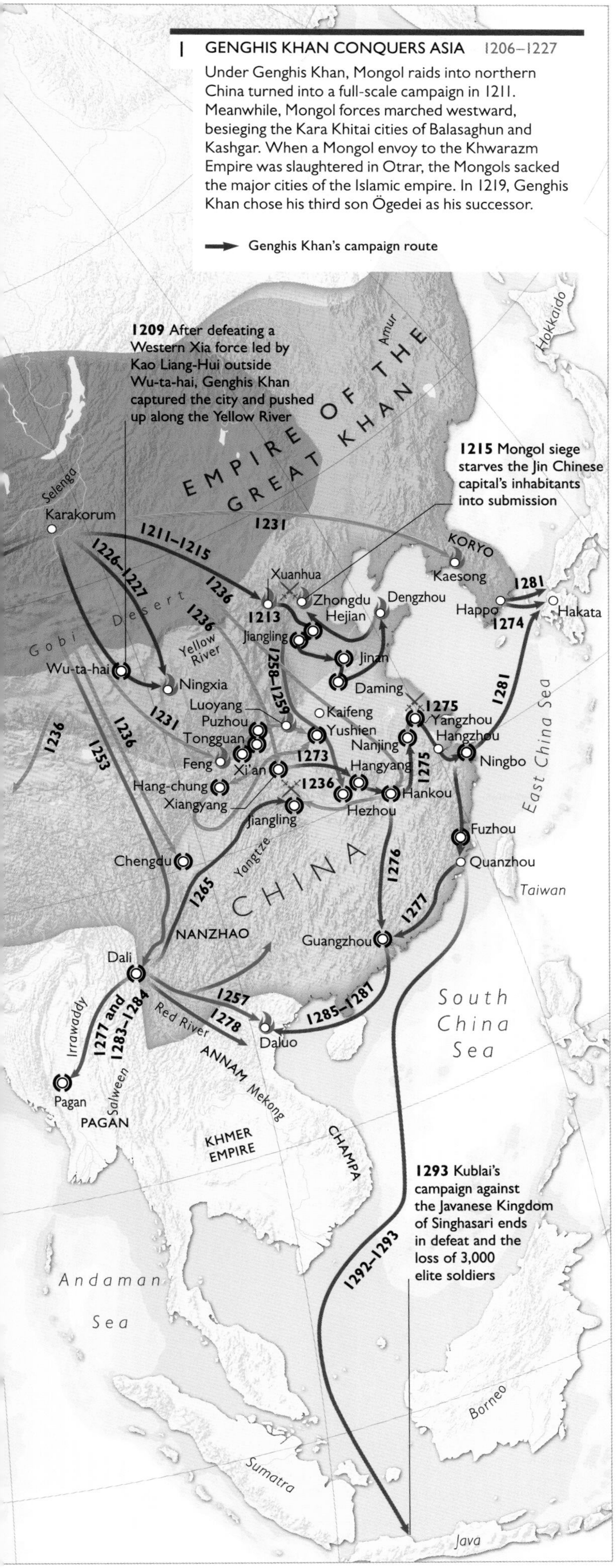

| GENGHIS KHAN CONQUERS ASIA 1206–1227

Under Genghis Khan, Mongol raids into northern China turned into a full-scale campaign in 1211. Meanwhile, Mongol forces marched westward, besieging the Kara Khitai cities of Balasaghun and Kashgar. When a Mongol envoy to the Khwarazm Empire was slaughtered in Otrar, the Mongols sacked the major cities of the Islamic empire. In 1219, Genghis Khan chose his third son Ögedei as his successor.

➡️ Genghis Khan's campaign route

1209 After defeating a Western Xia force led by Kao Liang-Hui outside Wu-ta-hai, Genghis Khan captured the city and pushed up along the Yellow River

1215 Mongol siege starves the Jin Chinese capital's inhabitants into submission

EMPIRE OF THE GREAT KHAN

Karakorum · Selenga · Amur · Hokkaido

1211–1215 · 1226–1227 · 1231 · 1236

Gobi Desert

KORYO · Kaesong · 1281 · Hakata · Happo · 1274

Xuanhua · Zhongdu · Hejian · Dengzhou · 1213 · Jiangling · Yellow River · Jinan · Daming · 1258–1259 · Kaifeng · Yushien · 1275 · Yangzhou · Hangzhou · 1281 · Nanjing · Ningbo · Hangyang · 1275 · 1273 · 1236 · Hankou · 1236 · Hezhou · Fuzhou · Quanzhou

Wu-ta-hai · Ningxia · Luoyang · Puzhou · Tongguan · 1231 · Feng · Xi'an · Hang-chung · Xiangyang · Jiangling · Yangtze · 1265 · Chengdu · 1253 · 1236 · 1236

CHINA · East China Sea · Taiwan

NANZHAO · Guangzhou · 1276 · 1277

Dali · 1257 · 1285–1287 · South China Sea

Irrawaddy · 1277 and 1283–1284 · 1278 · Daluo · Red River · ANNAM · Salween · Mekong · CHAMPA · Andaman Sea

PAGAN · Pagan · KHMER EMPIRE

1293 Kublai's campaign against the Javanese Kingdom of Singhasari ends in defeat and the loss of 3,000 elite soldiers

1292–1293 · Borneo · Sumatra · Java

THE MONGOL CONQUESTS

The Mongols were a mix of Mongolian and Turkic-speaking tribes who united under the leadership of Temujin in the early 13th century. From their homeland in modern-day Mongolia, the fierce Mongol warriors then swept across Asia and Europe, creating the largest land empire in history.

Chosen as the Mongol leader at a tribal meeting in 1206, Temujin took the name Genghis Khan (meaning universal ruler) and united all the tribes under his leadership. In command of a formidable army of warriors on horseback, Genghis Khan organized his army and embarked on a conquest that lasted more than 20 years and resulted in the majority of Asia falling under his rule.

In 1211, Mongol armies invaded northern China, raiding and sacking many Chinese cities. In a long and hard-fought battle, the Mongols took the Chinese capital, Zhongdu, and forced the Jin emperor to flee south.

In 1218, Genghis Khan defeated the Kara Khitai Empire in central Asia after besieging the capital Balasaghun. He then redirected his army against the Islamic world and overwhelmed the lands of the Khwarazm Shah, wreaking great destruction upon the cities of Bukhara and Samarkand. The Mongol army's expertise at traversing long distances and fighting on horseback, combined with its brutal reputation, struck terror into most adversaries. Although Genghis Khan died in 1227, while on a campaign in China, the empire continued to grow under his son Ögedei, who eliminated the Jin Empire in China in 1234 and also fought campaigns in Russia and eastern Europe. The expansion of the empire slowed after Ögedei died in 1241 and ended in 1260 following the Mongols' first major defeat by the army of the Mamluk Sultanate (1250–1517) at Ain Jalut in Palestine. Soon afterward, the empire fragmented, with separate khans ruling China, Persia, central Asia, and the Russian Principalities.

A century later, a last Mongol resurgence took place under Timur—ruler of a Mongol principality in Transoxiana (a remnant of the Chagatai Khanate). He briefly conquered a vast territory across central Asia but was unable to consolidate the empire.

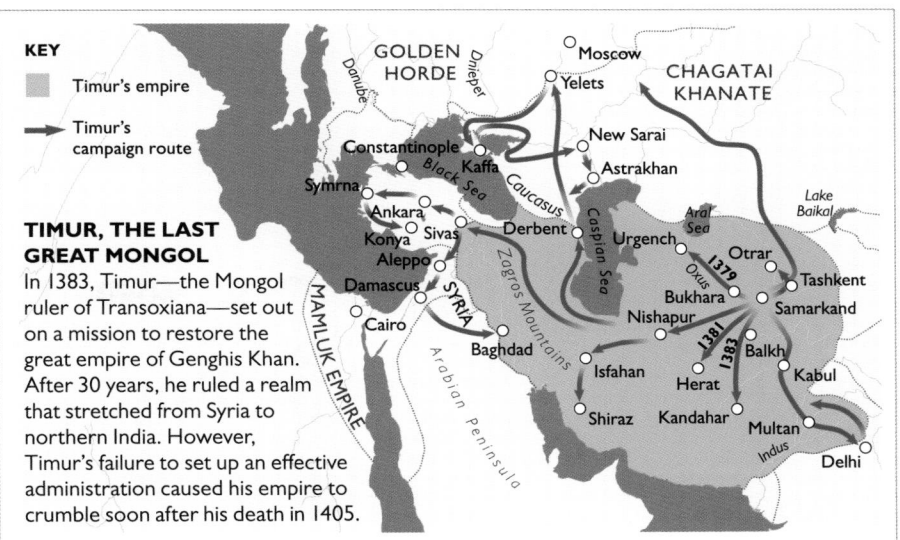

KEY

Timur's empire

Timur's campaign route

TIMUR, THE LAST GREAT MONGOL
In 1383, Timur—the Mongol ruler of Transoxiana—set out on a mission to restore the great empire of Genghis Khan. After 30 years, he ruled a realm that stretched from Syria to northern India. However, Timur's failure to set up an effective administration caused his empire to crumble soon after his death in 1405.

GOLDEN HORDE · Moscow · CHAGATAI KHANATE · Danube · Dnieper · Yelets · New Sarai · Constantinople · Kaffa · Black Sea · Astrakhan · Caucasus · Symrna · Ankara · Aral Sea · Lake Baikal · Konya · Sivas · Derbent · Urgench · 1379 · Otrar · Aleppo · Caspian Sea · Bukhara · Tashkent · Damascus · SYRIA · Zagros Mountains · Oxus · Nishapur · 1381 · Samarkand · Cairo · Baghdad · 1383 · Balkh · MAMLUK EMPIRE · Arabian Peninsula · Isfahan · Herat · Kabul · Shiraz · Kandahar · Multan · Indus · Delhi

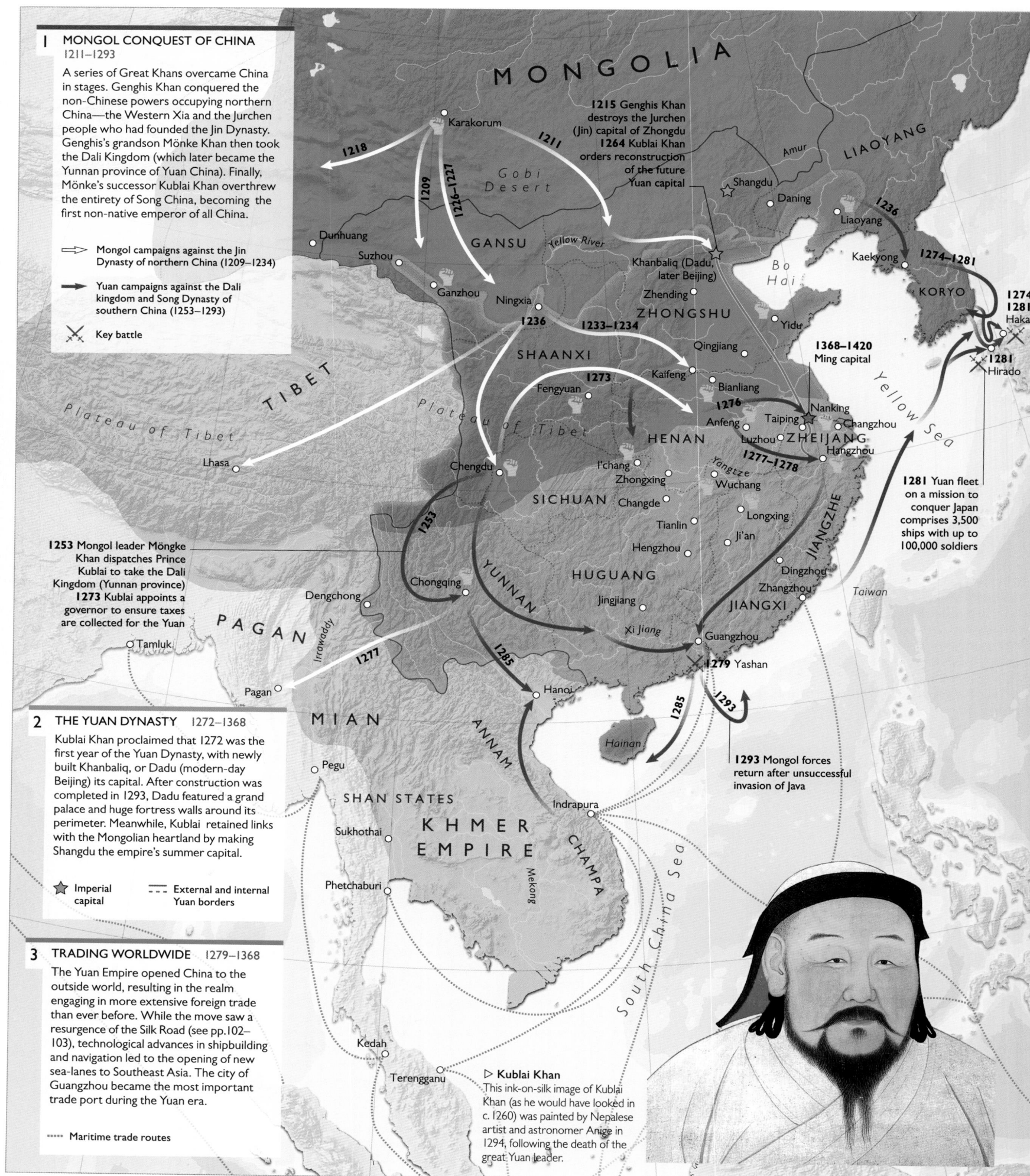

1 MONGOL CONQUEST OF CHINA 1211–1293

A series of Great Khans overcame China in stages. Genghis Khan conquered the non-Chinese powers occupying northern China—the Western Xia and the Jurchen people who had founded the Jin Dynasty. Genghis's grandson Mönke Khan then took the Dali Kingdom (which later became the Yunnan province of Yuan China). Finally, Mönke's successor Kublai Khan overthrew the entirety of Song China, becoming the first non-native emperor of all China.

⇨ Mongol campaigns against the Jin Dynasty of northern China (1209–1234)

→ Yuan campaigns against the Dali kingdom and Song Dynasty of southern China (1253–1293)

✕ Key battle

1253 Mongol leader Mönke Khan dispatches Prince Kublai to take the Dali Kingdom (Yunnan province)
1273 Kublai appoints a governor to ensure taxes are collected for the Yuan

2 THE YUAN DYNASTY 1272–1368

Kublai Khan proclaimed that 1272 was the first year of the Yuan Dynasty, with newly built Khanbaliq, or Dadu (modern-day Beijing) its capital. After construction was completed in 1293, Dadu featured a grand palace and huge fortress walls around its perimeter. Meanwhile, Kublai retained links with the Mongolian heartland by making Shangdu the empire's summer capital.

★ Imperial capital

--- External and internal Yuan borders

3 TRADING WORLDWIDE 1279–1368

The Yuan Empire opened China to the outside world, resulting in the realm engaging in more extensive foreign trade than ever before. While the move saw a resurgence of the Silk Road (see pp.102–103), technological advances in shipbuilding and navigation led to the opening of new sea-lanes to Southeast Asia. The city of Guangzhou became the most important trade port during the Yuan era.

····· Maritime trade routes

1215 Genghis Khan destroys the Jurchen (Jin) capital of Zhongdu
1264 Kublai Khan orders reconstruction of the future Yuan capital

1368–1420 Ming capital

1281 Yuan fleet on a mission to conquer Japan comprises 3,500 ships with up to 100,000 soldiers

1293 Mongol forces return after unsuccessful invasion of Java

▷ **Kublai Khan**
This ink-on-silk image of Kublai Khan (as he would have looked in c. 1260) was painted by Nepalese artist and astronomer Anige in 1294, following the death of the great Yuan leader.

MONGOLIA
Karakorum
Gobi Desert
Yellow River
GANSU
Dunhuang
Suzhou
Ganzhou
Ningxia
ZHONGSHU
SHAANXI
Fengyuan
Chengdu
SICHUAN
Changde
Tianlin
Hengzhou
HUGUANG
Jingjiang
Chongqing
Dengchong
YUNNAN
Xi Jiang
Tamluk
PAGAN
Irrawaddy
Pagan
MIAN
Pegu
SHAN STATES
Sukhothai
KHMER EMPIRE
Phetchaburi
Mekong
Kedah
Terengganu
South China Sea

LIAOYANG
Amur
Shangdu
Daning
Liaoyang
Kaekyong
KORYO
Bo Hai
Khanbaliq (Dadu, later Beijing)
Zhending
Yidu
Qingjiang
Kaifeng
Bianliang
Anfeng
Luzhou
Taiping
Nanking
Changzhou
ZHEIJANG
Hangzhou
HENAN
I'chang
Zhongxing
Wuchang
Longxing
Ji'an
JIANGZHE
Dingzhou
Zhangzhou
JIANGXI
Guangzhou
Yashan
Hainan
Hanoi
ANNAM
CHAMPA
Indrapura
Taiwan
Yellow Sea
Hakat
Hirado

Plateau of Tibet
TIBET
Lhasa
Plateau of Tibet

1218
1209
1226–1227
1211
1236
1233–1234
1273
1236
1276
1277–1278
1253
1277
1285
1285
1293
1279
1274–1281
1274, 1281
1281
1236

4 LUCKLESS IN JAPAN 1274–1281

In 1274, Kublai Khan dispatched a fleet to conquer Japan. Despite scoring some early victories, the Mongols were forced to retreat when a storm destroyed hundreds of ships, many of which were flat-bottomed river vessels. A second invasion in 1281 met a similar fate, as the Mongol armada was unable to penetrate the Japanese defense wall and perished when it was struck by a typhoon.

INVASION ROUTES
→ 1274   ⚔ Key battle, 1274
→ 1281

5 THE GRAND CANAL 1281–1293

The Yuan rounded up 4 million peasants to work on a new, direct route for the Grand Canal, the oldest parts of which dated to the 6th century BCE. The laborers carved a passage hundreds of miles long through hill country, linking the capital to Hangzhou. This allowed grain transportation to the north, further disenfranchizing the populace.

— Grand Canal

6 RED TURBAN REBELLION 1351–1368

A series of floods and droughts in the 1340s was interpreted by the Chinese as divine signs of the Yuan having lost the "Mandate of Heaven." Revolts broke out across the realm and gave rise to the Red Turban Rebellion. Led by Zhu Yuanzhang, the rebels drove out the Yuan court and seized the capital in 1368.

✊ Provincial capital affected by peasant revolt

7 EARLY MING 1368–1398

Zhu Yuanzhang became the Hongwu emperor—the first ruler of the Ming Dynasty, which would rule China for the next three centuries. He took personal control of the organs of government and restored order throughout the country. He instituted public work projects and introduced reforms to redistribute land to the peasants.

▬ Ming Empire   ★ Imperial capital

RISE AND FALL OF THE YUAN EMPIRE

The Mongols eliminated the Jin Empire in 1234 and took control of northern China. Under the leadership of Kublai Khan, the Yuan Empire conquered the southern Song lands in 1279. After ruling China for 89 years, the Yuan Dynasty fell to peasant revolts and was replaced by the native Chinese Ming Dynasty.

KEY
■ Yuan Empire to 1279
■ Yuan expansion 1280–1368
■ Area under loose or temporary Yuan control

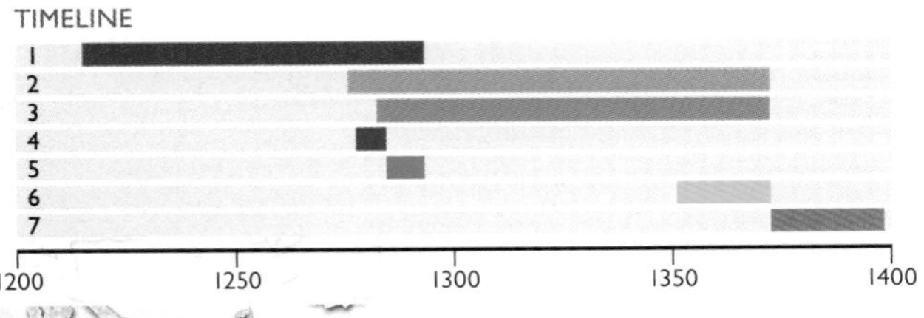

TIMELINE
1 2 3 4 5 6 7
1200 1250 1300 1350 1400

YUAN CHINA TO THE EARLY MING

In 1272, Genghis Khan's grandson, Kublai Khan, founded China's first foreign-led empire, the Yuan, and 9 years later, he wrested control of the whole realm. However, a system of rule that repressed the Chinese eventually gave rise to widespread rebellion that led to the empire's downfall 89 years later.

Kublai Khan ruled China as an independent realm of the Mongol Empire. He enforced a rigid racial hierarchy, placing the Mongols at the top while denying the Chinese any roles in the government or the military.

Kublai made Dadu (Beijing) the Yuan capital, encouraged trade links with the outside world, and brought paper money into common circulation. Kublai's successors, however, faced a populace that was increasingly aggrieved over rising inflation and the oppressive taxes borne out of the dynasty's discriminatory social policies. Moreover, the arrival of the Black Death in the 1330s (see pp.114–115), along with a spate of natural disasters, wrought great hardship upon the poorer classes. From the 1340s, revolts broke out in every province, giving rise to a movement known as the Red Turban Rebellion, led by Zhu Yuanzhang.

In 1368, Zhu seized Dadu and expelled the Mongol rulers. He founded the Ming Dynasty and introduced reforms that improved the prospects of the peasant classes.

"… one can conquer the empire on horseback, but one cannot govern it on horseback."

KUBLAI KHAN, YUAN DYNASTY EMPEROR, 1271–1294

MARCO POLO TRAVELS TO CHINA
Mongol control of Eurasia ushered in a period of peace and stability, known as "Pax Mongolica," which allowed Italian merchant and explorer Marco Polo to embark along the Silk Road on a trade mission to China. According to his travel writings, Marco Polo spent 17 years in China serving emperor Kublai Khan as a government official.

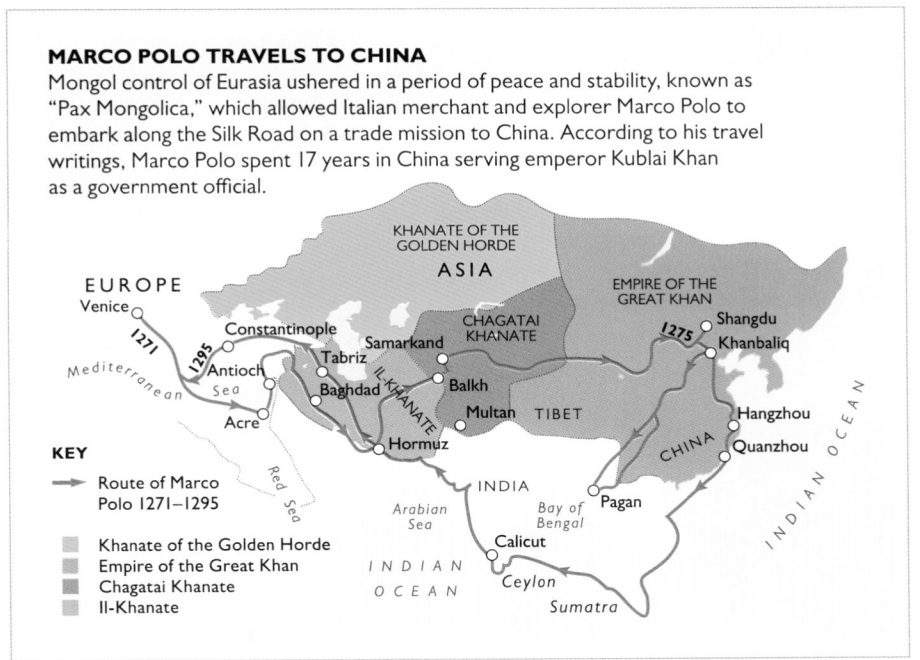

KEY
→ Route of Marco Polo 1271–1295
■ Khanate of the Golden Horde
■ Empire of the Great Khan
■ Chagatai Khanate
■ Il-Khanate

TEMPLE STATES OF SOUTHEAST ASIA

The kingdoms that emerged in Southeast Asia from the start of the 1st millennium CE were strongly influenced by their powerful neighbors. Forms of government and religious ideas were imported via trade routes from India, while China's diplomatic and commercial strength shaped the formation of states in the east.

Organized states appeared in Southeast Asia around the 2nd century CE, with the Indian-influenced kingdom of Funan in Cambodia's Mekong Delta among the earliest. They imported key ideas from India, most notably in art, government, and religion. Buddhism reached the Mon kingdom of Burma (modern-day Myanmar) by the late 3rd century and Funan by 375. Hinduism, too, spread rapidly, reaching Borneo by 400 and becoming the favored religion of the Angkor kingdom (in modern-day Cambodia). Rulers took on the characteristics of god-kings (sometimes using the title *cakravartin*, or universal ruler, borrowed from India) and built lavish capitals adorned with Buddhist and Hindu temples. While Indian cultural influence predominated in the west, direct Chinese political influence touched the eastern states. These sent diplomatic missions to Tang China and, in the case of Vietnam,

suffered direct military interventions. By the 9th century, a constellation of large states had emerged from Pagan in Myanmar, to Champa and Angkor in Cambodia, and Dai Viet in modern Vietnam. The Sailendra Empire of Srivijaya, based on Sumatra, dominated the Indonesian archipelago.

In 1287, the Mongols invaded (see pp.130–131) and captured Pagan. Invasion and growth of new competitors, notably the Dvaravati kingdoms of Thailand, shook the stability of the temple kingdoms. By the late 15th century, Angkor, Pagan, Champa, and Srivijaya had all collapsed, leaving a fractured system of regional states by the time Europeans reached the region a century later.

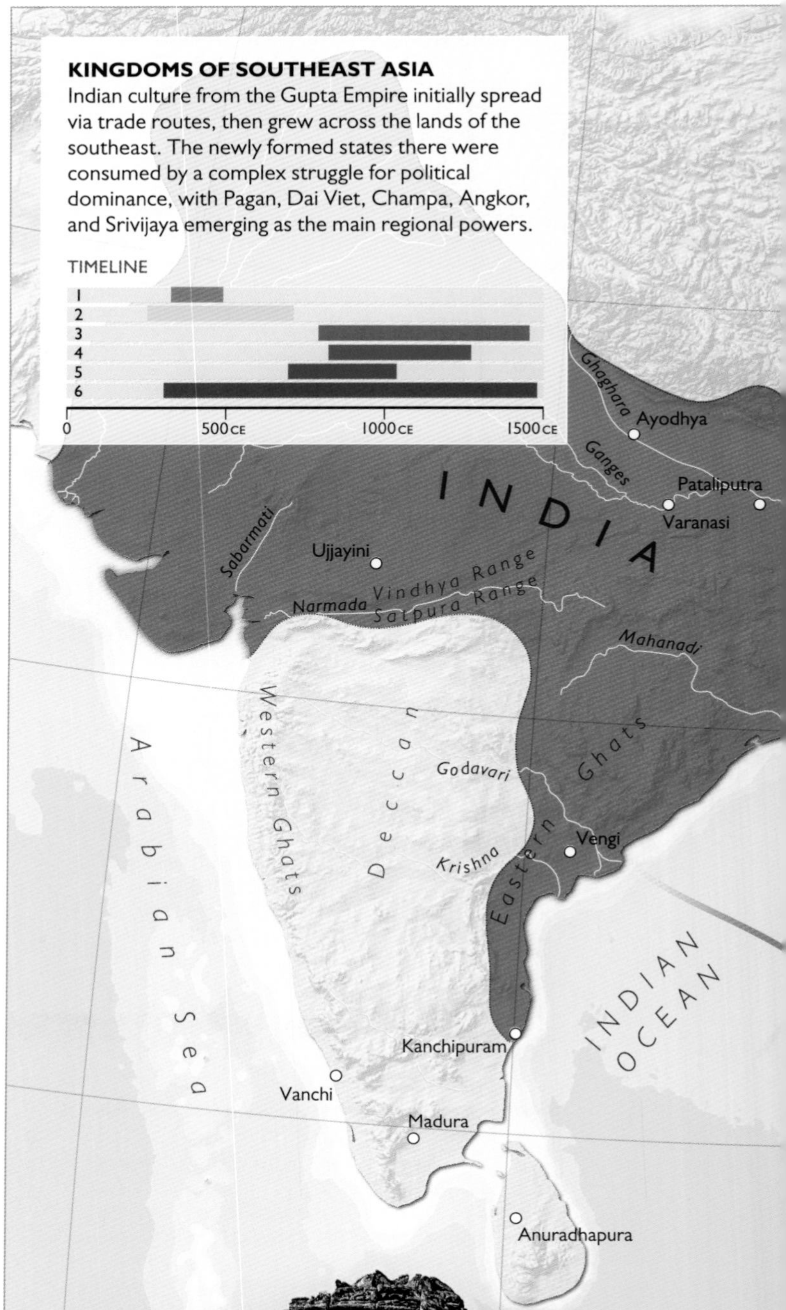

▷ **Pyramid temple**
The Bayon temple at Angkor was built c. 1200 for Jayavarman VII, one of the empire's kings. Some of its towers feature carvings of Jayavarman's face, while others have faces of Buddhist gods.

HINDUISM
RELIGIOUS INFLUENCE ACROSS SOUTHEAST ASIA

Hinduism developed in the 2nd millennium BCE, when its most ancient texts, the *Rig-Veda* hymns, were composed. The worship of many gods—all aspects of a single divine truth—within a temple-based system produced an extremely diverse religion. By the time of the Gupta Empire in the 3rd century CE, the principal forms of Hinduism were Vaishnavism (focused on the worship of Vishnu) and Sivaism (worship of Shiva, the god of creation and destruction), both of which spread widely in Southeast Asia.

Hindu carvings
This 10th-century temple shows the influence of Sivaism in Angkor.

KINGDOMS OF SOUTHEAST ASIA

Indian culture from the Gupta Empire initially spread via trade routes, then grew across the lands of the southeast. The newly formed states there were consumed by a complex struggle for political dominance, with Pagan, Dai Viet, Champa, Angkor, and Srivijaya emerging as the main regional powers.

TIMELINE

1
2
3
4
5
6

0   500 CE   1000 CE   1500 CE

Ghaghara
Ayodhya
Ganges
Pataliputra
Varanasi

INDIA

Sabarmati
Ujjayini
Narmada Vindhya Range
Salpura Range
Mahanadi

Western Ghats
Deccan
Godavari
Krishna
Eastern Ghats
Vengi

Arabian Sea

Kanchipuram
Vanchi
Madura

INDIAN OCEAN

Anuradhapura

1 GUPTA EMPIRE 320–500

Founded by Chandra Gupta I in 320, the Gupta Empire became wealthy from trade with Southeast Asia. Merchants carried Indian culture and religion overland and across maritime routes around Malaysia. Continual warfare to subdue rebellious provinces, and defeat at the hands of Hephthalite Hun invaders in 455, hastened the empire's decline and disappearance in the mid-6th century.

■ Maximum extent of Gupta Empire c. 550

→ Indian influence

2 THE KINGDOM OF FUNAN 243–700

Funan, the earliest recorded state in the region of Southeast Asia, appeared around the 2nd century in the Mekong Delta. It maintained close trading links with China through an emporium at Oc Eo on the coast, sending an embassy there in 243. Although Buddhism was strong in the kingdom, Chinese records describe a king called Chan-t'an who sent tribute in 357 as a Hindu.

■ Areas influenced by India

3 THE RISE AND FALL OF ANGKOR 802–1431

The Kingdom of Angkor began in 802, when Jayavarman II proclaimed himself *cakravartin* and founded a new capital near the later site of Angkor. Subsequent kings established new royal cities nearby, each adorned with Hindu temples. Jayavarman VII (r. 1181–1218) instead promoted Buddhism, but Angkor returned to Hinduism and survived until its collapse in the 15th century.

■ Core area of Angkor

■ Outermost limit of Angkor

4 THE BUDDHIST KINGDOM OF PAGAN 849–1287

Pagan was established in 849 by Burmese-speaking people. Its power grew until, in 1044, Anawrahta brought much of modern Burma under his control, finally defeating the Mon of Thaton in 1057. His descendants ruled for two centuries, but alienation of land to support its temples weakened Pagan, and it fell easily to the Mongols in 1287.

■ Core area of Pagan

■ Outermost limit of Pagan

5 THE MARITIME STATE OF SRIVIJAYA 671–1045

Unlike the land-based states, Srivijaya depended on control of maritime routes and domination of trading ports and cities for its success. Based at Palembang on Sumatra, Srivijaya had close links with China and sent frequent embassies there. The appearance in the 11th century of rivals in Java, notably Kadiri, ended Srivijaya's empire.

■ Core area of Srivijaya   ■ Core area of Kadiri

■ Outermost limit of Srivijaya   ■ Outermost limit of Kadiri

6 CHAMPA AND DAI VIET c. 300–1471

The Cham people established the Hindu kingdom of Champa in southern Vietnam in the 4th century. They waged frequent wars against their northern neighbors the Vietnamese, who overran their capital Vijaya in 1471. The Vietnamese Dai Viet kingdom developed in a region long overshadowed by China, achieving independence under Ngo Quyen in 939.

■ Core area of Champa   ■ Core area of Dai Viet

■ Outermost limit of Champa   ■ Outermost limit of Dai Viet

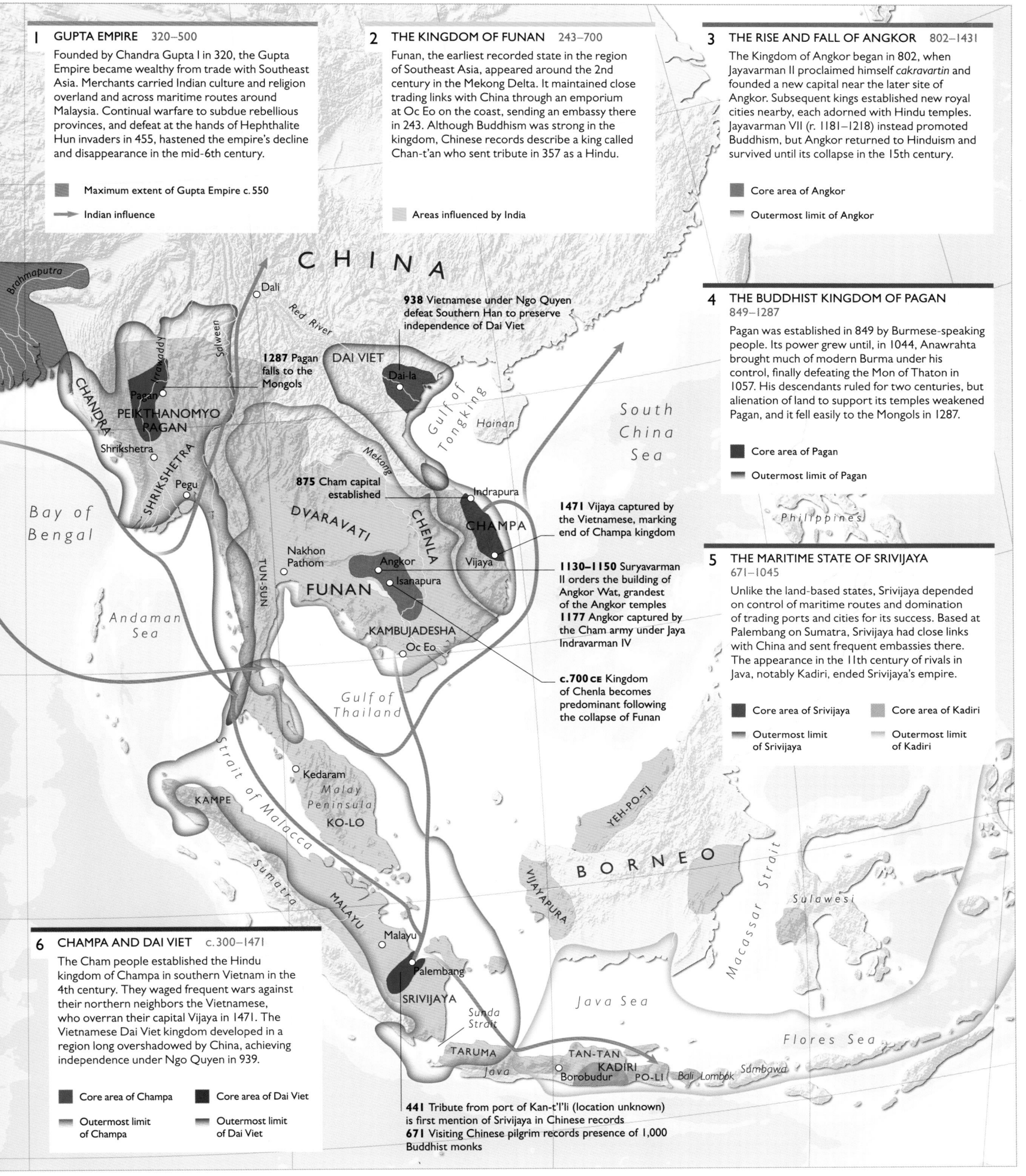

938 Vietnamese under Ngo Quyen defeat Southern Han to preserve independence of Dai Viet

1287 Pagan falls to the Mongols

875 Cham capital established

1471 Vijaya captured by the Vietnamese, marking end of Champa kingdom

1130–1150 Suryavarman II orders the building of Angkor Wat, grandest of the Angkor temples
1177 Angkor captured by the Cham army under Jaya Indravarman IV

c.700 CE Kingdom of Chenla becomes predominant following the collapse of Funan

441 Tribute from port of Kan-t'l'li (location unknown) is first mention of Srivijaya in Chinese records
671 Visiting Chinese pilgrim records presence of 1,000 Buddhist monks

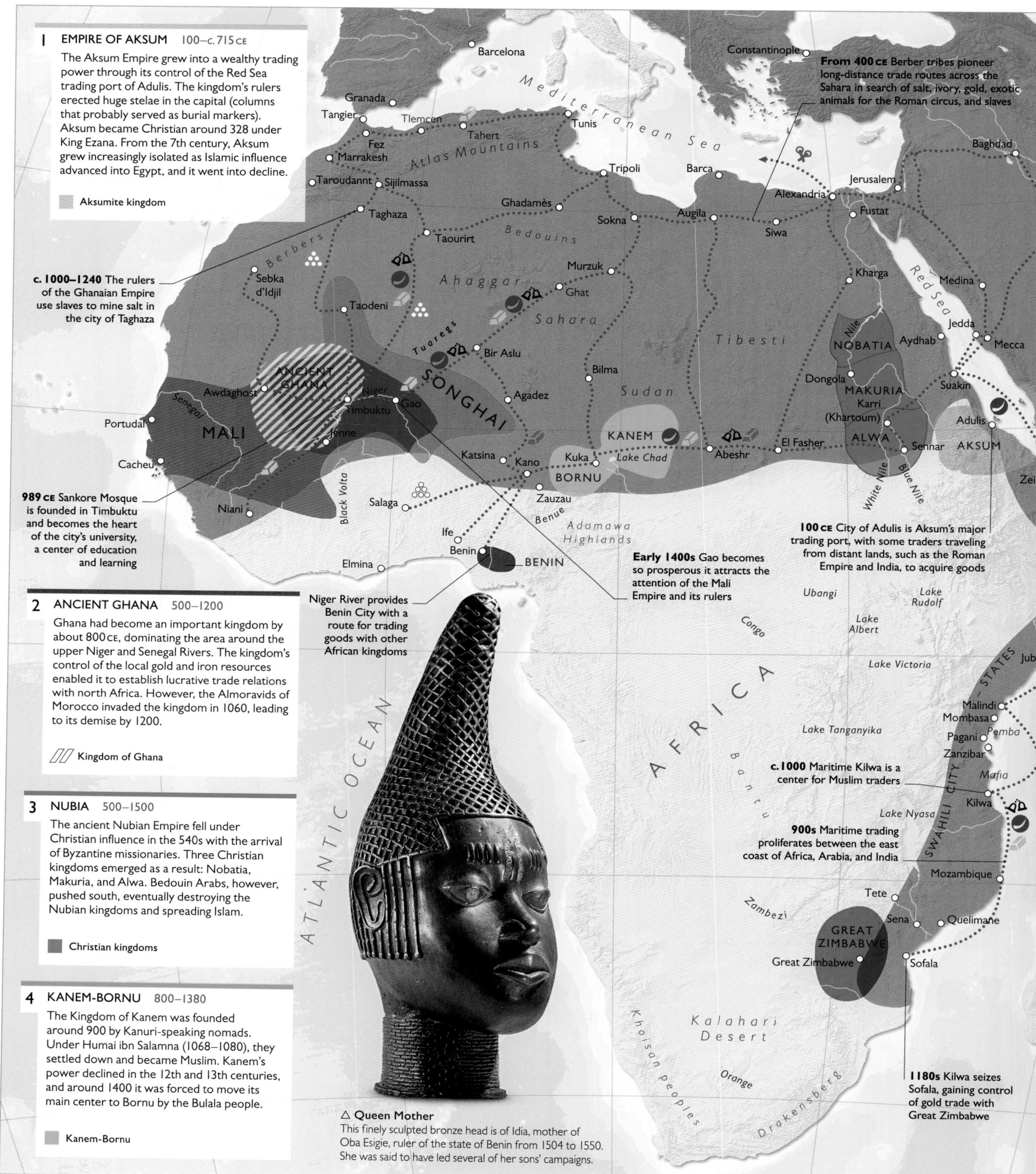

1 EMPIRE OF AKSUM 100–c.715 CE

The Aksum Empire grew into a wealthy trading power through its control of the Red Sea trading port of Adulis. The kingdom's rulers erected huge stelae in the capital (columns that probably served as burial markers). Aksum became Christian around 328 under King Ezana. From the 7th century, Aksum grew increasingly isolated as Islamic influence advanced into Egypt, and it went into decline.

▢ Aksumite kingdom

c. 1000–1240 The rulers of the Ghanaian Empire use slaves to mine salt in the city of Taghaza

989 CE Sankore Mosque is founded in Timbuktu and becomes the heart of the city's university, a center of education and learning

2 ANCIENT GHANA 500–1200

Ghana had become an important kingdom by about 800 CE, dominating the area around the upper Niger and Senegal Rivers. The kingdom's control of the local gold and iron resources enabled it to establish lucrative trade relations with north Africa. However, the Almoravids of Morocco invaded the kingdom in 1060, leading to its demise by 1200.

▨ Kingdom of Ghana

3 NUBIA 500–1500

The ancient Nubian Empire fell under Christian influence in the 540s with the arrival of Byzantine missionaries. Three Christian kingdoms emerged as a result: Nobatia, Makuria, and Alwa. Bedouin Arabs, however, pushed south, eventually destroying the Nubian kingdoms and spreading Islam.

▢ Christian kingdoms

4 KANEM-BORNU 800–1380

The Kingdom of Kanem was founded around 900 by Kanuri-speaking nomads. Under Humai ibn Salamna (1068–1080), they settled down and became Muslim. Kanem's power declined in the 12th and 13th centuries, and around 1400 it was forced to move its main center to Bornu by the Bulala people.

▢ Kanem-Bornu

From 400 CE Berber tribes pioneer long-distance trade routes across the Sahara in search of salt, ivory, gold, exotic animals for the Roman circus, and slaves

100 CE City of Adulis is Aksum's major trading port, with some traders traveling from distant lands, such as the Roman Empire and India, to acquire goods

Early 1400s Gao becomes so prosperous it attracts the attention of the Mali Empire and its rulers

Niger River provides Benin City with a route for trading goods with other African kingdoms

c. 1000 Maritime Kilwa is a center for Muslim traders

900s Maritime trading proliferates between the east coast of Africa, Arabia, and India

1180s Kilwa seizes Sofala, gaining control of gold trade with Great Zimbabwe

△ **Queen Mother**
This finely sculpted bronze head is of Idia, mother of Oba Esigie, ruler of the state of Benin from 1504 to 1550. She was said to have led several of her sons' campaigns.

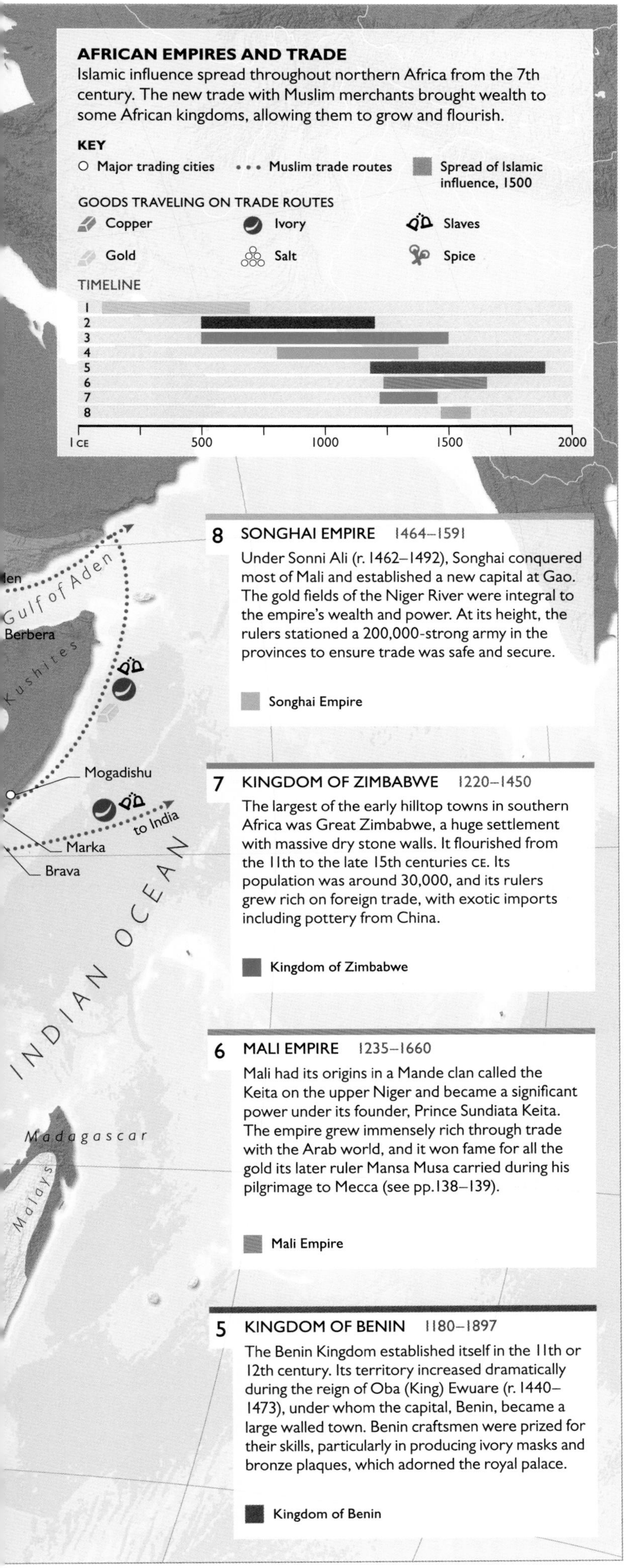

AFRICAN EMPIRES AND TRADE

Islamic influence spread throughout northern Africa from the 7th century. The new trade with Muslim merchants brought wealth to some African kingdoms, allowing them to grow and flourish.

KEY

○ Major trading cities • • • Muslim trade routes ▨ Spread of Islamic influence, 1500

GOODS TRAVELING ON TRADE ROUTES

Copper ◖ Ivory ⚖ Slaves

Gold ⚛ Salt 🗲 Spice

TIMELINE

1
2
3
4
5
6
7
8

1 CE — 500 — 1000 — 1500 — 2000

AFRICAN PEOPLES AND EMPIRES

By 1000 CE, Africa's great range of environments and differing access to natural resources had led to a huge diversity of societies. State formation accelerated in the Middle Ages, a process in part provoked by the spread of Islam into the continent.

Africa's cultures ranged from the Islamic caliphates in the north to hunter-gatherer bands in the southern Kalahari Desert, with chiefdoms and complex trading states in between. Islam spread into east Africa and was carried by Muslim merchants into west Africa. States that already existed there, such as Ghana, became rich, and their rulers were able to extend their sway across the Sahel belt, south of the Sahara. Increased wealth also sparked competition for resources. Ghana suffered attacks from the Almoravids of Morocco in the mid-11th century and was finally snuffed out by the rival Sahel state of Mali, which was in turn supplanted by Songhai in the mid-14th century. By this time, a new Islamic sultanate had arisen at Borno, in modern Chad, sustained by its control of salt mines in the desert basins.

Not all state formations were the result of Islamic influence, however. In the northeast, a variety of Christian kingdoms formed in the aftermath of the breakup of Aksum in the late first millennium CE. The kingdom of Zimbabwe, and the iron-working kingdom of Benin in west Africa, which flourished from the 14th century, both imported artifacts and raw materials from abroad but were not subject to direct Islamic influence.

"They exchanged gold until they depressed its value in Egypt and caused its price to fall."

MANSA MUSA DESCRIBED BY ARAB HISTORIAN AL-UMARI, C. 1350

8 SONGHAI EMPIRE 1464–1591

Under Sonni Ali (r. 1462–1492), Songhai conquered most of Mali and established a new capital at Gao. The gold fields of the Niger River were integral to the empire's wealth and power. At its height, the rulers stationed a 200,000-strong army in the provinces to ensure trade was safe and secure.

▨ Songhai Empire

7 KINGDOM OF ZIMBABWE 1220–1450

The largest of the early hilltop towns in southern Africa was Great Zimbabwe, a huge settlement with massive dry stone walls. It flourished from the 11th to the late 15th centuries CE. Its population was around 30,000, and its rulers grew rich on foreign trade, with exotic imports including pottery from China.

▨ Kingdom of Zimbabwe

6 MALI EMPIRE 1235–1660

Mali had its origins in a Mande clan called the Keita on the upper Niger and became a significant power under its founder, Prince Sundiata Keita. The empire grew immensely rich through trade with the Arab world, and it won fame for all the gold its later ruler Mansa Musa carried during his pilgrimage to Mecca (see pp.138–139).

▨ Mali Empire

5 KINGDOM OF BENIN 1180–1897

The Benin Kingdom established itself in the 11th or 12th century. Its territory increased dramatically during the reign of Oba (King) Ewuare (r. 1440–1473), under whom the capital, Benin, became a large walled town. Benin craftsmen were prized for their skills, particularly in producing ivory masks and bronze plaques, which adorned the royal palace.

▨ Kingdom of Benin

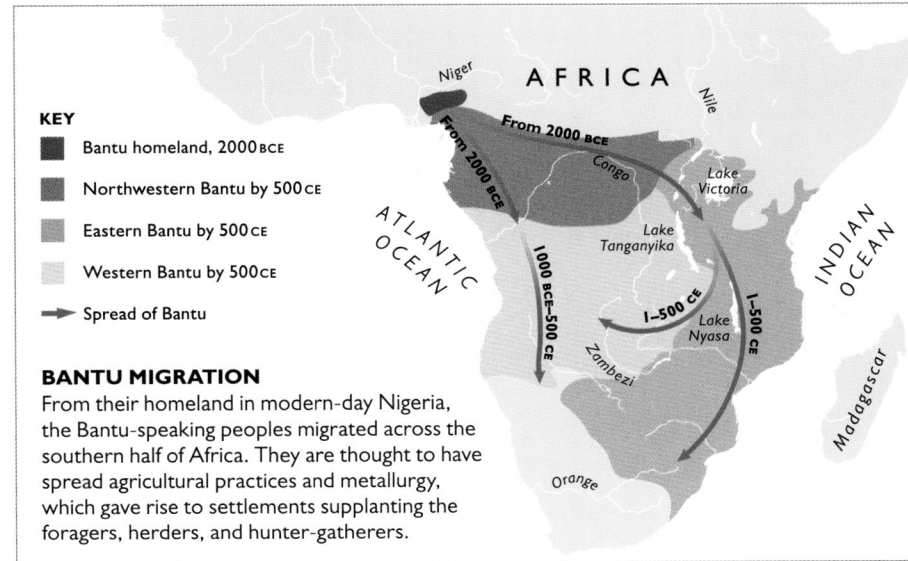

KEY

▨ Bantu homeland, 2000 BCE

▨ Northwestern Bantu by 500 CE

▨ Eastern Bantu by 500 CE

▨ Western Bantu by 500 CE

➡ Spread of Bantu

BANTU MIGRATION

From their homeland in modern-day Nigeria, the Bantu-speaking peoples migrated across the southern half of Africa. They are thought to have spread agricultural practices and metallurgy, which gave rise to settlements supplanting the foragers, herders, and hunter-gatherers.

On his way
This 17th-century print gives an impression of the sheer scale of Mansa Musa's caravan. He was said to have brought 60,000 followers—including 12,000 slaves—and 80 camels to carry the vast quantity of gold needed to fund his expedition.

MANSA MUSA

In 1324, Mansa Musa, the ruler of Mali, made a pilgrimage to Mecca that became famous for its lavishness. The vast quantities of gold the king brought with him were a sign of the prosperity of Islamic west Africa.

Islam was brought to central Africa by merchants and by the 11th century had reached west Africa, where a series of kingdoms grew rich on trade in gold and slaves. By the early 14th century, the Sundjata Kingdom of Mali, ruled by Mansa Musa (r. 1312–1337), had become the most powerful kingdom in west Africa. Musa extended its boundaries farther, reaching as far as northern Nigeria and Timbuktu.

△ **Great mosque**
One of Africa's greatest Islamic monuments, the Djingareyber Mosque was built in 1327 by Abu Ishaq al-Sahili, an architect Musa met in Mecca.

The famous pilgrim

As a show of his power, in 1324, Musa set off to perform his duty as a devout Muslim by undertaking the *hajj*, or pilgrimage to Mecca, taking with him thousands of followers and chests full of gold. His spending was so extravagant that it caused a sudden inflation of prices in Cairo, and when he paid back his debts on his return, the price of gold plummeted. He brought Islamic scholars and architects back with him, founding dozens of Quranic schools and encouraging the growth of a university at Timbuktu, which had more than 1,000 students. The fame of his pilgrimage caused Mali to become known even in Europe. However, after his death, the Sundjata Kingdom went into decline, collapsing in 1433 after Timbuktu fell to the Songhai Empire of Gao (see pp.136–137).

△ **Wealth and fame**
Mansa Musa, holding a golden scepter and a gold nugget, is prominent in west Africa in this atlas compiled in Spain in 1325. News of his lavish spending, which included a gift of 50,000 dinars to Egypt's sultan, spread far beyond the Islamic world.

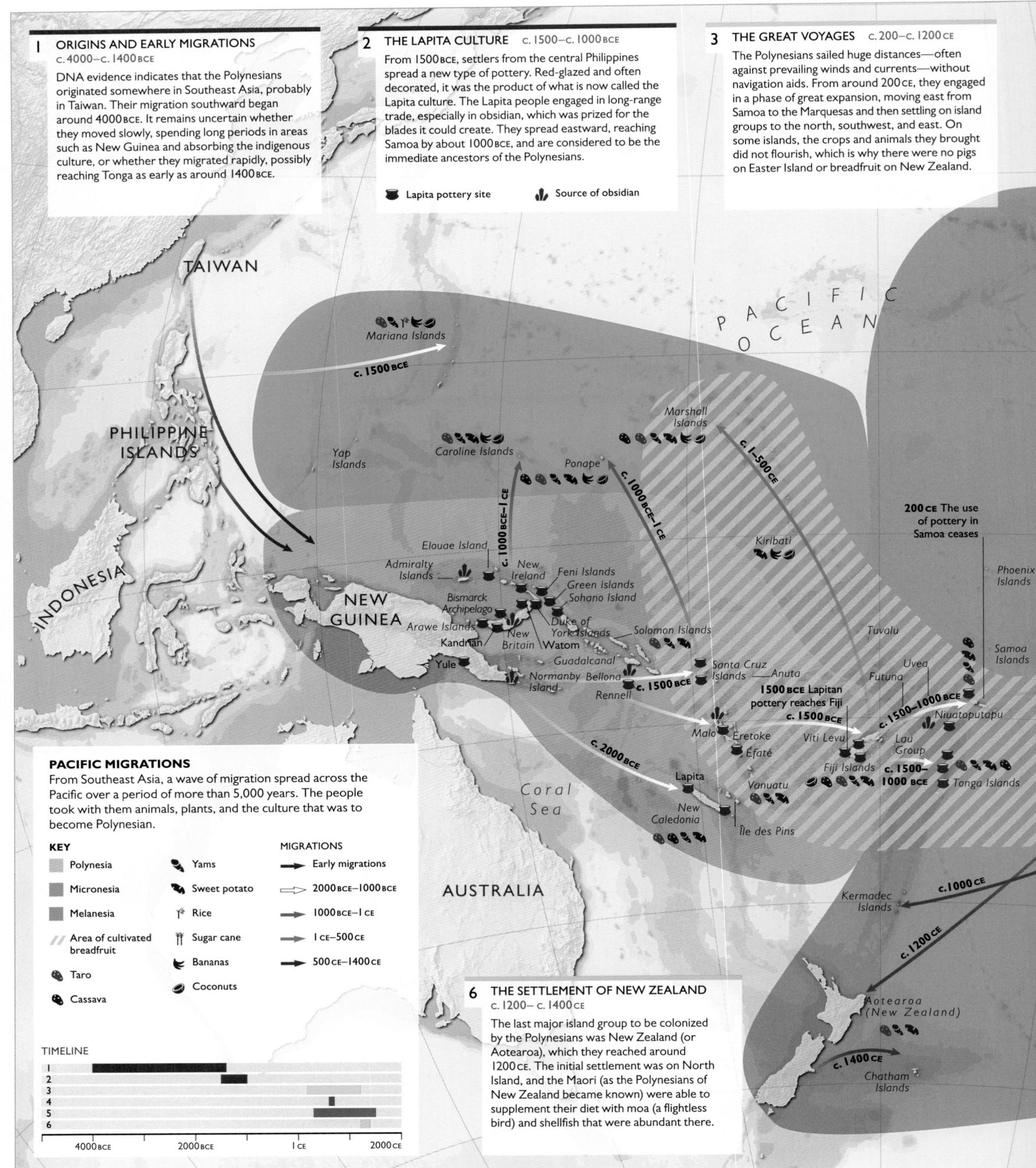

1 | ORIGINS AND EARLY MIGRATIONS c.4000–c.1400 BCE

DNA evidence indicates that the Polynesians originated somewhere in Southeast Asia, probably in Taiwan. Their migration southward began around 4000 BCE. It remains uncertain whether they moved slowly, spending long periods in areas such as New Guinea and absorbing the indigenous culture, or whether they migrated rapidly, possibly reaching Tonga as early as around 1400 BCE.

2 | THE LAPITA CULTURE c.1500–c.1000 BCE

From 1500 BCE, settlers from the central Philippines spread a new type of pottery. Red-glazed and often decorated, it was the product of what is now called the Lapita culture. The Lapita people engaged in long-range trade, especially in obsidian, which was prized for the blades it could create. They spread eastward, reaching Samoa by about 1000 BCE, and are considered to be the immediate ancestors of the Polynesians.

🪔 Lapita pottery site   🌿 Source of obsidian

3 | THE GREAT VOYAGES c.200–c.1200 CE

The Polynesians sailed huge distances—often against prevailing winds and currents—without navigation aids. From around 200 CE, they engaged in a phase of great expansion, moving east from Samoa to the Marquesas and then settling on island groups to the north, southwest, and east. On some islands, the crops and animals they brought did not flourish, which is why there were no pigs on Easter Island or breadfruit on New Zealand.

PACIFIC MIGRATIONS

From Southeast Asia, a wave of migration spread across the Pacific over a period of more than 5,000 years. The people took with them animals, plants, and the culture that was to become Polynesian.

KEY

▨ Polynesia	🥔 Yams
▨ Micronesia	🍠 Sweet potato
▨ Melanesia	🌾 Rice
▨ Area of cultivated breadfruit	🍴 Sugar cane
🥥 Taro	🍌 Bananas
🥔 Cassava	🥥 Coconuts

MIGRATIONS

➡ Early migrations
⇨ 2000 BCE–1000 BCE
→ 1000 BCE–1 CE
→ 1 CE–500 CE
➡ 500 CE–1400 CE

6 | THE SETTLEMENT OF NEW ZEALAND c.1200–c.1400 CE

The last major island group to be colonized by the Polynesians was New Zealand (or Aotearoa), which they reached around 1200 CE. The initial settlement was on North Island, and the Maori (as the Polynesians of New Zealand became known) were able to supplement their diet with moa (a flightless bird) and shellfish that were abundant there.

TIMELINE

	4000 BCE	2000 BCE	1 CE	2000 CE
1				
2				
3				
4				
5				
6				

Map labels:
TAIWAN · PHILIPPINE ISLANDS · INDONESIA · NEW GUINEA · AUSTRALIA · PACIFIC OCEAN · Coral Sea

Mariana Islands — c. 1500 BCE
Marshall Islands — c. 1–500 CE
Caroline Islands · Yap Islands · Ponape — c. 1000 BCE–1 CE
Kiribati
200 CE The use of pottery in Samoa ceases
Phoenix Islands
Elouae Island · Admiralty Islands — c. 1000 BCE–1 CE
New Ireland · Feni Islands · Green Islands · Sohano Island
Bismarck Archipelago · Duke of York Islands · Watom
Arawe Islands · Kandrian · New Britain · Yule
Normanby Island · Guadalcanal · Bellona · Rennell
Santa Cruz Islands · Anuta — c. 1500 BCE
Solomon Islands
Tuvalu · Uvea · Futuna
Samoa Islands
1500 BCE Lapitan pottery reaches Fiji — c. 1500 BCE
Niuatoputapu
Malo · Eretoke · Éfaté · Viti Levu · Lau Group — c. 1500–1000 BCE
Fiji Islands — c. 1500–1000 BCE
Tonga Islands
Vanuatu · Lapita · New Caledonia · Île des Pins — c. 2000 BCE
Kermadec Islands — c. 1000 CE
c. 1200 CE
Aotearoa (New Zealand) — c. 1400 CE
Chatham Islands

4 THE SETTLEMENT OF TAHITI   c. 600–c. 700 CE

The Polynesians reached Tahiti around 600 CE. The society that they founded there became layered, with classes of chiefs (*ari'i*), lesser chiefs and landowners (*ra'atira*), and commoners (*manahune*) that did not intermarry. They built great stone cult platforms (*marae*) for the worship of their gods and developed new technologies, such as fishing gear and adzes with tangs to make attaching hafts easier.

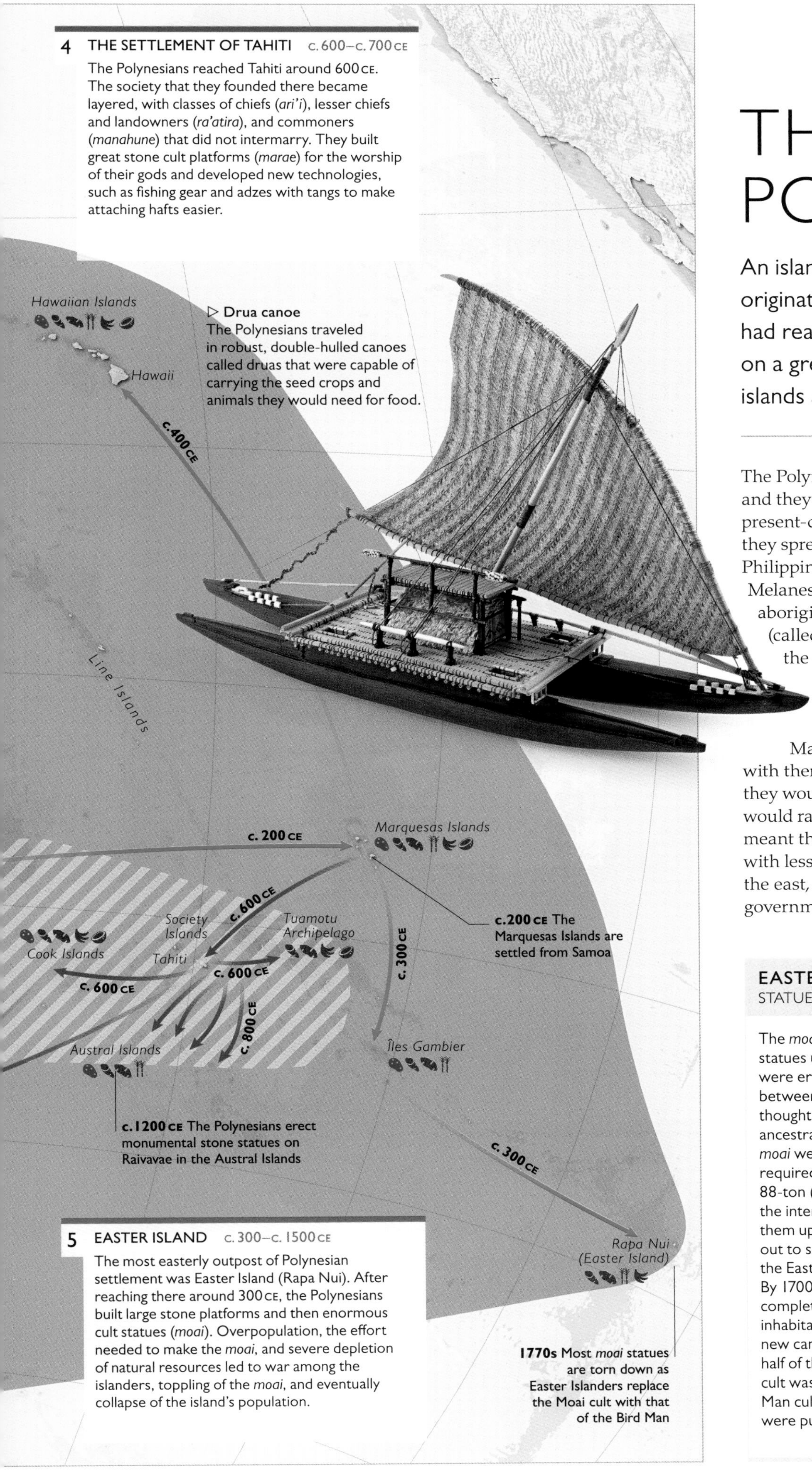

Hawaiian Islands

Hawaii

c. 400 CE

▷ **Drua canoe**
The Polynesians traveled in robust, double-hulled canoes called *druas* that were capable of carrying the seed crops and animals they would need for food.

Line Islands

c. 200 CE   Marquesas Islands

Society Islands   c. 600 CE   Tuamotu Archipelago

Cook Islands   Tahiti   c. 600 CE

c. 600 CE

c. 800 CE

Austral Islands   Îles Gambier

c. 300 CE

c. 300 CE

c. 200 CE The Marquesas Islands are settled from Samoa

c. 1200 CE The Polynesians erect monumental stone statues on Raivavae in the Austral Islands

5 EASTER ISLAND   c. 300–c. 1500 CE

The most easterly outpost of Polynesian settlement was Easter Island (Rapa Nui). After reaching there around 300 CE, the Polynesians built large stone platforms and then enormous cult statues (*moai*). Overpopulation, the effort needed to make the *moai*, and severe depletion of natural resources led to war among the islanders, toppling of the *moai*, and eventually collapse of the island's population.

Rapa Nui (Easter Island)

1770s Most *moai* statues are torn down as Easter Islanders replace the Moai cult with that of the Bird Man

THE POLYNESIANS

An island people of the central Pacific, the Polynesians originated in Southeast Asia. By around 1000 BCE, they had reached Tonga and Samoa. They then embarked on a great migration to reach previously unpopulated islands as distant as Easter Island and New Zealand.

The Polynesians' original ancestors probably came from Taiwan, and they spoke Austronesian languages similar to those heard in present-day Indonesia and the Philippines. From about 4000 BCE, they spread southward and eastward, passing through the Philippines and areas settled more than 20,000 years earlier by Melanesians (an ethnic group related to modern Australian aboriginals). The eastward spread of their early culture (called Lapita) to Tonga and Samoa can be traced through the remains of its distinctive red-glazed pottery.

The Polynesians developed double-hulled voyaging canoes with balancing outriggers that allowed them to reach distant island groups, including the Cook and Marquesas islands, Hawaii, and New Zealand. They took with them taro, yams, sweet potatoes, breadfruit, and bananas that they would cultivate on the islands, and chickens and pigs they would raise for meat. The far-flung nature of their island settlement meant that their societies diverged significantly from one another, with less stratified societies to the west and more complex ones to the east, especially in Hawaii, where a monarchy and centralized government emerged.

EASTER ISLAND *MOAI*
STATUES OF THE SPIRITS

The *moai*, monumental stone statues up to 33 ft (10 m) high, were erected on Easter Island between 1200 and 1600. They are thought to represent protective ancestral spirits. More than 900 *moai* were erected, but the effort required to quarry and haul 88-ton (80-tonne) blocks from the interior of the island and to set them up on *ahau* (platforms) facing out to sea was a major drain on the Easter Islanders' resources. By 1700, the island was almost completely deforested, and its inhabitants could not even build new canoes to fish. In the second half of the 18th century, the Moai cult was superseded by the Bird Man cult, and the *moai* statues were pulled down.

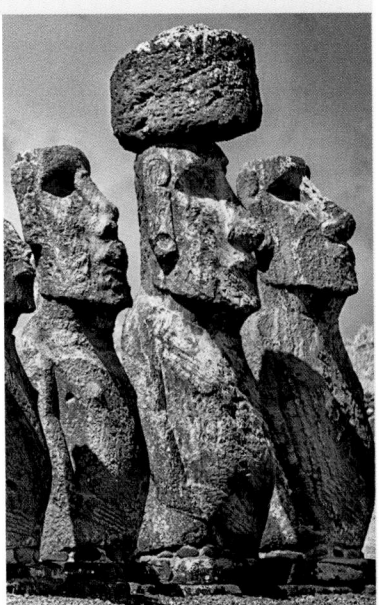

NORTH AMERICAN CULTURES

From 500 to 1500, many diverse cultures flourished in North America, including complex chiefdoms. Various nomadic groups turned to farming, including the Puebloan cultures in the southwest, evolving into large communities that traded extensively. Meanwhile, a new wave of Mound Builder cultures emerged to the east.

The ancient cultures of North America were shaped largely by the environment and available food resources.

In the southwest, the adoption of corn followed by the development of irrigation practices—as conditions became drier around 1000 BCE—forced previously nomadic groups to adopt complex social structures to ensure their survival, giving rise to the early Puebloan settlements. By 400 CE, these settlements had developed into complexes of cliff-dwellings or small towns, which clustered around a large centre featuring low platform mounds and ceremonial ball courts (which hint at Mesoamerican influences). These communities made pottery and basketware, and also mined turquoise, which they traded with the great Mesoamerican cities to the south. Several distinct cultures emerged, and each dominated at different times and in different regions of the southwest.

Elsewhere, the introduction of corn, later supplemented by beans, led to the birth of the Mississippian Mound Builder cultures, following the decline of the Adena and Hopewell (see pp. 52–53). The various Mississippian subgroups flourished between 800 and 1500, each ruled by chiefs residing in fortified centers featuring mounds that served as foundations for temples. Some Mississippian centers grew into towns, the largest of which, Cahokia, thrived from 1050 to 1250. With up to 20,000 inhabitants, these settlements each had a palisaded center, ringed by large earthen platform mounds.

> "… a group of mounds… at a distance resembling enormous haystacks scattered through a meadow"
>
> WRITER HENRY MARIE BRACKENRIDGE ON SEEING CAHOKIA, 1811

MESA VERDE
GREAT ANCIENT PUEBLOAN SETTLEMENT

From about 700 CE, many of the Ancient Puebloans of the southwest began constructing settlements high in the cliffs, which offered protection. The largest of these was Mesa Verde, comprising 4,500 residential sites, of which 600 were cliff dwellings: villages built into the giant alcoves of the mesa walls. By about 1200, the population of Mesa Verde proper reached about 30,000 people, most of whom lived in dense settlements at the heads of the area's canyons.

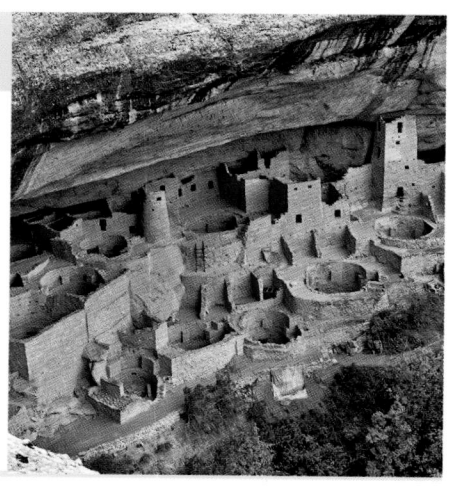

◁ **Warrior relief**
This Mississippian copper ornament depicting a warrior or a chief in relief was unearthed in the Caddoan settlement at Spiro, which thrived between 800 and 1450.

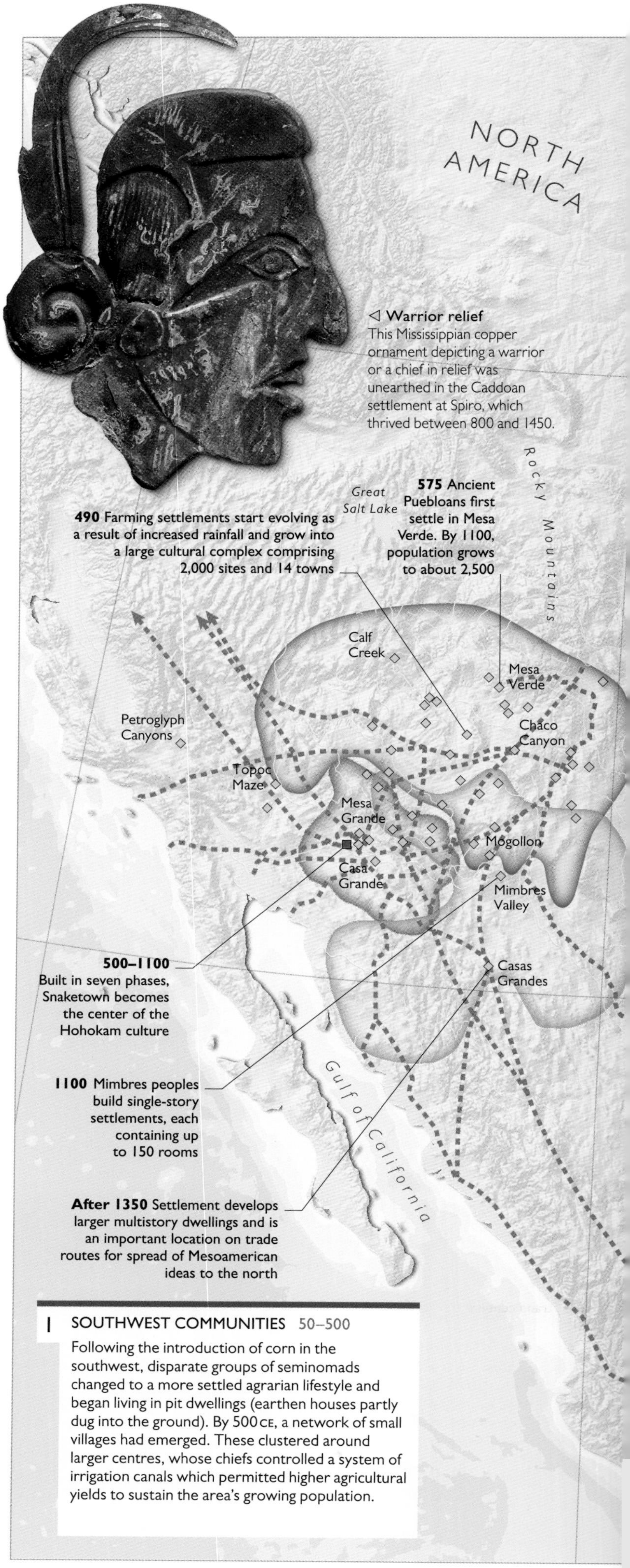

NORTH AMERICA

490 Farming settlements start evolving as a result of increased rainfall and grow into a large cultural complex comprising 2,000 sites and 14 towns

575 Ancient Puebloans first settle in Mesa Verde. By 1100, population grows to about 2,500

Great Salt Lake

Rocky Mountains

Calf Creek

Petroglyph Canyons

Mesa Verde

Chaco Canyon

Topoc Maze

Mesa Grande

Mogollon

Casa Grande

Mimbres Valley

Casas Grandes

Gulf of California

500–1100 Built in seven phases, Snaketown becomes the center of the Hohokam culture

1100 Mimbres peoples build single-story settlements, each containing up to 150 rooms

After 1350 Settlement develops larger multistory dwellings and is an important location on trade routes for spread of Mesoamerican ideas to the north

SOUTHWEST COMMUNITIES 50–500

Following the introduction of corn in the southwest, disparate groups of seminomads changed to a more settled agrarian lifestyle and began living in pit dwellings (earthen houses partly dug into the ground). By 500 CE, a network of small villages had emerged. These clustered around larger centres, whose chiefs controlled a system of irrigation canals which permitted higher agricultural yields to sustain the area's growing population.

2 THE MOGOLLON 250–1350

Small hamlets comprising several pithouses made up the earliest Mogollon villages. Settlements were built near mountain streams or along ridges, offering defense from raiders. The Mogollon made distinctive red-on-brown ceramics with intricate designs. A subgroup of the Mogollon culture, the Mimbres, made pottery with beautiful black-on-white geometric patterns.

▬ Area of influence

3 THE HOHOKAM 300–1450

Between 1100 and 1450, the Hohokam people built a settlement at Snaketown featuring a series of large mounds. The settlement was home to about 1,000 people and also had two ball courts—similar to those of Mesoamerican cultures, from whom they imported exotic products such as copper bells and macaws.

▬ Area of influence   ■ Hohokam center

4 CHACO CANYON 700–1500

The peoples of the southwest began to build complexes of houses set into sheltered rock-faces. The Ancient Puebloans constructed towns, notably at Chaco Canyon, with an extensive road network connecting them. They managed water resources carefully, but around 1130, overpopulation, aggravated by droughts, strained the area's resources and the Chaco culture collapsed.

▬ Area of influence

5 MIDDLE MISSISSIPPIAN 600–1400

From 600 CE, peoples in the Midwest started shifting to farming corn, beans, and squash. By 1000 they had organized a complex settlement-based society, typically featuring large ceremonial mounds encircled by ditches and ramparts. The largest was based in Cahokia, where about 100 earth mounds were grouped around open plazas.

▮ Area of Influence   ◖ Temple mound site

6 LATE MISSISSIPPIAN MOUND CULTURES 1000–1600

After 1000 CE, corn cultivation spread widely throughout the east, giving rise to a variety of temple mounds subcultures. It is thought that the subgroups were organized as chiefdoms composed of people with either "elite" or "commoner" social ranking. The Mississippians did not have writing, but representations of their beliefs were preserved in engravings on stone figurines, shells, ceramic designs, effigy smoking pipes, and stone tablets.

CULTURAL AREA AND TEMPLE MOUND SITE

◖ Oneota		◖ Caddoan
◖ Fort Ancient		◖ South Appalachian
◖ Plaquemine		

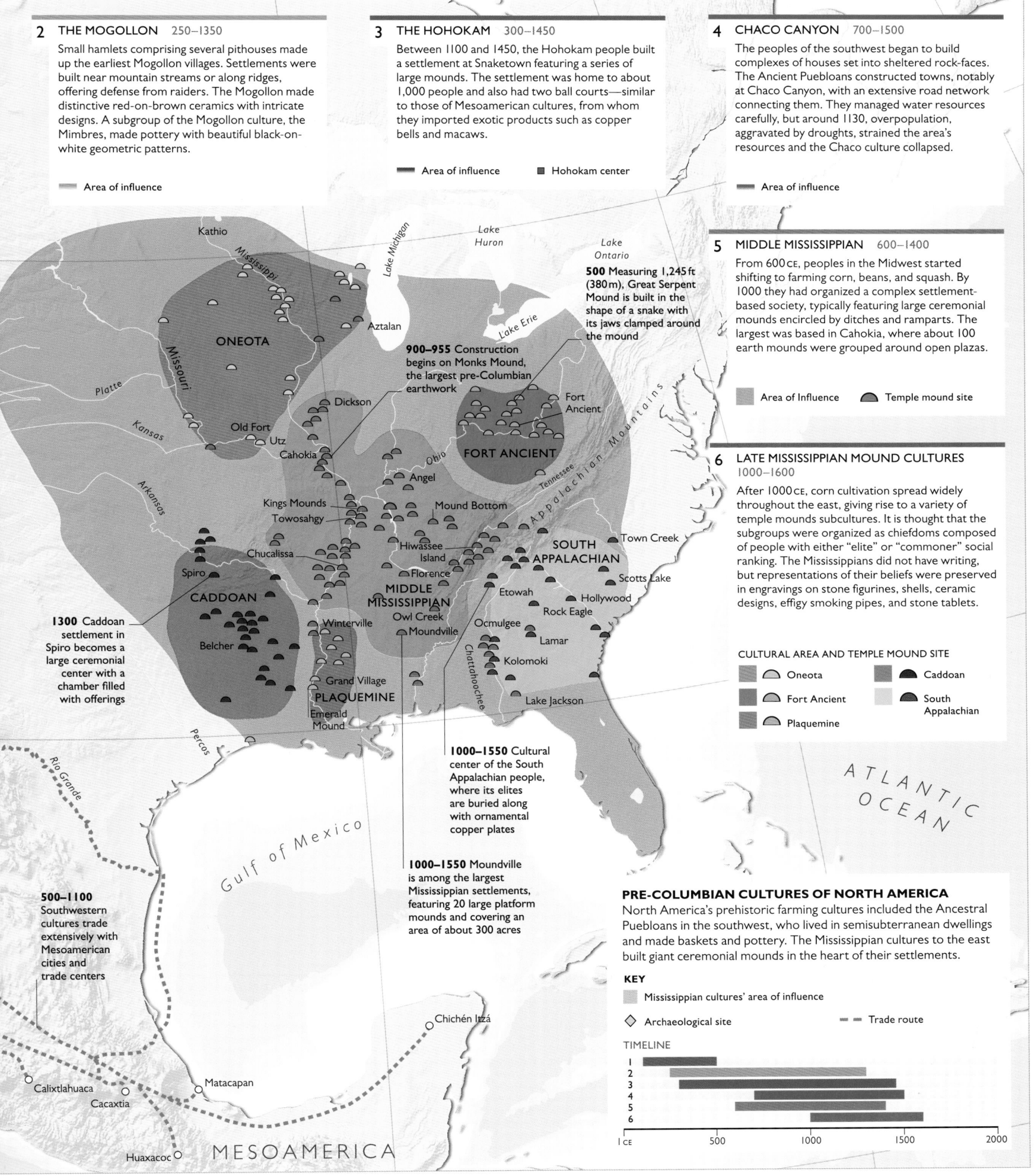

500 Measuring 1,245 ft (380 m), Great Serpent Mound is built in the shape of a snake with its jaws clamped around the mound

900–955 Construction begins on Monks Mound, the largest pre-Columbian earthwork

1300 Caddoan settlement in Spiro becomes a large ceremonial center with a chamber filled with offerings

500–1100 Southwestern cultures trade extensively with Mesoamerican cities and trade centers

1000–1550 Cultural center of the South Appalachian people, where its elites are buried along with ornamental copper plates

1000–1550 Moundville is among the largest Mississippian settlements, featuring 20 large platform mounds and covering an area of about 300 acres

PRE-COLUMBIAN CULTURES OF NORTH AMERICA

North America's prehistoric farming cultures included the Ancestral Puebloans in the southwest, who lived in semisubterranean dwellings and made baskets and pottery. The Mississippian cultures to the east built giant ceremonial mounds in the heart of their settlements.

KEY

▮ Mississippian cultures' area of influence

◇ Archaeological site   ---- Trade route

TIMELINE

AZTEC AND INCA EMPIRES

Two large empires emerged in the Americas in the 14th century. In Mesoamerica, the Aztec culture grew into a major civilization, famous for its tribute system, warfare, art, and architecture. Meanwhile, starting in Peru's Cuzco valley, the Inca people created a vast realm along the Andes and asserted their rule using a sophisticated bureaucracy and a sprawling network of roads.

The Aztecs originally settled on an island in Lake Texcoco and founded the city of Tenochtitlan in 1325. The culture privileged the training of a warrior elite, and within half a century amassed a formidable army. Following the Triple Alliance—a partnership the Aztecs formed with the cities of Texcoco and Tlacopan—the Aztecs engaged in a phase of conquests. Their army invaded neighboring communities, overthrew the local chieftains, and turned these territories into vassals. Aztec officials were then appointed to ensure that tributes—the main source of revenue for the empire—as well as captives for human sacrifice were sent to the capital, where the rulers pooled the resources into building monuments and artworks.

The Incas emerged as the predominant group in Peru's Cuzco valley after settling in the region in about 1250, developing techniques to farm on mountain terraces. The Incas began a phase of conquests in 1438; by the early 1500s, they had overthrown powerful neighbors the Chimú and the Chancas and extended their rule to Quito in the north and the Araucanian desert of Chile to the south. The Incas instituted a strong administrative structure and built a complex road network to help them govern the vast empire.

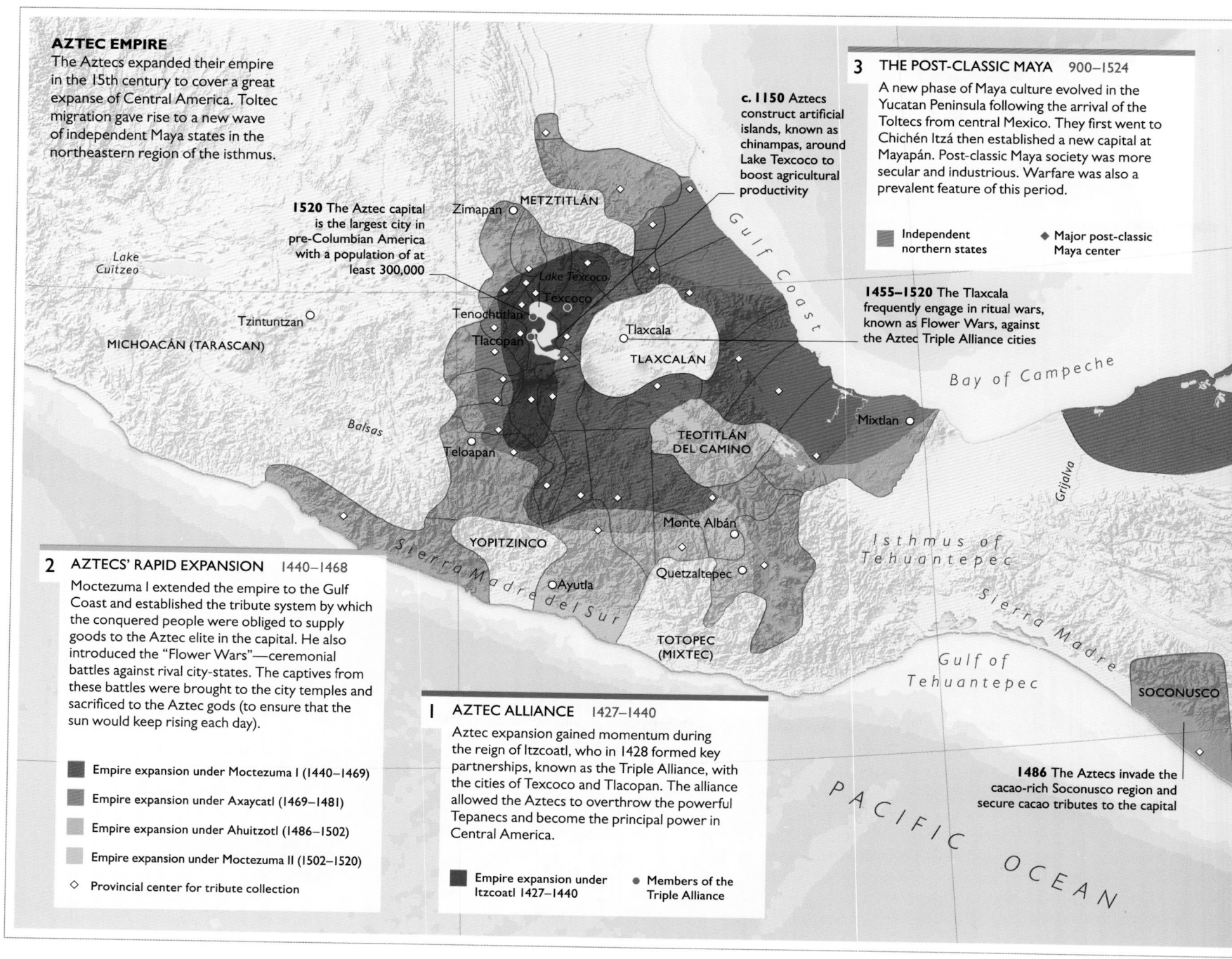

AZTEC EMPIRE
The Aztecs expanded their empire in the 15th century to cover a great expanse of Central America. Toltec migration gave rise to a new wave of independent Maya states in the northeastern region of the isthmus.

c. 1150 Aztecs construct artificial islands, known as chinampas, around Lake Texcoco to boost agricultural productivity

1520 The Aztec capital is the largest city in pre-Columbian America with a population of at least 300,000

3 THE POST-CLASSIC MAYA 900–1524
A new phase of Maya culture evolved in the Yucatan Peninsula following the arrival of the Toltecs from central Mexico. They first went to Chichén Itzá then established a new capital at Mayapán. Post-classic Maya society was more secular and industrious. Warfare was also a prevalent feature of this period.

■ Independent northern states
◆ Major post-classic Maya center

1455–1520 The Tlaxcala frequently engage in ritual wars, known as Flower Wars, against the Aztec Triple Alliance cities

2 AZTECS' RAPID EXPANSION 1440–1468
Moctezuma I extended the empire to the Gulf Coast and established the tribute system by which the conquered people were obliged to supply goods to the Aztec elite in the capital. He also introduced the "Flower Wars"—ceremonial battles against rival city-states. The captives from these battles were brought to the city temples and sacrificed to the Aztec gods (to ensure that the sun would keep rising each day).

■ Empire expansion under Moctezuma I (1440–1469)
■ Empire expansion under Axaycatl (1469–1481)
■ Empire expansion under Ahuitzotl (1486–1502)
■ Empire expansion under Moctezuma II (1502–1520)
◇ Provincial center for tribute collection

1 AZTEC ALLIANCE 1427–1440
Aztec expansion gained momentum during the reign of Itzcoatl, who in 1428 formed key partnerships, known as the Triple Alliance, with the cities of Texcoco and Tlacopan. The alliance allowed the Aztecs to overthrow the powerful Tepanecs and become the principal power in Central America.

■ Empire expansion under Itzcoatl 1427–1440
● Members of the Triple Alliance

1486 The Aztecs invade the cacao-rich Soconusco region and secure cacao tributes to the capital

AZTEC AND INCA CONQUESTS

The Aztec and Inca Empires, as well as the independent post-classic Maya states, were the largest urban civilizations in Central and South America before the Europeans' arrival in the 16th century. In particular, the Aztecs and Incas were territorial and embarked on a phase of conquests to absorb other societies and extend their rule over a larger area.

KEY

○ Major urban centers

TIMELINE

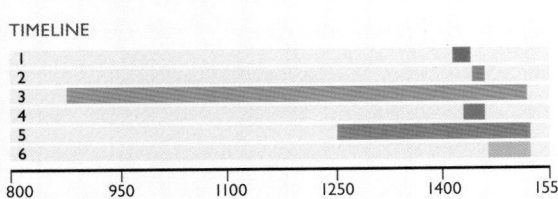

1						
2						
3						
4						
5						
6						

800   950   1100   1250   1400   1550

INCA EMPIRE

At its height, the Inca Empire extended from modern Ecuador to the southern city of Talca in modern-day Chile. A vast network of roads connected the major Inca cities.

PACIFIC OCEAN

---

4   THE BIRTH OF THE INCA EMPIRE   1438–1471

Led by Cusi Yupanqui, in 1438 the Incas defeated the Chancas, who had attacked the Inca stronghold in Cuzco. Yupanqui took the name Pachacutec and became the Sapa Inca (Inca ruler). He then waged a series of wars that resulted in Inca expansion and culminated with victory in Chan Chan, the capital of the Chimú civilization, in 1470.

■ Empire expansion under Pachacutec (1438–1471)

☐ Chimú civilization

1471 The sacred Huari site of Pachacamac is taken over by the Incas. A temple dedicated to the Inca sun deity is built

c.1470 Incas conquer the Chimú capital Chan Chan and bring back many craftsmen to work on Inca constructions in Cuzco

1438 Inca ruler Yupanqui defeats the Chancas to control the Cuzco valley and further expand the Inca Empire

Map locations: Quito, Latacunga, Amabato, Ríobamba, Ingapirca, Tomebamba, Tumbes, Saraguro, Sullana, Piura, Huancabamba, Chiquitoy, Cajamarca, Chan Chan, Huaylas, Huarás, Huánuco, Pumpo, Tarma, Paramonga, Jauja, Machu Picchu, Pachacamac, Huamanga, Vitcos, Ollantaytambo, Incawasi, Tambo Colorado, Cuzco, Huaitará, Vilcási, Abancay, Ayaviri, Ica, Andahuaylas, Hatuncolla, Nazca, Chucuito, Chuquiabo, Acari, Juli, Tiahuanaco, Atico, Pomata, Cotopachi, Paria, Hualla Tampu, Cochabamba, Tupiza, Catarpe, Tilcara, Mount Acay, La Paya, Copiapó, Pucará de Andagalá, Chilecito, Ranchillos, Santiago, Talca

Geographic labels: Napo, Amazon Basin, Amazon, Marañón, Juruá, Purus, Ucayali, Andes, Madeira, Madre de Dios, Mamoré, Lake Titicaca, Altiplano, Lake Poopó, Atacama Desert, Araucanian Desert, Salado, Maule

---

5   INCA CAPITAL   1250–1525

The Sapa Inca ruled the empire from Cuzco, which sat at the center of a 12,500 mile (20,000 km) road network. The Sapa Inca imposed a realm-wide taxation system (paid in kind), controlled trade, and drew on a large peasant labor force for construction projects.

— Imperial roads   ☆ Inca capital

---

6   EXPANDING SOUTH   1471–1525

Under Tupac Yupanqui (1471–1493) and Huaya Capac (1493–1525), the Inca completed the conquest of Ecuador and pushed far south into modern Chile. With the prospect of sharing the plunder won in subsequent conquests, male captives often became Inca soldiers, which further strengthened Inca dominance. At its height, the Inca Empire ruled as many as 12 million people.

■ Inca expansion under Tupac Yupanqui (1471–1493)

☐ Inca expansion under Huayna Capac (1493–1525)

1224 City is abandoned by the Toltecs. A people known as the Uicil-abnal, which later takes the name Itzá, settles in the desolate city

c.1200 Mayapán becomes a vast and powerful Maya political center

Map locations (Maya): Mayapán, Chichén Itzá, Isla de Cozúmel, Uxmal, Yucatan Peninsula, Tayasal, Zacaleu, Utatlán, Mixco Viejo, Iximché, Gulf of Honduras, Usumacinta, Motagua, Sierra Madre

▷ **Serpent mask of Tlaloc**
This turquoise mosaic mask in the form of two intertwined serpents is associated with Tlaloc, the Aztec god of rain, water, and earthly fertility.

THE EARLY MODERN WORLD

AS HORIZONS WIDENED IN 1450–1700, CONTACT BETWEEN EAST AND WEST MADE TRADE AND CULTURAL EXCHANGE GLOBAL AND THE WORLD RECOGNIZABLY MODERN.

THE EARLY MODERN WORLD

Between 1450 and 1700, European explorers reached the Americas and began to explore maritime routes around Africa into Asia. Military and scientific revolutions in Europe also enabled its leading powers to encroach on non-European territories.

△ **Competing for souls**
This 1614 painting by the Dutch artist Adriaen van de Venne is symbolic of the religious rivalry that divided Europe. Here, the "catch" of the Protestants (to the left) is depicted as greater than that of their Catholic rivals.

In 1450, a politically fragmented Europe exerted little influence outside its borders—France and England were still at war, Spain was divided, and the trading city-states of Italy seemed to be the continent's most dynamic powers. It was the impulse to trade that eventually revolutionized Europe's position in the world.

Discovering new worlds

Portuguese mariners inched around the African coastline in search of new routes to the lucrative spice markets of Asia—succeeding in 1498, when Vasco da Gama's fleet reached the Indian port of Calicut (now Kozhikode). By then, however, an even more astonishing discovery had been made—Christopher Columbus had stumbled upon a Caribbean island in 1492. This had opened up the Americas, which had been isolated from the rest of the world for millennia.

Spanish adventurers poured across the Atlantic into the Americas, toppling the native Aztec and Inca Empires with surprising ease. They established the first European colonial empire and sent back treasures and silver, which contributed to inflation in Spain but also boosted the country's Habsburg rulers' ability to fight continental wars. This was an invaluable asset at a volatile time; the

religious unity of western Europe had broken down after the German priest Martin Luther had made protests in 1517 against corruption in the Roman Catholic Church. This had prompted a series of reformers to establish alternative Protestant churches, which in turn provoked a spasm of religious warfare. Matters came to a head with the outbreak of the Thirty Years' War in 1618, which pitched German Catholic and Protestant princes against each other and brought in armies from France, the Habsburg Empire, and Sweden that criss-crossed the continent and left it utterly devastated.

Wars in Europe

The arrival of gunpowder warfare heralded the beginnings of European standing armies, trained in the use of firearms and operating in units far larger than ever before. This military revolution in the 16th century immeasurably enhanced the powers of European monarchs but raised the risks of warfare. England suffered the consequences of civil war when tension between an autocratic monarch and a resentful parliament burst into conflict—resulting in the execution of King Charles I in 1649

◁ **Art flourishes in India**
This beautiful edition of the *Divan*, the collected works of the popular 14th-century Persian poet Hafiz, was compiled in Mughal India—a rich period for both visual art and literature.

EXPLORATION AND SCHISM

The Early Modern period was one of profound transformation. European explorers reached the New World in 1492, precipitating the collapse of previously dominant societies. Although European traders also reached the spice-producing areas of Asia by rounding Africa, the footholds they established there were much more modest. Europe itself was racked by religious conflicts marred by violence that only ended after a century of warfare.

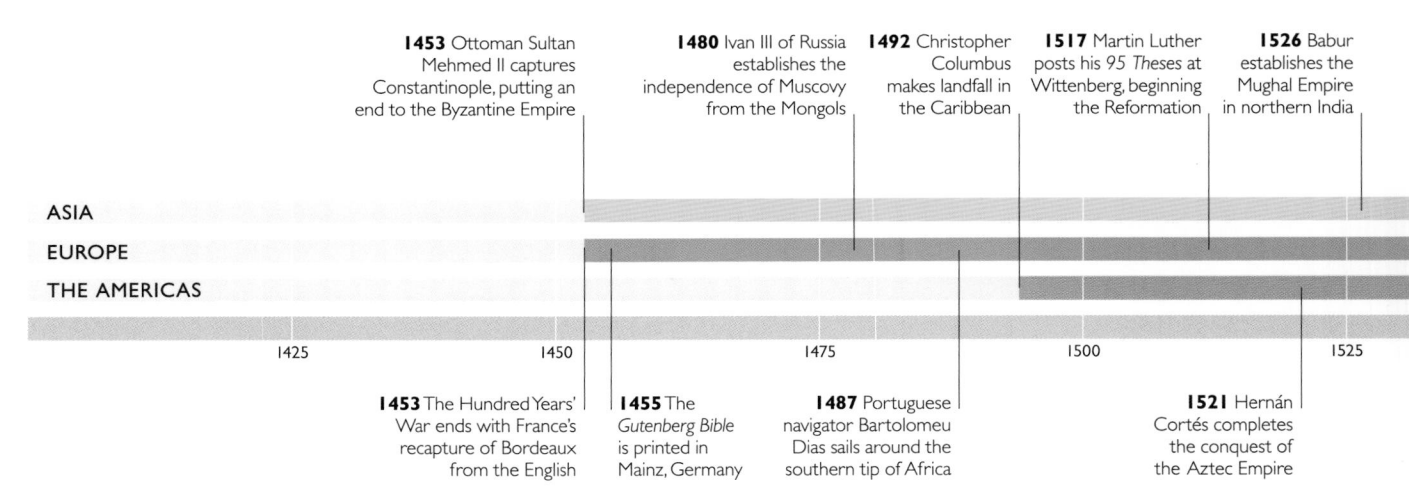

1453 Ottoman Sultan Mehmed II captures Constantinople, putting an end to the Byzantine Empire

1480 Ivan III of Russia establishes the independence of Muscovy from the Mongols

1492 Christopher Columbus makes landfall in the Caribbean

1517 Martin Luther posts his *95 Theses* at Wittenberg, beginning the Reformation

1526 Babur establishes the Mughal Empire in northern India

ASIA

EUROPE

THE AMERICAS

1425   1450   1475   1500   1525

1453 The Hundred Years' War ends with France's recapture of Bordeaux from the English

1455 The *Gutenberg Bible* is printed in Mainz, Germany

1487 Portuguese navigator Bartolomeu Dias sails around the southern tip of Africa

1521 Hernán Cortés completes the conquest of the Aztec Empire

◁ **Way of the warrior**
During Japan's Edo, or Tokugawa, period, samurai warriors had gained a high ranking in a rigidly followed caste system. This military armor of a samurai warrior dates from the 19th century.

and the establishment of a republic for 12 years, the only one in Britain's history. By the time monarchy was restored in 1660, Britain faced new rivals: a resurgent France under Louis XIV, and the infant Dutch Republic, whose traders displaced the Portuguese and the Spanish in parts of Asia.

Further expansion

France and Britain extended their competition to the Americas, where they ate away at the Portuguese and Spanish duopoly. They also began to encroach upon Asia, but here they faced strong rivals.

The Ottoman Empire had expanded to occupy the whole of Turkey and much of the Middle East and North Africa. The Safavid Empire brought a golden age to Persia (modern Iran), while the Mughals seized Delhi in 1526 and had conquered most of the Indian subcontinent by 1700. In China, the Ming and Qing Dynasties, both socially

"The church needs a reformation ... it is the work of God alone ..."

MARTIN LUTHER, GERMAN THEOLOGIAN

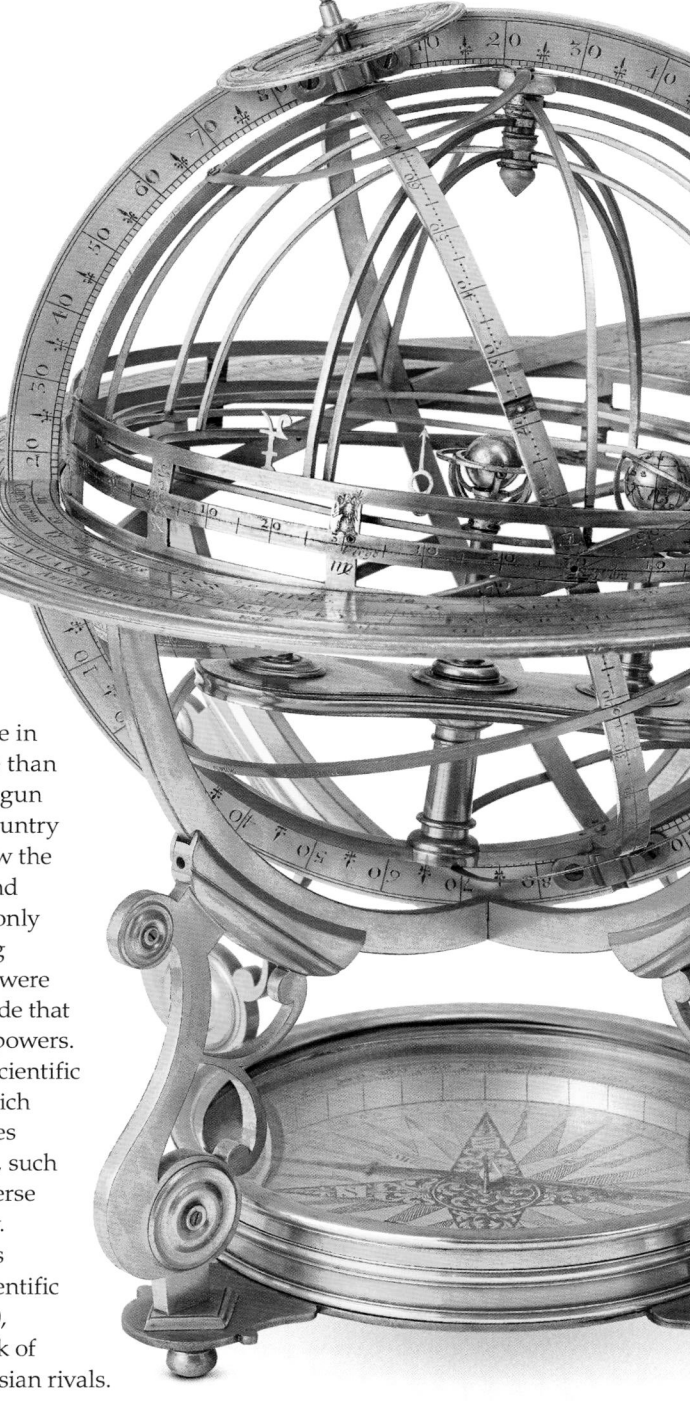

▷ **Celestial model**
With the Sun at its center, this model, called an armillary sphere, was used to represent the positions of celestial objects.

and diplomatically conservative, regarded the foreigners—who came in increasing numbers—as little more than irritants. In Japan, however, the shogun Tokugawa, who had reunited the country in 1600 after a long civil war, foresaw the dangers posed by foreign powers and gradually excluded them, allowing only the Dutch to persist in a tiny trading enclave off Nagasaki. The Japanese were thus protected from the European tide that began to wash against other Asian powers. They were also insulated from the scientific revolution that began in Europe, which overturned centuries-old orthodoxies and paved the way for new theories, such as Copernicus's Sun-centered Universe and Isaac Newton's work on gravity. As Europe's military power grew, its economic reach widened and its scientific resourcefulness burgeoned. By 1700, European powers stood on the brink of pulling definitively ahead of their Asian rivals.

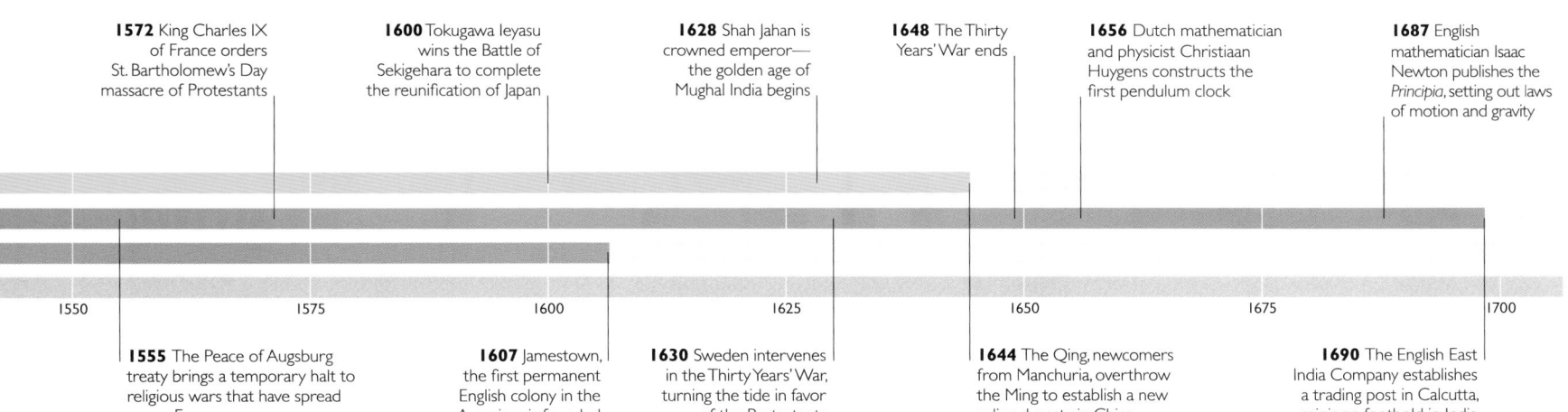

1572 King Charles IX of France orders St. Bartholomew's Day massacre of Protestants

1600 Tokugawa Ieyasu wins the Battle of Sekigehara to complete the reunification of Japan

1628 Shah Jahan is crowned emperor—the golden age of Mughal India begins

1648 The Thirty Years' War ends

1656 Dutch mathematician and physicist Christiaan Huygens constructs the first pendulum clock

1687 English mathematician Isaac Newton publishes the *Principia*, setting out laws of motion and gravity

1550　　　　1575　　　　1600　　　　1625　　　　1650　　　　1675　　　1700

1555 The Peace of Augsburg treaty brings a temporary halt to religious wars that have spread across Europe

1607 Jamestown, the first permanent English colony in the Americas, is founded

1630 Sweden intervenes in the Thirty Years' War, turning the tide in favor of the Protestants

1644 The Qing, newcomers from Manchuria, overthrow the Ming to establish a new ruling dynasty in China

1690 The English East India Company establishes a trading post in Calcutta, gaining a foothold in India

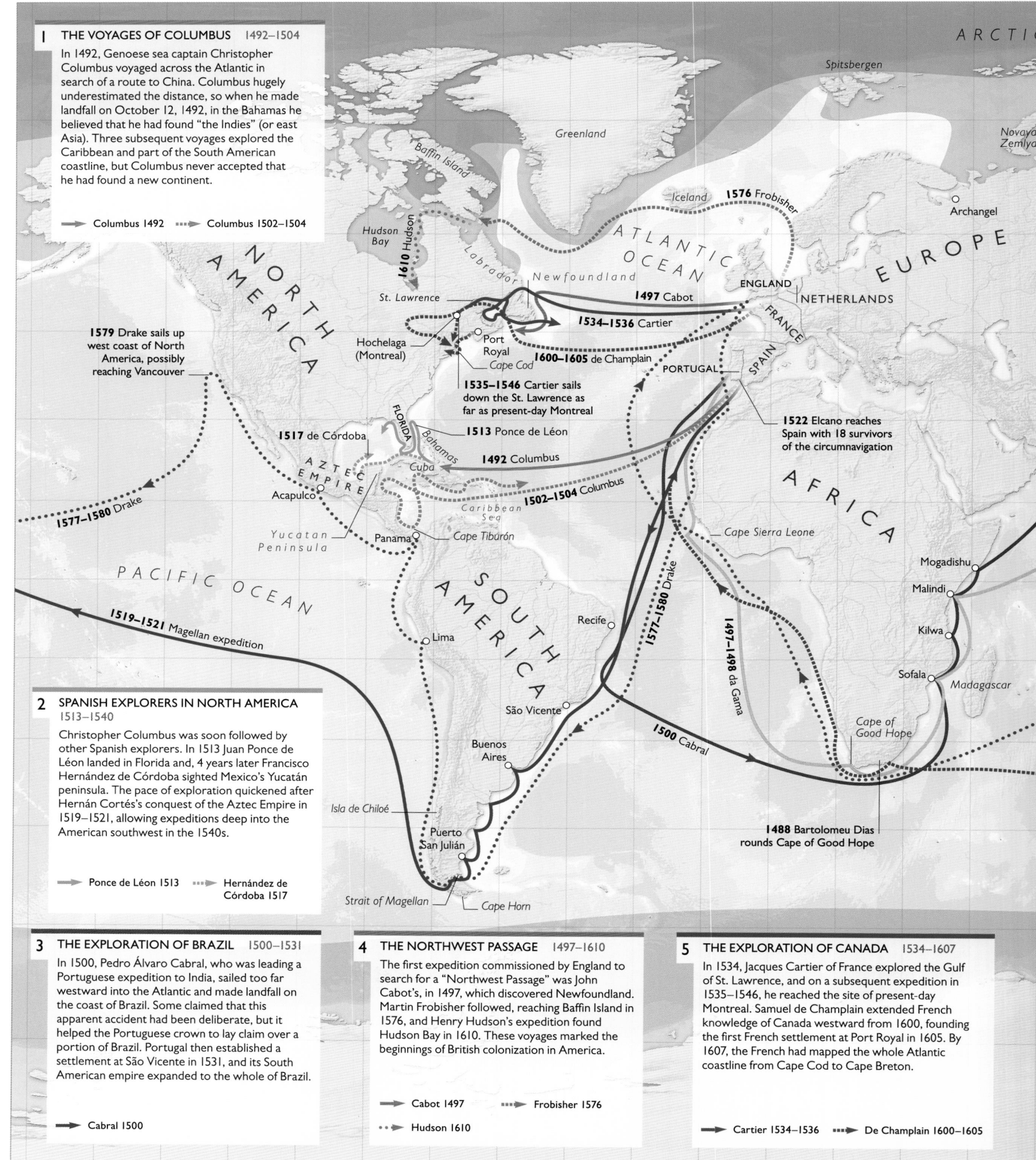

1 THE VOYAGES OF COLUMBUS 1492–1504

In 1492, Genoese sea captain Christopher Columbus voyaged across the Atlantic in search of a route to China. Columbus hugely underestimated the distance, so when he made landfall on October 12, 1492, in the Bahamas he believed that he had found "the Indies" (or east Asia). Three subsequent voyages explored the Caribbean and part of the South American coastline, but Columbus never accepted that he had found a new continent.

→ Columbus 1492   ▪▪▶ Columbus 1502–1504

2 SPANISH EXPLORERS IN NORTH AMERICA 1513–1540

Christopher Columbus was soon followed by other Spanish explorers. In 1513 Juan Ponce de Léon landed in Florida and, 4 years later Francisco Hernández de Córdoba sighted Mexico's Yucatán peninsula. The pace of exploration quickened after Hernán Cortés's conquest of the Aztec Empire in 1519–1521, allowing expeditions deep into the American southwest in the 1540s.

→ Ponce de Léon 1513   ▪▪▶ Hernández de Córdoba 1517

3 THE EXPLORATION OF BRAZIL 1500–1531

In 1500, Pedro Álvaro Cabral, who was leading a Portuguese expedition to India, sailed too far westward into the Atlantic and made landfall on the coast of Brazil. Some claimed that this apparent accident had been deliberate, but it helped the Portuguese crown to lay claim over a portion of Brazil. Portugal then established a settlement at São Vicente in 1531, and its South American empire expanded to the whole of Brazil.

→ Cabral 1500

4 THE NORTHWEST PASSAGE 1497–1610

The first expedition commissioned by England to search for a "Northwest Passage" was John Cabot's, in 1497, which discovered Newfoundland. Martin Frobisher followed, reaching Baffin Island in 1576, and Henry Hudson's expedition found Hudson Bay in 1610. These voyages marked the beginnings of British colonization in America.

→ Cabot 1497   ▪▪▶ Frobisher 1576
▪▪▪ Hudson 1610

5 THE EXPLORATION OF CANADA 1534–1607

In 1534, Jacques Cartier of France explored the Gulf of St. Lawrence, and on a subsequent expedition in 1535–1546, he reached the site of present-day Montreal. Samuel de Champlain extended French knowledge of Canada westward from 1600, founding the first French settlement at Port Royal in 1605. By 1607, the French had mapped the whole Atlantic coastline from Cape Cod to Cape Breton.

→ Cartier 1534–1536   ▪▪▶ De Champlain 1600–1605

Map labels: ARCTIC, Spitsbergen, Novaya Zemlya, Greenland, Baffin Island, Iceland, 1576 Frobisher, Archangel, ATLANTIC OCEAN, EUROPE, Hudson Bay, 1610 Hudson, Labrador, Newfoundland, ENGLAND, NETHERLANDS, St. Lawrence, 1497 Cabot, FRANCE, NORTH AMERICA, 1534–1536 Cartier, Hochelaga (Montreal), Port Royal, 1600–1605 de Champlain, PORTUGAL, SPAIN, Cape Cod, 1535–1546 Cartier sails down the St. Lawrence as far as present-day Montreal, 1579 Drake sails up west coast of North America, possibly reaching Vancouver, 1522 Elcano reaches Spain with 18 survivors of the circumnavigation, 1513 Ponce de Léon, FLORIDA, 1517 de Córdoba, Bahamas, 1492 Columbus, AZTEC EMPIRE, Cuba, Acapulco, 1577–1580 Drake, Caribbean Sea, 1502–1504 Columbus, AFRICA, Yucatan Peninsula, Panama, Cape Tiburón, Cape Sierra Leone, Mogadishu, Malindi, PACIFIC OCEAN, SOUTH AMERICA, Recife, 1577–1580 Drake, 1497–1498 da Gama, Kilwa, 1519–1521 Magellan expedition, Lima, Sofala, Madagascar, São Vicente, 1500 Cabral, Cape of Good Hope, Buenos Aires, Isla de Chiloé, Puerto San Julián, 1488 Bartolomeu Dias rounds Cape of Good Hope, Strait of Magellan, Cape Horn

OCEAN

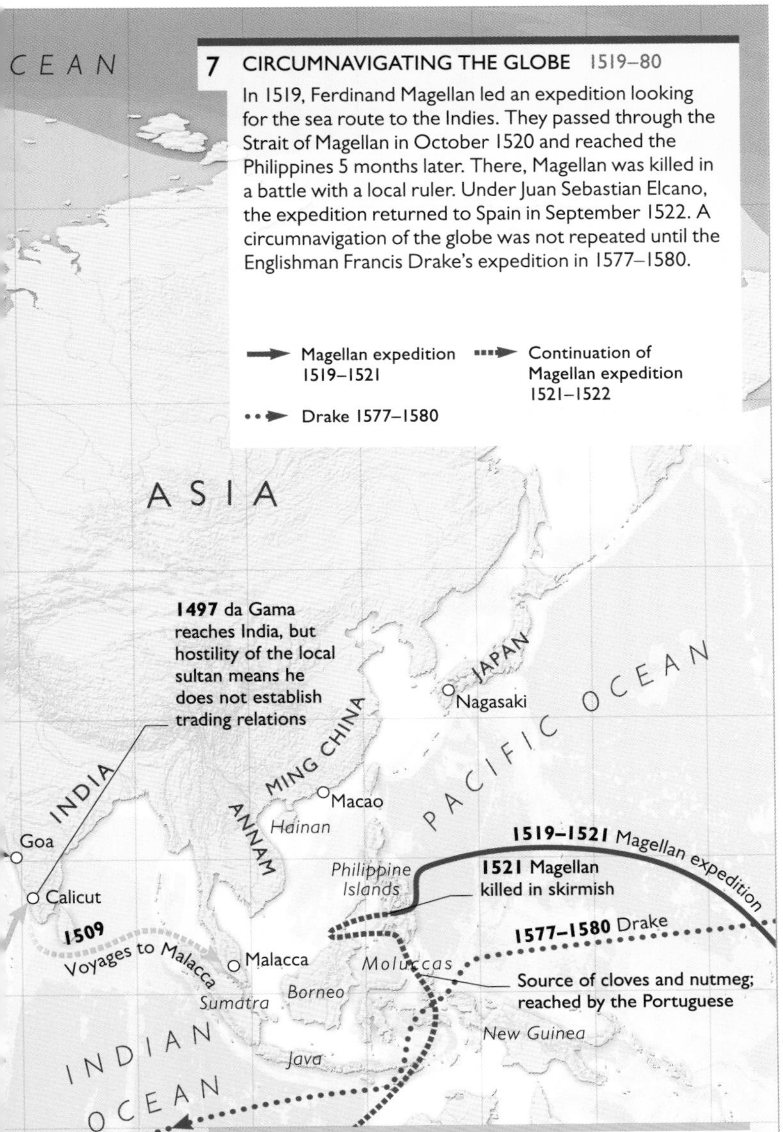

7 CIRCUMNAVIGATING THE GLOBE 1519–80

In 1519, Ferdinand Magellan led an expedition looking for the sea route to the Indies. They passed through the Strait of Magellan in October 1520 and reached the Philippines 5 months later. There, Magellan was killed in a battle with a local ruler. Under Juan Sebastian Elcano, the expedition returned to Spain in September 1522. A circumnavigation of the globe was not repeated until the Englishman Francis Drake's expedition in 1577–1580.

⟶ Magellan expedition 1519–1521
⟶ Continuation of Magellan expedition 1521–1522
⟶ Drake 1577–1580

ASIA

1497 da Gama reaches India, but hostility of the local sultan means he does not establish trading relations

JAPAN
Nagasaki

INDIA

MING CHINA

Macao
Hainan

PACIFIC OCEAN

Goa

Calicut

ANNAM

Philippine Islands

1519–1521 Magellan expedition

1521 Magellan killed in skirmish

1577–1580 Drake

1509
Voyages to Malacca

Malacca
Borneo
Sumatra
Java

Moluccas

Source of cloves and nutmeg; reached by the Portuguese

New Guinea

INDIAN OCEAN

1521–1522 continuation of Magellan expedition

6 THE CIRCUMNAVIGATION OF AFRICA 1488–1512

By 1488, the Portuguese exploration of Africa's coast had reached the southernmost tip of the continent, when Bartolomeu Dias rounded it and entered the Indian Ocean. In 1497–1498, Vasco da Gama went even further, succeeding in opening up a direct trade route to Asia, by sailing up Africa's east coast and then across to Calicut in India. Before long, the Portuguese had attained the sources of spices—the most valuable of luxury goods—reaching Malacca in 1509 and the Moluccas in 1512.

⟶ da Gama 1497–1498
⟶ Voyages to Malacca 1509

EUROPEAN EXPLORATION

A series of spectacular voyages by European explorers in the late 15th and early 16th centuries opened up vast new areas of the globe to European trade. These would lead to European colonization.

KEY

▮ Extent of summer pack ice

▮ Additional extent of winter pack ice

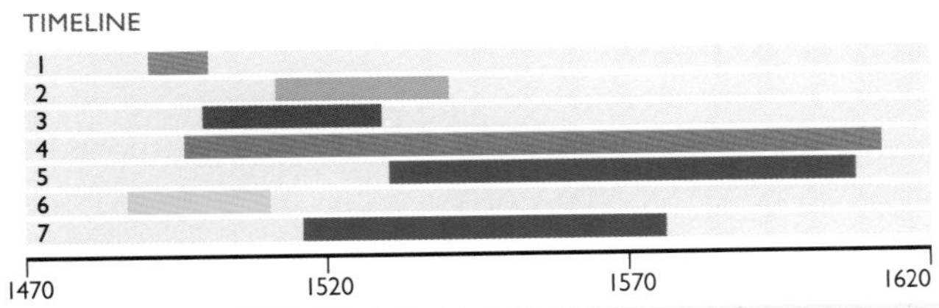

TIMELINE

1
2
3
4
5
6
7

1470   1520   1570   1620

VOYAGES OF EXPLORATION

The 15th and 16th centuries saw a massive increase in the reach of European nations. Voyages set out in search of new routes to exploit the trade in luxury goods. Portuguese explorers pushed eastward, their Spanish counterparts voyaged west, and soon the English, French, and Dutch joined the scramble to find new lands.

The breakup of the Mongol Empire in the 14th century and expansion of the Ottoman Turks in the eastern Mediterranean blocked the Silk Road, which had been the traditional conduit for trade from Europe to east Asia. Maritime nations on Europe's western coasts began to explore alternative routes by which to access the rich east Asian trade in luxuries and, in particular, spices. From the mid-1420s Portuguese-sponsored voyages edged around the west coast of Africa. It took until 1497, however, for the Portuguese captain Vasco da Gama to circumnavigate Africa and reach the markets of India. By then, the Spanish-sponsored voyage of Christopher Columbus had encountered the coastline of the Americas. The Portuguese established a toehold in Brazil by 1500, and British and French expeditions tried to locate the "Northwest Passage" to access Asia by sailing north around North America.

More ambitious voyages yet circumnavigated the globe, beginning with that led by the Portuguese explorer Ferdinand Magellan in 1519. The consequences of these voyages were profound. Parts of the world that had had little or no communication with each other were now linked by trading routes and by networks of trading outposts. These were either directly state-controlled or governed by great trading corporations such as the British and Dutch East India Companies (founded in 1600 and 1602). Soldiers and settlers soon followed since what had originally been an effort to secure trading routes became the precursor to the establishment of global European empires.

△ **A new world**
This late-17th-century engraving by the Flemish-German publisher Theodor de Bry depicts Christopher Columbus arriving in the Americas and is part of a series that portrayed famous explorers surrounded by allegorical scenes.

SPANISH CONQUESTS IN THE AMERICAS

In the first half of the 16th century, the Spanish established a vast empire in the Americas. Their conquest of the rich native cultures of Mexico and Peru between 1519 and 1533 encouraged Spanish explorers to seize further large tracts of territory. They established an empire that remained in Spanish hands until a series of nationalist revolts in the 1800s.

Following Columbus's discovery of the Americas in 1492, initial Spanish efforts were focused on the Caribbean. However, there were few resources to exploit, and the collapse of the native population pushed Spanish adventurers onto the mainland. The conquest of the Aztec Empire by Hernán Cortés from 1519–1521 and of the Inca Empire of Peru by Francisco Pizarro from 1531–1533 (see pp.154–155) transformed the prospects for the Spanish possessions in the Americas. Christian missionaries soon followed in the wake of the conquistadors and made large numbers of converts among the Aztecs and Inca, whose central religious hierarchy had been swept away. These rich, centralized territories fell rapidly into the hands of the conquistadors and formed the nucleus from which

further Spanish expeditions fanned out across the continent—penetrating into Colombia and Venezuela in 1537–1543 and northward into Florida and the southwest of the modern United States in the 1540s. The Spanish brought new diseases to the Americas (such as smallpox), and the native population had declined to around one-tenth its former level by 1600. However, throughout the 16th century there was also an influx of around 100,000 European settlers, the importation of African slaves to work plantations, and the discovery of rich silver deposits (in Peru in 1545 and in Mexico in 1546). The Spanish empire thrived and developed a distinctive colonial society that lasted until Spanish rule was overthrown by revolutionary nationalists in the early 19th century.

THE TREATY OF TORDESILLAS (1493–1529)

Spain and Portugal were very confident in their future pursuits of new lands. In 1493, the Spanish persuaded Pope Alexander VI to issue an edict, or decree, that set a dividing line to avoid disputes over any new territories either country might discover. After Portuguese lobbying, the Treaty of Tordesillas (1494) pushed the line westward, which placed Brazil within their sector. The Treaty of Zaragoza (1529) established an antimeridian demarcating Spanish and Portuguese territory in east Asia.

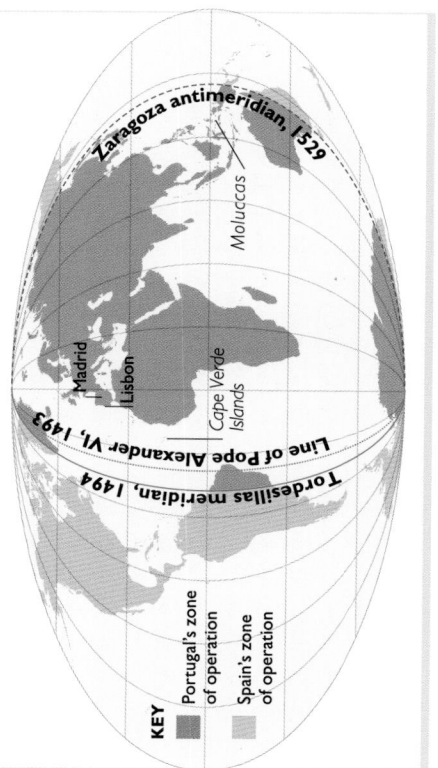

Zaragoza antimeridian, 1529

Moluccas

Madrid
Lisbon

Cape Verde
Islands

Line of Pope Alexander VI, 1493

Tordesillas meridian, 1494

KEY
Portugal's zone of operation
Spain's zone of operation

"I and my companions suffer from a disease of the heart, which can only be cured with gold."

HERNÁN CORTÉS, CONQUEROR OF MEXICO, c.1520

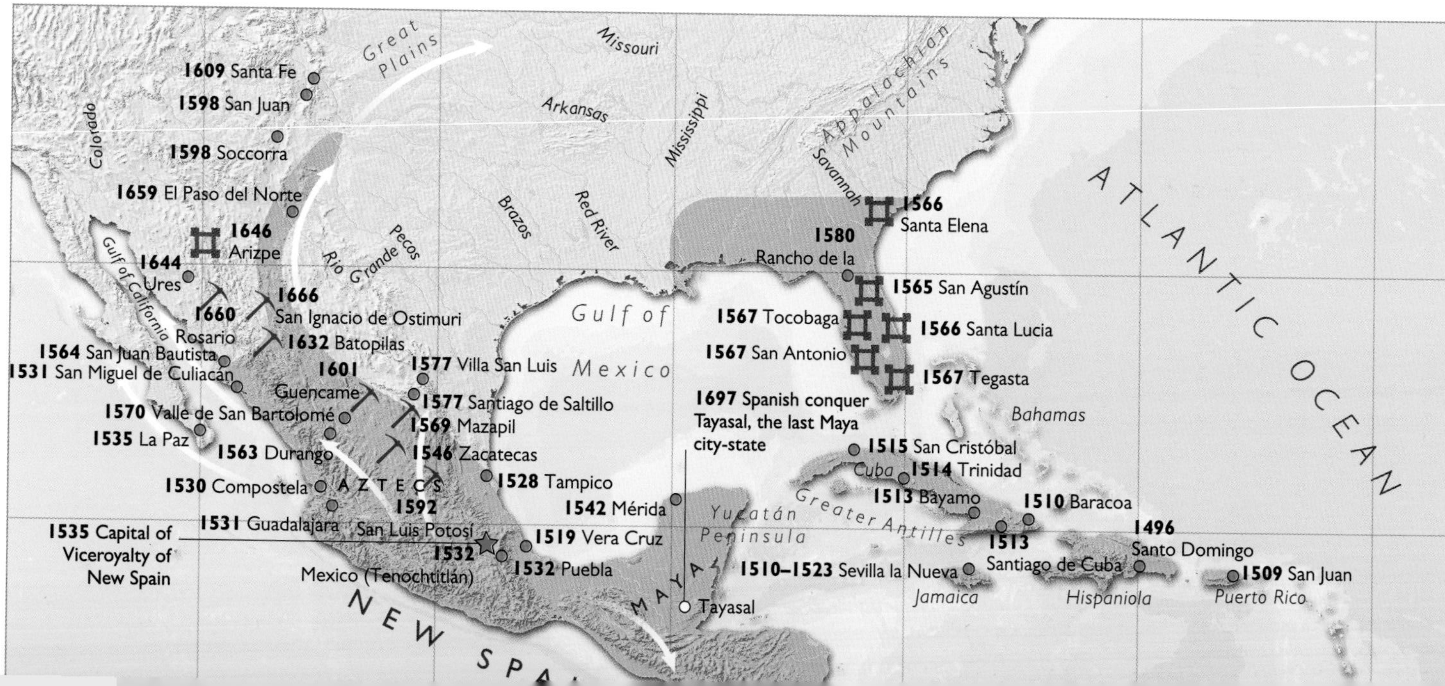

1 CORTÉS AND MEXICO 1519–1524

The expedition of Hernán Cortés to Mexico in 1519 overwhelmed the rich Aztec Empire within 3 years. The centralized nature of the empire meant that the Spanish acquired all of its resources and tribute-bearing provinces, providing them with a base from which to move southward into the Yucatán Peninsula by 1524.

2 THE CONQUEST OF THE MAYA 1527–1697

The Maya of the Yucatán Peninsula were politically fragmented, and so the Spanish conquistadors had to reduce each Maya city-state individually. Francisco de Montejo began the process in 1527, but the only made significant progress in the 1540s. The last Maya city, Tayasal, finally fell to the Spanish in 1697.

ATLANTIC OCEAN

1509 San Juan
Puerto Rico

1510 Baracoa
Santo Domingo
1513
Santiago de Cuba
Hispaniola
1496
Jamaica

1566
Santa Elena
1565 San Agustín
1566 Santa Lucia
1567 Tegasta

1580
Rancho de la

1515 San Cristóbal
1514 Trinidad
1513 Bayamo
Cuba

Bahamas

1567 Tocobaga
1567 San Antonio

1697 Spanish conquer
Tayasal, the last Maya
city-state

Appalachian Mountains
Savannah

Greater Antilles

Mississippi

Missouri

Arkansas

Red River

Brazos

Gulf of Mexico

Yucatán Peninsula

Tayasal
MAYA

1542 Mérida

1519 Vera Cruz
1528 Tampico
1532 Puebla
1532
Mexico (Tenochtitlán)
AZTECS
San Luis Potosí
1546 Zacatecas
1569 Mazapil
1577 Santiago de Saltillo
1577 Villa San Luis
1601
1632 Batopilas
San Ignacio de Ostimuri
1660
1666
1644
1646
Arizpe
Ures

Great Plains

Colorado

Pecos

Rio Grande

Gulf of California

NEW SPAIN

1609 Santa Fe
1598 San Juan
1598 Soccorra
1659 El Paso del Norte

1564 San Juan Bautista
1531 San Miguel de Culiacán
Rosario
1570 Valle de San Bartolomé
1535 La Paz
1563 Durango
1530 Compostela
1531 Guadalajara
1535 Capital of Viceroyalty of New Spain

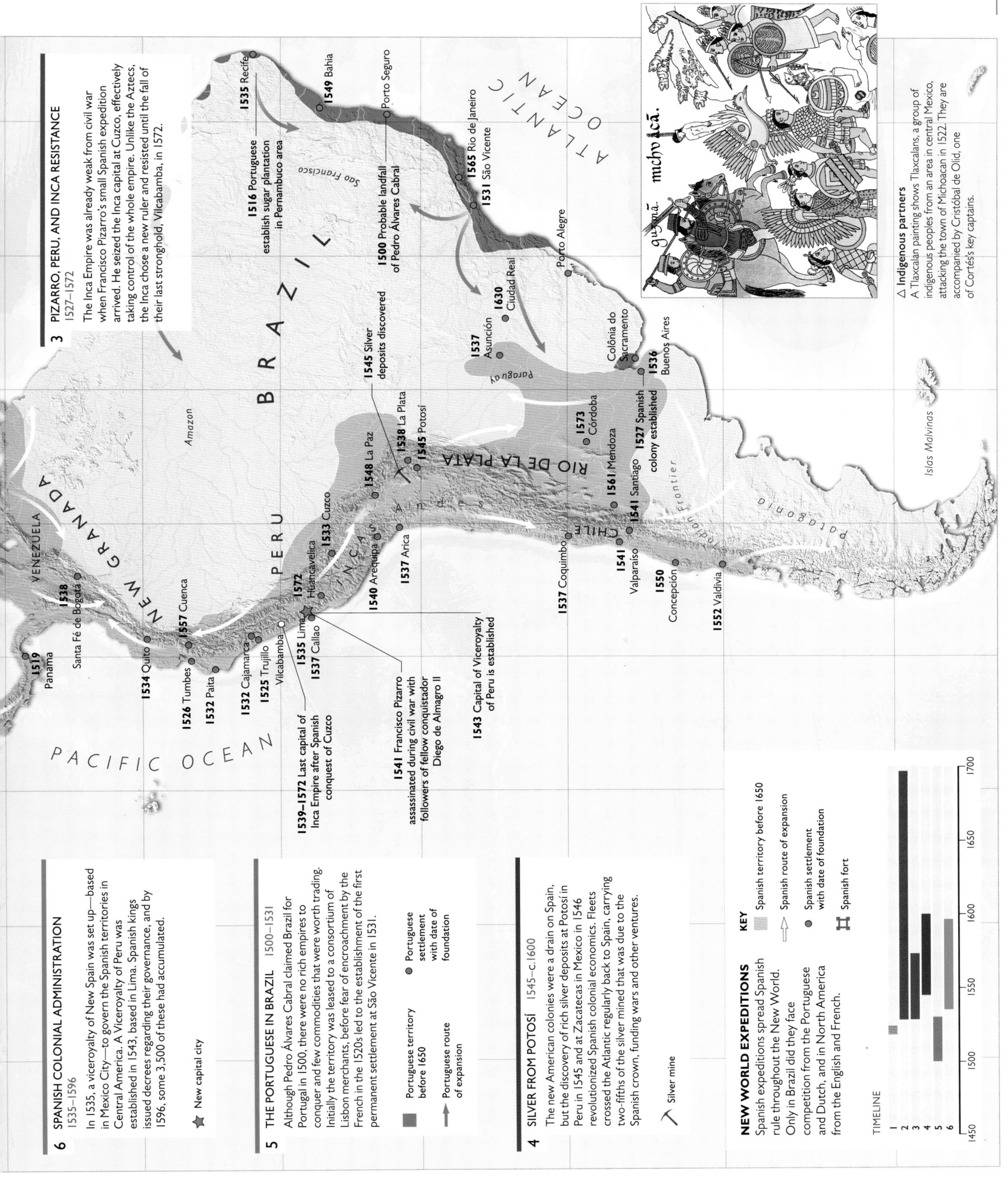

3 PIZARRO, PERU, AND INCA RESISTANCE
1527–1572

The Inca Empire was already weak from civil war when Francisco Pizarro's small Spanish expedition arrived. He seized the Inca capital at Cuzco, effectively taking control of the whole empire. Unlike the Aztecs, the Inca chose a new ruler and resisted until the fall of their last stronghold, Vilcabamba, in 1572.

6 SPANISH COLONIAL ADMINISTRATION
1535–1596

In 1535, a viceroyalty of New Spain was set up—based in Mexico City—to govern the Spanish territories in Central America. A Viceroyalty of Peru was established in 1543, based in Lima. Spanish kings issued decrees regarding their governance, and by 1596, some 3,500 of these had accumulated.

★ New capital city

5 THE PORTUGUESE IN BRAZIL 1500–1531

Although Pedro Álvares Cabral claimed Brazil for Portugal in 1500, there were no rich empires to conquer and few commodities that were worth trading. Initially the territory was leased to a consortium of Lisbon merchants, before fear of encroachment by the French in the 1520s led to the establishment of the first permanent settlement at São Vicente in 1531.

■ Portuguese territory before 1650

→ Portuguese route of expansion

● Portuguese settlement with date of foundation

4 SILVER FROM POTOSÍ 1545–c.1600

The new American colonies were a drain on Spain, but the discovery of rich silver deposits at Potosí in Peru in 1545 and at Zacatecas in Mexico in 1546 revolutionized Spanish colonial economics. Fleets crossed the Atlantic regularly back to Spain, carrying two-fifths of the silver mined that was due to the Spanish crown, funding wars and other ventures.

⟂ Silver mine

NEW WORLD EXPEDITIONS

Spanish expeditions spread Spanish rule throughout the New World. Only in Brazil did they face competition from the Portuguese and Dutch, and in North America from the English and French.

KEY

▨ Spanish territory before 1650

⇨ Spanish route of expansion

● Spanish settlement with date of foundation

⌗ Spanish fort

TIMELINE
1450 · 1500 · 1550 · 1600 · 1650 · 1700

△ **Indigenous partners**
A Tlaxcalan painting shows Tlaxcalans, a group of indigenous peoples from an area in central Mexico, attacking the town of Michoacan in 1522. They are accompanied by Cristóbal de Olid, one of Cortés's key captains.

gu5mã. michvlcã.

Map labels:

ATLANTIC OCEAN
PACIFIC OCEAN
BRAZIL
PERU
INCA
NEW GRANADA
VENEZUELA
CHILE
RÍO DE LA PLATA
Andes
Amazon
São Francisco
Paraguay
Patagonia
Indian Frontier
Islas Malvinas

1519 Panamá
Santa Fé de Bogotá
1538
1557 Cuenca
1534 Quito
1526 Tumbes
1532 Paita
1532 Cajamarca
1525 Trujillo
Vilcabamba
1535 Lima
1537 Callao
1572 Huancavelica
1533 Cuzco
1540 Arequipa
1537 Arica
1548 La Paz
1538 La Plata
1545 Potosí
1545 Silver deposits discovered
1630 Ciudad Real
1537 Asunción
1573 Córdoba
1561 Mendoza
1527 Spanish colony established
1536 Buenos Aires
Colônia do Sacramento
Porto Alegre
1541 Santiago
1541
1550 Concepción
1537 Coquimbo
Valparaíso
1552 Valdivia
1565 Rio de Janeiro
1531 São Vicente
Porto Seguro
1549 Bahia
1516 Portuguese establish sugar plantation in Pernambuco area
1500 Probable landfall of Pedro Álvares Cabral
1535 Recife

1539–1572 Last capital of Inca Empire after Spanish conquest of Cuzco

1541 Francisco Pizarro assassinated during civil war with followers of fellow conquistador Diego de Almagro II

1543 Capital of Viceroyalty of Peru is established

THE SPANISH IN AMERICA

Within 25 years of their arrival, the Spanish ruled a vast colonial empire in the Americas. Their astonishing success was enabled by exploitation of the political weakness of indigenous empires, superior weaponry, and the diseases that came in their wake.

△ **Soldier-explorer**
Hernán Cortés had a reputation for ruthlessness. After founding the city of Vera Cruz, he burned his ships to prevent his forces from turning back.

The principal indigenous empires of the Americas, the Aztec of Mexico and the Inca of Peru (see pp.144–145), were highly centralized and dependent on rigid hierarchies and a deeply ingrained respect for their rulers—the Aztec *Tlatoani* in the capital Tenochtitlan and the Sapa Inca in Cuzco. These empires expanded rapidly by conquest in the 14th and 15th centuries, and their hold on recently conquered or peripheral peoples was fragile. When the Spanish arrived in Mexico in 1519 and in Peru in 1531, the Aztec and Inca leaders underestimated the threat they posed.

In Mexico, the Spanish formed alliances with dissenting groups, and in Peru, rapid and ruthless action led to the capture of the Sapa Inca, Atahualpa. Leaderless, the indigenous empires rapidly collapsed—a process accelerated by epidemics of diseases brought by the Spanish, to which native Americans had no resistance. Once embedded, the invaders—known as conquistadors—proved impossible to remove. A constant supply of ambitious yet landless men with military training from the Iberian Peninsula allowed the Spanish to absorb the Maya of Central America in the 1540s–1550s, push into southern North America, and extend into Amazonian South America. Financed by silver, which was discovered in Peru in 1545, and ruled through viceroys, the Spanish empire in South America would last for over 250 years (see pp.152–153).

CORTÉS'S CAMPAIGNS

Nov 1519 Cortés first enters Tenochtitlan

Dec 1520–Aug 1521 Cortés returns to Tenochtitlan and finally completes recapture

Spanish conquistador Hernán Cortés and his force of 600 men entered the Aztec capital Tenochtitlan in November 1519 and took the *Tlatoani* Montezuma captive. Although the Spanish were expelled with heavy losses in June 1520, they returned and took the city after an 8-month siege, putting an end to the Aztec Empire.

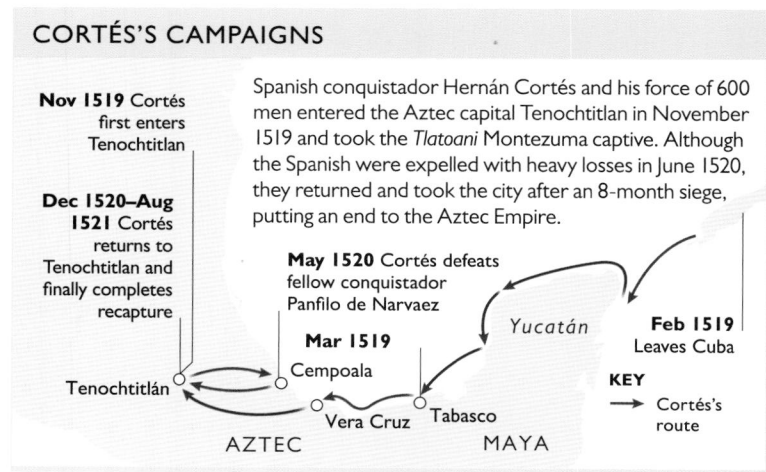

May 1520 Cortés defeats fellow conquistador Panfilo de Narvaez

Mar 1519 Cempoala

Yucatán

Feb 1519 Leaves Cuba

Tenochtitlán

Vera Cruz · Tabasco

AZTEC

MAYA

KEY
→ Cortés's route

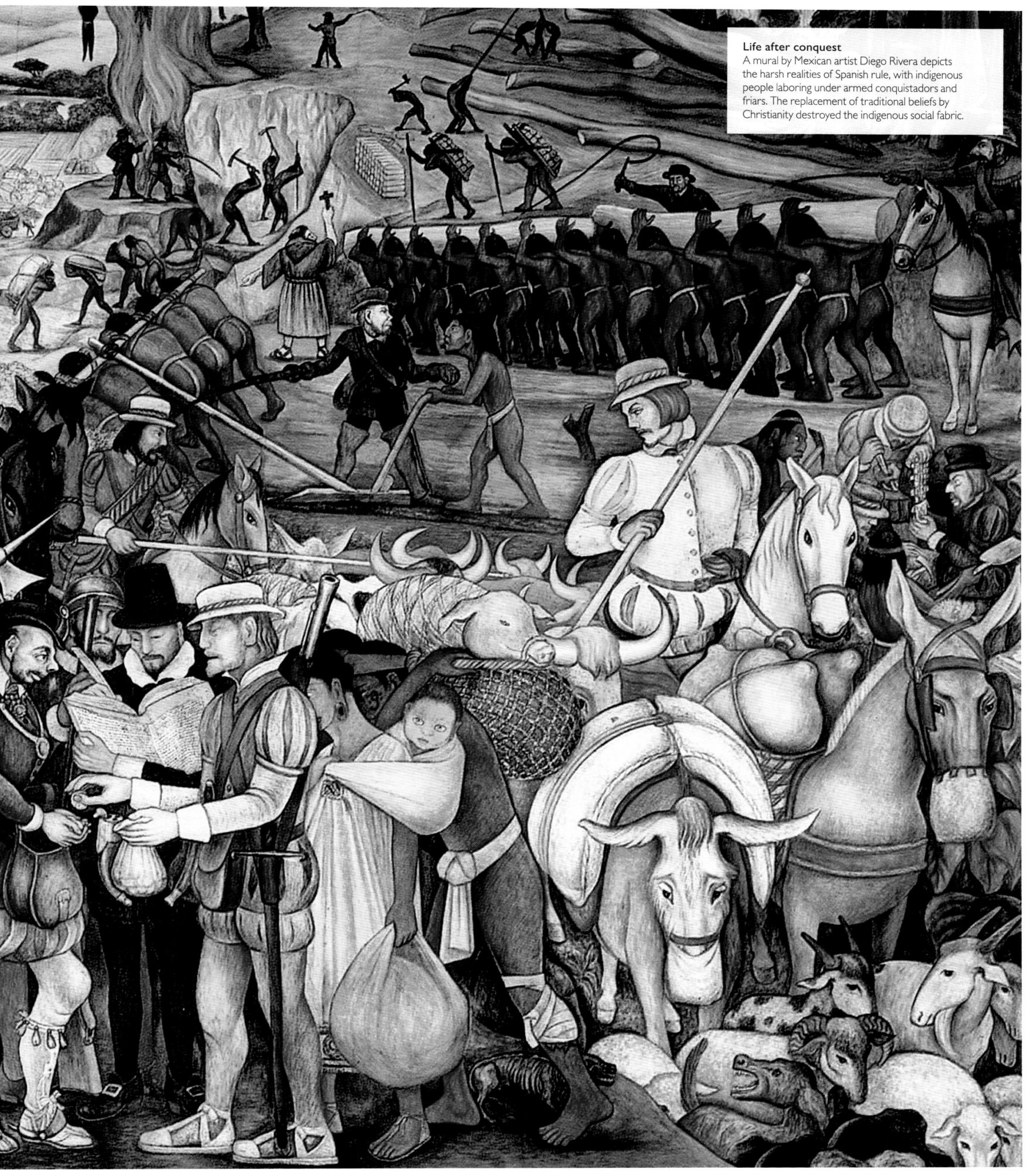

Life after conquest
A mural by Mexican artist Diego Rivera depicts the harsh realities of Spanish rule, with indigenous people laboring under armed conquistadors and friars. The replacement of traditional beliefs by Christianity destroyed the indigenous social fabric.

THE COLONIZATION OF NORTH AMERICA

The Europeans first successfully colonized North America in the early 17th century. While the French and Spanish colonies depended on their crowns for orders, the English colonies—founded by a mix of religious dissidents, merchant companies, and royal initiatives—operated at arm's length, gaining an advantage over their rivals.

In 1585, Sir Walter Raleigh attempted to found Roanoke as the first English colony of the New World, but the colony failed. The first successful English colony was Jamestown, founded in 1607. A century later, around 200,000 British migrants had arrived, and the number of British colonies in America had grown to 13. European slave traders also brought close to 175,000 African slaves to America to work on the plantations.

French settlers laid down roots in Quebec, Canada, in 1608, and started populating the St. Lawrence River basin and the accessible inland areas. They established forts as far south as New Orleans, stoking a rivalry with the British that erupted in war in 1689. Meanwhile, the Spanish were unable to develop their fledgling colony in Florida or to capitalize on their explorations of the American Southwest, which had begun in the 1520s. Growing European presence disturbed local power structures, and Native American groups eventually fought to reclaim their lost land, beginning a phase of conflict that would last for almost three centuries. By the mid-1700s, tension was also increasing between the colonists themselves and their overseas rulers in Britain.

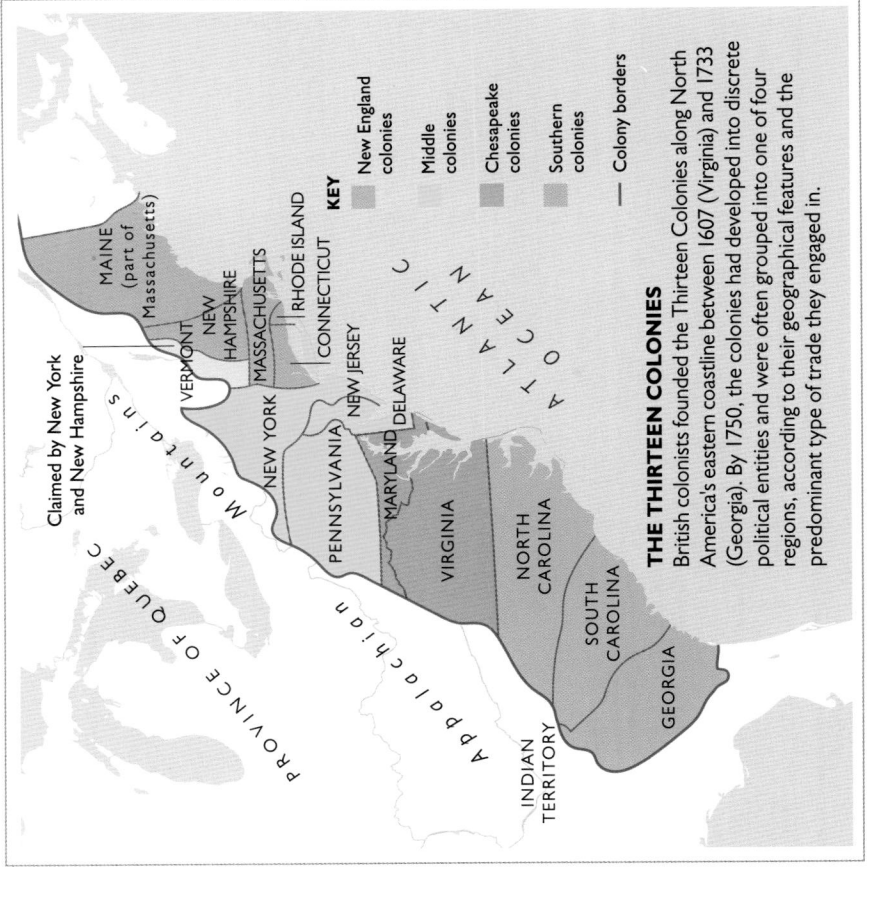

THE THIRTEEN COLONIES

British colonists founded the Thirteen Colonies along North America's eastern coastline between 1607 (Virginia) and 1733 (Georgia). By 1750, the colonies had developed into discrete political entities and were often grouped into one of four regions, according to their geographical features and the predominant type of trade they engaged in.

KEY
- New England colonies
- Middle colonies
- Chesapeake colonies
- Southern colonies
- — Colony borders

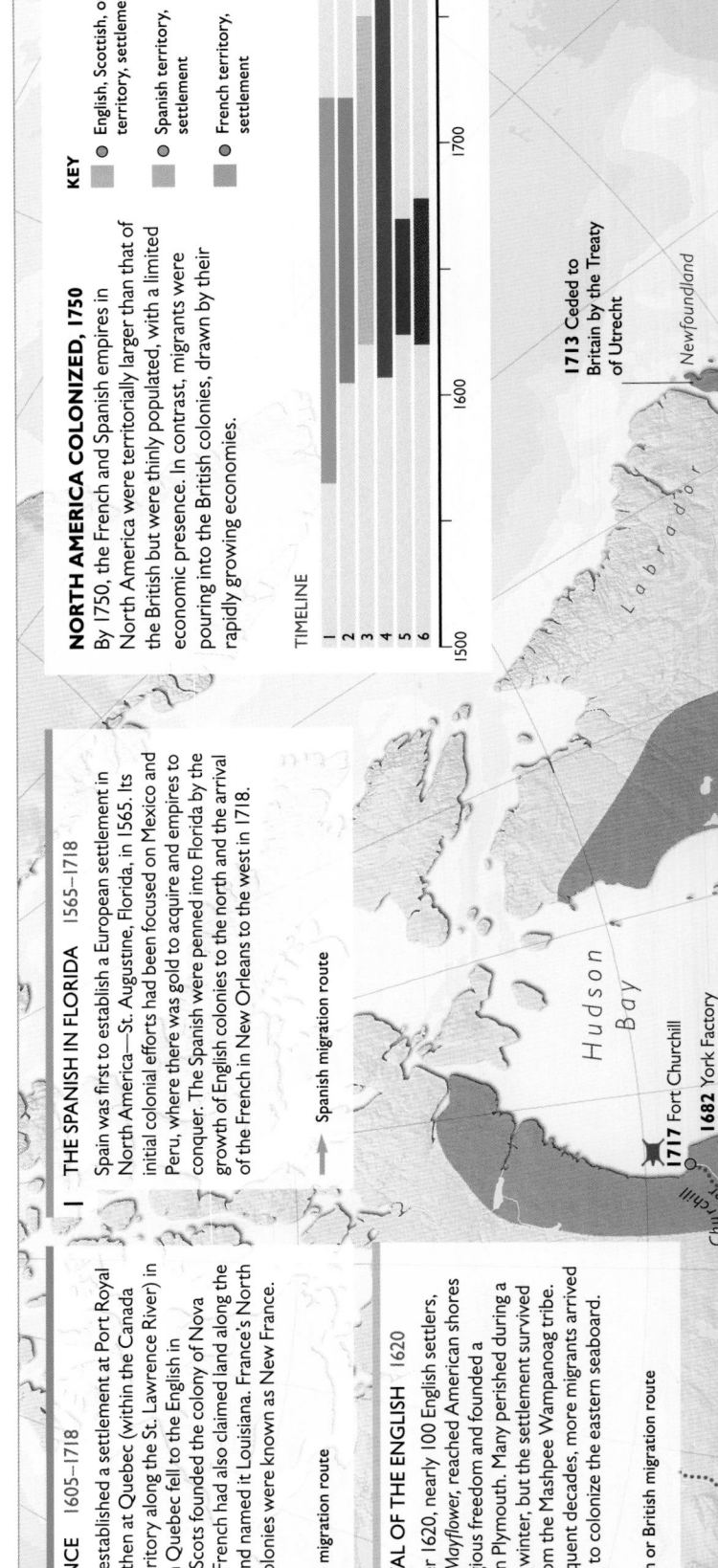

NORTH AMERICA COLONIZED, 1750

By 1750, the French and Spanish empires in North America were territorially larger than that of the British but were thinly populated, with a limited economic presence. In contrast, migrants were pouring into the British colonies, drawn by their rapidly growing economies.

KEY
- English, Scottish, or British territory, settlement
- Spanish territory, settlement
- French territory, settlement

TIMELINE
1500 | 1600 | 1700 | 1800

1 THE SPANISH IN FLORIDA 1565–1718

Spain was first to establish a European settlement in North America—St. Augustine, Florida, in 1565. Its initial colonial efforts had been focused on Mexico and Peru, where there was gold to acquire and empires to conquer. The Spanish were penned into Florida by the growth of English colonies to the north and the arrival of the French in New Orleans to the west in 1718.

→ Spanish migration route

2 NEW FRANCE 1605–1718

The French established a settlement at Port Royal in 1605 and then at Quebec (within the Canada colony—territory along the St. Lawrence River) in 1608. When Quebec fell to the English in 1629–1632, Scots founded the colony of Nova Scotia. The French had also claimed land along the Mississippi and named it Louisiana. France's North American colonies were known as New France.

→ French migration route

3 THE ARRIVAL OF THE ENGLISH 1620

In December 1620, nearly 100 English settlers, aboard the *Mayflower*, reached American shores seeking religious freedom and founded a settlement in Plymouth. Many perished during a difficult first winter, but the settlement survived with help from the Mashpee Wampanoag tribe. Over subsequent decades, more migrants arrived from Britain to colonize the eastern seaboard.

→ English or British migration route

1600–1700 French migrants arrive at a rate of 100 per year

6 EUROPEAN–NATIVE AMERICAN CONFLICTS 1620–1678

Rising tensions between the Europeans and local indigenous groups inevitably exploded into fighting, beginning with the First Anglo-Powhatan War around Jamestown in 1620. The most grave one was King Philip's War, fought from 1675 to 1678 between the Wampanoag and the English, which resulted in the burning of many towns and the death of about 3,000 Native Americans.

➤ Conflict with Native Americans

1600–1700 British migrants arrive at a rate of 2,000 per year

5 COLONIES IN THE CARIBBEAN 1624–1670

Following in the footsteps of Spain—France and England both began to claim territory in the Caribbean islands. Both nations established settlements on the Island of St. Kitt's in 1624, and the English acquired Barbados in 1627. By the 1660s, around 40,000 European settlers had arrived in the Caribbean, many as indentured servants. However, by then, the slave trade was underway as thousands of Africans were shipped over to work on the new sugar plantations.

→ Route of slave trade

4 TRADING COLONIES 1607–1776

British trading colonies began profiting after 1617 once they ventured into tobacco farming. They also found viable commodities in the exploitation of furs and fisheries in the north. The Crown sought to control this trade and passed a series of laws forbidding the American colonies from trading with anyone but England. However, the laws inflamed the hostilities of American colonists and eventually sowed the seeds of revolution (see pp.190–191).

- 🌿 Tobacco
- 🌲 Fisheries
- ✶ Fur trading post
- ···· Fur trade routes

▽ The Pilgrim Fathers

This hand-colored woodcut shows the arrival of the settlers of Plymouth, Massachusetts, in 1620. The term "Pilgrim Fathers" only entered into common usage two centuries later.

Map labels:

Gulf of St. Lawrence · Cape Breton Island · ACADIA · NOVA SCOTIA · NEW ENGLAND · CANADA · NEW FRANCE · PAYS D'EN HAUT · LOUISIANA · INDIAN TERRITORY · Great Plains · Rocky Mountains · Gulf of Mexico · Caribbean Sea · West Indies · NEW SPAIN · VICEROYALTY OF NEW SPAIN · VICEROYALTY OF NEW GRANADA · MOSQUITO COAST · BELIZE · Yucatan Peninsula

1605 Port Royal
1691 Plymouth absorbed into Massachusetts Bay colony
1608 Quebec
1608 Founded by French; occupied by English Canada Company in 1629–1632; attacked again by English in 1690
1642 Montreal
1630 Boston
1664 Albany
1620 Plymouth · Newport · New York
1682 Philadelphia
1607 Jamestown · Roanoke Island
1664 Dutch colony of New Amsterdam captured by the English
1733 Richmond
1672 Charleston
1733 Savannah
1565 St. Augustine
1718 New Orleans
1670 Fort Albany
1668 Rupert House
1671 Moose Factory
1717 Fort Kaministiquia
1697 Michilimackinac
1701 Detroit
1700 The Illinois Post
1609 Santa Fe

Lake Winnipeg · Lake Superior · Lake Michigan · Lake Huron · Lake Erie · Lake Ontario · Lake Champlain
Ottawa River · Mississippi River · Missouri River · Ohio River · Arkansas River · Rio Grande · Colorado River

1635 Martinique
1627 Barbados
1592 Trinidad
1635 Guadeloupe
1664 St. Lucia
1650 Grenada
1632 Antigua
1508 Puerto Rico · San Juan
Danish Virgin Islands
1496 Santo Domingo · Hispaniola · SAINT-DOMINGUE
1659 French colony established
1567 Caracas
Curaçao · Bonaire · Aruba
1532 Cartagena
1519 Panama
Cuba
1511 Havana
Jamaica **1509–1655**
1655 · **1665** Captured by Britain from Spain
1629 Bahamas
1525 Trujillo
1542 Mérida
1521 Mexico City
1519 Veracruz · Tampico

1587 First English colony founded by Walter Raleigh but disappears by 1590

1600–1700 About 1,500 slaves are imported per year to British territories

1600–1700 Spanish migrants arrive at a rate of 2,500 migrants per year

1535 The Spanish establish the capital of the Viceroyalty of New Spain at Mexico City during their conquest of South America (see pp.152–153).

THE AGE OF EXCHANGE

Human migration across the world and the resulting exchange of food crops and animals started in Neolithic times, but it was not until 1492, when European explorers reached the New World (the Americas), that a biological exchange had such dramatic effects.

The domestication of crops occurred independently in various areas around the world between 11,000 BCE and 6000 BCE. Among the "founder crops" that formed the cornerstone of early agriculture, wheat was the first to be cultivated on a large scale in western Asia in about 9500 BCE, and rice emerged as a staple crop in east Asia 1,500 years later. Farming communities in the Americas, meanwhile, domesticated an entirely different set of crops owing to their complete isolation from the Old World (Africa, Asia, and Europe).

When European explorers reached the Americas in the late 15th century (see pp.150–151), the Old and New Worlds began to embark on an unprecedented level of biological exchange, in what would become known as the Columbian Exchange. Old World staples such as wheat, rice, pigs, cattle, and horses were introduced to the Americas, while New World foods such as tomatoes, corn, potatoes, and cassava were exported to the rest of the world. Tobacco and the furs of animals native to the Americas became highly profitable commodities that allowed settlers to finance their new colonies. However, not all aspects of the Columbian Exchange were positive. Disease traveled between the two worlds, with syphilis crossing into Europe and Old World diseases such as smallpox, measles, and influenza spreading to the Americas, decimating the native population. Consequently, European plantation owners replaced their depleted Native American workforce with slaves procured from Africa—leading to the displacement and deaths of tens of millions.

THE HORSE
THE IMPACT OF THE HORSE ON NATIVE AMERICAN TRIBES

Horses were reintroduced to the Americas in the late 15th century, when Christopher Columbus brought a herd of 25 animals with him on his second voyage to the continent. By 1750, the animal had dispersed into an area of 10 states known as the Great Plains and revolutionized the lives of the people living there. Almost overnight, Plains Indians found a superior animal with which to hunt their main food staple, buffalo.

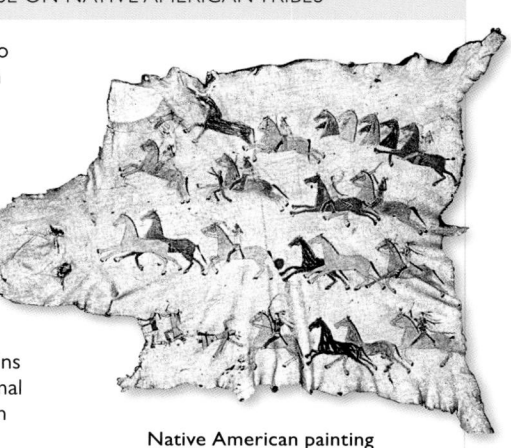

Native American painting

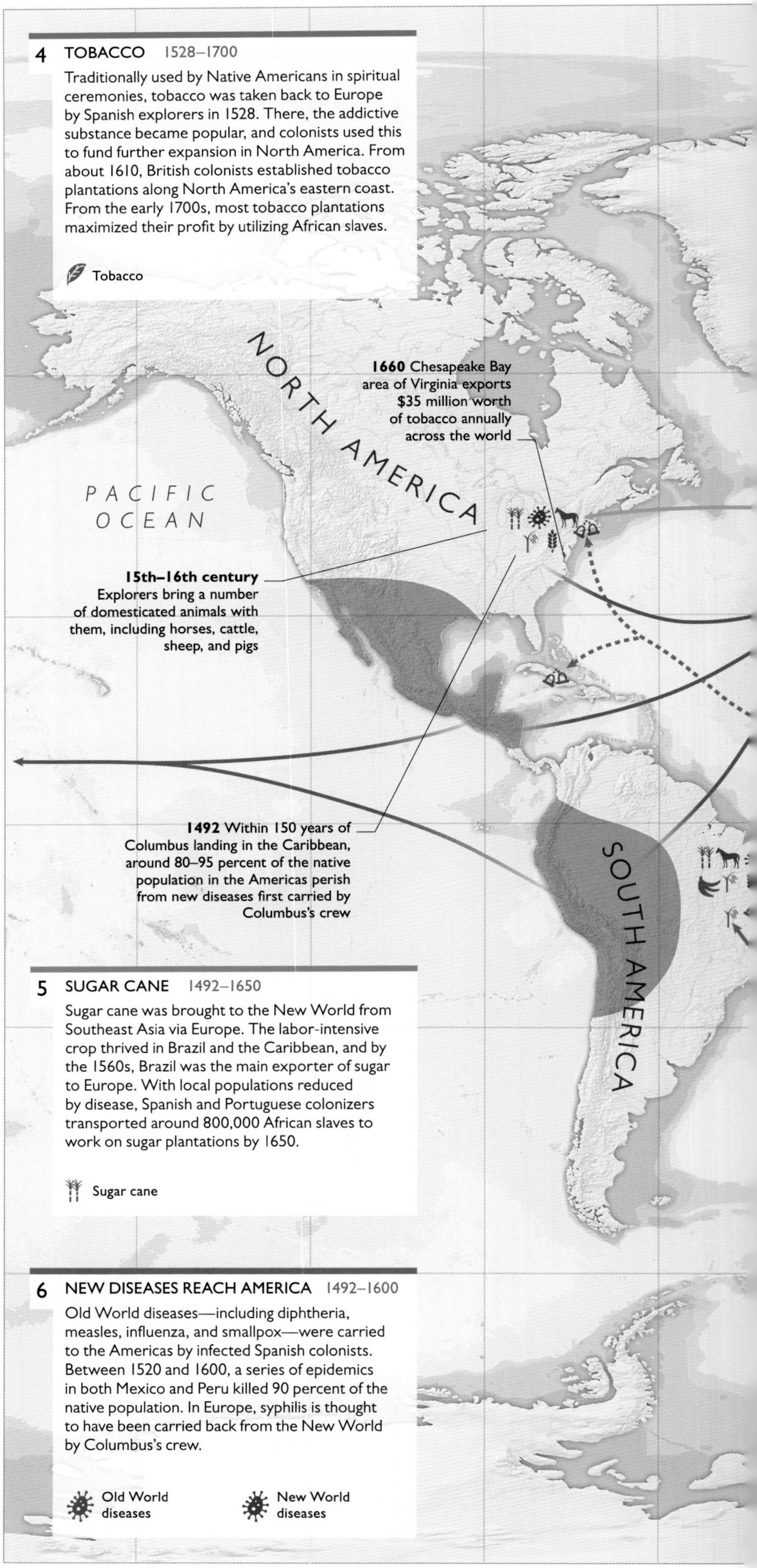

---

4 TOBACCO 1528–1700

Traditionally used by Native Americans in spiritual ceremonies, tobacco was taken back to Europe by Spanish explorers in 1528. There, the addictive substance became popular, and colonists used this to fund further expansion in North America. From about 1610, British colonists established tobacco plantations along North America's eastern coast. From the early 1700s, most tobacco plantations maximized their profit by utilizing African slaves.

🌿 Tobacco

1660 Chesapeake Bay area of Virginia exports $35 million worth of tobacco annually across the world

NORTH AMERICA

PACIFIC OCEAN

15th–16th century Explorers bring a number of domesticated animals with them, including horses, cattle, sheep, and pigs

1492 Within 150 years of Columbus landing in the Caribbean, around 80–95 percent of the native population in the Americas perish from new diseases first carried by Columbus's crew

SOUTH AMERICA

---

5 SUGAR CANE 1492–1650

Sugar cane was brought to the New World from Southeast Asia via Europe. The labor-intensive crop thrived in Brazil and the Caribbean, and by the 1560s, Brazil was the main exporter of sugar to Europe. With local populations reduced by disease, Spanish and Portuguese colonizers transported around 800,000 African slaves to work on sugar plantations by 1650.

🌿 Sugar cane

---

6 NEW DISEASES REACH AMERICA 1492–1600

Old World diseases—including diphtheria, measles, influenza, and smallpox—were carried to the Americas by infected Spanish colonists. Between 1520 and 1600, a series of epidemics in both Mexico and Peru killed 90 percent of the native population. In Europe, syphilis is thought to have been carried back from the New World by Columbus's crew.

❋ Old World diseases   ❋ New World diseases

3 POTATOES 1570–1774

Indigenous to South America, the potato was first brought to Europe in the late 16th century. The potato was slow to spread across Europe, as many were suspicious of the new plant, but eventually it was accepted. It played a key role in decreasing outbreaks of food shortages; King Frederick II of Prussia, for example, ordered large-scale potato cultivation following a famine in 1774.

🥔 Potatoes

2 HORSES 1493–1800

First domesticated in central Asia between 4000 BCE and 2000 BCE, horses later spread to Europe. They were reintroduced to the Americas in the late 15th century, although they did not become widespread until the 17th century. The Plains Indians were among the first people to obtain and use horses. Colonists relied on the animal's mobility in wars against local populations.

🐴 Horses

1 RICE 1500–1690

Rice was introduced to Europe between the 8th and 10th centuries, having first been domesticated in Asia approximately 10,000 years ago. It was also separately domesticated in Africa around 3,000 years ago. Rice from both continents was taken to the Americas by European explorers from the early 16th century, and the crop reached South Carolina by 1690.

🌾 Rice

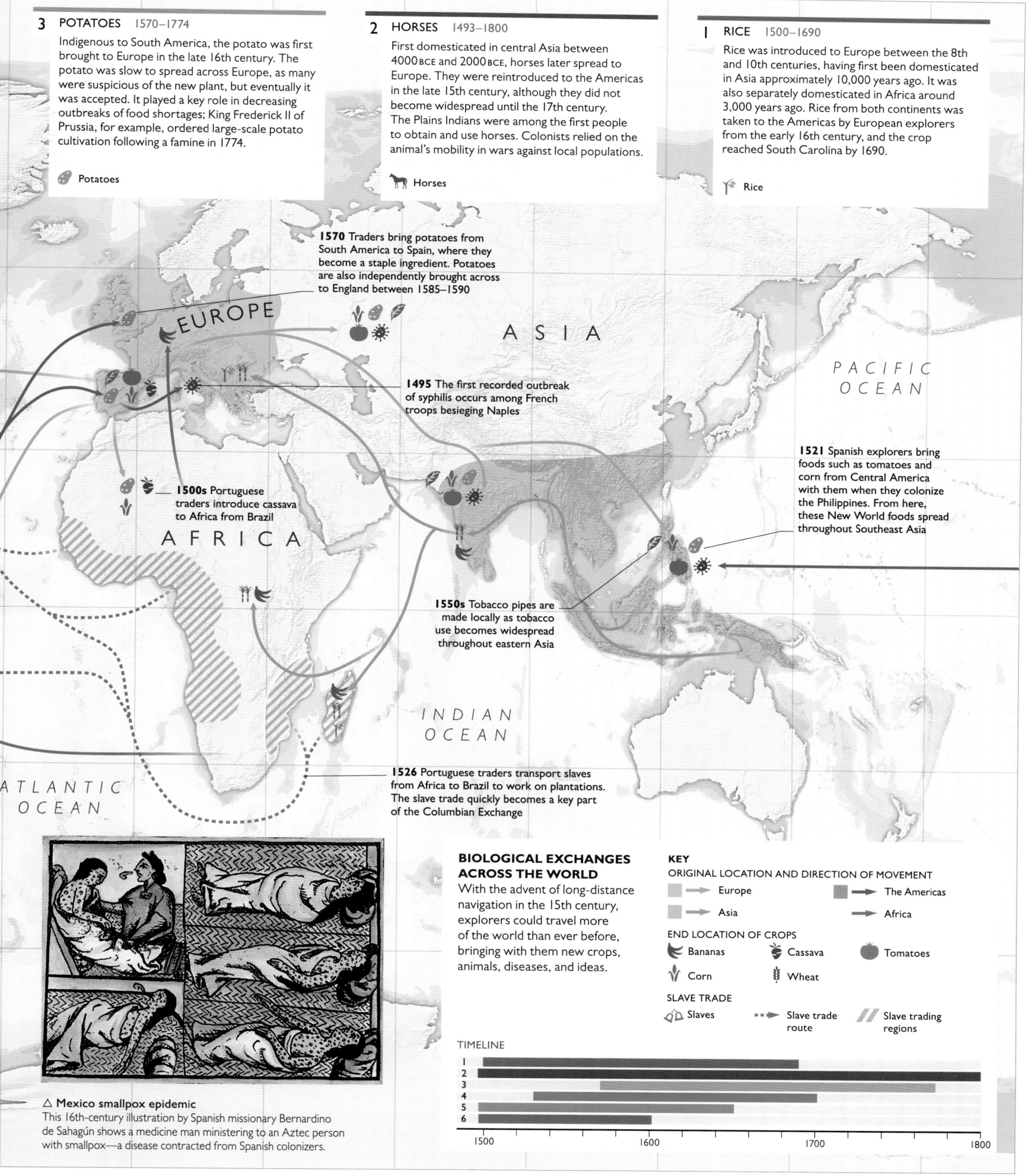

1570 Traders bring potatoes from South America to Spain, where they become a staple ingredient. Potatoes are also independently brought across to England between 1585–1590

1495 The first recorded outbreak of syphilis occurs among French troops besieging Naples

1521 Spanish explorers bring foods such as tomatoes and corn from Central America with them when they colonize the Philippines. From here, these New World foods spread throughout Southeast Asia

1500s Portuguese traders introduce cassava to Africa from Brazil

1550s Tobacco pipes are made locally as tobacco use becomes widespread throughout eastern Asia

1526 Portuguese traders transport slaves from Africa to Brazil to work on plantations. The slave trade quickly becomes a key part of the Columbian Exchange

EUROPE · ASIA · AFRICA · PACIFIC OCEAN · INDIAN OCEAN · ATLANTIC OCEAN

△ **Mexico smallpox epidemic**
This 16th-century illustration by Spanish missionary Bernardino de Sahagún shows a medicine man ministering to an Aztec person with smallpox—a disease contracted from Spanish colonizers.

BIOLOGICAL EXCHANGES ACROSS THE WORLD

With the advent of long-distance navigation in the 15th century, explorers could travel more of the world than ever before, bringing with them new crops, animals, diseases, and ideas.

KEY

ORIGINAL LOCATION AND DIRECTION OF MOVEMENT

Europe · The Americas · Asia · Africa

END LOCATION OF CROPS

🍌 Bananas · Cassava · 🍅 Tomatoes · Corn · Wheat

SLAVE TRADE

Slaves · Slave trade route · Slave trading regions

TIMELINE

1500 · 1600 · 1700 · 1800

THE RENAISSANCE

In 15th-century Italy, a revival of interest in classical learning and secular studies, along with a flowering of artistic production, gave rise to the Renaissance (meaning "rebirth"). The movement soon spread to northern Europe, reshaping the continent's cultural landscape.

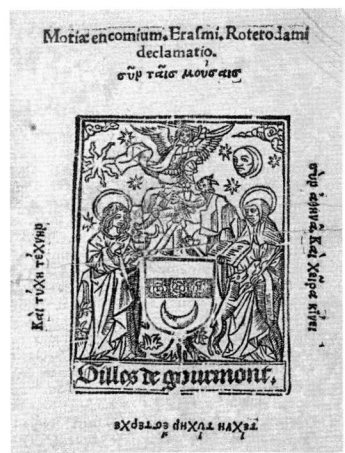

△ Daring satire
Written in 1509 by Desiderius Erasmus, *In Praise of Folly* pokes fun at some of the excesses of the contemporary Catholic Church and ends with a call for a return to a purer sense of Christian morality.

Knowledge of classical authors had declined in Europe after the fall of the Roman Empire in the 5th century, although Latin and Greek texts, particularly those dealing with law and the philosophy of Aristotle, had been rediscovered in the 11th and 12th centuries. This renewal, however, was based within the church and focused on a narrow curriculum designed for the education of clerics. Fourteenth-century Italy was made up of dozens of independent city-states. Most of these, such as Florence and Venice, were republics governed by their more prosperous

citizens, made wealthy by the late medieval growth in trade and industry. The growth in secular wealth, uncontrolled by monarchs or the Catholic Church, slowly created a class of patrons whose interests inclined more toward the promotion of their own cities than praise for the Church.

Rediscovering the past

An awareness of past glories led to a thirst to recover the knowledge that had made the Roman Empire great. Scholars such as Poggio Bracciolini scoured the archives of monasteries looking for new texts—a search that yielded eight new speeches by the orator Cicero and a manuscript of the *Ten Books on Architecture* by Marcus Vitruvius Pollio. Although he served as papal secretary, Bracciolini formed part of a new humanist movement, which placed human nature—and not just God—at the center of its studies, encouraging a wider approach to education.

Artistic renaissance

Accompanying humanism was a new interest in the production of literature in vernacular languages, rather than Latin, which had been the medium of almost all

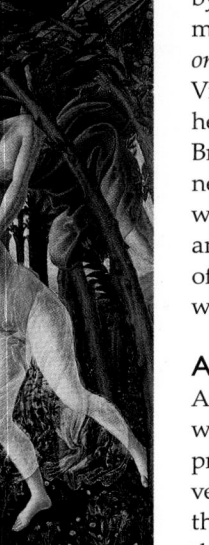

▷ Patronage in art
Florentine artist Sandro Botticelli painted *Primavera* (meaning "Spring") for a member of Florence's ruling Medici family. With its portrayal of Venus, the Three Graces, and Mercury, the painting is typical of the works of art commissioned by rich Italian patrons during the Renaissance.

EUROPE'S REBIRTH

Although there had been periods of cultural renewal in the 9th and 12th centuries, the Renaissance—which began in Italy in the 15th century—was remarkable in the breadth of artistic, literary, educational, and political endeavors it touched. Its first stirrings occurred in the 14th century, with paintings by artists such as Giotto di Bondone, and it continued to exert influence well into the 17th century. However, the key events of this movement took place in the 125 years from around 1400.

1345 Italian writer Francesco Petrarca (or Petrarch) rediscovers some letters written by the Roman politician and writer Cicero; their publication is credited with helping to initiate the Renaissance

1401 Florentine artist Lorenzo Ghiberti is commissioned to cast new doors for Florence cathedral's baptistry

LITERATURE

ARCHITECTURE

EDUCATION

PAINTING AND SCULPTURE

1360   1380   1400

1348–1353 Giovanni Bocaccio writes *The Decameron*, one of the best early works of Italian prose

1417 Bracciolini unearths a manuscript of *De Rerum Natura* ("Of the Nature of Things") by ancient Roman philosopher Lucretius

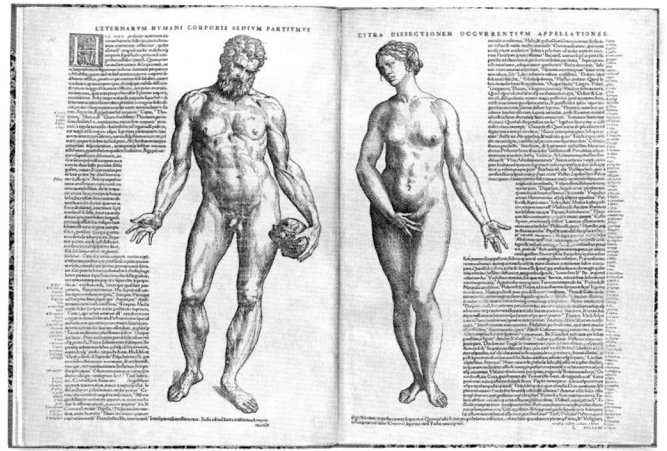

◁ **A revolution in anatomy**
The central illustration of Flemish anatomist Andreas Vesalius's *Epitome*, which was published in 1543, shows human anatomy in great detail. Vesalius revolutionized the study of the human body.

> *"The first thing I shall do as soon as the money arrives … buy some Greek authors; after that, I shall buy clothes."*

DESIDERIUS ERASMUS, DUTCH SCHOLAR, 1498

scholarship for centuries. The Florentine poet Dante Alighieri was a pioneer in this; his *Divine Comedy* (1320) virtually invented the Italian literary language. By the 16th century, vernacular literatures had been firmly established in many countries, producing works as vibrant as the plays of William Shakespeare in England and the philosophy of Michel de Montaigne in France. The Dutch scholar Desiderius Erasmus pioneered a critical approach to historical analysis and penned *In Praise of Folly*, a satirical attack on religious superstition. An increase in literacy among the affluent and the invention of printing in the 1450s all helped loosen the hold of the Church—whose near-monopoly on the dissemination of manuscripts and on education provided in Europe's universities and theological schools had done much to stifle dissent. This in turn paved the way for the Reformation—a movement that questioned the excesses of the Church, as well as Catholic doctrine. By the 15th century, the wealthy patrons of the Italian city-states had begun to enrich their home towns with tangible signs of the new learning.

Italian artists had been experimenting since the early 14th century with new techniques, seeking to endow their work with a fresher and more realistic approach. Florentine artists such as Masaccio, who developed expertise in portraying nature and a depth in landscapes, were followed by generations of painters such as Sandro Botticelli, Leonardo da Vinci, and Raphael, whose works are considered among the greatest masterpieces in artistic history. Sculptors produced pieces of public art, such as the statue of David created by Michelangelo, which was placed outside the seat of Florence's city government. Architects, too, advanced their crafts, most notably Filippo Brunelleschi, who designed the *Duomo* at Florence, the largest masonry dome ever constructed.

Culmination of the movement

The movement spread rapidly, as Flemish masters such as Jan van Eyck and German scholars like Rudolph Agricola produced works inspired by advances in Italy. Its influence also extended to political thought, as Florentine historian Niccolò Machiavelli wrote a series of works examining how rulers should best govern. By the latter part of the 16th century, Italy's wealth and power had declined in comparison to other rising states such as France, England, and the Dutch Republic, and as its status as a cultural powerhouse waned, the Renaissance drew to a close.

▽ **Architectural feat**
Florence's cathedral, the *Duomo*, started in 1296, was still incomplete in 1418 when Filippo Brunelleschi won the competition to design its dome. He used innovative techniques to spread the dome's weight across the vast span.

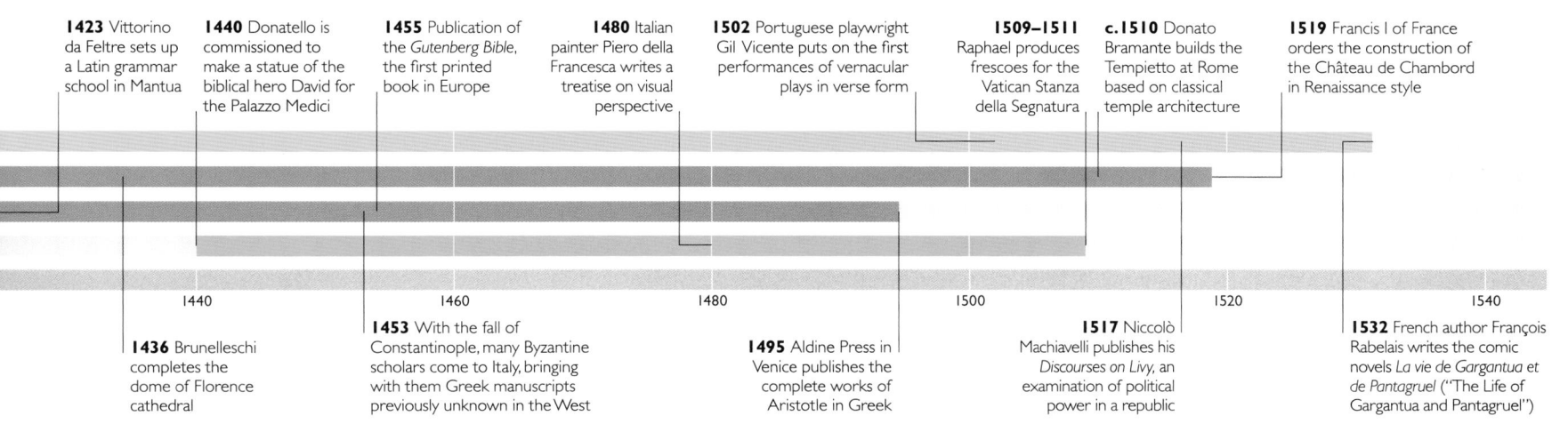

1423 Vittorino da Feltre sets up a Latin grammar school in Mantua

1440 Donatello is commissioned to make a statue of the biblical hero David for the Palazzo Medici

1455 Publication of the *Gutenberg Bible*, the first printed book in Europe

1480 Italian painter Piero della Francesca writes a treatise on visual perspective

1502 Portuguese playwright Gil Vicente puts on the first performances of vernacular plays in verse form

1509–1511 Raphael produces frescoes for the Vatican Stanza della Segnatura

c.1510 Donato Bramante builds the Tempietto at Rome based on classical temple architecture

1519 Francis I of France orders the construction of the Château de Chambord in Renaissance style

1440 — 1460 — 1480 — 1500 — 1520 — 1540

1436 Brunelleschi completes the dome of Florence cathedral

1453 With the fall of Constantinople, many Byzantine scholars come to Italy, bringing with them Greek manuscripts previously unknown in the West

1495 Aldine Press in Venice publishes the complete works of Aristotle in Greek

1517 Niccolò Machiavelli publishes his *Discourses on Livy*, an examination of political power in a republic

1532 French author François Rabelais writes the comic novels *La vie de Gargantua et de Pantagruel* ("The Life of Gargantua and Pantagruel")

THE COLONIAL SPICE TRADE

The discovery of a sea route from Europe to India in the late 15th century resulted in several European countries swiftly establishing fortified trading posts along the coast of sub-Saharan Africa and in south Asia. In doing so, these countries gained access to sources of spices—a product highly prized in European markets.

During medieval times, Asian spices such as nutmeg, cloves, and pepper reached Europe via overland routes and in doing so passed through the hands of many traders, which accounted for their high price. The aim of European exploration around the coastline of Africa was to find a route that would bypass Muslim-controlled areas of Asia and secure direct access to the sources of these spices.

Vasco Da Gama's pioneering voyage around Africa in 1497–1498 led to Portuguese fleets establishing posts in Mozambique (1505), Goa (1510), Hormuz (1515), and Malacca (1511). Spain, by contrast, largely confined itself

to outposts in the Philippines (1565). Under Afonso de Albuquerque's governorship (1509–1515), Portugal took control of trade in the Indian Ocean but was superseded in 1609 by the Dutch, who established posts in the Moluccas (later known as the Spice Islands).

Britain, too, was attracted by the lucrative returns promised by the spice trade but, unable to break the Dutch monopoly in the Moluccas, turned its attention to India. From 1613, Britain's commercial arm, the British East India Company, set up a series of trading posts and factories in India and gained a foothold that would form the nucleus of its empire in the 18th century.

> "Nutmeges be good for them which have cold in their head and doth comforte the syght and the brain."
>
> ANDREW BORDE, FROM *DYETARY OF HELTH*, 1452

AMBOINA MASSACRE 1623
DUTCH MEASURES TO PROTECT THE SPICE TRADE

By 1621, the Dutch East India Company (VOC) fully controlled the islands in the Moluccas, gaining a monopoly on spices, such as nutmeg, mace, cloves, and pepper, that were cultivated exclusively in the region. In February 1623, the Dutch company allegedly foiled a terrorist plot by British merchants to infiltrate Amboina Island (now Ambon) and sieze the fort. The Dutch proceeded to arrest the guilty party (which also included Japanese and Portuguese personnel employed by the VOC), of which 20 were subsequently tortured and executed for acts against Dutch sovereignty.

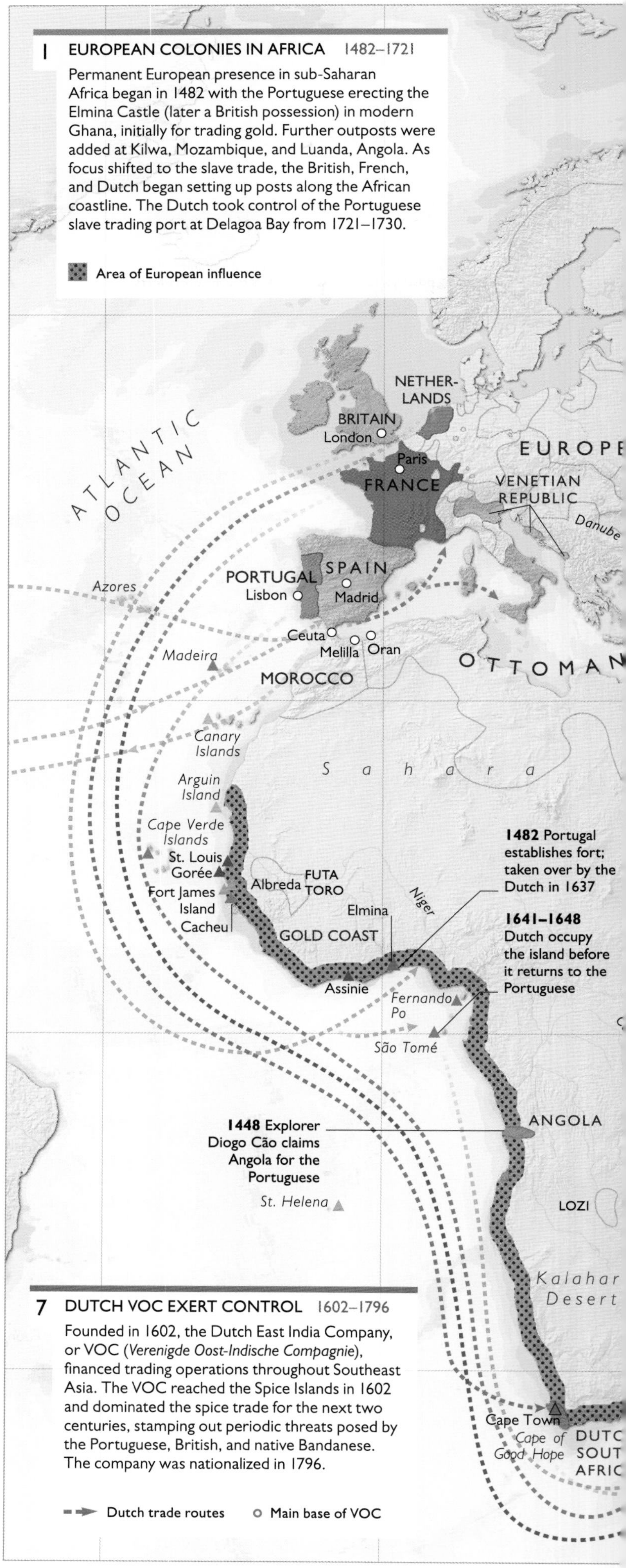

1 EUROPEAN COLONIES IN AFRICA 1482–1721

Permanent European presence in sub-Saharan Africa began in 1482 with the Portuguese erecting the Elmina Castle (later a British possession) in modern Ghana, initially for trading gold. Further outposts were added at Kilwa, Mozambique, and Luanda, Angola. As focus shifted to the slave trade, the British, French, and Dutch began setting up posts along the African coastline. The Dutch took control of the Portuguese slave trading port at Delagoa Bay from 1721–1730.

Area of European influence

1482 Portugal establishes fort; taken over by the Dutch in 1637

1641–1648 Dutch occupy the island before it returns to the Portuguese

1448 Explorer Diogo Cão claims Angola for the Portuguese

7 DUTCH VOC EXERT CONTROL 1602–1796

Founded in 1602, the Dutch East India Company, or VOC (*Verenigde Oost-Indische Compagnie*), financed trading operations throughout Southeast Asia. The VOC reached the Spice Islands in 1602 and dominated the spice trade for the next two centuries, stamping out periodic threats posed by the Portuguese, British, and native Bandanese. The company was nationalized in 1796.

Dutch trade routes   Main base of VOC

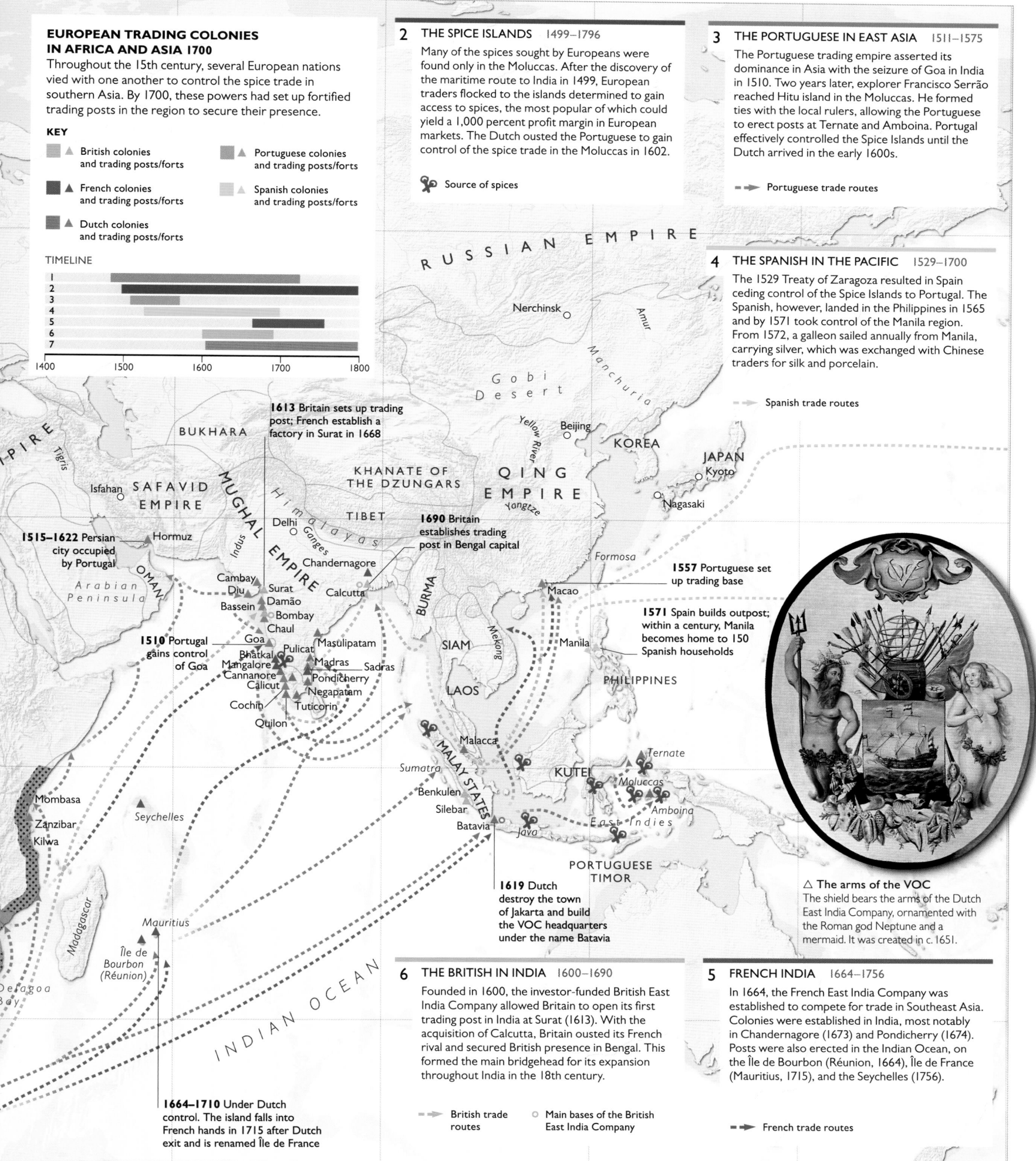

EUROPEAN TRADING COLONIES IN AFRICA AND ASIA 1700

Throughout the 15th century, several European nations vied with one another to control the spice trade in southern Asia. By 1700, these powers had set up fortified trading posts in the region to secure their presence.

KEY

- ▲ British colonies and trading posts/forts
- ▲ French colonies and trading posts/forts
- ▲ Dutch colonies and trading posts/forts
- ▲ Portuguese colonies and trading posts/forts
- ▲ Spanish colonies and trading posts/forts

TIMELINE

1
2
3
4
5
6
7

1400   1500   1600   1700   1800

2 THE SPICE ISLANDS 1499–1796

Many of the spices sought by Europeans were found only in the Moluccas. After the discovery of the maritime route to India in 1499, European traders flocked to the islands determined to gain access to spices, the most popular of which could yield a 1,000 percent profit margin in European markets. The Dutch ousted the Portuguese to gain control of the spice trade in the Moluccas in 1602.

🐾 Source of spices

3 THE PORTUGUESE IN EAST ASIA 1511–1575

The Portuguese trading empire asserted its dominance in Asia with the seizure of Goa in India in 1510. Two years later, explorer Francisco Serrão reached Hitu island in the Moluccas. He formed ties with the local rulers, allowing the Portuguese to erect posts at Ternate and Amboina. Portugal effectively controlled the Spice Islands until the Dutch arrived in the early 1600s.

➡ Portuguese trade routes

4 THE SPANISH IN THE PACIFIC 1529–1700

The 1529 Treaty of Zaragoza resulted in Spain ceding control of the Spice Islands to Portugal. The Spanish, however, landed in the Philippines in 1565 and by 1571 took control of the Manila region. From 1572, a galleon sailed annually from Manila, carrying silver, which was exchanged with Chinese traders for silk and porcelain.

➡ Spanish trade routes

1613 Britain sets up trading post; French establish a factory in Surat in 1668

1690 Britain establishes trading post in Bengal capital

1515–1622 Persian city occupied by Portugal

1510 Portugal gains control of Goa

1557 Portuguese set up trading base

1571 Spain builds outpost; within a century, Manila becomes home to 150 Spanish households

RUSSIAN EMPIRE

Gobi Desert

Manchuria

Amur

Nerchinsk

BUKHARA

SAFAVID EMPIRE

Isfahan

Tigris

Hormuz

OMAN

Arabian Peninsula

MUGHAL EMPIRE

Indus

Ganges

Delhi

Himalayas

TIBET

KHANATE OF THE DZUNGARS

QING EMPIRE

Yangtze

Yellow River

Beijing

KOREA

JAPAN

Kyoto

Nagasaki

Macao

Formosa

Cambay
Diu
Surat
Damão
Bassein
Bombay
Chaul
Chandernagore
Calcutta
Goa
Bhatkal
Mangalore
Cannanore
Calicut
Pulicat
Masulipatam
Madras
Sadras
Pondicherry
Negapatam
Cochin
Tuticorin
Quilon

BURMA

SIAM

LAOS

Mekong

Manila

PHILIPPINES

Malacca

Sumatra

MALAY STATES

Benkulen
Silebar
Batavia

Java

KUTEI

Ternate

Moluccas

Amboina

East Indies

PORTUGUESE TIMOR

Mombasa
Zanzibar
Kilwa

Seychelles

Madagascar

Mauritius

Île de Bourbon (Réunion)

Delagoa Bay

INDIAN OCEAN

△ **The arms of the VOC**
The shield bears the arms of the Dutch East India Company, ornamented with the Roman god Neptune and a mermaid. It was created in c.1651.

1619 Dutch destroy the town of Jakarta and build the VOC headquarters under the name Batavia

1664–1710 Under Dutch control. The island falls into French hands in 1715 after Dutch exit and is renamed Île de France

6 THE BRITISH IN INDIA 1600–1690

Founded in 1600, the investor-funded British East India Company allowed Britain to open its first trading post in India at Surat (1613). With the acquisition of Calcutta, Britain ousted its French rival and secured British presence in Bengal. This formed the main bridgehead for its expansion throughout India in the 18th century.

➡ British trade routes
○ Main bases of the British East India Company

5 FRENCH INDIA 1664–1756

In 1664, the French East India Company was established to compete for trade in Southeast Asia. Colonies were established in India, most notably in Chandernagore (1673) and Pondicherry (1674). Posts were also erected in the Indian Ocean, on the Île de Bourbon (Réunion, 1664), Île de France (Mauritius, 1715), and the Seychelles (1756).

➡ French trade routes

PRINTING

The invention of the printing press revolutionized the spread of knowledge. Books that previously had to be laboriously copied by hand could now be printed in the hundreds or thousands for a wider market.

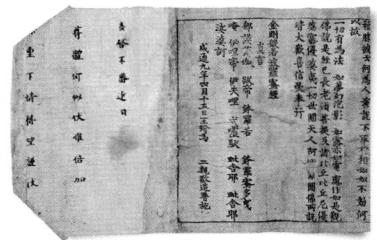

△ **Antique print**
This is a page from the *Diamond Sutra*, the world's oldest dated printed book. It was produced in 868 CE using wood-block printing techniques, and rediscovered in western China in 1907.

Printing was not a new technology. Engraved wooden blocks had been used for printing in east Asia since the 2nd century CE. In 1041, Chinese inventor Bi Sheng came up with movable type, which meant new pages could be composed rapidly without having to engrave a new block each time. However, the key innovation in printing came in 1439 with German printer Johannes Gutenberg's printing press. By using a long lever and a screw to press down on paper laid over a wooden tray in which inked type was arrayed, it could accurately create printed sheets at a rate of more than 200 per hour.

Reaching a wider audience

Gutenberg set up his printing press in Mainz, Germany, in the early 1440s, and by 1455, he had produced his *Forty-two-line Bible,* one of the most famous works ever printed. From here, the technique spread quickly, and by 1500, around 60 German towns had printing presses. Printing reached Italy in 1465, France in 1470, and England by 1476. It made larger editions of books practical, helping the new humanist ideas that were emerging as part of the Renaissance (see pp.104–105) to spread more rapidly. Cheaper in the long run to produce than handwritten manuscripts, these editions were affordable to wider social groups and helped advance literacy. Although Gutenberg could not have known it, he had unleashed a knowledge revolution.

Relation:
Aller Fürnemmen/vnd gedenckwürdigen Historien / so sich hin vnnd wider in Hoch vnnd Nieder Teutschland / auch in Franckreich / Italien / Schott vnd Engelland / Hisspanien / Hungern / Polen / Siebenbürgen / Wallachey / Moldaw / Türckey / etc. Inn diesem 1609. Jahr verlauffen vnd zutragen möchte.

Alles auff das trewlichst wie ich solche bekommen vnd zu wegen bringen mag / in Truck verfertigen will.

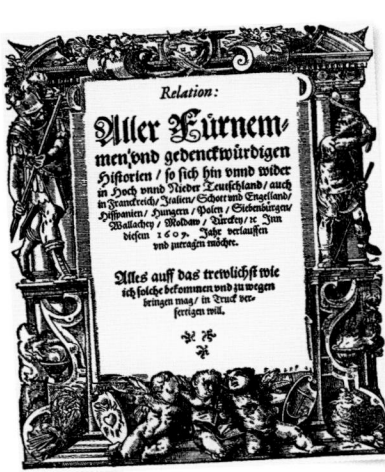

◁ **World's first newspaper**
Relation Aller Fürnemmen und Gedenckwürdigen Historien (Collection of all Distinguished and Commemorable News), probably the world's first newspaper, was printed by German publisher Johann Carolus at Strasbourg in 1605.

"The present book of the Psalms … has been fashioned by an ingenious invention of printing …"

FROM THE PSALMS PRINTED BY FUST AND SCHOEFFER, 1457

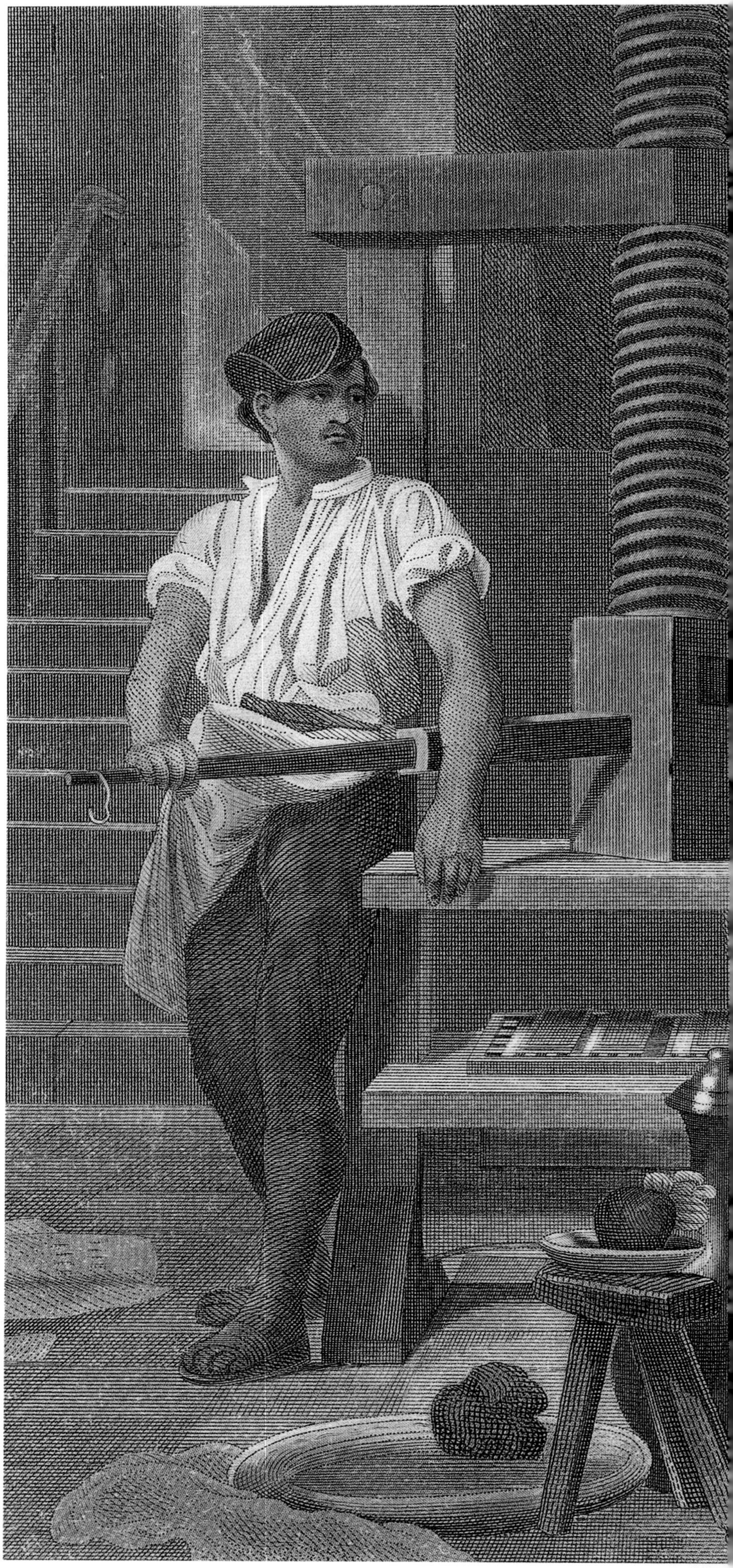

THE REFORMATION

Long-standing dissatisfaction at the conduct of the Roman Catholic Church led to a schism in 1517, causing Reformed (or Protestant) churches to spring up throughout Europe. A period of hostility followed as Catholic states tried to reassert papal authority.

In 1517, Martin Luther, a German Augustinian friar, composed his *Ninety-five Theses*—a tract condemning many of the practices of the Roman Catholic Church. The Church's hostile reaction forced Luther to reject the Catholic hierarchy and adopt a new theological position. He attracted large numbers of supporters, who formed the nucleus of the Reformed churches which proliferated throughout the German states. Once German princes began supporting this movement, a series of religious wars broke out. Amid the hostilities, more radical Protestant reformers appeared, such as Calvin in Switzerland, while

> *"A simple layman armed with Scripture is greater than the mightiest pope without it."*
>
> MARTIN LUTHER, 1519

the English and Swedish kings either rejected papal authority or even adopted Protestantism, increasing the geographical spread of Reformed churches. In 1542, the Catholic church council at Trent strengthened the education of the clergy and clamped down on its more dubious practices, and in 1555, a peace agreement was brokered at Augsburg, granting limited religious tolerance to Protestants. The peace, however, was brittle at best, and renewed religious conflict broke out in France in the 1560s and simmered elsewhere, too, before exploding anew in 1618 in the Thirty Years' War (see pp.168–169).

ST. BARTHOLOMEW'S DAY MASSACRE
A BLOODY EPISODE IN FRENCH HISTORY

On August 24, 1572, on the instruction of the Queen Mother, King Charles IX of France ordered the assassination of Huguenot Protestant leaders in Paris. Among those marked for death was the Huguenot leader, Admiral Gaspard de Coligny, who was brutally beaten and thrown out of his bedroom window just before dawn. The act set off a wave of mass fanaticism as Catholic mobs took to the streets and massacred 10,000–20,000 Protestants throughout the country.

RELIGIOUS MAP OF EUROPE

A powerful force of revivalism swept across Europe following Martin Luther's attack on the Roman Catholic Church in 1517. Secular rulers in Germany and Scandinavia established Protestantism along Lutheran lines. Calvinism became dominant in the Netherlands, Scotland, and Eastern Europe, while Anglicanism emerged in England.

KEY

- ■ Catholic majority areas 1555
- ■ Protestant majority areas 1555
- ▬ Frontier of the Roman Holy Empire c. 1570

TIMELINE

	1500	1520	1540	1560	1580	1600
1						
2						
3						
4						
5						
6						
7						

1 THE *NINETY-FIVE THESES* 1517–1521

Martin Luther pinned his *Ninety-five Theses*, to the door of Wittenberg Castle Church in October 1517. The document listed 95 complaints against the Church and adopted new theological positions on topics such as salvation and the interpretation of communion. The tract caused a huge stir throughout Europe, and led to his excommunication by the Catholic Church in 1521.

- Birthplace of Lutheranism
- ➡ Spread of Lutheranism
- ▬ Lutheran areas

2 CATHOLIC-PROTESTANT CONFLICT 1530–1555

In 1530, the Holy Roman Emperor Charles V ordered all Protestant churches to abandon their reforms, sparking a series of wars in the 1540s and 1550s. Eventually, peace was brokered in 1555 at Augsburg, Germany, with the Catholic Church agreeing to accept Protestantism but only in those German states that had already adopted the religion.

- 🤝 Site of Augsburg Agreement

3 RELIGIOUS CONFLICT IN FRANCE 1534–1598

Religious wars initially broke out in 1534 after King Francis I (r. 1515–1537) tried to repress Protestantism on French soil. On St. Bartholomew's Day in 1572, thousands of Protestants, known as Huguenots, were massacred in Paris. In 1598, Henri IV (r. 1589–1610), a former Huguenot, issued the Edict of Nantes, which tolerated Protestantism in France. Protestants also faced persecution in London and Rome.

- ✝ Site of persecution
- 🤝 Edict of Nantes
- ● Huguenot centers

4 CALVINISM 1540–1600

The French theologian John Calvin established a Protestant community in Geneva in the 1540s. His movement advanced a theology more radical than that of Luther, emphasizing God's sovereignty and the doctrine of predestination. Calvinism spread rapidly in France, the German states, the Netherlands, Scotland, and many parts of central Europe.

- ▬ Calvinism
- ➡ Spread of Calvinism

ATLANTIC OCEAN

PORTUGAL

Lisbon

SPAIN

Seville

5 THE CHURCH OF ENGLAND 1531–1534

The Reformation made little headway in England until King Henry VIII (r. 1509–1547) quarreled with the Papacy over his decision to divorce (an act forbidden by Catholic canon law) his wife, Catherine of Aragon. He rejected papal supremacy and established in 1534, through the Act of Supremacy, the Church of England and introduced Protestantism to England.

— Church of England

6 THE REFORMATION IN SWEDEN 1523–1544

As Lutheran ideas spread across Sweden, King Gustavus Vasa (r. 1523–1560) sought to establish a national church, still in communion with the papacy. However, following an assembly led by reformer Olavus Petri at Västeras in 1527, Catholic Church property was seized. In 1544, Sweden was officially declared a Protestant nation.

✦ Site of Västeras assembly

7 THE COUNTER-REFORMATION 1545–1563

The three sessions held by the General Council of Trent between 1545 and 1563 was the high point of the Catholic Reformation. The Church hierarchy upheld papal supremacy and core Catholic doctrines, but reformed education of the clergy and banned abuses such as the sale of Indulgences—where a penitent was able to gain absolution for a monetary contribution.

✦ Site of Council of Trent

1559 Calvinist reformer John Knox returns to Scotland, beginning the Reformation there

1527 Church synod disendows monasteries, weakening the Catholic Church

1593 Swedish Church becomes Lutheran and adopts the Augsburg Confession of Faith

1521 Imperial Diet orders Luther to recant; Luther's refusal forces him to go into hiding

1572 St. Bartholomew's Day Massacre of Protestants aggravates religious civil war in France

1545 First session of Catholic Church Council opens the Counter-Reformation

1536 Protestant reformer John Calvin publishes his *Institutes of the Christian Religion*

1555 Peace of Augsburg determines that religion in German states be determined by their ruling power

SCOTLAND
Edinburgh
IRELAND
Dublin
York
London
ENGLAND
North Sea
NETHERLANDS
Hamburg
DENMARK–NORWAY
Copenhagen
SWEDEN
Västeras
Stockholm
Uppsala
RUSSIA
Riga
Berlin
PRUSSIA
POLAND–LITHUANIA
Wittenberg
SMALL GERMAN STATES
Worms
Prague
AUSTRIA
Cracow
Rouen
Meaux
Paris
Nantes
Orléans
Troyes
Bourges
FRANCE
Cognac
Bordeaux
FRANCHE COMTÉ
SWISS CONFEDERATION
Zürich
Augsburg
HUNGARY
Buda
Debrecen
MOLDAVIA
Lyon
Geneva
Toulouse
Avignon
Aix
Saragossa
Barcelona
SAVOY
Milan
Trent
Genoa
Venice
Florence
Papal States
Rome
Adriatic Sea
OTTOMAN EMPIRE
Belgrade
TRANSYLVANIA
WALLACHIA
Balearic Islands
Mediterranean Sea
Naples
SARDINIA

▷ **Martin Luther**
German theologian Martin Luther forever changed Christianity when he began the Protestant Reformation in 16th-century Europe.

Descent into chaos
As Sebastien Vrancx records in his 1620 painting, widespread looting and plundering by soldiers was rife during the Thirty Years' War—by both sides—and there are numerous first-hand accounts of the atrocities committed.

THE THIRTY YEARS' WAR

When war broke out in 1618, it concerned the rights of Protestant minorities in Bohemia. But the fighting spread, pitting the Catholic rulers of Austria, Bavaria, and the Holy Roman Empire against German Protestant princes and, eventually, several foreign powers.

The Peace of Augsburg in 1555 (see pp.166–167) led to an agreement that each ruler in the Holy Roman Empire should be able to choose between Catholicism or Protestantism as their realm's religion, but a simmering tension still existed between Catholics and Protestants.

The pressure finally boiled over in 1617, when Catholic zealot Ferdinand, Archduke of Styria, was named as King of Bohemia, a primarily Protestant realm. Bohemian Protestants feared for their religious freedom and revolted in May 1618. The conflict that then erupted spread across Greater Bohemia. Imperial forces, supported by Spain, eventually crushed the rebellion at the Battle of White Mountain (1620) and enforced Catholicism as the Bohemian state religion.

Over several years, resentment of the Catholic regime grew and set the stage for neighboring Protestant states to wage war against the empire, starting with Denmark (1625–1629), followed by Sweden (1630–1635), and finally France (1635–1648), which, though Catholic, fought on the Protestant side.

The Thirty Years' War was one of the most intensely fought and devastating wars in European history and reduced the empire's population of 20–25 million by one-third. Peace would finally be brokered in 1648, bringing about an end to widespread Protestant discrimination and the European Wars of Religion.

▷ **King of Sweden (r. 1611–1632)**
Gustavus led his country to military supremacy during the Thirty Years' War, smashing the Imperial army at Breitenfeld in 1631 (right) and overrunning much of Germany and Bohemia. His death during Sweden's victory at the Battle of Lützen in 1632 slowed Sweden's progress.

"All the things that happened in this robber-war can barely be described."

PETER THIELE, EYEWITNESS ACCOUNT

BRITISH CIVIL WARS

In the 1640s and early 1650s, the British Isles were engulfed in a series of intertwined wars, as a king with tendencies to be an absolute monarch tried to take on Parliament. What resulted was a short-lived republican revolution, during which radical political groups pushed for radical social and political reforms.

By the 16th century, it had become customary that English monarchs had to seek parliamentary approval for most taxation. Charles I had to pay for wars against France and Spain in 1636–1637 and Scotland in 1639–1640, but until 1640, he resorted to expedients that did not need parliamentary approval, such as Ship Money, an antiquated naval tax. He avoided summoning Parliament from 1629 to 1640, which led to suspicions that he wanted to dispense with it. Meanwhile, a tide of Puritanism, a radical religious strain that opposed the traditional hierarchy of the Church of England, was rising. Parliament

insisted on stronger powers, which complicated negotiations with the king, and in 1642, war broke out between royalists and parliamentarians.

In the First Civil War, parliamentary armies under the guidance of Oliver Cromwell left the royalist side utterly defeated. The king turned to the Scots during the Second Civil War, but a Scottish-backed invasion failed. Charles was tried and executed, then his son, Charles II, was defeated in the Third Civil War. Political radicals then installed an English Republic which, slightly moderated under the rule of Oliver Cromwell as Lord Protector, lasted until 1660.

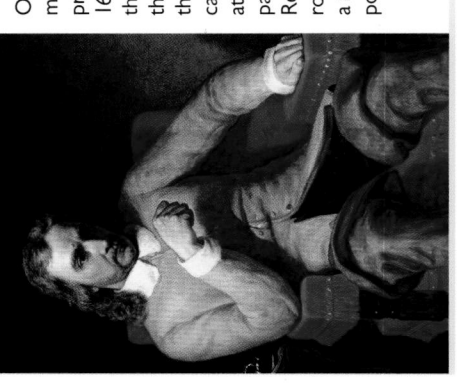

OLIVER CROMWELL
1599–1658

Oliver Cromwell was a Puritan who became a member of parliament (MP) in 1628. He rose to prominence in Britain during the Civil Wars. In 1645, Cromwell became second in command of the New Model Army. This radically new army thrived on its focus on a person's ability, rather than social standing. It was based on light armed cavalry, which greatly increased its speed of attack. Cromwell rose to commander of the parliamentary army in 1650. During the English Republic, he was appointed Lord Protector, a role with quasi-monarchical powers, to stem a rising tide of radicalism. He occupied this position until his death.

"I shall go from a corruptible to an incorruptible Crown, where no disturbance can be."

CHARLES I'S LAST WORDS BEFORE HIS EXECUTION, 1649

PARLIAMENTARY UPRISING

Struggles between king and Parliament led to three Civil Wars, which involved England, Scotland, Wales, and Ireland and ended with a short-lived English Republic. The king gradually lost land to Parliament, leaving him with only isolated strongholds.

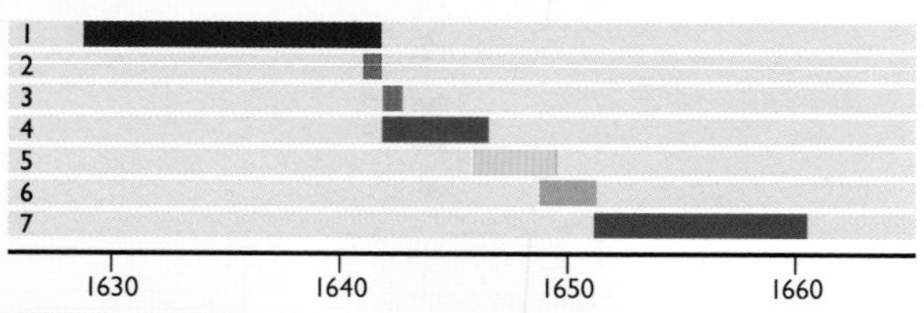

TIMELINE

1 2 3 4 5 6 7

1630   1640   1650   1660

✗ Events leading to Civil War

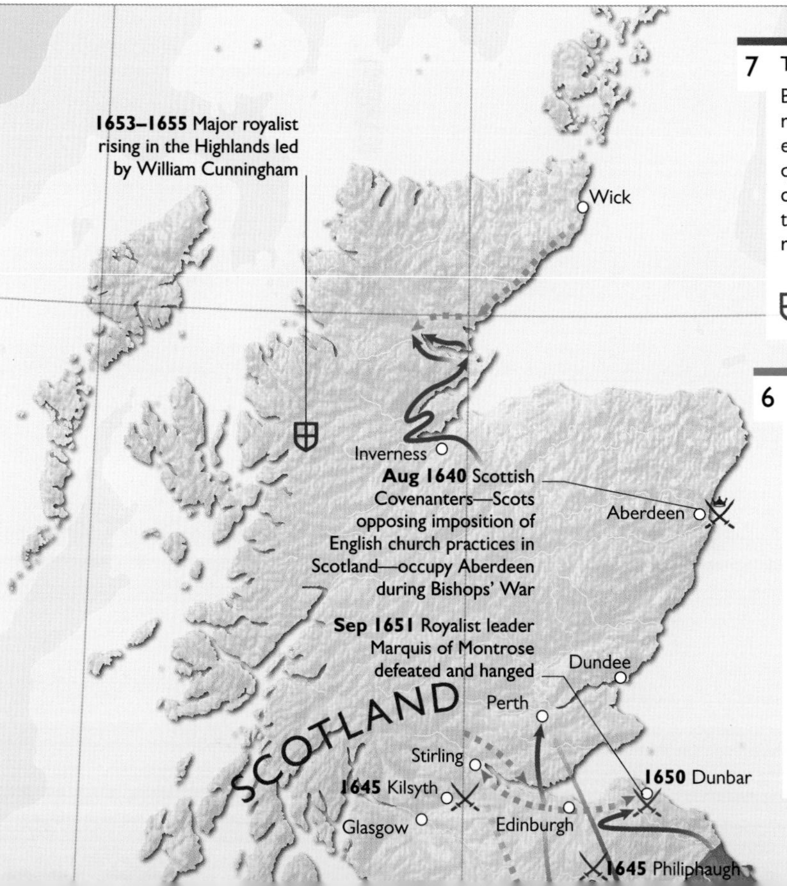

1 THE BREAKDOWN OF ROYAL AUTHORITY 1629–1642

Charles I's financial difficulties worsened with the 1639–1640 "Bishops' War" in Scotland, caused by his attempt to impose a Church of England prayer-book on the Scots. When he was eventually forced to summon Parliament to pay for it, a decade of grievances burst out, and a tussle between king and Parliament erupted. After a failed attempt to force Parliament's hand, the king fled north, fearing for his safety. When he raised the Royal Standard at Nottingham in August 1642, the Civil Wars had begun.

7 THE ENGLISH REPUBLIC 1652–1660

By 1652, Cromwell was the leading parliamentarian, but radical opponents such as Levellers (who favored social equality) came to the fore. In 1654, Cromwell took up the quasi-monarchical position of Lord Protector to stem chaos. His son, Richard, succeeded him in 1658, but by then the English Republic was rudderless, and Charles II returned from exile to restore the monarchy in 1660.

⊞ Key events during the English Republic

6 THE FINAL CIVIL WAR 1649–1651

From 1642–1649, much of Ireland was controlled by the Irish Catholic Confederation. Charles I's son, Charles II, turned to the Confederates for help in restoring the monarchy. Under the Marquis of Ormonde, the royalist army attempted to eliminate Cromwell's army, but were crushed in 1649. The royalists then made a new pact with the Scottish Presbyterians, but, after a final race toward London, they were defeated at Worcester in 1651.

Parliamentary/
Protestant-controlled
areas, Ireland 1642–1649

→ Royalist campaigns
of the Third Civil War

⋯▶ Parliamentary
campaigns of the
Third Civil War

✗ Battles of the
Third Civil War

SCOTLAND

Wick

Inverness

Aberdeen

Aug 1640 Scottish
Covenanters—Scots
opposing imposition of
English church practices in
Scotland—occupy Aberdeen
during Bishops' War

Sep 1651 Royalist leader
Marquis of Montrose
defeated and hanged

1653–1655 Major royalist
rising in the Highlands led
by William Cunningham

Dundee

Perth

Stirling

Glasgow

Kilsyth 1645

Edinburgh

1650 Dunbar

1645 Philiphaugh

Aug 1640 Scottish Covenanters occupy Newcastle after the Battle of Newburn

1644 Attempt by Prince Rupert, a royalist commander, to relieve York ends in defeat

Aug 22, 1642 King raises the Royal Standard, signaling start of the Civil War

May 1646 Charles I surrenders to the Scots

1651 Cromwell's parliamentary forces combine at Warwick and advance to Worcester

1648 Colchester

1648 Maidstone

1648 Dover

May 1660 Charles II lands to resume the crown of England

1642 First pitched battle of the war ends inconclusively

1649 Leveller mutiny

1642 Turnham Green London

1643, 1644 Newbury

1643 Cheriton

Nov 1640 Charles II summons the Long Parliament

Jan 1642 Charles I enters House of Commons Chamber to arrest opponents

Jan 1649 Charles I executed

Apr 1649 Leveller mutiny by soldiers stationed in Bishopsgate

Newcastle

Castle Bolton

Marston Moor

Sandal Castle

Newark

Nottingham

Ashby-de-la-Zouch

1645 Naseby

Lichfield

Warwick

Carlisle

Hulme

Uttoxeter

Worcester

Edgehill

Burford

Donnington Castle

1643 Roundaway Down

Langford House

1643 Lansdown

Bristol

1645 Langport

Raglan

1643 Parliamentary forces repulse royalists to regain initiative in southern England

1643 Sir Ralph Hopton wins royalist victory, opening way to Devon

Braddock Down **1643**

South Molton

ENGLAND

WALES

SOMERSET

DEVON

CORNWALL

East Anglia

Preston

Lathom

Aug 17, 1648 Scottish Presbyterian-royalist army defeated

1649 Drogheda sacked by Cromwell, causing large numbers of civilian casualties

Aug 25, 1648 Last Scottish cavalry surrender

1651 Charles II flees into exile after last army supporting him is defeated at Worcester

1642 Defeat of an Irish Confederate army by an English force at Liscarrol means Cork will be a royalist and Protestant stronghold

Jul 1643 Captured by royalist forces

Sep 1645 Surrenders to Parliament

1655 Royalist uprising under Colonel Penruddock crushed

Coleraine

1649 Londonderry

1652 Irish leaders of royalist forces and civilians deemed disloyal to the English Commonwealth have lands confiscated

Dublin

Drogheda

Rathmines

1649 Defeat of Marquis of Ormonde ends chances of royalist revival in Ireland

1650 Clonmel

Liscarrol

Cork

IRELAND

2 FIRST CIVIL WAR BEGINS 1642

The first, inconclusive engagement of the war took place at Edgehill in October 1642. Neither parliamentary nor royalist forces initially had effective leadership, and the king missed the chance of a thrust from Oxfordshire into London to put an early end to the war. Instead, the country divided into a patchwork of areas supporting either side; in the West, Cornwall was initially royalist and Somerset parliamentarian.

■ Area controlled by the king late 1643
■ Area controlled by Parliament late 1643

✕ Battles of First Civil War (1642–1646)

3 THE ROYALIST RESURGENCE 1643

1643 saw fragmentary fighting in which the royalists made strategic gains. Sir Ralph Hopton emerged victorious in the West Country after the Battle of Braddock Down in January, and by July, the royalists had captured Bristol. The north, too, fell largely into the hands of the royalists. Only in East Anglia, where Oliver Cromwell was in command, did Parliament hold its own.

■ Area controlled by the king late 1643
■ Area controlled by Parliament late 1643

✕ Battles of Royalist Resurgence 1643

▽ **Walking to the scaffold**
Flanked by soldiers, King Charles I takes a final walk through St. James's Park on his way to his execution on January 30, 1649.

4 PURITANS AND PRESBYTERIANS 1643–1646

Many parliamentarians held Puritan beliefs; Puritanism was a strict form of Protestantism. Scotland was mostly Presbyterian, another type of Protestantism, so in 1643, the parliamentary leadership turned to the Scots for aid and in return agreed that the English Church would be reformed on Presbyterian lines. Parliamentary victories led to the fall of most formerly royalist regions.

■ Area controlled by the king late 1645
■ Area controlled by Parliament late 1645
⊞ Royalist strongholds in areas controlled by Parliament late 1645

5 A SECOND CIVIL WAR 1646–1649

In 1646, Charles surrendered himself to the Scots, but was handed over to Parliament, marking the end of the First Civil War. In 1647, the king secretly negotiated a treaty with the Scots, and they invaded England on his behalf. Under Cromwell, the strong New Model Army had emerged, which won key victories of the war and defeated the king's army at Preston in 1648. The king was tried and executed.

⇢ Royalist campaigns of the Second Civil War
→ Parliamentary campaigns of the Second Civil War
✕ Battles of the Second Civil War

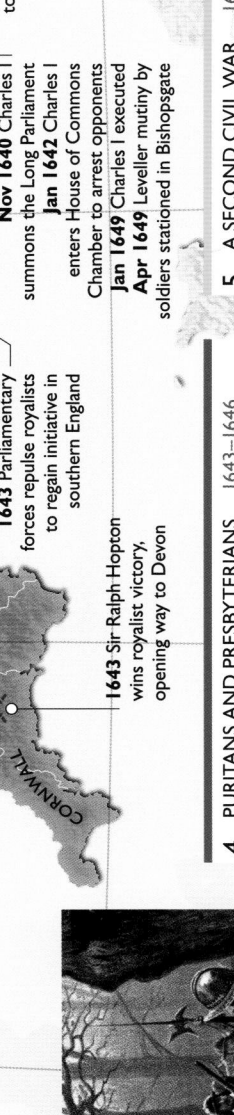

1 THE CONQUEST OF THE BALKANS
1453–1495

After taking Constantinople in 1453, Mehmed II claimed the remaining Byzantine possessions, finally seizing Morea in 1460. He conquered Serbia in 1454 and annexed Bosnia in 1463. Moldavia and the Republic of Ragusa both yielded peacefully to the Ottomans and became tributary states. Only a failed siege of Belgrade in 1456 halted Ottoman advances further west.

→ Major campaigns   ◎ Siege

2 SELIM CLAIMS THE CALIPHATE   1512–1520

Sultan Selim I (r. 1512–1520) began his conquest of Mamluk-ruled Syria and Egypt in 1516. His army swept away the resistance at Aleppo and Damascus and proclaimed victory by hanging the Mamluk caliph at the Gates of Cairo (1517). By gaining guardianship of the Islamic holy cities of Medina and Mecca, the Ottomans effectively became the fourth major Caliphate after the Rashiduns, Umayyads, and the Abbasids.

→ Major campaigns of Selim I   ✗ Ottoman victory

◁ Suleyman I holds court
This 16th-century Ottoman miniature depicts Suleyman the Magnificent receiving an ambassador from the vassal Hungarian state in 1556.

3 SULEYMAN THE MAGNIFICENT   1520–1566

Suleyman I, better known as Suleyman the Magnificent (r. 1520–1566), ruled the empire during the height of its power. In 1526, he routed the Hungarians at Mohács, reducing the country to a vassal state. The Austrian Habsburg ruler Ferdinand I attempted to recapture the state, but the Ottomans struck back by besieging Vienna in 1529. Suleyman failed to take the Habsburg city, but he remained overlord of Hungary.

→ Major campaigns of Suleyman I   ◎ Siege
✗ Major victory

4 OTTOMANS' NAVAL WARFARE   1522–1571

In 1522, the Ottoman navy expelled the Knights of St. John (a Crusader army) from Rhodes and, in 1529, captured Algiers. Following the Ottoman's assault on Cyprus in 1570, European powers formed the Holy League. A year later, the League's fleet, led by Don Juan of Austria, crushed the Ottomans at Lepanto, ending Ottoman naval dominance in the eastern Mediterranean.

→ Major naval campaigns   ✗ Major victory
– – ▶ Christian counteroffensive   ✗ Major defeat
◎ Siege

Map labels

NORWAY
SWEDEN
DENMARK
POMERANIA
UNITED PROVINCES
SMALL GERMAN STATES
BRANDENBURG
SPANISH NETHERLANDS
HOLY ROMAN EMPIRE
SAXONY
POLAND-LITHUANIA
RUSSIAN EMPIRE
EASTERN UKRAINE
AUSTRIA
BAVARIA
SALZBURG
FRANCHE COMTÉ
SWISS CONFEDERATION
FRANCE
MILAN
SAVOY
REP OF GENOA
PORTUGAL
SPAIN
Madrid
Lisbon
Fez
Oran
MOROCCO
ALGIERS
Algiers
TUNIS
Tunis
Djerba
Tripoli
TRIPOLI
EGYPT
PAPAL STATES
FLORENCE
NAPLES
Otranto
SARDINIA
Sicily
Malta
VENETIAN REPUBLIC
Venice
BOSNIA
SERBIA
WALLACHIA
MOLDAVIA
Jassy
TRANSYLVANIA
HUNGARY
Buda
Vienna
Esztergom (Gran)
Szigetvár
Mohács
Belgrade
Sofia
Edirne (Adrianople)
Constantinople
OTTOMAN EMPIRE
ANATOLIA
Athens
MOREA
Monemvasia
Preveza
Lepanto
Rhodes
Cyprus
Crete
Black Sea
Mediterranean Sea
KHANATE OF THE CRIMEA
Azov
Kaffa (Kefe)
CIRCASSIA
GEORGIAN STATES
Caucasus
Don
Dniester
Dnieper
Danube
Nile
BUJAK
JEDISAN
Trebizond
Taurus Mountains
SYRIA
Aleppo
Tripoli
Damascus
Jerusalem
Alexandria
Cairo
Suez
REPUBLIC OF RAGUSA

Map annotations

1475 Khanate of the Crimea becomes an Ottoman tributary state

1504 Moldavia becomes an Ottoman tributary state

1541 Hungary is annexed by the Ottomans

1461 Ottomans capture Byzantine stronghold of Trebizond

1366–1453 Ottoman capital

1453 Ottomans make Constantinople their capital, renaming it Istanbul

1516 Aleppo

1516 Damascus

1517 Ottoman conquest of Cairo signals collapse of the Mamluk Sultanate—in control of Egypt and Syria since 1250

1565 A 3-month Ottoman siege fails to dislodge Crusader army, the Knights of St. John

1460 Ottomans capture the Byzantine territory of Morea (Peloponnese)

1683
1529
1543
1526, 1541
1566
1456
1521
1566
1538
1687
1571
1540
1522
1569
1574
1560
1551
1541

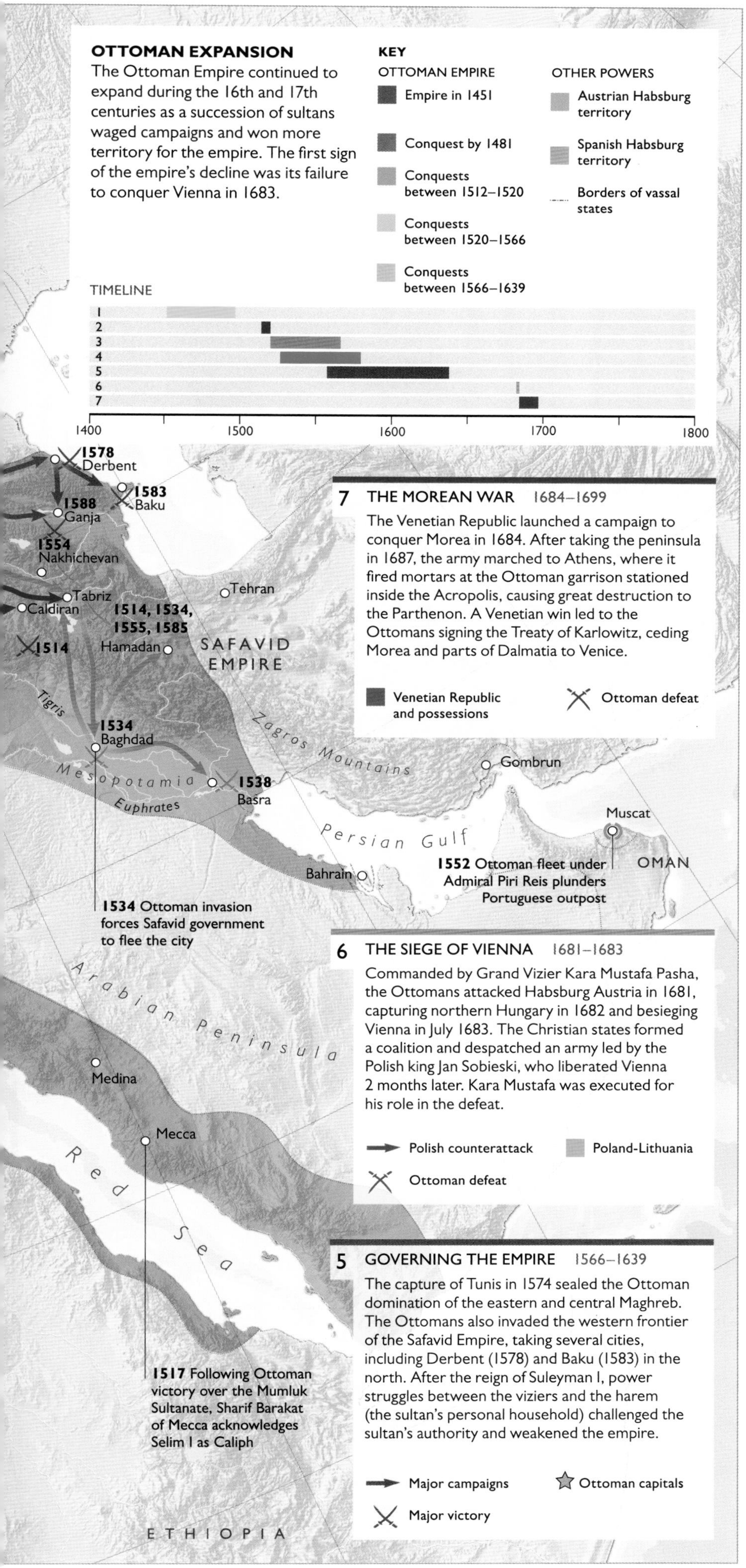

OTTOMAN EXPANSION

The Ottoman Empire continued to expand during the 16th and 17th centuries as a succession of sultans waged campaigns and won more territory for the empire. The first sign of the empire's decline was its failure to conquer Vienna in 1683.

KEY

OTTOMAN EMPIRE

- Empire in 1451
- Conquest by 1481
- Conquests between 1512–1520
- Conquests between 1520–1566
- Conquests between 1566–1639

OTHER POWERS

- Austrian Habsburg territory
- Spanish Habsburg territory
- Borders of vassal states

TIMELINE

1
2
3
4
5
6
7

1400　　1500　　1600　　1700　　1800

1578 Derbent
1583 Baku
1588 Ganja
1554 Nakhichevan
Tehran
Tabriz
1514, 1534, 1555, 1585
Caldiran
1514 Hamadan
SAFAVID EMPIRE
Zagros Mountains
Tigris
1534 Baghdad
Mesopotamia
Euphrates
1538 Basra
Gombrun
Persian Gulf
Muscat
Bahrain
1552 Ottoman fleet under Admiral Piri Reis plunders Portuguese outpost
OMAN
1534 Ottoman invasion forces Safavid government to flee the city
Arabian Peninsula
Medina
Mecca
Red Sea
1517 Following Ottoman victory over the Mumluk Sultanate, Sharif Barakat of Mecca acknowledges Selim I as Caliph
ETHIOPIA

7　THE MOREAN WAR　1684–1699

The Venetian Republic launched a campaign to conquer Morea in 1684. After taking the peninsula in 1687, the army marched to Athens, where it fired mortars at the Ottoman garrison stationed inside the Acropolis, causing great destruction to the Parthenon. A Venetian win led to the Ottomans signing the Treaty of Karlowitz, ceding Morea and parts of Dalmatia to Venice.

- Venetian Republic and possessions
- ✕ Ottoman defeat

6　THE SIEGE OF VIENNA　1681–1683

Commanded by Grand Vizier Kara Mustafa Pasha, the Ottomans attacked Habsburg Austria in 1681, capturing northern Hungary in 1682 and besieging Vienna in July 1683. The Christian states formed a coalition and despatched an army led by the Polish king Jan Sobieski, who liberated Vienna 2 months later. Kara Mustafa was executed for his role in the defeat.

- → Polish counterattack
- Poland-Lithuania
- ✕ Ottoman defeat

5　GOVERNING THE EMPIRE　1566–1639

The capture of Tunis in 1574 sealed the Ottoman domination of the eastern and central Maghreb. The Ottomans also invaded the western frontier of the Safavid Empire, taking several cities, including Derbent (1578) and Baku (1583) in the north. After the reign of Suleyman I, power struggles between the viziers and the harem (the sultan's personal household) challenged the sultan's authority and weakened the empire.

- → Major campaigns
- ★ Ottoman capitals
- ✕ Major victory

REIGN OF THE OTTOMANS

The 15th century heralded an era of expansion for the Ottoman Empire, in which it extended its domain in the Balkans, Syria, and Egypt. At the pinnacle of its power, the empire posed a challenge to western Europe, forcing Christian states to form alliances to protect their lands.

With the capture of the Byzantine capital, Constantinople, in 1453, the Ottoman Empire consolidated its position as the principal Islamic power of the modern era. Sultan Mehmed II (r. 1444–1446 and 1451–1481) proceeded to annex the remnants of Byzantium, lands in the northern Balkans and eastern Anatolia, and bolstered the sultanate's power by earning revenues from these new conquests. In 1481, the Ottomans sent shock waves across western Europe by launching an attack on Otranto in southern Italy, but Mehmed's untimely death a year later put a stop to the campaign.

Successor Bayezid II (r. 1481–1512) made further gains in the Balkans, and Selim I's (r. 1512–1520) conquest of Egypt and the Holy Lands allowed him to lay claim to the caliphate and claim preeminence among Muslim rulers. Suleyman the Magnificent (r. 1520–1566) ruled an empire at the height of its power, notably invading Hungary in 1526. The Habsburg rulers proved an obdurate foe, but still most of the country was lost to the Ottomans.

From the mid-16th century, the authority of the sultanate began to diminish as internal power wranglings led to military officials taking greater regional control while government ministers, notably the grand vizier, rose to power. Although Murad IV (r. 1623–1640) and Mehmed IV (r. 1648–1687) made fitful attempts at reform, their efforts proved largely ineffectual. The Ottoman Empire's increasingly dysfunctional leadership was evident in its failed siege of Vienna in 1683, and defeat marked the start of its decline.

OTTOMAN ARCHITECTURE
BYZANTINE INSPIRATION

After the conquest of Constantinople, Sultan Mehmed II headed to the Hagia Sophia church—the centrepiece of the former Byzantine capital—and converted it to a mosque. The majesty of the building inspired great Ottoman architects such as Sinan, who went on to design mosques with soaring domes, vast open interiors, and multiple minarets, such as the Sülemaniye mosque (1558) in Istanbul.

Hagia Sophia
This 16th-century painting shows the church of Hagia (Saint) Sophia transformed into a mosque.

EAST MEETS WEST

The arrival of Europeans in the Indian Ocean in the 15th century began a 200-year-long period in which western travelers, goods, and ideas reached Asia in increasing numbers. In turn, information about the continent and its powerful indigenous empires filtered back to Europe.

△ **Trading hub**
This 1665 painting shows the Dutch flag flying over the trading station of the Dutch East India Company at Hooghly in Bengal, India. Dutch ships can be seen navigating the Ganges.

Before the late 15th century, European knowledge of Asia had been minimal, derived mainly from the observations of the Venetian merchant Marco Polo about the Mongol Empire. It was the desire to acquire spices such as nutmeg, pepper, cinnamon, and cloves—prized for their culinary and medicinal uses—that drew Europeans to Asia once more. Spices were expensive and could only be sourced along overland routes controlled by the Chinese, Mughal, and Ottoman Empires.

To Asia by sea

The Italian explorer Christopher Columbus sailed westward across the Atlantic in 1492 in an attempt to reach India and China. However, it was the Portuguese captain Vasco da Gama who finally reached Calicut (modern-day Kozhikode) on India's Malabar Coast in 1498 by sailing around Africa and then eastward into the Indian Ocean. Thereafter, the Portuguese returned in greater force and established a series of trading posts across southern Asia: at Goa, India, in 1510; in Malacca on the Malay peninsula in 1511; and in the Moluccas, in modern-day Indonesia, in 1512.

The Portuguese soon lost ground to other European rivals—notably the Dutch, who began to encroach on the Moluccas in 1599, and the English, who established a trading post at Surat in India in 1612. By then, however, Portugal had acquired a trading post at Macao, China, from where European missionaries and merchants traveled into China and Japan. In China, Jesuit missionaries (members of the Catholic order of the Society of Jesus) under the leadership of Matteo Ricci adopted many Chinese customs, including their dress, and established a presence at the Ming court in Beijing. Although they made few converts and only secured formal toleration of Christianity in 1692, the missionaries introduced China to European astronomical, medical, and mathematical ideas. In turn, knowledge of China was transmitted back to the West,

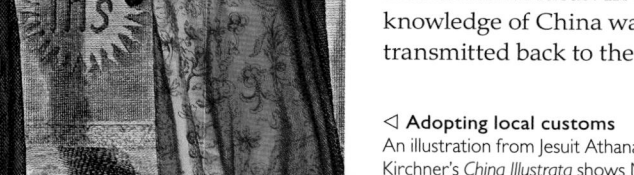

◁ **Adopting local customs**
An illustration from Jesuit Athanasius Kirchner's *China Illustrata* shows Matteo Ricci (left) and another Christian missionary dressed in Chinese-style robes that made their acceptance at the imperial court easier.

MISSIONARIES AND MERCHANTS

The arrival of Vasco da Gama in India was followed by the setting up of Portuguese forts in south and Southeast Asia. From these, traders and missionaries traveled into Asia, particularly India, Japan, and China. By the mid-17th century, the Portuguese had largely been supplanted by the Dutch and the British. Although their missionary effort was less notable than that of the Portuguese, their merchants helped to spread European ideas into Asia and transmit knowledge about Asia to the West.

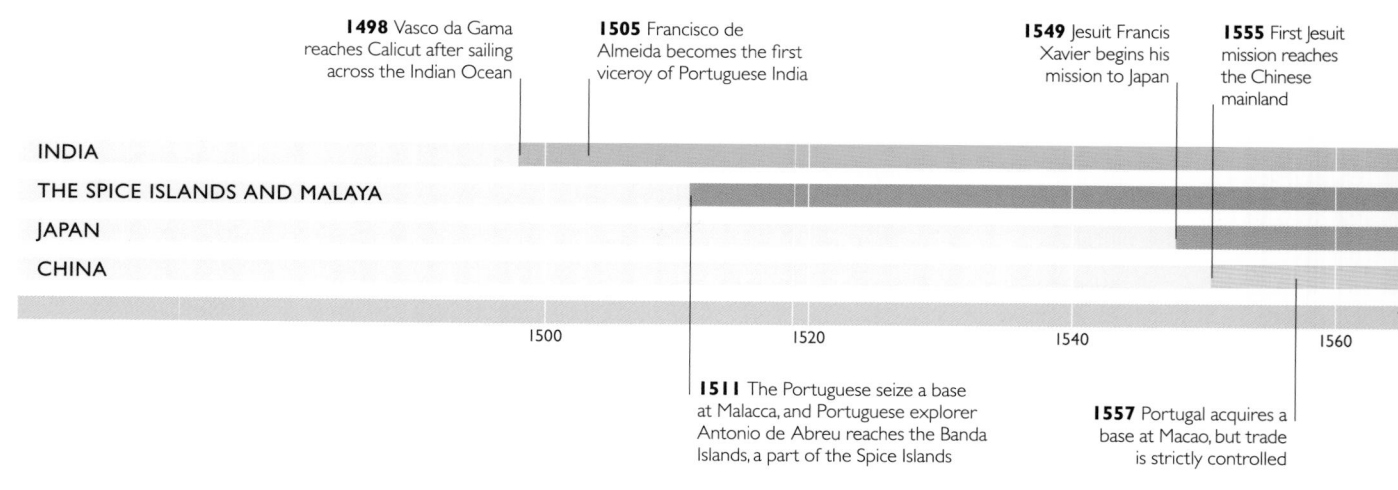

1498 Vasco da Gama reaches Calicut after sailing across the Indian Ocean

1505 Francisco de Almeida becomes the first viceroy of Portuguese India

1549 Jesuit Francis Xavier begins his mission to Japan

1555 First Jesuit mission reaches the Chinese mainland

INDIA

THE SPICE ISLANDS AND MALAYA

JAPAN

CHINA

1500   1520   1540   1560

1511 The Portuguese seize a base at Malacca, and Portuguese explorer Antonio de Abreu reaches the Banda Islands, a part of the Spice Islands

1557 Portugal acquires a base at Macao, but trade is strictly controlled

◁ **Painting foreigners**
This painting from the 16th–17th century showing a Portuguese expedition arriving in Japan is in the Nanban style, a Japanese school of art that specialized in the depiction of foreigners and foreign themes.

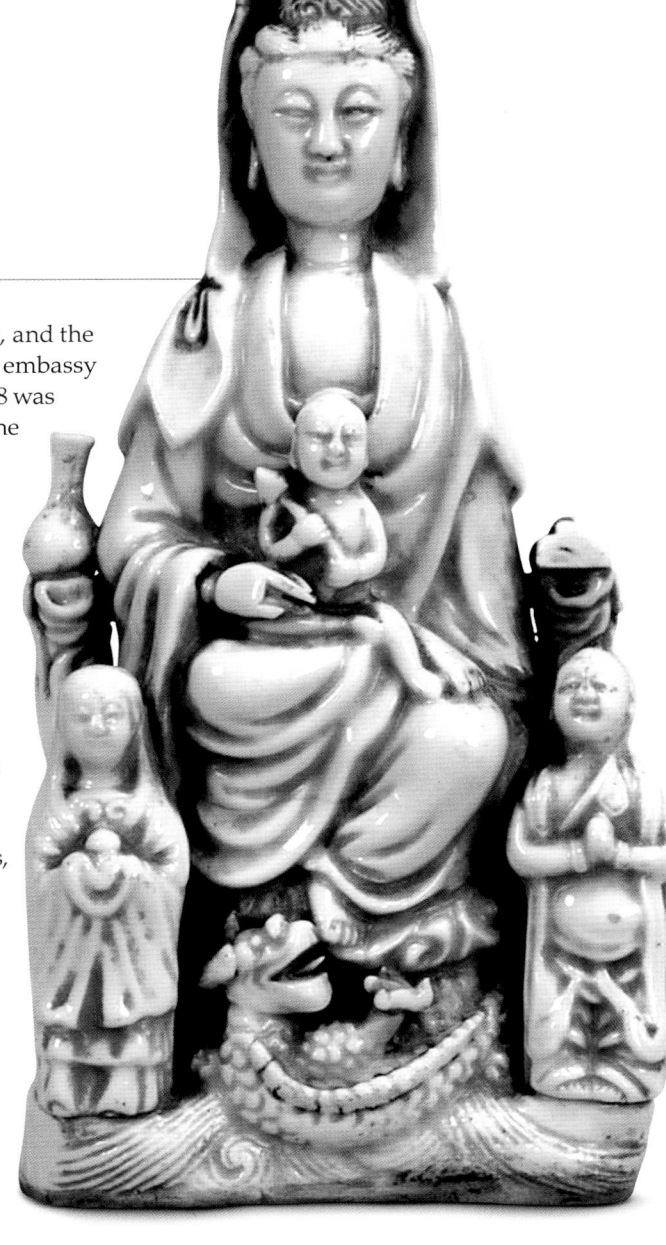

in works such as the *China Illustrata* (1667), compiled by the Jesuit Athanasius Kirchner, which reproduced Chinese texts for a European audience for the first time.

Japan in the 16th century was mired in internal wars. The shipwreck of two Portuguese sailors in 1543 introduced modern firearms into Japan, increasing the bloodiness of the civil wars. The Jesuit Francis Xavier established a mission in 1549, and its converts included the daimyo lord Omura Sumitada, who gave the Portuguese the site of Nagasaki in 1571, from where they operated a growing trading network.

Although European goods were valued, and the Portuguese introduced copper-plate engraving and painting in oils and watercolors to the Japanese, the increasing number of Christian converts worried the Tokugawa shoguns who ruled Japan after 1600. The Shimabara Revolt of 1637, an uprising that included many Japanese Roman Catholics, proved to be the final straw. Christianity was savagely repressed and the Portuguese expelled; henceforth, the only contact allowed with Europeans was through a trading enclave off Nagasaki run by the Dutch.

Trade and diplomacy in India

In India, rather than winning converts, the English sought to expand their trade by gaining access to the principal centers of power, which in the north meant the court of the Mughals. Although the English East India Company acquired Fort St. George (modern-day Chennai) in 1641 and Fort William (modern-day Kolkata) in 1690, they avoided large-scale political commitments that would exhaust their resources.

Trade, though, required knowledge, and the English diplomat Sir Thomas Roe's embassy to the Mughal court from 1615–1618 was one of many that reported back on the topography, customs, and politics of India. Indians traveling to the west were limited to servants and *lascars* (seamen of Indian origin) aboard company vessels, though a few high-status Indians also traveled.

By then, the terms of engagement between Asia and Europe were changing. Within a century, the British would directly occupy much of India, the Ottoman Empire would begin to fragment, the Qing Empire would become dependent on trade with Europeans, and Japan would cut itself off from the outside world. East and West, though, would be inextricably intertwined in an increasingly globalized world.

▷ **Camouflaged piety**
This Japanese ivory figurine depicts the Virgin Mary as Kannon, the Buddhist goddess of mercy, a pretense made necessary by the outlawing of Christianity in Japan from 1614.

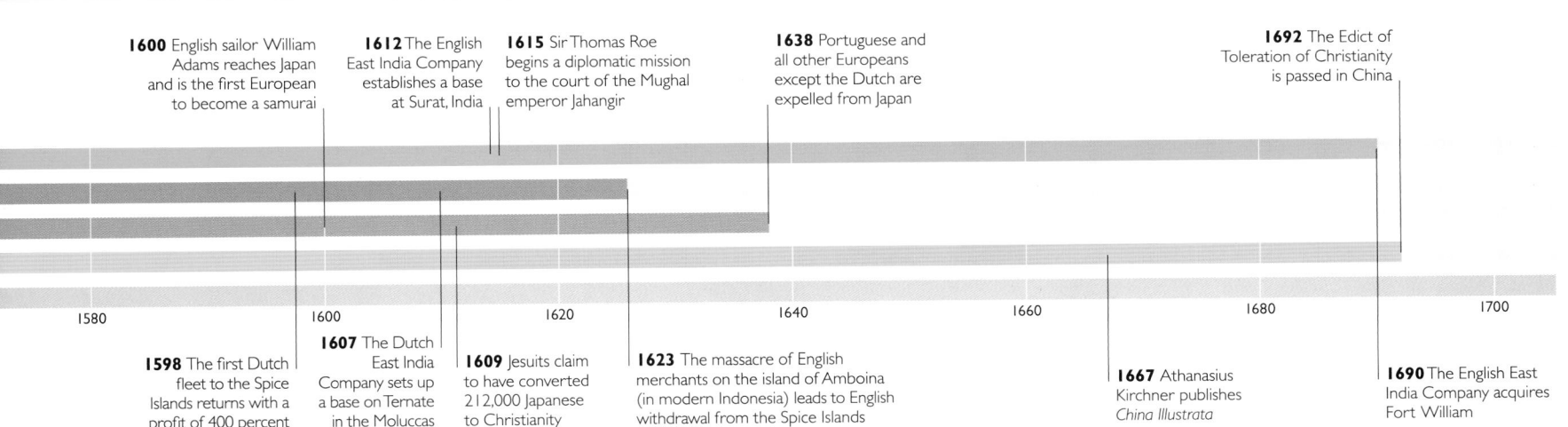

1600 English sailor William Adams reaches Japan and is the first European to become a samurai

1612 The English East India Company establishes a base at Surat, India

1615 Sir Thomas Roe begins a diplomatic mission to the court of the Mughal emperor Jahangir

1638 Portuguese and all other Europeans except the Dutch are expelled from Japan

1692 The Edict of Toleration of Christianity is passed in China

1598 The first Dutch fleet to the Spice Islands returns with a profit of 400 percent

1607 The Dutch East India Company sets up a base on Ternate in the Moluccas

1609 Jesuits claim to have converted 212,000 Japanese to Christianity

1623 The massacre of English merchants on the island of Amboina (in modern Indonesia) leads to English withdrawal from the Spice Islands

1667 Athanasius Kirchner publishes *China Illustrata*

1690 The English East India Company acquires Fort William

1580   1600   1620   1640   1660   1680   1700

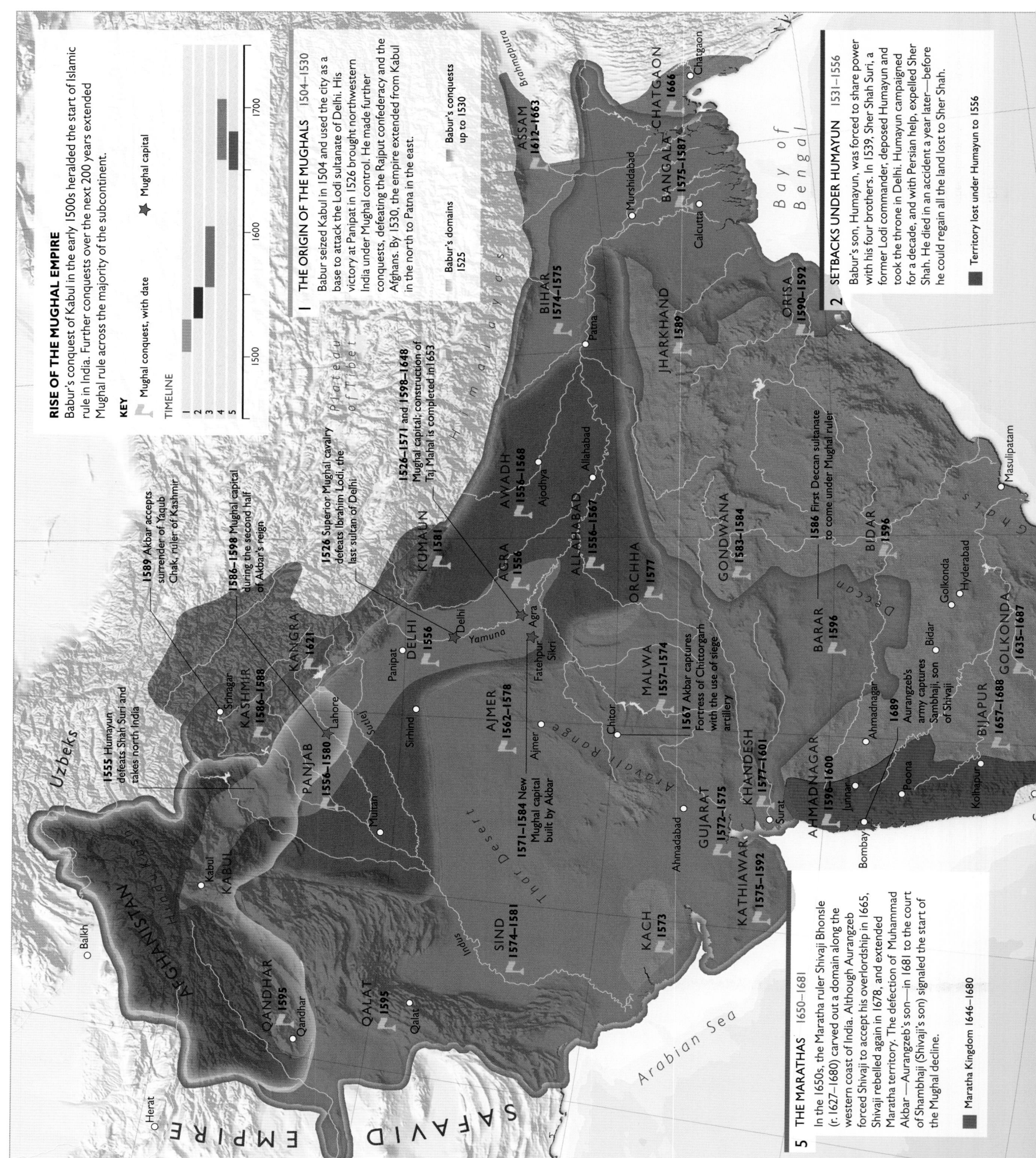

RISE OF THE MUGHAL EMPIRE

Babur's conquest of Kabul in the early 1500s heralded the start of Islamic rule in India. Further conquests over the next 200 years extended Mughal rule across the majority of the subcontinent.

KEY

★ Mughal conquest, with date
★ Mughal capital

TIMELINE

1
2
3
4
5

1500   1600   1700

1 | THE ORIGIN OF THE MUGHALS 1504–1530

Babur seized Kabul in 1504 and used the city as a base to attack the Lodi sultanate of Delhi. His victory at Panipat in 1526 brought northwestern India under Mughal control. He made further conquests, defeating the Rajput confederacy and the Afghans. By 1530, the empire extended from Kabul in the north to Patna in the east.

Babur's domains 1525

Babur's conquests up to 1530

2 | SETBACKS UNDER HUMAYUN 1531–1556

Babur's son, Humayun, was forced to share power with his four brothers. In 1539, Sher Shah Suri, a former Lodi commander, deposed Humayun and took the throne in Delhi. Humayun campaigned for a decade, and with Persian help, expelled Sher Shah. He died in an accident a year later—before he could regain all the land lost to Sher Shah.

Territory lost under Humayun to 1556

5 | THE MARATHAS 1650–1681

In the 1650s, the Maratha ruler Shivaji Bhonsle (r. 1627–1680) carved out a domain along the western coast of India. Although Aurangzeb forced Shivaji to accept his overlordship in 1665, Shivaji rebelled again in 1678, and extended Maratha territory. The defection of Muhammad Akbar—Aurangzeb's son—in 1681 to the court of Shambhaji (Shivaji's son) signaled the start of the Mughal decline.

Maratha Kingdom 1646–1680

1555 Humayun defeats Shah Suri and takes north India

1589 Akbar accepts surrender of Yaqub Chak, ruler of Kashmir

1586–1598 Mughal capital during the second half of Akbar's reign

1526 Superior Mughal cavalry defeats Ibrahim Lodi, the last sultan of Delhi

1526–1571 and 1598–1648 Mughal capital: construction of Taj Mahal is completed in 1653

1571–1584 New Mughal capital built by Akbar

1567 Akbar captures Fortress of Chittorgarh with the use of siege artillery

1586 First Deccan sultanate to come under Mughal rule

1689 Aurangzeb's army captures Sambhaji, son of Shivaji

Map labels

Uzbeks

Balkh

AFGHANISTAN
QANDHAR 1595
Qandhar
Qalat
QALAT 1595
Kabul
KABUL

Herat

SAFAVID EMPIRE

Srinagar
KASHMIR 1586–1588
KANGRA 1621
Lahore
PANJAB 1556–1580
Multan
Sutlej
Sirhind
Indus
SIND 1574–1581
KACH 1573
KATHIAWAR 1575–1592
Ahmadabad
GUJARAT 1572–1575
Surat
Bombay
KHANDESH 1577–1601

Himalayas
Plateau of Tibet
KUMAUN 1581
Panipat
DELHI 1556
Delhi
Yamuna
AGRA 1556
Agra
Fatehpur Sikri
AJMER 1562–1578
Ajmer
Thar Desert
Aravalli Range
Chitor
MALWA 1557–1574
Brahmaputra
ASSAM 1612–1663
BANGALA 1575–1587
CHATGAON 1666
Chatgaon
Bay of Bengal
Murshidabad
Calcutta
BIHAR 1574–1575
Patna
AWADH 1556–1568
Ajodhya
ALLAHABAD 1556–1567
Allahabad
ORCHHA 1577
JHARKHAND 1589
ORISA 1590–1592
GONDWANA 1583–1584
Deccan
BARAR 1596
BIDAR 1596
Bidar
Hyderabad
Golkonda
GOLKONDA 1635–1687
AHMADNAGAR 1596–1600
Junnar
Poona
Ahmadnagar
BIJAPUR 1657–1688
Kolhapur
Masulipatam
Arabian Sea

MUGHAL INDIA

In the 1520s, the Mughals, a Muslim group from central Asia, founded an empire in northern India that expanded over the next 150 years to cover most of the subcontinent. A succession of Mughal rulers presided over a culture whose rich legacy includes grand architectural pieces such as the Taj Mahal and the Red Fort in Delhi.

In 1526, Babur, a descendant of the Mongol warlord Timur, defeated the Lodi sultan of Delhi, conquered a swathe of northern India, and founded the Mughal dynasty. During his reign, he doubled the size of the empire through further conquests. Babur's son and successor, Humayun, however, lost Mughal territories to rival Sher Shah Suri— and lived in exile for 15 years before enlisting the help of Safavid Persia to regain the throne shortly before his death in 1556. It was Humayun's son, Akbar (r. 1556–1605), who secured the empire's future, extending its boundaries to the south and east,

establishing a well-organized and secular government that brought unity to the realm. The next two Mughal rulers, Jahangir (r. 1605–1627) and Shah Jahan (r. 1628–1658), presided over brilliant courts and marked the empire's golden age. Shah Jahan's passion for grand architecture led to the building of the Taj Mahal in Agra and the grand mosque, Jama Masjid, in Delhi, but his overzealous military campaigns also drained the empire's wealth. Under Aurangzeb (r. 1658–1707), the empire extended deep into southern India, but his harsher religious policies alienated many Hindu rulers, giving rise to local revolts, such as that of the Marathas, causing imperial borders to start fraying. The encroaching European powers took advantage of the instability and further eroded Mughal power, and by the early 1800s, Mughal rule extended scarcely beyond the suburbs of Delhi.

"Miracles occur in the temples of every creed."

AKBAR THE GREAT, FROM AKBARNAMA, c. 1603

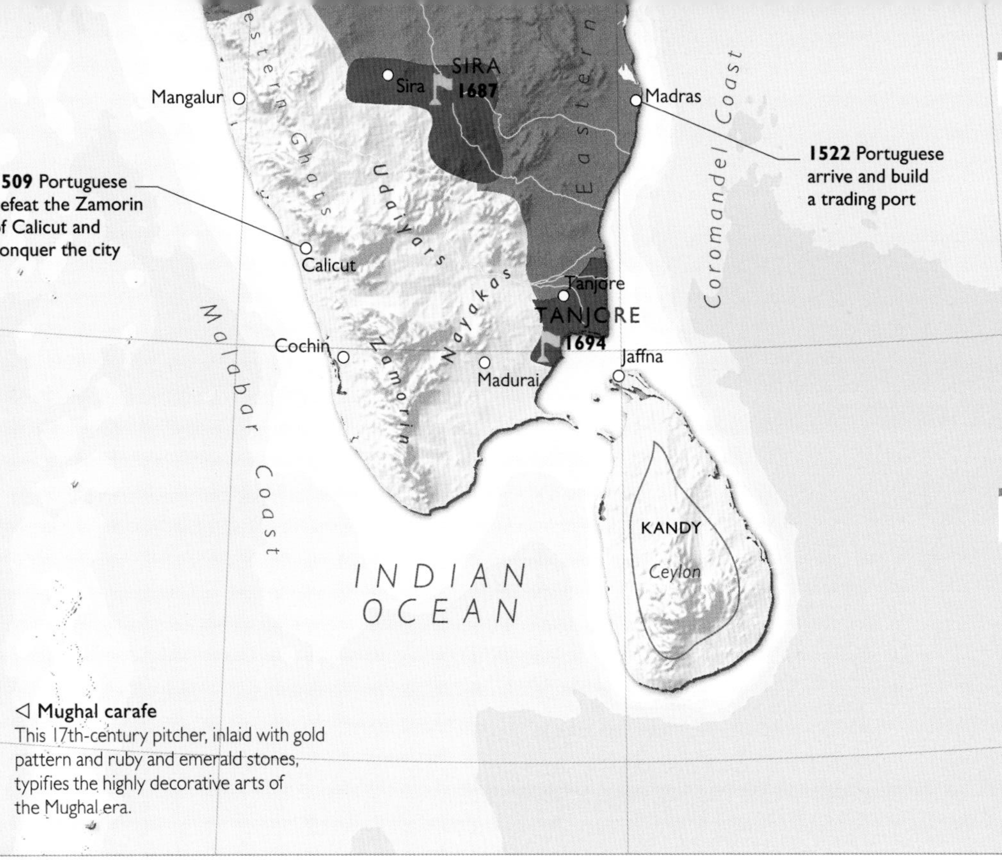

3 THE EMPIRE UNDER AKBAR   1556–1605

Seventeen-year-old Akbar came to power after the death of his father, Humayun. Akbar not only restored the Mughal Empire's old boundaries but also expanded the empire through conquests, annexing Afghanistan, Kashmir, Sind, Gujarat, and Bengal, and pushed south into the Deccan. By abolishing the "jizya" tax on non-Muslims, he won the acceptance of the Hindu territories.

- Akbar's domains 1556
- Akbar's gains 1605

4 AURANGZEB'S REIGN   1658–1707

Aurangzeb seized the throne after a long civil war against his brothers. He reasserted Mughal power in many of the empire's territories, including Bengal, and also muted a Rajput revolt in 1680. He then annexed Koch Bihar, reclaimed the Deccan, and pushed the imperial boundary as far south as Tanjore. His promotion of Islam and restoration of the jizya tax alienated many Hindus.

- Areas brought under Mughal rule 1658–1707

1522 Portuguese arrive and build a trading port

1509 Portuguese defeat the Zamorin of Calicut and conquer the city

▽ **Mughal carafe**
This 17th-century pitcher, inlaid with gold pattern and ruby and emerald stones, typifies the highly decorative arts of the Mughal era.

SHAH JAHAN AND MUMTAZ
AN EMPEROR'S UNDYING LOVE

This miniature painting depicts the Mughal emperor Shah Jahan embracing his wife, Mumtaz Mahal, who he cherished over his two other wives. In 1631, Shah Jahan was left heartbroken after Mumtaz died during childbirth. The following year, he ordered the construction of the Taj Mahal in Agra—a white marble mausoleum, inlaid with gemstones—as a tribute to his beloved.

Coromandel Coast

Madras

Jaffna

KANDY
Ceylon

Eastern

Tanjore
TANJORE **1694**

Madurai

Nayaks

SIRA **1687**
Sira

INDIAN OCEAN

Udaiyars

Cochin
Zamorin
Calicut

Western Ghats

Mangalur

Malabar Coast

Between 1405 and 1433, Admiral Zheng He led seven state-sponsored naval missions, known as the "Ming Treasure Voyages," across the Indian Ocean. With a fleet comprising more than 200 ships and 27,800 crewmen, Zheng He sailed as far as Arabia and the east coast of Africa, establishing new trade links and extending China's commercial influence.

CHINA FROM THE MING TO THE QING

The Ming Dynasty (1368–1644) encouraged industry and foreign trade, heralding a renaissance in China's economy and technological development. However, from 1506, a succession of feckless rulers eroded Ming authority. When civil rebellion broke out across the land following a famine in the 1620s, the non-Han Chinese Jurchen (later known as Manchus) took their opportunity and ousted the beleaguered Ming to become China's new rulers.

The Ming governed the realm according to systems set up long ago by the Qin (see pp. 74–75). China's manufacturing blossomed under the Ming, encouraged by foreign trade. Under Emperor Yongle (r. 1403–1424), the Forbidden City was built in the new capital Beijing (which replaced Nanjing as the main seat of imperial residence). He also increased China's trade influence across Asia and Africa.

The later emperors lacked the same vision, which led to a gradual waning of Ming power. Emperor Xuande (r. 1425–1435) established a Grand Secretariat to streamline legislation and, in doing so, reduced the burden on his rule. The Ming suffered a blow in 1449 when the young Emperor Zhengtong (r. 1435–1449 and 1457–1464) was taken prisoner by Mongol tribes while leading a battle against them. The second half of the Ming era saw court officials displace the traditional bureaucracy, leading to factionalism and poor governance. The empire's fall was presaged in the 1620s by a severe famine, which triggered lawlessness and peasant rebellions across the realm.

In 1644, the Manchus seized Beijing. Initially, the Chinese ruling classes were excluded from government positions, leading to revolts, but reforms thereafter created stability for Qing rule under Emperors Shunzhi (r. 1644–1661) and Kangxi (r. 1661–1722).

1 GOLDEN AGE OF THE MING 1368–1435

The Ming engaged extensively in domestic and foreign trade, establishing major commercial centers predominantly along China's eastern coast. The country exported manufactured goods such as porcelain, silk cloth, and paper. During this period, the growth in international trade encouraged many Chinese people to settle in cities throughout Southeast Asia.

▲ Major trading center

2 FROM EMPEROR TO PRISONER 1449–1457

In 1449, Emperor Zhengtong was captured after leading an ill-advised war against the Mongols. He was released after a year but spent several years battling to return to the throne. Throughout Ming rule, measures were taken to reinforce the northern frontier against any Mongol invasion: the Great Wall was extended and then fortified with a series of garrisons and 1,200 watchtowers.

▲ Great Wall garrison

3 THE MING IN DECLINE 1506–1620

Emperor Zhengde (r. 1506–1521) adopted Confucianism—a system of ethics based on mutual responsibility. His successor Jianjing (r. 1521–1567), however, favored the more carefree, nature-based teachings of Daoism. In reaction, he left the governing to court officials and ignored the problem of Japanese pirate raids, devoting himself to sporting pastimes and hosting lavish Daoist ceremonies. Ming authority became even more ineffectual under Emperor Wanli (r. 1573–1620).

→ Japanese pirate raids

▨ Area affected by the pirate raids

1688 The Qing build a system of embankments and ditches, known as the Willow Palisade, to restrict Chinese movement into Manchu territory

MANCHURIA

Mukden
Liaodong

Willow Palisade

INNER MONGOLIA

LIAOYANG

Mongols

◁ **Chinese porcelain**
During the Ming era, expert potters used local clay and imported Persian cobalt to create beautifully decorated porcelain products. Manufactured only in China, porcelain goods became as highly prized as silk in European and Middle Eastern markets.

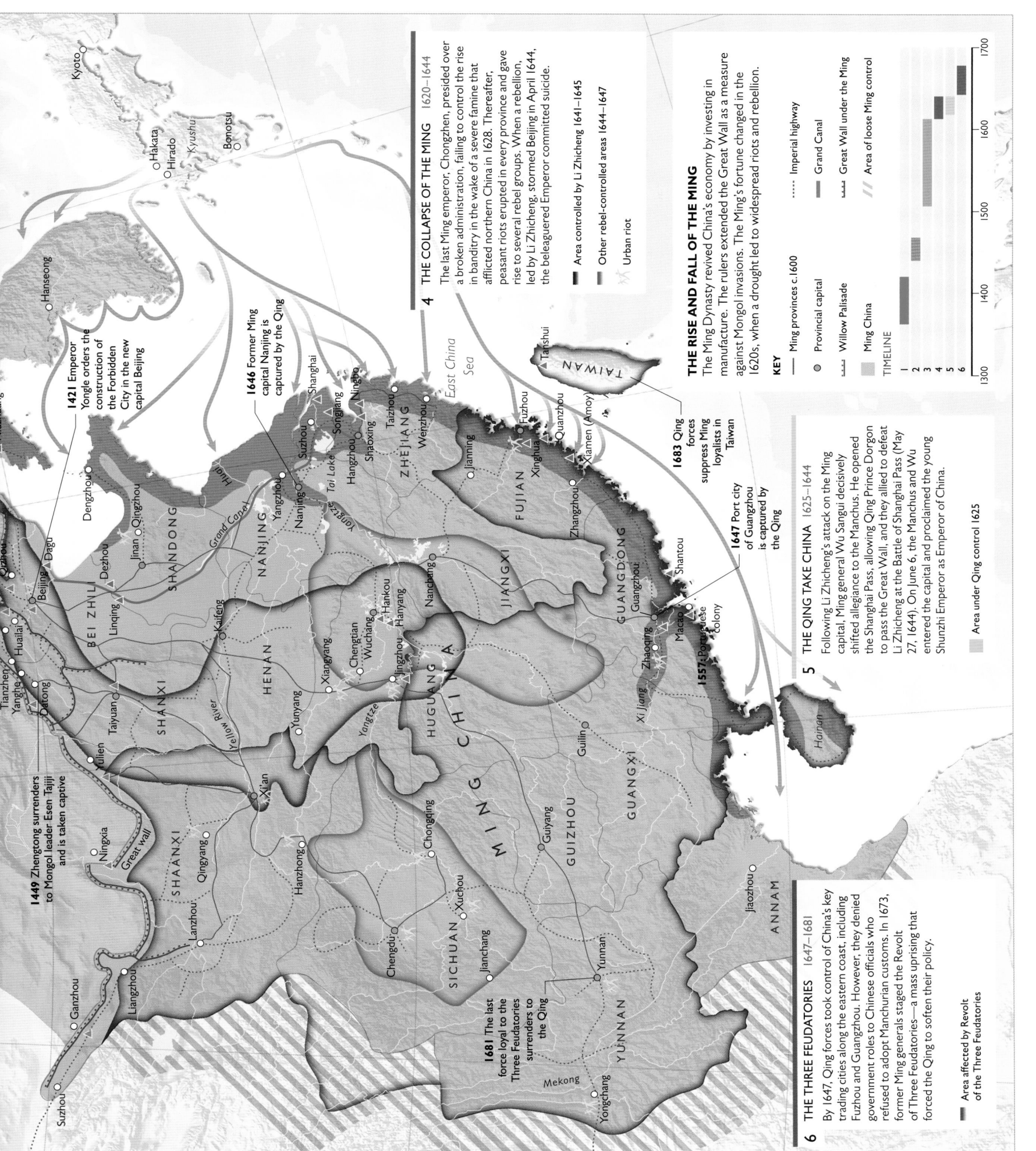

1421 Emperor Yongle orders the construction of the Forbidden City in the new capital Beijing

1646 Former Ming capital Nanjing is captured by the Qing

1449 Zhengtong surrenders to Mongol leader Esen Taijii and is taken captive

1683 Qing forces suppress Ming loyalists in Taiwan

1647 Port city of Guangzhou is captured by the Qing

1681 The last force loyal to the Three Feudatories surrenders to the Qing

4 THE COLLAPSE OF THE MING 1620–1644

The last Ming emperor, Chongzhen, presided over a broken administration, failing to control the rise in banditry in the wake of a severe famine that afflicted northern China in 1628. Thereafter, peasant riots erupted in every province and gave rise to several rebel groups. When a rebellion, led by Li Zhicheng, stormed Beijing in April 1644, the beleaguered Emperor committed suicide.

KEY
- ▬ Area controlled by Li Zhicheng 1641–1645
- ▬ Other rebel-controlled areas 1644–1647
- ⚔ Urban riot

THE RISE AND FALL OF THE MING

The Ming Dynasty revived China's economy by investing in manufacture. The rulers extended the Great Wall as a measure against Mongol invasions. The Ming's fortune changed in the 1620s, when a drought led to widespread riots and rebellion.

KEY
- ▬ Ming provinces c.1600
- ● Provincial capital
- ▬ Willow Palisade
- ▬ Ming China
- ‥‥‥ Imperial highway
- ▬ Grand Canal
- ▬ Great Wall under the Ming
- ⫻ Area of loose Ming control

TIMELINE

1300		1400		1500		1600	1700

1
2
3
4
5
6

5 THE QING TAKE CHINA 1625–1644

Following Li Zhicheng's attack on the Ming capital, Ming general Wu Sangui decisively shifted allegiance to the Manchus. He opened the Shanghai Pass, allowing Qing Prince Dorgon to pass the Great Wall, and they allied to defeat Li Zhicheng at the Battle of Shanghai Pass (May 27, 1644). On June 6, the Manchus and Wu entered the capital and proclaimed the young Shunzhi Emperor as Emperor of China.

- ▬ Area under Qing control 1625

6 THE THREE FEUDATORIES 1647–1681

By 1647, Qing forces took control of China's key trading cities along the eastern coast, including Fuzhou and Guangzhou. However, they denied government roles to Chinese officials who refused to adopt Manchurian customs. In 1673, former Ming generals staged the Revolt of Three Feudatories—a mass uprising that forced the Qing to soften their policy.

- ▬ Area affected by Revolt of the Three Feudatories

JAPAN UNIFIES UNDER THE TOKUGAWA

Following the Onin War (1467–1477) involving Japan's two most powerful families, the daimyos (provincial warlords) fought for supremacy, keeping the country in a state of civil unrest for almost a century. Peace came in stages as a succession of men assumed control, but it was Tokugawa Ieyasu who finally restored long-term stability, establishing a tightly controlled regime that would endure for 265 years.

A dispute between Japan's powerful Hosakawa and Yamana clans in 1467 erupted into a violent conflict over who should succeed Ashikaga Yoshimata as *shogun* (Japan's military commander). The resulting Onin War raged on for a decade, destroying the capital, Kyoto, and ended with the Yamana yielding.

With the two families left markedly weakened by the ravages of war, the daimyos saw their opportunity to sieze power. Japan was thus thrown into further turmoil as rival daimyo lords battled one another for supremacy. Daimyo Oda Nobunaga emerged victorious almost a century later, forming alliances to defeat his rivals in a campaign spanning 15 years. On the cusp of becoming Japan's new leader, however, Nobunaga was forced into committing suicide in June 1582, at the hands of his samurai general.

Nobunaga's former ally, Toyotomi Hideyoshi, fought for the next 8 years to defeat daimyos from the Katsuie, Shimazu, and Hojo clans to reunify Japan. His death from ill health in 1598 led to another series of battles, in which Tokugawa Ieyasu (r. 1603–1605) scored a decisive victory at Sekigahara (1600) and earned the title of shogun. Ieyasu introduced strict reforms, which were also enforced by his Tokugawa successors, to curb the powers of the daimyo lords. He also removed the growing threat of Christian wars on Japanese soil by limiting European presence in the port cities of Kyushu, thereby ensuring stability under Tokugawa rule.

> *"The strong manly ones in life are those who understand the meaning of the word patience."*
>
> TOKUGAWA IEYASU, FIRST TOKUGAWA SHOGUN, 1616

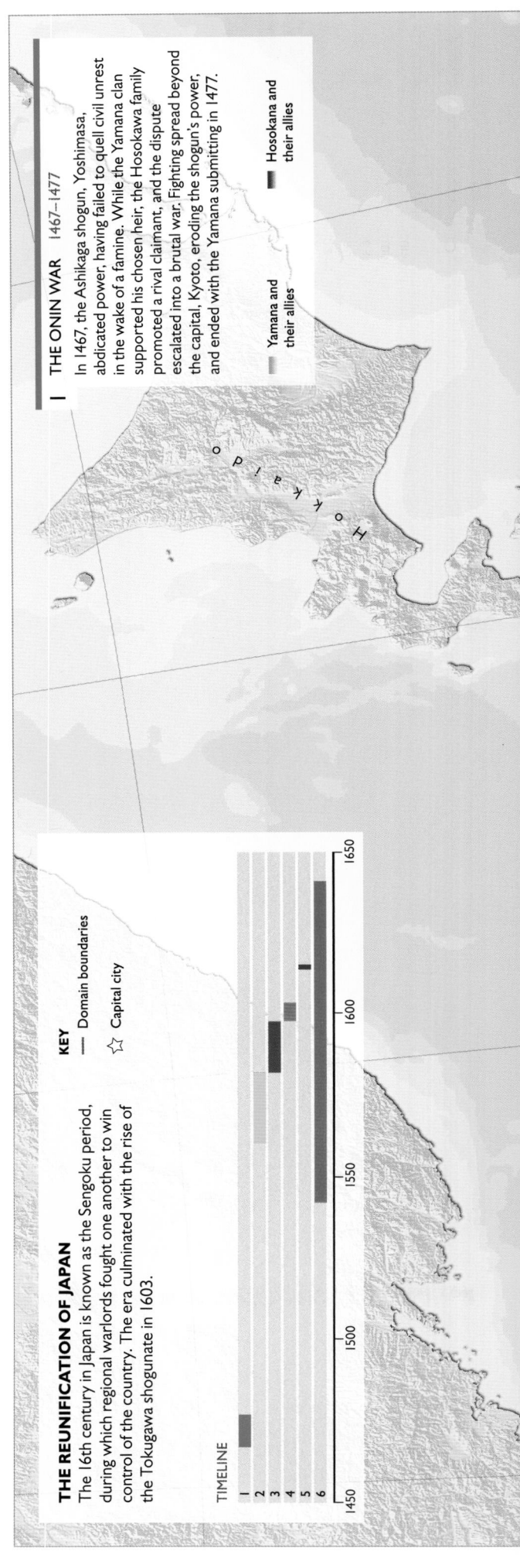

TOKUGAWA IEYASU
1543–1616

Inheritor of the minor Okazaki domain in eastern Mikawa Province (modern-day Aichi Prefecture), Tokugawa Ieyasu began his military training with the Imagawa family. He allied himself with the powerful forces of Oda Nobunaga first and then Toyotomi Hideyoshi and expanded his land holdings by defeating the neighboring Hojo family to the east. After Hideyoshi's death in 1603, Ieyasu became shogun to Japan's imperial court and founded the Tokugawa shogunate.

THE ONIN WAR   1467–1477

In 1467, the Ashikaga shogun, Yoshimasa, abdicated power, having failed to quell civil unrest in the wake of a famine. While the Yamana clan supported his chosen heir, the Hosokawa family promoted a rival claimant, and the dispute escalated into a brutal war. Fighting spread beyond the capital, Kyoto, eroding the shogun's power, and ended with the Yamana submitting in 1477.

■ Yamana and their allies
■ Hosokana and their allies

THE REUNIFICATION OF JAPAN

The 16th century in Japan is known as the Sengoku period, during which regional warlords fought one another to win control of the country. The era culminated with the rise of the Tokugawa shogunate in 1603.

KEY
— Domain boundaries
☆ Capital city

TIMELINE
1
2
3
4
5
6

1450 1500 1550 1600 1650

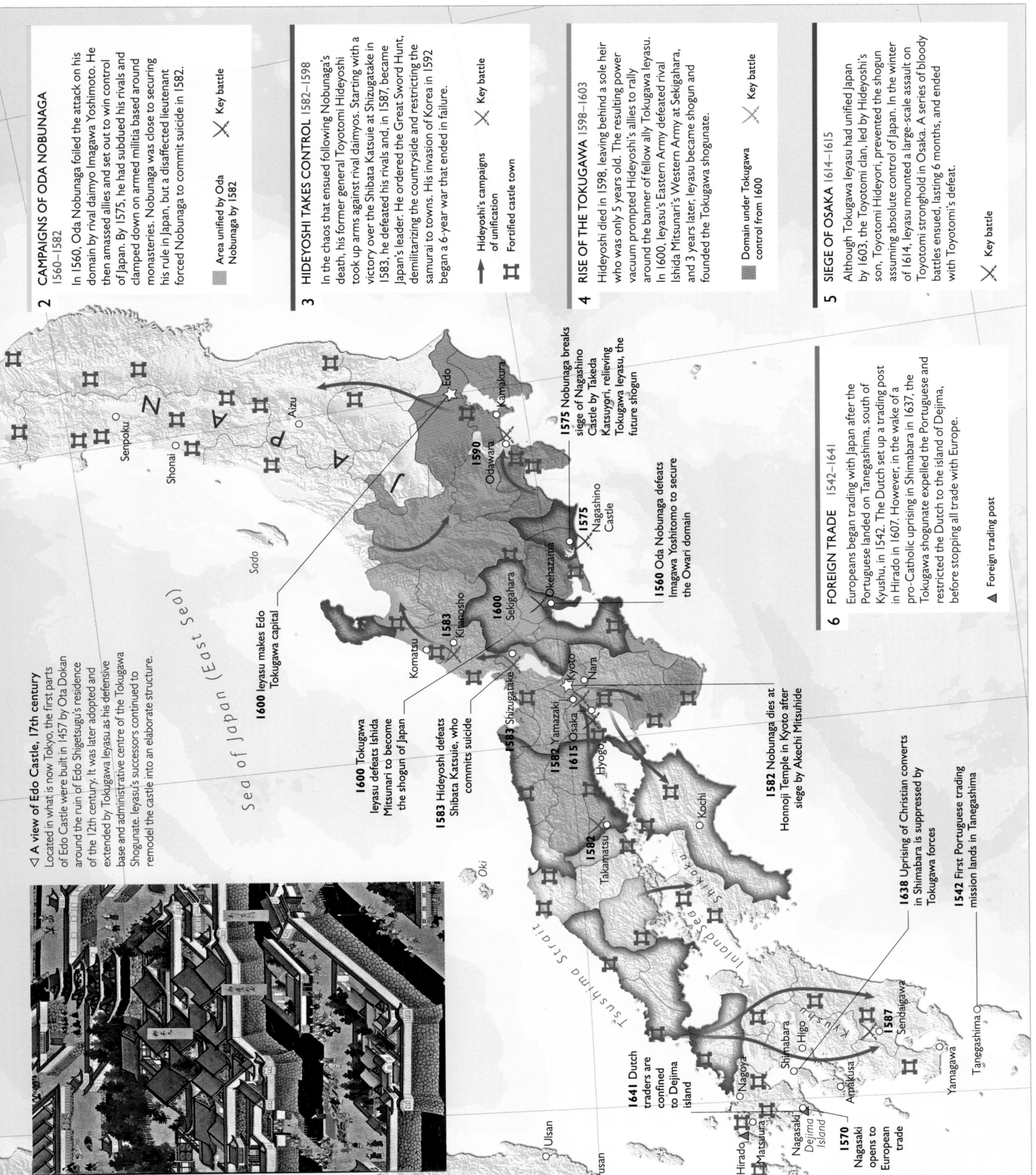

2 CAMPAIGNS OF ODA NOBUNAGA
1560–1582

In 1560, Oda Nobunaga foiled the attack on his domain by rival daimyo Imagawa Yoshimoto. He then amassed allies and set out to win control of Japan. By 1575, he had subdued his rivals and clamped down on armed militia based around monasteries. Nobunaga was close to securing his rule in Japan, but a disaffected lieutenant forced Nobunaga to commit suicide in 1582.

⬛ Area unified by Oda Nobunaga by 1582   ✕ Key battle

3 HIDEYOSHI TAKES CONTROL 1582–1598

In the chaos that ensued following Nobunaga's death, his former general Toyotomi Hideyoshi took up arms against rival daimyos. Starting with a victory over the Shibata Katsuie at Shizugatake in 1583, he defeated his rivals and, in 1587, became Japan's leader. He ordered the Great Sword Hunt, demilitarizing the countryside and restricting the samurai to towns. His invasion of Korea in 1592 began a 6-year war that ended in failure.

→ Hideyoshi's campaigns of unification   ✕ Key battle
卄 Fortified castle town

4 RISE OF THE TOKUGAWA 1598–1603

Hideyoshi died in 1598, leaving behind a sole heir who was only 5 years old. The resulting power vacuum prompted Hideyoshi's allies to rally around the banner of fellow ally Tokugawa Ieyasu. In 1600, Ieyasu's Eastern Army defeated rival Ishida Mitsunari's Western Army at Sekigahara, and 3 years later, Ieyasu became shogun and founded the Tokugawa shogunate.

⬛ Domain under Tokugawa control from 1600   ✕ Key battle

5 SIEGE OF OSAKA 1614–1615

Although Tokugawa Ieyasu had unified Japan by 1603, the Toyotomi clan, led by Hideyoshi's son, Toyotomi Hideyori, prevented the shogun assuming absolute control of Japan. In the winter of 1614, Ieyasu mounted a large-scale assault on Toyotomi stronghold in Osaka. A series of bloody battles ensued, lasting 6 months, and ended with Toyotomi's defeat.

✕ Key battle

6 FOREIGN TRADE 1542–1641

Europeans began trading with Japan after the Portuguese landed on Tanegashima, south of Kyushu, in 1542. The Dutch set up a trading post in Hirado in 1607. However, in the wake of a pro-Catholic uprising in Shimabara in 1637, the Tokugawa shogunate expelled the Portuguese and restricted the Dutch to the island of Dejima, before stopping all trade with Europe.

▲ Foreign trading post

◁ A view of Edo Castle, 17th century
Located in what is now Tokyo, the first parts of Edo Castle were built in 1457 by Ota Dokan around the ruin of Edo Shigetsugu's residence of the 12th century. It was later adopted and extended by Tokugawa Ieyasu as his defensive base and administrative centre of the Tokugawa Shogunate. Ieyasu's successors continued to remodel the castle into an elaborate structure.

1600 Ieyasu makes Edo Tokugawa capital

1600 Tokugawa Ieyasu defeats Ishida Mitsunari to become the shogun of Japan

1583 Hideyoshi defeats Shibata Katsuie, who commits suicide

1583 Shizugatake

1582 Yamazaki

1615 Osaka

1582 Nobunaga dies at Honnoji Temple in Kyoto after siege by Akechi Mitsuhide

1638 Uprising of Christian converts in Shimabara is suppressed by Tokugawa forces

1542 First Portuguese trading mission lands in Tanegashima

1641 Dutch traders are confined to Dejima island

1570 Nagasaki opens to European trade

1575 Nobunaga breaks siege of Nagashino Castle by Takeda Katsuyori, relieving Tokugawa Ieyasu, the future shogun

1575 Nagashino Castle

1590 Odawara

1560 Oda Nobunaga defeats Imagawa Yoshitomo to secure the Owari domain

1583 Kitanosho

1600 Sekigahara

1587 (Higo/Sendaigawa)

1582 Takamatsu

Edo · Kamakura · Aizu · Senpoku · Shonai · Nagoya · Kyoto · Nara · Osaka · Hyogo · Kochi · Takamatsu · Shimabara · Amakusa · Higo · Yamagawa · Tanegashima · Sendaigawa · Hirado · Matsuura · Nagasaki · Dejima Island · Ulsan · Pusan · Okehazama · Komatsu

Sea of Japan (East Sea)
Sado
Oki
Inland Sea
Tsushima Strait
Shikoku
Kyushu

Master and disciple
This 1892 painting by Italian painter Tito Lessi shows
Galileo Galilei (right), who became blind toward the end
of his life. Galileo is accompanied by his assistant Vincenzo
Viviani, who calculated the speed of sound in 1660 by
observing the sound and light flash from a cannon.

THE SCIENTIFIC REVOLUTION

In the mid-16th to late 17th centuries, scientists such as Nicolaus Copernicus, Galileo Galilei, and Isaac Newton inspired a revolution that overturned traditional views of the workings of nature and the Universe.

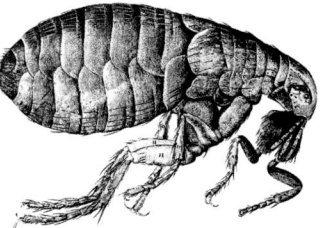

△ **Microscopic observation**
The English naturalist Robert Hooke produced this drawing of a flea in 1665 using the recently invented microscope—another instrument that helped advance scientific observation.

Before 1500, scholars had largely confined themselves to commentaries on the works of ancient writers such as Ptolemy, whose astronomical work in the 2nd century CE described an Earth-centric solar system. In 1543, dissatisfaction with Ptolemy's theory led Polish astronomer Nicolaus Copernicus to propose an alternative— he observed that Earth orbits the Sun. German astronomer Johannes Kepler refined the Copernican system and, in 1619, discovered that planetary orbits are elliptical and not circular. Copernicus's work encouraged others to base their theories on observation rather than orthodoxy. In 1609–1610, Italian astronomer Galileo Galilei discovered the four moons of Jupiter using the newly invented telescope. He also made huge advances in dynamics, establishing laws for the acceleration of falling bodies.

Far-ranging efforts

In the field of medicine, the direct observation of patients and dissection of corpses yielded new insights, such as the discovery of blood circulation in the human body by English physician William Harvey in 1628. The culmination of the scientific revolution came in the late 17th century with English mathematician Isaac Newton's three Laws of Motion and Theory of Gravity, which provided a mathematical explanation of planetary orbits. By then, the view that the Universe could be described in mechanical terms, by mathematical formulae rather than theological dogma, had been firmly established.

MAPPING THE WORLD

The voyages of European explorers in the 15th and 16th centuries inspired a revolution in mapping. The Netherlands became a center of expertise, where, in 1569, the Flemish cartographer Gerardus Mercator produced a world map using a new projection. This became the standard for maps for centuries to come.

THE DUTCH GOLDEN AGE

The Netherlands began to assert its independence from Spain in 1568; a golden age for the new country followed. Abroad, the Dutch East India Company out-competed other European nations in the Spice Islands (see pp.162–163) and constructed a maritime empire.

The revolt of the Netherlands against Spanish rule in 1568 initially devastated the main rebel areas in the north. On winning their independence, these areas became known as the Dutch Republic or United Provinces. After the country had recovered from the war, economic prosperity returned, and a "Regent" class emerged. Though wealthy, this class privileged the virtues of self-reliance and hard work, an ethic that their religious leaders applauded. Yet they also provided a pool of patrons in the fields of arts and sciences that made the first century of Dutch independence a golden era.

Together with early forms of maritime insurance, state banks, and stock exchanges, the Dutch Republic pioneered the joint stock company, in which investors pooled their risks (and shared equally in the profits). The most important, the Verenigde Oost-Indische Compagnie (the VOC, or Dutch East India Company), founded in 1602, exploited a favorable investment climate in the spice markets, which included a lack of state interference. The VOC captured Ambon in 1605, at the center of the spice production region of the Moluccas—also known as the Spice Islands—and it became the VOC headquarters from 1610–1619. The VOC expanded its network of forts and outposts until, by the 1660s, the Dutch had built an empire that stretched from Surinam in South America to Cape Town, Ceylon (modern Sri Lanka), and large parts of the Indonesian archipelago.

DUTCH GOLDEN AGE PAINTING
ART AFTER INDEPENDENCE

The growing wealth of the Dutch Republic meant that there were many rich mercantile families who could act as patrons, encouraging the flourishing artistic scene. Their lack of interest in religious subjects meant that the Netherlands' leading artists were masters in history paintings (Rembrandt van Rijn, 1606–1669), genre scenes (Johannes Vermeer, 1632–1675), landscapes (Jacob van Ruisdael, 1629–1682), and portraits (Frans Hals, 1582–1666).

Domestic art
Vermeer's *The Milkmaid* (c.1666) is typical of scenes of domestic tranquility favored by many Dutch patrons.

THE DUTCH EMPIRE

Throughout the 17th century, the Netherlands sought to expand its empire and had to compete with already well-established European empires, such as those of Spain and Portugal. The Dutch gained many possessions across the world, including the Moluccas in Indonesia, which helped develop their dominance in the spice trade.

KEY

Netherlands possessions or regions held temporarily by the Netherlands during 17th century

Spanish possessions 1700

Other European possessions 1700

TIMELINE
1
2
3
4

1550   1650   1750   1850

CANADA

1625 New Amsterdam is capital of New Netherland region on east coast of America

1664 Taken by British and renamed New York

1667 Ceded to Britain by Treaty of Breda

1655 New Sweden captured by Dutch

New Amsterdam (New York)

Dutch 1613–1664

Dutch 1655–1664

Jamestown

VICEROYALTY OF NEW SPAIN

PACIFIC OCEAN

Jamaica

West Indies

ESSEQUIBO DEMERARA
Dutch 1632–1676
BERBICE
SURINAM

Lima

VICEROYALTY OF PERU

INDEPENDENT NETHERLANDS

The Dutch revolt against Habsburg rule in the Spanish Netherlands broke out in 1568. It took 80 years for the seven, largely Protestant, provinces in the north to secure their independence and become the Dutch Republic (or the United Provinces). The southern provinces, which would later become Belgium and Luxembourg, were initially involved in the revolt but submitted to Spain.

KEY

Dutch Republic 1648

Spanish Netherlands

Bishopric of Liège

Holy Roman Empire

1575 Leiden University founded—the educator of many world-leading practitioners in science and technology

1579 Seven northern provinces sign the Union of Utrecht, joining forces against Spanish rule

Zuider Zee

North Sea

Lingen

Oldenzaal

Amsterdam

Groenlo

Leiden

Utrecht

HOLY ROMAN EMPIRE

DUTCH REPUBLIC 1648

Mörs

Antwerp

Cologne

Brussels

Maastricht

Rhine

SPANISH NETHERLANDS

BISHOPRIC OF LIÈGE

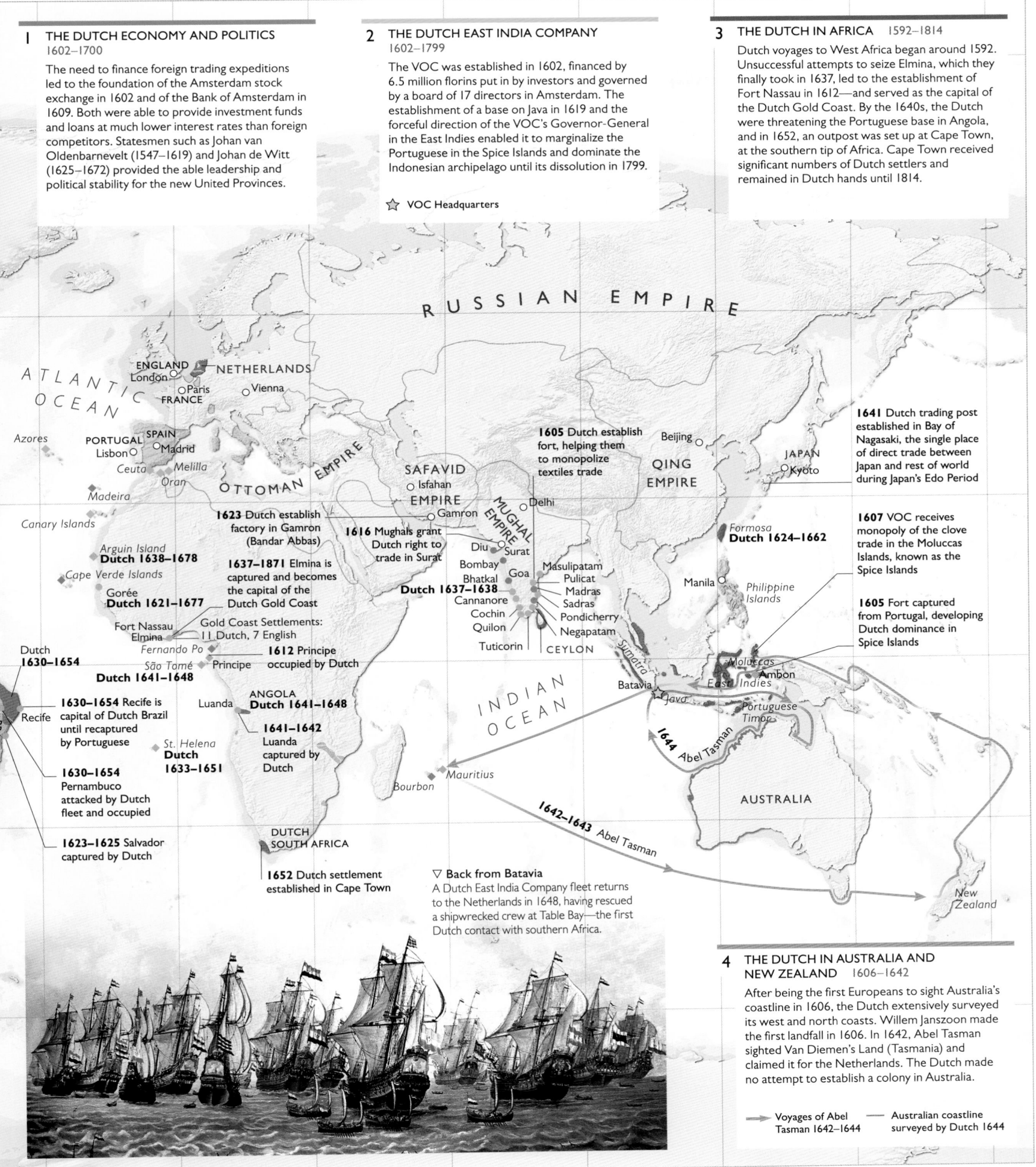

1 THE DUTCH ECONOMY AND POLITICS
1602–1700

The need to finance foreign trading expeditions led to the foundation of the Amsterdam stock exchange in 1602 and of the Bank of Amsterdam in 1609. Both were able to provide investment funds and loans at much lower interest rates than foreign competitors. Statesmen such as Johan van Oldenbarnevelt (1547–1619) and Johan de Witt (1625–1672) provided the able leadership and political stability for the new United Provinces.

2 THE DUTCH EAST INDIA COMPANY
1602–1799

The VOC was established in 1602, financed by 6.5 million florins put in by investors and governed by a board of 17 directors in Amsterdam. The establishment of a base on Java in 1619 and the forceful direction of the VOC's Governor-General in the East Indies enabled it to marginalize the Portuguese in the Spice Islands and dominate the Indonesian archipelago until its dissolution in 1799.

☆ VOC Headquarters

3 THE DUTCH IN AFRICA 1592–1814

Dutch voyages to West Africa began around 1592. Unsuccessful attempts to seize Elmina, which they finally took in 1637, led to the establishment of Fort Nassau in 1612—and served as the capital of the Dutch Gold Coast. By the 1640s, the Dutch were threatening the Portuguese base in Angola, and in 1652, an outpost was set up at Cape Town, at the southern tip of Africa. Cape Town received significant numbers of Dutch settlers and remained in Dutch hands until 1814.

RUSSIAN EMPIRE

ATLANTIC OCEAN

ENGLAND
London
Paris
FRANCE
Vienna

NETHERLANDS

Azores

PORTUGAL SPAIN
Lisbon Madrid
Ceuta
Melilla
Oran

OTTOMAN EMPIRE

SAFAVID EMPIRE
Isfahan

MUGHAL EMPIRE
Delhi
Gamron

QING EMPIRE

Beijing

JAPAN
Kyoto

1641 Dutch trading post established in Bay of Nagasaki, the single place of direct trade between Japan and rest of world during Japan's Edo Period

1605 Dutch establish fort, helping them to monopolize textiles trade

Madeira

Canary Islands

Arguin Island
Dutch 1638–1678

Cape Verde Islands

Gorée
Dutch 1621–1677

1623 Dutch establish factory in Gamron (Bandar Abbas)

1637–1871 Elmina is captured and becomes the capital of the Dutch Gold Coast

Fort Nassau
Elmina

Gold Coast Settlements:
11 Dutch, 7 English

Fernando Po
São Tomé
Principe

1612 Principe occupied by Dutch

Dutch **1641–1648**

Dutch **1630–1654**

Recife

BRAZIL

1630–1654 Recife is capital of Dutch Brazil until recaptured by Portuguese

1630–1654 Pernambuco attacked by Dutch fleet and occupied

1623–1625 Salvador captured by Dutch

Luanda

ANGOLA
Dutch 1641–1648

1641–1642 Luanda captured by Dutch

St. Helena
Dutch 1633–1651

DUTCH SOUTH AFRICA

1652 Dutch settlement established in Cape Town

1616 Mughals grant Dutch right to trade in Surat

Dutch **1637–1638**

Diu
Surat
Bombay
Bhatkal
Cannanore
Cochin
Quilon
Tuticorin

Goa

Masulipatam
Pulicat
Madras
Sadras
Pondicherry
Negapatam

CEYLON

INDIAN OCEAN

Mauritius

Bourbon

Formosa
Dutch 1624–1662

Manila

Philippine Islands

1607 VOC receives monopoly of the clove trade in the Moluccas Islands, known as the Spice Islands

1605 Fort captured from Portugal, developing Dutch dominance in Spice Islands

Sumatra

Batavia
Java

East Indies

Moluccas
Ambon

Portuguese Timor

1644 Abel Tasman

1642–1643 Abel Tasman

AUSTRALIA

New Zealand

▽ **Back from Batavia**
A Dutch East India Company fleet returns to the Netherlands in 1648, having rescued a shipwrecked crew at Table Bay—the first Dutch contact with southern Africa.

4 THE DUTCH IN AUSTRALIA AND NEW ZEALAND 1606–1642

After being the first Europeans to sight Australia's coastline in 1606, the Dutch extensively surveyed its west and north coasts. Willem Janszoon made the first landfall in 1606. In 1642, Abel Tasman sighted Van Diemen's Land (Tasmania) and claimed it for the Netherlands. The Dutch made no attempt to establish a colony in Australia.

→ Voyages of Abel Tasman 1642–1644
— Australian coastline surveyed by Dutch 1644

REVOLUTION AND INDUSTRY

IN 1700–1850, MUCH OF THE WORLD WAS REVOLUTIONIZED BY NEW SCIENTIFIC AND POLITICAL IDEAS. PERHAPS THE MOST FAR-REACHING CHANGE, HOWEVER, WAS THE INDUSTRIAL REVOLUTION.

THE AGE OF REVOLUTION

The era from 1700 to 1850 could be called by many names—the age of empire, of industry, of nation-states, of Enlightenment, or of Romanticism and Nationalism. It was all these and more—it was the Age of Revolution, which formed the modern world.

▽ **Fight to the finish**
In one of the decisive naval battles of the Seven Years' War, the British took control of the French fortress of Louisbourg (in modern Canada) in July 1758. The victory enabled the British to take over the French North American capital of Quebec the next year.

The overriding and underlying force of this period in world history was growth. An explosion in world population went hand in hand with innovations that, in turn, resulted in a growth in productivity, trade, economies, urbanization, agriculture and industry, literacy and education, and media and technology, among others. The end result was the expansion of some empires and the toppling of others, as different political entities and systems tried—and sometimes failed—to cope with the sudden growth. Some nations thrived, often with brutal economic and human ramifications, as with the British exploitation of global resources, which was underpinned by the slave trade, or with the expansion of the US farther into the North American continent (see pp.260–261). Others, from east Asia to western Europe, failed to cope with the pressure, unleashing revolutions with long-term effects.

△ **Party in Boston**
Of all the tea chests thrown into the harbor at the Boston Tea Party in 1773 by Americans protesting against British rule, this is the only chest to have survived.

Reshaping the world
The early 18th century saw change on several fronts. Innovations in agriculture, industry, and other kinds of technology prompted colonization by European settlers in America, Asia, Australia, and New Zealand. The consequences for indigenous populations were horrific—for example, the expansion of the US into Native American territory, or the genocide of Aboriginal peoples in Australia. Advances in technology meant that the scale and lethality of conflicts grew exponentially, whether in Europe where

GROWING CONNECTIONS

As the connections between different parts of the world increased, populations grew, and travel and communication became easier. The consequences were seen in the movement of people, a change in the scale of world economies, and political developments within and between nations, including global conflicts. It was a period that saw immense strides in the development of human understanding of nature and the subsequent ability to control and exploit it.

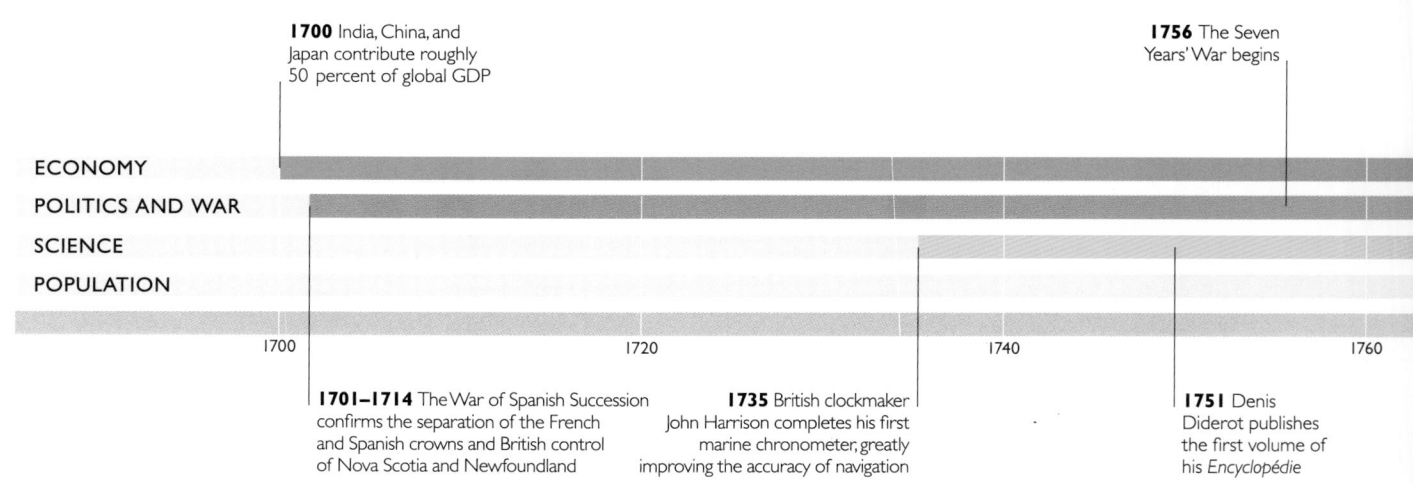

1700 India, China, and Japan contribute roughly 50 percent of global GDP

1756 The Seven Years' War begins

ECONOMY

POLITICS AND WAR

SCIENCE

POPULATION

1700   1720   1740   1760

1701–1714 The War of Spanish Succession confirms the separation of the French and Spanish crowns and British control of Nova Scotia and Newfoundland

1735 British clockmaker John Harrison completes his first marine chronometer, greatly improving the accuracy of navigation

1751 Denis Diderot publishes the first volume of his *Encyclopédie*

◁ **Heads up**
An 18th-century etching depicts French revolutionaries displaying the heads of the guards killed during the storming of the Bastille on July 14, 1789—one of the great symbolic acts of the French Revolution.

the Napoleonic Wars (see pp.208–211) saw the mobilization of huge armies; in New Zealand, where muskets transformed traditional Maori warfare; in India where small European forces were able to defeat larger local forces; or in Africa, where slaving empires flourished due to new weapons.

Global impacts

The 18th century saw the world's first global war, when the Seven Years' War (see pp.192–193), fought between European powers, spread to theaters around the world—from North America to Southeast Asia. As networks of trade and finance reached into every corner of the world, the consequences could be felt everywhere: on the plains of the American Midwest, where coast-to-coast railroads led to economic growth but also wiped out buffalo herds that sustained indigenous ways of life; across Africa, where the slave trade resulted in massive depopulation; and in south Asia, where British imperialism eventually resulted in the thorough dislocation of local economies and trade. In China, problems with currency and trade in commodities led to the Opium Wars; while in Australasia, colonial land grabs resulted in the depletion of indigenous populations.

Such immense transformations inevitably had profound political consequences. In Europe and the Americas, growing middle and artisan classes pushed for change, by revolution if necessary, so that the period 1700–1850 saw a slew of revolutionary conflicts, with the American and French revolutions of the 18th century and the nationalist and

political revolutions of the early 19th century in South America. The greatest upheavals came in China, where the 19th century saw near-constant unrest as the country failed to cope with economic, technological, and political changes in the world.

By 1850, the world was vastly richer overall but with greater inequality than ever before. Despite celebrated advances in politics, society, and culture, with revolutionary, liberation, and emancipation movements, the Enlightenment, and the Scientific Revolution, it was the global sum of human misery that had grown most of all. Achievements in industry, trade, technology, and culture had been built on foundations of exploitation, slavery, genocide, and injustice.

▷ **Map of the future**
This map was drawn during the Lewis and Clark Expedition (1804–1806), which helped open North America to settlement and accelerated the expansion of the US.

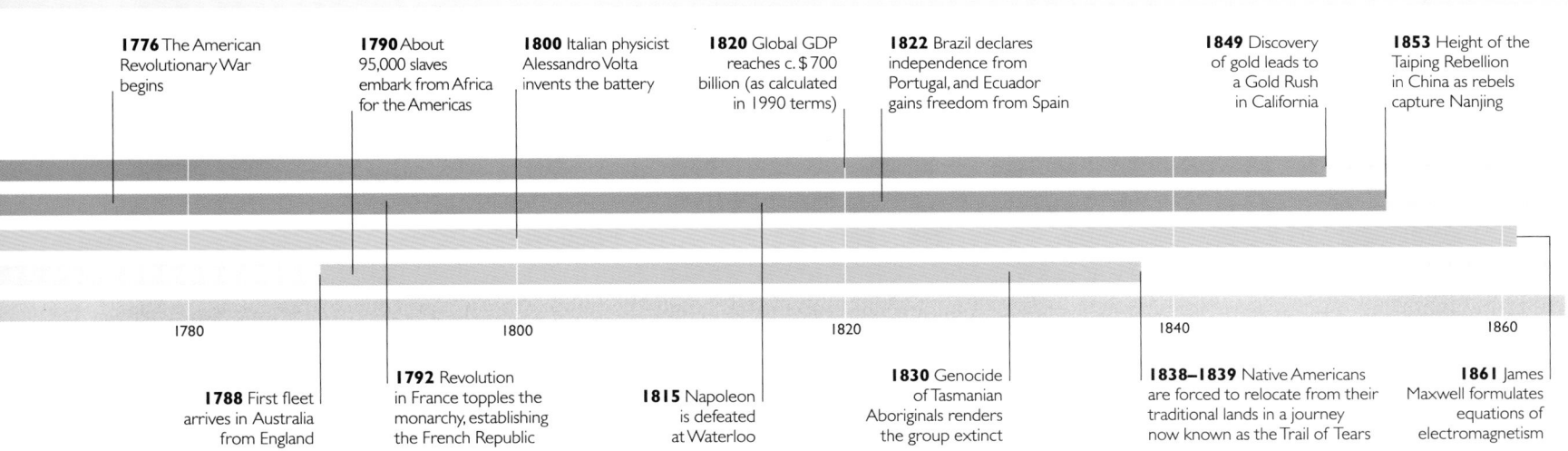

1776 The American Revolutionary War begins

1790 About 95,000 slaves embark from Africa for the Americas

1800 Italian physicist Alessandro Volta invents the battery

1820 Global GDP reaches c. $700 billion (as calculated in 1990 terms)

1822 Brazil declares independence from Portugal, and Ecuador gains freedom from Spain

1849 Discovery of gold leads to a Gold Rush in California

1853 Height of the Taiping Rebellion in China as rebels capture Nanjing

1780   1800   1820   1840   1860

1788 First fleet arrives in Australia from England

1792 Revolution in France topples the monarchy, establishing the French Republic

1815 Napoleon is defeated at Waterloo

1830 Genocide of Tasmanian Aboriginals renders the group extinct

1838–1839 Native Americans are forced to relocate from their traditional lands in a journey now known as the Trail of Tears

1861 James Maxwell formulates equations of electromagnetism

1 FRENCH VIE FOR DOMINATION 1700–1750

French colonists claimed, and began to settle, a vast expanse of North America—from the Mississippi Delta in the south to the northeastern coastline, with the fur trade forming the mainstay of their economy. By 1750, rising tension over British encroachment into Midwestern territories abutting the Great Plains had resulted in the French erecting a series of forts. They also formed friendly relations with tribes such as the Huron and Odawa to help them fight the British threat.

⚏ French forts   ▲ French trading posts

1704

1708

1704–1708 French raid British colonies during Queen Anne's War

1745 French fortress of Louisbourg falls to Americans during King George's War

1710 British troops take the Acadian capital of Port Royal, renaming it Annapolis Royal

1745 French forces and their Native American allies raid and destroy the village of Saratoga, killing up to 100 inhabitants

1774 The First Continental Congress is held in Philadelphia, in which the colonies decide to boycott British imports as a protest against the 1773 Tea Act

1758 Fort Louisbourg

△ **The Boston Tea Party**
In response to new British tax laws, including the Tea Act and the Stamp Act (a tax on paper), revolutionaries disguised as Native Americans destroyed the valuable tea cargo of British East India Company ships.

2 QUEEN ANNE'S WAR 1702–1713

Allied with Native American groups, French colonists raided British settlements in the New England colonies. In retaliation, the British captured the key French fortress of Port Royal in the French colony of Acadia. Following the war, mainland Acadia, Hudson Bay, and Newfoundland were ceded to Britain under the 1713 Treaty of Utrecht. Part of Acadia became Nova Scotia, so named due to its brief period as a Scottish colony in 1629–1632 (see p.156).

→ French campaign

➔ British campaign

⋯▶ French and Native American campaign

✕ French raid

3 THE IROQUOIS CONFEDERACY 1600–1779

In 1722, the Tuscarora tribe, displaced from the Carolinas by European settlement, became the sixth member of a league of nations known as the Iroquois Confederacy, located in upper New York State. The Iroquois successfully defended their territory until 1779 when an American force carried out a systematic destruction of Iroquois settlement and crops.

▮ Iroquois Confederacy territory

4 WAR OF JENKINS' EAR 1739–1748

The conflict between the Spanish and English over the land between South Carolina and Florida had been simmering for a century. However, the hostilities found a new edge with English naval captain Robert Jenkins's claim that Spanish coast guards had pillaged his ship and cut off his ear (which he presented to Parliament), triggering a 9-year war with Spain, which eventually became mixed up with King George's War.

→ Spanish campaign

➔ British campaign

✕ Major battle

5 KING GEORGE'S WAR 1744–1748

In 1744, the French and British were at war in Europe, over the Austrian succession. King George's War was the name given to its French and British theater in North America. The war resulted in the British-American colonists taking Louisbourg on Cape Breton Island. However, under the terms of the 1748 peace treaty, the British returned Louisbourg to the French—a move that infuriated the American colonists.

→ French campaign

➔ British campaign

✕ Major battle

1700s The forts in fertile Illinois country (Kaskaskia, Cahokia, and Vincennes) became the grain garden of New France

Jul 1742 Spanish attempt to invade Georgia at the Battle of Bloody Marsh

1742

1740

6 THE FRENCH AND INDIAN WAR 1756–1762

With French military resources committed in Europe, British colonists took advantage, waging war on their French counterparts (see p.192). Key victories in Fort Louisbourg (1758), Quebec (1759), Fort Niagara (1759), and Montreal (1760), ended French territorial claims in North America, with France ceding Louisiana to Spain in the secret Treaty of Fontainebleau (1762).

✕ Major battle

Map labels: Bonavista, St. John, Newfoundland, Gulf of St. Lawrence, Cape Breton Island, ACADIA, NOVA SCOTIA, Halifax, Annapolis Royal (Port Royal), Quebec, Montreal, St. Lawrence, Lake Champlain, CANADA, NEW ENGLAND, Boston, Newport, Philadelphia, Richmond, Jamestown, South Carolina, Charleston, Savannah, Fort Frederica, San Agustin, Fort St. George, Fort St. Francis, Fort Piccolata, Florida, Appalachian Mountains, INDIAN TERRITORY, Ohio, Bloody Marsh, Gulf of Mexico, New Orleans, Mississippi, LOUISIANA, Vincennes, Cahokia, Kaskaskia, Lake Michigan, Detroit, Lake Erie, Niagara, Lake Ontario, Michilimackinac, Lake Huron, PAYS D'EN HAUT, Lake Superior, Fort Kaministikwia, Fort Albany, Eastmain, Rupert House, Moose Factory, James Bay, RUPERT'S LAND, Severn Factory, York Factory, Nelson, Churchill, Fort Churchill, Hudson Bay, Lake Winnipeg, Great Plains, Missouri, Rio Grande, BAHA[MAS]

1704 · 1708 · 1710 · 1707 · 1745 · 1759 · 1740

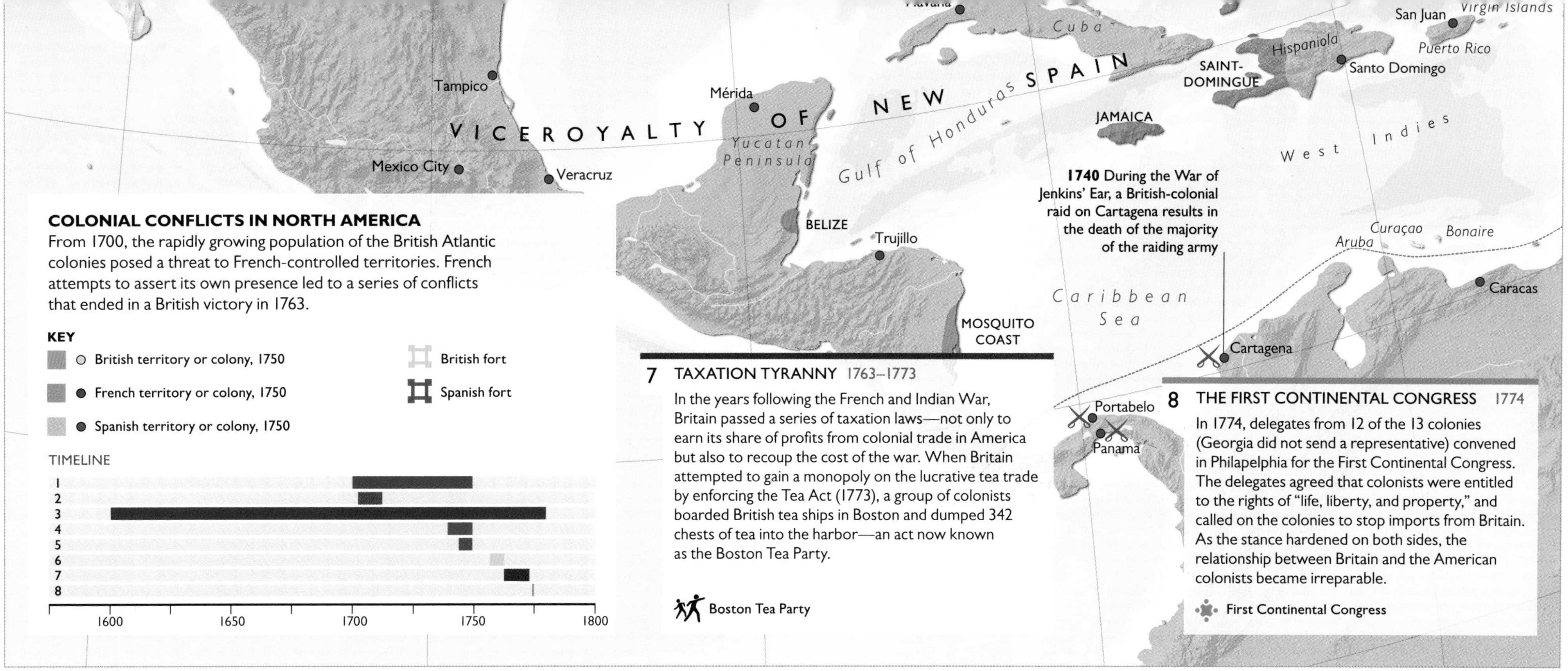

COLONIAL CONFLICTS IN NORTH AMERICA

From 1700, the rapidly growing population of the British Atlantic colonies posed a threat to French-controlled territories. French attempts to assert its own presence led to a series of conflicts that ended in a British victory in 1763.

KEY

- ○ British territory or colony, 1750
- ● French territory or colony, 1750
- ● Spanish territory or colony, 1750

British territory or colony, 1750 (fill)
French territory or colony, 1750 (fill)
Spanish territory or colony, 1750 (fill)

British fort
Spanish fort

TIMELINE

1
2
3
4
5
6
7
8

1600 1650 1700 1750 1800

1740 During the War of Jenkins' Ear, a British-colonial raid on Cartagena results in the death of the majority of the raiding army

7 TAXATION TYRANNY 1763–1773

In the years following the French and Indian War, Britain passed a series of taxation laws—not only to earn its share of profits from colonial trade in America but also to recoup the cost of the war. When Britain attempted to gain a monopoly on the lucrative tea trade by enforcing the Tea Act (1773), a group of colonists boarded British tea ships in Boston and dumped 342 chests of tea into the harbor—an act now known as the Boston Tea Party.

Boston Tea Party

8 THE FIRST CONTINENTAL CONGRESS 1774

In 1774, delegates from 12 of the 13 colonies (Georgia did not send a representative) convened in Philadelphia for the First Continental Congress. The delegates agreed that colonists were entitled to the rights of "life, liberty, and property," and called on the colonies to stop imports from Britain. As the stance hardened on both sides, the relationship between Britain and the American colonists became irreparable.

First Continental Congress

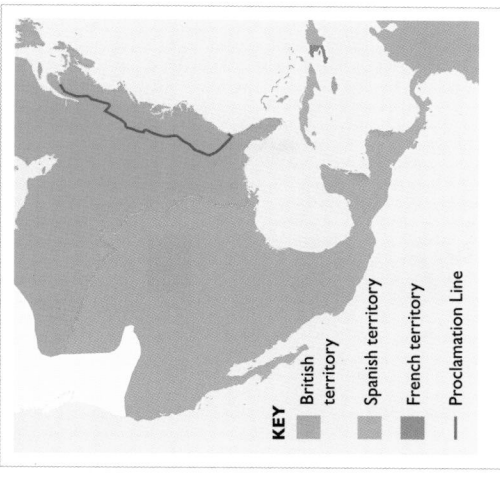

KEY

British territory
Spanish territory
French territory
Proclamation Line

NORTH AMERICA, 1763

The map of North America changed dramatically following British victory in the French and Indian War (1754–1760) as Britain wrested all lands east of the Mississippi from the French. Meanwhile, Spain gained nominal control over Louisiana and ceded Florida to the British. To appease Native American groups, the British government drew up the Proclamation Line of 1763, which forbade colonial settlement beyond the line of the Appalachian Mountains.

BATTLE FOR NORTH AMERICA

In the first half of the 18th century, North America became another theater for the expression of the imperial rivalries between France, Britain, and Spain. Britain would eventually triumph, but the cost of victory would sow the seeds of revolutionary sentiment into the hearts of the American colonists.

The population of Britain's North American colonies had reached 1.2 million by 1750—far outnumbering the 65,000 French and 20,000 or so Spanish colonists on the continent.

In contrast, the native population was in rapid decline, ravaged by displacement, massacres, and diseases borne from the Old World. For example, Native American numbers east of the Appalachians had dwindled from about 120,000 at the start of European colonization to just 20,000 in 1750. Moreover, the Native American groups struggled to find unity among themselves to help them withstand the tide of incomers. The French sought to contain the burgeoning British Atlantic colonies by strategically locating their own settlements

and forming alliances with Native Americans. The tactic gave rise to skirmishes but could not prevent the British colonies from extending their territory, displacing French colonists in the northeast, and destroying Spanish outposts that threatened to curtail their expansion to the south. The conflicts culminated in the French and Indian War (part of the Seven Years' War; see pp.192–193)—a bloody and costly campaign that earned the British a sweeping victory, and which all but ended French territorial claims on the continent. However, in the war's aftermath, the British government imposed laws and taxes to recoup the cost of the war, stoking resentment among colonists about being ruled from afar.

THE SEVEN YEARS' WAR

The outbreak of a conflict between Britain and France for colonial domination drew in allies on both sides. With hostilities extending from North America to India and from the Caribbean to Russia, this was the first war on a truly global scale.

The Seven Years' War pitted the alliance of Britain, Prussia, and Hanover against the alliance of France, Austria, Sweden, Saxony, Russia, and Spain. The war was driven by commercial and imperial rivalry, and by the antagonism between Prussia and Austria. In Europe, Prussia made a preemptive strike on Saxony in August 1756 after finding itself surrounded by enemies, once France had ended its ancient rivalry with Habsburg Austria and, along with Russia, formed a grand alliance. Britain aligned itself with Prussia, partly so that the British king could protect his German possession, Hanover, from the threat of a French takeover. However, Britain's main aim was to destroy France as a commercial rival, and its attack focused on the French navy and French colonies overseas, particularly in North America. Heavily committed to the European cause, France had few resources to spare for its colonies and consequently suffered substantial losses in North America, the Caribbean, west Africa, and also India (see pp.224–225). Fought simultaneously on five continents, the Seven Years' War culminated in 1763 with Britain emerging as the world's largest colonial power.

> *"While we had France for an enemy, Germany was the scene to employ and baffle her arms."*
>
> WILLIAM PITT, BRITISH PRIME MINISTER, 1762

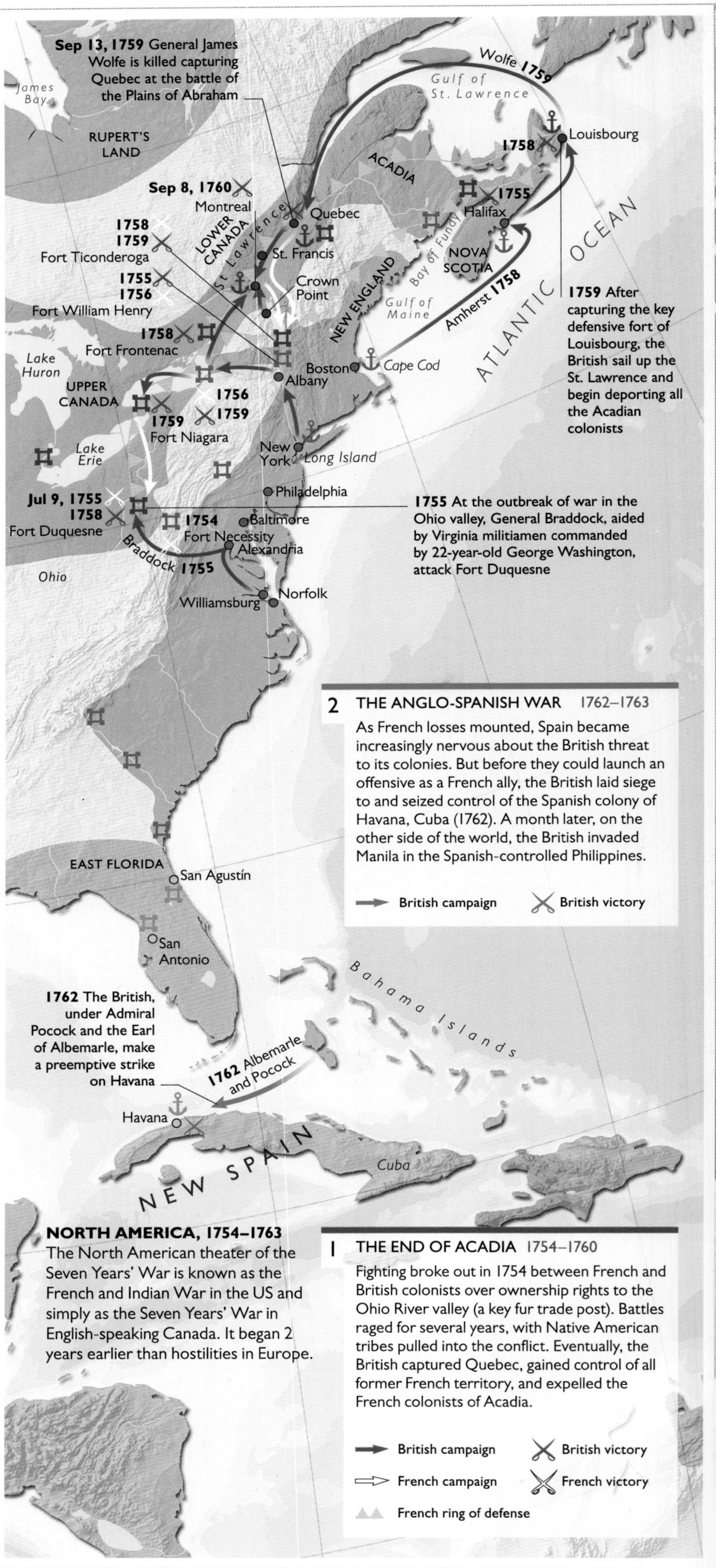

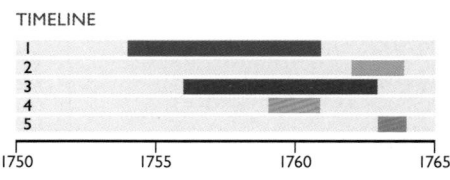

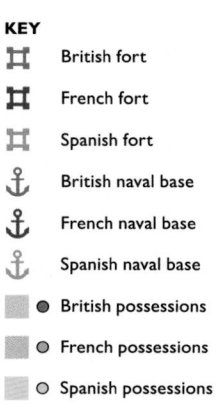

Sep 13, 1759 General James Wolfe is killed capturing Quebec at the battle of the Plains of Abraham
James Bay
RUPERT'S LAND
Wolfe 1759
Gulf of St. Lawrence
Louisbourg
1758
ACADIA
1755
Halifax
Sep 8, 1760
Montreal
Quebec
LOWER CANADA
St. Lawrence
1758
1759
Fort Ticonderoga
St. Francis
NOVA SCOTIA
Bay of Fundy
1755
1756
Crown Point
NEW ENGLAND
Gulf of Maine
Amherst 1758
ATLANTIC OCEAN
Fort William Henry
1759 After capturing the key defensive fort of Louisbourg, the British sail up the St. Lawrence and begin deporting all the Acadian colonists
1758
Fort Frontenac
Lake Huron
Boston
Albany
Cape Cod
UPPER CANADA
1756
1759
1759
Fort Niagara
New York
Long Island
Lake Erie
Philadelphia
Jul 9, 1755
1758
Fort Duquesne
1754
Fort Necessity
Baltimore
Alexandria
Braddock 1755
1755 At the outbreak of war in the Ohio valley, General Braddock, aided by Virginia militiamen commanded by 22-year-old George Washington, attack Fort Duquesne
Ohio
Williamsburg
Norfolk
EAST FLORIDA
San Agustín
San Antonio
Bahama Islands
1762 The British, under Admiral Pocock and the Earl of Albemarle, make a preemptive strike on Havana
1762 Albemarle and Pocock
Havana
Cuba
NEW SPAIN

2 THE ANGLO-SPANISH WAR 1762–1763

As French losses mounted, Spain became increasingly nervous about the British threat to its colonies. But before they could launch an offensive as a French ally, the British laid siege to and seized control of the Spanish colony of Havana, Cuba (1762). A month later, on the other side of the world, the British invaded Manila in the Spanish-controlled Philippines.

British campaign — British victory

NORTH AMERICA, 1754–1763

The North American theater of the Seven Years' War is known as the French and Indian War in the US and simply as the Seven Years' War in English-speaking Canada. It began 2 years earlier than hostilities in Europe.

1 THE END OF ACADIA 1754–1760

Fighting broke out in 1754 between French and British colonists over ownership rights to the Ohio River valley (a key fur trade post). Battles raged for several years, with Native American tribes pulled into the conflict. Eventually, the British captured Quebec, gained control of all former French territory, and expelled the French colonists of Acadia.

British campaign — British victory
French campaign — French victory
French ring of defense

COLONIAL DOMINATION

The Seven Years' War tested the military might of European powers—France, Britain, and Spain—in North America as they fought for colonial supremacy. Fighting battles on two fronts, in Europe and in the colonies, strained both resources and colonists' loyalties.

TIMELINE

1
2
3
4
5
1750
1755
1760
1765

KEY

- British fort
- French fort
- Spanish fort
- British naval base
- French naval base
- Spanish naval base
- British possessions
- French possessions
- Spanish possessions

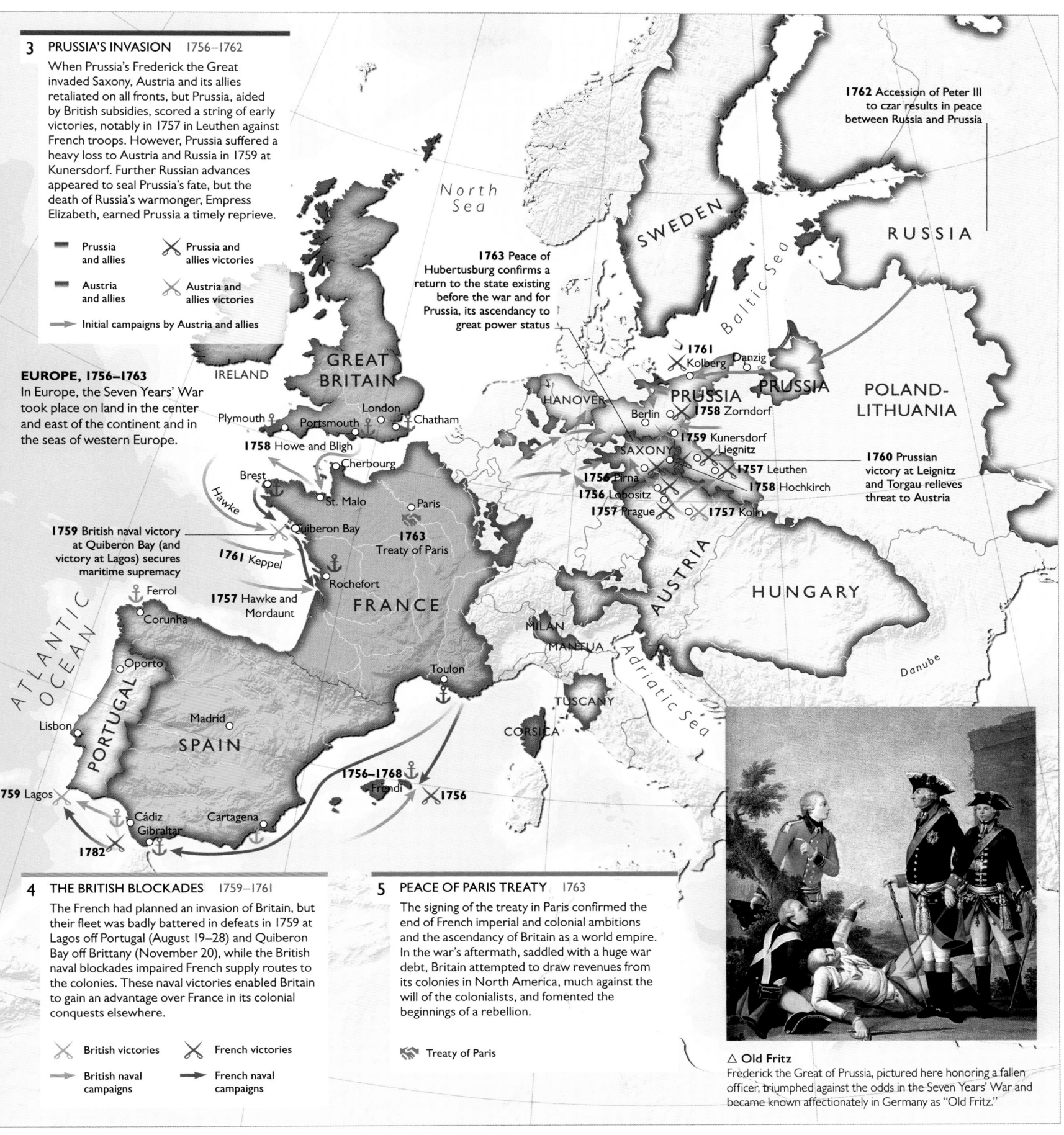

3 PRUSSIA'S INVASION 1756–1762

When Prussia's Frederick the Great invaded Saxony, Austria and its allies retaliated on all fronts, but Prussia, aided by British subsidies, scored a string of early victories, notably in 1757 in Leuthen against French troops. However, Prussia suffered a heavy loss to Austria and Russia in 1759 at Kunersdorf. Further Russian advances appeared to seal Prussia's fate, but the death of Russia's warmonger, Empress Elizabeth, earned Prussia a timely reprieve.

▬	Prussia and allies	
▬	Austria and allies	
✂	Prussia and allies victories	
✕	Austria and allies victories	
→	Initial campaigns by Austria and allies	

EUROPE, 1756–1763

In Europe, the Seven Years' War took place on land in the center and east of the continent and in the seas of western Europe.

1762 Accession of Peter III to czar results in peace between Russia and Prussia

1763 Peace of Hubertusburg confirms a return to the state existing before the war and for Prussia, its ascendancy to great power status

1761 Kolberg

Danzig

1758 Zorndorf

Berlin

1759 Kunersdorf
Liegnitz

1757 Leuthen
1758 Hochkirch

1756 Pirna
1756 Lobositz
1757 Prague
1757 Kolin

1760 Prussian victory at Leignitz and Torgau relieves threat to Austria

1758 Howe and Bligh

Plymouth
Portsmouth
London
Chatham

Cherbourg

Brest

Hawke

St. Malo
Paris

1763 Treaty of Paris

1759 British naval victory at Quiberon Bay (and victory at Lagos) secures maritime supremacy

Quiberon Bay

1761 Keppel

1757 Hawke and Mordaunt

Rochefort

FRANCE

Ferrol

Corunha

Oporto

Lisbon

PORTUGAL

Madrid

SPAIN

1759 Lagos

Cádiz
Gibraltar

Cartagena

1782

1756–1768 Fréndi

1756

Toulon

MILAN
MANTUA

TUSCANY

CORSICA

AUSTRIA

HUNGARY

Danube

Adriatic Sea

4 THE BRITISH BLOCKADES 1759–1761

The French had planned an invasion of Britain, but their fleet was badly battered in defeats in 1759 at Lagos off Portugal (August 19–28) and Quiberon Bay off Brittany (November 20), while the British naval blockades impaired French supply routes to the colonies. These naval victories enabled Britain to gain an advantage over France in its colonial conquests elsewhere.

✕	British victories	
✕	French victories	
→	British naval campaigns	
→	French naval campaigns	

5 PEACE OF PARIS TREATY 1763

The signing of the treaty in Paris confirmed the end of French imperial and colonial ambitions and the ascendancy of Britain as a world empire. In the war's aftermath, saddled with a huge war debt, Britain attempted to draw revenues from its colonies in North America, much against the will of the colonialists, and fomented the beginnings of a rebellion.

🤝 Treaty of Paris

△ **Old Fritz**
Frederick the Great of Prussia, pictured here honoring a fallen officer, triumphed against the odds in the Seven Years' War and became known affectionately in Germany as "Old Fritz."

THE AGRICULTURAL REVOLUTION

The term "Agricultural Revolution" is traditionally associated with the rapid increase in agricultural productivity from the early 18th to the mid-19th centuries. It began mainly in Britain and later spread throughout Europe, the US, and beyond.

△ **New land from the sea**
This illustration from 1705 is one of the most dramatic portrayals of the impact of land reclamation—the Dutch literally enlarged their nation by using dams and dikes to drain land that had previously been below sea level.

Beginning in the early 18th century, innovative British farmers adopted and adapted techniques, crops, and technologies from other parts of the world, particularly the Low Countries (modern-day Belgium and Holland), to achieve a dramatic increase in agricultural productivity. Between 1750 and 1850, grain productivity in Britain tripled, supporting a similar expansion of the population far beyond historically sustainable levels. Many of the practices and ideas involved may have been drawn from continental Europe, but by 1815, British agricultural productivity far outstripped that of any other European country. In the 19th century, these innovations spread across the developed world. The four pillars of this revolution in agriculture were: agricultural technology, such as seed drills and mechanization; crop rotation; selective breeding to improve livestock yields; and enclosure, reclamation, and other changes in land-use practices.

Innovation and mechanization

In 1701, English farmer and agronomist Jethro Tull developed an improved seed drill—a device that planted seeds in rows, making it easier to weed and tend the crop, and thus increasing labor efficiency. Although initially slow to catch on, the seed drill was emblematic of the potential of technology to greatly improve the productivity of both land and labor. In the US, Cyrus McCormick developed a machine called the reaper; in 1840, he was able to cut 12½ times more wheat with it in a day than was possible with a scythe.

Another source of increasing yields was the use of new crop types, such as high-yielding wheat and barley—which replaced low-yielding rye—and turnips, root vegetables that could be grown without impeding weed clearance. However, perhaps the greatest boost came by overcoming the factor that was primarily limiting yields: the level of biologically available nitrogen in the soil. Although they did not yet understand the underlying biology, farmers in the Low Countries had discovered that crops such as legumes and clover could improve soil fertility and reduce the need for land to be left fallow. This is because bacterial root nodules on such crops can fix, or assimilate, atmospheric nitrogen, fertilizing the soil even as they produce useful food and

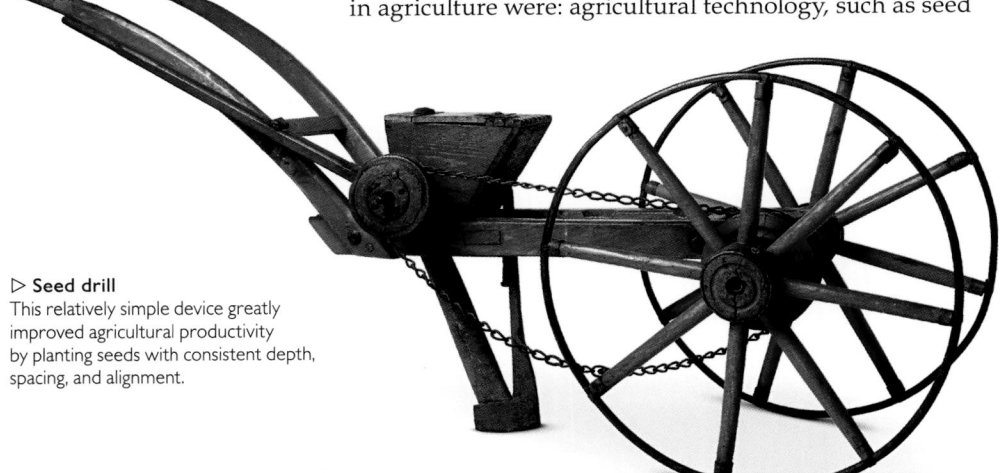

▷ **Seed drill**
This relatively simple device greatly improved agricultural productivity by planting seeds with consistent depth, spacing, and alignment.

DRIVING THE REVOLUTION

The introduction of high-yielding crop varieties, crop rotation, and the economic impact of nonfood cash crops were some of the primary drivers of the Agricultural Revolution. Other milestones included new livestock breeds and how they were brought to market. New areas of land were tilled in the New World even as land use was transformed in the Old World. Shifts in urban and rural demographics changed the labor force, while new technologies boosted productivity.

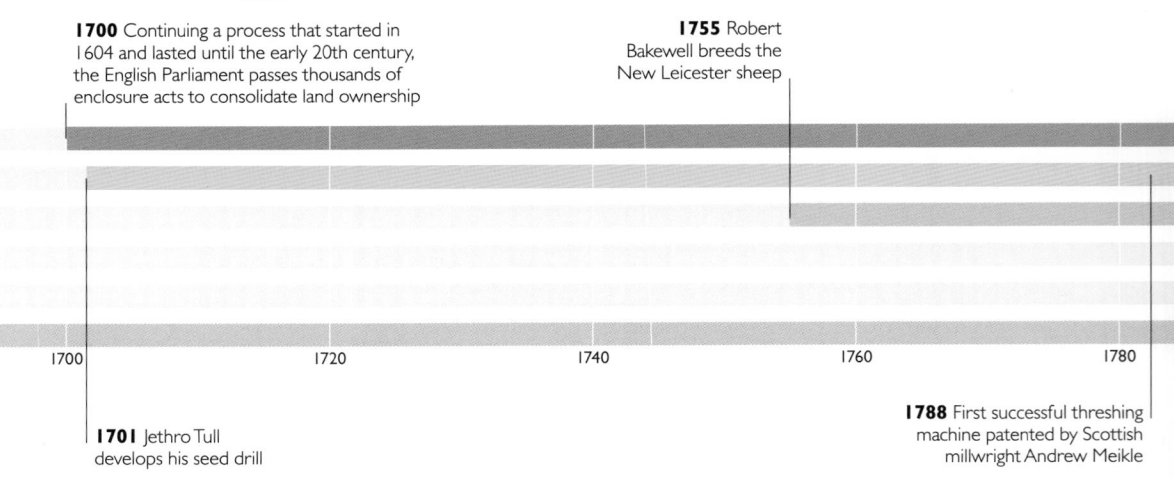

1700 Continuing a process that started in 1604 and lasted until the early 20th century, the English Parliament passes thousands of enclosure acts to consolidate land ownership

1755 Robert Bakewell breeds the New Leicester sheep

LAND
TECHNOLOGY
ANIMALS
CROPS
LABOR

| 1700 | 1720 | 1740 | 1760 | 1780 |

1701 Jethro Tull develops his seed drill

1788 First successful threshing machine patented by Scottish millwright Andrew Meikle

◁ **Bakewell's Leicester ram**
This engraving shows a Dishley or New Leicester ram, one of the products of Robert Bakewell's extensive program of selective breeding to create more productive livestock.

fodder crops. In Norfolk, for example, between 1700 and 1850, a switch to clover and the doubling of the cultivation area of legumes tripled the rate of nitrogen fixation.

Changing practices

Meanwhile, changes in the way livestock were reared (stall rearing instead of pasturing, for example) made it possible to collect manure to use as fertilizer. Together, such innovations increased wheat yields by about one-quarter between 1700 and 1800, and then by about half between 1800 and 1850. Eventually, scientific knowledge caught up with empirical wisdom to reveal nitrogen as the key element in fertilizers, and from the mid-19th century imported sources such as guano became important.

Better yields and cultivation of fodder plants resulted in an increase in livestock rearing, and selective breeding led to higher-yielding breeds. Breeds such as the Merino sheep, famous for its wool, radicalized Australian agriculture from 1807; by the 1850s, there were 39 sheep for every Australian.

> *"Agriculture not only gives riches to a nation, but the only riches she can call her own."*
>
> SAMUEL JOHNSON, ENGLISH ESSAYIST (1709–1784)

In Britain, enclosures—the fencing in of wasteland or common land to make it private property—increased the land available for intensive farming, as did the clearing of woodland, the reclamation of upland pastures, and the reclamation of fenland. From the mid-17th to the mid-19th centuries, nearly one-third of England's agricultural land was affected. Land that had previously been pasture became arable, as pasture was replaced by fodder crops, especially those produced in the crop rotation system. Crop rotation, especially when crops were planted in rows, meant that fields need not be left fallow to allow weeding.

The Agricultural Revolution laid the foundations for the Industrial Revolution (see pp.212–213). It sustained high levels of population growth and increased the productivity of land and workers, freeing up labor from agriculture and the countryside and driving the growth of cities and industrial workforces.

△ **Muck spreading**
This pleasant country scene somewhat obscures the true nature of the product being advertised—guano, or fertilizer made from bird droppings.

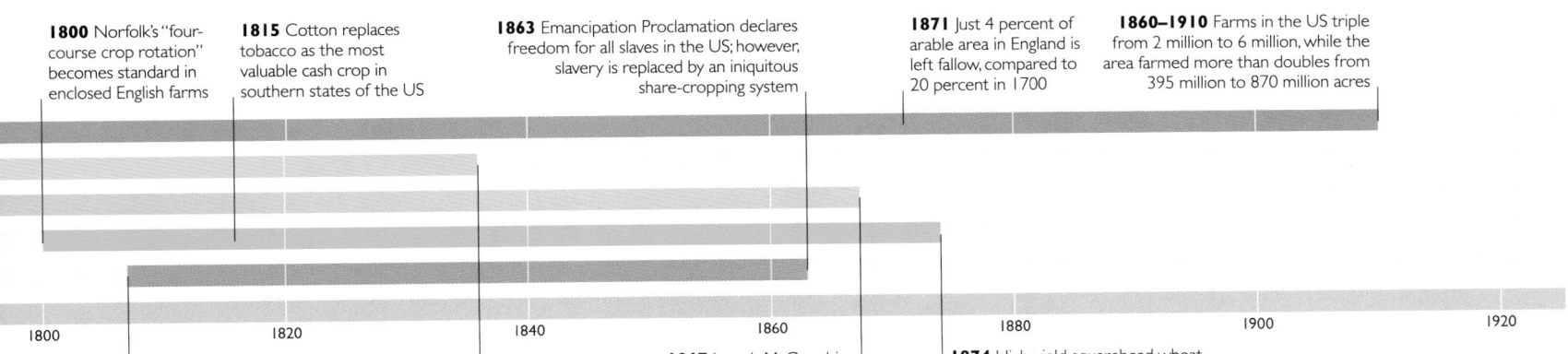

1800 Norfolk's "four-course crop rotation" becomes standard in enclosed English farms

1815 Cotton replaces tobacco as the most valuable cash crop in southern states of the US

1863 Emancipation Proclamation declares freedom for all slaves in the US; however, slavery is replaced by an iniquitous share-cropping system

1871 Just 4 percent of arable area in England is left fallow, compared to 20 percent in 1700

1860–1910 Farms in the US triple from 2 million to 6 million, while the area farmed more than doubles from 395 million to 870 million acres

1800   1820   1840   1860   1880   1900   1920

1807 October Edict ends serfdom in Prussia; serfdom in western Europe had mostly disappeared in the Middle Ages, but it would linger in Russia until 1861

1837 Cyrus McCormick patents mechanical reaper

1867 Joseph McCoy ships cattle from Abilene in Texas to slaughterhouses in Chicago, sparking the "Beef Bonanza"

1874 High-yield squarehead wheat bred by Scottish agronomist Patrick Sheriff arrives in Denmark, from where it will spread across Europe

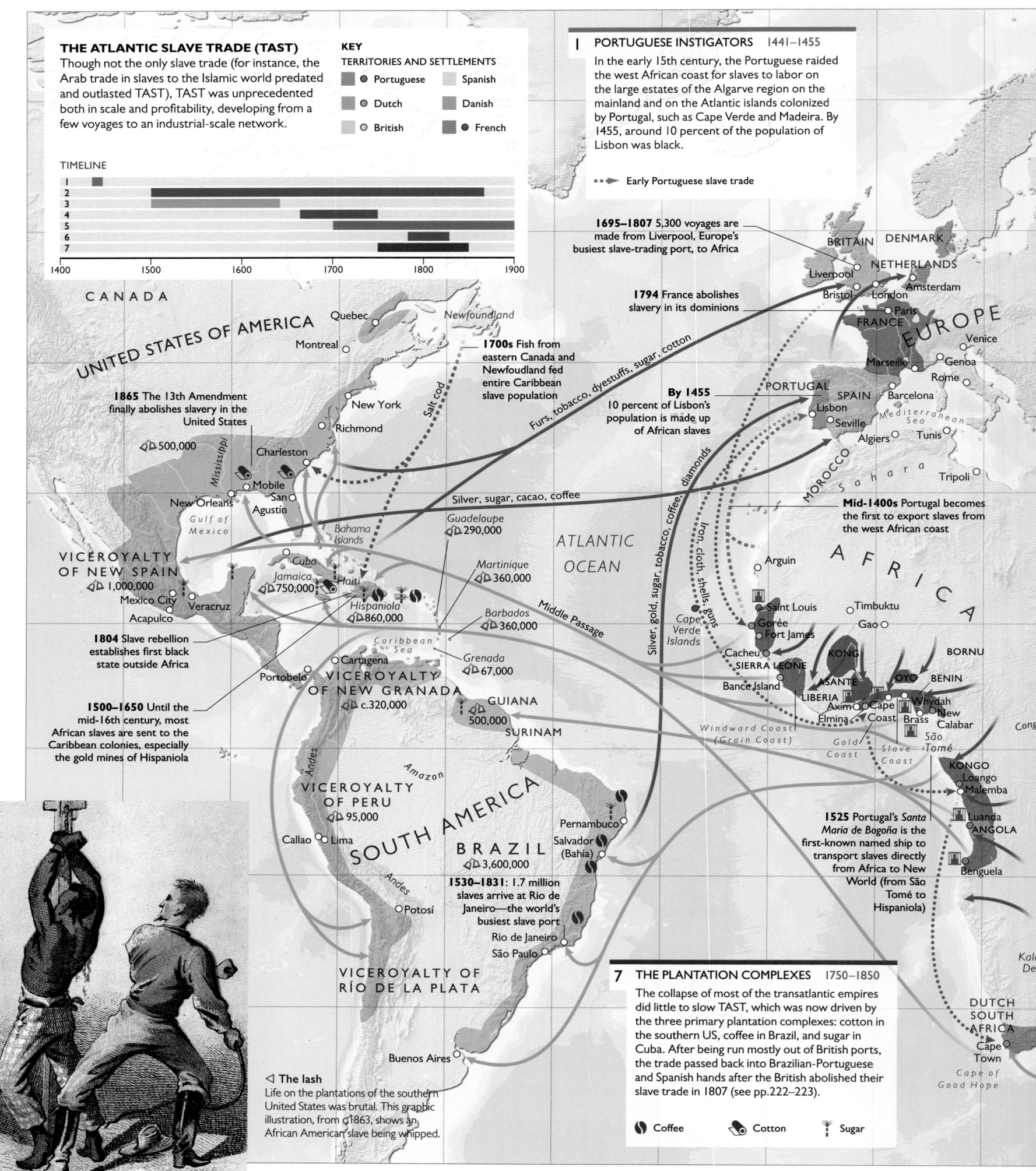

THE ATLANTIC SLAVE TRADE (TAST)
Though not the only slave trade (for instance, the Arab trade in slaves to the Islamic world predated and outlasted TAST), TAST was unprecedented both in scale and profitability, developing from a few voyages to an industrial-scale network.

KEY
TERRITORIES AND SETTLEMENTS
- Portuguese
- Dutch
- British
- Spanish
- Danish
- French

TIMELINE
1
2
3
4
5
6
7
1400 1500 1600 1700 1800 1900

1 PORTUGUESE INSTIGATORS 1441–1455
In the early 15th century, the Portuguese raided the west African coast for slaves to labor on the large estates of the Algarve region on the mainland and on the Atlantic islands colonized by Portugal, such as Cape Verde and Madeira. By 1455, around 10 percent of the population of Lisbon was black.

- - - → Early Portuguese slave trade

1695–1807 5,300 voyages are made from Liverpool, Europe's busiest slave-trading port, to Africa

1794 France abolishes slavery in its dominions

1700s Fish from eastern Canada and Newfoudland fed entire Caribbean slave population

By 1455 10 percent of Lisbon's population is made up of African slaves

Mid-1400s Portugal becomes the first to export slaves from the west African coast

1865 The 13th Amendment finally abolishes slavery in the United States

Furs, tobacco, dyestuffs, sugar, cotton

Silver, sugar, cacao, coffee

Iron, cloth, shells, guns

Silver, gold, sugar, tobacco, coffee, diamonds

Salt cod

Middle Passage

1525 Portugal's *Santa Maria de Bogoña* is the first-known named ship to transport slaves directly from Africa to New World (from São Tomé to Hispaniola)

CANADA

Quebec
Montreal
New York
Richmond
Charleston
Mobile
San Agustín
New Orleans
Mexico City
Acapulco
Veracruz
Portobelo
Cartagena
Callao
Lima
Potosí
Buenos Aires
Pernambuco
Salvador (Bahia)
Rio de Janeiro
São Paulo

UNITED STATES OF AMERICA

VICEROYALTY OF NEW SPAIN
1,000,000

1804 Slave rebellion establishes first black state outside Africa

1500–1650 Until the mid-16th century, most African slaves are sent to the Caribbean colonies, especially the gold mines of Hispaniola

Gulf of Mexico
Bahama Islands
Cuba
Jamaica 750,000
Haiti
Hispaniola 860,000
Guadeloupe 290,000
Martinique 360,000
Barbados 360,000
Grenada 67,000

Caribbean Sea

VICEROYALTY OF NEW GRANADA
c.320,000

GUIANA 500,000
SURINAM

VICEROYALTY OF PERU
95,000

Andes
Amazon
SOUTH AMERICA
BRAZIL 3,600,000

1530–1831: 1.7 million slaves arrive at Rio de Janeiro—the world's busiest slave port

VICEROYALTY OF RÍO DE LA PLATA

ATLANTIC OCEAN

BRITAIN DENMARK
NETHERLANDS
Liverpool
Bristol London Amsterdam
FRANCE Paris EUROPE
Venice
Marseille Genoa
Rome
PORTUGAL SPAIN Barcelona
Lisbon Mediterranean Sea
Seville
Algiers Tunis
MOROCCO Sahara Tripoli

AFRICA
Arguin
Cape Verde Islands
Saint Louis Timbuktu
Gorée Gao
Fort James
Cacheu KONG BORNU
SIERRA LEONE ASANTE OYO BENIN
Bance Island LIBERIA Whydah
Axim Cape Coast New Calabar
Elmina Brass
Windward Coast (Grain Coast) São Tomé
Gold Coast Slave Coast
KONGO
Loango
Malemba
Luanda ANGOLA
Benguela
Congo

DUTCH SOUTH AFRICA
Cape Town
Cape of Good Hope
Kala Des

7 THE PLANTATION COMPLEXES 1750–1850
The collapse of most of the transatlantic empires did little to slow TAST, which was now driven by the three primary plantation complexes: cotton in the southern US, coffee in Brazil, and sugar in Cuba. After being run mostly out of British ports, the trade passed back into Brazilian-Portuguese and Spanish hands after the British abolished their slave trade in 1807 (see pp.222–223).

- Coffee
- Cotton
- Sugar

◁ **The lash**
Life on the plantations of the southern United States was brutal. This graphic illustration, from c1863, shows an African American slave being whipped.

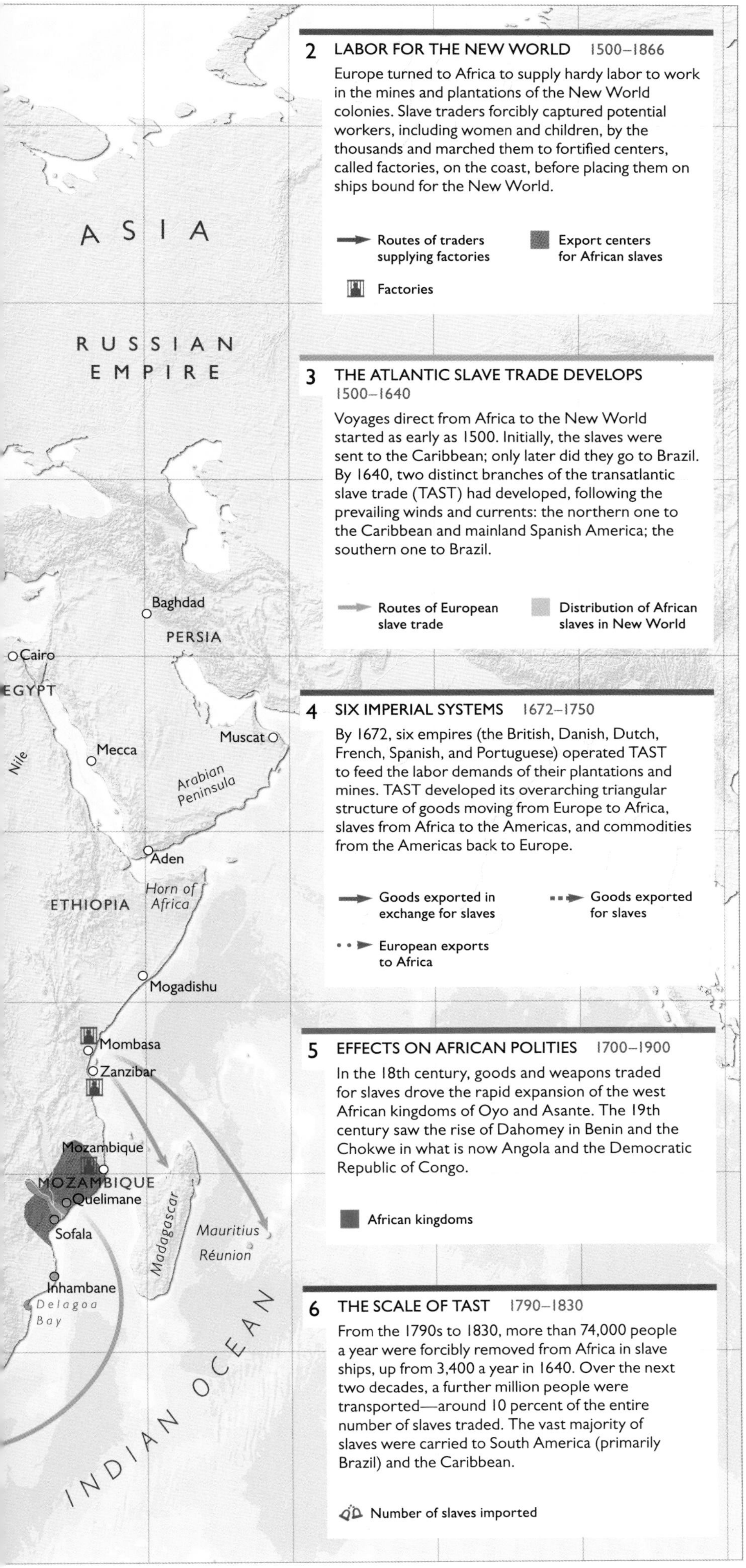

2 LABOR FOR THE NEW WORLD 1500–1866

Europe turned to Africa to supply hardy labor to work in the mines and plantations of the New World colonies. Slave traders forcibly captured potential workers, including women and children, by the thousands and marched them to fortified centers, called factories, on the coast, before placing them on ships bound for the New World.

→ Routes of traders supplying factories

Export centers for African slaves

Factories

3 THE ATLANTIC SLAVE TRADE DEVELOPS 1500–1640

Voyages direct from Africa to the New World started as early as 1500. Initially, the slaves were sent to the Caribbean; only later did they go to Brazil. By 1640, two distinct branches of the transatlantic slave trade (TAST) had developed, following the prevailing winds and currents: the northern one to the Caribbean and mainland Spanish America; the southern one to Brazil.

→ Routes of European slave trade

Distribution of African slaves in New World

4 SIX IMPERIAL SYSTEMS 1672–1750

By 1672, six empires (the British, Danish, Dutch, French, Spanish, and Portuguese) operated TAST to feed the labor demands of their plantations and mines. TAST developed its overarching triangular structure of goods moving from Europe to Africa, slaves from Africa to the Americas, and commodities from the Americas back to Europe.

→ Goods exported in exchange for slaves

▪▶ Goods exported for slaves

▪▪▶ European exports to Africa

5 EFFECTS ON AFRICAN POLITIES 1700–1900

In the 18th century, goods and weapons traded for slaves drove the rapid expansion of the west African kingdoms of Oyo and Asante. The 19th century saw the rise of Dahomey in Benin and the Chokwe in what is now Angola and the Democratic Republic of Congo.

African kingdoms

6 THE SCALE OF TAST 1790–1830

From the 1790s to 1830, more than 74,000 people a year were forcibly removed from Africa in slave ships, up from 3,400 a year in 1640. Over the next two decades, a further million people were transported—around 10 percent of the entire number of slaves traded. The vast majority of slaves were carried to South America (primarily Brazil) and the Caribbean.

Number of slaves imported

THE ATLANTIC SLAVE TRADE

The Atlantic slave trade was an international system of commerce and human misery that saw around 12.5 million people forcibly transported to the New World, and about 2 million killed in the process. The trade transformed the world economy and the nations involved.

Slavery was still a major feature of 15th-century life, especially in Iberia and Italy, with slaves coming from eastern Europe as well as Africa. Though slaves were often domestic servants, this provided a model when the colonization and exploitation of the New World got under way, as the intense demand for labor drove the development of one of the first global systems of large-scale commerce: a triangular system in which manufactured goods from Europe were traded for slaves in Africa, who were then transported to the New World and forced to produce raw materials to be shipped back to Europe.

Slave trading was immensely profitable, so much so that it may have underwritten the entire edifice of Western capitalism. Even as some of the nations that had profited the most sought to stamp out the trade, it continued at high volumes into the early part of the 19th century. The trade had profound effects on the populations and subsequent development of both exporting and importing regions and constituted one of the greatest forced migration events in history. It was an atrocity on an immense scale, the ramifications of which are still barely acknowledged today.

"The shrieks and groans rendered the whole scene of horror almost unimaginable."

FORMER SLAVE OLAUDAH EQUIANO, 1789

THE MIDDLE PASSAGE
THE JOURNEY AND THE DESTINATION

The journey across the Atlantic was the "middle" leg of the triangular trade and so was known as the Middle Passage. Slaves, most of whom had never before seen the sea, were shackled and tightly packed together, confined in horrific conditions for 6–8 weeks, or sometimes up to 13 weeks with adverse weather. Disease, murder, and suicide were rampant and 10–20 percent of slaves died on the voyage.

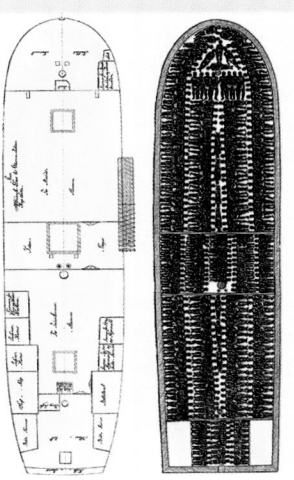

Packed together
This harrowing deck plan shows the unimaginable way in which slaves were packed together in the hold of a slave ship.

THE AMERICAN REVOLUTION

Also known as the American War of Independence, the American Revolution was the culmination of increasing tensions between Britain and its colonies in the Americas. The war pitted Patriots (who wanted independence) against Loyalists (who were loyal to the Crown) in a conflict that would forge a new nation in America.

Seeking to defray the costs of war debt, as well as the many expenses of securing the western frontier and protecting colonists from Native Americans, Britain looked to impose more taxation on its 13 colonies. The colonies, however, resented this repressive taxation, since they did not receive any direct representation in British Parliament in return. Fired by Enlightenment ideals of liberty and justice, many colonists resisted the acts of a distant Parliament, staging rebellious stunts such as the Boston Tea Party in 1773 and summoning a Continental Congress in 1774 to press for autonomous rights and liberties.

Growing tension between Patriots and foreign troops spilled over into war when the first shots were fired at Lexington, Massachusetts, in April 1775. The war was as much a civil conflict as a revolution; many colonists remained loyal to the Crown, and

Loyalist militia composed a significant portion of British forces. British efforts to crush George Washington's Patriot army in the north ended in a stalemate, yet the Patriots won key symbolic victories, such as their defeat of a column marched from Canada, which convinced the French to enter the war on the Patriots' side. When the British began to attack from the south, and after a crushing British victory at Charleston, the Revolution looked to be in danger, but slowly things changed in the Patriots' favor, and the British began to feel the strain of fighting a war from such a distance—orders, troops, and supplies could take months to cross the Atlantic. When the French fleet chased off British naval relief in 1781, Washington and his French allies were able to trap the British commander Charles Cornwallis in Yorktown, Virginia, and force the British to agree to a peace treaty.

THOMAS JEFFERSON
1743–1826

A lawyer and plantation owner from Virginia, Thomas Jefferson emerged as one of the prime intellectual powerhouses of the Patriot cause with his 1774 defense of American independence, *A Summary View of the Rights of British America*. He was asked to help write the Declaration of Independence, and his draft was adopted in 1776, with only minor changes. He went on to found the Democratic Party, serve as third president of the US, and oversee major expansion of US territory.

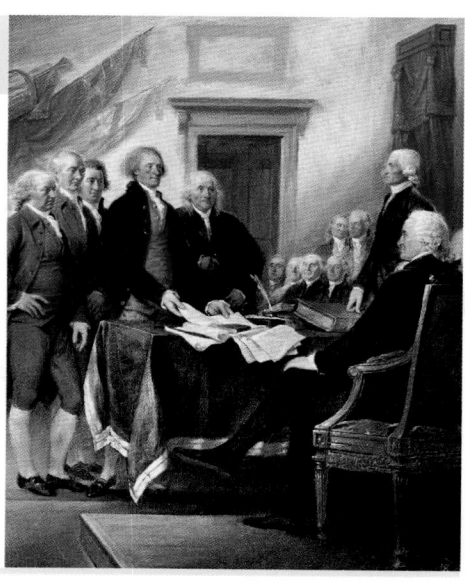

Declaring independence
Thomas Jefferson presents the Declaration of Independence to Congress.

VICTORIES AND LOSSES

The American Revolutionary War had three main phases: a northern phase, in which the British were unable to force a decisive victory; a southern phase, in which initial British gains were slowly reversed; and a central phase, in which the British were finally defeated.

KEY

MOVEMENTS, WITH DATE AND LEADER NAME
→ British   → French   → Patriots

VICTORIES
✗ British   ✗ French   ✗ US
✗ Indecisive outcomes

⊞ Fort   – – The Thirteen Colonies 1775   ···· State lines

TIMELINE
1
2
3
4
1770   1780   1790

Feb 1779 American commander George Clark leads an army of 170 men to lay siege to the British fort at Vincennes

Oct 1778 Hamilton

Illinois   Wabash   INDIAN   RESERVE

St. Louis   Cahokia   Vincennes   Harrodsbur

Kaskaskia   Alabama

4 BIRTH OF A NATION 1782–1783

With no realistic prospect of maintaining the war on American soil, the British were forced to recognize American independence. In the Treaty of Paris, the Americans won control of their waters and vast territories, which now extended as far west as the Mississippi River. The treaty was officially signed on September 3, 1783, and approved by the Continental Congress a few months later.

US border 1783

3 DEFEAT OF THE BRITISH 1781

In the final stages of the war, the focus shifted to the central region. Costly Pyrrhic victories for the British were followed by a decisive intervention by French naval forces from mid-1781. Washington and French General Rochambeau coordinated their forces to trap General Charles Cornwallis, leader of the British expeditionary force, in Yorktown, where he surrendered.

(O) Siege of Yorktown

CANADA

Georgian Bay

Lake Huron

QUEBEC

Montreal

Aug 1775 Montgomery

May 1776 Thomas

Quebec

DISTRICT OF MAINE *to Massachusetts*

Oct 1777 British General Burgoyne, marching south from Canada to cut off the rebellious northern colonies, suffers a devastating defeat at the Battles of Saragota

Ottawa

Fort Chambly
Fort St. John's

Jun 1777 Burgoyne

Sep 1775 Arnold

NEW HAMPSHIRE

Nov 1778 Following a violent storm that damages much of his fleet, French Admiral Charles-Hector d'Estaing departs for the West Indies—a great loss for the Patriots

Lake Ontario

Jun 1777 St. Leger

Fort Stanwix

Crown Point

Connecticut

Fort Oswego

Saratoga

Cherry Valley

Bennington

Concord
Cambridge
Lexington
Boston

Jun 1775 Patriots show their determination at the fierce Battle of Bunker Hill, near Boston; the British are forced to evacuate Boston

Fort Niagara

Jul 1778 Butler

NEW YORK

Albany **MASSACHUSETTS**
Providence

Nov 1778 d'Estaing

RHODE ISLAND

Lake Erie

Dec 1776 Washington crosses the Delaware and scores a symbolic victory, having suffered a series of defeats in and around New York

Hartford

May/Jun 1781 Rochambeau

Fort Detroit

Sep 1777 Gates

Hudson

West Point
White Plains

CONNECTICUT

New Haven
New London
Newport

1 WAR IN THE NORTH 1775–1780

American Patriots faced an experienced British army, but they proved their mettle in initial battles in Massachusetts. General George Washington marshaled his inexperienced Patriot troops through a difficult campaign, avoiding decisive defeats to reach a stalemate in the north, and scoring two morale-boosting successes: Trenton (1776) and at the Battles of Saratoga (1777).

☐ Northern colonies

Fort Malden

Wilkes Barre

PENNSYLVANIA

New York

Sep 1778 Washington

Jul 1776 Howe

UPPER OHIO FRONTIER

Fort Pitt (or Pittsburg)

Germantown

Princeton
Monmouth
Trenton

Fort Henry

Redstone Fort

Philadelphia
NEW JERSEY

Aug 1781 de Barras

Jul 1778 d'Estaing

Jul 1778–Feb 1779 Clark

Wilmington

DELAWARE

Jul 1777 Howe

Aug 1781 Hood/Graves

KENTUCKY FRONTIER

Mar 1781 Costly win proves a Pyrrhic victory for the British

VIRGINIA

Potomac

Lafayette

1781 Washington

MARYLAND

Chesapeake Bay

2 WAR IN THE SOUTH 1778–1781

The British opened a new front in the south in 1778 and scored a major victory with the capture of Charleston in 1780. But the Patriots refused to give in, and slowly the tide turned against the Loyalists, culminating in an important Patriot victory at Cowpens, South Carolina, in January 1781, which proved that the British southern strategy could be countered.

☐ Southern colonies

Oct 1763 The British issue a proclamation line, declaring lands to the west off limits to colonists, to prevent further expansion into Native American territories

Charlottesville

Jul 1781 Tarleton
Richmond
Petersburg

Bedford

Williamsburg
Yorktown
Norfolk

Aug 1781 de Grasse

Oct 1781 Cornwallis surrenders at Yorktown, effectively ending the war and leading to American independence from Britain

Sep 1781 French fleet chases off British fleet at the Battle of the Capes, depriving Cornwallis of naval support and trapping him in Yorktown

Jan 1781 Patriot victory at Cowpens

NORTH CAROLINA

Guilford

Jul/Aug 1780 Gates

Apr 1781 Greene

Ramsay's Mill

May 1781 Cornwallis

Roanoke

Mar 1781 Morgan/Greene

Charlotte

Cowpens

Cheraw

Cape Fear

Wilmington

Cape Hatteras

▽ Heading for success
On Christmas Day 1776, Washington's Patriot army crossed the Delaware River to make a surprise attack at Trenton, as commemorated in this 1851 painting by Emanuel Leutze.

Fort Ninety Six

Pee Dee

Camden

SOUTH CAROLINA

Balfour

Augusta

Feb 1779 Lincoln

Jan 1780 Clinton/Cornwallis

Dec 1778 Campbell

Prevost

GEORGIA

Charleston

Savannah

Mar–May 1780 Major British victory in Charleston threatens to cost the Patriots the south

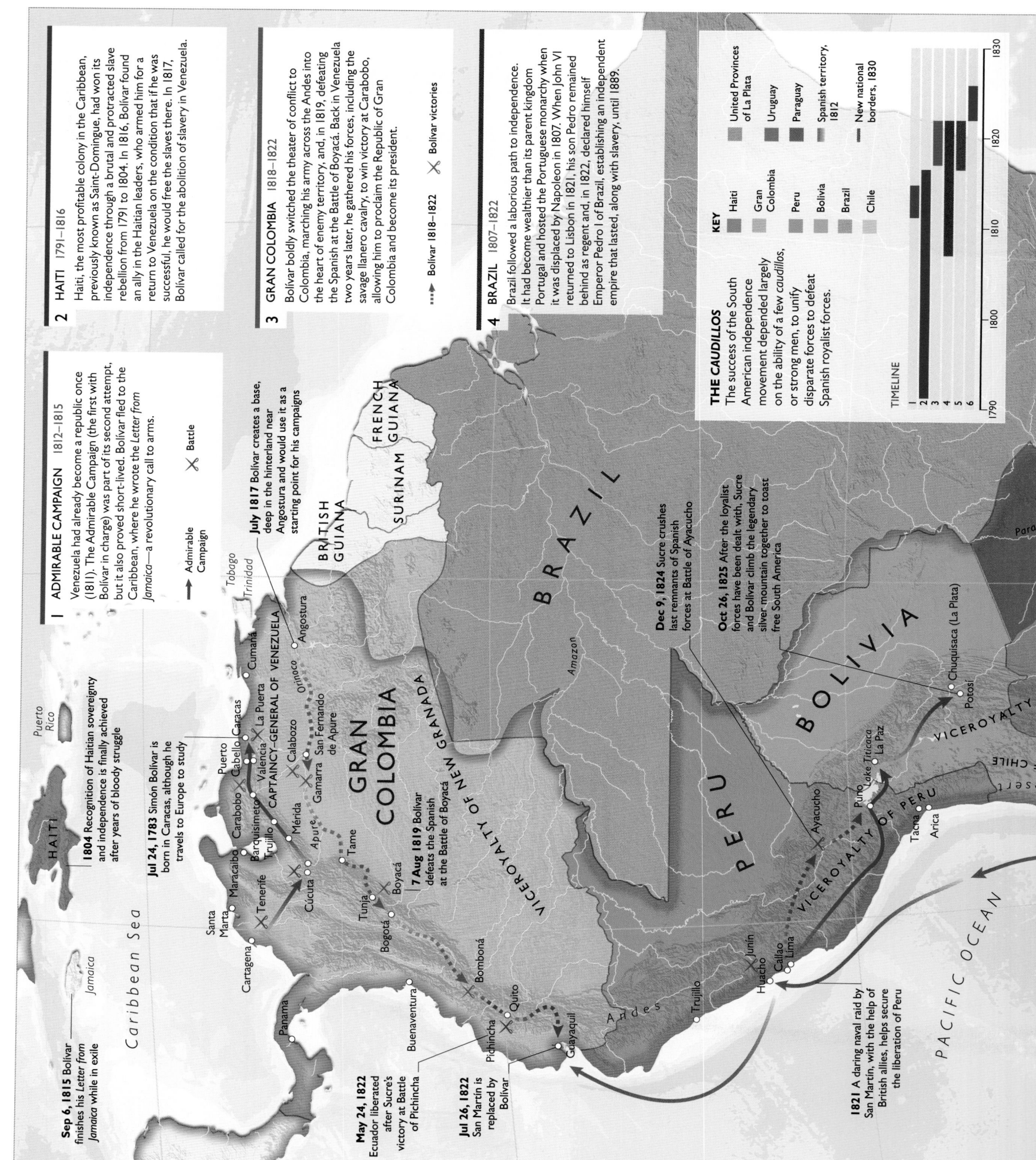

1 ADMIRABLE CAMPAIGN 1812–1815

Venezuela had already become a republic once (1811). The Admirable Campaign (the first with Bolívar in charge) was part of its second attempt, but it also proved short-lived. Bolívar fled to the Caribbean, where he wrote the *Letter from Jamaica*—a revolutionary call to arms.

→ Admirable Campaign

✕ Battle

2 HAITI 1791–1816

Haiti, the most profitable colony in the Caribbean, previously known as Saint-Domingue, had won its independence through a brutal and protracted slave rebellion from 1791 to 1804. In 1816, Bolívar found an ally in the Haitian leaders, who armed him for a return to Venezuela on the condition that if he was successful, he would free the slaves there. In 1817, Bolívar called for the abolition of slavery in Venezuela.

3 GRAN COLOMBIA 1818–1822

Bolívar boldly switched the theater of conflict to Colombia, marching his army across the Andes into the heart of enemy territory, and, in 1819, defeating the Spanish at the Battle of Boyacá. Back in Venezuela two years later, he gathered his forces, including the savage llanero cavalry, to win victory at Carabobo, allowing him to proclaim the Republic of Gran Colombia and become its president.

┈┈▶ Bolívar 1818–1822   ✕ Bolívar victories

4 BRAZIL 1807–1822

Brazil followed a laborious path to independence. It had become wealthier than its parent kingdom Portugal and hosted the Portuguese monarchy when it was displaced by Napoleon in 1807. When John VI returned to Lisbon in 1821, his son Pedro remained behind as regent and, in 1822, declared himself Emperor Pedro I of Brazil, establishing an independent empire that lasted, along with slavery, until 1889.

THE CAUDILLOS

The success of the South American independence movement depended largely on the ability of a few *caudillos*, or strong men, to unify disparate forces to defeat Spanish royalist forces.

KEY

- Haiti
- Gran Colombia
- Peru
- Bolivia
- Brazil
- Chile
- United Provinces of La Plata
- Uruguay
- Paraguay
- Spanish territory, 1812
- New national borders, 1830

TIMELINE

1790 1800 1810 1820 1830

1
2
3
4
5
6

Sep 6, 1815 Bolívar finishes his *Letter from Jamaica* while in exile

1804 Recognition of Haitian sovereignty and independence is finally achieved after years of bloody struggle

Jul 24, 1783 Simón Bolívar is born in Caracas, although he travels to Europe to study

July 1817 Bolívar creates a base, deep in the hinterland near Angostura and would use it as a starting point for his campaigns

7 Aug 1819 Bolívar defeats the Spanish at the Battle of Boyacá

Dec 9, 1824 Sucre crushes last remnants of Spanish forces at Battle of Ayacucho

Oct 26, 1825 After the loyalist forces have been dealt with, Sucre and Bolívar climb the legendary silver mountain together to toast free South America

May 24, 1822 Ecuador liberated after Sucre's victory at Battle of Pichincha

Jul 26, 1822 San Martín is replaced by Bolívar

1821 A daring naval raid by San Martín, with the help of British allies, helps secure the liberation of Peru

Puerto Rico

HAITI

Jamaica

Caribbean Sea

Santa Marta

Cartagena

Panama

Buenaventura

Tenerife

Maracaibo

Barquisimeto

Trujillo

Carabobo

Puerto Cabello

Valencia

La Puerta

Caracas

CAPTAINCY-GENERAL OF VENEZUELA

Cumaná

Angostura

Orinoco

Calabozo

Mérida

Cúcuta

Apure

San Fernando de Apure

Gamarra

Tame

GRAN COLOMBIA

Tunja

Boyacá

Bogotá

Bomboná

Quito

Pichincha

Guayaquil

VICEROYALTY OF NEW GRANADA

Andes

Tobago

Trinidad

BRITISH GUIANA

FRENCH GUIANA

SURINAM

BRAZIL

Amazon

Paraguay

BOLIVIA

PERU

VICEROYALTY OF PERU

Chuquisaca (La Plata)

Potosí

VICEROYALTY OF CHILE

La Paz

Lake Titicaca

Puno

Ayacucho

Junín

Callao

Lima

Huacho

Trujillo

Tacna

Arica

Desert

PACIFIC OCEAN

SOUTH AMERICAN INDEPENDENCE

South American desire for independence from distant Iberian overlords was driven mainly by the creole (American-born) elite and put into action by a handful of charismatic and dynamic revolutionary generals. In the Spanish colonies, after a rocky start in the north, liberation from Spanish rule swept across the continent from south and north, while Brazil forged its own path to independence.

At the start of the 19th century, South America was simmering with political, economic, and racial tension. Creoles—those born in the Americas, often with mixed heritage—controlled most of the wealth and the plantations that produced it. Overall political power, however, came from the Iberian Peninsula, representing distant imperial authority that restricted trade and industry. The creoles resented this imposition but feared the consequences that revolution might bring; their fears were heightened by the example of Haiti, a former French colony in which slaves had staged the only successful slave uprising in the New World.

The tension between patriots and out-of-touch European rulers and those loyal to them resembled that in prerevolutionary North America, and it would be stoked by men like Simón Bolívar—leading creoles who were steeped in the the liberal nationalism emerging in Europe.

When Napoleon invaded Spain and Portugal in 1808 and 1809 and toppled or exiled the royal families of those countries, contact between Spain and Portugal and their colonies was cut. All the ingredients for revolution were present.

Initial attempts to proclaim republican independence were thwarted by the defeat of Napoleon and the restoration of the Spanish crown, which triggered aggressive action to reclaim the colonies. In 1815, the Spanish restored royal control in Venezuela and New Granada. Bolívar went into exile in Jamaica and Haiti, but the impetus of independence would not be checked. In the south, San Martín liberated Chile and Peru, while in the north Bolívar and his lieutenant Sucre liberated Colombia and Ecuador, finally chasing Spanish royalist forces out of South America for good in December 1824.

SIMÓN BOLÍVAR
1783–1830

The greatest hero of the South American liberation movement, Bolívar was born to a wealthy family in Caracas (in what is now Venezuela). He spent time in Europe, where he absorbed liberal ideas, and returned to South America fired with revolutionary zeal. A brilliant military strategist, he won a string of key victories against royalist forces but post-independence was unable to realize his dream of pan-Latin American unification.

1811 Paraguay declares itself independent from what would become Argentina

1813 Uruguay declares itself independent from what would become Argentina

1817 San Martín leads his army across the Andes in his campaign to liberate Chile from Spanish rule

1810 Rio de la Plata declares independence from Spain, but Buenos Aires is unable to maintain control of the outlying provinces

ATLANTIC OCEAN

PARAGUAY

URUGUAY

Montevideo

Paraná

RÍO DE LA PLATA

UNITED PROVINCES OF LA PLATA

Córdoba

Tucumán

Mendoza

Santiago

Valparaíso

Maipú

Cancha Rayada

Talca

Concepción

Talcahuano

CHILE

CAPTAINCY-GENERAL

Andes

Paso de los Patos

Chacabuco

Buenos Aires

Patagonia

Atacama

△ **The Battle of Chacabuco**
In 1817, General José de San Martín secured a famous victory at the Battle of Chacabuco after surprising Spanish forces by marching his army across the Andes.

---

6 SUCRE, BOLÍVAR, AND PERU 1822–26

Bolívar and his most able general, Antonio José de Sucre, moved south, liberating Ecuador in 1822 after Sucre's victory at Pinchincha, and taking possession of Peru after San Martín retired from the field. Sucre defeated the Spanish forces at the Battle of Ayacucho in 1824. By 1826 all Spanish territory had been liberated.

→ Bolívar 1823–26   ✕ Bolívar and Sucre victories

┈┈► Sucre 1824

5 SAN MARTÍN AND O'HIGGINS 1817–22

In southern South America, revolutionary armies under José de San Martín and Bernardo O'Higgins achieved daring victories over Spanish forces, first at Chacabuco (1817) and then in Peru (1821) after a surprise naval attack. O'Higgins became leader of Chile, while San Martín gave way to Bolívar after meeting him in Guayaquil in 1822.

→ San Martín or O'Higgins 1820–22   ✕ San Martín and O'Higgins victories

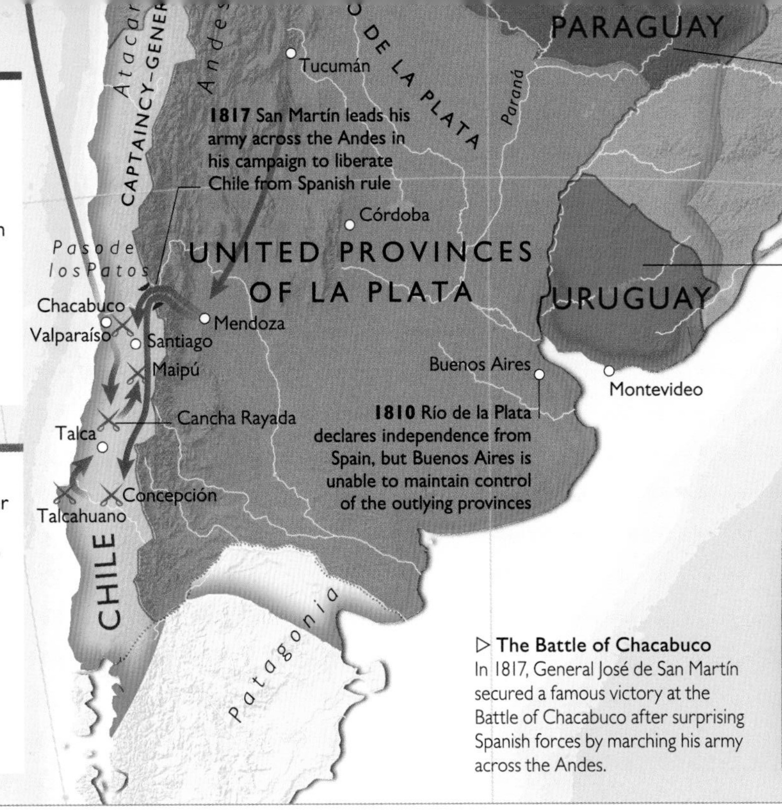

THE ENLIGHTENMENT

Spanning the mid-17th to early 19th centuries, the Enlightenment was a period in which thinkers championed reason over superstition and made significant advances in the sciences, arts, politics, economics, and religion.

△ **Enlightened empress**
As well as modernizing and expanding the Russian Empire during her 34-year rule, Empress Catherine the Great championed Enlightenment ideas and advanced state education for women.

Also known as the Age of Reason, the Enlightenment blossomed in pockets across the Western world, advocating rationalism and religious tolerance over superstition and sectarianism.

In Germany, it took the shape of a philosophical and literary movement, known as the *Aufklärung*, which helped invigorate literature and philosophy in eastern Europe. In France, the movement was associated with *philosophes*—men of letters, science, and philosophy—starting with René Descartes and including Voltaire and Jean-Jacques Rousseau, among others. Their ideas combined rationalism with a desire to bring about social change and overcome inequality and injustice. Their belief in the supremacy of reason, religious tolerance, and constitutional governments formed a critique of a dogmatic church and absolute monarchy in France. Their writings provided an intellectual basis for the French Revolution. The US Founding Fathers drew inspiration from them when framing the constitution of their new nation.

In England, the Enlightenment included thinkers such as John Locke and Thomas Paine, who in turn influenced poets, as well as writers such as Mary Wollstonecraft. In Scotland, the movement flourished in and around Edinburgh between 1750 and 1800 thanks to writers such as David Hume and Adam Smith. This Age of Reason encouraged not only literary realism and the growth of the novel, but also created a cultural reaction in the form of Romanticism—an artistic and literary movement in the late 18th century (see pp.216–217).

THE EXPANSION OF RATIONAL THOUGHT

"Rationalist hotspots" in Europe ranged from Stockholm to Lisbon and from Dublin to St. Petersburg. In the United States, they included Boston and Philadelphia. The increasing communication between these centers allowed rapid exchange of ideas, mirroring the development of international trade.

KEY
● Main centers of the Enlightenment

Edinburgh · Stockholm · St Petersburg · Dublin · Copenhagen · London · Amsterdam · Paris · Berlin · Vienna · Lisbon

Learning from Voltaire
The guests at this Paris salon in 1755 include Denis Diderot and Jean Le Rond d'Alembert. The *philosophes* are gathered around a bust of Voltaire to hear a reading of one of his plays, in which blind force and barbarism are defeated by genius and reason.

THE FATE OF NATIVE AMERICANS

Native American societies across North America were transforming even before direct contact with the United States, but the young nation's increasing belief that westward expansion was its destiny would bring drastic change—two centuries of brutal conflict and near-eradication of America's native peoples.

In 1783, the United States became a sovereign nation, no longer bound by the limitations on settlement imposed by Britain. This newfound freedom inspired in the American settlers a belief that they were the natural inheritors of the continent, giving birth to the empowering phrase "manifest destiny" (see below), which drove their expansion westward.

By 1790, about 500,000 settlers had laid down roots west of the original Thirteen States (see pp.156–157). The expansion gained momentum during the next 50 years as explorers ventured westward in wagon trains or sailed to the Pacific Coast to join the Gold Rush. Pioneers paved the way for migrants to settle on the western coast, especially after railroads replaced the wagon trails. By 1860, approximately 16 million colonists had migrated and settled west of the Appalachians, their arrival displacing and disenfranchising the 250,000 or so Native Americans in the Great Plains and the West.

Many indigenous groups fought for their lands and mounted some notable defenses, but it was only a matter of time before their resistance was crushed by the might and momentum of this Euro-American expansion. By 1890, the remaining Native Americans who had survived the wars were forced out of their homes and herded into specially designated sites called reservations, which amounted to a little more than 2 percent of the area of the United States.

> *"Kill them all, big and little: nits make lice."*
>
> JOHN CHIVINGTON, US COLONEL, 1864

MANIFEST DESTINY
THE RIGHT TO COLONIZE

Coined in 1845, the term "manifest destiny" encompassed the belief in American settlers of their divine right to inhabit and "civilize" the whole expanse of the continent. Although the hunger for land and opportunities in the west had long been features of American colonization, after independence, it evolved into a sense of continental entitlement that drove mass migration westward. In his painting *American Progress* (1872), John Gast depicts Columbia—a personification of the US—leading settlers westward. The figure strings a telegraph wire, implying that the settlers are bringing "light" to the west.

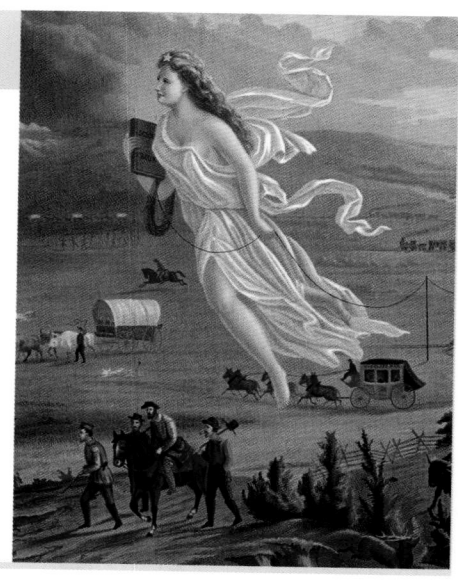

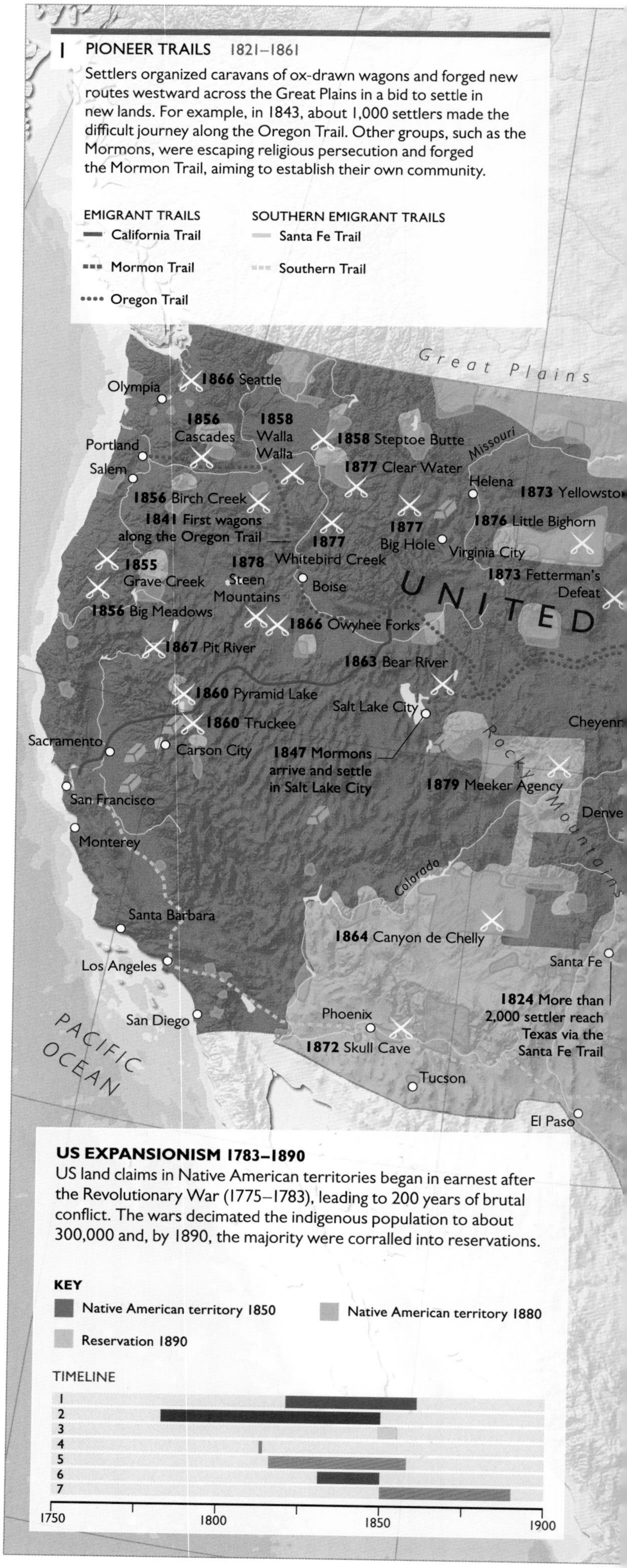

PIONEER TRAILS 1821–1861

Settlers organized caravans of ox-drawn wagons and forged new routes westward across the Great Plains in a bid to settle in new lands. For example, in 1843, about 1,000 settlers made the difficult journey along the Oregon Trail. Other groups, such as the Mormons, were escaping religious persecution and forged the Mormon Trail, aiming to establish their own community.

EMIGRANT TRAILS
— California Trail
••• Mormon Trail
•••• Oregon Trail

SOUTHERN EMIGRANT TRAILS
— Santa Fe Trail
••• Southern Trail

Great Plains

Olympia ✕ 1866 Seattle
Portland
Salem
1856 Cascades
1858 Walla Walla
1858 Steptoe Butte
1877 Clear Water
Helena
1873 Yellowstone
1856 Birch Creek
1841 First wagons along the Oregon Trail
1877
1877 Big Hole
1876 Little Bighorn
Virginia City
1855 Grave Creek
1878 Whitebird Creek
Steen Mountains
Boise
1873 Fetterman's Defeat
1856 Big Meadows
UNITED
1866 Owyhee Forks
1867 Pit River
1863 Bear River
1860 Pyramid Lake
Salt Lake City
Cheyenne
1860 Truckee
Sacramento
Carson City
1847 Mormons arrive and settle in Salt Lake City
1879 Meeker Agency
San Francisco
Denver
Monterey
Santa Barbara
1864 Canyon de Chelly
Santa Fe
Los Angeles
1824 More than 2,000 settler reach Texas via the Santa Fe Trail
PACIFIC OCEAN
San Diego
Phoenix
1872 Skull Cave
Tucson
El Paso

US EXPANSIONISM 1783–1890

US land claims in Native American territories began in earnest after the Revolutionary War (1775–1783), leading to 200 years of brutal conflict. The wars decimated the indigenous population to about 300,000 and, by 1890, the majority were corralled into reservations.

KEY
■ Native American territory 1850
■ Native American territory 1880
■ Reservation 1890

TIMELINE

1
2
3
4
5
6
7

1750   1800   1850   1900

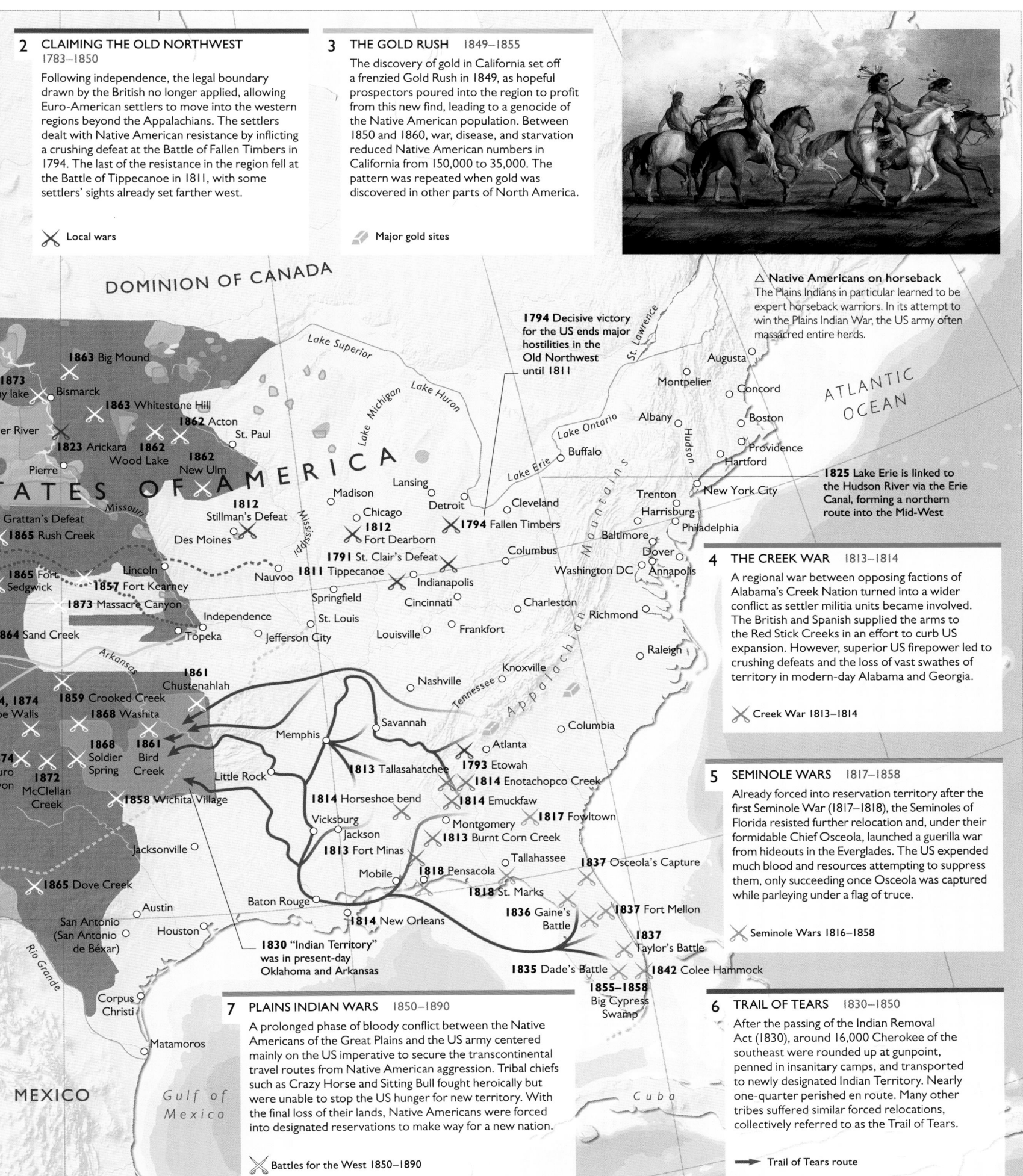

2 CLAIMING THE OLD NORTHWEST
1783–1850

Following independence, the legal boundary drawn by the British no longer applied, allowing Euro-American settlers to move into the western regions beyond the Appalachians. The settlers dealt with Native American resistance by inflicting a crushing defeat at the Battle of Fallen Timbers in 1794. The last of the resistance in the region fell at the Battle of Tippecanoe in 1811, with some settlers' sights already set farther west.

✗ Local wars

3 THE GOLD RUSH   1849–1855

The discovery of gold in California set off a frenzied Gold Rush in 1849, as hopeful prospectors poured into the region to profit from this new find, leading to a genocide of the Native American population. Between 1850 and 1860, war, disease, and starvation reduced Native American numbers in California from 150,000 to 35,000. The pattern was repeated when gold was discovered in other parts of North America.

▱ Major gold sites

△ **Native Americans on horseback**
The Plains Indians in particular learned to be expert horseback warriors. In its attempt to win the Plains Indian War, the US army often massacred entire herds.

1794 Decisive victory for the US ends major hostilities in the Old Northwest until 1811

1825 Lake Erie is linked to the Hudson River via the Erie Canal, forming a northern route into the Mid-West

4 THE CREEK WAR   1813–1814

A regional war between opposing factions of Alabama's Creek Nation turned into a wider conflict as settler militia units became involved. The British and Spanish supplied the arms to the Red Stick Creeks in an effort to curb US expansion. However, superior US firepower led to crushing defeats and the loss of vast swathes of territory in modern-day Alabama and Georgia.

✗ Creek War 1813–1814

5 SEMINOLE WARS   1817–1858

Already forced into reservation territory after the first Seminole War (1817–1818), the Seminoles of Florida resisted further relocation and, under their formidable Chief Osceola, launched a guerilla war from hideouts in the Everglades. The US expended much blood and resources attempting to suppress them, only succeeding once Osceola was captured while parleying under a flag of truce.

✗ Seminole Wars 1816–1858

7 PLAINS INDIAN WARS   1850–1890

A prolonged phase of bloody conflict between the Native Americans of the Great Plains and the US army centered mainly on the US imperative to secure the transcontinental travel routes from Native American aggression. Tribal chiefs such as Crazy Horse and Sitting Bull fought heroically but were unable to stop the US hunger for new territory. With the final loss of their lands, Native Americans were forced into designated reservations to make way for a new nation.

✗ Battles for the West 1850–1890

6 TRAIL OF TEARS   1830–1850

After the passing of the Indian Removal Act (1830), around 16,000 Cherokee of the southeast were rounded up at gunpoint, penned in insanitary camps, and transported to newly designated Indian Territory. Nearly one-quarter perished en route. Many other tribes suffered similar forced relocations, collectively referred to as the Trail of Tears.

➡ Trail of Tears route

Map labels

DOMINION OF CANADA

Lake Superior
Lake Michigan
Lake Huron
Lake Ontario
Lake Erie

St. Lawrence
Hudson

ATLANTIC OCEAN

TATES OF AMERICA

Missouri
Mississippi
Arkansas
Tennessee
Rio Grande

Appalachian Muntains

1863 Big Mound
1873 Stony lake
Bismarck
1863 Whitestone Hill
1876 Powder River
1862 Acton
St. Paul
1823 Arickara
1862 Wood Lake
1862 New Ulm
Pierre
1854 Grattan's Defeat
1865 Rush Creek
1865 Fort Sedgwick
1857 Fort Kearney
Lincoln
1873 Massacre Canyon
Independence
1864 Sand Creek
Topeka
Jefferson City
1861 Chustenahlah
1864, 1874 Adobe Walls
1859 Crooked Creek
1868 Washita
1874 lo Duro Canyon
1872 McClellan Creek
1868 Soldier Spring
1861 Bird Creek
1858 Wichita Village
Jacksonville
1865 Dove Creek
San Antonio (San Antonio de Béxar)
Austin
Houston
Corpus Christi
Matamoros
Little Rock

Madison
Chicago
Detroit
Cleveland
Lansing
Des Moines
Nauvoo
Springfield
St. Louis
Louisville
Cincinnati
Frankfort
1812 Stillman's Defeat
1812 Fort Dearborn
1791 St. Clair's Defeat
1811 Tippecanoe
Indianapolis
Columbus
1794 Fallen Timbers
Washington DC

Augusta
Montpelier
Concord
Albany
Boston
Buffalo
Providence
Hartford
Trenton
New York City
Harrisburg
Philadelphia
Baltimore
Dover
Annapolis
Charleston
Richmond
Raleigh
Knoxville
Nashville
Columbia

Memphis
Savannah
Atlanta
1793 Etowah
1813 Tallasahatchee
1814 Enotachopco Creek
1814 Emuckfaw
1814 Horseshoe bend
1817 Fowltown
Vicksburg
Montgomery
1813 Burnt Corn Creek
Jackson
1813 Fort Mims
Tallahassee
Mobile
1818 Pensacola
1837 Osceola's Capture
1818 St. Marks
Baton Rouge
1836 Gaine's Battle
1837 Fort Mellon
1814 New Orleans
1837 Taylor's Battle
1830 "Indian Territory" was in present-day Oklahoma and Arkansas
1835 Dade's Battle
1842 Colee Hammock
1855–1858 Big Cypress Swamp

MEXICO
Gulf of Mexico
Cuba

THE FRENCH REVOLUTION

The French Revolution was actually a series of revolutions accompanied by pan-continental war. Three revolutionary forces converged to drive the transformation of the French state: a liberal aristocratic and bourgeois movement that brought about constitutional change; a popular revolutionary mob in the streets of Paris; and an agrarian revolt by peasants across the country.

In 1789, Louis XVI convoked the Estates-General (for the first time in 175 years) as he sought financial reforms to alleviate France's huge debt. The Estates-General was the Ancien Régime's representative assembly, made up of three estates: clergy (First Estate); nobility (Second Estate); and commoners (Third Estate). In May 1789, the majority Third Estate insisted on greater voting rights. When they were refused, they broke away to form the National Assembly. This triggered a period of great change: a constitutional monarchy was created; and the Declaration of the Rights of Man was drafted, defining a single set of individual and collective rights for all men.

The Assembly, formed out of the National Assembly, pushed through a new constitution and other major reforms, such as the end of feudalism. Factional struggles between the Girondists on the one hand and the Jacobins, headed by Robespierre,

Marat, and Danton, on the other, dominated the Assembly.

The threat posed to France's neighbors by a revolutionary state exporting its ideals prompted a reactionary coalition against France. With enemy armies pressing on all sides and domestic counterrevolutionary uprisings, the revolutionaries panicked. The Revolution descended into a second, extremist phase known as the Reign of Terror. In July 1794, the Jacobins were overthrown in the Thermidor coup, and this instituted the third phase of the Revolution, with the more moderate Directory taking power in October 1795 and attempting to restore the liberal, constitutional values of the first phase. By November 1799, however, enemy armies once more threatened the survival of the Republic, and a coup engineered by Bonaparte to make himself First Consul is traditionally held to mark the end of the Revolution and the start of the Napoleonic era.

DECLARATION OF THE RIGHTS OF MAN
PRINCIPLES OF THE REVOLUTION

The Declaration of the Rights of Man and Citizen was a statement of the principles of the Revolution, establishing the sovereignty of the people and the principle of "liberty, equality, and fraternity." Louis XVI was forced to accept it in the 1791 constitution. The painting shows an officer of the National Guard swearing an oath of allegiance before the Altar of the Convention.

THE FRENCH REVOLUTION 1789–1795

Not everyone accepted the Revolution. Counterrevolutionary centers sprang up, but counterrevolutionaries were crushed. France went to war to spread its revolutionary ideals. Napoleon's successful Italian campaign in 1796 set him on the path to power.

KEY

■ French territory 1789

TIMELINE

2 THE NATIONAL ASSEMBLY 1789–1791

The National Assembly abolished feudalism, adopted the Declaration of the Rights of Man, and proclaimed a new, constitutional monarchy. In June 1791, the king was caught fleeing Paris, and radical sentiment was further inflamed when moderates were blamed for the "massacre of the Champ de Mars" on July 17, in which the National Guard fired upon a crowd in Paris, killing up to 50 civilians.

☠ Massacre

3 THE TUMULT SPREADS ABROAD 1792–1794

Shock waves rippled across Europe, sparking both revolutionary feeling (the Austrian Netherlands revolted and declared independence as Belgium) and reactionary opposition (neighboring monarchies formed the First Coalition to restore the French monarchy). The Revolutionary Wars began, with France going to war with Austria, Prussia, and most of its neighbors. Panic grew inside France, and the revolution became more extreme.

⚔ French victory   ⚔ French defeat

➡ Offensives by French forces 1792–1794

⇢ Offensives by coalition forces 1792–1794

■ Territories annexed by France 1792–1797

○ Brest

4 THE REPUBLIC 1792–1793

The Parisian mob, fearful that Louis XVI was in league with the Prussians, stormed the Tuileries Palace and locked up the royal family. The monarchy was abolished, a republic declared, and a new Year One proclaimed. The Jacobin Convention took over, promulgating in 1792 an Edict of Fraternity espousing the export of revolutionary ideals, and in 1793, the king was executed.

5 LEVÉE EN MASSE 1792–1794

Forced mass military conscription prompted a counterrevolutionary uprising in the Vendée and elsewhere. Combined with the threat from a British landing at Toulon, this prompted the Convention in August 1793 to issue a decree of levée en masse—total mobilization of the entire population. The Vendée risings were brutally suppressed and the foreign armies thrown back.

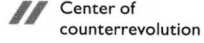 Center of counterrevolution   ▬ War in the Vendée

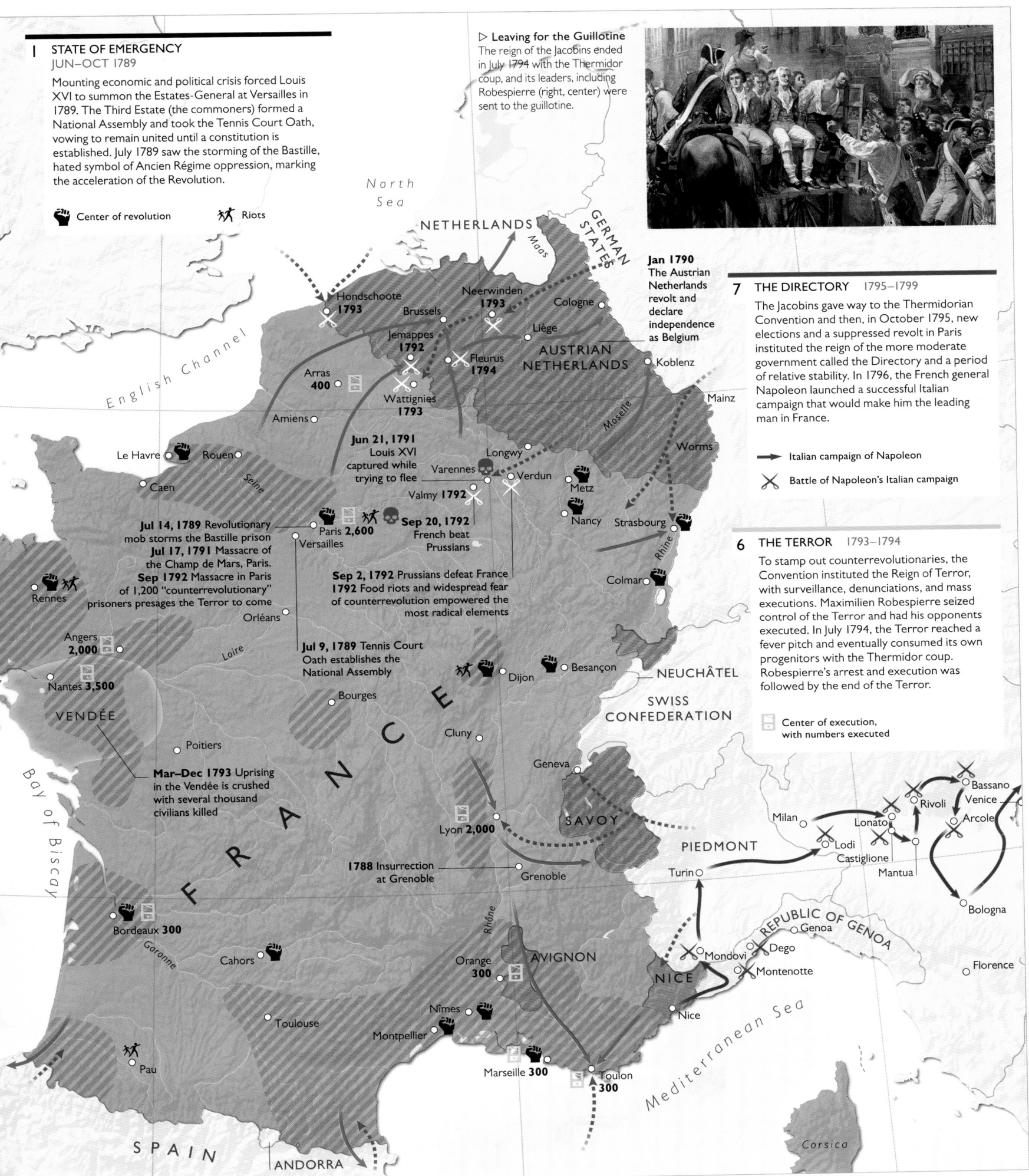

1 STATE OF EMERGENCY
JUN–OCT 1789

Mounting economic and political crisis forced Louis XVI to summon the Estates-General at Versailles in 1789. The Third Estate (the commoners) formed a National Assembly and took the Tennis Court Oath, vowing to remain united until a constitution is established. July 1789 saw the storming of the Bastille, hated symbol of Ancien Régime oppression, marking the acceleration of the Revolution.

✊ Center of revolution   🏃 Riots

▷ Leaving for the Guillotine
The reign of the Jacobins ended in July 1794 with the Thermidor coup, and its leaders, including Robespierre (right, center) were sent to the guillotine.

7 THE DIRECTORY 1795–1799

The Jacobins gave way to the Thermidorian Convention and then, in October 1795, new elections and a suppressed revolt in Paris instituted the reign of the more moderate government called the Directory and a period of relative stability. In 1796, the French general Napoleon launched a successful Italian campaign that would make him the leading man in France.

→ Italian campaign of Napoleon
✗ Battle of Napoleon's Italian campaign

6 THE TERROR 1793–1794

To stamp out counterrevolutionaries, the Convention instituted the Reign of Terror, with surveillance, denunciations, and mass executions. Maximilien Robespierre seized control of the Terror and had his opponents executed. In July 1794, the Terror reached a fever pitch and eventually consumed its own progenitors with the Thermidor coup. Robespierre's arrest and execution was followed by the end of the Terror.

🗃 Center of execution, with numbers executed

Jan 1790 The Austrian Netherlands revolt and declare independence as Belgium

Jun 21, 1791 Louis XVI captured while trying to flee

Jul 14, 1789 Revolutionary mob storms the Bastille prison
Jul 17, 1791 Massacre of the Champ de Mars, Paris.
Sep 1792 Massacre in Paris of 1,200 "counterrevolutionary" prisoners presages the Terror to come

Sep 20, 1792 French beat Prussians

Sep 2, 1792 Prussians defeat France
1792 Food riots and widespread fear of counterrevolution empowered the most radical elements

Jul 9, 1789 Tennis Court Oath establishes the National Assembly

Mar–Dec 1793 Uprising in the Vendée is crushed with several thousand civilians killed

1788 Insurrection at Grenoble

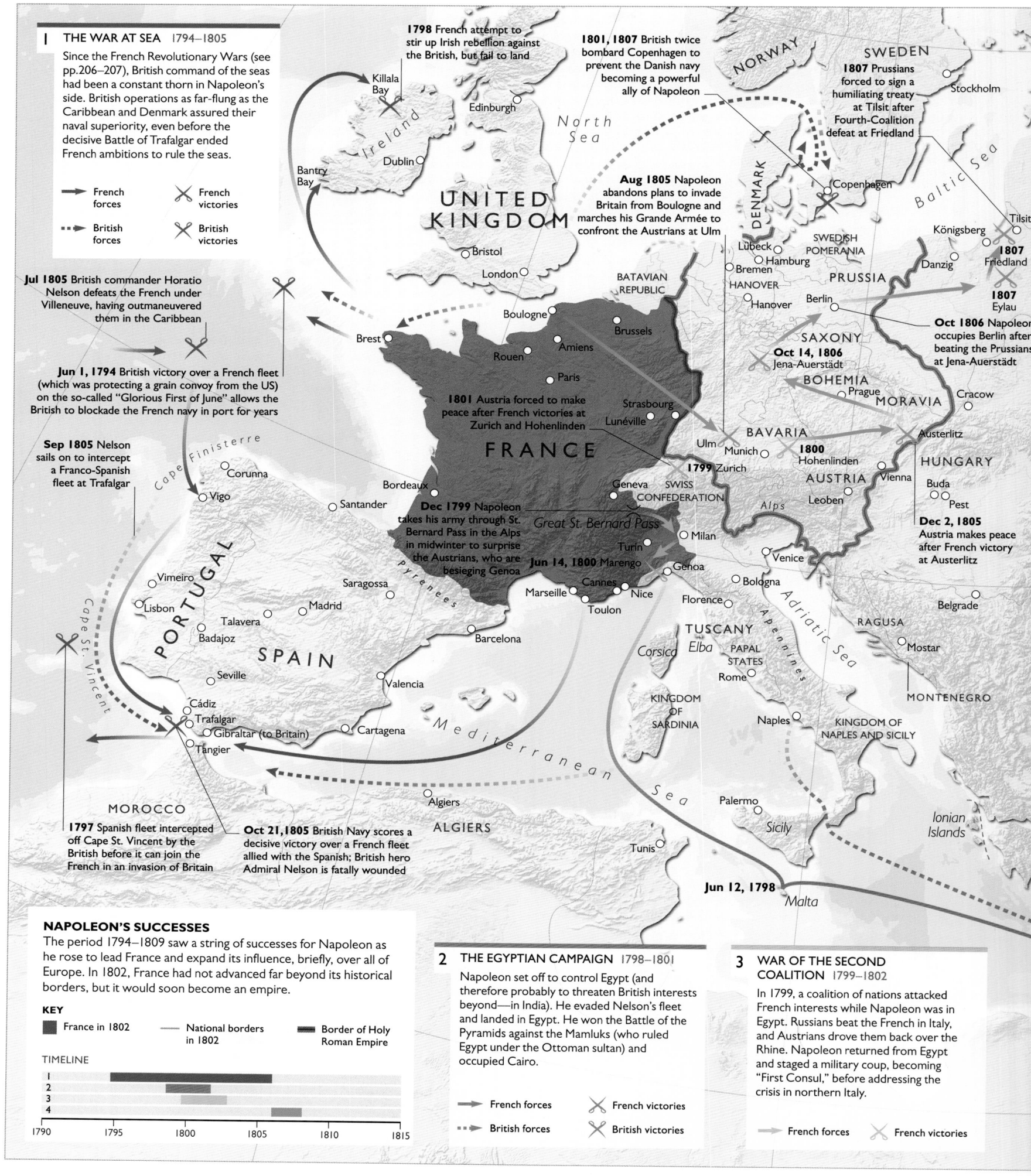

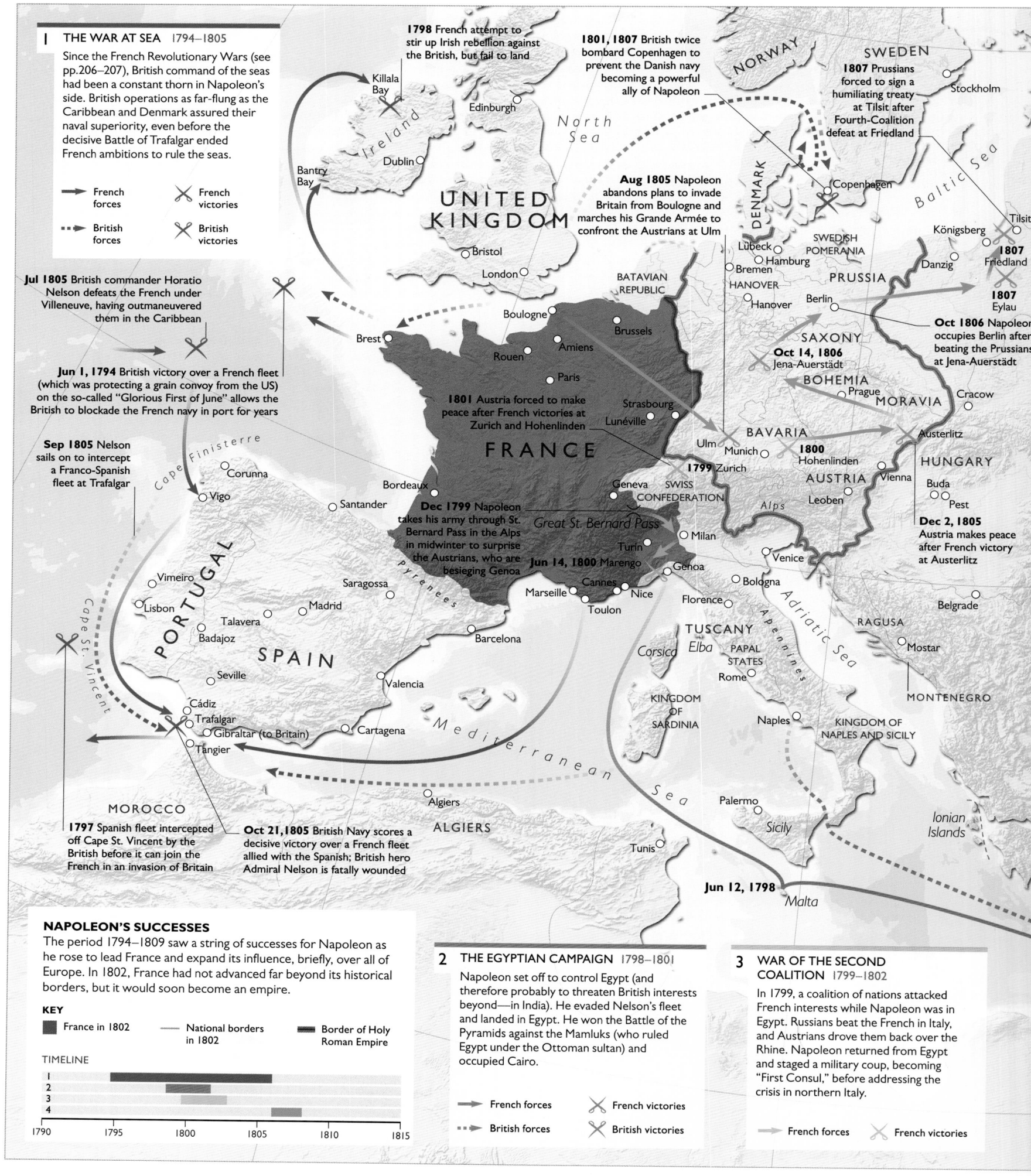

1 THE WAR AT SEA 1794–1805

Since the French Revolutionary Wars (see pp.206–207), British command of the seas had been a constant thorn in Napoleon's side. British operations as far-flung as the Caribbean and Denmark assured their naval superiority, even before the decisive Battle of Trafalgar ended French ambitions to rule the seas.

→ French forces ✕ French victories
┄➤ British forces ✕ British victories

1798 French attempt to stir up Irish rebellion against the British, but fail to land

1801, 1807 British twice bombard Copenhagen to prevent the Danish navy becoming a powerful ally of Napoleon

1807 Prussians forced to sign a humiliating treaty at Tilsit after Fourth-Coalition defeat at Friedland

Aug 1805 Napoleon abandons plans to invade Britain from Boulogne and marches his Grande Armée to confront the Austrians at Ulm

Jul 1805 British commander Horatio Nelson defeats the French under Villeneuve, having outmaneuvered them in the Caribbean

Jun 1, 1794 British victory over a French fleet (which was protecting a grain convoy from the US) on the so-called "Glorious First of June" allows the British to blockade the French navy in port for years

Sep 1805 Nelson sails on to intercept a Franco-Spanish fleet at Trafalgar

1801 Austria forced to make peace after French victories at Zurich and Hohenlinden

Oct 14, 1806 Jena-Auerstädt

Oct 1806 Napoleon occupies Berlin after beating the Prussians at Jena-Auerstädt

1807 Eylau

1800 Hohenlinden

1799 Zurich

Dec 1799 Napoleon takes his army through St. Bernard Pass in the Alps in midwinter to surprise the Austrians, who are besieging Genoa

Jun 14, 1800 Marengo

Dec 2, 1805 Austria makes peace after French victory at Austerlitz

1797 Spanish fleet intercepted off Cape St. Vincent by the British before it can join the French in an invasion of Britain

Oct 21, 1805 British Navy scores a decisive victory over a French fleet allied with the Spanish; British hero Admiral Nelson is fatally wounded

Jun 12, 1798

NAPOLEON'S SUCCESSES

The period 1794–1809 saw a string of successes for Napoleon as he rose to lead France and expand its influence, briefly, over all of Europe. In 1802, France had not advanced far beyond its historical borders, but it would soon become an empire.

KEY
■ France in 1802 — National borders in 1802 ■ Border of Holy Roman Empire

TIMELINE
1790 1795 1800 1805 1810 1815

2 THE EGYPTIAN CAMPAIGN 1798–1801

Napoleon set off to control Egypt (and therefore probably to threaten British interests beyond—in India). He evaded Nelson's fleet and landed in Egypt. He won the Battle of the Pyramids against the Mamluks (who ruled Egypt under the Ottoman sultan) and occupied Cairo.

→ French forces ✕ French victories
┄➤ British forces ✕ British victories

3 WAR OF THE SECOND COALITION 1799–1802

In 1799, a coalition of nations attacked French interests while Napoleon was in Egypt. Russians beat the French in Italy, and Austrians drove them back over the Rhine. Napoleon returned from Egypt and staged a military coup, becoming "First Consul," before addressing the crisis in northern Italy.

→ French forces ✕ French victories

NAPOLEON'S EMPIRE, 1812
At its greatest extent in 1812, Napoleon's domain included most of Europe. Only Britain consistently opposed him.

KEY
- French Empire
- French client states
- Independent allies
- Countries at war with Napoleon

4 WARS OF THE THIRD AND FOURTH COALITIONS
1805–1807

Austria joined a British-financed anti-French coalition that already included Russia, Sweden, and the Kingdom of Naples. After heavy defeats, Austria agreed on peace terms with France and Russia and retreated to Poland. France created the Confederation of the Rhine, as a client state, in the ashes of the Holy Roman Empire. Prussia was threatened by this and made war with France, which ended in Prussian defeat and the creation of another client, the Duchy of Warsaw (Poland), from former Austrian and Prussian lands.

- → French forces
- ✗ French victories

1798 Ottoman sultan declares jihad on Napoleon in response to his invasion of Egypt

Mar 1799 Undeterred by losing his fleet, Napoleon presses on and besieges the Ottomans at Acre, who resist him with the help of British guns

Aug 1798 In the Battle of the Nile, Nelson destroys the French fleet, crippling Napoleon's Egyptian campaign

Apr 1799 Napoleon wins a battle on his retreat to Egypt

Jul 21, 1798 Napoleon defeats the Mamluk rulers of Egypt and captures Cairo

MOLDAVIA — WALLACHIA — Bucharest — Varna — Constantinople — Smyrna — OTTOMAN EMPIRE — Crete — Cyprus — Beirut — Damascus — Acre — Jaffa — Gaza — Jerusalem — Alexandria — EGYPT — Cairo — to Aswan

NAPOLEON ADVANCES

Napoleon established his reputation as leader of the French Revolutionary Army with his bold, unexpected maneuvers against Austria in Italy (1796–1797). By 1804, 10 years after France's republican revolution, he had crowned himself emperor. By 1809, he had complete control of central Europe.

From the maelstrom of the French Revolutionary Wars, Napoleon Bonaparte emerged as a young, ambitious general. Among his early remarkable successes, he pushed the armies of Austria and the kingdom of Sardinia out of northern Italy (1796–1797). Austrian forces retreated all the way back to Vienna, leaving northern Italy in the hands of the French. By 1809, Napoleon had absorbed the southern Netherlands (Batavia), the west bank of the Rhine, and a large part of Italy into French territory. He had created client states under French control (for example, the Confederation of the Rhine). He had placed family members on thrones all over Europe, married Marie Louise of Austria, and made Prussia and Austria reluctant allies.

Throughout, Britain remained at war with Napoleon. The British established naval superiority, and it was naval power that thwarted Napoleon's ambitions in Egypt and the Middle East. Napoleon retaliated by isolating Britain with a trade blockade called the Continental System. Its aim of destroying British commerce failed, however, as it was impossible to enforce compliance throughout Europe, from Portugal to Russia.

◁ **The man and the myth**
Jacques-Louis David's equestrian portrait (1800–1801), which pictured Napoleon crossing the Alps, fed into the leader's desired image of a classical hero.

"In war there is but one favorable moment; the great art is to seize it!"

NAPOLEON BONAPARTE, 1804

NAPOLEON BONAPARTE
1769–1821

Napoleon rose to prominence during the French Revolution and led several successful campaigns during the French Revolutionary Wars. As Napoleon I, he was endorsed by the Pope as Emperor of the French 1804–1814, and again in 1815 (see pp.210–211). Napoleon dominated European and global affairs for more than a decade while leading France against a series of coalitions in the Napoleonic Wars. He won most of these wars and the vast majority of his battles, building an empire that ruled over continental Europe before its final collapse in 1815.

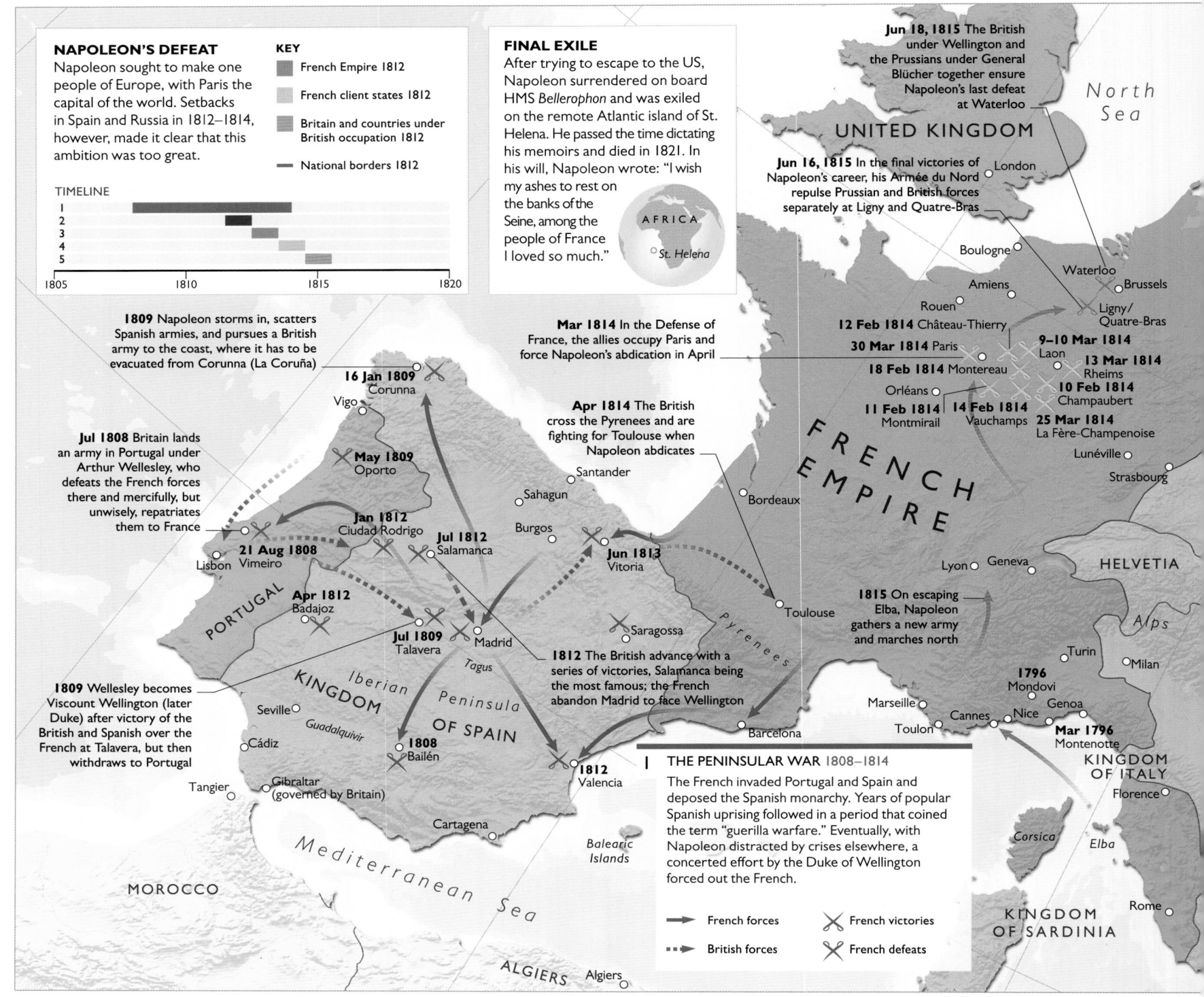

NAPOLEON'S DEFEAT
Napoleon sought to make one people of Europe, with Paris the capital of the world. Setbacks in Spain and Russia in 1812–1814, however, made it clear that this ambition was too great.

KEY
- French Empire 1812
- French client states 1812
- Britain and countries under British occupation 1812
- National borders 1812

TIMELINE
1805 1810 1815 1820
1 2 3 4 5

FINAL EXILE
After trying to escape to the US, Napoleon surrendered on board HMS *Bellerophon* and was exiled on the remote Atlantic island of St. Helena. He passed the time dictating his memoirs and died in 1821. In his will, Napoleon wrote: "I wish my ashes to rest on the banks of the Seine, among the people of France I loved so much."

AFRICA
St. Helena

Jun 18, 1815 The British under Wellington and the Prussians under General Blücher together ensure Napoleon's last defeat at Waterloo

North Sea

UNITED KINGDOM

Jun 16, 1815 In the final victories of Napoleon's career, his Armée du Nord repulse Prussian and British forces separately at Ligny and Quatre-Bras

London

1809 Napoleon storms in, scatters Spanish armies, and pursues a British army to the coast, where it has to be evacuated from Corunna (La Coruña)

Mar 1814 In the Defense of France, the allies occupy Paris and force Napoleon's abdication in April

Boulogne
Amiens
Waterloo
Brussels
Ligny/Quatre-Bras

16 Jan 1809 Corunna
Vigo

12 Feb 1814 Château-Thierry
30 Mar 1814 Paris
18 Feb 1814 Montereau
Orléans
11 Feb 1814 Montmirail
14 Feb 1814 Vauchamps
9–10 Mar 1814 Laon
13 Mar 1814 Rheims
10 Feb 1814 Champaubert
25 Mar 1814 La Fère-Champenoise
Lunéville
Strasbourg

Jul 1808 Britain lands an army in Portugal under Arthur Wellesley, who defeats the French forces there and mercifully, but unwisely, repatriates them to France

May 1809 Oporto

Apr 1814 The British cross the Pyrenees and are fighting for Toulouse when Napoleon abdicates

Santander
Sahagún
Burgos
Bordeaux

F R E N C H   E M P I R E

Jan 1812 Ciudad Rodrigo
Jul 1812 Salamanca
Jun 1813 Vitoria

21 Aug 1808 Vimeiro
Lisbon

Apr 1812 Badajoz

PORTUGAL

Jul 1809 Talavera
Madrid
Tagus

1812 The British advance with a series of victories, Salamanca being the most famous; the French abandon Madrid to face Wellington

Saragossa
Toulouse

Lyon
Geneva
HELVETIA

Alps

1815 On escaping Elba, Napoleon gathers a new army and marches north

1809 Wellesley becomes Viscount Wellington (later Duke) after victory of the British and Spanish over the French at Talavera, but then withdraws to Portugal

Iberian Peninsula
KINGDOM OF SPAIN
Seville
Guadalquivir
Cádiz

1808 Bailén

Tangier
Gibraltar (governed by Britain)

1812 Valencia

Barcelona
Marseille
Toulon

1796 Mondovi
Turin
Milan

Genoa
Cannes
Nice

Mar 1796 Montenotte

KINGDOM OF ITALY
Florence

Cartagena
Balearic Islands

THE PENINSULAR WAR 1808–1814
The French invaded Portugal and Spain and deposed the Spanish monarchy. Years of popular Spanish uprising followed in a period that coined the term "guerilla warfare." Eventually, with Napoleon distracted by crises elsewhere, a concerted effort by the Duke of Wellington forced out the French.

Corsica
Elba

MOROCCO

Mediterranean Sea

KINGDOM OF SARDINIA
Rome

French forces
British forces
French victories
French defeats

ALGIERS
Algiers

NAPOLEON'S DOWNFALL

Napoleon's efforts to dominate Europe took him to the far eastern and western ends of the continent. After failing to control Spain, Portugal, and Russia, he was met and defeated by a coalition of nations in central Europe. He was exiled first to Elba, then to far-off St. Helena.

Napoleon's 1806–07 defeat of Prussia and the Fourth Coalition (see pp.208–209) seemed to consolidate his hold over Europe, but Britain had not made peace, and he would not rest. His strategy to defeat Britain—a trade blockade called the Continental System—needed the cooperation of Spain, Portugal, and Russia. The Spanish monarchy was sympathetic, but a French army invaded Portugal in 1807 to force the Portuguese hand, and soon also replaced the Spanish king to assert direct control in Spain as well.

In May 1809, a popular revolt in Madrid spread across Spain and began a guerilla war that Napoleon came to know as his "Spanish ulcer." Although the French leader took matters into his own hands early on and chased the British out of Spain, he was distracted by a new declaration of war by Austria. He beat the Austrians at Wagram, but with huge losses—the cost of controlling Europe was beginning to mount. Napoleon's plans unraveled more profoundly when he

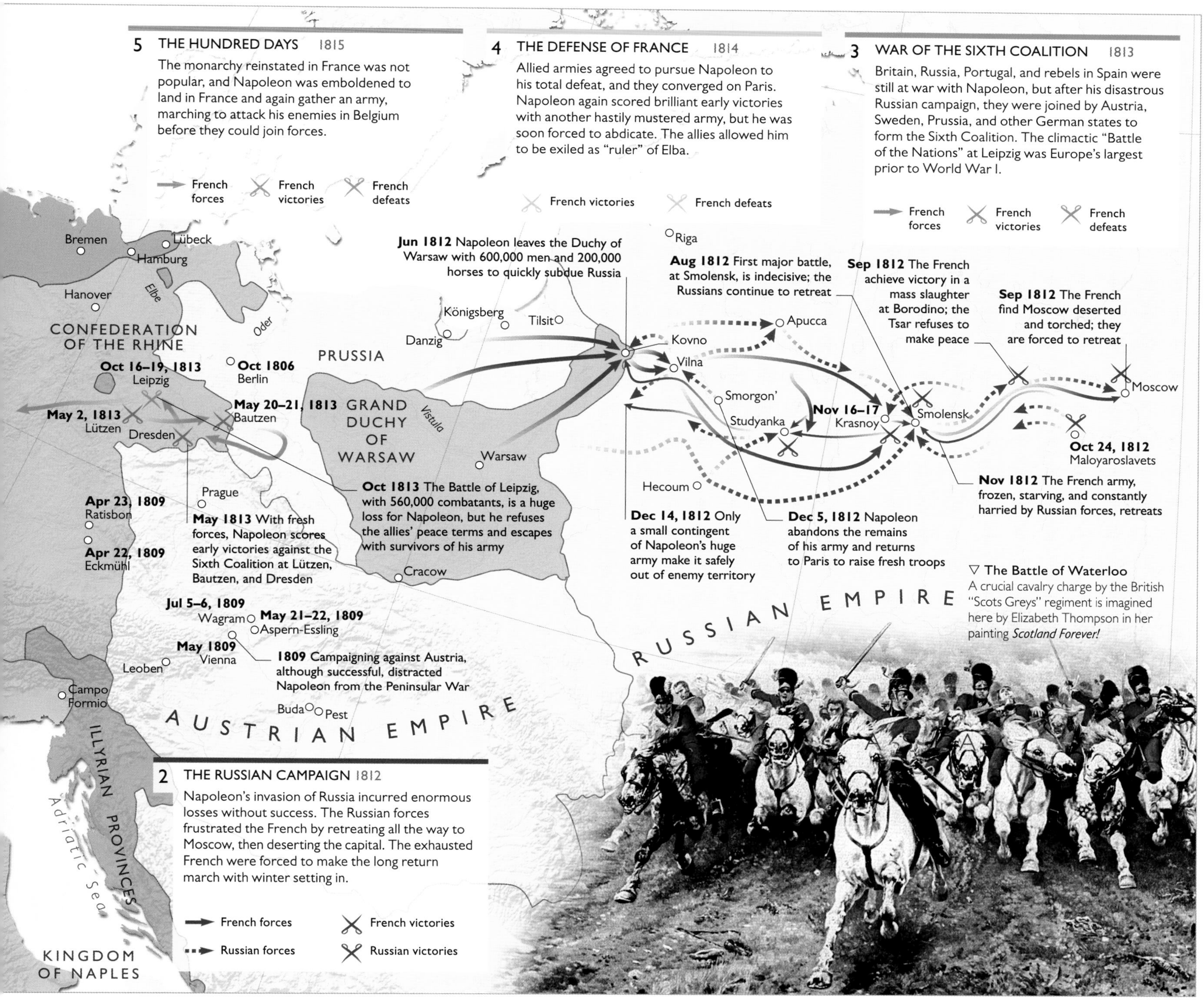
5 THE HUNDRED DAYS 1815
The monarchy reinstated in France was not popular, and Napoleon was emboldened to land in France and again gather an army, marching to attack his enemies in Belgium before they could join forces.
French forces
French victories
French defeats
4 THE DEFENSE OF FRANCE 1814
Allied armies agreed to pursue Napoleon to his total defeat, and they converged on Paris. Napoleon again scored brilliant early victories with another hastily mustered army, but he was soon forced to abdicate. The allies allowed him to be exiled as "ruler" of Elba.
French victories
French defeats
3 WAR OF THE SIXTH COALITION 1813
Britain, Russia, Portugal, and rebels in Spain were still at war with Napoleon, but after his disastrous Russian campaign, they were joined by Austria, Sweden, Prussia, and other German states to form the Sixth Coalition. The climactic "Battle of the Nations" at Leipzig was Europe's largest prior to World War I.
French forces
French victories
French defeats
Bremen
Lübeck
Hamburg
Hanover
Elbe
Oder
CONFEDERATION OF THE RHINE
Oct 16–19, 1813 Leipzig
Oct 1806 Berlin
PRUSSIA
May 2, 1813 Lützen
Dresden
May 20–21, 1813 Bautzen
GRAND DUCHY OF WARSAW
Vistula
Warsaw
Königsberg
Tilsit
Danzig
Jun 1812 Napoleon leaves the Duchy of Warsaw with 600,000 men and 200,000 horses to quickly subdue Russia
Riga
Aug 1812 First major battle, at Smolensk, is indecisive; the Russians continue to retreat
Sep 1812 The French achieve victory in a mass slaughter at Borodino; the Tsar refuses to make peace
Sep 1812 The French find Moscow deserted and torched; they are forced to retreat
Apucca
Kovno
Vilna
Smorgon'
Studyanka
Nov 16–17 Krasnoy
Smolensk
Moscow
Oct 24, 1812 Maloyaroslavets
Hecoum
Nov 1812 The French army, frozen, starving, and constantly harried by Russian forces, retreats
Dec 14, 1812 Only a small contingent of Napoleon's huge army make it safely out of enemy territory
Dec 5, 1812 Napoleon abandons the remains of his army and returns to Paris to raise fresh troops
Prague
Apr 23, 1809 Ratisbon
Apr 22, 1809 Eckmühl
May 1813 With fresh forces, Napoleon scores early victories against the Sixth Coalition at Lützen, Bautzen, and Dresden
Oct 1813 The Battle of Leipzig, with 560,000 combatants, is a huge loss for Napoleon, but he refuses the allies' peace terms and escapes with survivors of his army
Cracow
Jul 5–6, 1809 Wagram
May 21–22, 1809 Aspern-Essling
May 1809 Vienna
1809 Campaigning against Austria, although successful, distracted Napoleon from the Peninsular War
Leoben
Campo Formio
Buda
Pest
RUSSIAN EMPIRE
AUSTRIAN EMPIRE
ILLYRIAN PROVINCES
Adriatic Sea
KINGDOM OF NAPLES
2 THE RUSSIAN CAMPAIGN 1812
Napoleon's invasion of Russia incurred enormous losses without success. The Russian forces frustrated the French by retreating all the way to Moscow, then deserting the capital. The exhausted French were forced to make the long return march with winter setting in.
French forces
Russian forces
French victories
Russian victories

▽ **The Battle of Waterloo**
A crucial cavalry charge by the British "Scots Greys" regiment is imagined here by Elizabeth Thompson in her painting *Scotland Forever!*

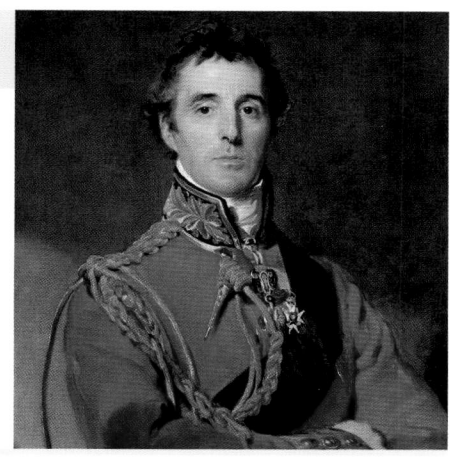

when he attempted to force the cooperation of Russia, which had been persuaded by Britain to renounce the Continental System. In 1812, he invaded Russia with a vast army but retreated with a few ragged, emaciated survivors. The other European powers saw their chance and assembled the largest anti-French coalition yet, which pursued him eventually to Paris and forced him into exile. Although Napoleon escaped for a final flourish at Waterloo, his time was over.

> *"I used to say of him [Napoleon] that his presence on the field made the difference of 40,000 men."*
>
> ARTHUR WELLESLEY, DUKE OF WELLINGTON, 1831

DUKE OF WELLINGTON
1769–1852

Irish-born Arthur Wellesley, later the Duke of Wellington, first distinguished himself fighting the Kingdom of Mysore and the Marathas (people from Maharashtra state) in India. His success in the Peninsular War made him a British national hero, a status enhanced by his leading role in the defeat of Napoleon at Waterloo in 1815. Usually a cautious general, he was also capable of bold attacking strokes, as at Salamanca in 1812. He was never careless of his men's lives and took only necessary risks.

THE INDUSTRIAL REVOLUTION

Industrialization is probably the single greatest event in world economic history, at least since the advent of agriculture several millennia earlier. The process, which began in the late 18th century, had far-reaching consequences that would reshape the world.

△ **Slave to the machine**
This engraving celebrating American inventor Eli Whitney's cotton gin also reveals the human suffering and exploitation that helped to make the Industrial Revolution possible.

▽ **Flying shuttles**
Patented by John Kay in England in 1733, these shuttles drew threads back and forth on mechanical looms, halving the labor force required to produce cloth.

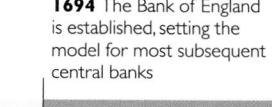

Before the late 18th century, the Western world's economy was largely static. Although it periodically expanded as populations grew, this population growth tended to outstrip the carrying capacity of the economy, leading to famine, disease, or war and resulting in population crashes followed by economic contraction.

However, from the late 18th century, economic growth broke free of this trap and began to rise continually. What changed was that the efficiency of the economy began to increase relentlessly. Known as the Industrial Revolution, this transformation began in Britain and then spread to the rest of the world.

The Industrial Revolution was not a single event but a series of changes that took place in a piecemeal fashion in different places and different parts of the economy at different times. Some of these changes had already begun well before the 18th century. For example, a miniature revolution in the manufacture of woolen textiles, thanks to water-mill technology, can be traced to the 13th century.

Labor, materials, and technology

Industrialization was underpinned by population growth and enabled by the Agricultural Revolution (see pp.194–195), which had dramatically increased agricultural efficiency and output. Another contributor was slavery. The abuse and exploitation of slave labor in the New World drove an explosive growth in the production of raw cotton to fuel the dynamic textile industries of the era. Slavery also enabled large-scale production of sugar, tobacco, and other raw materials. The profits from the trade contributed to the growing financial might of Europe, and later the US, underwriting the injections of capital that helped transform cottage industries into global ones.

The Industrial Revolution was also powered by changes in technology. The invention of the steam engine provided the power for the textile mills and other factory machinery. The need to fuel these engines created an increased demand for coal that could be met because of improved mining and better distribution, first by canal and later by rail. In the later part of the revolution, improvements in steel-making provided an impetus to change as stronger, more versatile kinds of steel began to replace iron.

A global phenomenon

Although the revolution began in Britain, it was not long before it spread throughout Europe and to America. Industrialization was readily adopted in countries with enthusiastic entrepreneurs and governments open to change. In the US, iron production and shipbuilding

SEEDING INDUSTRIALIZATION

The Industrial Revolution involved a complex set of factors. Demographics—the growth and distribution of population—influenced the supply of raw materials and demand for products. This in turn drove developments in finance, which provided the capital needed by industries. Innovations in communication, power, and transportation—inspired by new materials and the rising social and economic demand—led to a dramatic boost in productivity.

FINANCE

DEMOGRAPHICS

INNOVATION

TRADE

TRANSPORTATION

1694 The Bank of England is established, setting the model for most subsequent central banks

1750 Global population of about 715 million, mostly concentrated in south and east Asia, will almost double over the next century with the most growth in Europe and the Americas

1720 The South Sea Bubble, rampant speculation in a British Company granted a monopoly to trade with South America, causes a financial crisis

| 1690 | 1710 | 1730 | 1750 |

◁ **The Barton Aqueduct**
Part of a coal-shipping canal network that made Francis Egerton, the Duke of Bridgewater, a fortune when completed in 1761, this aqueduct helped to transport raw material from the duke's mines to market at a vastly reduced cost.

were the first industries to undergo transformation. In Europe, Belgium and Prussia led the way as the French Revolution initially stalled development in France. A fresh wave of industrialization followed German unification in the 1870s, and by 1900, industrial output in Germany and the US had overtaken that in Britain.

The consequences of industrialization

With better transportation, it was no longer necessary to build factories close to the sources of raw materials. Industries were built in cities, and urban populations grew rapidly. In 1800, there were 28 cities in Europe with populations over 100,000; by 1848, there were 45 such cities. However, conditions for urban workers were harsh. Wages were low, living standards were poor, and inequality grew, especially during the early part of the revolution.

As the revolution progressed, new patterns of trade emerged. Improvements in transportation, combined with the invention of communication technologies such as the telegraph, led to a rise in global trade. In turn, trade fueled

further growth as raw materials could be sourced more cheaply and markets for finished products expanded. The Industrial Revolution has many echoes in the present—not least, the changes in climate we are now experiencing, the onset of which can be traced to the increased use of fossil fuels such as coal in the very first wave of industrialization.

▽ **Bessemer converters**
The Bessemer process, which used vast furnaces such as those installed at the Krupp Steel Works at Essen in Germany, transformed industrial output in Europe.

> *"The process of industrialization is necessarily painful."*
>
> E. P. THOMPSON, BRITISH HISTORIAN, FROM *THE MAKING OF THE ENGLISH WORKING CLASS*, 1963

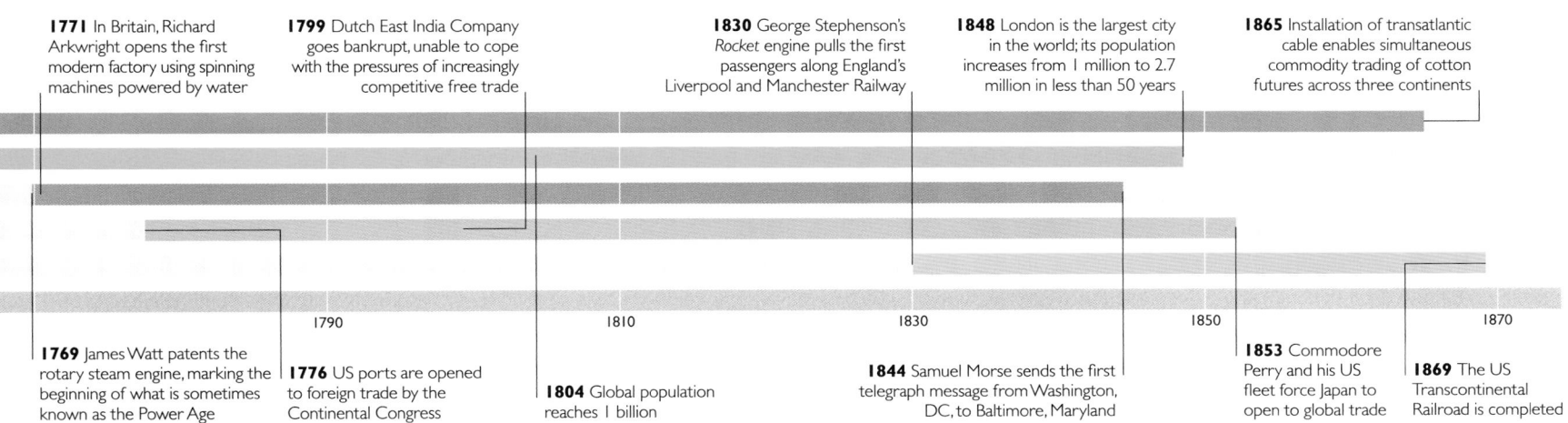

1771 In Britain, Richard Arkwright opens the first modern factory using spinning machines powered by water

1799 Dutch East India Company goes bankrupt, unable to cope with the pressures of increasingly competitive free trade

1830 George Stephenson's *Rocket* engine pulls the first passengers along England's Liverpool and Manchester Railway

1848 London is the largest city in the world; its population increases from 1 million to 2.7 million in less than 50 years

1865 Installation of transatlantic cable enables simultaneous commodity trading of cotton futures across three continents

1790   1810   1830   1850   1870

1769 James Watt patents the rotary steam engine, marking the beginning of what is sometimes known as the Power Age

1776 US ports are opened to foreign trade by the Continental Congress

1804 Global population reaches 1 billion

1844 Samuel Morse sends the first telegraph message from Washington, DC, to Baltimore, Maryland

1853 Commodore Perry and his US fleet force Japan to open to global trade

1869 The US Transcontinental Railroad is completed

JAMES WATT
1736–1819

Born in Greenock, Scotland, in 1736, inventor and engineer James Watt is chiefly remembered for his improvements to steam engine technology. Watt worked to make Thomas Newcomen's 1712 steam engine more efficient by creating a separate condensing chamber to prevent loss of steam. Watt patented his invention in 1769.

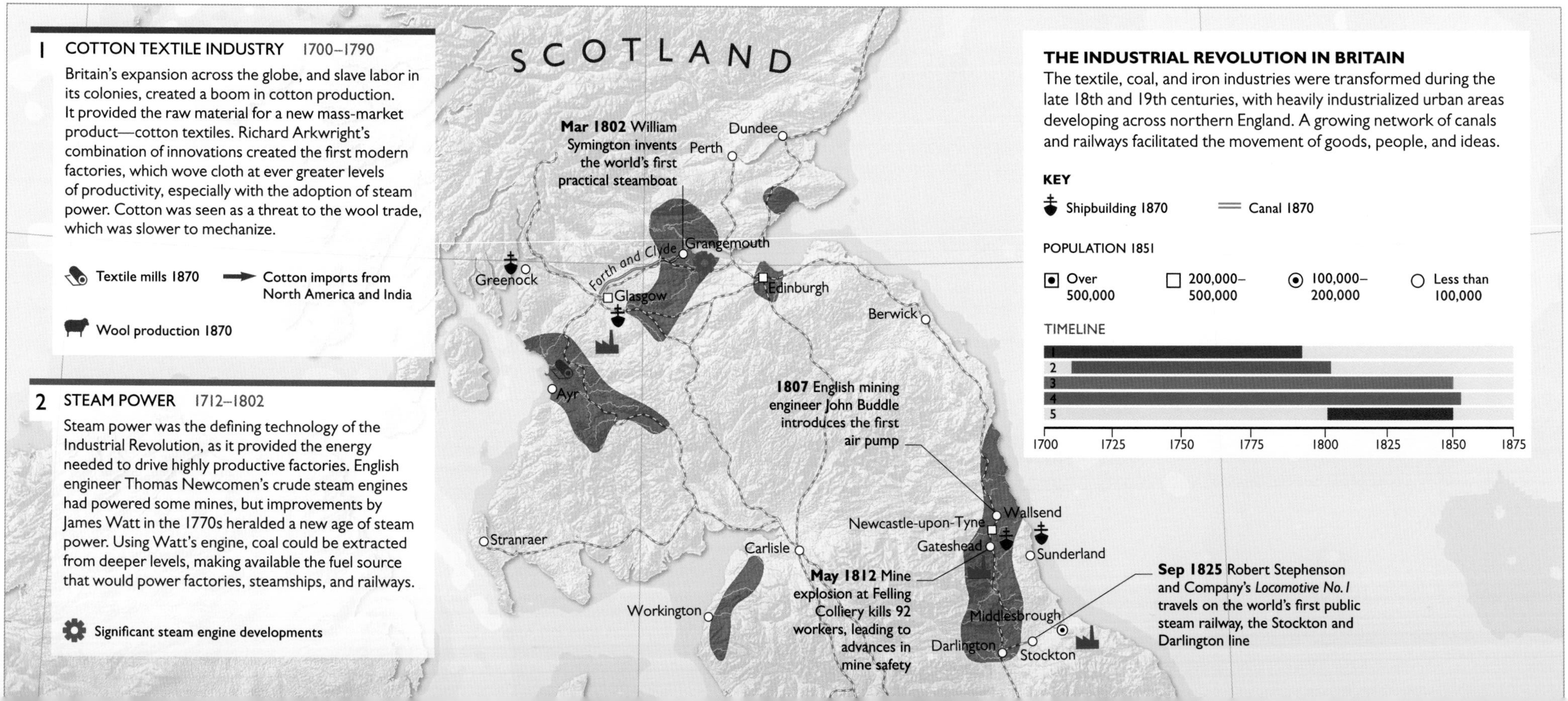

INDUSTRIAL BRITAIN

The Industrial Revolution, which began in Britain in the late 18th century, was a period of rapid development in industry that led to changes in politics, society, and the economy. It was in Britain that many of the technological advances occurred that would drive mechanization, urbanization, and capitalism, and lead to the growth of industries such as cotton, coal, and iron.

Many factors contributed to the start of the Industrial Revolution in Britain, as well as to its rapid progression. One significant cause was the Agricultural Revolution (see pp.194–195), which saw improvements to the farming process. Agricultural production became more efficient, and Britain was able to sustain a larger workforce. Fewer agricultural workers were needed to work on the land, and many were now able to move to urban areas to find work in the new factories. The political system in Britain was also conducive to rapid industrialization. As a nation now dependent on trading across the globe, the British government took steps to encourage commercial innovation, such as introducing laws

to protect intellectual property rights. The geographical location of Britain was a key factor, allowing it to communicate and trade with the rest of the world. Britain also had an abundance of natural resources, such as water to power mills and factories, coal to burn for energy, and ores to smelt for metals, which proved invaluable.

Combined with these factors, a series of important technological innovations in the 18th and early 19th century, funded by an increasingly wealthy middle class, revolutionized many industrial processes. By the end of the 19th century, Britain was transformed from a predominantly rural society into an urban one, and almost every aspect of daily life had been altered.

THE INDUSTRIAL REVOLUTION IN BRITAIN

The textile, coal, and iron industries were transformed during the late 18th and 19th centuries, with heavily industrialized urban areas developing across northern England. A growing network of canals and railways facilitated the movement of goods, people, and ideas.

KEY

⚓ Shipbuilding 1870   ═ Canal 1870

POPULATION 1851

◉ Over 500,000   □ 200,000– 500,000   ◉ 100,000– 200,000   ○ Less than 100,000

TIMELINE

1700	1725	1750	1775	1800	1825	1850	1875

2
3
4
5

---

1 COTTON TEXTILE INDUSTRY 1700–1790

Britain's expansion across the globe, and slave labor in its colonies, created a boom in cotton production. It provided the raw material for a new mass-market product—cotton textiles. Richard Arkwright's combination of innovations created the first modern factories, which wove cloth at ever greater levels of productivity, especially with the adoption of steam power. Cotton was seen as a threat to the wool trade, which was slower to mechanize.

🏭 Textile mills 1870   → Cotton imports from North America and India

🐑 Wool production 1870

2 STEAM POWER 1712–1802

Steam power was the defining technology of the Industrial Revolution, as it provided the energy needed to drive highly productive factories. English engineer Thomas Newcomen's crude steam engines had powered some mines, but improvements by James Watt in the 1770s heralded a new age of steam power. Using Watt's engine, coal could be extracted from deeper levels, making available the fuel source that would power factories, steamships, and railways.

⚙ Significant steam engine developments

SCOTLAND

Greenock

Mar 1802 William Symington invents the world's first practical steamboat

Grangemouth

Forth and Clyde Canal

Glasgow

Ayr

Stranraer

Dundee

Perth

Edinburgh

Berwick

Carlisle

Workington

Newcastle-upon-Tyne

Wallsend

Gateshead

Sunderland

Middlesbrough

Darlington

Stockton

1807 English mining engineer John Buddle introduces the first air pump

May 1812 Mine explosion at Felling Colliery kills 92 workers, leading to advances in mine safety

Sep 1825 Robert Stephenson and Company's Locomotive No.1 travels on the world's first public steam railway, the Stockton and Darlington line

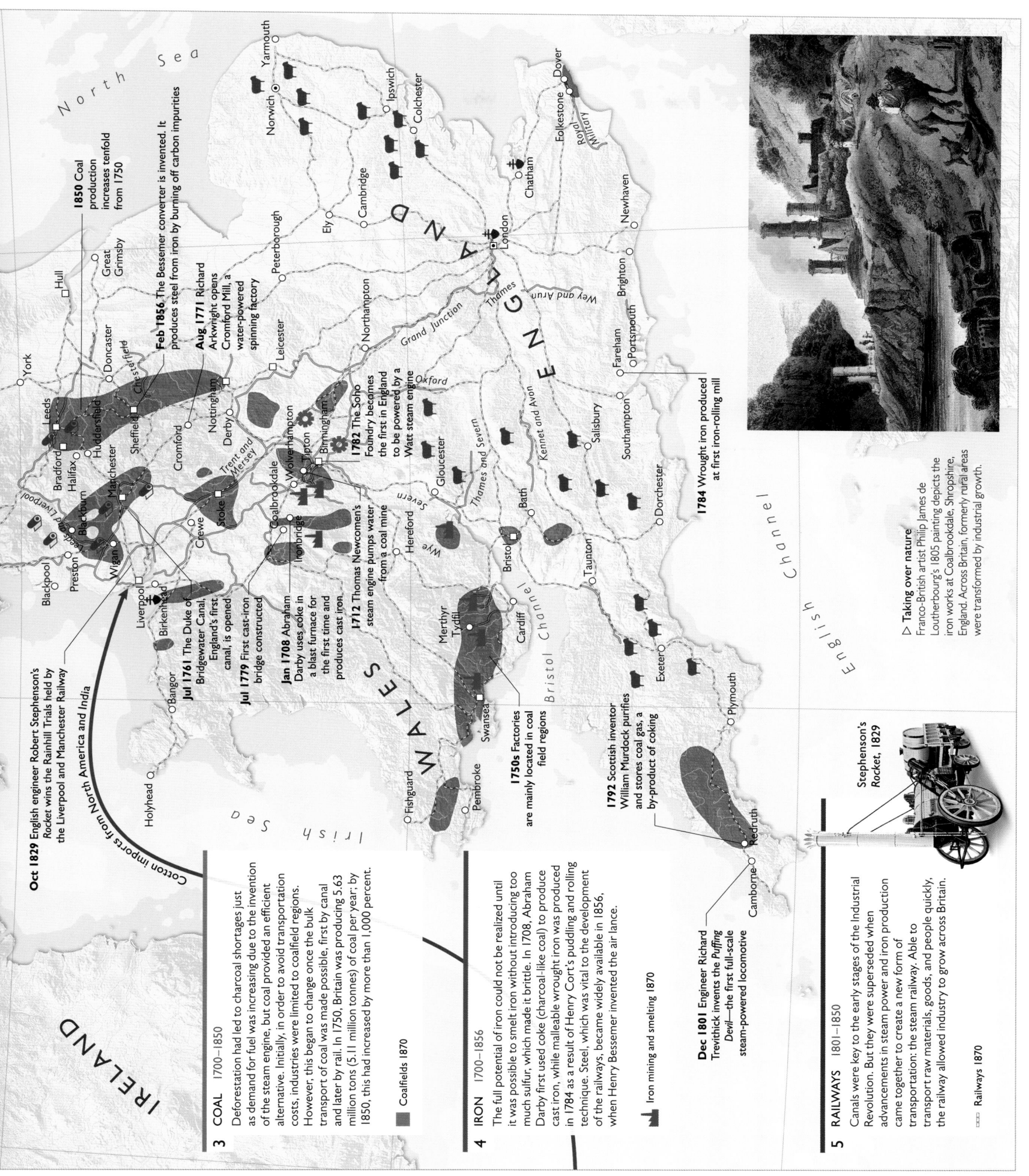

1850 Coal production increases tenfold from 1750

Feb 1856 The Bessemer converter is invented. It produces steel from iron by burning off carbon impurities

Aug 1771 Richard Arkwright opens Cromford Mill, a water-powered spinning factory

1782 The Soho Foundry becomes the first in England to be powered by a Watt steam engine

1784 Wrought iron produced at first iron-rolling mill

1712 Thomas Newcomen's steam engine pumps water from a coal mine

Jan 1708 Abraham Darby uses coke in a blast furnace for the first time and produces cast iron.

Jul 1779 First cast-iron bridge constructed

Jul 1761 The Duke of Bridgewater Canal, England's first canal, is opened

Oct 1829 English engineer Robert Stephenson's *Rocket* wins the Rainhill Trials held by the Liverpool and Manchester Railway

Cotton imports from North America and India

1750s Factories are mainly located in coal field regions

1792 Scottish inventor William Murdock purifies and stores coal gas, a by-product of coking

Dec 1801 Engineer Richard Trevithick invents the *Puffing Devil*—the first full-scale steam-powered locomotive

Stephenson's *Rocket*, 1829

△ **Taking over nature**
Franco-British artist Philip James de Loutherbourg's 1805 painting depicts the iron works at Coalbrookdale, Shropshire, England. Across Britain, formerly rural areas were transformed by industrial growth.

3 COAL 1700–1850

Deforestation had led to charcoal shortages just as demand for fuel was increasing due to the invention of the steam engine, but coal provided an efficient alternative. Initially, in order to avoid transportation costs, industries were limited to coalfield regions. However, this began to change once the bulk transport of coal was made possible, first by canal and later by rail. In 1750, Britain was producing 5.63 million tons (5.11 million tonnes) of coal per year; by 1850, this had increased by more than 1,000 percent.

■ Coalfields 1870

4 IRON 1700–1856

The full potential of iron could not be realized until it was possible to smelt iron without introducing too much sulfur, which made it brittle. In 1708, Abraham Darby first used coke (charcoal-like coal) to produce cast iron, while malleable wrought iron was produced in 1784 as a result of Henry Cort's puddling and rolling technique. Steel, which was vital to the development of the railways, became widely available in 1856, when Henry Bessemer invented the air lance.

▲ Iron mining and smelting 1870

5 RAILWAYS 1801–1850

Canals were key to the early stages of the Industrial Revolution. But they were superseded when advancements in steam power and iron production came together to create a new form of transportation: the steam railway. Able to transport raw materials, goods, and people quickly, the railway allowed industry to grow across Britain.

▭ Railways 1870

ROMANTICISM AND NATIONALISM

Romanticism and Nationalism were intertwined cultural and political movements that spread across the Western world from the late 18th to the early 20th centuries, emphasizing emotion and patriotism over reason and cosmopolitanism.

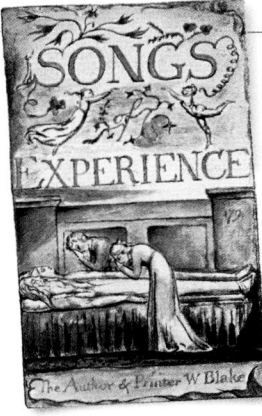

△ **Early Romantic poetry**
The title page of the 1794 poem *Songs of Experience* was written, illustrated, and hand-printed by William Blake—a key early proponent of both Romanticism and Nationalism.

Romanticism was a cultural movement that began in the late 18th century and affected art, literature, music, theater, and politics. It was a reaction against the rationalism of the Enlightenment (see pp.202–203) and insisted on the primacy of imagination and emotion. The Romantics were fascinated with nature and its relationship with the human psyche. This led to the belief that a land and its people shared a special bond, hence the Romantic enthusiasm for folk culture and legends.

Romanticism became a driving force for the emerging Nationalist movement, which declared the nation state to be the defining unit in politics, culture, language, and history. Aspirations for nationhood, as opposed to sprawling dynasties such as the Austro-Hungarian Empire, became bound up with liberal aspirations for greater rights for citizens.

Romantic Nationalism and culture

Culture was to be at the forefront of Romantic Nationalism, celebrating the unifying legends and arts of traditional culture and creating new ones. Writers collected folk tales and made up their own in literature, drama, and national epics. Painters sought to capture characteristic scenes or create nationalist allegories. Composers incorporated folk songs and country dances into their music, produced stirring new anthems, and, at their most ambitious, sought to create what German composer Richard Wagner called a *Gesamtkunstwerk*, or "total work of art"—a synthesis of arts in the service of the soul of the nation.

Romantic Nationalism shaped the world order in the early 20th century. It can be credited with the creation of independent states in Europe and the birth of populist movements that resulted in claims of supremacy based on ethnic identities. For example, in Germany, the notion of racial superiority of Germans over other peoples contributed to the rise of Nazism.

◁ **Influential composer**
Richard Wagner's *Ring Cycle* of operas was based on Germanic legends and is seen as the high point of Romanticism. It was embraced by German Nationalists as a potential foundational myth.

Revolutionary sentiments
French artist Eugène Delacroix's painting *Liberty Leading The People* (1830), based on an uprising he witnessed, is a classic example of Romantic Nationalist art, symbolizing the revolutionary power of liberal, nationalist aspiration.

THE REVOLUTIONS OF 1848

Frustration was growing at the failure of the European ruling classes to modernize or to answer the aspirations of a wealthier population for greater liberties and rights to nationhood. Tension boiled over in 1848 as a string of revolts and rebellions flared up across the continent, prompting a bloody, reactionary backlash.

The Congress of Vienna in 1815, after the Napoleonic Wars (see pp.208–211), was supposed to create a lasting European settlement. Statesmen from the powers that had brought down Napoleonic France gathered at Vienna to decide how to redraw the borders of Europe. The resulting agreement was essentially conservative: an attempt to stamp out nationalism, a movement centerd on the concept of the nation as a legitimate and necessary political and cultural unit, the rise of which, in France, had shattered the old order of Europe. And, for 30 years, it succeeded.

However, major change in the years following the congress continued and even accelerated. The population of Europe had increased by 50 percent since 1800, and it had urbanized rapidly, with the number of cities having populations over 100,000 increasing from 28 in 1800 to 45 in 1848. In the political arena, the preservation of the Holy Alliance empires—Prussia, Russia, and, especially, Austria—had come at the cost of suppressing and frustrating awakening nationalist sentiment, particularly in Germany, Poland, and Italy.

Social and economic changes had led to the rapid growth of the middle classes. Such growth fostered liberal sentiments that fueled an appetite for change, with demands for greater representation and freedoms—including the freedom for nations to self-determine.

On Europe's borders, the crumbling of the Ottoman Empire lent impetus to Balkan drives for self-determination, with the Serbs gaining autonomy in 1817 and the Greeks in 1821 (see pp.266–267). Revolutionary sentiment that had convulsed Europe in the Napoleonic era stirred once more, and the growing demand for a more liberal political order meant that many parts of Europe were like a tinderbox, waiting for a spark.

SOWING SEEDS FOR THE FUTURE
THE SIGNIFICANCE OF THE 1848 REVOLUTIONS

The 1848 Revolutions ended in failure, harsh repression, and disillusionment among liberals, but they did leave crucial legacies. They led to the formation of different political groups; accelerated the abolition of serfdom and feudal systems; and stimulated political awareness among the masses. Widespread dreams of nationalism may have been stifled momentarily, but they had not been quashed entirely: both Italy and Germany were unified by 1871 (see pp.264–265). The nationalist mood can be seen in this painting from 1860: Germania is seen holding a shield and sword, defending the Rhine River.

△ **Down with the monarchy**
This 19th-century illustration shows people burning the French throne in the Place de la Bastille during the 1848 Revolution in France.

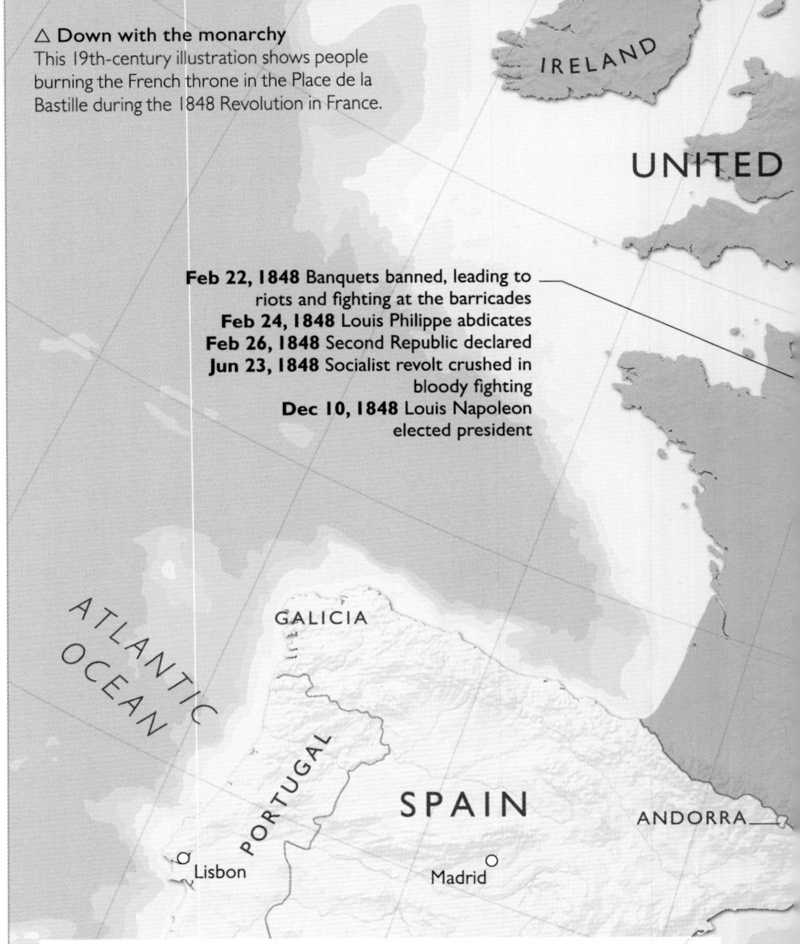

IRELAND

UNITED

Feb 22, 1848 Banquets banned, leading to riots and fighting at the barricades
Feb 24, 1848 Louis Philippe abdicates
Feb 26, 1848 Second Republic declared
Jun 23, 1848 Socialist revolt crushed in bloody fighting
Dec 10, 1848 Louis Napoleon elected president

ATLANTIC OCEAN

GALICIA

PORTUGAL

SPAIN

ANDORRA

○ Lisbon   ○ Madrid

EUROPE AFTER THE CONGRESS OF VIENNA
Exhausted by decades of revolutionary turmoil, the great powers of Europe had agreed at the Congress of Vienna a geopolitical dispensation that often cut across linguistic and nationalistic lines, brewing trouble for the future.

KEY

▬ German Confederation	▬ Other countries subject to 1848 revolts
▮ Prussia	— Frontiers 1848
▮ Small German states	

TIMELINE

1
2
3
4
5
6

JAN 1848   JULY   JAN 1849   JULY   JAN 1850

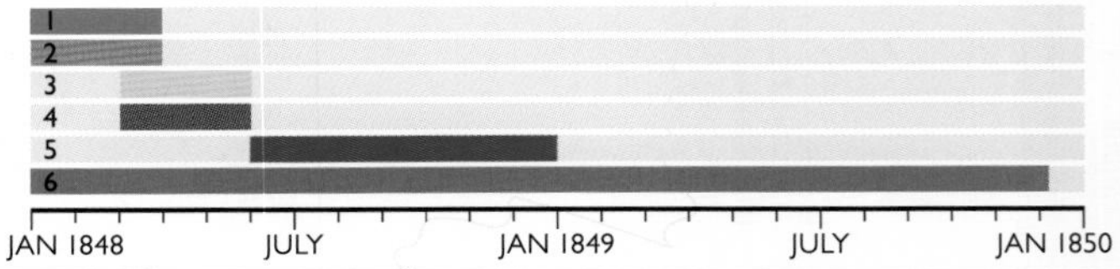

1 OUTBREAK OF REVOLUTION IN FRANCE AND SICILY JAN–MAR 1848

In Palermo, Sicily, a revolt broke out against the Spanish Borbón king Ferdinand II, and it soon spread to Naples. In France, King Louis-Philippe suppressed public meetings, triggering riots in Paris. The mob was fired upon, Louis-Philippe fled, and the Second Republic was declared. Unrest erupted across France as workers took to the streets.

🚩 Nationalist revolution   ✊ Republican revolution

👑 Abdication of monarch

2 THE FIRE CATCHES JAN–MAR 1848

Revolutionary sentiment spread across Italy. The Milanese rose up and drove the Austrian soldiers, under Marshal Radetzky, out of the city, appealing to the Piedmontese King, Charles Albert, to take them under his protection. Venice declared itself a Republic and had the support of a number of surrounding cities, including Treviso and Udine, while Parma revolted. Charles Albert declared war on Austria but lacked allies to win.

🚩 Nationalist revolution   ✊ Republican revolution

3 A UNITED GERMAN NATION MAR–MAY 1848

The death of King Christian VIII of Denmark in January ignited the Schleswig-Holstein question (see pp.264–265) and prompted an outpouring of pan-German nationalism, with demands for unification under a liberal constitution. Nationalist assemblies in Berlin and Frankfurt called on the Prussian king to unite Germany, and revolts flared up across the German Confederation.

🚩 Nationalist revolution   👑 Abdication of monarch

4 THE ESTABLISHMENT HANGS IN THE BALANCE MAR–MAY 1848

The fate of the establishment hung in the balance as the forces of reaction fought to cling on. Revolution in Vienna forced foreign minister Metternich to resign and the Emperor to flee; a liberal constitution was granted. Imperial forces crushed a pan-Slav conference in Prague but failed to prevent nationalist uprisings in Hungary.

🚩 Nationalist revolution   👑 Establishment victory

👑 Abdication of monarch

5 REACTION ASCENDANT JUN–DEC 1848

Reactionary forces turned the tide. In France, the newly elected Assembly proved to be reactionary, resulting in riots in Limoges and elsewhere and a bloodily suppressed socialist uprising in Paris. Imperial forces subdued Vienna in June but failed to crush the Hungarian uprising. In Italy, Austrian forces crushed the Piedmontese at Custoza in July.

👑 Establishment victory

6 REPUBLICANISM DEFEATED 1848–1849

Republican risings in the Rhineland and southern Germany were put down after the Prussian king refused to unite Germany under his aegis. Rome, where Garibaldi had proclaimed a republic, held out for a month but was defeated by an army sent from France, where Louis Napoleon had been elected president. Republican outposts in Venice and Tuscany were also crushed, as was the Hungarian uprising.

👑 Establishment victory   ✊ Republican revolution

Map labels and annotations:

Edinburgh
North Sea
SWEDEN
Jan 1848 King Christian VIII of Denmark dies
Baltic Sea
St. Petersburg
DENMARK
SCHLESWIG-HOLSTEIN
Copenhagen
Bornholm
KINGDOM
Hamburg
Danzig
EAST PRUSSIA
Amsterdam
THE NETHERLANDS
HANOVER
London
Brussels
PRUSSIA
Berlin
Jun 1848 Bloody repression by Habsburg troops ends efforts for constitutional reform
BELGIUM
PRUSSIA
RUSSIA
Warsaw
Frankfurt
SAXONY
Mar 12, 1848 Metternich resigns
Paris
Prague
POLAND
Mar 20, 1848 Uprising in Poland
May Uprising suppressed by Prussian troops
BAVARIA
Stuttgart
BOHEMIA
Cracow
WÜRTTEMBERG
GALICIA
Mar 15, 1848 Outbreak of revolution; Hungary granted independence
Oct 1949 Hungarians defeated
BADEN
BAVARIA
Munich
Vienna
AUSTRIA
FRANCE
May–June 1848 Revolution suppressed
Geneva
SWITZERLAND
Buda
Pest
Mar 23, 1848 King Charles Albert declares war on Austria
Aug 6, 1848 Austrian forces retake Milan
HUNGARY
Jul 24–25, 1848 Austrian forces defeat Piedmontese revolt
Milan
Custoza
Venice
TRANSYLVANIA
MOLDAVIA
Mar 23, 1848 Republic declared
Aug 28, 1849 Retaken by Austria
PIEDMONT
MODENA
SAN MARINO
Sebastopol
PARMA
WALLACHIA
MONACO
LUCCA
TUSCANY
PAPAL STATES
BOSNIA
Belgrade
Bucharest
Corsica
SERBIA
Black Sea
Rome
MONTENEGRO
MACEDONIA
Sardinia
Naples
OTTOMAN EMPIRE
Nov 1848 Pope flees
Feb 1849 Garibaldi declares Republic
Jul 1849 Republic defeated
THE TWO SICILIES
Salonica
Corfu
GREECE
Republican rings in the Rhineland
Mediterranean Sea
Palermo
Ionian Islands
Athens
Sicily
Jan 12, 1848 Revolution breaks out
Mar 25, 1848 Sicilian parliament declares independence
May 15, 1848 Bourbon troops retake Sicily
TUNISIA
Malta

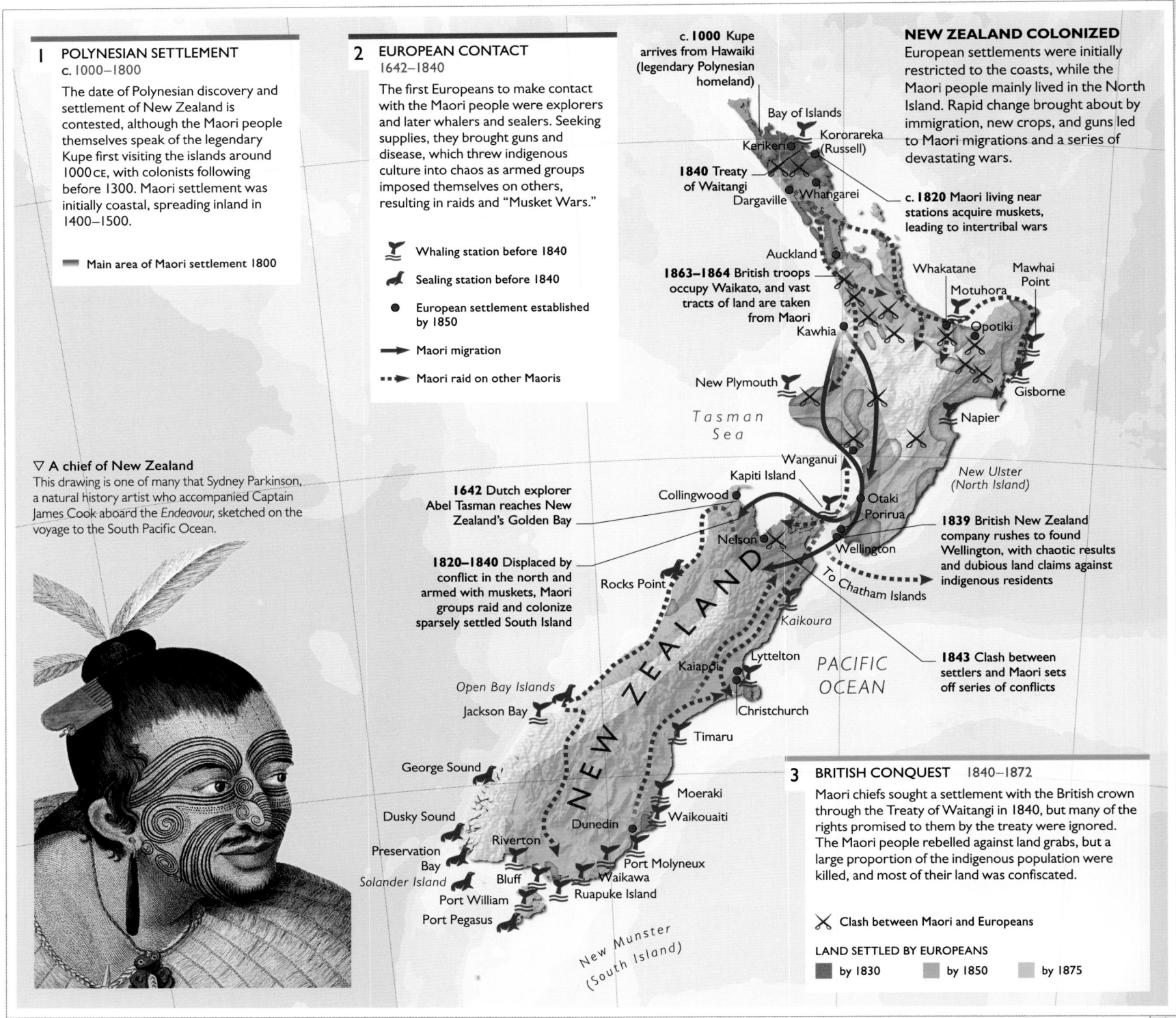

1 POLYNESIAN SETTLEMENT
c. 1000–1800

The date of Polynesian discovery and settlement of New Zealand is contested, although the Maori people themselves speak of the legendary Kupe first visiting the islands around 1000 CE, with colonists following before 1300. Maori settlement was initially coastal, spreading inland in 1400–1500.

▬ Main area of Maori settlement 1800

2 EUROPEAN CONTACT
1642–1840

The first Europeans to make contact with the Maori people were explorers and later whalers and sealers. Seeking supplies, they brought guns and disease, which threw indigenous culture into chaos as armed groups imposed themselves on others, resulting in raids and "Musket Wars."

⌃ Whaling station before 1840

🦭 Sealing station before 1840

● European settlement established by 1850

→ Maori migration

┅► Maori raid on other Maoris

NEW ZEALAND COLONIZED
European settlements were initially restricted to the coasts, while the Maori people mainly lived in the North Island. Rapid change brought about by immigration, new crops, and guns led to Maori migrations and a series of devastating wars.

c. 1000 Kupe arrives from Hawaiki (legendary Polynesian homeland)

Bay of Islands

Kororareka (Russell)

Kerikeri

1840 Treaty of Waitangi

Dargaville

Whangarei

c. 1820 Maori living near stations acquire muskets, leading to intertribal wars

Auckland

1863–1864 British troops occupy Waikato, and vast tracts of land are taken from Maori

Whakatane

Mawhai Point

Motuhora

Kawhia

Opotiki

New Plymouth

Gisborne

Napier

Tasman Sea

Wanganui

New Ulster (North Island)

Kapiti Island

Collingwood

Otaki

Porirua

1839 British New Zealand company rushes to found Wellington, with chaotic results and dubious land claims against indigenous residents

Nelson

Wellington

Rocks Point

To Chatham Islands

Kaikoura

Lyttelton

Kaiapoi

PACIFIC OCEAN

1843 Clash between settlers and Maori sets off series of conflicts

Open Bay Islands

Christchurch

Jackson Bay

Timaru

George Sound

Moeraki

Waikouaiti

Dusky Sound

Dunedin

Preservation Bay

Riverton

Port Molyneux

Solander Island

Bluff

Waikawa

Port William

Ruapuke Island

Port Pegasus

New Munster (South Island)

NEW ZEALAND

⌃ **A chief of New Zealand**
This drawing is one of many that Sydney Parkinson, a natural history artist who accompanied Captain James Cook aboard the *Endeavour*, sketched on the voyage to the South Pacific Ocean.

1642 Dutch explorer Abel Tasman reaches New Zealand's Golden Bay

1820–1840 Displaced by conflict in the north and armed with muskets, Maori groups raid and colonize sparsely settled South Island

3 BRITISH CONQUEST 1840–1872

Maori chiefs sought a settlement with the British crown through the Treaty of Waitangi in 1840, but many of the rights promised to them by the treaty were ignored. The Maori people rebelled against land grabs, but a large proportion of the indigenous population were killed, and most of their land was confiscated.

✕ Clash between Maori and Europeans

LAND SETTLED BY EUROPEANS
■ by 1830   ■ by 1850   ▢ by 1875

NEW ZEALAND AND AUSTRALIA

Motives ranging from whaling to exiling criminals drove European colonization of New Zealand and Australia. This had shocking and often tragic consequences for the indigenous peoples, including warfare and genocide.

Settlement of the land now known as Australia dates back to the earliest days of modern humanity (see pp.18–19). After that, remoteness led to relative cultural isolation for both Australia and for its southern neighbor New Zealand—probably the last habitable place on Earth to be settled by humans.

This would change with the increasing technological reach and territorial appetite of European powers, particularly Britain, in the 18th and 19th centuries. To these powers, the unknown lands of the Antipodes appeared as a blank canvas upon which all manner of colonial and imperial fantasies could be projected. In fact, they were home to a diverse range of cultures and

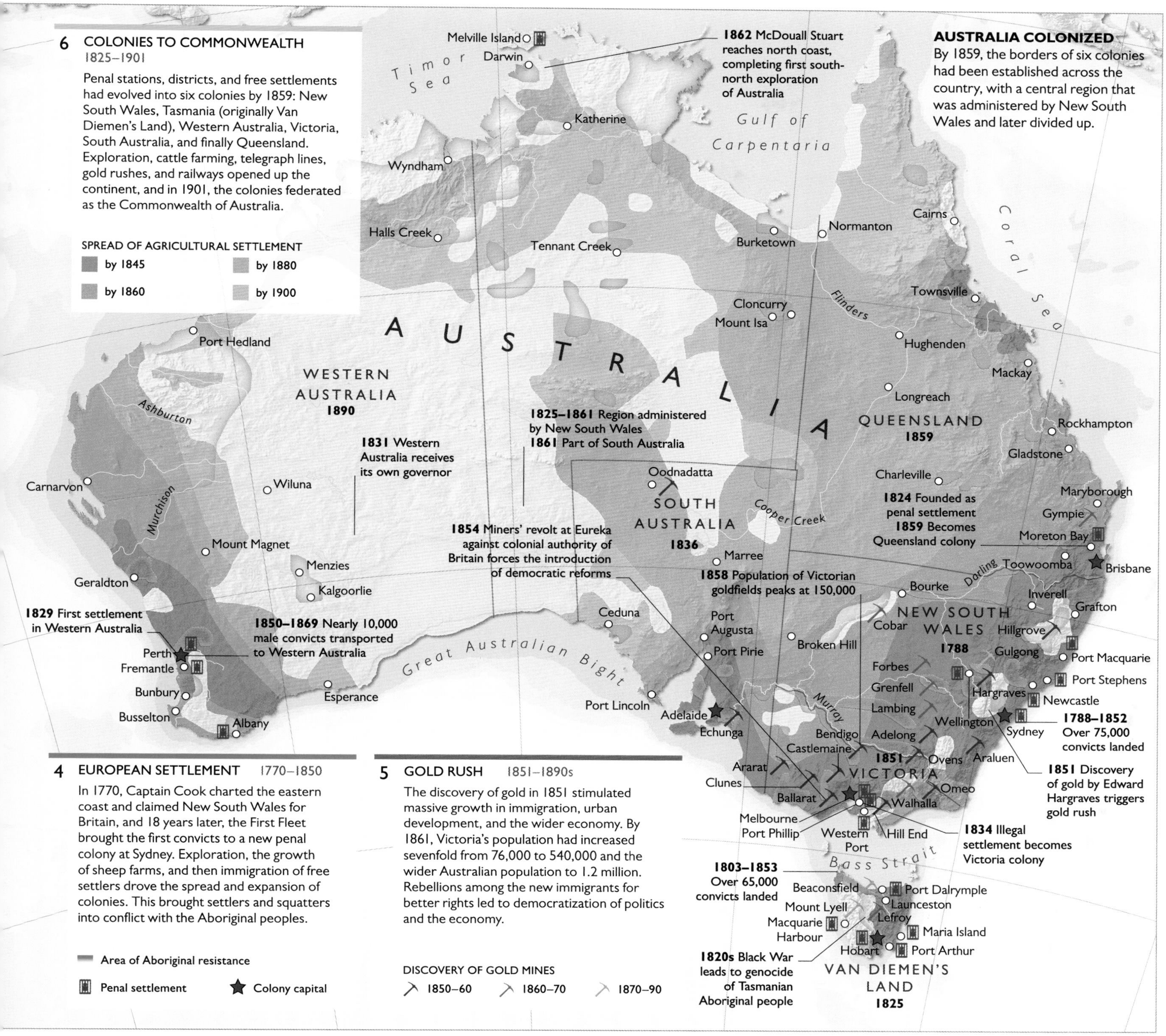

6 COLONIES TO COMMONWEALTH
1825–1901

Penal stations, districts, and free settlements had evolved into six colonies by 1859: New South Wales, Tasmania (originally Van Diemen's Land), Western Australia, Victoria, South Australia, and finally Queensland. Exploration, cattle farming, telegraph lines, gold rushes, and railways opened up the continent, and in 1901, the colonies federated as the Commonwealth of Australia.

SPREAD OF AGRICULTURAL SETTLEMENT
- by 1845
- by 1880
- by 1860
- by 1900

AUSTRALIA COLONIZED

By 1859, the borders of six colonies had been established across the country, with a central region that was administered by New South Wales and later divided up.

1862 McDouall Stuart reaches north coast, completing first south-north exploration of Australia

Melville Island

Darwin

Timor Sea

Gulf of Carpentaria

Katherine

Wyndham

Halls Creek

Tennant Creek

Normanton

Burketown

Cairns

Coral Sea

Townsville

Hughenden

Cloncurry
Mount Isa

Flinders

QUEENSLAND
1859

Longreach

Mackay

Rockhampton

Gladstone

Port Hedland

WESTERN
AUSTRALIA
1890

Ashburton

1831 Western Australia receives its own governor

1825–1861 Region administered by New South Wales
1861 Part of South Australia

Charleville

Maryborough

Oodnadatta

SOUTH
AUSTRALIA
1836

Cooper Creek

1824 Founded as penal settlement
1859 Becomes Queensland colony

Gympie

Moreton Bay

Carnarvon

Wiluna

Murchison

1854 Miners' revolt at Eureka against colonial authority of Britain forces the introduction of democratic reforms

Marree

Toowoomba

Darling

Brisbane

Mount Magnet

1858 Population of Victorian goldfields peaks at 150,000

Inverell

Geraldton

Menzies

Kalgoorlie

1850–1869 Nearly 10,000 male convicts transported to Western Australia

Ceduna

Port Augusta

Bourke

Cobar

NEW SOUTH
WALES
1788

Grafton

Hillgrove

1829 First settlement in Western Australia

Perth

Fremantle

Port Pirie

Broken Hill

Gulgong

Port Macquarie

Port Stephens

Bunbury

Esperance

Great Australian Bight

Port Lincoln

Forbes

Grenfell

Hargraves

Newcastle

Busselton

Albany

Adelaide

Echunga

Lambing

Bendigo

Adelong

Wellington

Sydney

1788–1852 Over 75,000 convicts landed

Murray

1851 Discovery of gold by Edward Hargraves triggers gold rush

Araluen

4 EUROPEAN SETTLEMENT 1770–1850

In 1770, Captain Cook charted the eastern coast and claimed New South Wales for Britain, and 18 years later, the First Fleet brought the first convicts to a new penal colony at Sydney. Exploration, the growth of sheep farms, and then immigration of free settlers drove the spread and expansion of colonies. This brought settlers and squatters into conflict with the Aboriginal peoples.

- Area of Aboriginal resistance
- Penal settlement
- ★ Colony capital

5 GOLD RUSH 1851–1890s

The discovery of gold in 1851 stimulated massive growth in immigration, urban development, and the wider economy. By 1861, Victoria's population had increased sevenfold from 76,000 to 540,000 and the wider Australian population to 1.2 million. Rebellions among the new immigrants for better rights led to democratization of politics and the economy.

DISCOVERY OF GOLD MINES
- 1850–60
- 1860–70
- 1870–90

Castlemaine

Ararat

Clunes

Ballarat

Melbourne
Port Phillip

Western
Port

1851

VICTORIA

Ovens

Omeo

Walhalla

Hill End

1834 Illegal settlement becomes Victoria colony

1803–1853 Over 65,000 convicts landed

1820s Black War leads to genocide of Tasmanian Aboriginal people

Beaconsfield

Mount Lyell

Macquarie
Harbour

Port Dalrymple

Launceston

Lefroy

Hobart

Maria Island

Port Arthur

VAN DIEMEN'S
LAND
1825

Bass Strait

---

societies. European arrivals in New Zealand began with sealing and whaling stations, where foreign ships could harvest resources, make repairs, and resupply. In Australia, the new arrivals began with the transportation of convicts from Britain and Ireland to penal colonies. The British soon took advantage in regions where the climate was familiar and introduced crops and livestock from home to drive a rapid colonial expansion. Growing numbers of new settlers increased the demand for land and also introduced firearms and unfamiliar diseases to the native peoples. These factors contributed to the severe decline of the populations of both the Maori people in New Zealand and the Aboriginal peoples in Australia.

EUROPEAN COLONIZATION

European settlement of New Zealand and Australia began slowly in the late 18th and early 19th centuries, but accelerated rapidly in the mid-19th century, with consequences for indigenous peoples inhabiting the land that settlers appropriated for farming.

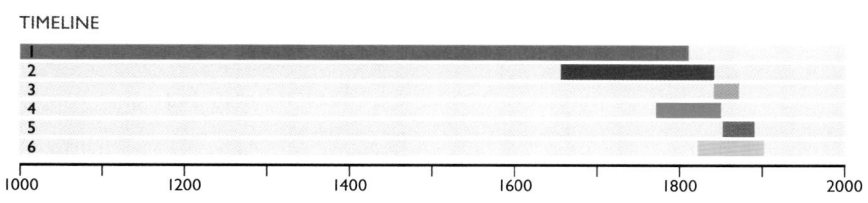

TIMELINE

1000   1200   1400   1600   1800   2000

THE ABOLITION OF SLAVERY

The explosive economic growth that brought European powers to global ascendancy was driven in large part by slavery. However, from the 18th century, a long process to abolish the global slave trade was set in motion.

△ **Anti-slavery crusaders**
The British Anti-slavery Society, whose emblem is seen here, was a major force in the battle over abolition.

The abolition movement, or abolitionism, was a moral, social, and political campaign to ban the slave trade. It was distinct from, but related to, the movement to emancipate slaves. Abolitionism first took shape among the Quakers, a Protestant Christian group, who in 1787 in Britain set up the Committee for the Abolition of the Slave Trade.

The cause's success was checked when the movement associated itself with radical sentiments following the French Revolution in 1789. Public fears about reprisals that might follow abolition were also stoked by a revolt among Haitian slaves in 1791–1804. Nonetheless, skillful use of propaganda, and alliances with evangelical Christians and women's groups helped abolitionism gain ground. Although the slave trade was abolished by a Bill of Parliament in Britain in 1807, followed by other European nations such as France, Spain, and Portugal, the practice of slavery continued in many colonies.

The enactment of anti-slavery legislation in Europe boosted the cause of emancipation in America's northern states, fed by a religious revival known as the Second Great Awakening and by voters' resentment of "fugitive slave" laws. Increasing radical responses by both pro- and anti-abolitionists that ensued in the US helped tip the dispute over slavery into civil war (see pp.170–171).

THE ABOLITION OF SLAVERY AROUND THE WORLD

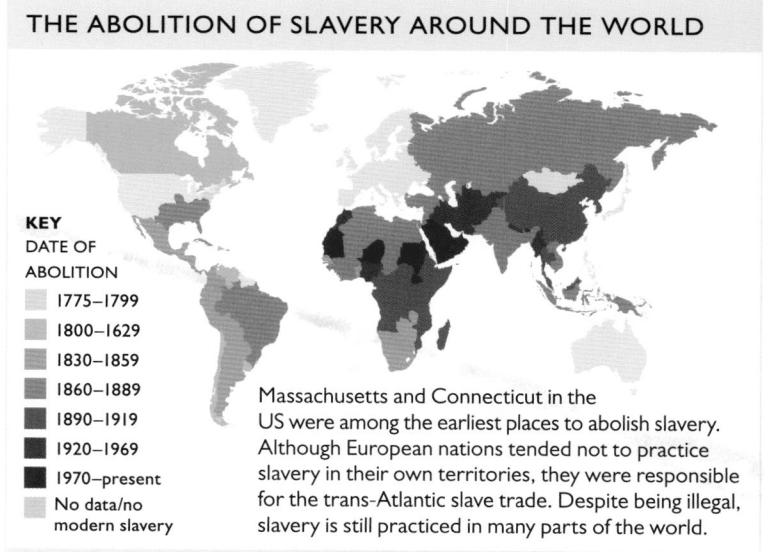

KEY
DATE OF ABOLITION
- 1775–1799
- 1800–1629
- 1830–1859
- 1860–1889
- 1890–1919
- 1920–1969
- 1970–present
- No data/no modern slavery

Massachusetts and Connecticut in the US were among the earliest places to abolish slavery. Although European nations tended not to practice slavery in their own territories, they were responsible for the trans-Atlantic slave trade. Despite being illegal, slavery is still practiced in many parts of the world.

The ceremony of Bois-Caiman
A legendary voodoo ceremony that has become part of the foundation myth of Haiti is depicted here by Haitian painter Andre Normil. The island nation was the site of perhaps the only successful slave rebellion in history.

RISE OF BRITISH POWER IN INDIA

From initial footholds in the southeast and Bengal, the power of the British East India Company, a corporate concern with imperial pretensions, spread across all of India, conquering territory and winning fealty through guile, brutality, and arrogance. Eventually, almost the entire subcontinent came under Company control.

European nations had been trading extensively with India since the 16th century, and by the late 17th century, five European powers had trading ports in the subcontinent. Among them was the British East India Company, a commercial organization first chartered in 1600 to profit from trade with the Moluccas (or Spice Islands) in Southeast Asia. Rebuffed by the Dutch, the British East India Company focused instead on trade in textiles and spices with south India, where it had won trading concessions with the Mughal Empire.

Under the Mughals (see pp.176–177), India was a developed, sophisticated polity, with a strong military and wealth and population outstripping that of Europe. However, the collapse of Mughal rule in the 18th century led to the rise of a mosaic of princely states, confederations, and small kingdoms. With no major, unifying power in India, imperialistic and mercantile European powers had the opportunity to exploit the subcontinent, and it would be the British that took it. Faced with foreign competitors and sometimes hostile hosts, the East India Company developed its own military force to strengthen and protect its interests. Over about the next 100 years, the Company first overcame its competitors and then widened its control of territory, trade, and power in India, using a combination of diplomacy, bribery, and force.

In consolidating its power, the Company faced formidable opponents, including the French, the sultans of Mysore, the Maratha Confederacy, the Sikh kingdom, and the Afghans. The Company was not always victorious, but it was relentless, and it eventually controlled all of India. However, in the wake of a bloody revolt (see pp.244–245), the Company was effectively abolished in 1858. Its possessions and forces were taken over by the British government, and direct colonial rule began.

SIR ROBERT CLIVE
1725–1774

Commonly known as Clive of India, Robert Clive played a key role in establishing the power of the British East India Company in the subcontinent, gaining honors and wealth in the process. After leading several successful military actions—notably defeat of a French and Mughal force at Plassey in 1757—he twice served as Governor of Bengal (1758–1760, 1765–1767). He returned to England in 1767 and died—possibly by suicide—7 years later in London.

A meeting of allies
Robert Clive meeting Mir Jafar after the Battle of Plassey. Mir Jafar supported Clive in the battle and was made Nawab of Bengal in return for his support.

1 THE FRENCH THREATEN BRITISH POWER
1740–1746

The Dutch and French had their own India companies, which initially vied with the British for supremacy. Dutch ambitions were ended after defeat by forces of the state of Travancore at Colachel in 1741, but in 1746, the French took Madras from the British and then defeated an Indian army, establishing European military supremacy in the subcontinent.

✕ Battle   ● French colony

GROWTH OF BRITISH TERRITORY
From its early 19th-century strongholds in the southeast and northeast, Britain gained increasing territorial control through piecemeal acquisition of lands in central and western India and by means of a network of protectorates and vassal states.

KEY

- British territory, 1805
- British gains by 1838
- British gains by 1857
- Princely state or protectorate
- **1856** Date gained by Britain

TIMELINE

1 2 3 4 5 6

1750   1800   1850

6 LAST DAYS OF THE EAST INDIA COMPANY
1839–1857

As the Company sought to extend control to the northwest, it fought a series of conflicts in the Punjab and Afghanistan. In 1856, the Company annexed Oudh, which precipitated a revolt in 1857 that eventually led to the British government taking direct control of India. The Company was finished, and the era of the British Raj had begun.

✕ Battle

5 MARATHA WARS 1775–1818

Three conflicts between the British and the Maratha Confederacy of Hindu princes (1775–1782, 1803–1805, 1817–1818) effectively marked the last stand for indigenous power against British hegemony over India. As in the Mysore Wars, sometimes humiliating reverses for the British were followed by victories and gradual extension and consolidation of East India Company control.

━━ Maratha territory 1785   ✕ Battle

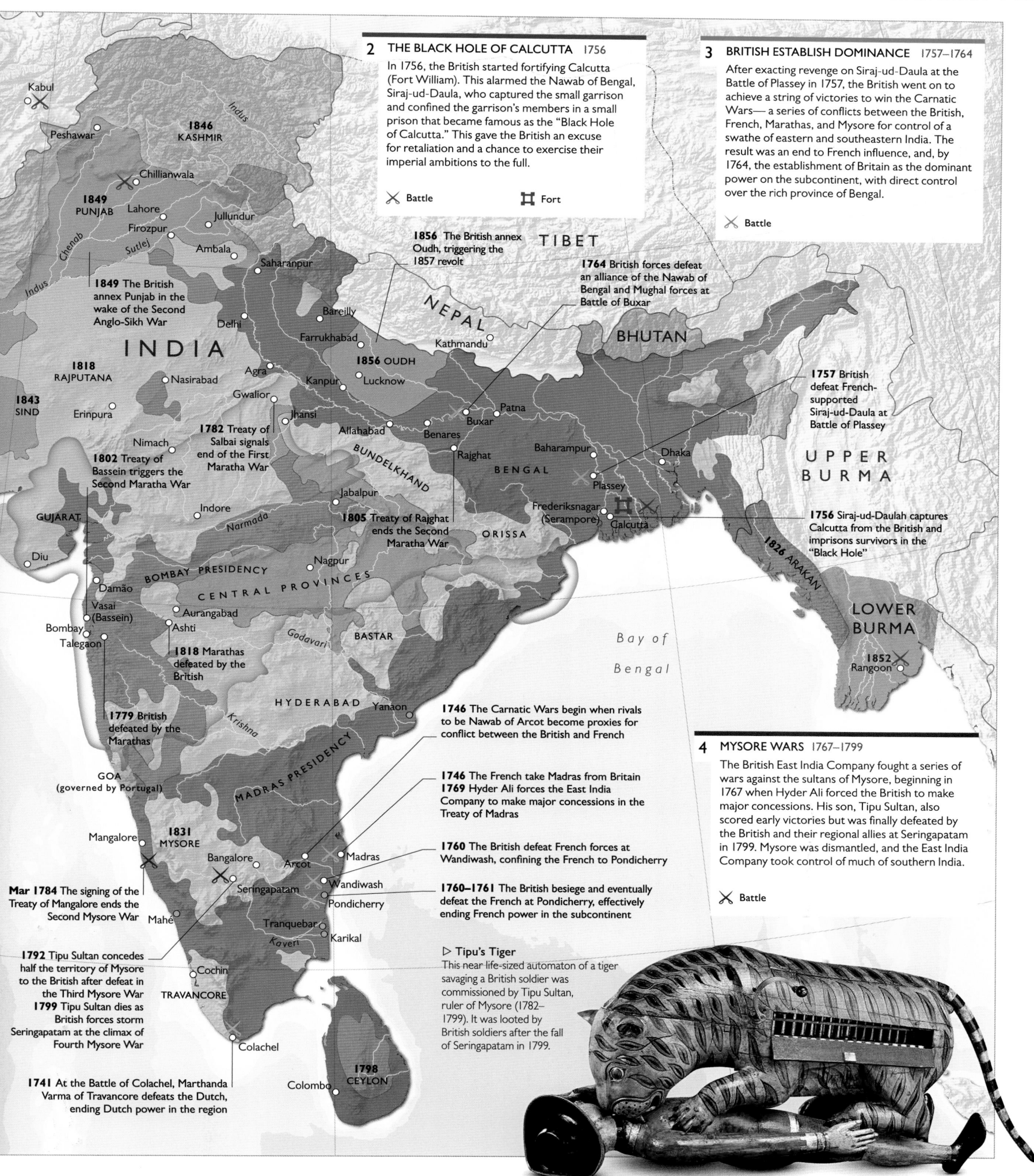

2 THE BLACK HOLE OF CALCUTTA 1756

In 1756, the British started fortifying Calcutta (Fort William). This alarmed the Nawab of Bengal, Siraj-ud-Daula, who captured the small garrison and confined the garrison's members in a small prison that became famous as the "Black Hole of Calcutta." This gave the British an excuse for retaliation and a chance to exercise their imperial ambitions to the full.

⚔ Battle   ⊟ Fort

3 BRITISH ESTABLISH DOMINANCE 1757–1764

After exacting revenge on Siraj-ud-Daula at the Battle of Plassey in 1757, the British went on to achieve a string of victories to win the Carnatic Wars— a series of conflicts between the British, French, Marathas, and Mysore for control of a swathe of eastern and southeastern India. The result was an end to French influence, and, by 1764, the establishment of Britain as the dominant power on the subcontinent, with direct control over the rich province of Bengal.

⚔ Battle

4 MYSORE WARS 1767–1799

The British East India Company fought a series of wars against the sultans of Mysore, beginning in 1767 when Hyder Ali forced the British to make major concessions. His son, Tipu Sultan, also scored early victories but was finally defeated by the British and their regional allies at Seringapatam in 1799. Mysore was dismantled, and the East India Company took control of much of southern India.

⚔ Battle

1846 KASHMIR

1849 The British annex Punjab in the wake of the Second Anglo-Sikh War

1849 PUNJAB

1856 The British annex Oudh, triggering the 1857 revolt

1764 British forces defeat an alliance of the Nawab of Bengal and Mughal forces at Battle of Buxar

1857 British defeat French-supported Siraj-ud-Daula at Battle of Plassey

INDIA

1818 RAJPUTANA

1843 SIND

1856 OUDH

1782 Treaty of Salbai signals end of the First Maratha War

1802 Treaty of Bassein triggers the Second Maratha War

1805 Treaty of Rajghat ends the Second Maratha War

1756 Siraj-ud-Daulah captures Calcutta from the British and imprisons survivors in the "Black Hole"

1779 British defeated by the Marathas

1818 Marathas defeated by the British

1852 Rangoon

LOWER BURMA

UPPER BURMA

1826 ARAKAN

TIBET

NEPAL

BHUTAN

GOA (governed by Portugal)

1831 MYSORE

Mar 1784 The signing of the Treaty of Mangalore ends the Second Mysore War

1792 Tipu Sultan concedes half the territory of Mysore to the British after defeat in the Third Mysore War
1799 Tipu Sultan dies as British forces storm Seringapatam at the climax of Fourth Mysore War

TRAVANCORE

1741 At the Battle of Colachel, Marthanda Varma of Travancore defeats the Dutch, ending Dutch power in the region

1798 CEYLON

1746 The Carnatic Wars begin when rivals to be Nawab of Arcot become proxies for conflict between the British and French

1746 The French take Madras from Britain
1769 Hyder Ali forces the East India Company to make major concessions in the Treaty of Madras

1760 The British defeat French forces at Wandiwash, confining the French to Pondicherry

1760–1761 The British besiege and eventually defeat the French at Pondicherry, effectively ending French power in the subcontinent

BOMBAY PRESIDENCY

CENTRAL PROVINCES

BUNDELKHAND

BENGAL

ORISSA

BASTAR

HYDERABAD

MADRAS PRESIDENCY

Bay of Bengal

▷ **Tipu's Tiger**
This near life-sized automaton of a tiger savaging a British soldier was commissioned by Tipu Sultan, ruler of Mysore (1782–1799). It was looted by British soldiers after the fall of Seringapatam in 1799.

THE OPIUM WARS

In the early 1800s, opium was being illegally imported into China (mainly by Britain), which eventually sparked confrontations over foreign trade. China's rulers, the Qing Dynasty, badly misjudged their strength in relation to Britain, which used "gunboat diplomacy" to force China to open to international trade.

The Chinese imperial court viewed trade as a favor bestowed on foreign tributaries; the British, in contrast, viewed it as the lifeblood of international relations and a way to exploit their colonies. Specifically, the British were seeking to monetize their colonization of India, and they saw opium as the key. India produced high-grade cash crop opium, which could be sold in China for silver, which was promptly swapped for tea—a valuable commodity for the domestic British market. The only problem with the arrangement was that it was illegal to sell opium to China. The trade fed massive corruption and a huge black economy, at the same time as contributing to monetary problems that the Qing were suffering

linked to inflation. Tension inevitably flared, boiling over into confrontations between the Chinese and the British, which the latter were happy to exploit.

The "gunboat diplomacy" that followed saw China lose a series of battles across two wars, with the Qing forced to make severe concessions in what became known as the "unequal treaties." These stoked resentment in China and inflicted lasting humiliation that even today affects Chinese relations with Western powers. The damage to the prestige of the Qing Dynasty undermined their mandate to rule, instigating the series of colossal rebellions that would convulse and eventually destroy imperial China (see pp.252–253).

THE OPIUM TRADE
CHINA'S ADDICTION, BRITAIN'S FINANCIAL GAIN

Poppy plants were grown and the seeds dried (see below) in factories in India. Produced and processed by the quasi-governmental British East India Company, the opium was then imported to China by private merchants, allowing the British to wash their hands of the trade's illegality. Chests of opium were unloaded onto floating warehouses off the coast of Guangzhou, where Chinese smugglers bought it with silver and shipped it upriver, paying bribes and spreading corruption to get around official prohibitions.

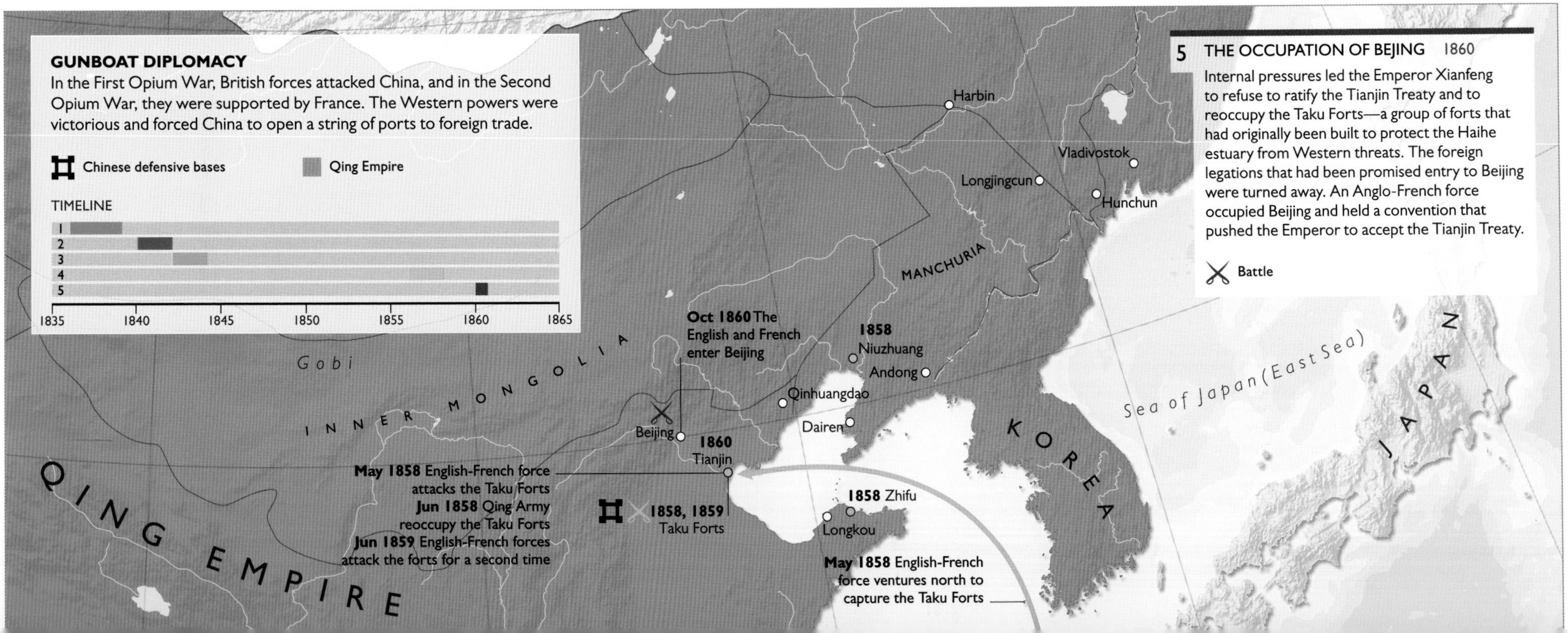

GUNBOAT DIPLOMACY

In the First Opium War, British forces attacked China, and in the Second Opium War, they were supported by France. The Western powers were victorious and forced China to open a string of ports to foreign trade.

Chinese defensive bases

Qing Empire

TIMELINE

1	2	3	4	5

1835 1840 1845 1850 1855 1860 1865

May 1858 English-French force attacks the Taku Forts

Jun 1858 Qing Army reoccupy the Taku Forts

Jun 1859 English-French forces attack the forts for a second time

5 THE OCCUPATION OF BEIJING 1860

Internal pressures led the Emperor Xianfeng to refuse to ratify the Tianjin Treaty and to reoccupy the Taku Forts—a group of forts that had originally been built to protect the Haihe estuary from Western threats. The foreign legations that had been promised entry to Beijing were turned away. An Anglo-French force occupied Beijing and held a convention that pushed the Emperor to accept the Tianjin Treaty.

✕ Battle

Vladivostok
Hunchun
Harbin
Longjingcun
MANCHURIA
1858
Niuzhuang
Andong
Qinhuangdao
Dairen
1858 Zhifu
Longkou

May 1858 English-French force ventures north to capture the Taku Forts

Oct 1860 The English and French enter Beijing

1860
Beijing
Tianjin

1858, 1859 Taku Forts

KOREA

Sea of Japan (East Sea)

JAPAN

GOBI

INNER MONGOLIA

QING EMPIRE

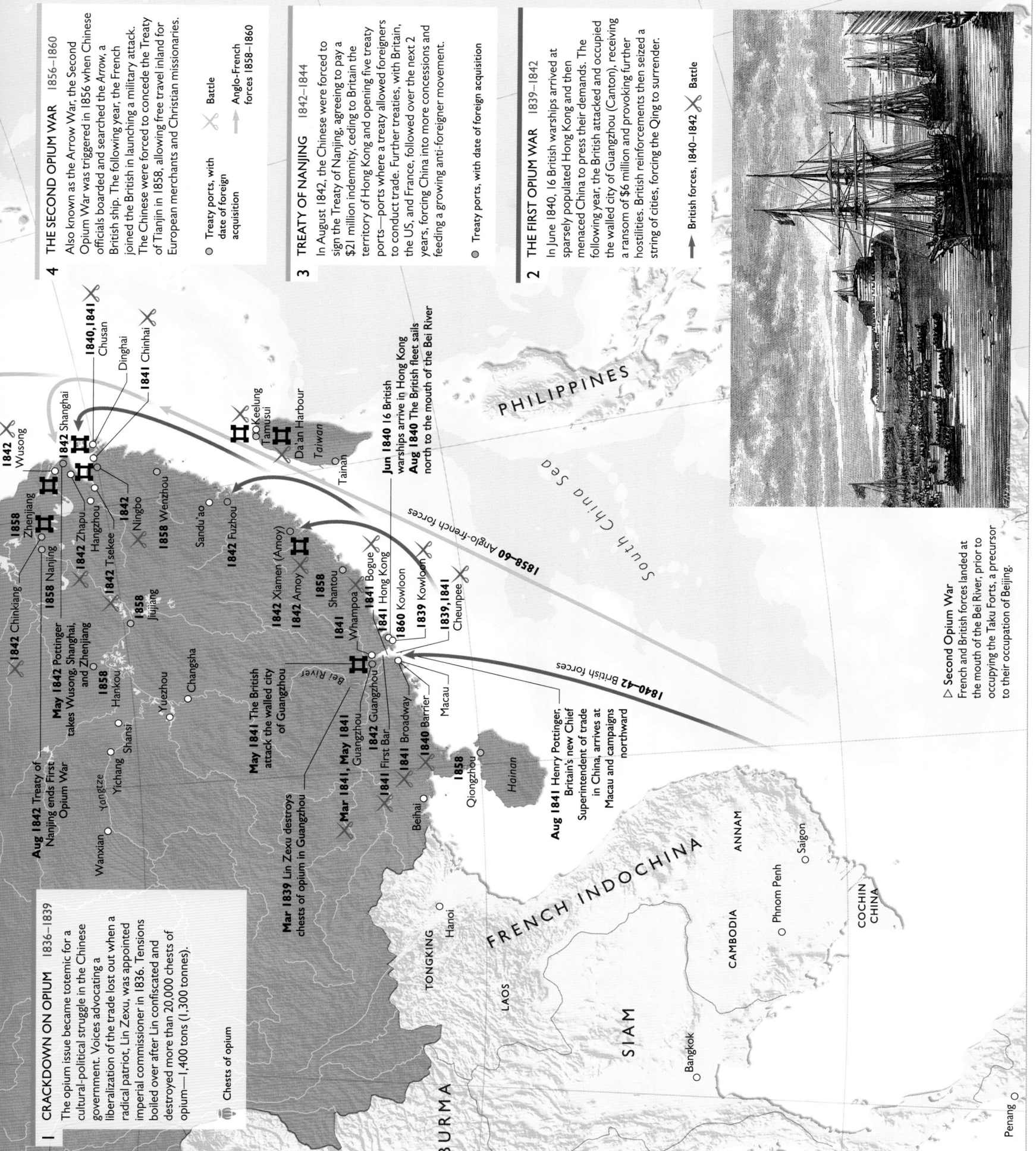

1 CRACKDOWN ON OPIUM 1836–1839

The opium issue became totemic for a cultural-political struggle in the Chinese government. Voices advocating a liberalization of the trade lost out when a radical patriot, Lin Zexu, was appointed imperial commissioner in 1836. Tensions boiled over after Lin confiscated and destroyed more than 20,000 chests of opium—1,400 tons (1,300 tonnes).

⊕ Chests of opium

4 THE SECOND OPIUM WAR 1856–1860

Also known as the Arrow War, the Second Opium War was triggered in 1856 when Chinese officials boarded and searched the Arrow, a British ship. The following year, the French joined the British in launching a military attack. The Chinese were forced to concede the Treaty of Tianjin in 1858, allowing free travel inland for European merchants and Christian missionaries.

◉ Treaty ports, with date of foreign acquisition

✗ Battle

→ Anglo-French forces 1858–1860

3 TREATY OF NANJING 1842–1844

In August 1842, the Chinese were forced to sign the Treaty of Nanjing, agreeing to pay a $21 million indemnity, ceding to Britain the territory of Hong Kong and opening five treaty ports—ports where a treaty allowed foreigners to conduct trade. Further treaties, with Britain, the US, and France, followed over the next 2 years, forcing China into more concessions and feeding a growing anti-foreigner movement.

◉ Treaty ports, with date of foreign acquisition

2 THE FIRST OPIUM WAR 1839–1842

In June 1840, 16 British warships arrived at sparsely populated Hong Kong and then menaced China to press their demands. The following year, the British attacked and occupied the walled city of Guangzhou (Canton), receiving a ransom of $6 million and provoking further hostilities. British reinforcements then seized a string of cities, forcing the Qing to surrender.

→ British forces, 1840–1842

△ Second Opium War
French and British forces landed at the mouth of the Bei River, prior to occupying the Taku Forts, a precursor to their occupation of Beijing.

Map labels

1840,1841 Chusan
Dinghai
1841 Chinhai
1842 Shanghai
1842 Wusong
1858 Zhenjiang
1858 Nanjing
1842 Zhapu
Hangzhou
1842 Tsekee
Ningbo
1858 Wenzhou
Sandu'ao
1842 Fuzhou
Keelung
Tamsui
Da'an Harbour
Taiwan
Tainan
Jun 1840 16 British warships arrive in Hong Kong
Aug 1840 The British fleet sails north to the mouth of the Bei River
1858 Jiujiang
Changsha
Yuezhou
Hankou
Shansi
Yichang
Yangtze
Wanxian
Aug 1842 Treaty of Nanjing ends First Opium War
May 1842 Pottinger takes Wusong, Shanghai, and Zhenjiang
1842 Chinkiang
1858 Chinkiang
1858 Hankou
1842 Xiamen (Amoy)
1842 Amoy
1858 Shantou
May 1841 The British attack the walled city of Guangzhou
Mar 1839 Lin Zexu destroys chests of opium in Guangzhou
Bei River
1841 Bogue
1841 Whampoa
1841 Hong Kong
1842 Guangzhou
Mar 1841, May 1841 Guangzhou
1842 First Bar
1841 Broadway
1840 Barrier
1860 Kowloon
1839,1841 Cheunpee
1839,1841 Kowloon
Macau
1858 Qiongzhou
Beihai
Hainan
Aug 1841 Henry Pottinger, Britain's new Chief Superintendent of trade in China, arrives at Macau and campaigns northward

1858–60 Anglo-french forces
1840–42 British forces

South China Sea
PHILIPPINES

BURMA
SIAM
Bangkok
LAOS
TONGKING
Hanoi
FRENCH INDOCHINA
CAMBODIA
Phnom Penh
ANNAM
Saigon
COCHIN CHINA
Penang

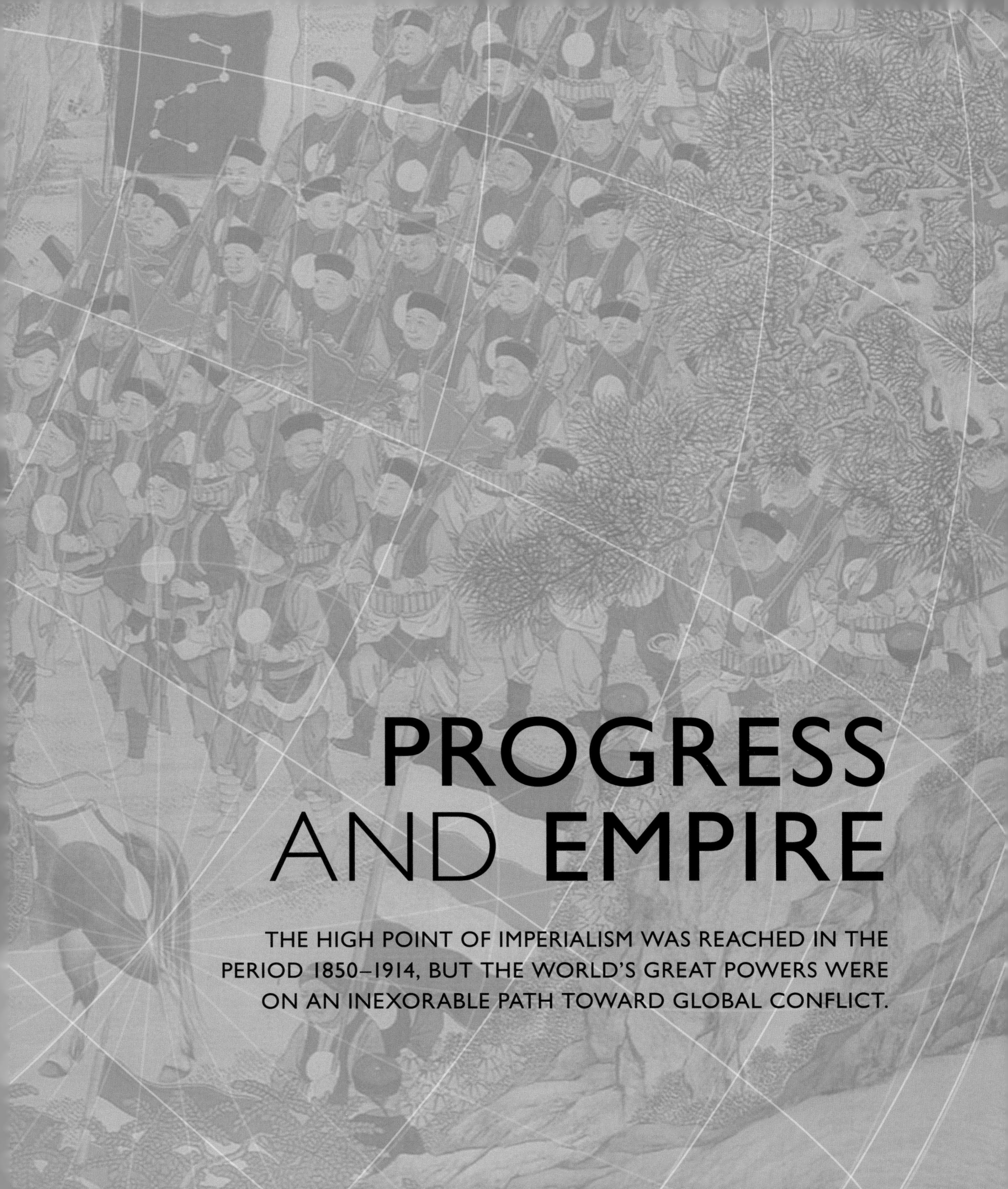

PROGRESS AND EMPIRE

THE HIGH POINT OF IMPERIALISM WAS REACHED IN THE PERIOD 1850–1914, BUT THE WORLD'S GREAT POWERS WERE ON AN INEXORABLE PATH TOWARD GLOBAL CONFLICT.

CITIES AND INDUSTRY

Industrialization shaped every aspect of life in the 19th century. It not only affected where and how people lived, and how they traveled and communicated with each other, but also helped shape public health, politics, and people's attitudes.

△ **Unequal world**
Poverty was rife in many cities, as this photograph of a child in Paris from 1900 illustrates.

Industrialization became a global phenomenon in the second half of the 19th century. Where the industrial advances at the end of the 18th and beginning of the 19th centuries had predominantly benefited Britain (see pp.212–215), the development of heavy industry based on coal, iron, and steel, and the transport revolution of the mid-19th century, reshaped the world.

As western Europe, Japan, Russia, and the US all began to industrialize rapidly from 1870, they experienced huge social, cultural, and population changes. The world's population grew as land reform and modern farming methods—the utilization of chemical fertilizers, steel tools, and steam-powered machinery—helped sustain more people. Millions moved from the countryside into the cities seeking employment and opportunities. In 1800, 5 percent of the world's population lived in urban areas; by 1925, that figure had reached 20 percent, and in the industrialized regions of Europe and the US, 71.2 percent of the population lived in cities. Millions took advantage of the improved transportation offered by oceangoing steamships to migrate overseas (see pp.238–239). The immigrants who traveled

to find gold in the US, Canada, South Africa, and Australia contributed to the creation of a world in which all but a few currencies were convertible to gold. The gold standard—a monetary system that backed paper money with gold—in turn facilitated international trade, stimulating new markets for industrial products and creating a period of great financial stability. The people made rich by industrialization sought new avenues for investment, feeding a wave of imperial activity that saw Africa carved up by the European nations, the ancient Chinese Empire come under threat, and Latin America brought within the spheres of influence of Britain and the US.

△ **New horizons**
In this photograph from 1906, immigrants crowd the decks of an Atlantic liner as it approaches Ellis Island—the gateway to a new, better life in the US. Third-class passengers would remain at Ellis Island until they passed health and legal checks.

The modern city

Society developed in multifarious ways in the 19th century—industrialization fueled the gap between the rich and the poor but also created a middle class comprising lawyers, doctors, businessmen, merchants, civil servants, shopkeepers, and clerks. While a generation of tycoons became wealthy on the back of industry and investment, in the cities where their workers lived, poverty, pollution, and diseases—such as dysentery, tuberculosis, rickets, and cholera—were rife. Work itself involved long hours in hazardous conditions, and many

CITIES OF THE INDUSTRIAL AGE

The technological developments of the 19th century brought with them profound changes in the size and distribution of the world's population. There was a shift away from rural to city life in the industrialized West. Europe outdid Asia for the first time in terms of the number and size of its cities. The population grew rapidly, particularly in Europe. Modern transportation meant that the overspill from Europe's cities could move easily to the high-rise cities in the US.

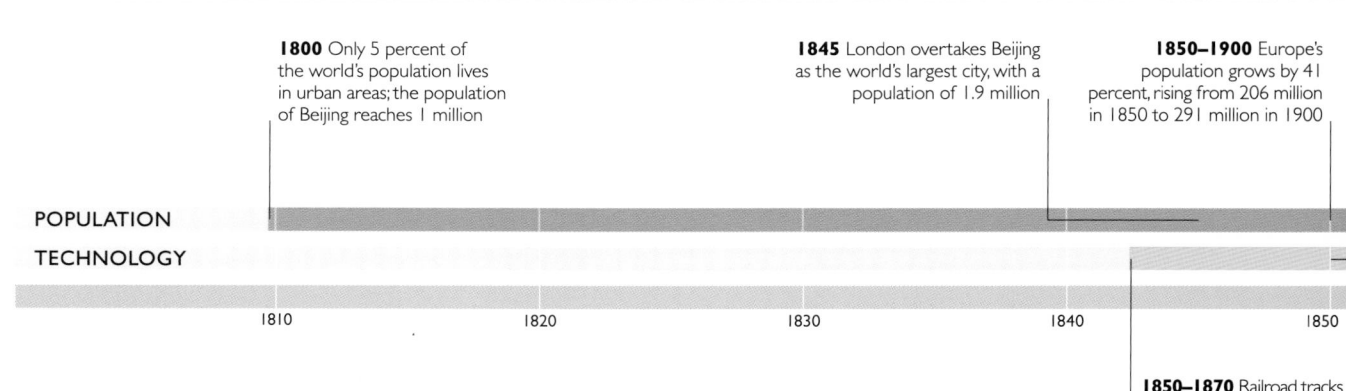

1800 Only 5 percent of the world's population lives in urban areas; the population of Beijing reaches 1 million

1845 London overtakes Beijing as the world's largest city, with a population of 1.9 million

1850–1900 Europe's population grows by 41 percent, rising from 206 million in 1850 to 291 million in 1900

POPULATION

TECHNOLOGY

1810   1820   1830   1840   1850

1843 The first steamship crosses the Atlantic; by 1907, the crossing takes just 4.5 days

1850–1870 Railroad tracks in Europe grow from 15,000 miles (24,000 km) in 1850 to 64,000 miles (103,000 km) in 1870

◁ **Cleaning up**
British engineer Sir Joseph William Bazalgette (top right) surveys work on London's sewers. His sanitation systems transformed public health in cities around the world.

children had to work. Yet the cities also provided the means to combat this inequality and solve some of the ills of industrialized society. Migrants from rural areas and other countries arrived into a melting pot of social classes and ethnic backgrounds. Social and religious taboos broke down, and the exchange of ideas gave rise to movements for social change. Various workers' unions came into existence campaigning for better pay and improved working conditions. The demands for suffrage for both men and women also began to increase. Charitable organizations proliferated as both wealthy philanthropists and Christian societies such as the Salvation Army sought to meet the city populations' physical and spiritual needs. A deeper understanding of poverty combined with political activism ensured that by the 20th century, Germany and Britain—the most industrialized nations— had in place the beginnings of a welfare system that would care for the elderly and the sick.

By then, industry and the wealth it generated had also begun to solve some of the practical problems of city life. Steel construction made high-rise living and working a reality; steel-framed buildings provided a way for offices and accommodations to be erected swiftly and made the best use of limited space by reaching upward. The development of modern sanitation—the use of iron tanks and steam-powered pumping stations—saved city dwellers from the horrors of diseases such as cholera. Underground transportation meant that workers could move swiftly around the city, and connections with the railroads meant they could escape the city for the suburbs. The speed and breadth of technological change in the 19th century was unprecedented, and even the telecommunication revolution of the 20th century could not match the impact of industrialization on modern society.

> *"It is from the midst of this putrid sewer that the greatest river of human industry springs up ..."*
>
> ALEXIS DE TOCQUEVILLE, FRENCH HISTORIAN, FROM *VOYAGES EN ANGLETERRE ET IRLANDE* (JOURNEYS TO ENGLAND AND IRELAND), 1835

△ **Gold rush**
A presidential election poster from 1900 shows US President William McKinley held aloft on a gold coin, celebrating the prosperity of the Gold Standard era.

1875 London is the first city to reach a population of 4 million

1900 US population reaches 76.2 million; it was just 5.3 million in 1800

1925 Mass immigration makes New York the largest city in the world, with a population of more than 5 million

1860   1870   1880   1890   1900   1910   1920

1858 The first transatlantic telegraph cables are laid

1863 The world's first underground railroad opens in London

1875 London's modern sewage system is completed; it transforms public health there

1855–1885 English inventor Henry Bessemer and British metallurgist Sidney Gilchrist Thomas transform steel production; the first steel-framed skyscraper is completed in Chicago in 1885

1913 Global steel output reaches 38 million tons (34 million tonnes) a year

1927 World population reaches 2 billion; it has doubled in 120 years

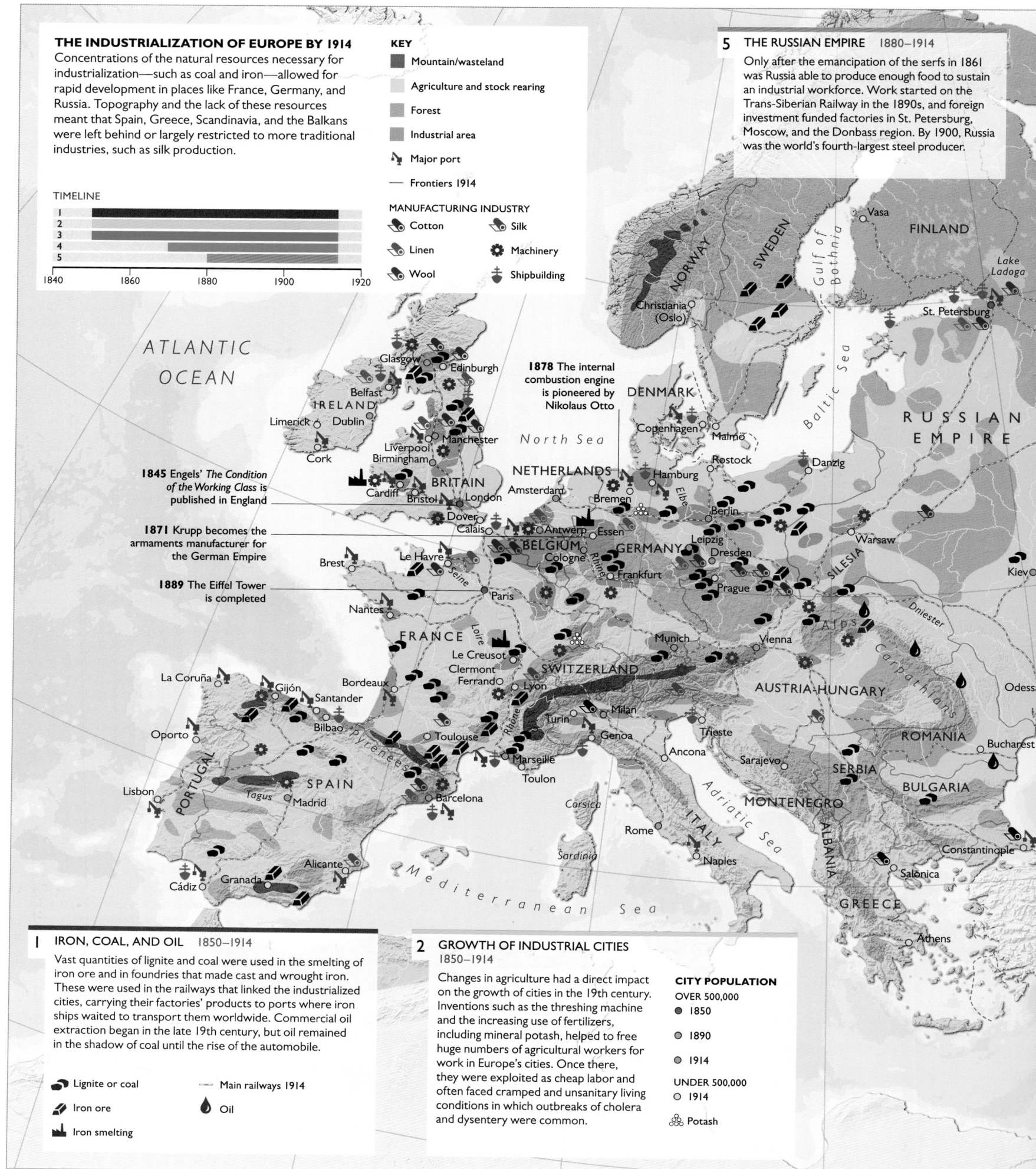

THE INDUSTRIALIZATION OF EUROPE BY 1914

Concentrations of the natural resources necessary for industrialization—such as coal and iron—allowed for rapid development in places like France, Germany, and Russia. Topography and the lack of these resources meant that Spain, Greece, Scandinavia, and the Balkans were left behind or largely restricted to more traditional industries, such as silk production.

KEY

Mountain/wasteland

Agriculture and stock rearing

Forest

Industrial area

Major port

— Frontiers 1914

MANUFACTURING INDUSTRY

Cotton   Silk

Linen   Machinery

Wool   Shipbuilding

TIMELINE

1
2
3
4
5

1840   1860   1880   1900   1920

5 THE RUSSIAN EMPIRE 1880–1914

Only after the emancipation of the serfs in 1861 was Russia able to produce enough food to sustain an industrial workforce. Work started on the Trans-Siberian Railway in the 1890s, and foreign investment funded factories in St. Petersburg, Moscow, and the Donbass region. By 1900, Russia was the world's fourth-largest steel producer.

1878 The internal combustion engine is pioneered by Nikolaus Otto

1845 Engels' *The Condition of the Working Class* is published in England

1871 Krupp becomes the armaments manufacturer for the German Empire

1889 The Eiffel Tower is completed

1 IRON, COAL, AND OIL 1850–1914

Vast quantities of lignite and coal were used in the smelting of iron ore and in foundries that made cast and wrought iron. These were used in the railways that linked the industrialized cities, carrying their factories' products to ports where iron ships waited to transport them worldwide. Commercial oil extraction began in the late 19th century, but oil remained in the shadow of coal until the rise of the automobile.

Lignite or coal   — Main railways 1914

Iron ore   Oil

Iron smelting

2 GROWTH OF INDUSTRIAL CITIES 1850–1914

Changes in agriculture had a direct impact on the growth of cities in the 19th century. Inventions such as the threshing machine and the increasing use of fertilizers, including mineral potash, helped to free huge numbers of agricultural workers for work in Europe's cities. Once there, they were exploited as cheap labor and often faced cramped and unsanitary living conditions in which outbreaks of cholera and dysentery were common.

CITY POPULATION

OVER 500,000
1850
1890
1914

UNDER 500,000
1914

Potash

INDUSTRIALIZED EUROPE

From 1850, Britain's position as the unchallenged leader of industrialization was threatened as other countries, notably the US and Germany, began to modernize. The industrializing nations of this second revolution pioneered technologies that helped change the world.

In 1851, Great Britain held the Great Exhibition, a showcase of the achievements of British industry, at the Crystal Palace in London's Hyde Park. It marked the pinnacle of Britain's industrial dominance. Britain's success had been built on the mechanization of the textile industry and leadership in the iron industry. But, by 1850, much of northern Europe was catching up, building factories and developing their own exploitation of mineral resources, such as coal and iron. In the second half of the 19th century, social and political changes in Germany, the United States, Russia, and Japan sparked a new wave of industrialization, and the industrial balance shifted in their favor. World industrial output from 1870 to 1914 increased at an extraordinary rate: coal production rose by 650 percent; steel by 2,500 percent; and steam engine capacity by over 350 percent.

This second industrial revolution brought significant innovations in engineering and science: the internal combustion engine, petroleum, communication technologies, armaments, and chemicals all played a part. It also brought new opportunities for the wealthy nations of the West to extend their influence through investment and control of industrial knowledge. However, the developed nations of the late 19th century also had to contend with an increasingly educated and informed urban working class, ready to fight for their rights to better living and working conditions.

EMPIRE AND INDUSTRIALIZATION

The pace of industrialization was, in many countries, determined by the interests of colonial powers. In South America, European investment helped to build railways and shipyards to facilitate exports of coffee and meat. In India—which was both a source of raw materials and a market for Britain's industrial goods—the British saw little to be gained from industrialization.

KEY

- ▦ Major industrial regions c.1914
- ⚙ Heavy machinery
- Iron and steel
- Textile production

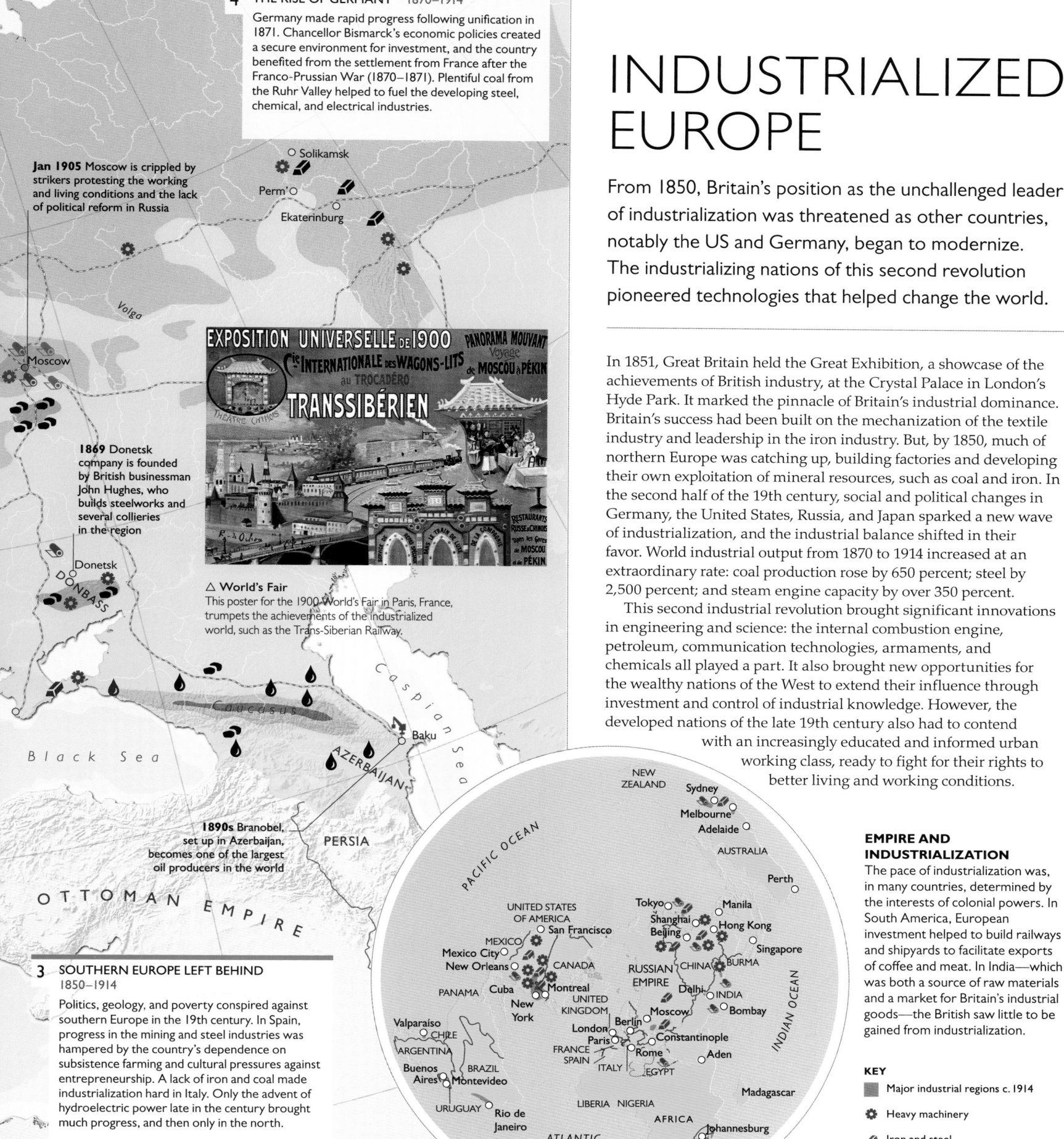

4 THE RISE OF GERMANY 1870–1914
Germany made rapid progress following unification in 1871. Chancellor Bismarck's economic policies created a secure environment for investment, and the country benefited from the settlement from France after the Franco-Prussian War (1870–1871). Plentiful coal from the Ruhr Valley helped to fuel the developing steel, chemical, and electrical industries.

Jan 1905 Moscow is crippled by strikers protesting the working and living conditions and the lack of political reform in Russia

1869 Donetsk company is founded by British businessman John Hughes, who builds steelworks and several collieries in the region

△ **World's Fair**
This poster for the 1900 World's Fair in Paris, France, trumpets the achievements of the industrialized world, such as the Trans-Siberian Railway.

1890s Branobel, set up in Azerbaijan, becomes one of the largest oil producers in the world

3 SOUTHERN EUROPE LEFT BEHIND
1850–1914
Politics, geology, and poverty conspired against southern Europe in the 19th century. In Spain, progress in the mining and steel industries was hampered by the country's dependence on subsistence farming and cultural pressures against entrepreneurship. A lack of iron and coal made industrialization hard in Italy. Only the advent of hydroelectric power late in the century brought much progress, and then only in the north.

SOCIALISM AND ANARCHISM

Socialist ideas of common ownership of resources and production had a long history. However, socialism developed as a political theory in the 1840s; it spread across the world in several forms, including a variant taken up by anarchists.

△ **Fathers of socialism**
A statue of Karl Marx (left) and Friedrich Engels stands in the Marx-Engels Forum, a public park in Berlin, Germany.

In 1848, German thinkers Karl Marx and Friedrich Engels published *The Communist Manifesto,* suggesting that workers would inevitably revolt against capitalists and move toward communism—public ownership and control of production and resources.

The ideas quickly spread. At a meeting in London in 1864, an influential federation of labor groups called the First International was founded. In 1871, the Paris Commune created the world's first, albeit short-lived, socialist government. By 1872, socialists were divided over how to achieve their aims.

While moderates developed political parties to work within the parliamentary system, radicals turned to anarchism—a philosophy that deems all governments unnecessary. Anarchism took many forms; some were peaceful, but others came to be associated with terrorism. By the early 1900s, anarchists had bombed several western cities and assassinated King Umberto I of Italy and US President William McKinley.

A revolutionary direction

Socialism took another path in Russia when Vladimir Lenin proposed that workers needed a Revolutionary Party to lead them to communism. In 1922, Russia formed the Union of Soviet Socialist Republics (USSR)—a socialist state that finally collapsed in 1991.

△ **Violent display of anarchy**
A contemporary illustration shows the anarchist Leon Czolgosz shooting US President William McKinley while the president greets visitors at the Pan-American Exposition in Buffalo, New York, on September 6, 1901. The president died 8 days later.

Paris's Bloody Week
This print shows Paris burning after the French National Guard set fire to the Paris Commune's headquarters on May 24, 1871. More than 20,000 supporters of the Commune were killed in the "Bloody Week."

1 CANAL CONSTRUCTION 1825–1914

The Industrial Revolution fueled a boom in canal building that created thousands of miles of new inland waterways and dramatically reduced journey times along the world's trade routes. The Panama and Suez Canals were impressive feats of engineering, but costly; over 5,000 workers died constructing the $375-million Panama Canal, and 120,000 died building the $100-million Suez Canal.

🛶 Major Canals

2 THE ELECTRIC TELEGRAPH 1844–1914

The electric telegraph allowed messages to travel hundreds of miles. Undersea telegraph cables revolutionized global communication. The first, laid across the Atlantic, cut the time for a message from Europe to reach the US from days to hours. Poor reception on the first cable meant that messages were transmitted at 0.1 words a minute. Undersea cables soon connected the world.

— Underwater telegraph cable route

3 MASS TRANSIT IN THE CITIES 1863–1914

In January 1863, London became the first city to run trains underground. The network transported 38,000 passengers on its first day alone, and its success prompted other cities to develop their own. The underground trains boosted the economy by introducing a more efficient way to transport increasing numbers of workers across the cities.

🚇 Underground train systems

1858 First transatlantic telegraph cable laid between Ireland and Newfoundland
1866 The SS Great Eastern steamship lays a second, more reliable cable

August 1858 Queen Victoria sends first transatlantic telegraph message to President Buchanan; it takes 17 hours to arrive

1895 Manchester Ship Canal links Manchester to the Irish Sea and makes the city one of Britain's busiest ports

1895 Kiel Canal links the North Sea to the Baltic Sea, saving a 288-mile (463-km) journey around Jutland

1863 First underground train system opens in London

1825 Erie Canal links New York and Atlantic coast to the Great Lakes

1901 The United States' first underground railway opens

1907 Mauritania sets new record by crossing the Atlantic in 4.5 days

1896 Glasgow
1863 London
1900 Paris
1912 Hamburg
1902 Berlin
1896 Budapest
1896 Rome
1904 Athens

1896 Continental Europe's first underground system opens in Budapest

Railroads transport beef cattle from western grasslands to the populated east coast

1901 Boston
1904 New York
1907 Philadelphia
1844 Samuel Morse sends first electric telegraph message in the US

1900 The Paris Metro's first line opens less than 2 years after construction began

1869 Steamships gain a competitive edge from the faster route offered by the Suez Canal, which is not open to sailing ships

1914 Panama Canal completed—the fastest route between the Atlantic and Pacific Oceans

◁ **The Paris Metro**
This French cartoon from 1886 mocks plans for an above-ground railway system in Paris; the city's underground railway opened in 1990

1876 First successful export of refrigerated meat from Argentina

1913 Buenos Aires
1913 Buenos Aires' Subte becomes first underground system in Latin America

4 THE ADVENT OF OCEAN-GOING STEAMSHIPS 1830–1914

Steamships crossed the Atlantic from the early 1830s. Improvements to ships and their engines in the middle of the century increased the distances they could travel before recoaling, reducing journey times. Steamships were larger and could carry more cargo and passengers, making long-distance trade far more profitable.

- - - North Atlantic shipping route
···· Other shipping routes

5 TECHNOLOGY AND EXPORT 1876–1914

New, refrigerated ships and the spread of railways opened up new export markets. Cattle raised in America or Australia and New Zealand were sent by train to processing plants on the coast, from which ships carried the meat around the world. Refrigeration also boosted fruit exports, giving rise to the "banana republics" of Central America.

Major rail networks c.1914 | Lamb and mutton | Beef cattle
Fruit | Tea

Map labels: CANADA, NORTH AMERICA, USA, Prince Rupert, Portland, San Francisco, Los Angeles, Chicago, Montreal, Washington, New Orleans, MEXICO, Mexico City, CUBA, PANAMA, Guayaquil, Callao, SOUTH AMERICA, BRAZIL, Pará (Belém), Bahia (Salvador), Rio de Janeiro, Valparaíso, Santiago, CHILE, ARGENTINA, URUGUAY, Montevideo, Buenos Aires, ATLANTIC OCEAN, UNITED KINGDOM, EUROPE, GERMAN EMPIRE, FRANCE, SPAIN, ITALY, AUSTRIA-HUNGARY, Moscow, Rome, Istanbul, OTTOMAN EMPIRE, EGYPT, Arabian Peninsula, Karachi, Aden, AFRICA, Conakry, LIBERIA, Lagos, NIGERIA, Luanda, Mombasa, BRITISH EAST AFRICA, INDIAN OCEAN, Walvis, Beira, MADAGASCAR, Johannesburg, Lourenço Marques, CAPE COLONY, NATAL, Cape Town, Durban

THE IMPACT OF ADVANCES

Technological advances in shipbuilding, electric telegraphy, mass transit, canal construction, the railways, and refrigeration contributed to the economic revolution in the 19th century, helping create a worldwide trading system.

TIMELINE

1						
2						
3						
4						
5						
1820	1840	1860	1880	1900	1920	

RUSSIAN EMPIRE

ASIA

CHINA

PACIFIC OCEAN

Vladivostok

Tokyo

Shanghai

1866 The steamship *Agamemnon* successfully sails from London to China with only one stop, substantially outpacing sailing ships on the route

BURMA

Calcutta

Hong Kong

Manila

Singapore

1870 Cables between Singapore and Darwin in north Australia complete a telegraphic link between Britain and its farthest dominions

Darwin

Broome

AUSTRALIA

Brisbane

Perth

Adelaide

Melbourne

Sydney

Auckland

NEW ZEALAND

Napier

1880 Refrigerated beef and mutton is successfully shipped 15,000 miles (24,000 km) from Australia to London

Dunedin

1879 The *Dunedin* successfully transports the first full cargo of refrigerated meat from New Zealand to London

TRANSPORT AND COMMUNICATIONS

In the 19th century, transport and communications were transformed. In turn, they transformed the world's economy by improving productivity in the cities, speeding up intercontinental communication, and increasing trade profits. Developments in refrigeration and the railways created new export opportunities.

Advances in technology made the world a much smaller place. The sailing ships that had, for centuries, plied the long-distance routes around the globe gave way to steamships capable of carrying more cargo more quickly and profitably. In the 1830s, steamer journeys across the Atlantic took 17 days. Continued steam engine improvements made the ships even faster and by 1910, transatlantic journey times had been reduced to just 5 days. The shortcuts provided by the great Canals built during the 19th and early 20th centuries allowed ships to bypass notoriously dangerous passages like those around the Cape of Africa and the tip of South America. And as journeys became less risky, insurance costs came down and profits increased further. By the end of the 19th century, even the farthest-flung corners of the world were participating in the global economy. Once refrigeration had been mastered, frozen beef, lamb, and mutton from as far afield as New Zealand and the tip of South America, along with fruit from South Africa and Central America, were crossing the oceans to feed the hungry workforces of Europe's and North America's industrial cities. Electric telegraphy and mass transportation systems ensured that the wheels of commerce in the cities turned smoothly.

"Cunard's liners and the electric telegraph, are ... signs that ... there is a mighty spirit working among us."

CHARLES KINGSLEY, FROM HIS NOVEL *YEAST* (1851)

SAMUEL MORSE
1791–1872

A successful artist born in Massachusetts in 1791, Samuel Morse began working on improving electric telegraphy in the 1830s after hearing about the newly invented electromagnet on a ship home from Europe. Morse's design used a single telegraph wire to send messages. He created a system for encoding messages, known as Morse Code, using short and long electrical signals to represent letters. These signals were then sent along the wire to a stylus operated by an electromagnet that embossed the code onto a moving paper tape. He completed America's first electric telegraph line in 1844.

MASS MIGRATIONS

In the 19th century, millions left their home countries in search of stability, freedom, and employment. As they left the Old World behind, flowing out from Russia, Europe, China, and India, the younger countries of the Americas and Australasia saw their populations boom.

The political, social, and economic changes wrought by the Industrial Revolution, coupled with new forms of mass transportation, caused a huge surge in migration in the 19th century. Newly mechanized industries demanded a concentration of labor on a scale never seen before. A ready supply of migrant labor was to be found among those fleeing economic hardship in Europe, India, and China. And with political upheaval and anti-Semitism in central Europe and the Russian Empire swelling the ranks of those seeking a new life, more than 80 million people left their country of origin in the 19th and early 20th centuries.

Many headed for the rapidly industrializing coastal regions of the United States, due to the end of the Civil War and the opening up of Native American land to new settlers. The emerging economies of South America drew millions from southern Europe, and hundreds of thousands were attracted by the promise of riches in the gold rush towns of Australia, Canada, and South Africa. That so many could travel so far was a result of the advances brought by the Industrial Revolution: the railroads, faster and safer ships, and new routes through the Panama and Suez Canals.

▷ *The Last of England*, 1855
This painting by the English artist Ford Madox Brown shows the apprehension on the faces of emigrants bound for an uncertain future in the gold fields of Australia.

THE AMERICAN DREAM 1800–1914

Over 50 million migrants traveled to North America in the 19th century, the majority of them to the United States, as wave after wave left their homes for the economic opportunities and political and religious freedom offered by the "land of the free." They initially came from northern Europe—Germany, Scandinavia, Britain, and Ireland—but from 1880, migrants from southern Europe, particularly Italy, began to arrive in large numbers.

1882 The US passes the Chinese Exclusion Act, stopping labor immigration from China

1860–1920 More than 5 million European migrants travel to Canada

1850–1880 Tens of thousands of Chinese laborers come to work in Peru's guano, sugar, and cotton industries

1888 Slavery is abolished in Brazil, triggering a large influx of immigrants

Panama Canal 1914

JEWISH MIGRATION (1880–1914)

The 19th century brought persecution to the world's largest Jewish population, in Russia. When the assassination of Alexander II in 1881 prompted years of government-sanctioned pogroms, the Jews flooded out of Russia, heading for the Holy Land. Some Jews moved toward western Europe and were soon joined by those fleeing anti-Semitism in the Ottoman Empire.

CANADA ● 105,000
USA ● 2 million
CENTRAL AND SOUTH AMERICA ● 14,000
ARGENTINA ● 113,000
PALESTINE ● 70,000
SOUTH AFRICA ● 43,000

KEY
- Major concentration of Jews in the Russian Empire
- Region with emigrating Jewish population
- Region with substantial Jewish immigration
- ● Gateway city
- → Jewish migrations
- ● Number of Jewish immigrants 1880–1914

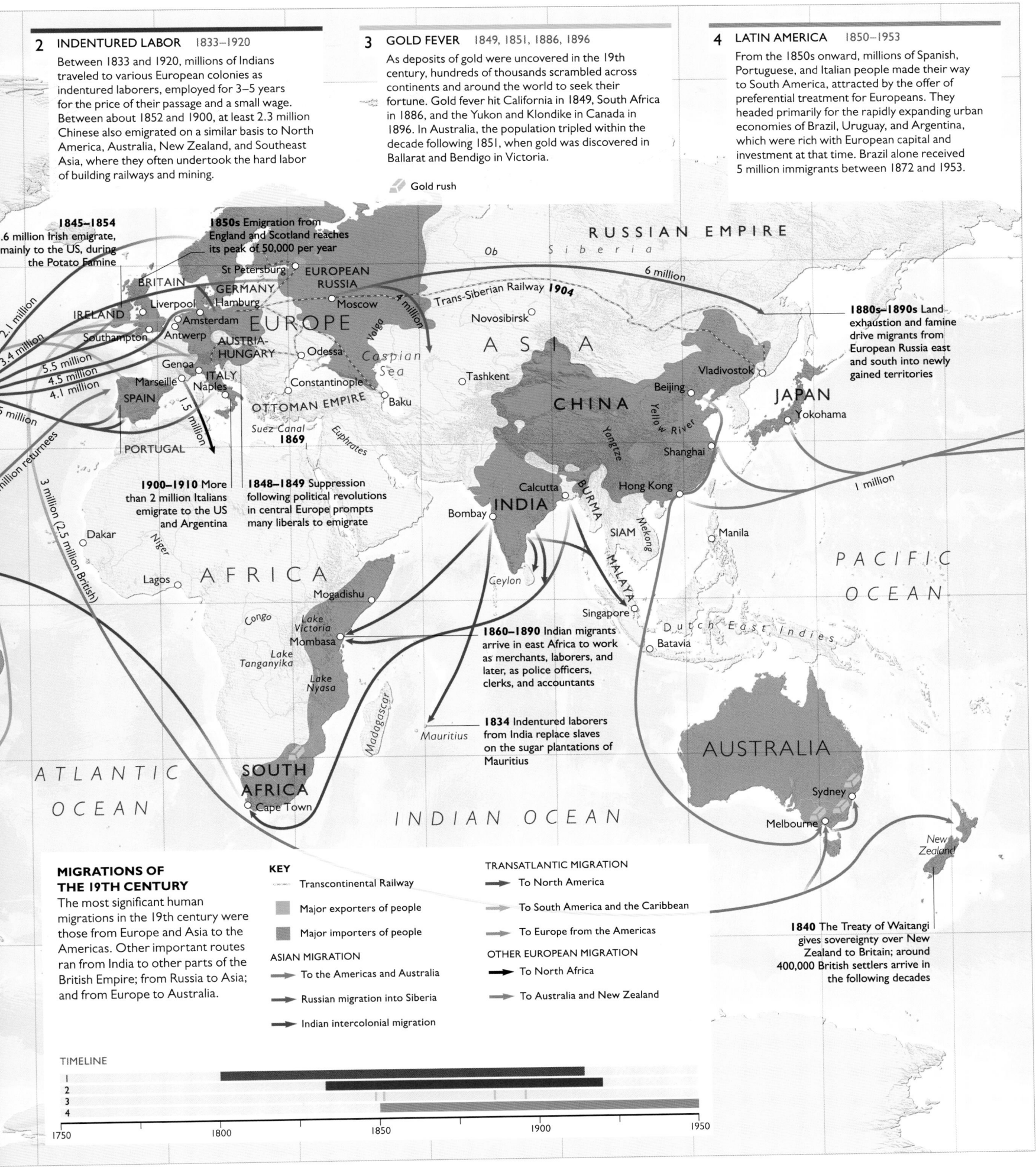

2 INDENTURED LABOR 1833–1920

Between 1833 and 1920, millions of Indians traveled to various European colonies as indentured laborers, employed for 3–5 years for the price of their passage and a small wage. Between about 1852 and 1900, at least 2.3 million Chinese also emigrated on a similar basis to North America, Australia, New Zealand, and Southeast Asia, where they often undertook the hard labor of building railways and mining.

3 GOLD FEVER 1849, 1851, 1886, 1896

As deposits of gold were uncovered in the 19th century, hundreds of thousands scrambled across continents and around the world to seek their fortune. Gold fever hit California in 1849, South Africa in 1886, and the Yukon and Klondike in Canada in 1896. In Australia, the population tripled within the decade following 1851, when gold was discovered in Ballarat and Bendigo in Victoria.

Gold rush

4 LATIN AMERICA 1850–1953

From the 1850s onward, millions of Spanish, Portuguese, and Italian people made their way to South America, attracted by the offer of preferential treatment for Europeans. They headed primarily for the rapidly expanding urban economies of Brazil, Uruguay, and Argentina, which were rich with European capital and investment at that time. Brazil alone received 5 million immigrants between 1872 and 1953.

1845–1854 .6 million Irish emigrate, mainly to the US, during the Potato Famine

1850s Emigration from England and Scotland reaches its peak of 50,000 per year

2.1 million
3.4 million
5.5 million
4.5 million
4.1 million
5 million
1.5 million
million returnees
3 million (2.5 million British)

Trans-Siberian Railway **1904**

6 million

4 million

1880s–1890s Land exhaustion and famine drive migrants from European Russia east and south into newly gained territories

1 million

1900–1910 More than 2 million Italians emigrate to the US and Argentina

1848–1849 Suppression following political revolutions in central Europe prompts many liberals to emigrate

Suez Canal **1869**

1860–1890 Indian migrants arrive in east Africa to work as merchants, laborers, and later, as police officers, clerks, and accountants

1834 Indentured laborers from India replace slaves on the sugar plantations of Mauritius

RUSSIAN EMPIRE
Ob · Siberia
St Petersburg · EUROPEAN RUSSIA
BRITAIN · GERMANY · Hamburg · Moscow
Liverpool · Amsterdam · Novosibirsk
IRELAND · Antwerp · EUROPE
Southampton · AUSTRIA-HUNGARY · Volga
Genoa · Odessa · Caspian Sea
Marseille · ITALY · Constantinople · Tashkent
SPAIN · Naples · Baku
OTTOMAN EMPIRE · Euphrates
PORTUGAL

ASIA · CHINA · Beijing · Vladivostok · JAPAN
Yellow River · Yokohama
Yangtze · Shanghai
Calcutta · Hong Kong
INDIA · BURMA
Bombay · SIAM · Manila
Ceylon · MALAYA · Mekong
Singapore

Dakar · Niger · AFRICA
Lagos · Congo · Lake Victoria · Mombasa · Mogadishu
Lake Tanganyika
Lake Nyasa
Madagascar · Mauritius
SOUTH AFRICA · Cape Town

Dutch East Indies · Batavia
PACIFIC OCEAN

AUSTRALIA
Sydney
Melbourne
New Zealand

ATLANTIC OCEAN
INDIAN OCEAN

1840 The Treaty of Waitangi gives sovereignty over New Zealand to Britain; around 400,000 British settlers arrive in the following decades

MIGRATIONS OF THE 19TH CENTURY

The most significant human migrations in the 19th century were those from Europe and Asia to the Americas. Other important routes ran from India to other parts of the British Empire; from Russia to Asia; and from Europe to Australia.

KEY

- - - Transcontinental Railway

Major exporters of people

Major importers of people

ASIAN MIGRATION
→ To the Americas and Australia
→ Russian migration into Siberia
→ Indian intercolonial migration

TRANSATLANTIC MIGRATION
→ To North America
→ To South America and the Caribbean
→ To Europe from the Americas

OTHER EUROPEAN MIGRATION
→ To North Africa
→ To Australia and New Zealand

TIMELINE

1
2
3
4

1750 · 1800 · 1850 · 1900 · 1950

THE AGE OF IMPERIALISM

In the 19th century, forces of imperialism reshaped the world, as nations sought to gain control of overseas territories that would provide valuable resources, space for growing populations, and power in a competitive world.

△ **Ravaging their colonies**
Contemporary cartoons frequently satirized the plundering nature of imperialism. In this American cartoon from 1885, Germany, England, and Russia grab pieces of Africa and Asia.

The middle of the 19th century witnessed a dramatic shift in European overseas expansion. For centuries, European activities overseas had been dominated by trade and the creation of a chain of staging posts, by which the riches of the East could be brought to Europe. However, this changed in the 1870s. Countries everywhere scrambled to annex new territories and strengthen their control over existing colonies, and new nations competed with the old colonial powers. By 1900, the world was largely imperial, setting the stage for World War I.

Reasons for imperialism

The shift from colonialism to imperialism was largely driven and facilitated by industrialization (see pp.232–233), which required vast amounts of raw materials. Imperialism gave nations control over raw materials, access to labor and huge new markets, and plenty of investment opportunities.

The colonies offered ample chances for those hoping to make their fortune, and some countries—mainly Britain and France—needed space for their growing populations. The desire to become a "Great Power" also nudged many countries to expand. European countries were keen to reassert themselves or carve out new identities. Britain hoped to recover its stature after losing its American colonies, France wanted to rebuild its power, and Russia continued its push eastward into the weakening Qing Empire in China. From the 1860s, the young nations of Germany, Italy, and the US sought to become world powers. Emerging from centuries of

isolation, Japan, too, was keen to gain access to the resources it lacked and living space for its people, while being painfully aware that it was itself vulnerable to imperialism.

In addition to the economic and political benefits of imperialism, there was also a belief in the superiority of the white man. As scientists sought to apply Charles Darwin's theory of evolution to humankind, the perceived "advanced" state of Western society was used to justify imperialism. Many Westerners felt that they had a moral duty to Christianize "native" cultures. It was an attitude neatly summed up in Kipling's 1899 poem "The White Man's Burden," which exhorted Americans to colonize the Philippines. It spoke of a white man's moral obligation to rule the nonwhite peoples, or the "other," and encourage their economic, cultural, and social progress.

Building empires

The huge empires built in the 19th century were largely made possible by the advances brought about by industrialization. Modern medicine, such as the discovery of quinine as a treatment for malaria, meant that Europeans could push farther than ever before into lands rife with tropical disease. Modern communications, such as railways and telegraph lines, allowed large areas to be easily

◁ **Resisting imperialism**
Zulu chief Cetshwayo kaMpande led his warriors against the British in 1879. His defeat removed a major threat to British colonial interests in South Africa.

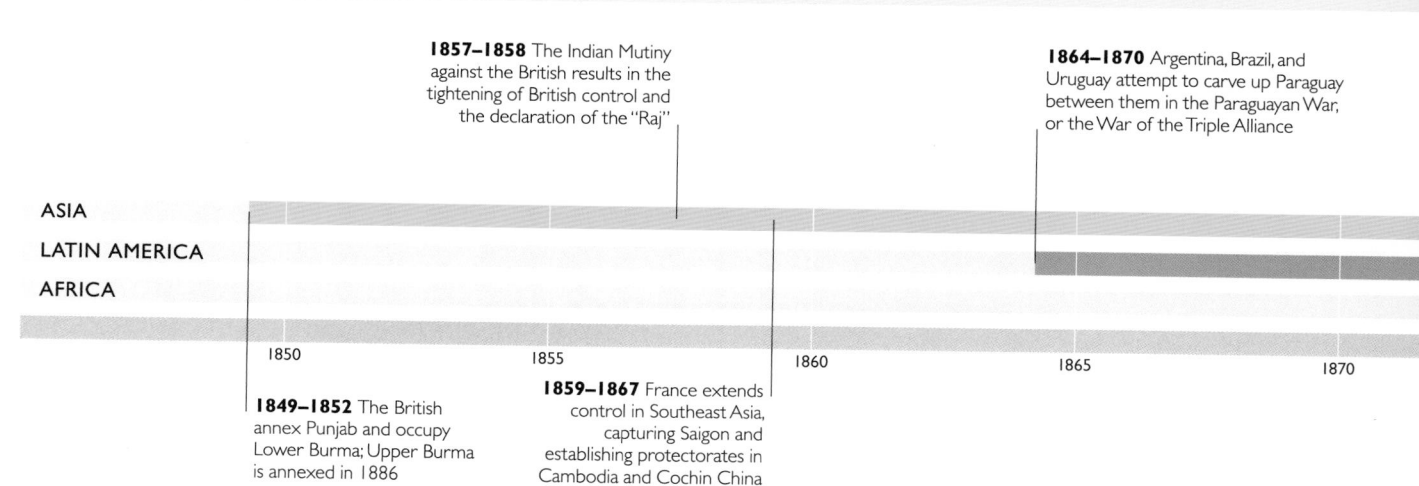

THE IMPERIAL WORLD

Patterns of imperial activity varied around the world. While the colonization of Africa was marked by a scramble in which almost all major European countries took part, India and Southeast Asia were mainly dominated by the British and French, respectively. The decaying Qing Empire provided easy pickings for Japan and Russia. While Britain and the US sought to bring Latin America within their spheres of influence, Latin American countries also embarked on their own expansionist ventures.

1857–1858 The Indian Mutiny against the British results in the tightening of British control and the declaration of the "Raj"

1864–1870 Argentina, Brazil, and Uruguay attempt to carve up Paraguay between them in the Paraguayan War, or the War of the Triple Alliance

ASIA

LATIN AMERICA

AFRICA

1850   1855   1860   1865   1870

1849–1852 The British annex Punjab and occupy Lower Burma; Upper Burma is annexed in 1886

1859–1867 France extends control in Southeast Asia, capturing Saigon and establishing protectorates in Cambodia and Cochin China

◁ **Soft imperialism**
Built with British expertise, using British materials, the Retiro Railway Station in Buenos Aires is an example of how imperial influence extended beyond official colonies through cultural, financial, and industrial means.

controlled. New mechanized weaponry made it possible to suppress local resistance; this also meant that brutality was a frequent companion of imperialism.

Even countries that were not directly colonized came under the influence of imperialist nations. For example, in Latin America, political and economic intervention helped secure American and British influence in the region. Cultural influence helped the imperialist nations to embed their lifestyles and aspirations both in their colonies and beyond.

"I am an anti-imperialist. I am opposed to having the eagle put its talons on any other land."

MARK TWAIN, WRITER,
NEW YORK HERALD, 1900

▽ **Military might**
Japan destroyed Russia's Baltic Fleet at the Battle of Tsushima in 1905 during the Russo-Japanese War. Japan's victory was proof of her increasing military and imperial power and of Russia's growing weakness.

1876 Queen Victoria is proclaimed the Empress of India

1884–1899 Germany creates German New Guinea after annexing territories in the Pacific

1889–1896 Italy establishes its first colony in Eritrea but is kept out of Abyssinia by the armies of King Menelik II at the Battle of Adwa

1895 France creates the federation of French West Africa, comprising eight territories

1895–1898 The Venezuela Crisis—a border dispute between British Guyana and Venezuela—justifies US intervention in the region

1904–1905 Japan defeats Russia to become the first non-European nation to defeat a great European power

1875   1880   1885   1890   1895   1900   1905

1876 A scramble for Africa begins when Belgian King Leopold II begins colonizing Congo

1884–1886 Germany acquires parts of southwest Africa, present-day Togo, and Cameroon. It agrees to share east Africa with Britain

1894–1895 Japan gains control of China's Liaodong peninsula and annexes Formosa (modern-day Taiwan)

1898 Victory in the Spanish-American War gives the US Cuba and Puerto Rico

1899–1902 The Second Anglo-Boer War gives Britain control of South Africa, paving the way for the creation of the British Union of South Africa in 1910

THE NEW IMPERIALISM

The 19th century saw a remarkable wave of imperial activity as freedom from war, the second wave of the Industrial Revolution, and the emergence of new countries fueled the land grab of most of Africa, the Pacific, and southern Asia among European powers.

In 1830, the European colonies were in retreat. The French, British, and Spanish had been swept out of the Americas in a wave of revolution. Only Russia, with its vast empire in north and central Asia, and Britain, holding Canada, Australia, and India, retained significant territory. However, conditions were ripe for the emergence of renewed imperial activity and new forms of imperialism.

Britain made a cautious start. Many of its acquisitions—Singapore (1819), Malacca (1824), Hong Kong (1842), Natal (1843), and Lower Burma (1852)—were driven by a desire to secure the trade routes to the East Indies and protect its position in India. France acquired Algeria (1830s) and Tahiti and the Marquesas in the South Pacific (1840s), then gained a foothold in Indochina (1858–1859).

By 1870, Europeans had not yet penetrated Africa's interior, and much of Indochina and China remained untouched, but this was not to last far beyond 1880, when the Second Industrial Revolution created a strong demand for raw materials and markets. By then, the unified countries of Germany and Italy—along with the US and Japan—were eager to challenge the older colonial powers. In the last 20 years of the century, the European nations carved up almost all of Africa, while in Asia, the weakness of the Qing Dynasty allowed the French, British, Russians, and Japanese to extend their influence deep into China. Between 1880 and 1914, Europe added 8.5 million square miles (20.7 million sq km) to its overseas possessions, and Britain and France ruled more than 500 million people between them.

OVERCOMING RESISTANCE
FORCE AND TRICKERY IN THE COLONIES

Colonists faced almost constant pressure from local uprisings. In Indochina, for example, the French were engaged in a guerilla war from 1883–1913. Brute force was the usual response—the Herero rising against the Germans in Southwest Africa in 1904 ended in genocide—but trickery played a part, too, as Cecil Rhodes showed when in 1888, he deceived King Lobengula into signing away mining rights for his territory in Matabeleland.

Cecil Rhodes with the Matabeles
Rhodes, prime minister of Britain's Cape Colony, confronts the Matabele in this contemporary illustration.

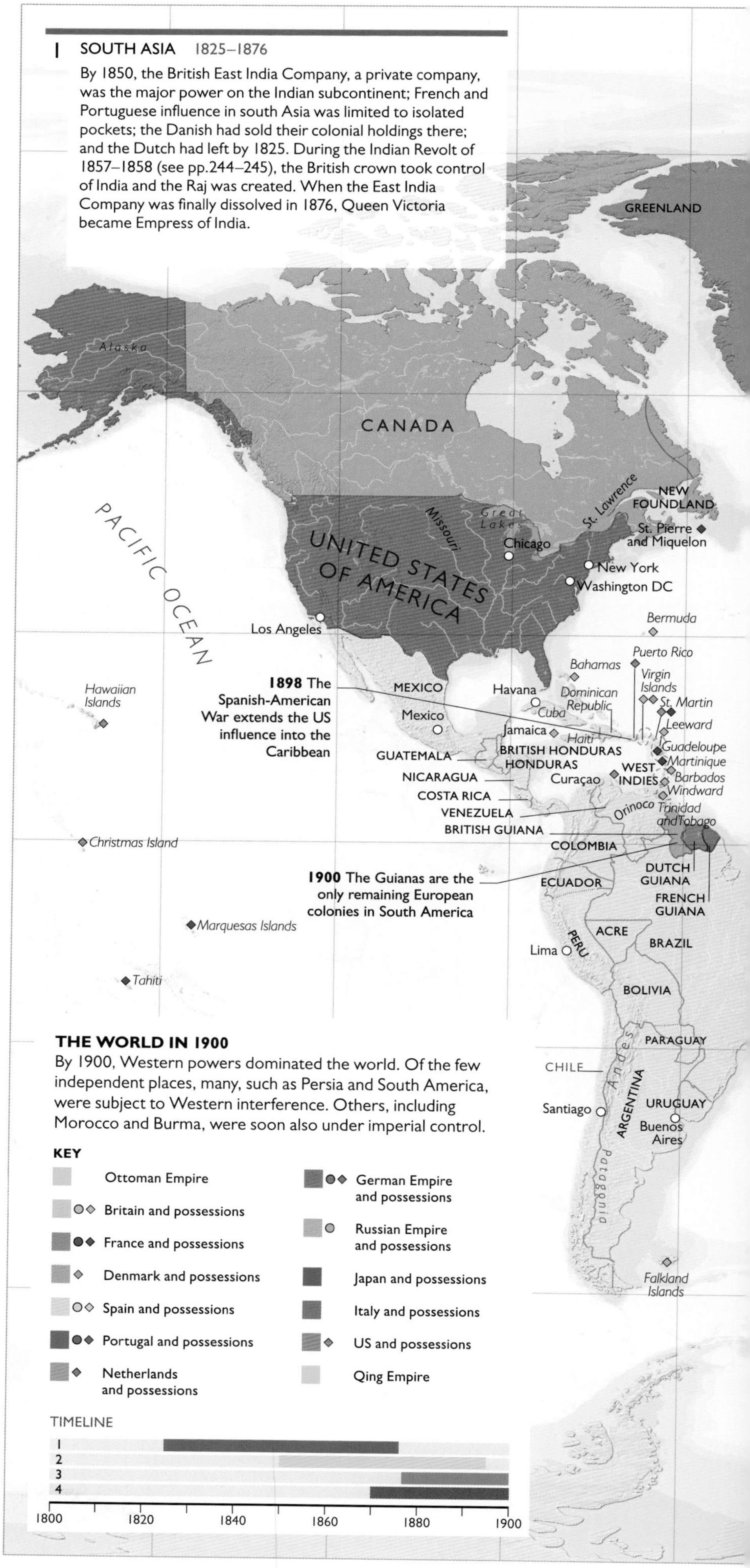

SOUTH ASIA 1825–1876

By 1850, the British East India Company, a private company, was the major power on the Indian subcontinent; French and Portuguese influence in south Asia was limited to isolated pockets; the Danish had sold their colonial holdings there; and the Dutch had left by 1825. During the Indian Revolt of 1857–1858 (see pp.244–245), the British crown took control of India and the Raj was created. When the East India Company was finally dissolved in 1876, Queen Victoria became Empress of India.

1898 The Spanish-American War extends the US influence into the Caribbean

1900 The Guianas are the only remaining European colonies in South America

THE WORLD IN 1900

By 1900, Western powers dominated the world. Of the few independent places, many, such as Persia and South America, were subject to Western interference. Others, including Morocco and Burma, were soon also under imperial control.

KEY

Ottoman Empire		○◆ German Empire and possessions	
○◆ Britain and possessions			
●◆ France and possessions		○ Russian Empire and possessions	
◆ Denmark and possessions		Japan and possessions	
○◆ Spain and possessions		Italy and possessions	
●◆ Portugal and possessions		◆ US and possessions	
◆ Netherlands and possessions		Qing Empire	

TIMELINE

1800 — 1820 — 1840 — 1860 — 1880 — 1900

Map labels: GREENLAND, CANADA, Alaska, UNITED STATES OF AMERICA, Great Lakes, Missouri, St. Lawrence, Chicago, NEW FOUNDLAND, St. Pierre and Miquelon, New York, Washington DC, Bermuda, Los Angeles, PACIFIC OCEAN, Hawaiian Islands, MEXICO, Mexico, Havana, Cuba, Bahamas, Puerto Rico, Virgin Islands, Dominican Republic, St. Martin, Haiti, Jamaica, Leeward, GUATEMALA, BRITISH HONDURAS, HONDURAS, Guadeloupe, Martinique, WEST INDIES, Barbados, NICARAGUA, Curaçao, Windward, COSTA RICA, VENEZUELA, Orinoco, Trinidad and Tobago, BRITISH GUIANA, Christmas Island, COLOMBIA, DUTCH GUIANA, ECUADOR, FRENCH GUIANA, ACRE, Marquesas Islands, PERU, Lima, BRAZIL, Tahiti, BOLIVIA, PARAGUAY, CHILE, Andes, Santiago, ARGENTINA, URUGUAY, Buenos Aires, Patagonia, Falkland Islands

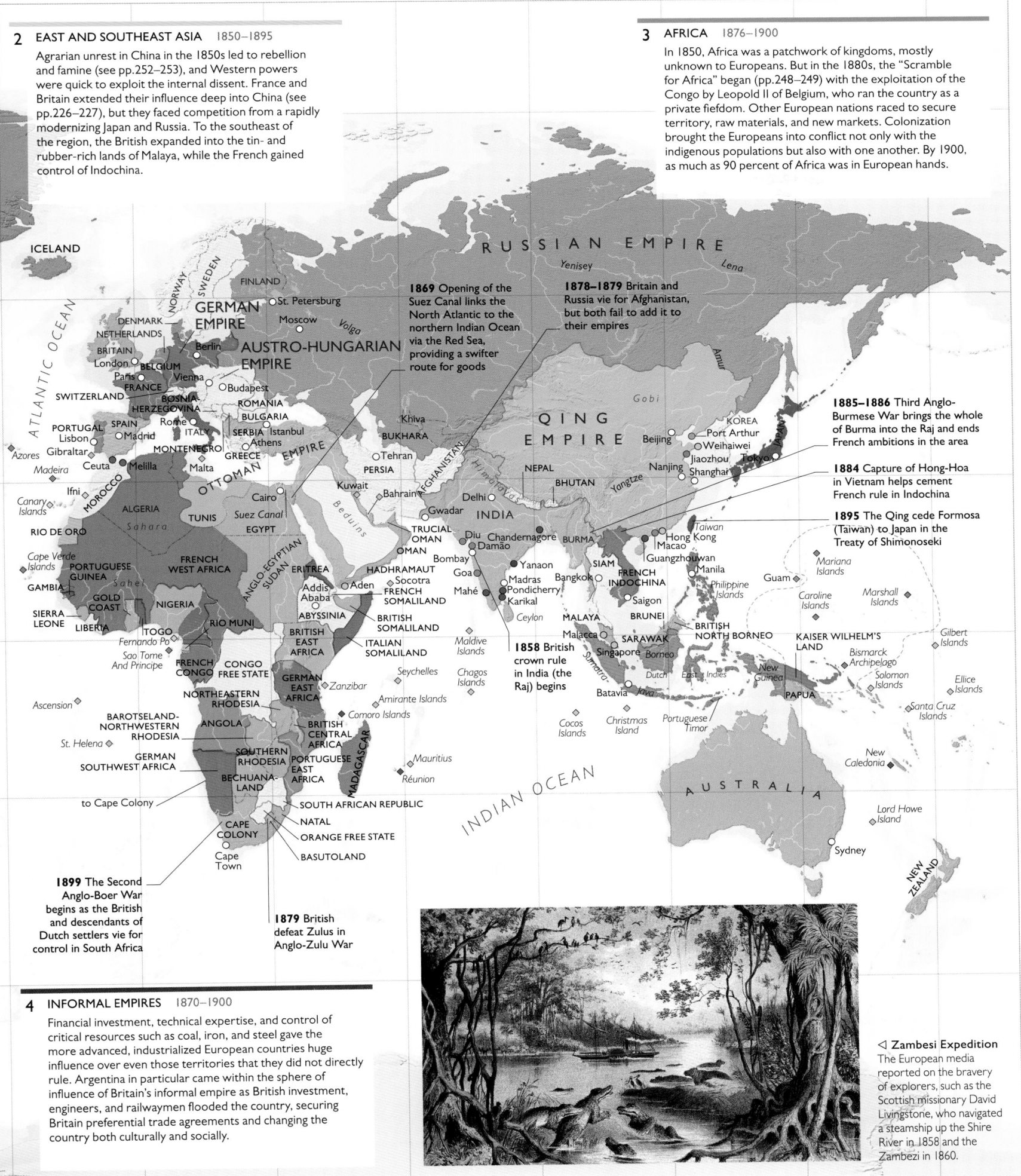

2 EAST AND SOUTHEAST ASIA 1850–1895

Agrarian unrest in China in the 1850s led to rebellion and famine (see pp.252–253), and Western powers were quick to exploit the internal dissent. France and Britain extended their influence deep into China (see pp.226–227), but they faced competition from a rapidly modernizing Japan and Russia. To the southeast of the region, the British expanded into the tin- and rubber-rich lands of Malaya, while the French gained control of Indochina.

3 AFRICA 1876–1900

In 1850, Africa was a patchwork of kingdoms, mostly unknown to Europeans. But in the 1880s, the "Scramble for Africa" began (pp.248–249) with the exploitation of the Congo by Leopold II of Belgium, who ran the country as a private fiefdom. Other European nations raced to secure territory, raw materials, and new markets. Colonization brought the Europeans into conflict not only with the indigenous populations but also with one another. By 1900, as much as 90 percent of Africa was in European hands.

1869 Opening of the Suez Canal links the North Atlantic to the northern Indian Ocean via the Red Sea, providing a swifter route for goods

1878–1879 Britain and Russia vie for Afghanistan, but both fail to add it to their empires

1885–1886 Third Anglo-Burmese War brings the whole of Burma into the Raj and ends French ambitions in the area

1884 Capture of Hong-Hoa in Vietnam helps cement French rule in Indochina

1895 The Qing cede Formosa (Taiwan) to Japan in the Treaty of Shimonoseki

1858 British crown rule in India (the Raj) begins

1899 The Second Anglo-Boer War begins as the British and descendants of Dutch settlers vie for control in South Africa

1879 British defeat Zulus in Anglo-Zulu War

4 INFORMAL EMPIRES 1870–1900

Financial investment, technical expertise, and control of critical resources such as coal, iron, and steel gave the more advanced, industrialized European countries huge influence over even those territories that they did not directly rule. Argentina in particular came within the sphere of influence of Britain's informal empire as British investment, engineers, and railwaymen flooded the country, securing Britain preferential trade agreements and changing the country both culturally and socially.

◁ **Zambesi Expedition**
The European media reported on the bravery of explorers, such as the Scottish missionary David Livingstone, who navigated a steamship up the Shire River in 1858 and the Zambezi in 1860.

RESISTANCE AND THE RAJ

In 1857–1858, a revolt by Indian soldiers threatened to force the British out of India. Instead, the British increased their control, creating the Raj under the direct rule of Queen Victoria.

Unrest was growing in India in the 1850s. Indians were worried about British expansionism and feared forced conversion to Christianity, suspecting that the British were trying to undermine traditional culture.

In 1857, a rumor spread among the sepoys (native soldiers) employed by the British. They came to believe that cartridges for the new Enfield rifles, which had to be opened with the teeth, were greased with cow or pig fat. This caused offense to both Hindus, who believed cows were sacred, and Muslims, who thought pigs were unclean. In spite of British reassurances that the cartridges were free from animal fat, the sepoys on parade at Meerut on May 10, 1857, refused to use them and mutinied.

△ **Enfield rifle cartridges**
Rumors about the fat used to grease the new Enfield rifle cartridges sparked a mutiny among India's sepoys, which developed into a wide-reaching Indian Revolt.

The mutiny quickly developed into a general revolt, spreading through Bengal, Oudh, and the Northwest Provinces as local princes, such as Nana Sahib and Lakshmi Bai, the Rani of Jhansi, tried to drive out the British. After atrocities on both sides, the British succeeded in quelling the rebellion by the end of 1858. Their position in India was totally changed. The East India Company was abolished, and the last ruler of the Mughal line, Bahadur Shah Zafar, was tried for treason and exiled, opening the way for direct rule by the British over India. The British Raj had been born.

THE REVOLT OF 1857–1858

From Meerut, the mutiny soon spread to other sepoy regiments around India and to the general populace. Some princely states remained neutral or loyal to the British, while others seized the chance to rebel. The revolt remained largely centered in northern India.

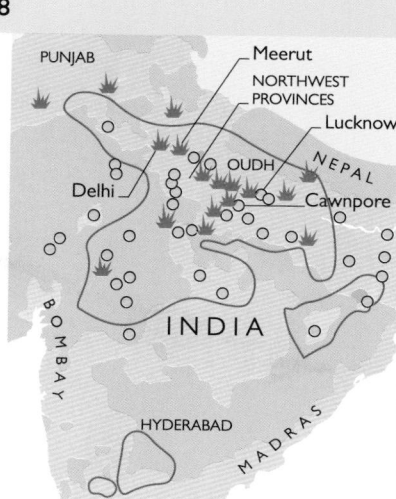

PUNJAB
Meerut
NORTHWEST PROVINCES
Lucknow
Delhi
OUDH
NEPAL
Cawnpore
BOMBAY
INDIA
HYDERABAD
MADRAS

KEY

British India
Princely states
— Areas affected by the revolt
○ Posts at which Indian troops mutinied
🔥 Main centers of rebellion

The Siege of Lucknow
Part of the British administrative headquarters, or Residency, in Lucknow, the Chattar Manzil palace was besieged by rebel forces for several months. The siege was eventually broken by the British in March 1858.

△ **The *Petropavlovsk* sinks**
Russia clashed with Japan over rival imperial ambitions in Manchuria and Korea. The battleship *Petropavlovsk*, shown in this illustration, was a casualty of the Russo-Japanese War in 1904.

1854–1855 The Siege of Sevastopol ends Russia's attempt to expand its territories in the Black Sea region

1 THE CONQUEST OF SIBERIA 1600–1812

Russia first tried to find a sea passage from the Arctic to the Pacific Ocean. When this failed, it turned to conquering Siberia in order to gain access to the Pacific coast and to win control over its land, minerals, and fur trade. Military forays and massacres, as well as diseases brought in by Russian trappers and traders, subdued the indigenous peoples. By 1650, Russia had colonized the whole of north Asia. Russia then reached North America, where it founded colonies in Alaska (1784) and California (1812).

2 EXPANSION TO THE WEST 1768–1815

For centuries, the Swedish Empire and the Polish-Lithuanian Commonwealth had limited Russia's western territory. However, the military reforms of two czars, Ivan V and Peter the Great, helped to bring much of Poland and Lithuania into the empire by 1795. Success against Sweden in the Finnish War (1808–1809) gave Russia the Grand Duchy of Finland. A final shuffle of Polish territories after the Napoleonic Wars (1803–1815) defined the western limits of the Russian Empire.

3 THE BLACK SEA AND CRIMEA 1768–1856

Under Empress Catherine the Great, Russia moved toward the Black Sea, securing the independence of the Crimean Khanate from the Ottoman Empire in the Russo-Turkish War (1768–1774) and then annexing it in 1783. By 1815, Russia had gained control of the entire northern shore of the Black Sea, and finally it had a warm-water port. Russia's attempt to occupy the Balkans, however, was swiftly suppressed in the Crimean War (1853–1856).

⚓ New Russian port

4 CENTRAL ASIA AND "THE GREAT GAME" 1830–1895

As Russia moved south and Britain moved north from its power base in India, a series of political and diplomatic confrontations known as "The Great Game" played out, as each side tried to expand its influence in Afghanistan and its surrounding countries. Ultimately, Afghanistan became a buffer zone, but Russia was able to annex the valuable lands of Bukhara, Khiva, and Samarkand.

🚩 Acquired by Russia during "The Great Game"   ▮ Afghanistan

5 RUSSIA AND MANCHURIA 1858–1914

From 1858, a weakening Qing Empire ceded Outer Manchuria to Russia—an area from which it had previously been excluded by the Treaty of Nerchinsk (1689). Russia founded Vladivostok, a relatively ice-free port and, in 1898, leased the Liaodong Peninsula from China, gaining the warm-water port of Port Arthur. Alarmed by Japan's growing interest in China, Russia occupied southern Manchuria but was defeated in the Russo-Japanese War (1904–1905) and abandoned its imperial ambitions in the area.

⚓ New Russian port

1808 The Treaty of Tilsit between Russia and France allows Russia to move against their common enemy—Sweden—and annex Finland

1709 Swedish defeat in the Battle of Poltava marks beginning of Russian supremacy in eastern Europe

19th century Russia conquers the Caucasus from the Persian Empire

Sep 1895 The Pamir Boundary Commission protocols define the border between Afghanistan and the Russian Empire

SWEDEN

FINLAND

Barents Sea

Severnaya Zemlya

Novaya Zemlya

Baltic Sea

St. Petersburg

POLISH-LITHUANIAN COMMONWEALTH

Moscow

Poltava

CRIMEAN KHANATE

Sevastopol

Black Sea

Ural'sk

Kazan

Perm

Samara

Yekaterinburg

Ural Mountains

Ob'

TOBOL'SK

1594 Surgut

YENISEYSK

1587 Tobol'sk

Yenisey

RUSSIAN

1743 Orenburg

1730

1731

1734

1716 Omsk

Irtysh

1619 Yeniseysk

1604 Tomsk

1628 Krasnoyarsk

Astrakhan

Caucasus

URAL'SK

1824

TURGAY

AKMOLINSK

TOMSK

1652 Irkuts

Baku

Caspian Sea

Aral Sea

Volga

Ural

1824

Syr Darya

1854

SEMIPALATINSK

1864

1718 Semipalatinsk

Altai Mountains

1912–21 URYANKHAI

TRANSCASPIAN

1873 KHIVA

Khiva

Amu Darya

1873

SYR DARYA

1864

Lake Balkhash

1871 SEMIRECH'YE

Tehran

Ashkhabad

Bukhara

1868–1870 SAMARKAND

Samarkand

1868 BUKHARA

Tashkent

TURKESTAN

FERGHANA

1871–1881 ILI

Tien Shan

MONGOL

PERSIA

AFGHANISTAN

Kabul

1895

Pamirs

Hindu Kush

Himalayas

Takla Makan Desert

XINJIANG

INDIA

TIBET

QING EMPIRE

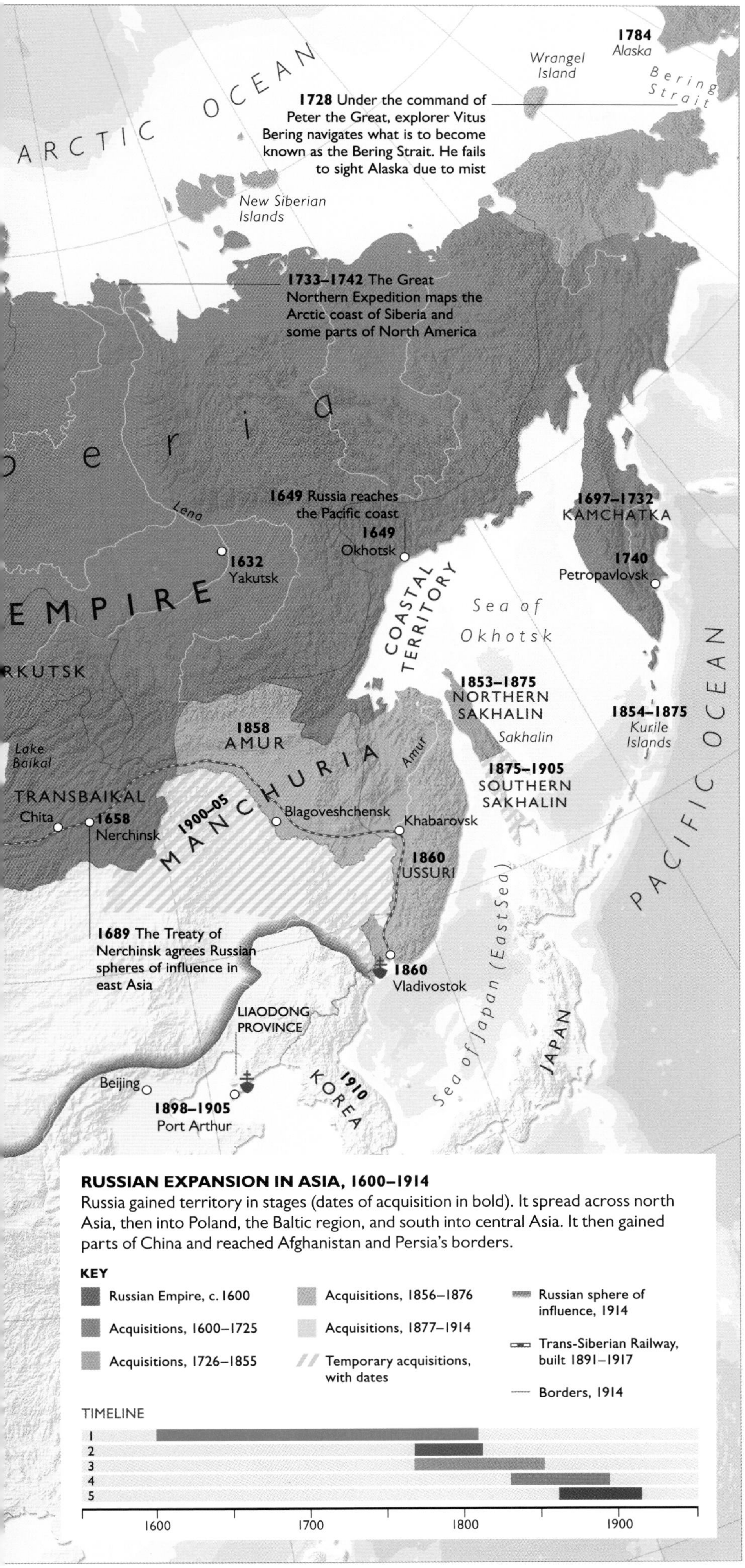

1784 Alaska

1728 Under the command of Peter the Great, explorer Vitus Bering navigates what is to become known as the Bering Strait. He fails to sight Alaska due to mist

Wrangel Island

Bering Strait

ARCTIC OCEAN

New Siberian Islands

1733–1742 The Great Northern Expedition maps the Arctic coast of Siberia and some parts of North America

Siberia

EMPIRE

Lena

1649 Russia reaches the Pacific coast
1649 Okhotsk

1632 Yakutsk

RKUTSK

1697–1732 KAMCHATKA

1740 Petropavlovsk

COASTAL TERRITORY

Sea of Okhotsk

1858 AMUR

Lake Baikal

Amur

1853–1875 NORTHERN SAKHALIN

Sakhalin

1854–1875 Kurile Islands

1875–1905 SOUTHERN SAKHALIN

TRANSBAIKAL
Chita **1658** Nerchinsk

MANCHURIA **1900–05**

Blagoveshchensk

Khabarovsk

1860 USSURI

PACIFIC OCEAN

1689 The Treaty of Nerchinsk agrees Russian spheres of influence in east Asia

1860 Vladivostok

Sea of Japan (East Sea)

LIAODONG PROVINCE

Beijing

1910 KOREA

JAPAN

1898–1905 Port Arthur

RUSSIAN EXPANSION IN ASIA, 1600–1914

Russia gained territory in stages (dates of acquisition in bold). It spread across north Asia, then into Poland, the Baltic region, and south into central Asia. It then gained parts of China and reached Afghanistan and Persia's borders.

KEY

Russian Empire, c.1600	Acquisitions, 1856–1876	Russian sphere of influence, 1914
Acquisitions, 1600–1725	Acquisitions, 1877–1914	Trans-Siberian Railway, built 1891–1917
Acquisitions, 1726–1855	Temporary acquisitions, with dates	Borders, 1914

TIMELINE

1
2
3
4
5

1600　　1700　　1800　　1900

RUSSIAN EMPIRE EXPANDS

From 1600, Russia set out on a mission to expand its territory. It conquered Siberia, reached North America, drove deep into central Asia, and gained a foothold in the Black Sea region. By the 19th century, Russia's sizeable empire had begun to alarm Europe.

In 1600, the Czardom of Russia spread from the Ural Mountains in the east to the edge of the great Polish-Lithuanian Commonwealth in the west. It was, however, effectively landlocked; the Arctic Ocean was often frozen, and the Baltic Sea was controlled by Russia's enemy, Sweden. Consequently, Russia's expansion over the next 400 years was driven, to a great extent, by the search for a warm-water port that would allow it to house a fleet to rival the French and British navies and that would provide access to international trade.

Russia seized Siberia by conquest, but the growth of the empire was largely achieved by a process of accretion. Territories occupied by Russian migrants were slowly incorporated into the empire, and as the older powers—such as the Polish-Lithuanian Commonwealth, the Ottoman Empire in central Asia, and the Qing Empire in China—weakened, Russia simply took over. Russia's attempts at more aggressive expansion in the Balkans, Manchuria, and to the north of Afghanistan met with varying degrees of success, and, in the end, the limits of Russia's empire were defined by other imperial powers.

"Russia has only two allies: her army and her fleet."

ALEXANDER III, EMPEROR OF RUSSIA, c.1890

IVAN IV VASILYEVICH
1530–1584

The Grand Prince of Moscow from 1533–1547, Ivan IV Vasilyevich (also known as "the Terrible") became the first czar of Russia in 1547. A brutal autocrat, his rule is considered to mark the beginning of the Russian Empire, as he set about bringing Russia's aristocracy under his autocratic rule and uniting their lands under a central administration. By the time of his death in 1584, Ivan had not only united Russia's princedoms but also conquered Kazan, Astrakhan, and parts of Siberia, setting the foundation for a vast empire that would span much of Europe and Asia.

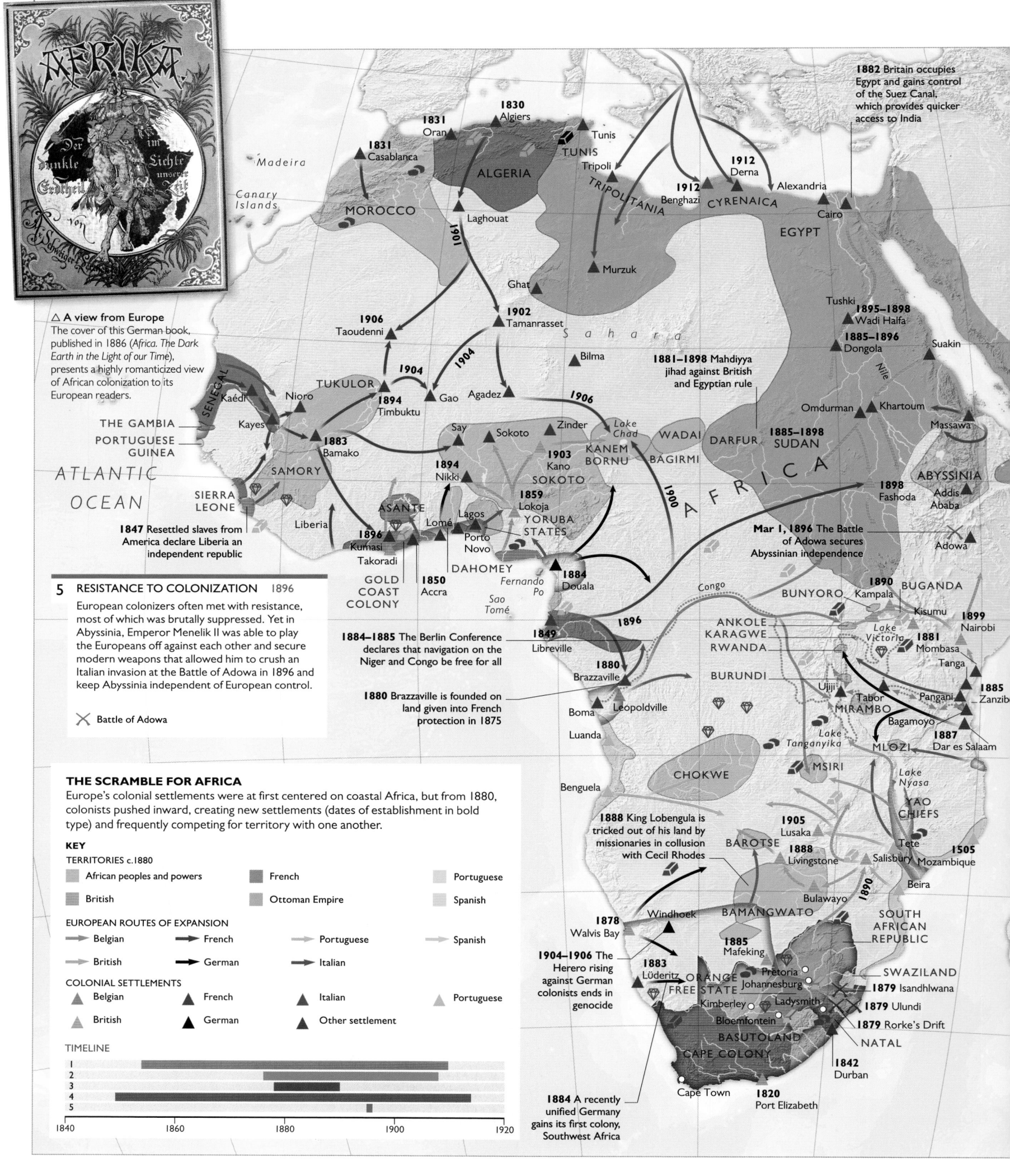

1882 Britain occupies Egypt and gains control of the Suez Canal, which provides quicker access to India

1830 Algiers
1831 Oran
1831 Casablanca
TUNIS
Tunis
Tripoli
1912 Derna
1912 Benghazi
CYRENAICA
Alexandria
Cairo
TRIPOLITANIA
MOROCCO
ALGERIA
Laghouat
1901
Murzuk
EGYPT
Ghat

Madeira
Canary Islands

1906 Taoudenni
1902 Tamanrasset
Sahara
Bilma
Tushki
1895–1898 Wadi Halfa
1885–1896 Dongola
Suakin

△ **A view from Europe**
The cover of this German book, published in 1886 (*Africa. The Dark Earth in the Light of our Time*), presents a highly romanticized view of African colonization to its European readers.

1904
1904
TUKULOR
Nioro
1894 Timbuktu
Gao
Agadez
1906
1881–1898 Mahdiyya jihad against British and Egyptian rule
Omdurman
Khartoum
Massawa

THE GAMBIA
PORTUGUESE GUINEA
SENEGAL
Kaédi
Kayes
Say
Sokoto
Zinder
Lake Chad
WADAI
1885–1898 SUDAN
DARFUR

ATLANTIC OCEAN

SAMORY
1883 Bamako
1894 Nikki
1903 Kano
SOKOTO
KANEM BORNU
BAGIRMI
1900
A F R I C A
ABYSSINIA
Addis Ababa
1898 Fashoda

SIERRA LEONE
Liberia
1847 Resettled slaves from America declare Liberia an independent republic

1896 Kumasi
Takoradi
ASANTE
Lomé
Lagos
Porto Novo
1859 Lokoja
YORUBA STATES
Mar 1, 1896 The Battle of Adowa secures Abyssinian independence
Adowa ✕

GOLD COAST COLONY
1850 Accra
DAHOMEY
Sao Tomé
Fernando Po
1884 Douala
Congo
BUNYORO
1890 Kampala
BUGANDA
Kisumu
1899 Nairobi

5 RESISTANCE TO COLONIZATION 1896

European colonizers often met with resistance, most of which was brutally suppressed. Yet in Abyssinia, Emperor Menelik II was able to play the Europeans off against each other and secure modern weapons that allowed him to crush an Italian invasion at the Battle of Adowa in 1896 and keep Abyssinia independent of European control.

✕ Battle of Adowa

1884–1885 The Berlin Conference declares that navigation on the Niger and Congo be free for all

1880 Brazzaville is founded on land given into French protection in 1875

1849 Libreville
1896
1880 Brazzaville
ANKOLE KARAGWE RWANDA
BURUNDI
Lake Victoria
1881 Mombasa
Tanga
Ujiji
Tabor
MIRAMBO
Pangani
1885 Zanzibar
Bagamoyo
1887 Dar es Salaam
Boma
Leopoldville
Luanda
Lake Tanganyika
MLOZI

THE SCRAMBLE FOR AFRICA

Europe's colonial settlements were at first centered on coastal Africa, but from 1880, colonists pushed inward, creating new settlements (dates of establishment in bold type) and frequently competing for territory with one another.

Benguela
CHOKWE
MSIRI
Lake Nyasa
YAO CHIEFS
Tete
1505 Mozambique

1888 King Lobengula is tricked out of his land by missionaries in collusion with Cecil Rhodes

1905 Lusaka
BAROTSE
1888 Livingstone
Salisbury
Beira

KEY

TERRITORIES c.1880

▨ African peoples and powers	▨ French	▨ Portuguese
▨ British	▨ Ottoman Empire	▨ Spanish

EUROPEAN ROUTES OF EXPANSION

→ Belgian	→ French	→ Portuguese	→ Spanish
→ British	→ German	→ Italian	

COLONIAL SETTLEMENTS

▲ Belgian	▲ French	▲ Italian	▲ Portuguese
▲ British	▲ German	▲ Other settlement	

1878 Walvis Bay
Windhoek
BAMANGWATO
Bulawayo
1890
SOUTH AFRICAN REPUBLIC

1904–1906 The Herero rising against German colonists ends in genocide

1883 Lüderitz
1885 Mafeking
ORANGE FREE STATE
Pretoria
Johannesburg
SWAZILAND
1879 Isandhlwana
1879 Ulundi
1879 Rorke's Drift
Kimberley
Ladysmith
Bloemfontein
NATAL
BASUTOLAND
CAPE COLONY
1842 Durban
Cape Town
1820 Port Elizabeth

1884 A recently unified Germany gains its first colony, Southwest Africa

TIMELINE

1
2
3
4
5

1840   1860   1880   1900   1920

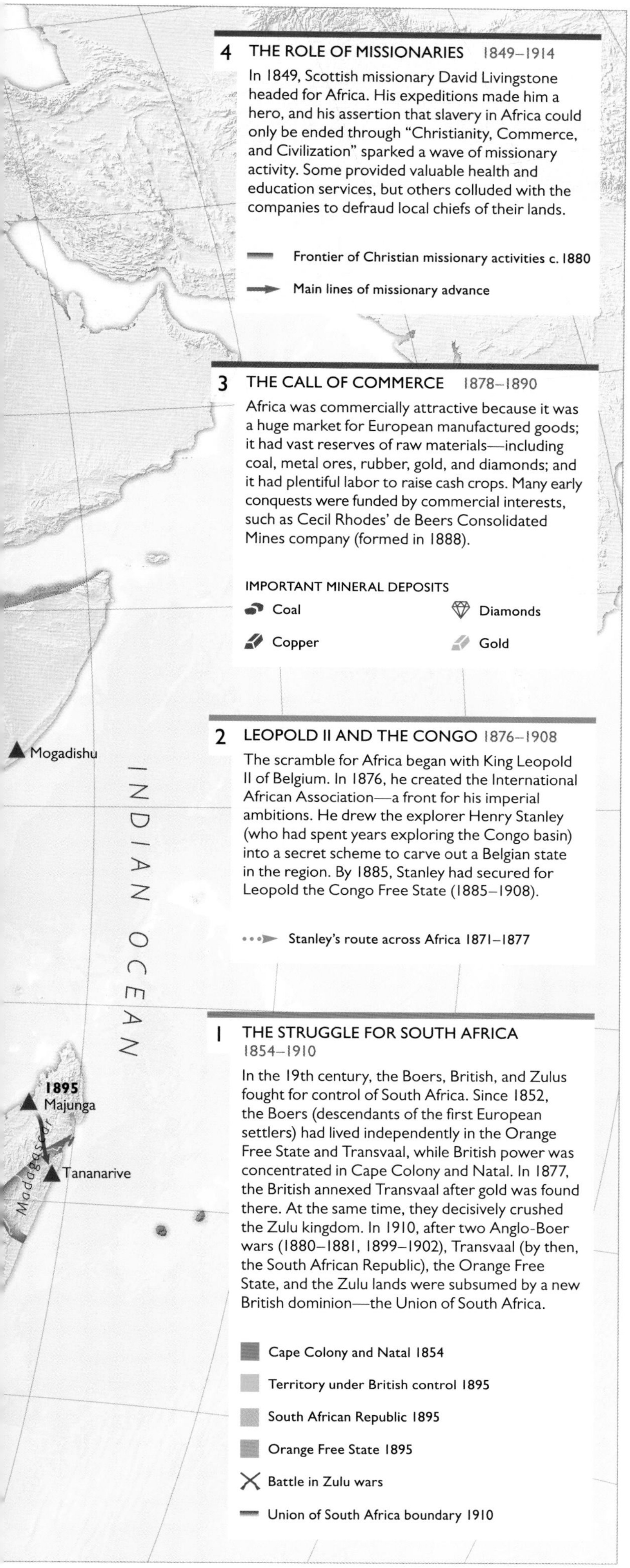

4 THE ROLE OF MISSIONARIES 1849–1914

In 1849, Scottish missionary David Livingstone headed for Africa. His expeditions made him a hero, and his assertion that slavery in Africa could only be ended through "Christianity, Commerce, and Civilization" sparked a wave of missionary activity. Some provided valuable health and education services, but others colluded with the companies to defraud local chiefs of their lands.

— Frontier of Christian missionary activities c. 1880

→ Main lines of missionary advance

3 THE CALL OF COMMERCE 1878–1890

Africa was commercially attractive because it was a huge market for European manufactured goods; it had vast reserves of raw materials—including coal, metal ores, rubber, gold, and diamonds; and it had plentiful labor to raise cash crops. Many early conquests were funded by commercial interests, such as Cecil Rhodes' de Beers Consolidated Mines company (formed in 1888).

IMPORTANT MINERAL DEPOSITS

🪨 Coal   💎 Diamonds

⛏ Copper   🪙 Gold

2 LEOPOLD II AND THE CONGO 1876–1908

The scramble for Africa began with King Leopold II of Belgium. In 1876, he created the International African Association—a front for his imperial ambitions. He drew the explorer Henry Stanley (who had spent years exploring the Congo basin) into a secret scheme to carve out a Belgian state in the region. By 1885, Stanley had secured for Leopold the Congo Free State (1885–1908).

•••► Stanley's route across Africa 1871–1877

1 THE STRUGGLE FOR SOUTH AFRICA 1854–1910

In the 19th century, the Boers, British, and Zulus fought for control of South Africa. Since 1852, the Boers (descendants of the first European settlers) had lived independently in the Orange Free State and Transvaal, while British power was concentrated in Cape Colony and Natal. In 1877, the British annexed Transvaal after gold was found there. At the same time, they decisively crushed the Zulu kingdom. In 1910, after two Anglo-Boer wars (1880–1881, 1899–1902), Transvaal (by then, the South African Republic), the Orange Free State, and the Zulu lands were subsumed by a new British dominion—the Union of South Africa.

■ Cape Colony and Natal 1854

■ Territory under British control 1895

■ South African Republic 1895

■ Orange Free State 1895

✕ Battle in Zulu wars

— Union of South Africa boundary 1910

Mogadishu

INDIAN OCEAN

1895 Majunga

Madagascar

Tananarive

AFRICA COLONIZED

In 1880, only a few European colonies dotted the African coastline. Much of the north was formally part of the Ottoman Empire, but most of Africa was free of direct control from outside. By 1914, nine-tenths of the continent had been divided between seven nations, each hungry for resources and keen to build their empires.

The shifting balance of power in Europe in the 19th century was to have lasting consequences for Africa, as nationalist, liberal, and commercial interests converged in an orgy of colonization. Having lost their American colonies, Spain and Portugal also lost influence in Africa, but Britain and France were ready to build their empires after the Napoleonic wars, and the newly unified nations of Italy and Germany sought to bolster their international standing. Tales from African explorers about diamonds, gold, copper, and coal stirred Europe's commercial interest, so when news reached Europe in the 1880s that the Belgian king, Leopold II, had made a grab for the Congo, the race to conquer Africa's interior began.

Competition between the colonizers nearly resulted in conflict, so the Berlin Conference (1884–1885) was called to settle claims and set rules for partition. Missionaries, companies, and military forces all played a part in the colonization process, but it was also made possible by technological and scientific advances that came out of the Industrial Revolution. Steamships—and the discovery of effective antimalarial treatments—allowed Europeans to navigate deep into the continent's interior. The weapons of local peoples were no match for the breech-loading rifle, and within 20 years, Africa had been carved up by European powers with little regard for the traditions of the indigenous peoples.

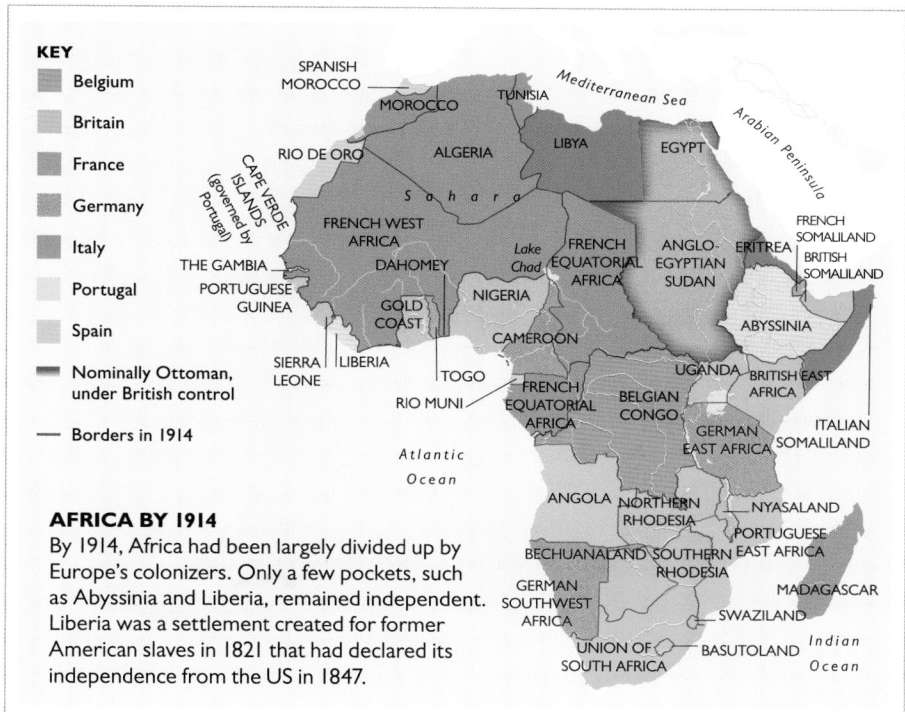

AFRICA BY 1914

By 1914, Africa had been largely divided up by Europe's colonizers. Only a few pockets, such as Abyssinia and Liberia, remained independent. Liberia was a settlement created for former American slaves in 1821 that had declared its independence from the US in 1847.

KEY

■ Belgium
■ Britain
■ France
■ Germany
■ Italy
■ Portugal
■ Spain
— Nominally Ottoman, under British control
— Borders in 1914

FOREIGN POWERS IN CHINA

By the mid-19th century, the Qing Empire in China was facing internal strife, as well as pressure from foreign powers. Anger against growing foreign dominance erupted in the Boxer Rebellion, but it was swiftly repressed by a coalition of foreign forces. The subsequent war reparations crippled the empire.

Two hundred years of Qing rule had created a vast empire that flourished economically. Foreign traders were granted access to only one port, Canton (modern Guangzhou), but requests for further concessions were rebuffed.

Western merchants began to bribe officials and pay for goods with opium, which damaged the Chinese economy and led to a rise in opium addiction. The First Opium War (see pp.226–227) resulted in the transfer of Hong Kong and other ports to Britain, and over the next decades, parts of the empire fell under the influence of Britain, France, Russia, Germany, Japan, and the US.

△ **Assassination of Baron Ketteler**
In revenge for his having beaten and shot a boy suspected of being a Boxer, German diplomat Baron Clemens von Ketteler was murdered in Beijing on June 20, 1900. His assassin was later beheaded.

The Boxer Rebellion

By 1900, anger at foreign control of trade and at Christian missionary activity made many Chinese join a secret group known as the Society of Righteous and Harmonious Fists. Popularly called "Boxers," its members began attacking Westerners and Chinese Christians.

In June 1900, Qing forces and the Boxers besieged the foreign legations in Peking (Beijing). Soldiers from an eight-nation alliance lifted the siege 55 days later, and then demanded war reparations. Damaged by its failure to expel the foreigners and by internal rebellions, the Qing Dynasty could not prevent further losses to foreign powers or stop the spread of revolutionary ideas. In 1912, the last emperor abdicated and China became a republic.

△ **The Peking Protocol**
Having defeated the Boxers, the foreign powers demanded in the Peking Protocol (1901) that China punish the government officials involved in the uprising, pay reparations equivalent to $330 million, and allow foreign troops to be stationed there.

Storming the Imperial Palace
On August 14, 1900, a multinational force, including British, American, and Japanese soldiers, broke the siege of the Imperial Palace in Peking (modern Beijing) by Qing forces and Boxer rebels.

DECLINE OF QING CHINA

The richest and most populous state in the world, Qing China should have been a major presence on the world stage competing with Western powers. Instead, however, it underwent a long decline from the mid-1800s, racked with rebellions and civil wars and repeatedly carved up by foreign military adventures.

The Qing Dynasty was founded by a clan of Manchurians who had seized the Chinese empire and, under a series of forceful emperors (see pp.178–179), enlarged it with conquests in central Asia. But their failure to modernize had exacerbated a series of problems that afflicted China in the 19th century, including population growth and the constant threat of famine; problems with the money supply; failure to open the economy to foreign trade; and failure to keep pace with the technology and military power of foreign states that wanted to impose trade liberalization, and possibly even carve up China between themselves (see pp.250–251).

The humiliations inflicted as a result of the Opium Wars (see pp.226–227) had severely damaged the authority of the Qing and centralized government. In the resulting power vacuum, there flourished corruption, smuggling, and "secret societies"—networks of local leaders and low-ranking nobility with diverse cultural, political, and economic agendas. The threat of rebellion was relentless, and the ground was fertile for mass movements to galvanize resistance to the Qing. This feverish atmosphere would spark the greatest civil war in history and eventually bring to an end the Qing Dynasty and millennia of imperial rule.

> *"Heaven sees as the people see; Heaven hears as the people hear … China is weak, the only thing we can depend on is the hearts of the people."*
>
> DOWAGER EMPRESS CIXI DURING THE BOXER REBELLION, 1899–1901

PUYI
1906–1967

The turbulent life of the last Emperor of China traced the history of 20th-century China. Puyi became emperor in 1908, aged only 2, but was forced to abdicate in 1912 as a result of the Xinhai revolution. He was briefly restored as puppet emperor by a warlord in 1917 and again by the Japanese in 1934. Later, he was captured by the Soviets, then handed over to the Chinese Communists after World War II and reeducated to be a common citizen. He died in Beijing in 1967.

Emperor Puyi as a child
Puyi (seen here aged 3) was proclaimed the Xuantong Emperor by his great-aunt, the Dowager Empress Cixi.

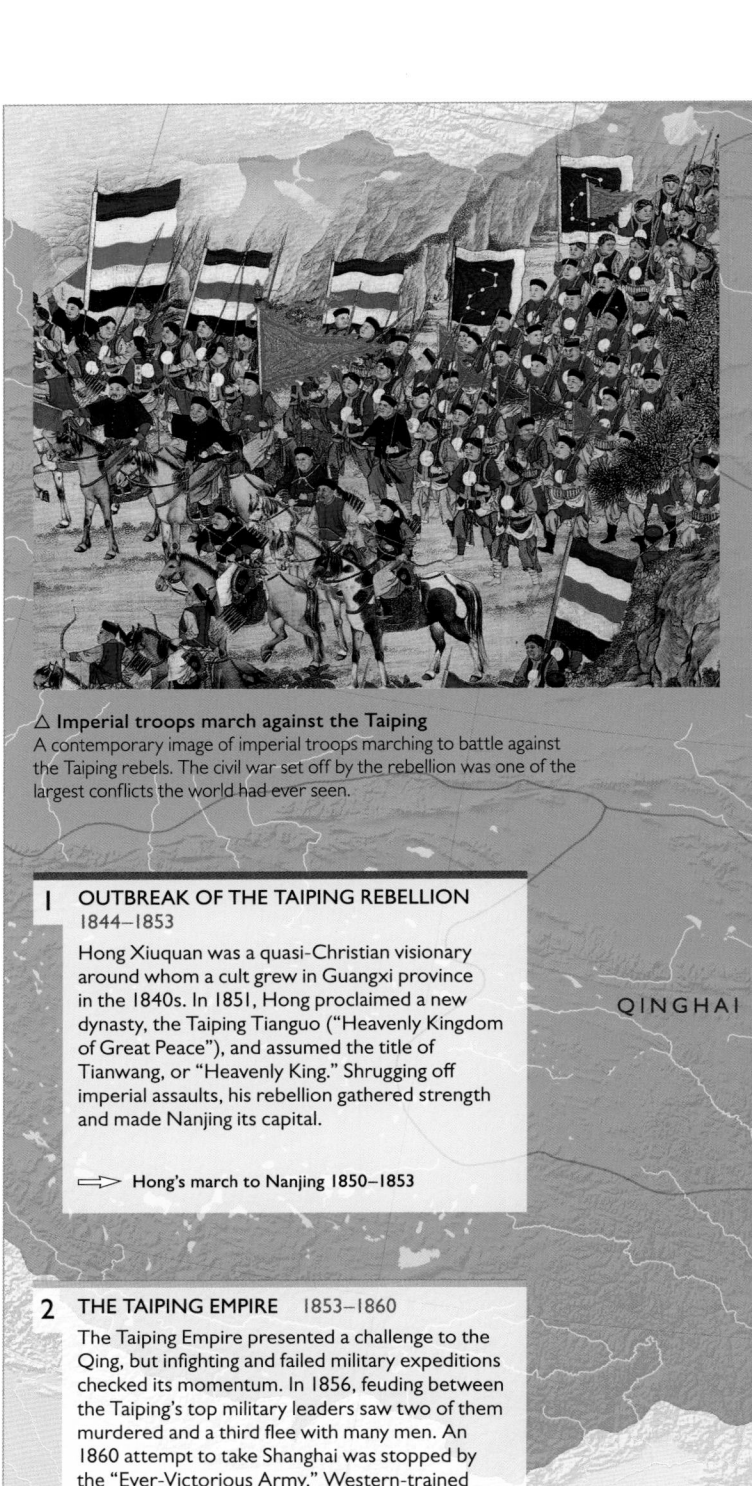

△ **Imperial troops march against the Taiping**
A contemporary image of imperial troops marching to battle against the Taiping rebels. The civil war set off by the rebellion was one of the largest conflicts the world had ever seen.

QINGHAI

1 OUTBREAK OF THE TAIPING REBELLION
1844–1853

Hong Xiuquan was a quasi-Christian visionary around whom a cult grew in Guangxi province in the 1840s. In 1851, Hong proclaimed a new dynasty, the Taiping Tianguo ("Heavenly Kingdom of Great Peace"), and assumed the title of Tianwang, or "Heavenly King." Shrugging off imperial assaults, his rebellion gathered strength and made Nanjing its capital.

⇨ Hong's march to Nanjing 1850–1853

2 THE TAIPING EMPIRE   1853–1860

The Taiping Empire presented a challenge to the Qing, but infighting and failed military expeditions checked its momentum. In 1856, feuding between the Taiping's top military leaders saw two of them murdered and a third flee with many men. An 1860 attempt to take Shanghai was stopped by the "Ever-Victorious Army," Western-trained and led troops fighting for the Qing.

◼ Area controlled by rebels c.1861   ⟶ Unsuccessful northern campaign 1853–1855

THE END OF IMPERIAL RULE
The power of the Qing Dynasty started to decline significantly from the 1840s, and a series of uprisings finally ended their rule in 1911–1912.

KEY
◼ Qing Empire 1850

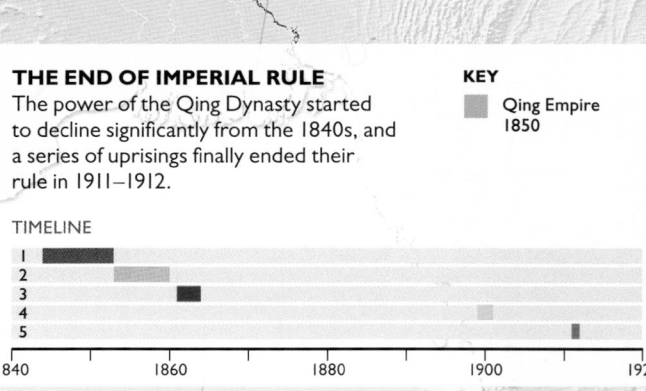

TIMELINE

1 2 3 4 5

1840   1860   1880   1900   1920

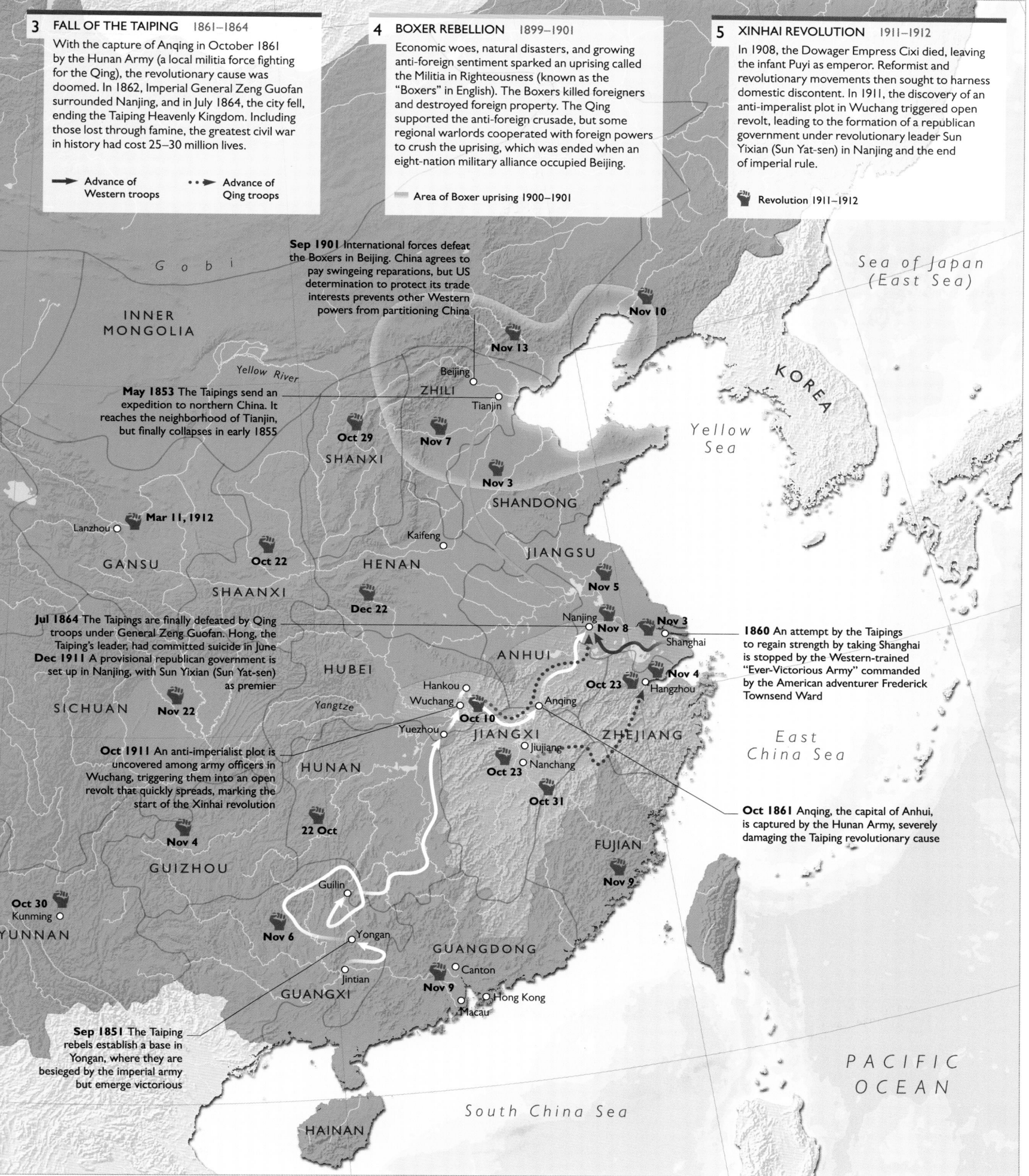

3 FALL OF THE TAIPING 1861–1864

With the capture of Anqing in October 1861 by the Hunan Army (a local militia force fighting for the Qing), the revolutionary cause was doomed. In 1862, Imperial General Zeng Guofan surrounded Nanjing, and in July 1864, the city fell, ending the Taiping Heavenly Kingdom. Including those lost through famine, the greatest civil war in history had cost 25–30 million lives.

➡ Advance of Western troops   ⬦⬦➤ Advance of Qing troops

4 BOXER REBELLION 1899–1901

Economic woes, natural disasters, and growing anti-foreign sentiment sparked an uprising called the Militia in Righteousness (known as the "Boxers" in English). The Boxers killed foreigners and destroyed foreign property. The Qing supported the anti-foreign crusade, but some regional warlords cooperated with foreign powers to crush the uprising, which was ended when an eight-nation military alliance occupied Beijing.

Area of Boxer uprising 1900–1901

5 XINHAI REVOLUTION 1911–1912

In 1908, the Dowager Empress Cixi died, leaving the infant Puyi as emperor. Reformist and revolutionary movements then sought to harness domestic discontent. In 1911, the discovery of an anti-imperialist plot in Wuchang triggered open revolt, leading to the formation of a republican government under revolutionary leader Sun Yixian (Sun Yat-sen) in Nanjing and the end of imperial rule.

✊ Revolution 1911–1912

Sep 1901 International forces defeat the Boxers in Beijing. China agrees to pay swingeing reparations, but US determination to protect its trade interests prevents other Western powers from partitioning China

May 1853 The Taipings send an expedition to northern China. It reaches the neighborhood of Tianjin, but finally collapses in early 1855

Jul 1864 The Taipings are finally defeated by Qing troops under General Zeng Guofan. Hong, the Taiping's leader, had committed suicide in June
Dec 1911 A provisional republican government is set up in Nanjing, with Sun Yixian (Sun Yat-sen) as premier

Oct 1911 An anti-imperialist plot is uncovered among army officers in Wuchang, triggering them into an open revolt that quickly spreads, marking the start of the Xinhai revolution

Sep 1851 The Taiping rebels establish a base in Yongan, where they are besieged by the imperial army but emerge victorious

1860 An attempt by the Taipings to regain strength by taking Shanghai is stopped by the Western-trained "Ever-Victorious Army" commanded by the American adventurer Frederick Townsend Ward

Oct 1861 Anqing, the capital of Anhui, is captured by the Hunan Army, severely damaging the Taiping revolutionary cause

JAPAN TRANSFORMED

The restoration of the Meiji ("enlightened rule") emperor in 1868 kick-started a process of modernization that would see Japan transformed from an isolationist, feudal country to an outward-looking industrial nation with an educated population and an army and navy ready to defend and strengthen its position in the world.

By 1850, Japan had endured 200 years of isolation under the Tokugawa shogunate (see pp.180–181). The country was weak compared to foreign powers and was forced to accept unfavorable treaties that undermined its sovereignty.

An alliance of samurai from Japan's western domains began to coalesce around the imperial court in Kyoto, and by 1868 sought to restore imperial power and to modernize Japan. The shogun, Tokugawa Yoshinobu, resigned in an attempt to maintain peace but could not prevent the clash between imperial and government forces in the Boshin War of 1868–1869. The imperial faction won the conflict, securing the emperor's position, although not his personal

power. A group of ambitious young samurai took control of the country and soon began to implement profound reform. They asked the feudal lords to give up their domains in favor of a centralized state, placed the nation's defense in the hands of a new imperial army and navy, and promoted rapid industrialization to transform Japan's economic base.

It was little wonder that many of the older samurai from the most powerful clans balked at the changes and rebelled in 1877. The rebellion (known after its origin in Satsuma Domain) failed, but it forced a reassessment of reform, ensuring that Japanese values were not lost in the race to modernize.

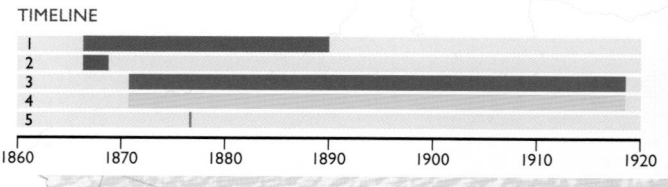

MODERNIZATION OF JAPAN

The modernization of Japan progressed swiftly between 1868 and 1918, as the new government swept away feudal structures and established power bases during the Boshin War and Satsuma Rebellion, paving the way for rapidly developing industrial areas and increasing urbanization.

TIMELINE

2 BOSHIN WAR 1868–1869

Civil war broke out between imperial forces and troops loyal to the ex-shogun, Tokugawa Yoshinobu, when Yoshinobu was stripped of all titles and land. The imperial troops won the war's first battle, at Fushimi on January 27, 1868. They then moved east to secure Edo's surrender, before heading north to Hokkaido to defeat the remaining government supporters at Hakodate in June 1869.

→ Route of imperial army   ✕ Battle, with date

▨ Imperial alliance

1 MODERNIZATION OF THE ARMY AND NAVY
1868–1890

The Meiji government's determination to modernize the military cut across the privileges of Japan's warrior class, the samurai. In 1869, their fleets were subsumed by the new Imperial Japanese Navy, and in 1873, their exclusive right to bear arms was broken by the introduction of conscription. Many samurai became officers in the new regime, where their discipline helped to create the most powerful military force in Asia by the 1890s.

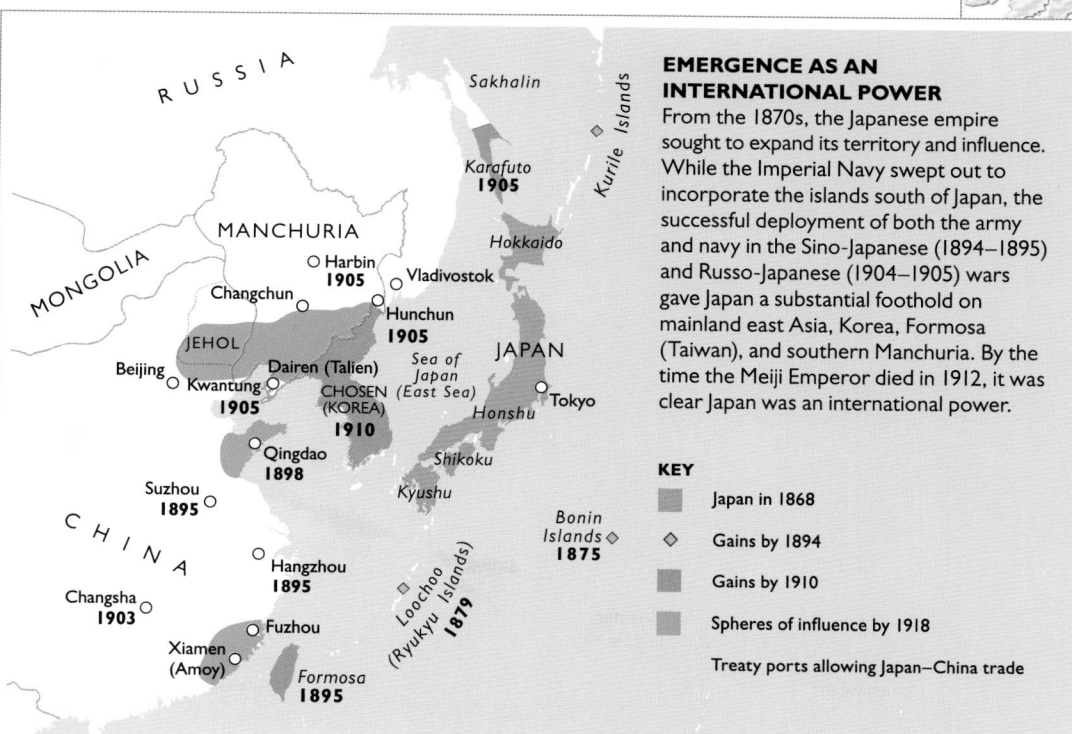

EMERGENCE AS AN INTERNATIONAL POWER

From the 1870s, the Japanese empire sought to expand its territory and influence. While the Imperial Navy swept out to incorporate the islands south of Japan, the successful deployment of both the army and navy in the Sino-Japanese (1894–1895) and Russo-Japanese (1904–1905) wars gave Japan a substantial foothold on mainland east Asia, Korea, Formosa (Taiwan), and southern Manchuria. By the time the Meiji Emperor died in 1912, it was clear Japan was an international power.

KEY

▨ Japan in 1868

◇ Gains by 1894

▨ Gains by 1910

▨ Spheres of influence by 1918

Treaty ports allowing Japan–China trade

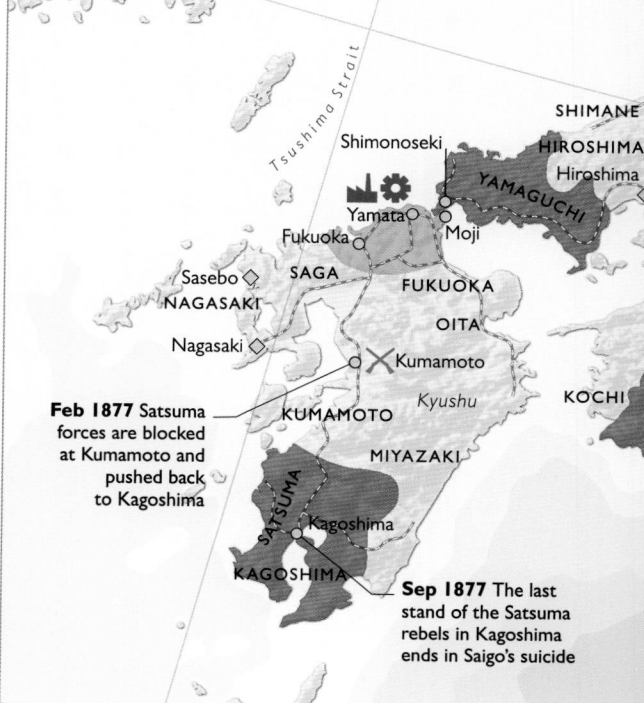

Feb 1877 Satsuma forces are blocked at Kumamoto and pushed back to Kagoshima

Sep 1877 The last stand of the Satsuma rebels in Kagoshima ends in Saigo's suicide

3 INDUSTRIALIZATION 1871–1918

The abolition of feudalism in Japan freed millions of people to choose their occupation and move around the country. The government encouraged industrialization, building railway and shipping lines and telegraph and telephone systems, as well as opening mines; shipyards; and munitions, glass, textile, and chemical factories. Many of these were privatized when a European-style banking system was introduced in 1882, leaving the government free to invest in education and the armed forces.

MODERNIZATION UNDER THE MEIJI

- ▨ Main industrial areas by 1918
- ▭▭▭ Railways built 1868–1918

TRADITIONAL INDUSTRIES

- Ceramics
- Textiles
- Silk

INDUSTRIES DEVELOPED AFTER 1868

- Manufacturing
- Machine-building
- Shipbuilding
- Chemicals

4 URBAN GROWTH 1871–1918

By 1871, all of Japan's ancient feudal domains, loyal to the local lord, had been reorganized into prefectures, each with a chief executive answerable to the central government. Initially, Japan's urban prefectures—Tokyo, Osaka, and Kyoto—lost population as people adjusted to the new regime and migrated to other areas. However, by 1883, the work offered through industrialization was driving population growth in the urban prefectures and in emerging cities such as Kobe, Yokohama, Nagasaki, and Hiroshima.

- ◇ City of over 500,000 in 1918
- ▢ City of over 100,000 in 1918
- ○ Other major city

1871 Akita is one of the prefectures—the divisions of the new centralized state created when the feudal domains are abolished

Oct 1868–May 1869 Hakodate is besieged by imperial forces in the final stage of the Boshin War

Jun 27, 1869

Jan 1868 Meiji Restoration begins at the imperial court in Kyoto

Jan 27, 1868

Jan 1868 The city of Edo is renamed Tokyo

1868 The port of Yokohama is developed for the export of silk, predominantly to Britain

1871 Japan's first domestically produced warship, *Seiki*, is completed at Yokosuka Shipyards

5 SATSUMA REBELLION 1877

Some samurai felt that the spirit of Japan was being destroyed by rapid reforms. In February 1877, Saigo Takamori, a key figure in the restoration who disliked the changes that were being pressed on the emperor, marched from his base in Satsuma (now part of Kagoshima prefecture) with an army of samurai. They were heading for Tokyo, but their advance was blocked by the Imperial Army at Kumamoto. Forced back to Kagoshima, the rebels were finally defeated in September.

- ✕ Battle

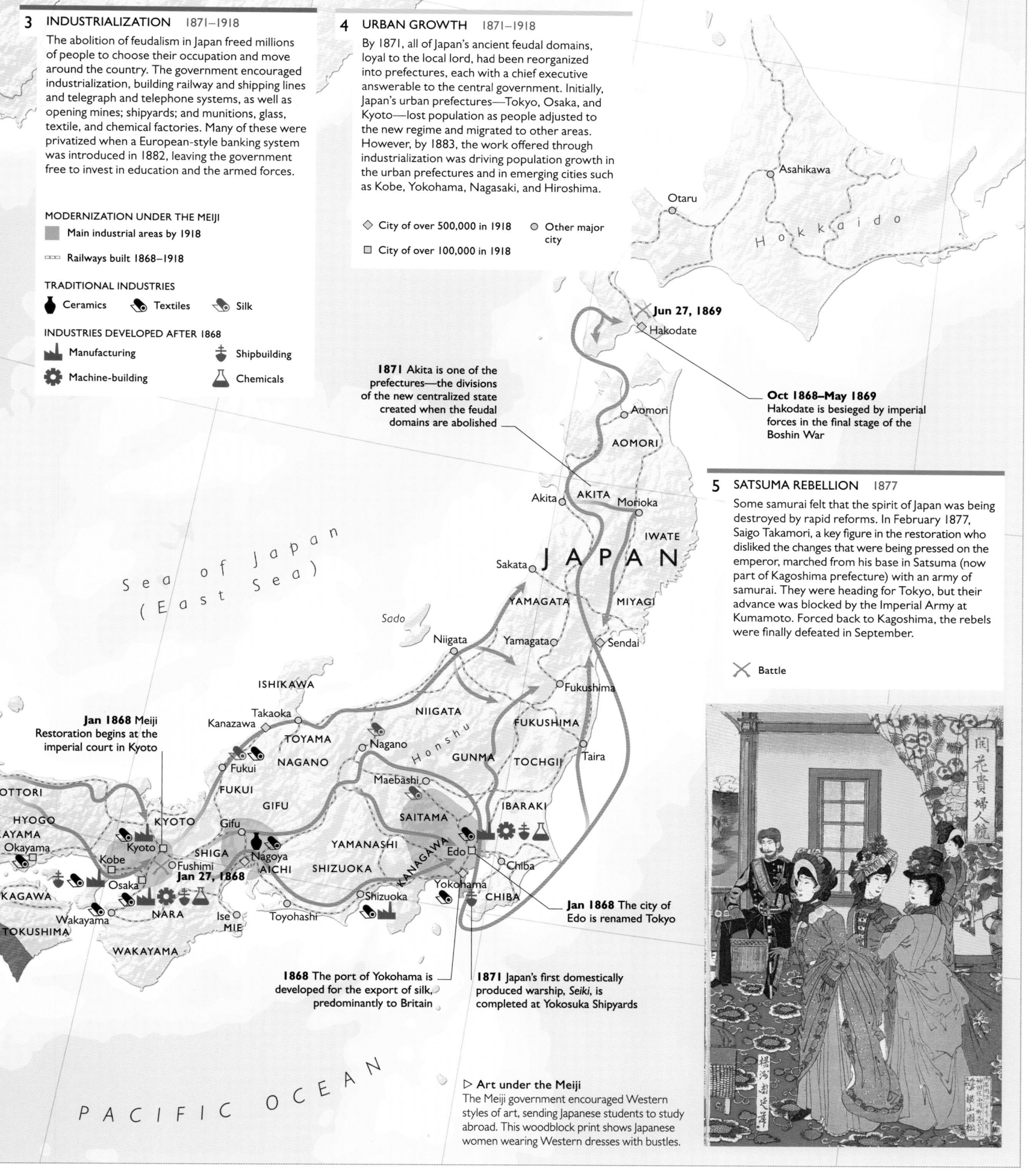

▷ **Art under the Meiji**
The Meiji government encouraged Western styles of art, sending Japanese students to study abroad. This woodblock print shows Japanese women wearing Western dresses with bustles.

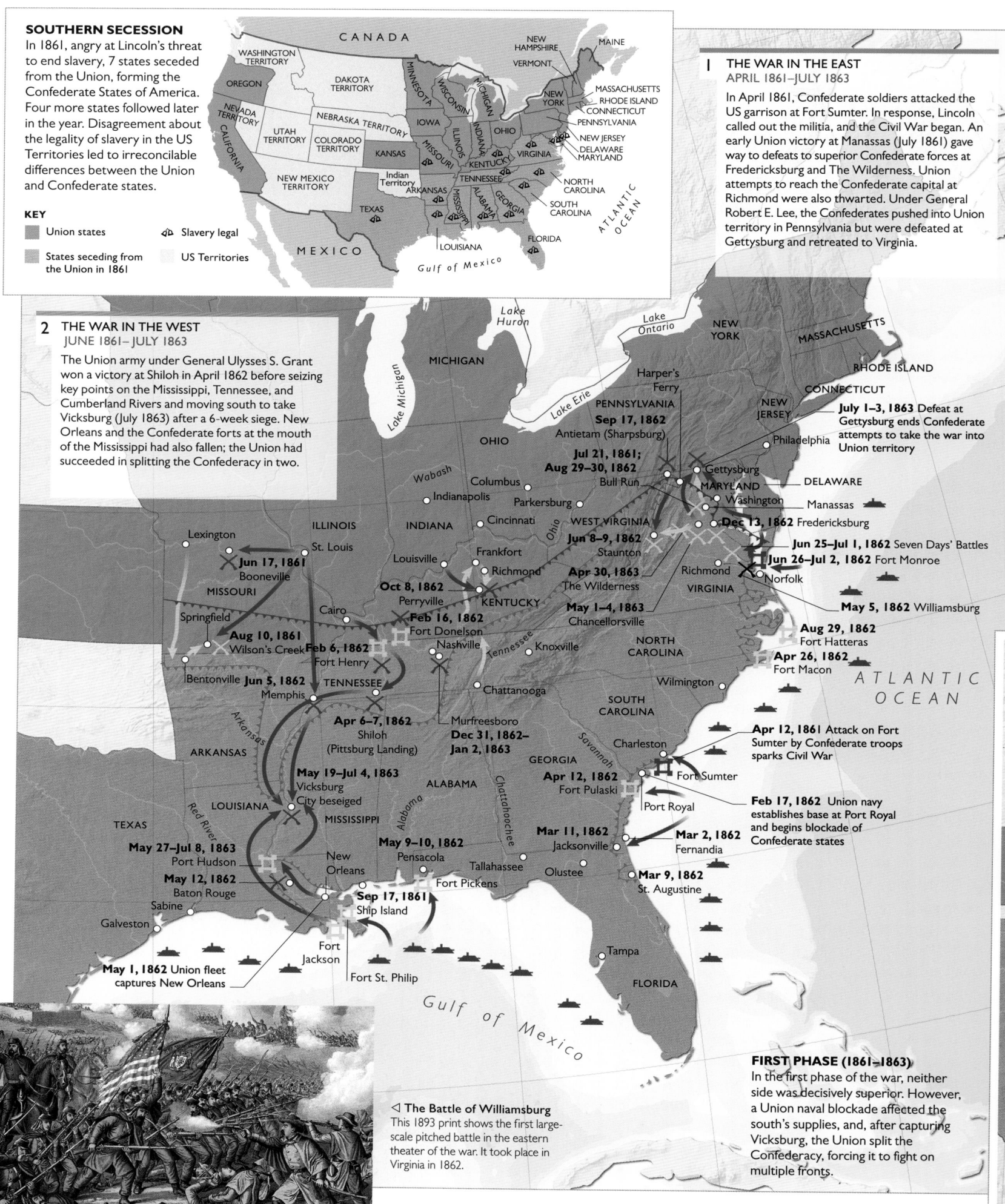

SOUTHERN SECESSION

In 1861, angry at Lincoln's threat to end slavery, 7 states seceded from the Union, forming the Confederate States of America. Four more states followed later in the year. Disagreement about the legality of slavery in the US Territories led to irreconcilable differences between the Union and Confederate states.

KEY

- Union states
- States seceding from the Union in 1861
- ⚔ Slavery legal
- US Territories

2 THE WAR IN THE WEST
JUNE 1861– JULY 1863

The Union army under General Ulysses S. Grant won a victory at Shiloh in April 1862 before seizing key points on the Mississippi, Tennessee, and Cumberland Rivers and moving south to take Vicksburg (July 1863) after a 6-week siege. New Orleans and the Confederate forts at the mouth of the Mississippi had also fallen; the Union had succeeded in splitting the Confederacy in two.

1 THE WAR IN THE EAST
APRIL 1861–JULY 1863

In April 1861, Confederate soldiers attacked the US garrison at Fort Sumter. In response, Lincoln called out the militia, and the Civil War began. An early Union victory at Manassas (July 1861) gave way to defeats to superior Confederate forces at Fredericksburg and The Wilderness. Union attempts to reach the Confederate capital at Richmond were also thwarted. Under General Robert E. Lee, the Confederates pushed into Union territory in Pennsylvania but were defeated at Gettysburg and retreated to Virginia.

July 1–3, 1863 Defeat at Gettysburg ends Confederate attempts to take the war into Union territory

Sep 17, 1862 Antietam (Sharpsburg)

Jul 21, 1861; Aug 29–30, 1862 Bull Run

Dec 13, 1862 Fredericksburg

Jun 8–9, 1862 Staunton

Apr 30, 1863 The Wilderness

May 1–4, 1863 Chancellorsville

Jun 25–Jul 1, 1862 Seven Days' Battles

Jun 26–Jul 2, 1862 Fort Monroe

May 5, 1862 Williamsburg

Aug 29, 1862 Fort Hatteras

Apr 26, 1862 Fort Macon

Jun 17, 1861 Booneville

Aug 10, 1861 Wilson's Creek

Feb 6, 1862 Fort Henry

Feb 16, 1862 Fort Donelson

Oct 8, 1862 Perryville

Jun 5, 1862 Memphis

Apr 6–7, 1862 Shiloh (Pittsburg Landing)

Dec 31, 1862– Jan 2, 1863 Murfreesboro

May 19–Jul 4, 1863 Vicksburg City beseiged

Apr 12, 1861 Attack on Fort Sumter by Confederate troops sparks Civil War

Apr 12, 1862 Fort Pulaski

Feb 17, 1862 Union navy establishes base at Port Royal and begins blockade of Confederate states

Mar 11, 1862 Jacksonville

Mar 2, 1862 Fernandia

May 9–10, 1862 Pensacola

Mar 9, 1862 St. Augustine

May 27–Jul 8, 1863 Port Hudson

May 12, 1862 Baton Rouge

Sep 17, 1861 Ship Island

May 1, 1862 Union fleet captures New Orleans

◁ **The Battle of Williamsburg**
This 1893 print shows the first large-scale pitched battle in the eastern theater of the war. It took place in Virginia in 1862.

FIRST PHASE (1861–1863)

In the first phase of the war, neither side was decisively superior. However, a Union naval blockade affected the south's supplies, and, after capturing Vicksburg, the Union split the Confederacy, forcing it to fight on multiple fronts.

NORTH VERSUS SOUTH

In two phases, 1861–1863 and 1864–1865, the north's Union forces moved on several fronts into the Confederate states. Although isolated by the north's naval blockade and often outnumbered, the Confederates won several victories but were ultimately beaten by the Union's superior power.

KEY

UNION FORCES

■ Union states 1861	⊞ Union fort	→ Union movement
⬥ Union naval blockade	✕ Union victory	

UNION FRONT LINE

▲▲▲ 1861	▲▲▲ 1862	✕ Inconclusive battle
▲▲▲ Dec 1863	▲▲▲ Dec 1864	**Apr 26, 1865** Date of battle or attack

CONFEDERATE FORCES

■ Confederate states 1861	⊞ Confederate fort
✕ Confederate victory	→ Confederate movement

TIMELINE

1
2
3
4

1860   1861   1862   1863   1864   1865   1866

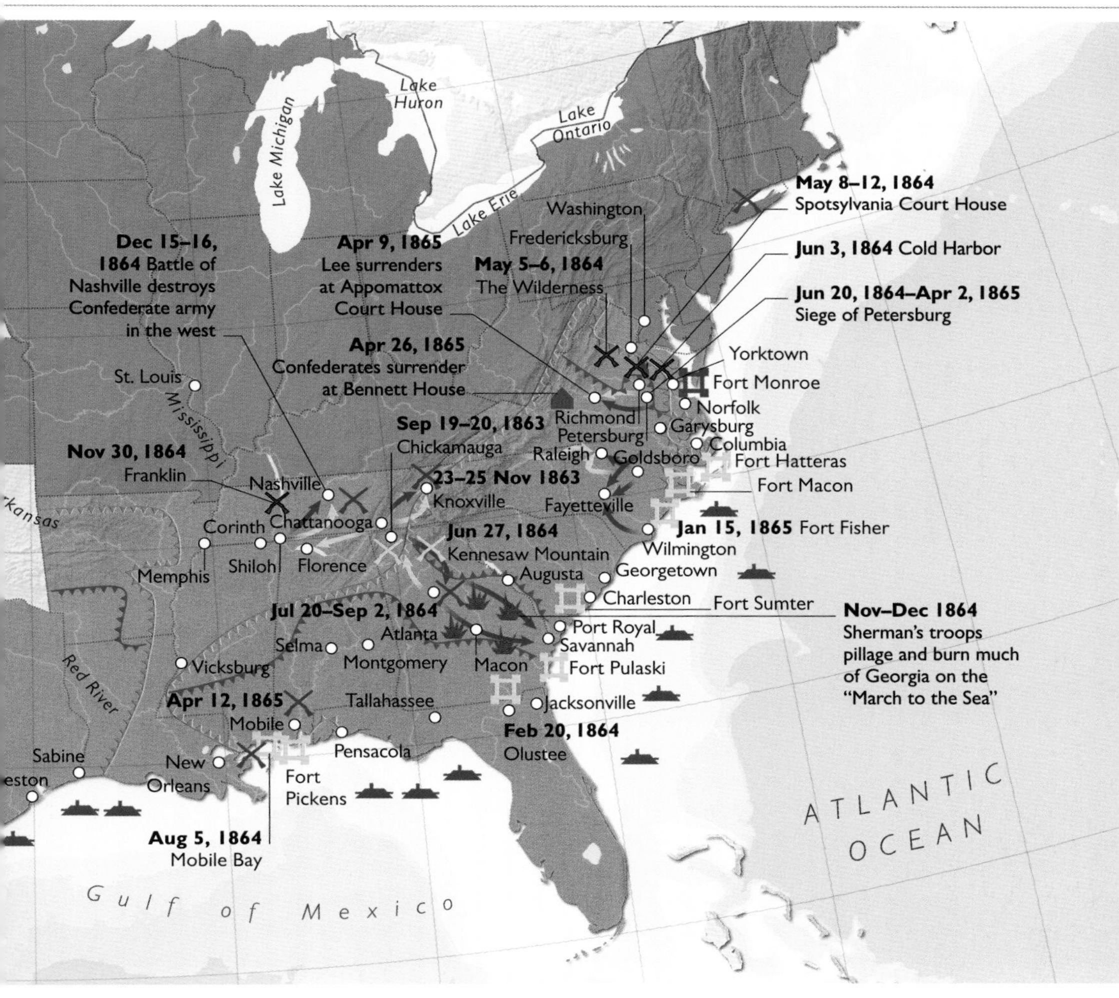

THE CIVIL WAR

The American Revolution created the United States, but it was the Civil War of 1861–1865 that decided its future, forging a nation under one government and ensuring that freedom and equality remained its guiding principles, albeit at a terrible human cost.

After independence in 1783, the US developed into two regions. The rich, libertarian north was dominated by industry and finance, while the south relied on farming driven by slave labor and was anxious about the north's desire to restrict slave ownership. By 1860, the US—composed of 18 "free" states and 15 "slave" states—was just about held together by the Democratic Party, but after the party split in 1859, and Abraham Lincoln was elected president in 1860 on an antislavery platform, the Union collapsed. Several southern states seceded to form the Confederate States of America, and civil war followed. The Confederate armies put up fierce resistance, and it was 4 years before the north's forces finally prevailed. By the time the war ended in April 1865, about 650,000 men had died. Yet America's slaves had also been emancipated, and the states reunited under a supreme federal government.

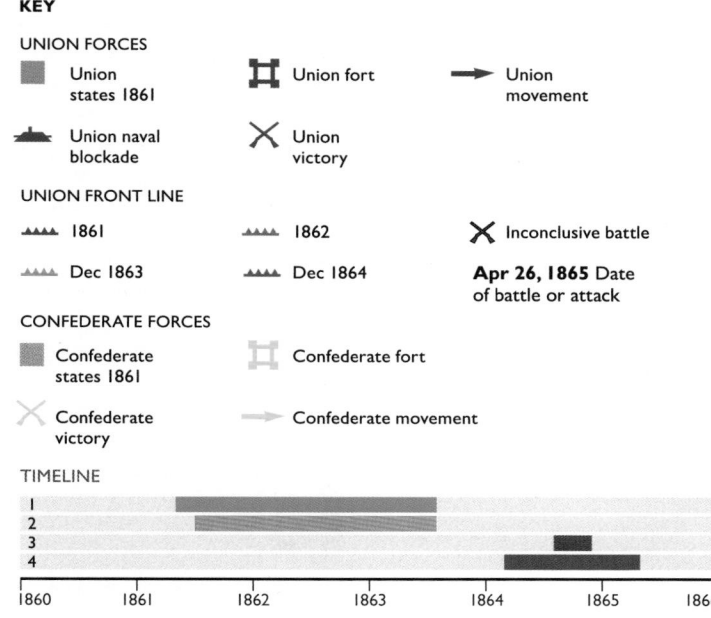

Dec 15–16, 1864 Battle of Nashville destroys Confederate army in the west

Apr 9, 1865 Lee surrenders at Appomattox Court House

Apr 26, 1865 Confederates surrender at Bennett House

May 5–6, 1864 The Wilderness

May 8–12, 1864 Spotsylvania Court House

Jun 3, 1864 Cold Harbor

Jun 20, 1864–Apr 2, 1865 Siege of Petersburg

Nov 30, 1864 Franklin

Sep 19–20, 1863 Chickamauga

23–25 Nov 1863 Knoxville

Jun 27, 1864 Kennesaw Mountain

Jan 15, 1865 Fort Fisher

Jul 20–Sep 2, 1864 Atlanta

Apr 12, 1865 Mobile

Feb 20, 1864 Olustee

Nov–Dec 1864 Sherman's troops pillage and burn much of Georgia on the "March to the Sea"

Aug 5, 1864 Mobile Bay

Lake Michigan, Lake Huron, Lake Ontario, Lake Erie, Washington, Fredericksburg, Yorktown, Fort Monroe, Norfolk, Richmond, Petersburg, Garysburg, Raleigh, Goldsboro, Columbia, Fort Hatteras, Fort Macon, Fayetteville, Wilmington, Georgetown, Charleston, Fort Sumter, St. Louis, Mississippi, Nashville, Corinth, Chattanooga, Memphis, Shiloh, Florence, Selma, Montgomery, Macon, Port Royal, Savannah, Fort Pulaski, Vicksburg, Tallahassee, Jacksonville, Red River, Pensacola, New Orleans, Fort Pickens, Sabine, Charleston, Gulf of Mexico, ATLANTIC OCEAN

SECOND PHASE (1864–1865)

After defeats at Vicksburg and Gettysburg, the Confederates were increasingly outnumbered and outfought by Union forces under Generals Sherman and Grant. In April 1865, Confederate resistance collapsed, ending the war.

3 GENERAL SHERMAN'S ADVANCE
JULY–DECEMBER 1864

In 1864, the Union targeted Atlanta, an important Confederate rail and commercial center, which General William Sherman besieged from July 1864. Its capture in September boosted the north's morale and helped win Lincoln a second term in office. Sherman then marched south to Savannah and the sea, operating deep in enemy territory without supply lines and destroying Confederate infrastructure, industry, and property as he went.

✦ Destruction by Sherman's forces

4 THE END OF THE WAR FEBRUARY 1864–APRIL 1865

During 1864, General Grant was put in command of all Union armies. After a series of bloody battles, he forced General Lee's Confederate army into defensive positions around Richmond and Petersburg. On April 9, 1865, Lee fled to Appomattox and surrendered. Soon after, 89,000 Confederate soldiers surrendered at Bennett House, North Carolina, effectively bringing the war to an end.

▲ Bennett House

At home in her laboratory
French-Polish physicist Marie Curie received
two Nobel Prizes for her work on radioactivity.
Renowned for her efforts at the front during World
War I and for her research into cancer treatments,
her contribution to medical science is invaluable.

SCIENCE AND INNOVATION

In the 19th century, new techniques and improvements in laboratory equipment enabled scientists to make important advances that changed our understanding of the world and revolutionized public health.

△ **Founder of microbiology**
In the 1860s, French biologist Louis Pasteur proved that decay and disease were caused by microbes, or germs; this knowledge changed the course of medicine.

The roots of many of the things that define modern life—such as plastics, fiber optics, and radar—can be traced back to the 19th century. Yet, perhaps the most important discoveries of the time were in the field of medicine. In 1869, Russian chemist Dmitri Mendeleev developed the periodic table, a framework for understanding chemical elements and their reactions. Knowledge of chemistry quickly advanced, creating a new a pharmaceutical industry, and soon the use of synthetic drugs, such as aspirin and barbiturates, became commonplace.

Medical breakthroughs

The discovery of X-rays (1895), radiation (1896), and the radioactive elements polonium and radium (1898) revolutionized medical treatment. Radiography made diagnoses more accurate, and radiation therapies were developed for cancer. Combined with the discovery of the electron (1897) and of the source of radioactivity (1901), these findings also paved the way for nuclear power. Louis Pasteur's theory that microorganisms were the transmitters of disease radicalized approaches to disease control. Vaccines for cholera, anthrax, rabies, diphtheria, and typhoid soon followed. Deaths from infection were much reduced by the introduction of carbolic to disinfect both operation theaters and surgeons. Together, these advances contributed to a population explosion in the early 20th century.

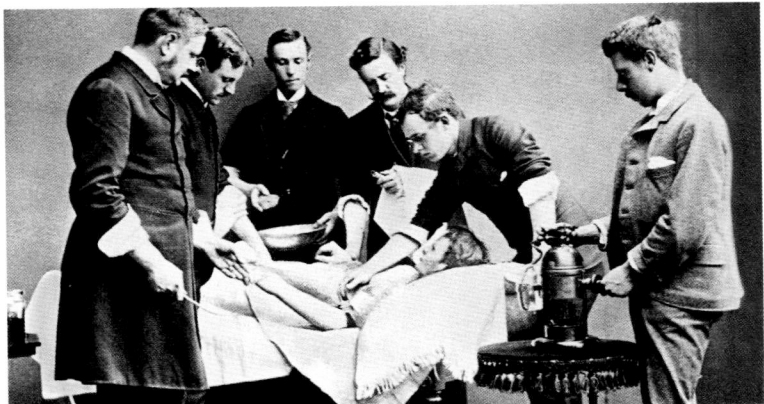

Safer surgery
Building on Pasteur's work, English surgeon Joseph Lister introduced carbolic acid (phenol) to clean wounds and sterilize surgical equipment. His promotion of antiseptic surgery dramatically reduced postoperative infections.

EXPANSION OF THE US

US territory grew in the 19th century through the agencies of war, political agreement, and annexation. Settlement by migrants helped bring new areas into cultivation, while rapid industrialization from the 1870s fueled urbanization and population growth.

In 1800, the borders of the United States reached only to the Mississippi River, but the next 100 years saw a swift westward expansion as Britain withdrew its claim on Oregon Country and the US annexed Texas and defeated Mexico in the war of 1846–1848. By 1900, the country stretched from the Atlantic to the Pacific and covered an area of almost 3 million sq miles (7.8 million sq km).

The promise of cheap land attracted immigrants from abroad who settled alongside American frontiersmen and women. In 1890, the US Census declared the frontier closed—there were no longer any continuous unsettled areas in the west. By then, America's cattle barons were driving their herds to railheads that supplied growing cities in the east, where industrialization was taking hold. By 1900, the US was producing more steel than Britain and Germany combined. Cities such as Chicago—just a small town in 1837—had grown into metropolises of more than 1 million people. New York's Ellis Island had become a key entry point for millions of migrants to America's vast cities. The industrial boom of the late 19th century made millions of dollars for a few, but it was punctuated by periods of depression that boded ill for America's rapidly growing population.

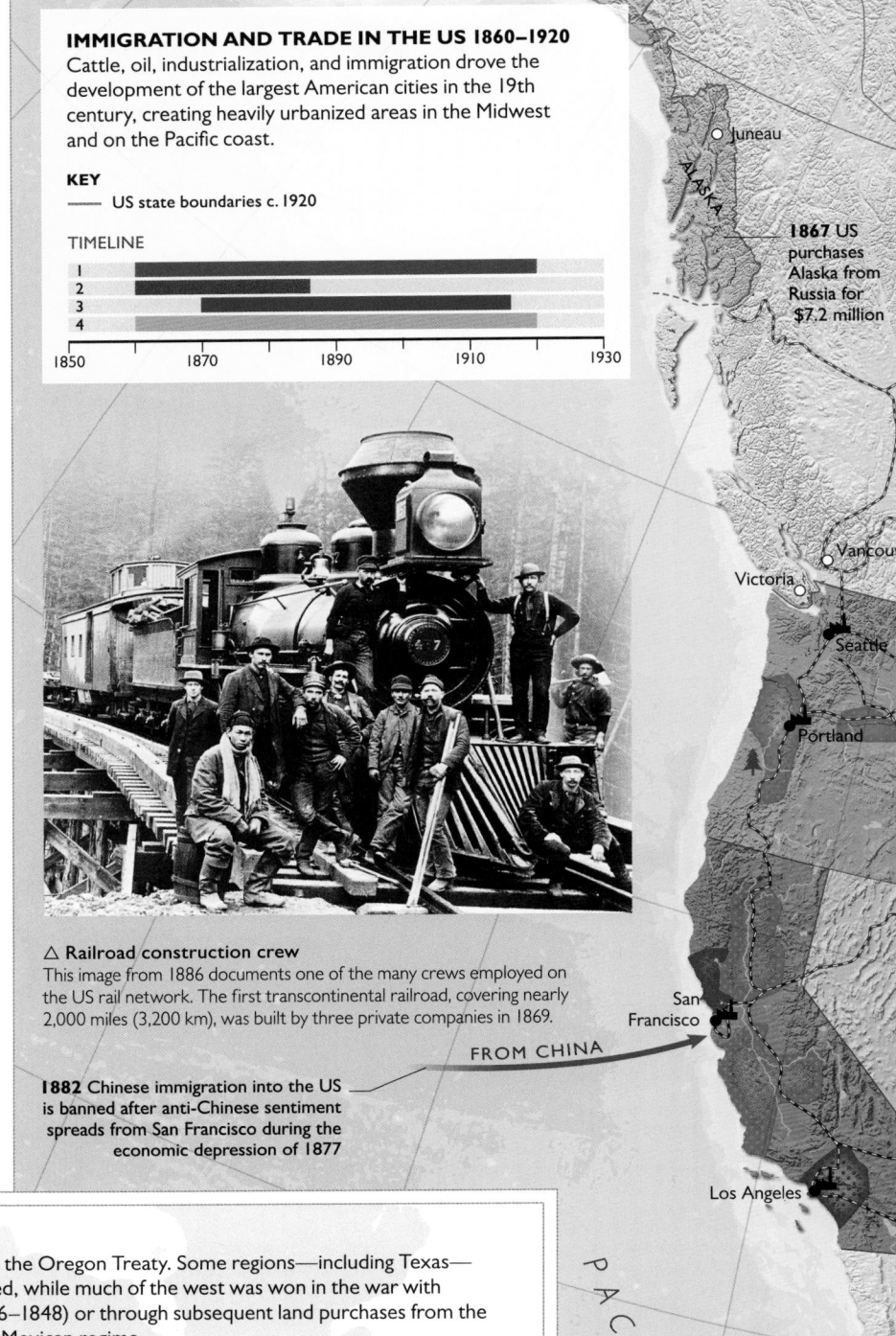

IMMIGRATION AND TRADE IN THE US 1860–1920

Cattle, oil, industrialization, and immigration drove the development of the largest American cities in the 19th century, creating heavily urbanized areas in the Midwest and on the Pacific coast.

KEY

—— US state boundaries c. 1920

TIMELINE

1
2
3
4

1850   1870   1890   1910   1930

1867 US purchases Alaska from Russia for $7.2 million

△ **Railroad construction crew**
This image from 1886 documents one of the many crews employed on the US rail network. The first transcontinental railroad, covering nearly 2,000 miles (3,200 km), was built by three private companies in 1869.

FROM CHINA

1882 Chinese immigration into the US is banned after anti-Chinese sentiment spreads from San Francisco during the economic depression of 1877

Juneau
ALASKA
Vancouver
Victoria
Seattle
Portland
San Francisco
Los Angeles

PACIFIC OCEAN

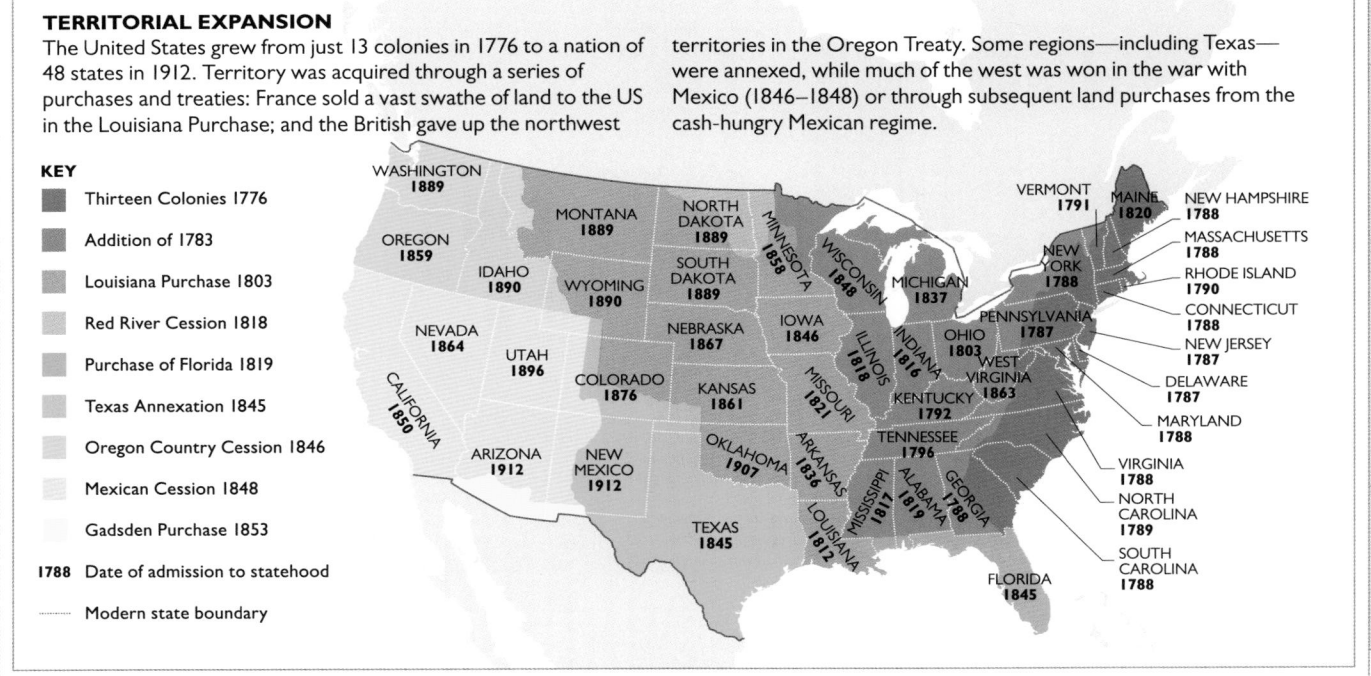

TERRITORIAL EXPANSION

The United States grew from just 13 colonies in 1776 to a nation of 48 states in 1912. Territory was acquired through a series of purchases and treaties: France sold a vast swathe of land to the US in the Louisiana Purchase; and the British gave up the northwest territories in the Oregon Treaty. Some regions—including Texas—were annexed, while much of the west was won in the war with Mexico (1846–1848) or through subsequent land purchases from the cash-hungry Mexican regime.

KEY

- Thirteen Colonies 1776
- Addition of 1783
- Louisiana Purchase 1803
- Red River Cession 1818
- Purchase of Florida 1819
- Texas Annexation 1845
- Oregon Country Cession 1846
- Mexican Cession 1848
- Gadsden Purchase 1853

1788 Date of admission to statehood

---- Modern state boundary

WASHINGTON 1889
OREGON 1859
MONTANA 1889
NORTH DAKOTA 1889
MINNESOTA 1858
IDAHO 1890
WYOMING 1890
SOUTH DAKOTA 1889
WISCONSIN 1848
MICHIGAN 1837
VERMONT 1791
MAINE 1820
NEW HAMPSHIRE 1788
NEW YORK 1788
MASSACHUSETTS 1788
RHODE ISLAND 1790
NEVADA 1864
UTAH 1896
NEBRASKA 1867
IOWA 1846
ILLINOIS 1818
INDIANA 1816
OHIO 1803
PENNSYLVANIA 1787
CONNECTICUT 1788
NEW JERSEY 1787
CALIFORNIA 1850
COLORADO 1876
KANSAS 1861
MISSOURI 1821
KENTUCKY 1792
WEST VIRGINIA 1863
DELAWARE 1787
MARYLAND 1788
ARIZONA 1912
NEW MEXICO 1912
OKLAHOMA 1907
ARKANSAS 1836
TENNESSEE 1796
MISSISSIPPI 1817
ALABAMA 1819
GEORGIA 1788
VIRGINIA 1788
NORTH CAROLINA 1789
SOUTH CAROLINA 1788
TEXAS 1845
LOUISIANA 1812
FLORIDA 1845

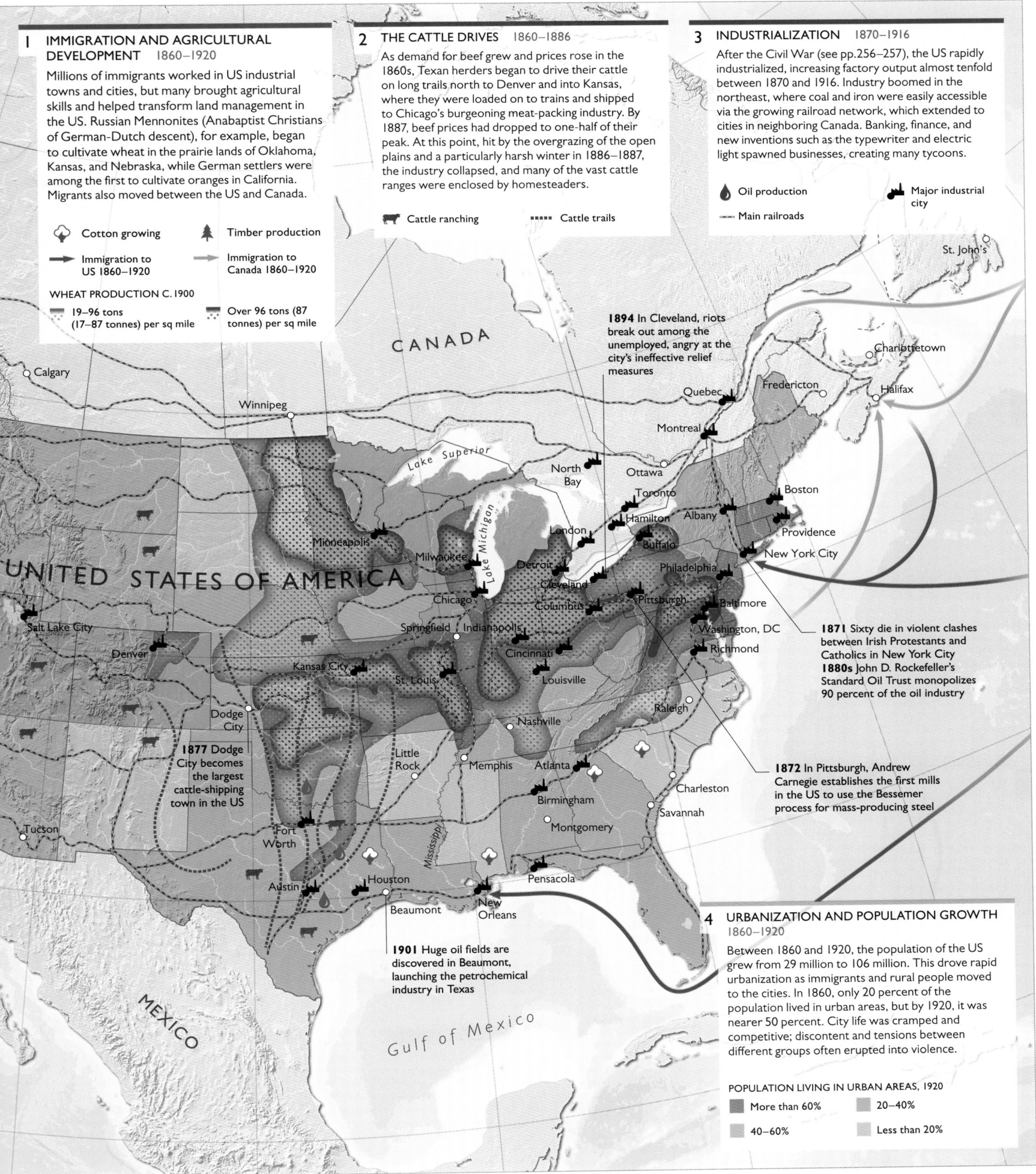

1 IMMIGRATION AND AGRICULTURAL DEVELOPMENT 1860–1920

Millions of immigrants worked in US industrial towns and cities, but many brought agricultural skills and helped transform land management in the US. Russian Mennonites (Anabaptist Christians of German-Dutch descent), for example, began to cultivate wheat in the prairie lands of Oklahoma, Kansas, and Nebraska, while German settlers were among the first to cultivate oranges in California. Migrants also moved between the US and Canada.

Cotton growing

Timber production

Immigration to US 1860–1920

Immigration to Canada 1860–1920

WHEAT PRODUCTION C. 1900

19–96 tons (17–87 tonnes) per sq mile

Over 96 tons (87 tonnes) per sq mile

2 THE CATTLE DRIVES 1860–1886

As demand for beef grew and prices rose in the 1860s, Texan herders began to drive their cattle on long trails north to Denver and into Kansas, where they were loaded on to trains and shipped to Chicago's burgeoning meat-packing industry. By 1887, beef prices had dropped to one-half of their peak. At this point, hit by the overgrazing of the open plains and a particularly harsh winter in 1886–1887, the industry collapsed, and many of the vast cattle ranges were enclosed by homesteaders.

Cattle ranching

Cattle trails

3 INDUSTRIALIZATION 1870–1916

After the Civil War (see pp.256–257), the US rapidly industrialized, increasing factory output almost tenfold between 1870 and 1916. Industry boomed in the northeast, where coal and iron were easily accessible via the growing railroad network, which extended to cities in neighboring Canada. Banking, finance, and new inventions such as the typewriter and electric light spawned businesses, creating many tycoons.

Oil production

Major industrial city

Main railroads

1894 In Cleveland, riots break out among the unemployed, angry at the city's ineffective relief measures

1871 Sixty die in violent clashes between Irish Protestants and Catholics in New York City
1880s John D. Rockefeller's Standard Oil Trust monopolizes 90 percent of the oil industry

1872 In Pittsburgh, Andrew Carnegie establishes the first mills in the US to use the Bessemer process for mass-producing steel

1877 Dodge City becomes the largest cattle-shipping town in the US

1901 Huge oil fields are discovered in Beaumont, launching the petrochemical industry in Texas

4 URBANIZATION AND POPULATION GROWTH 1860–1920

Between 1860 and 1920, the population of the US grew from 29 million to 106 million. This drove rapid urbanization as immigrants and rural people moved to the cities. In 1860, only 20 percent of the population lived in urban areas, but by 1920, it was nearer 50 percent. City life was cramped and competitive; discontent and tensions between different groups often erupted into violence.

POPULATION LIVING IN URBAN AREAS, 1920

More than 60%

20–40%

40–60%

Less than 20%

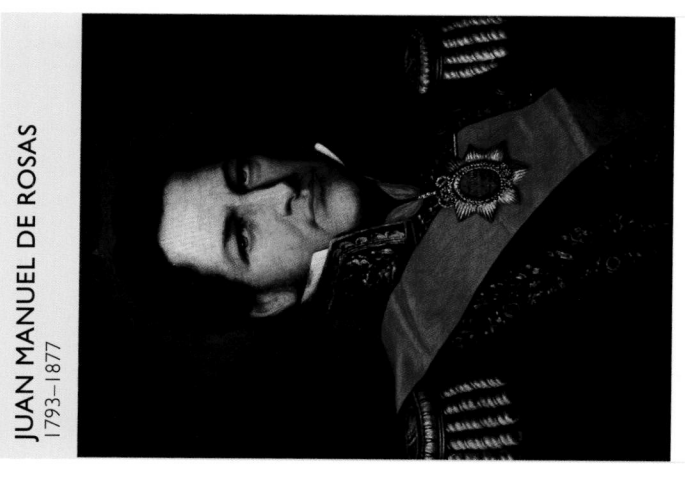

JUAN MANUEL DE ROSAS
1793–1877

A charismatic but brutal military dictator, Juan Manuel de Rosas was the archetypal *caudillo*. As governor of Buenos Aires province, Rosas controlled all of Argentina for 17 years and extended the country's territories deep into Patagonia through a violent campaign against the indigenous people there. Ousted from power by a rival general in 1852, he fled to England and died there in 1877.

INDEPENDENT LATIN AMERICA

The decades following liberation in Latin America were marked by the appearance of successive military dictators, civil wars, and battles between states over resources and territories. The shadow of imperialism continued to hang over the region, too, as financial investment and military intervention secured American and British influence.

In the aftermath of liberation, many countries in South America saw power seized by *caudillos*, military dictators such as José Antonio Páez in Venezuela and Juan Manuel de Rosas in Argentina. Civil wars were common as new dictators fought for leadership, as happened in Mexico in 1910. Border disputes were also common as the young states sought to extend their territory or gain control of valuable natural resources. Bolivia and Peru both lost lands to Chile

in the War of the Pacific, fought over the Atacama Desert's nitrates, which were used in fertilizers and explosives. Brazil, Bolivia, and Argentina took almost half of Paraguay's territory in Latin America's bloodiest war. The region's economies depended on the export of raw materials and food to feed Europe's burgeoning industries and consumer markets: coffee and rubber from Brazil; copper and tin from Chile and Peru; and salted and frozen meat from Argentina. Access to the Atlantic trade routes gave Argentina in particular an advantage, and the country developed rapidly. Yet foreign power lingered in the region. It was evident in the United States' interference in Central America and the Caribbean—where it annexed Puerto Rico and occupied or made Protectorates of many other countries—and in the large profits made by British and American firms investing in the region's railways and mines.

"I'd rather die on my feet, than live on my knees."

ATTRIBUTED TO EMILIANO ZAPATA, 1913

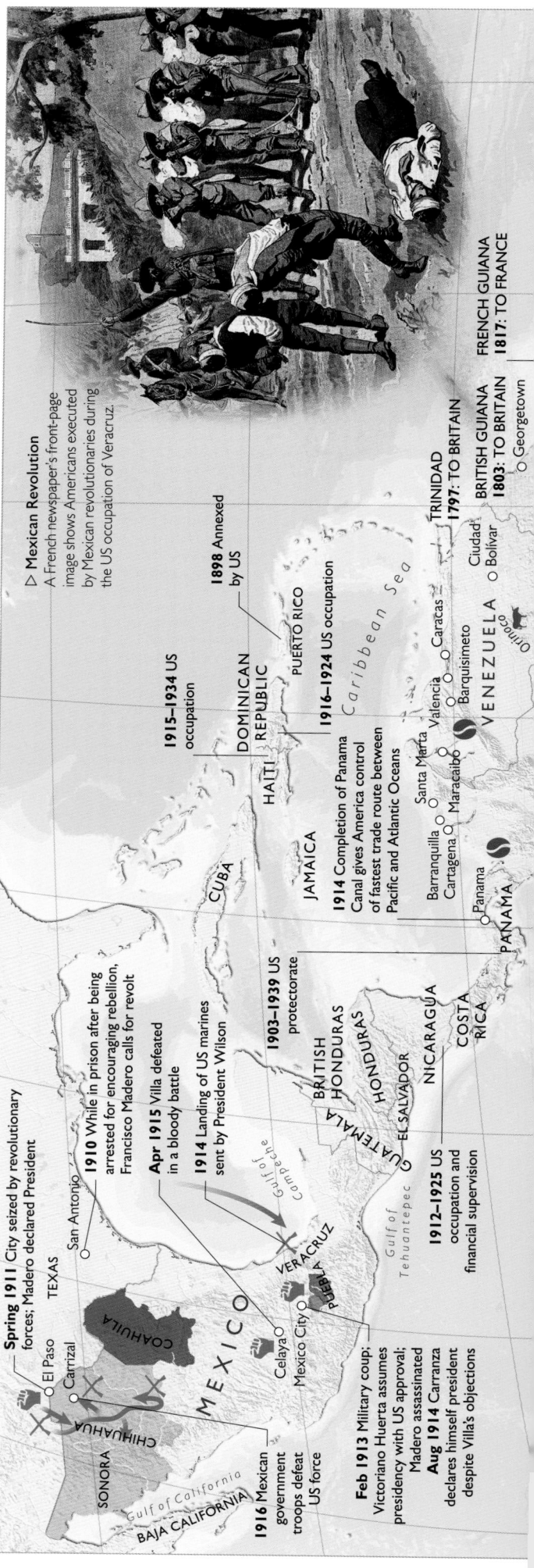

▷ **Mexican Revolution**
A French newspaper's front-page image shows Mexican revolutionaries executed by Americans during the US occupation of Veracruz.

Map labels and regions

BRAZIL
Planalto do Mato Grosso
PACIFIC OCEAN
COLOMBIA
ECUADOR
PERU
BOLIVIA
Andes
PARAGUAY
URUGUAY
ARGENTINA
CHILE
Patagonia
Tierra del Fuego
ACRE
TARAPACÁ
ATACAMA
BUENOS AIRES

Place names
Maceió, Bahia (Salvador), Santa Cruz, Minas Novas, Diamantina, Belo Horizonte, Ouro Prêto, Victoria, Rio de Janeiro, São Paulo, Pará (Belém), Xingu, Santarém, Manáos, Topajós, Madeira, Amazon, Rio Negro, Goyaz, Pirapora, Porto Alegre, Rio Grande, Corrientes, Montevideo, Colonia, La Plata, Rosario, Córdoba, Mar del Plata, Bahia Blanca, Neuquén, Santa Cruz, Corumbá, Santa Cruz, Potosí, La Paz, Lake Titicaca, Lake Poopó, Cuzco, Pisco, Lima, Callao, Islas de Chincha, Mollendó, Tacna, Arica, Iquique, Tocopilla, Punta de Angamos, Antofagasta, Caldera, Copiapó, La Serena, Talca, Viña del Mar, Valparaíso, Santiago, Mendoza, Tucumán, Salta, Catamarca, Concepción, Valdivia, Puerto Montt, Punta Arenas, Quito, Cuenca, Guayaquil, Tumbes, Iquitos, Putumayo, Trujillo, Yungay, Salta, Talta, Río Negro, Uruguay, Paraná, Paraguay

Timeline annotations (map)

Dec 27, 1865 Paraguayans invade Brazil and attack the Brazilian garrison at Nova Coimbra fort

Dec 21–22, 1868 Battle of Lomas Valentinas

1870–1914 Brazil's economy becomes heavily dependent on coffee exports

Apr 1866 Argentina's President Mitre invades southwest Paraguay

Jun 11, 1865 Brazilian navy defeats Paraguayan flotilla in Battle of Riachuelo on the Paraná River near Corrientes

1884 Work begins on development of Buenos Aires port, funded by the British Barings Bank

1850–1914 Argentina's largely British-built railways make large-scale beef exports possible

1870–1914 Tin becomes Bolivia's main export

1890–1920 Manáos flourishes as center of rubber boom in Amazon region

1884 Tacna and Arica conquered by Chile
1929 Tacna area awarded to Peru, Arica area to Chile

Oct 20, 1883 Peru and Chile sign Treaty of Ancon; Tarapacá area ceded to Chile

Oct 8, 1879 Sinking of a Peruvian ironclad, the *Huáscar*, gives Chile control of the sea

Feb 14, 1879 Chilean armed forces occupy Antofagasta

1878 Bolivia demands more taxes from the Chilean Antofagasta Nitrate Company working in the Atacama

1881–1884 Lima and Callao occupied by Chilean forces

1890–1920 (Manáos)

KEY
— 1930 international borders
▪▪▪ Railways

AFTER INDEPENDENCE
Latin America was marked by civil war, competition for resources, and interference from outside, all of which determined its future development.

TIMELINE
1, 2, 3, 4, 5 (1840–1920)

5 CENTRAL AMERICA, THE CARIBBEAN, AND THE UNITED STATES 1895–1920
In 1898, the Spanish-American War finally ended Spanish rule in Latin America. Prefaced by America's support for Cuba's revolt against Spain in 1895, the war left America in possession of Cuba and Puerto Rico and secured its influence in the Caribbean and Central America. The US then intervened across the region in Honduras, Guatemala, Nicaragua, the Dominican Republic, and, crucially, Panama.

4 EXPORT AND INVESTMENT 1850–1920
As the world entered a second phase of industrialization at the end of the 19th century, South America experienced a series of export booms in nitrates, rubber, copper, and tin. South America also became a major coffee producer, and British investment in the region's railways and ports made wheat and beef viable export products.

Major ports
Beef
Nitrates
Rubber
Tin
Coffee

3 THE MEXICAN REVOLUTION 1910–1917
In 1910, Francisco Madero challenged Mexico's dictator for the presidency and called for revolution. Armies under Pascual Orozco, Pancho Villa, and Emiliano Zapata all attacked government positions. Successive presidents failed to pacify the country, and the US intervened militarily. A new constitution was agreed on in 1917, and Venustiano Carranza became President.

AREA OF LEADERSHIP
Venustiano Carranza
Pancho Villa
Emiliano Zapata
Francisco Madero
US/Mexican clash
Major incident in revolution
Route of US expedition

1 THE PARAGUAYAN WAR 1864–1870
In 1864, Paraguay was pitted against an alliance of Argentina, Brazil, and Uruguay set on conquest. Outnumbered 10 to 1, Paraguay's army was destroyed at the Battle of Lomas Valentinas in 1868. Guerrilla war rumbled on until 1870, but ultimately Paraguay lost around 54,000 square miles (140,000 square km) of territory and around half its population in the conflict.

Battle
Former Paraguay

2 WAR OF THE PACIFIC 1879–1883
In 1879, Bolivia, Chile, and Peru went to war over control of the Atacama Desert's nitrate deposits. Chile landed an army at Antofagasta, taking the Bolivian coastline and the southern provinces of Peru. Chilean troops then sailed to attack Lima, and the city was occupied by a Chilean force between 1881 and 1884.

Chile before 1874
Gained from Bolivia
Gained from Peru
Conquered by Chile
Battle

▷ **Battling hussars**
A painting by German artist Christian Sell the Elder shows a clash between French and German cavalry in the Franco-Prussian War.

UNIFICATION OF ITALY AND GERMANY

After 1835, powerful German and Italian leaders emerged who contested Austrian power and—in a rapid succession of political and military campaigns from 1850 to 1870—created the unified nations of Italy and Germany.

TIMELINE

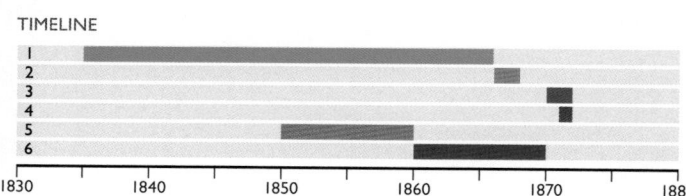

1 AUSTRIA CHALLENGED 1835–1866

In 1863, Bismarck engineered an alliance with Austria to claim the provinces of Schleswig and Holstein from Denmark. By October 1864, Schleswig belonged to Prussia and Holstein to Austria. The arrangement was unworkable because Holstein was isolated and hemmed in by Prussia. When Austria sought a resolution to the issue, Prussia used it as a pretext for conflict, beginning the Seven Weeks' War (1866).

▬ Boundary of German Confederation of 1815

→ Austro-Prussian forces in Denmark 1864

■ Prussia in 1815

Sep 1, 1870 Prussia captures Napoleon III at the Battle of Sedan

1871 Prussians march through France to besiege and occupy Paris

May 1871 The French cede Alsace-Lorraine to Germany in the Treaty of Frankfurt

4 UNIFICATION AND EMPIRE 1871

As a result of the war, France lost the region of Alsace-Lorraine to Germany and was forced to pay compensation. The now unified German states adopted a new imperial constitution, with William I as kaiser (emperor). The empire, with Prussia firmly in control, comprised 26 states.

▬ Boundary of German Empire 1871

GERMANY UNIFIED

German unification was achieved in several stages that saw Prussia free the north German states from Austrian authority and then defeat Austria and France to create a new empire in 1871.

Jul 3, 1866 The Battle of Sadowa gives Prussia a decisive victory over Austria in the Seven Weeks' War

2 THE NORTH GERMAN CONFEDERATION 1866–1867

Prussia defeated Austria in the Seven Weeks' War. Prussia kept the territories it had won in the conflict and formed a North German Confederation, in which each state kept its own laws and sent an elected representative to a federal parliament.

─ Prussian armies in Seven Weeks' War 1866

✕ Battle

■ Prussian gains by 1866

■ Other states in North German Confederation 1867

■ Other German states 1866–1867

■ Austro-Hungarian Empire 1867

3 FRANCO-PRUSSIAN WAR 1870–1871

Another great power, France, viewed Prussia's growing status with concern. Bismarck engineered a political situation that provoked the French emperor, Napoleon III, into declaring war. This prompted the southern German states to ally with the Northern Confederation. The Germans crushed their French enemies, captured Napoleon III, and took Paris in 1871.

→ Prussian invasion of France 1870–1871

✕ Battle

Map labels:
DENMARK · SWEDEN · Baltic Sea · Copenhagen · SCHLESWIG-HOLSTEIN · Königsberg · Hamburg · Bremen · Rostock · MECKLENBURG · POMERANIA · Danzig · WEST PRUSSIA · EAST PRUSSIA · RUSSIA · The Hague · Amsterdam · NETHERLANDS · HANOVER · Elbe · P R U S S I A · Berlin · BRANDENBURG · Oder · POSEN · Posen · Brussels · BELGIUM · WESTPHALIA · Cologne · Rhine · THURINGIAN STATES · Breslau · Meuse · Leipzig · SAXONY · SILESIA · Luxembourg · Prague · BOHEMIA · Sadowa · Sedan · Nuremberg · Karlsruhe · BAVARIA · Strassburg · Stuttgart · BADEN · WÜRTTEMBERG · HOHENZOLLERN · Munich · Danube · Vienna · Basle · FRANCE · SWITZERLAND · AUSTRIA · HUNGARY · ITALY

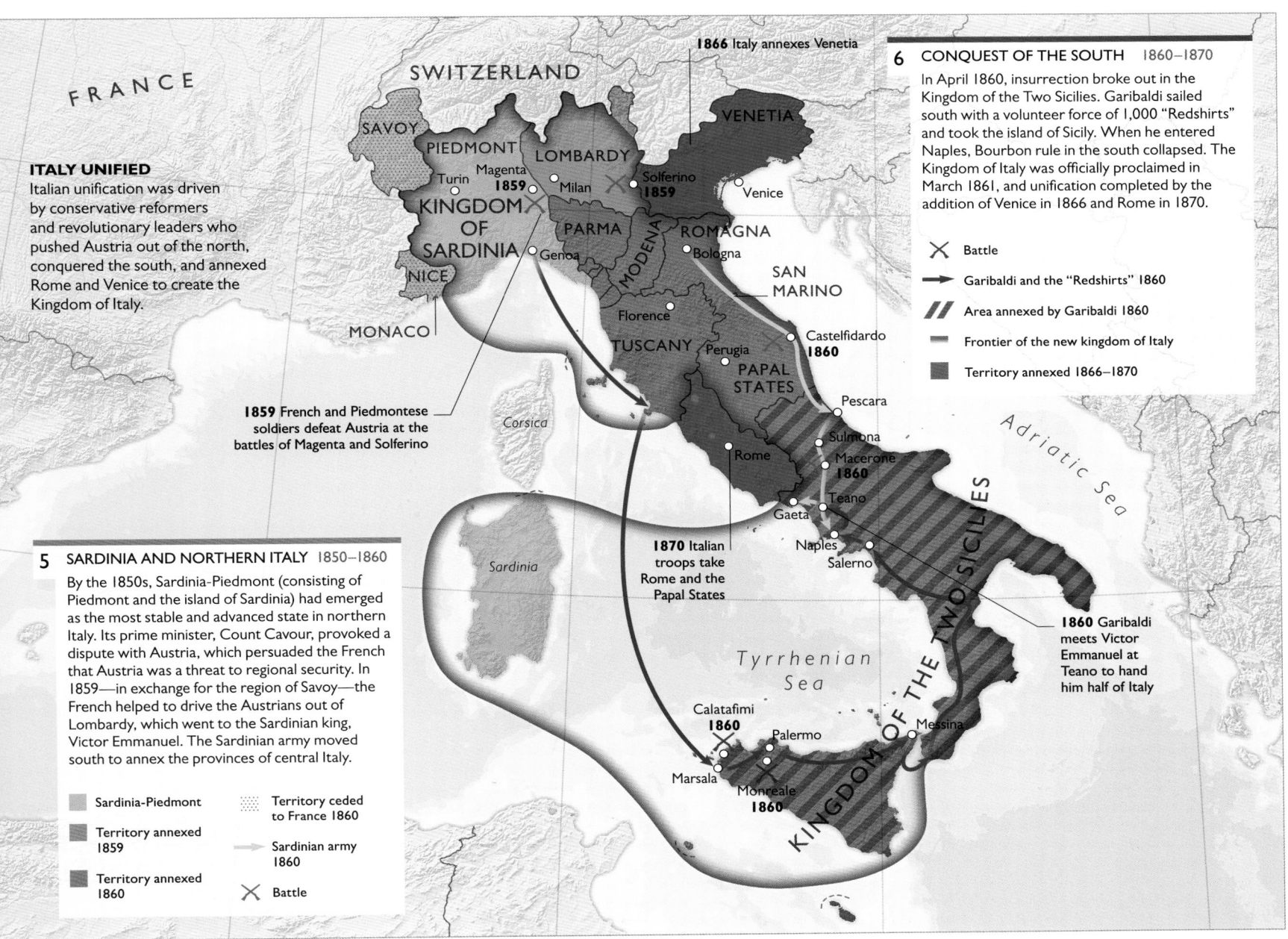

1866 Italy annexes Venetia

ITALY UNIFIED
Italian unification was driven by conservative reformers and revolutionary leaders who pushed Austria out of the north, conquered the south, and annexed Rome and Venice to create the Kingdom of Italy.

6 CONQUEST OF THE SOUTH 1860–1870

In April 1860, insurrection broke out in the Kingdom of the Two Sicilies. Garibaldi sailed south with a volunteer force of 1,000 "Redshirts" and took the island of Sicily. When he entered Naples, Bourbon rule in the south collapsed. The Kingdom of Italy was officially proclaimed in March 1861, and unification completed by the addition of Venice in 1866 and Rome in 1870.

✕ Battle

→ Garibaldi and the "Redshirts" 1860

⫽ Area annexed by Garibaldi 1860

▬ Frontier of the new kingdom of Italy

▮ Territory annexed 1866–1870

1859 French and Piedmontese soldiers defeat Austria at the battles of Magenta and Solferino

1870 Italian troops take Rome and the Papal States

1860 Garibaldi meets Victor Emmanuel at Teano to hand him half of Italy

5 SARDINIA AND NORTHERN ITALY 1850–1860

By the 1850s, Sardinia-Piedmont (consisting of Piedmont and the island of Sardinia) had emerged as the most stable and advanced state in northern Italy. Its prime minister, Count Cavour, provoked a dispute with Austria, which persuaded the French that Austria was a threat to regional security. In 1859—in exchange for the region of Savoy—the French helped to drive the Austrians out of Lombardy, which went to the Sardinian king, Victor Emmanuel. The Sardinian army moved south to annex the provinces of central Italy.

▮ Sardinia-Piedmont

▮ Territory annexed 1859

▮ Territory annexed 1860

⣿ Territory ceded to France 1860

→ Sardinian army 1860

✕ Battle

GERMANY AND ITALY UNIFIED

In 1850, Germany and Italy were fragmented. Germany was a loose confederation of states dominated by Austria, while Italy was a mixture of duchies and kingdoms with little direction. By 1870, through war, diplomacy, and a certain amount of political machination, both had been unified into new nations.

A wave of popular nationalism followed the Napoleonic Wars (see pp.208–211). In 1848–1849, this erupted in a series of republican revolutions (see pp.218–219), which began in Sicily and extended across much of Europe. These revolts were repressed by armies loyal to their respective goverments; and popular fervor had largely dissipated by the 1850s, leaving the German and Italian states as fragmented as ever.

The yoke of unification was, however, taken up by conservative reformers in both Italy and Germany in the 1860s. Afraid of revolution from below, they took control of reform from above, seeing in unification a chance to curb Austro-Hungarian power and carve out strong new kingdoms.

After the Napoleonic Wars, Prussia was one of a confederation of 39 states under the leadership of Austria. It was the only one of these states powerful enough to compete with Austria-Hungary for control of the fiercely independent German principalities, so it took the lead on unification. In 1864, Prussia, led by its formidable prime minister, Otto von Bismarck, made its move against Austria. Within 7 years, through a combination of war, political maneuvering, and luck, the threat to unification posed by both Austria and France had been neutralized, and Bismarck had forged a unified German empire. Bismark became the first chancellor of the Empire in 1871.

In Italy, following the failure of Giuseppe Mazzini's nationalist revolution in 1848, the prime minister of Sardinia-Piedmont, Count Cavour, steered the process of unification. By allying with France against the Austrians in northern Italy and harnessing the talents of the great nationalist revolutionary Giuseppe Garibaldi to secure the south, Cavour was able to create a unified kingdom by 1860.

5 THE SECOND BALKAN WAR 1913

In June 1913, tension over the division of Macedonia turned to war when the Bulgarians attacked Greek and Serbian positions in the region. When Romanian and Ottoman forces invaded Bulgaria, looking for gains of their own, Bulgaria soon sued for peace, and Macedonia was largely divided between Greece and Serbia.

- Serbian gain 1913
- Greek gain 1913
- Romanian gain 1913
- Bulgarian gain 1913
- Montenegrin gain 1913
- ✕ Battles

1878 Treaty of Berlin puts Bosnia-Herzegovina under Austria-Hungary's control, although it remains an Ottoman possession

Oct 7, 1908 Serbia mobilizes its troops and demands Novi Pazar region as compensation

1878 Enlarged by the treaty of San Stefano, Serbia becomes independent

1878 Romania becomes independent and gains Dobruja

Sep 30, 1913 Treaty of Bucharest ends Second Balkan War

Dec 1877 Ottoman garrison at Pleven submits after being besieged by Russian and Romanian force for 5 months

Oct 6, 1908 Austria-Hungary annexes Bosnia-Herzegovina

Mar 1821 Greek revolutionaries in Moldavia occupy Jassy and call on all Greeks and Christians to rise up against the Ottomans

Jul 10, 1913 Romanians occupy Varna

Oct 5, 1908 Prince Ferdinand of Bulgaria declares Bulgaria's independence

1878–1885 Treaty of Berlin returns Eastern Rumelia to Ottoman Empire, but Bulgaria reclaims it in 1885

1878 Montenegro doubles its territory and gains independence

Oct 23–24, 1912 Serbian army defeats Ottomans at Battle of Kumanovo and joins forces with Montenegrins to enter Skopje

Jun 30–Jul 8, 1913 Bulgarian army defeated by Serbs at Battle of Bregalnica

Oct 19–20, 1912 Greek army defeats Ottomans and captures Yanitza

May 21, 1864 Britain transfers the Ionian islands to Greece as a gesture of support for King George I

Jul 19–21, 1913 Greek victory against the Bulgarians at the Battle of Kilkis

Oct 21, 1912 The Bulgarians defeat the main Ottoman forces in Thrace and reach Constantinople

Jan 1878 Russians take Edirne, then known as Adrianople
Mar 26, 1913 Edirne falls to the Bulgarians
Jul 23, 1913 Ottomans force Bulgarians out of Edirne

Mar 1878 Treaty of San Stefano ends Russo-Turkish War

Jul 1908 Young Turks establish a constitutional government in Constantinople and begin program of reform

4 THE FIRST BALKAN WAR 1912–1913

In 1912, Russia encouraged Serbia, Bulgaria, Greece, and Montenegro to band together and take Macedonia from Turkey. Montenegro declared war on Turkey and was joined by the other league nations. By May 1913, the war was over and the Ottoman Empire had lost most of its remaining European territories, including Albania.

- ✕ Significant Ottoman defeats
- Albania 1913

Jul 1881 Ottoman Empire cedes Thessaly to Greece following the Russo-Turkish War

Mar 6, 1913 Janina falls to the Greeks

3 BOSNIA CRISIS 1908

Fearing that the Young Turks in Constantinople might reinvigorate Turkey, Austria-Hungary decided to annex Bosnia and Herzegovina. When Serbia demanded that they receive compensation for the annexation, Russia supported their claim. But when Austria—backed by Germany—threatened to invade Serbia, Russia was forced to back down and accept the annexation.

- ✕ The Bosnia Crisis
- Annexation border

Oct 20, 1827 British, French, and Russian naval fleets destroy the Egyptian fleet supporting the Ottomans

Aug 1826 Ottoman forces capture Athens

Jan 1822 Greek National Assembly declares Greece a free and independent state

AUSTRO-HUNGARIAN EMPIRE

RUSSIAN EMPIRE

MOLDAVIA

Jassy

ROMANIA

DOBRUJA

Bucharest

Danube

BOSNIA-HERZEGOVINA

Belgrade

SERBIA

Sarajevo

DALMATIA

Pleven

BULGARIA

Varna

Novi Pazar

MONTENEGRO

Cetinje

Sofia

EASTERN RUMELIA

Üsküb (Skopje)

Kumanovo

Bregalnica

ALBANIA

Tirana

MACEDONIA

Yanitza

Kilkis

Kurdzhali

Edirne

Constantinople

THRACE

Yesilköy (San Stefano)

ITALY

Janina

Ionian Islands

Ionian Sea

THESSALY

Athens

Aegean Sea

Epidaurus

Navarino

Mediterranean Sea

Crete

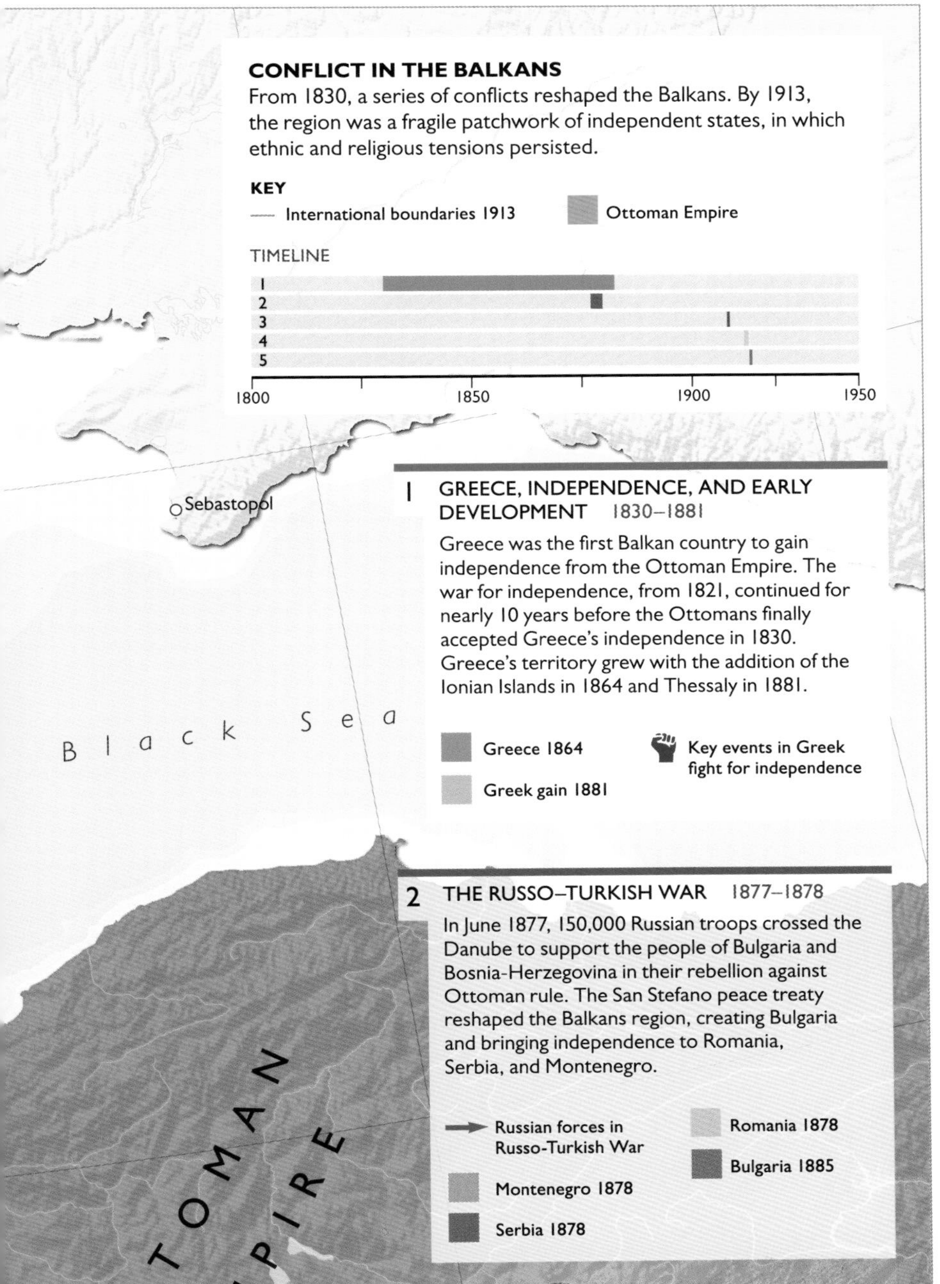

CONFLICT IN THE BALKANS

From 1830, a series of conflicts reshaped the Balkans. By 1913, the region was a fragile patchwork of independent states, in which ethnic and religious tensions persisted.

KEY

— International boundaries 1913   ▨ Ottoman Empire

TIMELINE

1	
2	
3	
4	
5	

1800   1850   1900   1950

Sebastopol

Black Sea

1 GREECE, INDEPENDENCE, AND EARLY DEVELOPMENT 1830–1881

Greece was the first Balkan country to gain independence from the Ottoman Empire. The war for independence, from 1821, continued for nearly 10 years before the Ottomans finally accepted Greece's independence in 1830. Greece's territory grew with the addition of the Ionian Islands in 1864 and Thessaly in 1881.

▨ Greece 1864

▨ Greek gain 1881

✊ Key events in Greek fight for independence

2 THE RUSSO–TURKISH WAR 1877–1878

In June 1877, 150,000 Russian troops crossed the Danube to support the people of Bulgaria and Bosnia-Herzegovina in their rebellion against Ottoman rule. The San Stefano peace treaty reshaped the Balkans region, creating Bulgaria and bringing independence to Romania, Serbia, and Montenegro.

→ Russian forces in Russo-Turkish War

▨ Montenegro 1878

▨ Serbia 1878

▨ Romania 1878

▨ Bulgaria 1885

OTTOMAN EMPIRE

Anatolia

▷ **Bulgarian attack**
In this 1913 painting, Czech artist Jaroslav Věšín shows the fierceness with which the Bulgarians fought the Turks in the First Balkan War.

BALKAN WARS

A wave of nationalism swept through the Balkans in the 19th century. As the Balkan countries coalesced and gained independence—often under the influence of the Great Powers—ethnic and religious diversity created conflict, feeding the instability in the region.

The Balkans in the 19th and early 20th centuries endured a series of conflicts as Ottoman power receded and the peoples of the region fought for independence. In 1830, Greece broke away from the Ottoman Empire. There were further conflicts, at the expense of the Ottomans, over the next 80 years. The Great Powers of Russia, Britain, and Austria-Hungary all played a part in these conflicts and regarded the region with an uneasy mix of ambition and anxiety. Russia supported Slavic nationalism, hoping that the Bulgarians, Montenegrins, Bosnians, and Serbs would provide it with allies. Austria-Hungary watched the emergence of Serbia with concern, aware that its own population of Serbs might make a claim for independence. And Britain, wary of Russian influence in the region, sought to bolster the Greeks. But for all their involvement in peace treaties and territory division, the Great Powers could not solve the problem at the heart of the Balkans: the region's ethnic groups would not be separated neatly into nations. By 1914, Turkey may have lost all but a small part of its European possessions, but few were happy with the outcome of 70 years of struggle. The two Balkan Wars alone resulted in more than half a million casualties, and the conflicts pushed the Great Powers closer to a European war.

"A … peninsula filled with sprightly people … who had a splendid talent for starting wars."

C.L. SULZBERGER, FROM *A LONG ROW OF CANDLES*, 1969

EDIRNE
THE IMPORTANCE OF ADRIANOPLE

The city of Edirne (formerly known as Adrianople) was one of the largest in the Ottoman Empire. It guarded the route to Constantinople, the capital of the Ottoman Empire, so was of vital strategic importance to the Ottomans. Heavily fortified with a network of trenches, fences, and 20 massive concrete forts, the fortress at Edirne was believed to be unassailable; its capture by the Bulgarians in 1913 was a huge blow to Ottoman confidence.

Flight from Edirne, 1913
A stream of foreigners flees the Bulgarian attack on Edirne.

1 GERMANY, AUSTRIA-HUNGARY, AND RUSSIA 1871–1918

Germany negotiated alliances with Austria-Hungary and Russia to limit or prevent war. The defensive Austro-German alliance, later joined by Italy (creating the Triple Alliance), prevented Austria siding with Russia in any attack on Germany; Romania secretly joined in 1883. The Three Emperors' Alliance helped to ease the tension between Russia and Austria over the Balkans and isolated France.

● Austro-German alliance 1879–1918

◆ Three Emperors' Alliance 1881–1887

⬠ Triple Alliance 1882–1915

2 THE DEVELOPMENT OF THE TRIPLE ENTENTE 1894–1907

After the Three Emperors' Alliance collapsed, Bismarck arranged the Reinsurance Treaty between Germany and Russia. In 1890, Kaiser Wilhelm II refused to renew this treaty, leaving Russia free to ally with France. The Franco-Russian alliance provided reassurances of mutual military support. Britain sought to limit threats to her Empire, and in 1904 allied with France, and then in 1907 with Russia, creating what was called the Triple Entente.

■ Franco-Russian alliance 1894–1917

▲ Anglo-Russian Entente 1907

★ Entente Cordiale 1904

1887–1890 Germany agrees to Reinsurance Treaty with Russia, guaranteeing neutrality in any war with a third power, excluding France and Austria

1909–1910 Tsar Nicholas II commits around 1 million rubles to construction of a military air force

1907 Construction begins on Rosyth naval dockyard

1907 Britain reorganizes its army to create Expeditionary Force of 160,000 troops and a volunteer, part-time force of 300,000 Territorials

1903 Krupp's dockyard in Kiel completes the first fully functioning U-boat

1910 First aviation school opens in Gatchina

Feb 1906 Launch of HMS *Dreadnought*, the first "all-big-gun" battleship, fuels naval race

Mar 1908 Germany launches its first "all-big-gun" dreadnought battleship, SMS *Nassau*

1898–1912 German naval laws signal Germany's ambition to build a navy to rival Britain's

1883–1916 Romania secretly joins the Triple Alliance with Germany, Austria-Hungary, and Italy

1908 Austria-Hungary annexes Bosnia, driving Serbia closer to Russia

1839 Treaty of London guarantees Belgian neutrality and commits Austria, Belgium, France, the German Confederation, the Netherlands, Russia, and Britain to military intervention if neutrality is breached

1882 Italy joins the Austro-German alliance to create the Triple Alliance

1881–1895 Serbia associates with the Triple Alliance through the Austro-Serb alliance

1906 Britain supports France over Morocco at the Algeciras Conference, and the two countries begin talks on a military alliance

1905–1906 Germany tests the strength of the Anglo-French Entente by recognizing Morocco as independent

NORWAY

SWEDEN

St. Petersburg

DENMARK

Kiel

North Sea

NETHERLANDS

BELGIUM

Wilhelmshaven

Berlin

GERMANY

Warsaw

RUSSIAN EMPIRE

Baltic Sea

BRITAIN

Rosyth

London

Chatham

Brussels

Portsmouth

Plymouth

Paris

Munich

AUSTRIA-HUNGARY

ROMANIA

ATLANTIC OCEAN

Brest

FRANCE

SWITZERLAND

Trieste

Genoa

ITALY

Belgrade

Sarajevo

SERBIA

MONTENEGRO

BULGARIA

Constantinople

Toulon

ALBANIA

Taranto

GREECE

OTTOMAN EMPIRE

PORTUGAL

SPAIN

Algeciras

Tangier

MOROCCO to France

ALGERIA to France

TUNISIA to France

LIBYA to Italy

EGYPT

Mediterranean Sea

THE BALANCE OF POWER IN EUROPE

European relations from 1871 were marked by a shifting pattern of alliances designed initially to keep the peace. From 1890, the balance of power was disrupted by an alliance between Russia and France, which threatened the Central Powers, and by the build-up of military power across Europe.

- Allied Powers 1914
- Central Powers 1914
- Neutral states 1914
- Joined Allied Powers during war
- Joined Central Powers during war

TIMELINE

1
2
3
4

1870   1880   1890   1900   1910   1920

---

3 ARMS BUILD-UP   1898–1914

Alongside shifting alliances, Europe was building its military capacity; Britain already had the largest navy in the world. Vast numbers of men were conscripted into Europe's armies, and advances in military technology meant that more money was spent on the armies and navies, creating a volatile mix of militarism and mutual suspicion.

1 ICON = 100,000 COMBATANTS

- Allied Powers' army strength
- Central Powers' army strength
- Allied Powers' naval bases
- Central Powers' naval bases

---

4 ALLIANCES ON THE EVE OF THE WAR   1914

By the time war broke out in 1914, Europe was divided into two well-armed camps: the Allied Powers, formed of the Entente Powers—Great Britain, France, and Russia—and Montenegro; and the Central Powers of Germany, Austria-Hungary, and Italy. Throughout the war, more countries joined each side.

▽ **HMS Dreadnought**
This British ship—more powerful, faster, and with more firepower than any seen before—ushered in a new class of battleship.

1907 Britain and Russia settle disputes over spheres of influence in Persia and create the Triple Entente with France

PERSIA

THE EVE OF WORLD WAR

War between the Great Powers—Austria-Hungary, Britain, France, Germany, Italy, and Russia—was prevented throughout the late 19th century by a series of defensive alliances. However, those alliances were eroded by the crises in the Balkans in the early 20th century and by the rise of militarism.

Since the end of the Napoleonic War in 1815, Europe had maintained a delicate balance of power. The creation of Germany in 1871 (see pp.264–265) brought a powerful new force into play. Yet instead of breaking the balance of power, Germany was instrumental in maintaining it for many years. Under the leadership of Otto von Bismarck, Germany set about allying with the more conservative powers in Europe—Austria-Hungary and Russia. This ensured that the other two would remain neutral if any one of them took military action against any nonallied country, and if Russia attacked Austria, it would have to face Germany as well.

As tensions in the Balkans increased (see pp.266–267), so did the tensions between the Great Powers. Russia moved to ally with France, and Austria's annexation of Bosnia in 1908 humiliated Russia and pushed it closer to Austria's nemesis, Serbia. By then, an arms race had begun that saw millions of marks, pounds, rubles, and francs poured into military reorganization and new technology. In 1913 alone, Germany spent $140 million on its military and Britain spent $106 million. By 1914, the bond that prevented a major war had been broken, and Europe was divided into two heavily armed blocs, primed for war.

"England, France, and Russia have conspired … to wage a war of annihilation against us."

KAISER WILHELM II, MEMORANDUM WRITTEN JULY 30, 1914

OTTO VON BISMARCK
(1815–1898)

Architect of the unification of Germany and its rise as a major power, Otto von Bismarck guided Germany's fate, first as chief minister of Prussia (1862–1890) and then as chancellor of the German Empire (1871–1890). His skilled diplomacy ensured that there was no major European conflict in the late 19th century; he created an alliance with Austria-Hungary and also kept friendly relations with Russia. However, Kaiser Wilhelm II came to the throne in 1888 with a more aggressive desire to lead the German Empire toward global power, and in 1890, he forced von Bismarck's resignation. Without his hand to steady international relations, Europe moved inexorably toward war.

THE
MODERN
WORLD

WORLD WARS, UNPRECEDENTED TECHNOLOGICAL AND ECONOMIC
DEVELOPMENT, AND EXPLOSIVE POPULATION GROWTH HAVE MADE
THE 20TH AND 21ST CENTURIES THE MOST EVENTFUL IN HISTORY.

THE MODERN WORLD

The early 20th century was dominated by extraordinary developments in technology, economics, and new ideologies that transformed societies. However, demands for national independence and a better way of life destroyed old structures, leading to unprecedented violence and turbulence before a new world order was formed.

△ **The face of nationalism**
A Bosnian nationalist, Gavrilo Princip shot Austrian Archduke Franz Ferdinand on June 28, 1914. The event catapulted the Great Powers into World War I, a century-defining conflict that caused the downfall of empires.

By the dawn of the 20th century, the old had begun giving way to the new. Although new empires were still being formed in South Africa, Korea, and elsewhere, some established empires were in turmoil as people demanded emancipation from oppression and political exclusion. In Russia, thousands marched against Czar Nicholas II, demanding reform, while the czar's forces were being routed by the Japanese in the Russo-Japanese War. Around the same time, imperial China was crumbling under the pressure of European imperialism and internal strife. By 1912, China had done away with the Qing Dynasty and become a republic.

In 1908, the vast Ottoman Empire was shaken when the Young Turks (a Turkish nationalist party) revolted and brought in a constitution and multiparty politics. Taking advantage of these unsettled affairs, a league of Balkan states—Serbia, Bulgaria, Greece, and Montenegro—went to war with Turkey and then squabbled over the spoils, leading to yet another war.

Constant turmoil

The assassination of the Austrian Archduke Franz Ferdinand by a radical nationalist, Gavrilo Princip, in Sarajevo, Bosnia, set off World War I (see pp. 274–275). Lasting 4 long years, the war became a stalemate at an incalculable cost—a generation of young men was mown down as deadly technological advances saw aircraft, poison gas, tanks, and submarines deployed on a mass scale. By the third year of World

◁ **The cost of war**
Passchendaele (the Third Battle of Ypres) was fought in 1917. It cost the Allies 300,000 lives and brought them a gain of a meager 5 miles (8 km). It became a byword for the utter futility of war.

TROUBLED TIMES

The early part of the 20th century was dominated by conflict; the timeline shown here ends with the ominous build-up to yet another world war. Unlike Europe and east Asia, North America avoided major turbulence until its involvement in World War I. However, its stock market collapse in 1929 was one of the most damaging events in its, and the world's, history. Despite the convulsions of the period, this era was also one of great technological innovation and productivity.

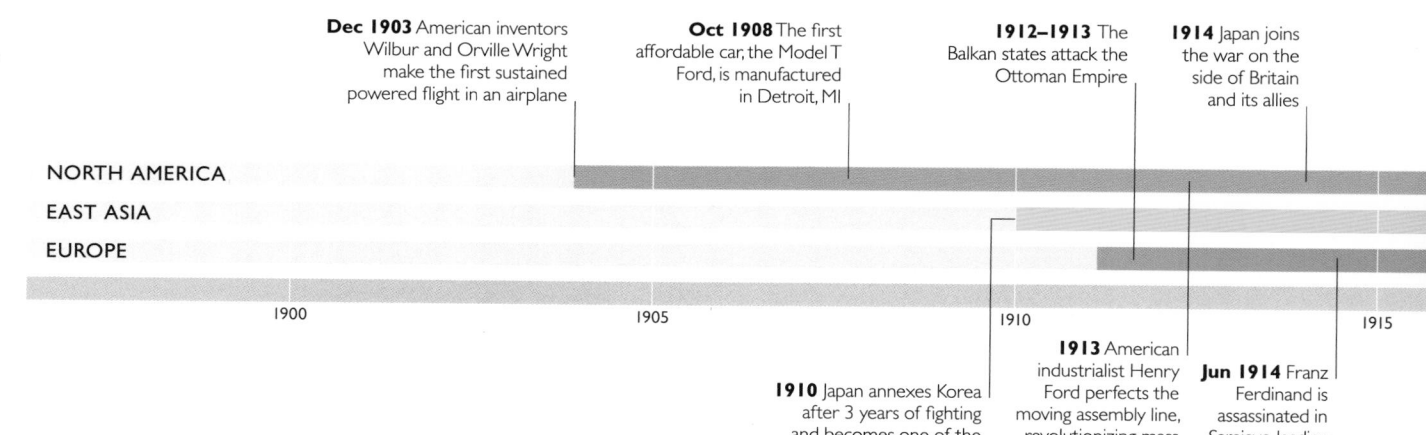

Dec 1903 American inventors Wilbur and Orville Wright make the first sustained powered flight in an airplane

Oct 1908 The first affordable car, the Model T Ford, is manufactured in Detroit, MI

1912–1913 The Balkan states attack the Ottoman Empire

1914 Japan joins the war on the side of Britain and its allies

NORTH AMERICA

EAST ASIA

EUROPE

1900   1905   1910   1915

1910 Japan annexes Korea after 3 years of fighting and becomes one of the world's leading powers

1913 American industrialist Henry Ford perfects the moving assembly line, revolutionizing mass production

Jun 1914 Franz Ferdinand is assassinated in Sarajevo, leading to World War I

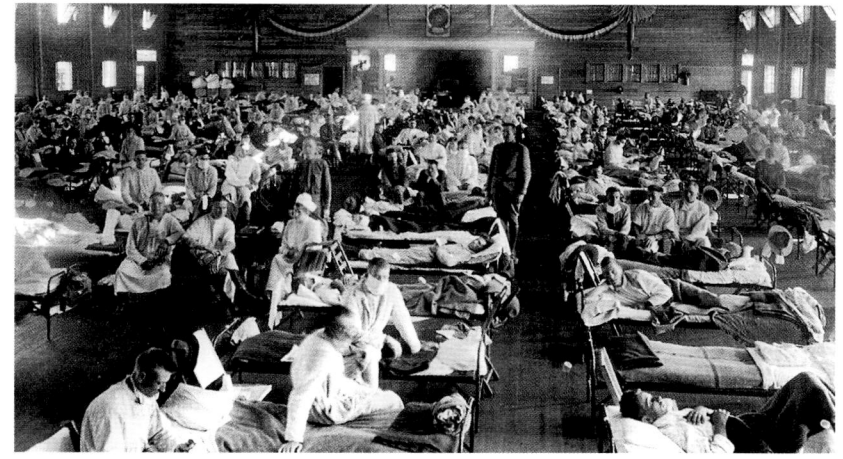

◁ **Worldwide epidemic**
An outbreak of Spanish flu in 1918–19 infected around 500 million people and killed up to 50 million. Starting in the US, it became a global catastrophe.

War I, Russia was in tatters. Into this chaos stepped revolutionary Vladimir Lenin, who saw his Bolshevik Party to power. By 1919, the Russian, Austrian, and German empires had collapsed. The Ottoman Empire was the last great casualty of the war—the Treaty of Sèvres was signed in 1920, and the empire was dismantled.

Meanwhile, around Easter 1916, an armed uprising in Dublin set southern Ireland on a path to independence from British rule, and the Irish Free State was founded in 1922.

Global repercussions

The US had followed an isolationist policy at the start of the war but was drawn into the conflict by German submarine attacks on their commercial ships. During and after the war, Americans embraced and invested heavily in technology, pioneering methods of assembly-line production. Women, who had contributed so much to the war effort, had been granted the right to vote in 1918 in the UK, Austria, Germany, and Canada. Most American women were given the same right in 1920. However, the good times came to a grinding halt with the Stock Market Crash of 1929.

The Great Depression that followed (see pp.286–287) led to mass unemployment and strikes. It became a global crisis, leading to poverty on an unprecedented scale. The 1930s were haunted by violent political extremism. China, in turmoil due to a civil war, was also under attack from Japan. In Germany, more than 40 percent of industrial workers were unemployed. Already hit severely by the collapse of world trade, a starving Germany suffered, and the time was ripe for an ambitious

Adolf Hitler to form the Nationalist Socialist (Nazi) Party. With his promise to restore Germany's status as a great power, he was poised to assume total control.

Totalitarianism and the seeds of war

Other European nations, too, became seduced by right-wing politics and propaganda. While Germany had *der Führer* (Adolf Hitler), Italy had *il Duce* (Benito Mussolini) and fascist-leaning Spaniards had *el Caudillo* (Francisco Franco). In July 1936, Franco's forces fought the forces of the Spanish Left in a brutal civil war. Aided by Hitler and Mussolini, Franco was victorious in this precursor to the next global war. World War I—called the Great War—was supposed to have been the conflict to end all conflicts. Instead, the peace treaty that followed in 1919—the Treaty of Versailles—redrew the map of Europe, breeding discontent and resentment. Together with the Great Depression, it paved the way for the world's bloodiest conflict yet—World War II (see pp.294–295).

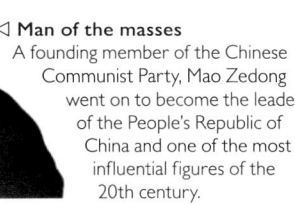

◁ **Man of the masses**
A founding member of the Chinese Communist Party, Mao Zedong went on to become the leader of the People's Republic of China and one of the most influential figures of the 20th century.

△ **Germany on fire**
The mysterious fire of the German parliament building on February 27, 1933, was a key moment in Nazi history, acting as a stepping-stone to the total dictatorship of Adolf Hitler.

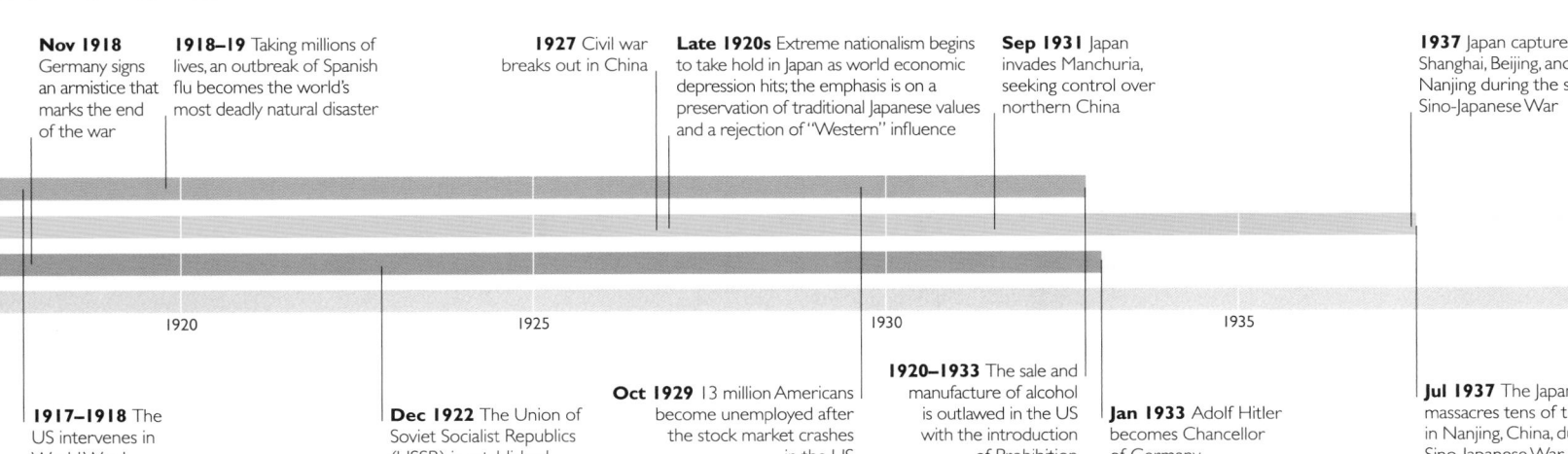

Nov 1918 Germany signs an armistice that marks the end of the war

1918–19 Taking millions of lives, an outbreak of Spanish flu becomes the world's most deadly natural disaster

1927 Civil war breaks out in China

Late 1920s Extreme nationalism begins to take hold in Japan as world economic depression hits; the emphasis is on a preservation of traditional Japanese values and a rejection of "Western" influence

Sep 1931 Japan invades Manchuria, seeking control over northern China

1937 Japan captures Shanghai, Beijing, and Nanjing during the second Sino-Japanese War

1920   1925   1930   1935   1940

1917–1918 The US intervenes in World War I

Dec 1922 The Union of Soviet Socialist Republics (USSR) is established

Oct 1929 13 million Americans become unemployed after the stock market crashes in the US

1920–1933 The sale and manufacture of alcohol is outlawed in the US with the introduction of Prohibition

Jan 1933 Adolf Hitler becomes Chancellor of Germany

Jul 1937 The Japanese army massacres tens of thousands in Nanjing, China, during the Sino-Japanese War

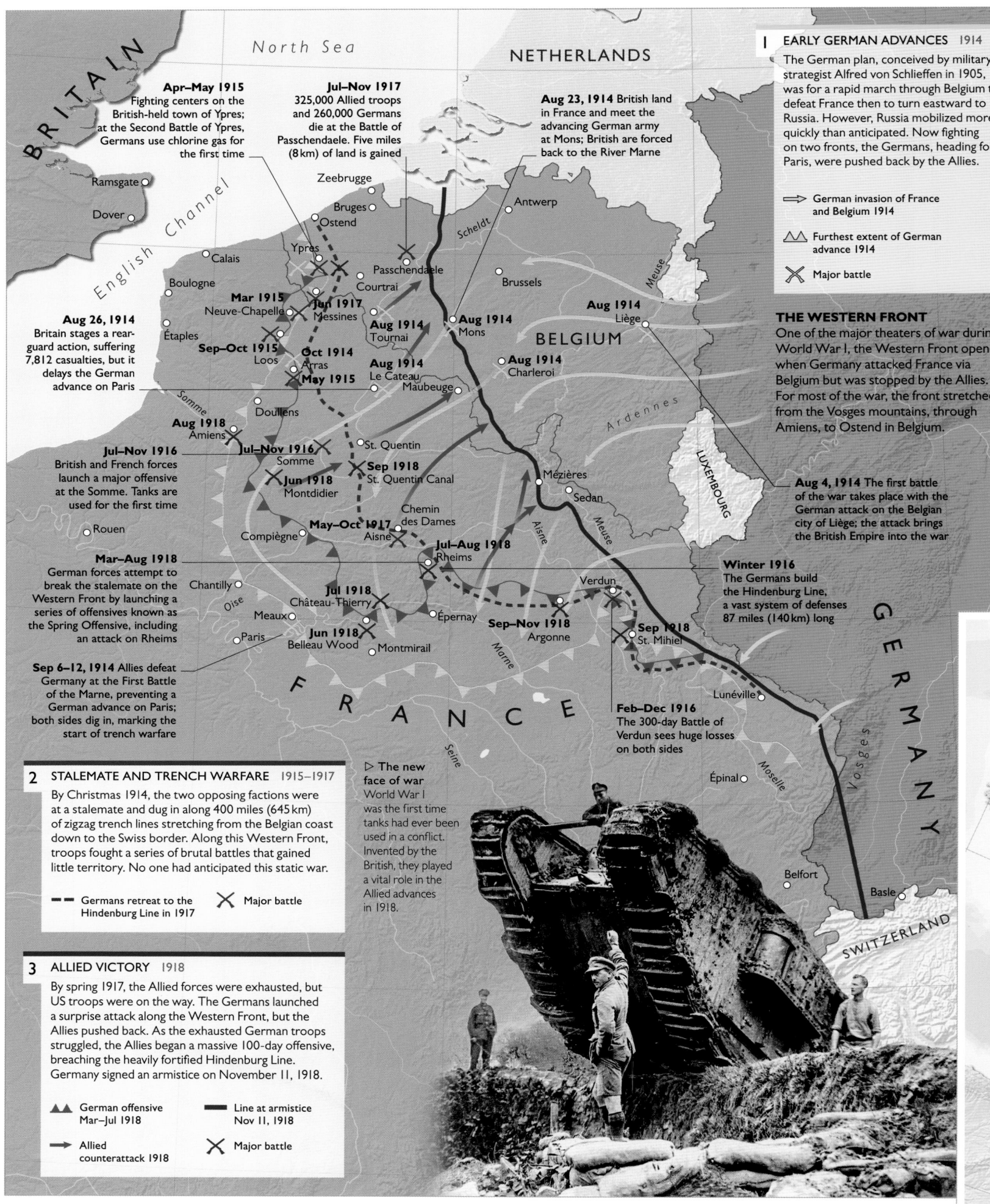

1 EARLY GERMAN ADVANCES 1914
The German plan, conceived by military strategist Alfred von Schlieffen in 1905, was for a rapid march through Belgium to defeat France then to turn eastward to Russia. However, Russia mobilized more quickly than anticipated. Now fighting on two fronts, the Germans, heading for Paris, were pushed back by the Allies.

⇒ German invasion of France and Belgium 1914

⋀⋀ Furthest extent of German advance 1914

✕ Major battle

THE WESTERN FRONT
One of the major theaters of war during World War I, the Western Front opened when Germany attacked France via Belgium but was stopped by the Allies. For most of the war, the front stretched from the Vosges mountains, through Amiens, to Ostend in Belgium.

Aug 4, 1914 The first battle of the war takes place with the German attack on the Belgian city of Liège; the attack brings the British Empire into the war

Winter 1916 The Germans build the Hindenburg Line, a vast system of defenses 87 miles (140 km) long

Apr–May 1915 Fighting centers on the British-held town of Ypres; at the Second Battle of Ypres, Germans use chlorine gas for the first time

Jul–Nov 1917 325,000 Allied troops and 260,000 Germans die at the Battle of Passchendaele. Five miles (8 km) of land is gained

Aug 23, 1914 British land in France and meet the advancing German army at Mons; British are forced back to the River Marne

Aug 26, 1914 Britain stages a rear-guard action, suffering 7,812 casualties, but it delays the German advance on Paris

Jul–Nov 1916 British and French forces launch a major offensive at the Somme. Tanks are used for the first time

Mar–Aug 1918 German forces attempt to break the stalemate on the Western Front by launching a series of offensives known as the Spring Offensive, including an attack on Rheims

Sep 6–12, 1914 Allies defeat Germany at the First Battle of the Marne, preventing a German advance on Paris; both sides dig in, marking the start of trench warfare

Feb–Dec 1916 The 300-day Battle of Verdun sees huge losses on both sides

2 STALEMATE AND TRENCH WARFARE 1915–1917
By Christmas 1914, the two opposing factions were at a stalemate and dug in along 400 miles (645 km) of zigzag trench lines stretching from the Belgian coast down to the Swiss border. Along this Western Front, troops fought a series of brutal battles that gained little territory. No one had anticipated this static war.

– – Germans retreat to the Hindenburg Line in 1917   ✕ Major battle

3 ALLIED VICTORY 1918
By spring 1917, the Allied forces were exhausted, but US troops were on the way. The Germans launched a surprise attack along the Western Front, but the Allies pushed back. As the exhausted German troops struggled, the Allies began a massive 100-day offensive, breaching the heavily fortified Hindenburg Line. Germany signed an armistice on November 11, 1918.

⋀⋀ German offensive Mar–Jul 1918   ▬ Line at armistice Nov 11, 1918

→ Allied counterattack 1918   ✕ Major battle

▷ **The new face of war**
World War I was the first time tanks had ever been used in a conflict. Invented by the British, they played a vital role in the Allied advances in 1918.

WORLD WAR I

World War I was one of the defining events of the 20th century. Bound by the chains of interlocking alliances and provoked by the massive buildup of battleships and weaponry, governments sent their armies off to face a new kind of warfare.

On June 28, 1914, Archduke Franz Ferdinand, heir to the Austrian throne, was assassinated in Sarajevo, Bosnia. Blaming their bitter rival, Austria-Hungary declared war on Serbia. Events quickly escalated, and the wider system of alliances (see pp.268–269) got drawn into the war. Russia hurried to the aid of Serbia, while Germany, coming to the support of Austria-Hungary, declared war on both Russia and France. When Germany, on its way to France, invaded neutral Belgium on August 4, 1914, Britain declared war on Germany. Stalemate quickly followed. The Germans, British, and French dug a

network of trenches stretching from the Swiss border to the North Sea, and with modern weaponry, the Western Front became a killing field. On the more fluid Eastern Front, the better-equipped German army defeated the Russians, and in December 1917 Russia signed an armistice. The arrival of the US into the war in April 1917 turned the tide in the Allies' favor, and following a series of brutal battles, an armistice was agreed on November 11, 1918. At the start of the war, both the Central Powers and the Allies had been convinced it would be short and decisive; neither was prepared for this long war of attrition.

WAR ON TWO FRONTS

World War I was fought largely on the Western Front (in western Europe) and the Eastern Front (in eastern Europe), although countries from around the world were gradually pulled into the conflict. There were two opposing alliances: the Central Powers (Germany and Austria-Hungary) and the Allies (Russia, France, and Britain). Despite early German successes, the Allies achieved victory in November 1918.

KEY

- Central Powers
- Allies
- Russian Empire

TIMELINE

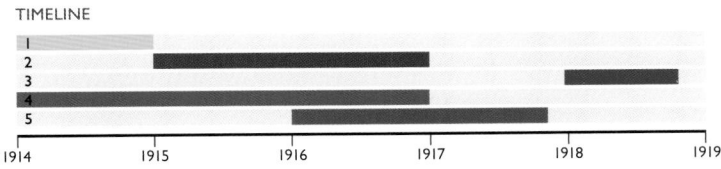

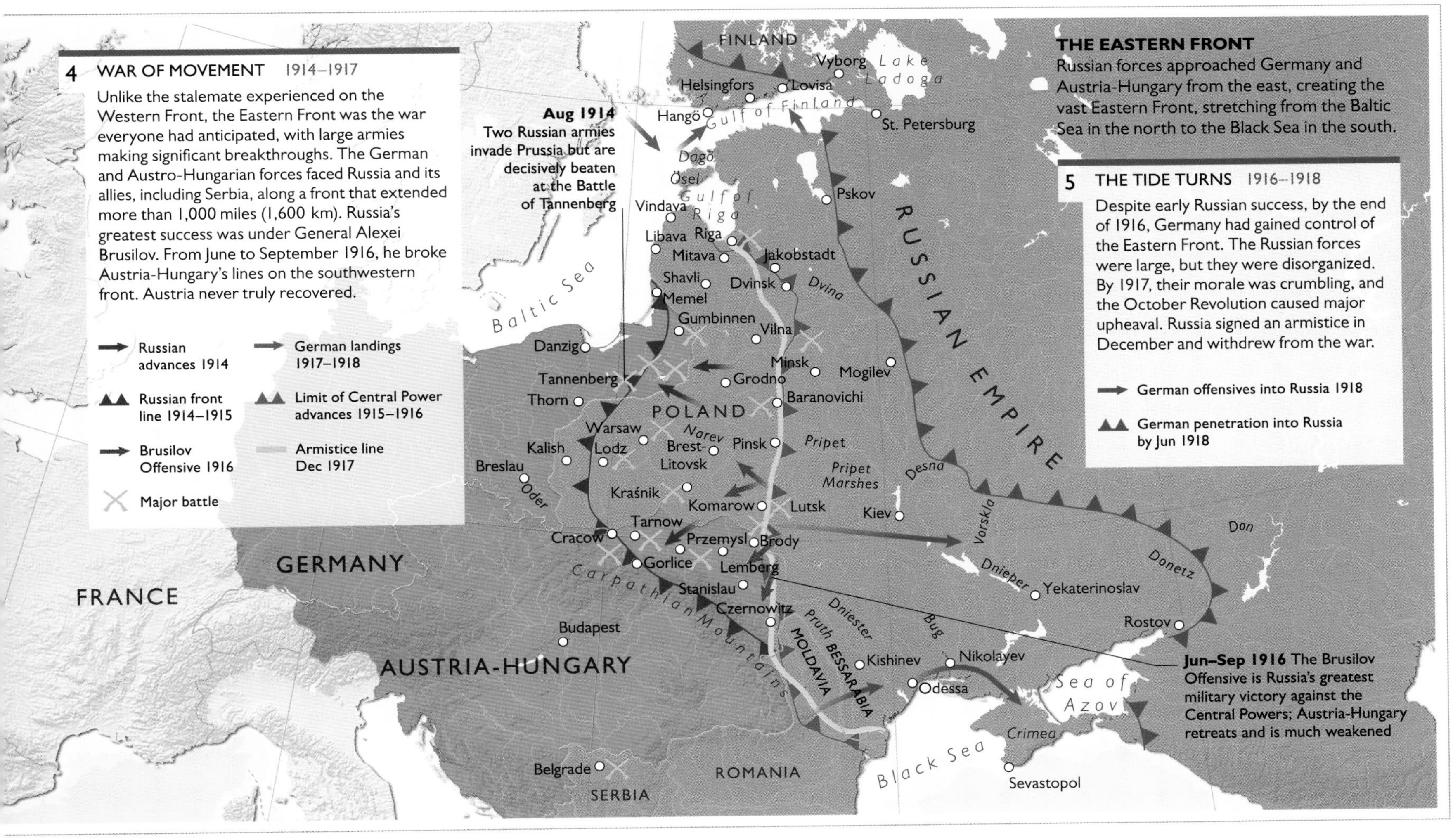

4 WAR OF MOVEMENT 1914–1917

Unlike the stalemate experienced on the Western Front, the Eastern Front was the war everyone had anticipated, with large armies making significant breakthroughs. The German and Austro-Hungarian forces faced Russia and its allies, including Serbia, along a front that extended more than 1,000 miles (1,600 km). Russia's greatest success was under General Alexei Brusilov. From June to September 1916, he broke Austria-Hungary's lines on the southwestern front. Austria never truly recovered.

- → Russian advances 1914
- ▲▲ Russian front line 1914–1915
- → Brusilov Offensive 1916
- ✕ Major battle
- → German landings 1917–1918
- ▲▲ Limit of Central Power advances 1915–1916
- — Armistice line Dec 1917

THE EASTERN FRONT

Russian forces approached Germany and Austria-Hungary from the east, creating the vast Eastern Front, stretching from the Baltic Sea in the north to the Black Sea in the south.

5 THE TIDE TURNS 1916–1918

Despite early Russian success, by the end of 1916, Germany had gained control of the Eastern Front. The Russian forces were large, but they were disorganized. By 1917, their morale was crumbling, and the October Revolution caused major upheaval. Russia signed an armistice in December and withdrew from the war.

- → German offensives into Russia 1918
- ▲▲ German penetration into Russia by Jun 1918

Aug 1914 Two Russian armies invade Prussia but are decisively beaten at the Battle of Tannenberg

Jun–Sep 1916 The Brusilov Offensive is Russia's greatest military victory against the Central Powers; Austria-Hungary retreats and is much weakened

THE TRENCHES

Much of the fighting in World War I was characterized by the mud and blood of the trenches. The prolonged stalemate between trench-bound enemies was marked by mass killings over just a few yards of land.

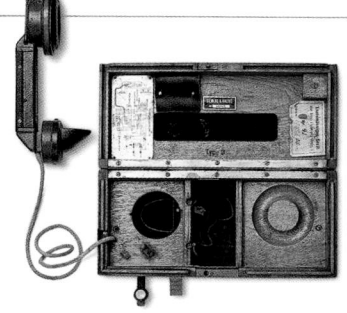

△ **Lines of communication**
Telephones were used extensively to give orders directly to front-line troops. A web of telephone and telegraph wires crisscrossed the battlefields.

The German advance across France was halted in the early fall of 1914. Confronted with deadly machine guns, mortars, and howitzers, both sides reached for their spades to dig rudimentary trenches, from where they could both defend and attack. The era of modern trench warfare had begun.

By mid-October 1914, two lines of trenches faced each other in a meandering line that ran from the Swiss border in the south to the North Sea. It became known as the Western Front. The early Allied trenches were crude and shallow. The German trenches, on the other hand, were more solidly built and on higher ground. Some even had electricity and toilets. Sandbags, wire mesh, and wooden frames were brought in to reinforce the walls.

The human cost

Life in the trenches was appalling. They were filled with rats, flies, and lice and prone to flooding. Frightened young men stood in knee-deep mud waiting for the call to go "over the top." Casualty rates were high, not only from major battles such as Passchendaele (July–November 1917), but also from the ever-present threats of sniper fire, random shells, and poison gas. Diseases, such as typhoid and trench foot, put many out of action. The constant bombardment and sound of enemy fire led to the diagnosis of a new condition called "shell shock," which prompted a range of disabling psychosomatic conditions.

For soldiers trapped in the trenches, there was no way out. Deserters were shot and malingerers penalized. Trench warfare in World War I resulted in a 4-year-long impasse, with soldiers dying from not just new weaponry but horrific living conditions.

△ **Crossing the trenches**
German troops clamber over the top of their trenches and advance across no-man's land—the area that separated the enemy trenches—toward British lines. Soldiers marched into the guns and were mown down in droves.

Battle of the Somme
While a soldier from the 11th Cheshire Regiment keeps watch during the Battle of the Somme (July–November 1916), his comrades catch what sleep they can amid the rubble of their trench.

THE WIDER WAR

Although the main theater of battle during World War I (1914–1918) was in Europe, the conflict extended across the globe. It was shaped by the major European powers, spreading through a series of alliances, as well as through their empires and colonies.

World War I originated in central Europe. However, since many of the European belligerents were colonial powers, they had valuable assets and troops stationed all over the globe. Millions of soldiers were recruited from colonized countries and brought in to fight on the front lines. As the war spread, new fronts opened up in the Balkans, Mesopotamia, Anatolia (modern Turkey), East Africa, and Salonika. Italy joined the war on the side of the Allies in May 1915, and a series of brutal battles were fought along its border with Austria-Hungary.

In the Balkans, already a volatile region, loyalties were divided. In September 1918, Allied forces attacked from northern Greece, eventually liberating Serbia. The entry of the Turkish Ottoman Empire as an ally of Germany in fall 1914 had brought the Middle East into the conflict. The Turks had initial successes against the British, but struggled against Russia in the Caucasus. In 1916, a widespread Arab uprising against Ottoman rule helped the British cause by tying up Ottoman forces. By the time Turkey sued for an armistice in October 1918, the centuries-old empire had collapsed.

"We were casting them by thousands into the fire to the worst of deaths."

T. E. LAWRENCE, BRITISH MILITARY OFFICER

T. E. LAWRENCE
1888–1935

One of the most iconic figures of World War I, Thomas Edward Lawrence—popularly known by his nickname, Lawrence of Arabia—was an Arabic-speaking British archaeologist who traveled and worked in the Middle East. During World War I, he joined the British army and became an intelligence officer in Cairo, Egypt. His daring raids made him an international legend. Lawrence developed a deep sympathy for the Arabs living under Turkish rule and worked for their emancipation. He died in England in a motorcycle accident in 1935.

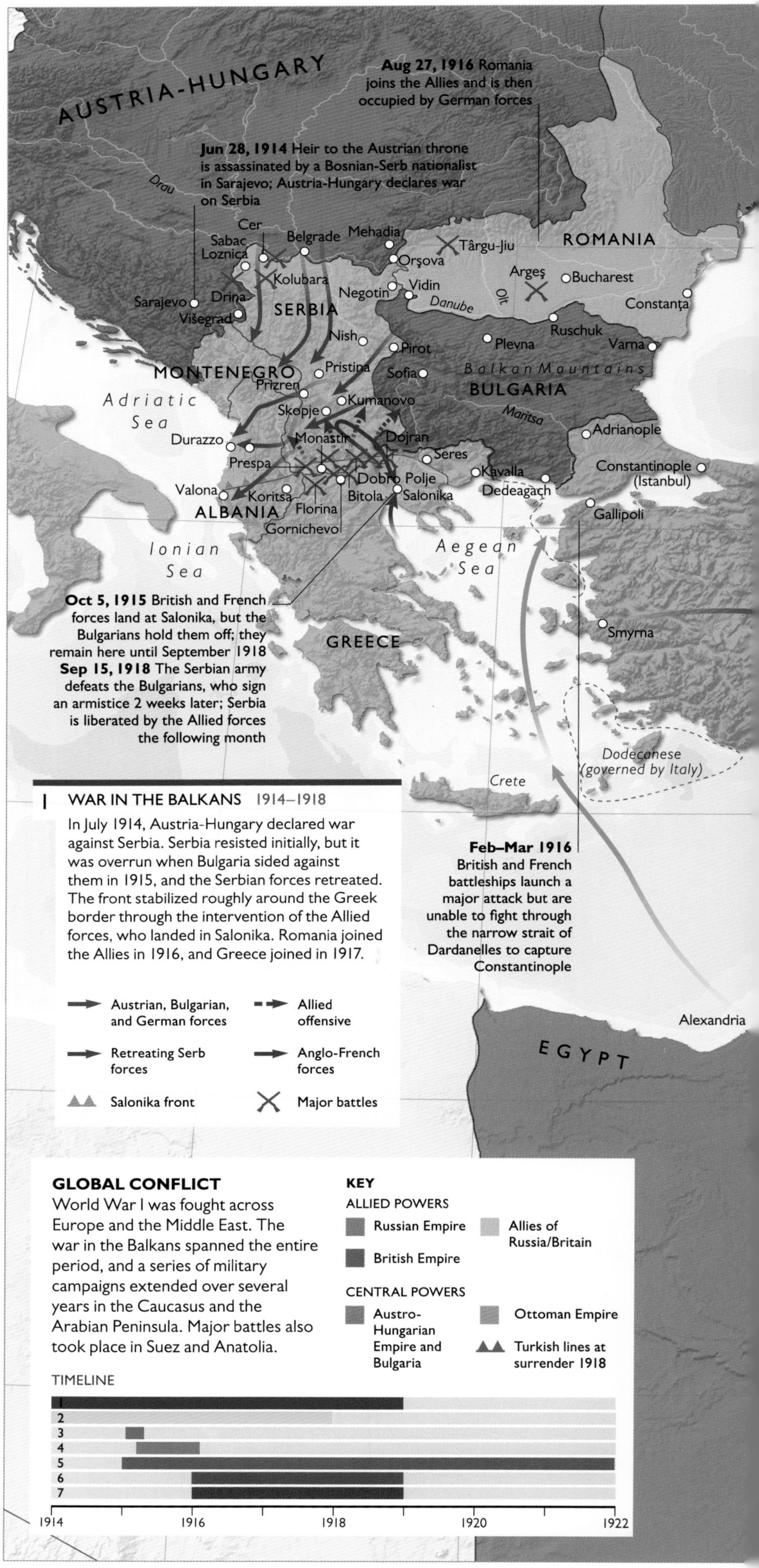

Aug 27, 1916 Romania joins the Allies and is then occupied by German forces

Jun 28, 1914 Heir to the Austrian throne is assassinated by a Bosnian-Serb nationalist in Sarajevo; Austria-Hungary declares war on Serbia

Oct 5, 1915 British and French forces land at Salonika, but the Bulgarians hold them off; they remain here until September 1918
Sep 15, 1918 The Serbian army defeats the Bulgarians, who sign an armistice 2 weeks later; Serbia is liberated by the Allied forces the following month

WAR IN THE BALKANS 1914–1918

In July 1914, Austria-Hungary declared war against Serbia. Serbia resisted initially, but it was overrun when Bulgaria sided against them in 1915, and the Serbian forces retreated. The front stabilized roughly around the Greek border through the intervention of the Allied forces, who landed in Salonika. Romania joined the Allies in 1916, and Greece joined in 1917.

- Austrian, Bulgarian, and German forces
- Allied offensive
- Retreating Serb forces
- Anglo-French forces
- Salonika front
- Major battles

Feb–Mar 1916 British and French battleships launch a major attack but are unable to fight through the narrow strait of Dardanelles to capture Constantinople

GLOBAL CONFLICT

World War I was fought across Europe and the Middle East. The war in the Balkans spanned the entire period, and a series of military campaigns extended over several years in the Caucasus and the Arabian Peninsula. Major battles also took place in Suez and Anatolia.

KEY
ALLIED POWERS
- Russian Empire
- British Empire
- Allies of Russia/Britain

CENTRAL POWERS
- Austro-Hungarian Empire and Bulgaria
- Ottoman Empire
- Turkish lines at surrender 1918

TIMELINE

1914 1916 1918 1920 1922

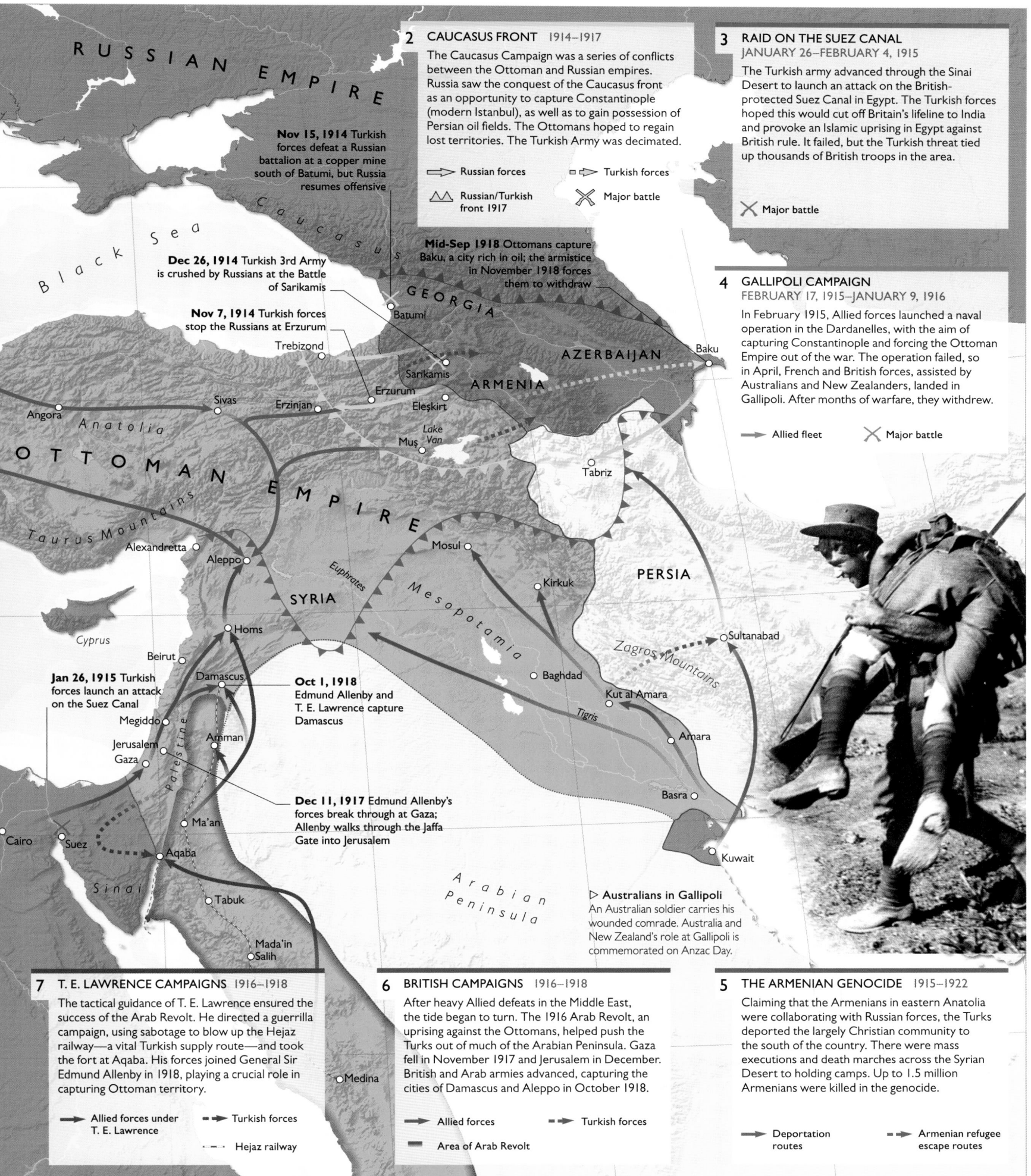

RUSSIAN EMPIRE

Nov 15, 1914 Turkish forces defeat a Russian battalion at a copper mine south of Batumi, but Russia resumes offensive

2 CAUCASUS FRONT 1914–1917

The Caucasus Campaign was a series of conflicts between the Ottoman and Russian empires. Russia saw the conquest of the Caucasus front as an opportunity to capture Constantinople (modern Istanbul), as well as to gain possession of Persian oil fields. The Ottomans hoped to regain lost territories. The Turkish Army was decimated.

⇨ Russian forces ▫⇨ Turkish forces

⋀⋀ Russian/Turkish front 1917 ✕ Major battle

3 RAID ON THE SUEZ CANAL
JANUARY 26–FEBRUARY 4, 1915

The Turkish army advanced through the Sinai Desert to launch an attack on the British-protected Suez Canal in Egypt. The Turkish forces hoped this would cut off Britain's lifeline to India and provoke an Islamic uprising in Egypt against British rule. It failed, but the Turkish threat tied up thousands of British troops in the area.

✕ Major battle

Mid-Sep 1918 Ottomans capture Baku, a city rich in oil; the armistice in November 1918 forces them to withdraw

Dec 26, 1914 Turkish 3rd Army is crushed by Russians at the Battle of Sarikamis

Nov 7, 1914 Turkish forces stop the Russians at Erzurum

Black Sea

Caucasus

GEORGIA

Batumi

Trebizond

AZERBAIJAN

Baku

Sarikamis

ARMENIA

Erzurum

Eleşkirt

Angora

Sivas

Erzinjan

Erzurum

Anatolia

Muş

Lake Van

4 GALLIPOLI CAMPAIGN
FEBRUARY 17, 1915–JANUARY 9, 1916

In February 1915, Allied forces launched a naval operation in the Dardanelles, with the aim of capturing Constantinople and forcing the Ottoman Empire out of the war. The operation failed, so in April, French and British forces, assisted by Australians and New Zealanders, landed in Gallipoli. After months of warfare, they withdrew.

➡ Allied fleet ✕ Major battle

Tabriz

OTTOMAN EMPIRE

Taurus Mountains

Alexandretta

Aleppo

Euphrates

Mosul

Kirkuk

PERSIA

SYRIA

Mesopotamia

Homs

Cyprus

Beirut

Zagros Mountains

Sultanabad

Damascus

Baghdad

Kut al Amara

Jan 26, 1915 Turkish forces launch an attack on the Suez Canal

Oct 1, 1918 Edmund Allenby and T. E. Lawrence capture Damascus

Megiddo

Palestine

Amman

Tigris

Amara

Jerusalem

Gaza

Ma'an

Dec 11, 1917 Edmund Allenby's forces break through at Gaza; Allenby walks through the Jaffa Gate into Jerusalem

Basra

Cairo

Suez

Aqaba

Kuwait

Sinai

Tabuk

Arabian Peninsula

▷ **Australians in Gallipoli**
An Australian soldier carries his wounded comrade. Australia and New Zealand's role at Gallipoli is commemorated on Anzac Day.

Mada'in Salih

7 T. E. LAWRENCE CAMPAIGNS 1916–1918

The tactical guidance of T. E. Lawrence ensured the success of the Arab Revolt. He directed a guerrilla campaign, using sabotage to blow up the Hejaz railway—a vital Turkish supply route—and took the fort at Aqaba. His forces joined General Sir Edmund Allenby in 1918, playing a crucial role in capturing Ottoman territory.

➡ Allied forces under T. E. Lawrence
⇢ Turkish forces
┉ Hejaz railway

Medina

6 BRITISH CAMPAIGNS 1916–1918

After heavy Allied defeats in the Middle East, the tide began to turn. The 1916 Arab Revolt, an uprising against the Ottomans, helped push the Turks out of much of the Arabian Peninsula. Gaza fell in November 1917 and Jerusalem in December. British and Arab armies advanced, capturing the cities of Damascus and Aleppo in October 1918.

➡ Allied forces ⇢ Turkish forces
▬ Area of Arab Revolt

5 THE ARMENIAN GENOCIDE 1915–1922

Claiming that the Armenians in eastern Anatolia were collaborating with Russian forces, the Turks deported the largely Christian community to the south of the country. There were mass executions and death marches across the Syrian Desert to holding camps. Up to 1.5 million Armenians were killed in the genocide.

➡ Deportation routes
⇢ Armenian refugee escape routes

4 CIVIL WAR BREAKS OUT 1917–1922

Although the Bolsheviks had gained power, they were a minority in Russia. Lenin started the "Red Terror"—a campaign of intimidation against anyone thought to be a threat to the regime—which was carried out by the new Bolshevik secret police, the Cheka. Meanwhile, a violent civil war broke out between the Bolsheviks (the "Reds") and anti-Bolshevik forces, including the White Army, formed of Tsarist supporters and military officers. Russia's former allies—Britain, France, and the US—supported the Whites, fearing the spread of communism.

3 RUSSIA PULLS OUT OF WORLD WAR I 1917–1918

The new Bolshevik government, led by Lenin, signed an armistice with the Central Powers (see p.275) in December 1917. The terms, which were harsh on Russia, were formalized in the Treaty of Brest-Litovsk in March 1918. Russia relinquished control of the Baltic States and Ukraine and was forced to pay 6 billion German marks in reparations. Anger at these losses fueled opposition to the Bolsheviks.

■ Russian boundary after Treaty of Brest-Litovsk 1918

2 INDEPENDENT REPUBLICS 1917–1921

The Russian Empire was ethnically diverse, and calls for self-determination had been growing among non-Russian nationalities. After the revolution, Finland, Estonia, Poland, Latvia, Lithuania, and Ukraine declared independence, while Armenia, Azerbaijan, and Georgia formed a short-lived republic. Faced with financial crisis and militarily weak, Ukraine and the Caucasus states were later reabsorbed into the USSR.

▧ Countries declaring independence from Russia 1917–1918

➤ Temporarily independent from Russia 1917–1921

Feb 1919–Oct 1920 With growing Bolshevik success in the civil war, Lenin seeks to gain back lost territory in Poland. After initial success, the Bolsheviks are defeated at the Battle of Warsaw

Dec 18, 1918 France, an ally of the Whites, enters the civil war by sending troops to Odessa

Apr 8, 1919 Allied forces lose Odessa to the Red Army

Nov 7–17, 1920 The Siege of Perekop leads to another Red victory, and the Red Army occupy the Crimea

Apr 10–13, 1918 At the Battle of Yekaterinodar, the first major battle between the two armies, the commander of the White Army is killed in combat

Mar 1918 Russia moves the state capital to Moscow (from Petrograd), after German soldiers march through Russia virtually unopposed

Jul 16–17, 1918 Tsar Nicholas II is shot by the Bolsheviks, along with his wife, five children, and four royal staff members

Aug 1918 Allied forces offer support to the leader of the White Army, Admiral Alexander Kolchak, who sets up his government in Omsk

Sep 5–10, 1918 The White Army, allied with the Czechs, suffer a defeat at the Battle of Kazan

Map labels: SWEDEN, Stockholm, FINLAND, Baltic Sea, Revel (Tallinn), ESTONIA, LATVIA, LITHUANIA, Warsaw, POLAND, Minsk, Pskov, Novgorod, Petrograd (St. Petersburg), Petrozavodsk, Archangel, Barents Sea, Novaya Zemlya, Vitebsk, Mogilev, Tver, Vologda, Smolensk, Moscow, Yaroslavl, Kostroma, Ivanovo, Zhytomyr, Gomel, Kaluga, Tula, Orel, Nizhny Novgorod, Vyatka, Ural Mountains, Ob, U S S R, Siberia, Kiev, UKRAINE, Voronezh, Tambov, Kazan, Perm, ROMANIA, Kishinev, Poltava, Nikolayev, Kharkov, Penza, Saratov, Samara, Yekaterinburg, Tobolsk, BULGARIA, Odessa, Perekop, Rostov-on-Don, Novocherkassk, Tsaritsyn (Stalingrad), Ufa, Orenburg, Omsk, Tomsk, Krasnoyarsk, Yenisey, Sevastopol, Simferopol, Krasnodar (Yekaterinodar), Astrakhan, Black Sea, TURKEY, Batum, Kars, GEORGIA, ARMENIA, AZERBAIJAN, Baku, SYRIA, Tabriz, Caspian Sea, Aral Sea, Khiva, Lake Balkhash, Tannu-Tuva, MONGO, Bukhara, Tashkent, CHINA, IRAQ, PERSIA, Volga

5 COSSACK ATTACK 1917–1920

The Cossacks, a group who formed self-governing communities, rose to fight against the Bolsheviks, and many anti-Bolsheviks fled to join them in southern Russia. United with the Whites, the Cossacks put the Bolsheviks on the defensive along the Southern Front, wrecking their lines of communication, laying siege to the port city of Tsaritsyn from 1918–1920, and briefly occupying the city of Voronezh in September 1919.

■ Don Cossacks   ▧ Kuban Cossacks

6 BOLSHEVIK ADVANCES 1917–1922

Although the Whites had the support of many countries outside of Russia, the Bolsheviks had a brilliant tactical leader in Leon Trotsky and were better organized. Crucially, they had control of the industrial cities of Moscow and Petrograd, which included much of Russia's railroad network. When the civil war ended in October 1922, the Bolsheviks had total control of Russia.

✕ Bolshevik battles   — Bolshevik territories 1919

7 USSR FOUNDED DECEMBER 1922

After the civil war, the country was in tatters. Around 6 million peasants had died from famine between 1921 and 1922, and there was rioting in many cities. Lenin suffered a stroke in May 1922. In December 1922, the Union of Soviet Socialist Republics (USSR) was established, based on one-party rule. Lenin died in 1924, worried about political infighting in his party. His legacy, however, was the world's first socialist state.

■ USSR 1922

OCTOBER REVOLUTION OCTOBER 1917

When Lenin returned to Russia in fall 1917, having been in hiding in Finland, he urged immediate action. The Red Guards seized control of Petrograd, and on October 26, 1917, guards at the Winter Palace—the seat of the Provisional Government—willingly surrendered. Power passed to the Bolsheviks, with Lenin establishing a Marxist one-party state after closing down the Russian Constituent Assembly in January 1918.

● Towns where Bolsheviks gained control

May 1918
Allied forces guard the Trans-Siberian Railway to protect their war supplies from Bolshevik attacks and to keep the railway running

Jan 1919
Troops from Allied nations are sent to fight with the Whites, largely in Siberia, through the city of Vladivostok

Khabarovsk

Blagoveshchensk

Lake Baikal

Chita

Vladivostok

Ulan Bator

Lena

Sea of Okhotsk

Bering Sea

KOREA

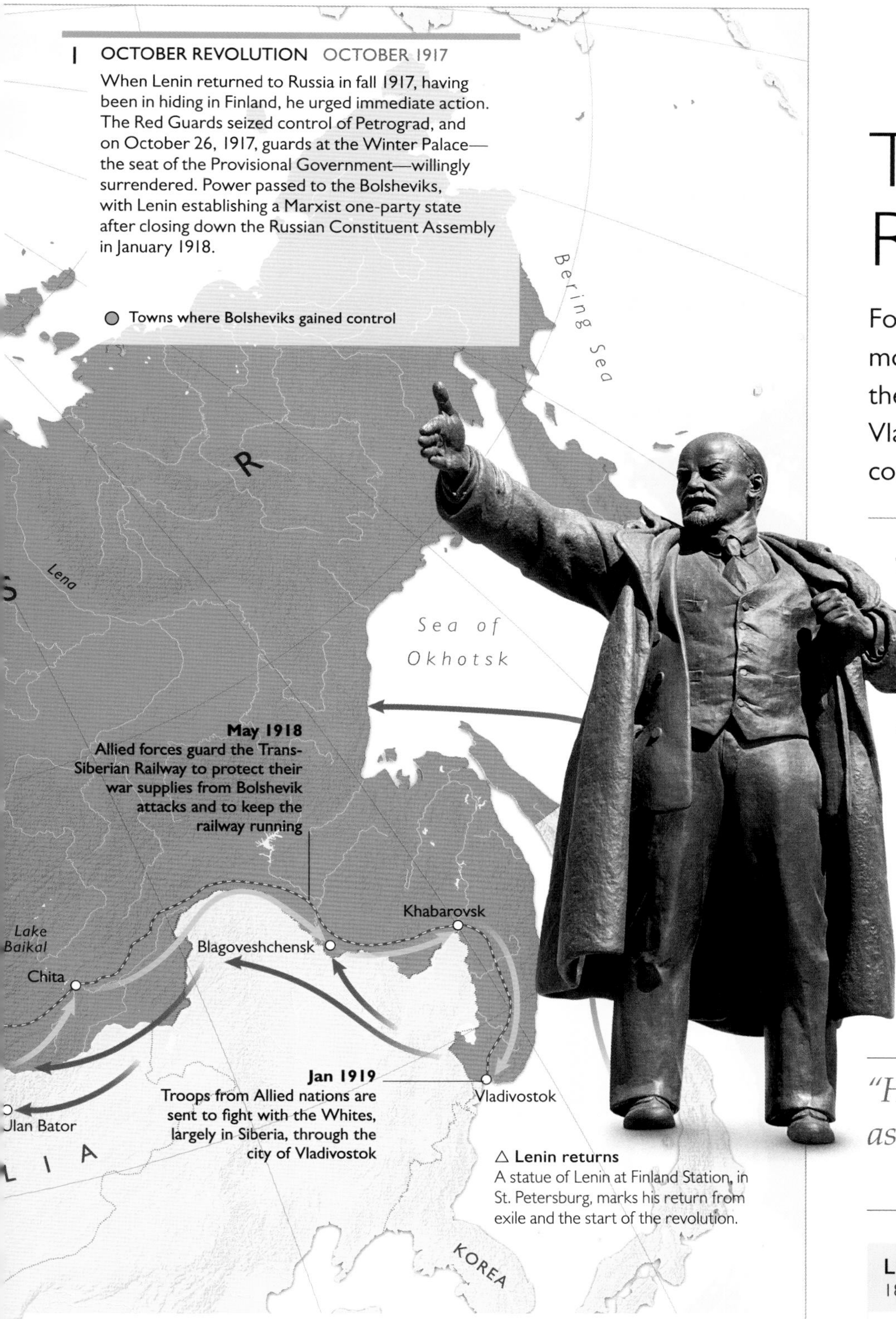

△ **Lenin returns**
A statue of Lenin at Finland Station, in St. Petersburg, marks his return from exile and the start of the revolution.

THE RUSSIAN REVOLUTION

For centuries, the Russian Empire was ruled by absolute monarchs, or Tsars. However, in one tumultuous year, the people of Russia rose up to topple Tsarist rule. Vladimir Lenin's communist party, the Bolsheviks, took control and set the stage for the creation of the USSR.

The outbreak of World War I in 1914 briefly united a discontented Russia, but the war did not go well. Huge military losses and food shortages led to increasing resentment against Tsar Nicholas II. On February 23, 1917, a riot broke out in Petrograd, led by women who had waited hours for bread. The riot grew into a general strike. The Tsar was forced to abdicate in March 1917, and a provisional government was put in charge, but it was weak. Meanwhile, the Petrograd Soviet of Workers' and Soldiers' Deputies, a council pushing for change, grew in popularity. Lenin, the leader of the Bolshevik faction of the Russian Social Democratic Party, who was in exile for Marxist activities, returned to Russia, convinced it was the time to implement his ideas. However, the Provisional Government leader, Alexander Kerensky, banned the Bolsheviks and ordered the arrest of Lenin, who fled to Finland. By August 1917, the Bolsheviks had taken control of the Petrograd Soviet. Sensing victory, Lenin returned home in the fall, certain that the Bolsheviks could seize power.

"History will not forgive us if we do not assume power now."

VLADIMIR LENIN, REVOLUTIONARY, SEPTEMBER 1917

COUNTRY IN TURMOIL

Russia experienced extreme turbulence from February 1917 to the founding of the USSR in 1922. In a country battered by World War I, the end of the monarchy, revolution, civil war, and famine, Lenin emerged as virtual dictator.

KEY

→ Bolshevik forces

⇒ White Army forces

→ Allied forces

⊷ Railway

TIMELINE

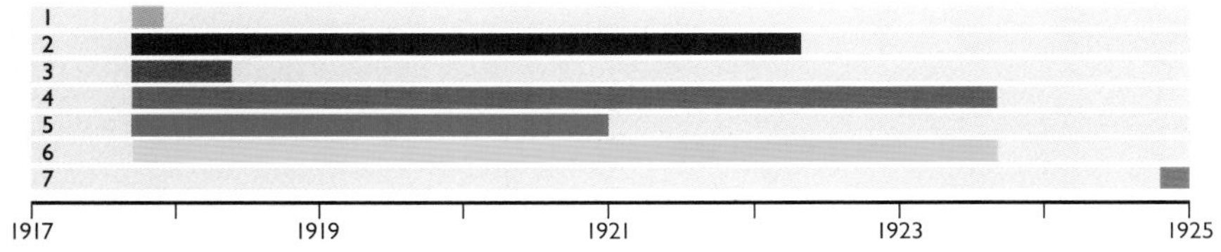

1
2
3
4
5
6
7

1917   1919   1921   1923   1925

LEON TROTSKY
1879–1940

Originally a member of the Mensheviks—a faction of the Russian socialist movement in opposition to the Bolsheviks—Leon Trotsky was in exile in the US for anti-war activities when the Tsar was overthrown in March 1917. He returned to Russia and joined the Bolshevik Party. Trotsky helped to organize the October Revolution and form the Red Army, which he then commanded in the Russian Civil War (1917–1922). After Lenin's death in 1924, he clashed with Joseph Stalin. Trotsky was exiled again in 1929 and found asylum in Mexico. In 1940, he was fatally stabbed by a Stalinist assassin.

POLITICAL EXTREMISM

World War I left a poisonous legacy. Several nations—including Germany, Italy, and Spain—looked for solutions to their problems in political extremism.

△ **The birth of fascism**
Charismatic Italian dictator Benito Mussolini inspired thousands at mass rallies. His stiff-armed salute became a symbol of fascism.

After World War I, Europe saw a rise in communism, triggering the emergence of extreme right-wing groups. People turned to leaders willing to assume political authority, and Benito Mussolini, who coined the term "fascism" to describe his right-wing movement, became Italy's military dictator in 1922.

Mussolini's mass rallies and use of propaganda influenced Adolf Hitler, the rising star of Germany's Right and leader of the National Socialist German Workers (Nazi) Party, which was openly racist, anti-Semitic, and anti-communist. The 1930s became a period of extreme turbulence. The Great Depression (see pp.286–287) led to a global economic crisis. Both communism and fascism offered answers to hungry, unemployed people. Authoritarian governments came to power in central and eastern Europe, and democracy was in decline.

Crisis and conflict

In Germany, as Nazi groups battled communists and against a backdrop of economic crisis, Hitler assumed power in 1933. The Spanish Civil War (see pp.292–293) epitomized the antipathy between fascists and the left. Italy and Germany supported fascist General Francisco Franco and used the war to test new weapons and strategies against the Republican government, which was supported with supplies and advisers by the USSR. Europe was once again choosing sides and forming alliances.

▷ **Bombing Guernica**
The bombing of the Basque town of Guernica, Spain, on April 26, 1937 during the Spanish Civil War was carried out by the Nazis in support of General Francisco Franco.

"The truth is that men are tired of liberty."

BENITO MUSSOLINI, ITALIAN DICTATOR, 1934

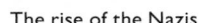

The rise of the Nazis
Nazi leader Adolf Hitler addresses a rally of paramilitary SA (*Sturmabteilung*) troops in Germany in 1933. Such larger-than-life displays built up support for the Nazi Party to fever pitch.

6 IRELAND 1916–1922

The outbreak of World War I interrupted a political crisis in Britain over Ireland's future. The failure to resolve this crisis first caused a wartime insurrection (the Easter Rising, 1916), then a War of Independence (1919–1921), when Irish separatists fought to establish an independent Irish Republic. The partition of Ireland in 1922 into Northern Ireland and the Irish Free State led to further unrest.

■ Irish Free State 1922

7 GERMAN LOSSES 1918–1919

The terms set out against Germany by the 1919 Treaty of Versailles were punitive. One-eighth of its prewar territory was lost, including land in Poland, Denmark, Belgium, and France. It was stripped of its colonial possessions, its armed forces were reduced, and its merchant fleet confiscated. Germany was made to pay war reparations, provoking bitter, long-lasting resentment.

— German border 1918

1920 Russia recognizes Finnish independence in the Treaty of Tartu

1922 Ireland is divided into two parts: the six mainly Protestant counties of Ulster become Northern Ireland and are subordinate to London

1921 Under the Treaty of Riga, Russia pledges to respect Latvia's independence

1920 Estonia is liberated from Russia following the Estonian War of Independence

1923 The borders of Poland are finally settled

1920 A peace treaty is signed between Lithuania and Soviet Russia after the Lithuanian War of Independence

1918 The region of Bessarabia is added to Romania

5 COLLAPSE AND DIVISION OF AUSTRIA-HUNGARY 1918–1923

After the Habsburg regime collapsed in 1918, new national states were created in Austria, Hungary, and Czechoslovakia. Habsburg territories were also absorbed by the new states of Poland and Yugoslavia. The Austrian army was restricted and reparations imposed, and Hungary lost two-thirds of its old land, principally to Yugoslavia and Romania.

— Austria-Hungary border 1914

1919 Treaty of St.-Germain sets the borders for the new state of Austria

4 PALESTINE 1922–1947

In 1922, the British were formally given the mandate to govern the region, having pledged to establish a home for Jews in Palestine. The Arabs rose up against the British, and many were killed in the Arab Revolt (1936–1939). The influx of Jewish refugees from Nazi-occupied territories, and the suggestion from the United Nations that Palestine be divided into Arab and Jewish states, exacerbated tensions. Civil war broke out in 1947 (see pp.332–333).

□ Mandatory Palestine 1922

1918 The Kingdom of the Serbs, Croats, and Slovenes is formed from parts of the old Austro-Hungarian Empire and Serbia. It is renamed Yugoslavia in 1929

1919 Greece occupies Smyrna, leading to war between Greece and Turkey

3 TURKEY 1922–1923

The Turkish War of Independence (1919–1922) saw Atatürk and a rebel army fight against the Ottoman sultan and the proxies of the Allied forces. Following the nationalists' victory, a new government was set up in Ankara, and the Treaty of Sèvres was abandoned. The Treaty of Lausanne (1923) legitimized the newly independent Turkish Republic and marked the end of the Ottoman Empire.

■ Turkey after Treaty of Sèvres 1920
□ Restored to Turkey after Treaty of Lausanne 1923
□ Annexed by Turkey 1921

2 BRITISH AND FRENCH MANDATES 1920–1946

The Treaty of Sèvres, signed in August 1920, divided parts of the defeated Ottoman Empire into British and French control. The Ottoman government accepted the treaty. However, it was rejected by Turkish nationalists, led by Mustafa Kemal Atatürk, who were determined to drive out foreign armies. In Egypt (a British protectorate), the diminishing British military presence after the war allowed the nationalist Wafd Party to launch a revolution. Limited independence was gained in February 1922.

■ French mandate
■ British mandate
□ British protectorate

1922 The growing popular support of the nationalistic Wafd Party prompts Britain to grant Egypt limited independence

AFTER WORLD WAR I

The postwar period saw territorial winners and losers. Russia lost the most, with Germany close behind. Many of the old empires had fallen, except for Britain and France, which retained influence and colonies worldwide.

KEY
- New states
- National borders 1923

TIMELINE

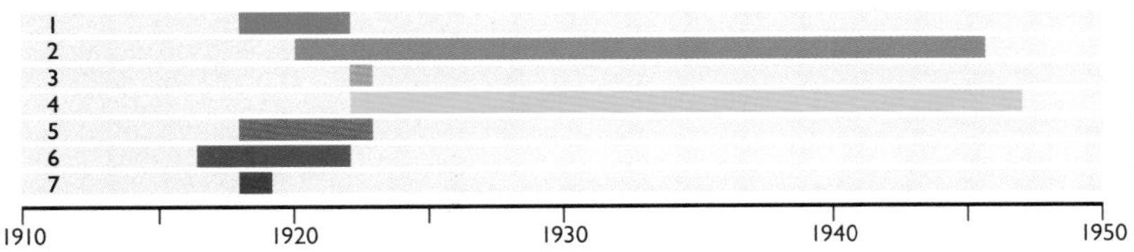

	1910	1920	1930	1940	1950
1					
2					
3					
4					
5					
6					
7					

△ **The Wafd Party**
Members of the Egyptian nationalist party, the Wafd Party, gather in 1936. The party was instrumental in gaining independence.

I RUSSIAN LOSSES 1918–1922

The Bolshevik regime could not hold on to its new empire. In the 1918 Treaty of Brest-Litovsk, Russia recognized the independence of the Baltic States, Ukraine, Georgia, and Finland. Ukraine and Georgia both joined the USSR in 1922, and the Baltic States did not achieve true independence until the 1920s.

Russian border 1918

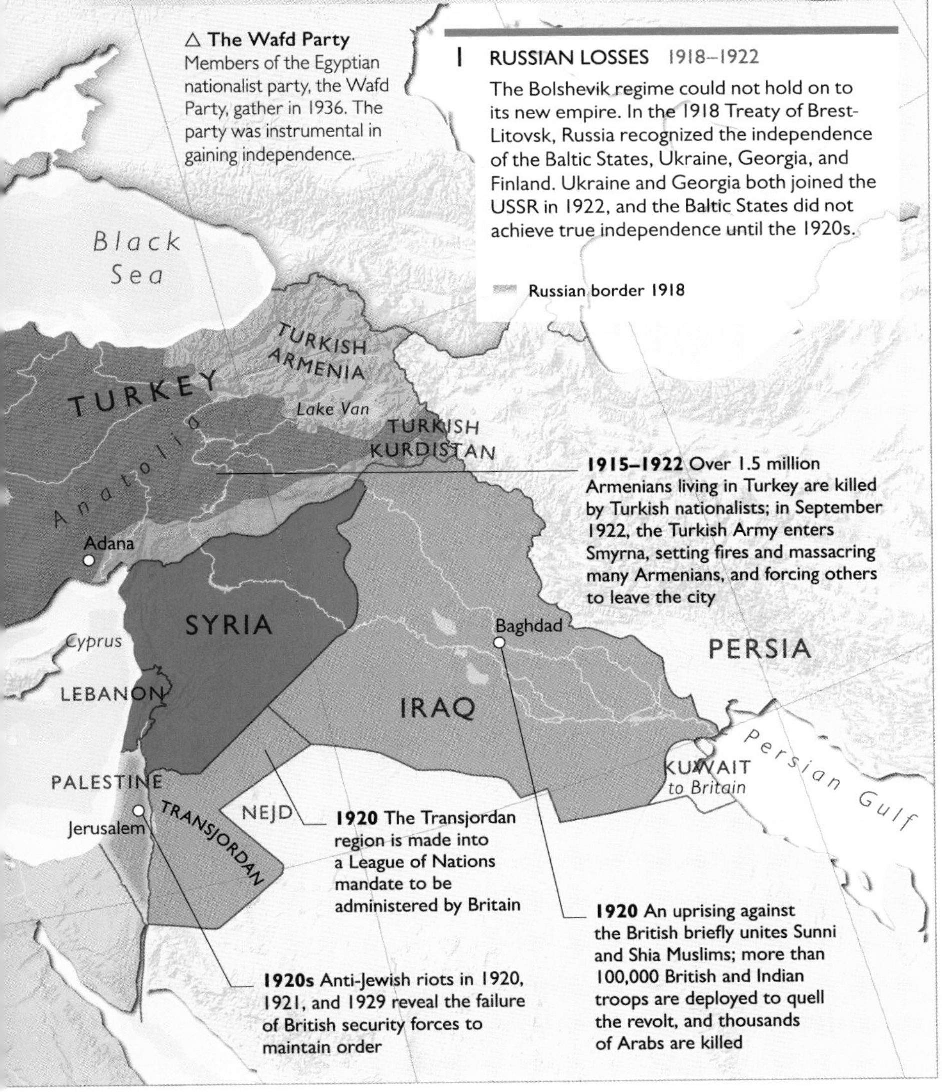

1915–1922 Over 1.5 million Armenians living in Turkey are killed by Turkish nationalists; in September 1922, the Turkish Army enters Smyrna, setting fires and massacring many Armenians, and forcing others to leave the city

1920 The Transjordan region is made into a League of Nations mandate to be administered by Britain

1920 An uprising against the British briefly unites Sunni and Shia Muslims; more than 100,000 British and Indian troops are deployed to quell the revolt, and thousands of Arabs are killed

1920s Anti-Jewish riots in 1920, 1921, and 1929 reveal the failure of British security forces to maintain order

Map labels: USSR, Black Sea, TURKEY, Anatolia, TURKISH ARMENIA, Lake Van, TURKISH KURDISTAN, Adana, Cyprus, SYRIA, LEBANON, Baghdad, PERSIA, IRAQ, PALESTINE, Jerusalem, TRANSJORDAN, NEJD, KUWAIT to Britain, Persian Gulf

AFTERMATH OF THE GREAT WAR

By the end of World War I, the political landscape of Europe and the Middle East had changed forever. Centuries-old empires and dynasties had collapsed, borders were redrawn, new nation-states were created, and the seeds of future conflict were sown.

World War I had a profound effect on global politics, bringing to an end three powerful monarchies—Germany, Russia, and Austria-Hungary. The victorious Allies assembled at the 1919 Paris Peace Conference to draw up a settlement. The main result was the Treaty of Versailles, which punished Germany harshly. Austria-Hungary, Turkey, and Bulgaria also suffered losses, while Italy, which had entered the war in 1915, was given former Habsburg lands in northern Italy. Also to gain were nine new nation-states created in Europe. The Middle East was also hugely impacted by the war. In 1916, the Sykes-Picot Agreement set out the intention to divide the Ottoman Empire's Middle Eastern territory between British and French zones of control. In many areas, the act of being placed under British or French control in 1920 fueled nationalist sentiments.

The victors of World War I hoped to build a lasting peace, but disputes rumbled on across the globe, and mass unemployment, bitter ideological divisions, fanatical nationalism, and the threat of communism created escalating international tension.

> *"This [the Treaty of Versailles] is not peace. It is an armistice for 20 years."*
>
> FERDINAND FOCH, FRENCH GENERAL, JUNE 28, 1919

THE LEAGUE OF NATIONS
1920–1946

Proposed by US President Woodrow Wilson, the League of Nations was an international organization set up in Geneva in 1920 to preserve peace. Conflict was to be settled by negotiation; diplomacy; and, if necessary, sanctions. The league relied on international goodwill, but Germany and Russia were excluded, and the US Senate refused to ratify US membership. In 1946, the league was replaced by the United Nations.

President Wilson arrives in Italy to discuss founding the League of Nations.

THE GREAT DEPRESSION

The US stock market crash in October 1929 was part of a worldwide economic recession that crippled the future of an entire generation. As people lost faith in democracy, new extremist politics gained popularity, setting the stage for the horrors of World War II.

The US recovered quickly after World War I. Factories used in the war effort switched to making consumer goods, and industrial growth doubled in the 1920s. Thousands of Americans invested in the stock market, often using borrowed money. A boom time, it became known as the "Roaring Twenties." However, by mid-1929, there were signs of trouble. Unemployment was rising, and car sales had dipped. The crisis broke on October 24, when the stock market dropped by 11 percent. Panic set in, and over the next 6 days, the market crashed. One-quarter of the US working population became unemployed. In mid-1932, Franklin Roosevelt replaced Herbert Hoover as president and pledged a "New Deal" of social and economic reforms.

The Great Depression spread around the globe, leading to massive poverty. The only country not adversely affected was the USSR. In Germany, the US's demand for outstanding loans to be repaid further impoverished the country, fueling the popularity of Adolf Hitler's National Socialist (Nazi) Party.

"There may be a recession in stock prices, but not anything in the nature of a crash."

IRVING FISHER, US ECONOMIST, SEPTEMBER 5, 1929

1 STOCK MARKET CRASH AND STRIKES 1929–1934

Approximately $25 billion was lost in the 1929 crash. People became bankrupt, factories closed, trade collapsed, wages fell, and homelessness soared. There were strikes and riots across the country as workers sought protection offered by the unions, as well as greater involvement of the US government in the economy.

Strikes

May–Jul 1934 Dock workers go on strike at ports in San Francisco, as well as all other West Coast ports, shutting down about 2,000 miles (3,200 km) of coastline

1931–1932 Miners strike in Harlan County, Kentucky; like many strikes at the time, it turns violent

Jul–Aug 1934 Textile workers strike in Huntsville, Alabama; the strike spreads from the south of the country to the north, becoming one of the biggest industrial strikes in US history

Oct 1929 The financial bubble bursts, and panic hits Wall Street in New York; banks close, bankrupting millions overnight

2 LATIN AMERICA 1929–1933

After the crash, some of Latin America saw a drop of over 70 percent in exports to the US. In Colombia, this hit its coffee, banana, and oil markets. Brazil's coffee economy also suffered. In Cuba, reliant on its sugar exports, the impact was devastating. Chile, which exported nitrate and copper, was one of the worst-hit countries. Argentina and Venezuela, however, recovered relatively quickly.

1931–1932 In Chile, copper exports collapse, and the value of sodium nitrate exports to the US drops from $21 million to $1.4 million

1929–1930 In Argentina, exports of wheat and beef drop by more than two-thirds, and inflation increases; subsequent political instability leads to a military dictatorship

THE DUST BOWL

In 1932, severe droughts hit the US from Texas to the Dakotas. Exposed topsoil turned to dust, and without windbreaks such as trees, high winds churned the dust into huge storms. Settlers and livestock choked on the dirt. Farmers, already hit by the Great Depression, were forced to migrate west to California, where regular harvests meant more jobs. Many rode along Route 66, which became known as the "road to opportunity."

KEY

- Area of severe damage
- Other areas damaged by dust storms
- → Migration route

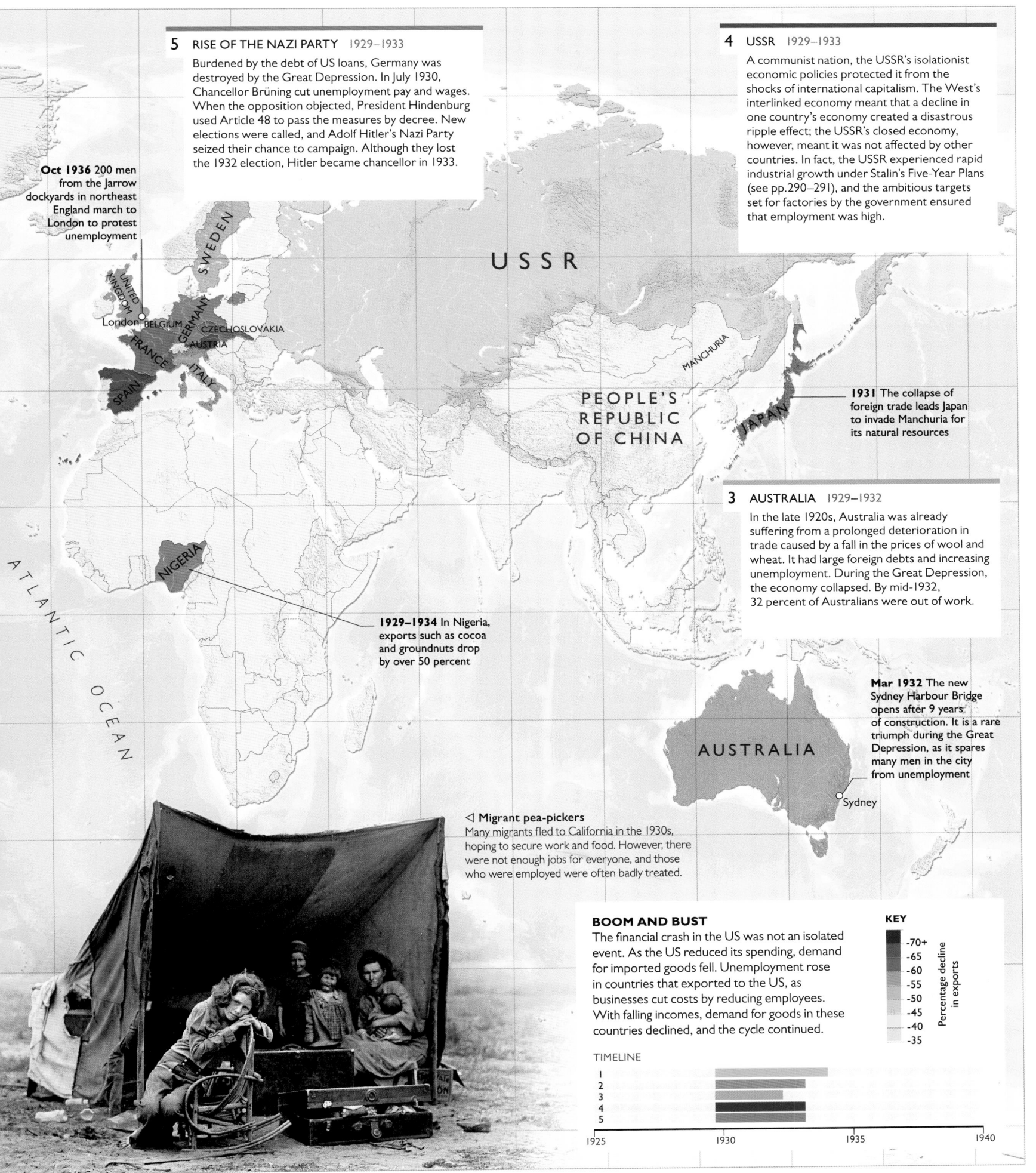

5 RISE OF THE NAZI PARTY 1929–1933

Burdened by the debt of US loans, Germany was destroyed by the Great Depression. In July 1930, Chancellor Brüning cut unemployment pay and wages. When the opposition objected, President Hindenburg used Article 48 to pass the measures by decree. New elections were called, and Adolf Hitler's Nazi Party seized their chance to campaign. Although they lost the 1932 election, Hitler became chancellor in 1933.

Oct 1936 200 men from the Jarrow dockyards in northeast England march to London to protest unemployment

4 USSR 1929–1933

A communist nation, the USSR's isolationist economic policies protected it from the shocks of international capitalism. The West's interlinked economy meant that a decline in one country's economy created a disastrous ripple effect; the USSR's closed economy, however, meant it was not affected by other countries. In fact, the USSR experienced rapid industrial growth under Stalin's Five-Year Plans (see pp.290–291), and the ambitious targets set for factories by the government ensured that employment was high.

1931 The collapse of foreign trade leads Japan to invade Manchuria for its natural resources

3 AUSTRALIA 1929–1932

In the late 1920s, Australia was already suffering from a prolonged deterioration in trade caused by a fall in the prices of wool and wheat. It had large foreign debts and increasing unemployment. During the Great Depression, the economy collapsed. By mid-1932, 32 percent of Australians were out of work.

1929–1934 In Nigeria, exports such as cocoa and groundnuts drop by over 50 percent

Mar 1932 The new Sydney Harbour Bridge opens after 9 years of construction. It is a rare triumph during the Great Depression, as it spares many men in the city from unemployment

◁ **Migrant pea-pickers**
Many migrants fled to California in the 1930s, hoping to secure work and food. However, there were not enough jobs for everyone, and those who were employed were often badly treated.

BOOM AND BUST

The financial crash in the US was not an isolated event. As the US reduced its spending, demand for imported goods fell. Unemployment rose in countries that exported to the US, as businesses cut costs by reducing employees. With falling incomes, demand for goods in these countries declined, and the cycle continued.

KEY

Percentage decline in exports

-70+
-65
-60
-55
-50
-45
-40
-35

TIMELINE

1
2
3
4
5

1925   1930   1935   1940

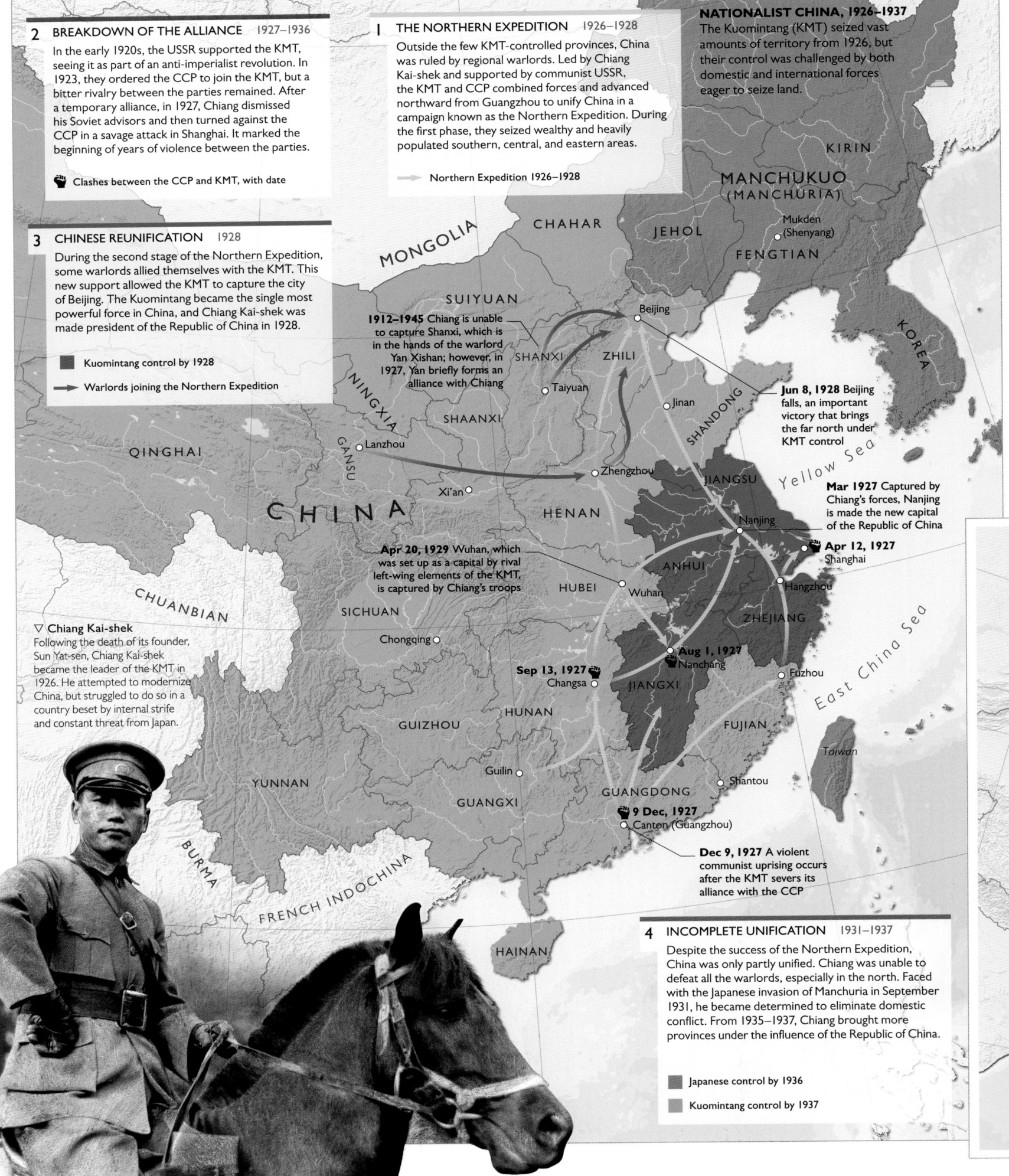

2 BREAKDOWN OF THE ALLIANCE 1927–1936

In the early 1920s, the USSR supported the KMT, seeing it as part of an anti-imperialist revolution. In 1923, they ordered the CCP to join the KMT, but a bitter rivalry between the parties remained. After a temporary alliance, in 1927, Chiang dismissed his Soviet advisors and then turned against the CCP in a savage attack in Shanghai. It marked the beginning of years of violence between the parties.

✊ Clashes between the CCP and KMT, with date

3 CHINESE REUNIFICATION 1928

During the second stage of the Northern Expedition, some warlords allied themselves with the KMT. This new support allowed the KMT to capture the city of Beijing. The Kuomintang became the single most powerful force in China, and Chiang Kai-shek was made president of the Republic of China in 1928.

◼ Kuomintang control by 1928

➡ Warlords joining the Northern Expedition

1 THE NORTHERN EXPEDITION 1926–1928

Outside the few KMT-controlled provinces, China was ruled by regional warlords. Led by Chiang Kai-shek and supported by communist USSR, the KMT and CCP combined forces and advanced northward from Guangzhou to unify China in a campaign known as the Northern Expedition. During the first phase, they seized wealthy and heavily populated southern, central, and eastern areas.

➡ Northern Expedition 1926–1928

NATIONALIST CHINA, 1926–1937

The Kuomintang (KMT) seized vast amounts of territory from 1926, but their control was challenged by both domestic and international forces eager to seize land.

1912–1945 Chiang is unable to capture Shanxi, which is in the hands of the warlord Yan Xishan; however, in 1927, Yan briefly forms an alliance with Chiang

Jun 8, 1928 Beijing falls, an important victory that brings the far north under KMT control

Mar 1927 Captured by Chiang's forces, Nanjing is made the new capital of the Republic of China

Apr 20, 1929 Wuhan, which was set up as a capital by rival left-wing elements of the KMT, is captured by Chiang's troops

Apr 12, 1927 Shanghai

Aug 1, 1927 Nanchang

Sep 13, 1927 Changsa

9 Dec, 1927 Canton (Guangzhou)

Dec 9, 1927 A violent communist uprising occurs after the KMT severs its alliance with the CCP

▽ **Chiang Kai-shek**
Following the death of its founder, Sun Yat-sen, Chiang Kai-shek became the leader of the KMT in 1926. He attempted to modernize China, but struggled to do so in a country beset by internal strife and constant threat from Japan.

4 INCOMPLETE UNIFICATION 1931–1937

Despite the success of the Northern Expedition, China was only partly unified. Chiang was unable to defeat all the warlords, especially in the north. Faced with the Japanese invasion of Manchuria in September 1931, he became determined to eliminate domestic conflict. From 1935–1937, Chiang brought more provinces under the influence of the Republic of China.

◼ Japanese control by 1936

◼ Kuomintang control by 1937

CHINA AND NATIONALISM

When its last emperor abdicated in 1912 (see pp.252–253), China was torn apart as warlords and China's Nationalist Party rushed to fill the void. After Japan was given territory in China in 1919, political unrest grew, leading to the emergence of the Communist Party. Years of fighting between the two parties and Japan followed, which carried on during the wider conflict of World War II.

The years following the fall of the Qing Dynasty were tumultuous. Regional warlords fought among themselves for territory, and the Nationalist Party, the Kuomintang (KMT) (Guomindang in modern Pinyin)—which had helped to overthrow the Qing Dynasty—battled them for control. After Japan was given land in China following the Paris Peace Conference (1919), a radical group known as the May Fourth Movement demanded change, and the Chinese Communist Party (CCP) emerged.

In 1924, the KMT set up a government in Guangzhou and built up an army. In 1926, the new leader, Chiang Kai-shek, then began a military campaign to crush the warlords and unite China. The CCP initially helped, but in 1927, fearing a power struggle, Chiang turned against them, massacring communists in Shanghai. This outburst led to years of civil war (see pp.310–311). The KMT and the CCP came to an uneasy truce in 1937, when Japan invaded the country and began seizing territory.

CHINA
During the first half of the 20th century, China experienced constant turbulence, with battles fought against regional warlords in attempts to unify the vast nation, frequent struggles between the nationalist and communist parties, and the ever-present threat of Japanese invasion.

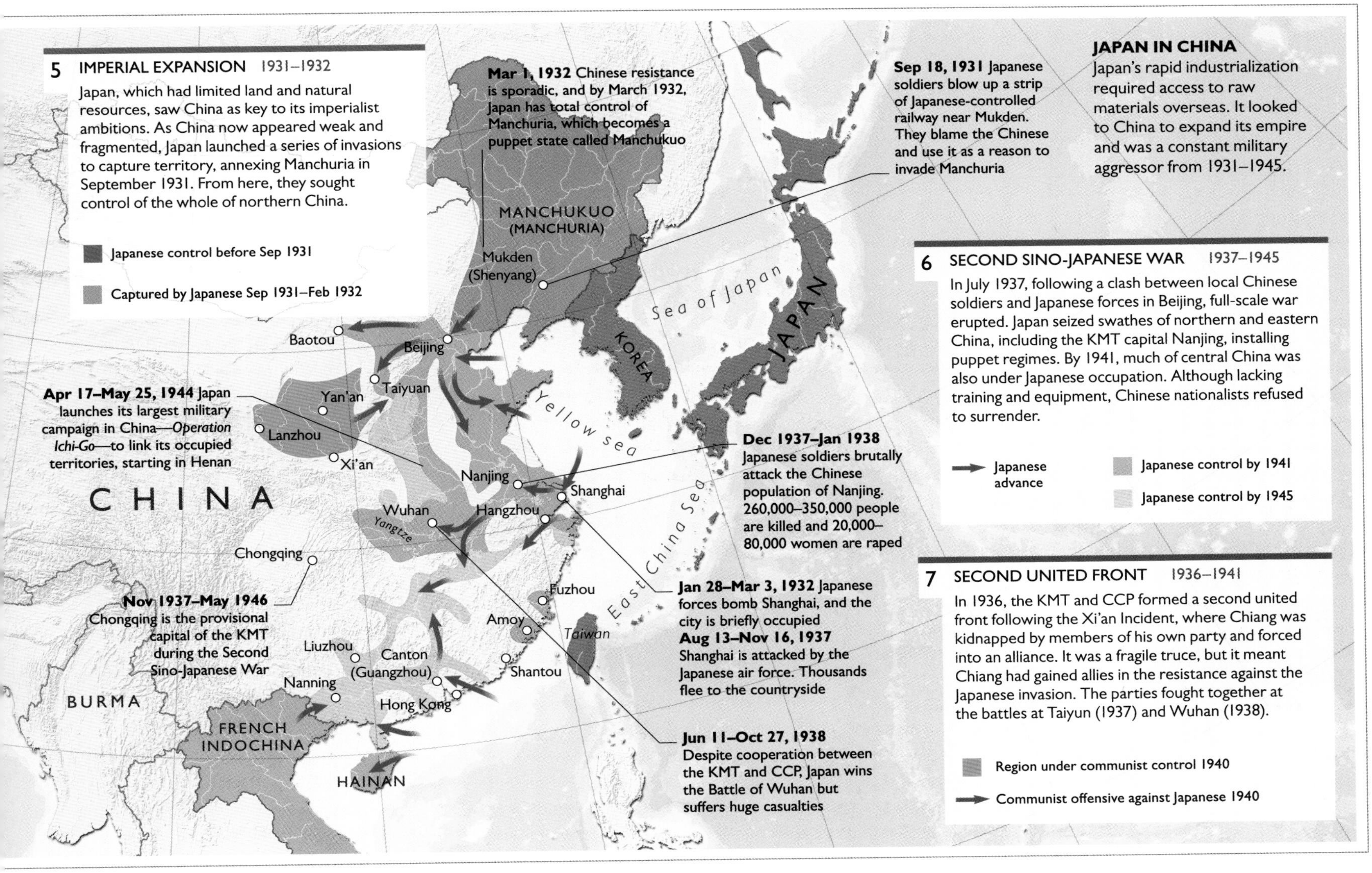

TIMELINE
1
2
3
4
5
6
7
1925
1930
1935
1940
1945

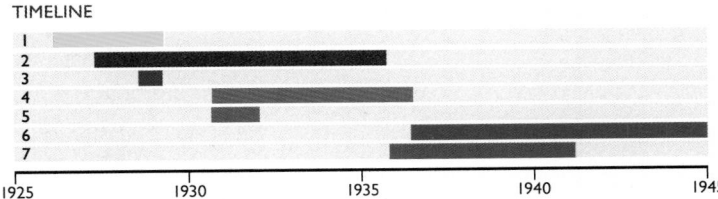

5 IMPERIAL EXPANSION 1931–1932
Japan, which had limited land and natural resources, saw China as key to its imperialist ambitions. As China now appeared weak and fragmented, Japan launched a series of invasions to capture territory, annexing Manchuria in September 1931. From here, they sought control of the whole of northern China.
Japanese control before Sep 1931
Captured by Japanese Sep 1931–Feb 1932
Mar 1, 1932 Chinese resistance is sporadic, and by March 1932, Japan has total control of Manchuria, which becomes a puppet state called Manchukuo
Sep 18, 1931 Japanese soldiers blow up a strip of Japanese-controlled railway near Mukden. They blame the Chinese and use it as a reason to invade Manchuria
JAPAN IN CHINA
Japan's rapid industrialization required access to raw materials overseas. It looked to China to expand its empire and was a constant military aggressor from 1931–1945.
MANCHUKUO (MANCHURIA)
Mukden (Shenyang)
Sea of Japan
JAPAN
KOREA
Baotou
Beijing
Taiyuan
Yan'an
Lanzhou
Xi'an
Yellow Sea
Nanjing
Shanghai
Hangzhou
Wuhan
Yangtze
CHINA
Chongqing
East China Sea
Fuzhou
Amoy
Taiwan
Shantou
Liuzhou
Canton (Guangzhou)
Nanning
Hong Kong
BURMA
FRENCH INDOCHINA
HAINAN
Apr 17–May 25, 1944 Japan launches its largest military campaign in China—*Operation Ichi-Go*—to link its occupied territories, starting in Henan
Dec 1937–Jan 1938 Japanese soldiers brutally attack the Chinese population of Nanjing. 260,000–350,000 people are killed and 20,000–80,000 women are raped
Nov 1937–May 1946 Chongqing is the provisional capital of the KMT during the Second Sino-Japanese War
Jan 28–Mar 3, 1932 Japanese forces bomb Shanghai, and the city is briefly occupied
Aug 13–Nov 16, 1937 Shanghai is attacked by the Japanese air force. Thousands flee to the countryside
Jun 11–Oct 27, 1938 Despite cooperation between the KMT and CCP, Japan wins the Battle of Wuhan but suffers huge casualties
6 SECOND SINO-JAPANESE WAR 1937–1945
In July 1937, following a clash between local Chinese soldiers and Japanese forces in Beijing, full-scale war erupted. Japan seized swathes of northern and eastern China, including the KMT capital Nanjing, installing puppet regimes. By 1941, much of central China was also under Japanese occupation. Although lacking training and equipment, Chinese nationalists refused to surrender.
Japanese advance
Japanese control by 1941
Japanese control by 1945
7 SECOND UNITED FRONT 1936–1941
In 1936, the KMT and CCP formed a second united front following the Xi'an Incident, where Chiang was kidnapped by members of his own party and forced into an alliance. It was a fragile truce, but it meant Chiang had gained allies in the resistance against the Japanese invasion. The parties fought together at the battles at Taiyun (1937) and Wuhan (1938).
Region under communist control 1940
Communist offensive against Japanese 1940

1 GULAGS 1917–1953

Gulags—concentration camps for prisoners—were created under Lenin but proliferated under Stalin. They housed a range of convicts, who were exploited to open up remote and forbidding areas of the country, such as the Arctic north and the Siberian east. The population of the gulag camps reached its height in the late 1940s, but the system was run down under Stalin's successors.

⚒ Gulag ▬ Isolation camp region

2 COLLECTIVIZATION 1927–1953

Stalin deemed Soviet agricultural methods outdated, as they produced too little food for a growing urban population. From 1927, Stalin instigated collectivization, uniting small farms into larger collectives. Food production eventually grew, and labor was freed for industry. Few farms volunteered, and terror was used to coerce them into handing over their land. Millions were starved, persecuted, or sent to gulags. By 1939, 99 percent of land was collectivized.

3 INDUSTRIALIZATION 1928–1953

Stalin's main ambition was industrialization on a massive scale. Over 12 million people moved from rural areas to the new factories and towns that had been built or extensively remodeled between 1928–1932. They were attracted by the promise of higher wages and training. Life for workers was brutal, but Stalin achieved his goal; under the first Five-Year Plan, which ended in 1934, there was a 50 percent increase in industrial output.

⬤ New or remodeled towns

Nov 1923 The Solovki prison camp is opened on an island in the White Sea. Political opponents and criminals are incarcerated here

Mar 1918 Fearing invasion from the West, Lenin moves the capital city farther east, to Moscow. It undergoes extensive modernization, including the building of the subway system

1921 Novosibirsk is reconstructed after damage done by the Russian Civil War. It becomes the major industrial center in Siberia

1945 After World War I, Kiev becomes a major industrial center

1929 Under Stalin's Five-Year Plans, iron ore-rich Magnitogorsk is extensively remodeled and becomes a one-industry city

1931 Karlag is one of the largest labor camps. Its prisoners include scientists, doctors, artists, and political figures

◁ **"No room for kulaks"**
This Soviet poster from 1930 denounces kulaks as the opponents of the collective farm. People were encouraged to believe that kulaks were the enemy of the working class.

4 FAMINE 1932–1933

Grain grown on the collectives was given to the city workforce, leaving little for rural peasants. Hardest hit by famine was the north Caucasus, the Volga region, southern Russia, central Russian Asia, and above all the Ukraine, known as the Soviet "breadbasket." Millions died in the Holodomor ("hunger death"), as Stalin used famine to break Ukrainian resistance to farm reform.

🍂 Famine

5 DEPORTATIONS 1942–1945

Stalin enforced mass deportations of entire peoples deemed "anti-Soviet." These groups were relocated to underpopulated, inhospitable areas of the country. During World War II, he deported about a dozen nationalities from western regions of the USSR to central Asia, accusing them of collaboration with the invading Nazi army.

→ Deportations 1942–1945

▬ Areas depopulated by deportations

Map labels: FRANCE, DENMARK, SWEDEN, WEST GERMANY, EAST GERMANY, ITALY, AUSTRIA, CZECHOSLOVAKIA, POLAND, HUNGARY, YUGOSLAVIA, ROMANIA, BULGARIA, TURKEY, FINLAND, ESTONIA, LATVIA, LITHUANIA, EAST PRUSSIA, KARELIA, Kaliningrad, Leningrad, Archangel, Moscow, Kiev, Odessa, CRIMEAN TARTARS, KALMYK, KARACHAY, MESKHETIAN, CHECHEN, Black Sea, Caspian Sea, Caucasus, VOLGA GERMANS, Molotoy, Sverdlovsk, Magnitogorsk, Omsk, Novosibirsk, Krasnoyarsk, KRASLAG, NORYL LAG, Ural Mountains, Aral Sea, Lake Balkash, Alma-Ata, TANNU TUVA, MOLDAVIA, AFGHANISTAN, IRAN, CHINA, MON

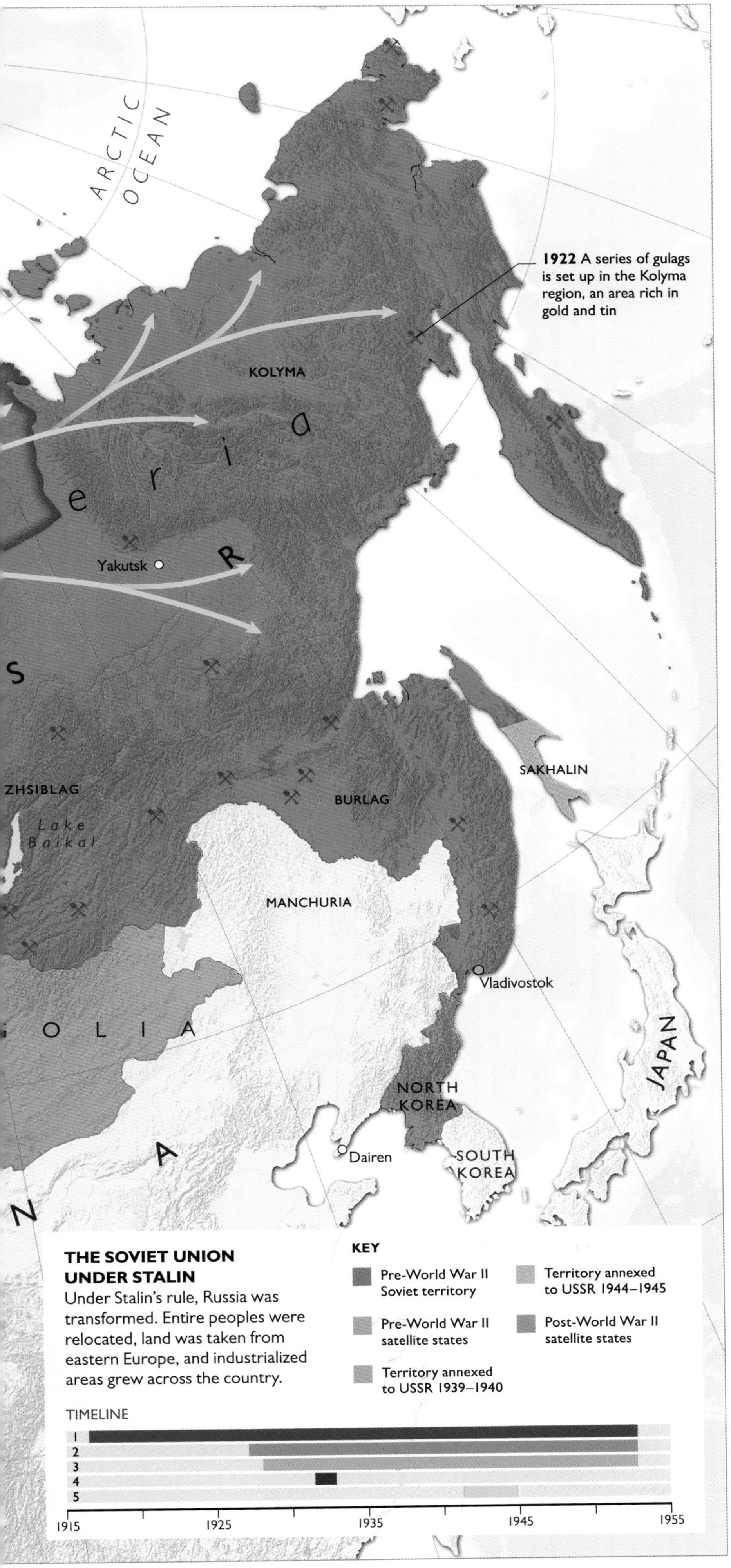

1922 A series of gulags is set up in the Kolyma region, an area rich in gold and tin

ARCTIC OCEAN

KOLYMA

Yakutsk

Siberia

USSR

ZHSIBLAG

Lake Baikal

BURLAG

SAKHALIN

MANCHURIA

Vladivostok

MONGOLIA

CHINA

JAPAN

Dairen

NORTH KOREA

SOUTH KOREA

THE SOVIET UNION UNDER STALIN

Under Stalin's rule, Russia was transformed. Entire peoples were relocated, land was taken from eastern Europe, and industrialized areas grew across the country.

KEY

- ◼ Pre-World War II Soviet territory
- ◼ Pre-World War II satellite states
- ◼ Territory annexed to USSR 1939–1940
- ◼ Territory annexed to USSR 1944–1945
- ◼ Post-World War II satellite states

TIMELINE

	1915	1925	1935	1945	1955
1					
2					
3					
4					
5					

SOVIET UNION UNDER STALIN

With civil war at an end by 1922, Joseph Stalin had ambitions to transform the newly formed Soviet Union into an industrialized, modern society. He achieved extraordinary economic growth for Russia but became one of the most brutal tyrants of the 20th century.

After the death of Vladimir Lenin in 1924, Stalin manipulated his way to becoming leader of the USSR. Stalin wanted to transform the country into an international power, but this required rapid industrial growth. To achieve this, he launched a series of Five-Year Plans, starting in 1928. He began by taking farms from wealthy peasant landowners (kulaks), combining them into vast farms to be run collectively, providing more crops for the population. When these measures were resisted, he unleashed a wave of terror across the countryside. Millions of kulaks were deported, sent to labor camps, or deliberately starved when their grain was seized.

Ever fearful of dissent, Stalin launched a campaign of terror from 1936–1938 to wipe out anyone who might oppose him. During this "Great Terror," the gulag concentration camp system was expanded, with hundreds of thousands executed after a brief trial. Meanwhile, Stalin promoted himself as the "Father of the People." He rallied his troops against a German invasion in World War II (see pp.296–297), and after the war, he expanded communism beyond the USSR. By the 1950s, a modern Russia had emerged, but at a terrible cost.

"The death of one man is a tragedy. The death of a million is a statistic."

JOSEPH STALIN
1878–1953

Joseph Stalin began his rise to power in 1905, when he befriended Vladimir Lenin. His political career was quite unpredictable; in 1917, he had been a minor figure in the Bolshevik Revolution, but when he was made General Secretary of the Party in 1922, he used this role to expand his power. Once leader, he set about making the USSR a great industrial power. He used propaganda to build a cult of personality, which reached its peak during World War II, when he led the USSR to victory over Germany. After the war, Stalin led the USSR into a Cold War with its former allies.

THE SPANISH CIVIL WAR

The Spanish Civil War (1936–1939) epitomized the struggle between the old and new political orders. A prequel to World War II, it ushered in a new and horrific form of warfare that would come to define future conflicts in the 20th century.

Spain in the 1930s was a divided country, split between Church and State, rich and poor, town and countryside. Politics was also polarized. On one side was the left-wing Popular Front (Republicans), made up of socialists, communists, liberals, and anarchists. On the other side was the right-wing National Front (Nationalists), supported by the Falange (a Spanish fascist party), monarchists, and some Catholics.

On February 16, 1936, the Republicans narrowly won a general election. Fearing a communist revolution, General Francisco Franco, a career army officer and one of the Nationalist leaders, launched a military uprising in Spanish Morocco and across southwestern Spain. Pro-government groups rallied against the Nationalist rebels, but Franco received significant help from Nazi Germany and Fascist Italy, both keen to stop the spread of communism in Europe. By November 1936, Franco's troops had made it to the outskirts of Madrid, where support for the Republicans was strong. Unable to capture the city, the Nationalists laid siege to Madrid for two and a half years.

The Republicans continued to control eastern Spain and much of the southeast. However, Franco's forces were better coordinated, and areas under Republican control gradually shrank. The Nationalist victory at the Battle of Teruel (December 1937–February 1938) was a turning point in the war, and at the Battle of the Ebro (July–November 1938), the Republican troops were all but wiped out. By spring 1939, the bitter conflict was over, and Franco's government was recognized by most of Europe.

> "Better to die on one's feet than to live on one's knees."
>
> DOLORES IBARRURI, REPUBLICAN, JULY 18, 1936

GENERAL FRANCO
1892–1975

Born into a military family, General Francisco Franco became the youngest general in the Spanish Army in 1926. Franco led the Nationalist forces to victory in the Spanish Civil War, and then became the head of state in Spain from 1939 until his death in 1975. Although he sympathized with the Axis powers, Franco kept Spain out of World War II, and under his rule, the country became more industrialized and prosperous. However, he was a ruthless military dictator who presided over a totalitarian regime.

1 THE START OF THE WAR JULY 1936

The Civil War began on July 17, 1936, when Nationalist forces based in Spanish Morocco launched a coup against the newly elected Republican government. Franco assumed command of the Army of Africa—a Moroccan-based group of professional soldiers—on July 19. From July 27, Franco's army was flown from Morocco to Spain by German and Italian forces, and fighting soon spread through southwest Spain.

→ Nationalist forces   ✕ Major battles

⇢ Republican forces

2 FOREIGN INTERVENTION SEPTEMBER 1936

A total of 27 countries, including Britain, France, the USSR, Germany, and Italy, signed a nonintervention pact in September 1936. However, the ideological nature of the war gave it an international element. The Nationalists were aided by soldiers and equipment supplied by Fascist Italy and Nazi Germany. The Republicans were supported by the communist governments of Russia and Mexico, as well as by volunteers from International Brigades. These were groups of left-wing fighters who came from all over the world to fight in a war they saw as a struggle against extreme nationalism and tyranny.

⛴ German support   ⛴ USSR support

⛴ Italian support

Aug 22, 1936 Portugal allows German ships to dock at Lisbon and from there dispatch war supplies into Nationalist territory

3 CIVILIAN ATROCITIES 1936–1939

During the course of the war, both sides committed atrocities against civilians. The Republicans targeted anyone believed to be right wing, including teachers, lawyers, mayors, and landowners. Hatred of the Church meant that many churches were ransacked. Meanwhile, in Guernica, Franco's forces undertook a brutal attack on civilians from the air. This extreme violence stunned the international community.

✝ Republican violence   ✋ Nationalist violence

Porto

Lisbon

PORTUGAL

▽ **Preparing to attack**
Republican soldiers prepare mortar shells to fire at the Nationalist army in 1936. The Nationalists were organized and well-armed.

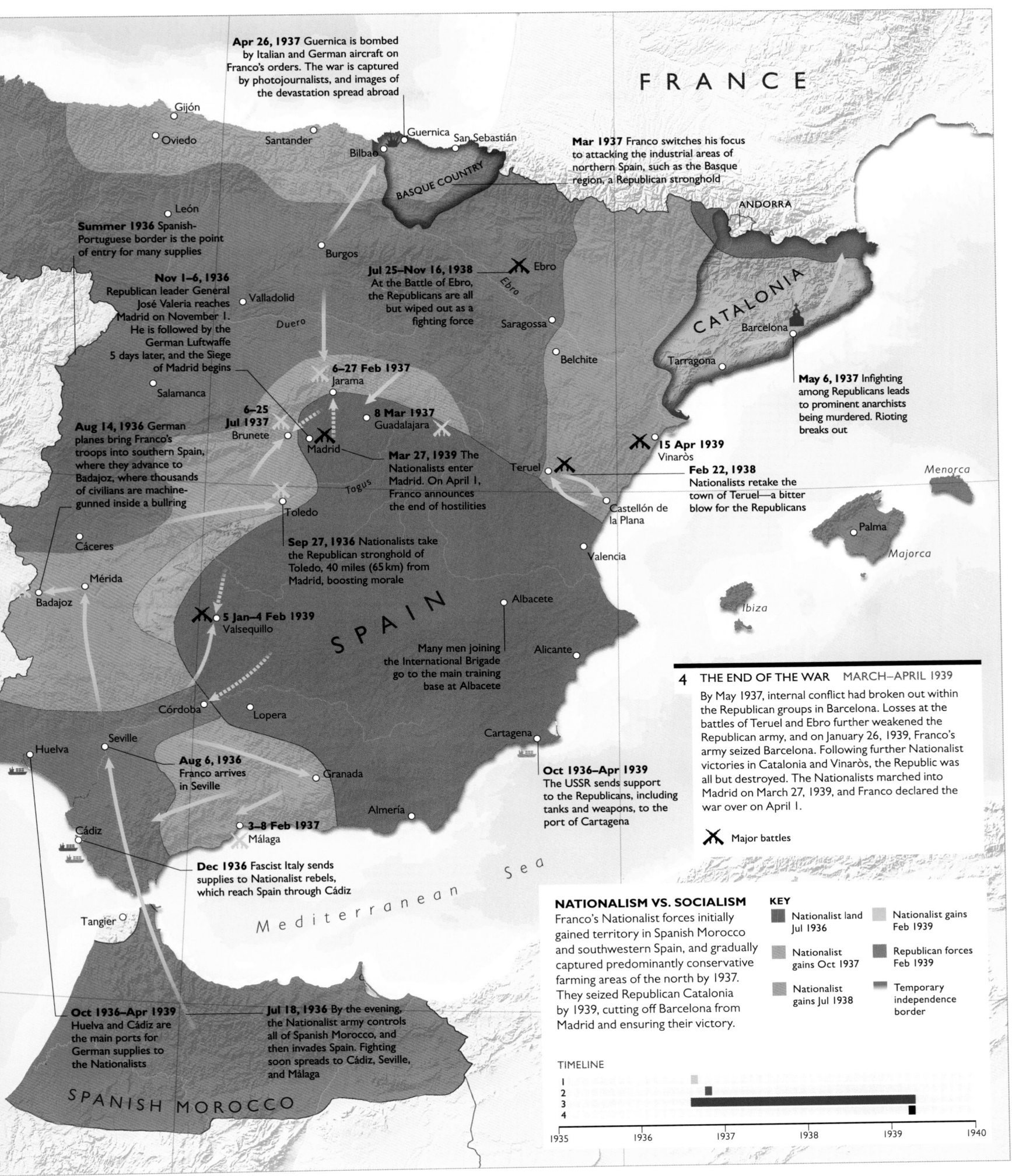

FRANCE

Apr 26, 1937 Guernica is bombed by Italian and German aircraft on Franco's orders. The war is captured by photojournalists, and images of the devastation spread abroad

Gijón
Oviedo
Santander
Guernica
San Sebastián
Bilbao

BASQUE COUNTRY

Mar 1937 Franco switches his focus to attacking the industrial areas of northern Spain, such as the Basque region, a Republican stronghold

ANDORRA

León

Summer 1936 Spanish-Portuguese border is the point of entry for many supplies

Burgos

Jul 25–Nov 16, 1938 At the Battle of Ebro, the Republicans are all but wiped out as a fighting force

Ebro

Ebro

CATALONIA

Nov 1–6, 1936 Republican leader General José Valeria reaches Madrid on November 1. He is followed by the German Luftwaffe 5 days later, and the Siege of Madrid begins

Valladolid

Duero

Saragossa

Barcelona

Belchite

Tarragona

May 6, 1937 Infighting among Republicans leads to prominent anarchists being murdered. Rioting breaks out

6–27 Feb 1937 Jarama

Salamanca

6–25 Jul 1937 Brunete

8 Mar 1937 Guadalajara

Aug 14, 1936 German planes bring Franco's troops into southern Spain, where they advance to Badajoz, where thousands of civilians are machine-gunned inside a bullring

Madrid

Mar 27, 1939 The Nationalists enter Madrid. On April 1, Franco announces the end of hostilities

Teruel

15 Apr 1939 Vinaròs

Feb 22, 1938 Nationalists retake the town of Teruel—a bitter blow for the Republicans

Menorca

Cáceres

Tagus

Toledo

Castellón de la Plana

Sep 27, 1936 Nationalists take the Republican stronghold of Toledo, 40 miles (65 km) from Madrid, boosting morale

Valencia

Palma

Mérida

Badajoz

Majorca

Albacete

S P A I N

5 Jan–4 Feb 1939 Valsequillo

Ibiza

Many men joining the International Brigade go to the main training base at Albacete

Alicante

Córdoba

Lopera

Cartagena

---

4 THE END OF THE WAR MARCH–APRIL 1939

By May 1937, internal conflict had broken out within the Republican groups in Barcelona. Losses at the battles of Teruel and Ebro further weakened the Republican army, and on January 26, 1939, Franco's army seized Barcelona. Following further Nationalist victories in Catalonia and Vinaròs, the Republic was all but destroyed. The Nationalists marched into Madrid on March 27, 1939, and Franco declared the war over on April 1.

✕ Major battles

Seville

Aug 6, 1936 Franco arrives in Seville

Granada

Oct 1936–Apr 1939 The USSR sends support to the Republicans, including tanks and weapons, to the port of Cartagena

Huelva

Almería

3–8 Feb 1937 Málaga

Cádiz

Dec 1936 Fascist Italy sends supplies to Nationalist rebels, which reach Spain through Cádiz

Mediterranean Sea

Tangier

NATIONALISM VS. SOCIALISM

Franco's Nationalist forces initially gained territory in Spanish Morocco and southwestern Spain, and gradually captured predominantly conservative farming areas of the north by 1937. They seized Republican Catalonia by 1939, cutting off Barcelona from Madrid and ensuring their victory.

KEY

■ Nationalist land Jul 1936

■ Nationalist gains Oct 1937

■ Nationalist gains Jul 1938

■ Nationalist gains Feb 1939

■ Republican forces Feb 1939

— Temporary independence border

Oct 1936–Apr 1939 Huelva and Cádiz are the main ports for German supplies to the Nationalists

Jul 18, 1936 By the evening, the Nationalist army controls all of Spanish Morocco, and then invades Spain. Fighting soon spreads to Cádiz, Seville, and Málaga

S P A N I S H   M O R O C C O

TIMELINE

1
2
3
4

1935   1936   1937   1938   1939   1940

WORLD WAR II

A European and Asian conflict that became a global war, World War II (1939–1945) was the most brutal conflict in history, engulfing the world in a struggle over ideology and national sovereignty. It was also the costliest war in terms of human life—at least 55 million people were killed in battle, in concentration camps, and in bombed-out cities. The war marked a watershed in world history.

The treaties meant to bring peace after World War I (see pp. 274–275) sowed the seeds for future conflict. Germany was made to pay substantial war reparations. In 1923, the currency collapsed, impoverishing millions, and in 1929–1932, the Great Depression (see pp.286–287) plunged Germany into severe recession. Here, and elsewhere in Europe, people were disenchanted with liberal politics and weak governments that polarized political opinion into the Right and Left. Right-wing politics prevailed in Italy, Germany, and Japan—known collectively as the Axis powers, although each had its own ambitions for territorial expansion.

The Axis aggression

Japan invaded Manchuria then attacked the rest of China; Italy overran Abyssinia (modern Ethiopia); and in Germany, Adolf Hitler pursued his plans to unite all German-speaking people in one country. In March 1938, Germany annexed Austria. The German-speaking districts of Czechoslovakia—the Sudetenland—were occupied next. In September 1939, Hitler invaded Poland, convinced that Britain and France would do nothing. To his surprise, both countries declared war.

The invasion of Poland lasted just over a month. Hitler put aside his hatred of communists to work in cooperation with the Soviets, who attacked Poland from the east. The world watched in shock as Germany attacked Denmark and Norway then France, Belgium, and the Netherlands. Within 6 weeks, France had fallen. Hitler then turned his sights on Britain. His plans to invade were abandoned, however, after the *Luftwaffe*—the German air force—failed to win the Battle of Britain (1940).

Total war

The European War became a world war. In June 1940, Italy declared war on Britain and France. "Total War" was brought to civilians when bombing raids pulverized European cities. With men joining the army, women were recruited to work on farms and in factories. Europe experienced food shortages, which led to food rationing. Despite having signed strategic pacts with the USSR in the past, Germany invaded Russia in June 1941, and Britain gained a new ally.

As German troops swept into the USSR, they inflicted a campaign of extermination against communists. Then, in December 1941, the US entered the war after its naval

△ **Japanese ambitions**
Determined to become a major colonial power, Japan built up the largest navy in the Pacific Ocean. This recruitment poster seeks pilots for its aircraft carriers.

▽ **Paris under siege**
Seen here in front of the iconic Eiffel Tower, Adolf Hitler, flanked by German officials, takes a tour of conquered Paris in June 1940, marking the end of the French Campaign.

THEATERS OF CONFLICT

World War II became a global war but had two main theaters—Europe and the Pacific. In Europe, the war started with the Western Front as the German "blitzkrieg" swept through Western Europe into France. The Eastern Front opened when Germany turned on the USSR. The Pacific theater, fought over by the Allies and Japan, stretched throughout eastern China and Southeast Asia, including the Pacific Ocean and its islands. The role of the US in this arena was pivotal.

Sep 1, 1939 Germany invades Poland; Britain and France declare war on Germany 2 days later

May 1940 Germany invades Belgium, the Netherlands, and then France; France surrenders in June

Mar 31–Nov 27, 1941 The Allies take Tobruk in Libya and resist German attacks

EUROPE

AFRICA AND ITALY

THE PACIFIC

1939

1940

1941

Aug–Sep 1940 The Battle of Britain is fought between the British and German air forces, but the failure to defeat the British compels Hitler to abandon plans to invade England

Dec 7, 1941 The US enters the war as Japan attacks Pearl Harbor, Hawaii

◁ **Gateway of death**
Millions of unsuspecting Jews arrived by train at the infamous death camp, Auschwitz-Birkenau, where they were gassed. It became a memorial site after the war.

base at Pearl Harbor in the Hawaiian Islands was attacked by Japan. Japan won quick victories in the Pacific and dominated the region. In North Africa, British troops struggled against German and Italian forces. By the summer of 1942, Hitler was at the height of his power, but in November, the German General Erwin Rommel was stopped at El Alamein in Egypt. Soviet victories at Stalingrad and Kursk in 1943 destroyed the German sixth army, which was forced to surrender. This defeat marked the beginning of a retreat that was to end in Berlin.

The tide turns

A strategy was devised by the Allies—Britain, France, the US, and the USSR—in 1943 to free Europe. While the USSR drove the Germans back in the east, and the British and Americans advanced through Italy, a huge Allied force landed in Normandy in June 1944. Almost a year later, it reached the River Elbe in northern Germany. As Soviet troops took Berlin, Hitler committed suicide on April 30, 1945. Germany surrendered a week later. The war was over in Europe but not in the Pacific, where Americans fought island by island. Japan finally surrendered soon after Hiroshima and Nagasaki were destroyed by American atomic bombs in August 1945 (see pp.306–307).

World War II changed the world forever. New military technology had shown the capacity for massive destruction, with U-boats, jet aircraft, and, ultimately, nuclear bombs. Germany's Nazis displayed new, efficient, and horrific methods of mass killing in their genocide of almost 6 million Jews. Countries went bankrupt, major cities were destroyed, and the great European empires were on their last legs. Representatives of 50 nations met in 1945 to form the United Nations in the hope that out of this devastation, a new era of international understanding could begin.

▽ **Bombed city**
Ferocious bombing raids on major cities defined WWII. This 1945 photograph shows the German city of Dresden, which was among the last to be destroyed in the war.

Feb 1942 Singapore falls to the Japanese

Mid-1942 The mass murder of Jews begins at Auschwitz as part of Hitler's "Final Solution"

Sep 8, 1943 Italy surrenders and signs an armistice; immediately after, German troops occupy the rest of Italy

1944 Soviet offensive gathers pace in Eastern Europe

Jun 6, 1944 D-day: the Allied invasion of France; Paris is liberated in August

May 8, 1945 VE Day: the Germans surrender to the Allies unconditionally

Aug 15, 1945 VJ Day: Japan formally surrenders following the destruction of Hiroshima and Nagasaki

1943

1944

1945

1946

Jun 1942 American naval victory in the Battle of Midway marks a turning point in the Pacific

Jul 1942–Nov 1943 Germany suffers a major setback at the Battle of Stalingrad and also at El Alamein

May 1943 Major Allied victories in North Africa enable the launch of Italy's invasion and end the Africa Campaign

Jan 1944 Allies land at Anzio, Italy, and in March bomb a monastery at Monte Cassino, suspecting it to be a German observation post

Jan 27, 1945 Auschwitz liberated by Soviet troops

Apr 1945 Russians reach Berlin; Hitler commits suicide; Mussolini is killed by Italian partisans

8 THE BATTLE OF STALINGRAD
AUGUST 1942–FEBRUARY 1943

A new Axis offensive in 1942 brought them to the industrial city of Stalingrad. In one of the largest and bloodiest battles of the war, almost 800,000 civilians and soldiers were killed. It ended with a humiliating German surrender, and this marked a turning point in WWII.

◎ Siege

7 INVASION OF THE SOVIET UNION
JUNE–DECEMBER 1941

Germany, along with its Axis allies, attacked the Soviet Union with 4 million troops, on a front of almost 1,000 miles. In 3 months, the invaders had almost reached Moscow and Leningrad, but here they failed to win complete victories. The advance was halted in December 1941.

◎ Siege

6 BRITAIN UNDER ATTACK
JULY 1940–MAY 1941

Hitler's plans to invade Britain were scuppered when Germany failed to beat Britain in the skies in 1940. Hitler switched to bombing Britain's cities, but he abandoned the campaign in May 1941 in favor of invading the Soviet Union.

✹ German bombing raids

5 ITALY'S CAMPAIGNS
JUNE 1940–FEBRUARY 1942

Italy invaded southern France in June 1940, keen to profit from German successes and to give Italy a place at any later peace conference. To gain control of the Mediterranean, Mussolini then attacked British and British Empire forces in north Africa and attempted to invade Greece. The Italians were repelled in both Egypt and Greece, and Hitler had to divert German troops in support of his ally.

→ Italian advance   ▪▪▶ Allied offensive

AXIS CONQUESTS 1939–1943

Germany launched offensives in both eastern and western Europe, while Italy advanced in the Mediterranean. German forces used armor and aircraft to great effect.

KEY

- ■ Axis powers
- ■ Axis satellites
- ■ Axis conquests 1939
- ■ Axis conquests 1940
- ■ Axis conquests 1941
- ■ Allied powers
- → German advance
- ▽ Airborne attacks

TIMELINE

1 2 3 4 5 6 7 8

1939 | 1940 | 1941 | 1942 | 1943 | 1944

Apr 1940 German forces enter Norwegian waters, starting a two-month conflict that ends in defeat for the Allies

Apr 9, 1940 German paratroopers land in Norway. It is the first airborne attack in history

Sep 1941–Jan 1944 The 900-day Siege of Leningrad by German forces results in over 1 million civilian deaths

Sep 7, 1940–May 16, 1941 Hitler bombs Britain's cities, in an offensive known as The Blitz

Jul 10–Sep 6, 1940 During the Battle of Britain, the Luftwaffe (German airforce) target airfields and ports along the English Channel

May–Jun 1940 335,000 British and French soldiers are evacuated from Dunkirk

Jun 14, 1940 German forces occupy Paris

Sep 1–27, 1939 Polish forces attempt to defend Warsaw but are outgunned

Sep 17, 1939 Soviet forces attack Poland from the east

1940 To Hungary

1940 To Bulgaria

Apr 6, 1941 Germany invades Yugoslavia, allowing it to attack, and ultimately seize, Greece

Oct 1940 Italy attacks Greece via Albania, which it had annexed in 1939, but the invasion fails

Jan 1941 Allied forces seize the key port of Tobruk from Italian forces

Sep 13, 1940 A second Italian offensive into British-occupied Egypt is a failure

ICELAND

Petsamo

Narvik

Faeroe Islands

Åndalsnes

Shetland Islands

North Sea

SWEDEN

NORWAY

Oslo

Stavanger

FINLAND

Helsinki

Suomussalmi

Leningrad

ESTONIA

LATVIA

LITHUANIA

Glasgow

Belfast

IRELAND

BRITAIN

Liverpool

Manchester Hull

Birmingham

Bristol Coventry

Plymouth

Southampton London

Dunkirk

NETHER-LANDS

Rotterdam

Copenhagen

DENMARK

Hamburg

Essen

Berlin

Danzig

Königsberg

EAST PRUSSIA

Wilno

BELGIUM GERMANY

Warsaw

POLAND

Kiev

Paris

Sedan

LUXEMBOURG

Prague

BOHEMIA AND MORAVIA

Cracow

Lwów

UKRAINE

Orléans

FRANCE

Munich

Linz

Vienna

SLOVAKIA

Bratislava

Budapest

HUNGARY

Vichy

SWITZERLAND

Lyon

AUSTRIA (OSTMARK)

Alps

Milan

VICHY FRANCE

Pyrenees

Marseille

Madrid

SPAIN

Balearic Islands

Corsica

Rome

Sardinia

ITALY

Zagreb

CROATIA

Sarajevo

Belgrade

YUGOSLAVIA

ROMANIA

Ploeşti

Bucharest

BULGARIA

Tirana

ALBANIA

GREECE

Istanbul

Aegean Sea

Ankara

SPANISH NORTH AFRICA

Atlas Mountains

MOROCCO ALGERIA

TUNISIA

Tunis

Sicily

Malta

Athens

Crete

Mediterranean Sea

Tripoli

LIBYA

Benghazi

El Agheila

Tobruk Sidi Barrani

Alexandria

Cairo

EGYPT

Nile

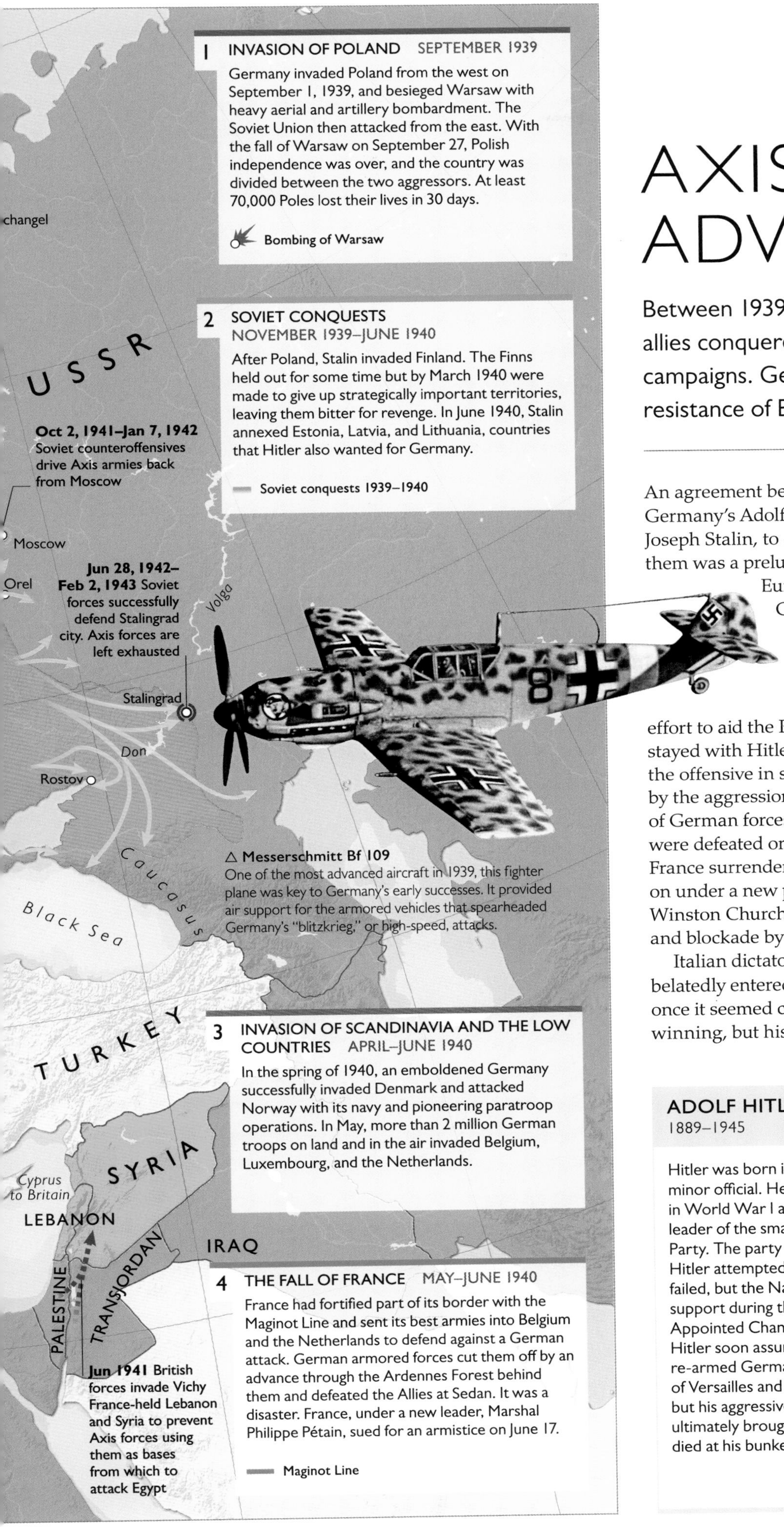

AXIS POWERS ADVANCE

Between 1939 and 1942, the armies of Nazi Germany and its Axis allies conquered most of mainland Europe in a series of lightning campaigns. Germany was denied total victory by the stubborn resistance of Britain and the Soviet Union.

An agreement between two dictators, Germany's Adolf Hitler and Soviet ruler Joseph Stalin, to divide Poland between them was a prelude to World War II in Europe. When the Germans invaded Poland, Britain and France declared war on Germany but made no practical effort to aid the Poles. The initiative stayed with Hitler, who again took the offensive in spring 1940. Outclassed by the aggression and professionalism of German forces, the Allied armies were defeated on the Western Front. France surrendered, but Britain fought on under a new prime minister, Winston Churchill, surviving air attack and blockade by German submarines.

Italian dictator Benito Mussolini belatedly entered the war in June 1940, once it seemed clear Germany was winning, but his forces were of lamentably poor quality. Hitler was drawn into fighting in the Mediterranean zone to save his ally from humiliating defeat by the British.

Hitler's long-term goal, however, had always been to establish the Germans as a master race controlling the Slav lands to the east, so in June 1941, he ordered the invasion of the Soviet Union. He was joined by his allies: Italy, the second Axis power; Finland, which had recently lost land to the Soviets in their conflict of 1939–1940; and Hungary, Romania, and Slovakia, whose right-wing governments became allied to the Axis powers and were pressured into joining the Soviet invasion. Despite further victories that saw his armies occupy vast tracts of Soviet territory, by the end of 1942, it seemed that Hitler had overreached himself. The era of German triumphs came to an end at the Battle of Stalingrad in 1943.

1 INVASION OF POLAND SEPTEMBER 1939

Germany invaded Poland from the west on September 1, 1939, and besieged Warsaw with heavy aerial and artillery bombardment. The Soviet Union then attacked from the east. With the fall of Warsaw on September 27, Polish independence was over, and the country was divided between the two aggressors. At least 70,000 Poles lost their lives in 30 days.

— Bombing of Warsaw

2 SOVIET CONQUESTS NOVEMBER 1939–JUNE 1940

After Poland, Stalin invaded Finland. The Finns held out for some time but by March 1940 were made to give up strategically important territories, leaving them bitter for revenge. In June 1940, Stalin annexed Estonia, Latvia, and Lithuania, countries that Hitler also wanted for Germany.

— Soviet conquests 1939–1940

Oct 2, 1941–Jan 7, 1942 Soviet counteroffensives drive Axis armies back from Moscow

Jun 28, 1942–Feb 2, 1943 Soviet forces successfully defend Stalingrad city. Axis forces are left exhausted

△ **Messerschmitt Bf 109**
One of the most advanced aircraft in 1939, this fighter plane was key to Germany's early successes. It provided air support for the armored vehicles that spearheaded Germany's "blitzkrieg," or high-speed, attacks.

3 INVASION OF SCANDINAVIA AND THE LOW COUNTRIES APRIL–JUNE 1940

In the spring of 1940, an emboldened Germany successfully invaded Denmark and attacked Norway with its navy and pioneering paratroop operations. In May, more than 2 million German troops on land and in the air invaded Belgium, Luxembourg, and the Netherlands.

Jun 1941 British forces invade Vichy France-held Lebanon and Syria to prevent Axis forces using them as bases from which to attack Egypt

4 THE FALL OF FRANCE MAY–JUNE 1940

France had fortified part of its border with the Maginot Line and sent its best armies into Belgium and the Netherlands to defend against a German attack. German armored forces cut them off by an advance through the Ardennes Forest behind them and defeated the Allies at Sedan. It was a disaster. France, under a new leader, Marshal Philippe Pétain, sued for an armistice on June 17.

— Maginot Line

ADOLF HITLER
1889–1945

Hitler was born in Austria, the son of a minor official. He fought in the German army in World War I and after the war became leader of the small National Socialist (Nazi) Party. The party came to prominence after Hitler attempted a coup in 1923; the coup failed, but the Nazis went on to attract mass support during the Great Depression. Appointed Chancellor of Germany in 1933, Hitler soon assumed dictatorial powers. He re-armed Germany in defiance of the Treaty of Versailles and set out to dominate Europe, but his aggressive policies led to a war that ultimately brought disaster to Germany. He died at his bunker in Berlin in April 1945.

1 GHETTOS 1939–1942

Under Nazi occupation, Jewish people living in small towns and villages were transferred to ghettos set up within the cities. The Nazis established more than 1,000 ghettos in Poland and the Soviet Union alone. Starvation and disease were rife due to food shortages and poor sanitation. In 1942, after the Nazis decided to kill the Jews, the Germans destroyed many of the ghettos and deported the Jews to death camps.

✡ Ghettos

2 POLITICAL CONTROL 1939–1945

Nazi Germany persuaded Hungary, Romania, and Bulgaria to accede to the Tripartite Pact as Axis allies. In Slovakia, Norway, and Croatia, puppet regimes were installed—these countries had their own government but with restricted autonomy and Nazi commissioners in residence. In unoccupied France, the Vichy regime was forced to accept the terms of a German-imposed armistice.

🏯 Puppet regimes

3 LABOR CONSCRIPTION 1940–1945

In all the countries occupied, Germany controlled labor and industry for its war effort; the free deployment of labor was prohibited. Laborers were issued with workbooks and either worked in plants in the occupied countries or were sent to Germany. By the end of 1944, about 8.2 million foreign civilians and prisoners of war, as well as 700,000 concentration camp prisoners, were workers in the German Reich.

✗ Forced labor conscription

7 EXTERMINATION CAMPS 1942–1945

Dedicated death camps did not come into operation until 1942, when the Nazis implemented a policy to exterminate the Jews of Europe. Most victims were killed immediately upon their arrival, in the gas chambers, but a minority were kept as slave labor. Roma people, communists, homosexuals, and other "undesirables" were included in the mass murder.

☠ Extermination camps

6 MASS KILLINGS 1941–1943

During the invasion of the Soviet Union, the Nazis deliberately slaughtered large groups of Jews. Einsatzgruppen (mobile killing units) followed the German army as it advanced; they went directly to the home communities of Jews and massacred them. Other massacres, such as Kragujevac in Serbia and Lidice in Bohemia-Moravia, were carried out as reprisals for the killing of Nazi officials by local resistance fighters.

☠ Site and date of massacre

5 CONCENTRATION CAMPS 1933–1945

The Nazis established concentration camps in Germany on coming to power in 1933. Designed for the imprisonment of enemies of the state, concentration camps were not initially set up to kill, but victims died by starvation and physical exhaustion. Some of these camps were later converted into extermination camps, such as Majdanek in Poland, which was originally built for Soviet prisoners of war.

☠ Concentration camps

Feb 1942 Vidkun Quisling, a Norwegian Nazi, is installed as head of a puppet regime. His name becomes synonymous with "traitor"

Oct 1939 The first ghetto in Poland is established

1941 More than 20,000 Dutch people die of starvation after farmers are forced to hand over produce to Germany

Dec 1941 First death camp opens at Chelmno

Nov 30 and Dec 8–9, 1941 At least 26,000 Jews are shot by German killing squads

1941 Riga

1943 Kaunas

1943 Khatyn

1940–1944 Eighty percent of Belgian children suffer rickets due to malnutrition

1940 Luxembourg is absorbed into Germany

1942 Lidice

Jun 1944 More than 220,000 Jews are expelled from their homes in Budapest

1941 Babi Yar (Kiev)

Sep 29–30, 1941 More than 30,000 Ukrainian Jews are shot in Babi Yar ravine

Jun 22, 1940 France signs an armistice that preserves a degree of sovereignty in unoccupied southern France, until Germany takes full control in November 1942 after losses in French North Africa

1933 First concentration camp is built at Dachau

1941 Kragujevac

Oct 20, 1941 2,300 Serbian males are executed at Kragujevac

Apr 1941 An anti-Axis coup in Yugoslavia prompts Germany to invade the country and set up the "Independent State of Croatia" as a puppet

1941–1944 Greece is plundered for the German war machine, and supplies are blocked by the British. An estimated 300,000 die of starvation by the end of the war

ATLANTIC OCEAN

IRELAND — Dublin

BRITAIN — London

NETHERLANDS

BELGIUM — Drancy, Paris

OCCUPIED FRANCE

FRANCE — Vichy, Bordeaux

VICHY FRANCE — Marseille, Toulon

SPAIN

PORTUGAL

NORWAY — Oslo

SWEDEN — Stockholm

DENMARK — Copenhagen

FINLAND — Helsinki

KARELIA

Leningrad

Baltic Sea

REICHSKOMMISSARIAT OSTLAND — Jungerhof, Minsk, Maly Trostinets, Bialystok

NORD

REICHSKOMMISSARIAT UKRAINE

GERMANY — Hamburg, Bergen Belsen, Ravensbruck, Sachsenhausen, Essen, Berlin, Buchenwald, Flossenburg, Dachau, Munich

SUDETENLAND

POLAND — Warsaw, Chelmno, Treblinka, Lublin, Gross-Rosen, Majdanek, Sobibor, Belzec, Lwów, Cracow, Auschwitz-Birkenau

Luxembourg

Theresienstadt

BOHEMIA AND MORAVIA

SLOVAKIA — Bratislava

AUSTRIA (OSTMARK) — Vienna, Mauthausen

HUNGARY — Budapest

Bozen, Trieste, Milan, Fossoli

ITALY — Rome

Corsica, Sardinia, Sicily

SWITZERLAND

CROATIA, YUGOSLAVIA

SERBIA — Belgrade, Zagreb

MONTENEGRO — Sofia

ROMANIA — Bucharest

BULGARIA

DEMOTIKA

ALBANIA — Tirane

SALONIKA

GREECE — Athens

Mediterranean Sea

FRENCH NORTH AFRICA

MALTA

Dodecanese Islands

Crete

THE GREATER GERMAN REICH

By 1942, the Axis powers and their satellites dominated Europe. Germany and Italy placed some regions under military occupation, while others were absorbed to create the "Greater German Reich."

KEY

- Greater German Reich 1942
- Areas occupied by Germany and Finland
- Italy and areas occupied by Italy
- Axis satellites
- Temporary Axis satellite
- Allied territories

TIMELINE

1
2
3
4
5
6
7

1932 1934 1936 1938 1940 1942 1944 1946

Moscow

MITTE

1941 Kharkov

U S S R

Stalingrad

SÜD

△ **Holocaust survivors**
The Soviet army discovered the Nazi death camps as they advanced through eastern Europe in 1944–1945, including Auschwitz-Birkenau in southern Poland, where the children in this photo were found.

1941–1944 Approximately 2.6 million Soviet prisoners die of starvation and disease in German captivity. The people of occupied USSR are forced to eat dogs and rats and cook their food in paraffin

Caucasus

Black Sea

TURKEY

4 THE BATTLE FOR FOOD 1940–1945

At least 20 million people died of starvation during World War II. Hitler sought to create a Reich that was self-sufficient and independent of world trade. He regarded the whole of Eastern Europe as an industrial site and a food source and was prepared to let its people starve in his pursuit of Lebensraum (living space) for German-speaking peoples. In other parts of Europe, Jews and non-Germans were starved, either by deliberate German policy or by Allied blockades.

SYRIA

Major food shortages

Cyprus

OCCUPIED EUROPE

The Axis occupation of a large area of Europe in World War II brought hardship or death to many millions of the continent's inhabitants. The brutal experience of Nazi rule, and resistance to it, had profound effects on European politics and society.

The German victories early in the war were met with a mixed response in the defeated nations. In all countries, there were both anti-Nazi resistance fighters and also collaborators—those who accepted defeat and sought a role in the new German-dominated Europe. In some places, such as Croatia, Lithuania, and Ukraine, the Nazis were initially welcomed as liberators. The French government, based at Vichy, was a willing collaborator for the Germans.

Some German officials dreamed of a New Order in which all of Europe would flourish under German leadership, but Nazi leader Adolf Hitler was interested only in domination and exploitation. In practice, the Nazis simply plundered the conquered countries for their resources of food and labor, treating collaborators with contempt and suppressing opposition with terror. The worst suffering was in eastern Europe, where Hitler planned to reduce the Slavic peoples to servile status and colonize the land with German settlers in order to achieve his ultimate goal of gaining more Lebensraum (living space) for German-speaking peoples. Germany's borders were expanded and redrawn to create the Greater German Reich (realm). One-fifth of Poland's people were killed during the war, including most of its Jewish population. The only check to the Nazis' extermination of the Jews of Europe was their need to keep Jewish prisoners alive for use as slave labor.

ARMED RESISTANCE
1940 ONWARD

The hardships of life under Nazi rule inspired armed resistance movements, backed by the Allies. The largest of these forces fought in Poland, Yugoslavia, the western Soviet Union, and northern Italy after German occupation in 1943. Communists played a leading role, and in some places, notably Yugoslavia, there was bitter conflict between communist and noncommunist resistance fighters. Armed resistance in France was limited in scale but essential to French pride.

Russian resistance
Women and girls in the occupied western Soviet Union practice shooting guns in a trench in order to defend themselves.

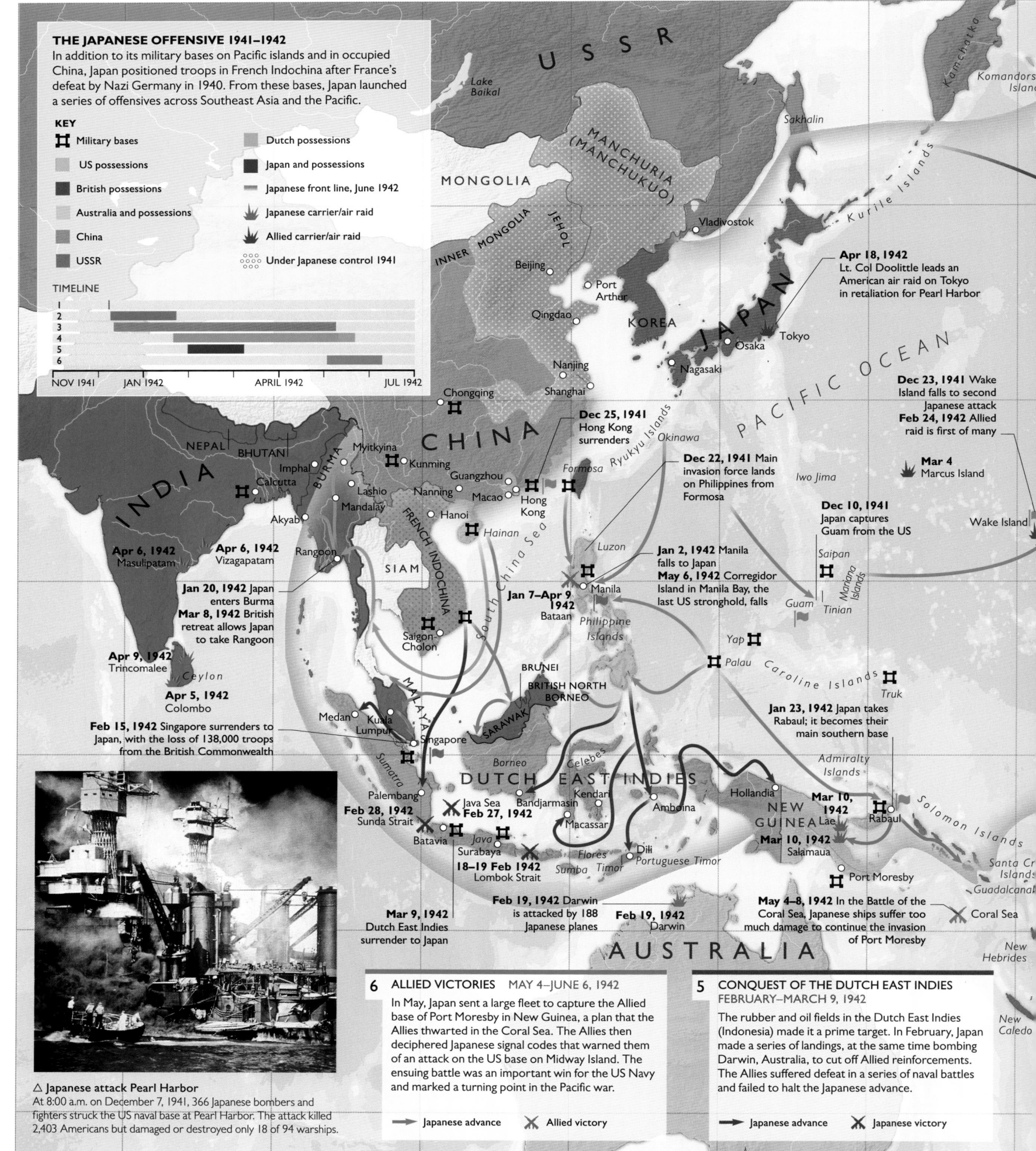

THE JAPANESE OFFENSIVE 1941–1942

In addition to its military bases on Pacific islands and in occupied China, Japan positioned troops in French Indochina after France's defeat by Nazi Germany in 1940. From these bases, Japan launched a series of offensives across Southeast Asia and the Pacific.

KEY

- ✪ Military bases
- US possessions
- British possessions
- Australia and possessions
- China
- USSR
- Dutch possessions
- Japan and possessions
- Japanese front line, June 1942
- Japanese carrier/air raid
- Allied carrier/air raid
- Under Japanese control 1941

TIMELINE

NOV 1941   JAN 1942   APRIL 1942   JUL 1942

Apr 18, 1942 Lt. Col Doolittle leads an American air raid on Tokyo in retaliation for Pearl Harbor

Dec 23, 1941 Wake Island falls to second Japanese attack
Feb 24, 1942 Allied raid is first of many

Mar 4 Marcus Island

Dec 22, 1941 Main invasion force lands on Philippines from Formosa

Dec 10, 1941 Japan captures Guam from the US

Apr 6, 1942 Masulipatam
Apr 6, 1942 Vizagapatam

Jan 20, 1942 Japan enters Burma
Mar 8, 1942 British retreat allows Japan to take Rangoon

Apr 9, 1942 Trincomalee

Apr 5, 1942 Colombo

Feb 15, 1942 Singapore surrenders to Japan, with the loss of 138,000 troops from the British Commonwealth

Jan 2, 1942 Manila falls to Japan
May 6, 1942 Corregidor Island in Manila Bay, the last US stronghold, falls

Jan 7–Apr 9 1942 Bataan

Jan 23, 1942 Japan takes Rabaul; it becomes their main southern base

Mar 10, 1942 Lae

Mar 10, 1942 Salamaua

Feb 28, 1942 Sunda Strait
Feb 27, 1942 Java Sea

18–19 Feb 1942 Lombok Strait

Feb 19, 1942 Darwin is attacked by 188 Japanese planes

Feb 19, 1942 Darwin

Mar 9, 1942 Dutch East Indies surrender to Japan

May 4–8, 1942 In the Battle of the Coral Sea, Japanese ships suffer too much damage to continue the invasion of Port Moresby

---

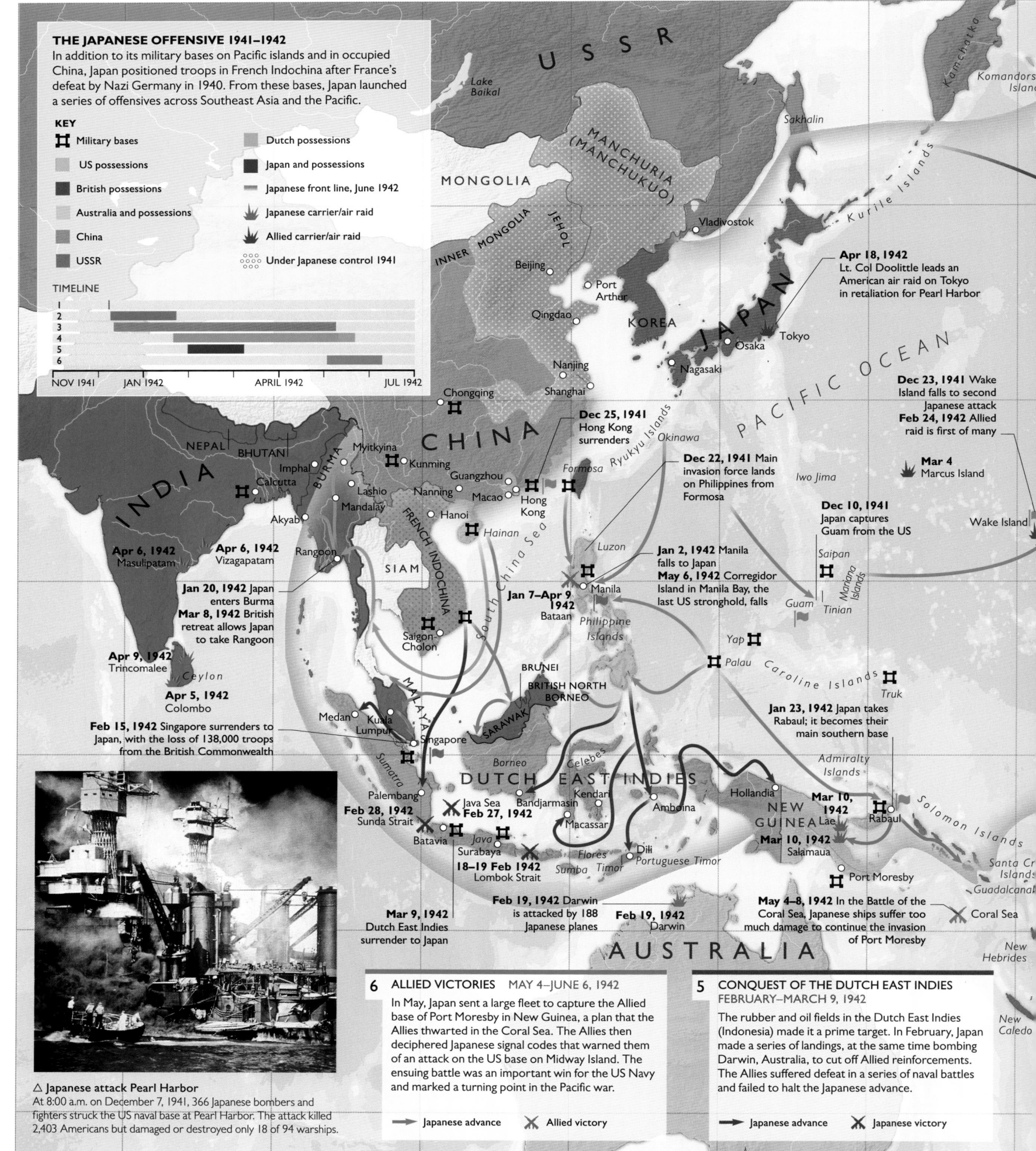

△ **Japanese attack Pearl Harbor**
At 8:00 a.m. on December 7, 1941, 366 Japanese bombers and fighters struck the US naval base at Pearl Harbor. The attack killed 2,403 Americans but damaged or destroyed only 18 of 94 warships.

---

6 ALLIED VICTORIES MAY 4–JUNE 6, 1942

In May, Japan sent a large fleet to capture the Allied base of Port Moresby in New Guinea, a plan that the Allies thwarted in the Coral Sea. The Allies then deciphered Japanese signal codes that warned them of an attack on the US base on Midway Island. The ensuing battle was an important win for the US Navy and marked a turning point in the Pacific war.

→ Japanese advance   ✕ Allied victory

5 CONQUEST OF THE DUTCH EAST INDIES
FEBRUARY–MARCH 9, 1942

The rubber and oil fields in the Dutch East Indies (Indonesia) made it a prime target. In February, Japan made a series of landings, at the same time bombing Darwin, Australia, to cut off Allied reinforcements. The Allies suffered defeat in a series of naval battles and failed to halt the Japanese advance.

→ Japanese advance   ✕ Japanese victory

Jun 6–7, 1942 The Japanese take Attu and Kiska in the Aleutian Islands off Alaska, the only American soil they occupied

Aleutian Islands ⌗ Dutch Harbor

ttu *Kiska*

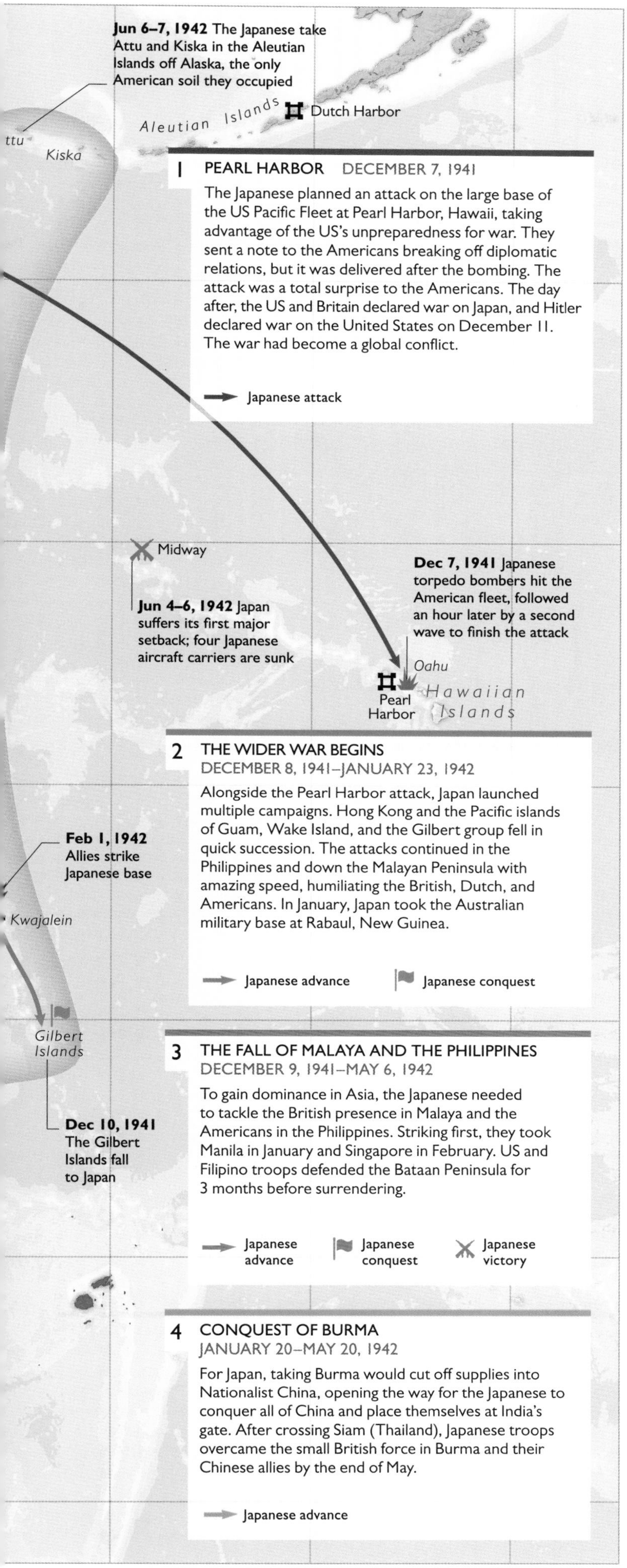

1 PEARL HARBOR   DECEMBER 7, 1941

The Japanese planned an attack on the large base of the US Pacific Fleet at Pearl Harbor, Hawaii, taking advantage of the US's unpreparedness for war. They sent a note to the Americans breaking off diplomatic relations, but it was delivered after the bombing. The attack was a total surprise to the Americans. The day after, the US and Britain declared war on Japan, and Hitler declared war on the United States on December 11. The war had become a global conflict.

→ Japanese attack

✕ Midway

Dec 7, 1941 Japanese torpedo bombers hit the American fleet, followed an hour later by a second wave to finish the attack

Jun 4–6, 1942 Japan suffers its first major setback; four Japanese aircraft carriers are sunk

Oahu
⌗ *Hawaiian*
Pearl *Islands*
Harbor

2 THE WIDER WAR BEGINS
DECEMBER 8, 1941–JANUARY 23, 1942

Alongside the Pearl Harbor attack, Japan launched multiple campaigns. Hong Kong and the Pacific islands of Guam, Wake Island, and the Gilbert group fell in quick succession. The attacks continued in the Philippines and down the Malayan Peninsula with amazing speed, humiliating the British, Dutch, and Americans. In January, Japan took the Australian military base at Rabaul, New Guinea.

Feb 1, 1942 Allies strike Japanese base

Kwajalein

→ Japanese advance   ⚑ Japanese conquest

Gilbert Islands

3 THE FALL OF MALAYA AND THE PHILIPPINES
DECEMBER 9, 1941–MAY 6, 1942

To gain dominance in Asia, the Japanese needed to tackle the British presence in Malaya and the Americans in the Philippines. Striking first, they took Manila in January and Singapore in February. US and Filipino troops defended the Bataan Peninsula for 3 months before surrendering.

Dec 10, 1941 The Gilbert Islands fall to Japan

→ Japanese advance   ⚑ Japanese conquest   ✕ Japanese victory

4 CONQUEST OF BURMA
JANUARY 20–MAY 20, 1942

For Japan, taking Burma would cut off supplies into Nationalist China, opening the way for the Japanese to conquer all of China and place themselves at India's gate. After crossing Siam (Thailand), Japanese troops overcame the small British force in Burma and their Chinese allies by the end of May.

→ Japanese advance

THE WAR IN THE PACIFIC

In 1931, Japan began a project to establish an extensive empire in Asia by occupying northeast China, then launching a full-scale invasion of the country in 1937. This brought Japan into conflict with the United States and the European colonial powers in the region and, in 1941, the war extended to Southeast Asia and the Pacific.

Throughout 1941, the United States tried to force Japan to abandon its invasion of China (see pp.288–289) using a policy of economic blockade. The Japanese responded with a risky plan for a wider war. Their attack on the American naval base at Pearl Harbor, Hawaii, was designed to cripple the US Pacific Fleet, leaving the Japanese Imperial Navy in command of the ocean while the Japanese army conquered Southeast Asia, the source of raw materials such as rubber and oil. Initially, the plan worked brilliantly, but the "sneak attack" on Pearl Harbor created such outrage in the US that any future compromise or peace based on acceptance of Japanese domination of Asia became inconceivable. The US entered World War II as a result.

Although Nazi Germany declared war on the United States in support of Japan, the conflicts in the Pacific and Europe remained essentially separate. Japan's defeat of the European colonial powers in Southeast Asia, especially the fall of British Singapore, was a fatal blow to white racial prestige in Asia. But the Japanese proved exploitative rulers and won little support from other Asian peoples in their "Co-Prosperity Sphere." American victory in the naval battle of Midway in June 1942 marked the end of the period of rapid Japanese expansion.

"Before we're through with them, the Japanese language will be spoken only in hell."

US VICE ADMIRAL HALSEY ON THE PEARL HARBOR ATTACK, 1941

GENERAL DOUGLAS MACARTHUR
1880–1964

When he was appointed US Army Commander in Southeast Asia in 1941, Douglas MacArthur already had a distinguished military career behind him, including service in World War I and a spell as US Chief of Staff. Forced to evacuate the Philippines in 1942, he famously promised "I shall return," a promise he kept in 1944. As Allied supreme commander, he received the Japanese surrender in 1945 (see pp.302–303) and played a leading role in Japan's postwar political reconstruction. Commanding UN forces in the Korean War (see pp.316–317) from 1950, MacArthur quarreled with US government policy and President Truman relieved him of his duties in 1951.

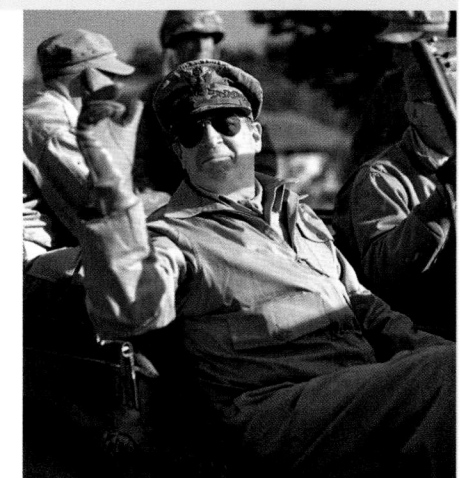

GERMANY DEFEATED

Confronted by the combined strength of the US, the Soviet Union, and Britain, Germany was overwhelmed in the later stages of World War II. The scale of destruction mounted through the war, leaving Europe a continent of ruins and refugees.

The tide of war turned decisively against Nazi Germany and its Axis allies in the course of 1943. On the Eastern Front, Soviet armies, victorious at Stalingrad (see pp.296–297), began an unstoppable advance westward that would eventually carry them all the way to Berlin. In the Atlantic, the menace of German U-boats was overcome after years of heavy losses of shipping. US troops entered the war against Germany by landing in North Africa. Meeting up with the British in Tunisia, they crossed the Mediterranean to invade Sicily and Italy, bringing about the downfall of Germany's ally Benito Mussolini. But Nazi leader Adolf Hitler remained defiant even after the Western Allies invaded Normandy, France, in summer 1944. Surviving an attempted assassination, Hitler led a fight to the finish. The alliance between the Western powers and the Soviet Union held firm in pursuit of unconditional surrender. After a hard-fought struggle for command of the air, the US and British air forces devastated German cities. In spring 1945, Allied troops, invading Germany from east and west, took possession of a ruined country as Hitler committed suicide in his Berlin bunker.

"We have a new experience. We have victory—a remarkable and definite victory."

WINSTON CHURCHILL, ON EL ALAMEIN VICTORY, 1942

WINSTON CHURCHILL
1874–1965

In May 1940, maverick Conservative politician Winston Churchill took power in Britain at the head of a coalition government. His rousing speeches and fighting spirit sustained morale in Britain, and he worked tirelessly to maintain good relations with his fellow Allied powers, the US and the Soviet Union, during World War II. He was voted out of office in an election 2 months after victory in Europe in 1945.

THE ALLIED INVASION OF EUROPE 1942–1945

Victories in North Africa in 1942 provided the Allies with a base from which to invade Italy in 1943. The following year, the Western Allies began an offensive in western Europe while the Soviet army attacked from the east, closing in on Germany.

KEY

AXIS
- Under Axis control by 1942
- German offensive from 1942
- Areas occupied by Germany by Nov 1942
- Axis satellites

ALLIES
- Allied territory 1942
- Allied offensive 1942–1943
- Allied offensive 1944
- Allied offensive 1945
- Allied victory

TIMELINE

1 2 3 4 5 6

1941 1942 1943 1944 1945 1946

6 GERMANY ON THE ROPES MAR–MAY 1945

In the last months of the war, despite tough resistance, Germany suffered only defeats. US troops crossed the Rhine into Germany in March 1945 and proceeded to capture Hanover and Nuremberg. Meanwhile, Soviet forces launched a huge offensive through Poland and eventually captured Berlin on April 30.

5 INVASION OF NORMANDY JUN–JUL 1944

On June 6, 1944, the Allies invaded northern France in what was the largest amphibious attack in history. Five Allied divisions landed on five French beaches, but progress was slow because of thick hedgerows and a fierce German defense. With this invasion, the Allies forced Hitler to fight on two fronts: in both western and eastern Europe.

→ D-Day landings

4 STRATEGIC BOMBING 1944–1945

During 1944, the bombing of German cities became a significant strategy for the Allies. Attacks on oil supplies and oil fields devastated the German war effort. Some 400,000 German civilians were killed and many cities annihilated. Hitler responded by firing V-1 cruise missiles and V-2 rockets on London.

- Cities severely bombed by Allies
- City severely bombed by Germans

May 24, 1943 Admiral Dönitz withdraws German U-boats from the North Atlantic after huge losses

Nov 1942 Allied forces make landings in Morocco and Algeria as part of Operation Torch, a campaign to take control of North Africa

ATLANTIC OCEAN

PORTUGAL

Lisbon

Gibraltar to Britain

Casablanca

MOROCCO

◁ **D-Day landings**
A US landing craft approaches Omaha Beach in Normandy, France, on June 6, 1944. Although the Allied invasion succeeded, nearly 3,000 US soldiers were killed or injured during the landing.

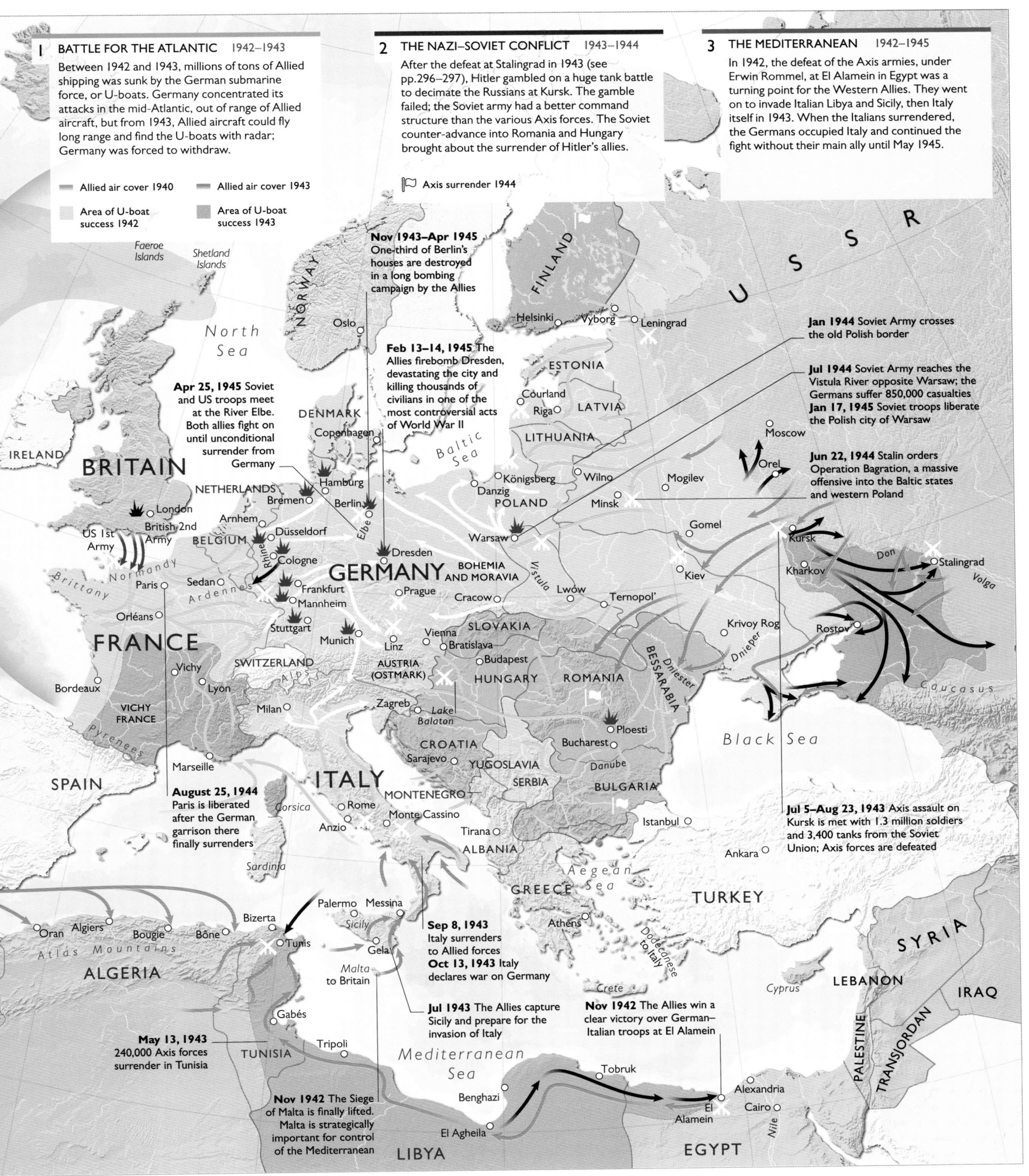

1 BATTLE FOR THE ATLANTIC 1942–1943

Between 1942 and 1943, millions of tons of Allied shipping was sunk by the German submarine force, or U-boats. Germany concentrated its attacks in the mid-Atlantic, out of range of Allied aircraft, but from 1943, Allied aircraft could fly long range and find the U-boats with radar; Germany was forced to withdraw.

— Allied air cover 1940   — Allied air cover 1943

Area of U-boat success 1942   Area of U-boat success 1943

2 THE NAZI–SOVIET CONFLICT 1943–1944

After the defeat at Stalingrad in 1943 (see pp.296–297), Hitler gambled on a huge tank battle to decimate the Russians at Kursk. The gamble failed; the Soviet army had a better command structure than the various Axis forces. The Soviet counter-advance into Romania and Hungary brought about the surrender of Hitler's allies.

🏴 Axis surrender 1944

3 THE MEDITERRANEAN 1942–1945

In 1942, the defeat of the Axis armies, under Erwin Rommel, at El Alamein in Egypt was a turning point for the Western Allies. They went on to invade Italian Libya and Sicily, then Italy itself in 1943. When the Italians surrendered, the Germans occupied Italy and continued the fight without their main ally until May 1945.

Nov 1943–Apr 1945 One-third of Berlin's houses are destroyed in a long bombing campaign by the Allies

Feb 13–14, 1945 The Allies firebomb Dresden, devastating the city and killing thousands of civilians in one of the most controversial acts of World War II

Apr 25, 1945 Soviet and US troops meet at the River Elbe. Both allies fight on until unconditional surrender from Germany

Jan 1944 Soviet Army crosses the old Polish border

Jul 1944 Soviet Army reaches the Vistula River opposite Warsaw; the Germans suffer 850,000 casualties

Jan 17, 1945 Soviet troops liberate the Polish city of Warsaw

Jun 22, 1944 Stalin orders Operation Bagration, a massive offensive into the Baltic states and western Poland

August 25, 1944 Paris is liberated after the German garrison there finally surrenders

Jul 5–Aug 23, 1943 Axis assault on Kursk is met with 1.3 million soldiers and 3,400 tanks from the Soviet Union; Axis forces are defeated

Sep 8, 1943 Italy surrenders to Allied forces

Oct 13, 1943 Italy declares war on Germany

Jul 1943 The Allies capture Sicily and prepare for the invasion of Italy

Nov 1942 The Allies win a clear victory over German–Italian troops at El Alamein

May 13, 1943 240,000 Axis forces surrender in Tunisia

Nov 1942 The Siege of Malta is finally lifted. Malta is strategically important for control of the Mediterranean

Faeroe Islands — Shetland Islands — NORWAY — North Sea — Oslo — DENMARK — Copenhagen — Baltic Sea — FINLAND — Helsinki — Vyborg — Leningrad — ESTONIA — Courland — Riga — LATVIA — LITHUANIA — Moscow — Königsberg — Wilno — Mogilev — U S S R — Orel — IRELAND — BRITAIN — London — British 2nd Army — US 1st Army — Normandy — Brittany — Paris — Sedan — Ardennes — Orléans — FRANCE — Hamburg — Bremen — Berlin — Arnhem — NETHERLANDS — BELGIUM — Düsseldorf — Cologne — Rhine — Elbe — Dresden — GERMANY — Frankfurt — Mannheim — Stuttgart — Munich — Linz — Prague — BOHEMIA AND MORAVIA — Danzig — POLAND — Warsaw — Vistula — Minsk — Gomel — Kiev — Kursk — Kharkov — Don — Stalingrad — Volga — Krivoy Rog — Rostov — Dnieper — Caucasus — Lwów — Ternopol' — Cracow — SLOVAKIA — Vienna — Bratislava — Budapest — AUSTRIA (OSTMARK) — HUNGARY — ROMANIA — BESSARABIA — Dniester — Black Sea — Vichy — Lyon — SWITZERLAND — Alps — Bordeaux — VICHY FRANCE — Pyrenees — Milan — Zagreb — Lake Balaton — CROATIA — Sarajevo — YUGOSLAVIA — SERBIA — Ploesti — Bucharest — Danube — BULGARIA — Istanbul — Ankara — TURKEY — SPAIN — Marseille — Corsica — ITALY — Rome — Anzio — MONTENEGRO — Monte Cassino — Tirana — ALBANIA — Sardinia — GREECE — Aegean Sea — Athens — Dodecanese to Italy — Palermo — Messina — Sicily — Gela — Oran — Algiers — Bougie — Bône — Bizerta — Tunis — Malta to Britain — Crete — Cyprus — LEBANON — SYRIA — IRAQ — Atlas Mountains — ALGERIA — Gabés — TUNISIA — Tripoli — Mediterranean Sea — Benghazi — El Agheila — LIBYA — Tobruk — El Alamein — Alexandria — Cairo — Nile — EGYPT — PALESTINE — TRANSJORDAN

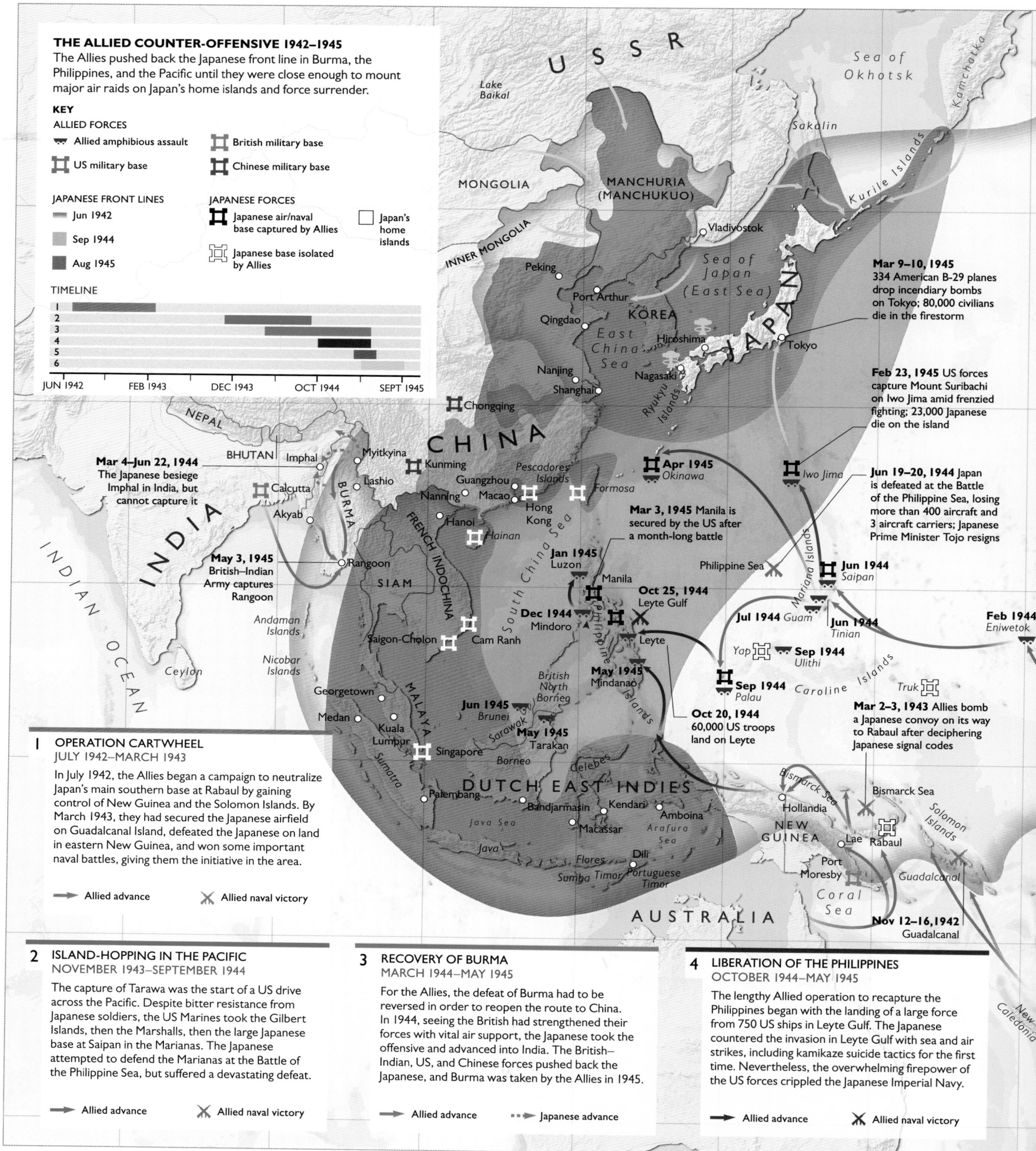

THE ALLIED COUNTER-OFFENSIVE 1942–1945
The Allies pushed back the Japanese front line in Burma, the Philippines, and the Pacific until they were close enough to mount major air raids on Japan's home islands and force surrender.

KEY

ALLIED FORCES
- Allied amphibious assault
- US military base
- British military base
- Chinese military base

JAPANESE FRONT LINES
- Jun 1942
- Sep 1944
- Aug 1945

JAPANESE FORCES
- Japanese air/naval base captured by Allies
- Japanese base isolated by Allies
- Japan's home islands

TIMELINE
1
2
3
4
5
6
JUN 1942   FEB 1943   DEC 1943   OCT 1944   SEPT 1945

Mar 9–10, 1945 334 American B-29 planes drop incendiary bombs on Tokyo; 80,000 civilians die in the firestorm

Feb 23, 1945 US forces capture Mount Suribachi on Iwo Jima amid frenzied fighting; 23,000 Japanese die on the island

Jun 19–20, 1944 Japan is defeated at the Battle of the Philippine Sea, losing more than 400 aircraft and 3 aircraft carriers; Japanese Prime Minister Tojo resigns

Mar 4–Jun 22, 1944 The Japanese besiege Imphal in India, but cannot capture it

May 3, 1945 British–Indian Army captures Rangoon

Mar 3, 1945 Manila is secured by the US after a month-long battle

Jan 1945 Luzon

Oct 25, 1944 Leyte Gulf

Jun 1944 Saipan

Jul 1944 Guam

Jun 1944 Tinian

Feb 1944 Eniwetok

Dec 1944 Mindoro

Sep 1944 Ulithi

Jun 1945 Brunei

May 1945 Tarakan

May 1945 Mindanao

Sep 1944 Palau

Oct 20, 1944 60,000 US troops land on Leyte

Mar 2–3, 1943 Allies bomb a Japanese convoy on its way to Rabaul after deciphering Japanese signal codes

Nov 12–16, 1942 Guadalcanal

1 OPERATION CARTWHEEL
JULY 1942–MARCH 1943

In July 1942, the Allies began a campaign to neutralize Japan's main southern base at Rabaul by gaining control of New Guinea and the Solomon Islands. By March 1943, they had secured the Japanese airfield on Guadalcanal Island, defeated the Japanese on land in eastern New Guinea, and won some important naval battles, giving them the initiative in the area.

→ Allied advance   ✕ Allied naval victory

2 ISLAND-HOPPING IN THE PACIFIC
NOVEMBER 1943–SEPTEMBER 1944

The capture of Tarawa was the start of a US drive across the Pacific. Despite bitter resistance from Japanese soldiers, the US Marines took the Gilbert Islands, then the Marshalls, then the large Japanese base at Saipan in the Marianas. The Japanese attempted to defend the Marianas at the Battle of the Philippine Sea, but suffered a devastating defeat.

→ Allied advance   ✕ Allied naval victory

3 RECOVERY OF BURMA
MARCH 1944–MAY 1945

For the Allies, the defeat of Burma had to be reversed in order to reopen the route to China. In 1944, seeing the British had strengthened their forces with vital air support, the Japanese took the offensive and advanced into India. The British–Indian, US, and Chinese forces pushed back the Japanese, and Burma was taken by the Allies in 1945.

→ Allied advance   ⇢ Japanese advance

4 LIBERATION OF THE PHILIPPINES
OCTOBER 1944–MAY 1945

The lengthy Allied operation to recapture the Philippines began with the landing of a large force from 750 US ships in Leyte Gulf. The Japanese countered the invasion in Leyte Gulf with sea and air strikes, including kamikaze suicide tactics for the first time. Nevertheless, the overwhelming firepower of the US forces crippled the Japanese Imperial Navy.

→ Allied advance   ✕ Allied naval victory

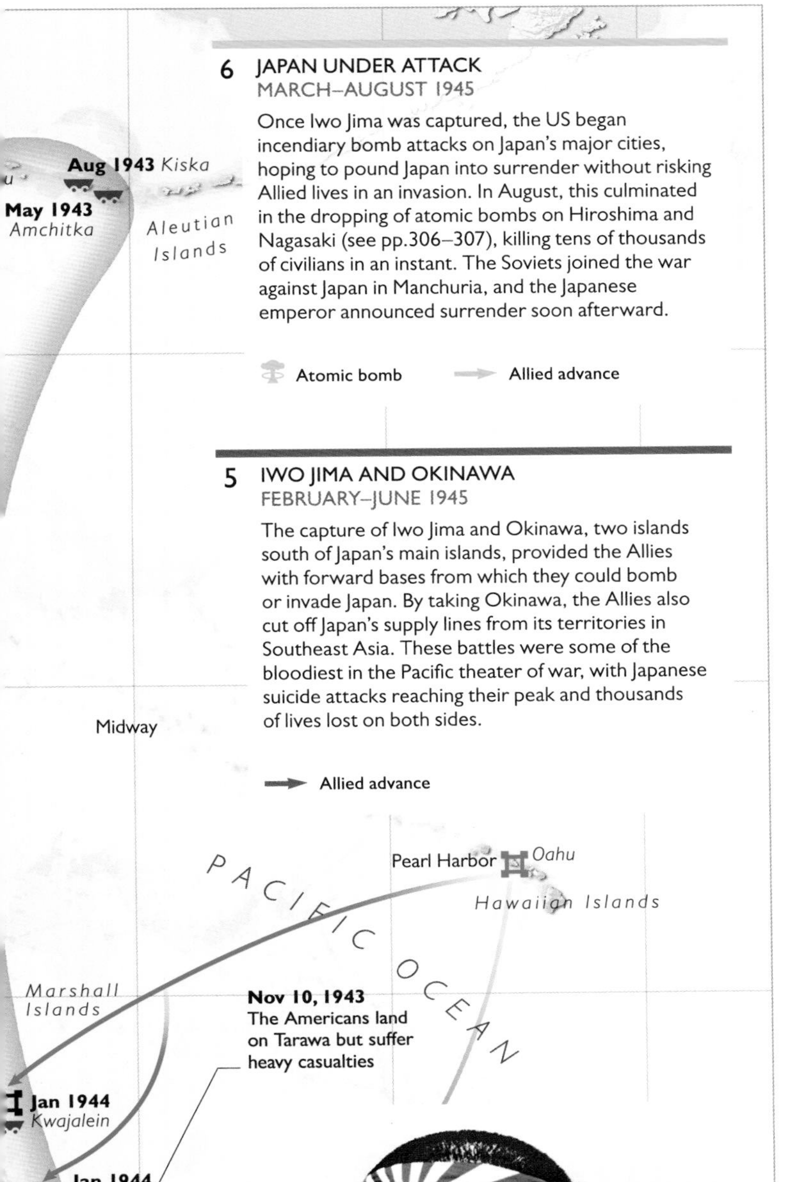

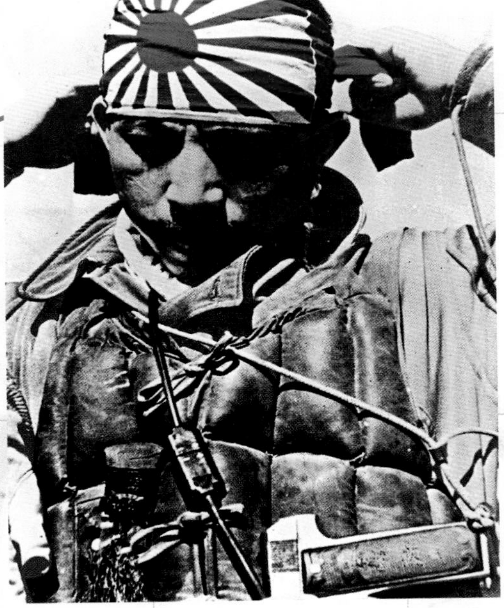

Aug 1943 Kiska
May 1943 Amchitka
Aleutian Islands
Midway
Pearl Harbor
Oahu
Hawaiian Islands
PACIFIC OCEAN
Marshall Islands
Nov 10, 1943
The Americans land on Tarawa but suffer heavy casualties
Jan 1944 Kwajalein
Jan 1944 Majuro
Tarawa
Nov 1943
Gilbert Islands

6 JAPAN UNDER ATTACK
MARCH–AUGUST 1945

Once Iwo Jima was captured, the US began incendiary bomb attacks on Japan's major cities, hoping to pound Japan into surrender without risking Allied lives in an invasion. In August, this culminated in the dropping of atomic bombs on Hiroshima and Nagasaki (see pp.306–307), killing tens of thousands of civilians in an instant. The Soviets joined the war against Japan in Manchuria, and the Japanese emperor announced surrender soon afterward.

Atomic bomb — Allied advance

5 IWO JIMA AND OKINAWA
FEBRUARY–JUNE 1945

The capture of Iwo Jima and Okinawa, two islands south of Japan's main islands, provided the Allies with forward bases from which they could bomb or invade Japan. By taking Okinawa, the Allies also cut off Japan's supply lines from its territories in Southeast Asia. These battles were some of the bloodiest in the Pacific theater of war, with Japanese suicide attacks reaching their peak and thousands of lives lost on both sides.

Allied advance

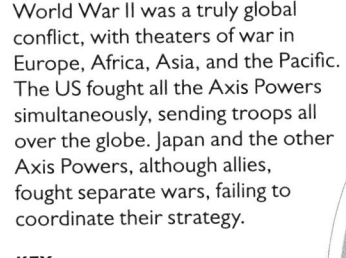

△ **Kamikaze pilot**
A Japanese pilot prepares for a suicide mission by donning a headband bearing the ensign of the Japanese Imperial Navy. Committed to the idea of "victory or death," Japanese men volunteered to crash aircraft loaded with explosives deliberately into enemy targets.

JAPAN DEFEATED

Mobilizing its superior industrial resources and manpower, the United States overcame extremely determined Japanese resistance in a series of fierce battles in the Pacific from 1942 to 1945. Japan's cities were laid waste by American bombing, and its imperial government was forced to sign a humiliating surrender.

By mid-1942, Japan had established a far-flung defensive perimeter in the Pacific to protect its conquests in Asia. Hard fighting continued in China and Burma, but the outcome of the war was decided by an American thrust "island-hopping" across the Pacific, bringing the US within reach of Japan itself. A massive American shipbuilding program created a powerful fleet of aircraft carriers, while the US Marines developed an unprecedented expertise in seaborne landings. From Tawara to Okinawa, each island was defended by Japanese soldiers to the last man, but the Japanese Imperial Navy was destroyed in a series of large-scale sea battles. Outclassed Japanese aviators were compelled to use "kamikaze" suicide tactics to attack the American fleet, but with limited effect.

By the summer of 1945, it was clear that Japan had lost the war. The Japanese government was split between those who wanted to fight to the death and those who wished to seek a peace deal that might preserve some element of independence. The Americans, however, demanded unconditional surrender. In August, the United States destroyed the cities of Hiroshima and Nagasaki with atom bombs, and the Soviet Union, previously neutral, attacked Japanese forces in Manchuria. The Japanese government finally bowed to the inevitable and surrendered.

"The war situation has developed not necessarily to Japan's advantage."

EMPEROR HIROHITO, SURRENDER BROADCAST, AUGUST 15, 1945

GLOBAL WARFARE
World War II was a truly global conflict, with theaters of war in Europe, Africa, Asia, and the Pacific. The US fought all the Axis Powers simultaneously, sending troops all over the globe. Japan and the other Axis Powers, although allies, fought separate wars, failing to coordinate their strategy.

KEY

Maximum extent of Japanese expansion in Asia/Pacific

Maximum extent of Axis Powers in Europe/USSR

MOVEMENT OF AXIS TROOPS

German — Japanese

MOVEMENT OF ALLIED TROOPS

British — American

British Commonwealth — Soviet

NEW ZEALAND
AUSTRALIA
PACIFIC OCEAN
INDIAN OCEAN
JAPAN
CHINA
UNITED STATES OF AMERICA
CANADA
ARCTIC OCEAN
USSR
INDIA
EUROPE
AFRICA
SOUTH AFRICA
ATLANTIC OCEAN

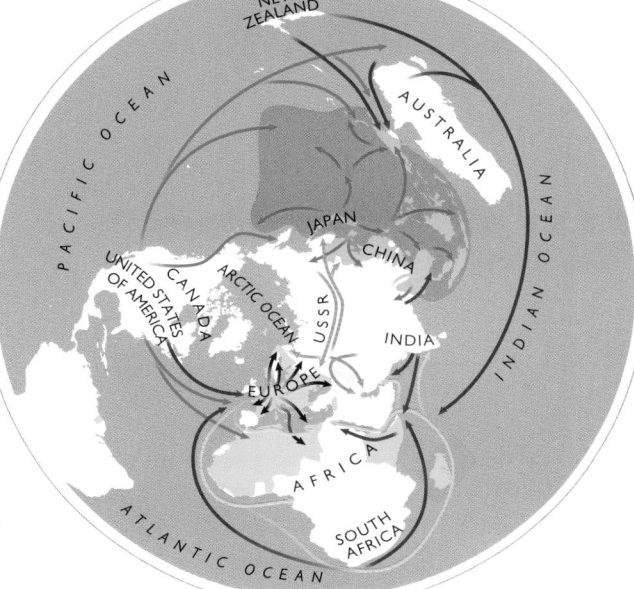

Hiroshima destroyed
Within seconds of detonation of the first atomic bomb, the city of Hiroshima lay in ruins. Nearly 70,000 people are believed to have died immediately. Here, the shattered Nagarekawa Methodist Church stands out.

HIROSHIMA AND NAGASAKI

In August 1945, the US dropped the world's first atomic bombs on the Japanese cities of Hiroshima and Nagasaki in a bid to end World War II. It led the world to a new, and controversial, nuclear age. For Japan, its impact was cataclysmic.

On May 10, 1945, 3 days after Germany had surrendered to the Allies and ended the war in Europe, a group of US scientists and military personnel met in Los Alamos, New Mexico. The top minds within the Manhattan Project—the American effort to build an atomic bomb— focused on how to end Japanese resistance in the Pacific. The island-hopping strategy adopted by the US Navy had brought B-29 bombers within range of the Japanese archipelago, and they carried out massive aerial bombing attacks. Yet Japan refused to surrender. US president Harry Truman authorized the use of two atomic weapons against Japan, believing it would be a less bloody way to secure surrender than an invasion.

The final attack

At the meeting at Los Alamos in May, the experts had deliberated on which Japanese cities to attack. The targets needed to have some military significance. Four cities,

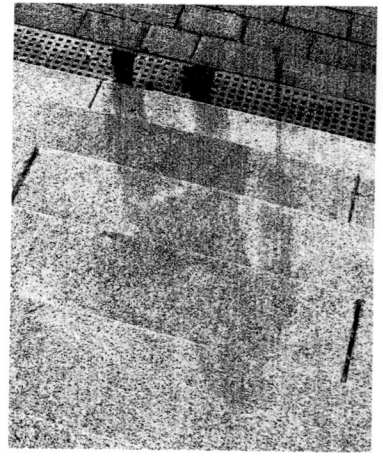

△ **Human shadow**
The intense heat of the detonation in Hiroshima left "shadows" of people and objects exactly as they were at 8:15 a.m. on August 6, 1945.

including Hiroshima and Nagasaki, were chosen. Over the summer of 1945, Japanese attempts to negotiate a formula for surrender were rebuffed by the Allies. Then, on July 28, 1945, a demand from the Allies to surrender unconditionally or face destruction was rejected by the Japanese high command.

On August 6, 1945, the crew of the *Enola Gay*, the B-29 bomber assigned to drop the first bomb on Hiroshima, took off. At 8:15 a.m., "Little Boy" was dropped. Three days later, the US dropped "Fat Man" on Nagasaki. Estimates of people killed in the two bombings range as high as 246,000. On August 15, 1945, Japan surrendered. More atomic bombs were planned, although Japan's emperor was also influenced by the Soviet invasion of Manchuria and the starvation that was already widespread. The surrender was formalized on board the USS *Missouri* on September 2, 1945.

The bombings had helped to hasten the end of WWII but launched a nuclear arms race between the US and the Soviet Union that lasted until the 1990s.

▽ **"Fat Man"**
Nicknamed Fat Man, the atomic bomb dropped on Nagasaki on August 9, 1945, created winds of 620 mph (1,000 km/h) and temperatures of 12,700°F (7,050°C).

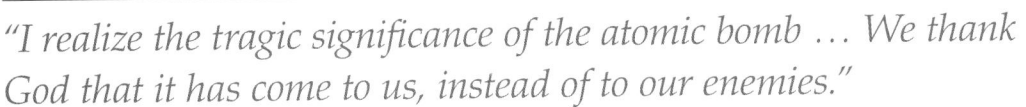

"I realize the tragic significance of the atomic bomb … We thank God that it has come to us, instead of to our enemies."

HARRY S TRUMAN, US PRESIDENT, AUGUST 9, 1945

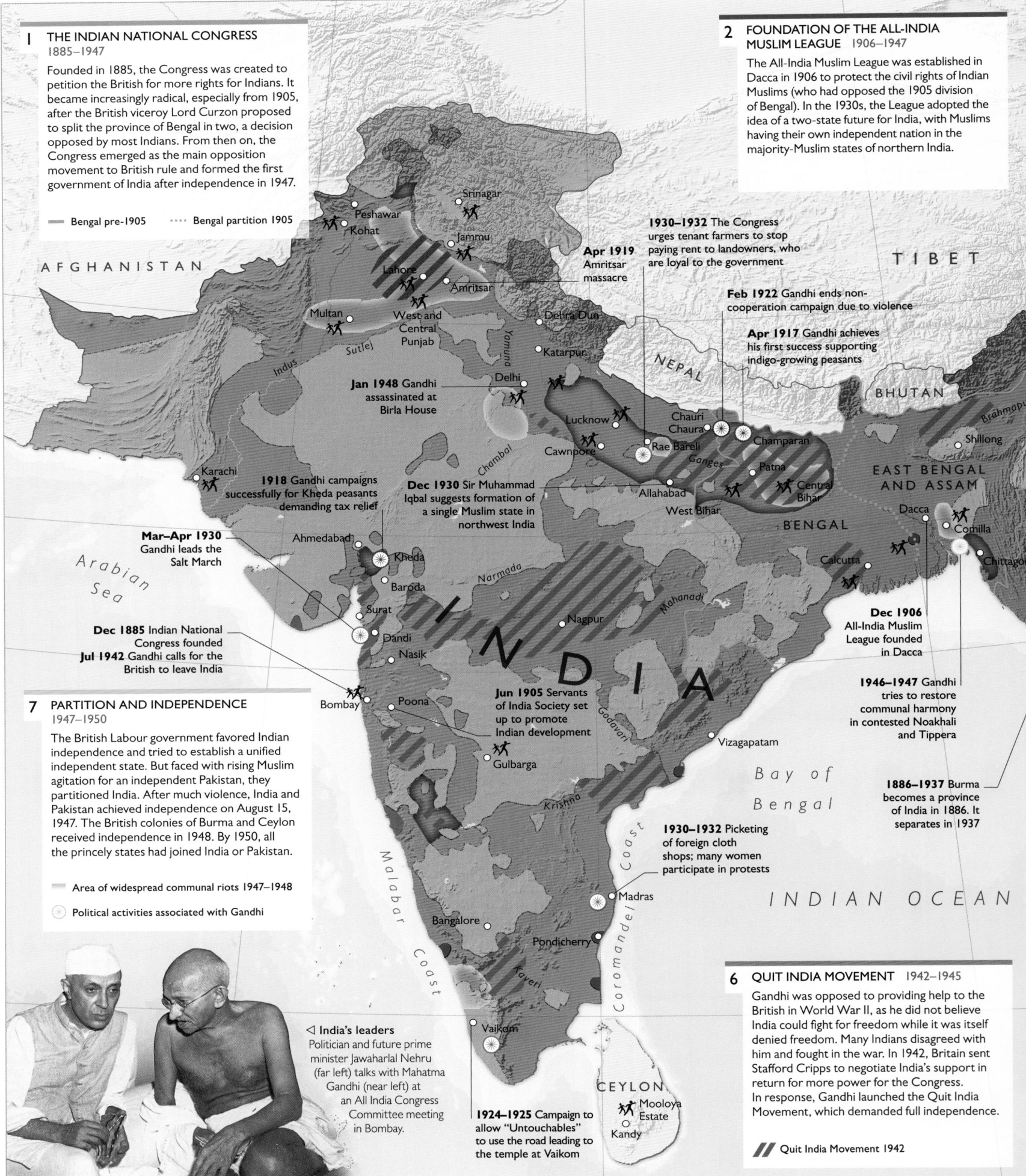

1 THE INDIAN NATIONAL CONGRESS
1885–1947

Founded in 1885, the Congress was created to petition the British for more rights for Indians. It became increasingly radical, especially from 1905, after the British viceroy Lord Curzon proposed to split the province of Bengal in two, a decision opposed by most Indians. From then on, the Congress emerged as the main opposition movement to British rule and formed the first government of India after independence in 1947.

—— Bengal pre-1905   ···· Bengal partition 1905

2 FOUNDATION OF THE ALL-INDIA MUSLIM LEAGUE 1906–1947

The All-India Muslim League was established in Dacca in 1906 to protect the civil rights of Indian Muslims (who had opposed the 1905 division of Bengal). In the 1930s, the League adopted the idea of a two-state future for India, with Muslims having their own independent nation in the majority-Muslim states of northern India.

1930–1932 The Congress urges tenant farmers to stop paying rent to landowners, who are loyal to the government

Apr 1919 Amritsar massacre

Feb 1922 Gandhi ends non-cooperation campaign due to violence

Apr 1917 Gandhi achieves his first success supporting indigo-growing peasants

Jan 1948 Gandhi assassinated at Birla House

1918 Gandhi campaigns successfully for Kheda peasants demanding tax relief

Dec 1930 Sir Muhammad Iqbal suggests formation of a single Muslim state in northwest India

Mar–Apr 1930 Gandhi leads the Salt March

Dec 1885 Indian National Congress founded
Jul 1942 Gandhi calls for the British to leave India

Dec 1906 All-India Muslim League founded in Dacca

1946–1947 Gandhi tries to restore communal harmony in contested Noakhali and Tippera

1886–1937 Burma becomes a province of India in 1886. It separates in 1937

Jun 1905 Servants of India Society set up to promote Indian development

1930–1932 Picketing of foreign cloth shops; many women participate in protests

7 PARTITION AND INDEPENDENCE
1947–1950

The British Labour government favored Indian independence and tried to establish a unified independent state. But faced with rising Muslim agitation for an independent Pakistan, they partitioned India. After much violence, India and Pakistan achieved independence on August 15, 1947. The British colonies of Burma and Ceylon received independence in 1948. By 1950, all the princely states had joined India or Pakistan.

—— Area of widespread communal riots 1947–1948

⊙ Political activities associated with Gandhi

◁ **India's leaders**
Politician and future prime minister Jawaharlal Nehru (far left) talks with Mahatma Gandhi (near left) at an All India Congress Committee meeting in Bombay.

1924–1925 Campaign to allow "Untouchables" to use the road leading to the temple at Vaikom

6 QUIT INDIA MOVEMENT 1942–1945

Gandhi was opposed to providing help to the British in World War II, as he did not believe India could fight for freedom while it was itself denied freedom. Many Indians disagreed with him and fought in the war. In 1942, Britain sent Stafford Cripps to negotiate India's support in return for more power for the Congress. In response, Gandhi launched the Quit India Movement, which demanded full independence.

// Quit India Movement 1942

AFGHANISTAN · TIBET · NEPAL · BHUTAN · Arabian Sea · Bay of Bengal · INDIAN OCEAN · INDIA · BENGAL · EAST BENGAL AND ASSAM · CEYLON · Malabar Coast · Coromandel Coast

Peshawar · Kohat · Srinagar · Jammu · Lahore · Amritsar · Multan · West and Central Punjab · Dehra Dun · Katarpur · Delhi · Lucknow · Cawnpore · Chauri Chaura · Rae Bareli · Champaran · Shillong · Allahabad · Central Bihar · West Bihar · Patna · Dacca · Comilla · Calcutta · Chittagong · Karachi · Ahmedabad · Kheda · Baroda · Surat · Dandi · Nasik · Bombay · Poona · Nagpur · Gulbarga · Vizagapatam · Madras · Bangalore · Pondicherry · Vaikom · Mooloya Estate · Kandy

Sutlej · Indus · Yamuna · Chambal · Ganges · Brahmaputra · Narmada · Mahanadi · Godavari · Krishna · Kaveri

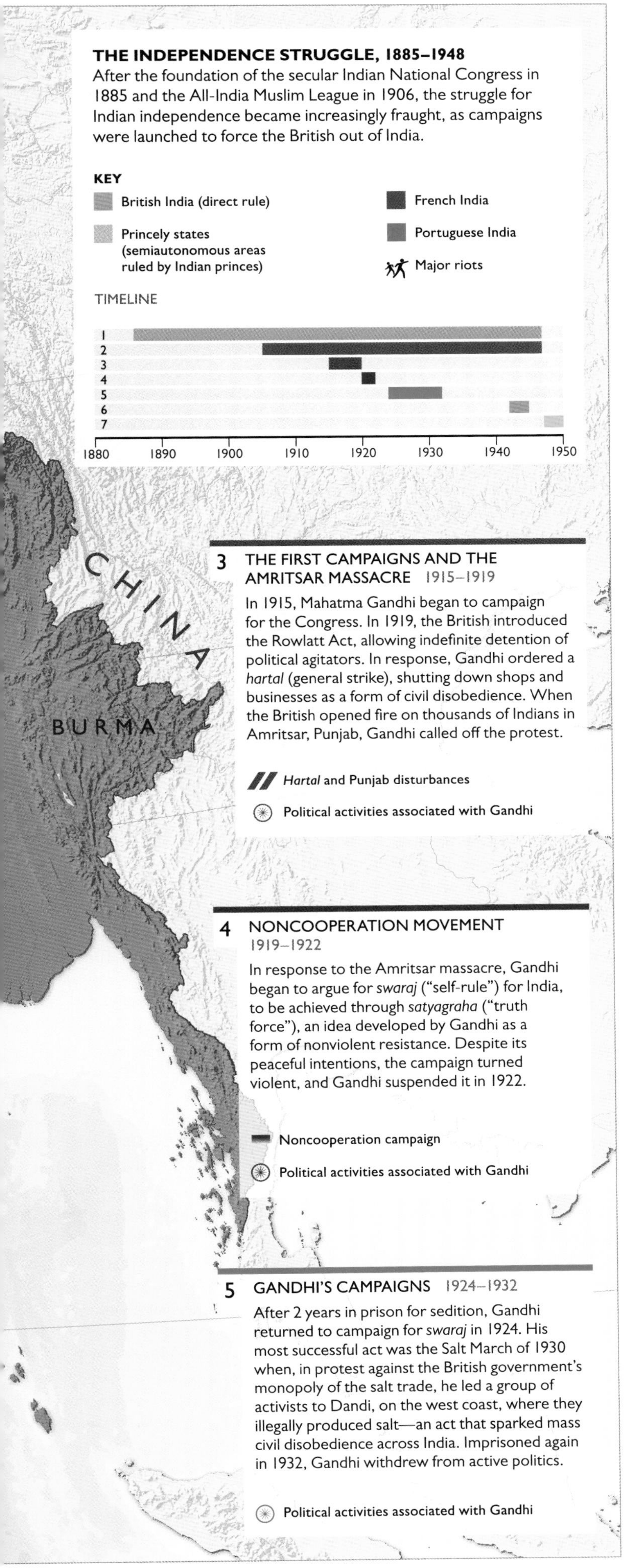

THE INDEPENDENCE STRUGGLE, 1885–1948

After the foundation of the secular Indian National Congress in 1885 and the All-India Muslim League in 1906, the struggle for Indian independence became increasingly fraught, as campaigns were launched to force the British out of India.

KEY

British India (direct rule)	French India
Princely states (semiautonomous areas ruled by Indian princes)	Portuguese India
	Major riots

TIMELINE

1
2
3
4
5
6
7

1880   1890   1900   1910   1920   1930   1940   1950

3 THE FIRST CAMPAIGNS AND THE AMRITSAR MASSACRE 1915–1919

In 1915, Mahatma Gandhi began to campaign for the Congress. In 1919, the British introduced the Rowlatt Act, allowing indefinite detention of political agitators. In response, Gandhi ordered a *hartal* (general strike), shutting down shops and businesses as a form of civil disobedience. When the British opened fire on thousands of Indians in Amritsar, Punjab, Gandhi called off the protest.

/// *Hartal* and Punjab disturbances

⊛ Political activities associated with Gandhi

4 NONCOOPERATION MOVEMENT 1919–1922

In response to the Amritsar massacre, Gandhi began to argue for *swaraj* ("self-rule") for India, to be achieved through *satyagraha* ("truth force"), an idea developed by Gandhi as a form of nonviolent resistance. Despite its peaceful intentions, the campaign turned violent, and Gandhi suspended it in 1922.

▬ Noncooperation campaign

⊛ Political activities associated with Gandhi

5 GANDHI'S CAMPAIGNS 1924–1932

After 2 years in prison for sedition, Gandhi returned to campaign for *swaraj* in 1924. His most successful act was the Salt March of 1930 when, in protest against the British government's monopoly of the salt trade, he led a group of activists to Dandi, on the west coast, where they illegally produced salt—an act that sparked mass civil disobedience across India. Imprisoned again in 1932, Gandhi withdrew from active politics.

⊛ Political activities associated with Gandhi

PARTITION OF INDIA

The campaign to end British rule over its Indian empire was one of the most successful such movements in colonial history. Although marked with occasional and often appalling violence, the campaign stressed nonviolent resistance based on the beliefs of one of its most inspirational leaders, politician and activist Mahatma Gandhi.

Britain's efforts to hold on to India were undermined by a massacre of unarmed Indians by British troops in Amritsar, Punjab, in 1919. In response, Gandhi initiated a nonviolent, non-cooperation campaign for independence, which was led mainly by the secular Indian National Congress. However, the religious divide within India, between Hindus and Muslims, complicated matters. The All-India Muslim League began to campaign for an independent Muslim state called Pakistan, which would be created through partition.

After Britain declared war on Germany in 1939 on behalf of India—without consulting Indian leaders—the Congress launched the Quit India Movement, calling for civil disobedience to upset the British war effort. By 1945, Britain was economically drained by the war, and the government began to plan for withdrawal from India. It supported partition reluctantly and, amid a crisis that saw millions of Hindu and Muslim refugees cross the new borders, the divided empire finally achieved its independence on August 15, 1947.

"At the stroke of the midnight hour, when the world sleeps, India will awake to life and freedom."

JAWAHARLAL NEHRU, INDIA'S 1ST PRIME MINISTER, AUGUST 14, 1947

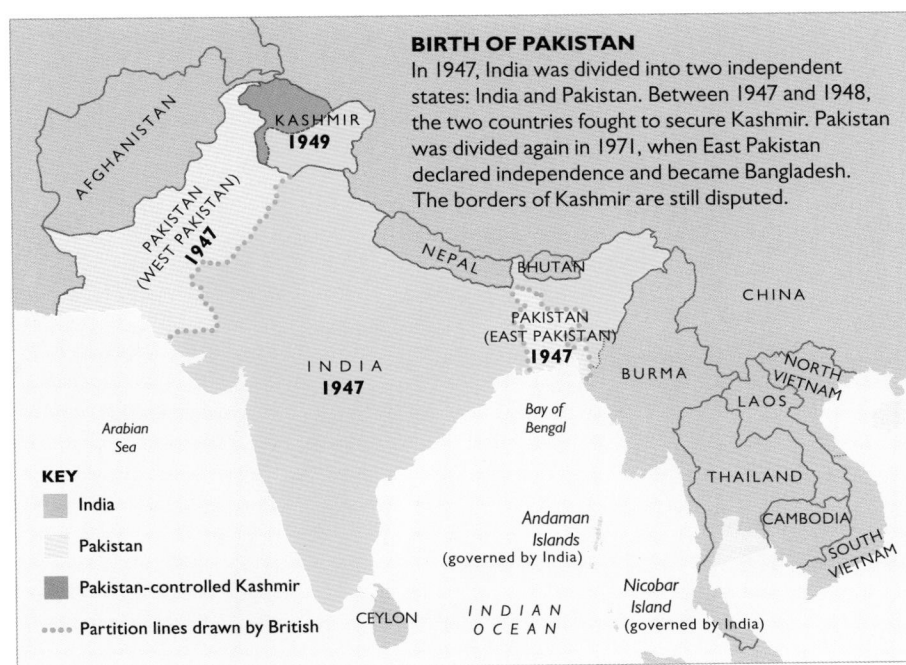

BIRTH OF PAKISTAN

In 1947, India was divided into two independent states: India and Pakistan. Between 1947 and 1948, the two countries fought to secure Kashmir. Pakistan was divided again in 1971, when East Pakistan declared independence and became Bangladesh. The borders of Kashmir are still disputed.

KEY

	India
	Pakistan
	Pakistan-controlled Kashmir
····	Partition lines drawn by British

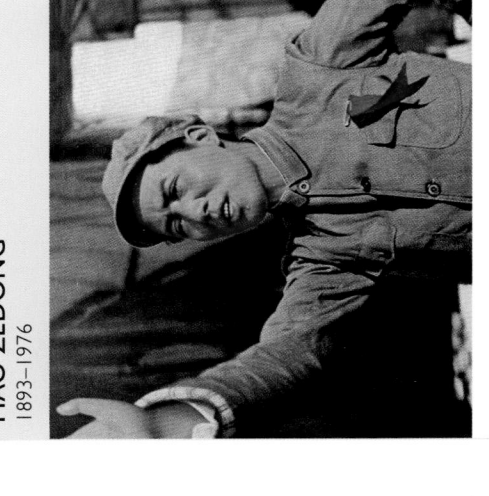

MAO ZEDONG
1893–1976

THE FOUNDING OF COMMUNIST CHINA

Between 1927 and 1949, an ideological divide split China, as Mao Zedong's Communist Party fought China's Nationalist Party for the future of the country. Eventually, after years of civil war, Japanese occupation, and World War II, Mao emerged as ruler of a new communist China.

The Chinese Communist Party (CCP) was set up in Shanghai on July 23, 1921. At first, it collaborated with China's Nationalist Party, the Kuomintang (KMT), but the alliance was severed in 1927, when the KMT, under the rule of a new leader, anti-communist Chiang Kai-shek, turned on their rivals (see pp.288–289). The KMT destroyed the communists in all major cities, and the CCP was forced to retreat to Jiangxi province in southern China, where they established the Soviet Republic of China in 1931. In 1934, they were forced to abandon their base when they were surrounded by KMT forces. Under the guidance of the future Chairman of the Soviet Republic of China, Mao Zedong, the fragments of the Communist Party

undertook the "Long March"—a year-long trek to the northern province of Shaanxi. It was a good strategic base, being both far away from the KMT and close to supply routes from the USSR.

Japanese invasion during World War II briefly forced the CCP and KMT to collaborate again to some extent. After the war, US negotiators tried to reconcile the two parties, but civil war broke out. The KMT had early victories, but the CCP gained the support of the rural peasantry, and their army swelled. They quickly gained ground by splitting the KMT forces into isolated pockets. By 1949, the Kuomintang had collapsed. On October 1, 1949, Mao announced the establishment of the People's Republic of China.

The ruler of communist China from 1949 until his death in 1976, Mao Zedong trained as a teacher in Hunan before traveling to Peking (Beijing). While working as a librarian at Peking University, he became a communist, and he helped to found the Communist Party in 1921. In 1934, Mao guided 86,000 communists on the Long March. He became chairman of the party in 1943. As leader, he modernized China, but his radical policies were ruthless and ambitious and caused huge loss of life.

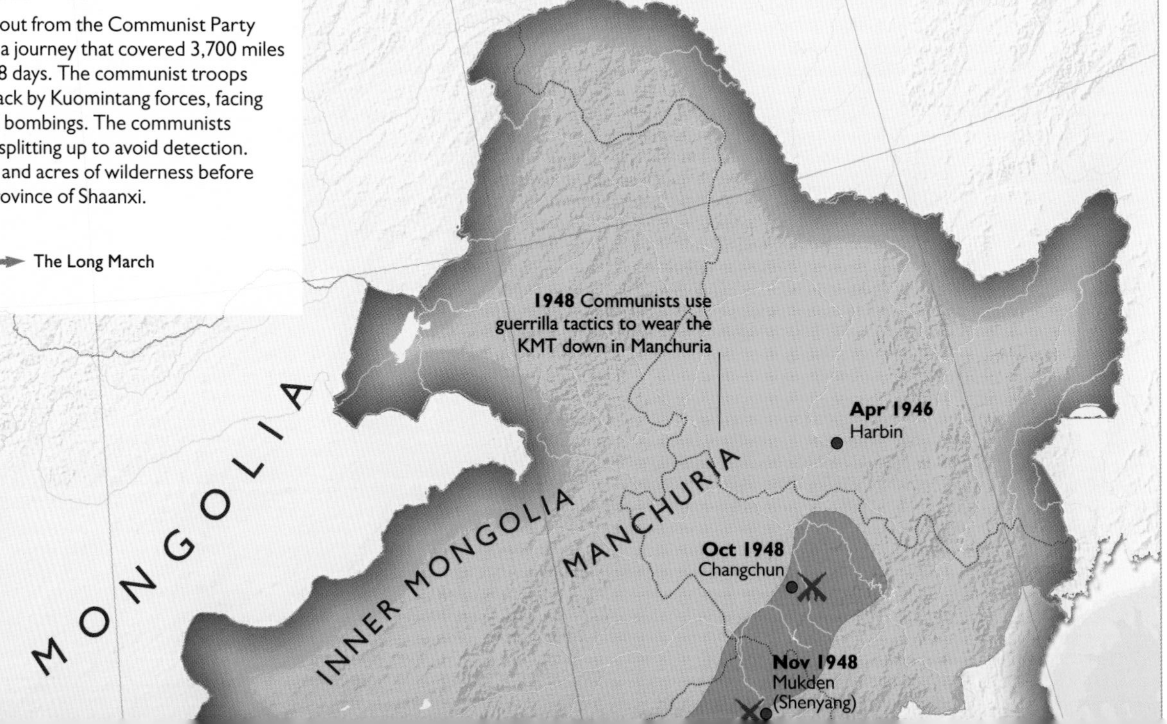

1948 Communists use guerrilla tactics to wear the KMT down in Manchuria

Apr 1946
Harbin

Oct 1948
Changchun

Nov 1948
Mukden
(Shenyang)

MANCHURIA

INNER MONGOLIA

MONGOLIA

Gobi

I **THE LONG MARCH**
OCTOBER 1934–OCTOBER 1935

Some 86,000 troops set out from the Communist Party base in Ruijin, Jiangxi, on a journey that covered 3,700 miles (6,000 km) and lasted 368 days. The communist troops were under constant attack by Kuomintang forces, facing machine-gun attacks and bombings. The communists traveled mostly at night, splitting up to avoid detection. They crossed mountains and acres of wilderness before reaching the northern province of Shaanxi.

Communist centers 1934

→ The Long March

▽ **Chairman Mao Zedong**
People gather to celebrate the end of the Chinese Civil War and the founding of the People's Republic of China in this propaganda poster from 1949.

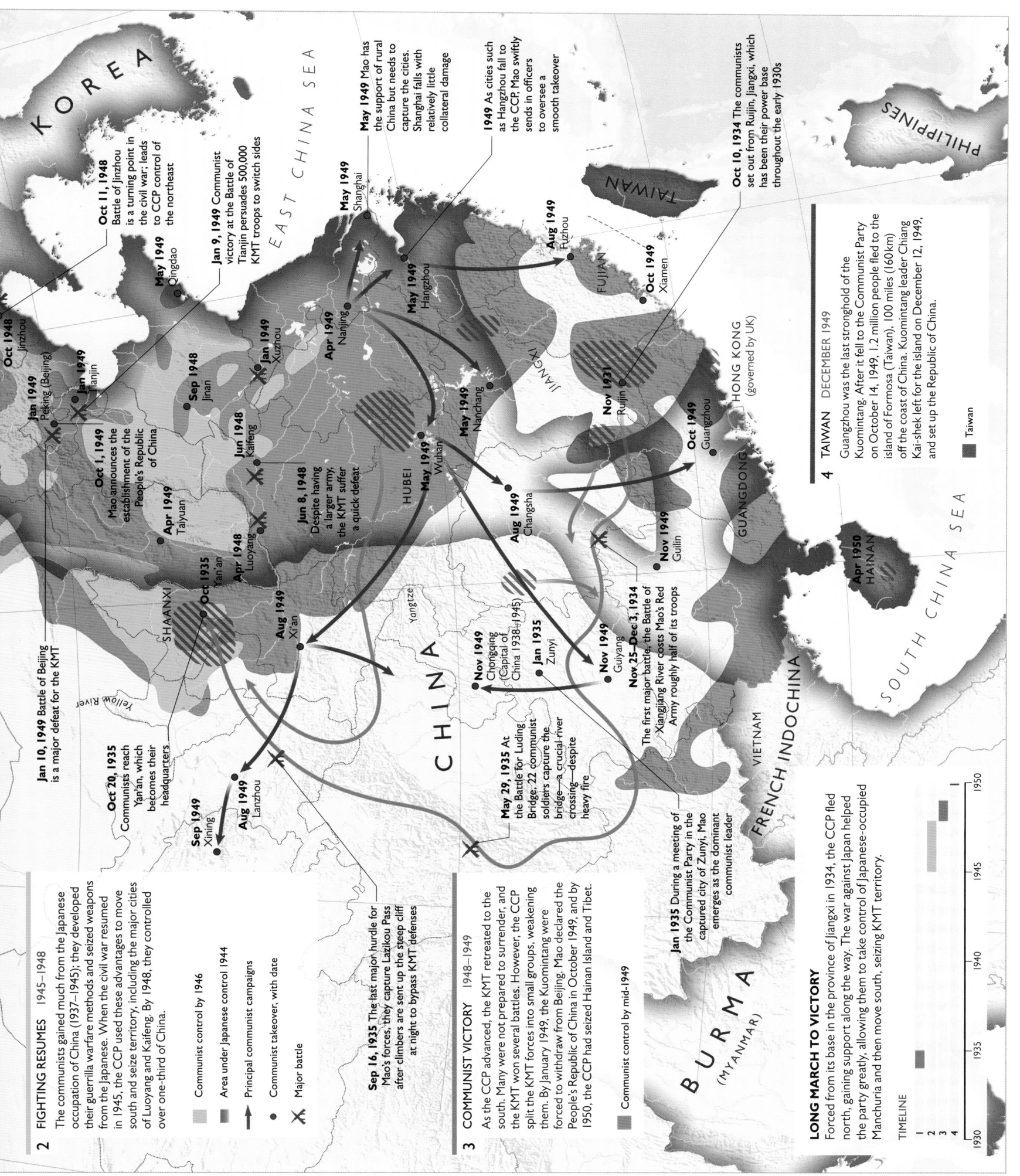

2 FIGHTING RESUMES 1945–1948

The communists gained much from the Japanese occupation of China (1937–1945); they developed their guerrilla warfare methods and seized weapons from the Japanese. When the civil war resumed in 1945, the CCP used these advantages to move south and seize territory, including the major cities of Luoyang and Kaifeng. By 1948, they controlled over one-third of China.

Oct 11, 1948 Battle of Jinzhou is a turning point in the civil war; leads to CCP control of the northeast

May 1949 Qingdao

Jan 9, 1949 Communist victory at the Battle of Tianjin persuades 500,000 KMT troops to switch sides

May 1949 Mao has the support of rural China but needs to capture the cities. Shanghai falls with relatively little collateral damage

1949 As cities such as Hangzhou fall to the CCP, Mao swiftly sends in officers to oversee a smooth takeover

Oct 10, 1934 The communists set out from Ruijin, Jiangxi, which has been their power base throughout the early 1930s

May 1949 Shanghai

Aug 1949 Fuzhou

May 1949 Hangzhou

Oct 1949 Xiamen

Apr 1949 Nanjing

Jan 1949 Xuzhou

Jan 1949 Peking (Beijing)

Jan 1949 Tianjin

Oct 1948 Jinzhou

Jan 10, 1949 Battle of Beijing is a major defeat for the KMT

Sep 1948 Jinan

Jun 1948 Kaifeng

Oct 1, 1949 Mao announces the establishment of the People's Republic of China

Apr 1949 Taiyuan

Apr 1948 Luoyang

Jun 8, 1948 Despite having a larger army, the KMT suffer a quick defeat

May 1949 Wuhan

May 1949 Nanchang

Nov 1931 Ruijin

Oct 1949 Guangzhou

Oct 1935 Yan'an

Aug 1949 Changsha

Nov 1949 Guilin

Apr 1950 HAINAN

Oct 20, 1935 Communists reach Yan'an, which becomes their headquarters

Aug 1949 Xi'an

Nov 1949 Chongqing (Capital of China 1938–1945)

Jan 1935 Zunyi

Nov 1949 Guiyang

Nov 25–Dec 3, 1934 The first major battle, the Battle of Xiangjiang River costs Mao's Red Army roughly half of its troops

Sep 16, 1935 The last major hurdle for Mao's forces; they capture Lazikou Pass after climbers are sent up the steep cliff at night to bypass KMT defenses

Aug 1949 Lanzhou

Sep 1949 Xining

May 29, 1935 At the Battle for Luding Bridge, 22 communist soldiers capture the bridge—a crucial river crossing—despite heavy fire

Jan 1935 During a meeting of the Communist Party in the captured city of Zunyi, Mao emerges as the dominant communist leader

- Communist control by 1946
- Area under Japanese control 1944
- Principal communist campaigns
- Communist takeover, with date
- Major battle

3 COMMUNIST VICTORY 1948–1949

As the CCP advanced, the KMT retreated to the south. Many were not prepared to surrender, and the KMT won several battles. However, the CCP split the KMT forces into small groups, weakening them. By January 1949, the Kuomintang were forced to withdraw from Beijing. Mao declared the People's Republic of China in October 1949, and by 1950, the CCP had seized Hainan Island and Tibet.

- Communist control by mid-1949

4 TAIWAN DECEMBER 1949

Guangzhou was the last stronghold of the Kuomintang. After it fell to the Communist Party on October 14, 1949, 1.2 million people fled to the island of Formosa (Taiwan), 100 miles (160km) off the coast of China. Kuomintang leader Chiang Kai-shek left for the island on December 12, 1949, and set up the Republic of China.

- Taiwan

LONG MARCH TO VICTORY

Forced from its base in the province of Jiangxi in 1934, the CCP fled north, gaining support along the way. The war against Japan helped the party greatly, allowing them to take control of Japanese-occupied Manchuria and then move south, seizing KMT territory.

TIMELINE
1 2 3 4
1930 1935 1940 1945 1950

SUPERPOWERS

By the end of World War II, two of the Allies—the US and USSR—had emerged as the world's dominant powers. Owing to their military might and global political influence, they became known as "superpowers." The ideological gulf that separated them generated regular conflict in the era of the Cold War.

△ **Powerful weapon**
On November 1, 1952, the US detonated the first hydrogen bomb, code named Ivy Mike. It was 1,000 times more powerful than the atomic bombs dropped on Hiroshima and Nagasaki.

The USSR had been an unexpected ally in World War II, and Britain and the US made common cause with Stalin's dictatorship in the overthrow of Hitler's European "New Order." As the Red Army advanced into eastern Europe, it became clear that Stalin wanted to dominate the region politically, an ambition that drove a wedge between the wartime allies and opened the way to what was christened the Cold War. The first major conflict came over the future of Berlin, which was inside the Soviet zone of Germany but was controlled by all four major allies: Britain, the US, France, and the USSR. In 1948, Stalin tried to cut Berlin off from the West in order to incorporate it fully in the Communist bloc, but a Western relief effort that came to be known as the Berlin Airlift brought food and supplies to West Berliners, and after 318 days, Stalin abandoned the blockade. The battle line between the two super-powers was now clear.

Growing tensions
By the time of the Berlin crisis, both the USSR and the US had come to realize that there was now no possibility of peaceful collaboration. Soviet influence rapidly spread, and with the triumph of

communism in China, North Korea, and North Vietnam, it seemed likely that Soviet power would pose a profound threat to the West. In the US, a wave of anti-communism was unleashed in the early 1950s as the American public came to realize that the Soviet superpower represented a menace to American interests. When communist North Korea invaded the South, the US used its influence in the United Nations to organize an alliance to contain the threat.

The Korean War was only one of a number of proxy wars in which the US and the USSR looked to enhance their global influence as the new superpowers.

At the core of American and Soviet superpower status was the possession of a large arsenal of nuclear weapons. By 1953, both states had tested the hydrogen bomb, whose destructive power eclipsed the atomic bombs dropped on Japan in 1945. As the stockpiles of bombs built up, no other state could match the military potential of the superpowers. Competition between them was symbolized by the Space Race, in which each side sought to outdo the other. The USSR successfully launched the *Sputnik 1* satellite in 1957 and boasted the first man in space, the first woman in space, and the first spacewalk. Only with the American success in sending a manned mission to the Moon in 1969 did the race

△ **Anti-communist propaganda**
The outbreak of war in Korea brought the Cold War to east Asia. Propaganda produced during the period was used to antagonize South Koreans against the communists.

DEADLY RIVALRY
In 1945, the emergence of the US and USSR as superpowers was founded on their capacity to build, test, and accumulate nuclear weapons in massive quantities. The Cold War, so called because no direct military action was taken, led to deep divisions and animosity between the two countries and their respective allies. The threat of nuclear annihilation was constant, but after the Cuban Missile Crisis in 1962, the rivalry between the two nations played out in the Space Race.

Aug 1945 The US drops atomic bombs on the Japanese cities of Hiroshima and Nagasaki, starting the nuclear arms race

Aug 29, 1949 The Soviet Union tests its first nuclear bomb, and the arms race escalates

Jun 24, 1950 The Korean War begins: North Korea invades the south, with Stalin's support

Mid-1950s The USSR and its affiliated communist nations in eastern Europe begin talks for forming the Warsaw Pact, ultimately signed in May 1955

NUCLEAR WEAPONS
THE COLD WAR
THE SPACE RACE

1945

1950

Jun 24, 1948–May 12, 1949 The first major crisis of the Cold War occurs—Stalin blockades Berlin; an effort from various countries saves Berliners from starvation

Apr 4, 1949 NATO is formed between the US and other western nations

◁ **Concrete divide**
An East German worker makes repairs to the hastily built Berlin Wall—a 28-mile (45-km) scar that cut through the German capital, dividing east from west.

"Mankind must put an end to war or war will put an end to mankind."

JOHN F. KENNEDY, US PRESIDENT, 1961

become more equal. The nuclear confrontation in the 1950s did not provoke war between the two superpowers because neither side could risk retaliation. But in 1962, to counter the stationing of American missiles in Turkey, Nikita Khrushchev, the Soviet leader, authorized the establishment of Soviet missile sites in Cuba, the site of Castro's pro-Soviet revolution. In the end, the USSR backed down from President Kennedy's ultimatum to end the project, and a more serious crisis was averted.

The coming of détente

From the Cuban crisis onward, the two superpowers looked for ways to reduce the nuclear risks. A so-called "red telephone" line was installed between leaders in Moscow and Washington so that they could communicate directly during a crisis. In August 1963, the first Test Ban Treaty was signed, and in 1972, talks between the two superpowers produced SALT I, the first serious effort to scale back the nuclear arsenals. Although

both superpowers continued to spend heavily on defense and to play out political battles between them in other parts of the world, there emerged a greater willingness to talk and to avoid the open hostility of the 1940s and 1950s. When the Soviet bloc collapsed in 1989–1991, the USSR's status as a superpower disappeared. By the 1990s, the US was, for the time being, the sole superpower.

▽ **The American dream**
This Cadillac convertible epitomizes the growing prosperity of America's middle class, asserting capitalism as superior to communism.

Feb 17, 1958 The Campaign for Nuclear Disarmament (CND) is formed; its iconic emblem becomes one of the most recognized in the world

May 5, 1961 Alan Shepard, flying on *Freedom 7*, becomes the first American in space

Aug 13, 1961 Barbed wire is put up as the first stage of construction of the Berlin Wall, which splits east Berlin from west

Mar 18, 1965 Soviet cosmonaut Alexei Leonov makes the first spacewalk in history, beating American rival Ed White by almost 3 months

Jul 1, 1968 The Non-Proliferation Treaty is signed to make countries holding nuclear weapons commit to a cautious undertaking to disarm

1960   1965   1970

Oct 4, 1957 The USSR launches the world's first man-made satellite, *Sputnik I*; it takes 98 minutes to orbit Earth

Apr 12, 1961 Soviet cosmonaut Yuri Gagarin becomes the first human to travel in space in his spacecraft, *Vostok I*

May 25, 1961 US president John F. Kennedy pledges to the American public to put the first man on the Moon

Oct 16, 1962 The Cuban Missile Crisis begins—a tense stand-off between the US and USSR in Cuba brings the world to the brink of nuclear war

Jul 20, 1969 American astronaut Neil Armstrong becomes the first man to walk on the Moon; the historic event is watched live on television worldwide

THE COLD WAR

After World War II ended in 1945, bitter rivalry between the US and the USSR dominated international affairs and led to many global crises. Known as the Cold War, this period of extreme political tension, which lasted for almost half a century, was as much a conflict of ideology and influence as military action.

The US and the USSR emerged from World War II as the most powerful victors. Although formerly allies, the two nations had major political and economic disagreements about the world's future, with the US promoting democracy and capitalism and the USSR supporting communism. By 1949, communist regions had emerged throughout eastern Europe, and China had emerged as a communist state, intensifying international division. The Western nations set up the North Atlantic Treaty Organization (NATO) military alliance, and the Soviet bloc responded with the Warsaw Pact. Competition escalated as first the US, then the USSR, acquired and tested nuclear weapons, initially to be delivered by aircraft, later by missiles and submarines (see pp.324–325).

The Cold War never developed into a direct war because the threat of nuclear retaliation was too great. However, armed conflicts between proxy countries across the globe became frequent. The USSR would back smaller, non-nuclear communist regimes, while the US would retaliate by supporting anti-communist forces in the same conflict. Few countries avoided taking sides, although some did remain nonaligned.

This new style of war was not just a military conflict, however; scientific, technological, cultural, and propaganda wars between the two superpowers were intense. Despite the antagonism between the two major powers, the Cold War did keep a kind of peace in place for almost half a century, although at huge cost to those nations where the conflict became "hot."

> *"Whether you like it or not, history is on our side. We will bury you."*
>
> NIKITA KHRUSHCHEV, SOVIET PREMIER, NOVEMBER 18, 1956

GERMANY DIVIDED

After World War II, the four victorious allies divided Germany and its capital, Berlin, between them. In 1949, the US, French, and British merged their sectors to form West Germany, with a new capital in Bonn; East Germany and East Berlin remained under Soviet control. In 1961, the East Germans built a wall to separate the communist East from capitalist West Berlin.

KEY

▦ Control point

- - - Railway line

— Major road

Map labels: North Sea, Baltic Sea, Hamburg, Berlin, West Berlin, East Berlin, WEST GERMANY, EAST GERMANY, POLAND, Bonn, Dresden, Frankfurt, FRANCE, Munich

FOUNDATION OF NATO 1949–2017

In the wake of World War II, in 1949, the US, Canada, and 10 European nations signed the North Atlantic Treaty, which established NATO. It was a defensive military alliance that promised to provide mutual assistance if one nation were to be attacked. Greece and Turkey joined in 1952, West Germany in 1955, and Spain in 1982. After the end of the Cold War, NATO expanded into eastern Europe to become an alliance of 29 states.

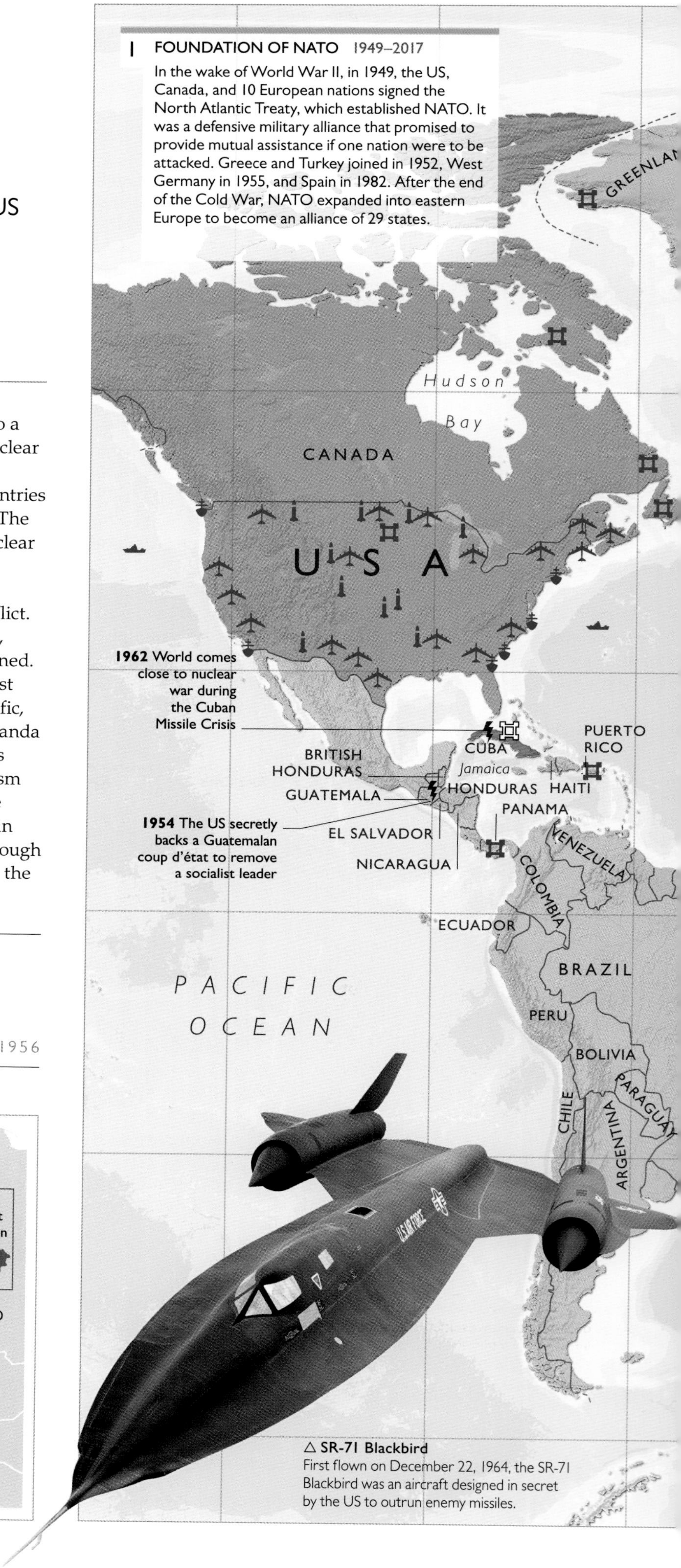

1962 World comes close to nuclear war during the Cuban Missile Crisis

1954 The US secretly backs a Guatemalan coup d'état to remove a socialist leader

Map labels: GREENLAND, Hudson Bay, CANADA, U S A, BRITISH HONDURAS, GUATEMALA, EL SALVADOR, NICARAGUA, CUBA, Jamaica, HONDURAS, HAITI, PANAMA, PUERTO RICO, VENEZUELA, COLOMBIA, ECUADOR, BRAZIL, PERU, BOLIVIA, CHILE, ARGENTINA, PARAGUAY, PACIFIC OCEAN

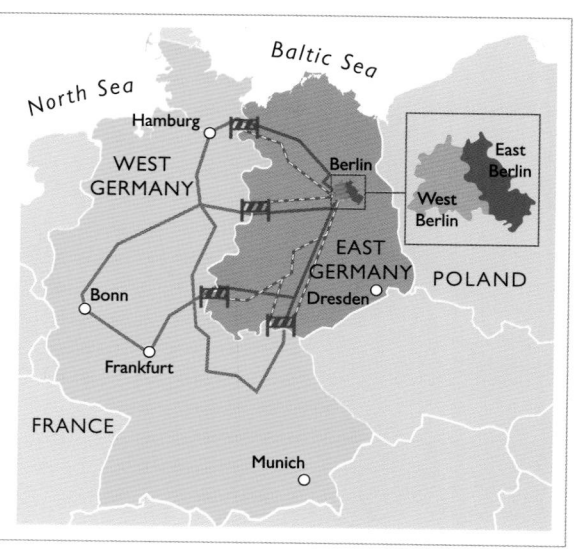

△ **SR-71 Blackbird**
First flown on December 22, 1964, the SR-71 Blackbird was an aircraft designed in secret by the US to outrun enemy missiles.

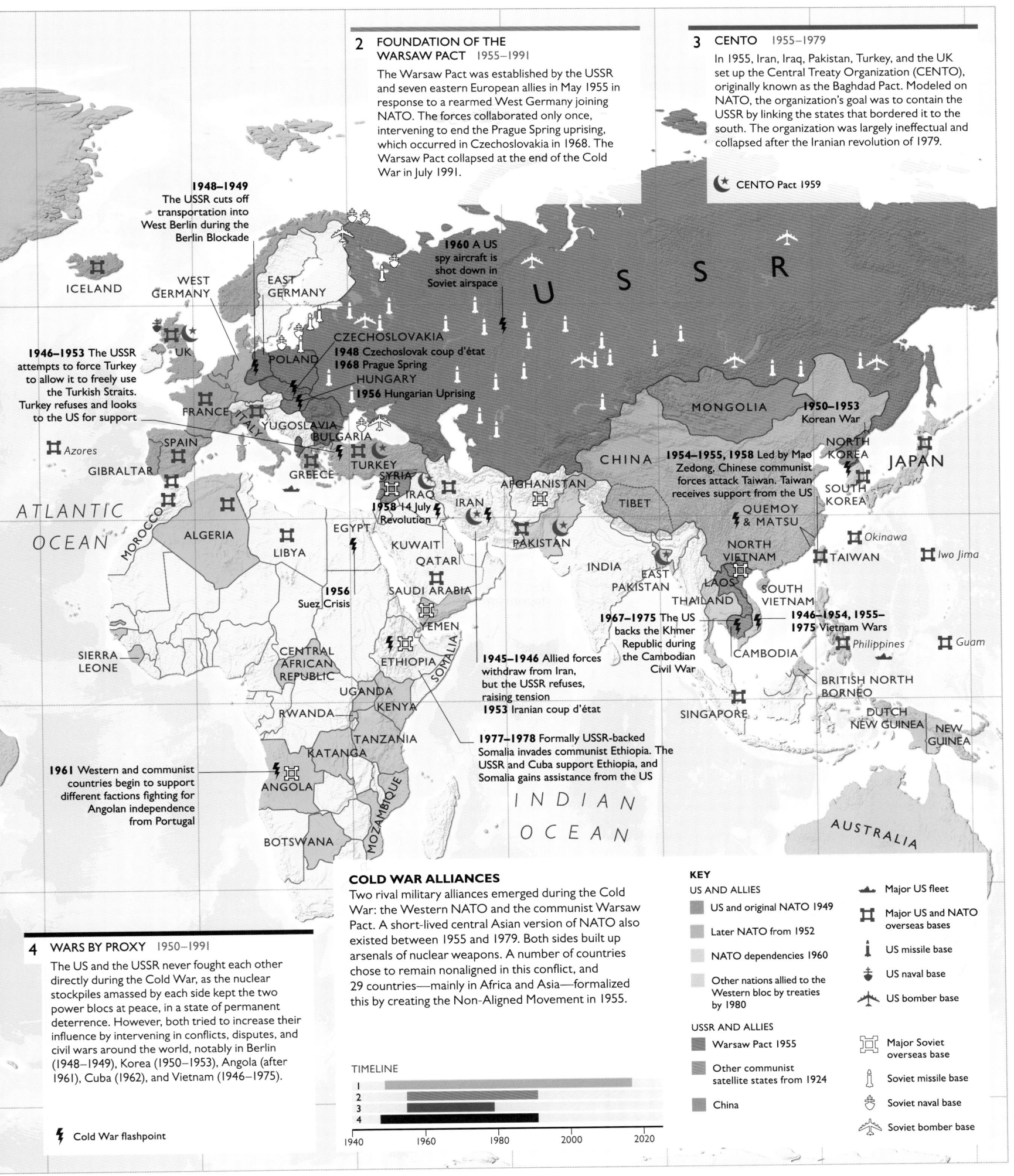

2 FOUNDATION OF THE WARSAW PACT 1955–1991

The Warsaw Pact was established by the USSR and seven eastern European allies in May 1955 in response to a rearmed West Germany joining NATO. The forces collaborated only once, intervening to end the Prague Spring uprising, which occurred in Czechoslovakia in 1968. The Warsaw Pact collapsed at the end of the Cold War in July 1991.

3 CENTO 1955–1979

In 1955, Iran, Iraq, Pakistan, Turkey, and the UK set up the Central Treaty Organization (CENTO), originally known as the Baghdad Pact. Modeled on NATO, the organization's goal was to contain the USSR by linking the states that bordered it to the south. The organization was largely ineffectual and collapsed after the Iranian revolution of 1979.

☾ CENTO Pact 1959

1948–1949 The USSR cuts off transportation into West Berlin during the Berlin Blockade

1960 A US spy aircraft is shot down in Soviet airspace

1946–1953 The USSR attempts to force Turkey to allow it to freely use the Turkish Straits. Turkey refuses and looks to the US for support

1948 Czechoslovak coup d'état
1968 Prague Spring
1956 Hungarian Uprising

1950–1953 Korean War

1954–1955, 1958 Led by Mao Zedong, Chinese communist forces attack Taiwan. Taiwan receives support from the US

1958 14 July Revolution

1956 Suez Crisis

1967–1975 The US backs the Khmer Republic during the Cambodian Civil War

1946–1954, 1955–1975 Vietnam Wars

1945–1946 Allied forces withdraw from Iran, but the USSR refuses, raising tension
1953 Iranian coup d'état

1977–1978 Formally USSR-backed Somalia invades communist Ethiopia. The USSR and Cuba support Ethiopia, and Somalia gains assistance from the US

1961 Western and communist countries begin to support different factions fighting for Angolan independence from Portugal

COLD WAR ALLIANCES

Two rival military alliances emerged during the Cold War: the Western NATO and the communist Warsaw Pact. A short-lived central Asian version of NATO also existed between 1955 and 1979. Both sides built up arsenals of nuclear weapons. A number of countries chose to remain nonaligned in this conflict, and 29 countries—mainly in Africa and Asia—formalized this by creating the Non-Aligned Movement in 1955.

4 WARS BY PROXY 1950–1991

The US and the USSR never fought each other directly during the Cold War, as the nuclear stockpiles amassed by each side kept the two power blocs at peace, in a state of permanent deterrence. However, both tried to increase their influence by intervening in conflicts, disputes, and civil wars around the world, notably in Berlin (1948–1949), Korea (1950–1953), Angola (after 1961), Cuba (1962), and Vietnam (1946–1975).

⚡ Cold War flashpoint

KEY

US AND ALLIES
- US and original NATO 1949
- Later NATO from 1952
- NATO dependencies 1960
- Other nations allied to the Western bloc by treaties by 1980

USSR AND ALLIES
- Warsaw Pact 1955
- Other communist satellite states from 1924
- China

- Major US fleet
- Major US and NATO overseas bases
- US missile base
- US naval base
- US bomber base
- Major Soviet overseas base
- Soviet missile base
- Soviet naval base
- Soviet bomber base

TIMELINE
1940 1960 1980 2000 2020

A WAR WITHOUT WINNERS

The Korean War engulfed the whole of the Korean peninsula, as first the North Korean, then the UN, and then the Chinese armies swept up and down the peninsula. At the end of the war in 1953, the original border between the two countries remained roughly the same.

TIMELINE

KEY		
NORTH KOREA GAINS 1950		
Jul 4		Aug 5
Jul 25		Sep 15
SOUTH KOREA		
Pusan Perimeter		

1 THE NORTH KOREAN ATTACK
JUNE–SEPTEMBER 1950

At dawn on June 25, 1950, North Korean troops launched a surprise attack across the 38th parallel against South Korea, rapidly capturing the South's capital, Seoul, and reaching almost to the south coast. By mid-September 1950, South Korea was reduced to a small pocket of land in the southeast corner of the peninsula known as the Pusan Perimeter.

→ Main axis of North Korean attack
⋯⋯ Extent of North Korean advance Sep 15, 1950
★ Capital city
✕ Major battle

2 THE UN RESPONSE
SEPTEMBER–OCTOBER 1950

In response to the North Korean invasion, the UN Security Council, boycotted by the USSR, recommended member states support South Korea. In September 1950, UN troops led by US General MacArthur landed at Inchon and then Pusan, in the south. Fearing encirclement, the North's troops withdrew. The UN troops then headed north to capture the capital Pyongyang and neared Chosan on the frontier with China.

→ UN counter-attack
★ Capital city
✕ Major battle
▬ US fleet
➤ UN landings
⋯⋯ Extent of UN advance Nov 25, 1950

3 THE CHINESE INVASION
OCTOBER 1950–JANUARY 1951

China warned the US that it would intervene to support North Korea if troops crossed the 38th parallel. After UN troops crossed this divide, Chinese volunteers began to cross the frontier in October 1950. The main Chinese army crossed the border in November and pushed the UN forces southward, retaking Seoul and establishing a new frontline across the south of the peninsula.

→ Chinese attack
⋯⋯ Extent of Chinese advance Jan 26, 1951
✕ Major battle

4 STALEMATE JANUARY 1951–JULY 1953

In the second half of January 1951, UN forces responded to the Chinese invasion, successfully containing two major Chinese attacks before launching a successful push northward in May 1951. What had been a mobile war now became static, and by November 1951, the war stabilized along a defensive line slightly north of the 38th parallel. Limited fighting continued for 2 years, until July 1953, when a ceasefire was agreed upon.

⇒ UN counter-attack
▬▬ Ceasefire line Jul 27, 1953

Nov 25, 1950 Farthest advance of UN troops toward the Chinese border

Oct 19, 1950 Pyongyang captured by UN forces

Sep 15, 1950 40,000 UN troops plus 7,000 South Korean troops launch amphibious assault at Inchon and bombard the city before recapturing Seoul and heading north

Nov 26–Dec 13, 1950 UN forces are encircled by Chinese troops at the Battle of Chosin Reservoir

Jul 27, 1953 An armistice line is established close to the 38th parallel

East Sea (Sea of Japan)

Yellow Sea

38th parallel

CHINA

NORTH KOREA

SOUTH

Chongjin
Kimchaek
Tanchon
Hyesan
Changbai
Yalu
Marpo
Kangye
Amu
Chosan
Sinuiju
Dandong
Hungnam
Wonsan
Kosong
Pyongyang
Haeju
Panmunjom
Seoul
Wonju
Inchon
Ulchin

Sep 16, 1950 US troops head north from the Pusan Perimeter

Sep 16–Oct 24, 1950 UN reinforcements arrive from Japan

J A P A N

Strait

Korea

Pohang

Taegu

Pusan

Tsushima (governed by Japan)

Sep 15, 1950 Southern limit of North Korea's advance

KOREA

Taejon

Kunsan

Kwangju

Mokpo

▽ **The victims of war**
A young Korean girl and her baby brother stand in front of an M-26 tank in June 1951. About 2.5 million Korean civilians were killed or wounded during the war, and many were made homeless.

KOREAN WAR

The Cold War became "hot" in June 1950, when North Korean forces attacked South Korea in an attempt to unite the Korean peninsula under communist control. The war continued for 3 years, with the Chinese supporting the North and the US the South; the expected confrontation between the USSR and the US never happened.

In 1945, at the end of World War II, the US and USSR occupied the Japanese colony of Korea. They divided the country along the 38th parallel, with Soviet forces taking control of the north and the US the south. The intention was to rule jointly for 5 years until Korea became independent, but disagreements between the two countries about Korea's future solidified the division. Both North Korea and South Korea held their own separate elections in 1948, and the USSR and US withdrew their troops the following year. However, North Korea intended to unify the peninsula under communist rule, and with tacit Soviet support, but no promise

of troops, it attacked South Korea in June 1950. The invasion was unexpected, enabling the North Korean troops to occupy almost the entire peninsula. US, South Korean, and Allied troops, endorsed by the UN, responded from July. The frontline then changed as UN troops headed north, only to be met in November by a Chinese invasion. By the middle of 1951, there was a stalemate, which resulted in an agreed armistice in July 1953 to withdraw forces either side of the 38th parallel. That armistice remains in force, as no permanent peace treaty has been signed to end the war.

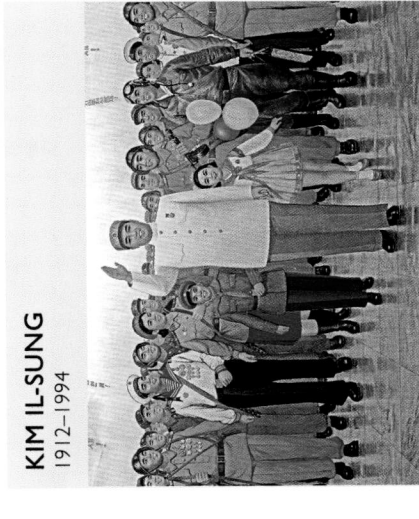

KIM IL-SUNG
1912–1994

Born near Pyongyang, Kim Il-Sung was the leader of North Korea from 1948 until his death in 1994. He became involved in communism as a student and in the 1930s joined an anti-Japanese guerrilla group. In 1940, he traveled to the USSR and later became a major in the Soviet Army. At the end of World War II, he returned to Korea intent on creating a unified communist nation.

1 THE PHILIPPINES 1935–1946

The US had acquired the Philippines from Spain after success in the 1898 Spanish–American War. The islands were granted Commonwealth or autonomous status in 1935, but were then occupied by the Japanese between 1941 and 1945. After liberation, the Philippines became an independent republic on July 4, 1946.

2 INDONESIA 1945–1949

The Indonesian National Party proclaimed the country's independence from the Netherlands on August 17, 1945. After much fighting between the two countries, as well as a communist insurrection, independence was achieved on December 27, 1949, although constitutional links remained with the Dutch crown until 1956.

3 FRENCH INDOCHINA 1945–1954

At the end of Japanese occupation in 1945, the Viet Minh nationalist independence coalition, led by Ho Chi Minh, occupied Hanoi and proclaimed a provisional government. The French tried to restore colonial rule, leading to war in 1946. They were defeated, and on July 20, 1954, they granted independence to Cambodia, Laos, and Vietnam.

CHINA

TAIWAN

Macao **1999**   Hong Kong **1997**

BURMA **1948**

Dien Bien Phu

LAOS **1954**

Hanoi

Gulf of Tongking

Hainan

Yangon (formerly Rangoon)

Bay of Bengal

THAILAND

1954 French suffer massive defeat at hands of General Giap and the Viet Minh at Dien Bien Phu

Andaman Islands to India

Andaman Sea

CAMBODIA **1954**

VIETNAM **1954**

1954 Vietnam is divided in two at the Geneva Accords, with both parts being granted independence

South China Sea

Manila

Philippine Sea

PACIFIC OCEAN

Nicobar Islands to India

Phnom Penh

Saigon (Ho Chi Minh City)

Gulf of Siam

PHILIPPINES

Sulu Sea

1946

1984 Brunei gains independence from the UK as an independent sultanate

BRITISH NORTH BORNEO (SABAH) **1963**

BRUNEI **1984**

1965 Having joined Malaysia in 1963, Singapore then leaves to become an independent island republic in 1965

MALAYA **1957**

M A L A Y S I A

SARAWAK **1963**

Celebes Sea

SINGAPORE **1963**

Borneo

Celebes

Sumatra

I N D O N E S I A

1949

Java Sea

Banda Sea

Java

Flores

EAST TIMOR **2002**

Sumba   *Timor*

1975 Indonesia occupies the Portuguese colony of East Timor, which gains its independence in 2002

Timor Sea

6 HONG KONG AND MACAO 1997–1999

In 1997, with the end of Britain's 99-year lease on the New Territories, Hong Kong was handed back to China. Portugal then returned Macao to Chinese rule in 1999, abolishing the last remaining European colony in Asia. The age of European colonialism in Asia was now over.

● Hong Kong   △ Macao

5 NEW GUINEA 1949–1975

After occupation by Australia in World War I, the northeastern half of New Guinea became an Australian mandate. It remained under Australia's control until 1975, when it became independent as Papua New Guinea. Western New Guinea had been a Dutch colony, but in 1963, it became part of Indonesia under the name of Irian Jaya.

AUSTRALIA

END OF COLONIAL RULE

The imperial powers that had colonies in Southeast Asia slowly granted their former lands independence after the end of World War II, starting with the US in the Philippines in 1946, and ending with Portugal handing over Macao to China in 1999. The transition was often violent, with fighting particularly intense in Indonesia and French Indochina.

KEY

- UK
- France
- Netherlands
- US
- Portugal
- Australia
- ⚑ Independence from colonial rule

TIMELINE

1
2
3
4
5
6

1920　1940　1960　1980　2000

△ **The fight for independence**
Protesters gather in 1975 to support an East Timor independence party. Having gained independence from Portugal in November 1975, East Timor was then occupied by Indonesia 9 days later.

Jayapura

IRIAN JAYA 1963

TERRITORY OF NEW GUINEA

PAPUA NEW GUINEA 1975

TERRITORY OF PAPUA

New Guinea

1963 Netherlands hands over Irian Jaya to Indonesia

Coral Sea

Port Moresby

4 MALAYA 1948–1963

The Japanese occupation of Malaya (1942–1945) stirred up nationalist sentiment, prompting the British to set up the Federation of Malaya in 1948. The federation united the territories and guaranteed the rights of the Malay people. It gained full independence in 1957. In 1963, the new state of Malaysia was formed, including the Federation of Malaya and the British colonies of Sarawak, Sabah, and Singapore.

DECOLONIZATION OF SOUTHEAST ASIA

In 1945, all of Southeast Asia, except Thailand, was nominally under colonial control. However, it was a time of great change; within 30 years, former empires had disappeared, and what had previously been colonies were replaced by independent states. The final colonial relics were handed over at the end of the 20th century.

During World War II, the Japanese invaded Southeast Asia, driving out the colonial powers. In 1945, at the end of the war, the colonial powers returned. However, their right to rule was now seriously challenged, as they were seen to have been weak in the face of Japanese aggression. Nationalist sentiments, stirred up by the Japanese occupation, were on the rise. Indonesian nationalists proclaimed independence even before the Dutch had time to return to Indonesia, and the Viet Minh, a Vietnamese independence group, surprised the French with their own declaration. One by one, the imperial powers started to leave the region.

The US was the first to go, leaving the Philippines peacefully in 1946, followed by the Dutch from Indonesia in 1949, after much fighting. The French left Indochina in 1954, after losing a major battle in Vietnam, then the British left Malaya between 1957 and 1963, their departure complicated by a communist uprising. The merged state of Papua New Guinea gained its independence from Australia in 1975, while Brunei gained its independence from Britain in 1984. After the British departed from Hong Kong in 1997, Macao—the last European colony in Asia—was handed over by the Portuguese to China in 1999. The colonial era was over.

"You can kill ten of my men for every one I kill of yours. But even at those odds, you will lose and I will win."

HO CHI MINH, VIETNAM'S LEADER, TO FRENCH COLONIALISTS, 1946

SUKARNO
1901–1970

Sukarno was a charter member of the Indonesian National Party, which was formed in 1927. He was jailed for political activities in 1929, and then spent 13 of the next 15 years in prison or exile. Politically astute during the Japanese occupation of 1942–1945, he emerged as the de facto president of Indonesia in November 1945. Sukarno steered Indonesia to independence in 1949, and gained great prestige as leader of the nonaligned Bandung Conference in 1955. His increasingly authoritarian tendencies and confrontation with Malaya caused him to lose power to the army leader General Muhammad Suharto in 1967.

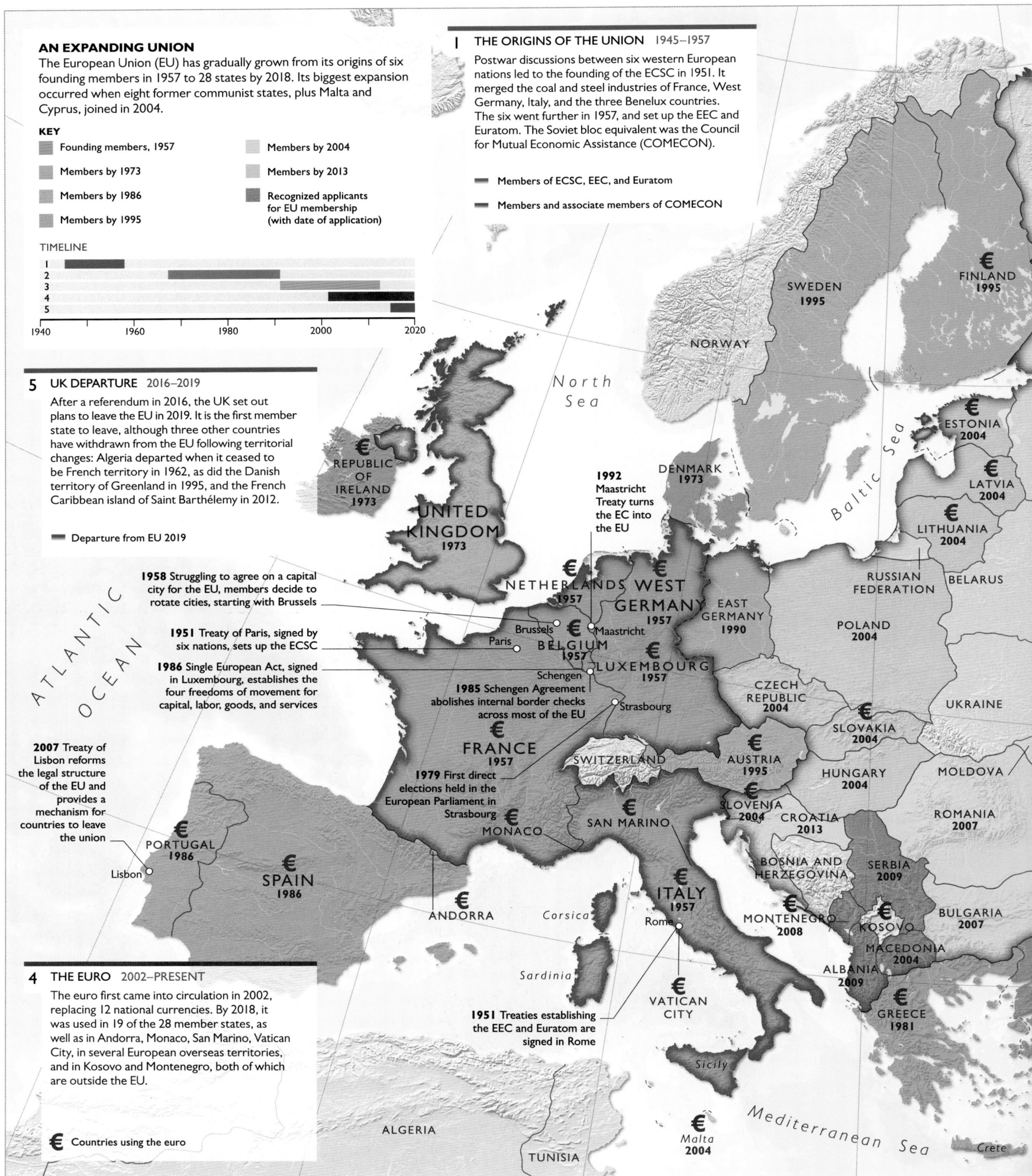

AN EXPANDING UNION

The European Union (EU) has gradually grown from its origins of six founding members in 1957 to 28 states by 2018. Its biggest expansion occurred when eight former communist states, plus Malta and Cyprus, joined in 2004.

KEY

- Founding members, 1957
- Members by 1973
- Members by 1986
- Members by 1995
- Members by 2004
- Members by 2013
- Recognized applicants for EU membership (with date of application)

TIMELINE

1 | 2 | 3 | 4 | 5

1940 | 1960 | 1980 | 2000 | 2020

1 THE ORIGINS OF THE UNION 1945–1957

Postwar discussions between six western European nations led to the founding of the ECSC in 1951. It merged the coal and steel industries of France, West Germany, Italy, and the three Benelux countries. The six went further in 1957, and set up the EEC and Euratom. The Soviet bloc equivalent was the Council for Mutual Economic Assistance (COMECON).

- Members of ECSC, EEC, and Euratom
- Members and associate members of COMECON

5 UK DEPARTURE 2016–2019

After a referendum in 2016, the UK set out plans to leave the EU in 2019. It is the first member state to leave, although three other countries have withdrawn from the EU following territorial changes: Algeria departed when it ceased to be French territory in 1962, as did the Danish territory of Greenland in 1995, and the French Caribbean island of Saint Barthélemy in 2012.

- Departure from EU 2019

1958 Struggling to agree on a capital city for the EU, members decide to rotate cities, starting with Brussels

1951 Treaty of Paris, signed by six nations, sets up the ECSC

1986 Single European Act, signed in Luxembourg, establishes the four freedoms of movement for capital, labor, goods, and services

1985 Schengen Agreement abolishes internal border checks across most of the EU

1992 Maastricht Treaty turns the EC into the EU

2007 Treaty of Lisbon reforms the legal structure of the EU and provides a mechanism for countries to leave the union

1979 First direct elections held in the European Parliament in Strasbourg

1951 Treaties establishing the EEC and Euratom are signed in Rome

4 THE EURO 2002–PRESENT

The euro first came into circulation in 2002, replacing 12 national currencies. By 2018, it was used in 19 of the 28 member states, as well as in Andorra, Monaco, San Marino, Vatican City, in several European overseas territories, and in Kosovo and Montenegro, both of which are outside the EU.

€ Countries using the euro

Map labels

North Sea
Baltic Sea
ATLANTIC OCEAN
Mediterranean Sea

NORWAY
SWEDEN 1995
FINLAND 1995
ESTONIA 2004
LATVIA 2004
LITHUANIA 2004
RUSSIAN FEDERATION
BELARUS
POLAND 2004
REPUBLIC OF IRELAND 1973
UNITED KINGDOM 1973
DENMARK 1973
NETHERLANDS 1957
WEST GERMANY 1957
EAST GERMANY 1990
Brussels
Maastricht
BELGIUM 1957
LUXEMBOURG 1957
Schengen
Paris
Strasbourg
CZECH REPUBLIC 2004
UKRAINE
SLOVAKIA 2004
FRANCE 1957
SWITZERLAND
AUSTRIA 1995
HUNGARY 2004
MOLDOVA
SLOVENIA 2004
CROATIA 2013
ROMANIA 2007
SAN MARINO
MONACO
BOSNIA AND HERZEGOVINA
SERBIA 2009
PORTUGAL 1986
Lisbon
SPAIN 1986
ANDORRA
Corsica
ITALY 1957
Rome
MONTENEGRO 2008
KOSOVO
MACEDONIA 2004
BULGARIA 2007
VATICAN CITY
ALBANIA 2009
GREECE 1981
Sardinia
Sicily
ALGERIA
TUNISIA
Malta 2004
Crete

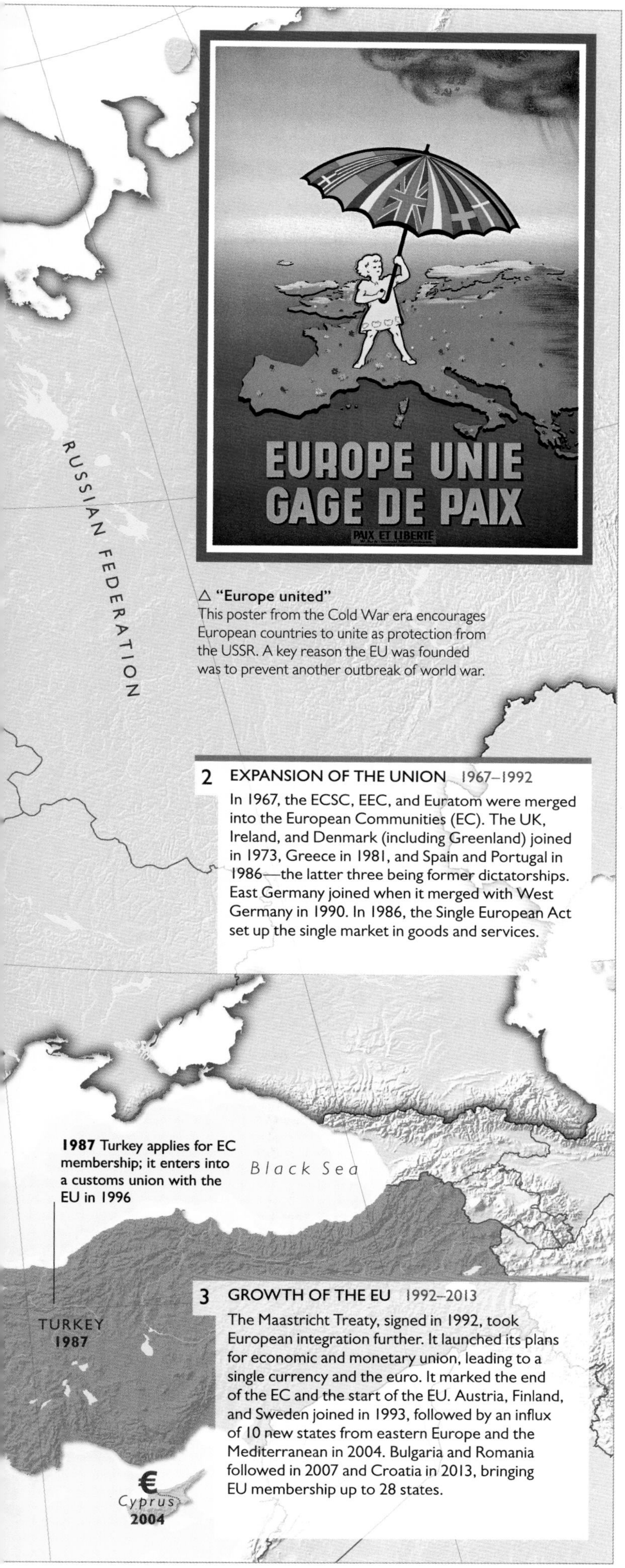

△ **"Europe united"**
This poster from the Cold War era encourages European countries to unite as protection from the USSR. A key reason the EU was founded was to prevent another outbreak of world war.

RUSSIAN FEDERATION

2 EXPANSION OF THE UNION 1967–1992
In 1967, the ECSC, EEC, and Euratom were merged into the European Communities (EC). The UK, Ireland, and Denmark (including Greenland) joined in 1973, Greece in 1981, and Spain and Portugal in 1986—the latter three being former dictatorships. East Germany joined when it merged with West Germany in 1990. In 1986, the Single European Act set up the single market in goods and services.

1987 Turkey applies for EC membership; it enters into a customs union with the EU in 1996

Black Sea

TURKEY
1987

3 GROWTH OF THE EU 1992–2013
The Maastricht Treaty, signed in 1992, took European integration further. It launched its plans for economic and monetary union, leading to a single currency and the euro. It marked the end of the EC and the start of the EU. Austria, Finland, and Sweden joined in 1993, followed by an influx of 10 new states from eastern Europe and the Mediterranean in 2004. Bulgaria and Romania followed in 2007 and Croatia in 2013, bringing EU membership up to 28 states.

€
Cyprus
2004

EUROPEAN UNITY

Since the end of the Roman Empire in 476 CE, the dream of a united Europe has existed in some form or other. In 1951, following the mass devastation of World War II, six western European nations began a process that would ultimately lead to a political and economic union of 28 member states.

World War II was the third time in 70 years that France and Germany had been at war with one another. To end this age-old conflict, and to confront the extreme nationalism that had so recently devastated Europe, French and West German politicians began to plan a new future together. In the 1951 Treaty of Paris, they merged their coal and steel industries with those of Italy and the three Benelux countries (the Netherlands, Luxembourg, and Belgium), forming the European Coal and Steel Community (ECSC). This union was a precursor to the European Economic Community (EEC) and the European Atomic Energy Community (Euratom), which were established by the same six countries in the Treaty of Rome in 1957. From then on, the competencies and the membership of the EEC grew. In 1967, it was renamed the European Communities (EC), and in 1992 it became the European Union (EU). Waves of new members joined after 1973, and in 2002 a single currency, the euro, was introduced by 12 member states. All EU member states have been at peace with each other since joining the organization, and membership is coveted by former communist states in the Balkans. Only a few European nations are outside the Union. However, 40 years of expansion were dashed in 2016 when the UK announced plans to leave the EU.

> *"The coming together of the nations of Europe requires the elimination of the age-old opposition of France and Germany."*
>
> ROBERT SCHUMAN, FRENCH FOREIGN MINISTER, MAY 9, 1950

ROBERT SCHUMAN
1886–1963

One of the founding fathers of the EU, Robert Schuman was born a German national in Luxembourg. His mother was from Luxembourg, and his father, who came from Alsace, was French at birth but became German when the region was annexed by Germany in 1871. In 1919, when Alsace was reunited with France after World War I, Robert Schuman became a French national. As French foreign minister, he helped to set up the Council of Europe in 1949, to enhance human rights, and, together with French economist Jean Monnet, he was a guiding light in setting up the European Coal and Steel Community (ECSC) in 1951—the forerunner of the EU.

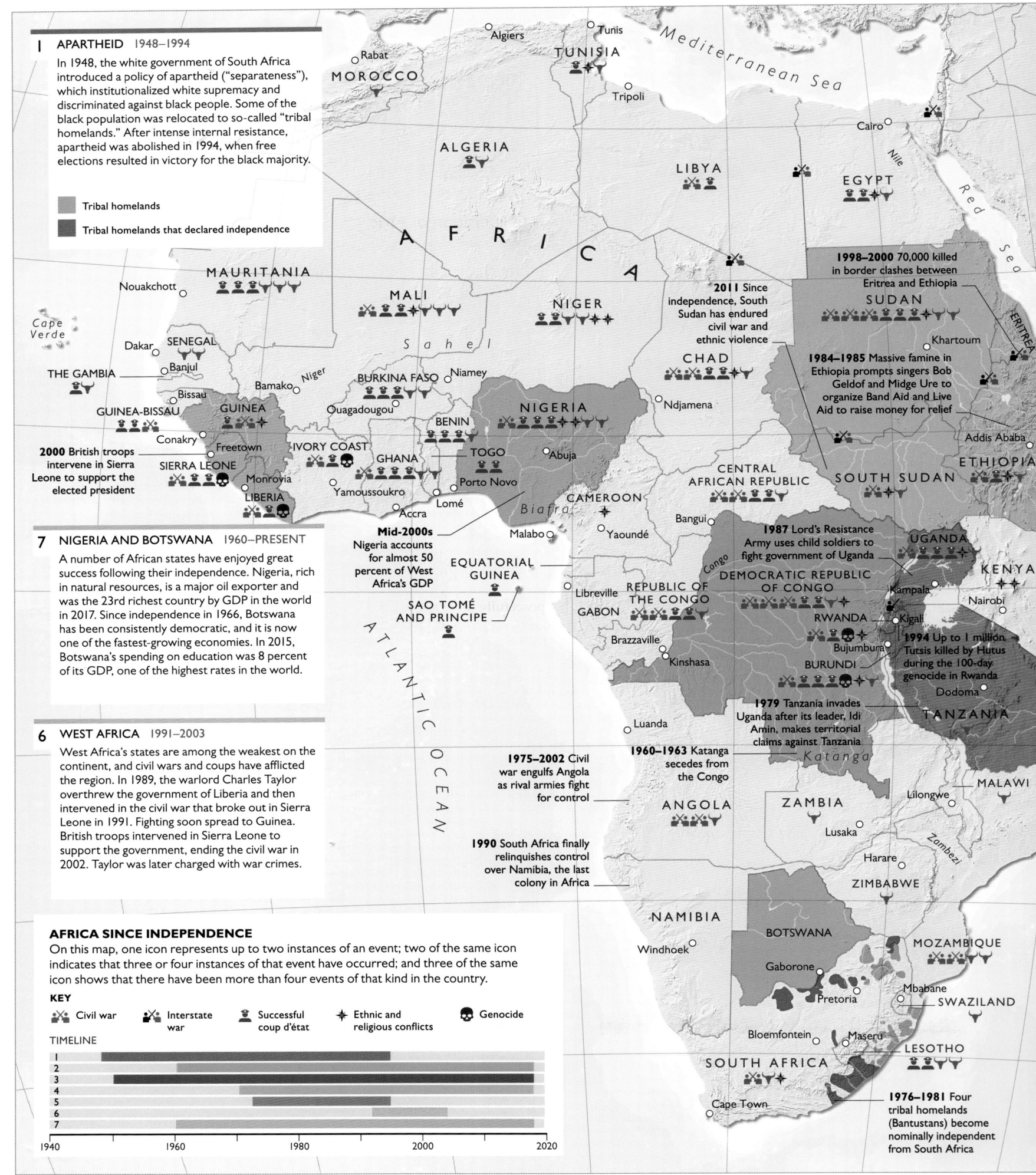

1 APARTHEID 1948–1994

In 1948, the white government of South Africa introduced a policy of apartheid ("separateness"), which institutionalized white supremacy and discriminated against black people. Some of the black population was relocated to so-called "tribal homelands." After intense internal resistance, apartheid was abolished in 1994, when free elections resulted in victory for the black majority.

- Tribal homelands
- Tribal homelands that declared independence

7 NIGERIA AND BOTSWANA 1960–PRESENT

A number of African states have enjoyed great success following their independence. Nigeria, rich in natural resources, is a major oil exporter and was the 23rd richest country by GDP in the world in 2017. Since independence in 1966, Botswana has been consistently democratic, and it is now one of the fastest-growing economies. In 2015, Botswana's spending on education was 8 percent of its GDP, one of the highest rates in the world.

6 WEST AFRICA 1991–2003

West Africa's states are among the weakest on the continent, and civil wars and coups have afflicted the region. In 1989, the warlord Charles Taylor overthrew the government of Liberia and then intervened in the civil war that broke out in Sierra Leone in 1991. Fighting soon spread to Guinea. British troops intervened in Sierra Leone to support the government, ending the civil war in 2002. Taylor was later charged with war crimes.

AFRICA SINCE INDEPENDENCE

On this map, one icon represents up to two instances of an event; two of the same icon indicates that three or four instances of that event have occurred; and three of the same icon shows that there have been more than four events of that kind in the country.

KEY

- Civil war
- Interstate war
- Successful coup d'état
- Ethnic and religious conflicts
- Genocide

TIMELINE

Map labels and annotations:

1998–2000 70,000 killed in border clashes between Eritrea and Ethiopia

2011 Since independence, South Sudan has endured civil war and ethnic violence

1984–1985 Massive famine in Ethiopia prompts singers Bob Geldof and Midge Ure to organize Band Aid and Live Aid to raise money for relief

2000 British troops intervene in Sierra Leone to support the elected president

Mid-2000s Nigeria accounts for almost 50 percent of West Africa's GDP

1987 Lord's Resistance Army uses child soldiers to fight government of Uganda

1994 Up to 1 million Tutsis killed by Hutus during the 100-day genocide in Rwanda

1979 Tanzania invades Uganda after its leader, Idi Amin, makes territorial claims against Tanzania

1975–2002 Civil war engulfs Angola as rival armies fight for control

1960–1963 Katanga secedes from the Congo

1990 South Africa finally relinquishes control over Namibia, the last colony in Africa

1976–1981 Four tribal homelands (Bantustans) become nominally independent from South Africa

2 DEMOCRATIC REPUBLIC OF CONGO
1960–PRESENT

The DR Congo's independence in 1960 created a series of crises. The mineral-rich province of Katanga, hoping to secede, broke out in violence, and the recently elected Prime Minister Patrice Lumumba called on the USSR for support. Fearing communist influence in Africa, the US encouraged Congolese President Joseph Kasa-Vubu to depose Lumumba. The chief of staff of the army, Joseph-Désiré Mobutu, then launched a coup against both leaders, installing a new government. He assumed power in 1965, ruling the country (which he renamed Zaire in 1971) as a dictator.

3 FAMINE 1950–PRESENT

While famine has affected parts of the continent for centuries, from the 1950s, increasingly severe desertification; the effects of climate change, such as droughts; and problems caused by civil war caused famine to become more frequent across much of Africa. Millions have died, despite the intervention of international aid agencies.

🐂 Famine

4 EAST AFRICA 1970–PRESENT

From 1970–1993, Eritrea fought a long war to free itself from Ethiopia, which had taken control of it following World War II. It eventually won its independence, becoming a one-party repressive state. South Sudan fought for independence from Sudan from 1989–2005, becoming the world's newest state in 2011, when it peacefully gained independence. Central government in Somalia has collapsed since 1991 as rival warlords and Islamic groups have battled for control.

5 GREAT LAKES REGION 1972–1994

Conflict has affected much of the Great Lakes region. In 1979, Tanzania invaded Uganda to expel the tyrannical leader Idi Amin, after he tried to annex the Kagera Region in Tanzania. In Rwanda and Burundi, rivalry between two ethnic groups, the Hutu and the Tutsi, has led to ongoing conflict. A genocidal attack by Hutus against Tutsis in Rwanda in 1994 resulted in up to 1 million deaths. Many refugees fled to the DR Congo, where fighting continued.

▽ **A new dawn**
The election of Nelson Mandela as the first black president of South Africa in 1994 marked the end of apartheid, in force since 1948.

DECOLONIZATION OF AFRICA

The liberation of Africa from European rulers created 54 independent nations, many of them unprepared for the tasks of government and administration. Their recent history has been varied; while some continue to struggle with war and famine, others have been successful politically, socially, and economically.

The move toward decolonization and independence from Europe began in the 1950s, when colonies began to demand self-rule. At that time, only Egypt, Ethiopia, Liberia, and South Africa were independent nations. Libya was the first to gain its independence, in 1951 (from France and the UK), followed by Tunisia and Morocco (from France) and Sudan (from the UK) in 1956. From then on, new African countries appeared almost annually. Most gained independence peacefully, although French resistance to Algerian independence led to a brutal civil war from 1954–1962, and Portugal's refusal to hand over its five African colonies led to wars of revolt until 1974. A white-minority revolt in Rhodesia (which became Zimbabwe) delayed its independence from the UK until 1980.

By 1990, every country in Africa was independent, but many faced problems, including numerous changes of government through civil wars, coups d'état, and military dictatorships, as well as issues such as widespread poverty and famine. However, many countries are now experiencing success, including economic growth, increasing political stability, and social reform.

> *"The best way of learning to be an independent sovereign state is to be an independent sovereign state."*
>
> KWAME NKRUMAH, FIRST PRESIDENT OF GHANA, IN A SPEECH TO THE LEGISLATIVE ASSEMBLY, MAY 18, 1956

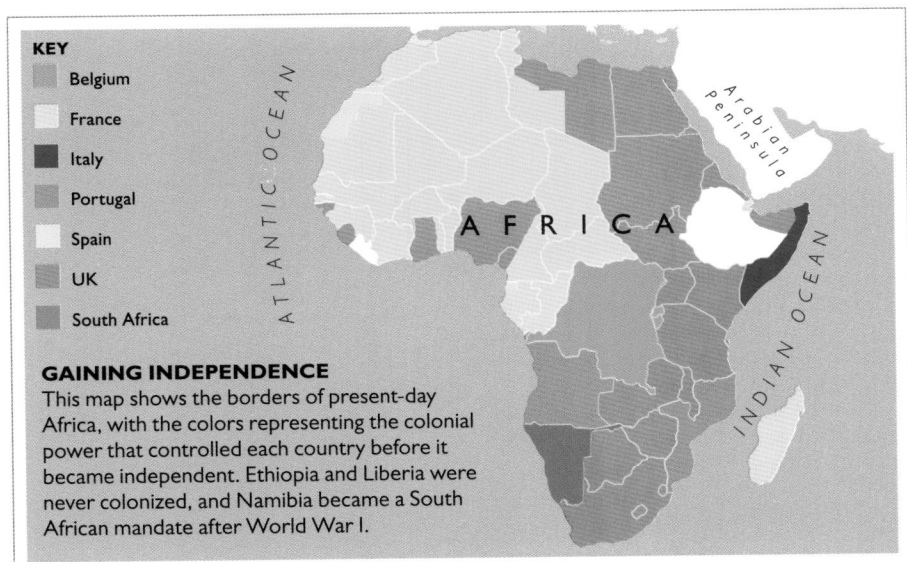

KEY

- Belgium
- France
- Italy
- Portugal
- Spain
- UK
- South Africa

GAINING INDEPENDENCE
This map shows the borders of present-day Africa, with the colors representing the colonial power that controlled each country before it became independent. Ethiopia and Liberia were never colonized, and Namibia became a South African mandate after World War I.

SAUDI ARABIA

JIBOUTI

SOMALILAND

Ogaden

PUNTLAND

SOMALIA

Mogadishu

1990s Somaliland and Puntland both declare their independence from Somalia

OMOROS

Mayotte to France

MADAGASCAR

Antananarivo

ROCKETS AND THE SPACE RACE

The development of the nuclear bomb and rocket technology during World War II triggered a postwar arms race between the US and the USSR. As the Cold War escalated, this race also headed into space, as each side used its rocket technology to travel to the Moon and beyond.

On September 8, 1944, Germany deployed the world's first long-range ballistic missile, the V-2 rocket. It was a devastating weapon, capable of traveling up to 200 miles (320 km) and reaching a top speed of 3,580 mph (5,760 kph). A few months earlier, it had also accidentally become the first artificial object to reach outer space when a test launch went wrong, and the rocket headed vertically off its launch site. From this military beginning emerged the technology both to carry intercontinental ballistic nuclear warheads to their distant targets and to power spacecraft and satellites into space.

At the end of World War II, and with the Cold War escalating (see pp.314–315), the US and the USSR scrambled to seize as much of this new German technology as possible. Some of the German scientists who had developed the V-2 rocket were recruited by the US to work on its military and space programs, while the Soviets based their missile program on the German rocket technology they had seized when they took over eastern Germany in 1945. The superpowers now began to fight a war on two fronts. A nuclear arms race started, with the US and the USSR each amassing enough weaponry to destroy the Earth many times over. Only the certainty of mutual destruction prevented all-out war. In a war that was as much about propaganda as weaponry, a race to reach space also began, with each country fighting to earn the international honor of having one of their men become the first person on the Moon.

PROPAGANDA
SOVIET POSTER

The US and the USSR used propaganda to promote their political ideology—capitalism or communism—and to criticize the beliefs of their enemy. Both superpowers were eager to send the first person into space because whoever achieved this victory would be able to use it for propaganda purposes and prove the superiority of their technology. This poster celebrates the USSR's victory, which came in 1961, when it sent Yuri Gagarin into space.

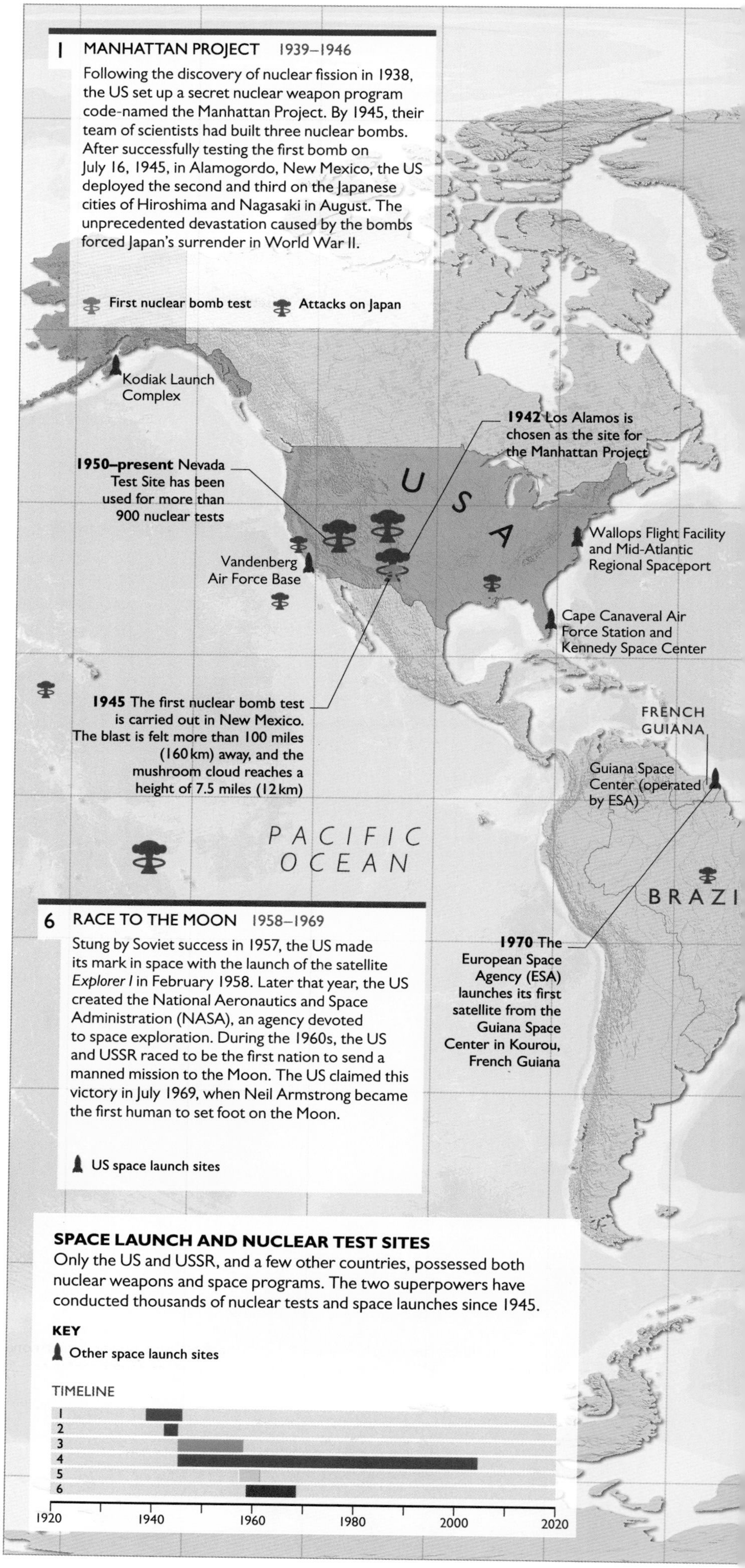

1 MANHATTAN PROJECT 1939–1946

Following the discovery of nuclear fission in 1938, the US set up a secret nuclear weapon program code-named the Manhattan Project. By 1945, their team of scientists had built three nuclear bombs. After successfully testing the first bomb on July 16, 1945, in Alamogordo, New Mexico, the US deployed the second and third on the Japanese cities of Hiroshima and Nagasaki in August. The unprecedented devastation caused by the bombs forced Japan's surrender in World War II.

☁ First nuclear bomb test   ☁ Attacks on Japan

Kodiak Launch Complex

1942 Los Alamos is chosen as the site for the Manhattan Project

1950–present Nevada Test Site has been used for more than 900 nuclear tests

Vandenberg Air Force Base

Wallops Flight Facility and Mid-Atlantic Regional Spaceport

Cape Canaveral Air Force Station and Kennedy Space Center

1945 The first nuclear bomb test is carried out in New Mexico. The blast is felt more than 100 miles (160 km) away, and the mushroom cloud reaches a height of 7.5 miles (12 km)

FRENCH GUIANA

Guiana Space Center (operated by ESA)

PACIFIC OCEAN

BRAZIL

6 RACE TO THE MOON 1958–1969

Stung by Soviet success in 1957, the US made its mark in space with the launch of the satellite *Explorer I* in February 1958. Later that year, the US created the National Aeronautics and Space Administration (NASA), an agency devoted to space exploration. During the 1960s, the US and USSR raced to be the first nation to send a manned mission to the Moon. The US claimed this victory in July 1969, when Neil Armstrong became the first human to set foot on the Moon.

1970 The European Space Agency (ESA) launches its first satellite from the Guiana Space Center in Kourou, French Guiana

⚓ US space launch sites

SPACE LAUNCH AND NUCLEAR TEST SITES

Only the US and USSR, and a few other countries, possessed both nuclear weapons and space programs. The two superpowers have conducted thousands of nuclear tests and space launches since 1945.

KEY

⚓ Other space launch sites

TIMELINE

	1920	1940	1960	1980	2000	2020
1						
2						
3						
4						
5						
6						

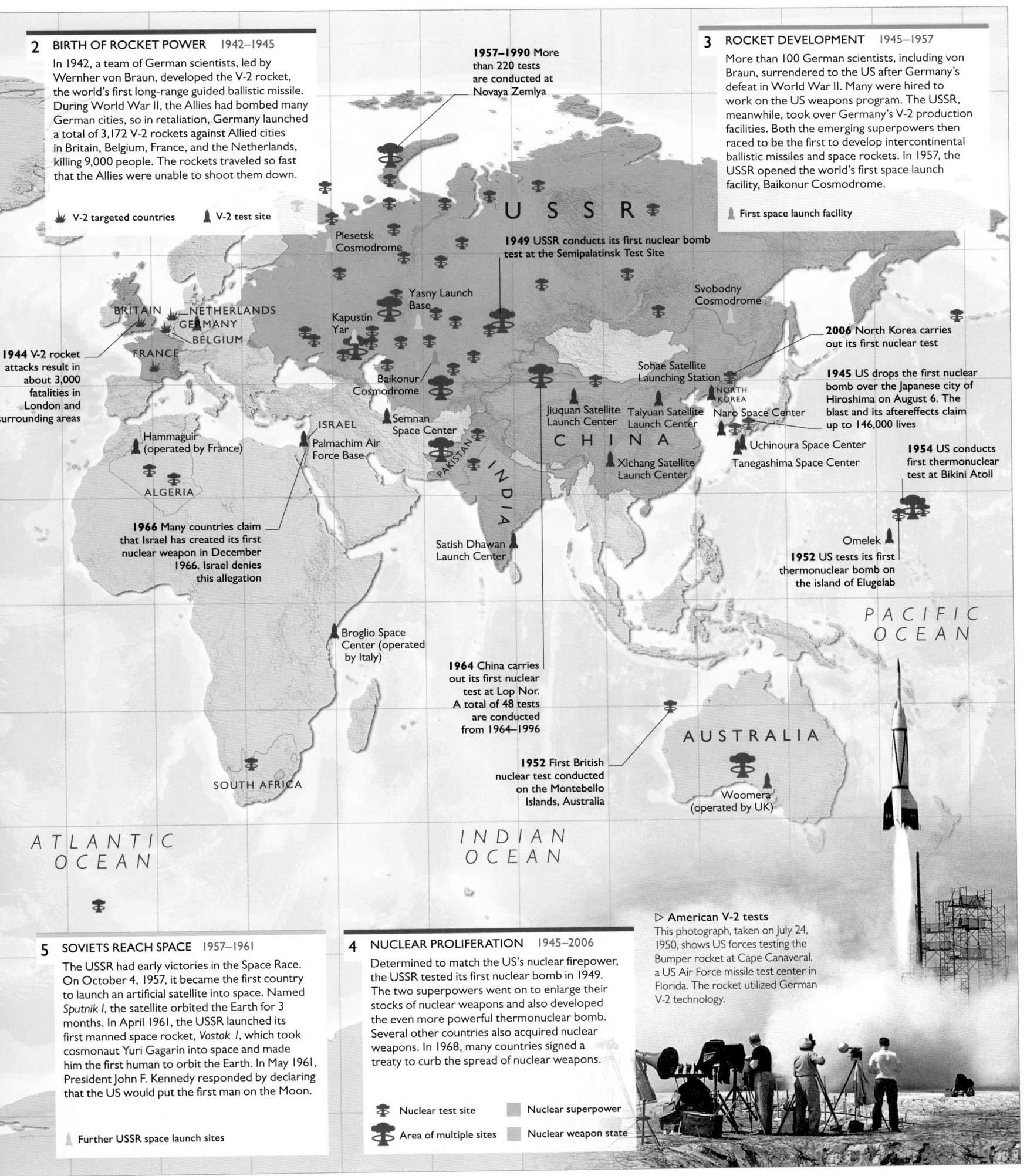

2 BIRTH OF ROCKET POWER 1942–1945

In 1942, a team of German scientists, led by Wernher von Braun, developed the V-2 rocket, the world's first long-range guided ballistic missile. During World War II, the Allies had bombed many German cities, so in retaliation, Germany launched a total of 3,172 V-2 rockets against Allied cities in Britain, Belgium, France, and the Netherlands, killing 9,000 people. The rockets traveled so fast that the Allies were unable to shoot them down.

- ✦ V-2 targeted countries
- ▲ V-2 test site

1957–1990 More than 220 tests are conducted at Novaya Zemlya

1949 USSR conducts its first nuclear bomb test at the Semipalatinsk Test Site

Plesetsk Cosmodrome

Yasny Launch Base

Kapustin Yar

Baikonur Cosmodrome

Semnan Space Center

Hammaguir (operated by France)

1944 V-2 rocket attacks result in about 3,000 fatalities in London and surrounding areas

ISRAEL
Palmachim Air Force Base

1966 Many countries claim that Israel has created its first nuclear weapon in December 1966. Israel denies this allegation

Satish Dhawan Launch Center

Broglio Space Center (operated by Italy)

1964 China carries out its first nuclear test at Lop Nor. A total of 48 tests are conducted from 1964–1996

3 ROCKET DEVELOPMENT 1945–1957

More than 100 German scientists, including von Braun, surrendered to the US after Germany's defeat in World War II. Many were hired to work on the US weapons program. The USSR, meanwhile, took over Germany's V-2 production facilities. Both the emerging superpowers then raced to be the first to develop intercontinental ballistic missiles and space rockets. In 1957, the USSR opened the world's first space launch facility, Baikonur Cosmodrome.

- ▲ First space launch facility

Svobodny Cosmodrome

2006 North Korea carries out its first nuclear test

1945 US drops the first nuclear bomb over the Japanese city of Hiroshima on August 6. The blast and its aftereffects claim up to 146,000 lives

Sohae Satellite Launching Station

NORTH KOREA

Naro Space Center

Jiuquan Satellite Launch Center

Taiyuan Satellite Launch Center

Xichang Satellite Launch Center

Uchinoura Space Center

Tanegashima Space Center

1954 US conducts first thermonuclear test at Bikini Atoll

Omelek

1952 US tests its first thermonuclear bomb on the island of Elugelab

PACIFIC OCEAN

AUSTRALIA

1952 First British nuclear test conducted on the Montebello Islands, Australia

Woomera (operated by UK)

ATLANTIC OCEAN

INDIAN OCEAN

▷ **American V-2 tests**
This photograph, taken on July 24, 1950, shows US forces testing the Bumper rocket at Cape Canaveral, a US Air Force missile test center in Florida. The rocket utilized German V-2 technology.

5 SOVIETS REACH SPACE 1957–1961

The USSR had early victories in the Space Race. On October 4, 1957, it became the first country to launch an artificial satellite into space. Named *Sputnik I*, the satellite orbited the Earth for 3 months. In April 1961, the USSR launched its first manned space rocket, *Vostok 1*, which took cosmonaut Yuri Gagarin into space and made him the first human to orbit the Earth. In May 1961, President John F. Kennedy responded by declaring that the US would put the first man on the Moon.

- ▲ Further USSR space launch sites

4 NUCLEAR PROLIFERATION 1945–2006

Determined to match the US's nuclear firepower, the USSR tested its first nuclear bomb in 1949. The two superpowers went on to enlarge their stocks of nuclear weapons and also developed the even more powerful thermonuclear bomb. Several other countries also acquired nuclear weapons. In 1968, many countries signed a treaty to curb the spread of nuclear weapons.

- ☢ Nuclear test site
- ☁ Area of multiple sites
- ▨ Nuclear superpower
- ▨ Nuclear weapon state

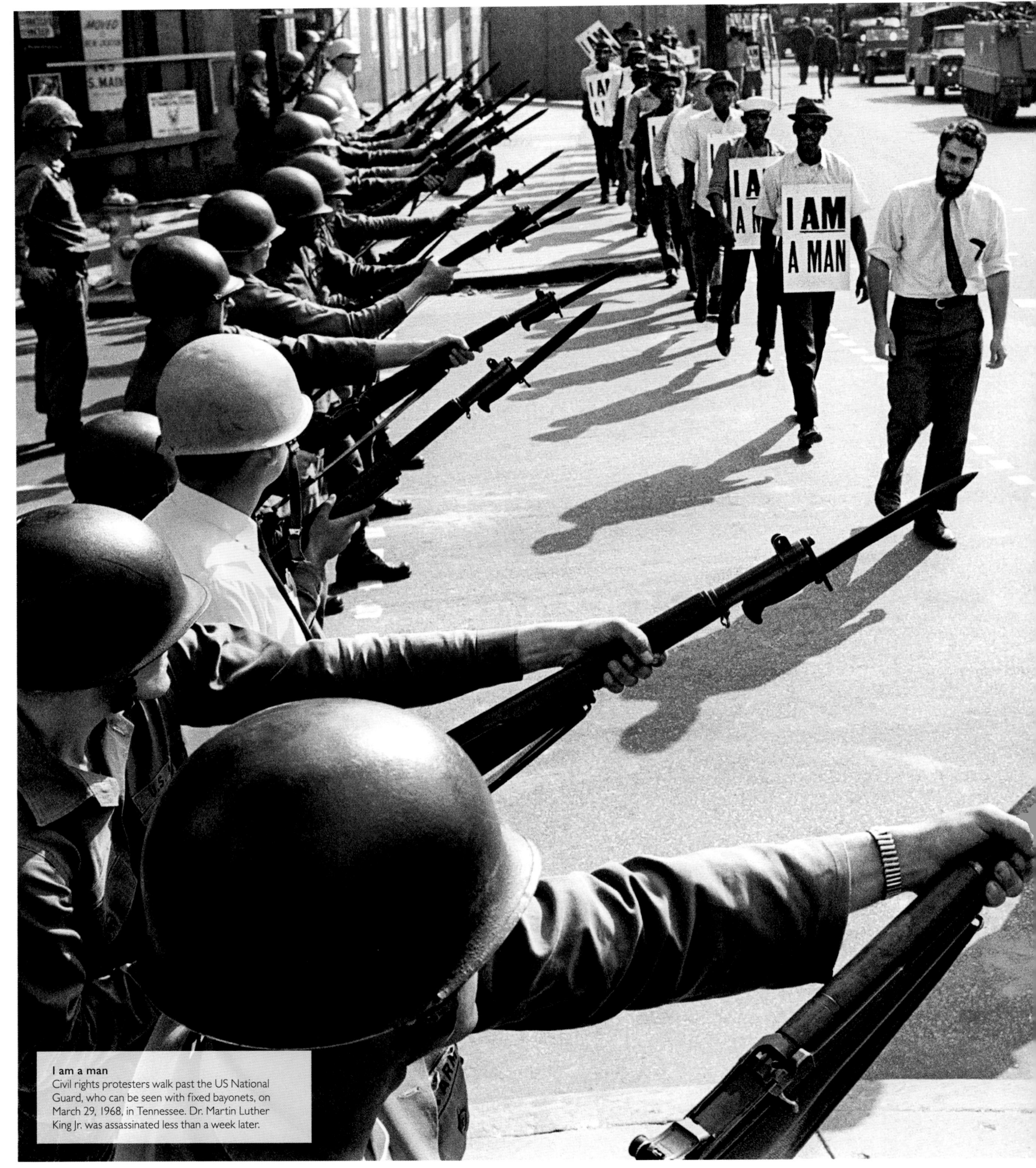

I am a man
Civil rights protesters walk past the US National Guard, who can be seen with fixed bayonets, on March 29, 1968, in Tennessee. Dr. Martin Luther King Jr. was assassinated less than a week later.

CIVIL RIGHTS AND STUDENT REVOLTS

Activists have campaigned for human rights since the turn of the 20th century. In the 1960s, the US and France in particular saw popular pressure for reform.

From the abolition of slavery to voting rights for women, social movements have been an instrument of change across the world. The US in the 1950s was a country riddled with racial inequality. In December 1955, Rosa Parks, a black civil rights activist, refused to give up her seat on a bus to a white passenger in Alabama. Her arrest sparked the modern civil rights movement. In August 1963, Dr. Martin Luther King Jr., a leading proponent of civil rights in the US, gave an inspiring speech to about 250,000 protesters, setting out his vision of a country free of prejudice. Segregation was abolished in 1964; the following year, all black people were given voting rights.

The year 1968 became the year of revolutions. Even as there were massive demonstrations in the US against the Vietnam War, student riots in Paris over poor university campus facilities spread across France. About 8 million workers joined the students and went on strike, calling for change. This was the defining moment of a year that saw young people across the Western world protest against outmoded bureaucracies, oppressive regimes, racial and gender inequality, and prejudice against sexual minorities. Although the protests in France died down, the events of 1968 inspired a generation.

△ **French May**
A poster proclaims the "beginning of a long struggle" during the civil unrest spearheaded by students in May 1968 in France.

DESEGREGATION IN THE AMERICAN SOUTH

In the 1950s, many aspects of life were still racially segregated in the southern states of the US. The states identified on this map all enforced segregation until 1957. By 1964, they had begun to desegregate to varying degrees.

KEY
AFRICAN AMERICANS IN SCHOOLS WITH WHITES, 1964

- 0–1%
- 1.5–6%
- 28–60%

GENERAL GIÁP
1911–2013

Vo Nguyen Giáp is considered to be one of the greatest military strategists of the 20th century, having mastered both conventional and guerrilla war tactics. Leading the Viet Minh resistance against Japanese occupation of Vietnam during World War II, he also led North Vietnamese forces against the French and then the US. His victory at Dien Bien Phu, in March–May 1954, is seen as one of the greatest military victories in modern history.

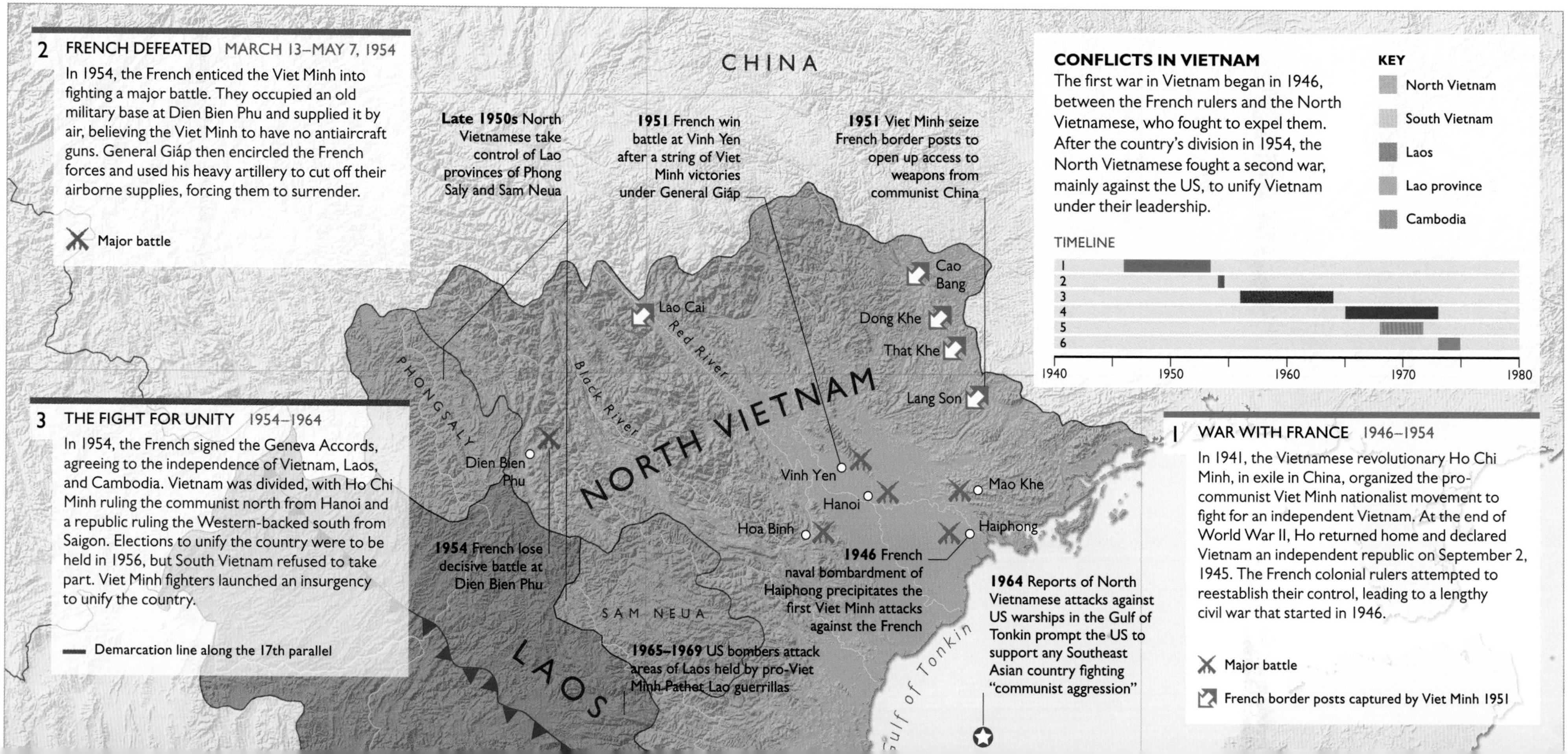

THE VIETNAM WARS

The two major wars in Vietnam after World War II were by far the most violent conflicts in Southeast Asia in the 20th century. Between them, they lasted almost 30 years and involved several major global powers. Although Vietnam had declared its independence in 1945, it was not fully achieved until 1975, once all foreign forces had left and the country was unified.

Fighting in Vietnam began when the Japanese occupied the French-ruled colony during World War II. The Viet Minh, a nationalist organization, led the resistance from 1941. After Japan was defeated in 1945, the French returned to Vietnam, and again the Viet Minh took up arms against the foreign forces. The ensuing and protracted war between Vietnam and France—known as the First Indochina War—began in 1946 and ended in the decisive defeat of the French at Dien Bien Phu in 1954. The now-independent Vietnam was then divided into the communist north and republican south. After a

partial lull, fighting broke out again in 1956, as the North Vietnamese fought to unite the country under their leadership. The war that then erupted—called the Second Indochina War, or the Vietnam War—was in many ways a proxy struggle within the global context of the Cold War, with the US supporting South Vietnam, and the USSR and China on the side of North Vietnam. The war also spread into Laos and Cambodia. Eventually, in the face of defeat, the US negotiated its way out of the war in 1973, paving the way for an eventual North Vietnamese victory and reunification of Vietnam in 1975.

CONFLICTS IN VIETNAM

The first war in Vietnam began in 1946, between the French rulers and the North Vietnamese, who fought to expel them. After the country's division in 1954, the North Vietnamese fought a second war, mainly against the US, to unify Vietnam under their leadership.

KEY

- North Vietnam
- South Vietnam
- Laos
- Lao province
- Cambodia

TIMELINE

	1940	1950	1960	1970	1980
1					
2					
3					
4					
5					
6					

1 WAR WITH FRANCE 1946–1954

In 1941, the Vietnamese revolutionary Ho Chi Minh, in exile in China, organized the pro-communist Viet Minh nationalist movement to fight for an independent Vietnam. At the end of World War II, Ho returned home and declared Vietnam an independent republic on September 2, 1945. The French colonial rulers attempted to reestablish their control, leading to a lengthy civil war that started in 1946.

✕ Major battle

🔄 French border posts captured by Viet Minh 1951

2 FRENCH DEFEATED MARCH 13–MAY 7, 1954

In 1954, the French enticed the Viet Minh into fighting a major battle. They occupied an old military base at Dien Bien Phu and supplied it by air, believing the Viet Minh to have no antiaircraft guns. General Giáp then encircled the French forces and used his heavy artillery to cut off their airborne supplies, forcing them to surrender.

✕ Major battle

3 THE FIGHT FOR UNITY 1954–1964

In 1954, the French signed the Geneva Accords, agreeing to the independence of Vietnam, Laos, and Cambodia. Vietnam was divided, with Ho Chi Minh ruling the communist north from Hanoi and a republic ruling the Western-backed south from Saigon. Elections to unify the country were to be held in 1956, but South Vietnam refused to take part. Viet Minh fighters launched an insurgency to unify the country.

— Demarcation line along the 17th parallel

Map labels

CHINA

1951 Viet Minh seize French border posts to open up access to weapons from communist China

Late 1950s North Vietnamese take control of Lao provinces of Phong Saly and Sam Neua

1951 French win battle at Vinh Yen after a string of Viet Minh victories under General Giáp

1954 French lose decisive battle at Dien Bien Phu

1946 French naval bombardment of Haiphong precipitates the first Viet Minh attacks against the French

1964 Reports of North Vietnamese attacks against US warships in the Gulf of Tonkin prompt the US to support any Southeast Asian country fighting "communist aggression"

1965–1969 US bombers attack areas of Laos held by pro-Viet Minh Pathet Lao guerrillas

NORTH VIETNAM

LAOS

PHONGSALY

SAM NEUA

Cao Bang

Dong Khe

That Khe

Lang Son

Mao Khe

Haiphong

Vinh Yen

Hanoi

Hoa Binh

Lao Cai

Red River

Black River

Dien Bien Phu

Gulf of Tonkin

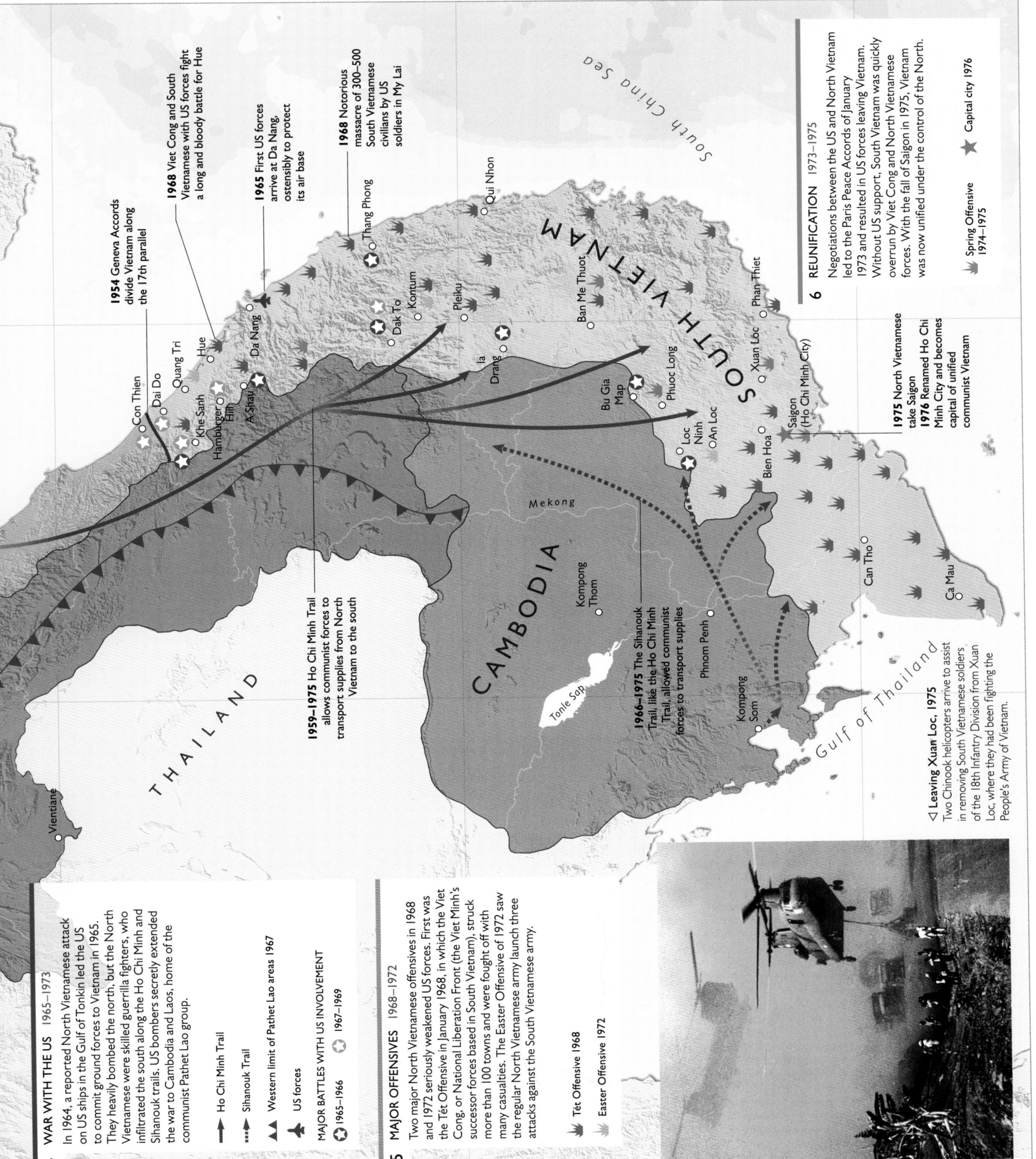

1954 Geneva Accords divide Vietnam along the 17th parallel

1968 Viet Cong and South Vietnamese with US forces fight a long and bloody battle for Hue

1965 First US forces arrive at Da Nang, ostensibly to protect its air base

1968 Notorious massacre of 300–500 South Vietnamese civilians by US soldiers in My Lai

1959–1975 Ho Chi Minh Trail allows communist forces to transport supplies from North Vietnam to the south

1966–1975 The Sihanouk Trail, like the Ho Chi Minh Trail, allowed communist forces to transport supplies

1975 North Vietnamese take Saigon
1976 Renamed Ho Chi Minh City and becomes capital of unified communist Vietnam

South China Sea

SOUTH VIETNAM

CAMBODIA

THAILAND

Mekong

Tonle Sap

Gulf of Thailand

Hainan

Vientiane · Thang Phong · Qui Nhon · Con Thien · Dai Do · Quang Tri · Hue · Khe Sanh · Hamburger Hill · A Shau · Da Nang · Dak To · Kontum · Pleiku · Ia Drang · Ban Me Thuot · Bu Gia Map · Phuoc Long · Loc Ninh · An Loc · Xuan Loc · Phan Thiet · Bien Hoa · Saigon (Ho Chi Minh City) · Kompong Thom · Phnom Penh · Kompong Som · Can Tho · Ca Mau

6 REUNIFICATION 1973–1975
Negotiations between the US and North Vietnam led to the Paris Peace Accords of January 1973 and resulted in US forces leaving Vietnam. Without US support, South Vietnam was quickly overrun by Viet Cong and North Vietnamese forces. With the fall of Saigon in 1975, Vietnam was now unified under the control of the North.

⇘ Spring Offensive 1974–1975   ★ Capital city 1976

4 WAR WITH THE US 1965–1973
In 1964, a reported North Vietnamese attack on US ships in the Gulf of Tonkin led the US to commit ground forces to Vietnam in 1965. They heavily bombed the north, but the North Vietnamese were skilled guerrilla fighters, who infiltrated the south along the Ho Chi Minh and Sihanouk trails. US bombers secretly extended the war to Cambodia and Laos, home of the communist Pathet Lao group.

→ Ho Chi Minh Trail
⇢ Sihanouk Trail
▲▲ Western limit of Pathet Lao areas 1967
✈ US forces

MAJOR BATTLES WITH US INVOLVEMENT
✪ 1965–1966   ✪ 1967–1969

5 MAJOR OFFENSIVES 1968–1972
Two major North Vietnamese offensives in 1968 and 1972 seriously weakened US forces. First was the Tét Offensive in January 1968, in which the Viet Cong, or National Liberation Front (the Viet Minh's successor forces based in South Vietnam), struck more than 100 towns and were fought off with many casualties. The Easter Offensive of 1972 saw the regular North Vietnamese army launch three attacks against the South Vietnamese army.

⇘ Tét Offensive 1968
⇘ Easter Offensive 1972

◁ **Leaving Xuan Loc, 1975**
Two Chinook helicopters arrive to assist in removing South Vietnamese soldiers of the 18th Infantry Division from Xuan Loc, where they had been fighting the People's Army of Vietnam.

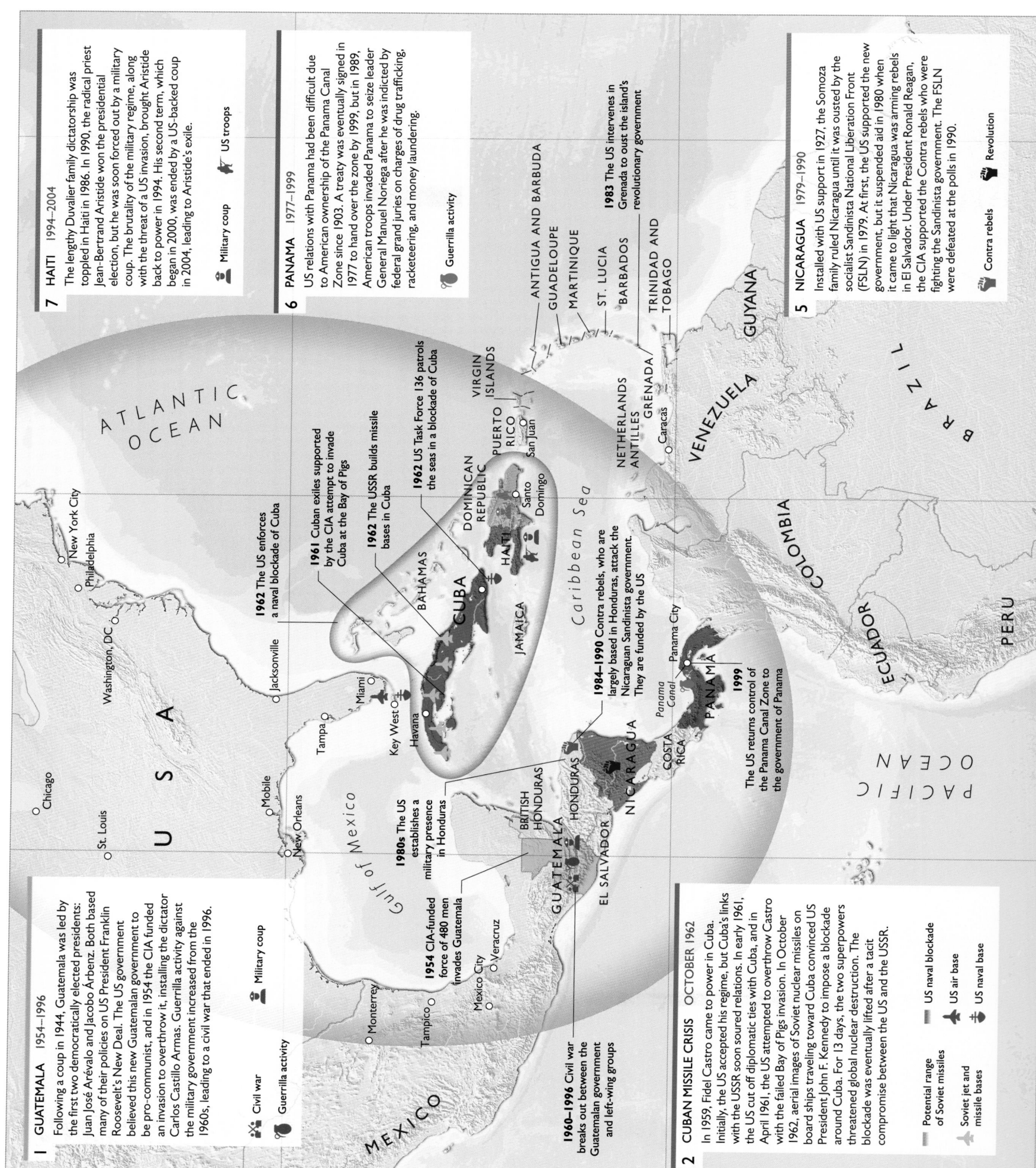

7 HAITI 1994–2004

The lengthy Duvalier family dictatorship was toppled in Haiti in 1986. In 1990, the radical priest Jean-Bertrand Aristide won the presidential election, but he was soon forced out by a military coup. The brutality of the military regime, along with the threat of a US invasion, brought Aristide back to power in 1994. His second term, which began in 2000, was ended by a US-backed coup in 2004, leading to Aristide's exile.

🛬 Military coup 　 🪖 US troops

6 PANAMA 1977–1999

US relations with Panama had been difficult due to American ownership of the Panama Canal Zone since 1903. A treaty was eventually signed in 1977 to hand over the zone by 1999, but in 1989, American troops invaded Panama to seize leader General Manuel Noriega after he was indicted by federal grand juries on charges of drug trafficking, racketeering, and money laundering.

🐍 Guerrilla activity

5 NICARAGUA 1979–1990

Installed with US support in 1927, the Somoza family ruled Nicaragua until it was ousted by the socialist Sandinista National Liberation Front (FSLN) in 1979. At first, the US supported the new government, but it suspended aid in 1980 when it came to light that Nicaragua was arming rebels in El Salvador. Under President Ronald Reagan, the CIA supported the Contra rebels who were fighting the Sandinista government. The FSLN were defeated at the polls in 1990.

👊 Contra rebels 　 👊 Revolution

1 GUATEMALA 1954–1996

Following a coup in 1944, Guatemala was led by the first two democratically elected presidents: Juan José Arévalo and Jacobo Árbenz. Both based many of their policies on US President Franklin Roosevelt's New Deal. The US government believed this new Guatemalan government to be pro-communist, and in 1954 the CIA funded an invasion to overthrow it, installing the dictator Carlos Castillo Armas. Guerrilla activity against the military government increased from the 1960s, leading to a civil war that ended in 1996.

⚔ Civil war 　 🛬 Military coup

🐍 Guerrilla activity

2 CUBAN MISSILE CRISIS OCTOBER 1962

In 1959, Fidel Castro came to power in Cuba. Initially, the US accepted his regime, but Cuba's links with the USSR soon soured relations. In early 1961, the US cut off diplomatic ties with Cuba, and in April 1961, the US attempted to overthrow Castro with the failed Bay of Pigs invasion. In October 1962, aerial images of Soviet nuclear missiles on board ships traveling toward Cuba convinced US President John F. Kennedy to impose a blockade around Cuba. For 13 days, the two superpowers threatened global nuclear destruction. The blockade was eventually lifted after a tacit compromise between the US and the USSR.

▬ Potential range of Soviet missiles

✈ Soviet jet and missile bases

🚢 US naval blockade

✈ US air base

⚓ US naval base

1954 CIA-funded force of 480 men invades Guatemala

1980s The US establishes a military presence in Honduras

1960–1996 Civil war breaks out between the Guatemalan government and left-wing groups

1984–1990 Contra rebels, who are largely based in Honduras, attack the Nicaraguan Sandinista government. They are funded by the US

1999 The US returns control of the Panama Canal Zone to the government of Panama

1962 The US enforces a naval blockade of Cuba

1961 Cuban exiles supported by the CIA attempt to invade Cuba at the Bay of Pigs

1962 The USSR builds missile bases in Cuba

1962 US Task Force 136 patrols the seas in a blockade of Cuba

1983 The US intervenes in Grenada to oust the island's revolutionary government

ATLANTIC OCEAN

Caribbean Sea

Gulf of Mexico

PACIFIC OCEAN

MEXICO

U S A

BRAZIL

VENEZUELA

GUYANA

COLOMBIA

ECUADOR

PERU

New York City
Philadelphia
Washington, DC
Jacksonville
Chicago
St. Louis
Mobile
New Orleans
Tampa
Miami
Key West
Havana
Monterrey
Mexico City
Tampico
Veracruz
BAHAMAS
CUBA
JAMAICA
HAITI
DOMINICAN REPUBLIC
Santo Domingo
PUERTO RICO
San Juan
VIRGIN ISLANDS
BRITISH HONDURAS
GUATEMALA
EL SALVADOR
HONDURAS
NICARAGUA
COSTA RICA
PANAMA
Panama City
Panama Canal
Caracas
ANTIGUA AND BARBUDA
GUADELOUPE
MARTINIQUE
ST. LUCIA
BARBADOS
TRINIDAD AND TOBAGO
GRENADA
NETHERLANDS ANTILLES

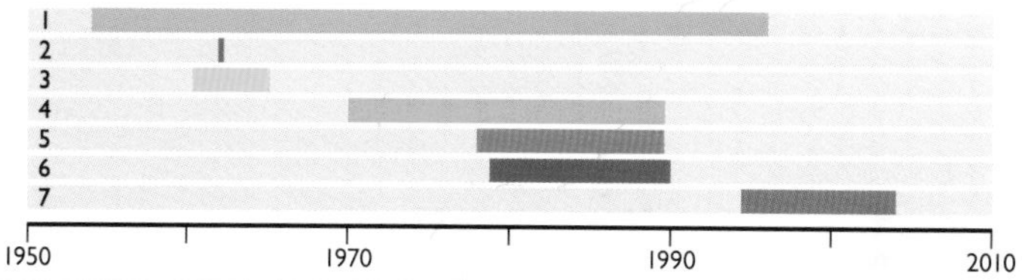

US INTERVENTIONS IN LATIN AMERICA

Since the 19th century, the US's foreign policies in Central and South America have been geared toward protecting its business interests in the region. Fearful of communist influence, the US has often become involved—covertly and otherwise—in Latin American politics.

In 1823, US President James Monroe announced a formal doctrine that any efforts by nations to take control of independent states in the American continent would be viewed as "the manifestation of an unfriendly disposition toward the United States." Over a century later, this doctrine enabled the US to exert control over its southern neighbors during the Cold War (see pp.314–315) in order to prevent the spread of communism in the region. As a result, there is barely a country in the region that has remained unaffected in some way by American intervention. Elected governments have been overthrown in Guatemala, Chile, and Haiti; a left-wing government was undermined in Nicaragua; democratic uprisings have been quashed in El Salvador and the Dominican Republic; and authoritarian governments have been supported in Honduras and elsewhere. US military intervention to overthrow the convicted drug trafficker and leader of Panama General Manuel Noriega, as well as to bring a recently deposed government back to power in Haiti, reinforces the picture of the US engaging actively in Latin American politics.

The effect on the countries invaded or influenced by the US has been considerable, with many enduring long periods of military or authoritarian rule. The end of the Cold War in 1991, and the resumption of relations between the US and Cuba in 2015 after 54 years, led to a revival of multiparty democracies. These changes also increased political and economic stability in the region, despite a long-running civil war in Colombia and upheavals in socialist Venezuela.

CHE GUEVARA
1928–1967

Born in 1928 to a left-wing, middle-class Argentine family, Ernesto Guevara—later known by the nickname Che, meaning "friend"—was a Marxist revolutionary and the leader of the guerrilla army during the Cuban Revolution. As a student, he took two motorcycle journeys around Latin America; the appalling conditions he saw, which he attributed to the capitalist US exploiting Latin America, consolidated his revolutionary ideas.

---

4 CHILE 1970–1989

In 1970, Salvador Allende became the President of Chile—the first Marxist to be elected through open elections. Opposition groups soon declared his rule unconstitutional, and he was overthrown by General Augusto Pinochet in a military coup supported by the CIA in 1973. Pinochet's anti-communist dictatorship was marked by numerous human rights violations, but he held on to power until 1989.

◀ Military coup

US INTERVENTION IN CENTRAL AND SOUTH AMERICA

Since the end of World War II, the US has intervened in numerous Central and South American nations, overthrowing elected governments and supporting right-wing or military alternatives. Its interventions in Cuba almost brought the world to the brink of nuclear war.

TIMELINE

1
2
3
4
5
6
7

1950   1970   1990   2010

◁ **Revolution in Cuba**
Communist rebel leader Fidel Castro and his army celebrate. Castro overthrew the dictatorship of Fulgencio Batistá to come to power in Cuba in 1957. Castro then ruled Cuba as a one-party socialist state for the next 50 years.

---

3 DOMINICAN REPUBLIC 1961–1965

After the assassination of dictatorial President Rafael Trujillo in 1961, a left-wing democratic government under Juan Bosch led the Dominican Republic. Bosch was overthrown in a military coup in September 1963, but a pro-Bosch revolt soon broke out. Concerned that this situation was similar to events in Cuba, US President Lyndon Johnson sent in troops to crush the uprising and allow a repressive government to take power.

◀ Military coup   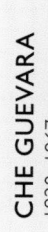 US troops

---

BOLIVIA

CHILE

ARGENTINA

○ Santiago

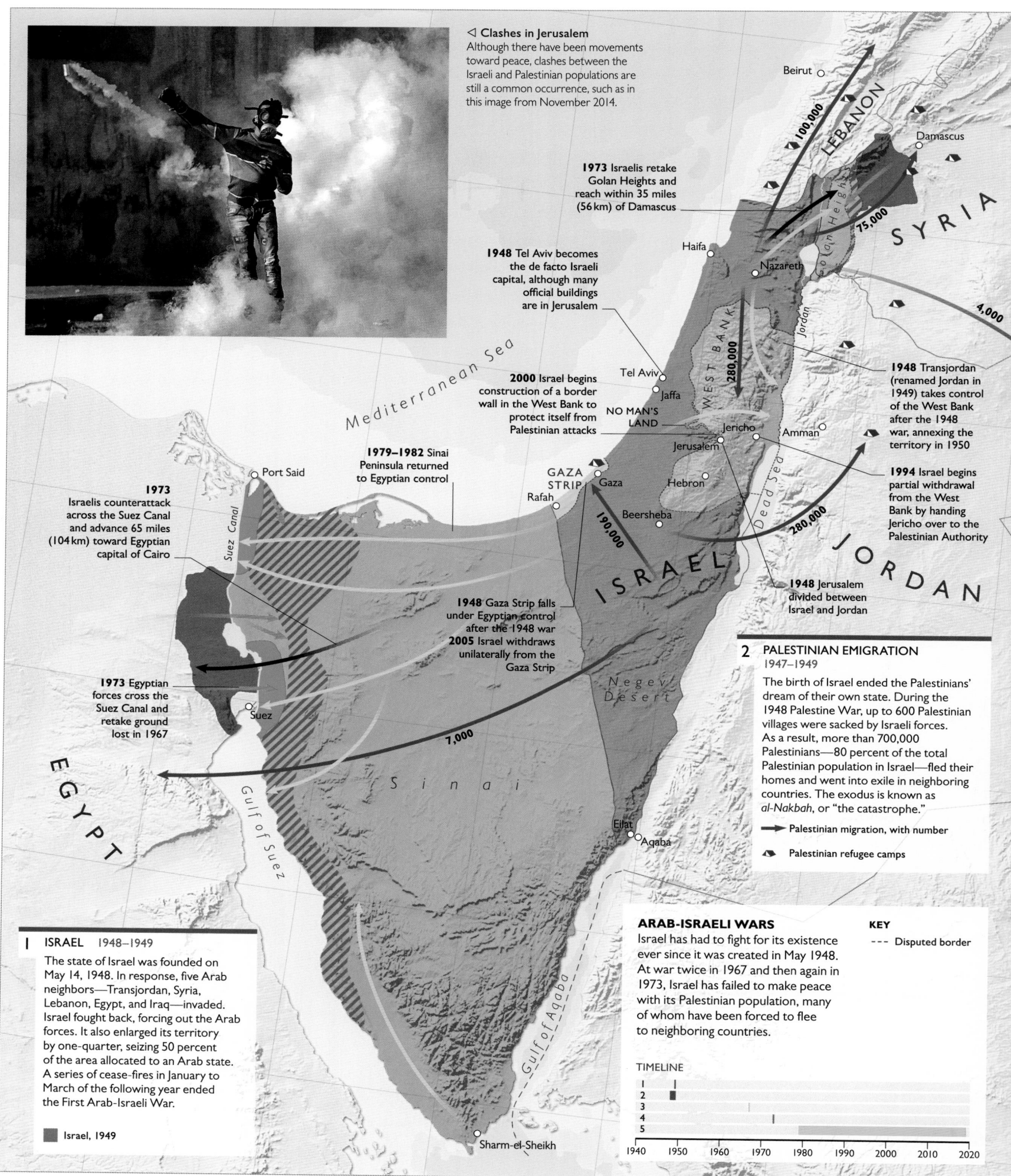

◁ **Clashes in Jerusalem**
Although there have been movements toward peace, clashes between the Israeli and Palestinian populations are still a common occurrence, such as in this image from November 2014.

1973 Israelis retake Golan Heights and reach within 35 miles (56 km) of Damascus

1948 Tel Aviv becomes the de facto Israeli capital, although many official buildings are in Jerusalem

2000 Israel begins construction of a border wall in the West Bank to protect itself from Palestinian attacks

1979–1982 Sinai Peninsula returned to Egyptian control

1973 Israelis counterattack across the Suez Canal and advance 65 miles (104 km) toward Egyptian capital of Cairo

1948 Gaza Strip falls under Egyptian control after the 1948 war
2005 Israel withdraws unilaterally from the Gaza Strip

1973 Egyptian forces cross the Suez Canal and retake ground lost in 1967

1948 Transjordan (renamed Jordan in 1949) takes control of the West Bank after the 1948 war, annexing the territory in 1950

1994 Israel begins partial withdrawal from the West Bank by handing Jericho over to the Palestinian Authority

1948 Jerusalem divided between Israel and Jordan

Beirut

Damascus

Haifa

Nazareth

Tel Aviv

Jaffa

NO MAN'S LAND

Jericho

Jerusalem

Amman

GAZA STRIP

Gaza

Hebron

Rafah

Beersheba

Port Said

Suez Canal

Suez

Eilat

Aqaba

Mediterranean Sea

Sinai

Negev Desert

Dead Sea

Gulf of Suez

Gulf of Aqaba

Sharm-el-Sheikh

LEBANON

SYRIA

WEST BANK

Golan Heights

Jordan

ISRAEL

JORDAN

EGYPT

100,000
75,000
4,000
280,000
190,000
280,000
7,000

2 PALESTINIAN EMIGRATION
1947–1949

The birth of Israel ended the Palestinians' dream of their own state. During the 1948 Palestine War, up to 600 Palestinian villages were sacked by Israeli forces. As a result, more than 700,000 Palestinians—80 percent of the total Palestinian population in Israel—fled their homes and went into exile in neighboring countries. The exodus is known as *al-Nakbah*, or "the catastrophe."

→ Palestinian migration, with number

◣ Palestinian refugee camps

1 ISRAEL 1948–1949

The state of Israel was founded on May 14, 1948. In response, five Arab neighbors—Transjordan, Syria, Lebanon, Egypt, and Iraq—invaded. Israel fought back, forcing out the Arab forces. It also enlarged its territory by one-quarter, seizing 50 percent of the area allocated to an Arab state. A series of cease-fires in January to March of the following year ended the First Arab-Israeli War.

■ Israel, 1949

ARAB-ISRAELI WARS

Israel has had to fight for its existence ever since it was created in May 1948. At war twice in 1967 and then again in 1973, Israel has failed to make peace with its Palestinian population, many of whom have been forced to flee to neighboring countries.

KEY

- - - Disputed border

TIMELINE

	1940	1950	1960	1970	1980	1990	2000	2010	2020
1									
2									
3									
4									
5									

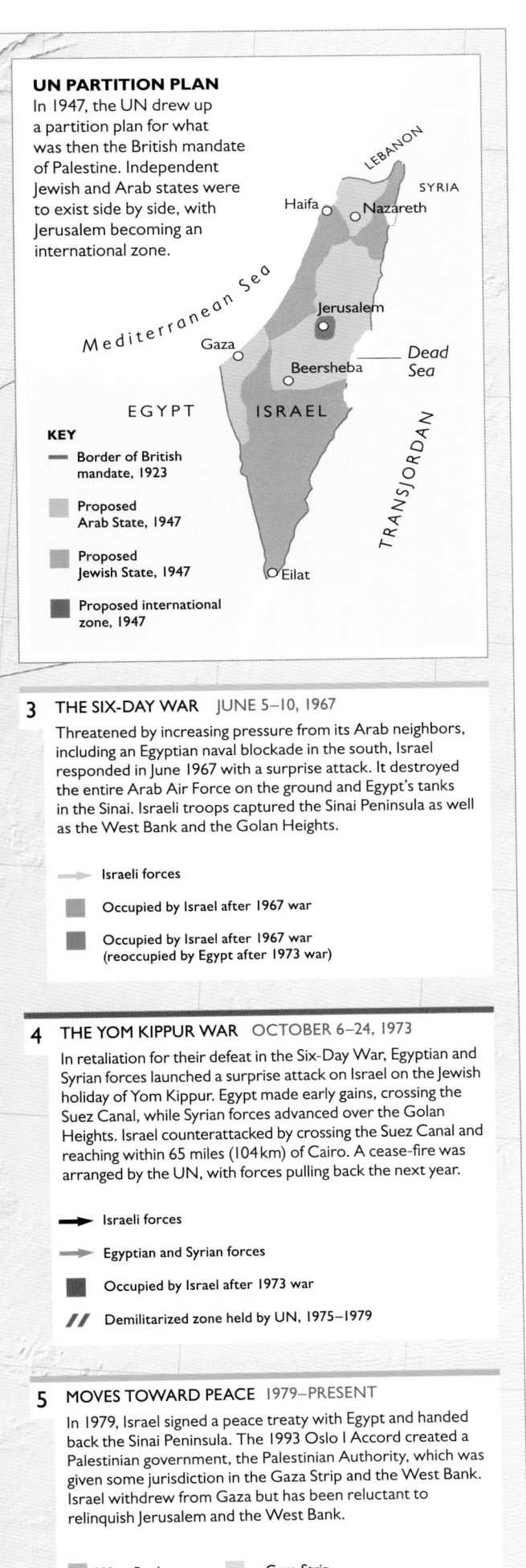

UN PARTITION PLAN
In 1947, the UN drew up a partition plan for what was then the British mandate of Palestine. Independent Jewish and Arab states were to exist side by side, with Jerusalem becoming an international zone.

KEY
— Border of British mandate, 1923

Proposed Arab State, 1947

Proposed Jewish State, 1947

Proposed international zone, 1947

3 THE SIX-DAY WAR JUNE 5–10, 1967
Threatened by increasing pressure from its Arab neighbors, including an Egyptian naval blockade in the south, Israel responded in June 1967 with a surprise attack. It destroyed the entire Arab Air Force on the ground and Egypt's tanks in the Sinai. Israeli troops captured the Sinai Peninsula as well as the West Bank and the Golan Heights.

→ Israeli forces

Occupied by Israel after 1967 war

Occupied by Israel after 1967 war (reoccupied by Egypt after 1973 war)

4 THE YOM KIPPUR WAR OCTOBER 6–24, 1973
In retaliation for their defeat in the Six-Day War, Egyptian and Syrian forces launched a surprise attack on Israel on the Jewish holiday of Yom Kippur. Egypt made early gains, crossing the Suez Canal, while Syrian forces advanced over the Golan Heights. Israel counterattacked by crossing the Suez Canal and reaching within 65 miles (104 km) of Cairo. A cease-fire was arranged by the UN, with forces pulling back the next year.

→ Israeli forces

→ Egyptian and Syrian forces

Occupied by Israel after 1973 war

∥ Demilitarized zone held by UN, 1975–1979

5 MOVES TOWARD PEACE 1979–PRESENT
In 1979, Israel signed a peace treaty with Egypt and handed back the Sinai Peninsula. The 1993 Oslo I Accord created a Palestinian government, the Palestinian Authority, which was given some jurisdiction in the Gaza Strip and the West Bank. Israel withdrew from Gaza but has been reluctant to relinquish Jerusalem and the West Bank.

West Bank   Gaza Strip

ISRAEL AND THE MIDDLE EAST

A Jewish population has existed in Palestine for centuries, but the founding of the Zionist Organization in 1897 marked new efforts to create a Jewish homeland in the region. The state of Israel created such a place but sparked a series of wars.

In November 1947, the United Nations, the overseers of the British mandate over Palestine (see pp.284–285), decided to partition the territory into independent Palestinian and Jewish states, in part as a response to Jewish displacement after the Holocaust. As a result of this declaration, violence broke out between the two sides, and British control broke down. The plan was abandoned, and the British ended their mandate over Palestine on May 14, 1948. The head of the Jewish Agency and future prime minister David Ben-Gurion then immediately declared the foundation of the independent state of Israel. Israeli forces promptly captured swathes of Palestinian territory and drove many of its people into exile in nearby countries. Israel's Arab neighbors became involved in the conflict, while Israel successfully fought back.

After decades of turmoil, both sides began to make steps toward peace. In 1979, Egypt and Israel signed a peace treaty, with Egypt recognizing the state of Israel and Israeli forces withdrawing from occupied Sinai. In 1993, Israel signed an accord with the Palestinian Liberation Organization—which for the first time recognized the existence of Israel—and began to disengage from the Gaza Strip and the West Bank. However, Israel's intention to cede land for peace has proved difficult to put into practice, with the result that relations with Palestinians remain fraught.

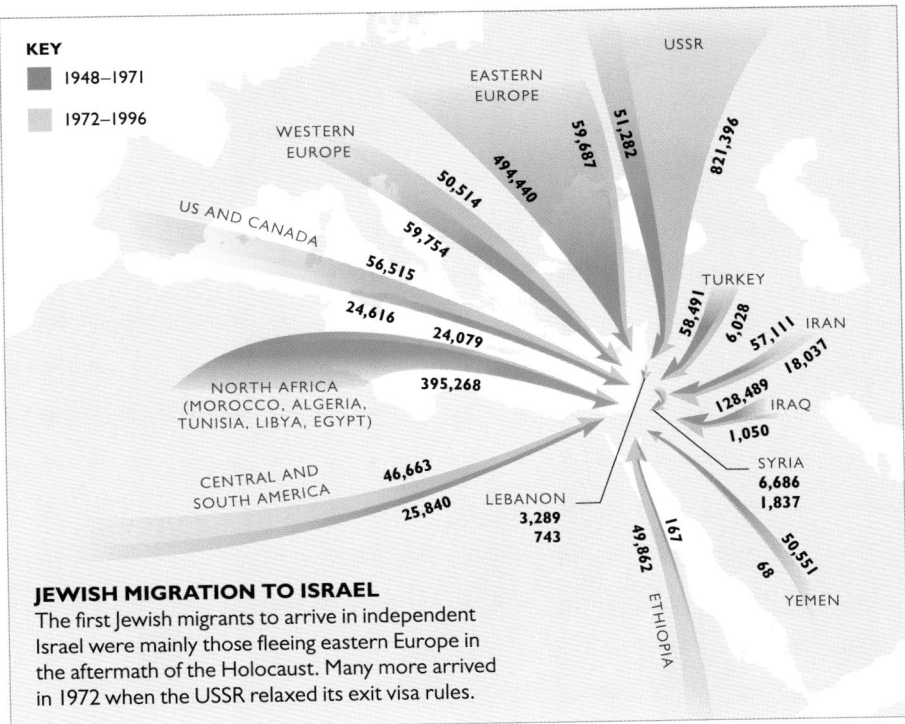

KEY
1948–1971

1972–1996

JEWISH MIGRATION TO ISRAEL
The first Jewish migrants to arrive in independent Israel were mainly those fleeing eastern Europe in the aftermath of the Holocaust. Many more arrived in 1972 when the USSR relaxed its exit visa rules.

ECONOMIC BOOM AND ENVIRONMENTAL COST

The world has seen staggering economic growth during the 20th and 21st centuries, leading to unprecedented wealth. The subsequent environmental damage to the planet, however, has led many experts to call for urgent action to prevent an irreversible global crisis.

△ Fuel crisis
A sign at a service station informs the public of fuel shortage during the 1973 oil crisis, when oil-producing Arab countries placed an embargo on exports.

In 1944, before World War II had even concluded, delegates from 44 countries met to restructure the world's international finance systems with a focus on introducing a stable system of exchange rates and rebuilding war-damaged economies in Europe. The International Monetary Fund (IMF) was set up to facilitate international currency exchange, and the World Bank was established to make long-term loans to hard-hit nations. In 1947, the US introduced the Marshall Plan, pumping billions of dollars of investment into western Europe. This helped to restore confidence in the world economy and led to extraordinary growth.

Japan in particular benefited from these initiatives, and the country invested in steel and coal, shipbuilding, and car production, turning to high-tech products in the 1960s. Other Asian countries, such as Taiwan, Singapore, Malaysia, and South Korea, copied the Japanese model. This collective success became known as "Asian tiger economics."

Crisis and recovery

In 1973, Egypt and Syria invaded Israel, and the Organization of Arab Petroleum Exporting Countries (OAPEC) stopped oil being exported to any country supporting Israel. Oil prices tripled, and industrial output

◁ Booming city
The Hong Kong night is illuminated by its many skyscrapers. The city is just one of the outstanding economic success stories in Southeast Asia.

THE PRICE OF SUCCESS

Changes to the world economy after World War II led to rapid economic growth. Awareness of the environmental cost lagged far behind the boom. Publicity about damaging oil spills, pesticides, and pollution led to the first global climate conference in 1979. By this time, economic growth was bringing lower air quality and industrial waste and depleting natural resources. The continuing rise in population has caused particular concern and intensified efforts to tackle global warming and secure food and water supplies.

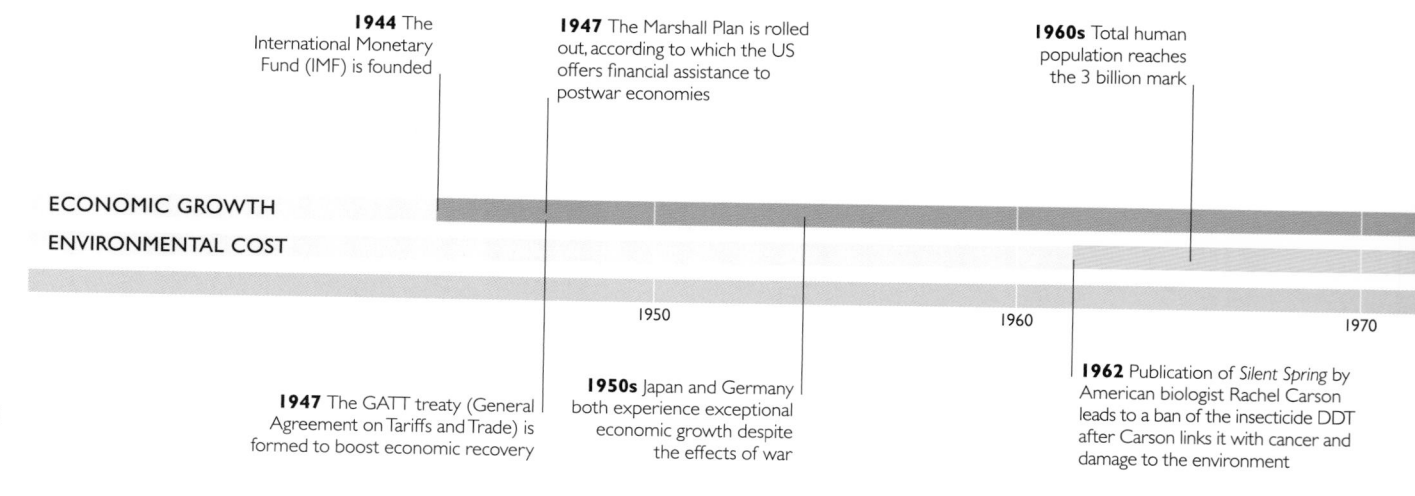

1944 The International Monetary Fund (IMF) is founded

1947 The Marshall Plan is rolled out, according to which the US offers financial assistance to postwar economies

1960s Total human population reaches the 3 billion mark

ECONOMIC GROWTH

ENVIRONMENTAL COST

1950

1960

1970

1947 The GATT treaty (General Agreement on Tariffs and Trade) is formed to boost economic recovery

1950s Japan and Germany both experience exceptional economic growth despite the effects of war

1962 Publication of *Silent Spring* by American biologist Rachel Carson leads to a ban of the insecticide DDT after Carson links it with cancer and damage to the environment

◁ **Toxic air**
A coal-fired power plant in England expels pollutants and greenhouse gases. Stricter air-pollution rules in Europe have sounded the death knell for energy production from coal.

in many countries dropped. The embargo lasted until 1974. The oil crisis led to a worldwide global recession, and in response, many countries changed their economic policies.

Control passed from the state to the private sector, and deregulation became the new driving force, allowing free trade to open up. China moved to allow private enterprise and rapidly developed the trappings of capitalism. Over the coming decades, it would become one of the world's largest and most influential economies. India was influenced by the success of the Asian tiger economies, while Brazil and Mexico also embarked on economic reform, drastically improving living standards. The reunification of West and East Germany in 1990 resulted in a new major force in the world economy. Despite a devastating financial crisis in 2008, the world, it seemed, had never been richer.

Environmental cost

This economic success came at a price. On October 31, 2011, the United Nations (UN) announced the birth of the 7 billionth person on Earth, heightening concern about the planet's capacity to support so many people. More crops were needed to feed the growing population, and more resources were needed to support the lifestyle of more affluent citizens. Urbanization and population growth strained the environment, and scientists found evidence that human activity is to blame for recent climate change (global warming).

> *"Population growth is straining the Earth's resources to the breaking point."*
>
> AL GORE, FORMER US VICE PRESIDENT

Developing nations were urged to reduce carbon emissions, thought to affect climate change, yet in 2015, India was opening a coal mine a month to lift its 1.3 billion citizens out of poverty. Developing nations objected to being told by developed nations to curb their ambitions for growth. In the 2000s, the world saw record levels of rainfall, as well as severe drought, melting icecaps, and natural disasters. Scientists warned that humans could pass the threshold beyond which climate change would be irreversible. With 7 billion people on the planet, the drain on natural resources was inevitable. In 2015, world leaders signed the Paris Climate Accord, and 196 nations adopted the first global climate deal, limiting global warming to 3.6°F (2°C).

Today, the UN estimates that by 2050, the global population will reach 9.7 billion. While the last two centuries have brought astonishing opportunities and wealth, challenges from war, pollution, and inequality remain grave.

▽ **Catching the sun**
Around 70,000 solar panels in the Nevada Desert provide 25 percent of the power used at the Nellis Air Force Base. It is the largest solar power plant in the western hemisphere; such projects are held up as models for renewable energy.

1973–1974 The oil crisis creates global recession, leading to new economic policies

1979 The first World Climate Conference is held in Geneva

1980s Phenomenal growth is seen in China's economy

Oct 3, 1990 East and West Germany unite, and Germany begins its rise from being the "sick man of Europe" into an economic powerhouse

2007–2011 A global financial crisis, which begins in the US, brings many of the world's financial systems close to collapse

2008 China's economic growth inflicts more than a trillion yuan's worth of damage on its environment each year, increasing pressure on planners to slow China's breakneck speed of development

2017 Total global wealth reaches $280 trillion

1980

1990

2000

2010

2020

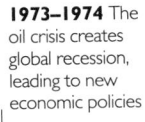

1975 France, Italy, Germany, Japan, Britain, and the US form a Group of Six (G6) to develop international trade

1992 At the Earth Summit in Rio de Janeiro, governments agree on the United Framework Convention on Climate Change

1997 Under the Kyoto Protocol, developed nations pledge to reduce carbon emissions by an average of 5 percent by 2008–2012

2007 The IPCC (Intergovernmental Panel on Climate Change) and former US vice president Al Gore receive the Nobel Peace Prize for their work on climate change

2009 China overtakes the US as the world's biggest greenhouse gas emitter—although the US remains well ahead on a per-capita basis

2017 Nations unite in their commitment to tackle global warming after the US pulls out of the Paris Climate Accord

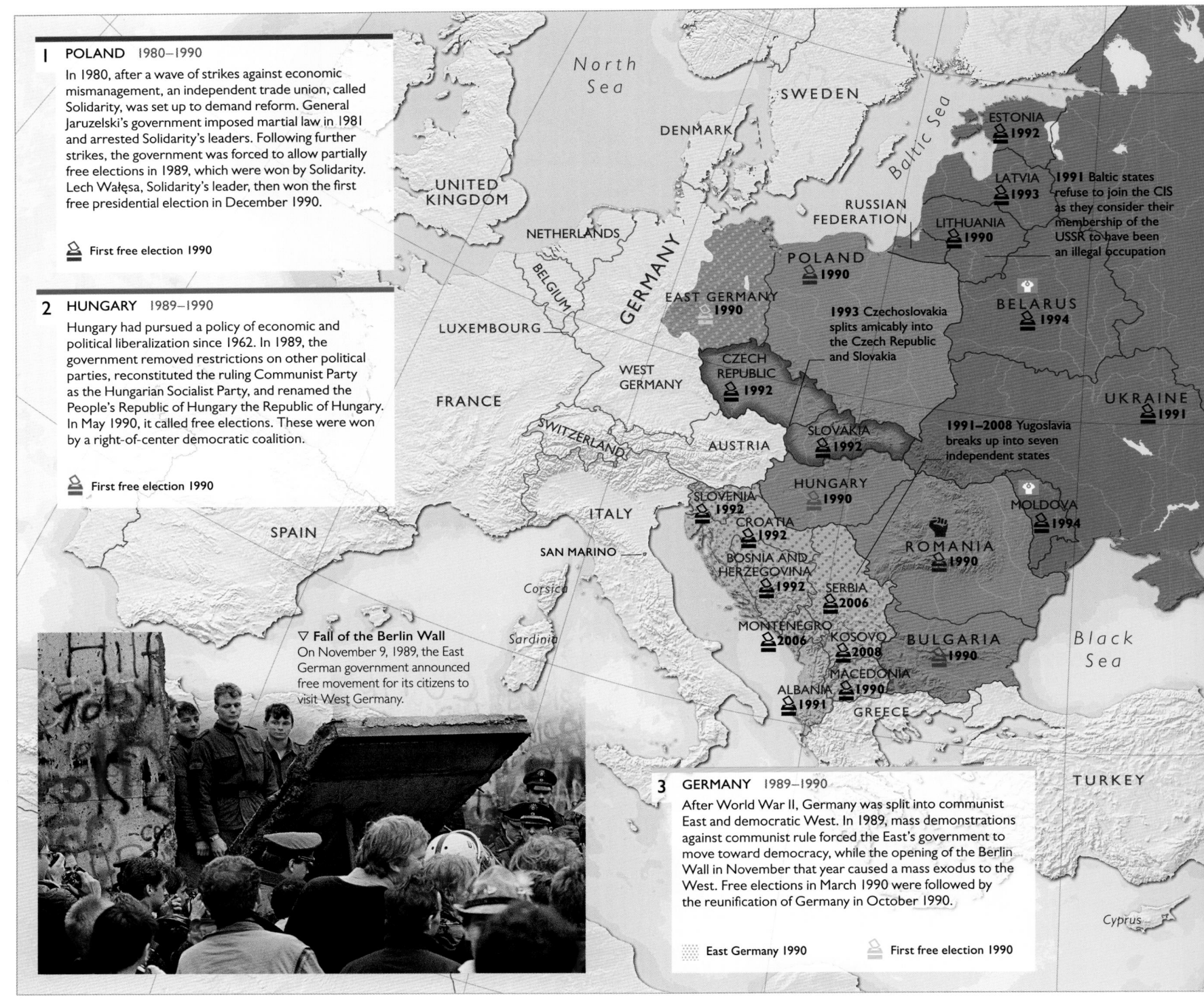

1 POLAND 1980–1990

In 1980, after a wave of strikes against economic mismanagement, an independent trade union, called Solidarity, was set up to demand reform. General Jaruzelski's government imposed martial law in 1981 and arrested Solidarity's leaders. Following further strikes, the government was forced to allow partially free elections in 1989, which were won by Solidarity. Lech Wałęsa, Solidarity's leader, then won the first free presidential election in December 1990.

First free election 1990

2 HUNGARY 1989–1990

Hungary had pursued a policy of economic and political liberalization since 1962. In 1989, the government removed restrictions on other political parties, reconstituted the ruling Communist Party as the Hungarian Socialist Party, and renamed the People's Republic of Hungary the Republic of Hungary. In May 1990, it called free elections. These were won by a right-of-center democratic coalition.

First free election 1990

▽ **Fall of the Berlin Wall**
On November 9, 1989, the East German government announced free movement for its citizens to visit West Germany.

3 GERMANY 1989–1990

After World War II, Germany was split into communist East and democratic West. In 1989, mass demonstrations against communist rule forced the East's government to move toward democracy, while the opening of the Berlin Wall in November that year caused a mass exodus to the West. Free elections in March 1990 were followed by the reunification of Germany in October 1990.

East Germany 1990   First free election 1990

1991 Baltic states refuse to join the CIS as they consider their membership of the USSR to have been an illegal occupation

1993 Czechoslovakia splits amicably into the Czech Republic and Slovakia

1991–2008 Yugoslavia breaks up into seven independent states

THE COLLAPSE OF COMMUNISM

The fall of communism in Europe and the dissolution of the USSR were among the most momentous events in modern history. Yet they were also among the least predicted, because it was internal weaknesses, rather than external pressures, that brought about their end. Change came quickly, and the effects were long-lasting.

The election of Mikhail Gorbachev as General Secretary of the Soviet Communist Party in March 1985 promised much-needed reforms in the USSR. He began to restructure the state and pledged economic and political change. Dissidents were released from prison, and private enterprise was encouraged. Crucially, in 1988, he declared the abandonment of the Brezhnev Doctrine, formulated in 1968 by Leonid Brezhnev, under which the USSR asserted its right to intervene militarily in the internal affairs of other communist countries in order to maintain strict communist rule. Relinquishing this doctrine gave the green light to eastern European communist nations to begin political reforms, as they now became aware that they could not rely on Soviet help to maintain their oppressive rule if opposition arose. As the eastern European nations, led by Poland and then Hungary, began to liberalize their political structures, the USSR came under pressure from its increasingly rebellious republics.

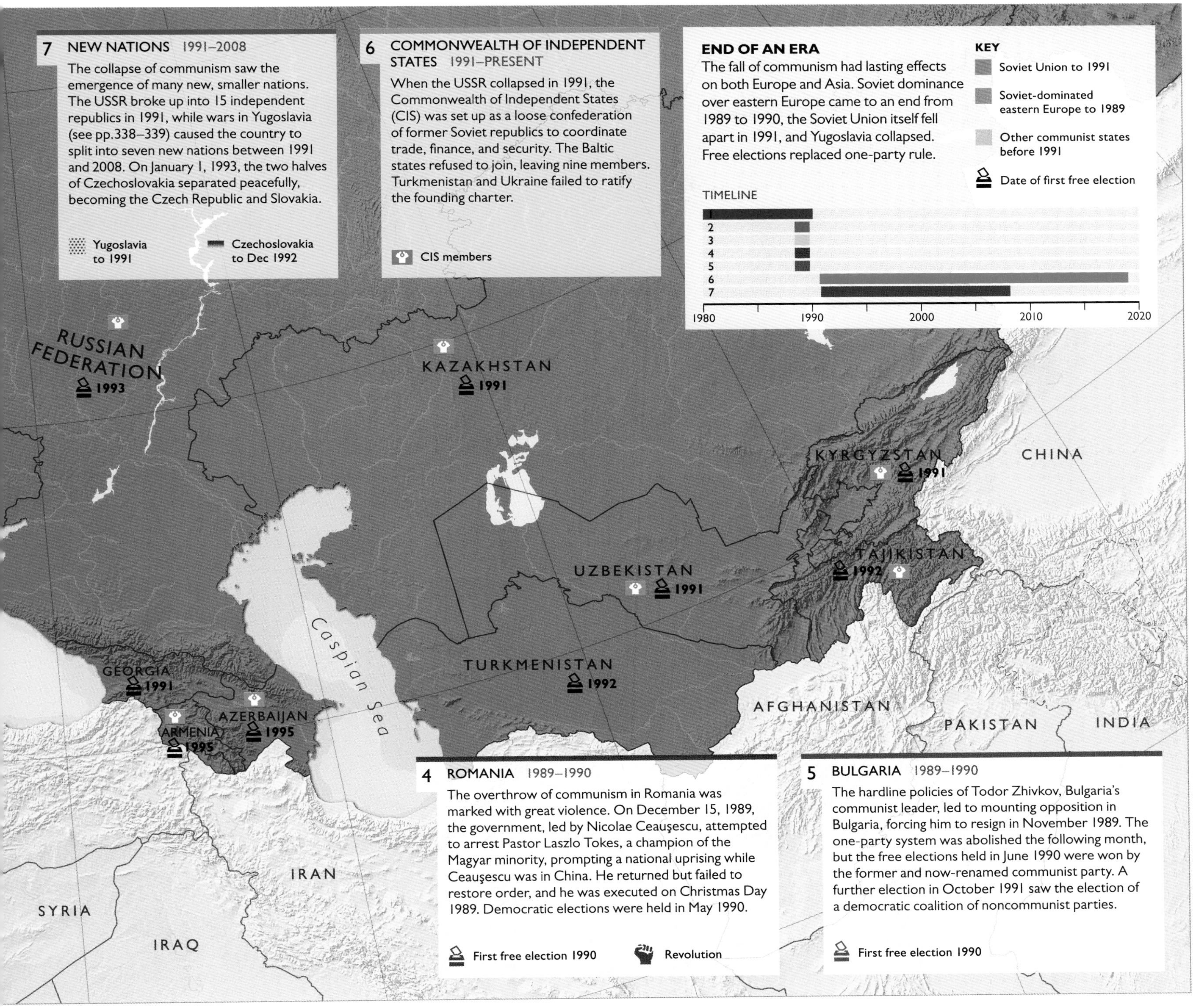
RUSSIAN FEDERATION
1993
KAZAKHSTAN
1991
KYRGYZSTAN
1991
CHINA
TAJIKISTAN
1992
UZBEKISTAN
1991
TURKMENISTAN
1992
GEORGIA
1991
ARMENIA
1995
AZERBAIJAN
1995
Caspian Sea
AFGHANISTAN
PAKISTAN
INDIA
IRAN
SYRIA
IRAQ
TIMELINE
1
2
3
4
5
6
7
1980
1990
2000
2010
2020

7 NEW NATIONS 1991–2008

The collapse of communism saw the emergence of many new, smaller nations. The USSR broke up into 15 independent republics in 1991, while wars in Yugoslavia (see pp.338–339) caused the country to split into seven new nations between 1991 and 2008. On January 1, 1993, the two halves of Czechoslovakia separated peacefully, becoming the Czech Republic and Slovakia.

Yugoslavia to 1991 — Czechoslovakia to Dec 1992

6 COMMONWEALTH OF INDEPENDENT STATES 1991–PRESENT

When the USSR collapsed in 1991, the Commonwealth of Independent States (CIS) was set up as a loose confederation of former Soviet republics to coordinate trade, finance, and security. The Baltic states refused to join, leaving nine members. Turkmenistan and Ukraine failed to ratify the founding charter.

CIS members

END OF AN ERA

The fall of communism had lasting effects on both Europe and Asia. Soviet dominance over eastern Europe came to an end from 1989 to 1990, the Soviet Union itself fell apart in 1991, and Yugoslavia collapsed. Free elections replaced one-party rule.

KEY

- Soviet Union to 1991
- Soviet-dominated eastern Europe to 1989
- Other communist states before 1991
- Date of first free election

4 ROMANIA 1989–1990

The overthrow of communism in Romania was marked with great violence. On December 15, 1989, the government, led by Nicolae Ceauşescu, attempted to arrest Pastor Laszlo Tokes, a champion of the Magyar minority, prompting a national uprising while Ceauşescu was in China. He returned but failed to restore order, and he was executed on Christmas Day 1989. Democratic elections were held in May 1990.

First free election 1990 — Revolution

5 BULGARIA 1989–1990

The hardline policies of Todor Zhivkov, Bulgaria's communist leader, led to mounting opposition in Bulgaria, forcing him to resign in November 1989. The one-party system was abolished the following month, but the free elections held in June 1990 were won by the former and now-renamed communist party. A further election in October 1991 saw the election of a democratic coalition of noncommunist parties.

First free election 1990

Gorbachev tried to restructure the Soviet Union as calls grew in the Baltic states and elsewhere for full independence, but he was opposed by demonstrations in Ukraine and by the Russian Federation leader, Boris Yeltsin. Fatally weakened by an attempted communist coup in August 1991 and a decisive vote for Ukrainian independence in December, Gorbachev was forced to resign as president on Christmas Day 1991. The next day, the USSR itself was disbanded, and Soviet communism—founded in 1917—had ended.

"The threat of world war is no more."

MIKHAIL GORBACHEV, SOVIET PRESIDENT, MAKING HIS FAREWELL SPEECH ENDING THE USSR, DECEMBER 1991

PERESTROIKA AND GLASNOST

RUSSIAN POLICIES

Mikhail Gorbachev became General Secretary of the Soviet Communist Party in 1985 and President of the USSR in 1990. Aiming to secure warmer relations with the West, he set out two new policies: *perestroika* (liberal economic restructuring) and *glasnost* (political openness).

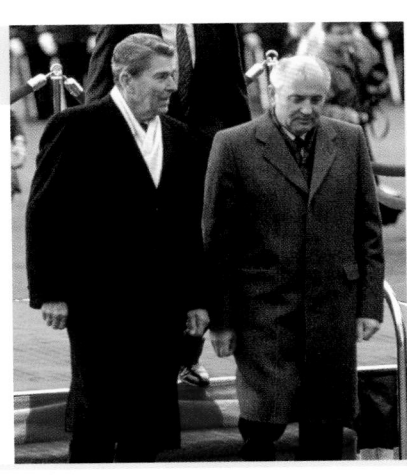

West meets East
Mikhail Gorbachev (right) met US President Ronald Reagan (left) several times to improve East–West relations.

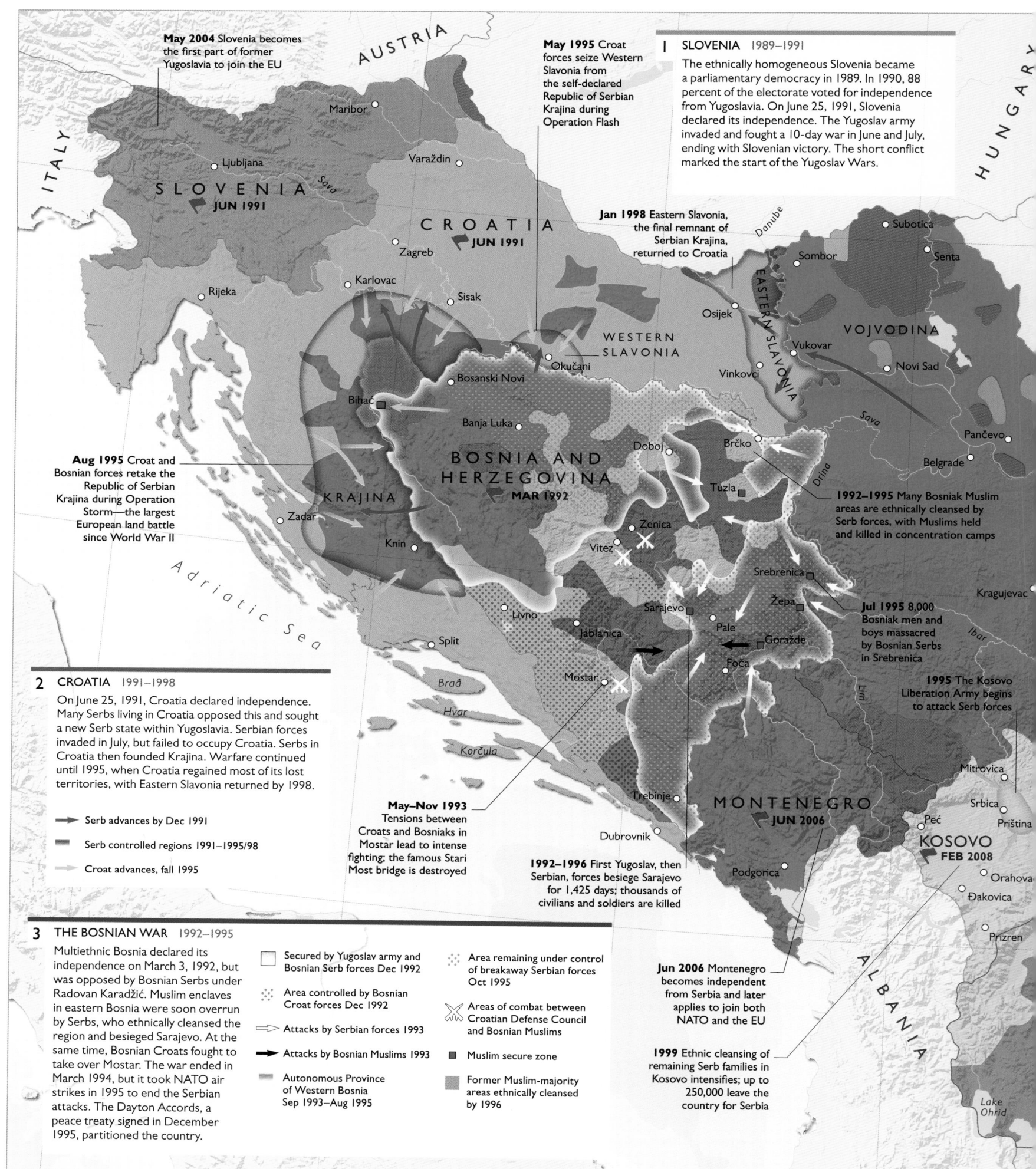

May 2004 Slovenia becomes the first part of former Yugoslavia to join the EU

May 1995 Croat forces seize Western Slavonia from the self-declared Republic of Serbian Krajina during Operation Flash

I SLOVENIA 1989–1991

The ethnically homogeneous Slovenia became a parliamentary democracy in 1989. In 1990, 88 percent of the electorate voted for independence from Yugoslavia. On June 25, 1991, Slovenia declared its independence. The Yugoslav army invaded and fought a 10-day war in June and July, ending with Slovenian victory. The short conflict marked the start of the Yugoslav Wars.

Jan 1998 Eastern Slavonia, the final remnant of Serbian Krajina, returned to Croatia

Aug 1995 Croat and Bosnian forces retake the Republic of Serbian Krajina during Operation Storm—the largest European land battle since World War II

1992–1995 Many Bosniak Muslim areas are ethnically cleansed by Serb forces, with Muslims held and killed in concentration camps

Jul 1995 8,000 Bosniak men and boys massacred by Bosnian Serbs in Srebrenica

1995 The Kosovo Liberation Army begins to attack Serb forces

2 CROATIA 1991–1998

On June 25, 1991, Croatia declared independence. Many Serbs living in Croatia opposed this and sought a new Serb state within Yugoslavia. Serbian forces invaded in July, but failed to occupy Croatia. Serbs in Croatia then founded Krajina. Warfare continued until 1995, when Croatia regained most of its lost territories, with Eastern Slavonia returned by 1998.

→ Serb advances by Dec 1991

▬ Serb controlled regions 1991–1995/98

→ Croat advances, fall 1995

May–Nov 1993 Tensions between Croats and Bosniaks in Mostar lead to intense fighting; the famous Stari Most bridge is destroyed

1992–1996 First Yugoslav, then Serbian, forces besiege Sarajevo for 1,425 days; thousands of civilians and soldiers are killed

Jun 2006 Montenegro becomes independent from Serbia and later applies to join both NATO and the EU

1999 Ethnic cleansing of remaining Serb families in Kosovo intensifies; up to 250,000 leave the country for Serbia

3 THE BOSNIAN WAR 1992–1995

Multiethnic Bosnia declared its independence on March 3, 1992, but was opposed by Bosnian Serbs under Radovan Karadžić. Muslim enclaves in eastern Bosnia were soon overrun by Serbs, who ethnically cleansed the region and besieged Sarajevo. At the same time, Bosnian Croats fought to take over Mostar. The war ended in March 1994, but it took NATO air strikes in 1995 to end the Serbian attacks. The Dayton Accords, a peace treaty signed in December 1995, partitioned the country.

☐ Secured by Yugoslav army and Bosnian Serb forces Dec 1992

⋮ Area controlled by Bosnian Croat forces Dec 1992

⇨ Attacks by Serbian forces 1993

➡ Attacks by Bosnian Muslims 1993

▬ Autonomous Province of Western Bosnia Sep 1993–Aug 1995

⋮ Area remaining under control of breakaway Serbian forces Oct 1995

✕ Areas of combat between Croatian Defense Council and Bosnian Muslims

■ Muslim secure zone

▬ Former Muslim-majority areas ethnically cleansed by 1996

ETHNIC COMPOSITION OF YUGOSLAVIA

Yugoslavia was a multiethnic nation, comprising five main groups of people—Bosniaks, Croats, Macedonians, Serbs, and Slovenes—as well as substantial minorities of Albanians, Bulgarians, Hungarians, and Romanians. Most groups were mainly Roman Catholic or Orthodox, while the majority of Bosniaks were Muslims.

KEY

- Serb and Montenegrin
- Croat
- Bosniak (after 1996 "ethnic cleansing")
- Slovene
- Albanian
- Macedonian
- Hungarian
- Bulgarian
- Romanian

TIMELINE

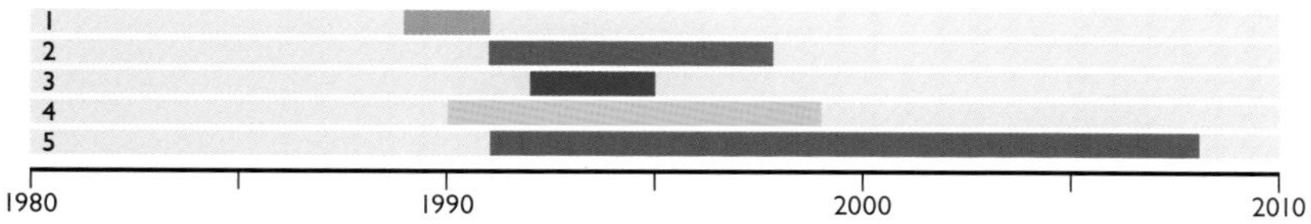

1
2
3
4
5

1980   1990   2000   2010

△ **Bosniak refugees**
Millions of Bosniak Muslims were displaced during the Bosnian War (1992–1995) as Serbian forces carried out ethnic cleansing. In this photograph, a man and his two grandchildren rest at a United Nations refugee camp in Kladanj.

5 THE FINAL BREAK-UP 1991–2008

Unlike other former republics, Macedonia achieved its independence peacefully in September 1991, with the Yugoslav army withdrawing 9 months later. Serbia and Montenegro formed the Federal Republic of Yugoslavia in 1992, renamed Serbia and Montenegro in 2003. In June 2006, Montenegro became independent from Serbia. Finally, Kosovo declared itself independent from Serbia in 2008.

🏳 Independence

Sep 1991 Macedonia (known officially as the Former Yugoslav Republic of Macedonia, in recognition of Greece's dispute over its name) declares independence

4 KOSOVO 1990–1999

Majority Albanian Kosovo declared its independence in 1990, but it did not receive international recognition. The Kosovo Liberation Army began to fight the Serbs in 1995, leading to full-scale war in February 1998. More than 1 million Albanian Kosovars fled and thousands more were killed before a NATO bombing campaign in 1999 forced Serbian forces to depart.

Kosovo Liberation Army (KLA) stronghold
→ Serb forces 1999

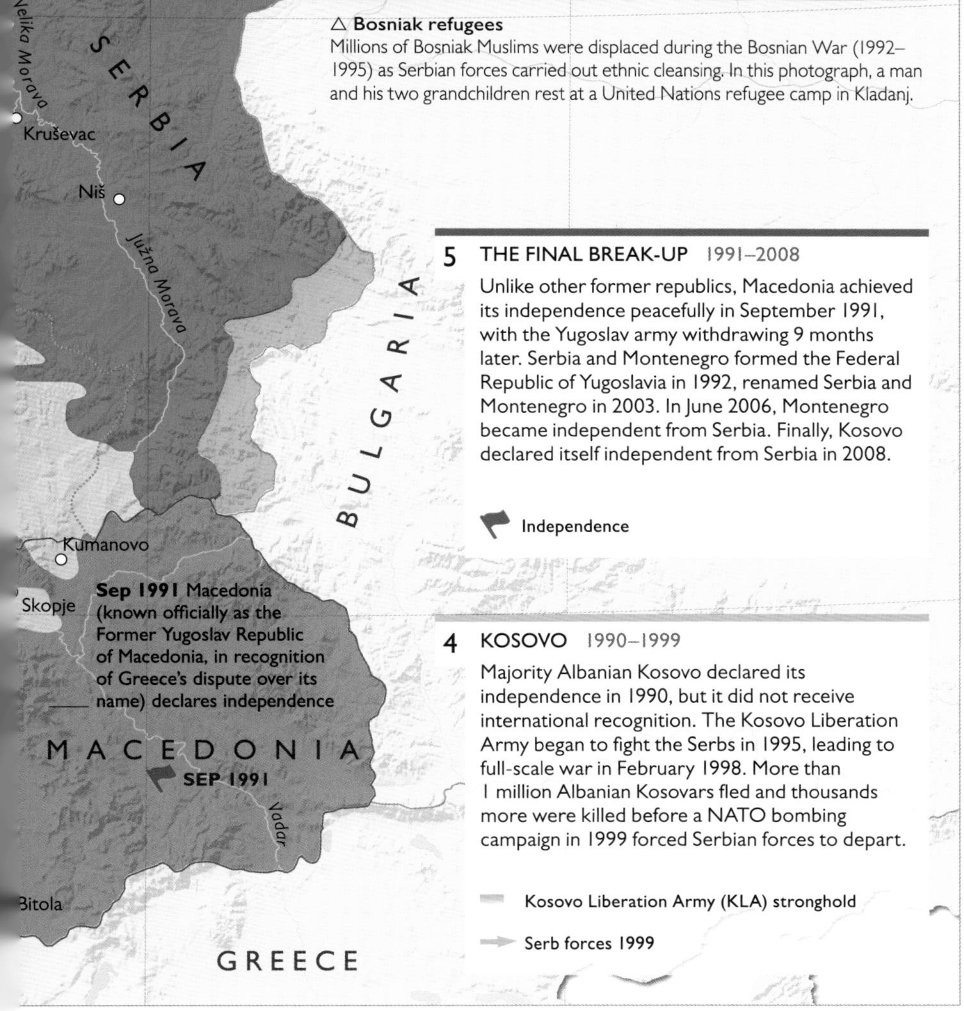

WAR IN YUGOSLAVIA

In the 1990s, the multiethnic but unified Socialist Federal Republic of Yugoslavia fell apart in the bloodiest series of wars fought in Europe since World War II.

Under the rule of leader Josip Broz Tito (1892–1980), Yugoslavia was a federation of six socialist republics, with two autonomous provinces inside Serbia. After Tito's death, a Serbian nationalist revival, led by Slobodan Milošević, started the country's disintegration by opposing Slovenian and Croatian independence in June 1991. Yugoslav (Serbian) forces moved in, and over the next decade, the nationalist drive to reorganize the territory along ethnic lines led to mass killings of civilians and other atrocities, giving the world a new phrase: "ethnic cleansing."

The conflict spread to Bosnia in 1992, where Serbs ethnically cleansed large areas of Bosniak Muslims. A fragile peace was eventually reached in 1995 with the signing of the Dayton Accords. The final tragedy was fought out in Kosovo, as Serbs tried to crush an uprising by the Kosovo Liberation Army. NATO stepped in, forcing the Serbs out of Kosovo in 1999. By 2008, seven new states had emerged from the once-unified country. The conflicts cost 140,000 lives and displaced nearly 4 million people.

"No country of people's democracy has so many nationalities as this country has."

JOSIP BROZ TITO, LEADER OF YUGOSLAVIA, 1948

BREAK-UP OF YUGOSLAVIA

In 1946, Yugoslavia became a federation consisting of six socialist republics, with Kosovo and Vojvodina being autonomous provinces of Serbia. By 2008, all six republics and Kosovo were independent states, with Vojvodina remaining an autonomous province of Serbia.

KEY

- Socialist Federal Republic of Yugoslavia
- Autonomous provinces

GLOBALIZATION

Globalization—the free movement of goods, people, money, knowledge, and culture around the world—was once seen as the answer to worldwide poverty, but inequality and political instability have led to a populist backlash.

Globalization is not a recent phenomenon. Countries have traded with each other for thousands of years; yet after World War II, technological advances, together with the lowering of trade barriers and the communication revolution, transformed the way nations interacted.

Globalization promoted economic growth in developing countries, yet in practice this often meant that industries would move from rich countries, where labor was expensive, to poor countries, where it was cheaper. Multinational corporations became increasingly global, locating production plants overseas in order to take advantage of lower costs and taxes. The growth of the internet allowed people to conduct business across the globe without leaving their office. International trade in goods, services, and financial capital became more widespread than ever before, further driven by China's decision to open its economy to the world in the late 80s and by the collapse of the Soviet bloc in the early 90s.

△ **Taking to the streets**
Following demonstrations in Seattle in 1999, subsequent WTO meetings in cities around the world became a focus for similar protests, sometimes involving confrontations between security forces and demonstrators.

Reactions and protests

A backlash against globalization had begun in the early 90s. It intensified in November 1999 as protesters in Seattle, Washington, took to the streets at the World Trade Organization (WTO) conference. Once applauded by economists, globalization was now fiercely contested as widening the gap between the rich and poor. Ordinary people were portrayed as victims of ruthless corporate domination, with large corporations exploiting the poor in search of new profits. The debate continues today, as political parties advancing protectionist and anti-immigration policies, including a return to local economies, have found wide support across much of the Western world.

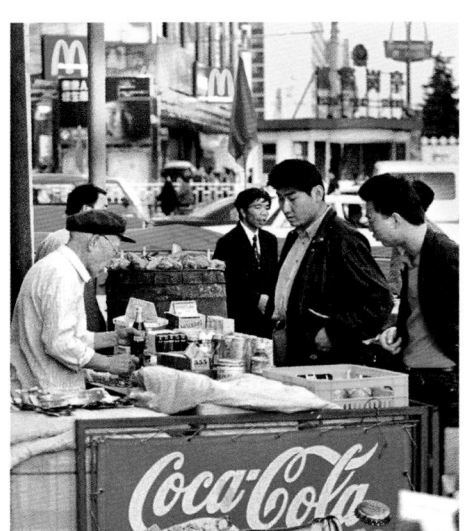

◁ **Advertising in Asia**
The logos of global corporations have become ubiquitous, even in countries such as China that were until relatively recently closed to foreign trade.

High-productivity industry
With its high-tech production lines, the Japanese car company Nissan's investment in the UK has transformed the UK's car industry. Nissan's factory (seen here) in Sunderland, UK, is regarded as a success story of globalization.

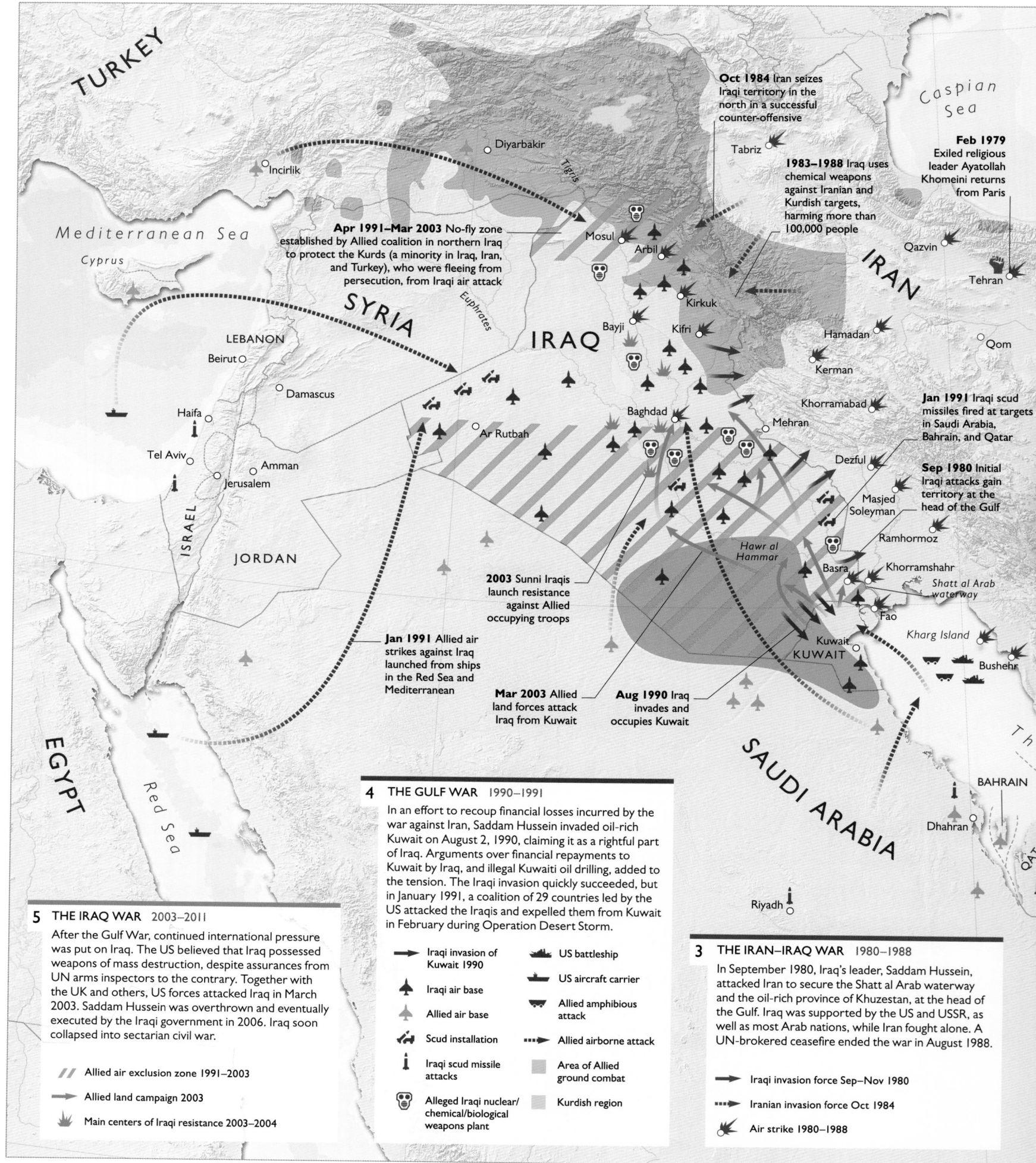

Oct 1984 Iran seizes Iraqi territory in the north in a successful counter-offensive

Feb 1979 Exiled religious leader Ayatollah Khomeini returns from Paris

1983–1988 Iraq uses chemical weapons against Iranian and Kurdish targets, harming more than 100,000 people

Apr 1991–Mar 2003 No-fly zone established by Allied coalition in northern Iraq to protect the Kurds (a minority in Iraq, Iran, and Turkey), who were fleeing from persecution, from Iraqi air attack

Jan 1991 Iraqi scud missiles fired at targets in Saudi Arabia, Bahrain, and Qatar

Sep 1980 Initial Iraqi attacks gain territory at the head of the Gulf

2003 Sunni Iraqis launch resistance against Allied occupying troops

Jan 1991 Allied air strikes against Iraq launched from ships in the Red Sea and Mediterranean

Mar 2003 Allied land forces attack Iraq from Kuwait

Aug 1990 Iraq invades and occupies Kuwait

Mediterranean Sea
Cyprus
Caspian Sea
Red Sea
Shatt al Arab waterway
Hawr al Hammar
Kharg Island

TURKEY · SYRIA · LEBANON · IRAQ · IRAN · ISRAEL · JORDAN · EGYPT · SAUDI ARABIA · KUWAIT · BAHRAIN · QATAR

Incirlik · Diyarbakir · Tabriz · Qazvin · Tehran · Mosul · Arbil · Kirkuk · Bayji · Kifri · Hamadan · Qom · Beirut · Damascus · Haifa · Tel Aviv · Jerusalem · Amman · Ar Rutbah · Baghdad · Mehran · Khorramabad · Kerman · Dezful · Masjed Soleyman · Ramhormoz · Basra · Khorramshahr · Fao · Kuwait · Busherh · Dhahran · Riyadh

4 THE GULF WAR 1990–1991

In an effort to recoup financial losses incurred by the war against Iran, Saddam Hussein invaded oil-rich Kuwait on August 2, 1990, claiming it as a rightful part of Iraq. Arguments over financial repayments to Kuwait by Iraq, and illegal Kuwaiti oil drilling, added to the tension. The Iraqi invasion quickly succeeded, but in January 1991, a coalition of 29 countries led by the US attacked the Iraqis and expelled them from Kuwait in February during Operation Desert Storm.

5 THE IRAQ WAR 2003–2011

After the Gulf War, continued international pressure was put on Iraq. The US believed that Iraq possessed weapons of mass destruction, despite assurances from UN arms inspectors to the contrary. Together with the UK and others, US forces attacked Iraq in March 2003. Saddam Hussein was overthrown and eventually executed by the Iraqi government in 2006. Iraq soon collapsed into sectarian civil war.

/ / Allied air exclusion zone 1991–2003

→ Allied land campaign 2003

🌿 Main centers of Iraqi resistance 2003–2004

→ Iraqi invasion of Kuwait 1990
▲ Iraqi air base
▲ Allied air base
🚙 Scud installation
⚓ Iraqi scud missile attacks
☠ Alleged Iraqi nuclear/chemical/biological weapons plant

⛴ US battleship
🚢 US aircraft carrier
🚤 Allied amphibious attack
- - -> Allied airborne attack
▨ Area of Allied ground combat
▨ Kurdish region

3 THE IRAN–IRAQ WAR 1980–1988

In September 1980, Iraq's leader, Saddam Hussein, attacked Iran to secure the Shatt al Arab waterway and the oil-rich province of Khuzestan, at the head of the Gulf. Iraq was supported by the US and USSR, as well as most Arab nations, while Iran fought alone. A UN-brokered ceasefire ended the war in August 1988.

→ Iraqi invasion force Sep–Nov 1980

- - -> Iranian invasion force Oct 1984

🌿 Air strike 1980–1988

Apr 1980 A US helicopter, used to rescue 63 hostages held in the US embassy in Tehran, crashes in Tabas

○ Tabas

— Shiraz

△ **On patrol**
During Operation Desert Storm (1991), US and Saudi fighter aircraft patrolled the skies over Kuwait as oil wells set alight by Iraqi forces burned freely below them.

IRAN AND THE GULF WARS

The resurgence of Shia Islam in Iran after the revolution of 1979, and the establishment of a Shia clerical government in Tehran, unsettled the Middle East. Between 1980 and 2003, three major wars took place in the Persian Gulf, all of them involving Iraq.

In 1980, Saddam Hussein, the leader of Iraq (which was dominated by Sunnis, although the majority of Iraqis were Shias), invaded neighboring Iran, still in turmoil after a revolution, to gain land and access to Iranian oil reserves. Thus began a long, bloody, but inconclusive war, which also involved many other countries. This conflict ended when the UN brokered a ceasefire in 1988, which brought to an end the longest conventional war of the 20th century.

Two years later, in what is known as the Gulf War, Saddam invaded Kuwait in order to gain its oil reserves to rebuild his military war machine. A US-led coalition of 29 countries, including many of Iraq's Arab neighbors, evicted the Iraqis from Kuwait in 1991, although Saddam Hussein remained in power. After the war, Iraq was subject to economic and military sanctions. It was also suspected of stockpiling weapons of mass destruction. Despite UN weapons inspectors failing to find such weapons, the US and Britain used their possible existence as justification to attack and invade Iraq in 2003, together with Australia, Poland, Spain, Italy, and Denmark. Unlike the Gulf War, the invasion was not supported by the UN. US forces carried out a search for Saddam, who had fled into hiding, and he was captured in December 2003. The coalition handed him over to Iraqi authorities in June 2004, and in 2006, he was tried and executed by an Iraqi Special Tribunal. Iraq then collapsed into sectarian chaos and civil war, further destabilizing an already unstable region. A civil war in Syria, which broke out in 2011, added to the turmoil in the Middle East, as rival Sunni and Shia forces fought it out.

1 THE IRANIAN REVOLUTION 1979

Resistance against the autocratic rule of the Shah of Iran led to demonstrations in the holy city of Qom in 1977 and 1978. Riots soon spread to the capital, Tehran, with demonstrators calling for the return of the exiled Shia religious leader Ayatollah Khomeini. The Shah eventually fled Iran in January 1979; Khomeini set up a religious government, one of only two theocracies in the world alongside the Vatican City.

✊ Revolution in Tehran

Abu Dhabi ○

U.A.E.

2 IRAN AFTER THE REVOLUTION
1979–PRESENT

The new government of Iran, led by Ayatollah Khomeini, became the world's first Shia government. It adopted strong anti-American and anti-Israeli policies and supported radical Shia groups, such as Hezbollah in Lebanon and, more recently, pro-government forces fighting in the Syrian civil war.

SHIA POPULATIONS
Although most of the world's Muslims are Sunni, about 12 percent are Shias. Shias form a majority in Iran, Iraq, Azerbaijan, and Bahrain, with sizeable minorities elsewhere in the Middle East. This map indicates the percentages of Shia Muslims in each country.

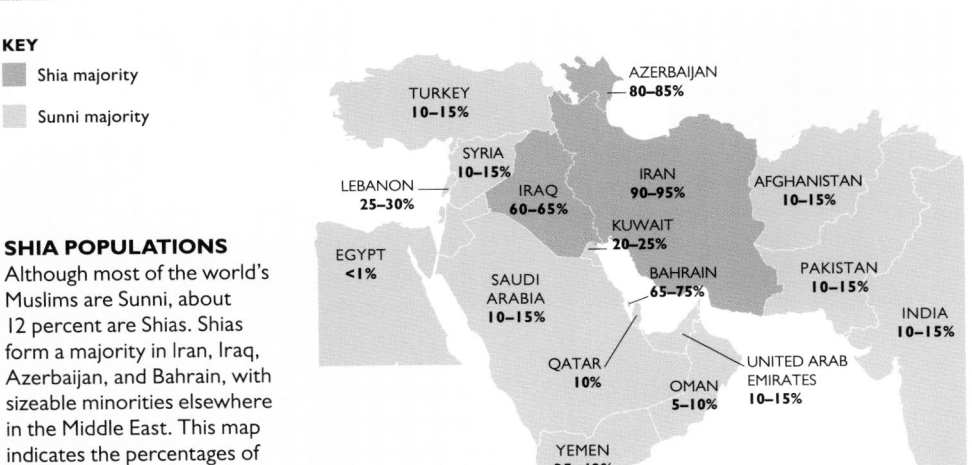

KEY
▓ Shia majority
░ Sunni majority

AZERBAIJAN 80–85%
TURKEY 10–15%
SYRIA 10–15%
LEBANON 25–30%
IRAQ 60–65%
IRAN 90–95%
AFGHANISTAN 10–15%
EGYPT <1%
KUWAIT 20–25%
SAUDI ARABIA 10–15%
BAHRAIN 65–75%
PAKISTAN 10–15%
INDIA 10–15%
QATAR 10%
OMAN 5–10%
UNITED ARAB EMIRATES 10–15%
YEMEN 35–40%

THE COMMUNICATION REVOLUTION

Advances in technology have brought about profound changes in the social, economic, and political landscape. Nowhere has the impact been felt more than in the field of communications, which is transforming every aspect of our daily lives.

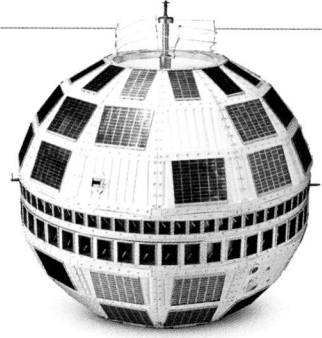

△ **Space Age communication**
The world's first active communication satellite, Telstar 1 was jointly built by the US, French, and British broadcasting agencies.

Until World War II, communications had been limited to messages sent by mail or by telegraph and telephone. During World War II, a surge in new thinking resulted in the forerunner of digital computers—the Electronic Numerical Integrator and Calculator (ENIAC).

The invention of the transistor in 1947 and the microchip in 1958 led to electronic components becoming smaller. Advances in rocket technology allowed satellites to be sent into orbit. In 1962, the Telstar 1 satellite was launched, sending telephone calls, fax messages, and TV signals flying through space.

During the Cold War, the US Defense Department was concerned about how it might communicate during a nuclear attack. This led to the creation of the Advanced Research Projects Agency Network (ARPANET) in 1969, a system of four computers communicating using standard protocols. By the 1980s, greater and more integrated use of computers, adoption of the ARPANET protocols, and advances in communications methods resulted in a widely available and global network of computers: the Internet. The smartphone made the internet a mobile resource. Social networking had an impact on education, healthcare, and culture. It was also used by protesters during the Arab Spring (2011) and has since become an inherent part of politics.

◁ **A connected world**
Smartphones have become an integral part of people's lives. They are not only used to navigate and send messages, but also to record and share moments on social media platforms.

"The information highway will transform our culture ... as Gutenberg's press did the Middle Ages."

BILL GATES, FROM *THE ROAD AHEAD*, 1995

Booting up
Unveiled on February 14, 1946, ENIAC—the first fully programmable computer—was originally devised to measure the trajectory of a shell. It weighed 27 tons (24 tonnes) and was filled with 20,000 vacuum tubes; 7,200 diodes; and several miles of wiring.

POPULATION AND ENERGY

After 1950, two of the main problems that faced the world were rising population and increasing energy consumption. Although population growth varies across the continents, the world's total population passed 3 billion in 1960 and then 7 billion in 2011.

China has the largest population in the world, and from 1970–2000, the country's population increased by 50 percent—an addition of more than 444 million people, more than the total population of the US in the year 2000 (282 million).

In 1950, poor, preindustrialized countries had high birth and death rates, but as they developed, first the death rate declined (particularly in infancy) due to better health care and nutrition, and then the birth rate declined in response to lower infant mortality. In the developed world, where these processes had already happened during industrialization, the population barely increased in the late 20th century, unless it was affected by immigration or inflows of migrant workers. In Africa, rapidly rising populations placed an ever-increasing strain on the countries' limited resources, including water, grazing land, and energy.

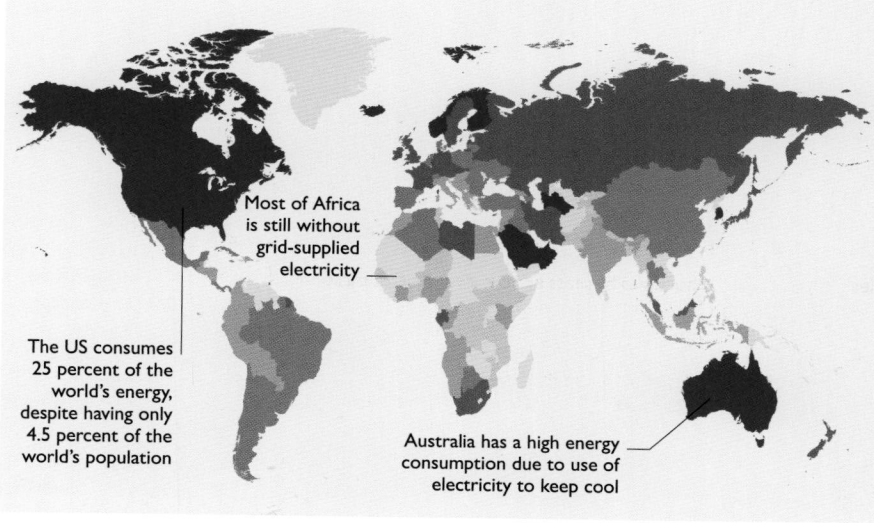

▷ **Abu Dhabi luxury**
The United Arab Emirates is a prosperous, oil-rich country. It has one of the highest levels of energy use, due to the luxury lifestyle led by its people and use of energy to keep cool in the high temperatures.

THE AMERICAS 1950–2010

In this period, two-thirds of the total population of the Americas lived in just three countries: the US, Mexico, and Brazil. Both the US and Canada supported immigration, increasing their populations, while emigration from the Caribbean islands kept their populations largely static.

1951–2001 Pro-immigration policies more than double Canada's population

1990–2010 Foreign-born population of the US doubles from 20 to 40 million due to immigration

1960 Brazil's rate of population increase begins to decline as rising prosperity causes falls in birth and death rates

1950 Argentina has one of the continent's lowest population growth rates due to its low birth rate

WORLD ENERGY USE

Energy use varies greatly from country to country. In 2014, wealthy, developed, and oil-rich nations used 50 times more energy per capita than the poorest nations. Latitude was also an important factor, with high-latitude countries, such as Canada, using more energy to keep warm.

ENERGY USE PER CAPITA, 2014

KG of oil equivalent

0	500	1000	2,500	5,000 +
0	4	7	18	36 +

Barrel of oil equivalent

No data

Most of Africa is still without grid-supplied electricity

The US consumes 25 percent of the world's energy, despite having only 4.5 percent of the world's population

Australia has a high energy consumption due to use of electricity to keep cool

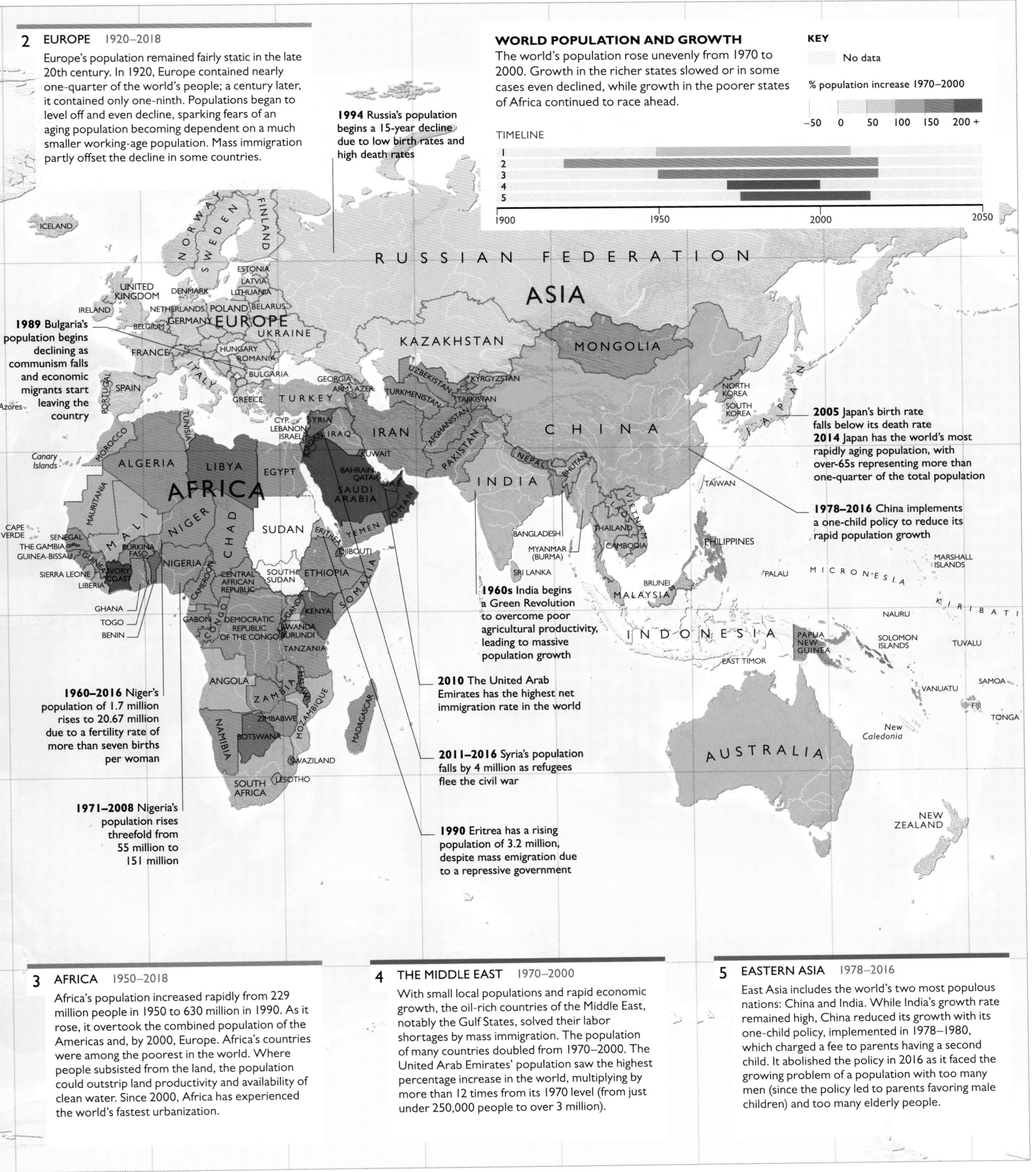

2 EUROPE 1920–2018

Europe's population remained fairly static in the late 20th century. In 1920, Europe contained nearly one-quarter of the world's people; a century later, it contained only one-ninth. Populations began to level off and even decline, sparking fears of an aging population becoming dependent on a much smaller working-age population. Mass immigration partly offset the decline in some countries.

1994 Russia's population begins a 15-year decline due to low birth rates and high death rates

WORLD POPULATION AND GROWTH

The world's population rose unevenly from 1970 to 2000. Growth in the richer states slowed or in some cases even declined, while growth in the poorer states of Africa continued to race ahead.

KEY

No data

% population increase 1970–2000

-50 0 50 100 150 200 +

TIMELINE

1
2
3
4
5

1900   1950   2000   2050

RUSSIAN FEDERATION

ASIA

ICELAND

NORWAY
SWEDEN
FINLAND

UNITED KINGDOM
IRELAND
DENMARK
NETHERLANDS
BELGIUM
GERMANY
EUROPE
POLAND
BELARUS
UKRAINE
ESTONIA
LATVIA
LITHUANIA

1989 Bulgaria's population begins declining as communism falls and economic migrants start leaving the country

FRANCE
HUNGARY
ROMANIA
BULGARIA
ITALY
GEORGIA
ARM. AZER.
KAZAKHSTAN
MONGOLIA

SPAIN
PORTUGAL
Azores
GREECE
TURKEY
TURKMENISTAN
UZBEKISTAN
KYRGYZSTAN
TAJIKISTAN

CYP.
LEBANON
ISRAEL
SYRIA
IRAQ
KUWAIT
IRAN
AFGHANISTAN
PAKISTAN
CHINA
NORTH KOREA
SOUTH KOREA
JAPAN

Canary Islands
MOROCCO
TUNISIA

2005 Japan's birth rate falls below its death rate
2014 Japan has the world's most rapidly aging population, with over-65s representing more than one-quarter of the total population

ALGERIA
LIBYA
EGYPT
BAHRAIN
QATAR
SAUDI ARABIA
UAE
OMAN

AFRICA
MAURITANIA
MALI
NIGER
CHAD
SUDAN
ERITREA
YEMEN
NEPAL
BHUTAN
INDIA
TAIWAN

CAPE VERDE
SENEGAL
THE GAMBIA
GUINEA-BISSAU
GUINEA
SIERRA LEONE
LIBERIA
BURKINA FASO
IVORY COAST
NIGERIA
DJIBOUTI
SOMALIA
BANGLADESH
MYANMAR (BURMA)
SRI LANKA
THAILAND
CAMBODIA
VIETNAM

1978–2016 China implements a one-child policy to reduce its rapid population growth

GHANA
TOGO
BENIN
GABON
CAMEROON
CENTRAL AFRICAN REPUBLIC
SOUTH SUDAN
ETHIOPIA
CONGO
DEMOCRATIC REPUBLIC OF THE CONGO
UGANDA
KENYA
RWANDA
BURUNDI
TANZANIA

PHILIPPINES
MICRONESIA
PALAU
MARSHALL ISLANDS
KIRIBATI

1960s India begins a Green Revolution to overcome poor agricultural productivity, leading to massive population growth

MALAYSIA
BRUNEI
INDONESIA
NAURU
SOLOMON ISLANDS
TUVALU
PAPUA NEW GUINEA
EAST TIMOR

1960–2016 Niger's population of 1.7 million rises to 20.67 million due to a fertility rate of more than seven births per woman

ANGOLA
ZAMBIA
MALAWI
MOZAMBIQUE
NAMIBIA
ZIMBABWE
BOTSWANA
MADAGASCAR
SWAZILAND
LESOTHO
SOUTH AFRICA

2010 The United Arab Emirates has the highest net immigration rate in the world

VANUATU
SAMOA
FIJI
TONGA
New Caledonia
AUSTRALIA

2011–2016 Syria's population falls by 4 million as refugees flee the civil war

NEW ZEALAND

1971–2008 Nigeria's population rises threefold from 55 million to 151 million

1990 Eritrea has a rising population of 3.2 million, despite mass emigration due to a repressive government

3 AFRICA 1950–2018

Africa's population increased rapidly from 229 million people in 1950 to 630 million in 1990. As it rose, it overtook the combined population of the Americas and, by 2000, Europe. Africa's countries were among the poorest in the world. Where people subsisted from the land, the population could outstrip land productivity and availability of clean water. Since 2000, Africa has experienced the world's fastest urbanization.

4 THE MIDDLE EAST 1970–2000

With small local populations and rapid economic growth, the oil-rich countries of the Middle East, notably the Gulf States, solved their labor shortages by mass immigration. The population of many countries doubled from 1970–2000. The United Arab Emirates' population saw the highest percentage increase in the world, multiplying by more than 12 times from its 1970 level (from just under 250,000 people to over 3 million).

5 EASTERN ASIA 1978–2016

East Asia includes the world's two most populous nations: China and India. While India's growth rate remained high, China reduced its growth with its one-child policy, implemented in 1978–1980, which charged a fee to parents having a second child. It abolished the policy in 2016 as it faced the growing problem of a population with too many men (since the policy led to parents favoring male children) and too many elderly people.

TIMELINE

PREHISTORY 15 MYA–3000 BCE

◁ **Acheulean handaxe**
Dating from around 1.5 MYA–800,000 BCE, this handaxe was made by hammering flakes off a piece of flint.

c. 15 MYA
The first hominids, or great apes, appear—they are ancestors of gorillas, chimpanzees, orangutans, and humans.

c. 7.2 MYA
Sahelanthropus tchadensis arises; this hominid species, known only from vestigial fossil remains found in Chad in 2001–2002, is the earliest known member of the Hominini subfamily, a small group that includes humans but excludes the other living great apes.

c. 3.6 MYA
Footprints found in volcanic ash in east Africa indicate that the hominin *Australopithecus afarensis* is walking upright by this time; it has a brain about one-third the size of a modern human's and thumb-opposed hands, potentially enabling the use of tools. Other findings, including that of the partial female skeleton discovered in Ethiopia in 1974 and nicknamed Lucy (dated c.3.2 MYA), indicate that the species lived in family groups.

c. 3.3 MYA
The date of stone tools found at the Lomekwi archaeological site in Kenya—the oldest yet discovered; they mark the start of the Paleolithic or Old Stone Age (which ends around 15,000–10,000 years ago). At Dikika in Ethiopia, the remains of a 3-year-old *Australopithecus* female confirm that the species is adapted both for bipedalism

600
million years ago. The time when multicellular life evolved on Earth.

(walking on two feet) and for tree-climbing. This increased mobility facilitates the move from forests to open savanna, opening up new opportunities for hunting and food gathering.

c. 2.8 MYA
A mandible fragment from this time is found in the Afar region of Ethiopia in 2013; it is currently the earliest fossil assigned to the genus *Homo*, to which the modern human species belongs.

2.4–1.4 MYA
Paranthropus boisei, a hominin species distinguished by its large jaws and cheek teeth and powerful jaw muscles, inhabits the Olduvai Gorge region of east Africa. The jaws earn the species its nickname of "Nutcracker Man."

c. 1.9 MYA
The date of remains found in the 1950s at Olduvai Gorge in Tanzania by Louis and Mary Leakey, to which they will give the name *Homo habilis* ("Handy man"); some anthropologists have since queried the attribution, putting the fossils in the *Australopithecus* genus instead.

c. 1.8 MYA
Homo erectus evolves, with a bigger brain than *Homo habilis*. Food remains indicate that the species was omnivorous, but with a higher proportion of meat in its diet than other primates. Fossilized remains

of *Homo erectus*, its Asian variant, indicate that the species spread quickly across Eurasia; specimens discovered at Dmanisi in Georgia and dating from this time are currently considered the earliest hominin remains found outside of Africa.

c. 1.5 MYA–800,000 BCE
Oval and pear-shaped handaxes of the type known as Acheulean spread from Africa to south and west Asia and Europe; the first remains of the axes are identified in St. Acheul, near Amiens, France, in 1859. One of the characteristic tools of Stone Age people, their dispersal is closely associated with the diffusion of *Homo erectus*.

c. 700,000–200,000 BCE
Homo heidelbergensis spreads through Africa, Europe, and western Asia. First described from remains found near Heidelberg in Germany in 1908, the species has a bigger brain than *Homo erectus* and uses more developed tools; it is the first early human species to build shelters. The Neanderthal population is thought to have evolved from this line.

c. 500,000 BCE
Fire and a wide range of stone tools are in use by human ancestors in China, as evidenced by remains found in a cave at Zhoukhoudian, near Beijing, in the 1920s ("Peking Man").

c. 400,000 BCE
Neanderthals appear; remains of the group have been found in Europe and western Asia. Shorter and stockier than other hominins, the Neanderthals will in time interbreed with *Homo* species, contributing to the DNA of modern humans.

c. 300,000 BCE
Hominin fossils found at Jebel Irhoud, Morocco, in 2017 that have been dated to this time are the earliest known examples of *Homo sapiens*—anatomically modern humans. The species is distinguished by a high, thin-walled cranium, a steep forehead, and a flat, vertical face with a protruding chin.

c. 180,000–80,000 BCE
The first dispersals of *Homo sapiens* out of Africa are documented by finds in the Levant from 194,000–177,000 BCE and in China from 120,000–80,000 BCE.

c. 170,000 BCE
The estimated date for the existence of "Mitochondrial Eve"—the most recent common ancestor of all living humans as traced back through the matrilineal

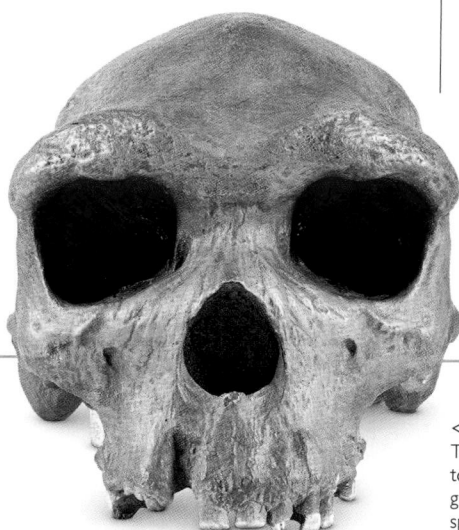

◁ *Homo heidelbergensis* **skull**
This species prevailed from around 700,000 to 200,000 BCE; its members lived in cooperative groups and hunted large animals using wooden spears set with stone spearheads.

▷ **Chauvet Cave art (replica)**
Animal images drawn in charcoal on the walls of the Chauvet Cave in southern France date back at least 30,000 years. A replica of the cave has been built to preserve the vulnerable originals.

genetic line (so-called because the DNA used in this analysis is from subcellular mitochondria, which are inherited only from mother to daughter).

c. 80,000–40,000 BCE
Genetic evidence suggests *Homo sapiens* dispersed through the Middle East and along the southern coast of Asia, possibly after the Toba event.

c. 75,000 BCE
The estimated date of the Toba supereruption—a volcanic event centered on what is now Lake Toba in Sumatra, Indonesia; the event may have caused a "global winter" affecting hominin populations across the world.

c. 65,000 BCE
The date of the earliest archaeological sites in Australia—evidence of the ancestors of today's Aboriginal population; they are thought to have traveled by island-hopping through Indonesia, suggesting that boats were in use by this time.

c. 45,000 BCE
The earliest "European early modern human" remains date back to this time. This population of *Homo sapiens* was named Cro-Magnon when it was discovered in a rock shelter of this name in the Dordogne, France, in 1868.

c. 43,000 BCE
Aurignacian tool-making techniques, characterized by parallel-sided stone blades (rather than the previous flakes) and finely worked bone and antler points, spread across eastern Europe, reaching the west of the continent between 40,000 and 33,000 BCE. The peoples would travel long distances to find suitable tool-making materials.

c. 40,000 BCE
Hand stencils are painted in caves in Sulawesi, Indonesia; they are thought to be the oldest human markings, predating European cave art. At about this time, the Neanderthals are thought to have died out in Europe.

c. 35,000 BCE
The Venus of Hohle Fels, an image carved out of mammoth ivory and found in a cave in southern Germany, is the earliest known of the Venus figurines, which are statuettes of (mostly) female figures thought to have been fertility symbols.

c. 30,000 BCE
The first settlers arrive in Japan and in the Solomon Islands in Oceania. In sites around Europe, the earliest evidence of grindstones being used to mill wild cereal grains dates from this time.

c. 24,500 BCE
The last glaciation (commonly called the Ice Age) of the current Quaternary geological era is at its peak.

c. 24,000–14,000 BCE
Estimated date range for the settling of North America by hunter-gatherers crossing from Siberia over the Beringia land bridge that spanned what is now the Bering Strait; since archaeological evidence is sparsely distributed across North America, the date is speculative.

c. 18,000 BCE
Ceramic fragments found in southern China indicate that pottery is being produced by this time.

c. 15,000 BCE
The estimated date of the cave paintings found at Lascaux in the Dordogne region of France.

c. 14,700 BCE
The first evidence of dog remains buried beside humans (found in a quarry in a suburb of Bonn, Germany) strongly indicates that dogs had been domesticated by this time.

c. 14,000 BCE
The Jomon culture, distinguished by cord-marked pottery, is established in Japan.

c. 13,000 BCE
The Clovis culture, named for the site in New Mexico where it was first identified and characterized by distinctive bone and ivory tools, makes its appearance. Clovis remains have been found from Oregon down to Chile; they are associated with a hunter-gatherer lifestyle that included hunting mammoths, bison, mastodon, sloths, and tapirs. It was once regarded as the first Native American culture, ancestral to developments throughout North and South America, but earlier, non-Clovis sites have now been found.

c. 12,000 BCE
The earliest Saharan rock art depicts rhinos, aurochs (wild cattle), antelopes, and other animals pursued by the region's hunter-gatherers.

c. 11,000 BCE
Rock paintings are created in Pedra Furada, Brazil, seemingly representing a tradition that differs from the Clovis culture.

c. 10,500 BCE
Cattle are first domesticated in Mesopotamia and in what is now Pakistan. DNA evidence suggests that one evolutionary line of living domestic cattle may have arisen from a herd of aurochs near the village of Çayönü Tepesi, in southeastern Turkey, near the modern border with Iraq.

c. 10,200 BCE
The start for the Neolithic, or New Stone Age, according to the ASPRO chronology of the Middle East. The Neolithic will see the birth of farming and the widespread domestication of animals; it ends with the adoption of metal tools, ushering in the Bronze Age.

c. 10,000 BCE
The last glaciation of the present Quaternary Era ends, marking the start of Earth's current warmer interglacial period. By this time, sheep are being domesticated in Mesopotamia. Radio carbon dating of stone tools found near campfire remains indicate that hunter-gatherer communities are by now settled in the Valley of Mexico.

32
The percentage of land covered by ice in the last glaciation.

c. 9500 BCE
Farming is underway in the Fertile Crescent lands of the Levant and Mesopotamia; evidence shows wheat, barley, peas, and lentils all being cultivated. The ensuing Agricultural Revolution will in time lead to a surge in the world's population as food supplies become more reliable and widespread.

c. 9000 BCE
Circles of stone pillars are erected at Göbekli Tepe, a site in eastern Turkey; these are currently the earliest known megaliths. Corn is first domesticated at about this time, in southern Mexico. The land bridge linking Siberia and North America finally disappears beneath the waters of the Bering Strait as sea levels rise following the retreat of the Ice Age glaciers.

c. 8700 BCE
The first copper tools are in use, made from naturally occurring deposits of the metal.

△ **Saharan rock art**
This painting, made in red iron oxide in the Acacus Mountains, Libya, dates back to 12,000 BCE; it shows a hunt in progress.

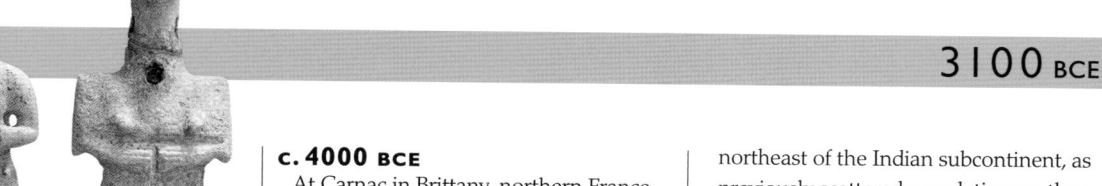

▷ **Cycladic figurines**
The Cycladic islands in the Aegean Sea were settled by people from Anatolia from about 3200 BCE; they shaped the marble they found there into clean-lined anthropomorphic figurines.

3100 BCE

c. 8200 BCE

Rice is being cultivated in the Pearl River region of China and spreads to the Yellow and Yangtze valleys; millet is also being grown in China by this time. Some experts estimate that rice was domesticated as early as 13,500 BCE.

c. 8000 BCE

Settled since c.10,000 BCE by hunter-gatherers attracted by its freshwater spring, Jericho (in modern-day Palestine) has by now become a fortified town of at least 300 inhabitants who support themselves by growing emmer wheat, barley, and pulses; the town is surrounded by a wall (which may have afforded some protection against flooding). A defensive tower 28 ft (8.5 m) in height is built within the walls.

c. 7000 BCE

Çatal Höyük is flourishing in Anatolia as a large settlement with an estimated population of 7,000.

c. 6500 BCE

Lead beads found at Çatal Höyük represent evidence of metal smelting.

c. 5500 BCE

The first known smelted copper objects date from this time; the earliest bronze objects, made of a copper–arsenic alloy, also appear. A painted disk found in Kuwait and assigned to this period has the earliest known depiction of a ship under sail. The Tărtăria tablets, discovered at a Neolithic site in Romania, bear symbols considered by some archeologists to be the world's earliest form of writing.

c. 5050 BCE

The Chinchorro people of northern Chile are the first culture known to mummify their dead.

c. 5000 BCE

Lower Mesopotamia, between the Tigris and Euphrates Rivers, is populated by a west Asian people called the Sumerians; over the next two millennia Sumer will become, along with Egypt, the Indus Valley, and coastal Peru, the seat of one of the world's earliest urban civilizations, developing masonry and pottery and building the towns of Uruk and Eridu.

c. 4500 BCE

Bones and carved images of horses found in graves in the Volga River region of central Russia suggest that horses have been domesticated there by this time. Finds from Serbia show tin-alloy bronze objects making their first appearance. Obsidian, prized by Neolithic tool-makers for its hardness and sharp edges, is being traded by now in Mesopotamia.

c. 4000 BCE

At Carnac in Brittany, northern France, the world's largest accumulation of megaliths is growing; eventually (by about 3300 BCE), it will incorporate more than 3,000 separate standing stones. Austronesians from Taiwan or the Philippines begin their Pacific migration.

c. 3600 BCE

Neolithic farmers in Malta, possibly from Sicily, build the temple complex at Skorba. In Mesopotamia, symbols representing numbers are being impressed on clay tablets as a way of keeping accounts—an early form of writing that will eventually develop into cuneiform.

c. 3500 BCE

Evidence from Mesopotamia, the North Caucasus region, and eastern Europe shows wheeled vehicles coming into use at about this time; the earliest schematic depiction of a four-wheeled wagon is on the Bronocice Pot, dated to around 3400 BCE and found in Southern Poland. In Crete, the Minoan civilization is starting to take shape.

c. 3300 BCE

Approximate start of the Bronze Age in the Middle East, when bronze begins supplementing stone for tool-making and other uses. The Indus Valley civilization starts to develop in the northeast of the Indian subcontinent, as previously scattered populations gather into permanent settlements that will eventually become fortified towns.

c. 3200 BCE

Newgrange, a circular mound 280 ft (85 m) wide and containing tunnels and chambers, is constructed in Ireland; its exact purpose is unclear, but it probably has a ritual function. The Cycladic culture is spreading across the islands of the Aegean Sea; it is known for its flat female statuettes made out of the local white marble.

c. 3150 BCE

The Narmer Palette is produced. It is an inscribed tablet depicting the unification of Upper and Lower Egypt under the ruler of that name (also known as Menes), who will establish the nation's First Dynasty. It bears some of the earliest known hieroglyphic writing.

3114 BCE

In Mesoamerica, the first date in the Mayan Long Count Calendar.

c. 3100 BCE

Europe's most complete Neolithic village, Skara Brae, is built, indicating that settled communities have formed in the Orkney Islands to the north of Scotland. The site is revealed after the islands are battered by a storm in 1850.

 ft (3.6 m). The height of the defensive wall built around the settlement of Jericho by around 8000 BCE.

▷ **Skara Brae, Orkney**
Skara Brae, occupied around 3100 BCE, is a settlement of circular one-room dwellings made from stone slabs. The houses would have been roofed with straw or turf.

THE ANCIENT WORLD 3000 BCE—500 CE

3000 BCE

c. 3000 BCE
In Sumer (modern Iraq and Kuwait), around a dozen city-states are flourishing, among them Lagash and Uruk (which has a population of more than 50,000 by this time, making it the largest city in the world). The cities trade with Anatolia, Syria, Dilmun (modern Bahrain), and Elam on the eastern coast of the Persian Gulf (now part of modern-day Iran). In southern Siberia, the Afanasevo Culture of cattle-, sheep-, and goat-herders is established. The first phase of the Stonehenge complex in southern England is built—a circular ditch and bank; construction on the site will continue through the next millennium.

c. 2900 BCE
In China, the Longshan Culture, centered on the lower Yellow River valley, is producing sophisticated, thin-walled black pottery; millet is the main crop and pigs the principal source of meat. In South America, the Norte Chico people build monumental centers on the coast of Peru; Aspero, at the mouth of the Supe Valley, boasts platform mounds endowed with plazas, terraces, and ceremonial buildings.

c. 2700 BCE
The legendary Gilgamesh rules Uruk; his exploits, richly mythologized, are the basis of one of the world's first literary works, the *Epic of Gilgamesh* (c. 2100 BCE).

c. 2630 BCE
Djoser, the first pharaoh of Egypt's Old Kingdom, orders the building of the Step Pyramid at Saqqara as his burial place.

c. 2600 BCE
Objects found in the Royal Cemetery of Ur include the Standard of Ur, a wooden box inlaid with shell, limestone, and lapis lazuli mosaics depicting scenes of feasting and of warfare, including war chariots.

c. 2575 BCE
Pharaoh Khufu (known to later Greeks as Cheops) builds the Great Pyramid of Giza, the oldest of the Seven Wonders of the Ancient World.

c. 2500 BCE
The Indus Valley civilization is at its peak, with the cities of Harappa and Mohenjo-Daro supporting populations of 25,000–40,000 and boasting sophisticated civic facilities and urban planning. In Europe, the Bell Beaker Culture, identified by its distinctive pottery, is flourishing at scattered sites in the west and center of the continent.

c. 2450 BCE
A conflict between the Sumerian city-state of Lagash and its neighbor, Umma, is the first to be historically documented, on the Stele of the Vultures, fragments of which are now preserved in the Louvre Museum, Paris.

◁ **Hero overpowering a lion**
This sculpture of a lion-taming spirit, recovered from the throne room of the palace of Assyrian king Sargon II, is believed to depict Gilgamesh (king of Uruk around 2700 BCE).

▽ **Stonehenge, Amesbury, England**
The neolithic monument of Stonehenge was built in several stages, beginning in 3000 BCE. The stones at its center were erected in about 2500 BCE and then rearranged some 300 years later.

2050 BCE

c. 2334–2279 BCE
Sargon of Akkad conquers Sumer, joining it with his own kingdom to create the world's first empire. He will go on to win further territory from the Hurrians and Elamites in what is now eastern Turkey and western Iran.

c. 2300 BCE
The Bronze Age Unetice culture—named for an archaeological site northwest of Prague, where its remains were uncovered—starts to spread across central Europe. Its people live in straw-thatched wooden houses with storage pits used as granaries and produce handsome metal goods that serve as status symbols for the nobility.

c. 2205 BCE
According to Chinese tradition, the Xia Dynasty, is established under Yu the Great. He is known in legend for holding back the floodwaters of the Yellow River.

c. 2193 BCE
Gutians from the Zagros Mountains overrun Akkad and Sumer, putting an end to the Akkadian Empire.

140
miles (225 km). The distance over which 25-ton stones were hauled to Stonehenge.

c. 2180 BCE
Egypt's Old Kingdom comes to an end as central control disintegrates, ushering in the First Intermediate Period, a time of strife when separate power bases emerge in Upper and Lower Egypt.

c. 2100 BCE
Semitic-speaking Amorites from northern Syria begin to infiltrate into Mesopotamia, possibly driven by drought.

c. 2050 BCE
King Ur-Nammu reunites Sumer, establishing the powerful Third Dynasty of Ur (also called the Sumerian Renaissance); ziggurats (stepped monuments) are built during his reign, and the world's oldest surviving legal code bears his name. In Egypt, Pharaoh Mentuhotep reunites a divided land in 2134 BCE, starting the Middle Kingdom period.

c. 2000 BCE

A rich civilization develops on the island of Crete, centered on the palace complex at Knossos. On the Greek mainland, the Achaeans move into the northern Peloponnese. In Britain, the main stages of construction of Stonehenge are by now complete, while people of the Wessex culture, distinguished by their barrow burials and rich grave goods, have spread widely across central and southern England and are trading extensively with continental Europe.

c. 1960 BCE

Under Pharaoh Amenemhet I, Middle Kingdom Egypt extends its southern frontier as far as the Second Cataract of the River Nile, which is now submerged by Lake Nasser.

c. 1940 BCE

Despite the building of fortifications, the city of Ur falls to Elamites from eastern Iran, who take its last ruler, Ibbi-Sin, into captivity, ending the Third Dynasty; the loss of the city is commemorated in the "Lament for Ur,"

a 438-line Sumerian poem inscribed on a tablet that is found by archaeologists at Nippur. The defeat marks the end of the golden age of Sumer, whose population has shrunk, as the irrigated lands on which it depended have been affected by salinity.

c. 1900 BCE

Assyria emerges as a major power, with its capital at Assur in the Upper Tigris Valley of northern Mesopotamia. Under the ruler Shamshi-Adad I, the Great Royal Palace is built, and the temple of Assur is enlarged with a ziggurat.

282

The number of laws enshrined in the Code of Hammurabi, king of Babylon.

◁ **Minoan fresco**
Painted on the east wall of the Minoan palace at Knossos in around 1400 BCE, the fresco depicts bull-leaping, which was possibly a ceremonial practice demonstrating bravery.

◁ **Hittite goddess**
The large pantheon of the Hittites, who created an empire in Anatolia from c.1600–1180 BCE, included many gods appropriated from neighboring cultures.

2000–1450 BCE

Hammurabi transforms his capital, Babylon, from a small city-state into the center of a large state that extends over much of Mesopotamia.

c. 1750 BCE
The Erlitou Culture is flourishing in northern China; it is distinguished by the production of elaborate bronze vessels, including two-handled, legged cauldrons known as dings.

c. 1700 BCE
The Indus Valley civilization collapses, probably because of the gradual drying up of the Saraswati River; the cities of Harappa and Mohenjo Daro are abandoned.

c. 1640 BCE
Speaking a Semitic language and worshipping the storm god Baal, chariot-borne Hyksos move into Egypt. The Middle Kingdom comes to an end and the country enters the Second Intermediate Period, a time of famine and political strife.

c. 1600 BCE
A cataclysmic volcanic eruption on the Greek island of Thera (modern Santorini) has profound effects on the neighboring lands; Knossos and other ceremonial centers on Crete are badly damaged, and though they will later be rebuilt, Minoan civilization will never regain its former glory. The Shang Dynasty under King Tang replaces the Xia, establishing its rule over China's northern plains.

c. 1595 BCE
Hittite invaders from Anatolia sack Babylon, by then a small city-state; Kassites from the Zagros Mountains take advantage of the situation to establish a dynasty that will rule for the next 375 years.

c. 1800 BCE
The truncated defensive towers known as *nuraghi* are built across all of Sardinia.

c. 1754 BCE
Hammurabi, the sixth ruler of the Amorite First Babylonian Dynasty, issues a celebrated law code; which covers subjects ranging from wage rates and the legal liability to inheritance, sexual conduct, and divorce. Over the course of his 42-year reign, from 1792 to 1750 BCE,

c. 1550 BCE
A Hurrian-speaking people establish the kingdom of Mitanni in northern Syria and southeast Anatolia; in the centuries to come, it will develop into a major regional power.

1532 BCE
Ahmose of Thebes drives the Hyksos out of Lower Egypt, reunifying the country and establishing the New Kingdom. During this period Egyptian power reaches its greatest extent.

c. 1500 BCE
Indo-Iranian Aryans begin to migrate in large numbers into the north of the Indian subcontinent; the Vedas, the oldest Hindu scriptures, will take shape under the auspices of these people over the ensuing Vedic Period (to 600 BCE). In the Pacific Ocean, the Lapita culture is flourishing in Vanuatu, Fiji, Samoa, and Tonga, laying the foundations for subsequent Polynesian and Micronesian cultures.

1470 BCE
Hatshepsut, the best-known of Egypt's female pharaohs and the woman who commissioned the celebrated Deir el-Bahari mortuary temple as her last resting place,

sends a major trading expedition to the Land of Punt, somewhere to the south, on the Red Sea.

1456 BCE
Egypt's Pharaoh Thutmose III defeats a coalition of Canaanite states at the Battle of Megiddo, in what is now northern Israel; Tuthmose will go on to restore Egyptian dominance in the area and to expand Egyptian imperial control to its greatest extent.

c. 1450 BCE
Shaushtatar, the ruler of Mittani, invades Assyria and sacks its capital, Assur. By this time, the Karasuk culture, known only from its burials, has replaced the Andronovo culture in southeastern Siberia; its people are farmers and horse riders who practice metalwork on a large scale.

25,000
The population of the Indus Valley city of Harappa at its height in the Bronze Age.

▷ **The mortuary temple of Hatshepsut**
Located near the Valley of the Kings on the west bank of the Nile, the colonnaded temple (reconstructed in the 20th century) took 15 years to build during Hatshepsut's reign (1478–1458 BCE).

▷ **Tutankhamun with Ankhesenpaaten**
Tutankhamun, who reigned in 1332–1323 BCE, is pictured with his wife under the rays of Aten (the radiant disk of the Sun) in this detail on the gilded wooden throne found in his tomb.

1400–701 BCE

c. 1400 BCE

The Olmecs, Mesoamerica's first major civilization, flourish in south-central Mexico. Noted for their monumental sculpted heads, the Olmecs practice such enduring innovations as ritual bloodletting and play an often lethal Mesoamerican game, involving a heavy rubber ball. Around this time, Crete is occupied by Mycenaeans from the Greek mainland, who adopt many Minoan customs and adapt the Minoan Linear A script for their own use.

1392 BCE

Assyria breaks free of its subjection to the kingdom of Mitanni, inaugurating the Middle Assyrian state, which endures until 1056 BCE.

1353–1336 BCE

Akhenaten, the "heretic pharaoh," reigns in Egypt. He does away with the worship of the traditional Egyptian gods and instead introduces a short-lived monotheistic cult that is dedicated to Aten, or the radiant disk of the Sun; to further the religious revolution, he eventually moves the nation's capital from Thebes to a new site at el-Amarna called Akhetaten, "Horizon of the Aten."

c. 1332–1323 BCE

Under the boy-king Tutankhamun, Akhenaten's controversial religious reforms are reversed, and Egypt soon returns to the worship of its old gods; the dead pharaoh's name is removed from monuments, and attempts are made to erase his memory from the historical record.

c. 1274 BCE

Hittite forces led by Muwatalli II halt an Egyptian advance under Rameses II at the Battle of Kadesh (fought near the modern Syrian–Lebanese border), ending an attempt by the pharaoh to reassert control over Canaan; it is thought to be one of the largest chariot battles ever fought.

c. 1220 BCE

Assyrian king Tukulti-Ninurta I captures Babylon, putting an end to the Kassite Dynasty that had ruled the city for more than 350 years.

c. 1210 BCE

Under the Shutrukid Dynasty, Elam (a civilization based in present-day Iran) is at the height of its power; its armies raid deep into Mesopotamia to carry back trophies to its capital, Susa.

c. 1200 BCE

By this time, the Phoenician people, based on the eastern coast of the Mediterranean Sea, are using a 22-letter alphabet, made up entirely of consonants. The Middle East enters a period of major change, known as the Bronze Age Collapse, with the Hittite Empire breaking up under attack from Phrygian and Assyrian invaders, while in Greece, the overthrow of the Mycenaean culture ushers in a prolonged dark age; some scholars believe that this time of troubles provided the backdrop for later Homeric legends of the Trojan War. In Mesoamerica, the Olmecs are at their zenith, with major ceremonial centers at San Lorenzo, Tres Zapotes, and La Venta.

c. 1175 BCE

Egyptian forces under Rameses III repel an attempted invasion by a coalition called (in Egyptian sources) the Sea Peoples—possibly the same assailants who had caused the downfall of the Hittite Empire, though their precise identity remains obscure; subsequent to their defeat, some of the Sea Peoples are thought to have settled in the southern Levant.

c. 1100 BCE

Hillfort construction is now well advanced at many sites across western Europe. In India, ironworking has reached the Ganges Plain. In Greece, the Dorian people, distinguished by their Doric dialect, are moving east and south from their original homeland in the mountains of Epirus (near the modern Greek border with Albania) to settle the Peloponnese.

c. 1056 BCE

The Middle Assyrian state suffers significant reverses on the death of King Ashurbelkala, following an uprising against his rule that allowed Aramean tribes to press in from Syria on its western borders.

c. 1046 BCE

According to Chinese tradition, King Wu defeats Zhou, the last ruler of the Shang Dynasty, at Muye in east-central China, starting the Zhou Dynasty, the longest-lasting in Chinese history.

50

tons. The weight of the largest of the Olmec heads found at the La Cobata archaeological site.

▷ **Prisoners of Sennacherib**
This relief from the palace of Sennacherib in Nineveh (in modern-day Iraq) records prisoners taken from Lachish, in Judah; by the Assyrians in 701 BCE.

c. 1000 BCE

The Phoenician civilization is at its peak, with major centers at Tyre and Sidon on the Levantine coast and a network of trading stations located around the Mediterranean Sea. In the Biblical lands, tradition holds that David is ruler of the joint kingdoms of Israel and Judah, following the death of King Saul at the Battle of Gilboa. In Mesoamerica, the Mayan people are starting to establish themselves in the Yucatán peninsula.

970–931 BCE

The traditional dates given for the reign of Solomon as king of Israel and Judah, after succeeding his father David, who

c. 900 BCE

By this time, the Vedic Aryans are living as settled farmers, forming kingdoms in northern India—first Kuru, then Panchala and Videha. In Greece, the (perhaps legendary) lawgiver Lycurgus gives Sparta the communistic form of military-minded government for which it would become lastingly famous; his laws promote the values of equality, military fitness, and austerity among all members of society.

814 BCE

Carthage is founded on the North African coast as a colony of the Phoenician city-state of Tyre.

"Let me not then die ingloriously and without a struggle, but let me first do some great thing that shall be told among men hereafter."

HOMER, FROM THE *ILIAD*, c. 750 BCE

dies after reigning for 40 years. Celebrated for his wisdom, Solomon builds Jerusalem's First Temple and hosts a visit from the Queen of Sheba (thought to be Saba, a nation spanning the southern lands of the Red Sea).

c. 800 BCE

Following the end of the Greek dark age, the population expands, smaller settlements come together to form influential city-states, and colonies begin to appear on the Mediterranean and Black Sea coasts. In Italy, the Villanovan culture of the area north of Rome introduces iron to the Italian peninsula; it will develop into the powerful and wealthy Etruscan civilization. To the north, the Hallstatt culture has replaced the earlier Urnfield culture in central and western Europe; supported by farming and skilled in metalworking, its tribal societies are increasingly stratified under an elite of warrior chieftains, but also trade widely, both locally and with the Mediterranean lands.

◁ **Olmec head**
The Olmecs, whose civilization began to flourish around 1400 BCE, were accomplished sculptors. They are best known for the colossal male heads that they carved from basalt boulders.

776 BCE

The traditional date of the first Olympic Games, held at Olympia, Greece's wealthiest religious center.

c. 771 BCE

The capital of the Zhou Dynasty is moved from Zhongzhou to Chengzhou, marking the beginning of the Spring and Autumn period of Chinese history; it takes its name from the *Spring and Autumn Annals*, an ancient chronicle of the official history of the state of Lu over a 250-year period, which is traditionally claimed to have been compiled by Confucius.

753 BCE

The traditional date for the foundation of Rome by Romulus.

c. 750 BCE

In Greece, the *Iliad* and the *Odyssey*, epic poems traditionally attributed to Homer, are written down; these works provide the basis of Greek education and culture throughout the Classical age and become hugely influential in the Renaissance, when they are rediscovered by 14th-century scholars in Italy. The mound-building Adena Culture spreads from its center in the Ohio Valley across the eastern woodlands of North America.

c. 744 BCE

The crown of Assyria is seized by Pul, who takes the name Tiglath-Pileser III. He introduces extensive political, civil, and military reforms throughout his reign. The Nubian ruler Piye conquers Egypt, establishing the 25th or Kushite Dynasty, which will control the country until it is conquered by the Assyrians in 671 BCE.

733 BCE

Settlers from Corinth found Syracuse as a Greek colony on the Sicilian coast.

c. 720 BCE

Sargon II, ruler of Assyria, conquers the kingdom of Israel, forcing large numbers of Israelites into exile and giving rise to legends of the 10 lost tribes.

c. 701 BCE

Assyrian king Sennacherib invades Judah and besieges Jerusalem to collect a tribute from its ruler Hezekiah.

330

ft (100 m). The diameter of the largest extant earthworks made by the Adena Culture.

700 BCE

c. 700 BCE
In Assyria, King Sennacherib builds an aqueduct and creates a garden for his palace in Nineveh by cutting irrigation channels from the rock. The screw pump (attributed to Archimedes) is in use for irrigation by this time, as are water clocks. Eastern Europe sees the arrival of nomadic Scythians from Central Asia. In Greece, the first city-states make their appearance. Agricultural villages spread in southeastern North America.

689 BCE
Sennacherib destroys Babylon, razing its temples and walls and diverting canals to flood the site.

671 BCE
Memphis in Egypt falls to the Assyrian king Esarhaddon, the youngest son of Sennacherib.

668 BCE
Assurbanipal, the son of Esarhaddon, comes to the Assyrian throne; the empire reaches its greatest extent during his reign.

663 BCE
Assyrian troops sack Thebes after repelling a Nubian invasion of Egypt. Temple treasures that had been collected over the past 14 centuries are looted.

660 BCE
According to legend, Jimmu, the first emperor of Japan, ascends to the throne. In mythology, he is a descendant of the sun goddess Amaterasu.

c. 660 BCE
Corcyra (on Corfu) defeats Corinth in the earliest recorded naval battle between Greek city-states.

c. 650 BCE
The first coins are minted, in the kingdom of Lydia, in Anatolia. The Age of Tyrants—aristocrats who seize absolute power without legal right—begins in many Greek cities, especially in the Peloponnese.

c. 630 BCE
Sparta wages war against the Messenians, conquering most of the southern Peloponnese by 600 BCE.

43
The number of years that Nebuchadnezzar II survived on the throne of the Neo-Babylonian Empire.

Colonists from the island of Thera found Cyrene in Libya, the first of five Greek cities in the region. The poet Sappho is born on the island of Lesbos. Only one of her poems—"Ode to Aphrodite" survives in complete form.

626 BCE
Nabopolassar secures Babylon's independence from Assyria and founds the Neo-Babylonian Empire. He makes Babylon his capital and rules over Babylonia for the next 20 years.

c. 624 BCE
Thales of Miletus, a leading philosopher, mathematician, and astronomer, is born. He is among the first great thinkers to use theories and hypotheses to explore the nature of natural phenomena and is celebrated as one of the Seven Sages of Greece.

621 BCE
Draco drafts Athens' first written code of law, replacing the previous reliance on oral law; Draconian law will in later times become legendary for the severity of its punishments.

616 BCE
Tarquinius Priscus (Tarquin the Elder) becomes the first Etruscan king of Rome. Construction begins on the Cloaca Maxima, one of the world's earliest sewage systems, and on the Circus Maximus, Rome's first stadium for chariot racing.

612 BCE
The Assyrian Empire crumbles with the sacking of Nineveh and Nimrud by its former vassals, including the Medes and Babylonians. The city of Nineveh becomes depopulated.

609 BCE
King Josiah is killed in battle against Pharaoh Necho II of Egypt, triggering the fall of the Kingdom of Judah.

c. 605 BCE
Birth of Nebuchadnezzar II, who will become the greatest and most powerful of the Neo-Babylonian emperors.

604 BCE
Traditional date for the birth of Lao Tzu, founder of the Chinese religion Taoism.

c. 600 BCE
With the collapse of the Assyrian Empire, much of the Middle East falls to the Medes, whose homeland lies in northwestern Iran. The Neo-Babylonian

◁ **The Palace of King Sennacherib**
The rooms and courtyards of the Assyrian palace at Nineveh (built around 700 BCE) were decorated with carved stone panels showing hunting and other scenes.

▷ **Warring States dagger**
The Warring States period of Chinese history, which began in 475 BCE, was a time of great cultural richness, producing objects such as this decorated dagger.

Empire retains power in Mesopotamia. The first known map of the world is made in Babylon. Ironworking technology reaches Zhou China. The first Upanishads, central texts of the Hindu religion, are usually assigned to this period. Greek settlers found a colony at Massalia on the Mediterranean coast, which eventually develops into the port of Marseilles.

597 BCE
First conquest of Judah by Nebuchadnezzar II of Babylon.

594 BCE
Solon becomes archon (ruler) of Athens; in reforming its laws, he recasts land ownership, protects the property rights of the poor, and bans debt slavery.

587 BCE
Following a revolt in Judah, Nebuchadnezzar II of Babylon destroys Jerusalem's temple and sends the Israelites into exile, the start of the "Babylonian Captivity."

585 BCE
Death of the Biblical prophet Jeremiah, in exile in Egypt. According to historian Herodotus, the Greek astronomer Thales of Miletus predicts a solar eclipse.

573 BCE
The prosperous Phoenician city of Tyre falls to the army of Nebuchadnezzar II after a 13-year siege.

c. 570 BCE
Pythagoras, the Greek philosopher and mathematician, is born on the island of Samos.

563 BCE
Traditional birthdate for Siddhartha Gautama, the Buddha (though some scholars place it at c. 448 BCE). He is born into a royal family in the village of Lumbini in present-day Nepal.

561 BCE
The mental decline and death of Nebuchadnezzar II signals the end of the period of Babylonian greatness.

c. 560 BCE
Croesus succeeds to the throne of Lydia (in western Anatolia) and begins its expansion. He reigns for the next 14 years.

c. 559 BCE
Cyrus the Great comes to power in Persia. In 550 BCE, he defeats the Medes and founds the Persian Empire—which becomes the largest empire yet created.

551 BCE
Birth of Confucius, whose *Analects* provide the central philosophy of the Chinese way of life. In Persia, Zoroastrianism is the main religion.

547 BCE
Cyrus defeats Croesus, the last king of Lydia. Greek philosopher Anaximander, propounder of an evolutionary theory that life developed from creatures living in the oceans, dies.

539 BCE
Cyrus quashes a rebellion in Babylon; the Babylonian empire is absorbed by Persia. Cyrus allows the Israelites exiled in Babylon to return home.

534 BCE
Tarquinius Superbus becomes Rome's last king; the Etruscans are at their height.

530 BCE
Cyrus the Great dies; his son Cambyses II succeeds him as ruler of Persia.

525 BCE
Cambyses II defeats Pharaoh Psammiticus III at the Battle of Pelusium and annexes Egypt.

522–486 BCE
Darius I (the Great) rules Persia, after succeeding Cambyses; under his sway, the Persian Empire will reach its greatest extent. He is succeeded by Xerxes.

c. 520 BCE
Birth of the Greek poet Pindar, whose odes are known for their rich imagery.

509 BCE
The Romans expel Tarquinius Superbus and set up a republic, with Lucius Junius Brutus and Collatinus as the first two annually elected consuls.

507 BCE
Cleisthenes establishes democratic government in Athens.

c. 500 BCE
Bronze coins appear in China. Ironworking spreads to Southeast Asia and east Africa. India's caste system is in place, and the *Puranas* and parts of the epic *Mahabharata* are composed. Nok Culture flourishes in west Africa (centered in modern Nigeria). In Mesoamerica, the Zapotecs use hieroglyphic writing.

499–491 BCE
Greek cities in Ionia, western Anatolia, revolt against Persian rule; their uprising is suppressed.

496 BCE
Rome defeats the Etruscan-led Latin League at Lake Regillus and signs its first treaty with Carthage.

491 BCE
Death of Bimbisara of Magadha, patron of the Buddha and founder of a northern Indian empire.

490 BCE
Greeks led by the prominent Athenian Miltiades defeat the Persians at the Battle of Marathon, ending the first Persian invasion of Greece.

480 BCE
Xerxes' invasion marks the end of the Archaic Period in Greece. In the Classical Period (480–323 BCE), Greece will be dominated in turn by Athens, Sparta, and Macedonia, and Greek culture will reach its peak.

480–479 BCE
Persian forces, sent by Xerxes, invade Greece, overcome resistance at the pass of Thermopylae, and take Athens. However, the Persian navy is defeated at Salamis (480 BCE) and Mycale (479 BCE), and the Spartan leader Pausanias routs their army at Plataea (479 BCE).

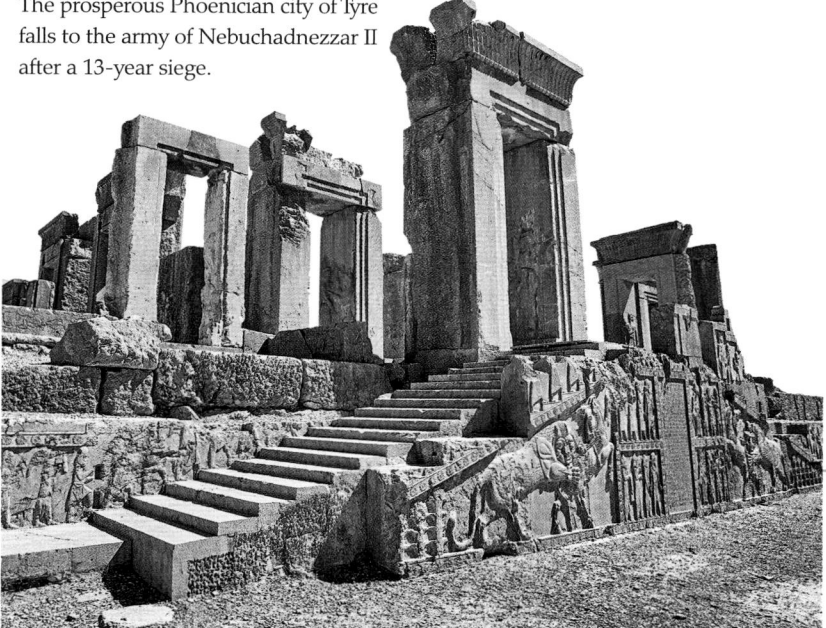

◁ **Persian winter palace**
Darius (ruled 522–486 BCE) initiated many building projects in Persia. His winter palace in Persepolis was one of the few buildings at the site to escape destruction by Alexander the Great.

◁ **Monte Albán**
One of the oldest of Mesoamerican cities, Monte Albán (built c. 450 BCE) was the center of Zapotec Culture, which then dominated much of the territory of the modern state of Oaxaca, Mexico.

478 BCE

c. 478 BCE
Athens founds the Delian League of city-states to counter Sparta's Peloponnesian League.

475 BCE
China enters the Warring States period (to 221 BCE), in which seven leading states jostle for supremacy.

c. 450 BCE
The Celtic La Tène culture emerges in central Europe, eventually supplanting the Halstatt culture; Celts expand their territory east and south and into the British Isles. Steppe nomads are buried with spectacular grave goods at Pazyryk and Noin-Ula in Siberia. In Mexico, the construction of the Zapotec city of Monte Albán begins.

449 BCE
Greece's Persian Wars come to an end after 41 years when Artaxerxes I, the king of Persia, recognizes the independence of the Greek city-states in the Peace of Callias.

447–432 BCE
The ruler of Athens, Pericles, builds a new Parthenon to replace the temple destroyed by the Persians.

c. 445 BCE
Nehemiah rebuilds the walls of Jerusalem, still under Persian rule.

438 BCE
The Greek sculptor Phidias supervises the completion of sculptures designed to decorate the Acropolis in Athens; they will later become known as the Elgin Marbles.

431–404 BCE
The Peloponnesian War leads to the destruction of the Athenian League by Sparta and its allies.

c. 427 BCE
Birth of the Greek philosopher Plato.

c. 424 BCE
Herodotus, the Greek writer known as the "Father of History," dies. He is best known for his work *The Histories*, a critical examination of the origins of the Greco-Persian Wars.

404 BCE
Egypt emerges from Persian rule under Amyrtaeus, the sole pharaoh of the 28th Dynasty.

399 BCE
In Greece, the philosopher Socrates is sentenced to death for corrupting the minds of Athenian youth.

c. 390 BCE
Celtic Gauls settled in northern Italy defeat the Romans at the Battle of the Allia and capture and sack Rome, holding the city for several months.

c. 385 BCE
In Greece, Plato writes his seminal philosophical text, the *Symposium*.

"Wonder is the feeling of a philosopher, and philosophy begins in wonder."

PLATO, QUOTING SOCRATES IN HIS *THEAETETUS*, c. 369 BCE

---

c. 401–399 BCE
The soldier and philosopher Xenophon of Athens leads an army of 10,000 Greek mercenaries, supporting a Persian rebellion from Babylon to the Black Sea, an exploit chronicled in his *Anabasis*.

c. 400 BCE
Celtic Gauls cross the Alps and settle in northern Italy. Carthage dominates in the western Mediterranean. In Mesoamerica, the Olmec civilization is seriously affected by environmental changes and enters its final phase, while the Zapotecs flourish in Monte Albán. The Moche Culture emerges in Peru. Ironworking develops in Korea.

c. 380 BCE
The Chu become dominant among China's Warring States.

371 BCE
The Theban general Epaminondas wins the Battle of Leuctra against Sparta; Thebes remains the dominant power in Greece until his death in battle in 362 BCE.

c. 370 BCE
Mahapadma Nanda founds the Nanda Dynasty in Magadha, north India.

359–336 BCE
Philip II rules Macedonia and wins control of most of Greece.

356 BCE
Shang Yang, chancellor of the western Chinese state of Qin, makes wide-ranging reforms to create a powerful centralized kingdom.

343–342 BCE
A Persian invasion puts an end to Egypt's independence and dethrones the last native line of pharaohs.

341–338 BCE
Rome defeats and dissolves the Latin League, moving closer to complete dominance of central Italy.

336 BCE
Philip of Macedon is murdered; he is succeeded by his son Alexander III, who forces other Greek states into submission (335), then crosses into Anatolia (334) to confront the Persians.

332 BCE
Alexander III (the Great) conquers Egypt and founds Alexandria, one of many new cities across his empire.

331 BCE
At Gaugamela, Alexander defeats Darius III, and the Persian Empire falls to him; his army burns its capital, Persepolis.

326 BCE
Alexander pushes east into India, extending his realm to the Indus River before his troops force him to turn back.

323 BCE
Alexander the Great dies of a fever in Babylon; his vast empire begins to disintegrate as his generals fight for dominance. Egypt falls to Ptolemy Soter, who founds the Ptolemaic Dynasty.

321–297 BCE
Chandragupta Maurya founds the Mauryan Dynasty, which goes on to create the largest empire in Indian history.

◁ **Lion Capital of Ashoka**
This capital topped one of the many columns erected across the Mauryan Empire by Ashoka (268–232 BCE); its design was adopted in 1950 as the official emblem of India.

160 BCE

312 BCE
Rome's first aqueduct is built by Appius Claudius; he also begins the Appian Way, the first of Rome's network of roads across Italy.

311 BCE
Seleucus establishes control of Babylon, going on to create the Seleucid Empire by conquering the former Median and Persian lands of Alexander's empire.

c. 300 BCE
Alexander's empire is partitioned between the Seleucid, Antigonid, Attalid, and Ptolemaic Dynasties. Rice farming reaches Japan from China. The Greek mathematician Euclid lays out the basic principles of geometry in his treatise, the *Elements*.

298–290 BCE
Rome defeats its Samnite enemies in south-central Italy, extending its territory across Italy to the Adriatic.

c. 287 BCE
China's northern states build frontier defenses to keep out Eurasian nomads.

280–275 BCE
Pyrrhus of Epirus lands in Italy and defeats the forces of Rome. The Romans regroup, and he returns to Greece.

c. 268–232 BCE
Ashoka, the Mauryan emperor of India, greatly expands his territories and promotes the Buddhist concept of *dharma* across his empire.

264–241 BCE
The First Punic War between Rome and Carthage ends after 23 years with Rome in control of almost the entire Italian peninsula and Sicily.

c. 250 BCE
Arsaces founds the kingdom of Parthia in lands southeast of the Caspian Sea.

221–210 BCE
In China, the state of Qin conquers the last of its rivals. Its ruler takes the title of Qin Shi Huang, "First Emperor" of a united China; after his death, he is buried in a vast mausoleum with an army of 8,000 terracotta soldiers.

1,200 ft (366 m). The length of the largest geoglyph motifs made by the Nazca.

218–203 BCE
In the Second Punic War, Carthaginian general Hannibal crosses the Alps and defeats the Romans at Lake Trasimene and Cannae. Roman forces regroup under Quintus Curtius Maximus, and Hannibal is ultimately defeated at Zama.

c. 218 BCE
Qin Shi Huang starts construction of what is to become the Great Wall of China, the purpose of which is to keep out invaders from the north. The wall is extended to a length of 1,400 miles (2,250 km) by later dynasties.

206 BCE
Liu Bang conquers the Qin to establish the Han Dynasty, whose rule (to 220 CE) is seen as the golden age of China.

c. 200 BCE
The Middle Yayoi Period (200–100 BCE) in Japan sees a big increase in population. In Ptolemaic Egypt, Alexandria becomes a major center of Greek trade, culture, and learning. In eastern North America,

Ohio's Adena Culture is developing into the Hopewell Culture. To the south in Mesoamerica, the Mayan civilization emerges as small communities on Mexico's Pacific Coast migrate northward to form larger states. The Nazca in Peru create mysterious geoglyphs—long lines in the desert.

197 BCE
A Roman army defeats Philip V of Macedon at Cynoscephalae in Thessaly, driving him back to his own kingdom.

c. 185 BCE
Pushyamitra, Hindu founder of the Shunga Dynasty, takes power in India, assassinating the last Mauryan ruler and persecuting Buddhists.

183 BCE
To avoid falling into Roman hands, Hannibal commits suicide in the Bithynian town of Libyssa.

171–138 BCE
Mithridates I conquers Greek-ruled kingdoms in Persia, establishing the Parthian Empire.

168 BCE
Macedon is defeated by Roman forces at Pydna and is divided by the conquerors into four separate republics.

167–160 BCE
Judah Maccabee and his brothers rebel against the growing influence of Greek culture (Hellenization) of Judea under Antiochus IV, reestablishing traditional Judaism and rededicating the Temple in Jerusalem before Judah's death in battle.

◁ **Alexander defeats Darius III**
This Roman mosaic, made around 100 BCE in the city of Pompeii, depicts the battle in 331 BCE between the armies of Alexander the Great and Darius III.

▷ **Scene with Emperor Wu**
In this silk painting from a history of Chinese emperors, Wu Ti (Han Emperor, 141–87 BCE) welcomes a man of letters.

149 BCE

150,000 Estimated casualties in the fall of Carthage, which is seen by some historians as the first genocide.

149–146 BCE
The Third Punic War between Rome and Carthaginian forces ends in the total destruction of Carthage.

148–146 BCE
After a series of defeats by Rome, Macedonia is annexed and becomes a Roman province.

142 BCE
Having freed Jerusalem from Seleucid rule, the Maccabees make it the capital of the Hasmonaean kingdom; the dynasty rules Judea until 63 BCE.

121–91 BCE
Under Mithridates II, the Parthian Empire reaches its greatest extent.

107–104 BCE
The Roman general Marius reforms the army, allowing poor citizens to become soldiers.

105 BCE
In Africa, Roman forces defeat Jugurtha, ruler of Numidia. In Gaul, Germanic Cimbri raiders overcome a Roman army at Arausio, causing panic in Rome itself until their ultimate defeat at Vercellae in 101 BCE.

c. 101 BCE
China's Han Empire reaches its largest extent under Emperor Wu; the Silk Road carries trade across central Asia to the Mediterranean world, stretching from the Han capital at Chang'an to Antioch (in modern-day Turkey).

c. 100 BCE
Celtic hill forts in western Europe are developed into fortified settlements. Trade links grow between China, Southeast Asia, and India. The Buddhist complex at Sanchi in India—commissioned by Emperor Ashoka in the 3rd century BCE, and famous for its Great Stupa—nears its present form.

91–89 BCE
The Social War—a conflict between the Roman Republic and several cities in Italy—breaks out, driven by discontent over the failure of Rome to give its allies Roman citizenship; this is finally granted to most Italian communities in 88 BCE.

88–82 BCE
Civil war between patricians and populists in Rome ends with the victorious general and statesman Sulla defeating his rivals and having himself declared dictator.

73–71 BCE
Spartacus, a former Roman slave and gladiator, originally from Thrace, leads a revolt (later known as the Third Servile War) that is brutally put down by Roman troops under Crassus and Pompey; Spartacus himself is killed in the fighting.

64–63 BCE
The Catiline Conspiracy to seize power in Rome ends as the consul, Cicero, has its leader Catilina put to death.

"Fortune … can bring about great changes in a situation through very slight forces."

JULIUS CAESAR, FROM *COMMENTARIES ON THE CIVIL WAR*, 68 BCE

63 BCE
Defeated in the last of three wars he has fought against Rome since 89 BCE, Mithridates IV, king of Pontus (a state on the coast of the Black Sea, founded by a Persian dynasty), kills himself.

60 BCE
Julius Caesar, Pompey, and Crassus form a political alliance, sharing power in Rome as the First Triumvirate. Their union lasts until the death of Crassus in battle against the Parthians in 53 BCE.

58–50 BCE
In a series of brilliant campaigns, Julius Caesar conquers Gaul for Rome.

55–44 BCE
Julius Caesar invades Britain to carry out an armed reconnaissance.

52 BCE
Pompey is declared sole consul in Rome after a vote taken in the Centuriate Assembly of the Roman Republic.

49 BCE
Ordered by the Roman Senate to disband his army, Caesar instead crosses the River Rubicon, starting a civil war in Italy. In a decisive battle at Pharsalus in the following year, Caesar defeats Pompey's larger army. Pompey flees to Egypt, where he is murdered in 48 BCE

44 BCE
Just 2 months after he is declared "dictator in perpetuity," Caesar is assassinated on March 15 by republican conspirators led by Brutus, Decimus, and Longinus.

43 BCE
Roman politician and general Mark Antony forms the Second Triumvirate with Lepidus and Octavian.

42 BCE
At Philippi in Macedonia, Antony and Octavian defeat the forces of Brutus and Cassius, who both commit suicide.

36 BCE
Mark Antony marries Cleopatra, ruler of Egypt, although he is already married to Octavian's sister.

◁ **Baths of Antoninus, Carthage**
After the destruction of Punic Carthage in 146 BCE, the Romans built their own city there. It becomes extremely wealthy, supporting the construction of the largest baths in north Africa.

70 CE

32–30 BCE
The Roman Senate declares war
against Cleopatra. Octavian's navy,
commanded by Marcus Vipsanius
Agrippa, defeats the combined fleets of
Antony and Cleopatra off Actium on
the Ionian Sea. The two retreat to Egypt,
where both commit suicide in 30 BCE.
Egypt becomes a Roman province.

27 BCE
Octavian becomes Rome's first emperor,
adopting the title Augustus.

c. 19 BCE
The poet Virgil completes his epic poem
the *Aeneid*.

4 BCE
The probable date of the birth of Jesus
Christ at Bethlehem.

c. 1 CE
By now, the Roman Empire includes
around one-seventh of the world's
population. Nabateans allied with
Rome control trade in the Red Sea.
The Buddhist religion spreads across
southeast Asia.

9
An alliance of Germanic tribes defeats
a Roman army in the Teutoburg Forest,
frustrating Augustus's attempts to
extend his empire to the River Elbe. In
China, Emperor Wang Mang introduces
radical reforms that provoke revolts; he
is killed in one of these revolts in 23.

125,000
Size of the Roman
legionary forces under
Emperor Tiberius.

14
Augustus dies
after a 40-year
reign as emperor
and is succeeded by
his stepson, Tiberius.

25
Guangwu seizes power in China,
establishing the Later (or Eastern)
Han Dynasty, which will rule the
country until 220.

c. 30
Jesus Christ is crucified on the orders of
Pontius Pilate, procurator of the Roman
province of Judea.

37
Caligula succeeds Tiberius as emperor,
reigning until his assassination in 41.

43
Emperor Claudius orders the Roman
invasion of Britain.

c. 50
The Yuezhi, a formerly nomadic people
settled in Bactria, north of the Hindu
Kush mountains in present-day
Afghanistan, lay the foundations of the
Kushan Empire. They will eventually
control much of northern India.

54
Nero becomes Rome's emperor on
Claudius's death.

64
Much of Rome is destroyed in a great
fire that reportedly burns for more than
1 week. Nero blames the disaster
on the city's Christians, starting a
general persecution.

66–70
A Jewish revolt against Rome
culminates in the capture and
destruction of Jerusalem in 70.

▷ **Augustus of Prima Porta**
This marble statue, dating from the 1st century CE,
shows Augustus, the first Roman Emperor. It was
found in the villa occupied by his wife after
Augustus's death in 14.

▷ **Villa of the Mysteries, Pompeii**
Though buried by ash in the eruption of Vesuvius in 79, the Villa sustained little damage. This fresco on its wall may depict the ceremony of initiation into the cult of Dionysus.

77

20 ft (6 m).

The depth of the ash that fell on Pompeii after the eruption of Vesuvius.

77
The Roman author Pliny the Elder starts work on his *Natural History*, planned as an encyclopedic survey of all areas of knowledge.

79
In southern Italy, Mount Vesuvius erupts, burying the cities of Pompeii and Herculaneum.

91
The Chinese general Ban Chao is given the title Protector of the Western Regions for his work in extending Chinese control over Turkestan and the Tarim Basin; his conquests will later allow increased trade with the West along the Silk Road.

98–116
Under the rule of Emperor Trajan, the Roman Empire

reaches its greatest extent. Following their victorious campaigns in Dacia, north of the Danube, and Parthia, the Romans annexe Armenia, Mesopotamia, and Assyria.

c. 100
Teotihuacan, in the Valley of Mexico, is the largest urban center in Mesoamerica. In Peru, the Moche Culture is rising to prominence.

105
Chinese sources credit Cai Lun with the invention of the paper-making process.

c. 115
Tacitus writes his *Annals*, recounting the history of Rome from the accession of Tiberius to the death of Nero.

117
Hadrian, a cousin of Emperor Trajan, ascends to the imperial throne in Rome.

122–127
Following a visit to Britain by the emperor, Hadrian's Wall is built to protect the Roman Empire's northernmost frontier.

c. 127–150
Kanishka the Great vastly expands the Kushan Empire through north-central India, facilitating the transmission of his Buddhist beliefs into China.

132–135
Simon bar Kokhba leads a Jewish revolt against Roman rule in Judea; after its suppression, Jews are barred from Jerusalem. In China, in 132, Zhang Heng invents a device for registering Earth tremors—the first seismometer.

c. 150
In Alexandria, a Roman province in Egypt, Ptolemy writes the work that will become known as the *Almagest*. This

astronomical compendium dominates thinking about the structure of the universe for more than a millennium. Ptolemy's other great work, *Geography*, similarly sums up the geographical knowledge of his time.

161–180
Marcus Aurelius reigns as the last of the five "Good Emperors" of late 1st- and 2nd-century Rome. A philosopher as well as a military leader, his *Meditations* reflect his Stoic view of life.

180
Commodus succeeds his father Marcus Aurelius, with whom he had co-reigned since 177. His reign is marked by conspiracies and an increasingly dictatorial approach, culminating in his assassination in 192.

184
The rebellion of the Yellow Turbans— peasants so called for their distinctive headbands—breaks out in China in reaction to famine in the countryside and the corrupt rule of court eunuchs. The rising is largely contained by 185, although pockets of resistance continue to flare up for a further 20 years.

c. 200
Jewish scholars assemble the Mishnah, a collection of Rabbinic oral traditions that will become the first of the two components of the Talmud.

c. 210
Death of Galen, physician to several Roman emperors, whose collected writings will dominate Western medical thinking for the next 1,300 years.

◁ **Moche vessel**
The Moche Culture, which became prominent in Peru from around 100, is known for its portrait vessels, which feature detailed, expressive human heads or figures.

212
Roman Emperor Caracalla issues the Antonine Constitution, granting citizenship to all freemen throughout the Empire.

c. 220
The Han Dynasty comes to an end in China, which then enters the Three Kingdoms period (220–280), in which power is divided between the Wei in the north, the Shu in the west, and the Wu in the south of the country. The Three Kingdoms period is among the bloodiest in Chinese history.

224
Ardashir defeats and kills the last king of Parthia, going on to establish the Sassanid Dynasty in Persia.

c. 225
On the death of Pulumavi IV, the territory of the Andhra (or Satavahana) Dynasty, based in the Deccan region of west-central India, fragments into five separate smaller kingdoms.

235
The murder of Emperor Alexander Severus at the hands of mutinous troops inaugurates a period of decline in Rome, which will see more than 20 emperors over the next 50 years; Germanic tribes threaten Rome's frontiers along the Danube and Rhine, invading Italy itself in 259.

238
The port of Histria near the mouth of the River Danube is ravaged by Goth invaders—their first recorded incursion into the lands of the Roman Empire.

c. 245
Chinese sources report a flourishing state (or collection of city-states) at Funan in the Mekong Delta region of what is now Vietnam.

c. 250
Established in Mesoamerica for at least two millennia, the Maya civilization enters its Classic period (to 900), in which city-states and trade flourish. The lodestone compass comes into use in China.

251
The Roman Emperor Decius is defeated and killed by Goth forces under Cniva at Abritus, south of the Danube (in what is now Bulgaria).

268
A Roman army under Emperor Gallienus (also known as Claudius II) defeats a Goth coalition at the Battle of Naissus (near Nis in present-day Serbia), temporarily removing the threat to the empire from the nomadic tribes.

2,000,000
Population of the Maya civilization in its Classic period, which begins around 250.

270
Zenobia, queen of Palmyra (a wealthy Syrian city that is a tributary to the Roman Empire), conquers Roman Arabia and annexes Egypt. She adds part of Anatolia to her empire and declares independence from Rome.

272
Emperor Aurelian crushes the Palmyran revolt, capturing Zenobia, who lives out the rest of her life in exile in Rome. After a further rebellion in 273, the city of Palmyra is destroyed.

274
Mani, the founder of the Manichaean sect (which preaches a philosophy of dualism, a belief in the forces of light and darkness), dies in prison in Persia; his followers later maintain that he was crucified.

280
Sima Yan of the kingdom of Wei defeats Eastern Wu forces. He reunites China under the Western Jin Dynasty, which itself soon falls into a crisis of succession.

284
After rising through the ranks of the army, Diocletian becomes Roman emperor. His 21-year reign brings stability to a realm that has experienced a century of relative decline.

286
Diocletian appoints Maximian as co-emperor, with responsibility for the west, while Diocletian himself concentrates his efforts on the empire's troubled eastern frontier.

c. 300
Chinese records mention a kingdom called Yamatai, ruled by a priest-queen named Himiko (meaning "sun-child"), in Japan; the location of the kingdom is unknown. Buddhism continues to spread across southeast Asia. The first Polynesian settlers reach the Hawaiian archipelago.

301
Tiridates III makes Christianity the state religion of Armenia—the first country to accept it as such.

◁ **Zenobia and her maid**
This relief from Palmyra depicts Queen Zenobia (who invaded Rome's territories in the east in 270) together with her maid, in the guises of the goddesses Ishtar and Tyche.

303

303–313
Diocletian unleashes a wave of persecution against Christians in the Roman Empire.

311
Xiongnu nomads capture Luoyang, capital of China's Jin Dynasty, and take the Chinese emperor prisoner. In the ensuing years, invaders set up 16 separate kingdoms in northern China, confining imperial power to the south.

312
Constantine defeats his imperial rival Maxentius at the Battle of the Milvian Bridge, winning undisputed power in Rome. In the following year (313), he issues the Edict of Milan, which orders toleration of the Christian faith and permits the establishment of churches across the empire.

> *"We make a ladder of our vices, if we trample those same vices underfoot."*
>
> ST AUGUSTINE OF HIPPO, c.420

c. 320–335
Chandragupta I expands his small kingdom by annexing neighboring states and marrying strategically. He creates the Gupta Empire, stretching across northern and western India.

324
Emperor Constantine orders the construction of Constantinople on the Bosphorus strait between Europe and Asia, taking over the site of the Greek city of Byzantium. In 330, the city is consecrated as the new capital of the Empire, replacing Rome.

325
The Council of Nicaea—the first ecumenical council of the Christian Church—is convened by Emperor Constantine. It codifies Christian beliefs and establishes the Nicene Creed as the hallmark of orthodoxy.

c. 350
In Africa, the city of Meroë—capital of Kush, a long-lasting and powerful kingdom in the Sudan—disappears from the historical record. In Ethiopia, Aksum becomes the first African kingdom to officially adopt Christianity.

361–363
Emperor Julian seeks to reestablish traditional pagan beliefs in place of Christianity as the Roman Empire's official religion. On his death in battle against the Persian Sassanians, the empire is divided into eastern and western portions, the east under Valens and the west under Valentinian I.

c. 370
Hun nomads arrive in Europe in large numbers, migrating from lands north of the Black Sea.

376
Driven south by the invading Huns, Visigothic tribes cross the River Danube into the Roman Empire. Initially accepted, they rebel against harsh treatment and defeat and kill the eastern emperor Valens at the Battle of Adrianople in 378.

◁ **Tikal sculpture**
This vase, embellished with jadeite, is in the form of a man wearing a Mayan feather headdress. It dates from around 450 in the Classic period of Mayan civilization.

496

380–415
In India, Chandragupta II conquers the Saka rulers of the Gujarat region of eastern India, expanding the Gupta Empire to its greatest extent. His reign is notable for a flowering of art, literature, and science.

386
The Tuoba people establish the Northern Wei Dynasty in north China, around the Yellow River delta.

389–392
Theodosius I—the last emperor to rule over both the eastern and western halves of the Roman Empire—proscribes the last elements of paganism and bans the rituals of the Olympics in Ancient Greece, making Christianity (as defined by the Nicene Creed) the official religion of the empire.

399–412
The Buddhist monk Faxian travels on foot from China to India, collecting texts and writing an account of his journey.

c. 400
Christianity is introduced to Ireland. Hinduism continues its spread through southeast Asia. India's two great epics, the *Ramayana* and the *Mahabharata*, are taking on their final form.

402
Emperor Honorius transfers the capital of the western Roman Empire from Milan to Ravenna, which is considered easier to defend.

406
Germanic Vandals cross the River Rhine into Gaul, under pressure from Huns invading from the east. In 409, they move on into Spain.

407
Most Roman legions are withdrawn from Britain to participate in Rome's civil wars. Emperor Honorius subsequently tells Britons to look to their own defenses.

410
Vandal forces under Alaric sack Rome for 3 days, a pivotal event in the fall of the Roman Empire.

421–422
Theodosius II goes to war with the Sassanid emperor over the persecution of Christians in Persia.

426
St Augustine of Hippo publishes his philosophical work *The City of God*.

429
The Vandals cross from their adopted homeland in Spain to north Africa, where they establish a kingdom that will last for a century, until it succumbs to forces of the Byzantine Empire.

435
Under pressure from the Huns, the eastern Roman emperor signs the Treaty of Margus, in which the Romans agree to pay a higher annual tribute to the Huns. There is sporadic warfare for the next 8 years as the Romans fail to keep to its terms.

439
The Northern Wei Dynasty succeeds in unifying northern China. During their rule, Buddhism becomes firmly established in the region, and the Yungang Grottoes are constructed.

c. 450
Angles and Saxons have started to settle in eastern England following the withdrawal of the Roman legions. Slav peoples are raiding and settling in the Balkans. In Mesoamerica, Tikal (in modern Guatemala) is the dominant Mayan city-state. The mausoleum of Galla Placidia is the earliest example of Christian mosaic in Ravenna (in Italy).

451
The Roman general Aetius—in a coalition with the Visigothic forces of Theoderic I—turns back a Hun invasion of Gaul led by Attila at the Battle of the Catalaunian Fields, fought in what is now northern France.

453
Constantinople wins ecclesiastical supremacy over its rival Alexandria at the Council of Chalcedon (now within the city of Istanbul), establishing itself as second only to Rome in the hierarchy of the Christian Church.

455
Vandal forces sack Rome for a second time, destroying its aqueducts and looting treasures from the city. Anglo-Saxon encroachment sends the Celtic Britons westward into Wales, to Ireland, and across the English Channel into what is today called Brittany.

c. 470
After the death of Attila in 453, the Hun empire begins to disintegrate. In India, the Gupta Empire is in decline following the death of Skandagupta in 467.

476
The last Roman emperor, Romulus Augustulus, is deposed. Odoacer, a German commander of Rome's army, replaces him as King of Italy.

484
Peroz I, ruler of Sassanian Persia, is killed in battle against the Hephthalite Huns (a Central Asian people based around Bactria), who force the empire to pay them tribute.

486
Clovis, founder of the Frankish kingdom, defeats the last Roman ruler in Gaul at Soissons.

488–493
An Ostrogothic army invades Italy, taking Ravenna in 493. At a banquet arranged to celebrate the subsequent peace treaty, the Ostrogoth leader Theodoric kills Odoacer, replacing him as King of Italy.

496
The Franks extend their rule into northeastern Gaul. Their leader, Clovis, converts to Christianity.

◁ *The Battle of Milvian Bridge* (detail)
Painted in 1517–1524 by Giulio Romano, this work depicts the battle in 312 between the Roman Emperors Constantine I and Maxentius.

THE MIDDLE AGES 500–1450

c. 500
In the Americas, the Huari state is on the rise in the Andean highlands, and the city of Teotihuacan is at the peak of its influence in Mesoamerica; the Moche state is in decline following catastrophic floods. In Africa, ironworking is spreading across the southern half of the continent. Hinduism is gaining adherents in Indonesia.

507
The Frankish leader Clovis defeats Visigoth forces at Campus Vogladensis (near modern Tours), driving the invaders south into the Iberian Peninsula.

511
On the death of Clovis, the Frankish kingdom is divided into four parts among his sons.

517
Emperor Wu of the Liang Dynasty converts to Buddhism, introducing the religion to central China.

527
Justinian becomes emperor in Constantinople. In his 38-year reign (which ends in 565), the Byzantine Empire will reach its greatest extent.

528
The Byzantine emperor Justinian orders a revision of existing Roman law, which is set out in the *Codex Justinianus*, published in 534.

c. 530
A coalition of princes succeeds in driving the Ephthalites, or White Huns (tribes originating from the region around Bactria), out of India.

531
Khusrow I ascends the Persian throne. In his 48-year reign (to 579), the Sassanian Empire will reach its peak.

533–534
Justinian's general Belisarius defeats the Vandals, winning back North Africa for the Byzantine Empire.

534
The Northern Wei kingdom in the north of China splits into eastern and western halves, neither of which survives beyond the year 557.

c. 535
Benedict of Nursia draws up his guidance for monastic life, *The Rule of St. Benedict*, which will influence Western monasticism to the present day. Extreme weather, probably triggered by a volcanic eruption in the tropics, affects large areas of the Northern Hemisphere, causing drought in Mesoamerica and perhaps triggering the decline of the city of Teotihuacan.

535
Sent by Justinian, Byzantine general Belisarius invades the Ostrogoth kingdom of Italy, capturing their capital of Ravenna in 540; however, resistance continues until 553.

c. 552
Monks smuggle silkworms out of China to Byzantine lands, enabling the beginning of silk production in the West. Buddhism is introduced to Japan by Korean monks.

553
Silla, one of the three ancient kingdoms of Korea, defeats a neighboring realm to become the dominant power in the Korean peninsula.

554
Forces dispatched by Justinian establish a Byzantine presence in southern Spain.

562
The Avars, a Mongol people who have migrated westward into Europe, establish a kingdom in the lower Danube Basin region. In Mesoamerica, the city-state of Tikal is defeated by forces from Caracol (now in Belize).

568
Germanic Lombards under their ruler Alboin invade and conquer northern Italy, establishing their own kingdom there by 572.

c. 570
Birth of the Prophet Muhammad at Mecca in Arabia.

1,104 miles
(1,776 km). The length of China's Grand Canal; it is the world's longest artificial waterway.

retain a Byzantine presence in the Balkans. He succeeds, but Roman rule over the Balkans collapses soon after his overthrow in 602.

593
Appointed as regent by his aunt, the Empress Suiko, the ardently Buddhist Prince Shotoku sets out to establish centralized government in Japan.

597
Dispatched from Rome by Pope Gregory the Great, the monk Augustine reaches England, taking on the task of

"The principal division of the law of persons is as follows, namely, that all men are either free or slaves."

EMPEROR JUSTINIAN, FROM *CODEX JUSTINIANUS*, 534

581
General Yang Jian seizes power over the Northern Zhou lands, governing as Emperor Wen of the new Sui Dynasty; he goes on to restore Chinese rule over the northern part of the country after 400 years of division.

592–602
Maurice (Byzantine emperor in 582–602) launches a series of campaigns against the Avars and Slavs, aiming to

converting the Anglo-Saxon settlers in the south. He is received by King Ethelbert of Kent and establishes an archbishopric at Canterbury.

c. 600
Tibet emerges as a unified state under the rule of Songtsen Gampo, who is traditionally credited with introducing Buddhism to his kingdom. In America, the Plains hunters are adopting the bow and arrow.

◁ **Emperor Justinian**
This 6th-century relief panel is believed to show a triumphant Justinian. The woman holding his foot symbolizes nature submitting to the great emperor, who reigned from 528.

656

◁ **Prince Shotoku**
A wooden sculpture from the Kamakura Period (1185–1333) depicts a young Prince Shotoku, regent of Japan from 593.

601–609
China's Grand Canal, begun in the previous century, is greatly extended, reaching Beijing in the north and Huangzhou in the south.

602
China's Emperor Wen takes advantage of civil war to crush the native Early Lý Dynasty and restore Chinese rule.

606–647
Harsha of the Pushyabhuti Dynasty builds an empire in northern India, uniting the states of the Gangetic Plain from his capital, Kanauj.

607–627
Hostilities break out again between the Byzantine Empire and Sassanian Persia, which extends its territory in Syria, Mesopotamia, Palestine, and Egypt. The prolonged campaigns will weaken both powers, reducing their ability to resist the coming Arab onslaught.

610
Heraclius accedes to the Byzantine throne and sets about rebuilding its administration; Greek replaces Latin as the language of the empire.

616
The Vandals expel the Byzantines from southern Spain.

618
Following the murder of its last emperor, the Sui Dynasty in China is replaced by the Tang, who will rule the country for the next three centuries.

622
Muhammad and his followers leave his hometown of Mecca for Medina. Known as the Hegira, the migration marks the start of the Muslim calendar.

624
Muhammad defeats the Meccans at the Battle of Badr, a turning point in the establishment of the Muslim faith.

626
A combined attack by Avars, Slavs, and Sassanian Persians fails to take Constantinople, the Byzantine capital.

628
The Indian mathematician Brahmagupta introduces the concept of zero as a number in its own right.

630
The city of Mecca surrenders to the forces of Muhammad.

632
On the death of Muhammad, the new Muslim caliphate starts under Abu Bakr.

633
The Chalukya rulers of an empire in south-central India defeat Harsha's forces at the Narmada River, frustrating his attempts to annex the Deccan.

634
Umar, a senior companion of the Prophet Muhammad, succeeds Abu Bakr as Muslim caliph.

635
Nestorian missionaries (those following the doctrine of the patriarch Nestorius) bring Christianity to China.

636
Fired up by their new Islamic faith, Arab forces erupt out of Arabia into Byzantine Syria, taking Damascus. They also confront the Sassanian Empire, defeating a Persian army at the Battle of al-Qadisiya and winning control of all Mesopotamia (modern Iraq).

639
The Frankish kingdom fractures, with power increasingly passing—in the following decades—from short-lived kings to the mayors of the palace.

642
Alexandria falls to the Arabs, completing their conquest of Byzantine Egypt. That year, they also decisively defeat the Sassanian emperor at the Battle of Nehavend in southern Iran.

651
Yazdegerd III, the deposed last Sassanian emperor, is killed, ending the dynasty.

656–661
The Caliphate of Ali is marked by civil war in the Muslim community; Ali is defeated and assassinated in 661. The split between Ali's followers and opponents lives on to the present day in the division between Shia and Sunni.

▷ **The Death of King Dagobert I**
A manuscript illustration presents a deathbed scene in which the Frankish king, Dagobert, divides his empire between his sons Sigeburt and Clovis in 639.

▷ **The Lindisfarne Gospels**
The title page of St. John's Gospel displays the meticulous design of the Lindisfarne Gospels, which are believed to be the work of just one artist–monk, Eadfrith, in the period around 715.

661

661
On the death of Ali, Muawiyah—the victor of the Muslim civil war—establishes the Umayyad Caliphate. The dynasty, based in Damascus, will rule the Muslim world until 750 and become one of the largest empires in history.

664
British churches accept the Roman, rather than the Celtic, form of Christianity at the Synod of Whitby.

668
The kingdom of Silla establishes control over the entire Korean peninsula after Chinese forces are expelled.

679
Bulgars conquer territory around the mouth of the River Danube from the Byzantines, establishing the first Bulgarian Empire.

687
Pepin II unites the Frankish lands under his rule, going on to expand their control into Germanic territories to the north and east.

695
In the Mayan lands of Mesoamerica, Tikal reestablishes its preeminence with a decisive victory over the rival city-state of Calakmul.

698
Islamic forces take Carthage, the last Byzantine stronghold in Africa.

700
In Mesoamerica, Monte Alban is in decline, while Teotihuacan has by now been sacked and abandoned. In Peru, the Moche state is also on the wane. In west Africa, the kingdom of Ghana is established about this time.

702
A Berber uprising against the new Arab rulers of North Africa is put down savagely; the Berbers accept Islam.

708
Empress Genmei of Japan establishes Japan's first official currency; 2 years later, she moves her official residence to Nara, which becomes the new capital of Japan.

711
Under a Berber commander, Arab forces invade southern Spain; within 2 years, the lands of the former Visigothic kingdom are almost entirely under Muslim control.

713
Xuanzong becomes emperor of China, starting a 43-year reign that will start as a golden age but eventually deteriorate into corruption and civil war.

714
In India, Arab forces complete the conquest of Sindh and the lower Indus Valley, pushing the expansion of Islam almost to its furthest extent.

c. 715
The Lindisfarne Gospels are created in Anglo-Saxon Northumbria, part of a cultural flourishing of the northern kingdom.

716–717
Byzantine Emperor Leo III the Isaurian (so-called for his Syrian birth) repels a third Arab siege of Constantinople with the help of the recently developed incendiary weapon known as Greek fire.

718
Christian forces defeat a Muslim army at Covadonga in the Asturias region of northern Spain—a victory cited in Spanish sources as the start of the 700-year struggle to reconquer the peninsula for the Christian faith.

724–749
The reign of Emperor Shomu, a devout Buddhist, marks the high point of Japan's Nara period (710–794).

726
Emperor Leo III issues the first of a series of edicts against the veneration of images, launching the Iconoclastic ("image-breaking") movement that will divide the Byzantine Empire for the next 117 years.

732
The Franks under Charles Martel defeat Arab forces at the Battle of Tours, halting their northward expansion into Europe.

740
Leo III defeats Arab forces besieging Akroinon, halting further Islamic expansion into Anatolia. He renames Akroinon Nikopolis ("City of Victory").

750
After their victory at the Battle of the Zab (in present-day Iraq), the Abbasids displace the Umayyads as rulers of the greater part of the Arab world. Lombard forces capture Ravenna, ending the Byzantine presence in northern Italy.

c. 750
On the American continent, the Toltecs begin to move into the Valley of Mexico, while the power of the city-state of Tiwanaku (in what is now Bolivia) is at its peak. In Africa, trade across the Sahara Desert is on the rise.

751
Arab forces halt Chinese expansion westward with a victory at the Battle of the Talas River, near Samarkand.

755
A rebellion breaks out against Tang rule in China; it is led by An Lushan, a general who declares himself Emperor of a new Yan Dynasty. An Lushan is assassinated by his own son in 757, and the Yan state is finally extinguished in 763.

29

Percentage of the world's population under the Umayyad Caliphate at its height—a total of 62 million people.

◁ **Emperor Xuanzong**
This 13th-century painting shows Xuanzong, the ninth ruler of the Tang Dynasty, who reigned from 713 to 756.

756
Abd al-Rahman establishes the Caliphate of Córdoba in southern Spain; as a member of the deposed Umayyad Dynasty, he refuses to acknowledge the suzerainty of the Abbasids in Syria, creating an independent, breakaway state on the Iberian Peninsula.

757
Krishna I of the rising Rashtrakuta Dynasty wins control of much of west-central India from the declining Chalukyas. In England, Offa becomes king of the central kingdom of Mercia, ruling until 796; during his reign, he gives his name to Offa's Dyke, a defensive earthwork protecting his western border against the Welsh.

762
The Abbasid ruler al-Mansur orders the construction of Baghdad on the banks of the River Tigris as the new capital of the Caliphate.

771
Charlemagne becomes sole ruler of the Frankish kingdom.

774
Charlemagne conquers the Lombard kingdom in north Italy.

780
Hyegong, king of Silla, is assassinated at the end of a lengthy civil war, plunging the Korean kingdom into a period of prolonged upheaval.

782
Charlemagne imposes a law code on the Germanic West Saxons, prescribing death for anyone refusing to abandon paganism. Despite frequent rebellions, Frankish rule will subsequently be confirmed.

786–809
Harun al-Rashid reigns as Abbasid Caliph. He brings the Abbasid Caliphate to its peak of power and influence.

789
The Idrisids establish an Arab-Berber dynasty in the lands that will become Morocco. They embrace the Shia branch of Islam.

c. 790
The Tibetan Empire reaches its greatest extent, ruling a realm stretching from modern Afghanistan to western China.

793
Scandinavian Vikings launch their first shipborne raids, crossing the North Sea to sack the monastery of Lindisfarne off the Northumbrian coast of England.

794
In Japan, Emperor Kanmu moves his capital to Kyoto, starting the Heian Period that will see the imperial court at its peak.

c. 800
In Mesoamerica, the Mayan city-states of the southern lowlands are in decline. The cultivation of corn is widespread in North America, and the first farming cultures are developing in the southwest; the mound-building Mississippian Culture is in a formative stage. In Africa, Kilwa Kisiwani is becoming a significant trading center on an archipelago off the Somali coast.

800
On Christmas Day, Charlemagne is crowned Holy Roman Emperor by Pope Leo III in Rome, in recognition of his services in spreading the Christian faith. His reign is marked by a flourishing of culture—the Carolingian Renaissance.

802
In Cambodia, Jayavarman II stages a consecration ceremony to celebrate the independence of his kingdom of Kambuja from Java—an event traditionally seen as marking the birth of the Khmer Empire.

813
Baghdad is besieged and sacked in the course of an Abbasid civil war.

814
Death of Charlemagne; he is succeeded by his son Louis the Pious.

150 miles
(240 km). The length of Offa's Dyke on the English–Welsh border.

817
Louis the Pious divides his empire between his three sons, who are expected to serve as co-rulers with him during his lifetime. The lion's share of the empire goes to his eldest, Lothair.

c. 820
The Buddhist temple complex at Borobodur in Java is completed.

827
An Arab army invades Sicily from North Africa, setting in train the Islamic conquest of the island.

831
Louis the Pious charges the monk Ansgar, Archbishop of Hamburg, with the mission of bringing Christianity to the Scandinavian lands.

836
The Abbasid ruler al-Mutasim orders the construction of a new capital for the Caliphate at Samarra, north of Baghdad.

840
The Uighur Khanate, which has ruled over a large part of eastern Asia for almost a century, falls apart in famine and civil war. The Kirghiz, another Turkic people, take control of its lands.

841
A Viking fleet sails up the River Liffey in Ireland, establishing a settlement where the city of Dublin will eventually grow.

◁ **Bust of Emperor Charlemagne**
This 14th-century gilt and silver bust is a reliquary that includes part of the skull of Charlemagne, who was crowned Emperor in 800.

Chichen Itza, in the eastern portion of the Yucatán state in Mexico, was an important Mayan city. The site was developed from around 750, and it became a regional capital in the 10th century.

841

842
In China, the Tang Emperor Wuzong launches a wave of religious persecutions, closing many Buddhist temples and monasteries and proscribing the Manichaean faith, condemning its priests to death.

843
The Treaty of Verdun ends 3 years of warfare in the Carolingian lands following the death of Louis the Pious (in 840); it confirms the division of the empire into three separate kingdoms: east, central, and west, ruled by the dead ruler's three sons.

845
Viking raiders led by the chieftain Ragnar Lodbrok sail up the River Seine to Paris; they are prevented from besieging the city by the payment of a tribute.

846
Saracen raiders attack Rome, sacking Old St. Peter's Basilica but failing to penetrate the city walls.

c. 850
In India, the future Chola kingdom is beginning to take shape in the south, while in Burma, Pagan starts to develop into as a small city-state that will grow over the next two centuries into the capital of the Pagan Empire. In the Mayan lands of Mesoamerica, Chichen Itza has become a major regional capital, while farther south, in what is now Peru, the Chimú people found Chan Chan, which will in time become the largest city in pre-Columbian South America.

858
Kenneth I MacAlpin, who is traditionally held to be the first king of the Scots, dies from a tumor.

859
A chronicle reports the presence of Varangians (Vikings) in northern Russia; they demand tribute from the local Slavic and Finnish tribes. To the west, other Viking groups attack major cities, including Cologne, Paris, and the Carolingian capital of Aachen. Meanwhile in the Mediterranean, shipborne raiders attack ports as far east as Anatolia.

862
Rurik emerges as the leader of the Varangians, establishing a dynasty that will rule over much of western Russia.

865–866
Danish invaders occupy the kingdom of Northumbria in northern England, establishing their capital at York.

867
Basil I usurps the Byzantine throne, establishing the Macedonian Dynasty that will rule until 1056; he will expand the empire to its greatest extent since the Muslim conquests.

868
Sent as Abbasid governor to Egypt, Ahmad ibn Tulun sets up his own independent Tulunid Dynasty, which will govern Egypt and the Levant until the Abbasids reassert control in 905.

869
A Danish force conquers the English kingdom of East Anglia, killing its ruler Edmund the Martyr (who is later venerated as St. Edmund).

873
Norse settlers arrive in Iceland, establishing a base at Reykjavik. In China, Huang Chao leads a rebellion that will severely weaken the ruling Tang Dynasty; before his eventual defeat and death in 884, the rebel leader's forces will temporarily control the southern port of Guangzhou and the imperial capital Chang'an (modern Xi'an).

◁ **Viking ship**
This model of the Oseberg Ship (which was recovered from a Viking burial mound in Norway) shows the type of vessel used in Viking raids. This oak ship would have been rowed by 30 men, reaching speeds of up to 10 knots (18.5 kph).

954

878
At the Battle of Edington, Alfred, ruler of the southern kingdom of Wessex, defeats the Danish army ravaging southern England; in the ensuing peace negotiations, the Danish leader Guthrum agrees to convert to Christianity. Danish power in England will subsequently be restricted to the Danelaw, a swathe of land stretching southeast from the Scottish border to the Thames estuary.

882
Rurik's successor, Oleg, founds the Rus' state in the lands along the Dnieper River, establishing Kiev as its capital.

885–886
Paris resists a prolonged siege by tens of thousands of Vikings.

887
Charles the Fat, who had briefly brought the three parts of Charlemagne's empire back together under his control, is deposed; the Frankish Empire will never again be reunited.

895
Under their leader Arpad, Magyar (Hungarian) tribes cross the Carpathian Mountains to settle in the lands of present-day Hungary.

897
The last king of the Pallava Dynasty dies in battle against the Cholas, who will rule a kingdom in southern India for the next four centuries.

899
The Qarmatians, a religious group with Shia affiliations, establish a republic in eastern Arabia, breaking away from Abbasid control. Death of Alfred the Great, king of Wessex; he is succeeded by his son, Edward, who repels a challenge from his cousin Æthelwold.

c. 900
In Korea, the kingdom of Silla is in steep decline. In North America, farming villages are beginning to appear in the Great Plains region, while in the southwest the Hohokam Culture farmers are digging irrigation channels for their crops. In Mesoamerica, in the wake of the collapse of Teotihuacan, the Toltec people found a state with its capital at Tula in the Valley of Mexico. In South America, the Sican state, centered on the Lambayeque Valley, comes to dominate northern Peru; it maintains its position until its conquest by the Chimú people in the 14th century.

907
The last emperor of the declining Tang Dynasty is deposed and China splits into the interregnum of the Five Dynasties and Ten Kingdoms period.

909
Taking advantage of Berber discontent with Abbasid rule, the Shia Fatimids establish control over a kingdom on the central North African coast.

910
The abbey of Cluny is founded in the Burgundy region of eastern France. Following a strict interpretation of Benedictine rule, it becomes the focus of a monastic reform movement.

911
Charles the Simple cedes land in Normandy to the Vikings, who have settled there, in exchange for their

930
The Althing, the world's first parliament, is established in Iceland; it begins as an outdoor assembly where the country's leaders meet to decide on new laws and to dispense justice.

934
The Shia Buwayhids capture Shiraz, which will become the capital of an empire stretching across Iran and Iraq.

937
Athelstan defeats a combined force of Ireland-based Vikings, Welsh, and Scots at the Battle of Brunanburh, fought in northern England; his victory is sometimes seen as marking the birth of a united English nation.

938
The Vietnamese win independence from Chinese control.

"Remember what punishments befell us ... when we did not cherish learning ..."

ALFRED THE GREAT, KING OF WESSEX, c. 890

---

promise to accept the Christian faith and to protect France from further Norse raids. Their leader Rollo becomes the first Duke of Normandy.

918
Taejo founds the Goryeo Dynasty, which will unify Korea by 936 and rule the country for the next four centuries.

919
Henry the Fowler, previously Duke of Saxony, becomes King of East Francia, uniting the two realms and replacing the previous Frankish line of rulers with his own Ottonian Dynasty; his accession is generally held to mark the start of the medieval German state.

939–967
Reign of Krishna III, the last great ruler of the Rashtrakuta Dynasty, who will preside over a realm covering much of India and patronize poetry.

945
The Buwayhids take Baghdad, making the Abbasid caliphs their vassals.

c. 950
In Mesoamerica, the Mixtecs sack the Zapotec capital of Monte Albán.

954
Eric Bloodaxe, the last Viking king of York, is driven out of the city by the Anglo-Saxon King Eadred.

◁ **Charles III (the Fat)**
This 13th-century statue in Aachen shows Charles, the great-great-grandson of Charlemagne. He was crowned Holy Roman Emperor in 881; his fall in 887 marked the end of Charlemagne's empire.

◁ **Emperor Taizu**
This silk hanging scroll depicts Zhao Kuangyin, who around 960 became the first ruler of the Song Dynasty.

955–1056

through his many military successes. His reign is generally considered to mark the start of the Polish state.

969
The Fatimids of central North Africa conquer Egypt and found the city of Cairo as their new capital. In the same year, Byzantine forces recapture the city of Antioch from its Muslim rulers.

973
Birth of al-Biruni in the Khwarezm region of central Asia; of Iranian descent, he will prove to be one of the great scholars and polymaths of the age,

955
Otto I of East Francia defeats the Magyars at Lechfeld, halting their westward expansion.

c. 960
Following an army mutiny, general Zhao Kuangyin becomes ruler of the Later Zhou territories in China. In the course of a 19-year reign, he will win control of the whole of China, ending the Five Dynasties and Ten Kingdoms period and uniting the whole nation under his Song Dynasty.

962
Otto I, "The Great," is crowned Holy Roman Emperor by the pope in Rome, reviving the empire in the west.

963
In Greece, the monk Athanasios founds the monastery of Great Lavra on Mount Athos; it remains the largest of several communities on the holy mountain.

c. 965
Harald Bluetooth, king of Denmark, becomes the first Scandinavian ruler to convert to Christianity.

966
King Mieszko I of Poland is baptized as a Christian. During his long reign (960–992), he greatly expands Poland's frontiers, both through diplomacy and

66,000 lb (30,000 kg). The amount of silver paid by King Cnut as Danegeld to ward off further Viking raids.

988
Vladimir, ruler of Kiev, accepts Eastern Orthodox Christianity as the religion of his people. Following his baptism, he will marry the sister of the Byzantine Emperor Basil II, sealing an alliance between the two realms.

993
Rajaraja I, ruler of the Chola kingdom in southern India, invades Sri Lanka, capturing the northern part of the island from a native dynasty; he builds a giant Hindu Temple in Thanjavur.

> *"Such is the passing that you must leave,*
> *All men must die, and it is vain to grieve."*
>
> FERDOWSI, FROM *SHANAMA*, 1010

doing important work in astronomy, mathematics, physics, geography, and history before his death in 1048.

980
Birth of the scholar Avicenna (ibn-Sina) in the Bukhara region of central Asia; he is best remembered for his medical works, the *Book of Healing* and the *Canon of Medicine*.

986
Norse settlers led by Erik the Red arrive in Greenland, founding two colonies on its southwest coast.

987
Hugues Capet is elected King of the Franks, starting the Capetian line of French kings.

999
Bukhara, capital of the Samanid Dynasty (which had ruled Iran and much of central Asia for more than a century), falls to the Turkic Qarakhanids. Mahmud of Ghazni, newly crowned emir of that Afghan city, takes advantage of the Samanid collapse to start building an empire of his own.

c. 1000
In Africa, Islamic influence is spreading in the northwest

of the continent and also around Kilwa Kisiwani on the east coast. In South America, the cities of Tiwanaku and Huari are abandoned by this time. In North America, Norse colonists from Greenland establish a settlement on the coast of Newfoundland that will survive for only about 20 years.

1001
Stephen I, later canonized as St. Stephen, becomes the first committedly Christian king of Hungary, doing much to establish the faith in the course of his 38-year reign. In Poland, Griezno has become the seat of the country's first archbishopric. In India, Mahmud of Ghazni wins a victory over a Hindu army at the Battle of Peshawar, opening up northern India to Muslim expansion.

1010
The Persian poet Ferdowsi completes the *Shanama* (*Book of Kings*), a work that will become Iran's national epic.

1011
The Cathedral of St. Sophia is founded in Kiev.

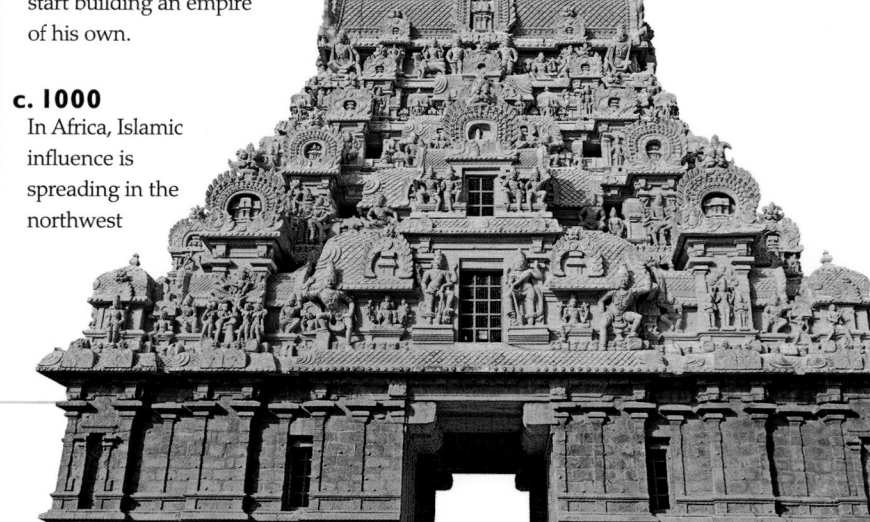

▷ **Brihadishwara Temple, Thanjavur**
This huge temple in Tamil Nadu was built under king Rajaraja I of the Chola Empire. It was classified as a UNESCO World Heritage Site in 2016.

▷ **King Cnut**
A 15th-century stained-glass panel at Canterbury Cathedral shows Cnut, the Danish warrior-king who ruled England in 1016–1035; he became a generous patron of the church.

1013
Sveyn Forkbeard, king of Denmark, conquers England.

1014
Byzantine Emperor Basil II completes his subjugation of the Bulgarian people on the empire's western frontier; he will become known as "the Bulgar-slayer" for the brutality of the conquest.

1016
Sveyn's son, Cnut, becomes king of England. He will also come to rule Denmark and Norway, creating a short-lived North Sea Empire.

1017
Rajaraja's son Rajendra I sacks Sri Lanka's capital Anuradhapura, extending Chola control over the island.

c. 1020
In Japan, Lady Murasaki Shikibu completes *The Tale of Genji*, sometimes described as the world's first novel.

1025
The Chola ruler Rajendra I launches naval raids on Srivijaya, on the island of Sumatra, and on Pegu in Burma.

1028
Empress Zoe ascends the Byzantine throne, starting a reign that will last for 22 years.

1031
After years of infighting and civil strife, the Umayyad Caliphate of Córdoba disintegrates into a number of separate states when its last ruler is overthrown.

1032–1034
The Holy Roman Emperor Conrad II annexes Provence and the kingdom of Burgundy. He founds the Salian Dynasty that rules over the empire for the next century.

1033–1044
Korea builds the "Thousand Li Wall" to defend the kingdom's northern frontier against the Khitans.

1038
Tibetan-speaking Tanguts launch an attack on northwest China, establishing their own Western Xia kingdom, which will survive until 1227.

1040
The Seljuk Turks defeat a Ghaznavid army at the Battle of Dandanaqan, establishing an independent central Asian empire under their leader Tughril Beg.

1044
Anawrahta becomes ruler of Pagan in what is now Myanmar. In the course of his 32-year reign, he will lay the foundations of the Pagan Empire and come to be considered the founder of the Burmese nation.

1045
The Byzantines take control of Armenia.

1046
Holy Roman Emperor Henry III summons a church council at Sutri in Italy to end faction-fighting in the Catholic Church.

1048
Birth of Omar Khayyam, Persian mathematician, astronomer, and poet.

c. 1050
In North America, the Mound Builder Mississippian Culture is now firmly entrenched in the lands around the central Mississippi River valley. In the southwest, the Ancestral Puebloans are creating complex settlements at sites including Mesa Verde and Chaco Canyon, featuring ceremonial sites known as *kivas*.

1053
Having entered southern Italy as mercenaries over the preceding decades, the Normans defeat the combined forces of the papacy and the Holy Roman Emperor at Civitate, taking Pope Leo IX prisoner. At the Treaty of Melfi 6 years later, the papacy finally recognizes Norman rule in the region.

1054
The schism between the Roman Catholic and Eastern Orthodox branches of Christianity becomes permanent after the Pope and the Patriarch of Constantinople mutually excommunicate each other.

Yaroslav the Wise, the Grand Prince of Rus', dies, leading to a division of the Kievan kingdom.

1055
The Seljuks conquer Baghdad, driving out the Buwayhid rulers; their leader Tughril Beg is made Sultan by the Caliph.

1056
Abu Bakr ibn Umar becomes leader of the Almoravids, creating a Berber Muslim dynasty based in Morocco that will rule much of western North Africa and southern Spain for the next 90 years from its capital of Marrakech, which is founded in 1062.

◁ **Anawrahta, King of Burma**
A statue at Mandalay Fort shows Anawrahta, who founded an empire centered on Pagan, an ancient settlement in the Mandalay Region of modern Myanmar. The empire lasted until 1287.

1057

1057
Anawrahta conquers the Mon people of what is now Myanmar, absorbing them into the Pagan Empire.

c. 1063
Construction starts on St. Mark's Basilica, Venice; the church is consecrated in 1093.

1064
The Seljuk ruler Alp Arslan invades Byzantine Armenia, sacking its capital Ani and massacring the inhabitants.

1066
William the Conqueror invades England, defeating and killing the English leader Harold Godwinson at the Battle of Hastings. Harold, England's last Anglo-Saxon king, had defeated a Norwegian invasion force at Stamford Bridge just 19 days before.

1069
Wang Anshi becomes chancellor of Song China, initiating a program of reforms that will divide the nation. His New Policies will be largely abandoned after the death of his patron, Emperor Shenzong, in 1086.

c. 1070
The influence of Islam spreads in sub-Saharan Africa, carried by traders from the Maghreb; the Kanem rulers of Chad convert to the Islamic faith at about this time.

1071
The Seljuks defeat the Byzantines at Manzikert, and their victory gives them control over much of Anatolia; in 1077, Sultan Suleyman will establish the Sultanate of Rum (so-called because the territory was originally "Roman") in the conquered lands.

1075–1122
The Investiture Controversy sets the papacy and the Holy Roman Emperor at odds over who should have the right to appoint bishops.

c. 1076
The Almoravids of Morocco secure control of the Empire of Ghana.

1077
Excommunicated by Pope Gregory VII in the bitter opening years of the Investiture Controversy, Holy Roman Emperor Henry IV goes to the castle of Canossa in northern Italy to do penance, standing in the snow in a hair shirt for 3 days before Gregory finally agrees to lift the excommunication.

1081
Robert Guiscard, ruler of Norman southern Italy and Sicily, invades the Balkans, defeating the Byzantine Emperor Alexius I outside Durazzo.

1086
William the Conqueror commissions the Domesday Book, a detailed survey of landholdings across much of England and Wales that will be used to assess tax liabilities.

1088–1094
The Chinese inventor Su Song creates a celebrated 40 ft (12 m) astronomical clock in Kaifeng, north-central China.

1091
The Normans complete the conquest of Sicily, first attempted 30 years earlier.

230ft (70 m).
The length of the Bayeaux tapestry—a record of events leading up to the Norman conquest of England.

c. 1094
Hassan-i-Sabbah founds the Assassins sect of Shia extremists, known for their violent, stealthy tactics; with a number of hilltop strongholds, adherents of the martial sect later become feared by Christian Crusaders, who name Hassan-i-Sabbah "Old Man of the Mountains."

1095
At the Council of Clermont, Pope Urban II launches the First Crusade to retake the Holy Land from Islamic control.

1098
Crusader forces take Antioch in Syria, which the Sicilian Norman Bohemond I later claims as his own principality.

1150 ▷

▷ **Southern Song ceramics**
The Song tradition of producing exquisite ceramics continued under the Southern Song (1127). Some items were so valued that they were used to pay taxes to the imperial court.

1099
The Crusaders capture Jerusalem, establishing a Christian presence in the lands of the Levant.

c. 1100
In Europe, towns are expanding and guilds of artisans and craftsmen are springing up to represent the interests of their members. In France, the *Song of Roland* is taking final shape as the first major work of French literature and one of the earliest epics of chivalry.

1115
Abbot (later Saint) Bernard founds the monastery of Citeaux in northeastern France, which will become the mother-house of the Cistercian Order. In northern China, the Jurchen chieftain Aguda proclaims the Jin Dynasty, declaring war against the neighboring Khitan-led Liao state.

1119
Crusaders in Jerusalem found the military Order of the Knights Templar.

condemns simony (the sale of church offices) and promotes clerical celibacy.

1126–1127
Jurchen forces capture the Song capital Kaifeng, and with it the Northern Song emperor; Song rule continues in the south from the Southern Song capital of Hangzhou. In Syria, Imad ad-Din Zengi becomes *atabeg* (governor) of Mosul, launching conquests that will bring him into conflict with the crusader states.

1135
On the death of Henry I, civil war breaks out in England between rival claimants to the throne, Henry's nephew Stephen of Blois and the king's daughter Matilda.

c. 1136
Geoffrey of Monmouth writes his *History of the Kings of Britain*, which will do much to popularize the legend of King Arthur.

1139
Afonso I wrests Portugal from fealty to the kingdom of León, establishing it as an independent kingdom.

c. 1140
Anna Comnena writes the *Alexiad*, a history of the life and reign of her father, the Byzantine Emperor Alexius I Comnenus (who reigned 1081–1118 BCE).

1144
Zengi conquers the Crusader state of Edessa, triggering the Second Crusade. In France, the Basilica of St. Denis, near Paris, is the first to be built in the Gothic style of architecture.

1147
Afonso I takes Lisbon from Muslim control with the help of a Christian fleet en route for the Second Crusade. Another Crusade is proclaimed in north Germany against the pagan Wends, a Slavic people. In Morocco, the Almohads overthrow the Almoravids, taking their capital of Marrakech; over the next 12 years, they will extend their rule over most of North Africa.

1150
Forces of the eastern Iranian Ghurid Dynasty sack Ghazni, capital of the Ghaznavid Empire. In Mesoamerica, the Toltec city of Tula, long in decline, is destroyed. In Europe, universities are developing in Oxford and Paris. Magnetic compasses are being used for navigation in Song China.

"My father's deeds … do not deserve to be consigned to Forgetfulness …"

ANNA COMNENA, FROM THE *ALEXIAD*, c.1140

1113
A papal bull (decree) recognizes the foundation of the crusading Order of the Hospital of St. John in Jerusalem, known as the Hospitallers; the order is charged with the care and defense of the Holy Land. In Cambodia, Suryavarman II ascends the Khmer throne; in his long reign (to 1150), he will oversee the construction of the Hindu temple complex of Angkor Wat.

1122
The Investiture Controversy ends at the Concordat of Worms in a compromise that divides the right to appoint bishops and high ecclesiastical functionaries between the Church and lay rulers.

1123
Pope Callixtus II convokes the First Lateran Council to counter lay influence in ecclesiastical matters; the Council

37

The number of years it took 300,000 workers and 6,000 elephants to build Angkor Wat.

◁ **Angkor Wat**
The construction of this monumental moated temple in northern Cambodia was initiated by Suryavarman II, Khmer king from 1113 to 1150.

◁ **Basilica of St. Denis**
Completed in 1144, this church in the city of St. Denis (now a suburb of Paris) was the resting place of Louis VII – who died in 1180 – and all but three French kings.

1152

1152
Frederick Barbarossa is elected King of Germany at Aachen. Three years later, in 1155, he will become King of Italy and Holy Roman Emperor.

1154
The son of Geoffrey of Anjou and Matilda (daughter of Henry I of England)—and already one of the greatest landholders in France—Henry II becomes the first Angevin king of England, sparking centuries of strife between the English and French crowns. In the Middle East, Nur ad-Din, son of the *atabeg* Zengi, annexes Damascus, uniting all Syria north of the crusader states under his control.

1156
Frederick Barbarossa creates the Duchy of Austria as a counterweight to its neighbor Bavaria.

1167
Sixteen cities in the Lombardy region of north Italy form the Lombard League to resist attempts by Frederick Barbarossa to restrict their freedoms.

1170
In England, Thomas Becket, the Archbishop of Canterbury, is murdered in his cathedral following a drawn-out dispute with King Henry II over ecclesiastical independence.

> *"The Law teaches that the universe was invented and created by God, and that it did not come into being by chance or by itself."*
>
> IBN RUSHD, FROM *THE DECISIVE TREATISE*, c.1190

1156–1159
The Hogen (1156) and Heiji (1159) rebellions over issues of succession and the transfer of political power shake imperial Japan; they boost the influence of the samurai (warrior) class and set the rival military clans—the Minamoto and the Taira—against one another. The result is the downfall of the Taira and the establishment of a Minamoto shogunate in 1192.

1162
Frederick Barbarossa destroys Milan after subduing it in successive campaigns stretching over two decades.

1171
Saladin, vizir of Egypt, seizes power on the death of the last Fatimid sultan, renouncing its former Shia allegiance; he will later realign Egypt with the Abbasid caliphs in Baghdad.

1173
Muhammad of Ghur captures the former Ghaznavid capital of Ghazni; he will use it as a base from which to build a central Asian empire.

1176
The Lombard League's forces defeat Frederick Barbarossa at Legnano.

1180
The death of Louis VII of France, who oversaw the foundation of the University of Paris and the Second Crusade.

1181
Jayavarman VII becomes Khmer king, rallying his people against the Cham (Vietnamese) and founding the new capital of Angkor Thom.

1185
The Minamoto fleet defeats Taira forces in the naval Battle of Dannoura, fought off the southern tip of Honshu in Japan; in the wake of the battle, the Minamoto leader Yoritomo will establish the shogun system of military rule.

1186
Muhammad of Ghur's forces take Lahore, the last remaining stronghold of the former Ghaznavid Empire, executing its ruler and so ending the Ghaznavid Dynasty.

1187
Saladin routs a crusader army at Hattin, going on to recapture Jerusalem from the Christians.

1189–1192
The forces of the Third Crusade attempt to win back Jerusalem. One of its leaders, Frederick Barbarossa, drowns in Turkey on his way to the Holy Land (1190). The other, England's Richard the Lionheart, takes Cyprus and Acre and wins the Battle of Arsuf (1191) before signing a peace treaty with Saladin that leaves Jerusalem in Muslim hands but guarantees Christians access to the city.

1190
Jayavarman VII's Khmers conquer the Vietnamese kingdom of Champa.

1191
A Japanese monk introduces Zen Buddhism (derived from Chan, a Chinese variant of Mahayana Buddhism) to Japan. The intuitive, fearless path of Zen appeals to the powerful Japanese samurai class.

1192
The Ghurid general Qutb al-Din conquers Delhi and starts the construction of the Qutb Minar minaret.

1194
The Holy Roman Emperor Henry VI conquers Norman-ruled Sicily.

1198
Ibn Rushd (often westernized to Averroes) dies in Marrakesh. He was an Andalusian Muslim philosopher and polymath who did much to preserve the heritage of Plato and Aristotle.

c. 1200
The Chimú people establish themselves in the northern coastal valleys of Peru, while farther inland the Inca, under Manco Capac, are a growing presence around Cuzco, which will become their capital. The Icelandic sagas—stories exploring history, genealogy, and conflict—inspired by the history of Norse settlers in Iceland, are taking shape. Great Zimbabwe is a powerful presence in southern Africa. The Buddhist faith is dying out in northern India, its original heartland.

30,000 The number of soldiers in Saladin's victorious army at the Battle of Hattin on July 4, 1187.

◁ **Coin of Henry VI**
This 12th-century German coin is struck with an image of Henry VI, the son of Emperor Frederick Barbarossa. Henry became Holy Roman Emperor in 1191, and King of Sicily in 1194.

1204
The army of the Fourth Crusade diverts from its original target of Jerusalem to besiege and sack Christian Constantinople, replacing the emperor with the crusaders' own Latin dynasty.

1206
Having united the Mongol tribes, Temujin is acknowledged as their leader, assuming the title of Genghis Khan. In India, the former slave Qutb ud-Din Aibak founds the Delhi Sultanate; his dynasty (the Mamluk Dynasty) will rule until 1290, while the Sultanate itself will last until 1526. Under the Mamluks, the Quwwat-ul-Islam mosque in Delhi is built.

1208
Pope Innocent III proclaims the Albigensian Crusade against Cathar heretics in southern France.

1209
Founded by St. Francis of Assisi, the Franciscan Order of mendicant monks receives papal approval.

1210
Military victories give the Turkic rulers of the Khwarazm Dynasty a short-lived empire that stretches from the Persian Gulf deep into central Asia; it will fall to Genghis Khan's Mongols by 1220.

1211–1234
Mongol forces conquer the Jin Empire of northern China, capturing their capital Zhongdu (Beijing) in 1215.

1212
Christian forces under Alfonso VIII of Castile defeat the Almohad Muslims at Las Navas de Tolosa, a major step in the Christian Reconquista (reconquest) of Spain.

1215
In England, King John signs the Magna Carta to appease rebellious barons, accepting limitations on royal power.

1217–1221
The Fifth Crusade targets Muslim Egypt but fails to make lasting gains.

1220
Frederick II is Holy Roman Emperor.

1226
Frederick II commissions the Teutonic Knights to forcibly convert the pagan Prussians to Christianity.

780

The length in years of the Reconquista—the recapture of Iberia from Moorish occupation.

1227
Genghis Khan dies while campaigning against rebel Tanguts in China.

1228–1229
Leading the Sixth Crusade, Frederick II regains Jerusalem for the crusader states by peaceful diplomacy.

1232
The papacy sets up the Inquisition as a tool to combat heresy.

1237
Frederick II defeats forces of the Lombard League at Cortenuova in northern Italy.

1240
Alexander Nevsky's victory at the Battle of the River Neva halts Swedish expansion eastward into Russia. Two years later, he will defeat the Teutonic Knights at Lake Peipus.

1241
The north German ports of Hamburg and Lübeck form an alliance, presaging the development of the Hanseatic League, which will dominate Baltic trade for the next three centuries. Mongol forces strike deep into Europe, annexing Russian principalities, winning decisive victories in Poland and Hungary, and only turning back on news of the death of the Great Khan Ögedei, Genghis Khan's son and successor.

◁ **The capture of Jerusalem by Saladin**
A 15th-century miniature shows the surrender of Jerusalem to Saladin after a short siege in 1187. The loss of the city triggered the launch of the Third Crusade in 1189.

◁ **The Battle of the Neva**
This illustration from a 16th-century chronicle of Russian history shows a scene from The Battle of the Neva in 1240, which occurred during the invasion of Russia by Swedish forces.

1243

24

The number of years spent by Marco Polo traveling to and around Asia, where he befriended Kublai Khan.

1243
The Seljuk sultanate of Rum in Anatolia becomes a Mongol vassal state.

1248–1254
In the Seventh Crusade, King Louis IX (later canonized as St. Louis) of France invades Egypt but is defeated, captured, and ransomed.

1250
On the death of Egypt's last Ayubbid ruler, the sultan's Mamluk slave-soldiers seize power in their own name, founding the Mamluk Sultanate.

1256
Hostilities break out between the Italian trading ports of Venice and Genoa, signaling the start of a struggle for commercial dominance that will last for more than a century. Hulegu founds the Mongol Ilkhanate Empire in Persia.

1257
Mongol forces under Möngke invade the Song lands of southern China.

1258
Hulegu's Ilkhans sack Baghdad and put an end to the Abbasid Caliphate, executing the last caliph.

1259
On the death of the Great Khan Möngke, the Mongol domains across Europe and Asia start to divide into four separate khanates: the Ilkhans in Persia and adjoining lands; the Golden Horde in Russia; the Chaghatai Khanate in central Asia; and the Chinese lands where, in 1271, Kublai Khan will establish the Yuan Dynasty.

1260
The Mamluks defeat a Mongol army at Ain Jalut in Palestine.

1261
The Byzantines reconquer Constantinople from the Latin Dynasty that had ruled it since the time of the Fourth Crusade. In Egypt, the Mamluk Sultan Baybars reestablishes the Caliphate, now based in Cairo.

1265–1274
The philosopher Thomas Aquinas writes his *Summa Theologiae*, attempting to reconcile Christian belief with Aristotelian philosophy.

1266
Norway gives up the Outer Hebrides and the Isle of Man to the kingdom of Scotland in the Treaty of Perth.

1269
Italian Marco Polo, just 6 years old, embarks on an epic expedition to Asia with his father and uncle. He later records his adventures in *The Travels of Marco Polo* (c.1300).

1270
Yekuno Amlak establishes the Solomonic Dynasty, which will rule Ethiopia until the deposition of Emperor Haile Selassie in 1974. In Egypt, Louis IX dies of dysentery while besieging Tunis on the Eighth Crusade.

1272
Kublai Khan moves the capital of his newly established Yuan Empire to Beijing, which he calls Dadu.

1278–1279
Kublai Khan completes the conquest of the Song realm, becoming the first non-native ruler of a united China. In India, the Chola kingdom finally comes to an end following a string of military defeats.

1281
The second of two attempted invasions of Japan by Kublai Khan (the first was in 1274) is thwarted in part by a typhoon, known to later Japanese as the kamikaze or "divine wind."

1287
Mongol forces invade Myanmar, putting an end to the Pagan Empire.

1290
The Teutonic Knights finally subjugate the last southern Baltic pagan tribes.

1291
Acre, the only remaining Christian stronghold in the Holy Land, falls to the Mamluks, extinguishing the Crusader presence in the Levant.

1295
The Ilkhans convert to Islam, aligning with the faith of most of their subjects.

c. 1300
Introduced by traders from the Middle East, Islam spreads through the Indonesian islands and the Malay peninsula, replacing Buddhism and Hinduism.

▷ **Kublai Khan**
This 13th-century portrait depicts the leader of the Mongol Empire and founder of Yuan Dynasty that governed China from 1261 to 1368.

c. 1308
Italian poet Dante Alighieri begins work on the *Divine Comedy*, completing it a year before his death in 1321. It is considered one of the most significant literary works of the Middle Ages.

1309
After his election in 1305, French Pope Clement V moves the seat of the papacy to Avignon in France, where it will remain until 1377.

1312
The Knights Templar are brutally suppressed by Philip IV of France; following the loss of the Holy Land, their fellow military order the Hospitallers have, 2 years earlier, established a new base on the Greek island of Rhodes. In Africa, Mansa Musa ascends to the throne of Mali; he becomes legendarily rich in gold and uses this wealth to strengthen the country's cultural centers, particularly Timbuktu, which he annexes in 1324. Egyptian Mamluks occupy the Christian kingdom of Makuria in Nubia and try to impose Islam, inaugurating a period of civil strife.

1313
Ozbeg Khan ascends to the throne of the Golden Horde (a Mongol Khanate) and accepts Islam as the state religion, banning shamanism and other non-Islamic religious practices.

67
The number of years that the papacy was based in the French city of Avignon.

1314
A Scots army led by Robert the Bruce defeats a much larger English force led by Edward II at Bannockburn, guaranteeing Scotland's status as an independent nation.

1324
Osman I, ruler of a small enclave in Anatolia, dies. His realm will be the first home of the Ottoman Dynasty, named for him.

1325
The Aztecs found their capital city, Tenochtitlán, on an island in Lake Texcoco, where modern Mexico City now stands. In India, Muhammad bin Tughluq becomes ruler of the Delhi Sultanate; during his 26-year reign, he suppresses multiple rebellions and the sultanate reaches its greatest extent.

1326
The Ottomans, under Osman I's son, Orhan, capture Bursa in Anatolia from the Byzantines.

1331
Stephen Dushan becomes King of Serbia; before his death in 1355, he will build an empire in southeastern Europe.

1333
In the Kemmu Restoration, Emperor Go-Daigo of Japan overthrows the Kamakura shogunate, temporarily restoring imperial power

1336
Harihara I establishes the Hindu Vijayanagara Empire, which will dominate the Deccan Plateau region in southern India for the next two centuries.

1337
The Hundred Years' War breaks out when Edward III of England refuses to do feudal homage for his continental

"I came into a place void of all light, which bellows like the sea in tempest, when it is combated by warring winds."

DANTE ALIGHIERI, FROM THE *DIVINE COMEDY*, c.1308

possessions to Philip VI of France; sporadic fighting between the two nations will continue until 1453.

1347
First recorded in Asia in 1331, the plague known as the Black Death reaches Europe.

1348–1353
In Italy, Boccaccio writes the *Decameron*, which frames 100 tales told by a group of people escaping the Black Death.

1350
Hayam Wuruk becomes raja of Majapahit, based on the Indonesian island of Java; in his 39-year reign, the empire will reach its greatest extent, stretching from the Malay Peninsula through the Philippines.

1351
The Red Turban revolt breaks out in the Yangtze River region of China, directed against the Mongol Yuan Dynasty. The Ayutthaya kingdom is founded; the Thai nation will eventually develop from this kingdom.

1354
Ottoman forces capture the Gallipoli peninsula in Thrace from the Byzantine Empire, giving the Turkish dynasty its first foothold in Europe.

1356
A decree called the Golden Bull fixes the procedure for the election of Holy Roman Emperors, omitting any mention of a papal role—a significant step in the centuries-old power struggle between Church and State.

▷ **Mamluk cavalry**
An illustration from the 14th-century *Complete Instructions in the Practices of Military Art* shows the cavalry of the Mamluks—the dynasty that ruled over Egypt and Syria from 1250 to 1517.

Der Tod zum Pabst. Der Tod zum Kaiser. Der Tod zur Kaiserin. Der Tod zum König.

Der Tod zum Grafen. Der Tod zum Abt. Der Tod zum Ritter. Der Tod zum Juristen.

Der Tod zum Kaufmann. Der Tod zur Aebtissin. Der Tod zum Krüppel. Der Tod zum Waldbruder.

Der Tod zum Schultheiss. Der Tod zum Blutvogt. Der Tod zum Narren. Der Tod zum Krämer.

Der Tod zum Bauer. Der Spiegel aller Welt. Der Tod zum Maler.

1368

1368
The Black Death has, by now, killed more than one-third of Europe's population. In China, rebel leader Zhu Yuanzhang captures Beijing from the collapsing Mongol Yuan Dynasty, forcing them to retreat to the central Asian steppe; he takes power as Hongwu, first emperor of the new Ming Dynasty.

1370
Timur the Lame (Tamberlane) wins control of the Chagatai Khanate; in the 35 years until his death in 1405, he will defeat forces of the Mamluk Dynasty in Egypt, the Delhi Sultanate in India, and the emergent Ottoman Empire, building a short-lived central Asian empire from his capital of Samarkand; the empire splits into warring factions after his death. Construction of the Bastille, a fortress in Paris, is begun; its function is to defend Paris from the approach of English forces during the Hundred Years' War.

1371
An Ottoman army under the Sultan Murad I defeats Byzantine forces at the Battle of Maritsa and conquers most of the Balkans.

1375
The Chimú take control of the Lambayeque Valley of northern Peru from their Late Sican neighbors.

1378
The Catholic Church's Western Schism gets underway, with rival popes established in Rome and Avignon; it will not be healed until 1417.

1380
Russia's Prince Dmitri defeats the forces of the Golden Horde at Kulikovo; although not decisive (Moscow will be sacked 2 years later), the battle marks a turning point in the struggle to free the country from Mongol rule.

◁ *The Basel Dance of Death*
This 19th-century watercolor is a copy of a fresco in a Basel church that records death dancing with victims of the Black Death, the plague that ravaged Europe in the mid-14th century.

▷ **Aztec vase**
This polychrome ceramic vase depicting Tlaloc, god of rain, is from the Main Temple of Tenochtitlán—a settlement that grew into the largest and most powerful city in Mesoamerica in the 15th century.

1381
In England, the Peasants' Revolt against serfdom and high taxes is suppressed. Theologian John Wycliffe translates the Bible into English.

1382
In Egypt, the ruling Bahri Mamluks are succeeded by the Burji Dynasty, another group of Mamluks.

1386
Foundation of the University of Heidelberg, the oldest such institution in Germany. Construction begins on Milan's cathedral; it is not completed for another 500 years.

1386–1400
Geoffrey Chaucer writes the *Canterbury Tales*, a long poem in Middle English that follows the journey of a group of pilgrims from London to St. Thomas Becket's shrine at Canterbury Cathedral. The story becomes very popular in its time.

1387
After resisting attempts at forcible conversion for more than a century, Lithuania, Europe's last pagan realm, voluntarily accepts Christianity.

1389
Invading Ottoman forces defeat a Serbian army at Kosovo, reducing Serbia to vassal status in the following years.

1396
The Ottomans defeat a crusader army raised from across Europe at Nicopolis in Bulgaria, putting an end to the Second Bulgarian Empire.

1397
The Kalmar Union unites the Swedish, Norwegian, and Danish crowns in an attempt to counter the growing power of the Germanic Hanseatic League. In Italy, the Medici Bank is founded in Florence; over the next century, it will become the largest financial institution in all of Europe.

1398
Timur defeats the army of the Delhi Sultanate and sacks Delhi, leaving it in ruins.

c. 1400
On the Malay Peninsula, Malacca is founded by Parameswara, the last Raja of Temasek (Singapore); over the ensuing century, it becomes a major port for east–west trade.

1402
Timur takes Ankara, capturing the Ottoman Sultan Bayezid I, who dies in captivity the following year.

1405
The Ming Yongle Emperor dispatches the first of seven "treasure voyages" launched over the next 28 years; these maritime expeditions extend Chinese influence as far as east Africa and the Persian Gulf.

50,000,000
The estimated number of people killed by the Black Death in the 14th century.

1407–1424
Chinese forces occupy Dai Ngu (modern-day Vietnam) and attempt to integrate it into their empire, but they are eventually beaten back by Le Loi, founder of the Le Dynasty.

1415
King John I captures Ceuta on the North African coast, making it Portugal's first African possession. In central Europe, the religious reformer Jan Hus is burned at the stake as a heretic, sparking the rebel Hussite movement. In France, English forces under Henry V win the Battle of Agincourt, gaining the initiative in the Hundred Years' War.

1417
The Council of Constance ends the Western Schism, in which two men simultaneously claimed to be pope.

1419
In the Defenestration of Prague, Hussite demonstrators throw seven city council members to their death out of a window of the city's New Town Hall, sparking the Hussite Wars.

c. 1425
Under the rule of Philip the Good, Duke of Burgundy from 1419 to 1467, the Low Countries in general, and Bruges in particular, become centers of the arts; Bruges is home to Jan van Eyck, who paints the *Arnolfini Portrait* in 1434.

1428
In the Valley of Mexico, the Aztecs enter the Triple Alliance with the city-states of Texcoco and Tlacopan; they will come to dominate the coalition, which in time will form the basis of the Aztec Empire.

1429
In France, Joan of Arc, aged just 19, relieves the siege of Orleans; even though she is captured and burned at the stake in 1431, her intervention proves a turning point for the French forces in the Hundred Years' War.

1431
Long in decline, Angkor is sacked by Ayutthaya raiders; by the end of the century, the former Khmer capital will be largely abandoned.

1434
Gil Eanes sails past Cape Bojador, opening up the coast of west Africa to exploration by Portuguese sailors; they benefit from the development of three-masted ships, as well as from the patronage of Prince Henry the Navigator.

1436
Completion of the dome of Florence Cathedral, engineered by Filippo Brunelleschi, concludes 140 years of construction.

1438
Pachacuti becomes ruler of the Incas; in his 34-year reign, he transforms a small kingdom in the valley of Cuzco into a major regional presence.

1440
Frederick III is the first Habsburg to be crowned Holy Roman Emperor; the title remains in the family thereafter until its abolition in 1806.

▷ **Joan of Arc**
This illustration shows the "Maid of Orléans," sword in hand. A hero to the French, she was canonized in 1920 by Pope Benedict XV.

THE EARLY MODERN WORLD 1450–1700

1450

c. 1450–1629
The Mwene Mutapa Empire dominates southeast Africa from its capital in Zimbabwe. Rich in gold, copper, and ivory, it controls the lucrative trade routes from the interior to the Arab kingdoms on the east coast, attracting Portuguese traders who settle in Mozambique from 1505.

1453
The Byzantine Empire falls when the Ottoman Turks capture Constantinople and expand their territory into the Balkans and Greece. The Hundred Years' War (1337–1453) ends when France recaptures Bordeaux, leaving Calais as England's only possession in France; the French retake it in 1558.

1454–1455
The Gutenberg Bible is printed in Mainz, Germany; it is the world's first mass-produced book and the first major book to be produced on a printing press with movable metal type.

1455–1485
The Wars of the Roses: civil war ensues as the rival Plantagenet houses of Lancaster and York (symbolized respectively by a red and a white rose) vie for the English throne; the dynastic struggle ends when Henry Tudor seizes the throne as Henry VII, founding the Tudor Dynasty.

1462–1505
Ivan III (the Great), Grand Prince of Muscovy, consolidates and triples the extent of his domain; he breaks the power of the Golden Horde, which had dominated eastern Europe for 200 years.

1467–1477
The Onin War leads to a century of civil strife—the Warring States period—as Japan's regional magnates (daimyo) seek to destroy their rivals.

1468
The Songhai Empire under Sonni Ali annexes the city of Timbuktu and the remnants of the Mali Empire, creating a vast empire and becoming the leading power in west Africa.

1469
Isabella of Castile marries Ferdinand of Aragon, creating a Christian Spain that dominates 16th-century Europe. Birth of Niccolò Machiavelli, Italian diplomat and philosopher, who argues in *The Prince* (1532) that the state should promote the common good, irrespective of any moral evaluation of its acts.

c. 1470
The Chimor kingdom of Peru's Chimú people, famous for its metalwork, textiles, and pottery, is conquered by the Inca king Pachacuti; the Inca Empire extends about 2,500 miles (c. 4,000 km).

▷ **Chimor ceremonial knife**
This gold knife is adorned with an image of Naymlap, legendary founder of the Sican civilization that preceded the Chimor kingdom in coastal Peru; the Chimor fell to the Inca from around 1470.

180
The print run of the Gutenberg Bible. Only 21 complete copies are known to exist today.

1473
The Aztec emperor Axayacatl conquers the city-state of Tlatelolco; he expands and consolidates the Aztec Empire.

1477
Charles the Bold, Duke of Burgundy, dies; his territories are split between the Austrian Habsburg Empire and the Kingdom of France, but disputes over them continue for centuries.

1482
Portugal builds São Jorge da Mina (Elmina Castle) on the Gold Coast, giving Europe its first settlement in sub-Saharan Africa and allowing Portugal to monopolize west Africa's gold trade. Sandro Botticelli paints *Primavera* (*Spring*), a masterpiece of the Italian Renaissance.

1487
The Aztec Great Temple in Tenochtitlán is rebuilt for the sixth time; it opens with the ritual sacrifice of up to 5,000 people.

1488
Portuguese navigator Bartolomeu Dias becomes the first European to round the Cape of Good Hope at the tip of southern Africa; his expedition opens the sea route to India via the Atlantic and Indian Oceans.

1492
The Reconquista of Spain is completed by the capture of Granada, the last Moorish territory in Spain; Muslims and Jews are expelled from Spain. Supported by the Spanish crown, Genoese explorer Christopher Columbus crosses the Atlantic, believing he can reach China and the East Indies; instead, he lands in the West Indies and "discovers" the New World. Martin of Bohemia creates the oldest surviving globe, the *Erdapfel* ("Earth apple"); the Americas are not shown.

1494
The Treaty of Tordesillas settles a dispute between Spain and Portugal over New World discoveries. Charles VIII of France claims Naples, sparking the Italian Wars (1494–1559) between France and Spain over control of Italy.

1497
Under the commission of Henry VII of England, Venetian navigator John Cabot sails from Bristol in search of Asia; instead, he discovers the mainland of North America, paving the way for the English exploration and settlement of the continent.

1497–1498
Portugal's Vasco da Gama is the first European to reach India via the Cape of Good Hope; his route transforms trade between Europe and Asia.

1498
Columbus reaches South America on his third voyage to the New World, thereby discovering a new continent.

1500
Leading a fleet of 13 ships into the western Atlantic Ocean, Pedro Alvares Cabral sights Brazil and claims it for Portugal. Spanish navigator Vicente Yáñez Pinzón discovers the mouth of

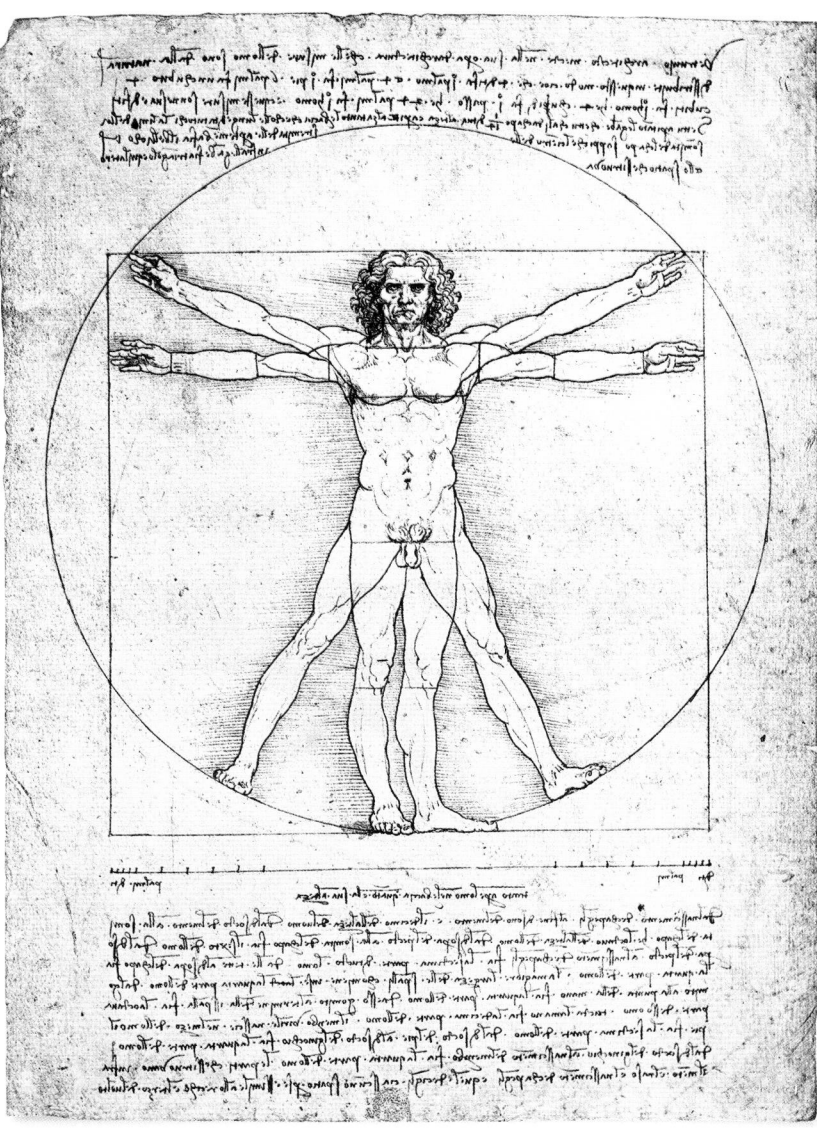

◁ *Vitruvian Man*
This ink drawing was made around 1490 by Leonardo da Vinci to illustrate the perfect geometry of human proportions. The artist went on to create the *Mona Lisa* in 1503–1506.

the Amazon River. New Zealand's Maori Culture enters its classic period, characterized by finely made bone tools and weapons, elaborate wood carvings, textiles, tattoos, some of the biggest war canoes ever built, and a move away from nomadism toward settlement in large hilltop forts and earthworks; this society is only disrupted by the introduction of metal technologies by Europeans arriving in 1642.

1501

Ismail I becomes Shah of Persia and founds the Safavid Dynasty, which rules Iran for over 200 years; he seizes Baghdad, makes Isfahan his capital, and extends the eastern frontier of the empire to Afghanistan and the edge of the Mughal Empire.

1501–1502

Florentine explorer Amerigo Vespucci reaches the coast of Brazil and continues southward to discover that Columbus had not reached the eastern edge of Asia, but a separate continent. In 1507, cartographer Martin Waldseemüller names it America, after Vespucci.

1502

The slave trade between Europe, west Africa, and the Americas begins with a shipment of African slaves sent to Cuba to work in the Spanish settlements.

1503–1506

Leonardo da Vinci paints the *Mona Lisa*, one of the most famous works of the Renaissance; Michelangelo finishes his statue of David.

1510–1511

Afonso de Albuquerque conquers Goa and captures Malacca, laying the foundations of Portuguese hegemony in maritime Southeast Asia.

1513

Spain makes first contact with mainland North America when Juan Ponce de León reaches Florida. He is the first to encounter and describe the Gulf Stream, a powerful current important for ships navigating the Atlantic.

1514

Ottoman forces crush the Safavid Persians at the Battle of Chaldiran, northwest Iran; Sultan Selim I then annexes eastern Anatolia and northern Mesopotamia and conquers large territories in Syria and Egypt, securing almost all the Muslim holy places in southwest Asia.

1517

The Reformation begins when the German monk and theologian Martin Luther publishes his *Ninety-five Theses* in Wittenberg. These challenge the authority of the pope, sparking a revolt that leads to a permanent split between Catholics and Protestants.

1519

Spanish explorer Hernán Cortés lands in Mexico; he captures the Aztec capital Tenochtitlán with the help of Indian allies in 1521; Spain begins its domination of Central America. Charles I, the Habsburg king of Spain, is elected Holy Roman Emperor as Charles V.

1520

Aztec populations crash when Europeans bring smallpox to the Americas; in the next 100 years, around 20 million people, or 90 percent of the population of the New World, are killed by diseases from Europe.

1522

Financed by King Charles I of Spain to find a navigable route around the tip of South America to the Spice Islands (Maluku Islands), Portuguese explorer Ferdinand Magellan completes the first circumnavigation of the globe, though he dies during the voyage.

1526

Babur, a descendent of Mongol warlord Timur, founds the Mughal Empire in northern India; he defeats the Afghan sultan of Delhi, Ibrahim Lodi, and ushers in a new era of order, prosperity, and artistic achievement.

1527

Charles V's imperial troops sack Rome, crushing the papal Holy League and bringing Italy under Spanish rule. In South America, a smallpox epidemic devastates the Inca people of Cuzco.

1529

The Peace of Cambrai provides a break in the Italian Wars; France relinquishes its rights in Italy, Flanders, and Artois; the Holy Roman Emperor, Charles V, renounces his claims to Burgundy. In the Adal Sultanate (present-day Somalia), the imam and general Ahmad ibn Ghazi leads a rebellion against the Ethiopian Christian Empire.

▷ **Emperor Babur**
This detail from an illustration in *Baburnama* (the autobiography of Babur) shows the great Mughal emperor in his camp on his way to conquer Kabul around 1526.

1529–1593

1529–1566
The failed siege of Vienna by the Ottoman sultan Suleiman the Magnificent in 1529 stops the advance of the Ottoman Empire in central Europe. The reign of the sultan is marked by an artistic and cultural revival, advances in the law, and the expansion of Ottoman sovereignty in the Middle East and North Africa.

1531–1533
Spanish conquistador Francisco Pizarro sails from Panama to conquer Peru; in 1533, he captures, ransoms, and executes the Inca emperor Atahualpa, then conquers the Inca capital, Cuzco.

1534
Ignatius Loyola founds the Jesuits, a Catholic missionary order. Henry VIII of England puts himself at the head of the Church of England, after the pope refuses to allow him to divorce his first wife, Katherine of Aragon. Jacques Cartier explores Newfoundland and the Gulf of St. Lawrence, preparing the way for the French colonization of Canada.

1536
The Act of Union formally unites Wales and England. Henry VIII executes his second wife, Anne Boleyn; he starts the dissolution of the monasteries in order to seize their wealth and suppress opposition to the Church of England.

60
The percentage of world silver production coming from Potosí, Bolivia, in the late 16th century.

CLARISSIMUS ET DOCTISSIMUS DOCTOR NICOLAUS COPERNICUS TORUNENSIS CANONICUS WARMIENSIS ASTRONOMUS INCOMPARABILIS

1537
Jane Seymour gives birth to Henry VIII's long-awaited male heir (the future Edward VI).

1541
Francis Xavier leads a Jesuit mission to Southeast Asia that reaches Goa, the Spice Islands, China, and Japan. The Protestant reformer John Calvin settles in Geneva and steers the city toward a strict Christian rule.

1543
Polish astronomer Nicolaus Copernicus publishes *On the Revolutions of the Heavenly Spheres*, outlining his theory that Earth revolves around the Sun. Andreas Vesalius's *On the Fabric of the Human Body* provides the foundation of modern medicine through its use of evidence provided by human dissection.

1545–1563
The Council of Trent instigates the Counter-Reformation in response to the threat from Protestantism, agreeing to reform and remodel the Catholic Church. The Spanish discover huge silver deposits in Potosí, Bolivia, much of which is minted into coins known as "pieces of eight."

1547
Ivan IV, Grand Prince of Moscow, is proclaimed czar of Russia in. Under his rule, Russia expands east into Siberia and south and takes control of the trade routes to Central Asia; he destroys the Russian *boyars* (hereditary nobility) in his attempt to centralize Russia, earning himself the epithet "the Terrible."

1550
Jesuits reach Brazil and go on to create a network of mission villages, known as *reducciones*, which act as a buffer between Spanish and Portuguese territories in South America.

1552–1555
The Holy Roman Emperor, Charles V, is driven out of Germany by Henri II of France and Maurice of Saxony; he only just evades capture, but is forced to agree to the Peace of Augsburg, which allows German princes to adopt either Lutheranism or Catholicism as the official faith of their state.

1556
Akbar succeeds his father Humayun as Mughal emperor in India at age 14; he rules for nearly 50 years, expanding Mughal power and presiding over a time of cordial Hindu–Muslim relations.

1558
Elizabeth I, the daughter of Henry VIII and Anne Boleyn, becomes Queen of England; she rules until 1603.

1561
St. Basil's Cathedral in Moscow's Red Square is consecrated. It is the city's tallest building.

1565
Spain founds its first colony in the Philippines on Cebu Island.

1568–1648
In the Dutch Revolt, seven northern, predominantly Protestant provinces of the Low Countries rebel against the rule of the Catholic King Philip II of Spain. The United Provinces assert their independence, becoming the Dutch Republic in 1588; the southern provinces remain under Spanish rule.

▷ **Toyotomi Hideyoshi**
Hideyoshi, pictured here around 1600, rose through the ranks of the army and eventually took control of the military, unifying Japan in 1591 after centuries of civil strife.

1569
Flemish cartographer Gerardus Mercator creates the first world map to reflect the true compass bearing of every landmass; his projection remains widely used.

1570
The Vijayanagar Empire in southern India goes into decline after the Battle of Talikota; it finally collapses in 1646.

1571
Fought in the waters off southwestern Greece, the naval Battle of Lepanto is the last major battle between galley ships; it gives the forces of the Christian Holy League their first victory against the Ottoman Turks, halting Ottoman expansion in the Mediterranean.

1572
More than 3,000 Protestant Huguenots are massacred in Paris on August 24, and up to 20,000 are killed across France

1580
A Spanish force claims the Portuguese crown for Philip II of Spain following the death of the young king Sebastian of Portugal in battle against Morocco; Spain becomes a formidable power.

1585
Spain receives the first commercial shipment of cacao beans from the New World; Europe soon acquires a taste for chocolate. England's first colony in North America is founded by Sir Walter Raleigh on Roanoke Island; colonists arrive in 1587 but it is abandoned in 1590. It is known as the Lost Colony.

1587
Elizabeth I sends Francis Drake to raid Portuguese and Spanish ships and ports; his fleet enters Cadiz harbor, southern Spain, and destroys 30 Spanish ships and thousands of tons of supplies.

"The advantage of time and place in all practical actions is half a victory …"

SIR FRANCIS DRAKE, 1588

in the following weeks. It is the worst atrocity in the French Wars of Religion, a 36-year-long conflict between Roman Catholics and Huguenots, which claims an estimated 3 million lives.

1573
Oda Nobunaga overthrows the Ashikaga shogunate (1338–1573) and unites half of Japan under his rule.

1576
At the Battle of Rajmahal, Mughal forces defeat the Sultanate of Bengal in north India and annex the region. The last Sultan of Bengal, Daud Khan Karrani, is captured and executed.

1588
The Spanish Armada, under the command of the Duke of Medina Sidonia, sets out to conquer England for Philip II and the Roman church. It is defeated by terrible weather and the superior tactics and technology of the English fleet, led by Lord Charles Howard and Sir Francis Drake.

1588–1629
Shah Abbas I ("the Great") rules Safavid Persia. The kingdom he inherits is riven by internal disputes and beset by foreign enemies. Abbas, however, restores Persia to formidable power; regains territory from the Ottomans,

Portuguese, and Mughals; creates a beautiful new capital in Isfahan; and encourages trade with Dutch and English merchants, while carpet weaving becomes a national industry.

1589
The world's first industrial machine is designed and built by English clergyman William Lee; its function is to knit stockings.

1590
The Treaty of Constantinople ends the Ottoman-Safavid War; Persia accepts the Ottoman frontiers, which extend to the Caucasus and the Caspian Sea.

c. 1590
Dutch eyewear-maker Zacharias Janssen creates the first compound optical microscope.

1591
The Songhai Empire in the western Sahel enters a period of decline after the death of Askia Daud. Toyotomi Hideyoshi unifies all of Japan under his authority; he moves his power base to Edo (Tokyo) and bans Christianity.

1592
Japan invades Korea but is kept at bay by the Korean fleet and intervention by China; Japan makes several more attempts over the following years.

1593–1606
Habsburgs and Ottomans clash in Hungary and the Balkans. A 13-year-long conflict is fought over territories in Transylvania, Moldavia, and Wallachia; the war—often called The Long Turkish War—costs numerous lives but is ultimately indecisive.

130

The number of ships in the Spanish Armada. They carried more than 30,000 men.

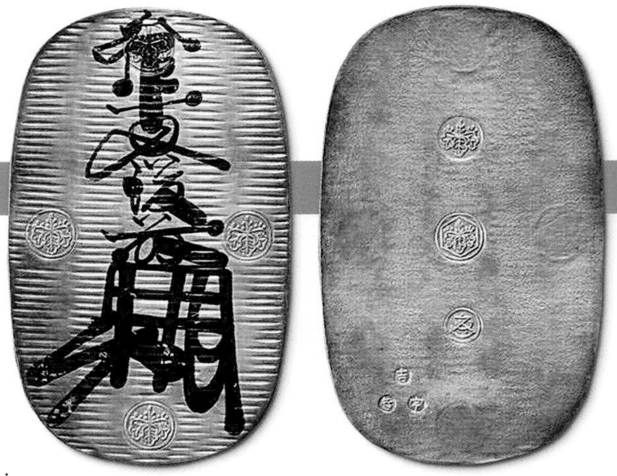

▷ **Japanese gold koban**
Oval coins made from gold and silver were used under the Tokugawa shogunate, which began around 1603 and lasted until the Boshin War of 1868–1888.

1597–1631

c. 1597
The first edition of Shakespeare's tragic romance *Romeo and Juliet* is published in two quarto editions. It is likely that the play was written in 1590–1595.

1598
The Edict of Nantes marks the end of the French Wars of Religion (1562–1598); it allows the Calvinist Protestants (Huguenots) to practice their religion freely and awards them substantial rights. Henri IV seeks to heal the religious divisions in France by uniting the country in a war against Spain.

1600
Tokugawa Ieyasu wins the Battle of Sekigahara to gain control of Japan; the Tokugawa shogunate rules Japan in the Edo Period (1603–1868), an isolationist era in which European missions are violently suppressed. The English East India Company is granted a Royal Charter for trade in the East Indies; it goes on to gain control of substantial areas in India and China and becomes a formidable force in the British Empire. The Yoruba kingdom of Oyo in southern Nigeria develops into one of the most powerful empires in the region.

1602
The Dutch East India Company is founded and granted a tax-free monopoly of Asian trade; it forces the Portuguese out of the Spice Islands in 1605 and creates a powerful trading empire that dominates world trade for the next two centuries.

1603
James VI of Scotland succeeds Elizabeth I as James I, uniting the crowns of England and Scotland.

1604
James VI of Scotland (also James I of England) commissions the Authorized Version of the Bible, which remains one of the world's most used translations of the work. Italian scientist Galileo Galilei observes a supernova and concludes that the universe is able to change.

△ **King Gustavus Adolphus**
This 17th-century painting by Strasbourg-born painter Johann Walter shows Gustavus Adolphus of Sweden at the battle of Breitenfeld in 1631. The king died in battle the following year.

1606
Portuguese (or Galician) navigator Luís Vaez de Torres is the first European to sight Australia. While searching for new trading islands in the east (particularly for the "great land of New Guinea") the Dutch navigator Willem Janszoon lands on the north Australian coast, near what is now the town of Weipa.

1607
The Virginia Company of London establishes the first permanent English settlement in North America in Jamestown, Virginia.

1608
Dutch eyewear-makers invent the telescope, which is used by Galileo Galilei in systematic observations of the night sky; he observes the Milky Way, the Moon, and Jupiter's moons orbiting the planet—findings that later challenge the model of the Universe. Quebec is founded in New France, Canada, by French explorer and cartographer Samuel de Champlain; European demand for beaver and other exotic animal pelts drives French, Dutch, and British expeditions across North America.

1609–1619
German astronomer Johannes Kepler publishes his laws of planetary motion, describing the planets' elliptical orbits around the Sun.

1612
Russia repulses Polish invaders in the Battle of Moscow. The first Romanov czar, Mikhail, is elected in 1613, ending the 15-year interregnum known as the Time of Troubles.

1616
Prominent Manchu chieftain Nurhaci claims the title Great Jin (Khan) of China and declares war on Ming rule in 1618; his descendants found the Qing Dynasty in 1644.

1618
Bohemia's Protestants revolt against Habsburg rule, igniting the Thirty Years' War, which develops from a religious war into a destructive conflict between the major powers of Europe and claims the lives of 8 million people. Jamestown in Virginia receives its first shipment of African slaves.

1620
The Pilgrim Fathers—a group of Puritan colonists—sail from Plymouth, England, aboard the *Mayflower*. They arrive near Boston in November; after Native Americans help them survive the winter, they found the Plymouth Colony.

1621
The settlers from the *Mayflower* celebrate their first harvest in America by eating turkey with the local natives.

1622
Algonquian-speaking Native Americans of the Powhatan Confederacy attack the English colony at Jamestown; more than 300 settlers die.

1624
Cardinal Richelieu becomes King Louis XIII of France's chief minister; he is set on destroying the Huguenots, the power of the French nobles, and the military might of the Habsburgs.

1625
The Dutch found the colony of New Amsterdam (modern New York); they pay the Lenape tribe just 60 guilders (around $1,000) for Manhattan Island.

1628–1629
The English parliament's Petition of Right gives English citizens the right to be protected from overreaches in royal authority; it is one of several measures designed to curb royal power. King Charles dismisses the English parliament in 1629 and rules without it for 11 years.

1631
Sweden's king, Gustavus Adolphus, enters the Thirty Years' War and crushes the army of the Holy Roman Emperor.

102
The number of passengers aboard the *Mayflower* on its voyage across the Atlantic.

◁ **Return to Amsterdam**
This 1599 painting by Hendrick Cornelisz Vroom depicts the second of several Dutch voyages made to the east in search of trade before the formation of the Dutch East India Company in 1602.

◁ **English Civil War helmet**
Lobster-tailed helmets were worn by soldiers on both sides during the English Civil War (1642–1651).

1632

19

The number of years taken to complete the construction of the Taj Mahal in Agra.

1632

Two of the 17th century's greatest thinkers are born: the Dutch philosopher Baruch Spinoza (1632–1677), whose rationalist approach lays the foundations for the Enlightenment; and Englishman John Locke (1632–1704), whose political liberalism influences both the Enlightenment and the Constitution of the United States.

1633

In Japan, the Shogun Tokugawa Iemitsu pursues isolationist policies. He forbids all travel abroad, except for highly restricted voyages by ships to China and Korea; books from abroad are banned; and overseas traders are expelled from the country (except for the Dutch, who are allowed to retain a base near Nagasaki). This period of Japanese isolation will last until 1853. In the Mughal Empire, Shah Jahan ends the tradition of religious tolerance by ordering the destruction of all recently built Hindu temples.

1633–1637

Tulip mania in Holland provides the first example of an economic bubble; prices for tulip bulbs rise dramatically before collapsing, bankrupting many investors.

1634

Work begins on the Taj Mahal, a huge marble mausoleum on the bank of the river Yamuna in Agra. It is commissioned by Shah Jahan in memory of his wife Mumtaz Mahal and is completed in 1653.

1635

France enters the Thirty Years' War against Habsburg Spain in 1635 and the Holy Roman Empire in 1636.

1636

The first institute for advanced learning in North America is founded in Cambridge, Massachusetts. Two years later it is given the name Harvard College in honor of the Reverend John Harvard, a prominent benefactor.

1638

The Ottomans under sultan Murad IV retake Baghdad from the Safavids and are granted Mesopotamia by the Treaty of Qasr-i-Shirin in 1639, ending the Ottoman-Safavid conflict. Galileo formulates the law of falling bodies, which states that bodies of the same material falling through the same medium go at the same speed, regardless of mass.

1642

Dutchman Abel Tasman claims Tasmania for the Dutch, but Maori warriors prevent him from claiming New Zealand. Dutch artist Rembrandt van Rijn paints *The Night Watch*.

1644–1651

Charles I of England's insistence on the "Divine Right" of kings to rule without consulting Parliament triggers the British Civil Wars; Parliamentarians (Roundheads) are set against Royalists (Cavaliers); Charles is convicted of treason for fighting a war against Parliament and beheaded in 1649; Oliver Cromwell heads the new English Commonwealth, and in 1651 his New Model Army defeats Charles's son (Charles II) at Worcester, ending the wars.

1644

China's Ming Dynasty falls to the Manchus, who install the first Qing emperor in Beijing and gain control of all China by 1681.

▷ **Louis XIV**
This 1701 painting shows France's "Sun King," who was crowned in 1654 and took direct rule over France in 1661 after the death of his Chief Minister.

▷ **Emperor Aurangzeb**
This 17th-century painting depicts the Mughal Emperor Aurangzeb, who ruled from 1658, being carried on a palanquin, accompanied by a royal hunting party.

1673

1644–1647
Witchfinder General Matthew Hopkins zealously examines, tortures, and executes hundreds of people accused of witchcraft in the east of England.

1647–1648
The French physicist Blaise Pascal demonstrates the existence of atmospheric pressure and shows that it decreases at higher altitudes.

1648
The Peace of Westphalia brings an end to the Thirty Years' War—a turbulent period of European history—but fatally undermines the authority of the Holy Roman Emperor.

1648–1653
Civil war (the Fronde rebellion) breaks out in France after years of war and peasant uprisings; the monarchy survives, but the protests against royal power are a sign of things to come.

1652
The Dutch East India Company founds Cape Town, South Africa, as a resupply port for company ships trading with Asia. The first of three Anglo-Dutch naval wars (1652–1654, 1665–1667, and 1672–1674) breaks out over control of the seas and shipborne trade.

1656
Oliver Cromwell petitions for Jews to be allowed to return to England; they had been expelled more than 350 years earlier under King Edward I following their demonization as anti-Christian murderers and moneylenders.

1658
Cromwell's reconquest of Ireland and the subsequent "Plantation" (the confiscation of territory and its granting to "Planters") sees two-thirds of Irish land in English or Scottish hands; it creates a long-lasting hatred of the English in Ireland.

1658–1707
The Mughal Empire reaches its greatest extent during the reign of Aurangzeb; he rules over approximately 160 million subjects and controls all but the tip of India's subcontinent.

1659
The Franco-Spanish War ends with the Peace of the Pyrenees; France takes Spain's place as Europe's major power, a position embodied by Louis XIV ("the Sun King") and his lavish court.

1660
The English Restoration returns Charles II to the throne following the collapse of the Commonwealth. The Royal Society is founded in London by royal charter in 1662; dedicated to advancing the understanding of science, it is the oldest scientific society in the world still in existence.

1661
Louis XIV assumes personal rule of France on the death of Cardinal Mazarin, declaring he will rule without a chief minister. Italian physician Marcello Malpighi's rese into the tissues of the human body provides the foundation for the science of microscopic anatomy, paving the way for advances in physiology, embryology, and practical medicine.

1664
The Second Anglo-Dutch War begins; the following year, the Dutch director-general of New Amsterdam peacefully yields the colony to the British.

1665
The Kingdom of Kongo in central Africa is plunged into 40 years of civil war. English physicist Robert Hooke provides a name for the smallest units of life that he observes through his compound microscope, calling them "cells."

1666
The Great Fire of London ravages the city for 4 days, destroying more than 13,000 houses and 87 churches.

1668
Spain finally recognizes Portuguese independence. The War of Devolution (1667–1668) ends with the Treaty of Aix-la-Chapelle; a triple alliance of England, Sweden, and the Dutch forces France to abandon its claims to the Spanish Netherlands. Charles II receives Bombay from his Portuguese bride and leases it to the English East India Company. The Bank of Sweden is founded; it is the world's oldest central bank.

c. 1670
The Empire of Mali collapses, after dominating west Africa for 400 years.

1672
English physicist Isaac Newton publishes the results of his experiments into the nature of light.

1672–1678
The Franco-Dutch War begins as Louis XIV invades the Dutch Republic with the support of England and Sweden; the war ends with the Dutch losing New Amsterdam (New York) to England (for a second time) and France gaining territories in the Spanish Netherlands.

1673
Louis Joliet and Jacques Marquette confirm that the Mississippi reaches the Gulf of Mexico, not the Pacific. Gabriel Arthur crosses the Appalachians via the Cumberland Gap—the main route west in the 18th century.

> *"The State, in choosing men to serve it, takes no notice of their opinions. If they be willing faithfully to serve it, that satisfies."*
>
> OLIVER CROMWELL, 1644

72
The number of years that Louis XIV occupied the French throne—the longest reign of any European monarch.

▷ **Peter the Great**
This portrait was made in 1715 by the French artist Jean-Marc Nattier, while the Russian leader was staying in Amsterdam.

1674–1699

6'8"
(200 cm). The exceptional height of Peter I (the Great), Czar of All Russia.

c. 1674
Dutch scientist and businessman Antonie van Leeuwenhoek is the first to observe and describe microbes—including protists and bacteria—through a microscope. He calls these tiny organisms "animalcules."

1675–1676
In North America, Metacomet ("King Philip"), chief of the Wampanoag, together with Mohawks of the Iroquois Confederacy, attacks English settlements in New England; the Treaty of Casco agrees to provide tribes with an annual measure of corn for each family settled on Native American lands.

1675–1711
St. Paul's Cathedral in London is rebuilt to a design by architect Christopher Wren, following the Great Fire of 1666.

1678
John Bunyan writes his Christian allegory, *The Pilgrim's Progress*.

1680
The Pueblo people in the colony of New Mexico rebel against the Spanish after the colonizers attempt to crush local religious practices and force Catholism on them. The Spanish retreat but, led by Pedro de Vargas, return to reconquer the Pueblos in 1692.

1682
English Quaker and philosopher William Penn founds Philadelphia, Pennsylvania. Robert de La Salle reaches the mouth of the Mississippi River and claims Louisiana for France. Louis XIV moves the French court from Paris to the palace at Versailles, which he enlarges into one of the largest residences in the world, as a symbol of his absolute power as French monarch. Peter I ("the Great") becomes Czar of All Russia; determined to modernize and reshape Russia as a western European power, he builds a new capital at St. Petersburg, abolishes the titles of *boyars* (nobles), centralizes government, reforms Russian society, restructures the army, builds a navy, and vastly expands the empire.

1683
The Polish king Jan III Sobieski lifts the Ottoman siege of Vienna at the Battle of Kahlenberg; Ottoman power in the Balkans collapses, and Sobieski is hailed as the savior of Christendom. The Qing Empire conquers Taiwan, bringing it under Chinese rule.

1685
After almost a century of tolerance, the Edict of Fontainebleau—issued by Louis XIV—makes Protestantism illegal in France; thousands of Huguenots flee to England, the Dutch Republic, and Prussia.

1686
The League of Augsburg (or Grand Alliance) is formed by England, the United Provinces of the Netherlands, and the Austrian Habsburgs to block Louis XIV's expansion plans in the Nine Years' War (1688–1697).

1687
English physicist Isaac Newton publishes his three-volume work *Philosophiæ Naturalis Principia Mathematica*, a cornerstone of scientific thought. In it, he states his universal law of gravity and his three laws of motion.

1688
In the Glorious Revolution, James II, the last Catholic king of England, Scotland, and Ireland, is overthrown by a union of English Parliamentarians and his own son-in-law, the Dutch prince William of Orange; William is then crowned William III and rules as joint monarch with his wife, Mary; James flees to France, lands in Ireland in 1689, and is defeated at the Battle of the Boyne in 1690. Aphra Behn, one of England's first professional writers, makes an early protest against slavery in her novel, *Oroonoko*. Explorer and navigator William Dampier is the first Englishman to visit Australia.

1689
The Treaty of Nerchinsk settles the border between China and Russia.

1690
The Qing Dynasty begins its conquest of Outer Mongolia (modern Mongolia); by the end of the 18th century, the Chinese empire has almost doubled in size.

1692
The city of Salem, Massachusetts is gripped by witchfinding hysteria; 20 people are convicted and executed for witchcraft.

> *"To explain all nature is too difficult a task for any one man or even for any one age. 'Tis much better to do a little with certainty …"*
>
> ISAAC NEWTON, 1704

◁ **Newton's telescope**
This is a replica of the first reflecting telescope made by Sir Isaac Newton and shown to the Royal Society in 1668. It uses a concave mirror, rather than a lens, to gather light.

1693

A massive earthquake devastates Sicily, southern Italy, and Malta; as many as 60,000 people are killed. The first women's magazine in English, "The Ladies' Mercury," is published in London; it runs for only 4 weeks.

1694

The Bank of England is established; it becomes the central banker for England's private banks, transforming the country's ability to finance wars and imperial expansion.

1696

Having moved its main Bengal trading station to Calcutta in 1690, the English East India Company starts building a large base, Fort William, on the bank of the River Hooghly.

1698

English engineer Thomas Savery patents the first steam-powered engine, which he designs to pump water from mine workings and to towns and cities. He demonstrates the machine to the Royal Society in London the following year.

1699

In response to religious repression under the Mughals, Guru Gobind Singh introduces the five Ks, the five outward signs of Sikhism, and charges his followers with the mission to secure Sikh rule in the Punjab.

60,000

The number of people killed in the 1693 earthquake in southern Italy.

▷ **Emperor Kangxi**
Painted on silk, this portrait shows the Qing leader Kangxi, who greatly enlarged the empire from 1600 and encouraged the spread of Western education in China.

REVOLUTION AND INDUSTRY 1700–1850

1700

1700–1721
A coalition led by Russia and including Poland and Denmark launches an attack on Sweden (the dominant power in the Baltic), beginning the Great Northern War; after 21 years of conflict, Sweden cedes the Baltic ports to Russia in the Treaty of Nystad and Russia emerges as a major power in the region.

as king of England, Scotland, and Ireland in place of William III and his wife Mary. This leads to the War of the Spanish Succession (1701–1714).

1704
The first edition of *The Boston News-Letter*, North America's oldest continuously published newspaper, is

> *"Generally speaking, the errors in religion are dangerous; those in philosophy only ridiculous."*
>
> DAVID HUME, FROM *A TREATISE OF HUMAN NATURE*, 1738–1740

1700
The Spanish king, Charles II, bequeaths his territories to Philip of Anjou, grandson of Louis XIV, the reigning French king; the rest of Europe is alarmed by the increase in French power.

1701
Jethro Tull invents the horse-drawn seed drill, an innovation in the Agricultural Revolution that raises British agricultural productivity in the 17th–19th centuries. Osei Tutu, ruler of Kumasi (in modern Ghana) leads the Asante confederation in west Africa to independence from the Denkyira nation; he takes the name Asantehene and uses his people's military prowess and the Atlantic coastal trade to triple the new state's territories and build a powerful empire.

1701
The English and Dutch ally to support Austria's claim to the Spanish throne and prevent unification of the French and Spanish thrones under the Bourbons Louis XIV and Philip of Anjou; Louis XIV sends an army to the Spanish Netherlands to defend them from the English and Dutch and recognizes James Francis Edward Stuart (the "Old Pretender"), son of the exiled James II,

published; it is subsidized and approved by the British governor. Boston emerges as the principal port for the Atlantic slave trade in the New World.

1705
British astronomer Edmond Halley is the first to predict a comet's return; when the comet returns exactly when he said it would, in 1758, it is named after him. The Husaynid Dynasty comes to power in Tunis, north Africa; it rules until 1957.

1707
Mughal India begins to decline following the death of the emperor Aurangzeb. The Acts of Union unite Scotland and England in the United Kingdom of Great Britain.

1709
Shipwrecked sailor Alexander Selkirk is discovered after 5 years alone on an island in the south Pacific; his story is probably one of the inspirations for Daniel Defoe's novel, *Robinson Crusoe*.

1712
British inventor Thomas Newcomen's improved version of Savery's steam engine is installed in a tin mine; Newcomen's engine was only bettered in 1775 by Thomas Watt's steam engine. Japan publishes its first encyclopedia, *Waka Sansai Zue*.

1713–1714
The Treaties of Utrecht (1713) and Rastatt (1714) end the War of the Spanish Succession and seek to balance power in Europe by separating the French and Spanish crowns; the Spanish Netherlands are ceded to Austria, and Britain receives Newfoundland, Nova Scotia, and Gibraltar.

1714
The Dutch-Polish scientific instrument maker Daniel Gabriel Fahrenheit invents the mercury thermometer; he sets the interval between the freezing and boiling points of water as 180 degrees, with 0 degrees being the temperature of a mixture of ice, water, and ammonium chloride.

1715
Following the death of Queen Anne (r. 1702–1714), the British crown passes to the elector of Hannover, George I. The Jacobite Rebellion, a Scottish Catholic attempt to restore the Stuarts to the throne, fails; Prince James Francis Edward Stuart flees to France. Louis XIV dies after ruling France for 72 years.

1715–1717
The Spanish in Texas encourage the Yamasee and other tribes of Native Americans to attack the British colonists in South Carolina.

1717
Handel's *Water Music*, a masterpiece of the Baroque period, is performed for the first time, on the River Thames in London. English pirate Edward Teach, known as Blackbeard, begins plundering ships in the Caribbean; in 1718, his alliance of pirates blockades Charleston, South Carolina, and takes the crew and passengers of the *Crowley* hostage, demanding the payment of a ransom.

1720
The War of the Quadruple Alliance ends. Austria, Britain, the Dutch Republic (United Provinces), and France succeed in forcing Philip V of Spain to abandon his claim to Sicily and Sardinia; however, Spain regains territory in Pensacola, Florida, and in the north of Spain (from France), and Texas is confirmed as a Spanish possession. It becomes fashionable among young English noblemen to visit Italy on the Grand Tour. In Venice, the artist Canaletto finds customers for his views of the canals among the English tourists.

1720–1721
Qing warriors oust the Zunghar Mongols from Tibet; they install Kelzang Gyatso as the 7th Dalai Lama, and Tibet remains under Chinese protection until 1912.

1721
The Russian Senate and Synod proclaim Peter the Great Emperor of All the Russias; many of Europe's rulers fear he will assert his authority over them.

200,000
The number of slaves carried by British ships in the 1710s and 1720s.

▷ **Fahrenheit's thermometer**
This 18th-century mercury thermometer is engraved with the Fahrenheit scale. On the reverse side is the signature of its inventor.

◁ **Piazza San Marco, Venice**
This view, painted around 1730 by Antonio Canal, better known as Canaletto, was a favorite of young gentlemen taking the Grand Tour from the 1720s.

Dutch explorer Jakob Roggeveen discovers Easter Island and explores some of the Samoan islands.

1722

Ghilzai Afghans rout Persian forces outside Isfahan, take the city, and assume control of the Persian Empire; in 1729, the Safavid Shah Tahmasp II recovers Isfahan with the help of the Afsharid Persians led by Nader Shah.

1724

The Kingdom of Dahomey in west Africa (now southern Benin) becomes the main supplier of slaves to European traders. Louis XIV's Code Noir, created for France's Caribbean territories, is introduced in Louisiana: it stipulates basic rights for slaves, but also legitimizes cruel punishments.

1725

Italian composer Antonio Vivaldi publishes *The Four Seasons*. In China, the *Imperial Encyclopedia*—10,000 volumes in length—is completed.

1727

Coffee begins to be cultivated in the Caribbean and South America. The Portuguese create the first coffee plantation in Brazil.

1728

Hindu Marathas defeat the Nizam of Hyderabad in the Palkhed Campaign; the campaign establishes Maratha supremacy over the Deccan plateau in southern India. Russia commissions the Danish-born cartographer Vitus Bering to explore the Siberian coast; he navigates the strait (now called the Bering Strait) that separates Siberia from Alaska.

1729

A rise in opium addiction prompts China to ban the sale and smoking of opium, which Britain is bringing from India to trade for Chinese goods; opium smugglers continue to cause problems for China into the 19th century.

1730

The Arabian state of Oman drives the Portu guese from the Kenyan and Tanzanian coasts and expands its dominions in east Africa by gaining control of Zanzibar.

1733

The last of the Thirteen Colonies established by Britain on North America's Atlantic coast is founded and named Georgia. In England, John Kay patents the flying shuttle for looms, which revolutionizes the textile industry. Prussia's army becomes the fourth largest in Europe after King Frederick William I introduces military service.

1735

English carpenter and clockmaker John Harrison creates the marine chronometer, a portable clock capable of keeping time at sea; it enables navigators to work out longitude at sea, considerably improving the safety of long-distance voyages.

1735–1738

Swedish botanist Carl Linnaeus publishes *Systema Naturae* on taxonomy—the science of identifying, naming, and classifying organisms. In 1749, he outlines his system of binomial classification, which uses two Latin names to identify an organism uniquely .

1736

Nader Shah deposes the last Safavid rulers in Persia and takes power himself; he founds the Afsharid Dynasty. French explorer and scientist Charles Marie de La Condamine sends samples of the flexible material, rubber, long-used by the Maya, to Paris.

1737

The Marathas extend their control over northern India at the expense of the Mughal Empire.

1738

David Hume, Scottish economist and empiricist, argues that there can be no knowledge beyond experience in his *Treatise on Human Nature*.

1739

Nader Shah's Persian force occupies Delhi and carries off the riches of the Mughal Empire, including the Koh-i-Noor diamond; Persia now controls all land north and west of the Indus River. The Treaty of Belgrade ends the Austro–Turkish War (1737–1739) and stabilizes the Ottomans' position in the Balkans. French-Canadian brothers Pierre and Paul Mallet open up a route from the Mississippi River to Santa Fe (New Mexico) in the first known crossing by a European of North America's Great Plains. The Viceroyalty of New Granada is created from territory now occupied by Panama, Venezuela, Colombia, and Equador.

1740

The rabbi Baal Shem Tov develops Hasidism in Poland; it is a mystical, revivalist Jewish movement that remains as an influential subgrouping within ultra-orthodox Judaism.

▷ **Nader Shah**
This contemporary painting depicts Nader Shah, the powerful Persian ruler whose military successes included the capture of Delhi in 1739.

◁ *Messiah*, original score
Handel reportedly wrote the 259-page score of his great work in about 4 weeks in 1741; it was first performed in the following year.

1742

1742
German composer George Frederic Handel's Baroque masterpiece *Messiah* is performed for the first time, in Dublin; it has its London premiere almost a year later. George II personally commands a British army in battle (against the French, in the War of the Austrian Succession); he is the last British monarch ever to do so.

1743
In an attempt to reach the Pacific coast, French brothers Louis Joseph and Francois de La Vérendrye become the first Europeans to see the Rocky Mountains, in Wyoming.

1744
Muslim theologian Muhammad ibn Abd al-Wahhab founds the Salafi movement, a conservative strand of Sunni Islam that advocates a return to fundamentals; he forms an alliance with the family of Muhammad ibn Saud that has lasted over 250 years in Saudi Arabia.

1745–1746
A second Jacobite rebellion again fails in its attempt to return the Stuarts to power in Britain; the Scottish highlanders supporting the "Young Pretender" (Prince Charles Edward Stuart, or "Bonnie Prince Charlie") are massacred by British troops at Culloden.

1747
The murder of Nader Shah, weakens the Persian Empire; Ahmad Shah Durrani breaks with Persia and creates the Durrani Empire, the last Afghan empire, which is the precursor of the modern state of Afghanistan. In west Africa, the kingdom of Dahomey (within present-day Benin) is invaded by the Yoruba of the Oyo Empire and forced to pay tribute.

1748
The Afghans invade Punjab. The Peace of Aix-la-Chapelle ends the War of the Austrian Succession (1740–1748); Maria Theresa, daughter of Holy Roman Emperor Charles VI, is finally confirmed as heir to the Habsburg lands.

1749
The kingdom of Mysore rises to prominence in south India. British Lieutenant General Edward Cornwallis founds the town of Halifax in Nova Scotia.

1750
The Treaty of Madrid defines the boundary between Spanish and Portuguese colonies in the New World; it recognizes the extent of Portuguese settlement in Brazil.

1751–1772
French philosopher Denis Diderot publishes his *Encyclopédie*—a catalog of human knowledge, including science, philosophy, politics, and religion—with the intention of helping people to think for themselves; it is a defining work of the Enlightenment.

1752
Diplomat, writer, publisher, and scientist Benjamin Franklin invents the lightning rod; it is one of his many innovations, which also include the Franklin stove, bifocal glasses, swimming fins, and the urinary catheter.

1755
The Great Lisbon Earthquake—and the accompanying tsunami—almost destroy the Portuguese city. The earthquake kills 60,000–100,000 people, making it one of the deadliest in history.

1756–1763
Frederick the Great of Prussia marches into Saxony, beginning the Seven Years' War, in which Hanover, Britain, and Prussia clash with France, Austria, Russia, Saxony, Spain, and Sweden.

8.5

Estimated strength of the Great Lisbon Earthquake on the Richter Scale.

1757
Robert Clive ("Clive of India") wins Bengal for the British East India Company at the Battle of Plassey. Prussia wins control of Silesia from Austria at the Battle of Leuthen.

1757–1759
William Pitt (later called "the Elder" to distinguish him from his son, who was also a notable politician) becomes Secretary of State in Britain and is the architect of the conquest of French possessions around the world; Britain

▷ *An Incident in the Rebellion of 1745*
This painting by Anglo-Swiss artist David Morier depicts the charge of the highlanders against the British infantry at the Battle of Culloden.

▷ **Benjamin Franklin**
An engraving of the American inventor playfully references his 1752 experiments with lightning, suggesting a conductor in an umbrella.

1764

takes Fort Duquesne in Pennsylvania, Senegal in west Africa, and the French Caribbean island of Guadeloupe from France. In 1759, General Wolfe captures Quebec and much of French Canada for Britain.

1759
The French are defeated by an Anglo–Prussian force at Minden, north Germany; the succession of British victories over the French in the Seven Years' War is described as the *Annus Mirabilis* (year of miracles).

1760
Rebellion spreads after a group of slaves led by Takyi, an enslaved Fante chief from west Africa, overruns plantations in the British colony of Jamaica; it is months before the revolt is suppressed. China's Qing Empire extends into Mongolia after a series of campaigns launched by the Qianlong Emperor.

1761
In India, the Maratha Empire is defeated by Afghans. The British seize Pondicherry, destroying French power in India.

1762
Catherine the Great is proclaimed Empress of Russia; her reign is characterized by wide-ranging reform and territorial expansion. In his book, *The Social Contract*, the French political philosopher Jean-Jacques Rousseau questions the relationship between governments and the governed, attesting that "Man is born free, and everywhere he is in chains"; his writing exerts great influence on the Enlightenment, the French Revolution, and the Romantic movement.

1763
The Seven Years' War ends with British naval supremacy asserted over France and Spain; taxes are raised to pay the national debt incurred in the war, fueling discontent in Britain and in its colonies. Rio de Janeiro becomes the capital of the State of Brazil, part of the Portuguese Empire.

1764
English weaver James Hargreaves invents the "Spinning Jenny," which increases cloth production eightfold.

◁ **Independence Hall**
The Assembly Room in this building in Philadelphia, Pennsylvania, is where the Declaration of Independence was adopted on July 4, 1776.

1768

1768
Russia wins the right to free navigation in the Black Sea in the Russo–Turkish War. English explorer and navigator James Cook sails from Plymouth aboard the vessel HMS *Endeavour* in his first voyage to the Pacific; he reaches New Zealand in 1769 and charts its entire coastline; he reaches mainland Australia in 1770, names Botany Bay, and begins charting the east coast. In Egypt, Ali Bey al-Kabir deposes the Ottoman governor and invades Syria, briefly securing the independence of what had previously been the Mamluk sultanate; the Ottomans regain control by 1773. Spanish Franciscan friars begin building a chain of missions along the Californian coast, founding the main west coast cities in North America, including San Francisco and Los Angeles.

1769–1771
The Industrial Revolution begins when Scottish inventor James Watt patents his version of the steam engine and British industrialist and inventor Richard Arkwright opens the first factory—a water-powered textile mill. The Industrial Revolution transforms the global economy, replacing the rural agricultural economies that exist in many countries with ones based on manufactured goods made in factories clustered in cities.

1772
Austria, Prussia, and Russia partition Poland, taking around one-third of its land and half its population.

1773
Captain Cook, aboard HMS *Resolution*, circumnavigates the continent of Antarctica during his second voyage to the southern hemisphere. In America, merchants dump a valuable cargo of tea into Boston Harbor as a protest against British taxes and governance; the incident becomes known as the Boston Tea Party. Britain responds by issuing the "Intolerable Acts" (1774), authorizing punitive measures against the 13 colonies; the colonies respond by boycotting British goods and trade.

1775–1783
The Revolutionary War (also called the American War of Independence) begins with a skirmish at Lexington between British troops (known as "redcoats") and local militiamen; George Washington is appointed commander-in-chief of the colonial forces. Britain's George III rejects the colonies' Olive Branch Petition and declares that the colonies are in revolt.

1776
The Declaration of Independence of the United States is signed on July 4; drafted by Thomas Jefferson, it asserts that all men are equal and have the right to "life, liberty and the pursuit of happiness," but enslaved Africans are excluded.

the Atlantic. Spain and the Dutch Republic support the American cause. Captain Cook is the first European to make contact with the Hawaiian Islands; he is killed there in a dispute over a boat. French chemist Antoine Lavoisier names oxygen and identifies its role in combustion.

1779
Boer (Dutch-speaking) settlers in South Africa clash with Xhosa tribes; it is the start of around 100 years of conflict between settlers and the indigenous peoples of the Eastern Cape.

1780–1782
Tupac Amaru II, a descendent of the last Inca ruler, leads around 75,000 Peruvian Indians and Creoles in an unsuccessful rebellion against Spanish colonial rule.

> *"The God who gave us life gave us liberty at the same time; the hand of force may destroy, but cannot disjoin them."*
>
> THOMAS JEFFERSON, 1774

1777
In the Treaty of San Ildefonso, Spain retains Uruguay but cedes the Amazon basin to the Portuguese.

1778
France formally recognizes the United States and enters the Revolutionary War against the British, sending a fleet across

1780
In the US, Pennsylvania secures the freedom of children born to slaves in the state in the future; the model is slowly adopted in other northern states.

1781
George Washington and his French allies defeat the British at Yorktown, and British General Charles Cornwallis surrenders after this last major battle in the Revolutionary War. German philosopher Immanuel Kant publishes

▷ **Shark-tooth knife**
This ceremonial Maori knife was collected in New Zealand during one of Captain Cook's voyages.

▷ *Dream of the Red Chamber*
This painting presents a scene from *Dream of the Red Chamber* (1791), one of China's Four Great Classical Novels.

17,000

The number of enemies of the French Revolution executed during the Reign of Terror.

his *Critique of Pure Reason*, a hugely influential attempt to answer the question, "What can we know?"

1782
The Treaty of Salbai ends the first of the three wars fought between the British East India Company and the Maratha Empire, ushering in a period of peace.

1783
Crimea is annexed by the Russian Empire under Catherine the Great. The first manned flight of a hot air balloon, designed by the Montgolfier brothers, is made in Paris. Britain recognizes American independence in the Treaty of Paris.

1784
The India Act allows the British East India Company to retain control of trade in India, but political matters are handled by three directors directly responsible to the British government.

1787
Sierra Leone, west Africa, is colonized by settlers who have freed themselves from slavery in America; the Society for the Abolition of the Slave Trade is founded in Britain. The US Constitution is drafted; it is ratified the following year. American inventor John Fitch runs trials of his steamboat on the Delaware River; he goes on to operate the first steamboat service in the US.

1788
The first convicts are transported to the British penal colony in Botany Bay, Australia; nearly 60,000 people settle in Australia over the next 50 years.

1789
George Washington becomes the first president of the United States. The French Revolution begins: the newly formed revolutionary National Assembly vows to produce a constitution; a Parisian mob storms the Bastille prison on July 14. Smallpox brought to Australia by the Europeans decimates the aboriginal population of Port Jackson, Botany Bay, and Broken Bay. Fletcher Christian leads a mutiny on HMS *Bounty*; Captain Bligh is cast adrift.

1790
Pemulwuy and his son Tedbury lead Aboriginal resistance around the Sydney area in Australia in a guerrilla campaign that lasts several years.

1791
Louis XVI attempts to flee Paris but is caught at Varennes; he is returned to the city and imprisoned in Tuileries Palace.

Amendments to the US Constitution included in the Bill of Rights include the freedom of religion. Cao Xueqin publishes his semiautobiographical work, *Dream of the Red Chamber*, which is considered one of China's Four Great Classical Novels (the others being *Romance of the Three Kingdoms*, *Journey to the West*, and *Water Margin*). Austrian composer Wolfgang Amadeus Mozart conducts the orchestra at the premiere of his opera *The Magic Flute* in Vienna.

1792
The French monarchy is abolished and the First French Republic declared. France declares war on Austria, Prussia, and Piedmont; fearful of the spread of revolution, the Netherlands, Spain, Austria, Prussia, Portugal, Sardinia, and Naples, and later Britain, form the First Coalition to fight France in a war that lasts until 1797.

1793
Louis XVI and his wife Marie Antoinette are executed in Paris; the Committee of Public Safety launches a "Reign of Terror" to eliminate enemies of the Revolution. American inventor Eli Whitney patents the cotton gin, which speeds up cotton processing and increases production in the American south. The Fugitive Slave Laws are passed in the United States; they allow southern slave owners to recover escaped slaves from northern states.

1794
France abolishes slavery in its colonies following the Haiti Revolution led by Toussaint Louverture.

1795
Following an unsuccessful uprising against Imperial Russia and the Kingdom of Prussia led by Tadeusz Kościuszko, Poland ceases to exist; its remaining territories are partitioned between Russia, Austria, and Prussia. The British seize the Cape Colony from the Dutch in South Africa.

1796
Edward Jenner pioneers the use of vaccines, inoculating a boy against smallpox by infecting him with the milder cowpox.

1796–1804
The White Lotus Rebellion in central China contributes to the decline of the Qing Dynasty. The White Lotus is a secretive political and religious movement with its roots in ancient Buddhist traditions.

10
The duration in minutes of the first flight ever made in a hot air balloon; it took place on September 19, 1783.

▷ **The Naked Maja**
Painted by Goya in 1797–1800, *The Naked Maya* (and a clothed companion piece) were commissioned by Manuel Godoy, a royal minister.

1797

200

Years that Jane Austen's *Pride and Prejudice* has remained in print.

1797–1800
Spain's Francisco de Goya paints *The Naked Maja*; he is later brought before the Spanish Inquisition on a charge of moral depravity but escapes prosecution.

1798
In the Wexford uprising, the Society of United Irishmen challenges British rule in Ireland and seeks political reform. An alliance, led by Britain, Austria, and Russia, forms to fight against France; it leads to the War of the Second Coalition (1799–1802). The British navy under Horatio Nelson defeats the French fleet at the Battle of the Nile after a French army commanded by Napoleon Bonaparte invades Egypt.

1799
Napoleon overthrows the French Revolutionary Directory government

and makes himself First Consul. Britain defeats and partitions Mysore in southern India. The Rosetta Stone is discovered by Napoleon's troops in Egypt; it holds the key to understanding Egyptian hieroglyphics.

c. 1800
Romanticism—which emphasizes inspiration, subjectivity, and the individual— emerges in Europe as an artistic, literary, and philosophical form in reaction to the rationalism of the 18th-century Enlightenment; German Romantic composer Ludwig van Beethoven finishes the *Moonlight Sonata* in 1801.

1801
The Act of Union links Britain and Ireland in a United Kingdom.

1801–1804
British mining engineer Richard Trevithick develops the first steam railway locomotive. His engine pulls a train in February 1804.

1803–1805
France sells its territories between the Mississippi River and the Rocky Mountains to the US in the Louisiana Purchase; the territory is extended south to New Orleans in 1804. The Lewis and Clark expedition crosses the western US and reaches the Pacific coast in 1805.

1804
Napoleon assumes the title Emperor of France; the Napoleonic Code declares all men equal and ends hereditary nobility. Uthman dan

Fodio creates the Sokoto Caliphate in west Africa after conquering the Hausa kingdoms; the caliphate is one of the largest states in Africa until defeated by the British in 1903 and abolished.

1805
Admiral Nelson and the British fleet defeat the Franco–Spanish fleet at the Battle of Trafalgar; France is victorious against Russia and Austria at the Battle of Austerlitz.

1805–1807
Britain, Sweden, Russia, Austria, and Prussia counter Napoleon's ambitions in the War of the Third Coalition.

1806
Napoleon abolishes the Holy Roman Empire and defeats Prussia; he attempts to deny the British trade through blockades called the Continental System.

1807
The Third Coalition ends when Russia switches sides and allies with France. The Slave Trade Act abolishes the slave trade in the British Empire.

1808
Napoleon declares his brother, Joseph Bonaparte, the new king of Spain, triggering the Peninsular War (to 1814) with the allied powers of Britain, Spain, and Portugal.

1810
The Mexican War of Independence (to 1821) begins a series of revolts against Spanish rule. Russia withdraws from Napoleon's Continental System and recommences trade with Britain.

1812
Napoleon invades Russia and goes on, after several victories over the Russian army, to occupy Moscow; his troops, however, are forced into a brutal retreat during the winter. Britain and the United States clash in the War of 1812; British troops set fire to the White House in Washington, D. C.

1812–1813
Egyptian forces retake Medina, Jeddah, and Mecca from the Wahhabi; Ottoman rule is reinstated in the area. The English paleontologist Mary Anning discovers the first complete ichthyosaur skeleton in Lyme Regis; her observations of fossils deeply influence scientific understanding of prehistoric life.

1813
In a turning point in the Napoleonic Wars, France is defeated at the Battle of the Nations (Leipzig) by an allied force of Britain, Prussia, and Russia. Simón Bolívar invades Venezuela and captures Caracas; he is proclaimed Libertador (Liberator). English novelist Jane Austen publishes *Pride and Prejudice*.

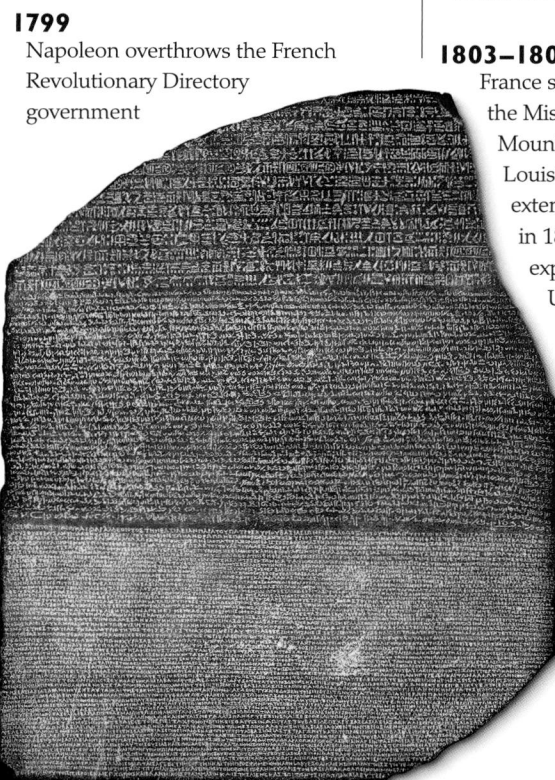

◁ **The Rosetta Stone**
Originating in Egypt in the 2nd century BCE, the Rosetta Stone was rediscovered in 1799. It is inscribed with Egyptian hieroglyphs, Egyptian demotic script, and Greek (top to bottom).

▷ **Napoleon's retreat**
This contemporary painting records the disastrous retreat of Napoleon's forces from Moscow in 1812, during which the starving troops were relentlessly harried by the Russian army.

1814

Paris is occupied by Anti-French allies who force Napoleon to abdicate and exile him to Elba; Louis XVI's brother, Louis XVIII, is placed on the French throne. After years of war, the balance of power in Europe is settled by the Congress of Vienna (1814–1815).

1815

Napoleon escapes from Elba, gathers an army, and marches to Paris at the start of the "Hundred Days" of his return to power. He is defeated at the Battle of Waterloo by British and Prussian forces under the Duke of Wellington and

Gebhard Leberecht von Blücher. Napoleon is exiled to St. Helena, where he dies in 1821; the French monarchy is again restored under Louis XVIII.

1816

The United Provinces of South America (modern-day Argentina) declares its independence from Spain. Shaka becomes chief of the Zulu nation and builds a powerful state in southern Africa.

1818

Spanish rebels defeat Spanish royalists at the Battle of Maipu and secure Chile's independence from Spain.

1819

Spain cedes Florida to the United States and settles the boundary between the Viceroyalty of New Spain and the US; Spain is soon forced to accept the loss of its colonies in Central and South America. Simón Bolívar becomes the first president of the new Republic of Gran Colombia, following independence from Spain. British colonial administrator Stamford Raffles founds the city of Singapore; it gives the British East India Company a base in the Malay peninsula from which to challenge Dutch dominance of the trading routes between China and India.

1820

The Khedive of Egypt, Muhammad Ali, orders an invasion of Sudan; the campaign brings him a vast empire.

1821–1822

Spain acknowledges Mexico's independence. Simón Bolívar secures Venezuela's independence in 1821, and Panama, Colombia, and Ecuador join it to form Gran Colombia, while José de San Martín proclaims an independent Peru. British scientist Michael Faraday creates the first electric motor; 10 years later, he discovers electromagnetic induction and builds the first electric generator.

C.R.

1822

1822
British mathematician Charles Babbage designs the first programmable computer, a calculator he calls a "difference engine." The Empire of Brazil becomes independent of Portugal.

1823
Joseph Smith starts to record revelations he claims were given to him in a vision by the Angel Moroni, creating what becomes the *Book of Mormon*; he founds the Church of Christ (later the Church of the Latter-Day Saints) in 1831. Costa Rica, Guatemala, El Salvador, Nicaragua, and Honduras declare their independence as a federal republic, the United Provinces of Central America.

1824–1825
José de Sucre wins Bolivia's independence from Spain at the Battle of Ayacucho in 1824. The following year,

George Stephenson and his son Robert open the first railway line to use a steam locomotive to pull passenger trains; it runs between Stockton and Darlington in northeast England.

1825–1832
Alexander Pushkin publishes *Eugene Onegin* in serial form; this novel in verse form becomes a classic of Russian literature.

1826
French inventor Joseph-Nicéphore Niépce makes the earliest surviving photographic prints.

1827
At the Battle of Navarino off the Peloponnese, Britain, France, and Russia sink three-quarters of the Ottoman fleet when the Ottomans refuse to give Greece its independence.

> *"Devoured by all crimes and extinguished by ferocity, the Europeans will not deign to conquer us."*
>
> SIMÓN BOLÍVAR, 1830

1828
Brazil and Argentina recognize Uruguay's independence. Russia acquires Armenia and declares war on the Ottomans.

1830
The French take control of Algeria. The French Bourbon monarch, Charles X, is replaced with his cousin Louis-Philippe, Duke of Orléans, in the July Revolution in Paris. Belgium demands independence from the Netherlands. Calls for political reform throughout Europe follow amid a wave of rebellion and social unrest. Native Americans are forcibly expelled from the southeast of the US after the Indian Removal Act strips them of rights; they head west along the "Trail of Tears" to Oklahoma. Simón Bolívar dies of tuberculosis.

1830–1832
Japanese artist Katsushika Hokusai produces his masterful woodblock print *Under the Wave off Kanagawa*.

1831
Belgium becomes independent and elects Leopold I as king.

1832
The Great Powers formally recognize Greek independence from the Ottoman Empire; the London Conference creates

the Greek monarchy, and in May, Prince Otto of Bavaria becomes the first modern king of Greece as Otto I.

1833
The Slave Emancipation Act bans slavery throughout the British Empire. The British Parliament passes the Factory Act, prohibiting the employment of children under the age of 9. Britain pushes the Argentinians out of the Falkland Islands (Las Malvinas) and begins settling British farmers there.

1835–1840
Around 12,000 Boers from Cape Colony make the "Great Trek" into the South African interior; the majority settle in what becomes Orange Free State, Transvaal, and Natal.

1836
At the Battle of the Alamo, around 200 Texan rebels attempt to hold off a Mexican army of several thousand; they are defeated, but soon Mexico has to recognize the independent Republic of Texas. The first wagon train taking settlers west heads out along the Oregon Trail; in 1841, wagon trains reach California.

1837
Queen Victoria ascends the throne of the United Kingdom, beginning a reign that lasts over 60 years.

2,500
Tons of opium imported into China in the year 1838.

◁ **Simón Bolívar**
This painting puts Bolívar, the "Liberator" of South America, into the famous pose in which Napoleon was pictured by French artist Jacques-Louis David in 1801. Bolívar died in 1830.

◁ *Under the Wave off Kanagawa*
Hokusai's most famous print, made in 1830–1832, is part of a series entitled *Thirty-Six Views of Mount Fuji*. The mountain is visible in the hollow of the wave.

1850 ▷

4

The number of words in the first telegraph message: "What hath God wrought?"

---

leader Abd al-Qadir, bringing an end to the Algerian war of independence.

1848
Karl Marx and Friedrich Engels publish *The Communist Manifesto*. Europe is wracked by political upheaval in the "Year of Revolution"; France overthrows the monarchy to form the Second Republic with Louis-Napoleon Bonaparte, as president. The California Gold Rush (1848–1855) begins when gold is found at Sutter's Mill.

1850
The Taiping Rebellion begins in China; it lasts 14 years, claims 20 million lives, and irrevocably damages the authority of the Qing Dynasty.

1838
Guatemala, Honduras, and Nicaragua become independent states. The slaughter of around 3,000 Zulus at the Battle of Blood River in southern Africa allows the Dutch Voortrekkers to establish the Republic of Natal.

1839
British artist J. M. W. Turner exhibits *The Fighting Téméraire*, in which he uses the scrapping of a ship that fought at the Battle of Trafalgar as an allegory of the decline of British naval power.

1839–1840
The First British colonists arrive in New Zealand.

1839–1842
Britain seeks to curb Russia's growing influence over Afghanistan in the First Anglo-Afghan War. China and Britain clash over trade and the British import of opium into China; Britain's superior navy wins this First Opium War; China opens five "treaty ports" to foreign trade and cedes Hong Kong.

1840
American artist and inventor Samuel Morse patents the electric telegraph in the US; he sends the first message in 1844. The formation of the Magnetic Telegraph Company in 1845 sees the technology spread quickly across the US; the first transatlantic telegraph cable is laid in 1858.

1841
The first operation using diethyl ether as an anesthetic is performed; its efficacy is later publicly demonstrated by William Morton at the Massachusetts General Hospital. In 1846, chloroform is first used as a medical anesthetic.

1842
Disputes surrounding the US–Canadian border are finally settled by the Webster–Ashburton Treaty.

1843
The British annex Natal; many Boers do not recognize British rule and trek over the mountains into the Orange Free State and Transvaal provinces.

1845–1854
The Irish potato crop fails due to blight and poor weather, causing the Great Famine. More than a million people die from starvation and associated diseases, but many more emigrate over the years that follow, leaving Ireland severely depopulated.

1846
US commodore James Biddle moors two warships in Edo Bay in an attempt to open up trade with Japan; however, Japan refuses to open its ports to foreign merchants. The US–Mexican War begins after the US annexes Texas (1845); Mexico surrenders in 1847 and cedes a vast swathe of territory to the United States. Danish philosopher Søren Kierkegaard (1813–1855) publishes *Concluding Unscientific Postscript to Philosophical Fragments*, a work that stresses the individual's unique position as self-determining agent and is a forerunner of existentialism. The French capture resistance

▷ **Queen Victoria's crown**
The Imperial State Crown, encrusted with precious stones, was made for the coronation of Queen Victoria in London in 1838.

PROGRESS AND EMPIRE 1850–1914

1851
The Great Exhibition, held in London's Crystal Palace, showcases goods and manufacturers from around the world to over 6 million visitors. Gold is discovered in Australia; in the next 10 years, 500,000 immigrants arrive.

1852
The British recognize the independent Boer republic of Transvaal in South Africa; the Orange Free State is recognized in 1854.

1853–1856
In the Crimean War, Britain, France, and the Ottomans curb Russia's ambitions in the Balkans; Sevastopol is besieged for a year; terrible losses among the French and British prompt Florence Nightingale to organize military nursing services.

1855–1856
Innovations by Britain's Henry Bessemer and Robert Mushet make the mass production of steel possible.

1856–1858
A mutiny by native troops against their British officers develops into an Indian Revolt; it is crushed by the British, who exile the last Mughal emperor and place India under the direct control of the British crown, ushering in the period known as the Raj (to 1947).

1856–1860
In the Second Opium War, Britain and France invade China and force it to open more ports to trade and to legalize opium imports.

1858–1870
The unification of Italy develops out of the Risorgimento movement: France and Piedmont-Sardinia join to end Austrian rule in northern Italy, and Garibaldi secures the south; Victor Emmanuel II is declared king in 1861.

> "All happy families resemble one another, but each unhappy family is unhappy in its own way."
>
> LEO TOLSTOY, FROM *ANNA KARENINA*, 1877

1859
Charles Darwin publishes *On the Origin of Species by Means of Natural Selection*, outlining his theory of evolution.

1859–1867
France captures Saigon (1859) and establishes protectorates in Cambodia (1863) and Cochin China (1867).

1860–1900
Thousands of Pacific Islanders are coerced or tricked into working as laborers in Peru, Australia, and Fiji.

1861
Russia abolishes serfdom. Abraham Lincoln, an abolitionist, becomes president of the United States; states in the south assert their right to own slaves in defiance of the federal government; seven secede from the Union to form a Confederacy. The Civil War begins with a Confederate attack at Fort Sumter. French chemist Louis Pasteur's experiments demonstrate that airborne microbes cause decay and disease.

1862
In the Civil War, there are Union victories at Shiloh and Antietam and a Confederate victory at the second Battle of Bull Run. Otto von Bismarck becomes prime minister of Prussia; he reforms the army and masterminds the unification of Germany in 1871.

1863
President Lincoln abolishes slavery in the south with the Emancipation Proclamation; the Union takes Vicksburg; Confederate general Robert E. Lee pushes into Pennsylvania, but is defeated at Gettysburg. Having been forced to open Japan to trade with the West, Emperor Komei orders the expulsion of "barbarians" from Japan.

1864
General Ulysses S. Grant becomes commander-in-chief of the Union forces; in the "March to the Sea," Union troops under the command of General William T. Sherman destroy railway lines and towns from Atlanta to Savannah, Georgia. The Paraguayan

president Francisco Solano López starts the War of the Triple Alliance, or Paraguayan War, against Brazil, Argentina, and Uruguay that will kill more than half of Paraguay's population.

1865
The Civil War ends, and General Lee surrenders on 9 April: at the end of the war, 625,000 men are dead and 500,000 are injured. Confederate supporter John Wilkes Booth assassinates President Lincoln on April 14 at Ford's Theatre in Washington, D.C. British surgeon Joseph Lister pioneers modern antiseptics.

1865–1869
Russian novelist Leo Tolstoy publishes *War and Peace*, which draws on his own experiences in the Crimean War (1853–1856).

1866
Prussia crushes Austria in the Seven Weeks War; Austria is excluded from Germany. Austrian monk Gregor Mendel's study of plant hybrids lays the foundations for the science of genetics.

1867
Prussia leads a North German Confederation of 22 states. Franz Josef I is crowned king of Hungary and rules the "dual monarchy" of Austria-Hungary. German social theorist and founder of modern communism Karl Marx publishes *Das Kapital*, outlining his theory of class struggle. The US buys the territory of Alaska from Russia for the sum of $7.2 million.

1868
The Tokugawa shogunate in Japan ends with the restoration of imperial power under Emperor Meiji; his reign (to 1912) sees Japan end its isolationism, implement constitutional government, and modernize.

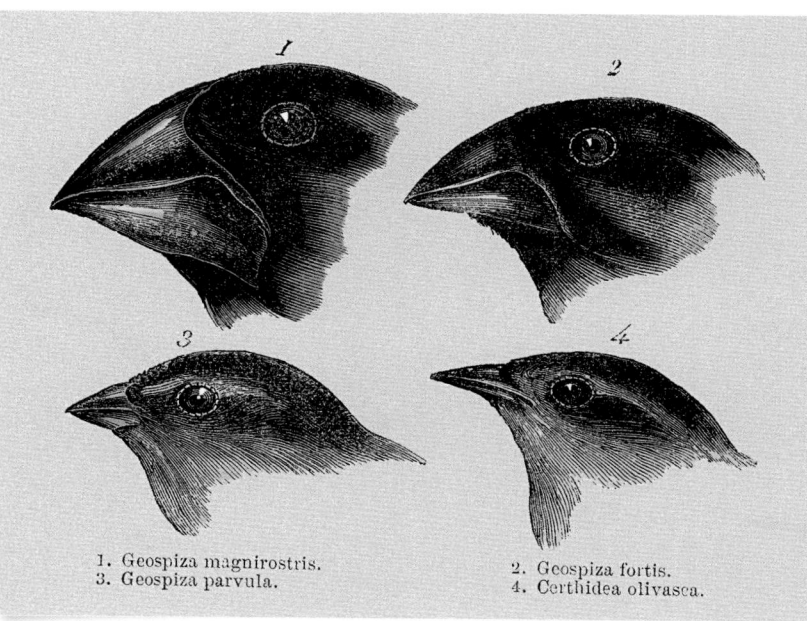

1. Geospiza magnirostris.
2. Geospiza fortis.
3. Geospiza parvula.
4. Certhidea olivasea.

◁ **Darwin's finches**
Comparative studies of the beak shape and size of different species of finch on the Galápagos Islands contributed to Darwin's theory of evolution, which was set out in his treatise of 1859.

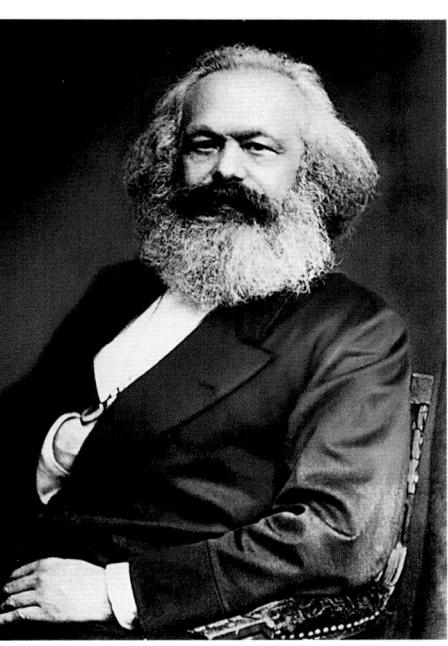

1885

1869
In Australia, the Act for "Protection and Management of Aboriginal Natives" gives the government extensive powers over the lives of aboriginals.

1870
Freed slaves in the US are given the right to vote by the Fifteenth Amendment to the Constitution.

1870–1871
The Franco-Prussian War precipitates the collapse of the French monarchy and the creation of the Third Republic; Wilhelm I of Prussia becomes Emperor of Germany, Bismarck its chancellor. The revolutionary Paris Commune demands independence; Paris is blockaded for 6 weeks before government forces violently suppress the commune.

1872
Denmark's Hans Christian Andersen publishes the last installment of his *Fairy Tales*. Cetshwayo succeeds Mpande as Zulu paramount chief; he leads his warriors against the British in 1879, but is captured at Ulundi and exiled to England.

1874
French impressionists, including Claude Monet and Paul Cézanne, hold their first exhibition in Paris. Alexander Graham Bell patents the telephone.

1875–1876
Russian composer Pyotr Ilyich Tchaikovsky writes *Swan Lake*; German composer Richard Wagner's four-opera *Ring Cycle* is first staged in Bayreuth.

1876
Lt. Colonel George Custer and his troops are killed by Sioux and Cheyenne warriors at the Battle of Little Bighorn in the Indian Wars. Britain's Queen Victoria is proclaimed Empress of India.

1877
The British annex Transvaal in South Africa when gold is found there.

1877–1878
The Balkans are reshaped when a Russian-led coalition wins the Russo-Turkish War; Bulgaria, Serbia, Romania, and Montenegro all gain independence from the Ottoman Empire.

1878
Joseph Swan patents the electric bulb in Britain; Thomas Edison soon develops electric lighting for public use.

1880–1881
In the First Anglo-Boer War, Boers in Transvaal rebel against British rule and succeed in establishing the South African Republic.

1881
Mohammed Ahmed proclaims himself the Mahdi in Sudan and begins an 18-year war against the Khedivate of Egypt and later the British in Egypt. The French occupy Tunisia. The "Czar Liberator" Alexander II is assassinated; an anti-Jewish pogrom in Russia follows, forcing many Jews to flee to western Europe, the US, and Palestine.

1882
Germany, Austria-Hungary, and Italy form the Triple Alliance against France. The British occupy Egypt after the Anglo–Egyptian War between Britain and Egyptian and Sudanese forces.

1884
General Gordon begins to evacuate the British from Sudan; he dies when Mahdist forces break their 10-month-

20,000
People killed when the French army suppressed the Paris Commune.

long siege of Khartoum and massacre the Egyptian garrison and 4,000 Sudanese civilians in January 1885.

1884–1885
European powers meet at the Berlin Conference to agree on the rules of colonization in Africa.

1885
German engineers Gottlieb Daimler and Karl Benz independently build the first automobiles powered by an internal combustion engine. The Indian National Congress is the first modern nationalist movement to emerge in the British Empire in Africa and Asia.

▷ **Custer's last stand**
General Custer makes a brave stand, with guns in both hands, as his soldiers go down in defeat, in this romanticized 1889 lithograph of the Battle of the Little Bighorn in Montana, June 25, 1876.

1888

1888–1889
Emperor Pedro II frees Brazil's remaining slaves but refuses to compensate their owners; in 1889, he is overthrown in a coup, and Brazil becomes a republic.

1889
The Eiffel Tower opens in Paris on the centenary of the French Revolution. Dutch artist Vincent van Gogh paints *The Starry Night*, a landmark of the Post-Impressionist movement.

1890
The Battle of Wounded Knee brings an end to the Indian Wars between the Great Plains Native American tribes and the US Army (1854–1890). In West Kimberley, Australia, the aboriginal resistance fighter Jandamarra declares war on European invaders and prevents them settling for 6 years.

1891
German philosopher Friedrich Nietzsche declares "God is dead" in *Thus Spake Zarathustra*. Work begins on the Trans-Siberian Railway connecting Moscow and Vladivostock.

1893
New Zealand is the first country to grant voting rights to women. Sigmund Freud and Joseph Breuer publish *On the Physical Mechanism of Hysterical Phenomena*, a founding work in the emerging field of psychoanalysis.

1894–1895
Japan gains Formosa (Taiwan) and China recognizes Korean independence after the First Sino–Japanese War.

1894–1897
In the Hamidian massacres, around 250,000 are killed in anti-Christian pogroms, directed primarily against Armenians, in the Ottoman Empire.

1895
French brothers Auguste and Nicolas Lumière show the first motion picture, lasting 46 seconds, in Paris. Italian inventor Guglielmo Marconi builds the first wireless, paving the way for the development of radio technology. German physicist Wilhelm Röntgen discovers X-rays.

1896
Emperor Menelik II secures Ethiopia's independence by defeating an invading Italian army at the Battle of Adowa.

1896–1898
The Yukon and Klondike gold rushes fuel a short-lived boom around Dawson City, Canada.

> *"All our scientific and philosophic ideals are altars to unknown gods."*
>
> WILLIAM JAMES, LECTURE AT HARVARD UNIVERSITY, 1884

1898
In the Spanish–American War, Spain cedes Puerto Rico, Guam, and the Philippines to the US and grants Cuba independence; the US annexes Hawaii.

1899
In Colombia, 100,000 die in the War of a Thousand Days.

1899–1902
In the Second Anglo–Boer War, thousands of Boer women and children die in British camps; British "scorched earth" attacks force the Boers to recognize British sovereignty in South Africa.

1900
Waves of immigrants swell the population of the US to around 75 million. Southern Nigeria becomes a British protectorate when French rivals begin to threaten British traders in the Niger Delta. In China, Qing power weakens: Chinese nationalists known as "Boxers" besiege European and US legations in Beijing until an international relief force captures the city in 1901; Russia occupies southern Manchuria. German physicist Max Planck outlines his quantum theory, that radiation comes in discrete packets (quanta) of energy.

1901
Oil is struck at Spindletop in Texas; the US becomes the world's leading oil producer and benefits from the first modern consumer boom. Six colonies in Australian federate to form the Commonwealth of Australia; the Immigration Restriction Act bars people of non-European descent from settling in the country; the policy remains in place until 1950. The death of Britain's Queen Victoria ends a 63-year reign. Italian composer Giuseppe Verdi dies, and thousands line the streets of Milan for his funeral.

1902
US philosopher William James publishes *The Varieties of Religious Experience*, exploring the nature of religion.

1903
In the US, Brothers Wilbur and Orville Wright make the first controlled, sustained flight of a powered aircraft. In Britain, suffragettes Emmeline and Christabel Pankhurst found the Women's Social and Political Union, which advocates the use of civil disobedience to secure the vote for women. Marie Curie wins the Nobel Prize for her work on radioactivity and the discovery of radium.

1904
Britain and France sign a series of agreements, known as the Entente Cordiale; Russia joins them in the Triple Entente in 1907.

1904–1905
Japan and Russia clash over Manchuria in the Russo–Japanese War; Russia is forced to leave Manchuria.

1905
Political and social unrest in the Russian Empire forces Czar Nicholas II to sign the October Manifesto, authorizing the creation of an elected legislature (the Duma). Norway secures independence

◁ **The Starry Night**
In 1889, Vincent van Gogh painted this view from the window of his room at the Saint-Paul asylum in Saint-Rémy. The turbulence in his mind is reflected in the expressive color and form of the work.

◁ **English suffragettes**
This 1908 photograph shows the suffragettes Emmeline Pankhurst and her daughter Christabel after leaving Bow Street police station in London, where they had been imprisoned.

when the union between the kingdoms of Norway and Sweden (of 1814) is dissolved. The German physicist Albert Einstein describes the relationship between space and time in his special theory of relativity; his general theory of relativity in (1915) explains the effect of gravity on spacetime.

1905–1907
The Maji-Maji rebellion threatens German settlers in East Africa.

1906
Britain launches HMS *Dreadnought*, a new class of battleship and a major development in the arms race with Germany. Mahatma Gandhi develops *satyagraha*, his policy of civil disobedience and passive resistance to be used against British rule in India.

1907
The self-governing colonies of Australia, Canada, and New Zealand are given the status of dominions of the British Empire. Belgian-American Leo Baekeland invents Bakelite, an early plastic. The rebuilt Great Mosque at Djenné in Mali is the world's largest clay building.

1908
The Young Turks—a Turkish nationalist party—demand reform in the Ottoman Empire; Austria-Hungary annexes Bosnia-Herzegovina, and Bulgaria wins recognition of its independence. The first Model T cars are produced at Ford's factory in Michigan.

1909
US Navy engineer Robert Peary claims to have reached the North Pole.

1910
In Portugal, revolutionaries depose King Manuel II and declare a republic. China invades Tibet and deposes the 13th Dalai Lama; it is a short occupation, and Tibet is independent by 1912. Japan annexes Korea. The Union of South Africa is founded as a dominion of the British Empire; it becomes a sovereign republic in 1961. The first Hollywood film is made: D. W. Griffith's *Old California*.

1910–1915
American geneticist Thomas Hunt Morgan's study of *Drosophila melanogaster* fruit flies confirms the link between the inheritance of a specific trait with a particular chromosome.

1910–1920
The Mexican Revolution leads to a new constitution (1917), presidential elections (1920), and agrarian, educational, and political reform.

1911–1912
A revolutionary alliance overthrows the Qing in China; the last emperor Puyi abdicates; Sun Yat-sen becomes the first president of the new Chinese Republic and forms the Kuomintang (Nationalist Party). Italy invades the Turkish province of Libya; it retains control there until 1947. US marines are sent to Honduras to protect American interests. In December, Norwegian explorer Roald Amundsen becomes the first man to reach the South Pole; a month later, British explorer Robert Falcon Scott's expedition reaches the pole, but none of the team survive the return journey. New Zealand-born Ernest Rutherford discovers the atomic nucleus. Later, in 1919, he successfully splits the atom in the world's first artificially created nuclear reaction. US archaeologist Hiram Bingham reaches the lost Inca city of Machu Picchu.

1912
The luxury liner RMS *Titanic* sinks on her maiden voyage after hitting an iceberg; 1,513 passengers and crew perish. German geophysicist Alfred Wegener uses fossil evidence and rock formations as the basis for his theory of continental drift, paving the way for the understanding of plate tectonics. Indian polymath Rabindranath Tagore publishes *Gitanjali*; it earns him a Nobel Prize.

1912–1913
The Balkan League, backed by Russia and comprising Serbia, Bulgaria, Greece, and Montenegro, defeats the Ottoman Empire in the First Balkan War; the Ottomans lose their remaining territory in Europe. In the Second Balkan War (1913), Greece and Serbia defeat Bulgaria to gain Macedonia; Serbia's increasing power and alliance with Russia alarm Austria-Hungary and Germany.

1913
Russian composer Igor Stravinsky's avant-garde ballet *The Rite of Spring* causes a sensation and near riot at its premiere in Paris. Danish physicist Niels Bohr describes the structure of the atom. The Ford Motor Company in the US installs the world's first moving assembly line; by 1927, there is one car for every six Americans. British suffragette Emily Davison dies when she throws herself under the king's horse at the Epsom Derby. Unionists in Ulster create the Ulster Volunteer Force to block Ireland gaining more autonomy (Home Rule) from the British; in response, the Irish Volunteers are formed in Dublin.

▷ **Model T Ford**
Mass production of Henry Ford's vehicle made driving affordable. More than 15 million of the cars were produced between 1908 and 1927.

THE MODERN WORLD 1914–PRESENT

1914

1914

The Panama Canal opens, connecting the Pacific and Atlantic Oceans. Austrian Archduke Franz Ferdinand is assassinated in Sarajevo on June 28, 1914, by a Bosnian-Serb revolutionary hoping to end Austro-Hungarian rule in Bosnia and Herzegovina; his death ignites World War I. Austria-Hungary declares war on Serbia on July 28; Russia mobilizes in Serbia's defense. Germany declares war on Russia and France on August 1 and implements the Schlieffen Plan, invading France in the hope of swiftly shutting down the war on the Western Front. Britain declares war on Germany and sends the British Expeditionary Force to France; it drives the Germans back in the Battle of the Marne; the Germans begin digging trenches that eventually total 25,000 miles (40,000 km) in length. Russia invades Austria and East Prussia but is defeated at Tannenberg. The Ottoman Empire enters the war in October. British troops invade Turkish-ruled Iraq and German East Africa. Japan joins the war, attacking German holdings in China and the Pacific.

1,197

Number who died in the sinking of the ocean liner RMS *Lusitania* in 1915.

1915

The US occupies Haiti (to 1934) and the Dominican Republic (1916–1924), securing American influence in the region. Germany begins unrestricted submarine warfare, sinking all ships on sight, but temporarily halts the operation after the sinking of the liner RMS *Lusitania* threatens to bring the US into the war. Germany makes the first use of poison gas at the Second Battle of Ypres. Allied troops land at Gallipoli and attempt to end the Turkish blockade in the Dardanelles; they suffer almost 250,000 casualties and begin to evacuate in December. Italy revokes the Triple Alliance, abandons neutrality, and declares war on Austria-Hungary. Countries across Europe abandon the Gold Standard; currency is no longer convertible into gold. The Armenian genocide begins when the Ottoman Empire rounds up Armenians suspected of harboring sympathy for the Russians; by 1923, 1.5 million Armenians have been killed or left to die in concentration camps.

1916

The British crush the nationalist Easter Rising in Ireland. Great Britain introduces conscription for all men aged 18–41. Huge offensives result in mass casualties (400,000 at Verdun, more than a million at the Somme), with little territory gained on the Western Front. The British Grand Fleet and the German High Sea Fleet clash off the coast of Denmark in the Battle of Jutland, the only major naval battle in World War I. Arab nationalists revolt against the Ottoman Empire when Hussein bin Ali, Sharif of Mecca, proclaims himself leader of the Muslim

world with the intention of creating a unified Arab state. The Sykes–Picot agreement between Britain and France agrees on how the Middle East will be divided in the event of the Ottoman Empire's defeat. Jeannette Rankin is the first woman elected to the US Congress.

1917

The Russian Revolution erupts in food riots, strikes, and a military mutiny; Czar Nicholas II abdicates, and a provisional government is formed. Bolsheviks under Vladimir Ilyich Lenin and Leon Trotsky seize power; civil war breaks out. In March, the US enters World War I after discovering German foreign minister Arthur Zimmerman's telegram urging Mexico to reclaim Texas, New Mexico, and Arizona. The British

◁ **The last emperor of Russia**
Czar Nicholas II of Russia, pictured here with his family in 1913, was forced to abdicate in 1917. The family was imprisoned and executed on the orders of Bolshevik leader Vladimir Lenin.

1923

Germany becomes a republic. Charles I abdicates, ending the Habsburg monarchy in Austria–Hungary. Female suffrage is granted to British women over 30. Constance Markievicz becomes Britain's first female member of parliament.

"Politics begin where the masses are, not where there are thousands, but where there are millions; that is where serious politics begins."

VLADIMIR ILYICH LENIN, 1918

begin a new push at Ypres; fought in a sea of mud, the campaign ends in slaughter at Passchendaele in Flanders, but at the Battle of Cambrai, the British use of massed tanks provides a way to break the stalemate of trench warfare. The Balfour Declaration, made without consulting Britain's Arab allies, signals Britain's support for a Jewish homeland in Palestine. The first Pulitzer Prizes are awarded in the US.

1918
Czar Nicholas II and his family are shot near Yekaterinburg. Russia exits World War I, losing Poland, Ukraine, Belarus, Finland, and the Baltic states in the Treaty of Brest-Litovsk with the Central Powers. The Allies check Germany's Spring Offensive and launch a counter-offensive, which breaches the defenses of the Hindenburg Line. The war ends as the Ottoman Empire signs an armistice on October 30, Austria on November 3, and Germany on November 11; total casualties number around 37 million, including 15 million dead. Kaiser Wilhelm II abdicates;

585,000
The number of Allied and German troops killed at Passchendaele.

1918–1919
More than 50 million die during the Spanish influenza global pandemic.

1919
The Paris Peace Conference dismantles the German, Austrian, and Ottoman Empires; the Treaty of Versailles imposes war reparations on Germany, set at 132 billion Deutsche Marks in 1921, and restricts its military power. The Weimar Republic is established in Germany. Lenin establishes the Communist International (known as Comintern) to promote communism worldwide. Benito Mussolini founds the Fascist party in Italy to combat socialism. British aviators John Alcock and Arthur Whitten Brown make the first nonstop transatlantic flight. In the Irish War of Independence (to 1922), the Irish Republican Army mounts a campaign against the British government's forces, who are known from the color of their uniforms as "Black and Tans."

1920
The US begins Prohibition (a ban on the production and sale of alcohol). Russia's Red Army is driven back outside Warsaw after its invasion of Poland. The League of Nations is established to prevent conflicts by committing members to collective security and disarmament. Women in the US are enfranchised through the 19th amendment to the Constitution, adopted on August 18.

1921
Six million perish in Russia's famine; victorious in the civil war, Lenin begins to rebuild Russia's economy with the New Economic Policy, allowing a return to private enterprise. The Communist Party of China (CPC) is founded.

1922
The former Russian Empire becomes the Union of Soviet Socialist Republics (USSR). Britain declares Egypt an independent kingdom but retains a military presence to protect the Suez Canal. In Italy, Mussolini and his Blackshirts threaten to march on Rome and seize power; to avoid conflict, King Victor Emmanuel III makes Mussolini prime minister and head of a Fascist government. The British Empire, the largest empire in history, reaches its greatest extent; it covers one-quarter of the world's land. The African National

Congress is formed to combat discrimination against blacks in South Africa. Writer James Joyce publishes his experimental novel *Ulysses* in Paris. British archaeologist Howard Carter uncovers the tomb of Tutankhamun in Egypt. The British Broadcasting Company (BBC) is founded. The Anglo-Irish treaty (signed 1921) ends the Irish War of Independence; it divides Ireland into the Irish Free State and Northern Ireland, with separate parliaments in Dublin and Belfast; William Cosgrave becomes the Irish Free State's first prime minister. Ireland erupts in civil war (to 1923) over the Anglo-Irish Treaty.

1923
After securing Turkish independence in the Turkish War of Liberation (from 1919), President Mustafa Kemal (Ataturk) begins reforming the Turkish republic into a modern secular state. The Treaty of Lausanne settles the long conflict between the Ottoman Empire and France, Britain, Italy, Japan, Greece, and Romania and sets the borders of the Turkish Republic. Germany is crippled by war reparations payments and hyperinflation; the German currency reaches 242 million marks to the dollar; Adolf Hitler, leader of the National Socialist (Nazi) Party, is imprisoned after attempting to grab power in the Munich Beer Hall putsch; while in jail, he writes *Mein Kampf*. Miguel Primo de Rivera leads a military coup in Spain and becomes dictator.

◁ **The Battle of Cambrai**
A British tank is upturned and trapped in an enemy trench in France in 1917. The battle was an early example of tank warfare, although the machines proved unreliable.

◁ **Funerary mask of Tutankhamun**
The discovery by Howard Carter in 1922 of Tutankhamun's intact tomb caused a worldwide sensation. Tutankhamun was an Egyptian pharaoh who ruled from around 1332 to 1323 BCE.

◁ The first televised images
This photograph shows an image on the screen of John Logie Baird's pioneering television system in 1926. The face is that of Baird's business partner, Oliver Hutchinson.

1924–1936

1924

Vladimir Lenin dies and Joseph Stalin becomes leader of the Soviet Union after an intense power struggle with Leon Trotsky, Lev Kamenev, and Grigory Zinoviev (who were all members of the first Politburo, founded in 1917). Mahatma ("Great Soul") Gandhi becomes leader of India's National Congress and drives the campaign for an end to the British Raj.

1925

Mussolini becomes dictator in Italy and takes the title *Il Duce* (The Leader). Nationalists in Syria and Lebanon revolt against the French mandate to prepare the countries for self-rule. The Locarno Pact (signed in Switzerland) guarantees peace between Germany, France, Belgium, Britain, and Italy; it restores relations with Germany as a precursor to Germany joining the League of Nations in 1926. The Geneva Protocol prohibits the use of chemical and biological weapons; the US and Japan reject the agreement.

1926

In China, Chiang Kai-shek succeeds Sun Yat-sen as leader of the Chinese Nationalist Party (Kuomintang). Scottish inventor John Logie Baird gives the first public demonstration of television. Reza Khan Pahlavi becomes shah of Iran and begins to modernize the country; his dynasty rules until 1979. Military coups overthrow the governments in Poland and Portugal.

1927

Chiang Kai-shek purges Chinese communists in the Shanghai massacre. In the Soviet Union, Leon Trotsky is expelled from the Communist Party on Stalin's orders and exiled (1929); he is assassinated in Mexico in 1940 by a Spanish-born agent of the NKVD (the organization that what would later become the Soviet Secret Police). American aviator Charles Lindbergh makes the first solo flight across the Atlantic. *The Jazz Singer*, starring Al Jolson and directed by Alan Crosland, is the first talking motion picture. Oil is discovered in Iraq.

1928

Stalin's Five Year Plan (the first of many Soviet plans) aims to transform the Soviet Union through rapid industrialization and the collectivization of farms. Kuomintang forces take Beijing and declare the Nationalist Government of China with Chiang Kai-shek as Chairman; Mao Zedong leads communist resistance in remote rural areas. Penicillin, the first antibiotic, is discovered by Scottish biologist and pharmacologist Alexander Fleming.

1929

Riots in Palestine see Arabs attack Jewish immigrants. The Kenyan politician Jomo Kenyatta travels to London to press the Kikuyu Central Association's demands for equality in Kenya. The Stock Market Crash bursts the American stock market bubble, plunging the world into the Great Depression, which lasts until the late 1930s. American astronomer Edwin

Hubble calculates that the Universe is expanding and has more than 100 billion galaxies. Belgian cartoonist Hergé publishes the first Tintin comic strip, *Tintin in the Land of the Soviets*. The BBC runs trials on its first TV broadcasts.

1930

Hundreds of thousands of peasants are sent to gulags (forced labor camps) for resisting the Soviet Union's mass collectivization of farms. The Vietnamese Communist Party is founded by Ho Chi Minh. Thousands join Gandhi's Salt March to protest against government

monopolies and British rule in India; Gandhi and around 60,000 others are arrested.

1930

Mass unemployment and political extremism follow the collapse of the world economy: Hitler's Nazi party becomes the second largest political party in Germany; an army revolt brings autocrat Getúlio Vargas to power in

> *"Nonviolence is the first article of my faith. It is the last article of my faith."*
>
> MAHATMA GANDHI, 1922

Brazil. Ras Tafari becomes Emperor of Ethiopia, taking the name Haile Selassie; in Jamaica, the cult of Rastafarianism views Ras Tafari as the Black Messiah.

1931

In Spain, King Alfonso abdicates after elections return a Republican government. Japan occupies Manchuria; in 1934 it installs Puyi (China's last emperor) as emperor of the new state, which is known as Manchukuo. The

▷ Hitler's Brownshirts
Hitler is pictured surrounded by members of the "Storm Detachment," or Brownshirts, who provided him with close protection and disrupted the campaigns of his opponents.

British Commonwealth is formalized by the Statute of Westminster. Belgian astronomer Georges Lemaître argues that quantum theory supports the idea that the universe came into being from the explosion of a "primeval atom" holding all mass and energy; his ideas are later developed into the Big Bang Theory. The Empire State Building opens in New York.

1932

Britain terminates its mandate in Iraq, and the kingdom becomes independent; Ibn Sa'ūd unifies the dual kingdoms of Hejaz and Najd in the new Kingdom of Saudi Arabia. Paraguay and Bolivia go to war over control of the Gran Chaco lowland plain; Paraguay wins, but by 1935, more than 85,000 have died. With more than 12 million people unemployed in the US, newly elected president Franklin D. Roosevelt promises "a new deal" to salvage the economy. In Germany, the Nazis become the largest party in fresh elections to the Reichstag but continue to be excluded from government. American aviator Amelia Earhart becomes the first woman to fly solo across the Atlantic; she disappears over the Pacific in 1937 while attempting to fly around the world.

1932–1933

Soviet collectivization results in the "Great Famine"; 6–8 million peasants die over the winter, including 4–5 million in Ukraine.

2,500,000

The number of people who fled the Great Plains during the years of the US Dust Bowl.

1933

Adolf Hitler is appointed Chancellor of Germany and soon creates a one-party state in which opposition is brutally suppressed by the SS and Gestapo. A nationwide boycott of Jewish shops and businesses begins; the first Nazi concentration camp opens at Dachau; in a crackdown on "un-German" culture, students burn books and Germany's famous school of modern art and architecture, the Bauhaus, is closed. Germany quits the League of Nations. The World Economic Conference fails to agree to global measures to alleviate the Depression. Japan leaves the League of Nations after it declares the occupation of Manchuria illegal.

1934

Hitler authorizes the execution of members of the Nazi Party's paramilitary wing, the Storm Detachment (or Brownshirts), in the Night of the Long Knives; President Hindenburg dies and Hitler becomes *Führer* (leader). The Nazis are banned in Austria by its dictatorial chancellor Engelbert Dollfuss; he is assassinated by Nazis. The Soviet Union joins the League of Nations.

1934–1935

In the Long March, Mao Zedong and his communist forces retreat around 6,000 miles (10,000 km) from the Jiangxi Soviet (a communist base formed in 1931) to Yan'an, evading Chiang Kai-shek's nationalist forces.

1934–1937

Thousands of destitute farmers migrate west to California from the Great Plains after drought, intensive farming, and giant dust storms strip the land of topsoil in the 1932 Dust Bowl disaster.

1935–1939

The US passes several Neutrality Acts that seek to maintain American isolationism and prevent the country from being drawn into foreign conflicts.

1935

Hitler builds Germany's army through conscription (banned by the Treaty of Versailles); the Nuremberg Laws deprive Jews of German citizenship and ban marriage between Jews and non-Jews. Emperor Haile Selassie leads resistance to Italian invasion of Ethiopia; economic sanctions are imposed on Italy.

1936

Germany moves troops unopposed into the demilitarized Rhineland; Britain and France begin expanding their armed forces. Italy annexes Ethiopia; Haile Selassie warns "It is us today; it will be you tomorrow. " With the Anti-Comintern Pact, Germany and Japan declare their hostility to communism and agree that neither country will make any treaties with the USSR; Spain and Italy join the pact in 1937, forming the basis of the Axis Powers. Stalin begins the Great Purge of the Communist party, government officials, army leaders, intellectuals, and peasants with a series of show trials of "Old Bolsheviks;" between 680,000 and 2 million people are killed over the next 2 years. Spain is thrown into Civil War when General Francisco Franco leads a nationalist revolt against the newly elected left-wing Popular Front government. The Nationalists are backed by Germany and Italy, while the Republicans are backed by the Soviet Union and supported by International Brigades of volunteers from Europe and North America; the Nationalists prevail in 1939, and Franco becomes dictator.

◁ *Spirit of St. Louis*
Charles Lindbergh piloted this single-engined aircraft on his flight from New York to Paris in 1927. He was the first to cross the Atlantic from west to east. It took 33 hours and 30 minutes.

1936–1943

1936–1939

Arabs in Palestine revolt against the British administration of the Palestine Mandate; they demand an end to unrestricted Jewish immigration; plans to resolve the crisis by partitioning Palestine between Arabs and Jews have to be abandoned, and the British agree to restrict Jewish immigration.

1937

Japan invades northern China, sparking the Second Sino-Japanese War, which continues throughout World War II; by 1938, Japanese troops have captured Nanjing, Shanghai, Hankou, and Guangzhou, massacring more than 1,000,000 civilians and using rape as an instrument of war in the "Rape of Nanjing"; resistance comes from both the Kuomintang and the communist 8th Route Army. Brazil's President Vargas uses the threat of a communist coup to create a new constitution, the Estado Novo (New State), giving himself dictatorial powers. Pablo Picasso paints the gigantic *Guernica*, a response to the German bombing of the town of Guernica in northern Spain during the Spanish Civil War. The German-built *Hindenburg*, then the world's largest airship, explodes on arrival in the US.

The British engineer Frank Whittle successfully runs trials on his turbojet engine; it is used in Britain's first jet aircraft, tested in 1941.

1938

In the *Anschluss* (unification), German troops march on Vienna and annex Austria in direct contravention of the peace terms of 1919. Hoping to avoid war, Britain and France continue their policy of appeasement and allow Germany to annex Sudetenland from Czechoslovakia. On November 9, *Kristallnacht* (the Night of Broken Glass), the Nazis orchestrate attacks on Jewish homes, businesses, and schools in Germany and Austria.

> *"Never in the field of human conflict was so much owed by so many to so few."*
>
> WINSTON CHURCHILL, 1940

▷ **Star of David badge**
Following a decree issued by the German Reich in 1941, all Jews over the age of 6 were forced to wear this badge, inscribed with the word "Jude" (German for "Jew").

Japan declares its intention to create a New Order in East Asia, essentially acknowledging its imperial ambitions; the US begins to finance Chiang Kai-shek's resistance to Japan.

1939
World War II begins: Germany invades Czechoslovakia; Britain and France guarantee Polish independence; Hitler and Mussolini sign the Pact of Steel military alliance; the Soviet Union and Germany sign the Molotov-Ribbentrop nonaggression pact (named after the foreign ministers of the two nations); Germany invades Poland on

September 1; Britain and France declare war 2 days later. Poland is partitioned by the Soviet Union and Germany. The Soviet Union attacks Finland. Merchant ships crossing the Atlantic begin to sail in convoy; 114 Allied ships are sunk in the first year of war.

1940
Germany unleashes the *Blitzkrieg* (lightning war) on Europe: Denmark, Norway, the Netherlands, Belgium, Luxembourg, and France are invaded. Britain evacuates 338,000 men from the beaches of Dunkirk, France. France surrenders; the French government

under Marshal Pétain relocates to Vichy; Charles de Gaulle positions himself as the figurehead of the French Resistance. Italy declares war on Britain and France. Britain's Royal Air Force (RAF) blocks the German *Luftwaffe*'s attack in the Battle of Britain, forcing Hitler to abandon plans to invade Britain. Germany begins the mass transportation of prisoners to the Auschwitz concentration camp in southern Poland. The *Luftwaffe* begin mass bombing raids on British cities; the Blitz lasts until 1941; Allied bombers retaliate with raids on Germany. The US restricts sales of iron and oil to Japan in an attempt to curb Japanese aggression; the US Pacific Fleet is moved to Pearl Harbor, Hawaii. The British hold off the Italian invasion of Egypt. Japan, Germany, and Italy form an alliance in the Tripartite Pact.

1941
Germany begins Operation Barbarossa: 3 million troops invade the USSR and advance on Leningrad, besieging the city; by December, the Germans are exhausted and forced to retreat from Moscow. Japan annexes Indochina. Japan bombs the US fleet in Pearl Harbor on December 7 and invades the Philippines and European colonies in Southeast Asia, securing control of the Pacific; the US enters the war.

1942
At the Wannsee Conference in Berlin, senior Nazi officials are briefed on the systematic deportation and extermination of Jews across Europe; by 1945, 6 million Jews have been killed.

A US victory against the Imperial Japanese Navy at the Battle of Midway in the Pacific proves a turning point in the war in the Pacific. Japan begins construction of the Burma–Thailand railway using British, Australian, and Dutch prisoners of war and native laborers; within 3 years, more than 100,000 of them die under appalling conditions. In the Battle of Stalingrad (to 1943), Germans capture the city but are encircled by Soviet troops; few survive the freezing conditions during the siege, and the German defeat is a turning point in the war; more than 1.7 million soldiers are killed, wounded, or captured in the battle. In North Africa, German troops under Erwin Rommel reach the borders of Egypt; defeated by the British at El Alamein, and under pressure from advancing Allied troops, the Axis Powers in Africa surrender (1943). The Quit India campaign sees leaders of the Indian National Congress imprisoned.

1943
Jews in the Warsaw Ghetto resist German efforts to transport them; 13,000 die in the uprising, and most of the remaining 50,000 Jews are shipped to Nazi death camps. At Kursk, the Soviets win the largest tank battle in history. US and British troops invade Sicily; Mussolini is removed from power, and Italy surrenders.

1,000
The number of Jewish synagogues burned on *Kristallnacht*.

◁ *Guernica, 1937*
Pablo Picasso painted this violent, mural-sized masterpiece in response to the deliberate bombing by Nazi aircraft of civilians in the Basque village of Guernica.

▷ **The Potsdam Conference**
Clement Attlee of Great Britain, President Harry S. Truman of the US, and Soviet Premier Joseph Stalin (seated from left to right) pose at the Potsdam Conference in Germany in 1945.

1944

1944

The 900-day siege of Leningrad is lifted. Polish troops break the German defensive line in Italy at Monte Cassino; the Allies take Rome. The Allies launch an invasion of occupied France, landing more than 130,000 troops in Normandy on D-Day (June 6); over the coming weeks, more than 3 million Allied troops land in France. Hitler survives an assassination attempt by officers and high officials. General Charles de Gaulle's Free French forces and resistance fighters liberate Paris on August 25. Japanese naval pilots start to mount *kamikaze* suicide attacks on US naval forces in the Pacific. At the Battle of the Bulge in the Ardennes, Hitler launches Germany's final offensive;

German tanks break through the American front line but are defeated in a counterattack; the German troops retreat to Germany.

1945

British Prime Minister Winston Churchill, US president Franklin D. Roosevelt, and Soviet premier Joseph Stalin meet at Yalta to discuss Europe's postwar reorganization. The Red Army takes Poland and marches on Berlin. Hitler commits suicide, and the war in Europe ends when Germany surrenders on May 8. At the Potsdam Conference, Germany, Austria, Berlin, and Vienna are divided into four occupation zones, and parts of Poland, Finland, Romania, Germany, and the Balkans are assigned

to Soviet control. Rather than invade Japan, the US drops the world's first atomic bombs on the Japanese cities of Hiroshima on August 6 and Nagasaki on August 9; Japan surrenders on August 15, ending the war in the Pacific. The Nuremberg trials of leading Nazi war criminals begin. Vietnam is declared an independent republic by Ho Chi Minh ("He Who Enlightens"), leader of the Viet Minh nationalist coalition. The president of the Indian National Congress, Jawaharlal Nehru, demands full independence from Britain. Fifty-one countries sign the newly created United Nations (UN) Charter for the promotion of peace, security, cooperation, and self-determination of nations.

1946

Churchill refers to an "iron curtain" falling across Europe as communist governments are set up in Yugoslavia (1945), Bulgaria and Albania (1946), Poland and Romania (1947), Czechoslovakia (1948), and Hungary (1949). China's communists and nationalists resume civil war. France recognizes Vietnam, Cambodia, and Laos as autonomous states, but resistance to colonial authority soon triggers the First Indochina War (1946–1954).

1947

India becomes independent; to avoid civil war between Hindus and Muslims, a new state (Pakistan) is created in the Muslim-majority areas in the northwest

and northeast of India, 1,000 miles (1,600 km) apart; widespread violence nonetheless follows partition as Muslims flee India and Hindus leave Pakistan. The United States' European Recovery Plan, or Marshall Plan, aims to help Europe's shattered economies recover, thus ensuring a market for American exports and making the spread of communism in western Europe less likely. The UN proposes to divide Palestine into separate Jewish and Arab states. The sound barrier is broken for the first time by American test pilot Chuck Yeager in a Bell X-1 aircraft.

1948

Gandhi is shot and killed by a Hindu fanatic. The South African government begins to increase the amount of legislation that supports its policy of apartheid; the Population Registration Act (1950) makes it compulsory for people to carry a pass identifying their racial group. The state of Israel is proclaimed; soon after, it repulses an invasion by five Arab states (Egypt, Iraq, Lebanon, Syria, and Transjordan) in the First Arab–Israeli War (to 1949). In the first crisis of the Cold War, the Soviet Union blockades Berlin, hoping to force the West to withdraw from West Berlin. Burma and Ceylon become independent. Korea is partitioned into

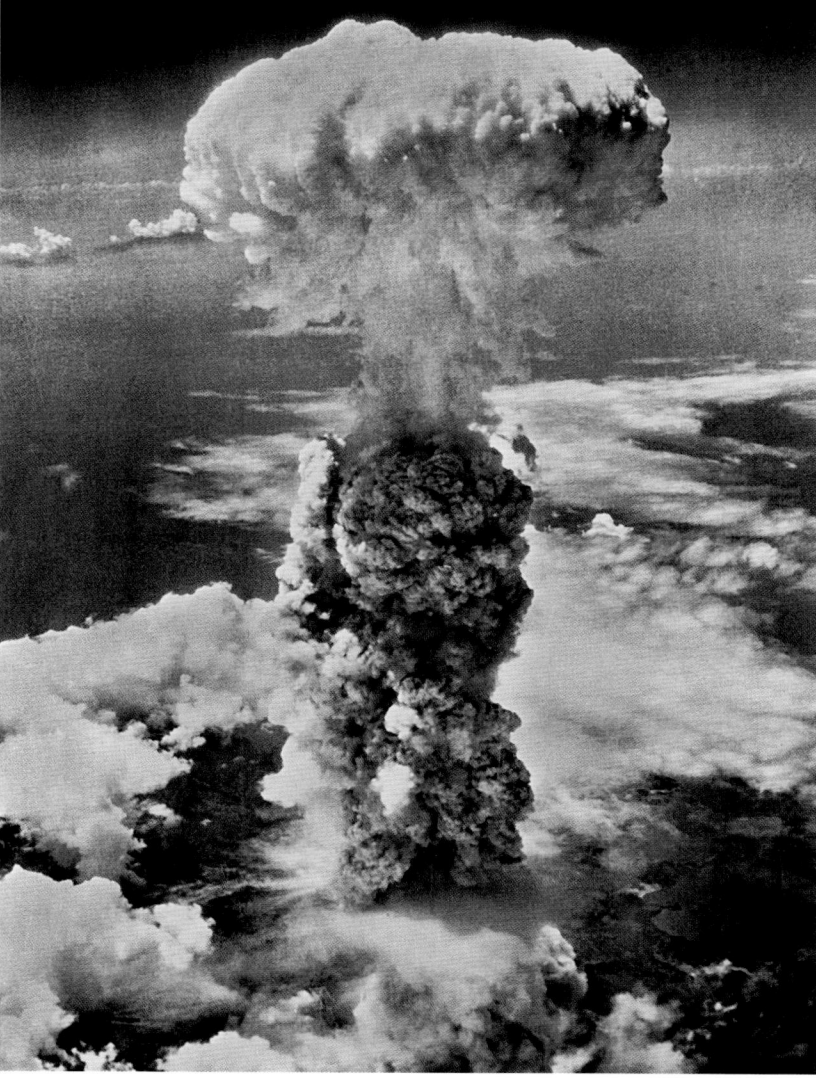

> *"The seeds of totalitarian regimes are nurtured by misery and want."*
>
> PRESIDENT HARRY S. TRUMAN, 1947

◁ **The bombing of Hiroshima**
On August 6, 1945, an American B-29 bomber dropped an atomic bomb over the city of Hiroshima; approximately 80,000 people were killed in the initial blast alone.

the Republic of Korea in the south and the Democratic People's Republic in the north. Communists in Malaya begin a guerrilla war against British colonial rule; the Malayan Emergency (1948–1960) continues for 3 years after Malaya gains independence (1957). The Universal Declaration of Human Rights is adopted by the United Nations. The World Health Organization (WHO) is set up in Geneva, Switzerland.

1949

Germany is divided into East and West; East Germany is part of the Communist Bloc. Twelve nations join in the North Atlantic Treaty Organization (NATO), a military alliance for mutual defense. Eire becomes the Republic of Ireland. The Soviet Union tests its first atomic bomb. After 4 years of war, the Dutch are forced to accept the independence of the East Indies (Indonesia). The Communists emerge victorious in China's civil war; Mao Zedong declares the People's Republic of China; Chiang Kai-shek and the remnants of the nationalist Republic of China government flee to Taiwan. Following the Arab–Israeli War, the Gaza Strip is controlled by Egypt and the West Bank of the River Jordan by Jordan.

1950

Senator Joseph McCarthy begins his investigation into alleged Communist activity in the US; over the next 4 years, many people—including prominent Hollywood actors and writers—are accused and blacklisted. The Korean War (to 1953) begins when North Korea invades South Korea; in the first major armed confrontation of the Cold War, US and UN troops support the South, while the Soviet Union and China back the North. Tibet is incorporated into the People's Republic of China, but formally remains autonomous under the Dalai Lama.

1951

Mohammad Mosaddegh is appointed prime minister of Iran and nationalizes the oil industry; 2 years later, a US-sponsored coup to replace Mosaddegh fails.

1952

East Germany tightens control of its border with West Germany in an attempt to stop the flow of its citizens to the West. Gamal Abdel Nasser seizes power in a military coup in Egypt. Britain drafts troops into Kenya to deal with the anti-colonial Mau Mau Rebellion (to 1960). At Bikini Atoll in the Pacific, the US tests the first hydrogen bomb.

1953

Stalin dies; under his successor, Nikita Khrushchev, there is a thaw in relations between Russia and the West. The shah returns to Iran after Mosaddegh is ejected in a coup; US and UK support strengthens the shah's position as he reprivatizes the oil industry. In the UK, Francis Crick and

10 megatons of TNT. The yield of the first hydrogen bomb. It is 100 times more powerful than the Hiroshima bomb.

James Watson build on the work of Rosalind Franklin and Maurice Wilkins and discover the double helix structure of DNA (deoxyribonucleic acid), the molecule that governs heredity. New Zealand explorer Edmund Hillary and Sherpa Tenzing Norgay scale Mount Everest, the world's highest mountain.

1954

French rule in Indochina collapses: Vietnam is partitioned into Ho Chi Minh's Democratic Republic of Vietnam in the north and the State of Vietnam in the south; Laos and Cambodia also become independent. The first nuclear-powered submarine, USS *Nautilus*, is launched. CERN, the European Organization for Nuclear Research, is established in Geneva, Switzerland, to examine the fundamental structure of the universe.

1955

The Eastern Bloc counters NATO with its own military alliance, the Warsaw Pact. Juan Perón is ousted as president in Argentina. Rosa Parks becomes an inspirational figure in the US Civil Rights movement when she breaks Alabama's race laws by refusing to give up her seat on a bus to a white man. The Vietnam War (to 1975) begins: South Vietnam rejects reunification with communist North Vietnam; Viet Minh sympathizers, or "Viet Cong" (Vietnamese Communists), in the South begin an insurgency; the US offers support to Ngo Dinh Diem's government in South Vietnam.

1956

Soviet troops invade Hungary when Prime Minister Imre Nagy withdraws from the Warsaw Pact and asks the UN to recognize Hungary as a neutral state. Egypt's President Nasser nationalizes the Suez Canal; British and French forces occupy the canal but are forced to withdraw, a sign of their declining power. Decolonization continues as France withdraws from Morocco and Tunisia and Britain withdraws from Sudan.

▷ **The conquest of Everest**
Sir Edmund Hillary and Tenzing Norgay are photographed on Mount Everest on May 28, 1953; they reach the summit the next day.

◁ The beginning of the jet age
Entering service with Pan American Airlines in 1958, the Boeing 707 replaced an earlier generation of piston-engined airliners, making international air travel safer and more affordable.

1957

1957
Six countries join the European Economic Community (EEC), created by the Treaty of Rome. The USSR launches the *Sputnik 1* satellite and begins the Space Age. President Sukarno of Indonesia nationalizes Dutch businesses, expels all Dutch nationals, and imposes martial law. Sudan and Ghana are the first British colonies in Africa to gain independence.

1958
Forced industrialization in Mao's "Great Leap Forward" plunges China into one of history's worst famines; over 35 million are worked, starved, or beaten to death. General de Gaulle is elected president of the Fifth Republic in France. NASA (North American Space Agency) is established. The Boeing 707 begins commercial flights across the Atlantic, revolutionizing air travel.

1959
The Cuban Revolution makes Fidel Castro the first communist head of state in the Americas. The Dalai Lama and 80,000 Tibetans flee to India when China takes full control of Tibet. North Vietnamese guerrillas invade South Vietnam; two US soldiers are killed. The US gains its 49th and 50th states: Alaska and Hawaii.

1960
In Africa, 12 French colonies, Congo (Belgian), and Nigeria and Somalia (British) gain independence. The Organization of the Petroleum Exporting Countries (OPEC) is founded to coordinate policy and provide members with economic and technical aid. John F. Kennedy becomes US president.

Civil war (to 1964) breaks out in the Congo; the UN is nearly bankrupted by its attempts to restore order there. The South African government begins the forced resettlement of black South Africans to so-called "black homelands." The US physicist Theodore H. Maiman builds the first laser.

1961
The Soviet rocket *Vostok 1* carries Yuri Gagarin into space. American troops begin to arrive in South Korea. South Africa withdraws from the British Commonwealth and becomes a republic. In the Bay of Pigs invasion, US-trained Cuban exiles invade Cuba, aiming to overthrow Castro's government; they are soon defeated. East German troops build the Berlin Wall; it eventually extends over 100 miles (160km), dividing the city and encircling West Berlin.

1962
Algeria, Uganda, Jamaica, and Trinidad and Tobago become independent. The first communication satellite, *Telstar I*, relays international telephone calls and transmits its first television signals from Europe to the US. Nuclear war between the US and the Soviet Union is narrowly avoided during the Cuban Missile Crisis.

1963
The Test Ban Treaty, signed by the US, USSR, and UK, ends nuclear testing in the atmosphere. At the March on Washington, civil rights leader Martin Luther King Jr. addresses 250,000 protesters. President Kennedy is assassinated in Dallas; Lee Harvey Oswald is arrested, but is shot soon after. Singapore, Sarawak, and Sabah join the 11 states of the Federation of Malaya to create Malaysia. Jomo Kenyatta becomes prime minister, then president, of a fully independent Kenya.

1964
The UN sends troops to Cyprus (which has been independent from Britain since 1960) after civil war breaks out between the Greek and Turkish populations; Turkish Cypriots are confined to small enclaves of the island. US President Lyndon B. Johnson signs the Civil Rights Act into law, creating equal rights for all, regardless of race, religion, or color. Nelson Mandela, leader of the anti-apartheid Spear of the Nation movement, is sentenced to life imprisonment in South Africa for conspiring to overthrow the state.

"Palestine is the cement that holds the Arab world together, or it is the explosive that blows it apart."

YASSER ARAFAT, 1974

1965
The US begins bombing North Vietnam in the hope that Ho Chi Minh will stop Viet Cong operations in South Vietnam; 500,000 US troops land in South Vietnam. Pakistani troops invade the Indian zone in Kashmir; the UN intervenes to secure a ceasefire.

1966
Mao's Cultural Revolution aims to rid China of "impure elements;" by 1976, much of China's cultural heritage is destroyed in the process.

1967
Indonesia, Malaysia, the Philippines, Singapore, and Thailand form the Association of Southeast Asian Nations (ASEAN). Martial law is imposed in Greece after a military coup. Israel seizes Sinai, the Gaza Strip, West Bank, Golan Heights, and Jerusalem in the Six-Day (or Arab–Israeli) War. One million Igbo people flee Hausa violence for eastern Nigeria, which secedes as Biafra; civil war ensues, and Biafra is reincorporated into Nigeria in 1970. Australian Aborigines are finally given full citizenship rights.

▷ The assassination of JFK
President Kennedy and his wife smile at the crowds lining their motorcade route in Dallas, Texas, on November 22, 1963, just minutes before the president is assassinated.

▷ **Moon landings**
Apollo 11 Lunar Module pilot Buzz Aldrin walks on the surface of the Moon on July 20, 1969. Aldrin and Armstrong spent less than 22 hours on the lunar surface.

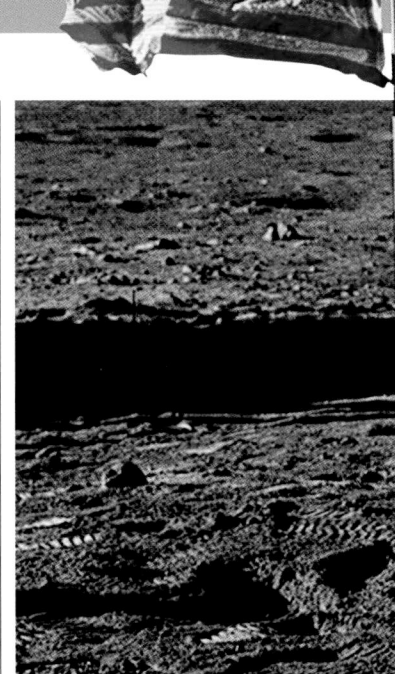

1968

The Viet Cong capture the majority of South Vietnam's towns and villages in the Tet Offensive; the US public is convinced that the Vietnam War is unwinnable. Martin Luther King Jr. is assassinated in Memphis; his death sparks race riots across the US. Warsaw Pact troops invade Czechoslovakia and crush the Prague Spring reform movement. Saddam Hussein plays a prominent role in helping the socialist Ba'ath party seize power in Iraq.

1969

Yasser Arafat becomes leader of the Palestine Liberation Organization (PLO). Mu'ammar al-Gaddafi deposes King Idris and forms the Libyan Arab Republic. Sectarian violence escalates in Northern Ireland; the Troubles continue until 1998. American astronauts Neil Armstrong and Buzz Aldrin are the first men on the Moon.

1970

The Nuclear Non-Proliferation Treaty, ratified by the US, the Soviet Union, Britain, and 40 other countries, aims to prevent the spread of nuclear weapons.

1971

Idi Amin seizes power in Uganda. India supports the Mukti Bahini in the War of Liberation in East Pakistan; East Pakistan becomes the independent state of Bangladesh. Qatar becomes independent from Britain. The People's Republic of China joins the UN.

1972

On Bloody Sunday, British troops open fire on Catholic demonstrators in Londonderry, Northern Ireland; support for the Irish Republican Army grows. Palestinian terrorists kill members of Israel's team at the Munich Olympics. In the Philippines, President Ferdinand Marcos imposes martial law.

1973

US troops finally withdraw from Vietnam. The IRA begins bombing targets in mainland Britain. In the US-backed military coup led by General Augusto Pinochet, Chile's Marxist president Salvador Allende commits suicide (or is murdered) after delivering a farewell speech over the radio. In the Yom Kippur (or October) War, Israel repulses Arab attacks led by Egypt and Syria; OPEC embargoes oil exports to the US and the Netherlands, Israel's main supporters, causing oil shortages and spiraling inflation; oil-importing countries begin to find other sources of oil and invest in coal, gas, and nuclear power. Denmark, Ireland, and the UK join the EEC. Mohammad Daoud Khan seizes power and establishes the Republic of Afghanistan. Companies IBM and Xerox develop prototype personal computers, and the first telephone call from a handheld cellphone is made in the US.

1974

Democracy is restored in Portugal when a bloodless coup brings an end to the dictatorial Estado Novo regime. Portugal's African colonies gain independence: Guinea Bissau in 1974; Cape Verde, Angola, Mozambique, and São Tomé and Príncipe in 1975. Turkish troops occupy northeast Cyprus; Greek Cypriots flee to the south, and the country is partitioned. US President Richard Nixon resigns after being implicated in the Watergate bugging scandal. English scientist Stephen Hawking outlines his theory on black hole radiation, known as "Hawking radiation." Isabel Péron succeeds her husband in Argentina and is Latin America's first female president.

1975

The fall of Saigon to North Vietnamese troops ends the Vietnamese War; North and South Vietnam are reunified in 1976. Civil war breaks out in Lebanon (to 1990). Pol Pot's Khmer Rouge seizes power in Cambodia and begins a reign of terror in which, by 1979, over 1 million people are killed. Civil war (to 2002) erupts in Angola between US-funded guerrillas and South African troops and communist guerrillas funded by the USSR and supported by Cuban troops. Indonesia invades East Timor; decades of guerrilla resistance and brutal suppression follow. The monarchy is restored in Spain when General Franco dies; Juan Carlos I is king.

10 The number of people to have landed on the surface of the Moon since the *Apollo 11* mission of 1969.

◁ **Khomeini in Iran**
Ayatollah Khomeini waves to supporters after his
return to Tehran in February 1979. He declares an
Islamic republic and is appointed Iran's political and
religious leader for life.

◁ **Khomeini in Iran**
Ayatollah Khomeini waves to supporters after his
return to Tehran in February 1979. He declares an
Islamic republic and is appointed Iran's political and
religious leader for life.

1976

1,000,000 The estimated number of people on both sides killed during the Iran–Iraq War of 1980–1988.

1976

Chairman Mao dies; the Gang of Four (who controlled the government in line with Mao's wishes) are arrested, two are sentenced to death, the others are imprisoned. Syrian peacekeeping troops enter Lebanon. In Soweto, South Africa, 176 people are killed in clashes with the police during anti-apartheid protests.

1977

Prominent black rights activist Steve Biko is tortured to death in prison in South Africa. Pakistan's Prime Minister Zulfikar al Bhutto is overthrown in a military coup; accused of conspiracy, he is executed in 1978. Mengistu Haile Mariam takes control of the Dergue (ruling body) in Ethiopia and begins to build a communist state.

1978

Israeli troops enter Lebanon; the Camp David Accords pave the way for the Egypt–Israel Treaty in 1979. In Afghanistan, Daoud is assassinated and an unstable regime takes over. Vietnamese troops invade Cambodia; in 1979, the Khmer Rouge is overthrown; civil war in Cambodia continues until 1991, when Vietnam withdraws. The first "test-tube baby" is born following conception by *in vitro* fertilization (IVF). Numerous strikes by public sector workers in Britain create the "winter of discontent."

1979

Idi Amin's brutal regime in Uganda is overthrown; he dies in exile in Saudi Arabia in 2003. The US-backed Somoza regime in Nicaragua is overthrown by left-wing Sandinistas; their opponents, backed by the CIA, form a militia known as the Contras. In Iran, an Islamic revolution sees Ayatollah Khomeini return to Iran when the shah is ousted; he leads the Islamic Republic of Iran until his death in 1989; Iranian militants seize 63 hostages from Tehran's US embassy. Soviet troops invade Afghanistan to suppress an Islamist revolt (to 1989) by US-armed guerrilla Mujaheddin forces; 6 million refugees flee to Iran and Pakistan. Panama regains control of the Panama Canal Zone; it gains control of the canal itself in 1999. Saddam Hussein becomes President of Iraq with absolute power.

1980

Rhodesia becomes independent as Zimbabwe; Robert Mugabe becomes Prime Minister. Saddam Hussein's Iraq invades Iran; the Iran–Iraq war (to 1988) results in huge casualties on both sides. The US ends aid to Nicaragua and funds the Contras in Honduras. Polish dockyard strikers form Solidarność, a trade union independent of Communist Party control that swiftly develops, under Lech Wałęsa, into a political movement. The WHO ensures smallpox is the first infectious disease to be eradicated.

1981

President Anwar Sadat of Egypt is assassinated by Muslim terrorists angry at the peace agreement with Israel. Pope John Paul II and US president Ronald Reagan are both shot, but survive. The US hostage crisis in Tehran ends after 444 days, when Iran releases 52 hostages. King Juan Carlos survives a military coup, in which rebels hold members of the Spanish parliament hostage. AIDS (Acquired Immune Deficiency Syndrome) is first identified in the US; scientists identify the HIV virus responsible for AIDS in 1984. The first "keyhole" surgery is performed. Polish government imposes martial law.

1982

Argentinian troops invade the Falkland Islands; a British task force brings the war to an end after 10 weeks; Argentine dictator Leopold Galtieri resigns. Israel invades Lebanon and besieges Beirut, forcing the PLO to move its headquarters to Tunis; militant group Hezbollah emerges in Lebanon and aims to establish an Islamic state there. In Poland, the trade union Solidarność is banned and its leaders arrested.

1983

Tamil Tigers seeking an independent state begin a war in Sri Lanka; they are defeated in 2009. Sudan imposes Sharia law, prompting civil war between the Christian south and Muslim north; South Sudan becomes independent when the war ends in 2005. Terrorists in Lebanon bomb the US embassy in Beirut and the French and US peacekeeping headquarters. The USSR shoots down a Korean airliner it mistakes for a US spy plane. US troops invade Grenada after a Marxist coup raises concerns about the spread of communism; constitutional government is restored in 1984. General Noriega becomes dictator in Panama.

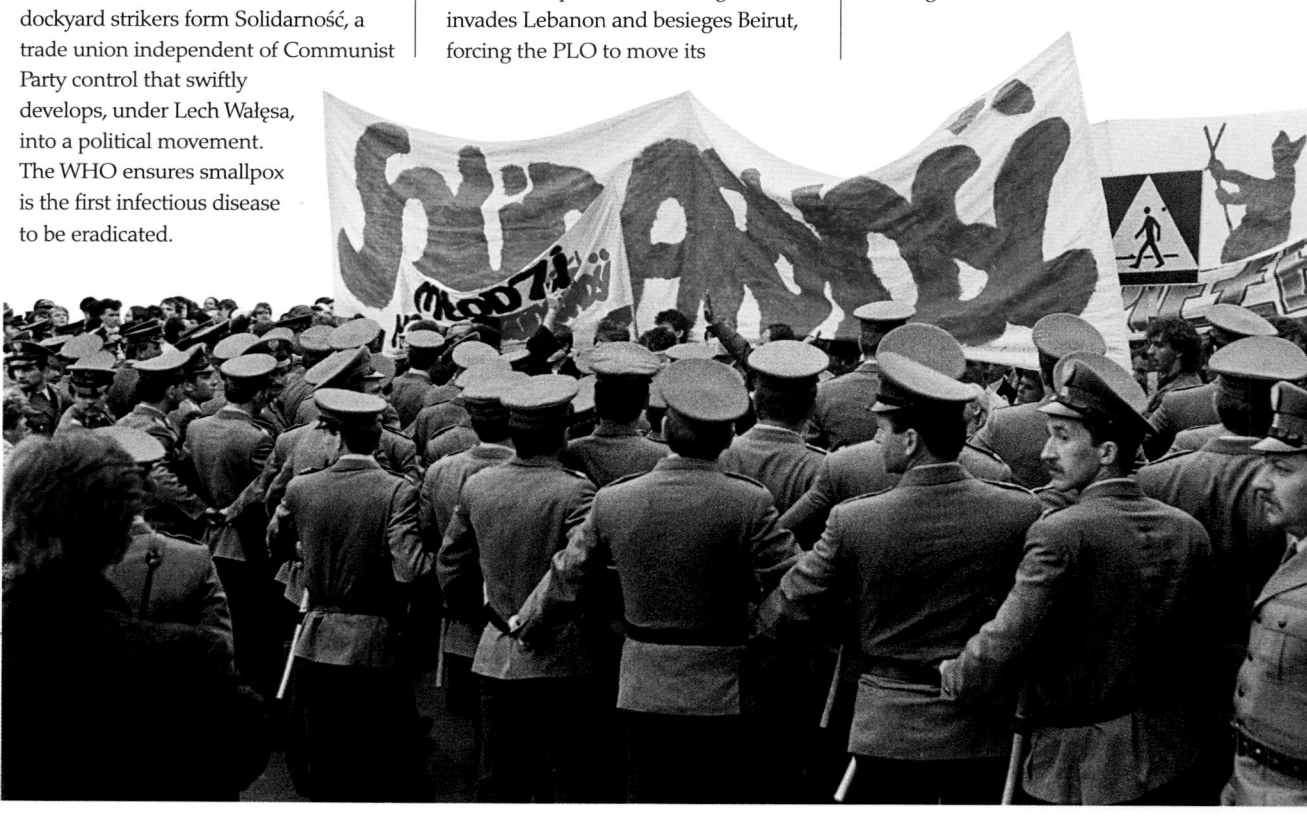

▷ **Polish Solidarity**
Polish police block demonstrators supporting the trade union Solidarność (Solidarity), which has become a national movement of resistance backed by the Roman Catholic Church.

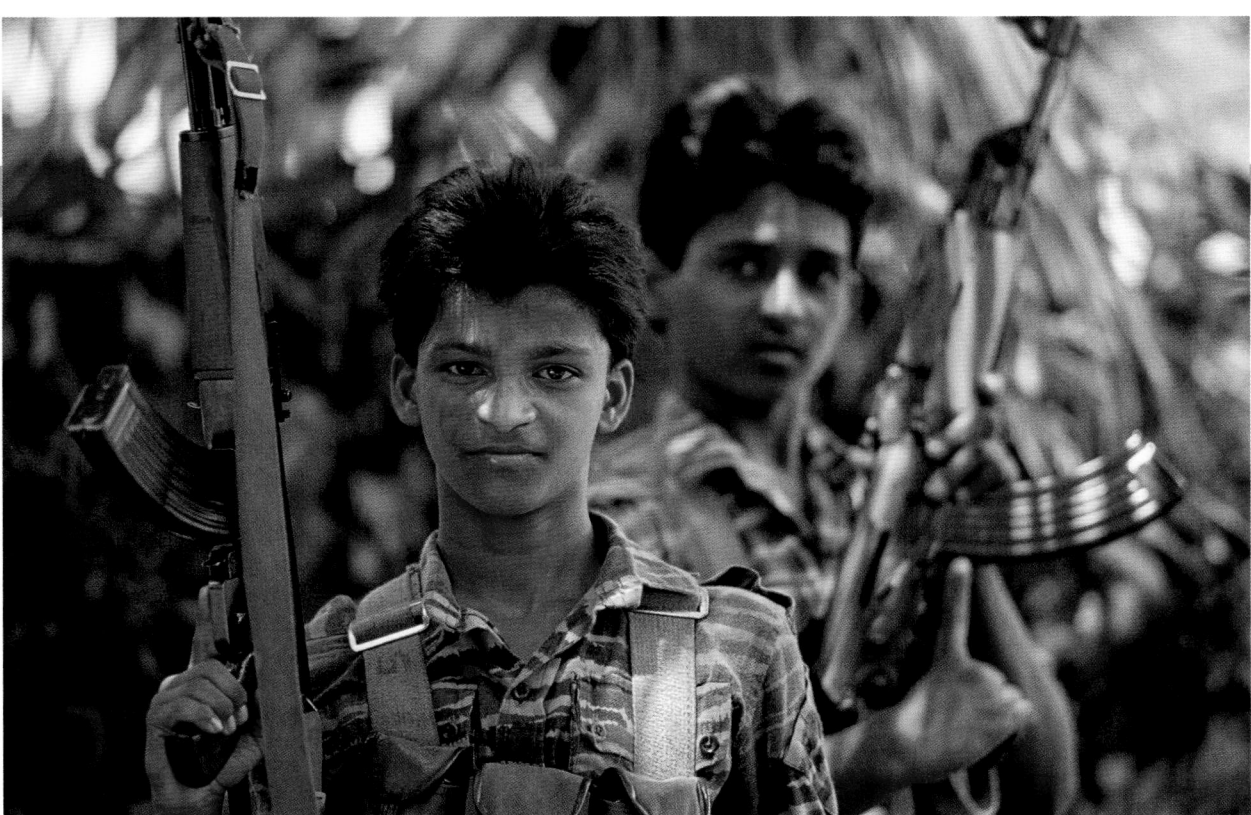

◁ Tamil Tigers
Many young men and boys joined the Tamil Tigers fighting for an independent Tamil homeland in the north of Sri Lanka.

1990

9 billion light-years. The distance of the farthest star detected by the Hubble Space Telescope.

Solidarność is leg alized and Lech Wałęsa becomes Poland's first postcommunist president in 1990; communist regimes fall in Czechoslovakia, Hungary, Bulgaria, Romania, and East Germany; citizens breach the Berlin Wall, symbolically ending the Cold War. Democracy is restored in Chile with the collapse of Pinochet's military regime and election of Patricio Aylwin. British engineer Sir Tim Berners-Lee outlines his concept for a World Wide Web. US troops invade Panama City and capture General Noriega after blasting rock music at the Vatican embassy where he was taking shelter; in the US, he is jailed for drug trafficking and money laundering.

1984–1985
The Ethiopian famine is one of the 20th century's deadliest disasters, as more than 400,000 people die and millions are left destitute; civil war hampers international relief efforts.

1984
India's prime minister Indira Gandhi orders troops to oust Sikh extremists occupying a complex at Amritsar that includes the Golden Temple (the center of the Sikh religion); she is assassinated by her own Sikh bodyguards soon after. Toxic methyl isocyanate gas leaks from the Union Carbide pesticide plant in Bhopal, India; 500,000 people are exposed and 2,000 die as a result.

1985
In the USSR, Mikhail Gorbachev is elected Executive President; his policies of *glasnost* (openness) and *perestroika* (restructuring) bring Russia closer to the US and Europe. In the UK, a miners' strike ends after 11 months; prime minister Margaret Thatcher succeeds in breaking the power of the industrial unions. A hole in the ozone layer over Antarctica is discovered.

1986
Ferdinand Marcos, dictator of the Philippines, flees after being defeated in the election. The US responds to a terrorist attack on US soldiers in Berlin believed to have been ordered by Libya by bombing Tripoli. Radioactive contamination spreads across Europe after an explosion at the Chernobyl

"The essence of perestroika lies in the fact that it unites socialism with democracy ..."

MIKHAIL GORBACHEV, FROM *PERESTROIKA*, 1987

nuclear power plant in Ukraine. The US and Commonwealth impose limited economic sanctions on South Africa in protest against apartheid.

1987
The US and USSR sign the INF (Intermediate-range Nuclear Forces) Treaty. Palestinians fight against Israeli occupation of the West Bank and Gaza in the First Intifada (to 1993). On Black Monday, the US stock market experiences its worst crash since 1929.

1988
A bomb aboard PanAm flight 103 explodes over Lockerbie, Scotland, killing 270 people; Libya accepts responsibility in 2003. Osama bin Laden founds the terrorist organization al-Qaeda. Cuban and South African troops withdraw from Angola and Namibia. Martial law is imposed in

Burma, which is renamed Myanmar; opposition leaders, including Aung San Suu Kyi, are imprisoned.

1989
More than 1 million protesters gather in Tiananmen Square, Beijing, to call for economic and political reform; over 3,000 are killed and 10,000 injured when Chinese troops and tanks open fire. Soviet troops withdraw from Afghanistan. A series of revolutions tears down the Iron Curtain: in Poland,

1990
In South Africa, President F. W. de Klerk lifts the ban on the African National Congress (ANC), frees Nelson Mandela, and repeals the remaining apartheid laws (1991). Namibia gains independence from South Africa. UN forces are sent to the Persian Gulf after Iraq invades Kuwait. East and West Germany are reunited as the Federal Republic of Germany. The Hubble Space Telescope (HST) goes into orbit 340 miles (547 km) above Earth's atmosphere. Aung San Suu Kyi's party wins the election in Myanmar, but she is kept under house arrest. The Sandinis tas are defeated in free elections in Nicaragua; Daniel Ortega is replaced by Violeta Barrios de Chamorro.

1991–2004

1991
UN forces expel Iraqi troops from Kuwait in the First Gulf War. The Paris Peace Accords end the Cambodian–Vietnamese War. The USSR is dissolved, breaking into 15 countries; Russia, Ukraine, and Belarus form the Commonwealth of Independent States (CIS). Boris Yeltsin is elected first president of the Russian Federation. Yugoslavia disintegrates, and the region descends into a series of civil wars: Slovenia and Croatia declare their independence; Slovenia repels the Serb-dominated Yugoslav People's Army in the Ten-Day War; fighting in Croatia ends in 1995. Mengistu flees Ethiopia when the Ethiopian People's Revolutionary Democratic Front takes control; he is later sentenced to death for crimes against humanity. Civil war (to 2002) breaks out in Algeria between the government and various Islamic militant groups.

1992
The Maastricht Treaty creates the European Union (EU) and commits its 12 signatory states to common citizenship and common economic and defense policies. Bosnia and Herzegovina seek independence from the remnant of Yugoslavia, sparking the Bosnian War (to 1995); Radovan Karadžić's policy of ethnic cleansing results in the systematic destruction of 296 Bosnian Muslim villages and the execution of at least 3,000 Muslims around Srebrenica; in 2016, Karadžić is found guilty of genocide. Mujaheddin rebels oust president Najibullah in Afghanistan; the fundamentalist Muslim Taliban are strengthened. Sectarian violence in India sees Hindus destroy the Babri mosque in Ayodhya; 12 bombs are detonated in Mumbai in response in 1993.

1993
Czechoslovakia splits peacefully into the Czech Republic and Slovakia. Israel and the PLO sign the Oslo Accords; they agree to mutual recognition and set out the principles for Palestinian autonomy. Prince Sihanouk is elected head of state in Cambodia.

1994
In Rwanda, civil war leads to genocide: Hutu extremists massacre 800,000 Tutsis; 2 million Hutus flee to neighboring countries. Nelson Mandela becomes the country's first black president in South Africa's first democratic elections. Russian troops enter the Muslim-dominated region of Chechnya; after a disastrous war, Russia is forced to offer Chechnya almost complete autonomy (1996). The US invades Haiti to restore Jean-Bertrand Aristide to power. In

> "Never, never, and never again shall it be that this beautiful land will again experience the oppression of one by another …"
>
> NELSON MANDELA, 1994

Ireland, a ceasefire is declared by the IRA and Protestant paramilitaries; it is broken in 1995, when the IRA bombs Canary Wharf, London. The Channel Tunnel linking Britain and France opens.

1995
A Gulf War veteran plants a bomb in Oklahoma City that kills 168 people. Israeli prime minister Yitzhak Rabin is assassinated shortly after winning the Nobel Peace Prize with Yasser Arafat and Shimon Perez. UN peacekeepers pull out of Somalia, having failed to secure the end of the civil war. The US Department of Defense completes the first operational satellite-based GPS (Global Positioning System).

1996
Taliban rebels capture Kabul and declare Afghanistan a fundamentalist Islamic state; Osama bin Laden returns to Afghanistan. Israeli shells kill over 100 civilians in Lebanon; Hezbollah is accused of using civilians as human shields. Created in Scotland, Dolly the sheep is the first mammal to be cloned from an adult cell.

1997
Tutsi rebels attack Hutu refugee camps in Zaire; Laurent Kabila ends dictator Mobutu Sese Seko's 32-year rule, and Zaire is renamed the Democratic Republic of Congo.

Hong Kong returns to China when Britain's 99-year lease expires. A major financial crisis in Asia leads to an economic slump in many developing countries and the wider world. Industrialized nations agree to cut carbon dioxide and other greenhouse gas emissions to combat global warming in the Kyoto Protocol. Kofi Annan is the first black African to be appointed secretary-general of the UN.

1998
The Good Friday agreement ends the Troubles in Northern Ireland and provides the region with devolved government. India and Pakistan begin tests of nuclear weapons. Serbs and ethnic Albanians clash in Kosovo. The financial crisis deepens: Indonesia's economy collapses, and President Suharto resigns; the price of oil drops, contributing to Russia's economic difficulties. In Africa, war breaks out between Eritrea and Ethiopia (to 2000), and the Democratic Republic of Congo descends into civil war again. US missiles hit al-Qaeda targets in Afghanistan and Sudan. US and Britain bomb Iraq after it ceases to cooperate with UN inspectors looking for weapons of mass destruction.

1999
Serbian ethnic cleansing of Kosovan Albanians is halted by NATO bombing; Serbian president Slobodan Milosovic is later charged with

31.4
miles (50.5 km). The length of the Channel Tunnel linking England and France.

▷ **Nelson Mandela victorious**
Mandela became the first nonwhite head of state in South Africa after his party, the African National Congress, won the election of 1994.

▷ 9/11
Hijacked United Airlines Flight 175 from Boston crashes into the south tower of the World Trade Center and explodes at 9:03 a.m. on September 11, 2001, in New York City.

500 mph

(800 kph). The speed of the devastating tsunami in the Indian Ocean in 2004.

---

war crimes, but dies in prison in 2006. East Timor votes to secede from Indonesia; anti-independence rebels supported by the Indonesian military attack civilians; independence is granted in 2002. General Pervez Musharraf seizes control in Pakistan. Russian forces reassert Russian control over Chechnya after Chechen rebels begin to attack Russian targets. President Yeltsin resigns, leaving former KGB agent Vladimir Putin as acting president. Portugal returns Macau to Chinese control more than 430 years after Portugal first leased the territory (1557).

2000
Vladimir Putin wins the presidential election in Russia. Israel pulls out of South Lebanon after 22 years of occupation. More than 3,000 Israelis and Palestinians are killed in the Second Intifada. Bashar al-Assad becomes president of Syria. The first crew arrives at the International Space Station (ISS).

2001
On September 11, 2,996 people are killed in four al-Qaeda terror attacks in the US. The US declares a "war on terrorism" and, with the UK, attacks targets in Afghanistan thought to be harboring Osama bin Laden; the war in Afghanistan ends in 2014. China has the fastest-growing economy in the world and is admitted to the World Trade Organization.

2002
US President George W. Bush describes the countries of Iraq, Iran, and North Korea as the "axis of evil." The Euro is introduced in 12 European countries. Civil war in Sierra Leone and Angola ends. In the US-led invasion of Afghanistan, the Taliban are swept from power. In Bali, 200 are killed when Islamist terrorists bomb a club. Over 100 die when Chechen militants besiege a Moscow theater. US troops return to the Gulf when Iraq denies that it has weapons of mass destruction.

2003
Civil war erupts in Darfur, west Sudan. The State Union of Serbia and Montenegro emerges as Yugoslavia ceases to exist. The Iraq War begins as a US-led coalition invades Iraq and topples Saddam Hussein's government; it struggles to stabilize the country and contain insurgency. Scientists publish the results of the Human Genome Project, identifying the DNA sequence of a full set of human chromosomes. The SARS virus, a new form of pneumonia, spreads globally.

2004
In Madrid, Islamic terrorists place bombs on commuter trains, killing 191. Ten countries join the EU, most of them former communist states in eastern Europe. An earthquake of magnitude 9.1–9.3 off Sumatra triggers the most destructive tsunami in history; more than 200,000 people in 11 countries across the Indian Ocean and Southeast Asia lose their lives; millions are made homeless. Chechen rebels take a school hostage in Beslan, southern Russia; more than 300 people are killed.

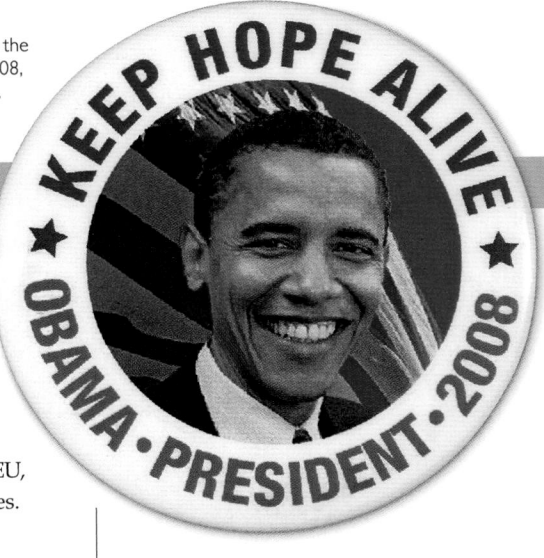

▷ **Obama campaign button**
Democrat Barack Obama was elected as the 44th President of the United States in 2008, winning 59.2 percent of the popular vote.

2005–2018

6.9 trillion dollars. The value wiped off global stock markets in the 2008 crash; it is the largest fall in history.

2005
Mahmoud Abbas becomes president of the Palestinian Authority after the death of Yasser Arafat. Syria withdraws from Lebanon, and Israel withdraws from Gaza. In London, 52 people die when Islamist suicide bombers target public transportation. In Ireland, the Provisional IRA announces that it will cease its armed campaign and pursue its goals through peaceful political means. In the US, the city of New Orleans is devastated by Hurricane Katrina; in Pakistan, an earthquake kills more than 70,000 people in Kashmir.

2006
In Palestine, Hamas—the Sunni-Islamist fundamentalist organization—wins the parliamentary elections. In the month-long Lebanon War, Hezbollah captures two Israeli soldiers; Israel responds with air and rocket strikes on south Lebanon; the UN brokers a ceasefire, and an international force occupies south Lebanon. North Korea begins its testing of nuclear weapons. Serbia and Montenegro split into separate nations. Basque separatist organization ETA announces a ceasefire, ending 40 years of terrorist activity.

2007
In occupied Iran, sectarian violence between Sunni and Shia militias escalates. Political enemies the DUP and Sinn Fein agree to share power in the Northern Ireland Assembly. Pratibha Patil becomes the first female President of India. Russia cuts oil supplies to Poland, Germany, and Ukraine during a dispute with Belarus.

2007–2011
A global recession follows the collapse of the Lehman Brothers investment bank; banks worldwide face insolvency and throttle lending. Bulgaria and Romania join the EU, which now has 27 member states.

2008
Barack Obama becomes the United States' first African-American president. Kosovo declares independence from Serbia. Nepal becomes a republic after abolishing the monarchy. Russia invades the Russian enclaves of South Ossetia and Abkhazia in Georgia. Australia's prime minister apologizes to the "Stolen Generations" of indigenous children removed from their families.

2009
Israel invades Gaza to halt rocket attacks by Hamas; it withdraws 3 weeks later. Russia ends military operations in Chechnya; jihadists remain active in the region. A global pandemic of swine flu kills 17,000.

2010
In Haiti, around 230,000 people die in a devastating earthquake. The International Monetary Fund (IMF) and EU bail out the Greek and Irish economies with huge loans, but insist on the introduction of severe austerity measures. Myanmar's military regime releases pro-democracy leader Aung San Suu Kyi. Argentina's economic crisis sees the country go through five presidents in 1 month. The nonprofit WikiLeaks organization publishes more than 90,000 classified reports about US involvement in the war in Afghanistan. An explosion at the Deepwater Horizon oil rig spills 200 million gallons of oil into the Gulf of Mexico.

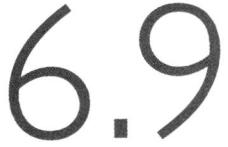

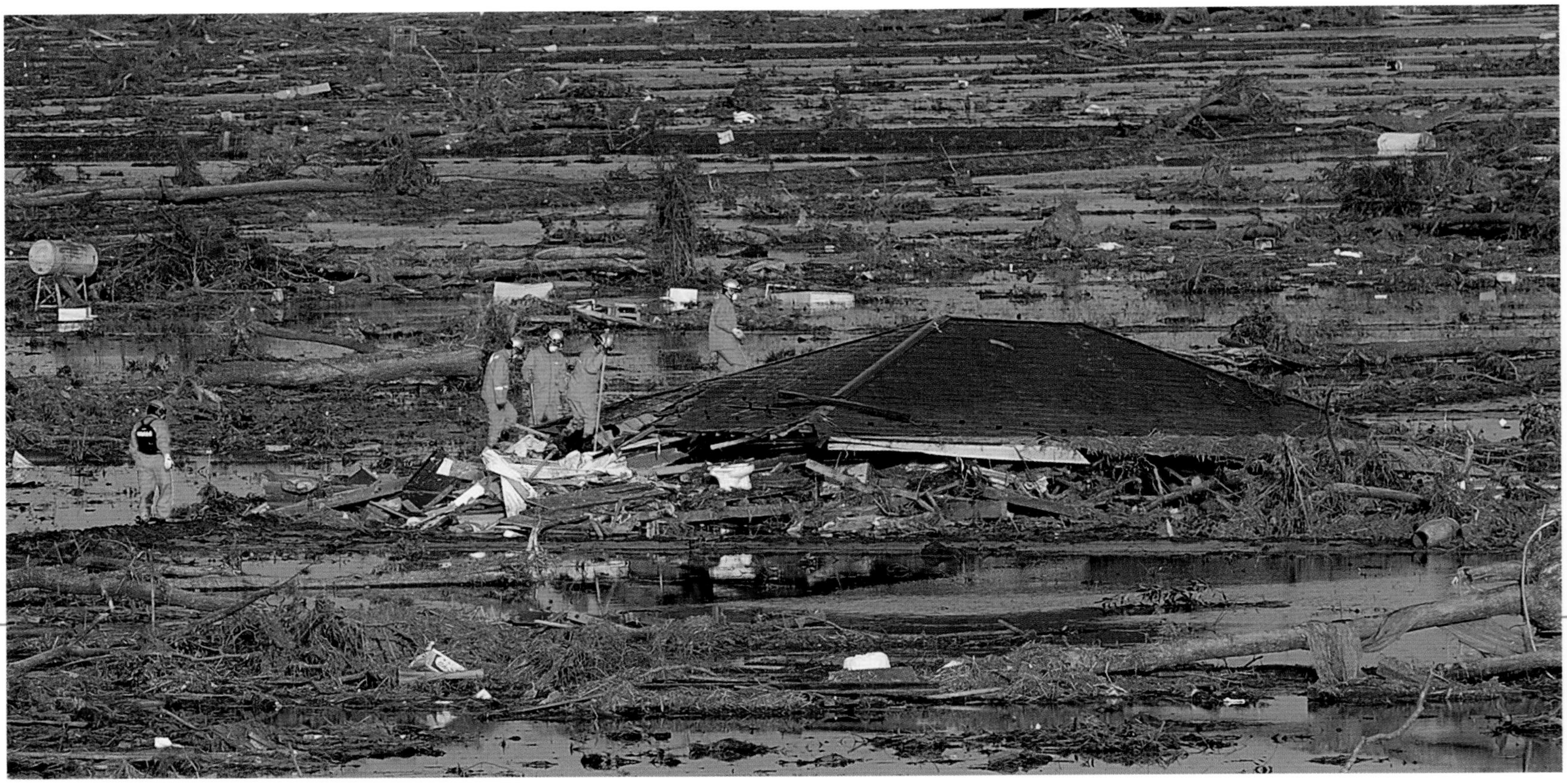

▷ **The fall of President Mugabe**
People in Zimbabwe take to the streets in 2017, demanding that Robert Mugabe resign as President—a post he had held for 37 years.

2011

In the Arab Spring, pro-democracy rebellions erupt across North Africa and the Middle East: in Egypt, President Hosni Mubarak hands power to the army after mass protests; in Libya, Mu'ammar al-Gaddafi's regime is toppled, but civil war follows; in Syria, civil war begins with a violent crackdown on civilian dissenters. South Sudan becomes independent of Sudan, but ethnic tensions fuel civil war in 2013. Osama bin Laden is killed by US special forces in Pakistan. The war in Iraq ends, and US troops withdraw. Three fission reactors at Fukushima Nuclear Power Plant in Japan melt down after being damaged by a tsunami that kills 20,000.

2012

Mohammed Morsi of the Muslim Brotherhood wins Egypt's presidential elections. Schoolgirl, blogger, and human rights activist Malala Yousafzai is shot and wounded by the Taliban in Pakistan; she survives and becomes the youngest Nobel laureate in 2014. In Africa, civil war breaks out in the Central African Republic; there are coups in Mali and Guinea-Bissau. Austrian skydiver Felix Baumgartner, diving from a helium balloon 24 miles (39 km) above Earth, is the first person to break the sound barrier without any machine assistance.

2013

French forces intervene against Islamist insurgents fighting the government in northern Mali. Syria's government pledges to hand over its chemical weapons for destruction after denying responsibility for a chemical attack on Ghouta. Violence breaks out in Egypt after President Morsi is ousted in a military coup. A shopping mall in Nairobi, Kenya, is attacked by fundamentalist Islamist militants belonging to the al-Shabaab group.

2014

The Ebola virus kills 11,000 people in west Africa by 2016. In Ukraine, the pro-Russian president is ousted; Russia invades eastern Ukraine and annexes Crimea; the US imposes sanctions on Russia. Israel launches air strikes on Gaza; a ground offensive follows. In Nigeria, Islamic extremist group Boko Haram kidnaps 276 schoolgirls. Civil war resumes in Libya: the democratically elected government in Tobruk faces Islamist factions in Tripoli and Benghazi. The terrorist group Islamic State of Iraq and the Levant (ISIL, also known as ISIS or Daesh) occupies territory in northern Iraq and Syria; more than 3 million refugees flee to neighboring countries.

2015

Egypt begins air strikes targeting ISIL in Libya. A Saudi-led Arab coalition begins military intervention in Yemen, attacking Iranian-backed Houthi rebels in the south. Al-Shabaab shoots 148 people, mainly students, at Garissa University in Kenya. Iran agrees to limit its nuclear program if sanctions are eased. Russia begins air strikes against ISIL and anti-government forces in Syria. ISIL destroys ancient sites in Syria and is responsible for multiple attacks across the world. The Paris Accord commits nearly 200 countries to reducing carbon emissions. The Zika fever epidemic begins in Brazil and rapidly spreads throughout the Americas, causing worldwide alarm. Surgeons in New York perform the first full facial transplant.

2016

The United Kingdom votes to leave the European Union. Barack Obama is the first US president to visit Cuba since 1928. In November, Donald Trump becomes US President; within months, he is embroiled in an investigation into alleged collusion with Russia. Islamist terror continues, with multiple attacks in France, Germany, and Belgium. Fifty-two years of conflict in Colombia ends when the government and the Revolutionary Armed Forces of Colombia–People's Army (FARC) agree a peace deal.

2017

President Trump's decision to pull out of the Paris Accord to combat climate change makes the US the only country in the world not to be part of the agreement. A military coup forces Robert Mugabe to resign after 37 years as President of Zimbabwe. Islamist terror attacks continue in Europe in Manchester, London, Barcelona, Turkey, France, Germany, Russia, and Belgium.

North Korea fires a ballistic missile across Japan and continues its nuclear testing; international condemnation is followed by increased sanctions. More than 20 million people face starvation and famine in Yemen, Somalia, South Sudan, and Nigeria. Reports emerge that the Syrian government has dropped toxic gas on a rebel-held town; the US launches a missile strike on the Syrian air base at Sharyat. The autonomous region of Catalonia declares independence, but Spain refuses to recognize it; Catalan leaders are arrested. Thousands of Rohingya Muslims flee Myanmar after experiencing systematic violence, amounting to ethnic cleansing.

2018

In China, the government brings in a change to the constitution that lifts term limits for its leaders; the sitting president Xi Jinping effectively becomes "President for Life." In Russia, Vladimir Putin is elected as president for a fourth term. North Korean leader Kim Jong-un crosses into South Korea to meet with President Moon Jae-in; he is the first North Korean leader to cross the Demilitarized Zone since its creation in 1953. The United States, together with the UK and France, bombs Syrian military bases in response to a chemical attack launched by Bashar al-Assad on civilians in Ghouta. Social media company Facebook is rocked by scandal relating to its sharing of personal data.

"A girl has the power to go forward in her life. And she's not only a mother, she's not only a sister, she's not only a wife."

MALALA YOUSAFZAI, 2014

◁ **Tragedy in Japan**
A magnitude-9 earthquake shakes northeastern Japan, unleashing a savage tsunami that destroys 250,000 buildings. It is thought to be the costliest natural disaster in history.

INDEX

Page numbers in **bold** refer
to main entries.

ACKNOWLEDGMENTS

Dorling Kindersley would like to thank the following people for their help in the preparation of this book: Ann Baggaley, Carron Brown, Thomas Booth, Chris Hawkes, Cecile Landau, and Justine Willis for editorial assistance; Chrissy Barnard, Amy Child, Phil Gamble, and Renata Latipova for design assistance; Steve Crozier for image retouching; Katie John for proofreading; and Helen Peters for indexing.

DK India would like to thank Arpita Dasgupta, Tina Jindal, Rupa Rao, and Isha Sharma for editorial assistance; Simar Dhamija and Meenal Goel for design assistance; Ashutosh Ranjan Bharti, Deshpal Dabas, Mohammad Hassan, Zafar Ul Islam Khan, and Lokamata Sahu for cartographic assistance; Shanker Prasad and Mohd Rizwan for DTP assistance.

The publisher would like to thank the following for their kind permission to reproduce their photographs: (Key: a-above; b-below/bottom; c-center; f-far; l-left; r-right; t-top)

2 Alamy Stock Photo: Science History Images. **4 Getty Images:** De Agostini Picture Library (tr). **Robert Gunn:** Courtesy of Jawoyn Association (tl). **5 Alamy Stock Photo:** The Granger Collection (tr). **Getty Images:** Photo Josse / Leemage (tl). **6 Alamy Stock Photo:** Paul Fearn (tr). **The Metropolitan Museum of Art:** Gift of John Stewart Kennedy, 1897 (tl). **7 Getty Images:** Galerie Bilderwelt (tl). **8–9 Bridgeman Images:** Pictures from History. **10-11 Robert Gunn:** Courtesy of Jawoyn Association. **12 Alamy Stock Photo:** The Natural History Museum (tl). **Getty Images:** DEA / G. Dagli Orti / De Agostini (c). **13 Bridgeman Images:** Caves of Lascaux, Dordogne, France (cr). **Science Photo Library:** ER Degginger (tl). **14 Alamy Stock Photo:** Puwadol Jaturawutthichai (crb). **Dorling Kindersley:** Oxford Museum of Natural History (ca). **15 akg-images:** CDA / Guillemot (cr). **Science Photo Library:** John Reader (tr). **17 Alamy Stock Photo:** Chronicle (br); Paul Fearn (c). **18 Getty Images:** Kerry Lorimer (cl). **18–19 Robert Gunn:**

Courtesy of Jawoyn Association. **21 Alamy Stock Photo:** Phil Degginger (cl). **22 © CNRS Photothèque:** © C. Jarrige (cb). **Dorling Kindersley:** The Museum of London (cla). **23 akg-images:** Bible Land Pictures / Jerusalem Photo by: Z.Radovan (t). **Alamy Stock Photo:** blickwinkel (cr). **24 Getty Images:** DEA / G. Dagli Orti / De Agostini (c). **26 Getty Images:** DEA / A. De Gregorio / De Agostini (bl). **27 Alamy Stock Photo:** www.BibleLandPictures.com (bl). **28–29 Getty Images:** De Agostini Picture Library. **30 Dorling Kindersley:** University of Pennsylvania Museum of Archaeology and Anthropology (cla). **Getty Images:** Kitti Boonnitrod (cra). **31 Alamy Stock Photo:** World History Archive (tc). **Getty Images:** Leemage (crb). **32 Bridgeman Images:** Iraq Museum, Baghdad (br). **33 Dreamstime.com:** Kmiragaya (br). **35 Getty Images:** Art Media / Print Collector (bl). **36 Alamy Stock Photo:** Heritage Image Partnership Ltd (br). **Dorling Kindersley:** The University of Aberdeen (bl). **37 Alamy Stock Photo:** Kylie Ellway (br). **39 Getty Images:** DEA / G. Nimatallah / De Agostini (tc, br). **40 Alamy Stock Photo:** World History Archive (c). **42 Getty Images:** DEA / G. Dagli Orti / De Agostini (bl). **42–43 Getty Images:** De Agostini Picture Library. **44 Getty Images:** Nathan Benn (bl). **45 Getty Images:** Dea / A. Dagli Orti / DeAgostini (cla). **46 Alamy Stock Photo:** imageBROKER (cl). **Bridgeman Images:** Musee des Antiquites Nationales, St. Germain-en-Laye, France (cr). **47 Alamy Stock Photo:** robertharding (crb); The Print Collector (tl). **48 Getty Images:** Dea / G. Dagli Orti / DeAgostini (bl). **49 Alamy Stock Photo:** MuseoPics - Paul Williams (bl). **50 akg-images:** Erich Lessing (bc). **51 Bridgeman Images:** (br). **52 Getty Images:** Ernesto Benavides / AFP (tr). **53 Getty Images:** Werner Forman / Universal Images Group (br). **54–55 Alamy Stock Photo:** Lanmas. **54 Alamy Stock Photo:** Peter Horree (bc); North Wind Picture Archives (cla). **57 Bridgeman Images:** Pictures from History (c). **58 Getty Images:** CM Dixon / Print Collector (clb). **59 Bridgeman Images:** Werner Forman Archive (br). **60 Getty Images:** Leemage (bl). **62 Alamy Stock Photo:** Konstantinos Tsakalidis (cla). **Dorling Kindersley:** The University of Aberdeen (c). **63 Getty Images:** Michael Dunning (tl). **Photo Scala, Florence:** courtesy of the Ministero Beni e Att. Culturali e del Turismo (cr). **64 Alamy**

Stock Photo: ART Collection (bc). **65 Getty Images:** DEA / G. Nimatallah / De Agostini (cr). **66 Getty Images:** DEA / G. Dagli Orti / De Agostini (crb). **68 Getty Images:** Dea / A. Dagli Orti / De Agostini (bc). **69 Getty Images:** Chris Hellier / Corbis (br). **70 Alamy Stock Photo:** Angelo Hornak (cl). **70–71 Alamy Stock Photo:** MCLA Collection. **73 Alamy Stock Photo:** Dinodia Photos (bl); Robert Preston Photography (tr). **74 Getty Images:** UniversalImagesGroup (bl). **76 Alamy Stock Photo:** David Davis Photoproductions (cl); Yong nian Gui (bl). **76–77 Alamy Stock Photo:** Oleksiy Maksymenko Photography. **78 Alamy Stock Photo:** Granger Historical Picture Archive (cl). **81 Getty Images:** DEA Picture Library (ca, br). **82 Bridgeman Images:** Pictures from History (crb). **84 Bridgeman Images:** Pictures from History / David Henley (bl). **86 akg-images:** André Held (bc). **87 123RF.com:** Lefteris Papaulakis (bc).**88–89 Getty Images:** Photo Josse / Leemage. **90 Alamy Stock Photo:** Ian Dagnall (c). **Dreamstime.com:** Sean Pavone / Sepavo (cla). **91 Alamy Stock Photo:** ART Collection (tl). **Bridgeman Images:** Ancient Art and Architecture Collection Ltd. (cr). **93 Getty Images:** Werner Forman / Universal Images Group (bl); Universal History Archive (br). **94 123RF.com:** Mikhail Markovskiy (br). **Bridgeman Images:** Private Collection / Archives Charmet (bl). **96 akg-images:** Pictures From History (bc). **97 The Metropolitan Museum of Art:** Theodore M. Davis Collection, Bequest of Theodore M. Davis, 1915 (tr). **98 Getty Images:** Kristin Piljay (bc). **Michael Czytko, www.finemodelships.com:** (crb). **100 Alamy Stock Photo:** Pere Sanz (cl). **100–101 Getty Images:** DEA Picture Library. **103 Alamy Stock Photo:** Granger Historical Picture Archive (br). **Getty Images:** Photo Josse / Leemage (tl). **105 Alamy Stock Photo:** Kumar Sriskandan (br). **Getty Images:** Leemage (tl). **107 Getty Images:** Photo Josse / Leemage (br). **108 Bridgeman Images:** Basilica di San Giovanni Battista, Monza, Italy / Alinari (cla). **Getty Images:** CM Dixon / Print Collector (cb). **109 Alamy Stock Photo:** Granger Historical Picture Archive (r); Chris Pancewicz (tl). **111 Alamy Stock Photo:** The Picture Art Collection (br). **113 Getty Images:** Ann Ronan Pictures / Print Collector (br). **RMN:** RMN-Grand Palais (Cluny Museum - National Museum of the Middle Ages) / Jean-Gilles Berizzi (c). **115 Alamy Stock Photo:** Pictorial Press Ltd (tl). **116–117 Bridgeman Images:** Musee Conde, Chantilly, France. **117 Bridgeman Images:** Pictures from History (bc). **Getty Images:** Imagno (cr). **119 Alamy Stock Photo:** Everett Collection Inc (tl). **120 akg-images:** (c). **122 Alamy Stock Photo:** MCLA Collection (bc). **123 Alamy Stock Photo:** Jon Bower Spain (crb). **124 Bridgeman Images:** De Agostini Picture Library / G. Dagli Orti (cl, cra). **125 Alamy Stock Photo:** Ariadne Van Zandbergen (tl); ephotocorp (crb). **127 Alamy Stock Photo:** Images & Stories (br). **128 akg-images:** Pansegrau (tl). **129 Getty Images:** DEA Picture Library (br). **130 Getty Images:** Heritage Images (bl). **132 Alamy Stock Photo:** Pictorial Press Ltd (br). **134 Getty Images:** photographer (br); photo by Pam Susemiehl (bl). **136 Getty Images:** Werner Forman / Universal Images Group (bc). **138–139 Getty Images:** Print Collector. **139 Bridgeman Images:** Bibliotheque Nationale, Paris, France (br). **Getty Images:** Werner Forman / Universal Images Group (cra). **141 Alamy Stock Photo:** Regula Heeb-Zweifel (br). **Museum of New Zealand Te Papa Tongarewa:** (c). **142 Alamy Stock Photo:** Science History Images (tr). **Getty Images:** Mladen Antonov (bc). **145 Alamy Stock Photo:** Peter Horree (bl).**146–147 Alamy Stock Photo:** The Granger Collection. **148 Alamy Stock Photo:** Peter Horree (tl). **149 Dorling Kindersley:** Maidstone Museum and Bentliff Art Gallery (tl); Whipple Museum of History of Science, Cambridge (cr). **151 Alamy Stock Photo:** The Granger Collection (br). **153 Alamy Stock Photo:** INTERFOTO (tr). **154 Getty Images:** Fine Art Images / Heritage Images (cl). **154–155 Photo Scala, Florence:** Photo Schalkwijk / Art Resource / © Banco de México Diego Rivera Frida Kahlo Museums Trust, Mexico, D.F. / © DACS 2018. **157 Getty Images:** adoc-photos (br). **158 Bridgeman Images:** Granger (bc). **159 Alamy Stock Photo:** The Granger Collection (bl). **160 Alamy Stock Photo:** World Photo Collection (c). **Bridgeman Images:** British Library, London, UK / © British Library Board. All Rights Reserved (cla). **161 Bridgeman Images:** (cr). **Wellcome Images http://creativecommons.org/licenses/by/4.0/:** (tl). **162 Bridgeman Images:** Pictures from History (bc). **163 Getty Images:** PHAS / UIG (crb). **164–165 Alamy Stock Photo:** Science History Images. **164 Alamy Stock Photo:** Falkensteinfoto (bl). **Bridgeman Images:** British Library, London, UK (cl). **166 Getty Images:** DEA / G. Dagli Orti / De Agostini (bc). **167 Alamy Stock Photo:** FineArt (br). **168–169 Bridgeman Images:** Deutsches Historisches Museum, Berlin, Germany / © DHM. **169 Getty Images:** DEA Picture Library (br). **170 Getty Images:** DEA / G. Nimatallah / De Agostini (cla). **171 Getty Images:** The Print Collector (br). **172 Getty Images:** De Agostini Picture Library (bl). **173 Bridgeman Images:** Private Collection / Archives Charmet (br). **174 Alamy Stock Photo:** Peter Horree (tl). **Bridgeman Images:** Private Collection (c). **175 Alamy Stock Photo:** Heritage Image Partnership Ltd (c). **Getty Images:** DEA / G. Dagli Orti / Deagostini (tl). **177 akg-images:** (bl). **Alamy Stock Photo:** Dinodia Photos (tr). **178 Bridgeman Images:** (tl). **Getty Images:** DEA / A. C. Cooper (br). **180 Getty Images:** De Agostini Picture Library (tl). **181 Bridgeman Images:** Pictures from History (bl). **182–183 Getty Images:** Fine Art Images / Heritage Images. **183 Alamy Stock Photo:** Pictorial Press Ltd (ca). **Library of Congress, Washington, D.C.:** map55000728 (br). **184 Rijksmuseum, Amsterdam:** Purchased with the support of the Rembrandt Association (bc). **185 Alamy Stock Photo:** Peter Horree (bl).**186–187 The Metropolitan Museum of Art:** Gift of John Stewart Kennedy, 1897. **188 Alamy Stock Photo:** Science History Images (cl). **Boston Tea Pary Ships & Museum, Historic Tours of America, Inc:** (cra). **189 Alamy Stock Photo:** Art Collection 2 (cr); Science History Images (tl). **190 Getty Images:** Edward Gooch (tr). **193 akg-images:** (br). **194 Dorling Kindersley:** Museum of English Rural Life, The University of Reading (clb). **Rijksmuseum, Amsterdam:** (tl). **195 Alamy Stock Photo:** The Protected Art Archive (cr). **Getty Images:** Photo12 / UIG (tl). **196 Getty Images:** Universal History Archive (bl). **197 Alamy Stock Photo:** North Wind Picture Archives (br). **198 Yale University Art Gallery:** (bc). **199 The Metropolitan Museum of Art:** Gift of John Stewart Kennedy, 1897 (br). **201 Getty Images:** De Agostini Picture Library (tc); UniversalImagesGroup (tr). **202 Bridgeman Images:** Museum of Art, Serpukhov, Russia (cl). **202–203 Bridgeman Images:** Musee National du Chateau de Malmaison, Rueil-Malmaison, France. **204 Library of Congress, Washington, D.C.:** LC-DIG-ppmsca-09855 (bc). **205 Getty Images:** Photo Josse / Leemage (tr). **206 Bridgeman Images:** Private Collection (bc). **207 Bridgeman Images:** Galerie Dijol, Paris, France (tr). **209 Getty Images:** John Parrot / Stocktrek Images (br); Peter Willi (clb). **211 Getty Images:** Ann Ronan Pictures / Print Collector (crb); Fine Art Images / Heritage Images (br). **212 Alamy Stock Photo:** North Wind Picture Archives (tl). **Getty Images:** Science & Society Picture Library (clb). **213 Getty Images:** Science & Society Picture Library (tl); ullstein bild Dtl. (cr). **214 Getty Images:** Science & Society Picture Library (tl). **215 Alamy Stock Photo:** Heritage Image Partnership Ltd (tr). **Dorling Kindersley:** National Railway Museum, York / Science Museum Group (crb). **216 Alamy Stock Photo:** AF archive (bl); Granger Historical Picture Archive (cl). **216–217 Getty Images:** Photo Josse / Leemage. **218 Bridgeman Images:** Bibliotheque Nationale, Paris, France / Archives Charmet (tr). **Getty Images:** Fine Art Images / Heritage Images (bc). **220 Getty Images:** Universal History Archive (clb). **222–223 Provenance , Galerie Nader Pétion Ville Haiti:** Collection Of Mr. Jean Walnard Dorneval , Arcahaie Haiti. **222 Rex by Shutterstock:** The Art Archive (cl). **224 Alamy Stock Photo:** Peter Horree (bc). **225 akg-images:** Pictures From History (br). **226 Alamy Stock Photo:** Science History Images (tc). **227 Getty Images:** PHAS / UIG (tr). **228–229 Alamy Stock Photo:** Paul Fearn. **230 Alamy Stock Photo:** Everett Collection Historical (c). **Rex by Shutterstock:** Roger-Viollet (cla). **231 Alamy Stock Photo:** Pictorial Press Ltd (cr). **Getty Images:** W. Brown / Otto Herschan (tl). **233 akg-images:** (c). **234 Alamy Stock Photo:** Granger Historical Picture Archive (bl). **Getty Images:** Schöning / ullstein bild (cl). **234–235 Bridgeman Images:** Musee de la Ville de Paris, Musee Carnavalet, Paris, France. **236 Getty Images:** Stefano Bianchetti (clb). **237 Getty Images:** Stock Montage / Hulton Archive (br). **238 Getty Images:** DEA Picture Library / DeAgostini (cb). **240 Alamy Stock Photo:** Pictorial Press Ltd (cb); The Granger Collection (cla). **241 Alamy Stock Photo:** INTERFOTO (c). **Getty Images:** Sean Sexton (tr). **242 Bridgeman Images:** © Look and Learn (bc). **243 Getty Images:** Hulton Archive (br). **244 Dorling Kindersley:** © The Board of Trustees of the Armouries (cl). **244–245 Getty Images:** Popperfoto. **246 Getty Images:** UniversalImagesGroup (tl). **247 Getty Images:** Sovfoto / UIG (br). **248 akg-images:** Pictures From History (tl). **250 Alamy Stock Photo:** Photo 12 (bl). **Rex by Shutterstock:** Universal History Archive (c). **250–251 Rex by Shutterstock:** Granger. **252 Alamy Stock Photo:** Everett Collection Historical (bc); Paul Fearn (tr). **255 Alamy Stock Photo:** Artokoloro Quint Lox Limited (br). **256 Getty Images:** Buyenlarge (bl). **258–259 Getty Images:** Bettmann. **259 Alamy Stock Photo:** The Granger Collection (c). **Getty Images:** Bettmann (br). **260 Getty Images:** Bettmann (cr). **262 Alamy Stock Photo:** Paul Fearn (tl). **Getty Images:** Leemage (tr). **264 akg-images:** (tl). **267 Alamy Stock Photo:** Chronicle (br); Paul Fearn (bc). **269 Getty Images:** Culture Club (br); ullstein bild Dtl. (bl). **270–271 Getty Images:** Galerie Bilderwelt. **272 Alamy Stock Photo:** Paul Fearn (cla); Pictorial Press Ltd (cl). **273 Alamy Stock Photo:** Science History Images (tl). **Getty Images:** Sovfoto / UIG (cb); Universal History Archive (cr). **274 Alamy Stock Photo:** Universal Art Archive (br). **276 Dorling Kindersley:** Imperial War Museum, London (cla). **Getty Images:** Buyenlarge (bl). **276–277 Getty Images:** UniversalImagesGroup. **278 Alamy Stock Photo:** Granger Historical Picture Archive (bc). **279 Getty Images:** Time Life Pictures (crb). **281 Alamy Stock Photo:** Paul Fearn (br). **282 Getty Images:** Keystone (cl); Universal History Archive (bl). **282–283 Mary Evans Picture Library. 285 Alamy Stock Photo:** Photo 12 (br). **Getty Images:** Keystone-France (cla). **287 Alamy Stock Photo:** Science History Images (bl). **288 Alamy Stock Photo:** Granger Historical Picture Archive (bl). **290 Bridgeman Images:** Pictures from History / Woodbury & Page (bl). **291 Getty Images:** Print Collector (br). **292 Alamy Stock Photo:** Pictorial Press Ltd (bc). **Getty Images:** Keystone-France (br). **294 Bridgeman Images:** Pictures from History (cr). **Getty Images:** Bettmann (cl). **295 Alamy Stock Photo:** dpa picture alliance (crb). **Getty Images:** Bettmann (tl). **297 Alamy Stock Photo:** 502 collection (cl). **Getty Images:** Hulton Archive (br). **299 akg-images:** (br). **Getty Images:** Galerie Bilderwelt (cla). **300 Getty Images:** Universal History Archive / UIG (bl). **301 Getty Images:** Bettmann (br). **302 Alamy Stock Photo:** Prisma by Dukas Presseagentur GmbH (br). **Getty Images:** Central Press (bl). **305 Getty Images:** Apic / Retired (bl). **306–307 Hiroshima Peace Memorial Museum:** Shigeo Hayashi. **306 Getty Images:** Universal History Archive / UIG (br). **307 Getty Images:** Prisma by Dukas (br). **308 Getty Images:** Central Press (bl). **310 Alamy Stock Photo:** age fotostock (br). **Getty Images:** Print Collector (tl). **312 Alamy Stock Photo:** Science History Images (cla). **Bridgeman Images:** Peter Newark Military Pictures (c). **313 akg-images:** (tl). **Dorling Kindersley:** Stewart Howman / Dream Cars (crb). **314 Getty Images:** jondpatton (br). **317 Alamy Stock Photo:** robertharding (tr). **Getty Images:** RV Spencer / Interim Archives (bl). **319 Alamy Stock Photo:** World History Archive (br); Penny Tweedie (cl). **321 Alamy Stock Photo:** Shawshots (tl). **Getty Images:** Jon Feingersh (br). **323 Getty Images:** Louise Gubb (bl). **324 Getty Images:** Science & Society Picture Library (bc). **325 Getty Images:** Science & Society Picture Library (br). **326–327 Getty Images:** Bettmann. **327 Getty Images:** Fototeca Storica Nazionale (cr). **328 Alamy Stock Photo:** World History Archive (tl). **329 Getty Images:** Dirck Halstead (br). **331 Getty Images:** Bettmann (tr, bl). **332 Getty Images:** Muammar Awad / Anadolu Agency (tl). **334 123RF.com:** danielvfung (cl). **Alamy Stock Photo:** ClassicStock (cla). **335 Alamy Stock Photo:** eye35.pix (tc); PJF Military Collection (crb). **336 Getty Images:** Gerard Malie (clb). **337 Getty Images:** Wally McNamee (br). **339 Getty Images:** David Turnley / Corbis / VCG (cl). **340–341 Getty Images:** James Sebright. **340 Getty Images:** Ulrich Baumgarten (bl). **Rex by Shutterstock:** Dennis M. Sabangan / EPA (ca). **343 U.S. Air Force:** (cl). **344 Getty Images:** Science & Society Picture Library (cl); Stefan Wermuth / AFP (bl). **344–345 Getty Images:** Jerry Cooke. **346 Getty Images:** Allan Baxter (cb). **348–349 Alamy Stock Photo:** Science History Images. **350 Dorling Kindersley:** Gary Ombler / Oxford Museum of Natural History (bl). **Getty Images:** Science & Society Picture Library (tr). **350–351 Alamy Stock Photo:** Andia (br). **352 Alamy Stock Photo:** blickwinkel (t). **353 Alamy Stock Photo:** Constantinos Iliopoulos (tl); Florian Neukirchen (br). **354–355 Getty Images:** Frans Sellies (b). **355 Getty Images:** DEA / G. Dagli Orti / De Agostini (tl). **356 Getty Images:** Leemage / UIG (bl). **357 Alamy Stock Photo:** RF Company (tr). **Getty Images:** DEA / Ara Guler / De Agostini (bc). **358 Getty Images:** Apic / Retired / Hulton Archive (tr). **359 Alamy Stock Photo:** Konstantin Kalishko (bl). **Getty Images:** Werner Forman / Universal Images Group (tr). **360 Alamy Stock Photo:** Lanmas (bl). **361 Alamy Stock Photo:** eFesenko (bl). **Bridgeman Images:** Christie's Images (tr). **362 Alamy Stock Photo:** Ariadne Van Zandbergen (tc). **363 123RF.com:** wrangel (tc). **Getty Images:** David Lees / Corbis/VCG (bl). **364 Alamy Stock Photo:** Nataliya Hora (bl). **Bridgeman Images:** Bibliotheque Nationale, Paris, France (tr). **365 Bridgeman Images:** Vatican Museums and Galleries, Vatican City (r). **366 Dorling Kindersley:** Dave Rudkin / Birmingham Museum and Art Galleries (bl). **Getty Images:** DEA / A. Dagli Orti / De Agostini (tr). **367 Getty Images:** DEA / G. Dagli Orti / De Agostini (bc). **368-369 Bridgeman Images:** Vatican Museums, Vatican City / Pictures from History (bl). **369 Getty Images:** Leemage / Corbis (tc). **370 Alamy Stock Photo:** MuseoPics - Paul Williams (bl). **371 Bridgeman Images:** Asian Art Museum, San Francisco / Pictures from History (tl); Brabant School, (15th century) / Bibliotheque de L'Arsenal, Paris, France / Archives Charmet (br). **372 Bridgeman Images:** Pictures from History (bl). **Getty Images:** Bettmann (tr). **373 Getty Images:** DEA / A. Dagli Orti / De Agostini (bl). **374 Alamy Stock Photo:** Heritage Image Partnership Ltd (bl). **374-375 Sam Nixon:** (t). **375 Bridgeman Images:** German School, (13th century) / Aachen Cathedral Treasury, Aachen, Germany / De Agostini Picture Library / A. Dagli Orti (bc). **376 Bridgeman Images:** Pictures from History (tl). **Getty Images:** Frédéric Soltan / Corbis (br). **377 Getty Images:** Print Collector (tr). **378 Bridgeman Images:** Pictures from History / David Henley (tl). **378-379 Alamy Stock Photo:** Peter Sumner (b). **379 Getty Images:** Heritage Images / Museum of East Asian Art (tr). **380 akg-images:** Hervé Champollion (tl). **381 Bridgeman Images:** German School, (12th century) / Germanisches Nationalmuseum, Nuremberg, Germany (tl). **Getty Images:** Photo Josse / Leemage / Corbis (bl). **382 Getty Images:** Heritage Images / Fine Art Images (tl, br). **383 akg-images:** Pictures From History (br). **384 akg-images:** (l). **385 Bridgeman Images:** De Agostini Picture Library / A. De Gregorio (tl). **Getty Images:** Kean Collection / Staff (br). **386 Bridgeman Images:** Museo del Oro, Lima, Peru (bl). **387 akg-images:** Roland and Sabrina Michaud (br). **Bridgeman Images:** The Stapleton Collection (tl). **388 Getty Images:** DEA / W. Buss / De Agostini (br); Leemage / Corbis (tl). **389 Alamy Stock Photo:** Paul Fearn (tr). **390 Bridgeman Images:** Pictures from History (tr). **390-391 Getty Images:** Heritage Images / Fine Art Images (bl). **391 Getty Images:** DEA Picture Library / De Agostini (tr). **392 Dorling Kindersley:** Richard Leeney / Maidstone Museum and Bentliff Art Gallery (tl). **Getty Images:** UniversalImagesGroup / Universal History Archive (br). **393 Alamy Stock Photo:** MCLA Collection (tc). **394 Bridgeman Images:** State Hermitage Museum, St. Petersburg, Russia (tr). **Getty Images:** Science & Society Picture Library (bl). **395 Getty Images:** Fine Art / VCG Wilson / Corbis (r). **396 Bridgeman Images:** Christie's Images (bc). **397 Getty Images:** Heritage Images / Fine Art Images (br); Photo Josse / Leemage / Corbis (tl). **398 Bridgeman Images:** Coram in the care of the Foundling Museum, London (tl). **Getty Images:** Apic / Retired / Hulton Archive (bl). **398-399 Alamy Stock Photo:** GL Archive (br). **400 Alamy Stock Photo:** Diego Grandi (tl). **Getty Images:** Werner Forman / UIG (b). **401 Bridgeman Images:** Pictures from History (tc). **402 Alamy Stock Photo:** The Print Collector (tr). **Getty Images:** DEA Picture Library / De Agostini (bl). **403 Alamy Stock Photo:** Falkensteinfoto (b). **404 Alamy Stock Photo:** Granger Historical Picture Archive (bl). **405 Alamy Stock Photo:** World History Archive (br). **Getty Images:** Historical Picture Archive / Corbis (tl). **406 Getty Images:** Print Collector (bl). **407 Getty Images:** Bettmann (tl); Historical / Corbis (br). **408 Getty Images:** Fine Art / VCG Wilson/Corbis (bl). **409 Dorling Kindersley:** Gary Ombler / R. Florio (br). **Getty Images:** Hulton Archive / Stringer (tl). **410 Getty Images:** Universal History Archive / UIG (b). **411 Alamy Stock Photo:** IanDagnall Computing (tl). **Getty Images:** UniversalImagesGroup (br). **412 Getty Images:** Keystone-France / Gamma-Keystone (b); Print Collector / Ann Ronan Pictures (tl). **413 Getty Images:** Universal History Archive / UIG (tr). **414-415 Bridgeman Images:** Museo Nacional Centro de Arte Reina Sofia, Madrid, Spain / © Succession Picasso / © DACS 2018 (bl). **415 Getty Images:** Galerie Bilderwelt (tr). **416 Getty Images:** Bettmann (tr); SuperStock (bl). **417 Alamy Stock Photo:** Granger Historical Picture Archive (b). **418 Getty Images:** Bettmann (bc); Museum of Flight Foundation / Corbis (tl). **419 Alamy Stock Photo:** Science History Images (tr). **420 Getty Images:** Bettmann (tl); Peter Turnley / Corbis/VCG (br). **421 Getty Images:** Roger Hutchings / Corbis (tl). **422 123RF.com:** paolo77 (tl). **Getty Images:** Per-Anders Pettersson (br). **423 Getty Images:** Spencer Platt / Staff (tr). **424 Alamy Stock Photo:** Granger Historical Picture Archive (tr). **Getty Images:** Mike Clarke / Staff (b). **425 Alamy Stock Photo:** Newscom (tr)

All other images © Dorling Kindersley

For further information see: www.dkimages.com

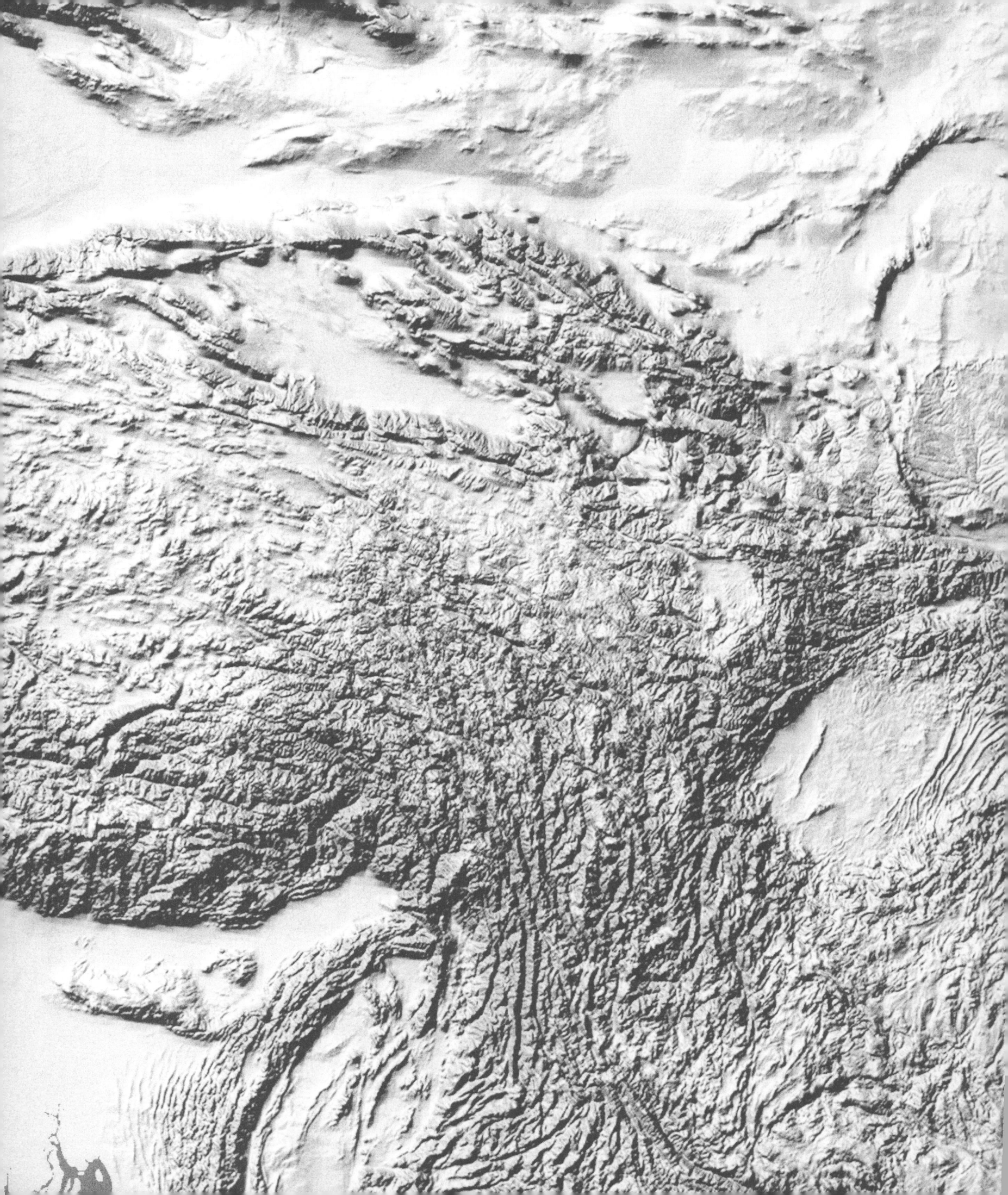

SMITHSONIAN

WORLD WAR II
MAP BY MAP

FOREWORD BY

PETER SNOW

10

THE SLIDE TO WAR 1918–1939

34

GERMANY TRIUMPHANT 1939–1941

CONTENTS

Penguin Random House

DK LONDON

Senior Editor Hugo Wilkinson
Project Editors Shashwati Tia Sarkar, Miezan van Zyl
Editor Polly Boyd
US Editors Megan Douglass, Lori Hand
Editorial Assistant Michael Clark
Project Assistant Briony Corbett
Managing Editor Angeles Gavira Guerrero
Associate Publishing Director Liz Wheeler
Publishing Director Jonathan Metcalf

Lead Senior Art Editor Duncan Turner
Senior Art Editor Sharon Spencer
Project Art Editor Steve Woosnam-Savage
Cartographer Ed Merritt
Jacket Design Development Manager Sophia MTT
Jacket Designer Surabhi Wadhwa
Jacket Editor Emma Dawson
Producer (Pre-production) Rob Dunn
Senior Producer Meskerem Berhane
Managing Art Editor Michael Duffy
Art Director Karen Self
Design Director Phil Ormerod

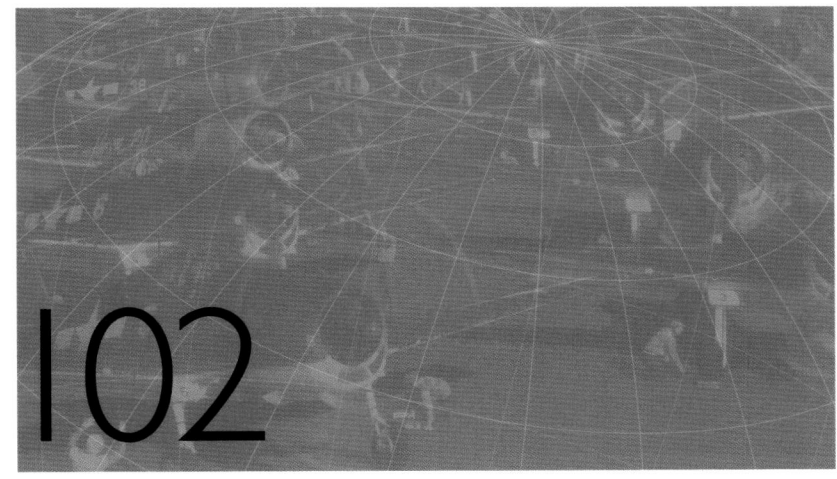

102

THE WIDENING WAR   1942

DK INDIA

Senior Editor Rupa Rao
Assistant Editors Aashirwad Jain, Sonali Jindal
Picture Researchers Akash Jain, Surya Sankash Sarangi
Picture Research Manager Taiyaba Khatoon
Jackets Editorial Coordinator Priyanka Sharma
Managing Editor Rohan Sinha
Managing Jackets Editor Saloni Singh
Pre-production Manager Balwant Singh
Cartographers Ashutosh Ranjan Bharti, Swati Handoo, Animesh Kumar Pathak
Cartography Manager Suresh Kumar

Lead Senior Art Editor Vaibhav Rastogi
Senior Art Editor Mahua Mandal
Project Art Editors Sanjay Chauhan, Anjali Sachar
Art Editors Rabia Ahmad, Mridushmita Bose, Debjyoti Mukherjee, Sonali Rawat Sharma
Managing Art Editor Sudakshina Basu
Senior Jackets Designer Suhita Dharamjit
Senior DTP Designers Harish Aggarwal, Vishal Bhatia, Jagtar Singh
Production Manager Pankaj Sharma

COBALT ID

Designer Darren Bland
Art Director Paul Reid
Editorial Director Marek Walisiewicz

CONTRIBUTORS

FOREWORD
Peter Snow CBE

CONSULTANT
Richard Overy, Professor of History, Exeter University

WRITERS
Simon Adams, Tony Allan, Kay Celtel, R.G. Grant, Jeremy Harwood, Philip Parker, Christopher Westhorp

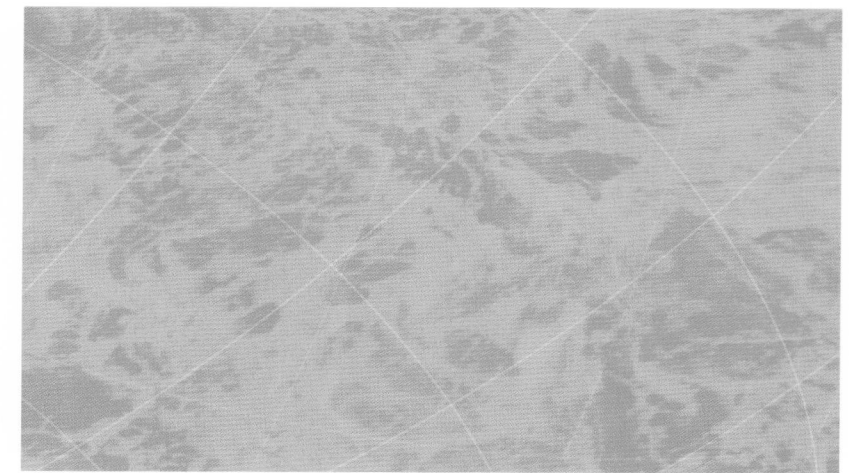

156

TURNING THE TIDE 1943–1944

First American Edition, 2019
Published in the United States by DK Publishing, 1745 Broadway, 20th Floor, New York, NY 10019

Copyright © 2019 Dorling Kindersley Limited
DK, a Division of Penguin Random House LLC
22 23 10 9 8 7 6
001-311581-Sep/2019
Foreword copyright © 2019 Peter Snow

DK books are available at special discounts when purchased in bulk for sales promotions, premiums, fund-raising, or educational use. For details, contact: DK Publishing Special Markets, 1745 Broadway, 20th Floor, New York, NY 10019 SpecialSales@dk.com

A catalog record for this book is available from the Library of Congress.
ISBN: 978-1-4654-8179-5

Printed and bound in UAE
A WORLD OF IDEAS:
SEE ALL THERE IS TO KNOW
www.dk.com

Smithsonian Institution

CURATOR

Dr. F. Robert van der Linden, Chairman, Aeronautics Department, National Air and Space Museum

SMITHSONIAN ENTERPRISES

Product Development Manager Kealy Gordon

Editorial Director Ellen Nanney

Vice President, Consumer Brigid Ferraro
and Education Products

Senior Vice President, Consumer Carol LeBlanc
and Education Products

224

ENDGAME AND AFTERMATH   1944–1955

SMITHSONIAN

Established in 1846, the Smithsonian—the world's largest museum and research complex—includes 19 museums and galleries and the National Zoological Park. The total number of artifacts, works of art, and specimens in the Smithsonian's collections is estimated at 154 million, the bulk of which is contained in the National Museum of Natural History, which holds more than 126 million specimens and objects. The Smithsonian is a renowned research center, dedicated to public education, national service, and scholarship in the arts, sciences, and natural history.

FOREWORD

This is the most compelling work of military geography I've ever seen. It's a testament to the titanic scale of the conflict of 1939–1945, which dwarfs all others in world history. The ferocity of World War II— the level of its violence and the cost in human life—almost defies description: up to 80 million deaths; some 20 million on the battlefield; and around three times more than that among civilians caught up in the firestorm of bombing and all-embracing warfare on land, sea, and air. What these maps explain in intricate detail is the mobility and speed with which mechanized armies could sweep across vast areas, and with which warships and aircraft could inflict destruction at ranges never before dreamed of.

No earlier conflict has demanded such comprehensive mapping. No other conflict has been as challenging to the cartographer. Each of the pivotal moments of the war is marked by more movement and the exercise of more industrial might than in any previous war. It is maps such as these that can help us to envisage the scope, the size, and the sheer pace of Hitler's blitzkrieg, which crushed the Low Countries and France in the spring of 1940. Other instances of mass mobility are illuminated for us—the see-sawing of the rival armies in North Africa in 1940–1943, the great leap across the Mediterranean by Montgomery's and Patton's armies from North Africa to Sicily and Italy, the lightning Nazi assault on Stalin's Soviet Union, and

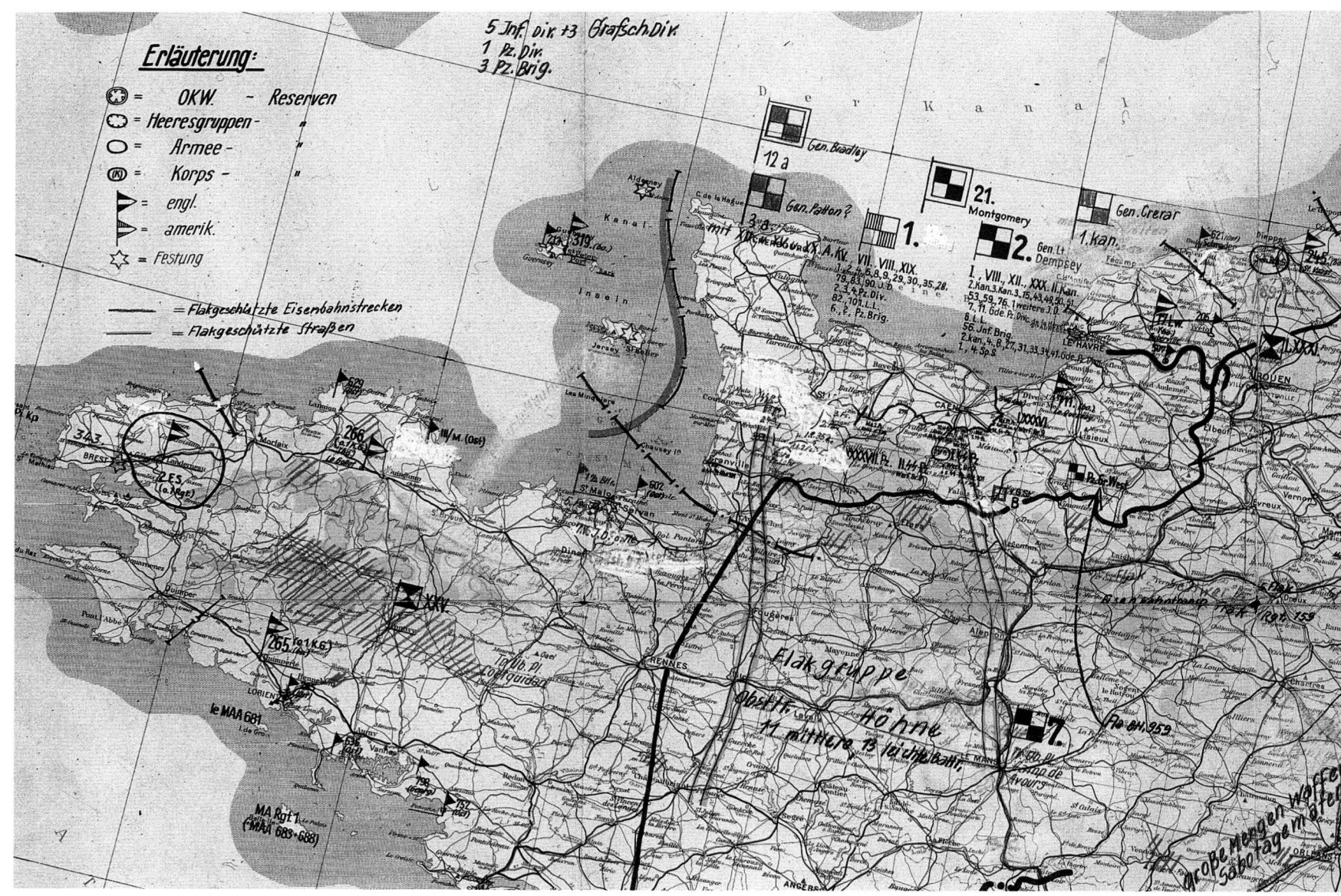

▽ **Contemporary map of action in Normandy**
This German situation map shows Axis and Allied troop movements in 1944. Following the Allied counterinvasion of France on D-Day, the two sides battled fiercely for control of territory in northern France, Belgium, and the Netherlands in what was to be one of the pivotal episodes of the war in Europe (see pp.190–191).

the astonishing turnaround after Stalingrad in 1942–1943. Perhaps most dramatically of all, we can see the greatest seaborne invasion of all time on D-Day in June 1944.

This book also reminds us that the war enveloped Asia. It describes the great naval battles of the Pacific that followed Japan's attack on Pearl Harbor on December 7, 1941. This was, in President Roosevelt's words, the "date which will live in infamy," propelling the US into the war. More than anything, it was the commitment of America's industrial might on the side of the Allies that spelled the end for Germany, Italy, and Japan. The set of maps describing the desperately hard-fought and costly series of battles that finally consumed Japan's short-lived

Pacific empire is an essential guide to the understanding of the massive task that confronted the US forces. This comprehensive picture of World War II is enhanced by further maps and features that illustrate the state of the world before and after the fighting, and the wider social, political, and economic aspects of the conflict. We also get a glimpse of the kind of mapping that was available to military commanders at the time. I've long been fascinated by the way good maps have helped me and other commentators explain the ups and downs of warfare. This book is right at the forefront of that great enterprise.

PETER SNOW, 2019

THE SLIDE TO WAR 1918—1939

MOUNTING TENSIONS AFTER WORLD WAR I LED TO INSTABILITY AND THE RISE OF EXTREMIST NATIONALISM IN EUROPE, WHILE CLASHES IN ASIA GATHERED MOMENTUM. A NEW GLOBAL WAR DREW NEAR.

△ **Nationalist propaganda**
This Spanish Civil War poster promotes the Nationalist cause. Fought between Republicans and Nationalists, the war epitomized the right–left divide that polarized Europe in the 1930s.

THE SEEDS OF WAR

The world of the 1920s and 1930s was scarred by ideological divisions, social conflicts, and economic collapse. Aggressive militarists intent on conquest rose to power in major states, notably Germany and Japan, and the clumsy efforts of liberal democracies to preserve the peace only precipitated a headlong rush to war.

It is a sad irony that the origins of World War II can be directly traced back to World War I, which was known as "the war to end war." This immensely destructive conflict bred a widespread popular longing for peace, but also left a heritage of grievance, insecurity, and instability. Germany in particular found it hard to come to terms with defeat, and the Versailles peace treaty, devised by the victorious powers in 1919, was bitterly resented by most Germans, who felt it was too punitive. The German Weimar Republic, the government founded in 1919, was weak, facing hyperinflation and armed revolts from both the right and the left.

From peace to rearmament

During the 1920s, there was encouraging evidence of recovery, with a marked improvement in international affairs. The League of Nations, set up in 1920

▷ **Japanese firepower**
The Type 92 heavy machine gun was one of the weapons adopted by Japan as it pursued military expansion in the 1930s.

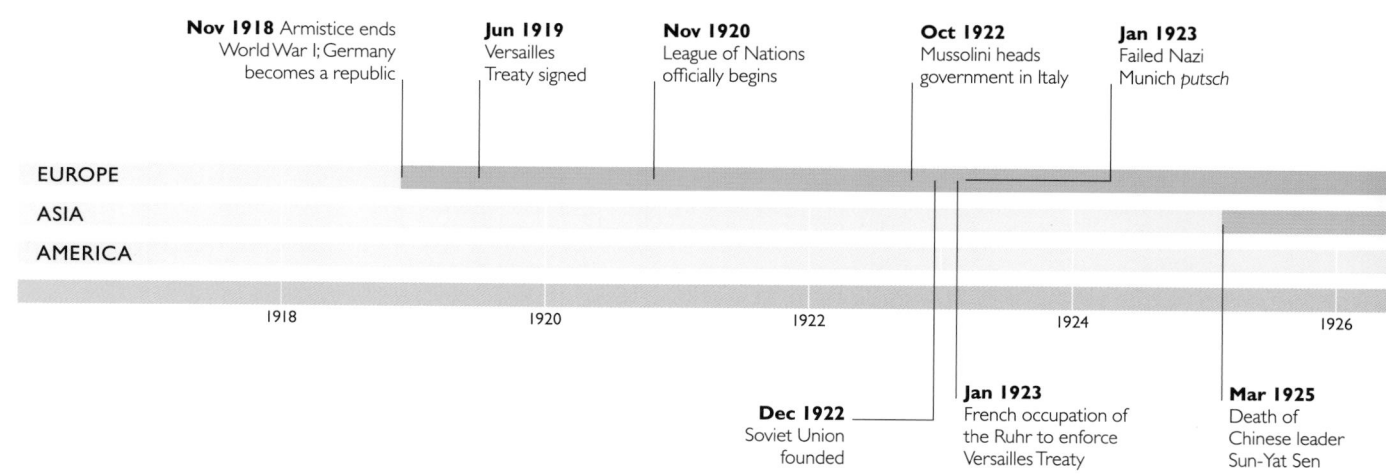

under the terms of the peace treaty, pursued ambitious plans for collective security and disarmament, although its authority was lessened by the refusal of the US to take part. After a crisis over enforcement of the Treaty of Versailles in 1923, Germany and France started making moves toward normalizing relations, but true stability proved elusive. The transformation of the former Russian Empire into the Soviet Union—a Communist state theoretically committed to world revolution—constituted a new unsettling factor in international politics. In Italy, also fatally destabilized by World War I, Fascist dictator Benito Mussolini took power. In China, Nationalists struggled to uphold a central government against Communists and warlords.

Hopes for a return to "normalcy" disappeared definitively with the onset of the Great Depression in 1929, after the Wall Street Crash. This crushing blow to the global economy had a devastating impact on a world riven by domestic and international tensions. As trade collapsed, major powers were tempted to seek economic security through political control of territory and resources. Faced with mass unemployment and falling living standards, many countries abandoned liberalism for authoritarian government. In Germany, the impact of the Depression turned Adolf Hitler's Nazi Party from a marginal extremist movement into a major

BETWEEN THE WARS

In Europe, a period of turmoil after the end of World War I was followed by relative stability in the mid-1920s. Then the onset of the Great Depression in 1929 propelled Hitler's rise to power in Germany. After that, German aggression led to crisis after crisis, until the fateful invasion of Poland that started World War II in Europe in September 1939. The Japanese invasion of China in 1937 had already led to war in Asia.

EUROPE

ASIA

AMERICA

Nov 1918 Armistice ends World War I; Germany becomes a republic

Jun 1919 Versailles Treaty signed

Nov 1920 League of Nations officially begins

Oct 1922 Mussolini heads government in Italy

Jan 1923 Failed Nazi Munich *putsch*

1918   1920   1922   1924   1926

Dec 1922 Soviet Union founded

Jan 1923 French occupation of the Ruhr to enforce Versailles Treaty

Mar 1925 Death of Chinese leader Sun-Yat Sen

◁ **Unopposed conquest**
Occupying Czechoslovakia without a fight, the German army parades through the streets of Prague before a sullen crowd in spring 1939.

political force. Marshaling German resentment against the Treaty of Versailles, Hitler linked solving Germany's economic problems to a reassertion of German military power. Within two years of Hitler becoming Chancellor of Germany in 1933, the country had embarked on open, full-scale rearmament. Meanwhile, in East Asia, an increasingly militarist Japan was tempted by Chinese weakness into encroachments that culminated in a full-scale invasion in 1937. Mussolini's Italy committed its own smaller-scale act of aggression with an invasion of Ethiopia in 1935. Revealed as impotent to prevent such breaches of world peace, the League of Nations faded into insignificance.

The lead-up to war
Britain and France, both liberal democracies, struggled to find an adequate response to the rise of naked aggression. They failed to take action when Hitler rearmed in defiance of the Treaty of Versailles. When civil war broke out in Spain in 1936, and Germany and Italy intervened on the side of right-wing rebels, the British and French stayed neutral, refusing to align with the ideologically opposed Soviet Union, which supported the Spanish government.

Belatedly, the democracies began to rearm, but they were desperate to avoid war with Germany, fearful of the possibly immediate effect of aerial bombardment. British prime minister Neville Chamberlain decided on a policy of appeasement, seeking to satisfy German grievances. In 1938, Hitler was allowed to absorb Austria and take the Sudetenland from Czechoslovakia. However, this was not enough for the Nazi leader. Instead, he actively desired war and conquest, making plans to reverse the verdict of World War I and establish German domination in Europe.

After Germany occupied Prague in March 1939, the British government decided to oppose any further Nazi expansionism. When Britain and France promised to assist Poland, Hitler's next target, a countdown to war began. Britain and France were still reluctant to ally with the Soviet Union. As they dallied, the Soviet dictator Joseph Stalin opted for a deal with Hitler, clearing the way for a German attack on Poland and the start of World War II.

"War is to man what motherhood is to woman ... I do not believe in perpetual peace."

BENITO MUSSOLINI, ITALIAN DICTATOR, 1939

▷ **The face of Fascism**
Italian Fascist leader Benito Mussolini set the model for the uniformed dictators who dominated Europe between the wars.

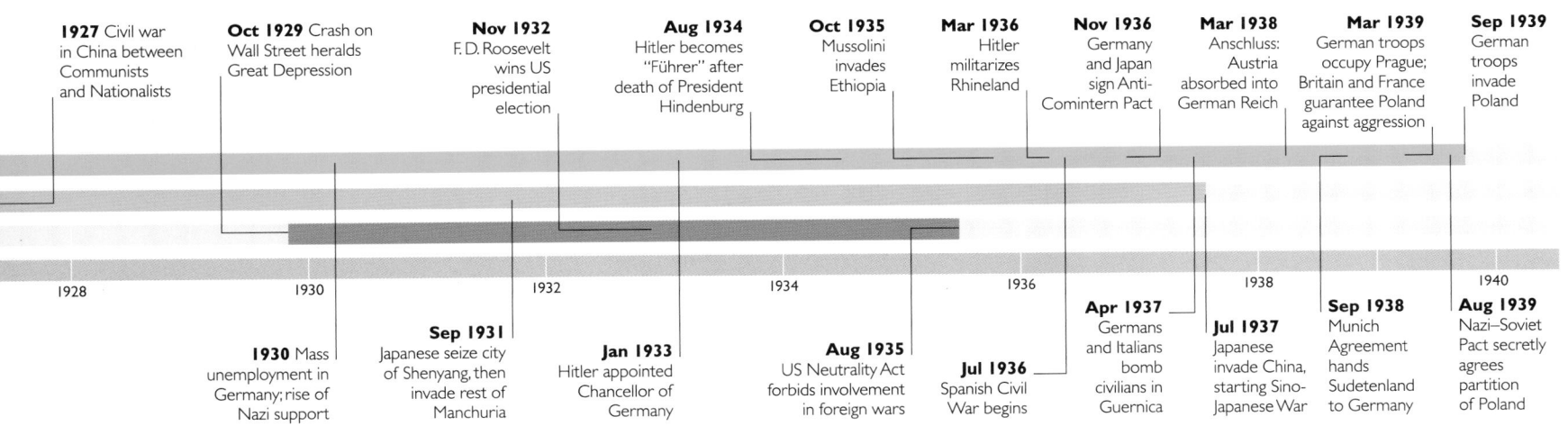

1927 Civil war in China between Communists and Nationalists

Oct 1929 Crash on Wall Street heralds Great Depression

Nov 1932 F. D. Roosevelt wins US presidential election

Aug 1934 Hitler becomes "Führer" after death of President Hindenburg

Oct 1935 Mussolini invades Ethiopia

Mar 1936 Hitler militarizes Rhineland

Nov 1936 Germany and Japan sign Anti-Comintern Pact

Mar 1938 Anschluss: Austria absorbed into German Reich

Mar 1939 German troops occupy Prague; Britain and France guarantee Poland against aggression

Sep 1939 German troops invade Poland

1928   1930   1932   1934   1936   1938   1940

1930 Mass unemployment in Germany; rise of Nazi support

Sep 1931 Japanese seize city of Shenyang, then invade rest of Manchuria

Jan 1933 Hitler appointed Chancellor of Germany

Aug 1935 US Neutrality Act forbids involvement in foreign wars

Jul 1936 Spanish Civil War begins

Apr 1937 Germans and Italians bomb civilians in Guernica

Jul 1937 Japanese invade China, starting Sino-Japanese War

Sep 1938 Munich Agreement hands Sudetenland to Germany

Aug 1939 Nazi–Soviet Pact secretly agrees partition of Poland

AVEZ VOUS PLACE DANS VOTRE COEUR POUR NOUS?

◁ War children
This poster from 1917 asks "Have you room in your hearts for us?," appealing on behalf of the many thousands of French children left fatherless by World War I. The scale of the casualties had far-reaching implications in the combatants' home countries.

1920 Russia recognizes Finnish independence in the Treaty of Tartu.

1920 Estonia is liberated from Russia following a short war of independence.

1921 After a Russian defeat outside Warsaw, Poland and Russia reach agreement on their common border.

1921 Russia recognizes Latvian independence under the Treaty of Riga.

1920 Poland annexes Wilno from Lithuania, which it gains by plebiscite in 1922.

1920 A peace treaty is signed between Russia and Lithuania.

1922 Ireland is divided between a mainly Catholic Free State and a mainly Protestant six-county entity in the north.

1916 Irish Republicans launch the Easter Rising in Dublin against British rule.

1919 Saarland is placed under League of Nations mandate until reunited with Germany by plebiscite in 1935.

1919 The former German city of Danzig becomes a Free City under the League of Nations.

1920 Teschen is partitioned between Poland and Czechoslovakia.

1923–1925 French and Belgian troops occupy the Ruhr after Germany fails to pay reparations.

1919 Rhineland is demilitarized until 1936.

1919 Alsace-Lorraine returns to France after 48 years of German rule.

1919 The Treaty of St.-Germain sets new borders for Austria.

6 EUROPE IN DISPUTE 1919–1925

The treaties that ended the war in Europe attempted to resolve many outstanding territorial disputes. Most involved returning lands lost in previous wars or addressing the issues of ethnic groups living on the "wrong" side of a new border. Plebiscites—public referendums—were called to allow local people the final say on their future government.

○ Areas of dispute   Plebiscites held

1920 The Treaty of Trianon settles new borders for Hungary.

1918 The Kingdom of the Serbs, Croats, and Slovenes is created from the Austro-Hungarian empire and Serbia; it is renamed Yugoslavia in 1929.

1918 Bessarabia is added to Romania.

1920–1922 Greeks occupy Eastern Thrace.

5 THE NEW TURKEY 1919–1923

Following an armistice with Ottoman Turkey in October 1918, the victorious Allies sought to partition the country in the 1920 Treaty of Sèvres. Turkish Nationalists under Mustafa Kemal rejected the treaty and gradually expelled the occupying Greek, Armenian, and French armies by 1922. The Ottoman sultanate was abolished and the new republic recognized by the 1923 Treaty of Lausanne, which approved Turkey's new borders.

Turkey after Treaty of Sèvres

Land restored to Turkey after Treaty of Lausanne, 1923

// Annexed by Turkey, 1921

4 THE BREAKUP OF THE GERMAN EMPIRE 1918–1923

At the end of the war, Kaiser Wilhelm II fled to the Netherlands, and Germany became a republic. The Treaty of Versailles in 1919 imposed punitive terms on Germany. Land was lost to Denmark, Belgium, France, and Poland; its empire was removed, its armed forces reduced, and its fleet confiscated. Germany was also made to pay war reparations.

— German border, 1918

Areas under League of Nations High Commissioners

👤 Ruhr under armed occupation

// Demilitarized Rhineland

1925 Greece and Bulgaria are in conflict over Macedonia.

1919 Greece occupies Smyrna, leading to war with Turkey until 1922.

SWEDEN

NORWAY

FINLAND

Petrograd

Åland Is.

ESTONIA   Pskov

LATVIA

LITHUANIA

Wilno

WHITE RUSSIA

North Sea

DENMARK

MEMEL TERRITORY

SCHLESWIG-HOLSTEIN

Danzig   EAST PRUSSIA

Allenstein

Marienwerder

POLISH CORRIDOR

UKRAINE

NORTHERN IRELAND

IRISH FREE STATE

Dublin

UNITED KINGDOM

NETHERLANDS

RUHR

BELGIUM

Eupen

LUXEMBOURG

GERMANY

UPPER SILESIA

POLAND

Brest-Litovsk

RHINELAND

ALSACE-LORRAINE

FRANCE

SWITZERLAND

BOHEMIA

CZECHOSLOVAKIA

RUTHENIA

Teschen

AUSTRIA   SLOVAKIA

CARINTHIA   Sopron

HUNGARY

TRANSYLVANIA

BESSARABIA

ROMANIA

SLOVENIA

KINGDOM OF SERBS, CROATS, AND SLOVENES

CROATIA

DALMATIA

BOSNIA-HERZEGOVINA

SERBIA

Corsica

ITALY

Adriatic Sea

MONTENEGRO

MACEDONIA

BULGARIA

EASTERN THRACE

SPAIN

ALBANIA

NORTHERN EPIRUS

WESTERN THRACE

GREECE

Smyrna

Baltic Sea

Dodecanese Is.

Crete

AFTER THE WAR

The borders of many European countries were redrawn after World War I, as empires collapsed and new countries were born. This new settlement was often violent, and left its own damaging legacy.

KEY

— National borders, 1923

TIMELINE

1
2
3
4
5
6

1915   1920   1925   1930

RUSSIA

1   END OF THE RUSSIAN EMPIRE   1917–1921

The February Revolution of 1917 that overthrew the Romanov Czar and the October Revolution that ended the provisional government led to a Communist takeover of Russia. The Bolshevik regime arranged a cease-fire with Germany in December 1917, and in March 1918 signed the Treaty of Brest-Litovsk, renouncing its claims on Finland, the Baltic provinces, Poland, and Ukraine.

1918 Russia signs the Treaty of Brest-Litovsk, giving up its claims on lands west of the Brest-Litovsk line.

▬ Russian border, December 1917

▦ Areas temporarily autonomous or independent

▪▪▪ Brest-Litovsk treaty line

2   THE BREAKUP OF THE AUSTRO-HUNGARIAN EMPIRE   1918–1920

The Hapsburg Empire's collapse led to three new states: Austria, Hungary, and Czechoslovakia. Former Austrian territory was added to Poland, Romania, and what later became Yugoslavia. Austria had to pay reparations, was forbidden to unite with Germany, and saw its army restricted. The old Kingdom of Hungary lost two-thirds of its land and many ethnic Hungarians to Romania and elsewhere.

▬ Austria-Hungary border, 1914

Rostov

Caucasus

GEORGIA

AZERBAIJAN

1915–1922 Around 1.5 million Turkish Armenians are killed by Turkish Nationalists.

Black Sea

ARMENIA

TURKISH ARMENIA

Lake Van

PERSIA

TURKEY

Anatolia

Ankara

TURKISH KURDISTAN

1923 Ankara becomes new capital of Republican Turkey.

3   EMERGING STATES   1918–1922

The collapse of the Ottoman, German, Russian, and Austro-Hungarian empires at the end of the war led to the formation of new states in central Europe: Estonia; Finland; Austria; Czechoslovakia; Poland; Hungary; Lithuania; Latvia; and the Kingdom of Serbs, Croats, and Slovenes. They were joined by the Irish Free State, which broke free from Britain in 1922 after a brutal civil war.

▦ New states created

Cyprus

THE LEGACY OF WORLD WAR I

The end of war in Europe in 1918 saw the collapse of four major empires. The map of the continent needed to be redrawn, and the future home of millions of people decided. As new states emerged and old conflicts were slowly resolved, the legacy of the war continued to be felt across Europe for many years.

The peace treaties that settled the future of Europe after 1919 were the result of numerous compromises between the "Big Four": the victorious Allied powers of the US, UK, France, and Italy. American president Woodrow Wilson wanted to forge a liberal peace settlement based on national self-determination, while French prime minister Georges Clemenceau wanted above all to ensure the future security of his country and make Germany pay for the war—a view that was shared by David Lloyd George, prime minister of Britain. The resulting treaties had the overall effect of pleasing no one, and left the people and governments of many countries profoundly dissatisfied with the outcome.

Territorial disputes continued to divide nations, notably in Eastern Europe, while actual fighting continued in Turkey until 1922. Many of the new states were crudely carved out of Austro-Hungary and the other old empires, while defeated Germany emerged as a shrunken republic and imperial Russia, excluded from the peace talks, became the world's first Communist state.

While some problems were addressed by the peace treaties, the legacy of the war had profound social, economic, and political consequences across Europe and Asia, and would become one of the defining causes of a new world war within 20 years.

"My home policy: I wage war. My foreign policy: I wage war. All the time I wage war."

GEORGES CLEMENCEAU, 1918

WRITING THE PEACE

The victorious Allied politicians and diplomats met in Paris in 1919 to draw up a series of treaties with the defeated Central Powers, each one named after the palaces, chateaux, and towns to the west of Paris where they were signed. The main treaty was signed with Germany at Versailles in June 1919, followed by St.-Germain-en-Laye with Austria in September 1919, Neuilly-sur-Seine with Bulgaria in November 1919, Trianon with Hungary in June 1920, and finally the abortive Sèvres treaty with Turkey in August 1920.

Signing the Treaty of Versailles

△ Giving peace a chance
This postcard in favor of Switzerland's membership of the League of Nations in 1920 reveals a mood of optimism.

2 MEMBERSHIP OF THE LEAGUE 1920–1939

The League had 42 founding members, and by 1934 its membership stood at 58. The US, Saudi Arabia, Yemen, Mongolia, Bhutan, and Nepal never joined. The USSR belonged only in 1934–1939, while Japan and Germany left in 1933, Italy in 1937, and Spain in 1939. As colonies and mandates were excluded from membership, most of Africa, Southeast Asia, and the Pacific went unrepresented in the League.

1932 Former Ottoman Iraq becomes the first (British) mandate to achieve independence.

1923 France acquires a mandate over former Ottoman Syria, including the future Lebanon.

1933 The New German chancellor Adolf Hitler quickly pulls Germany out of the League.

GREENLAND ☆

ICELAND

See panel

1932–34 The World Disarmament Conference meets in Geneva with representatives from 60 states but fails to make any progress.

1936 The League refuses to intervene in the Spanish Civil War despite pleas from the Republican government.

CANADA

1919 The US Senate refuses to ratify the Treaty of Versailles, thereby excluding the US from the League.

USA

PACIFIC OCEAN

MEXICO 1931

GUATEMALA 1920–36

EL SALVADOR 1924–37

HAITI

CUBA

DOMINICAN REPUBLIC 1924

HONDURAS 1920–36

NICARAGUA 1920–36

PANAMA

COSTA RICA 1920–25

VENEZUELA 1920–38

COLOMBIA

ECUADOR 1934

1923 Britain acquires a mandate over former Ottoman Palestine, and creates Transjordan (later Jordan) as an autonomous area.

1930 A League report leads to the Liberian government outlawing slavery.

PALESTINE   SYRIA   PERSIA
IRAQ   TRANSJORDAN

MOROCCO   LIBYA   EGYPT 1937

ALGERIA

FRENCH WEST AFRICA

BRITISH TOGO

LIBERIA

FRENCH TOGO

ANGLO-EGYPTIAN SUDAN

NIGERIA

UGANDA

RUANDA-URUNDI

ETHIOPIA 1923–1937

BELGIAN CONGO   KENYA

BRITISH CAMEROONS

TANGANYIKA

FRENCH CAMEROONS

NYASALAND

ANGOLA

NORTHERN RHODESIA

FRENCH EQUATORIAL AFRICA

SOUTHERN RHODESIA

MOZAMBIQUE

MADAGASCAR

BECHUANALAND

SOUTH-WEST AFRICA

SOUTH AFRICA

1 FOUNDING OF THE LEAGUE 1919

Established under the Treaty of Versailles of 1919 that ended World War I, the League of Nations met for the first time in Paris on January 10, 1920. It consisted of a General Assembly of all member states, an Executive Council limited to the major powers, and a permanent secretariat. All were based in Geneva, Switzerland. A Permanent Court of International Justice, sitting in The Hague in the Netherlands, judged disputes referred to it.

PERU 1920–39

BOLIVIA

CHILE 1920–38

BRAZIL 1920–26

1926 Brazil becomes the first founding member of the League to leave.

PARAGUAY 1920–35

ARGENTINA

URUGUAY

1935 The League imposes weak sanctions on Italy after its invasion of Ethiopia but fails to prevent Italian seizure of the country.

THE LEAGUE IN ACTION

Active from 1920 until its eventual replacement by the United Nations in 1946, the League became largely irrelevant at the outbreak of World War II.

KEY

■ Founder members and states	■ Possessions of member states	■ States and their possessions that withdrew or were expelled
■ Subsequent members, with dates of membership	■ Mandated territories	— Borders, 1930
	■ Non-member states	

TIMELINE

1					
2					
3					
4					
5					
6					
1910	1930	1950	1970	1990	

6 THE FAILURE OF THE LEAGUE 1930–1939

The League settled a number of disputes around the world, but it did not reduce the world's stock of armaments. Moreover, it significantly failed to halt the military expansions in Germany, Italy, and Japan that eventually led to World War II; the hostile actions of these nations went unpunished throughout the 1930s. Ultimately, the League's belief in collective security proved no match for states acting in their own national interests.

5 DRIVING DISARMAMENT 1926–1939

Under Article 8 of its founding covenant, the League aimed to reduce world armaments. In 1926 it set up a commission to prepare for a world conference on disarmament, which eventually met in Geneva in 1932 but effectively collapsed in 1933 when Hitler withdrew. Meanwhile the Kellogg–Briand Pact, an international treaty forged outside the League in 1928, sought but failed to outlaw conflict as an instrument of national policy.

3 THE MANDATE SYSTEM 1919–1990

After the defeat of Germany and Ottoman Turkey in World War I, their possessions in Africa, the Pacific, and the Middle East were ceded to the Allies under the authority of the League. Legal mandates allowed these lands to be administered on behalf of the League by member countries. The British mandate of Iraq became independent in 1932; the rest gained independence after World War II.

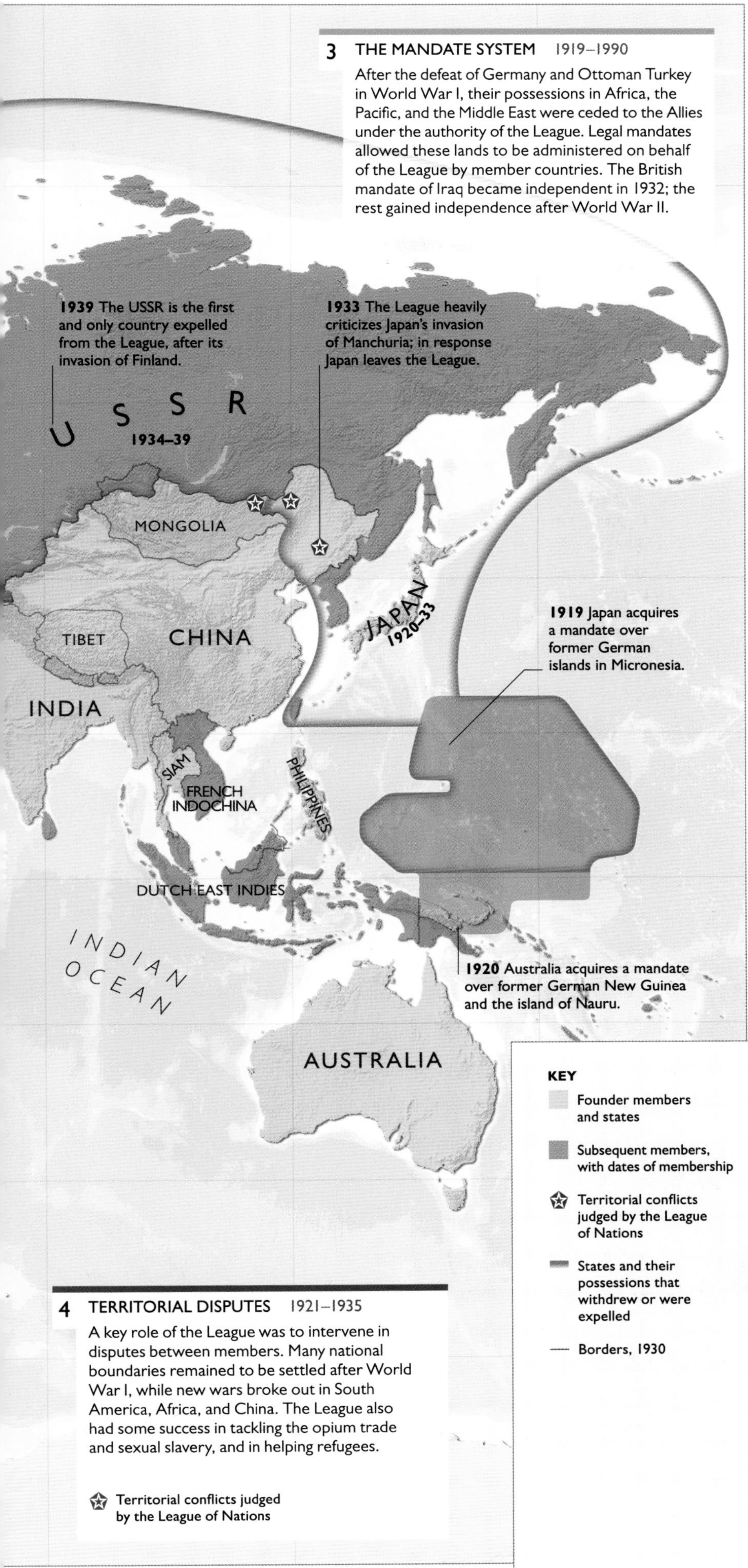

1939 The USSR is the first and only country expelled from the League, after its invasion of Finland.

1933 The League heavily criticizes Japan's invasion of Manchuria; in response Japan leaves the League.

U S S R
1934–39

MONGOLIA

TIBET   CHINA

INDIA

SIAM

FRENCH INDOCHINA

PHILIPPINES

DUTCH EAST INDIES

JAPAN
1920–33

1919 Japan acquires a mandate over former German islands in Micronesia.

INDIAN OCEAN

1920 Australia acquires a mandate over former German New Guinea and the island of Nauru.

AUSTRALIA

THE LEAGUE OF NATIONS

After the horrors of World War I, a group of countries conceived the idea of a League of Nations, the world's first-ever international organization whose primary mission would be to maintain world peace and avoid another catastrophic global war.

The name "League of Nations" was coined in 1914 by the British political scientist and pacifist Goldsworthy Lowes Dickinson, who drew up a draft diagram for its organization. As World War I progressed, leaders of the eventually victorious Allies began to clarify their war aims, agreeing that there should be some form of international organization created to prevent future wars. This idea was made explicit by American president Woodrow Wilson who, in January 1918, included in his Fourteen Points that were used to negotiate the end of the war a "league of nations to insure peace and justice."

The founding covenant of the League was written by the British diplomat Lord Robert Cecil and the South African statesman Jan Smuts, and was agreed during the 1919 Paris Peace Conference. To achieve world peace, the covenant pledged the League's support for disarmament, and it stated that its aim was to prevent wars through collective security, in which member states would respond collectively to any threats to world peace. The League would also extend international relations in the fields of finance, trade, and transportation, and help promote health and the struggle against drugs, prostitution, and slavery. Many of its lofty ambitions were thwarted, however, by member states acting in their own interests.

4 TERRITORIAL DISPUTES 1921–1935

A key role of the League was to intervene in disputes between members. Many national boundaries remained to be settled after World War I, while new wars broke out in South America, Africa, and China. The League also had some success in tackling the opium trade and sexual slavery, and in helping refugees.

⭐ Territorial conflicts judged by the League of Nations

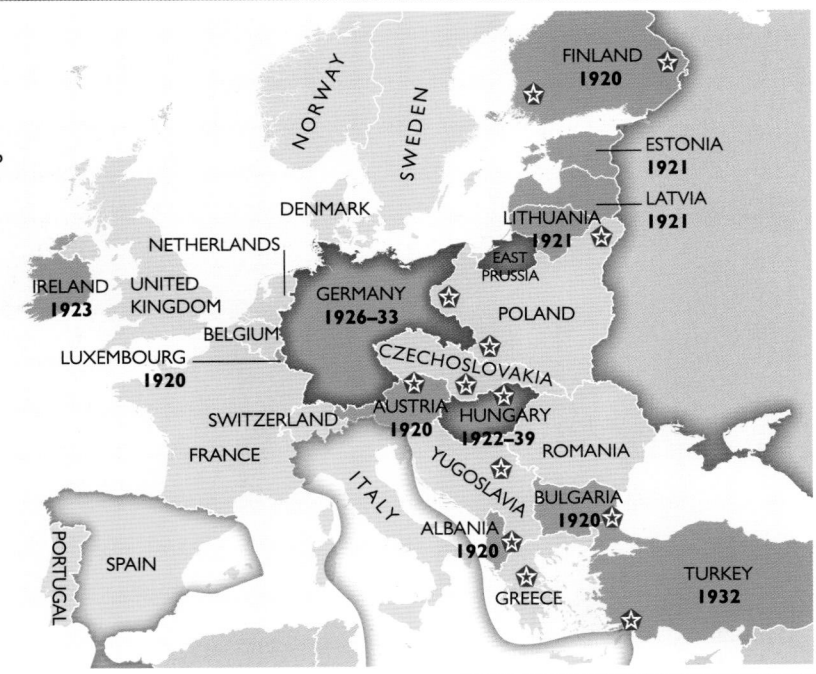

KEY

▢ Founder members and states

▢ Subsequent members, with dates of membership

⭐ Territorial conflicts judged by the League of Nations

▬ States and their possessions that withdrew or were expelled

—— Borders, 1930

NORWAY

SWEDEN

FINLAND 1920

DENMARK

ESTONIA 1921

LATVIA 1921

LITHUANIA 1921

NETHERLANDS

IRELAND 1923

UNITED KINGDOM

EAST PRUSSIA

GERMANY 1926–33

POLAND

BELGIUM

LUXEMBOURG 1920

CZECHOSLOVAKIA

SWITZERLAND

AUSTRIA 1920

HUNGARY 1922–39

ROMANIA

FRANCE

ITALY

YUGOSLAVIA

BULGARIA 1920

ALBANIA 1920

PORTUGAL

SPAIN

GREECE

TURKEY 1932

DIVIDED EUROPE

The interwar years saw the failure of democracy in most European nations as both Fascism and Communism gained ground. Strong, often dictatorial leaders took control of their countries.

KEY

Fascist regime

Communist regime

Other dictatorship

Right-wing activity

Strikes and riots during the 1930s

Over 20 percent unemployment by 1932

Percentage decrease in industrial output from 1929 to 1932

TIMELINE

1   2   3   4   5   6

1915   1920   1925   1930   1935   1940

6 SPAIN AND PORTUGAL 1931–1939

In Spain, the dictatorship of Primo de Rivera, which had begun in 1923, was replaced in 1931 by a republic that failed to gain widespread support. A brutal civil war in 1936–1939 led to the victory of the proto-Fascist Nationalists under General Franco. Portugal emerged from its limited role in World War I with a weak republican government, but by 1932 it had embraced the conservative and authoritarian ideologies of Antonio de Salazar, who became prime minister with almost dictatorial powers.

5 ECONOMIC DOWNTURN 1929–1939

The New York Stock Exchange crash (see box, right) led to an international financial crisis that crippled the economies of Europe. International economic collaboration broke down and was replaced by insular economic nationalism. This weakened some already fragile democratic governments, with many countries establishing Fascist or other dictatorial governments. Nationalist groups also gained popularity in democracies such as the Netherlands and France.

4 GERMANY AND AUSTRIA 1929–1939

Germany emerged from World War I defeated, divided, and demoralized. Its democratic Weimar government lacked popular support, and was debilitated by the financial crisis after 1929. The far-right Nazi party under Adolf Hitler pledged national renewal, taking power in January 1933 and establishing a one-party totalitarian state. The newly formed Austria was similarly weak, becoming an authoritarian state in 1933 before Nazi Germany annexed it in March 1938.

▽ The March on Rome

With the threat of civil war looming in Italy, Benito Mussolini and his Fascist Blackshirts marched on Rome October 28–29, 1922, leading to Mussolini's appointment as prime minister.

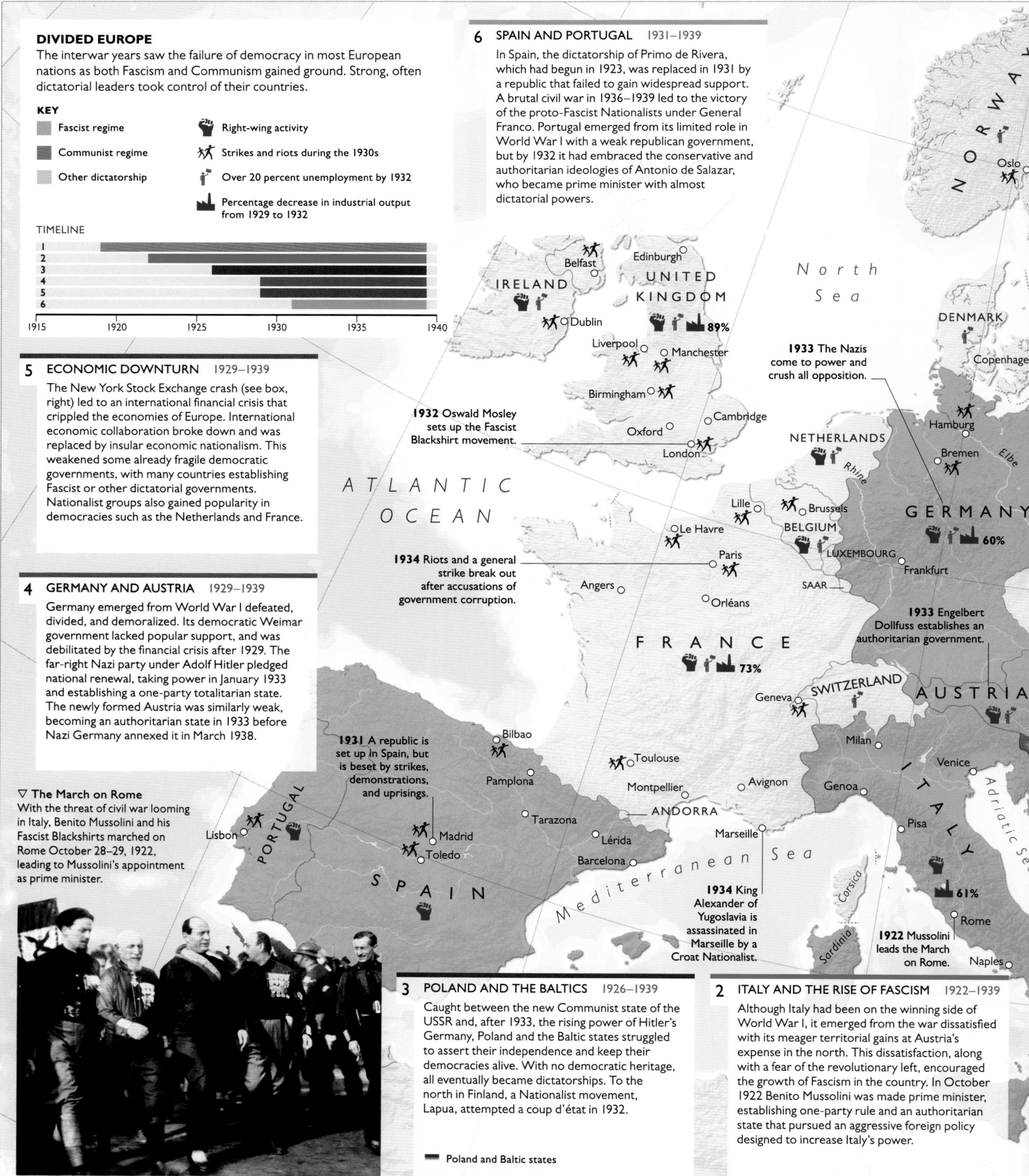

1932 Oswald Mosley sets up the Fascist Blackshirt movement.

1933 The Nazis come to power and crush all opposition.

1934 Riots and a general strike break out after accusations of government corruption.

1933 Engelbert Dollfuss establishes an authoritarian government.

1931 A republic is set up in Spain, but is beset by strikes, demonstrations, and uprisings.

1934 King Alexander of Yugoslavia is assassinated in Marseille by a Croat Nationalist.

1922 Mussolini leads the March on Rome.

3 POLAND AND THE BALTICS 1926–1939

Caught between the new Communist state of the USSR and, after 1933, the rising power of Hitler's Germany, Poland and the Baltic states struggled to assert their independence and keep their democracies alive. With no democratic heritage, all eventually became dictatorships. To the north in Finland, a Nationalist movement, Lapua, attempted a coup d'état in 1932.

— Poland and Baltic states

2 ITALY AND THE RISE OF FASCISM 1922–1939

Although Italy had been on the winning side of World War I, it emerged from the war dissatisfied with its meager territorial gains at Austria's expense in the north. This dissatisfaction, along with a fear of the revolutionary left, encouraged the growth of Fascism in the country. In October 1922 Benito Mussolini was made prime minister, establishing one-party rule and an authoritarian state that pursued an aggressive foreign policy designed to increase Italy's power.

NORWAY
Oslo
North Sea
DENMARK
Copenhagen
IRELAND
Belfast
Dublin
Liverpool
Edinburgh
UNITED KINGDOM
Manchester
Birmingham
Oxford
Cambridge
London
Hamburg
Bremen
Elbe
NETHERLANDS
Rhine
Brussels
BELGIUM
Lille
Le Havre
Paris
LUXEMBOURG
Frankfurt
SAAR
GERMANY 60%
89%
Angers
Orléans
FRANCE 73%
Geneva
SWITZERLAND
AUSTRIA
Milan
Bilbao
Toulouse
Pamplona
Montpellier
Avignon
Genoa
Venice
Adriatic Sea
ANDORRA
Marseille
Pisa
Tarazona
Lérida
Barcelona
ITALY 61%
PORTUGAL
Lisbon
Madrid
Toledo
SPAIN
Mediterranean Sea
Corsica
Sardinia
Rome
Naples
ATLANTIC OCEAN

EUROPE OF THE DICTATORS

The victors of World War I had been a coalition of democracies, but in the uncertain decades that followed, many European countries underwent major political upheaval. Economic problems only served to add to the instability of inter-war Europe.

After the end of the war in 1918 and the subsequent signing of various peace treaties, most European states—excepting the newly formed Communist state in Russia—were democracies. However, one by one these democratic regimes gave way to dictatorships. Italy was the first of these, when Mussolini took power in 1922, followed by Spain in 1923 and Poland in 1926. Democracy collapsed in the Baltic states between 1926 and 1934, while the Balkan states become dictatorships after 1929. The rise of Nazi rule after 1933 in Germany, and later in Austria, completed the picture.

"The Spanish national will was never freely expressed through the ballot box."

FRANCISCO FRANCO, 1938

This transformation was exacerbated by the economic crisis that swept across Europe after 1929. Rising unemployment and economic collapse undermined democratic governments and gave rise to right-wing and Fascist groups. These were often militaristic in structure and populist in appeal, providing their members with power that had not been available to them under democracy. By 1939, democratic rule existed only in Scandinavia, Britain and Ireland, France, the Benelux nations, and Switzerland. The rest of Europe was under dictatorial rule.

THE GREAT DEPRESSION

In October 1929, the long boom on the New York Stock Exchange came to a sudden end. American creditors began to call in foreign loans and the supply of international credit dried up. In response, the US government introduced tariffs in 1930 that restricted imports. Competitive protection by other countries followed, causing world trade to fall by almost two-thirds between 1929 and 1932. Prices and profits collapsed, output plummeted, and millions were left unemployed (right) and impoverished.

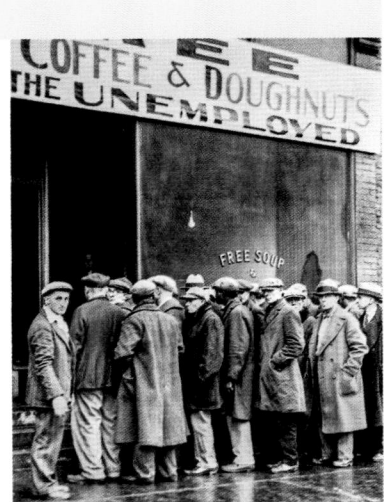

Map annotations

1934 Acting head of state Konstantin Päts declares a state of emergency, claiming that the right-wing Vaps movement is planning a coup.

1934 Three-time prime minister Karlis Ulmanis establishes an authoritarian dictatorship.

1926 A coup d'état sets up an authoritarian government under Antanas Smetona.

1926 Dissatisfied with Poland's unstable democratic governments, former military commander Josef Pilsudski comes out of retirement to stage a coup.

63%

1919 Admiral Horthy forms an authoritarian regency in the new kingdom.

1929 King Alexander appoints a royal dictatorship to end the fighting between Serbs and Croats.

1938 King Carol II takes dictatorial powers.

1936 King Boris III establishes a royal dictatorship.

1936 A right-wing dictatorship under General Metaxas takes power.

HUNGARY AND THE BALKANS 1919–1939

Following the collapse of the Austro-Hungarian and Ottoman empires at the end of World War I, new states emerged in the Balkans. Their governments were typically weak and were replaced by royal or military dictatorships; the growing influence of Nazi Germany led to the formation of far-right groups in the region. In Hungary, resentment over the loss of territory under the 1920 Treaty of Trianon led to closer ties with Nazi Germany.

▬ Balkan countries

Map labels: SWEDEN, FINLAND, Helsinki, Tallinn, Stockholm, ESTONIA, Baltic Sea, Riga, LATVIA, Danzig free port, LITHUANIA, EAST PRUSSIA, Wilno, Wagrowiec, POLAND, Warsaw, Krakow, CZECHOSLOVAKIA, U S S R, Budapest, ROMANIA, HUNGARY, Belgrade, Bucharest, Danube, YUGOSLAVIA, Black Sea, BULGARIA, Sofia, Tirana, ALBANIA, TURKEY, GREECE, Athens

HITLER AND NAZI GERMANY

Although Hitler's attempted *putsch* (or coup) in 1923 failed, by 1930 the Nazi party had become a force to be reckoned with in Germany. The economic depression that followed the Wall Street crash of 1929 was crucial in winning them nationwide support.

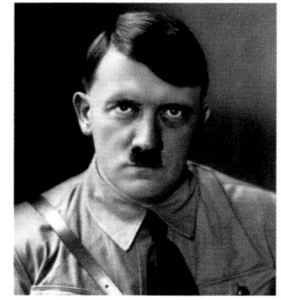

△ **The *Führer***
Adolf Hitler, in his uniform, poses for the camera. A picture of the *Führer* (leader) was a must in every German home.

Defeat in World War I had left Germany poor, resentful, and polarized between the political extremes of left and right. Many Germans were looking for strong, decisive leadership, which mainstream parties had failed to provide. Adolf Hitler emerged as leader of the National Socialist German Workers Party (NSDAP, known as the Nazi party) in the early 1920s, with great determination. As one commentator said, Hitler was "the living incarnation of the nation's yearning."

The Nazi program

Hitler's oratory was direct, aggressive, and uncompromising, as was his program. He pledged a national revolution that would restore German strength and dignity. His promises included an end to mass unemployment, abrogating the Treaty of Versailles, stopping the crippling war reparations Germany was forced to pay, and rebuilding the armed forces. Germany was listening. In the 1932 federal elections, the Nazis won 230 seats in the German *Reichstag* (parliament), making them the most powerful party in the country. After months of back room negotiations, in January 1933 a reluctant President Hindenburg was finally cajoled into appointing Hitler Chancellor. In March, the so-called Enabling Act gave Hitler emergency dictatorial powers. Its passage effectively marked the end of German democracy. The Nazis dubbed their new regime the Third Reich, or Third Empire, reflecting their ambitions.

JOSEPH GOEBBELS
1897–1945

Joseph Goebbels, a masterful orator, was one of Hitler's closest colleagues. In 1926, Hitler appointed Goebbels *Gauleiter* (district leader) of Berlin, and in 1933 promoted him to Propaganda Minister, with control over German radio, press, and cultural institutions. His propaganda sold the Nazi vision of German superiority and territorial expansion to the public.

Addressing the rally
The rally at Nuremberg, which was held annually from 1933 to 1938 and masterminded by the Propaganda Minister Joseph Goebbels, was a highlight of the Nazi year. Here, at the 1936 rally, massed troops at the Zeppelinfeld stadium listen attentively to Hitler's keynote speech.

CHINA IN TURMOIL

China between the two world wars was a country embroiled in internal conflict: its disunited provinces were ruled over by rival warlords and threatened by a growing Communist insurgency, while its national territory later came under attack from imperialist army forces from Japan.

The Chinese Revolution of 1911 began with a mutiny among troops in Wuchang in Hubei province, in central China. It rapidly led to the overthrow of the Manchu or Qing dynasty, whose autocratic rulers had controlled the country since 1644, and the formation of a republic in 1912. The first president of the republic, Yuan Shih-k'ai, tried to turn his office into a virtual dictatorship based on military force. However, on his death in 1916 China fragmented into a number of provincial military dictatorships run by local warlords who fought among themselves. Civil war raged throughout China until, under Chiang Kai-shek, China's

Nationalist Party, the Guomindang (GMD), was able to unite the east of the country by 1928. The GMD then slowly extended their control over the rest of the country by 1937.

Two forces emerged to oppose the Nationalists: the Chinese Communist Party (CCP), fighting for a social and economic revolution, and the Japanese army, intent on establishing an empire in China. The Communists were largely crushed in the cities in 1927, but the Japanese were a more formidable foe, absorbing the region of Manchuria in 1931 and the northern province of Jehol in 1932, and setting up a puppet state across northern China in 1935.

"We shall not lightly talk about sacrifice until we are driven to the last extreme which makes sacrifice inevitable."

CHIANG KAI-SHEK, 1935

CHIANG KAI-SHEK 1887–1975

Nationalist leader Chiang Kai-shek was born in Fenghua, a district of the city of Ningbo, in Zhejiang province. The son of a merchant, and a supporter of the new Chinese republic, he built up the Republican army and became commandant of the military school at Whampoa in 1924. His connections enabled him to take over the leadership of the Nationalist Guomindang (GMD) party and become commander-in-chief of the army in 1926. Despite successes against the warlords, Chiang's rule over China was never secure, as it was threatened by Communist insurgents and Japanese invasions. In 1949 he was defeated in the Chinese Civil War by the Chinese Communist Party (CCP) under Mao Zedong and retreated to Taiwan.

△ **Director of the masses**
Mao Zedong, leader of China's Communists, addresses followers during the Sino-Japanese war. In 1945, at the conflict's end, Mao commanded an army of over 1.2 million Chinese Communists.

1 THE NATIONALIST REVIVAL 1919–1937

Student demonstrations in Beijing in May 1919 initiated a wave of nationalist feeling across the country, which gave birth to the Chinese Communist Party (CCP) in 1921 and a revived Guomindang (GMD) in 1924. The GMD cooperated with the CCP and began a campaign of unification against warlord forces that culminated in the Northern Expedition of 1926–1928, which was led by Chiang Kai-shek. After its successful conclusion, the Communists were purged from power.

- ◻ Under direct control of the Nationalist government, 1928
- ◼ Nationalist territory, 1929–1934
- ◼ Nationalist territory, 1935–1937
- → Route of Northern Expedition
- ••▶ Pro-Nationalist forces

○ Juyan

Wuwei ○

Qinghai

Lanzh

2 JAPANESE INVASION OF MANCHURIA 1931

Responding to an act of provocation (which was staged by the Japanese army), Japanese forces invaded Manchuria on September 19, 1931, seizing the key city of Shenyang. They went on to take the whole of Manchuria, establishing the state of Manchukuo in 1932 with the former Chinese boy emperor Pu Yi Hsuan-t'ung as puppet emperor. The invasion and occupation of Manchuria marked the start of Japanese imperial expansion into northern and eastern China.

- ◼ Invaded by Japan, 1931
- → Japanese invasion

Luding ○

DISUNITED CHINA

Republican China was initially ruled by a number of local warlords and was only united under Nationalist control in 1937. By then China faced Japanese armed incursions in the north and east of the country.

TIMELINE

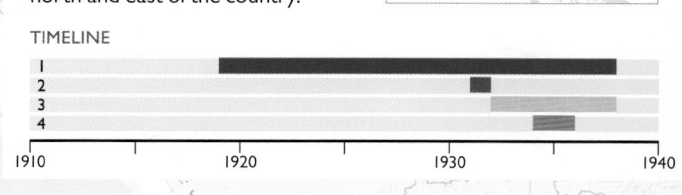

	1910	1920	1930	1940
1				
2				
3				
4				

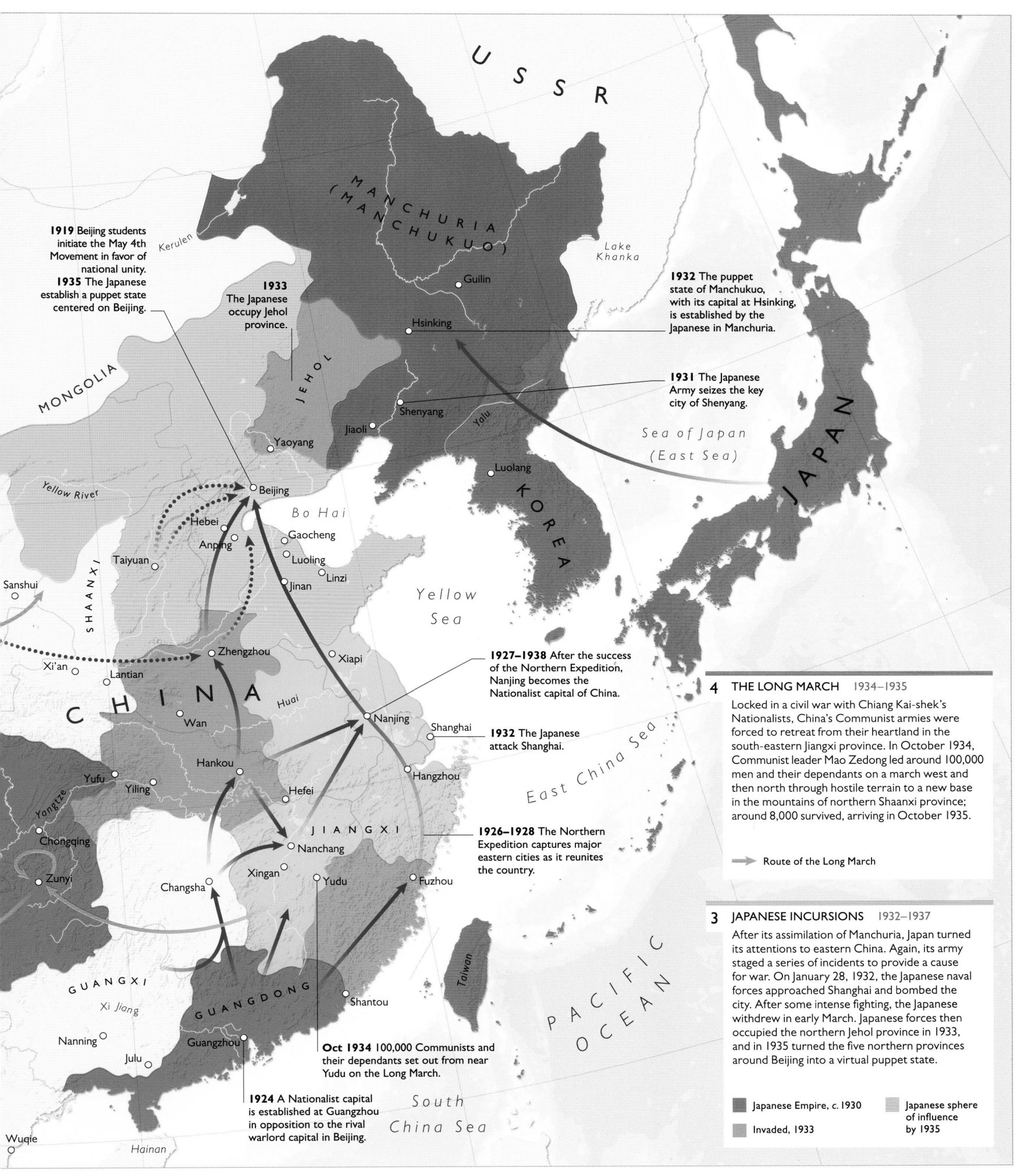

U S S R

MANCHURIA (MANCHUKUO)

Kerulen

Lake Khanka

1919 Beijing students initiate the May 4th Movement in favor of national unity.
1935 The Japanese establish a puppet state centered on Beijing.

MONGOLIA

1933 The Japanese occupy Jehol province.

Guilin

1932 The puppet state of Manchukuo, with its capital at Hsinking, is established by the Japanese in Manchuria.

Hsinking

J E H O L

1931 The Japanese Army seizes the key city of Shenyang.

Yaoyang

Jiaoli

Shenyang

Yalu

Luolang

Sea of Japan (East Sea)

K O R E A

J A P A N

Yellow River

Beijing

Bo Hai

S H A A N X I

Hebei

Anping

Gaocheng

Luoling

Linzi

Taiyuan

Jinan

Sanshui

Yellow Sea

Xi'an

Lantian

Zhengzhou

Xiapi

C H I N A

Huai

1927–1938 After the success of the Northern Expedition, Nanjing becomes the Nationalist capital of China.

Wan

Nanjing

Shanghai

1932 The Japanese attack Shanghai.

Hankou

Hefei

Hangzhou

East China Sea

Yufu

Yiling

Yangtze

Chongqing

J I A N G X I

1926–1928 The Northern Expedition captures major eastern cities as it reunites the country.

Zunyi

Nanchang

Xingan

Yudu

Fuzhou

Changsha

Shantou

Taiwan

G U A N G X I

Xi Jiang

G U A N G D O N G

Nanning

Guangzhou

Julu

Oct 1934 100,000 Communists and their dependants set out from near Yudu on the Long March.

P A C I F I C   O C E A N

1924 A Nationalist capital is established at Guangzhou in opposition to the rival warlord capital in Beijing.

South China Sea

Wuqie

Hainan

---

4   THE LONG MARCH   1934–1935

Locked in a civil war with Chiang Kai-shek's Nationalists, China's Communist armies were forced to retreat from their heartland in the south-eastern Jiangxi province. In October 1934, Communist leader Mao Zedong led around 100,000 men and their dependants on a march west and then north through hostile terrain to a new base in the mountains of northern Shaanxi province; around 8,000 survived, arriving in October 1935.

➤ Route of the Long March

---

3   JAPANESE INCURSIONS   1932–1937

After its assimilation of Manchuria, Japan turned its attentions to eastern China. Again, its army staged a series of incidents to provide a cause for war. On January 28, 1932, the Japanese naval forces approached Shanghai and bombed the city. After some intense fighting, the Japanese withdrew in early March. Japanese forces then occupied the northern Jehol province in 1933, and in 1935 turned the five northern provinces around Beijing into a virtual puppet state.

■ Japanese Empire, *c.* 1930

■ Invaded, 1933

■ Japanese sphere of influence by 1935

THE SPANISH CIVIL WAR

A prelude to World War II, the Spanish Civil War (1936–1939) was a bitter struggle between supporters of the democratically elected government and an emerging military dictatorship. Several other countries lent their support to each side.

During the 1930s, Spain was highly polarized, with major divisions between the church and state, urban and rural communities, liberal and conservative values, and the rich and poor. At one end of the political spectrum was the right-wing National Front (Nationalists), supported by the Falange (a Spanish Fascist party), monarchists, and some Catholics. At the other end was the left-wing Popular Front (Republicans), consisting of Communists, socialists, liberals, and anarchists.

The Republicans won the general election on February 16, 1936. Fearing a Communist revolution, the army officer and Nationalist leader General Francisco Franco launched a military uprising in Spanish Morocco and across south-western Spain. Pro-government groups fought against the Nationalist rebels, but Franco received significant help from Nazi Germany and Fascist Italy, both of which wanted to stop the spread of Communism in Europe. By November 1936, Franco's troops had reached the outskirts of Madrid—a Republican stronghold. Unable to capture the capital, the Nationalists besieged the city for over two years.

Although the Republicans continued to control eastern Spain and much of the south-east, Franco's forces were more organized and gradually took over areas previously under Republican control. The Nationalist victory at the Battle of Teruel (December 1937–February 1938) was a turning point in the war, and at the Battle of the Ebro (July–November 1938) the Republican troops were almost entirely eliminated. By spring 1939 the conflict was over, and Franco's government was accepted by most of Europe.

> *"… wherever I am there will be no Communism."*
>
> FRANCISCO FRANCO, QUOTED IN 1938

SPAIN IN WORLD WAR II

While Spain was a non-belligerent in World War II, it was not entirely neutral. Although Franco did not officially join the Axis alliance, he did support Germany by providing essential supplies and allowing thousands of Spaniards to volunteer in the Axis forces, albeit on condition that they did not fight the Western Allies. Spain and Germany came close to an alliance after the fall of France in June 1940, but Hitler considered Franco's demands too high and the two could not broker a deal. As the war progressed, Hitler considered an invasion of Spain, prompting Franco to move his forces to the border with France.

General Francisco Franco

---

1 THE WAR BEGINS JULY 1936

On July 17, 1936, Nationalist forces based in Spanish Morocco launched a coup against the newly elected Republican government. Franco took command of the Army of Africa—a Moroccan-based group of professional soldiers—on July 19. From July 27, Franco's army was flown from Morocco to Spain by German and Italian forces, and fighting soon spread through south-western Spain.

ATLANTIC OCEAN

2 INTERNATIONAL INTERVENTION 1936

Although 27 countries signed a non-intervention pact in September 1936, the ideological nature of the war gave it an international dimension. The Nationalists were aided by soldiers and equipment supplied by Fascist Italy and Nazi Germany. The Republicans were supported by the Communist government of Russia, and the government of Mexico, as well as by volunteers from International Brigades—left-wing fighters who came from all over the world to fight Fascism.

- German support
- Soviet support
- Italian support

Porto

Aug 22, 1936 Portugal allows German ships to dock at Lisbon and from there dispatch war supplies into Nationalist territory.

Lisbon

PORTUGAL

3 ATROCITIES AGAINST CIVILIANS 1936–1939

Both sides committed atrocities against civilians during the war. The Republicans targeted anyone believed to be right wing, including teachers, lawyers, mayors, and landowners, and they ransacked many churches. Meanwhile, the Nationalists persuaded the Nazis and Italians to carry out attacks from the air, including raids on Guernica and Barcelona, which was bombed by Italian aircraft that flew from the Balearic Islands.

- Republican violence
- Nationalist violence

▽ **Resisting the Nationalists**
The women's militia of the left-wing Popular Front march in Madrid in July 1936. A number of women fought in the Republican forces.

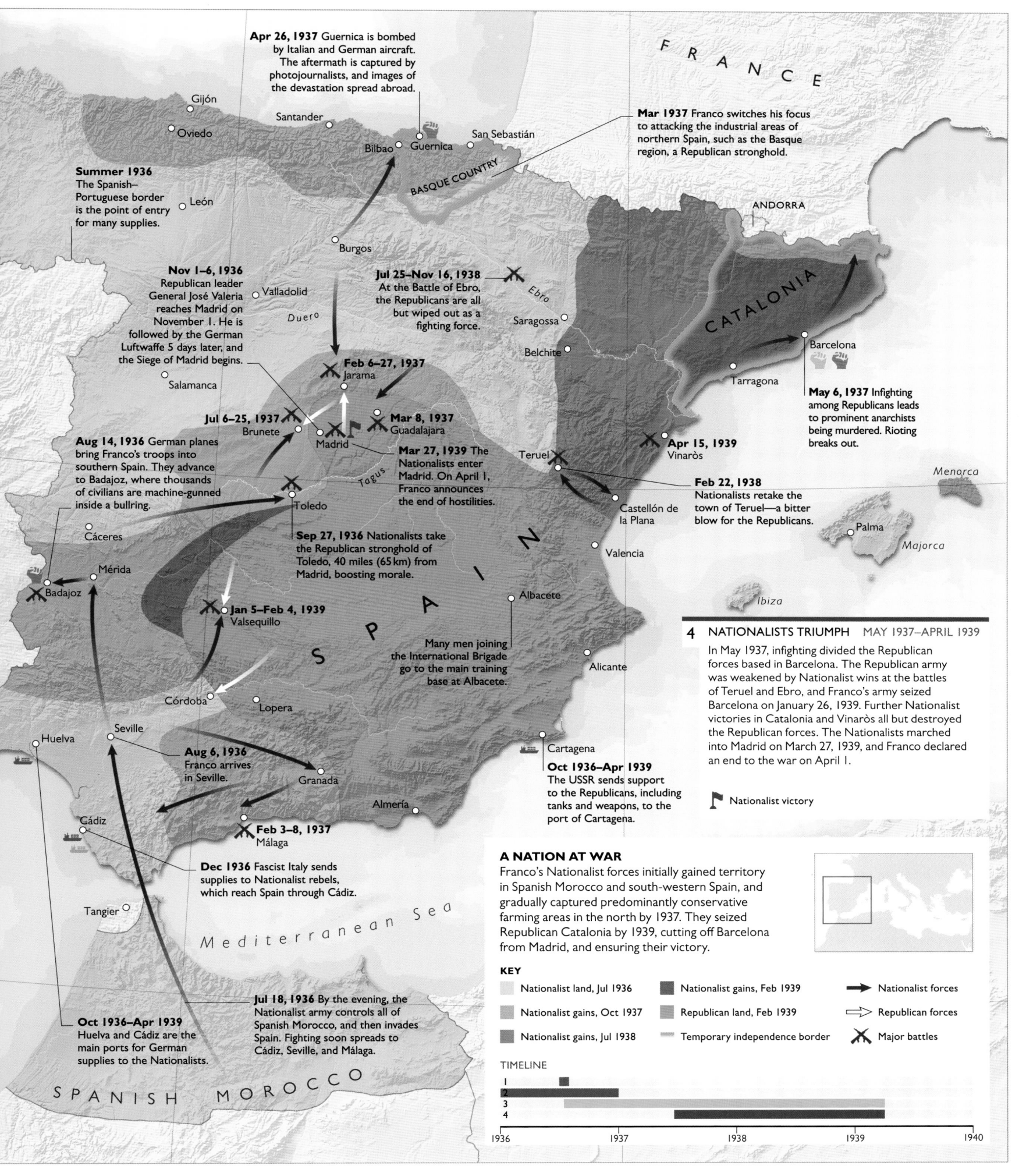

Apr 26, 1937 Guernica is bombed by Italian and German aircraft. The aftermath is captured by photojournalists, and images of the devastation spread abroad.

Mar 1937 Franco switches his focus to attacking the industrial areas of northern Spain, such as the Basque region, a Republican stronghold.

Summer 1936 The Spanish–Portuguese border is the point of entry for many supplies.

Nov 1–6, 1936 Republican leader General José Valeria reaches Madrid on November 1. He is followed by the German Luftwaffe 5 days later, and the Siege of Madrid begins.

Jul 25–Nov 16, 1938 At the Battle of Ebro, the Republicans are all but wiped out as a fighting force.

Jul 6–25, 1937 Brunete

Feb 6–27, 1937 Jarama

Mar 8, 1937 Guadalajara

Aug 14, 1936 German planes bring Franco's troops into southern Spain. They advance to Badajoz, where thousands of civilians are machine-gunned inside a bullring.

Mar 27, 1939 The Nationalists enter Madrid. On April 1, Franco announces the end of hostilities.

May 6, 1937 Infighting among Republicans leads to prominent anarchists being murdered. Rioting breaks out.

Apr 15, 1939 Vinaròs

Sep 27, 1936 Nationalists take the Republican stronghold of Toledo, 40 miles (65 km) from Madrid, boosting morale.

Feb 22, 1938 Nationalists retake the town of Teruel—a bitter blow for the Republicans.

Jan 5–Feb 4, 1939 Valsequillo

Many men joining the International Brigade go to the main training base at Albacete.

4 NATIONALISTS TRIUMPH MAY 1937–APRIL 1939

In May 1937, infighting divided the Republican forces based in Barcelona. The Republican army was weakened by Nationalist wins at the battles of Teruel and Ebro, and Franco's army seized Barcelona on January 26, 1939. Further Nationalist victories in Catalonia and Vinaròs all but destroyed the Republican forces. The Nationalists marched into Madrid on March 27, 1939, and Franco declared an end to the war on April 1.

🚩 Nationalist victory

Aug 6, 1936 Franco arrives in Seville.

Oct 1936–Apr 1939 The USSR sends support to the Republicans, including tanks and weapons, to the port of Cartagena.

Feb 3–8, 1937 Málaga

Dec 1936 Fascist Italy sends supplies to Nationalist rebels, which reach Spain through Cádiz.

A NATION AT WAR
Franco's Nationalist forces initially gained territory in Spanish Morocco and south-western Spain, and gradually captured predominantly conservative farming areas in the north by 1937. They seized Republican Catalonia by 1939, cutting off Barcelona from Madrid, and ensuring their victory.

Oct 1936–Apr 1939 Huelva and Cádiz are the main ports for German supplies to the Nationalists.

Jul 18, 1936 By the evening, the Nationalist army controls all of Spanish Morocco, and then invades Spain. Fighting soon spreads to Cádiz, Seville, and Málaga.

KEY

▢ Nationalist land, Jul 1936	▢ Nationalist gains, Feb 1939
▢ Nationalist gains, Oct 1937	▢ Republican land, Feb 1939
▢ Nationalist gains, Jul 1938	— Temporary independence border
→ Nationalist forces	⇨ Republican forces
✕ Major battles	

TIMELINE

```
1
2
3
4
1936   1937   1938   1939   1940
```

THE SINO-JAPANESE WAR

The Japanese attacked China in July 1937, marking the start of an eight-year war. The fighting was brutal; there were more than seven million military casualties on both sides and 17–22 million Chinese civilians lost their lives.

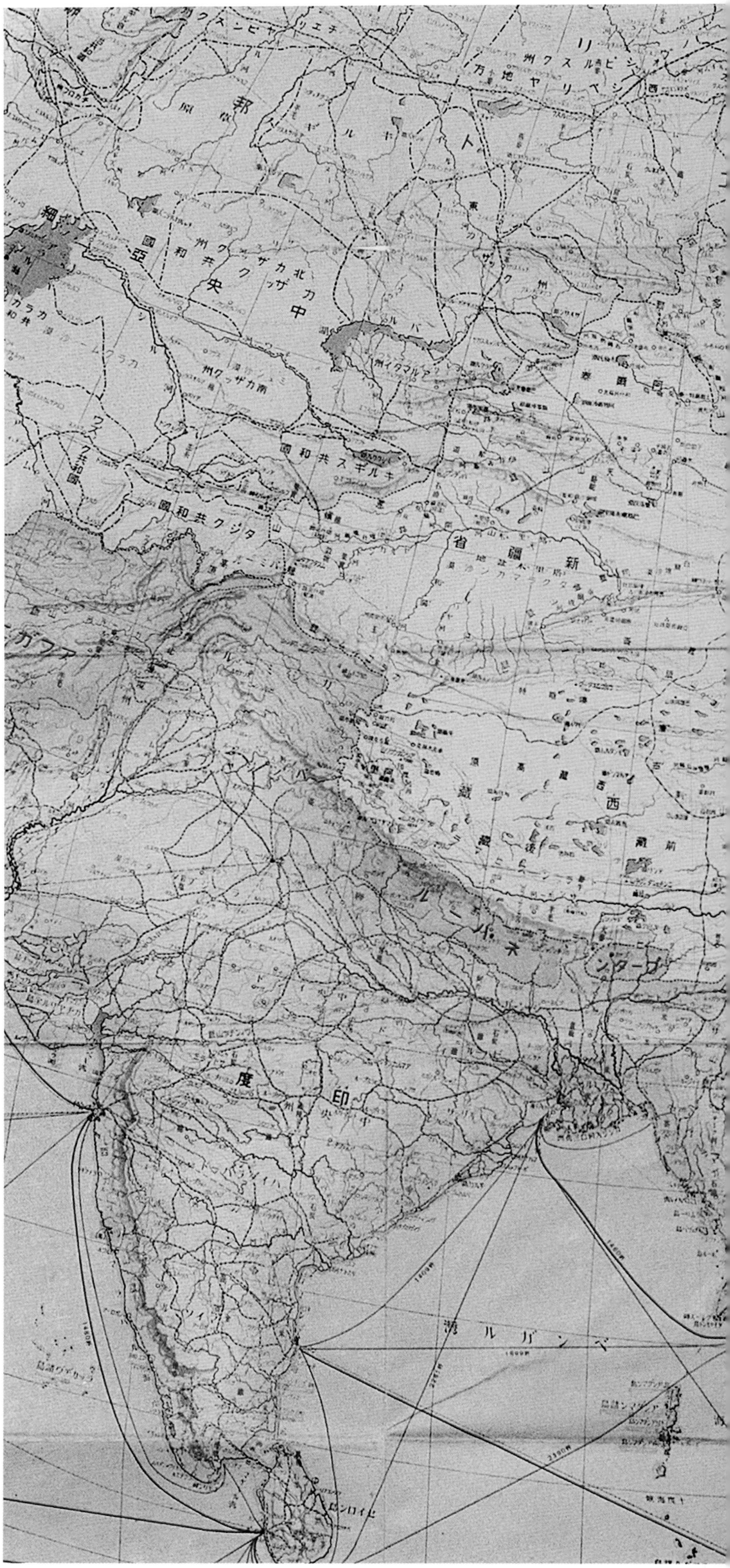

The hostilities that broke out in July 1937 were the culmination of a long-term Japanese aspiration to dominate China in order to gain access to raw materials, food, and labor. Having already captured Taiwan in 1895 (seen here in dark red), Manchuria in 1931, and Jehol province in 1933 (both seen in the right-hand pink area), Japan turned its attention to the rest of China. On July 7–9, 1937, the Japanese and Chinese exchanged fire over an incident involving a missing Japanese soldier at Wanping, 10 miles (16 km) south-west of Beijing. The Japanese opened fire on Marco Polo (Lugou) Bridge, a key access route to Beijing, and attacked Wanping. This skirmish developed into a major battle. Although a cease-fire was soon agreed, Japanese and Chinese forces continued to clash, leading to full-scale hostilities as the Japanese began to conquer northern China. Neither side officially declared war.

Invasion and expansion

Some Japanese forces then headed south; others landed on the east coast. In November they captured Shanghai after a three-month battle, and in December took Nanjing (both in the pink-tinted area on this map), where they perpetrated a major massacre. In 1938, they won a victory at Hankou against Chinese forces and Soviet volunteers led by Chiang Kai-shek. The four-month battle claimed around 1.2 million lives. These offensives were accompanied by the bombing of civilian targets, intended to destroy morale; Chongqing, for example, was bombed more than 200 times and had its center burned out. By 1941, Japan controlled much of eastern China and almost the entire coastline.

Chinese resistance

Despite these victories, the war turned into a stalemate. Chinese lines of communication stretched far into local territory, and Japan lacked the manpower to dominate the countryside. It was unable to defeat a major Communist guerrilla campaign in Shaanxi, nor could it repel two massive Nationalist and Communist counter-offensives, losing two major battles at Hankou and South Guangxi.

◁ **Massacre at Nanjing**
The Imperial Japanese Army entered Nanjing in January 1938. Up to 300,000 civilians are estimated to have been killed.

D.8.

Japanese empire map, c. 1939
The red areas of this map show Japan's empire in 1930 including Korea and Taiwan; the right-hand pink area shows conquests of 1931–1933, including Manchuria. The pink tint shows gains in China by 1937, and the orange tint shows gains made in 1938–1939.

GERMANY AND ITALY EXPAND

In the years following World War I, the governments of Fascist Italy and Nazi Germany both pursued expansionist policies aimed at enlarging their territories and overcoming the terms of the 1919 Versailles Treaty. At the time, they met with little opposition from other European nations.

Although Italy was on the winning Allied side in World War I, it emerged from the conflict with high casualties, a crippled, indebted economy, and few territorial gains. This fueled great resentment at home, which was among the many factors that propelled Benito Mussolini's National Fascist Party to power in 1922.

Mussolini sought to bolster the nation's standing by expanding Italy's territories in the Mediterranean and in Africa in an attempt to build a second Roman Empire. The conquests of Ethiopia (1935) and Albania (1939) were successful parts of this process.

Hitler also had imperial ambitions, believing that Germany required *Lebensraum* (living space) to survive.

When he came to power in 1933, he intended to avenge the Treaty of Versailles and create a remilitarized, pan-German state in central Europe. As Germany began to rearm in defiance of Versailles, the Saarland and Rhineland returned to full German control in 1935–1936, Austria was united with Germany in 1938, and Czechoslovakia was occupied and divided in 1938–1939.

In response to these expansionist policies, the European powers of Britain and France did little to defend Versailles, instead choosing to appease the dictators in the hope that this would keep the peace. However, the failure of appeasement by the spring of 1939 forced both countries to prepare for the inevitability of renewed war in Europe.

> *"It is not programs that are wanting for the salvation of Italy but men and will power."*
>
> BENITO MUSSOLINI, SPEECH MADE IN UDINE, 1920

ALLIED REARMAMENT

After World War I, Britain and France reduced their military capacities, but the rise of the Nazi Party in Germany in 1933 forced a rethink. After 1936 Britain began to produce a new generation of tanks and artillery pieces, new aircraft carriers and battleships, and to develop the Spitfire and Hawker Hurricane fighter aircraft. France built the defensive Maginot Line along its eastern border with Germany and modernized its air force, the biggest in the world at the time.

A British Spitfire production line

△ **Hitler in Austria, March 1938**
Following the Anschluss, Hitler traveled in triumph through Austria to Vienna, where he addressed 200,000 jubilant German Austrians in the Heldenplatz (Heroes' Square).

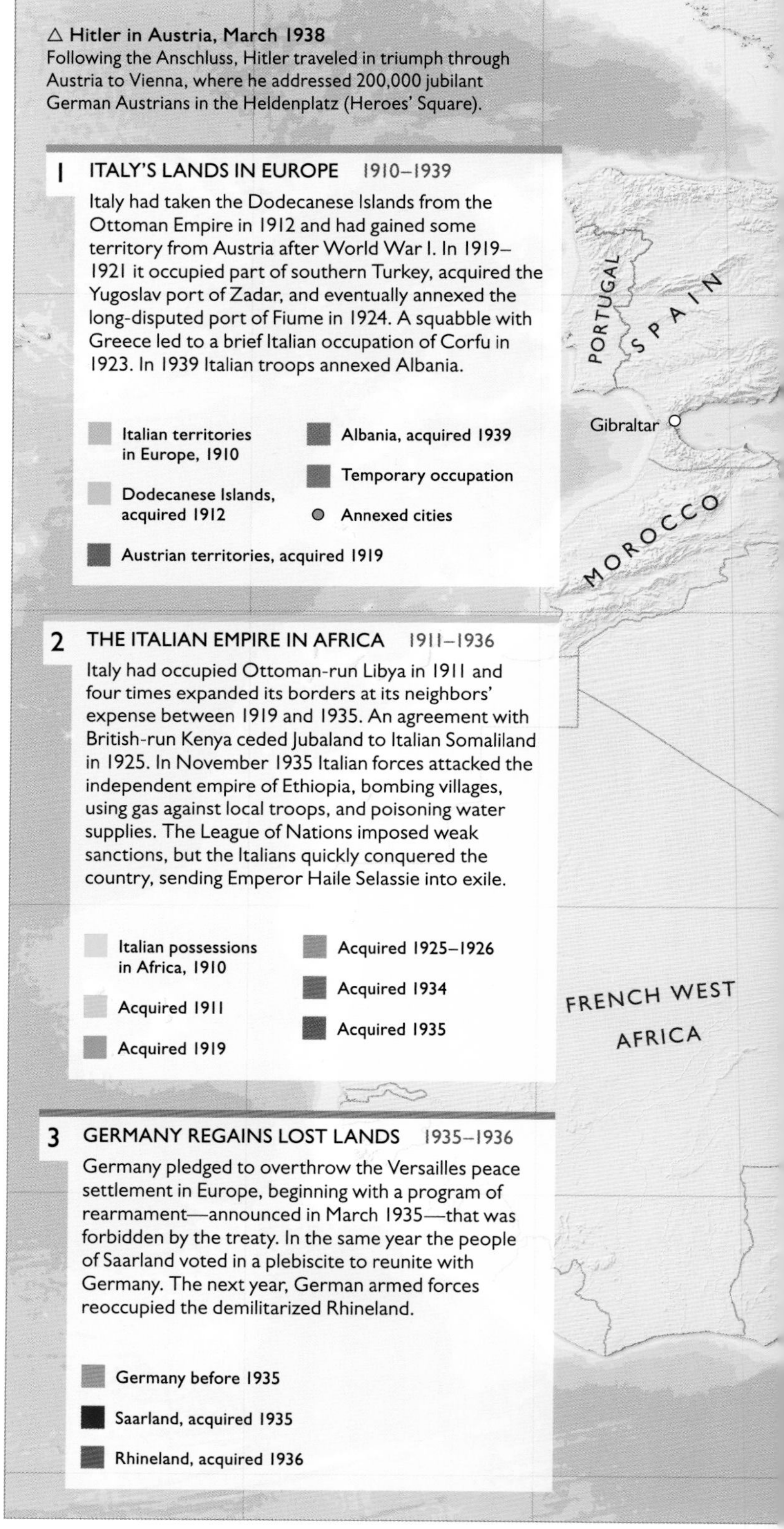

---

1 ITALY'S LANDS IN EUROPE   1910–1939

Italy had taken the Dodecanese Islands from the Ottoman Empire in 1912 and had gained some territory from Austria after World War I. In 1919–1921 it occupied part of southern Turkey, acquired the Yugoslav port of Zadar, and eventually annexed the long-disputed port of Fiume in 1924. A squabble with Greece led to a brief Italian occupation of Corfu in 1923. In 1939 Italian troops annexed Albania.

- Italian territories in Europe, 1910
- Dodecanese Islands, acquired 1912
- Austrian territories, acquired 1919
- Albania, acquired 1939
- Temporary occupation
- Annexed cities

---

2 THE ITALIAN EMPIRE IN AFRICA   1911–1936

Italy had occupied Ottoman-run Libya in 1911 and four times expanded its borders at its neighbors' expense between 1919 and 1935. An agreement with British-run Kenya ceded Jubaland to Italian Somaliland in 1925. In November 1935 Italian forces attacked the independent empire of Ethiopia, bombing villages, using gas against local troops, and poisoning water supplies. The League of Nations imposed weak sanctions, but the Italians quickly conquered the country, sending Emperor Haile Selassie into exile.

- Italian possessions in Africa, 1910
- Acquired 1911
- Acquired 1919
- Acquired 1925–1926
- Acquired 1934
- Acquired 1935

---

3 GERMANY REGAINS LOST LANDS   1935–1936

Germany pledged to overthrow the Versailles peace settlement in Europe, beginning with a program of rearmament—announced in March 1935—that was forbidden by the treaty. In the same year the people of Saarland voted in a plebiscite to reunite with Germany. The next year, German armed forces reoccupied the demilitarized Rhineland.

- Germany before 1935
- Saarland, acquired 1935
- Rhineland, acquired 1936

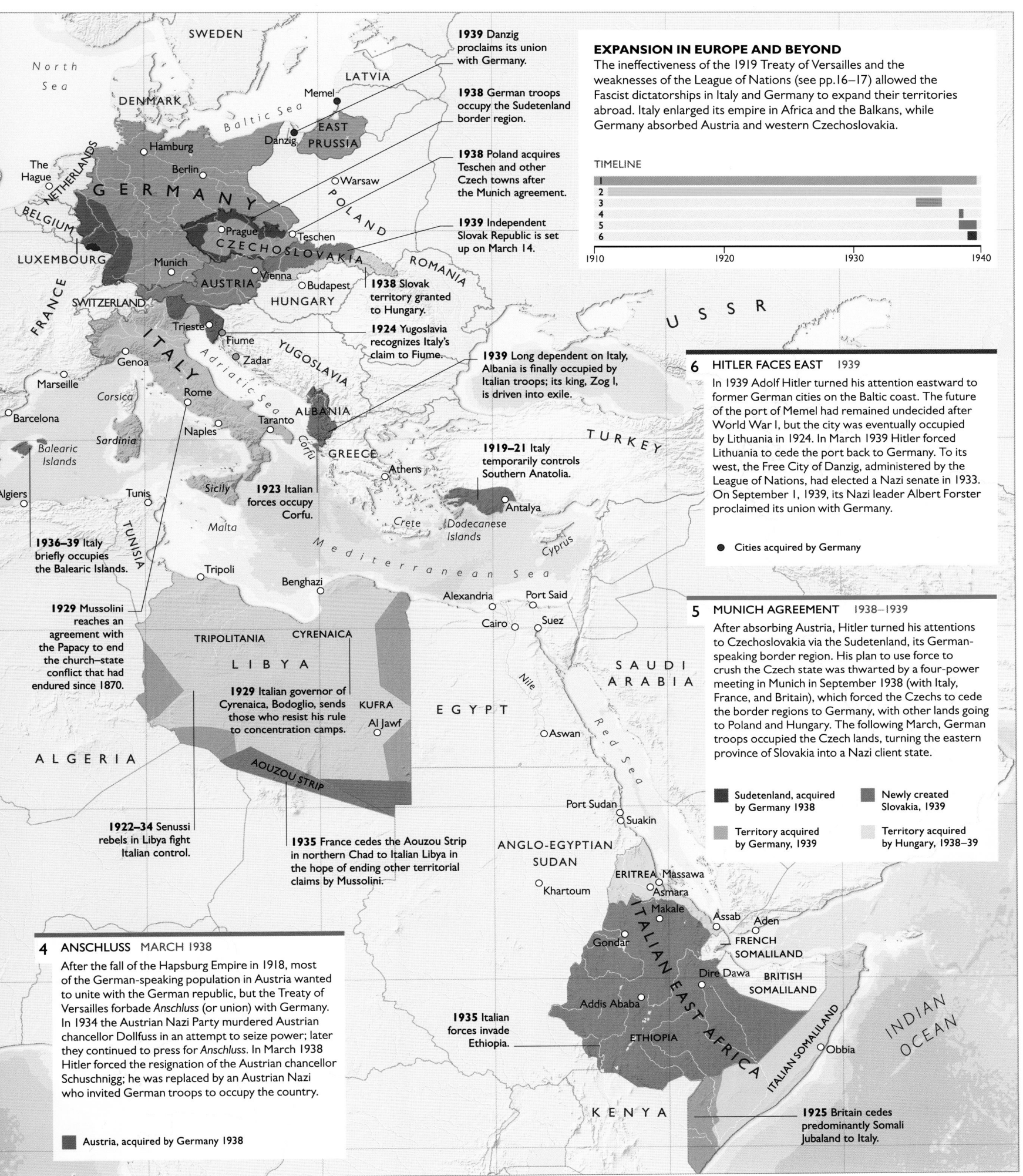

1939 Danzig proclaims its union with Germany.

1938 German troops occupy the Sudetenland border region.

1938 Poland acquires Teschen and other Czech towns after the Munich agreement.

1939 Independent Slovak Republic is set up on March 14.

1938 Slovak territory granted to Hungary.

1924 Yugoslavia recognizes Italy's claim to Fiume.

1939 Long dependent on Italy, Albania is finally occupied by Italian troops; its king, Zog I, is driven into exile.

1919–21 Italy temporarily controls Southern Anatolia.

1923 Italian forces occupy Corfu.

1936–39 Italy briefly occupies the Balearic Islands.

1929 Mussolini reaches an agreement with the Papacy to end the church–state conflict that had endured since 1870.

1929 Italian governor of Cyrenaica, Bodoglio, sends those who resist his rule to concentration camps.

1922–34 Senussi rebels in Libya fight Italian control.

1935 France cedes the Aouzou Strip in northern Chad to Italian Libya in the hope of ending other territorial claims by Mussolini.

1935 Italian forces invade Ethiopia.

1925 Britain cedes predominantly Somali Jubaland to Italy.

EXPANSION IN EUROPE AND BEYOND

The ineffectiveness of the 1919 Treaty of Versailles and the weaknesses of the League of Nations (see pp.16–17) allowed the Fascist dictatorships in Italy and Germany to expand their territories abroad. Italy enlarged its empire in Africa and the Balkans, while Germany absorbed Austria and western Czechoslovakia.

TIMELINE

1910   1920   1930   1940

6   HITLER FACES EAST   1939

In 1939 Adolf Hitler turned his attention eastward to former German cities on the Baltic coast. The future of the port of Memel had remained undecided after World War I, but the city was eventually occupied by Lithuania in 1924. In March 1939 Hitler forced Lithuania to cede the port back to Germany. To its west, the Free City of Danzig, administered by the League of Nations, had elected a Nazi senate in 1933. On September 1, 1939, its Nazi leader Albert Forster proclaimed its union with Germany.

●   Cities acquired by Germany

5   MUNICH AGREEMENT   1938–1939

After absorbing Austria, Hitler turned his attentions to Czechoslovakia via the Sudetenland, its German-speaking border region. His plan to use force to crush the Czech state was thwarted by a four-power meeting in Munich in September 1938 (with Italy, France, and Britain), which forced the Czechs to cede the border regions to Germany, with other lands going to Poland and Hungary. The following March, German troops occupied the Czech lands, turning the eastern province of Slovakia into a Nazi client state.

■ Sudetenland, acquired by Germany 1938	■ Newly created Slovakia, 1939
■ Territory acquired by Germany, 1939	■ Territory acquired by Hungary, 1938–39

4   ANSCHLUSS   MARCH 1938

After the fall of the Hapsburg Empire in 1918, most of the German-speaking population in Austria wanted to unite with the German republic, but the Treaty of Versailles forbade *Anschluss* (or union) with Germany. In 1934 the Austrian Nazi Party murdered Austrian chancellor Dollfuss in an attempt to seize power; later they continued to press for *Anschluss*. In March 1938 Hitler forced the resignation of the Austrian chancellor Schuschnigg; he was replaced by an Austrian Nazi who invited German troops to occupy the country.

■   Austria, acquired by Germany 1938

Synagogue ablaze
The main synagogue in Hanover, in northern Germany, was burned to the ground by Nazis on November 9, 1938. Jewish shops and dwellings in the city were also looted, and the furniture from homes was dragged into a square and burned.

KRISTALLNACHT

In November 1938, a 17-year-old Polish Jew, Herschel Grynszpan, assassinated Ernst vom Rath, a diplomat working at the German Embassy in Paris. This triggered a Nazi pogrom that would have disastrous consequences for Jews throughout the Third Reich.

In a matter of hours after vom Rath's death on November 9, Nazis throughout Germany went on a violent rampage, attacking synagogues and Jewish businesses and homes. The event came to be called *Kristallnacht* ("Crystal Night") for the shattered window glass that littered the streets. By the time the pogrom came to an end a day later, around 100 synagogues had been demolished and several hundred more severely damaged by fire. Many Jewish cemeteries had been desecrated, and at least 7,500 Jewish-owned shops had been sacked and looted.

△ **Mark of a Jew**
The pogrom had a lasting impact. By 1941, all Jews in Germany had to wear a yellow Star of David with the word *Jude* (Jew).

Cause and aftermath

Whether Hitler ever gave a specific order to launch the pogrom is uncertain. Goebbels, the Propaganda Minister, was quick to claim that the pogrom was an outburst of national anger in response to a cowardly attack. As well as inciting racial hatred through propaganda, the Nazis had institutionalized anti-semitism by teaching it in schools and introducing the Nuremberg Laws in 1935, which stripped Jews of German citizenship. Following the death of vom Rath, the Jews were fined one billion Reichsmarks and told to repair all the damage the pogrom had caused. About 30,000 Jewish men were arrested, most of whom were transported to concentration camps.

△ **Anti-Jewish boycott**
A Berlin shop window is vandalized during *Kristallnacht* with a poster warning shoppers not to buy from Jews. A correspondent in Berlin for the *Daily Telegraph* reported, "racial hatred and hysteria seemed to have taken complete hold of otherwise decent people."

COUNTDOWN IN EUROPE

In a frenzy of diplomatic activity before the war, nations formed alliances, offered guarantees, and—if not wishing to fight—proclaimed neutrality. The final piece of the jigsaw—the Nazi–Soviet Nonaggression Pact—was the most surprising diplomatic coup of the century.

The threat to world peace intensified through the 1930s as Germany and Italy expanded their imperial possessions in Europe, while to the east Japan entered into conflict with China (see pp.26–27). In response, the two major democracies in Europe—Britain and France—abandoned their policy of appeasing Hitler and Mussolini and moved to deterrence instead. On March 31, 1939, they made a guarantee to Poland that the western powers would come to its aid if the country was attacked, and extended similar assurances to Romania, Greece, and Turkey after the Italian annexation of Albania.

With the emergence of the two rival power blocs, several European nations grouped together to proclaim their neutrality, but such diplomatic alliances were nothing next to the announcement in August 1939 that the two ideological foes of Europe—Nazi Germany and the Communist USSR—had agreed a mutual nonaggression pact. Its secret clauses redrew the map of central and Eastern Europe and absorbed previously independent states into their two spheres of influence. With the safeguard of nonaggression, Hitler's Germany had now cleared the way for a successful invasion of Poland.

> *"In war, whichever side may call itself the victor, there are no winners, but all are losers."*
>
> NEVILLE CHAMBERLAIN, BRITISH PRIME MINISTER, 1938

JOSEPH STALIN 1879–1953

Born in Gori, Georgia, Josef Djugashvili was educated in a seminary but expelled for holding revolutionary views. Twice exiled by the Czarist government to Siberia, and from 1912 known as Stalin, or "Man of Steel," he helped Lenin during the October Revolution of 1917, becoming Commissar for Nationalities in the Bolshevik government. In 1922 he became General Secretary of the Party and used this to build his own power base. By the late 1920s he had established a dictatorship that lasted until his death in 1953.

A DIVIDED EUROPE

The rise of Nazi Germany and its alliance with Italy divided Europe into two camps. One group of nations attempted to remain neutral, while the USSR reached a surprising understanding with Nazi Germany.

TIMELINE

1	
2	
3	
4	
5	

1936   1937   1938   1939   1940   1941

1 THE AXIS POWERS 1936–1940

On November 1, 1936, after the signing of a new set of protocols with Germany, the Italian dictator Benito Mussolini proclaimed the establishment of a Rome–Berlin "Axis." Italy and Germany formalized their alliance in the Pact of Steel on May 22, 1939. Meanwhile, Germany and Japan had signed the Anti-Comintern Pact against the USSR on November 25, 1936, which Italy joined in 1937. The ties between Japan, Germany, and Italy, who came to be called the "Axis powers," were strengthened by the Tripartite Pact of September 27, 1940.

■ European Axis powers, May 1939

Glasgow
Belfast
IRELAND
Dublin
UNITED KINGDOM
London

ATLANTIC OCEAN

Nov 1938 Strikes take place in France amid tension between Communists and the far right.

Paris

FRANCE

2 COPENHAGEN DECLARATION
JULY 1938

In July 1938 Norway, Sweden, Denmark, the Netherlands, Belgium, Finland, and the three Baltic states of Estonia, Latvia, and Lithuania signed a declaration in the Danish capital, Copenhagen, stating that they would remain neutral in any forthcoming European war. Most of these states, except Belgium, had been neutral or not yet independent in World War I, and wished to avoid being drawn into a future conflict.

■ Signatories of Copenhagen Declaration

Jan 26, 1939 General Franco's Nationalist troops capture Barcelona.

PORTUGAL   SPAIN

Barcelona

Madrid

3 THE END OF APPEASEMENT 1939

After Germany broke the Munich Agreement of September 1938 (see pp.28–29) and occupied western Czechoslovakia, Britain and France offered guarantees to Poland (March 1939), Romania and Greece (April 1939), and Turkey (May 1939) that they would defend them from attack. With these guarantees in place, the German invasion of Poland in September 1939 triggered a declaration of war against Germany.

■ Allies and countries promised Allied assistance

Apr 1, 1939 Franco declares victory in Madrid, ending the Spanish Civil War.

1939 Denmark signs a ten-year nonaggression pact with Germany.

Jul 1938 A declaration of neutrality is signed by nine states in Copenhagen.

Aug 1939 Hitler issues ultimatum claiming sovereignty over Free City of Danzig.

May 22, 1939 The Pact of Steel is signed in Berlin.

Mar 22, 1939 Germany annexes the Baltic port of Memel from Lithuania.

1939 Originally assigned to Germany in the Nazi–Soviet Pact, Lithuania is later transferred to the Soviet sphere of influence.

1939 Under the Nazi–Soviet Pact, Poland is to be split between Germany and the USSR and wiped off the map.

Mar 1938 *Anschluss:* Hitler annexes Austria.

Nov 1, 1936 In a speech in Milan, Mussolini uses the term "Axis" to denote his alliance with Nazi Germany.

Apr 7, 1939 Italian forces invade Albania.

△ Hitler and the bear
In a critique of the pact between the USSR and Germany, this French satirical cartoon from 1939 depicts Hitler and the USSR—the "bear"—wrestling over a map of Europe. The pact was negotiated in secret and was met with shock across Europe when it was announced.

5 THE EFFECTS OF THE PACT   1939–1940

Secret clauses in the pact were to affect the fate of neighboring countries. Germany gained a free hand in western Poland and Lithuania, while the influence of the USSR was to prevail over eastern Poland, Finland, Estonia, Latvia, and the Romanian province of Bessarabia. A later secret agreement on September 28, 1939, extended German control further into eastern Poland while giving the USSR a free hand in Lithuania. All the secret clauses were implemented by summer 1940.

🤝 Victims of the Pact

4 THE NAZI–SOVIET NONAGGRESSION PACT   AUGUST 23, 1939

On August 23, 1939, the German and Russian foreign secretaries Joachim von Ribbentrop and Vyacheslav Molotov signed a nonaggression pact. The published terms included pledges to maintain neutrality if either country was at war. This marked a major change in policy: the USSR, let down by the Munich Agreement, was now willing to precipitate war between "the two imperialist camps"; and Germany wanted to avoid possible Soviet interference in its invasion of Poland.

🤝 Signatories to the Nonaggression Pact

GERMANY TRIUMPHANT 1939–1941

AS THE AXIS ARMIES SWEPT ACROSS EUROPE AND PUSHED INTO THE USSR, THE BALKANS, AND AFRICA, THE ALLIES FOUND THEMSELVES BATTLING FOR SURVIVAL ON ALL FRONTS.

WAR IN EUROPE

The triumph of German armies in the first phase of World War II made Adolf Hitler the master of continental Europe. Under the leadership of Winston Churchill, Britain successfully resisted a German aerial onslaught, but with no immediate prospect of more than mere survival.

△ **Fleeing civilians**
A Parisian family sets out in search of a safe haven as German forces approach the French capital in 1940. Two-thirds of the city's population fled in panic to the countryside.

When World War II broke out in September 1939, there were no cheering crowds as there had been in World War I. The British and French governments reluctantly entered a conflict that they had not wanted, and took no action to aid the Poles, on whose behalf they had declared war on Germany. Quickly defeated and divided between Nazi Germany and the Soviet Union, Poland was subjected to the mass killing of its educated elite, and its Jews were driven into ghettos. Britain and France rejected a peace offer from Hitler after his victory in Poland, but had no desire for military action. The French army based itself on the Maginot Line, the fortifications that were supposed to block a German invasion, while a British Expeditionary Force headed to northern France. However, little actually happened, except at sea. The lack of military action led to this period being dubbed the "phony war."

In Britain, preparations for conflict had been under way long before war was officially declared. Civil defense programs set up to cope with air raids were implemented immediately, and blackouts were introduced in cities, although expectations that Germany would undertake a swift aerial attack proved

mistaken. In British cities, children were evacuated days before the declaration of war, likewise the residents in France's frontier zone. By the time war broke out, Germany's economy had already been geared to war for over a year, and Britain and France had begun to rearm. Indeed, armaments programs and military conscription ended the mass unemployment of the interwar period.

Germany storms Europe

Some politicians, especially in France, would have preferred to fight the Soviet Union rather than Nazi Germany. They toyed with plans for intervention in support of Finland after it was attacked by the Soviets in the winter of 1939–1940. However, in spring 1940 this idea was abandoned as Germany took decisive and widespread military action. First, Hitler sent his armies northward into Denmark and Norway. He then followed this by launching a lightning offensive in France, Belgium, the Netherlands, and Luxembourg. Combining tanks and aircraft in fast-moving "Blitzkrieg" tactics, the Germans scored a series of astonishing victories. On the Western front, the French and British armies were routed in six weeks, although many soldiers escaped capture through the evacuation of Dunkirk in May–June 1940.

△ **Third Reich medal**
The Knight's Cross, introduced by Hitler in 1939, was awarded to German soldiers for acts of exceptional valor or skill in command.

HITLER TRIUMPHANT

Nazi Germany conquered most of northern Europe in three short campaigns: the first against Poland in September 1939, the second in Scandinavia beginning in April 1940, and the third in Western Europe in May–June 1940. However, after France surrendered, Hitler failed to pursue an invasion of Britain with equal energy and willpower. The Luftwaffe's air attacks caused extensive damage but were inconclusive. Meanwhile the US was increasingly drawn into supporting the British war effort.

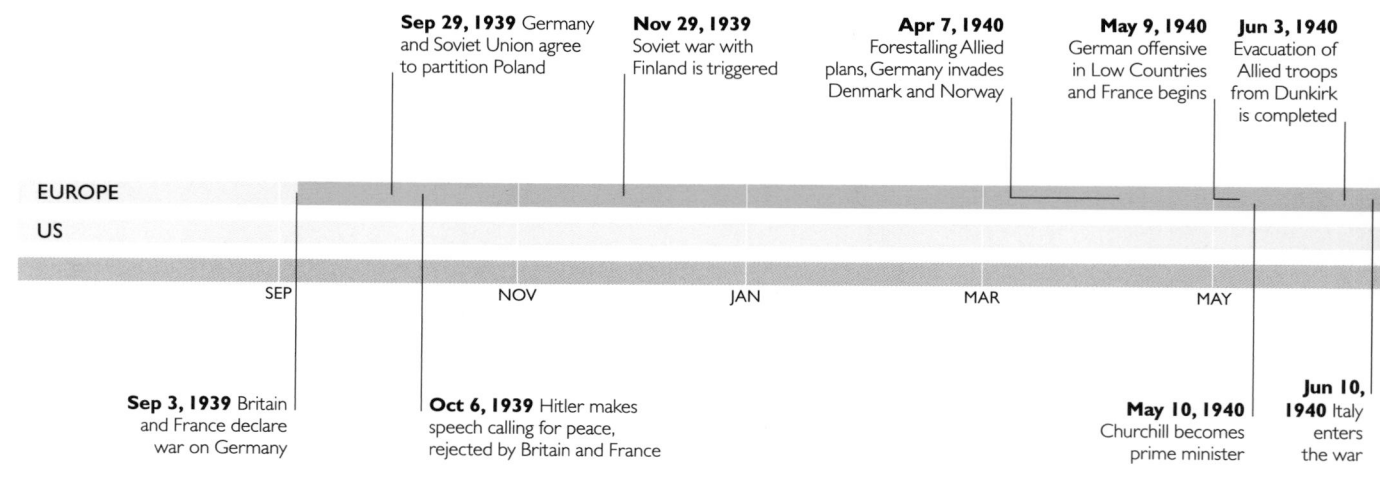

Sep 29, 1939 Germany and Soviet Union agree to partition Poland

Nov 29, 1939 Soviet war with Finland is triggered

Apr 7, 1940 Forestalling Allied plans, Germany invades Denmark and Norway

May 9, 1940 German offensive in Low Countries and France begins

Jun 3, 1940 Evacuation of Allied troops from Dunkirk is completed

EUROPE

US

SEP   NOV   JAN   MAR   MAY

Sep 3, 1939 Britain and France declare war on Germany

Oct 6, 1939 Hitler makes speech calling for peace, rejected by Britain and France

May 10, 1940 Churchill becomes prime minister

Jun 10, 1940 Italy enters the war

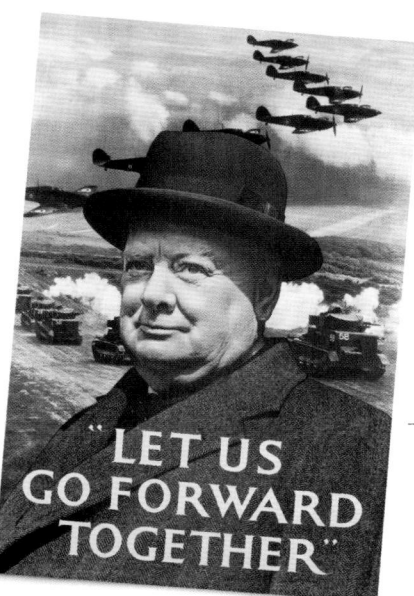

◁ Rallying support
Issued soon after Winston Churchill became prime minister in May 1940, this British poster was intended to encourage national unity.

"LET US GO FORWARD TOGETHER"

▽ Victory in Europe
Seen here at a parade on his 50th birthday a few months before the war, Hitler seemed to be fulfilling his promises in the war's early stages, as Poland and then France fell to the Nazis.

France's surrender a few weeks later was followed by the creation of the Vichy French government—a regime dedicated to collaboration with the Nazis. Hitler and his allies had control of almost all continental Europe.

In Britain, the recently appointed prime minister, Winston Churchill, resolved to fight on. In summer 1940, Germany fought for control of the air over southern England while preparing for a seaborne invasion. Known as the Battle of Britain, the aerial conflict ended in stalemate, and Hitler's invasion plans were abandoned. However, throughout the following fall and winter, Britain's cities were battered by German bombers attacking at night in the "Blitz." At sea, German U-boats took a heavy toll on merchant shipping.

There was little that Britain could do at this stage to take the war to its enemy. Instead, Churchill opted for "economic warfare," consisting of ineffectual attempts to bomb German cities from the air and stir up resistance in occupied Europe.

"What the world did not deem possible, the German people have achieved ..."

ADOLF HITLER, SPEECH, APRIL 6, 1941

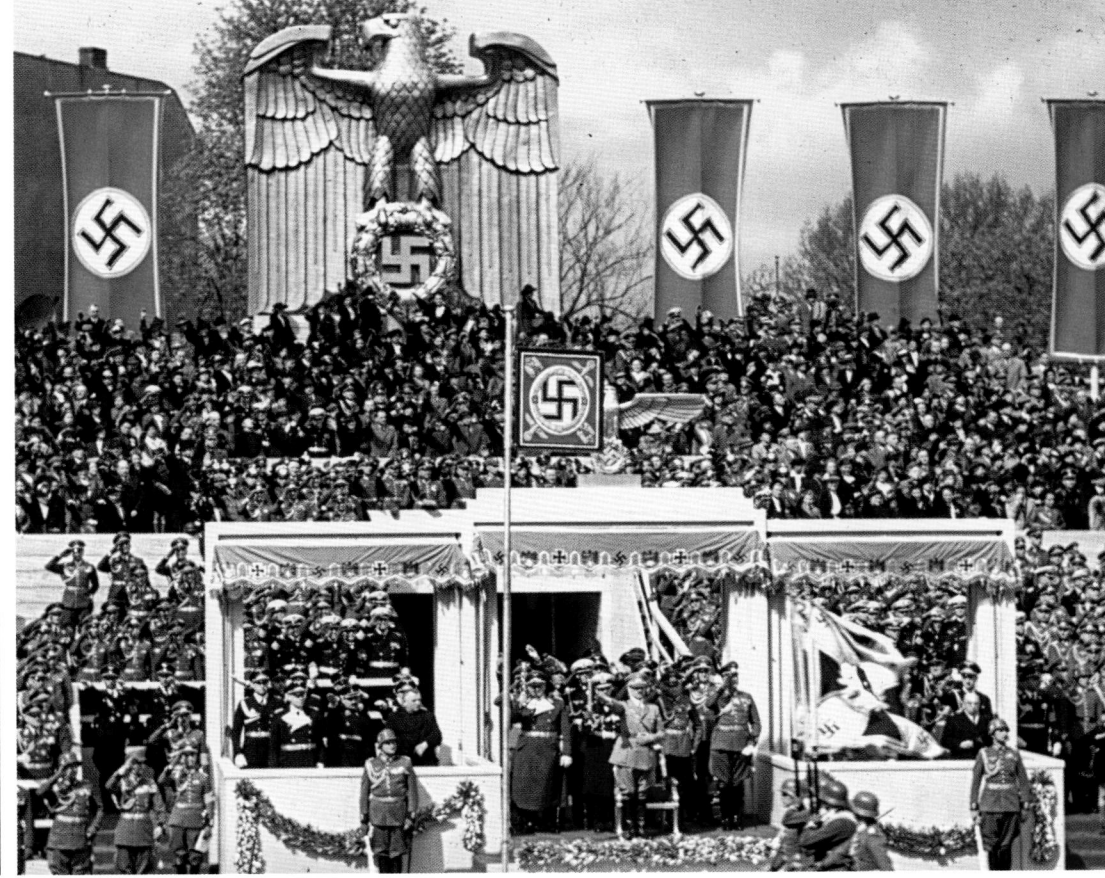

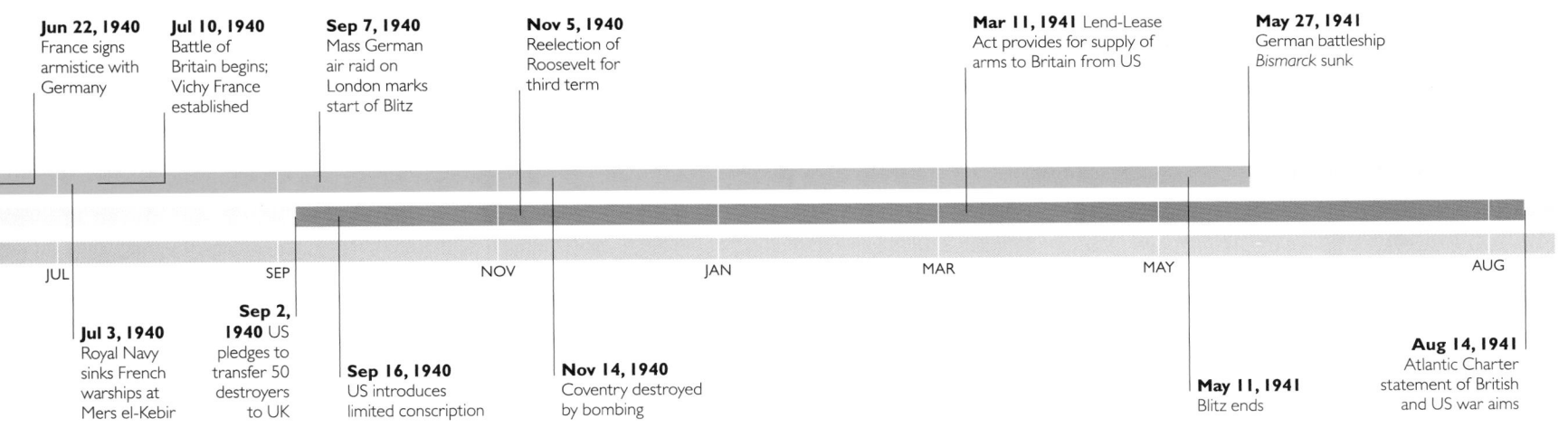

Jun 22, 1940
France signs armistice with Germany

Jul 10, 1940
Battle of Britain begins; Vichy France established

Sep 7, 1940
Mass German air raid on London marks start of Blitz

Nov 5, 1940
Reelection of Roosevelt for third term

Mar 11, 1941 Lend-Lease Act provides for supply of arms to Britain from US

May 27, 1941
German battleship *Bismarck* sunk

JUL · SEP · NOV · JAN · MAR · MAY · AUG

Jul 3, 1940
Royal Navy sinks French warships at Mers el-Kebir

Sep 2, 1940 US pledges to transfer 50 destroyers to UK

Sep 16, 1940
US introduces limited conscription

Nov 14, 1940
Coventry destroyed by bombing

May 11, 1941
Blitz ends

Aug 14, 1941
Atlantic Charter statement of British and US war aims

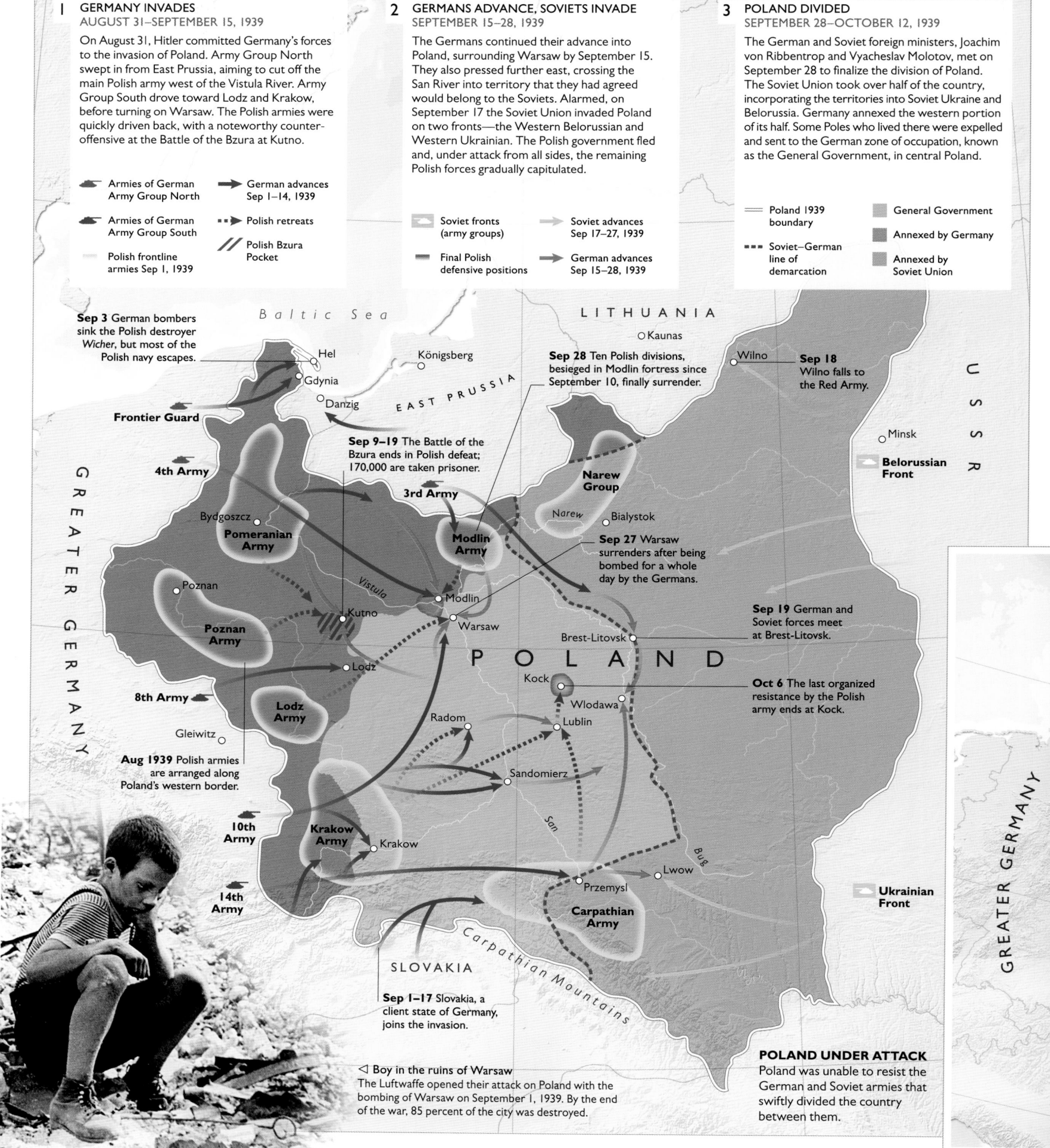

1 GERMANY INVADES
AUGUST 31–SEPTEMBER 15, 1939

On August 31, Hitler committed Germany's forces to the invasion of Poland. Army Group North swept in from East Prussia, aiming to cut off the main Polish army west of the Vistula River. Army Group South drove toward Lodz and Krakow, before turning on Warsaw. The Polish armies were quickly driven back, with a noteworthy counter-offensive at the Battle of the Bzura at Kutno.

- ◣ Armies of German Army Group North
- ◣ Armies of German Army Group South
- Polish frontline armies Sep 1, 1939
- ➤ German advances Sep 1–14, 1939
- ▪▪▶ Polish retreats
- ⫽ Polish Bzura Pocket

2 GERMANS ADVANCE, SOVIETS INVADE
SEPTEMBER 15–28, 1939

The Germans continued their advance into Poland, surrounding Warsaw by September 15. They also pressed further east, crossing the San River into territory that they had agreed would belong to the Soviets. Alarmed, on September 17 the Soviet Union invaded Poland on two fronts—the Western Belorussian and Western Ukrainian. The Polish government fled and, under attack from all sides, the remaining Polish forces gradually capitulated.

- ☁ Soviet fronts (army groups)
- ▬ Final Polish defensive positions
- ➤ Soviet advances Sep 17–27, 1939
- ➤ German advances Sep 15–28, 1939

3 POLAND DIVIDED
SEPTEMBER 28–OCTOBER 12, 1939

The German and Soviet foreign ministers, Joachim von Ribbentrop and Vyacheslav Molotov, met on September 28 to finalize the division of Poland. The Soviet Union took over half of the country, incorporating the territories into Soviet Ukraine and Belorussia. Germany annexed the western portion of its half. Some Poles who lived there were expelled and sent to the German zone of occupation, known as the General Government, in central Poland.

- ═ Poland 1939 boundary
- ▪▪▪ Soviet–German line of demarcation
- ▨ General Government
- ▨ Annexed by Germany
- ▨ Annexed by Soviet Union

Sep 3 German bombers sink the Polish destroyer *Wicher*, but most of the Polish navy escapes.

Sep 28 Ten Polish divisions, besieged in Modlin fortress since September 10, finally surrender.

Sep 18 Wilno falls to the Red Army.

Sep 9–19 The Battle of the Bzura ends in Polish defeat; 170,000 are taken prisoner.

Sep 27 Warsaw surrenders after being bombed for a whole day by the Germans.

Sep 19 German and Soviet forces meet at Brest-Litovsk.

Oct 6 The last organized resistance by the Polish army ends at Kock.

Aug 1939 Polish armies are arranged along Poland's western border.

Sep 1–17 Slovakia, a client state of Germany, joins the invasion.

Baltic Sea

LITHUANIA

○ Kaunas

○ Königsberg

○ Wilno

○ Minsk

EAST PRUSSIA

Hel
Gdynia
Danzig

Frontier Guard

4th Army

○ Bydgoszcz
Pomeranian Army

3rd Army

Narew Group

Narew

○ Bialystok

Modlin Army

○ Poznan
Poznan Army

Vistula

○ Kutno
○ Modlin
○ Warsaw

Belorussian Front

○ Brest-Litovsk

8th Army

○ Lodz
Lodz Army

P O L A N D

○ Kock
○ Wlodawa
○ Lublin

G R E A T E R   G E R M A N Y

○ Gleiwitz

10th Army

Krakow Army
○ Krakow

○ Radom

○ Sandomierz

San

○ Lwow

Bug

○ Przemysl

14th Army

Carpathian Army

U S S R

Ukrainian Front

GREATER GERMANY

SLOVAKIA

Carpathian Mountains

◁ **Boy in the ruins of Warsaw**
The Luftwaffe opened their attack on Poland with the bombing of Warsaw on September 1, 1939. By the end of the war, 85 percent of the city was destroyed.

POLAND UNDER ATTACK
Poland was unable to resist the German and Soviet armies that swiftly divided the country between them.

POLAND DESTROYED

Poland emerged from World War I as an independent state after more than 200 years of subjugation. However, it took just a few weeks in 1939 for Germany and the Soviet Union to crush Polish resistance, divide the country, and begin brutalizing its population.

After Germany's expansion into Austria and Czechoslovakia, Hitler determined to attack Poland to regain lost territory and create *Lebensraum* ("living space") for his people, turning Poland into a German satellite state. Under the terms of the cynical pact that he had negotiated with the Soviet Union in 1939 (see pp.32–33), Poland was to be partitioned between the two powers; this enabled Germany to attack Poland without the fear of Soviet intervention.

On September 1, German troops moved into the country. Although France and Britain declared war on Germany on September 3, they reneged on their promise to provide military aid to Poland, giving Hitler a free hand.

Within a week, German "Blitzkrieg" tactics had squeezed Polish forces into the heart of Poland. When the Soviet army invaded from the east on September 17, Poland's fate was sealed. With its forces trapped between two enemies, Poland capitulated on September 28. The country was split into three: one zone was annexed by Germany, one by Soviet Russia, and the third—the General Government—was occupied by the Germans.

INVASION AND OPPRESSION
Poland was destroyed in a matter of weeks from August 31 to October 12, 1939. The Poles were seen by their occupiers as an inferior people and suffered deeply under the oppressive regimes imposed upon them.

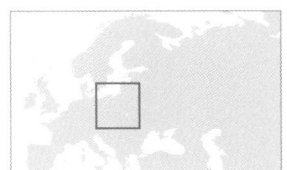

TIMELINE

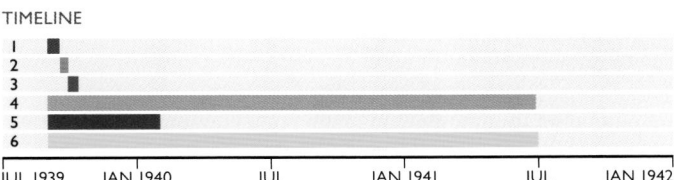

JUL 1939   JAN 1940   JUL   JAN 1941   JUL   JAN 1942

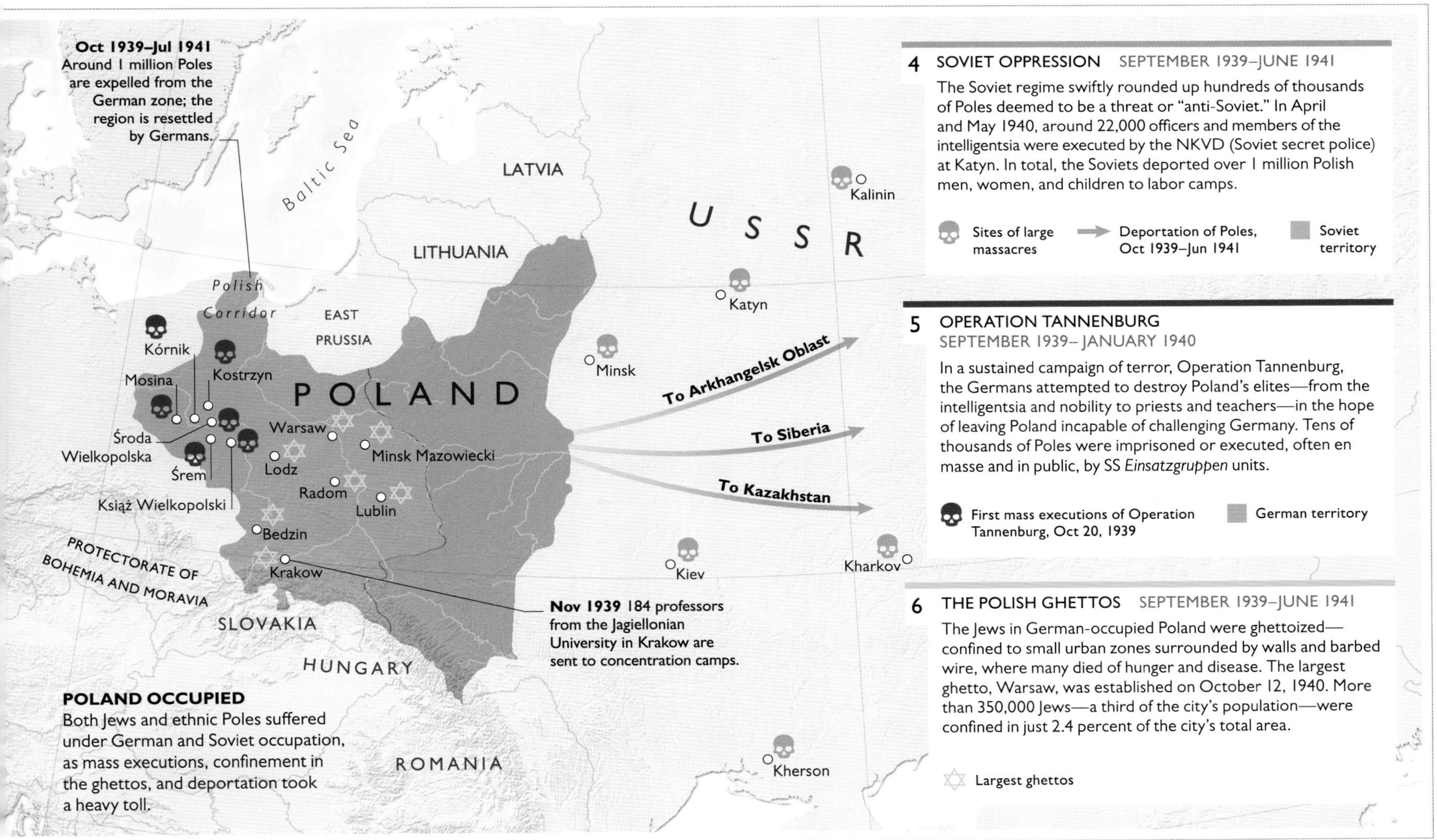

Oct 1939–Jul 1941
Around 1 million Poles are expelled from the German zone; the region is resettled by Germans.

LATVIA
Kalinin
LITHUANIA
U S S R
Baltic Sea
Polish Corridor
EAST PRUSSIA
Kórnik
Mosina   Kostrzyn
P O L A N D
Katyn
Minsk
To Arkhangelsk Oblast
Środa Wielkopolska   Warsaw
Śrem   Lodz   Minsk Mazowiecki
To Siberia
Książ Wielkopolski   Radom
Lublin
To Kazakhstan
Bedzin
PROTECTORATE OF BOHEMIA AND MORAVIA
Krakow
Kiev   Kharkov
SLOVAKIA
Nov 1939 184 professors from the Jagiellonian University in Krakow are sent to concentration camps.
HUNGARY
ROMANIA   Kherson

POLAND OCCUPIED
Both Jews and ethnic Poles suffered under German and Soviet occupation, as mass executions, confinement in the ghettos, and deportation took a heavy toll.

4 SOVIET OPPRESSION SEPTEMBER 1939–JUNE 1941
The Soviet regime swiftly rounded up hundreds of thousands of Poles deemed to be a threat or "anti-Soviet." In April and May 1940, around 22,000 officers and members of the intelligentsia were executed by the NKVD (Soviet secret police) at Katyn. In total, the Soviets deported over 1 million Polish men, women, and children to labor camps.

☠ Sites of large massacres   → Deportation of Poles, Oct 1939–Jun 1941   ▮ Soviet territory

5 OPERATION TANNENBURG
SEPTEMBER 1939– JANUARY 1940
In a sustained campaign of terror, Operation Tannenburg, the Germans attempted to destroy Poland's elites—from the intelligentsia and nobility to priests and teachers—in the hope of leaving Poland incapable of challenging Germany. Tens of thousands of Poles were imprisoned or executed, often en masse and in public, by SS *Einsatzgruppen* units.

☠ First mass executions of Operation Tannenburg, Oct 20, 1939   ▮ German territory

6 THE POLISH GHETTOS SEPTEMBER 1939–JUNE 1941
The Jews in German-occupied Poland were ghettoized—confined to small urban zones surrounded by walls and barbed wire, where many died of hunger and disease. The largest ghetto, Warsaw, was established on October 12, 1940. More than 350,000 Jews—a third of the city's population—were confined in just 2.4 percent of the city's total area.

✡ Largest ghettos

Emergency measures
Fearing mass air attacks, including the use of poison gas, once war had been declared, governments took measures to ensure that civil defense could be carried out in major cities. Here fire-fighters in gas masks carry out an exercise in Paris in 1939.

THE PHONY WAR

Although the Allies declared war against Germany on September 3, 1939, there was little fighting on land until spring 1940. This lull in hostilities became known as the "phony war."

△ **Safety precautions**
In this British government propaganda poster, an air raid warden warns a schoolboy that he should leave London. In total, 1.5 million schoolchildren and mothers with babies were evacuated from the city.

The lack of fighting in western Europe during this time suited both sides: the Germans feared an Allied attack while they were engaged against Poland, and the French and British needed time to build up their forces. While preparations were underway and wartime emergency powers were imposed at home, military action was very limited. The British Expeditionary Force (BEF) was deployed to France on September 4, 1939, but took up defensive positions, and a French offensive against the Germans in the Saar on September 7 lasted only five days. British bombers flew over Germany, but merely dropped propaganda leaflets aimed at undermining German morale.

Hitler made a peace offer to Britain on October 6, 1939, but after Britain rejected it he ordered his generals to prepare for an invasion of France and Belgium. Initial plans were unsatisfactory, and a harsh winter meant that the attack was postponed 29 times. Instead, in April 1940, the Germans invaded Denmark and Norway, ending the phony war.

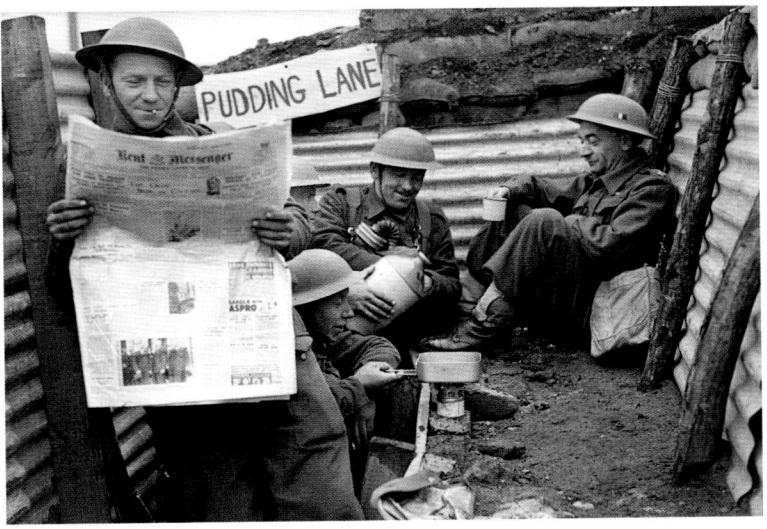

△ **Army in waiting**
The British Expeditionary Force was ordered into France on September 4, and within three weeks there were around 150,000 troops stationed there. Sent to the Franco-Belgian border, they had little to do for eight months but dig trenches and wait.

BATTLE OF THE RIVER PLATE

On the night of October 13–14, 1939, a German U-boat sank HMS *Royal Oak* at her berth in Scapa Flow, Britain's main naval base. The audacious attack was a blow to British morale, but just two months later the Royal Navy had claimed a victory against the odds in the first major naval battle of the war.

At the outbreak of war, Germany's naval strategy was to avoid direct combat between fleet units and instead use surface raiders and U-boats to sink Allied shipping wherever possible, severing Britain's maritime lifelines. Weeks before hostilities began, German warships and supply vessels went into the North and South Atlantic, and most of the U-boat fleet took up station in the North Sea and Atlantic approaches. There they awaited authorization to attack.

The flagship of the German navy (*Kriegsmarine*) was the *Admiral Graf Spee*, a fast, modern, heavily armed pocket battleship commanded by Hans Langsdorff. From late September to early December, *Graf*

Spee eluded detection and raided successfully, sinking nine Allied merchantmen totaling 55,000 tons (50,000 metric tons). The British and French navies organized hunting groups in areas throughout the North and South Atlantic, and in the early hours of December 13, *Graf Spee* was spotted. In the ensuing Battle of the River Plate, the smaller Royal Navy cruisers were able to harry *Graf Spee* and inflict damage that forced her to take refuge in a neutral port for repairs. The subsequent scuttling of *Graf Spee* was a major setback for the German navy, greatly undermining the original strategy of using its surface fleet to blockade British trade.

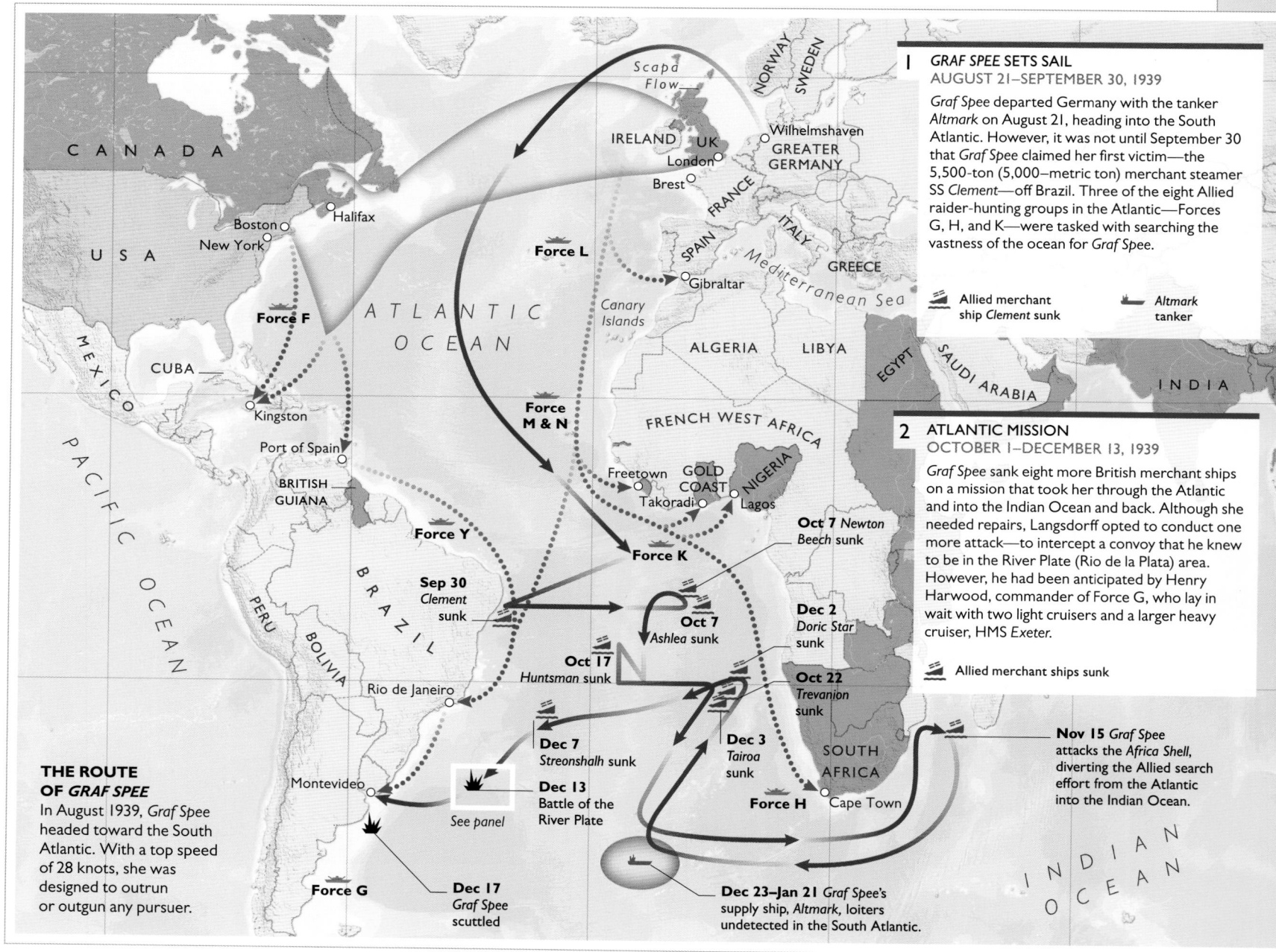

1 GRAF SPEE SETS SAIL
AUGUST 21–SEPTEMBER 30, 1939

Graf Spee departed Germany with the tanker *Altmark* on August 21, heading into the South Atlantic. However, it was not until September 30 that *Graf Spee* claimed her first victim—the 5,500-ton (5,000–metric ton) merchant steamer SS *Clement*—off Brazil. Three of the eight Allied raider-hunting groups in the Atlantic—Forces G, H, and K—were tasked with searching the vastness of the ocean for *Graf Spee*.

Allied merchant ship *Clement* sunk

Altmark tanker

2 ATLANTIC MISSION
OCTOBER 1–DECEMBER 13, 1939

Graf Spee sank eight more British merchant ships on a mission that took her through the Atlantic and into the Indian Ocean and back. Although she needed repairs, Langsdorff opted to conduct one more attack—to intercept a convoy that he knew to be in the River Plate (Rio de la Plata) area. However, he had been anticipated by Henry Harwood, commander of Force G, who lay in wait with two light cruisers and a larger heavy cruiser, HMS *Exeter*.

Allied merchant ships sunk

THE ROUTE OF GRAF SPEE
In August 1939, *Graf Spee* headed toward the South Atlantic. With a top speed of 28 knots, she was designed to outrun or outgun any pursuer.

Sep 30 Clement sunk

Oct 7 Ashlea sunk

Oct 7 Newton Beech sunk

Oct 17 Huntsman sunk

Oct 22 Trevanion sunk

Dec 2 Doric Star sunk

Dec 3 Tairoa sunk

Dec 7 Streonshalh sunk

Dec 13 Battle of the River Plate

Dec 17 Graf Spee scuttled

Nov 15 *Graf Spee* attacks the *Africa Shell*, diverting the Allied search effort from the Atlantic into the Indian Ocean.

Dec 23–Jan 21 *Graf Spee's* supply ship, *Altmark*, loiters undetected in the South Atlantic.

See panel

Force F, Force L, Force M & N, Force K, Force Y, Force G, Force H

6 GRAF SPEE SCUTTLED
DECEMBER 13/14–19, 1939

Graf Spee sheltered in the neutral port Montevideo and was permitted to stay until December 17 to make repairs and off-load her wounded. On December 15, a German officer thought he spotted British ships approaching, and Langsdorff became convinced that superior forces lay in wait. Unwilling to lose *Graf Spee*, he took her into the estuary, and at around 8pm on December 17 she was scuttled. On December 19, Captain Langsdorff shot himself dead in a hotel room.

5 GRAF SPEE WITHDRAWS
6:30AM–7:30AM DECEMBER 13, 1939

Torpedoes fired by the British forced *Graf Spee* to lay down a smokescreen and turn away. *Ajax* launched her spotter plane at 6:37am. She and *Achilles* were closing range, firing heavily, drawing *Graf Spee*'s main guns away from *Exeter*. *Ajax* was hit at 7:25am and had to turn east. *Graf Spee* was hit several dozen times and withdrew west into the River Plate Estuary.

✈ ••▸ *Ajax* reconnaissance aircraft

4 EXETER DAMAGED
6AM–6:30AM DECEMBER 13, 1939

The British force spotted *Graf Spee* shortly after 6am. The British doctrine on the engagement of a superior ship had been developed by Harwood himself a few years earlier: he duly divided his force into two—*Exeter* turning north-west and *Ajax* and *Achilles* north-east—to split the fire from the heavily armed ship. *Graf Spee* opened fire and concentrated her 11-in guns on *Exeter*, which, by 6:30am, had been hit three times, losing a turret and her Walrus spotter aircraft.

TORPEDO FIRE

🔫 ••▸ *Exeter*   🔫 ••▸ *Ajax*

🔫 ••▸ *Ajax* and *Achilles* combined

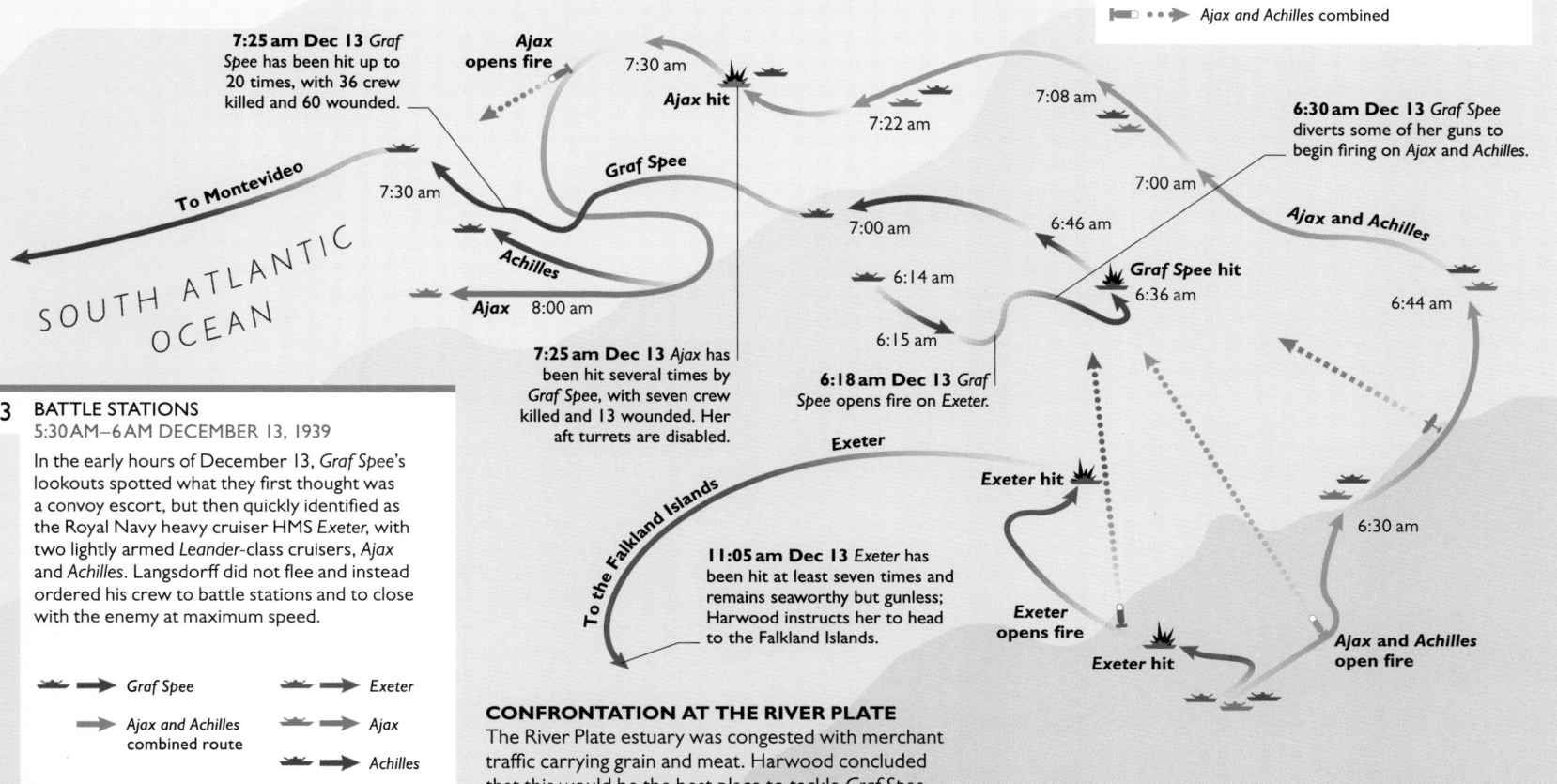

7:25am Dec 13 *Graf Spee* has been hit up to 20 times, with 36 crew killed and 60 wounded.

Ajax opens fire

7:30 am

Ajax hit

7:22 am

7:08 am

7:30 am

To Montevideo

7:30 am

Graf Spee

6:30am Dec 13 *Graf Spee* diverts some of her guns to begin firing on *Ajax* and *Achilles*.

7:00 am

Ajax and *Achilles*

SOUTH ATLANTIC OCEAN

Achilles

7:00 am

6:46 am

Ajax   8:00 am

6:14 am

Graf Spee hit
6:36 am

6:44 am

6:15 am

6:18am Dec 13 *Graf Spee* opens fire on *Exeter*.

7:25am Dec 13 *Ajax* has been hit several times by *Graf Spee*, with seven crew killed and 13 wounded. Her aft turrets are disabled.

3 BATTLE STATIONS
5:30AM–6AM DECEMBER 13, 1939

In the early hours of December 13, *Graf Spee*'s lookouts spotted what they first thought was a convoy escort, but then quickly identified as the Royal Navy heavy cruiser HMS *Exeter*, with two lightly armed *Leander*-class cruisers, *Ajax* and *Achilles*. Langsdorff did not flee and instead ordered his crew to battle stations and to close with the enemy at maximum speed.

Exeter

Exeter hit

6:30 am

11:05am Dec 13 *Exeter* has been hit at least seven times and remains seaworthy but gunless; Harwood instructs her to head to the Falkland Islands.

To the Falkland Islands

Exeter opens fire

Exeter hit

Ajax and **Achilles** open fire

━▸ *Graf Spee*   ━▸ *Exeter*

━▸ *Ajax* and *Achilles* combined route

━▸ *Ajax*

━▸ *Achilles*

CONFRONTATION AT THE RIVER PLATE
The River Plate estuary was congested with merchant traffic carrying grain and meat. Harwood concluded that this would be the best place to tackle *Graf Spee*.

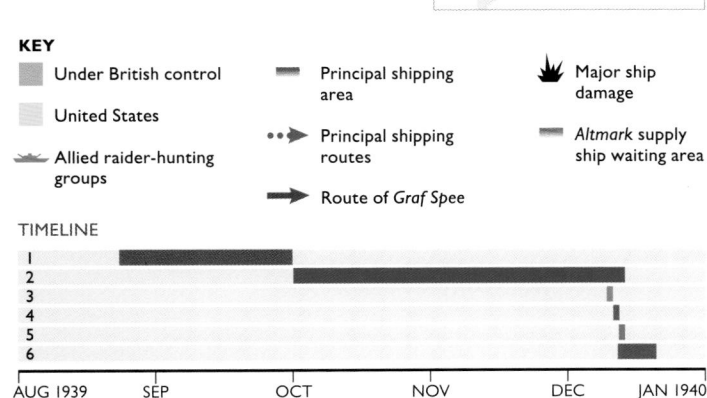

ATLANTIC HUNTING GROUNDS
Atlantic shipping routes were vital to Britain's global war effort. The German raiding campaign against this shipping required supply vessels and good luck to remain undetected for extended periods.

KEY

▮ Under British control

▮ United States

🛥 Allied raider-hunting groups

▬ Principal shipping area

••▸ Principal shipping routes

━▸ Route of *Graf Spee*

🕱 Major ship damage

▬ *Altmark* supply ship waiting area

TIMELINE

1
2
3
4
5
6

AUG 1939   SEP   OCT   NOV   DEC   JAN 1940

△ **Scuttling of *Admiral Graf Spee***
Charges set on the pocket battleship *Graf Spee* were detonated on the evening of December 17, 1939, to scuttle the ship. Her sinking was witnessed by a crowd of more than 20,000 onlookers.

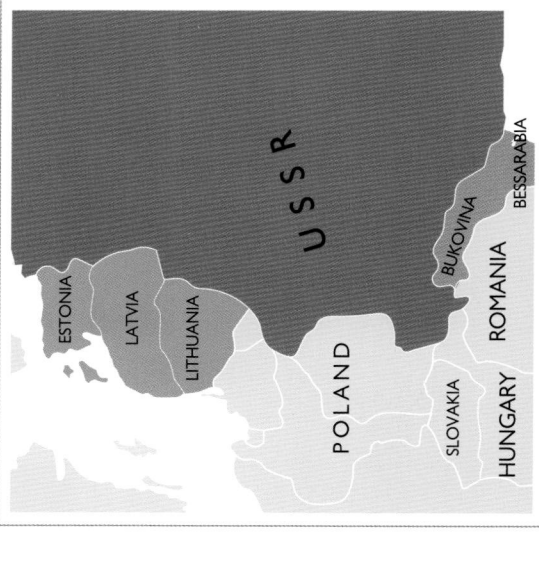

SOVIET ABSORPTION OF THE BALTIC AND BLACK SEA STATES

Following the Winter War, the Soviets annexed Estonia, Latvia, Lithuania, and parts of Romania—all areas recognized in the Molotov–Ribbentrop Pact as lying within the Soviet sphere of influence. These territories were incorporated into the Soviet Union as constituent republics in August 1940, and many of their residents, deemed "enemies of the people," were deported to Siberia or Kazakhstan.

KEY

▮ Annexed from the Baltic States

▮ Annexed from Romania

THE WINTER WAR IN FINLAND

The Soviet invasion of Finland in winter 1939 was met with ferocious resistance from a largely reservist Finnish army that was familiar with—and well trained for—the severe weather conditions. The damage inflicted by the Finns on their numerically superior enemy helped them negotiate a settlement that avoided their complete subjugation.

In the Molotov–Ribbentrop Pact of August 23, 1939, the Soviet Union and Germany secretly agreed to divide much of Europe between themselves in a way that anticipated the "territorial and political rearrangements" to come. According to this pact, the Baltic States and Finland fell into the Soviet sphere of influence, and it was not long before the Soviets demanded that Finland cede to them a number of strategically important territories on their shared border. Finland refused, and Stalin ordered an invasion, intending to install a compliant regime in Finland.

The Soviet attack began on November 30, 1939, and was undertaken initially by four armies of about 450,000 men. The plan was to reach Helsinki within three weeks. The main focus of the Soviet offensive was the Karelian Isthmus, where most of the Finnish Army was deployed along the Mannerheim Line—a series of fortifications, anti-tank ditches, and obstacles built over two decades to deter Soviet aggression. The Soviet build-up gave the Finns time to assemble around 250,000 men, who had been trained in the use of *motti* tactics—encircling and breaking up enemy formations into isolated pockets, then destroying them.

Stout resistance and damaging counter-attacks from the Finns stalemated the Soviets in most of Finland by the end of December. The highly mobile Finnish ski patrol units wreaked havoc behind Soviet formations. However, by early February, a reorganized Red Army converted its superiority in manpower and equipment into success on the battlefield. Hostilities ended on March 13, 1940, with Finland ceding around ten percent of its territory to the USSR.

△ **Finnish ski troopers**
Moving quickly through the forests, and equipped for the hostile conditions, Finnish ski patrols conducted successful missions against the Soviets.

ACTION IN THE ARCTIC NORTH
NOVEMBER 30–DECEMBER 15, 1939

Two divisions of the Soviet 14th Army attacked the Rybachy Peninsula and the arctic port of Petsamo from Murmansk on the Kola Peninsula. The Finns withdrew and the Soviets occupied the port to prevent any Allied landing. The Soviets resumed the offensive, pushing on to their objective—the town of Nautsi—but their progress was impeded by Finnish counterattacks. Nautsi was not captured until March 7.

KEY

✕ Finnish resistance

→ Soviet attacks

Dec 15–18, 1939
The Finns finally retreat from Salmijärvi, having counterattacked Soviet forces for two weeks.

Varanger Fjord

Rybachy Peninsula

Polyarnyy

Murmansk

Petsamo

Salmijärvi

Nautsi

Lapland

Tana

NORWAY

Harstad

SOVIET INVASION

The USSR invaded Finland with a huge army of around 450,000 men. However, they were confounded by a Finnish army that slowed their progress and inflicted heavy casualties until a peace deal ended the war.

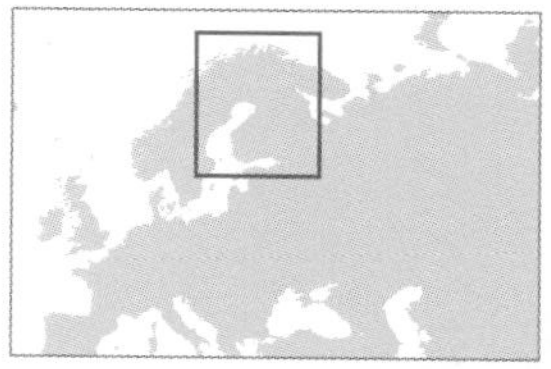

KEY

⇣ Soviet air raid

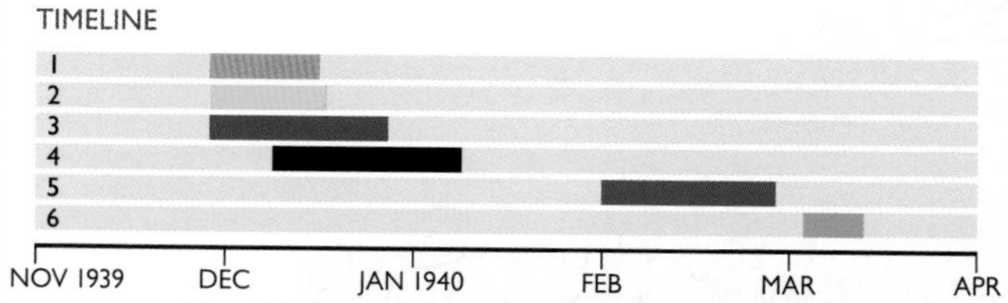

TIMELINE

NOV 1939 | DEC | JAN 1940 | FEB | MAR | APR

1 2 3 4 5 6

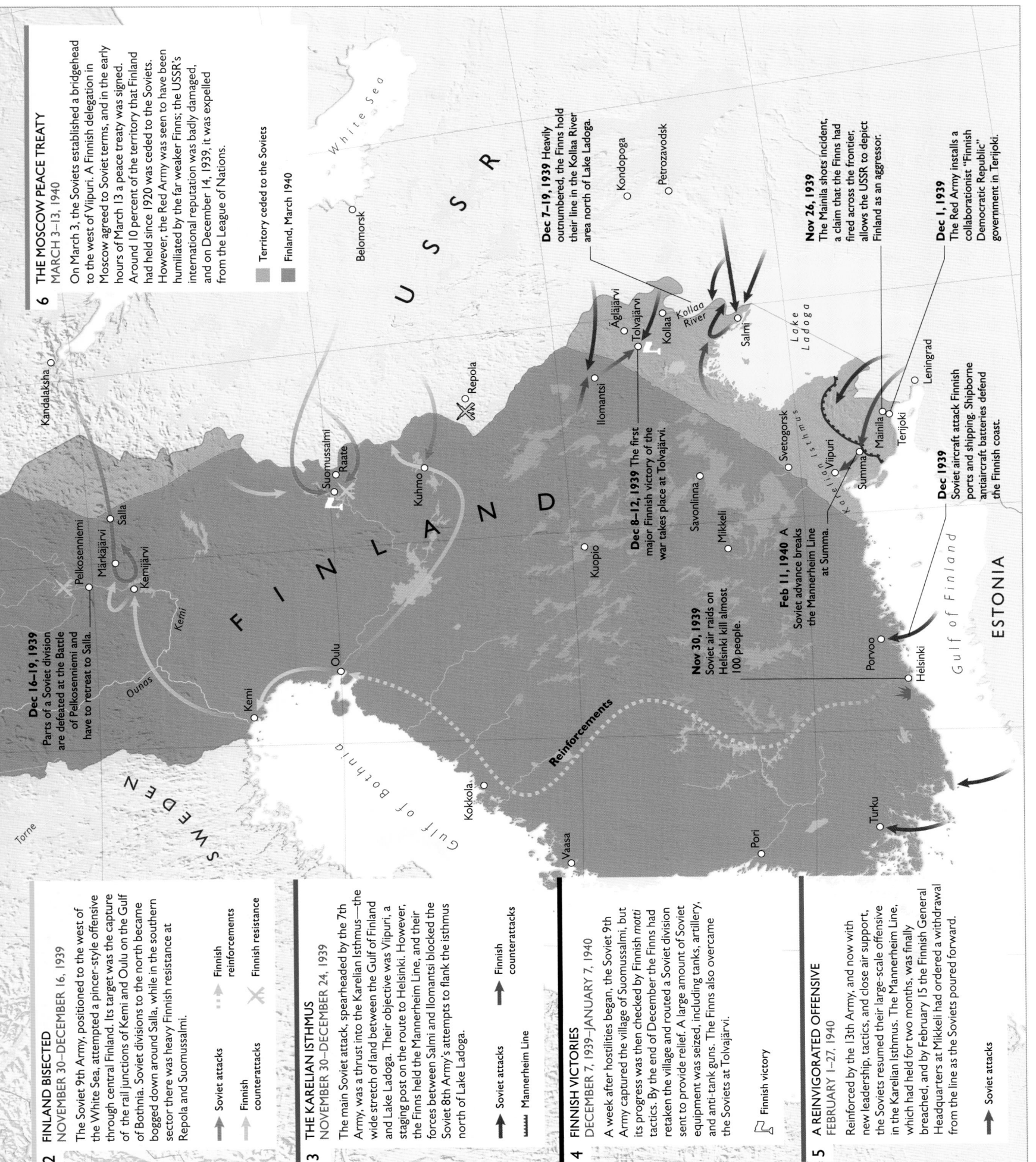

6 THE MOSCOW PEACE TREATY
MARCH 3–13, 1940

On March 3, the Soviets established a bridgehead to the west of Viipuri. A Finnish delegation in Moscow agreed to Soviet terms, and in the early hours of March 13 a peace treaty was signed. Around 10 percent of the territory that Finland had held since 1920 was ceded to the Soviets. However, the Red Army was seen to have been humiliated by the far weaker Finns; the USSR's international reputation was badly damaged, and on December 14, 1939, it was expelled from the League of Nations.

■ Territory ceded to the Soviets

■ Finland, March 1940

Dec 7–19, 1939 Heavily outnumbered, the Finns hold their line in the Kollaa River area north of Lake Ladoga.

Nov 26, 1939 The Mainila shots incident, a claim that the Finns had fired across the frontier, allows the USSR to depict Finland as an aggressor.

Dec 1, 1939 The Red Army installs a collaborationist "Finnish Democratic Republic" government in Terijoki.

Dec 8–12, 1939 The first major Finnish victory of the war takes place at Tolvajärvi.

Nov 30, 1939 Soviet air raids on Helsinki kill almost 100 people.

Feb 11, 1940 A Soviet advance breaks the Mannerheim Line at Summa.

Dec 1939 Soviet aircraft attack Finnish ports and shipping. Shipborne antiaircraft batteries defend the Finnish coast.

Dec 16–19, 1939 Parts of a Soviet division are defeated at the Battle of Pelkosenniemi and have to retreat to Salla.

Reinforcements

2 FINLAND BISECTED
NOVEMBER 30–DECEMBER 16, 1939

The Soviet 9th Army, positioned to the west of the White Sea, attempted a pincer-style offensive through central Finland. Its target was the capture of the rail junctions of Kemi and Oulu on the Gulf of Bothnia. Soviet divisions to the north became bogged down around Salla, while in the southern sector there was heavy Finnish resistance at Repola and Suomussalmi.

→ Soviet attacks
→ Finnish reinforcements
→ Finnish counterattacks
✕ Finnish resistance

3 THE KARELIAN ISTHMUS
NOVEMBER 30–DECEMBER 24, 1939

The main Soviet attack, spearheaded by the 7th Army, was a thrust into the Karelian Isthmus—the wide stretch of land between the Gulf of Finland and Lake Ladoga. Their objective was Viipuri, a staging post on the route to Helsinki. However, the Finns held the Mannerheim Line, and their forces between Salmi and Ilomantsi blocked the Soviet 8th Army's attempts to flank the isthmus north of Lake Ladoga.

→ Soviet attacks
→ Finnish counterattacks
⁙⁙⁙ Mannerheim Line

4 FINNISH VICTORIES
DECEMBER 7, 1939–JANUARY 7, 1940

A week after hostilities began, the Soviet 9th Army captured the village of Suomussalmi, but its progress was then checked by Finnish *motti* tactics. By the end of December the Finns had retaken the village and routed a Soviet division sent to provide relief. A large amount of Soviet equipment was seized, including tanks, artillery, and anti-tank guns. The Finns also overcame the Soviets at Tolvajärvi.

⌐ Finnish victory

5 A REINVIGORATED OFFENSIVE
FEBRUARY 1–27, 1940

Reinforced by the 13th Army, and now with new leadership, tactics, and close air support, the Soviets resumed their large-scale offensive in the Karelian Isthmus. The Mannerheim Line, which had held for two months, was finally breached, and by February 15 the Finnish General Headquarters at Mikkeli had ordered a withdrawal from the line as the Soviets poured forward.

→ Soviet attacks

Map labels: White Sea, USSR, Kandalaksha, Belomorsk, Kondopoga, Petrozavodsk, Repola, Salla, Pelkosenniemi, Märkäjärvi, Kemijärvi, Kemi, Kokkola, Vaasa, Pori, Turku, Oulu, Kuhmo, Suomussalmi, Raate, FINLAND, Kuopio, Savonlinna, Mikkeli, Ilomantsi, Ägläjärvi, Tolvajärvi, Kollaa, Kollaa River, Salmi, Lake Ladoga, Svetogorsk, Viipuri, Summa, Mainila, Terijoki, Leningrad, Karelian Isthmus, Porvoo, Helsinki, Gulf of Finland, ESTONIA, SWEDEN, Gulf of Bothnia, Torne, Ounas, Kemi, Kola Peninsula

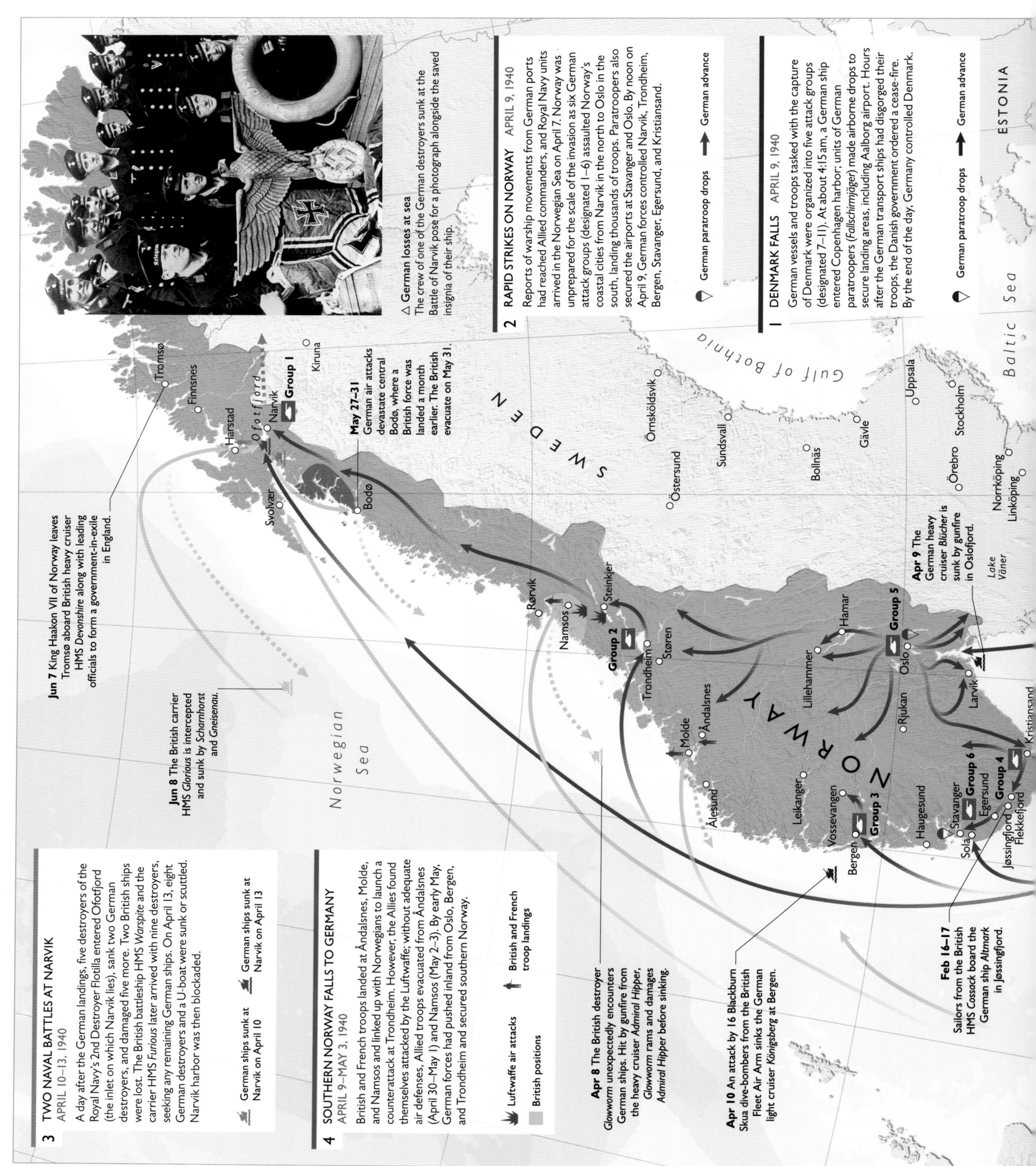

△ **German losses at sea**
The crew of one of the German destroyers sunk at the Battle of Narvik pose for a photograph alongside the saved insignia of their ship.

2 RAPID STRIKES ON NORWAY APRIL 9, 1940

Reports of warship movements from German ports had reached Allied commanders, and Royal Navy units arrived in the Norwegian Sea on April 7. Norway was unprepared for the scale of the invasion as six German attack groups (designated 1–6) assaulted Norway's coastal cities from Narvik in the north to Oslo in the south, landing thousands of troops. Paratroopers also secured the airports at Stavanger and Oslo. By noon on April 9, German forces controlled Narvik, Trondheim, Bergen, Stavanger, Egersund, and Kristiansand.

◑ German paratroop drops   → German advance

1 DENMARK FALLS APRIL 9, 1940

German vessels and troops tasked with the capture of Denmark were organized into five attack groups (designated 7–11). At about 4:15 am, a German ship entered Copenhagen harbor; units of German paratroopers (*Fallschirmjäger*) made airborne drops to secure landing areas, including Aalborg airport. Hours after the German transport ships had disgorged their troops, the Danish government ordered a cease-fire. By the end of the day, Germany controlled Denmark.

◑ German paratroop drops   → German advance

3 TWO NAVAL BATTLES AT NARVIK
APRIL 10–13, 1940

A day after the German landings, five destroyers of the Royal Navy's 2nd Destroyer Flotilla entered Ofotfjord (the inlet on which Narvik lies), sank two German destroyers, and damaged five more. Two British ships were lost. The British battleship HMS *Warspite* and the carrier HMS *Furious* later arrived with nine destroyers, seeking any remaining German ships. On April 13, eight German destroyers and a U-boat were sunk or scuttled. Narvik harbor was then blockaded.

⚓ German ships sunk at   ⚓ German ships sunk at
Narvik on April 10   Narvik on April 13

4 SOUTHERN NORWAY FALLS TO GERMANY
APRIL 9–MAY 3, 1940

British and French troops landed at Åndalsnes, Molde, and Namsos and linked up with Norwegians to launch a counterattack at Trondheim. However, the Allies found themselves attacked by the Luftwaffe; without adequate air defenses, Allied troops evacuated from Åndalsnes (April 30–May 1) and Namsos (May 2–3). By early May, German forces had pushed inland from Oslo, Bergen, and Trondheim and secured southern Norway.

▸ Luftwaffe air attacks   → British and French
troop landings

▨ British positions

Apr 8 The British destroyer *Glowworm* unexpectedly encounters German ships. Hit by gunfire from the heavy cruiser *Admiral Hipper*, *Glowworm* rams and damages *Admiral Hipper* before sinking.

Apr 10 An attack by 16 Blackburn Skua dive-bombers from the British Fleet Air Arm sinks the German light cruiser *Königsberg* at Bergen.

Feb 16–17 Sailors from the British HMS *Cossack* board the German ship *Altmark* in Jøssingfjord.

Jun 7 King Haakon VII of Norway leaves Tromsø aboard British heavy cruiser HMS *Devonshire* along with leading officials to form a government-in-exile in England.

Jun 8 The British carrier HMS *Glorious* is intercepted and sunk by *Scharnhorst* and *Gneisenau*.

May 27–31 German air attacks devastate central Bodø, where a British force was landed a month earlier. The British evacuate on May 31.

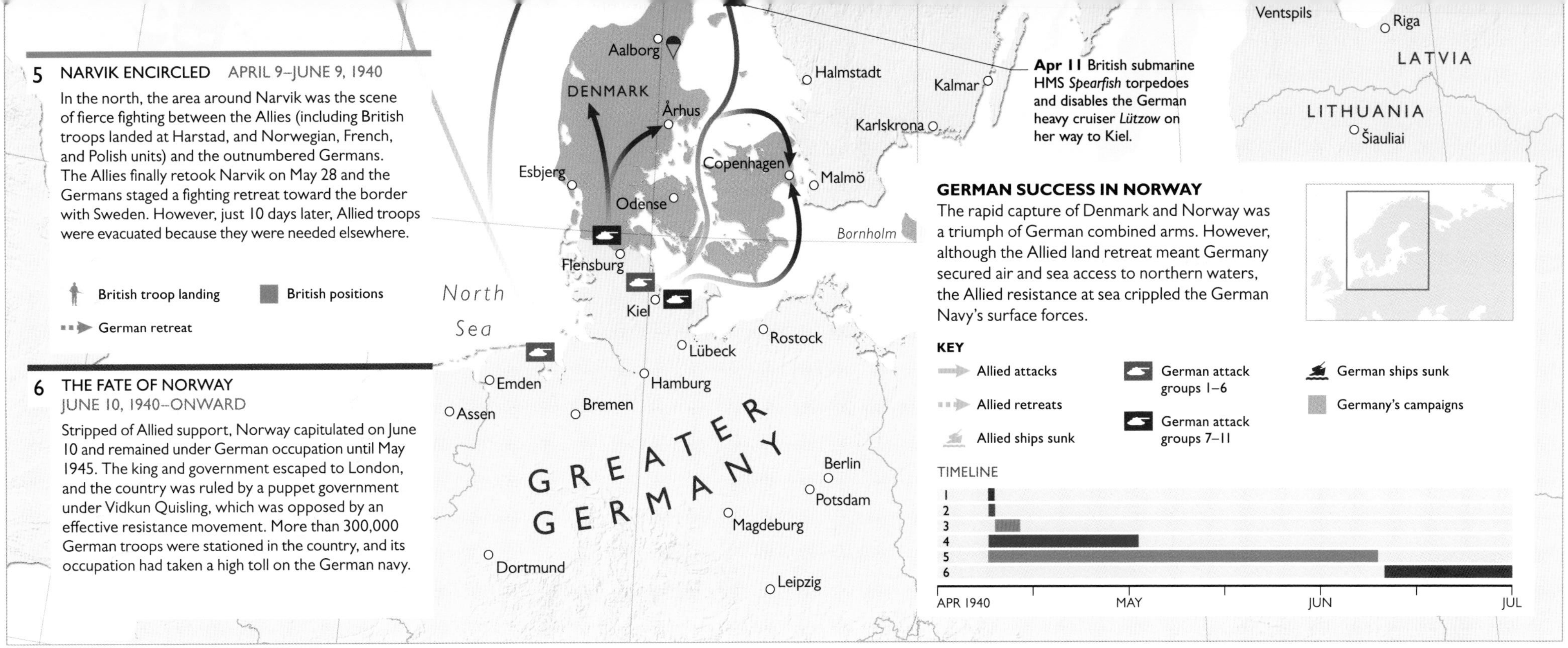

THE BATTLE FOR NORWAY

On March 1, 1940, Adolf Hitler signed the order for Operation Weserübung. The principal aim of this daring operation was to take control of Norway—a goal that also necessitated the occupation of Denmark. The invasion advanced Germany's aim of gaining greater access to the North Sea and provided a gateway to the Atlantic for its warships and submarines.

In July 1938, Norway and eight other countries declared their neutrality in any possible European conflict. Germany, in turn, agreed to respect Norway's integrity so long as its neutrality was not infringed by any other power. The peace was not to last.

Norway was of significant importance to Germany, not least because large quantities of iron ore from Sweden were shipped annually to Germany via the ice-free Norwegian port of Narvik. In addition, the German navy saw strategic advantages in establishing bases in Norway, because it would be far more difficult for an enemy to deny access to its long coastline than to blockade German ports.

The *Altmark* incident of February 1940 (see box, right) convinced Hitler that the British would not respect Norwegian neutrality. Fearing that the British would soon move to disrupt the vital trade in iron ore, the German high command planned an invasion of Norway, which began on April 9, 1940.

The focal point of the naval and land battles in Norway was the town of Narvik, which the Allies needed to occupy in order to retain a strategic foothold in Norway. The Allies decisively won the sea battles, with the German navy sustaining heavy losses. On land, however, the poorly equipped Allied troops were outnumbered and outgunned, and many were evacuated by the beginning of May. The Germans dominated the air through the Luftwaffe's 10th Air Corps (Fliegerkorps X), demonstrating the tactical importance of air superiority to achieving military aims on the modern battlefield.

The Allies abandoned their action in southern Norway after just three weeks, but fighting continued in the north, where the Norwegian and Allied forces eventually retook Narvik. However, German invasions in France and the Low Countries in May 1940 (see pp.48–49) dictated a withdrawal and evacuation because the remaining Allied soldiers were urgently needed elsewhere.

THE ALTMARK INCIDENT

From August to December 1939, the German supply ship *Altmark* (pictured below) refueled the warship *Admiral Graf Spee* during her raiding mission against Allied shipping in the South Atlantic (see pp.42–43). In January 1940, *Altmark* headed home, carrying prisoners from merchant ships sunk by *Admiral Graf Spee*. After neutral Norwegian destroyers prevented a Royal Navy interception, the British instructed the destroyer HMS *Cossack* to pursue *Altmark* into Jøssingfjord. On February 16, a boarding party armed with bayonets leaped onto *Altmark*, killing several guards but rescuing around 300 Allied POWs.

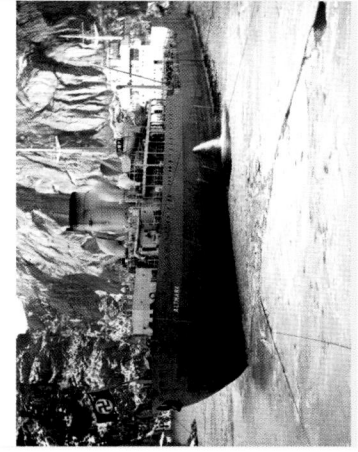

GERMAN SUCCESS IN NORWAY

The rapid capture of Denmark and Norway was a triumph of German combined arms. However, although the Allied land retreat meant Germany secured air and sea access to northern waters, the Allied resistance at sea crippled the German Navy's surface forces.

Apr 11 British submarine HMS *Spearfish* torpedoes and disables the German heavy cruiser *Lützow* on her way to Kiel.

KEY

- Allied attacks
- Allied retreats
- Allied ships sunk
- German attack groups 1–6
- German attack groups 7–11
- German ships sunk
- Germany's campaigns

TIMELINE

1
2
3
4
5
6

APR 1940 MAY JUN JUL

5 NARVIK ENCIRCLED   APRIL 9–JUNE 9, 1940

In the north, the area around Narvik was the scene of fierce fighting between the Allies (including British troops landed at Harstad, and Norwegian, French, and Polish units) and the outnumbered Germans. The Allies finally retook Narvik on May 28 and the Germans staged a fighting retreat toward the border with Sweden. However, just 10 days later, Allied troops were evacuated because they were needed elsewhere.

- British troop landing
- German retreat
- British positions

6 THE FATE OF NORWAY   JUNE 10, 1940–ONWARD

Stripped of Allied support, Norway capitulated on June 10 and remained under German occupation until May 1945. The king and government escaped to London, and the country was ruled by a puppet government under Vidkun Quisling, which was opposed by an effective resistance movement. More than 300,000 German troops were stationed in the country, and its occupation had taken a high toll on the German navy.

LATVIA
Riga
Ventspils

LITHUANIA
Šiauliai

Kalmar
Karlskrona
Halmstadt
Malmö
Copenhagen
Bornholm
Aalborg
Århus
DENMARK
Odense
Esbjerg
Flensburg
Kiel
Lübeck
Hamburg
Bremen
Emden
Assen
Dortmund
Rostock
Berlin
Potsdam
Magdeburg
Leipzig

GREATER GERMANY

North Sea

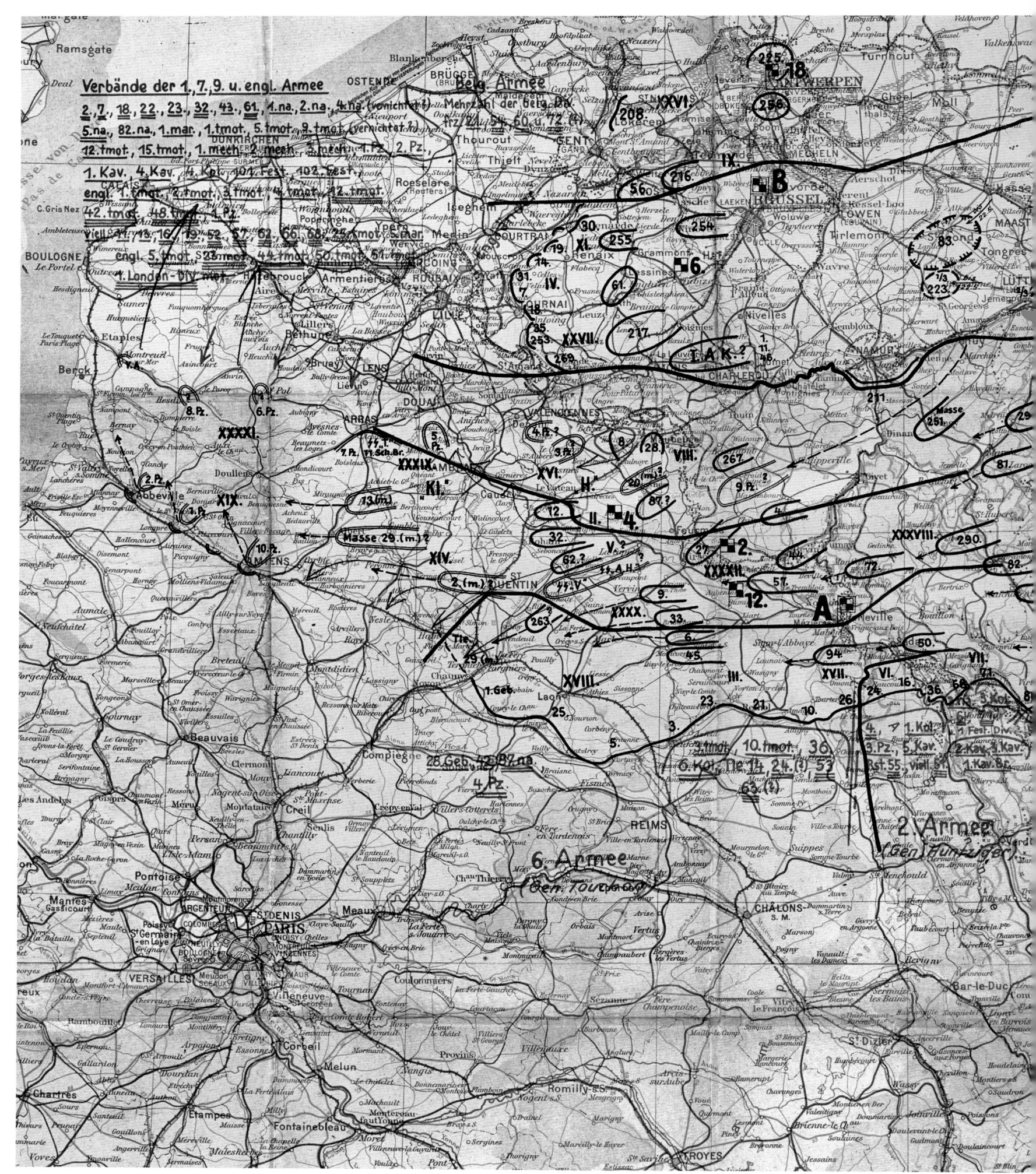

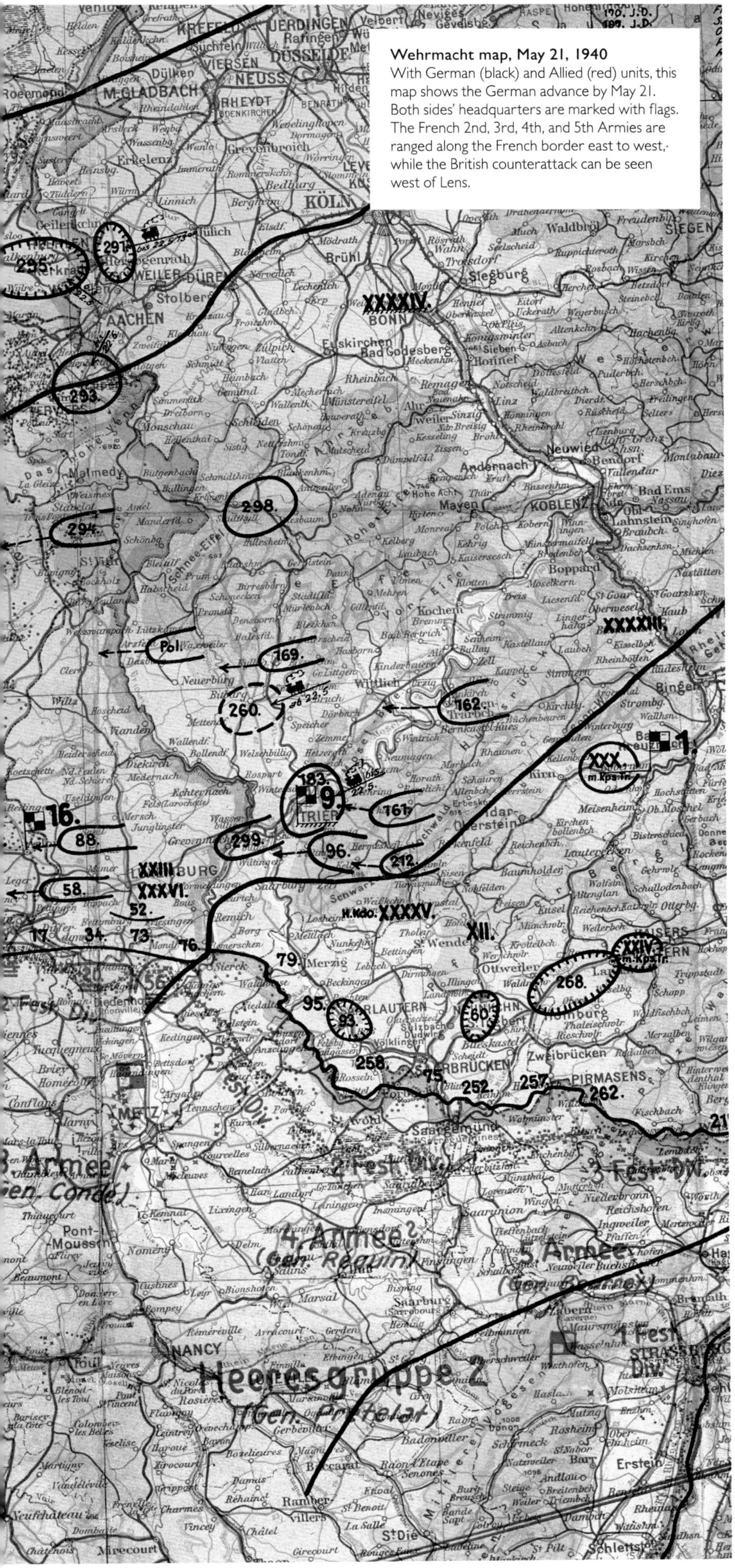

Wehrmacht map, May 21, 1940
With German (black) and Allied (red) units, this map shows the German advance by May 21. Both sides' headquarters are marked with flags. The French 2nd, 3rd, 4th, and 5th Armies are ranged along the French border east to west, while the British counterattack can be seen west of Lens.

THE GERMAN OFFENSIVE IN THE WEST

The Germans began their campaign in the west in May 1940. Within one day they had invaded the Low Countries, and within weeks they had swept across northern France to reach the Channel coast, trapping thousands of French and British soldiers around Dunkirk.

On May 10, Germany attacked the Netherlands, Belgium, and Luxembourg. Paratroopers were dropped in the Netherlands, taking key bridges and opening the way for ground forces. By May 12, German tanks had reached Rotterdam, which was heavily bombed by the Luftwaffe. The Dutch surrendered on May 14. In Belgium, German gliders dropped paratroopers onto the roof of Fort Eben-Emael, between Liège and Maastricht. They were joined by ground forces, which moved toward the British and French forces at the River Dyle in Belgium (see flag marked in Brussels). After 18 days of fighting, Belgium surrendered on May 28. Luxembourg surrendered in a matter of hours.

Breaching Allied defenses

British and French generals were sure that Germany could not penetrate France's fortified eastern border—the Maginot Line—or the densely forested Ardennes region. They were wrong. On May 12, panzer corps moved into the Ardennes and crossed the River Meuse at Sedan. This meant the Germans could advance to the Channel via the undefended countryside. To the south, the French fought to stop the Germans moving on Paris. However, Paris was not the goal, and on May 20 the Germans reached the Channel coast at Abbeville (center left) and trapped the Allies. The sole British tank division counterattacked Arras on May 21 (upper left), but to no avail. German forces pushed through Belgium, and panzers drew closer from the south and east. On May 20 Britain opted to evacuate its troops via Dunkirk.

▷ **German advance**
German infantry accompanied by a tank maneuver in the Ardennes in May 1940 during the Battle of France.

On land and in the air
Early in the German invasion of the USSR in June 1941, Heinkel III bombers fly over German motorized and infantry forces advancing in a column. It is likely this photo was manipulated for dramatic effect, possibly for propaganda.

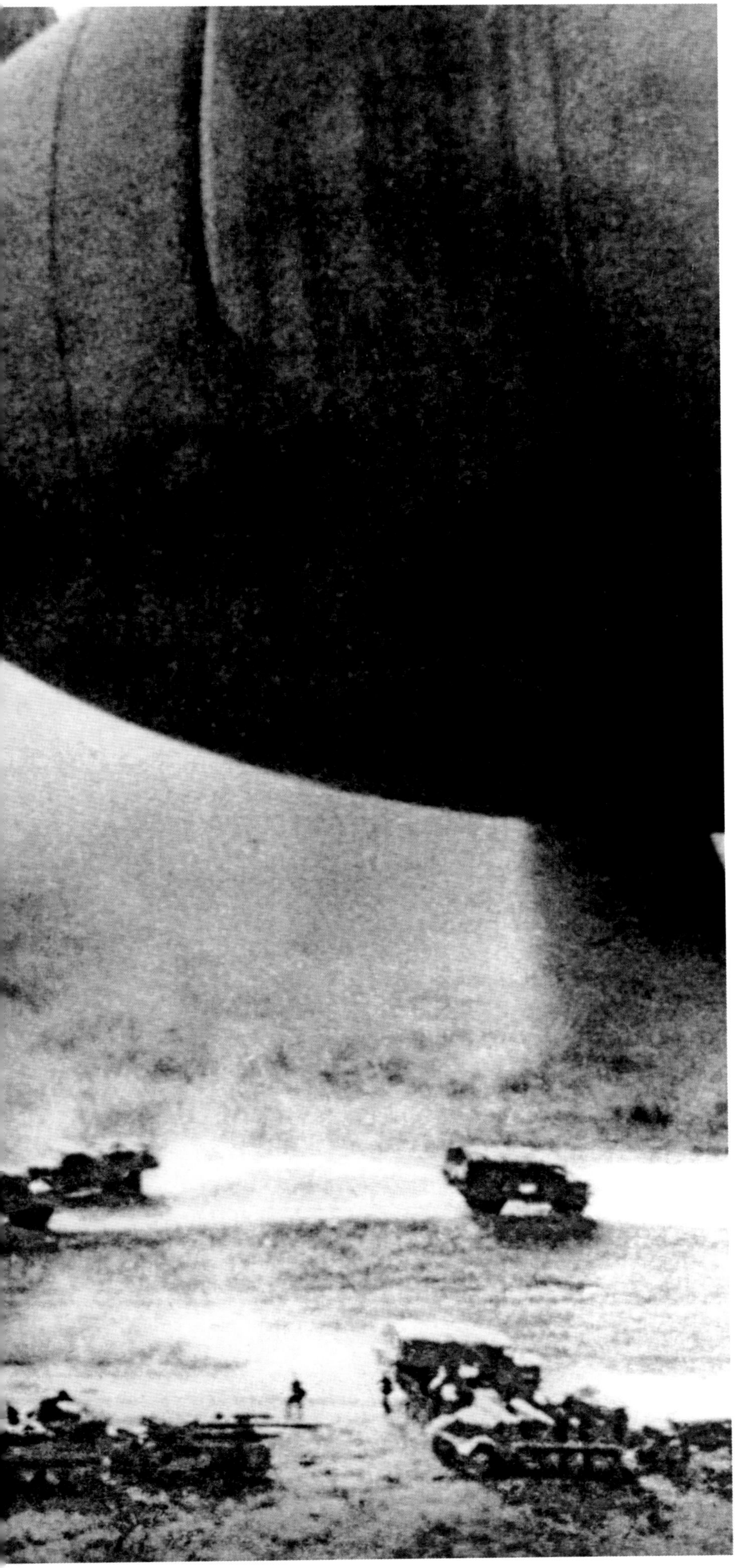

BLITZKRIEG

The incredible speed at which Germany overran Poland, France, and other countries in the opening stages of the war exposed the inadequacy of the Allies' preparations. These campaigns became known as Blitzkrieg ("lightning war"), as they were sudden, intense, and devastating.

During World War I, the German high command developed a tactic of using *Sturmtruppen* ("stormtroopers") to punch through gaps in the enemy's line, followed by heavier infantry. By World War II, advances in technology—including superior tanks, aircraft capable of ground support roles, and enhanced radio communications—meant the German Wehrmacht could develop this tactic further, unleashing combined arms offensives to penetrate enemy lines, then fan out to their rear and envelop them in a *Kessel* ("cauldron").

The effects of Blitzkrieg were striking. Poland was overwhelmed in September 1939, as was France in May 1940. The panzer corps sliced through the French army, reaching the Channel coast and cutting off much of the Allied army. Variants of Blitzkrieg, including employing airborne troops to disorient the enemy by seizing objectives in the rear, also helped Germany win rapid victories in Belgium, the Netherlands, and Norway from April to June 1940.

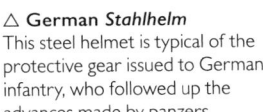

Lessons learned

Blitzkrieg tactics became less effective as Germany's opponents learned counter-measures, such as attacking the flanks of an advance, and sacrificing territory to avoid becoming trapped. This was one of several reasons why Germany's attack on the USSR in 1941 (see pp.90–91) failed disastrously.

△ **German *Stahlhelm***
This steel helmet is typical of the protective gear issued to German infantry, who followed up the advances made by panzers.

△ **Operation Barbarossa**
When they invaded the USSR in June 1941, Germany made rapid advances against the Red Army, trapping huge pockets of troops. However, over-extended supply lines and bad weather meant the advance stalled around Moscow in December.

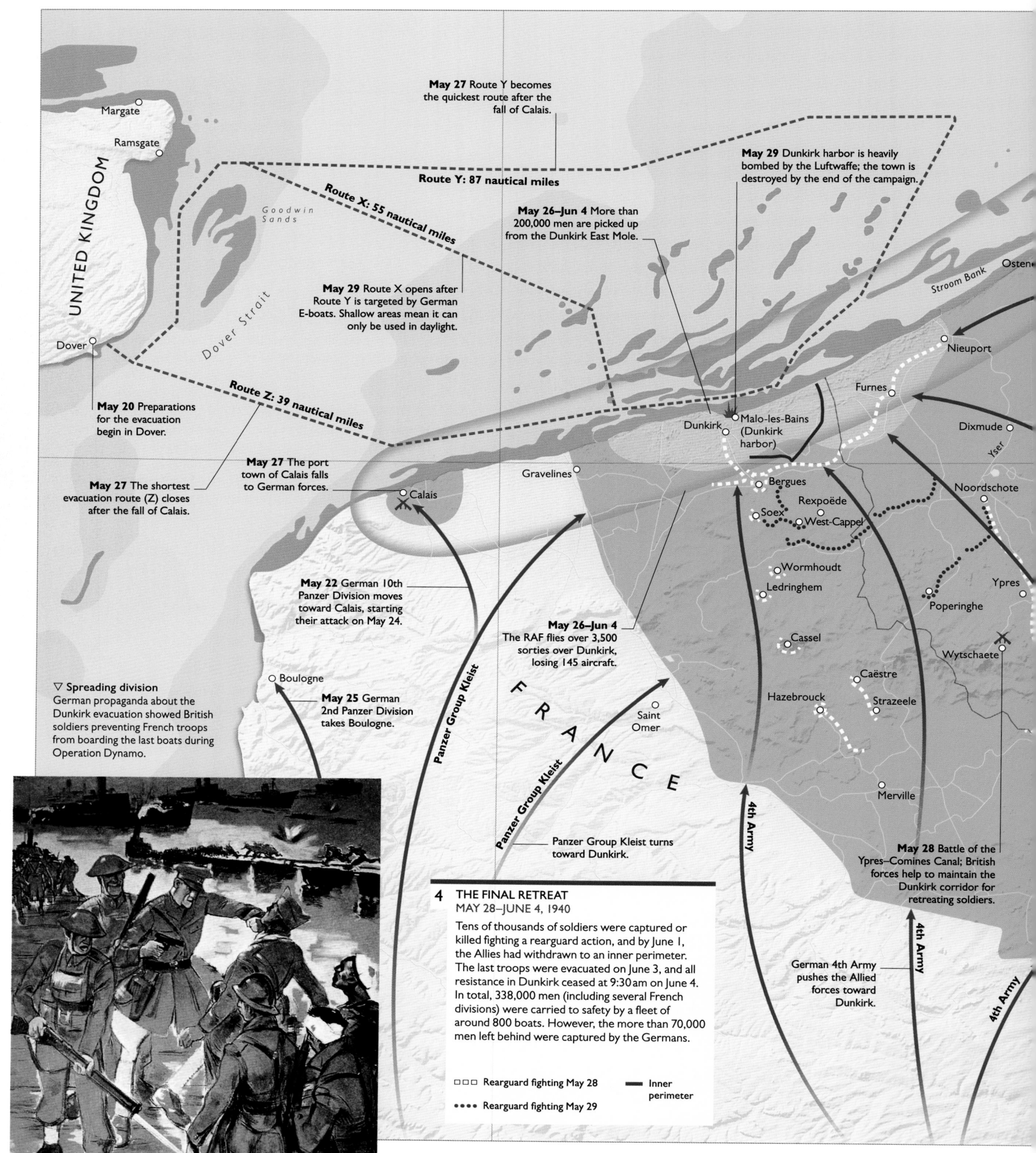

May 27 Route Y becomes the quickest route after the fall of Calais.

May 29 Dunkirk harbor is heavily bombed by the Luftwaffe; the town is destroyed by the end of the campaign.

Route Y: 87 nautical miles

Goodwin Sands

Route X: 55 nautical miles

May 26–Jun 4 More than 200,000 men are picked up from the Dunkirk East Mole.

May 29 Route X opens after Route Y is targeted by German E-boats. Shallow areas mean it can only be used in daylight.

Dover Strait

Stroom Bank

Osten

Nieuport

Route Z: 39 nautical miles

Furnes

May 20 Preparations for the evacuation begin in Dover.

Dixmude

Yser

Dunkirk

Malo-les-Bains (Dunkirk harbor)

May 27 The port town of Calais falls to German forces.

Gravelines

Noordschote

May 27 The shortest evacuation route (Z) closes after the fall of Calais.

Bergues

Calais

Soex

Rexpoëde

West-Cappel

Ypres

May 22 German 10th Panzer Division moves toward Calais, starting their attack on May 24.

Wormhoudt

Ledringhem

Poperinghe

May 26–Jun 4 The RAF flies over 3,500 sorties over Dunkirk, losing 145 aircraft.

Cassel

Wytschaete

Caëstre

▽ **Spreading division**
German propaganda about the Dunkirk evacuation showed British soldiers preventing French troops from boarding the last boats during Operation Dynamo.

Boulogne

May 25 German 2nd Panzer Division takes Boulogne.

F R A N C E

Panzer Group Kleist

Strazeele

Hazebrouck

Saint Omer

Merville

Panzer Group Kleist turns toward Dunkirk.

4th Army

May 28 Battle of the Ypres–Comines Canal; British forces help to maintain the Dunkirk corridor for retreating soldiers.

4 THE FINAL RETREAT
MAY 28–JUNE 4, 1940

Tens of thousands of soldiers were captured or killed fighting a rearguard action, and by June 1, the Allies had withdrawn to an inner perimeter. The last troops were evacuated on June 3, and all resistance in Dunkirk ceased at 9:30 am on June 4. In total, 338,000 men (including several French divisions) were carried to safety by a fleet of around 800 boats. However, the more than 70,000 men left behind were captured by the Germans.

German 4th Army pushes the Allied forces toward Dunkirk.

4th Army

▫▫▫ Rearguard fighting May 28   ▬ Inner perimeter

•••• Rearguard fighting May 29

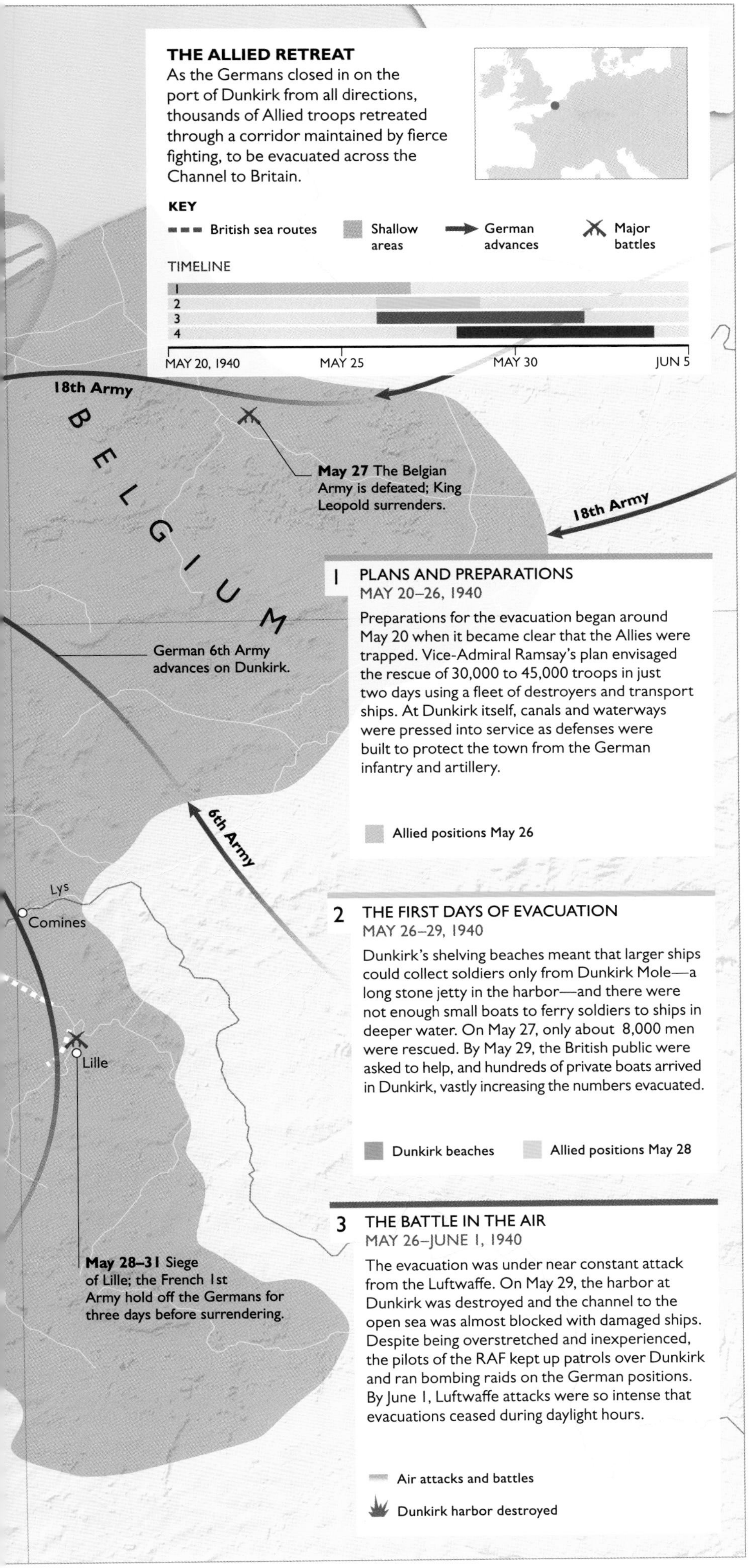

THE ALLIED RETREAT

As the Germans closed in on the port of Dunkirk from all directions, thousands of Allied troops retreated through a corridor maintained by fierce fighting, to be evacuated across the Channel to Britain.

KEY

- ▪▪▪ British sea routes
- ▪ Shallow areas
- → German advances
- ✕ Major battles

TIMELINE

	MAY 20, 1940	MAY 25	MAY 30	JUN 5
1				
2				
3				
4				

18th Army

BELGIUM

May 27 The Belgian Army is defeated; King Leopold surrenders.

18th Army

German 6th Army advances on Dunkirk.

6th Army

Lys

Comines

Lille

May 28–31 Siege of Lille; the French 1st Army hold off the Germans for three days before surrendering.

1 PLANS AND PREPARATIONS
MAY 20–26, 1940

Preparations for the evacuation began around May 20 when it became clear that the Allies were trapped. Vice-Admiral Ramsay's plan envisaged the rescue of 30,000 to 45,000 troops in just two days using a fleet of destroyers and transport ships. At Dunkirk itself, canals and waterways were pressed into service as defenses were built to protect the town from the German infantry and artillery.

▪ Allied positions May 26

2 THE FIRST DAYS OF EVACUATION
MAY 26–29, 1940

Dunkirk's shelving beaches meant that larger ships could collect soldiers only from Dunkirk Mole—a long stone jetty in the harbor—and there were not enough small boats to ferry soldiers to ships in deeper water. On May 27, only about 8,000 men were rescued. By May 29, the British public were asked to help, and hundreds of private boats arrived in Dunkirk, vastly increasing the numbers evacuated.

▪ Dunkirk beaches   ▪ Allied positions May 28

3 THE BATTLE IN THE AIR
MAY 26–JUNE 1, 1940

The evacuation was under near constant attack from the Luftwaffe. On May 29, the harbor at Dunkirk was destroyed and the channel to the open sea was almost blocked with damaged ships. Despite being overstretched and inexperienced, the pilots of the RAF kept up patrols over Dunkirk and ran bombing raids on the German positions. By June 1, Luftwaffe attacks were so intense that evacuations ceased during daylight hours.

▬ Air attacks and battles

✹ Dunkirk harbor destroyed

EVACUATING DUNKIRK

In just ten days from May 26 to June 4, 1940, 338,000 British and Allied troops were carried aboard a flotilla of boats and ships from Dunkirk to safety in Britain. Known as Operation Dynamo, it was the biggest military evacuation in history.

Barely one week after Hitler had ordered the invasion of France and the Low Countries, the German army had pushed the Allied forces into a corner of north-east France near the port of Dunkirk. Under attack from the Luftwaffe, the retreating soldiers of the British Expeditionary Force (BEF), together with their French, Canadian, and Belgian allies, faced roads blocked with vehicles and a flood of refugees. However, in one of the most pivotal decisions of the war, Hitler called a halt to the advance of his panzer divisions, giving the Allies sufficient breathing space to evacuate more than 330,000 men from the beaches of Dunkirk.

The evacuation was ordered by Winston Churchill and planned by logistics expert Vice-Admiral Bertram Ramsay from a room in the naval headquarters at Dover that once housed a dynamo (which gave the operation its name). It began on May 26. Even though the Germans did not launch a full-scale attack on the retreating Allies, the evacuation was accompanied by fierce fighting. Once on the beaches, soldiers often stood shoulder-deep in water, waiting for rescue, while the Germans bombed the sands from above.

Although the BEF left behind nearly all their equipment, the "miracle" of Dunkirk saved what Churchill called "the whole root and core and brain of the British Army" from a disastrous campaign. Without it, the Allied war effort would probably have collapsed.

THOSE LEFT BEHIND

Substantial Allied forces remained in France after the evacuation from Dunkirk; 35,000 French and as many British soldiers were forced to surrender. The majority were taken as POWs and forced to march for days before being transported to camps in Germany, where they remained for rest of the war. Several thousand French, British, and Canadian troops eluded capture, and by June 5 were ranged along the Somme, hoping to halt the German advance. Many were rescued in later evacuations.

Allied captives at Dunkirk

THE FALL OF FRANCE

After the evacuations at Dunkirk, the vastly outnumbered Allies fought fiercely but unsuccessfully to hold back Germany's advance into France. By June 22, 1940, France had signed an armistice and the country was split between the German-occupied north and Marshal Pétain's Vichy France.

On June 5, 1940, following the withdrawal of the British Expeditionary Forces, the Germans began the second stage of their invasion of France. Lacking significant British support (only one division, the 51st Highland, stayed in France), Maxime Weygand, chief of the Allied armies in France, was outgunned. With a depleted French army, he faced a near-impossible task—to defend a 560-mile (900-km) front from a German force of 10 panzer divisions and 130 infantry divisions.

Although their army fought fiercely, the French government was unwilling to commit to a long battle, abandoning Paris on June 10 and seeking an armistice on June 17. With the Allied forces in the west evacuating, the armies in the east surrounded, and forces in the center fragmenting as the Germans swept on, France capitulated on June 22.

In the Franco–German Armistice, France was divided, with the north and west under German occupation, and the south (nominally) under French sovereignty. Charles de Gaulle, then the French under-secretary of national defense and war, refused to accept the surrender and led the Free French from London. By the end of June 1940, France had lost half her huge army as prisoners of war or casualties. The Western Front remained closed for four years until the D-Day landings of June 1944.

> "Difficulty attracts the characterful man, for it is by grasping it that he fulfills himself."
>
> CHARLES DE GAULLE, *MEMOIRES DE GUERRE VOL 1, 1954*

DE GAULLE AND THE LONDON BROADCASTS

From a BBC studio in London, Charles de Gaulle broadcast a series of powerful speeches to the people of France in June 1940. He urged them to stand firm against the Germans: "Whatever happens, the flame of French resistance must not and shall not die." His words fanned the flames of resistance, but many of the French soldiers who had been evacuated from Dunkirk remained loyal to Vichy France and were unconvinced by De Gaulle's promises.

△ **Hitler in Paris**
One day after the armistice with France, Adolf Hitler visited Paris for the first and last time to celebrate the victory of his armies.

Jun 16–19 Over 30,000 Allied personnel evacuated from Brest.

Brest

Jun 16–19 The French fleet sails to North Africa.

St. Nazair

Jun 16–19 52,000 Allied troops evacuated.

1 THE OFFENSIVE BEGINS   JUNE 5–9, 1940

The German offensive, code named *Fall Rot*, began with an attack on the Allies between the city of Laon and the sea. After fierce fighting, German forces including panzer divisions broke through the Allied line and advanced on Rouen, crossing the Seine on June 9. Other forces moved south toward Paris or advanced on the River Aisne.

- - - German front line Jun 5
→ German advance

Bay of Biscay

2 THE CAPTURE OF PARIS AND MOVE SOUTH
JUNE 9–22, 1940

On June 9, the Germans moved on Paris. The government fled the city for Tours, where Churchill met the French leaders on June 11, encouraging them to continue the fight. However, the Germans marched unopposed into the largely empty capital on June 14. Their forces then poured south across central France while the French considered their options.

▭▭▭ German front line Jun 12
⇨ German advances

Jun 20–23 Polish troops evacuate from St.-Jean-de-Luz.

3 THE MAGINOT LINE COLLAPSES
JUNE 14–JULY 4, 1940

On June 14, at Saarbrucken, the German 1st Army broke through the Maginot Line—the defenses that the French had built in the 1930s to deter just such an attack—and then set about the forts to the east and west. The 7th Army breached the Line near Colmar soon after. Meanwhile, German panzers at the west end of the line headed southeast and reached the Swiss border, isolating the Maginot Line from the rest of France, and surrounding France's 5th and 8th Armies.

▮ Last French stronghold
▭▭▭ German front line Jun 22
⇨ German advances

SPAIN

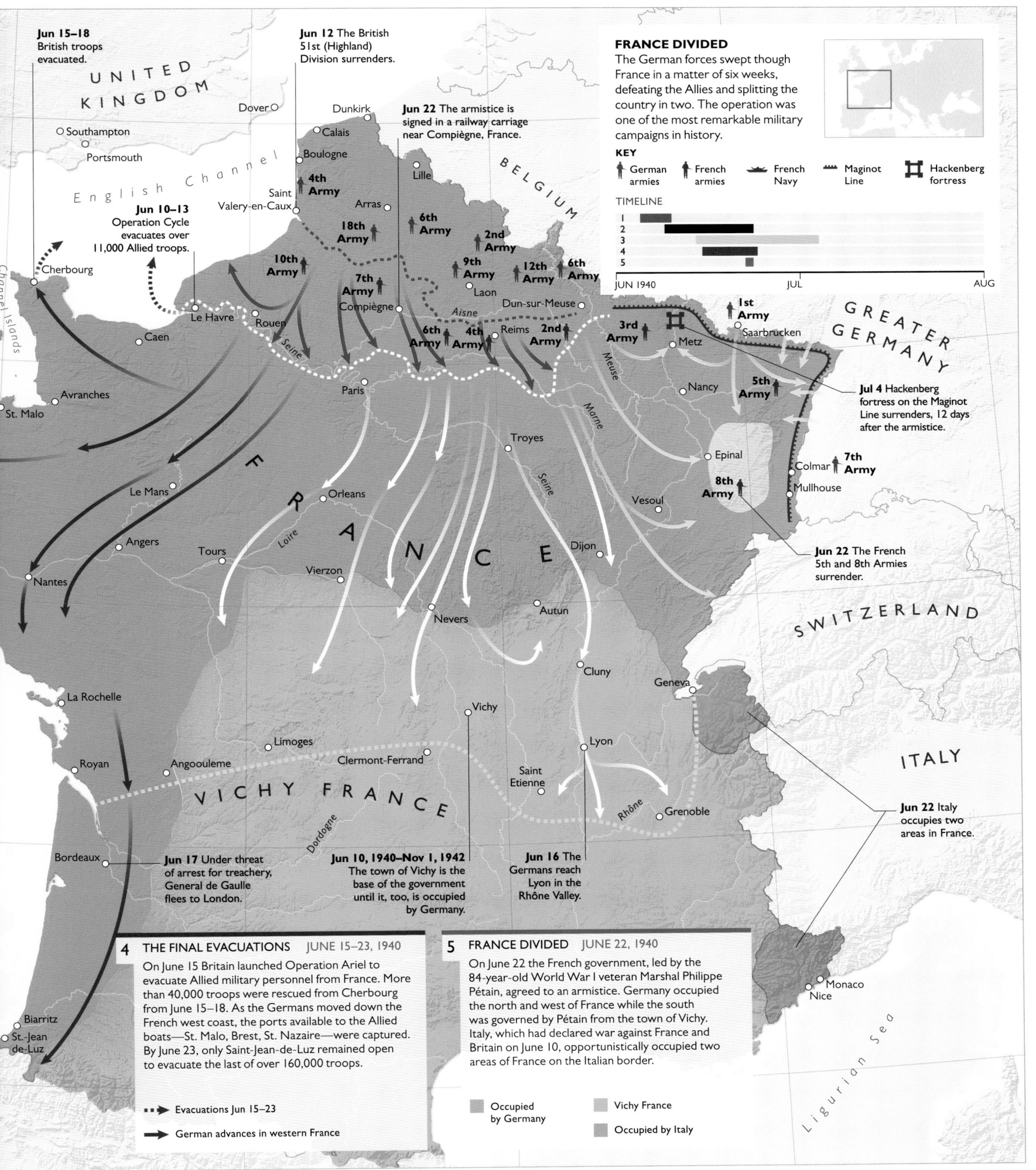

Jun 15–18 British troops evacuated.

UNITED KINGDOM

Dover

Southampton

Portsmouth

English Channel

Jun 10–13 Operation Cycle evacuates over 11,000 Allied troops.

Channel Islands

Cherbourg

Caen

Avranches

St. Malo

Le Havre

Rouen

Seine

Le Mans

Angers

Nantes

Tours

Orleans

Loire

Vierzon

F R A N C E

Jun 12 The British 51st (Highland) Division surrenders.

Calais

Dunkirk

Boulogne

Lille

Saint Valery-en-Caux

4th Army

Arras

18th Army

6th Army

10th Army

7th Army

Compiègne

Aisne

6th Army

4th Army

Laon

Paris

Jun 22 The armistice is signed in a railway carriage near Compiègne, France.

BELGIUM

2nd Army

Dun-sur-Meuse

Reims

2nd Army

Marne

Meuse

3rd Army

Metz

Nancy

1st Army

Saarbrucken

GREATER GERMANY

5th Army

Jul 4 Hackenberg fortress on the Maginot Line surrenders, 12 days after the armistice.

Epinal

8th Army

Colmar

7th Army

Mullhouse

Jun 22 The French 5th and 8th Armies surrender.

Troyes

Seine

Dijon

Vesoul

Nevers

Autun

Cluny

SWITZERLAND

Geneva

ITALY

La Rochelle

Limoges

Clermont-Ferrand

Vichy

Lyon

Royan

Angoouleme

VICHY FRANCE

Dordogne

Saint Etienne

Rhône

Grenoble

Jun 22 Italy occupies two areas in France.

Bordeaux

Jun 17 Under threat of arrest for treachery, General de Gaulle flees to London.

Jun 10, 1940–Nov 1, 1942 The town of Vichy is the base of the government until it, too, is occupied by Germany.

Jun 16 The Germans reach Lyon in the Rhône Valley.

Biarritz

St.-Jean de-Luz

Monaco

Nice

Ligurian Sea

FRANCE DIVIDED

The German forces swept though France in a matter of six weeks, defeating the Allies and splitting the country in two. The operation was one of the most remarkable military campaigns in history.

KEY

German armies | French armies | French Navy | Maginot Line | Hackenberg fortress

TIMELINE

1
2
3
4
5

JUN 1940   JUL   AUG

---

4   THE FINAL EVACUATIONS   JUNE 15–23, 1940

On June 15 Britain launched Operation Ariel to evacuate Allied military personnel from France. More than 40,000 troops were rescued from Cherbourg from June 15–18. As the Germans moved down the French west coast, the ports available to the Allied boats—St. Malo, Brest, St. Nazaire—were captured. By June 23, only Saint-Jean-de-Luz remained open to evacuate the last of over 160,000 troops.

┈┈▶ Evacuations Jun 15–23

───▶ German advances in western France

5   FRANCE DIVIDED   JUNE 22, 1940

On June 22 the French government, led by the 84-year-old World War I veteran Marshal Philippe Pétain, agreed to an armistice. Germany occupied the north and west of France while the south was governed by Pétain from the town of Vichy. Italy, which had declared war against France and Britain on June 10, opportunistically occupied two areas of France on the Italian border.

▣ Occupied by Germany

▣ Vichy France

▣ Occupied by Italy

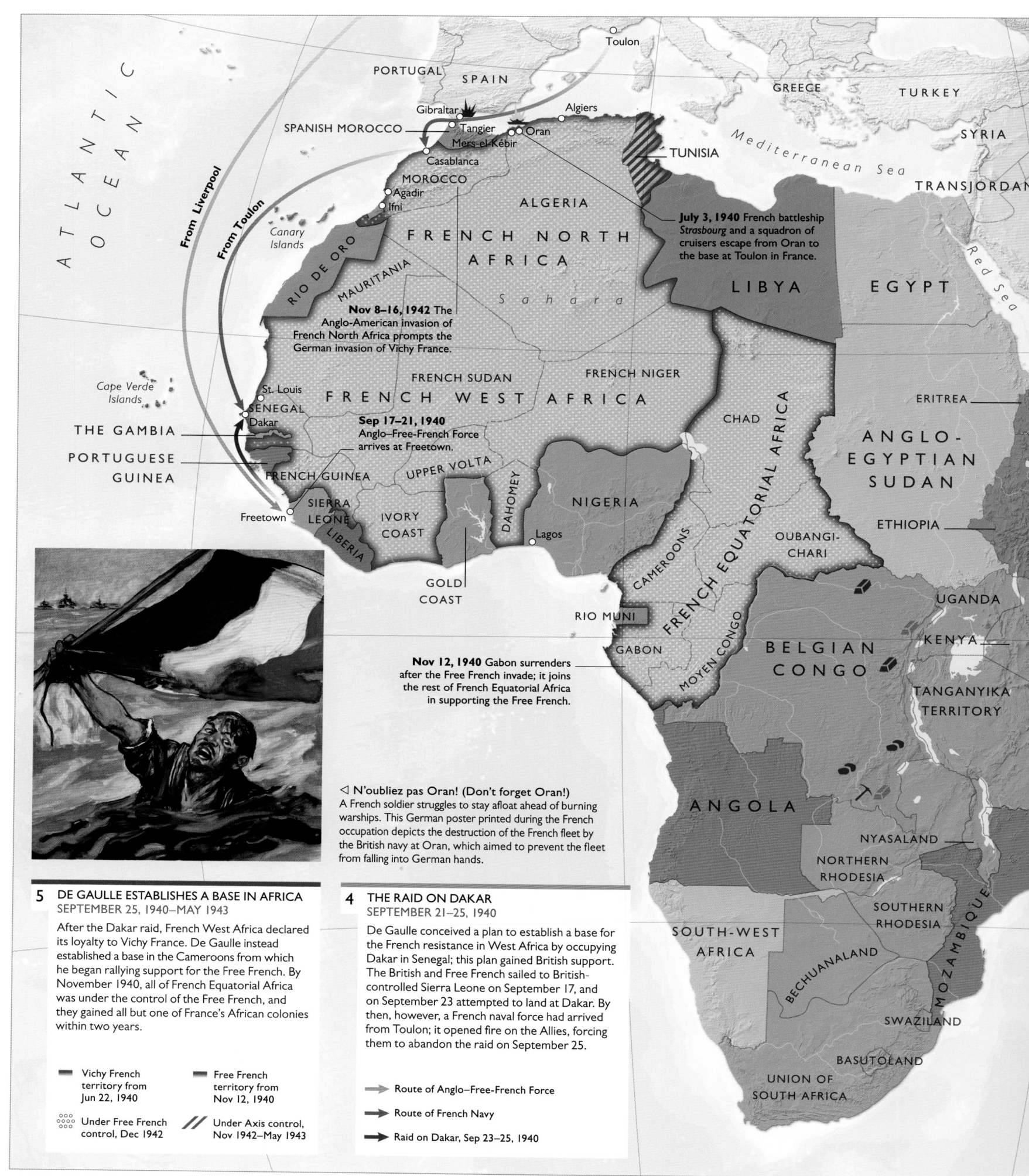

July 3, 1940 French battleship *Strasbourg* and a squadron of cruisers escape from Oran to the base at Toulon in France.

Nov 8–16, 1942 The Anglo-American invasion of French North Africa prompts the German invasion of Vichy France.

Sep 17–21, 1940 Anglo–Free-French Force arrives at Freetown.

Nov 12, 1940 Gabon surrenders after the Free French invade; it joins the rest of French Equatorial Africa in supporting the Free French.

◁ **N'oubliez pas Oran! (Don't forget Oran!)**
A French soldier struggles to stay afloat ahead of burning warships. This German poster printed during the French occupation depicts the destruction of the French fleet by the British navy at Oran, which aimed to prevent the fleet from falling into German hands.

5 DE GAULLE ESTABLISHES A BASE IN AFRICA
SEPTEMBER 25, 1940–MAY 1943

After the Dakar raid, French West Africa declared its loyalty to Vichy France. De Gaulle instead established a base in the Cameroons from which he began rallying support for the Free French. By November 1940, all of French Equatorial Africa was under the control of the Free French, and they gained all but one of France's African colonies within two years.

◼ Vichy French territory from Jun 22, 1940

◼ Free French territory from Nov 12, 1940

∘ Under Free French control, Dec 1942

⫽ Under Axis control, Nov 1942–May 1943

4 THE RAID ON DAKAR
SEPTEMBER 21–25, 1940

De Gaulle conceived a plan to establish a base for the French resistance in West Africa by occupying Dakar in Senegal; this plan gained British support. The British and Free French sailed to British-controlled Sierra Leone on September 17, and on September 23 attempted to land at Dakar. By then, however, a French naval force had arrived from Toulon; it opened fire on the Allies, forcing them to abandon the raid on September 25.

→ Route of Anglo–Free-French Force

→ Route of French Navy

→ Raid on Dakar, Sep 23–25, 1940

EUROPE'S AFRICAN COLONIES

Following the fall of France and Belgium, the race was on to secure their African colonies to the Allied cause and prevent war opening up on multiple fronts across the continent.

KEY

- British possessions
- Under British influence
- French possessions
- Spanish possessions
- Belgian possessions
- Portuguese possessions
- Italian possessions until 1941
- Independent

TIMELINE

1
2
3
4
5

1940 1941 1942 1943 1944 1945 1946

1 BELGIAN CONGO
MAY 1940–FEBRUARY 4, 1945

The Belgian Congo remained on the Allied side during the war. Administered by the Belgian government-in-exile in London, it provided the Allies with much-needed raw material, including gold, coal, copper, and uranium for America's atomic bomb program. Congolese troops also fought alongside the British in several African campaigns.

- Coal mines
- Shinkolobwe uranium mines
- Gold mines
- Copper mines

FRENCH SOMALILAND
Djibouti
BRITISH SOMALILAND
ITALIAN SOMALILAND

Dec 26, 1942 French Somaliland surrenders to the British after the Allied invasions of Madagascar and North Africa.

2 THE FRENCH FLEET   JULY 3, 1940

Concerned that the French fleet might fall under German control, the British sent a naval formation (Force H, based in Gibraltar) to intercept it. They made contact at Oran on July 3 and demanded that the French fleet surrender. The French admiral refused, and at 5:54pm Force H opened fire. In less than 15 minutes, the French battleship *Bretagne* had been sunk, several others had been damaged, and nearly 1,300 French servicemen had died.

- British Royal Navy Force H attack on the French Fleet

Sep 23, 1942 British forces capture Madagascar's capital after landing troops at Majunga and Tamatave.

MADAGASCAR
Tananarive (Antananarivo)

3 VICHY FRANCE BOMBS GIBRALTAR
JULY 18–SEPTEMBER 25, 1940

After the British attack on their fleet off the coast of Algeria, Vichy France broke off diplomatic relations with Britain. The Vichy regime authorized retaliatory bombing raids on the British territory of Gibraltar. On September 24 and 25, the Vichy French Air Force did serious damage to the British naval base and harbor, and sank a British armed trawler.

- French bombing raids on Gibraltar

INDIAN OCEAN

POWER STRUGGLES IN AFRICA

The French and Belgian colonial possessions in Africa represented both a threat and an opportunity to the Allies in 1940. If they could be kept out of Axis control, these territories promised vast resources of material and people for the Allied struggle.

After the fall of Belgium and France in June 1940 (see pp.54–55), Belgium's African possessions joined the Allied war effort. However, the position of France's colonies in Africa was more complex. Just as France itself was divided—into occupied France and Vichy France—so were the loyalties of her colonial possessions. The French colonists in Algeria stuck firmly by the Vichy regime, but others—such as Feliz Éboué, the governor of Chad—were disgusted by the Vichy capitulation and supported Charles de Gaulle's Free French. For de Gaulle, the colonies offered a huge reserve of troops with which he could build an army to regain France; however, they would also pose a threat to the Allies if they fell into Axis hands. These concerns prompted Allied attacks on the French Fleet in Algeria, and later on Madagascar (as well as Syria in the Middle East), and generated Allied support for de Gaulle's attempt to land at Dakar in French West Africa. Yet suspicion abounded: the French were wary of British ambition in Africa and the Middle East, and the Allies—along with many of the French who supported them—were unsure of de Gaulle's capabilities. Still, by November 1942, all but one of France's colonies in Africa and the Middle East had been successfully tied to the Allied cause.

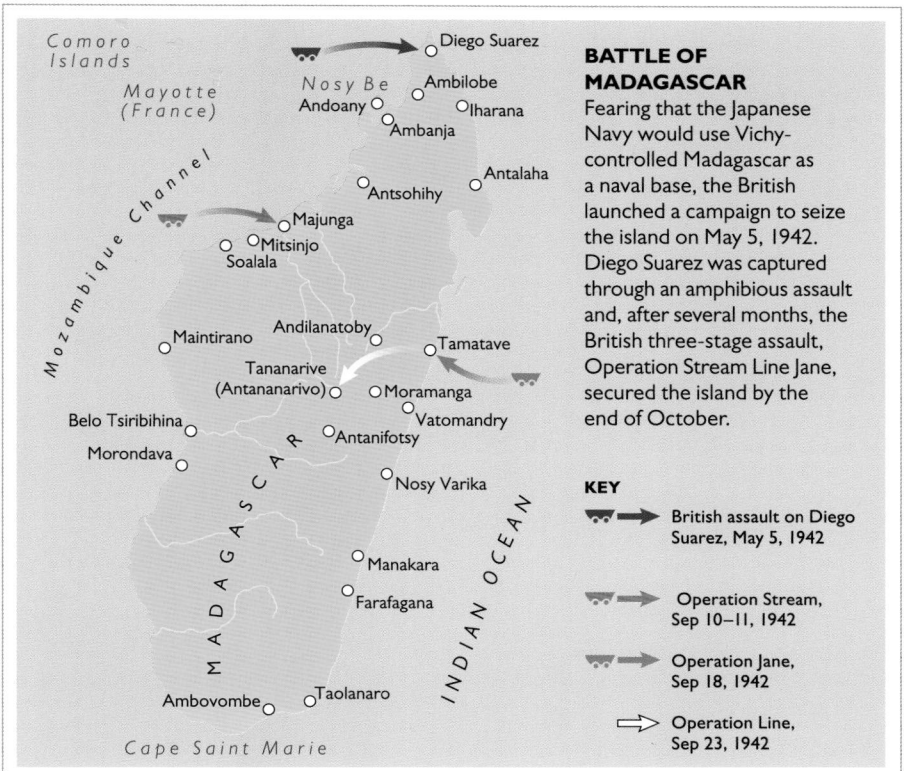

Comoro Islands
Mayotte (France)
Nosy Be
Andoany
Ambilobe
Diego Suarez
Iharana
Ambanja
Antalaha
Antsohihy
Majunga
Mitsinjo
Soalala
Maintirano
Andilanatoby
Tamatave
Tananarive (Antananarivo)
Moramanga
Vatomandry
Belo Tsiribihina
Antifotsy
Morondava
Nosy Varika
Manakara
Farafagana
Ambovombe
Taolanaro
Cape Saint Marie
Mozambique Channel
MADAGASCAR
INDIAN OCEAN

BATTLE OF MADAGASCAR

Fearing that the Japanese Navy would use Vichy-controlled Madagascar as a naval base, the British launched a campaign to seize the island on May 5, 1942. Diego Suarez was captured through an amphibious assault and, after several months, the British three-stage assault, Operation Stream Line Jane, secured the island by the end of October.

KEY

- British assault on Diego Suarez, May 5, 1942
- Operation Stream, Sep 10–11, 1942
- Operation Jane, Sep 18, 1942
- Operation Line, Sep 23, 1942

2 THE *KANALKAMPF* (CHANNEL BATTLE)
JULY–AUGUST 1940

The Luftwaffe's "nuisance raiders" tested Britain's aerial and sea defenses beginning in early July with large-scale daylight assaults on ports and shipping. British Spitfires and Hurricanes scrambled to confront the raiders in a series of dogfights over the sea-lanes. The Luftwaffe had some success in hampering British shipping but failed to establish air superiority over the Channel.

▬ Main areas of conflict, Aug 8–11, 1940

⚓ British naval ports

3 EAGLE ATTACKS AND THE "HARDEST DAY"
AUGUST 13–18, 1940

German High Command switched to focusing on RAF Fighter Command and its infrastructure. On August 13, dubbed *Adlertag* ("Eagle Day"), German raids destroyed 24 planes in the air and damaged 47 on the ground. This was the first of a series of daily attacks, code named *Adlerangriff* ("Eagle Attack"). The heaviest attacks came on August 18, known in Britain as the "hardest day."

■ "Hardest day" raids, Aug 18, 1940

✠ Luftwaffe headquarters

✈ Other Luftwaffe airfield

1 OPERATION SEA LION   JULY 1940

Hitler's plan, approved on July 16, envisaged a three-pronged assault across the Channel. The main thrust was to be delivered from the Pas-de-Calais region against the stretch of coastline west of Dover. A second prong, launched from Le Havre, would target Newhaven, Portsmouth, and the Isle of Wight, while a smaller force dispatched from Cherbourg was to land at Portland and embark on a cross-country march to Bristol.

🛩 German army group   ⛴ German corps

•••▶ Proposed invasion route   👤 German army

Aug 15 German aircraft based in Denmark and Norway attack sites in the north of England in one of the "Eagle attacks"; they meet heavy resistance and 75 planes are lost.

Aug 19 German bombers raid Liverpool, targeting the RAF's infrastructure.

Sep 7 German bombers target London.

Aug 13 German bombers hit RAF Eastchurch in the first of more than 1,500 sorties launched on "Eagle Day."

Jul 26 The British Admiralty suspends all traffic between Dover and Calais.

Aug 24 More than 100 are killed by bombing in Portsmouth.

Aug 30 The Spitfire base at Biggin Hill is hit by bombers.

Jul 4 Stuka dive bombers attack shipping in Portland harbor, sinking a converted merchantman.

Jun 30 Germany occupies the Channel Islands by landing a platoon of airmen at Guernsey's undefended airport.

4 COORDINATED DEFENSES
AUGUST 13–SEPTEMBER 16

The RAF divided coverage of Britain's airspace into four Groups, each split into sectors in which fighter activity was directed. Most of the action was over south-eastern England (under 11 Group), due principally to the limited effective range of the Luftwaffe's Messerschmitt Bf 109 escort fighters.

■ No.10 Group   ■ No.12 Group

■ No.11 Group   ■ No.13 Group

THE WAR IN THE SKIES

For a month in the summer of 1940, Britain withstood an onslaught from the Luftwaffe, seeking to take out the nation's air defenses in preparation for a seaborne invasion. The outcome of the battle put a halt to Hitler's plans for expansion in the west.

KEY

▬ High-level radar range	👓 Royal Observer Corps	■ Germany
▬ Low-level radar range	⚓ Anti-aircraft battery	■ Axis allies/occupation
		▬ German fighter range

TIMELINE

1
2
3
4
5
6

JUN 1940   JUL   AUG   SEP   OCT

6 A SWITCH OF TACTICS   SEPTEMBER 17, 1940

Hitler set a deadline of September 17 to determine whether to put his planned sea invasion of England into effect. As that date approached, it became clear that Göring's promised aerial supremacy had not been achieved, so Operation Sea Lion was indefinitely postponed. Instead the focus of the air war was switched to Britain's port cities as part of a strategy of air-sea blockade. The Blitz had begun.

5 RAF OPERATIONS
AUGUST 13–SEPTEMBER 16, 1940

More than 2,900 RAF pilots based at airfields around the UK served in the Battle of Britain: many were from Commonwealth countries or expatriates from territories occupied by the Nazis. Over four weeks of intensive activity, the RAF lost 915 aircraft, but more than 1,700 Luftwaffe planes were destroyed.

✈ RAF Fighter Command group headquarters

✈ Other RAF airfield

Ems

Amsterdam

NETHERLANDS

GREATER GERMANY

BELGIUM

LUXEMBOURG

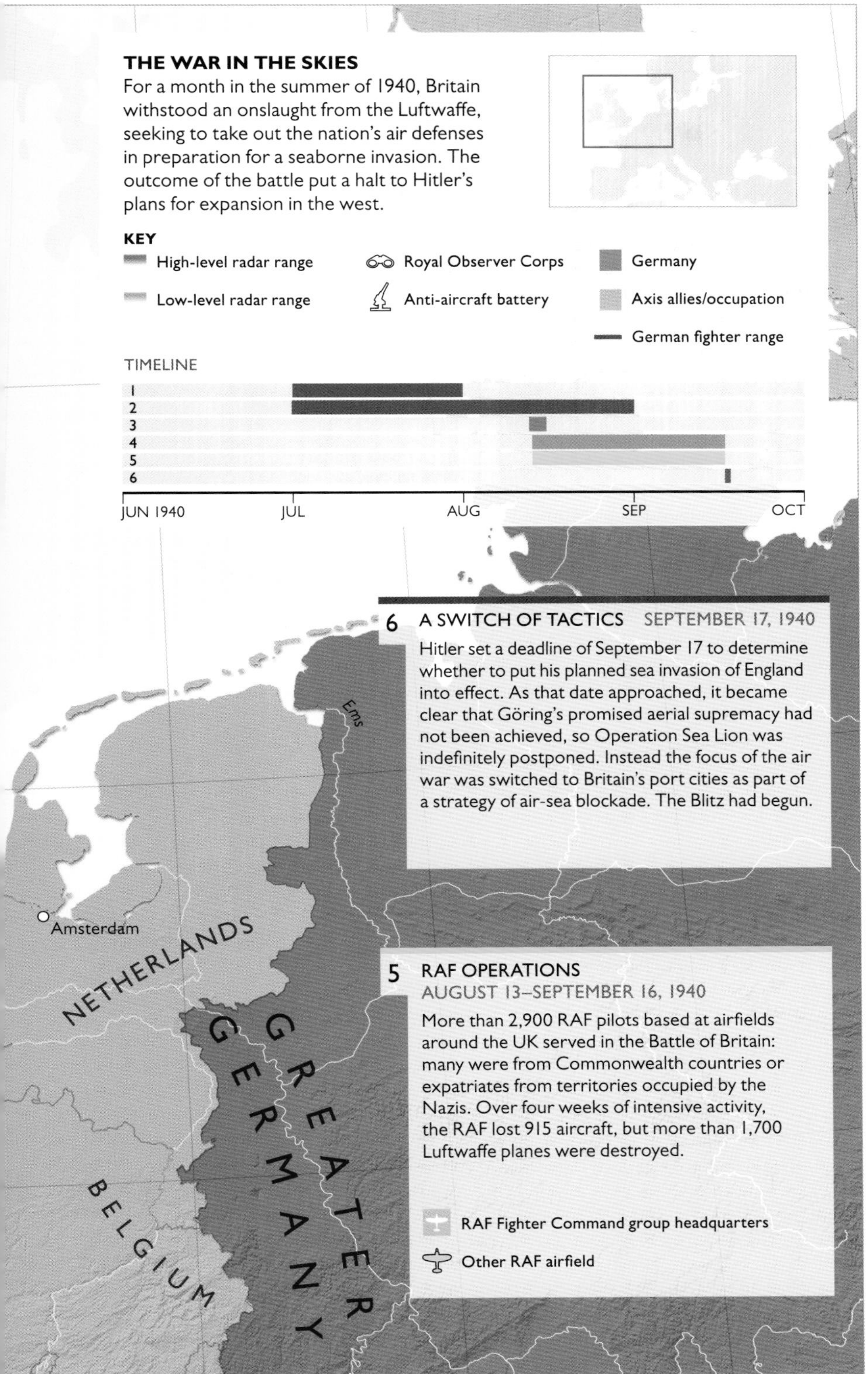

▷ The scramble
RAF Spitfire pilots rush to their aircraft in 1940. As well as British servicemen, many of the RAF's pilots were from a range of countries including South Africa, Australia, New Zealand, Poland, and Czechoslovakia.

THE BATTLE OF BRITAIN

After the fall of France, the British Empire stood alone against Nazi Germany. With his offer of peace rejected, Hitler planned an invasion of England. For this, he needed first to control the sea-lanes in the English Channel—and that meant commanding the skies above.

With Britain reeling after the fall of France (see pp.54–55), Hitler expected to impose a negotiated peace on his own terms. However, when Churchill made it clear that this was not an option, Hitler determined to force the nation to capitulate. Plans were drawn up for Operation Sea Lion—a coordinated shipborne assault on England's south coast. To make this happen, Hermann Göring, chief of the Luftwaffe, promised to eliminate Britain's Royal Air Force (RAF) within four weeks. The plan failed. In the years leading up to war, Britain had enhanced its air defenses with innovations such as radar and better coordination of aircraft from the ground. Meanwhile, signals intelligence including the top-secret Ultra decryptions (see pp.170–171) gave the RAF some advance knowledge of German plans—and, ultimately, Britain's Spitfire and Hurricane aircraft proved more than a match for German Messerschmitts in the dogfights over the Channel.

Thwarted in his attempt to subdue Britain's air defenses, Hitler turned instead to a strategy of bombing raids on British port cities, launching the nighttime Blitz on London and other industrial centers (see pp.60–61) as part of his air-sea blockade. However, Hitler's failure to defeat the RAF was perhaps his first major setback of the war, dealing a blow to his reputation for invincibility.

THE HAWKER HURRICANE

The Hurricane entered service in December 1937, and by August 1940 more than 2,300 had been delivered to the RAF. In the Battle of Britain they outnumbered Spitfires by almost two to one. Highly maneuverable, they brought down more enemy aircraft than any other British planes in the course of 1940. Over the following two years they were gradually replaced as dog-fighters by the more modern Spitfires.

Damage survey
A map of London shows the bomb damage caused to buildings in Bermondsey and Wapping. Black and purple indicate complete destruction or irreparable damage. Pink sites indicate severe damage that could be repaired, although repairs would be expensive.

THE BLITZ

In September 1940, Hitler made the fateful decision to switch the focus of Luftwaffe air attacks from RAF airfields to Britain's cities. His aim was to damage manufacturing centers and ports and to break civilian morale, forcing Churchill to sue for peace.

The Blitz (German for "lightning") was the word coined by the British press for the intense bombing campaign conducted by the Luftwaffe. The first attack over London on September 7, 1940, was followed by 57 consecutive nights of bombing raids on the capital, as well as raids on other major cities. The Blitz continued until May 1941.

Hitler still hoped to invade Britain, and bombing London was part of that plan, with the aim of softening up the British population. The fighting reached a climax on September 15, when waves of German planes launched an all-out attack on London but failed to achieve a decisive breakthrough. The devastating raid on Coventry on November 14–15 signaled that other industrial centers were also at risk. This single attack claimed the lives of 568 people and left around one-third of the city's houses uninhabitable. Over the next six months, the Luftwaffe carried out heavy raids on Belfast, Birmingham, Bristol, Cardiff, Clydebank, Hull, Manchester, Plymouth, Portsmouth, Sheffield, Southampton, and Swansea. Liverpool and Merseyside suffered the worst destruction of any area outside London, with 1,900 killed and 70,000 made homeless.

By May 1941, Hitler had turned his attention to the Soviet Union. The last major raid on London took place on May 10, when 1 sq mile (2.8 sq km) of the city center was set on fire and the Houses of Parliament took a dozen hits. Bombing continued to the end of the war, but not on the same scale.

The effects of the Blitz

During the campaign, there were 127 large-scale night raids (71 in London), during which some 50,700 tons (46,000 metric tons) of high explosives were dropped on Britain's cities, in addition to 110,000 incendiary bombs. The raids killed more than 43,000 civilians and destroyed or damaged two million homes. By February 1941, 1.37 million civilians had been evacuated from areas affected by the bombing.

Although the effects of the Blitz were devastating, Hitler's plan failed. British war production was reduced by no more than five percent during the Blitz, while popular morale, dented at times by the destruction, never collapsed.

▷ **Image of resistance**
This famous image shows St. Paul's Cathedral in London, lit up by fire and surrounded by smoke, during a night raid on December 29, 1940.

BRITAIN AT BAY

After France capitulated to Hitler in June 1940, the British Empire was the only major power fighting the Germans and Italians. While the Royal Air Force readied itself to battle the Luftwaffe for control of the skies, the British people prepared themselves for a German invasion.

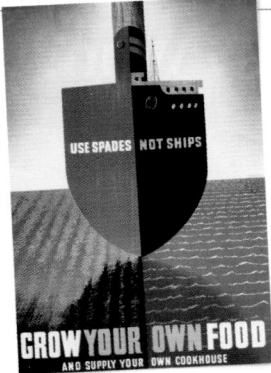

△ **Digging for victory**
This poster was part of a campaign to encourage the British to grow their own food. Garden plots sprang up in open spaces everywhere.

Even before France's surrender, the British government was making plans for the possibility of an invasion by Germany. On May 14, 1940, Anthony Eden, Prime Minister Winston Churchill's new Secretary of State for War, broadcast an appeal for part-time volunteers to fight alongside the army in the event of such an incursion. The response was immediate. Within 24 hours, some 250,000 men had enlisted in the Local Defense Volunteers; by the end of June, numbers had increased to nearly 1,500,000. In July, on the orders of Churchill, they were given the more martial-sounding title of the Home Guard.

An all-out effort

The country was preparing itself for total war. British factories and shipyards churned day and night manufacturing guns, tanks, aircraft, and warships. Gasoline had been rationed since the beginning of the war, and food rationing, which had begun in January 1940, was tightened. Butter, sugar, bacon, and ham were the first foods to be rationed, followed by preserves, syrup, golden syrup, cheese, tea, margarine, and cooking fats. Clothes were also rationed, and the government issued a pamphlet popularizing the slogan "Make Do and Mend."

The most significant shortage was that of manpower. In December 1941, the call-up age limits for men were reduced to 18 and raised to 51. Most revolutionary of all, women were conscripted. By the end of 1942, 10 million British women aged between 19 and 50 were registered for war work, many taking the place of men in the armed forces.

THE HOME GUARD AT WAR

The Home Guard were trained in small arms and anti-tank weapons to be used against an invading force; German orders were to shoot them out of hand. Some saw action in the Battle of Britain (see pp.58–59) manning anti-aircraft guns. Secret "Auxiliary Units" were trained in guerrilla warfare and sabotage.

Entertainment in wartime, 1940
During the Blitz, thousands sought refuge from the bombing in London's underground stations. Aldwych station was the first to develop into an air-raid shelter, with sleeping bunks and occasional concerts, as seen here, to boost morale.

THE U-BOAT WAR BEGINS

The German High Command used every means at its disposal to cut Britain's vital maritime supply routes. Its most effective weapon was the German submarine fleet, the U-boats, which was increasingly successful in attacking Atlantic shipping lanes from 1939 to 1941.

Germany's U-boats had played a major role in World War I, sinking almost 5,000 ships. From the start of the hostilities in 1939, Hitler looked again to the submarine fleet, commanded by Admiral Karl Dönitz (see p.168), to starve Britain into submission.

For a time the campaign came close to success, particularly after the fall of France and Norway opened up new ports from which the U-boats could operate. Germany's early successes persuaded Hitler to divert resources to submarine production. At first Britain was desperately short of warships to escort merchant shipping and of planes to provide air cover, and the Royal Canadian Navy played a vital role in protecting Atlantic shipping. However, the tide began to turn against the U-boats as the Allies improved their protective measures, developed technology to detect the raiders, and gained better intelligence about U-boat deployment. In 1939, the US established the Pan-American Security Zone, an area extending 300–1,000 nautical miles from the coast of the Americas in which the US Navy escorted merchant ships. After the US formally entered the war in 1941, the US Navy actively engaged German naval vessels in the Atlantic.

> *"The only thing that really frightened me during the war was the U-boat peril."*
>
> WINSTON CHURCHILL, *THE SECOND WORLD WAR*, 1949

THE *UNTERSEEBOOT* (U-BOAT)

Prohibited after World War I, German submarine construction recommenced in the mid 1930s. By 1939, 57 boats served under the skillful command of Admiral Karl Dönitz. Most were small, 825-ton (750-metric ton) Type VII (Sea Wolf) vessels, featuring a new diesel-electric propulsion system. The Type VIIC model had a top speed of 17 knots on the surface and 7.5 knots submerged, and carried 14 torpedoes or tube-launched mines.

U-boats at the port of Kiel

BATTLE OF THE ATLANTIC

The Atlantic Ocean became a battleground as Hitler attempted to cut Britain's supply lines. The Allies' ability to protect shipping with naval and air escorts was crucial. The map shows borders up to May 1941, before the invasion of the USSR (see pp.90–91) caused frontiers to fluctuate.

KEY

- Territory under Allied influence
- Territory under Axis control
- Territory under Vichy France
- Extent of Pan-American Security Zone
- Major convoy routes

TIMELINE

	1939	1940	1941	1942
1				
2				
3				
4				
5				

▽ **Sinking of HMS *Royal Oak*, 1939**
This painting depicts the attack on *Royal Oak*, anchored at Scapa Flow, Scotland, by German submarine U-47. The sinking, and the loss of 833 lives, was a huge blow to British morale.

Dec 11, 1941
The US plays a non-combatant role until Germany declares war on it, in support of Japan.

Oct 1939
Pan-American Security Zone established.

5 ALLIES GAIN A FORWARD BASE   JULY 1941

The British had established a garrison on (neutral) Iceland in May 1940, fearing that the island would be used by Germany. Aircraft from Iceland helped plug the gap in Allied air cover that had turned the mid-Atlantic into a favorite hunting ground for U-boat commanders. In July 1941, American forces took over defense of the island, freeing up British troops for service in North Africa.

— Extent of British air cover by Jul 1941

CANADA
LABRADOR
NEWFOUNDLAND
USA
Halifax
New York
Bermuda
Gulf of Mexico
Bahamas
CUBA
BRITISH HONDURAS
HONDURAS
Jamaica
HAITI
DOMINICAN REPUBLIC
NICARAGUA
Caribbean Sea
Puerto Rico
PAN-AMERICAN
Trinidad
VENEZUELA
BRITISH GUIANA
SURINAM
BRAZIL
FRENCH GUIANA

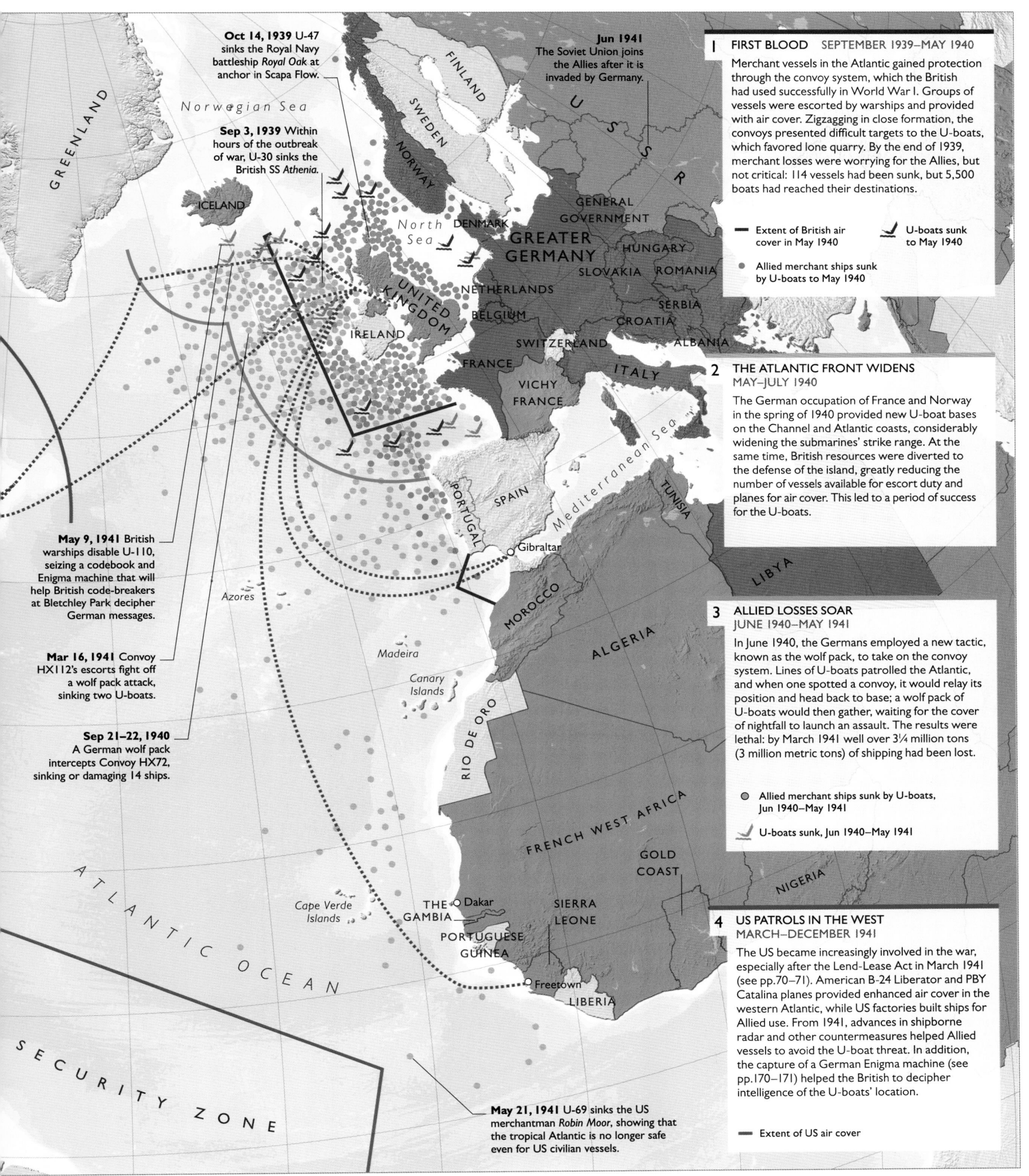

Oct 14, 1939 U-47 sinks the Royal Navy battleship *Royal Oak* at anchor in Scapa Flow.

Sep 3, 1939 Within hours of the outbreak of war, U-30 sinks the British SS *Athenia*.

Jun 1941 The Soviet Union joins the Allies after it is invaded by Germany.

May 9, 1941 British warships disable U-110, seizing a codebook and Enigma machine that will help British code-breakers at Bletchley Park decipher German messages.

Mar 16, 1941 Convoy HX112's escorts fight off a wolf pack attack, sinking two U-boats.

Sep 21–22, 1940 A German wolf pack intercepts Convoy HX72, sinking or damaging 14 ships.

May 21, 1941 U-69 sinks the US merchantman *Robin Moor*, showing that the tropical Atlantic is no longer safe even for US civilian vessels.

1 FIRST BLOOD SEPTEMBER 1939–MAY 1940

Merchant vessels in the Atlantic gained protection through the convoy system, which the British had used successfully in World War I. Groups of vessels were escorted by warships and provided with air cover. Zigzagging in close formation, the convoys presented difficult targets to the U-boats, which favored lone quarry. By the end of 1939, merchant losses were worrying for the Allies, but not critical: 114 vessels had been sunk, but 5,500 boats had reached their destinations.

— Extent of British air cover in May 1940

⚓ U-boats sunk to May 1940

● Allied merchant ships sunk by U-boats to May 1940

2 THE ATLANTIC FRONT WIDENS MAY–JULY 1940

The German occupation of France and Norway in the spring of 1940 provided new U-boat bases on the Channel and Atlantic coasts, considerably widening the submarines' strike range. At the same time, British resources were diverted to the defense of the island, greatly reducing the number of vessels available for escort duty and planes for air cover. This led to a period of success for the U-boats.

3 ALLIED LOSSES SOAR JUNE 1940–MAY 1941

In June 1940, the Germans employed a new tactic, known as the wolf pack, to take on the convoy system. Lines of U-boats patrolled the Atlantic, and when one spotted a convoy, it would relay its position and head back to base; a wolf pack of U-boats would then gather, waiting for the cover of nightfall to launch an assault. The results were lethal: by March 1941 well over 3¼ million tons (3 million metric tons) of shipping had been lost.

● Allied merchant ships sunk by U-boats, Jun 1940–May 1941

⚓ U-boats sunk, Jun 1940–May 1941

4 US PATROLS IN THE WEST MARCH–DECEMBER 1941

The US became increasingly involved in the war, especially after the Lend-Lease Act in March 1941 (see pp.70–71). American B-24 Liberator and PBY Catalina planes provided enhanced air cover in the western Atlantic, while US factories built ships for Allied use. From 1941, advances in shipborne radar and other countermeasures helped Allied vessels to avoid the U-boat threat. In addition, the capture of a German Enigma machine (see pp.170–171) helped the British to decipher intelligence of the U-boats' location.

— Extent of US air cover

3 IN SEARCH OF THE ENEMY
7:22PM MAY 23–5:50AM MAY 24, 1941

At 7:22pm on May 23, a lookout on the *Suffolk* spotted *Bismarck* and *Prinz Eugen*. Signals were sent to the *Hood* and *Prince of Wales* while *Suffolk* and *Norfolk* shadowed the German vessels at high speed through banks of fog and snow. *Hood* and *Prince of Wales* intercepted them at 5:30am. At 5:50am Commander Vice Admiral Holland, aboard *Hood*, closed range and directed *Hood* and *Prince of Wales* to open fire.

👓 German ships spotted

4 THE BATTLE OF THE DENMARK STRAIT
5:56–6:09AM MAY 24, 1941

The German ships returned fire, and a 15-in shell hit *Hood* near the main mast; she was struck by another shell before her aft magazines exploded. The ship sank with the loss of all but three of her crew. Following a brief lull, firing resumed; the *Prince of Wales* was hit, but she had also struck *Bismarck* and caused a fuel leak. At 6:03am, a damaged *Prince of Wales* disengaged and by 6:09am firing had ceased.

✗ Battle of Denmark Strait   ⚓ HMS *Hood* sunk

5 A NAVAL HUNT ON THE HIGH SEAS
MAY 24–25, 1941

Prinz Eugen slipped away to continue raiding while the *Bismarck*, in need of repair, continued south-west, shadowed by *Norfolk*, *Suffolk*, and *Prince of Wales*. Meanwhile, other British ships had joined the hunt. Near midnight, torpedo-armed Swordfish aircraft from *Victorious* attacked *Bismarck*, but caused little damage. Amid a long radio silence Lütjens gave the British the slip—until a message the next morning betrayed *Bismarck*'s bearings and reignited the chase.

➤ Torpedo   ✈ Fairey Swordfish biplanes

6 CLOSING IN FOR THE KILL   MAY 26

At about 10:30am on May 26 *Bismarck* was pinpointed by an RAF Catalina flying boat, but *King George V* and the battleship *Rodney* were about 130 miles (210km) behind the wounded giant. That evening, Gibraltar-based Force H caught up from the south, and 15 Swordfish from the British carrier *Ark Royal* struck *Bismarck* with torpedoes, crippling her rudders. As she floundered helplessly, her pack of pursuers closed in.

➤ Torpedo   ✈ Fairey Swordfish biplanes

7 THE END OF THE *BISMARCK*   MAY 27

By about 9am on May 27, the big guns from *Rodney* and *King George V* had neutralized the *Bismarck*'s eight 15-in guns. The cruisers *Norfolk* and *Dorsetshire* attacked. Despite hundreds of shell hits, the battered *Bismarck* remained afloat. The end came at about 10:39am when a torpedo from *Dorsetshire* coincided with explosive charges set in the boiler room by *Bismarck*'s crew. Only 115 men survived out of a crew of around 2,200.

➤ Torpedo   ⚓ *Bismarck* sunk

May 24 *Hood* is sunk; of 1,418 men, only three survive and are retrieved by the destroyer HMS *Electra*.

May 25 *Victorious* sets off for Iceland to refuel.

10:39 am May 27 The *Bismarck* sinks after a torpedo hit from the *Dorsetshire* and being scuttled by her crew.

May 25 *Repulse*, low on fuel, is forced to detach from the hunt for *Bismarck*.

3:06 am May 25 *Suffolk* loses contact with *Bismarck*, which turns to starboard, and behind her pursuers, to make her escape.

8 pm May 24 The British battleship *Rodney* and four destroyers, escorting the liner MV *Britannic* to Canada, are instructed by the Admiralty to join the hunt for *Bismarck*.

June 1 *Prinz Eugen* develops mechanical problems and returns to Brest. The threat in the Atlantic from the German surface fleet is over.

GREENLAND

Denmark Strait

ICELAND

Hvalfjördur

○ Reykjavík

○ Kulusuk

Ice Edge

○ Timmiarmiut

ATLANTIC OCEAN

◁ *Bismarck* in the Baltic
The battleship named after Chancellor Otto von Bismarck was commissioned into the Kriegsmarine in 1940. With a range of almost 9,000 nautical miles and armed with eight 15-in guns, she was a formidable foe.

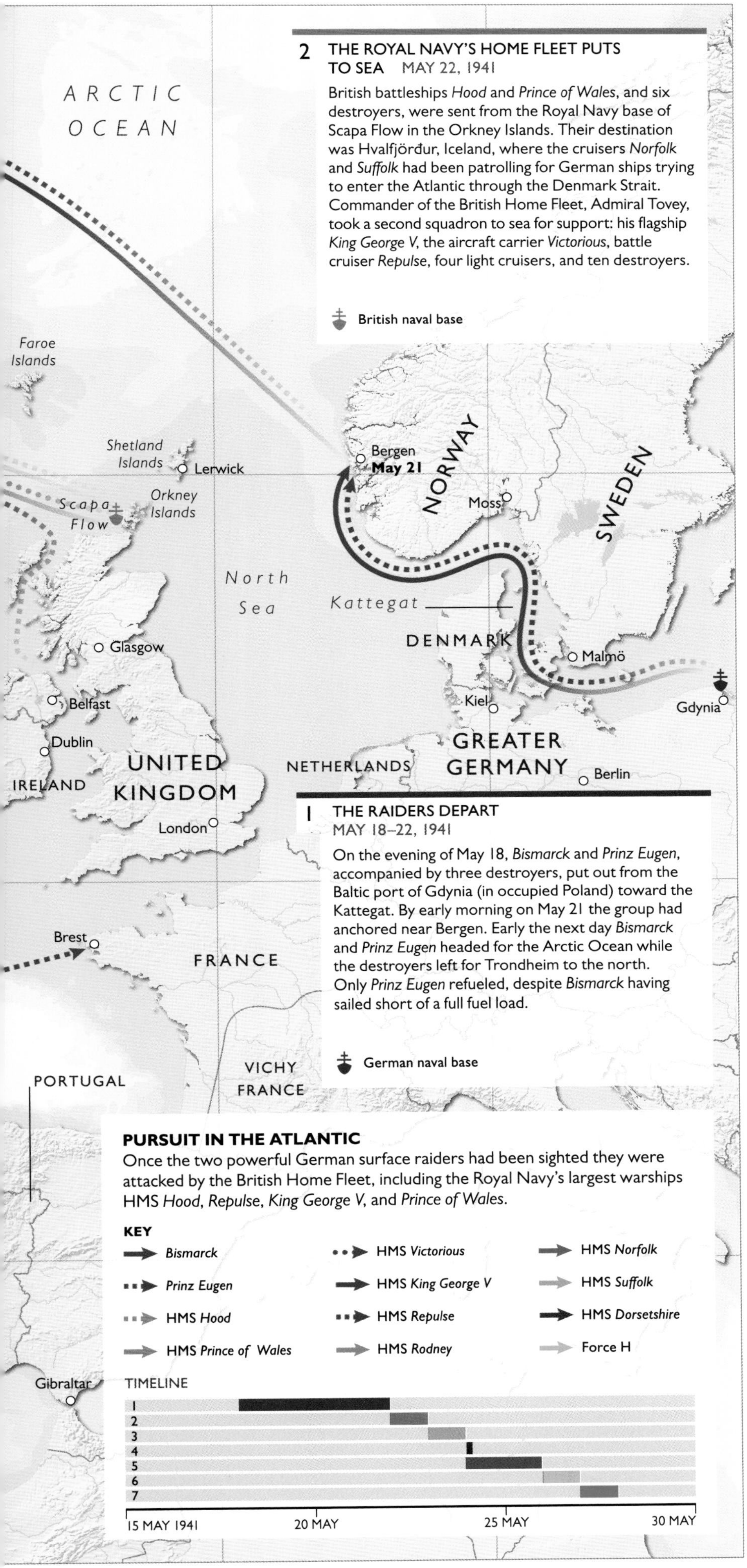

ARCTIC
OCEAN

2 THE ROYAL NAVY'S HOME FLEET PUTS TO SEA MAY 22, 1941

British battleships *Hood* and *Prince of Wales*, and six destroyers, were sent from the Royal Navy base of Scapa Flow in the Orkney Islands. Their destination was Hvalfjördur, Iceland, where the cruisers *Norfolk* and *Suffolk* had been patrolling for German ships trying to enter the Atlantic through the Denmark Strait. Commander of the British Home Fleet, Admiral Tovey, took a second squadron to sea for support: his flagship *King George V*, the aircraft carrier *Victorious*, battle cruiser *Repulse*, four light cruisers, and ten destroyers.

⚓ British naval base

Faroe
Islands

NORWAY

Bergen
May 21

Moss

SWEDEN

Shetland
Islands Lerwick

Orkney
Islands

Scapa
Flow

North
Sea

Kattegat

DENMARK

Glasgow

Malmö

Belfast

Kiel

Gdynia

Dublin

GREATER
GERMANY

IRELAND UNITED
KINGDOM NETHERLANDS

Berlin

London

1 THE RAIDERS DEPART
MAY 18–22, 1941

On the evening of May 18, *Bismarck* and *Prinz Eugen*, accompanied by three destroyers, put out from the Baltic port of Gdynia (in occupied Poland) toward the Kattegat. By early morning on May 21 the group had anchored near Bergen. Early the next day *Bismarck* and *Prinz Eugen* headed for the Arctic Ocean while the destroyers left for Trondheim to the north. Only *Prinz Eugen* refueled, despite *Bismarck* having sailed short of a full fuel load.

Brest

FRANCE

⚓ German naval base

PORTUGAL VICHY
FRANCE

PURSUIT IN THE ATLANTIC

Once the two powerful German surface raiders had been sighted they were attacked by the British Home Fleet, including the Royal Navy's largest warships HMS *Hood*, *Repulse*, *King George V*, and *Prince of Wales*.

KEY

➤ *Bismarck*	••➤ HMS *Victorious*	➤ HMS *Norfolk*
■■➤ *Prinz Eugen*	➤ HMS *King George V*	➤ HMS *Suffolk*
■■➤ HMS *Hood*	■■➤ HMS *Repulse*	➤ HMS *Dorsetshire*
➤ HMS *Prince of Wales*	➤ HMS *Rodney*	➤ Force H

Gibraltar

TIMELINE

1
2
3
4
5
6
7

15 MAY 1941   20 MAY   25 MAY   30 MAY

SINKING OF THE *BISMARCK*

On May 18, 1941, the German navy began Operation Rheinübung, part of the effort to isolate Britain by targeting merchant ships in the Atlantic. The vessels used in this operation were the heavy cruiser *Prinz Eugen* and the largest warship in the German fleet, *Bismarck*.

From January to March 1941, the German navy had deployed two battleships—*Scharnhorst* and *Gneisenau*—in the Atlantic under the command of Admiral Günther Lütjens. Maintained by supplies from support vessels and tankers, they destroyed or captured 22 Allied merchant ships. After the pair had to return to port for repairs, two new warships—*Prinz Eugen* and the formidable battleship *Bismarck*—were sent into the Atlantic under the same command with orders to continue the task.

On May 20, Allied intelligence sources in Scandinavia spotted the German ships as they made their way from the Baltic port of Gdynia. Four days later they were intercepted in the Denmark Strait, between Iceland and Greenland, by the British battle cruiser HMS *Hood* and the battleship HMS *Prince of Wales*. The ensuing battle was followed by an epic, three-day chase on the high seas, during which dozens of Allied warships converged on the *Bismarck*. Eventually, the *Bismarck* was sunk with the loss of around 2,100 men, including Günther Lütjens. In the aftermath, between June 3 and June 15 the Royal Navy sank or seized seven of the nine tankers and supply ships that had made raiding ventures into the Atlantic possible. Germany's hopes of conducting any similar operations in future had been gravely damaged.

AIRCRAFT CARRIERS IN WORLD WAR II

By the 1930s air power was eclipsing the battleship as the dominant weapon of naval warfare. At the time war broke out, aircraft carriers were a vital maritime offensive weapon, as combat aircraft could attack enemy ships at greater range than gun batteries and with a higher level of accuracy. However, once within range of the enemy, carriers were vulnerable to attacks themselves. Here a squadron of torpedo-armed Fairey Swordfish—also used in the attack on the *Bismarck*—prepares to launch from the British carrier HMS *Ark Royal* during the war.

THE END OF US NEUTRALITY

At the start of World War II, the US took a neutral position. However, President Franklin Roosevelt reversed this stance, rearming the US and increasing aid to Britain. By December 1941, the US was fully involved in the war.

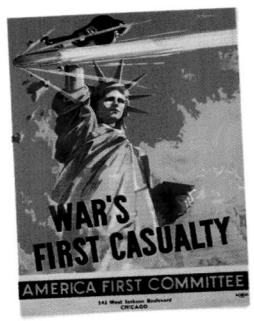

△ **Anti-war lobby**
Formed in 1940, the America First Committee lobbied against US intervention in Europe. It attracted 800,000 members.

The US's involvement in World War I had not been universally popular, and after the war ended, the US reduced its navy and army to fewer than 135,000 men. In 1937, it passed a Neutrality Act, forbidding the sale of arms to countries at war. However, as Germany and Japan became more aggressive, President Roosevelt sought to counter the powerful political voices that counseled keeping out of foreign conflicts.

The US takes up arms

After war broke out in September 1939, Roosevelt persuaded Congress to repeal the arms embargo, but recipients could only acquire arms with cash payments. He also ordered a major rearmament, buying 270 warships and increasing the army to over 1.6 million by December 1941. Roosevelt increased aid to Britain by the Lend-Lease Act (see pp.70–71), which allowed raw materials and military aid to go to the Allies on credit. After the Japanese attacked the US naval base at Pearl Harbor, Hawaii, in December 1941 (see pp.110–111), the neutralist sentiment vanished and the US joined the war.

△ **The Atlantic Charter meeting**
British prime minister Winston Churchill heads to Newfoundland, Canada, in August 1941, for a meeting with Roosevelt. The two leaders drew up a joint declaration known as the Atlantic Charter, which set out their goals for the war and its aftermath.

Marines prepare for war
New recruits undergo basic training at the
Parris Island Recruit Depot, South Carolina.
As part of Roosevelt's rearmament effort,
between 1939 and 1941 the Marines expanded
nearly four-fold.

LEND-LEASE

The Lend-Lease Act, passed by the US Congress in March 1941, provided assistance to Britain's war effort while allowing the US to maintain its neutrality. The policy ensured a flow of food, fuel, and matériel to Allied forces that the Axis powers could not match.

Following neutrality legislation in 1937, US companies could not export military goods to warring nations. However, President Roosevelt was committed to helping the fight against Fascism by all means short of war, and this sentiment underpinned policies such as the 1940 Destroyers for Bases Agreement, in which the US transferred destroyers to the British in exchange for land for US military bases. Lend-Lease was another such policy, under which the US could loan war matériel to the Allies. Roosevelt justified its implementation with a simple analogy—if a neighbor's house was on fire it was simply common sense to lend him a garden hose. Lend-Lease unlocked a wealth of supplies for the Allies, ranging

> *"We defend and we build a way of life, not for America alone, but for all mankind."*
>
> FRANKLIN D. ROOSEVELT, MAY 1940

from ordnance, oil, aircraft, tanks, and ships to tooth powder and salt cellars. The policy helped to save Britain, which was running desperately short of food and fuel in 1941. At first, the recipients were Britain and the Commonwealth countries, but within a year, Lend-Lease was providing aid to the Soviet Union and China. From 1942, it became increasingly significant as the war extended to the Pacific following the events of Pearl Harbor (see pp.110–111). By the end of the war, over $49 billion of American aid had been transported around the world to 40 countries.

US ISOLATIONISM IN WORLD WAR II

The US was determined to stay neutral in 1939. The country had suffered significant casualties in World War I, and debts owed by the Allies had caused resentment. There was little desire to become embroiled in another "foreign affair." However, knowing that the war threatened America's security, President Roosevelt worked to weaken the Neutrality Acts of the 1930s. With Lend-Lease, he hoped America could arm the fight for democracy while avoiding direct conflict.

President Franklin D. Roosevelt signing the Lend-Lease Act

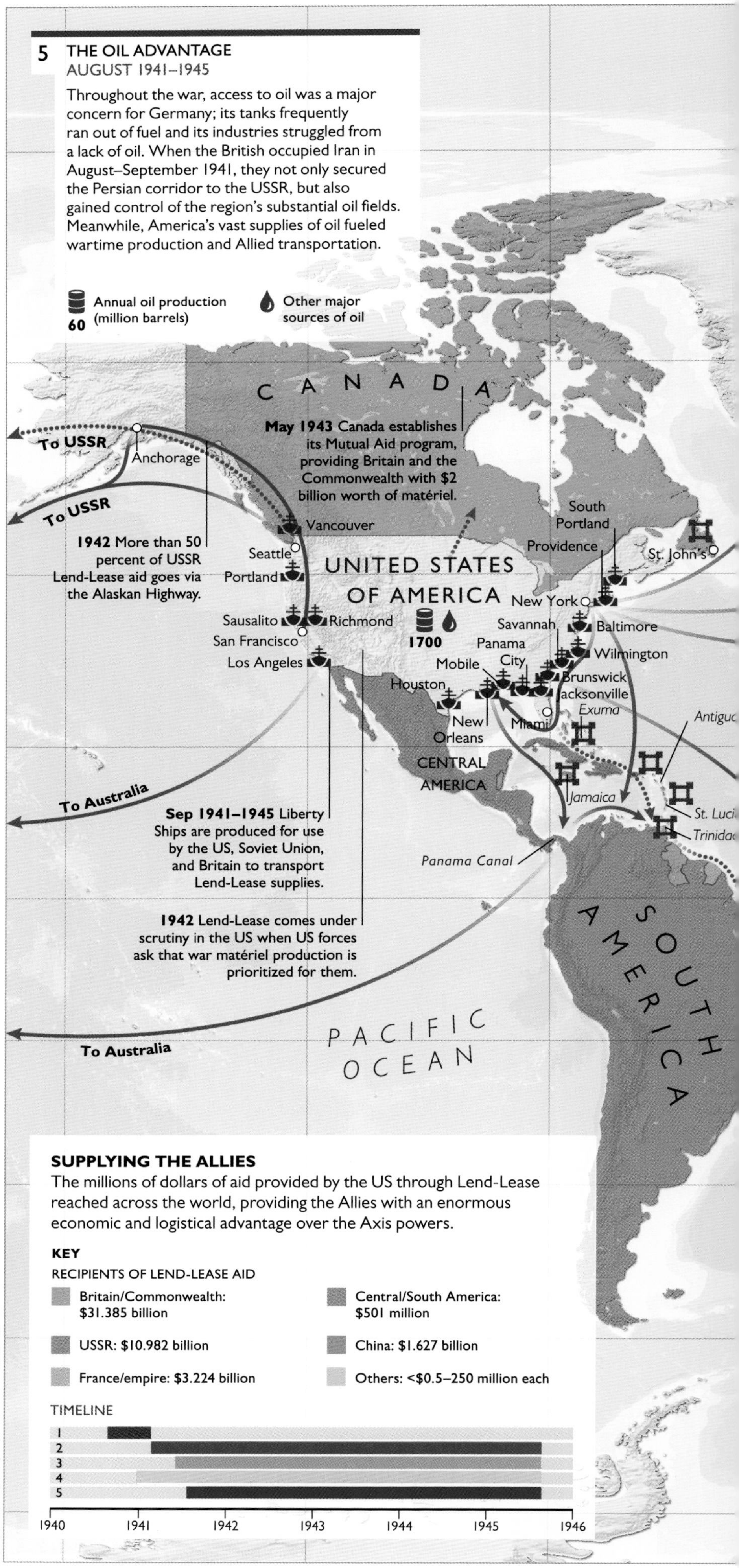

---

5 THE OIL ADVANTAGE
AUGUST 1941–1945

Throughout the war, access to oil was a major concern for Germany; its tanks frequently ran out of fuel and its industries struggled from a lack of oil. When the British occupied Iran in August–September 1941, they not only secured the Persian corridor to the USSR, but also gained control of the region's substantial oil fields. Meanwhile, America's vast supplies of oil fueled wartime production and Allied transportation.

🛢 Annual oil production (million barrels)
60

💧 Other major sources of oil

CANADA

May 1943 Canada establishes its Mutual Aid program, providing Britain and the Commonwealth with $2 billion worth of matériel.

To USSR — Anchorage

To USSR

1942 More than 50 percent of USSR Lend-Lease aid goes via the Alaskan Highway.

Vancouver
Seattle
Portland
Sausalito
San Francisco
Richmond
Los Angeles

1700

UNITED STATES OF AMERICA

South Portland
Providence
St. John's
New York
Savannah
Baltimore
Panama City
Wilmington
Mobile
Brunswick
Jacksonville
Houston
Exuma
New Orleans
Miami

CENTRAL AMERICA

Jamaica

Antigua
St. Lucia
Trinidad

Panama Canal

To Australia

Sep 1941–1945 Liberty Ships are produced for use by the US, Soviet Union, and Britain to transport Lend-Lease supplies.

1942 Lend-Lease comes under scrutiny in the US when US forces ask that war matériel production is prioritized for them.

SOUTH AMERICA

To Australia

PACIFIC OCEAN

SUPPLYING THE ALLIES

The millions of dollars of aid provided by the US through Lend-Lease reached across the world, providing the Allies with an enormous economic and logistical advantage over the Axis powers.

KEY

RECIPIENTS OF LEND-LEASE AID

- Britain/Commonwealth: $31.385 billion
- USSR: $10.982 billion
- France/empire: $3.224 billion
- Central/South America: $501 million
- China: $1.627 billion
- Others: <$0.5–250 million each

TIMELINE

	1940	1941	1942	1943	1944	1945	1946
1							
2							
3							
4							
5							

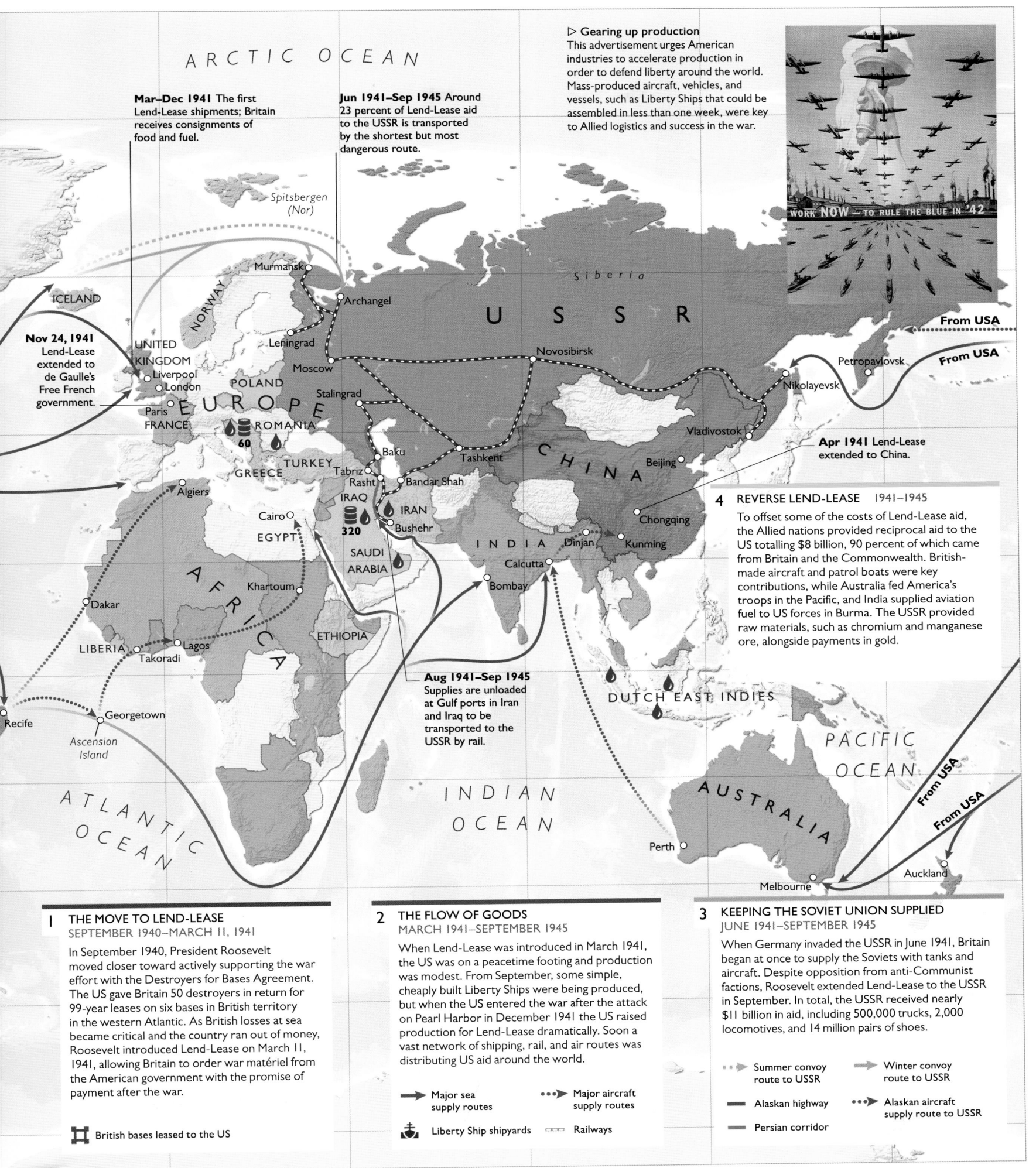

Mar–Dec 1941 The first Lend-Lease shipments; Britain receives consignments of food and fuel.

Jun 1941–Sep 1945 Around 23 percent of Lend-Lease aid to the USSR is transported by the shortest but most dangerous route.

▷ **Gearing up production**
This advertisement urges American industries to accelerate production in order to defend liberty around the world. Mass-produced aircraft, vehicles, and vessels, such as Liberty Ships that could be assembled in less than one week, were key to Allied logistics and success in the war.

WORK NOW – TO RULE THE BLUE IN '42

Nov 24, 1941 Lend-Lease extended to de Gaulle's Free French government.

Apr 1941 Lend-Lease extended to China.

Aug 1941–Sep 1945 Supplies are unloaded at Gulf ports in Iran and Iraq to be transported to the USSR by rail.

ARCTIC OCEAN
ATLANTIC OCEAN
INDIAN OCEAN
PACIFIC OCEAN

Spitsbergen (Nor)
Siberia
USSR
EUROPE
POLAND
UNITED KINGDOM
NORWAY
FRANCE
ROMANIA
GREECE
TURKEY
IRAQ
IRAN
SAUDI ARABIA
EGYPT
AFRICA
LIBERIA
ETHIOPIA
INDIA
CHINA
DUTCH EAST INDIES
AUSTRALIA

ICELAND
Murmansk
Archangel
Leningrad
Moscow
Novosibirsk
Petropavlovsk
Nikolayevsk
Vladivostok
Beijing
Liverpool
London
Paris
Stalingrad
Baku
Tabriz
Rasht
Bandar Shah
Bushehr
Tashkent
Chongqing
Kunming
Dinjan
Cairo
Khartoum
Dakar
Lagos
Takoradi
Calcutta
Bombay
Algiers
Recife
Georgetown
Ascension Island
Perth
Melbourne
Auckland

60
320

From USA

4 REVERSE LEND-LEASE 1941–1945

To offset some of the costs of Lend-Lease aid, the Allied nations provided reciprocal aid to the US totalling $8 billion, 90 percent of which came from Britain and the Commonwealth. British-made aircraft and patrol boats were key contributions, while Australia fed America's troops in the Pacific, and India supplied aviation fuel to US forces in Burma. The USSR provided raw materials, such as chromium and manganese ore, alongside payments in gold.

1 THE MOVE TO LEND-LEASE
SEPTEMBER 1940–MARCH 11, 1941

In September 1940, President Roosevelt moved closer toward actively supporting the war effort with the Destroyers for Bases Agreement. The US gave Britain 50 destroyers in return for 99-year leases on six bases in British territory in the western Atlantic. As British losses at sea became critical and the country ran out of money, Roosevelt introduced Lend-Lease on March 11, 1941, allowing Britain to order war matériel from the American government with the promise of payment after the war.

⌘ British bases leased to the US

2 THE FLOW OF GOODS
MARCH 1941–SEPTEMBER 1945

When Lend-Lease was introduced in March 1941, the US was on a peacetime footing and production was modest. From September, some simple, cheaply built Liberty Ships were being produced, but when the US entered the war after the attack on Pearl Harbor in December 1941 the US raised production for Lend-Lease dramatically. Soon a vast network of shipping, rail, and air routes was distributing US aid around the world.

→ Major sea supply routes
•••▸ Major aircraft supply routes
⚓ Liberty Ship shipyards
▭▭▭ Railways

3 KEEPING THE SOVIET UNION SUPPLIED
JUNE 1941–SEPTEMBER 1945

When Germany invaded the USSR in June 1941, Britain began at once to supply the Soviets with tanks and aircraft. Despite opposition from anti-Communist factions, Roosevelt extended Lend-Lease to the USSR in September. In total, the USSR received nearly $11 billion in aid, including 500,000 trucks, 2,000 locomotives, and 14 million pairs of shoes.

•••▸ Summer convoy route to USSR
— Alaskan highway
— Persian corridor
→ Winter convoy route to USSR
•••▸ Alaskan aircraft supply route to USSR

THE MEDITERRANEAN AND MIDDLE EAST

Italy's entry into World War II extended the conflict south into the Mediterranean region. After multiple failures by the Italian forces, Germany went to the rescue, and the Axis powers fought major tank battles against the British in the North African desert.

△ **Operation Compass**
In December 1940, British forces advanced to attack the Italians in the Western Desert, Egypt. Around 133,000 Italians were taken prisoner by British troops.

When war broke out in September 1939, Italy remained neutral, despite its alliance with Nazi Germany—a union grandiosely dubbed the "Pact of Steel." Knowing his country's military weakness, the Fascist dictator Benito Mussolini waited until the French were clearly beaten before declaring war on the Allies in June 1940. With France out of the picture, and Britain focused on its life-or-death struggle against Germany, it seemed an ideal opportunity for Italy to pursue its imperial ambitions around the Mediterranean.

In autumn 1940, Italy launched offensives from its North African colony, Libya, into Egypt, and from Albania (which they had occupied since spring 1939) into Greece. Despite Britain's desperate circumstances at that time, Winston Churchill was prepared to devote valuable resources to defend Egypt. Technically an independent, neutral country, it was in reality under British influence, and the Suez Canal was seen as a vital link to the British Empire in Asia. Maintaining a supply of oil from the Middle East was also a priority.

Poorly equipped and badly led, the Italian forces suffered disastrous defeats on all fronts. Italy quickly lost its East African colonies and most of Libya to the British, and was equally defeated by the Greeks. Although Hitler saw the Mediterranean and North Africa as distractions from more important matters, he sent German forces into the region to save Italy from disaster.

The Germans head southward

In spring 1941, having conquered Yugoslavia, German troops continued south into Greece and Crete in the last of their Blitzkrieg offensives; Britain sent forces to intervene. In North Africa, the arrival of the tanks of the Afrika Korps, led by the German general Erwin Rommel, placed Egypt under threat. There was heavy fighting between Britain and the Axis powers in the Western Desert. Meanwhile, the naval war in the Mediterranean centered on British efforts to block supplies to Rommel and keep a convoy route open between their bases at Gibraltar and Alexandria via Malta. Although the Royal Navy's warships were relatively well equipped, land-based Luftwaffe aircraft caused the British a lot of damage.

Britain's position was rendered more vulnerable by the hostile attitude of Francoist Spain and Vichy France, both

◁ **Parachutist's badge**
German airborne troops, marked by their distinctive badge, played a significant role in the Blitzkrieg offensives early in the war.

CHANGES IN FORTUNE
The war in the Mediterranean region had two distinct phases. From June 1940 to spring 1941, Italy suffered defeats on all fronts. Then the arrival of German air and land forces shifted the balance in favor of the Axis, although not decisively. Battered by British victories at Taranto, Italy, and Cape Matapan, Greece, the Italian navy could never control the Mediterranean. The British were frequently outfought by Rommel in North Africa, but mounted repeated counteroffensives.

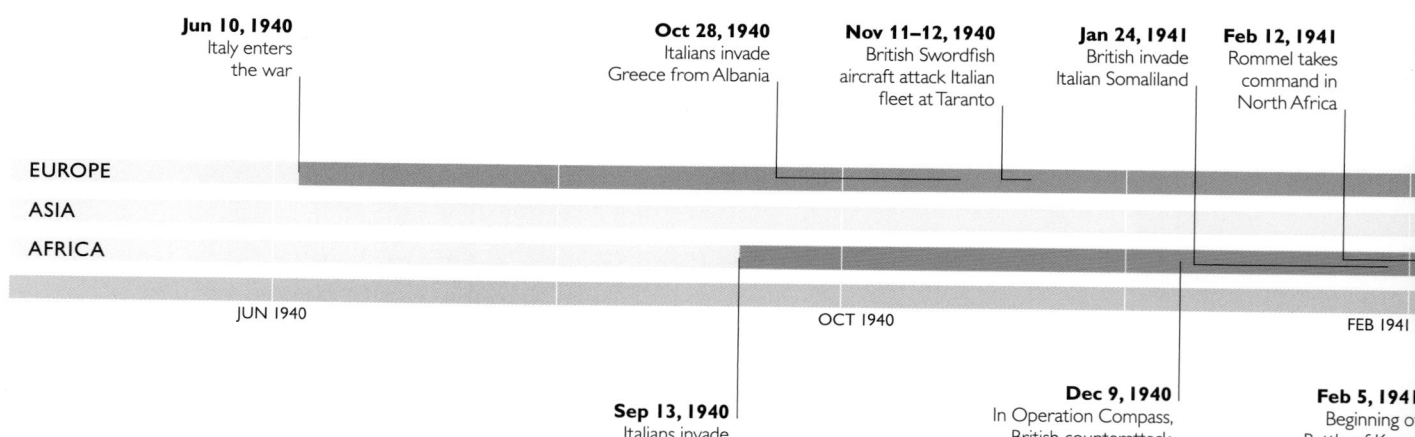

EUROPE
ASIA
AFRICA

Jun 10, 1940 Italy enters the war
Oct 28, 1940 Italians invade Greece from Albania
Nov 11–12, 1940 British Swordfish aircraft attack Italian fleet at Taranto
Jan 24, 1941 British invade Italian Somaliland
Feb 12, 1941 Rommel takes command in North Africa
Sep 13, 1940 Italians invade Egypt from Libya
Dec 9, 1940 In Operation Compass, British counterattack Italians in Egypt
Feb 5, 194▶ Beginning of Battle of Keren in Eritrea

JUN 1940   OCT 1940   FEB 1941

◁ **Greece conquered**
German troops raise the swastika on the Acropolis in Athens, having captured the Greek capital after a three-week campaign in April 1941.

officially neutral states, but leaning heavily toward collaboration with Nazi Germany. Colonies loyal to Vichy France controlled the western half of North Africa, but Britain succeeded in gaining Syria for the Free French (General De Gaulle's forces, which continued to fight with the Allies against the Axis powers after the fall of France). Generally, the British were successful in shoring up their position in the Middle East, securing the support of most Jewish settlers in Palestine, and bringing Iraq and Iran into line when their rulers leaned toward the Axis.

The Allies hold their own

Hitler never devoted sufficient resources to the Western Desert Campaign, or to the Mediterranean generally, to achieve decisive results. Malta was heavily bombed by German and Italian aircraft but was never invaded, despite being only 50 miles (80km) from Italy. This failure to seize an obvious prize was typical of an Axis policy that lacked resolute focus. For Britain, on the other hand, North Africa became very important strategically, because it was the only place where the enemy could be engaged on land. By 1942–1943, operations in the Mediterranean and North Africa were central to Allied strategy.

▷ **The Battle of Crete**
German paratroopers land in a mass assault on Crete in May 1941. Despite fierce local and Allied defense, the German forces captured the Greek island after 13 days of fighting.

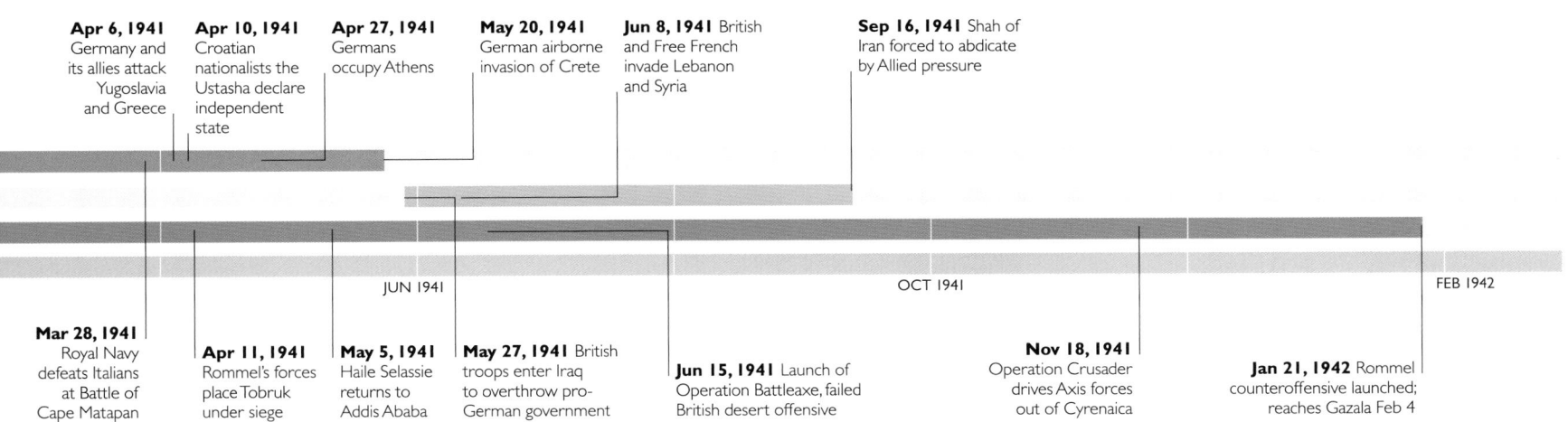

Apr 6, 1941 Germany and its allies attack Yugoslavia and Greece

Apr 10, 1941 Croatian nationalists the Ustasha declare independent state

Apr 27, 1941 Germans occupy Athens

May 20, 1941 German airborne invasion of Crete

Jun 8, 1941 British and Free French invade Lebanon and Syria

Sep 16, 1941 Shah of Iran forced to abdicate by Allied pressure

JUN 1941   OCT 1941   FEB 1942

Mar 28, 1941 Royal Navy defeats Italians at Battle of Cape Matapan

Apr 11, 1941 Rommel's forces place Tobruk under siege

May 5, 1941 Haile Selassie returns to Addis Ababa

May 27, 1941 British troops enter Iraq to overthrow pro-German government

Jun 15, 1941 Launch of Operation Battleaxe, failed British desert offensive

Nov 18, 1941 Operation Crusader drives Axis forces out of Cyrenaica

Jan 21, 1942 Rommel counteroffensive launched; reaches Gazala Feb 4

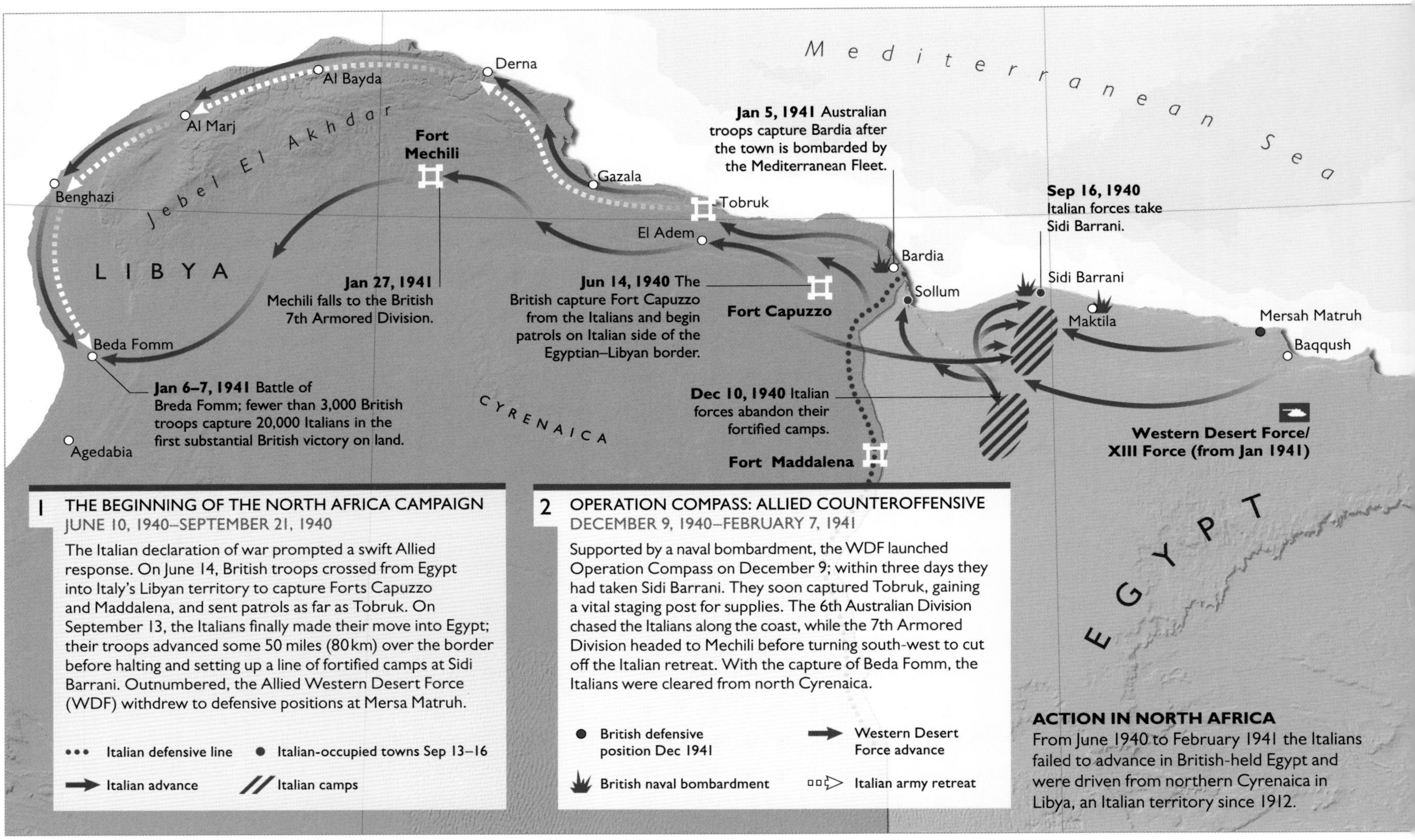

Derna

Al Bayda

Al Marj

Jan 5, 1941 Australian troops capture Bardia after the town is bombarded by the Mediterranean Fleet.

M e d i t e r r a n e a n S e a

Fort Mechili

Gazala

Tobruk

Sep 16, 1940 Italian forces take Sidi Barrani.

Benghazi

Jebel El Akhdar

El Adem

Bardia

LIBYA

Jan 27, 1941 Mechili falls to the British 7th Armored Division.

Jun 14, 1940 The British capture Fort Capuzzo from the Italians and begin patrols on Italian side of the Egyptian–Libyan border.

Fort Capuzzo

Sollum

Sidi Barrani

Maktila

Mersah Matruh

Baqqush

Beda Fomm

C Y R E N A I C A

Jan 6–7, 1941 Battle of Breda Fomm; fewer than 3,000 British troops capture 20,000 Italians in the first substantial British victory on land.

Dec 10, 1940 Italian forces abandon their fortified camps.

Western Desert Force/ XIII Force (from Jan 1941)

Agedabia

Fort Maddalena

E G Y P T

1 THE BEGINNING OF THE NORTH AFRICA CAMPAIGN
JUNE 10, 1940–SEPTEMBER 21, 1940

The Italian declaration of war prompted a swift Allied response. On June 14, British troops crossed from Egypt into Italy's Libyan territory to capture Forts Capuzzo and Maddalena, and sent patrols as far as Tobruk. On September 13, the Italians finally made their move into Egypt; their troops advanced some 50 miles (80 km) over the border before halting and setting up a line of fortified camps at Sidi Barrani. Outnumbered, the Allied Western Desert Force (WDF) withdrew to defensive positions at Mersa Matruh.

●●● Italian defensive line	● Italian-occupied towns Sep 13–16
➔ Italian advance	⫽ Italian camps

2 OPERATION COMPASS: ALLIED COUNTEROFFENSIVE
DECEMBER 9, 1940–FEBRUARY 7, 1941

Supported by a naval bombardment, the WDF launched Operation Compass on December 9; within three days they had taken Sidi Barrani. They soon captured Tobruk, gaining a vital staging post for supplies. The 6th Australian Division chased the Italians along the coast, while the 7th Armored Division headed to Mechili before turning south-west to cut off the Italian retreat. With the capture of Beda Fomm, the Italians were cleared from north Cyrenaica.

● British defensive position Dec 1941	➔ Western Desert Force advance
✹ British naval bombardment	▫▫▷ Italian army retreat

ACTION IN NORTH AFRICA
From June 1940 to February 1941 the Italians failed to advance in British-held Egypt and were driven from northern Cyrenaica in Libya, an Italian territory since 1912.

ITALY'S CAMPAIGNS IN AFRICA

Italian dictator Benito Mussolini saw the outbreak of war as an opportunity to pursue his imperial ambitions in Africa. He embarked on two disastrous campaigns against the British in Egypt, Anglo-Egyptian Sudan, and British Somaliland, which backfired and resulted in Italy's expulsion from northern Libya and Ethiopia.

Italy did not follow its Axis partner Germany into war in September 1939, but entered the conflict later, in June 1940, when Mussolini judged that the Allies would soon be defeated. His initial aim was to expand Italy's colonies in Libya, Ethiopia, Eritrea, and Italian Somaliland by taking territory from the British. With superior numbers in the air and on the ground, Italy posed a threat to Britain's positions in Anglo-Egyptian Sudan, Kenya, and the Horn of Africa, as well as British bases in Egypt and the vital supply route of the Suez Canal.

Italian forces invaded Sudan in early July 1940, but did not push deep into British territory, switching to assault British Somaliland in August, and then the Egyptian border in September. By the end of October, however, Italy had opened up a new front in Greece (pp.78–79) and did not appear to be planning new moves in Africa.

In December, the British launched Operation Compass against the Italian invaders in Egypt and then swept on through northern Libya, clearing the Italians out of the region in early February 1941. By then, British forces—supported by Ethiopian chieftains rallied by Emperor Haile Selassie—had launched counterattacks in East Africa. By May, only few pockets of Italian resistance remained.

ITALY'S EMPIRE
Italy's imperial ambitions were dealt a blow when its soldiers failed to make inroads in Egypt against the British, instead losing control of vital territory in Libya. The Italians were also driven from their East African colonies of Italian Somaliland, Eritrea, and the Ethiopian Empire, held since 1936.

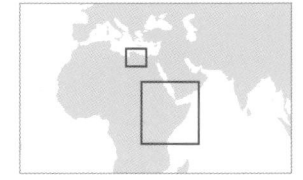

KEY

▦ Under British influence by Jun 1940	▦ French and French mandated territories Jun 1940	⬢⬟ Allied army units
▦ Italian Empire Jun 1940	⊡ Italian forts	✕ Major battles

TIMELINE

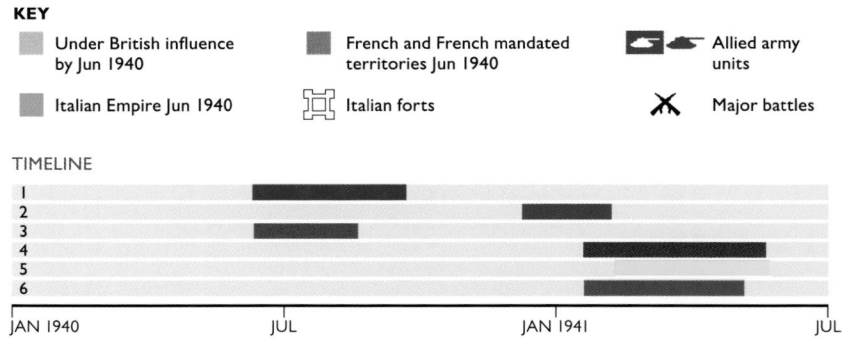

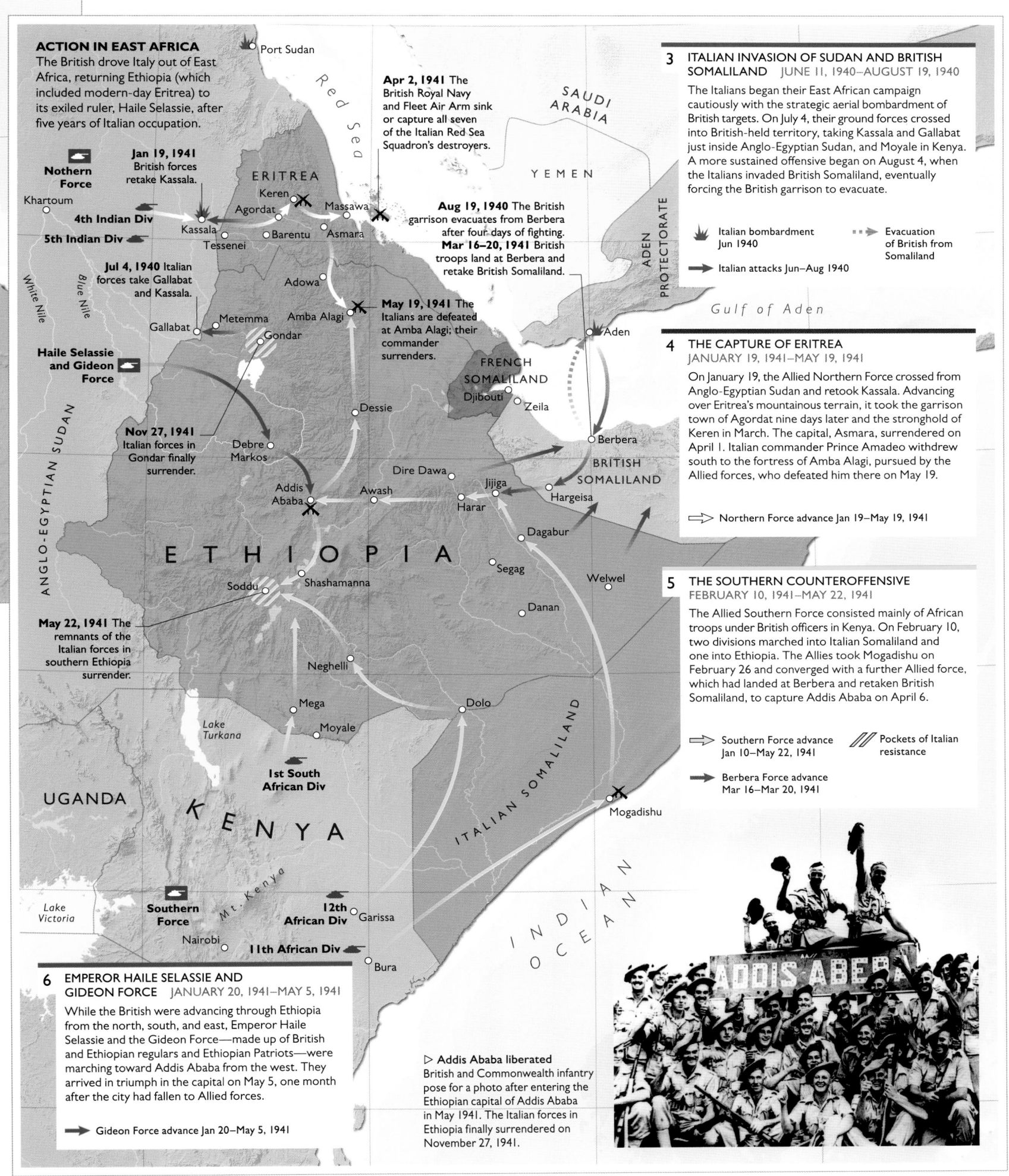

ACTION IN EAST AFRICA
The British drove Italy out of East Africa, returning Ethiopia (which included modern-day Eritrea) to its exiled ruler, Haile Selassie, after five years of Italian occupation.

Port Sudan

Nothern Force
Jan 19, 1941 British forces retake Kassala.

Khartoum

4th Indian Div
5th Indian Div

Kassala

Jul 4, 1940 Italian forces take Gallabat and Kassala.

Tessenei

White Nile
Blue Nile

Haile Selassie and Gideon Force

ANGLO-EGYPTIAN SUDAN

Gallabat
Metemma
Gondar

Nov 27, 1941 Italian forces in Gondar finally surrender.

Debre Markos

May 22, 1941 The remnants of the Italian forces in southern Ethiopia surrender.

Soddu
Shashamanna

ERITREA
Keren
Agordat
Barentu
Asmara
Adowa
Amba Alagi

Apr 2, 1941 The British Royal Navy and Fleet Air Arm sink or capture all seven of the Italian Red Sea Squadron's destroyers.

Massawa

Red Sea

SAUDI ARABIA

YEMEN

Aug 19, 1940 The British garrison evacuates from Berbera after four days of fighting.
Mar 16–20, 1941 British troops land at Berbera and retake British Somaliland.

May 19, 1941 The Italians are defeated at Amba Alagi; their commander surrenders.

Dessie

ADEN PROTECTORATE

Gulf of Aden

Aden

FRENCH SOMALILAND
Djibouti
Zeila

Berbera

BRITISH SOMALILAND

ETHIOPIA

Addis Ababa
Awash
Dire Dawa
Jijiga
Harar
Hargeisa
Dagabur

Segag
Welwel
Danan

Neghelli

Dolo

ITALIAN SOMALILAND

Lake Turkana

Mega
Moyale

1st South African Div

UGANDA

KENYA

Mt. Kenya

Lake Victoria

Southern Force
Nairobi

12th African Div
Garissa

11th African Div

Bura

INDIAN OCEAN

Mogadishu

3 ITALIAN INVASION OF SUDAN AND BRITISH SOMALILAND JUNE 11, 1940–AUGUST 19, 1940

The Italians began their East African campaign cautiously with the strategic aerial bombardment of British targets. On July 4, their ground forces crossed into British-held territory, taking Kassala and Gallabat just inside Anglo-Egyptian Sudan, and Moyale in Kenya. A more sustained offensive began on August 4, when the Italians invaded British Somaliland, eventually forcing the British garrison to evacuate.

🔺 Italian bombardment Jun 1940
➡ Italian attacks Jun–Aug 1940
⇢ Evacuation of British from Somaliland

4 THE CAPTURE OF ERITREA
JANUARY 19, 1941–MAY 19, 1941

On January 19, the Allied Northern Force crossed from Anglo-Egyptian Sudan and retook Kassala. Advancing over Eritrea's mountainous terrain, it took the garrison town of Agordat nine days later and the stronghold of Keren in March. The capital, Asmara, surrendered on April 1. Italian commander Prince Amadeo withdrew south to the fortress of Amba Alagi, pursued by the Allied forces, who defeated him there on May 19.

⇨ Northern Force advance Jan 19–May 19, 1941

5 THE SOUTHERN COUNTEROFFENSIVE
FEBRUARY 10, 1941–MAY 22, 1941

The Allied Southern Force consisted mainly of African troops under British officers in Kenya. On February 10, two divisions marched into Italian Somaliland and one into Ethiopia. The Allies took Mogadishu on February 26 and converged with a further Allied force, which had landed at Berbera and retaken British Somaliland, to capture Addis Ababa on April 6.

⇨ Southern Force advance Jan 10–May 22, 1941
➡ Berbera Force advance Mar 16–Mar 20, 1941
▨ Pockets of Italian resistance

6 EMPEROR HAILE SELASSIE AND GIDEON FORCE JANUARY 20, 1941–MAY 5, 1941

While the British were advancing through Ethiopia from the north, south, and east, Emperor Haile Selassie and the Gideon Force—made up of British and Ethiopian regulars and Ethiopian Patriots—were marching toward Addis Ababa from the west. They arrived in triumph in the capital on May 5, one month after the city had fallen to Allied forces.

➡ Gideon Force advance Jan 20–May 5, 1941

▷ **Addis Ababa liberated**
British and Commonwealth infantry pose for a photo after entering the Ethiopian capital of Addis Ababa in May 1941. The Italian forces in Ethiopia finally surrendered on November 27, 1941.

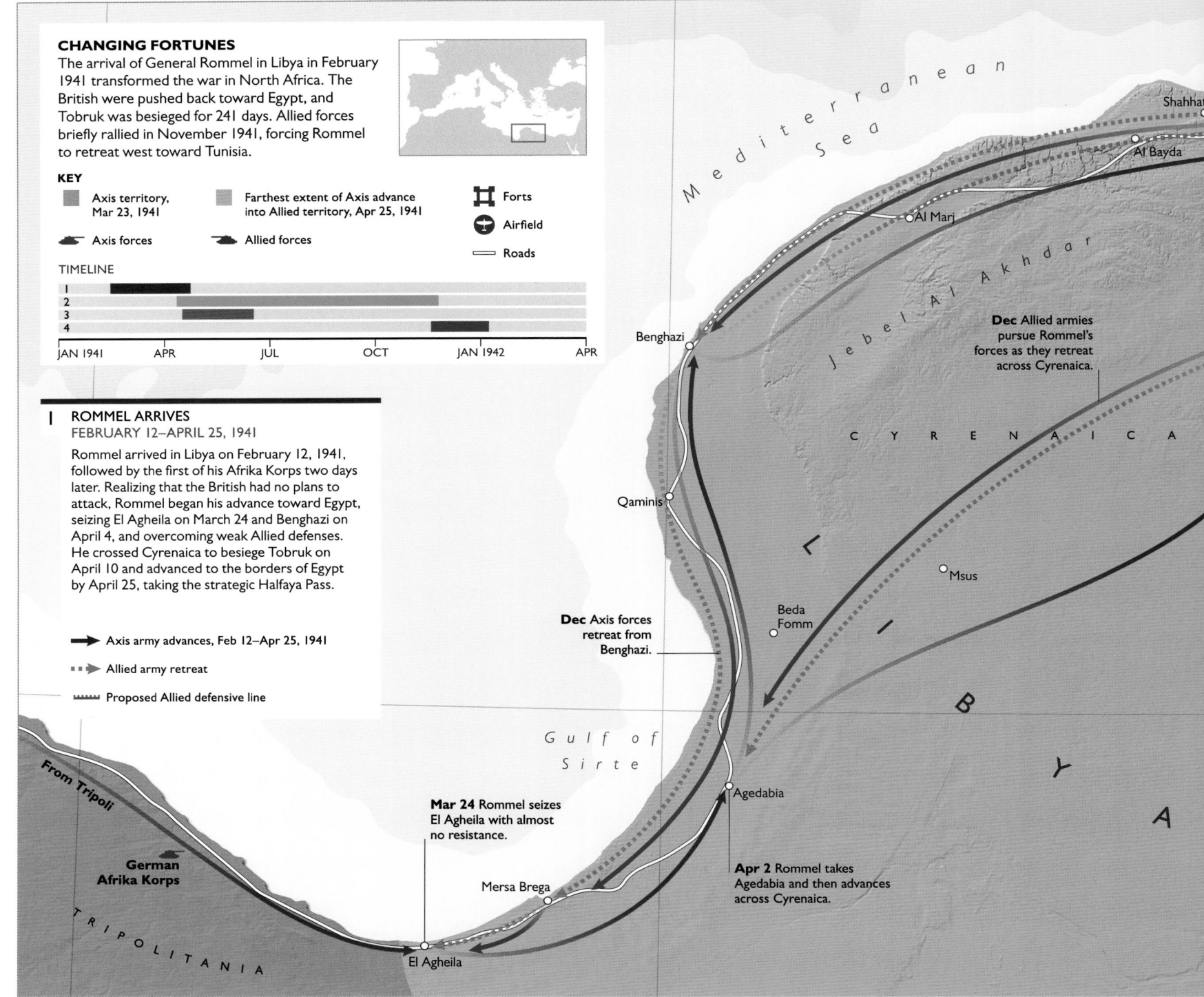

CHANGING FORTUNES

The arrival of General Rommel in Libya in February 1941 transformed the war in North Africa. The British were pushed back toward Egypt, and Tobruk was besieged for 241 days. Allied forces briefly rallied in November 1941, forcing Rommel to retreat west toward Tunisia.

KEY

- Axis territory, Mar 23, 1941
- Farthest extent of Axis advance into Allied territory, Apr 25, 1941
- Axis forces
- Allied forces
- Forts
- Airfield
- Roads

TIMELINE

1
2
3
4

JAN 1941　APR　JUL　OCT　JAN 1942　APR

I ROMMEL ARRIVES
FEBRUARY 12–APRIL 25, 1941

Rommel arrived in Libya on February 12, 1941, followed by the first of his Afrika Korps two days later. Realizing that the British had no plans to attack, Rommel began his advance toward Egypt, seizing El Agheila on March 24 and Benghazi on April 4, and overcoming weak Allied defenses. He crossed Cyrenaica to besiege Tobruk on April 10 and advanced to the borders of Egypt by April 25, taking the strategic Halfaya Pass.

→ Axis army advances, Feb 12–Apr 25, 1941
▪▪▪▶ Allied army retreat
⟆⟆⟆ Proposed Allied defensive line

Dec Allied armies pursue Rommel's forces as they retreat across Cyrenaica.

Dec Axis forces retreat from Benghazi.

Mar 24 Rommel seizes El Agheila with almost no resistance.

Apr 2 Rommel takes Agedabia and then advances across Cyrenaica.

Shahhat
Al Bayda
Al Marj
Benghazi
Qaminis
Msus
Beda Fomm
Agedabia
Mersa Brega
El Agheila
From Tripoli
German Afrika Korps

Mediterranean Sea
Jebel Al Akhdar
C Y R E N A I C A
L I B Y A
Gulf of Sirte
T R I P O L I T A N I A

ROMMEL ENTERS THE DESERT WAR

By February 1941, the Italians were struggling in their war against the Allies in North Africa. Their incursions into Egypt had failed, and they had been chased out of Cyrenaica in northern Libya. Hitler was anxious to save Italy from defeat and sent his favorite general, Erwin Rommel, with a German armored expeditionary force—the Afrika Korps—to rescue the situation.

Rommel's orders on arriving in Libya were to stand on the defensive and prevent any further Italian retreats, but the German general—who had proved his flair for tank warfare in France—had an instinct for attack. Knowing that the British forces facing him had been weakened by the diversion of troops to Greece (see pp.80–81), he launched a probing offensive in late March and found that his tanks could outmaneuver the British with ease.

Rommel soon began an eastward advance, forcing the Allies to retreat in disarray from Libya into Egypt. In early April, the 9th Australian Division found itself marooned in the port of Tobruk, surrounded by the enemy, and far behind the new front line. Rommel had orders to take Tobruk, but the Australian forces there, resupplied by sea, held a defensive perimeter against attack by superior German forces throughout the next six months. British counterattacks from Egypt in May and June failed to break the

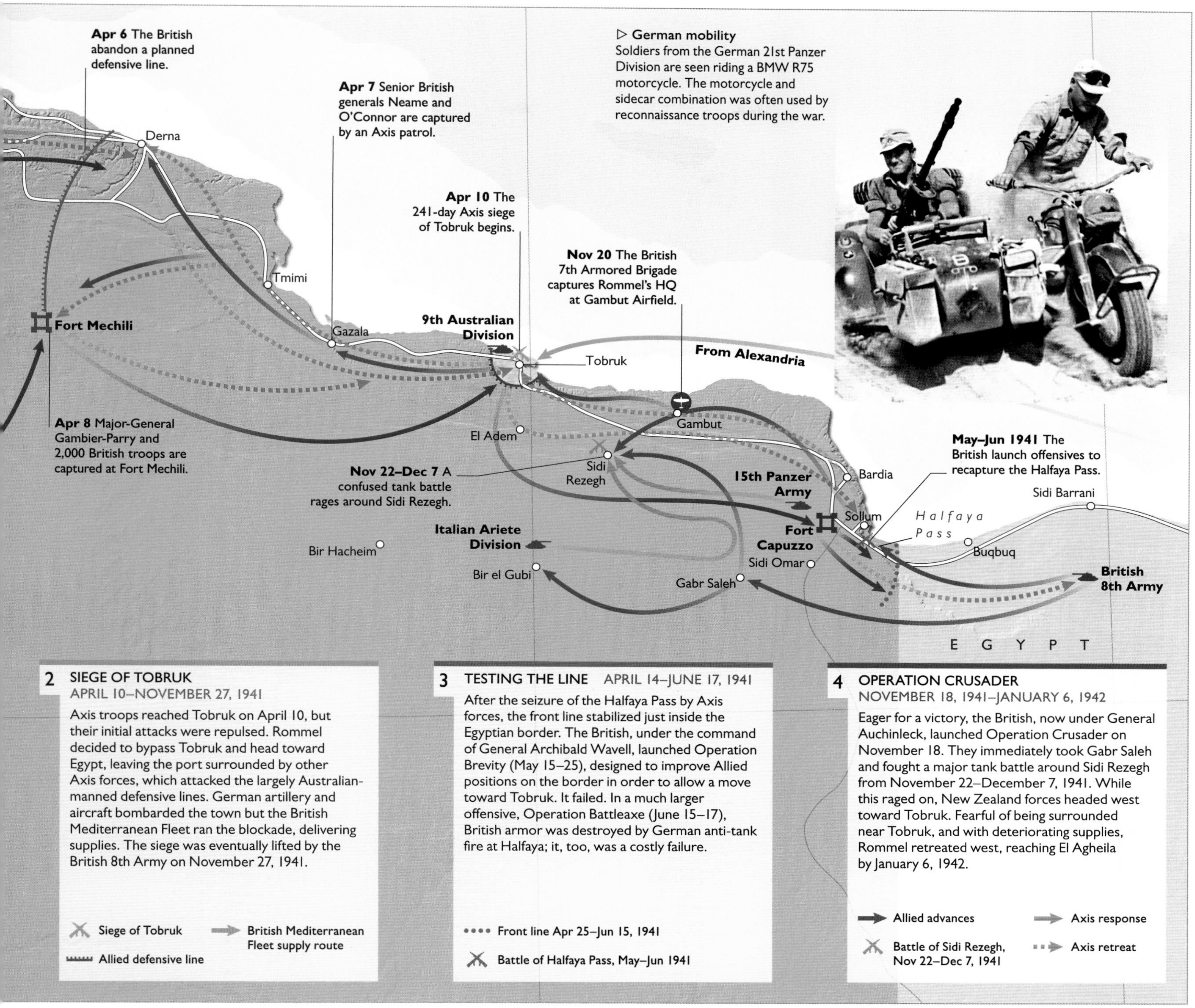

Apr 6 The British abandon a planned defensive line.

Derna

Apr 7 Senior British generals Neame and O'Connor are captured by an Axis patrol.

Tmimi

Apr 10 The 241-day Axis siege of Tobruk begins.

Gazala

9th Australian Division

Nov 20 The British 7th Armored Brigade captures Rommel's HQ at Gambut Airfield.

▷ **German mobility**
Soldiers from the German 21st Panzer Division are seen riding a BMW R75 motorcycle. The motorcycle and sidecar combination was often used by reconnaissance troops during the war.

Fort Mechili

Apr 8 Major-General Gambier-Parry and 2,000 British troops are captured at Fort Mechili.

El Adem

Tobruk

From Alexandria

Gambut

Nov 22–Dec 7 A confused tank battle rages around Sidi Rezegh.

Sidi Rezegh

15th Panzer Army

Bardia

May–Jun 1941 The British launch offensives to recapture the Halfaya Pass.

Sidi Barrani

Halfaya Pass

Italian Ariete Division

Bir Hacheim

Bir el Gubi

Fort Capuzzo

Sidi Omar

Gabr Saleh

Sollum

Buqbuq

British 8th Army

E G Y P T

---

2 SIEGE OF TOBRUK
APRIL 10–NOVEMBER 27, 1941

Axis troops reached Tobruk on April 10, but their initial attacks were repulsed. Rommel decided to bypass Tobruk and head toward Egypt, leaving the port surrounded by other Axis forces, which attacked the largely Australian-manned defensive lines. German artillery and aircraft bombarded the town but the British Mediterranean Fleet ran the blockade, delivering supplies. The siege was eventually lifted by the British 8th Army on November 27, 1941.

✕ Siege of Tobruk → British Mediterranean Fleet supply route

∿∿∿ Allied defensive line

3 TESTING THE LINE APRIL 14–JUNE 17, 1941

After the seizure of the Halfaya Pass by Axis forces, the front line stabilized just inside the Egyptian border. The British, under the command of General Archibald Wavell, launched Operation Brevity (May 15–25), designed to improve Allied positions on the border in order to allow a move toward Tobruk. It failed. In a much larger offensive, Operation Battleaxe (June 15–17), British armor was destroyed by German anti-tank fire at Halfaya; it, too, was a costly failure.

•••• Front line Apr 25–Jun 15, 1941

✕ Battle of Halfaya Pass, May–Jun 1941

4 OPERATION CRUSADER
NOVEMBER 18, 1941–JANUARY 6, 1942

Eager for a victory, the British, now under General Auchinleck, launched Operation Crusader on November 18. They immediately took Gabr Saleh and fought a major tank battle around Sidi Rezegh from November 22–December 7, 1941. While this raged on, New Zealand forces headed west toward Tobruk. Fearful of being surrounded near Tobruk, and with deteriorating supplies, Rommel retreated west, reaching El Agheila by January 6, 1942.

→ Allied advances ⟶ Axis response

✕ Battle of Sidi Rezegh, Nov 22–Dec 7, 1941 ⇢ Axis retreat

---

siege of Tobruk, and in July, a frustrated Churchill dismissed the area commander, General Archibald Wavell, replacing him with General Claude Auchinleck. The new commander was given substantial reinforcements, especially tanks, and the British desert forces—which included Australians, New Zealanders, Poles, South Africans, Indians, and Free French troops—were reorganized as the British 8th Army.

On November 18, Auchinleck took the offensive in Operation Crusader. Again the British armor was outfought by Rommel's more experienced tank commanders, but at a crucial moment Rommel lost contact with his enemy, advancing into empty desert while, further north, 8th Army infantry pressed towards Tobruk. The siege was lifted on November 27 and Rommel soon conducted a full-scale retreat, falling back as far as El Agheila—the first position he had captured from the British, the previous March.

FIELD MARSHAL ERWIN ROMMEL

Field Marshal Erwin Rommel (1891–1944) was one of the leading tank commanders of World War II, earning himself the nickname *der Wüstenfuchs*, "the Desert Fox," for his wily strategic command. His British adversaries admired his chivalry, and the war in North Africa has been called the "war without hate." Although a supporter of Adolf Hitler and the Nazi seizure of power in 1933, Rommel was a reluctant Nazi. In 1944 he was implicated in the July 20 plot to assassinate Hitler (see pp.196–197); he was allowed to take his own life rather than face trial.

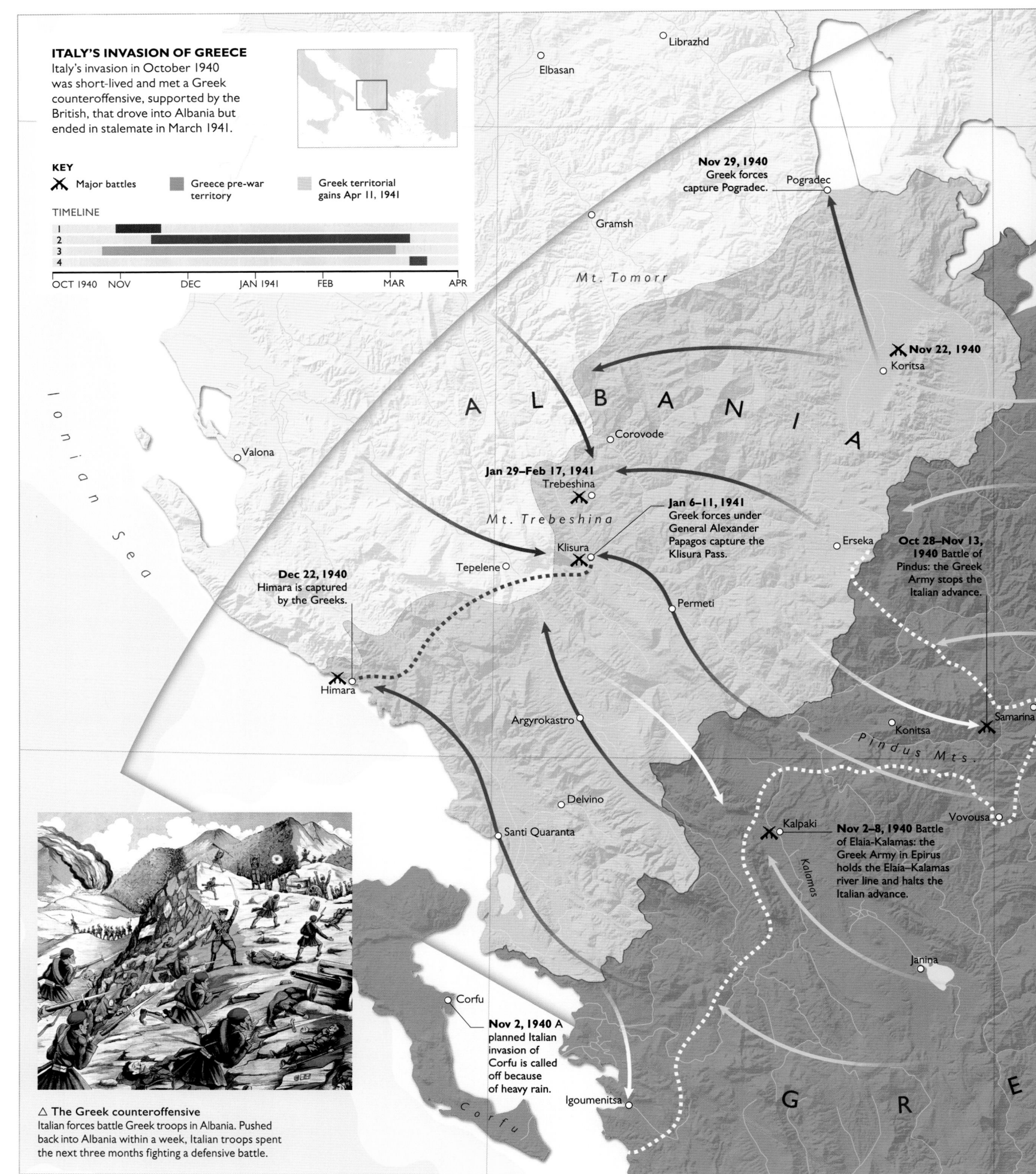

ITALY'S INVASION OF GREECE

Italy's invasion in October 1940 was short-lived and met a Greek counteroffensive, supported by the British, that drove into Albania but ended in stalemate in March 1941.

KEY

✗ Major battles

▬ Greece pre-war territory

▬ Greek territorial gains Apr 11, 1941

TIMELINE

1
2
3
4

OCT 1940 NOV DEC JAN 1941 FEB MAR APR

Nov 29, 1940
Greek forces capture Pogradec.

Pogradec

Librazhd

Elbasan

Gramsh

✗ Nov 22, 1940

Koritsa

Mt. Tomorr

A L B A N I A

Valona

Corovode

Jan 29–Feb 17, 1941
Trebeshina ✗

Mt. Trebeshina

Jan 6–11, 1941
Greek forces under General Alexander Papagos capture the Klisura Pass.

Klisura ✗

Erseka

Oct 28–Nov 13, 1940 Battle of Pindus: the Greek Army stops the Italian advance.

Tepelene

Permeti

Dec 22, 1940
Himara is captured by the Greeks.

Himara ✗

I o n i a n S e a

Argyrokastro

Konitsa

Samarina ✗

Pindus Mts.

Delvino

Vovousa

Santi Quaranta

Kalpaki ✗

Nov 2–8, 1940 Battle of Elaia-Kalamas: the Greek Army in Epirus holds the Elaia–Kalamas river line and halts the Italian advance.

Kalamas

Corfu

Nov 2, 1940 A planned Italian invasion of Corfu is called off because of heavy rain.

Janina

C o r f u

Igoumenitsa

G R E

△ **The Greek counteroffensive**
Italian forces battle Greek troops in Albania. Pushed back into Albania within a week, Italian troops spent the next three months fighting a defensive battle.

Map Legend (left column)

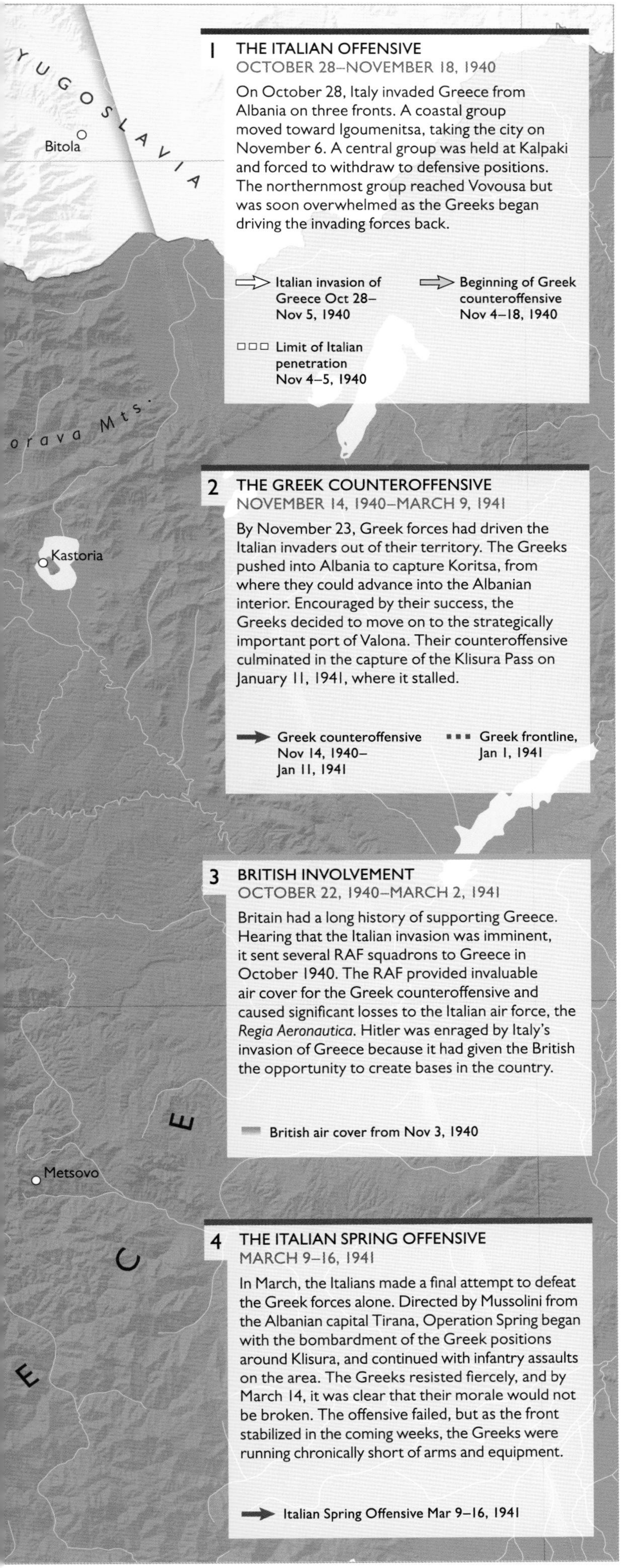

1 THE ITALIAN OFFENSIVE
OCTOBER 28–NOVEMBER 18, 1940

On October 28, Italy invaded Greece from Albania on three fronts. A coastal group moved toward Igoumenitsa, taking the city on November 6. A central group was held at Kalpaki and forced to withdraw to defensive positions. The northernmost group reached Vovousa but was soon overwhelmed as the Greeks began driving the invading forces back.

⇨ Italian invasion of Greece Oct 28– Nov 5, 1940

⇨ Beginning of Greek counteroffensive Nov 4–18, 1940

▢▢▢ Limit of Italian penetration Nov 4–5, 1940

2 THE GREEK COUNTEROFFENSIVE
NOVEMBER 14, 1940–MARCH 9, 1941

By November 23, Greek forces had driven the Italian invaders out of their territory. The Greeks pushed into Albania to capture Koritsa, from where they could advance into the Albanian interior. Encouraged by their success, the Greeks decided to move on to the strategically important port of Valona. Their counteroffensive culminated in the capture of the Klisura Pass on January 11, 1941, where it stalled.

➡ Greek counteroffensive Nov 14, 1940– Jan 11, 1941

▪▪▪ Greek frontline, Jan 1, 1941

3 BRITISH INVOLVEMENT
OCTOBER 22, 1940–MARCH 2, 1941

Britain had a long history of supporting Greece. Hearing that the Italian invasion was imminent, it sent several RAF squadrons to Greece in October 1940. The RAF provided invaluable air cover for the Greek counteroffensive and caused significant losses to the Italian air force, the *Regia Aeronautica*. Hitler was enraged by Italy's invasion of Greece because it had given the British the opportunity to create bases in the country.

▬ British air cover from Nov 3, 1940

4 THE ITALIAN SPRING OFFENSIVE
MARCH 9–16, 1941

In March, the Italians made a final attempt to defeat the Greek forces alone. Directed by Mussolini from the Albanian capital Tirana, Operation Spring began with the bombardment of the Greek positions around Klisura, and continued with infantry assaults on the area. The Greeks resisted fiercely, and by March 14, it was clear that their morale would not be broken. The offensive failed, but as the front stabilized in the coming weeks, the Greeks were running chronically short of arms and equipment.

➡ Italian Spring Offensive Mar 9–16, 1941

(Map labels: YUGOSLAVIA, Bitola, orava Mts., Kastoria, Metsovo)

THE GRECO-ITALIAN WAR

At war with the Allies since June 10, 1940, Italy had begun to fulfill its imperial ambitions with invasions of France, British Somaliland, and Egypt. In October 1940, it launched the invasion of Greece— a disastrous offensive that achieved nothing other than to test the relationship between Italy and Germany.

In October 1940, the Balkans were broadly pro-German, and Greece's own right-wing dictator—General Metaxas— had confirmed Greece's neutrality. This suited Hitler, because it allowed him to pursue his plans for the invasion of the Soviet Union without distraction. However, Mussolini had designs on Greece and was impatient for conquests to match those of his German allies.

Mussolini accused the Greeks of aiding the British in the Mediterranean, and on October 28 issued an ultimatum demanding free passage for his troops to occupy strategic points in Greek territory. When Metaxas rejected the ultimatum, Italy invaded from Albania.

The Italian forces crossed the border at three points, but were soon caught in bitter fighting with a fiercely patriotic and tenacious Greek army in the unforgiving terrain of the mountains along the Albanian–Greek border.

By early November, a Greek counteroffensive had pushed the Italians back into Albania, and the Greek army was soon advancing through the country. The counteroffensive halted by early January 1941, leaving the Italians to attempt one last offensive in March. It achieved little, but it did highlight the vulnerability of the Greek army, influencing Hitler's later decision to send his own armies into the region.

> *"We do not argue with those who disagree with us, we destroy them."*
>
> BENITO MUSSOLINI, 1936

ITALY'S IMPERIAL AMBITIONS

After its unification in the mid-19th century, Italy built a small empire that included the Dodecanese Islands and territories in East and North Africa. From the 1920s, Mussolini— whose Fascist Party was named after the bundle of wooden rods (or *fasces*) that was a symbol of Roman authority—sought to reclaim the glory of Ancient Rome. He gradually strengthened Italy's power in Libya, and conquered Ethiopia in 1935. Four years later, Albania was incorporated into Italy, and the invasion of Greece in 1940 was the next logical step in his plan to dominate the Mediterranean.

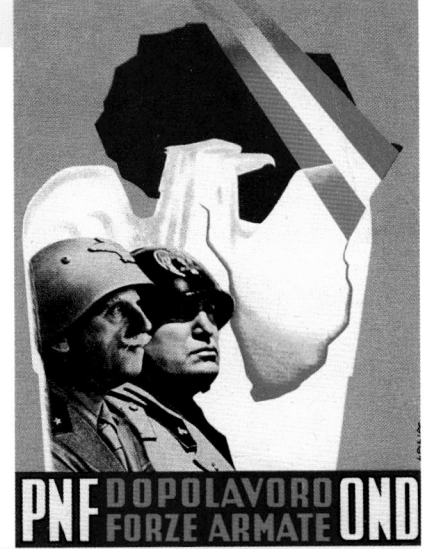

Italian imperial propaganda shows Mussolini and Vittorio Emanuele III superimposed on a graphic of Italy's planned African empire.

GERMANY PUSHES SOUTH

Italy's unsuccessful invasion of Greece forced Hitler to postpone his planned invasion of the USSR and concentrate on securing the Balkans. With the support of its regional allies, Germany invaded Yugoslavia and Greece in April 1941, taking both in under a month.

While Italy was fighting its ineffectual war with Greece (see pp.78–79), Hitler had been persuading and pressurizing the states in the Balkan region to join the defensive alliance known as the Tripartite Pact. By March 1, 1941, all the states except Yugoslavia and Greece had joined. German troops had begun to arrive in Romania and Hungary in November 1940, and—as the Italians prepared their counteroffensive against Greece in Albania—the German 12th Army moved into Bulgaria on March 2, 1941.

Alarmed by the arrival of German forces on Greece's borders, the British responded by sending an expeditionary force (W Force, named after its commander, Lieutenant-General Henry Maitland Wilson) from Egypt to Greece. On March 25, Yugoslavia yielded to pressure to join the Tripartite Pact, but a coup on March 27 gave power to a group of anti-Pact air force officers. When they signed a nonaggression pact with the Soviet Union and began talks with Britain about a Balkan coalition, Hitler immediately began planning the simultaneous invasion of Yugoslavia and Greece. The Yugoslav people were forced to defend a 1,000-mile (1,600-km) frontier with ill-equipped divisions numbering barely half the 50 fielded by Germany. Most of the Greek forces were in Albania, leaving only the Greek 2nd Army and W Force to defend the eastern route into Greece. On April 6, the Germans unleashed their blitzkrieg. By April 28, Yugoslavia had surrendered, and the Allies been driven out of Greece.

1 AXIS FORCES INVADE YUGOSLAVIA AND GREECE APRIL 6–9, 1941

The Axis campaign began on April 6 with air attacks on Belgrade and Piraeus, the port of Athens. These all but destroyed the Yugoslav air force and damaged the major British supply line into Greece. Ground forces then flooded across Yugoslavia's borders. Once Nis and Skopje had fallen, German troops crossed the Yugoslav border into Greece, capturing Salonika and trapping the Greeks defending the fortified Metaxas Line. When Monastir was captured on April 9, Yugoslavia was cut off from Greece.

🌿 Major Luftwaffe bombing targets

⇨ Axis advances Apr 6–9

〰 Metaxas Line

▨ Axis gains by Apr 9

2 FALL OF YUGOSLAVIA APRIL 10–17, 1941

The Axis forces squeezed Yugoslavia from all sides. The city of Zagreb fell on April 10 and the Yugoslav state of Croatia declared its independence—and its support for Italy. The Italians secured the coast of Yugoslavia, their forces moving in from Italy and Albania to meet at Dubrovnik. Meanwhile the Germans occupied Belgrade on April 13 before sweeping on to capture Yugoslavia's last major city, Sarajevo, along with its Army's Supreme Command. Yugoslavia surrendered on April 17.

➡ Axis advances Apr 10–17

THE EXPANSION OF THE TRIPARTITE PACT

On September 27, 1940, Germany, Italy (including Albania), and Japan had signed a defense alliance known as the Tripartite Pact. Unwilling to become embroiled in a war in the notoriously complex Balkan region, Hitler sought the support of the Balkan countries through diplomacy, and by the end of November 1940, Hungary, Romania, and Slovakia had all joined the Pact. Bulgaria joined on March 1, 1941. Threatened by the German, Hungarian, and Italian troops building up along its borders, Yugoslavia joined the pact on March 25. But on March 27, Yugoslavia revoked, forcing Germany to expand its invasion plans.

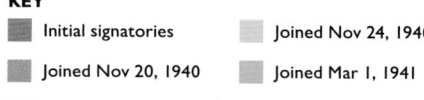

KEY

▓ Initial signatories	▨ Joined Nov 24, 1940
▓ Joined Nov 20, 1940	▨ Joined Mar 1, 1941
▓ Joined Nov 23, 1940	▨ Joined Mar 25, 1941

Jul 24, 1923 Turkey cedes Rhodes and Dodecanese Islands to Italy in treaty of Lausanne.

Apr 11–12 The Hungarian Army overruns part of northern Yugoslavia, which is then annexed by Hungary.

Hungarian 3rd Army

German XLI Panzer Corps

Apr 6 The German XIV Panzer Corps invades from Bulgaria; it reaches Belgrade on April 12.

Apr 17 The Yugoslav government is evacuated to Athens, before moving to London.

Italian 9th Army

Italian 11th Army

German XIV Panzer Corps

German 12th Army

German XL Motorized Corps

Greek 2nd Army

Greek 1st Army

British W Force

Apr 9 Trapped by the fall of Salonika, the Greek 2nd Army surrenders.

Apr 25 German paratroopers land in Corinth.

Apr 6–7 Piraeus is virtually destroyed by Luftwaffe bombing raids and the explosion of the British ammunition ship *Clan Fraser*.

THE AXIS CAMPAIGN IN THE BALKANS

Axis forces swiftly overwhelmed Yugoslavia and Greece in April 1941. The British were forced to retreat to Crete, leaving the entire Balkans in Axis hands.

KEY

▨ Axis territories, Apr 6, 1941		◣ Axis armies	◣ Allied armies

TIMELINE

1
2
3
4

APR 1, 1941   APR 15   MAY 1

△ Athens falls
German soldiers ride a Stug III assault gun in Athens, with the ruins of the Acropolis visible in the background. The first German forces—motorcycle troops—entered the city on April 27, 1941, and were followed by armor and infantry.

3 GREECE OVERRUN
APRIL 10–27, 1941

With the Germans threatening their rear from Monastir, the British W Force began to withdraw from the defensive Aliakmon Line on April 10, and pulled back to Mount Olympus. Over the next two weeks, the German forces pushed farther south, driving a wedge between W Force and the Greek 1st Army in Albania; by this time, the Italians had also retaken their Albanian territories. The Greek 1st Army surrendered on April 20.

┅┅┅ Aliakmon Line	•••• W Force position Apr 16
→ Axis advances Apr 10–27	

4 THE BRITISH EVACUATION
APRIL 20–28, 1941

Facing the advancing German forces alone, the British made plans to evacuate. W Force fell back to Thermopylae, where its commander, Lieutenant-General Henry Maitland Wilson, planned to fight a rearguard action to protect the withdrawing troops. Evacuations to Crete began on April 22. Three days later, German paratroopers landed at the Corinth Canal and crossed to Patras, driving the last Allied forces from the Peloponnesus.

⇢ British evacuation routes Apr 22–28	German paratrooper assault May 25
⚓ Main evacuation ports	

1 CRISIS IN IRAQ APRIL 1–MAY 6, 1941

On April 1, 1941, Iraq's pro-German prime minister, Rashid Ali, seized power. Determined to retain access to Iraq's oil, Britain landed the forces of the 10th Indian Division at Basra. Such a concentration of troops around Basra was not allowed under the terms of the Anglo–Iraqi Treaty (1930), and on April 30 Iraqi troops advanced on the RAF base at Habbaniyah, demanding an end to all British troop movements on the ground and in the air.

- Oil fields
- Oil pipelines
- RAF bases
- 10th Indian Division landings Apr 18–May 6
- Iraqi advance Apr 30

2 THE BRITISH TAKE CONTROL IN IRAQ MAY 2–30, 1941

The British responded by launching air strikes on the Iraqi forces on May 2. More Indian troops landed at Basra and an invading force—Habforce—set out from Palestine. It reached Habbaniyah on May 18, capturing Fallujah the next day. On May 27, Habforce and the forces at Basra advanced on Baghdad. Rashid Ali fled to Iran and, on May 30, an armistice was signed that restored the pro-British government of the Prince Regent Abd al-Ilah.

- Habforce advance on Habbaniyah May 11–18
- Allied advance on Baghdad May 27–30

3 FREE FRENCH AND BRITISH INVASION OF SYRIA AND LEBANON JUNE 8–JULY 12, 1941

On June 8, the British and Free French invaded Vichy French-controlled Syria and Lebanon to prevent the Germans using them as bases for attacks on Egypt. Troops moved in from Palestine, Transjordan, and Iraq, but hopes that the Vichy forces would capitulate faded as they put up strong resistance. By July 10, Damascus had fallen and the Allies were closing on Beirut, and the Vichy French sought an armistice. Fighting ceased on July 12.

- British forces advance Jun 8–Jul 12
- Free French advance Jun 8–Jul 12

CONFLICTS IN THE MIDDLE EAST

In 1941, the Allies moved swiftly to secure their access to resources in the Middle East and prevent Axis forces from gaining control of this oil-rich region.

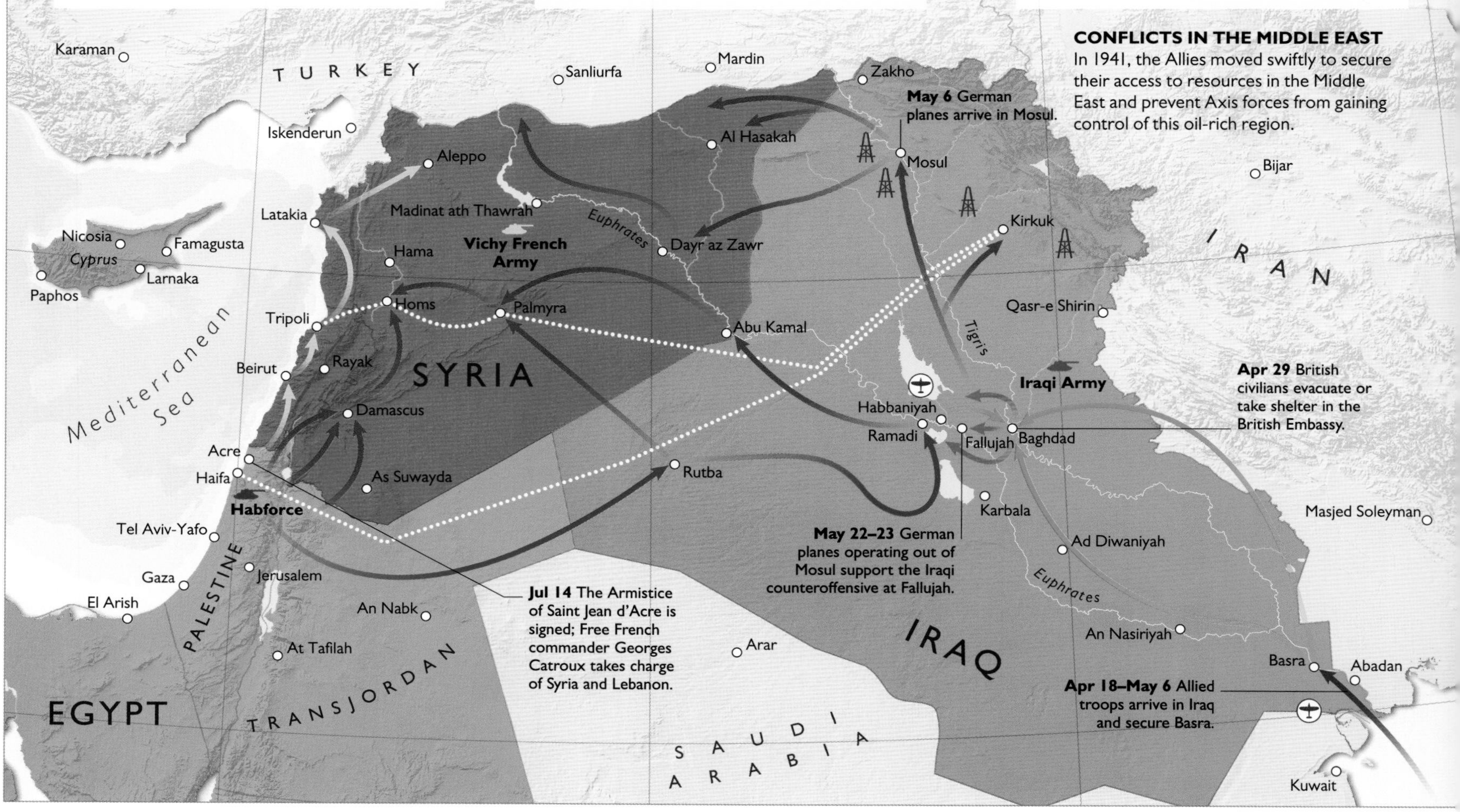

Karaman
TURKEY
Sanliurfa
Mardin
Zakho
May 6 German planes arrive in Mosul.
Iskenderun
Al Hasakah
Mosul
Aleppo
Bijar
Madinat ath Thawrah
Euphrates
Latakia
Nicosia
Famagusta
Cyprus
Larnaka
Paphos
Hama
Vichy French Army
Dayr az Zawr
Kirkuk
IRAN
Homs
Palmyra
Tripoli
Qasr-e Shirin
Abu Kamal
Tigris
Mediterranean Sea
Beirut
Rayak
SYRIA
Iraqi Army
Apr 29 British civilians evacuate or take shelter in the British Embassy.
Damascus
Habbaniyah
Ramadi
Fallujah
Baghdad
Acre
Haifa
As Suwayda
Rutba
Habforce
Karbala
Masjed Soleyman
Tel Aviv-Yafo
May 22–23 German planes operating out of Mosul support the Iraqi counteroffensive at Fallujah.
Ad Diwaniyah
Gaza
Jerusalem
PALESTINE
Euphrates
El Arish
An Nabk
Jul 14 The Armistice of Saint Jean d'Acre is signed; Free French commander Georges Catroux takes charge of Syria and Lebanon.
At Tafilah
Arar
IRAQ
An Nasiriyah
Basra
Abadan
EGYPT
TRANSJORDAN
Apr 18–May 6 Allied troops arrive in Iraq and secure Basra.
SAUDI ARABIA
Kuwait

THE ALLIES SECURE THE MIDDLE EAST

Between April and July 1941, Allied ground forces—supported by squadrons from the Royal Air Force and the Royal Australian Air Force—took control of Vichy Syria, Lebanon, and Iraq, creating a bloc that offered access to oil and protection for their other territories in the region.

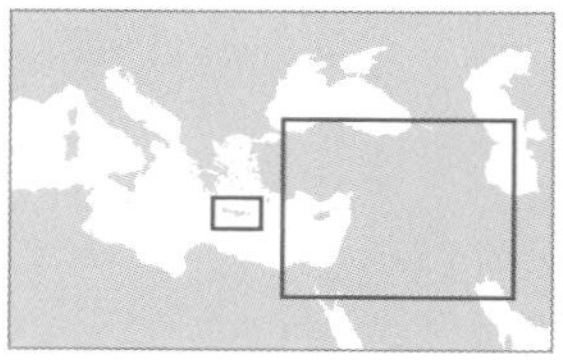

KEY

- British-controlled territory
- Axis-controlled territory
- Pro-Axis territory
- Vichy French Army
- British and Commonwealth forces
- Iraqi Army

TIMELINE

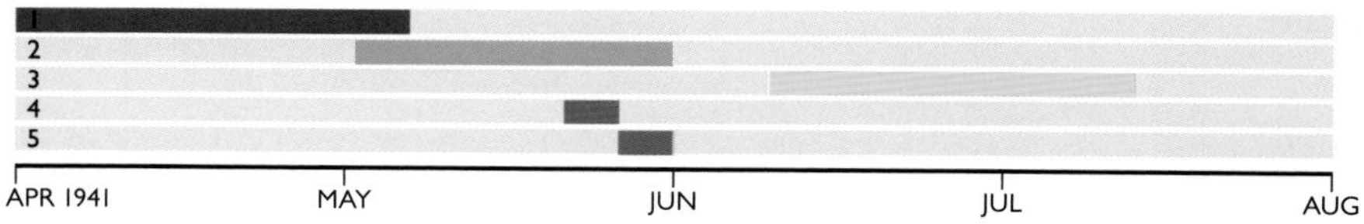

1
2
3
4
5
APR 1941
MAY
JUN
JUL
AUG

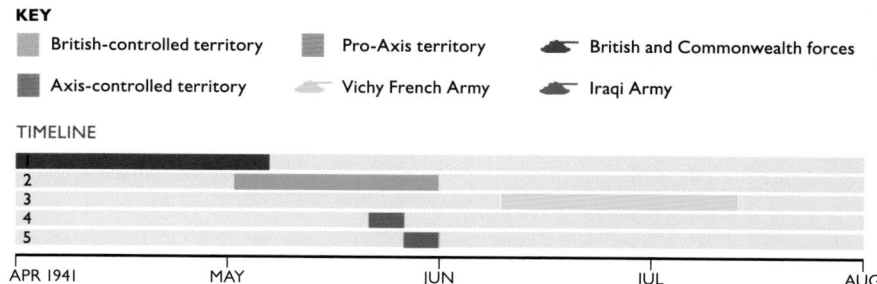

△ **British troops captured**
British troops surrender during the German invasion of Crete in May 1941. Code named Operation Mercury, the invasion involved the mass deployment of *Fallschirmjäger* (paratroopers).

THE MIDDLE EAST AND EASTERN MEDITERRANEAN

In 1941 the Allies faced a series of challenges that ended with Axis powers dominating the eastern Mediterranean. However, the Allies strengthened their position in the Middle East, securing oil and supply routes from Iraq to the USSR that would prove invaluable in the months to come.

The Allies experienced mixed fortunes in the Middle East and east Mediterranean in the first half of 1941. They were chased out of Greece by the German advance in April (see pp.80–81) and suffered a further humiliation in Crete in May. There, they were ousted by a surprise airborne assault, despite having known that the Germans had planned to invade since April. The loss of Crete deprived the Allied forces of around 16,000 men—either dead or captured—and cost the Royal Navy nine ships, with another 13 damaged. It was followed by more failure, when a British attempt to relieve Tobruk

in North Africa in June ended in disaster. Yet Hitler failed to capitalize on the dominance of the Mediterranean that the Axis powers had won through the conquest of the Balkans and Crete, and their success in North Africa. Instead, the Germans turned their attention to the Soviet Union.

The Allies were left to consolidate the gains they had begun to make in the Middle East. By mid-June, they had wrested control of Iraq from its pro-German leader, Rashid Ali, and had launched a successful invasion of Vichy-held Syria.

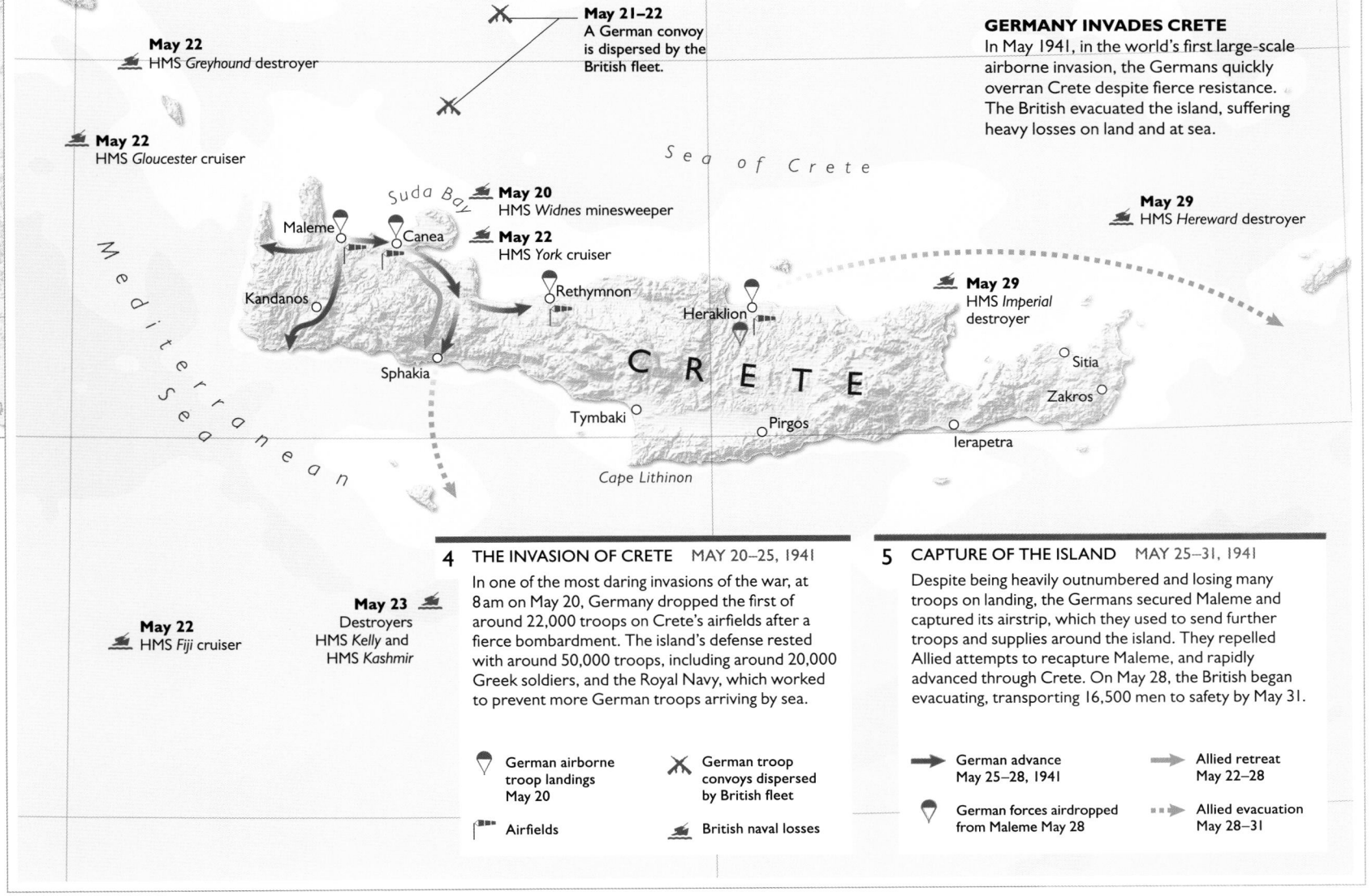

May 22
HMS *Greyhound* destroyer

May 21–22
A German convoy is dispersed by the British fleet.

May 22
HMS *Gloucester* cruiser

GERMANY INVADES CRETE
In May 1941, in the world's first large-scale airborne invasion, the Germans quickly overran Crete despite fierce resistance. The British evacuated the island, suffering heavy losses on land and at sea.

Sea of Crete

May 20
HMS *Widnes* minesweeper

May 22
HMS *York* cruiser

May 29
HMS *Hereward* destroyer

May 29
HMS *Imperial* destroyer

Suda Bay

Maleme — Canea

Kandanos

Rethymnon

Heraklion

Sitia

Zakros

Mediterranean Sea

Sphakia

Tymbaki

Pirgos

Ierapetra

C R E T E

Cape Lithinon

May 22
HMS *Fiji* cruiser

May 23
Destroyers
HMS *Kelly* and
HMS *Kashmir*

4 THE INVASION OF CRETE MAY 20–25, 1941
In one of the most daring invasions of the war, at 8am on May 20, Germany dropped the first of around 22,000 troops on Crete's airfields after a fierce bombardment. The island's defense rested with around 50,000 troops, including around 20,000 Greek soldiers, and the Royal Navy, which worked to prevent more German troops arriving by sea.

5 CAPTURE OF THE ISLAND MAY 25–31, 1941
Despite being heavily outnumbered and losing many troops on landing, the Germans secured Maleme and captured its airstrip, which they used to send further troops and supplies around the island. They repelled Allied attempts to recapture Maleme, and rapidly advanced through Crete. On May 28, the British began evacuating, transporting 16,500 men to safety by May 31.

⚲ German airborne troop landings May 20

✕ German troop convoys dispersed by British fleet

⌐▪▪ Airfields

⚓ British naval losses

➡ German advance May 25–28, 1941

⚲ German forces airdropped from Maleme May 28

⇨ Allied retreat May 22–28

▪▪▶ Allied evacuation May 28–31

Celeken

Caspian Sea

WAR IN THE MEDITERRANEAN

From Italy's entry into World War II until 1943, Allied and Axis forces were engaged in a naval battle for control of the Mediterranean. Each strove to destroy the other's supply lines while keeping their own open, and to inflict as much damage as possible on their enemy's ability to wage war at sea.

The Italians entered the war on June 10, 1940, with a totally modernized fleet, replete with fast new battleships, cruisers, and destroyers, which outmatched the British Royal Navy's capabilities in the Mediterranean. They harbored high ambitions in the region, wishing to oust Britain from Egypt—where British troops were stationed to protect the nation's financial and strategic interests—and extend Mussolini's "New Roman Empire" into Nice, Corsica, Tunisia, and the Balkans.

The British, meanwhile, sought to hold the three key points in the Mediterranean—Gibraltar, Malta, and the Suez Canal—that would allow them to keep open supply routes across the Mediterranean and support Greece and Turkey should they enter the war.

Malta, in particular, was crucial (see pp.86–87). Sitting at the gateway to the eastern Mediterranean, it provided a stopping point for Allied convoys and a base from which to attack the Axis supply routes to North Africa.

Air power was vital in keeping the convoys moving, and both sides were able to take advantage of the short distances from their bases in Europe and North Africa, and of the good visibility in the Mediterranean skies. The Italians, however, lacked a fleet air arm, while the British had several aircraft carriers operating in the area.

For much of the first year, the Allies had the upper hand in the Mediterranean, but in December 1941, they lost the advantage when the Italians destroyed several of their battleships.

> "This tiny island [Malta] is a vital feature in the defense of our Middle East position."
>
> HASTINGS ISMAY, BRITISH GENERAL, 1942

THE SUBMARINE WAR

British submarines played a vital role in disrupting the Axis supply lines across the Mediterranean, sinking over 440,000 tons (400,000 metric tons) of Axis shipping between January 1941 and December 1942. German U-boats joined Italian submarines in September 1941 and destroyed 12 merchant vessels, HMS *Ark Royal*, and HMS *Barham* before the end of the year. However, the U-boats were themselves in danger from the Allies' radar-equipped aircraft; none survived the war in the Mediterranean.

Destruction of HMS *Barham*

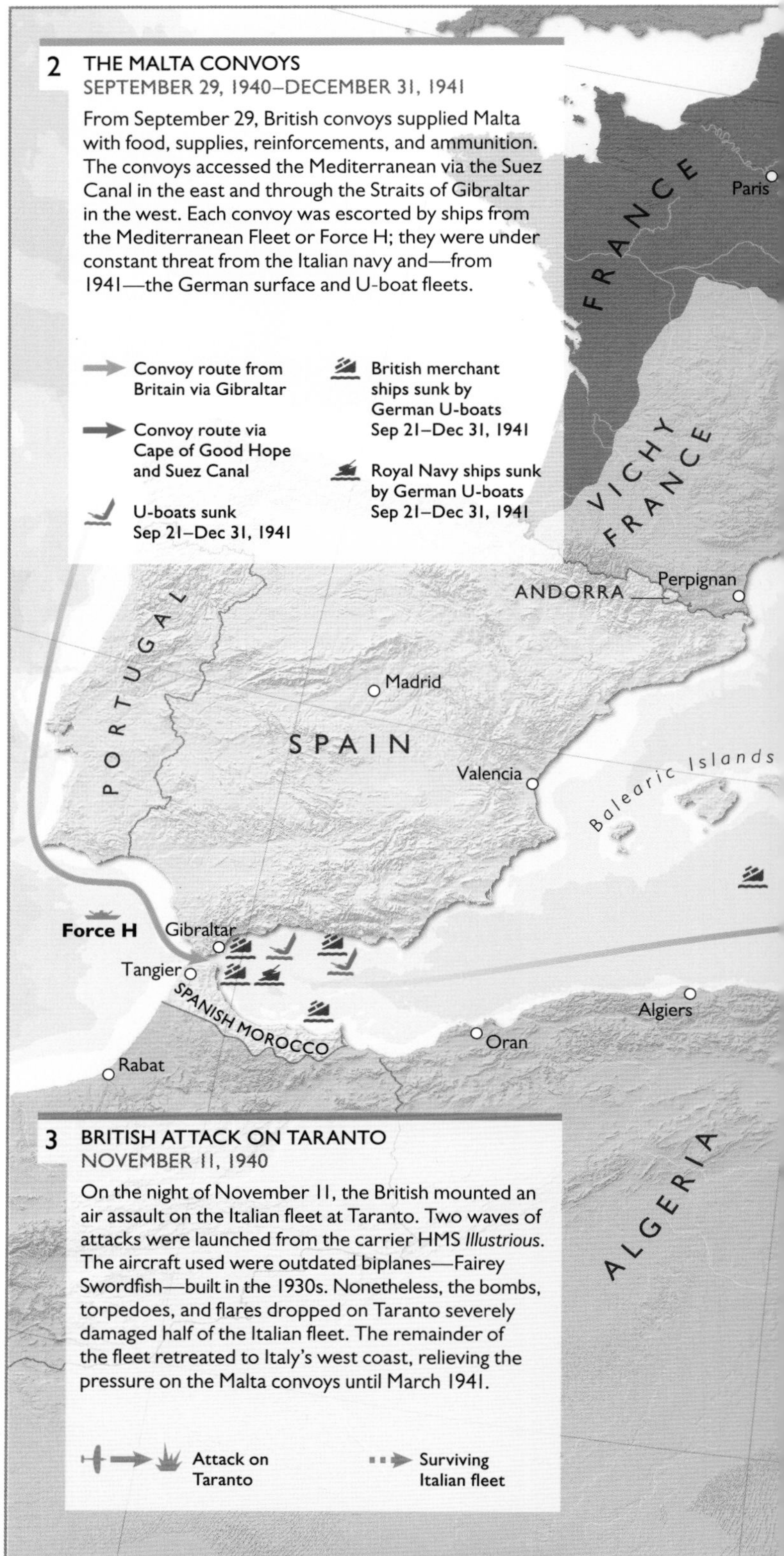

2 THE MALTA CONVOYS
SEPTEMBER 29, 1940–DECEMBER 31, 1941

From September 29, British convoys supplied Malta with food, supplies, reinforcements, and ammunition. The convoys accessed the Mediterranean via the Suez Canal in the east and through the Straits of Gibraltar in the west. Each convoy was escorted by ships from the Mediterranean Fleet or Force H; they were under constant threat from the Italian navy and—from 1941—the German surface and U-boat fleets.

- → Convoy route from Britain via Gibraltar
- → Convoy route via Cape of Good Hope and Suez Canal
- ↙ U-boats sunk Sep 21–Dec 31, 1941
- ↙ British merchant ships sunk by German U-boats Sep 21–Dec 31, 1941
- ↙ Royal Navy ships sunk by German U-boats Sep 21–Dec 31, 1941

3 BRITISH ATTACK ON TARANTO
NOVEMBER 11, 1940

On the night of November 11, the British mounted an air assault on the Italian fleet at Taranto. Two waves of attacks were launched from the carrier HMS *Illustrious*. The aircraft used were outdated biplanes—Fairey Swordfish—built in the 1930s. Nonetheless, the bombs, torpedoes, and flares dropped on Taranto severely damaged half of the Italian fleet. The remainder of the fleet retreated to Italy's west coast, relieving the pressure on the Malta convoys until March 1941.

- ⊹→ Attack on Taranto
- ⋯▶ Surviving Italian fleet

◁ **Air support**
A Fairey Swordfish biplane banks as it prepares to land on the British aircraft carrier HMS *Ark Royal*.

1 THE BATTLE OF THE MEDITERRANEAN BEGINS
JUNE 11–NOVEMBER 11, 1940

The Italians began the Battle of the Mediterranean with a bombing raid on Malta on June 11, and the British scored their first hit when they sank the Italian destroyer *Espero*, which was escorting a convoy to Benghazi on June 28. The first major clash between the Italian and British fleets occurred on July 9 at the Battle of Calabria. Neither side scored a decisive victory, and both avoided further large-scale action until November.

Italian bombing raid on Malta, Jun 11, 1940

British attack on Italian convoy

NAVAL BATTLES

The Mediterranean was the site of the largest conventional sea battles of the war outside the Pacific theater, as the British Royal Navy fought the Italian and German fleets for control of the convoy routes taking vital supplies and reinforcements to North Africa.

KEY

Areas controlled by Vichy France, 1940

Areas controlled by Italy, 1940

Areas under British influence, 1940

Areas controlled by Germany, 1940

Neutral / not yet involved in the war

Borders, Dec 1940

Major battles

British fleets

Italian fleet

TIMELINE

1, 2, 3, 4, 5, 6

JAN 1940   JUL   JAN 1941   JUL   JAN 1942

Italian fleet

9 Jul 1940 Calabria

Nov 27, 1941 Battle of Cape Spartivento; the Italians attack a convoy en route to Malta.

Nov 8–9, 1941 Battle of Duisburg Convoy; the Royal Navy sinks all seven merchant ships and a destroyer in a German convoy.

28–29 Mar 1941 Cape Matapan

Duisberg Convoy

Dec 13, 1941 Battle of Cape Bon; two Italian cruisers carrying supplies to the Luftwaffe in North Africa are sunk.

Mediterranean Fleet

Nov 25, 1941 HMS *Barham* is hit and sunk by three torpedoes; 862 die and 449 survive.

4 BATTLE OF CAPE MATAPAN
MARCH 28–29, 1941

On March 28, the Italians sent a small fleet to Crete to intercept British convoys that were carrying troops to Greece. However, the RAF spotted the Italian ships, and the British Mediterranean Fleet moved in from Alexandria and opened fire on their enemy. The battle lasted into the night, and the British sank three Italian cruisers, two destroyers, and damaged the battleship *Vittorio Veneto* in a significant victory, after which the Italian fleet avoided major battles.

→ Allied troop convoys to Greece

5 STRIKING THE AXIS CONVOYS
APRIL–DECEMBER 1941

The nine warships lost to the Luftwaffe during the defense and evacuation of Crete (see pp.82–83) in May 1941 highlighted just how vulnerable the British navy was in the eastern Mediterranean. However, the Allies continued to strengthen their position in the central Mediterranean, making several successful attacks on Axis convoys—particularly in the Battles of the Duisburg Convoy and Cape Bon—that left the Axis powers in North Africa short of fuel.

→ Axis convoy routes

6 THE AXIS POWERS IN THE ASCENDANT
DECEMBER 19–31, 1941

The Allies suffered a setback when ships returning to Alexandria ran into a minefield off the coast of Tripoli on December 19. Two ships were sunk and two were badly damaged, reducing the Allies' ability to threaten the Axis convoys. Later that day, the Italians disabled two battleships and damaged a destroyer in Alexandria harbor. While the Royal Navy recovered, the Italian fleet dominated the central and eastern Mediterranean.

✹ Italian minefield

Raid on Alexandria Dec 19, 1941

THE SIEGE OF MALTA

The British colony of Malta was strategically important to the Allies, who used the island as a base to attack the Axis forces' supply lines in the central Mediterranean. As a result, neutralizing the island became an Axis priority.

△ **Courage recognized**
Britain's King George VI awarded the George Cross to Malta in April 1942, in recognition of the population's remarkable bravery.

Following Mussolini's declaration of war on Britain on June 10, 1940, the Italian air force launched their first attacks on Malta. The capital city of Valletta, including its port (known as the Grand Harbor), and Hal Far (one of Malta's three airfields) were blitzed. The Luftwaffe soon joined the assault with further aerial bombing.

Starvation threat

The siege reached its climax in spring 1942, when the Germans decided to bomb and starve the island into submission. Food, fuel, and other essentials ran short as convoys trying to reach Valletta were decimated. Facing almost continual air raids, the islanders were housed in caves and tunnels that could withstand bombs, which helped them survive the repeated attacks. Eventually the Allies broke through Axis lines in August 1942 and delivered supplies to the besieged island. Operation Pedestal, as this convoy was known, suffered heavy casualties, but Malta was saved. By the time the siege ended in November 1942, the Axis air forces had attacked the island 3,343 times, winning Malta the unwanted distinction of being the most bombed place on Earth.

△ **Italian air attack on Malta**
An Italian Savoia-Marchetti SM.81 tri-motor bomber makes its bomb run over Malta's Grand Harbor naval base, in Valletta. The *Regia Aeronautica* (Italian air force) had 350 bombers ready for action only 20 minutes' flying time away from the island.

Under fire
Naval officers and ratings line the deck of the light cruiser HMS *Penelope*, moored in the Grand Harbor, Valletta. The ship's starboard side was so severely cratered by bomb splinters that the crew nicknamed the cruiser HMS *Pepperpot*.

GERMANY'S WAR WITH THE USSR

Hitler's invasion of the Soviet Union in June 1941 transformed the scale of the war in Europe. Despite putting almost four million soldiers into battle, the Germans failed to achieve the rapid victory they had hoped for.

△ **Soviet armor**
First deployed in 1941, the Soviet T-34 tank proved possibly the most effective armored vehicle of World War II. Over 60,000 were manufactured during the war.

In August 1939, Stalin made a nonaggression pact with Hitler. This allowed the Soviets to extend their territory westward—through the partition of Poland with Nazi Germany, and the occupation of Estonia, Lithuania, Latvia, and Bukovina, taken from Germany's ally Romania. Although Stalin behaved as a friendly neutral to Germany, providing vital supplies that sustained the German war effort, the Soviet economy and the Red Army were meanwhile being mobilized for war.

Planning Operation Barbarossa

For Hitler, no agreement with the Soviet Union could ever be other than temporary. His enduring hostility to Marxism, his belief in the racial inferiority of Slavs, and his aspiration to find *Lebensraum* ("room to live") for German settlers in the East made the Soviet Union a target for aggression. In December 1940, despite still being at war with Britain, Hitler decided to invade the Soviet Union, in a campaign known as Operation Barbarossa. The planning made plain the Nazis' intention to carry out mass murder of civilians, through killing squads and deliberate starvation. Joining the German forces were the armies of its allies, such as Romania, Hungary, and Italy, as well as ideologically motivated anticommunist volunteers from other countries, including France, Spain, and Portugal.

◁ **Ruthless warfare**
German infantry employ a flamethrower to clear a bunker during the invasion of the USSR in 1941. German soldiers had orders to fight especially fiercely against the Red Army.

GERMANY INVADES THE EAST

Invading the Soviet Union, Hitler's armies sought to destroy Stalin's Red Army in a series of massive encirclements. But German victories at Smolensk and Kiev, in which hundreds of thousands of Soviet soldiers were taken prisoner, failed to end Soviet resistance. Stopped outside Moscow in December, the Germans were driven back by a Soviet counteroffensive, but they were still in control of a vast area of Soviet territory, from the gates of Leningrad to the Crimea.

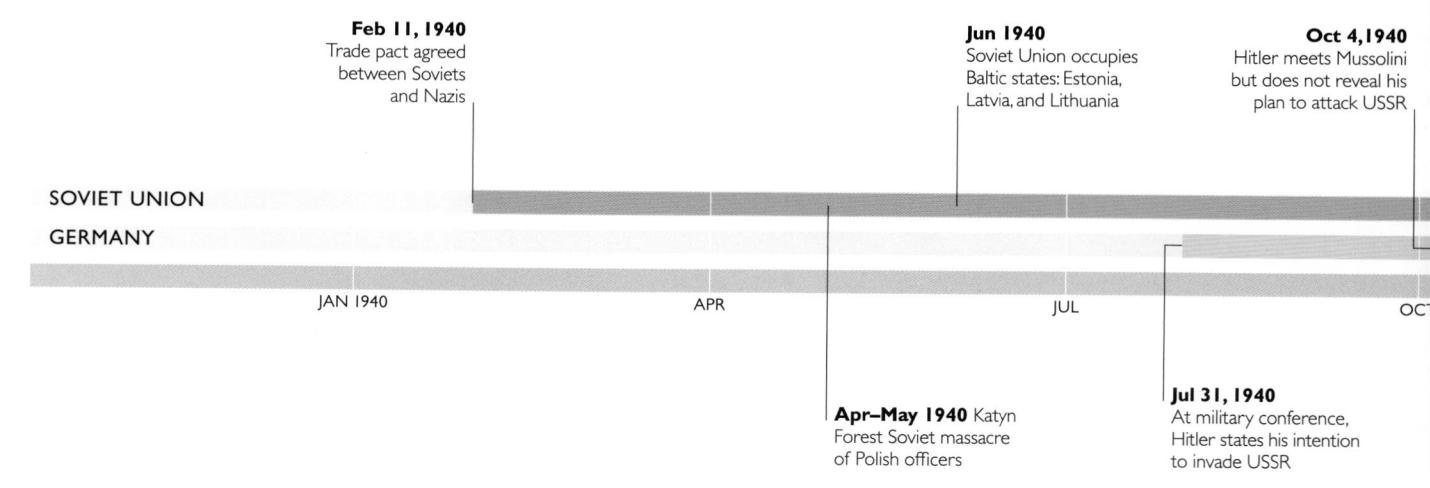

Feb 11, 1940 Trade pact agreed between Soviets and Nazis

Jun 1940 Soviet Union occupies Baltic states: Estonia, Latvia, and Lithuania

Oct 4, 1940 Hitler meets Mussolini but does not reveal his plan to attack USSR

SOVIET UNION

GERMANY

JAN 1940   APR   JUL   OC

Apr–May 1940 Katyn Forest Soviet massacre of Polish officers

Jul 31, 1940 At military conference, Hitler states his intention to invade USSR

◁ **Russian winter**
The Wehrmacht experienced great difficulty in coping with the extreme winter conditions encountered in the Soviet Union. In December 1941, a German officer recorded temperatures of –36.5°F (–38°C) outside Moscow.

Early successes for Germany

In 1941, the Soviet Union was not in a very strong military position. The world's first Communist state had achieved rapid industrialization under its dictator Joseph Stalin, but in 1937–1938, during Stalin's "Great Purge" campaign, a substantial percentage of senior Soviet army officers had been denounced as traitors and were shot, imprisoned, or dismissed. The Red Army's mediocre performance in the Winter War against Finland in 1939–1940 had confirmed suspicions that, despite its large size, the army might suffer from poor morale and leadership. Stalin's brutal rule had certainly alienated many of the Soviet people, especially in Ukraine, where a famine killed millions in the 1930s.

Despite ample warnings of an imminent invasion, Stalin's forces were not well deployed when the blow struck in June 1941. The first few months after the launch of Operation Barbarossa brought a series of catastrophic defeats for the Red Army, and Leningrad was placed under siege. The Germans were initially welcomed as liberators in many areas, such as Lithuania and western Ukraine, but brutal mistreatment soon alienated local populations.

The tide turns

After its initial panic, the Soviet regime held together, shifting its heavy industry eastward out of the invaders' reach, and using ruthless measures to compel its soldiers to fight in desperate counterattacks. They also received military supplies from the Allied forces. The Red Army held out against Germany in Moscow, thwarting Hitler's plans

> *"Communism is a colossal danger for our future …*
> *This is a war of annihilation."*
>
> ADOLF HITLER, SPEECH TO HIS SENIOR OFFICERS, MARCH 30, 1941

to take the capital within four months. By the time winter had set in, the German army had been significantly weakened and were ill-equipped to stand the perishingly cold weather conditions. A spirit of determination set in among the Soviet people. Meanwhile, in Germany, as the army's casualty list lengthened, civilian morale for the first time showed signs of wavering.

▽ **Prisoners of war**
During Operation Barbarossa over two million Soviet soldiers were taken prisoner. Few survived captivity, most dying of starvation, maltreatment, exposure, and disease.

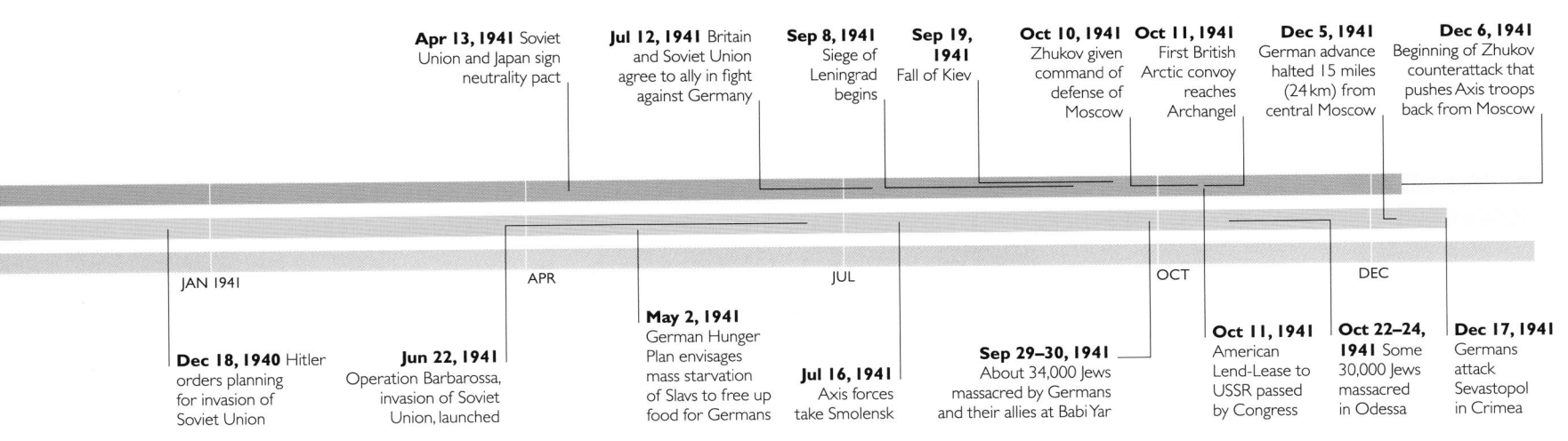

Apr 13, 1941 Soviet Union and Japan sign neutrality pact

Jul 12, 1941 Britain and Soviet Union agree to ally in fight against Germany

Sep 8, 1941 Siege of Leningrad begins

Sep 19, 1941 Fall of Kiev

Oct 10, 1941 Zhukov given command of defense of Moscow

Oct 11, 1941 First British Arctic convoy reaches Archangel

Dec 5, 1941 German advance halted 15 miles (24 km) from central Moscow

Dec 6, 1941 Beginning of Zhukov counterattack that pushes Axis troops back from Moscow

JAN 1941   APR   JUL   OCT   DEC

Dec 18, 1940 Hitler orders planning for invasion of Soviet Union

Jun 22, 1941 Operation Barbarossa, invasion of Soviet Union, launched

May 2, 1941 German Hunger Plan envisages mass starvation of Slavs to free up food for Germans

Jul 16, 1941 Axis forces take Smolensk

Sep 29–30, 1941 About 34,000 Jews massacred by Germans and their allies at Babi Yar

Oct 11, 1941 American Lend-Lease to USSR passed by Congress

Oct 22–24, 1941 Some 30,000 Jews massacred in Odessa

Dec 17, 1941 Germans attack Sevastopol in Crimea

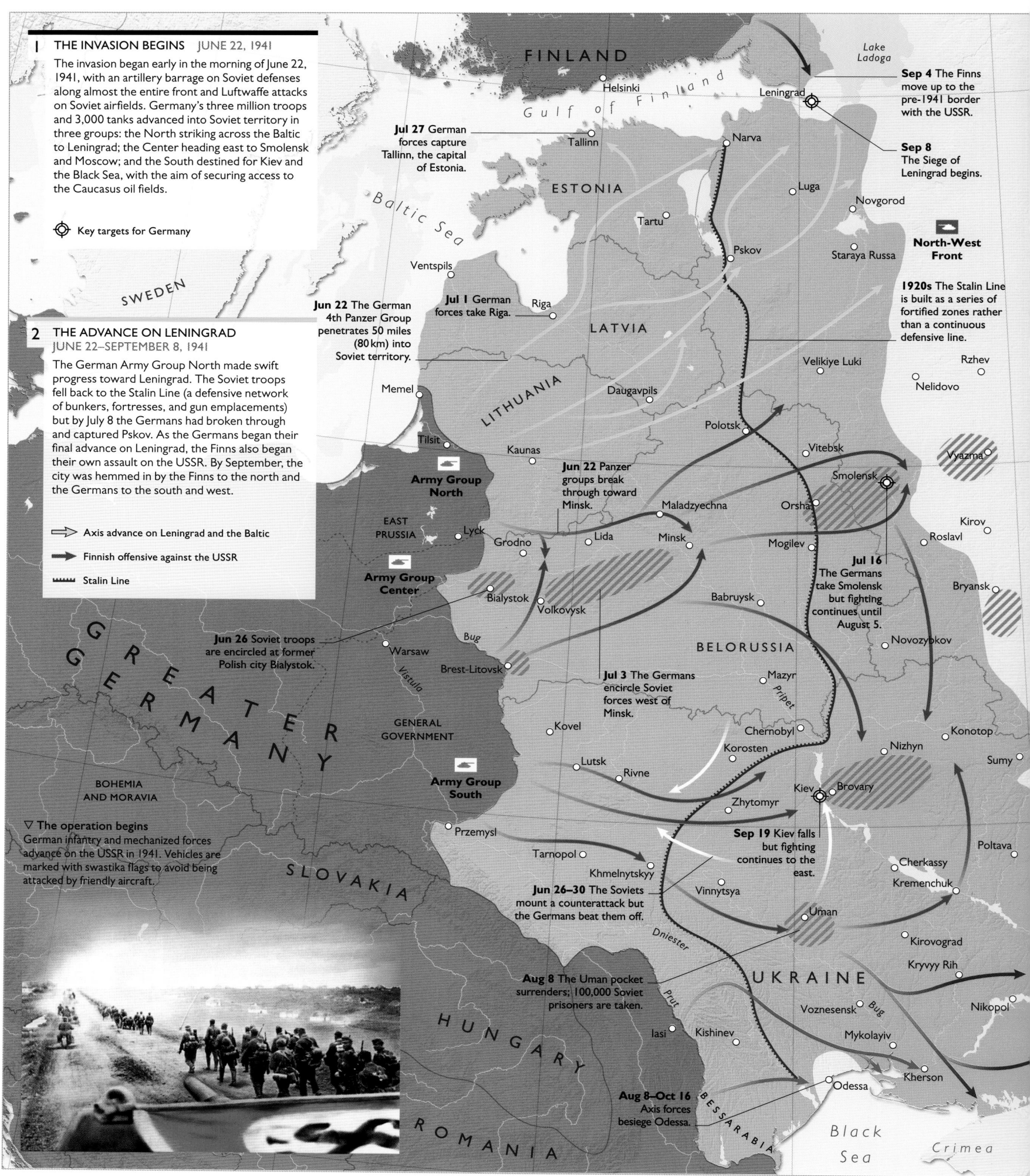

1 THE INVASION BEGINS JUNE 22, 1941

The invasion began early in the morning of June 22, 1941, with an artillery barrage on Soviet defenses along almost the entire front and Luftwaffe attacks on Soviet airfields. Germany's three million troops and 3,000 tanks advanced into Soviet territory in three groups: the North striking across the Baltic to Leningrad; the Center heading east to Smolensk and Moscow; and the South destined for Kiev and the Black Sea, with the aim of securing access to the Caucasus oil fields.

◎ Key targets for Germany

2 THE ADVANCE ON LENINGRAD
JUNE 22–SEPTEMBER 8, 1941

The German Army Group North made swift progress toward Leningrad. The Soviet troops fell back to the Stalin Line (a defensive network of bunkers, fortresses, and gun emplacements) but by July 8 the Germans had broken through and captured Pskov. As the Germans began their final advance on Leningrad, the Finns also began their own assault on the USSR. By September, the city was hemmed in by the Finns to the north and the Germans to the south and west.

⇨ Axis advance on Leningrad and the Baltic

➤ Finnish offensive against the USSR

〰 Stalin Line

▽ The operation begins
German infantry and mechanized forces advance on the USSR in 1941. Vehicles are marked with swastika flags to avoid being attacked by friendly aircraft.

Sep 4 The Finns move up to the pre-1941 border with the USSR.

Sep 8 The Siege of Leningrad begins.

Jul 27 German forces capture Tallinn, the capital of Estonia.

North-West Front

Jun 22 The German 4th Panzer Group penetrates 50 miles (80 km) into Soviet territory.

Jul 1 German forces take Riga.

1920s The Stalin Line is built as a series of fortified zones rather than a continuous defensive line.

Jun 22 Panzer groups break through toward Minsk.

Jul 16 The Germans take Smolensk but fighting continues until August 5.

Army Group North

Army Group Center

Jun 26 Soviet troops are encircled at former Polish city Bialystok.

Jul 3 The Germans encircle Soviet forces west of Minsk.

Army Group South

Sep 19 Kiev falls but fighting continues to the east.

Jun 26–30 The Soviets mount a counterattack but the Germans beat them off.

Aug 8 The Uman pocket surrenders; 100,000 Soviet prisoners are taken.

Aug 8–Oct 16 Axis forces besiege Odessa.

Map labels

FINLAND · Lake Ladoga · Helsinki · Gulf of Finland · Leningrad · Narva · Tallinn · ESTONIA · Luga · Novgorod · Tartu · Staraya Russa · Pskov · Ventspils · Baltic Sea · SWEDEN · Riga · LATVIA · Velikiye Luki · Rzhev · Nelidovo · Memel · Daugavpils · LITHUANIA · Polotsk · Vitebsk · Vyazma · Kaunas · Smolensk · Tilsit · Maladzyechna · Orsha · Kirov · EAST PRUSSIA · Lyck · Grodno · Lida · Minsk · Mogilev · Roslavl · Bialystok · Volkovysk · Babruysk · BELORUSSIA · Bryansk · Warsaw · Bug · Novozybkov · Brest-Litovsk · Mazyr · Pripet · GREATER GERMANY · Kovel · Chernobyl · Konotop · Vistula · Korosten · Nizhyn · GENERAL GOVERNMENT · Lutsk · Rivne · Kiev · Brovary · Sumy · BOHEMIA AND MORAVIA · Przemysl · Zhytomyr · Poltava · Tarnopol · Cherkassy · Khmelnytskyy · Vinnytsya · Kremenchuk · SLOVAKIA · Uman · Kirovograd · Dniester · Kryvyy Rih · Prut · UKRAINE · Nikopol · HUNGARY · Voznesensk · Bug · Iasi · Kishinev · Mykolayiv · BESSARABIA · Odessa · Kherson · ROMANIA · Black Sea · Crimea

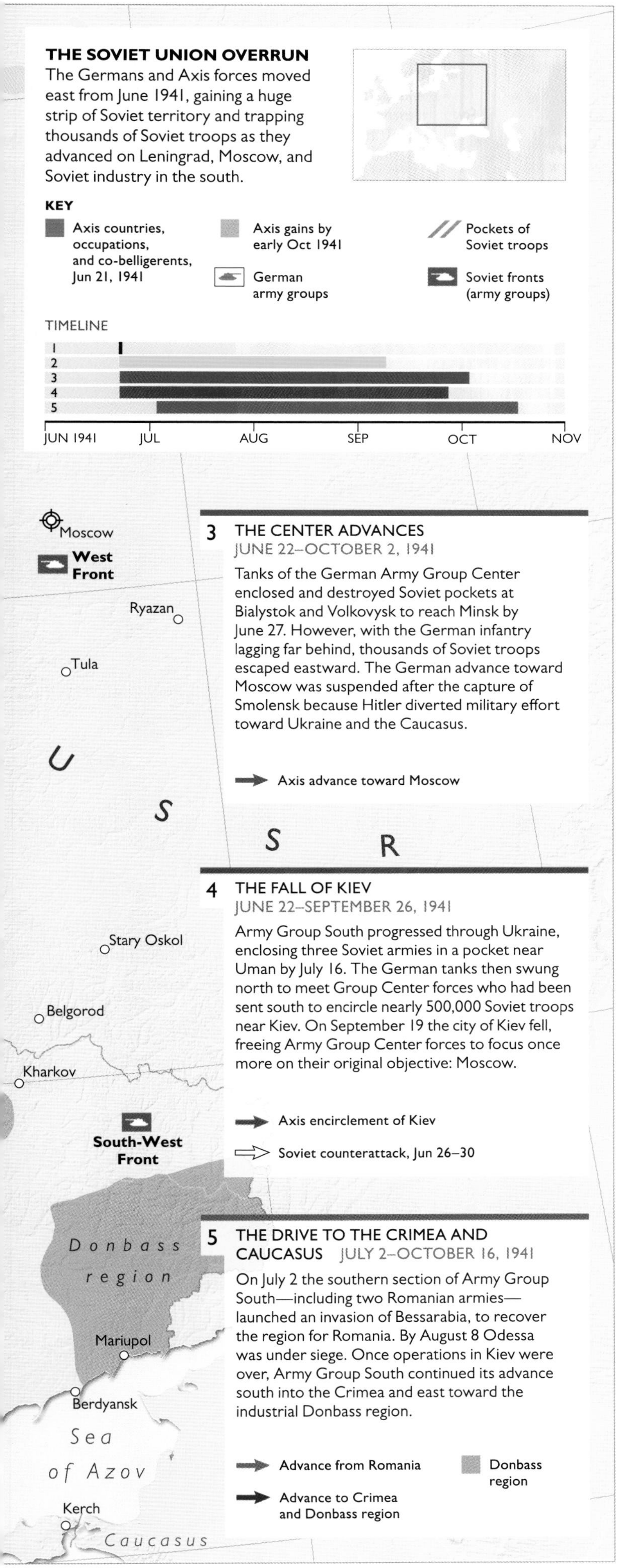

THE SOVIET UNION OVERRUN

The Germans and Axis forces moved east from June 1941, gaining a huge strip of Soviet territory and trapping thousands of Soviet troops as they advanced on Leningrad, Moscow, and Soviet industry in the south.

KEY

- ■ Axis countries, occupations, and co-belligerents, Jun 21, 1941
- ■ Axis gains by early Oct 1941
- // Pockets of Soviet troops
- ⬅ German army groups
- ◪ Soviet fronts (army groups)

TIMELINE

1
2
3
4
5

JUN 1941 — JUL — AUG — SEP — OCT — NOV

◎ Moscow
◪ **West Front**

Ryazan ○

○ Tula

U

S

S

R

3 THE CENTER ADVANCES
JUNE 22–OCTOBER 2, 1941

Tanks of the German Army Group Center enclosed and destroyed Soviet pockets at Bialystok and Volkovysk to reach Minsk by June 27. However, with the German infantry lagging far behind, thousands of Soviet troops escaped eastward. The German advance toward Moscow was suspended after the capture of Smolensk because Hitler diverted military effort toward Ukraine and the Caucasus.

➡ Axis advance toward Moscow

4 THE FALL OF KIEV
JUNE 22–SEPTEMBER 26, 1941

Army Group South progressed through Ukraine, enclosing three Soviet armies in a pocket near Uman by July 16. The German tanks then swung north to meet Group Center forces who had been sent south to encircle nearly 500,000 Soviet troops near Kiev. On September 19 the city of Kiev fell, freeing Army Group Center forces to focus once more on their original objective: Moscow.

○ Stary Oskol

○ Belgorod

○ Kharkov

◪ **South-West Front**

➡ Axis encirclement of Kiev
⇨ Soviet counterattack, Jun 26–30

Donbass region

○ Mariupol

○ Berdyansk

Sea of Azov

○ Kerch

Caucasus

5 THE DRIVE TO THE CRIMEA AND CAUCASUS JULY 2–OCTOBER 16, 1941

On July 2 the southern section of Army Group South—including two Romanian armies—launched an invasion of Bessarabia, to recover the region for Romania. By August 8 Odessa was under siege. Once operations in Kiev were over, Army Group South continued its advance south into the Crimea and east toward the industrial Donbass region.

➡ Advance from Romania
➡ Advance to Crimea and Donbass region
■ Donbass region

OPERATION BARBAROSSA

In June 1941, Hitler launched Operation Barbarossa, the invasion of Soviet territories. Ranged across a vast front that stretched 1,000 miles (1,600 km) from the Baltic to the Black Sea, Germany and its Axis allies advanced at an extraordinary pace, besieging Leningrad and reaching within striking distance of Moscow by early October.

The peace between Germany and the USSR that had been agreed in the Nazi–Soviet non-aggression pact of August 1939 (see pp.32–33) proved to be short-lived. Hitler believed the Slav people to be *Untermenschen* ("sub-humans") and wanted to take the USSR's vast territories for *Lebensraum* ("living space") for Germans. Operation Barbarossa, named after the Holy Roman Emperor who pursued German dominance in Europe, was Hitler's plan to invade the USSR with three million Germans and one million men from Axis Hungary, Romania, Slovakia, and Italy; Finland joined as a co-belligerent.

The German commanders were confident that Operation Barbarossa would be over quickly; they thought the Red Army was weak, and that German air power would provide a superior edge. The campaign did indeed start well: by July, the Germans had advanced 400 miles (640 km) and defeated large groups of Soviet forces around Minsk and Smolensk. The Red Army suffered enormous losses as Stalin refused to acknowledge the extent of the danger and willingly sacrificed men in defense of the cities.

By October, Kiev had fallen, Leningrad was surrounded with the help of the Finns (see pp.94–95), and Axis forces had reached the Crimea. However, the German troops were exhausted, their supply lines were stretched and, as they prepared to advance on Moscow, they were about to face the deadly cold of a Russian winter.

> *"The ideology that dominates us is in diametrical contradiction to that of Soviet Russia."*
>
> ADOLF HITLER, MAY 1935

STALIN'S PARANOIA AND PURGE OF THE ARMY

By the time of the German invasion in 1941, the Red Army was fatally short of experienced personnel; only a quarter of its officers had been in post for over a year. Paranoid about political opponents, Stalin had embarked on a Great Purge of the Communist party in 1936. By 1939, three of the five Marshals of the Soviet Union (right) were dead, along with hundreds of army officers.

GERMANY AND USSR AT HOME

Germany and the USSR both geared their economies to meet the demands of total war. The Soviets were more effective, manufacturing weapons that were cheaper and easier to make than those produced by the Germans.

△ **Fighting for the fatherland**
Armbands such as this were issued to members of the *Volkssturm* ("People's Militia"), a German militia formed of civilians conscripted into service.

The Soviet people suffered extreme deprivation as they fought what was christened the "Great Patriotic War." A ruthless focus on arms production meant that most civilians lived in near-starvation, working a 66-hour week while receiving half the rations of their German counterparts. At least 18 million civilians died, but a mixture of coercion, hatred for the "Fascist enemy," and Russian nationalism kept the people working.

In Germany, despite superior resources, production did not match the pace of the Soviets until the war industry was reorganized in 1942 (see pp.174–175). After this, German output rose steeply, with women playing an increasingly important role. Rationing was introduced from 1939, but privations increased from 1943 as Allied bombing raids intensified and disrupted food supplies. The civilian death toll rose, and millions were evacuated from German cities.

Dictatorships at war

The two totalitarian regimes both conducted forced population transfers. Germany imported more than 7 million civilians and prisoners of war from the occupied countries for forced labor, while the USSR transported hundreds of factories and their workers east beyond the Ural mountains to protect their war industry from the German advance in the west. Both regimes also exploited slave labor from concentration camps and gulags (Soviet prison camps).

▷ **Life goes on**
Young girls play with their dolls in a Munich street, undeterred by the shells stacked in front of their homes. As the Allied bombing raids increased in number and intensity, thousands of children were evacuated from German cities to keep them safe.

Komsomol workers' brigade
A forewoman of a Komsomol (All-Union Leninist Young Communist League) workers' brigade supervises rifle assembly at a Soviet military plant. Arms production in both the Soviet Union and Germany reached its peak in 1944.

THE SIEGE OF LENINGRAD

One of the most grueling blockades in history, the siege of Leningrad saw hundreds of thousands of civilians perish as the Germans and their Finnish allies encircled the city, bombarding and starving its people for 872 days.

The German army advanced on Leningrad in August 1941, two months after their invasion of the USSR. By September 8, the Germans in the south and the Finns in the north began closing in on the city. They severed all rail routes and land routes, cutting the city's supply lines.

In late September, Hitler changed tactics and issued orders to besiege Leningrad, to bombard and starve the people rather than accept surrender, and to raze the city to the ground. For over two years, heavy artillery fire and aerial bombing destroyed Leningrad's infrastructure, and an estimated 650,000 people died from artillery attacks, air raids, starvation, disease, and hypothermia.

Survival against the odds

Cut off from its major supply routes, Leningrad's survival depended entirely on Lake Ladoga to the northeast, the only means by which supplies could reach the city from elsewhere in the Soviet Union. Each summer, barges carried food, fuel, and munitions across the lake to the city. Each winter, when the lake froze over, provisions were driven across it on narrow and dangerous ice roads. Known as the "Road of Life," the route was also the main evacuation route for over one million civilians escaping the starving city. Soviet antiaircraft artillery and fighter planes protected the road against attack, but as the Germans regularly attacked convoys, travel was still dangerous.

Soviet forces made several attempts to break the blockade. An advance by the Leningrad and Volkhov Fronts in August–October 1942 ended in stalemate, but in Operation Iskra ("Spark") in January 1943 the Soviets broke through German lines to create a corridor to the city on the southern shore of Lake Ladoga. A railway was built in the corridor, providing faster transport than the Lake Lagoda routes. In January 1944, the Soviets finally broke the blockade. They drove out the Germans and recaptured the Moscow–Leningrad railway on January 27, ending the 872-day siege. In 1945, the city was awarded the Order of Lenin and in 1965 it was given the title the Hero City of the Soviet Union.

◁ **Attacking the city**
Soldiers of the Wehrmacht observe German attacks on Leningrad's defensive line in late 1941.

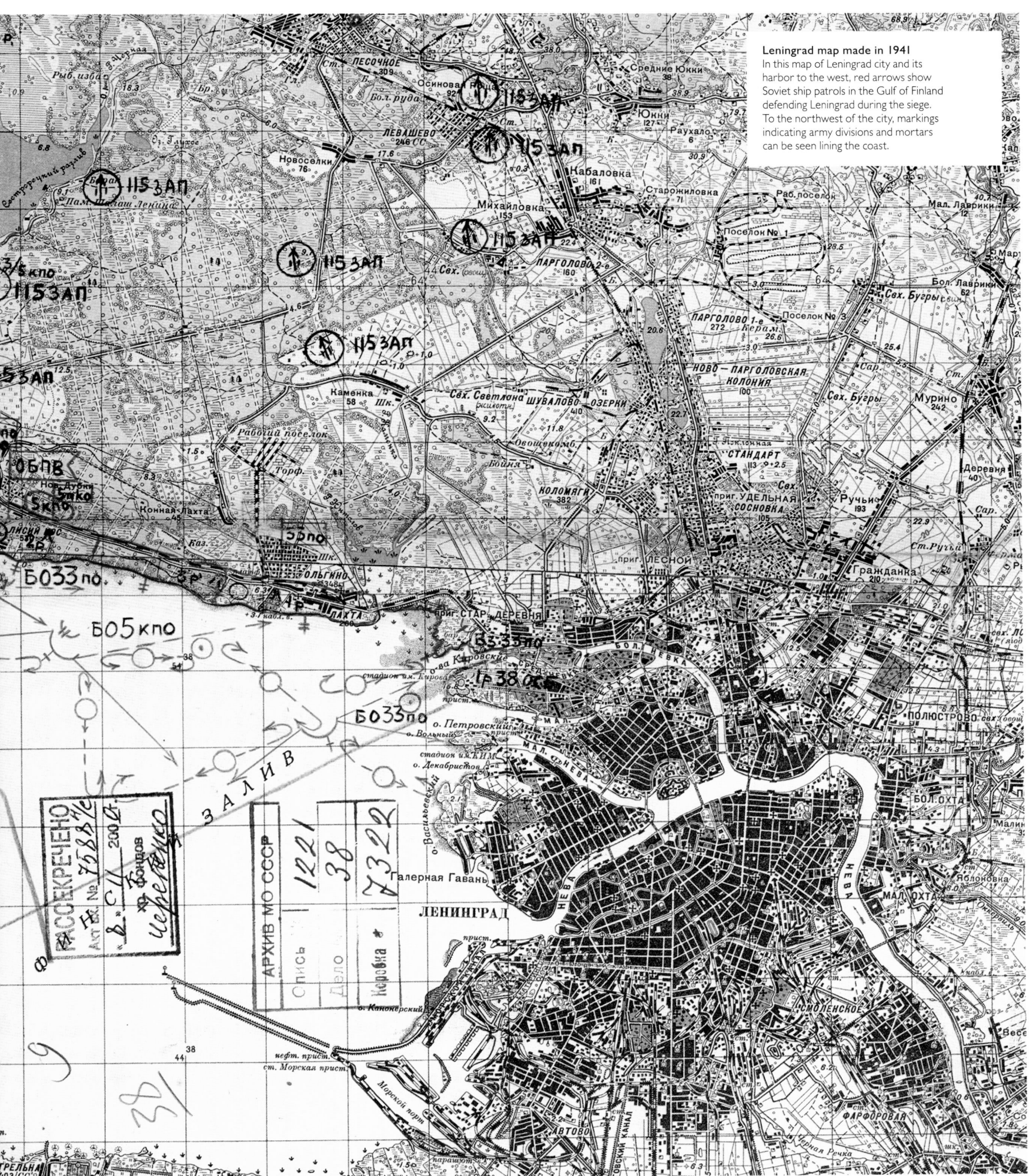

Leningrad map made in 1941
In this map of Leningrad city and its harbor to the west, red arrows show Soviet ship patrols in the Gulf of Finland defending Leningrad during the siege. To the northwest of the city, markings indicating army divisions and mortars can be seen lining the coast.

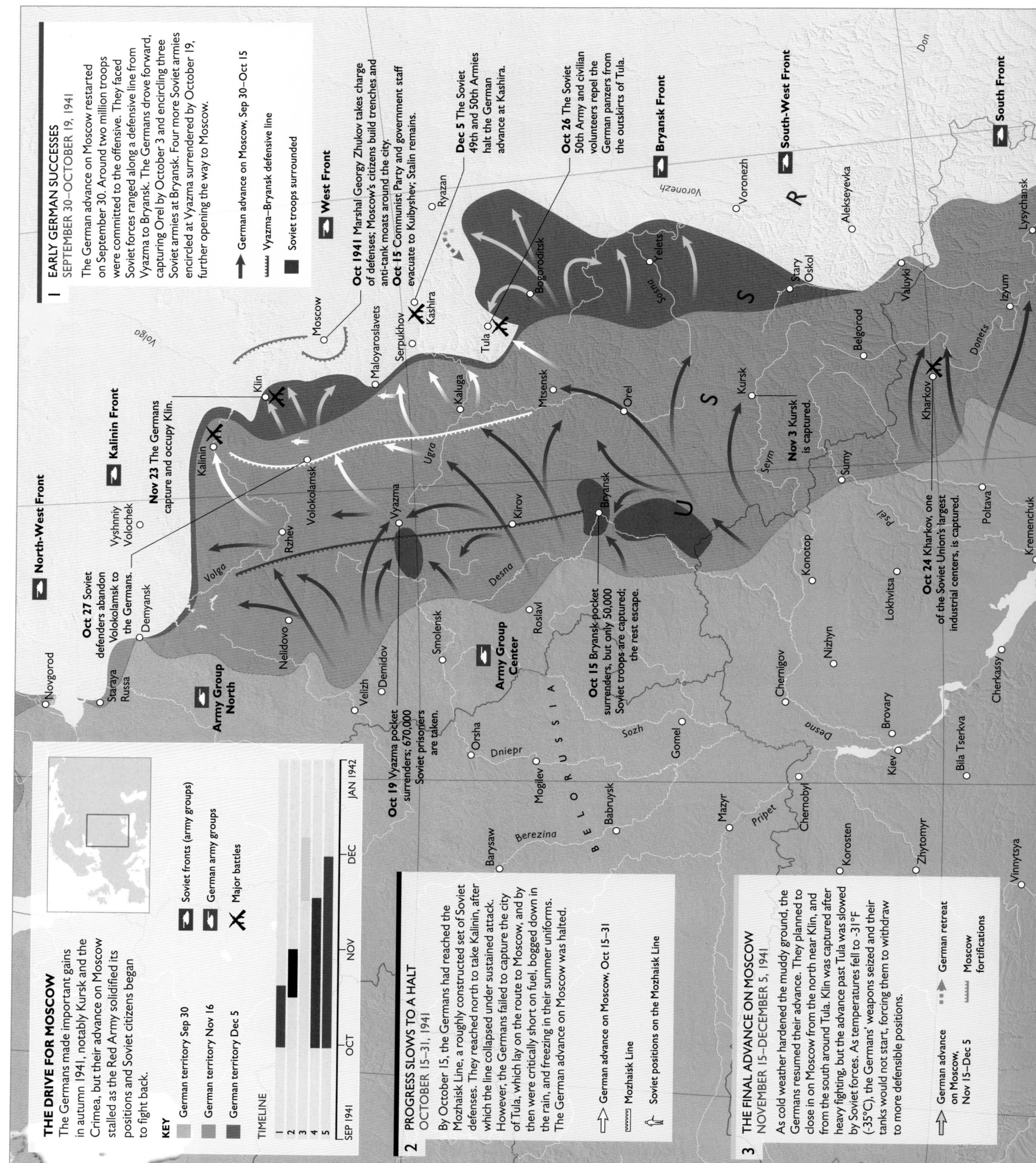

THE DRIVE FOR MOSCOW

The Germans made important gains in autumn 1941, notably Kursk and the Crimea, but their advance on Moscow stalled as the Red Army solidified its positions and Soviet citizens began to fight back.

KEY

1 ░ German territory Sep 30
2 ░ German territory Nov 16
3 ░ German territory Dec 5

◤ Soviet fronts (army groups)
◤ German army groups
✕ Major battles

TIMELINE

SEP 1941	OCT	NOV	DEC	JAN 1942

1 | EARLY GERMAN SUCCESSES
SEPTEMBER 30–OCTOBER 19, 1941

The German advance on Moscow restarted on September 30. Around two million troops were committed to the offensive. They faced Soviet forces ranged along a defensive line from Vyazma to Bryansk. The Germans drove forward, capturing Orel by October 3 and encircling three Soviet armies at Bryansk. Four more Soviet armies encircled at Vyazma surrendered by October 19, further opening the way to Moscow.

→ German advance on Moscow, Sep 30–Oct 15
⌐⌐⌐ Vyazma–Bryansk defensive line
◼ Soviet troops surrounded

Oct 1941 Marshal Georgy Zhukov takes charge of defenses; Moscow's citizens build trenches and anti-tank moats around the city.
Oct 15 Communist Party and government staff evacuate to Kuibyshev; Stalin remains.

Dec 5 The Soviet 49th and 50th Armies halt the German advance at Kashira.

Oct 26 The Soviet 50th Army and civilian volunteers repel the German panzers from the outskirts of Tula.

Nov 23 The Germans capture and occupy Klin.

Oct 27 Soviet defenders abandon Volokolamsk to the Germans.

Oct 19 Vyazma pocket surrenders; 670,000 Soviet prisoners are taken.

Oct 15 Bryansk pocket surrenders, but only 50,000 Soviet troops are captured; the rest escape.

Nov 3 Kursk is captured.

Oct 24 Kharkov, one of the Soviet Union's largest industrial centers, is captured.

⬒ North-West Front
⬒ Army Group North
⬒ West Front
⬒ Kalinin Front
⬒ Bryansk Front
⬒ South-West Front
⬒ South Front
⬒ Army Group Center

2 | PROGRESS SLOWS TO A HALT
OCTOBER 15–31, 1941

By October 15, the Germans had reached the Mozhaisk Line, a roughly constructed set of Soviet defenses. They reached north to take Kalinin, after which the line collapsed under sustained attack. However, the Germans failed to capture the city of Tula, which lay on the route to Moscow, and by then were critically short on fuel, bogged down in the rain, and freezing in their summer uniforms. The German advance on Moscow was halted.

→ German advance on Moscow, Oct 15–31
⌐⌐⌐ Mozhaisk Line
⬑ Soviet positions on the Mozhaisk Line

3 | THE FINAL ADVANCE ON MOSCOW
NOVEMBER 15–DECEMBER 5, 1941

As cold weather hardened the muddy ground, the Germans resumed their advance. They planned to close in on Moscow from the north near Klin, and from the south around Tula. Klin was captured after heavy fighting, but the advance past Tula was slowed by Soviet forces. As temperatures fell to –31°F (–35°C), the Germans' weapons seized and their tanks would not start, forcing them to withdraw to more defensible positions.

⇧ German advance on Moscow, Nov 15–Dec 5
⇡ German retreat
⌐⌐⌐ Moscow fortifications

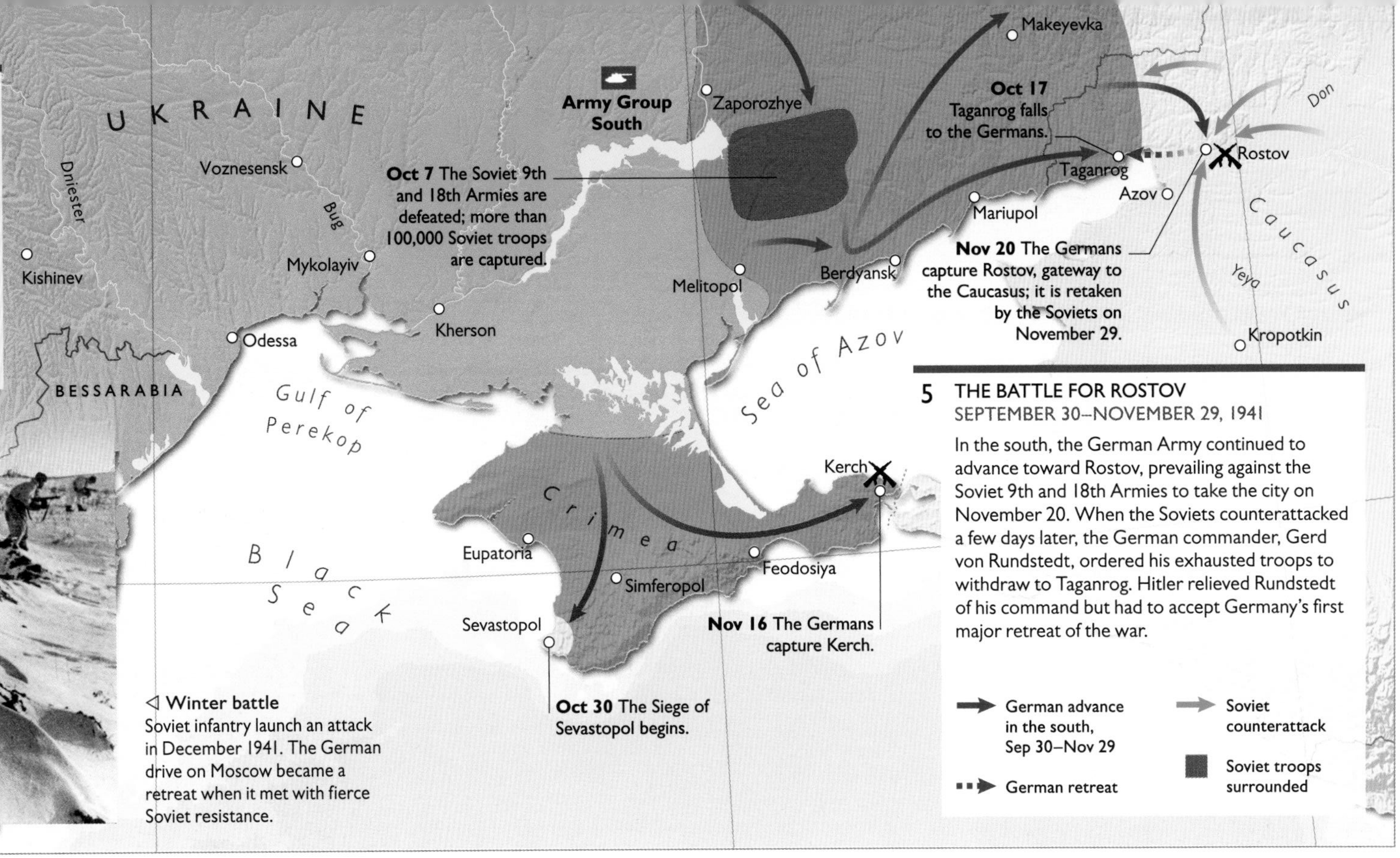

4 INTO THE CRIMEA
SEPTEMBER 30–NOVEMBER 16, 1941

Operation Barbarossa had seen the Germans reach the neck of the Crimean Peninsula, and by October 27 their 11th Army had taken control of the whole peninsula except Sevastopol and Kerch. The siege of Sevastopol lasted into July 1942, but Kerch was captured on November 16, providing Germany with another route into the Caucasus.

→ German advance in Crimea Sep 30–Nov 16

Oct 7 The Soviet 9th and 18th Armies are defeated; more than 100,000 Soviet troops are captured.

Oct 17 Taganrog falls to the Germans.

Nov 20 The Germans capture Rostov, gateway to the Caucasus; it is retaken by the Soviets on November 29.

Nov 16 The Germans capture Kerch.

Oct 30 The Siege of Sevastopol begins.

5 THE BATTLE FOR ROSTOV
SEPTEMBER 30–NOVEMBER 29, 1941

In the south, the German Army continued to advance toward Rostov, prevailing against the Soviet 9th and 18th Armies to take the city on November 20. When the Soviets counterattacked a few days later, the German commander, Gerd von Rundstedt, ordered his exhausted troops to withdraw to Taganrog. Hitler relieved Rundstedt of his command but had to accept Germany's first major retreat of the war.

→ German advance in the south, Sep 30–Nov 29

⇢ German retreat

↑ Soviet counterattack

■ Soviet troops surrounded

▽ **Winter battle**
Soviet infantry launch an attack in December 1941. The German drive on Moscow became a retreat when it met with fierce Soviet resistance.

THE GERMAN ADVANCE ON MOSCOW

After the success of Operation Barbarossa, Germany's invasion of the USSR, Hitler launched Operation Typhoon, a renewed push on Moscow. He believed it would be "the last, great, decisive battle of the war." The campaign, however, ended in a retreat that dealt a serious blow to Hitler's plan to destroy the Soviet Union.

During Operation Barbarossa (see pp.90–91), the Germans considered Moscow less important than other strategic targets. The push on the capital was delayed by the advance into the Ukraine for resources—a source of dispute between Hitler and his generals—and recommenced only in late September 1941, by which time the heavy rains were turning the roads into quagmires. This, along with fuel shortages and a failure to replace damaged tanks, slowed German progress and sapped morale. Moreover, it seemed that despite the capture of millions of Red Army troops, the USSR had millions more in reserve. The Red Army was regularly replenished, and even joined by civilian volunteers. By December 5, 1941, the Germans had failed to capture Moscow, and winter was upon them. Unprepared for the bitter cold and fatally overstretched against a determined Red Army, their casualties mounted. By Christmas that year, over 100,000 German soldiers had frostbite and over 250,000 had died.

In the south, meanwhile, the Germans had succeeded in taking the Crimea, but their advance on the Caucasus was hampered, as in the north, by overstretched supply lines and exhausted troops. When Red Army soldiers recaptured Rostov at the end of November, they highlighted just how vulnerable the Germans really were.

EVACUATION OF SOVIET INDUSTRIAL AREAS

The German advance threatened Soviet industries producing vital ammunition (pictured above) and other war materiel. In 1941, the Soviets began to evacuate factories and their workforces to safety in Siberia and beyond the Ural mountains. Over 1,500 large plants were relocated.

MASSACRES IN THE EAST

The German invasion of the Soviet Union in June 1941 brought millions more Jews under Hitler's control. Within weeks, special German units had begun to massacre the Russian Jews, killing up to one million in only five months.

△ **Head of the SS**
Heinrich Himmler was in charge of the *Einsatzgruppen*, and in 1941 he was tasked with implementing Hitler's "Final Solution" to exterminate all European Jews.

The German forces that invaded the USSR as part of Operation Barbarossa (see pp.90–91) were accompanied by *Einsatzgruppen*—special units of the SS tasked with exterminating the Jews who now lived in German-occupied territory. Four groups consisting of around 4,000 men fanned out across the Baltic States, Belorussia, and Ukraine. The killings began at Minsk on July 13, 1941, when over 1,000 Jews were shot, and accelerated as summer progressed. The death squads often used ravines on the edge of large towns, where Jews were shot and the bodies pushed over the edge and buried.

On September 26, the German military command in Kiev ordered the liquidation of the Jewish population. Over 33,000 Jews, believing they were being relocated out of the Kiev ghetto, were taken to the nearby Babi Yar ravine. There, an *Einsatzgruppe*, aided by Ukrainian collaborators, machine-gunned them down. It was the worst single massacre of a campaign that killed between 800,000 and one million Jews by the end of the year, when shootings were replaced by mobile gas vans and extermination camps using either carbon monoxide or hydrogen cyanide (Zyklon B).

△ **Operation Barbarossa**
A German armored unit moves forward during the early stages of Operation Barbarossa—the military invasion of the Soviet Union. The rapid advance of the German army trapped hundreds of thousands of Jews in Nazi-controlled territory.

MOSCOW SAVED

Soviet actions between December 1941 and April 30, 1942 brought them gains that relieved the pressure on Moscow. Their advance also threatened German lines of communication at Kharkov, and won a valuable toehold in Crimea.

KEY

- German army groups
- Soviet fronts (army groups)
- Territory held by Soviet army, Dec 5, 1941
- Regained by Soviets by Jan 1, 1942
- Regained by Soviets by April 30, 1942

TIMELINE

DEC 1941 | JAN 1942 | FEB | MAR | APR | MAY

1
2
3
4
5

4 THE IZYUM SALIENT
JANUARY 18–30, 1942

In eastern Ukraine, the armies of the Soviet South Front breached German lines on the Donets River and drove 62 miles (100km) toward the rear of the German forces and their communications center at Kharkov. Lacking reserves and logistical support, the Soviets were forced back by the end of January into a 38sq mile (100sq km) salient near Izyum, where they were at risk of being cut off.

➡ Soviet advance on Izyum

▨ Izyum salient

3 PARATROOPERS AND PARTISANS
JANUARY 18–APRIL 1, 1942

In a bid to encircle German forces in the Rzhev-Vyazma salient and cut their lines of communication, Soviet paratroopers were dropped behind German forces holding Vyazma from January 18. Although supported by Soviet partisans in the area and troops of the Kalinin and West Fronts, the Soviet forces soon found themselves encircled and engaged in a bitter struggle to close off the rear of the salient.

▨ German forces in Rzhev-Vyazma salient

↑ German counterattacks, Mar 1942

▨ Soviet airborne landings, Jan 1942

▨ Encircled Soviet partisan resistance

2 A RENEWED PUSH JANUARY–FEBRUARY 1942

From January 7, the Soviets renewed their offensive against the Germans, hoping to push them westward and force them to squander their reserves before the spring came. The Soviet high command planned a pincer movement to envelop Vyazma, Rzhev, and Smolensk. Soviet tanks and ski battalions from the North-West and Kalinin Fronts pushed south and south-west toward Velikiye Luki and Demidov. The West Front squeezed the German salient at Rzhev from the east, but failed to re-capture Vyazma.

⇨ Soviet counterattacks Jan–Feb 1942

1 THE COUNTEROFFENSIVE BEGINS
DECEMBER 5–31, 1941

On the night of December 5, the Soviets launched a huge counteroffensive. To drive the Germans back from Moscow, they concentrated on the salients to the north-west and south-east of the city, and liberated Klin by December 15. The German general Guderian's panzer group was nearly trapped near Tula as the Soviets re-took the area, but managed to escape to Bryansk. By the end of the year, Moscow was out of immediate danger.

➡ Soviet counterattacks, Dec 1941

⇢ German panzers retreat

Feb 23, 1942 Stalin addresses the Soviet people, promising to defeat the "Hitlerite" invaders.

Dec 26, 1941 German General Guderian is relieved of his command after retreating from Tula.

West Front
Bryansk Front
South-West Front
South Front
Volkhov Front
North-West Front
Kalinin Front
Leningrad Front
Army Group North
Army Group Center

Finland
Lake Onega
Lake Ladoga
Estonia
Tartu
Belorussia
Ukraine
U.S.S.R.

Leningrad
Luga
Novgorod
Staraya Russa
Tikhvin
Zaborie
Demyansk
Vyshniy Volochek
Kalinin
Klin
Moscow
Ryazan
Stalinogorsk
Bogoroditsk
Tula
Kaluga
Yelets
Kirov
Bryansk
Orel
Kursk
Voronezh
Stary Oskol
Alekseyevka
Valuyki
Belgorod
Sumy
Kharkov
Poltava
Cherkassy
Bila Tserkva
Kiev
Lokhvitsa
Konotop
Novozybkov
Roslavl
Smolensk
Demidov
Velizh
Velikiye Luki
Vitebsk
Mogilev
Babruysk
Barysaw
Minsk
Maladzyechna
Pripet
Mazyr
Chernobyl
Dniepr
Nelidovo
Rzhev
Vyazma

Volga
Don
Stalingrad
Izyum

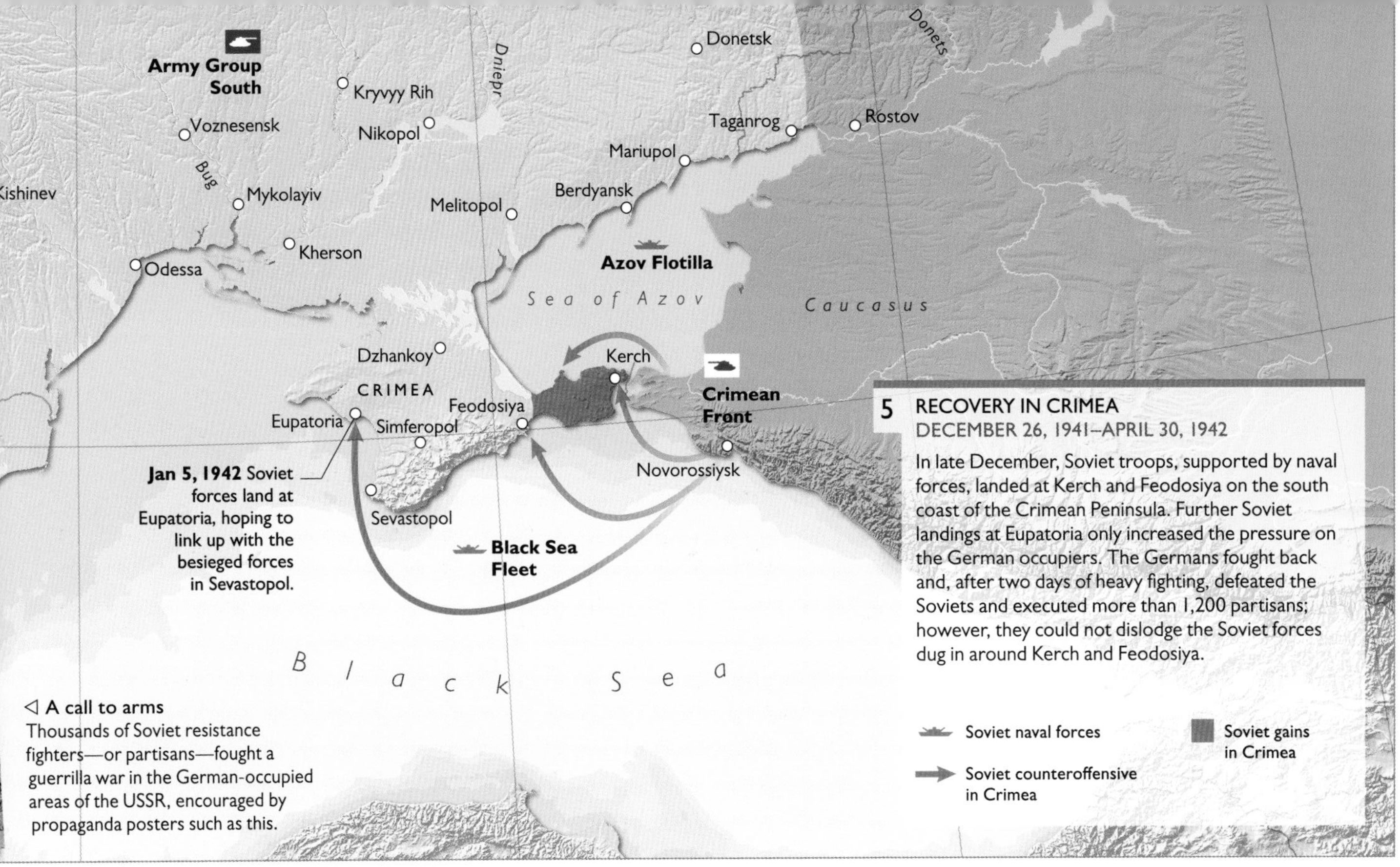

5 RECOVERY IN CRIMEA
DECEMBER 26, 1941–APRIL 30, 1942

In late December, Soviet troops, supported by naval forces, landed at Kerch and Feodosiya on the south coast of the Crimean Peninsula. Further Soviet landings at Eupatoria only increased the pressure on the German occupiers. The Germans fought back and, after two days of heavy fighting, defeated the Soviets and executed more than 1,200 partisans; however, they could not dislodge the Soviet forces dug in around Kerch and Feodosiya.

⟶ Soviet naval forces

⟶ Soviet counteroffensive in Crimea

▮ Soviet gains in Crimea

Jan 5, 1942 Soviet forces land at Eupatoria, hoping to link up with the besieged forces in Sevastopol.

△ **A call to arms**
Thousands of Soviet resistance fighters—or partisans—fought a guerrilla war in the German-occupied areas of the USSR, encouraged by propaganda posters such as this.

MARSHAL GEORGY ZHUKOV
1896–1974

One of Stalin's most capable commanders, Zhukov organized the defense of Leningrad and Moscow, and led the counterattack at Moscow in December 1941. At Stalingrad, his counteroffensive destroyed the German 6th Army in the city. It was Zhukov who accepted the German surrender in Berlin in 1945. He was made a Marshal of the Soviet Union in 1943, but was sidelined after the war because Stalin saw him as a threat.

THE RELIEF OF MOSCOW

The Soviets launched a counteroffensive against the German invaders in December 1941, making early gains at several points along the vast Eastern Front and freeing Moscow from immediate danger. However, they could not force a full retreat, and the front remained largely static from February 1942 until a new German offensive began in June.

In late September 1941, Hitler had aimed to take Moscow before the start of the bitter Russian winter (see pp.96–97). Despite German successes at Vyazma and Bryansk on the way to the capital, Soviet opposition forced the German armies to stall and dig in for the winter around Moscow. The German commanders assumed that the Red Army was as depleted as their own. Stalin, however, had armies in reserve in Siberia, most of which he brought forward to bolster the Soviet forces on the Eastern Front.

From December 5, the Soviet commanders launched a huge counteroffensive against the Germans, with operations running along the whole front. To the north, the Volkhov Front managed to regain the strategically important town of Tikhvin, which eased the supply routes to besieged Leningrad (see pp.94–95). Near Moscow,

the German salients around Klin and Tula were quickly pushed back, but it took longer to shift the Germans away from the center of the front. To the south, the Red Army re-took Kerch in Crimea and created a substantial salient at Izyum. The Germans, under orders to defend their positions, continued to fight and made several assaults in March; by April the Soviet counteroffensive had all but ground to a halt. Both sides had suffered huge casualties. The Soviet forces had advanced more than 62 miles (100km) in some places, but they had not been able to force the Germans into a general retreat or re-take the German communications centers at Vyazma and Kharkov. The Soviet failure to follow through their counteroffensive ultimately led to a successful German offensive in the south, and to the Battle of Stalingrad (see pp.148–153).

THE WIDENING
WAR 1942

THE US ENTERED THE WAR IN EUROPE AND THE PACIFIC, WHILE IN THE
EAST THE SOVIETS STEMMED THE GERMAN ADVANCE. MEANWHILE,
THE NAZIS REDOUBLED THEIR PERSECUTION OF THE JEWS.

AMERICA AND JAPAN GO TO WAR

In December 1941, Japan embarked on war with the US, which was blocking its imperial ambitions in Asia. Initial military victories left the Japanese in control of a wide area of Asia and the Pacific, but it faced a fierce US fight back.

△ **Man of influence**
Admiral Isoroku Yamamoto masterminded the surprise Japanese aircraft carrier attack on Pearl Harbor. However, he personally doubted that Japan could win a war against the US.

Throughout the 1930s, the US did not openly confront Japan about its increasing militarism in Asia, such as its invasion of China in 1937. However, following the rapid victory of Hitler's forces in Europe in 1940, Japan stepped up its aggression, recognizing the opportunity to seize Southeast Asia from the European colonial powers—the defeated French and Dutch, and the weakened British.

Hostilities on the rise

Increasingly committed to backing Britain against Nazi Germany, US President Roosevelt accepted responsibility for resisting Japan's expansion in Southeast Asia—a task the British could no longer perform. Japanese encroachment on French Indochina in 1940–1941 met an aggressive response from the US, which placed Japan under economic blockade and demanded that it abandon its ambitions to establish an empire in Asia.

Japan's response was to push ahead with a plan for the conquest of Southeast Asia. They believed a surprise attack on the US fleet at Pearl Harbor, Hawaii, would remove the US temporarily from the equation, allowing

Japan sufficient time to establish a far-flung defensive perimeter in the Pacific. The Japanese hoped their position would then be strong enough to deter the US from retaliation, leaving Japan securely in control of an Asian empire. However, this was a disastrous miscalculation. In reality, their surprise attack on Pearl Harbor on December 7, 1941, so outraged American popular opinion that the US was implacably committed to go to war against Japan and fight to the bitter end, regardless of cost or casualties. The following day, the US declared war against Japan.

Racial hatred of the Japanese was a feature of American attitudes to the Pacific War from the outset, and the mistreatment of Allied prisoners of war by the Japanese provided further fuel for anti-Japanese sentiment.

Germany declares war

Four days after the attack on Pearl Harbor, Hitler declared war on the US, bringing the US into the European conflict. Since Roosevelt saw US interests as more vitally threatened by the power of Nazi Germany than

◁ **Promoting war production**
A US propaganda poster links the Nazi swastika to the Japanese national flag, showing Germany and Japan as a common enemy.

JAPAN'S WAVE OF CONQUEST

For six months after the attack on Pearl Harbor, Japanese forces advanced victoriously through Southeast Asia and across the Pacific. Malaysia and Singapore, the Philippines, the Dutch East Indies, and Burma all fell to Japan, while landings in New Guinea threatened Australia. However, by the end of 1942 the battle of Midway and the extensive fighting at Guadalcanal, both in the Pacific, showed that the Americans were capable of defeating the Japanese both on land and at sea.

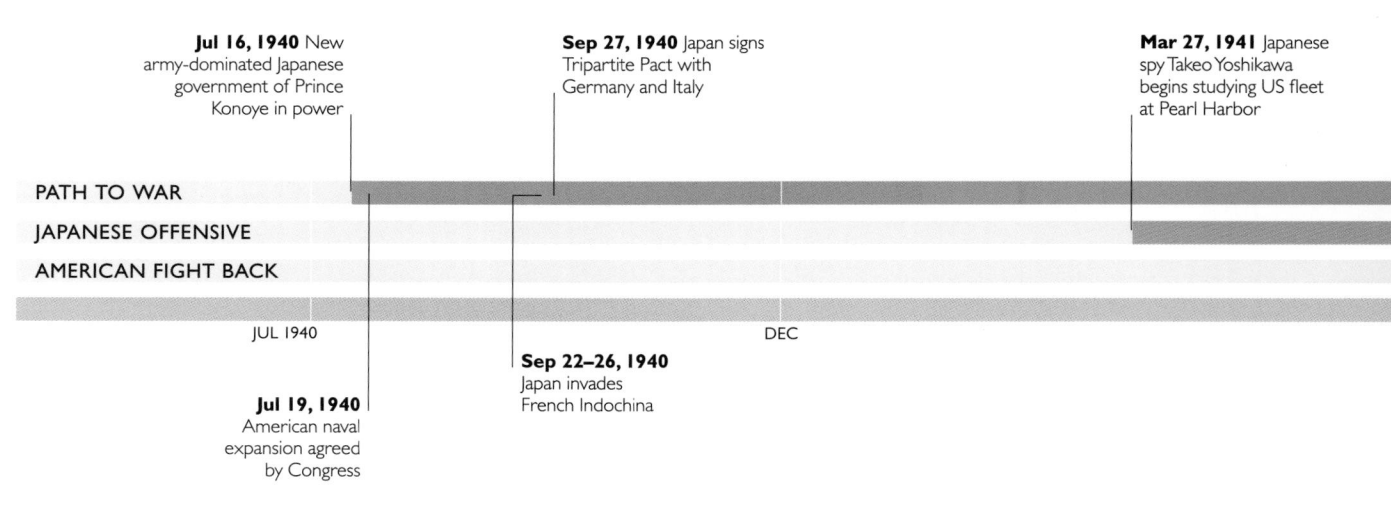

Jul 16, 1940 New army-dominated Japanese government of Prince Konoye in power

Sep 27, 1940 Japan signs Tripartite Pact with Germany and Italy

Mar 27, 1941 Japanese spy Takeo Yoshikawa begins studying US fleet at Pearl Harbor

PATH TO WAR

JAPANESE OFFENSIVE

AMERICAN FIGHT BACK

JUL 1940

DEC

Jul 19, 1940 American naval expansion agreed by Congress

Sep 22–26, 1940 Japan invades French Indochina

▷ **Zero fighter plane**
In 1941, the Japanese A6M Zero was probably the world's finest carrier-borne fighter, outclassing any aircraft operated by the US Navy.

▽ **Disaster at Pearl Harbor**
Fire spreads through the battleship USS *West Virginia* during the Japanese air strike at Pearl Harbor. Four American battleships were sunk in the attack.

"We will gain the inevitable triumph—so help us God."

PRESIDENT ROOSEVELT, DECEMBER 8, 1941

by Japanese aggression, he decided to prioritize the struggle against Germany in Europe, which slowed the American fight in the Pacific.

In contrast to the Western Allies, who established joint commands and strategies, Japan and Germany fought two totally separate wars. Japan remained at peace with the Soviet Union, Germany's bitterest enemy, until August 1945, when the Soviet Union declared war on Japan after Japan refused to capitulate.

Successes and failures

The initial Japanese offensives in Southeast Asia were very successful against the colonial empires, which lacked both morale and military strength. The spectacle of the British surrender at Singapore, in particular, delivered a fatal blow to European racial prestige. However, in British India only a minority of activists in the nationalist independence movement sided with Nazi Germany and Japan. Overall, the Japanese failed to capitalize on potential support from their fellow Asians, proving at least as exploitative and oppressive as the European colonialists they supplanted.

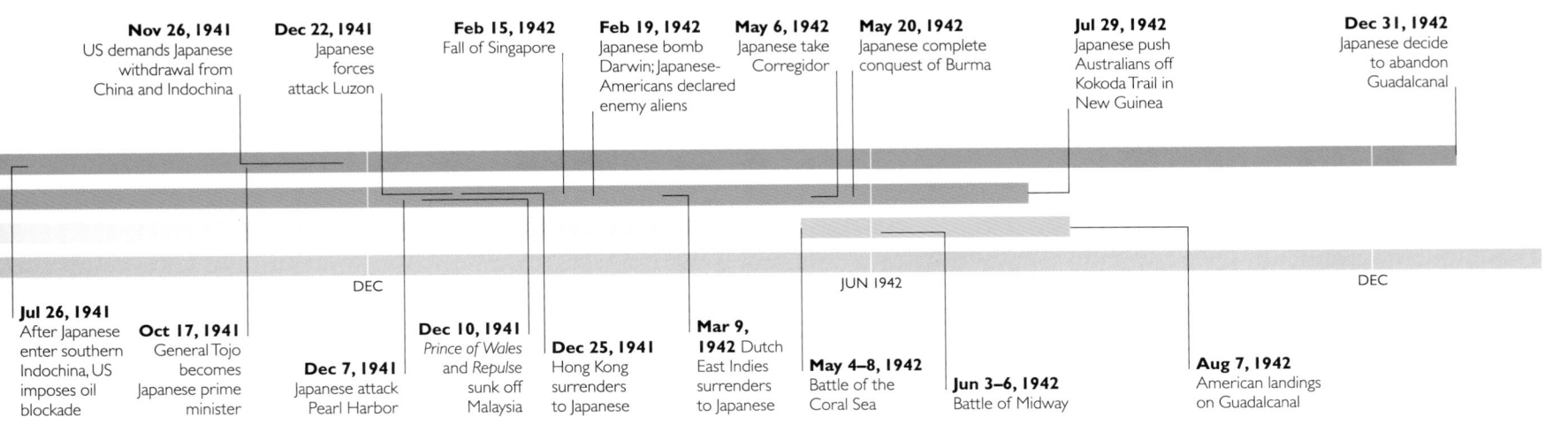

Nov 26, 1941 US demands Japanese withdrawal from China and Indochina

Dec 22, 1941 Japanese forces attack Luzon

Feb 15, 1942 Fall of Singapore

Feb 19, 1942 Japanese bomb Darwin; Japanese-Americans declared enemy aliens

May 6, 1942 Japanese take Corregidor

May 20, 1942 Japanese complete conquest of Burma

Jul 29, 1942 Japanese push Australians off Kokoda Trail in New Guinea

Dec 31, 1942 Japanese decide to abandon Guadalcanal

DEC

JUN 1942

DEC

Jul 26, 1941 After Japanese enter southern Indochina, US imposes oil blockade

Oct 17, 1941 General Tojo becomes Japanese prime minister

Dec 7, 1941 Japanese attack Pearl Harbor

Dec 10, 1941 *Prince of Wales* and *Repulse* sunk off Malaysia

Dec 25, 1941 Hong Kong surrenders to Japanese

Mar 9, 1942 Dutch East Indies surrenders to Japanese

May 4–8, 1942 Battle of the Coral Sea

Jun 3–6, 1942 Battle of Midway

Aug 7, 1942 American landings on Guadalcanal

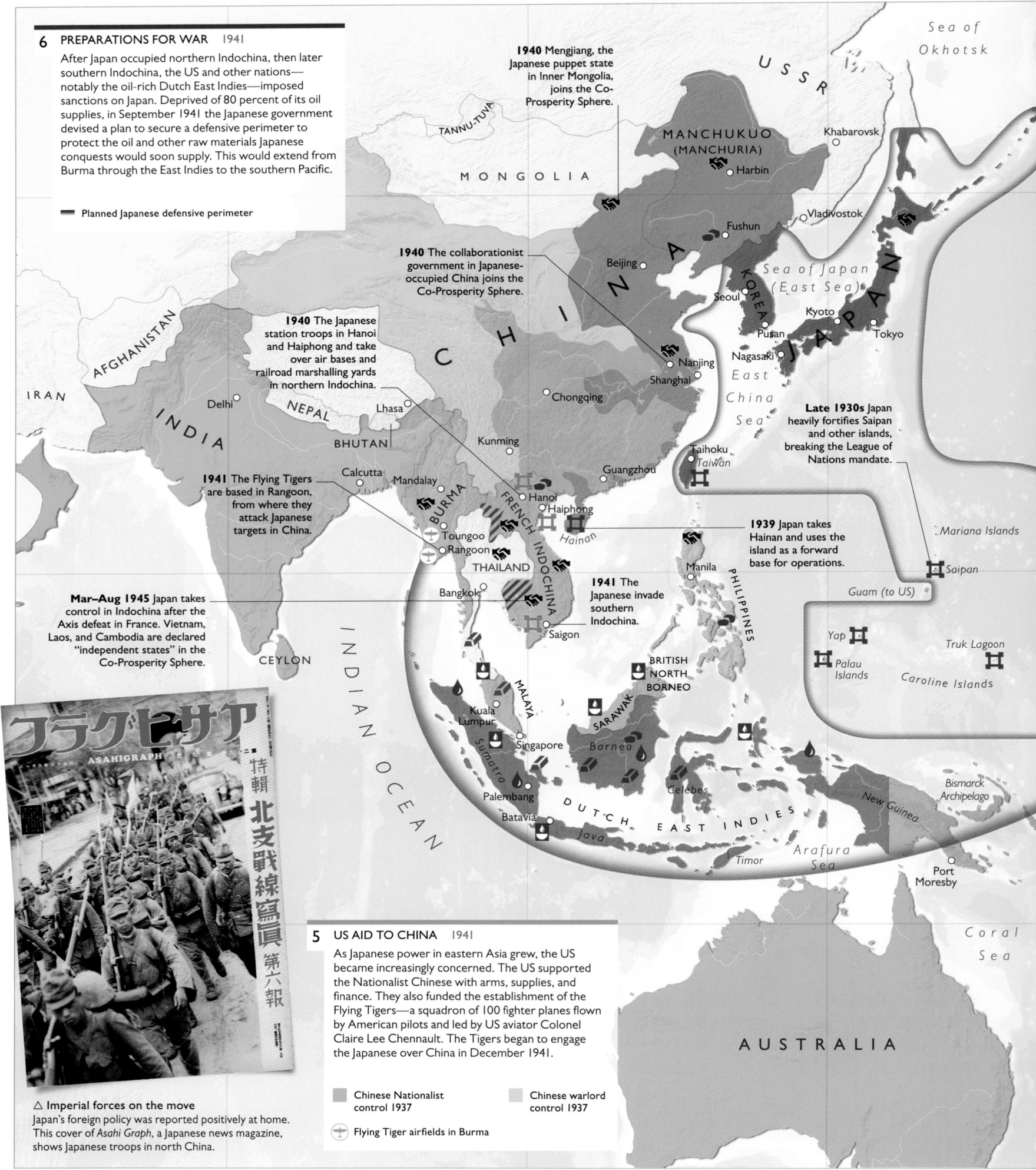

6 PREPARATIONS FOR WAR 1941

After Japan occupied northern Indochina, then later southern Indochina, the US and other nations—notably the oil-rich Dutch East Indies—imposed sanctions on Japan. Deprived of 80 percent of its oil supplies, in September 1941 the Japanese government devised a plan to secure a defensive perimeter to protect the oil and other raw materials Japanese conquests would soon supply. This would extend from Burma through the East Indies to the southern Pacific.

▬ Planned Japanese defensive perimeter

1940 Mengjiang, the Japanese puppet state in Inner Mongolia, joins the Co-Prosperity Sphere.

1940 The collaborationist government in Japanese-occupied China joins the Co-Prosperity Sphere.

1940 The Japanese station troops in Hanoi and Haiphong and take over air bases and railroad marshalling yards in northern Indochina.

Late 1930s Japan heavily fortifies Saipan and other islands, breaking the League of Nations mandate.

1941 The Flying Tigers are based in Rangoon, from where they attack Japanese targets in China.

1939 Japan takes Hainan and uses the island as a forward base for operations.

Mar–Aug 1945 Japan takes control in Indochina after the Axis defeat in France. Vietnam, Laos, and Cambodia are declared "independent states" in the Co-Prosperity Sphere.

1941 The Japanese invade southern Indochina.

Map labels

Sea of Okhotsk · USSR · TANNU-TUVA · MONGOLIA · MANCHUKUO (MANCHURIA) · Khabarovsk · Harbin · Vladivostok · Fushun · Beijing · CHINA · KOREA · Sea of Japan (East Sea) · Seoul · Kyoto · JAPAN · Pusan · Nagasaki · Tokyo · Nanjing · Shanghai · East China Sea · Chongqing · AFGHANISTAN · IRAN · INDIA · Delhi · NEPAL · Lhasa · BHUTAN · Kunming · Guangzhou · Taihoku / Taiwan · Mariana Islands · Calcutta · Mandalay · BURMA · FRENCH INDOCHINA · Hanoi · Haiphong · Hainan · Saipan · Guam (to US) · Toungoo · Rangoon · THAILAND · Manila · Bangkok · Saigon · PHILIPPINES · Yap · Truk Lagoon · CEYLON · Palau Islands · Caroline Islands · MALAYA · BRITISH NORTH BORNEO · Kuala Lumpur · Singapore · SARAWAK · Sumatra · Borneo · Celebes · Bismarck Archipelago · Palembang · Batavia · DUTCH EAST INDIES · New Guinea · Java · Timor · Arafura Sea · Port Moresby · INDIAN OCEAN · Coral Sea · AUSTRALIA

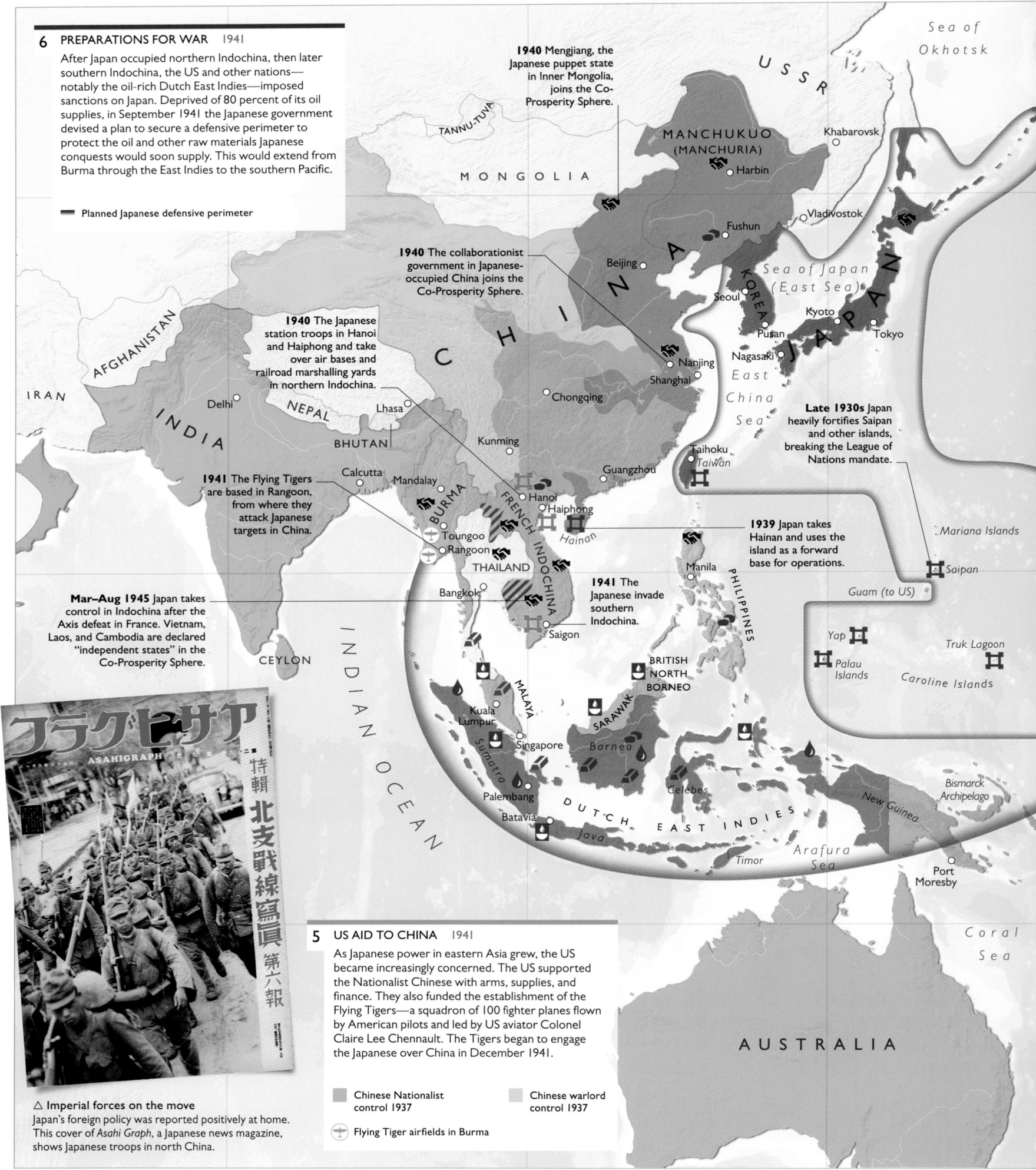

△ **Imperial forces on the move**
Japan's foreign policy was reported positively at home. This cover of *Asahi Graph*, a Japanese news magazine, shows Japanese troops in north China.

5 US AID TO CHINA 1941

As Japanese power in eastern Asia grew, the US became increasingly concerned. The US supported the Nationalist Chinese with arms, supplies, and finance. They also funded the establishment of the Flying Tigers—a squadron of 100 fighter planes flown by American pilots and led by US aviator Colonel Claire Lee Chennault. The Tigers began to engage the Japanese over China in December 1941.

⬛ Chinese Nationalist control 1937   ⬛ Chinese warlord control 1937

✈ Flying Tiger airfields in Burma

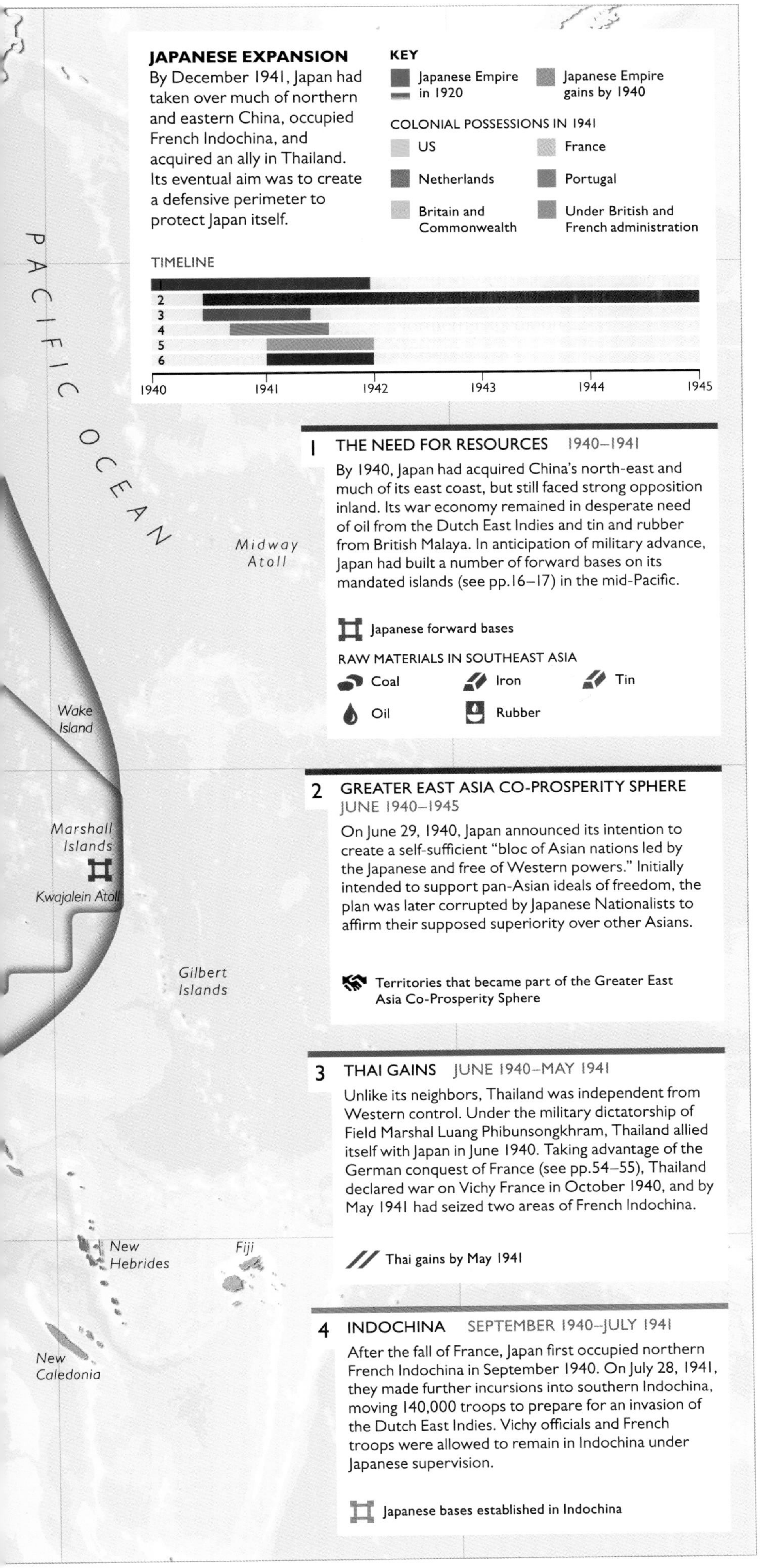

JAPANESE EXPANSION

By December 1941, Japan had taken over much of northern and eastern China, occupied French Indochina, and acquired an ally in Thailand. Its eventual aim was to create a defensive perimeter to protect Japan itself.

KEY

- ■ Japanese Empire in 1920
- ■ Japanese Empire gains by 1940

COLONIAL POSSESSIONS IN 1941

- US
- France
- Netherlands
- Portugal
- Britain and Commonwealth
- Under British and French administration

TIMELINE

	1940	1941	1942	1943	1944	1945
2						
3						
4						
5						
6						

---

1 THE NEED FOR RESOURCES   1940–1941

By 1940, Japan had acquired China's north-east and much of its east coast, but still faced strong opposition inland. Its war economy remained in desperate need of oil from the Dutch East Indies and tin and rubber from British Malaya. In anticipation of military advance, Japan had built a number of forward bases on its mandated islands (see pp.16–17) in the mid-Pacific.

⊞ Japanese forward bases

RAW MATERIALS IN SOUTHEAST ASIA

- Coal
- Iron
- Tin
- Oil
- Rubber

---

2 GREATER EAST ASIA CO-PROSPERITY SPHERE
JUNE 1940–1945

On June 29, 1940, Japan announced its intention to create a self-sufficient "bloc of Asian nations led by the Japanese and free of Western powers." Initially intended to support pan-Asian ideals of freedom, the plan was later corrupted by Japanese Nationalists to affirm their supposed superiority over other Asians.

🤝 Territories that became part of the Greater East Asia Co-Prosperity Sphere

---

3 THAI GAINS   JUNE 1940–MAY 1941

Unlike its neighbors, Thailand was independent from Western control. Under the military dictatorship of Field Marshal Luang Phibunsongkhram, Thailand allied itself with Japan in June 1940. Taking advantage of the German conquest of France (see pp.54–55), Thailand declared war on Vichy France in October 1940, and by May 1941 had seized two areas of French Indochina.

/// Thai gains by May 1941

---

4 INDOCHINA   SEPTEMBER 1940–JULY 1941

After the fall of France, Japan first occupied northern French Indochina in September 1940. On July 28, 1941, they made further incursions into southern Indochina, moving 140,000 troops to prepare for an invasion of the Dutch East Indies. Vichy officials and French troops were allowed to remain in Indochina under Japanese supervision.

⊞ Japanese bases established in Indochina

(Map labels: PACIFIC OCEAN, Midway Atoll, Wake Island, Marshall Islands, Kwajalein Atoll, Gilbert Islands, New Hebrides, Fiji, New Caledonia)

JAPANESE AMBITIONS

After the invasion of China, Japan looked elsewhere to expand its empire. By 1941, it became clear that Japan had substantial imperial and economic ambitions in Southeast Asia, particularly regarding the American and European colonies in the region.

Despite its size and its extensive empire, Japan had only limited access to vital raw materials. The oil, coal, steel, iron, and minerals it needed to drive its economy all had to be imported. Japan's conquest of Manchuria in 1931 (see pp.22–23) provided much-needed coal, but demand for oil, tin, and rubber had yet to be met. Japan's incursions into eastern Siberia in the 1930s were defeated by the USSR. The Japanese government thereafter looked toward the resource-rich European colonial territories in Southeast Asia.

Japan used discontent against the colonial powers to propose the Greater East Asia Co-Prosperity Sphere in 1940, promising "Asia for the Asiatics" and independence from oppression (see pp.222–223). Japan also allied with independent Thailand in June 1940, and began to plan for war in April–May 1941. It prepared for an invasion of Southeast Asia by occupying French Indochina in July 1941—an act that prompted an economic embargo of Japan by the Western powers. Faced with impending oil shortages and potential economic collapse, Japan prepared for a larger war, planning its conquests and its defense of a greatly enlarged empire.

> *"I fear we would become a third-class nation after two or three years if we just sat tight."*
>
> PRIME MINISTER HIDEKI TOJO, NOVEMBER 5, 1941

THE ECONOMIC EMBARGO AGAINST JAPAN

In order to deter Japanese military expansion in China and Southeast Asia, the US, Britain, and the Dutch East Indies restricted and then ended sales of oil, iron ore, and steel to Japan. Without oil, the Japanese military would have quickly ground to a halt. The Japanese referred to these embargoes as the ABCD (American-British-Chinese-Dutch) encirclement. In April 1941 they began to draw up plans to seize resource-rich Malaya and the Dutch East Indies.

Dutch soldiers destroy oil reserves in Java

Ready for battle
Cadets from the Imperial Naval Academy,
Etajima, near Hiroshima, undergo training
in September 1941. They were probably
prospective members of the *Kaigun Tokubetsu
Rikusentai*—the Japanese equivalent
of the Marines.

JAPAN GOES TO WAR

In July 1941, the US imposed sanctions on Japan in retaliation for their occupation of French Indochina, and Britain and the Dutch East Indies followed suit. For Japan, making concessions was not an option.

Faced with a trade embargo that threatened to strangle their economy, Japan's leaders came to the conclusion that war was the only option remaining open to them. As Admiral Osami Nagano, Chief of Staff of the Imperial Japanese Navy, declared in September 1941, "Since Japan is unavoidably

△ **Type 14 Nambu pistol**
This model was designed in 1925 and was used by officers of the Japanese army during World War II. It fired an 8mm round.

facing national ruin whether it decides to fight the United States or submit to its demands, it must by all means choose to fight." The Japanese leadership also believed that time was against them, and that the longer they delayed in mobilizing for war, the smaller their prospects of success would be.

The Japanese war plan

Japan's leaders planned to strike in Southeast Asia in order to win control of the US-held Philippines, the oil-rich Dutch East Indies, and the British colonies of Malaya and Singapore. The Japanese recognized that such a move would almost certainly provoke an armed response by American forces, and so decided to take preventative action by planning a surprise attack on the US Pacific Fleet at Pearl Harbor, Hawaii, on December 7, 1941 (see pp.110–111). The Japanese intention was that, by turning the central and southwestern Pacific into an impregnable military bastion, they would force the US into fighting an island-by-island war of attrition, the cost of which would break the Americans' will to fight. However, the reality of the situation proved to be very different.

HIDEKI TOJO
1884–1948

Born in Tokyo to a family of the former samurai caste, Hideki Tojo enlisted as a cadet in the Imperial Japanese Army in 1899 and rose to the rank of general. He went on to serve as prime minister of Japan from 1941 to 1944, and during this time he ordered the infamous attack on US forces at Pearl Harbor. At the end of the war he was arrested shortly after a botched suicide attempt and was tried for war crimes. He was executed in 1948.

PEARL HARBOR

US president Franklin D. Roosevelt called December 7, 1941, the day Japan attacked Pearl Harbor, "a date which will live in infamy." At the time, US negotiations with Japan were still in progress and no declaration of war had been made. The attack transformed the war from a European battle into a worldwide conflict.

Tensions between the US and Japan had been rising since the invasion of Manchuria in 1931 (see pp.22–23). The subsequent expansion of Japanese influence in the region put the US on alert and prompted it to move its Pacific Fleet to Pearl Harbor, Hawaii, in 1940, as a deterrent. When Japan took control of Indochina in mid-1941, the US ceased all exports to the country, so Japan set its sights on the oil-rich Dutch East Indies. The US opened negotiations with Japan that summer in an attempt to improve relations, but no agreement was reached. The Japanese Prime Minister Fumimaro Konoe resigned on October 16, to be replaced by a more hawkish military government under General Hideki Tojo. Final exchanges between the two sides

proved fruitless, and on December 1, Japanese Emperor Hirohito approved a "war against United States, Great Britain, and Holland."

Japanese strategists knew that the US base in Pearl Harbor was vulnerable and had made plans earlier in the year for a strike. Success would prevent the Pacific Fleet from interfering in the Japanese conquest of the Dutch East Indies and Malaya and buy time for Japan to increase its strength in the region. Japan hoped an attack would undermine American morale, forcing the US to seek a compromise peace. When the attack came, the Americans were unprepared, but the effect was the opposite of Japan's hopes. The US public became united behind a total war to the finish.

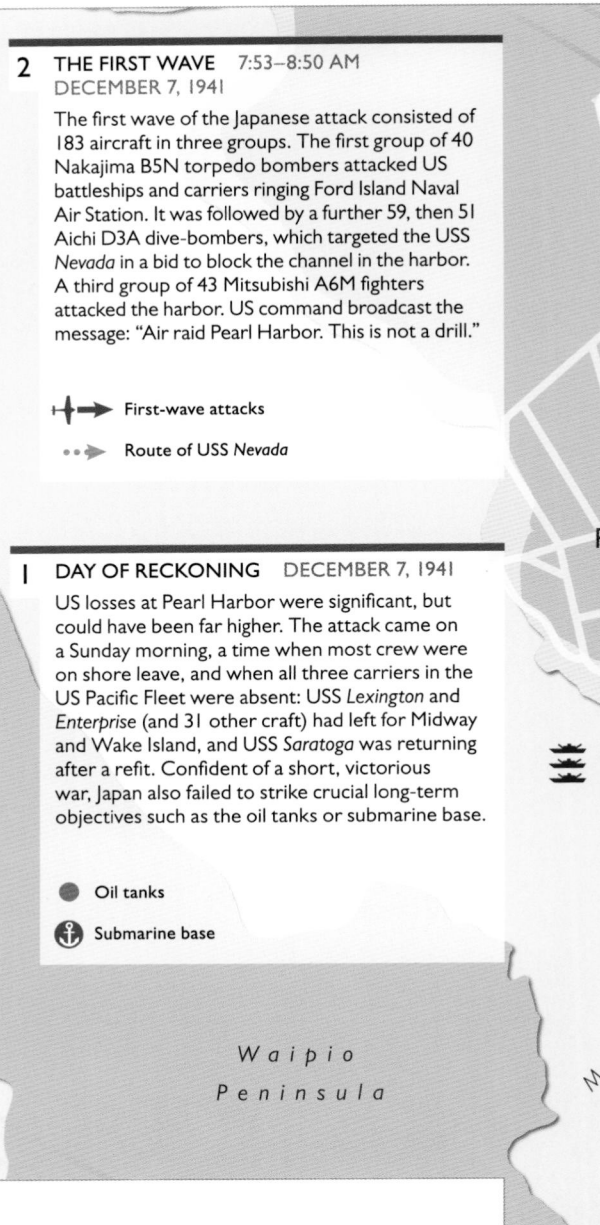

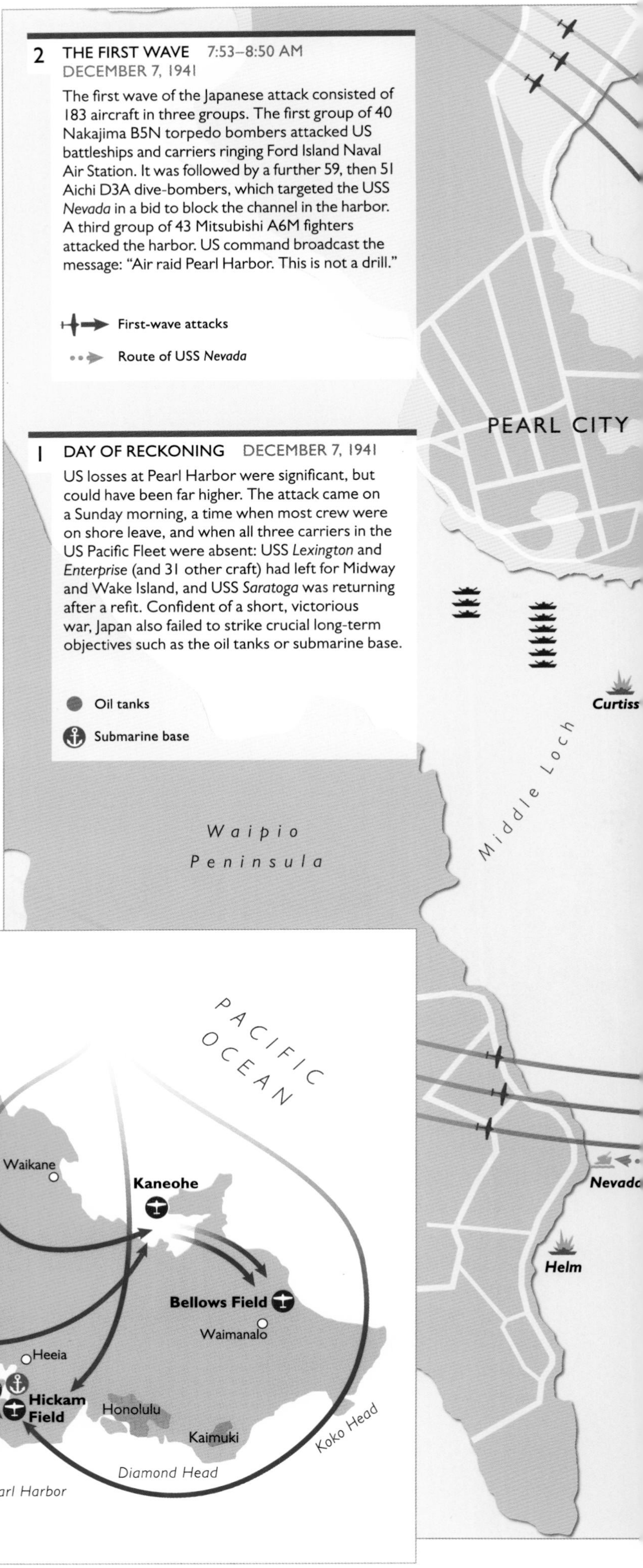

2 THE FIRST WAVE 7:53–8:50 AM
DECEMBER 7, 1941

The first wave of the Japanese attack consisted of 183 aircraft in three groups. The first group of 40 Nakajima B5N torpedo bombers attacked US battleships and carriers ringing Ford Island Naval Air Station. It was followed by a further 59, then 51 Aichi D3A dive-bombers, which targeted the USS *Nevada* in a bid to block the channel in the harbor. A third group of 43 Mitsubishi A6M fighters attacked the harbor. US command broadcast the message: "Air raid Pearl Harbor. This is not a drill."

�»→ First-wave attacks

•••➤ Route of USS *Nevada*

1 DAY OF RECKONING DECEMBER 7, 1941

US losses at Pearl Harbor were significant, but could have been far higher. The attack came on a Sunday morning, a time when most crew were on shore leave, and when all three carriers in the US Pacific Fleet were absent: USS *Lexington* and *Enterprise* (and 31 other craft) had left for Midway and Wake Island, and USS *Saratoga* was returning after a refit. Confident of a short, victorious war, Japan also failed to strike crucial long-term objectives such as the oil tanks or submarine base.

● Oil tanks

⚓ Submarine base

ROUTE OF THE ATTACK

The Japanese Striking Force, made up of six aircraft carriers carrying more than 400 aircraft, 14 other ships, and eight oil tankers, left the Kurile Islands in northern Japan on November 26 and assembled north of Hawaii. It was supported by 23 submarines from ports in mainland Japan. The plan was to launch two waves of air attacks, targeting not just the vessels in Pearl Harbor but also oil tanks, dockyards, air and naval bases, and military barracks across the island. The first wave of Japanese aircraft was detected by US radar, which mistook it for the scheduled arrival of six B-17 bombers from California.

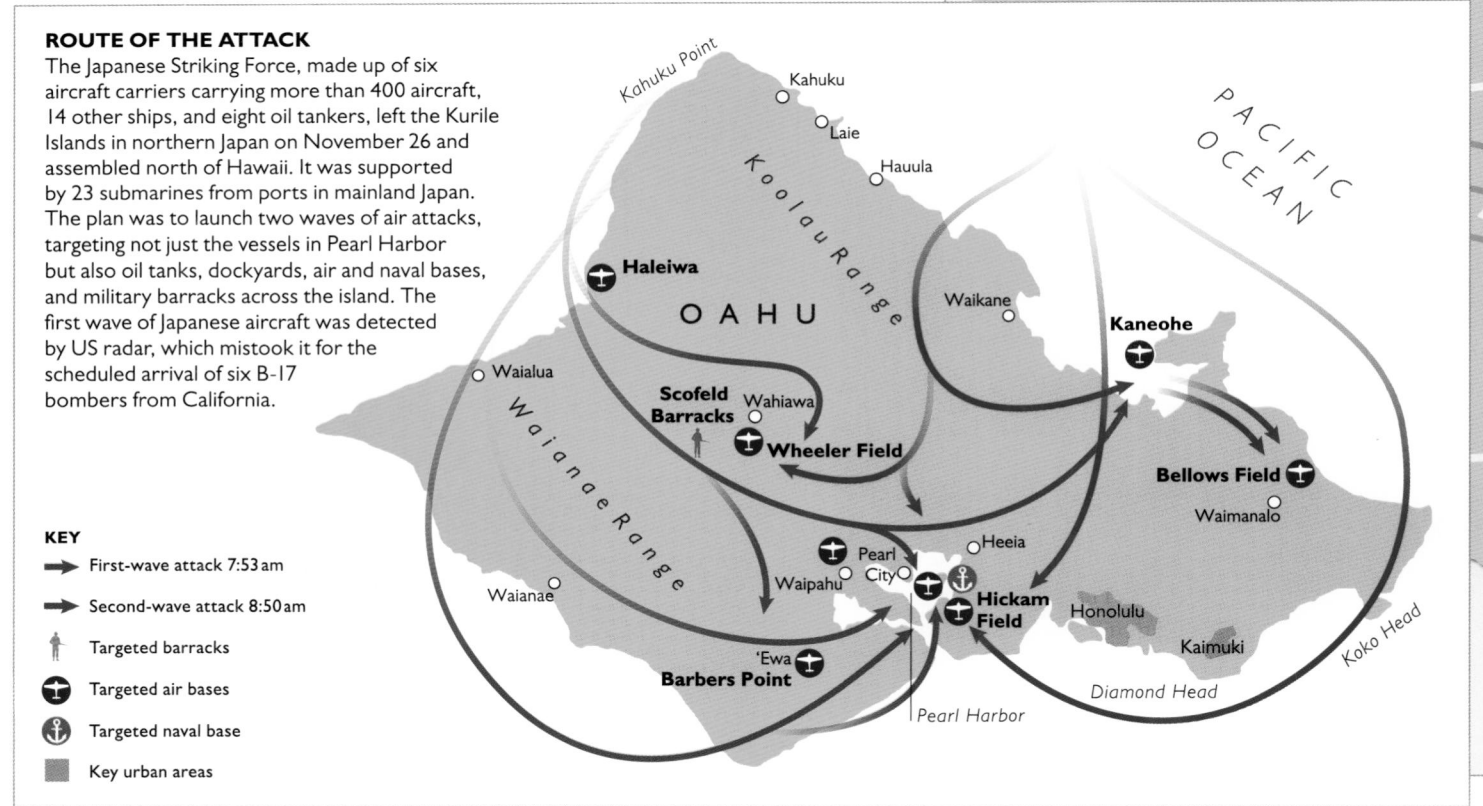

KEY

➤ First-wave attack 7:53 am

➤ Second-wave attack 8:50 am

🏃 Targeted barracks

⊕ Targeted air bases

⚓ Targeted naval base

▪ Key urban areas

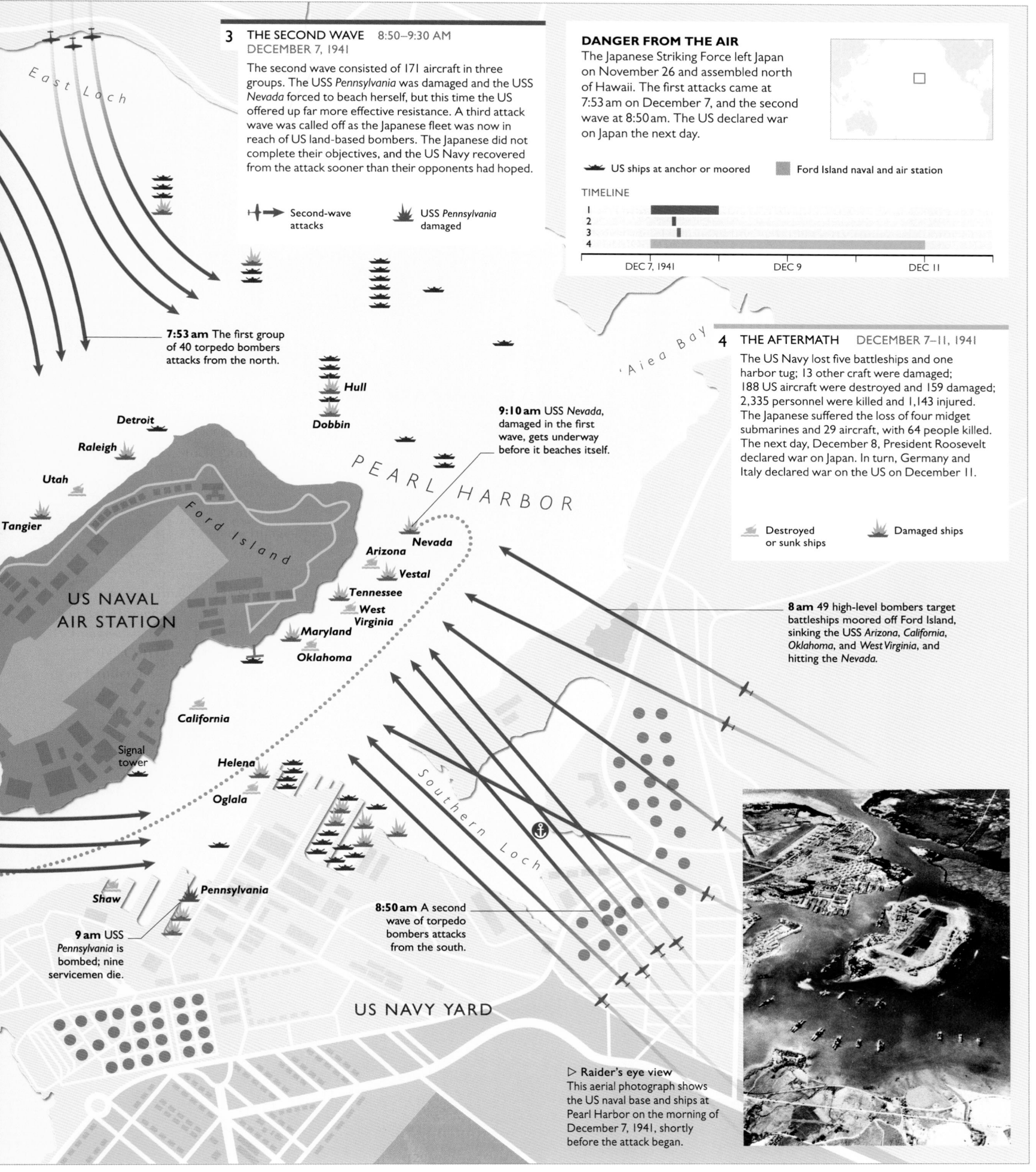

East Loch

3 THE SECOND WAVE 8:50–9:30 AM
DECEMBER 7, 1941

The second wave consisted of 171 aircraft in three groups. The USS *Pennsylvania* was damaged and the USS *Nevada* forced to beach herself, but this time the US offered up far more effective resistance. A third attack wave was called off as the Japanese fleet was now in reach of US land-based bombers. The Japanese did not complete their objectives, and the US Navy recovered from the attack sooner than their opponents had hoped.

⊢─► Second-wave attacks

🌿 USS *Pennsylvania* damaged

7:53 am The first group of 40 torpedo bombers attacks from the north.

Hull

Dobbin

9:10 am USS *Nevada*, damaged in the first wave, gets underway before it beaches itself.

Detroit

Raleigh

Utah

Tangier

Ford Island

US NAVAL AIR STATION

PEARL HARBOR

'Aiea Bay

Nevada

Arizona

Vestal

Tennessee

West Virginia

Maryland

Oklahoma

California

Signal tower

Helena

Oglala

Southern Loch

⚓

Shaw

Pennsylvania

9 am USS *Pennsylvania* is bombed; nine servicemen die.

8:50 am A second wave of torpedo bombers attacks from the south.

US NAVY YARD

DANGER FROM THE AIR
The Japanese Striking Force left Japan on November 26 and assembled north of Hawaii. The first attacks came at 7:53 am on December 7, and the second wave at 8:50 am. The US declared war on Japan the next day.

🌊 US ships at anchor or moored

⬛ Ford Island naval and air station

TIMELINE
1
2
3
4

DEC 7, 1941   DEC 9   DEC 11

4 THE AFTERMATH   DECEMBER 7–11, 1941

The US Navy lost five battleships and one harbor tug; 13 other craft were damaged; 188 US aircraft were destroyed and 159 damaged; 2,335 personnel were killed and 1,143 injured. The Japanese suffered the loss of four midget submarines and 29 aircraft, with 64 people killed. The next day, December 8, President Roosevelt declared war on Japan. In turn, Germany and Italy declared war on the US on December 11.

🚢 Destroyed or sunk ships

🌿 Damaged ships

8 am 49 high-level bombers target battleships moored off Ford Island, sinking the USS *Arizona, California, Oklahoma,* and *West Virginia,* and hitting the *Nevada.*

▷ **Raider's eye view**
This aerial photograph shows the US naval base and ships at Pearl Harbor on the morning of December 7, 1941, shortly before the attack began.

4 THE FALL OF HONG KONG
DECEMBER 8–25, 1941

The Japanese attacked the British colony Hong Kong just four hours after their assault on Pearl Harbor. After fierce fighting, Hong Kong surrendered on December 25. Many British and Commonwealth prisoners were massacred. The Japanese victory was symbolic—beating the British—rather than military, because Hong Kong had little strategic value. Neighboring Portuguese Macau was left neutral, although the Japanese installed a protectorate there in September 1943.

🏴 Japanese victory

5 ATTACKING THE EAST INDIES
DECEMBER 15, 1941–JANUARY 31, 1942

Three Japanese forces attacked the East Indies. The Western Force landed in British Sarawak on December 15 and launched attacks on Brunei, North Borneo, and the Dutch islands of Sumatra and Java. The Central Force, based at Davao in the Philippines, headed for Dutch Borneo, while the Eastern Force, also from Davao, attacked Dutch Celebes, Amboina, Timor, Bali, and eastern Java.

⚔ Japanese naval encounter

→ Japanese advances in the East Indies

🪂 Japanese paratroop drop

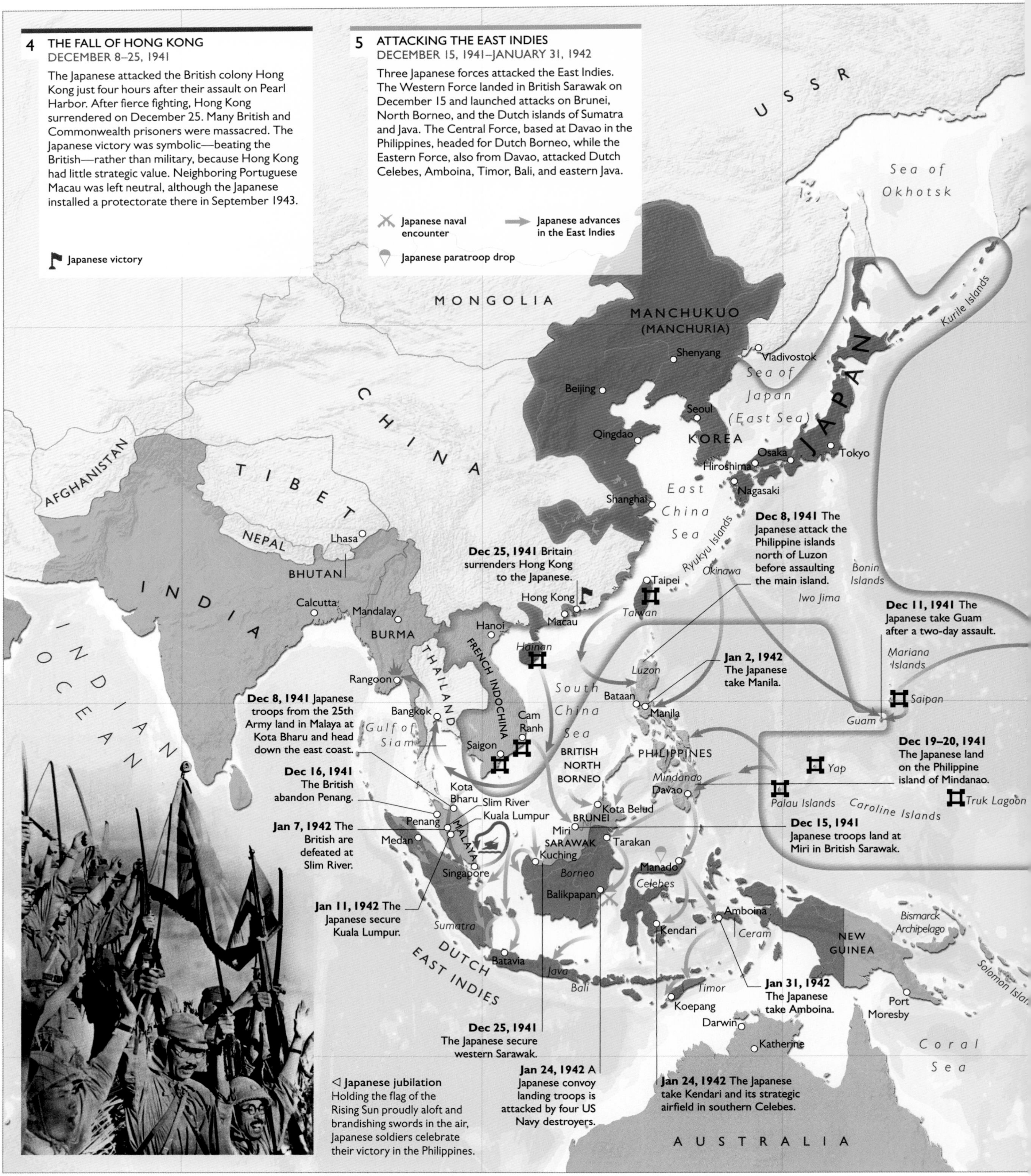

Dec 8, 1941 The Japanese attack the Philippine islands north of Luzon before assaulting the main island.

Dec 11, 1941 The Japanese take Guam after a two-day assault.

Dec 25, 1941 Britain surrenders Hong Kong to the Japanese.

Jan 2, 1942 The Japanese take Manila.

Dec 8, 1941 Japanese troops from the 25th Army land in Malaya at Kota Bharu and head down the east coast.

Dec 16, 1941 The British abandon Penang.

Jan 7, 1942 The British are defeated at Slim River.

Jan 11, 1942 The Japanese secure Kuala Lumpur.

Dec 19–20, 1941 The Japanese land on the Philippine island of Mindanao.

Dec 15, 1941 Japanese troops land at Miri in British Sarawak.

Dec 25, 1941 The Japanese secure western Sarawak.

Jan 24, 1942 A Japanese convoy landing troops is attacked by four US Navy destroyers.

Jan 31, 1942 The Japanese take Amboina.

Jan 24, 1942 The Japanese take Kendari and its strategic airfield in southern Celebes.

◁ **Japanese jubilation** Holding the flag of the Rising Sun proudly aloft and brandishing swords in the air, Japanese soldiers celebrate their victory in the Philippines.

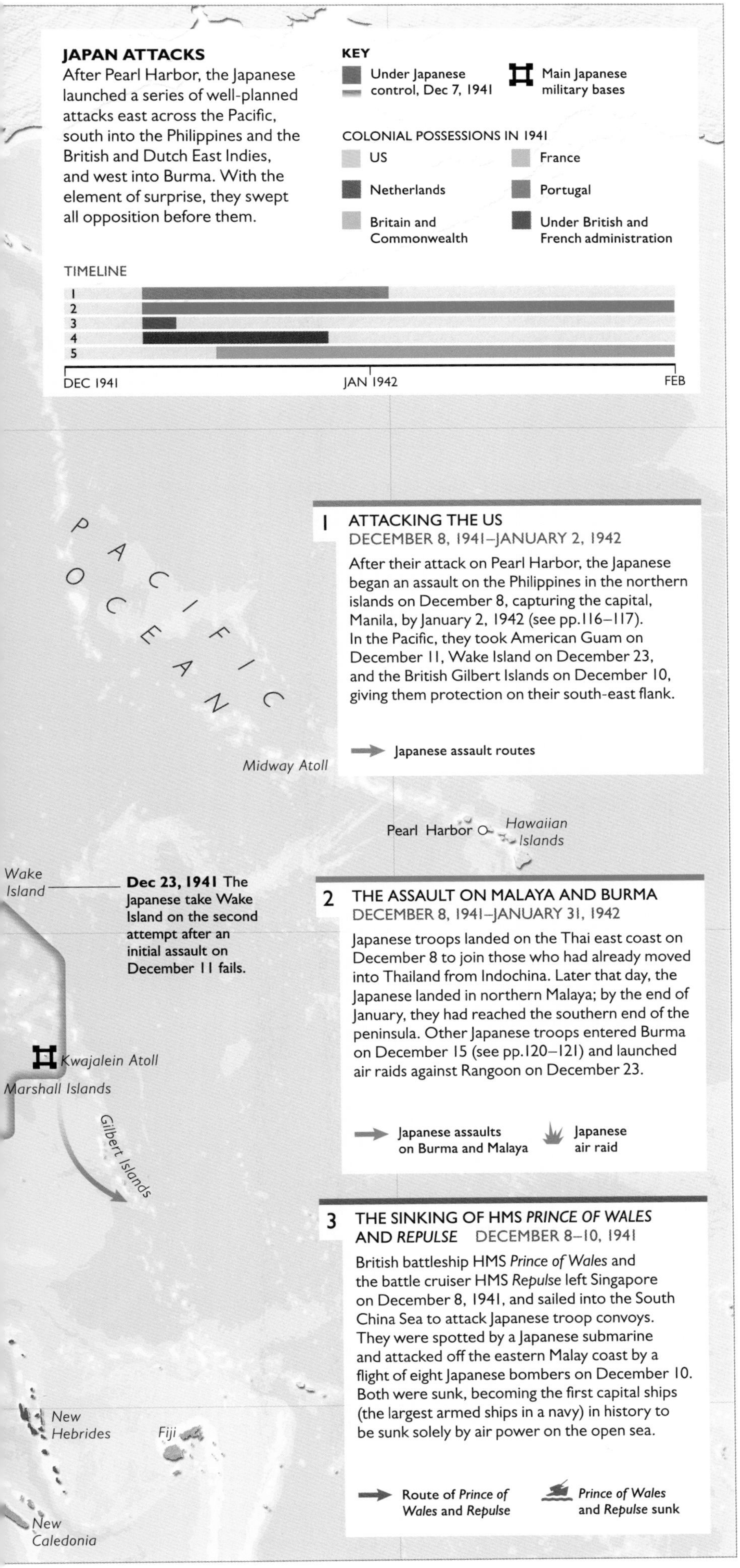

JAPAN ATTACKS

After Pearl Harbor, the Japanese launched a series of well-planned attacks east across the Pacific, south into the Philippines and the British and Dutch East Indies, and west into Burma. With the element of surprise, they swept all opposition before them.

KEY

- ■ Under Japanese control, Dec 7, 1941
- ⌗ Main Japanese military bases

COLONIAL POSSESSIONS IN 1941

- US
- France
- Netherlands
- Portugal
- Britain and Commonwealth
- Under British and French administration

TIMELINE

```
1
2
3
4
5
DEC 1941          JAN 1942          FEB
```

Midway Atoll

Wake Island

Dec 23, 1941 The Japanese take Wake Island on the second attempt after an initial assault on December 11 fails.

⌗ *Kwajalein Atoll*
Marshall Islands

Gilbert Islands

New Hebrides   *Fiji*

New Caledonia

Pearl Harbor ○ Hawaiian Islands

1 ATTACKING THE US
DECEMBER 8, 1941–JANUARY 2, 1942

After their attack on Pearl Harbor, the Japanese began an assault on the Philippines in the northern islands on December 8, capturing the capital, Manila, by January 2, 1942 (see pp.116–117). In the Pacific, they took American Guam on December 11, Wake Island on December 23, and the British Gilbert Islands on December 10, giving them protection on their south-east flank.

→ Japanese assault routes

2 THE ASSAULT ON MALAYA AND BURMA
DECEMBER 8, 1941–JANUARY 31, 1942

Japanese troops landed on the Thai east coast on December 8 to join those who had already moved into Thailand from Indochina. Later that day, the Japanese landed in northern Malaya; by the end of January, they had reached the southern end of the peninsula. Other Japanese troops entered Burma on December 15 (see pp.120–121) and launched air raids against Rangoon on December 23.

→ Japanese assaults on Burma and Malaya
↯ Japanese air raid

3 THE SINKING OF HMS *PRINCE OF WALES* AND *REPULSE*   DECEMBER 8–10, 1941

British battleship HMS *Prince of Wales* and the battle cruiser HMS *Repulse* left Singapore on December 8, 1941, and sailed into the South China Sea to attack Japanese troop convoys. They were spotted by a Japanese submarine and attacked off the eastern Malay coast by a flight of eight Japanese bombers on December 10. Both were sunk, becoming the first capital ships (the largest armed ships in a navy) in history to be sunk solely by air power on the open sea.

→ Route of *Prince of Wales* and *Repulse*
⚓ *Prince of Wales* and *Repulse* sunk

JAPANESE ADVANCES

The attack on Pearl Harbor on December 7, 1941, marked the start of a campaign by the Japanese to extend their control throughout Southeast Asia and the western Pacific. Within days, they had launched a series of daring amphibious and airborne assaults.

A few days before the events of Pearl Harbor (see pp.110–111), Japanese troops had moved through Thailand, positioning themselves for planned actions. On December 7, troop transports gathered in the Gulf of Siam ready for an assault on Malaya, which took place the next morning. The first attack on the Philippines occurred on the same day, with the British East Indies coming under attack a week later. By then, two British capital ships had been sunk in the South China Sea and Hong Kong was under assault. US-controlled Guam and Wake Island were quickly lost, the Dutch East Indies came under sustained attack in early January 1942, and by the end of January mainland Malaya was in Japanese hands.

American, British, and Dutch forces suffered heavy defeats, with many men taken prisoner or massacred by the Japanese. The Japanese attack was geographically wide, with air raids on Rangoon in Burma to the west and the capture of the Gilbert Islands in the Pacific to the east. It was also impeccably planned, with surprise and military experience giving the Japanese some easy victories.

"Japan was supreme, and we everywhere were weak and naked."

WINSTON CHURCHILL, *THE SECOND WORLD WAR*, 1950

THAILAND IN THE WAR

Thailand became increasingly authoritarian with the accession in 1938 of the pro-Fascist Luang Phibunsongkhram (right) as prime minister. A former field marshal who was pro-Japanese, Phibunsongkhram was pressured into allowing Japanese troops to pass through Thailand in late November 1941; however, on December 8 Japan issued an ultimatum and invaded anyway. Phibunsongkhram ordered an armistice and signed an alliance with Japan, undertaking to assist its war; he gained two states in Burma as a reward.

AMERICA AT WAR

With the onset of war, life in the US changed dramatically. Millions of men were conscripted, while at home industry geared up to provide necessities for the war effort, turning the country into what President Franklin D. Roosevelt christened "the arsenal of democracy."

△ **Patriotic duty**
A recruiting poster urges women to enroll as volunteer nurses. Around 74,000 served in the US Army and Navy in World War II.

Following the US's entry into the war in December 1941 (see pp.110–111), Roosevelt used a series of War Power Acts to reorganize the economy and industry for total war. Everyday life across the US changed. Meat, sugar, butter, canned goods, gasoline, fuel oil, clothes, and other commodities were all rationed, and civilians planted "victory gardens" to grow their own food. Americans were encouraged to save scrap metal for the war industries, and armament production soared. To fund the expense of waging a global war, US propaganda urged the public to buy war bonds and victory stamps. Meanwhile, anti-Japanese feeling led to the confinement of nearly 120,000 Japanese Americans in west-coast internment camps.

Changes in the workplace

To replace the men drafted into the armed forces, women joined the workplace in ever-increasing numbers. Many were enthusiastic about their new opportunities, some inspired by an advertisement that told them working in a war plant was "a lot more exciting than polishing the family furniture." The war also offered better jobs to thousands of African Americans, who moved from the south to work in the industrial cities of the north, midwest, and west. It was the start of the largest internal migration in US history. However, racial segregation was still in place, and race riots broke out in some urban centers.

HOLLYWOOD AT WAR

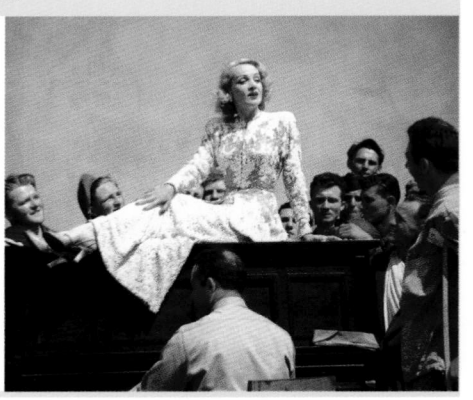

Hollywood played an important role in boosting national morale during the war. Film star and singer Marlene Dietrich (right), who in 1939 renounced her German citizenship and became a US citizen, often entertained the Allied troops. At home, Hollywood star power was used in the drive to raise funds for the war.

Replacing the men
A woman assembles the cowling for an engine of a B-25 bomber. By 1943, around 65 percent of workers in the aircraft industry were women. Their efforts helped the US produce more than 300,000 planes in the course of the war.

JAPAN INVADES THE PHILIPPINES

Following their attack on the US naval base at Pearl Harbor, Hawaii, Japanese troops began to land in the north of the US-held Philippine Islands on December 8, 1941. The US was now under attack across the Pacific Ocean and faced the most serious military challenge that it had known in a generation.

The Japanese began their campaign for the Philippines with heavy air attacks that neutralized US air power in the archipelago. Their first landings were met with little effective resistance, forcing the Commander of US Forces in the East, General Douglas MacArthur, to abandon the capital, Manila, and retreat west to fortify the Bataan Peninsula. Here the American and Filipino troops held out for four more months until forced to surrender on April 9, 1942. The final US redoubt on Corregidor Island fell the next month. The defeat was a blow to American morale, and the Philippine Islands would remain in Japanese hands until their gradual but bloody recovery after October 1944 (see pp.248–249).

The Japanese set up a Council of State to rule the islands until they declared them an independent republic, led by José Laurel, in October 1943. Most of the Filipino elite served the Japanese, but a successful resistance quickly arose, notably on Mindanao, the island furthest from Manila. By the end of the war, some 277 guerrilla units and about 260,000 people were in action. They were so effective that by the end of the war, the Japanese controlled only 12 of the 48 Philippine provinces.

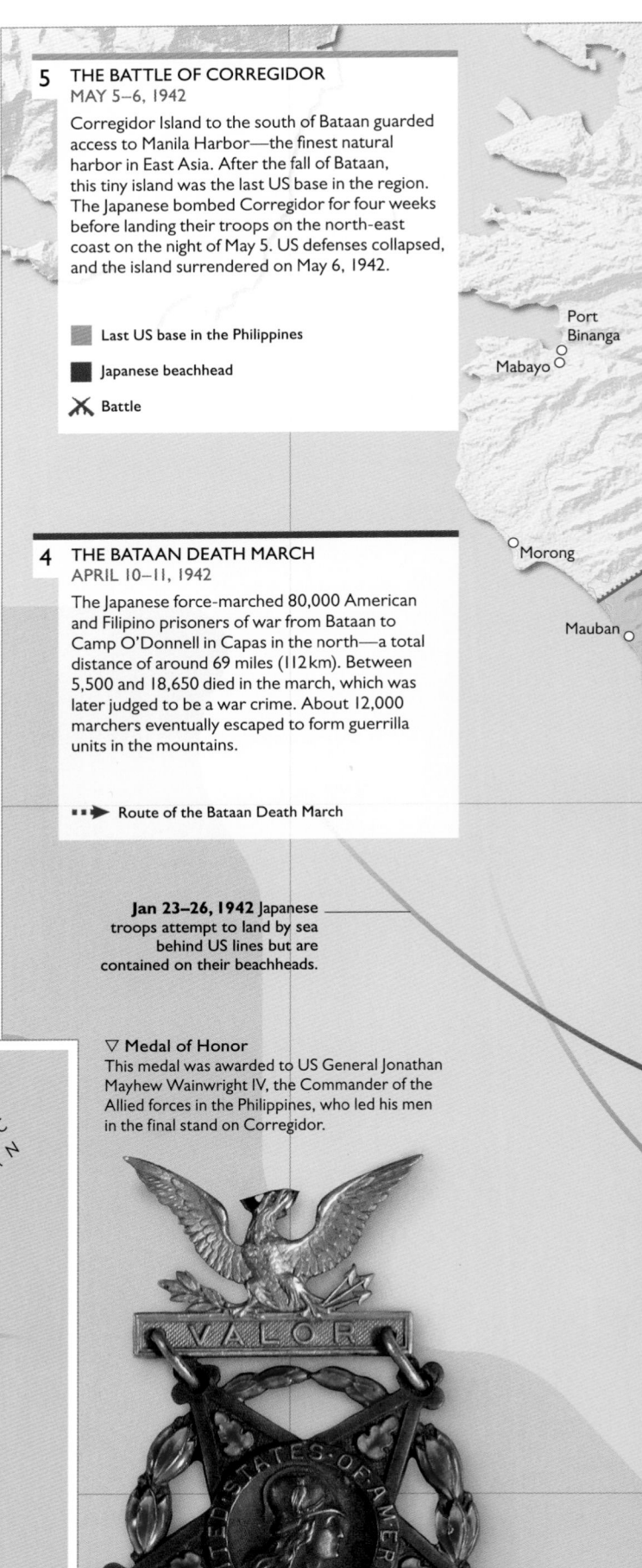

5 THE BATTLE OF CORREGIDOR
MAY 5–6, 1942

Corregidor Island to the south of Bataan guarded access to Manila Harbor—the finest natural harbor in East Asia. After the fall of Bataan, this tiny island was the last US base in the region. The Japanese bombed Corregidor for four weeks before landing their troops on the north-east coast on the night of May 5. US defenses collapsed, and the island surrendered on May 6, 1942.

- ▨ Last US base in the Philippines
- ▉ Japanese beachhead
- ✗ Battle

4 THE BATAAN DEATH MARCH
APRIL 10–11, 1942

The Japanese force-marched 80,000 American and Filipino prisoners of war from Bataan to Camp O'Donnell in Capas in the north—a total distance of around 69 miles (112 km). Between 5,500 and 18,650 died in the march, which was later judged to be a war crime. About 12,000 marchers eventually escaped to form guerrilla units in the mountains.

- ▪▪▶ Route of the Bataan Death March

Jan 23–26, 1942 Japanese troops attempt to land by sea behind US lines but are contained on their beachheads.

▽ **Medal of Honor**
This medal was awarded to US General Jonathan Mayhew Wainwright IV, the Commander of the Allied forces in the Philippines, who led his men in the final stand on Corregidor.

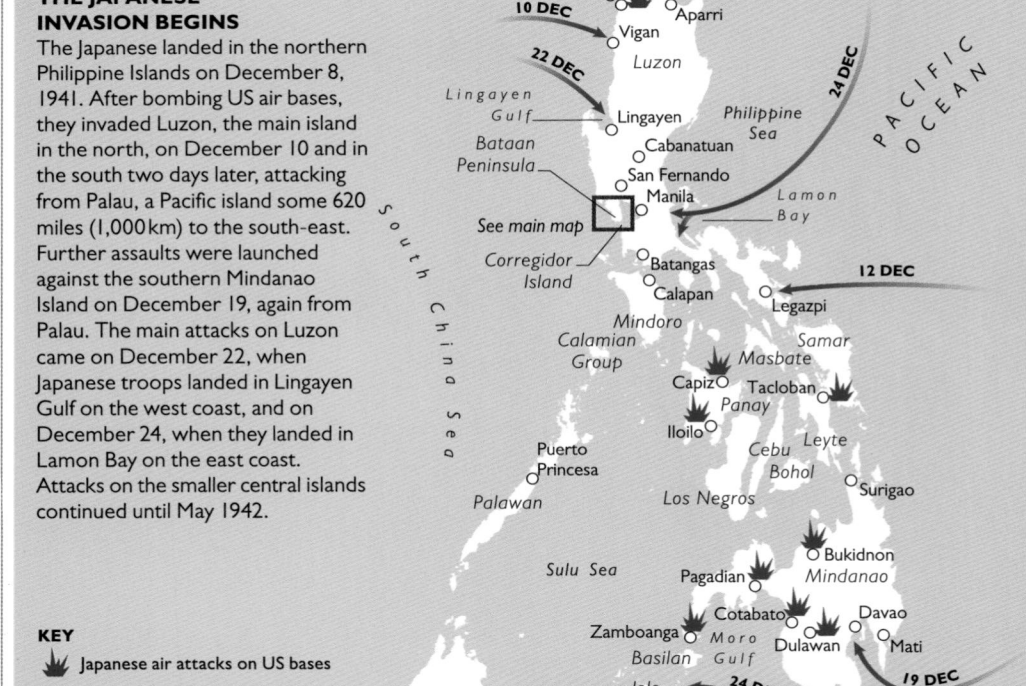

THE JAPANESE INVASION BEGINS

The Japanese landed in the northern Philippine Islands on December 8, 1941. After bombing US air bases, they invaded Luzon, the main island in the north, on December 10 and in the south two days later, attacking from Palau, a Pacific island some 620 miles (1,000 km) to the south-east. Further assaults were launched against the southern Mindanao Island on December 19, again from Palau. The main attacks on Luzon came on December 22, when Japanese troops landed in Lingayen Gulf on the west coast, and on December 24, when they landed in Lamon Bay on the east coast. Attacks on the smaller central islands continued until May 1942.

KEY
- ✹ Japanese air attacks on US bases
- ➜ Japanese landings

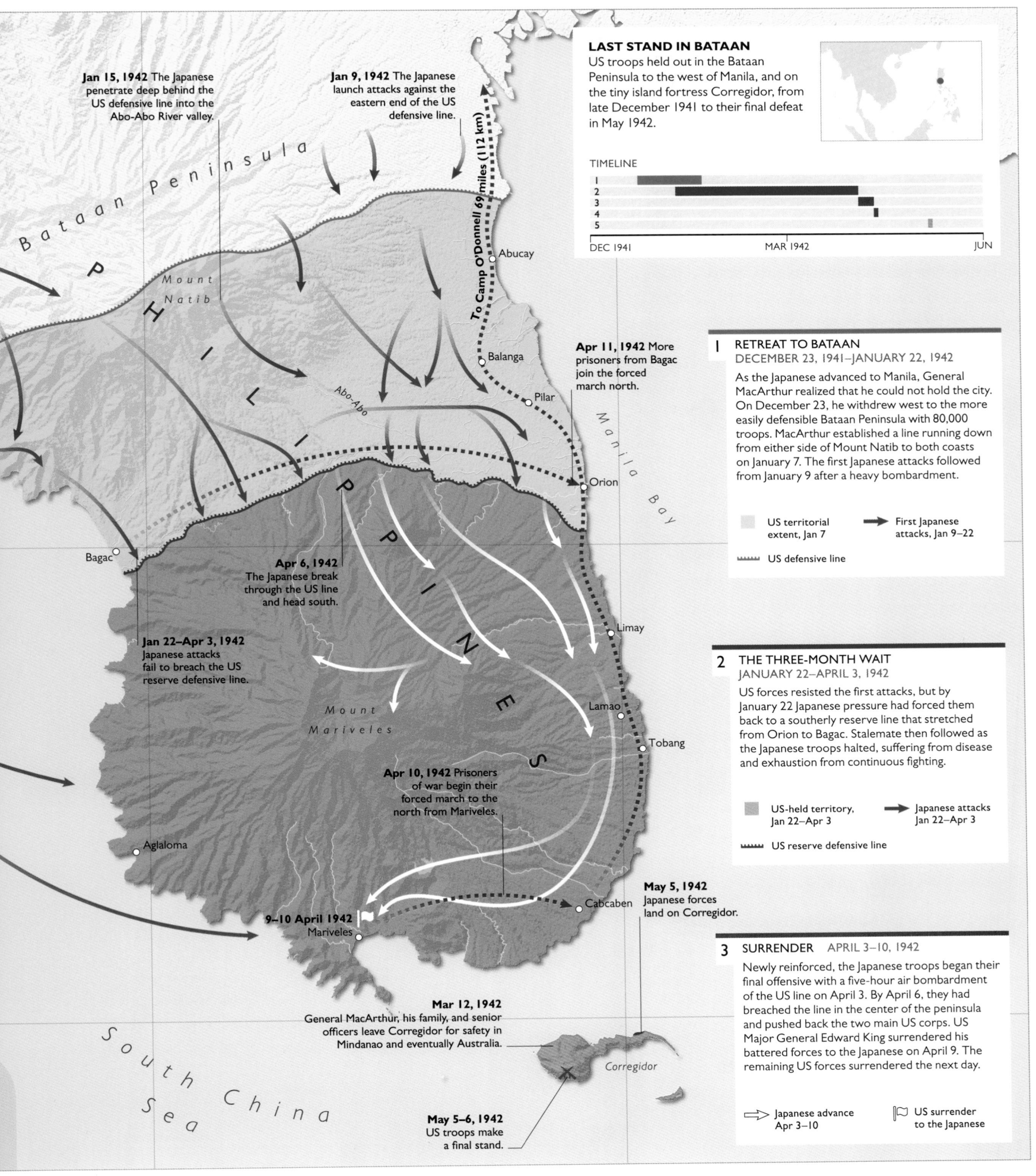

Jan 15, 1942 The Japanese penetrate deep behind the US defensive line into the Abo-Abo River valley.

Jan 9, 1942 The Japanese launch attacks against the eastern end of the US defensive line.

To Camp O'Donnell 69 miles (112 km)

Abucay

Balanga

Apr 11, 1942 More prisoners from Bagac join the forced march north.

Pilar

Orion

Bagac

Apr 6, 1942 The Japanese break through the US line and head south.

Jan 22–Apr 3, 1942 Japanese attacks fail to breach the US reserve defensive line.

Limay

Mount Mariveles

Lamao

Tobang

Apr 10, 1942 Prisoners of war begin their forced march to the north from Mariveles.

Aglaloma

9–10 April 1942 Mariveles

Cabcaben

May 5, 1942 Japanese forces land on Corregidor.

Mar 12, 1942 General MacArthur, his family, and senior officers leave Corregidor for safety in Mindanao and eventually Australia.

South China Sea

Corregidor

May 5–6, 1942 US troops make a final stand.

Bataan Peninsula

Mount Natib

Abo-Abo

Manila Bay

PHILIPPINES

LAST STAND IN BATAAN

US troops held out in the Bataan Peninsula to the west of Manila, and on the tiny island fortress Corregidor, from late December 1941 to their final defeat in May 1942.

TIMELINE

1			
2			
3			
4			
5			

DEC 1941   MAR 1942   JUN

1 RETREAT TO BATAAN
DECEMBER 23, 1941–JANUARY 22, 1942

As the Japanese advanced to Manila, General MacArthur realized that he could not hold the city. On December 23, he withdrew west to the more easily defensible Bataan Peninsula with 80,000 troops. MacArthur established a line running down from either side of Mount Natib to both coasts on January 7. The first Japanese attacks followed from January 9 after a heavy bombardment.

- US territorial extent, Jan 7
- → First Japanese attacks, Jan 9–22
- US defensive line

2 THE THREE-MONTH WAIT
JANUARY 22–APRIL 3, 1942

US forces resisted the first attacks, but by January 22 Japanese pressure had forced them back to a southerly reserve line that stretched from Orion to Bagac. Stalemate then followed as the Japanese troops halted, suffering from disease and exhaustion from continuous fighting.

- US-held territory, Jan 22–Apr 3
- → Japanese attacks Jan 22–Apr 3
- US reserve defensive line

3 SURRENDER APRIL 3–10, 1942

Newly reinforced, the Japanese troops began their final offensive with a five-hour air bombardment of the US line on April 3. By April 6, they had breached the line in the center of the peninsula and pushed back the two main US corps. US Major General Edward King surrendered his battered forces to the Japanese on April 9. The remaining US forces surrendered the next day.

- ⇨ Japanese advance Apr 3–10
- US surrender to the Japanese

SURRENDER AT SINGAPORE

The fall of the British colony of Singapore to the Japanese in February 1942 led to the largest surrender of British-led personnel in military history. It was described by prime minister Winston Churchill as the worst disaster ever to befall the British in wartime.

Japanese forces commanded by General Tomoyuki Yamashita had invaded British Malaya on December 8, 1941 (see pp.112–113). Through superior tactics and mobility they defeated the British and Commonwealth forces, and by January 30, 1942, had reached the Johore Strait at the southern tip of the Malay Peninsula. The exhausted Allied troops crossed to Singapore Island via a causeway, which they then partially destroyed in the hope of delaying Japanese progress. By this time though, the Japanese had reliable intelligence on the weak state of "Fortress Singapore," and invaded on February 9.

> "My attack on Singapore was a bluff—a bluff that worked."
>
> GENERAL TOMOYUKI YAMASHITA

Outgunned, outmaneuvered, and with inadequate air support—yet with more than twice the number of troops that the Japanese had—the British and Commonwealth forces were soon pushed back into Singapore city itself. They were forced into a humiliating surrender on February 15. It later became clear that while the British were running out of supplies in the last days of the battle, so were the Japanese, who were low on ammunition for their artillery. However, had the British commander Lieutenant-General Arthur Percival decided to fight on, victory would have been unlikely.

THE BRITISH NAVAL BASE IN SINGAPORE

Completed in 1939 at a staggering cost of $500 million, Singapore's naval base boasted what was then the largest dry dock in the world, the third-largest floating dock (below), and enough fuel tanks to support the entire British navy for six months. It was defended by heavy 15-in naval guns and also by airforce squadrons stationed at Tengah Air Base. Winston Churchill touted it as an impregnable fortress, the "Gibraltar of the East."

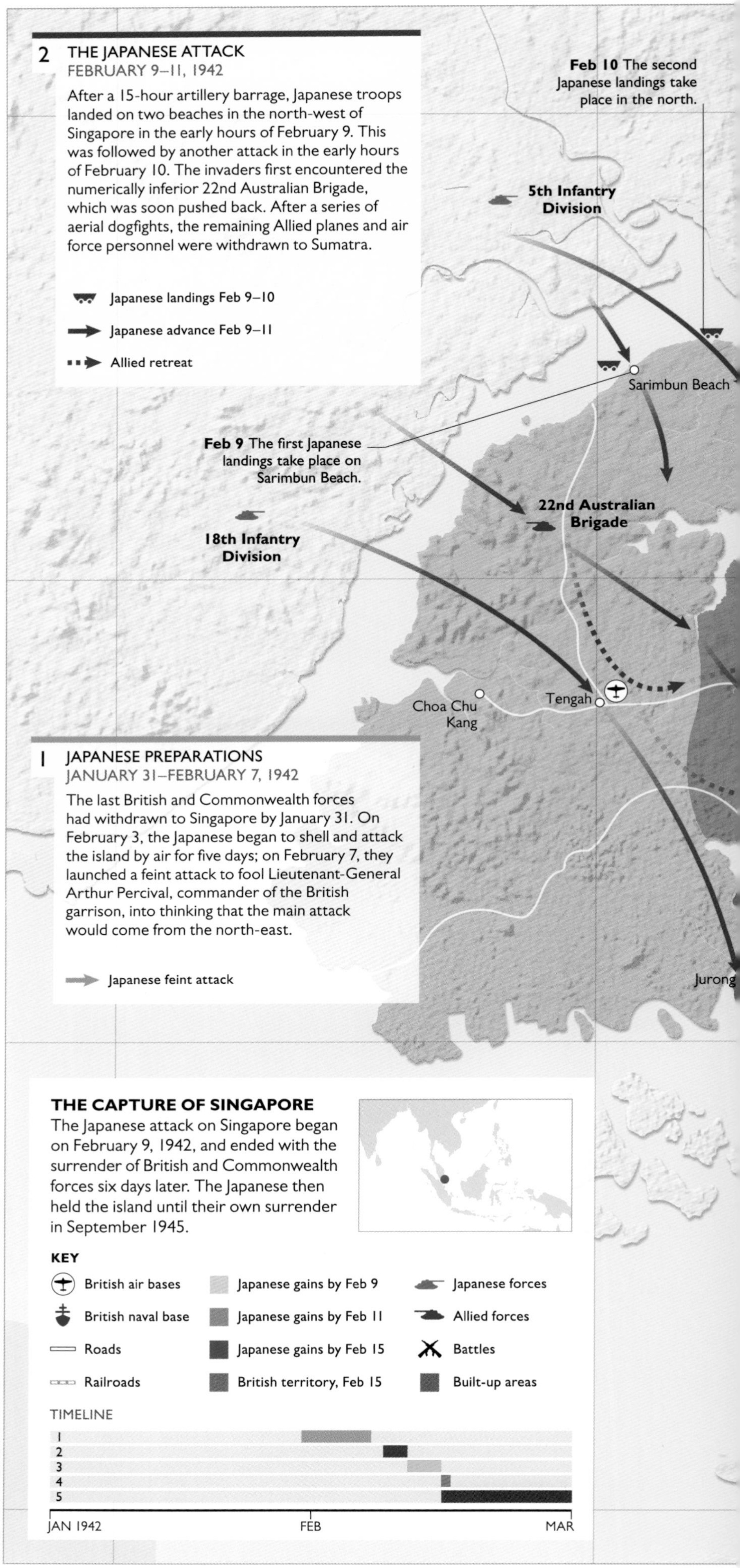

---

2 THE JAPANESE ATTACK
FEBRUARY 9–11, 1942

After a 15-hour artillery barrage, Japanese troops landed on two beaches in the north-west of Singapore in the early hours of February 9. This was followed by another attack in the early hours of February 10. The invaders first encountered the numerically inferior 22nd Australian Brigade, which was soon pushed back. After a series of aerial dogfights, the remaining Allied planes and air force personnel were withdrawn to Sumatra.

- Japanese landings Feb 9–10
- Japanese advance Feb 9–11
- Allied retreat

Feb 10 The second Japanese landings take place in the north.

5th Infantry Division

Sarimbun Beach

Feb 9 The first Japanese landings take place on Sarimbun Beach.

18th Infantry Division

22nd Australian Brigade

Choa Chu Kang

Tengah

1 JAPANESE PREPARATIONS
JANUARY 31–FEBRUARY 7, 1942

The last British and Commonwealth forces had withdrawn to Singapore by January 31. On February 3, the Japanese began to shell and attack the island by air for five days; on February 7, they launched a feint attack to fool Lieutenant-General Arthur Percival, commander of the British garrison, into thinking that the main attack would come from the north-east.

- Japanese feint attack

Jurong

THE CAPTURE OF SINGAPORE

The Japanese attack on Singapore began on February 9, 1942, and ended with the surrender of British and Commonwealth forces six days later. The Japanese then held the island until their own surrender in September 1945.

KEY

British air bases	Japanese gains by Feb 9	Japanese forces
British naval base	Japanese gains by Feb 11	Allied forces
Roads	Japanese gains by Feb 15	Battles
Railroads	British territory, Feb 15	Built-up areas

TIMELINE

1
2
3
4
5

JAN 1942   FEB   MAR

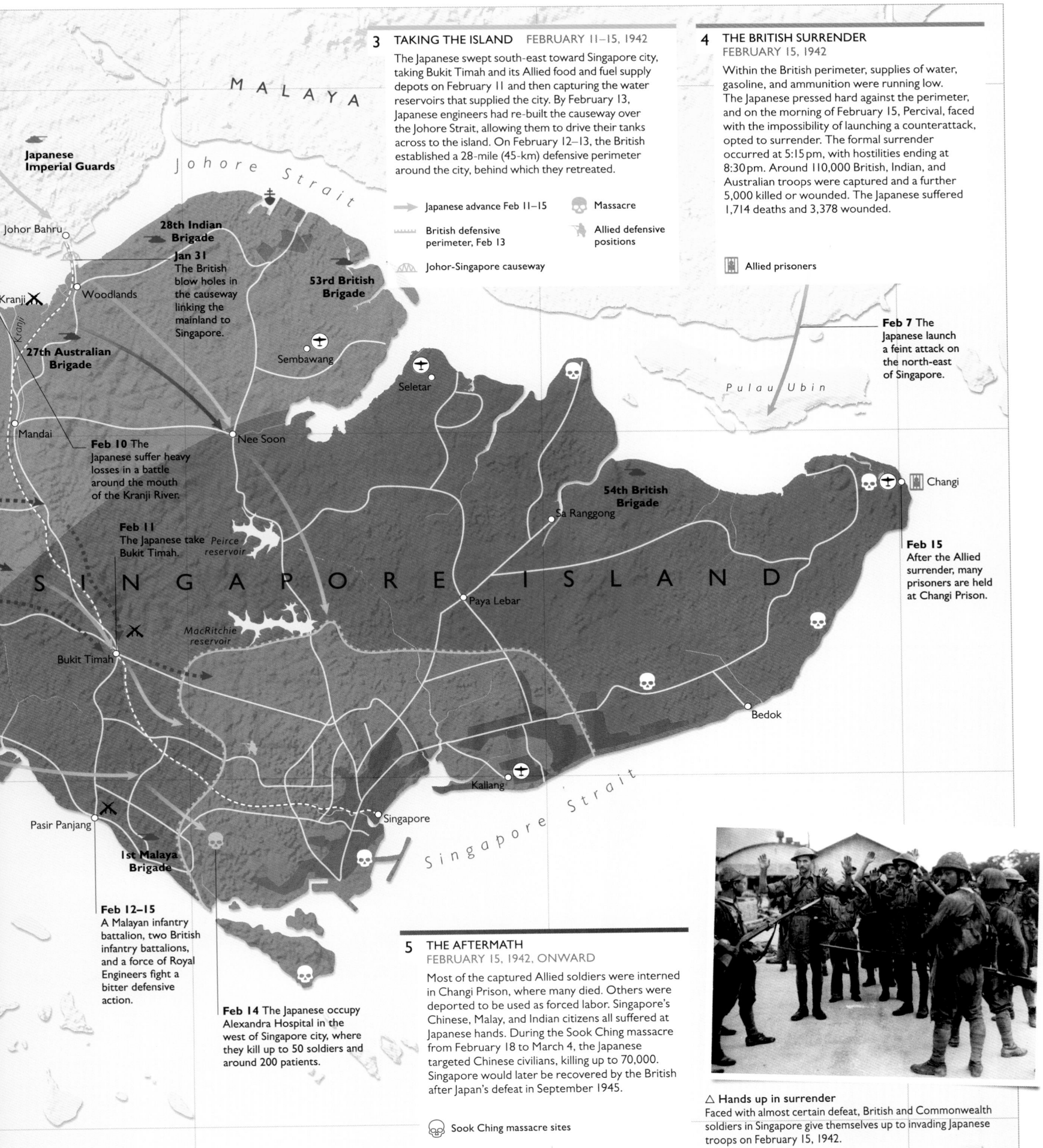

MALAYA

Johore Strait

Japanese Imperial Guards

Johor Bahru

28th Indian Brigade

Kranji

Woodlands

Jan 31
The British blow holes in the causeway linking the mainland to Singapore.

53rd British Brigade

Sembawang

27th Australian Brigade

Seletar

Mandai

Feb 10 The Japanese suffer heavy losses in a battle around the mouth of the Kranji River.

Nee Soon

Pulau Ubin

Feb 7 The Japanese launch a feint attack on the north-east of Singapore.

Feb 11 The Japanese take Bukit Timah.

Peirce reservoir

54th British Brigade

Sa Ranggong

Changi

SINGAPORE ISLAND

MacRitchie reservoir

Bukit Timah

Paya Lebar

Feb 15 After the Allied surrender, many prisoners are held at Changi Prison.

Pasir Panjang

Bedok

1st Malaya Brigade

Feb 12–15
A Malayan infantry battalion, two British infantry battalions, and a force of Royal Engineers fight a bitter defensive action.

Kallang

Singapore Strait

Singapore

Feb 14 The Japanese occupy Alexandra Hospital in the west of Singapore city, where they kill up to 50 soldiers and around 200 patients.

3 TAKING THE ISLAND FEBRUARY 11–15, 1942

The Japanese swept south-east toward Singapore city, taking Bukit Timah and its Allied food and fuel supply depots on February 11 and then capturing the water reservoirs that supplied the city. By February 13, Japanese engineers had re-built the causeway over the Johore Strait, allowing them to drive their tanks across to the island. On February 12–13, the British established a 28-mile (45-km) defensive perimeter around the city, behind which they retreated.

→ Japanese advance Feb 11–15

〰 British defensive perimeter, Feb 13

⛰ Johor-Singapore causeway

💀 Massacre

🏃 Allied defensive positions

4 THE BRITISH SURRENDER
FEBRUARY 15, 1942

Within the British perimeter, supplies of water, gasoline, and ammunition were running low. The Japanese pressed hard against the perimeter, and on the morning of February 15, Percival, faced with the impossibility of launching a counterattack, opted to surrender. The formal surrender occurred at 5:15 pm, with hostilities ending at 8:30 pm. Around 110,000 British, Indian, and Australian troops were captured and a further 5,000 killed or wounded. The Japanese suffered 1,714 deaths and 3,378 wounded.

🏛 Allied prisoners

5 THE AFTERMATH
FEBRUARY 15, 1942, ONWARD

Most of the captured Allied soldiers were interned in Changi Prison, where many died. Others were deported to be used as forced labor. Singapore's Chinese, Malay, and Indian citizens all suffered at Japanese hands. During the Sook Ching massacre from February 18 to March 4, the Japanese targeted Chinese civilians, killing up to 70,000. Singapore would later be recovered by the British after Japan's defeat in September 1945.

💀 Sook Ching massacre sites

△ **Hands up in surrender**
Faced with almost certain defeat, British and Commonwealth soldiers in Singapore give themselves up to invading Japanese troops on February 15, 1942.

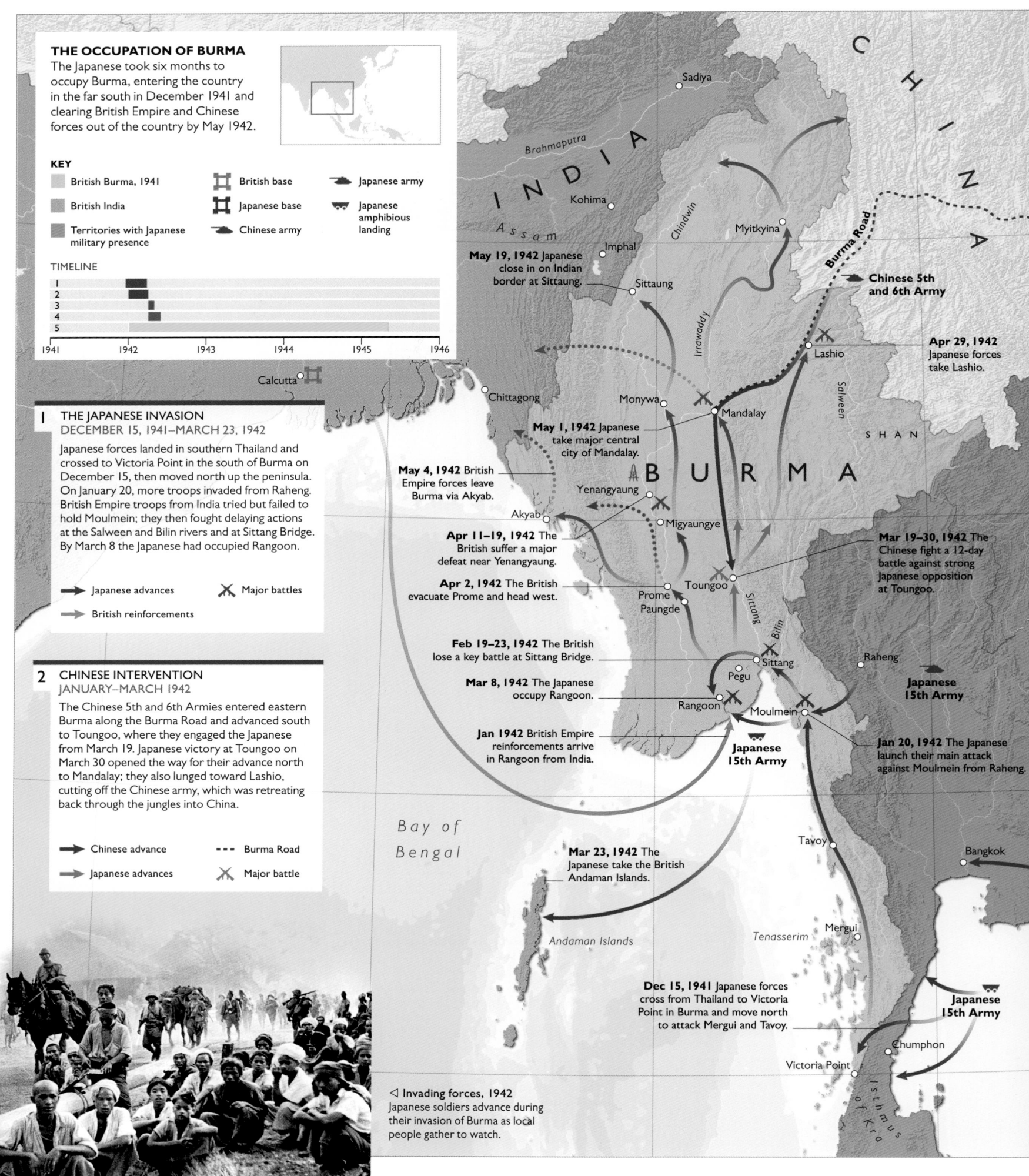

THE OCCUPATION OF BURMA

The Japanese took six months to occupy Burma, entering the country in the far south in December 1941 and clearing British Empire and Chinese forces out of the country by May 1942.

KEY

British Burma, 1941	British base	Japanese army
British India	Japanese base	Japanese amphibious landing
Territories with Japanese military presence	Chinese army	

TIMELINE

1
2
3
4
5

1941   1942   1943   1944   1945   1946

1   THE JAPANESE INVASION
DECEMBER 15, 1941–MARCH 23, 1942

Japanese forces landed in southern Thailand and crossed to Victoria Point in the south of Burma on December 15, then moved north up the peninsula. On January 20, more troops invaded from Raheng. British Empire troops from India tried but failed to hold Moulmein; they then fought delaying actions at the Salween and Bilin rivers and at Sittang Bridge. By March 8 the Japanese had occupied Rangoon.

Japanese advances   Major battles

British reinforcements

2   CHINESE INTERVENTION
JANUARY–MARCH 1942

The Chinese 5th and 6th Armies entered eastern Burma along the Burma Road and advanced south to Toungoo, where they engaged the Japanese from March 19. Japanese victory at Toungoo on March 30 opened the way for their advance north to Mandalay; they also lunged toward Lashio, cutting off the Chinese army, which was retreating back through the jungles into China.

Chinese advance   - - - Burma Road

Japanese advances   Major battle

May 19, 1942 Japanese close in on Indian border at Sittaung.

Chinese 5th and 6th Army

Apr 29, 1942 Japanese forces take Lashio.

May 1, 1942 Japanese take major central city of Mandalay.

May 4, 1942 British Empire forces leave Burma via Akyab.

Apr 11–19, 1942 The British suffer a major defeat near Yenangyaung.

Mar 19–30, 1942 The Chinese fight a 12-day battle against strong Japanese opposition at Toungoo.

Apr 2, 1942 The British evacuate Prome and head west.

Feb 19–23, 1942 The British lose a key battle at Sittang Bridge.

Mar 8, 1942 The Japanese occupy Rangoon.

Japanese 15th Army

Jan 1942 British Empire reinforcements arrive in Rangoon from India.

Jan 20, 1942 The Japanese launch their main attack against Moulmein from Raheng.

Japanese 15th Army

Bay of Bengal

Mar 23, 1942 The Japanese take the British Andaman Islands.

Andaman Islands

Tenasserim

Dec 15, 1941 Japanese forces cross from Thailand to Victoria Point in Burma and move north to attack Mergui and Tavoy.

Japanese 15th Army

◁ **Invading forces, 1942**
Japanese soldiers advance during their invasion of Burma as local people gather to watch.

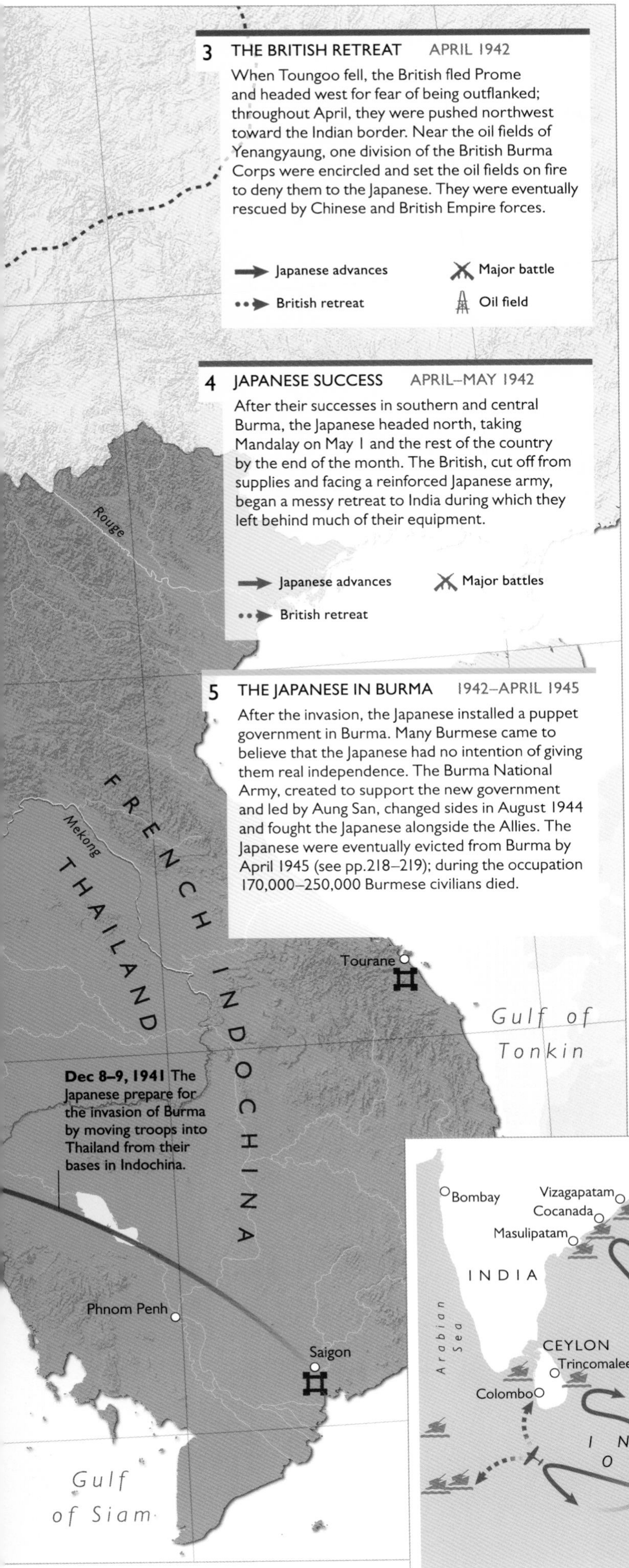

3 THE BRITISH RETREAT   APRIL 1942

When Toungoo fell, the British fled Prome and headed west for fear of being outflanked; throughout April, they were pushed northwest toward the Indian border. Near the oil fields of Yenangyaung, one division of the British Burma Corps were encircled and set the oil fields on fire to deny them to the Japanese. They were eventually rescued by Chinese and British Empire forces.

➡ Japanese advances   ✕ Major battle
••➤ British retreat   ⛏ Oil field

4 JAPANESE SUCCESS   APRIL–MAY 1942

After their successes in southern and central Burma, the Japanese headed north, taking Mandalay on May 1 and the rest of the country by the end of the month. The British, cut off from supplies and facing a reinforced Japanese army, began a messy retreat to India during which they left behind much of their equipment.

➡ Japanese advances   ✕ Major battles
••➤ British retreat

5 THE JAPANESE IN BURMA   1942–APRIL 1945

After the invasion, the Japanese installed a puppet government in Burma. Many Burmese came to believe that the Japanese had no intention of giving them real independence. The Burma National Army, created to support the new government and led by Aung San, changed sides in August 1944 and fought the Japanese alongside the Allies. The Japanese were eventually evicted from Burma by April 1945 (see pp.218–219); during the occupation 170,000–250,000 Burmese civilians died.

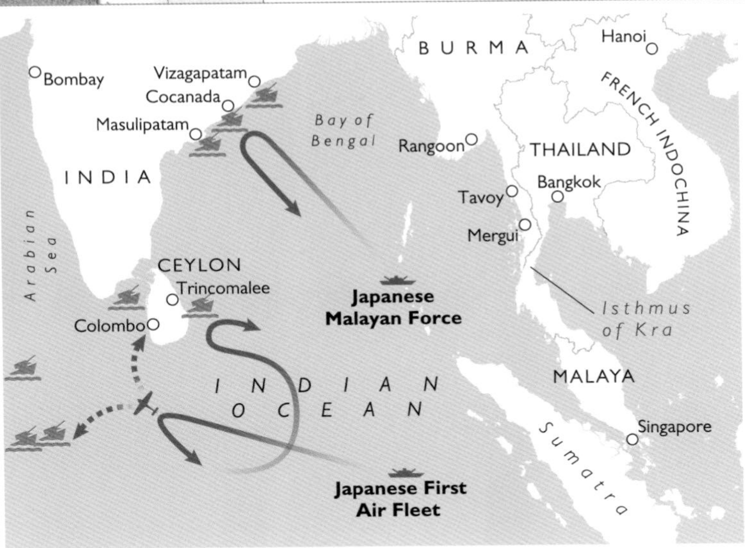

Dec 8–9, 1941 The Japanese prepare for the invasion of Burma by moving troops into Thailand from their bases in Indochina.

JAPAN TAKES BURMA

The conquest of the British colony of Burma extended the Japanese defensive perimeter to its westernmost point, and cut off Allied supply routes to China. The fighting was fierce and costly, and the result was a decisive Japanese victory in May 1942 that dealt yet another blow to the British after the fall of Singapore.

Japan wished to conquer Burma to gain access to its natural resources of oil, cobalt, and rice, and to gain a buffer zone to protect its planned conquests in Malaya and Singapore. It also wanted to close the Burma Road—a conduit for supplies for the Nationalist forces of Chiang Kai-shek, whom the Japanese had been fighting in China since 1937 (see pp.26–27). Many Burmese, who wished to see the end of British rule in their country, supported the invasion. Among them was Aung San, a Burmese activist, and the Thirty Comrades, who received military training from the Japanese and returned to form the Burma Independence Army.

The Japanese invasion began on December 15, 1941. The British Empire troops were no match for the battle-trained Japanese infantry, who exploited effective tactics and made good use of limited air resources. Delaying actions by the British and a major battle fought at Toungoo by a Chinese Nationalist army in March failed to stop the invaders; the British were forced out of the country by the end of May. Fearful that the Japanese would attack Ceylon, and so take control over the Indian Ocean, the British occupied Vichy-held Madagascar in May 1942 to prevent the Japanese establishing a submarine base there.

"Two brigades still east of the river fought to break through the great Sittang railway bridge. Then came tragedy."

WILLIAM SLIM, COMMANDER OF THE BRITISH BURMA CORPS, 1956

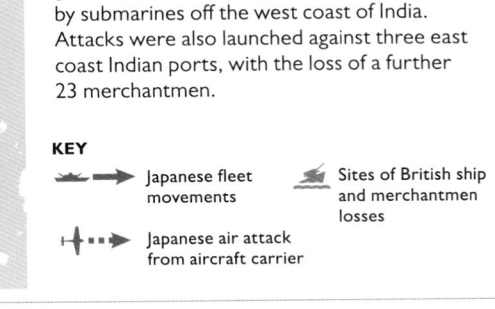

INDIAN OCEAN ATTACKS

On April 5, 1942, the Japanese launched an aircraft carrier attack against Colombo, Ceylon; this was followed by an assault on Trincomalee on April 9. Eight British naval ships and five merchantmen were sunk and more than 40 aircraft were lost; hundreds of servicemen and civilians were killed on the ground. Five more merchantmen were sunk by submarines off the west coast of India. Attacks were also launched against three east coast Indian ports, with the loss of a further 23 merchantmen.

KEY

⮕ Japanese fleet movements

⚓ Sites of British ship and merchantmen losses

✈••➤ Japanese air attack from aircraft carrier

War in Iraq
Sherman tank crews of the Indian 31st
Armored Division receive instruction on the
use of Browning machine guns in Iraq. They
had been sent to Iraq as part of operations
against the pro-Axis regime of Rashid Ali
in 1941 (see pp.82–83).

INDIA IN WORLD WAR II

Although India fought in the war to defend the British Empire, a Nationalist movement at home gained support, with the aim of shaking off British rule. The nation aided production of arms and raised 2.5 million volunteers, who fought in Europe, North Africa, and Asia.

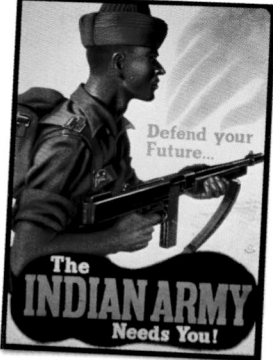

△ **Recruitment campaign**
The British government ran a highly successful campaign to encourage Indians to join the army, raising the largest volunteer force in history.

As part of the British Empire, India had little choice but to join the war. However, this was opposed by many Indian Nationalists, who withdrew their support from provincial governments that the British had established in 1935. There was also opposition from the "Quit India" movement, which was launched by Mahatma Gandhi in 1942 and called for the British to leave at once. The loss of rice imports from Burma after the Japanese invaded the former British colony, as well as the government's failure to improve food distribution, led in 1943 to a famine in Bengal in which three million died. Some Indians were so opposed to British rule that they fought for the Axis powers—mainly 13,000 troops of Subhash Chandra Bose's Indian National Army raised from prisoners of war.

Fighting for the British

Despite the opposition, the impact of Indians fighting for the Axis was slight compared to the loyalist Indian army, which expanded greatly, reaching 2.6 million members in 1945. Indian units were deployed widely—in Iraq, Ethiopia, North Africa, and Italy—but their main goals were to prevent the Japanese from crossing into India (1942–1944) and to defend Burma against the Japanese—an attempt that failed in spring 1942, but succeeded in 1944–1945, when they drove out the Japanese together with other Allied forces (see pp.218–219).

THE VOICE OF OPPOSITION

Gandhi (center) professed a nonviolence philosophy that led him to oppose India's involvement in the war, while other Nationalist leaders thought helping the British would achieve Indian independence more quickly. In 1942, his "Quit India" movement organized protests to encourage the British to leave. He was jailed for nearly two years.

JAPANESE SETBACKS

In early 1942, Japan sought to extend its defensive perimeter south and east across the Pacific. However, its plans were frustrated in an inconclusive naval battle in the Coral Sea, and its forces went on to suffer defeats in New Guinea.

Japan began its assaults on New Guinea, the Solomon Islands, and Australia from January 1942, and its determination to expand its defensive perimeter was heightened by the Doolittle Raid, a US bombing raid on Tokyo and other Japanese cities on April 18, 1942. While this attack did little damage, it made the Japanese realize the potential threat to their homeland.

To achieve their goals, the Japanese planned to capture Midway Atoll to the east (see pp.126–127) to deny its use to American bombers, to take the Australian base at Port Moresby in New Guinea to the south, and to extend their control over the Solomon Islands. This would isolate Australia from its ally, the US, and leave Allied nations and colonies in the region vulnerable.

The initial invasion of New Guinea and the Solomon Islands began favorably, but the assault against Port Moresby was stalled first by stalemate in the two-day Battle of the Coral Sea in May and then by the Japanese failure to seize the port via the overland Kokoda Trail in July. The Japanese had outrun their supply lines and were forced to retreat. The defeats suffered in and around New Guinea were the first major setbacks to Japanese expansion.

> *"Without a doubt ... the Coral Sea was the most confused battle area in world history."*
>
> US VICE ADMIRAL H. S. DUCKWORTH, 1972

ADMIRAL ISOROKU YAMAMOTO 1884–1943

Japanese Admiral Isoroku Yamamoto played a major role in Japan's naval battles in the Pacific Ocean. A student of Harvard University and twice naval attaché in Washington, he opposed war with the US and disagreed with the invasion of China in 1937. Nevertheless, he became an admiral in 1940 and planned the attacks on Pearl Harbor and Midway. He was heavily involved in the Battle of the Coral Sea.

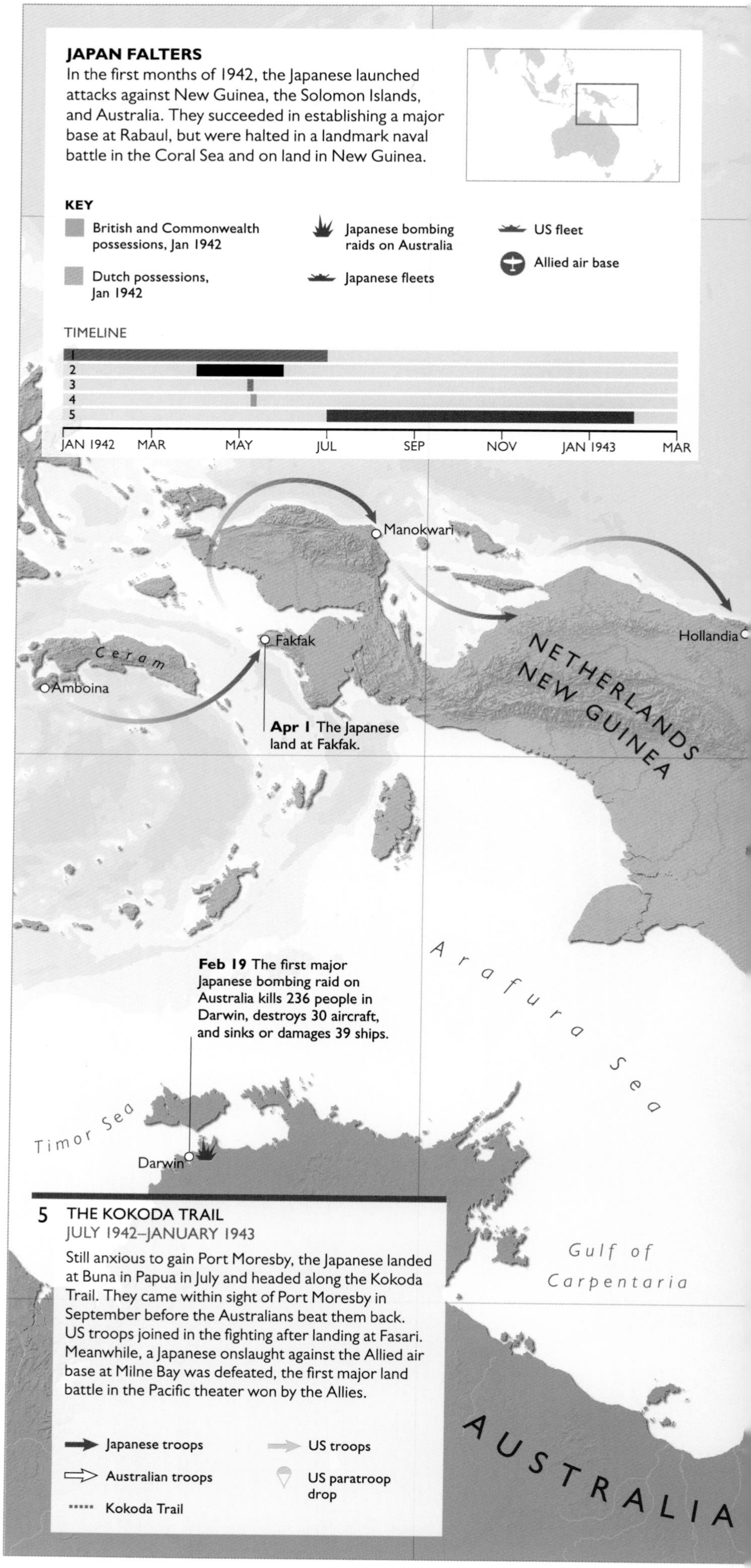

JAPAN FALTERS

In the first months of 1942, the Japanese launched attacks against New Guinea, the Solomon Islands, and Australia. They succeeded in establishing a major base at Rabaul, but were halted in a landmark naval battle in the Coral Sea and on land in New Guinea.

KEY

- British and Commonwealth possessions, Jan 1942
- Dutch possessions, Jan 1942
- Japanese bombing raids on Australia
- Japanese fleets
- US fleet
- Allied air base

TIMELINE

1
2
3
4
5

JAN 1942 · MAR · MAY · JUL · SEP · NOV · JAN 1943 · MAR

Manokwari

Hollandia

NETHERLANDS NEW GUINEA

Ceram

Fakfak

Amboina

Apr 1 The Japanese land at Fakfak.

Feb 19 The first major Japanese bombing raid on Australia kills 236 people in Darwin, destroys 30 aircraft, and sinks or damages 39 ships.

Arafura Sea

Timor Sea

Darwin

5 THE KOKODA TRAIL
JULY 1942–JANUARY 1943

Still anxious to gain Port Moresby, the Japanese landed at Buna in Papua in July and headed along the Kokoda Trail. They came within sight of Port Moresby in September before the Australians beat them back. US troops joined in the fighting after landing at Fasari. Meanwhile, a Japanese onslaught against the Allied air base at Milne Bay was defeated, the first major land battle in the Pacific theater won by the Allies.

- → Japanese troops
- ⇨ Australian troops
- ····· Kokoda Trail
- ⇒ US troops
- ⬠ US paratroop drop

Gulf of Carpentaria

AUSTRALIA

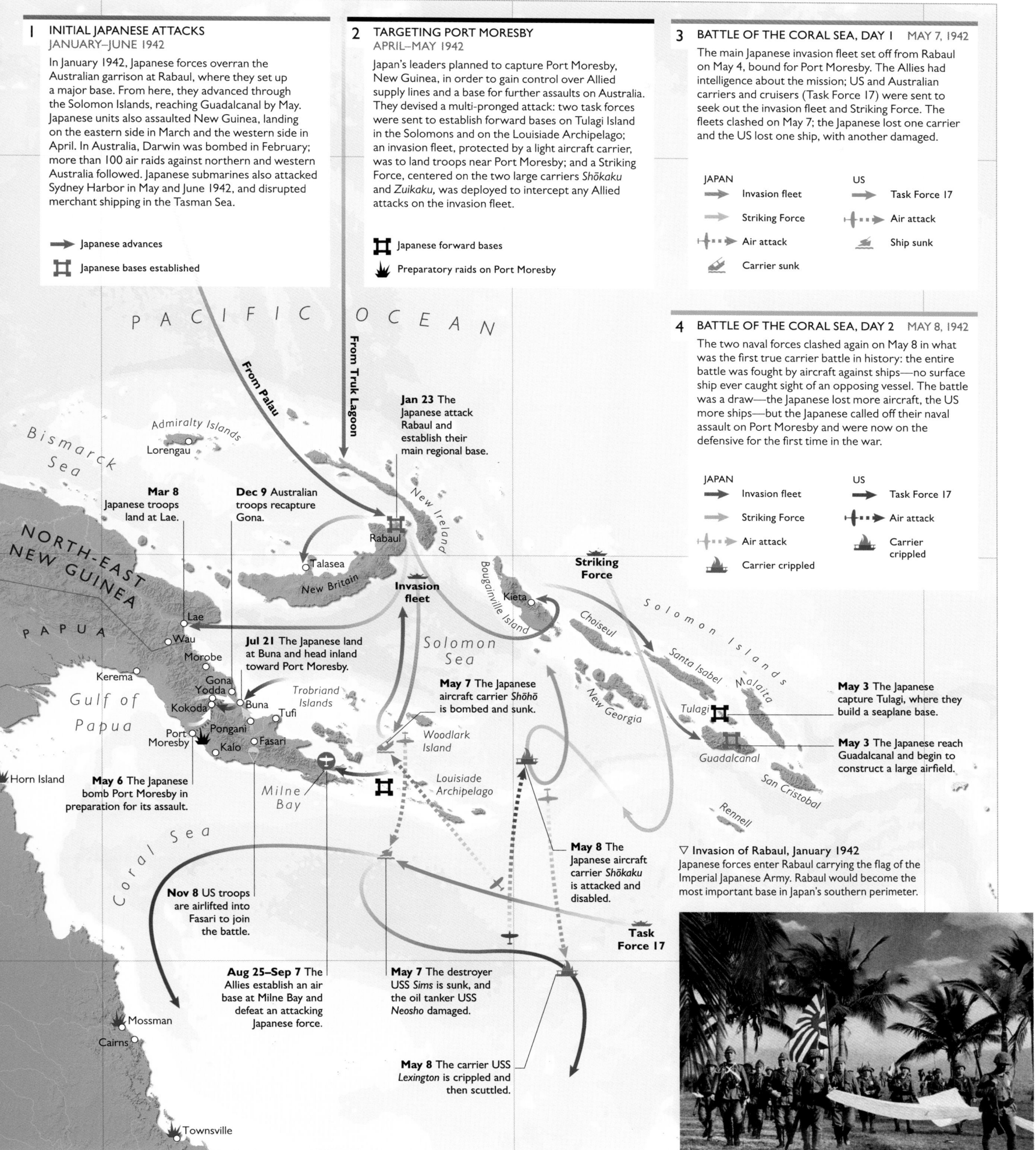

1 INITIAL JAPANESE ATTACKS
JANUARY–JUNE 1942

In January 1942, Japanese forces overran the Australian garrison at Rabaul, where they set up a major base. From here, they advanced through the Solomon Islands, reaching Guadalcanal by May. Japanese units also assaulted New Guinea, landing on the eastern side in March and the western side in April. In Australia, Darwin was bombed in February; more than 100 air raids against northern and western Australia followed. Japanese submarines also attacked Sydney Harbor in May and June 1942, and disrupted merchant shipping in the Tasman Sea.

→ Japanese advances

⊞ Japanese bases established

2 TARGETING PORT MORESBY
APRIL–MAY 1942

Japan's leaders planned to capture Port Moresby, New Guinea, in order to gain control over Allied supply lines and a base for further assaults on Australia. They devised a multi-pronged attack: two task forces were sent to establish forward bases on Tulagi Island in the Solomons and on the Louisiade Archipelago; an invasion fleet, protected by a light aircraft carrier, was to land troops near Port Moresby; and a Striking Force, centered on the two large carriers *Shōkaku* and *Zuikaku*, was deployed to intercept any Allied attacks on the invasion fleet.

⊞ Japanese forward bases

🜲 Preparatory raids on Port Moresby

3 BATTLE OF THE CORAL SEA, DAY 1 MAY 7, 1942

The main Japanese invasion fleet set off from Rabaul on May 4, bound for Port Moresby. The Allies had intelligence about the mission; US and Australian carriers and cruisers (Task Force 17) were sent to seek out the invasion fleet and Striking Force. The fleets clashed on May 7; the Japanese lost one carrier and the US lost one ship, with another damaged.

JAPAN	US
→ Invasion fleet	→ Task Force 17
→ Striking Force	✈ Air attack
✈ Air attack	⚓ Ship sunk
⚓ Carrier sunk	

4 BATTLE OF THE CORAL SEA, DAY 2 MAY 8, 1942

The two naval forces clashed again on May 8 in what was the first true carrier battle in history: the entire battle was fought by aircraft against ships—no surface ship ever caught sight of an opposing vessel. The battle was a draw—the Japanese lost more aircraft, the US more ships—but the Japanese called off their naval assault on Port Moresby and were now on the defensive for the first time in the war.

JAPAN	US
→ Invasion fleet	→ Task Force 17
→ Striking Force	✈ Air attack
✈ Air attack	⚓ Carrier crippled
⚓ Carrier crippled	

▽ Invasion of Rabaul, January 1942
Japanese forces enter Rabaul carrying the flag of the Imperial Japanese Army. Rabaul would become the most important base in Japan's southern perimeter.

Jan 23 The Japanese attack Rabaul and establish their main regional base.

Mar 8 Japanese troops land at Lae.

Dec 9 Australian troops recapture Gona.

Jul 21 The Japanese land at Buna and head inland toward Port Moresby.

May 6 The Japanese bomb Port Moresby in preparation for its assault.

Nov 8 US troops are airlifted into Fasari to join the battle.

Aug 25–Sep 7 The Allies establish an air base at Milne Bay and defeat an attacking Japanese force.

May 7 The Japanese aircraft carrier *Shōhō* is bombed and sunk.

May 8 The Japanese aircraft carrier *Shōkaku* is attacked and disabled.

May 3 The Japanese capture Tulagi, where they build a seaplane base.

May 3 The Japanese reach Guadalcanal and begin to construct a large airfield.

May 7 The destroyer USS *Sims* is sunk, and the oil tanker USS *Neosho* damaged.

May 8 The carrier USS *Lexington* is crippled and then scuttled.

PACIFIC OCEAN

From Palau

From Truk Lagoon

Bismarck Sea

Admiralty Islands

Lorengau

NORTH-EAST NEW GUINEA

PAPUA

Lae
Wau
Morobe
Kerema
Gona
Yodda
Kokoda
Buna
Tufi
Pongani
Port Moresby
Kalo
Fasari

Gulf of Papua

Horn Island

Talasea

New Britain

Rabaul

New Ireland

Invasion fleet

Trobriand Islands

Woodlark Island

Solomon Sea

Louisiade Archipelago

Milne Bay

Coral Sea

Bougainville Island

Striking Force

Kieta

Choiseul

New Georgia

Santa Isabel

Solomon Islands

Malaita

Tulagi

Guadalcanal

San Cristobal

Rennell

Task Force 17

Mossman

Cairns

Townsville

PIVOTAL PACIFIC BATTLE

The Battle of Midway was Japan's first naval defeat for centuries. It marked the ascendancy of carriers and their aircraft as the modern weapons with which to dominate the seas.

KEY

- Air raids
- Torpedo strikes
- Route of Japanese 1st Carrier Striking Force
- Japanese aircraft carriers sunk
- US aircraft carrier sunk

TIMELINE

2 JUN 1942   3 JUN   4 JUN   5 JUN

2
3
4
5
6

1 THE US NAVY LAYS AN AMBUSH
JUNE 2, 1942

By June 2, the US Navy's Task Forces 16 and 17 lay in an area of operations about 350 miles (560 km) north-east of Midway, from where their search planes scoured the ocean for the Japanese. The task forces were formed around three aircraft carriers: USS *Enterprise* and *Hornet*, which Yamamoto thought were in the Solomons; and USS *Yorktown*, which he believed sunk in the Coral Sea.

- US Task Force area of operations
- US Task Force 16: carriers *Enterprise* and *Hornet*, 152 aircraft, 6 cruisers, 9 destroyers
- US Task Force 17: carrier *Yorktown*, 73 aircraft, 2 cruisers, 5 destroyers

Jun 5 *Hiryū* is set ablaze; the crew abandons ship while Admiral Yamaguchi and Captain Kaku go down with their vessel.

Hiryū scuttled

5 pm

6:30 pm

Japanese 1st Carrier Striking Force

Sōryū sunk

Akagi scuttled

Jun 4–5 Route of carriers *Akagi*, *Sōryū*, *Kaga*, and *Hiryū*.

Kaga sunk

10:25 am

10:15 am

7:10 am

Jun 5 *Akagi* is scuttled at 5 am; Yamamoto calls off the operation against Midway and at midday the Japanese warships withdraw westward.

9:45 am

9:28 am

2 THE JAPANESE STRIKE MIDWAY
4:30–6:40 AM JUNE 4, 1942

The 1st Carrier Striking Force launched an air attack on Midway with 108 aircraft, holding back around half of its planes to deal with possible attacks by US naval forces. At 5:45 am the raiders were spotted and US interceptors scrambled. The Japanese failed to disable Midway's defenses in this attack, and around one-third of the Japanese aircraft were destroyed or damaged by US fighters and antiaircraft fire from the island.

- First air attack on Midway

3 CONFUSION IN THE JAPANESE FORCE
7:10–8:30 AM JUNE 4, 1942

US bombers from Midway attacked the Japanese 1st Carrier Striking Force with little effect. As the Japanese force changed course following reports of an approaching US naval force, planes began to return from Midway to land and refuel. Deck operations became confused, and planners were unsure whether to rearm aircraft with high-explosive bombs for a second sortie against Midway, or with torpedoes to repel a threat from the US Navy.

- US aircraft from Midway
- Japanese aircraft returning from Midway

PACIFIC OCEAN

4 A MOMENTOUS MORNING
9:20–10:30 AM JUNE 4, 1942

The 1st Carrier Striking Force was now targeted by torpedo planes from *Enterprise*, *Hornet*, and *Yorktown*, which were tackled by the faster Japanese Zero fighters. However, the Zeros, now out of position and low on ammunition, could not contain a later wave of attacks by dive-bombers. These hit the carriers *Kaga* and *Sōryū* (both sank later that day), the flagship *Akagi* (scuttled the next morning), two battleships, and a destroyer.

- *Yorktown* dive-bomber and torpedo aircraft
- *Enterprise* dive-bomber aircraft
- *Enterprise* torpedo aircraft
- *Hornet* torpedo aircraft

5 *YORKTOWN* BECOMES A CASUALTY
11:50 AM–3 PM JUNE 4, 1942

US radar detected planes from the carrier *Hiryū* approaching *Yorktown* from the west. The raiders were intercepted by US fighters, but several broke through and hit *Yorktown* at around noon with three bombs. By 2:30 pm the fires aboard *Yorktown* had been extinguished, but torpedo planes hit her again. By 3 pm *Yorktown* was listing and the order was issued to abandon ship. *Yorktown* finally sank on June 7.

- *Hiryū* dive-bomber aircraft
- *Hiryū* torpedo aircraft

6 THE CRIPPLING OF THE *HIRYU*
5 PM–6:30 PM JUNE 4, 1942

Hiryū had been located at 2:30 pm by a scout plane from *Yorktown*. Shortly after 5 pm 40 US dive-bombers attacked the Japanese carrier, which was defended by just a dozen fighters. *Hiryū* was hit many times and set ablaze (she was scuttled the next day). B-17s from Midway followed up the attack on the remains of the Japanese fleet, which was in retreat by June 5.

- US dive-bomber aircraft
- B-17 aircraft strike from Midway

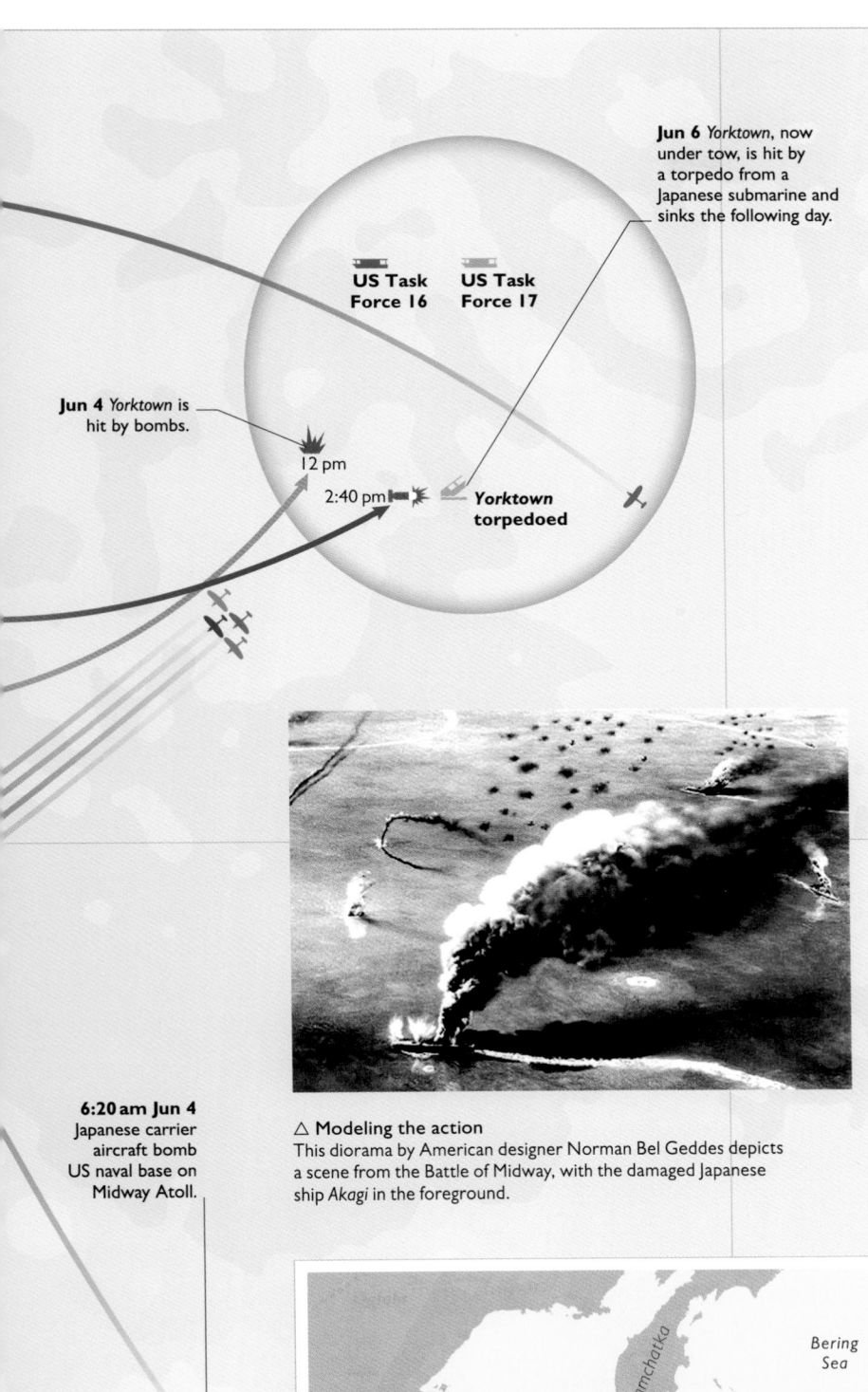

Jun 6 *Yorktown*, now under tow, is hit by a torpedo from a Japanese submarine and sinks the following day.

US Task Force 16

US Task Force 17

Jun 4 *Yorktown* is hit by bombs.

12 pm

2:40 pm

Yorktown torpedoed

6:20 am Jun 4 Japanese carrier aircraft bomb US naval base on Midway Atoll.

△ **Modeling the action**
This diorama by American designer Norman Bel Geddes depicts a scene from the Battle of Midway, with the damaged Japanese ship *Akagi* in the foreground.

THE BATTLE OF MIDWAY

In June 1942, the Japanese sought to neutralize US power in the Pacific by challenging the US in what they hoped would be a decisive naval engagement at Midway Atoll in the westernmost part of the Hawaiian archipelago.

After their attack on Pearl Harbor, the Japanese waged war for months in Southeast Asia and the Pacific. Their advance was only stemmed in May 1942 at the Battle of the Coral Sea (see pp.124–125), when they failed to seize Port Moresby. Alarmed by an American bombing raid on their cities, the Japanese decided to launch an attack on Midway—an island halfway across the Pacific. By mid-1942 the atoll was the most westerly US base in the central Pacific, and Japanese planners recognized its value as a fueling station for US vessels and aircraft.

Admiral Isoroku Yamamoto, commander-in-chief of the Japanese Combined Fleet, argued that Japan's defensive perimeter should be pushed eastward by capturing Midway and US islands in the western Aleutians. His plan involved luring part of the US fleet northward with an attack in the Aleutians, then attacking Midway from the north-west and south-west with three groups. He reasoned that this would draw out the US carrier fleet to be destroyed, but the US fleet knew of this plan, because code breaker Joseph Rochefort had cracked the Japanese cipher, JN-25. As Yamamoto had predicted, the encounter at Midway was decisive, but not in the way he had hoped: the battle marked the end of Japanese dominance in the Pacific.

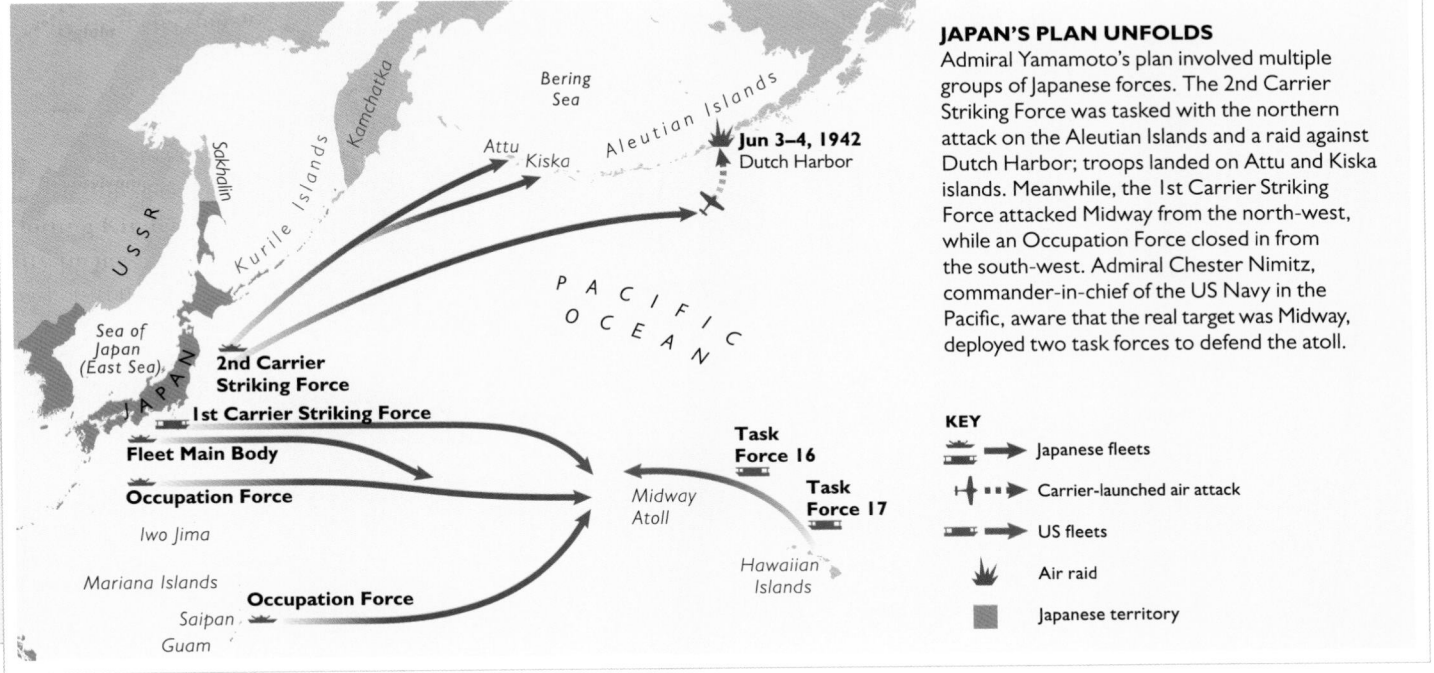

Midway Atoll

Bering Sea

Attu *Kiska* *Aleutian Islands*

Jun 3–4, 1942 Dutch Harbor

Kamchatka

Sakhalin

Kurile Islands

U S S R

P A C I F I C O C E A N

Sea of Japan (East Sea)

J A P A N

2nd Carrier Striking Force

1st Carrier Striking Force

Fleet Main Body

Occupation Force

Iwo Jima

Mariana Islands

Occupation Force

Saipan

Guam

Task Force 16

Task Force 17

Midway Atoll

Hawaiian Islands

JAPAN'S PLAN UNFOLDS
Admiral Yamamoto's plan involved multiple groups of Japanese forces. The 2nd Carrier Striking Force was tasked with the northern attack on the Aleutian Islands and a raid against Dutch Harbor; troops landed on Attu and Kiska islands. Meanwhile, the 1st Carrier Striking Force attacked Midway from the north-west, while an Occupation Force closed in from the south-west. Admiral Chester Nimitz, commander-in-chief of the US Navy in the Pacific, aware that the real target was Midway, deployed two task forces to defend the atoll.

KEY

Japanese fleets

Carrier-launched air attack

US fleets

Air raid

Japanese territory

Logistics map, December 1942
This map, made by the US 1st Marine Amphibious Corps, shows landing sites, anchorages, and tides. Henderson Field can be seen on the north coast, center-left.

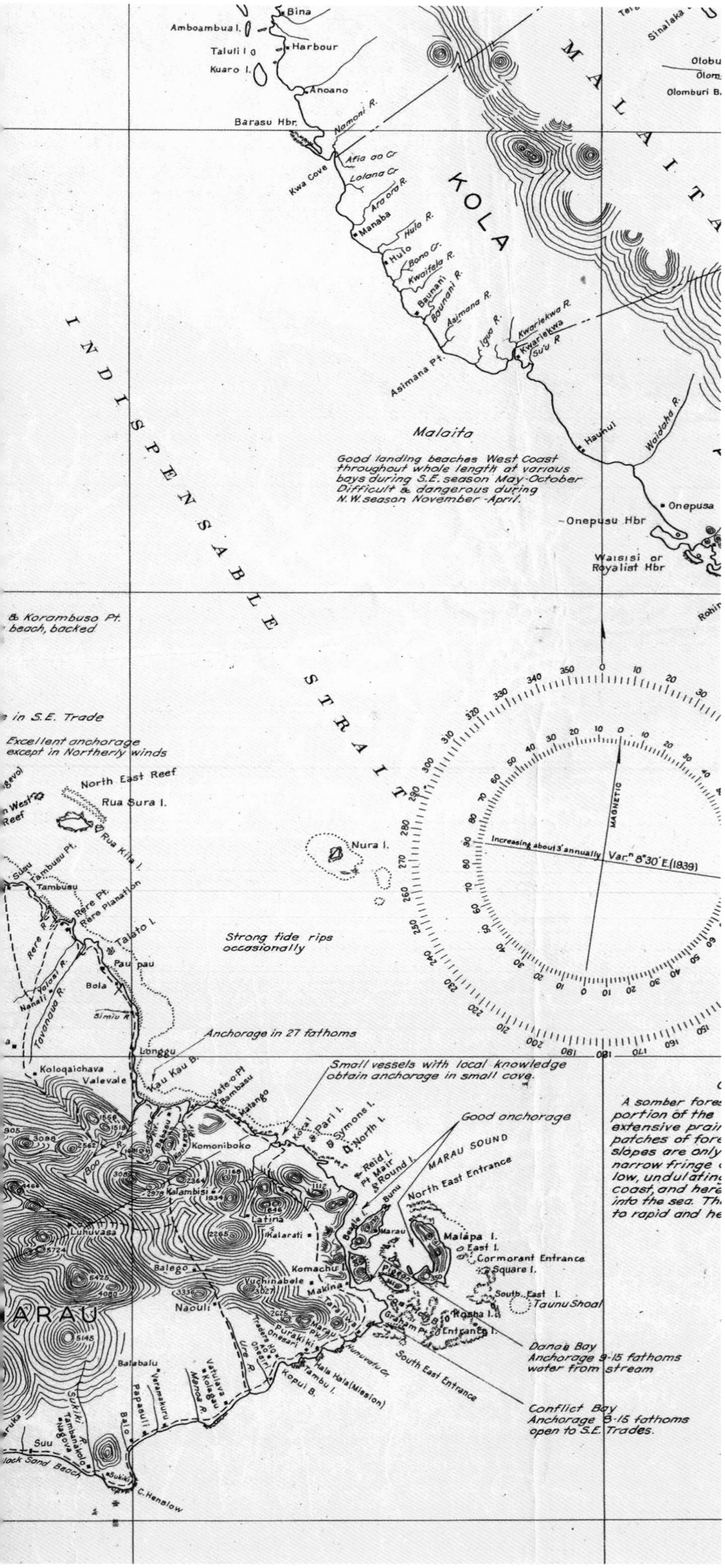

GUADALCANAL

In August 1942 the Allies went on the offensive in the Pacific War, landing on Japanese-held Guadalcanal in the Solomon Islands. Fierce battles raged on land and sea for six months until the Japanese withdrew.

The Japanese established a naval base in the southern Solomon Islands in May 1942 and in July began building an airfield on Guadalcanal. Seeing this as a threat to lines of communication between the US and Australia, the Allies assembled a force of US Marines and US and Australian warships to attack Guadalcanal and the nearby island of Tulagi to the north on August 7. The Japanese were caught by surprise, and 11,000 US Marines were put ashore on Guadalcanal almost unopposed. On the night of August 8–9, however, the Japanese navy counterattacked. Striking at the Allied naval force, they sank four cruisers in the battle of Savo Island, killing more than 1,000 seamen. The rattled Allied fleet withdrew, leaving the Marines ashore to fend for themselves without heavy equipment, which had not yet been landed.

The defense of Henderson Field

While the Japanese strove to organize troop landings to retake Guadalcanal, the US Marines completed construction of the airstrip on the north coast, named Henderson Field. Once US aircraft arrived two weeks after the initial landings, they could stop the Japanese navy operating around the island in daytime. The Japanese resorted to using fast destroyers to ferry troops from their base at Rabaul by night. Through this "Tokyo Express" they built up sufficient forces on Guadalcanal to launch serious attacks on the Marines' defensive perimeter around the airfield from mid-September. The Marines fought off a series of near-suicidal assaults through October, while mounting their own aggressive patrols into the hostile jungle terrain.

The final battles

The climax of the campaign came in mid-November. Japanese warships planned to sail in by night to bombard Henderson Field while transports landed fresh troops. The US Navy responded in force. In two nights of brutal, confused, close-range fighting in darkness, the Japanese lost two battleships and four other warships. The US Navy also suffered substantial losses, but the Japanese troop landings stopped. From here the Americans were able to reinforce their troops on Guadalcanal to 50,000 men. With no prospect of victory, Japan decided their resources would be better employed elsewhere. Troop withdrawals began, and the last Japanese forces left in early February 1943.

▷ **US landings**
Thousands of US Marines landed on the north coast between Koli Point and Lunga Point on August 7, 1942.

WAR IN EUROPE AND AFRICA

Throughout most of 1942, the outcome of the war against Hitler hung in the balance. However, by the year's end, Allied victories on the Eastern front and in the North African desert had decisively turned the tide, and Nazi Germany's era of conquests had ended.

After the US, Soviet Union, and Britain had united against Germany in 1941, the increase in economic resources and population were weighted heavily in favor of the Allies. However, bringing these resources to bear on the battlefield was no easy matter.

German successes

Militarily, the Germans were still capable of inflicting heavy defeats on their enemies. In the Soviet Union, Axis forces repulsed Soviet offensives and resumed their advance eastward, reaching the Volga and the Caucasus. By late summer 1942, Hitler's aim of crippling the Soviets' war effort by capturing their sources of oil supplies and arms production looked within sight.

Meanwhile, in Egypt's Western Desert, the German field marshal Erwin Rommel outfought the British, and by July had advanced to El Alamein, less than 70 miles (100 km) from Britain's major naval base at Alexandria. In the Atlantic, German U-boats attacked American coastal shipping and transoceanic convoys, threatening to block the movement of US arms and troops to the European theater, which depended entirely upon sea transport. Merchant convoys taking military aid to the Soviet Union through its Arctic ports also suffered heavy losses.

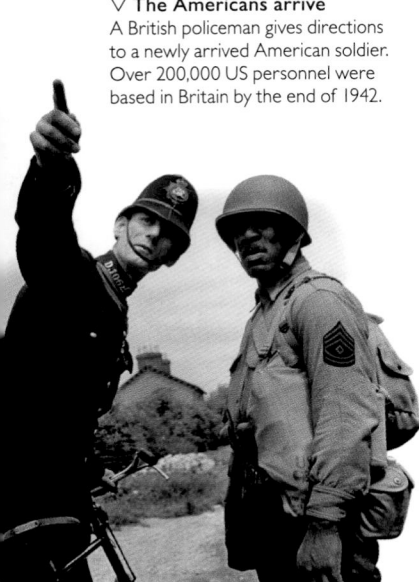

▽ **The Americans arrive**
A British policeman gives directions to a newly arrived American soldier. Over 200,000 US personnel were based in Britain by the end of 1942.

◁ **Call for collaboration**
A poster calls for Dutch volunteers to join the Nazis' elite force, the Waffen-SS. Recruits were sought from conquered countries with racially "Aryan" populations, including the Netherlands, Denmark, and Norway. Every nation in occupied Europe produced enthusiastic collaborators, who identified ideologically with the Nazis' racist and anticommunist beliefs.

Domination over cooperation

Throughout this period, the German hold on occupied Europe remained secure. Coastal raids and RAF bombing of cities were too ineffectual to have significant impact. In occupied countries, the Nazis crushed all opposition by force and exploited the resources to the maximum. The scale of resistance activity remained quite limited, despite the efforts of the British Special Operations Executive (SOE) and the growth of Communist-led partisan guerrilla groups after the Soviet Union's entry into the war.

Hitler also had plans for construction of a racially stratified New Order in Europe. In 1942, his policy to massacre all Jews (code named "the Final Solution") became organized into a coherent project to annihilate Europe's Jewish population. Extermination camps industrialized killing, the scale of which was limited only by the need to use Jews as slave labor. The same camps killed off Soviet prisoners of war, political opponents of Nazism, the Romany people, and homosexuals.

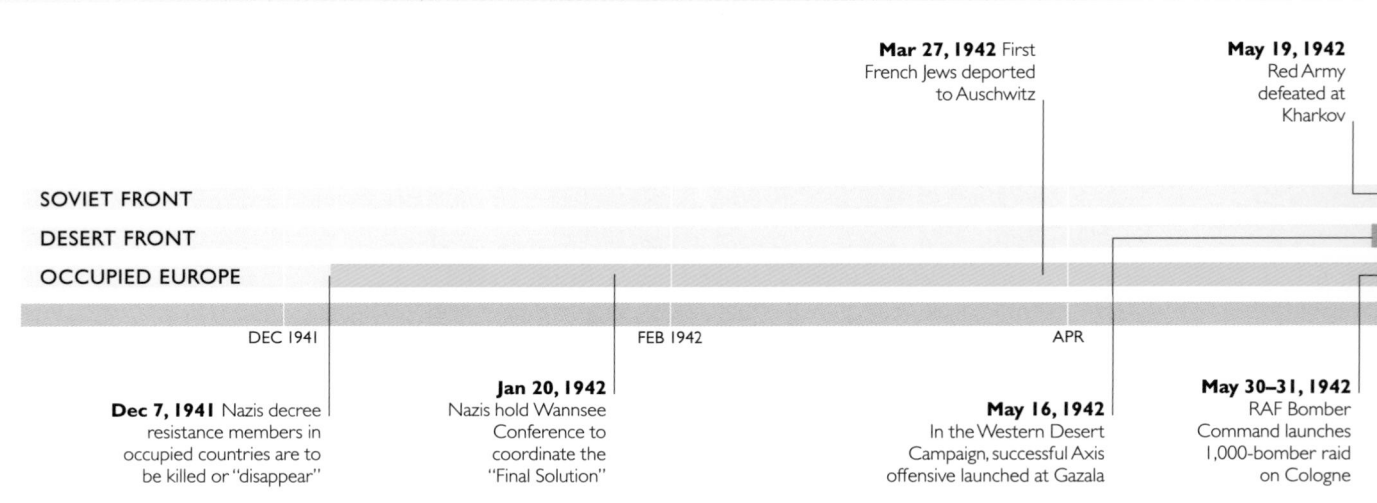

THE TURNING POINT

Throughout the first half of 1942, the Axis powers' victories continued. When German troops reached Stalingrad in August, it appeared another major success was in prospect, but instead the battle was a disaster for Hitler's forces. In North Africa, Field Marshal Rommel's Panzer Army was trapped between the British, who had recently been victorious at the Second Battle of El Alamein, and US troops, which landed in Operation Torch. Meanwhile, the sufferings of the people of Nazi-occupied Europe mounted.

SOVIET FRONT

DESERT FRONT

OCCUPIED EUROPE

DEC 1941   FEB 1942   APR

Mar 27, 1942 First French Jews deported to Auschwitz

May 19, 1942 Red Army defeated at Kharkov

Dec 7, 1941 Nazis decree resistance members in occupied countries are to be killed or "disappear"

Jan 20, 1942 Nazis hold Wannsee Conference to coordinate the "Final Solution"

May 16, 1942 In the Western Desert Campaign, successful Axis offensive launched at Gazala

May 30–31, 1942 RAF Bomber Command launches 1,000-bomber raid on Cologne

◁ **Decisive battle**
Red Army soldiers advance through the ruins of Stalingrad in 1943. The battle for the Soviet city—the largest conflict in World War II—ended in a crushing victory for Stalin's forces, transforming the war on the Eastern front.

Allied successes

Hitler's military strategy was based on the calculation that he could defeat the Soviet Union and so place Germany in an impregnable position in Europe before American strength was brought to bear. However, Soviet forces exhibited formidable resilience, despite suffering great losses of men, equipment, and territory. The encirclement and destruction of a German army at Stalingrad in the winter of 1942–1943 demonstrated that, at the very least, the Soviet Union was not going to be defeated soon.

While battle raged in Stalingrad, the British scored a decisive victory over Axis forces at El Alamein, in the North African desert. Largely responsible for Britain's success was General Bernard Montgomery—a commander who knew how to triumph over a more skillful opponent through patiently deployed material superiority. Meanwhile, landings in French North Africa gave US troops their first experience of fighting the Axis forces. By the end of 1942, US bomber aircraft had begun arriving at bases in Britain, and Allied leaders were discussing a future full-scale invasion of occupied Europe. For Germany, the years of victory were over and a long, tenacious struggle for survival against the odds lay ahead.

▷ **British on the offensive**
At the battle of El Alamein in October 1942, the infantry of Britain's 8th Army advanced to attack well-prepared Axis defensive positions. After lengthy fighting, General Rommel's army was driven into headlong retreat.

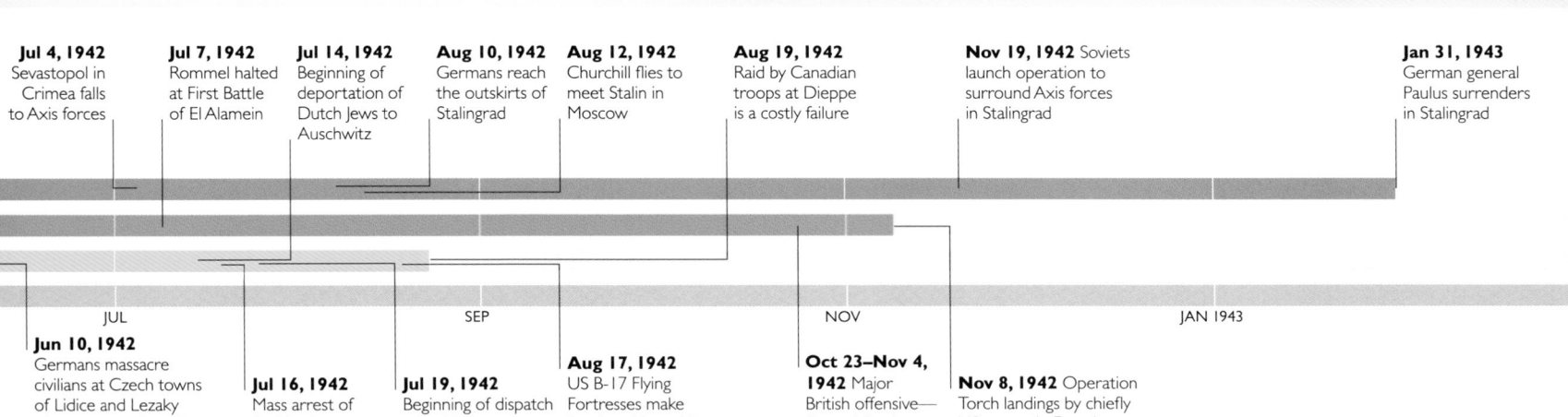

Jul 4, 1942 Sevastopol in Crimea falls to Axis forces

Jul 7, 1942 Rommel halted at First Battle of El Alamein

Jul 14, 1942 Beginning of deportation of Dutch Jews to Auschwitz

Aug 10, 1942 Germans reach the outskirts of Stalingrad

Aug 12, 1942 Churchill flies to meet Stalin in Moscow

Aug 19, 1942 Raid by Canadian troops at Dieppe is a costly failure

Nov 19, 1942 Soviets launch operation to surround Axis forces in Stalingrad

Jan 31, 1943 German general Paulus surrenders in Stalingrad

JUL   SEP   NOV   JAN 1943

Jun 10, 1942 Germans massacre civilians at Czech towns of Lidice and Lezaky after assassination of Heydrich in Prague

Jul 16, 1942 Mass arrest of Parisian Jews by French police

Jul 19, 1942 Beginning of dispatch of Polish Jews to extermination camps

Aug 17, 1942 US B-17 Flying Fortresses make first bombing raid in Europe

Oct 23–Nov 4, 1942 Major British offensive— Second Battle of El Alamein

Nov 8, 1942 Operation Torch landings by chiefly US troops in French North Africa

4 PAYING FOR THE WAR EFFORT
1942–1945

Occupied countries were forced to make direct financial contributions to support the German war effort. Worst affected was France, which had to pay all the costs of the occupying forces, amounting to about 80 million Reichmarks per day. In addition, the Nazi authorities seized a significant proportion of French food production, leading to severe rationing and widespread hunger, especially in the cities.

🪙 Total financial contribution to Germany (millions of Reichmarks)

5 THE FALL OF VICHY FRANCE
NOVEMBER 1942

After the German invasion of northern France in 1940, Hitler allowed the southern half of the country to remain in collaborationist French hands under the Vichy regime. The situation changed with the Allied landings in North Africa in November 1942, when French commanders struck deals with the Allies. Losing faith in the Vichy regime, Hitler extended direct German control over the whole country.

⫽⫽ Vichy France and territories until 1942   ▬ German-controlled France from Nov 1942

Feb 1, 1942 The collaborationist Vidkun Quisling is recognized by the Nazis as head of the government in Norway, but holds little real power.

Aug 29, 1943 The Danish government is dissolved by Germany and martial law is declared.

Jun 1941 Finland fights the USSR alongside Germany.

Aug 30, 1942 Occupied since 1940, Luxembourg is officially incorporated into Nazi Germany.

Sep 4, 1942 Under pressure from Germany, Pierre Laval, France's Vichy prime minister, orders compulsory work service for men and women of working age.

▽ **Enforcing Nazi rule**
As Germany's territories grew, it relied on the troops of the Waffen SS to control local populations. In doing so, they committed a number of atrocities, notably in Poland.

Nov 1942–Sep 1943 Italy occupies Corsica after the fall of Vichy France.

Sep 1943 Germany occupies Italy after Badoglio seeks an armistice with the Allies.

Aug 29, 1941 Following an uprising in Serbia, the German military command backs the foundation of the puppet Government of National Salvation.

Dec 1941 Widespread famine impacts Greece.

Map labels

NORWAY 🪙 2,940
SWEDEN
FINLAND
KARELIA
IRELAND ○ Dublin
ESTONIA
LATVIA ○ Riga
LITHUANIA
NORD
Smolensk
BELORUSSIA ○ Minsk
REICHSKOMMISSARIAT OSTLAND
North Sea
Baltic Sea
UNITED KINGDOM ○ London
DENMARK
Oslo
Copenhagen
Hamburg
Danzig ○ Königsberg
POLAND 🪙 2,175 ✕ 1.7 million
Warsaw
NETHERLANDS 🪙 10,078 ✕ 254,000
NORD
BELGIUM 🪙 5,840 ✕ 199,000
Heessen
Watenstedt-Salzgitter
Berlin
GREATER GERMANY
Radom
Lublin
VOLHYNIA-PODOLIA
REICHSKOMMISSARIAT UKRAINE
Kiev
Kirov
OCCUPIED FRANCE ○ Paris
LUXEMBOURG
Kladno
Kattowitz
Krakow
GENERAL GOVERNMENT
Zhytomyr
FRANCE 🪙 34,200 ✕ 646,000
ALSACE
Brüx
Pilsen
Prague
Ostrava
Krompachy
GALICIA
Pegnitz
BOHEMIA AND MORAVIA
Hayingen
AUSTRIA (OSTMARK)
Linz
🪙 2,020
SLOVAKIA ✕ 38,000
○ Vienna
Judenburg
Krieglach
Graz
HUNGARY ✕ 24,000
SWITZERLAND
Vichy
VICHY FRANCE
Milan
ROMANIA
CROATIA
YUGOSLAVIA ✕ 325,000
Belgrade
Bucharest
Corsica
Rome 🪙 13,300 ✕ 287,000
SERBIA 🪙 472
MONTENEGRO
Sofia
Sardinia
ITALY
ALBANIA
BULGARIA
DEMOTIKA
Istanbul
SALONIKA 🪙 95
GREECE
Sicily
Athens
FRENCH NORTH AFRICA
Mediterranean Sea
Dodecanese Islands
Crete

WAFFEN-ϟϟ
EINTRITT NACH VOLLENDETEM 17. LEBENSJAHR

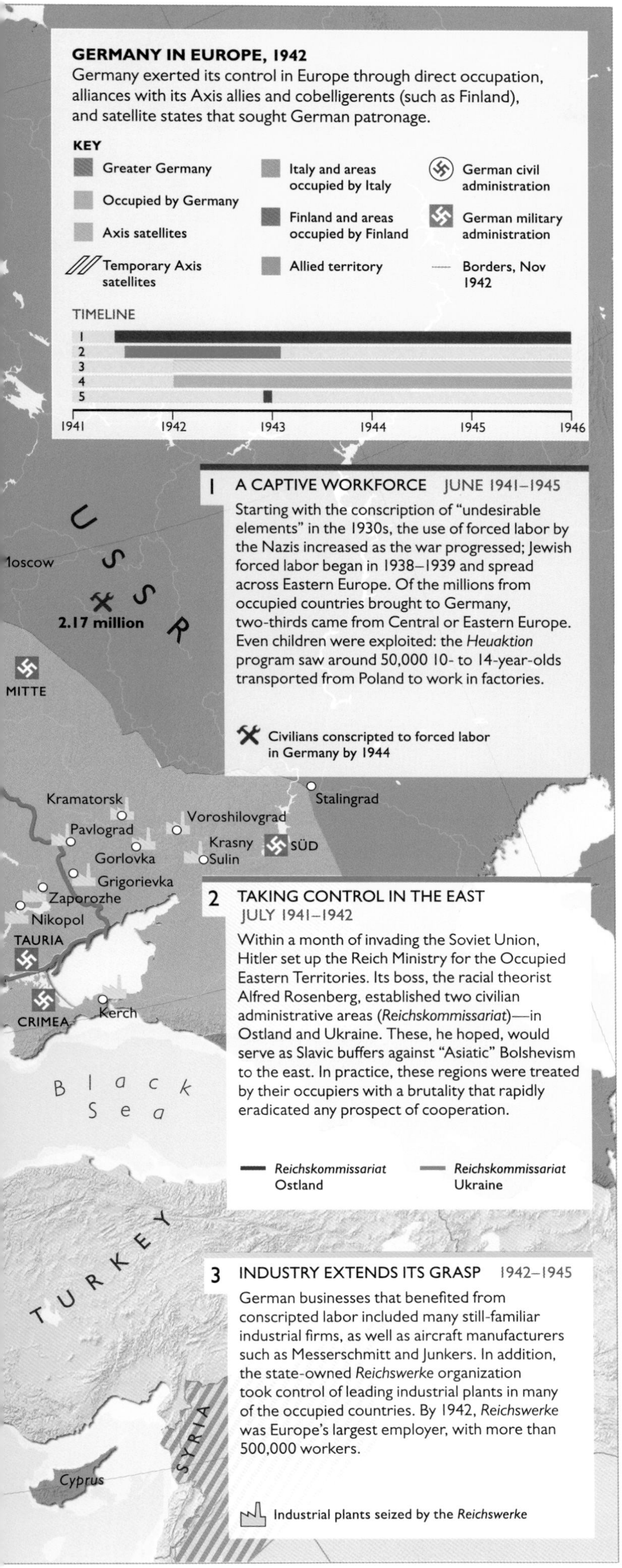

GERMANY IN EUROPE, 1942

Germany exerted its control in Europe through direct occupation, alliances with its Axis allies and cobelligerents (such as Finland), and satellite states that sought German patronage.

KEY

- Greater Germany
- Occupied by Germany
- Axis satellites
- /// Temporary Axis satellites
- Italy and areas occupied by Italy
- Finland and areas occupied by Finland
- Allied territory
- ⚙ German civil administration
- ⚙ German military administration
- --- Borders, Nov 1942

TIMELINE

1
2
3
4
5

1941 | 1942 | 1943 | 1944 | 1945 | 1946

Moscow

2.17 million

MITTE

1 A CAPTIVE WORKFORCE   JUNE 1941–1945

Starting with the conscription of "undesirable elements" in the 1930s, the use of forced labor by the Nazis increased as the war progressed; Jewish forced labor began in 1938–1939 and spread across Eastern Europe. Of the millions from occupied countries brought to Germany, two-thirds came from Central or Eastern Europe. Even children were exploited: the *Heuaktion* program saw around 50,000 10- to 14-year-olds transported from Poland to work in factories.

✖ Civilians conscripted to forced labor in Germany by 1944

Kramatorsk
Pavlograd
Gorlovka
Grigorievka
Zaporozhe
Nikopol
TAURIA
Voroshilovgrad
Stalingrad
Krasny
Sulin ⚙ SÜD

CRIMEA — Kerch

Black Sea

2 TAKING CONTROL IN THE EAST   JULY 1941–1942

Within a month of invading the Soviet Union, Hitler set up the Reich Ministry for the Occupied Eastern Territories. Its boss, the racial theorist Alfred Rosenberg, established two civilian administrative areas (*Reichskommissariat*)—in Ostland and Ukraine. These, he hoped, would serve as Slavic buffers against "Asiatic" Bolshevism to the east. In practice, these regions were treated by their occupiers with a brutality that rapidly eradicated any prospect of cooperation.

— Reichskommissariat Ostland
— Reichskommissariat Ukraine

TURKEY

SYRIA

Cyprus

3 INDUSTRY EXTENDS ITS GRASP   1942–1945

German businesses that benefited from conscripted labor included many still-familiar industrial firms, as well as aircraft manufacturers such as Messerschmitt and Junkers. In addition, the state-owned *Reichswerke* organization took control of leading industrial plants in many of the occupied countries. By 1942, *Reichswerke* was Europe's largest employer, with more than 500,000 workers.

⚒ Industrial plants seized by the *Reichswerke*

NEW ORDER IN EUROPE

At its peak, Greater Germany—Germany and the territories it had annexed—covered much of central Europe, and most other countries on the continent were either occupied by Germany or under its influence. Hitler had begun to fullfil his dream of creating *Lebensraum* ("living space") for the German "master race."

Countries occupied by Germany were treated with degrees of severity that reflected how closely their populations matched the Nazis' Aryan ideal. Norway and Denmark received relatively lenient treatment; Denmark kept its king and its government until mid-1943, when it was placed under military occupation.

The situation in Eastern Europe, however, was very different: the Nazis regarded the people there as inferior, or subject, races and treated them with brutality. The worst regimes were imposed on Poland, occupied USSR, and the Baltic states, where communities were evicted to create living space for ethnic German settlement.

Occupied territories were placed under the control of civilian administrations, headed by Nazi Party officials, or under military administrations. In either case, the countries were exploited financially, economically, and militarily in order to advance the German war effort. Occupied nations were forced to transfer large capital sums to Germany and to provide workers for German factories; when the number of volunteers was considered insufficient, forced labor was introduced on a huge scale. Such measures provoked active resistance movements (see pp.176–177), which the occupation authorities sought to suppress with extreme brutality.

> *"The year 1941 will be, I am convinced, the historical year of a great European New Order."*
>
> ADOLF HITLER, SPEECH AT THE BERLIN *SPORTPALAST*, 1941

ITALY AND *LO SPAZIO VITALE*

Just as *Lebensraum* was a key goal for Germany's Nazis, Italy's Fascists also sought their own living space (*Lo Spazio Vitale*), by expanding their national boundaries across the Mediterranean and into North Africa (see pp.74–75). Fueled by the racist ideologies of figures such as Giuseppe Bottai—who served as Italy's Minister of Education—they argued that Italy was the heir to ancient Rome. Their goal was to create "a new Empire in which Italians would illuminate the world with their art, educate it with their knowledge, and … their administrative technique and ability."

Giuseppe Bottai, Fascist politician during the early years of the war.

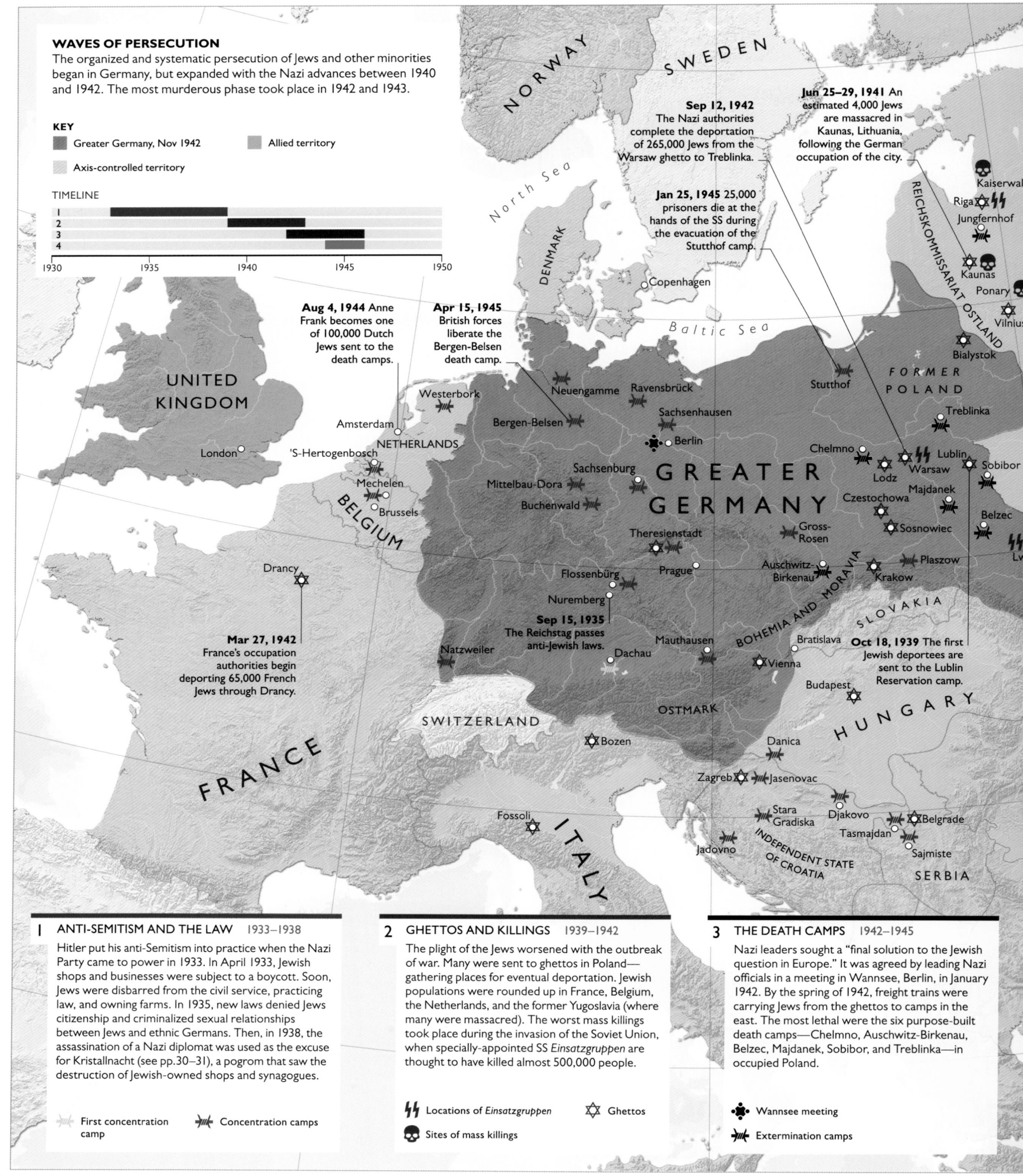

WAVES OF PERSECUTION

The organized and systematic persecution of Jews and other minorities began in Germany, but expanded with the Nazi advances between 1940 and 1942. The most murderous phase took place in 1942 and 1943.

KEY

- Greater Germany, Nov 1942
- Allied territory
- Axis-controlled territory

TIMELINE

1
2
3
4

1930   1935   1940   1945   1950

Sep 12, 1942 The Nazi authorities complete the deportation of 265,000 Jews from the Warsaw ghetto to Treblinka.

Jun 25–29, 1941 An estimated 4,000 Jews are massacred in Kaunas, Lithuania, following the German occupation of the city.

Jan 25, 1945 25,000 prisoners die at the hands of the SS during the evacuation of the Stutthof camp.

Aug 4, 1944 Anne Frank becomes one of 100,000 Dutch Jews sent to the death camps.

Apr 15, 1945 British forces liberate the Bergen-Belsen death camp.

Mar 27, 1942 France's occupation authorities begin deporting 65,000 French Jews through Drancy.

Sep 15, 1935 The Reichstag passes anti-Jewish laws.

Oct 18, 1939 The first Jewish deportees are sent to the Lublin Reservation camp.

Map labels: NORWAY, SWEDEN, North Sea, DENMARK, Copenhagen, Baltic Sea, REICHSKOMMISSARIAT OSTLAND, Kaiserwald, Riga, Jungfernhof, Kaunas, Ponary, Vilnius, Bialystok, FORMER POLAND, Stutthof, Treblinka, Neuengamme, Ravensbrück, Sachsenhausen, Chelmno, Lublin, Sobibor, Warsaw, Lodz, Majdanek, Belzec, Czestochowa, Sosnowiec, Lwow, Plaszow, Krakow, Gross-Rosen, Auschwitz-Birkenau, BOHEMIA AND MORAVIA, SLOVAKIA, Bratislava, Vienna, Budapest, HUNGARY, Mauthausen, OSTMARK, Dachau, Nuremberg, Flossenbürg, Prague, Theresienstadt, Buchenwald, Mittelbau-Dora, Sachsenburg, Berlin, GREATER GERMANY, Natzweiler, SWITZERLAND, Bozen, Danica, Zagreb, Jasenovac, Stara Gradiska, Djakovo, Tasmajdan, Belgrade, Sajmiste, SERBIA, Jadovno, INDEPENDENT STATE OF CROATIA, Fossoli, ITALY, FRANCE, Drancy, UNITED KINGDOM, London, Amsterdam, Westerbork, 'S-Hertogenbosch, NETHERLANDS, Mechelen, Brussels, BELGIUM, Bergen-Belsen

---

1 ANTI-SEMITISM AND THE LAW 1933–1938

Hitler put his anti-Semitism into practice when the Nazi Party came to power in 1933. In April 1933, Jewish shops and businesses were subject to a boycott. Soon, Jews were disbarred from the civil service, practicing law, and owning farms. In 1935, new laws denied Jews citizenship and criminalized sexual relationships between Jews and ethnic Germans. Then, in 1938, the assassination of a Nazi diplomat was used as the excuse for Kristallnacht (see pp.30–31), a pogrom that saw the destruction of Jewish-owned shops and synagogues.

⚞ First concentration camp
⚞ Concentration camps

2 GHETTOS AND KILLINGS 1939–1942

The plight of the Jews worsened with the outbreak of war. Many were sent to ghettos in Poland—gathering places for eventual deportation. Jewish populations were rounded up in France, Belgium, the Netherlands, and the former Yugoslavia (where many were massacred). The worst mass killings took place during the invasion of the Soviet Union, when specially-appointed SS *Einsatzgruppen* are thought to have killed almost 500,000 people.

⚡ Locations of *Einsatzgruppen*   ✡ Ghettos
☠ Sites of mass killings

3 THE DEATH CAMPS 1942–1945

Nazi leaders sought a "final solution to the Jewish question in Europe." It was agreed by leading Nazi officials in a meeting in Wannsee, Berlin, in January 1942. By the spring of 1942, freight trains were carrying Jews from the ghettos to camps in the east. The most lethal were the six purpose-built death camps—Chelmno, Auschwitz-Birkenau, Belzec, Majdanek, Sobibor, and Treblinka—in occupied Poland.

✦ Wannsee meeting
⚞ Extermination camps

THE HOLOCAUST

Hitler and his supporters saw the Jews as a worldwide enemy conspiring to undermine the German nation. The Nazi regime embarked on what became known as the Holocaust—the systematic persecution and murder of around six million European Jews.

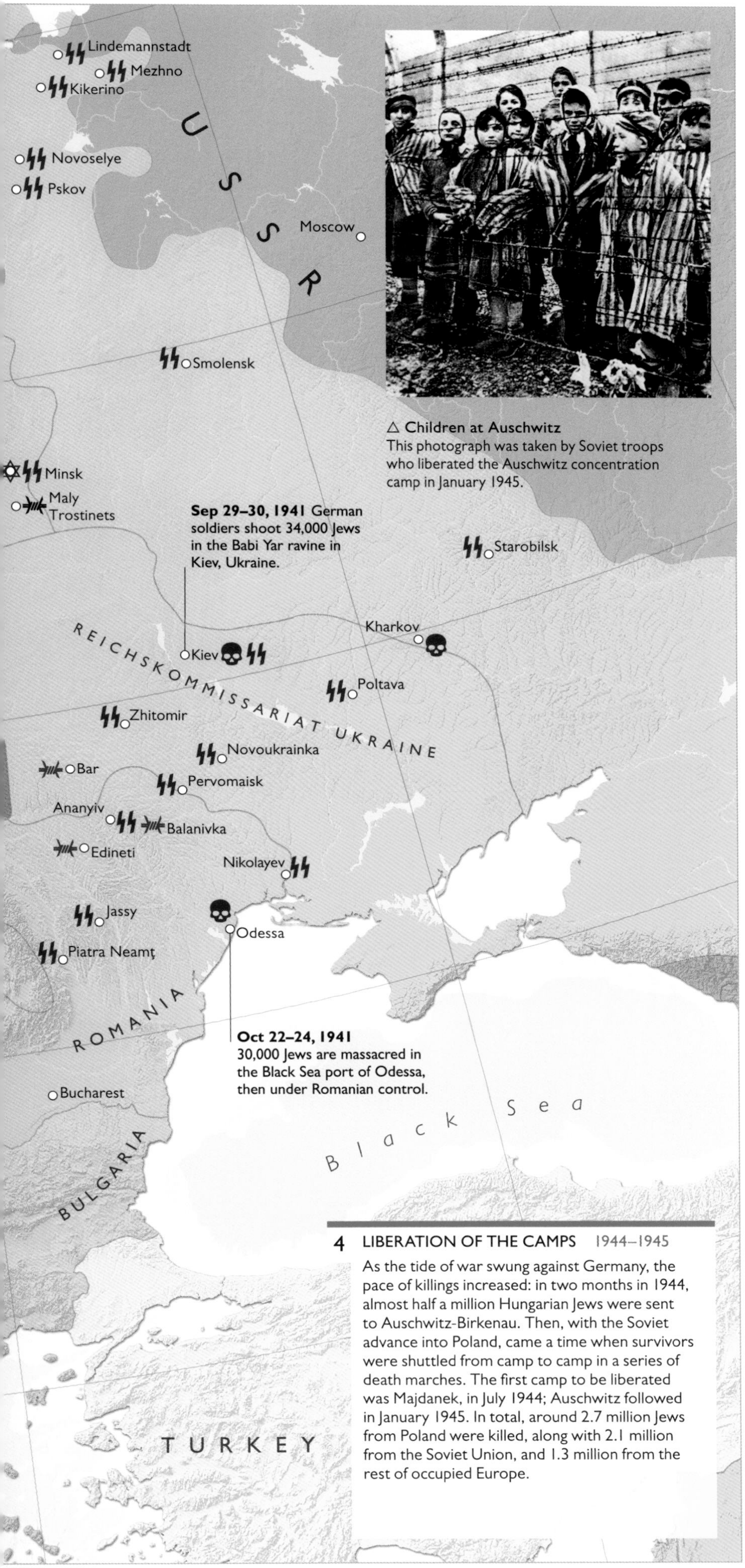

The Nazi rise to power had immediate consequences for Germany's Jews, who were treated from the start as racial outcasts. From 1935 onward they were denied citizenship and forbidden to marry or have sexual relations with people of "German blood." The policy was deliberately aimed at encouraging Jews to flee the country, and by 1938 about half the Jewish population had done just that.

With the outbreak of war, the situation deteriorated further. Ghettos were created in the occupied eastern lands where deportees could be resettled and controlled. During the drive eastward many Jewish populations were massacred, often in retaliation for isolated acts of resistance. From late 1941, new extermination centers were constructed—known as Operation Reinhard camps—where Jews were sent to the gas chambers or selected for grueling slave labor, through which thousands more were worked to death. The results were horrifying: when liberation finally came, an estimated two-thirds of Europe's pre-war Jewish population had been wiped out.

"The Holocaust was not only a Jewish tragedy, but also a human tragedy."

SIMON WIESENTHAL, HOLOCAUST SURVIVOR

OTHER PERSECUTED MINORITIES

Jews were not the only minority group persecuted by the Nazis. Their victims stretched from homosexual men and people with disabilities to Jehovah's Witnesses, Freemasons, and Catholic and Protestant dissidents. In terms of numbers, ethnic groups suffered the worst losses. Romani people faced the same genocidal threat as the Jews, while the Nazi assault on the Slavic peoples ended in the deaths of some 15 million Soviets and 3 million Poles.

Roma and Sinti women at Bergen-Belsen

△ **Children at Auschwitz**
This photograph was taken by Soviet troops who liberated the Auschwitz concentration camp in January 1945.

Sep 29–30, 1941 German soldiers shoot 34,000 Jews in the Babi Yar ravine in Kiev, Ukraine.

Oct 22–24, 1941
30,000 Jews are massacred in the Black Sea port of Odessa, then under Romanian control.

4 LIBERATION OF THE CAMPS 1944–1945

As the tide of war swung against Germany, the pace of killings increased: in two months in 1944, almost half a million Hungarian Jews were sent to Auschwitz-Birkenau. Then, with the Soviet advance into Poland, came a time when survivors were shuttled from camp to camp in a series of death marches. The first camp to be liberated was Majdanek, in July 1944; Auschwitz followed in January 1945. In total, around 2.7 million Jews from Poland were killed, along with 2.1 million from the Soviet Union, and 1.3 million from the rest of occupied Europe.

Map labels:
Lindemannstadt
Mezhno
Kikerino
Novoselye
Pskov
U S S R
Moscow
Smolensk
Minsk
Maly Trostinets
Starobilsk
Kharkov
REICHSKOMMISSARIAT UKRAINE
Kiev
Poltava
Zhitomir
Novoukrainka
Bar
Pervomaisk
Ananyiv
Balanivka
Edineti
Nikolayev
Jassy
Piatra Neamţ
Odessa
ROMANIA
Bucharest
BULGARIA
Black Sea
TURKEY

THE WARSAW GHETTO

In the 1930s, Warsaw was home to 375,000 Jews—the second largest single Jewish population in the world after New York. Following Germany's invasion of Poland in 1939, the Nazis imposed a multitude of restrictions on Jews, including their enforced relocation to a ghetto.

△ **Identification mark**
Jews in the Warsaw Ghetto were forced to wear a white armband featuring a blue Star of David on their right arm so they could be identified easily.

On October 12, 1940, all Jewish residents of Warsaw and others from outlying districts were forced to move to an area of just 1.3 sq miles (3.4 sq km) in the north of the city. High walls made of stone and barbed wire enclosed the ghetto, and armed guards kept watch; any Jew found outside the walls could be shot. In such a confined space, chronic overcrowding and malnutrition were rife. An estimated 400,000 Jews struggled daily for survival with an average of eight to ten people sharing a single room. The threat of starvation was constant, since the food rations were not sufficient to sustain life. Typhus and other deadly illnesses became endemic.

The Warsaw Ghetto Uprising

Mass deportations of Polish Jews to concentration camps and extermination camps began in July 1942. They resumed in January 1943 and again in early April. This time, the Jews fought back against the Germans, with Jewish resistance fighters giving battle for four weeks. However, they were vastly outnumbered, and the ghetto was incinerated and reduced to rubble. By the time the fighting ended on May 16, 7,000 Jews had been slaughtered on the streets and another 42,000 had been taken captive and deported. The Warsaw concentration camp complex was built on the site of the old ghetto.

THE NAZI CAMPS

Shown here on a contemporary map, concentration and extermination camps were spread throughout the territory of the Third Reich during World War II. Auschwitz-Birkenau in Poland became the most notorious: between 1.1 and 1.3 million Jews were sent there, and at least 960,000 were executed in the gas chambers. An estimated 750,000 perished at Treblinka, also in Poland.

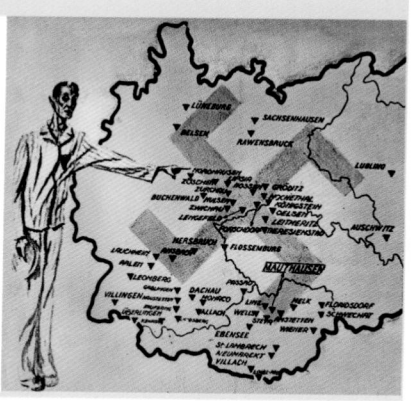

Nazi round-up
Terrified Jewish families are rounded up by Nazi troops in the Warsaw Ghetto prior to their forced deportation to concentration and extermination camps. Attempts by Jewish guerrillas to resist the Nazis ultimately ended in failure.

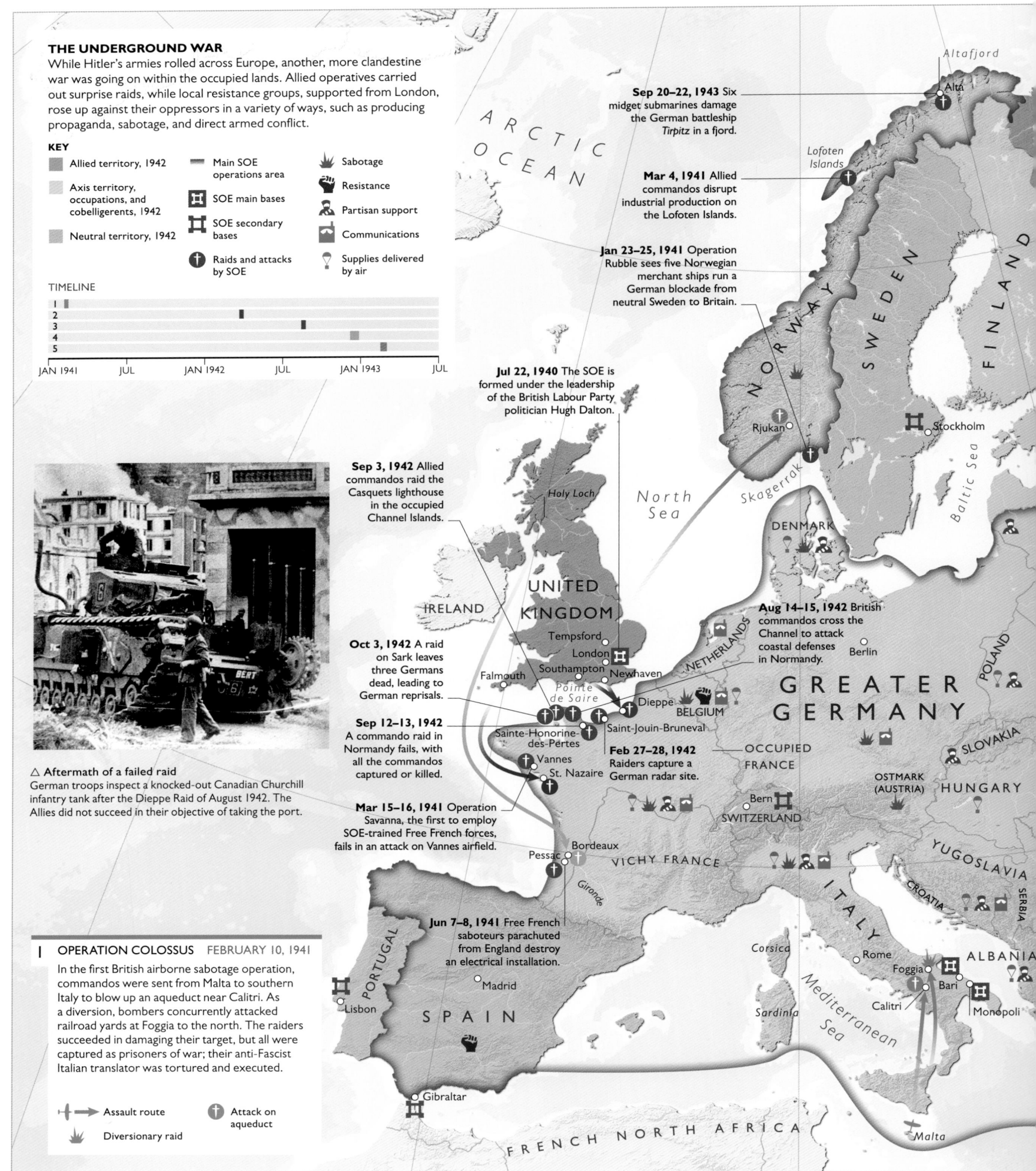

THE UNDERGROUND WAR

While Hitler's armies rolled across Europe, another, more clandestine war was going on within the occupied lands. Allied operatives carried out surprise raids, while local resistance groups, supported from London, rose up against their oppressors in a variety of ways, such as producing propaganda, sabotage, and direct armed conflict.

KEY

- Allied territory, 1942
- Axis territory, occupations, and cobelligerents, 1942
- Neutral territory, 1942
- Main SOE operations area
- SOE main bases
- SOE secondary bases
- Raids and attacks by SOE
- Sabotage
- Resistance
- Partisan support
- Communications
- Supplies delivered by air

TIMELINE

1		
2		
3		
4		
5		

JAN 1941   JUL   JAN 1942   JUL   JAN 1943   JUL

Sep 20–22, 1943 Six midget submarines damage the German battleship *Tirpitz* in a fjord.

Mar 4, 1941 Allied commandos disrupt industrial production on the Lofoten Islands.

Jan 23–25, 1941 Operation Rubble sees five Norwegian merchant ships run a German blockade from neutral Sweden to Britain.

Jul 22, 1940 The SOE is formed under the leadership of the British Labour Party politician Hugh Dalton.

Sep 3, 1942 Allied commandos raid the Casquets lighthouse in the occupied Channel Islands.

Oct 3, 1942 A raid on Sark leaves three Germans dead, leading to German reprisals.

Sep 12–13, 1942 A commando raid in Normandy fails, with all the commandos captured or killed.

Aug 14–15, 1942 British commandos cross the Channel to attack coastal defenses in Normandy.

Feb 27–28, 1942 Raiders capture a German radar site.

Mar 15–16, 1941 Operation Savanna, the first to employ SOE-trained Free French forces, fails in an attack on Vannes airfield.

Jun 7–8, 1941 Free French saboteurs parachuted from England destroy an electrical installation.

△ **Aftermath of a failed raid**
German troops inspect a knocked-out Canadian Churchill infantry tank after the Dieppe Raid of August 1942. The Allies did not succeed in their objective of taking the port.

OPERATION COLOSSUS   FEBRUARY 10, 1941

In the first British airborne sabotage operation, commandos were sent from Malta to southern Italy to blow up an aqueduct near Calitri. As a diversion, bombers concurrently attacked railroad yards at Foggia to the north. The raiders succeeded in damaging their target, but all were captured as prisoners of war; their anti-Fascist Italian translator was tortured and executed.

- Assault route
- Diversionary raid
- Attack on aqueduct

Map labels:
ARCTIC OCEAN
Altafjord — Alta
Lofoten Islands
NORWAY
SWEDEN
FINLAND
Baltic Sea
Rjukan
Stockholm
DENMARK
North Sea
Skagerrak
Holy Loch
IRELAND
UNITED KINGDOM
Tempsford
London
Southampton
Newhaven
Falmouth
Pointe de Saire
Dieppe
Saint-Jouin-Bruneval
NETHERLANDS
BELGIUM
Berlin
GREATER GERMANY
POLAND
SLOVAKIA
OSTMARK (AUSTRIA)
HUNGARY
Sainte-Honorine-des-Pertes
Vannes
St. Nazaire
OCCUPIED FRANCE
Bern
SWITZERLAND
YUGOSLAVIA
CROATIA
SERBIA
Pessac
Bordeaux
Gironde
VICHY FRANCE
ITALY
Corsica
Rome
Foggia
Bari
ALBANIA
PORTUGAL
Madrid
SPAIN
Sardinia
Calitri
Monopoli
Mediterranean Sea
Lisbon
Gibraltar
FRENCH NORTH AFRICA
Malta

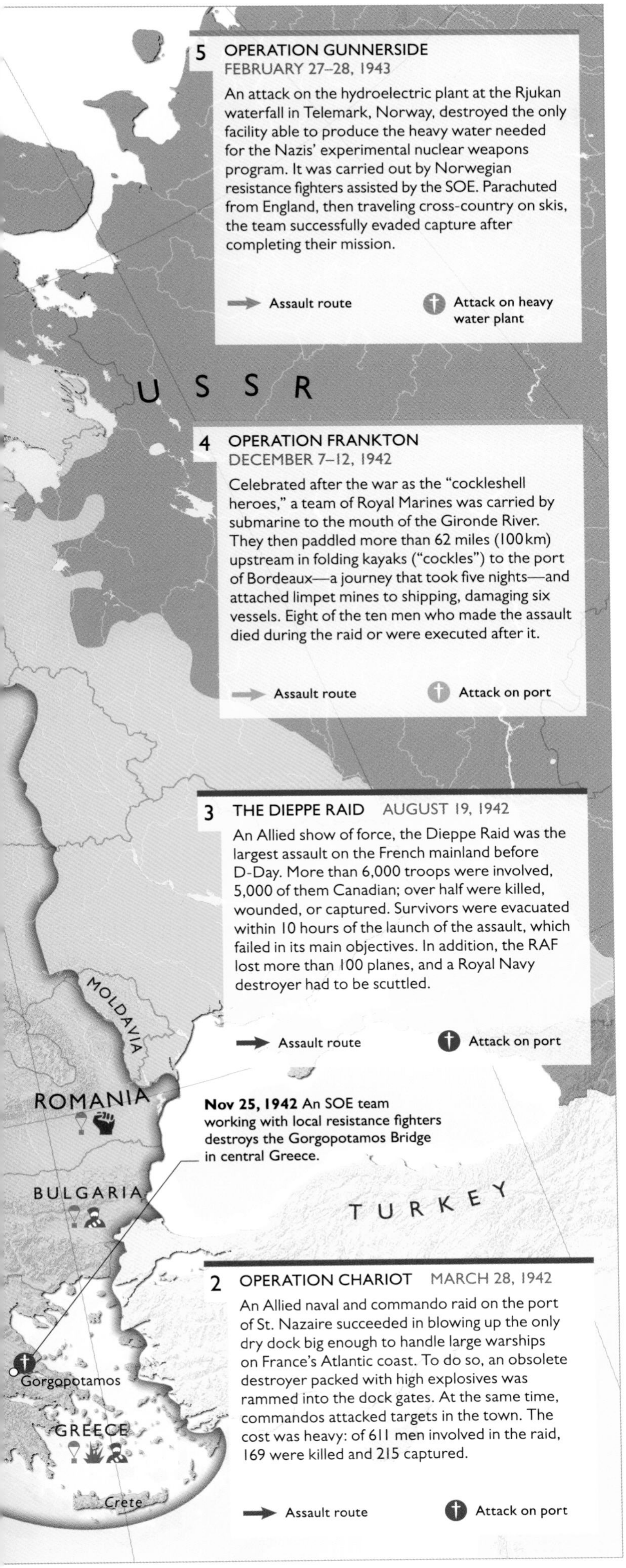

5 OPERATION GUNNERSIDE
FEBRUARY 27–28, 1943

An attack on the hydroelectric plant at the Rjukan waterfall in Telemark, Norway, destroyed the only facility able to produce the heavy water needed for the Nazis' experimental nuclear weapons program. It was carried out by Norwegian resistance fighters assisted by the SOE. Parachuted from England, then traveling cross-country on skis, the team successfully evaded capture after completing their mission.

→ Assault route   ✠ Attack on heavy water plant

4 OPERATION FRANKTON
DECEMBER 7–12, 1942

Celebrated after the war as the "cockleshell heroes," a team of Royal Marines was carried by submarine to the mouth of the Gironde River. They then paddled more than 62 miles (100km) upstream in folding kayaks ("cockles") to the port of Bordeaux—a journey that took five nights—and attached limpet mines to shipping, damaging six vessels. Eight of the ten men who made the assault died during the raid or were executed after it.

→ Assault route   ✠ Attack on port

3 THE DIEPPE RAID   AUGUST 19, 1942

An Allied show of force, the Dieppe Raid was the largest assault on the French mainland before D-Day. More than 6,000 troops were involved, 5,000 of them Canadian; over half were killed, wounded, or captured. Survivors were evacuated within 10 hours of the launch of the assault, which failed in its main objectives. In addition, the RAF lost more than 100 planes, and a Royal Navy destroyer had to be scuttled.

→ Assault route   ✠ Attack on port

Nov 25, 1942 An SOE team working with local resistance fighters destroys the Gorgopotamos Bridge in central Greece.

2 OPERATION CHARIOT   MARCH 28, 1942

An Allied naval and commando raid on the port of St. Nazaire succeeded in blowing up the only dry dock big enough to handle large warships on France's Atlantic coast. To do so, an obsolete destroyer packed with high explosives was rammed into the dock gates. At the same time, commandos attacked targets in the town. The cost was heavy: of 611 men involved in the raid, 169 were killed and 215 captured.

→ Assault route   ✠ Attack on port

RAIDS AND SUBVERSIONS

With much of Europe under Nazi control by mid-1940, Britain resorted to unconventional means of attacking the enemy. A secret body—the Special Operations Executive (SOE)—trained commandos in guerrilla tactics and employed special forces to conduct clandestine operations in occupied territory.

At a time when Hitler's plans for Europe seemed close to success, Britain's War Cabinet considered it important to take the offensive by staging surprise attacks on occupied territory. Sometimes these took the form of combined operations, with air, land, and naval forces working together. The first such raid, on the Lofoten Islands in Norway, was conducted successfully in March 1941. Other attacks followed, aimed at spreading fear along the coasts. The most ambitious was the assault on St. Nazaire in March 1942, the success of which encouraged Allied commanders to launch the disastrous Dieppe Raid five months later.

Meanwhile, from early 1941 onward the SOE had been coordinating espionage and sabotage activities in the occupied lands, as well as liaising with resistance movements across the continent (see pp.176–177). Some incursions were conducted by its own operatives, while others employed SOE-trained resistance fighters inserted back into their own homelands to carry out missions. The SOE's activities were sometimes controversial, as they risked triggering Nazi reprisals on local civilians. Yet by striking into the heart of occupied Europe, they kept the spirit of resistance alive and helped prepare the path for D-Day (see pp.186–187).

"In no previous war … have resistance forces been so closely harnessed to the main military effort."

US GENERAL DWIGHT D. EISENHOWER, 1945

MAJOR-GENERAL SIR COLIN GUBBINS
1896–1976

The SOE—also known as "Churchill's secret army"—was officially formed in 1940. The organization was shaped and then led by Colin Gubbins, the son of a British diplomat. Gubbins served with distinction in World War I, winning the Military Cross for rescuing wounded men under fire. He developed an interest in irregular warfare while serving in Russia and then Ireland in the immediate post-war years. In 1940, after service in the brief Norwegian campaign, he was seconded to the newly formed SOE, taking over as its head in 1943. There he coordinated the work of resistance groups in the occupied lands, playing a significant, if little-acknowledged, part in the victorious Allied war effort.

ARCTIC CONVOYS

Allied civilian sailors endured the dangers of extreme Arctic conditions and German air, surface, and U-boat fleets to bring more than 4½ million tons (4 million metric tons) of supplies to Soviet ports between 1941 and 1945. Around 3,000 men died and more than 100 ships were lost in the effort to keep the USSR in the war.

The German invasion of the USSR in June 1941 prompted Stalin to ask Britain and its allies for assistance in supplying the Soviet war effort. From August 1941, convoys undertook what Churchill called the "worst journey in the world," ferrying materiel needed in the war against Germany.

The most direct route took convoys through the Arctic Circle to the Soviet ports of Murmansk and Archangel. Passing close to German-held territory, they were within easy reach of the Luftwaffe and U-boats waiting in ambush, while in the Norwegian fjords, German warships—including the pride of the fleet, the *Tirpitz*—lay in wait.

The convoys faced gales, blizzards, and dense fog in the Arctic Ocean. In summer, they could follow a route that lay further from the Norwegian coast,

but this took them nearer to icebergs drifting into the sea lanes. In winter, the darkness offered cover but the sea ice forced the ships nearer their enemies. Thick ice formed over the vessels and had to be chipped away so that they did not capsize.

The first convoys suffered few losses, but Germany intensified its operations in 1942. The calamitous attack on convoy PQ-17 in July 1942 forced the Allies to improve the security of the convoys. The Allied decision to suspend the convoys while they prepared for Operation Torch (see pp.146–47) in September–December 1942 increased tension with the Soviets, who were desperately fighting for Stalingrad (see pp.150–151). Convoys resumed and ran until the end of the war, but bad feeling between the Eastern and Western Allies remained.

ROUTES TO THE USSR

The Arctic route to the USSR was the shortest, and accounted for almost 25 percent of Allied aid sent to the Soviet Union. However, Soviet ships voyaging from the west coast of the US carried 50 percent. The Soviets also ran a convoy route through the Bering Strait, supplying fuel for Lend-Lease aircraft being transferred from Alaska to Siberia.

KEY

→ Summer Arctic convoy route

→ Winter Arctic convoy route

→ Soviet convoy route

→ US/Soviet convoy route

PACIFIC OCEAN

Bering Strait

Vladivostok
Magadan
Anchorage

USA
CANADA
ARCTIC OCEAN
USSR
ASIA

Archangel
Murmansk

ATLANTIC OCEAN

Scapa Flow

EUROPE

PERIL ALL AROUND

Squeezed between the ice and the German navy, U-boats, and air bases along the coast of Norway, the Arctic route was the most dangerous supply route to the Soviet Union.

KEY

▨ Axis territories, occupations, and cobelligerents by end of 1942

▨ Allied territories by end of 1942

᠅ Extent of winter sea ice

⊕ German air bases

⚓ German naval and U-boat bases

⚓ Allied naval bases

TIMELINE

1 | 2 | 3 | 4 | 5

1941 | 1942 | 1943 | 1944 | 1945 | 1946

ATLANTIC OCEAN

Norwegian Sea

Jan Mayen Island

Reykjavík
ICELAND
Hvalfjörður

Aug 1941–Jun 1942 Convoys congregate at the Icelandic harbors of Reykjavík and Hvalfjörður before sailing to the USSR.

Aug 1941–May 1945 Convoys set off from numerous naval bases across the British Isles.

Loch Ewe

Scapa Flow

Bergen

Oban
Glasgow

Firth of Clyde

UNITED KINGDOM

IRELAND

Liverpool

Aug 12, 1941 The first convoy "Dervish" sets sail for Archangel via Iceland.

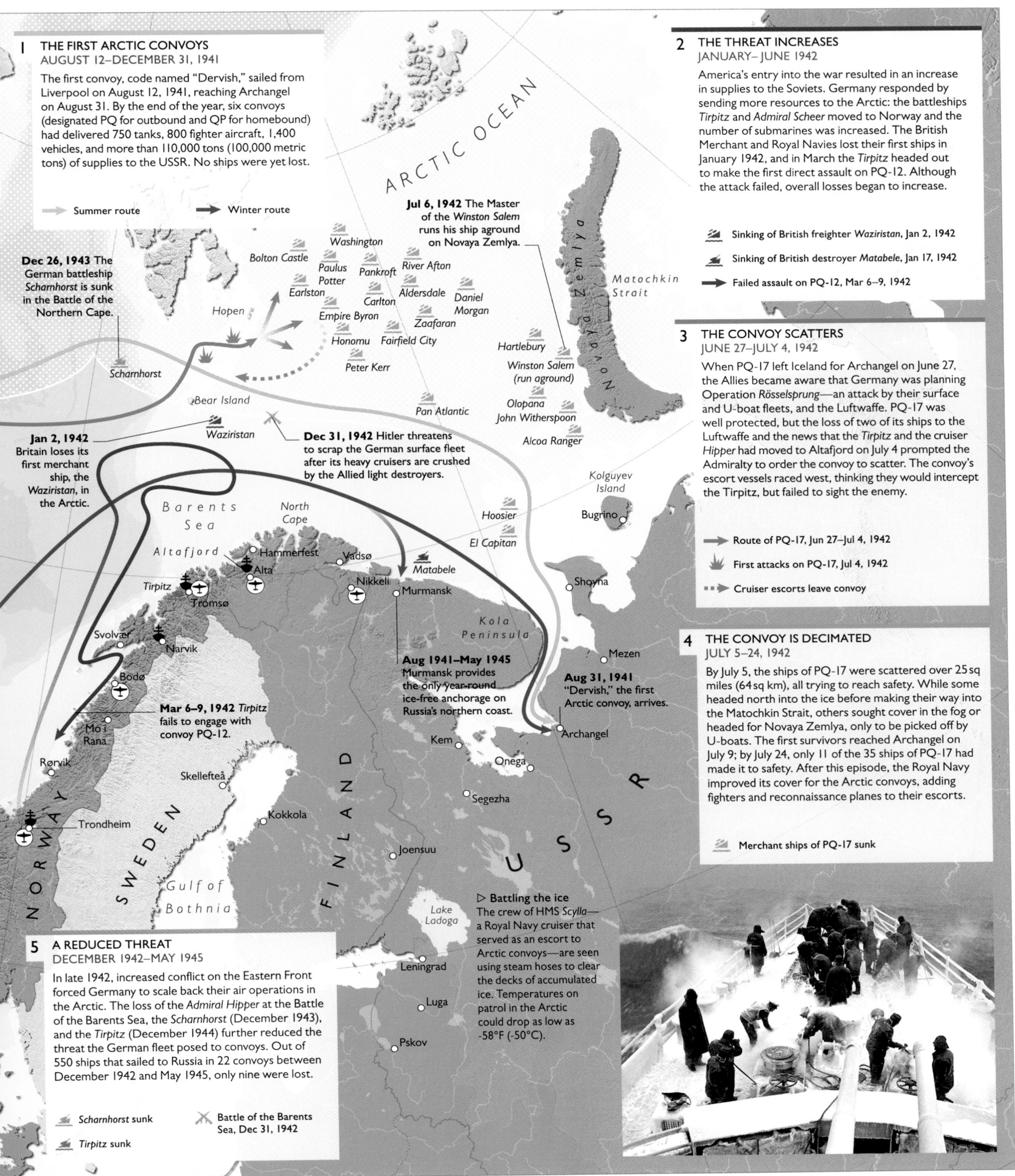

1 THE FIRST ARCTIC CONVOYS
AUGUST 12–DECEMBER 31, 1941

The first convoy, code named "Dervish," sailed from Liverpool on August 12, 1941, reaching Archangel on August 31. By the end of the year, six convoys (designated PQ for outbound and QP for homebound) had delivered 750 tanks, 800 fighter aircraft, 1,400 vehicles, and more than 110,000 tons (100,000 metric tons) of supplies to the USSR. No ships were yet lost.

→ Summer route   → Winter route

2 THE THREAT INCREASES
JANUARY– JUNE 1942

America's entry into the war resulted in an increase in supplies to the Soviets. Germany responded by sending more resources to the Arctic: the battleships *Tirpitz* and *Admiral Scheer* moved to Norway and the number of submarines was increased. The British Merchant and Royal Navies lost their first ships in January 1942, and in March the *Tirpitz* headed out to make the first direct assault on PQ-12. Although the attack failed, overall losses began to increase.

⛴ Sinking of British freighter *Waziristan*, Jan 2, 1942

⛴ Sinking of British destroyer *Matabele*, Jan 17, 1942

→ Failed assault on PQ-12, Mar 6–9, 1942

3 THE CONVOY SCATTERS
JUNE 27–JULY 4, 1942

When PQ-17 left Iceland for Archangel on June 27, the Allies became aware that Germany was planning Operation *Rösselsprung*—an attack by their surface and U-boat fleets, and the Luftwaffe. PQ-17 was well protected, but the loss of two of its ships to the Luftwaffe and the news that the *Tirpitz* and the cruiser *Hipper* had moved to Altafjord on July 4 prompted the Admiralty to order the convoy to scatter. The convoy's escort vessels raced west, thinking they would intercept the Tirpitz, but failed to sight the enemy.

→ Route of PQ-17, Jun 27–Jul 4, 1942

🌿 First attacks on PQ-17, Jul 4, 1942

⇢ Cruiser escorts leave convoy

4 THE CONVOY IS DECIMATED
JULY 5–24, 1942

By July 5, the ships of PQ-17 were scattered over 25 sq miles (64 sq km), all trying to reach safety. While some headed north into the ice before making their way into the Matochkin Strait, others sought cover in the fog or headed for Novaya Zemlya, only to be picked off by U-boats. The first survivors reached Archangel on July 9; by July 24, only 11 of the 35 ships of PQ-17 had made it to safety. After this episode, the Royal Navy improved its cover for the Arctic convoys, adding fighters and reconnaissance planes to their escorts.

⛴ Merchant ships of PQ-17 sunk

5 A REDUCED THREAT
DECEMBER 1942–MAY 1945

In late 1942, increased conflict on the Eastern Front forced Germany to scale back their air operations in the Arctic. The loss of the *Admiral Hipper* at the Battle of the Barents Sea, the *Scharnhorst* (December 1943), and the *Tirpitz* (December 1944) further reduced the threat the German fleet posed to convoys. Out of 550 ships that sailed to Russia in 22 convoys between December 1942 and May 1945, only nine were lost.

⛴ *Scharnhorst* sunk   ✕ Battle of the Barents Sea, Dec 31, 1942

⛴ *Tirpitz* sunk

Dec 26, 1943 The German battleship *Scharnhorst* is sunk in the Battle of the Northern Cape.

Jul 6, 1942 The Master of the *Winston Salem* runs his ship aground on Novaya Zemlya.

Jan 2, 1942 Britain loses its first merchant ship, the *Waziristan*, in the Arctic.

Dec 31, 1942 Hitler threatens to scrap the German surface fleet after its heavy cruisers are crushed by the Allied light destroyers.

Mar 6–9, 1942 *Tirpitz* fails to engage with convoy PQ-12.

Aug 1941–May 1945 Murmansk provides the only year-round ice-free anchorage on Russia's northern coast.

Aug 31, 1941 "Dervish," the first Arctic convoy, arrives.

Map labels

ARCTIC OCEAN

Novaya Zemlya

Matochkin Strait

Washington
Bolton Castle
Paulus Potter
Pankroft
River Afton
Earlston
Carlton
Aldersdale
Daniel Morgan
Empire Byron
Zaafaran
Honomu
Fairfield City
Peter Kerr
Hartlebury
Winston Salem (run aground)
Olopana
John Witherspoon
Pan Atlantic
Alcoa Ranger

Hopen

Scharnhorst

Bear Island

Waziristan

Barents Sea

North Cape

Altafjord
Hammerfest
Alta
Tirpitz
Tromsø
Svolvær
Narvik
Bodø
Mo i Rana
Rørvik
Trondheim

NORWAY
SWEDEN
FINLAND

Skellefteå
Kokkola
Joensuu

Gulf of Bothnia

Lake Ladoga

Leningrad
Luga
Pskov

Vadsø
Nikkeli
Matabele
Murmansk

Kola Peninsula

Kolguyev Island
Bugrino

Shoyna

Mezen

Hoosier
El Capitan

Kem
Onega
Segezha
Archangel

U S S R

▷ **Battling the ice**
The crew of HMS *Scylla*—a Royal Navy cruiser that served as an escort to Arctic convoys—are seen using steam hoses to clear the decks of accumulated ice. Temperatures on patrol in the Arctic could drop as low as -58°F (-50°C).

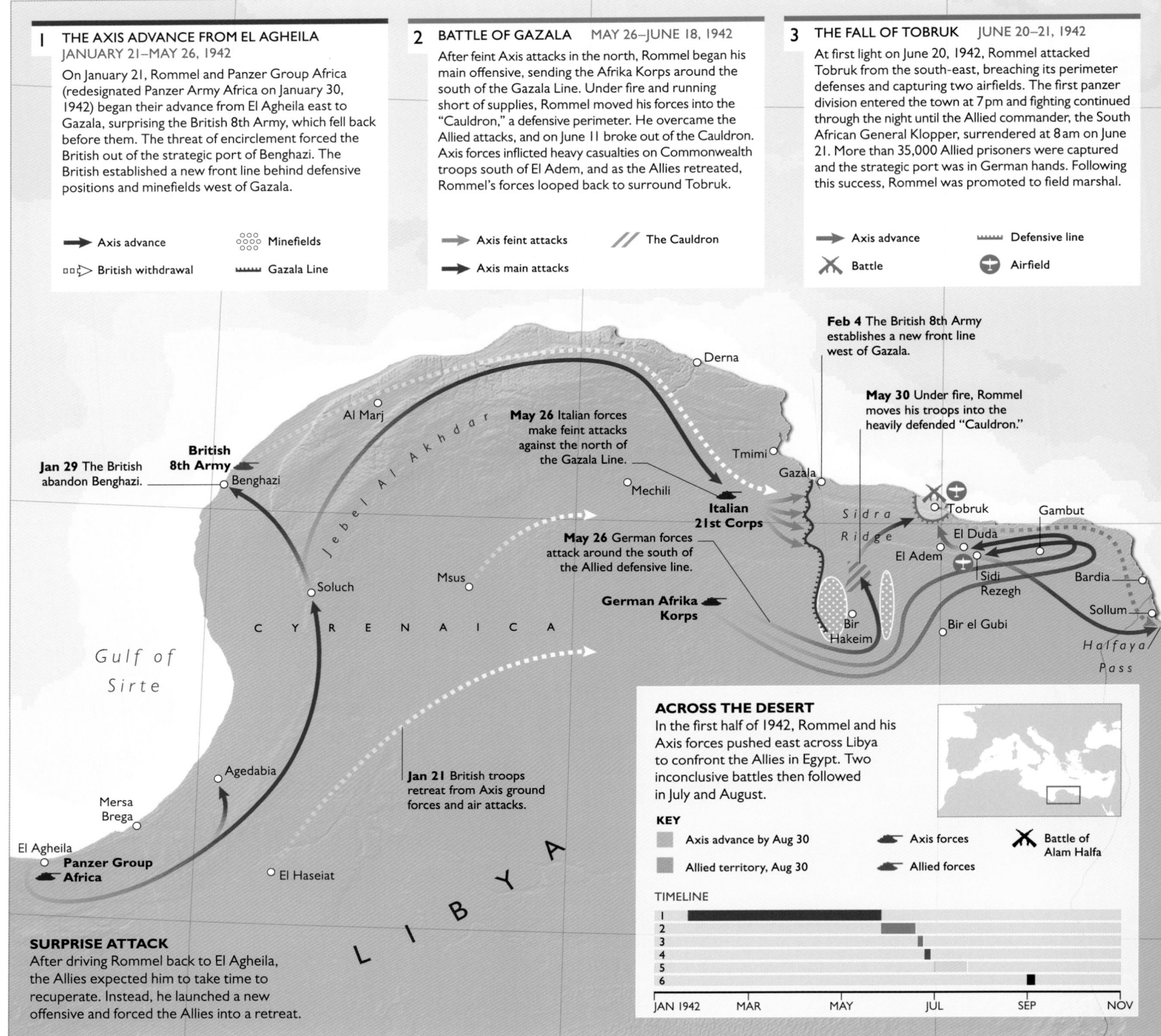

1 THE AXIS ADVANCE FROM EL AGHEILA
JANUARY 21–MAY 26, 1942

On January 21, Rommel and Panzer Group Africa (redesignated Panzer Army Africa on January 30, 1942) began their advance from El Agheila east to Gazala, surprising the British 8th Army, which fell back before them. The threat of encirclement forced the British out of the strategic port of Benghazi. The British established a new front line behind defensive positions and minefields west of Gazala.

→ Axis advance
⇢ British withdrawal
⊙ Minefields
ᴗᴗᴗ Gazala Line

2 BATTLE OF GAZALA   MAY 26–JUNE 18, 1942

After feint Axis attacks in the north, Rommel began his main offensive, sending the Afrika Korps around the south of the Gazala Line. Under fire and running short of supplies, Rommel moved his forces into the "Cauldron," a defensive perimeter. He overcame the Allied attacks, and on June 11 broke out of the Cauldron. Axis forces inflicted heavy casualties on Commonwealth troops south of El Adem, and as the Allies retreated, Rommel's forces looped back to surround Tobruk.

→ Axis feint attacks
→ Axis main attacks
// The Cauldron

3 THE FALL OF TOBRUK   JUNE 20–21, 1942

At first light on June 20, 1942, Rommel attacked Tobruk from the south-east, breaching its perimeter defenses and capturing two airfields. The first panzer division entered the town at 7pm and fighting continued through the night until the Allied commander, the South African General Klopper, surrendered at 8am on June 21. More than 35,000 Allied prisoners were captured and the strategic port was in German hands. Following this success, Rommel was promoted to field marshal.

→ Axis advance
✕ Battle
ᴗᴗᴗ Defensive line
⊕ Airfield

Feb 4 The British 8th Army establishes a new front line west of Gazala.

May 30 Under fire, Rommel moves his troops into the heavily defended "Cauldron."

Jan 29 The British abandon Benghazi.

May 26 Italian forces make feint attacks against the north of the Gazala Line.

May 26 German forces attack around the south of the Allied defensive line.

British 8th Army

Italian 21st Corps

German Afrika Korps

Derna

Al Marj

Jebel Al Akhdar

Tmimi

Gazala

Mechili

Sidra Ridge

Tobruk

Gambut

El Duda

El Adem

Sidi Rezegh

Bardia

Benghazi

Soluch

Msus

Bir el Gubi

Sollum

Halfaya Pass

C Y R E N A I C A

Bir Hakeim

Gulf of Sirte

Jan 21 British troops retreat from Axis ground forces and air attacks.

Agedabia

Mersa Brega

El Agheila

Panzer Group Africa

El Haseiat

L I B Y A

ACROSS THE DESERT
In the first half of 1942, Rommel and his Axis forces pushed east across Libya to confront the Allies in Egypt. Two inconclusive battles then followed in July and August.

KEY

▮ Axis advance by Aug 30
▮ Allied territory, Aug 30
◄ Axis forces
◄ Allied forces
✕ Battle of Alam Halfa

TIMELINE

	JAN 1942	MAR	MAY	JUL	SEP	NOV
1						
2						
3						
4						
5						
6						

SURPRISE ATTACK
After driving Rommel back to El Agheila, the Allies expected him to take time to recuperate. Instead, he launched a new offensive and forced the Allies into a retreat.

ROMMEL'S FINAL ADVANCE

By the start of 1942, the war in North Africa had seemingly turned against Rommel, but the man known as the "desert fox" countered with a new attack. He pushed the Allies into a retreat deep into Egypt, leading to confrontation at El Alamein.

By early January 1942, the Allied Operation Crusader (see pp.76–77) had forced Rommel all the way back from the Egyptian border to El Agheila, on Libya's Gulf of Sirte. This major retreat left the Axis forces (consisting of Italian and German corps) exhausted and their supply lines disrupted. The British assumed that Rommel would be unable to regain the initiative for some time, and so took the opportunity to refit their equipment and allow their troops time to relax. However, Rommel acted swiftly to restore his troops to fighting order and began to advance eastward on January 21, overrunning Benghazi on January 28 and Tmini by early February. The Allies regrouped behind the Gazala Line—a defensive barrier of minefields interspersed with small, fortified keeps—which ran from

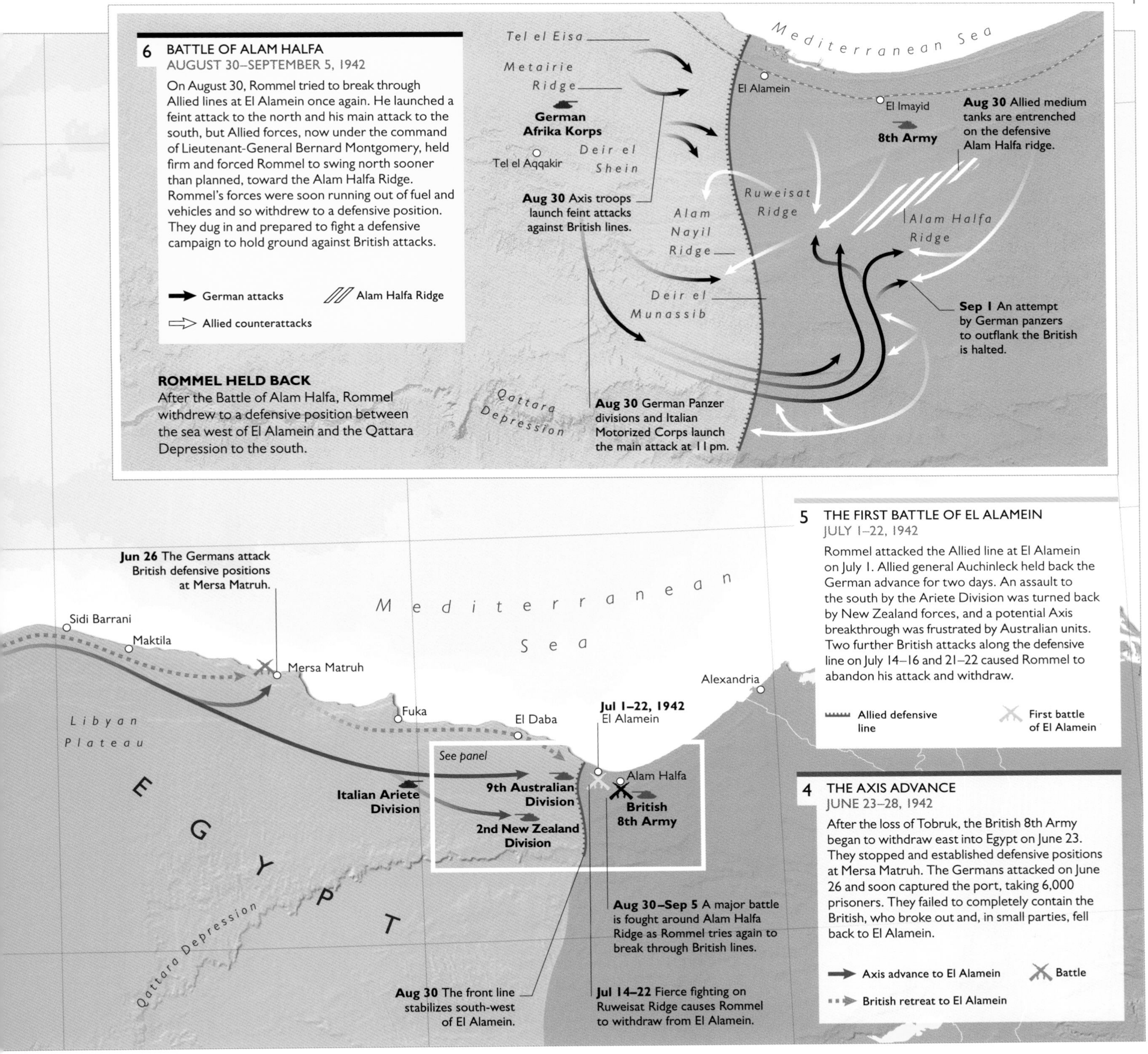

6 BATTLE OF ALAM HALFA
AUGUST 30–SEPTEMBER 5, 1942

On August 30, Rommel tried to break through Allied lines at El Alamein once again. He launched a feint attack to the north and his main attack to the south, but Allied forces, now under the command of Lieutenant-General Bernard Montgomery, held firm and forced Rommel to swing north sooner than planned, toward the Alam Halfa Ridge. Rommel's forces were soon running out of fuel and vehicles and so withdrew to a defensive position. They dug in and prepared to fight a defensive campaign to hold ground against British attacks.

➡ German attacks   ⫽ Alam Halfa Ridge

⇨ Allied counterattacks

ROMMEL HELD BACK

After the Battle of Alam Halfa, Rommel withdrew to a defensive position between the sea west of El Alamein and the Qattara Depression to the south.

Tel el Eisa
Metairie Ridge
German Afrika Korps
Tel el Aqqakir   Deir el Shein
Aug 30 Axis troops launch feint attacks against British lines.
Alam Nayil Ridge
Ruweisat Ridge
Deir el Munassib
Qattara Depression
Aug 30 German Panzer divisions and Italian Motorized Corps launch the main attack at 11pm.

El Alamein
El Imayid
8th Army
Aug 30 Allied medium tanks are entrenched on the defensive Alam Halfa ridge.
Alam Halfa Ridge
Sep 1 An attempt by German panzers to outflank the British is halted.

---

5 THE FIRST BATTLE OF EL ALAMEIN
JULY 1–22, 1942

Rommel attacked the Allied line at El Alamein on July 1. Allied general Auchinleck held back the German advance for two days. An assault to the south by the Ariete Division was turned back by New Zealand forces, and a potential Axis breakthrough was frustrated by Australian units. Two further British attacks along the defensive line on July 14–16 and 21–22 caused Rommel to abandon his attack and withdraw.

⸗⸗⸗ Allied defensive line   ⚔ First battle of El Alamein

4 THE AXIS ADVANCE
JUNE 23–28, 1942

After the loss of Tobruk, the British 8th Army began to withdraw east into Egypt on June 23. They stopped and established defensive positions at Mersa Matruh. The Germans attacked on June 26 and soon captured the port, taking 6,000 prisoners. They failed to completely contain the British, who broke out and, in small parties, fell back to El Alamein.

➡ Axis advance to El Alamein   ⚔ Battle

⫶⫶▶ British retreat to El Alamein

Jun 26 The Germans attack British defensive positions at Mersa Matruh.

Sidi Barrani
Maktila
Mersa Matruh
Mediterranean Sea
Libyan Plateau
Fuka
El Daba
Alexandria
Jul 1–22, 1942 El Alamein
See panel
Italian Ariete Division
9th Australian Division
Alam Halfa
British 8th Army
2nd New Zealand Division
E G Y P T
Qattara Depression

Aug 30 The front line stabilizes south-west of El Alamein.

Aug 30–Sep 5 A major battle is fought around Alam Halfa Ridge as Rommel tries again to break through British lines.

Jul 14–22 Fierce fighting on Ruweisat Ridge causes Rommel to withdraw from El Alamein.

---

the coast at Gazala to Bir Hakeim about 60 miles (95 km) to the south. Despite fierce resistance—particularly from the Free French forces at Bir Hakeim—and heavy losses on both sides, Rommel prevailed at the Battle of Gazala and forced the Allies to abandon their defensive line and retreat toward the Egyptian border.

By the middle of June, Axis forces had captured Tobruk and the Allies had fallen back to Mersa Matruh, which was itself overcome by the end of the month. The two sides confronted one another in Egypt in two inconclusive battles—El Alamein in July and Alam Halfa in August. Although Rommel had achieved his most impressive victories to date in North Africa, he had ultimately failed to break through Allied lines. His advance had been checked.

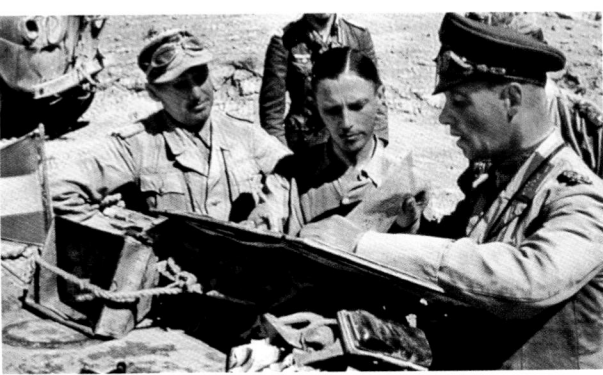

◁ **Battle instructions**
Erwin Rommel (on the right), the commander of the German and Italian forces in North Africa, gives directions to his officers.

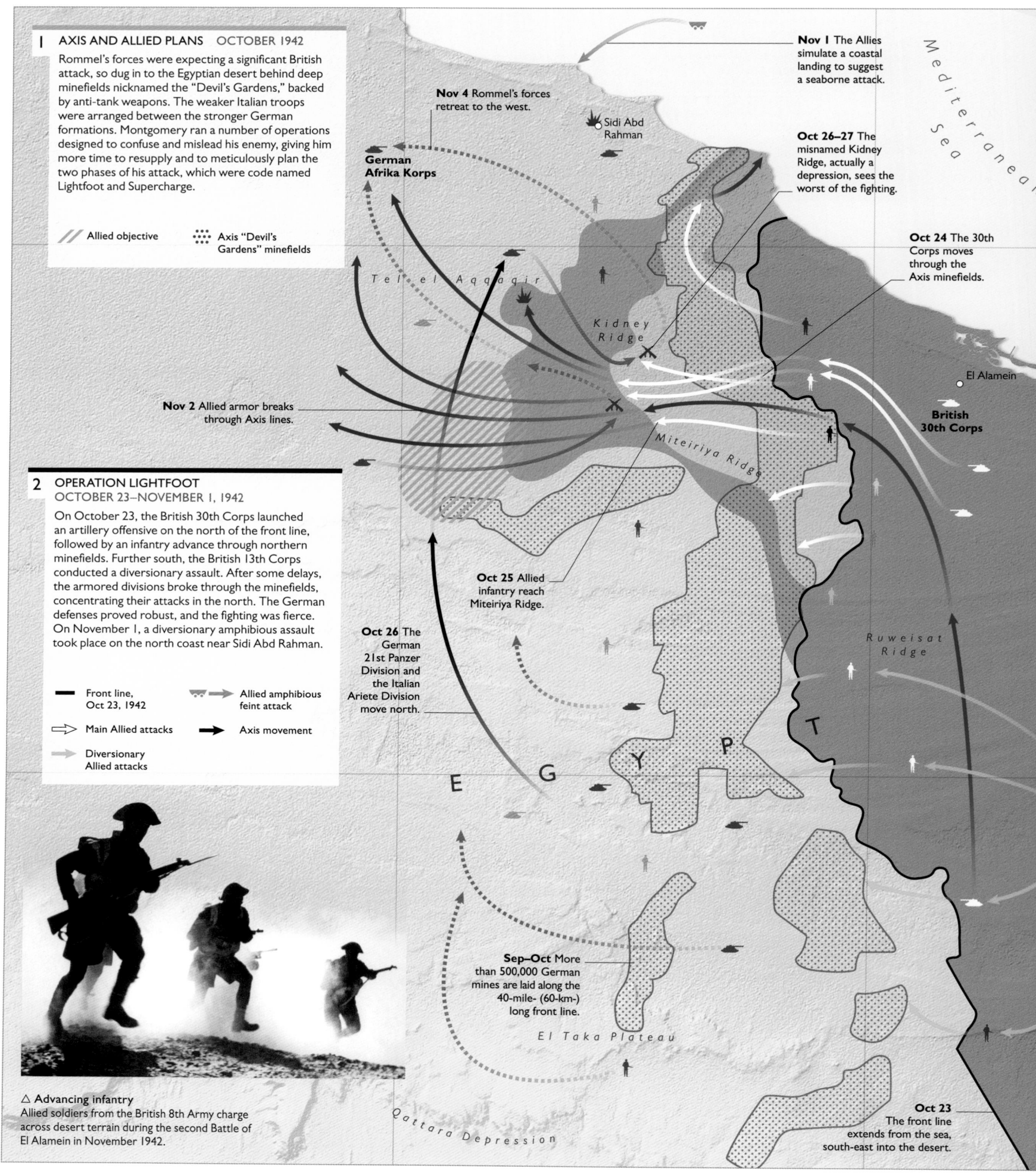

1 AXIS AND ALLIED PLANS OCTOBER 1942

Rommel's forces were expecting a significant British attack, so dug in to the Egyptian desert behind deep minefields nicknamed the "Devil's Gardens," backed by anti-tank weapons. The weaker Italian troops were arranged between the stronger German formations. Montgomery ran a number of operations designed to confuse and mislead his enemy, giving him more time to resupply and to meticulously plan the two phases of his attack, which were code named Lightfoot and Supercharge.

///// Allied objective   ⁘ Axis "Devil's Gardens" minefields

2 OPERATION LIGHTFOOT
OCTOBER 23–NOVEMBER 1, 1942

On October 23, the British 30th Corps launched an artillery offensive on the north of the front line, followed by an infantry advance through northern minefields. Further south, the British 13th Corps conducted a diversionary assault. After some delays, the armored divisions broke through the minefields, concentrating their attacks in the north. The German defenses proved robust, and the fighting was fierce. On November 1, a diversionary amphibious assault took place on the north coast near Sidi Abd Rahman.

▬▬▶	Front line, Oct 23, 1942	▭▭▶	Allied amphibious feint attack
⇨	Main Allied attacks	➡	Axis movement
➡	Diversionary Allied attacks		

△ **Advancing infantry**
Allied soldiers from the British 8th Army charge across desert terrain during the second Battle of El Alamein in November 1942.

Nov 1 The Allies simulate a coastal landing to suggest a seaborne attack.

Nov 4 Rommel's forces retreat to the west.

Oct 26–27 The misnamed Kidney Ridge, actually a depression, sees the worst of the fighting.

Sidi Abd Rahman

Oct 24 The 30th Corps moves through the Axis minefields.

German Afrika Korps

Tel el Aqqaqir

Kidney Ridge

El Alamein

Nov 2 Allied armor breaks through Axis lines.

Miteiriya Ridge

British 30th Corps

Oct 25 Allied infantry reach Miteiriya Ridge.

Oct 26 The German 21st Panzer Division and the Italian Ariete Division move north.

Ruweisat Ridge

Mediterranean Sea

Sep–Oct More than 500,000 German mines are laid along the 40-mile- (60-km-) long front line.

El Taka Plateau

E G Y P T

Oct 23 The front line extends from the sea, south-east into the desert.

Qattara Depression

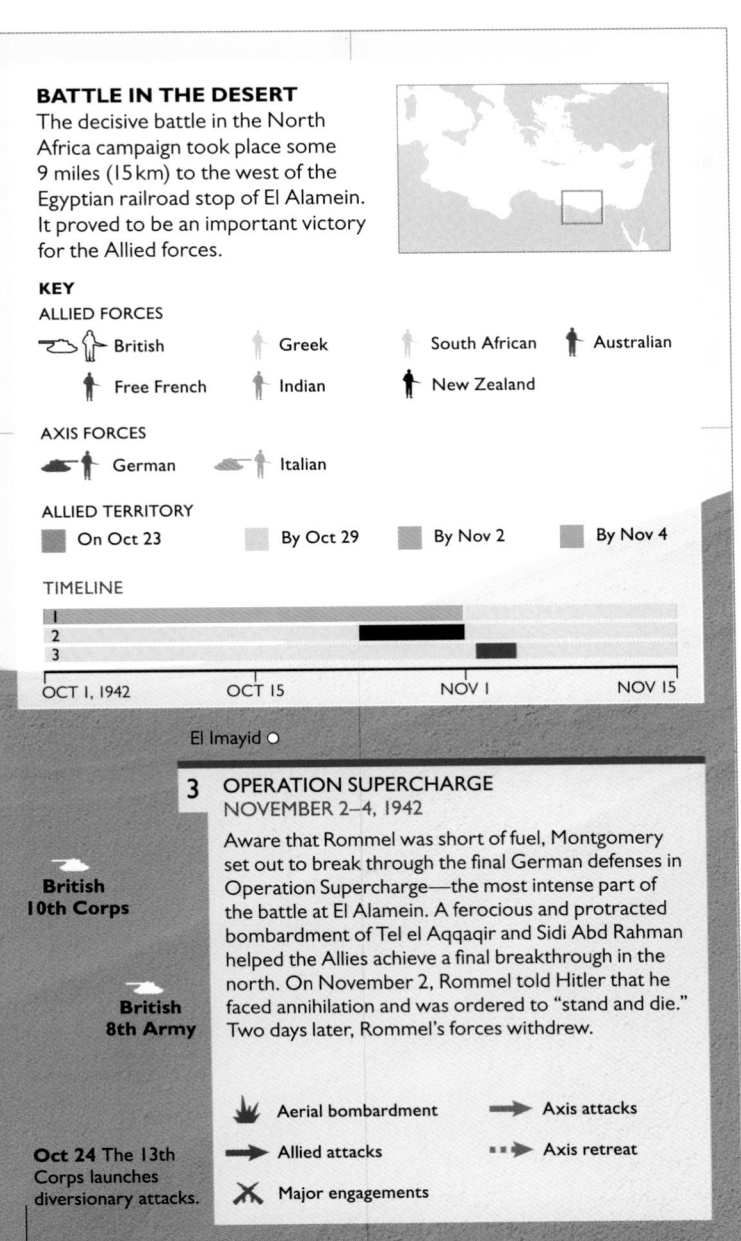

BATTLE IN THE DESERT

The decisive battle in the North Africa campaign took place some 9 miles (15 km) to the west of the Egyptian railroad stop of El Alamein. It proved to be an important victory for the Allied forces.

KEY

ALLIED FORCES

British   Greek   South African   Australian

Free French   Indian   New Zealand

AXIS FORCES

German   Italian

ALLIED TERRITORY

On Oct 23   By Oct 29   By Nov 2   By Nov 4

TIMELINE

1
2
3

OCT 1, 1942   OCT 15   NOV 1   NOV 15

El Imayid

3 OPERATION SUPERCHARGE
NOVEMBER 2–4, 1942

Aware that Rommel was short of fuel, Montgomery set out to break through the final German defenses in Operation Supercharge—the most intense part of the battle at El Alamein. A ferocious and protracted bombardment of Tel el Aqqaqir and Sidi Abd Rahman helped the Allies achieve a final breakthrough in the north. On November 2, Rommel told Hitler that he faced annihilation and was ordered to "stand and die." Two days later, Rommel's forces withdrew.

British 10th Corps

British 8th Army

Oct 24 The 13th Corps launches diversionary attacks.

Aerial bombardment   Axis attacks

Allied attacks   Axis retreat

Major engagements

SECOND BATTLE OF EL ALAMEIN

The key battle of the Western Desert Campaign took place around the Egyptian town of El Alamein from October to November 1942. It proved to be a watershed, stopping the Axis advance into Egypt, ending the threat to the Suez Canal, and forcing Rommel's troops, including the formidable Afrika Korps, to retreat into Tunisia.

After their failure to break through British lines at Alam Halfa in August 1942 (see pp.142–143), the Axis forces were on the defensive, and their supply lines were badly overstretched. However, General Montgomery did not immediately counterattack, choosing instead to build up his forces, gather intelligence, and further choke Axis supplies before launching an attack that he hoped would be decisive.

By October, the Axis forces were outnumbered and outgunned. The Allies fielded 195,000 men, 1,029 tanks, 435 armored cars, 900 artillery pieces, 1,451 anti-tank guns, and 750 aircraft. In response, the combined German and Italian forces numbered 116,000 men,

and were equipped with 547 tanks, 192 armored cars, 552 artillery pieces, and up to 1,060 anti-tank guns, as well as around 900 aircraft. The inevitable Allied attack finally came on October 23, 1942, with Rommel away in Germany for medical treatment; he returned to Africa on October 25. The Axis forces put up fierce resistance, but by November 4, Rommel was in retreat toward Tunisia. The Allies had won, and plans were underway to clear the Axis forces from Africa (see pp.146–147).

The second Battle of El Alamein was a turning point for the Western Allies and also a boost to flagging morale, as Britain celebrated a major success, the first for its land forces since 1939.

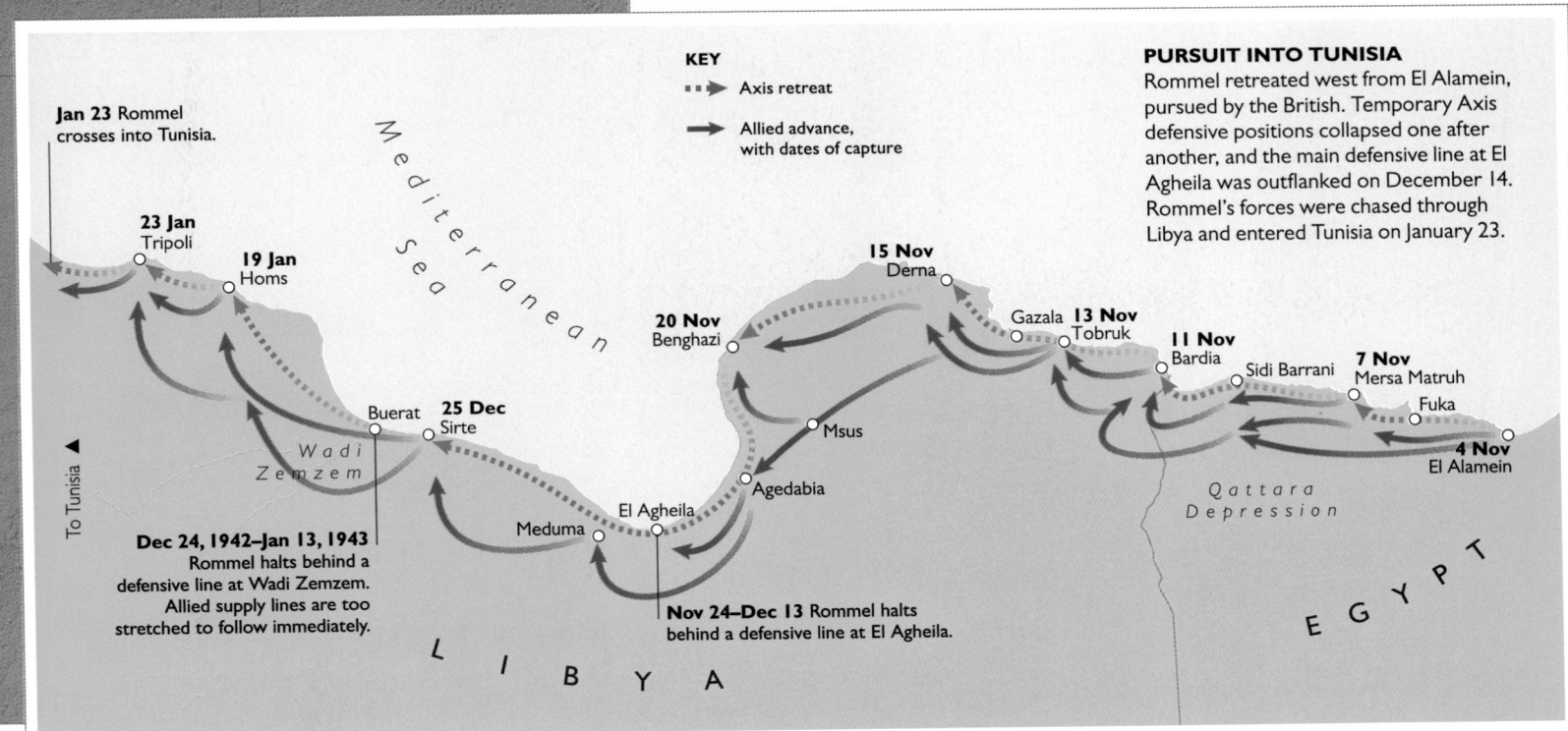

British 13th Corps

KEY

Axis retreat

Allied advance, with dates of capture

PURSUIT INTO TUNISIA

Rommel retreated west from El Alamein, pursued by the British. Temporary Axis defensive positions collapsed one after another, and the main defensive line at El Agheila was outflanked on December 14. Rommel's forces were chased through Libya and entered Tunisia on January 23.

Jan 23 Rommel crosses into Tunisia.

Mediterranean Sea

23 Jan Tripoli
19 Jan Homs
15 Nov Derna
20 Nov Benghazi
Gazala
13 Nov Tobruk
11 Nov Bardia
Sidi Barrani
7 Nov Mersa Matruh
Fuka
Buerat
25 Dec Sirte
Wadi Zemzem
Msus
4 Nov El Alamein
To Tunisia
Meduma
El Agheila
Agedabia
Qattara Depression

Dec 24, 1942–Jan 13, 1943 Rommel halts behind a defensive line at Wadi Zemzem. Allied supply lines are too stretched to follow immediately.

Nov 24–Dec 13 Rommel halts behind a defensive line at El Agheila.

L I B Y A

E G Y P T

OPERATION TORCH

Four days after German field marshal Rommel began his retreat from El Alamein in Egypt, US and British troops began to land in Morocco and Algeria. Known as Operation Torch, this campaign was intended to evict Axis forces from Africa and clear the way for the invasion of Italy.

The Soviet Union wanted its Western allies to open up a second front in Europe to relieve the pressure on the Red Army. The US backed a direct assault on occupied France, but Churchill argued for landings in Africa that would both reduce pressure on British and Commonwealth forces in Egypt and enable the Allies to clear North Africa of Axis troops. The Allies could then use Tunisia as a starting point from which to attack the Axis

through its most vulnerable member—Italy. Such a landing would also help safeguard passage for Allied vessels through the Mediterranean to the Suez Canal. US commanders opposed the British plan, and wanted a three-pronged attack across the English Channel. Roosevelt, however, saw the need for the campaign and ordered that Torch go ahead at the earliest possible date, much to the fury of US planners and the Soviets.

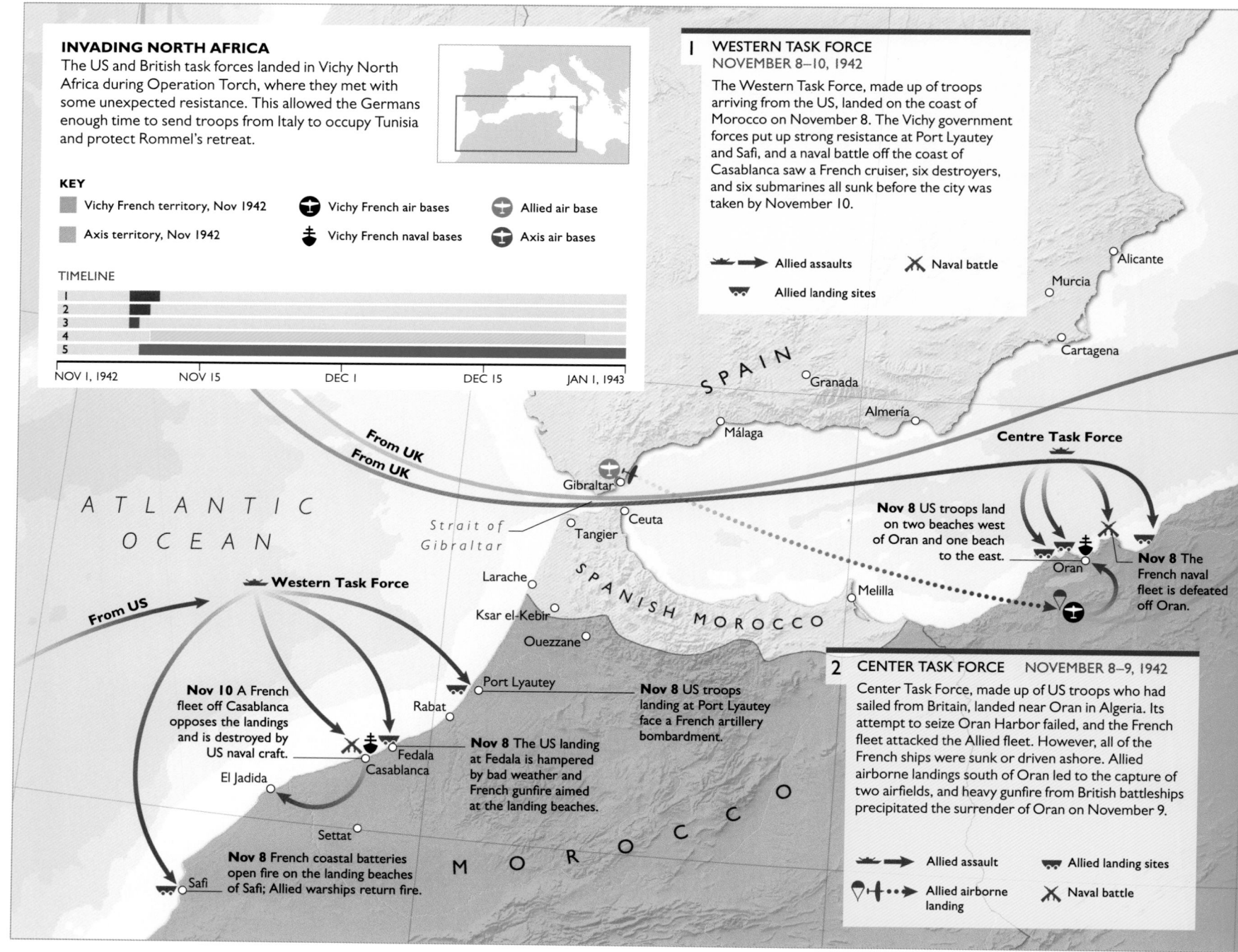

INVADING NORTH AFRICA
The US and British task forces landed in Vichy North Africa during Operation Torch, where they met with some unexpected resistance. This allowed the Germans enough time to send troops from Italy to occupy Tunisia and protect Rommel's retreat.

KEY

▓ Vichy French territory, Nov 1942 ⊕ Vichy French air bases ⊕ Allied air base

▓ Axis territory, Nov 1942 ⊕ Vichy French naval bases ⊕ Axis air bases

TIMELINE

NOV 1, 1942 — NOV 15 — DEC 1 — DEC 15 — JAN 1, 1943

1 | **WESTERN TASK FORCE**
NOVEMBER 8–10, 1942

The Western Task Force, made up of troops arriving from the US, landed on the coast of Morocco on November 8. The Vichy government forces put up strong resistance at Port Lyautey and Safi, and a naval battle off the coast of Casablanca saw a French cruiser, six destroyers, and six submarines all sunk before the city was taken by November 10.

→ Allied assaults   ✕ Naval battle

⊷ Allied landing sites

2 | **CENTER TASK FORCE**   **NOVEMBER 8–9, 1942**

Center Task Force, made up of US troops who had sailed from Britain, landed near Oran in Algeria. Its attempt to seize Oran Harbor failed, and the French fleet attacked the Allied fleet. However, all of the French ships were sunk or driven ashore. Allied airborne landings south of Oran led to the capture of two airfields, and heavy gunfire from British battleships precipitated the surrender of Oran on November 9.

→ Allied assault   ⊷ Allied landing sites

⊕┼∙∙∙ Allied airborne landing   ✕ Naval battle

Map labels:

ATLANTIC OCEAN

SPAIN — Granada, Almería, Málaga, Murcia, Alicante, Cartagena

Gibraltar — Strait of Gibraltar

Ceuta, Tangier, Larache, Ksar el-Kebir, Ouezzane

SPANISH MOROCCO — Melilla

From UK, From US

Western Task Force

Centre Task Force

Oran

Nov 8 US troops land on two beaches west of Oran and one beach to the east.

Nov 8 The French naval fleet is defeated off Oran.

Nov 8 US troops landing at Port Lyautey face a French artillery bombardment.

Port Lyautey, Rabat

Nov 10 A French fleet off Casablanca opposes the landings and is destroyed by US naval craft.

El Jadida, Fedala, Casablanca, Settat

Nov 8 The US landing at Fedala is hampered by bad weather and French gunfire aimed at the landing beaches.

Nov 8 French coastal batteries open fire on the landing beaches of Safi; Allied warships return fire.

Safi

MOROCCO

The planned landing areas on the North African coast were under the rule of Vichy France, which controlled tens of thousands of troops. The Allies were uncertain of what the Vichy leaders' response would be to an invasion and sent US Major General Mark Clark on a secret mission to Algiers to gauge their possible reaction. Despite the support of some individual generals, the Vichy governments in Morocco and Algeria opposed the landings, which consequently met with stiff resistance. A further drawback of landing in Morocco was that it was a considerable distance to Tunisia—the ultimate Allied target. As a result, German reinforcements were able to pour into Tunisia from Italy to protect Rommel's rear as he retreated following defeat at El Alamein (see pp.144–145).

"The only tough nut left is in your hands. Crack it open quickly."

EISENHOWER TO PATTON, CASABLANCA, 1943

THE END OF VICHY FRANCE

The failure of Vichy France to resist the Allied landings in North Africa convinced the Germans that it could no longer be trusted. On November 11, German and Italian troops occupied Vichy France and ended its independence. The Germans also launched Operation Lila to capture the units of the French fleet at Toulon and prevent them from sailing to join the Allies. However, the French navy scuttled almost their entire fleet at Toulon on November 27, before the Germans arrived in the port.

The French fleet is scuttled

---

5 THE DASH TO TUNIS NOVEMBER 9–DECEMBER 31, 1942

One day after Operation Torch, German forces began to land in Tunisia to protect Rommel's rear as he retreated west from El Alamein. British forces advancing from Bône encountered German patrols on November 18, and heavy fighting broke out as the Allies tried to seize Medjez el Bab. By the end of the year, the Germans had established a series of strongpoints and a front line was formed across northern Tunisia.

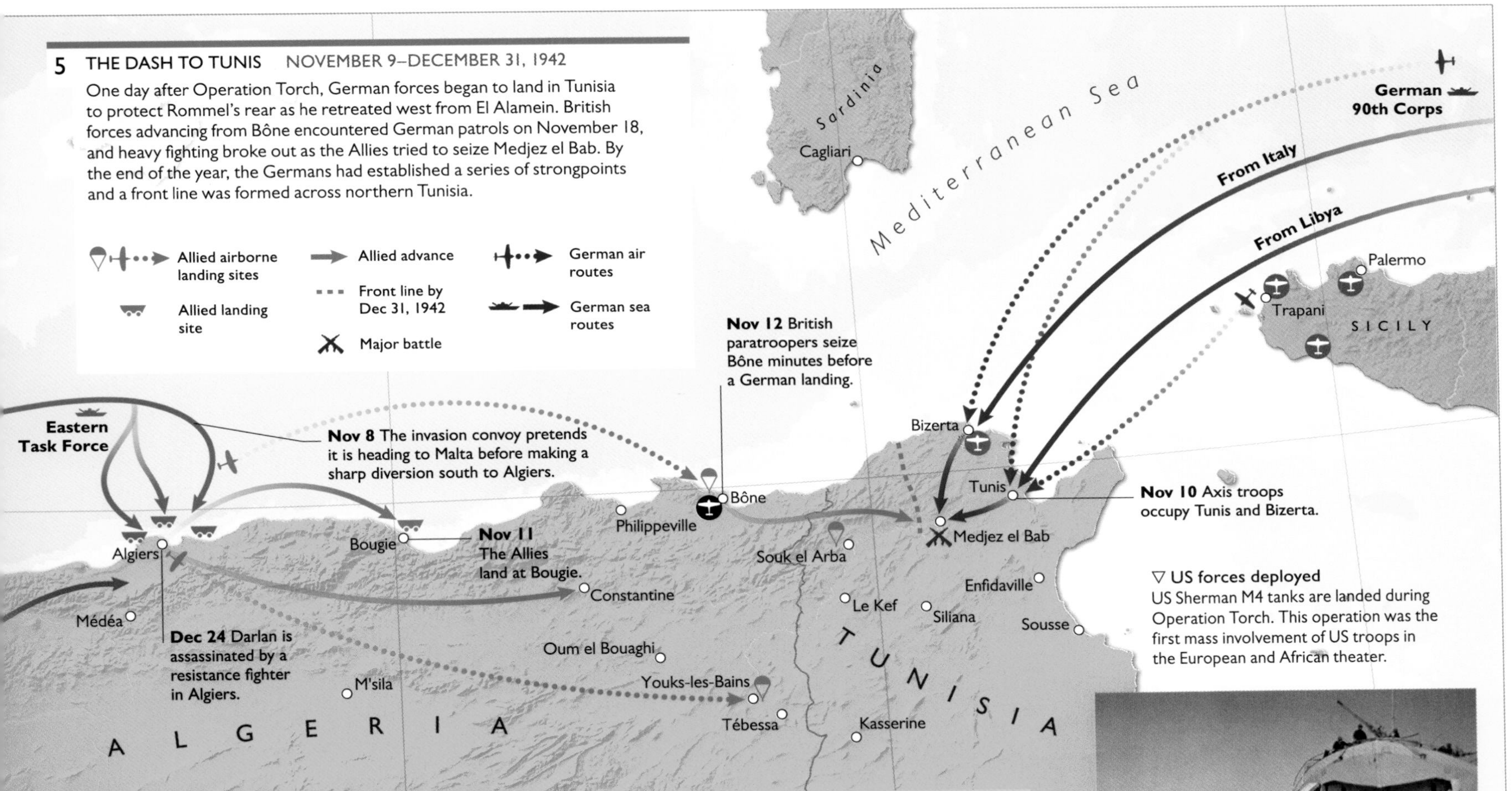

- Allied airborne landing sites
- Allied advance
- German air routes
- Allied landing site
- Front line by Dec 31, 1942
- German sea routes
- Major battle

German 90th Corps

From Italy

From Libya

Palermo

Trapani

SICILY

Nov 12 British paratroopers seize Bône minutes before a German landing.

Bizerta

Tunis

Nov 10 Axis troops occupy Tunis and Bizerta.

Eastern Task Force

Nov 8 The invasion convoy pretends it is heading to Malta before making a sharp diversion south to Algiers.

Bône

Philippeville

Medjez el Bab

Souk el Arba

Enfidaville

Algiers

Bougie

Nov 11 The Allies land at Bougie.

Constantine

Le Kef

Siliana

Sousse

Médéa

Dec 24 Darlan is assassinated by a resistance fighter in Algiers.

Oum el Bouaghi

M'sila

Youks-les-Bains

Tébessa

Kasserine

A L G E R I A

T U N I S I A

▽ **US forces deployed**
US Sherman M4 tanks are landed during Operation Torch. This operation was the first mass involvement of US troops in the European and African theater.

---

3 EASTERN TASK FORCE
NOVEMBER 8, 1942

Early on November 8, French Resistance fighters staged a coup d'état in Algiers. The 400 (mainly Jewish) fighters seized key targets in the Algerian capital. The British Eastern Task Force landed around Algiers later that morning and did not meet with much resistance from the French forces. The only fighting in the city took place by the harbor, when heavy French artillery prevented one British destroyer from landing its troops. The city surrendered to the Allies at 6pm.

- Allied assault
- Allied landing sites

4 THE AFTERMATH
NOVEMBER 10–DECEMBER 24, 1942

Admiral François Darlan, commander in chief of all Vichy French forces, happened to be in Algiers on a personal visit, attending to his sick son, when the Allied invasion of Morocco and Algeria took place. He convinced the French forces to give up their opposition to the invasion and signed an armistice with the Allies, folding his forces in with those of the Free French. However, many of the Free French criticized Darlan for his previous collaboration with the Axis powers, and he was assassinated by a resistance fighter on December 24.

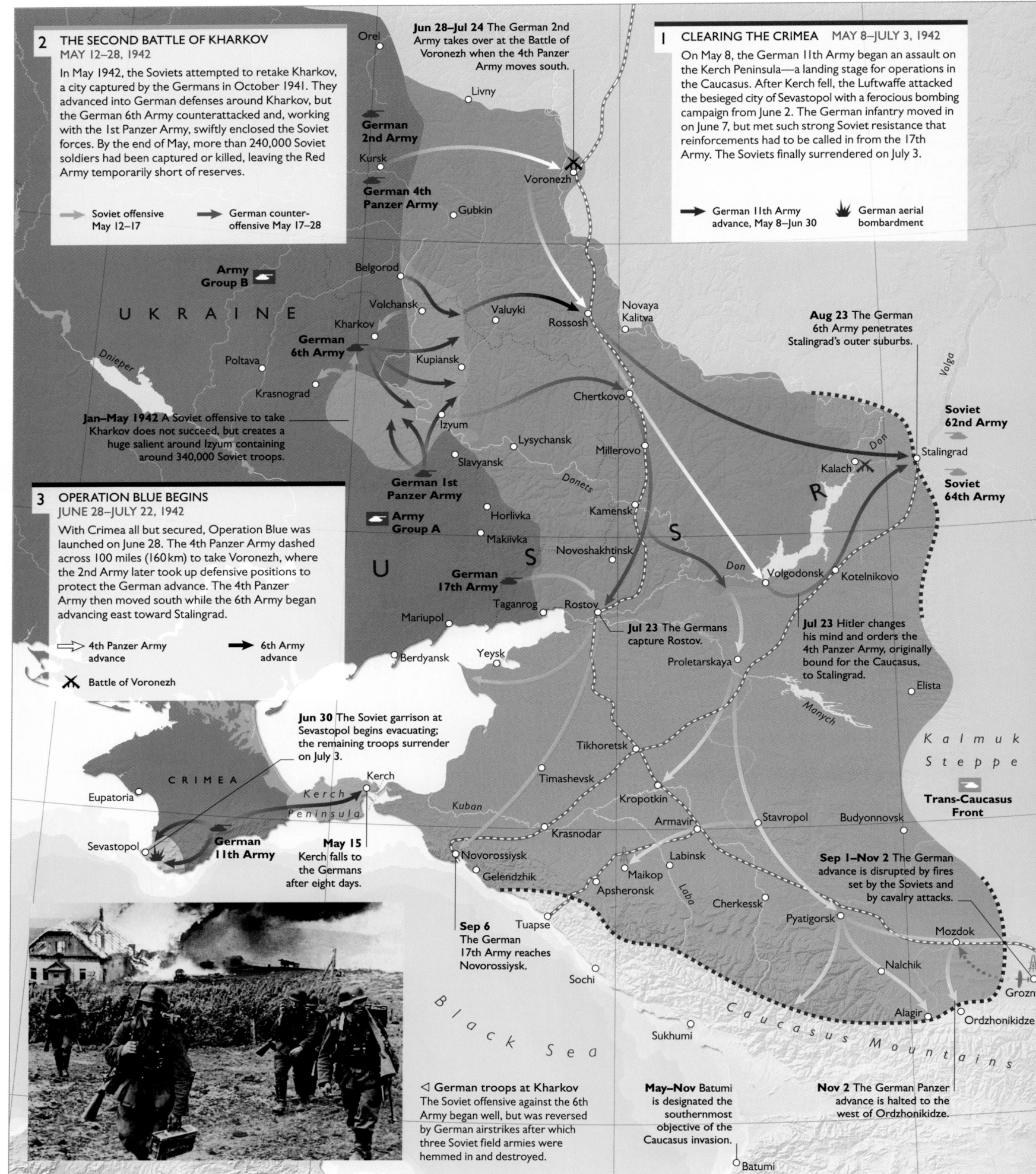

2 THE SECOND BATTLE OF KHARKOV
MAY 12–28, 1942

In May 1942, the Soviets attempted to retake Kharkov, a city captured by the Germans in October 1941. They advanced into German defenses around Kharkov, but the German 6th Army counterattacked and, working with the 1st Panzer Army, swiftly enclosed the Soviet forces. By the end of May, more than 240,000 Soviet soldiers had been captured or killed, leaving the Red Army temporarily short of reserves.

→ Soviet offensive May 12–17
→ German counter-offensive May 17–28

Jun 28–Jul 24 The German 2nd Army takes over at the Battle of Voronezh when the 4th Panzer Army moves south.

German 2nd Army

German 4th Panzer Army

1 CLEARING THE CRIMEA MAY 8–JULY 3, 1942

On May 8, the German 11th Army began an assault on the Kerch Peninsula—a landing stage for operations in the Caucasus. After Kerch fell, the Luftwaffe attacked the besieged city of Sevastopol with a ferocious bombing campaign from June 2. The German infantry moved in on June 7, but met such strong Soviet resistance that reinforcements had to be called in from the 17th Army. The Soviets finally surrendered on July 3.

→ German 11th Army advance, May 8–Jun 30
🗲 German aerial bombardment

Army Group B

U K R A I N E

German 6th Army

Jan–May 1942 A Soviet offensive to take Kharkov does not succeed, but creates a huge salient around Izyum containing around 340,000 Soviet troops.

3 OPERATION BLUE BEGINS
JUNE 28–JULY 22, 1942

With Crimea all but secured, Operation Blue was launched on June 28. The 4th Panzer Army dashed across 100 miles (160km) to take Voronezh, where the 2nd Army later took up defensive positions to protect the German advance. The 4th Panzer Army then moved south while the 6th Army began advancing east toward Stalingrad.

⇨ 4th Panzer Army advance
➡ 6th Army advance
✕ Battle of Voronezh

German 1st Panzer Army

Army Group A

U S S R

German 17th Army

Aug 23 The German 6th Army penetrates Stalingrad's outer suburbs.

Soviet 62nd Army

Soviet 64th Army

Jul 23 The Germans capture Rostov.

Jul 23 Hitler changes his mind and orders the 4th Panzer Army, originally bound for the Caucasus, to Stalingrad.

Jun 30 The Soviet garrison at Sevastopol begins evacuating; the remaining troops surrender on July 3.

C R I M E A

Kerch Peninsula

German 11th Army

May 15 Kerch falls to the Germans after eight days.

Sep 1–Nov 2 The German advance is disrupted by fires set by the Soviets and by cavalry attacks.

Kalmuk Steppe

Trans-Caucasus Front

Kuban

Sep 6 The German 17th Army reaches Novorossiysk.

Black Sea

Caucasus Mountains

◁ **German troops at Kharkov**
The Soviet offensive against the 6th Army began well, but was reversed by German airstrikes after which three Soviet field armies were hemmed in and destroyed.

May–Nov Batumi is designated the southernmost objective of the Caucasus invasion.

Nov 2 The German Panzer advance is halted to the west of Ordzhonikidze.

Places labeled on map: Orel, Livny, Kursk, Voronezh, Gubkin, Belgorod, Volchansk, Valuyki, Novaya Kalitva, Rossosh, Kharkov, Kupiansk, Poltava, Krasnograd, Chertkovo, Izyum, Lysychansk, Millerovo, Kalach, Stalingrad, Slavyansk, Kamensk, Horlivka, Makiivka, Novoshakhtinsk, Volgodonsk, Kotelnikovo, Taganrog, Rostov, Mariupol, Proletarskaya, Elista, Berdyansk, Yeysk, Tikhoretsk, Timashevsk, Kropotkin, Stavropol, Budyonnovsk, Armavir, Krasnodar, Labinsk, Novorossiysk, Gelendzhik, Maikop, Apsheronsk, Cherkessk, Pyatigorsk, Mozdok, Nalchik, Tuapse, Sochi, Sukhumi, Alagir, Ordzhonikidze, Grozny, Batumi, Eupatoria, Sevastopol, Kerch, Dnieper, Donets, Don, Manych, Laba, Volga

TWO-PRONGED ATTACK

Germany and its allies made spectacular gains from May to September 1942, reaching their furthest extent in the USSR. Split in two directions, however, their advance had halted by November.

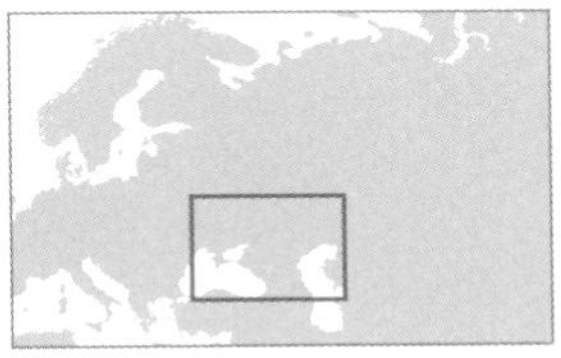

KEY

- ◄ Axis forces
- ◄ Soviet forces
- ▭▭ Main railroads

GERMAN-HELD TERRITORY

- ▮ on May 7
- ▮ by May 28
- ▮ by Jul 3
- ▮ by Jul 23
- ▮ by Nov 18 (farthest extent of advance in USSR)
- ■■■ Front line, Nov 18

TIMELINE

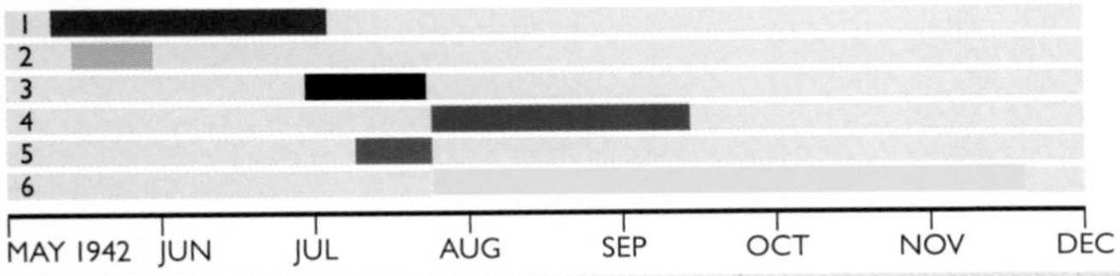

	MAY 1942	JUN	JUL	AUG	SEP	OCT	NOV	DEC
1								
2								
3								
4								
5								
6								

GERMAN ADVANCE TO STALINGRAD

The Germans launched a huge offensive in the southern USSR in the summer of 1942. Their target was the oil-rich Caucasus region, which they planned to seize after taking the cities in the Don River basin, the USSR's industrial heartland. They advanced rapidly, and by September had closed in on the city of Stalingrad.

Having failed to take Moscow (see pp.100–101), the Germans planned a new offensive that would bypass the capital. Operation Blue (*Fall Blau*) aimed to strike south-east to take the oil fields of the Caucasus, seizing the Red Army's vital fuel supplies for Germany, and also to capture Stalingrad, which would secure transport links into the Caucasus and protect the Germans' flank. Hitler also believed that the Soviets were near breaking point, and that one more major offensive would drive them to defeat.

First, the Germans needed to clear Crimea and the Kharkov area of Soviet forces, a task they achieved by early July. Once *Fall Blau* began, however, Hitler ordered simultaneous attacks on Stalingrad and the Caucasus. To achieve this, Army Group South (including Italian, Hungarian, and Romanian divisions) was split in two on July 7, 1942. Army Group A was to advance through the Caucasus and secure the Black Sea coast as far south as Batumi, while Army Group B was to move on Stalingrad.

Over the next months, resources were switched between the two offensives; by mid-September the Germans were spread across a vast area and neither army group had achieved its objective. Meanwhile, Stalin ordered the Red Army to defend Stalingrad at all costs (see pp.150–151).

> *"If we don't take Maikop and Grozny [oil fields in the Caucasus] then I must put an end to the war."*
>
> ADOLF HITLER, TO HIS GENERALS, JULY 23, 1942

Stalingrad Front

North Caucasus Front

6 INTO THE CAUCASUS
JULY 23–NOVEMBER 18, 1942

The 1st Panzer Army drove south, fanning out on a wide front, reaching the oil fields of Maikop and the town of Pyatigorsk on August 9. The 17th Army, meanwhile, was tasked with capturing the Black Sea coast, but became bogged down in the marshes and the rugged Caucasus foothills. As winter set in, the panzers' advance was also brought to a halt by fuel shortages and Soviet bombing raids.

- ⇨ 1st Panzer Army advance
- ⟶ 17th Army advance
- ⊢⊢⊢► Soviet bombing raids
- ⛏ Oil fields

5 THE CAPTURE OF ROSTOV   JULY 7–23, 1942

Tasked with taking the Caucasus, Army Group A began their campaign on July 7. The 1st Panzer Army (part of Group A) headed east to Chertkovo—a key point on the railroad from Moscow to Rostov—before turning south. It crossed the Don River on July 22 and advanced on Rostov, capturing the city the following day.

- ➡ 1st Panzer Army advance

Caspian Sea

Makhachkala ○
○ Buynaksk

4 THE ADVANCE ON STALINGRAD
JULY 23–SEPTEMBER 12, 1942

The 4th Panzer Army was ordered to stop its advance south and instead move on Stalingrad. The 6th Army's move toward Stalingrad met strong Soviet opposition at Kalach, which it overcame in mid-August. By September 12, German forces, now joined by the 4th Panzer Army, had surrounded Stalingrad on the west bank of the Volga River, and were preparing to take the city itself (see pp.150–151).

- ➡ 4th Panzer Army advance
- ➡ 6th Army advance
- ✕ Battle of Kalach, Jul 25–Aug 11

OIL IN THE CAUCASUS

The Caucasus had been an important oil-producing region since the start of the 20th century, and by 1940 the region was producing the majority of the Soviet Union's oil. In 1939–1940, the Soviets supplied oil to Nazi Germany, but the supply was cut off when the two countries went to war. In Operation Blue, Hitler was determined to capture the oil fields to fuel his war machine.

Oil derricks in the Caucasus

STALINGRAD UNDER SIEGE

One of the most colossal conflicts of the war, the Battle of Stalingrad became a symbol of Soviet patriotism as civilians fought alongside soldiers to defend the city street by street. The battle halted Germany's advance in the east, marking a turning point in the war.

In late August 1942, German Army Group B approached the industrial city of Stalingrad. The Luftwaffe rained bombs on the city before German ground forces entered in September. They met a fight that raged from street to street and house to house, and even descended into the sewers; the Germans dubbed it *Rattenkrieg* (Rat War). General Vasily Chuikov, commander of the Soviet 62nd Army, had his men "hug the enemy," fighting in such close proximity that the Germans could not exploit their superior air power and artillery.

The Soviet forces were steadily pressed back to the banks of the Volga River, but Stalin was willing to sacrifice huge numbers of people to serve his purposes and kept up reinforcements. The average life expectancy of a Soviet soldier in the battle was 24 hours; overall, there were around 1.1 million dead, wounded, and missing. Both sides were exhausted by mid-November, but the battle—which would continue until February 1943—had reached a turning point. The Red Army was about to launch a counteroffensive that would begin to turn the tide of the war (see pp.152–153).

"It is time to finish retreating. Not one step back!"

JOSEPH STALIN, ORDER NO. 227, JULY 28, 1942

"PAVLOV'S HOUSE"—A SYMBOL OF RESISTANCE

The Soviets turned ordinary buildings into "fortresses" in their defense of Stalingrad. A platoon of Soviet soldiers, led by Sergeant Yakov Pavlov, held this apartment building for two months against daily German assaults. They fortified it with minefields and barbed wire, dug trenches for supply lines, and placed machine guns at windows and an anti-tank gun on the roof to pick off approaching German forces.

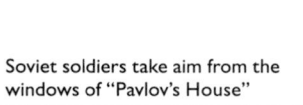

Soviet soldiers take aim from the windows of "Pavlov's House"

◁ **Soviet hero**
Red Army sniper Vasily Zaytsev (left) killed 225 Axis soldiers and officers, including 11 enemy snipers, between November 10 and December 17, 1942, during the Battle of Stalingrad.

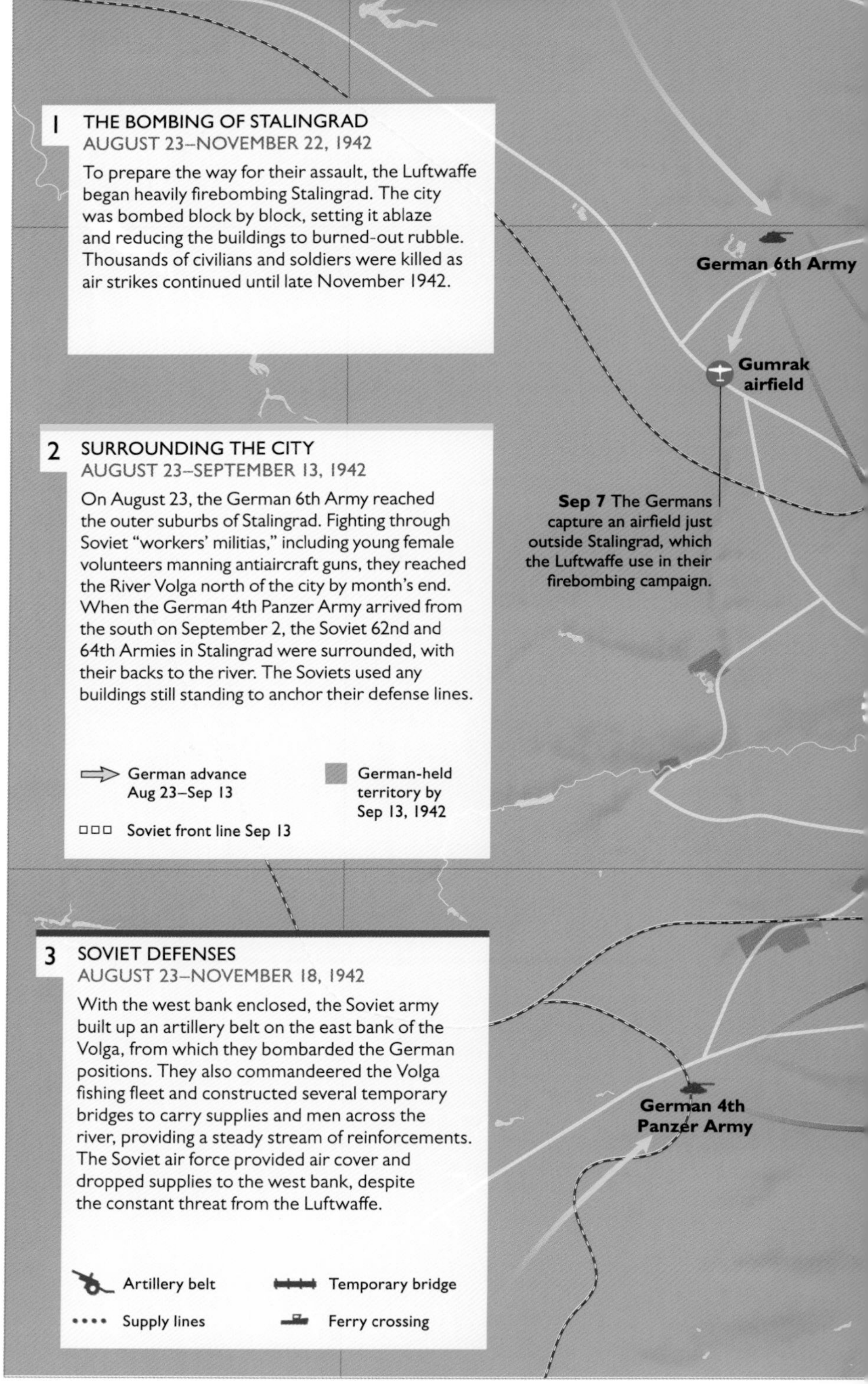

1 THE BOMBING OF STALINGRAD
AUGUST 23–NOVEMBER 22, 1942

To prepare the way for their assault, the Luftwaffe began heavily firebombing Stalingrad. The city was bombed block by block, setting it ablaze and reducing the buildings to burned-out rubble. Thousands of civilians and soldiers were killed as air strikes continued until late November 1942.

German 6th Army

Gumrak airfield

Sep 7 The Germans capture an airfield just outside Stalingrad, which the Luftwaffe use in their firebombing campaign.

2 SURROUNDING THE CITY
AUGUST 23–SEPTEMBER 13, 1942

On August 23, the German 6th Army reached the outer suburbs of Stalingrad. Fighting through Soviet "workers' militias," including young female volunteers manning antiaircraft guns, they reached the River Volga north of the city by month's end. When the German 4th Panzer Army arrived from the south on September 2, the Soviet 62nd and 64th Armies in Stalingrad were surrounded, with their backs to the river. The Soviets used any buildings still standing to anchor their defense lines.

➡ German advance Aug 23–Sep 13

▢ German-held territory by Sep 13, 1942

▢▢▢ Soviet front line Sep 13

3 SOVIET DEFENSES
AUGUST 23–NOVEMBER 18, 1942

With the west bank enclosed, the Soviet army built up an artillery belt on the east bank of the Volga, from which they bombarded the German positions. They also commandeered the Volga fishing fleet and constructed several temporary bridges to carry supplies and men across the river, providing a steady stream of reinforcements. The Soviet air force provided air cover and dropped supplies to the west bank, despite the constant threat from the Luftwaffe.

German 4th Panzer Army

Artillery belt | Temporary bridge

•••• Supply lines | Ferry crossing

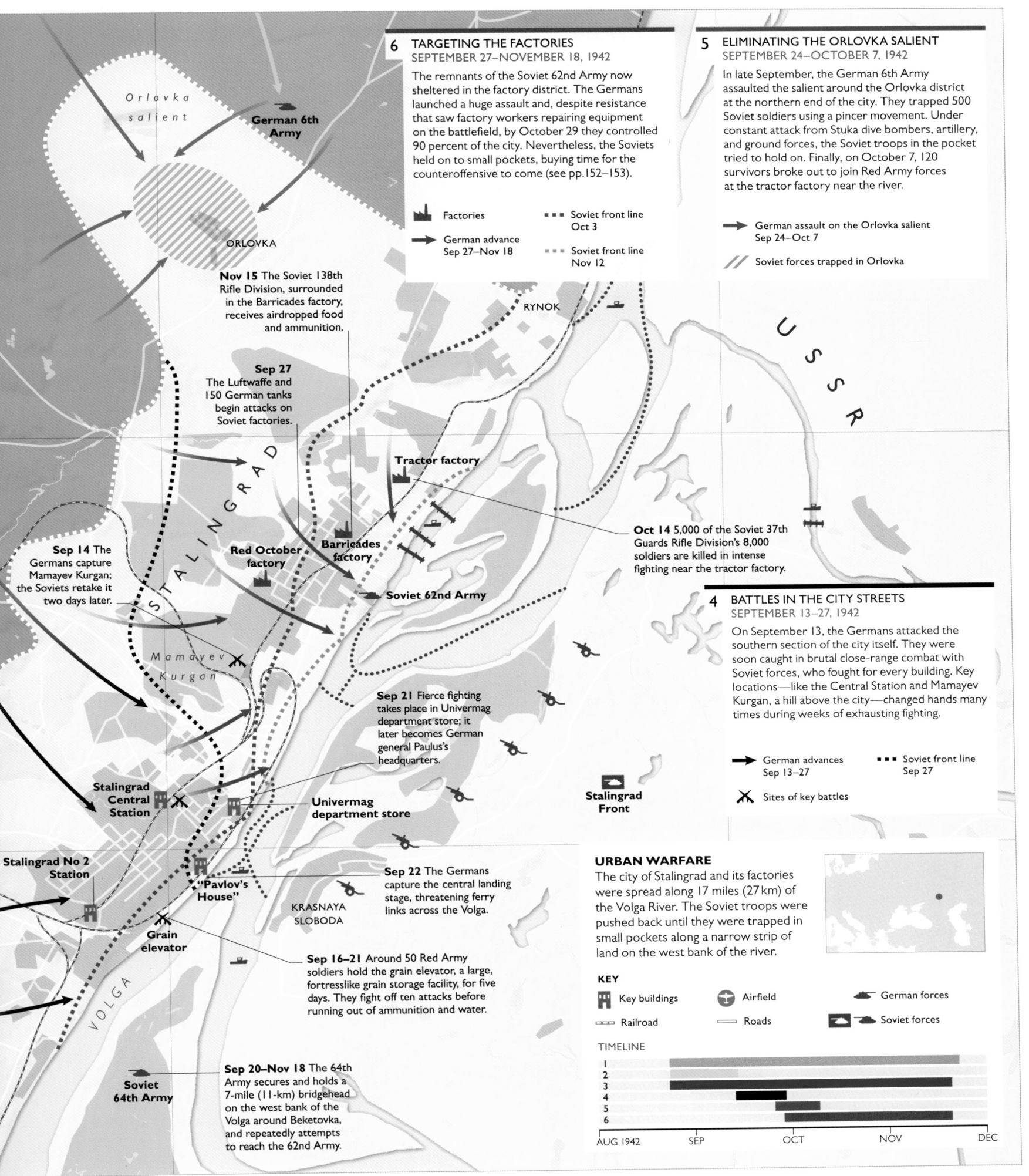

6 TARGETING THE FACTORIES
SEPTEMBER 27–NOVEMBER 18, 1942

The remnants of the Soviet 62nd Army now sheltered in the factory district. The Germans launched a huge assault and, despite resistance that saw factory workers repairing equipment on the battlefield, by October 29 they controlled 90 percent of the city. Nevertheless, the Soviets held on to small pockets, buying time for the counteroffensive to come (see pp.152–153).

🏭 Factories	▪▪▪ Soviet front line Oct 3
→ German advance Sep 27–Nov 18	▪▪▪ Soviet front line Nov 12

5 ELIMINATING THE ORLOVKA SALIENT
SEPTEMBER 24–OCTOBER 7, 1942

In late September, the German 6th Army assaulted the salient around the Orlovka district at the northern end of the city. They trapped 500 Soviet soldiers using a pincer movement. Under constant attack from Stuka dive bombers, artillery, and ground forces, the Soviet troops in the pocket tried to hold on. Finally, on October 7, 120 survivors broke out to join Red Army forces at the tractor factory near the river.

→ German assault on the Orlovka salient Sep 24–Oct 7

/// Soviet forces trapped in Orlovka

Nov 15 The Soviet 138th Rifle Division, surrounded in the Barricades factory, receives airdropped food and ammunition.

Sep 27 The Luftwaffe and 150 German tanks begin attacks on Soviet factories.

Sep 14 The Germans capture Mamayev Kurgan; the Soviets retake it two days later.

Oct 14 5,000 of the Soviet 37th Guards Rifle Division's 8,000 soldiers are killed in intense fighting near the tractor factory.

4 BATTLES IN THE CITY STREETS
SEPTEMBER 13–27, 1942

On September 13, the Germans attacked the southern section of the city itself. They were soon caught in brutal close-range combat with Soviet forces, who fought for every building. Key locations—like the Central Station and Mamayev Kurgan, a hill above the city—changed hands many times during weeks of exhausting fighting.

→ German advances Sep 13–27	▪▪▪ Soviet front line Sep 27
✕ Sites of key battles	

Sep 21 Fierce fighting takes place in Univermag department store; it later becomes German general Paulus's headquarters.

Sep 22 The Germans capture the central landing stage, threatening ferry links across the Volga.

Sep 16–21 Around 50 Red Army soldiers hold the grain elevator, a large, fortresslike grain storage facility, for five days. They fight off ten attacks before running out of ammunition and water.

Sep 20–Nov 18 The 64th Army secures and holds a 7-mile (11-km) bridgehead on the west bank of the Volga around Beketovka, and repeatedly attempts to reach the 62nd Army.

URBAN WARFARE

The city of Stalingrad and its factories were spread along 17 miles (27 km) of the Volga River. The Soviet troops were pushed back until they were trapped in small pockets along a narrow strip of land on the west bank of the river.

KEY

🏰 Key buildings	✈ Airfield	🚢 German forces
▭▭▭ Railroad	▭ Roads	🚢 Soviet forces

TIMELINE

1
2
3
4
5
6

AUG 1942   SEP   OCT   NOV   DEC

Map labels: Orlovka salient · German 6th Army · ORLOVKA · RYNOK · U S S R · Tractor factory · Red October factory · Barricades factory · Soviet 62nd Army · STALINGRAD · Mamayev Kurgan · Stalingrad Central Station · Univermag department store · Stalingrad No 2 Station · "Pavlov's House" · KRASNAYA SLOBODA · Grain elevator · VOLGA · Soviet 64th Army · Stalingrad Front

SOVIET VICTORY AT STALINGRAD

In November 1942, the Soviets launched an unexpected counteroffensive at Stalingrad—not pushing through the front line in the city itself, but encircling the city to cut off, then annihilate, the German army within. Following this victory, the Soviets went on to push the Germans out of the Caucasus and the Don River basin.

The Germans disregarded what limited intelligence they had about a major Soviet counteroffensive, believing that the Soviets could not have the men or equipment to mount such an attack. As a result, the speed and success of the Red Army assault in November 1942 came as a shock to them. The Soviets' plan was ingenious: they targeted Germany's allies, the weaker Romanian, Italian, and Hungarian armies that flanked the German 6th Army in Stalingrad and held the front line along the Don River. By November 23, the 6th Army was isolated from the stronger German forces to the west and south.

The Soviets then launched a series of operations to clear the Don basin and Caucasus. By the time the Red Army launched its final assault on Stalingrad in mid-January 1943, it had decimated the Germans' allies and retaken much of the territory lost to the German advance of 1942 (see pp.148–149). Hitler only averted further disaster by allowing Army Group A to retreat from the Caucasus. It had seemed as if the German retreat might turn into a rout, but by February the Soviet army was overstretched. A successful counterattack at Kharkov boosted German morale as they planned their next offensive (see pp.178–179).

> *"18,000 wounded without any supplies or dressings or drugs. Further defense senseless. Collapse inevitable."*
>
> GENERAL PAULUS, MESSAGE TO ADOLF HITLER, JANUARY 24, 1943

GERMAN ALLIES AT STALINGRAD

The Italian, Hungarian, and Romanian armies at Stalingrad were expected to protect the Germans' flanks and stabilize the front, but they were fatally overstretched and—as the Soviet marshal Zhukov noted—less well armed, less experienced, and less efficient at defense than the Germans. Having neglected to reinforce their positions along the Don River, Germany's allies provided an easy target for the Soviet counterattack.

Romanian POWs at Stalingrad

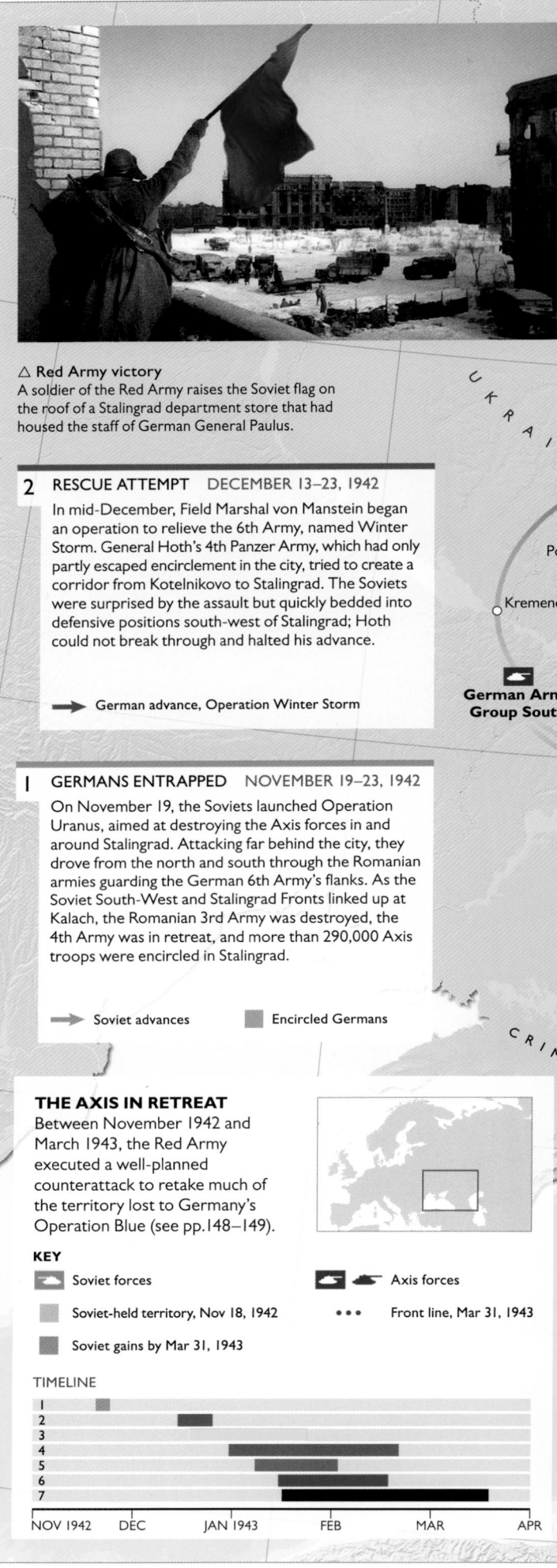

△ **Red Army victory**
A soldier of the Red Army raises the Soviet flag on the roof of a Stalingrad department store that had housed the staff of German General Paulus.

2 RESCUE ATTEMPT DECEMBER 13–23, 1942

In mid-December, Field Marshal von Manstein began an operation to relieve the 6th Army, named Winter Storm. General Hoth's 4th Panzer Army, which had only partly escaped encirclement in the city, tried to create a corridor from Kotelnikovo to Stalingrad. The Soviets were surprised by the assault but quickly bedded into defensive positions south-west of Stalingrad; Hoth could not break through and halted his advance.

→ German advance, Operation Winter Storm

Poltava

Kremenchuk

UKRAINE

Dnieper

German Army Group South

1 GERMANS ENTRAPPED NOVEMBER 19–23, 1942

On November 19, the Soviets launched Operation Uranus, aimed at destroying the Axis forces in and around Stalingrad. Attacking far behind the city, they drove from the north and south through the Romanian armies guarding the German 6th Army's flanks. As the Soviet South-West and Stalingrad Fronts linked up at Kalach, the Romanian 3rd Army was destroyed, the 4th Army was in retreat, and more than 290,000 Axis troops were encircled in Stalingrad.

→ Soviet advances ▪ Encircled Germans

CRIMEA

THE AXIS IN RETREAT
Between November 1942 and March 1943, the Red Army executed a well-planned counterattack to retake much of the territory lost to Germany's Operation Blue (see pp.148–149).

KEY

⬔ Soviet forces		⬔ Axis forces
▪ Soviet-held territory, Nov 18, 1942		••• Front line, Mar 31, 1943
▪ Soviet gains by Mar 31, 1943		

TIMELINE

1
2
3
4
5
6
7

NOV 1942 · DEC · JAN 1943 · FEB · MAR · APR

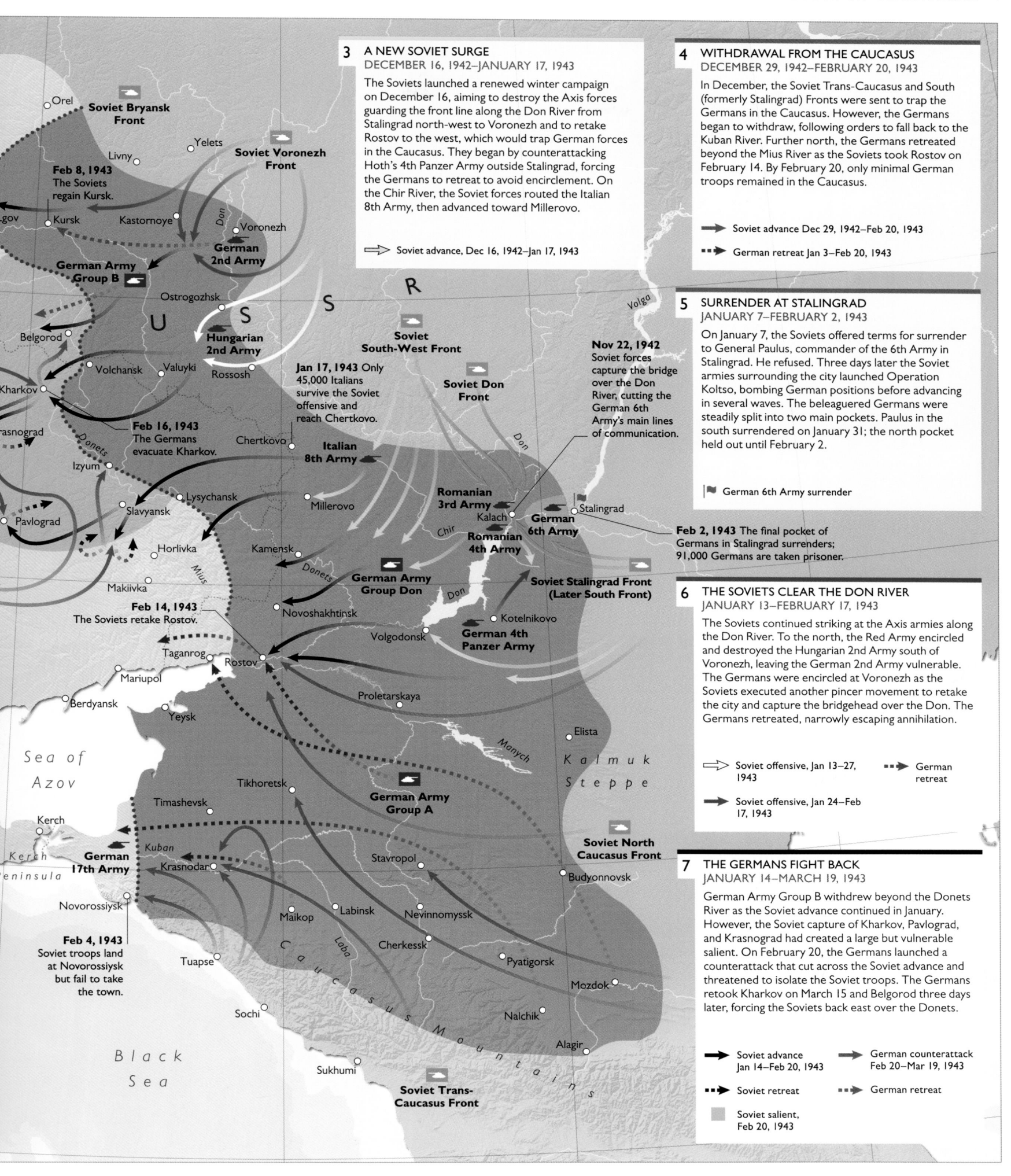

3 A NEW SOVIET SURGE
DECEMBER 16, 1942–JANUARY 17, 1943

The Soviets launched a renewed winter campaign on December 16, aiming to destroy the Axis forces guarding the front line along the Don River from Stalingrad north-west to Voronezh and to retake Rostov to the west, which would trap German forces in the Caucasus. They began by counterattacking Hoth's 4th Panzer Army outside Stalingrad, forcing the Germans to retreat to avoid encirclement. On the Chir River, the Soviet forces routed the Italian 8th Army, then advanced toward Millerovo.

⇨ Soviet advance, Dec 16, 1942–Jan 17, 1943

4 WITHDRAWAL FROM THE CAUCASUS
DECEMBER 29, 1942–FEBRUARY 20, 1943

In December, the Soviet Trans-Caucasus and South (formerly Stalingrad) Fronts were sent to trap the Germans in the Caucasus. However, the Germans began to withdraw, following orders to fall back to the Kuban River. Further north, the Germans retreated beyond the Mius River as the Soviets took Rostov on February 14. By February 20, only minimal German troops remained in the Caucasus.

➡ Soviet advance Dec 29, 1942–Feb 20, 1943

⇢ German retreat Jan 3–Feb 20, 1943

5 SURRENDER AT STALINGRAD
JANUARY 7–FEBRUARY 2, 1943

On January 7, the Soviets offered terms for surrender to General Paulus, commander of the 6th Army in Stalingrad. He refused. Three days later the Soviet armies surrounding the city launched Operation Koltso, bombing German positions before advancing in several waves. The beleaguered Germans were steadily split into two main pockets. Paulus in the south surrendered on January 31; the north pocket held out until February 2.

⎮ German 6th Army surrender

6 THE SOVIETS CLEAR THE DON RIVER
JANUARY 13–FEBRUARY 17, 1943

The Soviets continued striking at the Axis armies along the Don River. To the north, the Red Army encircled and destroyed the Hungarian 2nd Army south of Voronezh, leaving the German 2nd Army vulnerable. The Germans were encircled at Voronezh as the Soviets executed another pincer movement to retake the city and capture the bridgehead over the Don. The Germans retreated, narrowly escaping annihilation.

⇨ Soviet offensive, Jan 13–27, 1943   ⇢ German retreat

➡ Soviet offensive, Jan 24–Feb 17, 1943

7 THE GERMANS FIGHT BACK
JANUARY 14–MARCH 19, 1943

German Army Group B withdrew beyond the Donets River as the Soviet advance continued in January. However, the Soviet capture of Kharkov, Pavlograd, and Krasnograd had created a large but vulnerable salient. On February 20, the Germans launched a counterattack that cut across the Soviet advance and threatened to isolate the Soviet troops. The Germans retook Kharkov on March 15 and Belgorod three days later, forcing the Soviets back east over the Donets.

➡ Soviet advance Jan 14–Feb 20, 1943   ➡ German counterattack Feb 20–Mar 19, 1943

⇢ Soviet retreat   ⇢ German retreat

▨ Soviet salient, Feb 20, 1943

PRISONERS OF WAR

Millions of Allied and Axis solders were captured during World War II and sent to prisoner-of-war (POW) camps. Despite international agreements that were supposed to protect such prisoners, conditions in the camps could be dire.

Rapid advances made by the German army in the opening stages of the war meant that the Germans soon held several million French and Polish prisoners, and opened a network of camps to hold them. The invading Germans also encircled vast numbers of Soviet soldiers, and by December 1941 they had captured 3.2 million of them. However, the tables turned in Stalingrad in 1942, when the Germans experienced their first major defeat, and ultimately around 1.5 million German troops fell into Soviet hands.

△ **Bare necessities**
Prisoners had few possessions and so were forced to improvise, creating their own utensils such as this hand-carved spoon in a box with the prisoner's inmate number.

Variable conditions

The Geneva Convention of 1929 had laid down standards for captured POWs, but the Soviet Union had not signed it and Japan had not ratified it, so conditions in Soviet and Japanese camps during World War II were often appalling. The Germans generally treated prisoners from Britain, France, the US, and other western Allies according to the Geneva Convention, but not so the Soviets. As a result, almost 60 percent of Soviet POWs held by the Germans died, many of typhus, dysentery, exposure, or starvation.

Prisoners taken on the Western Front usually fared better: officers did not have to work, while rank-and-file soldiers were supposed to do work without military value, and the Red Cross dispatched 36 million food parcels to supplement their diet. Most were released soon after the war, although the last German POW held by the Soviet Union was not repatriated until 1956.

COLDITZ CASTLE

The Renaissance castle at Colditz in Saxony, Germany, was used by the German army from 1940 to detain POWs who had tried to escape from other camps. Security was tight, but escape attempts were rife, and a total of 30 prisoners managed to break out to freedom. One notable attempt involved a homemade glider.

Caught out in the cold
Prisoners were often at their most vulnerable immediately after capture, when they were transported to camps. Here, German soldiers taken in Alsace in January 1945 endure freezing conditions as they are moved from the frontline.

TURNING THE TIDE 1943–1944

WITH THE ALLIED INVASION OF NORMANDY, THE SOVIETS PRESSING FROM THE EAST, AND THE US CAMPAIGNING ACROSS THE PACIFIC, THE AXIS POWERS FACED THEIR HARDEST FIGHT YET.

GERMAN DEFIANCE

As 1943 progressed, it became increasingly evident that Nazi Germany would eventually be defeated. However, Hitler remained defiant, and the war continued in 1944 with unabated ferocity as the Allies pressed on toward the German homeland.

△ **Sicily landings**
British troops wade ashore during Operation Husky, the Allied invasion of Sicily, in July 1943. The invasion led to the overthrow of the Italian fascist dictator Benito Mussolini.

By 1943, superior manpower and industrial strength gave the Allies a huge advantage over Germany. Yet at crucial points in the war, the Germans came very close to major successes. In the battle of the Atlantic, the German submarine campaign inflicted almost unsustainable losses on Allied shipping before the Allies finally defeated the U-boat menace. On the Eastern front, Soviet forces won the battle of Kursk, but at huge cost. Germany suffered under the impact of British and US bombing, but losses on the Allied side were heavy as well. Even when Italy was invaded and sued for peace, the Germans were able to block the Allied advance northward.

Yet the most determined efforts of German fighting forces were eventually in vain. The Allies made sensible decisions to produce relatively simple equipment on a vast scale, and they had the manpower and organizational skills to put the arms into action effectively. The Germans had the best tanks and a great deal

of other superior technology, but despite this and their extensive use of slave labor, Germany could not match Allied industrial output.

Germany struggles to keep control

As conditions in Nazi-occupied Europe worsened, with food shortages and the mass conscription of men to work in German factories, armed resistance spread. This meant large numbers of German troops were needed to suppress subversive activities. Also, the Allied bombings forced Germany to devote substantial resources to home defense, as well as hampering arms production and fuel supplies.

As shown by their bombing of German cities, the Western Allies had learned the ruthlessness of total war. Their undertaking to pursue "unconditional surrender" committed them to the complete military defeat of Germany without negotiation or compromise. Hitler hoped the Allied countries would have a major disagreement, but despite ideological differences, the Soviet Union, Britain, and the US held together. Hitler also dreamed of a technological miracle—wonder weapons that would

◁ **King Tiger**
Introduced in 1944, the German Tiger II was the heaviest tank used in the war. Its thick armor gave good protection, giving it a considerable advantage over Allied tanks in head-on confrontations.

NAZI GERMANY'S CHANGING FORTUNES

In early 1943, the Germans remained in control of continental Europe, despite their surrender at Stalingrad. However, that summer the Allied invasion of Italy and the Soviet victory at Kursk placed German forces under mounting pressure. After Allied troops landed at Normandy in June 1944, while Soviet forces were advancing rapidly from the east, it appeared that Nazi resistance might collapse, even though Allied military progress faltered at the German frontiers.

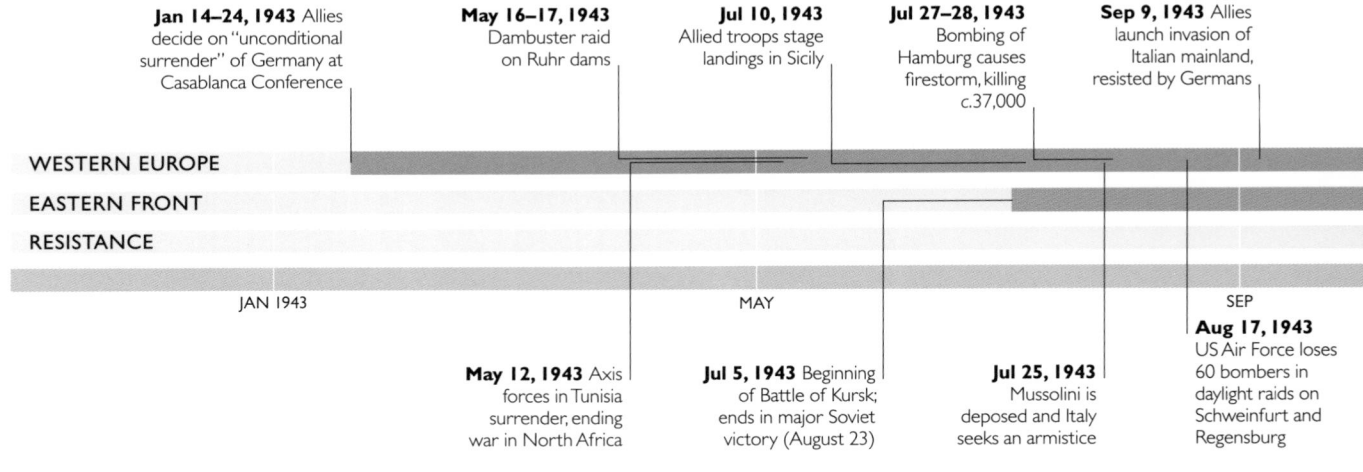

Jan 14–24, 1943 Allies decide on "unconditional surrender" of Germany at Casablanca Conference

May 16–17, 1943 Dambuster raid on Ruhr dams

Jul 10, 1943 Allied troops stage landings in Sicily

Jul 27–28, 1943 Bombing of Hamburg causes firestorm, killing c.37,000

Sep 9, 1943 Allies launch invasion of Italian mainland, resisted by Germans

WESTERN EUROPE

EASTERN FRONT

RESISTANCE

JAN 1943

MAY

SEP

May 12, 1943 Axis forces in Tunisia surrender, ending war in North Africa

Jul 5, 1943 Beginning of Battle of Kursk; ends in major Soviet victory (August 23)

Jul 25, 1943 Mussolini is deposed and Italy seeks an armistice

Aug 17, 1943 US Air Force loses 60 bombers in daylight raids on Schweinfurt and Regensburg

◁ Ruins of Warsaw
After suppressing an uprising by Polish resistance fighters in the summer of 1944, German troops systematically destroyed Warsaw, leaving four-fifths of the city in ruins.

"The free men of the world are marching together to Victory!"

GENERAL DWIGHT D. EISENHOWER, "ORDER OF THE DAY" STATEMENT, JUNE 5, 1944

▽ Liberation of Paris
US soldiers and Parisian women celebrate in front of the Eiffel Tower after the liberation of Paris in August 1944. The city had been under German occupation for four years.

transform the war. But although the Germans introduced flying bombs, rockets, and jet aircraft, the weapons were too little, too late to have any decisive impact.

The final stages

By summer 1944, the Soviets were advancing toward Germany from the east, while the Western Allies had invaded Normandy. However, the euphoria of liberation as Allied forces raced across France and Belgium that August was followed by frustration when they ground to a halt in the fall. The failure of a coup against Hitler left him securely in control and determined to fight to the end. Political conflicts came to the fore, with Communist-led partisan movements clashing with Nationalists and Fascists in Yugoslavia, Greece, and Italy.

The suffering across Europe in the latter stages of the war was tremendous. The extermination of Jews continued, and the Allied aerial bombing campaign took a heavy toll on civilians in German cities and elsewhere. Liberation from Nazi rule brought joy to many, but death or humiliation to those judged as traitors—from collaborators in France to Crimean Tatars subject to mass deportation in the USSR. Millions of ethnic German civilians from the Baltic and central Europe fled west in the face of the advancing Soviet armies. A post-war Europe scarred by ideological division, ruins, and refugees was already taking shape while the fighting approached its climax.

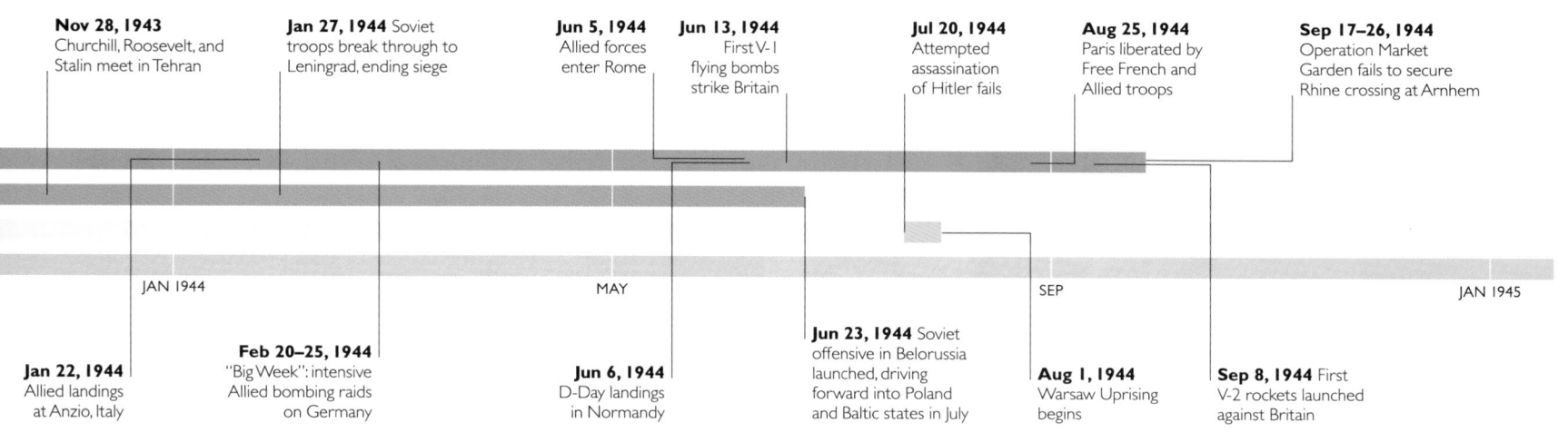

Nov 28, 1943
Churchill, Roosevelt, and Stalin meet in Tehran

Jan 27, 1944 Soviet troops break through to Leningrad, ending siege

Jun 5, 1944 Allied forces enter Rome

Jun 13, 1944 First V-1 flying bombs strike Britain

Jul 20, 1944 Attempted assassination of Hitler fails

Aug 25, 1944 Paris liberated by Free French and Allied troops

Sep 17–26, 1944 Operation Market Garden fails to secure Rhine crossing at Arnhem

JAN 1944

MAY

SEP

JAN 1945

Jan 22, 1944 Allied landings at Anzio, Italy

Feb 20–25, 1944 "Big Week": intensive Allied bombing raids on Germany

Jun 6, 1944 D-Day landings in Normandy

Jun 23, 1944 Soviet offensive in Belorussia launched, driving forward into Poland and Baltic states in July

Aug 1, 1944 Warsaw Uprising begins

Sep 8, 1944 First V-2 rockets launched against Britain

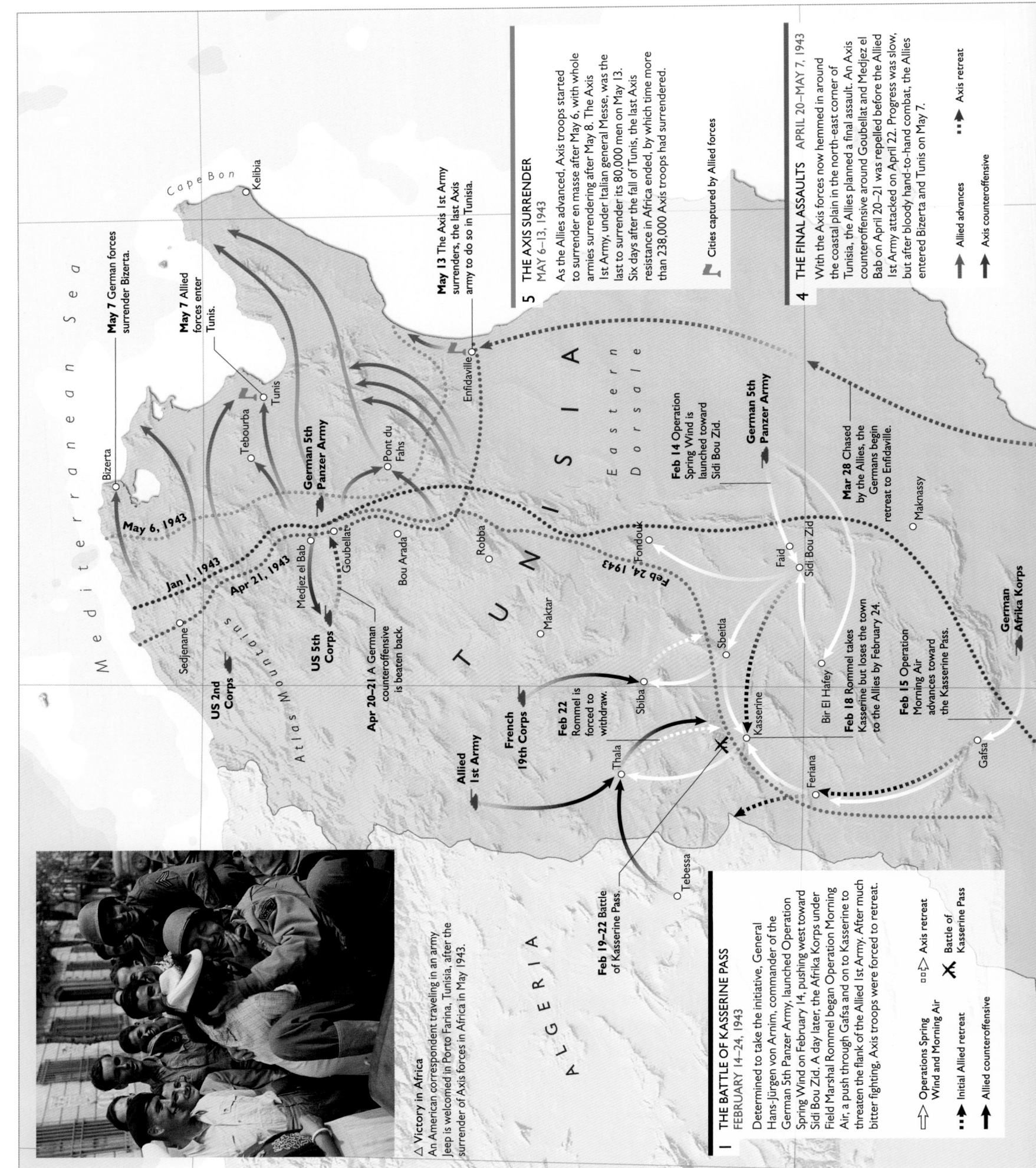

Mediterranean Sea

Cape Bon

Kelibia

May 7 German forces surrender Bizerta.

May 7 Allied forces enter Tunis.

May 13 The Axis 1st Army surrenders, the last Axis army to do so in Tunisia.

5 THE AXIS SURRENDER
MAY 6–13, 1943

As the Allies advanced, Axis troops started to surrender en masse after May 6, with whole armies surrendering after May 8. The Axis 1st Army, under Italian general Messe, was the last to surrender its 80,000 men on May 13. Six days after the fall of Tunis, the last Axis resistance in Africa ended, by which time more than 238,000 Axis troops had surrendered.

⌐ Cities captured by Allied forces

4 THE FINAL ASSAULTS   APRIL 20–MAY 7, 1943

With the Axis forces now hemmed in around the coastal plain in the north-east corner of Tunisia, the Allies planned a final assault. An Axis counteroffensive around Goubellat and Medjez el Bab on April 20–21 was repelled before the Allied 1st Army attacked on April 22. Progress was slow, but after bloody hand-to-hand combat, the Allies entered Bizerta and Tunis on May 7.

→ Allied advances   ⇢ Axis retreat

→ Axis counteroffensive

Bizerta

Tebourba

Tunis

German 5th Panzer Army

Pont du Fahs

Enfidaville

Eastern Dorsale

T U N I S I A

Feb 14 Operation Spring Wind is launched toward Sidi Bou Zid.

German 5th Panzer Army

Mar 28 Chased by the Allies, the Germans begin retreat to Enfidaville.

Maknassy

May 6, 1943

Jan 1, 1943

Apr 21, 1943

Medjez el Bab

Goubellat

US 5th Corps

German 5th Panzer Army

Apr 20–21 A German counteroffensive is beaten back.

Bou Arada

Robba

Maktar

Feb 24, 1943

Fondouk

Faid

Sidi Bou Zid

German Afrika Korps

Sedjenane

Atlas Mountains

US 2nd Corps

French 19th Corps

Feb 22 Rommel is forced to withdraw.

Sbiba

Sbeitla

Bir El Hafey

Feb 18 Rommel takes Kasserine but loses the town to the Allies by February 24.

Feb 15 Operation Morning Air advances toward the Kasserine Pass.

Allied 1st Army

Thala

Kasserine ✗

Feriana

Gafsa

Feb 19–22 Battle of Kasserine Pass.

Tebessa

1 THE BATTLE OF KASSERINE PASS
FEBRUARY 14–24, 1943

Determined to take the initiative, General Hans-Jürgen von Arnim, commander of the German 5th Panzer Army, launched Operation Spring Wind on February 14, pushing west toward Sidi Bou Zid. A day later, the Afrika Korps under Field Marshal Rommel began Operation Morning Air, a push through Gafsa and on to Kasserine to threaten the flank of the Allied 1st Army. After much bitter fighting, Axis troops were forced to retreat.

⇨ Operations Spring Wind and Morning Air

⇨⇢ Axis retreat   ✗ Battle of Kasserine Pass

···▶ Initial Allied retreat

→ Allied counteroffensive

A L G E R I A

△ **Victory in Africa**
An American correspondent traveling in an army jeep is welcomed in Porto Farina, Tunisia, after the surrender of Axis forces in Africa in May 1943.

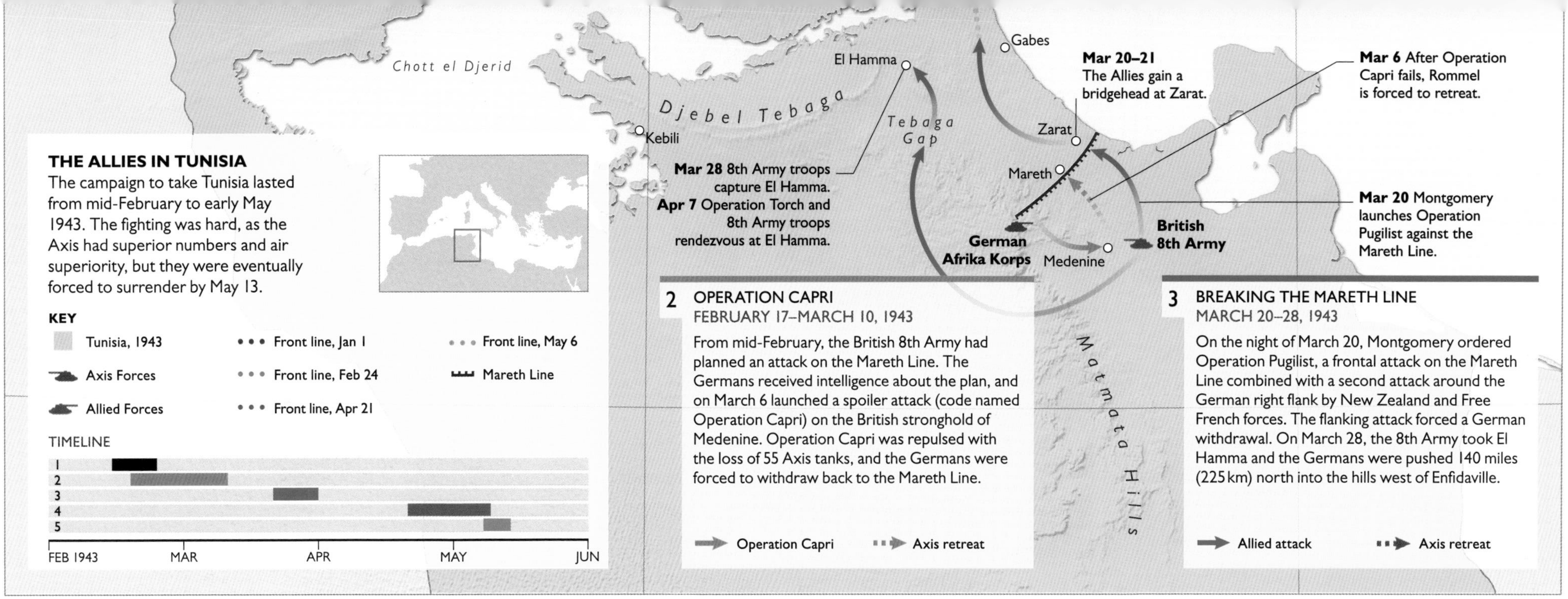

THE ALLIES IN TUNISIA

The campaign to take Tunisia lasted from mid-February to early May 1943. The fighting was hard, as the Axis had superior numbers and air superiority, but they were eventually forced to surrender by May 13.

KEY

- Tunisia, 1943
- Axis Forces
- Allied Forces
- ••• Front line, Jan 1
- ••• Front line, Feb 24
- ••• Front line, Apr 21
- ••• Front line, May 6
- ▬▬ Mareth Line

TIMELINE

1 2 3 4 5 — FEB 1943 · MAR · APR · MAY · JUN

Chott el Djerid

Mar 6 After Operation Capri fails, Rommel is forced to retreat.

Mar 20 Montgomery launches Operation Pugilist against the Mareth Line.

Mar 20–21 The Allies gain a bridgehead at Zarat.

British 8th Army

○ Gabes
○ Zarat
○ Mareth
○ Medenine
○ El Hamma
Tebaga Gap
Djebel Tebaga
○ Kebili
Matmata Hills

German Afrika Korps

Mar 28 8th Army troops capture El Hamma.
Apr 7 Operation Torch and 8th Army troops rendezvous at El Hamma.

→ Allied attack
→ Axis retreat
→ Operation Capri

2 OPERATION CAPRI
FEBRUARY 17–MARCH 10, 1943

From mid-February, the British 8th Army had planned an attack on the Mareth Line. The Germans received intelligence about the plan, and on March 6 launched a spoiler attack (code named Operation Capri) on the British stronghold of Medenine. Operation Capri was repulsed with the loss of 55 Axis tanks, and the Germans were forced to withdraw back to the Mareth Line.

3 BREAKING THE MARETH LINE
MARCH 20–28, 1943

On the night of March 20, Montgomery ordered Operation Pugilist, a frontal attack on the Mareth Line combined with a second attack around the German right flank by New Zealand and Free French forces. The flanking attack forced a German withdrawal. On March 28, the 8th Army took El Hamma and the Germans were pushed 140 miles (225 km) north into the hills west of Enfidaville.

VICTORY IN THE DESERT

Following the British victory at El Alamein to their east and the successful Allied landings of Operation Torch in Algeria and Morocco to their west, the Axis armies were forced to fight a defensive campaign in Tunisia. Resupplied and reinforced by air and by convoys arriving in Tunis, they dug in and prepared for a long battle.

A key goal of Operation Torch (see pp.146–147) had been to provide a route through Tunisia by which the Allies could attack Italy—the "soft underbelly" of the Axis, according to Churchill. In order to avoid Axis air attacks, Operation Torch had landed its forces some 500 miles (800 km) west of Tunis, and although they raced east across Algeria as soon as they landed, the Germans acted swiftly to reinforce their positions in Tunisia. The Vichy French governor of Tunisia, Admiral Jean-Pierre Esteva, allowed German aircraft to fly in additional troops, tanks (including the new Tiger tanks), artillery pieces, and other supplies. By the beginning of 1943, around 250,000

Axis troops had arrived in Tunisia, forming a substantial force. The Germans also benefited from the close proximity of their airfields in Sicily. Rommel's army, consisting of German and Italian corps, in retreat after the second Battle of El Alamein (see pp.144–145), was also in Tunisia, having taken up positions on the defensive Mareth Line—a former French colonial defensive line running 22 miles (35 km) from the coast to the mountains. The advances that Allied forces had made from Algeria since the Torch landings came to an end as they reached the Eastern Dorsale (the eastern extension of the Atlas Mountains), which effectively became the front line of the conflict in Tunisia.

January 1943 saw sporadic fighting on the long front as both sides struggled to resupply their forces. The Allies repulsed a significant Axis advance toward Kasserine in February 1943, and their attacks on the Mareth Line in March overwhelmed the Axis defenders. The Axis armies retreated toward north-east Tunisia, finally surrendering by May 13. The war in Africa was over.

> *"I want to impose on everyone that the bad times are over, they are finished!"*
>
> GENERAL BERNARD MONTGOMERY, 1942

THE 8TH ARMY

The British 8th Army was a multinational force. In addition to the UK, units came from Australia, New Zealand, India, South Africa, Rhodesia, Canada, Greece, and Poland, as well as a sizeable Free French contingent—a total of more than 220,000 men. For much of its operational life in North Africa and Italy, it was led by General Bernard Montgomery.

SUMMIT CONFERENCES

The global alliance that emerged in 1941 to oppose the Axis powers needed to make difficult strategic decisions. As a result, a series of summit meetings were arranged in 1943 to coordinate a joint Allied approach.

The Allies faced conflicting priorities. At a summit in Moscow in September 1941, they discussed the distribution of Lend-Lease Aid, the US scheme to help their allies by giving military supplies and raw materials on credit (see pp.70–71). This was followed in January 1943 by a conference in Morocco, attended by British prime minister Winston Churchill and US president Franklin D. Roosevelt. The two leaders decided on a combined bomber offensive against Germany, and on the policy of Germany's unconditional surrender. They also agreed a "Mediterranean First" strategy, prioritizing the defeat of Axis forces in North Africa and Italy over opening a new front in France.

△ **Soviet anti-German poster**
The shared goal of beating Germany encouraged Soviet collaboration with other powers.

Cairo and Tehran

In November 1943, the Allies met in Cairo and Tehran. In Cairo, Roosevelt, Churchill, and Chinese leader Chiang Kai-shek discussed strategies for the defeat of Japan, agreeing that an offensive against the Japanese in China took priority over recapturing Malaysia. In Tehran, Stalin joined the Allied leaders to discuss Poland, Japan, and more.

△ **Tehran conference**
Allied leaders Stalin, Roosevelt, and Churchill were all present at a conference in November 1943, held in the USSR's legation in Tehran. The leaders reached agreement over the invasion of occupied France and discussed the division of Germany.

Moroccan conference
President Roosevelt and Prime Minister Churchill speak to the press during the Casablanca Conference (code named "Symbol") in 1943. Germany's attack on Stalingrad prevented Joseph Stalin from attending the meeting.

SICILY AND ITALY INVADED

After the defeat of Axis forces in Tunisia, Axis-controlled southern Europe appeared vulnerable. Germany was led to believe that Allied interests lay in Sardinia or Corsica, but in January 1943 the Allies decided to invade Sicily. Six months later the invasion (Operation Husky) began.

In 1943, Axis forces on Sicily were under the command of General Alfredo Guzzoni. However, the only reliable troops in his 6th Army were two German divisions in Hans Hube's 14th Panzer Corps; Italy's own soldiers were poorly motivated.

The Allied forces for the invasion were Patton's US 7th Army and Montgomery's British and Commonwealth 8th Army, both under the overall command of Britain's General Harold Alexander. The initial plan was for the British to attack up the east coast, taking Catania and then Messina, with their flank and rear protected by the Americans. On August 5, the British took Catania, and by August 17 the Allies controlled Sicily. In late July, Mussolini was deposed and replaced as prime minister by Marshal Pietro Badoglio. When news broke on September 8 that Badoglio had agreed an armistice, the Germans seized Rome and effectively occupied Italy.

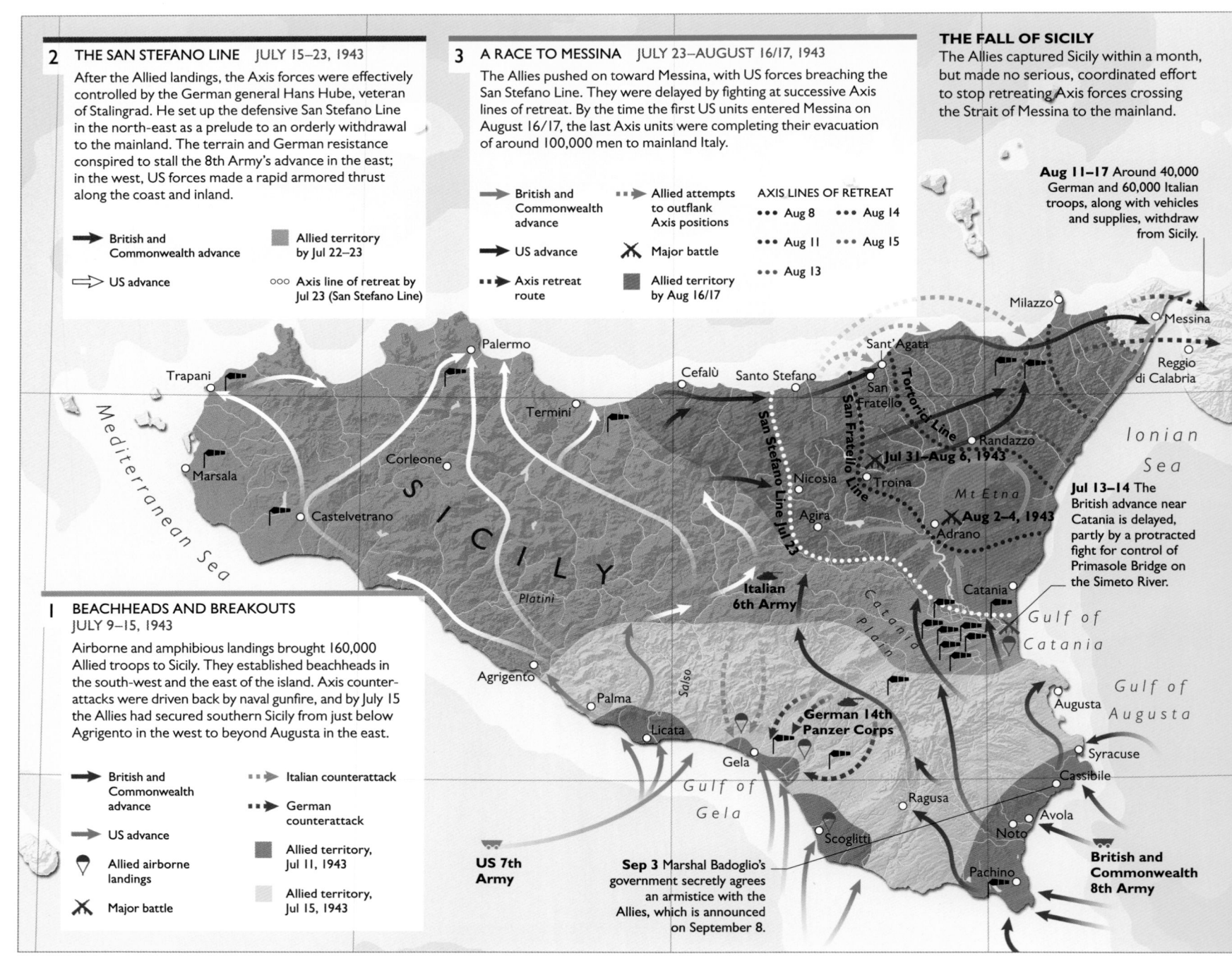

2 THE SAN STEFANO LINE JULY 15–23, 1943

After the Allied landings, the Axis forces were effectively controlled by the German general Hans Hube, veteran of Stalingrad. He set up the defensive San Stefano Line in the north-east as a prelude to an orderly withdrawal to the mainland. The terrain and German resistance conspired to stall the 8th Army's advance in the east; in the west, US forces made a rapid armored thrust along the coast and inland.

→ British and Commonwealth advance

⇨ US advance

▬ Allied territory by Jul 22–23

∘∘∘ Axis line of retreat by Jul 23 (San Stefano Line)

3 A RACE TO MESSINA JULY 23–AUGUST 16/17, 1943

The Allies pushed on toward Messina, with US forces breaching the San Stefano Line. They were delayed by fighting at successive Axis lines of retreat. By the time the first US units entered Messina on August 16/17, the last Axis units were completing their evacuation of around 100,000 men to mainland Italy.

→ British and Commonwealth advance

⇢ Allied attempts to outflank Axis positions

➤ US advance

✕ Major battle

⇢ Axis retreat route

▬ Allied territory by Aug 16/17

AXIS LINES OF RETREAT
••• Aug 8 ••• Aug 14
••• Aug 11 ••• Aug 15
••• Aug 13

THE FALL OF SICILY
The Allies captured Sicily within a month, but made no serious, coordinated effort to stop retreating Axis forces crossing the Strait of Messina to the mainland.

Aug 11–17 Around 40,000 German and 60,000 Italian troops, along with vehicles and supplies, withdraw from Sicily.

Jul 13–14 The British advance near Catania is delayed, partly by a protracted fight for control of Primasole Bridge on the Simeto River.

1 BEACHHEADS AND BREAKOUTS JULY 9–15, 1943

Airborne and amphibious landings brought 160,000 Allied troops to Sicily. They established beachheads in the south-west and the east of the island. Axis counter-attacks were driven back by naval gunfire, and by July 15 the Allies had secured southern Sicily from just below Agrigento in the west to beyond Augusta in the east.

→ British and Commonwealth advance

➤ US advance

⬙ Allied airborne landings

✕ Major battle

⇢ Italian counterattack

⇢ German counterattack

▬ Allied territory, Jul 11, 1943

▬ Allied territory, Jul 15, 1943

Sep 3 Marshal Badoglio's government secretly agrees an armistice with the Allies, which is announced on September 8.

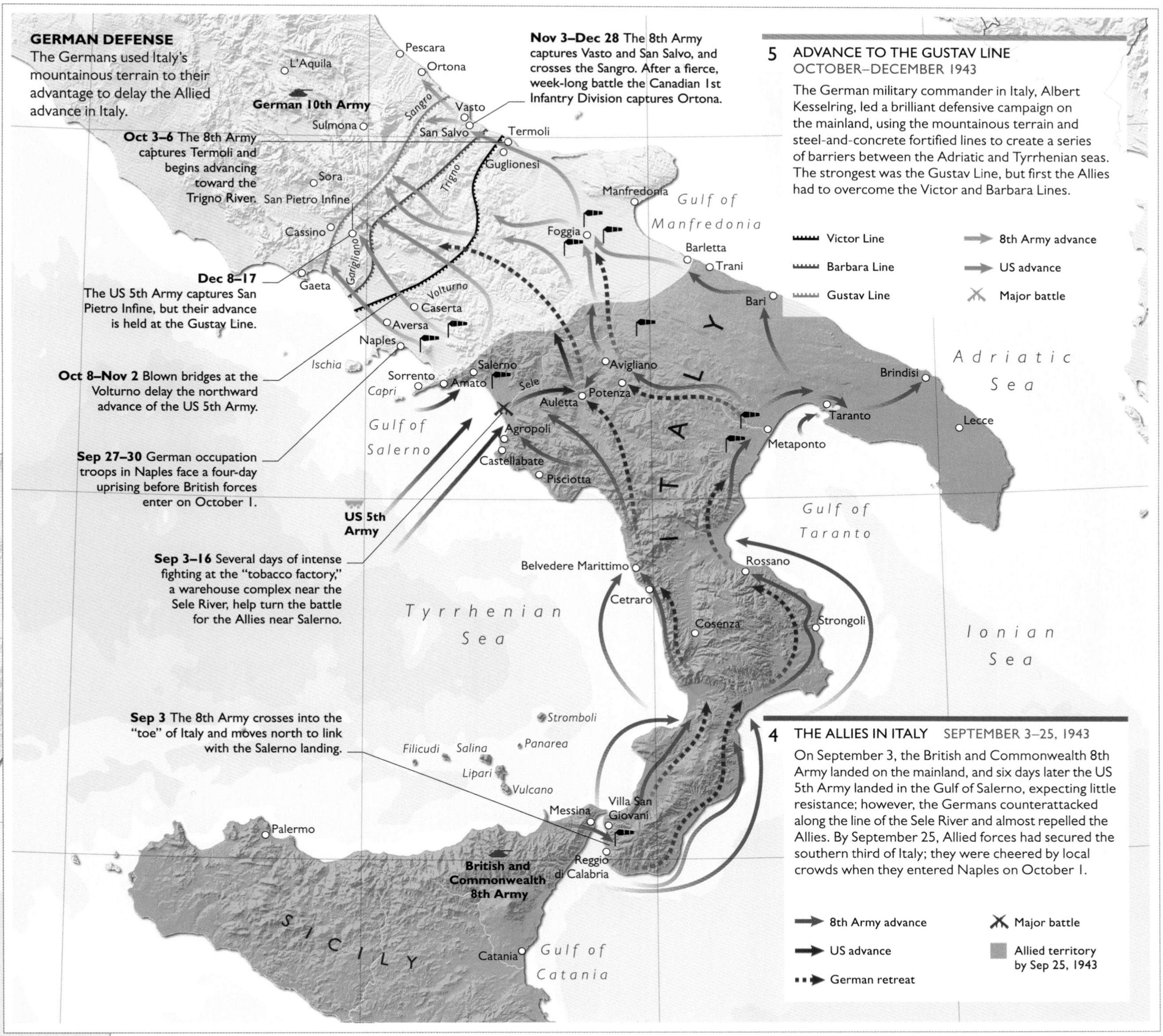
GERMAN DEFENSE
The Germans used Italy's mountainous terrain to their advantage to delay the Allied advance in Italy.
Nov 3–Dec 28 The 8th Army captures Vasto and San Salvo, and crosses the Sangro. After a fierce, week-long battle the Canadian 1st Infantry Division captures Ortona.
5 ADVANCE TO THE GUSTAV LINE
OCTOBER–DECEMBER 1943
The German military commander in Italy, Albert Kesselring, led a brilliant defensive campaign on the mainland, using the mountainous terrain and steel-and-concrete fortified lines to create a series of barriers between the Adriatic and Tyrrhenian seas. The strongest was the Gustav Line, but first the Allies had to overcome the Victor and Barbara Lines.
Victor Line
Barbara Line
Gustav Line
8th Army advance
US advance
Major battle
Oct 3–6 The 8th Army captures Termoli and begins advancing toward the Trigno River.
Dec 8–17 The US 5th Army captures San Pietro Infine, but their advance is held at the Gustav Line.
Oct 8–Nov 2 Blown bridges at the Volturno delay the northward advance of the US 5th Army.
Sep 27–30 German occupation troops in Naples face a four-day uprising before British forces enter on October 1.
US 5th Army
Sep 3–16 Several days of intense fighting at the "tobacco factory," a warehouse complex near the Sele River, help turn the battle for the Allies near Salerno.
Sep 3 The 8th Army crosses into the "toe" of Italy and moves north to link with the Salerno landing.
German 10th Army
British and Commonwealth 8th Army
Pescara
Ortona
L'Aquila
Sangro
Vasto
Sulmona
San Salvo
Termoli
Trigno
Guglionesi
Sora
San Pietro Infine
Manfredonia
Gulf of Manfredonia
Cassino
Foggia
Barletta
Trani
Gaeta
Garigliano
Volturno
Caserta
Bari
Aversa
Naples
Ischia
Salerno
Avigliano
Sorrento
Amato
Sele
Capri
Potenza
Auletta
ITALY
Brindisi
Adriatic Sea
Gulf of Salerno
Agropoli
Castellabate
Pisciotta
Taranto
Metaponto
Lecce
Gulf of Taranto
Rossano
Belvedere Marittimo
Cetraro
Tyrrhenian Sea
Cosenza
Strongoli
Ionian Sea
Stromboli
Panarea
Filicudi
Salina
Lipari
Vulcano
Villa San Giovanni
Messina
Palermo
Reggio di Calabria
SICILY
Catania
Gulf of Catania
4 THE ALLIES IN ITALY SEPTEMBER 3–25, 1943
On September 3, the British and Commonwealth 8th Army landed on the mainland, and six days later the US 5th Army landed in the Gulf of Salerno, expecting little resistance; however, the Germans counterattacked along the line of the Sele River and almost repelled the Allies. By September 25, Allied forces had secured the southern third of Italy; they were cheered by local crowds when they entered Naples on October 1.
8th Army advance
US advance
German retreat
Major battle
Allied territory by Sep 25, 1943

BREAKING THE AXIS

By transferring the campaign in the Mediterranean from North Africa to Italy, the Allies believed that General Harold Alexander's 15th Army Group could end the war by 1944.

KEY

British and Commonwealth forces

US forces

German forces

Italian forces

Airfields constructed by the Allies

TIMELINE

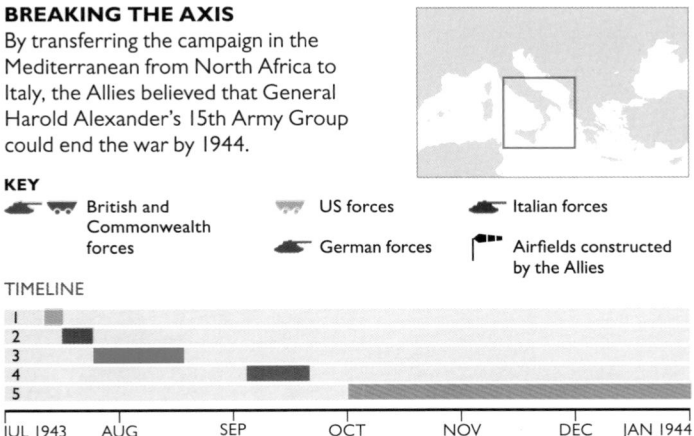

1
2
3
4
5
JUL 1943
AUG
SEP
OCT
NOV
DEC
JAN 1944

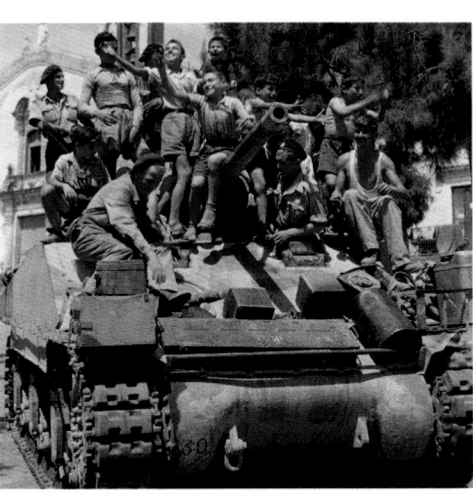

◁ **A warm welcome** Sicilian children join British soldiers on an M4 Sherman tank as the Allied forces are welcomed into Milo, in north-eastern Sicily, on August 15, 1943.

FROM ANZIO TO THE GOTHIC LINE

The Allies' campaign in Italy resumed in January 1944 with a long-held objective: to liberate Rome. They landed at Anzio, south of Rome, but their advance north was slowed by a series of defensive lines masterminded by German field marshal Albert Kesselring. The battles in Italy's mountainous terrain produced some of the toughest fighting of the war.

By the end of 1943, German forces in Italy had retreated to the fortified Gustav Line, also called the Winter Line. On this line lay Monte Cassino, a strategic location at the base of the Liri and Rapido river valleys that guarded Route 6—the road north to Rome.

Days before their first attack on Cassino, the Allies landed at Anzio, well behind the Gustav Line, in an attempt to outflank the Germans and cut their lines of communication. The US 6th Corps made an amphibious landing north of the Pontine Marshes, 35 miles (56km) from Rome. However, hesitation by the US commander at Anzio led to his units being hemmed in at the beachhead. At Cassino, a series of bloody and very costly Allied assaults began on January 24. Despite air support from Allied bombers flying from bases in North Africa, and later southern Italy, it took until May for the Allies to break through at Cassino.

The US 5th Army then pushed up the coast toward Anzio while the British 8th Army advanced up the Liri River—a combined attack that the Germans could not withstand. After five months of attrition, progress toward—and then beyond—Rome was achieved swiftly. However, the Germans withdrew skillfully, falling back behind the Trasimene and Arno Lines, which gave them time to create another well-fortified line, the Gothic Line, to the north. It was here, in August 1944, that the Allies paused again.

LIBERATION AND DIVISION

Rome was the first capital city to be liberated when the US 5th Army entered on June 4, 1944 (pictured). However, just two days later the Allies made the D-Day landings in Normandy (see pp.186–187), and within two months Allied troops in Italy had been redeployed. The US 6th Corps and the French Expeditionary Corps were transferred from the US 5th Army to the French Riviera for Operation Dragoon (see pp.194–195). These changes allowed German forces more time to make their retreat.

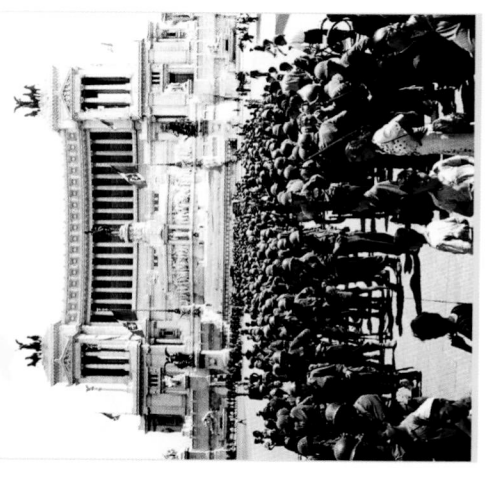

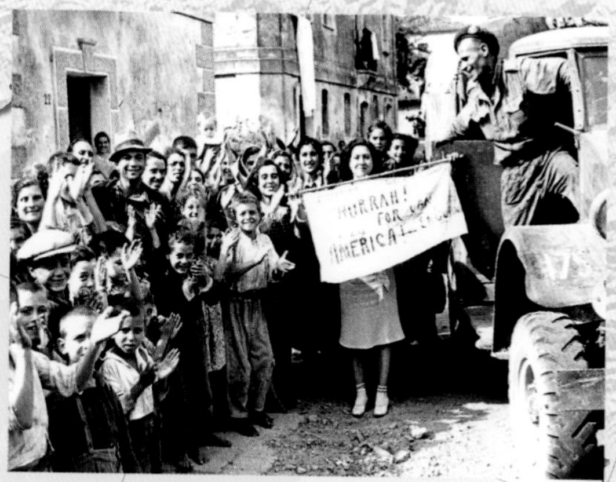
HURRAH! FOR ... AMERICA...

△ **Greeting the liberators**
A group of Italian townspeople welcome Allied troops. However, civilians often suffered most as the Allied, German, and partisan forces fought their way through Italy for nearly two years.

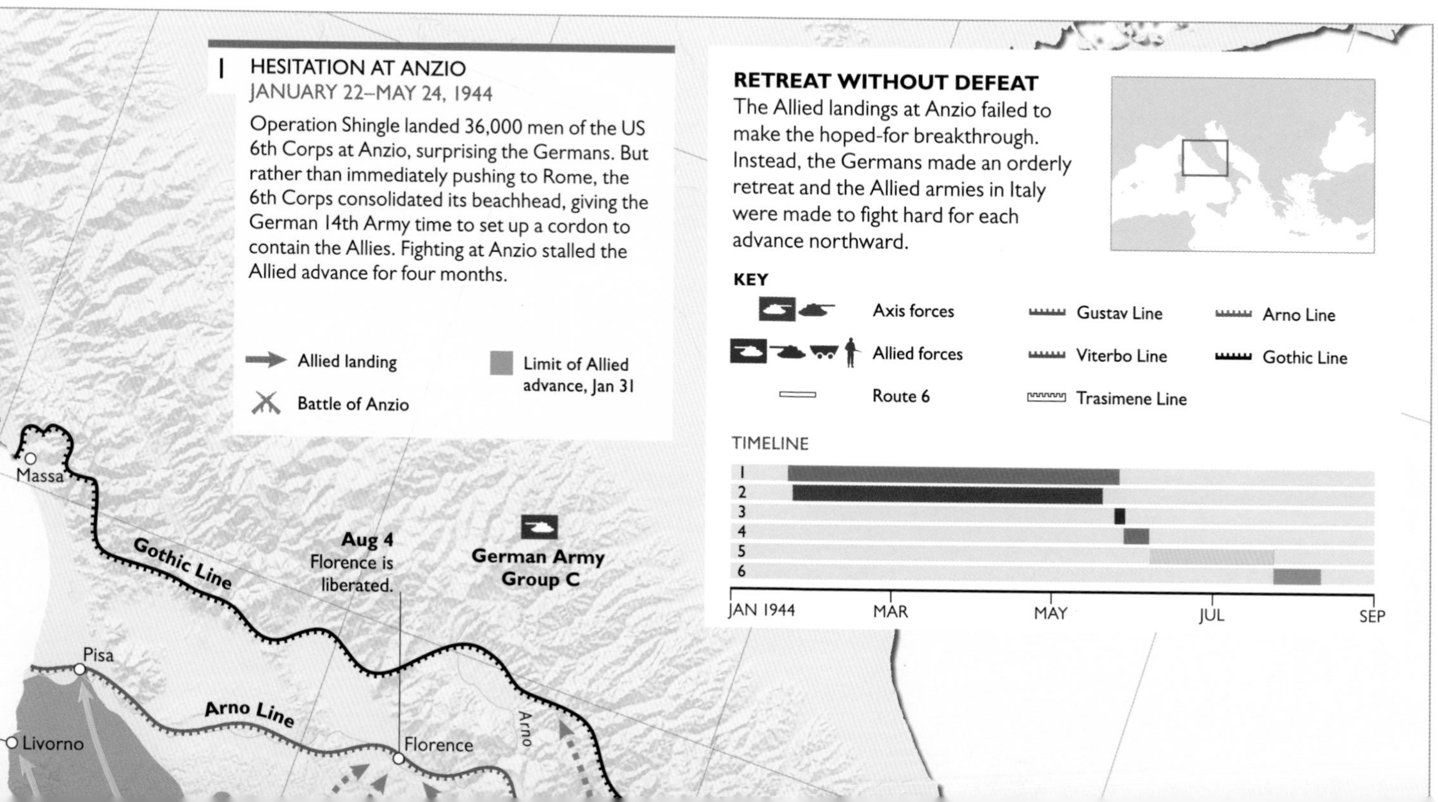
Massa
Gothic Line
Aug 4
Florence is liberated.
German Army Group C
Pisa
Jul 19 German troops abandon the port of Livorno, setting thousands of booby traps before they leave.
Livorno
Arno Line
Florence
Arno
KEY
Axis forces
Allied forces
Route 6
Gustav Line
Viterbo Line
Trasimene Line
Arno Line
Gothic Line
Allied landing
Battle of Anzio
Limit of Allied advance, Jan 31
TIMELINE
1
2
3
4
5
6
JAN 1944
MAR
MAY
JUL
SEP

1 HESITATION AT ANZIO
JANUARY 22–MAY 24, 1944

Operation Shingle landed 36,000 men of the US 6th Corps at Anzio, surprising the Germans. But rather than immediately pushing to Rome, the 6th Corps consolidated its beachhead, giving the German 14th Army time to set up a cordon to contain the Allies. Fighting at Anzio stalled the Allied advance for four months.

RETREAT WITHOUT DEFEAT

The Allied landings at Anzio failed to make the hoped-for breakthrough. Instead, the Germans made an orderly retreat and the Allied armies in Italy were made to fight hard for each advance northward.

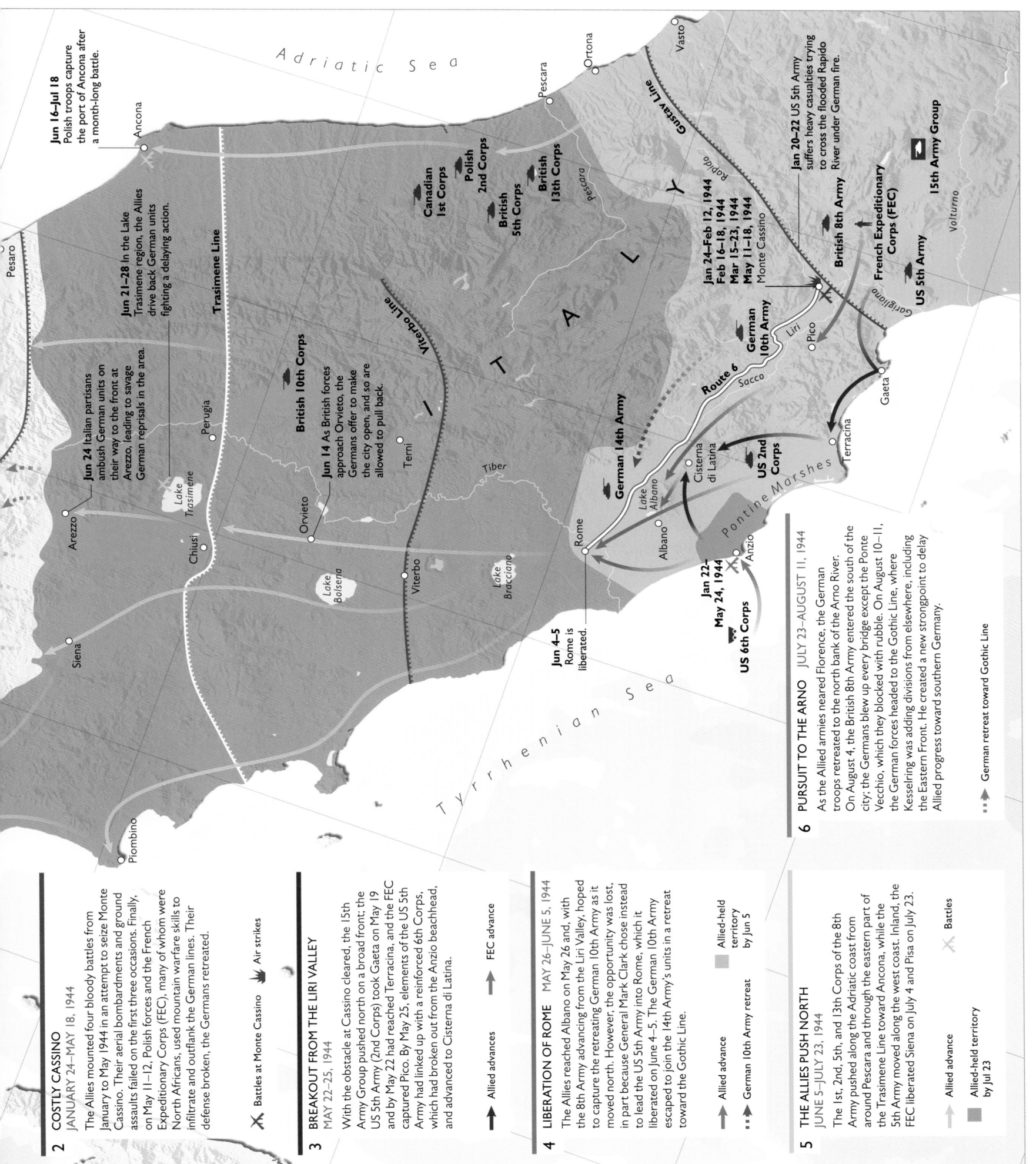

Adriatic Sea

Jun 16–Jul 18 Polish troops capture the port of Ancona after a month-long battle.

Ancona

Pesaro

Pescara

Ortona

Vasto

Gustav Line

Jun 21–28 In the Lake Trasimene region, the Allies drive back German units fighting a delaying action.

Rapido

Jan 20–22 US 5th Army suffers heavy casualties trying to cross the flooded Rapido River under German fire.

Pescara

Canadian 1st Corps

Polish 2nd Corps

British 5th Corps

British 13th Corps

Trasimene Line

Jun 24 Italian partisans ambush German units on their way to the front at Arezzo, leading to savage German reprisals in the area.

British 8th Army

French Expeditionary Corps (FEC)

15th Army Group

US 5th Army

Jan 24–Feb 12, 1944
Feb 16–18, 1944
Mar 15–23, 1944
May 11–18, 1944
Monte Cassino

Garigliano

Volturno

Perugia

Viterbo Line

British 10th Corps

Jun 14 As British forces approach Orvieto, the Germans offer to make the city open, and so are allowed to pull back.

Lake Trasimene

I T A L Y

Arezzo

Terni

German 10th Army

Liri

Pico

Route 6

Sacco

Gaeta

Chiusi

Siena

Orvieto

Tiber

German 14th Army

Terracina

Lake Bolsena

Viterbo

Lake Bracciano

Rome

Lake Albano

Cisterna di Latina

US 2nd Corps

Pontine Marshes

Anzio

Jun 4–5 Rome is liberated.

Albano

Jan 22– May 24, 1944

US 6th Corps

Piombino

Tyrrhenian Sea

6   PURSUIT TO THE ARNO JULY 23–AUGUST 11, 1944

As the Allied armies neared Florence, the German troops retreated to the north bank of the Arno River. On August 4, the British 8th Army entered the south of the city; the Germans blew up every bridge except the Ponte Vecchio, which they blocked with rubble. On August 10–11, the German forces headed to the Gothic Line, where Kesselring was adding divisions from elsewhere, including the Eastern Front. He created a new strongpoint to delay Allied progress toward southern Germany.

2   COSTLY CASSINO
JANUARY 24–MAY 18, 1944

The Allies mounted four bloody battles from January to May 1944 in an attempt to seize Monte Cassino. Their aerial bombardments and ground assaults failed on the first three occasions. Finally, on May 11–12, Polish forces and the French Expeditionary Corps (FEC), many of whom were North Africans, used mountain warfare skills to infiltrate and outflank the German lines. Their defense broken, the Germans retreated.

✕ Battles at Monte Cassino   ➵ Air strikes

3   BREAKOUT FROM THE LIRI VALLEY
MAY 22–25, 1944

With the obstacle at Cassino cleared, the 15th Army Group pushed north on a broad front; the US 5th Army (2nd Corps) took Gaeta on May 19 and by May 22 had reached Terracina, and the FEC captured Pico. By May 25, elements of the US 5th Army had linked up with a reinforced 6th Corps, which had broken out from the Anzio beachhead, and advanced to Cisterna di Latina.

➡ Allied advances   ➡ FEC advance

4   LIBERATION OF ROME   MAY 26–JUNE 5, 1944

The Allies reached Albano on May 26 and, with the 8th Army advancing from the Liri Valley, hoped to capture the retreating German 10th Army as it moved north. However, the opportunity was lost, in part because General Mark Clark chose instead to lead the US 5th Army into Rome, which it liberated on June 4–5. The German 10th Army escaped to join the 14th Army's units in a retreat toward the Gothic Line.

➡ Allied advance   ▨ Allied-held territory by Jun 5
┄➤ German 10th Army retreat

5   THE ALLIES PUSH NORTH
JUNE 5–JULY 23, 1944

The 1st, 2nd, 5th, and 13th Corps of the 8th Army pushed along the Adriatic coast from around Pescara and through the eastern part of the Trasimene Line toward Ancona, while the 5th Army moved along the west coast. Inland, the FEC liberated Siena on July 4 and Pisa on July 23.

➡ Allied advance   ✕ Battles
▨ Allied-held territory by Jul 23

┄➤ German retreat toward Gothic Line

DEFEAT OF THE U-BOATS

America's entry into the war began a new wave of U-boat activity in 1942 as the submarines hunted ships off the US east coast. Improved defenses soon drove the U-boats out into the mid-Atlantic, where they faced increasingly effective countermeasures by 1943.

After Germany declared war on the US in December 1941, the Atlantic Ocean became the theater for the early conflict between the nations. Admiral Karl Dönitz, commander of the German U-boat fleet, launched Operation Drumbeat to harass merchant ships moving along the US east coast. The first casualty was a British tanker, sunk on January 14, 1942, and by June of that year a total of 492 Allied ships had been lost, even though there were never more than a dozen German submarines operating in the area.

As the US improved its coastal defenses, the focus of the sea battle shifted to the mid-Atlantic, with additional attacks continuing in the Caribbean Sea. Germany poured ever-increasing resources into its submarine fleet and by November 1942, more than 80 U-boats were active in the Atlantic theater. That month was to prove the deadliest of all for the Allies, who lost over 88,000 tons (80,000 metric tons) of merchant shipping; the tally for the year 1942 amounted to over 6 million tons (5.4 million metric tons).

The tide of the war in the Atlantic turned in favor of the Allies in the spring of 1943. Faced by a real threat to Britain's oil supplies, the Allies deployed long-range aircraft equipped with improved radar, as well as hunting packs of anti-submarine vessels, typically escorted by small escort aircraft carriers. The tactic worked. In May 1943, when 41 U-boats were sunk, Admiral Dönitz unwillingly recalled all his vessels from the North Atlantic. Although they would return later, the U-boats never again presented the grave threat that they had in the early years of the war.

ADMIRAL KARL DÖNITZ 1891–1980

Karl Dönitz served as a submarine officer in World War I. In the mid 1930s he took charge of the clandestine program to rebuild Germany's U-boat fleet, which had been banned in 1919. Promoted to Rear-Admiral in 1939, he proved a skillful strategist—so much so that he was made Commander-in-Chief of the German navy in January 1943. For his loyalty, Hitler chose him as his successor, and he briefly served as Germany's head of state following the Führer's suicide in 1945.

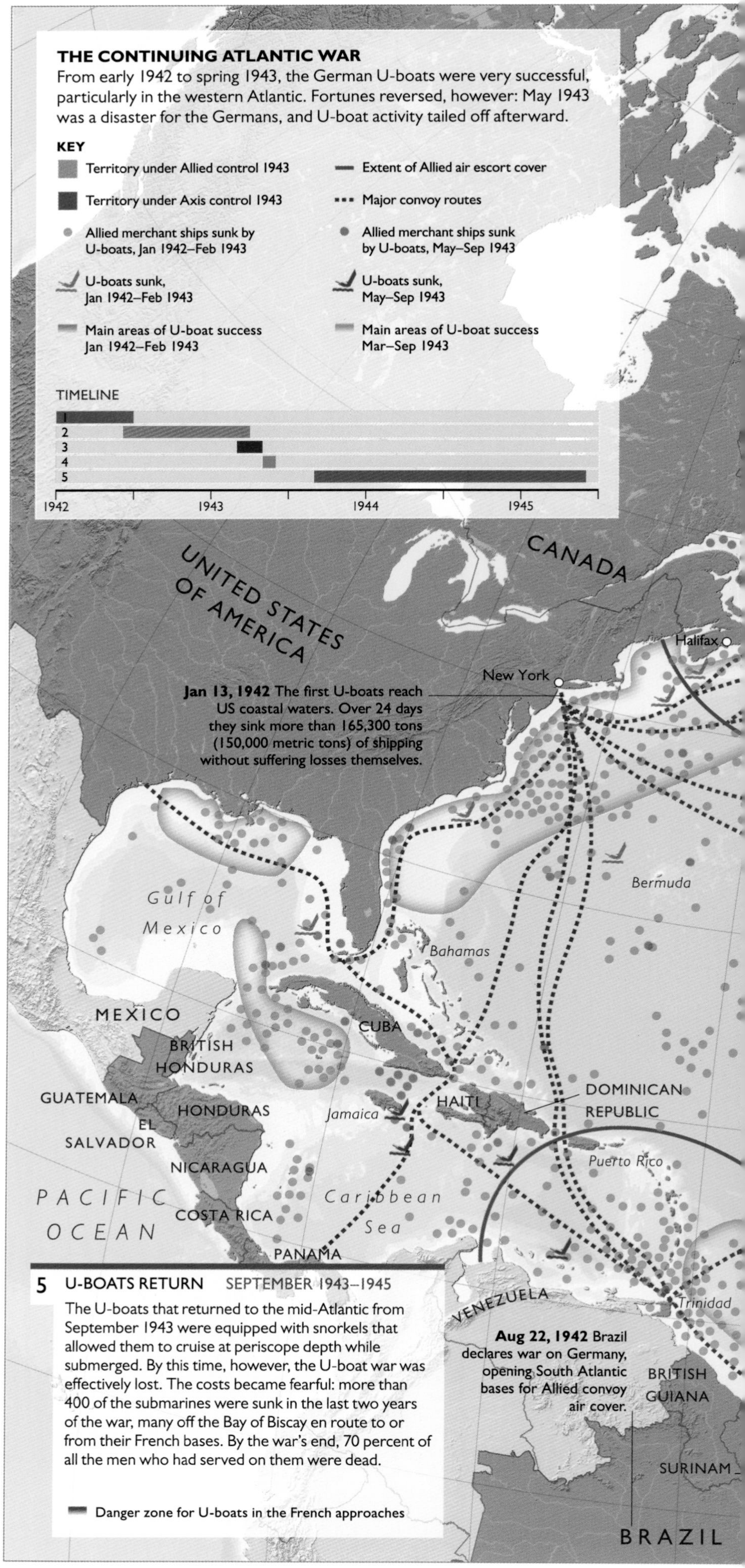

THE CONTINUING ATLANTIC WAR

From early 1942 to spring 1943, the German U-boats were very successful, particularly in the western Atlantic. Fortunes reversed, however: May 1943 was a disaster for the Germans, and U-boat activity tailed off afterward.

KEY

- Territory under Allied control 1943
- Territory under Axis control 1943
- Allied merchant ships sunk by U-boats, Jan 1942–Feb 1943
- U-boats sunk, Jan 1942–Feb 1943
- Main areas of U-boat success Jan 1942–Feb 1943
- Extent of Allied air escort cover
- Major convoy routes
- Allied merchant ships sunk by U-boats, May–Sep 1943
- U-boats sunk, May–Sep 1943
- Main areas of U-boat success Mar–Sep 1943

TIMELINE

1 2 3 4 5

1942 — 1943 — 1944 — 1945

Jan 13, 1942 The first U-boats reach US coastal waters. Over 24 days they sink more than 165,300 tons (150,000 metric tons) of shipping without suffering losses themselves.

CANADA

UNITED STATES OF AMERICA

Halifax

New York

Bermuda

Gulf of Mexico

Bahamas

MEXICO

CUBA

BRITISH HONDURAS

GUATEMALA

HONDURAS   Jamaica   HAITI

DOMINICAN REPUBLIC

EL SALVADOR

Puerto Rico

NICARAGUA

Caribbean Sea

PACIFIC OCEAN   COSTA RICA

PANAMA

5 U-BOATS RETURN   SEPTEMBER 1943–1945

The U-boats that returned to the mid-Atlantic from September 1943 were equipped with snorkels that allowed them to cruise at periscope depth while submerged. By this time, however, the U-boat war was effectively lost. The costs became fearful: more than 400 of the submarines were sunk in the last two years of the war, many off the Bay of Biscay en route to or from their French bases. By the war's end, 70 percent of all the men who had served on them were dead.

Trinidad

VENEZUELA

Aug 22, 1942 Brazil declares war on Germany, opening South Atlantic bases for Allied convoy air cover.

BRITISH GUIANA

SURINAM

- Danger zone for U-boats in the French approaches

BRAZIL

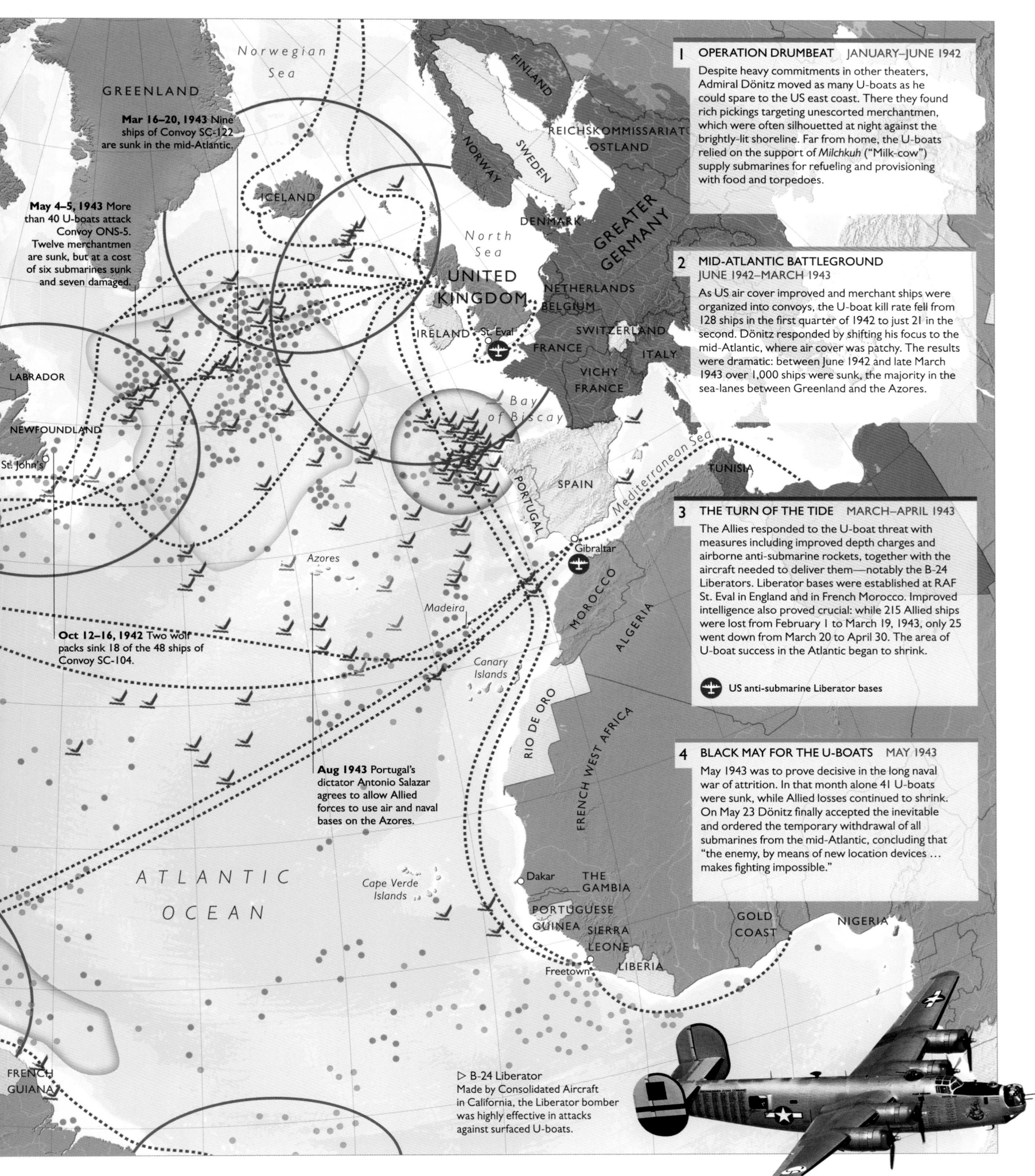

GREENLAND

Norwegian Sea

Mar 16–20, 1943 Nine ships of Convoy SC-122 are sunk in the mid-Atlantic.

ICELAND

FINLAND

NORWAY

SWEDEN

REICHSKOMMISSARIAT -OSTLAND

May 4–5, 1943 More than 40 U-boats attack Convoy ONS-5. Twelve merchantmen are sunk, but at a cost of six submarines sunk and seven damaged.

North Sea

DENMARK

GREATER GERMANY

UNITED KINGDOM

NETHERLANDS

BELGIUM

LABRADOR

IRELAND

St. Eval

SWITZERLAND

FRANCE

ITALY

VICHY FRANCE

NEWFOUNDLAND

Bay of Biscay

St. John's

Mediterranean Sea

PORTUGAL

SPAIN

TUNISIA

Azores

Gibraltar

MOROCCO

Madeira

ALGERIA

Oct 12–16, 1942 Two wolf packs sink 18 of the 48 ships of Convoy SC-104.

Canary Islands

RIO DE ORO

Aug 1943 Portugal's dictator Antonio Salazar agrees to allow Allied forces to use air and naval bases on the Azores.

FRENCH WEST AFRICA

ATLANTIC OCEAN

Cape Verde Islands

Dakar

THE GAMBIA

PORTUGUESE GUINEA

SIERRA LEONE

GOLD COAST

NIGERIA

Freetown

LIBERIA

FRENCH GUIANA

▷ **B-24 Liberator**
Made by Consolidated Aircraft in California, the Liberator bomber was highly effective in attacks against surfaced U-boats.

---

1 OPERATION DRUMBEAT JANUARY–JUNE 1942

Despite heavy commitments in other theaters, Admiral Dönitz moved as many U-boats as he could spare to the US east coast. There they found rich pickings targeting unescorted merchantmen, which were often silhouetted at night against the brightly-lit shoreline. Far from home, the U-boats relied on the support of *Milchkuh* ("Milk-cow") supply submarines for refueling and provisioning with food and torpedoes.

2 MID-ATLANTIC BATTLEGROUND JUNE 1942–MARCH 1943

As US air cover improved and merchant ships were organized into convoys, the U-boat kill rate fell from 128 ships in the first quarter of 1942 to just 21 in the second. Dönitz responded by shifting his focus to the mid-Atlantic, where air cover was patchy. The results were dramatic: between June 1942 and late March 1943 over 1,000 ships were sunk, the majority in the sea-lanes between Greenland and the Azores.

3 THE TURN OF THE TIDE MARCH–APRIL 1943

The Allies responded to the U-boat threat with measures including improved depth charges and airborne anti-submarine rockets, together with the aircraft needed to deliver them—notably the B-24 Liberators. Liberator bases were established at RAF St. Eval in England and in French Morocco. Improved intelligence also proved crucial: while 215 Allied ships were lost from February 1 to March 19, 1943, only 25 went down from March 20 to April 30. The area of U-boat success in the Atlantic began to shrink.

✈ US anti-submarine Liberator bases

4 BLACK MAY FOR THE U-BOATS MAY 1943

May 1943 was to prove decisive in the long naval war of attrition. In that month alone 41 U-boats were sunk, while Allied losses continued to shrink. On May 23 Dönitz finally accepted the inevitable and ordered the temporary withdrawal of all submarines from the mid-Atlantic, concluding that "the enemy, by means of new location devices … makes fighting impossible."

CODE-BREAKING

Both the Axis powers and the Allies devoted significant resources to breaking the ciphers used by governments and armed forces to conceal their communications. The Allies, in particular, achieved great success in this field.

Both sides stood to gain a huge advantage if they could intercept and decrypt enemy radio transmissions. However, gathering signals intelligence (SIGINT) was a complex and laborious process, made harder by machine-encoding devices such as Enigma (Germany), Typex (Britain), and Purple (Japan).

△ **Converting into code**
German soldiers encipher a message using an Enigma machine. Errors and shortcuts made by operators in a hurry often provided a way into the code.

The code war

In fall 1939, the British set up a specialist cryptography department, Ultra, at Bletchley Park, Buckinghamshire, staffed by civilian and military experts. By April 1941, these cryptographers, using electro-mechanic decoding devices called "bombes," could read transmissions from the German Luftwaffe, followed by variants of the code used by other German services.

This information was strategically vital, and included Rommel's intentions before El Alamein (see pp.76–77), German U-boat locations in the North Atlantic (see pp.64–65), and German deployments in Normandy before D-Day (see pp.186–189). However, the intelligence had to be used sparingly to prevent the Axis powers realizing the Enigma code had been broken. Elsewhere, the work of US code-breakers (MAGIC) on Japanese diplomatic codes and the JN-25 naval code yielded valuable intelligence in the Pacific theater, while German SIGINT on the Soviets was poor due to effective Soviet coding.

ENIGMA MACHINE

The German Enigma machine used a typewriter key attached to a series of rotating wheels (rotors), internal wiring, and a plugboard, which produced billions of variants for each letter depressed. In 1938, the Polish intelligence service provided information on the Enigma's construction, which proved key to cracking the code.

Code-breaking at Bletchley Park
Electronic devices, such as the Colossus (seen here in operation), allowed cryptographers to run multiple attempts to crack an Enigma message in a very short time. The Colossus could process 5,000 characters a second.

BOMBING BY DAY AND NIGHT

From 1942 onward, the RAF sought to stage a Blitz in reverse by pursuing the Strategic Bombing Offensive—an aerial campaign designed to shatter enemy morale. The arrival of the US 8th Air Force in England later that year further increased the pressure on Germany.

"The bomber will always get through," British politician Stanley Baldwin had opined in 1932, and this view was still widely held at the start of the war. Even though the Blitz's failure to destroy British morale contradicted this theory, the RAF looked to Bomber Command to take the fight to German soil. The British initially targeted military and industrial installations in nighttime raids, but these suffered from a lack of accuracy, so in 1942 they turned to the less discriminate "area bombing" that targeted industrial cities and their populations.

The US 8th Air Force units, which arrived in England in late 1942, favored a different strategy—precision bombing in daylight. However, this approach proved costly, with many aircraft lost to German fighters. In January 1943, the Allies agreed a joint policy in Casablanca (see pp.162–163), which prioritized attacks on enemy infrastructure. In the months that followed, the effectiveness of their raids improved with the introduction of new aircraft (notably the Avro Lancaster), better navigational aids, and the use of Pathfinder units to help locate targets. By the turn of the year, the Allies had the upper hand and the Luftwaffe had been forced onto the defensive.

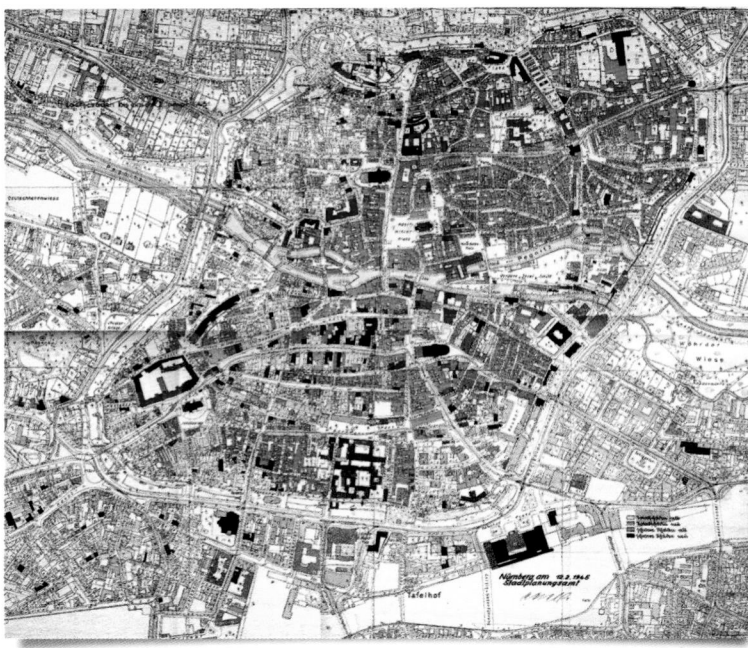

△ **Bomb damage in Nuremberg**
This German map from 1945 shows the new damage (dark red and black) to Nuremberg's old town after a huge Allied air raid on January 2, 1945. Bright red and blue areas show older damage from previous raids.

◁ **Attacks on infrastructure**
Allied bombers attack the German city of Ludwigshafen on the Rhine. The city was the site of important petrochemical plants during World War II.

Aug 17, 1942 USAAF flies its first mission over occupied Europe, targeting marshalling yards at Rouen.

THE WAR IN THE SKIES

After the failure of the Blitz, the Allies took the war to the skies over Germany. The arrival of US bombers from late 1942 tipped the balance in their favor, and even the sophisticated German air defenses of the Kammhuber Line could not stop the Allied attacks.

KEY

- Allied territory
- Axis territory, occupations, and cobelligerents
- Kammhuber Line
- Principal areas of German industry
- German night-fighter bases
- German shipyards
- Major RAF bomber bases
- Targets bombed by RAF
- Targets bombed by RAF and USAAF
- Major USAAF bomber bases
- Targets bombed by USAAF

TIMELINE

1
2
3
4
5
6

JAN 1942   JUL   JAN 1943   JUL   JAN 1944   JUL

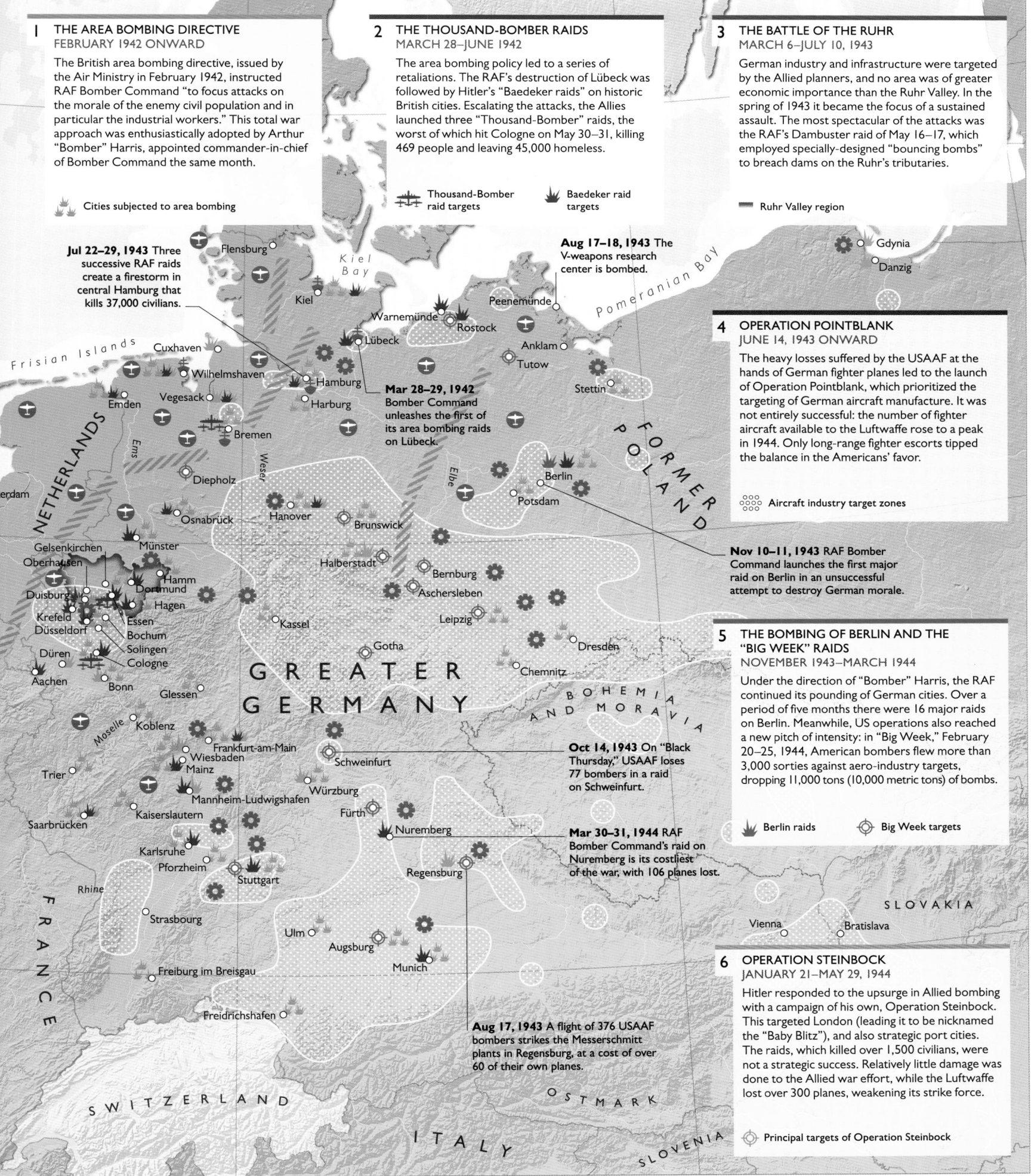

1 THE AREA BOMBING DIRECTIVE
FEBRUARY 1942 ONWARD

The British area bombing directive, issued by the Air Ministry in February 1942, instructed RAF Bomber Command "to focus attacks on the morale of the enemy civil population and in particular the industrial workers." This total war approach was enthusiastically adopted by Arthur "Bomber" Harris, appointed commander-in-chief of Bomber Command the same month.

🌱 Cities subjected to area bombing

2 THE THOUSAND-BOMBER RAIDS
MARCH 28–JUNE 1942

The area bombing policy led to a series of retaliations. The RAF's destruction of Lübeck was followed by Hitler's "Baedeker raids" on historic British cities. Escalating the attacks, the Allies launched three "Thousand-Bomber" raids, the worst of which hit Cologne on May 30–31, killing 469 people and leaving 45,000 homeless.

Thousand-Bomber raid targets   Baedeker raid targets

3 THE BATTLE OF THE RUHR
MARCH 6–JULY 10, 1943

German industry and infrastructure were targeted by the Allied planners, and no area was of greater economic importance than the Ruhr Valley. In the spring of 1943 it became the focus of a sustained assault. The most spectacular of the attacks was the RAF's Dambuster raid of May 16–17, which employed specially-designed "bouncing bombs" to breach dams on the Ruhr's tributaries.

— Ruhr Valley region

Jul 22–29, 1943 Three successive RAF raids create a firestorm in central Hamburg that kills 37,000 civilians.

Aug 17–18, 1943 The V-weapons research center is bombed.

Mar 28–29, 1942 Bomber Command unleashes the first of its area bombing raids on Lübeck.

4 OPERATION POINTBLANK
JUNE 14, 1943 ONWARD

The heavy losses suffered by the USAAF at the hands of German fighter planes led to the launch of Operation Pointblank, which prioritized the targeting of German aircraft manufacture. It was not entirely successful: the number of fighter aircraft available to the Luftwaffe rose to a peak in 1944. Only long-range fighter escorts tipped the balance in the Americans' favor.

Aircraft industry target zones

Nov 10–11, 1943 RAF Bomber Command launches the first major raid on Berlin in an unsuccessful attempt to destroy German morale.

5 THE BOMBING OF BERLIN AND THE "BIG WEEK" RAIDS
NOVEMBER 1943–MARCH 1944

Under the direction of "Bomber" Harris, the RAF continued its pounding of German cities. Over a period of five months there were 16 major raids on Berlin. Meanwhile, US operations also reached a new pitch of intensity: in "Big Week," February 20–25, 1944, American bombers flew more than 3,000 sorties against aero-industry targets, dropping 11,000 tons (10,000 metric tons) of bombs.

🌱 Berlin raids   ◎ Big Week targets

Oct 14, 1943 On "Black Thursday," USAAF loses 77 bombers in a raid on Schweinfurt.

Mar 30–31, 1944 RAF Bomber Command's raid on Nuremberg is its costliest of the war, with 106 planes lost.

6 OPERATION STEINBOCK
JANUARY 21–MAY 29, 1944

Hitler responded to the upsurge in Allied bombing with a campaign of his own, Operation Steinbock. This targeted London (leading it to be nicknamed the "Baby Blitz"), and also strategic port cities. The raids, which killed over 1,500 civilians, were not a strategic success. Relatively little damage was done to the Allied war effort, while the Luftwaffe lost over 300 planes, weakening its strike force.

◎ Principal targets of Operation Steinbock

Aug 17, 1943 A flight of 376 USAAF bombers strikes the Messerschmitt plants in Regensburg, at a cost of over 60 of their own planes.

SPEER AND THE WAR INDUSTRY

From 1942, Germany's war production effort became much more efficient under the direction of Albert Speer. As Minister of Armaments and Munitions, he increased output at a challenging time in the final years of the war.

△ **New plan for Berlin**
Speer surveys his plans for a redevelopment of Berlin, which Hitler commissioned in 1937. Most plans were abandoned due to the war.

In the early stages of the war, the German economy was not well mobilized for the needs of the armed forces; resources were not allocated efficiently, and the military interfered in production. Fritz Todt, a civil engineer who had supervised the construction of the Westwall fortifications along the Franco–German border, became Minister of Armaments and Munitions in 1940. He set in motion the reforms that would improve German industry, before dying in a plane crash in 1942.

Streamlining operations

Todt's replacement was architect and urban planner Albert Speer, who had designed the parade grounds for the Nuremberg rallies. Speer amalgamated military agencies to establish a central planning board, set up production committees for major weapons types, and excluded the armed forces from decisions about war production. He also used forced labor to boost production. As a result, despite Allied bombing offensives from 1943 onward, Speer tripled Germany's armaments production, enabling it to sustain the war into 1945. He was the only Nazi at the Nuremberg trials to admit guilt.

△ **Close associates**
Speer (far left) developed a close working relationship with Hitler, enabling Speer to secure necessary resources and overcome military objections to his industrial reorganizations. Here, he inspects a new weapons system with the Führer.

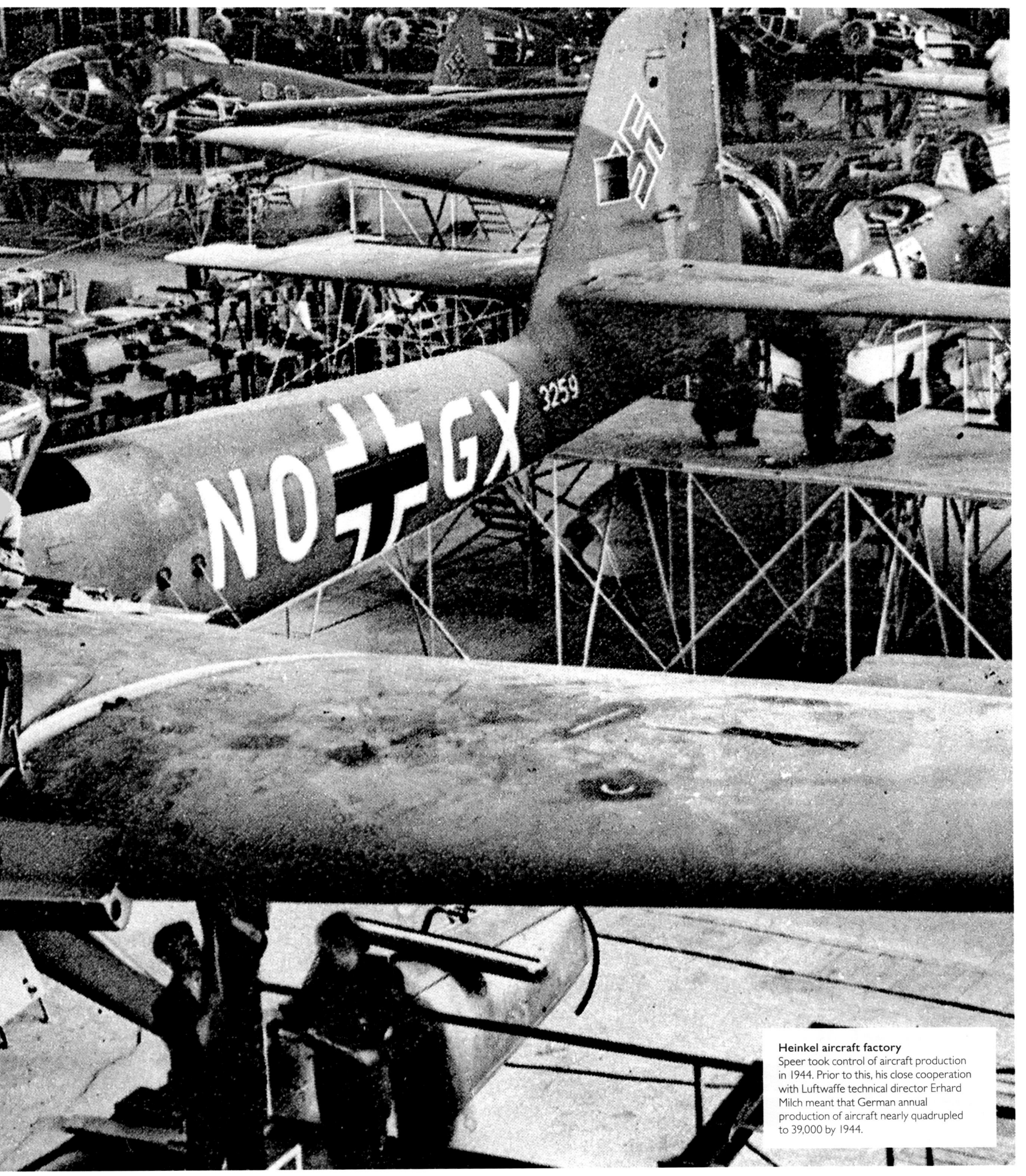

Heinkel aircraft factory
Speer took control of aircraft production in 1944. Prior to this, his close cooperation with Luftwaffe technical director Erhard Milch meant that German annual production of aircraft nearly quadrupled to 39,000 by 1944.

6 THE ITALIAN PARTISAN WAR
SEPTEMBER 1943–MAY 1945

The Italian resistance had its roots in anti-Fascist groups opposed to Mussolini before the war, but its activities expanded hugely after the Allied invasion in 1943 and the German occupation of the country. Nationalist, Communist, and Catholic groups combined to resist the invaders, often under the leadership of Italian former officers. In September 1943, the National Liberation Committee was founded to coordinate opposition to the Nazi forces.

🌿 Clashes between Germans and Partisan forces

7 THE DUTCH HUNGER WINTER
SEPTEMBER 1944–MAY 1945

In the Netherlands, underground fighters helped the Allies with intelligence and acts of sabotage. In 1944, with the southern half of the country already liberated, railroad workers went on strike, leading the Nazi authorities to retaliate by cutting off supply lines. The result was the Hunger Winter of 1944–1945, during which up to 20,000 people starved to death.

— Pre-war Netherlands → Main escape routes

👤 Major reprisal

△ **Fighting in the streets**
In August 1944, resistance members on the streets of Paris take aim from their makeshift barracks. At this time there were an estimated 100,000 members of the resistance across France.

5 POLISH RESISTANCE
NOVEMBER 1939–MAY 1945

Poland suffered more under Nazi occupation than any other country (see pp.38–39). Resistance centered on the Polish Home Army, loyal to the government in exile in London, and the pro-Communist People's Army. In August 1944 the Home Army launched an uprising in Warsaw (see pp.184–185) that was brutally crushed by Waffen-SS units, while the approaching Red Army was unable to assist. When it was over, the city was in ruins, and over 150,000 people were dead.

▭ Pre-war Poland ✊ Armed uprisings in Jewish ghettos

▨ Principal Polish Partisan areas 🌿 Clashes between Partisans and German forces 1941–1942

Jun 10, 1944 In retaliation for resistance activity in central France, Waffen-SS troops wipe out the entire population of the village of Oradour-sur-Glane.

4 NATIONAL LIBERATION FOR GREECE
MAY 1941–OCTOBER 1944

The Greek resistance movement was fractured between many different groups, who often fought among themselves and resisted attempts by the Allies to bring them together (see pp.202–203). The most successful was the Communist-inspired National Liberation Front (EAM), whose guerrilla forces won control of much of the mountainous interior of Greece. In March 1944, EAM set up the Political Committee of National Liberation, which became the de facto government of the liberated areas.

— Pre-war Greece ✊ Initial centers of resistance

May 9, 1944 Norwegian saboteurs blow up a train carrying mineral supplies for export to Germany.

May 27, 1942 SOE-trained Czech resistance fighters assassinate Nazi *Reichsprotektor* Reinhard Heydrich, triggering reprisals.

Mar 26, 1943 Polish resistance fighters free 25 captives from a Nazi prison van.

Jul 20, 1944 An attempt by Claus von Stauffenberg and other German officers to assassinate Hitler fails.

Feb 18, 1943 Nazi authorities break up the White Rose group.

Aug 29, 1944 Slovak resistance forces launch an armed uprising against Nazi troops occupying the country.

Jul 3, 1944 The Resistance declares a Free Republic of Vercors; the insurrection is viciously suppressed by the Germans.

Sep 27–30, 1943 Townspeople and resistance fighters join to drive out the occupying forces.

Mar 6, 1943 Yugoslav Partisans under Marshal Tito evade Axis forces by a strategic retreat in the Battle of the Neretva River.

ORKDAL · NORWAY · FINLAND · Bergen · Oslo · SWEDEN · Stavanger · REICHSKOMMISSARIAT OSTLAND · DENMARK · Silkeborg · Arhus · Herning · Copenhagen · NETHERLANDS · Rastenburg · Nowogródek · Nieswiez · UNITED KINGDOM · London · The Hague · Amsterdam · Berlin · Krynks · Bialystok · Warsaw · Treblinka · Kleck · Brussels · Radom · Sobibor · Lille · BELGIUM · GREATER GERMANY · Brest · Le Havre · Rouen · LUXEMBOURG · Paris · Luxembourg · Częstochowa · POLAND · OCCUPIED FRANCE · Metz · Prague · Będzin · Tarnów · Kladno · Strasbourg · Stefanau · SLOVAKIA · Munich · Oradour-sur-Glane · VICHY FRANCE · Beyssenac · SWITZERLAND · Bolzano · Marburg · HUNGARY · Coka · Petrila · Timişoara · Grenoble · Milan · Stari · Báctopolya · Aninoasa · SPAIN · Turin · Fossoli · Padua · Trieste · Petrovgrad · Belgrade · Lupeni · PORTUGAL · Vercors · Genoa · Bologna · Zasayi · ROMANIA · Madrid · La Spezia · Monte Battaglia · Šabac · Čačak · Zaječar · Toulouse · Marseille · Florence · YUGOSLAVIA · Neretva · Kruševac · Niš · Lisbon · Barcelona · Piombino · BULGARIA · Corsica · Rome · ITALY · Sofia · Plovadiv · Sardinia · Naples · Topollica · Tirane · ALBANIA · Salonika · FRENCH NORTH AFRICA · Sicily · GREECE · TUNISIA · Athens · Patras

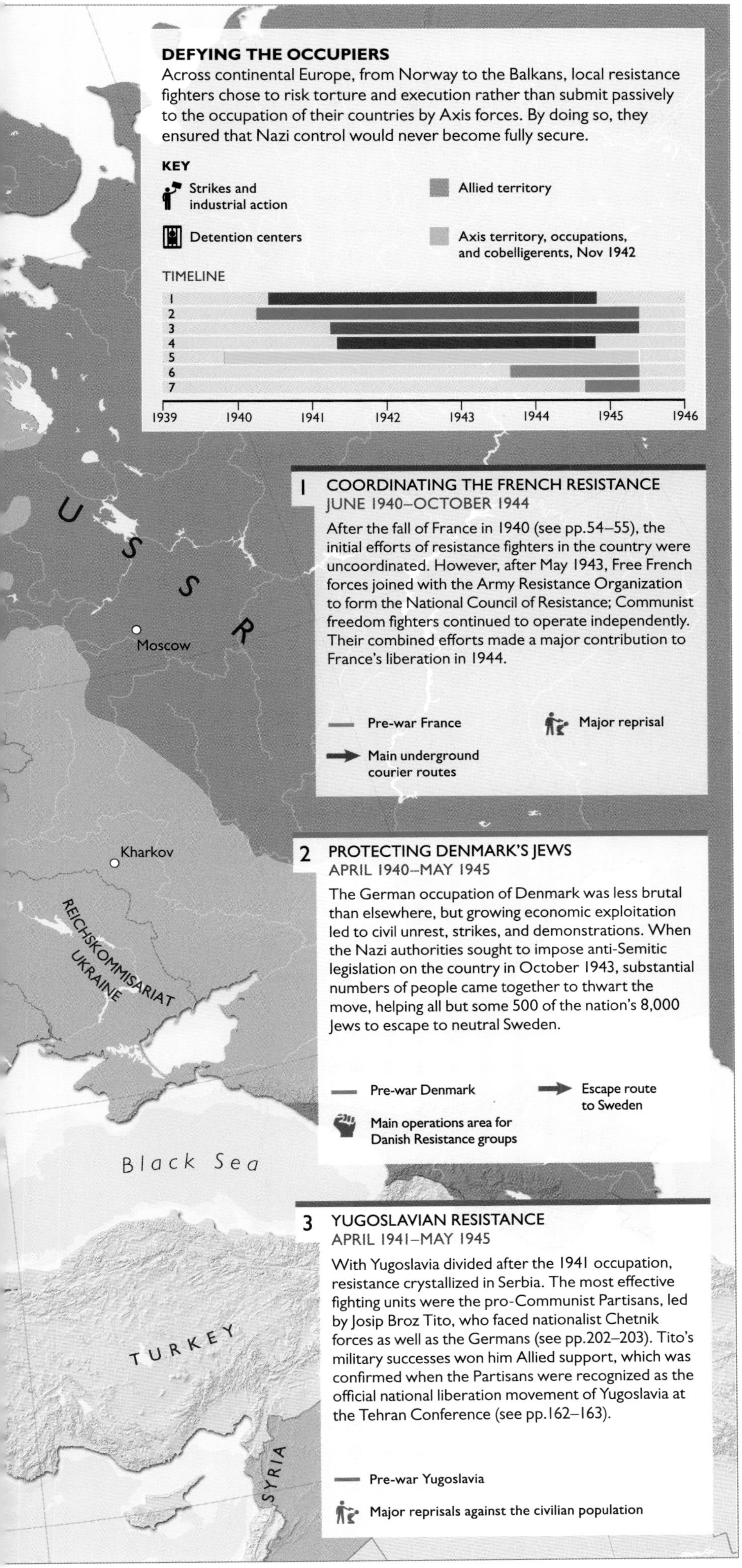

DEFYING THE OCCUPIERS

Across continental Europe, from Norway to the Balkans, local resistance fighters chose to risk torture and execution rather than submit passively to the occupation of their countries by Axis forces. By doing so, they ensured that Nazi control would never become fully secure.

KEY

- Strikes and industrial action
- Detention centers
- Allied territory
- Axis territory, occupations, and cobelligerents, Nov 1942

TIMELINE

1939 1940 1941 1942 1943 1944 1945 1946

1 COORDINATING THE FRENCH RESISTANCE
JUNE 1940–OCTOBER 1944

After the fall of France in 1940 (see pp.54–55), the initial efforts of resistance fighters in the country were uncoordinated. However, after May 1943, Free French forces joined with the Army Resistance Organization to form the National Council of Resistance; Communist freedom fighters continued to operate independently. Their combined efforts made a major contribution to France's liberation in 1944.

— Pre-war France

→ Main underground courier routes

Major reprisal

2 PROTECTING DENMARK'S JEWS
APRIL 1940–MAY 1945

The German occupation of Denmark was less brutal than elsewhere, but growing economic exploitation led to civil unrest, strikes, and demonstrations. When the Nazi authorities sought to impose anti-Semitic legislation on the country in October 1943, substantial numbers of people came together to thwart the move, helping all but some 500 of the nation's 8,000 Jews to escape to neutral Sweden.

— Pre-war Denmark

Main operations area for Danish Resistance groups

→ Escape route to Sweden

3 YUGOSLAVIAN RESISTANCE
APRIL 1941–MAY 1945

With Yugoslavia divided after the 1941 occupation, resistance crystallized in Serbia. The most effective fighting units were the pro-Communist Partisans, led by Josip Broz Tito, who faced nationalist Chetnik forces as well as the Germans (see pp.202–203). Tito's military successes won him Allied support, which was confirmed when the Partisans were recognized as the official national liberation movement of Yugoslavia at the Tehran Conference (see pp.162–163).

— Pre-war Yugoslavia

Major reprisals against the civilian population

RESISTANCE IN EUROPE

The brutality of Nazi rule led to the rise of resistance movements in every occupied country. These local groups received assistance, wherever possible, from Britain's Special Operations Executive (SOE), while the Soviet Union helped pro-Communist guerrillas in Eastern Europe.

Resistance groups often emerged spontaneously. Their operations took various forms, from passive opposition, such as that practiced in Germany by White Rose activists who distributed anti-Nazi pamphlets, to large-scale military activity. The mountainous terrain of the Balkans lent itself particularly well to the latter, and Yugoslavia and Greece experienced years of guerrilla warfare.

Elsewhere, opposition activities ranged from sabotage missions against military and industrial facilities to espionage and intelligence gathering. Sometimes local operatives carried out the actions, but the SOE (see pp.138–139) also inserted agents secretly by boat or parachute. Capture by the German authorities or collaborators usually meant torture and death, and successful ventures risked violent reprisals against the local population. However, such acts of resistance helped to divert valuable Axis resources from the two war fronts, as well as depleting the occupiers' morale. Equally important, resistance to the Nazi regime asserted human dignity in the face of oppression.

> *"France has lost a battle, but she has not lost the war."*
>
> GENERAL CHARLES DE GAULLE, 1940

RESISTANCE WRITING

Swaying public opinion was a vital part of the war effort: Vichy French authorities used propaganda to mobilize hostility to the resistance and the reprisals that they provoked. In response, resistance fighters set up underground newspapers that helped keep protest alive. In France there was *Libération* and *Combat* (edited by philosopher Albert Camus) and in Belgium *La Libre Belgique*, while in the Netherlands there were more than 1,000 publications.

Combat, May 29, 1944

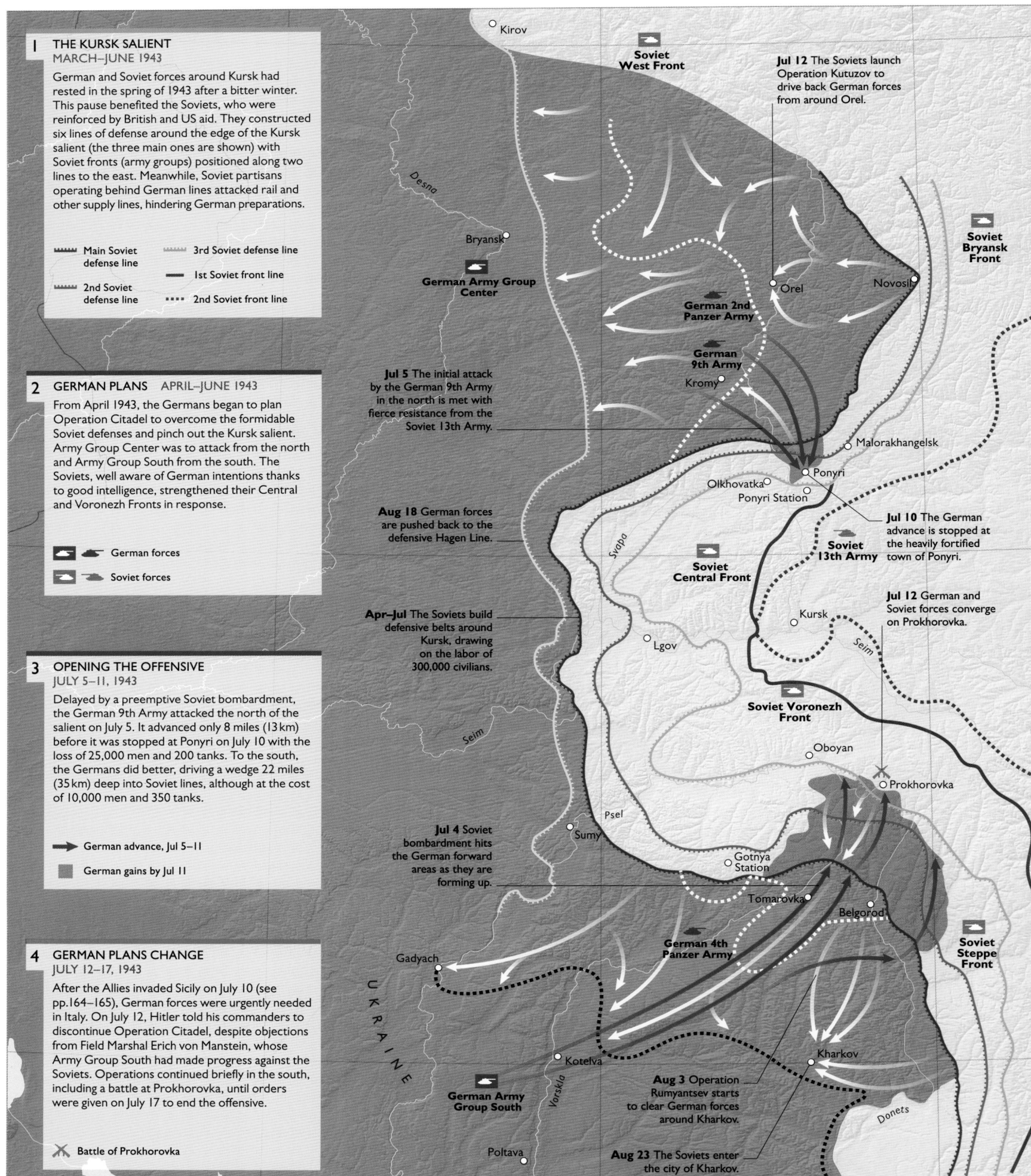

1 | THE KURSK SALIENT
MARCH–JUNE 1943

German and Soviet forces around Kursk had rested in the spring of 1943 after a bitter winter. This pause benefited the Soviets, who were reinforced by British and US aid. They constructed six lines of defense around the edge of the Kursk salient (the three main ones are shown) with Soviet fronts (army groups) positioned along two lines to the east. Meanwhile, Soviet partisans operating behind German lines attacked rail and other supply lines, hindering German preparations.

⌄⌄⌄⌄ Main Soviet defense line
⌄⌄⌄⌄ 2nd Soviet defense line
⌄⌄⌄⌄ 3rd Soviet defense line
━━━ 1st Soviet front line
┄┄┄ 2nd Soviet front line

2 | GERMAN PLANS APRIL–JUNE 1943

From April 1943, the Germans began to plan Operation Citadel to overcome the formidable Soviet defenses and pinch out the Kursk salient. Army Group Center was to attack from the north and Army Group South from the south. The Soviets, well aware of German intentions thanks to good intelligence, strengthened their Central and Voronezh Fronts in response.

◼ ◾ German forces
◼ ◾ Soviet forces

3 | OPENING THE OFFENSIVE
JULY 5–11, 1943

Delayed by a preemptive Soviet bombardment, the German 9th Army attacked the north of the salient on July 5. It advanced only 8 miles (13 km) before it was stopped at Ponyri on July 10 with the loss of 25,000 men and 200 tanks. To the south, the Germans did better, driving a wedge 22 miles (35 km) deep into Soviet lines, although at the cost of 10,000 men and 350 tanks.

➡ German advance, Jul 5–11
◼ German gains by Jul 11

4 | GERMAN PLANS CHANGE
JULY 12–17, 1943

After the Allies invaded Sicily on July 10 (see pp.164–165), German forces were urgently needed in Italy. On July 12, Hitler told his commanders to discontinue Operation Citadel, despite objections from Field Marshal Erich von Manstein, whose Army Group South had made progress against the Soviets. Operations continued briefly in the south, including a battle at Prokhorovka, until orders were given on July 17 to end the offensive.

✕ Battle of Prokhorovka

Kirov

Soviet West Front

Jul 12 The Soviets launch Operation Kutuzov to drive back German forces from around Orel.

Desna

Bryansk

Soviet Bryansk Front

German Army Group Center

Orel

Novosil

German 2nd Panzer Army

German 9th Army

Jul 5 The initial attack by the German 9th Army in the north is met with fierce resistance from the Soviet 13th Army.

Kromy

Malorakhangelsk

Aug 18 German forces are pushed back to the defensive Hagen Line.

Olkhovatka

Ponyri

Ponyri Station

Svapa

Soviet Central Front

Soviet 13th Army

Jul 10 The German advance is stopped at the heavily fortified town of Ponyri.

Apr–Jul The Soviets build defensive belts around Kursk, drawing on the labor of 300,000 civilians.

Kursk

Lgov

Jul 12 German and Soviet forces converge on Prokhorovka.

Seim

Soviet Voronezh Front

Oboyan

Prokhorovka

Seim

Psel

Jul 4 Soviet bombardment hits the German forward areas as they are forming up.

Sumy

Gotnya Station

Tomarovka

Belgorod

Soviet Steppe Front

Gadyach

German 4th Panzer Army

U
K
R
A
I
N
E

Kotelva

Vorskla

Aug 3 Operation Rumyantsev starts to clear German forces around Kharkov.

Kharkov

German Army Group South

Donets

Poltava

Aug 23 The Soviets enter the city of Kharkov.

A FORTIFIED SALIENT

The battle for control of the Kursk salient began on July 5, 1943, with a massive German onslaught that was at first held off by dense fortifications, then forced back by superior Soviet numbers.

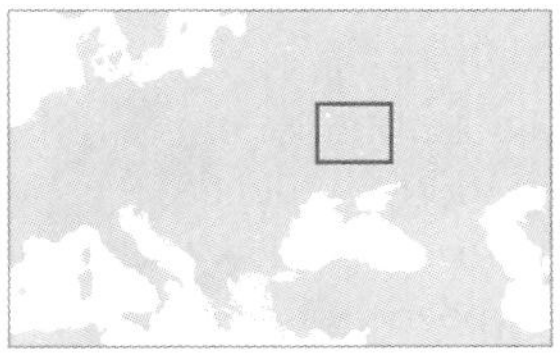

KEY

▨ German-held territory, Jul 4

TIMELINE

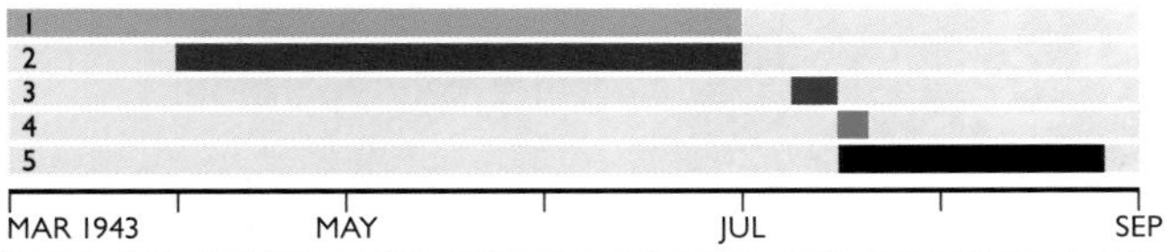

1			
2			
3			
4			
5			

MAR 1943   MAY   JUL   SEP

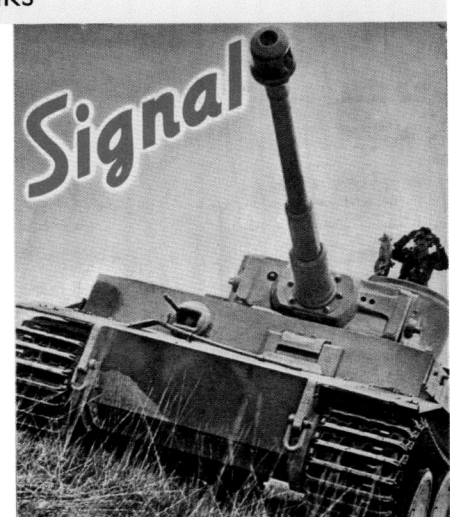

△ **Soviet counterattack**
Soviet troops follow their T-34 tanks during a counterattack near Kursk. The Soviets defended the salient with great bravery, often running close to German tanks to throw grenades under their tracks.

U   S   S   R

Apr–Jul Heavily defended front lines are drawn up, manned by the Soviet Central and Voronezh Fronts.

Soviet South-west Front

5 THE SOVIETS ADVANCE
JULY 12–AUGUST 23, 1943

As the Germans faltered, the Soviets attacked Army Group Center around Orel, north of Kursk, on July 12. The Germans were forced back across their defensive Hagen Line by August 18, and suffered huge losses. To the south, the Voronezh and Steppe Fronts advanced on August 3 and converged on Kharkov, forcing the Germans out by August 23.

⟹ Soviet advances		▫▫▫ Front line, Aug 5
ᗰᗰᗰ German Hagen Line		▰▰▰ Front line, Aug 23

THE BATTLE OF KURSK

In the summer of 1943, German forces in the USSR found themselves facing a huge, well-fortified Soviet salient around the city of Kursk, some 280 miles (450 km) south of Moscow. The resulting battle to remove the salient became a monumental clash of armor and was one of the largest tank battles of the war.

In early 1943, Soviet advances, combined with German retreats and counterattacks (see pp.152–153), resulted in a huge salient around Kursk. A vast, pivotal battle for the salient—an area of land 112 miles (180 km) wide and 62 miles (100 km) deep—followed in the summer, involving more than 8,000 tanks and 1.7 million men on both sides. Some 4,000 aircraft also played a vital role, both sides having recognized the effectiveness of air power—such as the lethal German Stuka dive-bomber— against tank armor.

The eventual Soviet victory at Kursk was a turning point in the war: it was the first time that a German strategic offensive had been halted before it could break through enemy lines; and it was Germany's final strategic offensive on the Eastern Front, where until now it had been dominant. From this point onward, Germany was on the defensive: the Wehrmacht had lost its armored supremacy, and the Luftwaffe had surrendered its dominance in the sky.

The Soviets' victory cost them three times more casualties than the Germans, but the losses were huge on both sides. Overall, more than 230,000 men were killed, missing, or wounded in battle, and more than 2,000 tanks and 600 aircraft were destroyed.

"The battle of Kursk ... and the liberation of Kiev, left Hitlerite Germany facing catastrophe."

VASILY IVANOVICH CHUIKOV, SOVIET GENERAL, 1968

RIVAL GERMAN AND SOVIET TANKS

The main Soviet tank at Kursk was the T-34 medium tank, supported by T-70 light tanks and Lend-Lease tanks supplied by the US and Britain. The Germans deployed mainly Panzer IV tanks, along with limited numbers of powerful Tiger heavy tanks and the new Panther medium tanks. The Panther suffered numerous technical problems during the battle and did not have enough firepower against enemy infantry; by contrast, the Soviets' highly mobile and rugged T-34 could be repaired quickly on the front line.

The powerful Tiger tank was heavily featured in propaganda as a symbol of German might

△ **Soviet momentum**
The Red Army launched new offensives in the wake of the Battle of Kursk. This propaganda poster, distributed in July 1943, reads "Over enemy land, forward to victory!"

5 LIBERATION OF CRIMEA
APRIL–MAY 1944

As the Soviets advanced through southern Ukraine, the German 17th Army became trapped in Crimea. The Soviets attacked Crimea on April 8, both from the north and from the east across the Sea of Azov. By May 9, Sevastopol's German garrison had surrendered, and the surviving Axis troops fled to Romania under heavy Soviet bomber and submarine attack.

→ Soviet attacks
🌿 Soviet bomber attacks
┅► German evacuation route

4 PUSHING AGAINST AXIS BORDERS
MARCH–APRIL 1944

By March 1944, Soviet forces had reached the border with Estonia. In the far south, they reached the Bug River in March and approached the border with Romania in April. The port of Odessa, Ukraine, was taken on April 10.

■ Encircled German forces
▨ Soviet-held territory by Mar 2, 1944
▨ Soviet-held territory by Apr 17, 1944

Jun 10, 1944 The Soviets breach Finnish defensive lines.

Mar 1, 1944 Soviets reach the Estonian border.

Jan 27, 1944 The lengthy siege of Leningrad is ended when the railroad line to Moscow is cleared.

Jan 19, 1944 Novgorod is recaptured by the Soviets.

🛩 **Leningrad Front**

🛩 **Volkhov Front**

🛩 **North-West Front**

Jan 19, 1944 Fearing encirclement, the German Army Group North is forced to retreat into Latvia.

🛩 **Kalinin Front**

Sep 25, 1943 The Soviets take Smolensk.

🛩 **West Front**

🛩 **Bryansk Front**

Army Group North 🛩

Army Group Center 🛩

🛩 **Center Front**

🛩 **Voronezh Front**

Nov 6, 1943 Kiev falls to the Soviets.

Sep 25, 1943 The Germans withdraw behind the Panther–Wotan Line.

🛩 **Steppes Front**

Sep 30, 1943 The Soviets begin to cross the Dnieper River along a 500-mile (800-km) front.

Apr 17, 1944 The Soviets occupy Tarnopol.

Army Group North Ukraine 🛩

Mar 15, 1944 Soviets reach the Bug River in southern Ukraine.

Apr 8, 1944 The Soviets cross into northern Crimea.

Army Group South Ukraine 🛩

Apr–May 1944 Romanian and German warships evacuate 113,000 Axis troops from Sevastopol in Crimea.

Army Group A 🛩

May 9, 1944 Sevastopol falls to the Soviets as the German garrison surrenders.

German 17th Army

FINLAND
Lake Ladoga
Helsinki
Gulf of Finland
Volkhov
Leningrad
Baltic Sea
Narva
ESTONIA
Lake Peipus
Luga
Novgorod
Tartu
Lake Ilmen
Staraya Russa
Valdai Hills
Pskov
Kalinin
Riga
LATVIA
Velikiye Luki
Rzhev
Moscow
Memel
LITHUANIA
Dvina
EAST PRUSSIA
Vyazma
Orsha
Maladzyechna
Smolensk
Kirov
GREATER GERMANY
Grodno
Bryansk
Orel
Białystok
Babruysk
BELORUSSIA
Kursk
Bug
Novozybkov
Warsaw
Brest-Litovsk
Pripet
Mazyr
Tula
Vistula
GENERAL GOVERNMENT
Kovel
Chernobyl
Konotop
Sumy
Belgorod
Lutsk
Korosten
Kharkov
Zhytomyr
Kiev
Lyutezh
Lubny
Donets
Tarnopol
Fastov
Cherkassy
Poltava
Chernivtsi
UKRAINE
Dnieper
HUNGARY
Dniester
Prut
Bug
Mariupol
Mykolaiv
ROMANIA
BESSARABIA
Odessa
Perekop
Sea of Azov
Kerch
CRIMEA
Novorossiysk
Sevastopol

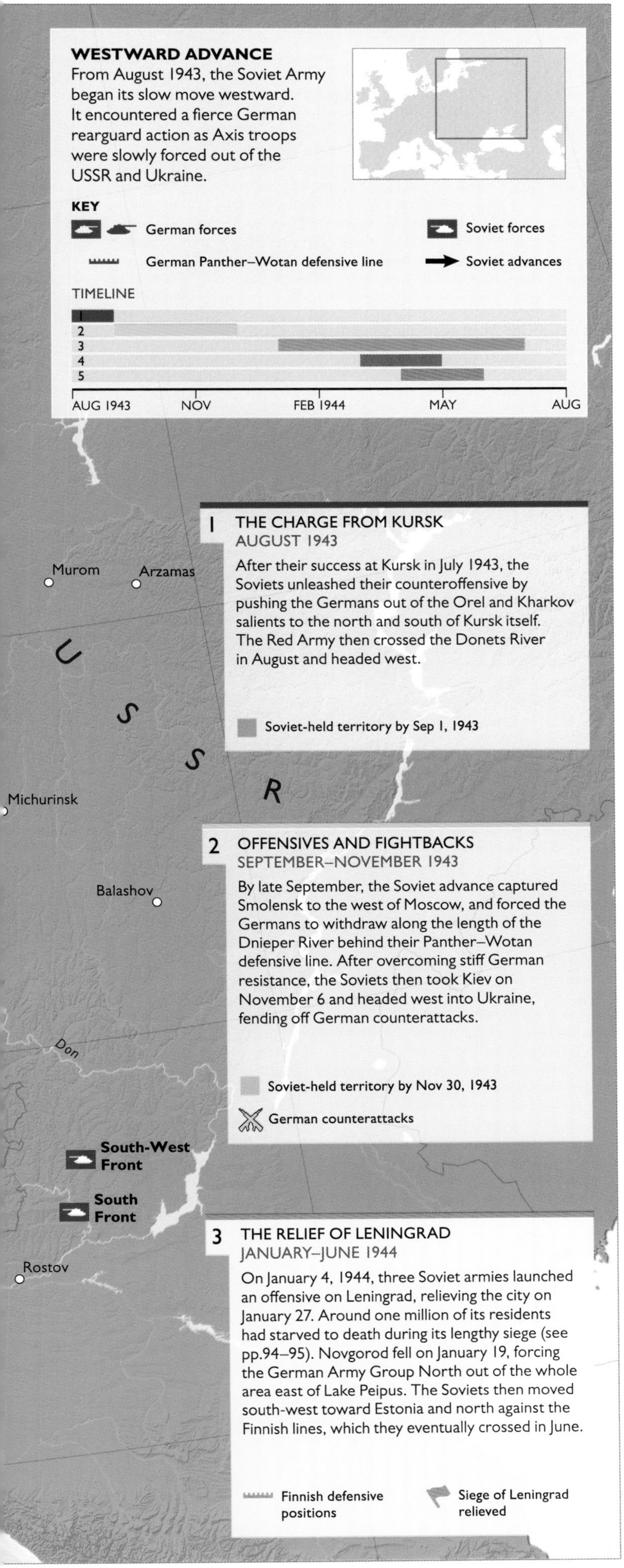

WESTWARD ADVANCE

From August 1943, the Soviet Army began its slow move westward. It encountered a fierce German rearguard action as Axis troops were slowly forced out of the USSR and Ukraine.

KEY

- German forces
- German Panther–Wotan defensive line
- Soviet forces
- Soviet advances

TIMELINE

	AUG 1943	NOV	FEB 1944	MAY	AUG
1					
2					
3					
4					
5					

Murom   Arzamas

U
S
S
R

Michurinsk

Balashov

Don

Rostov

1 THE CHARGE FROM KURSK
AUGUST 1943

After their success at Kursk in July 1943, the Soviets unleashed their counteroffensive by pushing the Germans out of the Orel and Kharkov salients to the north and south of Kursk itself. The Red Army then crossed the Donets River in August and headed west.

- Soviet-held territory by Sep 1, 1943

2 OFFENSIVES AND FIGHTBACKS
SEPTEMBER–NOVEMBER 1943

By late September, the Soviet advance captured Smolensk to the west of Moscow, and forced the Germans to withdraw along the length of the Dnieper River behind their Panther–Wotan defensive line. After overcoming stiff German resistance, the Soviets then took Kiev on November 6 and headed west into Ukraine, fending off German counterattacks.

- Soviet-held territory by Nov 30, 1943
- German counterattacks

South-West Front

South Front

3 THE RELIEF OF LENINGRAD
JANUARY–JUNE 1944

On January 4, 1944, three Soviet armies launched an offensive on Leningrad, relieving the city on January 27. Around one million of its residents had starved to death during its lengthy siege (see pp.94–95). Novgorod fell on January 19, forcing the German Army Group North out of the whole area east of Lake Peipus. The Soviets then moved south-west toward Estonia and north against the Finnish lines, which they eventually crossed in June.

- Finnish defensive positions
- Siege of Leningrad relieved

THE SOVIETS SWEEP FORWARD

The Soviet victory at the Battle of Kursk handed the initiative to the Red Army. It was now ready to attack the Germans on a wider front in order to push them out of the western USSR and Ukraine. The Germans never regained momentum in the east, and Hitler's ambitions for the USSR were crushed.

Following the huge Battle of Kursk (see pp.178–179), the Germans believed, despite their losses, that they had crippled the USSR, rendering it incapable of launching a counterattack. However, the Soviets regrouped quickly, and from summer 1943 German troops found themselves facing Soviet offensives on a front that stretched from Leningrad in the north to Crimea in the south.

In a series of major battles, with only a few setbacks, the Soviets fought their way to the western frontiers of the USSR by May 1944. The German forces on the Eastern Front were depleted due to the diversion of troops to Italy following the Allied landings there (see pp.164–165), but they nevertheless fought fiercely, giving ground grudgingly and at great cost to the enemy. They made tactical retreats behind new defensive lines built after the defeat at Kursk, particularly the Panther–Wotan Line.

Both sides suffered huge casualties, but the Soviets gained the upper hand: they lifted the 872-day siege of Leningrad; liberated Kiev, Smolensk, and Odessa; and cleared Crimea and its naval port Sevastopol of German forces. The way was now open for the Red Army to launch Operation Bagration (see pp.182–183) to clear the rest of the USSR of German troops and allow the Soviets to head into Eastern Europe.

"An extraordinary day. The entire city is waiting ... any moment now!"

VERA INBER, LENINGRAD CITIZEN, JANUARY 16, 1944

KONSTANTIN ROKOSSOVSKY, 1896–1968

After serving in World War I, Soviet and Polish officer Rokossovsky fought for the Bolsheviks in the Russian Civil War and soon climbed the ranks of the Red Army. He was imprisoned during Stalin's purges in the late 1930s, but was released in 1941 so the USSR could make use of his military skills. He gained fame for his defense of Moscow in 1941–1942 and his success at Stalingrad, where he led the Don Front in trapping the German 6th Army (see pp.152–153). He also played central roles at the Battle of Kursk and in Operation Bagration. It was Rokossovsky's army group that ended the war in north Germany (see pp.242–243). After the war, he became a member of the Communist Polish government.

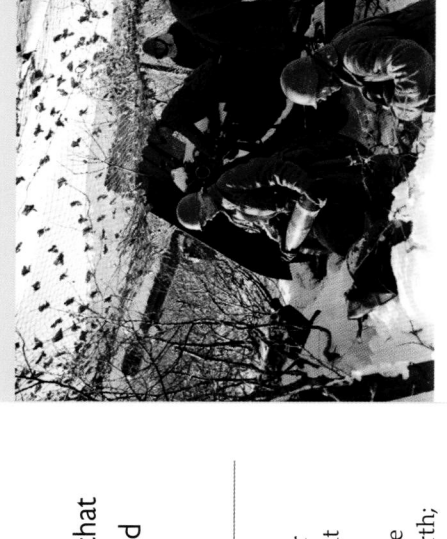

SOVIET MASKIROVKA

Maskirovka, meaning "camouflage" or "deception" in Russian, was a technique that the Soviets used with great success in Operation Bagration. They consistently misled the Germans about where they would attack along the broad front, positioning dummy armies, camouflaging trenches (see above), and sending false communications to suggest that the attack would come in Ukraine; in reality, Soviet troops were moving secretly and gradually by night to Belorussia. The Germans were deceived into moving their troops to the wrong locations on the Eastern Front.

OPERATION BAGRATION

Operation Bagration was the code name of the massive Soviet assault against German-occupied Belorussia that took place from June 22 to August 14, 1944. The assault, launched exactly three years after Germany invaded the USSR, involved millions of Soviet troops and was instrumental in bringing the war in Europe to an end.

Operation Bagration was named after Pyotr Ivanovich, Prince Bagration (1765–1812), a Russian general who had distinguished himself in the Napoleonic Wars by his use of innovative military tactics. The new campaign in his name was to be equally daring: it was intended to wipe out the German Army Group Center and clear German troops out of the western USSR.

In a series of brilliant but brutal assaults, striking where the Germans least expected, the Red Army swept all before it and advanced hundreds of miles in a couple of months. Soviet troops poured into the German-occupied areas of Belorussia, heading

north into Latvia and Lithuania, and west into Poland. A later operation in the south overran Romania and took Bulgaria out of the war. By the end of Bagration, Soviet troops were on the Vistula River in central Poland, facing Warsaw on the opposite bank; they were close to the shores of the Baltic Sea in the north; and they stood on the borders with Slovakia and Hungary in the south-west. Most threateningly for Germany, the Red Army was close to the eastern border of German East Prussia and the Third Reich itself.

The Soviet campaign was one of the largest Allied operations of the entire war, engaging more than 2.3 million Soviet troops and resulting in the destruction of the German Army Group Center. Losses on both sides were immense, with 180,000 Soviets killed or missing, and the Germans losing around 400,000 men, including nine generals killed and 22 captured. Up to 260,000 German troops were taken prisoner. Coming after German losses at Stalingrad (see pp.148–153) and then Kursk (see pp.178–179), Operation Bagration was another huge defeat for the German forces.

"The German troops now resemble a wounded beast which is compelled to crawl back to the frontiers of its lair ..."

JOSEPH STALIN, MAY 1, 1944

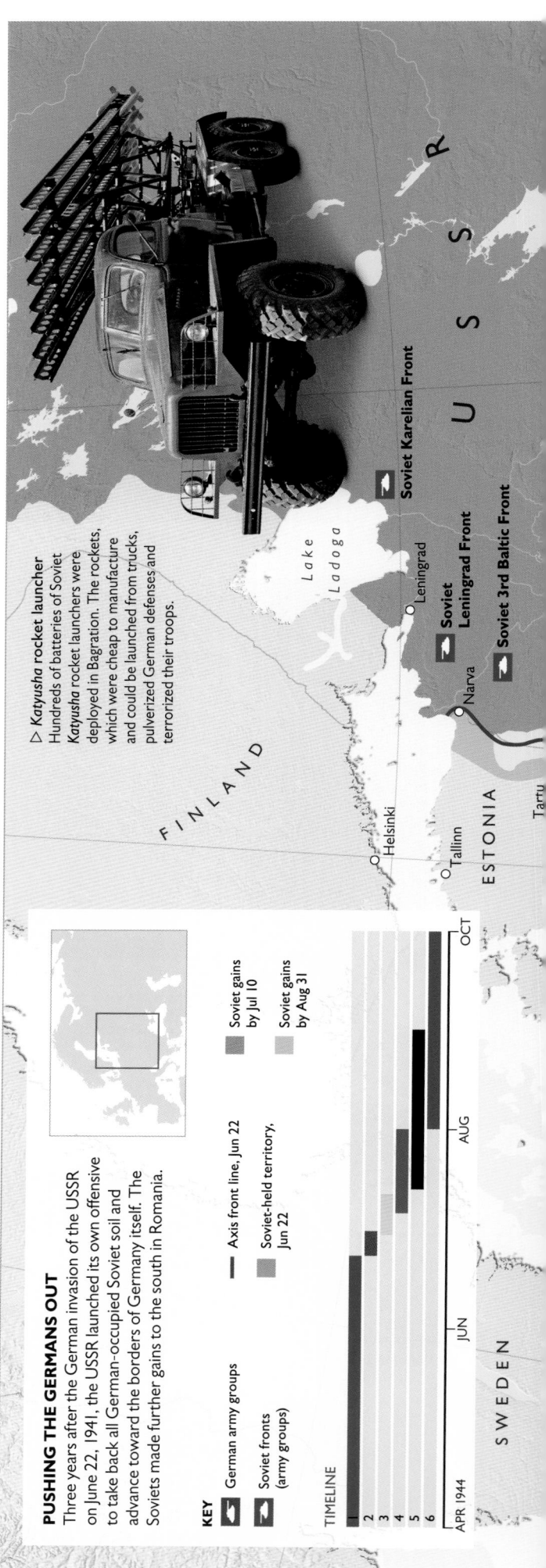

▷ **Katyusha rocket launcher**
Hundreds of batteries of Soviet *Katyusha* rocket launchers were deployed in Bagration. The rockets, which were cheap to manufacture and could be launched from trucks, pulverized German defenses and terrorized their troops.

Soviet Karelian Front

Soviet Leningrad Front

Soviet 3rd Baltic Front

PUSHING THE GERMANS OUT

Three years after the German invasion of the USSR on June 22, 1941, the USSR launched its own offensive to take back all German-occupied Soviet soil and advance toward the borders of Germany itself. The Soviets made further gains to the south in Romania.

KEY

⬆	German army groups
⬆	Soviet fronts (army groups)
—	Axis front line, Jun 22
■	Soviet-held territory, Jun 22
■	Soviet gains by Jul 10
■	Soviet gains by Aug 31

TIMELINE

APR 1944   JUN   AUG   OCT

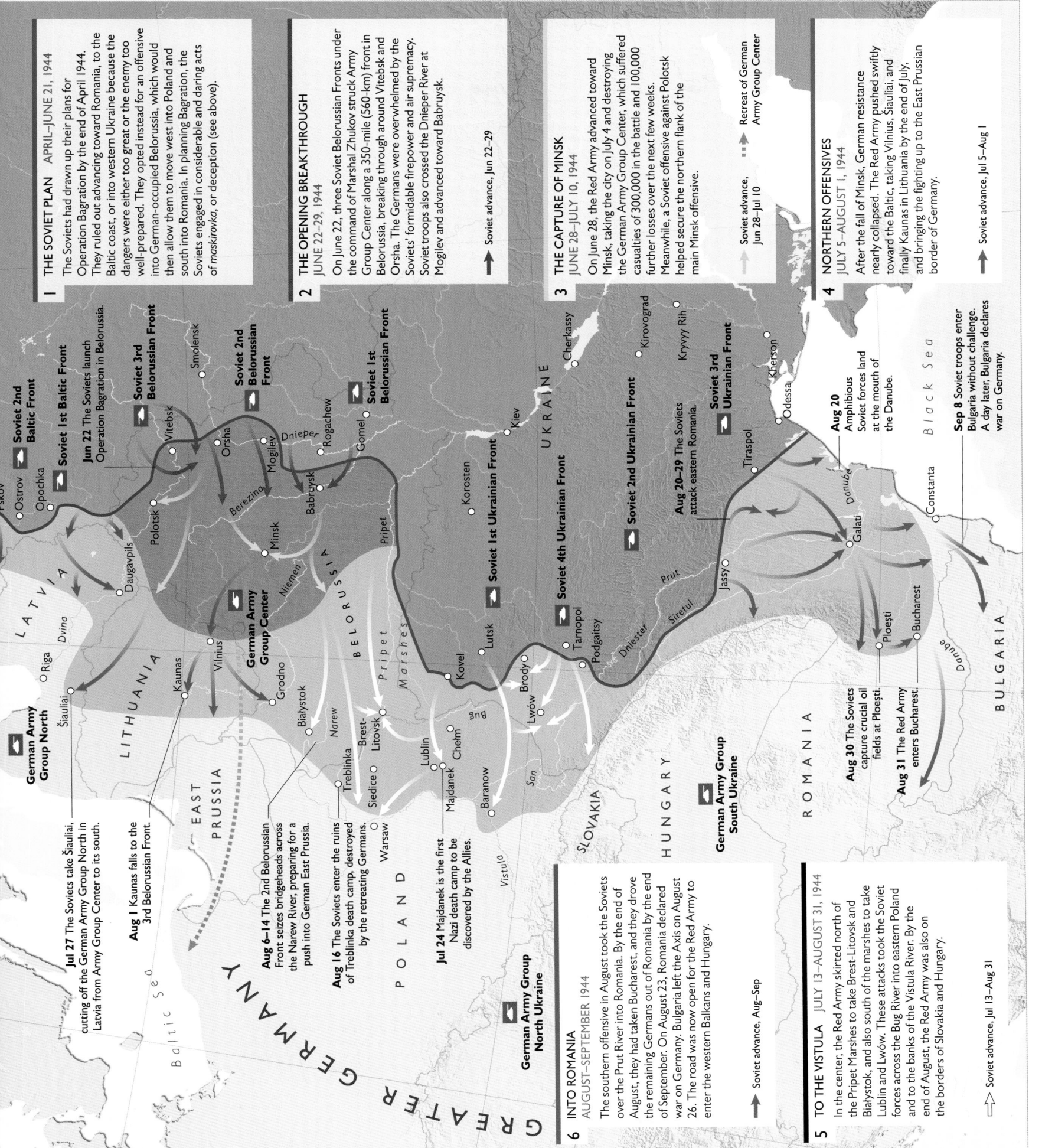

1 THE SOVIET PLAN APRIL–JUNE 21, 1944

The Soviets had drawn up their plans for Operation Bagration by the end of April 1944. They ruled out advancing toward Romania, to the Baltic coast, or into western Ukraine because the dangers were either too great or the enemy too well-prepared. They opted instead for an offensive into German-occupied Belorussia, which would then allow them to move west into Poland and south into Romania. In planning Bagration, the Soviets engaged in considerable and daring acts of *maskirovka*, or deception (see above).

→ Soviet advance, Jun 22–29

2 THE OPENING BREAKTHROUGH JUNE 22–29, 1944

On June 22, three Soviet Belorussian Fronts under the command of Marshal Zhukov struck Army Group Center along a 350-mile (560-km) front in Belorussia, breaking through around Vitebsk and Orsha. The Germans were overwhelmed by the Soviets' formidable firepower and air supremacy. Soviet troops also crossed the Dnieper River at Mogilev and advanced toward Babruysk.

→ Soviet advance, Jun 22–29

3 THE CAPTURE OF MINSK JUNE 28–JULY 10, 1944

On June 28, the Red Army advanced toward Minsk, taking the city on July 4 and destroying the German Army Group Center, which suffered casualties of 300,000 in the battle and 100,000 further losses over the next few weeks. Meanwhile, a Soviet offensive against Polotsk helped secure the northern flank of the main Minsk offensive.

→ Soviet advance, Jun 28–Jul 10   ···▷ Retreat of German Army Group Center

4 NORTHERN OFFENSIVES JULY 5–AUGUST 1, 1944

After the fall of Minsk, German resistance nearly collapsed. The Red Army pushed swiftly toward the Baltic, taking Vilnius, Šiauliai, and finally Kaunas in Lithuania by the end of July, and bringing the fighting up to the East Prussian border of Germany.

→ Soviet advance, Jul 5–Aug 1

5 TO THE VISTULA JULY 13–AUGUST 31, 1944

In the center, the Red Army skirted north of the Pripet Marshes to take Brest-Litovsk and Bialystok, and also south of the marshes to take Lublin and Lwów. These attacks took the Soviet forces across the Bug River into eastern Poland and to the banks of the Vistula River. By the end of August, the Red Army was also on the borders of Slovakia and Hungary.

→ Soviet advance, Jul 13–Aug 31

6 INTO ROMANIA AUGUST–SEPTEMBER 1944

The southern offensive in August took the Soviets over the Prut River into Romania. By the end of August, they had taken Bucharest, and they drove the remaining Germans out of Romania by the end of September. On August 23, Romania declared war on Germany. Bulgaria left the Axis on August 26. The road was now open for the Red Army to enter the western Balkans and Hungary.

→ Soviet advance, Aug–Sep

Jul 27 The Soviets take Šiauliai, cutting off the German Army Group North in Latvia from Army Group Center to its south.

Aug 1 Kaunas falls to the 3rd Belorussian Front.

Aug 6–14 The 2nd Belorussian Front seizes bridgeheads across the Narew River, preparing for a push into German East Prussia.

Aug 16 The Soviets enter the ruins of Treblinka death camp, destroyed by the retreating Germans.

Jul 24 Majdanek is the first Nazi death camp to be discovered by the Allies.

Aug 20 Amphibious Soviet forces land at the mouth of the Danube.

Sep 8 Soviet troops enter Bulgaria without challenge. A day later, Bulgaria declares war on Germany.

Aug 30 The Soviets capture crucial oil fields at Ploești.

Aug 31 The Red Army enters Bucharest.

Aug 20–29 The Soviets attack eastern Romania.

Jun 22 The Soviets launch Operation Bagration in Belorussia.

German Army Group North

German Army Group Center

German Army Group North Ukraine

German Army Group South Ukraine

Soviet 2nd Baltic Front

Soviet 1st Baltic Front

Soviet 3rd Belorussian Front

Soviet 2nd Belorussian Front

Soviet 1st Belorussian Front

Soviet 1st Ukrainian Front

Soviet 4th Ukrainian Front

Soviet 2nd Ukrainian Front

Soviet 3rd Ukrainian Front

GREATER GERMANY
Baltic Sea
LATVIA
LITHUANIA
EAST PRUSSIA
POLAND
BELORUSSIA
UKRAINE
SLOVAKIA
HUNGARY
ROMANIA
BULGARIA
Black Sea

Pskov, Ostrov, Opochka, Riga, Daugavpils, Šiauliai, Kaunas, Vilnius, Grodno, Bialystok, Narew, Brest-Litovsk, Siedlce, Treblinka, Warsaw, Lublin, Majdanek, Chełm, Baranow, Litovsk, Vistula, San, Bug, Lwów, Brody, Kovel, Lutsk, Korosten, Kiev, Tarnopol, Podgaitsy, Brody, Dniester, Prut, Siretul, Jassy, Tiraspol, Galați, Odessa, Kherson, Kryvyy Rih, Kirovograd, Cherkassy, Constanța, Bucharest, Ploești, Danube

Smolensk, Vitebsk, Orsha, Polotsk, Mogilev, Babruysk, Rogachev, Gomel, Dnieper, Berezina, Minsk, Niemen, Pripet, Pripet Marshes, Dvina, Divna

THE WARSAW UPRISING

In 1944, the main Polish resistance movement, the Home Army, embarked on an uprising to liberate their cities before the Soviets arrived. For nine weeks, resistance fighters battled the superior German forces.

△ **Insurgent's weapon**
Polish insurgents made thousands of weapons in secret factories, including copies of the British Sten Mark II submachine gun.

When the Soviets pushed the Germans back into Poland in July 1944, General Bor-Koromowski, commander of the Polish Home Army, decided to launch an operation to liberate Warsaw. With the Red Army approaching the Vistula river on August 1, 1944, about 37,000 Polish insurgents fell on the German garrison, which was caught off balance. Although lacking armaments—only one in seven had weapons—the resistance fighters rapidly took key parts of the city.

The Germans held key strategic positions such as railway stations, and on August 25 launched a counteroffensive. Some 20,000 heavily armed German troops, supported by aircraft, fought street battles with the Home Army. In the rubble of destroyed houses, and moving through makeshift tunnels, the Poles resisted for five weeks before surrendering on October 1. All this time, the Soviet army paused its offensive and offered no help, even denying the Western Allies access to airfields to resupply the insurgents. The Home Army lost 17,000 fighters and effectively disbanded, and Warsaw was destroyed on Hitler's orders. When the Soviets finally captured the city in January 1945, former resistance members were arrested, deported, or killed.

△ **Prisoners of war**
The suppression of the Warsaw Uprising was brutal; in the first few days, 40,000 civilians were massacred. The Home Army fought back fiercely, despite being outnumbered; here, German prisoners captured by the Polish resistance are forced to wear swastika-emblazoned shirts.

Fighting for liberty
Home Army fighters take shelter behind a makeshift barricade. Around 50 percent of Warsaw's buildings were destroyed during the German recapture of the city, and around 300,000 inhabitants became refugees.

THE D-DAY LANDINGS

On June 6, 1944, the largest seaborne invasion in history took place on the beaches of Normandy. Code named Operation Neptune, and usually referred to as D-Day, it began the liberation of France and the opening of another front in Europe.

At the Washington Conference of May 1943, the Allied leaders met to discuss their future strategy in Europe, and set a date of May 1944 for the invasion of France. Numerous sites for the offensive were considered. The obvious choice, an invasion across the narrowest part of the Channel to France's northernmost point, the Pas-de-Calais, was ruled out because it was the most heavily defended. Normandy was favored for the broad front it offered into central France.

The naval operations, led by British admiral Sir Bertram Ramsay, were described by historian Correlli Barnett as a "never surpassed masterpiece of planning" and involved a 6,939-strong invasion fleet. This consisted of 1,213 warships, 4,126 landing craft, 736 ancillary craft (including minesweepers), and 864 merchant vessels from eight different Allied navies, carrying 176,000 troops in all. German defenses consisted of around 50,000 troops and 170 artillery guns.

Allied planners identified the ideal conditions for the landings—low tide, clear skies, and a full moon—and suggested a window of June 5–7. Poor weather on June 5 delayed the landings by a day, but even so the seas remained rough when the invasion began in the early hours of June 6, 1944. A naval and aerial bombardment was followed by an airborne and amphibious assault by troops from the US, Britain, and Canada under the supreme command of US general Dwight D. Eisenhower.

THE DECEPTION PLAN

The Allies convinced Hitler that their attack would be centered on the Pas-de-Calais using a variety of methods. A bogus US 1st Army Group with fake tanks was created in south-east England. As the real invasion fleet headed for Normandy, naval launches headed to Calais and Boulogne towing barrage balloons to create radar echoes similar to those of troop ships. Dummy parachutists were also dropped in the area.

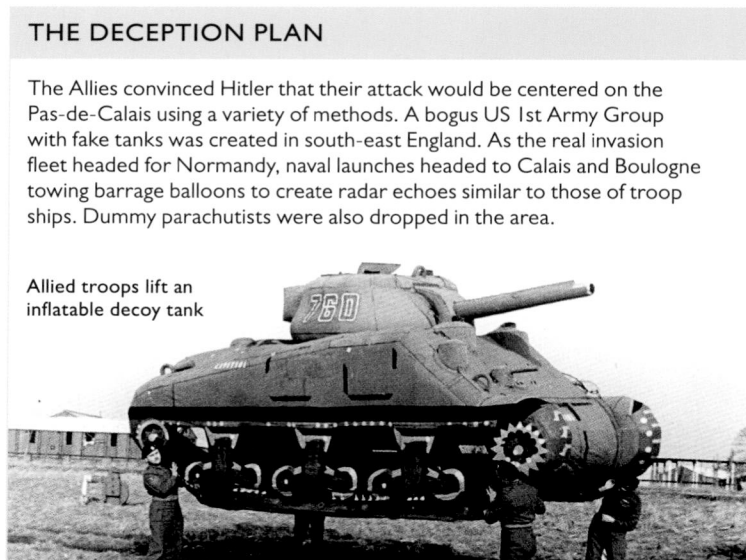

Allied troops lift an inflatable decoy tank

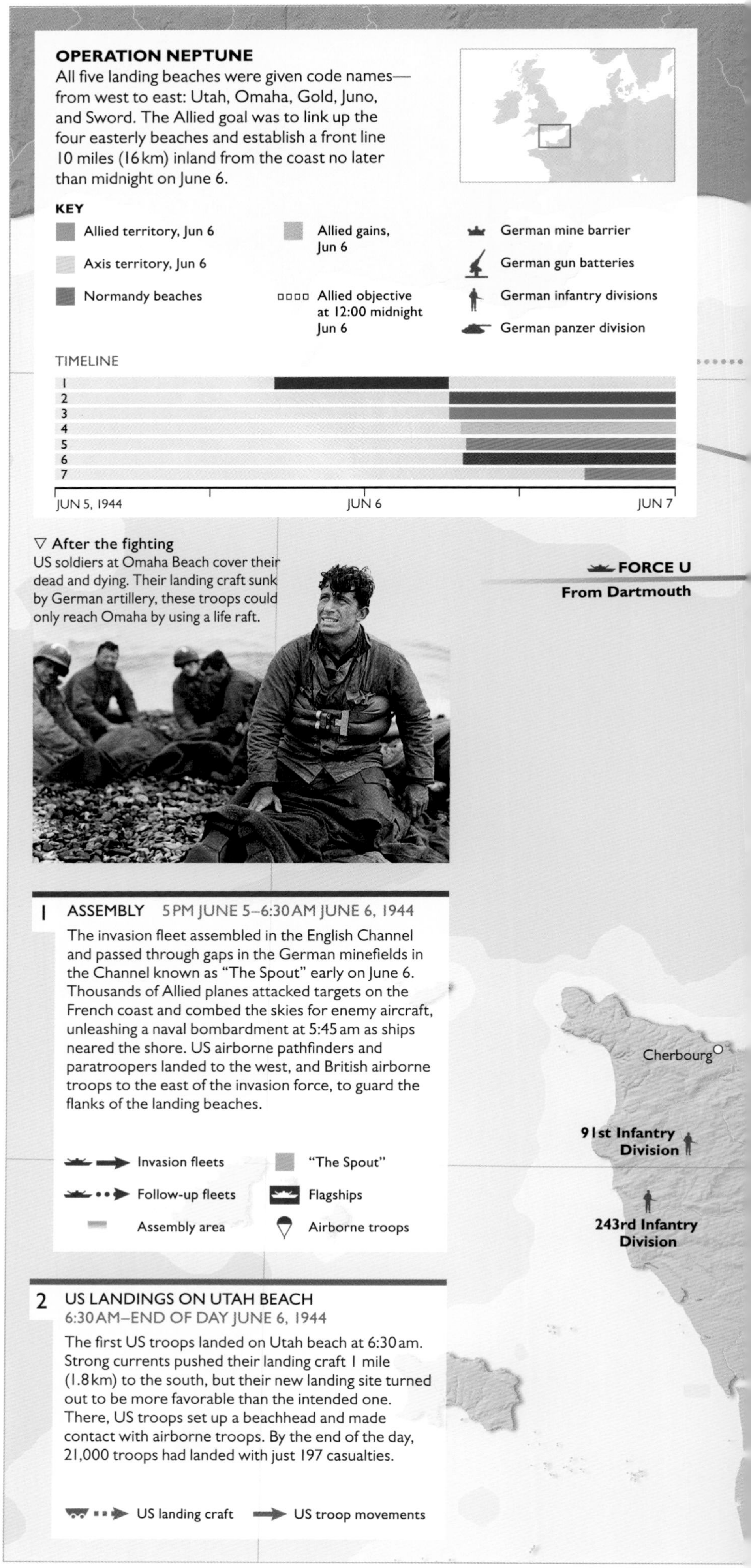

OPERATION NEPTUNE

All five landing beaches were given code names—from west to east: Utah, Omaha, Gold, Juno, and Sword. The Allied goal was to link up the four easterly beaches and establish a front line 10 miles (16km) inland from the coast no later than midnight on June 6.

KEY

- ◾ Allied territory, Jun 6
- ◾ Axis territory, Jun 6
- ◼ Normandy beaches
- ▨ Allied gains, Jun 6
- ⬚⬚⬚⬚ Allied objective at 12:00 midnight Jun 6
- 🪖 German mine barrier
- 🔫 German gun batteries
- 👤 German infantry divisions
- 🛡 German panzer division

TIMELINE

	JUN 5, 1944	JUN 6	JUN 7
1			
2			
3			
4			
5			
6			
7			

▽ **After the fighting**
US soldiers at Omaha Beach cover their dead and dying. Their landing craft sunk by German artillery, these troops could only reach Omaha by using a life raft.

FORCE U
From Dartmouth

1 ASSEMBLY 5PM JUNE 5–6:30AM JUNE 6, 1944

The invasion fleet assembled in the English Channel and passed through gaps in the German minefields in the Channel known as "The Spout" early on June 6. Thousands of Allied planes attacked targets on the French coast and combed the skies for enemy aircraft, unleashing a naval bombardment at 5:45 am as ships neared the shore. US airborne pathfinders and paratroopers landed to the west, and British airborne troops to the east of the invasion force, to guard the flanks of the landing beaches.

- ➤ Invasion fleets
- ⤍ Follow-up fleets
- ▬ Assembly area
- ▨ "The Spout"
- 🪖 Flagships
- ⦿ Airborne troops

Cherbourg ○

91st Infantry Division

243rd Infantry Division

2 US LANDINGS ON UTAH BEACH
6:30AM–END OF DAY JUNE 6, 1944

The first US troops landed on Utah beach at 6:30am. Strong currents pushed their landing craft 1 mile (1.8km) to the south, but their new landing site turned out to be more favorable than the intended one. There, US troops set up a beachhead and made contact with airborne troops. By the end of the day, 21,000 troops had landed with just 197 casualties.

- ⤍ US landing craft
- ➡ US troop movements

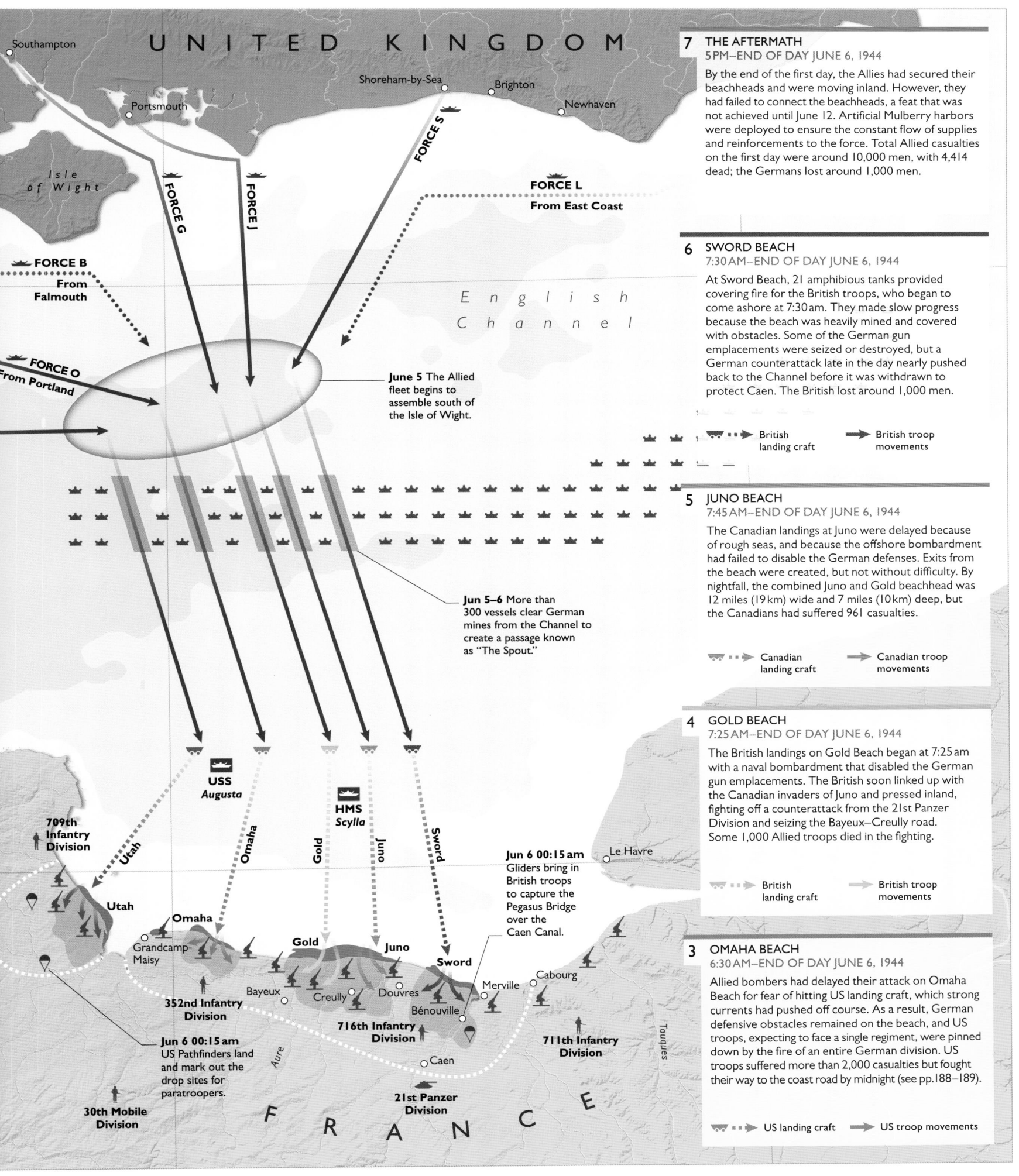

UNITED KINGDOM

Southampton

Portsmouth

Shoreham-by-Sea   Brighton

Newhaven

Isle of Wight

FORCE S

FORCE G

FORCE J

FORCE L
From East Coast

FORCE B
From Falmouth

English Channel

FORCE O
From Portland

June 5 The Allied fleet begins to assemble south of the Isle of Wight.

Jun 5–6 More than 300 vessels clear German mines from the Channel to create a passage known as "The Spout."

USS *Augusta*

HMS *Scylla*

709th Infantry Division

Utah

Omaha

Gold

Juno

Sword

Jun 6 00:15 am Gliders bring in British troops to capture the Pegasus Bridge over the Caen Canal.

Le Havre

Utah

Omaha

Gold

Juno

Sword

Grandcamp-Maisy

Bayeux

Creully

Douvres

Merville

Cabourg

Bénouville

352nd Infantry Division

716th Infantry Division

711th Infantry Division

Aure

Jun 6 00:15 am US Pathfinders land and mark out the drop sites for paratroopers.

30th Mobile Division

Caen

21st Panzer Division

Touques

FRANCE

---

7 THE AFTERMATH
5 PM–END OF DAY JUNE 6, 1944

By the end of the first day, the Allies had secured their beachheads and were moving inland. However, they had failed to connect the beachheads, a feat that was not achieved until June 12. Artificial Mulberry harbors were deployed to ensure the constant flow of supplies and reinforcements to the force. Total Allied casualties on the first day were around 10,000 men, with 4,414 dead; the Germans lost around 1,000 men.

6 SWORD BEACH
7:30 AM–END OF DAY JUNE 6, 1944

At Sword Beach, 21 amphibious tanks provided covering fire for the British troops, who began to come ashore at 7:30am. They made slow progress because the beach was heavily mined and covered with obstacles. Some of the German gun emplacements were seized or destroyed, but a German counterattack late in the day nearly pushed back to the Channel before it was withdrawn to protect Caen. The British lost around 1,000 men.

➤ British landing craft   ➤ British troop movements

5 JUNO BEACH
7:45 AM–END OF DAY JUNE 6, 1944

The Canadian landings at Juno were delayed because of rough seas, and because the offshore bombardment had failed to disable the German defenses. Exits from the beach were created, but not without difficulty. By nightfall, the combined Juno and Gold beachhead was 12 miles (19 km) wide and 7 miles (10 km) deep, but the Canadians had suffered 961 casualties.

➤ Canadian landing craft   ➤ Canadian troop movements

4 GOLD BEACH
7:25 AM–END OF DAY JUNE 6, 1944

The British landings on Gold Beach began at 7:25am with a naval bombardment that disabled the German gun emplacements. The British soon linked up with the Canadian invaders of Juno and pressed inland, fighting off a counterattack from the 21st Panzer Division and seizing the Bayeux–Creully road. Some 1,000 Allied troops died in the fighting.

➤ British landing craft   ➤ British troop movements

3 OMAHA BEACH
6:30 AM–END OF DAY JUNE 6, 1944

Allied bombers had delayed their attack on Omaha Beach for fear of hitting US landing craft, which strong currents had pushed off course. As a result, German defensive obstacles remained on the beach, and US troops, expecting to face a single regiment, were pinned down by the fire of an entire German division. US troops suffered more than 2,000 casualties but fought their way to the coast road by midnight (see pp.188–189).

➤ US landing craft   ➤ US troop movements

OMAHA BEACH

Of the five D-Day landings in Normandy on June 6, 1944, Omaha was the costliest for the Allies. Hampered by deep, rising water, and assaulted by heavy German fire from well-defended cliffs, around 2,400 US soldiers were killed or injured in the landing.

△ **Anti-tank mine**
The Normandy beaches were defended by mines such as this German T-42, devised to explode when a tank drove over it.

The US 1st and 29th Infantry Divisions were tasked with securing a beachhead 6 miles (10 km) long at Omaha beach, then linking up with other Allies landing at Utah beach to the west and Gold beach to the east.

The assault started at 6:35 am with a first wave of troops from the US 1st Infantry Division, but the operation did not go according to plan. The Allied bombers providing air cover missed their targets, and the naval gunfire was poorly directed. As soon as the landing craft hit the beach, the Germans defending the cliffs rained shell, mortar, and machine-gun fire on the US troops as they tried to disembark. Most of the amphibious tanks were swamped and sank in the heavy swell, as did the supporting artillery. Within minutes of the initial landing, one-third of the assault troops had become casualties. Lieutenant-General Omar N. Bradley had to make a snap decision on whether to continue the landings, or pull out and switch reinforcements to Utah beach. He chose to continue.

Gaining a foothold

The landing started to improve as the Americans, reinforced by a second wave from the 29th Infantry Division, slowly managed to move up the beach and toward the surrounding bluffs. A flotilla of Allied destroyers steamed close inshore to provide much-needed artillery support. By late afternoon, tanks and other vehicles were moving off the beach. Despite determined resistance by the German defenders, by the end of the day some 34,000 US troops had landed at Omaha beach and secured a beachhead.

COMMAND DIFFERENCES

The German response to the invasion was slowed by power struggles. Rommel (center) argued for a fight on the beaches, whereas Gerd von Rundstedt, his superior, planned for a counterattack when the Allies were ashore. However, the need for Hitler's permission delayed von Rundstedt's plan until the afternoon of D-Day.

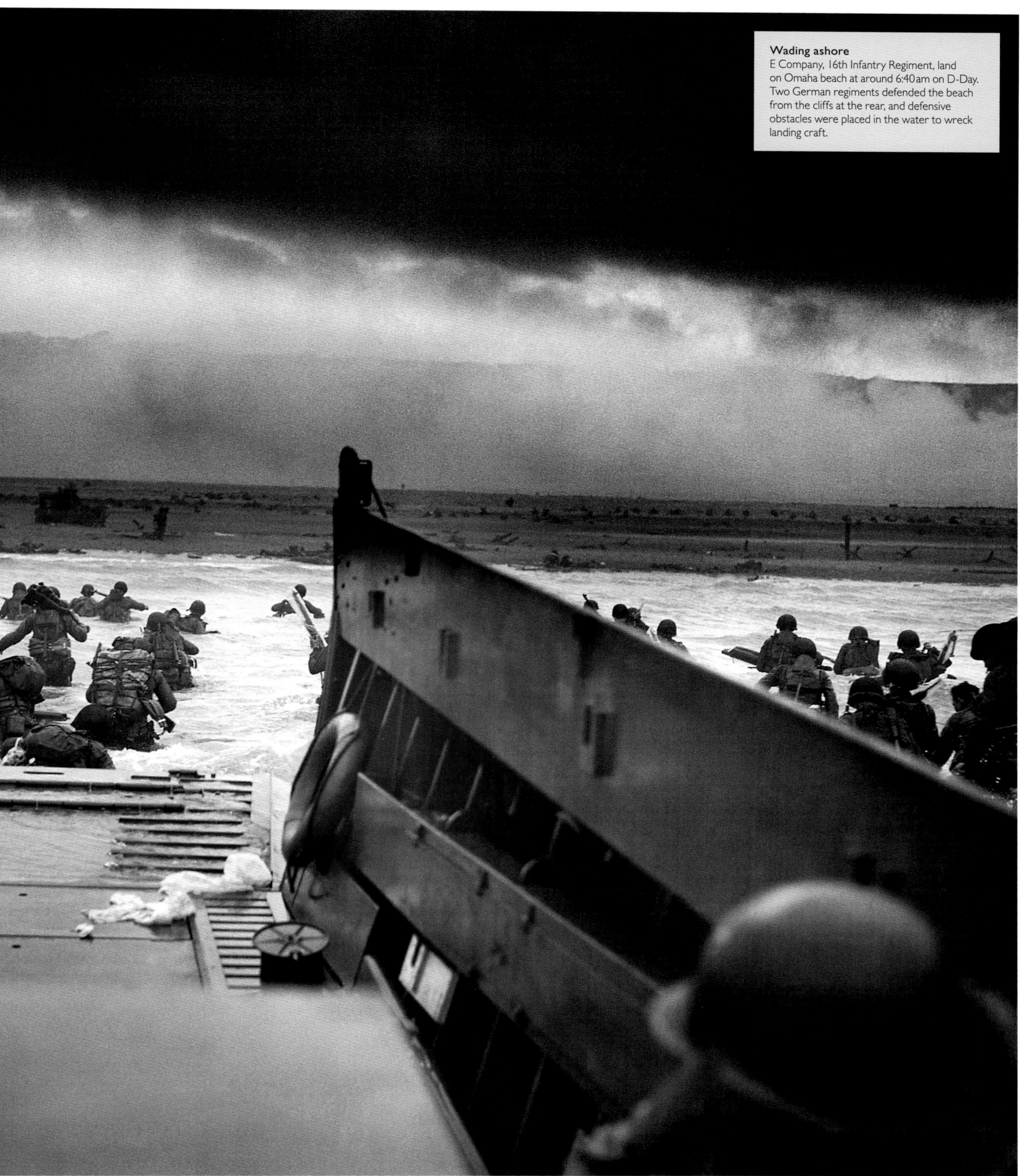

Wading ashore
E Company, 16th Infantry Regiment, land on Omaha beach at around 6:40 am on D-Day. Two German regiments defended the beach from the cliffs at the rear, and defensive obstacles were placed in the water to wreck landing craft.

Normandy bridgehead
This German situation map from August 1, 1944, shows the progress made by Allied forces (represented by red flags along the coast) by July 31, 1944. They have broken out of the bridgehead, but the advance is slowed by German defenses (shown as blue flags). Areas shaded in red show French resistance activities.

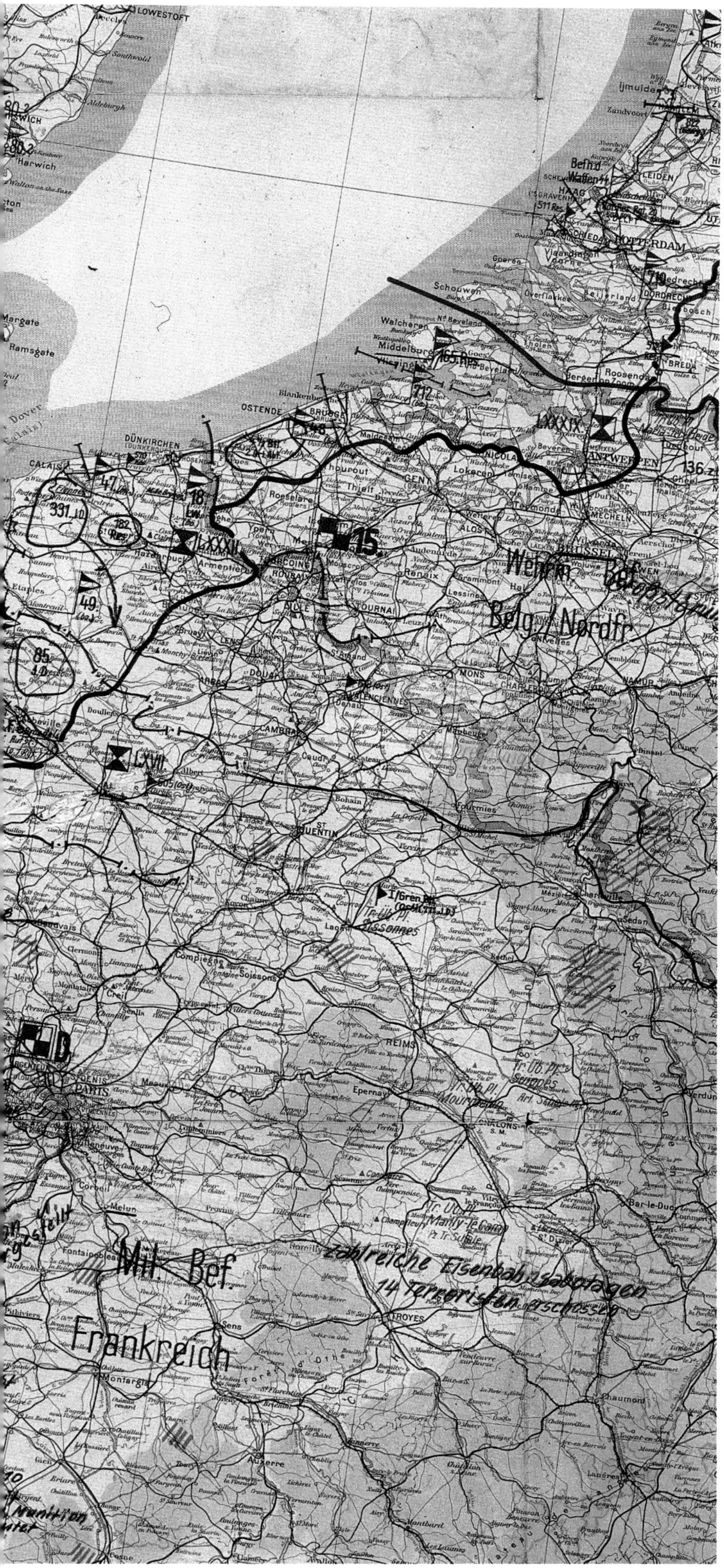

THE BATTLE OF NORMANDY

Some of the hardest fighting of the war took place in the two months after the D-Day landings. The Allies suffered around 100,000 casualties in a grueling struggle to break out of their bridgehead in Normandy.

The D-Day landings (see pp.186–187) put Allied troops ashore on the Normandy coast, but their progress inland stalled as elite panzer divisions rushed to Normandy, blocking their movement out of the bridgehead. The terrain favored the defenders, and bad weather reduced the effectiveness of Allied air power. According to Allied plans, the city of Caen, which is about 9 miles (14 km) from the coast, should have been swiftly captured by British and Canadian troops of the 2nd Army while the US 1st Army advanced west up the Cotentin Peninsula to seize the port of Cherbourg. In reality, the Americans did not take Cherbourg until three weeks after the landings and Caen was still firmly in German hands at the end of June. British general Bernard Montgomery, in command of Allied ground forces, was criticized by some US generals for the failure to make progress. A sense of crisis was also mounting on the German side; Hitler fired Field Marshal Gerd von Rundstedt as Commander-in-Chief West (headquartered with Army Group D in Paris) on July 1 after he called for a withdrawal from Normandy and an end to the war.

The Allied breakout

On July 18, after carpet-bombing by Allied air forces destroyed Caen and flattened much of its surrounding area, Montgomery launched Operation Goodwood, an offensive by three armored divisions east of the city. The British lost 300 tanks in the fighting and failed to break through the German lines. However, it drew the best German divisions away from the sector facing the US 1st Army. On July 25, the Americans launched Operation Cobra, overcoming much-weakened German resistance to break out toward Avranches. The US 3rd Army under General George Patton joined in the offensive, pouring through the gap opened in the enemy line. German tanks counterattacking on August 7 were destroyed by Allied ground-attack aircraft and US artillery. Much of the German army fleeing from Normandy escaped encirclement in the Falaise Pocket (see p.194–95), but the Allied path into France was now open.

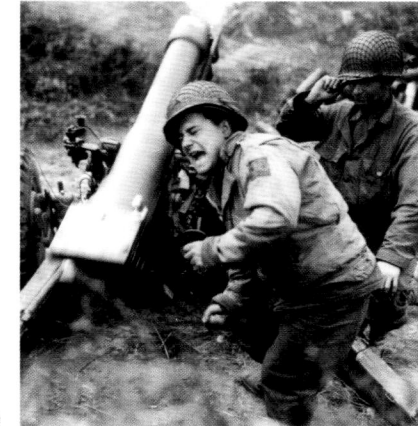

▷ **Heavy artillery**
US soldiers fire howitzer shells at German soldiers near the town of Carentan, on the Cotentin Peninsula.

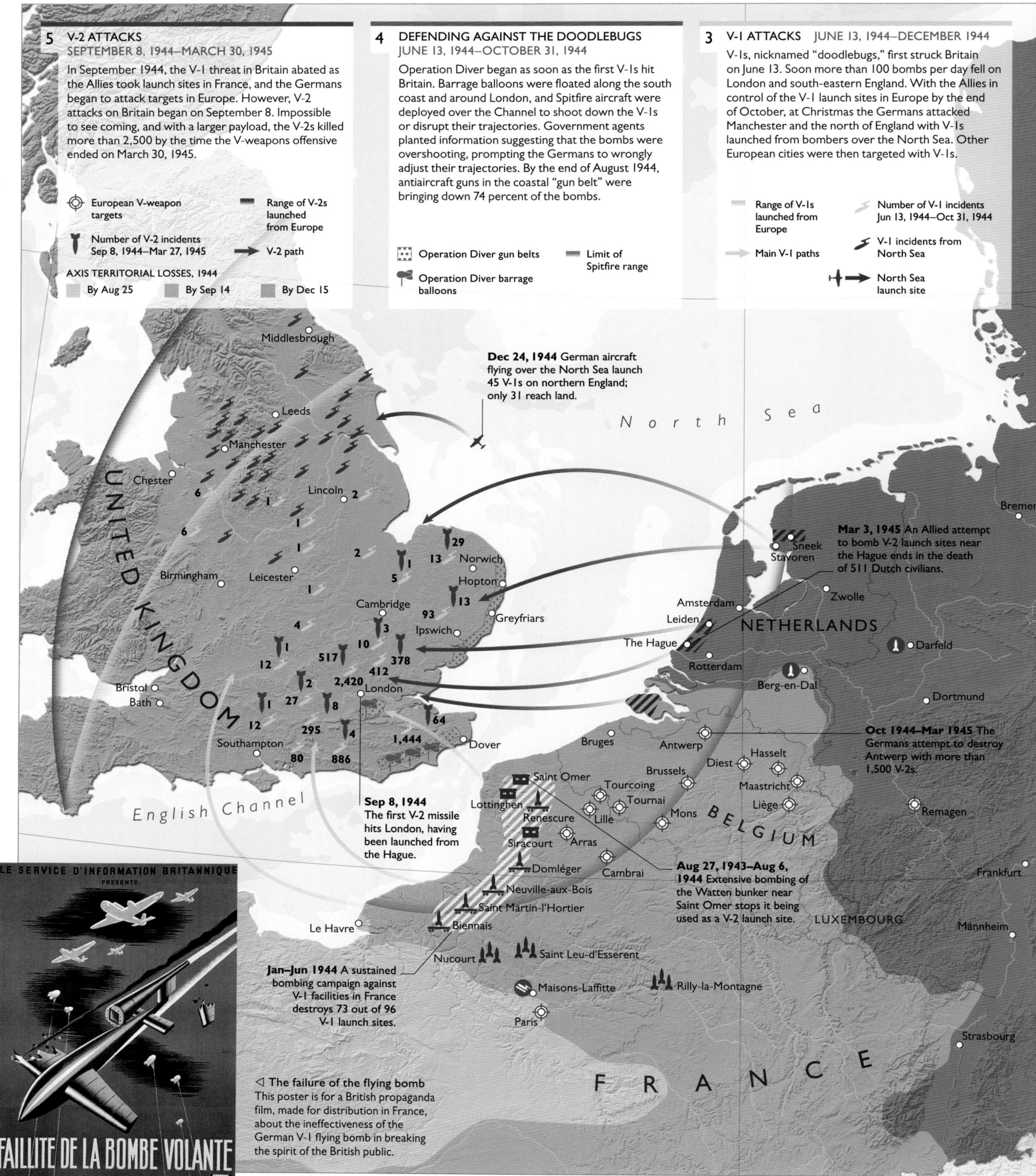

5 V-2 ATTACKS
SEPTEMBER 8, 1944–MARCH 30, 1945

In September 1944, the V-1 threat in Britain abated as the Allies took launch sites in France, and the Germans began to attack targets in Europe. However, V-2 attacks on Britain began on September 8. Impossible to see coming, and with a larger payload, the V-2s killed more than 2,500 by the time the V-weapons offensive ended on March 30, 1945.

- European V-weapon targets
- Number of V-2 incidents Sep 8, 1944–Mar 27, 1945
- Range of V-2s launched from Europe
- V-2 path

AXIS TERRITORIAL LOSSES, 1944
- By Aug 25
- By Sep 14
- By Dec 15

4 DEFENDING AGAINST THE DOODLEBUGS
JUNE 13, 1944–OCTOBER 31, 1944

Operation Diver began as soon as the first V-1s hit Britain. Barrage balloons were floated along the south coast and around London, and Spitfire aircraft were deployed over the Channel to shoot down the V-1s or disrupt their trajectories. Government agents planted information suggesting that the bombs were overshooting, prompting the Germans to wrongly adjust their trajectories. By the end of August 1944, antiaircraft guns in the coastal "gun belt" were bringing down 74 percent of the bombs.

- Operation Diver gun belts
- Operation Diver barrage balloons
- Limit of Spitfire range

3 V-1 ATTACKS   JUNE 13, 1944–DECEMBER 1944

V-1s, nicknamed "doodlebugs," first struck Britain on June 13. Soon more than 100 bombs per day fell on London and south-eastern England. With the Allies in control of the V-1 launch sites in Europe by the end of October, at Christmas the Germans attacked Manchester and the north of England with V-1s launched from bombers over the North Sea. Other European cities were then targeted with V-1s.

- Range of V-1s launched from Europe
- Main V-1 paths
- Number of V-1 incidents Jun 13, 1944–Oct 31, 1944
- V-1 incidents from North Sea
- North Sea launch site

Dec 24, 1944 German aircraft flying over the North Sea launch 45 V-1s on northern England; only 31 reach land.

Mar 3, 1945 An Allied attempt to bomb V-2 launch sites near the Hague ends in the death of 511 Dutch civilians.

Oct 1944–Mar 1945 The Germans attempt to destroy Antwerp with more than 1,500 V-2s.

Sep 8, 1944 The first V-2 missile hits London, having been launched from the Hague.

Aug 27, 1943–Aug 6, 1944 Extensive bombing of the Watten bunker near Saint Omer stops it being used as a V-2 launch site.

Jan–Jun 1944 A sustained bombing campaign against V-1 facilities in France destroys 73 out of 96 V-1 launch sites.

⊲ **The failure of the flying bomb** This poster is for a British propaganda film, made for distribution in France, about the ineffectiveness of the German V-1 flying bomb in breaking the spirit of the British public.

LE SERVICE D'INFORMATION BRITANNIQUE
PRÉSENTE:

FAILLITE DE LA BOMBE VOLANTE

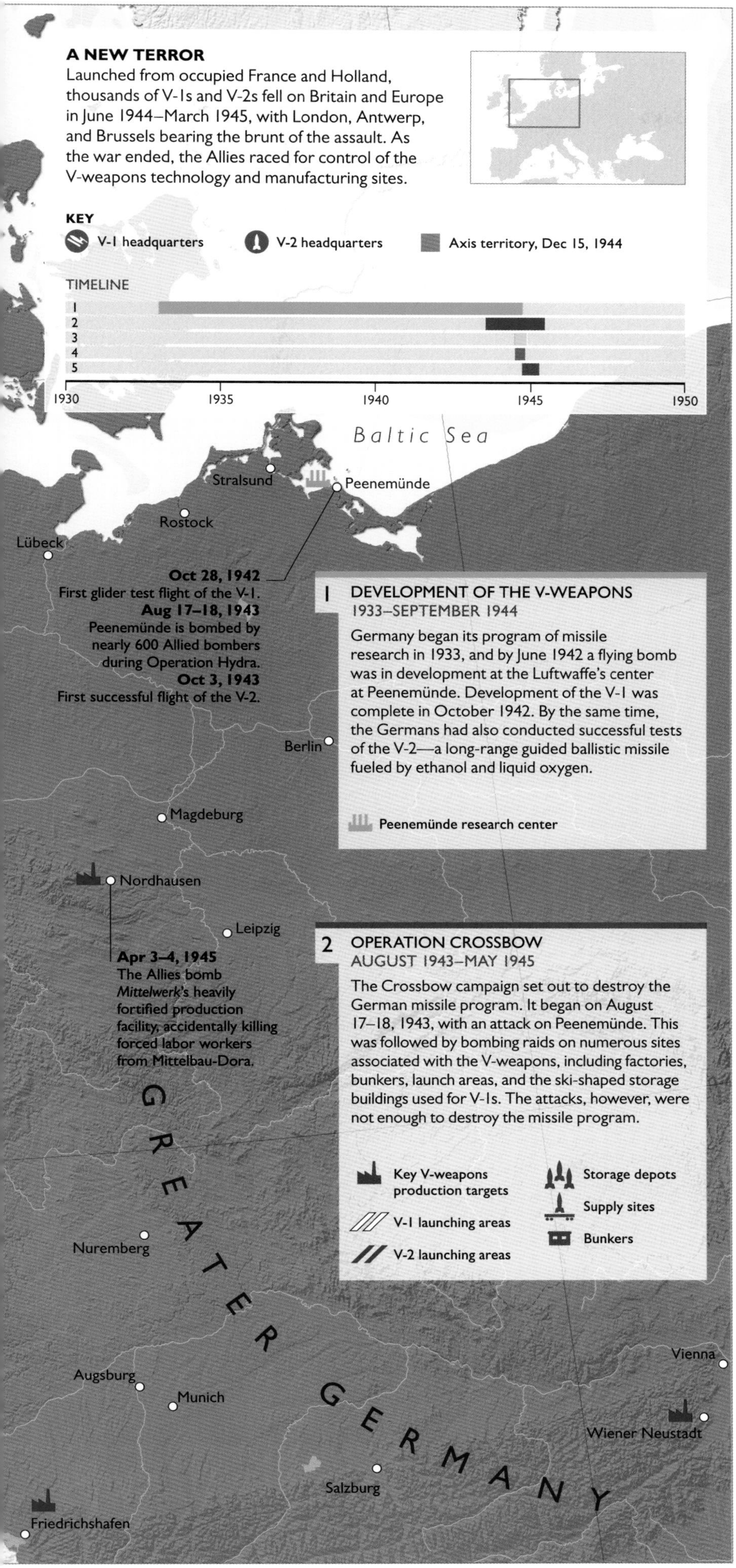

A NEW TERROR

Launched from occupied France and Holland, thousands of V-1s and V-2s fell on Britain and Europe in June 1944–March 1945, with London, Antwerp, and Brussels bearing the brunt of the assault. As the war ended, the Allies raced for control of the V-weapons technology and manufacturing sites.

KEY

⊘ V-1 headquarters ⬤ V-2 headquarters ▪ Axis territory, Dec 15, 1944

TIMELINE

```
1
2
3
4
5
1930      1935      1940      1945      1950
```

Baltic Sea

Stralsund — Peenemünde

Rostock

Lübeck

Oct 28, 1942
First glider test flight of the V-1.
Aug 17–18, 1943
Peenemünde is bombed by nearly 600 Allied bombers during Operation Hydra.
Oct 3, 1943
First successful flight of the V-2.

Berlin

Magdeburg

Nordhausen

Leipzig

Apr 3–4, 1945
The Allies bomb *Mittelwerk*'s heavily fortified production facility, accidentally killing forced labor workers from Mittelbau-Dora.

G R E A T E R   G E R M A N Y

Nuremberg

Augsburg

Munich

Salzburg

Vienna

Wiener Neustadt

Friedrichshafen

1 DEVELOPMENT OF THE V-WEAPONS
1933–SEPTEMBER 1944

Germany began its program of missile research in 1933, and by June 1942 a flying bomb was in development at the Luftwaffe's center at Peenemünde. Development of the V-1 was complete in October 1942. By the same time, the Germans had also conducted successful tests of the V-2—a long-range guided ballistic missile fueled by ethanol and liquid oxygen.

🏭 Peenemünde research center

2 OPERATION CROSSBOW
AUGUST 1943–MAY 1945

The Crossbow campaign set out to destroy the German missile program. It began on August 17–18, 1943, with an attack on Peenemünde. This was followed by bombing raids on numerous sites associated with the V-weapons, including factories, bunkers, launch areas, and the ski-shaped storage buildings used for V-1s. The attacks, however, were not enough to destroy the missile program.

🏭 Key V-weapons production targets

// V-1 launching areas

/// V-2 launching areas

🚀 Storage depots

⚓ Supply sites

▭ Bunkers

V-WEAPONS

In June 1944, the Germans began targeting Britain with new V-weapons (from *Vergeltungswaffen*, meaning "reprisal weapons" in response to Allied bombing). They succeeded—at first—in their goal of inflicting terror on the population and destroying infrastructure.

Rumors that Germany was developing long-range missiles were confirmed in 1943 when Polish intelligence agents smuggled details of the *Vergeltungswaffen* to the British. As well as terrorizing Allied civilians, these "wonder weapons" were intended to boost morale in Germany. The Allies responded with Operation Crossbow, intended to disrupt the production, transport, and launch of the weapons. Nevertheless, the first V-1 flying bombs fell on London in June 1944 and continued to affect a swathe of England throughout the summer. These simple steel and plywood missiles were powered by a pulse-jet that made a buzzing sound, which cut out when the bomb was about to fall. Thousands of Londoners fled the city, but they began to return when defensive countermeasures introduced in Operation Diver took effect, disabling or destroying nearly half of the 12,000 missiles fired. Those that did reach Britain caused 45,000 casualties.

The unleashing of the V-2—a large, fast, rocket-powered missile—in September 1944 added to the toll, both in Britain and in the cities targeted in Europe. As the Allies advanced through France to the Netherlands in March 1945, they knocked out German launch sites, and Europe was finally freed from the terror of the V-weapons.

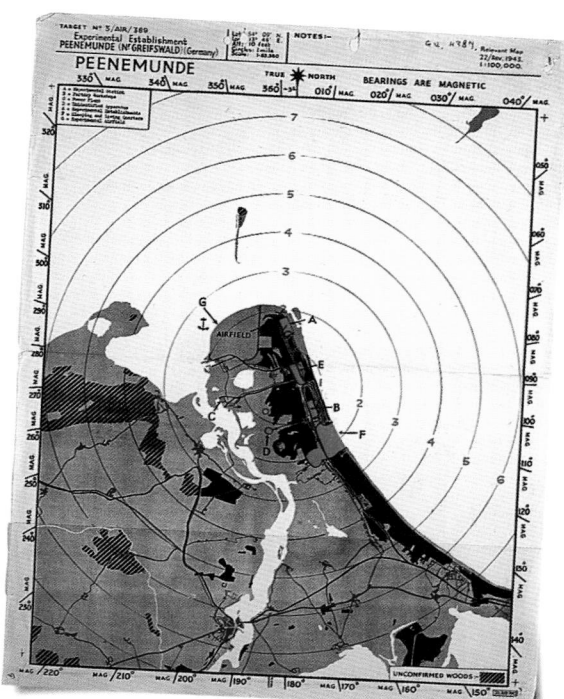

△ **The raid on Peenemünde**
This British map from 1943 shows the targets of Operation Hydra—the bombing raid on Peenemünde on the night of August 17–18, 1943. It forced the Germans to move V-2 production to the *Mittelwerk* factory.

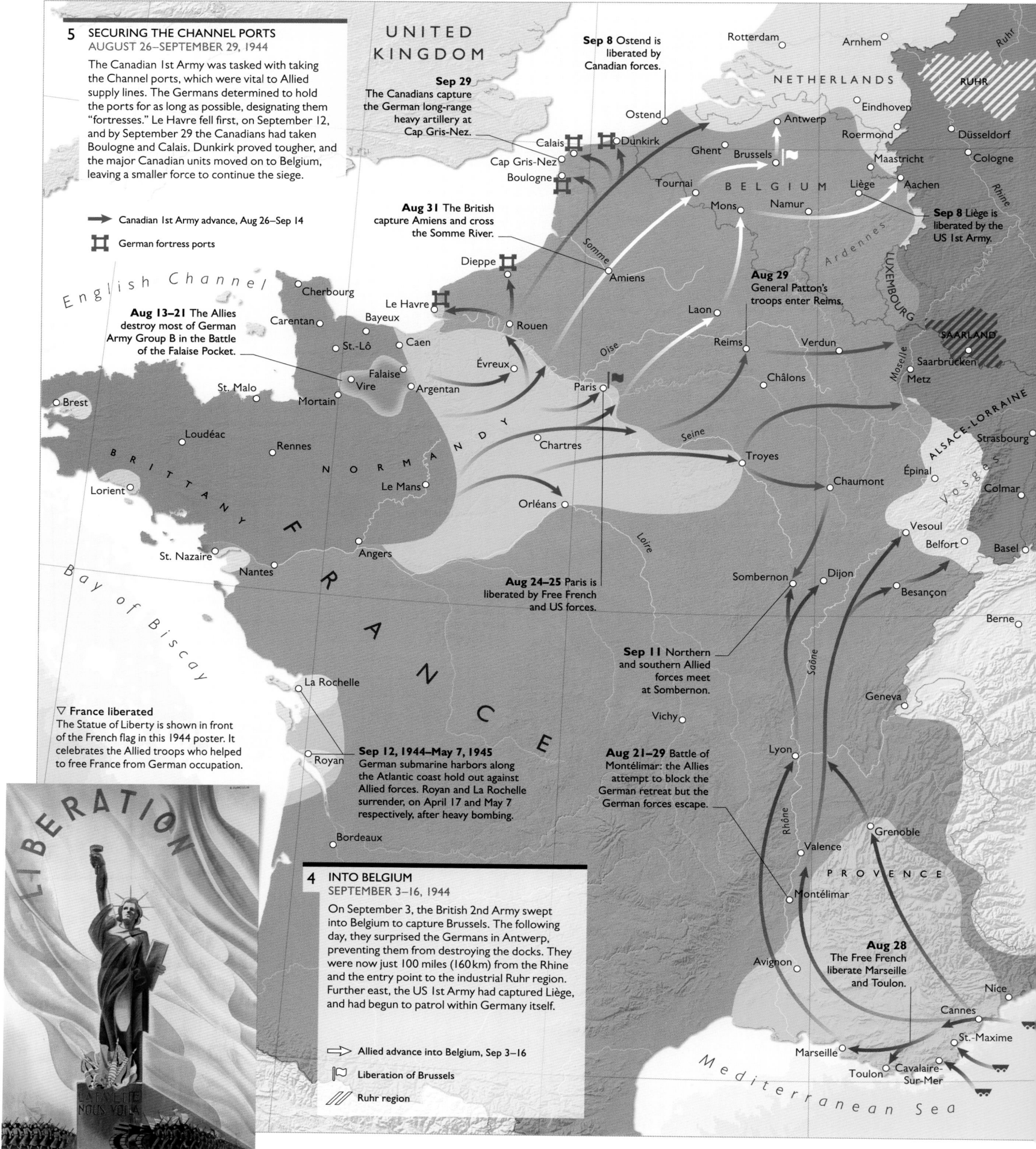

5 SECURING THE CHANNEL PORTS
AUGUST 26–SEPTEMBER 29, 1944

The Canadian 1st Army was tasked with taking the Channel ports, which were vital to Allied supply lines. The Germans determined to hold the ports for as long as possible, designating them "fortresses." Le Havre fell first, on September 12, and by September 29 the Canadians had taken Boulogne and Calais. Dunkirk proved tougher, and the major Canadian units moved on to Belgium, leaving a smaller force to continue the siege.

→ Canadian 1st Army advance, Aug 26–Sep 14

⊞ German fortress ports

Sep 29 The Canadians capture the German long-range heavy artillery at Cap Gris-Nez.

Sep 8 Ostend is liberated by Canadian forces.

Aug 31 The British capture Amiens and cross the Somme River.

Aug 13–21 The Allies destroy most of German Army Group B in the Battle of the Falaise Pocket.

Sep 8 Liège is liberated by the US 1st Army.

Aug 29 General Patton's troops enter Reims.

Aug 24–25 Paris is liberated by Free French and US forces.

Sep 11 Northern and southern Allied forces meet at Sombernon.

Sep 12, 1944–May 7, 1945 German submarine harbors along the Atlantic coast hold out against Allied forces. Royan and La Rochelle surrender, on April 17 and May 7 respectively, after heavy bombing.

Aug 21–29 Battle of Montélimar: the Allies attempt to block the German retreat but the German forces escape.

Aug 28 The Free French liberate Marseille and Toulon.

▽ **France liberated**
The Statue of Liberty is shown in front of the French flag in this 1944 poster. It celebrates the Allied troops who helped to free France from German occupation.

4 INTO BELGIUM
SEPTEMBER 3–16, 1944

On September 3, the British 2nd Army swept into Belgium to capture Brussels. The following day, they surprised the Germans in Antwerp, preventing them from destroying the docks. They were now just 100 miles (160km) from the Rhine and the entry point to the industrial Ruhr region. Further east, the US 1st Army had captured Liège, and had begun to patrol within Germany itself.

⇨ Allied advance into Belgium, Sep 3–16

⚑ Liberation of Brussels

/// Ruhr region

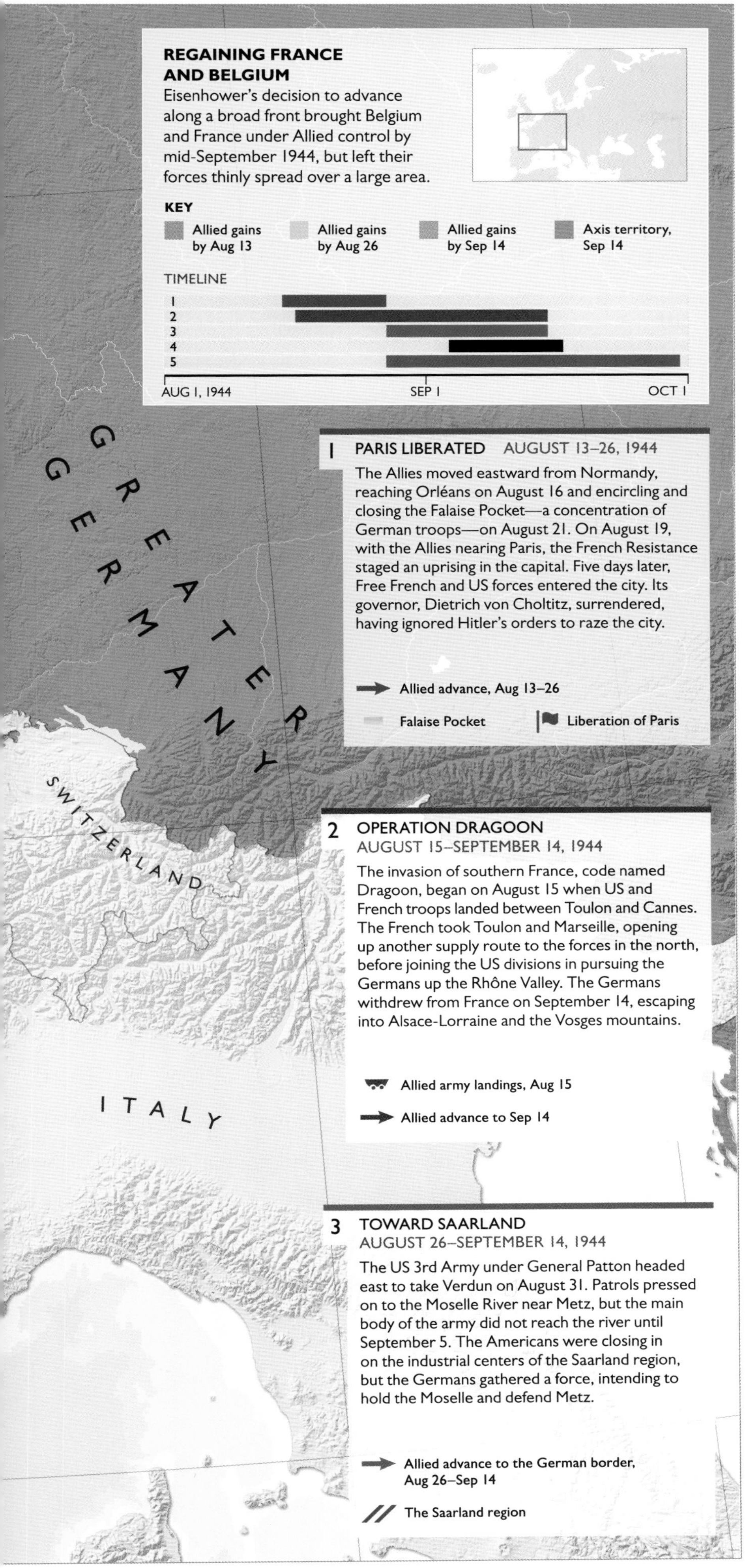

REGAINING FRANCE AND BELGIUM

Eisenhower's decision to advance along a broad front brought Belgium and France under Allied control by mid-September 1944, but left their forces thinly spread over a large area.

KEY

Allied gains by Aug 13	Allied gains by Aug 26	Allied gains by Sep 14	Axis territory, Sep 14

TIMELINE

1
2
3
4
5

AUG 1, 1944   SEP 1   OCT 1

GREATER GERMANY

SWITZERLAND

ITALY

1 PARIS LIBERATED AUGUST 13–26, 1944

The Allies moved eastward from Normandy, reaching Orléans on August 16 and encircling and closing the Falaise Pocket—a concentration of German troops—on August 21. On August 19, with the Allies nearing Paris, the French Resistance staged an uprising in the capital. Five days later, Free French and US forces entered the city. Its governor, Dietrich von Choltitz, surrendered, having ignored Hitler's orders to raze the city.

→ Allied advance, Aug 13–26

▭ Falaise Pocket   ⚑ Liberation of Paris

2 OPERATION DRAGOON AUGUST 15–SEPTEMBER 14, 1944

The invasion of southern France, code named Dragoon, began on August 15 when US and French troops landed between Toulon and Cannes. The French took Toulon and Marseille, opening up another supply route to the forces in the north, before joining the US divisions in pursuing the Germans up the Rhône Valley. The Germans withdrew from France on September 14, escaping into Alsace-Lorraine and the Vosges mountains.

⬛ Allied army landings, Aug 15

→ Allied advance to Sep 14

3 TOWARD SAARLAND AUGUST 26–SEPTEMBER 14, 1944

The US 3rd Army under General Patton headed east to take Verdun on August 31. Patrols pressed on to the Moselle River near Metz, but the main body of the army did not reach the river until September 5. The Americans were closing in on the industrial centers of the Saarland region, but the Germans gathered a force, intending to hold the Moselle and defend Metz.

→ Allied advance to the German border, Aug 26–Sep 14

// The Saarland region

THE BREAKOUT

Within three months of the D-Day landings, the Allies had broken out of Normandy, liberating France and most of Belgium. They swept eastward to reach the German border by the middle of September. However, a hard fight lay ahead.

In August, the Allied breakout from Normandy developed into a rout as their forces spread east, chasing the Germans from northern France. By the end of the month, they had cleared Brittany, reached the Loire, and moved as far as Troyes to the east. Paris was liberated, having been under Nazi control since June 1940, and General de Gaulle was installed in the city. Meanwhile, a French and US force had landed in Provence and begun to drive the Germans from the south.

The Allies disagreed on how best to proceed. British Field Marshal Bernard Montgomery wished to advance on a narrow front and push north-east through Belgium to reach the Ruhr Valley. However, US General Dwight Eisenhower—Supreme Commander of the Allied forces in Europe—rejected Montgomery's plan, favoring a "broad front" strategy in which troops would be deployed along the entire Western Front before driving into Germany. By mid-September, the Allies were stretched across a front from Antwerp in the north to the Swiss border near Belfort in the south. The British were poised to make a dramatic attempt to invade Germany through the Netherlands (see pp.198–199), while the US forces were within touching distance of the economically vital Saarland and Ruhr regions. However, both faced increasing German resistance.

> *"Steady, Monty. You can't speak to me like that. I'm your boss."*
>
> EISENHOWER TO MONTGOMERY, SEPTEMBER 10, 1944

THE RED BALL EXPRESS

For 83 days, from August 25 to November 16, 1944, convoys of trucks emblazoned with red balls and driven predominantly by African Americans carried food, fuel, and munitions along the road from Cherbourg to the Allied logistics base at Chartres. At its peak, the Red Ball Express operated nearly 6,000 vehicles, carrying 12,500 tons (11,300 metric tons) of supplies each day. The convoy system was abandoned once the port of Antwerp and the French railroad lines were re-opened and fuel pipes installed.

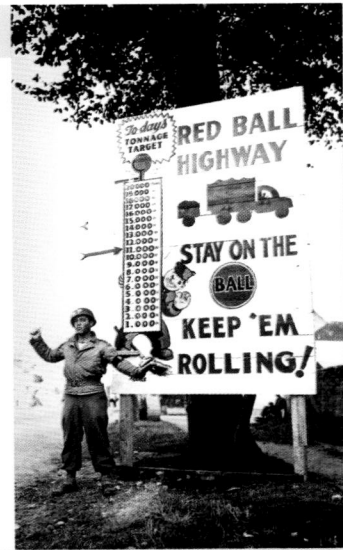

A US soldier on the Red Ball Highway

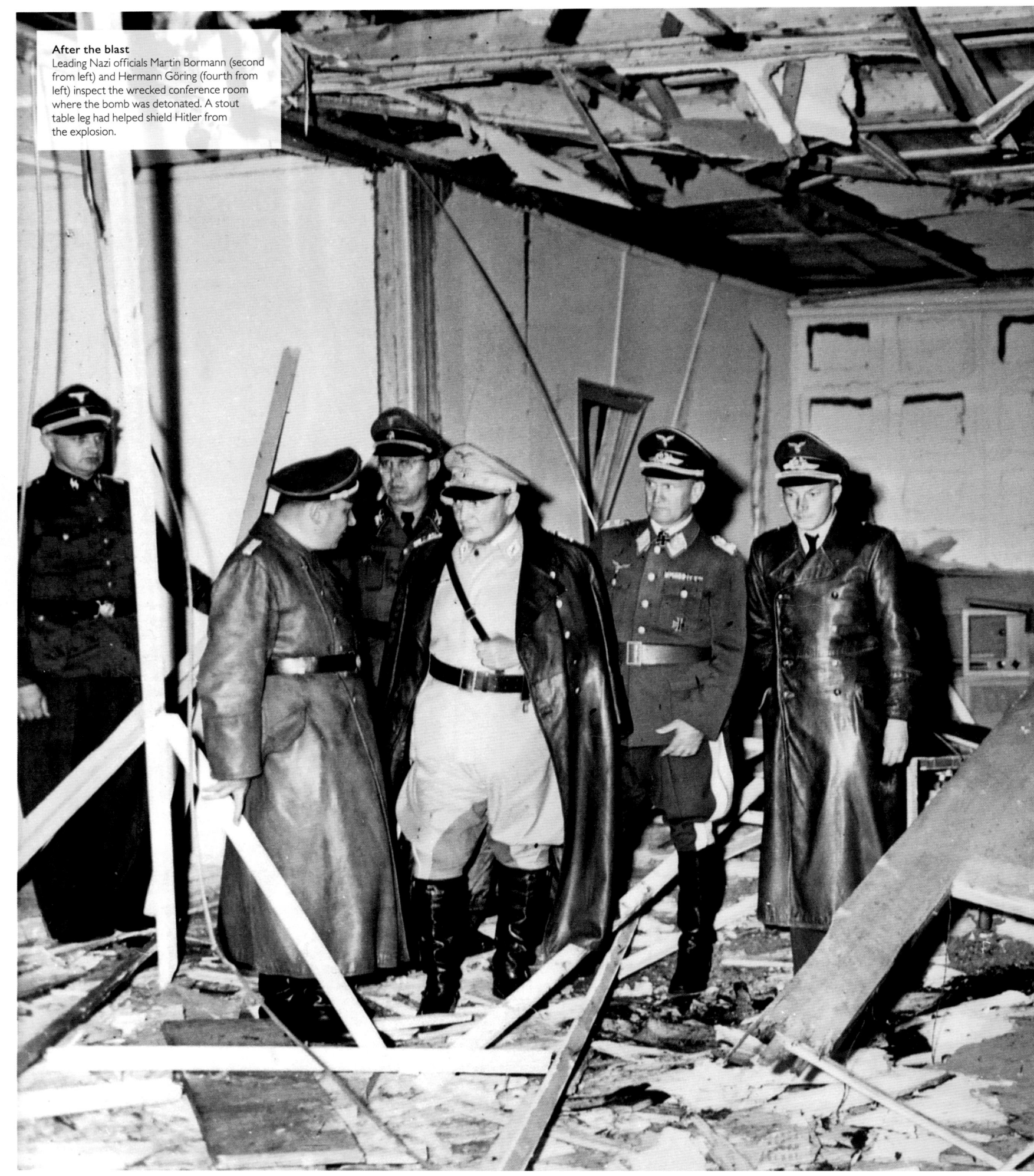

After the blast
Leading Nazi officials Martin Bormann (second from left) and Hermann Göring (fourth from left) inspect the wrecked conference room where the bomb was detonated. A stout table leg had helped shield Hitler from the explosion.

THE PLOT TO KILL HITLER

As the Allies drew closer on two fronts, within Germany a hostile faction plotted to overthrow Hitler and make peace. On July 20, 1944, there was an assassination attempt that came close to success.

Planned by a group of senior German military officers, the July Plot was set in motion when Colonel Claus von Stauffenberg planted a briefcase-bomb in a meeting at the "Wolf's Lair," Hitler's field headquarters in East Prussia. After the bomb went off, Stauffenberg flew to Berlin to claim that the SS had assassinated Hitler and order the German Replacement Army to overthrow the Nazi regime. However, Hitler was not dead. Although three other Nazis were killed, Hitler suffered only minor injuries.

△ **Key plotter**
After being severely injured in Tunisia in 1943, Stauffenberg joined other conspirators to save Germany from destruction.

The conspiracy fails

Not realizing that Hitler was still alive, the conspirators instructed the Replacement Army to arrest various officials; meanwhile, counter-orders were given by Hitler. When Major Otto Remer, acting on the conspirators' orders, arrived to arrest the Propaganda Minister Joseph Goebbels, he was informed by Goebbels that the Führer was still alive. To prove his point, Goebbels phoned Hitler, who spoke to Remer and ordered that he crush the rebellion immediately. Remer's troops moved on the War Ministry, where, after a brief gun battle, the conspirators surrendered. The leading figures were sentenced to death, with Stauffenberg shot that same evening.

▷ **Living to tell the tale**
Hitler greets Joseph Goebbels only hours after surviving the bomb blast that was intended to assassinate him. Following the attempted coup, more than 7,000 alleged conspirators were arrested; up to 5,000 ended up dead, either executed or forced to commit suicide.

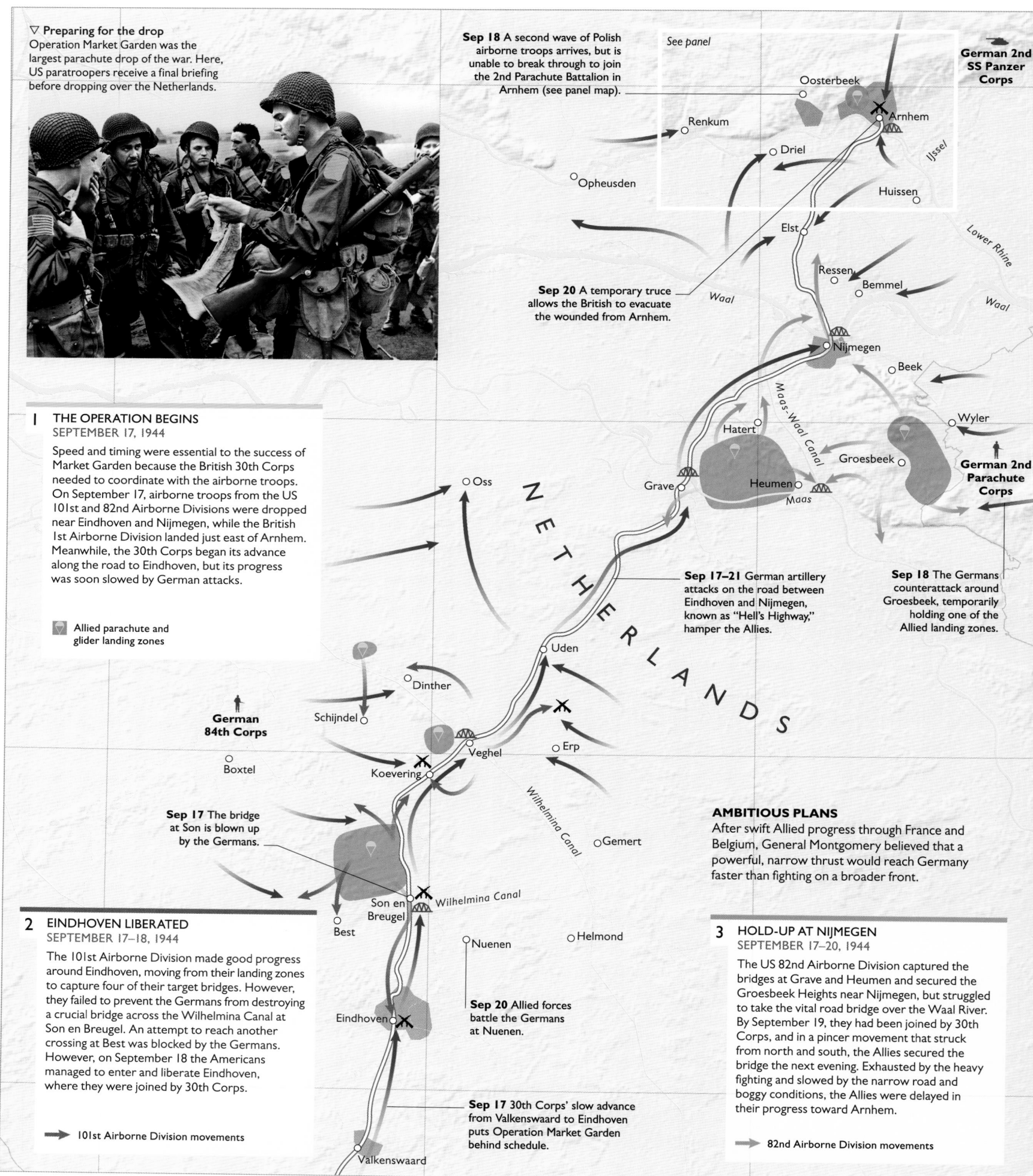

▽ **Preparing for the drop**
Operation Market Garden was the largest parachute drop of the war. Here, US paratroopers receive a final briefing before dropping over the Netherlands.

Sep 18 A second wave of Polish airborne troops arrives, but is unable to break through to join the 2nd Parachute Battalion in Arnhem (see panel map).

See panel

German 2nd SS Panzer Corps

Oosterbeek

Renkum

Driel

Arnhem

IJssel

Opheusden

Huissen

Elst

Ressen

Lower Rhine

Sep 20 A temporary truce allows the British to evacuate the wounded from Arnhem.

Bemmel

Waal

Waal

Nijmegen

Beek

1 THE OPERATION BEGINS
SEPTEMBER 17, 1944

Speed and timing were essential to the success of Market Garden because the British 30th Corps needed to coordinate with the airborne troops. On September 17, airborne troops from the US 101st and 82nd Airborne Divisions were dropped near Eindhoven and Nijmegen, while the British 1st Airborne Division landed just east of Arnhem. Meanwhile, the 30th Corps began its advance along the road to Eindhoven, but its progress was soon slowed by German attacks.

Maas-Waal Canal

Hatert

Wyler

Groesbeek

German 2nd Parachute Corps

Oss

Grave

Heumen

Maas

Sep 17–21 German artillery attacks on the road between Eindhoven and Nijmegen, known as "Hell's Highway," hamper the Allies.

Sep 18 The Germans counterattack around Groesbeek, temporarily holding one of the Allied landing zones.

 Allied parachute and glider landing zones

NETHERLANDS

Uden

Dinther

German 84th Corps

Schijndel

Boxtel

Koevering

Veghel

Erp

Wilhelmina Canal

Gemert

AMBITIOUS PLANS
After swift Allied progress through France and Belgium, General Montgomery believed that a powerful, narrow thrust would reach Germany faster than fighting on a broader front.

Sep 17 The bridge at Son is blown up by the Germans.

Son en Breugel

Wilhelmina Canal

Best

Nuenen

Helmond

2 EINDHOVEN LIBERATED
SEPTEMBER 17–18, 1944

The 101st Airborne Division made good progress around Eindhoven, moving from their landing zones to capture four of their target bridges. However, they failed to prevent the Germans from destroying a crucial bridge across the Wilhelmina Canal at Son en Breugel. An attempt to reach another crossing at Best was blocked by the Germans. However, on September 18 the Americans managed to enter and liberate Eindhoven, where they were joined by 30th Corps.

Sep 20 Allied forces battle the Germans at Nuenen.

Eindhoven

3 HOLD-UP AT NIJMEGEN
SEPTEMBER 17–20, 1944

The US 82nd Airborne Division captured the bridges at Grave and Heumen and secured the Groesbeek Heights near Nijmegen, but struggled to take the vital road bridge over the Waal River. By September 19, they had been joined by 30th Corps, and in a pincer movement that struck from north and south, the Allies secured the bridge the next evening. Exhausted by the heavy fighting and slowed by the narrow road and boggy conditions, the Allies were delayed in their progress toward Arnhem.

→ 101st Airborne Division movements

Sep 17 30th Corps' slow advance from Valkenswaard to Eindhoven puts Operation Market Garden behind schedule.

Valkenswaard

→ 82nd Airborne Division movements

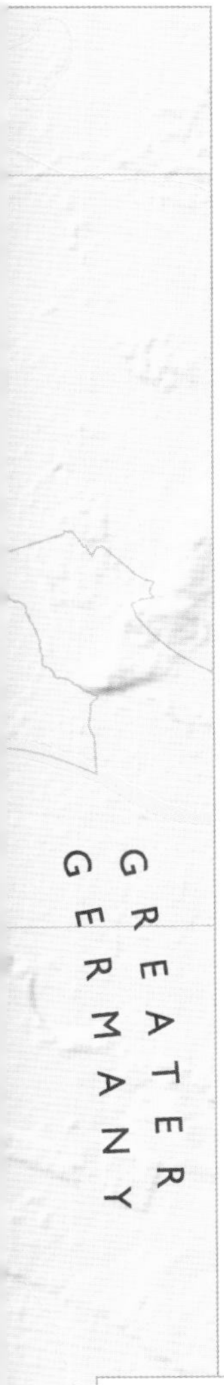

OPERATION MARKET GARDEN

In one of the boldest plans of the war, the Allies dropped thousands of troops behind enemy lines in the Netherlands, near the German border. This operation—designated Market Garden—aimed to clear a path for the Allies into Germany, but it turned out to be a costly failure.

By mid-September 1944, the Allies—sensing stiffening resistance—were desperate to break through into Germany. In a hastily conceived plan, Field Marshal Montgomery believed that he could push through the Netherlands and into Germany, bypassing the heavily defended Westwall, or Siegfried Line (see pp.200–201). On September 17–18, 35,000 airborne troops were delivered by glider and parachute to around Nijmegen, Eindhoven, and Arnhem. Their task was to secure bridges along the road between these cities; the British 30th Corps would then advance over this route and cross the Lower Rhine at Arnhem, after which the Allies would have easy access into Germany's industrial heartland in the Ruhr.

However, the Allies never managed to take the bridge over the Rhine at Arnhem, and after a week of bitter fighting, in which over 1,000 Allied troops died, they were forced to evacuate. Market Garden failed, wasting resources that would have been invaluable over the coming months, when the Allies tackled German defenses over a broader front.

A FLAWED PLAN

Montgomery planned to secure the bridges along the road from Eindhoven to Arnhem with airborne troops, creating a safe corridor for his ground forces. He anticipated little resistance.

KEY

→ Main German attacks

🚶🚗 German forces

➡ Advance of 30th Corps ground forces

▭ Road from Eindhoven to Arnhem

⩍ Key bridges

✕ Major battles

▨ Key urban areas

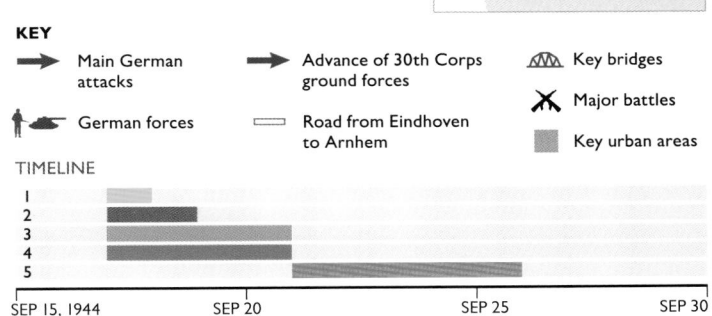

TIMELINE

1
2
3
4
5

SEP 15, 1944   SEP 20   SEP 25   SEP 30

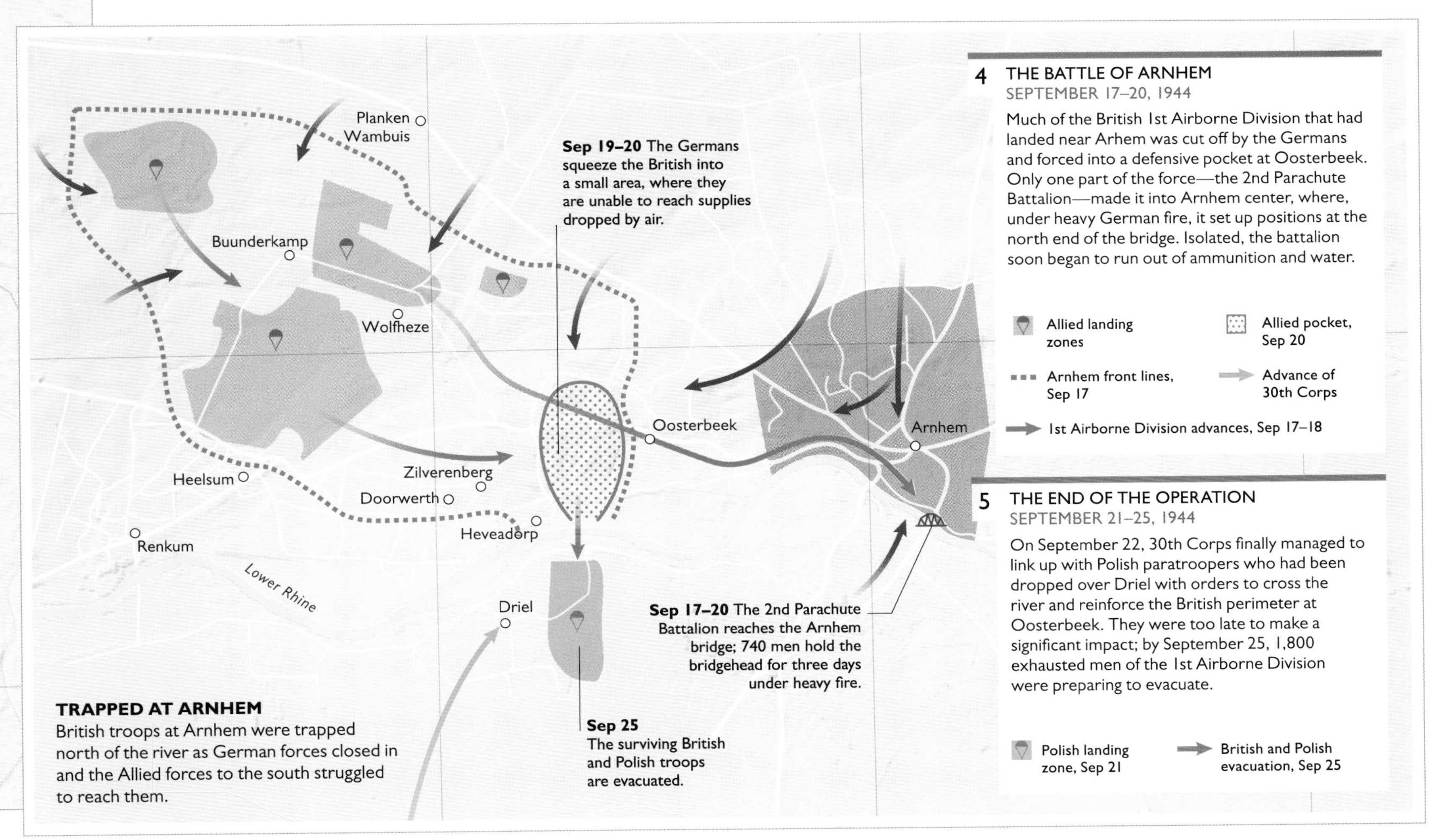

---

4 THE BATTLE OF ARNHEM
SEPTEMBER 17–20, 1944

Much of the British 1st Airborne Division that had landed near Arhem was cut off by the Germans and forced into a defensive pocket at Oosterbeek. Only one part of the force—the 2nd Parachute Battalion—made it into Arnhem center, where, under heavy German fire, it set up positions at the north end of the bridge. Isolated, the battalion soon began to run out of ammunition and water.

⬙ Allied landing zones

⬚ Allied pocket, Sep 20

∙∙∙ Arnhem front lines, Sep 17

⇨ Advance of 30th Corps

➡ 1st Airborne Division advances, Sep 17–18

Sep 19–20 The Germans squeeze the British into a small area, where they are unable to reach supplies dropped by air.

Planken
Wambuis

Buunderkamp

Wolfheze

Oosterbeek

Arnhem

Zilverenberg

Heelsum

Doorwerth

Heveadorp

Renkum

Lower Rhine

Driel

Sep 17–20 The 2nd Parachute Battalion reaches the Arnhem bridge; 740 men hold the bridgehead for three days under heavy fire.

5 THE END OF THE OPERATION
SEPTEMBER 21–25, 1944

On September 22, 30th Corps finally managed to link up with Polish paratroopers who had been dropped over Driel with orders to cross the river and reinforce the British perimeter at Oosterbeek. They were too late to make a significant impact; by September 25, 1,800 exhausted men of the 1st Airborne Division were preparing to evacuate.

⬙ Polish landing zone, Sep 21

➡ British and Polish evacuation, Sep 25

TRAPPED AT ARNHEM

British troops at Arnhem were trapped north of the river as German forces closed in and the Allied forces to the south struggled to reach them.

Sep 25
The surviving British and Polish troops are evacuated.

GREATER GERMANY

BATTLES AT GERMANY'S GATE

Weary from the Battle of Normandy and their advance across France, the Allies faced organized German resistance as they tried to cross the German border in late 1944. Although they made gains in Alsace–Lorraine and in Germany itself, exhausting campaigns in the Scheldt and Hürtgen Forest depleted their forces.

In Operation Market Garden (see pp.198–199) the Allies had failed to cross the Rhine and to establish an invasion route into Germany. This, together with their severely overstretched supply lines, lost the Allies the initiative they had won after their breakout from Normandy (see pp.194–195) and so their chances of bringing the war to an end in 1944. Instead, they spent the fall and early winter trying to breach German defenses along the borders in Belgium, the Netherlands, and France.

After a grueling battle, the Allies cleared the German defenses on the Scheldt Estuary in the Netherlands, opening up the port of Antwerp in Belgium as a supply route for their forces. However, to reach the Rhine River, the Allies now had to contend

with two formidable deterrents: the Westwall (or Siegfried Line), a 373-mile (600-km) German defensive line of bunkers, tank traps, and tunnels; and the increasingly cold, wet weather.

The US 7th Army and French 1st Army met with success on the southern end of the front, advancing toward the German industrial region of the Saarland and reducing the Germans in eastern France to a small pocket around Colmar; and the Canadians and British succeeded in bringing Antwerp back into operation. However, the Allies' aim to reach the Ruhr Valley, Germany's most economically important region, was hampered when the US 1st Army was defeated and suffered more than 33,000 casualties in a long battle in the Hürtgen Forest.

> *"In Hürtgen they just froze up hard; and it was so cold they froze up with ruddy faces."*
>
> ERNEST HEMINGWAY, *ACROSS THE RIVER AND INTO THE TREES*, 1950

▷ **Fallen bunker**
This bunker on Germany's Westwall defensive line has been destroyed by Allied armor-piercing weapons. In 1944, Hitler ordered a large-scale reinforcement of the line, but the bunkers became vulnerable to newly-developed Allied weaponry.

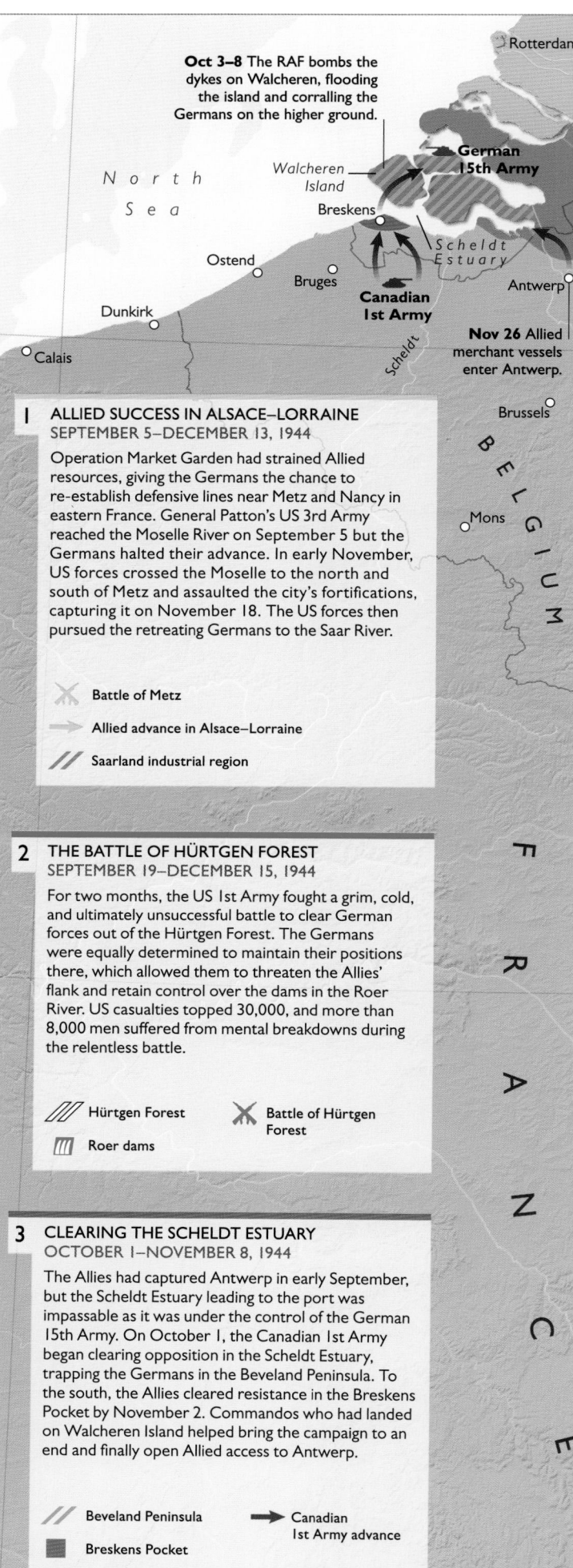

Oct 3–8 The RAF bombs the dykes on Walcheren, flooding the island and corralling the Germans on the higher ground.

Nov 26 Allied merchant vessels enter Antwerp.

North Sea · Rotterdam · Walcheren Island · German 15th Army · Breskens · Scheldt Estuary · Ostend · Bruges · Antwerp · Canadian 1st Army · Dunkirk · Calais · Scheldt · Brussels · BELGIUM · Mons · FRANCE

1 · ALLIED SUCCESS IN ALSACE–LORRAINE
SEPTEMBER 5–DECEMBER 13, 1944

Operation Market Garden had strained Allied resources, giving the Germans the chance to re-establish defensive lines near Metz and Nancy in eastern France. General Patton's US 3rd Army reached the Moselle River on September 5 but the Germans halted their advance. In early November, US forces crossed the Moselle to the north and south of Metz and assaulted the city's fortifications, capturing it on November 18. The US forces then pursued the retreating Germans to the Saar River.

✗ Battle of Metz

→ Allied advance in Alsace–Lorraine

/// Saarland industrial region

2 · THE BATTLE OF HÜRTGEN FOREST
SEPTEMBER 19–DECEMBER 15, 1944

For two months, the US 1st Army fought a grim, cold, and ultimately unsuccessful battle to clear German forces out of the Hürtgen Forest. The Germans were equally determined to maintain their positions there, which allowed them to threaten the Allies' flank and retain control over the dams in the Roer River. US casualties topped 30,000, and more than 8,000 men suffered from mental breakdowns during the relentless battle.

/// Hürtgen Forest

✗ Battle of Hürtgen Forest

▥ Roer dams

3 · CLEARING THE SCHELDT ESTUARY
OCTOBER 1–NOVEMBER 8, 1944

The Allies had captured Antwerp in early September, but the Scheldt Estuary leading to the port was impassable as it was under the control of the German 15th Army. On October 1, the Canadian 1st Army began clearing opposition in the Scheldt Estuary, trapping the Germans in the Beveland Peninsula. To the south, the Allies cleared resistance in the Breskens Pocket by November 2. Commandos who had landed on Walcheren Island helped bring the campaign to an end and finally open Allied access to Antwerp.

/// Beveland Peninsula

→ Canadian 1st Army advance

■ Breskens Pocket

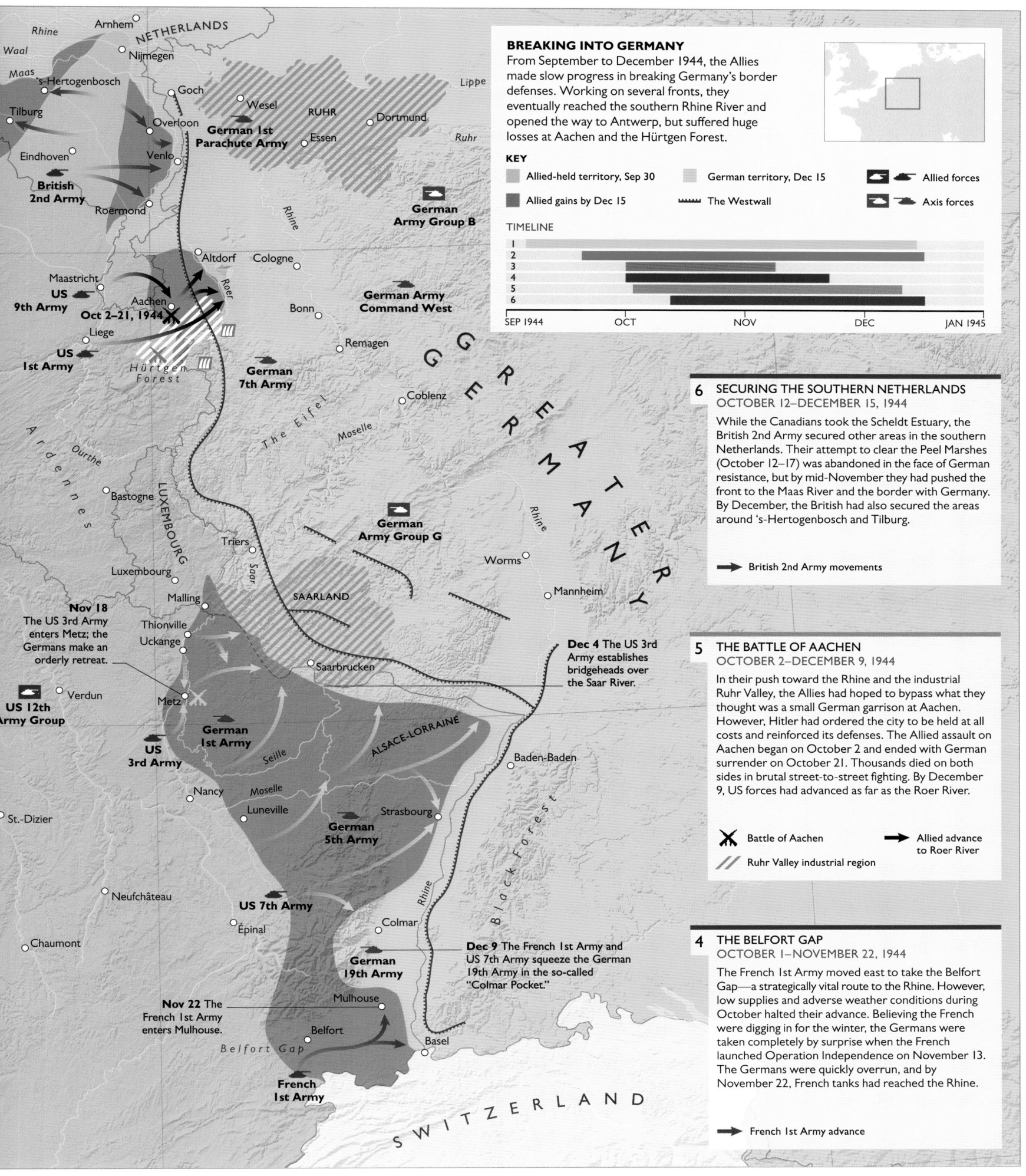

BREAKING INTO GERMANY

From September to December 1944, the Allies made slow progress in breaking Germany's border defenses. Working on several fronts, they eventually reached the southern Rhine River and opened the way to Antwerp, but suffered huge losses at Aachen and the Hürtgen Forest.

KEY

Allied-held territory, Sep 30	German territory, Dec 15	Allied forces
Allied gains by Dec 15	The Westwall	Axis forces

TIMELINE

1
2
3
4
5
6

SEP 1944   OCT   NOV   DEC   JAN 1945

6 SECURING THE SOUTHERN NETHERLANDS
OCTOBER 12–DECEMBER 15, 1944

While the Canadians took the Scheldt Estuary, the British 2nd Army secured other areas in the southern Netherlands. Their attempt to clear the Peel Marshes (October 12–17) was abandoned in the face of German resistance, but by mid-November they had pushed the front to the Maas River and the border with Germany. By December, the British had also secured the areas around 's-Hertogenbosch and Tilburg.

→ British 2nd Army movements

5 THE BATTLE OF AACHEN
OCTOBER 2–DECEMBER 9, 1944

In their push toward the Rhine and the industrial Ruhr Valley, the Allies had hoped to bypass what they thought was a small German garrison at Aachen. However, Hitler had ordered the city to be held at all costs and reinforced its defenses. The Allied assault on Aachen began on October 2 and ended with German surrender on October 21. Thousands died on both sides in brutal street-to-street fighting. By December 9, US forces had advanced as far as the Roer River.

✗ Battle of Aachen   → Allied advance to Roer River

⫽ Ruhr Valley industrial region

4 THE BELFORT GAP
OCTOBER 1–NOVEMBER 22, 1944

The French 1st Army moved east to take the Belfort Gap—a strategically vital route to the Rhine. However, low supplies and adverse weather conditions during October halted their advance. Believing the French were digging in for the winter, the Germans were taken completely by surprise when the French launched Operation Independence on November 13. The Germans were quickly overrun, and by November 22, French tanks had reached the Rhine.

→ French 1st Army advance

Map labels:
Rhine, Arnhem, NETHERLANDS, Waal, Maas, Nijmegen, Lippe, 's-Hertogenbosch, Goch, Tilburg, Wesel, RUHR, Dortmund, Overloon, German 1st Parachute Army, Essen, Ruhr, Eindhoven, Venlo, British 2nd Army, Roermond, German Army Group B, Altdorf, Cologne, Rhine, Maastricht, Roer, US 9th Army, Aachen, Oct 2–21, 1944, German Army Command West, Liege, Bonn, US 1st Army, Hürtgen Forest, Remagen, German 7th Army, The Eifel, Coblenz, Moselle, G R E A T E R G E R M A N Y, Ardennes, Ourthe, Bastogne, LUXEMBOURG, Triers, German Army Group G, Rhine, Worms, Luxembourg, Malling, Mannheim, Nov 18 The US 3rd Army enters Metz; the Germans make an orderly retreat., Thionville, Uckange, SAARLAND, Saarbrucken, Dec 4 The US 3rd Army establishes bridgeheads over the Saar River., Verdun, US 12th Army Group, Metz, German 1st Army, US 3rd Army, Seille, ALSACE-LORRAINE, Baden-Baden, Nancy, Moselle, Luneville, Strasbourg, St.-Dizier, German 5th Army, Black Forest, Neufchâteau, US 7th Army, Rhine, Chaumont, Épinal, Colmar, Dec 9 The French 1st Army and US 7th Army squeeze the German 19th Army in the so-called "Colmar Pocket.", German 19th Army, Nov 22 The French 1st Army enters Mulhouse., Mulhouse, Belfort, Belfort Gap, Basel, French 1st Army, SWITZERLAND

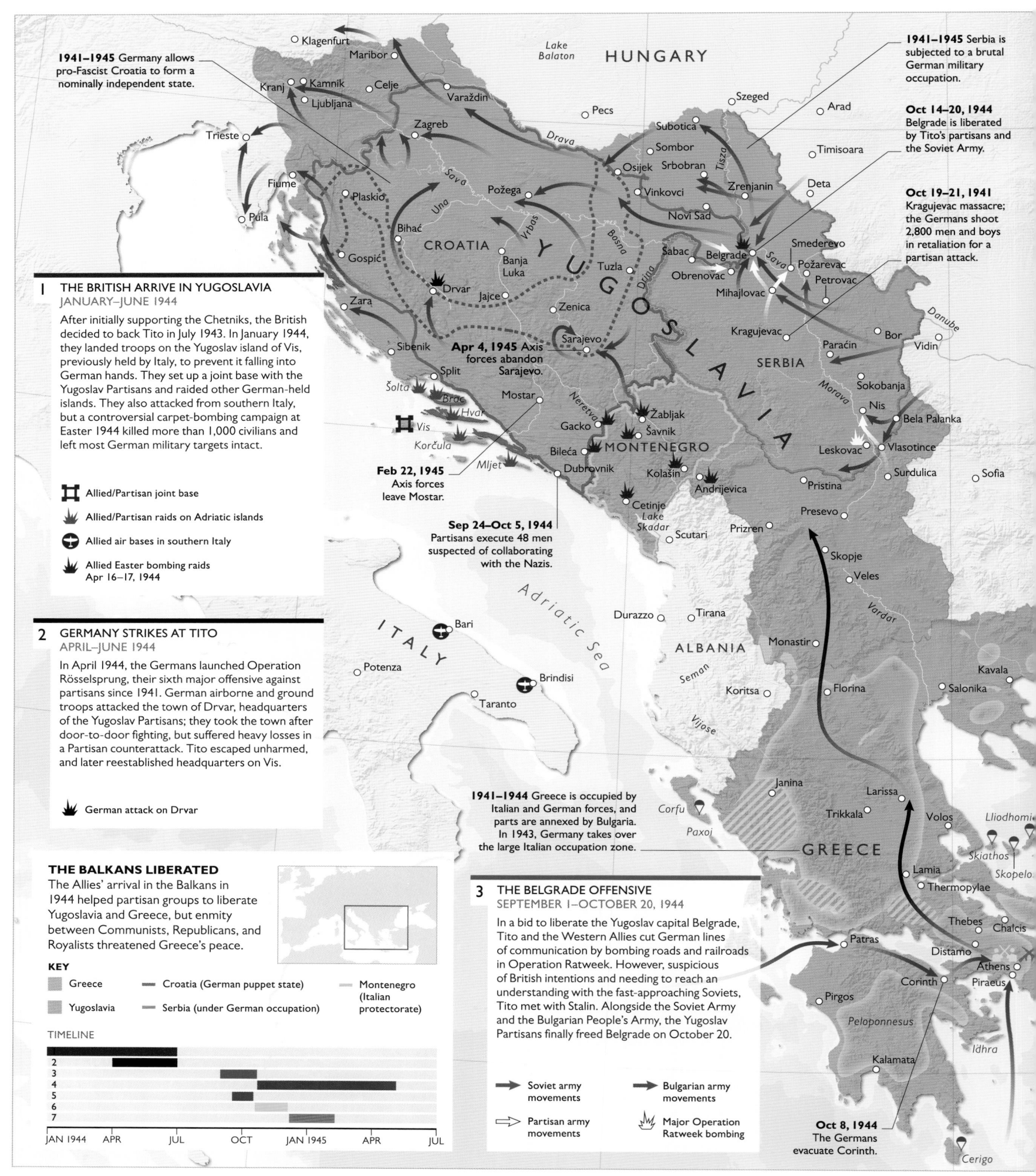

1941–1945 Germany allows pro-Fascist Croatia to form a nominally independent state.

1941–1945 Serbia is subjected to a brutal German military occupation.

Oct 14–20, 1944 Belgrade is liberated by Tito's partisans and the Soviet Army.

Oct 19–21, 1941 Kragujevac massacre; the Germans shoot 2,800 men and boys in retaliation for a partisan attack.

1 | THE BRITISH ARRIVE IN YUGOSLAVIA
JANUARY–JUNE 1944

After initially supporting the Chetniks, the British decided to back Tito in July 1943. In January 1944, they landed troops on the Yugoslav island of Vis, previously held by Italy, to prevent it falling into German hands. They set up a joint base with the Yugoslav Partisans and raided other German-held islands. They also attacked from southern Italy, but a controversial carpet-bombing campaign at Easter 1944 killed more than 1,000 civilians and left most German military targets intact.

- ⊞ Allied/Partisan joint base
- ☙ Allied/Partisan raids on Adriatic islands
- ✈ Allied air bases in southern Italy
- ☙ Allied Easter bombing raids Apr 16–17, 1944

Apr 4, 1945 Axis forces abandon Sarajevo.

Feb 22, 1945 Axis forces leave Mostar.

Sep 24–Oct 5, 1944 Partisans execute 48 men suspected of collaborating with the Nazis.

2 | GERMANY STRIKES AT TITO
APRIL–JUNE 1944

In April 1944, the Germans launched Operation Rösselsprung, their sixth major offensive against partisans since 1941. German airborne and ground troops attacked the town of Drvar, headquarters of the Yugoslav Partisans; they took the town after door-to-door fighting, but suffered heavy losses in a Partisan counterattack. Tito escaped unharmed, and later reestablished headquarters on Vis.

- ☙ German attack on Drvar

1941–1944 Greece is occupied by Italian and German forces, and parts are annexed by Bulgaria. In 1943, Germany takes over the large Italian occupation zone.

THE BALKANS LIBERATED

The Allies' arrival in the Balkans in 1944 helped partisan groups to liberate Yugoslavia and Greece, but enmity between Communists, Republicans, and Royalists threatened Greece's peace.

KEY

▨ Greece	▬ Croatia (German puppet state)	▬ Montenegro (Italian protectorate)
▨ Yugoslavia	▬ Serbia (under German occupation)	

TIMELINE

	JAN 1944	APR	JUL	OCT	JAN 1945	APR	JUL
2							
3							
4							
5							
6							
7							

3 | THE BELGRADE OFFENSIVE
SEPTEMBER 1–OCTOBER 20, 1944

In a bid to liberate the Yugoslav capital Belgrade, Tito and the Western Allies cut German lines of communication by bombing roads and railroads in Operation Ratweek. However, suspicious of British intentions and needing to reach an understanding with the fast-approaching Soviets, Tito met with Stalin. Alongside the Soviet Army and the Bulgarian People's Army, the Yugoslav Partisans finally freed Belgrade on October 20.

- ➡ Soviet army movements
- ➡ Bulgarian army movements
- ⇨ Partisan army movements
- ☙ Major Operation Ratweek bombing

Oct 8, 1944 The Germans evacuate Corinth.

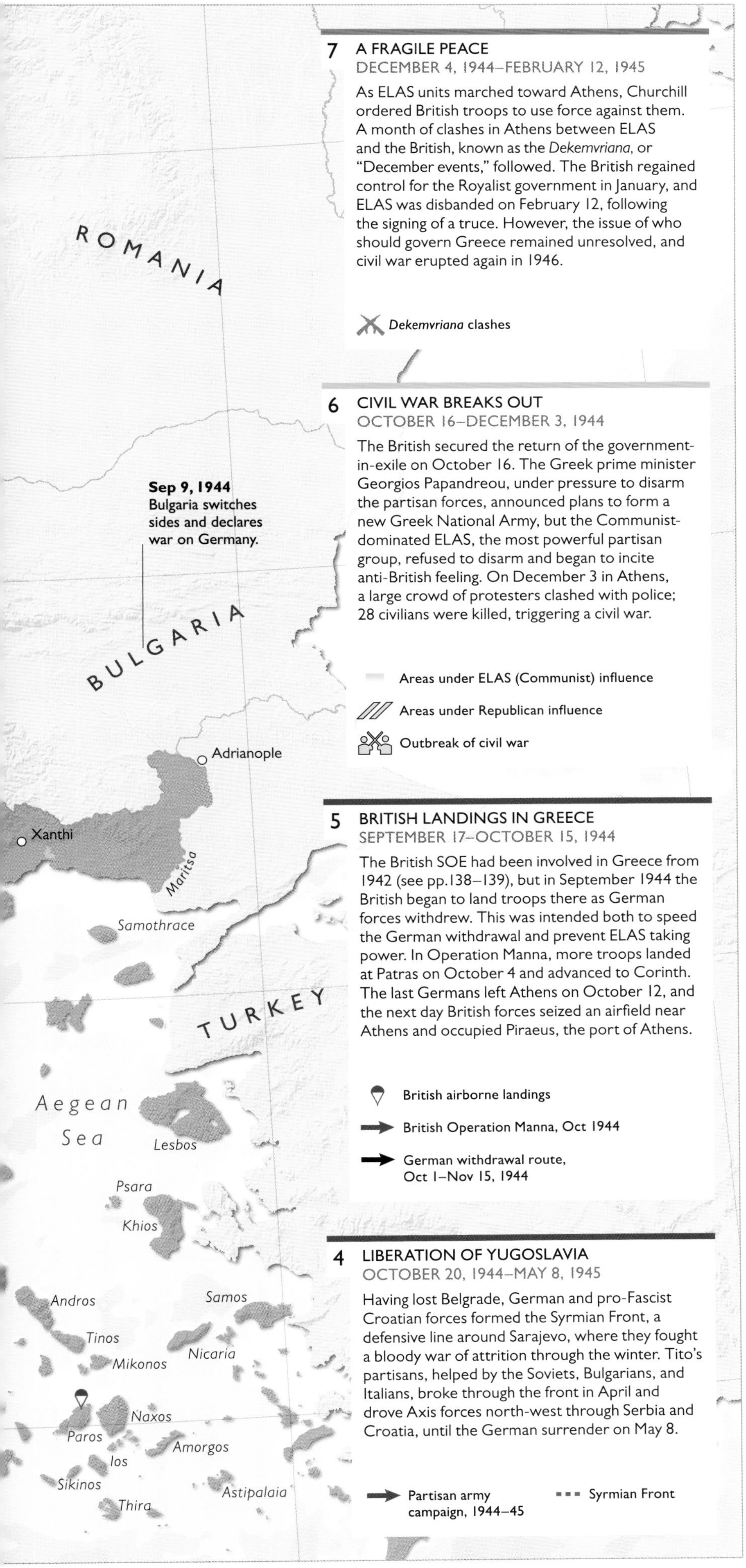

7 A FRAGILE PEACE
DECEMBER 4, 1944–FEBRUARY 12, 1945

As ELAS units marched toward Athens, Churchill ordered British troops to use force against them. A month of clashes in Athens between ELAS and the British, known as the *Dekemvriana*, or "December events," followed. The British regained control for the Royalist government in January, and ELAS was disbanded on February 12, following the signing of a truce. However, the issue of who should govern Greece remained unresolved, and civil war erupted again in 1946.

✕ *Dekemvriana* clashes

Sep 9, 1944
Bulgaria switches sides and declares war on Germany.

○ Adrianople

○ Xanthi

6 CIVIL WAR BREAKS OUT
OCTOBER 16–DECEMBER 3, 1944

The British secured the return of the government-in-exile on October 16. The Greek prime minister Georgios Papandreou, under pressure to disarm the partisan forces, announced plans to form a new Greek National Army, but the Communist-dominated ELAS, the most powerful partisan group, refused to disarm and began to incite anti-British feeling. On December 3 in Athens, a large crowd of protesters clashed with police; 28 civilians were killed, triggering a civil war.

⬚ Areas under ELAS (Communist) influence

⫽ Areas under Republican influence

⚔ Outbreak of civil war

5 BRITISH LANDINGS IN GREECE
SEPTEMBER 17–OCTOBER 15, 1944

The British SOE had been involved in Greece from 1942 (see pp.138–139), but in September 1944 the British began to land troops there as German forces withdrew. This was intended both to speed the German withdrawal and prevent ELAS taking power. In Operation Manna, more troops landed at Patras on October 4 and advanced to Corinth. The last Germans left Athens on October 12, and the next day British forces seized an airfield near Athens and occupied Piraeus, the port of Athens.

⛴ British airborne landings

➡ British Operation Manna, Oct 1944

➡ German withdrawal route, Oct 1–Nov 15, 1944

Samothrace

Aegean Sea

Lesbos

Psara

Khios

4 LIBERATION OF YUGOSLAVIA
OCTOBER 20, 1944–MAY 8, 1945

Having lost Belgrade, German and pro-Fascist Croatian forces formed the Syrmian Front, a defensive line around Sarajevo, where they fought a bloody war of attrition through the winter. Tito's partisans, helped by the Soviets, Bulgarians, and Italians, broke through the front in April and drove Axis forces north-west through Serbia and Croatia, until the German surrender on May 8.

➡ Partisan army campaign, 1944–45   ▪▪▪ Syrmian Front

Andros *Samos*

Tinos

Mikonos *Nicaria*

Paros *Naxos*

Ios *Amorgos*

Sikinos

Thira *Astipalaia*

ROMANIA

BULGARIA

Maritsa

TURKEY

GREECE AND YUGOSLAVIA

After Axis armies occupied Greece and Yugoslavia in 1941, partisan factions fought fiercely against them, but also against each other. As Axis control over the Balkans crumbled from 1943 onward, the Allies became embroiled in the complex politics of the region.

Following the invasion of the Balkans (see pp.80–81), Italy occupied most of Greece, while Yugoslavia—now divided into three states and with its remaining land annexed by its neighbors—was dominated by Germany. After Italy surrendered in September 1943 (see pp.164–165), the Germans occupied the whole region, but the approach of the Soviet Army in September 1944 (see pp.182–183) threatened to encircle them and they withdrew. At the same time, Churchill and Stalin agreed that Britain would have a free hand in Greece, while the USSR would have influence over the other Balkan nations.

In both countries, resistance to the occupying forces formed under competing groups. In Yugoslavia, Colonel Draža Mihailović led the Royalist Chetniks, and Josip Broz, known as Tito, led the Communist Yugoslav Partisans. By 1943, it was clear that Tito was more effective against the Germans, and when the Chetniks began collaborating with the Nazis against the Communists, Tito won Allied support. In Greece, Communist and Republican partisan groups shared mutual dislike of the British-supported Royalist government-in-exile. As liberation drew nearer, the British were alarmed by the increasing power of the Communist-dominated partisan group EAM and its armed wing, ELAS. Their attempts to broker a Greek government that would bring all factions together tipped into a civil war.

△ **Greek partisans on the move**
A line of partisans marches to join Allied forces in Greece in October 1944. Partisan forces in Greece and Yugoslavia offered a serious challenge to German troops, keeping them from joining Axis campaigns elsewhere.

WAR AGAINST JAPAN

In 1943–1944, the Japanese ground forces suffered a succession of defeats against the US, which had the advantages of a larger population and greater industrial capacity. The once-proud Imperial Japanese Navy was almost totally destroyed.

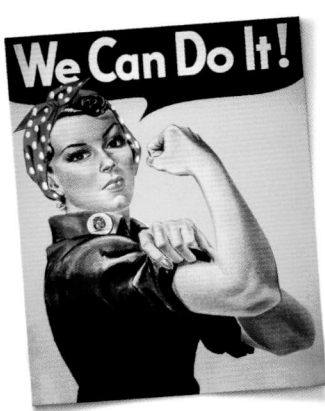

△ **Rosie the Riveter**
The name "Rosie the Riveter" was coined for American women working in heavy industry during World War II. This US propaganda poster exploits the stereotype to encourage the national effort for victory.

The feat of organization involved in the US's massive expansion in the production of arms, ships, and aircraft from 1942 onward was extraordinary. Business, the armed forces, and federal bureaucracy cooperated effectively to develop and manufacture the hardware needed to win the war. With US government spending quadrupling between 1941 and 1944, the unemployment of the Depression years was replaced by labor shortages. This had notable effects on American society. Women took jobs in heavy industry, and African Americans from the rural Deep South migrated to work in California and in northern cities—a population shift that provoked race riots in Detroit in summer 1943. The Roosevelt administration made tentative progress with desegregation of employment, but the US armed forces remained racially segregated.

Japan could not match the US's industrial output, nor the quality of its weapons. Despite the forced labor of Javanese, Korean, Chinese, and Allied prisoners of war, Japan was unable to fulfill its military and civilian manpower needs.

▷ **Amphibious landing**
US Marines go ashore on New Britain island, New Guinea, in December 1943. The use of landing craft and amphibious vehicles was a Marine speciality.

THE FIGHT FOR SUPREMACY

American "island-hopping" across the Pacific began in November 1943 at the Gilbert Islands and reached the Marianas in July 1944. The US offensive in the south-west Pacific led up to landings in the Philippines in October 1944, while the defeat of Japan's naval force left the Japanese exposed to potential invasion of their mainland. Meanwhile, fighting between Japan and China reached a new intensity, and the British advanced into Japanese-occupied Burma after repelling an attack on India.

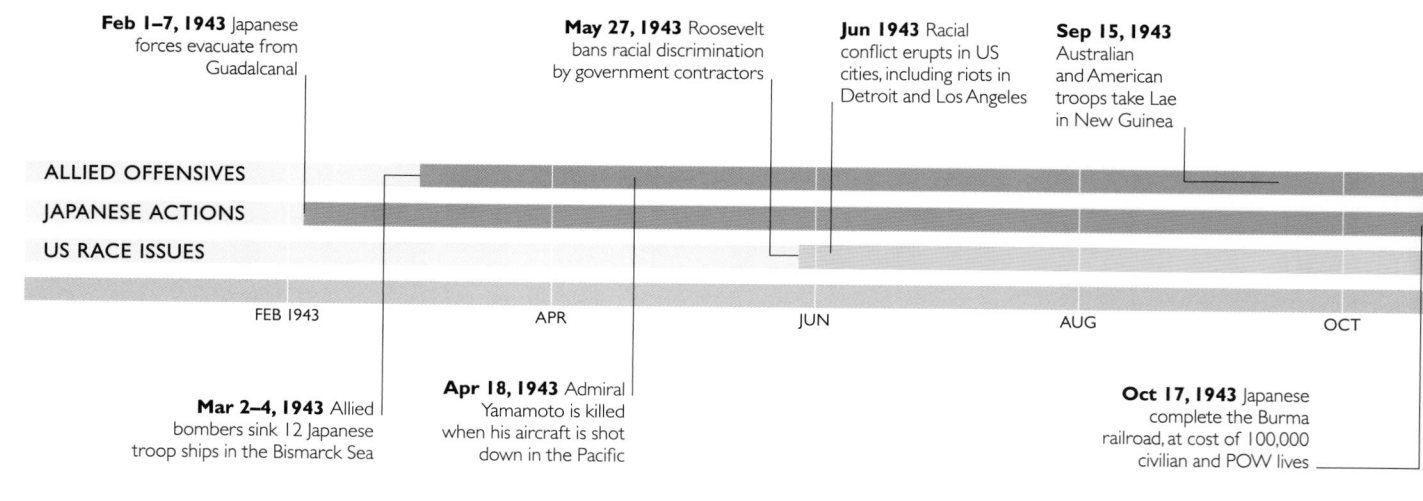

Feb 1–7, 1943 Japanese forces evacuate from Guadalcanal

May 27, 1943 Roosevelt bans racial discrimination by government contractors

Jun 1943 Racial conflict erupts in US cities, including riots in Detroit and Los Angeles

Sep 15, 1943 Australian and American troops take Lae in New Guinea

ALLIED OFFENSIVES

JAPANESE ACTIONS

US RACE ISSUES

FEB 1943　　　APR　　　JUN　　　AUG　　　OCT

Mar 2–4, 1943 Allied bombers sink 12 Japanese troop ships in the Bismarck Sea

Apr 18, 1943 Admiral Yamamoto is killed when his aircraft is shot down in the Pacific

Oct 17, 1943 Japanese complete the Burma railroad, at cost of 100,000 civilian and POW lives

◁ **Operations in China**
Japanese soldiers pose on their Type 97 medium tank during the 1944 Ichigo offensive in China. The operation showed the unbroken fighting strength of the Japanese army.

US strategy

US command in the Pacific War was divided between General Douglas MacArthur in the south-west Pacific sector, where the US Army predominated, and Admiral Chester Nimitz in the central and South Pacific, where the US Marines and the US Navy led the charge. Nimitz's island-hopping strategy across the central Pacific toward Japan proved most decisive. The Marines employed a range of new amphibious equipment in a series of landings on Japanese-held islands, which fell one by one, despite a defense-to-the-death mounted by their outnumbered garrisons. When the Japanese navy tried to intervene against the US landings on the Pacific island of Saipan in June 1944, it found that its carrier aircraft and pilots had ceased to be any match for their American opponents.

The Philippines campaign

Meanwhile, MacArthur's forces sidestepped Japanese strongpoints, such as Rabaul in New Guinea, to begin the reconquest of the Philippines. The naval battle of Leyte Gulf, fought during the Philippine landings in October 1944, destroyed the Japanese Imperial Navy as an effective fighting force.

Fighting spirit

Despite Japan's inferior military resources, there was no decline in its martial spirit. In spring 1944, Japanese troops from Burma invaded British India, and they mustered half a million men for one of the largest offensives of its long war in China. On the Pacific islands, US casualties mounted, and on Saipan, the Americans were shocked by the mass suicide of Japanese civilians and soldiers, who chose death over surrender. By autumn 1944, the US conquest of the Mariana Islands provided a Pacific base for America's new B-29 bombers to attack the Japanese mainland, and the balance of forces in favor of the US and its allies had become overwhelming.

▽ **Battle of Leyte Gulf**
Ships of the US Navy's Fast Carrier Task Force 38 sail in line astern at the battle of Leyte Gulf in October 1944. Deploying 36 carriers of all types, the US managed to regain the Philippines.

> *"I have returned. By the grace of Almighty God our forces stand again on Philippine soil ..."*
>
> GENERAL DOUGLAS MACARTHUR, SPEECH AT LEYTE, PHILIPPINES, OCTOBER 17, 1944

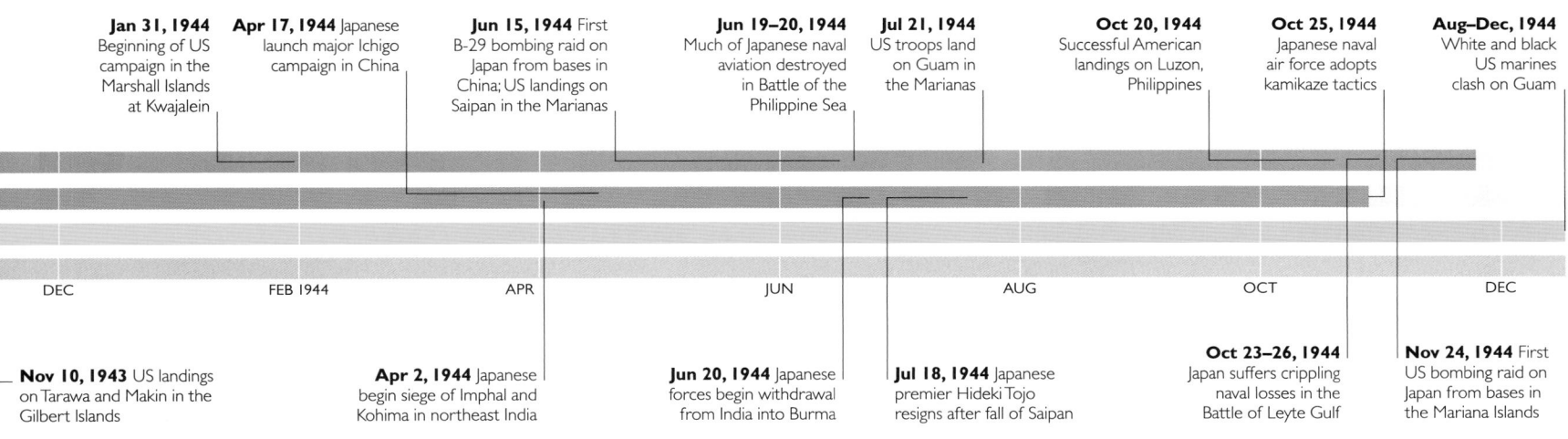

Jan 31, 1944 Beginning of US campaign in the Marshall Islands at Kwajalein

Apr 17, 1944 Japanese launch major Ichigo campaign in China

Jun 15, 1944 First B-29 bombing raid on Japan from bases in China; US landings on Saipan in the Marianas

Jun 19–20, 1944 Much of Japanese naval aviation destroyed in Battle of the Philippine Sea

Jul 21, 1944 US troops land on Guam in the Marianas

Oct 20, 1944 Successful American landings on Luzon, Philippines

Oct 25, 1944 Japanese naval air force adopts kamikaze tactics

Aug–Dec, 1944 White and black US marines clash on Guam

DEC | FEB 1944 | APR | JUN | AUG | OCT | DEC

Nov 10, 1943 US landings on Tarawa and Makin in the Gilbert Islands

Apr 2, 1944 Japanese begin siege of Imphal and Kohima in northeast India

Jun 20, 1944 Japanese forces begin withdrawal from India into Burma

Jul 18, 1944 Japanese premier Hideki Tojo resigns after fall of Saipan

Oct 23–26, 1944 Japan suffers crippling naval losses in the Battle of Leyte Gulf

Nov 24, 1944 First US bombing raid on Japan from bases in the Mariana Islands

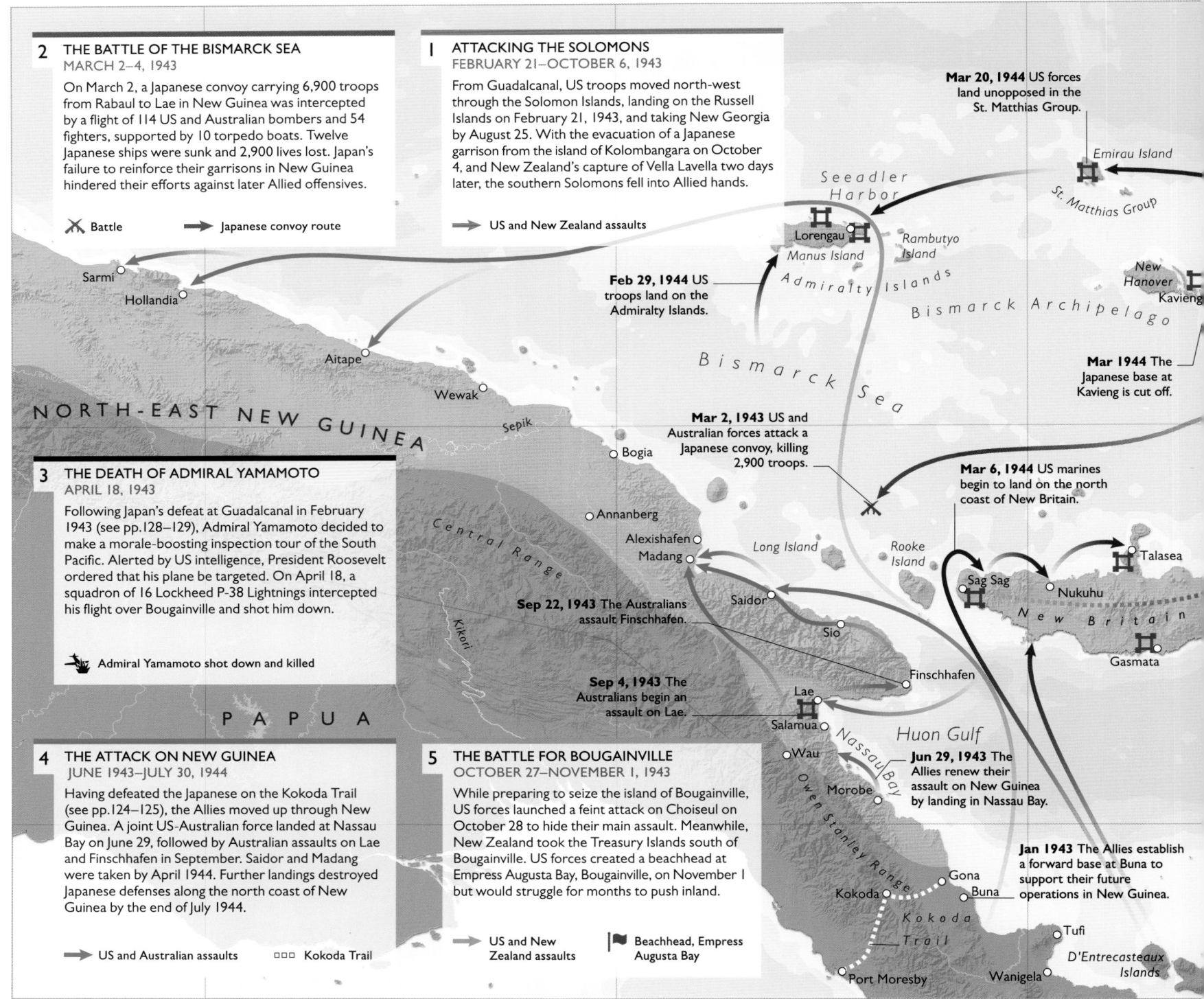

2 THE BATTLE OF THE BISMARCK SEA
MARCH 2–4, 1943

On March 2, a Japanese convoy carrying 6,900 troops from Rabaul to Lae in New Guinea was intercepted by a flight of 114 US and Australian bombers and 54 fighters, supported by 10 torpedo boats. Twelve Japanese ships were sunk and 2,900 lives lost. Japan's failure to reinforce their garrisons in New Guinea hindered their efforts against later Allied offensives.

✗ Battle   → Japanese convoy route

1 ATTACKING THE SOLOMONS
FEBRUARY 21–OCTOBER 6, 1943

From Guadalcanal, US troops moved north-west through the Solomon Islands, landing on the Russell Islands on February 21, 1943, and taking New Georgia by August 25. With the evacuation of a Japanese garrison from the island of Kolombangara on October 4, and New Zealand's capture of Vella Lavella two days later, the southern Solomons fell into Allied hands.

→ US and New Zealand assaults

Mar 20, 1944 US forces land unopposed in the St. Matthias Group.

Emirau Island

Seeadler Harbor

Feb 29, 1944 US troops land on the Admiralty Islands.

Lorengau
Manus Island
Rambutyo Island
Admiralty Islands

New Hanover
Kavieng

Bismarck Archipelago

Mar 1944 The Japanese base at Kavieng is cut off.

Sarmi
Hollandia

Aitape

Wewak

Bismarck Sea

Mar 2, 1943 US and Australian forces attack a Japanese convoy, killing 2,900 troops.

Mar 6, 1944 US marines begin to land on the north coast of New Britain.

NORTH-EAST NEW GUINEA

Sepik

Bogia

3 THE DEATH OF ADMIRAL YAMAMOTO
APRIL 18, 1943

Following Japan's defeat at Guadalcanal in February 1943 (see pp.128–129), Admiral Yamamoto decided to make a morale-boosting inspection tour of the South Pacific. Alerted by US intelligence, President Roosevelt ordered that his plane be targeted. On April 18, a squadron of 16 Lockheed P-38 Lightnings intercepted his flight over Bougainville and shot him down.

🛩 Admiral Yamamoto shot down and killed

Annanberg

Alexishafen
Madang

Central Range

Long Island

Rooke Island

Sag Sag
Nukuhu
Talasea

New Britain

Sep 22, 1943 The Australians assault Finschhafen.

Saidor

Sio

Gasmata

Kikori

Sep 4, 1943 The Australians begin an assault on Lae.

Finschhafen

Lae
Salamua

PAPUA

4 THE ATTACK ON NEW GUINEA
JUNE 1943–JULY 30, 1944

Having defeated the Japanese on the Kokoda Trail (see pp.124–125), the Allies moved up through New Guinea. A joint US-Australian force landed at Nassau Bay on June 29, followed by Australian assaults on Lae and Finschhafen in September. Saidor and Madang were taken by April 1944. Further landings destroyed Japanese defenses along the north coast of New Guinea by the end of July 1944.

→ US and Australian assaults   ▫▫▫ Kokoda Trail

5 THE BATTLE FOR BOUGAINVILLE
OCTOBER 27–NOVEMBER 1, 1943

While preparing to seize the island of Bougainville, US forces launched a feint attack on Choiseul on October 28 to hide their main assault. Meanwhile, New Zealand took the Treasury Islands south of Bougainville. US forces created a beachhead at Empress Augusta Bay, Bougainville, on November 1 but would struggle for months to push inland.

→ US and New Zealand assaults   ⚑ Beachhead, Empress Augusta Bay

Wau

Morobe

Jun 29, 1943 The Allies renew their assault on New Guinea by landing in Nassau Bay.

Nassau Bay

Huon Gulf

Owen Stanley Range

Jan 1943 The Allies establish a forward base at Buna to support their future operations in New Guinea.

Gona
Buna

Kokoda

Kokoda Trail

Tufi

D'Entrecasteaux Islands

Port Moresby
Wanigela

OPERATION CARTWHEEL

In early 1943, the Americans drew up a series of plans to challenge the Japanese in the south-west Pacific, known collectively as Operation Cartwheel. The objective was audacious: to advance through the Solomon Islands in the east and along New Guinea in the west in order to encircle and neutralize the major Japanese base at Rabaul in New Britain.

Operation Cartwheel was approved by US president Franklin D. Roosevelt and British prime minister Winston Churchill at the Casablanca Conference in January 1943 (see pp.162–163). Under the overall command of US general Douglas MacArthur, it consisted of 13 separate planned operations, of which 10 were undertaken and three were dropped because they were considered too costly. Cartwheel saw the movement of Allied forces in two large wings—one up the coast of New Guinea, the other up along the Solomon chain. The aim of this pincer action was to encircle Rabaul, a base that supported a large fleet of aircraft and gave the Japanese control of shipping in the south-west Pacific—a major obstacle to the eventual Allied goal of capturing the Philippines.

The Allied campaign aimed to avoid major concentrations of Japanese forces and focused instead on severing their lines of supply and communication, and on establishing airfields and bases to

▷ **Attack on Bougainville**
US troops on Bougainville on the perimeter of the 129th Infantry, 37th Division, advance in the cover of a tank in March 1944.

PRESSURIZING JAPAN

In a series of operations in the south-west Pacific that lasted for two years, US, Australian, and New Zealand forces slowly pushed the Japanese out of the Solomon Islands and New Guinea.

KEY

⊞ Japanese bases

Japanese-held territory, Feb 20, 1943

Allied territory, Feb 20, 1943

TIMELINE

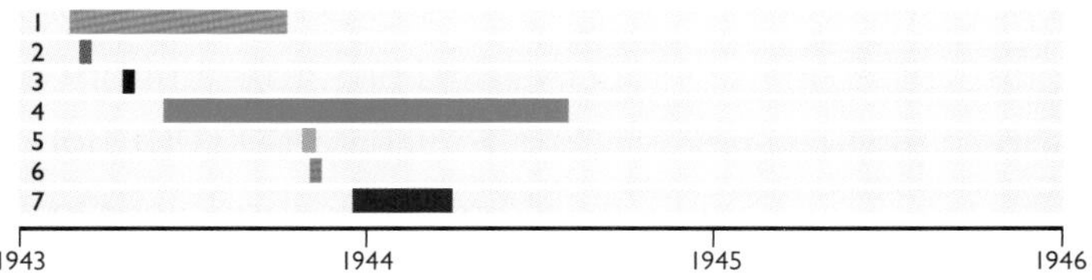

1
2
3
4
5
6
7

1943 1944 1945 1946

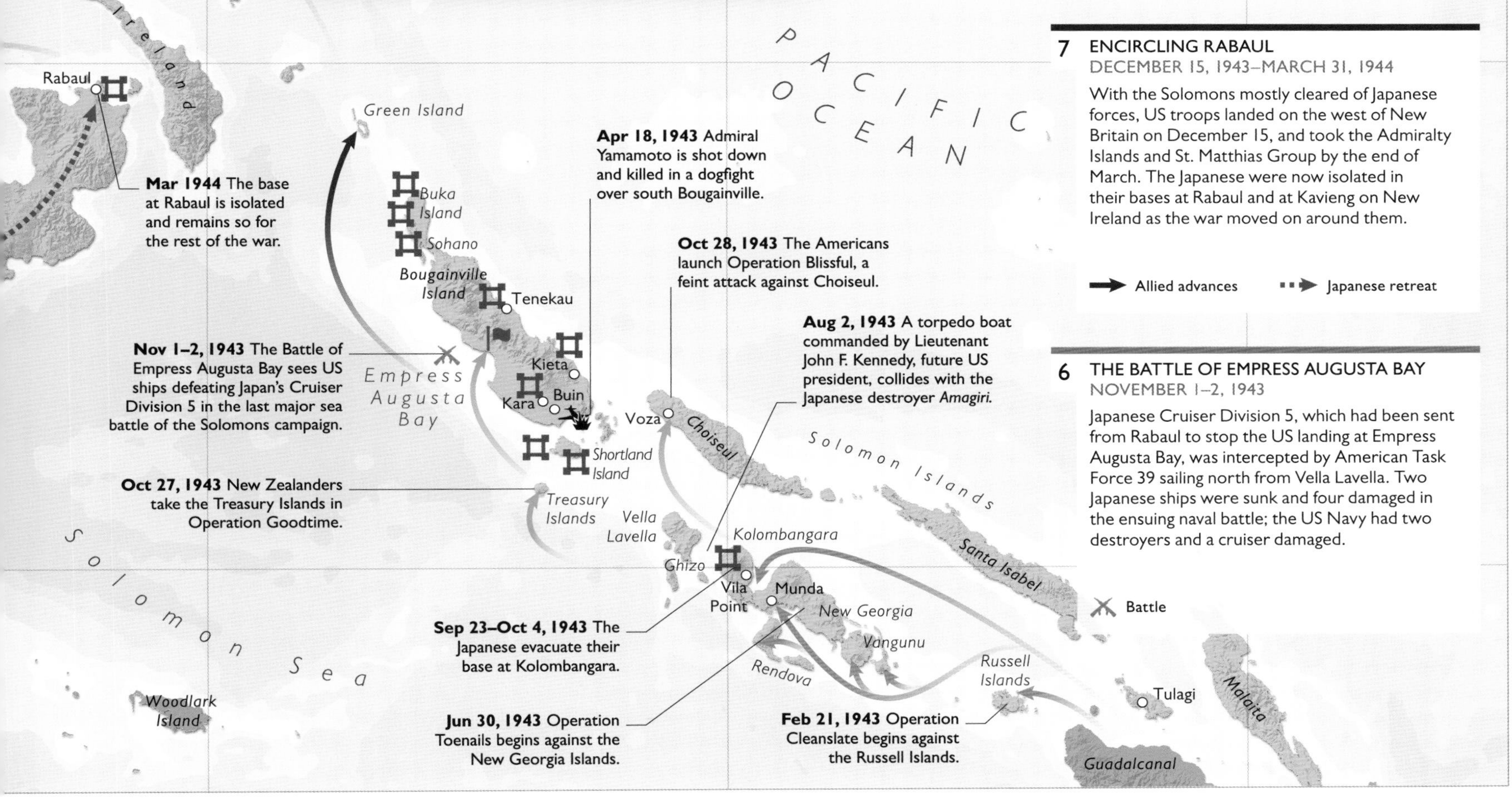

Rabaul

Mar 1944 The base at Rabaul is isolated and remains so for the rest of the war.

Green Island

New Ireland

Buka Island

Sohano

Bougainville Island

Tenekau

Nov 1–2, 1943 The Battle of Empress Augusta Bay sees US ships defeating Japan's Cruiser Division 5 in the last major sea battle of the Solomons campaign.

Empress Augusta Bay

Kieta

Kara Buin

Voza

Choiseul

Apr 18, 1943 Admiral Yamamoto is shot down and killed in a dogfight over south Bougainville.

Oct 28, 1943 The Americans launch Operation Blissful, a feint attack against Choiseul.

Aug 2, 1943 A torpedo boat commanded by Lieutenant John F. Kennedy, future US president, collides with the Japanese destroyer *Amagiri*.

Solomon Islands

Santa Isabel

Oct 27, 1943 New Zealanders take the Treasury Islands in Operation Goodtime.

Shortland Island

Treasury Islands *Vella Lavella*

Kolombangara

Ghizo

Vila Point Munda

New Georgia

Vangunu

PACIFIC OCEAN

7 ENCIRCLING RABAUL
DECEMBER 15, 1943–MARCH 31, 1944

With the Solomons mostly cleared of Japanese forces, US troops landed on the west of New Britain on December 15, and took the Admiralty Islands and St. Matthias Group by the end of March. The Japanese were now isolated in their bases at Rabaul and at Kavieng on New Ireland as the war moved on around them.

→ Allied advances   ▪▪▶ Japanese retreat

6 THE BATTLE OF EMPRESS AUGUSTA BAY
NOVEMBER 1–2, 1943

Japanese Cruiser Division 5, which had been sent from Rabaul to stop the US landing at Empress Augusta Bay, was intercepted by American Task Force 39 sailing north from Vella Lavella. Two Japanese ships were sunk and four damaged in the ensuing naval battle; the US Navy had two destroyers and a cruiser damaged.

✕ Battle

Solomon Sea

Woodlark Island

Sep 23–Oct 4, 1943 The Japanese evacuate their base at Kolombangara.

Jun 30, 1943 Operation Toenails begins against the New Georgia Islands.

Rendova

Feb 21, 1943 Operation Cleanslate begins against the Russell Islands.

Russell Islands

Tulagi

Malaita

Guadalcanal

support Allied logistics. Nevertheless, fighting throughout the campaign was intense, with the Japanese resisting all naval landings and fighting rearguard actions on many of the islands.

The Allies disrupted Japanese troop movements during the Battle of the Bismarck Sea in March 1943, and the shooting down of Admiral Yamamoto (see p.124), commander-in-chief of the Japanese Combined Fleet, severely dented Japanese morale. On reaching Rabaul, the Allies—much to General MacArthur's disapproval—opted not to attack in order to avoid unnecessary casualties, and instead surrounded and isolated the base, which remained in Japanese hands until the end of the war.

Cartwheel took more than a year to achieve, but its eventual success removed the Japanese from the south-west Pacific and allowed the Allies to start new campaigns against them in the Pacific islands to the north (see pp.210–211).

LOCKHEED P-38 LIGHTNING

The Lockheed P-38 Lightning— the aircraft that shot down Japan's Admiral Yamamoto—was a key American fighter aircraft produced in large numbers throughout the war. Used for bombing raids, night fighting, interception, escort, and reconnaissance work, it shot down more Japanese planes than any other aircraft during World War II. Its twin engines mounted on pods allowed it to carry heavier armaments than its competitors.

US AMPHIBIOUS WARFARE

In the Pacific, the campaigns were often fought over far-flung archipelagos. As a result, the US Marine Corps developed particular expertise in amphibious landings, which drove the Japanese from their island strongholds.

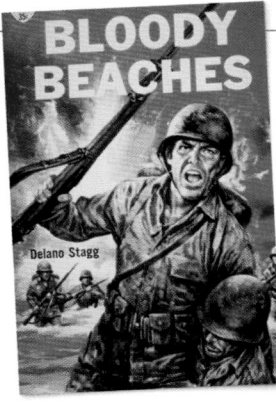

△ **War tales**
The Marine campaigns in the Pacific sparked a lively industry in books relating their exploits, such as this 1961 publication.

Following the Japanese attack on the US naval base at Pearl Harbor, Hawaii, in December 1941, the US joined World War II. It was clear from the start that the US Marine Corps—established during the American Revolution as the navy's land-fighting force—would be necessary to defend and recapture a series of island groups in the Pacific from the Japanese.

Marines on board

Although the Marines were involved in defensive campaigns early in the war, they came into their own in August 1942, when their special forces Raider battalions mounted highly effective raids during the invasion of Guadalcanal (see pp.128–129). In the island-hopping campaigns through the Marshall and Gilbert islands in 1943 (see pp.210–211), the Marines developed true amphibious assault capability, landing tanks and other assault vehicles. By 1945, the Marine Corps had expanded to six divisions, including parachute battalions and defense garrison battalions. They took part in most major operations, including the hard-fought battles for the Japanese islands of Iwo Jima (see pp.250–251) and Okinawa (see pp.254–255); at the latter, fierce resistance cost the Marines 3,440 dead and 15,487 wounded.

SPECIALIZED LANDING CRAFT

From mid-1943, the Marines used tank landing ships, with lowerable bow doors, to deliver tanks and other vehicles directly to beaches. Among the vehicles they carried was the Weasel—an armored troop carrier, which sometimes carried weapons and had tracks to prevent it becoming bogged down in wet sand.

An M29C Weasel

Beach landing
Marines wade ashore, their rifles held high above the water, at Cape Gloucester, on the island of New Britain, Papua New Guinea, in December 1943. The aim of the operation was to capture a Japanese airfield that dominated the island.

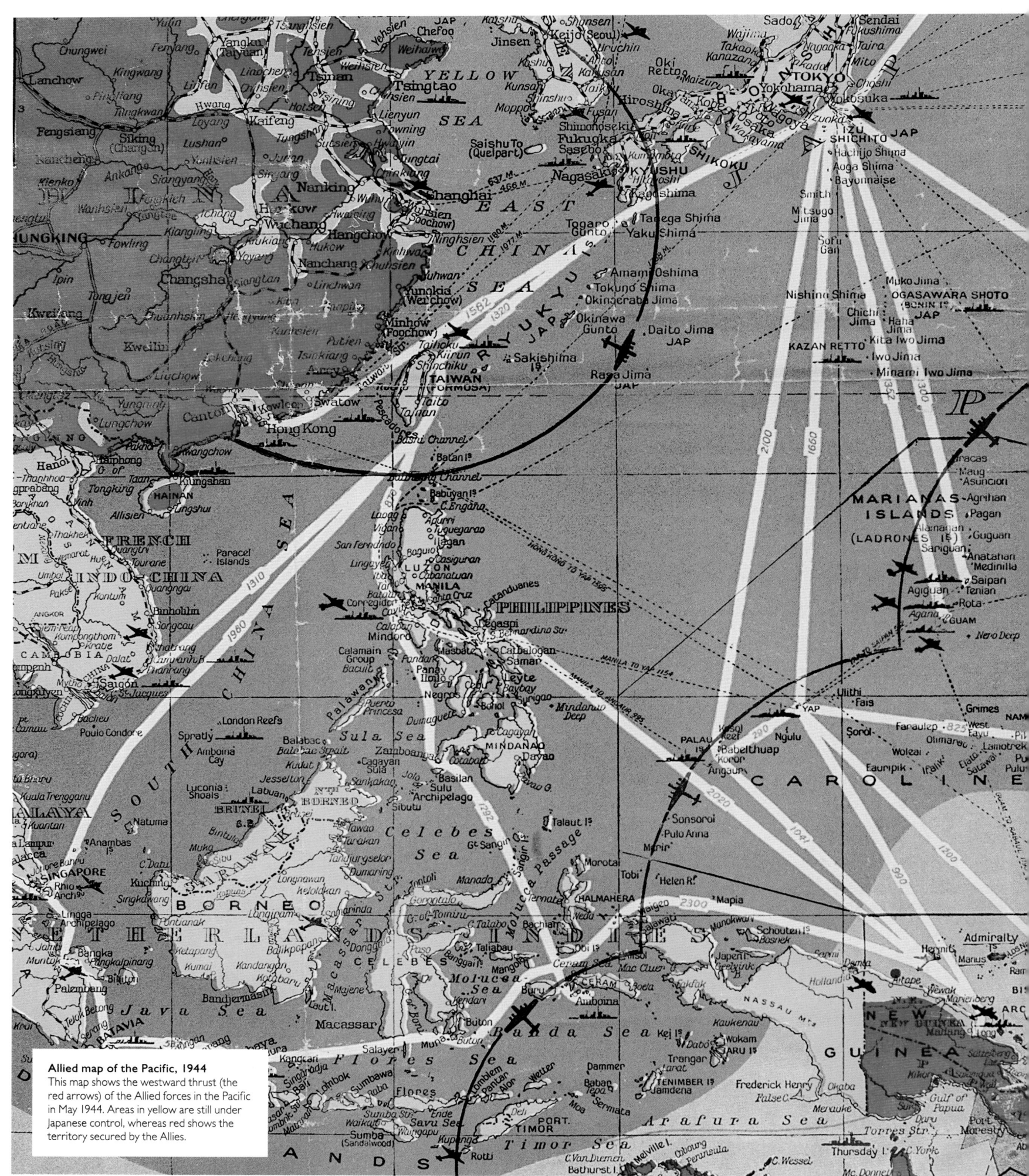

Allied map of the Pacific, 1944
This map shows the westward thrust (the red arrows) of the Allied forces in the Pacific in May 1944. Areas in yellow are still under Japanese control, whereas red shows the territory secured by the Allies.

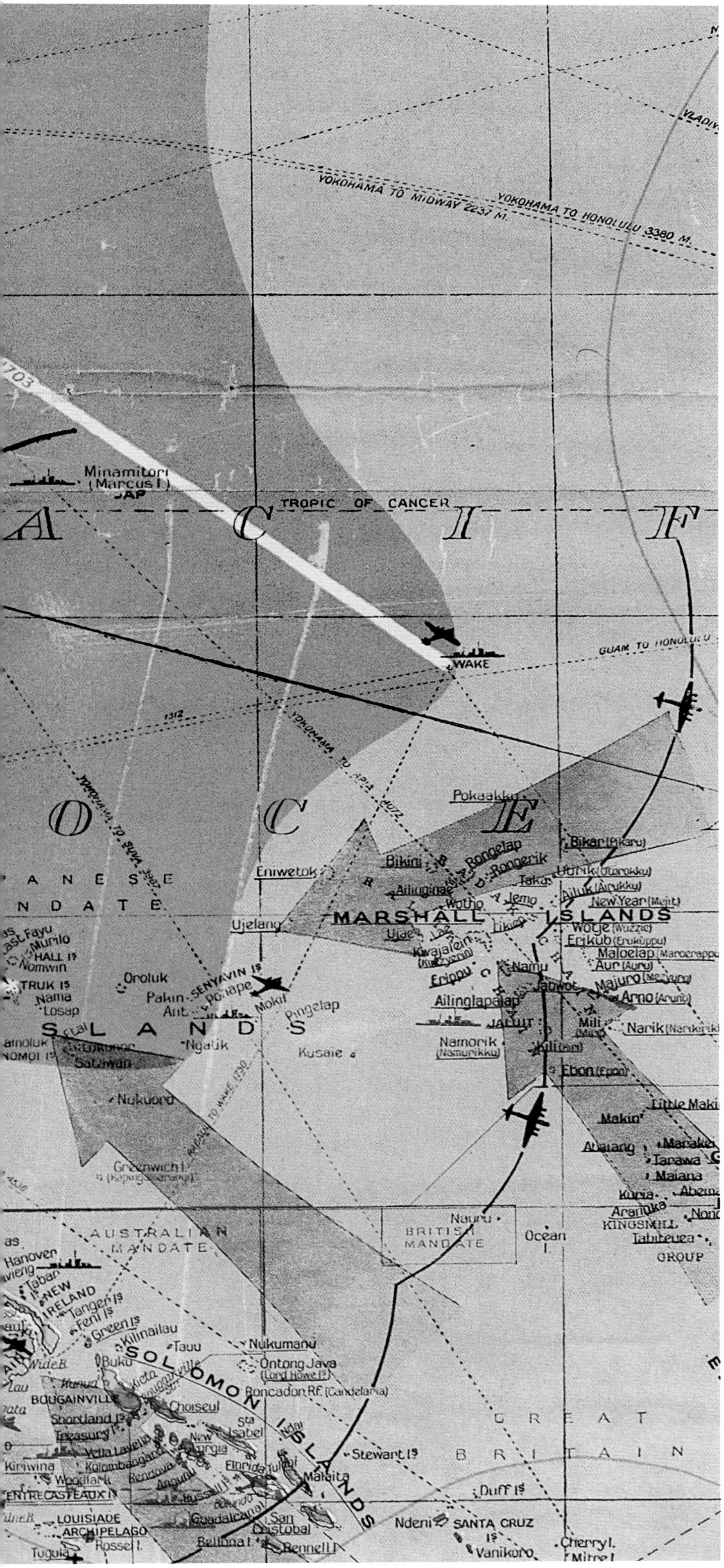

ISLAND-HOPPING IN THE PACIFIC

In autumn 1943, the US Navy and Marines initiated a drive across the central Pacific toward the Marianas. Advancing island by island, they took the war ever closer to the Japanese home islands, but at a heavy cost in lives.

Nearly two years after entering the war, the Japanese still held most of the far-flung defensive perimeter they had established in the Pacific (see pp.106–107), which stretched as far as the remote Gilbert and Marshall Islands (right-hand edge of the map). An American fightback in these islands was initially delayed by a lack of naval resources, but by November 1943, US Admiral Chester Nimitz was ready to take the offensive. Operation Cartwheel (see pp.206–207) was already under way in the Solomon Islands and New Guinea (bottom right on the map). Nimitz's first targets were Tarawa and Makin, tiny coral atolls in the Gilbert Islands. He was able to deploy a fleet of 17 aircraft carriers and 12 battleships—enough to prevent any major intervention by the Imperial Japanese Navy. The assault force possessed an array of landing craft and amphibious vehicles developed for Pacific operations.

Fierce defense

Tarawa was defended by fewer than 3,000 Japanese soldiers, but their commander, Rear Admiral Keiji Shibazaki, had strengthened the atoll's defenses. It took 18,000 US Marines four days to seize Tarawa, at a cost of over 1,000 dead and 2,000 wounded. The Japanese fought suicidally to the end; only 17 of the island's defenders survived. Another 66 US Army soldiers were killed in the simultaneous assault on Makin Atoll (Butaritari), while the navy lost 644 men when an escort carrier was sunk by a Japanese submarine. The scale of the casualties in taking such relatively minor objectives was a shock to the Americans.

The next targets were the Marshall Islands, which had been a Japanese mandate since 1920. The main fighting occurred at Eniwetok Atoll and Kwajalein Atoll. The Americans had learned lessons from Tarawa, but still suffered over 1,000 casualties. Further west, the major Japanese naval base at Truk (Chuuk) Lagoon in the Caroline Islands was devastated by US aircraft. Japan's defensive perimeter was disintegrating, and the path to the Mariana Islands (see pp.212–213) was opening up—with the eventual US aim of closing in on Japan itself.

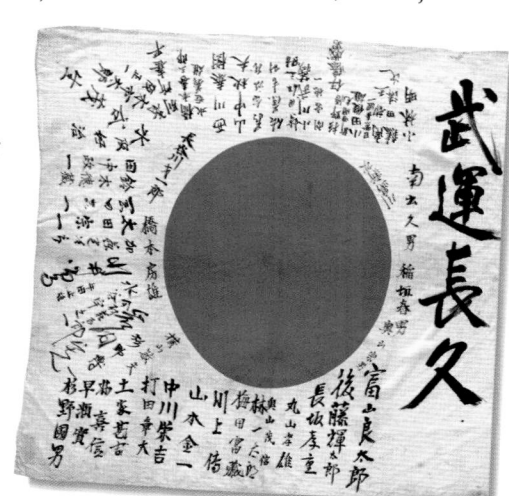

▷ **Japanese prayer flag**
Japanese soldiers in World War II sometimes wore or carried flags inscribed with prayers from their loved ones to bring them luck.

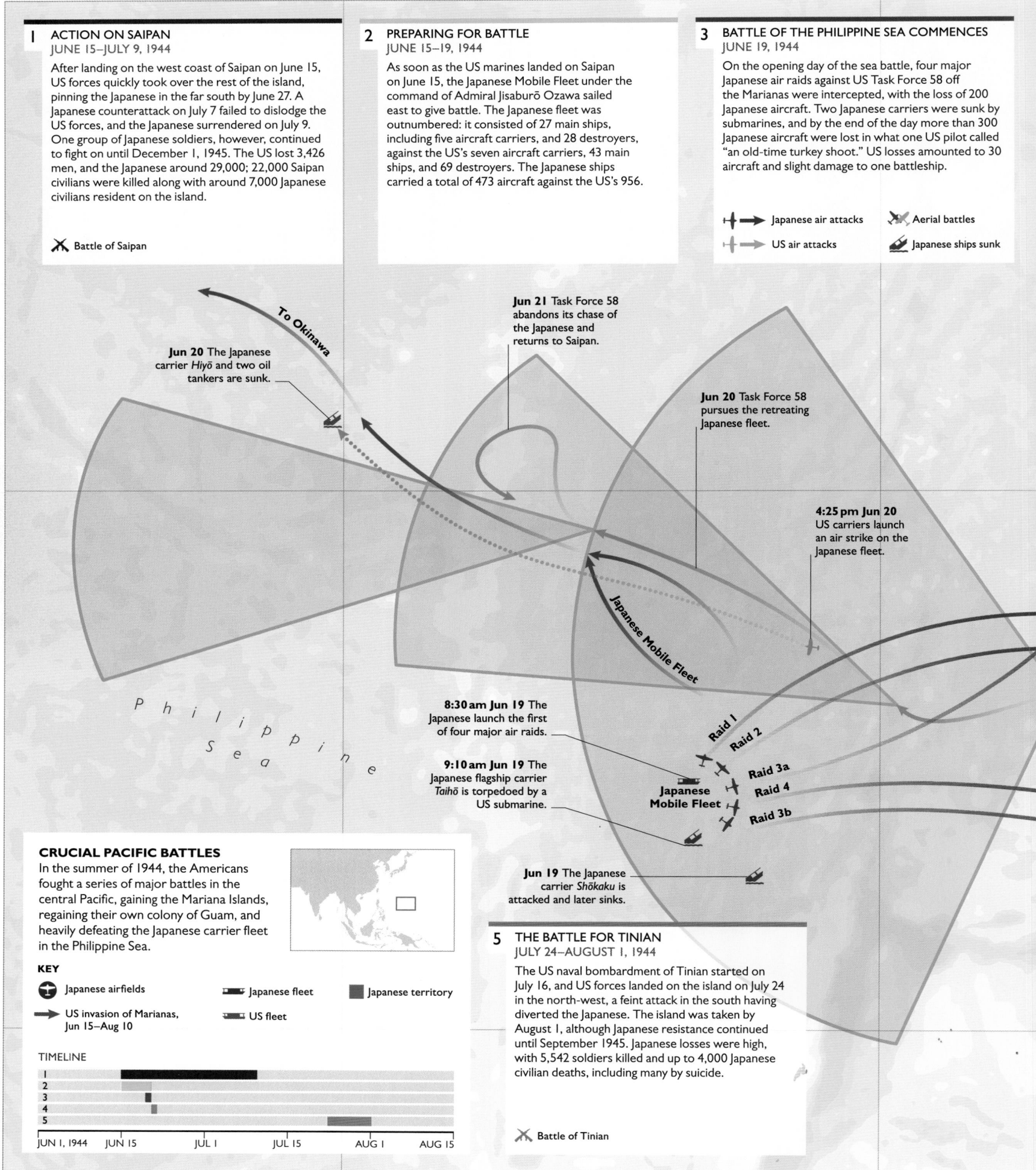

1 ACTION ON SAIPAN
JUNE 15–JULY 9, 1944

After landing on the west coast of Saipan on June 15, US forces quickly took over the rest of the island, pinning the Japanese in the far south by June 27. A Japanese counterattack on July 7 failed to dislodge the US forces, and the Japanese surrendered on July 9. One group of Japanese soldiers, however, continued to fight on until December 1, 1945. The US lost 3,426 men, and the Japanese around 29,000; 22,000 Saipan civilians were killed along with around 7,000 Japanese civilians resident on the island.

⚔ Battle of Saipan

2 PREPARING FOR BATTLE
JUNE 15–19, 1944

As soon as the US marines landed on Saipan on June 15, the Japanese Mobile Fleet under the command of Admiral Jisaburō Ozawa sailed east to give battle. The Japanese fleet was outnumbered: it consisted of 27 main ships, including five aircraft carriers, and 28 destroyers, against the US's seven aircraft carriers, 43 main ships, and 69 destroyers. The Japanese ships carried a total of 473 aircraft against the US's 956.

3 BATTLE OF THE PHILIPPINE SEA COMMENCES
JUNE 19, 1944

On the opening day of the sea battle, four major Japanese air raids against US Task Force 58 off the Marianas were intercepted, with the loss of 200 Japanese aircraft. Two Japanese carriers were sunk by submarines, and by the end of the day more than 300 Japanese aircraft were lost in what one US pilot called "an old-time turkey shoot." US losses amounted to 30 aircraft and slight damage to one battleship.

Japanese air attacks   ⚔ Aerial battles

US air attacks   Japanese ships sunk

Jun 21 Task Force 58 abandons its chase of the Japanese and returns to Saipan.

Jun 20 The Japanese carrier *Hiyō* and two oil tankers are sunk.

To Okinawa

Jun 20 Task Force 58 pursues the retreating Japanese fleet.

4:25 pm Jun 20 US carriers launch an air strike on the Japanese fleet.

Japanese Mobile Fleet

P h i l i p p i n e

S e a

8:30 am Jun 19 The Japanese launch the first of four major air raids.

9:10 am Jun 19 The Japanese flagship carrier *Taihō* is torpedoed by a US submarine.

Raid 1
Raid 2
Raid 3a
Raid 4
Raid 3b

Japanese Mobile Fleet

Jun 19 The Japanese carrier *Shōkaku* is attacked and later sinks.

CRUCIAL PACIFIC BATTLES

In the summer of 1944, the Americans fought a series of major battles in the central Pacific, gaining the Mariana Islands, regaining their own colony of Guam, and heavily defeating the Japanese carrier fleet in the Philippine Sea.

KEY

⊕ Japanese airfields

→ US invasion of Marianas, Jun 15–Aug 10

▬ Japanese fleet

▬ US fleet

■ Japanese territory

TIMELINE

1
2
3
4
5

JUN 1, 1944   JUN 15   JUL 1   JUL 15   AUG 1   AUG 15

5 THE BATTLE FOR TINIAN
JULY 24–AUGUST 1, 1944

The US naval bombardment of Tinian started on July 16, and US forces landed on the island on July 24 in the north-west, a feint attack in the south having diverted the Japanese. The island was taken by August 1, although Japanese resistance continued until September 1945. Japanese losses were high, with 5,542 soldiers killed and up to 4,000 Japanese civilian deaths, including many by suicide.

⚔ Battle of Tinian

▷ **Alert soldier**
Life magazine photographer W. Eugene Smith's iconic photo of US Army Sergeant Angelo Klonis was taken on Saipan during the fight to take the island from the Japanese.

BATTLE FOR THE MARIANAS

In June 1944, the greatest carrier battle of the war took place in the central Pacific in the Battle of the Philippine Sea. The Japanese were roundly defeated by the US Navy, losing the bulk of their carrier fleet and control of the strategically important Marianas. The US moved within striking distance of the Japanese home islands.

By February 1944, the Americans had secured the Gilbert and the Marshall Islands (see pp.210–211), and destroyed the Japanese base on Truk Lagoon in the Caroline Islands. The next US objective was to capture the Mariana Islands, notably the main Japanese bases on Saipan, Tinian, and Guam. Possession of these islands would provide the US with bases for a bombing campaign against the Japanese mainland and enable them to cut Japan off from the Philippines and its other gains in Southeast Asia— a loss that the Japanese could not allow to go unchallenged.

The US began its offensive in June 1944, with the landing of Marines on Saipan, supported by the 5th Fleet. The Japanese Mobile Fleet under Admiral Jisaburō Ozawa responded by attacking the US Navy, but was defeated by superior US tactics, intelligence, and technology in the two-day Battle of the Philippine Sea.

The Japanese suffered a crippling blow, losing three of their carriers along with 445 carrier-based aircraft and over 200 aircraft from the Marianas. They were left with a vastly reduced number of planes and aircrew with which to equip their remaining carriers.

The two-day naval battle that took place in the Philippine Sea was the last of the five major carrier-versus-carrier battles of the Pacific War, and the largest carrier battle in history.

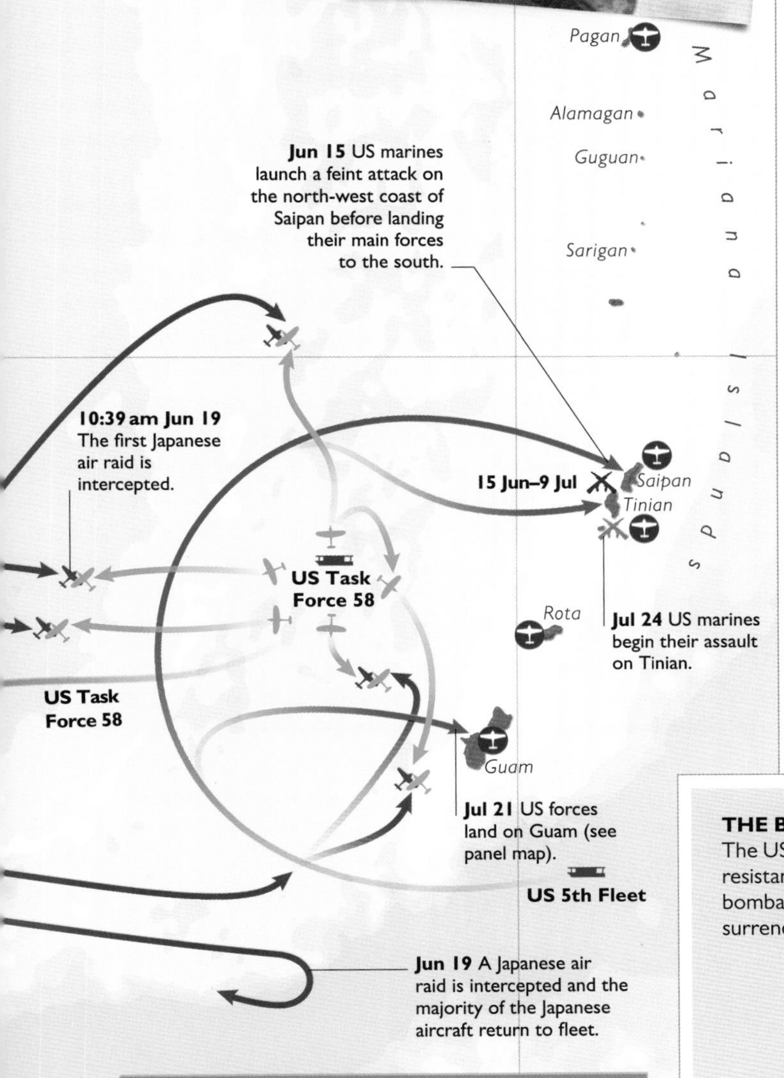

Pagan
Alamagan
Guguan
Sarigan

Mariana Islands

Jun 15 US marines launch a feint attack on the north-west coast of Saipan before landing their main forces to the south.

10:39 am Jun 19 The first Japanese air raid is intercepted.

15 Jun–9 Jul Saipan / Tinian

US Task Force 58

Rota

Jul 24 US marines begin their assault on Tinian.

US Task Force 58

Guam

Jul 21 US forces land on Guam (see panel map).

US 5th Fleet

Jun 19 A Japanese air raid is intercepted and the majority of the Japanese aircraft return to fleet.

4 THE BATTLE CONCLUDES JUNE 20, 1944

On the second day, the battle moved away from the Marianas west across the Pacific Ocean as the US fleet chased the Japanese. In the afternoon, US aircraft attacked and sank the Japanese carrier *Hiyō* and two oil tankers. Realizing that he had lost the battle, Admiral Ozawa retired his fleet to Okinawa.

◁ US search plane range
→ US fleet movements
╾┼╼ US air attack
→ Japanese fleet movements
↘ Japanese ships sunk

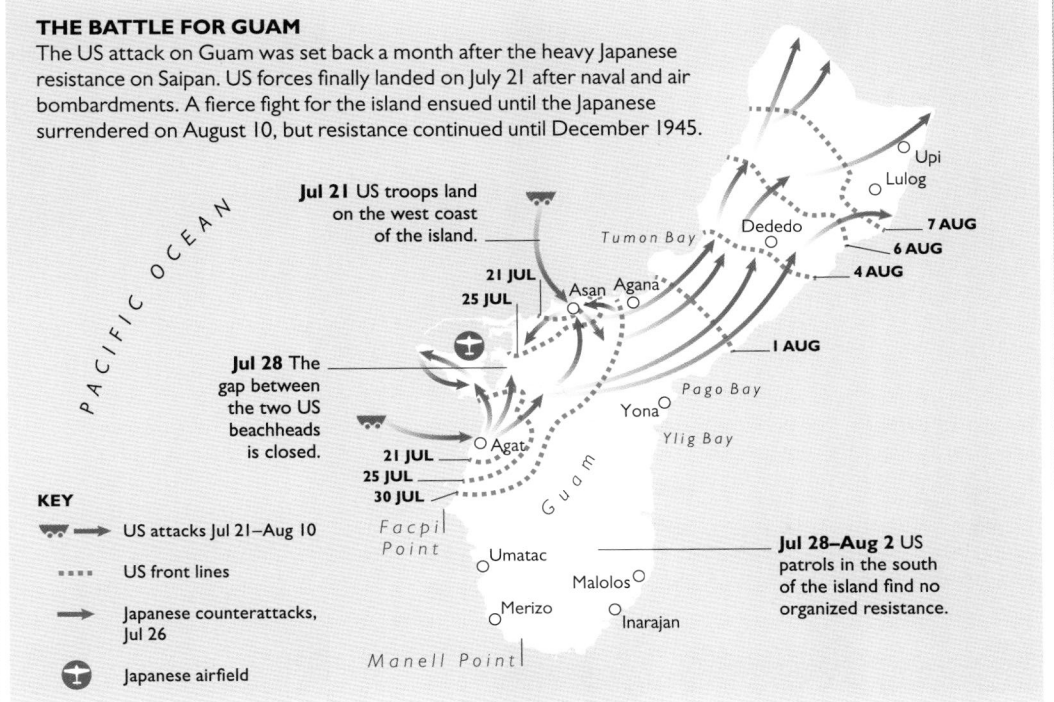

THE BATTLE FOR GUAM
The US attack on Guam was set back a month after the heavy Japanese resistance on Saipan. US forces finally landed on July 21 after naval and air bombardments. A fierce fight for the island ensued until the Japanese surrendered on August 10, but resistance continued until December 1945.

PACIFIC OCEAN

Jul 21 US troops land on the west coast of the island.

Tumon Bay — Dededo — **7 AUG**
Upi / Lulog
6 AUG
4 AUG

21 JUL / **25 JUL** — Asan / Agaña

1 AUG

Jul 28 The gap between the two US beachheads is closed.

Yona / *Pago Bay*
Ylig Bay

21 JUL / **25 JUL** / **30 JUL** — Agat

Guam

KEY
╾➤ US attacks Jul 21–Aug 10
···· US front lines
→ Japanese counterattacks, Jul 26
✈ Japanese airfield

Facpi Point
Umatac
Malolos
Merizo
Inarajan
Manell Point

Jul 28–Aug 2 US patrols in the south of the island find no organized resistance.

THE BATTLE OF LEYTE GULF

On March 11, 1942, US General Douglas MacArthur and his family left the Philippines after his forces were surrounded by Japanese troops. He famously stated that: "I came through and I shall return." On October 20, 1944, he fulfilled that vow when US troops landed on Leyte Island in the eastern Philippines.

After capturing most of the Mariana Islands (see pp.212–213), the US Joint Chiefs of Staff debated what move to make next. Some favored an attack on Taiwan—part of the Japanese Empire— or putting additional resources into the war in China, but General MacArthur successfully championed an attack on the Philippines. His personal affront was to be avenged.

US forces landed at Leyte Gulf in the Philippines on October 20, a move that caused the Japanese to summon much of their remaining navy to fend off the invasion. Allied fleets met the Japanese fleet in a series of engagements around the Philippines over the next three days.

Cumulatively, these engagements constituted the largest naval battle of the war. They involved 70 Japanese warships and 210 American and Australian vessels, and resulted in the shattering of Japanese sea power. The Japanese lost 28 ships and more than 300 aircraft; moreover, their ability to move oil and other key resources from Southeast Asia to their home islands was destroyed. In comparison, the US suffered far lighter losses of six ships and around 200 aircraft.

The US secured beachheads on Leyte and opened the road for their forces to recover the entire Philippine archipelago (see pp.248–249).

> *"Leyte was tantamount to the loss of the Philippines … I felt that it was the end."*
>
> ADMIRAL MITSUMASA YONAI, JAPANESE NAVY MINISTER, 1946

GENERAL DOUGLAS MACARTHUR

Douglas MacArthur (1880–1964) was Chief of Staff of the US Army from 1930 to 1935, before retiring from active service in 1937 to become military advisor to the Philippine government. Recalled to active duty in 1941 as commander of the US Army Forces in the Far East, he was forced out of the Philippines by the Japanese in 1942, returning in 1944 and officially accepting Japan's surrender in September 1945. His successes in World War II made him a hugely popular public figure in the US.

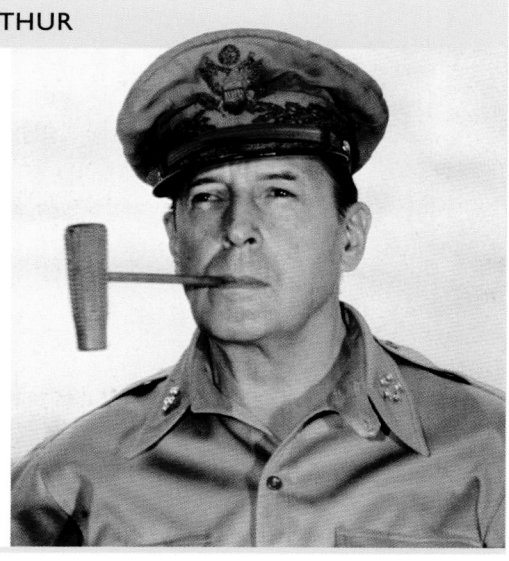

General Douglas MacArthur with his famous corn cob pipe

△ **Leyte liberated**
US soldiers and members of the US Coast Guard pose with a Japanese battle flag, which they captured while taking a beach on Leyte Island.

Japanese 2nd Striking Force

South China Sea

5 BATTLE OF CAPE ENGAÑO
OCTOBER 24–25, 1944

The Japanese sent a decoy carrier force to the north-east of the Philippines to lure the US fleet away from Leyte Gulf. Three US task groups sailed north to engage the carrier fleet. Though they lost the light carrier USS *Princeton*, sunk by land-based aircraft on October 24, the US groups sank four Japanese carriers and five other ships.

→ Japanese decoy carrier force movements

✗ Battle of Cape Engaño, Oct 25, 1944

→ US task force movements

⊢•▶ US air attacks from carrier task force

⚓ US aircraft carrier sunk

⚓ Japanese aircraft carrier sunk

4 THE BATTLE OF SURIGAO STRAIT
OCTOBER 24–25, 1944

Japanese Task Force C sailed east from Borneo into the Surigao Strait; it was soon followed there by the 2nd Striking Force, which had sailed from Taiwan to the north. The Japanese vessels encountered US and Australian cruisers, destroyers, and torpedo boats in the early hours of October 25. All but one of the seven vessels of Task Force C were destroyed before the Japanese withdrew, and most of the remaining fleet was sunk in later engagements around Leyte.

→ Japanese Task Force C

✗ Battle of Surigao Strait, Oct 25, 1944

→ Japanese 2nd Striking Force

Oct 23 US submarines sink Japanese cruisers *Atago* and *Maya* to the west of Palawan Island.

Palawan Passage

Palawan

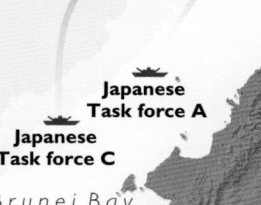
Japanese Task force A

Japanese Task force C

North Borneo

Brunei Bay

Brunei

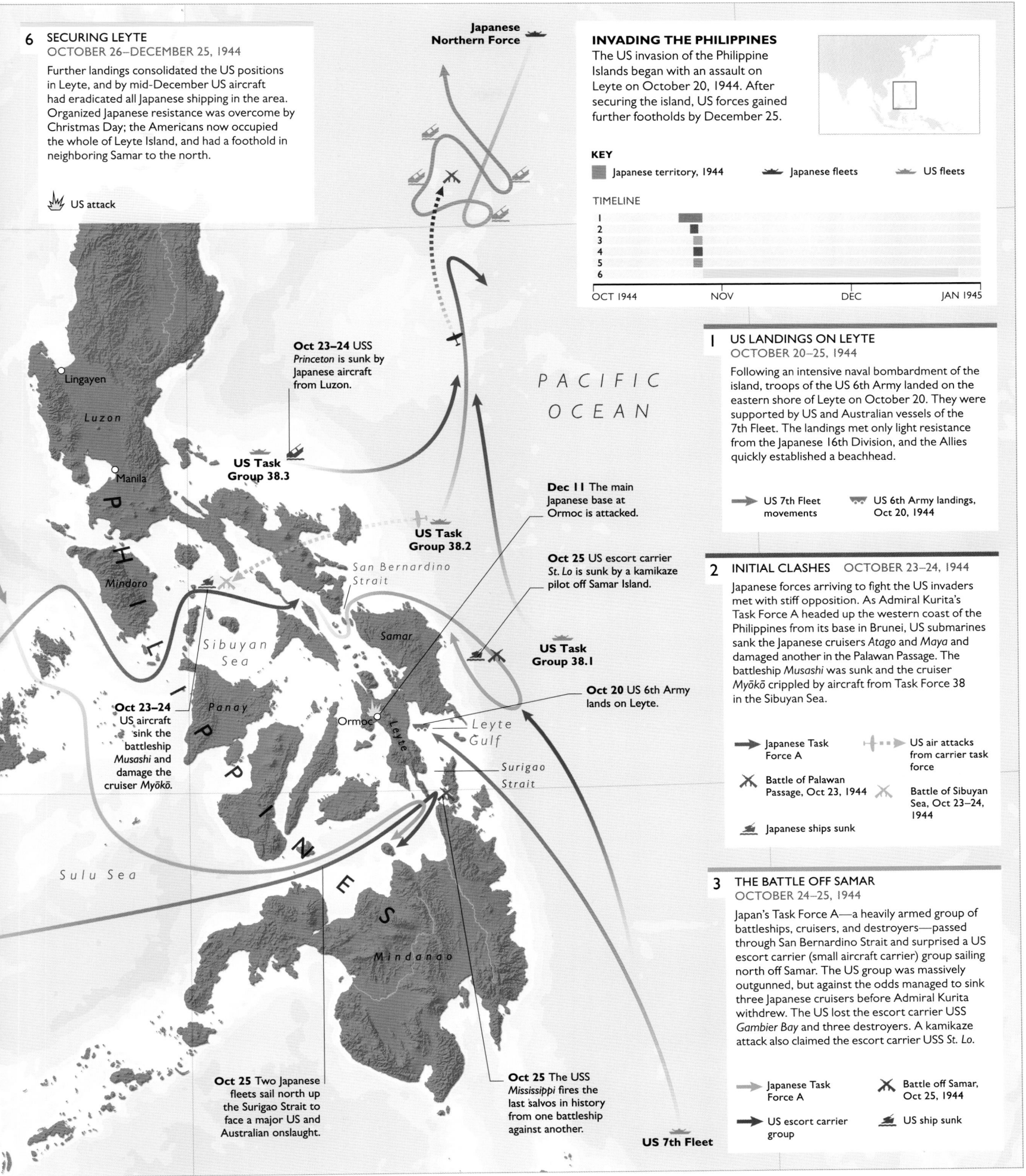

6 SECURING LEYTE
OCTOBER 26–DECEMBER 25, 1944

Further landings consolidated the US positions in Leyte, and by mid-December US aircraft had eradicated all Japanese shipping in the area. Organized Japanese resistance was overcome by Christmas Day; the Americans now occupied the whole of Leyte Island, and had a foothold in neighboring Samar to the north.

⚜ US attack

Japanese Northern Force

Oct 23–24 USS *Princeton* is sunk by Japanese aircraft from Luzon.

US Task Group 38.3

US Task Group 38.2

Dec 11 The main Japanese base at Ormoc is attacked.

Oct 25 US escort carrier *St. Lo* is sunk by a kamikaze pilot off Samar Island.

US Task Group 38.1

Oct 20 US 6th Army lands on Leyte.

Oct 23–24 US aircraft sink the battleship *Musashi* and damage the cruiser *Myōkō*.

Oct 25 Two Japanese fleets sail north up the Surigao Strait to face a major US and Australian onslaught.

Oct 25 The USS *Mississippi* fires the last salvos in history from one battleship against another.

US 7th Fleet

Lingayen
Luzon
Manila
PHILIPPINES
Mindoro
Sibuyan Sea
Panay
Samar
Ormoc
Leyte
Leyte Gulf
Surigao Strait
San Bernardino Strait
Sulu Sea
Mindanao

PACIFIC OCEAN

INVADING THE PHILIPPINES

The US invasion of the Philippine Islands began with an assault on Leyte on October 20, 1944. After securing the island, US forces gained further footholds by December 25.

KEY

▮ Japanese territory, 1944	⬤➤ Japanese fleets	⬤➤ US fleets

TIMELINE

1	
2	
3	
4	
5	
6	

OCT 1944 — NOV — DEC — JAN 1945

---

1 US LANDINGS ON LEYTE
OCTOBER 20–25, 1944

Following an intensive naval bombardment of the island, troops of the US 6th Army landed on the eastern shore of Leyte on October 20. They were supported by US and Australian vessels of the 7th Fleet. The landings met only light resistance from the Japanese 16th Division, and the Allies quickly established a beachhead.

➤ US 7th Fleet movements

US 6th Army landings, Oct 20, 1944

---

2 INITIAL CLASHES   OCTOBER 23–24, 1944

Japanese forces arriving to fight the US invaders met with stiff opposition. As Admiral Kurita's Task Force A headed up the western coast of the Philippines from its base in Brunei, US submarines sank the Japanese cruisers *Atago* and *Maya* and damaged another in the Palawan Passage. The battleship *Musashi* was sunk and the cruiser *Myōkō* crippled by aircraft from Task Force 38 in the Sibuyan Sea.

➤ Japanese Task Force A

US air attacks from carrier task force

✕ Battle of Palawan Passage, Oct 23, 1944

✕ Battle of Sibuyan Sea, Oct 23–24, 1944

Japanese ships sunk

---

3 THE BATTLE OFF SAMAR
OCTOBER 24–25, 1944

Japan's Task Force A—a heavily armed group of battleships, cruisers, and destroyers—passed through San Bernardino Strait and surprised a US escort carrier (small aircraft carrier) group sailing north off Samar. The US group was massively outgunned, but against the odds managed to sink three Japanese cruisers before Admiral Kurita withdrew. The US lost the escort carrier USS *Gambier Bay* and three destroyers. A kamikaze attack also claimed the escort carrier USS *St. Lo*.

➤ Japanese Task Force A

➤ US escort carrier group

✕ Battle off Samar, Oct 25, 1944

US ship sunk

KAMIKAZE TACTICS

In 1944, the Japanese military ordered suicide pilots—known as kamikaze—into action, in a desperate attempt to stem the tide of defeat. Thousands of volunteers enlisted to undertake crash-dive attacks with their planes, prepared to sacrifice their lives for Japan.

△ **Propaganda poster**
Japanese posters such as this one glorified kamikaze missions. Many young Japanese, often students, came forward to volunteer.

Toward the end of 1944, Japan was in a critical situation. The country had suffered catastrophic military defeats, both the navy and air force had lost their offensive capability, and a diminished economy meant resources were limited. The civilian population of Japan was mobilized for defense, but due to lack of funds some were armed only with bamboo spears.

Realizing that conventional bombing methods would not halt the advancing American forces, the Japanese high command attempted to decimate the US fleet by initiating mass suicide attacks. Named after the "divine wind" that, according to Japanese legend, had scattered an invading Mongol fleet in 1274, the kamikaze suicide bombers were the brainchild of Vice-Admiral Onishi Takijuro. Volunteer pilots were instructed to crash-dive planes laden with explosives, torpedoes, and full fuel tanks into Allied warships. The operation, code named Floating Chrysanthemum, drew upon the Japanese military tradition of death being more honorable and less shameful than defeat, capture, and surrender.

The first kamikaze attacks were launched against the American fleet on October 25, 1944, at the Battle of Leyte Gulf (see pp.214–215), and the attacks continued until the end of the war. In total, the use of kamikaze strikes resulted in the loss of 34 US ships, and a further 368 US vessels were badly damaged.

THE PILOTS

The average age of kamikazes was between 17 and 20 years old, and some of them had as few as 40 hours of flying experience before they were sent on their final mission. More than 2,500 kamikazes had sacrificed their lives by the end of World War II, and their success rate is estimated at around 19 percent.

Attack on USS *Bunker Hill*
US aircraft carrier *Bunker Hill* blazes after being attacked by two kamikazes off Okinawa on May 11, 1945. The two planes plunged into the carrier's flight deck, heavily damaging the ship and forcing it to retire for repair.

THE FIGHTBACK IN BURMA

Occupied by Japan in spring 1942, Burma was recaptured by British Empire troops toward the end of the war. The campaign was characterized by tactical innovation and fierce jungle fighting.

When the Japanese invaded Burma in 1942, they stopped at the border with British India, having achieved their goal to cut the Allied supply route from the port of Rangoon (shown here, right) to Nationalist China. Any attempt to recapture Burma by an advance from north-east India would involve fighting across formidable terrain of mountain and jungle. The difficulty of conducting such an offensive led the Allies to develop Long Range Penetration groups—specially trained infantry dropped into the jungle by parachute or glider. These groups—the British Chindits led by General Orde Wingate, and their American equivalents, Merrill's Marauders, under General Frank Merrill— operated for months behind Japanese lines in 1943–1944, carrying out guerrilla attacks on troops and communications.

In response, the Japanese mounted an offensive across the Indian border into Assam. Their 15th Army under General Renya Mutaguchi advanced swiftly northward in March 1944, surrounding more than 100,000 troops of the British Indian Army at Imphal. They also attacked Kohima on the road north of Imphal, where a garrison of 1,500 men came under siege on April 4. By the time the undernourished and disease-ridden Japanese troops were forced to withdraw into Burma in July, they had suffered more than 50,000 casualties.

The drive to Rangoon

The failed Assam invasion left the Japanese vulnerable to an Allied counteroffensive. British and Indian forces under General William Slim pressed southward from Imphal, crossing the Irrawaddy River south of Mandalay in February 1945. Meanwhile, Chinese Nationalist troops cleared the Japanese from north-eastern Burma. After Slim's forces captured Mandalay and the important road junction at Meiktila, they met determined counterattacks, but the balance of forces had swung against the Japanese. Burmese anti-colonialists, who had welcomed the Japanese in 1942, switched sides, and the Burma National Army joined in the British advance to Rangoon. The British secured the port city in May after amphibious landings.

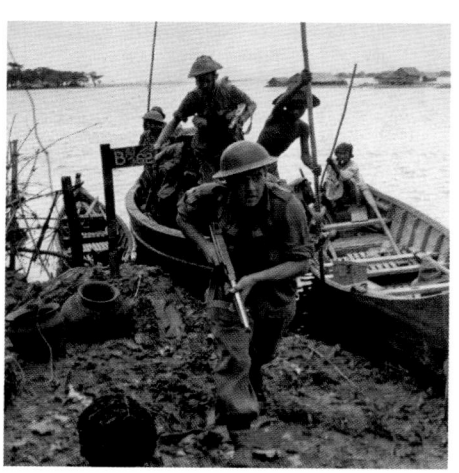

◁ Burma patrol
Allied soldiers search for Japanese soldiers. After May 1945, Japanese troops remained in Burma but their operations were of little significance.

Intelligence gathering, Rangoon
A map created by British Intelligence in April 1945 shows features of strategic importance in the Burmese port city of Rangoon. After capturing Mandalay in March 1945, the Allies sought to take Rangoon before the onset of the monsoon season in May.

◁ **Defending the Great Wall**
China's 8th Route Army fight Japanese invaders on a section of the Great Wall south of Futuyu. During the war, the 8th Route Army, operating largely in northern China, fought to establish guerrilla bases behind Japanese lines.

1 NATIONALIST CHINA 1940–1944

The Nationalists governed China from their capital at Chongqing (they had moved the capital inland from Nanjing in 1937). Corrupt, and losing support to the Communists, they fought an occasionally effective campaign against the Japanese, both with regular armies and by supporting guerrilla and bandit forces. They attempted to neutralize growing Communist strength by blockading Communist-held areas.

✊ Nationalist guerrilla and bandit forces

★ Nationalist capital

2 COMMUNIST CHINA 1940–1944

By 1940, relations between the Nationalists and Communists had broken down into conflict. In fall 1940, the Communist New 4th Army, surrounded by Nationalist forces in south Anhui, attacked, fighting a bitter battle in January 1941 known as the New 4th Army incident. It was not until early 1944 that a delicate truce was reestablished.

■ Communist zone

✖ New 4th Army incident

3 US SUPPORT 1941–1944

The US supported Chinese action against Japan by providing training to the Nationalist army. In addition, the USAF 14th Air Force maintained a number of air bases in the south from which they inflicted damage on Japanese positions in China and Taiwan, as well as on its shipping. Allied aircraft also brought supplies for the Nationalists via an air route from India known as "The Hump" (see panel, right).

✈ USAF 14th Air Force bases

⊢•••▶ The Hump air route

May 1944 The Japanese seize Henan province during the Ichigo offensive.

Jan 7–13, 1941 The New 4th Army incident brings the truce between Nationalists and Communists to an end.

Nov 2–Dec 20, 1943 Nationalist forces survive a major Japanese assault.

1937–1945 Chongqing serves as the Chinese Nationalist capital.

May 1944 Supplies from Dinjan in Assam, India, are carried to Kunming in Yunnan province via The Hump air route.

Mar 30, 1940 Anti-Communist defector Wang Ching-wei, backed by Japan, forms a puppet regime.

May 15–Sep 1942 The Japanese wage war in Zhejiang and Jiangxi provinces.

Dec 24, 1941–Jan 15, 1942 The Japanese are defeated in their offensive against Changsha.

Aug–Nov 1944 The Japanese seize Guilin and Liuzhou, creating a land bridge from China south to Indochina.

Map labels

U S S R
HEILONGJIANG
Blagoveshchensk
MANCHUKUO (MANCHURIA)
Yichun
Nomonhan
Harbin
Jixi
Songhua
Kirin
Changchun
Shenyang
MONGOLIA
Gobi
Jinzhou
Yingkou
Zhangjiakou
Lüshunkou
Seoul
KOREA
Beijing
Tianjin
Yellow River
Qingdao
Yellow Sea
C H I N A
Taiyuan
Zhengding
Weifang
Yan'an
Jinan
Luoyang
Zhengzhou
Xuzhou
Xi'an
H E N A N
Huai
Nanjing
Shanghai
Laohekou
Hankou
ANHUI
Hangzhou
Anking
ZHEJIANG
Chengdu
Chongqing
Lake Poyang
Changde
Lake Dongting
Nanchang
Changsha
JIANGXI
TIBET
Brahmaputra
Chihkiang
Hengyang
Suichuan
Fuzhou
NEPAL
BHUTAN
Dinjan
Guiyang
Lingling
Taipei
INDIA
BURMA
Yangtze
Guilin
Xiamen
Liuzhou
Guangzhou
Taiwan
Shantou
Kunming
Nanning
Macau
Hong Kong
Hanoi
Haikou
FRENCH INDOCHINA
Hainan
Vinh
THAILAND
South China Sea
PHILIPPINES

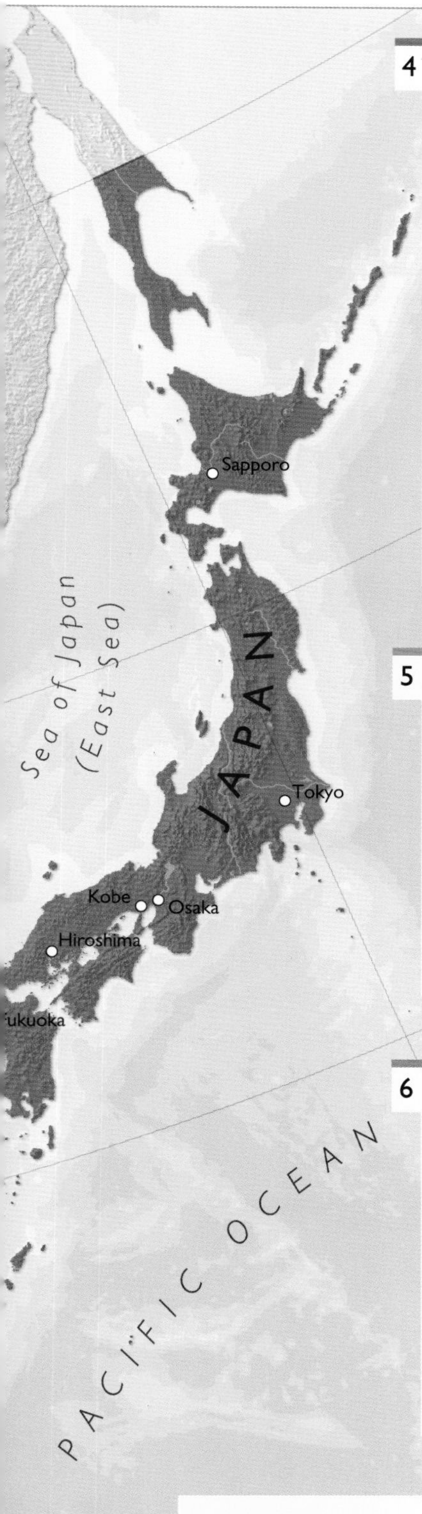

4 EARLY JAPANESE OFFENSIVES
DECEMBER 1941–SEPTEMBER 1942

The first major Japanese attack in China after Pearl Harbor began in late December 1941 and resulted in defeat at the hands of the Nationalists at Changsha. In May 1942, the Japanese launched an offensive in the provinces of Zhejiang and Jiangxi aimed at destroying US air bases and punishing the Chinese who supported US activity. More than 250,000 Chinese civilians were killed by Japanese biological weapons.

- ▮ Japan and its territories by 1941
- ▮ Japanese gains in China 1941–1942
- ▮ Other regions under Japanese control 1941–1942
- ✕ Battle site
- ➡ Japanese advances in Zhejiang–Jiangxi

5 STALEMATE JUNE 1942–DECEMBER 1943

Little action took place in China after mid-1942 as the Japanese focused on other goals in the Pacific. In 1943 they launched a series of "rice offensives"— attacks designed to battle-harden their new troops and to seize food supplies from the starving Chinese. However, with US help the Chinese managed to fight the Japanese to a stalemate at Changde, a battle in which the Japanese continued to use chemical weapons, including mustard gas.

- ✕ Battle site

6 OPERATION ICHIGO
APRIL 19–DECEMBER 31, 1944

In 1944 Japan launched its largest campaign in China to create a land bridge between its conquests in the east of the country and its gains in Indochina, and to eradicate the US air bases supporting B-29 Superfortress bombers. The Japanese fought three major battles with the Chinese. Losses were huge, with the Chinese suffering up to 700,000 casualties.

- ✕ Battle sites
- ⤢ Captured US air bases
- ▮ Territory held by the Japanese after Operation Ichigo

JAPANESE CHINA

By 1941, Japan controlled much of northern and eastern China. After sporadic fighting between Japanese and Nationalist Chinese, the Japanese made advances in the south and center during Operation Ichigo in 1944, with both sides suffering major casualties.

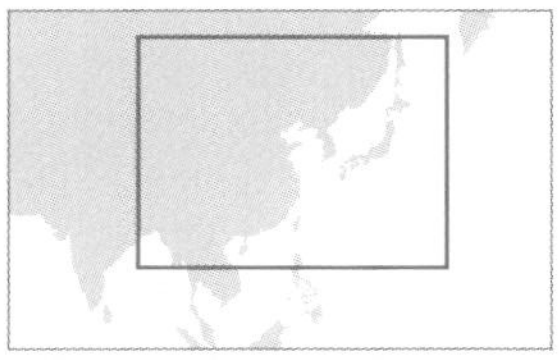

TIMELINE

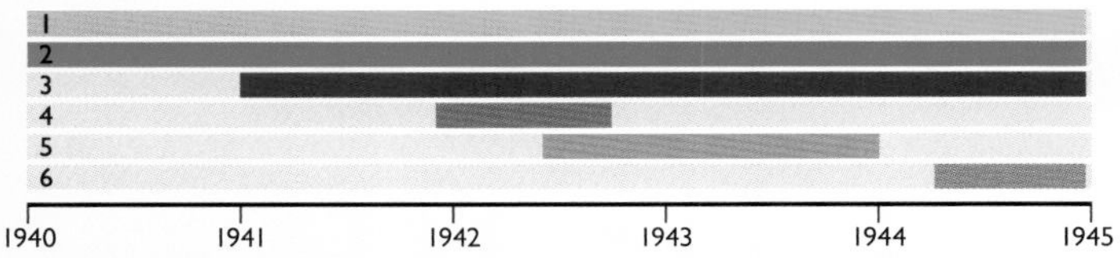

```
        1940    1941    1942    1943    1944    1945
1
2
3
4
5
6
```

CHINA AND JAPAN AT WAR

Despite a truce between China's Nationalist and Communist factions following the Japanese invasion in 1937, wartime China remained bitterly divided. Japan sought to capitalize on this, stretching its resources across China to wage an eight-year expansionist war.

While bitter fighting had raged between Chinese and Japanese forces since 1937, after the Japanese attack on Pearl Harbor in December 1941 the conflict became incorporated into the larger war that erupted in the Pacific. The US provided air and military support from India for the Nationalists, who managed to inflict several defeats on the Japanese, but the aid was never enough to turn the tide of the war in favor of the Chinese. Japan's offensives in the months following Pearl Harbor were sporadic, with attacks on US air bases in the south of China as well as the massacre of 250,000 civilians using biological agents such as cholera and typhoid. Further offensives in 1943 were also accompanied by chemical weapons. It was not until 1944 that Japan launched a huge offensive, Operation Ichigo, in which 500,000 troops attempted to carve out a path to Japanese-occupied Indochina and remove the threat from the US air bases used to bomb Japanese cities. The campaign was a success, and the Japanese largely kept the gains from Operation Ichigo until the end of the war.

"The Greater East Asian War was justified and righteous."

HIDEKI TOJO, FORMER JAPANESE PRIME MINISTER, 1946

FLYING THE HUMP

In 1942, the US set up an air route from Assam in India to supply Nationalist Chinese forces across the country. Nicknamed "The Hump" by pilots, it passed over the eastern end of the Himalayas, and was extremely dangerous due to consistently poor weather and a lack of charts and radio navigation aids. By August 1945, more than 728,000 tons (660,000 metric tons) of materiel had been flown in to China, with a great loss of Allied aircraft.

A US Army transport flies over the Himalayas

The bridge to Saigon
Japanese troops head into Saigon, in French
Indochina, in 1940 as part of an invasion that
secured the French colonies by 1941. The
French administered Indochina until March
1945, when the Japanese took control until
the war's end.

JAPANESE RULE IN EAST ASIA

Japan acquired an extensive colonial empire before and during World War II, in part to secure raw material supplies for its economy. Little political freedom was permitted in its colonies, and conditions were harsh.

Before World War I, Japan had annexed Taiwan and Korea, and it acquired former German Pacific islands as mandates after the war. In the 1930s it invaded Manchuria, large parts of eastern China, and Southeast Asia from 1940 (see pp.106–107). Where possible, the economies of these territories were shaped to supply Japan's war effort; steel production in Manchuria increased, agricultural output rose in Taiwan, and electricity production soared in Korea.

△ **Pan-Asian solidarity**
Japanese propaganda extolled the virtues of pan-Asian solidarity, such as on this poster, which promotes cooperation between Manchuria, Japan, and China.

Little consideration was given to local needs, and there were widespread food shortages. Many thousands of women were forced into sexual slavery as "comfort women" for the army. Japan also clamped down harshly on dissent. Allied prisoners of war (POWs) suffered greatly, including the 80,000 taken when Singapore fell in February 1942. The Japanese military code looked down on surrender, and Allied POWs routinely received minimal rations, were beaten, and were put to hard labor, including constructing the Burma railway, through 260 miles (420 km) of mountainous jungle. The death toll was high—of the 36,000 US troops taken prisoner by the Japanese, almost 40 percent died.

GREATER EAST ASIA CONFERENCE

In 1940, the Japanese government announced a Greater East Asia Co-Prosperity Sphere. Ostensibly a bloc of Asian powers to promote prosperity and political freedom, it was in reality completely directed by Japan. At its 1943 Conference in Tokyo, pro-Japanese leaders attended, such as Ba Maw of Burma (far left) and José P. Laurel of the Philippines (second from right).

ENDGAME AND AFTERMATH 1944–1955

AS THE WAR REACHED ITS FINALE IN EUROPE, THE US AND JAPAN INTENSIFIED THEIR BITTER STRUGGLE IN THE PACIFIC. THE DROPPING OF THE ATOMIC BOMB USHERED IN A NEW AND UNCERTAIN ERA.

ALLIED VICTORY IN EUROPE

Hitler's determination to fight to the finish condemned Germany to massive destruction in the final phase of the war in Europe. However, victory for the Allies was not achieved until Soviet troops raised the hammer and sickle flag over the ruins of Berlin.

△ **The face of war**
A soldier from an SS panzer division shows signs of combat exhaustion during the Battle of the Bulge in the winter of 1944–1945.

In December 1944, with the Allies closing in on Germany, Hitler made a last attempt to turn the tide of the war, launching a surprise offensive in the Ardennes, in Belgium, Luxembourg, and northeastern France. The initial success of this operation—named the Battle of the Bulge because of the bulging shape created when the Germans pushed through the Allied front line—was testimony to the remarkable tenacity of the German army, but Hitler's plan for a decisive breakthrough failed. The US troops held key positions and once poor weather had cleared, the Allies could resume their air attacks, which were having a decisive effect. Meanwhile, the Germans were running out of fuel.

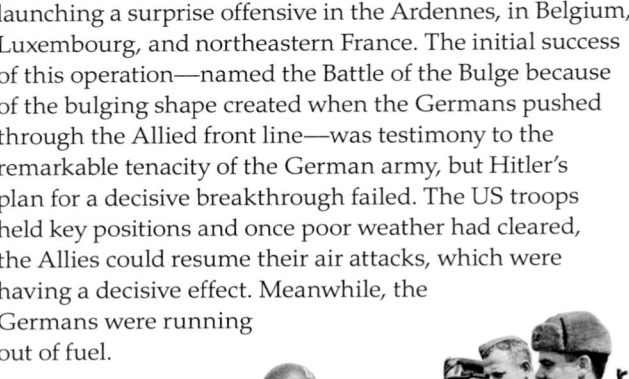

▷ **Meeting at Torgau**
US and Soviet troops meet in friendly fashion at Torgau, on the Elbe, as the Allies overrun Germany from east and west in April 1945.

False hopes

By January 1945, with the Ardennes offensive failing and Soviet troops ready to invade Germany from the east, the German position seemed hopeless. However, the Nazi regime retained the will to fight and many of its people remained loyal. While the Führer dreamed of miracles, young and old were marshalled for a final, desperate homeland defense. Hitler's remaining hope was for the Western Allies and the Soviet Union to have a major disagreement, but this did not happen. The Yalta conference of Allied leaders in February confirmed broad agreement on the immediate practical concerns of the wartime alliance, such as the military occupation of Germany, while skirting around more intractable future political issues. There was no "race for Berlin"; instead, the Western Allies were content to let the Soviets enjoy the honor—and suffer the casualties—involved in taking the city.

Carnage on an epic scale

The scale of the destruction and disruption in the last months of the war was staggering. The resumption of the Soviet advance in January 1945 triggered the mass evacuation of German civilians from East Prussia and the Baltic. Having won control of the air over Germany at great cost, the Allied air forces proceeded to destroy German towns and cities in attacks that no longer served any clear military purpose.

As Soviet forces fought their way into Berlin in late April, US and Soviet troops met at the Elbe River. The discovery of the Nazi death

THE THIRD REICH'S LAST STAND

The Ardennes operation, launched on December 16, 1944, was the German army's last offensive. The Soviet advance on Germany, which began in January 1945, carried the fighting deep into the country, and the Western Allies crossed the Rhine in March. The death of Roosevelt on April 12 gave Hitler a glimmer of hope, but it made no difference to the conduct of the war. Hostilities continued for a week after Hitler's suicide as surrenders were arranged on different fronts.

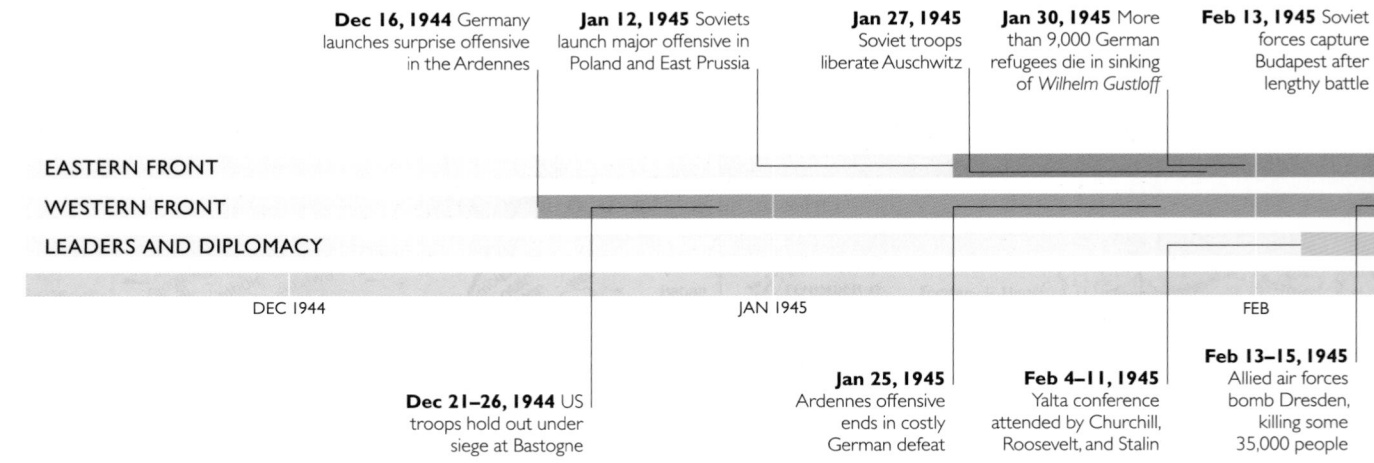

Dec 16, 1944 Germany launches surprise offensive in the Ardennes

Jan 12, 1945 Soviets launch major offensive in Poland and East Prussia

Jan 27, 1945 Soviet troops liberate Auschwitz

Jan 30, 1945 More than 9,000 German refugees die in sinking of *Wilhelm Gustloff*

Feb 13, 1945 Soviet forces capture Budapest after lengthy battle

EASTERN FRONT
WESTERN FRONT
LEADERS AND DIPLOMACY

DEC 1944   JAN 1945   FEB

Dec 21–26, 1944 US troops hold out under siege at Bastogne

Jan 25, 1945 Ardennes offensive ends in costly German defeat

Feb 4–11, 1945 Yalta conference attended by Churchill, Roosevelt, and Stalin

Feb 13–15, 1945 Allied air forces bomb Dresden, killing some 35,000 people

◁ **Mustang fighter**
The North American Mustang P-51 was a key aircraft in the war's final stages, acting as a long-range fighter escort for bombers and as a ground-attack aircraft armed with rockets and bombs.

▽ **Raising the flag**
As a symbol of Soviet victory, soldiers raise a flag over the Reichstag building amid the ruins of Berlin on May 2, 1945.

camps shocked the advancing Allied forces. A series of German surrenders began in Italy, where Mussolini met a grim end at the hands of Italian partisans on April 28. Two days later, Hitler died by suicide at his Berlin bunker, denouncing the German army and people as unworthy of his leadership. On May 8, the war in Europe was declared over.

Allied-occupied Germany

The victors of World War II reigned over a continent in ruins. Political conflicts between Communists and their enemies were already surfacing before the war ended: for example in Greece, where British intervention prevented Communist-led partisans from taking power. But in Germany itself, where prolonged Nazi resistance had been expected and feared, there was instead only the struggle to survive or, in the case of prominent Nazis, to escape retribution. The Allies carried out their plan for the four-way division of Germany, including Berlin, into military occupation zones, France having won the right to be included in the share-out. Occupation by the Soviet Union was, to say the least, an ambiguous "liberation" for many of the peoples of Central and Eastern Europe. However, despite the suffering that followed, Europe could at least now hope to move toward a brighter future.

> *"This is your victory! It is the victory of freedom in every land."*
>
> WINSTON CHURCHILL, SPEECH, MAY 8, 1945

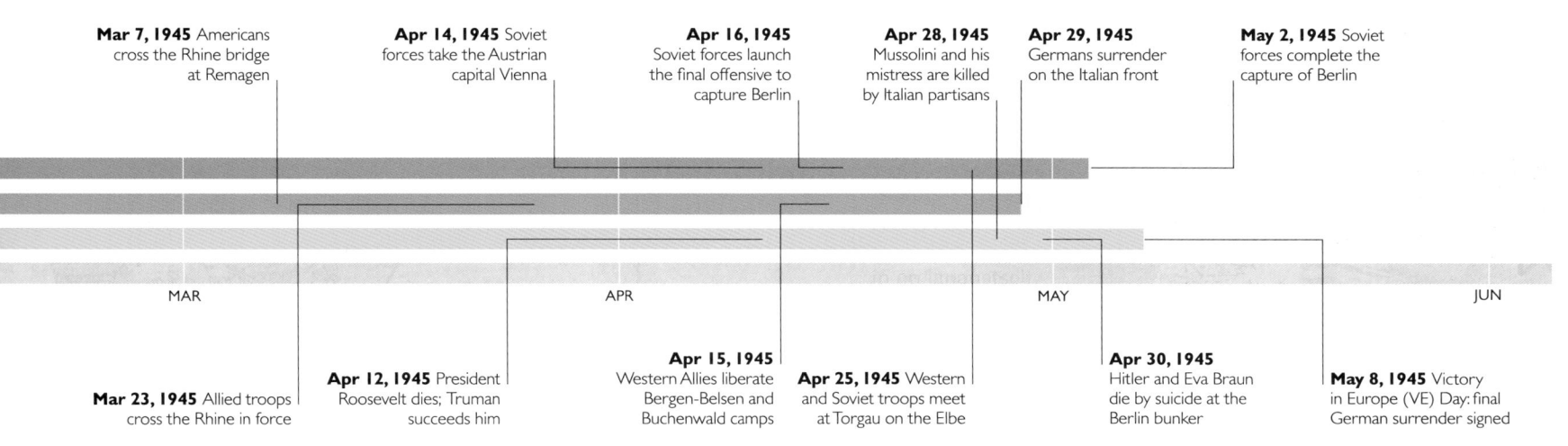

Mar 7, 1945 Americans cross the Rhine bridge at Remagen

Apr 14, 1945 Soviet forces take the Austrian capital Vienna

Apr 16, 1945 Soviet forces launch the final offensive to capture Berlin

Apr 28, 1945 Mussolini and his mistress are killed by Italian partisans

Apr 29, 1945 Germans surrender on the Italian front

May 2, 1945 Soviet forces complete the capture of Berlin

MAR APR MAY JUN

Mar 23, 1945 Allied troops cross the Rhine in force

Apr 12, 1945 President Roosevelt dies; Truman succeeds him

Apr 15, 1945 Western Allies liberate Bergen-Belsen and Buchenwald camps

Apr 25, 1945 Western and Soviet troops meet at Torgau on the Elbe

Apr 30, 1945 Hitler and Eva Braun die by suicide at the Berlin bunker

May 8, 1945 Victory in Europe (VE) Day: final German surrender signed

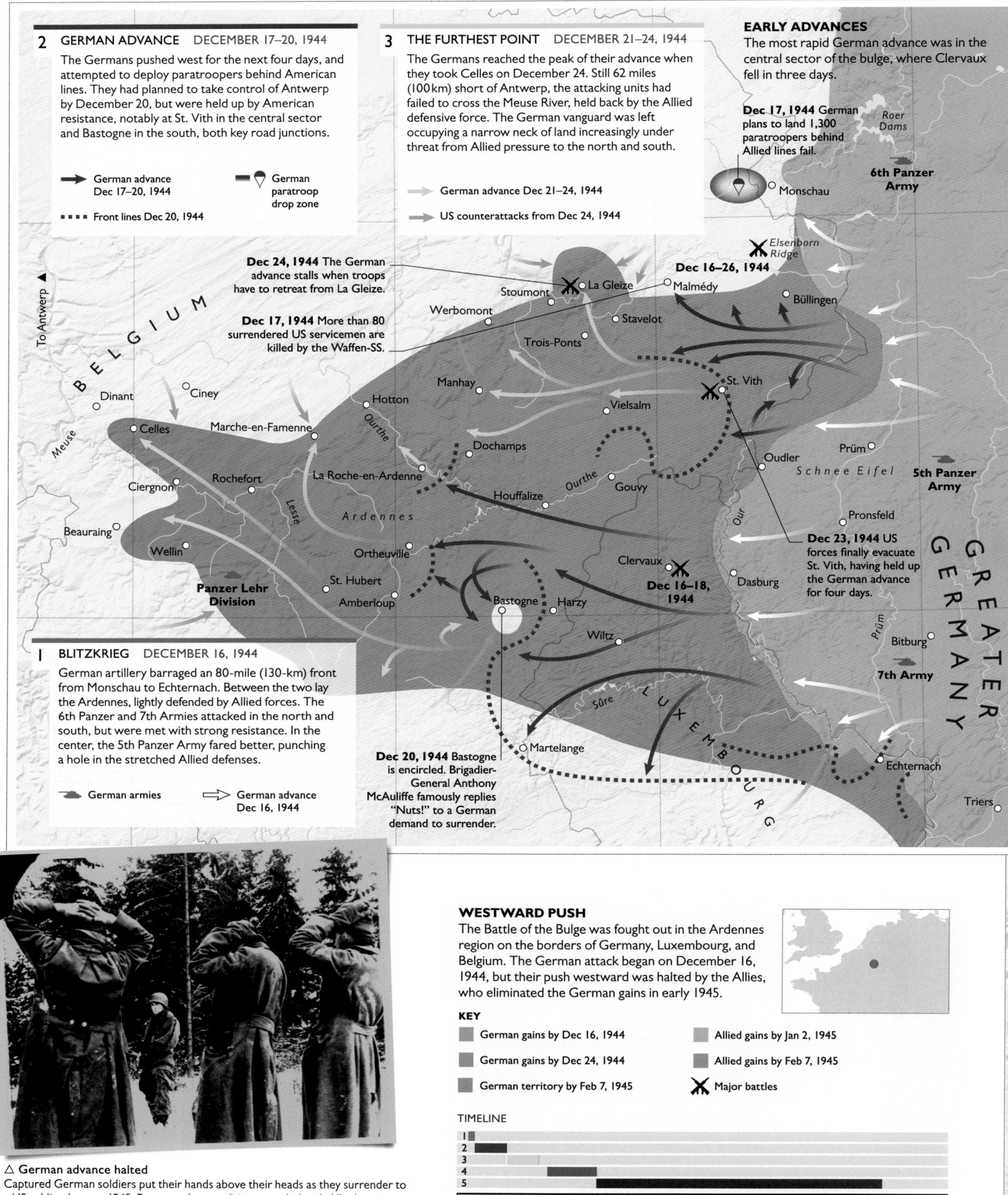

2 GERMAN ADVANCE DECEMBER 17–20, 1944

The Germans pushed west for the next four days, and attempted to deploy paratroopers behind American lines. They had planned to take control of Antwerp by December 20, but were held up by American resistance, notably at St. Vith in the central sector and Bastogne in the south, both key road junctions.

→ German advance Dec 17–20, 1944

▬● German paratroop drop zone

▪▪▪▪ Front lines Dec 20, 1944

3 THE FURTHEST POINT DECEMBER 21–24, 1944

The Germans reached the peak of their advance when they took Celles on December 24. Still 62 miles (100km) short of Antwerp, the attacking units had failed to cross the Meuse River, held back by the Allied defensive force. The German vanguard was left occupying a narrow neck of land increasingly under threat from Allied pressure to the north and south.

→ German advance Dec 21–24, 1944

→ US counterattacks from Dec 24, 1944

EARLY ADVANCES

The most rapid German advance was in the central sector of the bulge, where Clervaux fell in three days.

Dec 17, 1944 German plans to land 1,300 paratroopers behind Allied lines fail.

Dec 24, 1944 The German advance stalls when troops have to retreat from La Gleize.

Dec 17, 1944 More than 80 surrendered US servicemen are killed by the Waffen-SS.

Dec 23, 1944 US forces finally evacuate St. Vith, having held up the German advance for four days.

1 BLITZKRIEG DECEMBER 16, 1944

German artillery barraged an 80-mile (130-km) front from Monschau to Echternach. Between the two lay the Ardennes, lightly defended by Allied forces. The 6th Panzer and 7th Armies attacked in the north and south, but were met with strong resistance. In the center, the 5th Panzer Army fared better, punching a hole in the stretched Allied defenses.

◣ German armies ⇨ German advance Dec 16, 1944

Dec 20, 1944 Bastogne is encircled. Brigadier-General Anthony McAuliffe famously replies "Nuts!" to a German demand to surrender.

△ **German advance halted**
Captured German soldiers put their hands above their heads as they surrender to a US soldier, January 1945. Poor weather conditions coupled with Allied resistance at key junctions prevented the Germans reaching their goal.

WESTWARD PUSH

The Battle of the Bulge was fought out in the Ardennes region on the borders of Germany, Luxembourg, and Belgium. The German attack began on December 16, 1944, but their push westward was halted by the Allies, who eliminated the German gains in early 1945.

KEY

■ German gains by Dec 16, 1944

■ German gains by Dec 24, 1944

■ German territory by Feb 7, 1945

■ Allied gains by Jan 2, 1945

■ Allied gains by Feb 7, 1945

✕ Major battles

TIMELINE

1
2
3
4
5

DEC 15, 1944   JAN 1, 1945   JAN 15   FEB 1   FEB 15

BATTLE OF THE BULGE

Shaken by the Allies' advance on Germany, Hitler decided on a final gamble in winter 1944. His counter-offensive punched a deep wedge in Allied lines, leading Western newspapers to call it the Battle of the Bulge. It was the last major German offensive of the war, and the largest fought on the Western Front.

Desperate to regain the initiative in Europe, Hitler chose a move that startled even his own generals: an attack through the hilly, wooded Ardennes region bordering Germany to the port of Antwerp in Belgium, covering 112 miles (180 km). This action was intended to cut the Allied forces in two and disrupt their supplies. Allied commanders had discounted the possibility of such an attack, so the assault achieved almost total surprise. However, the German forces soon encountered exactly those problems the military planners had foreseen. Poor roads led to transportation bottlenecks and the winter weather made conditions difficult. Hitler's plan depended on an almost impossibly tight schedule, but his forces soon found themselves bogged down by the difficult terrain and held back by determined US resistance.

After three weeks, when it had become apparent that the planned breakthrough had not happened, Hitler ordered his troops back to Germany. The operation had been a huge failure. The killed and wounded on both sides numbered close to 100,000, and crucially Germany had also lost over 500 tanks and 1,000 aircraft.

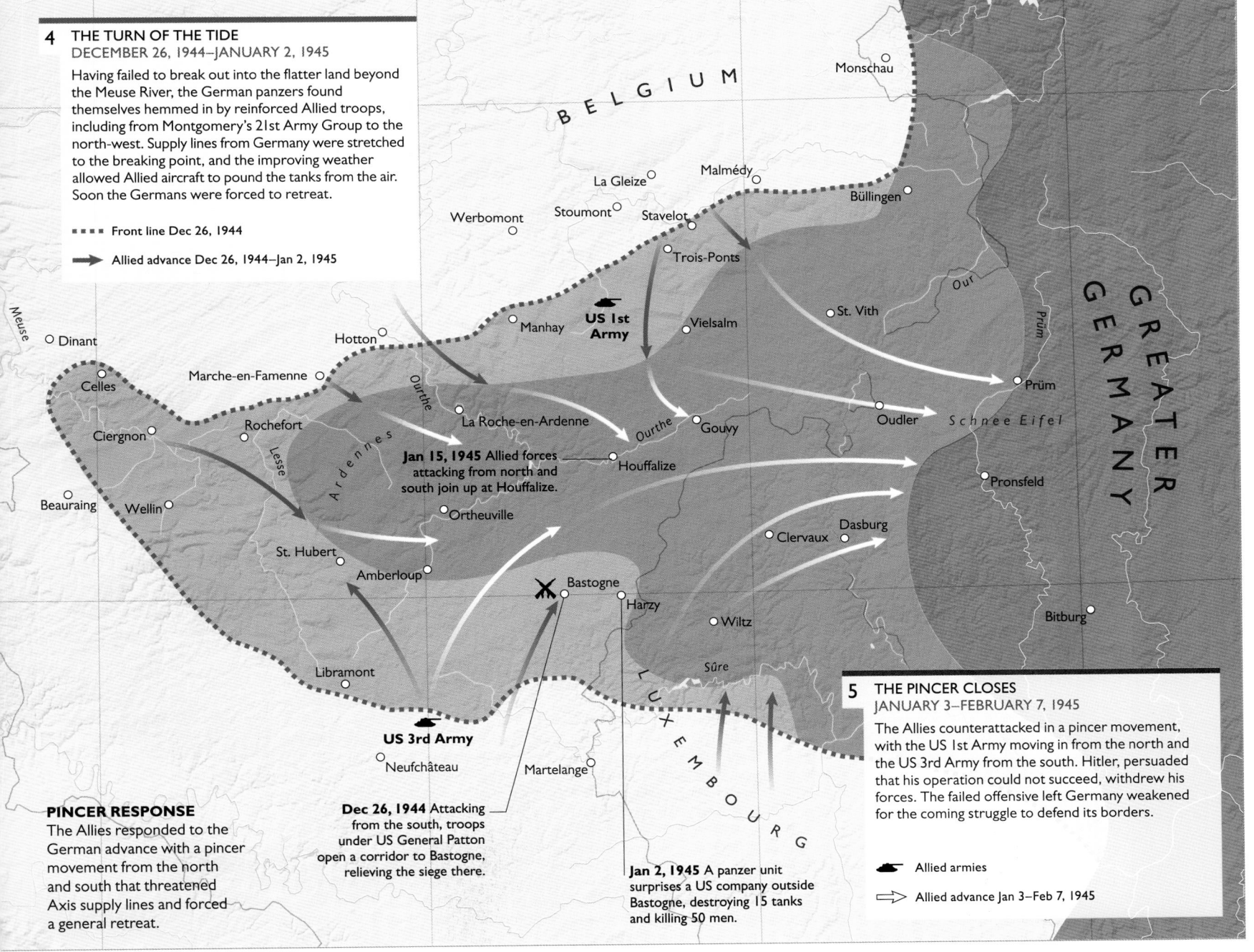

4 THE TURN OF THE TIDE
DECEMBER 26, 1944–JANUARY 2, 1945

Having failed to break out into the flatter land beyond the Meuse River, the German panzers found themselves hemmed in by reinforced Allied troops, including from Montgomery's 21st Army Group to the north-west. Supply lines from Germany were stretched to the breaking point, and the improving weather allowed Allied aircraft to pound the tanks from the air. Soon the Germans were forced to retreat.

▪▪▪▪ Front line Dec 26, 1944

➡ Allied advance Dec 26, 1944–Jan 2, 1945

Jan 15, 1945 Allied forces attacking from north and south join up at Houffalize.

PINCER RESPONSE
The Allies responded to the German advance with a pincer movement from the north and south that threatened Axis supply lines and forced a general retreat.

Dec 26, 1944 Attacking from the south, troops under US General Patton open a corridor to Bastogne, relieving the siege there.

Jan 2, 1945 A panzer unit surprises a US company outside Bastogne, destroying 15 tanks and killing 50 men.

5 THE PINCER CLOSES
JANUARY 3–FEBRUARY 7, 1945

The Allies counterattacked in a pincer movement, with the US 1st Army moving in from the north and the US 3rd Army from the south. Hitler, persuaded that his operation could not succeed, withdrew his forces. The failed offensive left Germany weakened for the coming struggle to defend its borders.

◄ Allied armies

⟹ Allied advance Jan 3–Feb 7, 1945

YALTA AND POTSDAM

In February 1945, the three Allied leaders—Roosevelt, Churchill, and Stalin—met at Yalta in Crimea to decide the fate of the post-war world. Five months later, the nations' leaders met again at Potsdam, near Berlin.

△ **Memorial for a leader**
The 1945 Yalta conference was a historical landmark, as this postage stamp from the former French colony of Togo, issued to mark Churchill's death in 1965, confirms.

One of the main aims of Yalta was to decide what should happen to Germany after the war. The Big Three—as Roosevelt, Churchill, and Stalin were known—agreed to divide the country into four occupation zones administered by the US, Britain, the USSR, and France, with control of Berlin split between the four powers. They agreed to establish a provisional government in Poland as a preliminary to holding elections. Similarly, the other freed peoples of Eastern Europe would be helped in setting up democratic regimes. Stalin agreed to join the war against Japan once Germany surrendered, and to join the UN.

Broken pledges

The Yalta agreements were initially heralded as a success, but the mood did not last. By the time they met again at Potsdam between July 7 and August 2, with Harry S Truman and Clement Attlee replacing Roosevelt and Churchill respectively, the tensions between the West and the USSR were obvious. Although the divided and disarmed state of Germany was confirmed, there was disagreement about the amount of reparations the Germans should pay. Refugees from the east were flooding westward, displaced by the adjustment of the Polish–German frontier in Poland's favor. Additionally, it was clear that Stalin, despite his promises, would not allow free elections to take place in the territories his armies had liberated.

THE POTSDAM DECLARATION

Following Potsdam, the US, UK, and China called for Japan's unconditional surrender, threatening "prompt and utter destruction" if it did not comply. Although Stalin was also present at the conference, the USSR and Japan had a treaty of nonaggression at the time, so he did not sign the declaration.

The Big Three
Winston Churchill, Franklin D. Roosevelt, and Joseph Stalin at the Yalta conference in February 1945. Roosevelt was suffering health problems at the time of the conference, and he died that year on April 12 in the US state of Georgia.

CROSSING THE RHINE

After driving back the German counteroffensive in the Ardennes, Allied forces met their next major challenge— fighting their way over the Rhine. They then spent a month advancing across Germany toward the Elbe to meet Soviet troops advancing from the east.

More than 1,310 ft (400 m) wide in places and fiercely defended on its eastern bank, the Rhine was a formidable barrier to Allied progress into Germany. The Supreme Commander of the Allied forces, General Eisenhower, made careful plans for a coordinated assault to storm across the river. In the end, the initial crossing took place almost by chance over a bridge at Remagen that German defenders had failed to blow up. The campaign then proceeded according to Eisenhower's plan, and by March 24 the Allies had established three substantial bridgeheads on the waterway's far bank.

> *"One of those rare and fleeting opportunities which occasionally arise in war."*
>
> GENERAL EISENHOWER ON THE CAPTURE OF REMAGEN

Germany now lay open before the Allies, but political considerations imposed a degree of caution. It had been agreed at Yalta (see pp.230–231) that the eastern approaches to Berlin were to remain in the Soviet zone, so instead of hastening toward the German capital, the Western Allied advance proceeded more haltingly. British troops uncovered horrors when they liberated the Bergen-Belsen concentration camp in mid-April, and US forces reached the Dachau camp two weeks later.

GENERAL GEORGE PATTON 1885–1945

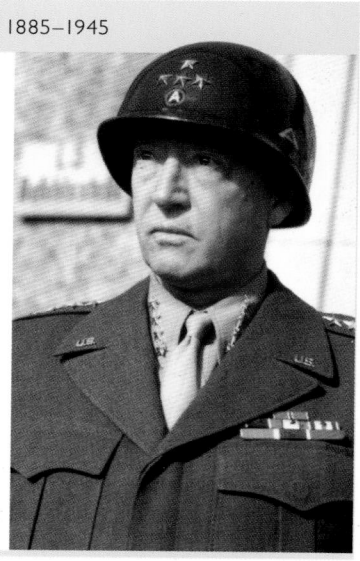

Born into a prosperous family in California, George Patton graduated from the US Military Academy at West Point in 1909. He represented his country in the modern pentathlon at the Stockholm Olympics in 1912 and pioneered the use of tanks by the US in World War I. He had already established a formidable fighting reputation in North Africa and Sicily before taking charge of the US 3rd Army early in 1944. Under his command the forces won a reputation for highly aggressive action.

PATHS THROUGH GERMANY

After crossing the Rhine, the way lay open for Allied armies to advance across central Germany and meet up with Soviet forces at the Elbe River.

KEY

German army groups	Allied gains by Dec 15, 1944
German armies	Allied gains by Mar 21, 1945
Allied army groups	Allied gains by Apr 18, 1945
Allied armies	Concentration camp
	Supplies delivered by air

TIMELINE

1
2
3
4
5
6
7

JAN 1945   FEB   MAR   APRIL   MAY   JUN

Apr 29–May 8 Food drops from Allied bombers help alleviate the suffering of Dutch civilians facing famine after the Hunger Winter of 1944–1945.

Amsterdam

Rotterdam   Rh

UNITED KINGDOM

British 21st Army Group

Brussels

BELGIUM

Lille

Seine

Reims

Loire

Troyes

FRANCE

1 TO THE RHINE'S BANK
JANUARY–MARCH 5, 1945

Before crossing the Rhine, Allied forces first had to clear the approaches to the river. The Canadian 1st Army advanced through the southern Netherlands; US 9th Army troops moved through München-Gladbach, their progress delayed as German troops flooded the Roer valley; and US 1st Army troops entered Cologne on the river's west bank on March 5, 1945.

Allied operations	Allied advances

2 THE BRIDGE AT REMAGEN
MARCH 7–21, 1945

On March 7, troops of the US 1st Army unexpectedly found the Ludendorff railroad bridge at Remagen still intact. They crossed the bridge under heavy enemy fire and established the first Allied bridgehead on the east bank of the Rhine. US engineers put additional pontoon bridges in place, and by March 21 more than 25,000 troops had crossed. Infuriated, Hitler had four officers executed for failing to prevent the breach.

Battle of Remagen	Bridgehead at Remagen

3 ACROSS THE RHINE
MARCH 22–25, 1945

The Remagen crossing preempted an Allied assault across the river planned for the night of March 23. The British 21st Army Group under Field Marshal Montgomery made a series of crossings in northern Germany, by which time General Patton had crossed at Oppenheim to the south. By March 25, two more substantial bridgeheads had been established.

Bridgeheads established March 23–25

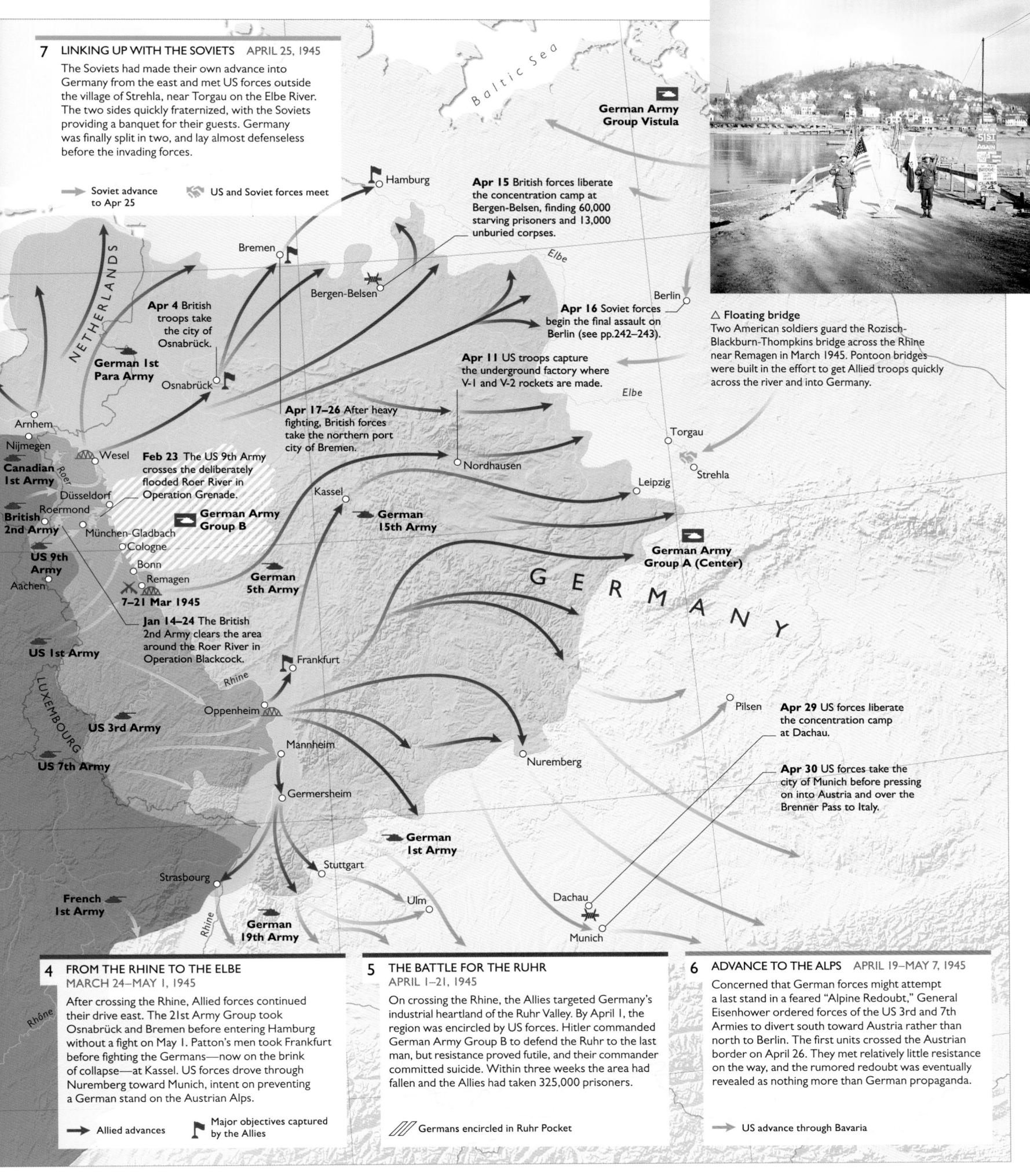

7 LINKING UP WITH THE SOVIETS APRIL 25, 1945

The Soviets had made their own advance into Germany from the east and met US forces outside the village of Strehla, near Torgau on the Elbe River. The two sides quickly fraternized, with the Soviets providing a banquet for their guests. Germany was finally split in two, and lay almost defenseless before the invading forces.

→ Soviet advance to Apr 25

🤝 US and Soviet forces meet

Baltic Sea

🛩 **German Army Group Vistula**

○ Hamburg

Apr 15 British forces liberate the concentration camp at Bergen-Belsen, finding 60,000 starving prisoners and 13,000 unburied corpses.

Bremen

Elbe

Bergen-Belsen

Berlin

Apr 16 Soviet forces begin the final assault on Berlin (see pp.242–243).

NETHERLANDS

Apr 4 British troops take the city of Osnabrück.

German 1st Para Army

Osnabrück

Apr 11 US troops capture the underground factory where V-1 and V-2 rockets are made.

Apr 17–26 After heavy fighting, British forces take the northern port city of Bremen.

Elbe

Torgau

○ Arnhem
Nijmegen

Wesel

Feb 23 The US 9th Army crosses the deliberately flooded Roer River in Operation Grenade.

Kassel

Nordhausen

Leipzig

Strehla

Canadian 1st Army

Düsseldorf
Roermond

German Army Group B

German 15th Army

🛩 **German Army Group A (Center)**

British 2nd Army

München-Gladbach
Cologne

US 9th Army

Bonn
Remagen

Aachen

7–21 Mar 1945

German 5th Army

G E R M A N Y

Jan 14–24 The British 2nd Army clears the area around the Roer River in Operation Blackcock.

Rhine

Frankfurt

Pilsen

Apr 29 US forces liberate the concentration camp at Dachau.

LUXEMBOURG

Oppenheim

US 3rd Army

Mannheim

Apr 30 US forces take the city of Munich before pressing on into Austria and over the Brenner Pass to Italy.

US 1st Army

US 7th Army

Nuremberg

Germersheim

German 1st Army

Strasbourg

Stuttgart

French 1st Army

Rhine

Ulm

Dachau

German 19th Army

Munich

Rhône

△ **Floating bridge**

Two American soldiers guard the Rozisch-Blackburn-Thompkins bridge across the Rhine near Remagen in March 1945. Pontoon bridges were built in the effort to get Allied troops quickly across the river and into Germany.

---

4 FROM THE RHINE TO THE ELBE
MARCH 24–MAY 1, 1945

After crossing the Rhine, Allied forces continued their drive east. The 21st Army Group took Osnabrück and Bremen before entering Hamburg without a fight on May 1. Patton's men took Frankfurt before fighting the Germans—now on the brink of collapse—at Kassel. US forces drove through Nuremberg toward Munich, intent on preventing a German stand on the Austrian Alps.

→ Allied advances

🚩 Major objectives captured by the Allies

5 THE BATTLE FOR THE RUHR
APRIL 1–21, 1945

On crossing the Rhine, the Allies targeted Germany's industrial heartland of the Ruhr Valley. By April 1, the region was encircled by US forces. Hitler commanded German Army Group B to defend the Ruhr to the last man, but resistance proved futile, and their commander committed suicide. Within three weeks the area had fallen and the Allies had taken 325,000 prisoners.

/// Germans encircled in Ruhr Pocket

6 ADVANCE TO THE ALPS APRIL 19–MAY 7, 1945

Concerned that German forces might attempt a last stand in a feared "Alpine Redoubt," General Eisenhower ordered forces of the US 3rd and 7th Armies to divert south toward Austria rather than north to Berlin. The first units crossed the Austrian border on April 26. They met relatively little resistance on the way, and the rumored redoubt was eventually revealed as nothing more than German propaganda.

→ US advance through Bavaria

GERMANY LOSES THE AIR WAR

The nature of the air war over Europe changed with the Allied landings in Normandy. The Luftwaffe was forced increasingly onto the defensive, and by late 1944, fuel shortages and loss of men and materiel had made it largely a spent force.

From mid-1944, the balance in the air war over Europe tipped decisively in the Allies' favor. This was in no small part due to the arrival in Europe of the P-51B Mustang—a fast fighter with enough range to provide effective cover for B-17 and B-24 bombers. Among the best fighters of the war, the P-51B could outperform the heavy fighters used by the Luftwaffe against the USAAF raiders, so Allied bombing raids became increasingly effective in disrupting German aircraft production and interrupting the development of new designs.

The Luftwaffe's activities were also curtailed by a chronic shortage of fuel caused by the Allied bombers' selective targeting of Germany's oil resources. By September 1944, the Luftwaffe had access to only 11,000 tons (10,000 metric tons) of octane each month instead of the 176,400 tons (160,000 metric tons) that it needed to fuel its operations. The USAAF mainly undertook the precision bombing of oil facilities, while the RAF under "Bomber" Harris turned their attention to the area bombing of cities.

Running out of legitimate strategic and industrial targets, the Allies dropped their bombs wherever they would cause maximum confusion to their enemy. In total, more than 350,000 German civilians were killed in Allied attacks; the rate of fatalities grew to 13,000 people a month from July 1944 to January 1945. The mass casualties of civilians that resulted in Hamburg, Dresden, Leipzig, Chemnitz, and other centers were controversial at the time, and have attracted growing criticism ever since.

THE P-51 MUSTANG

Originally designed by North American Aviation in 1940, the single-seater, long-range Mustang fighter took a major step forward in performance with the introduction of the B model, powered by a Rolls-Royce engine. From late 1943 onward, P-51Bs, along with the later C and D (shown here) models, were used as escorts on long-distance bombing raids, targeting German fighters and helping secure Allied victory in the skies.

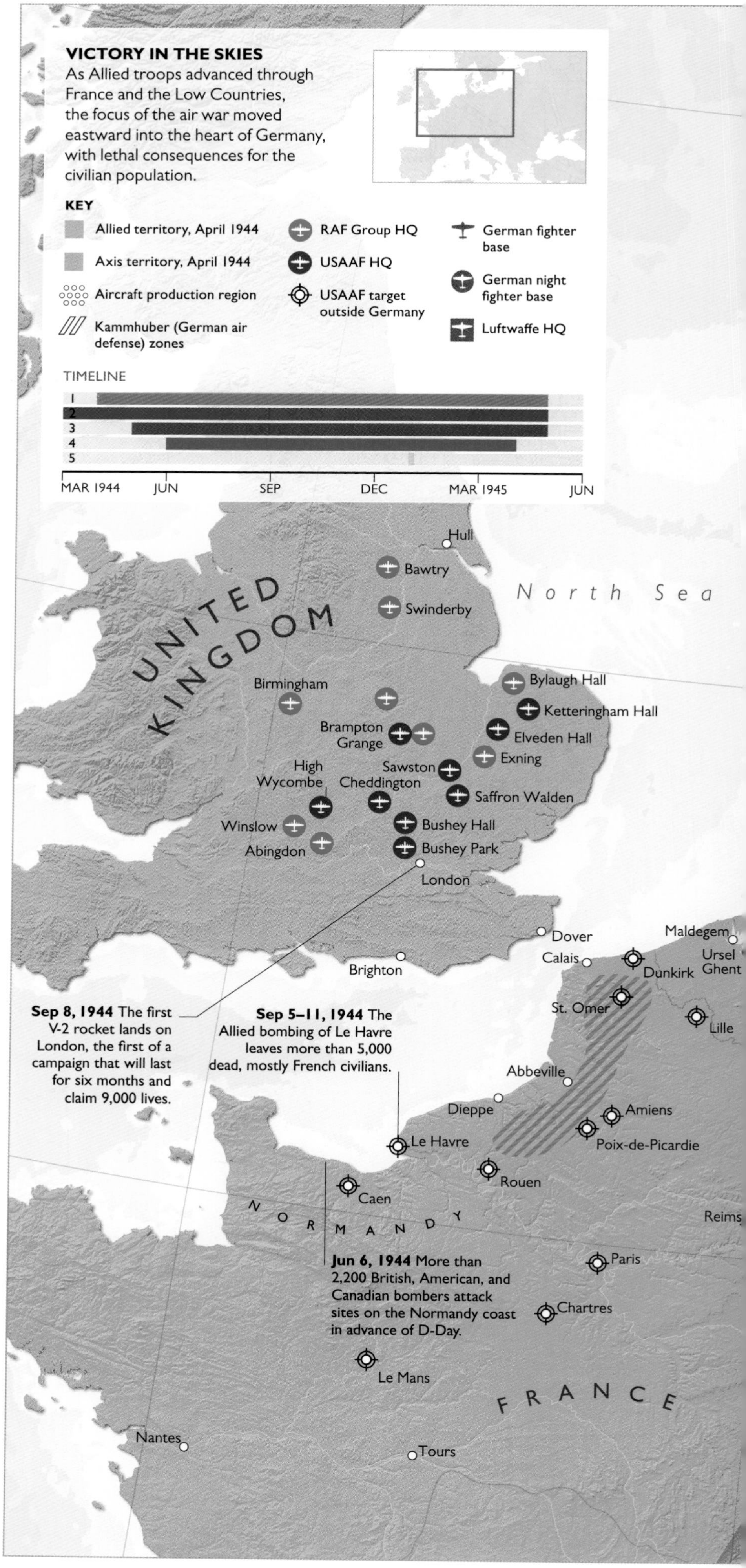

VICTORY IN THE SKIES

As Allied troops advanced through France and the Low Countries, the focus of the air war moved eastward into the heart of Germany, with lethal consequences for the civilian population.

KEY

- Allied territory, April 1944
- Axis territory, April 1944
- Aircraft production region
- Kammhuber (German air defense) zones
- RAF Group HQ
- USAAF HQ
- USAAF target outside Germany
- German fighter base
- German night fighter base
- Luftwaffe HQ

TIMELINE

1
2
3
4
5

MAR 1944   JUN   SEP   DEC   MAR 1945   JUN

Sep 8, 1944 The first V-2 rocket lands on London, the first of a campaign that will last for six months and claim 9,000 lives.

Sep 5–11, 1944 The Allied bombing of Le Havre leaves more than 5,000 dead, mostly French civilians.

Jun 6, 1944 More than 2,200 British, American, and Canadian bombers attack sites on the Normandy coast in advance of D-Day.

Map labels: Hull, Bawtry, Swinderby, North Sea, UNITED KINGDOM, Birmingham, Bylaugh Hall, Ketteringham Hall, Brampton Grange, Elveden Hall, Exning, High Wycombe, Sawston, Cheddington, Saffron Walden, Bushey Hall, Winslow, Bushey Park, Abingdon, London, Dover, Maldegem, Calais, Ursel Ghent, Dunkirk, Brighton, St. Omer, Lille, Abbeville, Amiens, Dieppe, Poix-de-Picardie, Le Havre, Rouen, Caen, NORMANDY, Reims, Paris, Chartres, Le Mans, FRANCE, Nantes, Tours

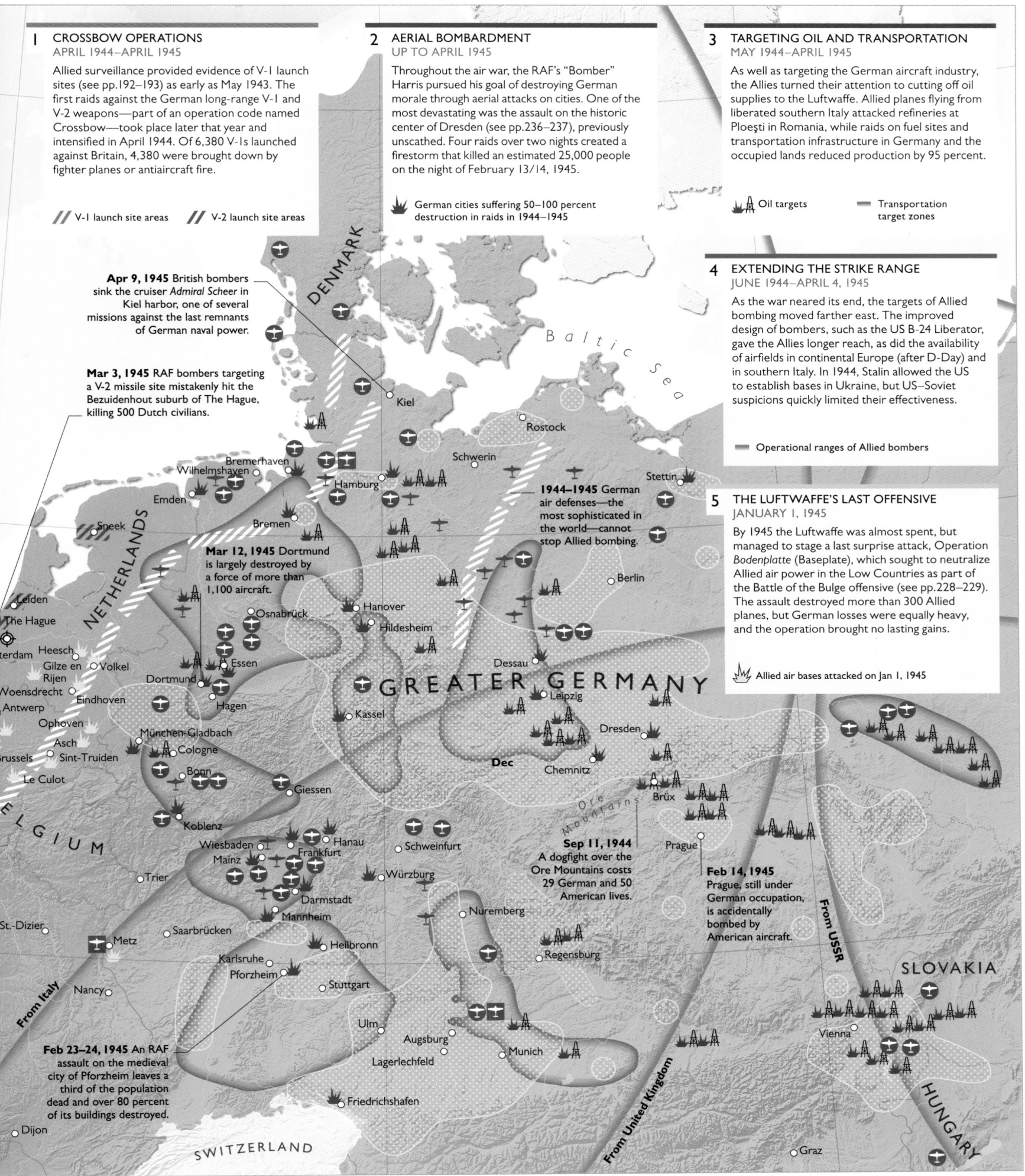

1 CROSSBOW OPERATIONS
APRIL 1944–APRIL 1945

Allied surveillance provided evidence of V-1 launch sites (see pp.192–193) as early as May 1943. The first raids against the German long-range V-1 and V-2 weapons—part of an operation code named Crossbow—took place later that year and intensified in April 1944. Of 6,380 V-1s launched against Britain, 4,380 were brought down by fighter planes or antiaircraft fire.

// V-1 launch site areas   // V-2 launch site areas

2 AERIAL BOMBARDMENT
UP TO APRIL 1945

Throughout the air war, the RAF's "Bomber" Harris pursued his goal of destroying German morale through aerial attacks on cities. One of the most devastating was the assault on the historic center of Dresden (see pp.236–237), previously unscathed. Four raids over two nights created a firestorm that killed an estimated 25,000 people on the night of February 13/14, 1945.

German cities suffering 50–100 percent destruction in raids in 1944–1945

3 TARGETING OIL AND TRANSPORTATION
MAY 1944–APRIL 1945

As well as targeting the German aircraft industry, the Allies turned their attention to cutting off oil supplies to the Luftwaffe. Allied planes flying from liberated southern Italy attacked refineries at Ploeşti in Romania, while raids on fuel sites and transportation infrastructure in Germany and the occupied lands reduced production by 95 percent.

Oil targets   Transportation target zones

4 EXTENDING THE STRIKE RANGE
JUNE 1944–APRIL 4, 1945

As the war neared its end, the targets of Allied bombing moved farther east. The improved design of bombers, such as the US B-24 Liberator, gave the Allies longer reach, as did the availability of airfields in continental Europe (after D-Day) and in southern Italy. In 1944, Stalin allowed the US to establish bases in Ukraine, but US–Soviet suspicions quickly limited their effectiveness.

Operational ranges of Allied bombers

5 THE LUFTWAFFE'S LAST OFFENSIVE
JANUARY 1, 1945

By 1945 the Luftwaffe was almost spent, but managed to stage a last surprise attack, Operation *Bodenplatte* (Baseplate), which sought to neutralize Allied air power in the Low Countries as part of the Battle of the Bulge offensive (see pp.228–229). The assault destroyed more than 300 Allied planes, but German losses were equally heavy, and the operation brought no lasting gains.

Allied air bases attacked on Jan 1, 1945

Apr 9, 1945 British bombers sink the cruiser *Admiral Scheer* in Kiel harbor, one of several missions against the last remnants of German naval power.

Mar 3, 1945 RAF bombers targeting a V-2 missile site mistakenly hit the Bezuidenhout suburb of The Hague, killing 500 Dutch civilians.

Mar 12, 1945 Dortmund is largely destroyed by a force of more than 1,100 aircraft.

1944–1945 German air defenses—the most sophisticated in the world—cannot stop Allied bombing.

Sep 11, 1944 A dogfight over the Ore Mountains costs 29 German and 50 American lives.

Feb 14, 1945 Prague, still under German occupation, is accidentally bombed by American aircraft.

Feb 23–24, 1945 An RAF assault on the medieval city of Pforzheim leaves a third of the population dead and over 80 percent of its buildings destroyed.

DENMARK
NETHERLANDS
BELGIUM
GREATER GERMANY
SWITZERLAND
SLOVAKIA
HUNGARY
Baltic Sea
Ore Mountains

From Italy
From United Kingdom
From USSR

Kiel
Rostock
Schwerin
Stettin
Bremerhaven
Wilhelmshaven
Hamburg
Emden
Bremen
Sneek
Berlin
Leiden
The Hague
Rotterdam
Heesch
Gilze en Rijen
Volkel
Woensdrecht
Eindhoven
Antwerp
Ophoven
Brussels
Asch
Sint-Truiden
Le Culot
Osnabrück
Hanover
Hildesheim
Dessau
Leipzig
Kassel
Dresden
Dortmund
Essen
Hagen
München-Gladbach
Cologne
Bonn
Chemnitz
Giessen
Brüx
Koblenz
Prague
Wiesbaden
Hanau
Schweinfurt
Mainz
Frankfurt
Trier
Würzburg
Darmstadt
St.-Dizier
Metz
Saarbrücken
Mannheim
Heilbronn
Nuremberg
Regensburg
Karlsruhe
Pforzheim
Stuttgart
Nancy
Ulm
Augsburg
Munich
Vienna
Lagerlechfeld
Dijon
Friedrichshafen
Graz

Dec

THE BOMBING OF DRESDEN

From around 10pm on February 13, 1945, until noon the following day, the historic city of Dresden in eastern Germany was subjected to one of the most intensive bombing raids of the war. The savage attack was sudden and unexpected, and the results were devastating.

Known as Operation Thunderclap, the attack began with 244 RAF Lancasters dropping more than 890 tons (810 tonnes) of high explosive and incendiary bombs on the center and inner suburbs of the city. After a 25-minute pause, a further 529 bombers arrived, dropping over 2,000 tons (1,800 tonnes) of bombs to fuel the firestorm the initial attack had kindled. The second attack lasted 40 minutes. By the time it ended, Dresden had been utterly devastated. The following morning, as the surviving residents stumbled into the streets to survey the damage, the air-raid sirens wailed again. Some 311 USAAF Flying Fortresses dropped a further 860 tons (770 tonnes) of bombs on the stricken city. Around 25,000 Dresdeners were killed.

△ **Air-raid warning**
A handheld air-raid siren of the type used in Dresden. The city's citizens had little warning of the initial attack.

A display of might

Whether such a destructive attack on Dresden was justified has provoked debate ever since. The Allies bombed eastern German cities in order to aid the Soviet advance and prevent a German retreat to an Alpine redoubt (or fortress). However, RAF Bomber Command's Arthur Harris briefed his aircrews to bomb densely packed residential zones, causing huge numbers of civilian deaths.

△ **The second attack**
Two months after the initial attack on Dresden by the RAF Lancasters, B-17 Flying Fortresses of the US 8th Air Force bombed Dresden by daylight on April 17, 1945. The aim of the mission was to sever the city's southeastern rail links. It was the final attack on Dresden, an ancient cathedral city that Germans referred to as "Florence on the Elbe."

Dresden in ruins
This view from the tower of Dresden's *Rathaus* (city hall) southward over the city reveals the extent of the destruction caused by Allied area bombing. Much of the city center remained rubble into the 1950s.

THE FINAL SOVIET ATTACK

In the final stage of the war in Europe, a series of hard-fought victories brought Soviet armies into the heart of central Europe and the Balkans, with major consequences for both the war and the continent itself.

The Red Army's advance of summer 1944 had cleared the Germans from Soviet soil and penetrated Poland, Romania, and the Baltic states. However, it stalled outside Warsaw while the Germans crushed an uprising by the Polish Home Army (see pp.184–185). To the south, Soviet forces invaded Bulgaria before taking the Yugoslav capital, Belgrade, with Josip Broz Tito's partisans. In Hungary, the Red Army beat a path to Budapest in December, but took almost two months to capture the city, which was defended by German and Hungarian forces.

Overwhelming forces

The final push into Germany began on January 12, 1945, with an offensive by Marshal Zhukov's 1st Ukrainian Front, joined two days later by Marshal Konev's 1st Belorussian Front (see right). With more than two million men and 4,000 tanks, the armies advanced almost 300 miles (500 km) by early February, with Zhukov penetrating the industrial area of Silesia, and Konev reaching the River Oder, less than 45 miles (70 km) east of Berlin. The Soviet advance liberated Auschwitz on January 27, and droves of German civilian refugees fled west, panicked by reports of Soviet atrocities. Zhukov halted at the Oder to resupply his army, while in the north the Soviets took control of East Prussia and the Baltic states. The Soviets began their final assault on April 16 (see pp.242–243). After four days Zhukov broke the defenses; by April 20 Berlin was encircled. On April 25, US and Soviet troops met triumphantly at Torgau on the Elbe.

△ **The Allies meet**
A lieutenant from the US 69th Infantry Division (in helmet) poses with soldiers from the Soviet 58th Guards Division in Torgau, Germany, in April 1945. The site would become the border of their future military occupation zones.

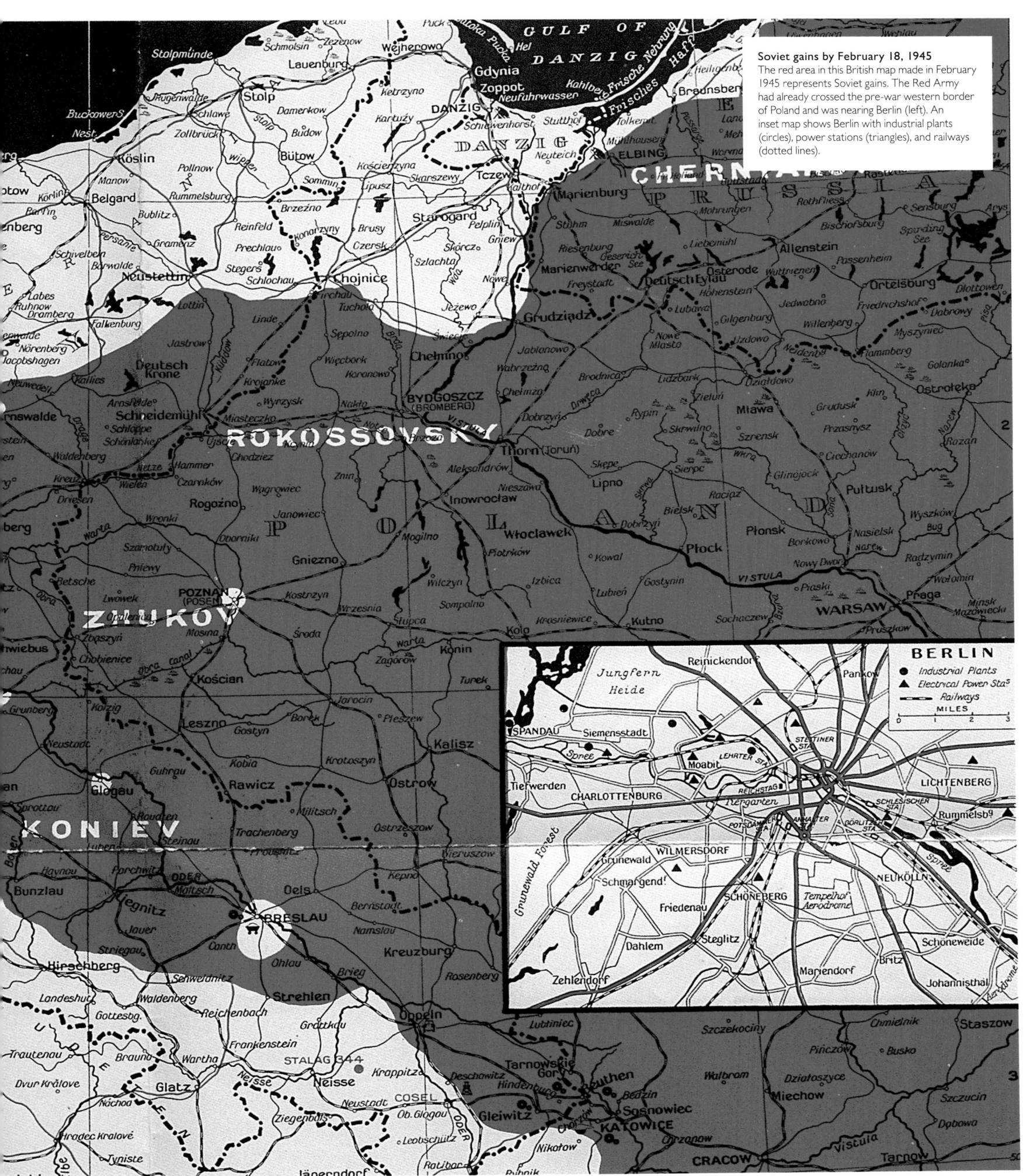

Soviet gains by February 18, 1945
The red area in this British map made in February 1945 represents Soviet gains. The Red Army had already crossed the pre-war western border of Poland and was nearing Berlin (left). An inset map shows Berlin with industrial plants (circles), power stations (triangles), and railways (dotted lines).

FINAL STRUGGLES IN ITALY

In 1944, the Allies pushed northward through Italy, eventually forcing the Germans behind the Gothic Line—a formidable defensive line that ran the width of the country. Following a winter of military stalemate, the Allies achieved a decisive breakthrough in spring 1945 that finally brought the war in Italy to an end.

German field marshal Albert Kesselring continued to frustrate the pursuing Allies by conducting a skillful defensive retreat. Under his orders, 15,000 slave laborers built the Gothic Line (also known as the Green Line)—a series of bunkers, anti-tank ditches, machine-gun posts, minefields, and other defenses. The location of the Gothic Line in the Apennine Mountains meant that the most viable places for the Allies to attack were along both coasts and at a few mountain passes—points that the Germans heavily defended. In September 1944, some Allied divisions broke through at the eastern end of the line, but otherwise the barrier held out

until the following spring, when the Allies launched a decisive offensive. The battle for the Gothic Line was one of the largest fought in the war, involving more than 1.2 million men.

As the Allies turned their focus to the Western Front after D-Day (see pp.186–187), the Italian campaign came to be seen as something of a sideshow. But for those involved, it was a long, punishing struggle that claimed the lives of around 250,000 soldiers and 150,000 noncombatants. Under Kesselring's orders, German troops responded brutally to any opposition, killing thousands of civilians in reprisal for partisan attacks or disobedience.

> *"A soldier's first duty is to obey, otherwise you might as well do away with soldiering."*
>
> FIELD MARSHAL ALBERT KESSELRING, 1946

ITALIAN PARTISANS

After the fall of Rome in June 1944 (see pp.166–167), some pro-Fascist Italian forces continued to fight alongside German troops. However, they were matched by the number of partisans fighting against the occupiers and against Mussolini's Italian Social Republic (the Republic of Salò: see Box 5). Italian partisans liberated many cities before the arrival of the Allies, including Milan, Genoa, and Turin. After the German forces were expelled, partisan groups executed thousands of collaborators.

Partisans enter the freed city of Milan on April 25, 1945

LAST STAND IN ITALY

The Germans pinned their last hopes of halting the Allied advance in Italy on their fortified Gothic Line. However, they could not contain the sustained attacks and were forced to capitulate in May 1945.

KEY

🛡 Allied forces   ☠ Massacres   // Areas of Italian partisan activity

TIMELINE

1 | 2 | 3 | 4 | 5

JUL 1944   SEP   NOV   JAN 1945   MAR   MAY   JUL

Zürich

Geneva

1 RETREAT TO THE GOTHIC LINE
AUGUST 1944

By early August, Allied forces had pushed the Germans as far north as the Arno River and had taken the city of Florence. The Germans withdrew behind the Gothic Line, a defensive line that stretched 200 miles (320km) between Italy's east and west coasts. The fortifications, which were 10 miles (16km) deep in some places, would be the last major line of defense for the Germans in Italy.

〰 Gothic Line   → Allied advance

✗ Battle   ▢ Allied territory by Aug 25, 1944

Novara

Vercelli

Turin

Alessandria

Mondovì

2 ALLIES BREACH THE GOTHIC LINE
AUGUST–DECEMBER 1944

The Allies gave the Germans every indication that they would assault the Gothic Line on the west coast, but the move was a feint to allow the British 8th Army to break through in the east, taking the port of Rimini. US forces made progress in the Apennine Mountains. The last Allied victory of 1944 came on December 5 with the capture of the east-coast city of Ravenna.

→ Allied advance   ▢ Allied territory by Dec 31, 1944

✗ Battles

San Remo

Ligurian Sea

3 WINTER STALEMATE
DECEMBER 1944–APRIL 9, 1945

The winter of 1944–1945 was harsh, and neither side made much progress. The inactivity enabled both sides to move forces to areas where they were needed more urgently. In March, the Allies bombed Axis-held Venice; the same month, Hitler promoted Kesselring to Commander-in-Chief on the Western Front. Morale dropped on both sides, as troops realized that the conflict in western Europe was taking priority over Italy.

▢ Allied territory by Apr 9, 1945   ✴ Allied air attack

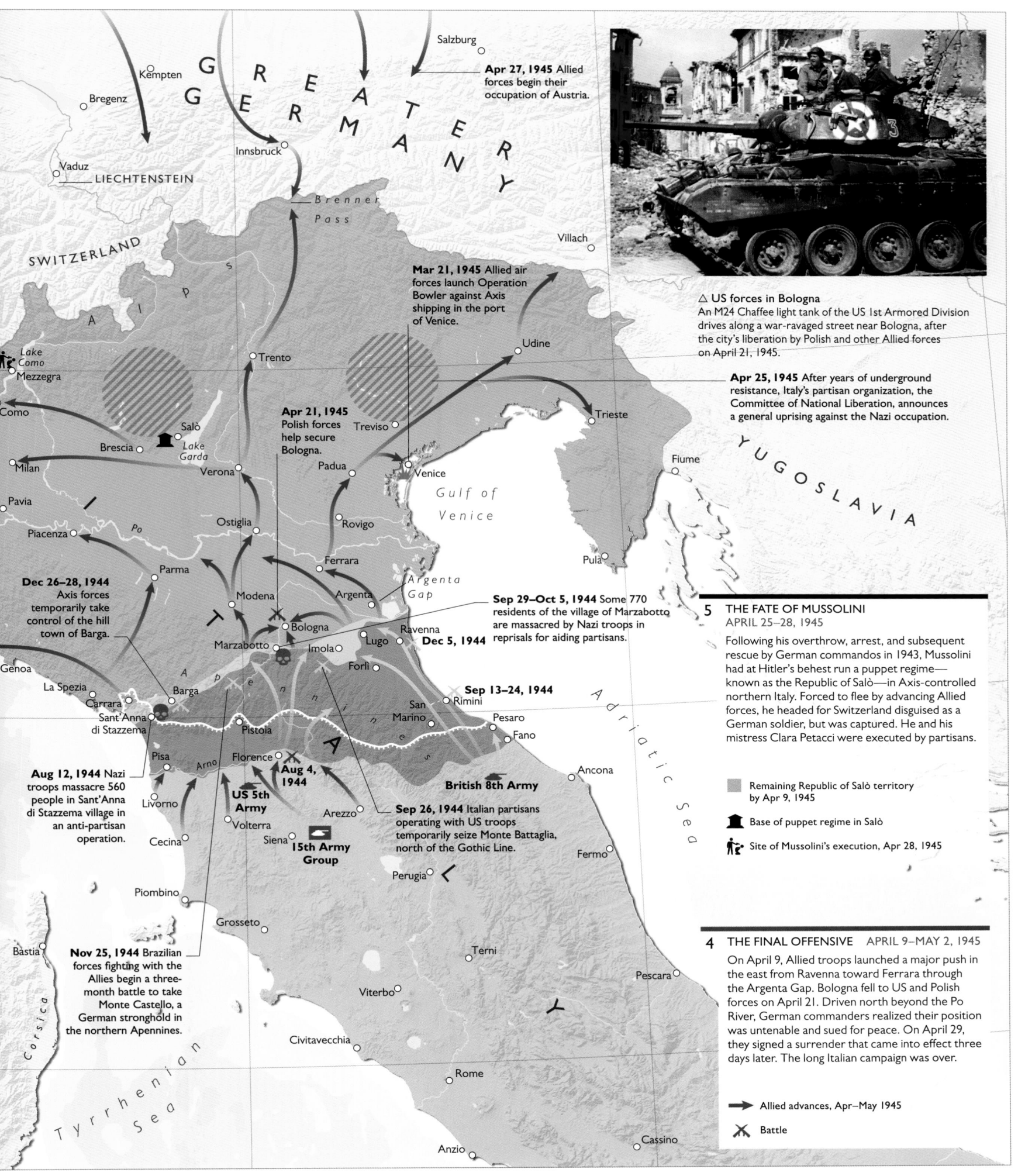

Apr 27, 1945 Allied forces begin their occupation of Austria.

Mar 21, 1945 Allied air forces launch Operation Bowler against Axis shipping in the port of Venice.

Apr 21, 1945 Polish forces help secure Bologna.

△ US forces in Bologna
An M24 Chaffee light tank of the US 1st Armored Division drives along a war-ravaged street near Bologna, after the city's liberation by Polish and other Allied forces on April 21, 1945.

Apr 25, 1945 After years of underground resistance, Italy's partisan organization, the Committee of National Liberation, announces a general uprising against the Nazi occupation.

Sep 29–Oct 5, 1944 Some 770 residents of the village of Marzabotto are massacred by Nazi troops in reprisals for aiding partisans.

Dec 26–28, 1944 Axis forces temporarily take control of the hill town of Barga.

Dec 5, 1944

Sep 13–24, 1944

5 THE FATE OF MUSSOLINI
APRIL 25–28, 1945

Following his overthrow, arrest, and subsequent rescue by German commandos in 1943, Mussolini had at Hitler's behest run a puppet regime—known as the Republic of Salò—in Axis-controlled northern Italy. Forced to flee by advancing Allied forces, he headed for Switzerland disguised as a German soldier, but was captured. He and his mistress Clara Petacci were executed by partisans.

▨ Remaining Republic of Salò territory by Apr 9, 1945

🏛 Base of puppet regime in Salò

👥 Site of Mussolini's execution, Apr 28, 1945

Aug 12, 1944 Nazi troops massacre 560 people in Sant'Anna di Stazzema village in an anti-partisan operation.

Aug 4, 1944

US 5th Army

15th Army Group

British 8th Army

Sep 26, 1944 Italian partisans operating with US troops temporarily seize Monte Battaglia, north of the Gothic Line.

Nov 25, 1944 Brazilian forces fighting with the Allies begin a three-month battle to take Monte Castello, a German stronghold in the northern Apennines.

4 THE FINAL OFFENSIVE   APRIL 9–MAY 2, 1945

On April 9, Allied troops launched a major push in the east from Ravenna toward Ferrara through the Argenta Gap. Bologna fell to US and Polish forces on April 21. Driven north beyond the Po River, German commanders realized their position was untenable and sued for peace. On April 29, they signed a surrender that came into effect three days later. The long Italian campaign was over.

➡ Allied advances, Apr–May 1945

✕ Battle

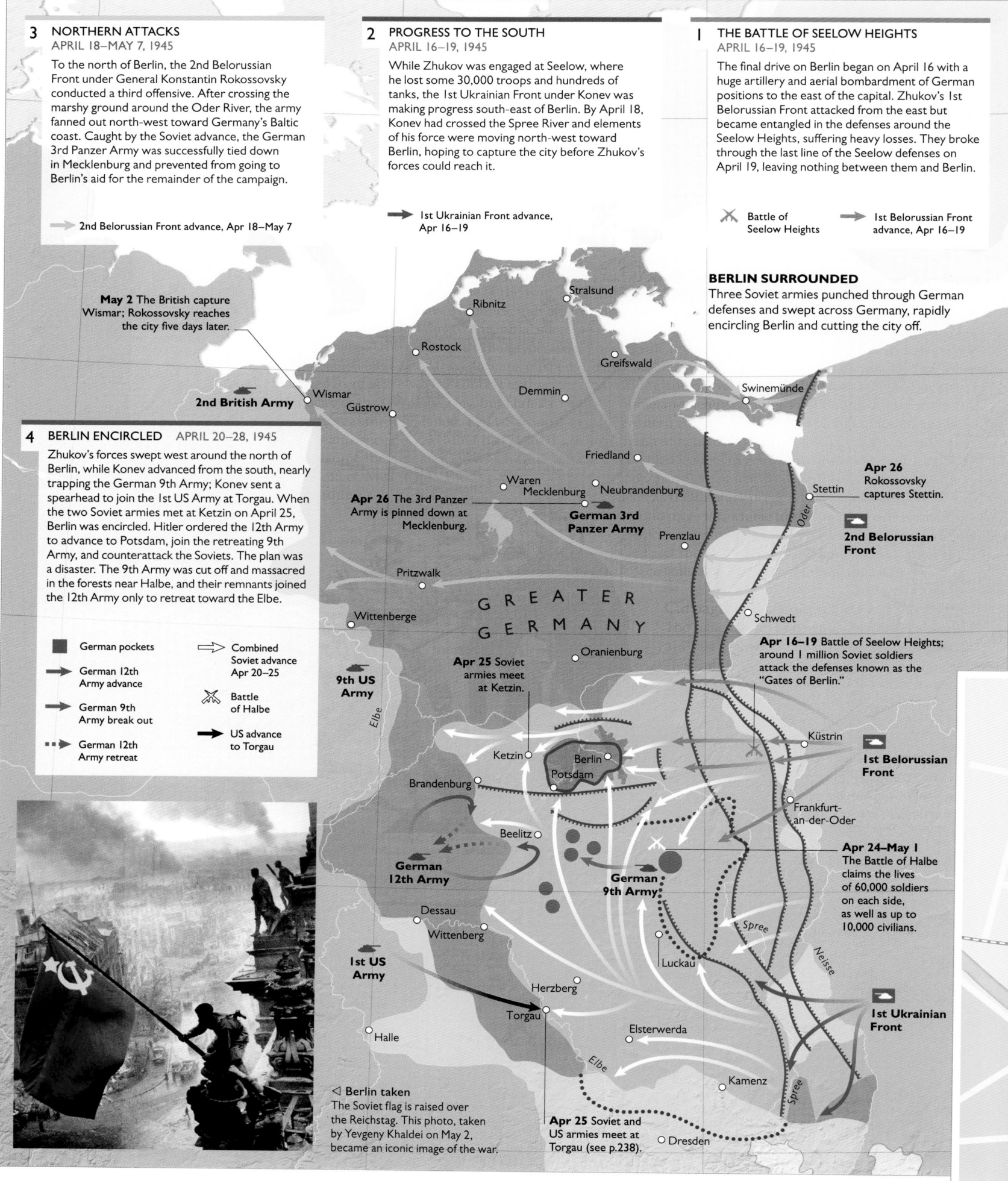

3 NORTHERN ATTACKS
APRIL 18–MAY 7, 1945

To the north of Berlin, the 2nd Belorussian Front under General Konstantin Rokossovsky conducted a third offensive. After crossing the marshy ground around the Oder River, the army fanned out north-west toward Germany's Baltic coast. Caught by the Soviet advance, the German 3rd Panzer Army was successfully tied down in Mecklenburg and prevented from going to Berlin's aid for the remainder of the campaign.

➡ 2nd Belorussian Front advance, Apr 18–May 7

2 PROGRESS TO THE SOUTH
APRIL 16–19, 1945

While Zhukov was engaged at Seelow, where he lost some 30,000 troops and hundreds of tanks, the 1st Ukrainian Front under Konev was making progress south-east of Berlin. By April 18, Konev had crossed the Spree River and elements of his force were moving north-west toward Berlin, hoping to capture the city before Zhukov's forces could reach it.

➡ 1st Ukrainian Front advance, Apr 16–19

1 THE BATTLE OF SEELOW HEIGHTS
APRIL 16–19, 1945

The final drive on Berlin began on April 16 with a huge artillery and aerial bombardment of German positions to the east of the capital. Zhukov's 1st Belorussian Front attacked from the east but became entangled in the defenses around the Seelow Heights, suffering heavy losses. They broke through the last line of the Seelow defenses on April 19, leaving nothing between them and Berlin.

⚔ Battle of Seelow Heights   ➡ 1st Belorussian Front advance, Apr 16–19

BERLIN SURROUNDED
Three Soviet armies punched through German defenses and swept across Germany, rapidly encircling Berlin and cutting the city off.

May 2 The British capture Wismar; Rokossovsky reaches the city five days later.

2nd British Army

4 BERLIN ENCIRCLED   APRIL 20–28, 1945

Zhukov's forces swept west around the north of Berlin, while Konev advanced from the south, nearly trapping the German 9th Army; Konev sent a spearhead to join the 1st US Army at Torgau. When the two Soviet armies met at Ketzin on April 25, Berlin was encircled. Hitler ordered the 12th Army to advance to Potsdam, join the retreating 9th Army, and counterattack the Soviets. The plan was a disaster. The 9th Army was cut off and massacred in the forests near Halbe, and their remnants joined the 12th Army only to retreat toward the Elbe.

■ German pockets
➡ German 12th Army advance
➡ German 9th Army break out
••• German 12th Army retreat
⇨ Combined Soviet advance Apr 20–25
⚔ Battle of Halbe
➡ US advance to Torgau

9th US Army

Apr 26 The 3rd Panzer Army is pinned down at Mecklenburg.

German 3rd Panzer Army

Apr 25 Soviet armies meet at Ketzin.

Apr 16–19 Battle of Seelow Heights; around 1 million Soviet soldiers attack the defenses known as the "Gates of Berlin."

Apr 26 Rokossovsky captures Stettin.

2nd Belorussian Front

1st Belorussian Front

Apr 24–May 1 The Battle of Halbe claims the lives of 60,000 soldiers on each side, as well as up to 10,000 civilians.

1st US Army

German 12th Army

German 9th Army

1st Ukrainian Front

Greifswald
Stralsund
Ribnitz
Rostock
Swinemünde
Demmin
Friedland
Waren
Mecklenburg
Neubrandenburg
Stettin
Wismar
Güstrow
Prenzlau
Pritzwalk
Schwedt
Wittenberge
GREATER GERMANY
Oranienburg
Küstrin
Ketzin
Berlin
Potsdam
1st Belorussian Front
Brandenburg
Frankfurt-an-der-Oder
Beelitz
Dessau
Wittenberg
Luckau
Spree
Herzberg
Torgau
Halle
Elsterwerda
Neisse
Kamenz
Spree
Elbe
Dresden

◁ **Berlin taken**
The Soviet flag is raised over the Reichstag. This photo, taken by Yevgeny Khaldei on May 2, became an iconic image of the war.

Apr 25 Soviet and US armies meet at Torgau (see p.238).

THE FALL OF BERLIN

In April 1945, the city of Berlin—already devastated by two years of Allied bombing—faced an overwhelming Red Army advance that drove the war in Europe to its bloody finale. The human cost was vast on both sides as vengeful Soviet troops attacked the German capital.

By mid-April 1945, the Red Army had amassed 2.5 million troops, 6,000 tanks, and more than 40,000 artillery pieces along the Oder and Neisse Rivers in preparation for their final assault on Berlin. Caught between the advancing British and American armies to the west and the Red Army's 200 divisions to the east were around 1 million German soldiers and 1,500 tanks. Many of the German soldiers were sick, wounded, or starving, but found themselves motivated to fight by their fear of what the Red Army might do in retribution for the millions of Soviet soldiers killed in the war.

Wishing to avoid a clash between the US and the Soviets, Eisenhower told Stalin that the US would not advance on Berlin. Stalin did not believe this and sped up his plans, pitting two generals—Konev and Zhukov—against each other in a race for the capital. Following a massive artillery bombardment of the city, the Red Army surrounded Berlin by April 25. Hitler, hiding in his bunker, pinned his hopes on a planned counterattack by his 9th and 12th Armies. It never came. Instead, the Red Army closed in and, as it tightened its grip on the city center, Hitler and Goebbels committed suicide. Berlin surrendered to the Soviets on May 2, and five days later the war in Europe was over.

GERMANY OVERRUN

Prevented from escaping westwards due to the advancing British and American armies, Germany's remaining armies were overwhelmed by the Red Army in just a few weeks from April to May 1945. By the time Berlin surrendered on May 2, Hitler had already been dead for two days.

KEY

British and US forces	German defensive lines
Soviet forces	Front lines of German counterattacks
German forces	German territory, 28 Apr

ALLIED TERRITORIAL GAINS

Apr 15	Apr 28
Apr 18	Urban areas
Apr 25	

TIMELINE

APR 15, 1945 APR 20 APR 25 APR 30 MAY 5 MAY 10

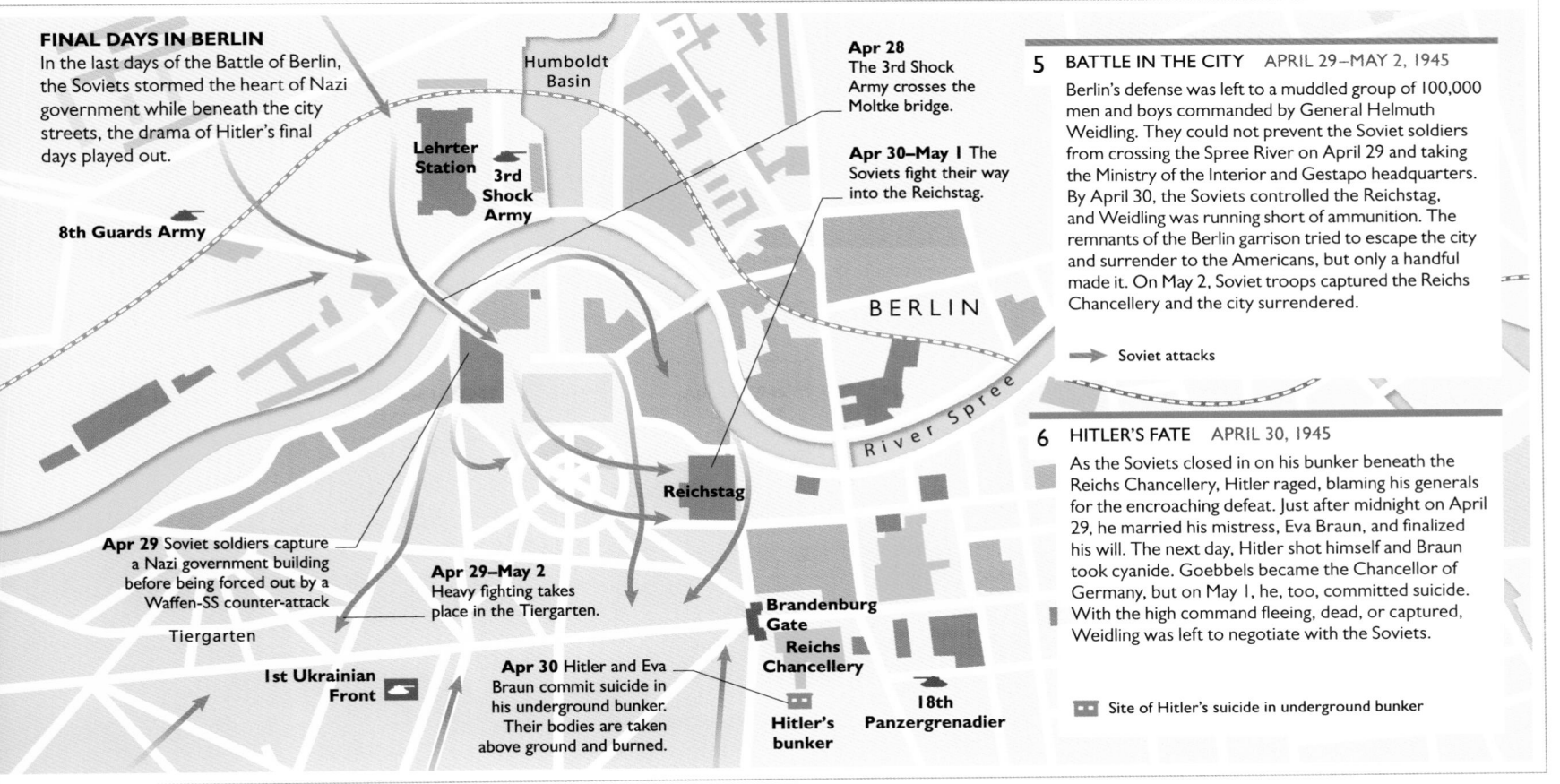

FINAL DAYS IN BERLIN
In the last days of the Battle of Berlin, the Soviets stormed the heart of Nazi government while beneath the city streets, the drama of Hitler's final days played out.

Humboldt Basin

Lehrter Station

3rd Shock Army

8th Guards Army

Apr 28 The 3rd Shock Army crosses the Moltke bridge.

Apr 30–May 1 The Soviets fight their way into the Reichstag.

BERLIN

Apr 29 Soviet soldiers capture a Nazi government building before being forced out by a Waffen-SS counter-attack

Tiergarten

Apr 29–May 2 Heavy fighting takes place in the Tiergarten.

River Spree

Reichstag

Soviet attacks

1st Ukrainian Front

Apr 30 Hitler and Eva Braun commit suicide in his underground bunker. Their bodies are taken above ground and burned.

Brandenburg Gate

Reichs Chancellery

Hitler's bunker

18th Panzergrenadier

5 BATTLE IN THE CITY APRIL 29–MAY 2, 1945

Berlin's defense was left to a muddled group of 100,000 men and boys commanded by General Helmuth Weidling. They could not prevent the Soviet soldiers from crossing the Spree River on April 29 and taking the Ministry of the Interior and Gestapo headquarters. By April 30, the Soviets controlled the Reichstag, and Weidling was running short of ammunition. The remnants of the Berlin garrison tried to escape the city and surrender to the Americans, but only a handful made it. On May 2, Soviet troops captured the Reichs Chancellery and the city surrendered.

6 HITLER'S FATE APRIL 30, 1945

As the Soviets closed in on his bunker beneath the Reichs Chancellery, Hitler raged, blaming his generals for the encroaching defeat. Just after midnight on April 29, he married his mistress, Eva Braun, and finalized his will. The next day, Hitler shot himself and Braun took cyanide. Goebbels became the Chancellor of Germany, but on May 1, he, too, committed suicide. With the high command fleeing, dead, or captured, Weidling was left to negotiate with the Soviets.

Site of Hitler's suicide in underground bunker

VE DAY

Germany's surrender on May 7, 1945, was celebrated across the Western world the following day. Hitler had killed himself in his bunker eight days previously, and war in Europe had finally ended.

△ **Special edition**
A commemorative edition of the UK magazine *Picture Post* celebrates VE Day. The magazine had previously campaigned against the Nazi regime.

On May 7, 1945, the Supreme Allied Commander, General Dwight D. Eisenhower, accepted the unconditional surrender of all German land, sea, and air forces at his headquarters in Reims, in northeastern France. In Britain, the news that the surrender document had been signed was broadcast that evening on the BBC. The following day, which was named Victory in Europe Day (usually abbreviated to VE Day), was declared a national holiday.

Celebrating victory

Even before the start of the official celebrations, the festivities began. In London, more than a million people took to the streets, while celebratory bonfires blazed the length and breadth of the country. Effigies of Hitler were burned on many of them. In America, the celebrations were slightly more subdued, primarily because the US was still mourning the death of President Franklin D. Roosevelt, who had died less than a month earlier. However, 15,000 policemen were still mobilized to control the huge crowds that had massed in Times Square, New York. There were also huge celebrations in Paris, with parades on the Champs-Élysées, and in France May 8 (*La fête de la Victoire*) continues to be a public holiday. In the USSR, however, because Stalin refused to recognize the signature at Reims and insisted on a formal surrender ceremony in Berlin on May 8, celebrations did not take place until May 9.

△ **Nazi downfall**
Soldiers from the US 7th Army fly the Stars and Stripes flag to celebrate victory, perched on what had been Hitler's viewing podium in the Luitpold Arena, Nuremberg, where the Nazi Party's infamous rallies had been held.

Dancing for joy
British girls dance with US GIs in London during the celebrations to mark the end of war in Europe. Thousands headed to Buckingham Palace, where Prime Minister Winston Churchill and the Royal Family greeted the ecstatic crowd.

DEFEAT OF JAPAN

By 1945, the eventual outcome of the war with Japan seemed inevitable. However, it was unclear how Japan's leaders could be brought to acknowledge defeat. In the end, the planned invasion of the Japanese mainland proved unnecessary, since the Allies' nuclear destruction of Hiroshima and Nagasaki was followed by Japan's surrender a few days later.

▽ **Targeting cities**
A US Army Air Forces map designates a key industrial target in Osaka, Japan. Over 200,000 Japanese were killed in non-nuclear strategic bombing.

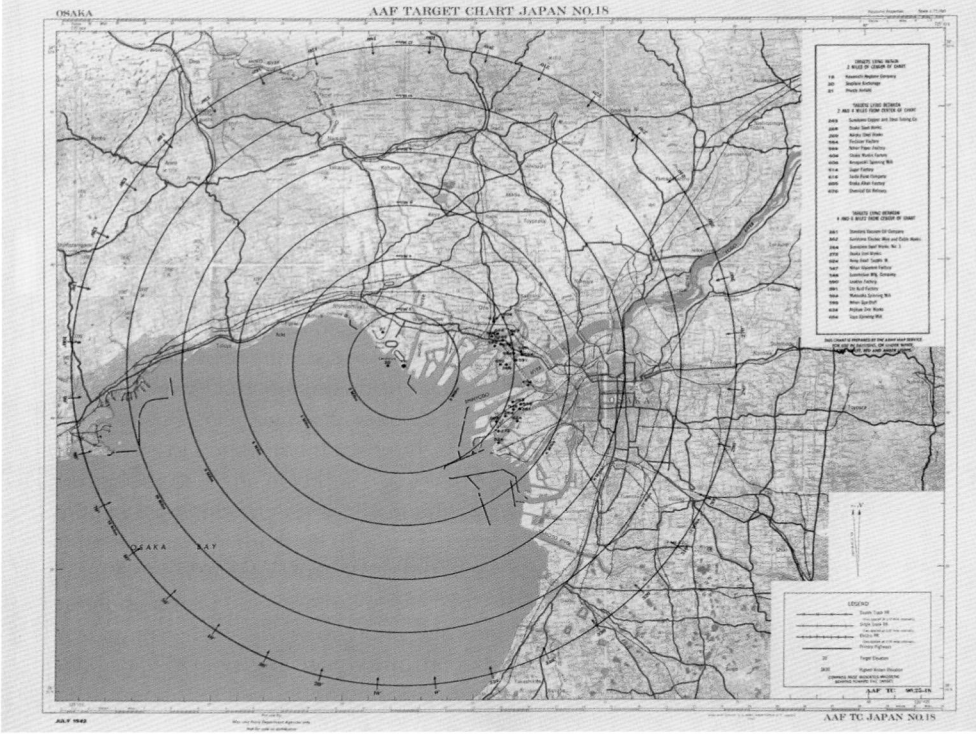

By any objective measure, Japan had already lost the war by spring 1945. US aircraft based on Pacific islands were carrying out mass raids against Japanese cities, and a naval blockade both starved the civilian population and crippled the nation's war machine through a lack of fuel and other supplies. Japan's overseas armies were giving up territory that they had conquered in Burma, the Philippines, and New Guinea.

When Germany surrendered in May 1945, it meant that the military resources of the Allies could now be transferred to the Pacific theater. However, the Japanese continued to show every sign of determination to fight to the last man, as exhibited in the fierce battles for Iwo Jima and Okinawa; indeed, America believed that the war against Japan could continue well into 1946. In June 1945, the US Army planned to land in Japan the following November, with follow-up landings in March 1946. The expectation was of heavy losses in prolonged campaigns.

△ **Display of might**
A propaganda poster boasts of Japanese air power. In reality, by 1945 Japan's aircraft were outnumbered and outclassed by those of their opponents.

Japan faces up to defeat

The Japanese leadership finally faced up to the certainty of defeat after the fall of Okinawa in June. Knowing the war was lost, the Japanese war council split into two factions known as the "peace" and "war" parties. The peace party sought some way to end the conflict that would leave Japan independent and unoccupied—a prospect that the Allies would probably never have accepted. The war party favored a fight to the death, devising a plan for

ENDGAME IN THE PACIFIC WAR

In the first half of 1945, the US suffered mounting casualties in fighting against resolute Japanese troops. Some 26,000 Americans were killed or wounded in the battle for the small island of Iwo Jima, and the subsequent capture of Okinawa cost the US over 50,000 casualties. In August, however, the dropping of atomic bombs on two Japanese cities, and a Soviet invasion of Manchuria, propelled the Japanese government into surrendering at last.

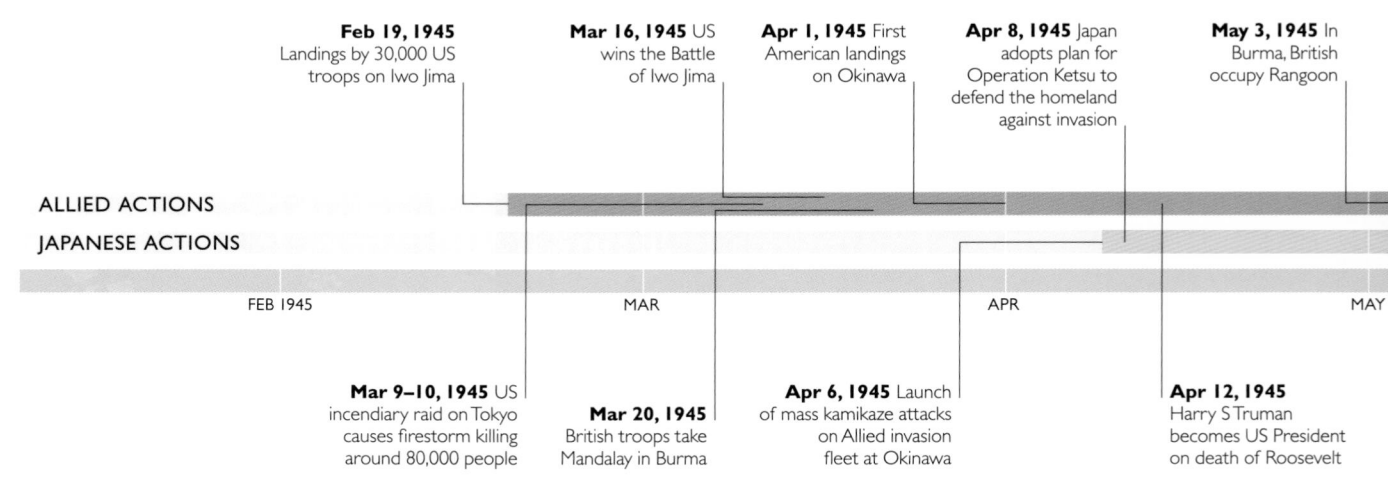

Feb 19, 1945 Landings by 30,000 US troops on Iwo Jima

Mar 16, 1945 US wins the Battle of Iwo Jima

Apr 1, 1945 First American landings on Okinawa

Apr 8, 1945 Japan adopts plan for Operation Ketsu to defend the homeland against invasion

May 3, 1945 In Burma, British occupy Rangoon

ALLIED ACTIONS

JAPANESE ACTIONS

FEB 1945   MAR   APR   MAY

Mar 9–10, 1945 US incendiary raid on Tokyo causes firestorm killing around 80,000 people

Mar 20, 1945 British troops take Mandalay in Burma

Apr 6, 1945 Launch of mass kamikaze attacks on Allied invasion fleet at Okinawa

Apr 12, 1945 Harry S Truman becomes US President on death of Roosevelt

◁ **Soviet offensive**
Motorized Soviet infantry advance into
Japanese-occupied Manchuria in August 1945.
The invasion of Manchuria by the Soviet Union
was a major factor in persuading Japan to
recognize the need for surrender.

the defense of the homeland involving the entire population in suicidal resistance, under the slogan "The Glorious Death of One Hundred Million." Emperor Hirohito leaned toward support of the peace party, but at this point no decisions were made. The peace party's hopes for a compromise deal with the Allies was unrealistic, and the war party remained adamant.

The dropping of the bomb

Unknown to all but a few, even in the Allied political and military leadership, the Manhattan Project had been pursuing development of the atomic bomb, initially intended for use against Germany. The new weapon was successfully tested the day before the opening of an Allied conference at Potsdam, Germany, one of the aims of which was to encourage the Soviet Union to join the war against Japan. Although some doubts were raised behind the scenes, vetoing the dropping of atomic bombs on Japanese cities was never seriously considered. The Potsdam Declaration, calling on Japan to surrender or face destruction, was issued before the bombing, but its threats were too vague to influence Japanese policy. In early August 1945, atomic bombs were dropped on Hiroshima and Nagasaki, and the Soviet Union declared war on Japan. Emperor Hirohito and the peace party finally surrendered, although even then Japanese officers tried to prevent the announcement from being broadcast.

▽ **Raising the flag**
A famous photograph shows US
Marines planting the Stars and Stripes
flag on Mount Suribachi on Iwo Jima in
March 1945. The capture of the Pacific
island took five weeks of intensive
fighting, and was one of the bloodiest
battles against Japan in World War II.

> *"Despite the best that has been done by everyone… the war situation has developed not necessarily to Japan's advantage.*
>
> EMPEROR HIROHITO, SURRENDER BROADCAST, AUGUST 15, 1945

Jun 22, 1945 Fighting on Okinawa ends with Allied victory

Jun 28, 1945 Fighting in the Philippines ends

Jul 16, 1945 Successful atomic bomb test conducted in New Mexico

Aug 6, 1945 Atomic bomb dropped on Hiroshima

Aug 9, 1945 Soviet troops invade Manchuria

Aug 15, 1945 Emperor Hirohito announces Japanese surrender

JUN   JUL   AUG   SEP   OCT

Jun 22, 1945 Emperor Hirohito tells his government it is necessary to pursue peace

Jul 17, 1945 Potsdam conference opens in Berlin

Jul 26, 1945 Potsdam Declaration calls on Japan to surrender or face "prompt and utter destruction"

Aug 9, 1945 Atomic bomb dropped on Nagasaki

Sep 2, 1945 Formal Japanese surrender at Tokyo on board USS *Missouri*

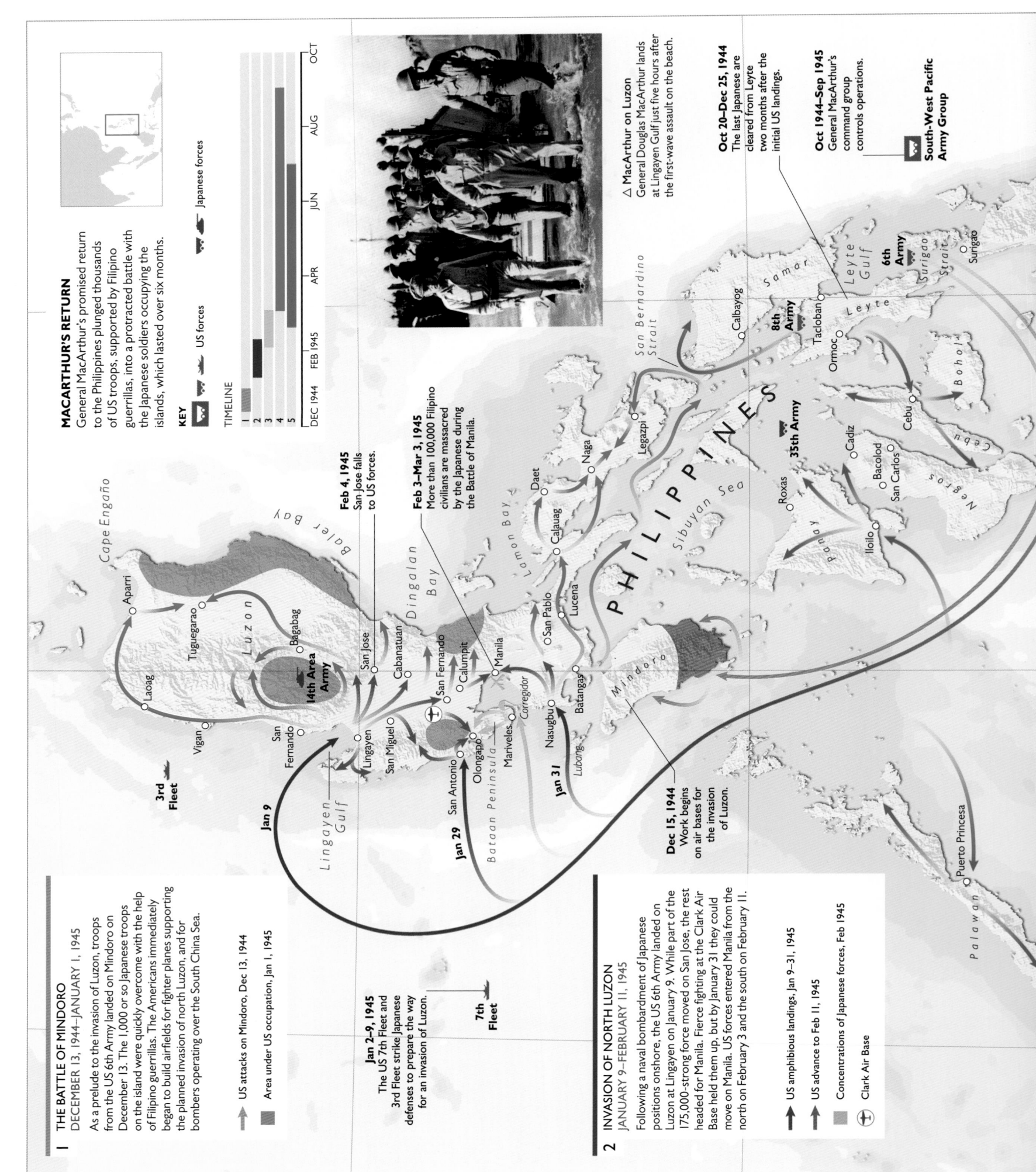

MACARTHUR'S RETURN

General MacArthur's promised return to the Philippines plunged thousands of US troops, supported by Filipino guerrillas, into a protracted battle with the Japanese soldiers occupying the islands, which lasted over six months.

KEY

US forces

Japanese forces

TIMELINE

DEC 1944   FEB 1945   APR   JUN   AUG   OCT

△ **MacArthur on Luzon**
General Douglas MacArthur lands at Lingayen Gulf just five hours after the first-wave assault on the beach.

Oct 20–Dec 25, 1944
The last Japanese are cleared from Leyte two months after the initial US landings.

Oct 1944–Sep 1945
General MacArthur's command group controls operations.

South-West Pacific
Army Group

---

1   THE BATTLE OF MINDORO
DECEMBER 13, 1944–JANUARY 1, 1945

As a prelude to the invasion of Luzon, troops from the US 6th Army landed on Mindoro on December 13. The 1,000 or so Japanese troops on the island were quickly overcome with the help of Filipino guerrillas. The Americans immediately began to build airfields for fighter planes supporting the planned invasion of north Luzon, and for bombers operating over the South China Sea.

→ US attacks on Mindoro, Dec 13, 1944

▨ Area under US occupation, Jan 1, 1945

Jan 2–9, 1945
The US 7th Fleet and 3rd Fleet strike Japanese defenses to prepare the way for an invasion of Luzon.

7th
Fleet

---

2   INVASION OF NORTH LUZON
JANUARY 9–FEBRUARY 11, 1945

Following a naval bombardment of Japanese positions onshore, the US 6th Army landed on Luzon at Lingayen on January 9. While part of the 175,000-strong force moved on San Jose, the rest headed for Manila. Fierce fighting at the Clark Air Base held them up, but by January 31 they could move on Manila. US forces entered Manila from the north on February 3 and the south on February 11.

→ US amphibious landings, Jan 9–31, 1945

→ US advance to Feb 11, 1945

▨ Concentrations of Japanese forces, Feb 1945

⊕ Clark Air Base

Feb 4, 1945
San Jose falls to US forces.

Feb 3–Mar 3, 1945
More than 100,000 Filipino civilians are massacred by the Japanese during the Battle of Manila.

Dec 15, 1944
Work begins on air bases for the invasion of Luzon.

3rd
Fleet

Jan 9

Jan 29

Jan 31

Place labels

Cape Engaño

Baler Bay

Dingalan Bay

Lamon Bay

Samar

Leyte Gulf

Leyte

Bohol

Cebu

Negros

Panay

Sibuyan Sea

San Bernardino Strait

Surigao Strait

Mindoro

Palawan

PHILIPPINES

Aparri
Tuguegarao
Bagabag
Laoag
Vigan
San Fernando
Lingayen
San Miguel
San Antonio
Olongapo
Mariveles
Corregidor
Bataan Peninsula
Lingayen Gulf
Luzon
14th Area Army
San Jose
Cabanatuan
San Fernando
Calumpit
Manila
Nasugbu
Batangas
Lubang
San Pablo
Lucena
Calauag
Daet
Naga
Legazpi
Roxas
Iloilo
Cadiz
Bacolod
San Carlos
Cebu
Calbayog
Tacloban
Ormoc
Surigao
Puerto Princesa

35th Army

6th Army

8th Army

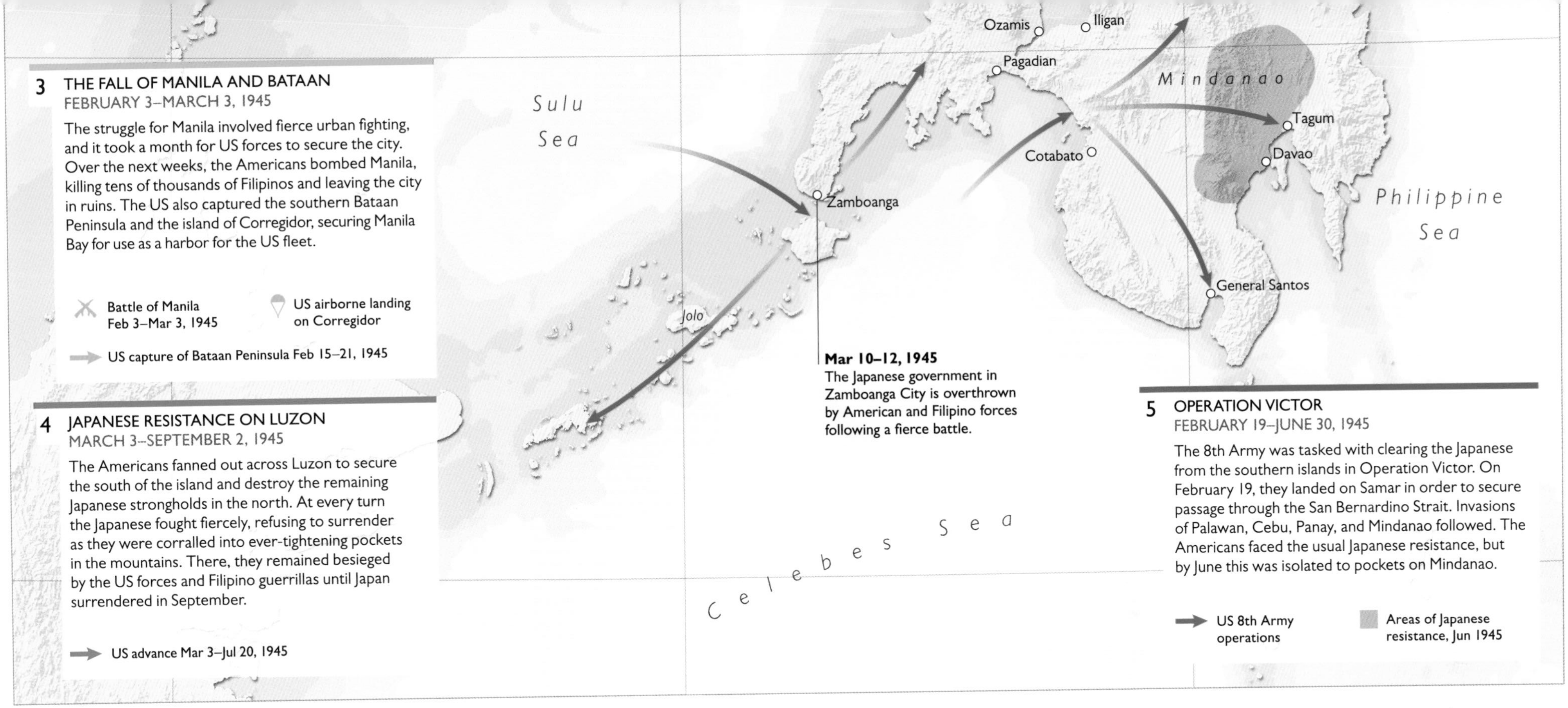

Philippine Sea

Sulu Sea

Celebes Sea

Mindanao

Tagum
Davao
General Santos
Iligan
Ozamis
Pagadian
Cotabato
Zamboanga
Jolo

3 THE FALL OF MANILA AND BATAAN
FEBRUARY 3–MARCH 3, 1945

The struggle for Manila involved fierce urban fighting, and it took a month for US forces to secure the city. Over the next weeks, the Americans bombed Manila, killing tens of thousands of Filipinos and leaving the city in ruins. The US also captured the southern Bataan Peninsula and the island of Corregidor, securing Manila Bay for use as a harbor for the US fleet.

✕ Battle of Manila
Feb 3–Mar 3, 1945

US airborne landing on Corregidor

⬆ US capture of Bataan Peninsula Feb 15–21, 1945

4 JAPANESE RESISTANCE ON LUZON
MARCH 3–SEPTEMBER 2, 1945

The Americans fanned out across Luzon to secure the south of the island and destroy the remaining Japanese strongholds in the north. At every turn the Japanese fought fiercely, refusing to surrender as they were corralled into ever-tightening pockets in the mountains. There, they remained besieged by the US forces and Filipino guerrillas until Japan surrendered in September.

⬆ US advance Mar 3–Jul 20, 1945

Mar 10–12, 1945
The Japanese government in Zamboanga City is overthrown by American and Filipino forces following a fierce battle.

5 OPERATION VICTOR
FEBRUARY 19–JUNE 30, 1945

The 8th Army was tasked with clearing the Japanese from the southern islands in Operation Victor. On February 19, they landed on Samar in order to secure passage through the San Bernardino Strait. Invasions of Palawan, Cebu, Panay, and Mindanao followed. The Americans faced the usual Japanese resistance, but by June this was isolated to pockets on Mindanao.

➡ US 8th Army operations

◼ Areas of Japanese resistance, Jun 1945

RETAKING THE PHILIPPINES

The US Navy's success in the Battle of Leyte Gulf in October 1944 was followed by a painful advance through the Philippine islands from January 1945 that cost the lives of more than 10,000 US soldiers, 200,000 Japanese soldiers, and 120,000 civilians. The campaign tied up US troops for longer than US General Douglas MacArthur expected, and with little strategic need.

Having broken the Imperial Japanese Navy's power in the Battle of Leyte Gulf (see pp.214–215), the US Navy saw little to gain in clearing the Japanese from the Philippine islands, with some strategists favoring a direct assault on Japan. General MacArthur, however, having promised to return after defeat in 1942, was set on retaking the Philippines. In January 1945, he began an invasion of the main island, Luzon, where around 250,000 soldiers of the Japanese 14th Area Army under the command of General Tomoyuki Yamashita were concentrated in the north around Manila, and on the high ground leading into the Bataan Peninsula.

The main invasion of Luzon began with landings by forces from the US 6th Army at Lingayen Gulf. The Filipino guerrillas were eager to take back control after the brutality of the Japanese regime and supported the Americans by striking the Japanese forces and carrying out reconnaissance activities. Still, progress was slow and brutal in the face of the Japanese refusal to surrender. Manila finally fell on March 3, 1945, by which time the US 8th Army had begun to move through the southern islands. In both north and south, the Americans were kept occupied until the end of the war.

"Have your troops hoist the colors to its peak, and let no enemy ever haul them down."

GENERAL DOUGLAS MACARTHUR, PHILIPPINES, 1945

NO SURRENDER

Hiroo Onoda (1922–2014) was one of several Japanese soldiers who remained hidden in the Philippines' jungles, unaware or not believing that the war had ended. Cut off from his unit on Lubang Island in 1945, Onoda refused to surrender until his former commanding officer traveled to the Philippines in 1974 and relieved him of duty (below).

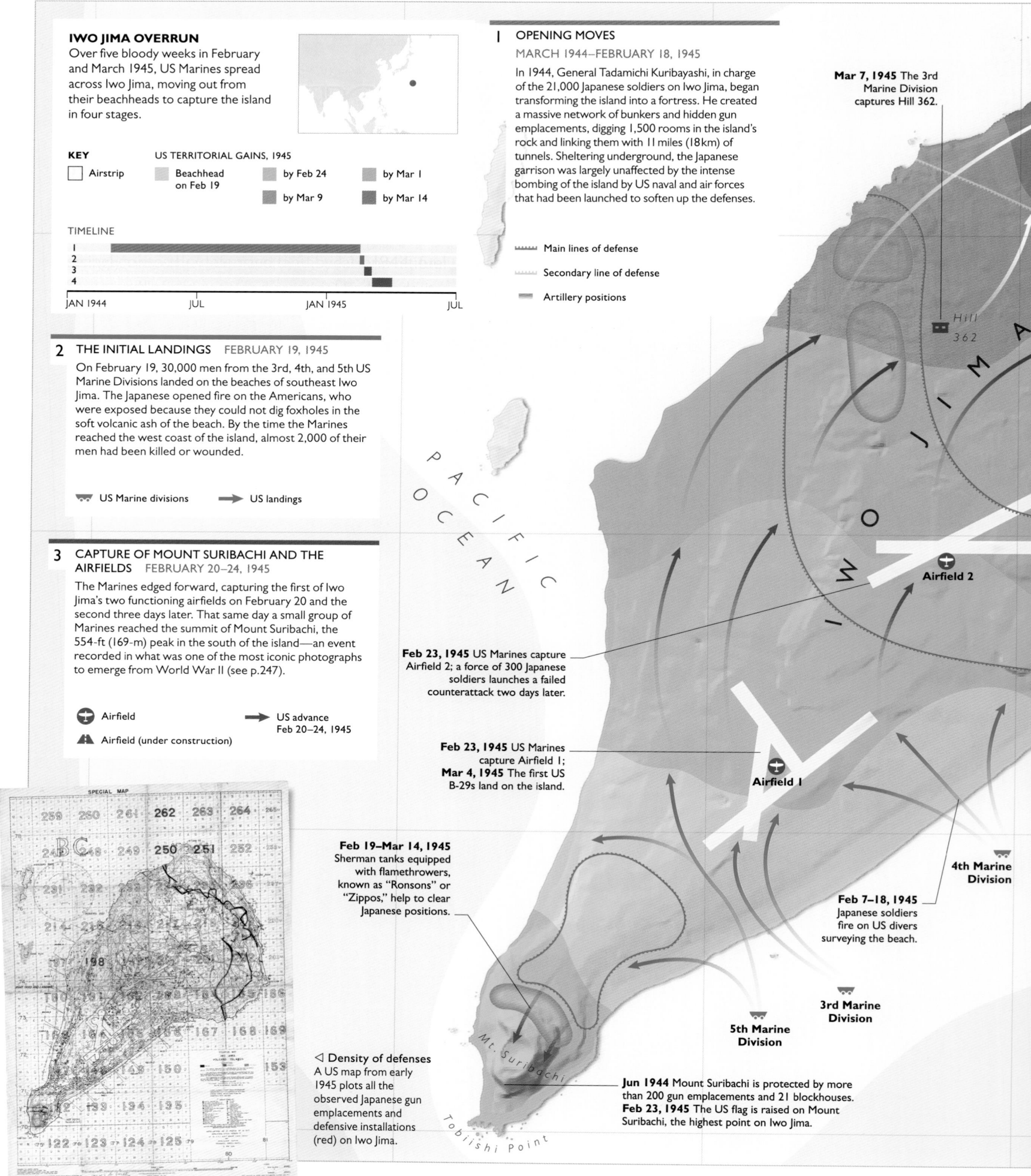

IWO JIMA OVERRUN

Over five bloody weeks in February and March 1945, US Marines spread across Iwo Jima, moving out from their beachheads to capture the island in four stages.

KEY

US TERRITORIAL GAINS, 1945

☐ Airstrip

▨ Beachhead on Feb 19

▨ by Feb 24

▨ by Mar 1

▨ by Mar 9

▨ by Mar 14

TIMELINE

1
2
3
4

JAN 1944   JUL   JAN 1945   JUL

1 OPENING MOVES
MARCH 1944–FEBRUARY 18, 1945

In 1944, General Tadamichi Kuribayashi, in charge of the 21,000 Japanese soldiers on Iwo Jima, began transforming the island into a fortress. He created a massive network of bunkers and hidden gun emplacements, digging 1,500 rooms in the island's rock and linking them with 11 miles (18km) of tunnels. Sheltering underground, the Japanese garrison was largely unaffected by the intense bombing of the island by US naval and air forces that had been launched to soften up the defenses.

⟞⟞⟞⟞ Main lines of defense

⟞⟞⟞⟞ Secondary line of defense

▬▬ Artillery positions

Mar 7, 1945 The 3rd Marine Division captures Hill 362.

2 THE INITIAL LANDINGS FEBRUARY 19, 1945

On February 19, 30,000 men from the 3rd, 4th, and 5th US Marine Divisions landed on the beaches of southeast Iwo Jima. The Japanese opened fire on the Americans, who were exposed because they could not dig foxholes in the soft volcanic ash of the beach. By the time the Marines reached the west coast of the island, almost 2,000 of their men had been killed or wounded.

⛟ US Marine divisions   ➝ US landings

3 CAPTURE OF MOUNT SURIBACHI AND THE AIRFIELDS FEBRUARY 20–24, 1945

The Marines edged forward, capturing the first of Iwo Jima's two functioning airfields on February 20 and the second three days later. That same day a small group of Marines reached the summit of Mount Suribachi, the 554-ft (169-m) peak in the south of the island—an event recorded in what was one of the most iconic photographs to emerge from World War II (see p.247).

✈ Airfield

▲ Airfield (under construction)

➝ US advance Feb 20–24, 1945

Feb 23, 1945 US Marines capture Airfield 2; a force of 300 Japanese soldiers launches a failed counterattack two days later.

Feb 23, 1945 US Marines capture Airfield 1; **Mar 4, 1945** The first US B-29s land on the island.

Feb 19–Mar 14, 1945 Sherman tanks equipped with flamethrowers, known as "Ronsons" or "Zippos," help to clear Japanese positions.

Feb 7–18, 1945 Japanese soldiers fire on US divers surveying the beach.

4th Marine Division

3rd Marine Division

5th Marine Division

◁ **Density of defenses**
A US map from early 1945 plots all the observed Japanese gun emplacements and defensive installations (red) on Iwo Jima.

SPECIAL MAP

Jun 1944 Mount Suribachi is protected by more than 200 gun emplacements and 21 blockhouses.
Feb 23, 1945 The US flag is raised on Mount Suribachi, the highest point on Iwo Jima.

Mt. Suribachi

Tobiishi Point

Airfield 2

Airfield 1

Hill 362

PACIFIC OCEAN

I W O   J I M A

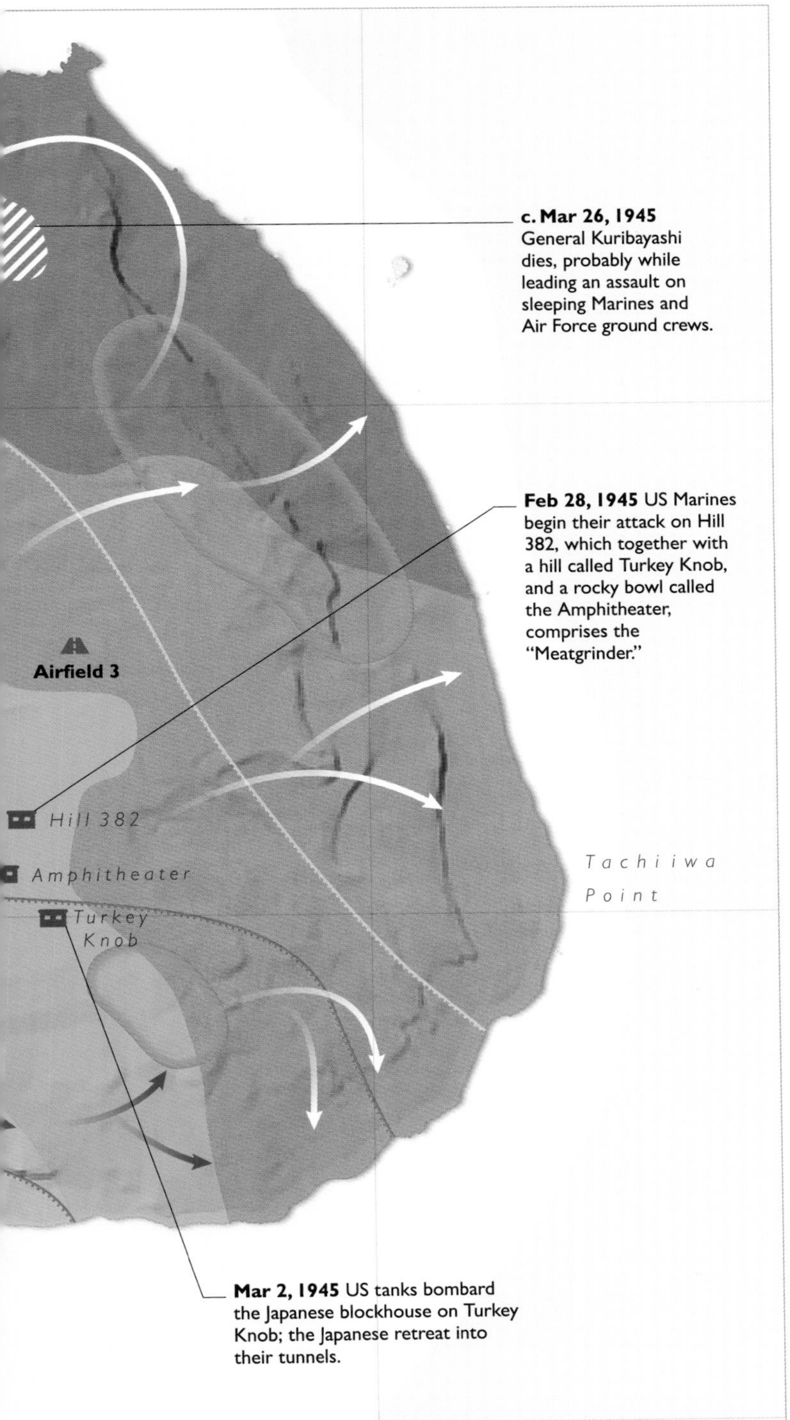

c. **Mar 26, 1945**
General Kuribayashi dies, probably while leading an assault on sleeping Marines and Air Force ground crews.

Feb 28, 1945 US Marines begin their attack on Hill 382, which together with a hill called Turkey Knob, and a rocky bowl called the Amphitheater, comprises the "Meatgrinder."

Airfield 3

🔲 *Hill 382*

▪ *Amphitheater*

🔲 *Turkey Knob*

Tachiiwa Point

Mar 2, 1945 US tanks bombard the Japanese blockhouse on Turkey Knob; the Japanese retreat into their tunnels.

---

4   NORTH TO THE "MEATGRINDER"
FEBRUARY 25–MARCH 26, 1945

The Marines moved slowly northward to attack the fortified ridges of Hill 362 and the area near Hill 382 known as the "Meatgrinder." Clearing the defenders, who were often hidden underground, was punishing work for the advancing US troops as there was little cover. By March 7, the Americans had taken both hills. On March 14, Iwo Jima was declared secure, although a few Japanese soldiers remained in isolated strongholds until the end of March.

➡ US advance Feb 24–Mar 1, 1945

⇨ US advance Mar 14, 1945

▱ Last Japanese stronghold until Mar 26, 1945

🔲 Heavy fortified terrain/high ground

IWO JIMA

The Japanese island of Iwo Jima, which lies some 800 miles (1,300 km) from mainland Japan, was a strategic target for the US. The Marines who took the island from the small number of Japanese forces based there in early 1945 encountered some of the bloodiest fighting of the Pacific War.

By the start of 1945, US forces had moved far west across the Pacific, reaching Leyte and Luzon in the Philippines and inflicting terrible damage on the Imperial Japanese Navy and its air force in the process. In February 1945, US Marines invaded the tiny Pacific island of Iwo Jima, a Japanese military base. Their aim was strategic: they wanted to secure the island's airfields, which would provide a base for Allied fighter planes needed to escort the bombers raiding Japan from the Marianas (see pp.252–53)—and for the B-29 bombers themselves.

The Japanese were aware of the impending threat and as a result had made their preparations: sending reinforcements to Iwo Jima, ordering the evacuation of its civilian population, and placing the island's defense into the hands of one of their most brilliant and experienced generals, Tadamichi Kuribayashi.

Lacking naval or air support and commanding a relatively small force, Kuribayashi knew that an American victory was near inevitable, but he was determined to make it as costly as possible, and to delay his enemy's advance. Instead of defending the island's landing beaches, he ordered the construction of a huge network of caves, tunnels, and pillboxes inland. The invading US troops on the surface—often without cover—were at the mercy of the defenders, who would suddenly emerge from their underground bunkers to launch attacks. Casualties were huge on both sides.

"Japan has started a war with a formidable enemy and we must brace ourselves accordingly."

GENERAL TADAMICHI KURIBAYASHI, 1944

FIGHT TO THE DEATH

Over 20,000 of the 21,000 Japanese soldiers on Iwo Jima died in the fighting while following the instructions set out in General Kuribayashi's six "Courageous Battle Vows." The vows pledged soldiers to defend the island with all their strength, to attack the enemy with suicidal bravery, to not die until they had killed at least ten enemy soldiers, and to continue fighting to the last man.

US Marines destroy a Japanese bunker on Iwo Jima

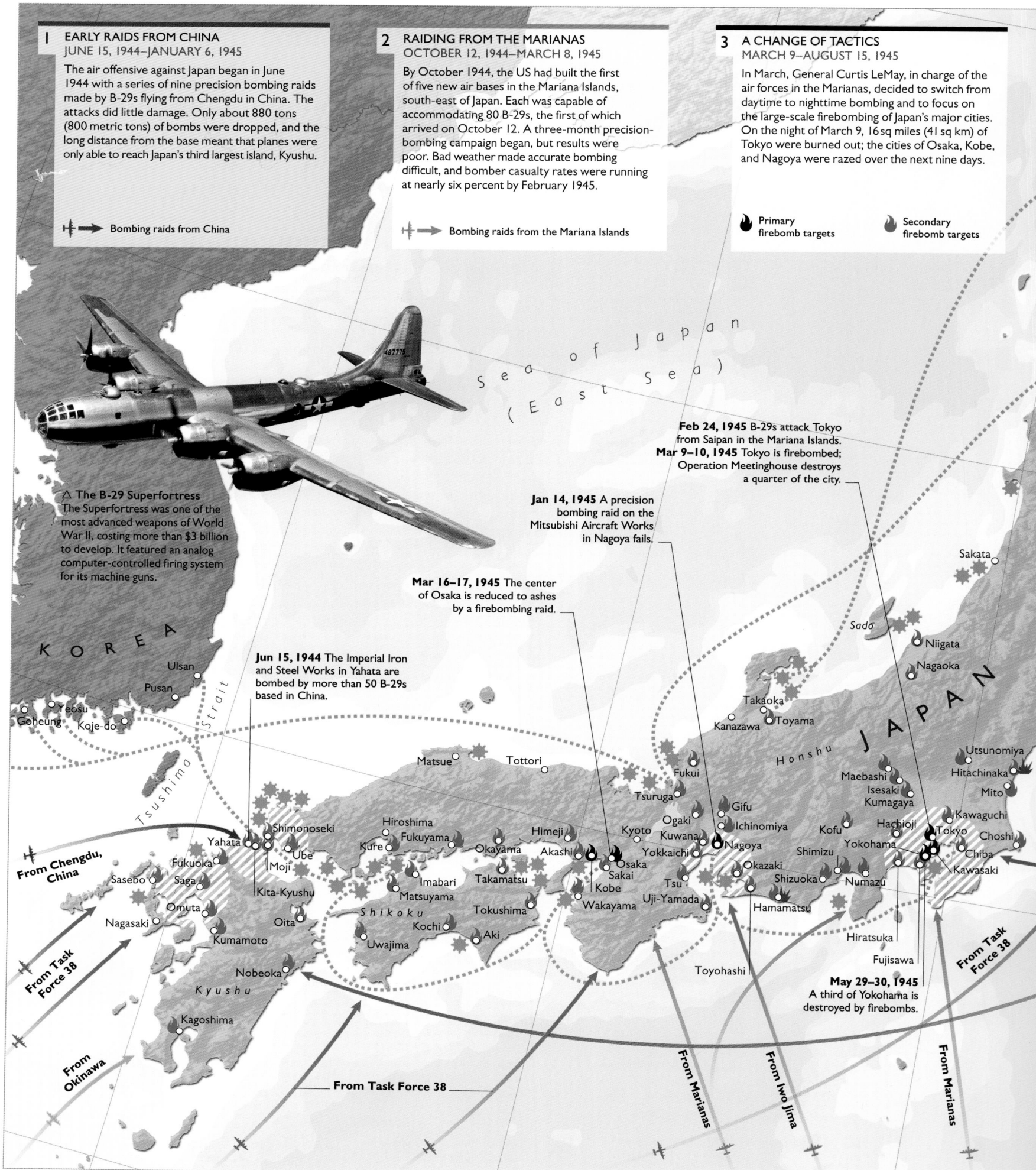

1 EARLY RAIDS FROM CHINA
JUNE 15, 1944–JANUARY 6, 1945

The air offensive against Japan began in June 1944 with a series of nine precision bombing raids made by B-29s flying from Chengdu in China. The attacks did little damage. Only about 880 tons (800 metric tons) of bombs were dropped, and the long distance from the base meant that planes were only able to reach Japan's third largest island, Kyushu.

⊢→ Bombing raids from China

2 RAIDING FROM THE MARIANAS
OCTOBER 12, 1944–MARCH 8, 1945

By October 1944, the US had built the first of five new air bases in the Mariana Islands, south-east of Japan. Each was capable of accommodating 80 B-29s, the first of which arrived on October 12. A three-month precision-bombing campaign began, but results were poor. Bad weather made accurate bombing difficult, and bomber casualty rates were running at nearly six percent by February 1945.

⊢→ Bombing raids from the Mariana Islands

3 A CHANGE OF TACTICS
MARCH 9–AUGUST 15, 1945

In March, General Curtis LeMay, in charge of the air forces in the Marianas, decided to switch from daytime to nighttime bombing and to focus on the large-scale firebombing of Japan's major cities. On the night of March 9, 16 sq miles (41 sq km) of Tokyo were burned out; the cities of Osaka, Kobe, and Nagoya were razed over the next nine days.

◆ Primary firebomb targets   ◆ Secondary firebomb targets

Sea of Japan (East Sea)

△ **The B-29 Superfortress**
The Superfortress was one of the most advanced weapons of World War II, costing more than $3 billion to develop. It featured an analog computer-controlled firing system for its machine guns.

Feb 24, 1945 B-29s attack Tokyo from Saipan in the Mariana Islands.
Mar 9–10, 1945 Tokyo is firebombed; Operation Meetinghouse destroys a quarter of the city.

Jan 14, 1945 A precision bombing raid on the Mitsubishi Aircraft Works in Nagoya fails.

Mar 16–17, 1945 The center of Osaka is reduced to ashes by a firebombing raid.

Jun 15, 1944 The Imperial Iron and Steel Works in Yahata are bombed by more than 50 B-29s based in China.

KOREA

Sakata
Sado
Niigata
Nagaoka

Ulsan
Pusan
Yeosu
Goheung   Koje-do

Takaoka
Kanazawa   Toyama

Honshu   JAPAN

Matsue   Tottori
Fukui
Utsunomiya
Tsuruga   Gifu   Maebashi   Hitachinaka
Ogaki   Ichinomiya   Isesaki   Mito
Kyoto   Kumagaya
Hiroshima   Kuwana   Kofu   Hachioji   Kawaguchi
Shimonoseki   Himeji   Yokkaichi   Nagoya   Tokyo
Yahata   Fukuyama   Akashi   Nagoya   Yokohama   Choshi
Kure   Okayama   Osaka   Tsu   Shimizu   Chiba
From Chengdu, China   Ube   Sakai   Okazaki   Shizuoka   Numazu   Kawasaki
Fukuoka   Moji   Kobe   Uji-Yamada   Hamamatsu
Sasebo   Saga   Kita-Kyushu   Imabari   Takamatsu   Wakayama
Omuta   Matsuyama   Tokushima   Hiratsuka
Nagasaki   Oita   Shikoku   Kochi   Aki   Fujisawa
Kumamoto   Uwajima   Toyohashi
From Task Force 38   Nobeoka   Kyushu

May 29–30, 1945 A third of Yokohama is destroyed by firebombs.

Kagoshima

From Okinawa

From Task Force 38
From Marianas
From Iwo Jima
From Marianas
From Task Force 38

Tsushima Strait

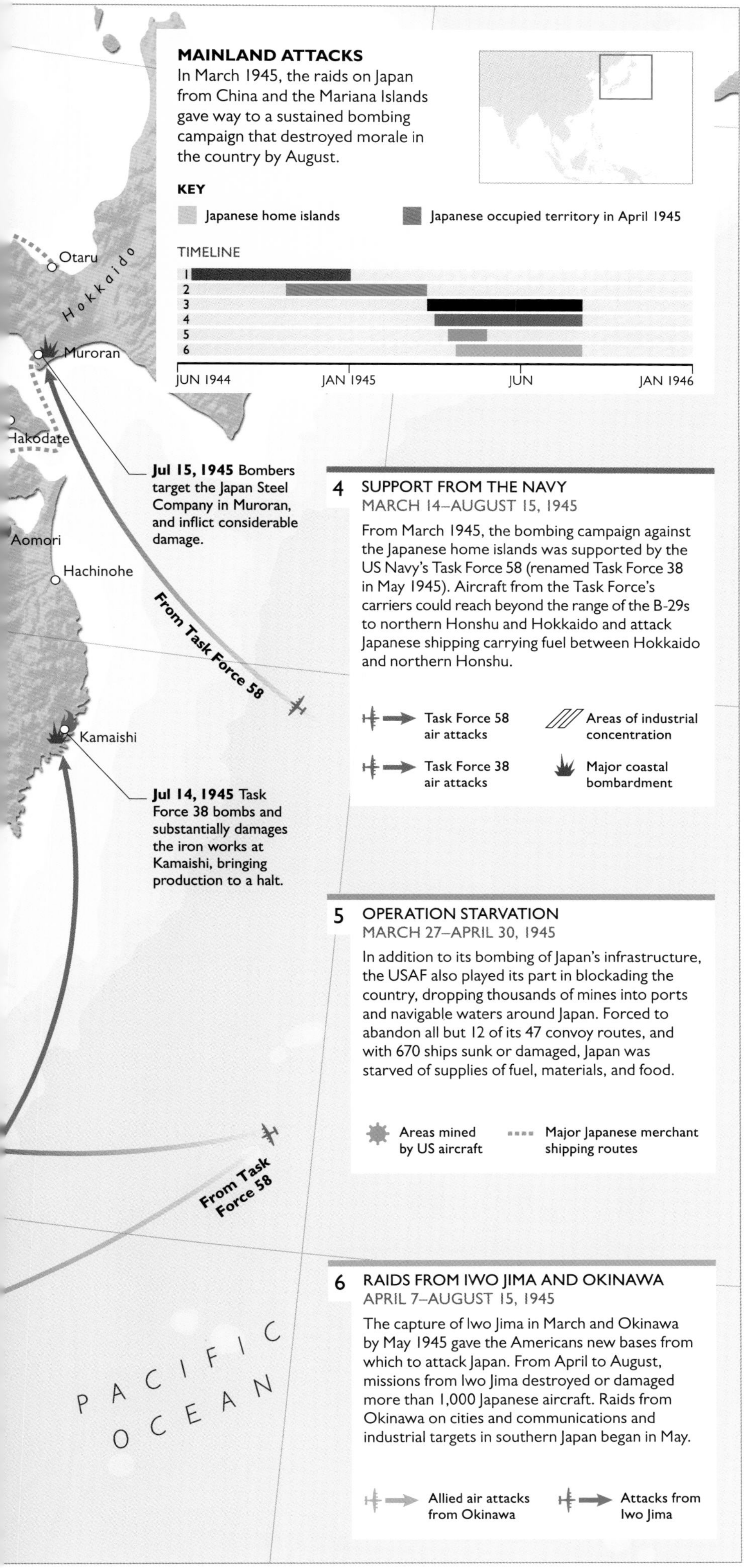

MAINLAND ATTACKS

In March 1945, the raids on Japan from China and the Mariana Islands gave way to a sustained bombing campaign that destroyed morale in the country by August.

KEY

☐ Japanese home islands   ◼ Japanese occupied territory in April 1945

TIMELINE

	JUN 1944	JAN 1945	JUN	JAN 1946
1				
2				
3				
4				
5				
6				

Jul 15, 1945 Bombers target the Japan Steel Company in Muroran, and inflict considerable damage.

Jul 14, 1945 Task Force 38 bombs and substantially damages the iron works at Kamaishi, bringing production to a halt.

Otaru
Hokkaido
Muroran
Hakodate
Aomori
Hachinohe
Kamaishi

From Task Force 58

From Task Force 58

PACIFIC OCEAN

4 SUPPORT FROM THE NAVY
MARCH 14–AUGUST 15, 1945

From March 1945, the bombing campaign against the Japanese home islands was supported by the US Navy's Task Force 58 (renamed Task Force 38 in May 1945). Aircraft from the Task Force's carriers could reach beyond the range of the B-29s to northern Honshu and Hokkaido and attack Japanese shipping carrying fuel between Hokkaido and northern Honshu.

�militaryicon→ Task Force 58 air attacks   /// Areas of industrial concentration

⊢⊢→ Task Force 38 air attacks   🌿 Major coastal bombardment

5 OPERATION STARVATION
MARCH 27–APRIL 30, 1945

In addition to its bombing of Japan's infrastructure, the USAF also played its part in blockading the country, dropping thousands of mines into ports and navigable waters around Japan. Forced to abandon all but 12 of its 47 convoy routes, and with 670 ships sunk or damaged, Japan was starved of supplies of fuel, materials, and food.

✳ Areas mined by US aircraft   ···· Major Japanese merchant shipping routes

6 RAIDS FROM IWO JIMA AND OKINAWA
APRIL 7–AUGUST 15, 1945

The capture of Iwo Jima in March and Okinawa by May 1945 gave the Americans new bases from which to attack Japan. From April to August, missions from Iwo Jima destroyed or damaged more than 1,000 Japanese aircraft. Raids from Okinawa on cities and communications and industrial targets in southern Japan began in May.

⊢⊢→ Allied air attacks from Okinawa   ⊢⊢→ Attacks from Iwo Jima

THE BOMBING OF JAPAN

In June 1944, the Allies began the aerial bombardment of Japan. Aimed initially at shutting down Japanese industrial production for its war machine and cutting off the country's supplies, the campaign turned into a devastating assault on Japan's cities.

The Allies had long realized that the aerial bombardment of Japan would be an essential element in bringing the Japanese Empire to its knees. Early in the Pacific War, the US had launched a mostly unsuccessful air raid on Japan from an aircraft carrier—the Doolittle Raid of April 18, 1942—but had not targeted the country since.

In early 1944, the US deployed the advanced B-29 Superfortress in the Pacific theater. The aircraft was capable of carrying 10 tons (9 metric tons) of bombs over long distances and was used from June 1944 until the end of the war in the sustained bombing of the Japanese home islands. The campaign began poorly; raids from China proved problematic, and precision bombing did little to disrupt Japanese industry. However, as the campaign progressed and the USAF changed tactics, carpet-bombing Japan's cities with napalm and incendiary bombs, the results were dramatic. By August, a third of Japan's buildings and more than 600 factories had been destroyed, tens of thousands of its citizens had been killed, millions were homeless, and Japanese morale was decimated.

"This fire left nothing but twisted, tumbled-down rubble in its path."

GENERAL CURTIS LEMAY ON THE BOMBING OF TOKYO

THE TOKYO FIRESTORM

On the night of March 9–10, 1945, the USAF unleashed Operation Meetinghouse on Tokyo. In a devastating raid, 279 B-29s dropped 1,665 tons (1,510 metric tons) of bombs on the capital city. These napalm or gasoline and white phosphorus incendiary bombs ignited on impact, setting fire to huge swathes of the city, including the densely populated dock districts. A quarter of Tokyo's buildings were destroyed, leaving one million people homeless, and at least 80,000 people were killed.

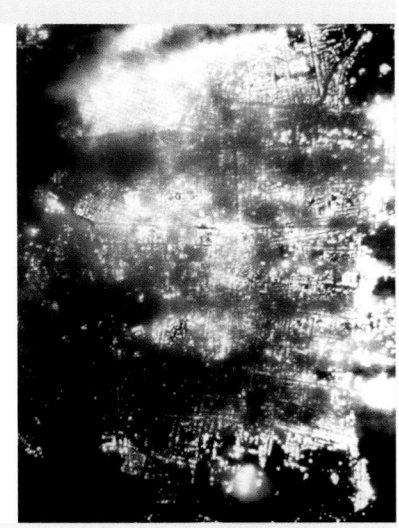

Tokyo ablaze

THE BATTLE OF OKINAWA

As the conflict in Europe was nearing its end, the US was still fighting a brutal war in the Pacific. Its planned conquest of the isolated island of Okinawa resulted in one of the bloodiest battles of the entire conflict, which earned the nickname "Typhoon of Steel."

With their assault on Iwo Jima still underway (see pp.250–251), US commanders began preparing for Operation Iceberg—the invasion of Okinawa, the largest island in the Ryukyu Archipelago. Just 60 miles (96 km) long and 20 miles (32 km) wide at its widest, Okinawa is equidistant from Taiwan, Japan, and China, and US strategists saw it as the ideal base for the final assaults on the main Japanese islands. Like Iwo Jima, Okinawa was heavily fortified, with artillery hidden in caves, and garrisoned by 100,000 men under Lieutenant General Ushijima Mitsuru.

Familiar with the fierce determination of the Japanese army and aware that losses in the battle would probably overtake those on Iwo Jima, the US began the campaign with a massive bombardment to soften up the island's defenses. This was followed by the US military's biggest amphibious landing of the Pacific War. Nonetheless, it took the US forces more than two months to capture the entire island. In the end 12,000 US soldiers, 100,000 Japanese soldiers, and 100,000 civilians died in a campaign that was made obsolete by the events at Hiroshima and Nagasaki (see pp.258–259).

> *"The Japanese bayonets were fixed; ours weren't. We used the knives …"*
>
> FORMER US MARINE WILLIAM MANCHESTER, 1987

CAUGHT IN THE CROSSFIRE

Both Japanese and American soldiers committed atrocities against civilians during the battle. The Japanese also confiscated the Okinawans' food, causing mass starvation. When an American victory seemed certain, thousands of Okinawans committed suicide under pressure from the government. Among the civilians killed on Okinawa were also many who had been forced to serve in the Japanese army.

A US Marine shares his rations with children on Okinawa

OKINAWA CAPTURED

In four broad phases extending from April 1 to June 21, the Americans gradually gained control of Okinawa. The battle for the island played out on land and at sea.

KEY

🚜 ⛴ Allied forces   ✈ Japanese airfields

UNDER US CONTROL 1945

■ Mar 31   ■ Apr 4   ■ Apr 21

■ May 12   ■ Jun 21

TIMELINE

	MAR 1945	APR	MAY	JUN	JUL
1					
2					
3					
4					
5					
6					

1 ALLIED PREPARATION
MARCH 18–31, 1945

Ahead of the invasion, Allied aircraft from carriers in Task Force 58 launched raids on Kyushu—the most south-westerly of Japan's main islands. They destroyed hundreds of Japanese aircraft, reducing the threat to the invasion of Okinawa. On March 26, US forces landed on the Kerama Islands west of Okinawa, which could be used as fleet anchorage, and on Keise Shima, from which artillery could provide fire support across most of southern Okinawa.

➡ Preliminary US landings

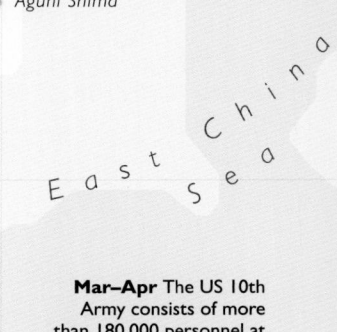

Aguni Shima

East China Sea

Mar–Apr The US 10th Army consists of more than 180,000 personnel at the start of the invasion.

US 10th Army ⛴

2 THE INVASION OF OKINAWA
APRIL 1–4, 1945

Troops of the US 10th Army landed at Hagushi on April 1. By the end of the day, 50,000 US soldiers were on Okinawa and had taken key targets, including airfields. Ultimately, 170,000 troops landed on the island. At first they faced little resistance as they moved inland; by April 4 they had divided the island in two.

➡ US landings and advance across Okinawa

🚢👤 Japanese forces on Apr 1

3 THE CONQUEST OF NORTH OKINAWA
APRIL 4–21, 1945

After taking south central Okinawa, General Buckner, commander of the US 10th Army, sent troops north. They encountered strong resistance from Japanese forces cornered in ridged, wooded terrain around Mount Yae in the Motobu Peninsula. By April 20, the US held the north, and had secured the islet of Ie Shima.

➡ US advance north

▬ Resistance around Mount Yae

Kerama Islands

Task Force 51

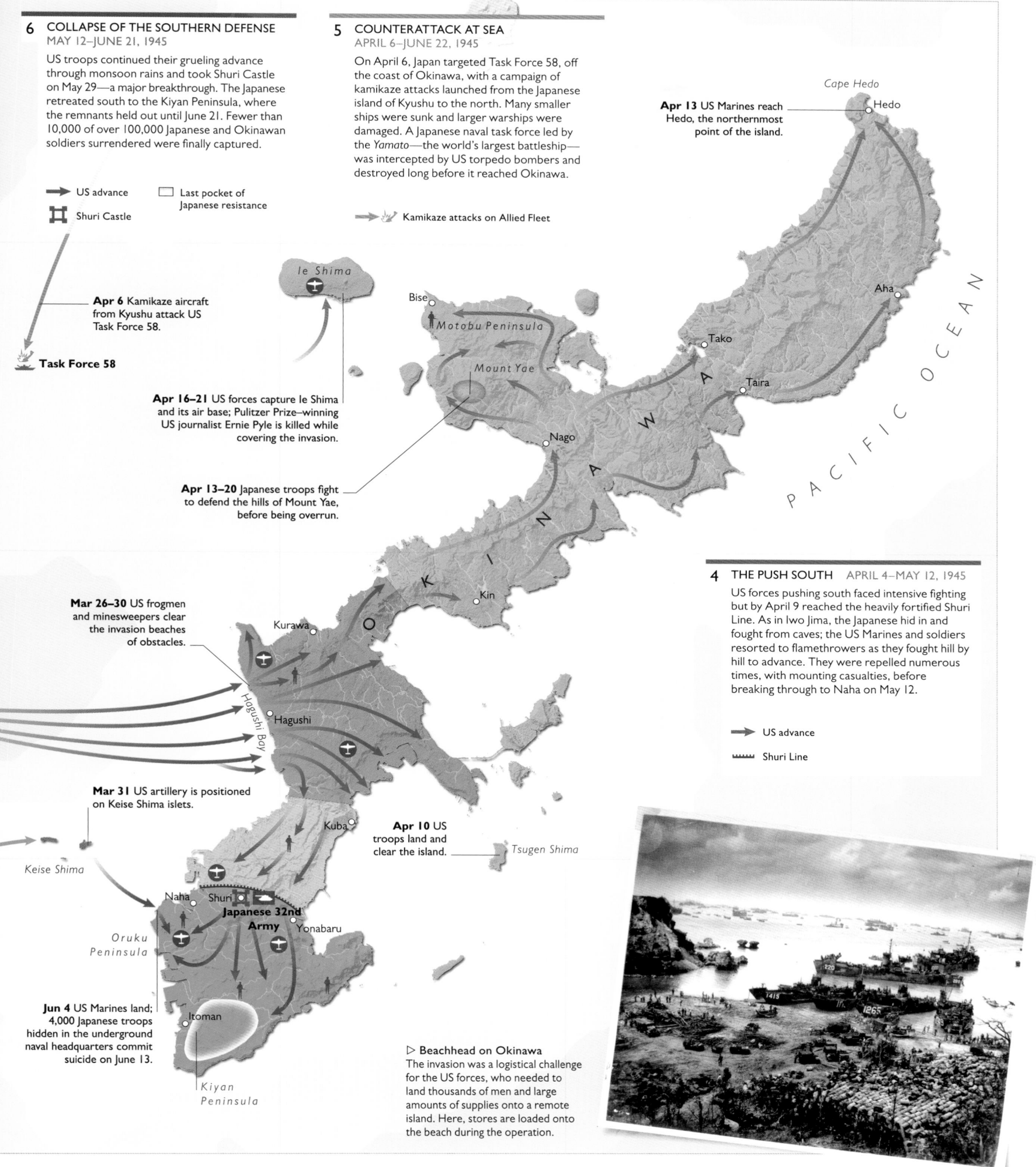

6 COLLAPSE OF THE SOUTHERN DEFENSE
MAY 12–JUNE 21, 1945

US troops continued their grueling advance through monsoon rains and took Shuri Castle on May 29—a major breakthrough. The Japanese retreated south to the Kiyan Peninsula, where the remnants held out until June 21. Fewer than 10,000 of over 100,000 Japanese and Okinawan soldiers surrendered were finally captured.

→ US advance

☐ Last pocket of Japanese resistance

⊞ Shuri Castle

5 COUNTERATTACK AT SEA
APRIL 6–JUNE 22, 1945

On April 6, Japan targeted Task Force 58, off the coast of Okinawa, with a campaign of kamikaze attacks launched from the Japanese island of Kyushu to the north. Many smaller ships were sunk and larger warships were damaged. A Japanese naval task force led by the *Yamato*—the world's largest battleship—was intercepted by US torpedo bombers and destroyed long before it reached Okinawa.

→ Kamikaze attacks on Allied Fleet

Apr 13 US Marines reach Hedo, the northernmost point of the island.

Apr 6 Kamikaze aircraft from Kyushu attack US Task Force 58.

Task Force 58

Apr 16–21 US forces capture Ie Shima and its air base; Pulitzer Prize–winning US journalist Ernie Pyle is killed while covering the invasion.

Apr 13–20 Japanese troops fight to defend the hills of Mount Yae, before being overrun.

Mar 26–30 US frogmen and minesweepers clear the invasion beaches of obstacles.

Mar 31 US artillery is positioned on Keise Shima islets.

Apr 10 US troops land and clear the island.

Jun 4 US Marines land; 4,000 Japanese troops hidden in the underground naval headquarters commit suicide on June 13.

4 THE PUSH SOUTH   APRIL 4–MAY 12, 1945

US forces pushing south faced intensive fighting but by April 9 reached the heavily fortified Shuri Line. As in Iwo Jima, the Japanese hid in and fought from caves; the US Marines and soldiers resorted to flamethrowers as they fought hill by hill to advance. They were repelled numerous times, with mounting casualties, before breaking through to Naha on May 12.

→ US advance

〰 Shuri Line

Cape Hedo · Hedo
Aha
Tako
Taira
Kin
Bise
Motobu Peninsula
Mount Yae
Ie Shima
Nago
Kurawa
Hagushi
Hagushi Bay
Keise Shima
Kuba
Tsugen Shima
Naha · Shuri
Japanese 32nd Army · Yonabaru
Oruku Peninsula
Itoman
Kiyan Peninsula

O K I N A W A

PACIFIC OCEAN

▷ **Beachhead on Okinawa**
The invasion was a logistical challenge for the US forces, who needed to land thousands of men and large amounts of supplies onto a remote island. Here, stores are loaded onto the beach during the operation.

MANHATTAN PROJECT

The Manhattan Project was one of several programs working on developing nuclear weapons in the 1940s, and it was the most successful. In July 1945, the project team detonated the world's first atomic bomb.

Knowledge about atomic physics developed very quickly. In 1896, French physicist Henri Becquerel discovered radioactivity, and by 1920, New Zealand-born physicist Ernest Rutherford had split the atom, and Danish physicist Niels Bohr had completed his atomic theory. With the discovery of nuclear fission by German

△ "Fat Man" replica
Code named "Fat Man," the atomic bomb that was dropped on the Japanese city of Nagasaki in August 1945 was even more powerful than the one used at Hiroshima.

scientists Otto Hahn and Fritz Strassman in 1938, the race to develop an atomic weapon had begun. The US-based Manhattan Project, set up in 1941, quickly outpaced the British program. In 1943, Britain's Tube Alloys program and the Manhattan Project merged, while the Allies successfully sabotaged Germany's atomic program with an attack on the Vemork heavy water plant (see pp.138–139).

The bomb as a reality

On July 16, 1945, the US army successfully detonated an atomic bomb at Almagordo, New Mexico. Churchill heard of the test through a note handed to him at the Potsdam Conference that said, "Babies satisfactorily born." The atomic bomb was now a reality, and was dropped to devastating effect on Japan in August of the same year, at Hiroshima and Nagasaki (see pp.258–259).

△ The beginning of the end
The world's first atomic bomb exploded at 5:29 am on July 16, 1945, in New Mexico, in an operation code named "Trinity."

▷ Team photo display
The Manhattan Project's team consisted of many scientists who had left Britain or fled Europe before or during the war.

Lawrence T. Abraham

Beverly J. Agnew

Groves

Samuel Paiz

Thomas H. Benoit

Helen Schneider

Mary Alice Nachtrieb

Enrico Fermi

Harold M. Agnew

Luis Alvarez

Athena V. Berry

Richard P. Feynman

Al Clark

R. Oppenheimer

Katherine Oppenheimer

Elinor Hempelmann

Marion L. Arnold

Leandro S. Ortiz

Viola M. Vigil

Elmer L. Hilton

John R. Von Neumann

Gladys Grinsel

Seth H. Neddermeyer

zel R. Greenbacker

Amadon Garcia

Sara Lea Peddicord

Gilbert J. Gutierrez

HIROSHIMA AND NAGASAKI

On August 6, 1945, a B-29 bomber dropped a nuclear weapon on Hiroshima that killed around 80,000 people instantly and left 70 percent of the city's buildings in ruins. A second bomb was dropped on Nagasaki three days later, claiming another 40,000 lives. The bombs helped to bring the Pacific war to an end, but at an appalling cost.

As the war in the west came to an end in May 1945, the Allied forces began drawing up plans to invade Japan. However, the Japanese had a large number of troops, along with a vast civilian militia, and US military planners feared that an invasion could result in a long-running conflict with extensive casualties on both sides. They considered using chemical and biological weapons, but, despite some opposition, President Truman made the decision to use nuclear weapons (see pp.256–257) against Japan.

Three nuclear bombs were built. The first prototype was tested over the New Mexico desert on July 16, 1945. The other two bombs were to be dropped on the cities of Hiroshima and Kokura, chosen for their industrial and military significance; however, poor weather conditions on the day of the attack resulted in one of the bombers diverting from Kokura to Nagasaki. The two explosions caused casualties on a vast scale, and their impact started a debate about the morality of nuclear weapons that still rages today.

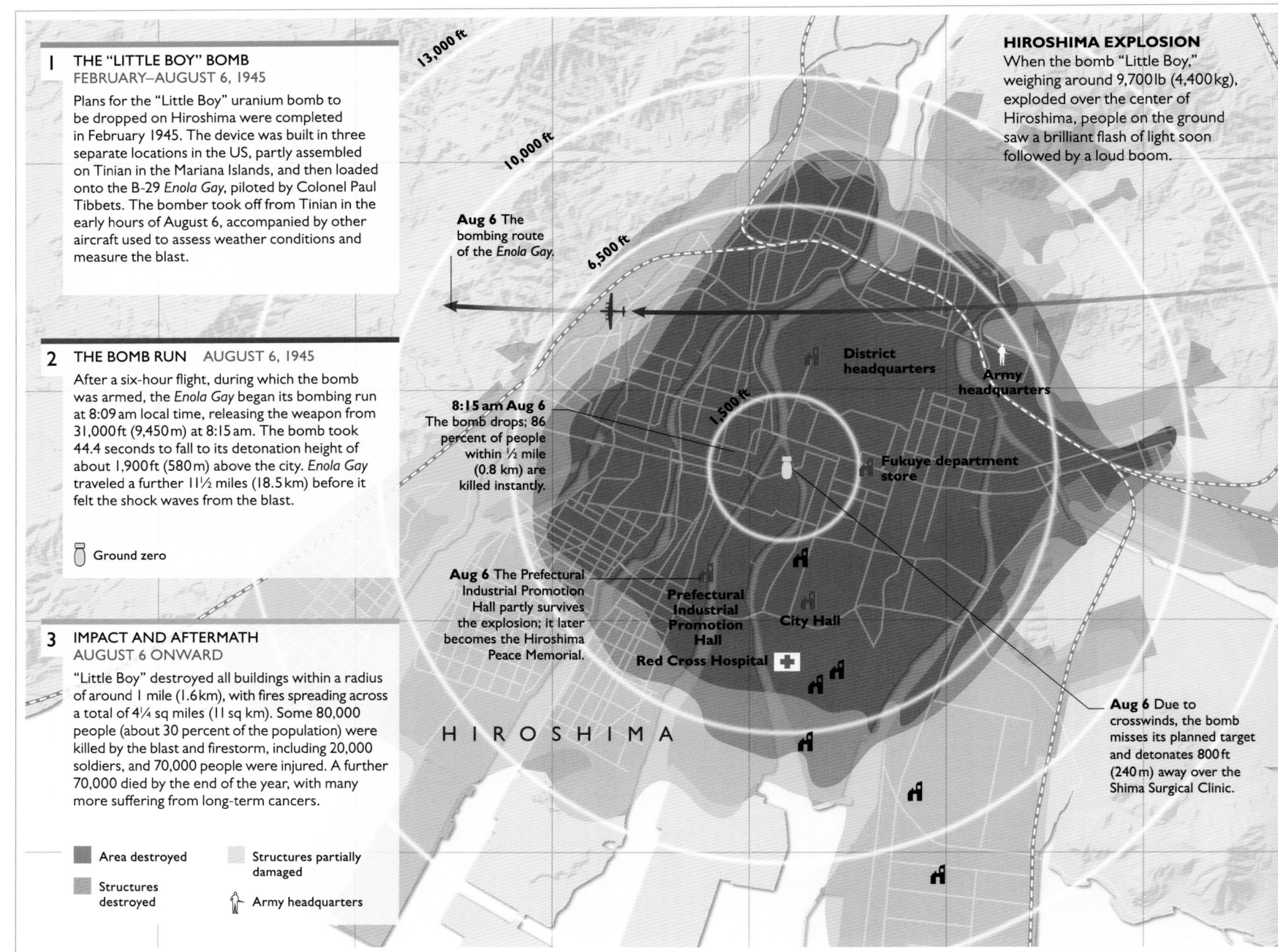

1 THE "LITTLE BOY" BOMB
FEBRUARY–AUGUST 6, 1945

Plans for the "Little Boy" uranium bomb to be dropped on Hiroshima were completed in February 1945. The device was built in three separate locations in the US, partly assembled on Tinian in the Mariana Islands, and then loaded onto the B-29 *Enola Gay*, piloted by Colonel Paul Tibbets. The bomber took off from Tinian in the early hours of August 6, accompanied by other aircraft used to assess weather conditions and measure the blast.

2 THE BOMB RUN   AUGUST 6, 1945

After a six-hour flight, during which the bomb was armed, the *Enola Gay* began its bombing run at 8:09 am local time, releasing the weapon from 31,000 ft (9,450 m) at 8:15 am. The bomb took 44.4 seconds to fall to its detonation height of about 1,900 ft (580 m) above the city. *Enola Gay* traveled a further 11½ miles (18.5 km) before it felt the shock waves from the blast.

▯ Ground zero

3 IMPACT AND AFTERMATH
AUGUST 6 ONWARD

"Little Boy" destroyed all buildings within a radius of around 1 mile (1.6 km), with fires spreading across a total of 4¼ sq miles (11 sq km). Some 80,000 people (about 30 percent of the population) were killed by the blast and firestorm, including 20,000 soldiers, and 70,000 people were injured. A further 70,000 died by the end of the year, with many more suffering from long-term cancers.

Area destroyed

Structures destroyed

Structures partially damaged

Army headquarters

13,000 ft

10,000 ft

6,500 ft

1,500 ft

Aug 6 The bombing route of the *Enola Gay*.

HIROSHIMA EXPLOSION
When the bomb "Little Boy," weighing around 9,700 lb (4,400 kg), exploded over the center of Hiroshima, people on the ground saw a brilliant flash of light soon followed by a loud boom.

District headquarters

Army headquarters

8:15 am Aug 6
The bomb drops; 86 percent of people within ½ mile (0.8 km) are killed instantly.

Fukuye department store

Aug 6 The Prefectural Industrial Promotion Hall partly survives the explosion; it later becomes the Hiroshima Peace Memorial.

Prefectural Industrial Promotion Hall

City Hall

Red Cross Hospital

HIROSHIMA

Aug 6 Due to crosswinds, the bomb misses its planned target and detonates 800 ft (240 m) away over the Shima Surgical Clinic.

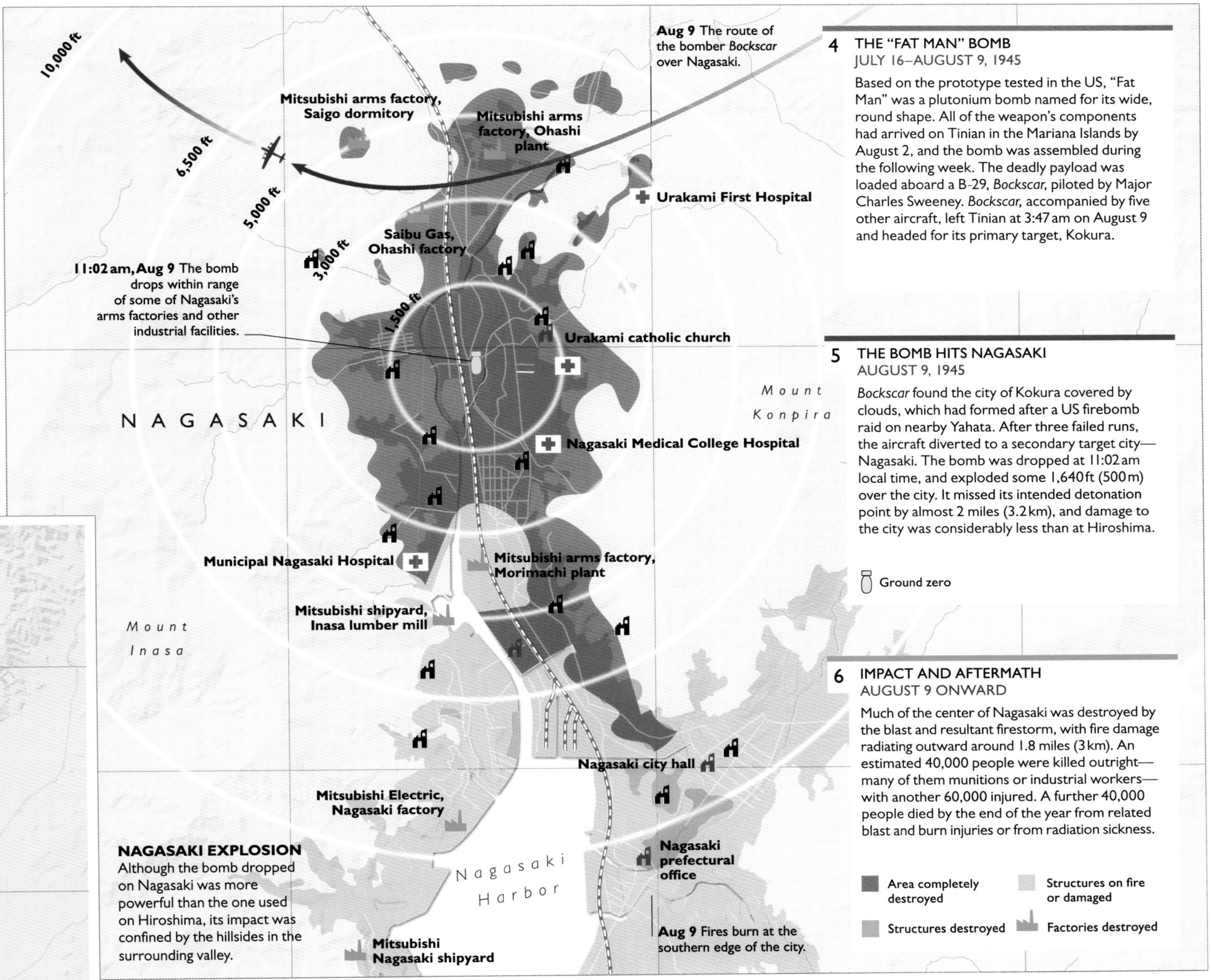

10,000 ft

6,500 ft

5,000 ft

Aug 9 The route of the bomber *Bockscar* over Nagasaki.

3,000 ft

Mitsubishi arms factory, Saigo dormitory

Mitsubishi arms factory, Ohashi plant

✚ **Urakami First Hospital**

1,500 ft

Saibu Gas, Ohashi factory

11:02 am, Aug 9 The bomb drops within range of some of Nagasaki's arms factories and other industrial facilities.

Urakami catholic church

Mount Konpira

N A G A S A K I

✚ **Nagasaki Medical College Hospital**

Municipal Nagasaki Hospital ✚

Mount Inasa

Mitsubishi arms factory, Morimachi plant

Mitsubishi shipyard, Inasa lumber mill

Nagasaki city hall

Mitsubishi Electric, Nagasaki factory

Nagasaki Harbor

Nagasaki prefectural office

NAGASAKI EXPLOSION
Although the bomb dropped on Nagasaki was more powerful than the one used on Hiroshima, its impact was confined by the hillsides in the surrounding valley.

Mitsubishi Nagasaki shipyard

Aug 9 Fires burn at the southern edge of the city.

4 THE "FAT MAN" BOMB
JULY 16–AUGUST 9, 1945

Based on the prototype tested in the US, "Fat Man" was a plutonium bomb named for its wide, round shape. All of the weapon's components had arrived on Tinian in the Mariana Islands by August 2, and the bomb was assembled during the following week. The deadly payload was loaded aboard a B-29, *Bockscar*, piloted by Major Charles Sweeney. *Bockscar*, accompanied by five other aircraft, left Tinian at 3:47 am on August 9 and headed for its primary target, Kokura.

5 THE BOMB HITS NAGASAKI
AUGUST 9, 1945

Bockscar found the city of Kokura covered by clouds, which had formed after a US firebomb raid on nearby Yahata. After three failed runs, the aircraft diverted to a secondary target city—Nagasaki. The bomb was dropped at 11:02 am local time, and exploded some 1,640 ft (500 m) over the city. It missed its intended detonation point by almost 2 miles (3.2 km), and damage to the city was considerably less than at Hiroshima.

▯ Ground zero

6 IMPACT AND AFTERMATH
AUGUST 9 ONWARD

Much of the center of Nagasaki was destroyed by the blast and resultant firestorm, with fire damage radiating outward around 1.8 miles (3 km). An estimated 40,000 people were killed outright—many of them munitions or industrial workers—with another 60,000 injured. A further 40,000 people died by the end of the year from related blast and burn injuries or from radiation sickness.

■ Area completely destroyed	▨ Structures on fire or damaged
▨ Structures destroyed	🏭 Factories destroyed

DESTRUCTION OF TWO CITIES

The bombs that flattened Hiroshima and Nagasaki were the first and last atomic weapons to be employed in war. Their impact killed tens of thousands of people instantly, with many more dying by the end of the year, and their use ushered in the nuclear age.

KEY

═ Road	◯ Radius of damage	✈ Bombing routes	
▭ Railroad	✚ Hospitals destroyed	▨ Built-up areas	
🏫 Schools destroyed	🏢 Buildings destroyed		

TIMELINE

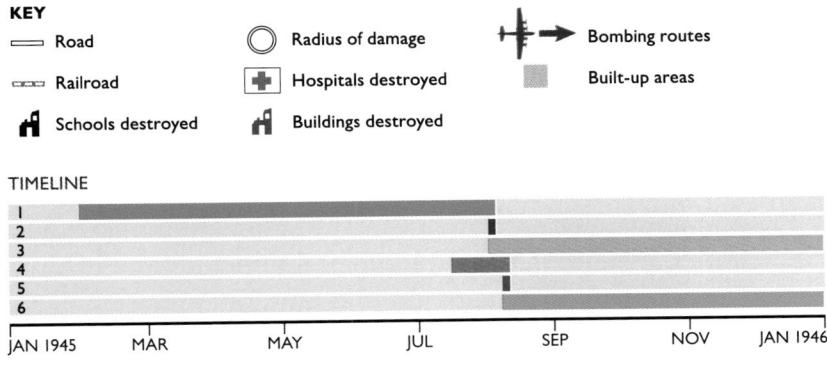

```
1
2
3
4
5
6
JAN 1945   MAR     MAY     JUL     SEP     NOV   JAN 1946
```

△ **Hiroshima after the blast**
A man stands in Hiroshima's ruins in the aftermath of the bombing. Unaware that there had been an attack, the Japanese military were puzzled by the ensuing radio silence from the city.

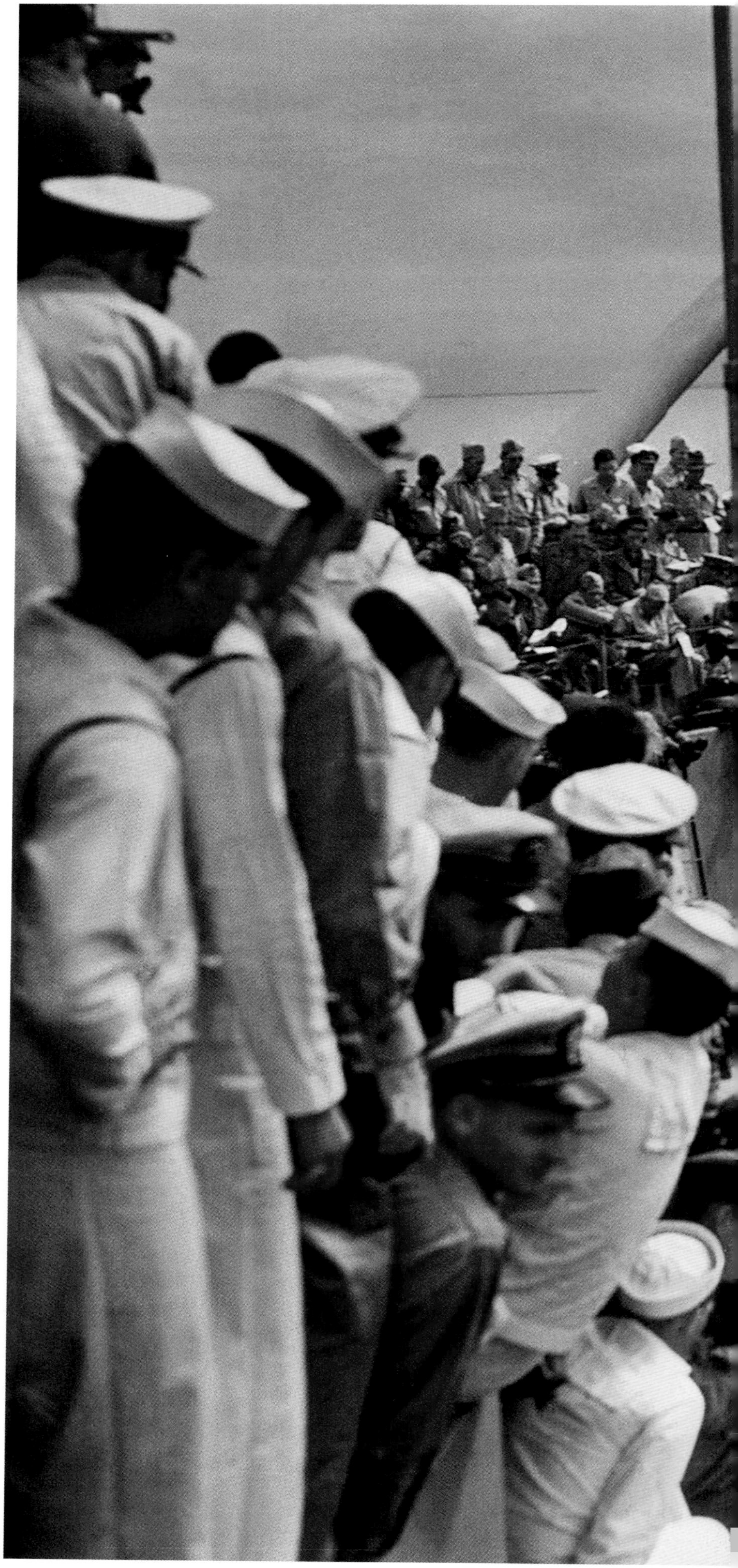

PEACE IN THE PACIFIC

Japan surrendered to the Allies on August 15, 1945, around three months after the capitulation of Axis forces in Europe. It brought World War II to an end, and prevented a US invasion of Japan's home islands that would almost certainly have cost many more lives.

THE STARS AND STRIPES
MEDITERRANEAN
PEACE AT LAST

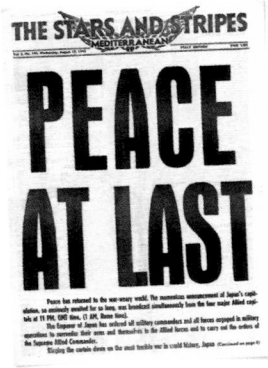

△ **Hot news**
The Stars and Stripes, the US military newspaper, splashes news of Japan's unconditional surrender and the end of the war.

While Japan's surrender is often attributed to the bombing of Hiroshima and Nagasaki (see pp.258–259), there were other elements involved. The Potsdam Declaration (see pp.230–231) had demanded unconditional Japanese surrender, and Japan's Supreme Council for the Direction of the War, or "Big Six," appealed to the USSR—secretly and unsuccessfully—to negotiate a surrender on more favorable terms. On August 6, the US dropped an atom bomb on Hiroshima, and a few days later they dropped another on Nagasaki. On August 8, the USSR declared war on Japan; the following day, Soviet forces began their invasion of Manchuria.

As the odds stacked up against Japan, Emperor Hirohito ordered the "Big Six" to accept the Allies' terms of surrender. A failed coup d'etat by pro-war factions ensued, and on August 15 Hirohito issued a radio broadcast declaring surrender. It was a crushing blow to the nation, and a few military personnel refused to accept it, fighting on for months and even years. US forces began occupying Japan on August 28, and the surrender ceremony took place on September 2.

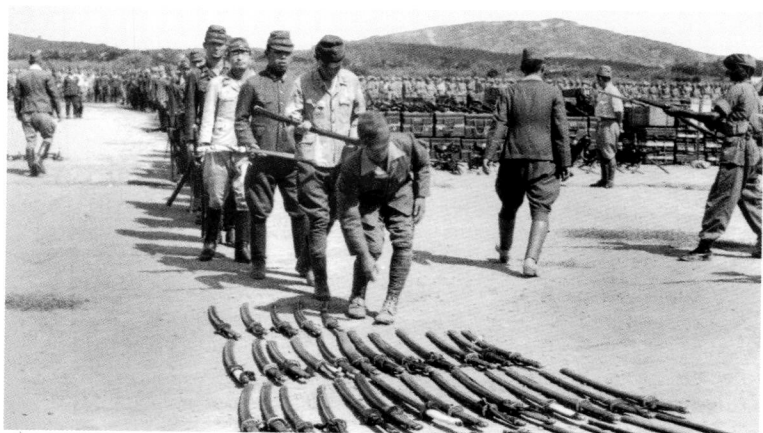

△ **Laying down of arms**
Japanese officers surrender their ceremonial samurai swords to soldiers of the 25th Indian Division at Kuala Lumpur, Malaya. In his capitulation speech, Emperor Hirohito had declared that if the Japanese continued to fight "it would not only result in an ultimate collapse and obliteration of the Japanese nation, but would lead to the total extinction of human civilization."

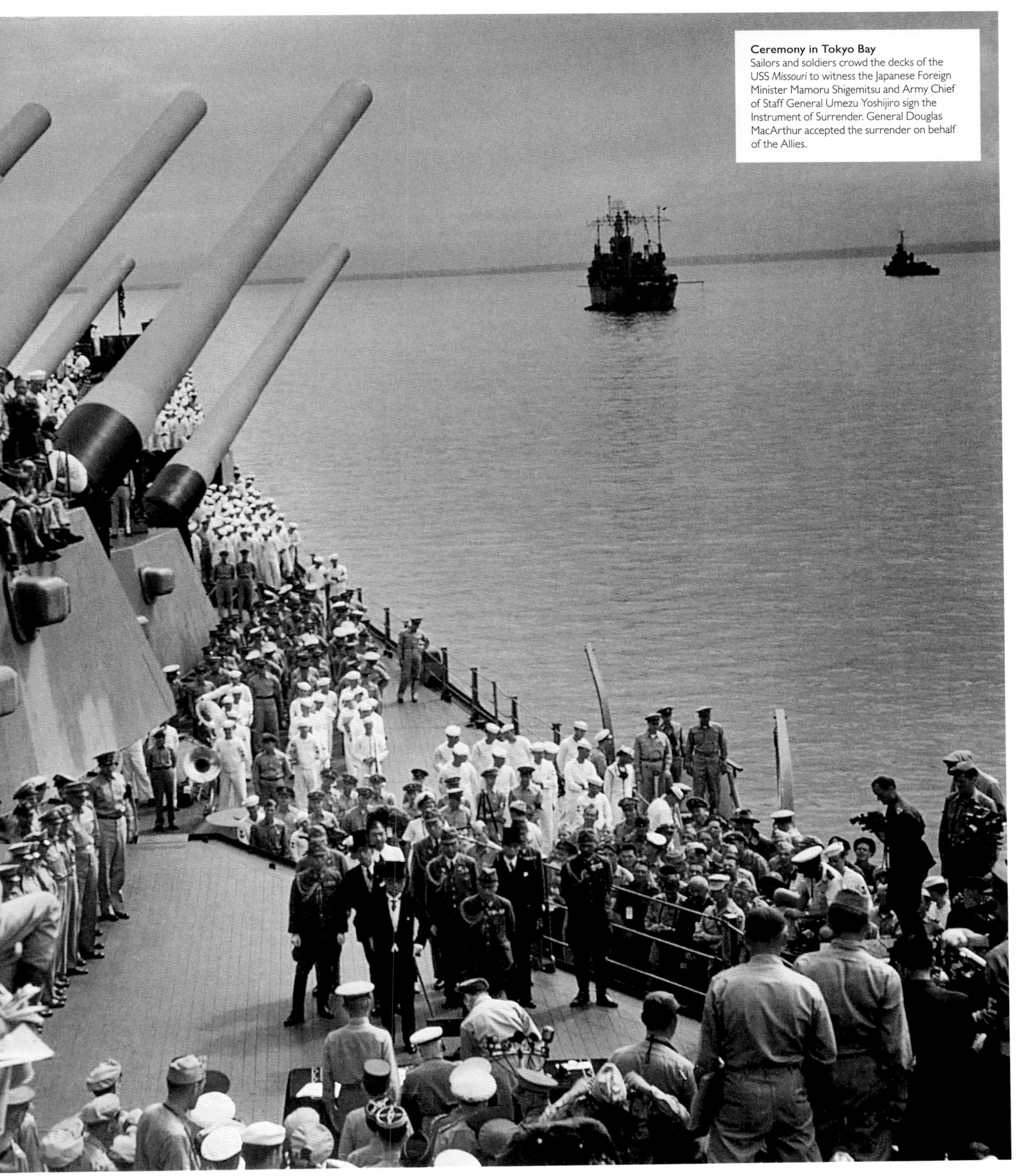

Ceremony in Tokyo Bay
Sailors and soldiers crowd the decks of the USS *Missouri* to witness the Japanese Foreign Minister Mamoru Shigemitsu and Army Chief of Staff General Umezu Yoshijiro sign the Instrument of Surrender. General Douglas MacArthur accepted the surrender on behalf of the Allies.

THE AFTERMATH OF WAR

The most destructive war in history, World War II was followed by a nuclear arms race between the US and the Soviet Union that created the potential for mass destruction on an unprecedented and almost unimaginable scale. Recovery from the material damage of the war was relatively swift, but achieving genuine peace proved an elusive goal.

△ **People on the move**
In the wake of World War II, there were at least 11 million civilian refugees throughout Europe who needed to find new homes.

Across most of Europe and Asia, World War II left a legacy of ruined cities and displaced lives. In contrast, the US was strengthened by the war, both economically and militarily, and became globally dominant. The Soviet Union had greatly extended its territory and possessed a formidable army, but it had suffered some of the worst damage of any country in the war, and could not compete with the US in economic strength. For Britain and France, although they had been on the winning side, the war had been humbling, and their imperial prestige would never be restored. By 1955, most countries in South and Southeast Asia had gained independence from colonial rule.

The Cold War sets in

The high ideals professed by the victors during World War II found embodiment in the United Nations and provided the basis for war crime trials of Nazi and Japanese leaders. However, the alliance between the Soviet Union and the Western powers soon fell apart, and Europe became divided by the "Iron Curtain," which separated the Soviet-dominated Communist East from the US-dominated capitalist West. By 1950, after the triumph of Mao Zedong in the Chinese Civil War, Communist societies stretched from Central Europe to the Pacific, while the US adopted the role of leader of the "Free World." As the US

◁ **Nuclear arms race**
The 1952 explosion of the first hydrogen bomb at Eniwetok Atoll, in the Pacific, further expanded the destructive power of nuclear arsenals.

EUROPE AND ASIA

Unable to agree on Germany's future, the Allies turned their temporary military occupation zones into separate states. The Soviet Union's zone became East Germany, and the Western powers' zones formed West Germany. Berlin remained divided between the four powers, but within East German territory. Later, West Germany integrated into NATO, and East Germany into the Warsaw Pact. Japan was only occupied by the Americans, and was reconstructed as a constitutional monarchy.

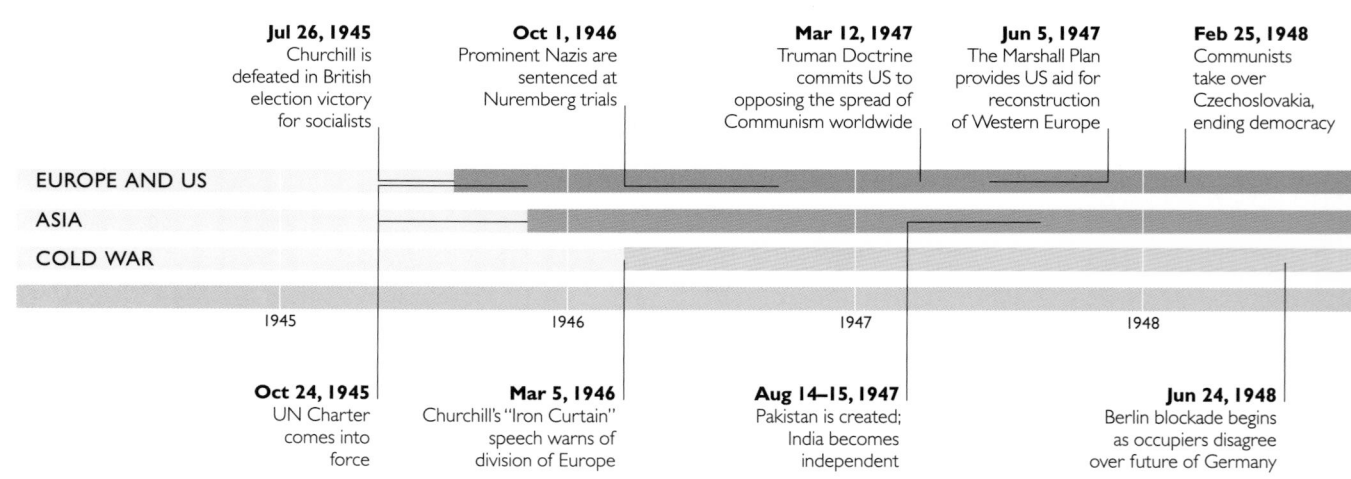

Jul 26, 1945
Churchill is defeated in British election victory for socialists

Oct 1, 1946
Prominent Nazis are sentenced at Nuremberg trials

Mar 12, 1947
Truman Doctrine commits US to opposing the spread of Communism worldwide

Jun 5, 1947
The Marshall Plan provides US aid for reconstruction of Western Europe

Feb 25, 1948
Communists take over Czechoslovakia, ending democracy

EUROPE AND US

ASIA

COLD WAR

1945   1946   1947   1948

Oct 24, 1945
UN Charter comes into force

Mar 5, 1946
Churchill's "Iron Curtain" speech warns of division of Europe

Aug 14–15, 1947
Pakistan is created; India becomes independent

Jun 24, 1948
Berlin blockade begins as occupiers disagree over future of Germany

◁ **Back on track**
The mass production of the Volkswagen (meaning "people's car") became a symbol of West Germany's economic and political recovery in the 1950s.

"Shall we put an end to the human race; or shall mankind renounce war?"

BERTRAND RUSSELL, THE RUSSELL–EINSTEIN MANIFESTO, 1955

and USSR (the "superpowers") engaged in a nuclear arms race, and the US fought the Chinese Communist troops in Korea, fears of an even more destructive World War III were only too real.

Economic recovery

Across the world, political recovery and economic reconstruction were surprisingly successful. As a global economy was restored (excluding the Communist states), there was no return to the mass unemployment of the Depression years, and in many countries, consumer demand was soon driving high growth rates. Japan and Germany had seen enough of the horrors of war and, unlike after World War I, there were no calls to avenge defeat. Japan was reestablished as a constitutional monarchy, and Hiroshima and Nagasaki were restored as flourishing cities. In West Germany, democracy took root, and industrial growth was rapid. Across much of Western Europe, forms of social democracy with mixed economies became standard. Progressive innovations included votes for women in France and the National Health Service in Britain.

The post-war world

The victorious powers fell far short of fulfilling the ideals they had expressed during the conflict. In the Soviet-controlled sphere—which included Albania, Bulgaria, Czechoslovakia, Hungary, East Germany, Poland, Romania, and Yugoslavia—prison camps and the denial of individual freedom negated the promise of liberation. Meanwhile, the US was prepared to support right-wing dictators serving the anticommunist cause, as in Francoist Spain and much of Latin America. For decades, the colonial powers still fought local wars against subject populations, while in the Middle East, the founding of Israel confirmed a chronic instability in the region. Instead of disarmament, there was a headlong race to expand both nuclear and conventional military arsenals. However, amid these conflicts and uncertainties, many individuals found a chance to build new lives in rapidly changing societies. The post-war world did not necessarily offer justice, peace, or security, but it did offer hope.

△ **Mao's China**
A poster celebrates the anniversary of the founding of Communist China, led by Chairman Mao Zedong. In the 1960s, about one third of the world's population lived under Communist rule.

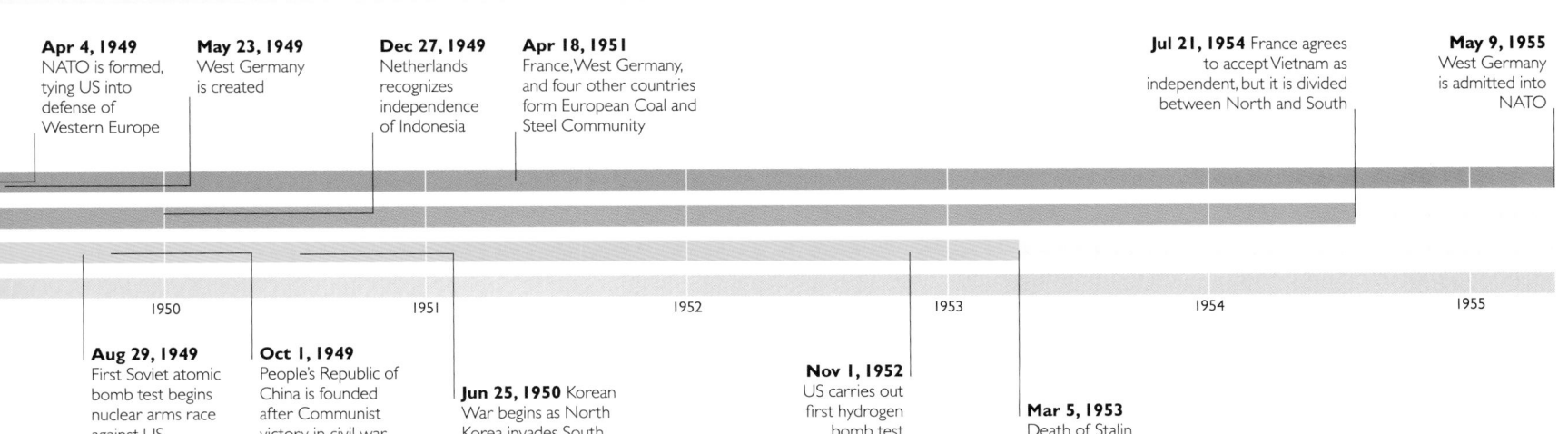

Apr 4, 1949 NATO is formed, tying US into defense of Western Europe

May 23, 1949 West Germany is created

Dec 27, 1949 Netherlands recognizes independence of Indonesia

Apr 18, 1951 France, West Germany, and four other countries form European Coal and Steel Community

Jul 21, 1954 France agrees to accept Vietnam as independent, but it is divided between North and South

May 9, 1955 West Germany is admitted into NATO

1950 1951 1952 1953 1954 1955

Aug 29, 1949 First Soviet atomic bomb test begins nuclear arms race against US

Oct 1, 1949 People's Republic of China is founded after Communist victory in civil war

Jun 25, 1950 Korean War begins as North Korea invades South

Nov 1, 1952 US carries out first hydrogen bomb test

Mar 5, 1953 Death of Stalin

4 THE BERLIN BLOCKADE AND AIRLIFT
JUNE 24, 1948–MAY 12, 1949

In 1948, the Western powers sparked the first major crisis in the Cold War when they introduced a new currency and ended rationing in their zones in Berlin as a prelude to creating a self-governing West Germany. The Soviets blockaded the city, hoping to starve the West out. Instead, over the next ten months, the Western Allies flew in large amounts of supplies to their sector. On May 12, 1949, the Soviets lifted the blockade.

Berlin blockade

5 NATO AND THE WARSAW PACT
APRIL 4, 1949–MAY 14, 1955

The Berlin crisis and the understanding that the USSR was most likely developing an atomic bomb prompted the Western European and American powers to sign a mutual defense pact—the North Atlantic Treaty—in April 1949. They also placed their defense forces under a joint NATO Command Organization. When West Germany joined NATO in May 1955, the USSR and its satellites signed their own defense treaty, the Warsaw Pact.

Founder-members of NATO, 1949 (with Canada and the US)

Signatories of the Warsaw Pact, 1955

1948–52 Britain receives the largest portion of aid from the Marshall Plan, around 26 percent of the total.

May 14, 1955 The Warsaw Pact pledges the USSR and its fellow Communist states to mutual cooperation and defense.

1945 Territory gained in East Prussia and the Baltic makes the USSR and Poland a formidable bloc.

1945 Poland gains control of German lands east of the Oder–Neisse Line.

Feb 1948 Czechoslovakia falls to Communism; the "iron curtain" is complete.

1945 Vienna is split into four occupation zones, plus one joint zone.

1948 Yugoslavia's Marshal Tito resents Soviet interference and breaks relations with Stalin.

1946–49 Civil War; British- and American-backed government forces fight and defeat the Greek Communist Party's army.

▷ **The Berlin airlift**
A plane delivers supplies to blockaded West Berlin in 1949. At the peak of the airlift, aircraft landed at Berlin's Tempelhof airport at a rate of one per minute.

ICELAND

ATLANTIC OCEAN

NORWAY

SWEDEN

FINLAND

Helsinki

Porkkala

Baltic Sea

ESTONIA

LATVIA

LITHUANIA

Kaliningrad

Minsk

EAST PRUSSIA

DENMARK

North Sea

UNITED KINGDOM

London

NETHERLANDS

Bremen

Berlin

Potsdam

EAST GERMANY

Leipzig

Warsaw

1947

POLAND

BELGIUM

Bonn

WEST GERMANY

Prague

1948

CZECHOSLOVAKIA

Paris

SAAR

Munich

Vienna

Budapest

1947

HUNGARY

ROMANIA

1947

SWITZERLAND

AUSTRIA

FRANCE

Trieste

Belgrade

Bucharest

YUGOSLAVIA

1945

SPAIN

PORTUGAL

ITALY

Corsica (France)

Rome

Sardinia (Italy)

BULGARIA

1946

Sofia

ALBANIA

1946

GREECE

Athens

Dodecanese Is. (Greece)

Mediterranean Sea

TUNISIA

Malta (Britain)

Crete (Greece)

THE IRON CURTAIN

After the end of World War II, Europe was divided by an ideological "iron curtain" that separated the Communist states of the East from the democracies of the West. The division deepened to create two economic and military blocs that existed at a tense stand-off for the next 40 years.

The goodwill between the USSR and its Western allies drained away toward the end of the war, and historic tensions between the powers began to resurface by the time the Allied leaders met to discuss the reorganization of Europe at Yalta in February 1945 (see pp.230–231).

As much of Eastern Europe fell into Communist hands over the next few years, the US gradually came to heed Churchill's warning—originally dismissed as warmongering—that an "iron curtain" was descending on Europe and that the West needed protection from the spread of Communism. Rivalry and antagonism between the former allies grew rapidly into the Cold War, a term originally coined by the English writer George Orwell. This war was expressed not through direct military conflict, but rather through general non-cooperation, propaganda, and economic measures, which created two opposed economic blocs—Western Europe and North America on one side, and the USSR and her satellite Communist states on the other.

The Cold War nearly tipped into armed conflict during the Berlin blockade in 1948. After this, both sides created mutual defense treaties—the North Atlantic Treaty and the Warsaw Pact—that successfully prevented war, despite later moments of crisis, such as the Cuban Missile Crisis in 1962. Relations between the two blocs would eventually thaw in the 1980s with the liberalization of the USSR under Mikhail Gorbachev.

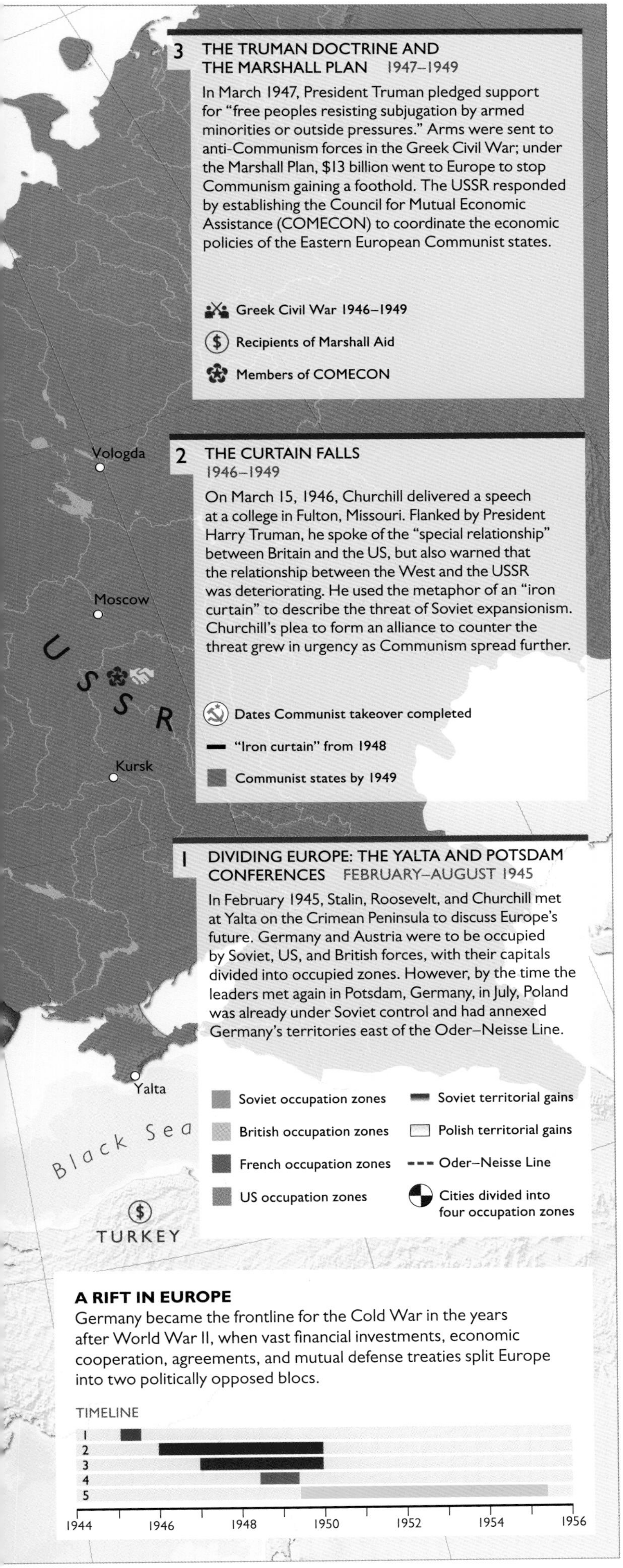
3 THE TRUMAN DOCTRINE AND THE MARSHALL PLAN 1947–1949
In March 1947, President Truman pledged support for "free peoples resisting subjugation by armed minorities or outside pressures." Arms were sent to anti-Communism forces in the Greek Civil War; under the Marshall Plan, $13 billion went to Europe to stop Communism gaining a foothold. The USSR responded by establishing the Council for Mutual Economic Assistance (COMECON) to coordinate the economic policies of the Eastern European Communist states.
Greek Civil War 1946–1949
Recipients of Marshall Aid
Members of COMECON
2 THE CURTAIN FALLS 1946–1949
On March 15, 1946, Churchill delivered a speech at a college in Fulton, Missouri. Flanked by President Harry Truman, he spoke of the "special relationship" between Britain and the US, but also warned that the relationship between the West and the USSR was deteriorating. He used the metaphor of an "iron curtain" to describe the threat of Soviet expansionism. Churchill's plea to form an alliance to counter the threat grew in urgency as Communism spread further.
Dates Communist takeover completed
"Iron curtain" from 1948
Communist states by 1949
1 DIVIDING EUROPE: THE YALTA AND POTSDAM CONFERENCES FEBRUARY–AUGUST 1945
In February 1945, Stalin, Roosevelt, and Churchill met at Yalta on the Crimean Peninsula to discuss Europe's future. Germany and Austria were to be occupied by Soviet, US, and British forces, with their capitals divided into occupied zones. However, by the time the leaders met again in Potsdam, Germany, in July, Poland was already under Soviet control and had annexed Germany's territories east of the Oder–Neisse Line.
Soviet occupation zones
British occupation zones
French occupation zones
US occupation zones
Soviet territorial gains
Polish territorial gains
Oder–Neisse Line
Cities divided into four occupation zones
Vologda
Moscow
USSR
Kursk
Yalta
Black Sea
TURKEY
A RIFT IN EUROPE
Germany became the frontline for the Cold War in the years after World War II, when vast financial investments, economic cooperation, agreements, and mutual defense treaties split Europe into two politically opposed blocs.
TIMELINE
1
2
3
4
5
1944
1946
1948
1950
1952
1954
1956

GERMANY: MAP OF THE OCCUPATION AREAS
KARTE DER BESATZUNGS-ZONEN
OST-PREUSSEN
HOLLAND
BELGIUM
BELGIEN
FRANCE
FRANKREICH
POLEN
CZECHOSLOVAKIA
TSCHECHOSLOWAKEI
AUSTRIA
OESTERREICH
SWITZERLAND
SCHWEIZ
HUNGARIA
UNGARN
LEGEND · ERKLÄRUNG
BOUNDARIES · GRENZEN:
ZONES · ZONEN:

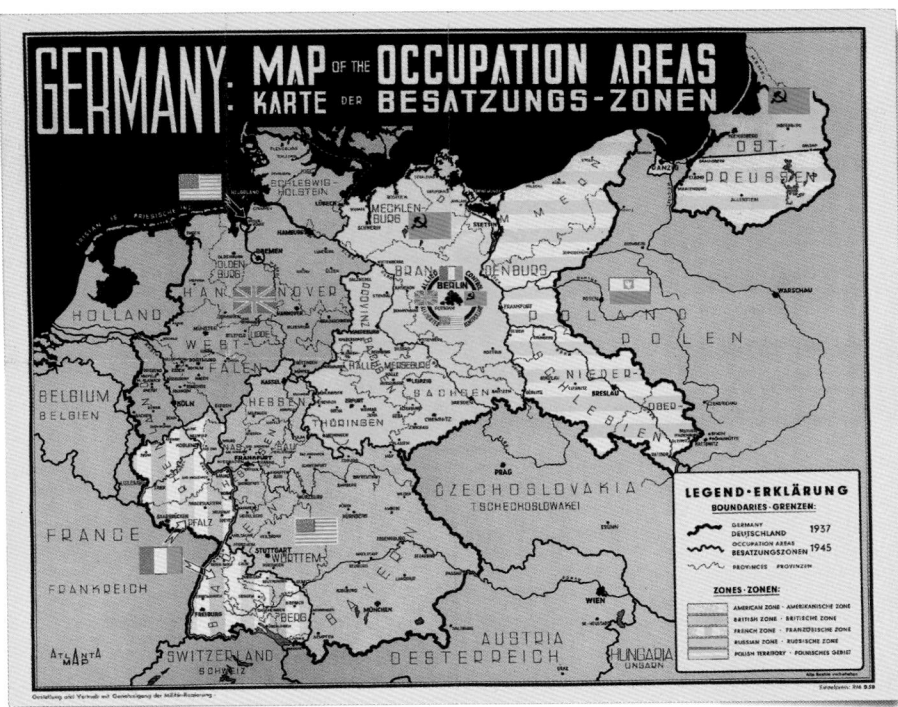

△ **Germany divided**
This map, produced in Frankfurt, Germany, in 1945, shows the division of the country into Occupation Zones. The symbol over Berlin shows the split of the city into four sectors.

THE CHINESE CIVIL WAR

After Japan's defeat in 1945, the uneasy wartime alliance between Chiang Kai-shek's Chinese Nationalist Party and Mao Zedong's Chinese Communist Party fell apart. The long battle for control of a unified China entered its final phase.

On September 9, 1945, a week after Japan's surrender ended World War II, Japanese forces in China (excluding those in Manchuria) surrendered to the Chinese Nationalist Party, or Guomindang (GMD), ending a merciless conflict that had lasted eight years (see pp.220–221). However, lingering political rivalries left China divided and would soon plunge the country into a bitter civil war.

The GMD government returned to power at its pre-war capital, Nanjing, but its perceived weakness and corruption caused its popularity to drop. Meanwhile, promises of land reform made by Mao's Chinese Communist Party (CCP) greatly appealed to the Chinese peasantry. Mao and Chiang Kai-shek met in Chongqing in an attempt to negotiate a peaceful way toward a united China, but despite the intervention of the US, war broke out. The GMD forces were numerically superior but had been weakened by years of war; they faced the Communists, who, during the wartime occupation, had supplemented their conventional army, which was renamed the People's Liberation Army (PLA).

Three campaigns were crucial to the PLA's victory: Liaoning-Shenyang, which drove the GMD from Manchuria; Huaihai, which destroyed the GMD stronghold of Xuzhou; and Pingjin, which led to Mao entering Beijing (then Beiping) on January 21, 1949. The GMD's then-capital Nanjing fell in April, and in December the GMD fled to Taiwan. One of the far-reaching effects of the war was the emergence of Communist China as a great power in the modern world.

MAO ZEDONG

Mao Zedong (1893–1976) was born into a well-off peasant family in Hunan, south-west China. He fought in the 1911 revolution, worked at the university in Beijing as a librarian, and became a founder member of the Chinese Communist Party in 1921. Later he returned to Hunan as a trade union organizer. He believed that the revolutionary movement could win mass support in China by radicalizing the peasantry rather than the urban industrial working class.

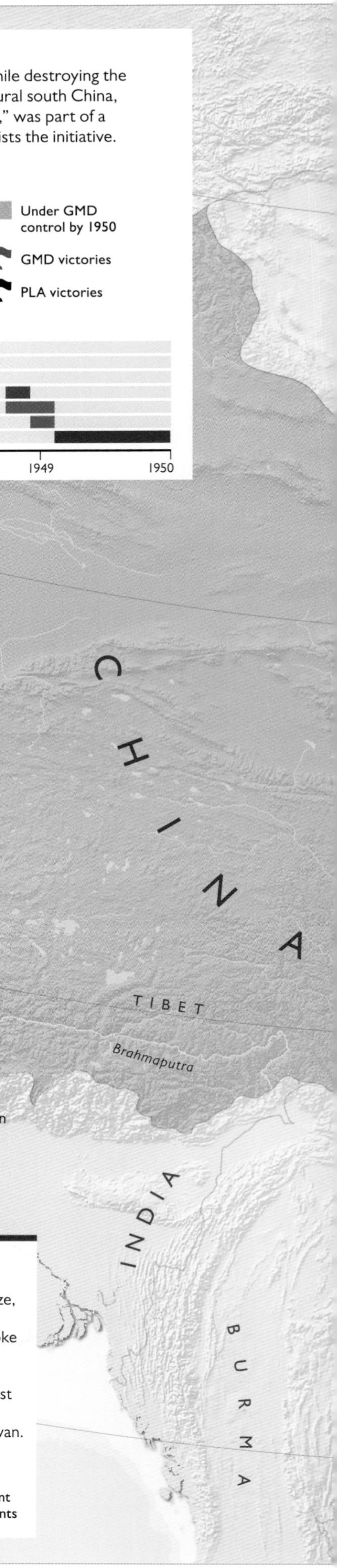

THE GROWTH OF RED CHINA

Mao's philosophy of war was self-preservation while destroying the enemy's will to fight. His use of guerrilla units in rural south China, able to "suddenly concentrate, suddenly disperse," was part of a strategy that, over time, would win the Communists the initiative.

KEY

UNDER COMMUNIST CONTROL

By 1946	By Jun 1948	Under GMD control by 1950
By Jun 1949	By 1950	GMD victories
Major railroads	Communist guerrilla operations 1945–49	PLA victories

TIMELINE

1 2 3 4 5 6 7

1946 1947 1948 1949 1950

△ Communist propaganda
In this CCP-issued poster, PLA soldier Dong Cunrui is shown sacrificing his life and blowing up an enemy bunker during the Chinese Civil War. The CCP often used the deaths of actual soldiers to stir up support for their cause.

董存瑞舍身炸碉堡

CHINA

TIBET

Brahmaputra

INDIA

BURMA

7 FROM NANJING TO SHANGHAI
JANUARY 1949–DECEMBER 1949

The PLA advanced to the north bank of the Yangtze, and on January 20 the GMD government began negotiations with Mao's politburo. When talks broke down, the PLA crossed the Yangtze; by April 23, Nanjing had surrendered. In May the PLA entered Hangzhou, Wuhu, and Shanghai, and advanced west and south. By late 1949, most of China was under Communist rule, and the GMD leaders fled to Taiwan.

→ PLA movements   GMD government aircraft movements

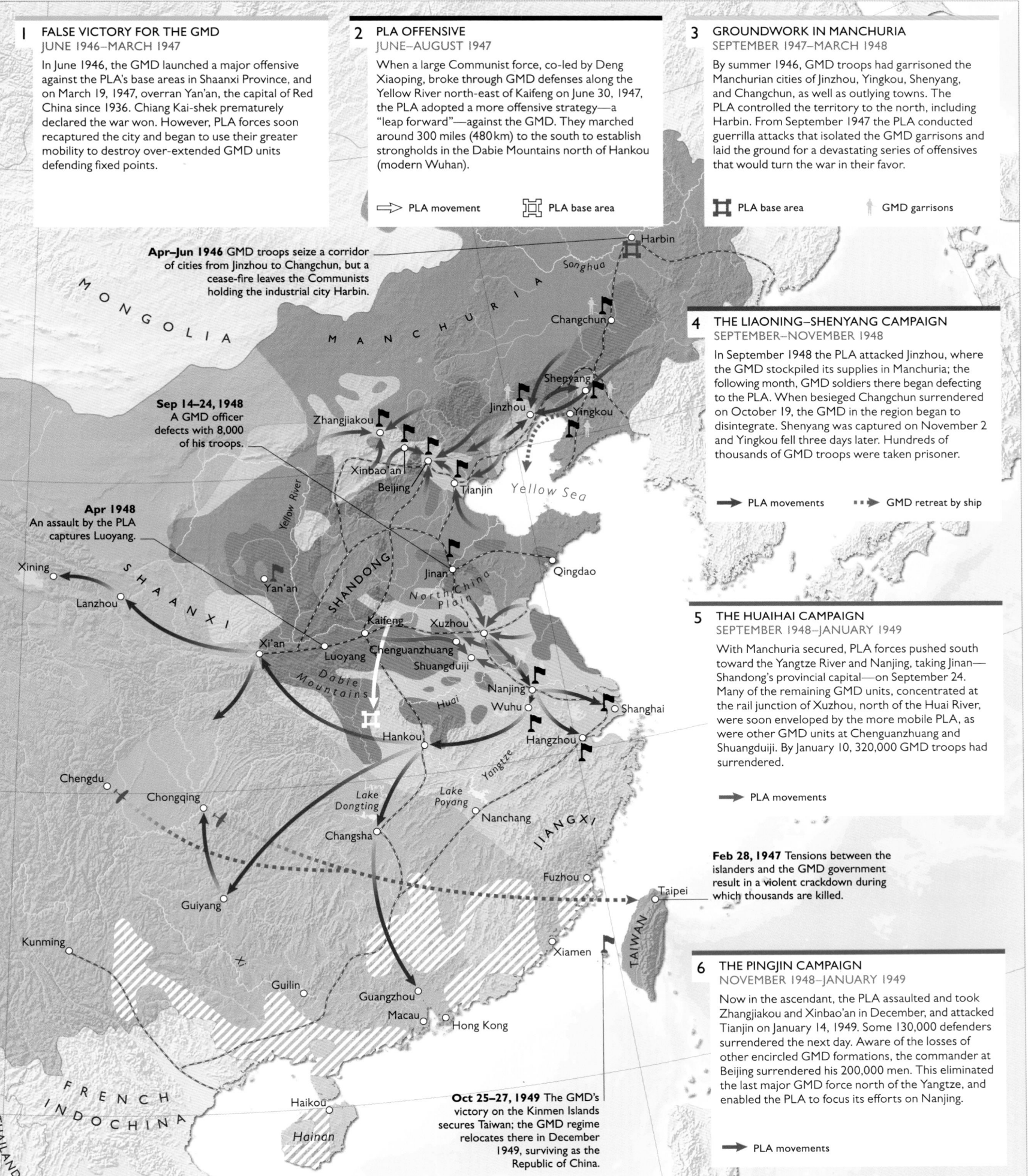

1 FALSE VICTORY FOR THE GMD
JUNE 1946–MARCH 1947

In June 1946, the GMD launched a major offensive against the PLA's base areas in Shaanxi Province, and on March 19, 1947, overran Yan'an, the capital of Red China since 1936. Chiang Kai-shek prematurely declared the war won. However, PLA forces soon recaptured the city and began to use their greater mobility to destroy over-extended GMD units defending fixed points.

2 PLA OFFENSIVE
JUNE–AUGUST 1947

When a large Communist force, co-led by Deng Xiaoping, broke through GMD defenses along the Yellow River north-east of Kaifeng on June 30, 1947, the PLA adopted a more offensive strategy—a "leap forward"—against the GMD. They marched around 300 miles (480km) to the south to establish strongholds in the Dabie Mountains north of Hankou (modern Wuhan).

⟹ PLA movement ⊞ PLA base area

3 GROUNDWORK IN MANCHURIA
SEPTEMBER 1947–MARCH 1948

By summer 1946, GMD troops had garrisoned the Manchurian cities of Jinzhou, Yingkou, Shenyang, and Changchun, as well as outlying towns. The PLA controlled the territory to the north, including Harbin. From September 1947 the PLA conducted guerrilla attacks that isolated the GMD garrisons and laid the ground for a devastating series of offensives that would turn the war in their favor.

⊞ PLA base area 👤 GMD garrisons

4 THE LIAONING–SHENYANG CAMPAIGN
SEPTEMBER–NOVEMBER 1948

In September 1948 the PLA attacked Jinzhou, where the GMD stockpiled its supplies in Manchuria; the following month, GMD soldiers there began defecting to the PLA. When besieged Changchun surrendered on October 19, the GMD in the region began to disintegrate. Shenyang was captured on November 2 and Yingkou fell three days later. Hundreds of thousands of GMD troops were taken prisoner.

➡ PLA movements ⇢ GMD retreat by ship

5 THE HUAIHAI CAMPAIGN
SEPTEMBER 1948–JANUARY 1949

With Manchuria secured, PLA forces pushed south toward the Yangtze River and Nanjing, taking Jinan—Shandong's provincial capital—on September 24. Many of the remaining GMD units, concentrated at the rail junction of Xuzhou, north of the Huai River, were soon enveloped by the more mobile PLA, as were other GMD units at Chenguanzhuang and Shuangduiji. By January 10, 320,000 GMD troops had surrendered.

➡ PLA movements

6 THE PINGJIN CAMPAIGN
NOVEMBER 1948–JANUARY 1949

Now in the ascendant, the PLA assaulted and took Zhangjiakou and Xinbao'an in December, and attacked Tianjin on January 14, 1949. Some 130,000 defenders surrendered the next day. Aware of the losses of other encircled GMD formations, the commander at Beijing surrendered his 200,000 men. This eliminated the last major GMD force north of the Yangtze, and enabled the PLA to focus its efforts on Nanjing.

➡ PLA movements

Apr–Jun 1946 GMD troops seize a corridor of cities from Jinzhou to Changchun, but a cease-fire leaves the Communists holding the industrial city Harbin.

Sep 14–24, 1948 A GMD officer defects with 8,000 of his troops.

Apr 1948 An assault by the PLA captures Luoyang.

Feb 28, 1947 Tensions between the islanders and the GMD government result in a violent crackdown during which thousands are killed.

Oct 25–27, 1949 The GMD's victory on the Kinmen Islands secures Taiwan; the GMD regime relocates there in December 1949, surviving as the Republic of China.

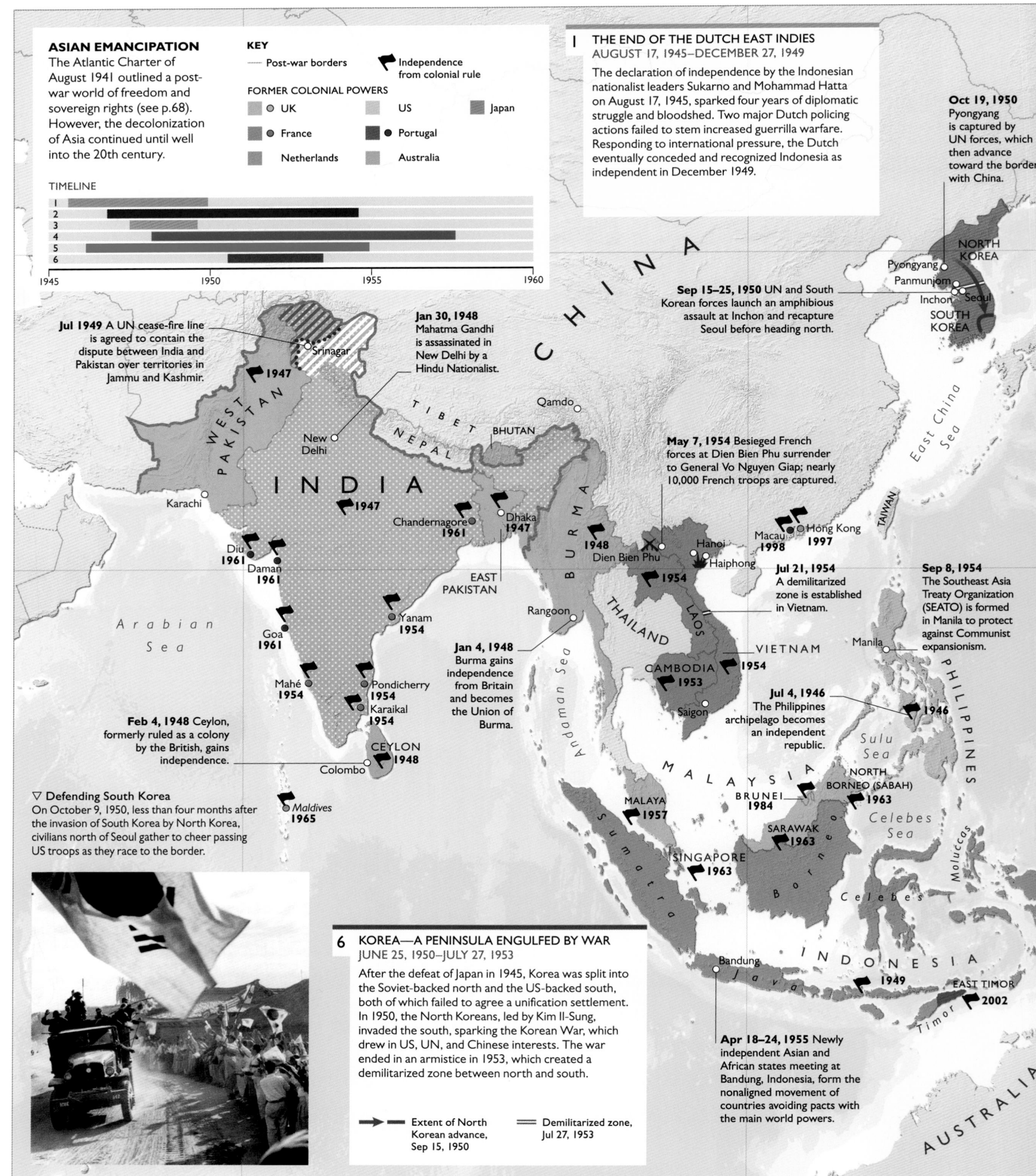

ASIAN EMANCIPATION
The Atlantic Charter of August 1941 outlined a post-war world of freedom and sovereign rights (see p.68). However, the decolonization of Asia continued until well into the 20th century.

KEY

— Post-war borders

▶ Independence from colonial rule

FORMER COLONIAL POWERS

UK
France
Netherlands
US
Portugal
Australia
Japan

TIMELINE

1
2
3
4
5
6

1945   1950   1955   1960

I THE END OF THE DUTCH EAST INDIES
AUGUST 17, 1945–DECEMBER 27, 1949

The declaration of independence by the Indonesian nationalist leaders Sukarno and Mohammad Hatta on August 17, 1945, sparked four years of diplomatic struggle and bloodshed. Two major Dutch policing actions failed to stem increased guerrilla warfare. Responding to international pressure, the Dutch eventually conceded and recognized Indonesia as independent in December 1949.

Oct 19, 1950 Pyongyang is captured by UN forces, which then advance toward the border with China.

Sep 15–25, 1950 UN and South Korean forces launch an amphibious assault at Inchon and recapture Seoul before heading north.

Jul 1949 A UN cease-fire line is agreed to contain the dispute between India and Pakistan over territories in Jammu and Kashmir.

Jan 30, 1948 Mahatma Gandhi is assassinated in New Delhi by a Hindu Nationalist.

May 7, 1954 Besieged French forces at Dien Bien Phu surrender to General Vo Nguyen Giap; nearly 10,000 French troops are captured.

Jul 21, 1954 A demilitarized zone is established in Vietnam.

Sep 8, 1954 The Southeast Asia Treaty Organization (SEATO) is formed in Manila to protect against Communist expansionism.

Jan 4, 1948 Burma gains independence from Britain and becomes the Union of Burma.

Jul 4, 1946 The Philippines archipelago becomes an independent republic.

Feb 4, 1948 Ceylon, formerly ruled as a colony by the British, gains independence.

▽ **Defending South Korea**
On October 9, 1950, less than four months after the invasion of South Korea by North Korea, civilians north of Seoul gather to cheer passing US troops as they race to the border.

Srinagar ▶ 1947

New Delhi

WEST PAKISTAN

Karachi

INDIA

Diu 1961
Daman 1961
Goa 1961

Chandernagore 1961

Dhaka 1947

EAST PAKISTAN

Yanam 1954

Mahé 1954
Pondicherry 1954
Karaikal 1954

CEYLON 1948
Colombo

Maldives 1965

TIBET
NEPAL
BHUTAN
Qamdo

BURMA
1948

Rangoon

THAILAND

Hanoi
Dien Bien Phu 1954
Haiphong

LAOS

CAMBODIA 1953

VIETNAM 1954

Saigon

Macau 1998
Hong Kong 1997

TAIWAN

East China Sea

NORTH KOREA
Pyongyang
Panmunjom
Inchon Seoul
SOUTH KOREA

CHINA

Andaman Sea

MALAYSIA

Manila

PHILIPPINES

1946

Sulu Sea

Celebes Sea

MALAYA 1957

BRUNEI 1984

NORTH BORNEO (SABAH) 1963

SARAWAK 1963

SINGAPORE 1963

Sumatra
Java
Borneo
Celebes
Moluccas

INDONESIA

1949

Bandung

Timor
EAST TIMOR 2002

AUSTRALIA

6 KOREA—A PENINSULA ENGULFED BY WAR
JUNE 25, 1950–JULY 27, 1953

After the defeat of Japan in 1945, Korea was split into the Soviet-backed north and the US-backed south, both of which failed to agree a unification settlement. In 1950, the North Koreans, led by Kim Il-Sung, invaded the south, sparking the Korean War, which drew in US, UN, and Chinese interests. The war ended in an armistice in 1953, which created a demilitarized zone between north and south.

Apr 18–24, 1955 Newly independent Asian and African states meeting at Bandung, Indonesia, form the nonaligned movement of countries avoiding pacts with the main world powers.

➤ Extent of North Korean advance, Sep 15, 1950

═ Demilitarized zone, Jul 27, 1953

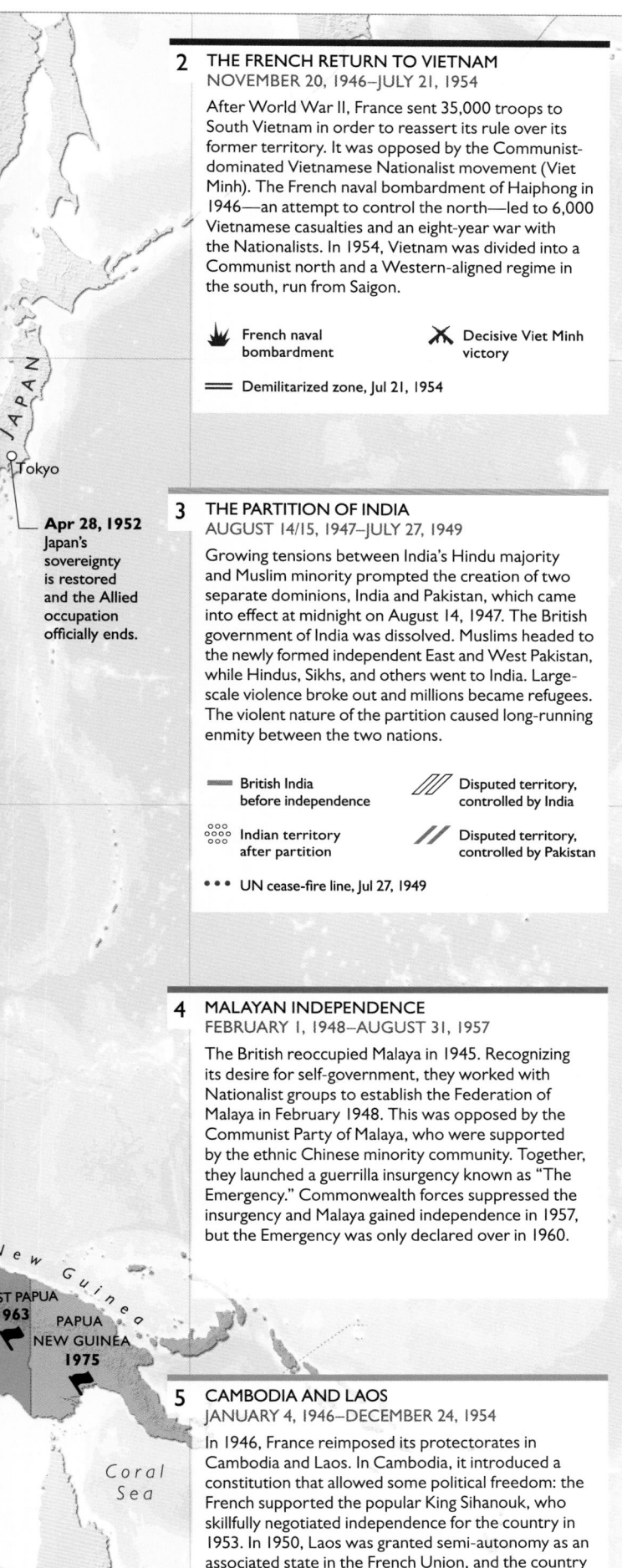

2 THE FRENCH RETURN TO VIETNAM
NOVEMBER 20, 1946–JULY 21, 1954

After World War II, France sent 35,000 troops to South Vietnam in order to reassert its rule over its former territory. It was opposed by the Communist-dominated Vietnamese Nationalist movement (Viet Minh). The French naval bombardment of Haiphong in 1946—an attempt to control the north—led to 6,000 Vietnamese casualties and an eight-year war with the Nationalists. In 1954, Vietnam was divided into a Communist north and a Western-aligned regime in the south, run from Saigon.

- 🔥 French naval bombardment
- ✕ Decisive Viet Minh victory
- ═══ Demilitarized zone, Jul 21, 1954

Apr 28, 1952
Japan's sovereignty is restored and the Allied occupation officially ends.

3 THE PARTITION OF INDIA
AUGUST 14/15, 1947–JULY 27, 1949

Growing tensions between India's Hindu majority and Muslim minority prompted the creation of two separate dominions, India and Pakistan, which came into effect at midnight on August 14, 1947. The British government of India was dissolved. Muslims headed to the newly formed independent East and West Pakistan, while Hindus, Sikhs, and others went to India. Large-scale violence broke out and millions became refugees. The violent nature of the partition caused long-running enmity between the two nations.

- ━━ British India before independence
- ⁄⁄⁄ Disputed territory, controlled by India
- ∘∘∘ Indian territory after partition
- ⁄⁄ Disputed territory, controlled by Pakistan
- ••• UN cease-fire line, Jul 27, 1949

4 MALAYAN INDEPENDENCE
FEBRUARY 1, 1948–AUGUST 31, 1957

The British reoccupied Malaya in 1945. Recognizing its desire for self-government, they worked with Nationalist groups to establish the Federation of Malaya in February 1948. This was opposed by the Communist Party of Malaya, who were supported by the ethnic Chinese minority community. Together, they launched a guerrilla insurgency known as "The Emergency." Commonwealth forces suppressed the insurgency and Malaya gained independence in 1957, but the Emergency was only declared over in 1960.

5 CAMBODIA AND LAOS
JANUARY 4, 1946–DECEMBER 24, 1954

In 1946, France reimposed its protectorates in Cambodia and Laos. In Cambodia, it introduced a constitution that allowed some political freedom: the French supported the popular King Sihanouk, who skillfully negotiated independence for the country in 1953. In 1950, Laos was granted semi-autonomy as an associated state in the French Union, and the country gained full independence four years later.

DECOLONIZATION OF ASIA

After the liberation of Japan's Asian colonies, many more Asian nations fought for independence. Anti-imperialist movements began to gain widespread popular legitimacy, and as a result many of the occupying powers were forced to reassess their old colonial outposts.

Japan's advance through Southeast Asia during World War II exposed the fragile hold that the Western powers had on their colonies. Even though the Allied powers emerged as victors in 1945, most were unwilling or unable to restore their colonial regimes.

A greatly weakened Britain was disinclined to defend its empire. Indian pressure for self-governance had grown since the foundation of the Indian National Congress in 1885, and for many it seemed inevitable that Britain would leave the subcontinent. Britain aimed to avert conflict by granting self-government, whereas the Netherlands and France tried to revive their empires in the East Indies and Indochina. This approach plunged both countries into wars that would prove to be unwinnable, and served as a warning to any outside power tempted to try to impose its will on the region.

The pattern of decolonization in Asia was affected not only by the countries involved, but also by shifting ideologies. Competing capitalist and Communist visions of society in a post-war world fueled the Cold War, which lasted for most of the 20th century (see pp.264–265). Fears surrounding Communist expansionism ignited war in the Korean peninsula in 1950, and would become a defining feature of Asia in this era.

> *"At the stroke of the midnight hour, while the world sleeps, India will awake to life and freedom."*
>
> JAWAHARLAL NEHRU, 1947

INDIAN INDEPENDENCE

The Indian National Congress (INC), the most influential group in the campaign for independence in India, was led by Mahatma Gandhi and Jawaharlal Nehru, both of whom had studied law in London. Under the leadership of Gandhi from 1921 to the mid-1930s the INC changed from an elite project to a mass movement of nonviolent civil disobedience. Nehru, who succeeded Gandhi as head of the party in 1929, rejected Dominion status, instead demanding full independence. He became India's first prime minister in 1947.

Nehru (left) and Gandhi meet in Bombay, India

New arrivals
Refugees from Eastern Europe, Turkey, and Tunisia prepare to go ashore at Haifa in early summer of 1949. In 1950 the Israeli Law of Return was passed, giving any Jew the legal right to settle in Israel.

THE CREATION OF ISRAEL

In 1917, Britain had pledged its support for "a national home for the Jewish people" in Palestine, in a statement now known as the Balfour Declaration. However, it was not until after World War II that Israel became a state.

After World War I, Britain controlled Palestine under the terms of the League of Nations mandate and aimed to create a home there for Jews. Since Arabs formed 90 percent of the population, many were opposed to the idea. Tensions escalated in the 1930s and 1940s when many Jews fleeing from the Nazis traveled to Palestine to seek a safe refuge.

△ **Commemorative stamp**
A 1949 stamp depicts the foundation of modern Tel Aviv. The city was established in 1909 by 60 Jewish families, 15 miles (24 km) northwest of Jerusalem.

Caught in the dispute between the Arabs and the Jews, Britain imposed strict quotas on Jewish immigration. Thousands of Jewish immigrants were imprisoned in British camps, and violence escalated. In 1947, the British government handed over control to the United Nations, which planned to partition Palestine and create one state for Arabs and another for Jews. However, the Arabs rejected the idea.

The first Arab–Israeli war

On May 14, 1948, the British mandate terminated and a Zionist organization proclaimed the establishment of the independent State of Israel. A military coalition of Arab states fought to gain control, but by the time a cease-fire was agreed in 1949, the Israelis had taken control of all the territories the UN had allocated to them, and made further gains at the expense of their Arab neighbors. Hundreds of thousands of Palestinian Arabs fled their homelands to become stateless refugees, while Israel held its first elections later that year.

VOYAGE OF THE EXODUS

Hundreds of would-be Jewish immigrants crowded the decks of the refugee ship SS *Exodus* in the port of Haifa, then part of Palestine, in July 1947. The British intercepted the ship as it tried to make an illicit landfall. The passengers were forcibly disembarked and then shipped back across the Mediterranean to France.

THE PRICE OF WAR

World War II affected most of the globe, and cost more than 50 million lives. The Eastern Front accounted for many of the military deaths, while the Holocaust, bombings, and land war left millions of civilians dead. In Europe, many survivors faced a desperate scramble to find homes in new places.

The human cost of World War II exceeded anything that came before it. Military casualty rates in north-west Europe in 1944–1945 matched—and sometimes exceeded—those of World War I, while the bitter war of attrition at the Eastern Front claimed further millions of lives. An unprecedented proportion of those who died in the war were civilians. Six million Jews, 130,000–200,000 Roma, and 250,000 disabled people died in the Nazi Holocaust, while the brutality of the Soviet, Nazi, and Japanese regimes added to the vast toll, as did the Allied bombing of cities in Germany and, most

destructively, in Japan. By the end of the war, Poland had lost 16 percent of its 1939 population, and the Soviet Union around 15 percent.

The human suffering did not end as the war came to a close. Millions of Germans who were living in Eastern Europe were forced to flee the advancing Red Army in 1944 and hundreds of thousands of them died from violence, malnutrition, or disease. And as Europe's boundaries were redrawn, the war's survivors faced the task of rebuilding their countries, their cities, and their lives in the midst of terrible devastation.

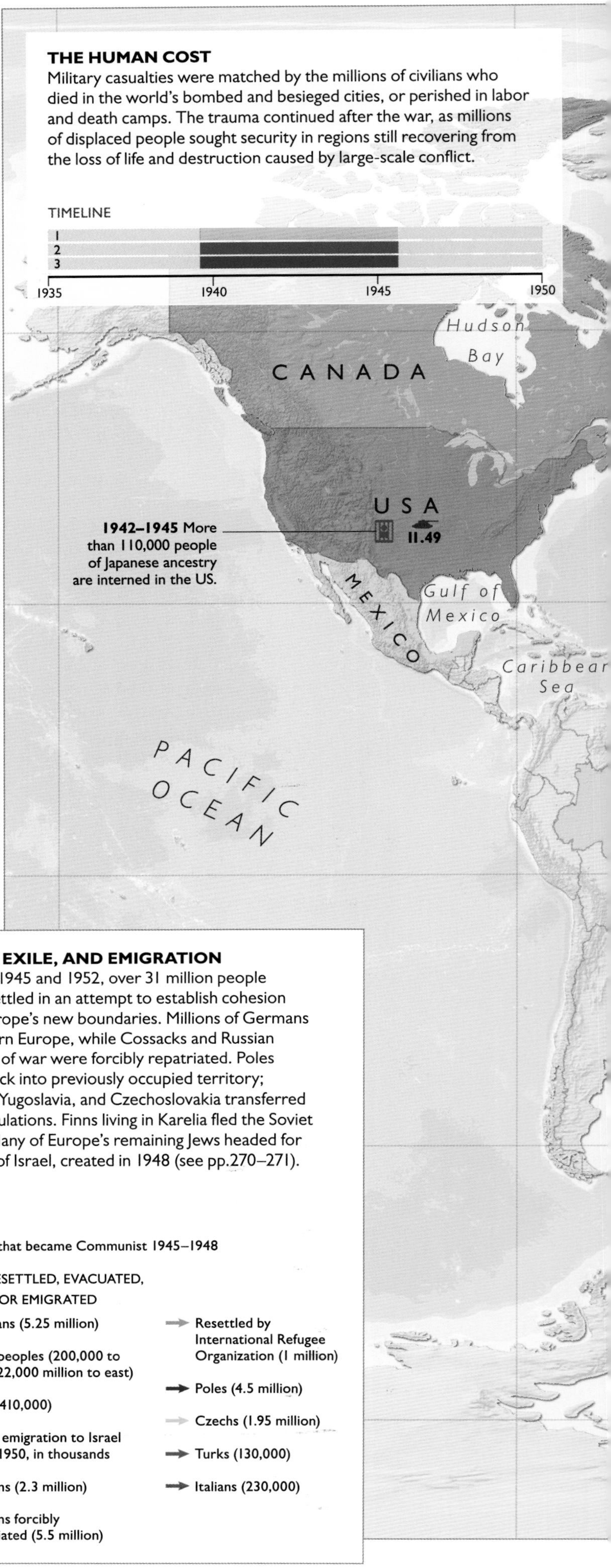

THE HUMAN COST

Military casualties were matched by the millions of civilians who died in the world's bombed and besieged cities, or perished in labor and death camps. The trauma continued after the war, as millions of displaced people sought security in regions still recovering from the loss of life and destruction caused by large-scale conflict.

TIMELINE

	1935	1940	1945	1950
1				
2				
3				

1942–1945 More than 110,000 people of Japanese ancestry are interned in the US.

11.49

CANADA

Hudson Bay

USA

MEXICO

Gulf of Mexico

Caribbean Sea

PACIFIC OCEAN

FLIGHT, EXILE, AND EMIGRATION

Between 1945 and 1952, over 31 million people were resettled in an attempt to establish cohesion within Europe's new boundaries. Millions of Germans fled Eastern Europe, while Cossacks and Russian prisoners of war were forcibly repatriated. Poles moved back into previously occupied territory; Hungary, Yugoslavia, and Czechoslovakia transferred small populations. Finns living in Karelia fled the Soviet regime. Many of Europe's remaining Jews headed for the state of Israel, created in 1948 (see pp.270–271).

KEY

▨ States that became Communist 1945–1948

PEOPLES RESETTLED, EVACUATED, EXPELLED, OR EMIGRATED

→ Germans (5.25 million)

→ Baltic peoples (200,000 to west, 22,000 million to east)

→ Finns (410,000)

✡ Jewish emigration to Israel 1945–1950, in thousands

→ Russians (2.3 million)

┄► Russians forcibly repatriated (5.5 million)

→ Resettled by International Refugee Organization (1 million)

→ Poles (4.5 million)

→ Czechs (1.95 million)

→ Turks (130,000)

→ Italians (230,000)

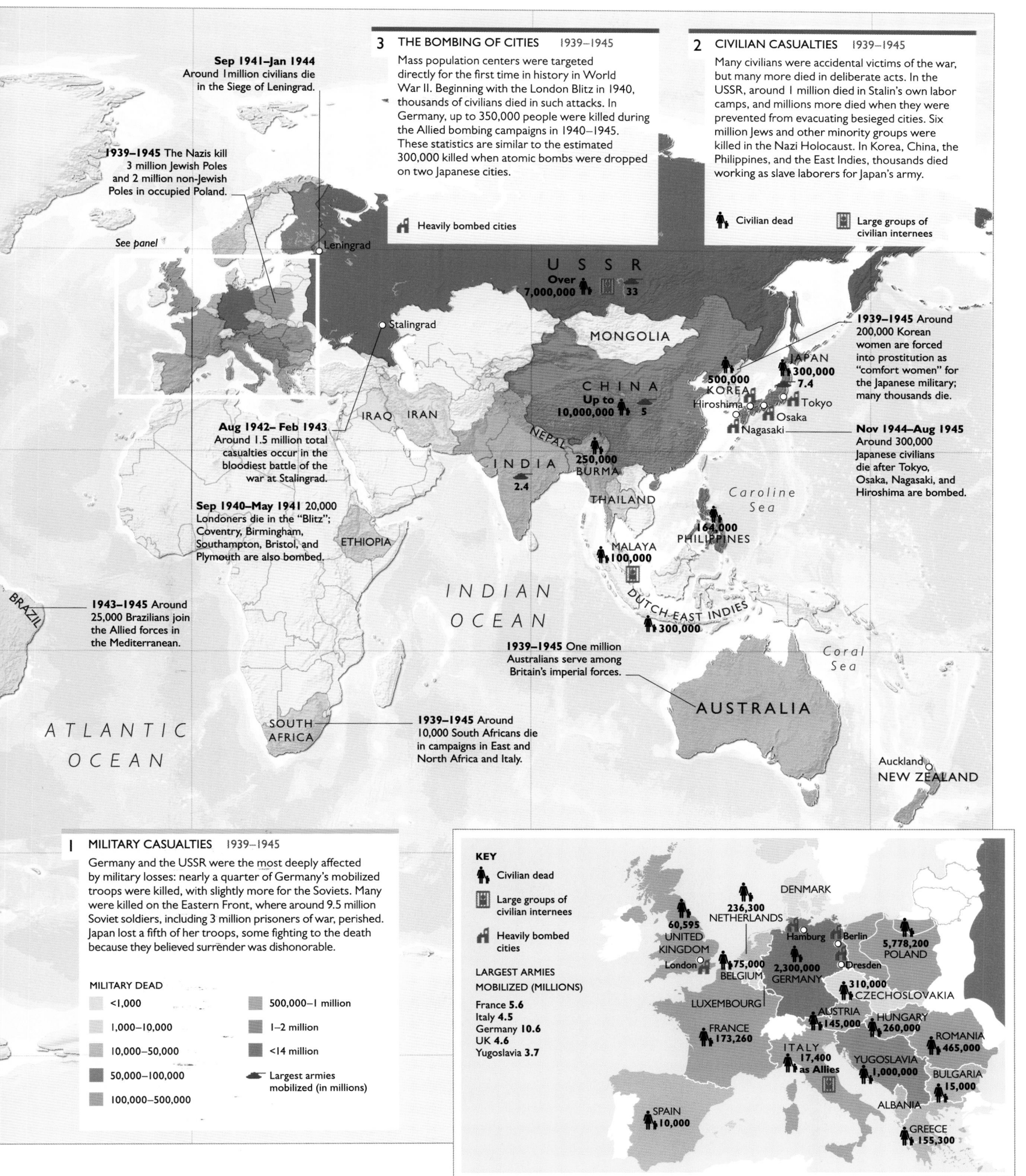

Sep 1941–Jan 1944 Around 1million civilians die in the Siege of Leningrad.

1939–1945 The Nazis kill 3 million Jewish Poles and 2 million non-Jewish Poles in occupied Poland.

See panel

3 THE BOMBING OF CITIES 1939–1945

Mass population centers were targeted directly for the first time in history in World War II. Beginning with the London Blitz in 1940, thousands of civilians died in such attacks. In Germany, up to 350,000 people were killed during the Allied bombing campaigns in 1940–1945. These statistics are similar to the estimated 300,000 killed when atomic bombs were dropped on two Japanese cities.

🏠 Heavily bombed cities

2 CIVILIAN CASUALTIES 1939–1945

Many civilians were accidental victims of the war, but many more died in deliberate acts. In the USSR, around 1 million died in Stalin's own labor camps, and millions more died when they were prevented from evacuating besieged cities. Six million Jews and other minority groups were killed in the Nazi Holocaust. In Korea, China, the Philippines, and the East Indies, thousands died working as slave laborers for Japan's army.

👥 Civilian dead   🏢 Large groups of civilian internees

Aug 1942– Feb 1943 Around 1.5 million total casualties occur in the bloodiest battle of the war at Stalingrad.

Sep 1940–May 1941 20,000 Londoners die in the "Blitz"; Coventry, Birmingham, Southampton, Bristol, and Plymouth are also bombed.

1943–1945 Around 25,000 Brazilians join the Allied forces in the Mediterranean.

USSR Over 7,000,000 — 33

1939–1945 Around 200,000 Korean women are forced into prostitution as "comfort women" for the Japanese military; many thousands die.

JAPAN 300,000 — 7.4

KOREA 500,000

CHINA Up to 10,000,000 — 5

250,000 BURMA

INDIA 2.4

164,000 PHILIPPINES

MALAYA 100,000

300,000 DUTCH EAST INDIES

Nov 1944–Aug 1945 Around 300,000 Japanese civilians die after Tokyo, Osaka, Nagasaki, and Hiroshima are bombed.

1939–1945 One million Australians serve among Britain's imperial forces.

1939–1945 Around 10,000 South Africans die in campaigns in East and North Africa and Italy.

1 MILITARY CASUALTIES 1939–1945

Germany and the USSR were the most deeply affected by military losses: nearly a quarter of Germany's mobilized troops were killed, with slightly more for the Soviets. Many were killed on the Eastern Front, where around 9.5 million Soviet soldiers, including 3 million prisoners of war, perished. Japan lost a fifth of her troops, some fighting to the death because they believed surrender was dishonorable.

MILITARY DEAD

<1,000	500,000–1 million
1,000–10,000	1–2 million
10,000–50,000	<14 million
50,000–100,000	Largest armies mobilized (in millions)
100,000–500,000	

KEY

👥 Civilian dead

🏢 Large groups of civilian internees

🏠 Heavily bombed cities

LARGEST ARMIES MOBILIZED (MILLIONS)

France 5.6
Italy 4.5
Germany 10.6
UK 4.6
Yugoslavia 3.7

DENMARK

236,300 NETHERLANDS

60,595 UNITED KINGDOM

London

Hamburg   Berlin

Dresden

5,778,200 POLAND

75,000 BELGIUM

2,300,000 GERMANY

310,000 CZECHOSLOVAKIA

LUXEMBOURG

AUSTRIA 145,000

HUNGARY 260,000

FRANCE 173,260

ITALY 17,400 as Allies

YUGOSLAVIA 1,000,000

ROMANIA 465,000

BULGARIA 15,000

ALBANIA

SPAIN 10,000

GREECE 155,300

REMEMBRANCE

The memory of World War II is kept alive by most of the participating countries, not only in ceremonies and monuments but also in each nation's particular view of the war and of the sacrifices made by both combatants and civilians.

△ **Makeshift memorial**
A hastily erected marker on a Normandy beach marks the grave of a US soldier killed during the D-Day landings in 1944.

Most Allied nations have an annual day of remembrance, including Veterans Day in the US, Anzac day in Australia and New Zealand, Victory Day in France and the Czech Republic, and Liberation Day in the Netherlands and Norway.

Russia commemorates victory on May 9 with parades and ceremonies. The war, specifically the period 1941–1945, is known as the Great Patriotic War, and its remembrance acknowledges the nation's huge sacrifice in lives. Among the events is the March of the Immortal Regiment, in which millions of citizens assemble carrying portraits and photographs of World War II veterans, victims, and survivors. Many countries also commemorate individual events. In the US, Pearl Harbor Remembrance Day takes place annually on the anniversary of the attack (see pp.110–111), while in Britain, Battle of Britain Day commemorates Fighter Command's victory over the Luftwaffe in 1940 (see pp.58–59).

Axis nations remember

In Japan, the war remains a controversial subject; nevertheless, the site of the Hiroshima bombing (see pp.258–259) is now the Hiroshima Peace Memorial Park. In Germany, remembrance of the war is characterized by somber reflection. Some former concentration camps are preserved as museums, and the Berlin monument to the Holocaust (right) serves as a stark reminder. In recent years, more open discussion of the war has been encouraged.

MUSIC FOR LENINGRAD

A native of Leningrad, the composer Dmitri Shostakovich wrote the first two movements of his monumental Symphony No. 7 in 1941, while the city was under siege by the Germans. Eventually safely evacuated, he christened the work the Leningrad Symphony to honor the city's heroic resistance. It premiered in 1942.

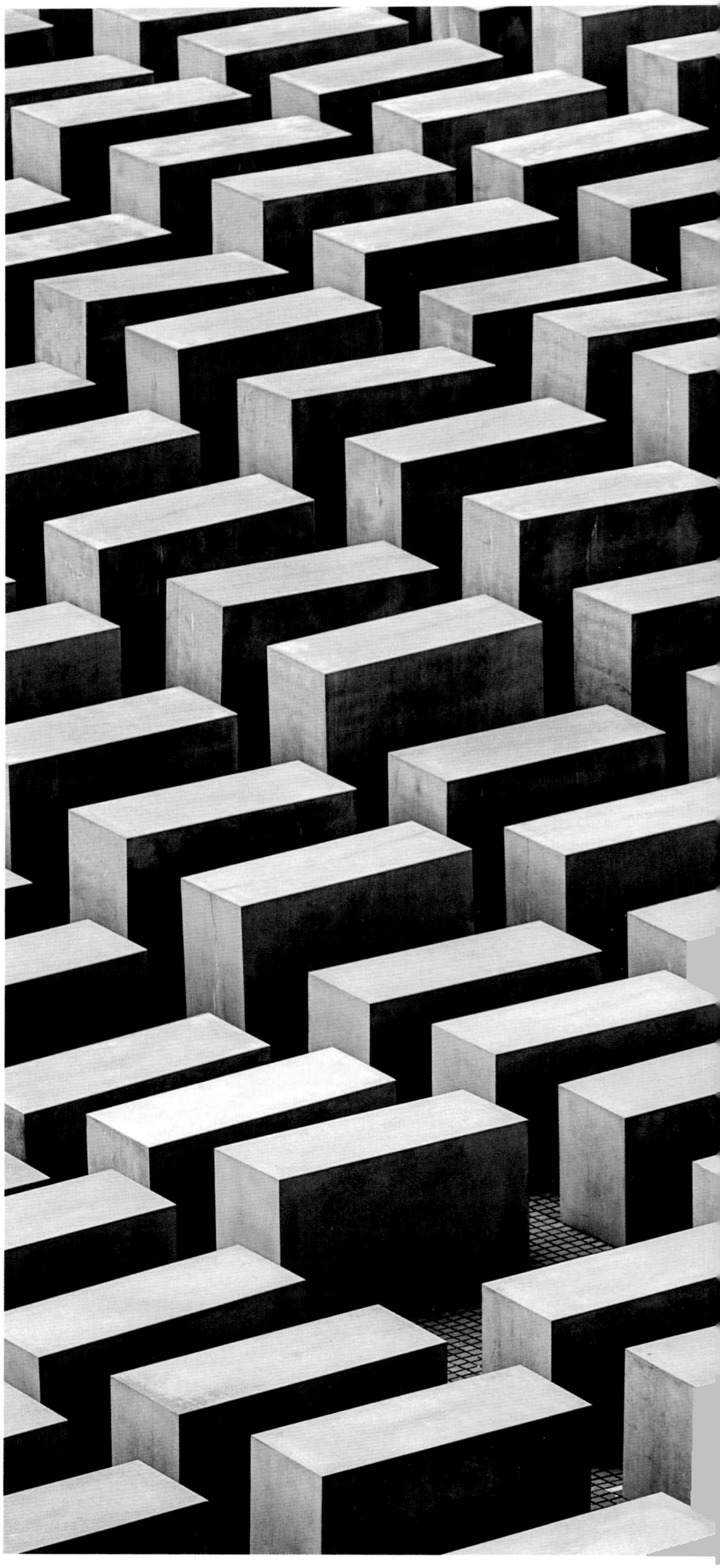

Holocaust memorial in Berlin
Designed by US architect Peter Eisenman and consisting of 2,711 concrete blocks, Berlin's "Memorial to the Murdered Jews of Europe" is often interpreted as representing an ordered system that has lost touch with reason.

GLOSSARY

Afrika Korps German expeditionary force, commanded by Erwin Rommel and sent to North Africa in spring 1941 to support the Italians following a string of defeats by the British. Later it was substantially reinforced to become Panzerarmee Afrika (Panzer Army Africa).

aircraft carrier Large naval vessel capable of launching and recovering aircraft, such as torpedo bombers, dive-bombers, and protective fighters.

Anschluss The absorption of Austria into Germany on March 13, 1938, the day after Hitler's troops marched into the country on the pretext of restoring order.

area bombing Blanket aerial bombardment of large urban areas.

armistice The temporary suspension of hostilities between warring countries so that negotiations for a formal peace agreement can take place.

army group The largest military land formation used in World War II, consisting of two or more armies serving under a single commander.

Atlantic Wall The massive coastal defenses the Germans built to repulse an Allied invasion of Western Europe.

Axis, Rome–Berlin The friendship pact agreed between Germany and Italy in November 1936, followed by the Pact of Steel, a formal military alliance in May 1939, and the Tripartite Pact, signed by Germany, Italy, and Japan in September 1940. Other Axis powers included Hungary, Romania, Slovakia, Bulgaria, and Croatia.

battalion Military unit typically consisting of between 300 and 800 soldiers, subdivided into companies and platoons. Battalions are commanded by lieutenant-colonels with a major as second-in-command. Generally, three or more battalions grouped together make up a regiment.

battleship An extremely large, heavily-armored warship, principally armed with large-caliber guns mounted in rotating turrets. Although vitally important to both the Allied and Axis powers, battleships proved highly vulnerable to air attack by carrier-borne aircraft.

beachhead An area close to the sea or a river that, when captured by attacking troops, is the foundation for a subsequent advance deeper into enemy-held territory.

"Big Six" The six members of the Japanese Imperial General Headquarters-Government Liaison Conference (later the Supreme Council for the Direction of the War): the Prime Minister, Minister for Foreign Affairs, Minister of War, Minister of the Navy, the Chief of the Army General Staff, and the Chief of the Naval General Staff.

Bletchley Park Headquarters of Britain's Government Code & Cypher School, tasked with decoding enemy military communications.

Blitz The Luftwaffe's mass bombing campaign against British cities, ports, and towns from September 1940 to May 1941.

Blitzkrieg As employed by the Germans, blitzkrieg ("lightning war") involved mass tank formations, supported by dive-bombers and motorized artillery, making a thrust forward on a narrow front.

Bomber Command The branch of the RAF specializing in bomber operations from 1936 to 1968.

bouncing bomb A spinning cylindrical bomb, invented by British engineer Barnes Wallis to destroy the Ruhr hydroelectric dams.

bridgehead *see* beachhead

brigade Military formation, typically consisting of three to six battalions plus supporting reconnaissance, artillery, engineers, supply, and transport elements.

BEF British Expeditionary Force. British troops sent to France in 1939.

capital ship One of a navy's most important warships. Traditionally a battleship or battle cruiser and, from 1942 onward, an aircraft carrier.

carpet bombing *see* area bombing

corps A military formation, consisting of two or more divisions and typically commanded by a lieutenant-general.

Desert Rats The nickname of the soldiers of the British 7th Armored Division during the fighting in the 1940–1943 North African campaign. It later was applied to the entire 8th Army.

division Military formation consisting of a team of all arms and services required to sustain independent operations. An army can have anything from four to ten divisions.

Eastern Front In World War II, the theater of war between the Axis powers and Finland—a co-belligerent—against the USSR. It took place in central and Eastern Europe, the Baltics, and the Balkans. In the former USSR this part of the war is known as the Great Patriotic War.

Einsatzgruppen Four battalion-sized mobile killing squads that targeted Jews and political enemies in territories occupied by Germany.

enfiladed Gunfire directed from a flanking point along the length of an enemy battle line.

escort carrier Smaller and slower than aircraft carriers, escort carriers were largely converted merchant ships carrying aircraft. They were principally tasked with escorting convoys carrying materiel and supplies.

Fighter Command Branch of the RAF specializing in fighter operations, founded in 1936. Integral in defeating the Luftwaffe during the Battle of Britain in 1940.

Free French French citizens who rallied to General Charles de Gaulle following his call for a continuation of the war after France's capitulation in June 1940.

front (Soviet) The Soviet equivalent of a Western army group. A front was generally made up of three to five armies, plus an army-size air wing to provide ground forces with aerial support.

Führer German word meaning leader. Hitler took it as a title in 1921 to signify his position as leader of the Nazi party.

Geneva Conventions Four political conventions, plus additional protocols, regulating the laws of war and allowing for the protection of POWs and civilians during war. First ratified in 1864, the Geneva Conventions were amended and extended in 1906, 1929, and 1949.

German high command Germany's military leadership, the *Oberkommando der Wehrmacht* ,was set up by Hitler in 1938 to help him establish undisputed control of the armed forces.

gulag Network of forced labor camps that operated in the USSR from the 1920s onward. Although the government agency administrating the gulags closed in 1960, forced labor in the USSR persisted for decades.

Habforce A British military force raised in Palestine in April 1941 and sent to relieve the RAF base at Habbaniyah in Iraq, before being besieged by rebel Iraqi forces.

howitzer A large artillery piece, generally with a comparatively short barrel, capable of firing shells at a high angle of elevation with a steep descent. Depending on the type of howitzer, range varied from around 5 miles (8 km) to 20 miles (30 km).

Imperial Japanese Navy Navy of the Empire of Japan from 1868 until 1945.

kamikaze Japanese pilots of World War II who, from October 1944, launched mass suicide attacks against Allied shipping.

Karelian Isthmus The stretch of land between the Gulf of Finland and Lake Lagoda where the Finns built the fortified Mannerheim Line.

Kriegsmarine The name by which the German navy was known from 1935 until the end of the war.

League of Nations Organization created after World War I to provide a forum for the resolution of international disputes.

Lebensraum A German word meaning "living space," the demand for which formed the basis for Nazi Germany's commitment to territorial expansion.

Lend-Lease US aid program initiated in March 1941 to guarantee the free supply of arms, ammunition, food, and other essential material, notably fuel, to Britain and subsequently to other allies.

legation Group of diplomats and other officials representing their government in a foreign country, but with less status than that of an embassy. A legation is headed by a minister as opposed to an ambassador.

Liberty ships Cargo ships, mass-produced in the US during World War II. Such ships were cheap and easy to build. In all, 2,711 were built, 200 being sunk by enemy action.

Lo Spazio Vitale The Italian equivalent of *Lebensraum*. Fascist Italy's aim was to establish dominance over North Africa and in the Mediterranean area.

Low Countries A collective term for Belgium, the Netherlands, and Luxembourg. Also known as the Benelux countries after the initial letters of their names.

Luftwaffe Officially created in 1935, Germany's Luftwaffe was the most modern air force in the world when war broke out in 1939.

materiel Collective word describing arms, ammunition, and military equipment and supplies in general.

Molotov–Ribbentrop Pact Nonaggression pact concluded by Soviet and German foreign ministers before the start of World War II that partitioned Poland between the two powers.

nautical mile Unit of measurement slightly greater than a land mile and equal to one minute of a degree of latitude.

Nazi party Abbreviated title of the *Nationalsozialistische Deutsche Arbeiterpartei* (National Socialist German Workers' Party).

partisans Members of the armed resistance groups that sprung up in Nazi-occupied territory during the war.

plebiscite A vote by which the people of a country expresses approval or disapproval of a specific proposal. After World War I and in the run-up to World War II, plebiscites were used in Europe to address the issues created by displaced populations.

pocket battleship A type of powerful heavy cruiser built by Germany in the 1930s. The Nazis built three in total: *Deutschland* (later renamed *Lutzow*), *Admiral Scheer*, and *Admiral Graf Spee*. Their main armament consisted of six 11-in guns.

POW Prisoner of war. A person, usually a combatant, held prisoner during an armed conflict.

putsch An illegal attempt to overthrow a government by force of arms. Hitler's so-called Beer Hall Putsch, which he launched against the Bavarian government in Munich in November 1923, though a failure, was a notable step along his road to power.

RAF Royal Air Force. Britain's air force, established in April 1918, and the world's oldest independent air force.

Red Army The Soviet government's army following the 1917 Bolshevik Revolution. The name was dropped in 1946.

Regia Aeronautica The Italian Royal Air Force, founded in 1923. Though on the surface numerically impressive, many of its aircraft were obsolete, and the ill-organized Italian aircraft industry failed to keep pace with its military losses.

regiment *see* battalion.

Reichskommissariat Administrative unit led by a Reichskommissar and tasked with governing regions of German-occupied Europe including the Netherlands, Norway, Belgium, and northern France. Five others were established in the east in a bid to break up the Soviet Union.

Reichstag The parliament of the Third Reich. Its role was largely ceremonial, unanimously approving Hitler's decisions.

Rhineland Area of western Germany along the River Rhine. Following World War I it was demilitarized by the terms of the 1925 Locarno Treaty.

Royal Navy The British navy, the strongest in the world at the start of World War II, fielding 15 battleships and battle cruisers, seven aircraft carriers, 66 cruisers, 184 destroyers, and 60 submarines.

ROC Royal Observer Corps. Civil defense organization tasked with plotting enemy aircraft movements over Britain during World War II.

Saarland Province of south-western Germany, administered by the League of Nations from 1920 to 1935.

salient A battlefield projection, also known as a bulge, surrounded by the enemy on multiple sides, making the troops holding it vulnerable to attack.

SOE Special Operations Executive. British secret intelligence organization tasked with aiding resistance movements in enemy-occupied territories and carrying out spying and sabotage activities.

SS *Schutzstaffel*. The elite paramilitary corps of the Nazi party. Led by Heinrich Himmler from 1929 onward.

SA *Sturmabteilung*. Otherwise known as the Brownshirts, the SA was the original paramilitary force of the Nazis that became gradually overshadowed by the SS.

sue for peace The initiation of negotiations for peace, usually a step taken by the losing party in an attempt to avoid an unconditional surrender.

task force A term coined by the US Navy in 1941 to describe naval units combined to undertake a specific military mission.

Third Reich The official name the Nazis gave Germany after coming to power in 1933. In their version of history the Holy Roman Empire, which lasted from 800 to 1806, constituted the First Reich, and the German Empire (1871–1918) constituted the Second Reich.

Treaty of Versailles The peace treaty that formally concluded World War I following the 1918 armistice between the Allies and Germany. Its contentious clauses on war guilt and its demand

for the payment of reparations caused lasting German resentment that helped fuel the rise of the Nazi party.

U-boats German submarines. While used to attack enemy warships, U-boats were primarily used to create a naval blockade of Allied shipping routes and to allow for commerce raiding.

United Nations International organization established in October 1945 with the aim of preventing future wars.

USAAF United States Army Air Forces. Formed in 1941 as the successor to the Army Air Corps. After the US entered World War II, its strength rose dramatically from just 4,000 aircraft to 75,000 by the end of the war.

Vichy France The name of the state set up under the leadership of Marshal Philippe Pétain to rule unoccupied France following the French surrender in June 1940. Its capital was the spa town of Vichy.

V-weapons The name coined by the Germans for the so-called "vengeance weapons" they deployed in 1944. They consisted of the V-1 pilotless flying bomb and the V-2 long-range rocket.

Waffen-SS The armed branch of the SS and the Wehrmacht's elite fighting formations. It was judged at the post-war Nuremberg trials to be a criminal organization due to its involvement in war crimes and crimes against humanity.

Wehrmacht The generic name for Germany's armed forces from 1935 to the end of the war. It consisted of the Herr (army), the Kriegsmarine (navy), and Luftwaffe (air force) with Hitler as the supreme commander.

Western Front In World War II, the theater of conflict taking place in Belgium, Denmark, Norway, France, Germany, Italy, Luxembourg, and the Netherlands.

INDEX

Page numbers in **bold** indicate main treatments of a topic

ACKNOWLEDGMENTS

Dorling Kindersley would like to thank the following people for their help in the preparation of this book: Phil Gamble for additional map design; Steve Crozier for image retouching; Garima Agarwal, Simar Dhamija, and Bianca Zambrea for design assistance; Jaypal Singh Chauhan for DTP assistance; Martyn Page and Kate Taylor for editorial assistance; Katie John for proofreading; and Helen Peters for indexing. Additional map references: maps courtesy of the USMA, Department of History; contains map data © OpenStreetMap contributors.

Editors' note: place names are mostly given in their contemporary forms, except China, where Pinyin Romanization is used. Tonnage is given in metric tonnes and US tons.

The publisher would like to thank the following for their kind permission to reproduce their photographs:

(Key: a-above; b-below/bottom; c-centre; f-far; l-left; r-right; t-top)

2 Dorling Kindersley: Wardrobe Museum, Salisbury. **4 Getty Images:** Bettmann (tl); Henry Guttmann Collection / Hulton Archive (tr). **4-5 Getty Images:** Ullstein bild Dtl.. **5 Getty Images:** Henry Guttmann Collection / Hulton Archive (tl); J. R. Eyerman / The LIFE Picture Collection (tr). **6 Getty Images:** Sgt Robert Howard / Hulton Archive (tl, tr). **6-7 Getty Images:** Ullstein bild Dtl.. **7 The US National Archives and Records Administration:** Photographer: Joe Rosenthal (tl). **8-9 John Calvin / www.wwii-photos-maps.com. 10-11 Getty Images:** Bettmann. **12 Getty Images:** Photo 12 / UIG (tl). **13 Getty Images:** De Agostini / Biblioteca Ambrosiana (cr); Popperfoto (tl). **14 Getty Images:** Swim ink 2 llc / Corbis Historical (tl). **15 Getty Images:** Universal History Archive / Universal Images Group (br). **16 Alamy Stock Photo:** Photo 12 (tl). **18 Getty Images:** Stefano Bianchetti / Corbis Historical (bl). **19 Alamy Stock Photo:** IanDagnall Computing (br). **20-21 Getty Images:** Bettmann. **20 Getty Images:** Bettmann (bc); Adoc-photos / Corbis Historical (cl). **22 Alamy Stock Photo:** Granger Historical Picture Archive (bc). **Getty Images:** Universal History Archive / Universal Images Group (tr). **24 Alamy Stock Photo:** Pictorial Press Ltd (bl). **Getty Images:** Ullstein bild Dtl. (br). **26 akg-images:** Pictures From History (bl). **26-27 Imperial War Museum. 28 akg-images:** (tr). **Getty Images:** Keystone / Hulton Archive (bc). **30-31 Bridgeman Images:** Pictures from History. **31 Bridgeman Images:** Pictures from History (br). **Dorling Kindersley:** By kind permission of The Trustees of the Imperial War Museum, London (cr). **32 Getty Images:** Print Collector / Hulton Archive (bc). **33 Getty Images:** Michael Nicholson / Corbis Historical

(tr). **34-35 Getty Images:** Henry Guttmann Collection / Hulton Archive. **36 Alamy Stock Photo:** Chronicle (tl); Heritage Image Partnership Ltd (c). **37 Getty Images:** Hugo Jaeger / Timepix / The Life Picture Collection (cr); IWM / Imperial War Museums (tl). **38 Wikipedia:** Julien Bryan (bl). **40-41 Getty Images:** Gaston Paris / Roger Viollet. **41 Alamy Stock Photo:** Hi-Story (c). **Getty Images:** Lt. L A Puttnam / IWM (br). **43 Alamy Stock Photo:** World History Archive (br). **44 Getty Images:** Bettmann (tr). **46 Getty Images:** Ullstein bild Dtl. (tl). **47 akg-images:** TT News Agency / SVT (tr). **48-49 Advanced Archival Associates Research. 49 Getty Images:** Ullstein bild Dtl. (br). **50-51 Alamy Stock Photo:** Everett Collection Historica. **51 Bridgeman Images:** Tallandier (br). **Dorling Kindersley:** Wardrobe Museum, Salisbury (cr). **52 Getty Images:** Culture Club / Hulton Archive (bl). **53 Getty Images:** Hulton-Deutsch / Corbis Historical (br). **54 Getty Images:** Adoc-photos / Corbis Historical (bc, tr). **56 Getty Images:** Photo Josse / Leemage / Corbis Historical (clb). **58 Rex by Shutterstock:** Associated Newspapers / Associated Newspapers (bc). **59 Getty Images:** IWM / Imperial War Museums (br). **60-61 London Metropolitan Archives. 61 Alamy Stock Photo:** Shawshots (br). **62 Alamy Stock Photo:** Pictorial Press Ltd (cla); Trinity Mirror / Mirrorpix (bc). **62-63 Getty Images:** Hulton-Deutsch Collection / Corbis. **64 Alamy Stock Photo:** Interfoto (bc); John Frost Newspapers (cr). **66 Getty Images:** Ullstein bild Dtl. (bc). **67 Alamy Stock Photo:** Trinity Mirror / Mirrorpix (crb). **68-69 Getty Images:** Bettmann. **68 Getty Images:** Capt. Horton / IWM (bl); Photo 12 / UIG (cl). **70 Alamy Stock Photo:** Everett Collection Inc (bc). **71 Getty Images:** Museum of Science and Industry, Chicago / Archive Photos (tr). **72 Getty Images:** Keystone-France / Gamma-Rapho (tl). **73 akg-images:** (r). **Getty Images:** Universal History Archive / UIG (tl). **75 Getty Images:** Haynes Archive / Popperfoto (br). **77 Getty Images:** Galerie Bilderwelt / Hulton Archive (tr); Michael Nicholson / Corbis Historical (br). **79 Getty Images:** Photo 12 / Universal Images Group (clb); Fototeca Storica Nazionale. / Hulton Archive (br). **81 akg-images:** (cr). **82 Bridgeman Images:** © SZ Photo / Scherl (br). **84 Getty Images:** Haynes Archive / Popperfoto (br); Bettmann (bl). **86-87 Getty Images:** Hulton Archive. **86 Alamy Stock Photo:** The Picture Art Collection (bl). **Getty Images:** Dan Burn-Forti / The Image Bank (cl). **88 Dorling Kindersley:** Musée des blindés, Saumur, France (tr). **Getty Images:** Galerie Bilderwelt (cl). **89 Getty Images:** Mondadori Portfolio (cr); Print Collector (t). **90 Alamy Stock Photo:** Pictorial Press Ltd (bl). **91 Getty Images:** Heritage Images / Hulton Archive (br). **92 Dorling Kindersley:** Wardrobe Museum, Salisbury (cl). **Getty Images:** Horace Abrahams / Hulton Archive (bc). **92-93 Getty Images:** TASS. **94 Getty Images:** Ullstein bild Dtl. (bl). **94-95 John Calvin / www.wwii-photos-maps.com. 97 Getty Images:** Ullstein bild Dtl. (bc); Alexander Ustinov / Hulton Archive (tc). **98-99 Getty Images:** TASS. **98 akg-images:** Ullstein bild (cla). **Getty Images:** ullstein bild Dtl. (bl). **101 akg-images:** Pictures From History (tc). **Getty Images:** Time & Life Pictures / The LIFE Picture Collection (bl). **102-103 Getty Images:** J. R. Eyerman / The LIFE Picture Collection. **104 akg-images:** (cb). **Alamy Stock Photo:** World History Archive (tl). **105 Dorling Kindersley:** Planes of Fame Air Museum, Chino, California (ca). **Getty Images:** Universal History Archive / UIG (cr). **106 Alamy Stock Photo:** Shawshots (bl). **107 Alamy Stock Photo:** Everett Collection Inc (br). **108-109 Getty Images:** The Asahi Shimbun. **109 Bridgeman Images:** Universal History Archive / UIG (br). **Dorling Kindersley:** Imperial War Museum, Duxford (cr). **111 Alamy Stock Photo:** Granger Historical Picture Archive (br). **112 Getty Images:** Keystone / Hulton Archive (bl). **113 Getty Images:** Dmitri Kessel / The LIFE Picture Collection (br). **114-115 Getty Images:** Alfred T. Palmer / Buyenlarge. **114 akg-images:** akg / John Parrot / Stocktrek Images (cl). **Getty Images:** PhotoQuest / Archive Photos (bc). **116 Bridgeman Images:** West Point Museum, New York, USA / Photo © Don Troiani (br). **118 Getty Images:** Carl Mydans / The LIFE Picture Collection (bl). **119 Getty Images:** Mondadori Portfolio (br). **120 Getty Images:** Bettmann (bl). **122-123 Getty Images:** IWM. **123 akg-images:**

GandhiServe India (br). **Getty Images:** Bettmann (c). **124 Alamy Stock Photo:** The Picture Art Collection (bc). **125 Alamy Stock Photo:** Historic Images (br). **127 Alamy Stock Photo:** Archivah (cl). **128-129 Alamy Stock Photo:** Hum Historical. **129 Getty Images:** Keystone / Hulton Archive (br). **130 Getty Images:** Photo 12 / UIG (ca); David E. Scherman / Time Life Pictures (clb). **131 akg-images:** (t). **Getty Images:** Sgt. Chetwyn / IWM (cr). **132 Bridgeman Images:** Deutsches Historisches Museum, Berlin, Germany / © DHM (bl). **133 Getty Images:** Ullstein bild Dtl. (br). **135 Alamy Stock Photo:** Pictorial Press Ltd (tc). **Bridgeman Images:** © Galerie Bilderwelt (br). **136-137 Alamy Stock Photo:** Pictorial Press Ltd. **136 akg-images:** Fototeca Gilardi (bc). **United States Holocaust Memorial Museum:** (cla). **138 Getty Images:** Keystone / Hulton Archive (cl). **139 Getty Images:** Evening Standard / Hulton Archive (br). **141 Alamy Stock Photo:** Pictorial Press Ltd (br). **143 Getty Images:** Jean Desmarteau / Gamma-Rapho (br). **144 Getty Images:** Universal History Archive / Universal Images Group (bl). **147 Bridgeman Images:** American Photographer, (20th century) / Private Collection / Peter Newark American Pictures (br). **Getty Images:** British Official Photo / The LIFE Picture Collection (tr). **148 akg-images:** (bl). **149 Getty Images:** Windmill Books / Universal Images Group (br). **150 Getty Images:** TASS (bc). **www.mediadrumworld.com:** (tc). **152 Getty Images:** Serge PlanTureux / Corbis Historical (bc). **www.mediadrumworld.com:** (tr). **154-155 Getty Images:** AFP Contributor. **154 Alamy Stock Photo:** Trinity Mirror / Mirrorpix (bc). **Dorling Kindersley:** Imperial War Museum, Duxford (c). **156-157 Getty Images:** Sgt Robert Howard / Hulton Archive. **158 Dorling Kindersley:** Musée des blindés, Saumur, France (cb). **Getty Images:** Popperfoto (tl). **159 Bridgeman Images:** Photo © AGIP (cr). **Getty Images:** Sovfoto / UIG (tl). **160 akg-images:** Stocktrek Images (bl). **161 akg-images:** Heritage-Images / The Print Collector (tr). **162-163 Alamy Stock Photo:** Granger Historical Picture Archive. **162 Alamy Stock Photo:** Peter Horree (ca). **Getty Images:** Lt. D C Oulds / IWM (bl). **165 Getty Images:** Lt. L Chetwyn / Imperial War Museums (bc). **166 akg-images:** (bc). **Bridgeman Images:** © Galerie Bilderwelt (tc). **168 akg-images:** (bl). **169 Getty Images:** aviation-images.com / Universal Images Group (br). **170-171 Getty Images:** Bletchley Park Trust / Sspl. **170 Alamy Stock Photo:** James King-Holmes (bc). **Getty Images:** Time Life Pictures / National Archives / The Life Picture Collection (ca). **172 Getty Images:** Hulton Deutsch / Corbis Historical (tr). **Wikipedia:** Stadt Nürnberg (bl). **174 Bridgeman Images:** SZ Photo / Sammlung Megele (cla). **Getty Images:** Ullstein bild Dtl. (bl). **174-175 Getty Images:** Roger Viollet. **176 Getty Images:** Robert Doisneau / Masters (tl). **177 Alamy Stock Photo:** John Frost Newspapers (br). **179 akg-images:** (br); Sputnik (cl). **180 Bridgeman Images:** Peter Newark Military Pictures (tl). **181 Alamy Stock Photo:** ITAR-TASS News Agency (br). **182 akg-images:** Sputnik (tl). **Dreamstime.com:** Yuri4u80 (tr). **184 Dorling Kindersley:** The Combined Military Services Museum (CMSM) (cla). **Getty Images:** Keystone Features / Hulton Archive (bl). **184-185 Getty Images:** Universal History Archive. **186 Bridgeman Images:** Colorized reproduction of original photograph by Walter Rosenblum, Omaha Beach Rescue, D-Day +1 / © Galerie Bilderwelt (cr). **Getty Images:** Roger Viollet (bl). **188-189 Getty Images:** Smith Collection / Gado. **188 akg-images:** (bc). **Dorling Kindersley:** By kind permission of The Trustees of the Imperial War Museum, London (cla). **190-191 John Calvin / www.wwii-photos-maps.com. 191 Getty Images:** Franklin / Hulton Archive (br). **192 Bridgeman Images:** French School, (20th century) / Private Collection / Archives Charmet (bl). **193 The National Archives:** (br). **194 akg-images:** Interfoto (bl). **196-197 TopFoto.co.uk:** Ullstein Bild. **196 Getty Images:** Interim Archives / Archive Photos (br). **197 Alamy Stock Photo:** History and Art Collection (cra). **Getty Images:** Heinrich Hoffmann / The Life Picture Collection (br). **198 Alamy Stock Photo:** Granger Historical Picture Archive (tl). **200 Getty Images:** Galerie Bilderwelt / Hulton Archive (bc). **203 Getty Images:** Mondadori Portfolio (br). **204 Bridgeman Images:** Private Collection / Peter Newark Pictures (cr).

Getty Images: Historical / Corbis Historical (tl). 205 Alamy Stock Photo: American Photo Archive (crb). Bridgeman Images: Pictures from History (t). 207 Alamy Stock Photo: Aviation history now (br). Getty Images: Time Life Pictures / The LIFE Picture Collection (tl). 208-209 Getty Images: Sgt Robert Howard / Hulton Archive. 208 Bridgeman Images: Private Collection / Peter Newark Pictures (cla). Dorling Kindersley: Musée des blindés, Saumur, France (bl). 210-211 Imperial War Museum. 213 Getty Images: W. Eugene Smith / The LIFE Picture Collection (tc). 214 Getty Images: Bettmann (bc); Keystone / Hulton Archive (tr). 216 Alamy Stock Photo: Hi-Story (cl). Getty Images: Hulton-Deutsch Collection / Corbis (bc). 216-217 Naval History and Heritage Command. 218-219 Imperial War Museum. 218 Getty Images: Keystone / Hulton Archive (bl). 220 Getty Images: Sovfoto / Universal Images Group (tl). 221 Getty Images: PhotoQuest / Archive Photos (br). 222-223 Getty Images: Roger Viollet. 223 Getty Images: Universal History Archive (br). Wikipedia: Manchukuo State Council of Emperor Kang-de Puyi (cra). 224-225 The US National Archives and Records Administration: Photographer: Joe Rosenthal. 226 Getty Images: Bettmann (c); Time Life Pictures (tl). 227 Bridgeman Images: Pictures from History (cr). Dorling Kindersley: Royal Airforce Museum, London (tl). 228 Getty Images: Time Life Pictures / The LIFE Picture Collection (bl). 230-231 akg-images: Heritage-Images / Keystone Archives. 230 Alamy Stock Photo: DBI Studio (cla). Getty Images: Hulton-Deutsch Collection / Corbis (bc). 232 Getty Images: PhotoQuest / Archive Photos (bc). 233 Getty Images: Galerie Bilderwelt / Hulton Archive (tr). 234 Getty Images: PhotoQuest / Archive Photos (bl). 236-237 akg-images: Picture-Alliance / ZB / Richard Peter sen.. 236 Alamy Stock Photo: Everett Collection Inc (bl). Imperial War Museum: (ca). 238-239 Imperial War Museum. 238 Getty Images: PhotoQuest / Archive Photos (bl). 240 akg-images: Fototeca Gilardi (bc). 241 Getty Images: Galerie Bilderwelt / Hulton Archive (tr). 242 akg-images: (c) Khaldei / Voller Ernst (bl). 244-245 Getty Images: Photo12 / UIG. 244 Getty Images: Hulton-Deutsch Collection / Corbis (bl); Picture Post / Hulton Archive (cla). 246 Getty Images: De Agostini Picture Library (tr). Stanford Libraries: (c). 247 Getty Images: Sovfoto / UIG (tl). The US National Archives and Records Administration: Photographer: Joe Rosenthal (c). 248 Getty Images: Carl Mydans / The LIFE Picture Collection (tc). 249 Getty Images: Jiji Press / AFP (tr). 250 Bridgeman Images: Museum of Fine Arts, Houston, Texas, USA / gift of Will Michels in honor of Jim and Erika Liu (bl). 251 Getty Images: W. Eugene Smith / The LIFE Picture Collection (br). 252 akg-images: (cla). 253 Getty Images: Time Life Pictures / The LIFE Picture Collection (br). 254 Getty Images: US Signal Corps / The LIFE Picture Collection (bc). 255 Getty Images: Time Life Pictures / The LIFE Picture Collection (br). 256-257 Alamy Stock Photo: Everett Collection Inc. 256 Alamy Stock Photo: DOD Photo (bl). Dorling Kindersley: Bradbury Science Museum, Los Alamos (ca). 259 Getty Images: The Asahi Shimbun (br). 260-261 Getty Images: MPI / Archive Photos. 260 Alamy Stock Photo: John Frost Newspapers (cl); Military Images (bl). 262 akg-images: (tl). Getty Images: Roger Viollet (cl). 263 Bridgeman Images: Universal History Archive / UIG (cr). Getty Images: Keystone-France / Gamma-Keystone (tl). 264 Alamy Stock Photo: Everett Collection Historical (bc). 265 David Rumsey Map Collection www.davidrumsey.com: (br). 266 Bridgeman Images: Pictures from History (bc). Getty Images: David Pollack / Corbis Historical (cr). 268 Alamy Stock Photo: Everett Collection Historical (bl). 269 Getty Images: Universal History Archive / Universal Images Group (br). 270-271 Magnum Photos: Robert Capa. 271 Alamy Stock Photo: Eddie Gerald (cr). Getty Images: Frank Shershel / GPO (br). 274-275 Alamy Stock Photo: DPA Picture Alliance. 274 akg-images: (bl). Getty Images: Popperfoto (cla)

Endpaper images: Front: akg-images: Back: akg-images: Ullstein bild.

All other images © Dorling Kindersley
For further information see: www.dkimages.com

SMITHSONIAN
BATTLES
MAP BY MAP

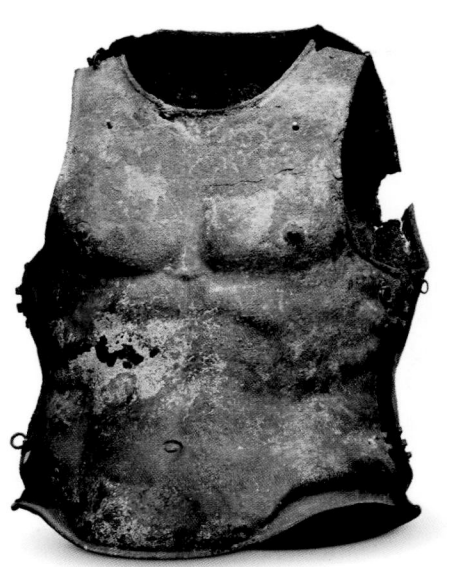

SMITHSONIAN
BATTLES
MAP BY MAP

FOREWORD BY
PETER SNOW

10

BEFORE 1000 CE

CONTENTS

Penguin
Random
House

DK LONDON

Senior Editor Hugo Wilkinson

Editors Tom Booth, Polly Boyd

Assistant Editor Michael Clark

US Editors Karyn Gerhard, Lori Hand

Managing Editor Angeles Gavira Guerrero

Associate Publishing Director Liz Wheeler

Publishing Director Jonathan Metcalf

Lead Senior Art Editor Duncan Turner

Senior Art Editor Sharon Spencer

Design Development Manager Sophia MTT

Jacket Designer Surabhi Wadhwa-Gandhi

Production Editor Gillian Reid

Senior Production Controller
Meskerem Berhane

Managing Art Editor Michael Duffy

Art Director Karen Self

Design Director Phil Ormerod

54

1000–1500

100

1500–1700

DK INDIA

Senior Editor Dharini Ganesh
Editors Ishita Jha, Priyanjali Narain
Picture Research Coordinator Sumita Khatwani
Picture Research Manager Taiyaba Khatoon
Senior Editorial Manager Rohan Sinha
Managing Art Editor Sudakshina Basu
Production Manager Pankaj Sharma
Pre-production Manager Balwant Singh
Editorial Head Glenda Fernandes
Design Head Malavika Talukder

Senior Art Editor Vaibhav Rastogi
Project Art Editor Anjali Sachar
Art Editors Mridushmita Bose, Rabia Ahmad
Senior Cartographers Subhashree Bharati, Mohammad Hassan
Cartographer Ashif
Cartography Manager Suresh Kumar
Senior Jackets Designer Suhita Dharamjit
Senior DTP Designers Harish Aggarwal, Vishal Bhatia
DTP Designer Nityanand Kumar

COBALT ID

Designer Darren Bland
Art Director Paul Reid
Editorial Director Marek Walisiewicz

CONTRIBUTORS

FOREWORD
Peter Snow CBE

CONSULTANT
Professor Philip Sabin, Professor of Strategic Studies, Kings College, London

WRITERS
Tony Allan, Kay Celtel, R.G. Grant, Philip Parker, Dr. Arrigo Velicogna

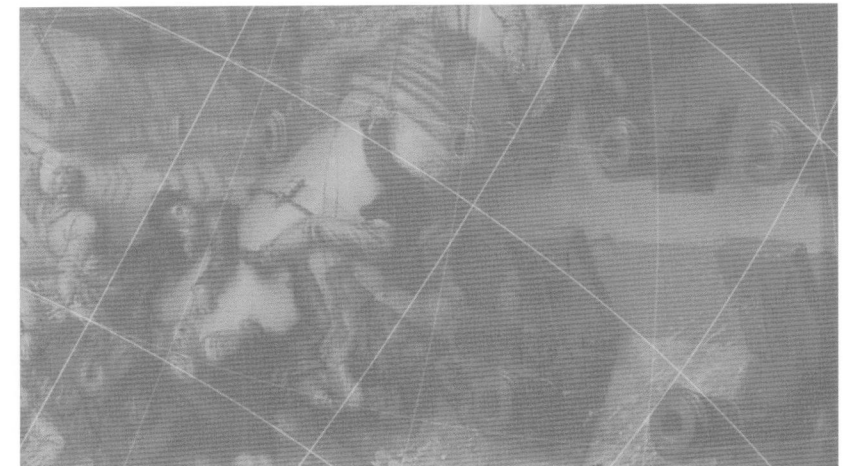

140

1700–1900

First American Edition, 2020
Published in the United States by DK Publishing
1745 Broadway, 20th Floor, New York, NY 10019

Copyright © 2021 Dorling Kindersley Limited
DK, a Division of Penguin Random House LLC

Foreword copyright © 2021 Peter Snow

22 23 24 25 10 9 8 7 6 5 4

001–319134–May/2021

A catalog record for this book is available from the Library of Congress.
ISBN 978-0-7440-2997-0

Printed and bound in United Arab Emirates

For the curious
www.dk.com

Smithsonian

CURATOR

Dr. F. Robert van der Linden, Curator of Air Transportation and Special Purpose Aircraft, Aeronautics Department, National Air and Space Museum

SMITHSONIAN ENTERPRISES

Product Development Manager Kealy Gordon

Director, Licensed Publishing Jill Corcoran

Divisional Merchandising Manager, E-Commerce and Direct-to-Consumer Janet Archer

President, Smithsonian Enterprises Carol LeBlanc

200

1900–PRESENT

SMITHSONIAN

Established in 1846, the Smithsonian is the world's largest museum and research complex, dedicated to public education, national service, and scholarship in the arts, sciences, and history. It includes 19 museums and galleries and the National Zoological Park. The total number of artifacts, works of art, and specimens in the Smithsonian's collection is estimated at 156 million.

DK books are available at special discounts when purchased in bulk for sales promotions, premiums, fund-raising, or educational use. For details, contact:
DK Publishing Special Markets,
1745 Broadway, 20th Floor, New York, NY 10019
SpecialSales@dk.com

FOREWORD

Wars and the battles that punctuate them are a timeless feature of human experience. Fighting is our ultimate means of resolving conflict when all else fails. Bloody though battles are, history cannot ignore them. This exceptional book illuminates the stories of the most important of those battles with a clarity I've never seen before. Only a map, the bird's eye view of a battle, can explain and illustrate the twists and turns of each contest.

All the battles in this meticulously designed volume are in their own way decisive. Some change the shape of the world map by shifting frontiers or deciding the rise and fall of nations. Others erupt within frontiers, marking the transformative moments in civil wars and revolutions. Marathon thwarted the awesome westward sweep of the Persians in 490 BCE; Ain Jalut blocked the Mongols in 1260; Tenochtitlan destroyed the Aztec empire and launched Mexico in 1521; Mohacs—in 1526—left most of Hungary under Ottoman

domination until their defeat at Vienna in 1683. The Battle of Britain and Stalingrad were two key deciding moments of World War II. Cromwell's victory at Naseby in 1645 changed England's government; Tokugawa Ieyasu's triumph at Sekigahara in 1600 propelled the Tokugawa shogunate into power in Japan for more than 250 years. Japan's defeat in World War II was decisively hastened by America's victory of Midway in 1942. Other battles light a different torch— the flare of great symbolic victories that become legends. Ethiopia's defeat of Italy at Adowa in 1896 lit the beacon of African resistance to colonialism. Kosovo Polje in 1389, although a defeat, is still celebrated in Serbia as a proud national symbol of resistance to a foreign invader.

This book also describes in unparalleled detail several key features of each battle. The arrows depicting movement on each map show how commanders responded to the chaos that soon ripped up carefully laid plans. German chief of staff Helmuth von

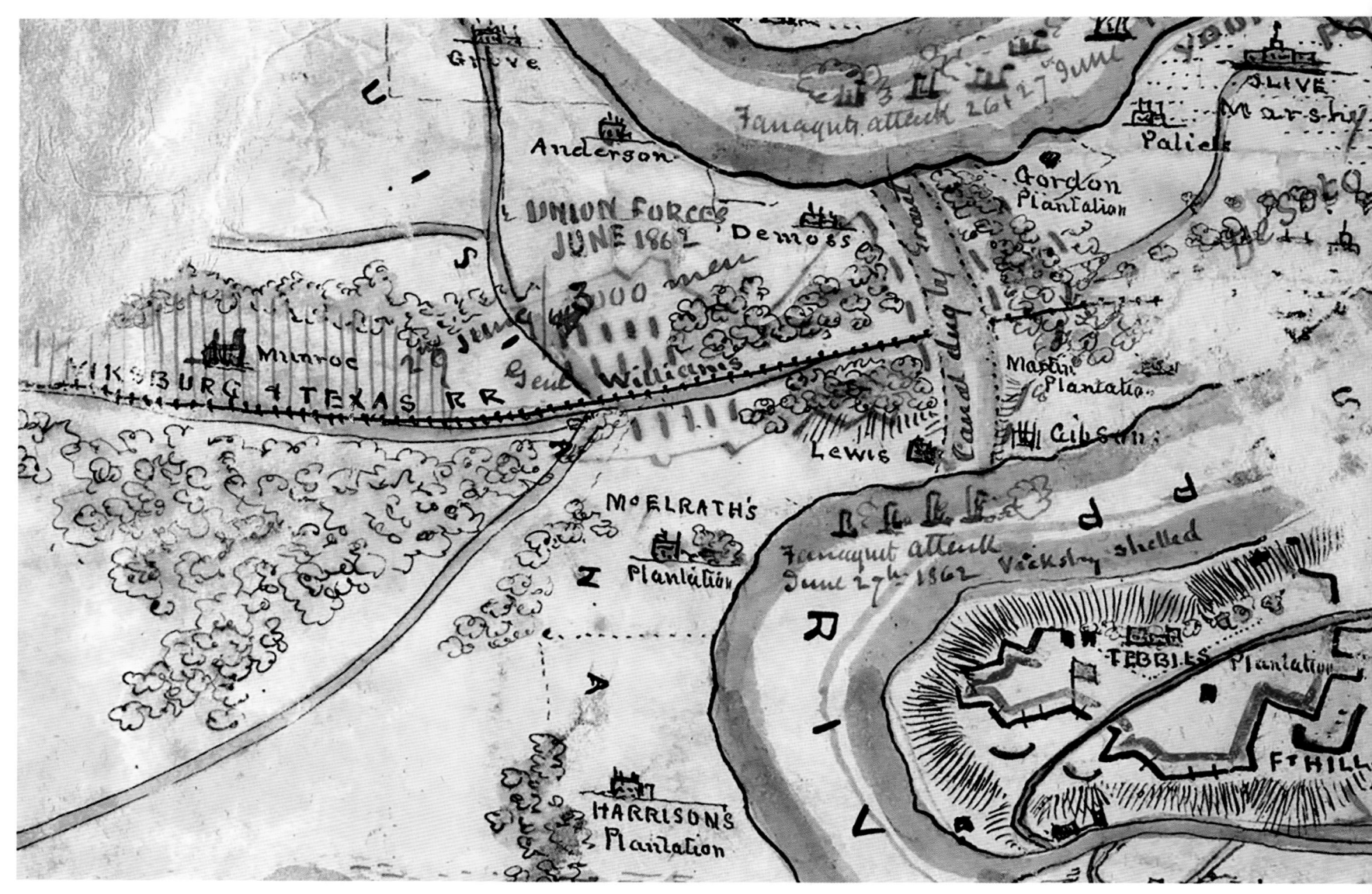

Moltke observed in 1871 that no plan for battle survives first contact with the enemy. Here we can see how great leadership by Frederick the Great at Leuthen in 1757 seized the opportunity to send a large force around his enemy's left flank and roll up the Austrian army. It's also easy to make out how the arrival of Gebhard Leberecht von Blücher's Prussian troops swooping down on Napoleon's right at Waterloo in 1815 helped decide one of the most pivotal battles in history. You can see the ridge at Crécy in 1346 that gave King Edward III of England the commanding view of the field that enabled him to tailor his tactics to achieve victory. At Austerlitz in 1805, the strategic importance of the Pratzen heights stormed by Napoleon's generals Vandamme and Saint-Hilaire is unmistakable.

Another striking feature of this parade of maps from century to century is how they describe the changing face of battle. For two millennia the battles are close-fought with sword, spear, and bow. Then, around the 14th century, we begin to discern how gunpowder widens the conflict. Babur's cannons were more than a match for the Indian elephants at Panipat in 1526. And finally the invention of the motor engine has tanks and armored cars dragging warfare out of the World War I trenches at Amiens in 1918 and unleashing them into the vast mobile battles at El Alamein in 1942 and Desert Storm in 1991.

If, as I fear, war persists as a permanent feature in the ebb and flow of civilization, this book will remain an essential guide to how its battles are won and lost.

PETER SNOW, 2020

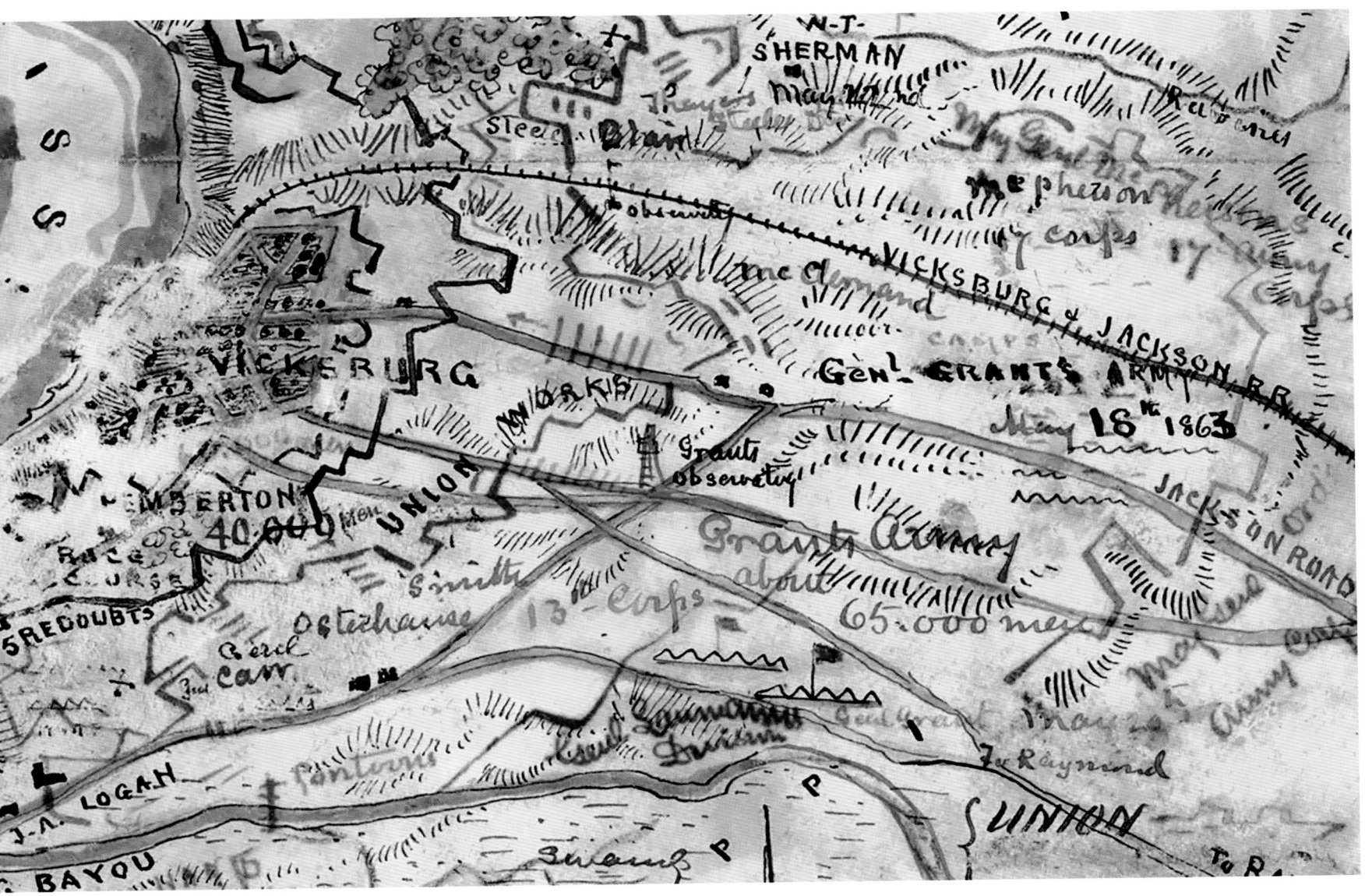

BEFORE
1000 CE

AS HUMAN CIVILIZATIONS GREW, SO ORGANIZED MILITARY
FORCES BEGAN TO DEVELOP. EMPIRES WERE WON AND LOST ON
THE BATTLEFIELD, WHILE SPECIALIZED TROOPS SUCH AS CAVALRY
AND CHARIOTEERS EMERGED TO FIGHT ALONGSIDE INFANTRY.

BEFORE 1000CE

The period up to 1000 CE saw the dawn of organized warfare. Armies gradually grew larger, and foot soldiers were complemented by cavalry and other arms. The largest states developed professional armies, but they were constantly challenged by newer forces who employed new weaponry, tactics, and modes of organization in battle.

△ **Egyptian sphinx**
The Sphinx is from the reign of Ramesses II (r.1279–1213 BCE), whose battle against the Hittites at Kadesh in 1274 BCE involved large chariot forces on each side.

The rise of cities in Mesopotamia by 3000 BCE created a need for specialized warriors to defend them against outsiders. By 1500 BCE, some city-states had become empires, and began to fight for territorial expansion. The Egyptians and Hittites, for example, vied for supremacy. They used chariots in battles, which provided greater mobility. Several centuries later, advances in metallurgy saw the spread of iron weaponry which was more lethal than bronze swords. The Assyrians developed siege engines by about 800 BCE, rendering even the most sturdy city walls vulnerable.

Citizen militia to professional soldiers

Empires grew larger, but the largest of them all, the Persian Achaemenid empire, found itself outmatched by smaller Greek city-states. The Greek hoplites—heavily armed infantry made up of citizens—wielded long spears in tight-knit rectangular formations known as phalanxes to defeat two Persian invasions in the 5th century BCE. This tactic set the pattern for warfare in the eastern Mediterranean for 300 years. Perfected

▷ **Death of a Roman emperor**
This Coptic icon depicts a vision of the 3rd-century Christian martyr Saint Mercurius killing the pagan emperor Julian, portraying his death as divine justice.

by the Macedonian king Alexander the Great, phalanxes were skilfully combined with cavalry and light infantry to conquer the Persian Empire in a series of campaigns from 334 to 323 BCE. However, the Macedonian phalanx, despite its improvements, proved unwieldy, falling victim to the latest Mediterranean military power, the Roman army.

From the 4th century BCE, the Romans combined political aggression with close-combat infantry tactics, conquering first Italy and then the entire Mediterranean region. The Roman legions were not unbeatable, but over the centuries they became increasingly well-trained and professional, annexing new provinces as far north as Britain and as far east as Syria, and overcoming almost all opposition. Gradually it became clear, however, that defending their long frontiers against barbarian raiders would not be sustainable.

Changing battlefields

China became a unified state in 221 BCE and faced a similar evolution. Internal warfare in the preceding years had led to large armies including many infantry and crossbowmen, significant naval forces, and a focus on clever strategy. The Chinese faced pressure along their northern borders from nomadic Xiongnu tribes, whose horse-mounted archers made them formidable foes.

BIRTH OF WARFARE

Organized warfare has its origins in Africa and the ancient Near East, where the Egyptians fought to expand their empire and quash rebellious states. Subsequently, the rise of iron weaponry saw warfare become increasingly efficient. Large-scale infantry formations were perfected by the Romans, birthing an empire that would only fall at the hands of Germanic tribes in 476 CE. The 8th century CE saw both Chinese and Frankish expansion, and the first Viking invasions of Britain.

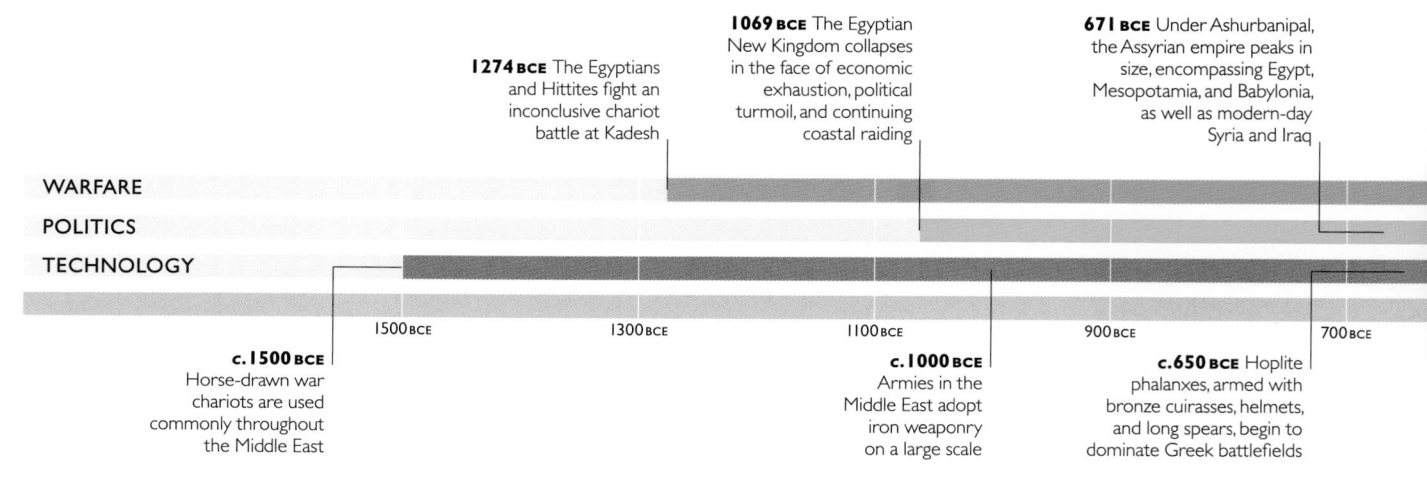

1274 BCE The Egyptians and Hittites fight an inconclusive chariot battle at Kadesh

1069 BCE The Egyptian New Kingdom collapses in the face of economic exhaustion, political turmoil, and continuing coastal raiding

671 BCE Under Ashurbanipal, the Assyrian empire peaks in size, encompassing Egypt, Mesopotamia, and Babylonia, as well as modern-day Syria and Iraq

WARFARE

POLITICS

TECHNOLOGY

1500 BCE   1300 BCE   1100 BCE   900 BCE   700 BCE

c.1500 BCE Horse-drawn war chariots are used commonly throughout the Middle East

c.1000 BCE Armies in the Middle East adopt iron weaponry on a large scale

c.650 BCE Hoplite phalanxes, armed with bronze cuirasses, helmets, and long spears, begin to dominate Greek battlefields

◁ Viking longships
The seafaring Vikings used swift longships to transport their armies along wide stretches of coastline or to sail upriver. Besides using the ships for raiding and invasions, the Vikings often fought sea battles among themselves.

"I have come not to make war on the Italians, but to aid the Italians against Rome."

HANNIBAL BARCA, 217 BCE

In the 620s, the Byzantine Empire, Rome's successor state in the east, lost a lot of territory to the Arab armies united by the new religion of Islam. Highly mobile and experienced in hit-and-run raids, these Arab forces soon adapted to the tactics required of larger armed formations. The peoples they conquered, such as the Persians and some Turkic tribes, became a source of military manpower for the Arab states, giving them an edge over their rivals.

While the Byzantine Empire managed to survive, the Roman Empire in the West deteriorated, giving way to a series of Germanic successor states by the 6th century. Initially these states retained the ethos of a nomadic warband, conceptualizing warfare as a clash of axes and spears until one side fled. However, they gradually cultivated sophisticated semipermanent forces.

The adoption of stirrups in Western Europe around 800 CE gave riders greater stability and reinforced the emerging dominance of heavily armored cavalry now that disciplined infantry had become scarce. They were the predecessors of the knights who would make up the backbone of armies by the 11th century.

Armies continued to face new waves of invaders, such as the Magyars in Hungary and the Vikings from Scandinavia. However, by 1000 CE, more centralized states, capable of resisting most invaders, began to consolidate in Europe.

▷ Striking fear into Rome
This 16th-century fresco shows the Carthaginians crossing the Alps in 218 BCE during the Second Punic War against Rome. Carthaginian leader Hannibal used war elephants to intimidate Roman soldiers and their horses.

490 BCE Athenian hoplites defeat a much larger Persian army at Marathon, ending the first Persian invasion of Greece

216 BCE Carthaginian general Hannibal defeats the Roman legions at Cannae during the Second Punic War

622 CE The prophet Mohammed moves from Mecca to Medina, beginning the Islamic era and a period of Arab conquests

634 CE Muslim armies defeat the Byzantine empire at Yarmuk, leading to the conquest of Syria and Palestine, and paving the way for the Arab conquest of north Africa

751 CE Tang armies from China are defeated by the Abbasid army at the River Talas, ending Chinese expansion westward of Central Asia

793 CE The first Viking raiders attack England, beginning a 250-year long period of attacks on the coastlines of northwestern Europe

500 BCE   300 BCE   100 BCE   100 CE   300 CE   500 CE   700 CE   900 CE

331 BCE Macedonian King Alexander the Great decisively defeats the Persian ruler Darius III at Gaugamela

c.200 BCE Roman legions adopt the improved *gladius hispaniensis* short sword

27 BCE Julius Caesar's adopted heir Octavian becomes the first Roman emperor

476 CE After a period of invasions, a Germanic general in Roman employ deposes the last Roman emperor in the West

581 CE The Sui dynasty reunites China after a period of fragmentation

771 CE Charlemagne becomes the Frankish ruler, and during his reign the kingdom expands to cover a large part of Western Europe

c.900 CE Gunpowder is discovered by Chinese alchemists. It is later utilized for fireworks and primitive firearms

△ **The Kadesh Treaty**
This Hittite clay tablet is a copy of the peace treaty that ended the war between Egypt and the Hittites in 1258 BCE. An Egyptian copy of the agreement has also survived to the present day.

The Hittites are allowed to withdraw east of the Orontes without pursuit by the Egyptian forces

The Hittite army is concealed by hills on the east bank of the Orontes River

Hittite army

Hittite army

Orontes

A

R

Y

S

○ Kadesh

Orontes

1,000 reserve Hittite chariots and possibly some infantry cross the Orontes to engage the Egyptians

Re Div

Amun Div

While marching toward Kadesh, the Egyptian Re division is surprised by the Hittite chariots attacking from across the river

The shattered remnants of the Re division are driven back upon the intact Amun division

From the Mediterranean coast

Orontes

Ne'arin troops

Egyptian Ne'arin soldiers arrive at Kadesh, having marched from the Mediterranean coast and enter the battle

The pharaoh's light chariots hurry out of the Egyptian camp to counter the Hittite onslaught

P l a i n   o f   K a d e s h

A CLASH OF EMPIRES

The Egyptian New Kingdom and the Hittite Empire had been vying for control of the eastern Mediterranean for the past two centuries. In 1274 BCE, Ramses II set out to reassert Egyptian dominance of the region.

KEY

EGYPTIANS		HITTITES	
🏛 Camp		🏛 Camp	
Forces		Forces	
🐎 Chariots		🐎 Chariots	

TIMELINE

MAY 1274 BCE	JUN 1274 BCE

1   HITTITES LAY AN AMBUSH   MAY 1274 BCE

Muwatallis set a trap for the Egyptians. Two of his agents fed Ramses with false information, claiming the Hittite army was nowhere near Kadesh. As a result, the pharaoh confidently advanced to establish a camp outside the city, while his army marched to join him in loose order. Hidden by the hills, the Hittites moved to attack the marching Egyptians' unprotected flank.

→ Arrival of the Egyptians

2   HITTITE CHARIOTS CHARGE

A Hittite force, estimated to number more than 2,500 chariots, forded the Orontes River and charged into the flank of the Re division, the second formation in the Egyptian line of march. Unprepared for this shock attack, the division was routed and scattered. The Hittites failed to take full advantage of their initial success, lingering to plunder the Egyptians' baggage.

→ Hittite chariot attack   ⇢ Re division scatters

3   RAMSES HEADS THE COUNTERATTACK

Even before the Hittite blow was struck, Ramses had received information of the proximity of the enemy. Ramses issued orders for the rear divisions to hasten their march, and prepared himself to enter battle. As the Hittites attacked the Amun division and threatened Ramses' camp, the pharaoh mounted a chariot and led his troops in a counvtercharge. The agile Egyptian chariots outmaneuvered their Hittite opponents and turned the tide of the battle.

→ Egyptian chariot attack

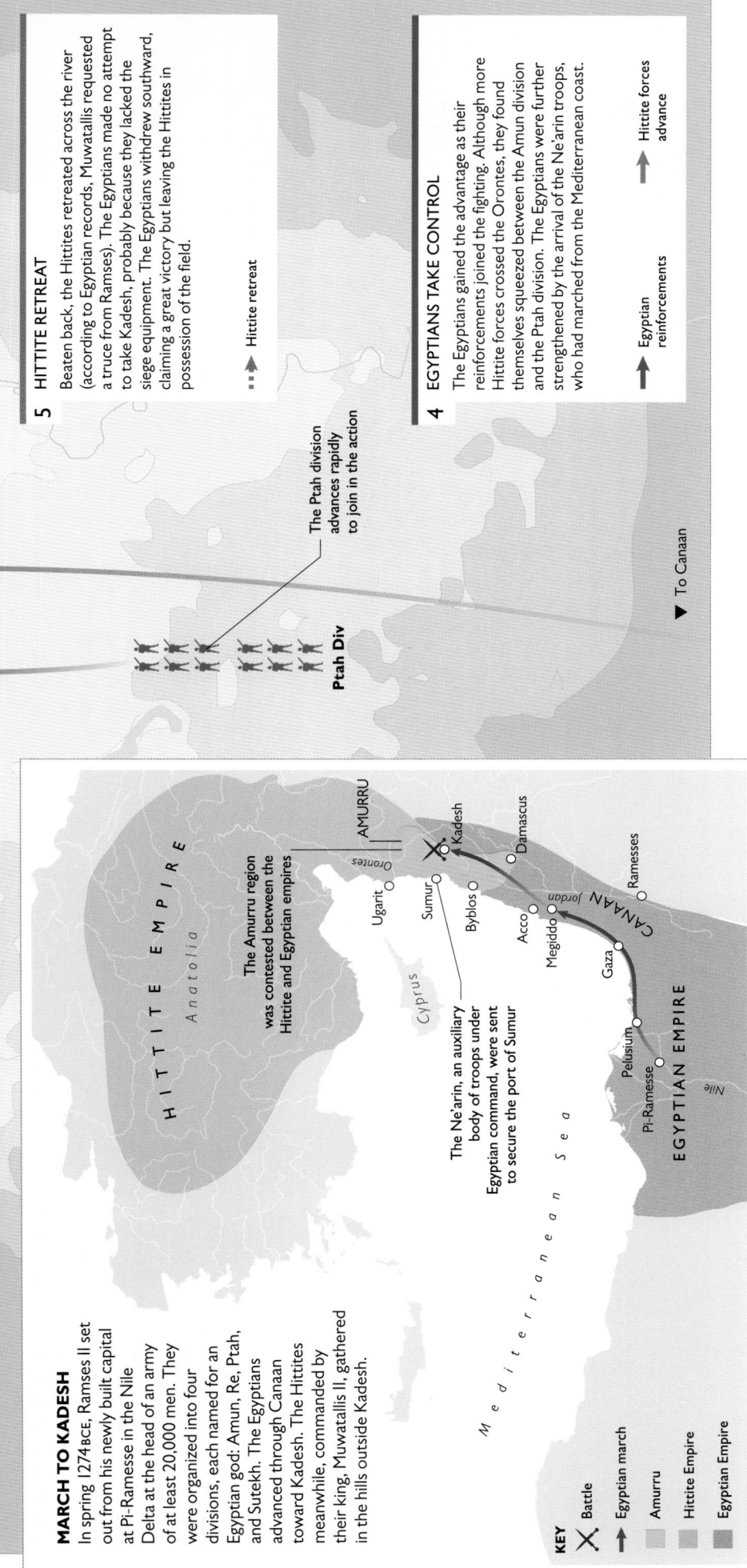

MARCH TO KADESH

In spring 1274 BCE, Ramses II set out from his newly built capital at Pi-Ramesse in the Nile Delta at the head of an army of at least 20,000 men. They were organized into four divisions, each named for an Egyptian god: Amun, Re, Ptah, and Sutekh. The Egyptians advanced through Canaan toward Kadesh. The Hittites meanwhile, commanded by their king, Muwatallis II, gathered in the hills outside Kadesh.

KEY

X Battle
→ Egyptian march
Amurru
Hittite Empire
Egyptian Empire

The Amurru region was contested between the Hittite and Egyptian empires

The Ne'arin, an auxiliary body of troops under Egyptian command, were sent to secure the port of Sumur

5 HITTITE RETREAT

Beaten back, the Hittites retreated across the river (according to Egyptian records, Muwatallis requested a truce from Ramses). The Egyptians made no attempt to take Kadesh, probably because they lacked the siege equipment. The Egyptians withdrew southward, claiming a great victory but leaving the Hittites in possession of the field.

➤ Hittite retreat

4 EGYPTIANS TAKE CONTROL

The Egyptians gained the advantage as their reinforcements joined the fighting. Although more Hittite forces crossed the Orontes, they found themselves squeezed between the Amun division and the Ptah division. The Egyptians were further strengthened by the arrival of the Ne'arin troops, who had marched from the Mediterranean coast.

→ Egyptian reinforcements
↑ Hittite forces advance

The Ptah division advances rapidly to join in the action

Ptah Div

▼ To Canaan

KADESH

More than 3,000 years ago, the Egyptian pharaoh Ramses II led an army into an area of Syria long contested with the Hittite Empire. The resulting clash between Egyptian and Hittite chariot forces, fought outside the city of Kadesh, is the earliest battle for which detailed information has survived.

Ramses II succeeded his father Seti I as ruler of the Egyptian New Kingdom in 1279 BCE. He inherited a long-running dispute with the Hittite Empire (based in Anatolia) over the possession of Amurru, a region in what is present-day northern Syria. Ramses conducted a successful offensive against the Hittites' allies in Amurru in 1275 BCE. The following year, he sought to repeat this exploit, taking as his target the walled city of Kadesh. But on this occasion, the Hittite ruler Muwatallis II responded by fielding an army that, in the words of an Egyptian chronicler, "covered the mountains and the valleys and were like locusts in their numbers."

Both the Egyptians and the Hittites depended on chariots for their elite shock force on the battlefield—the Hittites employing three-man chariots, the Egyptians lighter vehicles crewed by a horse driver and an archer. With about 5,000 chariots deployed, the fight that took place outside Kadesh in 1274 BCE is the largest chariot battle known to history. The most vivid account of the battle was written by the Egyptians, who claimed a heroic victory. Other evidence suggests it should be regarded as an inconclusive draw. Amurru remained in Hittite hands and fighting over the region intermittently continued. Sixteen years later, the border dispute between the two empires was settled by the world's earliest recorded international peace treaty, which was originally inscribed on a silver tablet. A period of relative peace would be maintained between the two powers for the following century.

RAMSES II
R. 1279–1213 BCE

Known by later Egyptians as the "Great Ancestor," Ramses II became ruler of the Egyptian New Kingdom in 1279 BCE. As well as fighting the Hittites, he launched successful campaigns against the Nubians to the south, and the Sherden sea pirates. Many of Ancient Egypt's finest temples were built during his 66-year-long reign, including Abu Simbel in southern Egypt.

CHARIOT WARFARE

Chariots dominated warfare from about 1800 to 600 BCE, and cultures ranging from the Celtic world and Carthage to India and China continued to use them for many centuries, especially until the 3rd century BCE.

△ **Assyrian forces**
This 7th-century BCE relief depicts a scene from the Battle of Til-Tuba (c.650 BCE). Elite warriors of the Assyrian army can be seen on board a chariot.

Carts pulled by onagers (Asian wild asses) and oxen were first used in what is today Europe and the Middle East in about 2500 BCE, and with them came early chariots. However, it was not until about 1800 BCE, with the domestication of horses and the invention of the spoked wheel, that war chariots became truly effective. Probably originating in Central Asia, they became a constant feature of wars fought in China, India, the Middle East, and also in the Aegean region and central Europe.

Chariot warfare reached its peak in the late Bronze (c.1550–1200 BCE) and early Iron (c.1200 BCE–550 BCE) ages. The Hittites, Mitanni, Egyptians, Canaanites, Assyrians, and Babylonians, all fielded armies that included thousands of chariots. The Egyptians and Canaanites tended to favor light, two-horse chariots that were easier to maneuver, but could only accommodate the driver and an archer. In contrast, other cultures such as Assyria, Carthage, India, and China used heavier, three- or four-horse chariots that could carry bigger crews, often including spearmen. War Chariots usually constituted the elite striking force of any army, and were supported by infantry, and later, by cavalry.

Cavalry on the rise

Toward the 8th century BCE, the use of war chariots declined as cavalry gained in popularity on the battlefield. Cavalry units were cheaper to recruit, equip, and train as well as easier to maintain. The Battle of Qarqar in the 9th century BCE is possibly the last time war chariots dominated the battlefield. Nevertheless chariots (including the infamous scythed version) appeared in battles for centuries after, and chariot racing later grew in popularity as a sport.

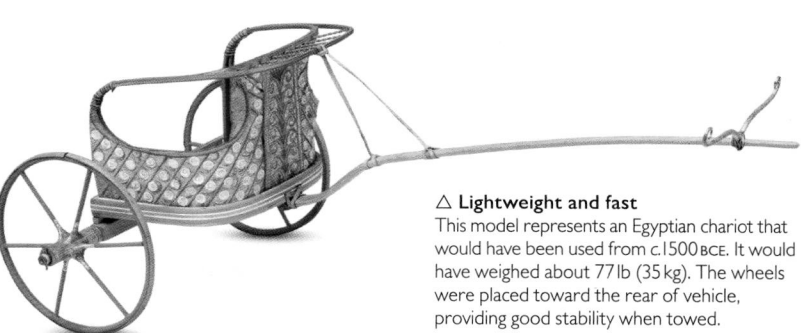

△ **Lightweight and fast**
This model represents an Egyptian chariot that would have been used from c.1500 BCE. It would have weighed about 77 lb (35 kg). The wheels were placed toward the rear of vehicle, providing good stability when towed.

The pharaoh in battle
This scene from a casket in the tomb
of Egyptian king Tutankhamun (r.1334–
1325 BCE) shows the king shooting arrows
at his enemies from his two-horse chariot.
He is accompanied by an infantry escort.

THE PERSIAN CAMPAIGN

The Persians set out to invade Greece in 492 BCE, but this expedition was abandoned after a storm destroyed their fleet. In 490 BCE, a second attempt was made under Datis and Artaphernes. The Persians sailed by a southerly route toward Eretria and Athens. Eretria was swiftly destroyed. The Persian army then re-embarked and landed at Marathon, 26 miles (42 km) northeast of Athens.

KEY

✕   Main battle

▓   Persian Empire

→   Persian fleet and army, 492 BCE

→   Persian fleet, 490 BCE

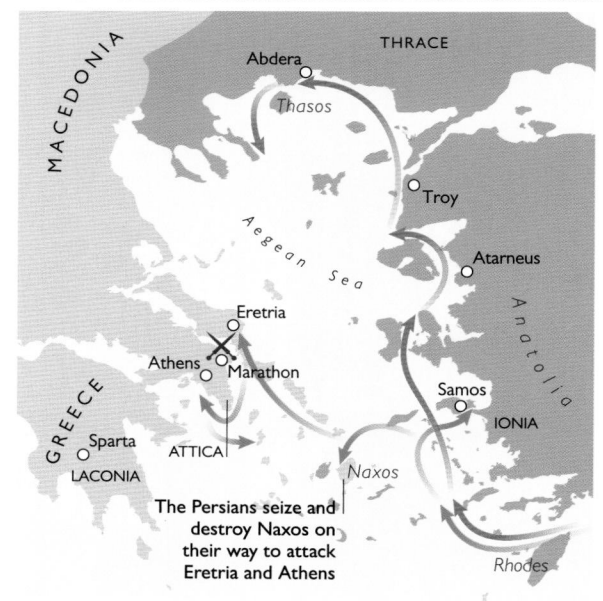

The Persians seize and destroy Naxos on their way to attack Eretria and Athens

SWIFT VICTORY

Marathon was not a large battle. Fought in a single day, it involved some 10,000 Greeks fighting 25,000 Persian troops. The victorious Greeks were hoplites, armored foot soldiers who fought at close quarters in a tight formation called the phalanx. Their tactics surprised the Persians, who preferred to fight at a distance with bows and javelins. The battle made the reputation of the Greek hoplites as fearsome infantry.

KEY

🏃   Greek troops

PERSIAN FORCES

🏰   Camp

🏃   Troops

🐎   Cavalry

🛶   Fleet

TIMELINE

SEP 12, 490 BCE	SEP 13, 490 BCE

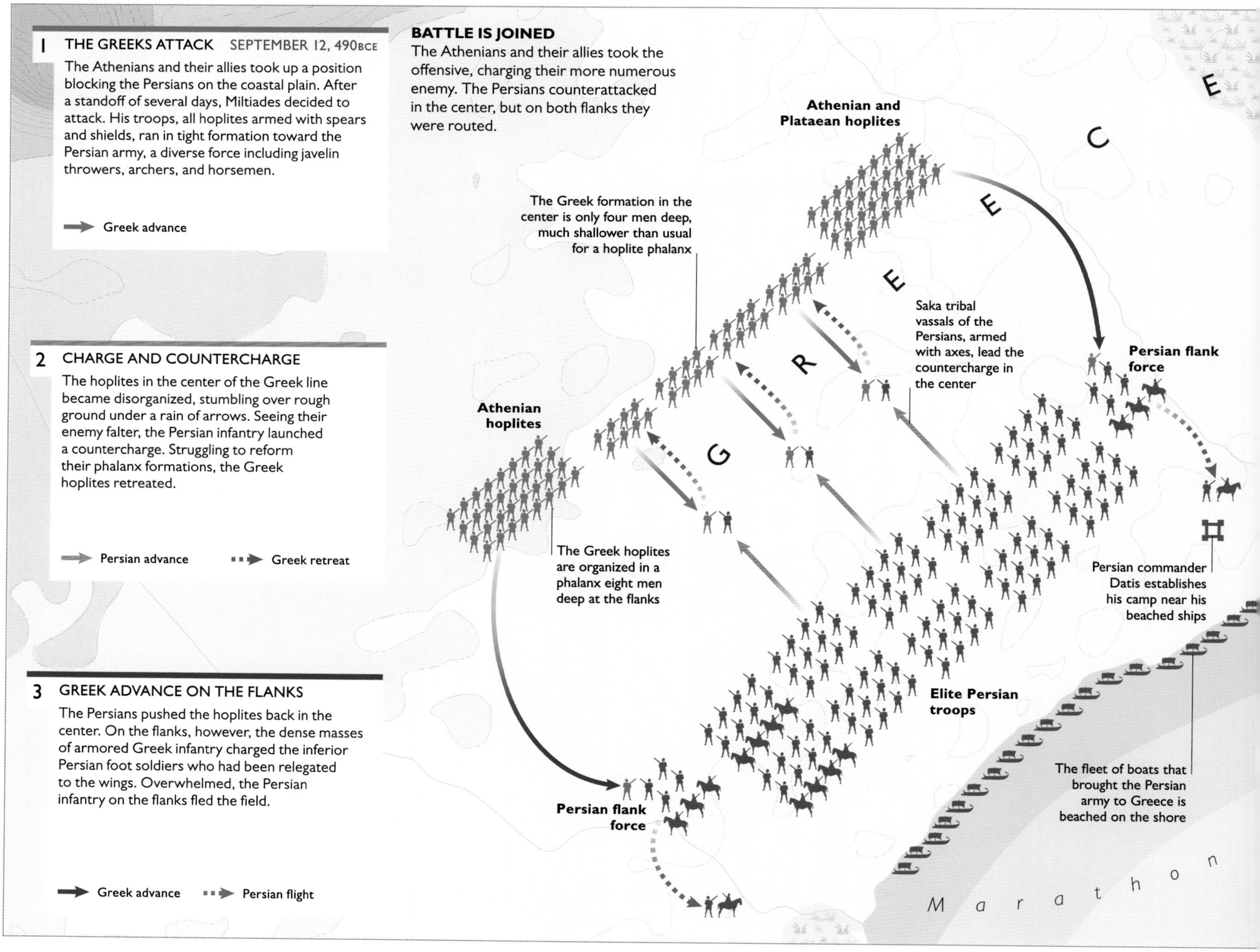

1   THE GREEKS ATTACK   SEPTEMBER 12, 490 BCE

The Athenians and their allies took up a position blocking the Persians on the coastal plain. After a standoff of several days, Miltiades decided to attack. His troops, all hoplites armed with spears and shields, ran in tight formation toward the Persian army, a diverse force including javelin throwers, archers, and horsemen.

→   Greek advance

2   CHARGE AND COUNTERCHARGE

The hoplites in the center of the Greek line became disorganized, stumbling over rough ground under a rain of arrows. Seeing their enemy falter, the Persian infantry launched a counastercharge. Struggling to reform their phalanx formations, the Greek hoplites retreated.

→   Persian advance   ▸▸▸   Greek retreat

3   GREEK ADVANCE ON THE FLANKS

The Persians pushed the hoplites back in the center. On the flanks, however, the dense masses of armored Greek infantry charged the inferior Persian foot soldiers who had been relegated to the wings. Overwhelmed, the Persian infantry on the flanks fled the field.

→   Greek advance   ▸▸▸   Persian flight

BATTLE IS JOINED

The Athenians and their allies took the offensive, charging their more numerous enemy. The Persians counterattacked in the center, but on both flanks they were routed.

Athenian and Plataean hoplites

The Greek formation in the center is only four men deep, much shallower than usual for a hoplite phalanx

Saka tribal vassals of the Persians, armed with axes, lead the countercharge in the center

Persian flank force

Athenian hoplites

The Greek hoplites are organized in a phalanx eight men deep at the flanks

Persian commander Datis establishes his camp near his beached ships

Elite Persian troops

Persian flank force

The fleet of boats that brought the Persian army to Greece is beached on the shore

Marathon

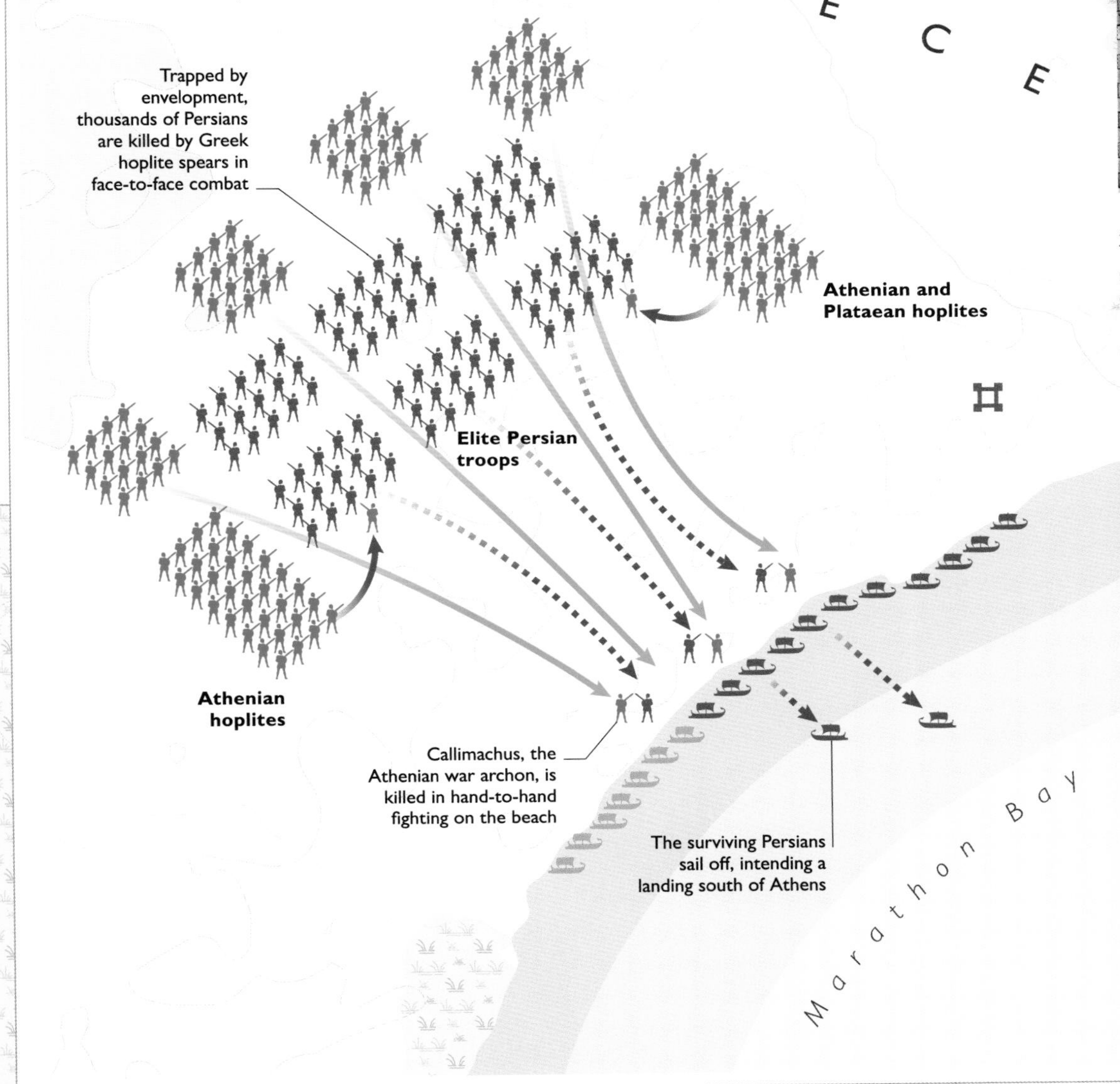

INVADERS ROUTED

With much of the Persian army trapped on a killing ground, those who could escape fled to their ships. Many drowned in the surrounding marshlands.

G R E E C E

Trapped by envelopment, thousands of Persians are killed by Greek hoplite spears in face-to-face combat

Athenian and Plataean hoplites

Elite Persian troops

Athenian hoplites

Callimachus, the Athenian war archon, is killed in hand-to-hand fighting on the beach

The surviving Persians sail off, intending a landing south of Athens

Marathon Bay

Marshland limits the usable battlefield to a plain between two streams

B a y

△ **Bodyguard of the Persian king**
This detail is from a frieze from the Palace of Darius in Susa (in modern-day Iran). At the time, Darius (r.522–486 BCE) ruled over a significant portion of the world's population.

5 THE PERSIANS DEFEATED

The Persians fled back toward their ships, which rapidly began to put to sea. There was fierce fighting on the beach with the pursuing Greeks, who seized seven Persian vessels. After the battle, the Greeks counted 6,400 Persian bodies left on the field. Greek sources claim that their own losses totaled no more than 200.

▪▪▪▶ Persian retreat ⟶ Greek pursuit

Persian ships seized by Greeks

4 ENVELOPMENT

The Athenian and Plataean hoplites on the wings resisted pursuing the routed Persian infantry, instead turning inward and attacking the exposed flanks of the Persian troops who had advanced against the Greek center. Threatened with envelopment, the Persians found themselves engaged in a close-quarters struggle for survival.

➡ Greek hoplites turn in

MARATHON

In 490 BCE, an army sent by Persian emperor Darius I invaded mainland Greece, going ashore at Marathon. Despite being heavily outnumbered, the soldiers of the Greek city-state of Athens and its allies from Plataea boldly engaged the Persian invasion force.

In the early 5th century BCE, the expanding Persian Achaemenid Empire controlled a vast area from Northern India to southeast Europe, and included among its subjects Ionian Greeks in western Anatolia (present-day western Turkey). The Greek city-states of Athens and Eretria supported an Ionian revolt against Persian rule that was crushed by Emperor Darius I in 494 BCE. It was Darius's resolve to punish the Athenians and Eretrians that motivated the Persian invasion of Greece in 490 BCE.

When the seaborne Persian army landed at Marathon, the Athenians marched out under leaders including Miltiades to confront the invaders at their landing ground. The Spartans,

the most militaristic of the Greeks, were urged to join the war but insisted they could not come immediately because they were engaged in sacred ceremonies. Only the small city of Plataea at the last moment sent troops to aid Athens.

The battle is known chiefly through the account of the Greek historian Herodotus, in which many details are obscure and some mythologized. News of the Greek victory is said to have been carried to Athens by the messenger Pheidippides, who ran 26 miles (42 km), giving the name to the modern marathon. A setback rather than a disaster for the Persians, the defeat delayed a full-scale invasion of Greece for another ten years.

THERMOPYLAE

Celebrated for acts of heroism and self-sacrifice, Thermopylae was a delaying action fought in Greece by a small body of Spartan-led Greek hoplites against a vast invading army of the Persian Empire. The Spartans held a mountain pass for three days against superior forces before being betrayed and overwhelmed.

In 480 BCE, the Persian Empire resumed its bid to conquer Greece, having temporarily abandoned its attempt ten years earlier, after the defeat of Darius I at the Battle of Marathon (see pp.18–19). Xerxes I (r. 486-465 BCE), his son and successor, led an army from Asia into Europe across the Hellespont (the Dardenelles Strait, in modern-day Turkey) on a bridge of boats, and advanced down the Greek coast accompanied by a large offshore fleet (see p.22). The Greek city-states, usually divided, agreed to cooperate in the face of this common threat. The city of Sparta sent 300 hoplites northward under King Leonidas to block the Persian advance, and other city-states sent contingents to join the Spartans. An army of about 7,000 Greeks took

a position in the Thermopylae pass, a narrow stretch of land between Mount Kallidromo and the sea on the east coast of central Greece. The Persian army they faced was huge; exact figures are unknown, but it is thought the army numbered more than 100,000 men.

Whether the fighting at Thermopylae significantly delayed the progress of the Persian invasion is open for debate. After the conflict, the Persian army occupied Athens and was overcome only when the naval defeat at Salamis (see pp.22–23) forced some of it to withdraw, with the remainder defeated at Plataea the following year. However, Thermopylae has legendary status in Greece as well as in wider European culture, where it became a symbol of supposed European moral superiority.

> "Eat your breakfast as if you are to eat your dinner in the other world."
>
> LEONIDAS OF SPARTA TO HIS MEN ON THE EVE OF BATTLE

SPARTAN HOPLITES

In ancient Greece, Sparta was the only city-state with full-time soldiers. Male Spartan citizens dedicated their lives to training for war, following an austere regime of exercise and military drills, while civilian work was carried out by slaves. Other Greeks, whose soldiers were part-time militia, were in awe of the abilities of the Spartan warriors. Their hardiness and discipline, as demonstrated at Thermopylae, made Sparta the dominant Greek city-state in land warfare, as Athens was at sea.

5th-century BCE drinking cup showing a hoplite fighting a Persian

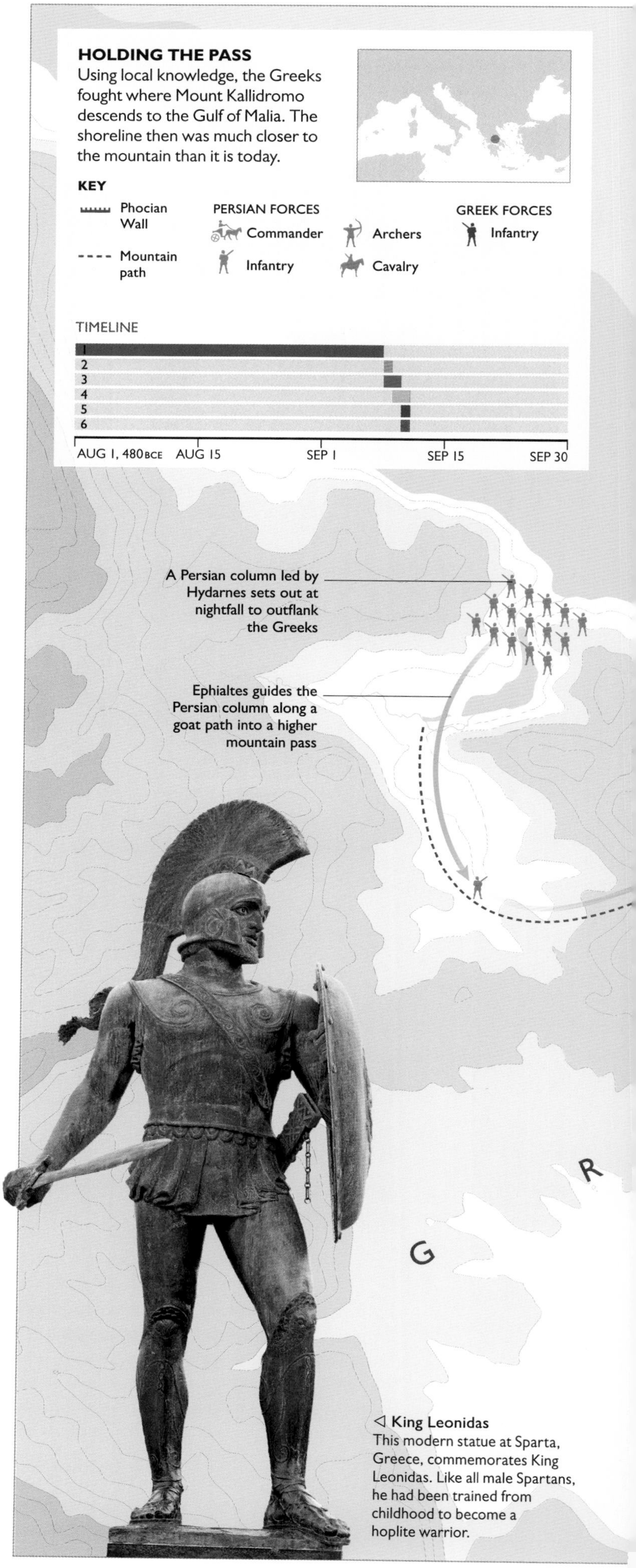

HOLDING THE PASS

Using local knowledge, the Greeks fought where Mount Kallidromo descends to the Gulf of Malia. The shoreline then was much closer to the mountain than it is today.

KEY

⎍⎍⎍ Phocian Wall	**PERSIAN FORCES**	**GREEK FORCES**
	🏇 Commander 🏹 Archers	🛡 Infantry
---- Mountain path	🛡 Infantry 🐎 Cavalry	

TIMELINE

1	2	3	4	5	6

AUG 1, 480 BCE   AUG 15   SEP 1   SEP 15   SEP 30

A Persian column led by Hydarnes sets out at nightfall to outflank the Greeks

Ephialtes guides the Persian column along a goat path into a higher mountain pass

◁ **King Leonidas**
This modern statue at Sparta, Greece, commemorates King Leonidas. Like all male Spartans, he had been trained from childhood to become a hoplite warrior.

1 PREPARING FOR BATTLE
AUGUST–EARLY SEPTEMBER 480 BCE

Knowing they would be heavily outnumbered by the Persians, the Greeks took up position at the narrowest point in the Thermopylae pass, the Middle Gate, where only a limited number of soldiers from either side would be able to engage at any one time. Nonetheless, when they saw the Persian army arrive, many of the Greek commanders argued for withdrawal.

→ Greeks take up position

2 OPENING CLASHES SEPTEMBER 8

After a four-day delay, Xerxes launched his army in a frontal attack. Thousands of archers delivered an opening barrage, which had little impact on the armored hoplites. Then Xerxes' infantry, the Medes and Cissians, swarmed forward but were slaughtered by the Greeks, drawn up in phalanx formation in front of the Phocian Wall. Reluctantly, Xerxes resolved to commit the Immortals, his crack troops, to the battle in the pass.

→ Persian advance   ⇢ Persian barrage

3 FIGHTING TO A STANDSTILL
SEPTEMBER 8–9

The 10,000 Persian Immortals attacked in waves. Leonidas rotated his troops, successively placing contingents from different cities in the frontline. At moments he staged fake retreats, drawing the Persians forward so the Greeks could punish them with counterattacks. Xerxes assumed that he must be wearing down Greek resistance, but renewed Persian attacks the following day were again repulsed with heavy losses.

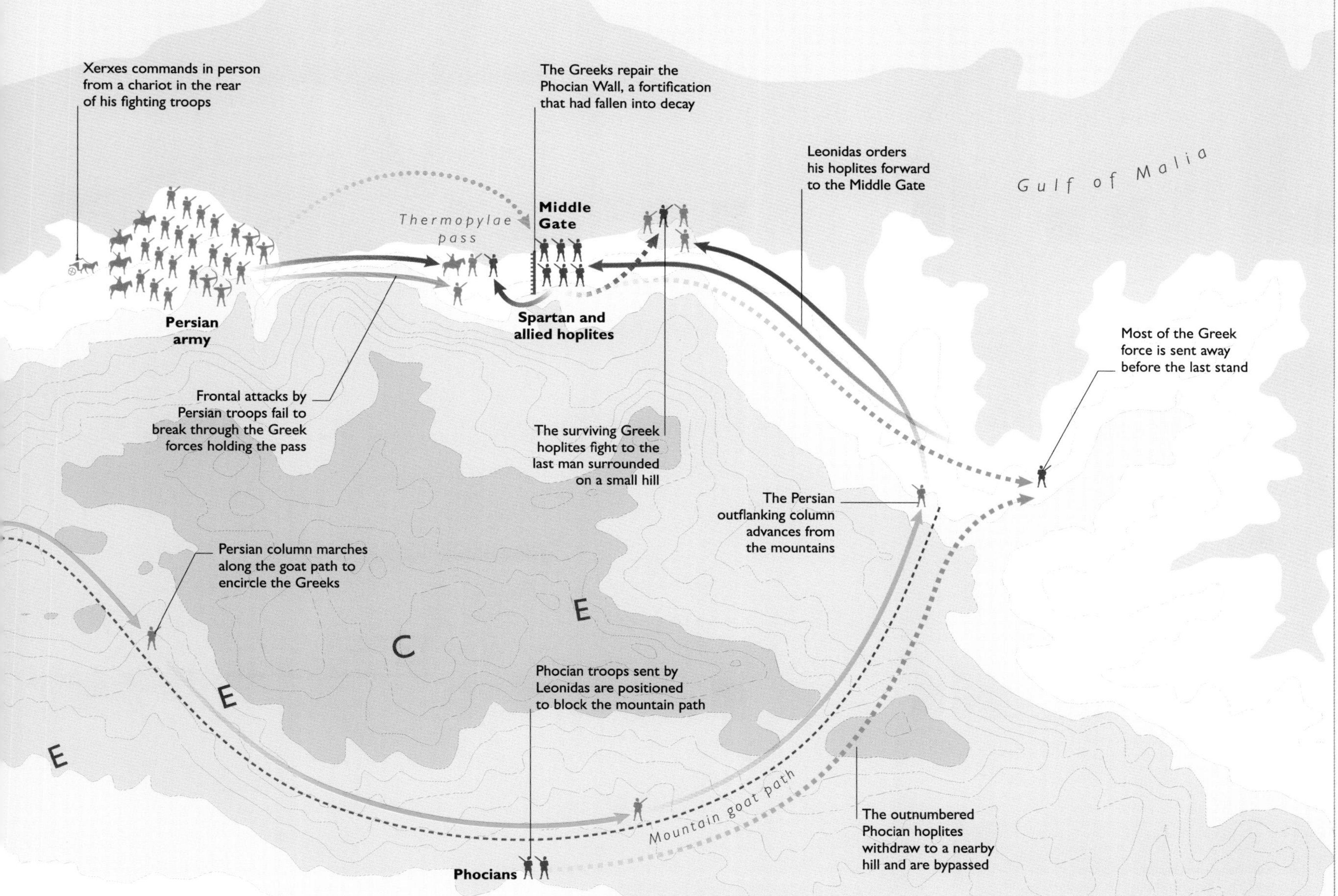

Xerxes commands in person from a chariot in the rear of his fighting troops

The Greeks repair the Phocian Wall, a fortification that had fallen into decay

Leonidas orders his hoplites forward to the Middle Gate

Gulf of Malia

Thermopylae pass

Middle Gate

Persian army

Spartan and allied hoplites

Frontal attacks by Persian troops fail to break through the Greek forces holding the pass

The surviving Greek hoplites fight to the last man surrounded on a small hill

Most of the Greek force is sent away before the last stand

The Persian outflanking column advances from the mountains

Persian column marches along the goat path to encircle the Greeks

G R E E C E

Phocian troops sent by Leonidas are positioned to block the mountain path

The outnumbered Phocian hoplites withdraw to a nearby hill and are bypassed

Mountain goat path

Phocians

6 LAST STAND AND AFTERMATH
SEPTEMBER 10

The surviving Spartans and Thespians carried Leonidas' body to a hill behind the Phocian Wall, where they fought to the death against the Persians. Only the Thebans surrendered. When the fighting was over, Xerxes had Leonidas' corpse decapitated and crucified as revenge for the losses he had inflicted. The Phocian Wall was dismantled and the Persian army continued their advance.

⇢ Spartans' and Thespians' last stand

5 DEATH OF LEONIDAS SEPTEMBER 10

Informed of the Persian outflanking move, Leonidas knew the battle was lost. Ordering most of his army to withdraw, he remained at the pass with his 300 Spartans, supported by 700 Thespians and 400 Thebans, to cover the retreat. At dawn he led his men out to meet the Persians on open ground. As Xerxes sent forward his cavalry and light infantry, Leonidas was killed by an arrow.

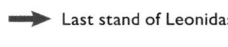

⇢ Main Greek force withdrawal   → Last stand of Leonidas

→ Persian attacks

4 THE GREEKS BETRAYED SEPTEMBER 9–10

The betrayal of the Greeks by a local man called Ephialtes gave Xerxes new hope. Ephialtes offered to guide the Persians along a goat path through the mountains leading to the rear of the Greek position. The Spartan King Leonidas had positioned 1,000 Phocian troops to defend it. Faced with 20,000 Persian infantry, however, the Phocians decided not to engage, and later withdrew.

→ Route of Persian outflanking maneuver   ⇢ Phocian retreat

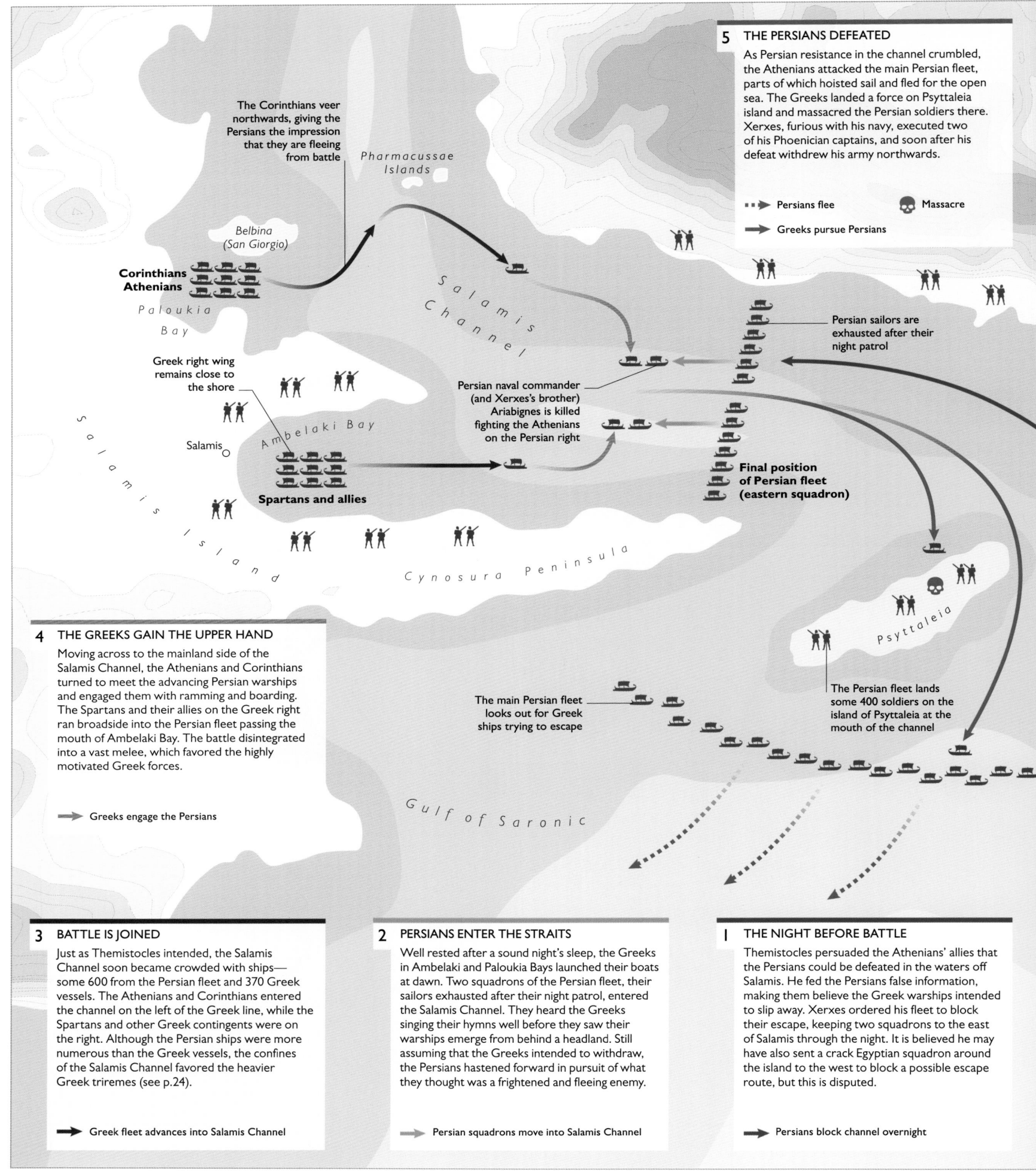

The Corinthians veer northwards, giving the Persians the impression that they are fleeing from battle

Pharmacussae Islands

Belbina (San Giorgio)

Corinthians
Athenians

Paloukia Bay

Salamis Channel

Greek right wing remains close to the shore

Ambelaki Bay

Salamis

Persian naval commander (and Xerxes's brother) Ariabignes is killed fighting the Athenians on the Persian right

Persian sailors are exhausted after their night patrol

Spartans and allies

Salamis Island

Cynosura Peninsula

Final position of Persian fleet (eastern squadron)

5 THE PERSIANS DEFEATED

As Persian resistance in the channel crumbled, the Athenians attacked the main Persian fleet, parts of which hoisted sail and fled for the open sea. The Greeks landed a force on Psyttaleia island and massacred the Persian soldiers there. Xerxes, furious with his navy, executed two of his Phoenician captains, and soon after his defeat withdrew his army northwards.

- ▸▸▸ Persians flee
- 💀 Massacre
- ➔ Greeks pursue Persians

The Persian fleet lands some 400 soldiers on the island of Psyttaleia at the mouth of the channel

Psyttaleia

4 THE GREEKS GAIN THE UPPER HAND

Moving across to the mainland side of the Salamis Channel, the Athenians and Corinthians turned to meet the advancing Persian warships and engaged them with ramming and boarding. The Spartans and their allies on the Greek right ran broadside into the Persian fleet passing the mouth of Ambelaki Bay. The battle disintegrated into a vast melee, which favored the highly motivated Greek forces.

➔ Greeks engage the Persians

The main Persian fleet looks out for Greek ships trying to escape

Gulf of Saronic

3 BATTLE IS JOINED

Just as Themistocles intended, the Salamis Channel soon became crowded with ships— some 600 from the Persian fleet and 370 Greek vessels. The Athenians and Corinthians entered the channel on the left of the Greek line, while the Spartans and other Greek contingents were on the right. Although the Persian ships were more numerous than the Greek vessels, the confines of the Salamis Channel favored the heavier Greek triremes (see p.24).

➔ Greek fleet advances into Salamis Channel

2 PERSIANS ENTER THE STRAITS

Well rested after a sound night's sleep, the Greeks in Ambelaki and Paloukia Bays launched their boats at dawn. Two squadrons of the Persian fleet, their sailors exhausted after their night patrol, entered the Salamis Channel. They heard the Greeks singing their hymns well before they saw their warships emerge from behind a headland. Still assuming that the Greeks intended to withdraw, the Persians hastened forward in pursuit of what they thought was a frightened and fleeing enemy.

➔ Persian squadrons move into Salamis Channel

1 THE NIGHT BEFORE BATTLE

Themistocles persuaded the Athenians' allies that the Persians could be defeated in the waters off Salamis. He fed the Persians false information, making them believe the Greek warships intended to slip away. Xerxes ordered his fleet to block their escape, keeping two squadrons to the east of Salamis through the night. It is believed he may have also sent a crack Egyptian squadron around the island to the west to block a possible escape route, but this is disputed.

➔ Persians block channel overnight

Mount
Aegaleos

Xerxes watches the action from a
vantage point on Mount Aegaleos
overlooking the strait (the exact
location is disputed)

A T T I C A

Piraeus

Initial position
of Persian fleet

SALAMIS

The huge naval battle fought off the island of Salamis in
480 BCE is considered a turning point in world history.
A decisive victory for the city-states of Greece over
the invading forces of the Persian ruler Xerxes I, it
secured the survival of Ancient Greek civilization.

△ Themistocles (c.524–459 BCE)
The great Athenian general and statesman
Themistocles had the strategic vision to
build up Greek naval capability. This led to
victory at Salamis and Greek dominance
over the Mediterranean region.

The Greek victory at Marathon in 490 BCE (see pp.18–19) had been a
dire insult to the Persian Empire. Ten years later, the Persian ruler
Xerxes led a second invasion of Greece, this time commanding much
larger land and sea forces. The Persians were able to assemble a
powerful navy from their subject peoples around the Mediterranean,
including the Phoenicians, the Egyptians, and the Ionian Greeks.
Anticipating an attack, the Greek city-states had made plans for a
joint defense, but relations between them were combative and unity
was precarious. In 482 BCE, Athens, inspired by the leadership of
Themistocles, embarked on a major shipbuilding program that
made the city the leading Greek power at sea.

Xerxes' power on land proved irresistible when he launched his
invasion in 480 BCE, but the battle at Salamis demonstrated the clear
superiority of the Athenians and their allies at sea. After the battle,
Xerxes withdrew from Greece with part of his army, leaving a
reduced force under Mardonius to complete the Persian conquest.
However, he was defeated the following year and the attempt to rule
Greece was abandoned. The following century was the golden age of
Greek civilization, centered on Athens, with high achievements in
philosophy, the arts, and political thought.

NAVAL SHOWDOWN
At Salamis, the oared galleys
of the Greek and Persian fleets
clashed in a narrow channel. The
Persians were outmaneuvered
and outfought by an enemy with
superior morale.

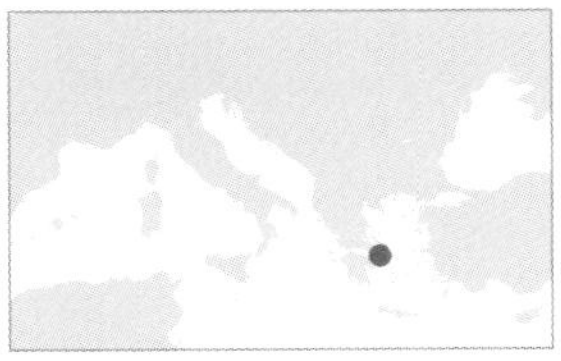

KEY
GREEKS

🏃 Land forces   ⚓ Port

🚣 Fleet

PERSIANS

🏃 Commander   🚩 Fleet

🚣 Land forces

TIMELINE

SEP 480 BCE   OCT 480 BCE

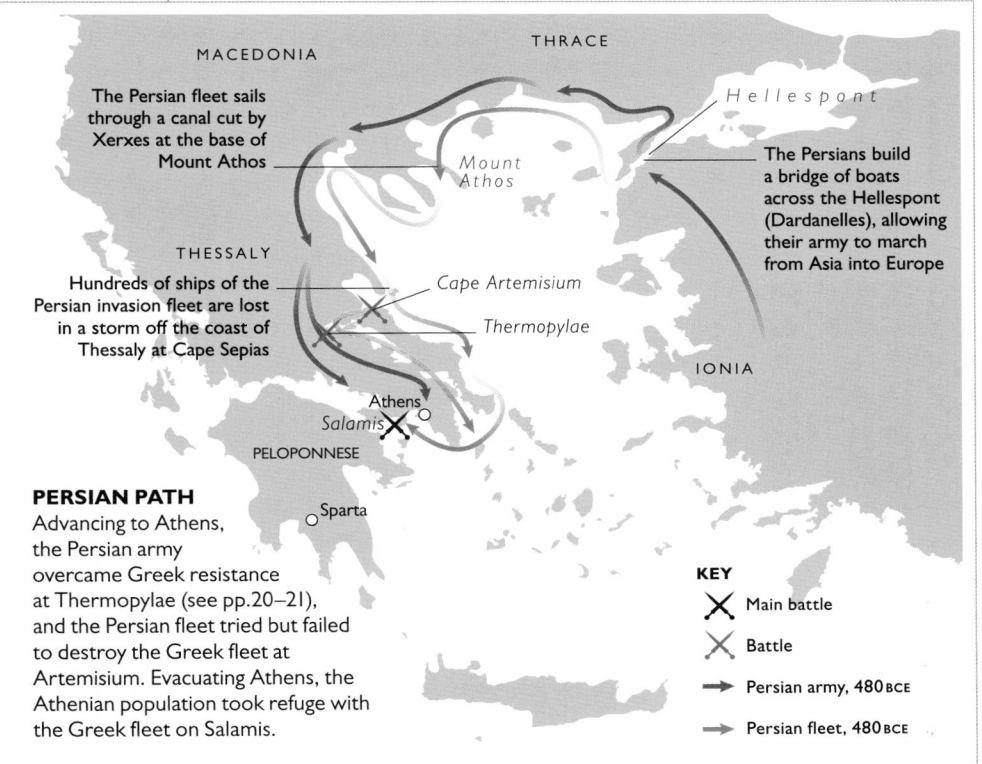

MACEDONIA   THRACE

The Persian fleet sails
through a canal cut by
Xerxes at the base of
Mount Athos

Mount
Athos

Hellespont

The Persians build
a bridge of boats
across the Hellespont
(Dardanelles), allowing
their army to march
from Asia into Europe

THESSALY

Cape Artemisium

Thermopylae

IONIA

Hundreds of ships of the
Persian invasion fleet are lost
in a storm off the coast of
Thessaly at Cape Sepias

Athens

Salamis

PELOPONNESE

PERSIAN PATH
Advancing to Athens,
the Persian army
overcame Greek resistance
at Thermopylae (see pp.20–21),
and the Persian fleet tried but failed
to destroy the Greek fleet at
Artemisium. Evacuating Athens, the
Athenian population took refuge with
the Greek fleet on Salamis.

Sparta

KEY

✕ Main battle

✕ Battle

→ Persian army, 480 BCE

→ Persian fleet, 480 BCE

ANCIENT GREEKS AT WAR

The Greek city-states of the Classical era developed a unique style of fighting, both on land and at sea. Their citizen-soldiers were widely regarded to be the finest infantry of their day, excelling in close-quarter combat.

Greek armies in the 5th and 4th centuries BCE centered around heavily armored foot soldiers known as hoplites. Wearing a bronze helmet, a cuirass (to protect the upper body), and greaves (to protect the legs), hoplites carried a large shield and used a spear as their primary weapon. Hoplites fought shoulder-to-shoulder in a phalanx, a tight formation usually eight ranks deep, with each man's shield covering the exposed side of his neighbor to the left.

△ **Hoplite helmet**
This 4th-century BCE bronze helmet would most likely have been ceremonial. It is decorated with a griffin, a mythical creature that is part-lion, part-eagle.

Often at war with one another, Greek city-states differed in military organization. In Sparta, all men underwent rigorous training from an early age, resulting in a hardened, disciplined infantry. In democratic Athens, however, military service was a part-time duty of free male citizens, and hoplites received very little formal training. Athenian citizens were expected to provide their own equipment, and those too poor to afford it volunteered to serve as oarsmen in the fleet instead. Slaves were used as light infantry skirmishers, supported by professional archers, slingers, and javelinmen.

All Greek citizen soldiers were highly motivated by attachment to their home city. When Greek cities fought one another, as in the Peloponnesian Wars (431–404 BCE), phalanx clashed with phalanx, shield to shield, in murderous close-quarter battles. The quality of Greek foot soldiers was widely appreciated and they were recruited as mercenaries by other countries, including Persia.

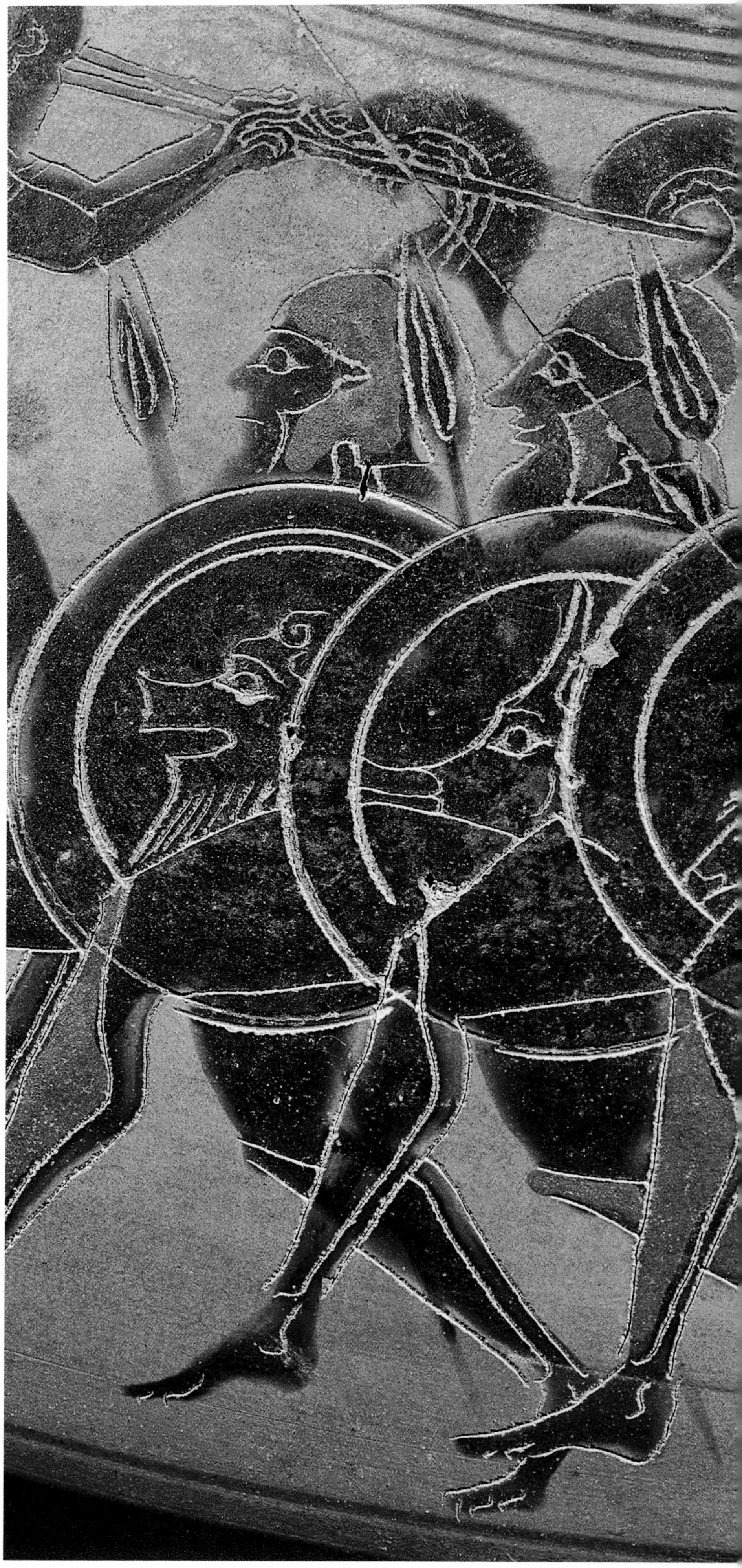

ATHENIAN TRIREMES

The Athenian trireme—shown here in a later illustration—was a swift, nimble warship rowed by about 170 oarsmen in three tiers. It carried a handful of fighting men, and mainly depended on the bronze-sheathed ram at its prow to sink enemy vessels by driving holes in them below the waterline.

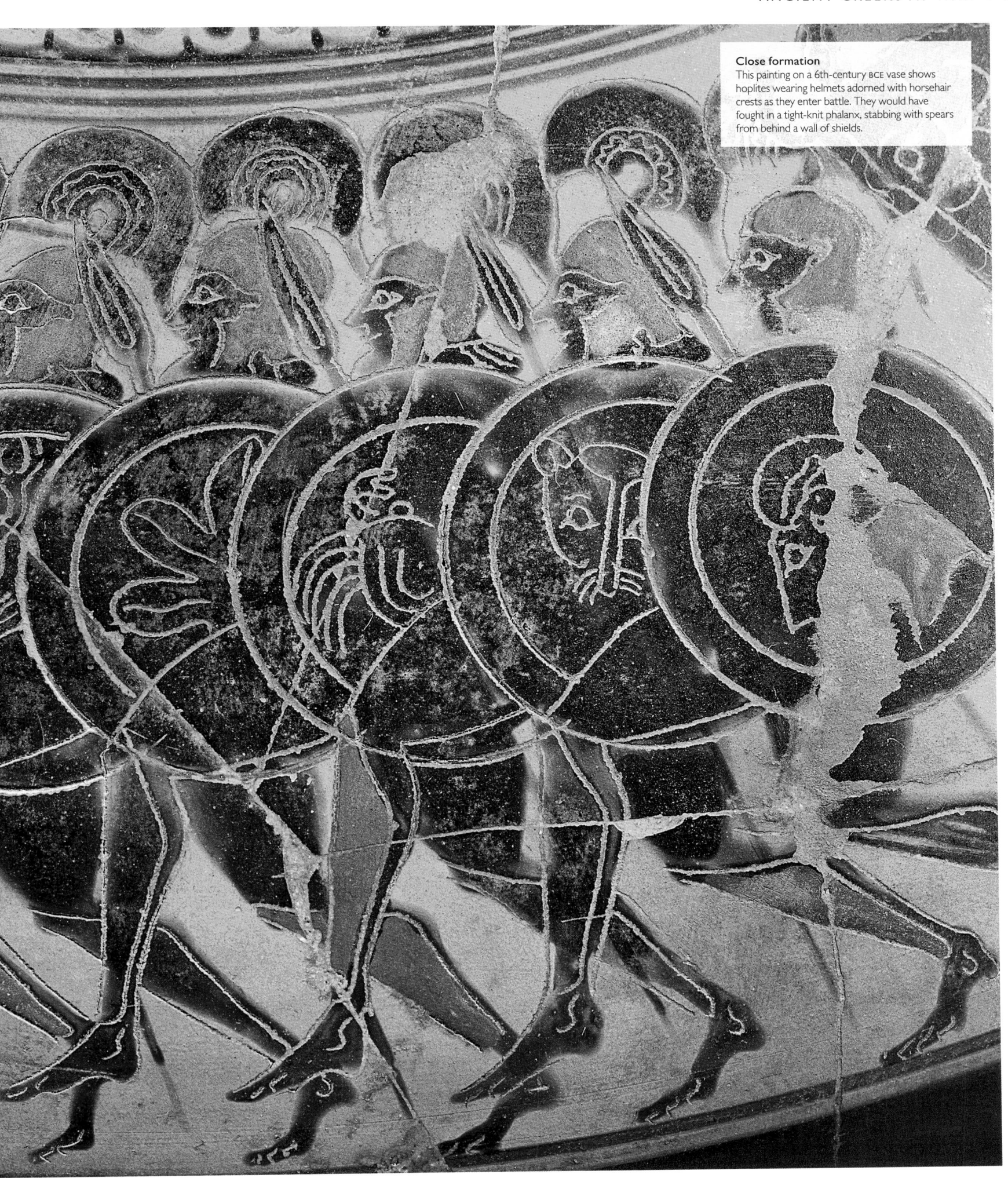

Close formation
This painting on a 6th-century BCE vase shows hoplites wearing helmets adorned with horsehair crests as they enter battle. They would have fought in a tight-knit phalanx, stabbing with spears from behind a wall of shields.

ISSUS

Fought in northern Syria in 333 BCE, the battle of Issus was a major victory for Alexander the Great over the larger forces of the Persian Empire. It allowed him to seize control of the eastern Mediterranean in preparation for an invasion of Persia itself.

In the 4th century BCE, Macedonia was a kingdom on Greece's northern border. Under King Philip II (r. 359–336 BCE), the Macedonians conquered Athens and the other city-states of Greece. Claiming leadership of the Greek world, Philip planned an attack on the Achaemenid Persian Empire, Greece's enemy. Philip's son Alexander inherited this project. Since its defeat in the Greco-Persian Wars of the 5th century BCE (see pp.18–25), the Persians had regained control of the Greek city-states of Anatolia. Alexander set out to liberate these cities and draw the Persian Great King, Darius III, into a major battle.

At the heart of Alexander's army were elite Macedonian cavalry and foot soldiers—the "Companions"—supported by horsemen from Macedonia's neighbor, Thessaly. Greeks from the city-states played a minor role—indeed, more Greeks fought in the Persian army, where they were employed as mercenary infantry. Alexander nonetheless saw himself as a crusader for the cause of Greek civilization. Instead of sating his ambitions, his victory at Issus stimulated him to envisage further ventures, which would eventually take him as far as India.

ALEXANDER OF MACEDON
356–323 BCE

Shown here in a mosaic depicting him at Issus, Alexander inherited the Macedonian throne from his father at the age of 20. He stamped his authority on the Greek city-states and pursued the conquest of the Persian Empire, which he achieved by 331 BCE. His military exploits continued in Central Asia and Northern India. He fell ill and died in Babylon at the age of 33.

> *"We of Macedon for generations past have been trained in the hard school of danger and war."*
>
> ALEXANDER THE GREAT, ADDRESSING HIS TROOPS AT ISSUS

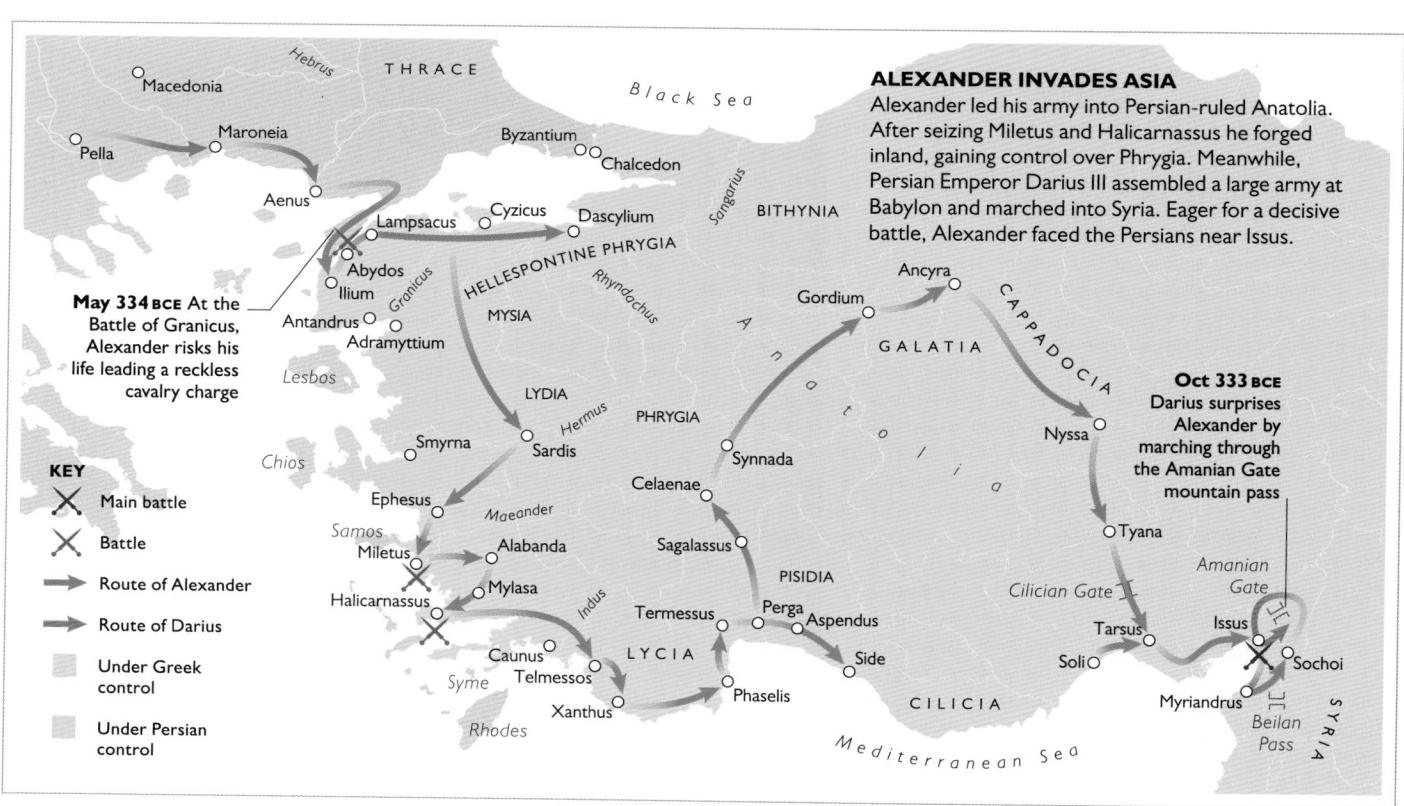

ALEXANDER INVADES ASIA
Alexander led his army into Persian-ruled Anatolia. After seizing Miletus and Halicarnassus he forged inland, gaining control over Phrygia. Meanwhile, Persian Emperor Darius III assembled a large army at Babylon and marched into Syria. Eager for a decisive battle, Alexander faced the Persians near Issus.

May 334 BCE At the Battle of Granicus, Alexander risks his life leading a reckless cavalry charge

Oct 333 BCE Darius surprises Alexander by marching through the Amanian Gate mountain pass

KEY
- ✕ Main battle
- ✕ Battle
- → Route of Alexander
- → Route of Darius
- Under Greek control
- Under Persian control

1 THE ARMIES LINE UP   NOVEMBER 5, 333 BCE

The rival armies met on a plain between the mountains and the sea, a restricted area that made it difficult for Darius to bring his superior numbers into play. The Persians took up a defensive position behind the River Pinarus, reinforced by a palisade. Darius commanded from a chariot at the rear, protected by his elite guard, the Immortals. Alexander, in contrast, led from the front, positioned at the head of his Companion cavalry on the Macedonian right.

2 BATTLE IS JOINED

Persian skirmishers tried to pass around the Macedonian right flank, but were blocked by Alexander's light infantry. Near the sea, Thessalian horsemen under Parmenion were attacked by Persian cavalry but held. The Macedonian phalanx crossed the river in the center, but became disordered and was outmatched by nimbler Greek mercenary hoplites.

→ Persian advance   → Macedonian advance

3 MACEDONIAN BREAKTHROUGH

With the battle going against him, Alexander launched a devastating charge on the Persian left. Riding at the head of his elite Companions, he shattered the Persian flank, scattering horsemen and light infantry. Turning inward, the Companion cavalry threatened to fight through to Darius himself.

→ Alexander's cavalry charge

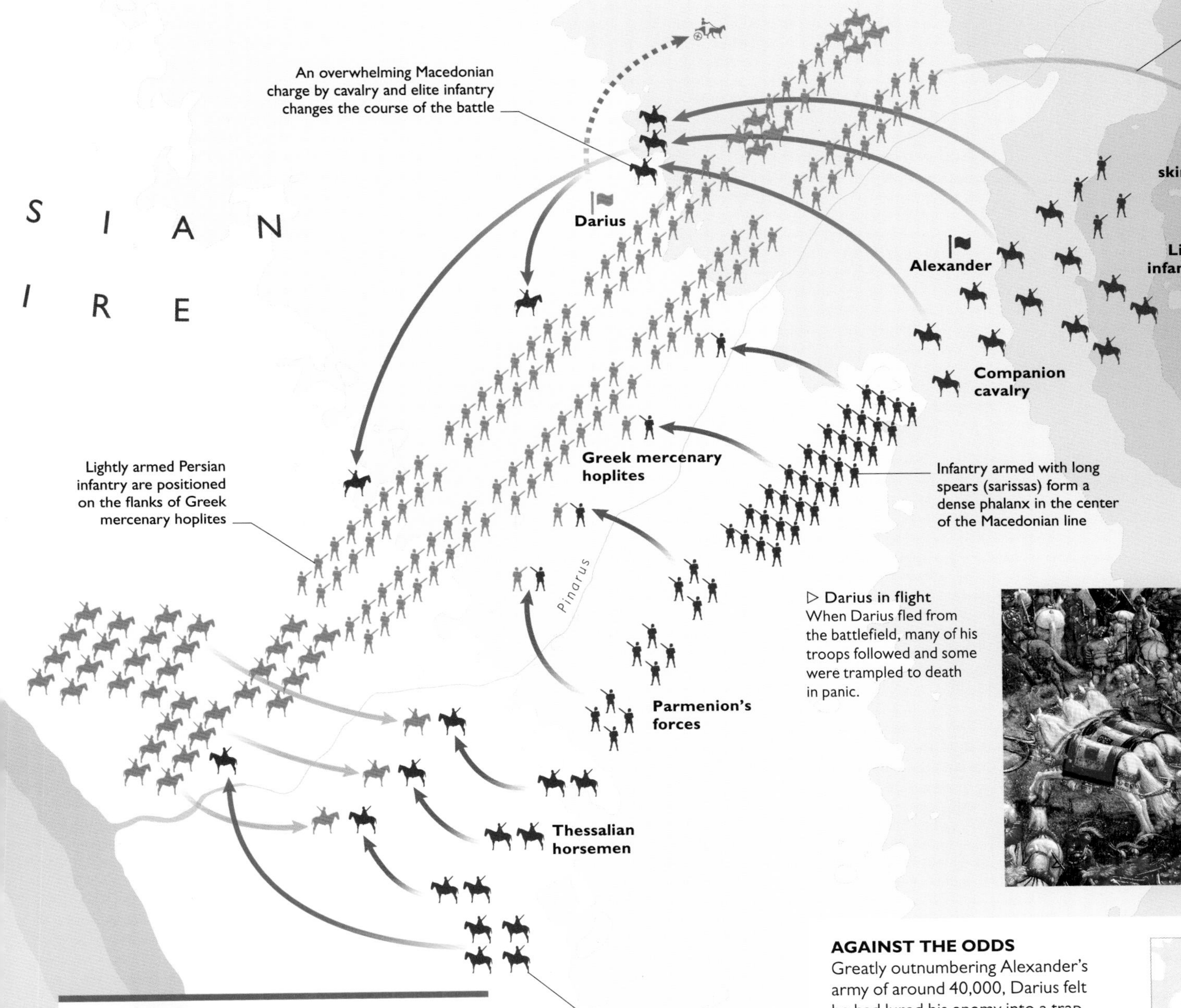

Thousands of Persian skirmishers advance through the mountains' foothills

Persian skirmishers

An overwhelming Macedonian charge by cavalry and elite infantry changes the course of the battle

Darius

Alexander

Light infantry

Companion cavalry

Lightly armed Persian infantry are positioned on the flanks of Greek mercenary hoplites

Greek mercenary hoplites

Infantry armed with long spears (sarissas) form a dense phalanx in the center of the Macedonian line

Pinarus

▷ Darius in flight
When Darius fled from the battlefield, many of his troops followed and some were trampled to death in panic.

Parmenion's forces

Thessalian horsemen

Parmenion, Alexander's second in command, controls the cavalry on the left flank

4 AFTERMATH

Parmenion's Thessalian horsemen counterattacked the Persian right flank, and the Greek mercenary hoplites found themselves surrounded. Darius fled the field and escaped eastward through the mountains, later changing from his chariot to horseback to speed his flight. Alexander was left in possession of Darius's treasure, as well as his wife and children.

→ Companion cavalry surrounds hoplites   → Thessalian cavalry counterattacks
∙∙▸ Darius flees

AGAINST THE ODDS

Greatly outnumbering Alexander's army of around 40,000, Darius felt he had lured his enemy into a trap. However, Alexander was confident that his veteran troops would carry the day.

KEY
PERSIAN FORCES
Commander   Troops   Cavalry

MACEDONIAN FORCES
Commander   Troops   Cavalry

TIMELINE

FRONTAL CONFLICT

Rejecting the option of a night attack, Alexander chose to confront the much larger Persian army in a set-piece battle on open ground. His confidence was justified.

KEY
MACEDONIAN FORCES

🏹 Infantry

🐎 Cavalry

📦 Camp and baggage train

PERSIAN FORCES

🏹 Infantry

🐎 Cavalry

🛡 Chariots

TIMELINE

SEP 29, 331 BCE   OCT 1, 331 BCE

ROUTE TO BATTLE

After his victory at Issus in 333 BCE, Alexander took the Persian-held cities of Tyre and Gaza. Occupying Egypt, he founded the new city of Alexandria as a base for Macedonian rule. In 331 BCE, he assembled an army at Tyre and marched east to meet Darius in battle at Gaugamela.

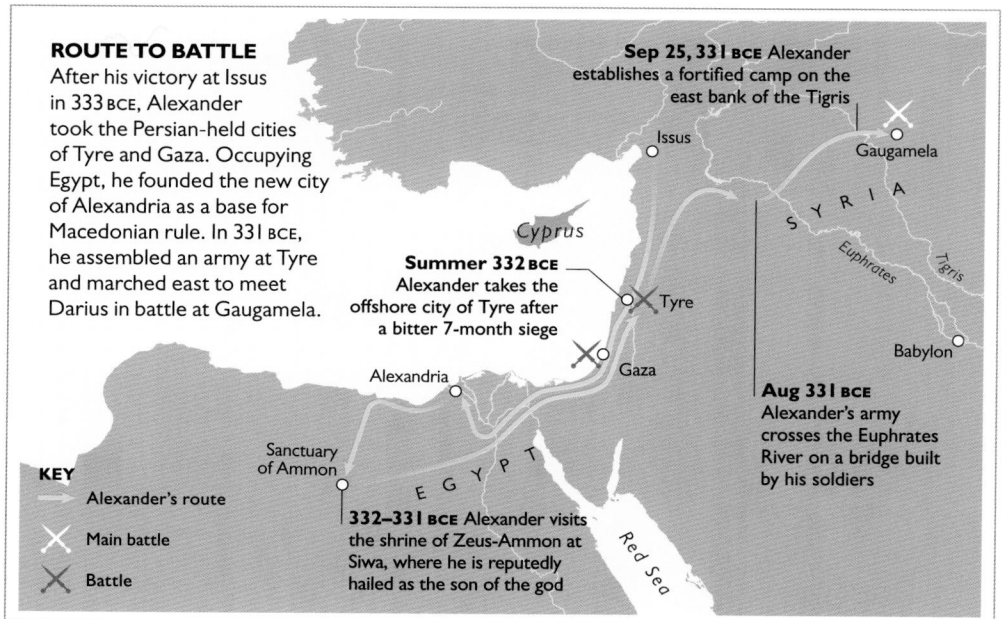

Sep 25, 331 BCE Alexander establishes a fortified camp on the east bank of the Tigris

Summer 332 BCE Alexander takes the offshore city of Tyre after a bitter 7-month siege

Aug 331 BCE Alexander's army crosses the Euphrates River on a bridge built by his soldiers

332–331 BCE Alexander visits the shrine of Zeus-Ammon at Siwa, where he is reputedly hailed as the son of the god

KEY

→ Alexander's route

✕ Main battle

✕ Battle

DARIUS ATTACKS

Before battle, Emperor Darius III had the ground cleared of rocks so he could deploy his war chariots to best effect, but Alexander's forces parried the initial chariot and cavalry onslaughts.

1   BATTLE IS JOINED
SEPTEMBER 29–OCTOBER 1, 331 BCE

Darius had drawn up his 100,000-strong forces on a broad plain as Alexander led his 47,000 men toward Gaugamela. On the morning of October 1, Alexander marched his army to meet Darius. The battle began with a charge by the Persian chariots, which were equipped with scythes on their wheels. They were repelled by Alexander's light troops armed with bows and javelins.

→ Persian chariot attack

2   FLANKING MANEUVER   OCTOBER 1

Darius ordered the Persian cavalry to outflank Alexander's forces, and instructed Bessus, the satrap of Bactria, to come around the Macedonian right wing and attack its phalanx from the back. However, Alexander's outnumbered forces resisted the Persian advance. Meanwhile, Alexander ordered his infantry, accompanied by the elite Companion cavalry, to advance on Darius's line at an oblique angle.

→ Persian cavalry advance

→ Macedonians counterattacks

→ Macedonian main advance

Parmenion's Thessalian cavalry is drawn away to the left

Parmenion

Mazaeus

Rear phalanx of auxiliaries

Phalanx

Darius's scythed chariots, as usual, fail to achieve success

Darius

Alexander places an auxiliary infantry phalanx in the rear to provide defense if his forces are outflanked and surrounded

Companion cavalry

Bessus

Alexander

Light cavalry and skirmishers bend back in the wings to defend Alexander's army against flanking Persian cavalry

Bactrian and Scythian cavalry try to pass around the right of the Macedonian line

P E R S I A N   E M P I R E

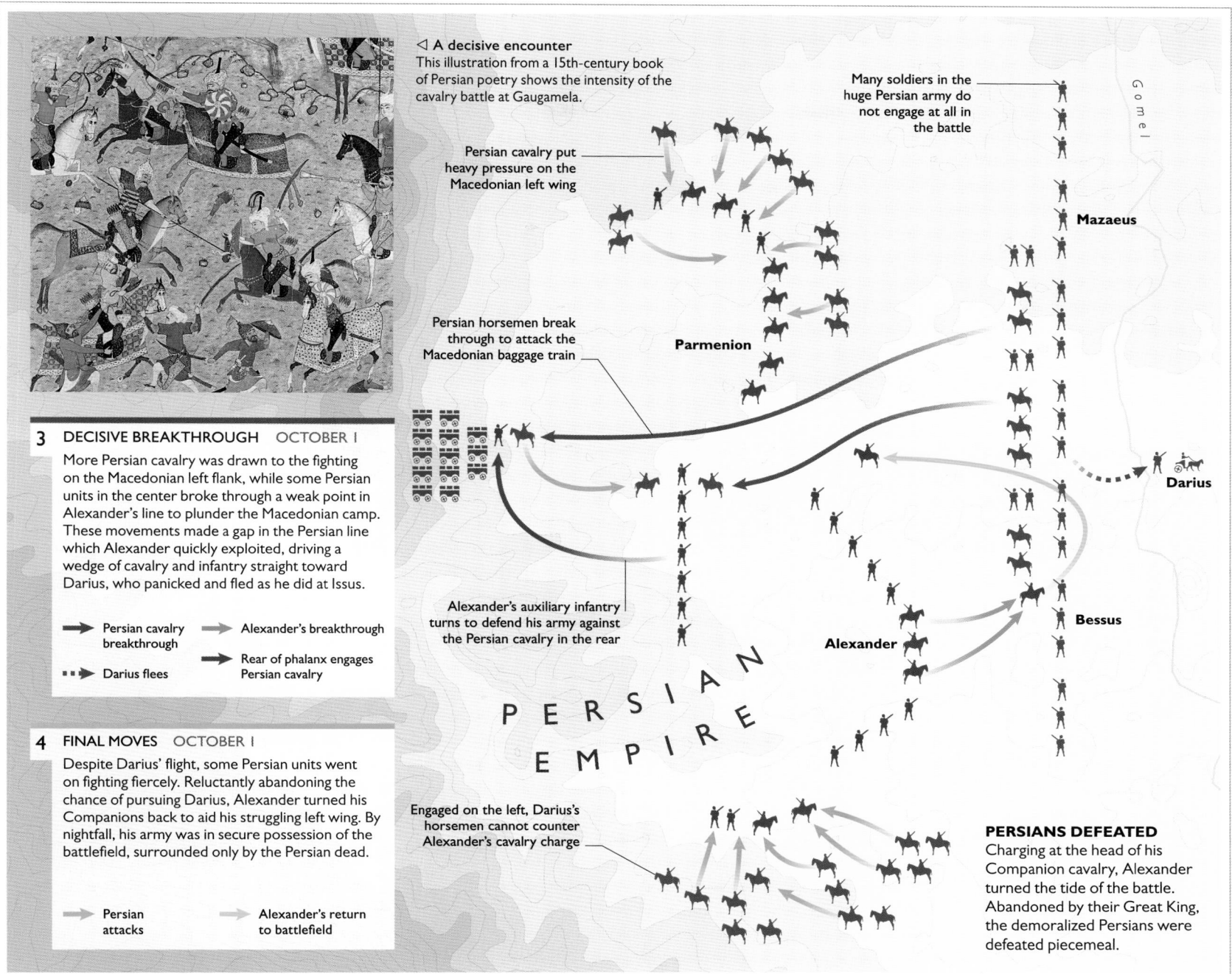

◁ **A decisive encounter**
This illustration from a 15th-century book of Persian poetry shows the intensity of the cavalry battle at Gaugamela.

Many soldiers in the huge Persian army do not engage at all in the battle

Mazaeus

Persian cavalry put heavy pressure on the Macedonian left wing

Persian horsemen break through to attack the Macedonian baggage train

Parmenion

Darius

3 DECISIVE BREAKTHROUGH   OCTOBER I

More Persian cavalry was drawn to the fighting on the Macedonian left flank, while some Persian units in the center broke through a weak point in Alexander's line to plunder the Macedonian camp. These movements made a gap in the Persian line which Alexander quickly exploited, driving a wedge of cavalry and infantry straight toward Darius, who panicked and fled as he did at Issus.

→ Persian cavalry breakthrough
⇢ Alexander's breakthrough
┅▶ Darius flees
→ Rear of phalanx engages Persian cavalry

Alexander's auxiliary infantry turns to defend his army against the Persian cavalry in the rear

Bessus

Alexander

4 FINAL MOVES   OCTOBER I

Despite Darius' flight, some Persian units went on fighting fiercely. Reluctantly abandoning the chance of pursuing Darius, Alexander turned his Companions back to aid his struggling left wing. By nightfall, his army was in secure possession of the battlefield, surrounded only by the Persian dead.

→ Persian attacks
→ Alexander's return to battlefield

PERSIAN EMPIRE

Engaged on the left, Darius's horsemen cannot counter Alexander's cavalry charge

PERSIANS DEFEATED
Charging at the head of his Companion cavalry, Alexander turned the tide of the battle. Abandoned by their Great King, the demoralized Persians were defeated piecemeal.

GAUGAMELA

The Battle of Gaugamela was a momentous victory for Macedonian conqueror Alexander the Great. Fought in 331 BCE in what is now Iraq, it completed the destruction of the powerful Achaemenid Persian Empire, which was brought under Alexander's rule.

After his defeat of the Persians at Issus in 333 BCE (see pp.26–27) and his occupation of Egypt (which had previously been conquered by the Persians), Alexander claimed to be successor to the pharaohs and became further persuaded of his own divine origins. Convinced of his superiority to the Persians in battle, he rejected generous peace offers from Emperor Darius III and sought a decisive showdown with his Persian foe. Alexander marched northeast to cross the headwaters of the Euphrates and Tigris, avoiding the predictability of the direct route along the Euphrates. Darius meanwhile raised another vast

army from all parts of his Asian domains and marched to meet Alexander. To make the most of his huge cavalry, he chose to fight on an open plain near the village of Gaugamela (in modern-day Dohuk, in Iraqi Kurdistan). He was routed. Pursuing the defeated Persian army, Alexander occupied Babylon and the ceremonial capital, Persepolis, which was destroyed by fire. After Darius was killed by his own satrap, Bessus, Alexander claimed the succession to the Persian throne, extending his empire through further campaigns into Central Asia and Northern India before his death in 323 BCE.

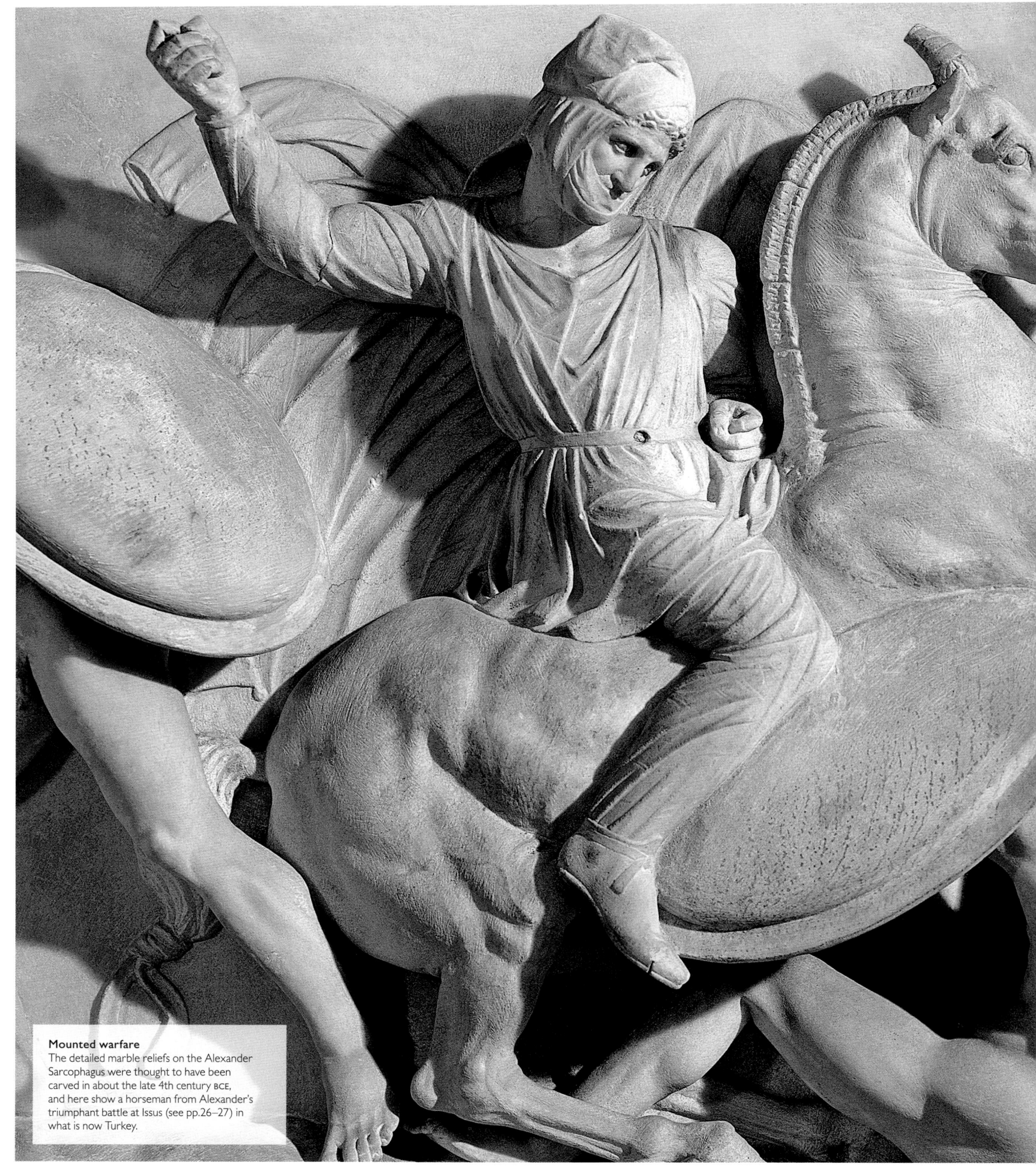

Mounted warfare
The detailed marble reliefs on the Alexander
Sarcophagus were thought to have been
carved in about the late 4th century BCE,
and here show a horseman from Alexander's
triumphant battle at Issus (see pp.26–27) in
what is now Turkey.

ALEXANDER'S ARMY

The Macedonian commander Alexander the Great (356–323 BCE) led one of the most successful armies in history, conquering the vast Persian Empire and campaigning deep into Central Asia and Northern India.

The strength of Alexander's army lay in its fusion of martial traditions from his native Macedonia with those of the Ancient Greek city-states (see pp.22–23). The Macedonians were a rough warrior people, whose horse-riding aristocracy regarded personal courage and individual prowess in battle as supreme values. From the Greeks, they learned the importance of disciplined infantry—foot soldiers fighting as a unified mass formation.

△ **Tribute to a legend**
Sculptors made many posthumous depictions of Alexander. This one dates from about two centuries after his death in 323 BCE.

Battle formation

Alexander led from the front, riding into battle at the head of his Companion cavalry, a mounted war band drawn from the Macedonian nobility. Numbering a few thousand, the Companions fought with a lance and a short, curved sword—the *kopis*. Always deployed on the right of the line—considered the place of honor—they acted as a shock attack force, charging into the heart of the enemy. Cavalry recruited from Thessaly, Macedonia's southern neighbor, rode on the left flank. The center of the battle line was occupied by trained, professional infantry in phalanxes of 256 men wielding long spears. Alexander's army also included foot soldiers with flexible roles, from the elite Macedonian *hypaspists* (shield-bearers) who were part of the right flank striking force along with the Companions, to various lightly equipped archers and skirmishers. This hybrid force, galvanized by its aggressive and charismatic leader, proved to be formidable on the battlefield.

MACEDONIAN PHALANX FORMATION

The Macedonian infantry fought in dense formations, up to 16 ranks deep and 16 wide. Each soldier in this phalanx was armed with a sarissa, a pike up to 20 ft (6 m) long, wielded with both hands. The raised sarissas of the rear ranks helped to deflect incoming arrows.

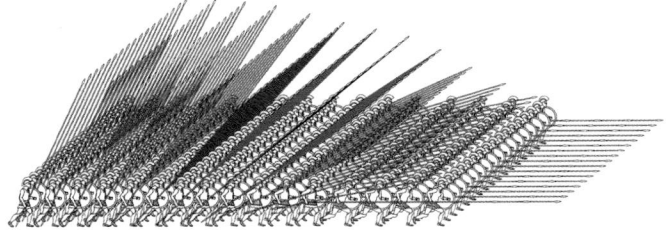

NAVAL TACTICS

Most warships of the Roman navy were cumbersome quinqueremes with three banks of oars, requiring a crew of 300 oarsmen. Armed with catapults hurling rocks or darts, each vessel carried more than 100 soldiers, whose objective was to board and capture enemy ships. The Carthaginians, better seamen in lighter quinqueremes, maneuvered to sink their opponents with the long rams at their prows.

Roman quinquereme

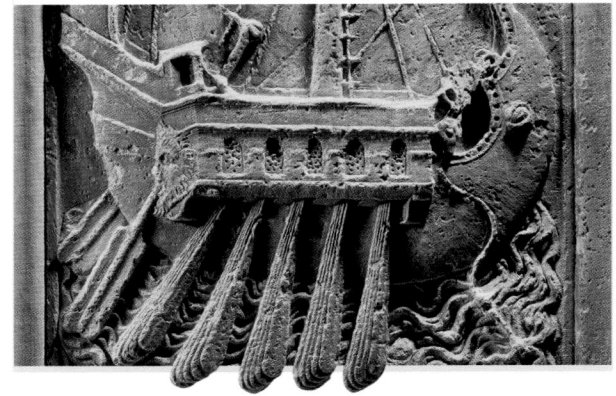

THE INVASION FORCE SETS OUT

The Roman fleet sailed from Ostia, near Rome, and embarked soldiers and horses at Phintias (Licata). Commanded by consuls Manlius Vulso and Atilius Regulus, the invasion force then set off westward along the Sicilian coast. The Carthaginian war fleet, commanded by Hamilcar and Hanno and roughly equal in number to the Romans, formed in a line blocking their path.

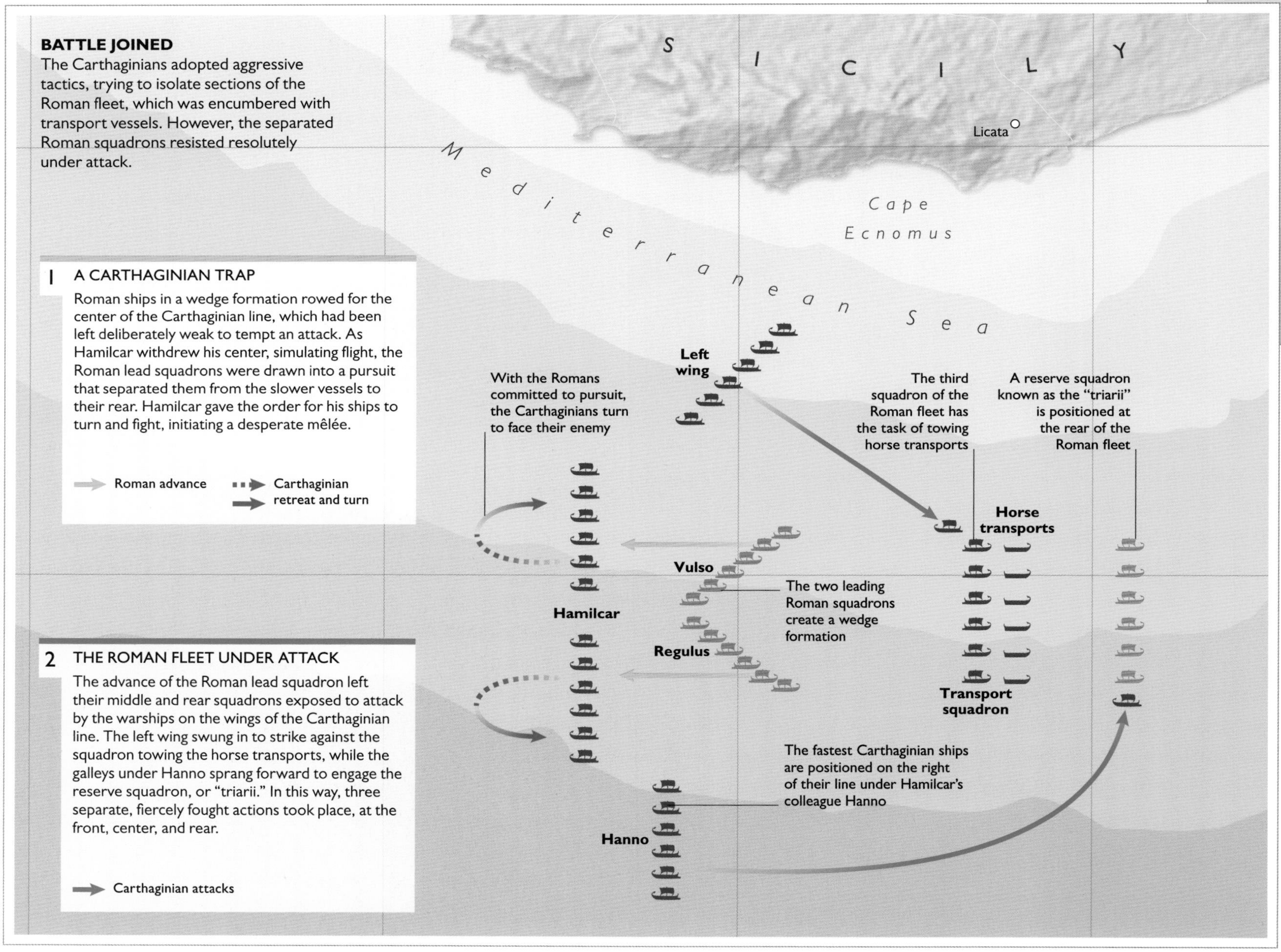

KEY

- ✕ Main battle
- → Carthaginian fleet
- → Roman fleet
- ▢ Carthaginian holdings
- ▢ Roman holdings
- ▢ Syracusan holdings

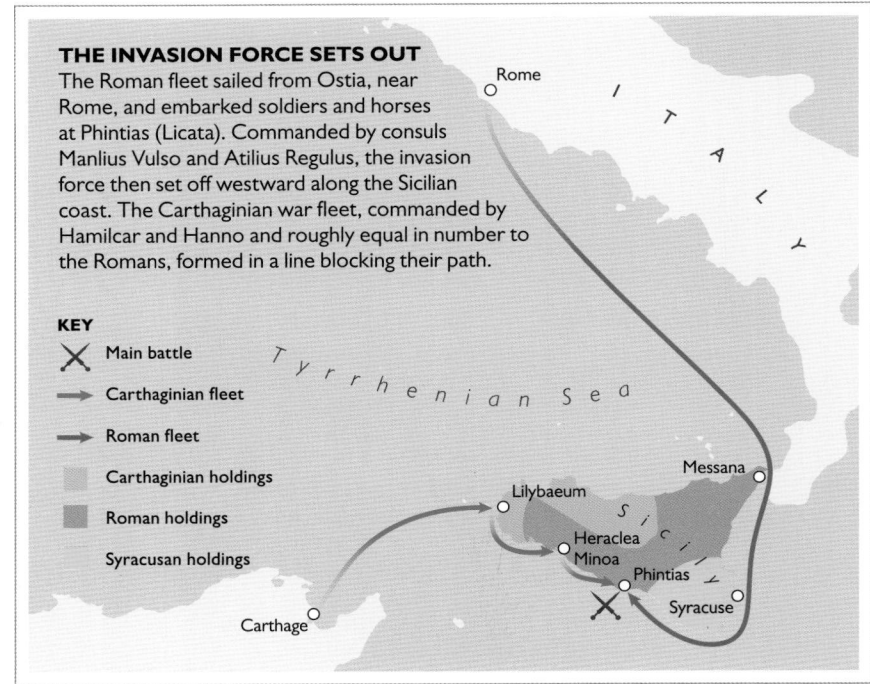

BATTLE JOINED

The Carthaginians adopted aggressive tactics, trying to isolate sections of the Roman fleet, which was encumbered with transport vessels. However, the separated Roman squadrons resisted resolutely under attack.

1 A CARTHAGINIAN TRAP

Roman ships in a wedge formation rowed for the center of the Carthaginian line, which had been left deliberately weak to tempt an attack. As Hamilcar withdrew his center, simulating flight, the Roman lead squadrons were drawn into a pursuit that separated them from the slower vessels to their rear. Hamilcar gave the order for his ships to turn and fight, initiating a desperate mêlée.

- → Roman advance
- ⇢ Carthaginian retreat and turn

2 THE ROMAN FLEET UNDER ATTACK

The advance of the Roman lead squadron left their middle and rear squadrons exposed to attack by the warships on the wings of the Carthaginian line. The left wing swung in to strike against the squadron towing the horse transports, while the galleys under Hanno sprang forward to engage the reserve squadron, or "triarii." In this way, three separate, fiercely fought actions took place, at the front, center, and rear.

- → Carthaginian attacks

With the Romans committed to pursuit, the Carthaginians turn to face their enemy

The third squadron of the Roman fleet has the task of towing horse transports

A reserve squadron known as the "triarii" is positioned at the rear of the Roman fleet

Left wing

Horse transports

Vulso

The two leading Roman squadrons create a wedge formation

Hamilcar

Regulus

Transport squadron

The fastest Carthaginian ships are positioned on the right of their line under Hamilcar's colleague Hanno

Hanno

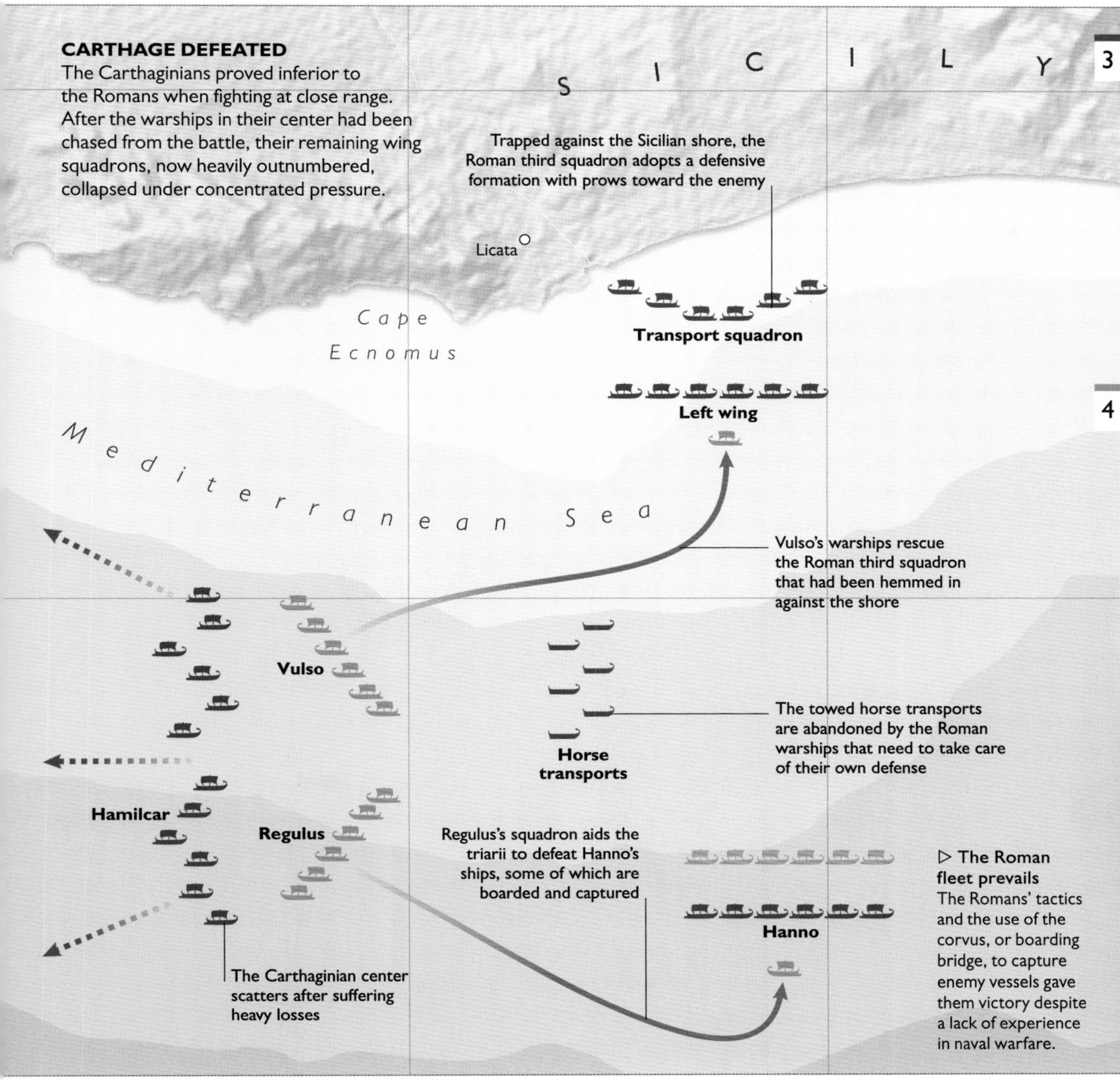

SICILY

CARTHAGE DEFEATED
The Carthaginians proved inferior to the Romans when fighting at close range. After the warships in their center had been chased from the battle, their remaining wing squadrons, now heavily outnumbered, collapsed under concentrated pressure.

Trapped against the Sicilian shore, the Roman third squadron adopts a defensive formation with prows toward the enemy

Licata

Cape Ecnomus

Mediterranean Sea

Transport squadron

Left wing

Vulso's warships rescue the Roman third squadron that had been hemmed in against the shore

Vulso

The towed horse transports are abandoned by the Roman warships that need to take care of their own defense

Horse transports

Hamilcar

Regulus

Regulus's squadron aids the triarii to defeat Hanno's ships, some of which are boarded and captured

Hanno

The Carthaginian center scatters after suffering heavy losses

3 THE ROMANS FIGHT BACK

The Roman lead squadrons won the upper hand in the mêlée provoked by Hamilcar's trap. As the warships in the center of the Carthaginian line scattered in flight, Regulus and Vulso were able to turn their ships to assist the hard-pressed squadrons behind them—the transport squadron forced back toward the Sicilian shore and the triarii battered by the ramming attacks of Hanno's skilfully rowed galleys.

- - ► Carthaginian retreat   ──► Roman attacks

4 A ROMAN VICTORY

Trapped between the Romans they were attacking and the lead squadrons under Regulus and Vulso returning from the center, the Punic fleet suffered heavy losses. In total, 64 Carthaginian warships were captured and 30 sunk, while the Romans lost 24 vessels. As the Carthaginians scattered, the Roman fleet returned to port for repair, to resume the invasion later. However, they later suffered heavy losses in storms.

▷ **The Roman fleet prevails**
The Romans' tactics and the use of the corvus, or boarding bridge, to capture enemy vessels gave them victory despite a lack of experience in naval warfare.

CAPE ECNOMUS

Fought in 256 BCE between the fleets of Carthage and the Roman Republic, Cape Ecnomus was one of the largest naval battles in history, with almost 700 ships and 300,000 men engaged. The Romans emerged victorious, winning overall command of the western Mediterranean Sea.

In the mid-3rd century BCE, the North African city of Carthage ruled an empire in the western Mediterranean based on trade and naval power. Its ascendancy was challenged by the rising Roman Republic, which had won control of Italy through the strength of its army. In the First Punic War (264–241 BCE) Carthage and Rome fought over Sicily, which had great strategic and economic value. Realizing that superiority on land would not suffice, the Romans built a navy almost from scratch. Knowing that they would never match Carthaginian

seamanship, they packed their ships with soldiers, devising a spiked wooden drawbridge known as a corvus to grapple and board enemy vessels.

In 256 BCE, with the war on Sicily stalemated, the Romans sent an army by sea to invade north Africa and attack Carthage. Attempting to block this invasion force off Cape Ecnomus, the Carthaginians suffered a crushing defeat. Although the invasion of north Africa was a failure, the Romans had won naval superiority and, as a result, were eventually able to win control of Sicily.

BATTLE FOR THE MEDITERRANEAN
At Ecnomus, the Carthaginians deployed all available naval resources to intercept the Roman force. Their defeat shifted the balance of regional power to Rome.

KEY

ROMAN				CARTHAGINIAN
Lead squadrons	Triarii	Transports		Carthaginian force

TIMELINE

256 BCE — 257 BCE

CANNAE

At the start of the Second Punic War (218–201 BCE), Carthaginian general Hannibal Barca led an army across the Alps to invade the territory of the Roman Republic. His invasion culminated in the annihilation of a Roman army at Cannae in 216 BCE, a masterpiece of battlefield tactics.

Carthage's defeat in the First Punic War (see pp.32–33) left the Roman Republic in control of Italy and Sicily; Carthage remained a major power in north Africa and southern Spain. In 221 BCE, 26-year-old Hannibal took command of the Carthaginian army in Spain and sought to avenge the defeat of his father, Hamilcar, in the First Punic War. In 219 BCE, Hannibal captured the Spanish city Saguntum, with which Rome had an alliance, prompting Rome to declare war. Hannibal led an invasion of Roman-ruled Italy, and won several battles culminating at Cannae, but

did not risk attacking Rome itself. Led by consuls including Fabius Maximus, the Romans refused to make peace and conducted a war of attrition, denying Hannibal any further battlefield triumphs. The Carthaginians remained in Italy for 15 years without a decisive battle. In 204 BCE, a Roman invasion of north Africa forced the Carthaginians to recall Hannibal's army; their defeat at Zama in 202 BCE forced Carthage into peace. Hannibal killed himself in exile in 182 BCE and Carthage was destroyed by the Romans after the Third Punic War in 149–146 BCE.

> *"Hannibal excelled as a tactician. No battle in history is a finer sample of tactics than Cannae."*
>
> THEODORE AYRAULT DODGE, US HISTORIAN, 1893

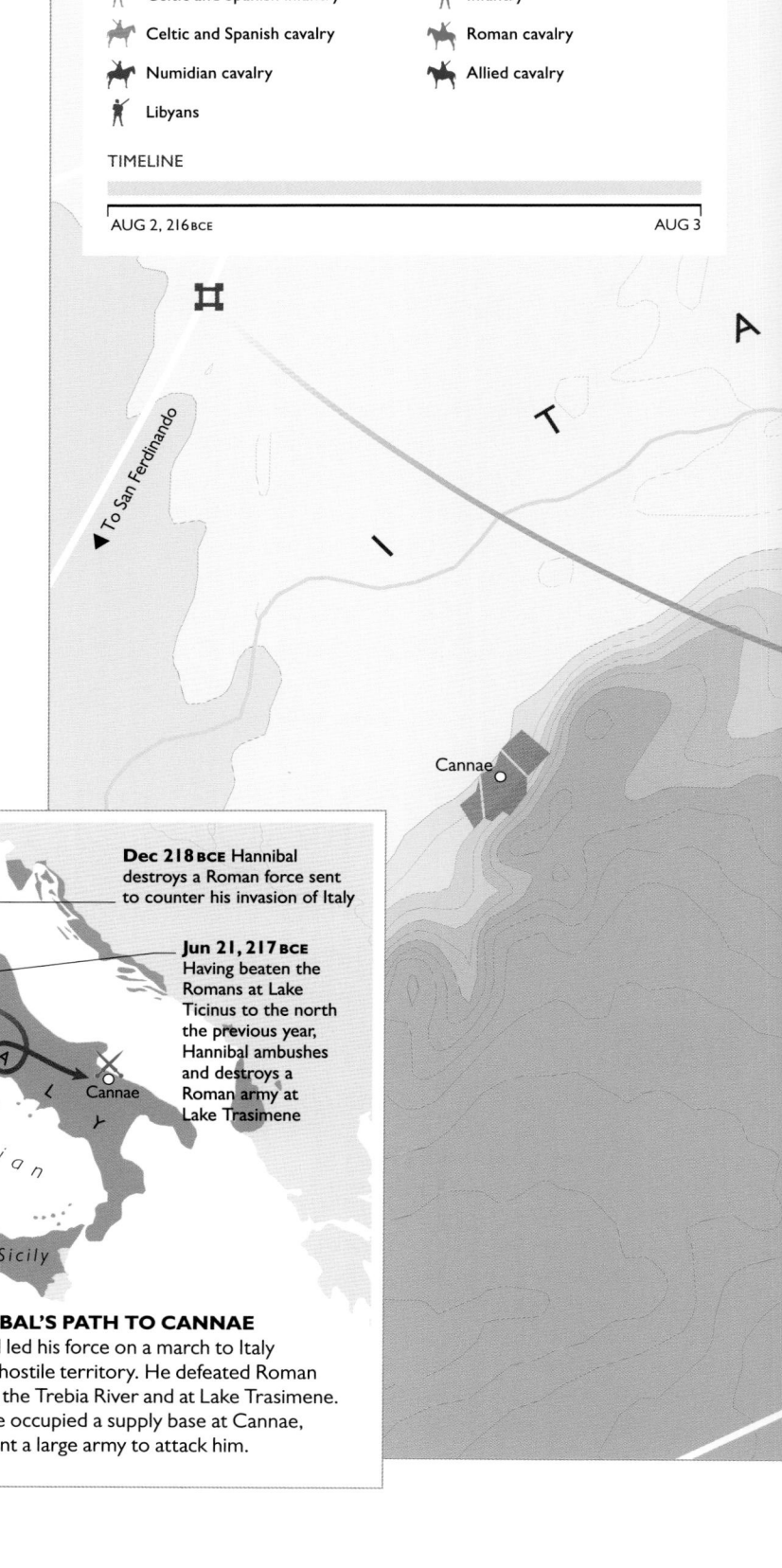

DOUBLE ENVELOPMENT

Military historians consider the battle of Cannae the classic example of a "double envelopment," the tactic in which an army outflanks both wings of its enemy's position, creating an inescapable trap.

KEY

■ Town

CARTHAGINIAN FORCES

⊞ Camp

Celtic and Spanish infantry

Celtic and Spanish cavalry

Numidian cavalry

Libyans

ROMAN FORCES

⊞ Camp

Infantry

Roman cavalry

Allied cavalry

TIMELINE

AUG 2, 216 BCE   AUG 3

To San Ferdinando

Cannae

KEY

✕ Main battle

✕ Battle

➔ Hannibal's route

▨ Carthage, 218 BCE

▨ Rome and allies, 218 BCE

Late summer 218 BCE Hannibal crosses the Rhône, fighting off Gallic tribesmen

Dec 218 BCE Hannibal destroys a Roman force sent to counter his invasion of Italy

Jun 21, 217 BCE Having beaten the Romans at Lake Ticinus to the north the previous year, Hannibal ambushes and destroys a Roman army at Lake Trasimene

Summer 218 BCE A Roman force lands at Massilia, but fails to intercept the Carthaginian army

Spring 218 BCE Hannibal sets out at the head of 90,000 infantry and 12,000 cavalry

Rhône

Massilia

Trebia

Corsica

Rome

Cannae

Ebro

Saguntum

SPAIN

New Carthage

Sardinia

Tyrrhenian Sea

Mediterranean Sea

Sicily

Carthage

AFRICA

ITALY

HANNIBAL'S PATH TO CANNAE

Hannibal led his force on a march to Italy through hostile territory. He defeated Roman forces at the Trebia River and at Lake Trasimene. When he occupied a supply base at Cannae, Rome sent a large army to attack him.

1 DEPLOYING FOR BATTLE
AUGUST 2, 216BCE

The Roman and Carthaginian armies camped on a plain alongside the River Aufidus. Early on the morning of August 2, the Romans, commanded by the consuls Aemilius Paullus and Terentius Varro, crossed the river to form a battle line in the constrained space between the river and the hills to the south. Hannibal, accepting the challenge, followed suit.

⟶ Carthaginians move into battle formation

⟶ Romans move into battle formation

2 HANNIBAL'S CRESCENT

Hannibal's force was made up of soldiers from different parts of the Carthaginian empire, including Celts, Spanish tribesmen, Numidians, and Libyans. While his cavalry was strong, his infantry was greatly outnumbered by the Romans. Hannibal arranged his infantry in a shallow crescent hoping to tempt the massed Roman infantry to attack at its center, where he had deployed his Spanish and his more expendable Celtic foot soldiers.

3 BATTLE JOINED

After some initial skirmishes, the Roman infantry pressed forward. The Celtic and Spanish center drew back, drawing the Roman infantry with them, while the heavy Libyan infantry to the left and right held its ground. Meanwhile, Hasdrubal's horsemen got the upper hand over the Roman heavy cavalry on the left flank, putting them to flight.

⟶ Roman infantry push forward

⟶ Carthaginian cavalry advance

⇢ Roman cavalry flee

⇢ Celtic and Spanish infantry draw back

4 ROMANS TRAPPED

The Roman infantry were surrounded on three sides as Hannibal's Libyan troops turned in against their flanks. As the Numidian horsemen on the right chased the Roman allied cavalry from the field, Hasdrubal's cavalry swung around to attack the Roman foot soldiers from the rear. The Roman infantry were destroyed, with few escaping.

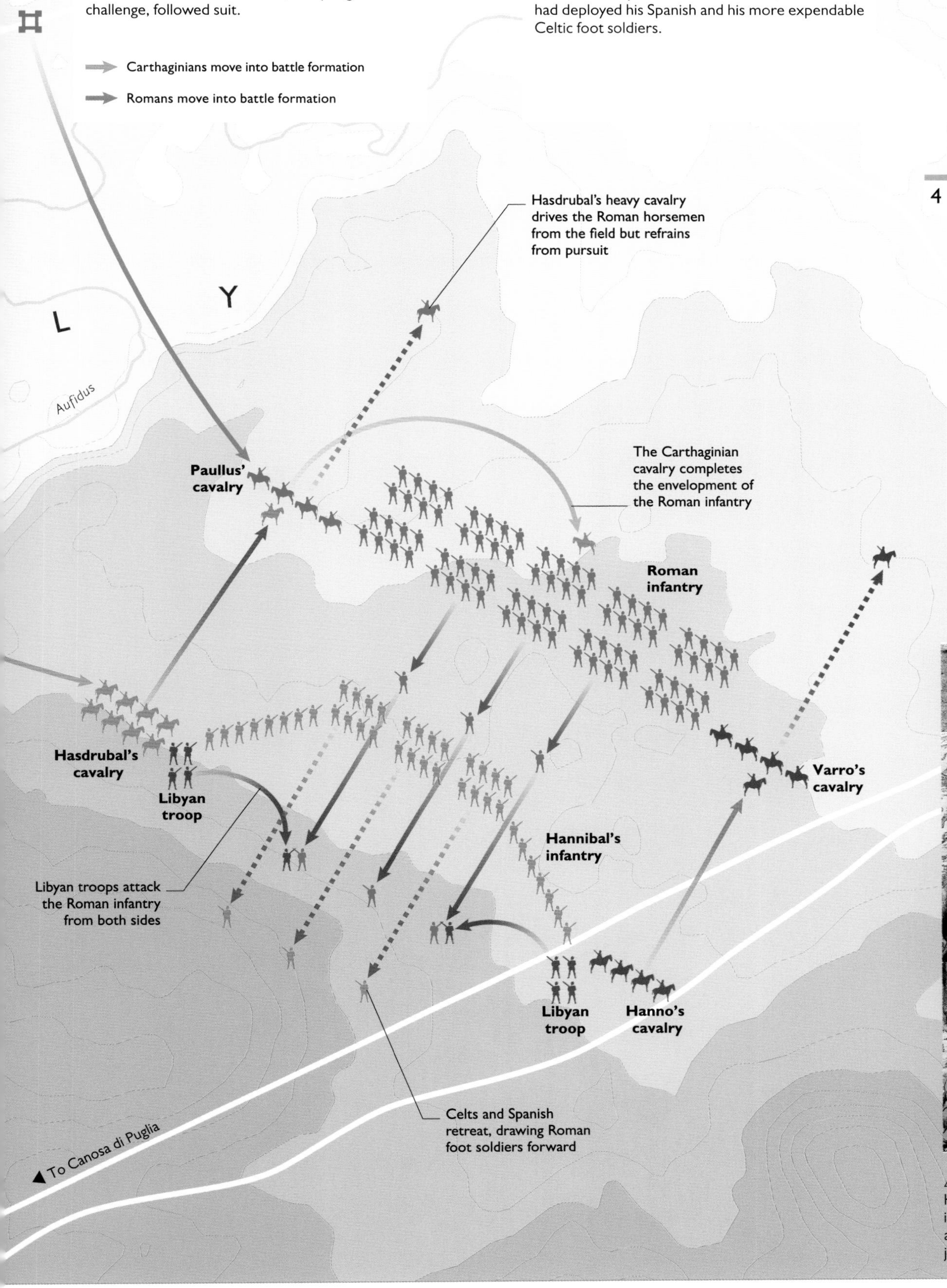

⟶ Romans push forward

⟶ Libyans push forward

⟶ Numidians push forward

⟶ Celts and Spanish push forward

⇢ Romans fall back

Hasdrubal's heavy cavalry drives the Roman horsemen from the field but refrains from pursuit

Aufidus

Paullus' cavalry

The Carthaginian cavalry completes the envelopment of the Roman infantry

Roman infantry

Hasdrubal's cavalry

Libyan troop

Varro's cavalry

Libyan troops attack the Roman infantry from both sides

Hannibal's infantry

Libyan troop

Hanno's cavalry

To Barletta ▶

Celts and Spanish retreat, drawing Roman foot soldiers forward

▲ To Canosa di Puglia

△ **Crossing the Alps**
Hannibal's epic crossing of the Alps, accompanied by his infantry, cavalry, mules, and an estimated 37 elephants, allowed him to avoid hostile land and naval forces on his journey to attack the Roman Republic.

ALESIA

The siege of Alesia in 52 BCE was the climax of Roman general Julius Caesar's campaign to conquer Gaul. Caesar encircled and destroyed an army of rebel Gallic tribesmen led by Vercingetorix, fighting off an attack by a relief force. As a result of Caesar's victory, Gaul fell under Roman domination for the following 500 years.

Covering present-day France, Belgium, Switzerland, and neighboring areas, Gaul was home to a number of Celtic tribes. Beginning in 58 BCE, Julius Caesar conquered these tribes in a series of campaigns, but his brutal treatment of the defeated provoked discontent. In the winter of 53–52 BCE, Vercingetorix, leader of the Arverni tribe, won the support of other Gallic tribes for an uprising. Caesar alleviated his supply shortage by seizing the fortified town of Avaricum, but when he attacked the Arverni capital of Gergovia, he was repelled. Vercingetorix attacked Caesar's marching army, but his cavalry were beaten back. Vercingetorix harassed the retreating Romans, but was defeated when he committed to a full-scale attack. He withdrew to a strong defensive position at the hill settlement of Alesia in eastern France.

Caesar knew, especially after Gergovia, that it would be foolish to assault the strong Gallic army in this hill position. Instead, he planned a siege to starve the Gauls. The legionaries enclosed Alesia in a 10-mile (16-km) siege line of ditches and ramparts of lumber and earth. Before it was completed, Vercingetorix dispatched horsemen to seek aid from other Gallic tribal leaders. Anticipating a counterattack from the

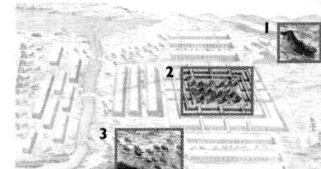
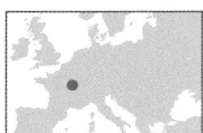

LOCATOR

rear, Caesar had a second circle of fortifications built outside the first, so his troops were defended from both sides. With forces of up to 80,000 men, the Gauls were soon short of food. To save supplies, Vercingetorix ordered the elderly, women, and children to leave. Caesar refused to allow them through Roman lines, letting them starve to death between the armies. In late September, a huge Gallic relief force arrived outside Alesia. The Romans were outnumbered, but their fortifications allowed them to repel successive Gallic assaults. The battle ended in a desperate all-out effort by the Gauls, which Caesar held off by inspiring his troops and sending his Germanic mercenary cavalry to attack from behind. The relief force was driven off and Vercingetorix surrendered.

THE FINAL BATTLE

The Gauls tried to lift the siege by coordinating a breakout attempt with an attack by the relief force outside. They identified a weak point in a Roman camp at the foot of Mount Réa. Seeing the Gauls threatening this position, Caesar led a counterattack and ordered his Germanic cavalry to strike the Gauls from the rear. The relief army dispersed in disarray.

KEY

ROMAN FORCES

⌇⌇⌇	Roman siege lines	🧍	Roman forces
⌇⌇⌇	Defensive trench	→	Caesar's movement
⊞	Roman camps	🐎	Germanic cavalry
		→	Germanic counterattack

GALLIC FORCES

⊞	Gallic relief force camp	🧍	Gallic forces
		→	Gallic advance

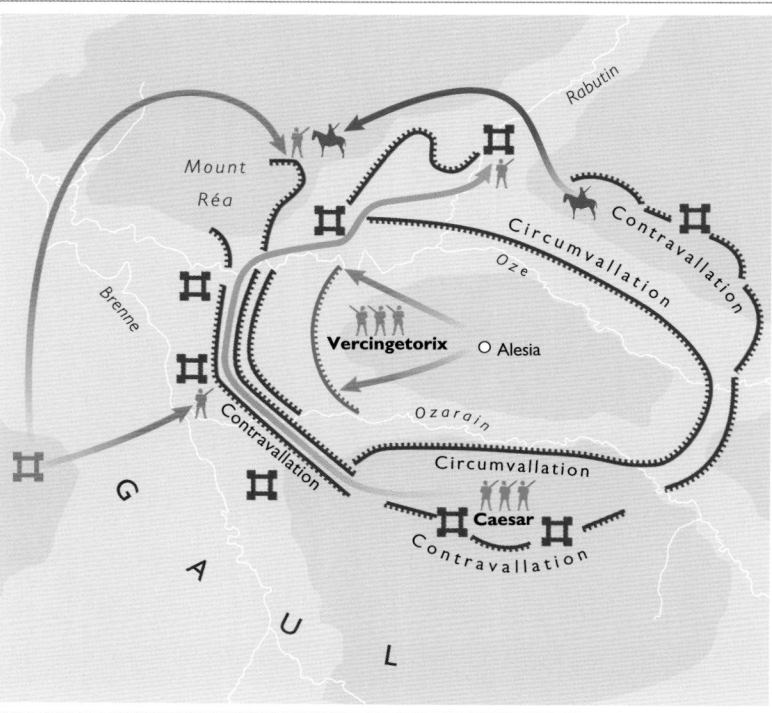

A. Infanterie de Vercingetorix de Vercingetorix divisée en tr faisant face de quatres côtes. D. l'Ennemi. E. Emplacement de la Cavalerie qui tourne la montagn

△ **The prelude to Alesia**
This 18th-century map shows an anachronistically formal portrayal of the failed attack on Caesar's marching army. The Gauls withdrew to Alesia, where they were besieged by Caesar's army.

▽ **Germanic cavalry**
Caesar made effective use of his Germanic horsemen during the campaign. Here, they prepare to counterattack the Gallic cavalry.

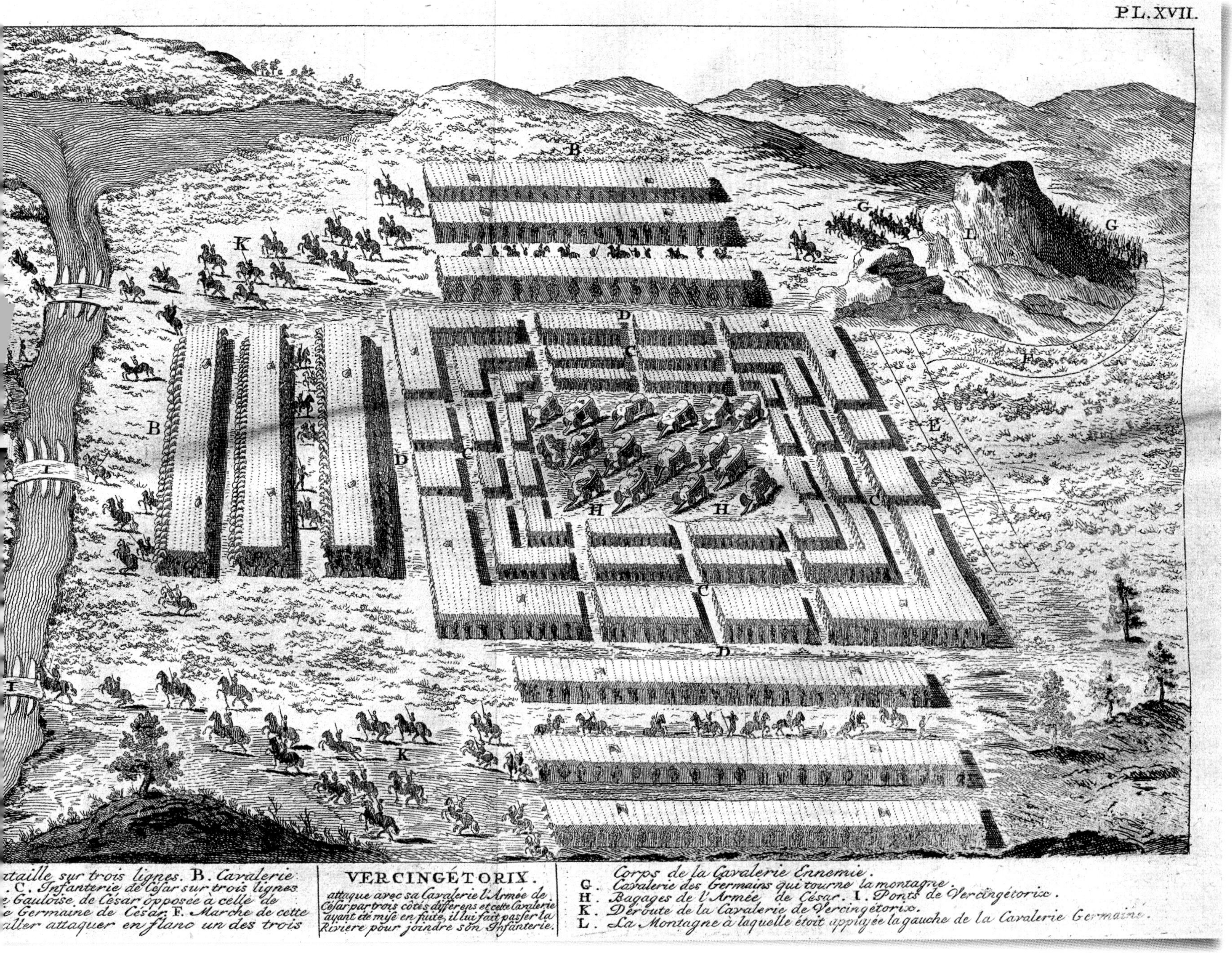

...taille sur trois lignes. B. Cavalerie
...C. Infanterie de César sur trois lignes
...Gauloise de César opposée à celle de
...Germaine de César. F. Marche de cette
...aller attaquer en flanc un des trois

VERCINGÉTORIX.

attaque avec sa Cavalerie l'Armée de
César par trois côtés differens et cette Cavalerie
ayant été mise en fuite, il lui fait passer la
Riviere pour joindre son Infanterie.

Corps de la Cavalerie Ennemie.
G. Cavalerie des Germains qui tourne la montagne
H. Bagages de l'Armée de César. I. Ponts de Vercingétorix.
K. Déroute de la Cavalerie de Vercingétorix.
L. La Montagne à laquelle étoit appuyée la gauche de la Cavalerie Germaine.

◁ **Defensive formation**
Caesar's army is shown in a defensive
square with its baggage train at the center.

△ **The Gauls flee**
Following their defeat by the Romans, the
Gallic cavalry fled back to their own lines.

Trajan's column
Erected in Rome in 113 CE to celebrate Emperor Trajan's victories on the Danube, Trajan's Column displays vivid images of life in the Roman army while on campaigns. Much of a legion's time was spent building walls, roads, and bridges.

ROMAN LEGIONS

Ancient Rome created and sustained one of the world's greatest empires through the power and efficiency of its army. Formidable in battle, Roman legionaries were also outstanding military engineers.

The Roman army was divided into legions of about 5,000 legionaries, and from the 1st century BCE became a fully professional force. Its soldiers were mostly men with Roman citizenship who signed up for 20 years of active service. Legionaries tended to come from the poorer classes, attracted by regular pay and the prospect of a grant of farmland when they retired. A legionary could rise to the rank of centurion and command 80 legionaries (a century). Each legion consisted of ten cohorts, each made up of six centuries. Legions were also supported by auxiliaries without Roman citizenship recruited from subjects of the empire. These noncitizens provided additional cavalry, supporting the legions' own 300 cavalry.

△ **Roman coin**
Augustus, the first Roman emperor, is seen above. During his reign, legionaries were paid 225 denarii a year.

Skilled force

Roman legionaries excelled as disciplined foot soldiers. Armed with two heavy javelins and a short sword, and well protected by a large shield, helmet, and cuirass, they were trained to fight flexibly in a variety of formations, and used various torsion catapults, from small "scorpions" to larger ballistae and one-armed onagers. Legionaries were not unbeatable in battle—they were especially vulnerable to mounted archers—but they were unmatched as engineers. Some of the siege works they built were remarkable in scale, including a spur and ramp to capture the mountain fortress of Masada in 73 CE. Legionaries also built most of the Roman road network as well as some great frontier fortifications, such as Hadrian's Wall in Britain.

THE *TESTUDO*

Named after the Latin word for tortoise, the *testudo* was a formation that Roman legionaries used when under attack by projectiles. Some of the men in the closely packed body raised their long shields to create a protective roof, like a tortoise's shell, while others formed a shield wall at the front and sides. The *testudo* was especially useful when facing massed enemy archers, allowing legionaries to approach the enemy through an otherwise deadly hail of arrows.

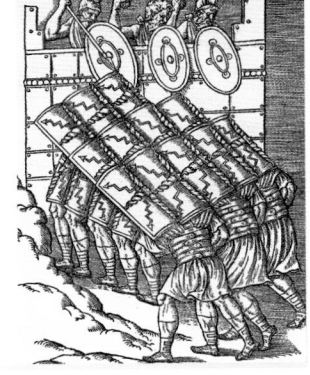

ACTIUM

The naval battle at Actium in 31 BCE was the climactic event in the struggle for power that followed the assassination of Roman dictator Julius Caesar by a group of senators in 44 BCE. At Actium, Caesar's adopted son Octavian defeated his rivals Mark Antony and Cleopatra, and was able to make himself the sole ruler of the Roman world.

In 43 BCE, Mark Antony, once Julius Caesar's most trusted general, set up a triumvirate (a political alliance) with Caesar's adopted son Octavian and the statesman Lepidus to rule over the Roman Republic. Over the following decade, this unstable arrangement was torn apart by rivalries. While Octavian held sway in Rome, Antony established a power base in the rich lands of the eastern Mediterranean, forming a political (and sexual) relationship with Egyptian ruler Cleopatra VII. In 32 BCE, Antony and Cleopatra assembled 19 legions and a large fleet at Actium, on the west coast of Greece. Antony was probably planning an invasion of Italy, but Octavian seized the initiative. The two forces confronted one another over the summer of 31 BCE, and Antony and Cleopatra finally opted for a naval battle to decide the issue, or to break out if this failed. They escaped, but their fates were sealed. The eastern Mediterranean fell to Octavian's forces, and in 30 BCE both Antony and Cleopatra committed suicide. Egypt came under Roman rule, and three years later Octavian was recognized as sole ruler of Rome.

THREATENED FROM LAND AND SEA

Antony and Cleopatra established their army and navy at Actium and other Greek bases in the fall of 32 BCE. In 31 BCE, Octavian's aggressive naval commander Marcus Vipsanius Agrippa raided key locations on the Greek coast with some success, and attempted to disrupt maritime supply shipments to Antony and Cleopatra's forces. Meanwhile, Octavian ferried an army from Italy to Epirus, and established his own camp opposite Actium.

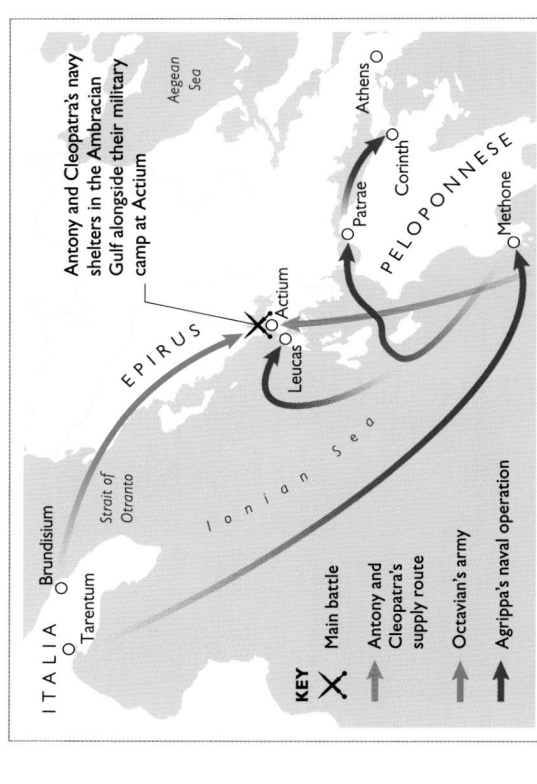

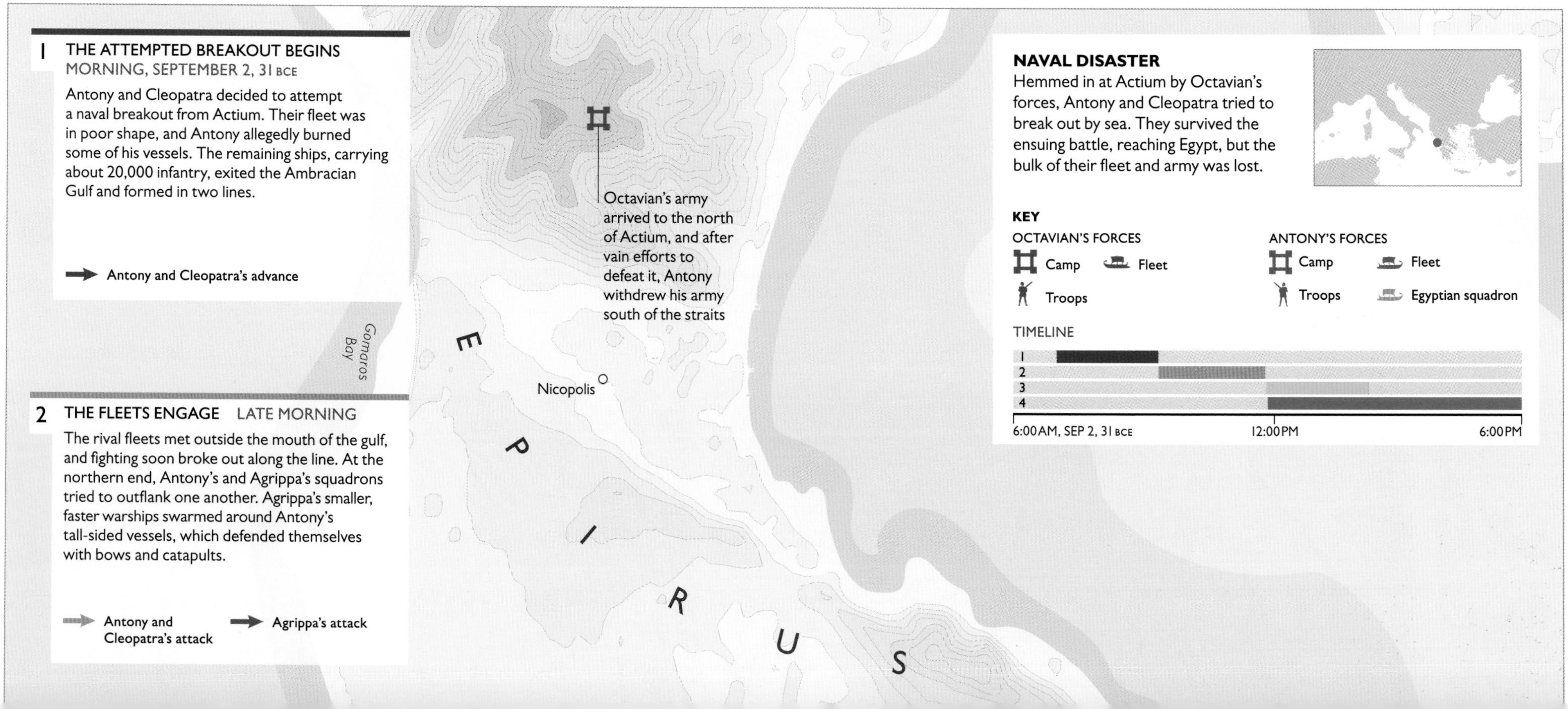

Antony and Cleopatra's navy shelters in the Ambracian Gulf alongside their military camp at Actium

Aegean Sea

Athens
Patrae   Corinth
PELOPONNESE
Actium
Leucas   Methone
EPIRUS
Ionian Sea
ITALIA
Tarentum
Brundisium
Strait of Otranto

KEY

✕ Main battle

↑ Antony and Cleopatra's supply route

↑ Octavian's army

↑ Agrippa's naval operation

NAVAL DISASTER

Hemmed in at Actium by Octavian's forces, Antony and Cleopatra tried to break out by sea. They survived the ensuing battle, reaching Egypt, but the bulk of their fleet and army was lost.

KEY

OCTAVIAN'S FORCES
⌂ Camp   ⛵ Fleet
🏃 Troops

ANTONY'S FORCES
⌂ Camp   ⛵ Fleet
🏃 Troops   ⛵ Egyptian squadron

TIMELINE

1
2
3
4

6:00AM, SEP 2, 31 BCE   12:00PM   6:00PM

Octavian's army arrived to the north of Actium, and after vain efforts to defeat it, Antony withdrew his army south of the straits

Nicopolis

E P I R U S

Gomaros Bay

1 THE ATTEMPTED BREAKOUT BEGINS
MORNING, SEPTEMBER 2, 31 BCE

Antony and Cleopatra decided to attempt a naval breakout from Actium. Their fleet was in poor shape, and Antony allegedly burned some of his vessels. The remaining ships, carrying about 20,000 infantry, exited the Ambracian Gulf and formed in two lines.

→ Antony and Cleopatra's advance

2 THE FLEETS ENGAGE LATE MORNING

The rival fleets met outside the mouth of the gulf, and fighting soon broke out along the line. At the northern end, Antony's and Agrippa's squadrons tried to outflank one another. Agrippa's smaller, faster warships swarmed around Antony's tall-sided vessels, which defended themselves with bows and catapults.

→ Antony and Cleopatra's attack   → Agrippa's attack

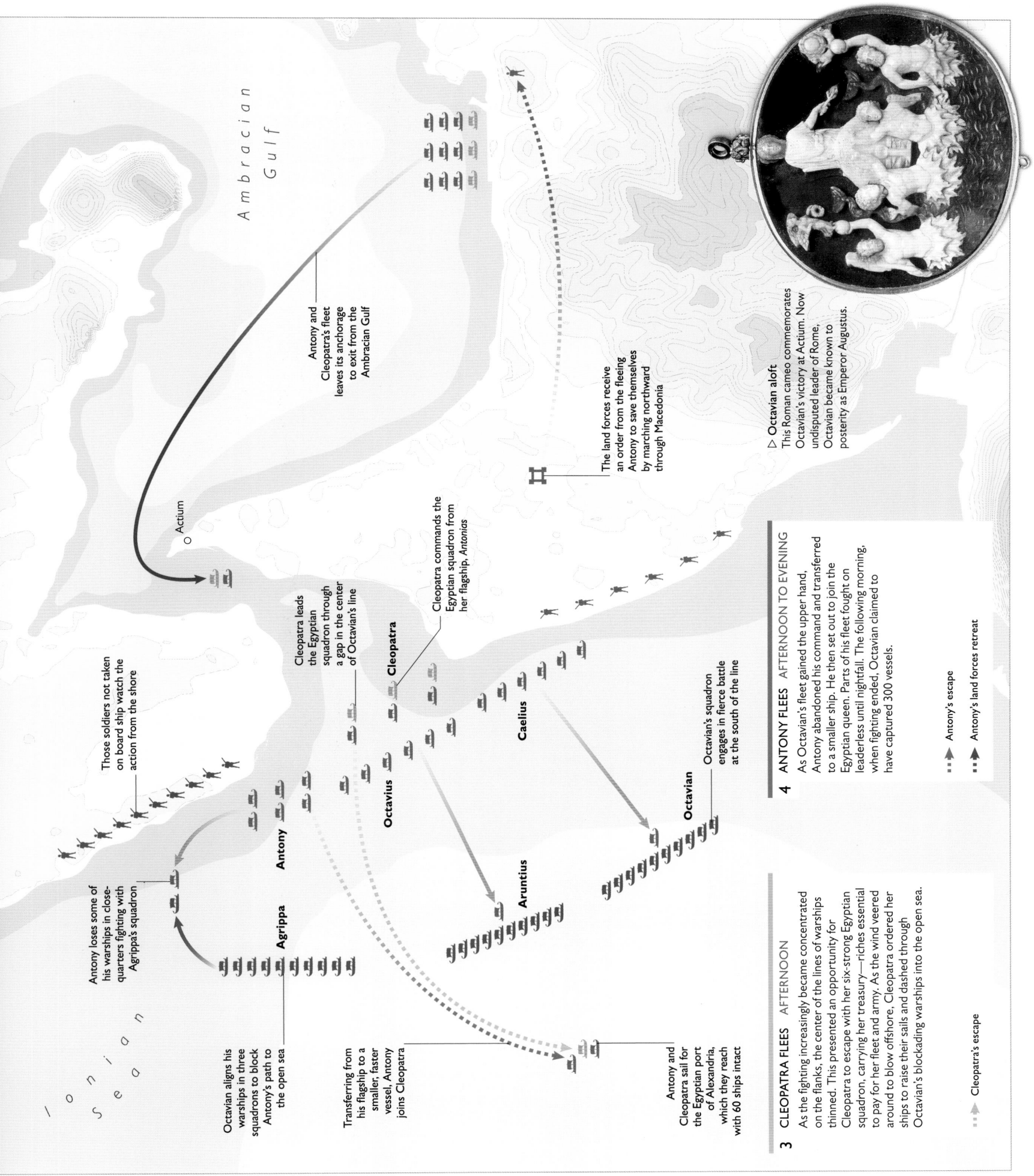

Ambracian Gulf

Ionian Sea

Actium

Antony and Cleopatra's fleet leaves its anchorage to exit from the Ambracian Gulf

The land forces receive an order from the fleeing Antony to save themselves by marching northward through Macedonia

Octavian aligns his warships in three squadrons to block Antony's path to the open sea

Those soldiers not taken on board ship watch the action from the shore

Antony loses some of his warships in close-quarters fighting with Agrippa's squadron

Agrippa

Antony

Cleopatra leads the Egyptian squadron through a gap in the center of Octavian's line

Cleopatra commands the Egyptian squadron from her flagship, *Antonias*

Cleopatra

Octavius

Caelius

Aruntius

Octavian

Octavian's squadron engages in fierce battle at the south of the line

Transferring from his flagship to a smaller, faster vessel, Antony joins Cleopatra

Antony and Cleopatra sail for the Egyptian port of Alexandria, which they reach with 60 ships intact

3 CLEOPATRA FLEES   AFTERNOON

As the fighting increasingly became concentrated on the flanks, the center of the lines of warships thinned. This presented an opportunity for Cleopatra to escape with her six-strong Egyptian squadron, carrying her treasury—riches essential to pay for her fleet and army. As the wind veered around to blow offshore, Cleopatra ordered her ships to raise their sails and dashed through Octavian's blockading warships into the open sea.

4 ANTONY FLEES   AFTERNOON TO EVENING

As Octavian's fleet gained the upper hand, Antony abandoned his command and transferred to a smaller ship. He then set out to join the Egyptian queen. Parts of his fleet fought on leaderless until nightfall. The following morning, when fighting ended, Octavian claimed to have captured 300 vessels.

▷ **Octavian aloft**
This Roman cameo commemorates Octavian's victory at Actium. Now undisputed leader of Rome, Octavian became known to posterity as Emperor Augustus.

→ Antony's escape

⇢ Antony's land forces retreat

⇢ Cleopatra's escape

TEUTOBURG FOREST

In September 9 CE, an army of Roman legionaries led by Publius Quinctilius Varus was ambushed and annihilated by Germanic tribal warriors in the forests of Saxony. This military disaster ensured that the Roman Empire never succeeded in extending its rule over Germany east of the Rhine.

In the early 1st century CE, during the reign of Emperor Augustus, the Romans embarked upon the conquest of northern Germany. By summer 9 CE, the legate Quinctilius Varus was campaigning in what is now Lower Saxony with an army of three legions, plus cavalry and tribal auxiliaries—German warriors recruited to fight for Rome. Varus was accompanied by the chief of the Cherusci tribe, Arminius, a German who was considered trustworthy and had been given Roman citizenship. Arminius had secretly organized a plot with other tribal leaders to destroy Varus's army. As the Romans marched westward toward their winter quarters, Arminius falsely informed Varus that a rebellion had broken out nearby. Turning to take action against the supposed rebels, the Romans were led into an ambush. Their massacre was soon avenged, but the Germanic tribes kept their independence and their devastating raids would eventually contribute to the collapse of the Roman Empire.

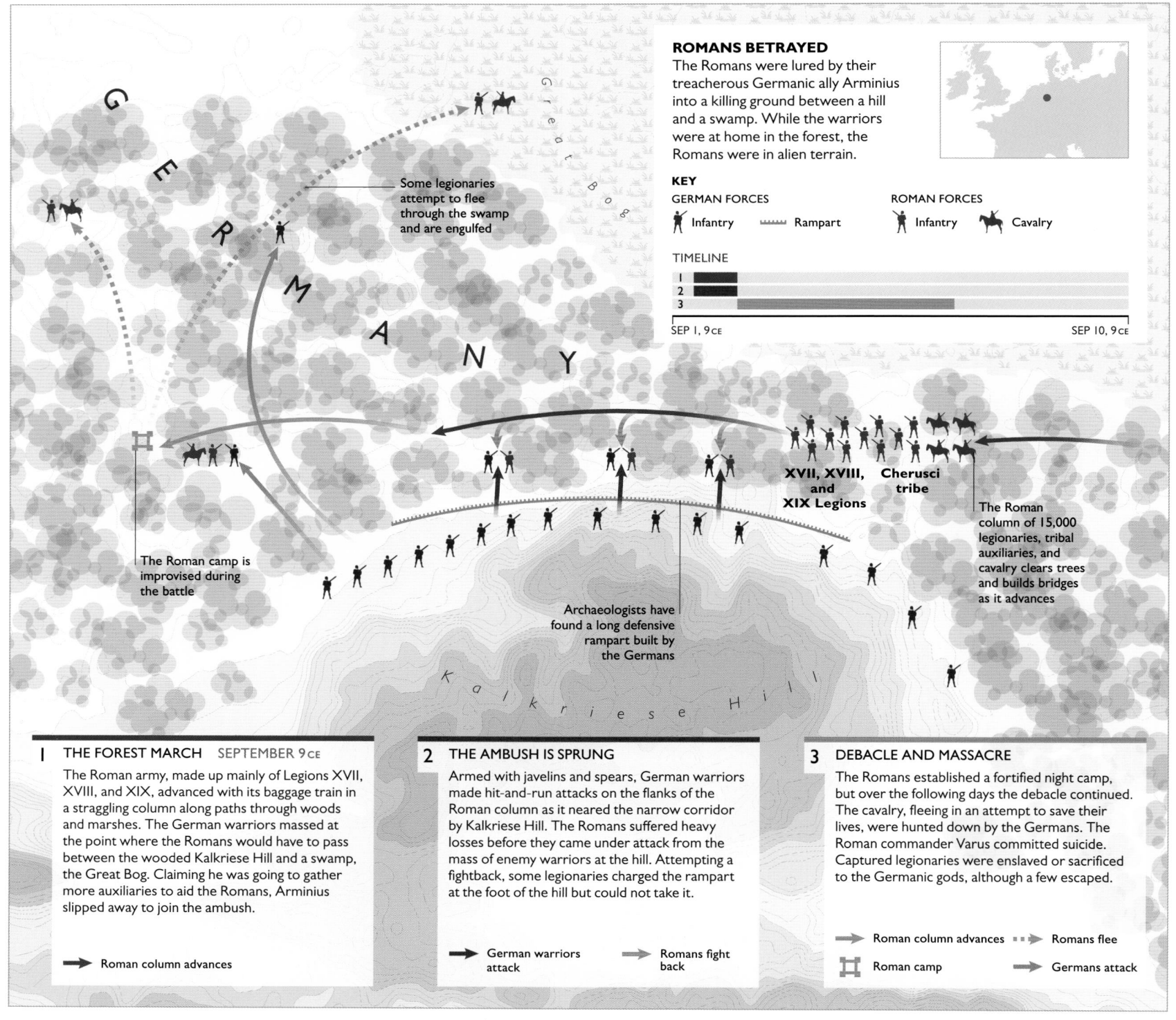

ROMANS BETRAYED

The Romans were lured by their treacherous Germanic ally Arminius into a killing ground between a hill and a swamp. While the warriors were at home in the forest, the Romans were in alien terrain.

KEY

GERMAN FORCES
- Infantry
- Rampart

ROMAN FORCES
- Infantry
- Cavalry

TIMELINE

1
2
3

SEP 1, 9 CE — SEP 10, 9 CE

Some legionaries attempt to flee through the swamp and are engulfed

Great Bog

GERMANY

The Roman camp is improvised during the battle

Archaeologists have found a long defensive rampart built by the Germans

XVII, XVIII, and XIX Legions — Cherusci tribe

The Roman column of 15,000 legionaries, tribal auxiliaries, and cavalry clears trees and builds bridges as it advances

Kalkriese Hill

1 THE FOREST MARCH SEPTEMBER 9 CE

The Roman army, made up mainly of Legions XVII, XVIII, and XIX, advanced with its baggage train in a straggling column along paths through woods and marshes. The German warriors massed at the point where the Romans would have to pass between the wooded Kalkriese Hill and a swamp, the Great Bog. Claiming he was going to gather more auxiliaries to aid the Romans, Arminius slipped away to join the ambush.

→ Roman column advances

2 THE AMBUSH IS SPRUNG

Armed with javelins and spears, German warriors made hit-and-run attacks on the flanks of the Roman column as it neared the narrow corridor by Kalkriese Hill. The Romans suffered heavy losses before they came under attack from the mass of enemy warriors at the hill. Attempting a fightback, some legionaries charged the rampart at the foot of the hill but could not take it.

→ German warriors attack
→ Romans fight back

3 DEBACLE AND MASSACRE

The Romans established a fortified night camp, but over the following days the debacle continued. The cavalry, fleeing in an attempt to save their lives, were hunted down by the Germans. The Roman commander Varus committed suicide. Captured legionaries were enslaved or sacrificed to the Germanic gods, although a few escaped.

→ Roman column advances ⇢ Romans flee
⌗ Roman camp → Germans attack

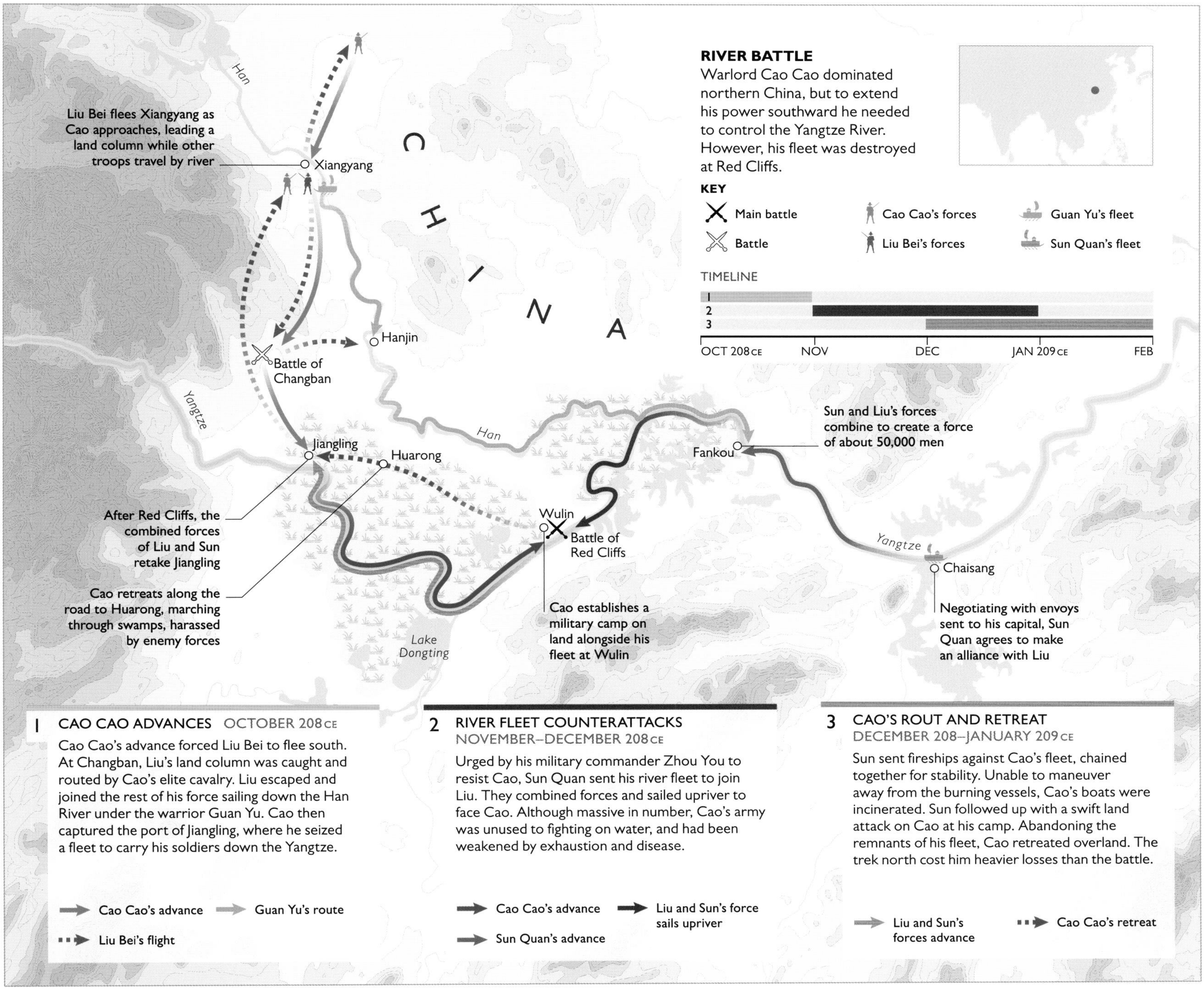

RIVER BATTLE

Warlord Cao Cao dominated northern China, but to extend his power southward he needed to control the Yangtze River. However, his fleet was destroyed at Red Cliffs.

KEY

✕ Main battle	👤 Cao Cao's forces	⛵ Guan Yu's fleet
⚔ Battle	👤 Liu Bei's forces	⛵ Sun Quan's fleet

TIMELINE

1					
2					
3					
OCT 208 CE	NOV	DEC	JAN 209 CE	FEB

Liu Bei flees Xiangyang as Cao approaches, leading a land column while other troops travel by river

CHINA

Han

Xiangyang

Hanjin

Battle of Changban

Yangtze

Jiangling

Huarong

Han

Wulin
Battle of Red Cliffs

Fankou

Yangtze

Chaisang

Sun and Liu's forces combine to create a force of about 50,000 men

Negotiating with envoys sent to his capital, Sun Quan agrees to make an alliance with Liu

Cao establishes a military camp on land alongside his fleet at Wulin

After Red Cliffs, the combined forces of Liu and Sun retake Jiangling

Cao retreats along the road to Huarong, marching through swamps, harassed by enemy forces

Lake Dongting

1 CAO CAO ADVANCES OCTOBER 208 CE

Cao Cao's advance forced Liu Bei to flee south. At Changban, Liu's land column was caught and routed by Cao's elite cavalry. Liu escaped and joined the rest of his force sailing down the Han River under the warrior Guan Yu. Cao then captured the port of Jiangling, where he seized a fleet to carry his soldiers down the Yangtze.

➔ Cao Cao's advance   ➔ Guan Yu's route

▪▪➔ Liu Bei's flight

2 RIVER FLEET COUNTERATTACKS NOVEMBER–DECEMBER 208 CE

Urged by his military commander Zhou You to resist Cao, Sun Quan sent his river fleet to join Liu. They combined forces and sailed upriver to face Cao. Although massive in number, Cao's army was unused to fighting on water, and had been weakened by exhaustion and disease.

➔ Cao Cao's advance   ➔ Liu and Sun's force sails upriver

➔ Sun Quan's advance

3 CAO'S ROUT AND RETREAT DECEMBER 208–JANUARY 209 CE

Sun sent fireships against Cao's fleet, chained together for stability. Unable to maneuver away from the burning vessels, Cao's boats were incinerated. Sun followed up with a swift land attack on Cao at his camp. Abandoning the remnants of his fleet, Cao retreated overland. The trek north cost him heavier losses than the battle.

➔ Liu and Sun's forces advance   ▪▪➔ Cao Cao's retreat

RED CLIFFS

A decisive episode in the civil war that split China in the final years of the Han dynasty, the battle of Red Cliffs was fought on and around the Yangtze River. The defeat of the feared warlord Cao Cao foiled his bid to unify China under his rule.

In 184 CE the Han dynasty, which had ruled China for almost 400 years, was undermined by a peasant revolt, the Yellow Turban rebellion. China became divided between warlords, the most successful of whom was the ruthless Cao Cao, who held sway in northern China. In 208 CE, he led an army reputed to be over 200,000 strong southward in pursuit of Liu Bei, a rival with a following of Han dynasty loyalists. Unable to match Cao's forces,

Liu formed an alliance with Sun Quan, a southern regional strongman who controlled much of the Yangtze River from Chaisang. Sun's military commander, Zhou Yu, masterminded the defeat of Cao at Red Cliffs, near modern-day Wuhan. The consequence of the battle, after further fighting, was the division of China in 220 CE into the "Three Kingdoms:" Wei (north of the Yangtze), Shu (in the southwest), and Wu (in the southeast).

△ **Cao Cao before the battle**
Cao Cao was an accomplished poet. Before the battle, he wrote *Short Song Style*, illustrated in this 19th-century Japanese woodblock print.

WAR IN ANCIENT CHINA

Organized warfare in China traces its roots to the Shang dynasty (c.1600 BCE–1046 BCE) and Zhou dynasty (1046–256 BCE). Wars were either fought between rival Chinese states, or for territorial expansion.

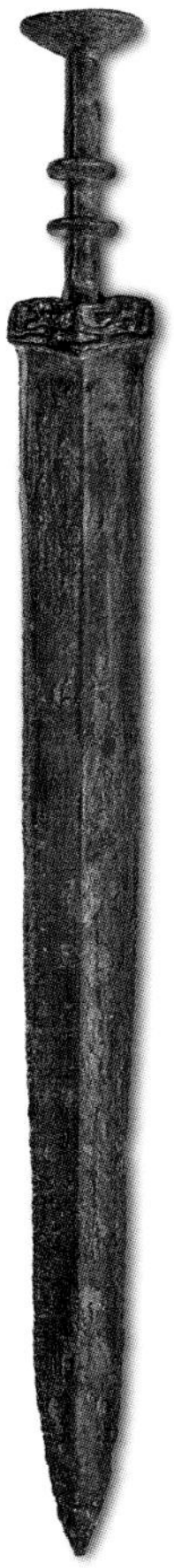

Shang and Zhou armies were built around a core of nobles on chariots and lightly armed slave-conscripts, continuing up to the Spring and Autumn Period (771–476 BCE). The bow was the main early weapon. Trained infantry with bows, dagger-axes, and crossbows appeared in the Warring States Period (476–221 BCE) alongside charioteers.

The age of horsemen

Cavalry began to replace chariots after the Warring States period. References to horse armor appeared in literary sources from the 3rd century, although it is thought to have been used centuries earlier than this. Non-Chinese mounted auxiliaries began to support Chinese cavalry in increasing numbers. By 306 CE, the central authority of the Jin dynasty had collapsed with the War of the Eight Princes, and the steppe tribes Xiongnu and Xianbei established kingdoms in Northern China. Armored lancer cavalry and horse archers became the dominant strike force of their armies, and this dominance continued in the Sui and Tang dynasties (581–907 CE).

Records suggest Chinese armies were larger than contemporary European ones, and were made up of semi-independent corps. Battle lines stretched for miles with extensive field fortifications. Rulers rarely went to battle, as defeat was associated with divine wrath.

◁ **Bronze sword**
Weapons such as this cast bronze sword from the Warring States Period were not just effective battlefield tools, but were also a status symbol for the bearer.

THE TERRA-COTTA ARMY

When Qin Shi Huang, the first Qin emperor, died in September 210 BCE, he was interred in a grand mausoleum near modern-day Xian. Along with him, a massive army of possibly tens of thousands of terra-cotta soldiers was buried in battle array. Several thousand of these figures have been unearthed by archaeologists. The terra-cotta army gives a rare glimpse at the uniform and equipment of Chinese armies of the time.

Tang tombs cavalry mural
The murals in the corridors and chambers of the subterranean tombs at the Qianling Mausoleum in modern-day Xian have remained mostly intact since 700–800 CE. This painting depicts armed men on horses, possibly in a hunting scene.

CTESIPHON

In 363 CE, Roman emperor Julian led an expedition against the Sassanid Persians in Mesopotamia (modern-day Iraq). Despite his victory at Ctesiphon, the overall campaign was disastrous. Julian was killed, and Rome was forced to accept a humiliating peace treaty. Julian's death ensured the continued dominance of Christianity in the Roman Empire.

The drawn-out conflict between the Roman and Persian empires flared up again in 359 CE, when the Persian ruler, Shapur II, set out to contest Roman control of Armenia and northern Mesopotamia. Aspiring to glory, the young Roman emperor, Julian, decided to strike back at the heart of Shapur's domains. Despite a victory at Ctesiphon, Julian's campaign failed and he was killed as his forces retreated. Shapur gained Mesopotamia for the Persian Empire and forced Rome to recognize Persian suzerainty over Armenia.

In 313 CE Julian's predecessor, Emperor Constantine, had accepted Christianity as a legitimate religion within the Roman Empire. Julian wanted to reverse the growing dominance of Christianity and restore pagan polytheism and neoplatonism. His death ended that mission and helped cement Christianity as the official state religion of Rome.

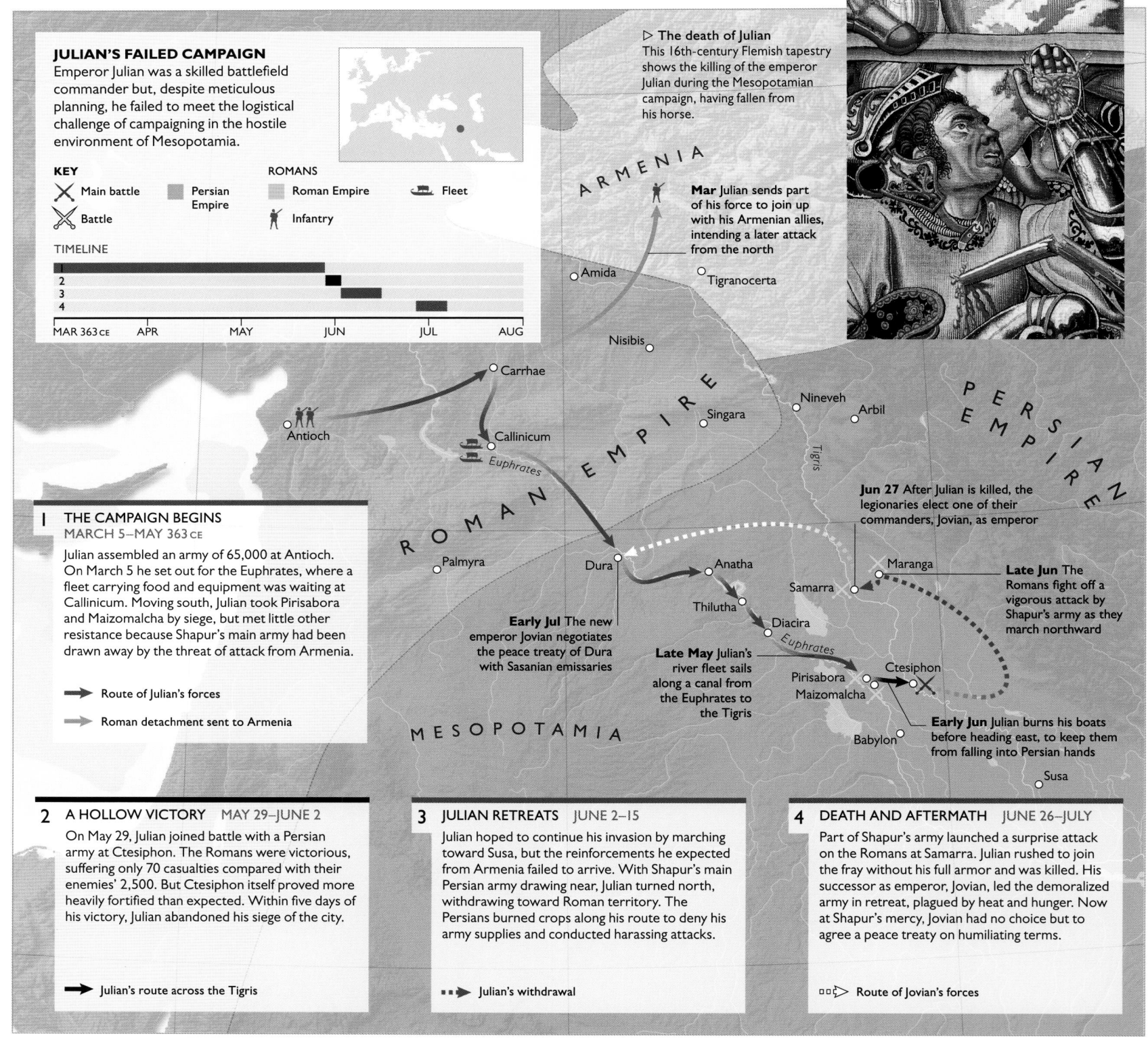

JULIAN'S FAILED CAMPAIGN
Emperor Julian was a skilled battlefield commander but, despite meticulous planning, he failed to meet the logistical challenge of campaigning in the hostile environment of Mesopotamia.

KEY

		ROMANS	
✗ Main battle	▨ Persian Empire	▨ Roman Empire	🚢 Fleet
⚔ Battle		🪖 Infantry	

TIMELINE

MAR 363 CE — APR — MAY — JUN — JUL — AUG

▷ **The death of Julian**
This 16th-century Flemish tapestry shows the killing of the emperor Julian during the Mesopotamian campaign, having fallen from his horse.

Mar Julian sends part of his force to join up with his Armenian allies, intending a later attack from the north

ARMENIA

Amida · Tigranocerta

Nisibis

Carrhae

Callinicum

Euphrates

ROMAN EMPIRE

Nineveh · Arbil
Singara

Tigris

PERSIAN EMPIRE

Palmyra

Dura · Anatha · Maranga

Thilutha · Samarra

Diacira · Euphrates

Jun 27 After Julian is killed, the legionaries elect one of their commanders, Jovian, as emperor

Late Jun The Romans fight off a vigorous attack by Shapur's army as they march northward

Early Jul The new emperor Jovian negotiates the peace treaty of Dura with Sasanian emissaries

Late May Julian's river fleet sails along a canal from the Euphrates to the Tigris

Pirisabora
Maizomalcha · Ctesiphon

Early Jun Julian burns his boats before heading east, to keep them from falling into Persian hands

Babylon

Susa

MESOPOTAMIA

1 THE CAMPAIGN BEGINS
MARCH 5–MAY 363 CE

Julian assembled an army of 65,000 at Antioch. On March 5 he set out for the Euphrates, where a fleet carrying food and equipment was waiting at Callinicum. Moving south, Julian took Pirisabora and Maizomalcha by siege, but met little other resistance because Shapur's main army had been drawn away by the threat of attack from Armenia.

➡ Route of Julian's forces
➡ Roman detachment sent to Armenia

Antioch

2 A HOLLOW VICTORY MAY 29–JUNE 2

On May 29, Julian joined battle with a Persian army at Ctesiphon. The Romans were victorious, suffering only 70 casualties compared with their enemies' 2,500. But Ctesiphon itself proved more heavily fortified than expected. Within five days of his victory, Julian abandoned his siege of the city.

➡ Julian's route across the Tigris

3 JULIAN RETREATS JUNE 2–15

Julian hoped to continue his invasion by marching toward Susa, but the reinforcements he expected from Armenia failed to arrive. With Shapur's main Persian army drawing near, Julian turned north, withdrawing toward Roman territory. The Persians burned crops along his route to deny his army supplies and conducted harassing attacks.

▪▪▶ Julian's withdrawal

4 DEATH AND AFTERMATH JUNE 26–JULY

Part of Shapur's army launched a surprise attack on the Romans at Samarra. Julian rushed to join the fray without his full armor and was killed. His successor as emperor, Jovian, led the demoralized army in retreat, plagued by heat and hunger. Now at Shapur's mercy, Jovian had no choice but to agree a peace treaty on humiliating terms.

▫▫▷ Route of Jovian's forces

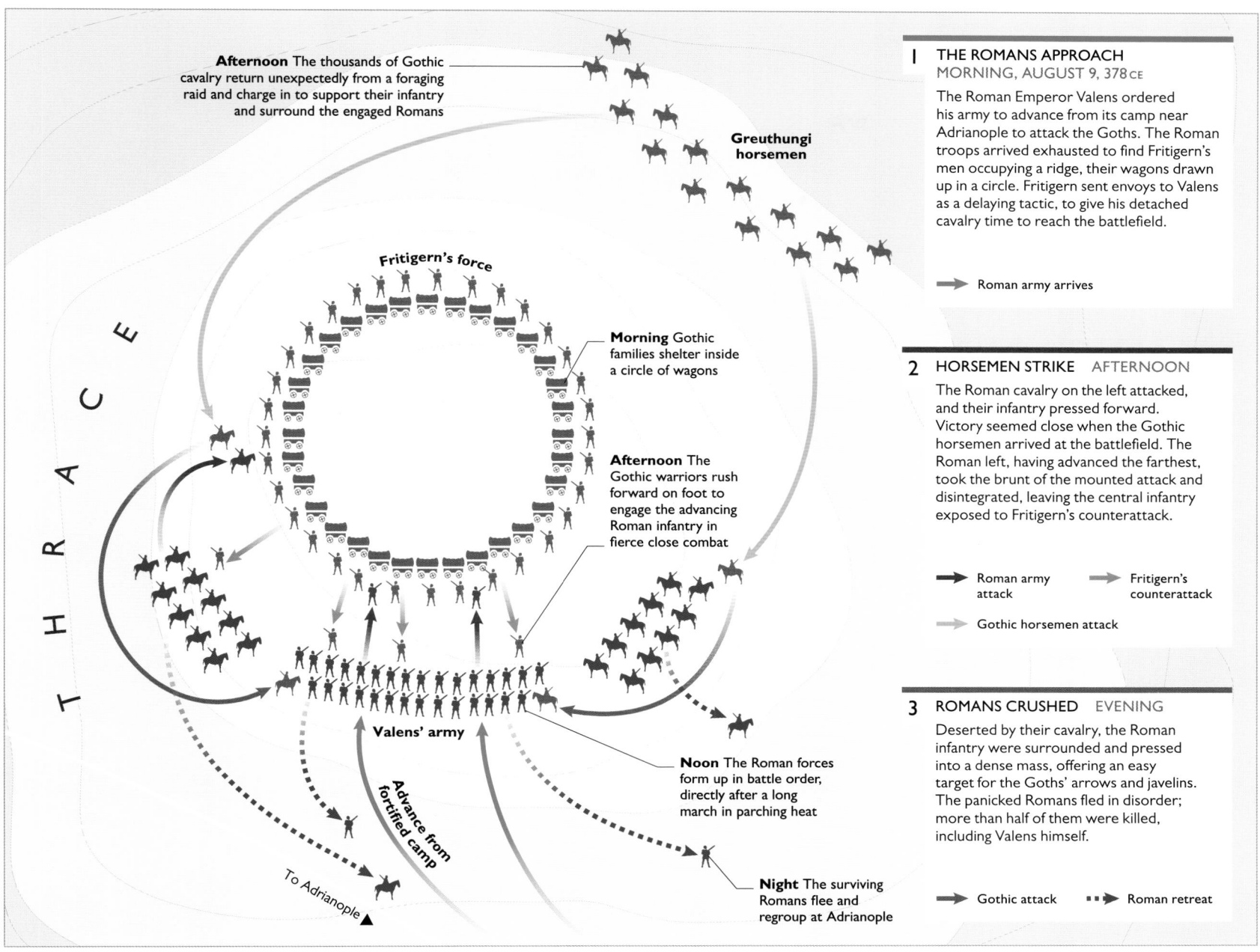

Afternoon The thousands of Gothic cavalry return unexpectedly from a foraging raid and charge in to support their infantry and surround the engaged Romans

Greuthungi horsemen

Fritigern's force

THRACE

Morning Gothic families shelter inside a circle of wagons

Afternoon The Gothic warriors rush forward on foot to engage the advancing Roman infantry in fierce close combat

Valens' army

Advance from fortified camp

To Adrianople

Noon The Roman forces form up in battle order, directly after a long march in parching heat

Night The surviving Romans flee and regroup at Adrianople

1 THE ROMANS APPROACH
MORNING, AUGUST 9, 378 CE

The Roman Emperor Valens ordered his army to advance from its camp near Adrianople to attack the Goths. The Roman troops arrived exhausted to find Fritigern's men occupying a ridge, their wagons drawn up in a circle. Fritigern sent envoys to Valens as a delaying tactic, to give his detached cavalry time to reach the battlefield.

→ Roman army arrives

2 HORSEMEN STRIKE AFTERNOON

The Roman cavalry on the left attacked, and their infantry pressed forward. Victory seemed close when the Gothic horsemen arrived at the battlefield. The Roman left, having advanced the farthest, took the brunt of the mounted attack and disintegrated, leaving the central infantry exposed to Fritigern's counterattack.

→ Roman army attack → Fritigern's counterattack

→ Gothic horsemen attack

3 ROMANS CRUSHED EVENING

Deserted by their cavalry, the Roman infantry were surrounded and pressed into a dense mass, offering an easy target for the Goths' arrows and javelins. The panicked Romans fled in disorder; more than half of them were killed, including Valens himself.

→ Gothic attack ▪▪▶ Roman retreat

ADRIANOPLE

Gothic tribal warriors, led by the chieftain Fritigern, crushed a Roman army outside Adrianople (in modern northwest Turkey) in 378 CE. The battle foreshadowed the decline of the Roman Empire, which would later see the "barbarian" tribes take control of Rome itself.

END OF ROMAN DOMINANCE
Valens was overconfident in his ability to conquer the "barbarians," advancing with inadequate preparation and reconnaissance. The battle was another stage in the gradual decline of the once dominant Roman infantry.

KEY

ROMAN FORCES		GOTHIC FORCES		
🚶 Infantry	🐎 Cavalry	🚶 Infantry	🐎 Cavalry	🛒 Wagon

TIMELINE

1	
2	
3	

6:00 AM, AUG 9, 378 CE   12:00 PM   6:00 PM   12:00 AM

In the 4th century CE, the Roman Empire faced pressure on its borders from migrants regarded as "barbarians." In 376 CE the Thervingi, a Germanic tribe of the group later known as Visigoths, were given permission to cross the border and settle in Thrace. However, the Thervingi were persecuted by local military authorities and, together with the Greuthungi, another Gothic tribe, they rose up in revolt and were soon threatening Constantinople (formerly Byzantium), the capital of the Eastern Roman Empire. After two years of running battles, the Roman eastern emperor Valens decided to take command himself and seek glory by crushing the Goths, without waiting for promised reinforcements from the western emperor Gratian. The defeat shook the Romans, but it had only limited consequences. Peace was restored in 382, with the Goths granted land in return for service in the Roman army. However, the battle prefigured later disaster—the sack of Rome by Visigoths in 410.

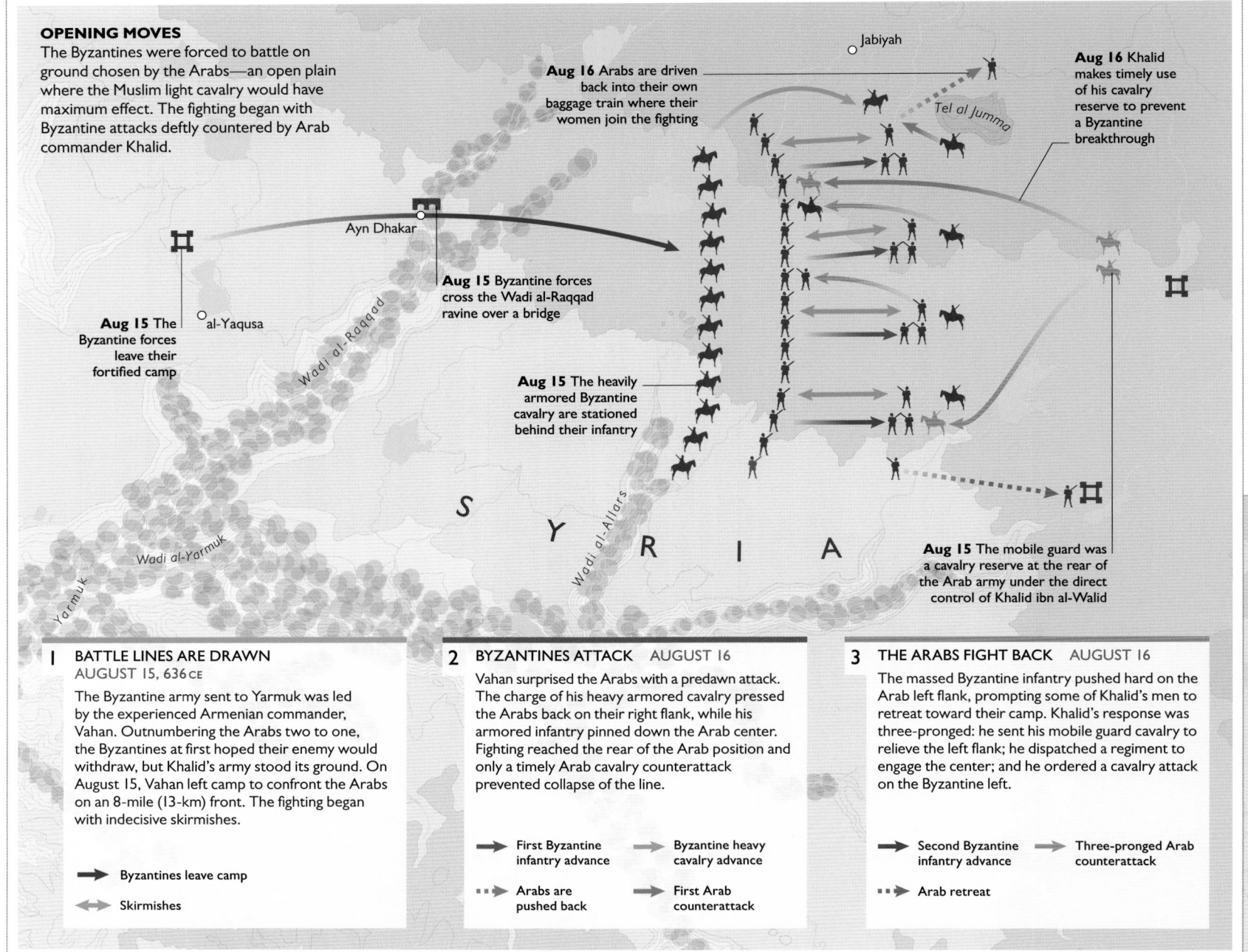

OPENING MOVES
The Byzantines were forced to battle on ground chosen by the Arabs—an open plain where the Muslim light cavalry would have maximum effect. The fighting began with Byzantine attacks deftly countered by Arab commander Khalid.

Aug 16 Arabs are driven back into their own baggage train where their women join the fighting

Aug 16 Khalid makes timely use of his cavalry reserve to prevent a Byzantine breakthrough

Jabiyah

Tel al Jumma

Ayn Dhakar

Aug 15 Byzantine forces cross the Wadi al-Raqqad ravine over a bridge

Aug 15 The Byzantine forces leave their fortified camp

al-Yaqusa

Wadi al-Raqqad

Aug 15 The heavily armored Byzantine cavalry are stationed behind their infantry

Wadi al-Allars

S Y R I A

Wadi al-Yarmuk

Yarmuk

Aug 15 The mobile guard was a cavalry reserve at the rear of the Arab army under the direct control of Khalid ibn al-Walid

---

1 BATTLE LINES ARE DRAWN
AUGUST 15, 636 CE

The Byzantine army sent to Yarmuk was led by the experienced Armenian commander, Vahan. Outnumbering the Arabs two to one, the Byzantines at first hoped their enemy would withdraw, but Khalid's army stood its ground. On August 15, Vahan left camp to confront the Arabs on an 8-mile (13-km) front. The fighting began with indecisive skirmishes.

→ Byzantines leave camp

↔ Skirmishes

2 BYZANTINES ATTACK AUGUST 16

Vahan surprised the Arabs with a predawn attack. The charge of his heavy armored cavalry pressed the Arabs back on their right flank, while his armored infantry pinned down the Arab center. Fighting reached the rear of the Arab position and only a timely Arab cavalry counterattack prevented collapse of the line.

→ First Byzantine infantry advance

→ Byzantine heavy cavalry advance

⇢ Arabs are pushed back

→ First Arab counterattack

3 THE ARABS FIGHT BACK AUGUST 16

The massed Byzantine infantry pushed hard on the Arab left flank, prompting some of Khalid's men to retreat toward their camp. Khalid's response was three-pronged: he sent his mobile guard cavalry to relieve the left flank; he dispatched a regiment to engage the center; and he ordered a cavalry attack on the Byzantine left.

→ Second Byzantine infantry advance

→ Three-pronged Arab counterattack

⇢ Arab retreat

YARMUK

The defeat of a Christian Byzantine Empire army in Syria in 636 CE marked the ascendancy of Arab forces inspired by the new religion of Islam. Over the following century, Muslim armies triumphed from Central Asia to the Atlantic.

At Nineveh in 627 CE, the Byzantine emperor, Heraclius, won a crushing victory over the Sasanid Persian Empire, apparently heralding a new era of Byzantine dominance in the Middle East. However, unnoticed by these warring empires, the tribes of Arabia were uniting under the banner of Islam, a religion based on the teachings of the prophet Mohammed. After Mohammed's death in 632, Arab armies left Arabia with a mission to spread their faith. Led by the gifted general Khalid ibn al-Walid, they seized Damascus from the Byzantines in 634. Heraclius responded to this challenge by assembling a large army at Antioch in northern Syria. As this force marched south, Khalid concentrated his smaller army by the Yarmuk River, preparing for a pitched battle.

Defeat at Yarmuk had a devastating effect on the Byzantine Empire. Although it endured for another eight centuries, much of its subsequent history is the record of a struggle for survival. The Sasanians suffered a decisive defeat at Qadisiyah later in 636. By 750, Arab armies had given the Damascus-based Umayyad Caliphate control of an empire that stretched from modern-day Pakistan to the Iberian peninsula.

al-Yaqusa

Wadi al-Yarm

Yarmuk

EXPANSION OF ISLAM

By the start of the Umayyad Caliphate in 661 CE, Arab armies controlled Persia, the Levant, and Egypt. Later conquests took them to Constantinople. North African Berbers, converted to Islam, invaded Iberia and threatened the kingdom of the Franks.

KEY

✕ Main battle

→ Muslim forces

▮ Frankish Kingdom

▮ Byzantine Empire

▮ Up to the death of Mohammed, 632

▮ The early caliphs, 632–61

▮ The Umayyads, 661–750

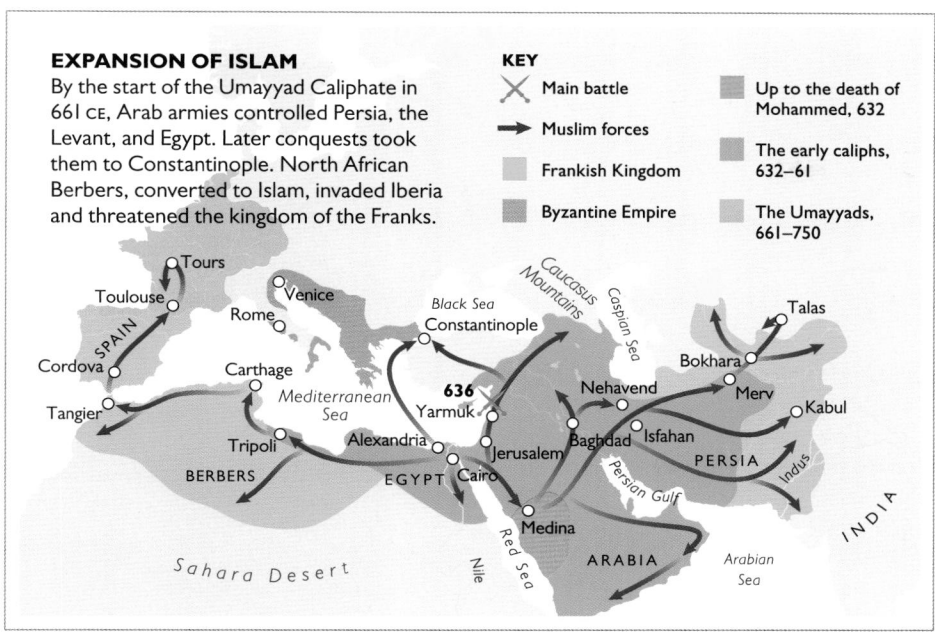

PITCHED BATTLE

At Yarmuk, the Arab commander Khalid ibn al-Walid drew the Byzantines into a pitched battle, which they preferred to avoid. His tactical skill and the quality of Arab cavalry won the six-day battle.

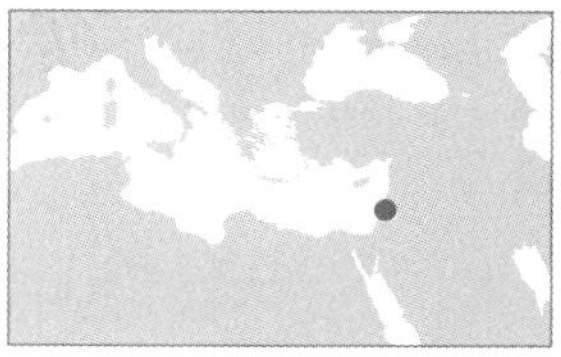

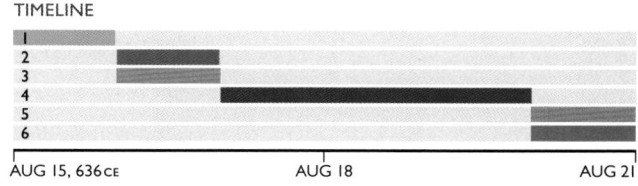

KEY

🏰 Bridge

BYZANTINE

⚔ Camp

🧍 Infantry

🐎 Cavalry

MUSLIM

⚔ Camp

🧍 Infantry

🐎 Cavalry

🐎 Cavalry reserve

TIMELINE

1			
2			
3			
4			
5			
6			

AUG 15, 636 CE   AUG 18   AUG 21

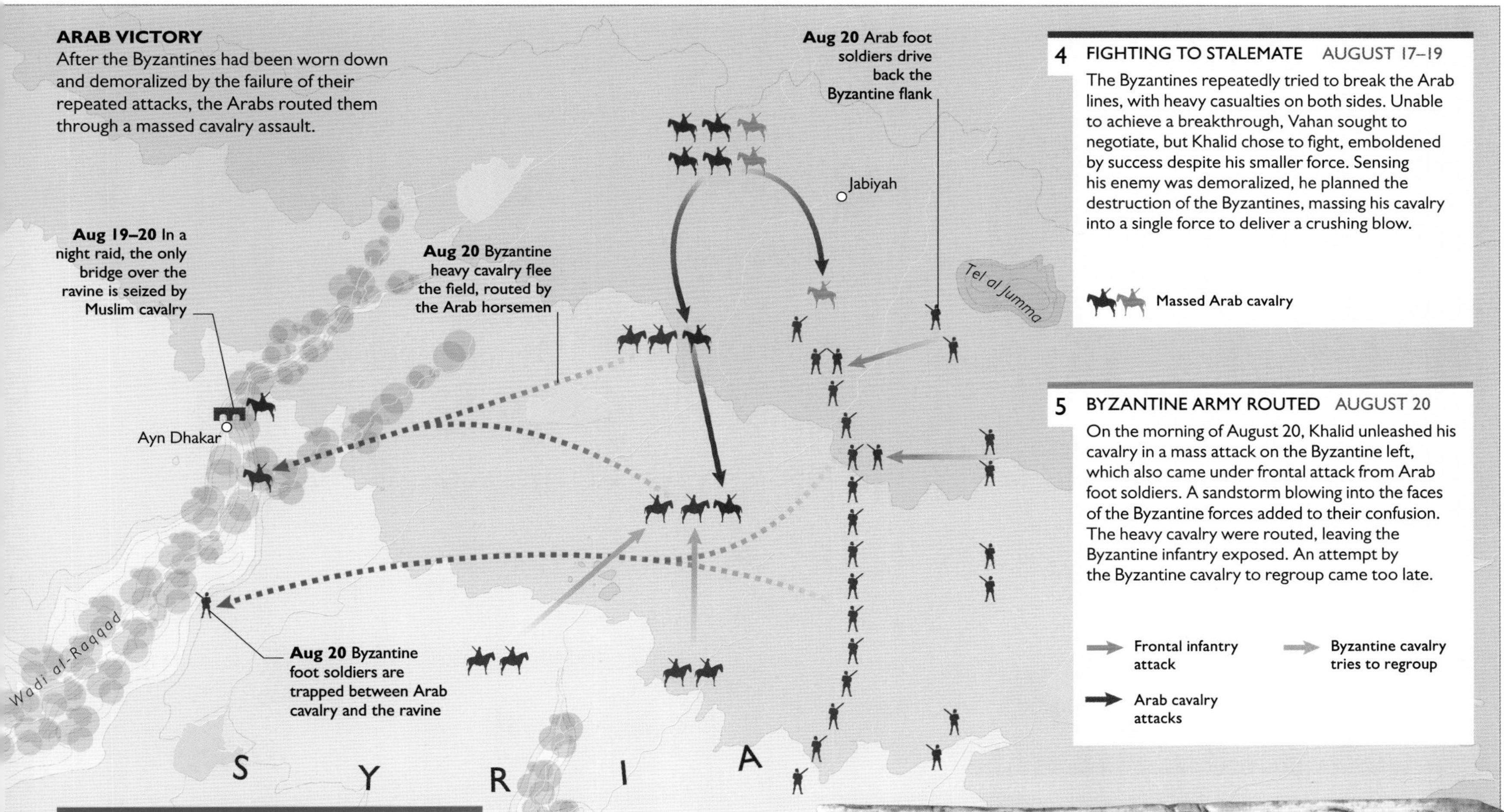

ARAB VICTORY

After the Byzantines had been worn down and demoralized by the failure of their repeated attacks, the Arabs routed them through a massed cavalry assault.

Aug 20 Arab foot soldiers drive back the Byzantine flank

Jabiyah

Tel al Jumma

Aug 19–20 In a night raid, the only bridge over the ravine is seized by Muslim cavalry

Aug 20 Byzantine heavy cavalry flee the field, routed by the Arab horsemen

Ayn Dhakar

Aug 20 Byzantine foot soldiers are trapped between Arab cavalry and the ravine

Wadi al-Raqqad

S Y R I A

Wadi al-Allan

4   FIGHTING TO STALEMATE   AUGUST 17–19

The Byzantines repeatedly tried to break the Arab lines, with heavy casualties on both sides. Unable to achieve a breakthrough, Vahan sought to negotiate, but Khalid chose to fight, emboldened by success despite his smaller force. Sensing his enemy was demoralized, he planned the destruction of the Byzantines, massing his cavalry into a single force to deliver a crushing blow.

🐎🐎   Massed Arab cavalry

5   BYZANTINE ARMY ROUTED   AUGUST 20

On the morning of August 20, Khalid unleashed his cavalry in a mass attack on the Byzantine left, which also came under frontal attack from Arab foot soldiers. A sandstorm blowing into the faces of the Byzantine forces added to their confusion. The heavy cavalry were routed, leaving the Byzantine infantry exposed. An attempt by the Byzantine cavalry to regroup came too late.

⟶ Frontal infantry attack

⟶ Arab cavalry attacks

⟶ Byzantine cavalry tries to regroup

6   BYZANTINE INFANTRY FLEE   AUGUST 20

With their left flank routed, many Byzantine soldiers fled the battlefield. By now, Khalid"s forces had taken control of the sole bridge over the deep Wadi al-Raqqad ravine; some Byzantine soldiers plunged to their deaths down its steep cliffs. Their commander, Vahan, was probably killed in the pursuit after the battle, which carried the Arab forces as far as Damascus.

▪▪▶ Byzantine infantry flee

▷ **Byzantine horsemen**
This 6th-century CE ivory carving depicts Byzantine cavalry and infantry. The armored horsemen were used to break through the enemy's lines and were typically armed with a bow, lance, and sword.

TOURS

Fought in central France in 732 CE, the Battle of Tours (or Poitiers) was a victory for the Christian Franks over the the Umayyad Caliphate. Had the Franks lost, more of Western Europe might have come under the dominance of Islam.

After crossing the straits of Gibraltar from north Africa in 711 CE, the armies of the Muslim Umayyad Caliphate conquered the Iberian peninsula and much of southern France. In 732, Abdul Rahman al-Ghafiqi, the emir of Cordoba, led an army north into the Christian Duchy of Aquitaine. Aquitaine's ruler, Duke Odo, fled and sought help from his old enemy the Franks under the effective leadership of Charles

Martel. Martel assembled an army to help Odo in return for Aquitaine accepting Frankish suzerainty. Abdul Rahman met the Frankish army when he was possibly en route to plunder the abbey at Tours; after his defeat, he abandoned campaigning for the year and withdrew. Although the battle was only one episode in the stagnation of Arab expansion, it remains symbolic of the defense of western Christendom.

△ *Grandes Chroniques de France*
This 15th-century depiction of the battle portrays the warriors anachronistically as contemporary knights, including the fleur-de-lis emblem for the Franks

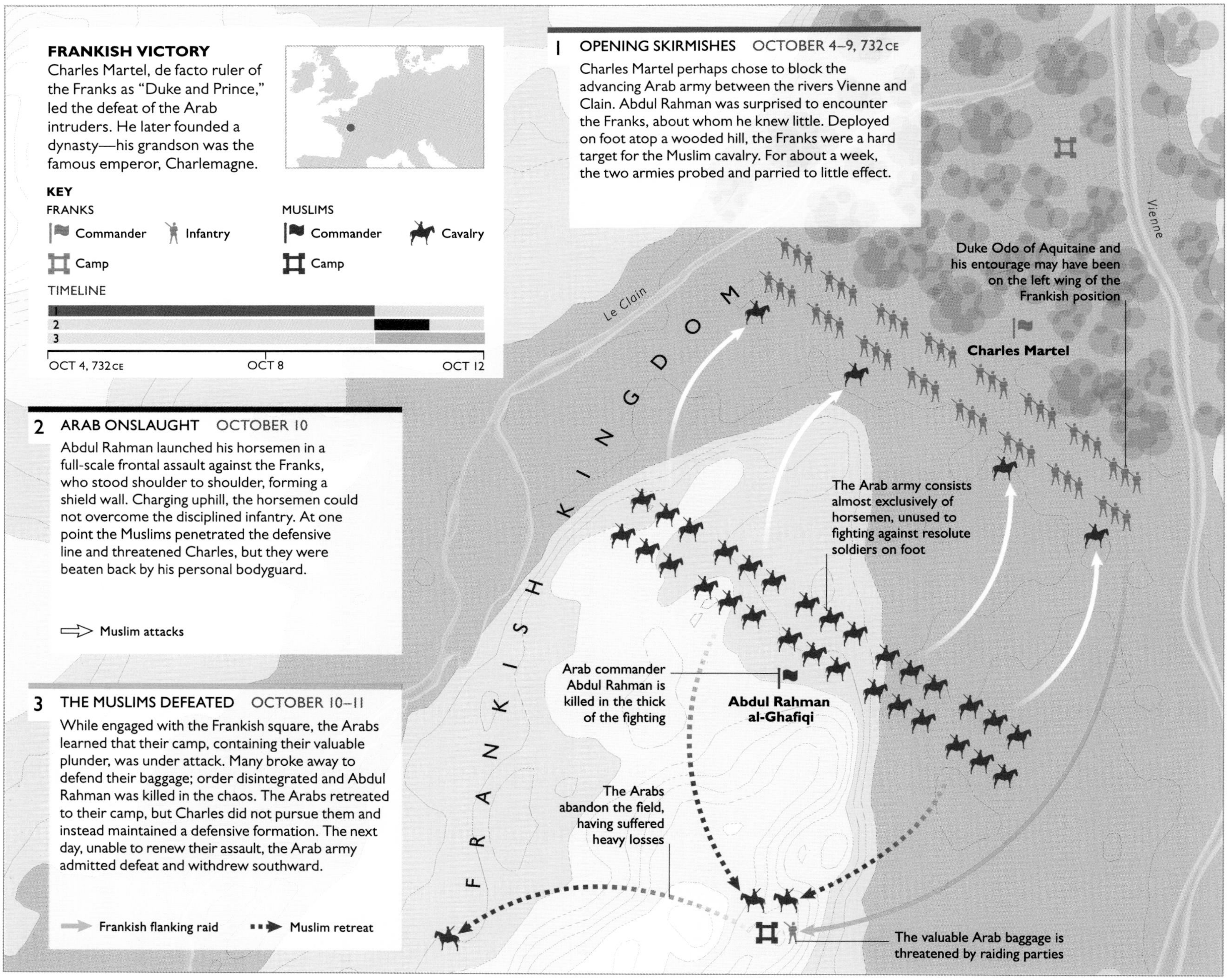

FRANKISH VICTORY

Charles Martel, de facto ruler of the Franks as "Duke and Prince," led the defeat of the Arab intruders. He later founded a dynasty—his grandson was the famous emperor, Charlemagne.

KEY

FRANKS

| | Commander | 🧍 Infantry

🏕 Camp

MUSLIMS

| | Commander | 🐎 Cavalry

🏕 Camp

TIMELINE

| 1 |
| 2 |
| 3 |

OCT 4, 732 CE   OCT 8   OCT 12

OPENING SKIRMISHES   OCTOBER 4–9, 732 CE

Charles Martel perhaps chose to block the advancing Arab army between the rivers Vienne and Clain. Abdul Rahman was surprised to encounter the Franks, about whom he knew little. Deployed on foot atop a wooded hill, the Franks were a hard target for the Muslim cavalry. For about a week, the two armies probed and parried to little effect.

2 ARAB ONSLAUGHT   OCTOBER 10

Abdul Rahman launched his horsemen in a full-scale frontal assault against the Franks, who stood shoulder to shoulder, forming a shield wall. Charging uphill, the horsemen could not overcome the disciplined infantry. At one point the Muslims penetrated the defensive line and threatened Charles, but they were beaten back by his personal bodyguard.

⇨ Muslim attacks

3 THE MUSLIMS DEFEATED   OCTOBER 10–11

While engaged with the Frankish square, the Arabs learned that their camp, containing their valuable plunder, was under attack. Many broke away to defend their baggage; order disintegrated and Abdul Rahman was killed in the chaos. The Arabs retreated to their camp, but Charles did not pursue them and instead maintained a defensive formation. The next day, unable to renew their assault, the Arab army admitted defeat and withdrew southward.

➡ Frankish flanking raid   ▪▪▪➤ Muslim retreat

Le Clain

Vienne

FRANKISH KINGDOM

Duke Odo of Aquitaine and his entourage may have been on the left wing of the Frankish position

Charles Martel

The Arab army consists almost exclusively of horsemen, unused to fighting against resolute soldiers on foot

Arab commander Abdul Rahman is killed in the thick of the fighting

Abdul Rahman al-Ghafiqi

The Arabs abandon the field, having suffered heavy losses

The valuable Arab baggage is threatened by raiding parties

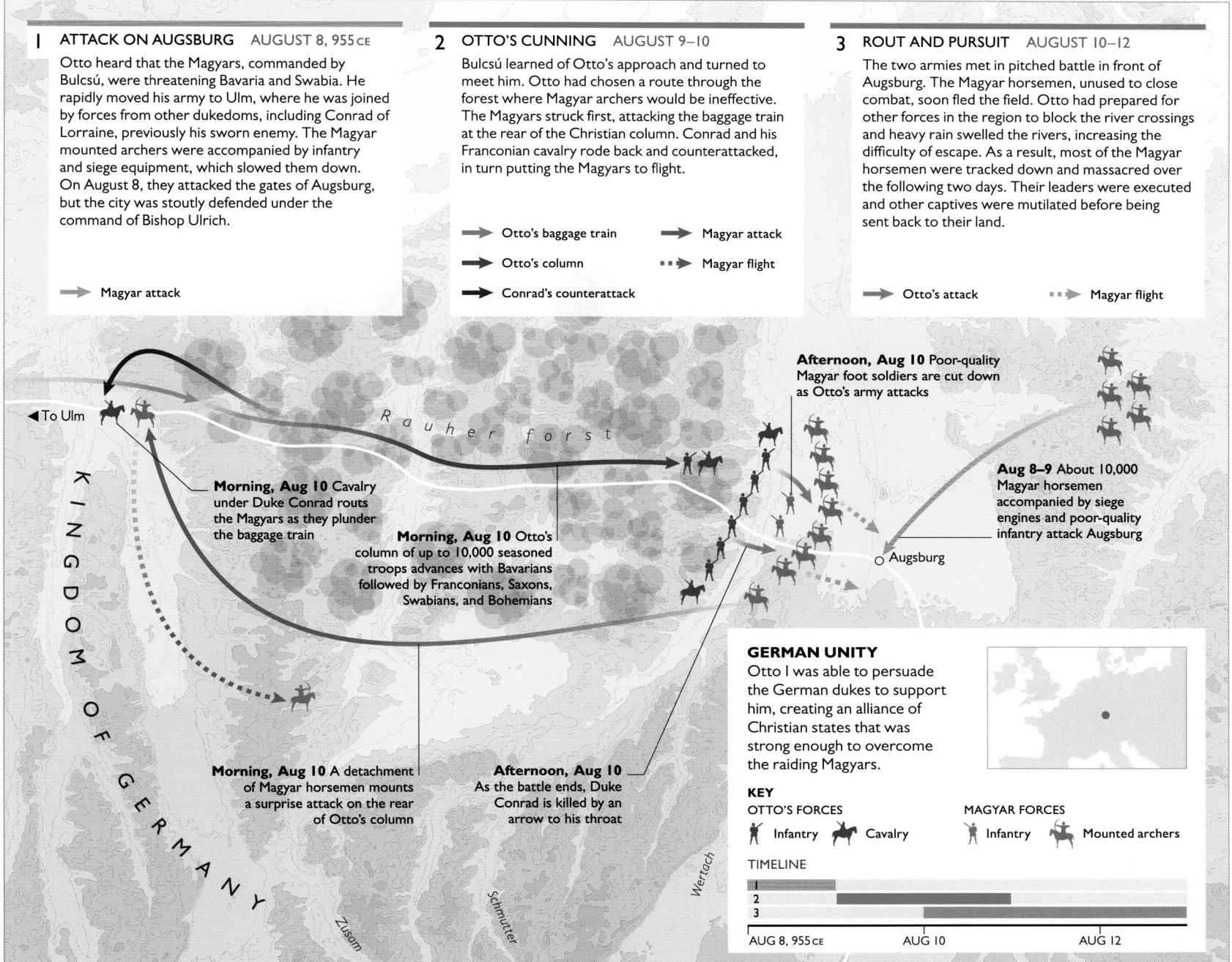

1 ATTACK ON AUGSBURG AUGUST 8, 955 CE

Otto heard that the Magyars, commanded by Bulcsú, were threatening Bavaria and Swabia. He rapidly moved his army to Ulm, where he was joined by forces from other dukedoms, including Conrad of Lorraine, previously his sworn enemy. The Magyar mounted archers were accompanied by infantry and siege equipment, which slowed them down. On August 8, they attacked the gates of Augsburg, but the city was stoutly defended under the command of Bishop Ulrich.

→ Magyar attack

2 OTTO'S CUNNING AUGUST 9–10

Bulcsú learned of Otto's approach and turned to meet him. Otto had chosen a route through the forest where Magyar archers would be ineffective. The Magyars struck first, attacking the baggage train at the rear of the Christian column. Conrad and his Franconian cavalry rode back and counterattacked, in turn putting the Magyars to flight.

→ Otto's baggage train
→ Otto's column
→ Conrad's counterattack
→ Magyar attack
⇢ Magyar flight

3 ROUT AND PURSUIT AUGUST 10–12

The two armies met in pitched battle in front of Augsburg. The Magyar horsemen, unused to close combat, soon fled the field. Otto had prepared for other forces in the region to block the river crossings and heavy rain swelled the rivers, increasing the difficulty of escape. As a result, most of the Magyar horsemen were tracked down and massacred over the following two days. Their leaders were executed and other captives were mutilated before being sent back to their land.

→ Otto's attack
⇢ Magyar flight

◀ To Ulm

KINGDOM OF GERMANY

Rauher forst

Afternoon, Aug 10 Poor-quality Magyar foot soldiers are cut down as Otto's army attacks

Morning, Aug 10 Cavalry under Duke Conrad routs the Magyars as they plunder the baggage train

Morning, Aug 10 Otto's column of up to 10,000 seasoned troops advances with Bavarians followed by Franconians, Saxons, Swabians, and Bohemians

Aug 8–9 About 10,000 Magyar horsemen accompanied by siege engines and poor-quality infantry attack Augsburg

Augsburg

Morning, Aug 10 A detachment of Magyar horsemen mounts a surprise attack on the rear of Otto's column

Afternoon, Aug 10 As the battle ends, Duke Conrad is killed by an arrow to his throat

Zusam

Schmutter

Wertach

GERMAN UNITY
Otto I was able to persuade the German dukes to support him, creating an alliance of Christian states that was strong enough to overcome the raiding Magyars.

KEY

OTTO'S FORCES		MAGYAR FORCES	
Infantry	Cavalry	Infantry	Mounted archers

TIMELINE

1	
2	
3	

AUG 8, 955 CE   AUG 10   AUG 12

LECHFELD

In 955 CE, an army led by German king Otto I defeated nomadic Magyar horsemen, who had been terrorizing Europe. The battle set Otto on course to become Holy Roman Emperor, and eventually led the Magyars to found the Christian kingdom of Hungary.

The Magyars were a nomadic steppe people who migrated to modern-day Hungary around 900 CE. Their horsemen repeatedly swept through Germany and other areas of Christian Europe to plunder towns and villages. The Magyars benefited from the break-up of the Carolingian Empire, which in the late 8th and early 9th century had united France, Germany, and northern Italy. Fragmented, these areas could not field an army capable of defeating the raiding horsemen. In 936 Otto I, Duke of Saxony, was crowned king of Germany. His ambition was to recreate Charlemagne's

empire. In 954, while Otto fought to assert his authority over rebellious German dukes, the Magyars raided unchecked. The following year they returned, intending to seize the wealthy city of Augsburg. Otto, who had persuaded the German dukes to follow his banner, was able to crush the invaders at Lechfeld, and went on to impose his rule on Italy as well as Germany. In 962, he was crowned Holy Roman Emperor by the pope. The Magyars, no longer able to mount profitable raids, became a settled people and converted to Christianity, founding the kingdom of Hungary in 1001.

DIRECTORY: BEFORE 1000 CE

SIEGE OF LACHISH

701 BCE

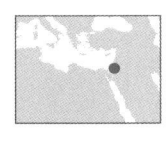

The Assyrian attack on the Judaean walled city of Lachish is the earliest siege about which detailed information is available. As the greatest military power in West Asia, Assyria claimed suzerainty over the Israelite Kingdom of Judah. In 701 BCE, its King Sennacherib (r.705–681) led an army to Judah to punish the Judaean king Hezekiah for rebelling against Assyrian authority.

Friezes carved on the walls of King Sennacherib's palace at Nineveh, in modern-day Iraq, show the siege techniques the Assyrians used against the Judaeans. The carvings portray archers and stone-slingers bombarding the defenders on the battlements as other soldiers were building an earthen ramp against one of the city walls. A wheeled siege engine with a ram was pushed up the ramp in order to break open the fortifications while soldiers scaled ladders to assault the walls. After the city was taken, the Assyrians exacted a fierce vengeance. The Nineveh friezes show Judaeans tortured and massacred, the city looted, and its population led into captivity. In the same year, however, Sennacherib failed to capture the Judaean capital city of Jerusalem.

△ Friezes at the Assyrian royal palace at Nineveh detailing scenes from the siege

THE SICILIAN EXPEDITION

415–413 BCE

The Athenian seaborne expedition to Sicily set sail in 415 BCE. It proved to be a turning point in the Peloponnesian War (431–404 BCE). The war was a prolonged struggle for supremacy between the two most powerful city-states in Ancient Greece: Athens and Sparta.

The Athenians targeted Syracuse, a Greek city in Sicily, that owed allegiance to the Spartans and provided them with a major part of their grain supply. The cautious Athenian commander Nicias eventually began a lengthy siege, and Athens accepted his request for major reinforcements. The Athenian fleet occupied Syracuse's Grand Harbor and the soldiers began building a surrounding wall to isolate the city. The wall, however, was never completed, and the Spartans succeeded in reinforcing the city's defenses. By 413 BCE, the tables had started to turn. The Athenians had begun to face a critical shortage of supplies and, in September, they decided to abandon the siege. However, the Spartans destroyed their fleet and in desperation Nicias attempted—in vain—to withdraw his land forces. Harassed by the enemy, the surviving Athenians finally surrendered. Athens fought on in the Aegean for nine years but was eventually blockaded into surrender.

THE CHANGPING CAMPAIGN

262–260 BCE

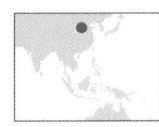

The kingdoms of Qin and Zhao were the strongest of the states into which China was divided in the 3rd century BCE. Both fielded massive armies of foot soldiers and cavalry. In 265 BCE, the Qin ruler Zhaoxiang attacked a town in Shandang, an area controlled by the weaker state of Han; the Zhao ruler Xiaucheng sent his forces to support Han. In 262 BCE, the Zhao army clashed with the Qin forces at Changping, in modern-day Shanxi province, and a stalemate ensued.

Xiaucheng replaced his cautious commander Lian Po with the more aggressive Zhao Kuo in 260 BCE. The new general led his army into a rash attack on the Qin's fortified position. The Qin commander Bai Qi used his cavalry to encircle the advancing Zhao army. After a 46-day-long siege and a number of failed breakout attempts, the Zhao army surrendered. Bai Qi massacred almost the entire force. Within 40 years, the Qin unified China under its First Emperor.

ZAMA

202 BCE

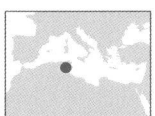

The Battle of Zama, in modern-day Tunisia, was the final encounter of the Second Punic War (218–201 BCE) fought between the Roman Republic and Carthage, a north African city-state. A Carthaginian army led by Hannibal had set out to invade Italy in 218 BCE. Hannibal occupied the south of Italy for more than a decade but failed to subdue Rome.

In 204 BCE, a Roman army under Publius Cornelius Scipio landed in north Africa and threatened Carthage. In desperation the Carthaginians recalled Hannibal's army from Italy. Hannibal advanced to meet Scipio, who confidently accepted battle.

The conflict opened with a charge by the Carthaginian war elephants. Harassed by skirmishers, the animals were driven off through corridors deliberately left open in the ranks of the Roman infantry. The foot soldiers then engaged in a brutal contest that resulted in heavy losses on both sides. Meanwhile, the Roman cavalry drove the Carthaginian horsemen far from the field. Returning from the pursuit, they attacked the Carthaginian infantry from the rear, initiating a rout. Hannibal's army was destroyed and Carthage accepted a humiliating peace. Hannibal was driven into exile, and Rome took a major stride toward creating an empire.

△ 17th-century tapestry depicting elephant-riding Carthaginians charging the Romans

PHARSALUS

AUGUST 9, 48 BCE

The Battle of Pharsalus was a key step in the quest by Roman general Julius Caesar to achieve supreme power in the Roman Republic. After years of successful campaigning against the Celtic tribes of Gaul (modern France and Belgium), in 49 BCE Caesar led his army across the River Rubicon into Italy and toward Rome, triggering a civil war. Pompey the Great, the most powerful figure in Rome at the time, withdrew to Greece, where he organized a new army. Caesar meanwhile defeated his old army in Spain.

The following year, Caesar sailed across the Adriatic Sea in pursuit of his rival. Pompey fared better than Caesar at an initial confrontation at Dyrrachium, but he failed to capitalize on his success. Short of supplies, Caesar marched into Thessaly, Greece, shadowed by Pompey's army, which outnumbered his forces by two to one. Pompey finally took the risk of engaging Caesar at Pharsalus. He planned to pin Caesar's veteran legionaries with his larger but inexperienced infantry and simultaneously send his superior cavalry, in a flanking move, to attack the legionaries from the rear. However, Caesar deployed skirmishers and

infantry reserves to repel the Pompeian cavalry while driving his legionaries relentlessly forward to crush the main body of his enemy's infantry. Pompey fled to Egypt, where he was murdered, and Caesar rose to be dictator of Rome before his assasinantion in 44 BCE.

▷ **Marble bust of Julius Caesar**

WUZHANG PLAINS

234 CE

After the fall of the Han dynasty in 220 CE, China was split between the warring kingdoms of Shu Han in the southwest, Sun Wu in the southeast, and Cao Wei in the north. The renowned Shu Han chancellor and general Zhuge Liang led a series of Northern Expeditions to attack Cao Wei. The battle fought on the Wuzhang Plains, in modern-day Shaanxi province, was the climax of his fifth and final northern campaign.

The large Shu Han army advanced to the River Wei, where they were confronted by the massed soldiers of the Cao Wei army already arrayed in defensive positions. After initial raids and skirmishes, the battle settled into a stalemate. Despite the provocations and insults hurled by Zhuge Liang,

the Cao Wei emperor Cao Rui prohibited his commander Sima Yi from engaging. Far from their supply base, the Shu Han soldiers turned to farming to keep themselves fed. The standoff continued for more than 100 days until Zhuge Liang died in his camp, exhausted by years of warfare, and the demoralized Shu Han army retreated. However, Sima Yi did not attack even during the withdrawal, fearing that the news of Zhuge Liang's death might be a deception.

The battle at Wuzhang Plains is celebrated by historians as an example of a victory achieved through the refusal to fight. Within 30 years of Cao Wei's bloodless triumph, Sima Yi's grandson founded the Jin Dynasty.

MILVIAN BRIDGE

OCTOBER 28, 312 CE

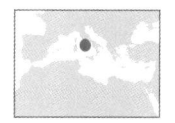

The clash at the Milvian Bridge between Constantine and Maxentius, rivals for power in the Roman Empire, was a key moment in the rise of Christianity as a world religion. In 306 CE, Constantine had been declared emperor in York, England, while in the same year Maxentius was proclaimed emperor in the city of Rome itself.

In 312, Constantine led an army to challenge Maxentius, who somewhat uncharacteristically accepted open battle near Rome. Maxentius's troops had their backs to the River Tiber, which was crossed by the partially dismantled Milvian Bridge and an improvised bridge of boats. Although Constantine was not a Christian at the time, later accounts claim that the night before the battle, he had a vision that convinced

him that fighting under the protection of the Christian God would bring him victory on the battlefield.

The battle that took place the following day was relatively brief. Constantine's infantry and cavalry charged, throwing Maxentius's forces into disarray. The latter's panicked soldiers attempted to withdraw to the city walls across the river, but were drowned as the bridge collapsed. Maxentius was among those killed. The next day, Constantine occupied the city of Rome and Maxentius's severed head was paraded through the streets. Constantine converted to Christianity during his subsequent reign, and the religion began its transformation from a repressed minority sect into the dominant religion of the Roman world.

THE SIEGE OF CONSTANTINOPLE

JULY 717–AUGUST 718 CE

The failure of the siege of Constantinople by the forces of the Arab Umayyad caliphate checked almost a century of Muslim expansion, and ensured the continued survival of the Christian Byzantine Empire for another seven centuries. The defense of the Byzantine capital was led by Emperor Leo the Isaurian, who had only recently usurped the throne in 717 CE (with Arab connivance). The Arab forces were led by the experienced general Maslama ibn Abd al-Malik. The city was besieged both by land and sea: a large army crossed the Hellespont from Asia while a fleet entered the Bosphorus.

However, the naval blockade was crippled by Byzantine ships armed with Greek fire, an early form of

flame-throwing weapon, and one against which the Muslims had no defense. As a result, through the hard winter of 717–718 CE, the city was amply supplied by sea, but the Arab besiegers suffered from food shortages, exposure to harsh weather, and the ravages of disease. In the spring, attempts to reinforce the siege failed as fresh Arab land and naval forces were intercepted and defeated by the Byzantines on their way to Constantinople. This, coupled with the intervention of the Bulgar army in the summer of 718, who attacked the Arabs from the north, convinced Maslama that he must withdraw. Constantinople would not fall into Muslim hands until much later, in 1453 (see p.96).

△ **Illustration from a 12th-century manuscript showing Byzantines in battle using Greek fire against enemy ships**

1000–1500

THE STATES THAT EMERGED FROM THE RUINS OF ANCIENT EMPIRES FOUGHT INCREASINGLY LARGE BATTLES, AND FORTRESSES AND SIEGE WARFARE BECAME A MAJOR FEATURE OF WARS. SLOWLY AT FIRST, GUNPOWDER WEAPONS ARRIVED AND BEGAN TO MAKE THEIR MARK, HERALDING THE FUTURE OF BATTLEFIELDS.

1000–1500

From 1000 CE onward, mounted warriors dominated battlefields, but territorial gains were won more often by siege warfare than field battles. Gradually, the balance shifted as the longbow, the pike, and the first gunpowder weapons made larger infantry-driven armies predominant among more centralized states.

By the 11th century, most European states relied on a central core of household troops for their defense. These troops were supported by a feudal system in which nobles provided the state with a number of mounted warriors in return for holding land, supplemented by peasant levies. Although the mounted knights made for a fearsome sight in battle, the infantry could resist cavalry attacks by presenting a wall of shields, as at the Battle of Hastings (see pp.58–59), or a bristling hedgehog of spears.

Feudal armies were only obliged to serve for periods of about 40 days and found it hard to assault strong fortifications directly. Stone forts and walled cities grew in number, particularly as a means to control newly conquered territory—for example in the Norman conquest of England after 1066. Sieges, using engines such as onagers—catapults that hurled heavy stones—portable siege towers, and battering rams were an essential part of medieval warfare, though starving out the defenders by blockading their supply lines often proved more effective.

The European states saw their first war of expansion during the Crusades, from the late 11th century. They found that

△ Archers at war
This 15th-century illumination from the *St. Albans Chronicle* shows English longbowmen repelling the attack of the French knights at the Battle of Agincourt in 1415 (see pp.90–91).

the Muslim armies' tactics of harrying the Crusader knights with mounted archers took away the shock induced by the imposing sight of an armored cavalry charge, and gained the Muslims victories, such as one at Hattin (see p.69) that eventually led to the reconquest of Jerusalem. However, both the Muslim and the Christian European states soon had to face an even more formidable foe in the Mongol empire (see pp.78–79). The Mongols' military organization, mounted archers, and ruthlessness won them a massive Eurasian empire, and devastated both the Muslim Abbasid Caliphate and eastern European states alike.

△ Siege engine
Medieval torsion catapults, such as this replica, could inflict serious casualties on the defenders of castles. However, unless striking at a weakened point, they were unlikely to create a breach in the castle's walls.

The rise of the infantry

In Europe, infantry began to assert itself on the battlefield. The spread of the crossbow and longbow (see pp.84–85) in the late 13th century gave foot soldiers greater attacking power, as they could now fire arrows capable of penetrating the chain armor of knights. This led to the development of plate armor, which, while stronger, was expensive and

SHIFTING ROLES

Although knights dominated the literature of the Middle Ages, infantry formed a vital part of armies. As states became more organized and new weaponry was developed, the armies came to rely at least as much on infantry as on the previously dominant mounted warriors. With increased resources, states fought larger battles, and civil wars between competing clans and factions became more common.

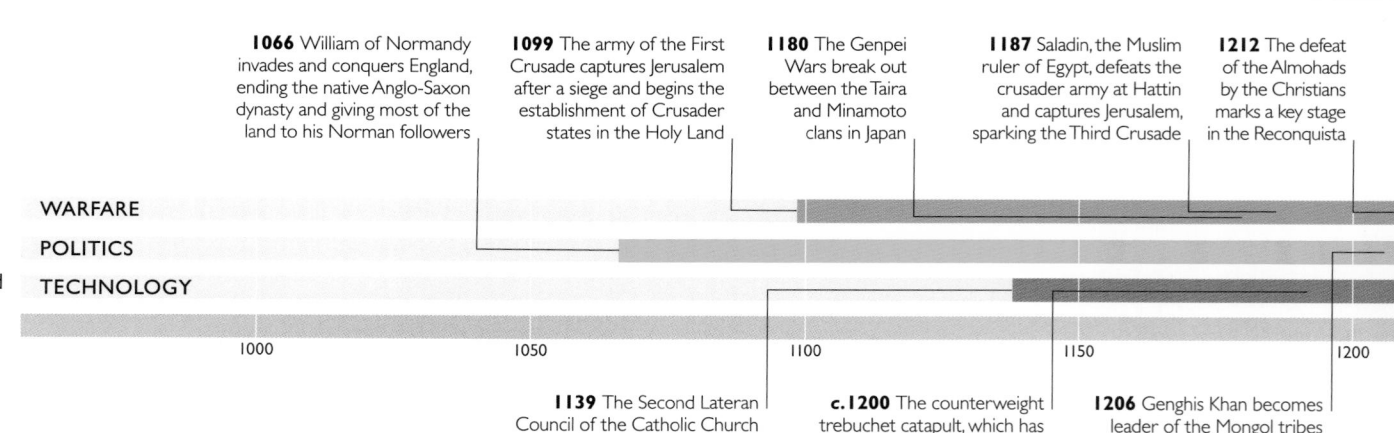

1066 William of Normandy invades and conquers England, ending the native Anglo-Saxon dynasty and giving most of the land to his Norman followers

1099 The army of the First Crusade captures Jerusalem after a siege and begins the establishment of Crusader states in the Holy Land

1180 The Genpei Wars break out between the Taira and Minamoto clans in Japan

1187 Saladin, the Muslim ruler of Egypt, defeats the crusader army at Hattin and captures Jerusalem, sparking the Third Crusade

1212 The defeat of the Almohads by the Christians marks a key stage in the Reconquista

WARFARE

POLITICS

TECHNOLOGY

| 1000 | 1050 | 1100 | 1150 | 1200 |

1139 The Second Lateran Council of the Catholic Church outlaws the use of bows and crossbows against Christians

c.1200 The counterweight trebuchet catapult, which has greater power and range than torsion catapults, is introduced

1206 Genghis Khan becomes leader of the Mongol tribes and begins campaigns against China and Central Asian powers

"By the disposition of God who orders all things, the art of war, the flower of knighthood, with horses and chargers of the finest, fell before… the common folk and foot soldiers of Flanders."

THE ANNALS OF GHENT, ACCOUNT OF THE BATTLE OF COURTRAI, 1302

△ **Heavy protection**
The sallet, with extended cheek protection and a flange at the back to guard the neck, became popular in the 15th century, with open-face versions also used by archers and crossbowmen.

unwieldy, and did not allow armored cavalry to regain the dominance in battle that they had once enjoyed. Armies raised by increasingly assertive towns could now win victories with pikes and spears. At Courtrai (see p.98), for example, the townspeople of Flanders defeated an army of French knights.

The Hundred Years War (1337–1453) between England and France saw a new style of mixed armies in which infantry predominated. While the French persisted at first with the old tactics of mounted charges, the English dismounted to meet them and their longbowmen exacted a terrible toll on the French nobility at Crécy (see pp.82–83) and Agincourt (see pp.90–91).

The bow and pike had only newly supplanted the lance and sword in battle when new gunpowder weapons began to appear that would ultimately replace them and revolutionize warfare. By the 1130s, the armies of China's Song dynasty had developed "fire-lances" which shot gunpowder-fueled projectiles. Their use soon became widespread, with larger versions employed during sieges. Gunpowder weapons appeared in Europe after 1326 as early cannons came in use in Italy. The development of cast-iron barrels and iron cannon balls by the 1450s meant cannons were able, for the first time, to destroy city walls. Although hand-held guns were still primitive and unwieldy, and traditional forms of warfare persisted in regions such as India and Japan, in Europe the battlefield stood on the edge of the gunpowder era.

▷ **Battle at sea**
In this 19th-century painting by Utagawa Kuniyoshi, the ghosts of the Japanese Taira clan defeated at the Battle of Dan-no-ura (see p.68) seek vengeance on a ship carrying the Minamoto clan victor Yoshitsune.

1314 Scottish king Robert Bruce defeats Edward II of England at Bannockburn to help secure the independence of Scotland

1337 The Hundred Years War breaks out between England and France

1415 English longbowmen inflict a devastating defeat on the French at Agincourt

1453 Constantinople falls to the Ottoman Sultan Mehmed II, bringing the Byzantine Empire to an end

1492 Granada's capture marks the end of the Reconquista and Spain returns to Christian rule

1250 1300 1350 1400 1450 1500

1279 Kublai Khan completes the conquest of southern China, bringing the whole country under the Mongol Yuan dynasty's rule

1346 The earliest significant use of war cannons in Europe takes place at the Battle of Crécy

1363 A law makes it obligatory for all Englishmen to practice using longbows every Sunday

c.1400 The invention of corned (grained) gunpowder makes cannons more reliable as they ignite more easily

HASTINGS

In late September 1066, Duke William of Normandy crossed the English Channel to assert his claim to the throne of England. Two weeks later, near Hastings, he defeated an Anglo-Saxon army that had just repelled another invasion in the north. The death of the English king Harold late in the battle crowned William's victory.

The death of the childless Edward the Confessor in January 1066 ignited a struggle for the succession to the English throne. Duke William of Normandy claimed that the late king had promised him the crown, while Harald Hardrada, king of Norway, maintained he had inherited a right to it from the Danish kings who preceded Edward. When the Anglo-Saxon nobility instead chose Harold Godwinson, Edward's brother-in-law, as king, both the other claimants planned invasions to secure their rights. Hardrada struck first, landing in the north with a force that included Harold's estranged brother Tostig. Although Hardrada won an initial victory at Fulford against the local Anglo-Saxon

earls, his death at Stamford Bridge on September 25 ended the threat of a Norwegian conquest.

Harold made a forced march south to resume his guard against the threatened Norman invasion, but learned that the Norman army had landed on the south coast in his absence. His death at the Battle of Hastings on October 14 (together with his brothers Leofwine and Gyrth, who might have succeeded him) left the English leaderless. An attempt to rally around Edgar the Aetheling, the remaining Anglo-Saxon prince, failed as he was too young to rule, and, after a slow march to London, William entered in triumph and was crowned king on Christmas Day.

TWIN INVASION

Harald Hardrada and Tostig landed and marched to York, where they defeated Earls Edwin and Morcar at the Battle of Fulford. Harold marched north rapidly and beat Hardrada at Stamford Bridge, but despite marching rapidly back to London, he was too late to interfere with Duke William's consolidation after his landing on September 28. In a bid to cut off William before he could strike out toward London, Harold met him at Hastings.

KEY

✕ Main battle

✕ Battle

➡ Norwegian forces

➡ Norman forces

➡ Harold marches north

➡ Harold intercepts William

Sep 20 Harald Hardrada and Tostig sail up the River Ouse and win a battle at Fulford

Sep 25 Hardrada and Tostig are killed at Stamford Bridge

End Sep–Oct 6 Harold marches his army over 200 miles (320 km) to London

Oct 6–7 Harold reaches London. Ignoring advice to wait for reinforcements, he moves south

Aug–Sep The crossing of Duke William's army is delayed by unfavorable winds

NORTHUMBRIA · Ouse · Stamford Bridge · North Sea · York · Fulford · Riccall · Nottingham · Leicester · EAST ANGLIA · WELSH PRINCIPALITIES · ENGLAND · MERCIA · Thames · London · WESSEX · SUSSEX · 14 OCT Hastings · Pevensey · English Channel · Saint-Valery-sur-Somme · NORMANDY · Dives-sur-Mer

NORMAN INVASION

William took a risk invading late in the summer: failure to win a quick victory would have left him isolated. In fact, his landing was uncontested and Harold's army engaged without reaching full strength.

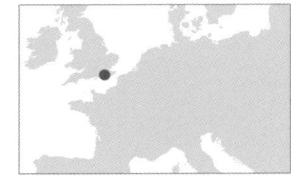

KEY

NORMANS
🚩 Commander
🧍 Infantry
🐎 Cavalry
🏹 Archers

ANGLO-SAXONS
🧍 English royal standard
🧍 Fyrd
🚩 Huscarls
🏹 Archers

TIMELINE

1 — 2 — 3 — 4 — 5 — 6

12:00AM, OCT 13, 1066 — 12:00AM, OCT 14 — 12:00AM, OCT 15

Malfosse

3 INITIAL NORMAN ATTACKS FAIL
MIDMORNING

After an initial volley from the archers, the Norman infantry charged up Senlac Hill with the cavalry following in support. However, the Norman arrows were ineffective against the wall of shields put up by the Anglo-Saxon infantry, and the successive charges lost momentum. The Anglo-Saxon line remained firm.

➡ Norman attacks   ┅➡ Norman retreat

2 THE NORMANS MOVE INTO POSITION
AROUND 9:00AM

William's army of about 8,000 men moved down from Telham Hill into the marshy valley bottom. He deployed his Norman troops in the center, with the Bretons, Angevins, and Poitevins on the left flank, and troops from Picardy and Flanders on the right. His archers took up position at the front of the line. Behind them were the infantry. Some 2,000 mounted knights—the backbone of William's force—took up the rear.

E

N

1 ANGLO-SAXON FORCES DEPLOY
OCTOBER 13–OCTOBER 14, 1066

Harold's gradually increasing army, some of whom had marched all the way from York, made camp near what is now Battle. In the morning, the Anglo-Saxon army, about 7,000 strong, deployed along Senlac Ridge. Harold's huscarls (elite troops bearing axes and protective armor) took up the center, while the more lightly equipped fyrd (local militia) were arranged on the wings. Harold's force had relatively few archers.

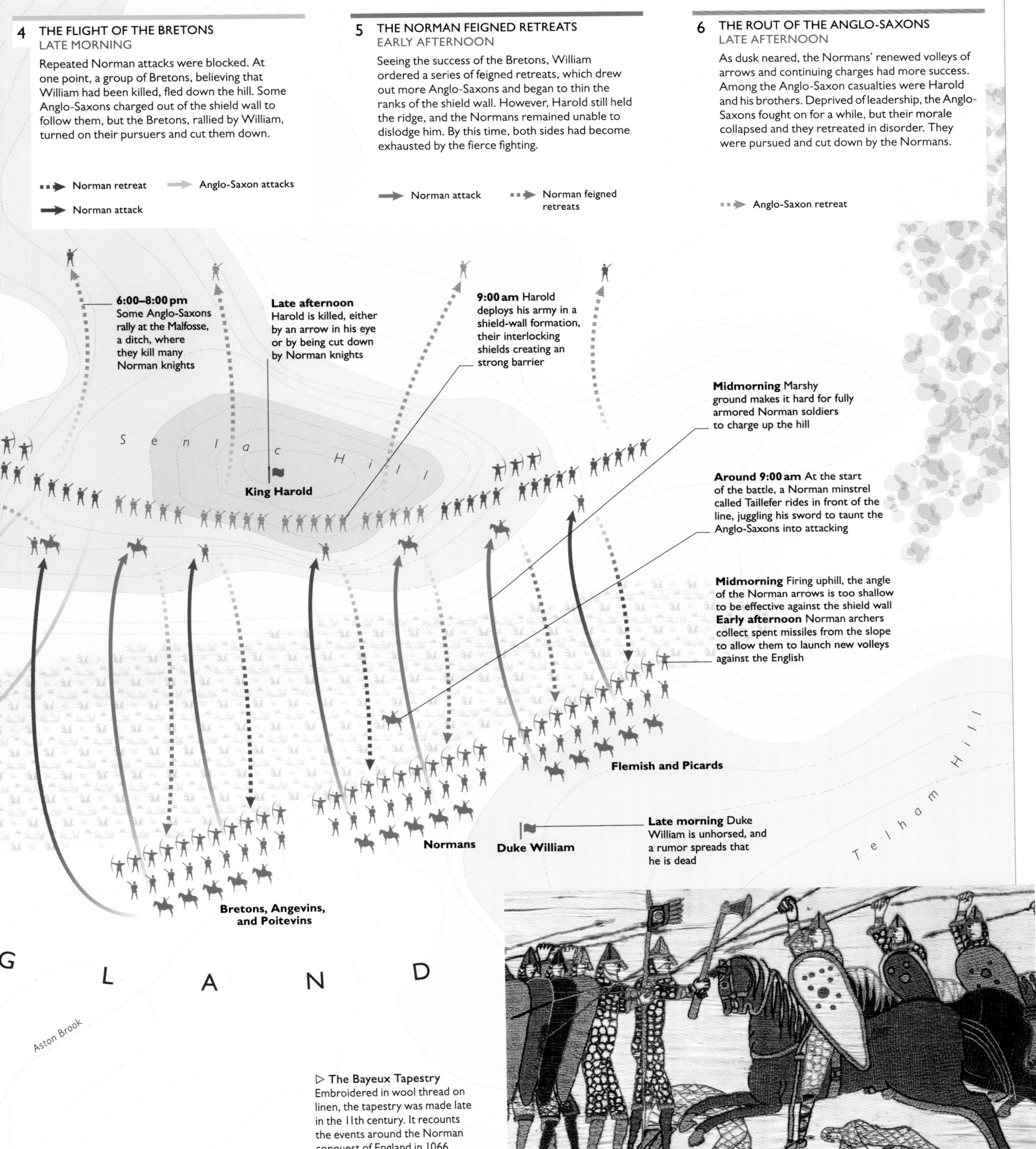

4 THE FLIGHT OF THE BRETONS
LATE MORNING

Repeated Norman attacks were blocked. At one point, a group of Bretons, believing that William had been killed, fled down the hill. Some Anglo-Saxons charged out of the shield wall to follow them, but the Bretons, rallied by William, turned on their pursuers and cut them down.

┄┄► Norman retreat   ➡ Anglo-Saxon attacks

━━► Norman attack

5 THE NORMAN FEIGNED RETREATS
EARLY AFTERNOON

Seeing the success of the Bretons, William ordered a series of feigned retreats, which drew out more Anglo-Saxons and began to thin the ranks of the shield wall. However, Harold still held the ridge, and the Normans remained unable to dislodge him. By this time, both sides had become exhausted by the fierce fighting.

➡ Norman attack   ┄┄► Norman feigned retreats

6 THE ROUT OF THE ANGLO-SAXONS
LATE AFTERNOON

As dusk neared, the Normans' renewed volleys of arrows and continuing charges had more success. Among the Anglo-Saxon casualties were Harold and his brothers. Deprived of leadership, the Anglo-Saxons fought on for a while, but their morale collapsed and they retreated in disorder. They were pursued and cut down by the Normans.

┄┄► Anglo-Saxon retreat

6:00–8:00 pm Some Anglo-Saxons rally at the Malfosse, a ditch, where they kill many Norman knights

Late afternoon Harold is killed, either by an arrow in his eye or by being cut down by Norman knights

9:00 am Harold deploys his army in a shield-wall formation, their interlocking shields creating an strong barrier

Midmorning Marshy ground makes it hard for fully armored Norman soldiers to charge up the hill

Around 9:00 am At the start of the battle, a Norman minstrel called Taillefer rides in front of the line, juggling his sword to taunt the Anglo-Saxons into attacking

Midmorning Firing uphill, the angle of the Norman arrows is too shallow to be effective against the shield wall

Early afternoon Norman archers collect spent missiles from the slope to allow them to launch new volleys against the English

Senlac Hill

King Harold

Flemish and Picards

Normans   **Duke William**

Late morning Duke William is unhorsed, and a rumor spreads that he is dead

Telham Hill

Bretons, Angevins, and Poitevins

G   L   A   N   D

Aston Brook

▷ **The Bayeux Tapestry**
Embroidered in wool thread on linen, the tapestry was made late in the 11th century. It recounts the events around the Norman conquest of England in 1066.

THE NORMANS

In 911 CE, Charles III of France granted the land of Normandy to Rollo, a Norseman, and his followers. Adopting French customs, they became the Normans and emerged as major players in medieval Europe.

In the Anglo-Saxon world, the Normans are usually associated with the Norman Conquest, the Battle of Hastings (see pp.58–59), the creation of the medieval kingdom of England, and the English king's claims on a part of France. However, they were also active in southern Italy and the Levant (modern-day western Asia).

△ **Combat helmet**
This is a typical Norman helmet with a nose guard, from the 12–13th centuries. Similar helmets were common in Western and Central Europe.

Expanding their horizons

The Norsemen went on to adopt Christianity and the French language, and also the French preference for mounted combat. Norman knights, either serving under their lords or as mercenaries, became a common feature of warfare in Europe. The Normans arrived in the Mediterranean as mercenaries for the Byzantine Empire, the Pope, and the local Lombard states. Under Robert Guiscard (c.1015–85), they carved out a large empire, at its height spanning southern Italy, Sicily, part of north Africa, and the western coast of Greece and Albania. Guiscard's son, Bohemond of Taranto, took part in the First Crusade (1096–99), claiming the principality of Antioch for himself in Syria.

Despite their fearsome reputation and impressive conquests, the Normans' power did not rest on superior weaponry, inexhaustible manpower, or innovative tactics. Their success stemmed instead from their renowned ferocity, drive and ambition, their determined castle-building, and the Norman princes' cunning and ability to exploit existing power dynamics in the lands they conquered and subsequently administered.

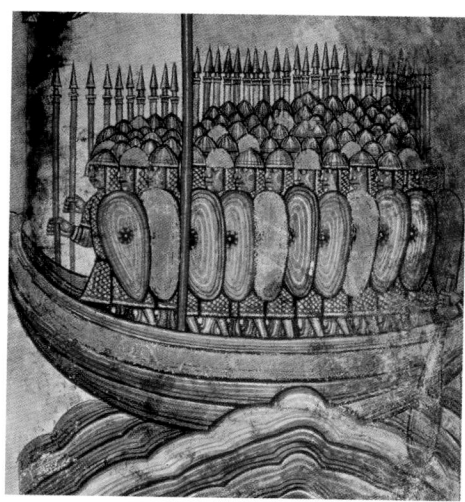

◁ **Crossing the Channel**
This 11th-century French manuscript shows Vikings sailing to attack a Breton town in 919 CE. They wear heavy armor and carry kite shields, as did the Normans who invaded England in the illustrator's century.

▷ **Clashing armies**
This 15th-century scene shows the Battle of Hastings. Although an 11th-century battle, this illustration also shows arms, armor, and troop types contemporary to the illustrator rather than the battle itself, with even the Saxons anachronistically using mounted knights.

MANZIKERT

In 1071, the Byzantine emperor, Romanos IV Diogenes, struck out at the Seljuq Turks who had been harrying his empire's eastern borders. He was defeated and captured at Manzikert, a battle that led to the loss of most of Anatolia to the Seljuqs.

After a military renaissance in the 10th and early 11th century that saw the Byzantine empire consolidate its eastern frontier, a series of weak emperors undermined its position. At the same time, the Seljuq Turks—a Muslim dynasty originating near the Aral Sea—emerged as a potent new threat in Anatolia. In 1068, Romanos Diogenes became emperor and began a series of reforms to strengthen the fractured Byzantine army. He led inconclusive campaigns into Armenia and Syria, and in 1069, made a treaty with the Seljuqs.

During negotiations for the renewal of this treaty in 1071, Romanos took the Seljuq sultan Alp Arslan by surprise, marching across Anatolia to capture territory held by the Seljuqs. On reaching Lake Van, he sent half of his forces—including the feared Varangian guard—under his general Joseph Tarchaneiotes to secure the fortress of Khilat, while he himself took Manzikert from its Turkish garrison.

When Alp Arslan heard of the Byzantine foray, he marched to Manzikert to confront Romanos. Lacking half his force, Romanos was captured. Even though the sultan released him after a week, Romanos's authority was undermined and he was deposed by his former allies, the Doukids. A decade-long civil war followed in Anatolia, allowing much of it to be overrun by the Seljuqs.

> *"Either I will achieve the goal or I will go as a martyr to Paradise."*
>
> ALP ARSLAN BEFORE THE BATTLE OF MANZIKERT

THE BYZANTINE EMPIRE

The Greek-speaking eastern provinces of the Roman empire survived the barbarian invasions of the 5th century CE to become the Byzantine empire, based in Constantinople. Although it lost north Africa to Arab attacks in the 7th century, it regained much of the Balkans from Slav invaders. The rise of new Muslim powers—first the Seljuqs and then the Ottomans—led to large territorial losses, and in 1453 Constantinople fell to the Ottoman sultan Mehmed II.

11th-century ivory panel showing Christ crowning Romanos IV

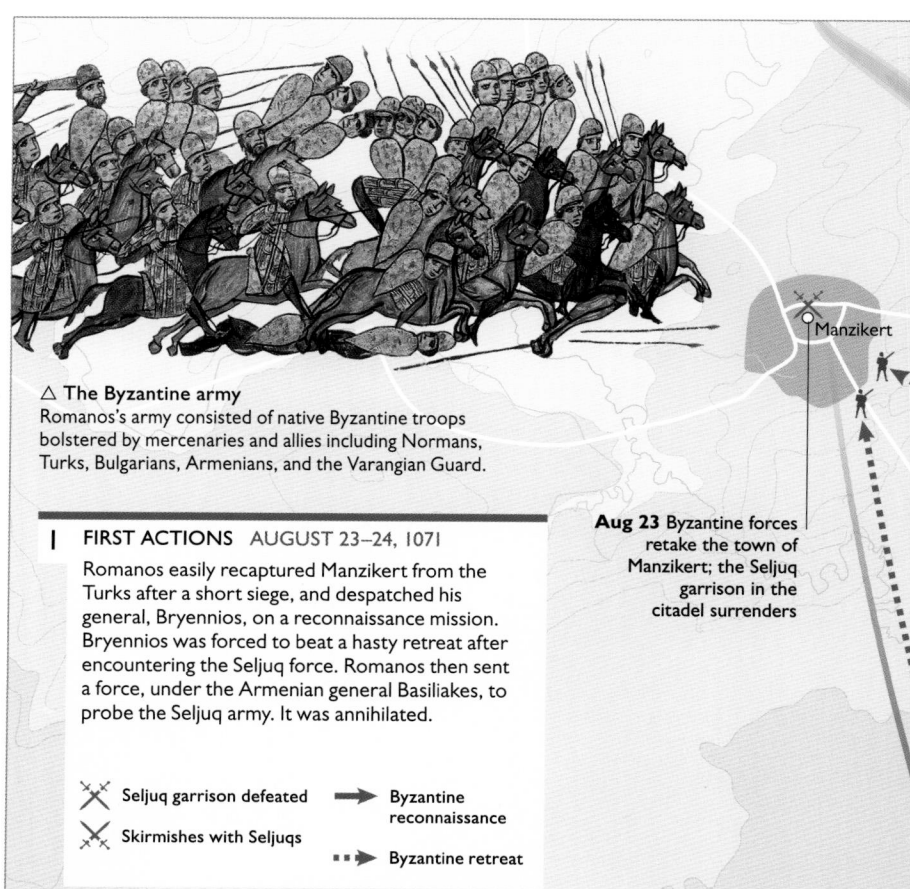

△ **The Byzantine army**
Romanos's army consisted of native Byzantine troops bolstered by mercenaries and allies including Normans, Turks, Bulgarians, Armenians, and the Varangian Guard.

I | FIRST ACTIONS AUGUST 23–24, 1071

Romanos easily recaptured Manzikert from the Turks after a short siege, and despatched his general, Bryennios, on a reconnaissance mission. Bryennios was forced to beat a hasty retreat after encountering the Seljuq force. Romanos then sent a force, under the Armenian general Basiliakes, to probe the Seljuq army. It was annihilated.

✕ Seljuq garrison defeated
✕ Skirmishes with Seljuqs
→ Byzantine reconnaissance
⇢ Byzantine retreat

Aug 23 Byzantine forces retake the town of Manzikert; the Seljuq garrison in the citadel surrenders

BYZANTINE–SELJUQ WARS

The Seljuqs, a nomadic Turkish group, began raiding the Byzantine empire in 1048, when they attacked the region near Trebizond. Under Sultan Alp Arslan, their attacks grew more severe and in 1064 Arslan captured the Armenian capital of Ani. In 1067–69, he took several key Byzantine towns in Anatolia and—though the Seljuqs were initially forced back—prompted Romanos's Manzikert campaign.

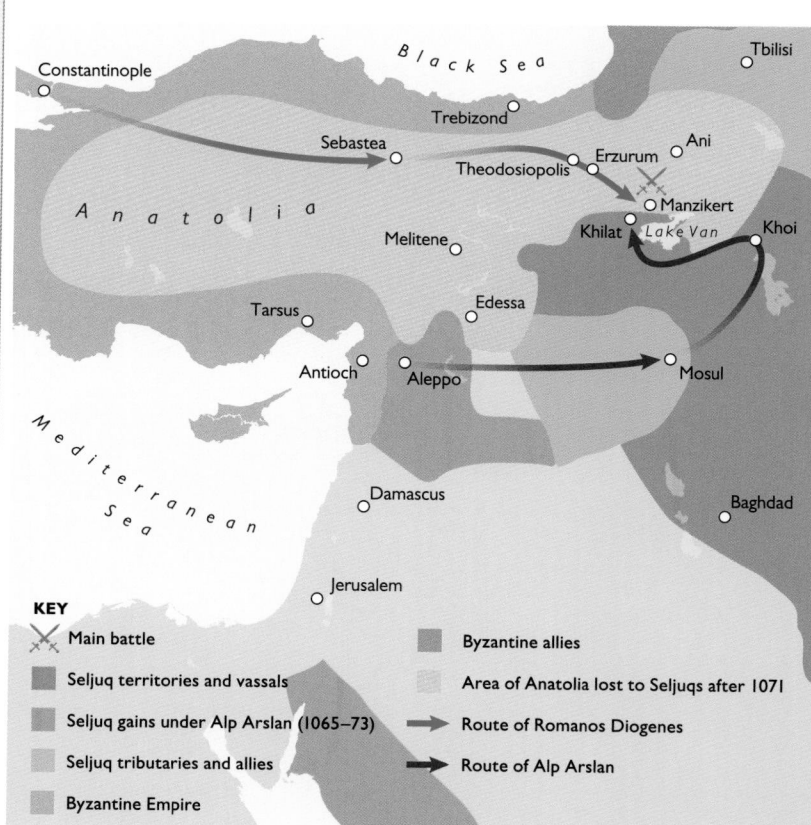

KEY

✕ Main battle

▨ Seljuq territories and vassals

▨ Seljuq gains under Alp Arslan (1065–73)

▨ Seljuq tributaries and allies

▨ Byzantine Empire

▨ Byzantine allies

▨ Area of Anatolia lost to Seljuqs after 1071

→ Route of Romanos Diogenes

→ Route of Alp Arslan

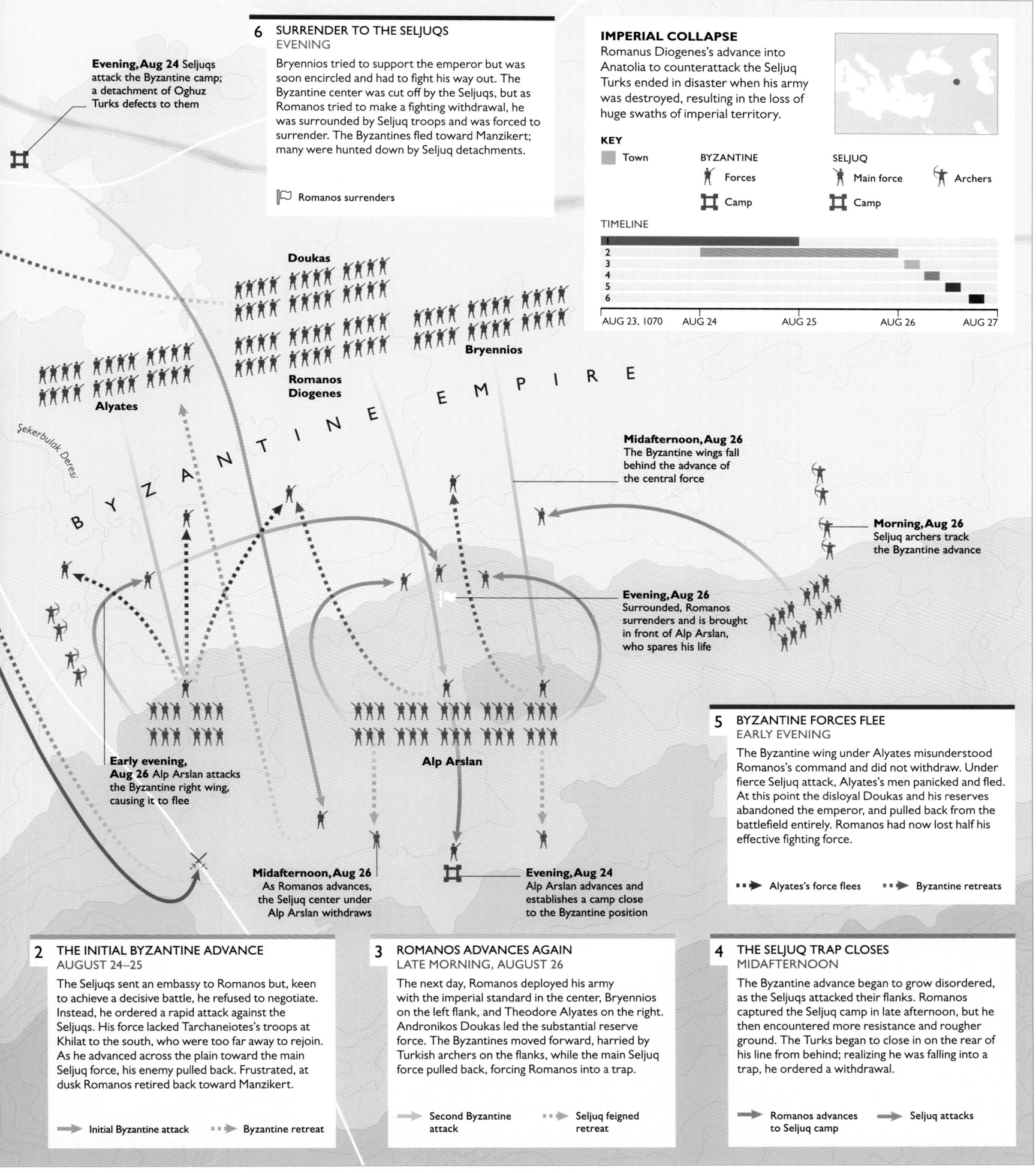

6 SURRENDER TO THE SELJUQS
EVENING

Bryennios tried to support the emperor but was soon encircled and had to fight his way out. The Byzantine center was cut off by the Seljuqs, but as Romanos tried to make a fighting withdrawal, he was surrounded by Seljuq troops and was forced to surrender. The Byzantines fled toward Manzikert; many were hunted down by Seljuq detachments.

⚐ Romanos surrenders

Evening, Aug 24 Seljuqs attack the Byzantine camp; a detachment of Oghuz Turks defects to them

IMPERIAL COLLAPSE
Romanus Diogenes's advance into Anatolia to counterattack the Seljuq Turks ended in disaster when his army was destroyed, resulting in the loss of huge swaths of imperial territory.

KEY

▨ Town	BYZANTINE	SELJUQ
	🧍 Forces	🧍 Main force 🏹 Archers
	▥ Camp	▥ Camp

TIMELINE

	AUG 23, 1070	AUG 24	AUG 25	AUG 26	AUG 27
1					
2					
3					
4					
5					
6					

Doukas

Bryennios

Romanos Diogenes

Alyates

Şekerbulak Deresi

B Y Z A N T I N E   E M P I R E

Midafternoon, Aug 26 The Byzantine wings fall behind the advance of the central force

Morning, Aug 26 Seljuq archers track the Byzantine advance

Evening, Aug 26 Surrounded, Romanos surrenders and is brought in front of Alp Arslan, who spares his life

Alp Arslan

Early evening, Aug 26 Alp Arslan attacks the Byzantine right wing, causing it to flee

Midafternoon, Aug 26 As Romanos advances, the Seljuq center under Alp Arslan withdraws

Evening, Aug 24 Alp Arslan advances and establishes a camp close to the Byzantine position

5 BYZANTINE FORCES FLEE
EARLY EVENING

The Byzantine wing under Alyates misunderstood Romanos's command and did not withdraw. Under fierce Seljuq attack, Alyates's men panicked and fled. At this point the disloyal Doukas and his reserves abandoned the emperor, and pulled back from the battlefield entirely. Romanos had now lost half his effective fighting force.

◼▸ Alyates's force flees   ◼▸ Byzantine retreats

2 THE INITIAL BYZANTINE ADVANCE
AUGUST 24–25

The Seljuqs sent an embassy to Romanos but, keen to achieve a decisive battle, he refused to negotiate. Instead, he ordered a rapid attack against the Seljuqs. His force lacked Tarchaneiotes's troops at Khilat to the south, who were too far away to rejoin. As he advanced across the plain toward the main Seljuq force, his enemy pulled back. Frustrated, at dusk Romanos retired back toward Manzikert.

➡ Initial Byzantine attack   ▸ Byzantine retreat

3 ROMANOS ADVANCES AGAIN
LATE MORNING, AUGUST 26

The next day, Romanos deployed his army with the imperial standard in the center, Bryennios on the left flank, and Theodore Alyates on the right. Andronikos Doukas led the substantial reserve force. The Byzantines moved forward, harried by Turkish archers on the flanks, while the main Seljuq force pulled back, forcing Romanos into a trap.

➡ Second Byzantine attack   ▸ Seljuq feigned retreat

4 THE SELJUQ TRAP CLOSES
MIDAFTERNOON

The Byzantine advance began to grow disordered, as the Seljuqs attacked their flanks. Romanos captured the Seljuq camp in late afternoon, but he then encountered more resistance and rougher ground. The Turks began to close in on the rear of his line from behind; realizing he was falling into a trap, he ordered a withdrawal.

➡ Romanos advances to Seljuq camp   ➡ Seljuq attacks

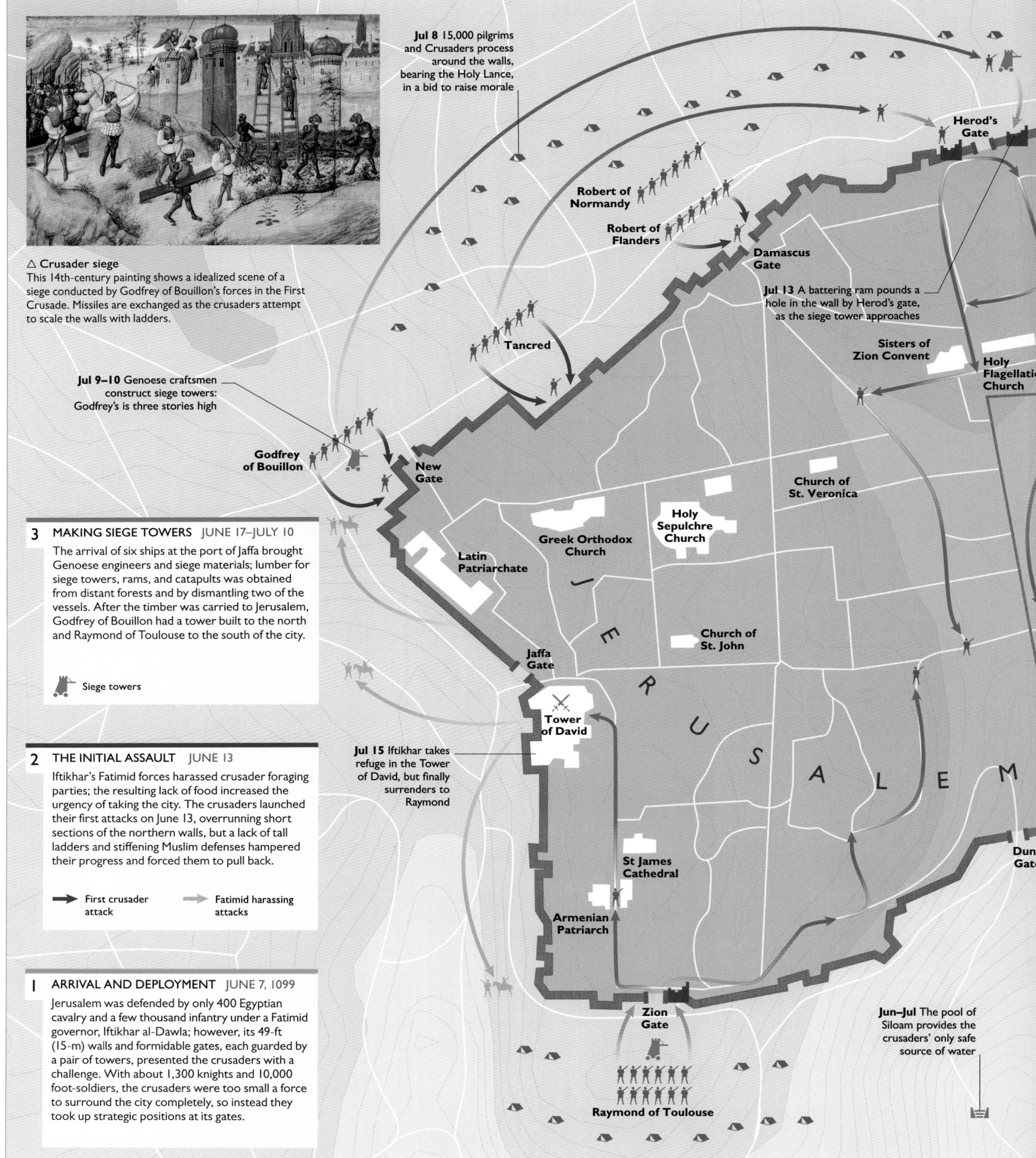

△ Crusader siege
This 14th-century painting shows a idealized scene of a siege conducted by Godfrey of Bouillon's forces in the First Crusade. Missiles are exchanged as the crusaders attempt to scale the walls with ladders.

Jul 8 15,000 pilgrims and Crusaders process around the walls, bearing the Holy Lance, in a bid to raise morale

Herod's Gate

Robert of Normandy

Robert of Flanders

Damascus Gate

Jul 13 A battering ram pounds a hole in the wall by Herod's gate, as the siege tower approaches

Sisters of Zion Convent

Holy Flagellation Church

Tancred

Jul 9–10 Genoese craftsmen construct siege towers: Godfrey's is three stories high

Godfrey of Bouillon

New Gate

Church of St. Veronica

Holy Sepulchre Church

Greek Orthodox Church

Latin Patriarchate

3 MAKING SIEGE TOWERS JUNE 17–JULY 10

The arrival of six ships at the port of Jaffa brought Genoese engineers and siege materials; lumber for siege towers, rams, and catapults was obtained from distant forests and by dismantling two of the vessels. After the timber was carried to Jerusalem, Godfrey of Bouillon had a tower built to the north and Raymond of Toulouse to the south of the city.

🏰 Siege towers

Jaffa Gate

Church of St. John

Tower of David

Jul 15 Iftikhar takes refuge in the Tower of David, but finally surrenders to Raymond

2 THE INITIAL ASSAULT JUNE 13

Iftikhar's Fatimid forces harassed crusader foraging parties; the resulting lack of food increased the urgency of taking the city. The crusaders launched their first attacks on June 13, overrunning short sections of the northern walls, but a lack of tall ladders and stiffening Muslim defenses hampered their progress and forced them to pull back.

→ First crusader attack

→ Fatimid harassing attacks

St James Cathedral

Armenian Patriarch

1 ARRIVAL AND DEPLOYMENT JUNE 7, 1099

Jerusalem was defended by only 400 Egyptian cavalry and a few thousand infantry under a Fatimid governor, Iftikhar al-Dawla; however, its 49-ft (15-m) walls and formidable gates, each guarded by a pair of towers, presented the crusaders with a challenge. With about 1,300 knights and 10,000 foot-soldiers, the crusaders were too small a force to surround the city completely, so instead they took up strategic positions at its gates.

Zion Gate

Dung Gate

Jun–Jul The pool of Siloam provides the crusaders' only safe source of water

Raymond of Toulouse

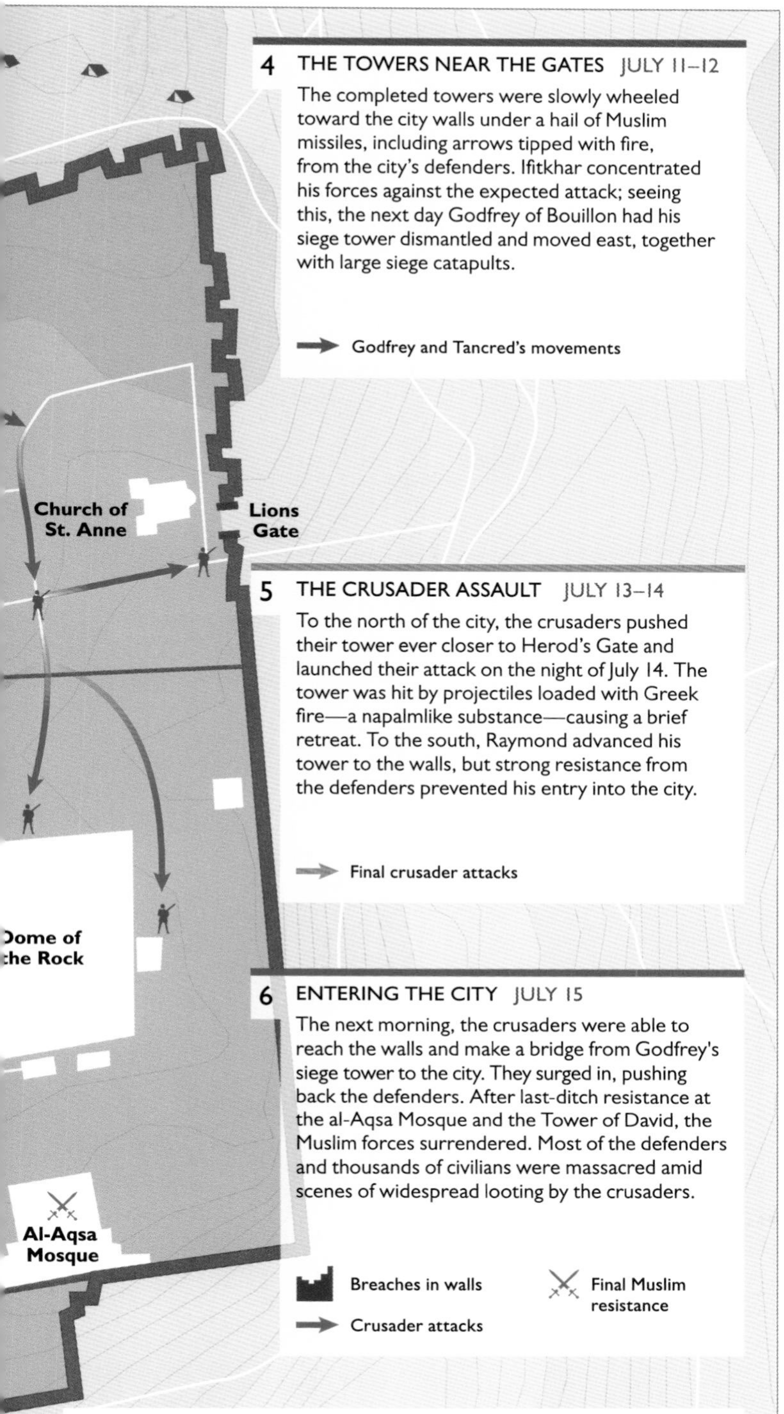

4 THE TOWERS NEAR THE GATES JULY 11–12

The completed towers were slowly wheeled toward the city walls under a hail of Muslim missiles, including arrows tipped with fire, from the city's defenders. Ifitkhar concentrated his forces against the expected attack; seeing this, the next day Godfrey of Bouillon had his siege tower dismantled and moved east, together with large siege catapults.

→ Godfrey and Tancred's movements

Church of St. Anne

Lions Gate

5 THE CRUSADER ASSAULT JULY 13–14

To the north of the city, the crusaders pushed their tower ever closer to Herod's Gate and launched their attack on the night of July 14. The tower was hit by projectiles loaded with Greek fire—a napalmlike substance—causing a brief retreat. To the south, Raymond advanced his tower to the walls, but strong resistance from the defenders prevented his entry into the city.

→ Final crusader attacks

Dome of the Rock

6 ENTERING THE CITY JULY 15

The next morning, the crusaders were able to reach the walls and make a bridge from Godfrey's siege tower to the city. They surged in, pushing back the defenders. After last-ditch resistance at the al-Aqsa Mosque and the Tower of David, the Muslim forces surrendered. Most of the defenders and thousands of civilians were massacred amid scenes of widespread looting by the crusaders.

Al-Aqsa Mosque

▮ Breaches in walls

✕ Final Muslim resistance

→ Crusader attacks

A CITY UNDER SIEGE

The crusaders lacked the supplies to conduct a long siege and the men to blockade Jerusalem's extensive walls. Their only hope was to make a breach with siege engines through which to enter the city.

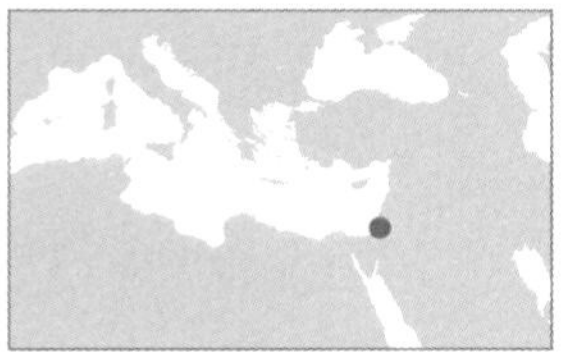

KEY

▢ Buildings	
〰 Pool of Siloam	

CRUSADER FORCES	FATIMID FORCES
♟ Infantry	♟ Infantry
⛺ Camps	🐎 Cavalry

TIMELINE

1
2
3
4
5
6

JUN 1, 1099 — JUN 15 — JUL 1 — JUL 15 — AUG 1

THE SIEGE OF JERUSALEM

The army of the First Crusade, which left its homelands in 1096 to recapture the Holy City of Jerusalem from its Muslim rulers, took nearly three years to reach its objective. Tired and short of supplies, the army succeeded in storming the city's walls, but the massacre of the defenders forever tarnished the crusaders' reputations.

In 1095, the Byzantine Emperor Alexios Komnenos appealed for help to repel the Muslim Seljuq Turks pressing against his borders. Pope Urban II responded, calling for a crusade to free Jerusalem from Muslim control. Thousands of knights under leaders including Godfrey of Bouillon, Bohemond of Taranto, and Count Raymond of Toulouse took up the cause, converging on Constantinople by April 1097. From there, they set out on an arduous journey across Anatolia. Attacks by Seljuqs cost them many men; the prolonged siege of Antioch and the need to garrison the towns

they captured drained many more. By the time they reached Jerusalem in June 1099, they were exhausted and demoralized, and Godfrey feared the expedition might collapse. However, in a last-ditch effort they successfully stormed the city walls. With Godfrey elected King of Jerusalem, they shattered an Egyptian army sent to retake the city in August 1099, and consolidated four crusader states based around Antioch, Tripoli, Edessa, and Jerusalem. It took nearly two centuries before Muslim rulers fully dislodged them.

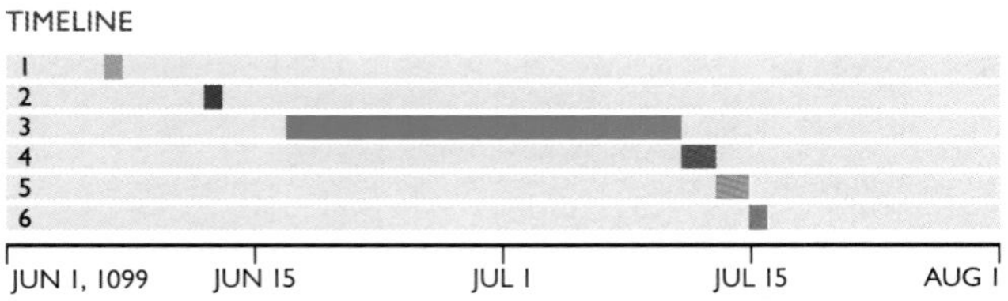

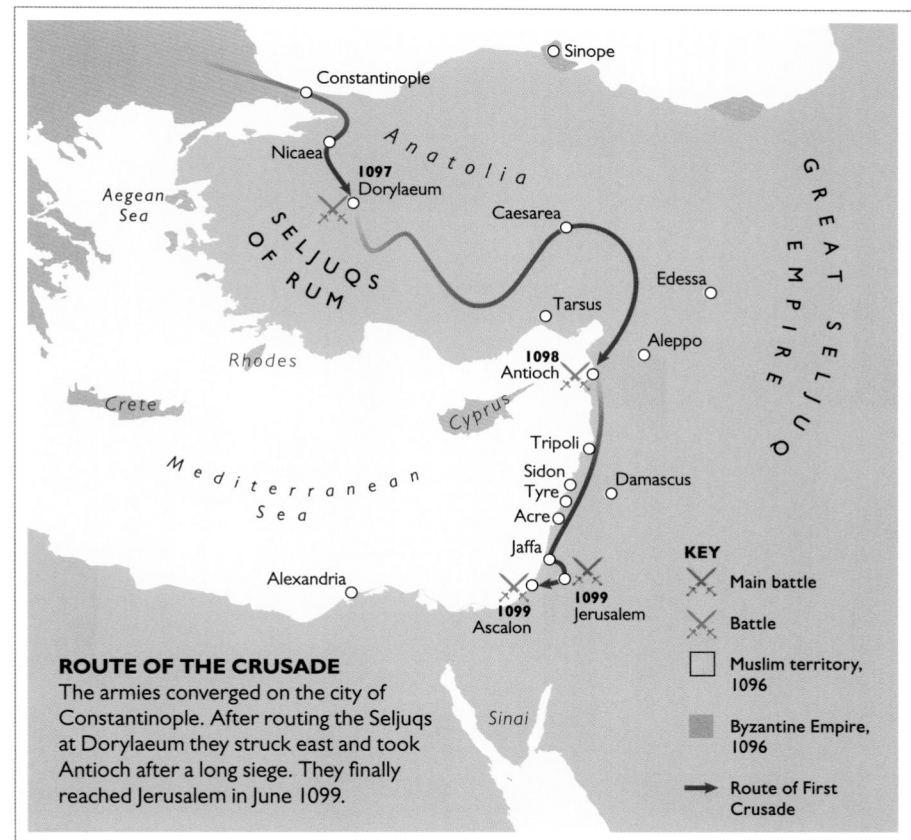

ROUTE OF THE CRUSADE

The armies converged on the city of Constantinople. After routing the Seljuqs at Dorylaeum they struck east and took Antioch after a long siege. They finally reached Jerusalem in June 1099.

KEY

✕ Main battle

✕ Battle

▢ Muslim territory, 1096

▮ Byzantine Empire, 1096

→ Route of First Crusade

LEGNANO

The Holy Roman Emperor Frederick Barbarossa's struggle to bring the restive towns of northern Italy to obedience came to a head at Legnano, near Milan, in 1176. There, the Italian infantry held firm against Frederick's knights, shattering their charge and dealing a devastating blow to the emperor's ambitions.

Frederick Barbarossa (or "Redbeard"), King of Germany and Holy Roman Emperor (r. 1155–1190), sought for many years to regain control over (and revenues from) the city states of northern Italy. In 1154, he launched the first of six expeditions to bring the cities back into the imperial fold and prevent them from drifting into the orbit of the Papacy. In 1167, with the support of Pope Alexander III, the cities formed an alliance known as the Lombard League. This prompted Frederick to invade Italy for a fifth time in 1174, but his campaign ended in disaster for him at Legnano.

Although he had some initial success with the capture of Susa and Asti, Frederick's siege of Alessandria failed in April 1175, and his campaign became bogged down in fruitless negotiations and abortive appeals for reinforcements from Germany. At long last, in May 1176, a force of only about 2,000 troops (consisting mainly of knights) crossed the Alps, and Frederick rode north with his own knights to meet them and lead them back toward his base at Pavia near Milan.

Unknown to Frederick, the Lombard League had assembled its forces and carroccio (see below) near Legnano. At the ensuing encounter, Frederick was defeated and almost lost his life. He was forced into signing a treaty with Alexander III and, ultimately, into recognizing the autonomy of the north Italian cities. The Italian infantry had not only won a famous victory against the imperial knights, but had secured their independent future.

> "It is not for the people to give laws to the prince, but to obey his mandate."
>
> FREDERICK BARBAROSSA, HOLY ROMAN EMPEROR

THE CARROCCIO

First adopted by Milan in the 12th century, the carroccio was a large wooden wagon used by northern Italian cities to carry symbols of their commune, such as battle standards, into combat. Drawn by oxen, it also carried a cross, an altar, and priests to celebrate Mass. A bell (called a martinella) and trumpeters accompanied it to give battle signals to the Lombard troops. The carroccio acted as a rallying point for the troops, and as its capture was regarded as a grave humiliation, it was always bitterly defended.

A 19th-century painting of the defense of the carroccio at Legnano

LOMBARD TRIUMPH

The Lombard League infantry showed what town militias could achieve against mounted knights. Caught between them and the Lombard cavalry, Frederick faced a humiliating defeat.

KEY

LOMBARD LEAGUE FORCES

Cavalry   Archers

Infantry

IMPERIAL FORCES

Cavalry

TIMELINE

1
2
3
4
5
6

4:00 AM, MAY 29, 1176   10:00 AM   4:00 PM

1 | MILANESE CAVALRY ATTACK THE IMPERIAL FORCE   AROUND DAWN, MAY 29, 1176

The Milanese positioned their infantry around their carroccio in a strategic location between Legnano and Borsano. Riding ahead of this position, 700 Milanese knights encountered Frederick's vanguard. The Milanese brushed aside this small imperial force, but Frederick was now aware of the presence of the Lombard League's army.

→ Lombard vanguard   → Imperial vanguard

To Borsano ◄

Early afternoon
Lombard forces arrive and join up with Milanese cavalry

◁ **Reliquary bust**
This gilded bronze bust of Frederick I was made in Aachen in the 12th century and used as a reliquary (a container for relics).

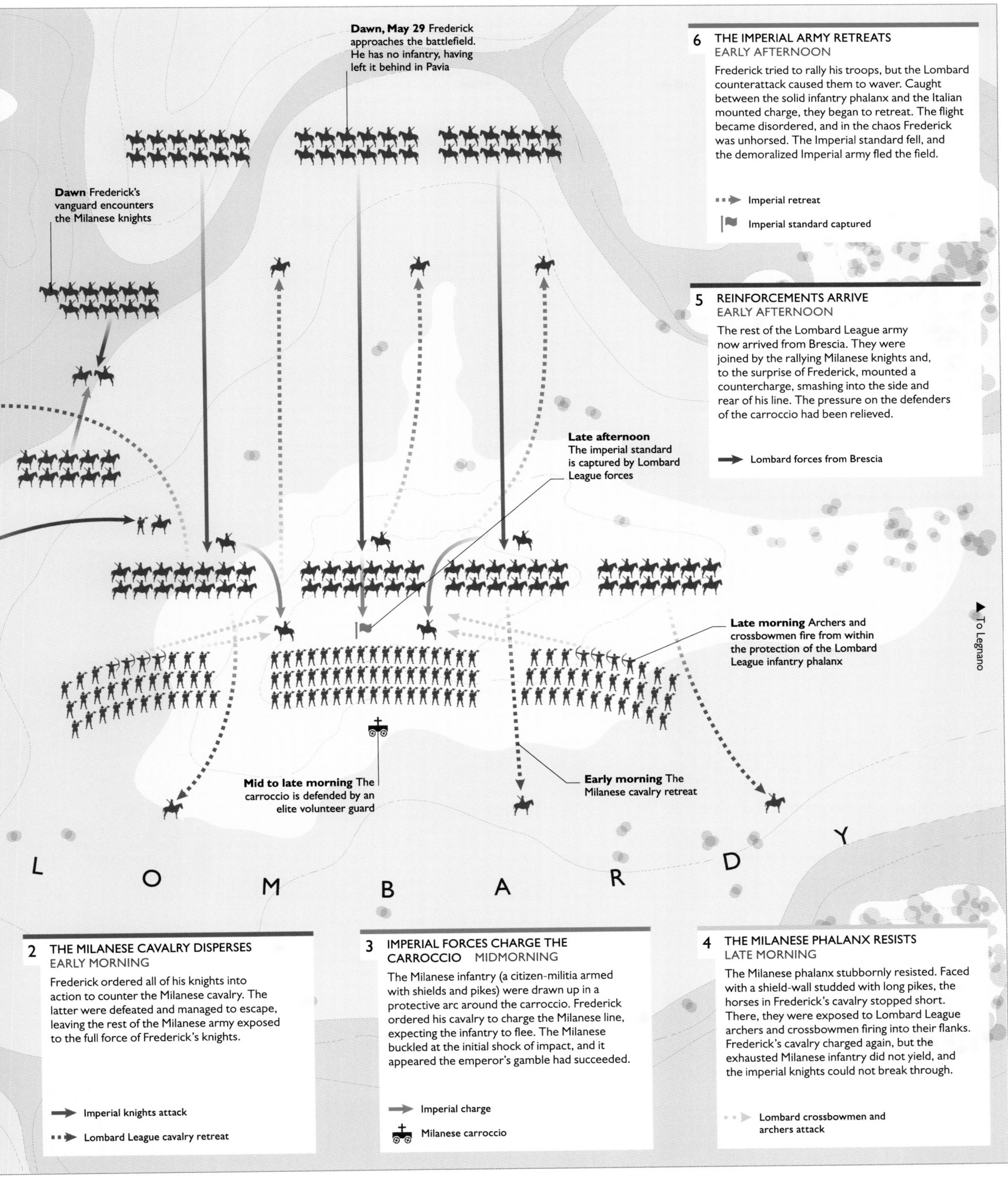

Dawn, May 29 Frederick approaches the battlefield. He has no infantry, having left it behind in Pavia

Dawn Frederick's vanguard encounters the Milanese knights

Late afternoon The imperial standard is captured by Lombard League forces

Late morning Archers and crossbowmen fire from within the protection of the Lombard League infantry phalanx

Mid to late morning The carroccio is defended by an elite volunteer guard

Early morning The Milanese cavalry retreat

▶ To Legnano

L O M B A R D Y

6 THE IMPERIAL ARMY RETREATS
EARLY AFTERNOON

Frederick tried to rally his troops, but the Lombard counterattack caused them to waver. Caught between the solid infantry phalanx and the Italian mounted charge, they began to retreat. The flight became disordered, and in the chaos Frederick was unhorsed. The Imperial standard fell, and the demoralized Imperial army fled the field.

▪▪▪▶ Imperial retreat

▐ Imperial standard captured

5 REINFORCEMENTS ARRIVE
EARLY AFTERNOON

The rest of the Lombard League army now arrived from Brescia. They were joined by the rallying Milanese knights and, to the surprise of Frederick, mounted a countercharge, smashing into the side and rear of his line. The pressure on the defenders of the carroccio had been relieved.

➡ Lombard forces from Brescia

2 THE MILANESE CAVALRY DISPERSES
EARLY MORNING

Frederick ordered all of his knights into action to counter the Milanese cavalry. The latter were defeated and managed to escape, leaving the rest of the Milanese army exposed to the full force of Frederick's knights.

➡ Imperial knights attack

▪▪▶ Lombard League cavalry retreat

3 IMPERIAL FORCES CHARGE THE CARROCCIO MIDMORNING

The Milanese infantry (a citizen-militia armed with shields and pikes) were drawn up in a protective arc around the carroccio. Frederick ordered his cavalry to charge the Milanese line, expecting the infantry to flee. The Milanese buckled at the initial shock of impact, and it appeared the emperor's gamble had succeeded.

➡ Imperial charge

⛪ Milanese carroccio

4 THE MILANESE PHALANX RESISTS
LATE MORNING

The Milanese phalanx stubbornly resisted. Faced with a shield-wall studded with long pikes, the horses in Frederick's cavalry stopped short. There, they were exposed to Lombard League archers and crossbowmen firing into their flanks. Frederick's cavalry charged again, but the exhausted Milanese infantry did not yield, and the imperial knights could not break through.

▪▪▸ Lombard crossbowmen and archers attack

2 THE TAIRA ATTACK   MIDMORNING

Advancing rapidly along the riptides, the Taira launched volleys of arrows into the Minamoto, and divided in an attempt to encircle Yoshitsune's fleet. Held back by the tides, the Minamoto were unable to maneuver. They maintained their lines, but their flanks begin to buckle under the attack. Grappling hooks brought the Taira ships alongside, and they engaged their foe in close-quarter fighting.

➡ Taira attack

1 THE MINAMOTO APPROACH
EARLY MORNING, APRIL 25, 1185

As the Minamoto fleet approached, it deployed in a line blocking the Shimonoseki Strait. The Taira commanders, including Tomomori, divided their ships into three squadrons. They hoped to use the riptides to launch an attack while the tidal current made it difficult for the Minamoto ships to respond effectively.

➡ Minamoto fleet arrives   ➡ Riptide

3 THE TIDE TURNS   11 AM–12 PM

Late in the morning, the tide turned against the Taira. This enabled Yoshitsune to launch a counterattack. At about the same time, Taguchi Shigeyoshi, one of the Taira commanders, defected, leaving a large gap in the Taira line and increasing the Minamoto's numerical advantage even more.

➡ Minamoto counterattack   ▪▪▶ Taira fleet pushed back

➡ Taira defectors

4 THE TAIRA ROUT   EARLY AFTERNOON

Shigeyoshi revealed the location of the emperor's ship to Yoshitsune, allowing the Minamoto to attack it directly. Under pressure, the Taira line fell apart and its commanders committed suicide. Tomomori plunged into the sea wrapped around an anchor, and the emperor Antoku's grandmother took him in her arms and jumped into the waters.

🚢 Emperor's ship

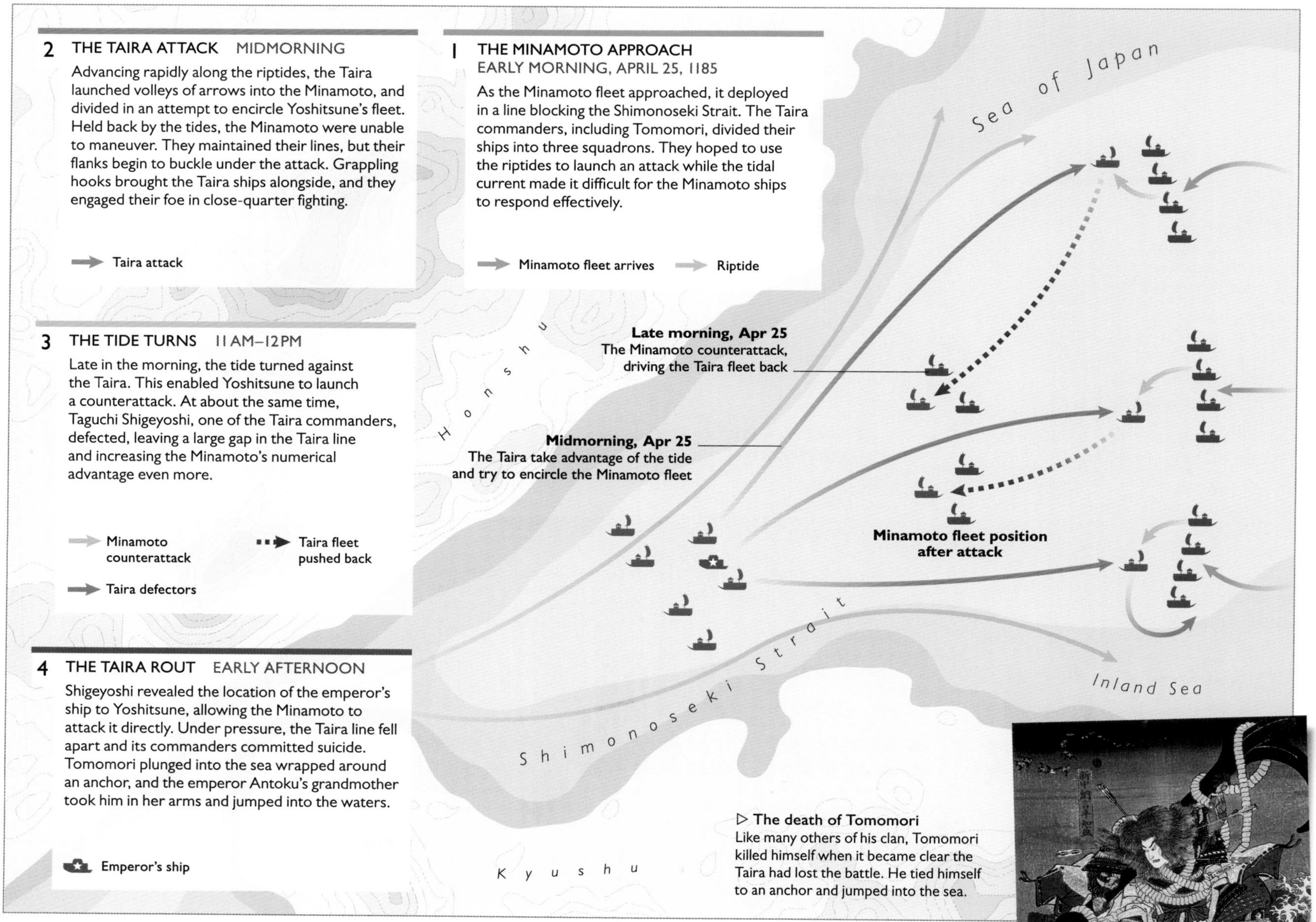

Sea of Japan

Honshu

Late morning, Apr 25
The Minamoto counterattack, driving the Taira fleet back

Midmorning, Apr 25
The Taira take advantage of the tide and try to encircle the Minamoto fleet

Minamoto fleet position after attack

Shimonoseki Strait

Inland Sea

Kyushu

▷ **The death of Tomomori**
Like many others of his clan, Tomomori killed himself when it became clear the Taira had lost the battle. He tied himself to an anchor and jumped into the sea.

DAN-NO-URA

A bitter civil war between the rival Taira and Minamoto clans came to an end in April 1185 at the naval battle of Dan-no-Ura. On the Shimonoseki Straits, the Taira fleet was soundly defeated, leaving Japan under the control of Minamoto no Yoritomo.

In 1180, Japan descended into civil war as the Minamoto clan tried to oust the rival Taira clan from their dominant position in the imperial capital, Kyoto. Three years later, they succeeded in dislodging the Taira, who fled to western Japan, together with five-year-old emperor Antoku. A split in the Minamoto clan between Minamoto no Yoshitsune and his cousin Yoshinaka allowed the Taira brief respite, but Yoshitsune's victory at Uji in early 1184 enabled him to reunite the clan. He pursued the Taira south, storming their

fortress of Ichi-no-Tani in March 1184, before forcing them to take to their fleet to escape. With no safe haven on land, the Taira were vulnerable to the pursuing Minamoto fleet, which caught them at Dan-no-Ura, on the narrow Shimonoseki Strait. The Taira suffered a crushing defeat—its fleet was destroyed and the young emperor and senior commanders were killed. In 1185, Minamoto no Yoritomo, Yoshitsune's elder half-brother, became effective ruler of Japan, and later the first shogun of the Kamakura Shogunate (1192–1333).

BATTLE ON THE STRAITS
The Shimonoseki Straits separate two of the main Japanese islands and are subject to strong riptides. The Taira clan hoped to use these tides to their advantage.

KEY

🚢 Taira fleet   ⛵ Minamoto fleet

TIMELINE

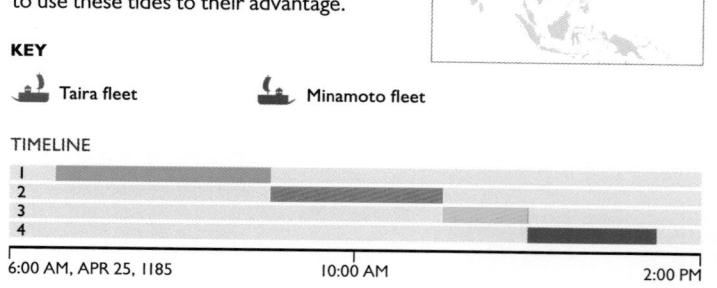

6:00 AM, APR 25, 1185   10:00 AM   2:00 PM

HATTIN

In July 1187, Guy de Lusignan, king of Jerusalem, set out to relieve the fortress of Tiberias, held under siege by Saladin. On the arid plain near Hattin, his army was surrounded and destroyed by the Ayyubid forces. Only months later, Saladin's armies would enter Jerusalem itself.

The crusader states of Palestine entered a period of decline in the 1180s. Few fresh recruits were coming from Europe, and Guy de Lusignan, the new king of Jerusalem, was only able to take the throne in 1186 following a damaging succession dispute. A recent truce with Saladin, the Ayyubid sultan of Egypt, broke down in early 1187 after Guy's ally Raynald of Châtillon raided a Muslim caravan traveling from Egypt to Syria. In retaliation, Saladin besieged the fortress at Tiberias on July 2, aiming to lure the crusaders to its rescue. In response, Guy mustered the crusader host at Sephoria, 19 miles (30 km) to the west of Tiberias, but ignored advice to stand fast and wait for Saladin to come to him. Instead, he headed on across the waterless plains. The resulting destruction of his army at Hattin two days later was a disaster for Guy and his kingdom. One by one, the crusader fortresses fell—Acre, Tiberias, Caesarea, Jaffa, and then, on October 2, 1187, the Holy City of Jerusalem. The shock was so profound it led to the calling of the Third Crusade to try to liberate it.

DESERT ENCOUNTER

Against the advice of his allies, Guy led the crusaders across the desert to confront Saladin. Exhausted and short of water, they were an easy target for Saladin's forces.

KEY

Crusader infantry   Crusader camp   Ayyubid infantry

Crusader cavalry   Springs   Ayyubid mounted archers

Ayyubid cavalry

TIMELINE

```
1
2
3
```
12:00 AM, JUL 3, 1187   12:00 PM   12:00 AM, JUL 4   12:00 PM

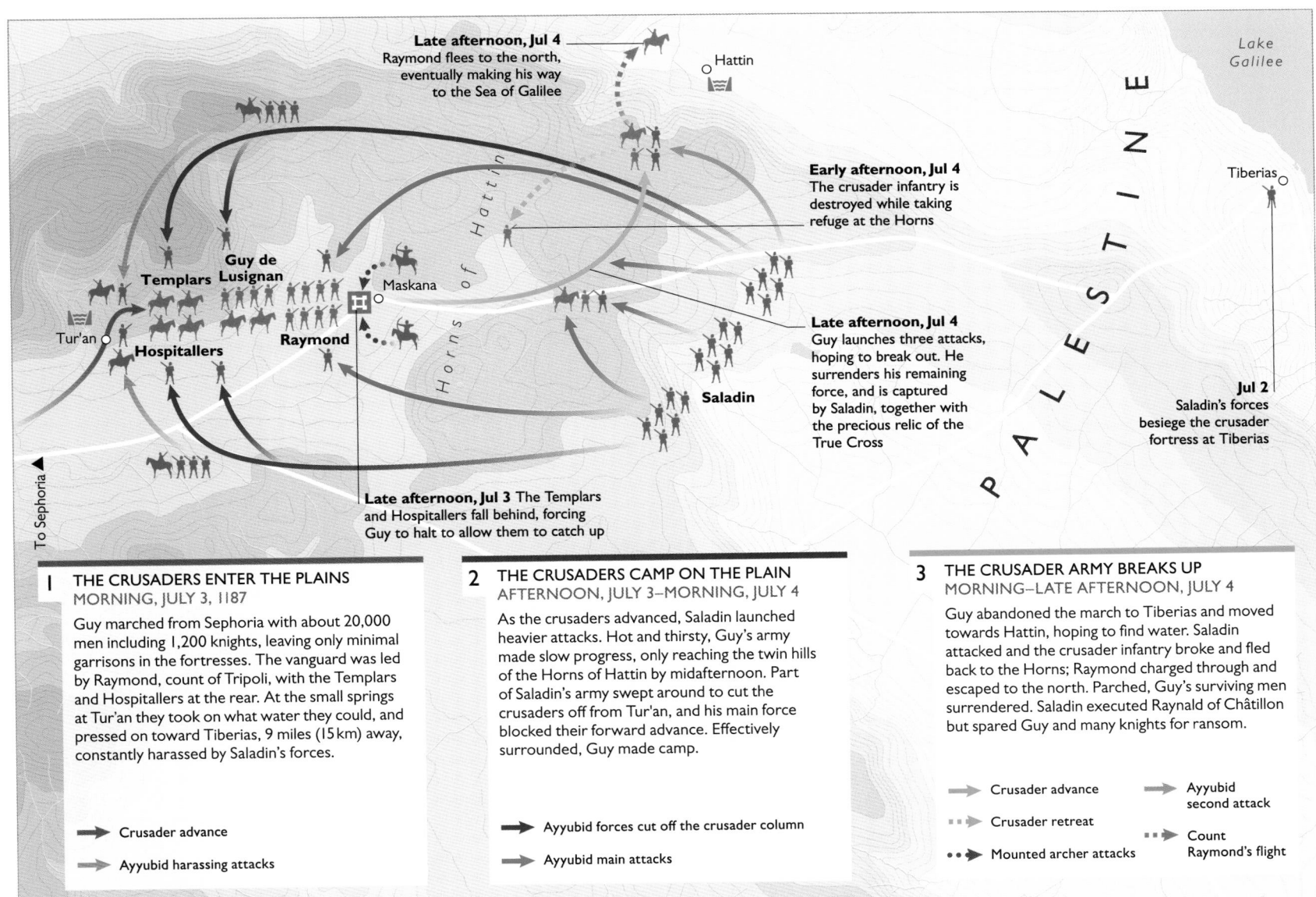

Late afternoon, Jul 4
Raymond flees to the north, eventually making his way to the Sea of Galilee

Hattin

Lake Galilee

Early afternoon, Jul 4
The crusader infantry is destroyed while taking refuge at the Horns

Tiberias

Guy de Lusignan

Templars

Maskana

Tur'an

Hospitallers

Raymond

Late afternoon, Jul 4
Guy launches three attacks, hoping to break out. He surrenders his remaining force, and is captured by Saladin, together with the precious relic of the True Cross

Saladin

Jul 2
Saladin's forces besiege the crusader fortress at Tiberias

To Sephoria

Horns of Hattin

P A L E S T I N E

Late afternoon, Jul 3 The Templars and Hospitallers fall behind, forcing Guy to halt to allow them to catch up

1 THE CRUSADERS ENTER THE PLAINS
MORNING, JULY 3, 1187

Guy marched from Sephoria with about 20,000 men including 1,200 knights, leaving only minimal garrisons in the fortresses. The vanguard was led by Raymond, count of Tripoli, with the Templars and Hospitallers at the rear. At the small springs at Tur'an they took on what water they could, and pressed on toward Tiberias, 9 miles (15 km) away, constantly harassed by Saladin's forces.

→ Crusader advance

→ Ayyubid harassing attacks

2 THE CRUSADERS CAMP ON THE PLAIN
AFTERNOON, JULY 3–MORNING, JULY 4

As the crusaders advanced, Saladin launched heavier attacks. Hot and thirsty, Guy's army made slow progress, only reaching the twin hills of the Horns of Hattin by midafternoon. Part of Saladin's army swept around to cut the crusaders off from Tur'an, and his main force blocked their forward advance. Effectively surrounded, Guy made camp.

→ Ayyubid forces cut off the crusader column

→ Ayyubid main attacks

3 THE CRUSADER ARMY BREAKS UP
MORNING–LATE AFTERNOON, JULY 4

Guy abandoned the march to Tiberias and moved towards Hattin, hoping to find water. Saladin attacked and the crusader infantry broke and fled back to the Horns; Raymond charged through and escaped to the north. Parched, Guy's surviving men surrendered. Saladin executed Raynald of Châtillon but spared Guy and many knights for ransom.

→ Crusader advance   → Ayyubid second attack

⋯→ Crusader retreat   •••→ Count Raymond's flight

•••→ Mounted archer attacks

ARSUF

Saladin appeared invincible to Christian Europe after his capture of Jerusalem in 1187. Four years later, King Richard I of England arrived in the Holy Land as part of the Third Crusade, which aimed to recapture the city. At Arsuf, the crusader armies dealt Saladin's forces a shattering blow and showed he could be defeated.

The capture of Jerusalem by the Muslim Ayyubid leader Saladin in 1187 was greeted with shock and outrage in Christian Europe. It led directly to the Third Crusade (1189–92), the aim of which was to retake the city and reconquer the Holy Land.

Initially, the crusade struggled: Emperor Frederick Barbarossa, the commander of the German contingent, was drowned in June 1190 while crossing Anatolia, and the French crusaders under Philip II had become bogged down in a siege at Acre starting in 1189—one of the crusaders' first objectives. It took the arrival of King Richard I ("the Lionheart") of England to hasten the final assault on the city,

which fell on July 12, 1191. Philip and Leopold went home, along with many French and German crusaders, and the slaughter of prisoners by the crusaders further infuriated Saladin.

Richard pressed south, hoping to take Jaffa as a base from which to assault Jerusalem. When the two forces finally met outside Arsuf, it was their first full encounter on the battlefield. The victory for Richard avenged Saladin's triumph at Hattin four years earlier (see p.69). However, complete victory remained elusive. Under ther terms of a treaty signed in September 1192, Christians would once more be allowed to visit Jerusalem. However, the city itself was to remain in Muslim hands.

> *"They shouted their shout of battle like one man... and through they rushed in one great charge."*
>
> BAHA-AL-DIN, DESCRIBING THE CRUSADERS, C.12TH CENTURY

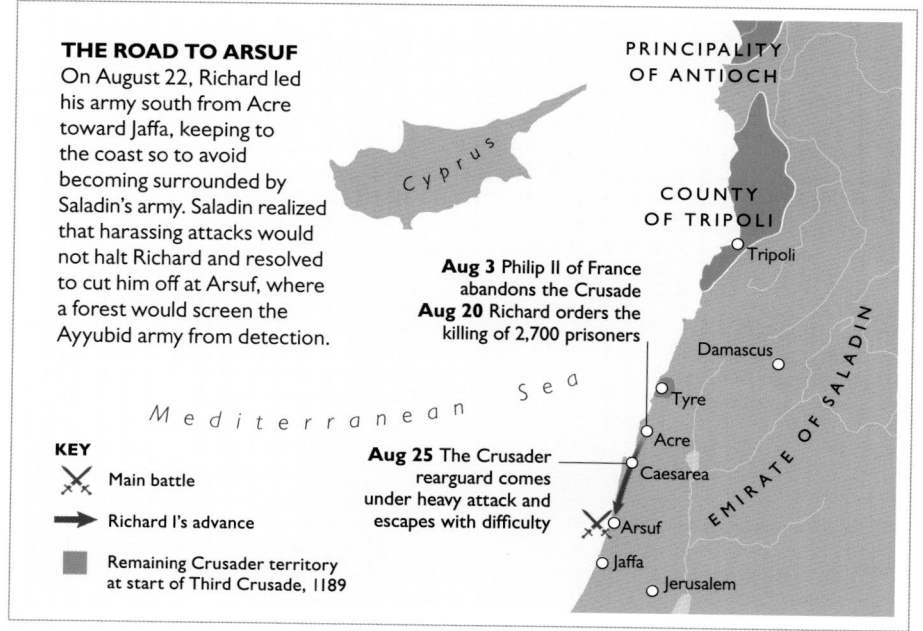

THE ROAD TO ARSUF
On August 22, Richard led his army south from Acre toward Jaffa, keeping to the coast so to avoid becoming surrounded by Saladin's army. Saladin realized that harassing attacks would not halt Richard and resolved to cut him off at Arsuf, where a forest would screen the Ayyubid army from detection.

PRINCIPALITY OF ANTIOCH

Cyprus

COUNTY OF TRIPOLI

Tripoli

Aug 3 Philip II of France abandons the Crusade
Aug 20 Richard orders the killing of 2,700 prisoners

Mediterranean Sea

Damascus

Tyre

Acre

Aug 25 The Crusader rearguard comes under heavy attack and escapes with difficulty

Caesarea

Arsuf

EMIRATE OF SALADIN

Jaffa

Jerusalem

KEY
✕ Main battle
➤ Richard I's advance
▮ Remaining Crusader territory at start of Third Crusade, 1189

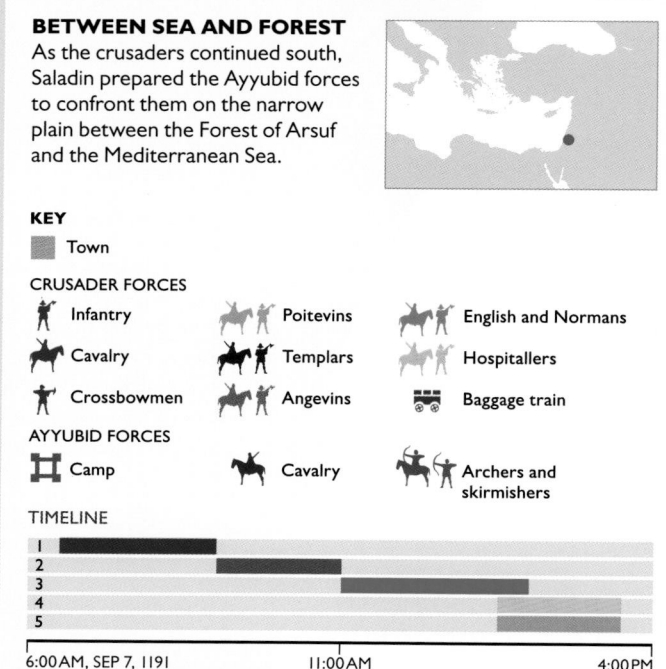

BETWEEN SEA AND FOREST
As the crusaders continued south, Saladin prepared the Ayyubid forces to confront them on the narrow plain between the Forest of Arsuf and the Mediterranean Sea.

KEY

▮ Town

CRUSADER FORCES

🏃 Infantry   🐎 Poitevins   🐎 English and Normans

🐎 Cavalry   🐎 Templars   🐎 Hospitallers

🏹 Crossbowmen   🐎 Angevins   🛒 Baggage train

AYYUBID FORCES

⊟ Camp   🐎 Cavalry   🏹 Archers and skirmishers

TIMELINE

1			
2			
3			
4			
5			

6:00AM, SEP 7, 1191   11:00AM   4:00PM

1 THE ARMIES PREPARE FOR BATTLE
EARLY MORNING, SEPTEMBER 7, 1191

With scouts reporting the presence of the Ayyubid army in the woodland, Richard formed his army of about 12,000 in a defensive formation, with the Knights Templar in the vanguard, the Poitevins, English, and Normans in the center, and the Knights Hospitaller in the rear. Each group was composed of both knights and protective infantry units.

➡ Crusader arrival

2 SALADIN LAUNCHES HARASSING ATTACKS
9:00–11:00AM

As the crusaders moved onto the plain of Arsuf, hoping to reach the town six miles away, Saladin unleashed a series of harassing attacks. Ayyubid foot archers launched volleys of arrows, while horse archers closed in to fire further volleys, before wheeling away in the hope of enticing some crusaders to break ranks and be cut down.

•••➤ ➡ Ayyubid harassing attacks

3 THE CRUSADER LEFT FLANK BUCKLES
11:00AM–2:00PM

With the crusader line holding firm, Saladin launched heavier attacks against the Hospitallers, in the rear of Richard's army. As they approached, the Ayyubids began to take casualties from Richard's crossbowmen. The Hospitaller Grand Master Garnier de Nablus pleaded with Richard to allow him to attack, but the English king insisted that the crusaders remain in formation until the enemy were exhausted.

➡ Ayyubid attacks

Mediterranean Sea

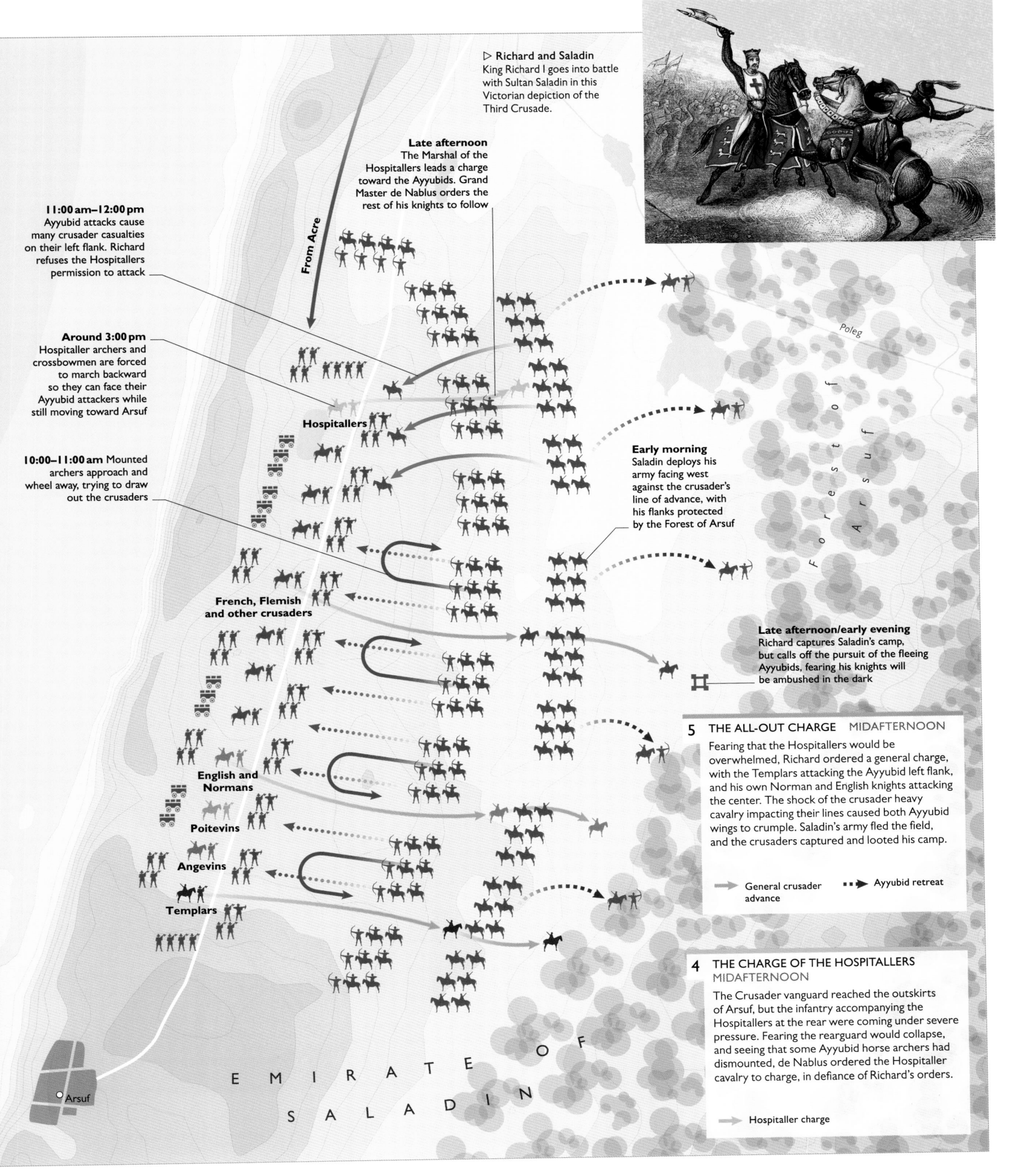

▷ **Richard and Saladin**
King Richard I goes into battle with Sultan Saladin in this Victorian depiction of the Third Crusade.

Late afternoon
The Marshal of the Hospitallers leads a charge toward the Ayyubids. Grand Master de Nablus orders the rest of his knights to follow

11:00 am–12:00 pm
Ayyubid attacks cause many crusader casualties on their left flank. Richard refuses the Hospitallers permission to attack

Around 3:00 pm
Hospitaller archers and crossbowmen are forced to march backward so they can face their Ayyubid attackers while still moving toward Arsuf

10:00–11:00 am Mounted archers approach and wheel away, trying to draw out the crusaders

From Acre

Hospitallers

Early morning
Saladin deploys his army facing west against the crusader's line of advance, with his flanks protected by the Forest of Arsuf

French, Flemish and other crusaders

Late afternoon/early evening
Richard captures Saladin's camp, but calls off the pursuit of the fleeing Ayyubids, fearing his knights will be ambushed in the dark

English and Normans

Poitevins

Angevins

Templars

Poleg

Forest of Arsuf

5 THE ALL-OUT CHARGE MIDAFTERNOON

Fearing that the Hospitallers would be overwhelmed, Richard ordered a general charge, with the Templars attacking the Ayyubid left flank, and his own Norman and English knights attacking the center. The shock of the crusader heavy cavalry impacting their lines caused both Ayyubid wings to crumple. Saladin's army fled the field, and the crusaders captured and looted his camp.

→ General crusader advance
▪▪▸ Ayyubid retreat

4 THE CHARGE OF THE HOSPITALLERS MIDAFTERNOON

The Crusader vanguard reached the outskirts of Arsuf, but the infantry accompanying the Hospitallers at the rear were coming under severe pressure. Fearing the rearguard would collapse, and seeing that some Ayyubid horse archers had dismounted, de Nablus ordered the Hospitaller cavalry to charge, in defiance of Richard's orders.

→ Hospitaller charge

E M I R A T E   O F

Arsuf

S A L A D I N

CRUSADERS AND SARACENS

The invasion of the Muslim-dominated eastern Mediterranean by crusaders from Western Europe led to a clash between two contrasting styles of warfare—Christian armored knights taking on nimble Muslim horsemen.

Known to the Christians as Saracens, the Muslim armies that resisted the Crusades (1095–1492) were mostly of Central Asian origin. They were fast-moving mounted warriors skilled in maneuvers and skirmishing. Often armed with composite bows, Saracen horsemen avoided close-quarters combat until they had worn the enemy down. Only then would they close in to deliver the *coup de grâce*. The crusader knights, wearing heavy armor, could not match the Saracens' mobility. The knights preferred cavalry charges and hand-to-hand fighting, which they prized as a supreme display of valor. The Muslim forces, on the other hand, favored tricking their enemy with feigned flight.

Clash of cultures

The crusaders partially adapted to Saracen tactics. They deployed foot soldiers to protect the mounted knights and Genoese crossbowmen (see pp.84–85) to counter the Saracen archers. Their heavy armor was unsuited to the heat but offered protection against arrows, and they reinforced the mystique of the knight by creating religious fighting orders such as the Templars. The Saracens also used armored cavalry in combination with light horse archers. The result was an asymmetric balance, with victories won by generalship and other factors.

◁ **Weapon of choice**
A two-edged sword was standard equipment for a Christian knight. It was an effective weapon whether used for stabbing or slashing.

RICHARD I 1157–99

Within a year of inheriting the English throne, King Richard I, also known as Richard the Lionheart, set off for Palestine on the Third Crusade (1189–92). He displayed great tactical skill and bravery while fighting the Saracen sultan Saladin at the battles of Arsuf (see pp.70–71) and Jaffa (1192), but failed to retake the city of Jerusalem, which was his primary objective. He returned to England in 1194 and was killed at a siege in France five years later.

Fighting off the enemy
This detail from a 12th-century illuminated manuscript shows Muslim warriors engaging with Christian knights at a siege during the First Crusade (1096–99). Saracen bowmen are seen firing arrows at the heavily armored crusaders trying to scale the walls of a town.

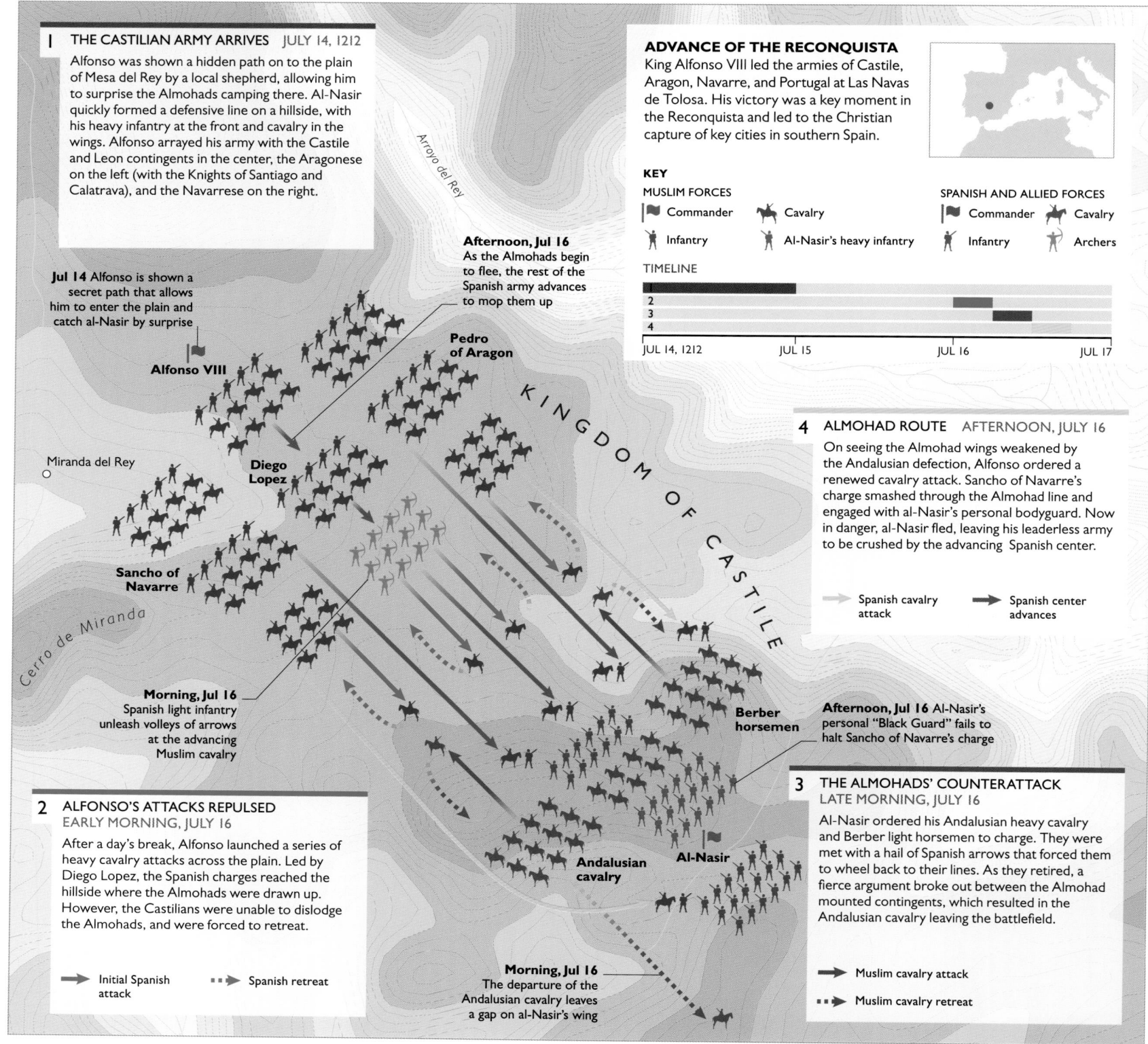

1 THE CASTILIAN ARMY ARRIVES JULY 14, 1212

Alfonso was shown a hidden path on to the plain of Mesa del Rey by a local shepherd, allowing him to surprise the Almohads camping there. Al-Nasir quickly formed a defensive line on a hillside, with his heavy infantry at the front and cavalry in the wings. Alfonso arrayed his army with the Castile and Leon contingents in the center, the Aragonese on the left (with the Knights of Santiago and Calatrava), and the Navarrese on the right.

ADVANCE OF THE RECONQUISTA
King Alfonso VIII led the armies of Castile, Aragon, Navarre, and Portugal at Las Navas de Tolosa. His victory was a key moment in the Reconquista and led to the Christian capture of key cities in southern Spain.

KEY

MUSLIM FORCES

Commander
Cavalry
Infantry
Al-Nasir's heavy infantry

SPANISH AND ALLIED FORCES

Commander
Cavalry
Infantry
Archers

TIMELINE

JUL 14, 1212   JUL 15   JUL 16   JUL 17

Arroyo del Rey

Jul 14 Alfonso is shown a secret path that allows him to enter the plain and catch al-Nasir by surprise

Afternoon, Jul 16
As the Almohads begin to flee, the rest of the Spanish army advances to mop them up

Alfonso VIII

Pedro of Aragon

Diego Lopez

Miranda del Rey

Sancho of Navarre

Cerro de Miranda

Morning, Jul 16
Spanish light infantry unleash volleys of arrows at the advancing Muslim cavalry

K I N G D O M   O F   C A S T I L E

Berber horsemen

Afternoon, Jul 16 Al-Nasir's personal "Black Guard" fails to halt Sancho of Navarre's charge

Andalusian cavalry

Al-Nasir

4 ALMOHAD ROUTE AFTERNOON, JULY 16

On seeing the Almohad wings weakened by the Andalusian defection, Alfonso ordered a renewed cavalry attack. Sancho of Navarre's charge smashed through the Almohad line and engaged with al-Nasir's personal bodyguard. Now in danger, al-Nasir fled, leaving his leaderless army to be crushed by the advancing Spanish center.

→ Spanish cavalry attack   → Spanish center advances

3 THE ALMOHADS' COUNTERATTACK
LATE MORNING, JULY 16

Al-Nasir ordered his Andalusian heavy cavalry and Berber light horsemen to charge. They were met with a hail of Spanish arrows that forced them to wheel back to their lines. As they retired, a fierce argument broke out between the Almohad mounted contingents, which resulted in the Andalusian cavalry leaving the battlefield.

→ Muslim cavalry attack   ▸▸▸ Muslim cavalry retreat

2 ALFONSO'S ATTACKS REPULSED
EARLY MORNING, JULY 16

After a day's break, Alfonso launched a series of heavy cavalry attacks across the plain. Led by Diego Lopez, the Spanish charges reached the hillside where the Almohads were drawn up. However, the Castilians were unable to dislodge the Almohads, and were forced to retreat.

→ Initial Spanish attack   ▸▸▸ Spanish retreat

Morning, Jul 16
The departure of the Andalusian cavalry leaves a gap on al-Nasir's wing

LAS NAVAS DE TOLOSA

In 1212, a coalition of Christian kings overwhelmed the caliph al-Nasir's Muslim army on the plains of Andalusia in a last-ditch charge. The victory marked a turning point in the Reconquista—the Christian reconquest of the Muslim lands in Spain.

The reign of King Alfonso VIII of Castile (r. 1158–1214) saw new Christian advances against southern Spain's Muslim emirates, which had fallen into disarray after the collapse of the ruling Almoravid dynasty in the 1140s. Alfonso pushed south, but his progress was stalled by the Almohads—a new Muslim power from Morocco. In 1211 Muhammad al-Nasir, the Almohad caliph, marched north from Seville, capturing the key fort of Salvatierra. The following Spring, Alfonso marched south to meet him, joined by the kings of Aragon and Navarre, and Portuguese and French allies. Alfonso waited until July to catch al-Nasir by surprise at Las Navas de Tolosa. The defeat of the Almohads led to rapid Christian gains; eventually Alfonso's grandson, Ferdinand III of Castile, seized Cordoba in 1236 and the Almohad capital of Seville in 1248.

MURET

While leading a crusade against the heretical Cathars in southwestern France in September 1213, the French knight and nobleman Simon de Montfort found himself outnumbered at the fortified town of Muret by a large force from Aragon and Toulouse. His daring sortie unexpectedly routed the Aragonese, killed their king, and dealt a blow to the Cathar cause.

In the 12th century, a heretical Christian movement known as Catharism (or Albigensianism) flourished in southwest France. It was supported by local nobles, who used it to assert independence from the north. In 1208, Pope Innocent III declared a crusade against the Cathars, known as the Albigensian Crusade. Many knights, led by Simon de Montfort, flocked to help. The crusaders captured a string of fortresses and began to crush the Cathars, but met stiffer resistance after Count Raymond VI of Toulouse defected to the Cathars, supported by King Peter II of Aragon. Raymond and Peter were defeated at Muret, but Catharism was not eliminated entirely, and it took the intervention of King Louis VIII of France in 1229 to agree to peace. After a brutal massacre at Montségur in 1244, Catharism disappeared as a significant force in France.

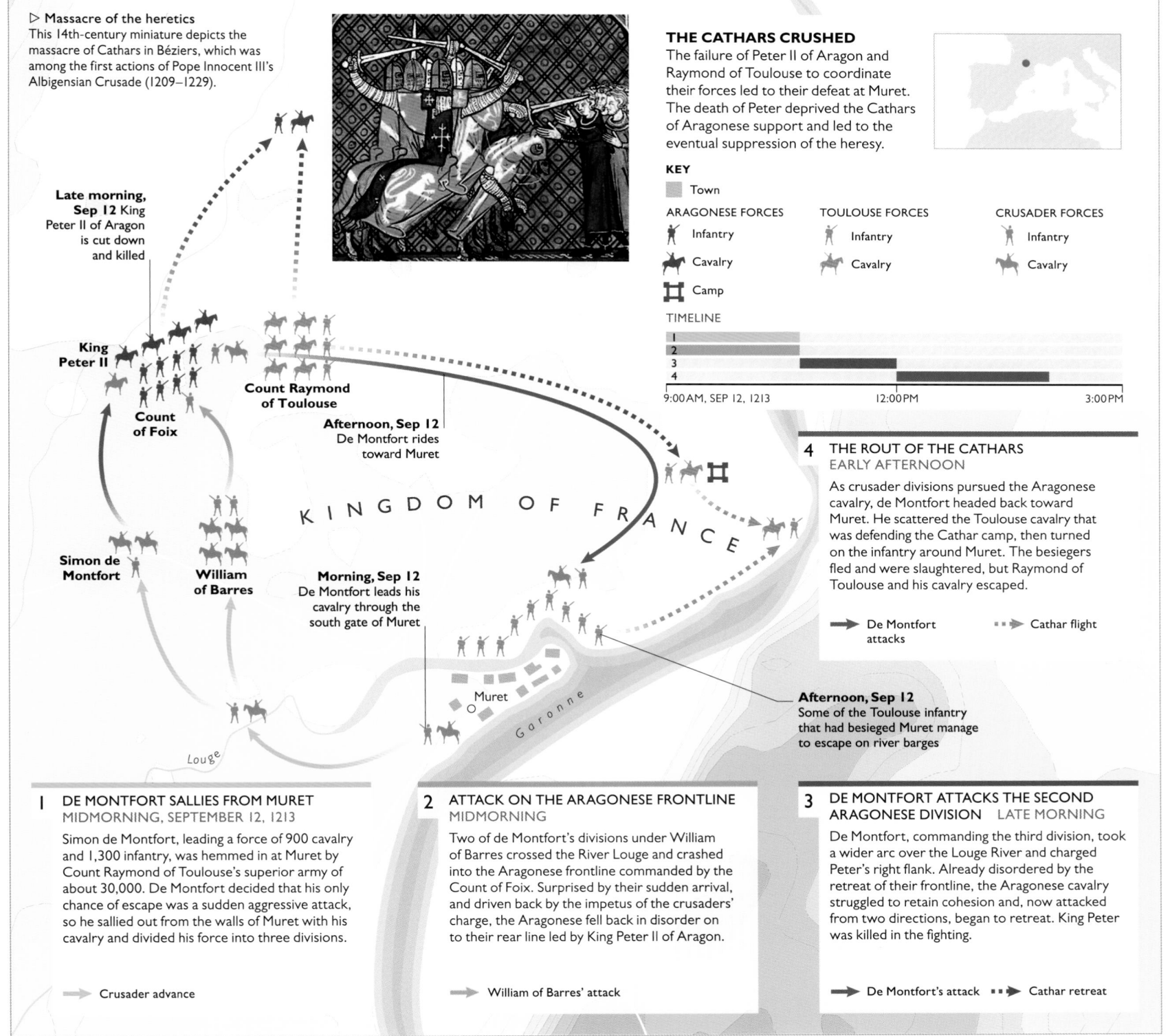

▷ **Massacre of the heretics**
This 14th-century miniature depicts the massacre of Cathars in Béziers, which was among the first actions of Pope Innocent III's Albigensian Crusade (1209–1229).

THE CATHARS CRUSHED
The failure of Peter II of Aragon and Raymond of Toulouse to coordinate their forces led to their defeat at Muret. The death of Peter deprived the Cathars of Aragonese support and led to the eventual suppression of the heresy.

KEY

▪ Town

ARAGONESE FORCES	TOULOUSE FORCES	CRUSADER FORCES
Infantry	Infantry	Infantry
Cavalry	Cavalry	Cavalry
Camp		

TIMELINE

9:00AM, SEP 12, 1213   12:00PM   3:00PM

Late morning, Sep 12 King Peter II of Aragon is cut down and killed

King Peter II

Count of Foix

Count Raymond of Toulouse

Afternoon, Sep 12
De Montfort rides toward Muret

Simon de Montfort

William of Barres

Morning, Sep 12
De Montfort leads his cavalry through the south gate of Muret

KINGDOM OF FRANCE

Muret

Louge

Garonne

4 THE ROUT OF THE CATHARS
EARLY AFTERNOON

As crusader divisions pursued the Aragonese cavalry, de Montfort headed back toward Muret. He scattered the Toulouse cavalry that was defending the Cathar camp, then turned on the infantry around Muret. The besiegers fled and were slaughtered, but Raymond of Toulouse and his cavalry escaped.

→ De Montfort attacks   ⇢ Cathar flight

Afternoon, Sep 12
Some of the Toulouse infantry that had besieged Muret manage to escape on river barges

1 DE MONTFORT SALLIES FROM MURET
MIDMORNING, SEPTEMBER 12, 1213

Simon de Montfort, leading a force of 900 cavalry and 1,300 infantry, was hemmed in at Muret by Count Raymond of Toulouse's superior army of about 30,000. De Montfort decided that his only chance of escape was a sudden aggressive attack, so he sallied out from the walls of Muret with his cavalry and divided his force into three divisions.

→ Crusader advance

2 ATTACK ON THE ARAGONESE FRONTLINE
MIDMORNING

Two of de Montfort's divisions under William of Barres crossed the River Louge and crashed into the Aragonese frontline commanded by the Count of Foix. Surprised by their sudden arrival, and driven back by the impetus of the crusaders' charge, the Aragonese fell back in disorder on to their rear line led by King Peter II of Aragon.

→ William of Barres' attack

3 DE MONTFORT ATTACKS THE SECOND ARAGONESE DIVISION LATE MORNING

De Montfort, commanding the third division, took a wider arc over the Louge River and charged Peter's right flank. Already disordered by the retreat of their frontline, the Aragonese cavalry struggled to retain cohesion and, now attacked from two directions, began to retreat. King Peter was killed in the fighting.

→ De Montfort's attack   ⇢ Cathar retreat

LIEGNITZ

In April 1241, Duke Henry II of Silesia faced an invading Mongol army outside the town of Liegnitz. Fooled by the classic mounted nomad tactic of a feigned retreat, his army was cut to pieces and the Duke killed. However, on the brink of conquering Poland and Hungary, the Mongols pulled back, saving Europe from further devastation.

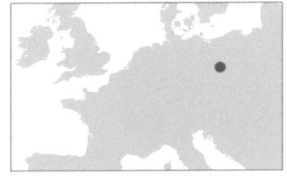

MONGOL INCURSION
Henry II's army faced the Mongols at Liegnitz, fearing that their enemy would soon be reinforced. They were defeated by Mongol mobility and superior tactics.

KEY

POLISH FORCES		MONGOL FORCES	
Commander	Infantry	Commander	Light cavalry
Cavalry		Heavy cavalry	

TIMELINE

APR 9, 1241   APR 10

In 1223, Genghis Khan (see p.78) invaded Russia. His horsemen raided towns and defeated the Cumans—a Turkic people who lived in the steppes along the Black Sea. They were granted sanctuary in Hungary by the king, Bela IV, and converted to Christianity.

The new Great Khan Ögodei invaded Russia again in 1237. He demanded the return of the Cumans, and in 1241 used King Bela's refusal as a pretext to invade Hungary. After sweeping through Russia, the Mongol army divided in two: commanders Batu Khan and Subotai were to attack Hungary directly, while a diversionary force under Baidar and Kadan was to strike north into Poland to stop the Hungarians and Poles from uniting.

The Mongols ravaged northern Poland and then turned south, sacking and burning the Polish capital Cracow in March 1241. The last force in Poland capable of stopping the Mongols was the 30,000-strong army of Henry II of Silesia. He decided to attack, unaware that assistance, in the form of 50,000 men under Wenceslas of Bohemia, was just two days' march away.

Henry's army was routed at Liegnitz (Legnica) on April 9, and two days later southern Mongol forces smashed the Hungarian army at Mohi. Poland and Hungary were only saved by the news of Ögodei's death in December, which ignited a power struggle among the Mongol commanders, causing them to pull their men back to Mongolia.

△ **Mongol superiority**
This detail from a 14th-century Silesian Codex depicts a scene from the battle, in which the agile mounted Mongol archers face heavy German and Polish cavalry.

THE MONGOL CAMPAIGN, 1237–42
The second Mongol invasion of Europe began in late 1237. Taking the Russian principalities by surprise, the cities of Vladimir, Moscow, and Tver were soon sacked. Then, in early 1241, Batu Khan (commander of the western part of the Mongol empire) sent his army through Kiev and across the Carpathians. In Galicia the force divided: one wing entered Poland to the north, and eventually met Duke Henry of Silesia at Liegnitz; the other wing went south and destroyed the Hungarians at the Battle of Mohi. The Mongol campaign ended with the pursuit by Kadan—the victor of Liegnitz—of King Bela IV of Hungary along the coast of Dalmatia and then through Bulgaria as the Mongols under Batu returned home in 1242.

KEY

- Main battle
- Mongol invasion, winter 1237–38
- Mongol invasion, 1241
- Campaign by Kadan, 1242
- Mongol return route

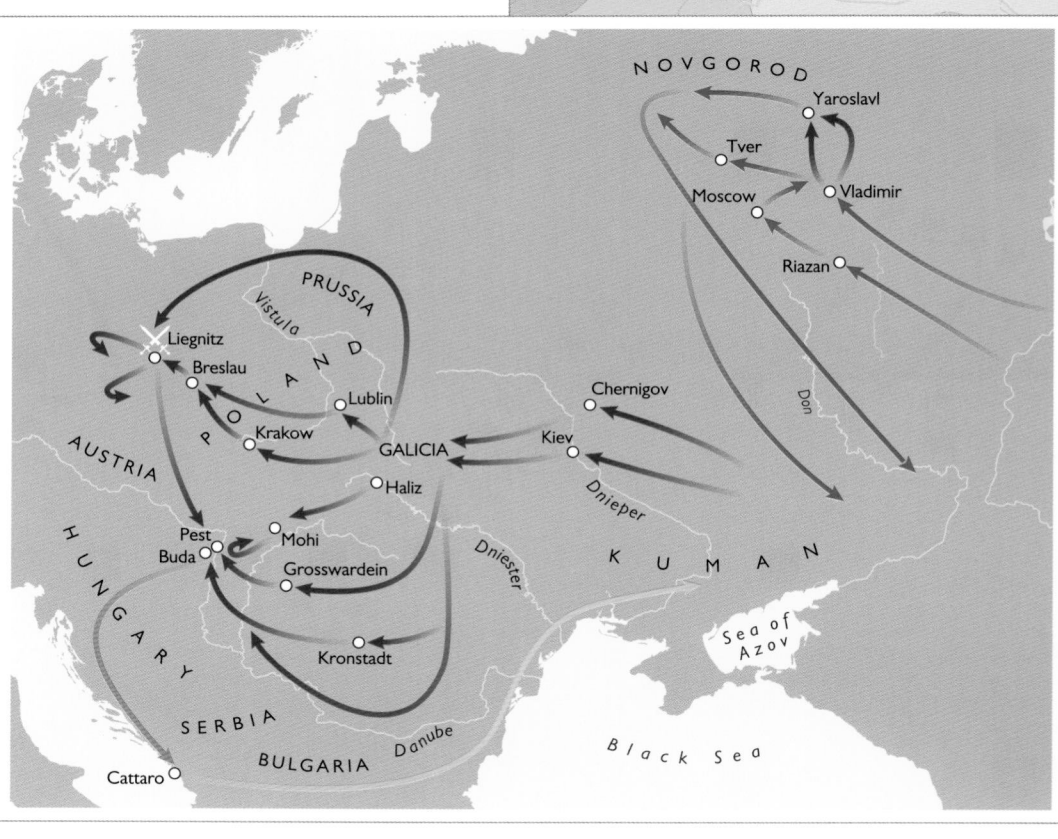

1 THE ARMIES DEPLOY APRIL 9, 1241

Henry approached the battlefield from Liegnitz to the northwest. He deployed his army in four squadrons: in the front were the elite German and Templar knights, along with less disciplined Polish levies and a force of Moravian miners. Two further groups of cavalry were commanded by Sulislaw of Cracow and Mieszko of Opole. Henry himself took up the rear. Facing them, Baidar and Kadan drew up their 20,000-strong force in a wide arc, with heavy cavalry at the center and lighter cavalry on the wings.

2 DUKE HENRY ATTACKS

Duke Henry ordered the cavalry in his first line to charge the Mongol center. As they surged forward, anticipating fierce close-quarters combat, they were met with a hail of arrows from the Mongol cavalry. The Mongol horsemen were highly skilled archers capable of hitting targets at 330 yards (300m). As the knights and their mounts crashed to the ground, the charge lost momentum and European cavalry wheeled around and returned to Henry's lines.

→ Polish attack   ▪▪▶ Polish retreat

3 THE SECOND ATTACK

Seeing the forward cavalry retreat, Sulislaw and Mieszko launched their attacks, charging toward the Mongol lines. As the Mongol vanguard pulled back, drawing the Poles further forward, the Mongol light cavalry began to close on the Poles from behind. At one point, a Mongol horseman began to shout in Polish "Run, Run!" The Poles, taken in by the ruse, turned and began to retreat.

→ Polish attack   ▪▪▶ Polish retreat
▫▫▷ Mongols' feigned retreat   → Mongols close in

4 THE TRAP SPRINGS

Witnessing the confusion in his forces, Duke Henry led his fourth squadron into battle. By this time, the Mongols had set another trap, lighting piles of reeds they had set in front of the Poles. The resulting pall of smoke blinded the Poles and added to their disarray. The Mongol wings closed in still further, cutting off any hope of an organized Polish retreat.

🔥 Mongols set fires   ⇨ Polish attack

5 THE DESTRUCTION OF DUKE HENRY'S ARMY

Continuing to suffer casualties from the Mongol archers, Duke Henry was now engaged at close-quarters by Mongol heavy cavalry. Several of his senior commanders were killed. Realizing he was trapped, the duke tried to break through the Mongol lines, but was struck in the arm with a spear and then beheaded by the jubilant Mongols.

→ Mongol attack

6 THE AFTERMATH APRIL 9

The few Polish and German cavalry who managed to break free of the encircling Mongols did not get far; most were picked off by the mobile Mongol light cavalry. Baidar and Kadan ordered that one ear be cut off each of the enemy dead; nine bags of ears were reportedly sent as trophies back to Batu Khan. Duke Henry's head was paraded on a spike around the walls of Liegnitz.

▪▪▶ Polish and German cavalry attempting to escape

Duke Henry

Mieszko

Strumień Księginicki

Germans and others

Mongol light cavalry

Księginice

POLAND

Sulislaw

Legnickie Pole

Mongol heavy cavalry

Biala Struga

Mongol light cavalry

The disorientated Poles attempt to flee, but most are caught by the Mongol cavalry

The Mongols raise a banner to signal their forces to mount a feigned retreat

The movement of Mongol reinforcements is hidden by smoke from the burning reeds

Mongol heavy cavalry

Baidar and Kadan

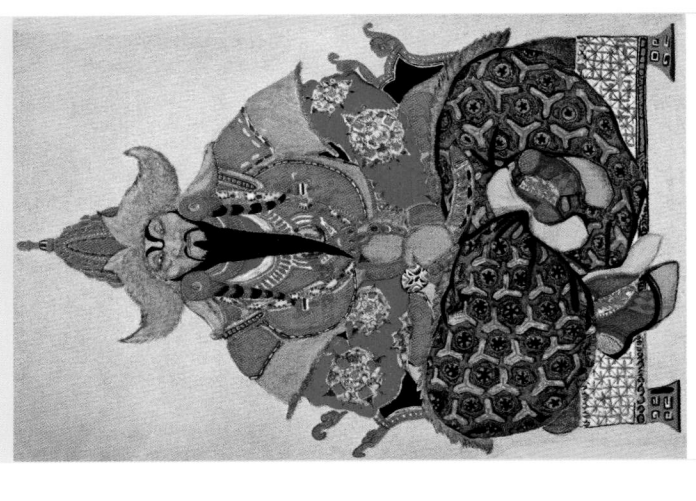

Better known as Genghis Khan ("universal ruler"), Temujin Borjigin was born to a family of minor chieftains. Over the years, he built his reputation as an aggressive warrior and skilled diplomat. With a formidable army, he embarked on a conquest that lasted more than 20 years and resulted in the entire Asian steppe and adjoining territories falling under his rule.

THE MONGOL EMPIRE

In 1206 CE Temujin, a Mongol chieftain took the name of Genghis Khan and united the Mongol tribes of the Central Asian steppes. These tribes, which had been subjects, raiders, interlopers, and mercenaries to imperial China for centuries, went on to create an empire spanning two centuries.

In the early 13th century, China was divided between the southern Song dynasty and the northern Jin Empire. Genghis Khan first allied himself with the Song against the Jin and their puppet Xia dynasty. He then moved west, his army conquering the Khwarazmian empire by the Caspian Sea and defeating a Russian coalition at the Kalka River in 1223. Mongol expansion did not end with the death of Genghis Khan in 1227. When the Song attempted to retake their former capitals from the defeated Jin, the Mongols turned on them and completed their conquest of China. Almost unstoppable, the Mongol armies spread westward, and in 1294 their empire, at its apex, stretched from the Yellow Sea to the Danube.

Essentially a cavalry force, the Mongol army combined heavily armored lancer cavalry and more numerous, lightly armored horsemen with composite bows. The Mongols were masters of mobile warfare and expert tacticians, and were a superior force to other armies of the time. Although the army primarily consisted of Mongol tribal warriors, it was supplemented by local auxiliaries, and the Mongol forces that invaded Japan in 1274 and 1281 included Chinese and Korean troops.

After Genghis Khan died, the sprawling empire had been divided into khanates (sub-empires) between his four sons, with Ögedei, the third son, succeeding his father as the Great Khan (ruler). This tradition of the Great Khans continued until Genghis' grandson Kublai Khan's death in 1294. The various khanates drifted apart, but continued to exert influence until the 15th century.

▽ **Central Asian quiver**
Possibly of Mongol origin, this ornate Central Asian quiver was designed to hold arrows used by mounted Mongol archers. They remained in use for centuries, with examples dating to the Qing dynasty (1644–1912).

Clashing armies
This reproduction from a 14th-century illustration probably shows Genghis Khan's army besieging a fortress in Western Xia. The Mongols learned siege warfare from the Chinese, and used giant catapults to hurl firebombs over battlements.

LAKE PEIPUS

The Teutonic Knights' eastward advance into the Novgorod Republic was finally halted on the ice of Lake Peipus in April 1242. There, Prince Alexander Nevsky defeated the invaders, preserving Eastern Orthodoxy from Catholic crusading zeal.

In 1198, Pope Innocent III reiterated his predecessor's call for a crusade against the pagan peoples of the eastern Baltic, marking the beginning of a long series of campaigns to convert them to Christianity. Having secured the Baltic lands, in 1240, the Teutonic Knights turned against the Republic of Novgorod (an Orthodox Christian state in northern Russia) and seized Pskov. It was retaken the following year by the 20-year-old Prince Alexander Nevsky, whom the Novgorodians had earlier banished due to tensions with the nobility. The Knights, led by Prince-Bishop Hermann of Dorpat, renewed the attack in March 1242, heading toward Novgorod. Alexander moved to intercept him, luring the crusaders onto the frozen waters of Lake Peipus, on the present-day Russian-Estonian border. His victory there halted the Teutonic Knights' efforts to absorb Novgorod, although their campaigns in Prussia and Lithuania continued into the early 15th century.

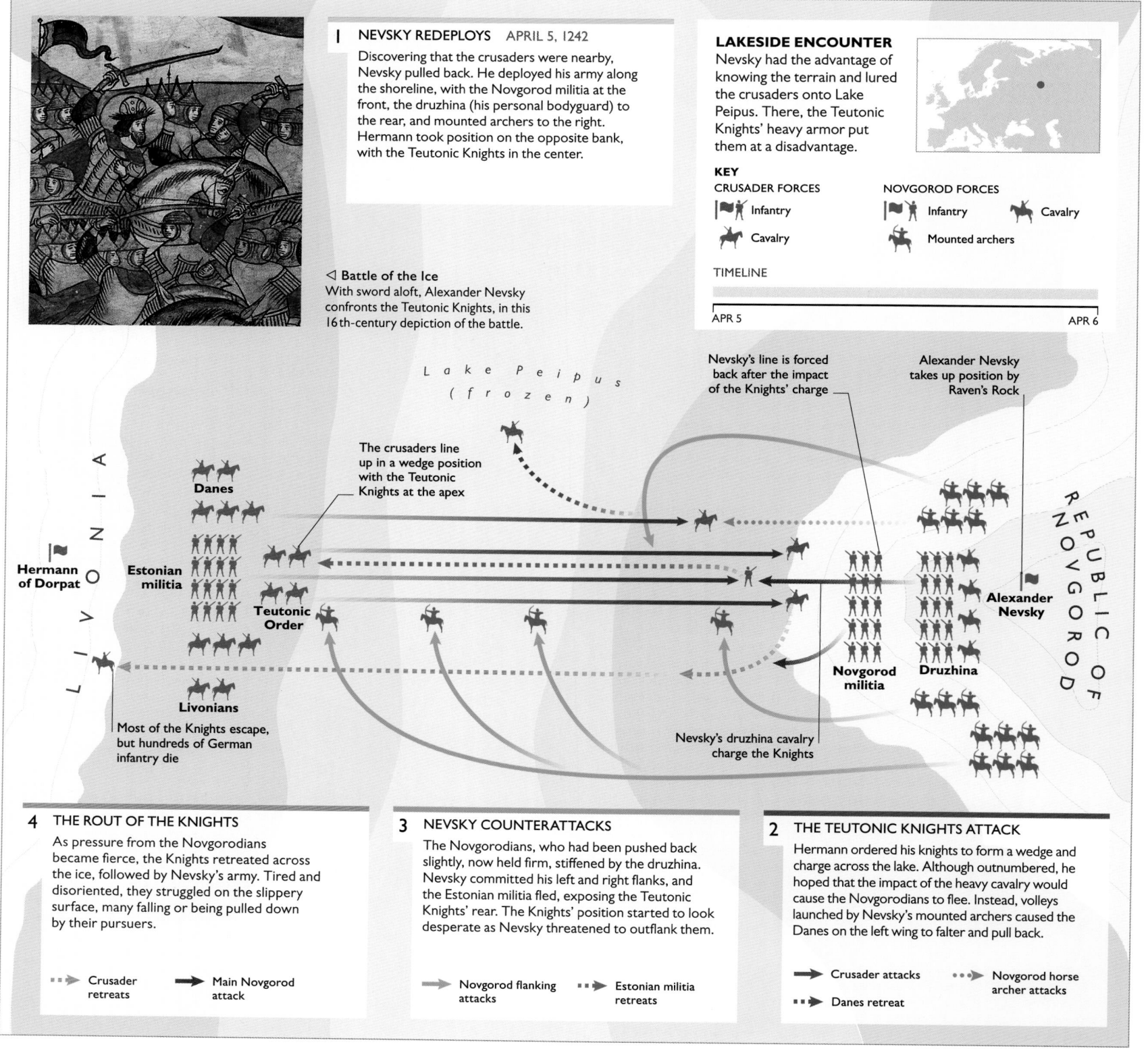

1 NEVSKY REDEPLOYS APRIL 5, 1242
Discovering that the crusaders were nearby, Nevsky pulled back. He deployed his army along the shoreline, with the Novgorod militia at the front, the druzhina (his personal bodyguard) to the rear, and mounted archers to the right. Hermann took position on the opposite bank, with the Teutonic Knights in the center.

◁ Battle of the Ice
With sword aloft, Alexander Nevsky confronts the Teutonic Knights, in this 16th-century depiction of the battle.

LAKESIDE ENCOUNTER
Nevsky had the advantage of knowing the terrain and lured the crusaders onto Lake Peipus. There, the Teutonic Knights' heavy armor put them at a disadvantage.

KEY

CRUSADER FORCES		NOVGOROD FORCES	
Infantry		Infantry	Cavalry
Cavalry		Mounted archers	

TIMELINE

APR 5   APR 6

Nevsky's line is forced back after the impact of the Knights' charge

Alexander Nevsky takes up position by Raven's Rock

Lake Peipus (frozen)

The crusaders line up in a wedge position with the Teutonic Knights at the apex

Danes

Hermann of Dorpat

Estonian militia

Teutonic Order

Livonians

Most of the Knights escape, but hundreds of German infantry die

Nevsky's druzhina cavalry charge the Knights

Alexander Nevsky

Novgorod militia

Druzhina

REPUBLIC OF NOVGOROD

LIVONIA

4 THE ROUT OF THE KNIGHTS
As pressure from the Novgorodians became fierce, the Knights retreated across the ice, followed by Nevsky's army. Tired and disoriented, they struggled on the slippery surface, many falling or being pulled down by their pursuers.

- - - ▸ Crusader retreats

⟶ Main Novgorod attack

3 NEVSKY COUNTERATTACKS
The Novgorodians, who had been pushed back slightly, now held firm, stiffened by the druzhina. Nevsky committed his left and right flanks, and the Estonian militia fled, exposing the Teutonic Knights' rear. The Knights' position started to look desperate as Nevsky threatened to outflank them.

⟶ Novgorod flanking attacks

- - - ▸ Estonian militia retreats

2 THE TEUTONIC KNIGHTS ATTACK
Hermann ordered his knights to form a wedge and charge across the lake. Although outnumbered, he hoped that the impact of the heavy cavalry would cause the Novgorodians to flee. Instead, volleys launched by Nevsky's mounted archers caused the Danes on the left wing to falter and pull back.

⟶ Crusader attacks

- - - ▸ Danes retreat

- - - ▸ Novgorod horse archer attacks

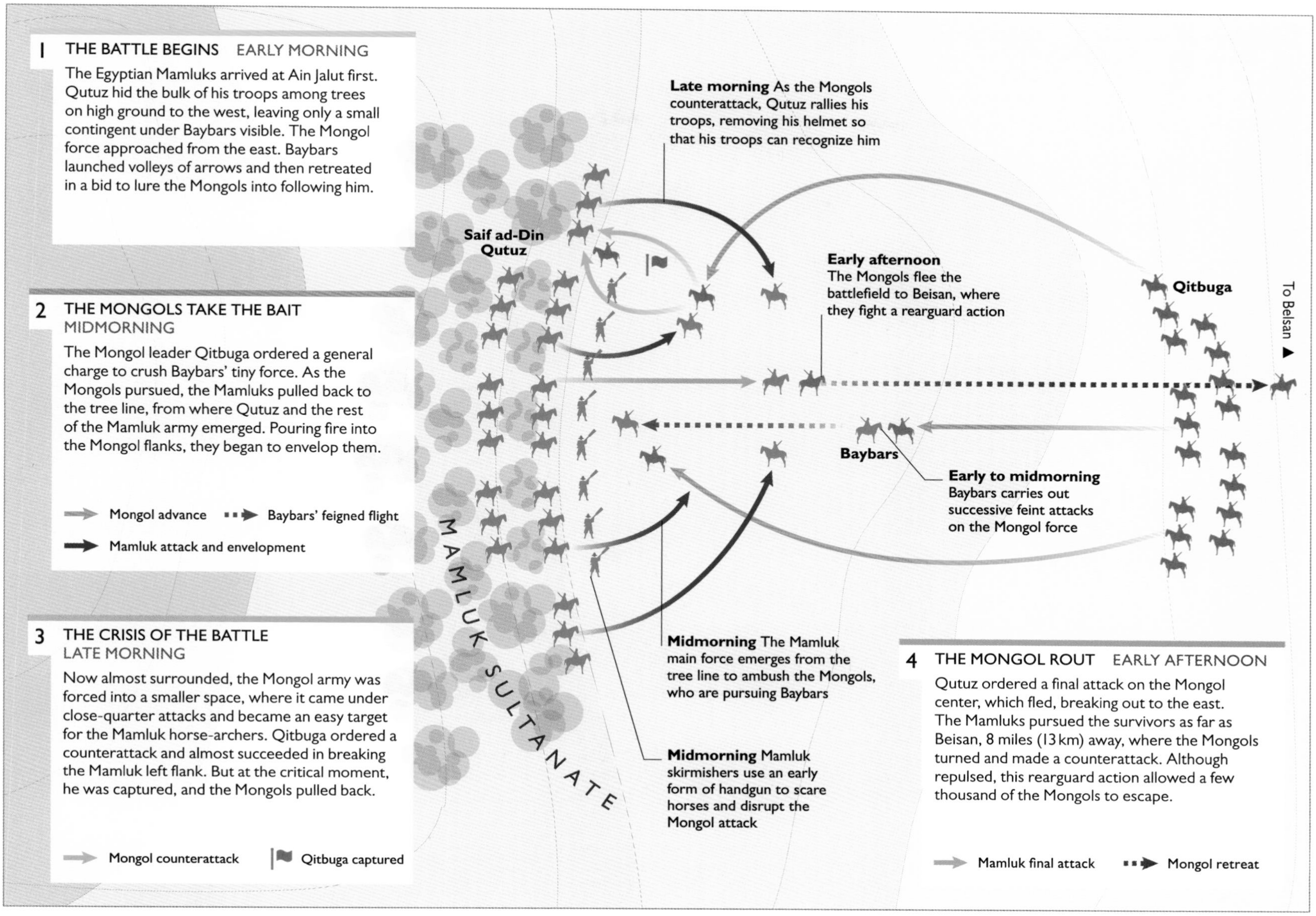

1 THE BATTLE BEGINS EARLY MORNING

The Egyptian Mamluks arrived at Ain Jalut first. Qutuz hid the bulk of his troops among trees on high ground to the west, leaving only a small contingent under Baybars visible. The Mongol force approached from the east. Baybars launched volleys of arrows and then retreated in a bid to lure the Mongols into following him.

2 THE MONGOLS TAKE THE BAIT MIDMORNING

The Mongol leader Qitbuga ordered a general charge to crush Baybars' tiny force. As the Mongols pursued, the Mamluks pulled back to the tree line, from where Qutuz and the rest of the Mamluk army emerged. Pouring fire into the Mongol flanks, they began to envelop them.

→ Mongol advance   ∙∙▶ Baybars' feigned flight

➜ Mamluk attack and envelopment

3 THE CRISIS OF THE BATTLE LATE MORNING

Now almost surrounded, the Mongol army was forced into a smaller space, where it came under close-quarter attacks and became an easy target for the Mamluk horse-archers. Qitbuga ordered a counterattack and almost succeeded in breaking the Mamluk left flank. But at the critical moment, he was captured, and the Mongols pulled back.

→ Mongol counterattack   ⚑ Qitbuga captured

Late morning As the Mongols counterattack, Qutuz rallies his troops, removing his helmet so that his troops can recognize him

Saif ad-Din Qutuz

Early afternoon The Mongols flee the battlefield to Beisan, where they fight a rearguard action

Qitbuga

To Beisan ▶

Baybars

Early to midmorning Baybars carries out successive feint attacks on the Mongol force

Midmorning The Mamluk main force emerges from the tree line to ambush the Mongols, who are pursuing Baybars

Midmorning Mamluk skirmishers use an early form of handgun to scare horses and disrupt the Mongol attack

MAMLUK SULTANATE

4 THE MONGOL ROUT EARLY AFTERNOON

Qutuz ordered a final attack on the Mongol center, which fled, breaking out to the east. The Mamluks pursued the survivors as far as Beisan, 8 miles (13 km) away, where the Mongols turned and made a counterattack. Although repulsed, this rearguard action allowed a few thousand of the Mongols to escape.

→ Mamluk final attack   ∙∙▶ Mongol retreat

AIN JALUT

In a little more than 50 years, the Mongols built a vast empire that dominated much of Asia. In 1260, their seemingly invincible army was defeated in battle at Ain Jalut, some 56 miles (90 km) north of Jerusalem. There, an Egyptian Mamluk army caught the Mongols in an ambush and cut them to pieces.

By 1256, the Mongols had already conquered much of Asia and Eastern Europe. That year, the Mongol Great Khan Möngke directed his brother Hülegü to launch a campaign against the Middle East and the Mamluk rulers of Egypt. His huge army took fortress after fortress, and in February 1258 stormed Baghdad, putting an end to the Abbasid Caliphate. In 1260, he sent an envoy to Qutuz, the Mamluk sultan, demanding Egypt's surrender. Qutuz refused and executed the envoys. At this point, Hülegü received news of Möngke's death, and an assembly was

called to elect a new Great Khan. Preoccupied with this (and aware that the Middle East offered little pasture for their horses), Hülegü pulled back most of his forces, leaving the remainder under the command of the general Qitbuga. Hearing of this, Qutuz marched north with his general, Baybars, to confront the Mongols.

The ensuing battle at Ain Jalut destroyed the Mongol reputation for invincibility and shifted the balance of power in favor of the Egyptian Mamluks, who went on to capture Damascus and Aleppo shortly after.

A FATEFUL AMBUSH

The Mamluks made use of hit-and-run tactics to provoke the Mongol troops into battle. The Mamluk general Baybars was familiar with the terrain and used this knowledge to set a fateful trap. Qutuz was later assassinated; Baybars took his place.

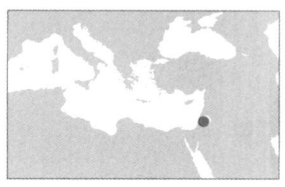

KEY

🐎 Mamluk cavalry   🏹 Mamluk hand-gunners   🐎 Mongol cavalry

TIMELINE

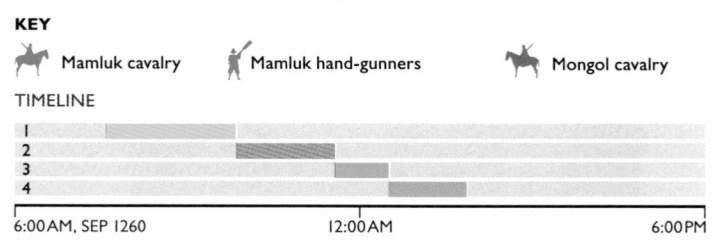

6:00 AM, SEP 1260   12:00 AM   6:00 PM

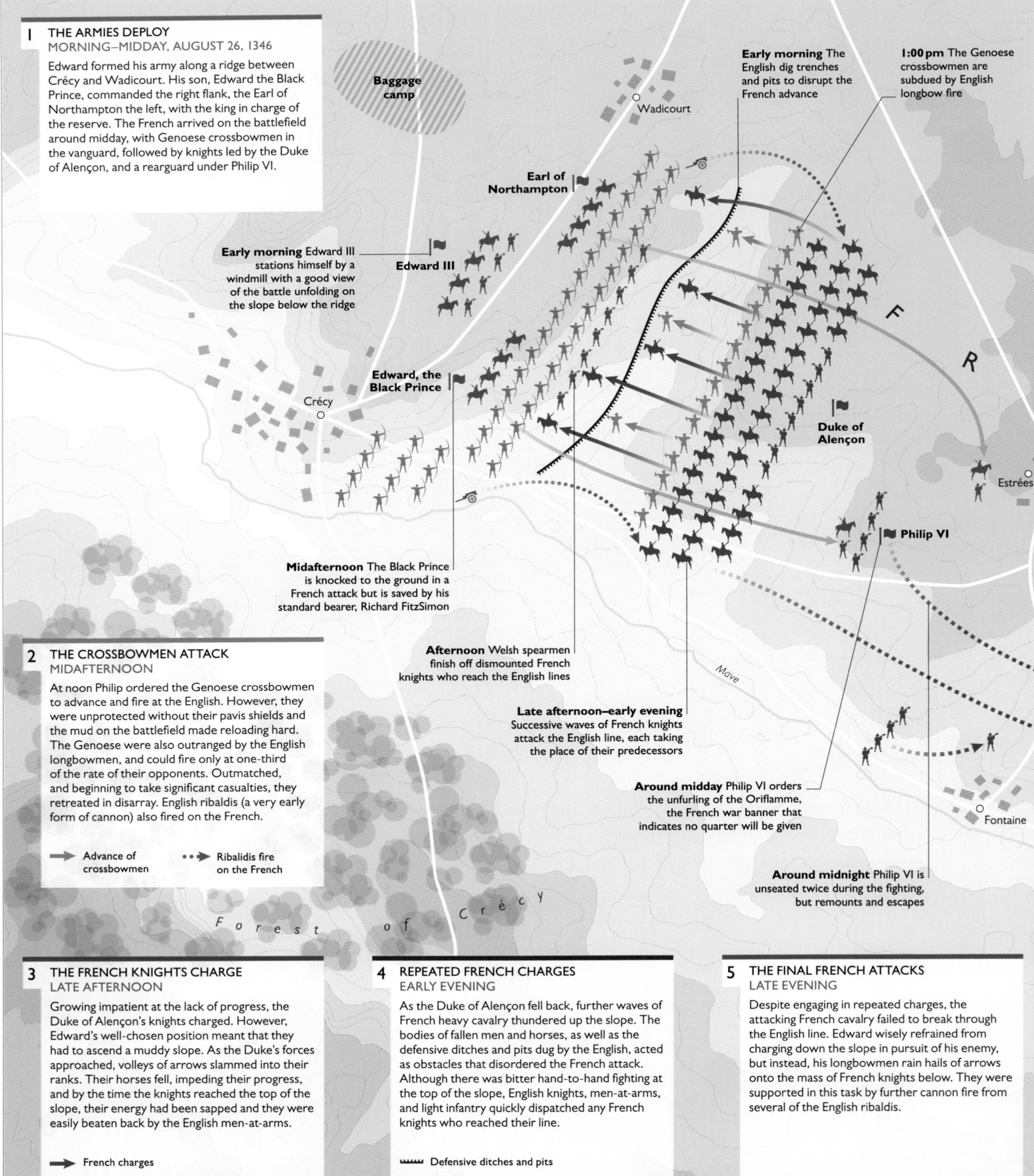

1 THE ARMIES DEPLOY
MORNING–MIDDAY, AUGUST 26, 1346

Edward formed his army along a ridge between Crécy and Wadicourt. His son, Edward the Black Prince, commanded the right flank, the Earl of Northampton the left, with the king in charge of the reserve. The French arrived on the battlefield around midday, with Genoese crossbowmen in the vanguard, followed by knights led by the Duke of Alençon, and a rearguard under Philip VI.

Early morning The English dig trenches and pits to disrupt the French advance

1:00 pm The Genoese crossbowmen are subdued by English longbow fire

Early morning Edward III stations himself by a windmill with a good view of the battle unfolding on the slope below the ridge

Earl of Northampton

Edward III

Edward, the Black Prince

Duke of Alençon

Crécy

Wadicourt

Baggage camp

Estrées

Philip VI

Mave

Fontaine

F R A

Midafternoon The Black Prince is knocked to the ground in a French attack but is saved by his standard bearer, Richard FitzSimon

Afternoon Welsh spearmen finish off dismounted French knights who reach the English lines

Late afternoon–early evening Successive waves of French knights attack the English line, each taking the place of their predecessors

Around midday Philip VI orders the unfurling of the Oriflamme, the French war banner that indicates no quarter will be given

Around midnight Philip VI is unseated twice during the fighting, but remounts and escapes

2 THE CROSSBOWMEN ATTACK
MIDAFTERNOON

At noon Philip ordered the Genoese crossbowmen to advance and fire at the English. However, they were unprotected without their pavis shields and the mud on the battlefield made reloading hard. The Genoese were also outranged by the English longbowmen, and could fire only at one-third of the rate of their opponents. Outmatched, and beginning to take significant casualties, they retreated in disarray. English ribaldis (a very early form of cannon) also fired on the French.

→ Advance of crossbowmen
••► Ribalidis fire on the French

Forest of Crécy

3 THE FRENCH KNIGHTS CHARGE
LATE AFTERNOON

Growing impatient at the lack of progress, the Duke of Alençon's knights charged. However, Edward's well-chosen position meant that they had to ascend a muddy slope. As the Duke's forces approached, volleys of arrows slammed into their ranks. Their horses fell, impeding their progress, and by the time the knights reached the top of the slope, their energy had been sapped and they were easily beaten back by the English men-at-arms.

→ French charges

4 REPEATED FRENCH CHARGES
EARLY EVENING

As the Duke of Alençon fell back, further waves of French heavy cavalry thundered up the slope. The bodies of fallen men and horses, as well as the defensive ditches and pits dug by the English, acted as obstacles that disordered the French attack. Although there was bitter hand-to-hand fighting at the top of the slope, English knights, men-at-arms, and light infantry quickly dispatched any French knights who reached their line.

⌇⌇⌇ Defensive ditches and pits

5 THE FINAL FRENCH ATTACKS
LATE EVENING

Despite engaging in repeated charges, the attacking French cavalry failed to break through the English line. Edward wisely refrained from charging down the slope in pursuit of his enemy, but instead, his longbowmen rain hails of arrows onto the mass of French knights below. They were supported in this task by further cannon fire from several of the English ribaldis.

△ The fall of the knight
This Flemish manuscript illumination from 1477 shows the fierce fighting at Crécy. The battle signaled the diminishing usefulness of knights on the battlefield, and marked the rise of England as a significant world power.

CRÉCY

England's victory against France at Crécy in August 1346 was won in large part by the longbow, a quick-firing weapon that decimated Philip VI of France's knights. The battle earned English king Edward III dominance over France in the early phases of the Hundred Years War—a long, intermittent struggle between the two powers.

Edward III's pursuit of his claim to the French throne led to the outbreak of war against France in 1337. Despite his naval victory at Sluys in 1340, Edward's campaigns were inconclusive until he landed in Normandy in July 1346 with a force of up to 15,000 men. Intent on conducting a *chevauchée* in northern France—terrorizing the region by raiding, burning, and pillaging— Edward attacked a series of northern towns. However, as he neared Paris an approaching French army forced him north, where his forces almost became trapped in the devastated lands south of the Somme river. On August 24, Edward forced a crossing of the river at Blanchetaque. Only then was he able to turn and face the French on terrain of his choice at Crécy.

Philip wrongly believed that his force's superior numbers—at least double those of the English—would prevail. Instead the battle claimed the lives of thousands of French knights and dozens of nobles, and opened the way to an English advance to Calais, which Edward's forces captured in 1347.

> *"Where the pride of the Norman had sway,*
> *The lions lord over the fray."*
>
> FROM "CRÉCY" BY FRANCIS TURNER PALGRAVE, 1881

N C E

6 THE FRENCH ROUT EVENING, AUGUST 26 TO MORNING, AUGUST 27

With the Duke of Alençon and other leaders dead, the French attacks weakened. Just after midnight Philip retreated with the remains of the reserve. The next morning, more French troops arrived at Crécy, but the English knights charged them down, inflicting still more casualties on the French, whose losses amounted to many thousands against only a few hundred English dead and wounded at most.

→ English final advance   ▪▪▶ French retreat

VICTORY FOR THE BOW

Edward III's triumph at Crécy was a turning point in the Hundred Years War. It allowed the English to set up a secure base around Calais and cemented the position of the longbow as a key battlefield weapon.

KEY

 Towns

ENGLISH FORCES

 Commanders	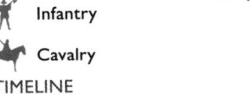 Artillery
Longbowmen	Baggage camp
Infantry	
Cavalry	

FRENCH FORCES

| Commanders |
| Genoese crossbowmen |
| Infantry |
| Cavalry |

TIMELINE

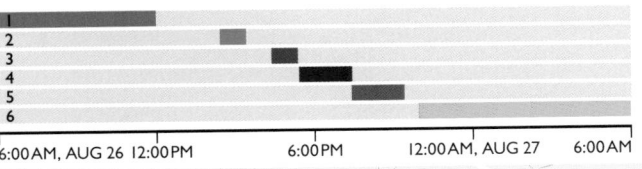

6:00AM, AUG 26 12:00PM   6:00PM   12:00AM, AUG 27   6:00AM

THE CRÉCY CAMPAIGN

Edward III's landing at Saint-Vaast-la-Hougue on July 12, 1346, took the French by surprise and at first he conducted his *chevauchée* unhindered. As Edward marched toward Paris, Philip VI raised a force to push the English north, where the French had blocked all crossings of the Somme. After overcoming the blockade, Edward met Philip at Crécy.

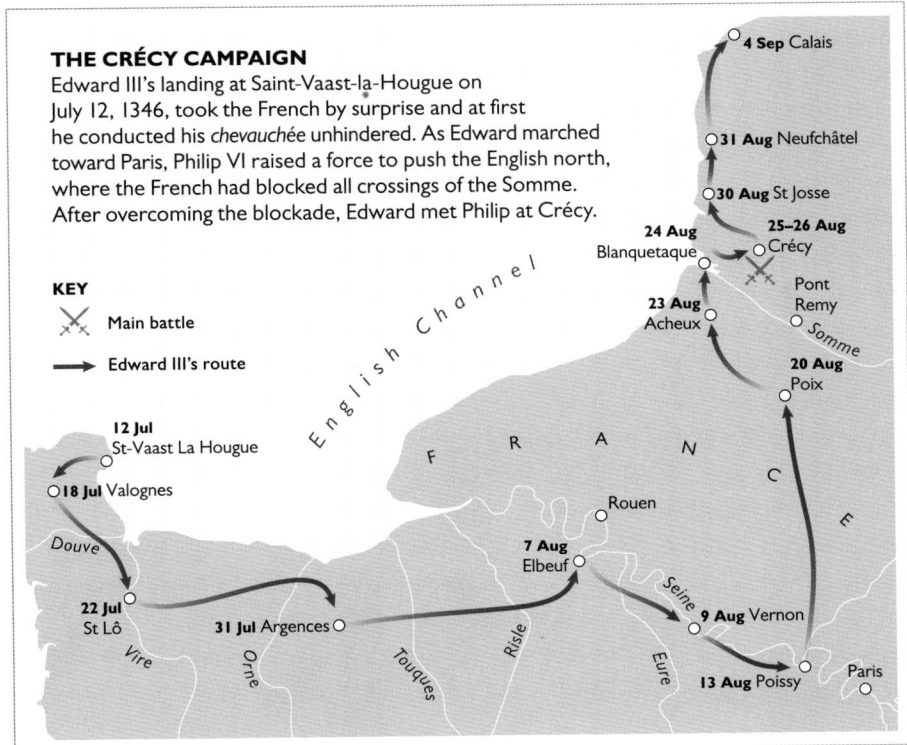

KEY

⚔ Main battle

→ Edward III's route

4 Sep Calais
31 Aug Neufchâtel
30 Aug St Josse
25–26 Aug Crécy
24 Aug Blanquetaque
Pont Remy
23 Aug Acheux
Somme
20 Aug Poix
English Channel
12 Jul St-Vaast La Hougue
18 Jul Valognes
Douve
Rouen
FRANCE
7 Aug Elbeuf
Seine
9 Aug Vernon
22 Jul St Lô
Vire
31 Jul Argences
Orne
Touques
Risle
Eure
13 Aug Poissy
Paris

△ **Archers at the Battle of Crécy**
At Crécy (see pp.82–83), Genoese crossbowmen clashed with Welsh and English longbowmen. Fought at longer range than shown here in Jean Froissart's *Chronicles*, the duel marked the effectiveness of the longbow, with the crossbowmen hampered by mud and a lack of shields and arrows.

▽ **14th-century painting of siege warfare**
This painting shows longbowmen's feathered arrows taking a heavy toll on the defenders. The crossbow was, in general, a superior siege weapon because it could be aimed more precisely, and bowmen could take cover while reloading.

KNIGHTS AND BOWMEN

Celebrated in chivalric romance, armored knights had the highest status among warriors in medieval Europe. However, on the battlefield, archers armed with longbows or crossbows often were more than a match for this military and social elite.

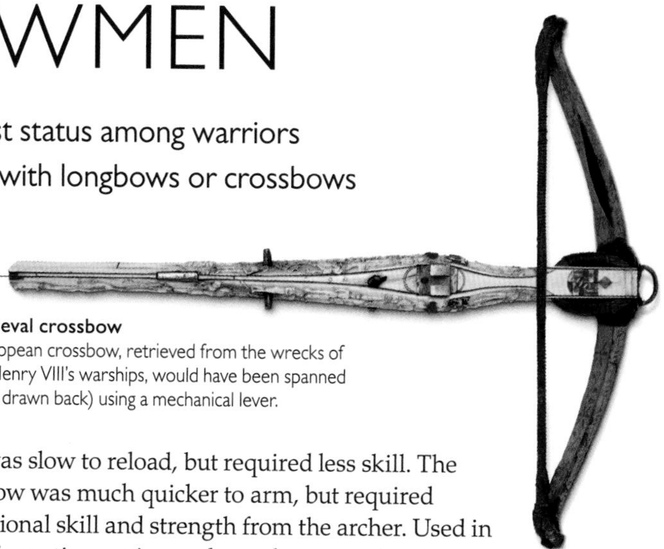

Armed with lances, swords, maces, and poleaxes, knights fought on foot as well as on horseback, and viewed battle as a test of personal courage and strength in close-quarter encounters with a worthy opponent. By contrast, archers, who fought largely from a distance, posed a direct threat to this chivalric concept of war. Any archer captured by enemy knights could expect to receive savage treatment. While several medieval popes banned the use of bows in warfare, this had little effect on the battlefield.

In battle, archers typically delivered the opening attack in preparation for a cavalry charge, using either crossbows or longbows. Many of the most accomplished crossbowmen hailed from Genoa, Italy, while Welsh and English longbowmen were the most feared troops in English armies. The crossbow was less successful in defense

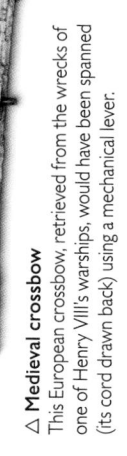

△ **Medieval crossbow**
This European crossbow, retrieved from the wrecks of one of Henry VIII's warships, would have been spanned (its cord drawn back) using a mechanical lever.

as it was slow to reload, but required less skill. The longbow was much quicker to arm, but required exceptional skill and strength from the archer. Used in mass formation against a charge by enemy knights, the impact of longbows was similar to machine-gun fire, with each archer shooting at least six arrows per minute. If helmets and plate armor protected knights from the arrows, the longbowmen aimed at their horses. In the 16th century, firearms replaced bows, putting an end to the dominance of knights and bowmen on the battlefield.

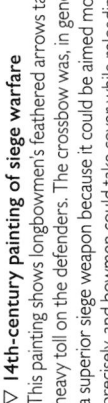

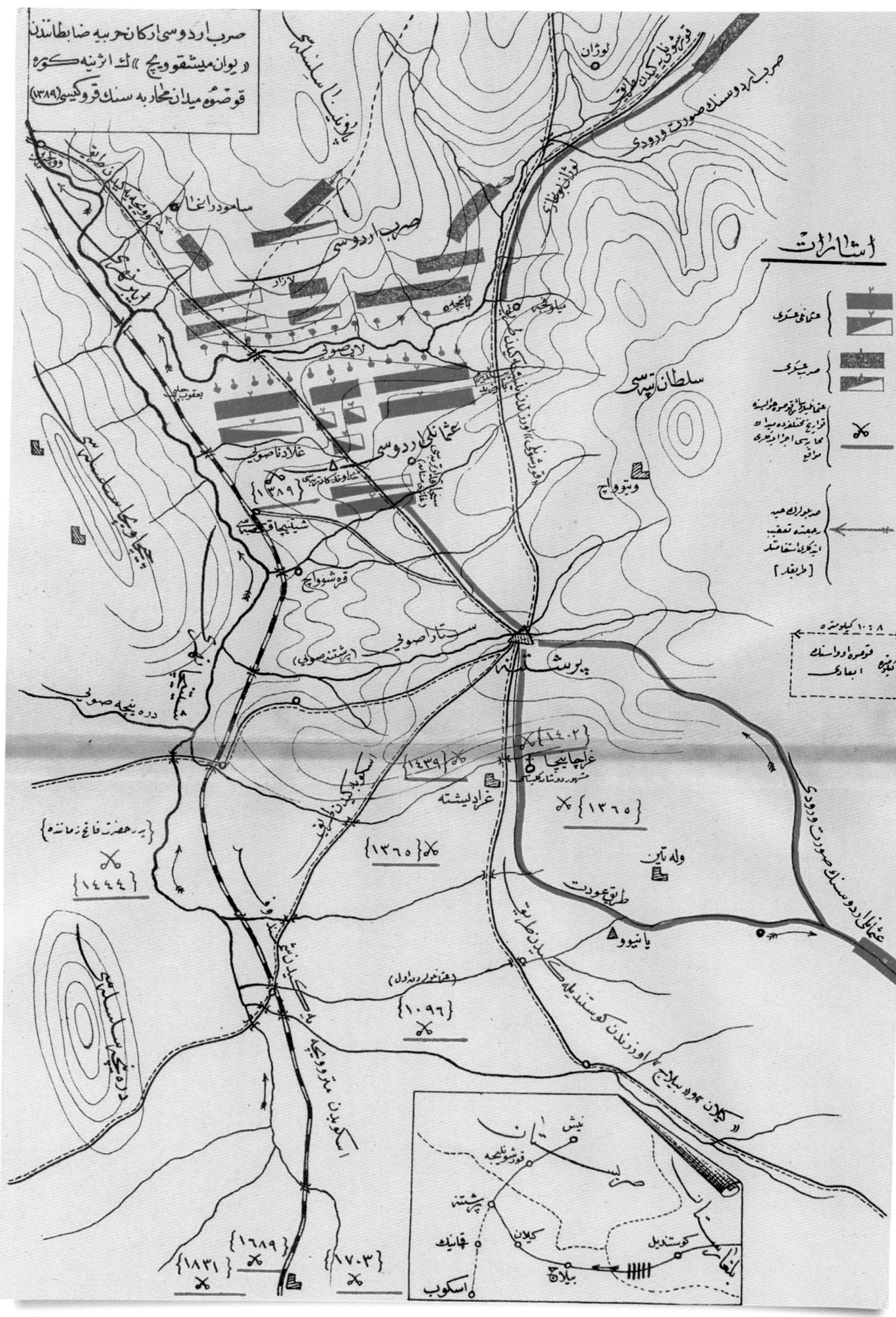

◁ **Rare Ottoman atlas**
Extracted from an atlas of Ottoman military maps published in 1908 by the Grand Vizier Ahmed Muhtar Pasha, the map shows the hilly topography around Kosovo Polje, as well as the advance of the two armies toward the battlefield.

▽ **Lazar's approach**
Lazar advances southwest from Niš, where the Allies had assembled. They include Vuk Branković, a Bosnian contingent sent by Bosnian king Tvrtko I, and smaller groups of Croatian Knights, Hospitallers, and Albanians.

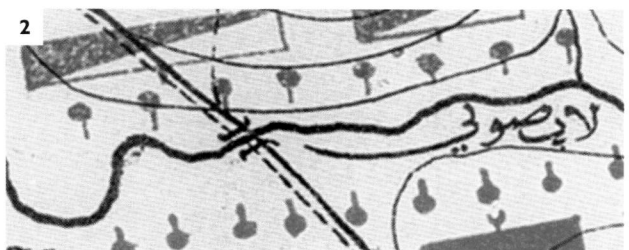

△ **Riverside defenses**
The River Lub, used as a defensive line by Lazar's Allied army. On the right, Lazar placed Brankovic and the main Serb contingent; in the center, he led the infantry; and on the left, Vukovic commanded the Bosnian allies.

▽ **Facing the enemy**
Murad and his 40,000-strong army, including elite Janissaries and European levies, arrived at Pristina on June 14. From there, they began to advance toward Kosovo to face Lazar's forces.

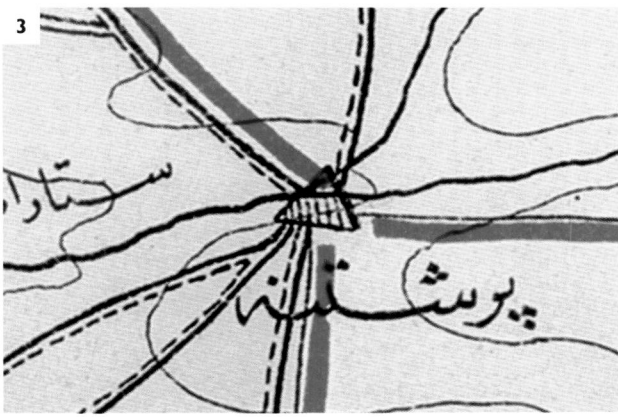

◁ **Ottoman left wing**
Yakub's left wing, made up of Anatolian (Asian) cavalry, faced an initial damaging charge from the Serbian cavalry. Yakub successfully counterattacked; he was later killed by his brother Bayezid when he inherited the throne.

KOSOVO POLJE

The clash in 1389 between Ottoman Sultan Murad I and the Serb Prince Lazar at Kosovo Polje ended in the death of both leaders. Losses on the Serbian side were so great that Serbia was fatally weakened and ultimately lost its independence to the Ottoman empire in 1459.

In spring 1389, Sultan Murad I, who had steadily expanded Ottoman possessions in the Balkans, gathered an army of up to 40,000 men and moved out of Bulgaria through Sofia into southern Kosovo. On June 15, Prince Lazar Hrebeljanović, ruler of the largest of Serbia's principalities, drew up his forces (which were significantly outnumbered by Murad's) on the north bank of the River Lub to face the Ottoman threat.

Although the battle began promisingly for the Serbs with an initial cavalry charge, the Ottoman counterattacks were strong. They ended in the death of Lazar, and accusations of treason against Branković, who fled the battle. The killing of Murad by a Serbian noble in the battle marred the Ottoman victory, but Bayezid, now sultan, sealed it by marrying Lazar's daughter and placing his son Stefan Lazarević on the throne as an Ottoman vassal. Gradually the Ottomans annexed parts of Serbia, seizing Skopje in 1392, and putting an end to Serbian independence altogether in 1459.

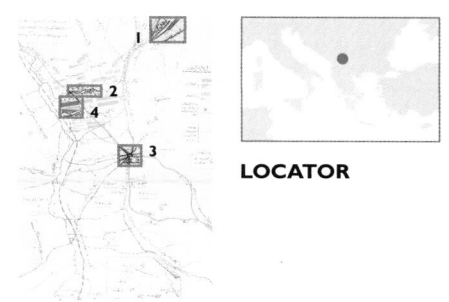

LOCATOR

"When fortune smiles 'tis easy to be good. Adversity reveals the hero's soul."

FROM AN ENGLISH TRANSLATION OF SERBIAN PLAY *THE MOUNTAIN WREATH*, 1847

CHAOTIC BATTLEFIELD
On the Ottoman left, Yakub stemmed Branković's assault. Bayezid meanwhile engaged the Bosnian contingent in bitter fighting. Now severely outnumbered, parts of the main Serbian contingent pulled back, leaving Lazar exposed. There he and many Serbian nobles died in a last stand.

KEY

Town

OTTOMAN FORCES

Cavalry — ⋯▶ Retreats

Infantry — ⊞ Camp

→ Attacks

ALLIED FORCES

Cavalry — → Attacks

Infantry — ⋯▶ Retreats

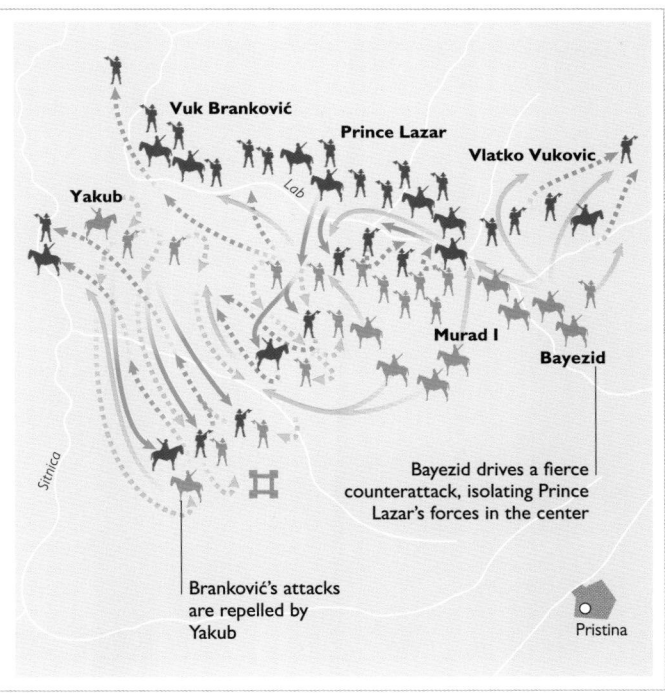

Vuk Branković · Prince Lazar · Vlatko Vukovic
Yakub · Murad I · Bayezid
Lab · Sitnica

Bayezid drives a fierce counterattack, isolating Prince Lazar's forces in the center

Branković's attacks are repelled by Yakub

Pristina

THE KNIGHTS' ASCENDANT

The early stages of battle favored the Teutonic Order, with the weight of its cavalry pushing back its enemy. However, the departure of a force of knights in pursuit of Tatars weakened its line.

I THE ARMIES ARRIVE
EVENING, JULY 14–6:00 AM, JULY 15, 1410

The Polish-Lithuanian army arrived the evening before the battle. The Teutonic Order reached the battlefield at about 6 am the next day, with Grand Master von Jungingen commanding 15 banners (units of roughly 200 men) at the rear. Ahead of him were vassal troops and the Order's artillery.

2 THE BATTLE DELAYED
6:00–9:00 AM, JULY 15

Jagiello delayed beginning the battle while he prayed for success in the chapel tent near the Polish camp. Von Jungingen mockingly sent him two swords as an encouragement to fight, but only in late morning did the Polish forces emerge, forming a left flank near Ludwigsdorf, with Vytautas's Lithuanians to their right, and the Tatars forming the right flank.

3 THE TATAR CHARGE 9:00–10:00 AM

Vytautas ordered the Tatars to charge the Order's left flank, and they were followed by his Lithuanian light cavalry. As the Tatars broke through the first rank, the second rank of knights counterattacked, causing the Tatars to flee. Four banners of the Order chased them off the field.

> ⟶ Tatars and Lithuanians advance
> ┅⟶ Tatars retreat, pursued by knights
> ⟶ Teutonic cavalry counterattacks

4 THE ORDER ADVANCES 10:00–11:00 AM

The Lithuanian light cavalry were pushed back, and retreated into the woods. Some Teutonic knights broke from their lines in pursuit, only to be decimated by a section of the Polish reserve. Meanwhile, von Jungingen ordered a general advance against the Polish forces, resulting in a hard-fought melee in the center.

> ┅⟶ Lithuanians pushed back
> ⟶ Polish resistance
> ⟶ Teutonic forces advance

5 THE POLES RALLY
11:00 AM–12:00 PM

The battle in the center was going in favor of the Teutonic Order until Jagiello ordered his cavalry reserves forward; he also deployed the third line of his army to reinforce the center and support his right wing. The Poles began to make some progress, pushing back the Teutonic knights on the Polish left flank, but with his last reserves deployed, Jagiello's position was still precarious.

> ⟶ Polish cavalry and third line advance

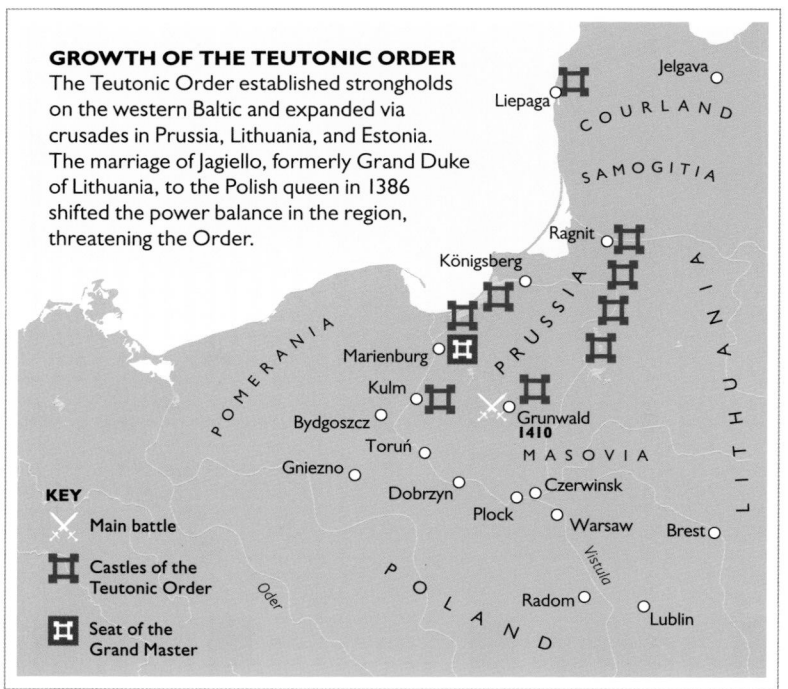

9:00 am The Teutonic knights' cannon fire only two shots before the Tatar cavalry reach them and kill the gunners

10:00 am Three Russian banners and some Polish cavalry hold the right flank after the retreat of the Lithuanians and Tatars

9:00 am Teutonic knights move back to allow the Poles to engage

Stebark (Tannenberg)

10:00 am Nine Banners of the Teutonic knights leave the battlefield in pursuit of the Lithuanians

von Jungingen

Grunwald

KINGDOM OF POLAND

Vytautas

Lake Lubien

Jagiello

Lodwigowo

6:00 am Polish cavalry and Royal Banner of Krakow assemble in the center

Ulnowo

11:00 am Von Jungingen leads a charge which almost captures the Royal Banner of Krakow

8:00 am Von Jungingen sends two swords to Jagiello to provoke him to attack

GROWTH OF THE TEUTONIC ORDER

The Teutonic Order established strongholds on the western Baltic and expanded via crusades in Prussia, Lithuania, and Estonia. The marriage of Jagiello, formerly Grand Duke of Lithuania, to the Polish queen in 1386 shifted the power balance in the region, threatening the Order.

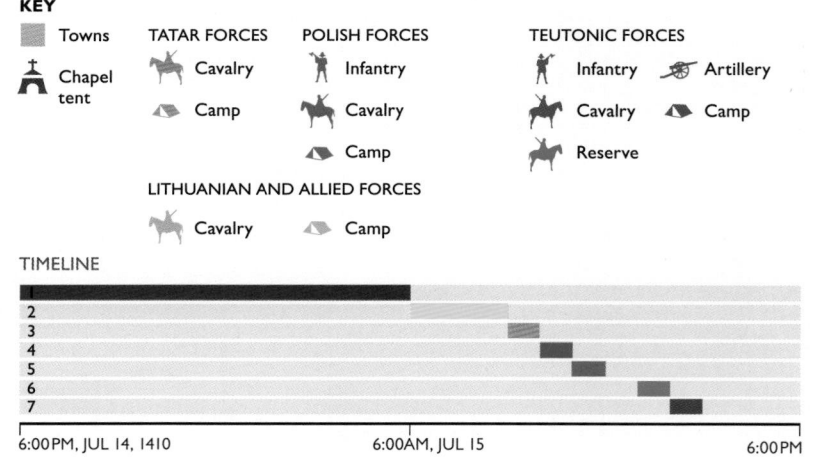

Jelgava
Liepaga
COURLAND
SAMOGITIA
Ragnit
Königsberg
PRUSSIA
Marienburg
Kulm
LITHUANIA
Bydgoszcz
Grunwald 1410
Toruń
MASOVIA
Gniezno
Dobrzyn
Plock
Czerwinsk
Warsaw
Brest
POLAND
Oder
Radom
Vistula
Lublin

KEY
> ✕ Main battle
> ⛫ Castles of the Teutonic Order
> ⛫ Seat of the Grand Master

THE END OF THE KNIGHTS

The military might of the Teutonic Order depended on its heavy cavalry. The loss of such a large part of its army at Grunwald compromised the Order's ability to defend its territories. It was forced to rely on expensive mercenaries, which contributed to the state's eventual decline and bankruptcy.

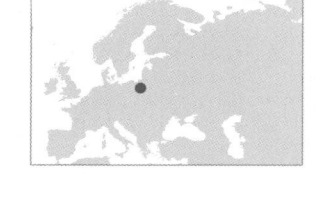

KEY

	TATAR FORCES	POLISH FORCES		TEUTONIC FORCES	
Towns	Cavalry	Infantry		Infantry	Artillery
Chapel tent	Camp	Cavalry		Cavalry	Camp
		Camp		Reserve	

LITHUANIAN AND ALLIED FORCES
Cavalry Camp

TIMELINE

1
2
3
4
5
6
7

6:00 PM, JUL 14, 1410   6:00 AM, JUL 15   6:00 PM

GRUNWALD

The Teutonic Order, a crusader state, tried to halt a Polish–Lithuanian invasion of their territory in 1410 at Grunwald (also known as the Battle of Tannenberg). The Teutonic knights were enveloped and decimated, ending their dominance of the western Baltic.

In 1409, after years of tension, conflict erupted between the Teutonic Order and Poland–Lithuania when the Polish king, Wladyslaw Jagiello, supported a revolt against the Order in the formerly Polish region of Samogitia. After inconclusive fighting, the Kings of Bohemia and Hungary brokered an armistice, but the belligerents used the brief peace to recruit allies. Wladyslaw's cousin Vytautas, Grand Duke of Lithuania, won the support of Tatars, Russians, and Moldavians, while the Grand Master of the Teutonic Order, Ulrich von Jungingen, drew knights from Western Europe.

Jagiello sent feint attacks north into Samogitia and west into Pomerania, combining his and Vytautas's armies, to conceal a huge main assault aimed at Marienburg, the Order's headquarters.

Jagiello's 40,000-strong force crossed the Vistula River on July 2, 1410, and von Jungingen—who made the mistake of dividing his army—rushed to the Drewenz River, the last obstacle in the way of Marienburg, so forcing his opponents east toward Grunwald.

The defeat at Grunwald was almost the end of the Order, with only a small part of the Teutonic force escaping back to Marienburg. However, as Jagiello did not follow them immediately, the new Grand Master, Heinrich von Plauen, had time to shore up the defenses at Marienburg and gather reinforcements. Jagiello withdrew, and in February 1411 he signed the Peace of Torun, giving him only a part of the Order's territory. Nonetheless, the Teutonic Order was broken as a force and eventually slipped into political irrelevance.

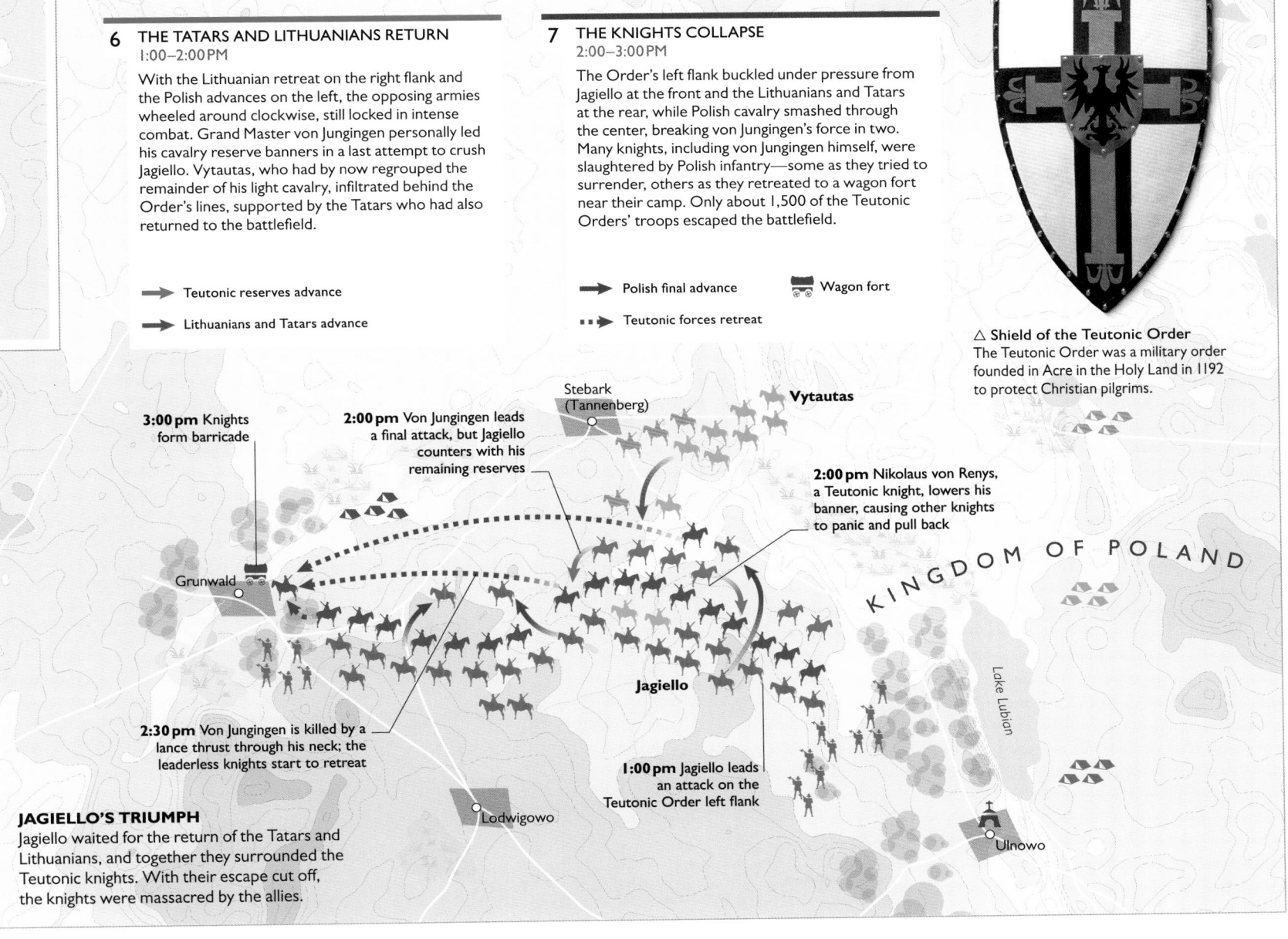

6 THE TATARS AND LITHUANIANS RETURN
1:00–2:00 PM

With the Lithuanian retreat on the right flank and the Polish advances on the left, the opposing armies wheeled around clockwise, still locked in intense combat. Grand Master von Jungingen personally led his cavalry reserve banners in a last attempt to crush Jagiello. Vytautas, who had by now regrouped the remainder of his light cavalry, infiltrated behind the Order's lines, supported by the Tatars who had also returned to the battlefield.

→ Teutonic reserves advance

→ Lithuanians and Tatars advance

7 THE KNIGHTS COLLAPSE
2:00–3:00 PM

The Order's left flank buckled under pressure from Jagiello at the front and the Lithuanians and Tatars at the rear, while Polish cavalry smashed through the center, breaking von Jungingen's force in two. Many knights, including von Jungingen himself, were slaughtered by Polish infantry—some as they tried to surrender, others as they retreated to a wagon fort near their camp. Only about 1,500 of the Teutonic Orders' troops escaped the battlefield.

→ Polish final advance

🛒 Wagon fort

▪▪▶ Teutonic forces retreat

△ **Shield of the Teutonic Order**
The Teutonic Order was a military order founded in Acre in the Holy Land in 1192 to protect Christian pilgrims.

3:00 pm Knights form barricade

2:00 pm Von Jungingen leads a final attack, but Jagiello counters with his remaining reserves

Stebark (Tannenberg)

Vytautas

2:00 pm Nikolaus von Renys, a Teutonic knight, lowers his banner, causing other knights to panic and pull back

KINGDOM OF POLAND

Grunwald

2:30 pm Von Jungingen is killed by a lance thrust through his neck; the leaderless knights start to retreat

Jagiello

Lake Lubian

1:00 pm Jagiello leads an attack on the Teutonic Order left flank

Lodwigowo

Ulnowo

JAGIELLO'S TRIUMPH
Jagiello waited for the return of the Tatars and Lithuanians, and together they surrounded the Teutonic knights. With their escape cut off, the knights were massacred by the allies.

AGINCOURT

In the summer of 1415, King Henry V of England invaded France to pursue his claim to the French throne. Two months later, he inflicted a devastating defeat on the French. Hampered by heavy mud and a narrow field, thousands of French men-at-arms perished in a hail of arrows from the English longbowmen.

King Henry V of England had inherited his great-grandfather Edward III's claim to the French throne, which provoked the Hundred Year's War between England and France in 1337. In 1414, he interrupted a 25-year-long truce between the two countries by demanding French recognition of his permanent right to Aquitaine, Normandy, and other English possessions in France, and the hand in marriage of Catherine, daughter of King Charles VI of France.

When the French rejected this, Henry assembled an army of about 12,000 men and landed at Harfleur in northern France in August 1415. The siege of the town proved protracted, and as winter approached, Henry decided that rather than return to England, he would turn toward English-held Calais. This delay allowed the French, led by Constable Charles d'Albret, to raise their own force, which blocked the English army from crossing the Somme, and forced them more than 60 miles (100 km) south to find an unguarded ford. Despite the advantage that d'Albret's maneuvering had secured (and his larger forces), the French army suffered a crushing defeat at Agincourt. The French leadership was decimated, and Charles VI was forced to consent to the Treaty of Troyes, which in 1420 agreed Henry V's marriage to Catherine and recognized him as heir to the French throne.

THE ENGLISH AND FRENCH ARMIES MEET

As Henry V's army made its way to the coast, the French assembled a large army. They finally intercepted the English forces near the village of Agincourt (Azincourt in French).

KEY

Towns	FRENCH FORCES	ENGLISH FORCES
	Mounted men-at-arms	Archers	Army
	Unmounted men-at-arms		Longbowmen

TIMELINE

1
2
3
4
5
6

OCT 24, 1415   OCT 25   OCT 26

△ **Pitched battle**
In this miniature from a 15th-century manuscript, the English army is shown attacking the defeated and fleeing French forces.

AN ENGLISH SHOW OF FORCE

Having taken Harfleur, Henry V decided to make a show of force by marching to Calais. With a French force blocking his way at Blanche-Taque, Henry was forced to turn south. Aiming to withdraw his depleted force to Calais, the French again blocked him north of Blangy.

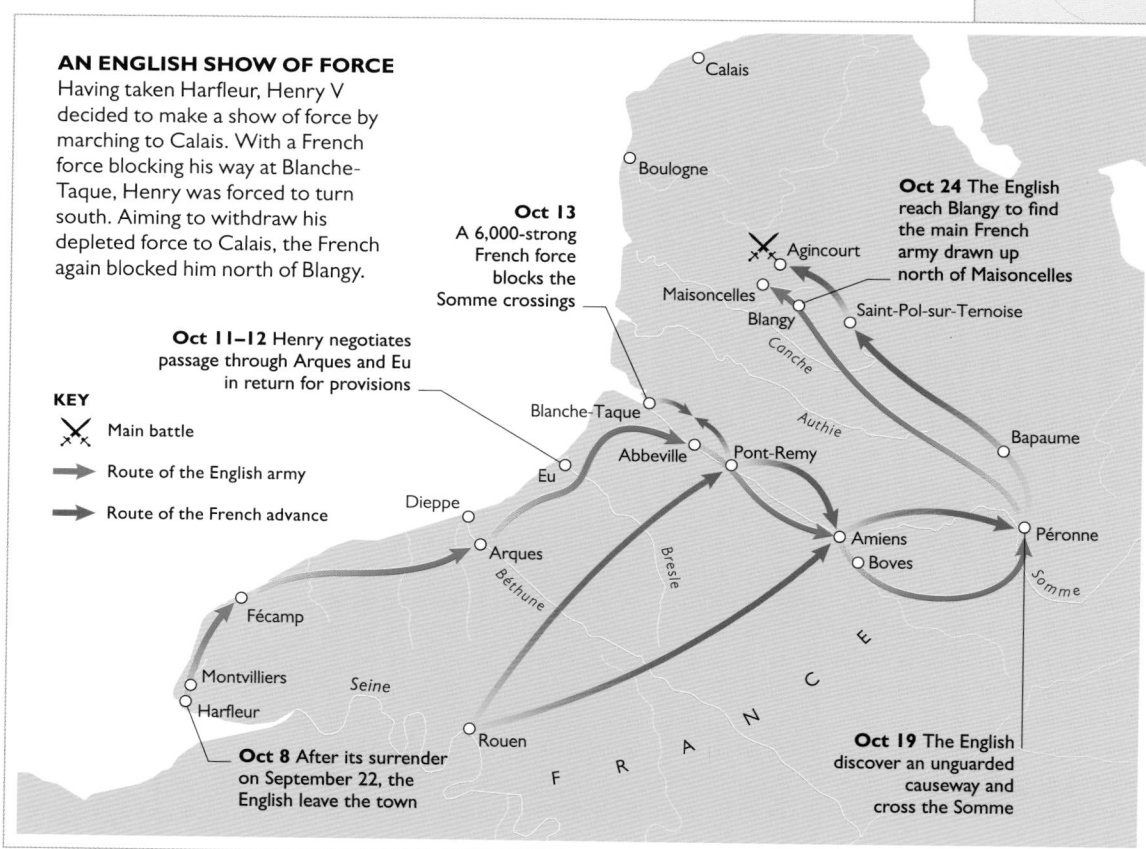

Oct 11–12 Henry negotiates passage through Arques and Eu in return for provisions

Oct 13 A 6,000-strong French force blocks the Somme crossings

Oct 24 The English reach Blangy to find the main French army drawn up north of Maisoncelles

Oct 19 The English discover an unguarded causeway and cross the Somme

Oct 8 After its surrender on September 22, the English leave the town

KEY

✕ Main battle

→ Route of the English army

→ Route of the French advance

Locations: Calais, Boulogne, Agincourt, Maisoncelles, Blangy, Saint-Pol-sur-Ternoise, Conche, Authie, Bapaume, Blanche-Taque, Abbeville, Pont-Remy, Eu, Dieppe, Amiens, Boves, Péronne, Arques, Béthune, Bresle, Somme, Fécamp, Montvilliers, Seine, Harfleur, Rouen

1   THE ARMIES DEPLOY
OCTOBER 24–8:00 AM, OCTOBER 25

Both armies arrived near the village of Agincourt on October 24. Early the next morning, the English deployed in a line, with Henry in the center, his cousin Edward Duke of York on the right, and Baron Camoys on the left. The French arrayed their force in three "battles," with most of the nobles in the vanguard, and the archers and crossbowmen in the second line.

→ English advance

2   THE LONGBOWMEN PREPARE
8:00 AM

Henry deployed his longbowmen on either flank. They set sharpened stakes protruding at an angle in the ground. This prevented horsemen from approaching, and gave the bowmen shelter from which they could launch volleys of arrows with a range of up to 650 ft (200 m). With the archers in place, the armies waited.

//// Line of stakes

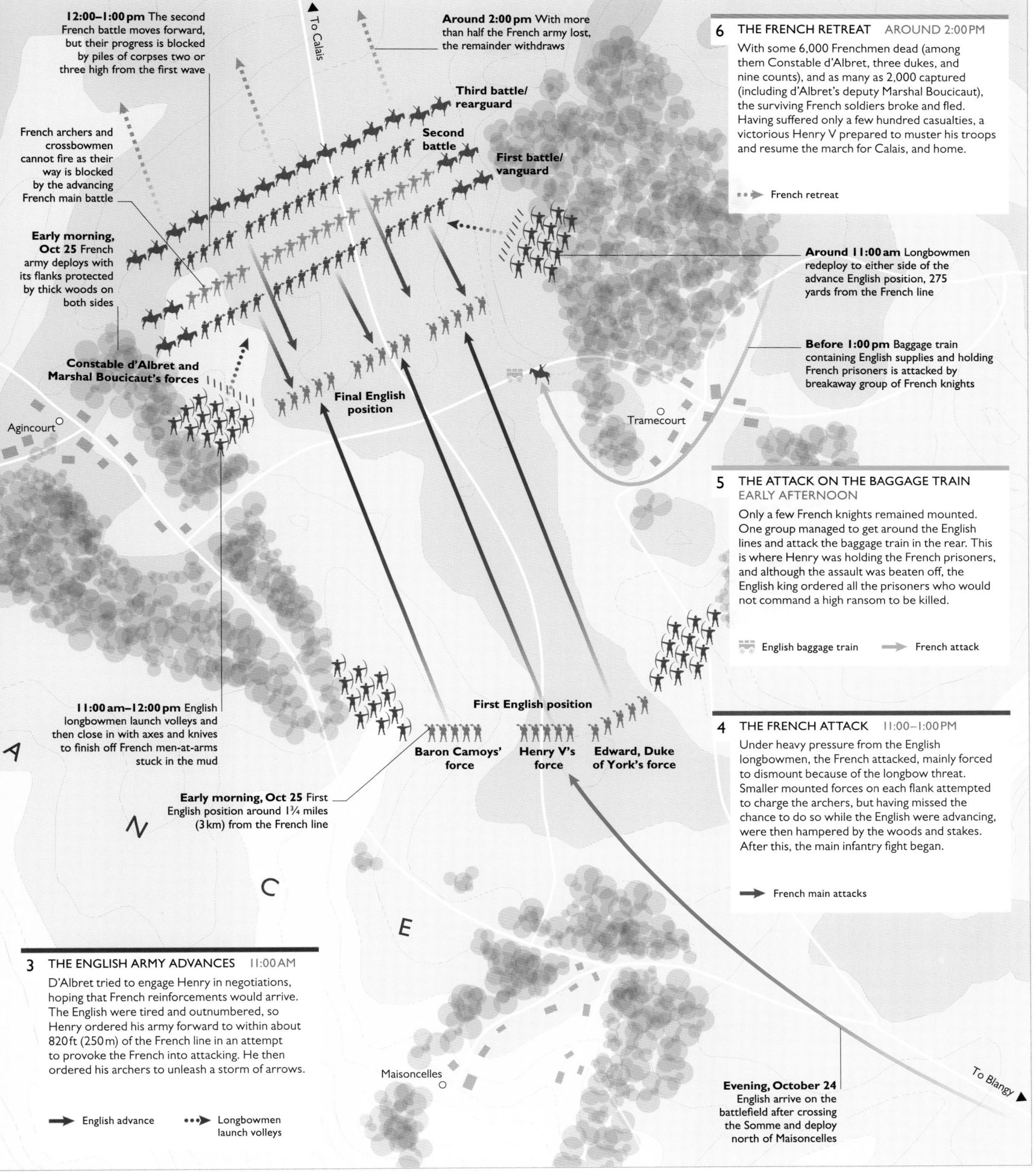

12:00–1:00 pm The second French battle moves forward, but their progress is blocked by piles of corpses two or three high from the first wave

French archers and crossbowmen cannot fire as their way is blocked by the advancing French main battle

Early morning, Oct 25 French army deploys with its flanks protected by thick woods on both sides

Constable d'Albret and Marshal Boucicaut's forces

Agincourt

11:00 am–12:00 pm English longbowmen launch volleys and then close in with axes and knives to finish off French men-at-arms stuck in the mud

Early morning, Oct 25 First English position around 1¾ miles (3 km) from the French line

Around 2:00 pm With more than half the French army lost, the remainder withdraws

Third battle/ rearguard

Second battle

First battle/ vanguard

Final English position

A
N
C
E

First English position

Baron Camoys' force   **Henry V's force**   **Edward, Duke of York's force**

Maisoncelles

To Calais

To Blangy

Tramecourt

---

6   THE FRENCH RETREAT   AROUND 2:00PM

With some 6,000 Frenchmen dead (among them Constable d'Albret, three dukes, and nine counts), and as many as 2,000 captured (including d'Albret's deputy Marshal Boucicaut), the surviving French soldiers broke and fled. Having suffered only a few hundred casualties, a victorious Henry V prepared to muster his troops and resume the march for Calais, and home.

‑‑‑▶   French retreat

Around 11:00 am Longbowmen redeploy to either side of the advance English position, 275 yards from the French line

Before 1:00 pm Baggage train containing English supplies and holding French prisoners is attacked by breakaway group of French knights

---

5   THE ATTACK ON THE BAGGAGE TRAIN
EARLY AFTERNOON

Only a few French knights remained mounted. One group managed to get around the English lines and attack the baggage train in the rear. This is where Henry was holding the French prisoners, and although the assault was beaten off, the English king ordered all the prisoners who would not command a high ransom to be killed.

🚃   English baggage train   ▶   French attack

---

4   THE FRENCH ATTACK   11:00–1:00PM

Under heavy pressure from the English longbowmen, the French attacked, mainly forced to dismount because of the longbow threat. Smaller mounted forces on each flank attempted to charge the archers, but having missed the chance to do so while the English were advancing, were then hampered by the woods and stakes. After this, the main infantry fight began.

▶   French main attacks

---

3   THE ENGLISH ARMY ADVANCES   11:00 AM

D'Albret tried to engage Henry in negotiations, hoping that French reinforcements would arrive. The English were tired and outnumbered, so Henry ordered his army forward to within about 820 ft (250 m) of the French line in an attempt to provoke the French into attacking. He then ordered his archers to unleash a storm of arrows.

▶   English advance   •••▶   Longbowmen launch volleys

Evening, October 24 English arrive on the battlefield after crossing the Somme and deploy north of Maisoncelles

SIEGE OF ORLÉANS

The successful defense of Orléans in 1428–29 was a turning point in the Hundred Years War between England and France, and came at a key moment at which the English seemed poised to win the war. The French victory resulted from the inspired intervention of Joan of Arc.

When the Treaty of Troyes was signed in 1420, the king of England was recognized as successor to the French throne, and the English and their allies controlled Paris and Reims. However, resistance continued, and in 1428 the Earl of Salisbury led an army to attack Orléans, a strategically important city on the River Loire.

On October 12, the English planned to storm the city across the bridge over the Loire defended by a fortified gatehouse, Les Tourelles. However, by the time the English took Les Tourelles on October 24, the defenders had rendered the bridge unusable. Two days later, Salisbury was fatally wounded and command devolved to the Earl of Suffolk, who abandoned the assault and built forts and earthworks for a long siege. Suffolk did not have enough troops for a total blockade, but by the new year the city's inhabitants were going hungry. In February, a 17-year-old peasant girl, Joan of Arc, began a journey to the Dauphin's court at Chinon.

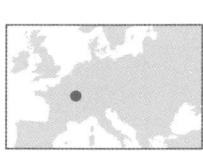

KEY

1 Joan of Arc and French forces entered the city with supplies on April 29.

2 St. Loup became the first English-held fort to fall to the French on May 4.

3 French troops forced the English from Les Tourelles gatehouse on May 7.

Claiming divine inspiration, she persuaded the leaders to let her attempt a relief of Orléans. Whether through her impact on morale or her tactical sense, she achieved the raising of the siege (see below), and set the stage for the expulsion of the English from France.

"Of the love or hatred God has for the English, I know nothing, but I do know that they will all be thrown out of France..."

ATTRIBUTED TO JOAN OF ARC, TRIAL RECORDS, 1431

THE RELIEF OF ORLÉANS
On April 29, 1429, Joan of Arc entered Orléans with vital supplies escorted by 500 soldiers, slipping through English lines from the east. Greeted rapturously by the people, she demanded action, but the French commander Jean de Dunois sought reinforcements before taking the English strongpoint at St. Loup on May 4. Two days later the French, with Joan in the forefront, crossed the river to attack the English fortified positions south of the city. After fierce fighting, the Augustines fell on May 6 and Les Tourelles the following day. The British abandoned the siege on May 8.

KEY
☒ English fortifications
➡ French army advances
⚔ French attacks

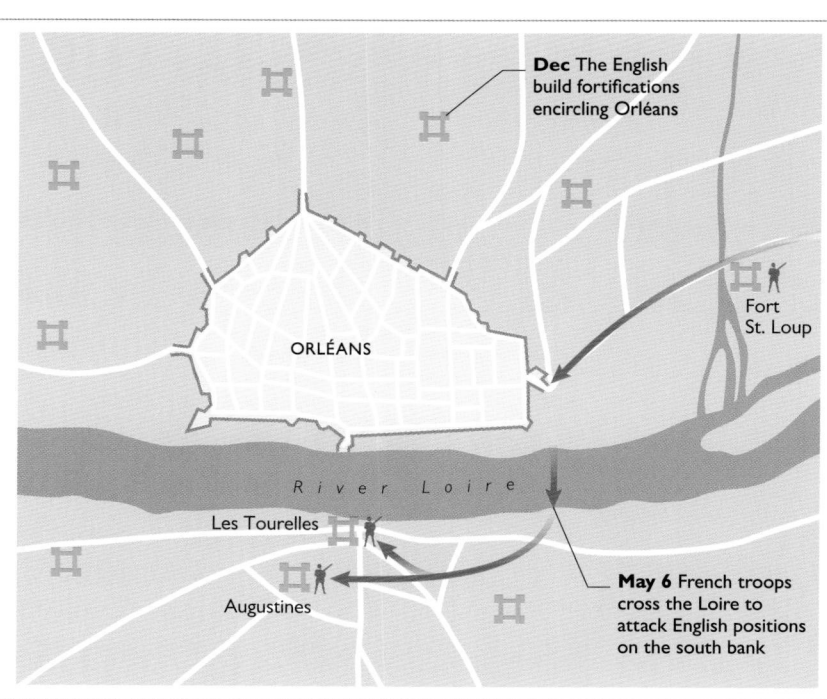

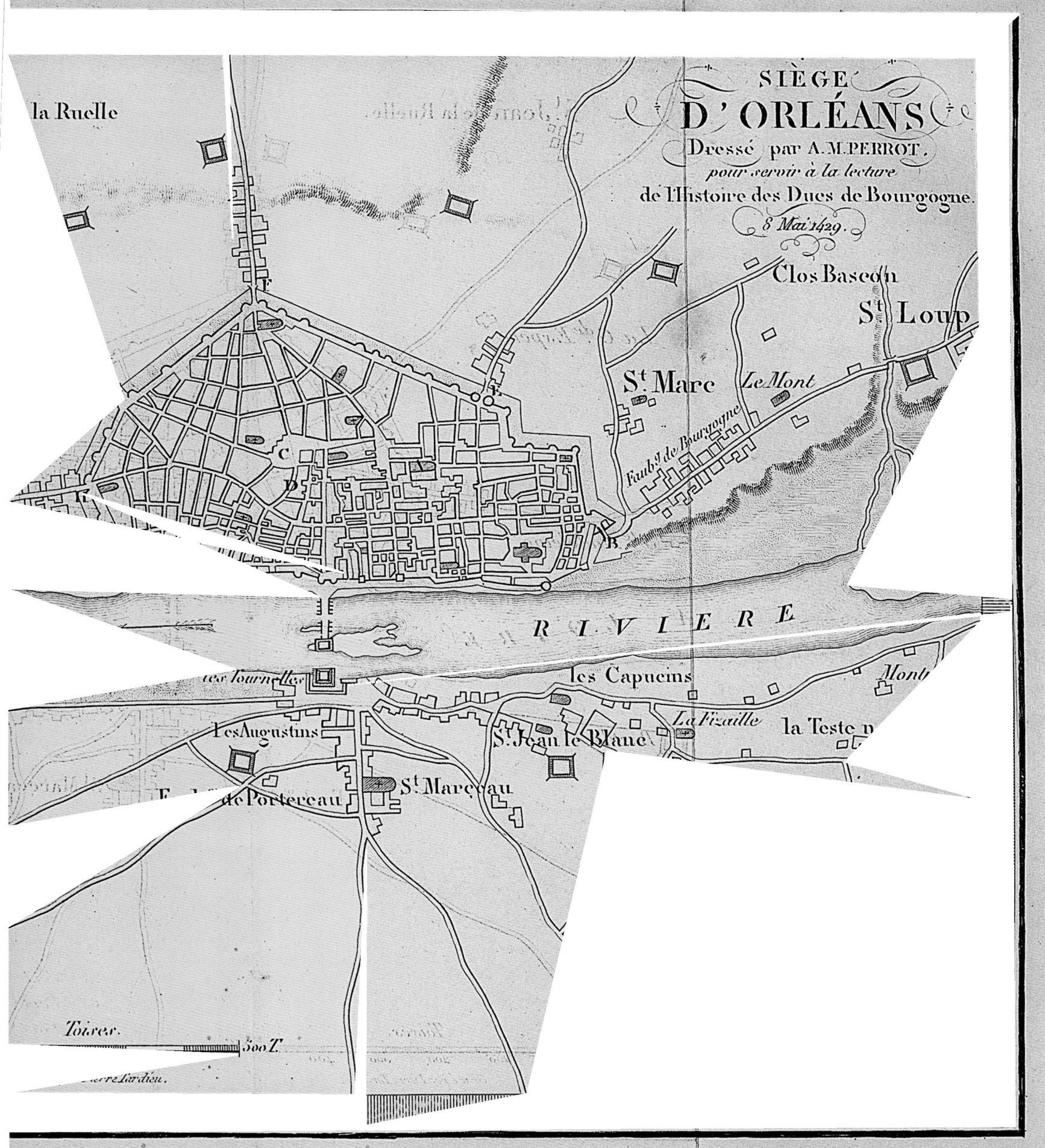

la Ruelle

SIÈGE
D'ORLÉANS
Dressé par A.M.PERROT.
pour servir à la lecture
de l'Histoire des Ducs de Bourgogne.
8 Mai 1429.

Clos Bascon

St Loup

St Marc   Le Mont

Faub⁵ de Bourgogne

C
D
B

RIVIERE

les Tournelles

les Capucins

Mont

Les Augustins

St Jean le Blanc

La Fizaille

la Teste

E.   de Portereau

St Marceau

Toises.

500 T.

Pierre Jardieu.

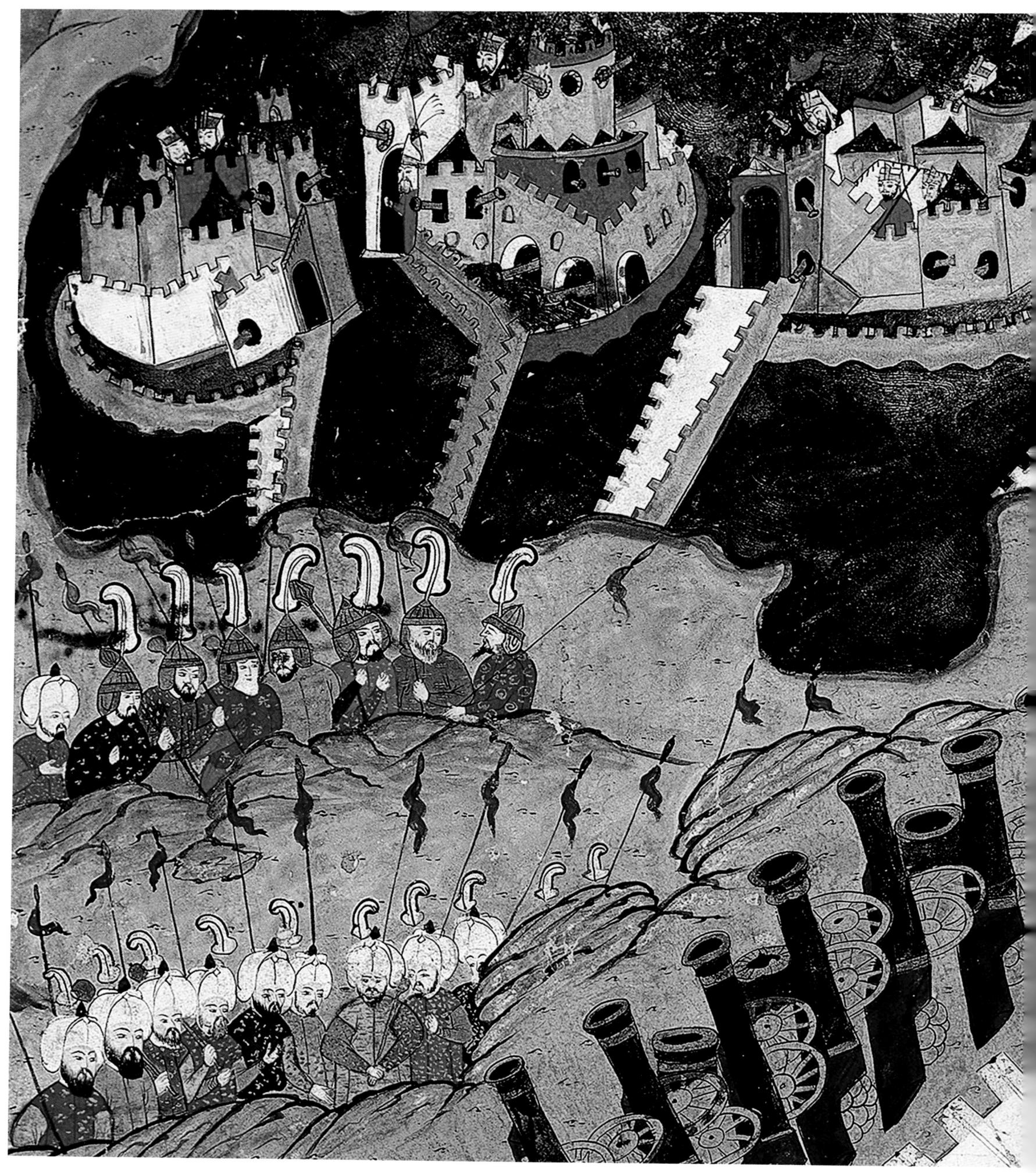

GUNPOWDER WEAPONS

In use in China as early as the 10th century, gunpowder-based weapons developed gradually. By 1500, the impact of these weapons transformed the tactics used in battles and sieges throughout Asia and Europe.

△ **Swivel gun**
In the 15th century European ships began mounting cannons, which at first comprised small guns such as this rotating weapon.

By the 13th century, knowledge of various gunpowder weapons—bombs, rockets, and incendiary devices—had reached Europe, and by 1346 English armies began deploying small cannons on the battlefield. From the late 14th century, several European empires competed to produce powerful siege guns. Called bombards, these cumbersome artillery pieces were highly effective against the stone walls of medieval cities and castles. Adopted by the Turkish Ottoman army, these bombards were used to breach Constantinople's previously impregnable walls in 1453 (see p.96). Field cannons and handguns developed in parallel with siege artillery. At Castillon, also in 1453, French cannons decimated charging English knights. Hand-held firearms took longer to develop; although unreliable and inaccurate, harquebuses and later muskets had begun to supplant bows in the early 16th century.

Changing tactics

Vulnerable to cannon and musket fire, the knight evolved into a lightly armored cavalryman wielding pistol and sword. In response to siege cannons, a new generation of low-lying, thick-walled, star-shaped forts was built across Europe with earth ramparts resistant to cannonballs and platforms for cannons to be used in defense.

△ **14th-century fire lance**
Invented in China, the fire lance was a gunpowder-filled tube attached to a spear, a one-shot fire weapon with a short range. This example is from Europe, although few were used in European warfare.

Siege of Szigetvár, 1566
The Ottoman Turks, the Safavid Persians, and the Mughals in India were known as "gunpowder empires" because of their use of cannons and muskets. This image depicts cannons in an Ottoman siege in Hungary.

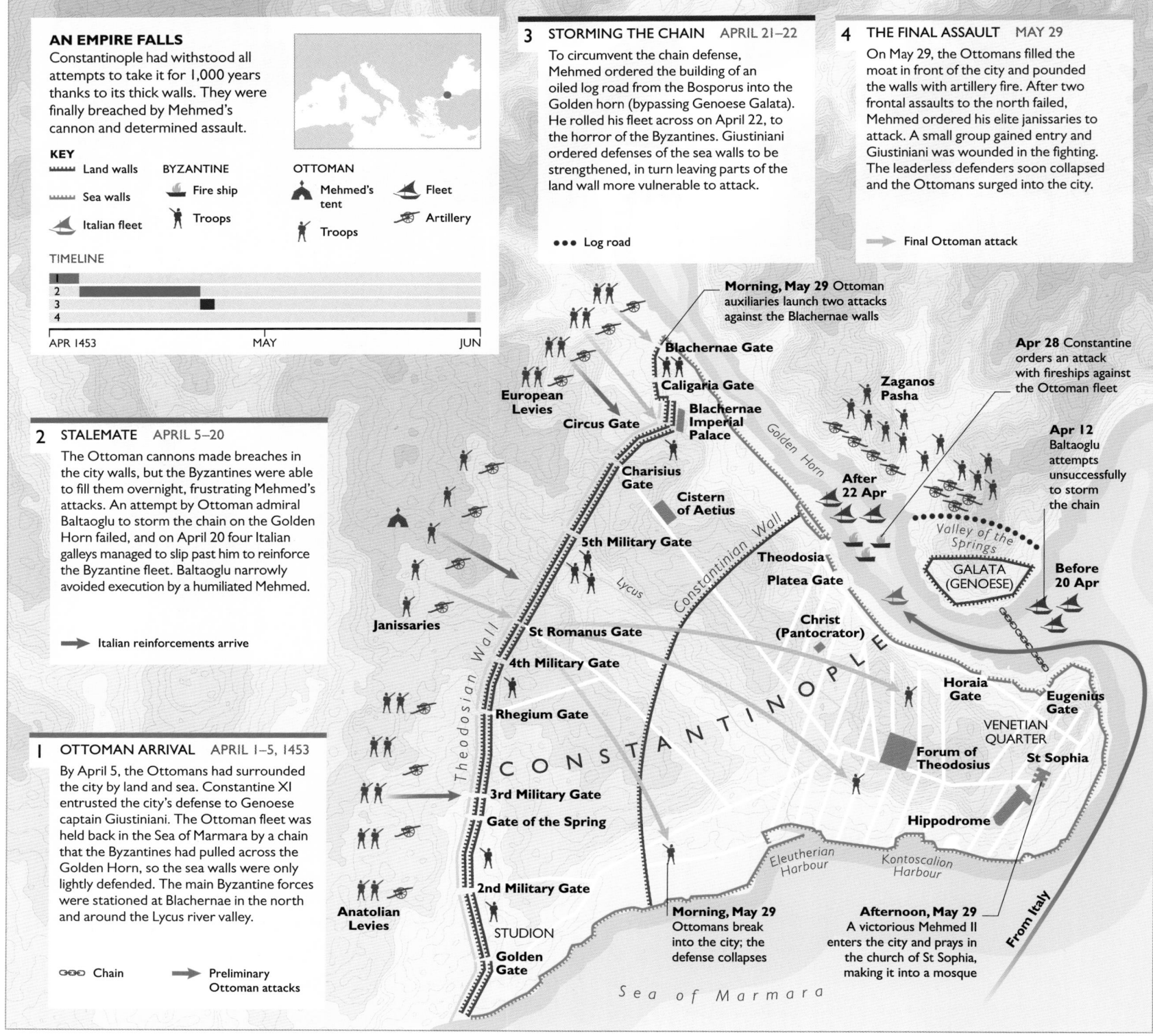

AN EMPIRE FALLS

Constantinople had withstood all attempts to take it for 1,000 years thanks to its thick walls. They were finally breached by Mehmed's cannon and determined assault.

KEY

- Land walls
- Sea walls
- Italian fleet

BYZANTINE
- Fire ship
- Troops

OTTOMAN
- Mehmed's tent
- Troops
- Fleet
- Artillery

TIMELINE

1
2
3
4

APR 1453   MAY   JUN

3 STORMING THE CHAIN APRIL 21–22

To circumvent the chain defense, Mehmed ordered the building of an oiled log road from the Bosporus into the Golden horn (bypassing Genoese Galata). He rolled his fleet across on April 22, to the horror of the Byzantines. Giustiniani ordered defenses of the sea walls to be strengthened, in turn leaving parts of the land wall more vulnerable to attack.

●●● Log road

4 THE FINAL ASSAULT MAY 29

On May 29, the Ottomans filled the moat in front of the city and pounded the walls with artillery fire. After two frontal assaults to the north failed, Mehmed ordered his elite janissaries to attack. A small group gained entry and Giustiniani was wounded in the fighting. The leaderless defenders soon collapsed and the Ottomans surged into the city.

→ Final Ottoman attack

2 STALEMATE APRIL 5–20

The Ottoman cannons made breaches in the city walls, but the Byzantines were able to fill them overnight, frustrating Mehmed's attacks. An attempt by Ottoman admiral Baltaoglu to storm the chain on the Golden Horn failed, and on April 20 four Italian galleys managed to slip past him to reinforce the Byzantine fleet. Baltaoglu narrowly avoided execution by a humiliated Mehmed.

→ Italian reinforcements arrive

1 OTTOMAN ARRIVAL APRIL 1–5, 1453

By April 5, the Ottomans had surrounded the city by land and sea. Constantine XI entrusted the city's defense to Genoese captain Giustiniani. The Ottoman fleet was held back in the Sea of Marmara by a chain that the Byzantines had pulled across the Golden Horn, so the sea walls were only lightly defended. The main Byzantine forces were stationed at Blachernae in the north and around the Lycus river valley.

Chain   → Preliminary Ottoman attacks

Morning, May 29 Ottoman auxiliaries launch two attacks against the Blachernae walls

Blachernae Gate

European Levies

Caligaria Gate

Circus Gate

Blachernae Imperial Palace

Zaganos Pasha

Apr 28 Constantine orders an attack with fireships against the Ottoman fleet

Charisius Gate

Cistern of Aetius

Golden Horn

Apr 12 Baltaoglu attempts unsuccessfully to storm the chain

5th Military Gate

After 22 Apr

Theodosia

Valley of the Springs

Janissaries

Lycus

Constantinian Wall

Platea Gate

GALATA (GENOESE)

Before 20 Apr

St Romanus Gate

Christ (Pantocrator)

CONSTANTINOPLE

4th Military Gate

Horaia Gate

Eugenius Gate

Rhegium Gate

Theodosian Wall

VENETIAN QUARTER

3rd Military Gate

Forum of Theodosius

St Sophia

Gate of the Spring

Hippodrome

Anatolian Levies

2nd Military Gate

Eleutherian Harbour

Kontoscalion Harbour

STUDION

Morning, May 29 Ottomans break into the city; the defense collapses

Afternoon, May 29 A victorious Mehmed II enters the city and prays in the church of St Sophia, making it into a mosque

From Italy

Golden Gate

Sea of Marmara

THE FALL OF CONSTANTINOPLE

In 1453, Ottoman Sultan Mehmed II moved to capture the Byzantine capital Constantinople. Its formidable walls resisted weeks of pummeling by Mehmed's artillery, but the city fell on May 29, putting an end to the Byzantine empire.

In 1451, Sultan Mehmed II ascended the Ottoman throne. Setting his sights on the capture of Constantinople, he built a fortress on the Bosphorus to throttle the sea-entrance to the Byzantine capital and assembled a 100-strong fleet and an army of 80,000 men. Equipped with huge Hungarian cannons, he marched against the walled city.

The Byzantine emperor Constantine XI had appealed for military help from western Christians, but his pleas had largely been ignored and he could muster only about 8,000 native defenders. Only the city walls, which had withstood attacks for more than 1,000 years, offered hope, but even they could not resist Mehmed's assault on May 29, 1453. Constantinople became the capital of the Ottoman empire and Mehmed and his successors pursued the conquest of the Balkans, reaching the gates of Vienna by 1529.

THE CONQUEST OF GRANADA

The reconquest of Muslim-held territory in the Iberian Peninsula by Spanish kingdoms stalled in the 13th century with stubborn defense by the Muslim Emirate of Granada. A campaign by Ferdinand of Aragon and Isabella of Castile culminated in the capture of Granada in 1492 and the expulsion of its Muslim population.

The hopes of Spain's Christian rulers that the Reconquista might be complete after the defeat of the Almohad caliphate at Las Navas de Tolosa (see p.75) were premature. Although Córdoba and Seville were retaken in 1236 and 1248, the Christian advance south faltered, and Muslim resistance concentrated in to their sole remaining territory, the Nasrid emirate of Granada.

The balance of power shifted with the marriage of Isabella of Castile and Ferdinand II of Aragon in 1469. The combined power of their kingdoms gave them greater leverage over a Nasrid dynasty, which had become divided by a struggle for power between the sultan, Boabdil, his father, Abū al-Hasan Alī, and his uncle, al-Zaghal. In 1483, Boabdil was captured by the Castilians; he was released on the condition that he would help the Spanish subdue and occupy those parts of Granada under the control of al-Zaghal. Fatally divided, the Nasrids could not offer coordinated resistance to the campaigns that culminated in Granada's capture in 1492, after which Boabdil was allowed to leave with his supporters, and religious freedoms were guaranteed.

THE END OF THE RECONQUISTA

Divisions in the last Muslim-held Emirate in Spain allowed Castile and Aragon to take most of its towns in a decade-long campaign from 1482, culminating in the fall of its capital, Granada, in 1492.

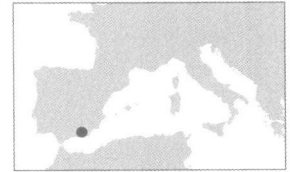

KEY

— Border of Granada   → Christian advances, 1482–92   ⚑ Towns captured by Christian forces

TIMELINE

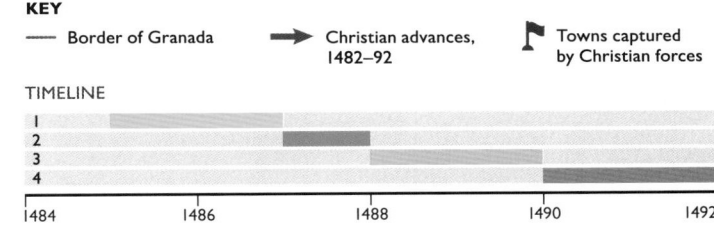

1484   1486   1488   1490   1492

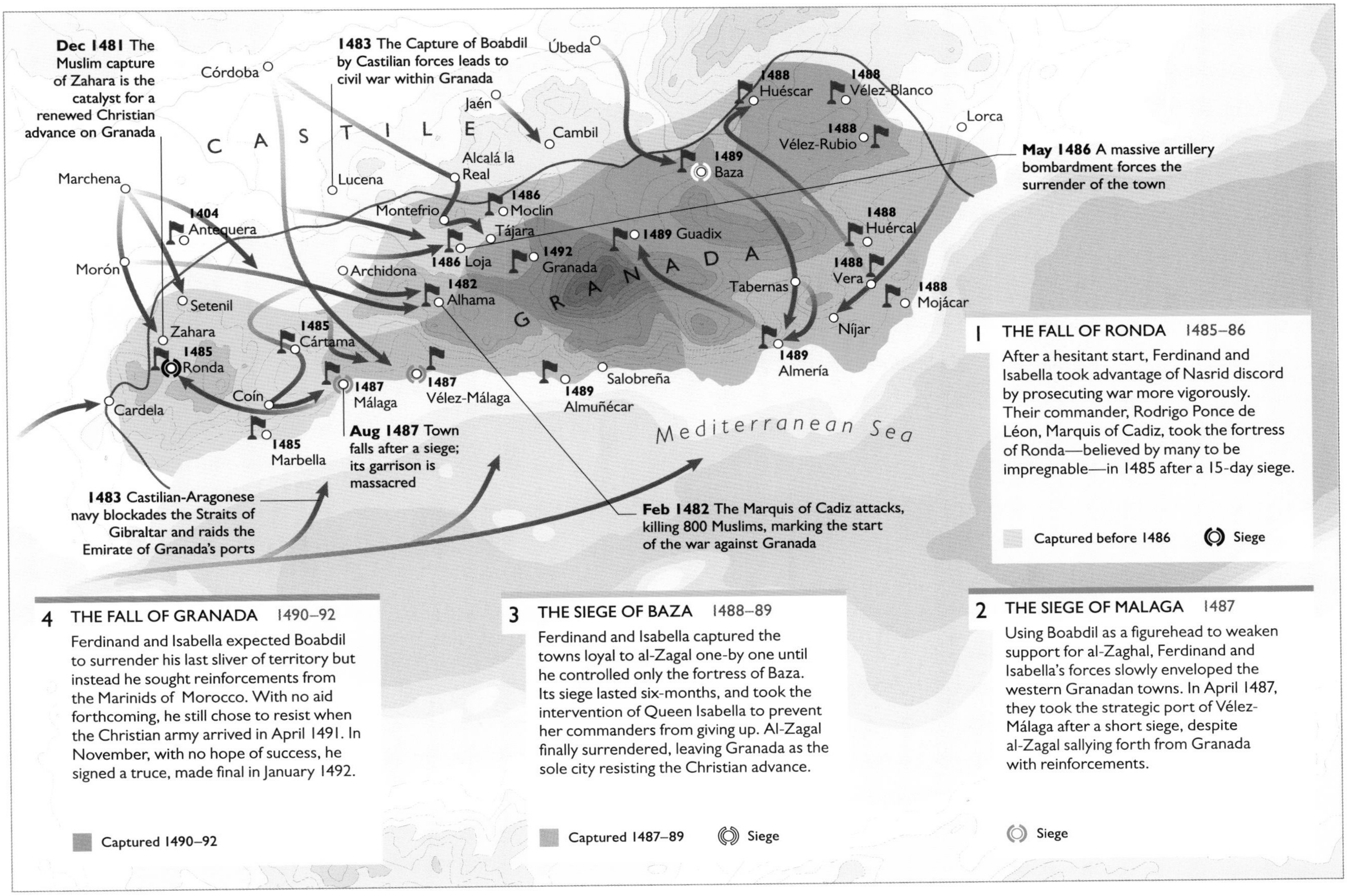

Dec 1481 The Muslim capture of Zahara is the catalyst for a renewed Christian advance on Granada

1483 The Capture of Boabdil by Castilian forces leads to civil war within Granada

Córdoba

Úbeda

CASTILE

Jaén

Cambil

Alcalá la Real

1488 Huéscar   1488 Vélez-Blanco

Lorca

1488 Vélez-Rubio

May 1486 A massive artillery bombardment forces the surrender of the town

Marchena

Lucena

1486 Moclin

1489 Baza

1404 Antequera

Montefrio   Tájara

1488 Huércal

Morón

Archidona

1486 Loja

1489 Guadix

1492 Granada

1488 Vera

Setenil

1482 Alhama

GRANADA

Tabernas

1488 Mojácar

Zahara
1485 Ronda

1485 Cártama

Níjar

1485 Coín

1487 Málaga

1487 Vélez-Málaga

1489 Salobreña

1489 Almería

Cardela

1485 Marbella

Aug 1487 Town falls after a siege; its garrison is massacred

1489 Almuñécar

Mediterranean Sea

1483 Castilian-Aragonese navy blockades the Straits of Gibraltar and raids the Emirate of Granada's ports

Feb 1482 The Marquis of Cadiz attacks, killing 800 Muslims, marking the start of the war against Granada

1 THE FALL OF RONDA 1485–86

After a hesitant start, Ferdinand and Isabella took advantage of Nasrid discord by prosecuting war more vigorously. Their commander, Rodrigo Ponce de Léon, Marquis of Cadiz, took the fortress of Ronda—believed by many to be impregnable—in 1485 after a 15-day siege.

☐ Captured before 1486   ◉ Siege

---

4 THE FALL OF GRANADA 1490–92

Ferdinand and Isabella expected Boabdil to surrender his last sliver of territory but instead he sought reinforcements from the Marinids of Morocco. With no aid forthcoming, he still chose to resist when the Christian army arrived in April 1491. In November, with no hope of success, he signed a truce, made final in January 1492.

■ Captured 1490–92

3 THE SIEGE OF BAZA 1488–89

Ferdinand and Isabella captured the towns loyal to al-Zagal one-by-one until he controlled only the fortress of Baza. Its siege lasted six-months, and took the intervention of Queen Isabella to prevent her commanders from giving up. Al-Zagal finally surrendered, leaving Granada as the sole city resisting the Christian advance.

▨ Captured 1487–89   ◉ Siege

2 THE SIEGE OF MALAGA 1487

Using Boabdil as a figurehead to weaken support for al-Zaghal, Ferdinand and Isabella's forces slowly enveloped the western Granadan towns. In April 1487, they took the strategic port of Vélez-Málaga after a short siege, despite al-Zagal sallying forth from Granada with reinforcements.

◎ Siege

DIRECTORY: 1000–1500

AL-MANSURAH

FEBRUARY 8–11, 1250

Al-Mansurah was a key battle of the Seventh Crusade (1248–54), the last major Christian attempt to wrest Palestine from Muslim control. Led by French king Louis IX, the crusaders launched a direct attack on Egypt, the seat of the Muslim Ayyubid dynasty that held Jerusalem. After capturing the Egyptian port of Damietta, the crusaders marched south toward Cairo. Their advance was blocked by the Ayyubid army encamped on the opposite side of a canal near the town of al-Mansurah.

The battle began when several hundred elite knights—the Knights Templar—led by Louis' brother Robert of Artois crossed the canal along with an English contingent headed by William of Salisbury, and launched a surprise attack on the Muslim camp. The Egyptians fled in disarray into the town. Instead of waiting for Louis to arrive with his crossbowmen and infantry, the knights impulsively pursued the enemy. Mamluk generals took command of the Egyptian forces and reorganized them to trap the enemy in the town's narrow streets. The crusaders were besieged from all sides and slaughtered. Both Robert of Artois and William of Salisbury were killed along with most of the Knights Templar.

What remained of Louis' main army repulsed repeated onslaughts, but unwisely disdained retreat. The Egyptians seized and destroyed several supply vessels of the crusaders. Short of food and decimated by disease, Louis' forces at last tried to retreat to Damietta in April, but were defeated and captured on the way. Many crusaders died, and Louis was ransomed for a huge sum.

▷ This 15th-century manuscript painting shows Muslim forces killing the crusaders

> *"I will assault your territory… my mind would not be changed."*
>
> LOUIS IX, IN A DECLARATION OF WAR TO THE EGYPTIAN SULTAN

XIANGYANG

1268–73

The five-year siege of Xiangyang, in present-day Hubei province in China, was a decisive event in the Mongol conquest of the country. By 1260, the Mongols had taken control of northern China, where their leader Kublai Khan had founded the Yuan dynasty, but the more populous and wealthy lands of southern China remained under the rule of the native Song dynasty. The geography of the region, with its large rivers and fortified cities, was unsuited to the traditional fighting techniques of Mongol steppe horsemen (see p.78). Identifying the fortified city of Xiangyang on the Han River as a key gateway to the south, Kublai placed it under siege in 1268. Despite the Mongols' complete inexperience in naval operations, Kublai assembled a fleet of 5,000 vessels to blockade the river. He brought in engineers from Persia to build siege equipment, including powerful stone-throwing counterweight trebuchets. Primitive incendiary and gunpowder devices added to the pressure on both sides' forces.

After many attempts to relieve the siege failed, the city surrendered in March 1273. The Song dynasty fell six years later, leaving Kublai Khan as the sole ruler of China.

COURTRAI

JULY 11, 1302

Also known as the Battle of the Golden Spurs, the medieval encounter fought outside the Flemish city of Courtrai, or Kortrijk, (in present-day Belgium) is famous as a victory of common Flemish foot soldiers against the French knights. The Flemings had risen in revolt against the occupation of their territory by the French king Philip IV. In the summer of 1302, a Flemish force besieged the French-held Courtrai castle. Philip sent an army under Count Robert II of Artois to suppress the revolt. The rival forces were roughly equal in number, with about 10,000 men, but the Flemings were mainly town militia and almost exclusively on foot, while the French included some 2,500 armored horsemen. The Flemings took up position behind streams and ditches on marshy ground. When the French horsemen charged, their mounts floundered and fell in the ditches. The Flemish infantry rushed forward, wielding pikes and spiked clubs known as *goedendags*, to murderous effect. Robert was among a thousand French nobles and knights who lost their lives. The victorious Flemings retrieved about 500 pairs of spurs from the battlefield, giving the battle its popular name.

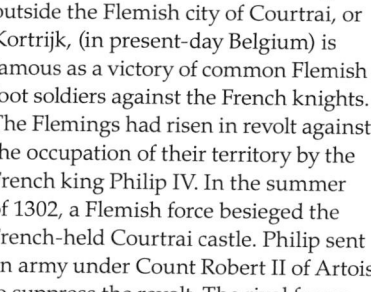

POITIERS

SEPTEMBER 19, 1356

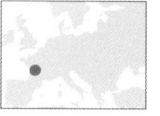

The Battle of Poitiers was a major defeat for France in the Hundred Years' War (see p.57) against England. A force of several thousand men led by Edward, the Prince of Wales, also known as the Black Prince, raided central France from English-ruled Aquitaine. The French king Jean II intercepted the raiders outside the city of Poitiers with a much larger army. The English could not evade without abandoning their hard-won plunder, so they decided to accept battle and to exploit the local defensive terrain, in particular a thick hedge through which the road south ran.

On September 19, Edward drew up his army for battle, his knights on foot and his longbowmen on the flanks.

A first wave of French knights attacked on horseback, but their mounts were cut down by the arrows of Edward's longbowmen. A second wave led by the Dauphin—Jean II's heir—advanced on foot and engaged the English in savage close-quarter fighting. Finally, as King Jean himself stepped forward to enter the fray, Edward ordered his forces to charge. A reserve of 200 mounted English knights rode around and attacked the French from the rear. Amid complete carnage, the king and many French nobles were captured. King Jean remained a prisoner in England until 1360, when France agreed a ransom of three million gold crowns in exchange for his safe return.

ANKARA

JULY 20, 1402

The Battle of Ankara was a contest between two outstanding military commanders: Ottoman sultan Bayezid I and the Turko-Mongol warrior Timur (Tamerlane). Based in Samarkand in Central Asia, Timur had conquered a vast swath of Asia, from Delhi to Damascus, earning a reputation for massacre and devastation. In 1402, he invaded Ottoman territory in Anatolia (modern-day Turkey). Bayezid led his forces eastward across the country to confront the intruder, but Timur outmaneuvered him, swerving behind the Ottoman army and occupying its former camp.

Bayezid's soldiers became exhausted and ran out of water when Timur diverted the nearby stream. Timur's steppe horsemen, armed with composite

bows, overwhelmed the slower-moving Turkish forces. Bayezid's Serbian vassals fought fiercely, but many of his other allies defected to Timur. Bayezid himself fled the battlefield with a cavalry escort but was captured. He died in captivity the following year, although legends of his imprisonment in a cage are dubious.

Timur died in 1405 while marching against China, and his short-lived empire quickly collapsed into civil war, but the Ottoman Empire was itself wracked by civil war until 1413, before reaching new heights under later sultans like Mehmed II (see p.96) and Suleyman I (see pp.112–17).

▽ A 16th-century painting depicting Bayezid I in Timur's captivity

NICOPOLIS

SEPTEMBER 25, 1396

△ Mounted Ottoman Turks attack the Christian knights at the Battle of Nicopolis

The crushing defeat of a Christian army in 1396 at present-day Nikopol in northern Bulgaria set the Ottoman Turks on course to create one of the world's biggest empires. Encroaching on southeast Europe, the Ottoman sultan Bayezid I threatened to attack the Christian kingdom of Hungary.

In response, the Hungarian king Sigismund gathered a multinational crusader army including French and Hospitaller knights, and besieged the Ottoman stronghold at Nicopolis. Bayezid led his army north to relieve the siege, accompanied by Serbian

knights who had become Ottoman vassals since the Battle of Kosovo in 1389 (see pp.86–87) His arrival surprised the crusaders, who hastily prepared for battle. Plagued by divided command and disputes over status, the Christian army attacked the Ottomans without knowing their strength or the disposition of their forces. Bayezid's disciplined army withstood the charge of the Christian knights before counter-attacking with devastating effect. Bayezid was merciless in victory, killing all enemy prisoners he took, except for those who could be profitably ransomed or enslaved.

BOSWORTH FIELD

AUGUST 22, 1485

The defeat of King Richard III at Bosworth Field in the English Midlands brought the Tudor dynasty to the throne of England. For 30 years, the royal houses of York and Lancaster had competed for power in the Wars of the Roses. The Yorkists appeared to have triumphed after victory at Tewkesbury in 1471, but the unpopularity of King Richard III provided an opportunity for the exiled Lancastrian Henry Tudor to bid for the throne. Sailing from France, Henry landed at Milford Haven in Wales and marched into England, gathering support along the way. Richard intercepted him near the town of Market Bosworth in Leicestershire.

Both armies fielded several thousand men. The king had the larger force, but their loyalty was uncertain. At the height

of the battle, Richard led his knights in a bold thrust toward Henry and his army. At that moment the powerful Stanley contingent switched sides and attacked Richard. He was surrounded and killed. Henry took power and became the first English monarch of the Tudor dynasty.

△ Plan showing the two armies positioned at Bosworth Field

1500–1700

EARLY GUNPOWDER WEAPONS UNDERWENT NUMEROUS
IMPROVEMENTS, AND ARMIES BECAME MORE STRUCTURED
AND PROFESSIONAL. WARS OF RELIGION AND SUCCESSION
TOOK PLACE ACROSS THE WORLD, WHILE WARSHIPS
DEVELOPED INTO LARGE SHIPS OF THE LINE DELIVERING
ENORMOUSLY INCREASED FIREPOWER.

1500–1700

The 16th and 17th centuries saw changes in war as gunpowder made the battlefield more lethal. In Asia, states fielded armies larger than ever in wars of territorial expansion, while increasingly professional armies fought religious and dynastic wars in Europe.

△ **Heavy protection**
This chainmail helmet was worn by Mughal cavalrymen in 16th-century India—a time in which mounted warriors were still a significant force on the battlefield.

Before 1500, combat mainly involved small armies of feudal levies and knights, but 200 years later, professional armies of thousands of uniformed soldiers, trained in military maneuvers, began to fight massive engagements. These armies were equipped with muskets and field artillery.

The introduction of gunpowder helped to provoke these changes. Handheld harquebuses and muskets became increasingly widespread, playing a growing role in battles as seen in engagements of the Italian Wars such as Cerignola in 1503 and Bicocca in 1522. Firing mechanisms were gradually refined from matchlock to wheellock and then flintlock. Firing rates and range also gradually improved. Together, this made traditional armored cavalry, armed with lances instead of firearms, unnecessary, and infantry began to dominate the battlefield alongside horsemen with little or no armor wielding swords and pistols. A parallel evolution

> *"War is not to be avoided, but is only put off to the advantage of others."*
>
> NICCOLÒ MACHIAVELLI, *THE PRINCE*, 1513

occurred in artillery, which had struggled to damage city walls in the 15th century. By 1600, field guns had grown in caliber to threaten all but the most formidable defenses. In response, engineers such as France's Sebastian le Prestre de Vauban and his Dutch counterpart, Menno van Coehoorn, improved the design of fortifications and advocated new techniques of siege warfare (see pp.148–49).

Combat turned back toward wars of maneuver—historically practiced by smaller armies—and the new infantry-driven armies grew larger. These massive forces required increasingly complex organization and training, and insignia and uniforms became a feature of military life. Formal military drills were introduced in the 1590s by the Dutch commander Maurice of Nassau.

Changing ways of war

The increased expense of such armies caused changes in the way countries were governed, leading to more centralization of power. Nations better equipped to fight did so with more

◁ **Channel encounter**
In this painting from c.1620, the Spanish Armada clash with Elizabeth I's forces in the English Channel in 1588 (see pp.120–21). The battle was the largest 16th-century naval confrontation in northern Europe and sparked a naval arms race.

NEW DEVELOPMENTS

The increasing pace of technological development in gunpowder armaments drove a military revolution in Europe. As the cost of warfare rose, states developed a greater ability to raise taxation that, in turn, enhanced their ability to wage wars, leading to further conflicts. Non-European powers adopted gunpowder weaponry as well. It enabled them, in some cases, to resist European encroachment on their territory, and in others, aided territorial expansion or fueled civil wars.

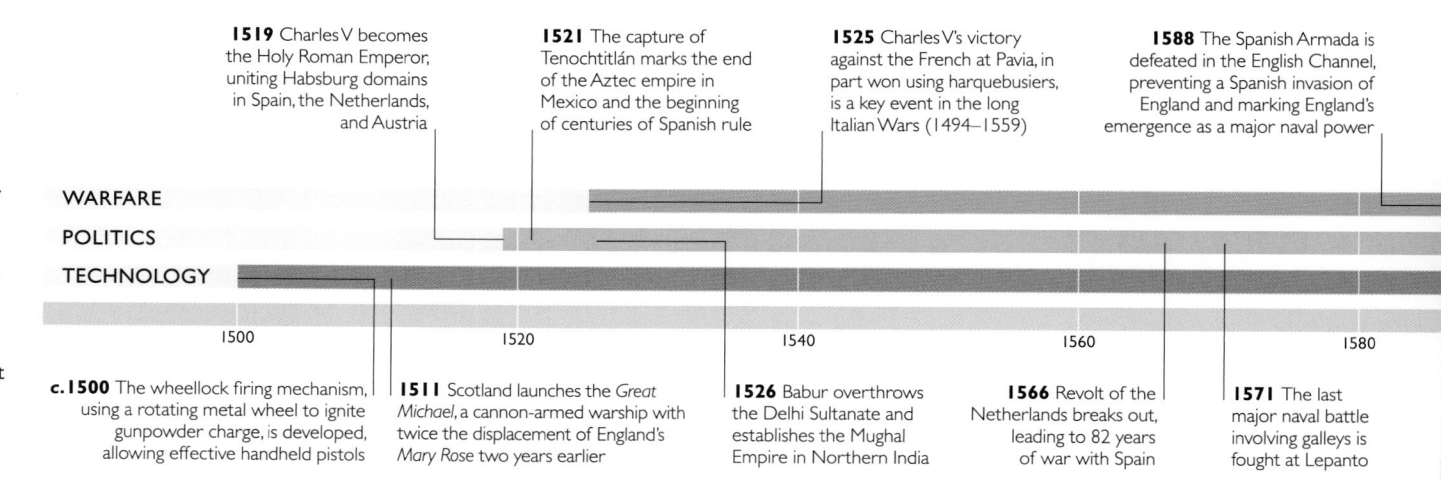

1519 Charles V becomes the Holy Roman Emperor, uniting Habsburg domains in Spain, the Netherlands, and Austria

1521 The capture of Tenochtitlán marks the end of the Aztec empire in Mexico and the beginning of centuries of Spanish rule

1525 Charles V's victory against the French at Pavia, in part won using harquebusiers, is a key event in the long Italian Wars (1494–1559)

1588 The Spanish Armada is defeated in the English Channel, preventing a Spanish invasion of England and marking England's emergence as a major naval power

WARFARE

POLITICS

TECHNOLOGY

| 1500 | 1520 | 1540 | 1560 | 1580 |

c.1500 The wheellock firing mechanism, using a rotating metal wheel to ignite gunpowder charge, is developed, allowing effective handheld pistols

1511 Scotland launches the *Great Michael*, a cannon-armed warship with twice the displacement of England's *Mary Rose* two years earlier

1526 Babur overthrows the Delhi Sultanate and establishes the Mughal Empire in Northern India

1566 Revolt of the Netherlands breaks out, leading to 82 years of war with Spain

1571 The last major naval battle involving galleys is fought at Lepanto

▷ **First shots**
Musketeers and pistol-wielding cavalry dominated at the Battle of the White Mountain (see p.128) in 1620, the first major battle of the Thirty Years War.

◁ **Failed king**
England's Charles I's attempt to fund his wars by raising tax without consulting with the Parliament ended in a civil war and his execution in 1649.

frequency. Europe was torn apart in a series of religious wars between Catholic and Protestant factions, culminating in the Thirty Years War (1618–48), in which as many as eight million soldiers and civilians died. Subsequently, religious warfare waned, but Europe became the scene of large-scale dynastic conflicts as monarchs such as Louis XIV of France sought territorial gains against Habsburg Spain and the Netherlands. Non-European powers, too, fought larger wars. The Ottoman Empire in Turkey, the Safavid Empire in Iran, and the Mughal Empire in India moved away from a dependence on feudal cavalry to develop centrally recruited forces, which owed primary allegiance to the rulers. Japan developed a military culture all of its own, based on the *daimyo* (warlords) and their samurai retainers, who engaged in a series of civil wars until the country was reunited under the Tokugawa shoguns from 1603.

Warfare at sea experienced equally profound changes. Warships in both Europe and Asia had been carrying a few small cannons since the 14th century, primarily for antipersonnel use, but from about 1500 the increasing deployment by European navies of heavy cannons changed the way naval battles were fought. Galleys with ranks of oarsmen, which fought in battles such as at Lepanto (see pp.118–19) were gradually replaced by ships of the line that fired broadsides through hinged gunports. Seafaring nations such as England, the Netherlands, and France spent massive sums on their navies, extending their rivalry to seaborne conflicts across the Atlantic and in the Indian Ocean. Just as on land, only the richest and well-organized states could compete militarily in a world where the cost of warfare was continually rising.

1600 Tokugawa victory at Sekigahara marks a key stage in the reestablishment of Japanese unity

1603 Tokugawa Ieyasu unites Japan after 150 years of civil war, beginning the Tokugawa shogunate

1632 Swedish king Gustavus Adolphus dies in battle as his forces win the Battle of Lützen against an army of the Holy Roman Empire

1645 The defeat of King Charles I's royalist forces against the Parliamentarian forces at Naseby leads to the end of the first phase of the English Civil War

1683 The defeat of the Ottomans at the Siege of Vienna marks the limit of their expansion out of the Balkans

1600   1620   1640   1660   1680   1700

c.1590 Paper cartridges become more widespread, making it easier to load muzzle-loading firearms, and increasing firing rates

c.1615 First "true" flintlock firing mechanism is developed, improving the efficiency and reliability of guns

1643 Accession of Louis XIV of France, whose 72-year reign marks an apogee in French power

1660 English monarchy is restored after 18 years of civil war and republican rule

1655–1703 Vauban builds a series of fortresses in France, adapted to the new era of long-range firearms and heavy artillery

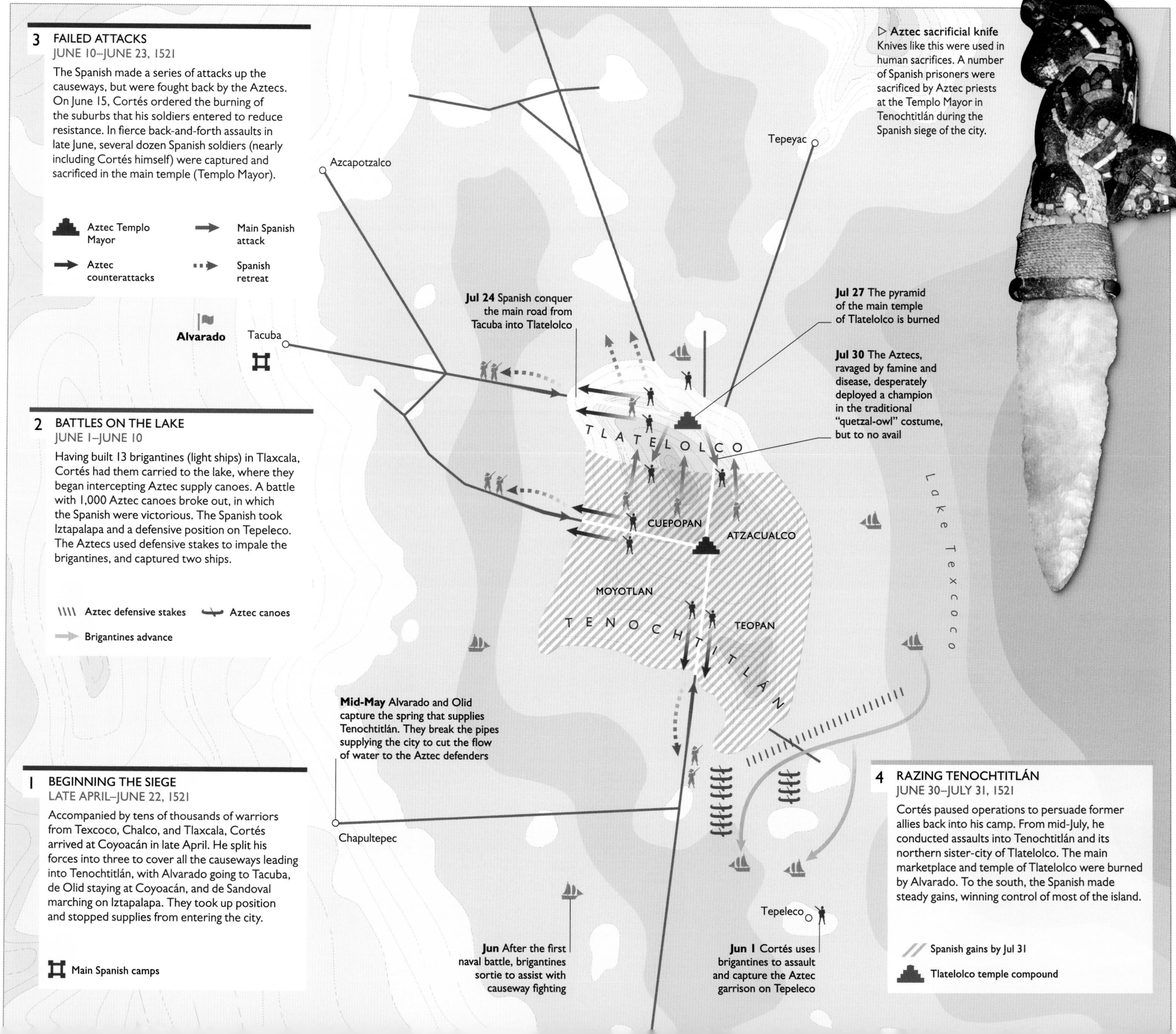

△ **Aztec sacrificial knife**
Knives like this were used in human sacrifices. A number of Spanish prisoners were sacrificed by Aztec priests at the Templo Mayor in Tenochtitlán during the Spanish siege of the city.

Lake Texcoco

Jul 27 The pyramid of the main temple of Tlatelolco is burned

Jul 30 The Aztecs, ravaged by famine and disease, desperately deployed a champion in the traditional "quetzal-owl" costume, but to no avail

4 RAZING TENOCHTITLÁN
JUNE 30–JULY 31, 1521

Cortés paused operations to persuade former allies back into his camp. From mid-July, he conducted assaults into Tenochtitlán and its northern sister-city of Tlatelolco. The main marketplace and temple of Tlatelolco were burned by Alvarado. To the south, the Spanish made steady gains, winning control of most of the island.

⟋⟋⟋ Spanish gains by Jul 31

Tlatelolco temple compound

Tepeyac

TLATELOLCO

ATZACUALCO

TEOPAN

CUEPOPAN

MOYOTLAN

TENOCHTITLÁN

Tepeleco

Jun 1 Cortés uses brigantines to assault and capture the Aztec garrison on Tepeleco

Azcapotzalco

Mid-May Alvarado and Olid capture the spring that supplies Tenochtitlán. They break the pipes supplying the city to cut the flow of water to the Aztec defenders

Chapultepec

Jun After the first naval battle, brigantines sortie to assist with causeway fighting

Jul 24 Spanish conquer the main road from Tacuba into Tlatelolco

3 FAILED ATTACKS
JUNE 10–JUNE 23, 1521

The Spanish made a series of attacks up the causeways, but were fought back by the Aztecs. On June 15, Cortés ordered the burning of the suburbs that his soldiers entered to reduce resistance. In fierce back-and-forth assaults in late June, several dozen Spanish soldiers (nearly including Cortés himself) were captured and sacrificed in the main temple (Templo Mayor).

⬛ Aztec Templo Mayor

↑ Main Spanish attack

↑ Aztec counterattacks

┅┅▶ Spanish retreat

Tacuba

⛩ Alvarado

2 BATTLES ON THE LAKE
JUNE 1–JUNE 10

Having built 13 brigantines (light ships) in Tlaxcala, Cortés had them carried to the lake, where they began intercepting Aztec supply canoes. A battle with 1,000 Aztec canoes broke out, in which the Spanish were victorious. The Spanish took Iztapalapa and a defensive position on Tepeleco. The Aztecs used defensive stakes to impale the brigantines, and captured two ships.

⫘⫘⫘ Aztec defensive stakes

↤ Aztec canoes

↑ Brigantines advance

1 BEGINNING THE SIEGE
LATE APRIL–JUNE 22, 1521

Accompanied by tens of thousands of warriors from Texcoco, Chalco, and Tlaxcala, Cortés arrived at Coyoacán in late April. He split his forces into three to cover all the causeways leading into Tenochtitlán, with Alvarado going to Tacuba, de Olid staying at Coyoacán, and de Sandoval marching on Iztapalapa. They took up position and stopped supplies from entering the city.

⌗ Main Spanish camps

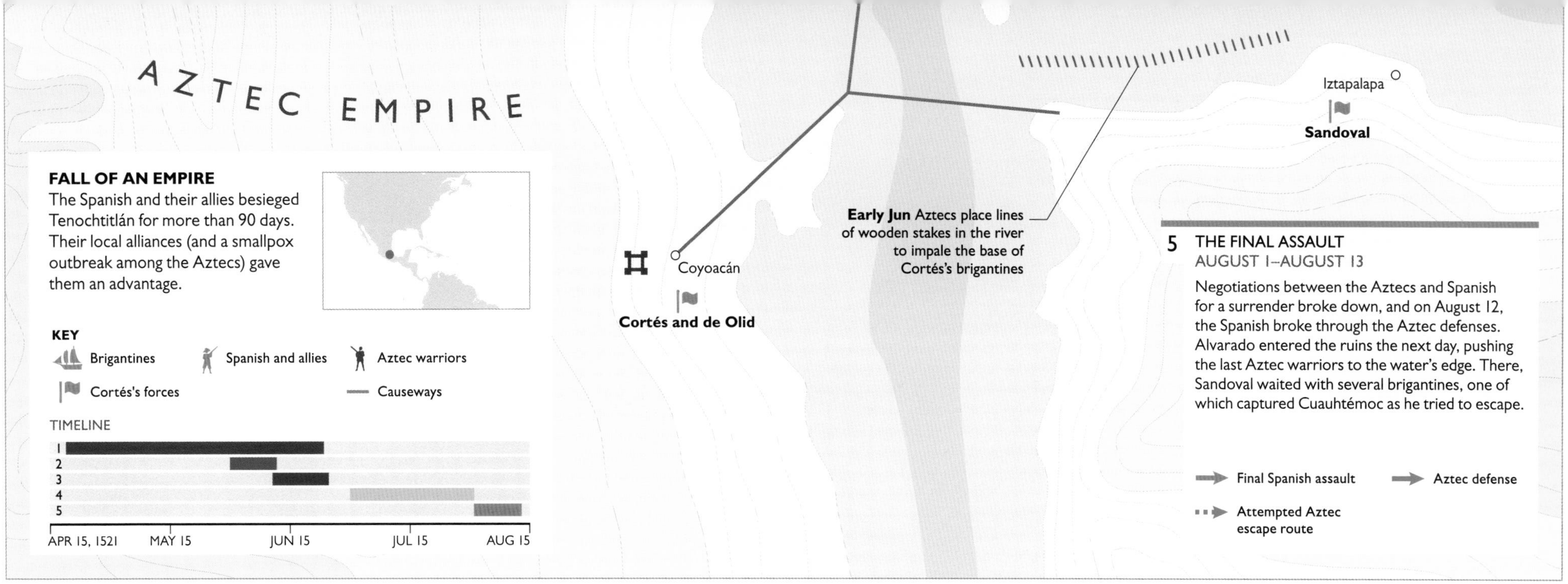

AZTEC EMPIRE

FALL OF AN EMPIRE

The Spanish and their allies besieged Tenochtitlán for more than 90 days. Their local alliances (and a smallpox outbreak among the Aztecs) gave them an advantage.

KEY

- Brigantines
- Cortés's forces
- Aztec warriors
- Causeways

TIMELINE

APR 15, 1521   MAY 15   JUN 15   JUL 15   AUG 15

○ Iztapalapa

Sandoval

Early Jun Aztecs place lines of wooden stakes in the river to impale the base of Cortés's brigantines

5   THE FINAL ASSAULT
AUGUST 1–AUGUST 13

Negotiations between the Aztecs and Spanish for a surrender broke down, and on August 12, the Spanish broke through the Aztec defenses. Alvarado entered the ruins the next day, pushing the last Aztec warriors to the water's edge. There, Sandoval waited with several brigantines, one of which captured Cuauhtémoc as he tried to escape.

→ Final Spanish assault
⤏ Attempted Aztec escape route
↑ Aztec defense

○ Coyoacán

Cortés and de Olid

THE SIEGE OF TENOCHTITLÁN

Hernán Cortés's invasion of Mexico in 1519 culminated in a three-month siege of the Aztec capital, Tenochtitlán. Despite ferocious resistance, the Spanish and their native allies seized the last stronghold in August 1521, leading to the collapse of the Aztec empire.

The landing of conquistador Hernán Cortés (see pp.106–107) near present-day San Juan de Ulúa in April 1519 prompted a wary but peaceful response from the Aztec emperor Moctezuma II. Although his force numbered little more than 600, Cortés swiftly recruited allies from the local peoples who resented Aztec rule, and marched to the Aztec capital Tenochtitlán, entering it on November 8. Although relations were initially cordial, they soon soured, and Cortés placed Moctezuma under house arrest, seeking to take direct control of the empire. The tactic failed and an anti-Spanish uprising broke out, during which Moctezuma was killed. On June 30,

1520, Cortés was driven from Tenochtitlán with huge losses. The Spanish army escaped to Tlaxcala, and it took almost 10 months to rebuild native alliances and return to Tenochtitlán, where the Aztecs had endured a smallpox epidemic.

The siege was protracted, lasting from May until August 1521, and the city's position on an island made direct attack difficult. But its near-destruction, the capture of the new emperor Cuauhtémoc, and the death or execution of much of the Aztec nobility shattered opposition to the Spanish. The fall of the city left them in control of the former Aztec empire and its rich resources for the next 300 years.

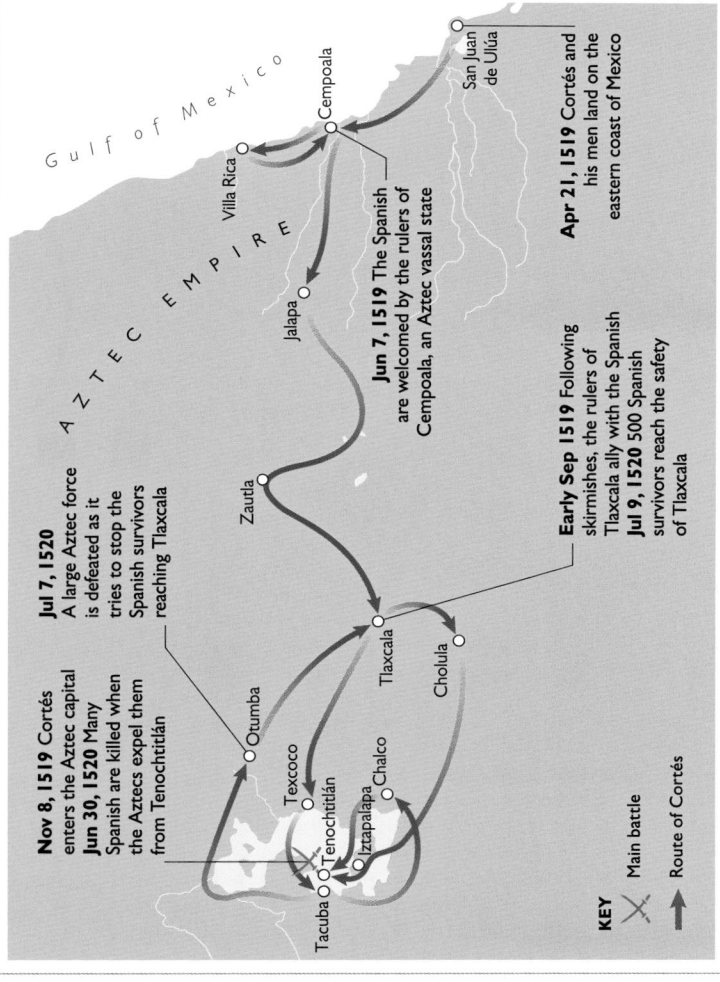

Gulf of Mexico

AZTEC EMPIRE

San Juan de Ulúa

Cempoala

Villa Rica

Jun 7, 1519 The Spanish are welcomed by the rulers of Cempoala, an Aztec vassal state

Apr 21, 1519 Cortés and his men land on the eastern coast of Mexico

Jalapa

Zautla

Otumba

Texcoco

Tenochtitlán

Tacuba

Iztapalapa

Chalco

Tlaxcala

Cholula

Nov 8, 1519 Cortés enters the Aztec capital
Jun 30, 1520 Many Spanish are killed when the Aztecs expel them from Tenochtitlán

Jul 7, 1520 A large Aztec force is defeated as it tries to stop the Spanish survivors reaching Tlaxcala

Early Sep 1519 Following skirmishes, the rulers of Tlaxcala ally with the Spanish
Jul 9, 1520 500 Spanish survivors reach the safety of Tlaxcala

KEY

✗ Main battle
→ Route of Cortés

THE MARCH ON TENOCHTITLÁN

After Cortés landed in April 1519, he proved adept at building alliances with the local Aztec people. The addition of the Tlaxcalans (long-standing rivals to the Aztecs) to the alliance made the Spanish a potent threat and aided their entry into Tenochtitlán in November. They were expelled eight months later, barely escaping across the city's causeways, and Cortés's forces were only saved from destruction in an ambush at Otumba by the inexperience of Aztecs in facing the Spanish cavalry in the open.

Load bearers
In this 16th-century illustration by artist Theodor de Bry, Spanish conquistadors can be seen exploiting the indigenous people by making them carry baggage and equipment.

THE SPANISH CONQUISTADORS

During the 16th century, small bands of Spanish nobles, soldiers, and assorted explorers launched countless expeditions in the New World, resulting in the Spanish conquest of large parts of the Americas.

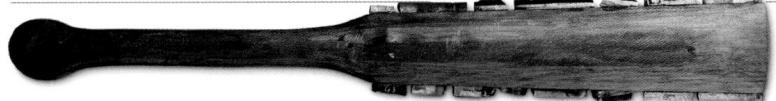

For a long time, the retelling of Spain's conquest of the Americas was dominated by the myth of invading soldiers with superior weapons toppling large but primitive indigenous empires. These conquerors, known as conquistadors, came with horses, steel swords, armor, pikes, and crossbows, and some harquebuses and light cannons—all unheard of in the Americas. In reality, while some of the armies they faced were equipped with basic stone weaponry, others were large, well trained, and part of sophisticated civilizations.

△ **Effective weapon**
The *macuahuitl*, a wooden club edged with obsidian blades, was one of the primary weapons of the Aztecs.

Cunning invaders

The conquest of Mexico in 1519–21 by Spanish soldier Hernán Cortés succeeded mainly due to his use of local allies and cunning diplomacy rather than advanced weapons (see pp.104–105). Cortés was fighting against an Aztec empire that had both a long list of enemies, and restless subjects. He also unwittingly took advantage of a smallpox epidemic that the Spaniards had brought with them. In some instances, however, such as Francisco Pizarro's conquest of the Inca empire in 1532–33 with only a tiny force, Spanish technology and organization played a more clear role in ensuring victory.

Technological superiority, however, did not protect conquistadors from weather, illness, hunger, and thirst, elements that saw many expeditions fail. Often, the ability of conquistadors to exploit existing divisions earned them lasting victories that reshaped the continent.

△ **Aztecs greet Cortés**
This 16th-century illustration by Dominican missionary Diego Durán shows Aztec ruler Montezuma II welcoming Hernán Cortés and his army. The Aztecs can be seen wearing simple cotton cloaks, while the armor-clad Spanish wield weapons.

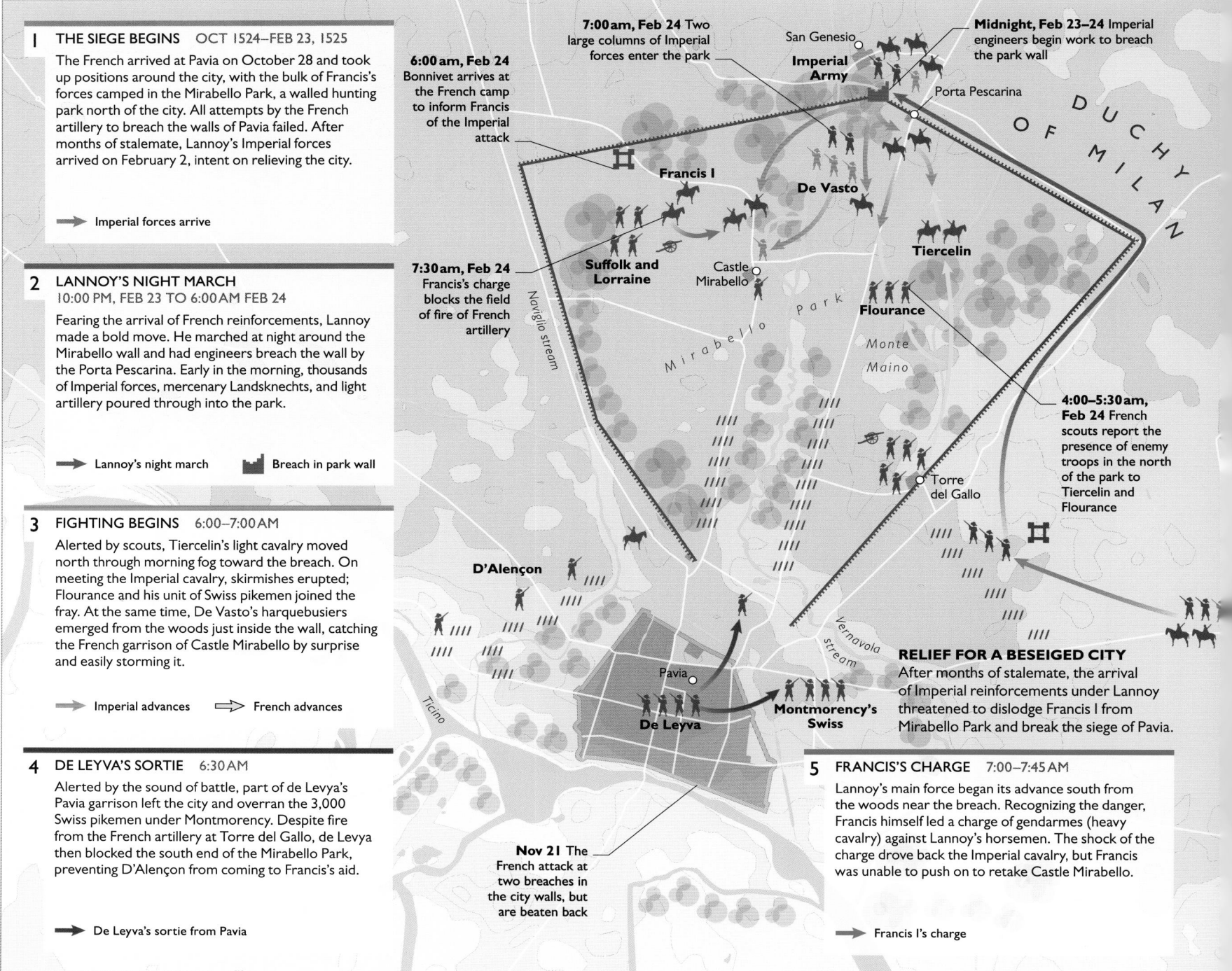

1 THE SIEGE BEGINS OCT 1524–FEB 23, 1525

The French arrived at Pavia on October 28 and took up positions around the city, with the bulk of Francis's forces camped in the Mirabello Park, a walled hunting park north of the city. All attempts by the French artillery to breach the walls of Pavia failed. After months of stalemate, Lannoy's Imperial forces arrived on February 2, intent on relieving the city.

→ Imperial forces arrive

2 LANNOY'S NIGHT MARCH
10:00 PM, FEB 23 TO 6:00 AM FEB 24

Fearing the arrival of French reinforcements, Lannoy made a bold move. He marched at night around the Mirabello wall and had engineers breach the wall by the Porta Pescarina. Early in the morning, thousands of Imperial forces, mercenary Landsknechts, and light artillery poured through into the park.

→ Lannoy's night march   ▉▊ Breach in park wall

3 FIGHTING BEGINS 6:00–7:00 AM

Alerted by scouts, Tiercelin's light cavalry moved north through morning fog toward the breach. On meeting the Imperial cavalry, skirmishes erupted; Flourance and his unit of Swiss pikemen joined the fray. At the same time, De Vasto's harquebusiers emerged from the woods just inside the wall, catching the French garrison of Castle Mirabello by surprise and easily storming it.

→ Imperial advances   ⇨ French advances

4 DE LEYVA'S SORTIE 6:30 AM

Alerted by the sound of battle, part of de Levya's Pavia garrison left the city and overran the 3,000 Swiss pikemen under Montmorency. Despite fire from the French artillery at Torre del Gallo, de Levya then blocked the south end of the Mirabello Park, preventing D'Alençon from coming to Francis's aid.

→ De Leyva's sortie from Pavia

7:00 am, Feb 24 Two large columns of Imperial forces enter the park

6:00 am, Feb 24 Bonnivet arrives at the French camp to inform Francis of the Imperial attack

Midnight, Feb 23–24 Imperial engineers begin work to breach the park wall

San Genesio

Imperial Army

Porta Pescarina

D U C H Y   O F   M I L A N

Francis I

De Vasto

Tiercelin

7:30 am, Feb 24 Francis's charge blocks the field of fire of French artillery

Suffolk and Lorraine

Castle Mirabello

Flourance

Naviglio stream

Mirabello Park

Monte Maino

4:00–5:30 am, Feb 24 French scouts report the presence of enemy troops in the north of the park to Tiercelin and Flourance

Torre del Gallo

D'Alençon

Ticino

Vernavola stream

Pavia

De Leyva

Montmorency's Swiss

RELIEF FOR A BESEIGED CITY

After months of stalemate, the arrival of Imperial reinforcements under Lannoy threatened to dislodge Francis I from Mirabello Park and break the siege of Pavia.

Nov 21 The French attack at two breaches in the city walls, but are beaten back

5 FRANCIS'S CHARGE 7:00–7:45 AM

Lannoy's main force began its advance south from the woods near the breach. Recognizing the danger, Francis himself led a charge of gendarmes (heavy cavalry) against Lannoy's horsemen. The shock of the charge drove back the Imperial cavalry, but Francis was unable to push on to retake Castle Mirabello.

→ Francis I's charge

PAVIA

Francis I of France's attempt to wrest control of northern Italy from the Habsburgs
foundered at Pavia in 1525 when a night march by Imperial troops caught him by surprise.
In a battle dominated for the first time by gunpowder weapons, his army was cut to pieces.

The Italian Wars of 1494–1559 were sparked by France's ambition to dominate northern Italy. In September 1524, Imperial Habsburg troops had been forced to retreat back into Italy after their failed siege of Marseilles; then in October 1524, Francis I began an offensive, first taking Milan with his 40,000-strong army, then pursuing the main Imperial force under Charles de Lannoy. He stopped to besiege the strategic town of Pavia, which was garrisoned by mercenaries under

Antonio de Leyva. However, the siege became deadlocked, allowing Lannoy to regroup, reinforce, and eventually outflank him when the Imperial forces arrived in early February. Francis was captured, imprisoned, and forced to sign a treaty waiving all French claims in Italy. He repudiated the treaty as soon as he was released, and forged a new anti-Habsburg alliance that included Henry VIII of England. The Italian Wars dragged on intermittently until 1559.

FRANCIS I DEFEATED

Francis I's invasion of northern Italy stalled at Pavia. The length of the siege allowed imperial reinforcements to reach the city and relieve its garrison. After a surprise night-march, they broke into the walled park where the main French force was stationed, taking advantage of the confusion to achieve the defeat of Francis's army.

KEY

〰〰〰 Mirabello Park wall   //// Defensive earthworks   ▨ Towns

FRENCH FORCES

⊟ Camp   🔫 Infantry   🐎 Cavalry   ⚙ Artillery

IMPERIAL FORCES

⊟ Camp   🔫 Infantry   🐎 Cavalry   🔫 Harquebusiers

TIMELINE

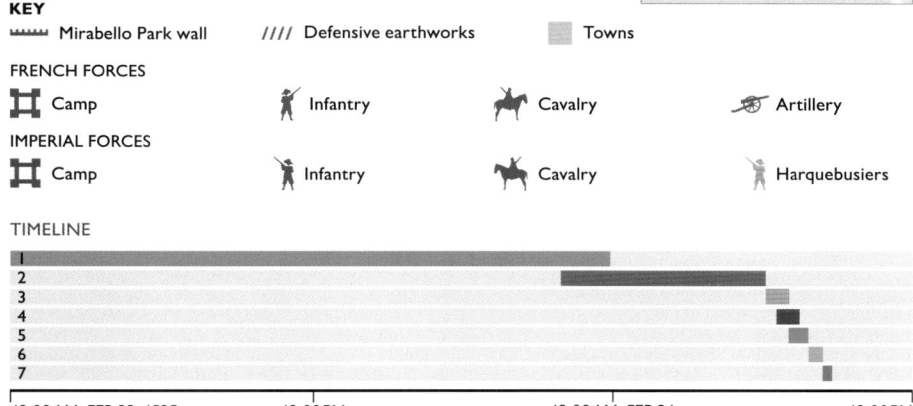

12:00 AM, FEB 23, 1525   12:00 PM   12:00 AM, FEB 24   12:00 PM

THE HARQUEBUS

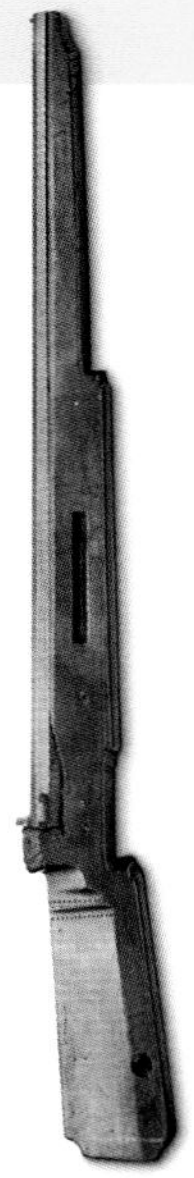

The harquebus appeared in Europe and the Ottoman Empire during the 15th century. It was a matchlock gun: a lit match was lowered by a trigger into a powder pan to spark the explosion. Its muzzle-loading mechanism was cumbersome, and damp made the powder too wet to ignite. The gun's weight meant it had to be fired resting on external support. However, these were the first guns to make a difference on the battlefield: they could inflict disruption and losses on cavalry and infantry, especially when volley fire was developed by the Ottomans, Ming Chinese, and Dutch.

An early harquebus

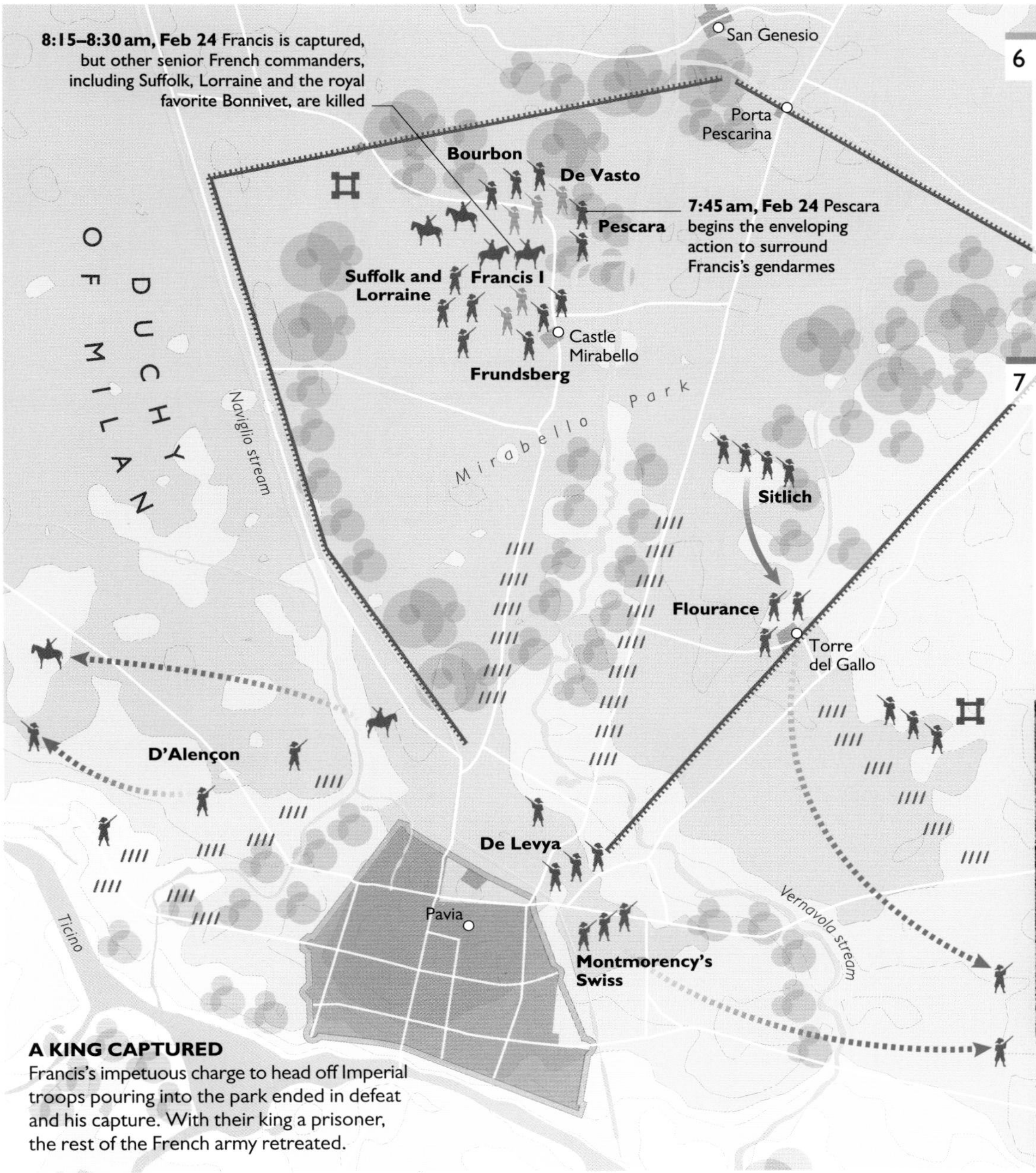

8:15–8:30 am, Feb 24 Francis is captured, but other senior French commanders, including Suffolk, Lorraine and the royal favorite Bonnivet, are killed

San Genesio

Porta Pescarina

7:45 am, Feb 24 Pescara begins the enveloping action to surround Francis's gendarmes

Bourbon

De Vasto

Pescara

Suffolk and Lorraine

Francis I

Castle Mirabello

Frundsberg

DUCHY OF MILAN

Naviglio stream

Mirabello Park

Sitlich

Flourance

Torre del Gallo

D'Alençon

De Levya

Pavia

Vernavola stream

Ticino

Montmorency's Swiss

A KING CAPTURED

Francis's impetuous charge to head off Imperial troops pouring into the park ended in defeat and his capture. With their king a prisoner, the rest of the French army retreated.

6 | THE GENDARMES DEFEATED 7:45–8:15 AM

Francis and his gendarmes gradually found themselves surrounded, with De Vasto's harquebusiers (see above) on one flank and Frundsberg's mercenary forces to the rear. Very few managed to break out, and most of them were slaughtered. Francis was captured, in one story exchanging courtesies with Lannoy himself.

7 | THE FRENCH ROUT 8:15–8:30 AM

As the Imperial attack continued, the French forces on the right were driven back via the Torre del Gallo; Montmorency and Flourance were both captured. Rather than engaging the enemy, the last coherent French force – that under D'Alençon – retreated from the battlefield once it had accepted inevitable defeat, so crowning the Imperial victory.

➡ Imperial advances   ┅➤ French retreat

△ **The French camp under attack**
This depiction of fighting in Mirabello Park is a detail from one of seven tapestries showing scenes from the battle, produced a few years afterward by Flemish artist Bernard van Orley.

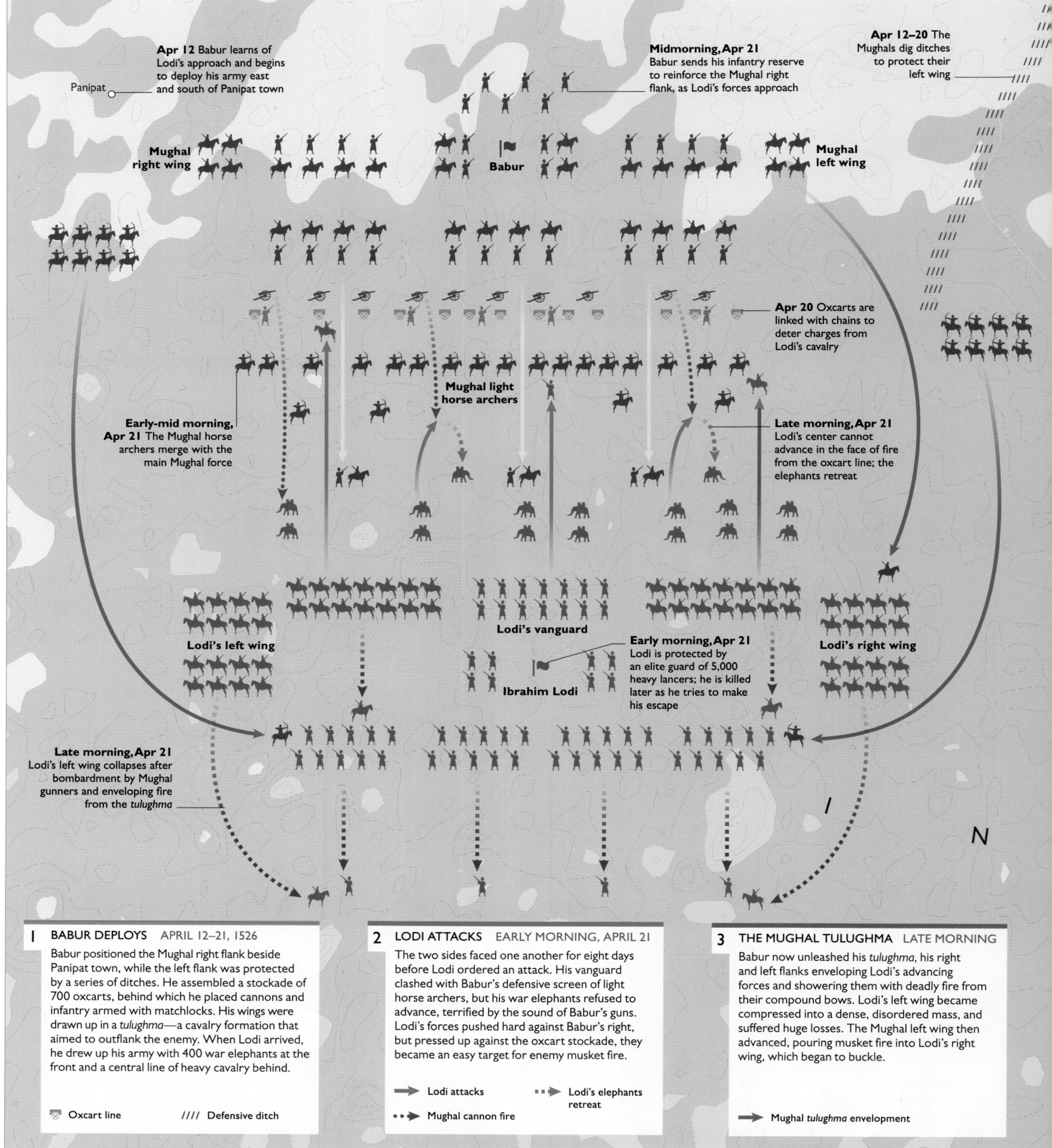

Panipat

Apr 12 Babur learns of Lodi's approach and begins to deploy his army east and south of Panipat town

Midmorning, Apr 21 Babur sends his infantry reserve to reinforce the Mughal right flank, as Lodi's forces approach

Apr 12–20 The Mughals dig ditches to protect their left wing

Mughal right wing

Babur

Mughal left wing

Apr 20 Oxcarts are linked with chains to deter charges from Lodi's cavalry

Early-mid morning, Apr 21 The Mughal horse archers merge with the main Mughal force

Mughal light horse archers

Late morning, Apr 21 Lodi's center cannot advance in the face of fire from the oxcart line; the elephants retreat

Lodi's vanguard

Lodi's left wing

Early morning, Apr 21 Lodi is protected by an elite guard of 5,000 heavy lancers; he is killed later as he tries to make his escape

Lodi's right wing

Ibrahim Lodi

Late morning, Apr 21 Lodi's left wing collapses after bombardment by Mughal gunners and enveloping fire from the *tulughma*

N

1 BABUR DEPLOYS APRIL 12–21, 1526

Babur positioned the Mughal right flank beside Panipat town, while the left flank was protected by a series of ditches. He assembled a stockade of 700 oxcarts, behind which he placed cannons and infantry armed with matchlocks. His wings were drawn up in a *tulughma*—a cavalry formation that aimed to outflank the enemy. When Lodi arrived, he drew up his army with 400 war elephants at the front and a central line of heavy cavalry behind.

⊞ Oxcart line   //// Defensive ditch

2 LODI ATTACKS EARLY MORNING, APRIL 21

The two sides faced one another for eight days before Lodi ordered an attack. His vanguard clashed with Babur's defensive screen of light horse archers, but his war elephants refused to advance, terrified by the sound of Babur's guns. Lodi's forces pushed hard against Babur's right, but pressed up against the oxcart stockade, they became an easy target for enemy musket fire.

→ Lodi attacks   ▪▪▶ Lodi's elephants retreat

•••▶ Mughal cannon fire

3 THE MUGHAL TULUGHMA LATE MORNING

Babur now unleashed his *tulughma*, his right and left flanks enveloping Lodi's advancing forces and showering them with deadly fire from their compound bows. Lodi's left wing became compressed into a dense, disordered mass, and suffered huge losses. The Mughal left wing then advanced, pouring musket fire into Lodi's right wing, which began to buckle.

→ Mughal *tulughma* envelopment

BABUR'S BRILLIANCE

Ibrahim Lodi's army boasted several hundred war elephants. They were no match, though, for Babur's Mughal army, which was armed with cannons and musketeers.

KEY

MUGHAL FORCES

- |▪ Commander
- 🏃 Infantry
- 🏃 Matchlock infantry
- 🐎 Cavalry
- 🐎 Mounted archers
- ⚬ Cannon

LODI FORCES

- |▪ Commander
- 🏃 Infantry
- 🐎 Cavalry
- 🐘 War elephants

TIMELINE

2	3	4

APR 12, 1526 APR 14 APR 16 APR 18 APR 20 APR 22

△ **Gunpowder against elephants**
Lodi's delay in launching his attack allowed Babur time to build his defenses and position his cannons and musketeers. Lodi's elephants were no match for Babur's firepower and battlefield fortifications.

PANIPAT

Through tactical brilliance and the use of gunpowder weapons, the Central Asian warlord Babur won a stunning victory against the Sultan of Delhi, Ibrahim Lodi, at Panipat in April 1526. He went on to conquer much of Northern India, founding the Mughal empire, which would last for the next three centuries.

Descended from the Mongol leaders Genghis Khan (see p.78) and Timur, Babur became ruler of Fergana (in present-day Uzbekistan) in 1494. He began to carve out a kingdom for himself, seizing Kabul in 1504. His ambitions, however, extended further, and from 1519 he sent several exploratory raids into the Punjab, which was ruled by Ibrahim Lodi, the Sultan of Delhi. Lodi's authority over his own nobles was weak, and some of them plotted his overthrow with Babur.

Seeing an opportunity, Babur raised an army of 10,000 men trained in the use of gunpowder weapons acquired from the Ottoman Turks. In November 1525, the army swept into Punjab, capturing Sialkot and Ambala, moving ever closer to Lodi's capital. Babur repelled a counterattack by Lodi's forces near the Yamuna river on April 2, 1526, but then heard that the Sultan's main force of 100,000 was approaching. He drew up at Panipat, 50 miles (85 km) north of Delhi, to face them.

Babur's tactical brilliance in combining nomad maneuverability with modern weaponry shattered his enemy's much larger army, and Lodi's death on the battlefield led to the rapid collapse of the Delhi sultanate. Within five years, Babur was master of Northern India. Although his son Humayun was deposed in 1540, the rule of his grandson Akbar (r. 1556–1605) saw the Mughal empire that Babur had founded reach its apogee and extend into central India.

4 LODI ROUTED MIDDAY

The Mughal center now advanced against the disorganized enemy force. Lodi attempted a cavalry charge in a bid to escape but was cut down as he fought his way through the Mughal lines. Leaderless, Lodi's army collapsed, and the reserve line—which had not yet been enveloped—disintegrated and fled. Lodi had suffered 15,000 casualties, four times the Mughal losses.

- ⇨ Secondary Mughal advance
- ▪▪▶ Lodi's army retreats

THE MUGHAL EMPIRE

Babur had planned to annex only the Punjab to his Kabul-based kingdom, but his unexpectedly decisive victory at Panipat allowed him to expand his control far to the south. Although Babur's son Humayun lost the empire, his grandson Akbar conducted a long series of campaigns that regained its core domains and expanded Mughal control as far south as Berar. His successors made further conquests, and by the death of Aurangzeb, the sixth Mughal emperor in 1707, only the tip of the subcontinent and a few European enclaves eluded Mughal rule.

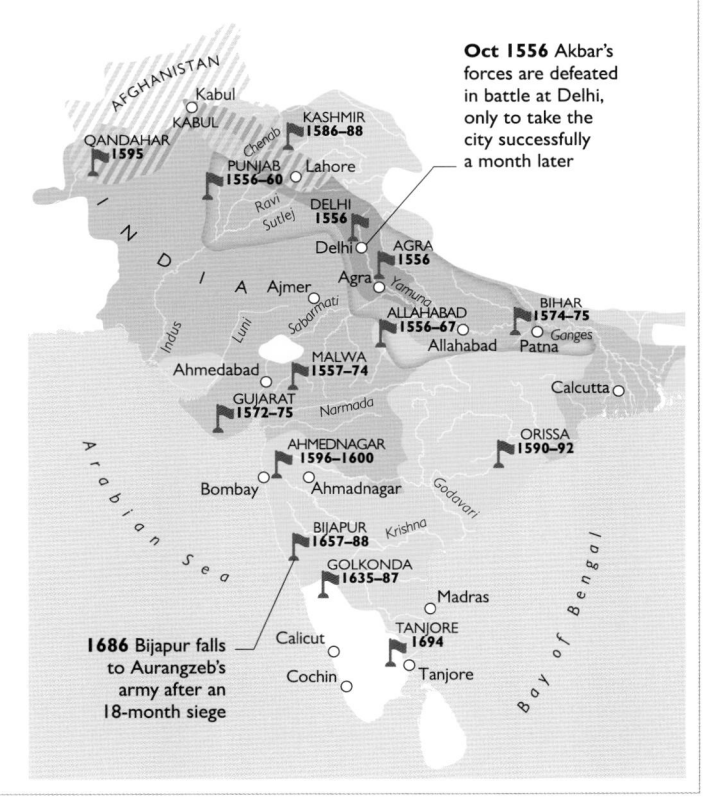

Oct 1556 Akbar's forces are defeated in battle at Delhi, only to take the city successfully a month later

1686 Bijapur falls to Aurangzeb's army after an 18-month siege

KEY

- /// Babur's Afghan kingdom
- ▬ Babur's conquests to 1539
- ▪ Mughal empire under Akbar, 1556
- Conquered by 1605
- Conquered by 1707
- ⚑ Regions acquired, with date

OTTOMAN GAINS

The Ottoman capture of Constantinople in 1453 was followed by advances in the Balkans. Only the Kingdom of Hungary stood between the Ottomans and the territory of the Austrian Habsburgs. After Mohács, Suleyman besieged Vienna in 1529 and annexed a broad swath of Hungary in 1541. This was the high tide of Ottoman expansion in the Balkans.

KEY

⚔ Main battle

Ottoman Empire and vassals, 1512

Ottoman Empire and vassals, 1639

Austrian Habsburg possessions

Spanish Habsburg possessions

— Frontier, c.1600

⚔ Ottoman victory

⚔ Ottoman defeat

THE JANISSARIES

The Janissaries, shown here being inspected by the Sultan, were the elite infantry of the Ottoman army. Born Christian, they were raised as Muslims and trained as warriors from a young age; their ability with firearms made them formidable. The expense of their salaries and their rebellious tendencies eventually led to their disbandment in 1807.

---

1 THE ARMIES ARRIVE
1:00 PM, AUGUST 29, 1526

The Hungarians arrived first at the north of the battlefield, their left flank protected by marshes. The Ottomans marched in battle formation for seven hours to face their enemy. The Hungarian troops under Pál Tomori charged the Rumelian contingent, which had arrived first; composed mostly of irregulars, the Rumelians fell back.

→ Initial Hungarian attack

⇢ Rumelian retreat

2 THE OTTOMANS REINFORCED
1:00–2:00 PM

The Rumelian retreat allowed Tomori almost to overrun Suleyman's position; Suleyman himself was struck by a bullet. However, more Ottoman units—including the elite janissaries—soon arrived to provide support. Turkish artillery positioned on a ridge overlooking the battlefield began to fire on Louis's frontline troops and his smaller artillery contingent.

→ Janissaries advance

3 THE HUNGARIAN ADVANCE AND REPULSE
2:00–3:00 PM

Tomori tried to exploit his success by charging the Ottoman guns, and Louis ordered the rest of his cavalry into action. However, the arrival of further Anatolian contingents soon gave the Ottomans overwhelming numerical superiority. The bloody close-quarters combat that ensued ended in the near destruction of the Hungarian infantry.

→ Hungarian advance

→ Arrival of Ottoman reinforcements

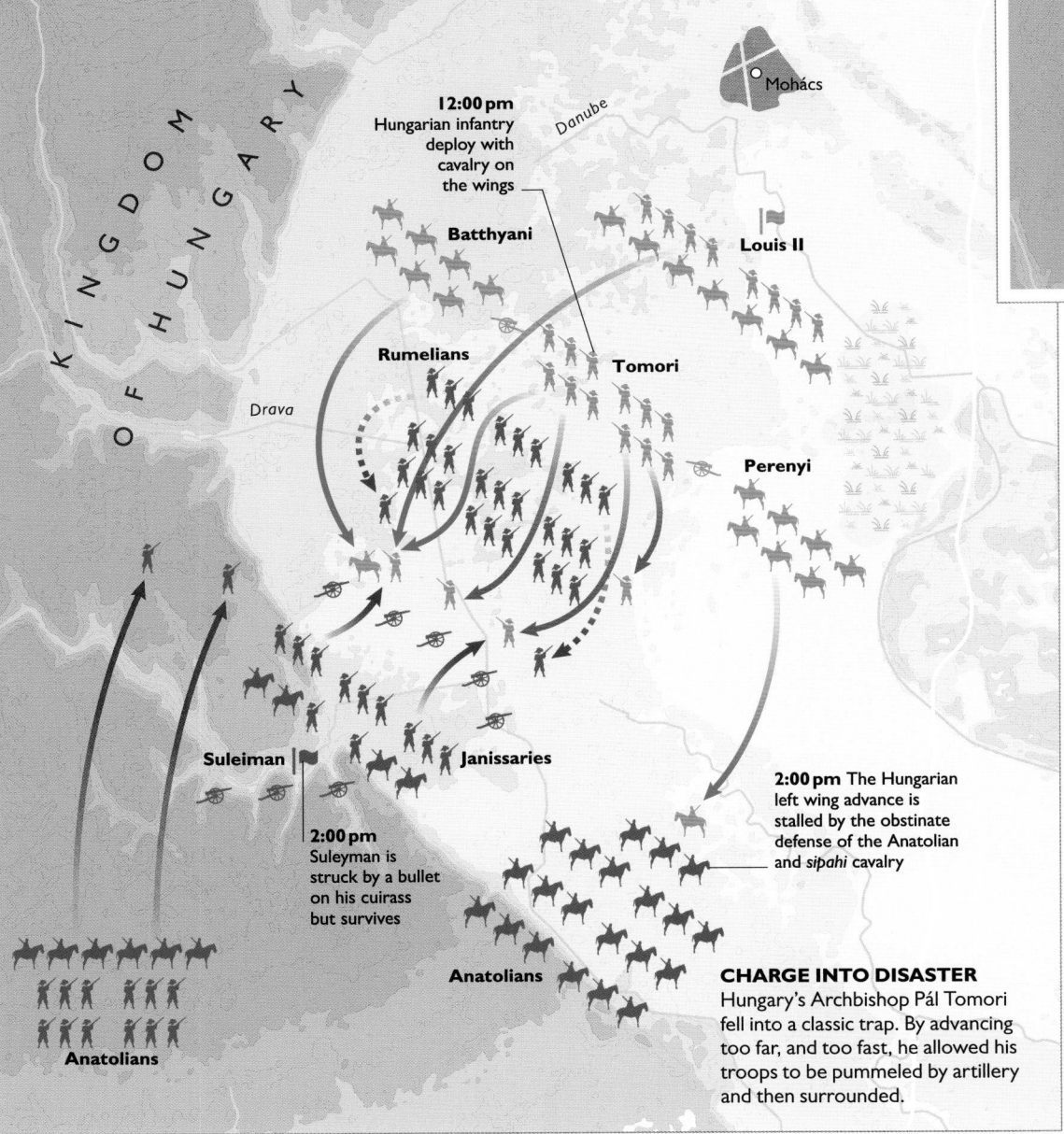

12:00 pm Hungarian infantry deploy with cavalry on the wings

Batthyani

Louis II

Rumelians

Tomori

Perenyi

Suleiman

Janissaries

2:00 pm Suleiman is struck by a bullet on his cuirass but survives

2:00 pm The Hungarian left wing advance is stalled by the obstinate defense of the Anatolian and *sipahi* cavalry

Anatolians

CHARGE INTO DISASTER

Hungary's Archbishop Pál Tomori fell into a classic trap. By advancing too far, and too fast, he allowed his troops to be pummeled by artillery and then surrounded.

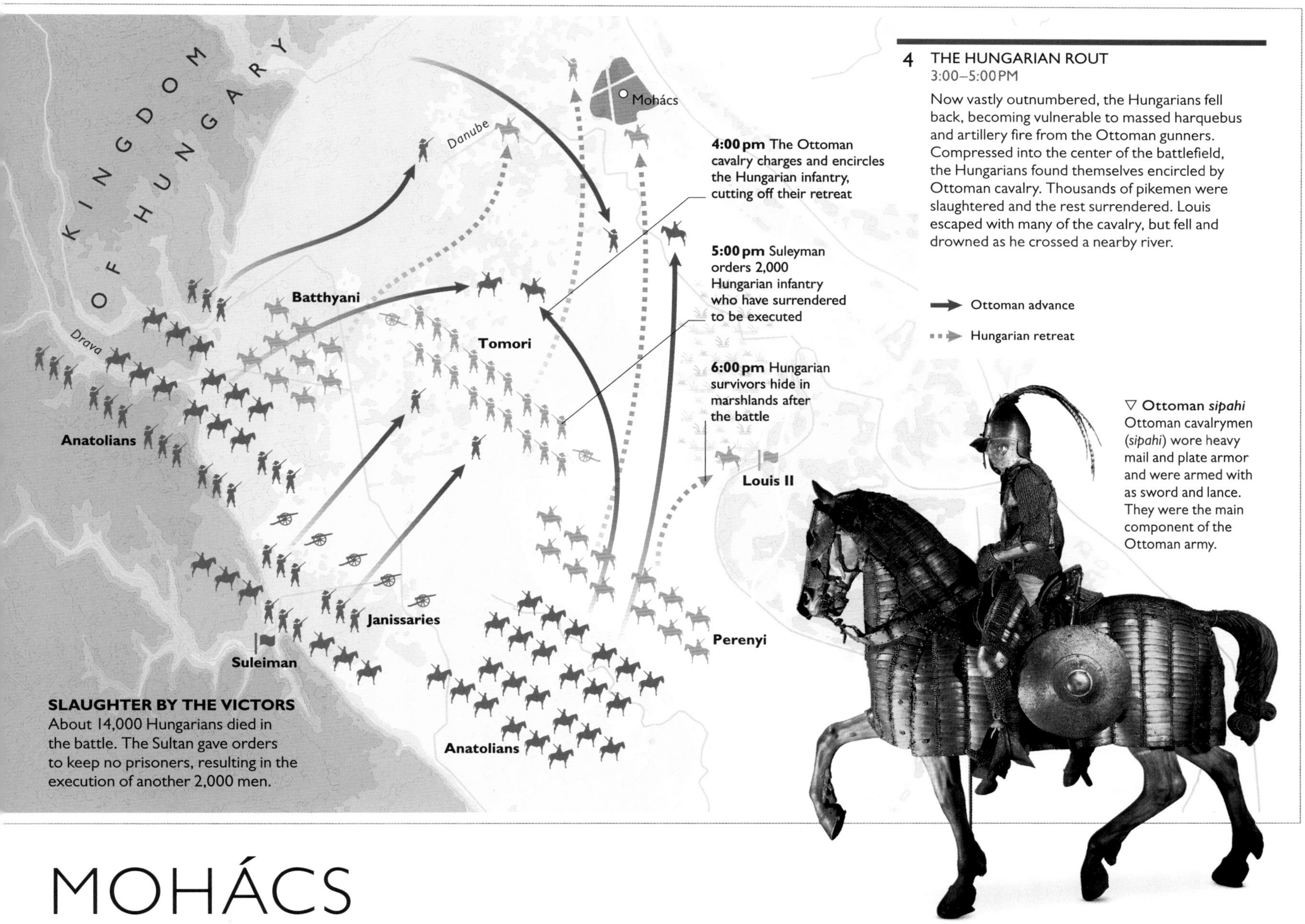

KINGDOM OF HUNGARY

Danube

○ Mohács

4:00 pm The Ottoman cavalry charges and encircles the Hungarian infantry, cutting off their retreat

Drava

Batthyani

Tomori

Anatolians

5:00 pm Suleyman orders 2,000 Hungarian infantry who have surrendered to be executed

6:00 pm Hungarian survivors hide in marshlands after the battle

Louis II

Janissaries

Perenyi

Suleiman

Anatolians

SLAUGHTER BY THE VICTORS
About 14,000 Hungarians died in the battle. The Sultan gave orders to keep no prisoners, resulting in the execution of another 2,000 men.

4 THE HUNGARIAN ROUT
3:00–5:00 PM

Now vastly outnumbered, the Hungarians fell back, becoming vulnerable to massed harquebus and artillery fire from the Ottoman gunners. Compressed into the center of the battlefield, the Hungarians found themselves encircled by Ottoman cavalry. Thousands of pikemen were slaughtered and the rest surrendered. Louis escaped with many of the cavalry, but fell and drowned as he crossed a nearby river.

➔ Ottoman advance

┅➤ Hungarian retreat

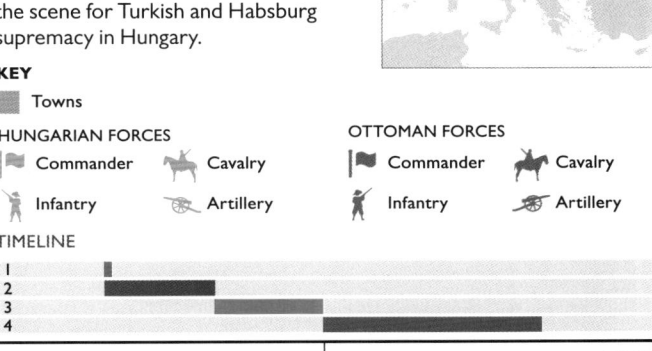

▽ **Ottoman *sipahi***
Ottoman cavalrymen (*sipahi*) wore heavy mail and plate armor and were armed with as sword and lance. They were the main component of the Ottoman army.

MOHÁCS

The defeat of Louis II's Hungarian army by Ottoman Sultan Suleyman the Magnificent at Mohács in 1526 was a disaster for his kingdom. With Louis dead and his force cut apart, Hungary was rapidly overrun by the Ottomans and ceased to exist as an independent nation.

By the 1520s, steady Ottoman expansion in the Balkans, which had begun with the capture of Gallipoli in 1354, was encroaching on the borders of Hungary. Weakened by a huge peasant revolt in 1514, and internal power struggles between its king Vladislaus II and powerful magnates, Hungary was in a vulnerable position when Louis II took the throne in 1516.

In 1521, Suleyman captured the strategically important city of Belgrade, a staging post to Hungary. Four years later he made an alliance with Francis I of France which effectively neutralized Hungary's possible allies in the West. In April the following year he set out from

Constantinople with a 50,000-strong force, while Louis tried to raise an army from a reluctant Hungarian nobility. Unsure of where Suleyman would strike, Louis held back at Buda, his capital, before advancing to meet defeat and his death at Mohács.

Suleyman failed to capitalize on his victory, delaying an advance to Buda. Instead, Hungary fell apart into rival kingdoms—the eastern part under Jan Zapolya, a Hungarian noble, and the west and Croatia ruled by Ferdinand I, the Holy Roman Emperor. Part of Zapolya's kingdom fell to the Ottomans in 1541, and Hungary would not emerge as an independent nation until 1918.

HUNGARY CRUSHED
The unexpectedly decisive nature of Suleyman's victory led to the rapid fall of the Hungarian monarchy and set the scene for Turkish and Habsburg supremacy in Hungary.

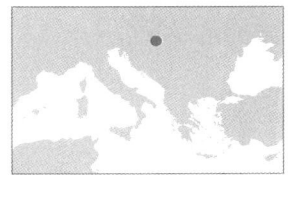

KEY

▮ Towns

HUNGARIAN FORCES		OTTOMAN FORCES	
⚑ Commander	🐎 Cavalry	⚑ Commander	🐎 Cavalry
🔱 Infantry	Artillery	🔱 Infantry	Artillery

TIMELINE

1
2
3
4

12:00 PM, AUG 29, 1526   3:00 PM   6:00 PM

Armed and equipped
This late 16th-century painting shows Ottoman sultan Selim II's (1524–74) army. On the left are the janissaries carrying muskets, while the cavalry, wielding shields and lances, can be seen on the right.

THE OTTOMAN ARMY

A key player in Europe and the Mediterranean basin for centuries, the Ottoman army was a terrifying professional force that displayed formidable military tactics from the 14th to the 18th centuries.

The Ottoman army was a large force with three distinct components. At its core was the central force, controlled, paid, and trained by the state. In the 17th century, the force consisted of tens of thousands of troops, mainly infantry, including the sultan's elite infantry bodyguard, the janissaries. These troops were usually long-term professionals, initially conscripted as slave-soldiers in the Turkish medieval tradition, but who were later recruited as volunteers. Supporting the central army was a larger feudal and provincial levy. The levies were mainly light cavalry, but included infantry as well. They were often poorly trained, ill-equipped, and unmotivated. The rest of the army was formed by auxiliary contingents from vassal states, either of Islamic or Christian faith, who participated in specific expeditions. They varied not only in quality, but also in the nature of their composition. While Tatars, Mamluks, and other Eastern forces often accompanied the army, other vassals were not uncommon. Serbian knights fought with the Ottomans at the Battle of Nicopolis (see p.97) in 1396, while Emeric Thököly's 20,000 catholic Hungarians fought with the Ottoman army in the second siege of Vienna in 1683.

△ **Skill and craftsmanship**
This 17th-century *hancer* (dagger) with a straight blade and an ornate ivory handle shows the superior craftsmanship of the Ottomans.

A skilled force

The Ottoman central force was mostly well-trained and equipped. The cavalry favored traditional weapons that were lighter than those of their European counterparts. Ottoman artillery was excellent and often employed in higher numbers than in European armies.

SÜLEYMAN I 1494–1566

Better known as Süleyman the Magnificent (r.1520–66), Süleyman I led the Ottoman Empire to its zenith. He led various battles during his reign, most notably the ones at Belgrade (1521), Rhodes (1522), and Mohács in Hungary (1526, see pp.112–13). However, his army lost at Vienna in 1529, followed by the Great Siege of Malta (see pp.116–17), which limited the Ottomans' reach into Western Europe. By the time he died, large parts of southeast Europe, the North African coast, and the Middle East were under Ottoman control.

THE SIEGE OF MALTA

The attempt by the Ottoman Sultan, Suleyman the Magnificent, to take the island of Malta from the Knights Hospitaller in 1565 was met with fierce resistance. Grand Master de Valette and his knights defended a line of fortresses for almost four months until a relieving fleet forced the Ottoman besiegers to withdraw.

By the mid-16th century, the Ottoman empire was threatening to penetrate the western Mediterranean. One bulwark against this was the Mediterranean island of Malta. Since 1530, the island had been a stronghold of the Knights Hospitaller, a Christian military order that lost its last base at Rhodes in 1522, and who countered attacks by Ottoman-backed corsairs (privateers) on Christian shipping. In 1551, the corsair Dragut responded by pillaging Gozo but failed to take the main island of Malta. After a Christian expedition against the corsair base at Tripoli was defeated at Djerba in 1560, it was only a matter of time before Suleyman ordered an attack on Malta to crush the Knights' resistance.

Jean de Valette, the Hospitaller Grand Master, prepared well, reinforcing the defenses of the island. When the assault finally came in May 1565, he was able to hold out long enough for a relief fleet to drive off the Ottoman expeditionary force. This revived Christian morale enough that a new alliance assembled and was able to defeat the Ottoman navy at Lepanto in 1571 (see pp.118–19).

> *"What men call sovereignty is worldly strife and constant war."*
>
> FROM A POEM BY SULEYMAN THE MAGNIFICENT, C.16TH CENTURY

1 THE ATTACK ON ST ELMO
MAY 24–JUNE 23, 1565

Ottoman commanders Piyale Pasha and Mustafa Pasha disagreed on strategy: Mustafa wanted to attack St. Michael, but he acceded to Piyale's wish to take St. Elmo first to allow his fleet to use Marsamxett harbor. The fort held off several massive assaults but fell on June 23. All 1,500 defenders died, but it cost the lives of 6,000 Ottomans and their supreme commander Dragut.

→ Ottoman attack

May 24
Ottoman troops advancing from Marsa take up a position around St. Elmo to begin the siege

2 ATTACK FROM THE SEA   JULY 15

Planning an attack on Fort St. Michael, Piyale had 100 boats carried across Mount Sceberras into the Grand Harbor so he could bypass the artillery at Fort St. Angelo. However, de Valette knew of the plan and built a palisade along the Senglea peninsula, preventing the enemy from landing. Many Ottoman boats were sunk by Maltese guns installed just above water level at Fort St. Angelo.

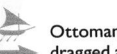 Ottoman boats dragged across land

Maltese palisade

3 ATTACK FROM THE LAND
JULY 15

While the Ottomans were attacking the Senglea peninsula from the sea, a contingent under Hassem, the Ottoman viceroy of Algiers, launched an assault on the peninsula's landward end. The land attack failed because Maltese reinforcements were able to cross onto the peninsula from neighboring Birgu, using a bridge made of wooden boats.

Bridge of boats   → Ottoman land assault

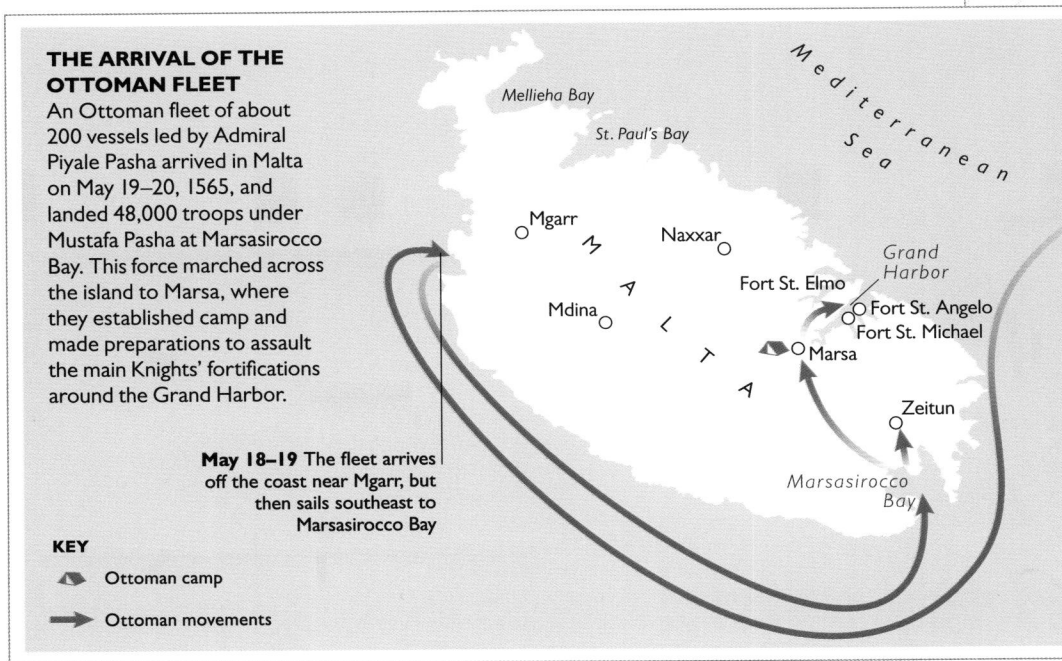

THE ARRIVAL OF THE OTTOMAN FLEET
An Ottoman fleet of about 200 vessels led by Admiral Piyale Pasha arrived in Malta on May 19–20, 1565, and landed 48,000 troops under Mustafa Pasha at Marsasirocco Bay. This force marched across the island to Marsa, where they established camp and made preparations to assault the main Knights' fortifications around the Grand Harbor.

May 18–19 The fleet arrives off the coast near Mgarr, but then sails southeast to Marsasirocco Bay

Mediterranean Sea

Mellieha Bay
St. Paul's Bay
Mgarr
Naxxar
MALTA
Mdina
Fort St. Elmo
Grand Harbor
Fort St. Angelo
Fort St. Michael
Marsa
Zeitun
Marsasirocco Bay
Corradin Heights

KEY
◣ Ottoman camp
→ Ottoman movements

△ **The Ottoman fleet arrives**
This 17th-century miniature from Istanbul shows the Ottoman fleet at Malta. Its arrival prompted many of Malta's islanders to take refuge in the island's walled cities.

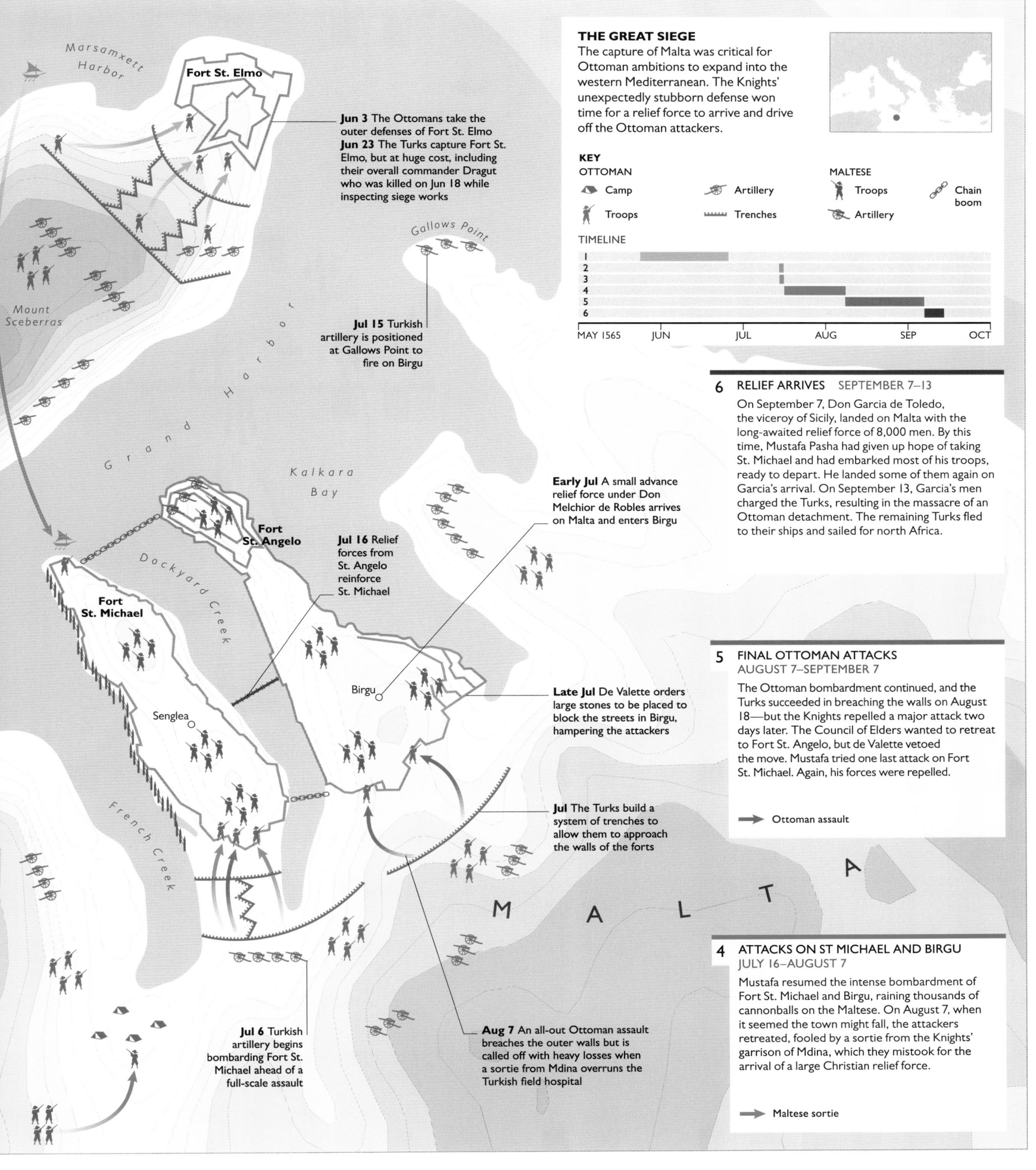

Fort St. Elmo

Jun 3 The Ottomans take the outer defenses of Fort St. Elmo

Jun 23 The Turks capture Fort St. Elmo, but at huge cost, including their overall commander Dragut who was killed on Jun 18 while inspecting siege works

Marsamxett Harbor

Gallows Point

Jul 15 Turkish artillery is positioned at Gallows Point to fire on Birgu

Mount Sceberras

Grand Harbor

Kalkara Bay

Early Jul A small advance relief force under Don Melchior de Robles arrives on Malta and enters Birgu

Fort St. Angelo

Dockyard Creek

Jul 16 Relief forces from St. Angelo reinforce St. Michael

Fort St. Michael

Birgu

Late Jul De Valette orders large stones to be placed to block the streets in Birgu, hampering the attackers

Senglea

French Creek

Jul The Turks build a system of trenches to allow them to approach the walls of the forts

M A L T A

Jul 6 Turkish artillery begins bombarding Fort St. Michael ahead of a full-scale assault

Aug 7 An all-out Ottoman assault breaches the outer walls but is called off with heavy losses when a sortie from Mdina overruns the Turkish field hospital

THE GREAT SIEGE

The capture of Malta was critical for Ottoman ambitions to expand into the western Mediterranean. The Knights' unexpectedly stubborn defense won time for a relief force to arrive and drive off the Ottoman attackers.

KEY

OTTOMAN

Camp

Troops

Artillery

Trenches

MALTESE

Troops

Artillery

Chain boom

TIMELINE

1					
2					
3					
4					
5					
6					

MAY 1565   JUN   JUL   AUG   SEP   OCT

6 RELIEF ARRIVES SEPTEMBER 7–13

On September 7, Don Garcia de Toledo, the viceroy of Sicily, landed on Malta with the long-awaited relief force of 8,000 men. By this time, Mustafa Pasha had given up hope of taking St. Michael and had embarked most of his troops, ready to depart. He landed some of them again on Garcia's arrival. On September 13, Garcia's men charged the Turks, resulting in the massacre of an Ottoman detachment. The remaining Turks fled to their ships and sailed for north Africa.

5 FINAL OTTOMAN ATTACKS
AUGUST 7–SEPTEMBER 7

The Ottoman bombardment continued, and the Turks succeeded in breaching the walls on August 18—but the Knights repelled a major attack two days later. The Council of Elders wanted to retreat to Fort St. Angelo, but de Valette vetoed the move. Mustafa tried one last attack on Fort St. Michael. Again, his forces were repelled.

➤ Ottoman assault

4 ATTACKS ON ST MICHAEL AND BIRGU
JULY 16–AUGUST 7

Mustafa resumed the intense bombardment of Fort St. Michael and Birgu, raining thousands of cannonballs on the Maltese. On August 7, when it seemed the town might fall, the attackers retreated, fooled by a sortie from the Knights' garrison of Mdina, which they mistook for the arrival of a large Christian relief force.

➤ Maltese sortie

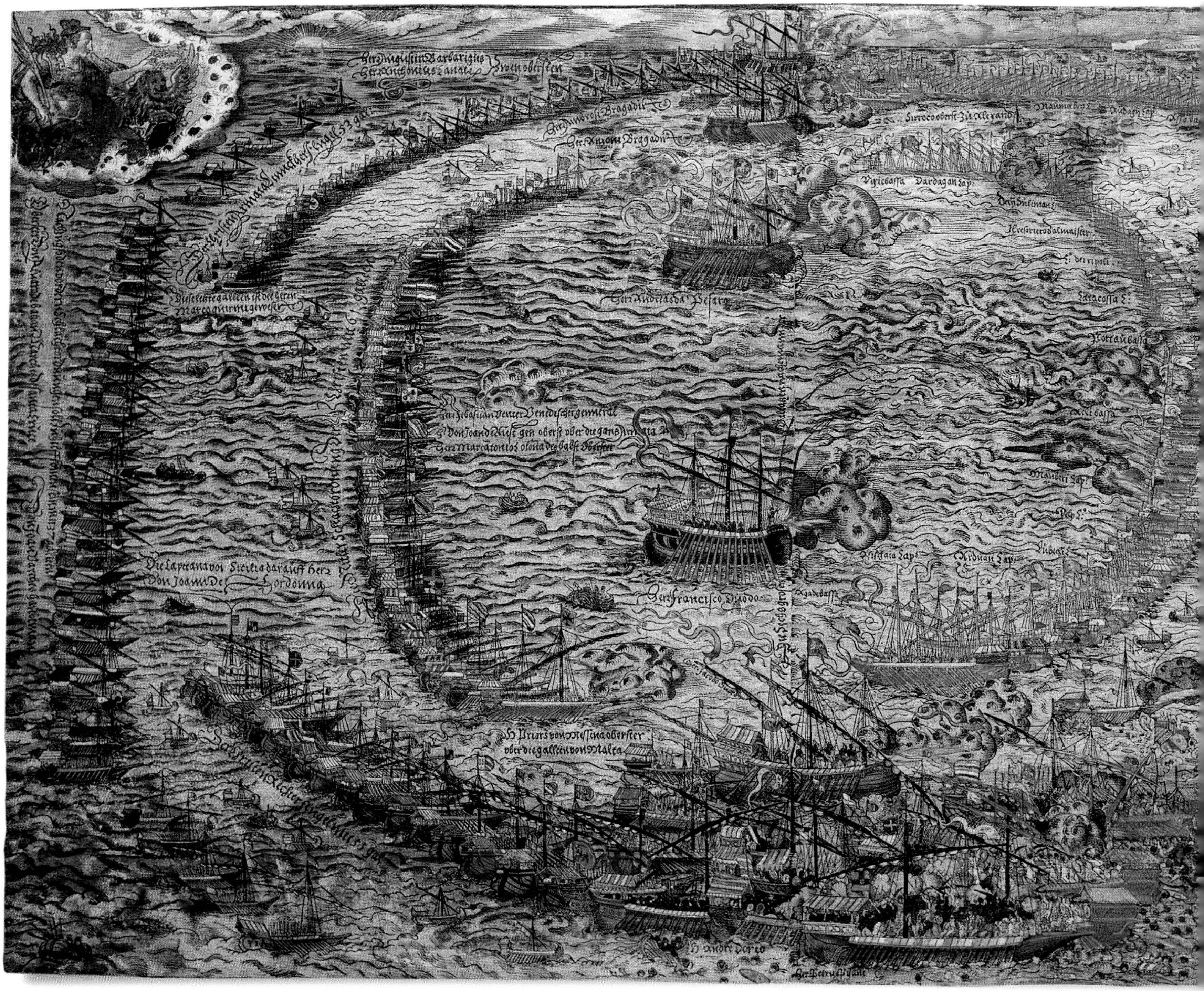

△ **Ships in formation**
This 16th-century colored, gold-embossed woodcut by Jacopo Amman von Jost depicts the beginning of the Battle of Lepanto, showing clearly the crescent formations of the Christian and Ottoman fleets, the huge galleasses billowing gunsmoke, and the flanks engaged in close-quarters combat.

▷ **The power of a city-state**
In the corner of the illustration, the symbols of Venice and Victory look out over the battle. The Republic of Venice used a winged lion as its symbol, while Victory is depicted as a female figure.

◁ **Heavy firepower**
The Venetian galleasses were large, heavily armed galleys powered by both sails and oars. Deployed across the front of the Christian fleet, these cumbersome ships were intended to fire on the enemy at close quarters.

▷ **Santa Cruz's reserves**
Commanded by the Spanish Marquess of Santa Cruz, the reserve squadron was vital to the Christian victory after they closed the dangerous gap which opened between the center and Doria's squadrons on the right.

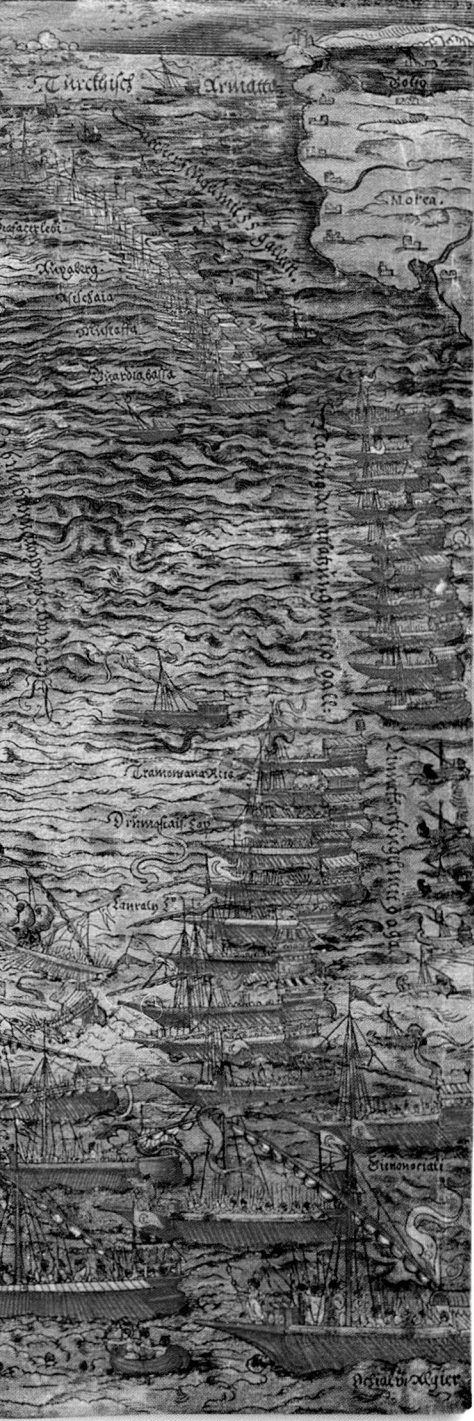

LEPANTO

At Lepanto, Don John of Austria led the Christian fleet against the Ottoman Turkish fleet of Ali Pasha. The last major battle in the West fought with rowing vessels, it shattered the myth of Ottoman invincibility. Although their fleet was rebuilt, it was soon overshadowed by new European naval technology.

In 1570, the Fourth Ottoman–Venetian War, or the War of Cyprus, broke out between the Ottoman Empire and the Republic of Venice. The Ottoman Turks invaded the Venetian-held Cyprus. By 1571, the pope had organized Christian states into a coalition— the Holy League. On September 16 that year, a large Holy League fleet led by Don John sailed from Sicily to relieve Cyprus (which fell before it could intervene).

Don John met the Turkish fleet under Ali Pasha near Lepanto on October 7. Both sides drew up in crescent formation. The Turkish fleet was larger, with more than 220 galleys and 56 galliots, but the Christian fleet was better armed and disciplined. Don John had 60,000 soldiers and oarsmen on more than 200 galleys, each with a heavy cannon in its bow, as well as smaller guns. He also had six Venetian 44-gun galleasses. The fleets engaged; as the ships locked together, the sea turned into a battlefield. Barbarigo and Suluk were

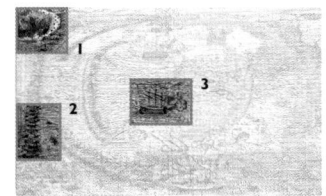
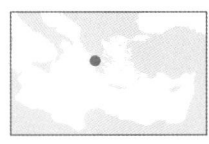

LOCATOR

killed; Ali Pasha's flagship *Sultana* was captured and Ali Pasha slain. Two hours later, the Christians had taken 117 galleys and 20 galliots, destroyed 50 other ships, and taken 10,000 prisoners. They also freed thousands of Christian galley slaves. Of the Turkish commanders, only Uluch Ali escaped, taking about a sixth of the original force to Constantinople. The battle stalled Ottoman expansion in the region and dented their fearsome naval reputation.

> *"… the heavy ordnance of the galleasses was more destructive than ever yet had been witnessed in naval gunnery…"*
>
> EDWARD SHEPHERD CREASY ON LEPANTO, *HISTORY OF THE OTTOMAN TURKS*, 1878

MELÉE IN THE SEA

On the Turkish right, Suluc's galleys rowed beyond the end of the Christian line. Barbarigo turned his bows to the shore, and engaged in close fighting until, with the help of Santa Cruz's reserves, Suluc retreated. In the center, Pasha Ali's galleys engaged Don John's ships. On the Turkish left, Uluch Ali drew Doria's squadron south, and attacked the gap in the Christian line. There was fierce fighting, but when Santa Cruz's reserves joined, the Turkish center collapsed.

KEY

- ⚓ Allied Christian fleet
- ⚓ Galleasses
- → Allied Christian advance
- ⚓ Turkish fleet
- → Turkish attack and retreat
- ▨ Shoals

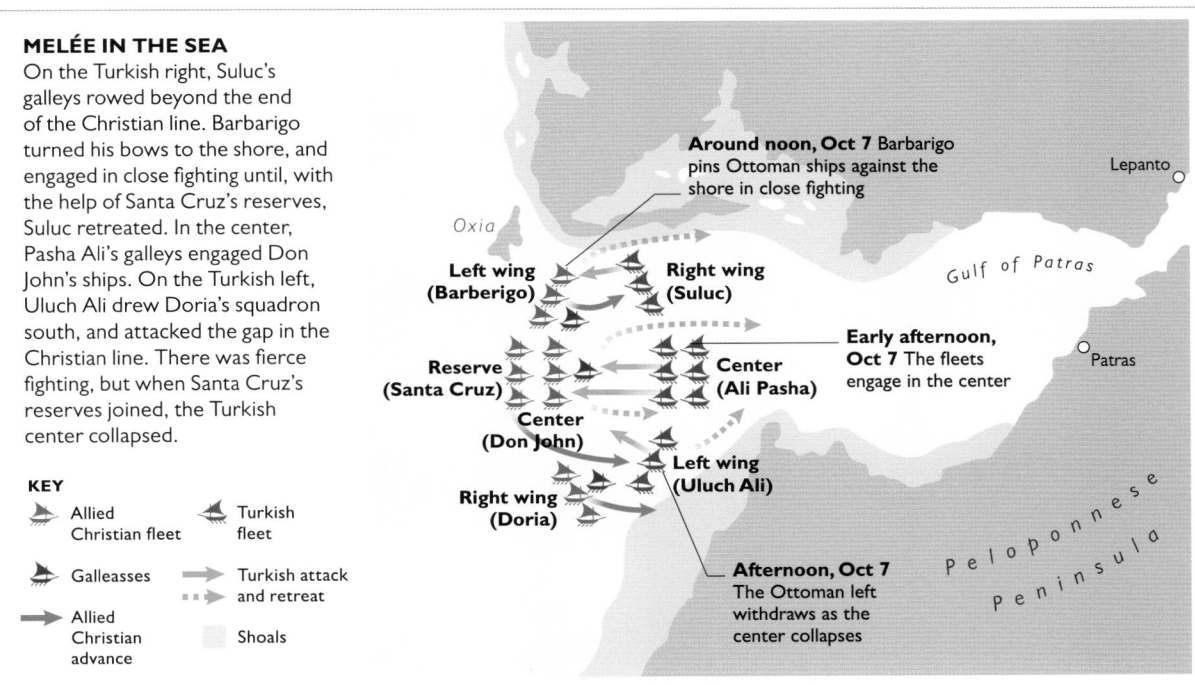

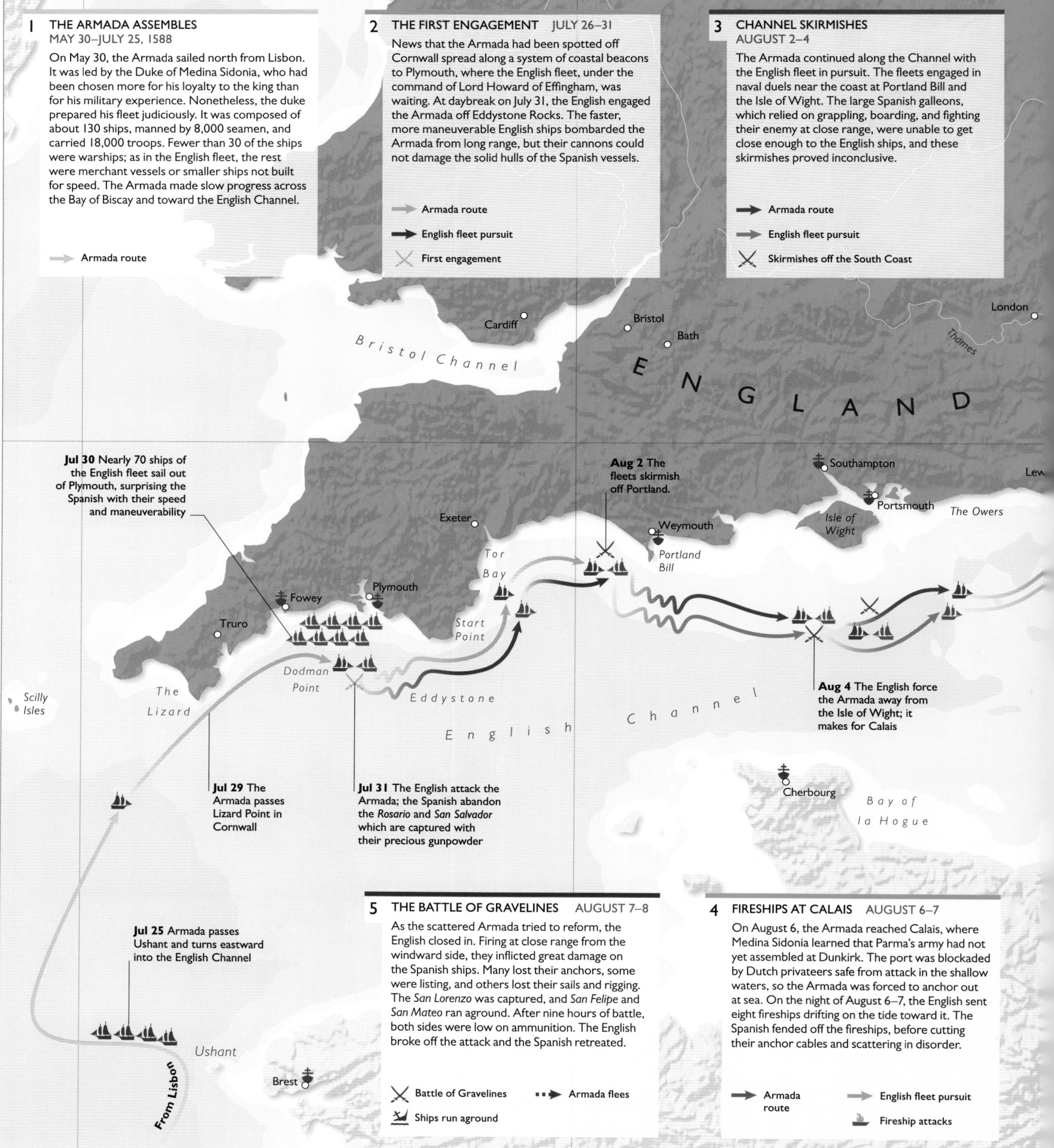

1 THE ARMADA ASSEMBLES
MAY 30–JULY 25, 1588

On May 30, the Armada sailed north from Lisbon. It was led by the Duke of Medina Sidonia, who had been chosen more for his loyalty to the king than for his military experience. Nonetheless, the duke prepared his fleet judiciously. It was composed of about 130 ships, manned by 8,000 seamen, and carried 18,000 troops. Fewer than 30 of the ships were warships; as in the English fleet, the rest were merchant vessels or smaller ships not built for speed. The Armada made slow progress across the Bay of Biscay and toward the English Channel.

→ Armada route

2 THE FIRST ENGAGEMENT JULY 26–31

News that the Armada had been spotted off Cornwall spread along a system of coastal beacons to Plymouth, where the English fleet, under the command of Lord Howard of Effingham, was waiting. At daybreak on July 31, the English engaged the Armada off Eddystone Rocks. The faster, more maneuverable English ships bombarded the Armada from long range, but their cannons could not damage the solid hulls of the Spanish vessels.

→ Armada route
→ English fleet pursuit
✕ First engagement

3 CHANNEL SKIRMISHES
AUGUST 2–4

The Armada continued along the Channel with the English fleet in pursuit. The fleets engaged in naval duels near the coast at Portland Bill and the Isle of Wight. The large Spanish galleons, which relied on grappling, boarding, and fighting their enemy at close range, were unable to get close enough to the English ships, and these skirmishes proved inconclusive.

→ Armada route
→ English fleet pursuit
✕ Skirmishes off the South Coast

Jul 30 Nearly 70 ships of the English fleet sail out of Plymouth, surprising the Spanish with their speed and maneuverability

Aug 2 The fleets skirmish off Portland.

Bristol Channel

Cardiff
Bristol
Bath
London
Thames

E N G L A N D

Southampton
Lew
Portsmouth *The Owers*
Isle of Wight
Exeter
Weymouth
Portland Bill
Tor Bay
Plymouth
Fowey
Truro
Start Point
Dodman Point
The Lizard
Eddystone
English Channel
Scilly Isles

Aug 4 The English force the Armada away from the Isle of Wight; it makes for Calais

Jul 29 The Armada passes Lizard Point in Cornwall

Jul 31 The English attack the Armada; the Spanish abandon the *Rosario* and *San Salvador* which are captured with their precious gunpowder

Cherbourg
Bay of la Hogue

Jul 25 Armada passes Ushant and turns eastward into the English Channel

Ushant
From Lisbon
Brest

5 THE BATTLE OF GRAVELINES AUGUST 7–8

As the scattered Armada tried to reform, the English closed in. Firing at close range from the windward side, they inflicted great damage on the Spanish ships. Many lost their anchors, some were listing, and others lost their sails and rigging. The *San Lorenzo* was captured, and *San Felipe* and *San Mateo* ran aground. After nine hours of battle, both sides were low on ammunition. The English broke off the attack and the Spanish retreated.

✕ Battle of Gravelines
⋯▶ Armada flees
⚓ Ships run aground

4 FIRESHIPS AT CALAIS AUGUST 6–7

On August 6, the Armada reached Calais, where Medina Sidonia learned that Parma's army had not yet assembled at Dunkirk. The port was blockaded by Dutch privateers safe from attack in the shallow waters, so the Armada was forced to anchor out at sea. On the night of August 6–7, the English sent eight fireships drifting on the tide toward it. The Spanish fended off the fireships, before cutting their anchor cables and scattering in disorder.

→ Armada route
→ English fleet pursuit
🔥 Fireship attacks

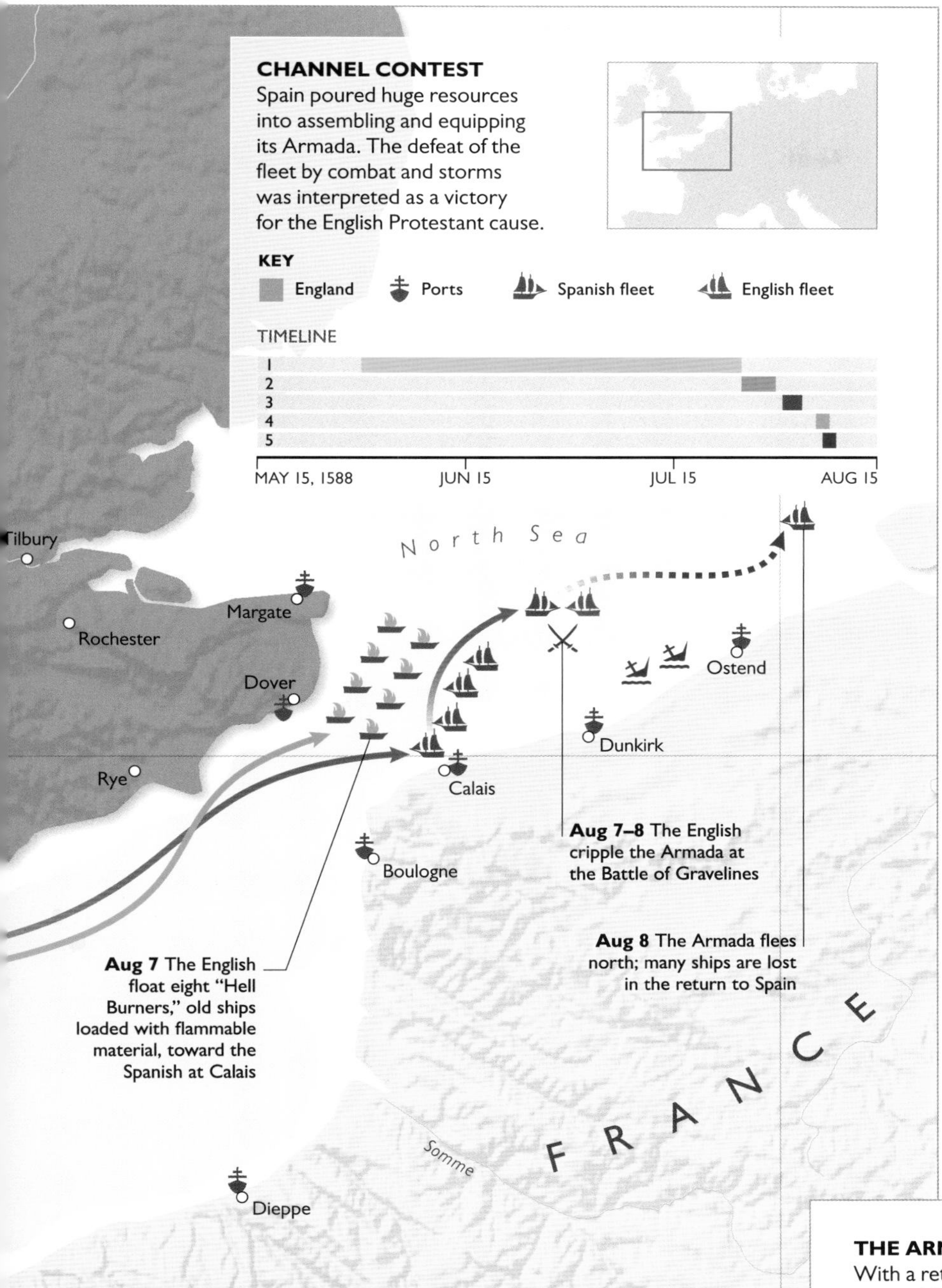

CHANNEL CONTEST
Spain poured huge resources into assembling and equipping its Armada. The defeat of the fleet by combat and storms was interpreted as a victory for the English Protestant cause.

KEY

▮ England	⚓ Ports	⛵ Spanish fleet	⛵ English fleet

TIMELINE

1
2
3
4
5

MAY 15, 1588   JUN 15   JUL 15   AUG 15

Tilbury

North Sea

Margate

Rochester

Dover

Ostend

Rye

Dunkirk

Calais

Aug 7–8 The English cripple the Armada at the Battle of Gravelines

Boulogne

Aug 8 The Armada flees north; many ships are lost in the return to Spain

Aug 7 The English float eight "Hell Burners," old ships loaded with flammable material, toward the Spanish at Calais

FRANCE

Somme

Dieppe

△ **A perilous crossing**
The progress of the Spanish was delayed by bad weather in the Bay of Biscay. This gave the English more time to prepare fortifications and set up a warning system of fire beacons.

THE SPANISH ARMADA

In 1588, King Philip II of Spain dispatched a vast fleet, the Armada, to invade England and remove Queen Elizabeth I from the throne. Harried through the Channel by English warships, the Armada was devastated by storms after fleeing the Battle of Gravelines.

In 1585, rivalry between the Catholic king of Spain, Philip II, and the Protestant queen of England, Elizabeth I, became an undeclared war. Philip had earlier been co-monarch of England through his marriage to Elizabeth's half-sister, Queen Mary I, who had died childless. Moreover, Philip was angry that Elizabeth was aiding Protestant rebels in the Spanish Netherlands, and that English privateers were raiding Spanish ships.

In spring 1587, Philip began assembling the "Great and Most Fortunate Navy" with which to depose Elizabeth. It was delayed by an English raid on Cadiz, and finally set sail from Lisbon with some 130 ships at the end of May 1588. The plan was for the Armada to journey east through the English Channel to rendezvous with 30,000 soldiers gathered by the Duke of Parma in the Spanish Netherlands, before going on to invade England. However, after facing the English fleet in the Channel, and failing to rendezvous with the Duke, the Armada was scattered at the Battle of Gravelines. Regrouping, it fled north to the Atlantic, where it was devastated by storms.

THE ARMADA FLEES
With a retreat down the Channel impossible, Medina Sidonia decided to turn northward and return to Spain by sailing around Scotland and Ireland. The English pursued the Armada to the Firth of Forth before heading home. Over the next weeks, tens of Spanish ships were shipwrecked around the Scottish and Irish coasts, and hundreds of sailors were killed after washing up in Ireland. Only about half of the Armada's ships returned to Spain.

Aug–Sep 1588 Many Spanish ships are blown off course and shipwrecked around the west coast of Scotland and Ireland

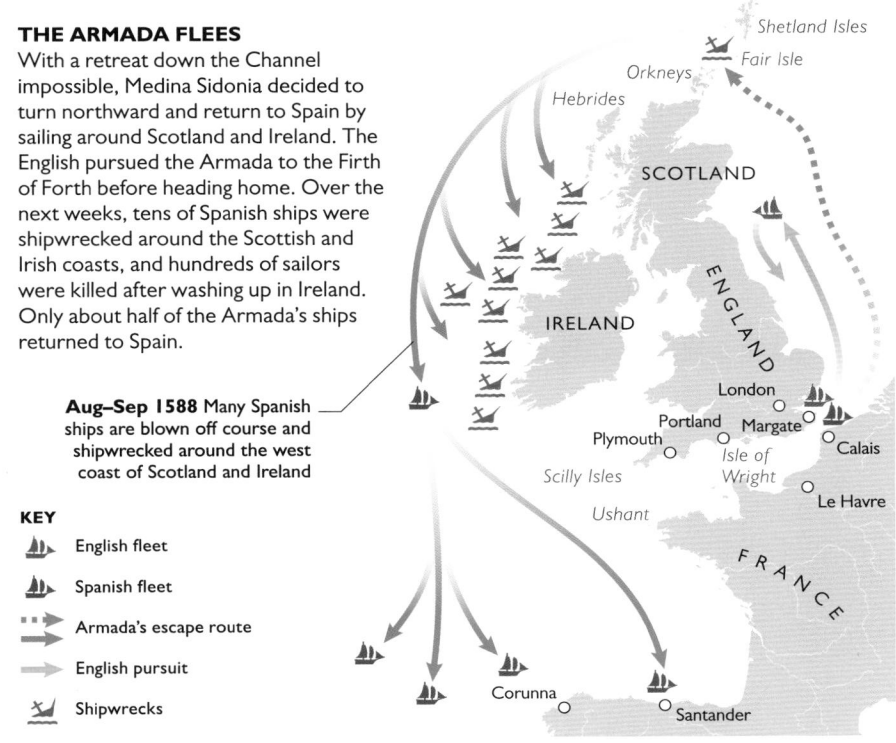

Shetland Isles

Fair Isle

Orkneys

Hebrides

SCOTLAND

IRELAND

ENGLAND

London

Portland   Margate

Plymouth

Isle of Wight

Calais

Scilly Isles

Le Havre

Ushant

FRANCE

Corunna

Santander

KEY

⛵	English fleet
⛵	Spanish fleet
┅►	Armada's escape route
━►	English pursuit
✕	Shipwrecks

Battle of Scheveningen (1653)
This 17th-century painting shows English and Dutch fleets using full-rigged galleons mounted with large broadside guns. *Brederode* (left), the Dutch flagship seen firing on the English ship, was armed with more than 50 guns.

GALLEYS AND GALLEONS

Between the 15th and 17th centuries, naval warfare saw not just a constant evolution in tactics, technology, and objectives, but also a growing expansion in the reach of European navies across the globe.

At the start of the 16th century, the sail-and-oar powered, sleek-hulled galley was the primary warship, supported by a smaller number of converted merchant vessels. This was the height of galley warfare, especially in the Mediterranean, where Christian nations warred between themselves and against the Ottoman Empire. Fleets, at times mustering hundreds of ships, clashed repeatedly during battle. The battle at Lepanto in 1571 (see pp.118–19) epitomized this, with hundreds of galleys lined up abreast and fighting mainly at close quarters.

△ **Bar shot**
This projectile was designed to damage sails and their rigging. The two halves extended and tumbled in flight.

The emergence of galleons

At the same time, especially outside the Mediterranean, converted seagoing merchant ships evolved into specially built warships. Known as galleons, these large vessels were powered by sail and carried numerous cannons; they were also better suited for longer voyages and rougher seas. Where galley warfare involved ramming and boarding, the heavily armed galleons used cannon fire from a distance, relying less heavily on boarding actions. By the end of the 17th century, they had become the dominant form of warship.

Galleys remained in use for some time in sheltered coastal waters, and were a part of Russian and Swedish navies in the Baltic Sea until the early 19th century. The superior firepower and endurance of galleons, however, made them increasingly dominant on the open sea, as seen in their leading role during the Spanish Armada campaign of 1588 (see pp.120–21), just 17 years after the Battle of Lepanto.

△ **Oar to sail**
Spanish artist Rafael Monleón's painting depicts a galleon (left) and a galley (right) from the 16th century. Galleys, propelled mainly by oars, had a long, slender hull. Galleons, on the other hand, were powered by sails and carried rows of guns on their decks.

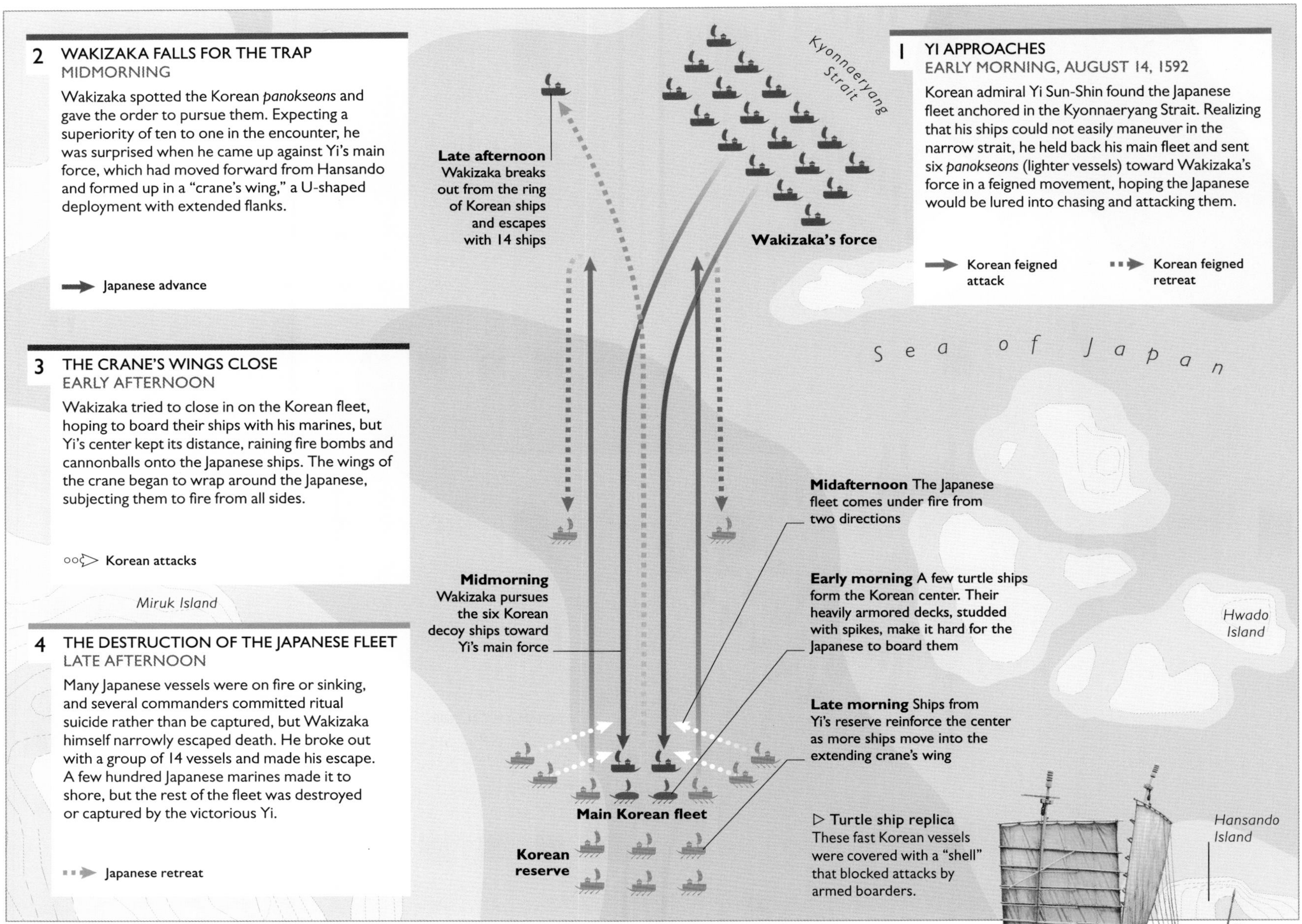

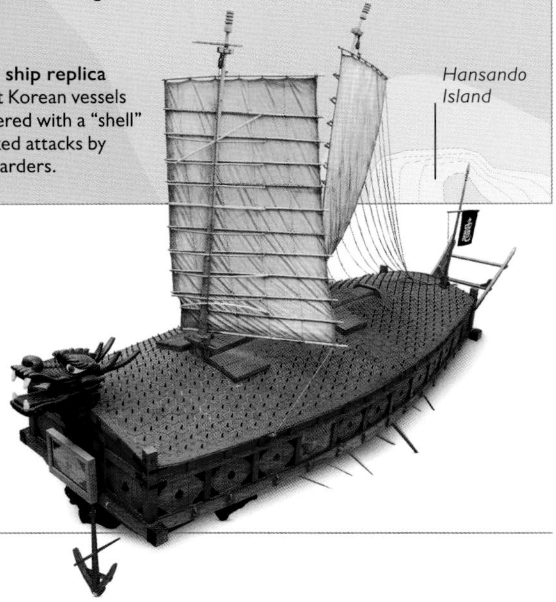

2 WAKIZAKA FALLS FOR THE TRAP
MIDMORNING

Wakizaka spotted the Korean *panokseons* and gave the order to pursue them. Expecting a superiority of ten to one in the encounter, he was surprised when he came up against Yi's main force, which had moved forward from Hansando and formed up in a "crane's wing," a U-shaped deployment with extended flanks.

➡ Japanese advance

3 THE CRANE'S WINGS CLOSE
EARLY AFTERNOON

Wakizaka tried to close in on the Korean fleet, hoping to board their ships with his marines, but Yi's center kept its distance, raining fire bombs and cannonballs onto the Japanese ships. The wings of the crane began to wrap around the Japanese, subjecting them to fire from all sides.

ᴏᴏⲥ▷ Korean attacks

Miruk Island

4 THE DESTRUCTION OF THE JAPANESE FLEET
LATE AFTERNOON

Many Japanese vessels were on fire or sinking, and several commanders committed ritual suicide rather than be captured, but Wakizaka himself narrowly escaped death. He broke out with a group of 14 vessels and made his escape. A few hundred Japanese marines made it to shore, but the rest of the fleet was destroyed or captured by the victorious Yi.

┅➡ Japanese retreat

Kyonnaeryang Strait

Late afternoon Wakizaka breaks out from the ring of Korean ships and escapes with 14 ships

Wakizaka's force

1 YI APPROACHES
EARLY MORNING, AUGUST 14, 1592

Korean admiral Yi Sun-Shin found the Japanese fleet anchored in the Kyonnaeryang Strait. Realizing that his ships could not easily maneuver in the narrow strait, he held back his main fleet and sent six *panokseons* (lighter vessels) toward Wakizaka's force in a feigned movement, hoping the Japanese would be lured into chasing and attacking them.

➡ Korean feigned attack   ┅➡ Korean feigned retreat

Sea of Japan

Midafternoon The Japanese fleet comes under fire from two directions

Early morning A few turtle ships form from the Korean center. Their heavily armored decks, studded with spikes, make it hard for the Japanese to board them

Hwado Island

Midmorning Wakizaka pursues the six Korean decoy ships toward Yi's main force

Late morning Ships from Yi's reserve reinforce the center as more ships move into the extending crane's wing

Main Korean fleet

Korean reserve

▷ **Turtle ship replica** These fast Korean vessels were covered with a "shell" that blocked attacks by armed boarders.

Hansando Island

HANSANDO

In the waters off Hansando Island, Korean admiral Yi Sun-Shin helped to resist the occupation of Korea launched by Japanese warlord Toyotomi Hideyoshi. He lured the Japanese into a trap, where his armored ships destroyed the enemy fleet.

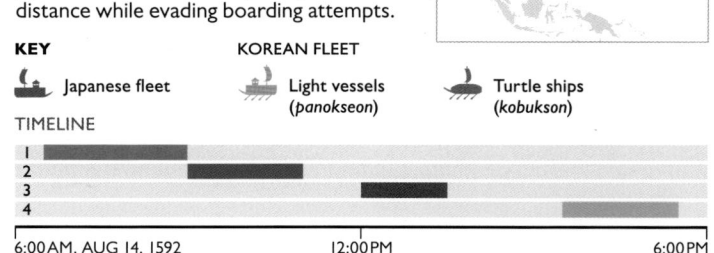

By 1592, warlord Toyotomi Hideyoshi had almost completed the reunification of Japan. As the country's de facto leader, he developed an aggressive foreign policy by which he hoped to subjugate Ming China. This prompted the occupation of most of Korea as a conduit for his armies.

The Korean fleet, however, remained intact, and its heavy cannons and armored "turtle ships" were a particular threat to the lighter Japanese vessels. Hideyoshi called on warlord Wakizaka Yasuharu to deal with

Korean admiral Yi Sun-Shin and his fleet. Wakizaka set sail with around 75 ships, without waiting for the reinforcements that would have given him a clear advantage.

The Korean fleet encountered the Japanese near Hansando Island on August 14, 1592, and soundly defeated them. Although the Japanese continued to advance in the aftermath of the battle, support for Korea from Ming China prompted Hideyoshi to agree a ceasefire and mutual withdrawal from most of Korea in May 1954.

NAVAL STRATEGY

Yi Sun-Shin skilfully lured the Japanese fleet into open water off Hansando Island where his ships could surround it and exploit the Japanese lack of cannon by firing from a distance while evading boarding attempts.

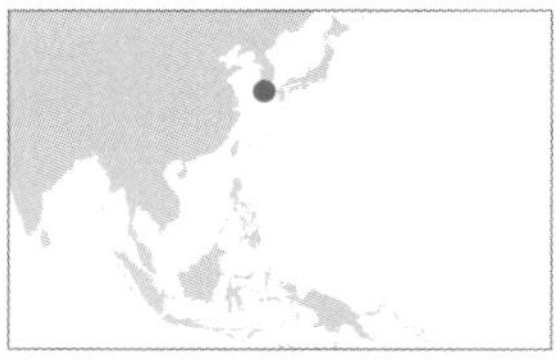

KEY

🚢 Japanese fleet

KOREAN FLEET
🛶 Light vessels (*panokseon*)
🛶 Turtle ships (*kobukson*)

TIMELINE

1			
2			
3			
4			

6:00AM, AUG 14, 1592   12:00PM   6:00PM

SEKIGAHARA

The bid by the feudal lord Tokugawa Ieyasu to achieve supremacy in Japan was opposed by a coalition led by Ishida Mitsunari, whose Western Army clashed with Tokugawa's Eastern Army at Sekigahara in October 1600. The defection of key parts of Mitsunari's force handed Ieyasu's forces a crushing victory and allowed him to establish a Tokugawa shogunate.

The death of Toyotomi Hideyoshi (see p.124) in 1598 meant that his lieutenant Tokugawa Ieyasu was now Japan's most important warlord. Brushing aside the regency of Hideyoshi's son Hideyori, Ieyasu began to cement his rule. He faced opposition, however, that coalesced around Ishida Mitsunari, a loyalist to Hideyori's cause. In preparation for conflict, both sides hurried to take strategic positions around the imperial capital Kyoto. Mitsunari's Western Army captured Fushimi Castle and Ogaki Castle, but the Eastern Army, meanwhile, took Gifu Castle. This prompted Mitsunari to redeploy to a defensive position near the village of Sekigahara, where the Eastern force confronted him on October 21. Ieyasu's decisive victory there shattered the Western alliance.

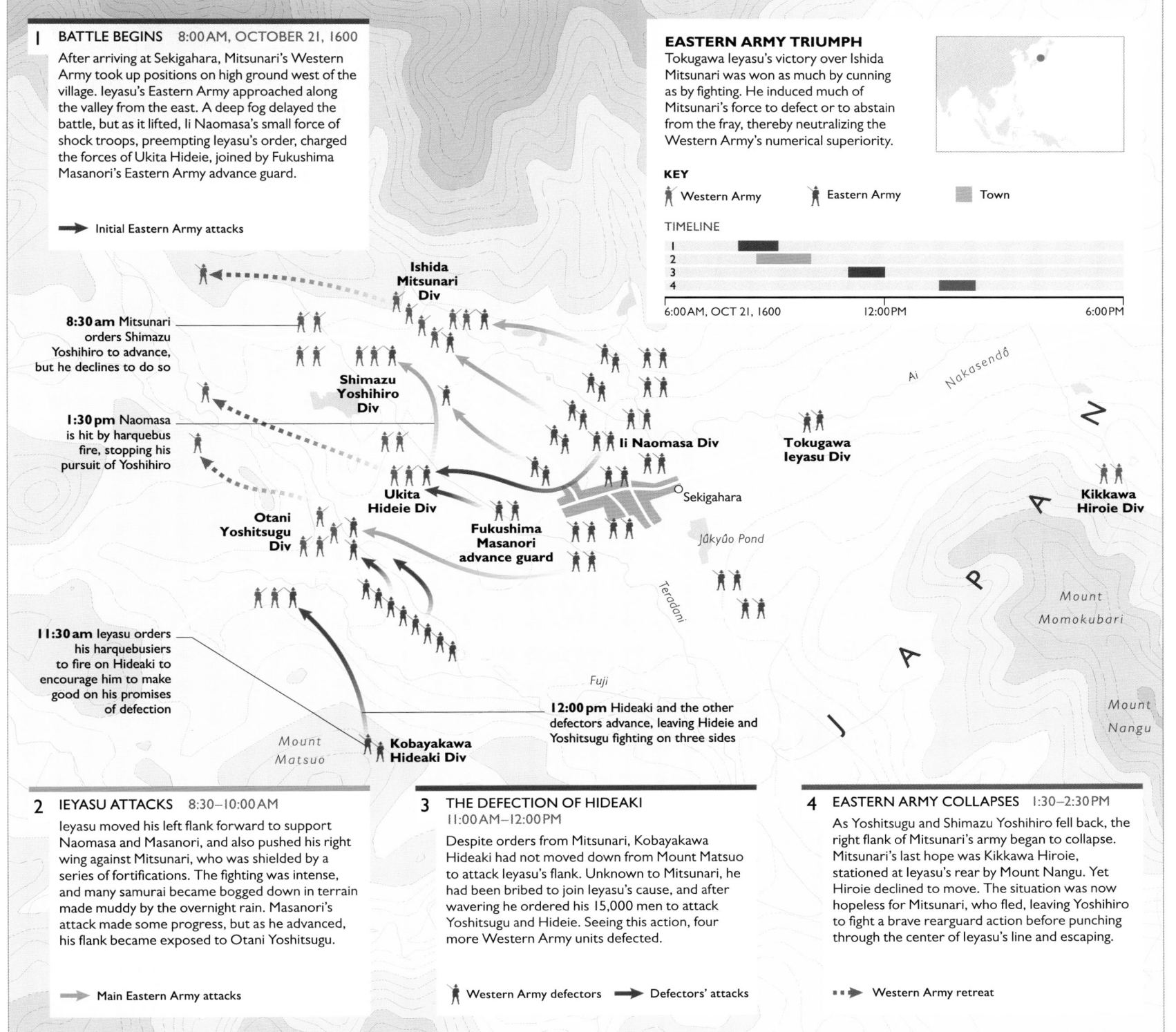

1 BATTLE BEGINS 8:00 AM, OCTOBER 21, 1600

After arriving at Sekigahara, Mitsunari's Western Army took up positions on high ground west of the village. Ieyasu's Eastern Army approached along the valley from the east. A deep fog delayed the battle, but as it lifted, Ii Naomasa's small force of shock troops, preempting Ieyasu's order, charged the forces of Ukita Hideie, joined by Fukushima Masanori's Eastern Army advance guard.

→ Initial Eastern Army attacks

EASTERN ARMY TRIUMPH

Tokugawa Ieyasu's victory over Ishida Mitsunari was won as much by cunning as by fighting. He induced much of Mitsunari's force to defect or to abstain from the fray, thereby neutralizing the Western Army's numerical superiority.

KEY

Western Army   Eastern Army   Town

TIMELINE

6:00 AM, OCT 21, 1600   12:00 PM   6:00 PM

8:30 am Mitsunari orders Shimazu Yoshihiro to advance, but he declines to do so

1:30 pm Naomasa is hit by harquebus fire, stopping his pursuit of Yoshihiro

11:30 am Ieyasu orders his harquebusiers to fire on Hideaki to encourage him to make good on his promises of defection

Ishida Mitsunari Div

Shimazu Yoshihiro Div

Ii Naomasa Div

Tokugawa Ieyasu Div

Ukita Hideie Div

Fukushima Masanori advance guard

Otani Yoshitsugu Div

Sekigahara

Jūkyūo Pond

Kikkawa Hiroie Div

Ai Nakasendō

Teradani

Mount Momokubari

Fuji

Mount Nangu

12:00 pm Hideaki and the other defectors advance, leaving Hideie and Yoshitsugu fighting on three sides

Mount Matsuo

Kobayakawa Hideaki Div

2 IEYASU ATTACKS 8:30–10:00 AM

Ieyasu moved his left flank forward to support Naomasa and Masanori, and also pushed his right wing against Mitsunari, who was shielded by a series of fortifications. The fighting was intense, and many samurai became bogged down in terrain made muddy by the overnight rain. Masanori's attack made some progress, but as he advanced, his flank became exposed to Otani Yoshitsugu.

→ Main Eastern Army attacks

3 THE DEFECTION OF HIDEAKI 11:00 AM–12:00 PM

Despite orders from Mitsunari, Kobayakawa Hideaki had not moved down from Mount Matsuo to attack Ieyasu's flank. Unknown to Mitsunari, he had been bribed to join Ieyasu's cause, and after wavering he ordered his 15,000 men to attack Yoshitsugu and Hideie. Seeing this action, four more Western Army units defected.

⚊ Western Army defectors   → Defectors' attacks

4 EASTERN ARMY COLLAPSES 1:30–2:30 PM

As Yoshitsugu and Shimazu Yoshihiro fell back, the right flank of Mitsunari's army began to collapse. Mitsunari's last hope was Kikkawa Hiroie, stationed at Ieyasu's rear by Mount Nangu. Yet Hiroie declined to move. The situation was now hopeless for Mitsunari, who fled, leaving Yoshihiro to fight a brave rearguard action before punching through the center of Ieyasu's line and escaping.

▪▪▶ Western Army retreat

Samurai legend
This 19th-century wooden plaque depicts Minamoto no Yoshitsune (left) being welcomed to Hokkaido by his subjects. Yoshitsune is considered to be one of Japan's greatest samurai warriors due to his heroics in the Genpei War.

SAMURAI AND SHOGUNS

As medieval Japan's power changed hands, a new warrior caste evolved as a hybrid military and police force—the samurai. They had become a staple of Japanese warfare and politics by the 12th century.

In the late 8th century CE, after fears of an impending invasion from Tang China had receded, the elaborate military forces of the Japanese imperial court stood down.

△ **Weapon of choice**
This long sword, or *katana*, was worn by samurai during the Edo period (1603–1868).

They were replaced by a new group of private military professionals called samurai, largely employed to deal with internal disturbances and police duties. Armed with bows and swords, samurai fought on horseback and rented their services to the court and the state when needed. In turn, they were remunerated in money and land deeds. This system prevailed during the Genpei War (see p.68), the two Mongol invasions of the 13th century, and the period of the two rival courts—the Nanbokucho period—from 1336 to 1392.

Changes in power

With the Onin War (1467–77) and the decline of centralized bureaucracy, the Sengoku era (1467–1615) saw the rise of a new power structure in Japan. The shogunate was a powerful national office for which the samurai dueled. Clan lords called *daimyo* had private retinues, which grew alongside their direct control over the farming estates, and they began to fight each other for possession of land rather than being mobilized by a central authority. This trend accelerated with the introduction of the Portuguese harquebus (see p.95) in 1543. This made it easy for warlords to field large armies with less training than archers. Shoguns and the dominant samurai warrior caste continued to rule Japan until the mid-19th century.

THE FEUDAL SYSTEM IN JAPAN

For most of the medieval period, the imperial court retained full control over lands and titles, and samurai could receive land deeds in exchange for services; however, these were not hereditary. As a result, the first few shoguns were agents of the court rather than autonomous lords. It was only in the 15th–16th centuries that samurai lords such as Uesugi Kenshin (1530–78, right) came to independently control specific provinces, and administered as well as defended them.

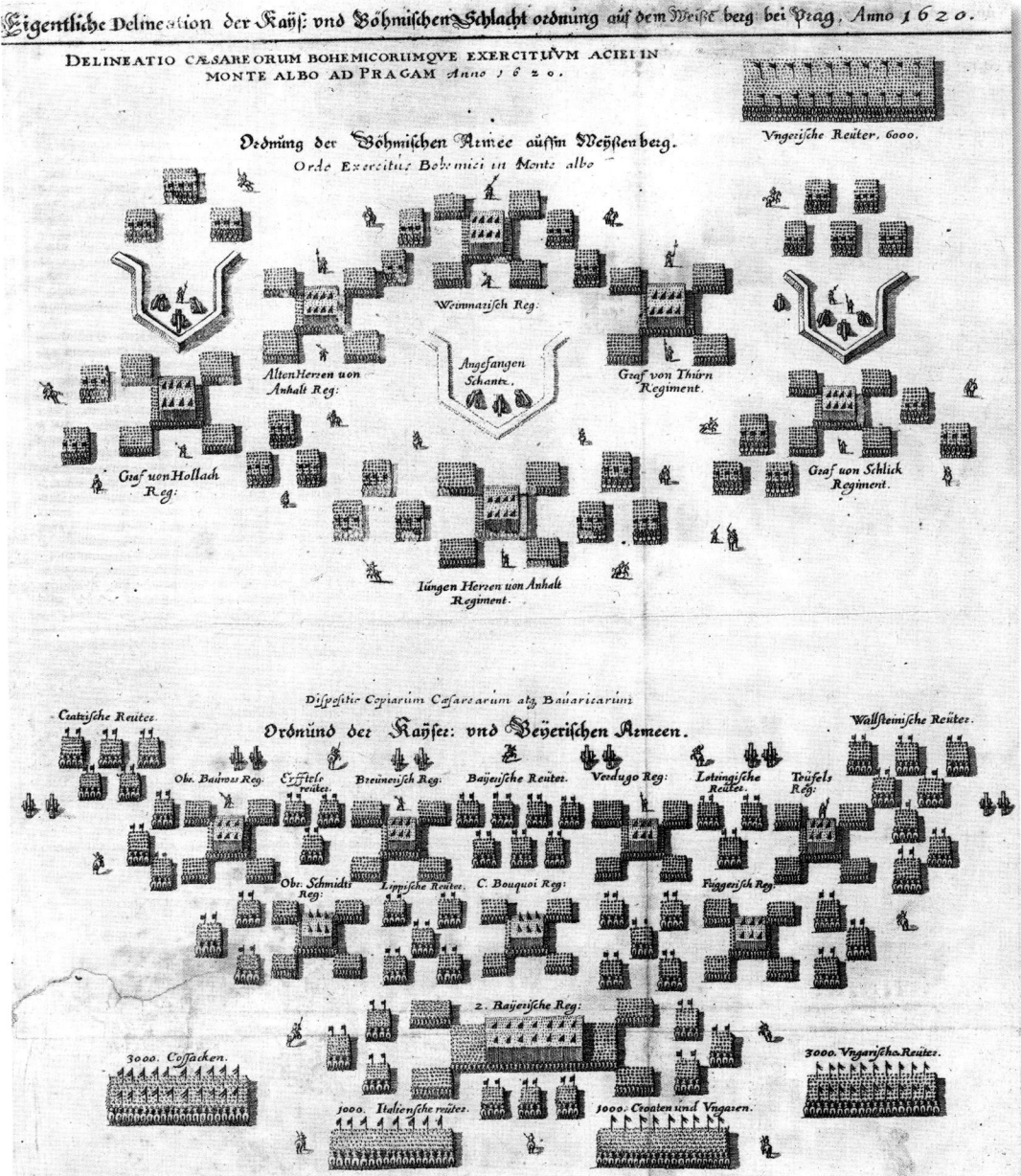

Ordnund der Kaÿse

△ **The "Apostles"**
The Catholic League had a dozen heavy guns they nicknamed the "12 Apostles." They fired at about 12:15 pm to signal the advance.

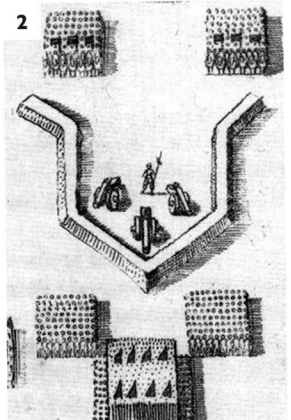

◁ **Stronghold**
The Bohemians dug in on the hillside above the plateau, and were partially protected by the walls of Prague's Star Palace.

▽ **Tercio**
The Catholic infantry formed in *tercios*—a formation of up to 3,000 infantry with pikes in the center and muskets concentrated in the sleeves on each of its four corners.

◁ **Initial positions**
This 1662 plan of the battle is from *Theatrum Europaeum*, a 21-volume history of German-speaking lands. It shows the positions of the Bohemian forces (above) and Imperial forces (below) at the start of the battle.

WHITE MOUNTAIN

On November 8, 1620, the Habsburg Holy Roman Empire won its first major victory over the Protestant Union in the Thirty Years War (1618–48) at White Mountain, near Prague in Bohemia. There the Bohemian army was routed and the Bohemian Revolt crushed.

In 1617, the Habsburg Ferdinand of Austria was crowned King of Bohemia and immediately began removing the religious freedoms of his Protestant subjects, which led to the Bohemian Revolt (1618–20). By 1620, Ferdinand, by then Holy Roman Emperor, was determined to end the revolt, and by November his Imperial forces had pushed the Bohemian army back to the outskirts of Prague.

On the morning of November 8, the dwindling Bohemian army assembled at White Mountain, a low plateau on the road to Prague, to face some 25,000 Imperial soldiers. On the right, the Catholic soldiers advanced, sweeping away the Protestant cavalry and charging the disintegrating enemy left. As the Bohemian flank crumbled, its cavalry charged the Imperial infantry. The cavalry was soon forced to retire, however, and the Bohemian infantry managed only one volley before it, too, fled toward Prague. The battle was over in less than two hours.

The Bohemian revolt ended after the rout at White Mountain; Prague fell and Bohemia was reabsorbed into the Holy Roman Empire. The Protestants would have to wait until the Battle of Breitenfeld (see pp.130–31) for their first major victory in the Thirty Years War.

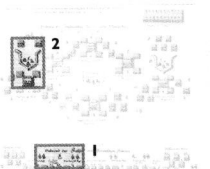

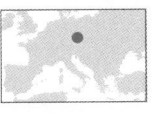

LOCATOR

THE SIEGE OF BREDA

The nine-month siege of Breda was one of Spain's greatest victories in the Eighty Years' War (1568–1648) fought over Dutch independence from Spanish rule. Spain's vast siege works were a marvel of military engineering, attracting visitors from across Europe.

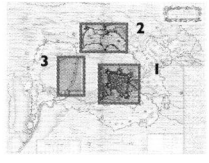 

In 1566, the Low Countries revolted against their Habsburg ruler, King Philip II of Spain, beginning the Dutch Revolt that would become the Eighty Years' War. In 1624, Spanish forces besieged Breda—a crucial fortress on the southern frontier of the United Provinces of the Netherlands, who had claimed independence from Spanish rule in 1581.

The Spanish general Ambrogio Spinola encircled Breda with a large army, aiming to starve it into submission. In less than a month, his men had built a complex network of siege works around the city. Both sides used the rivers and drains to flood fields or dry up navigable channels for tactical advantage. Spinola drove off two attempts to lift the siege before Breda's governor, Justin of Nassau, finally surrendered on June 5, 1625. Over half of the Dutch garrison of several thousand had died. Although the siege helped restore the Spanish army's reputation, Spanish resources were overstretched. Breda was retaken in 1637, and Spain was forced to recognize Dutch independence in 1648.

KEY

1 The bastion fortress of Breda had six major hornworks—smaller fortifications designed to slow the enemy's attack.

2 Spinola's lines of circumvallation consisted of the trenches, forts, and strongholds encircling Breda.

3 The Black Dyke was a causeway built by the Spanish to cross the flooded low-lying land.

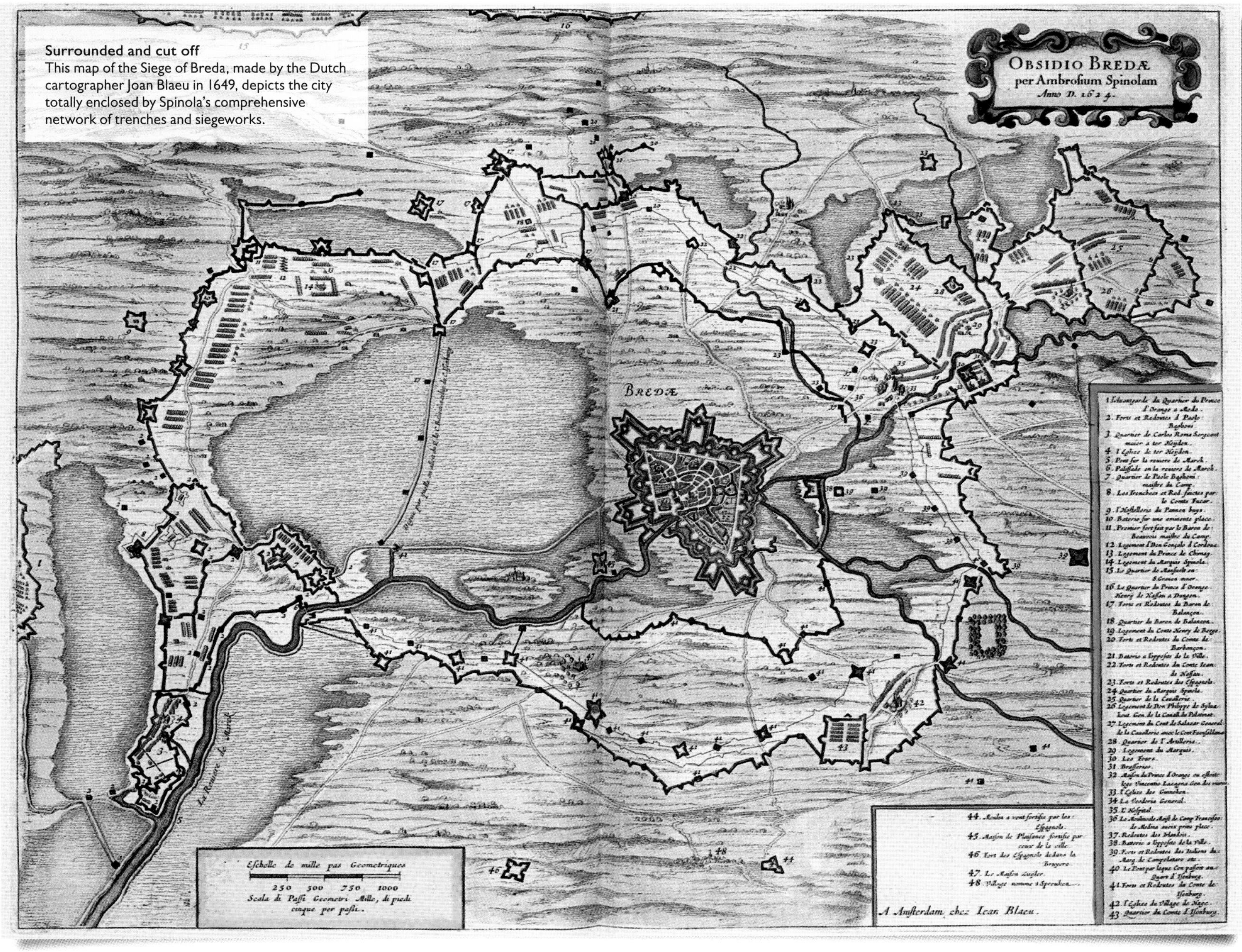

Surrounded and cut off
This map of the Siege of Breda, made by the Dutch cartographer Joan Blaeu in 1649, depicts the city totally enclosed by Spinola's comprehensive network of trenches and siegeworks.

BREITENFELD

The Swedish king Gustavus Adolphus established his reputation as a tactical genius in 1631 against Imperial Catholic forces at Breitenfeld. He shattered his foe's more traditional formations and revived the Protestant cause in the Thirty Years War.

The Thirty Years War began in Bohemia in 1618 as a Protestant revolt against attempts by Holy Roman Emperors Matthias (r. 1612 –19) and then Ferdinand II (r. 1619–37) to reimpose Catholicism. It spread to involve Spain, France, and opposing coalitions of German princes. By 1630, the Protestant cause was under pressure as the Imperial Catholic commander Tilly campaigned to mop up the last German princes still supporting it. However, the intervention of the Swedish ruler Gustavus Adolphus changed the balance of power. Gustavus enticed Johann Georg, elector of Saxony, into an alliance, and used the brutal sack of Magdeburg by Imperial troops in May 1631 to attract further allies. Sensing the danger, Tilly invaded Saxony, but before he had a chance to rendezvous with reinforcements at Jena, his 35,000-strong army encountered Gustavus at Breitenfeld, northwest of Leipzig. Gustavus's adaptability and his army's discipline won him a resounding victory. Further successes followed, leading to an upsurge in Protestant fortunes. However, Gustavus himself was killed at Lützen in 1632 and the war dragged on until 1648.

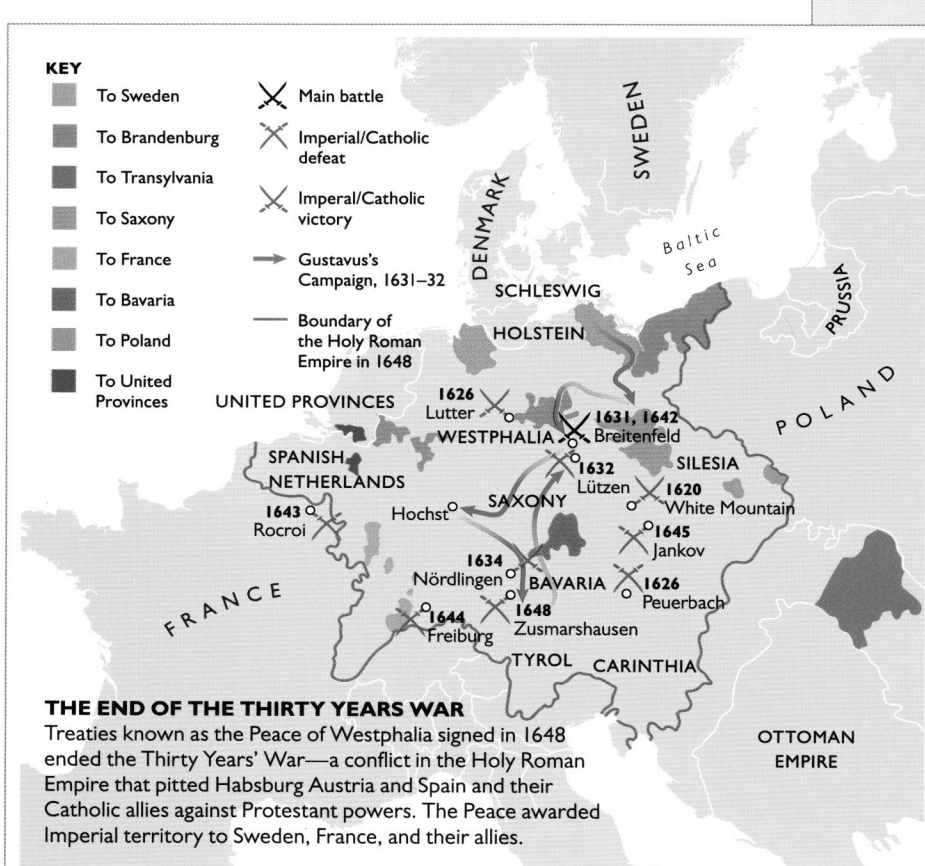

THE END OF THE THIRTY YEARS WAR
Treaties known as the Peace of Westphalia signed in 1648 ended the Thirty Years' War—a conflict in the Holy Roman Empire that pitted Habsburg Austria and Spain and their Catholic allies against Protestant powers. The Peace awarded Imperial territory to Sweden, France, and their allies.

KEY
- To Sweden
- To Brandenburg
- To Transylvania
- To Saxony
- To France
- To Bavaria
- To Poland
- To United Provinces

- ✕ Main battle
- ✕ Imperial/Catholic defeat
- ✕ Imperial/Catholic victory
- → Gustavus's Campaign, 1631–32
- — Boundary of the Holy Roman Empire in 1648

I THE DEPLOYMENT 9:00 AM–12:00 PM, SEPTEMBER 17, 1631

Gustavus deployed his 42,000-strong force just south of the Loberbach River and around the village of Podelwitz. Johann Georg's Saxons were on the left; the main Swedish cavalry on the right. Gustavus deployed his infantry in thin six-deep ranks. In contrast, Tilly drew up 17 *tercios*—unwieldy phalanxlike infantry units—at his center, with the cavalry under Pappenheim and Furstenberg at the wings.

Loberbach

Baner

2:00–3:00 pm Field guns integrated in Swedish infantry units fire grapeshot, devastating Pappenheim's Imperial cavalry

2:00–3:00 pm Pappenheim leads seven unsuccessful charges against Baner's lines

Pappenheim

◄ To Breitenfeld

FLEXIBLE TACTICS
Gustavus Adolphus' victory at Breitenfeld resulted from the greater mobility of his ranks and his ability to adapt tactics rapidly on the battlefield. The victory saved the Protestant cause in the Thirty Years War.

KEY

SWEDISH		IMPERIAL	
Commander	Cavalry	Commander	Cavalry
Infantry	Artillery	Infantry	Artillery

TIMELINE

9:00 AM, SEP 17   12:00 PM   3:00 PM   6:00 PM   9:00 PM

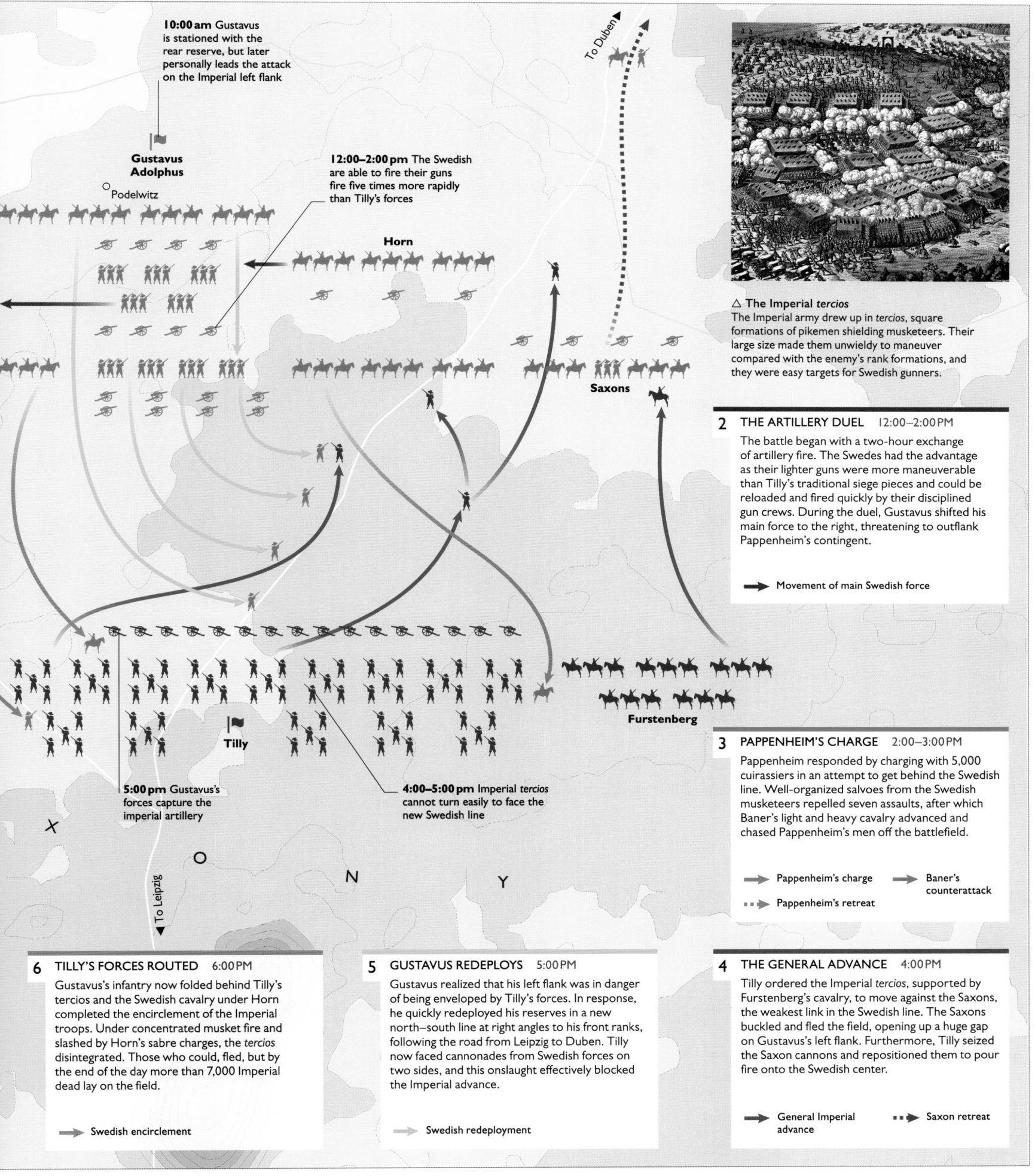

10:00 am Gustavus is stationed with the rear reserve, but later personally leads the attack on the Imperial left flank

Gustavus Adolphus

Podelwitz

12:00–2:00 pm The Swedish are able to fire their guns five times more rapidly than Tilly's forces

To Duben

Horn

Saxons

Furstenberg

Tilly

To Leipzig

5:00 pm Gustavus's forces capture the imperial artillery

4:00–5:00 pm Imperial *tercios* cannot turn easily to face the new Swedish line

△ **The Imperial *tercios***
The Imperial army drew up in *tercios*, square formations of pikemen shielding musketeers. Their large size made them unwieldy to maneuver compared with the enemy's rank formations, and they were easy targets for Swedish gunners.

2 THE ARTILLERY DUEL 12:00–2:00 PM

The battle began with a two-hour exchange of artillery fire. The Swedes had the advantage as their lighter guns were more maneuverable than Tilly's traditional siege pieces and could be reloaded and fired quickly by their disciplined gun crews. During the duel, Gustavus shifted his main force to the right, threatening to outflank Pappenheim's contingent.

→ Movement of main Swedish force

3 PAPPENHEIM'S CHARGE 2:00–3:00 PM

Pappenheim responded by charging with 5,000 cuirassiers in an attempt to get behind the Swedish line. Well-organized salvoes from the Swedish musketeers repelled seven assaults, after which Baner's light and heavy cavalry advanced and chased Pappenheim's men off the battlefield.

→ Pappenheim's charge   → Baner's counterattack

┅► Pappenheim's retreat

6 TILLY'S FORCES ROUTED 6:00 PM

Gustavus's infantry now folded behind Tilly's tercios and the Swedish cavalry under Horn completed the encirclement of the Imperial troops. Under concentrated musket fire and slashed by Horn's sabre charges, the *tercios* disintegrated. Those who could, fled, but by the end of the day more than 7,000 Imperial dead lay on the field.

→ Swedish encirclement

5 GUSTAVUS REDEPLOYS 5:00 PM

Gustavus realized that his left flank was in danger of being enveloped by Tilly's forces. In response, he quickly redeployed his reserves in a new north–south line at right angles to his front ranks, following the road from Leipzig to Duben. Tilly now faced cannonades from Swedish forces on two sides, and this onslaught effectively blocked the Imperial advance.

→ Swedish redeployment

4 THE GENERAL ADVANCE 4:00 PM

Tilly ordered the Imperial *tercios*, supported by Furstenberg's cavalry, to move against the Saxons, the weakest link in the Swedish line. The Saxons buckled and fled the field, opening up a huge gap on Gustavus's left flank. Furthermore, Tilly seized the Saxon cannons and repositioned them to pour fire onto the Swedish center.

→ General Imperial advance   ┅► Saxon retreat

PIKE AND MUSKET WARFARE

Bodies of pikemen and musketeers were the most characteristic feature of European battles from the 1500s to the late 17th century. Military tacticians were faced with the challenge of how best to combine the two.

Despite the unreliability of early gunpowder weapons, the idea of arming massed infantry with the harquebus and matchlock musket marked a bold step forward. Pikes, in contrast, were primitive arms that nevertheless retained their effectiveness against cavalry. From the 1470s, the Swiss had demonstrated the effectiveness of dense bodies of pikemen in battle not only for defense but also in attack (often described as "push of pike"), and adding musketeers to these ranks created the dominant fighting formations of the 16th century, such as the Spanish *tercios*. Cavalry, traditionally the elite arm of many forces, found itself no longer the dominant force on the battlefield.

Initially, musketeers were deployed in relatively small numbers to aid the pikemen, but by the 17th century commanders came to appreciate the potential of massed musketeers firing disciplined

△ **Matchlock musket**
An inaccurate and unreliable firearm, the matchlock was most effective when fired in disciplined volleys. This German musket dates from about 1580.

volleys. By the time of the English Civil Wars (1642–51), muskets regularly outnumbered pikes by two to one, and the firearm troops were organized in their own formations on the flanks of the pikemen. The cavalry charge, by horsemen armed with pistols and swords, also regained its potency. The introduction of flintlock muskets fitted with socket bayonets had made the pike obsolete by about 1700.

THE *LANDSKNECHT*

First raised in 1486–87, the *Landsknecht* were bands of mercenaries originally recruited to serve the Holy Roman Empire. Chiefly consisting of pikemen, their ranks also included firearm troops and elite soldiers wielding double-handed swords and halberds. The *Landsknecht* earned a fearsome reputation on and off the battlefield, their swaggering unruliness reflected in their colorful, ripped clothing. They played a prominent role in the Italian Wars (1494–1559) and, as *lansquenets*, in the French Wars of Religion (1562–98).

Fighting in formation
A battle scene painted by Pieter Snayers from the Eighty Years War, fought between the Dutch and the Spanish from 1568 to 1648, shows dense pike squares with borders of musketeers defying squadrons of pistol-armed cavalry.

NASEBY

The English Civil Wars (1642–51) were fought between Parliamentarians (supporters of Parliamentary rule) and Royalists (supporters of the absolutist king, Charles I). On June 14, 1645, the Parliamentarian New Model Army won a victory over Royalist forces at Naseby that proved to be a turning point in the conflict.

In 1642, relations between England's king, Charles I, and the country's parliament erupted into civil war. War had ravaged England for three years, when Sir Thomas Fairfax, commander-in-chief of Parliament's New Model Army (a recently formed army made up of professional soldiers) launched a siege of the Royalist city of Oxford in May 1645. The Royalist commander, Prince Rupert of the Rhine, responded by taking Leicester, a Parliamentarian stronghold 61 miles (99 km) to the north. Marching from Oxford with about 14,000 soldiers, Fairfax located the Royalists 26 miles (42 km) south of Leicester on June 12. With about 9,000 men, the Royalists withdrew, before deciding to make a stand near the village of Naseby on June 14.

Despite the disparity in their numbers, Parliament's victory was not inevitable. Prince Rupert was a seasoned soldier, and the New Model Army was relatively inexperienced. However, Rupert made two serious errors. First, he gave up an excellent defensive position in his eagerness to engage the enemy, thus ceding the choice of battleground to Fairfax and his second-in-command, Oliver Cromwell. Second, soon after the battle began, he led his cavalry in pursuit of the enemy cavalry, leaving the infantry unsupported at a crucial moment. Parliament's ensuing victory was devastating: 5,000 Royalists were taken prisoner, and the King lost many experienced officers. Parliament had won a decisive advantage in the war.

> *"The Earl of Carnwath took the King's Horse by the bridle [...] saying, Will you go upon your Death?"*
>
> SIR EDWARD WALKER, THE KING'S SECRETARY, C.17TH CENTURY

OLIVER CROMWELL
1599–1658

English military and political leader Oliver Cromwell is best known for making England a republic and leading the Commonwealth of England. In 1628, he became an MP and supported Parliament in its struggles against the King. When war broke out, he helped to build a strong professional army to fight on the Parliamentarian side. Cromwell was a self-taught soldier, and helped establish the New Model Army from scratch. From 1653 until his death five years later, he was Lord Protector, the head of state of the Commonwealth of England. After his death, the monarchy was restored, and Charles II became king.

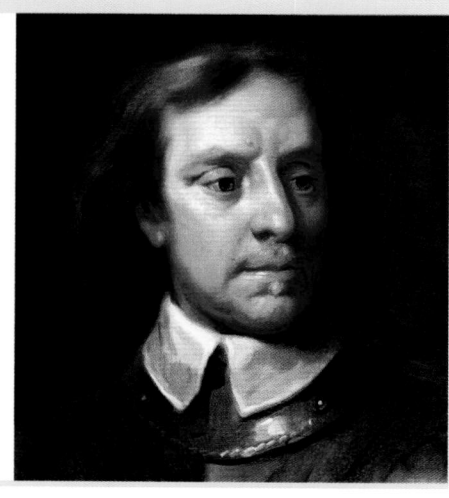

THE ROYALISTS ATTACK
Prince Rupert's Royalist forces chose to engage the Parliamentarian forces in battle. They took up position outside the village of Naseby, in the English East Midlands.

KEY

◼ Town

PARLIAMENTARIAN FORCES

Infantry · Musketeers · Cavalry · Commander

ROYALIST FORCES

Infantry · Commander · Cavalry

TIMELINE

1
2
3
4
5
6

JUN 14, 1645   12PM   JUN 15

1   THE ARMIES TAKE THEIR POSITIONS
EARLY MORNING, JUNE 14

In the early hours of June 14, Rupert discovered the enemy position. He gave up a commanding position and marched the Royalist army south to Naseby. Both armies adopted a formation with infantry in the center and cavalry on the wings, but the Parliamentarians also hid a regiment of dragoons on their left flank.

➡ Royalist forces arrive   ➡ Dragoons deployed behind hedgerows

Naseby Road

2   THE ROYALIST ADVANCE   AROUND 10:00AM

The Royalist infantry began their advance. In response, Skippon's infantry moved forward to meet them, exchanging only a single volley of musket fire with the Royalist infantry before the pikemen clashed. The more experienced Royalists pushed the Parliamentarians back in hand-to-hand combat, but could not break the line.

➡ Royalist infantry advance

➡ Parliamentarian infantry advance

3   PRINCE RUPERT'S CAVALRY CHARGE
10:00–10:30AM

Having exchanged fire with Okey's dragoons, Rupert's cavalry charged forward, attacking the Parliamentarian right flank, and engaging Ireton's cavalry in a fierce battle. Ireton had some success against the Royalists, but after half an hour many of his men were driven from the battlefield. Rupert's cavalry charged forward, reaching the Parliamentary baggage train.

➡ Prince Rupert's cavalry charge   ➡ Ireton's advance

🚛 Baggage train   ⇢ Ireton's flight

6 THE KING FLEES MIDAFTERNOON

Rupert finally rejoined the King, who was trying to rally Langdale's cavalry. Fairfax gathered up his infantry and cavalry to face the rump of the Royalists for one final assault. It never came. After one volley of musket fire from Okey's dragoons, the King's forces fled the field. The Parliamentarian forces pursued them and, despite Royalist attempts to rally, inflicted further slaughter, including that of female camp followers.

▪▪▪➤ Royalist retreat

▷ **Royalist cavalry**
The Royalist cavalry prepares to fight in this 18th-century depiction of the battle.

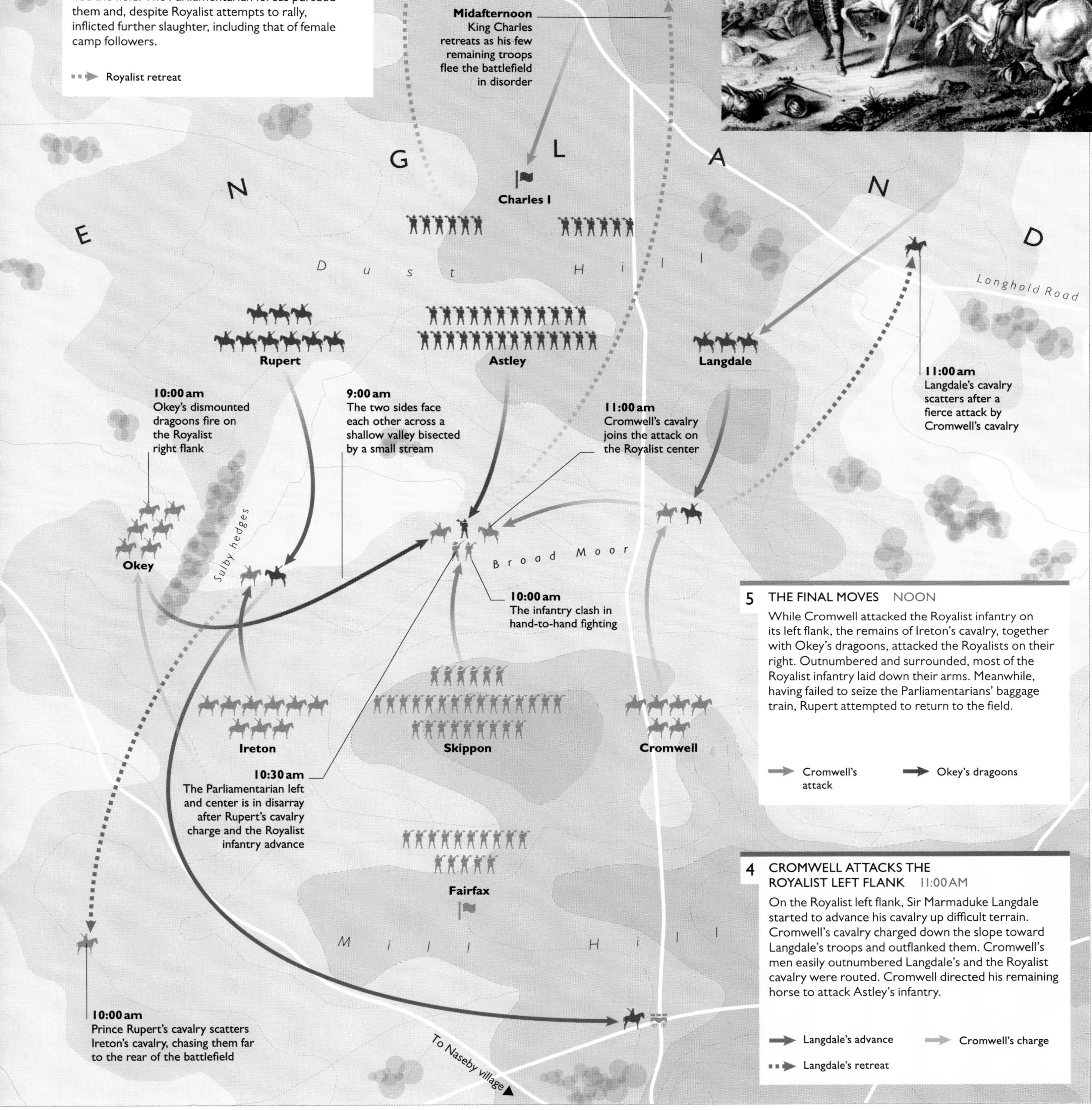

O Sibbertoft

Midafternoon
King Charles retreats as his few remaining troops flee the battlefield in disorder

E N G L A N D

D u s t   H i l l

Longhold Road

Charles I

Rupert

Astley

Langdale

10:00 am
Okey's dismounted dragoons fire on the Royalist right flank

9:00 am
The two sides face each other across a shallow valley bisected by a small stream

11:00 am
Cromwell's cavalry joins the attack on the Royalist center

11:00 am
Langdale's cavalry scatters after a fierce attack by Cromwell's cavalry

Okey

Sulby hedges

B r o a d   M o o r

10:00 am
The infantry clash in hand-to-hand fighting

5 THE FINAL MOVES NOON

While Cromwell attacked the Royalist infantry on its left flank, the remains of Ireton's cavalry, together with Okey's dragoons, attacked the Royalists on their right. Outnumbered and surrounded, most of the Royalist infantry laid down their arms. Meanwhile, having failed to seize the Parliamentarians' baggage train, Rupert attempted to return to the field.

➤ Cromwell's attack   ➤ Okey's dragoons

Ireton

Skippon

Cromwell

10:30 am
The Parliamentarian left and center is in disarray after Rupert's cavalry charge and the Royalist infantry advance

Fairfax

M i l l   H i l l

4 CROMWELL ATTACKS THE ROYALIST LEFT FLANK 11:00 AM

On the Royalist left flank, Sir Marmaduke Langdale started to advance his cavalry up difficult terrain. Cromwell's cavalry charged down the slope toward Langdale's troops and outflanked them. Cromwell's men easily outnumbered Langdale's and the Royalist cavalry were routed. Cromwell directed his remaining horse to attack Astley's infantry.

➤ Langdale's advance   ➤ Cromwell's charge
▪▪▪➤ Langdale's retreat

10:00 am
Prince Rupert's cavalry scatters Ireton's cavalry, chasing them far to the rear of the battlefield

To Naseby village ▲

THE SIEGE OF VIENNA

On September 12, 1683, John III Sobieski led an army to relieve the Ottoman Turkish siege of Vienna. Decided by reputedly the largest cavalry charge in history, Sobieski's victory heralded the end of Ottoman dominance in Eastern Europe.

Since 1664, the Habsburg-Ottoman borders in Hungary had enjoyed peace. When Hungarian Protestants and others led by Imre Thokoly rebelled against the Roman Catholic Habsburgs from 1681, they appealed to Ottoman Grand Vizier Kara Mustafa Pasha, who came to their aid with more than 100,000 men. On July 14, 1683, he besieged the Habsburg capital, Vienna. The city was well prepared, with strengthened walls, a bolstered garrison, and its suburbs razed so they could not provide cover. Turkish artillery had little impact on the city walls, but in time food supplies in Vienna ran low; disease afflicted both armies.

On September 11, Sobieski and Charles of Lorraine arrived with some 80,000 German and Polish soldiers. Under Sobieski, they assembled north and northwest of Vienna. On the morning of September 12, the army swept down on the Turkish encampments. Kara Mustafa diverted part of his forces from the siege while trying to take the city, but the Turkish resistance crumbled after Sobieski charged with about 18,000 horsemen. Under attack from all sides, including from the Vienna garrison, the Turks fled. Sobieski's victory set the stage for the reconquest of Hungary and marked the end of Ottoman expansion into Europe.

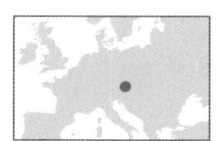

KEY

1 The star-shaped defenses held out just long enough against the Turks bombarding and mining them.

2 The Turks built an extensive network of siegeworks, including trenches allowing assault parties to get close to the walls.

3 Leopoldstadt island was taken by the Turks, but its bridges were destroyed and the river was too fast and deep to attack the main city.

> *"We have to save to-day, not a single city, but the whole of Christendom."*
>
> KING JOHN III SOBIESKI, QUOTED IN *THE SIEGES OF VIENNA BY THE TURKS*, 1879

ORDER OF BATTLE

During the morning of September 12, Charles of Lorraine's men on the allied left slowly but steadily advanced down the rough terrain on the east end of the Kahlenberg ridge, pushing the Turks back. Meanwhile the Ottoman Janissary and *Sipahi* units fiercely attacked the city. By late afternoon, Sobieski's men were formed up on the open ground on the allied right. Charles was pressing forward on the left, when Sobieski launched a large-scale cavalry attack and smashed through the Turkish lines.

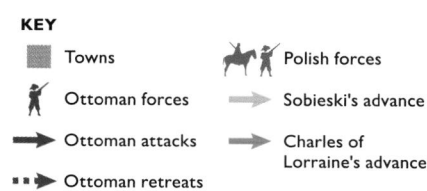

KEY

▪ Towns	🐎 Polish forces
🏹 Ottoman forces	→ Sobieski's advance
→ Ottoman attacks	→ Charles of Lorraine's advance
▪▪▶ Ottoman retreats	

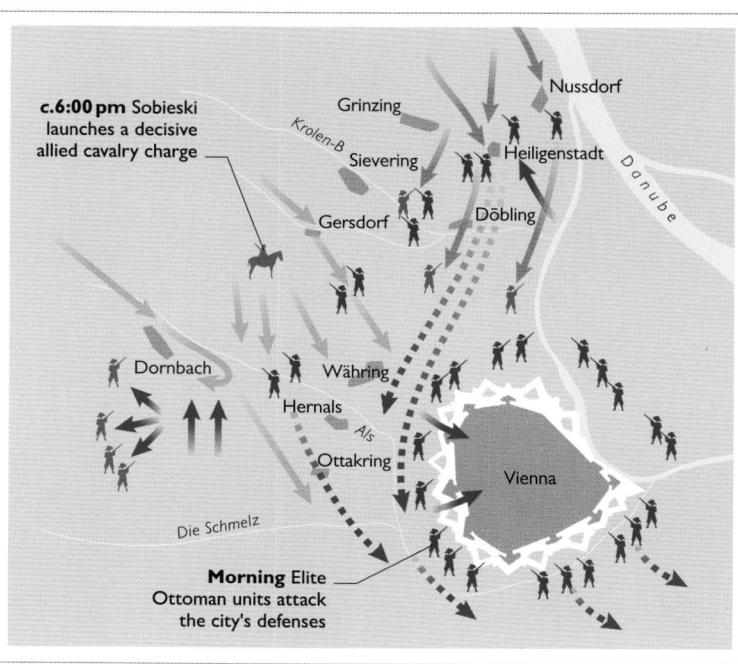

c.6:00 pm Sobieski launches a decisive allied cavalry charge

Nussdorf
Grinzing
Krolen-B
Sievering
Heiligenstadt
Danube
Gersdorf
Döbling
Dornbach
Währing
Hernals
Als
Ottakring
Vienna
Die Schmelz

Morning Elite Ottoman units attack the city's defenses

▷ **Relief of the siege**
In this contemporary Dutch engraving of the siege and battle of Vienna, the encampments of the Ottoman Turks can be seen ringing the star-shaped fortifications protecting Vienna. In the foreground are some of the many baggage camels used by the Turks.

Amstelodami apud Nicolaum Visscher
cum Privil. Ordin. General.

DIRECTORY: 1500–1700

MARIGNANO

SEPTEMBER 13–14, 1515

Between 1494 and 1559, France, Spain, and the Italian states fought for the control of Italy in a series of wars that involved much of Europe. In 1515, the conflict centered on the Duchy of Milan, then in the hands of the Old Swiss Confederacy (a loose federation of small independent states within the Holy Roman Empire). The French army, led by King Francis I, crossed the Alps with 72 cannons to retake Milan. The two armies met on September 13 at the village of Marignano (present-day Melegnano), southeast of Milan. The French, numbering about 30,000, outnumbered the Swiss who had little more than 20,000 soldiers, but they could not secure a victory. The following day, the French cannons continued to batter the advancing Swiss infantry, regarded as the best in Europe. It was only after the arrival of a Venetian force to reinforce the French that the Swiss finally withdrew. The French victory returned the Duchy of Milan to Francis I, and the Perpetual Peace Treaty, signed at Fribourg on November 29, 1516, ushered in several hundred years of close cooperation between the Swiss and the French.

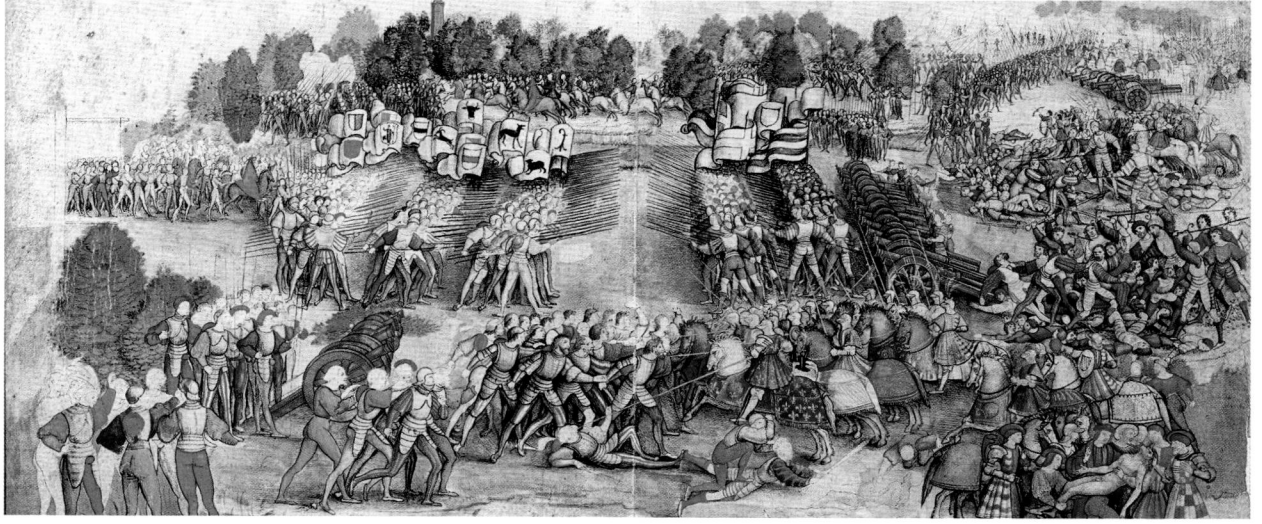

△ 16th-century pen-and-ink illustration of Marignano

RIDANIYA

22 JANUARY, 1517

The period following the conquest of Constantinople (see p.96) was marked by an Ottoman bid for expansion. Sultan Selim I pushed south to attack the Mamluk Sultanate, which ruled over Egypt as well as the holy cities of Mecca, Medina, and Jerusalem. After defeating the Mamluk forces at Marj Dabik, Syria, in 1516, Selim's army marched toward Cairo, Egypt.

The Mamluk sultan Tuman bay II and his army were entrenched at Ridaniya outside the city, and on 22 January the two sides clashed. The main body of the Ottoman force attacked the Mamluk troops and a cavalry force attacked their flank. Tuman reached Selim's tent with a group of men, and the Grand Vizier of the Ottoman Empire, Hadım Sinan Pasha, was killed in the ensuing action. However, Tuman's forces were eventually routed. While Tuman fled up the Nile, Selim took Cairo and captured Caliph Al-Mutawakkil II, the 17th and last caliph of the Mamluk Sultanate. Tuman continued guerrilla activities against the Ottomans until he was captured and hanged in April 1517. Selim went on to annex the entire Mamluk Sultanate to the Ottoman Empire.

ALCAZARQUIVIR

AUGUST 4, 1578

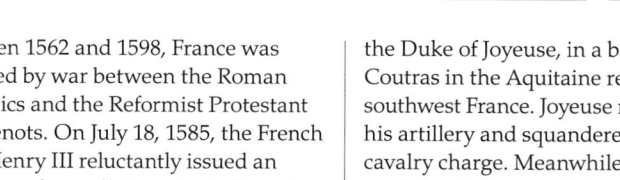

In 1578, Sebastian I of Portugal invaded Morocco to help Abu Abdallah Mohammed II regain power after he was deposed as sultan by his uncle, Abd Al-Malik I. On June 24, Sebastian sailed from the Algarve, carrying nearly 20,000 soldiers and considerable artillery to Portuguese Morocco. After landing south of Tangiers, he was joined by Abu Abdallah and 6,000 Moorish troops.

They marched into the interior, where they met Abd Al-Malik and his much larger army on August 4, at the Wadi al-Makhāzin near Ksar el-Kebir (Alcazarquivir). Abd Al-Malik drew up his forces on a broad front, with 10,000 cavalry on the wings and the Moors in the center. After exchanging several volleys of musket and artillery fire, the two sides advanced. The Portuguese flanks gave way as the Sultan's cavalry encircled them. After four hours of fighting, Sebastian and Abu Adbdallah's army was defeated—about 8,000 died, including King Sebastian and most of the Portuguese nobles, and almost all the rest were captured. The battle soon brought an end to the Aviz dynasty (1385–1580) in Portugal, and the kingdom was integrated into the Iberian Union under the Spanish Philippine dynasty for 60 years.

COUTRAS

OCTOBER 20, 1587

Between 1562 and 1598, France was wracked by war between the Roman Catholics and the Reformist Protestant Huguenots. On July 18, 1585, the French king Henry III reluctantly issued an edict banishing all Protestants from the kingdom, effectively declaring war against the Protestants and their figurehead, the Huguenot heir presumptive to the French throne, Henry of Navarre. Philip II of Spain fomented this tangled conflict by supporting the Catholic League under Henry of Lorraine, creating the "War of the Three Henrys." On October 20, 1587, Henry of Navarre met the royalist commander, the Duke of Joyeuse, in a battle at Coutras in the Aquitaine region in southwest France. Joyeuse mispositioned his artillery and squandered his first cavalry charge. Meanwhile, Navarre made excellent use of his artillery and drew up his troops with platoons of musketeers nestled within the cavalry squadrons as support. The royalist army was broken by a charge from the Protestant light cavalry, and Joyeuse was captured and executed. The battle was the first major Protestant victory in battle. Navarre took the throne in 1589 after Henry III died, but had to convert to Catholicism in 1593 to keep it.

MYONGYANG

SEPTEMBER 16, 1597

In a battle later known as the "Miracle of Myongyang," Admiral Yi Sunsin led the Korean Joseon Kingdom's navy to victory against the Japanese navy as it sought to take control of the Yellow Sea. The Korean fleet had been decimated by the Japanese at Chilchonryang earlier that year, and Yi is said to have had only 13 *panokseons* (cannon-armed vessels propelled by sails and oars) to face ten times as many Japanese warships.

The tactically brilliant Yi used his knowledge of the local conditions to change the odds. After holding off the Japanese at Oranpo, Yi withdrew to the Myongyang Strait, where the strong currents changed direction every three hours. When the Japanese fleet entered the Strait, it was carried toward the Yellow Sea, straight to where Yi's ships were waiting in the narrow passage to unleash a barrage of cannon fire and fire arrows. By the time the currents changed, the Japanese fleet was already in chaos. Japan lost about 30 ships and many of its officers in the battle, and the fleet commander Todo Takatora was wounded.

LÜTZEN

NOVEMBER 16, 1632

After victory at Breitenfeld (see pp.130–31), the Swedish king Gustavus Adolphus led the Allied forces of the Protestant Union and Sweden south to Bavaria (in southern Germany), where they were eventually pushed back by the Imperial Roman Catholic Army under commander Albrecht von Wallenstein. In September 1632, Wallenstein's forces invaded Saxony, and the two sides clashed at Lützen on November 16. Both forces were relatively evenly matched as they advanced through fog toward each other—each army had about 20,000

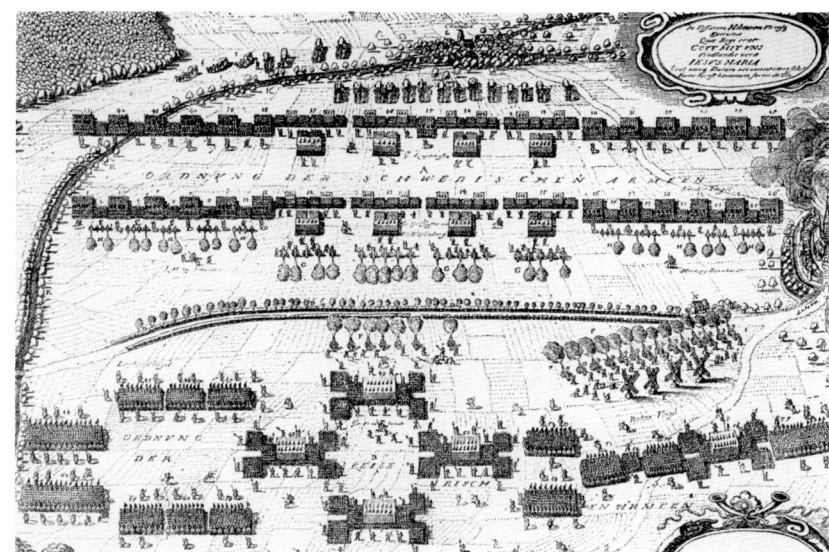

troops. The Swedes began well, driving forward on the right. Count Pappenheim arrived with Imperial reinforcements but was fatally wounded by a cannonball. In the early afternoon, as Gustavus Adolphus led a cavalry charge on the heavily engaged flank, he was separated from his men. He was shot several times, stabbed, and was found fallen from his horse. The rest of the Swedish line was repulsed by the Imperial center and right; determined to avenge their king, they returned to the fray and eventually captured the Imperial guns after bitter fighting. Wallenstein retreated under cover of night. The battle was one of the most important of the Thirty Years War (1618–48) and ended the Catholic threat to Saxony. However, with the death of Gustavus Adolphus, the "Lion of the North," the Protestant cause lost one of its most able leaders and Sweden lost the king who had overseen its rise as one of Europe's great powers.

◁ Plan showing the Protestant Swedish Army arrayed against the Roman Catholic Imperial Army at Lützen

SOLEBAY

JUNE 7, 1672

In April 1672, the English king Charles II declared war on the Dutch Republic. By early June 1672, the allied English and French fleets were anchored in Southwold Bay (also called Solebay) on the Suffolk coast in East England, under the command of the Duke of York. The Dutch fleet surprised them at dawn on June 7 with the wind in its sails. The allied ships hastily prepared for battle and struggled out to sea.

Whether a deliberate decision or due to a misunderstanding, the Comte d'Estrées, commanding the French fleet, steered the 30 French ships south and engaged only at long range, while most of the Dutch fleet focused its attacks on the 60 English ships. The *Royal James*, the flagship of the Earl of Sandwich, was raked with broadsides at point-blank range and then struck by a fire ship. The fighting ended at sunset with both fleets losing many men and having many ships damaged. Although inconclusive, the Battle of Solebay still ended Anglo-French plans to blockade the Dutch.

△ The burning of HMS *Royal James* in the battle

THE BOYNE

JULY 1, 1690

In the Glorious Revolution of 1688, the Catholic King of England and Ireland, James II, was deposed by his nephew and son-in-law, the Protestant William III, known as William of Orange. Determined to regain his crown, James landed in Ireland in 1689 with an under-equipped force of French troops and English, Scottish, and Irish volunteers. He quickly gained control of most of Ireland and moved to Dublin. In June 1690, William landed in Ulster and headed south with about 36,000 men, including professional soldiers from Holland and Denmark armed with modern flintlocks.

The two armies met on July 1, 1690, on the banks of the River Boyne, 30 miles (48km) north of Dublin. William sent a third of his men to cross the river at Roughgrange in a flanking maneuver, and James sent half his army to meet them. The two forces never engaged—they were kept apart by a swampy ravine throughout the battle. Meanwhile, William's elite Dutch Blue Guards drove back the Jacobite infantry at the Oldbridge ford. The Jacobite cavalry

△ Medal commemorating the battle

held them there until William's cavalry crossed the river, forcing the Jacobites to retreat. James fled to France, leaving his still largely intact army to fight a desperate rearguard action. After the battle, Dublin and Waterford soon capitulated and by the end of 1691, all of southern Ireland had been subdued. The battle marked the start of Ireland's social, political, and economic domination by the Protestant minority.

1700–1900

TECHNOLOGY BECAME EVER MORE IMPORTANT ON THE BATTLEFIELD, AS DID INCREASES IN PROFESSIONALISM AND THE USE OF CONSCRIPTION. THE FIRST TRULY GLOBAL WAR TOOK PLACE ACROSS EUROPE, INDIA, AND THE AMERICAS, WHILE THE INDUSTRIAL ERA BROUGHT VAST IMPROVEMENTS IN FIREPOWER.

1700–1900

Warfare changed radically in the 18th and 19th centuries. Professional armies and navies fought wars on a global scale, while massed conscripts clashed in their hundreds of thousands. The exploitation of new technologies and resources became just as important as fighting spirit.

△ **Imperial crest**
This silver-plated grenadier's cap plate shows the crest of Tsar Peter III, whose grandfather Peter the Great made Russia a reputable military power around 1700.

▽ **Doomed charge**
British painter Elizabeth Thompson depicts the charge of the Royal Scots Greys at Waterloo in her 19th-century painting *Scotland Forever*. The Scots overran a French infantry formation but were decimated by the reserve cavalry.

By 1700, European powers were still embroiled in the dynastic conflicts they had conducted for centuries. Although the Duke of Marlborough's Anglo-Austrian army that beat the French in 1714 during the War of the Spanish Succession was large compared to its predecessors, and the Duke himself was a military genius, the technology and tactics he deployed were generally similar to those used earlier.

The Seven Years' War (1756–63) signaled a change. Beginning as a territorial dispute between Austria and Prussia over Silesia (in present-day central Europe), it

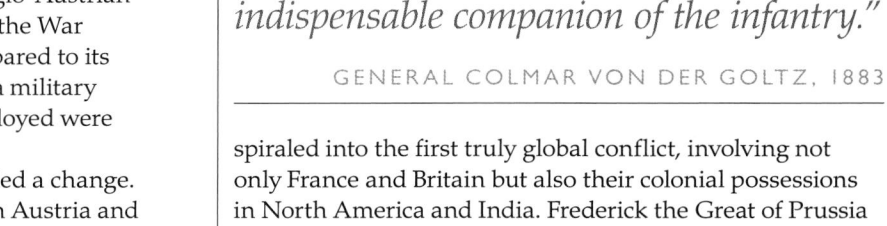

"Now, more than ever, the artillery is the indispensable companion of the infantry."

GENERAL COLMAR VON DER GOLTZ, 1883

spiraled into the first truly global conflict, involving not only France and Britain but also their colonial possessions in North America and India. Frederick the Great of Prussia honed his growing army into a formidable fighting force. His heavy infantry, drilled in rapid battlefield maneuvers, outfought their less well-drilled opponents. Aided by the king's tactical brilliance, they won stunning victories such as at Leuthen (see p.151) in 1757.

Large armies trained to perform traditional maneuvers proved to be of less use in North America, where the American colonies rose up against Britain over political rights and unjust taxation. With local knowledge and adept use of skirmishing tactics and long rifles, the Americans won a War of Independence in 1783. They also laid the framework for a new style of army, composed of citizen-soldiers, which the French adopted and refined after their own revolution in 1789. Within five years, the French army had become a million-strong force, and increasingly began to employ professional leaders to replace old aristocratic officers. Such a massive force required new tactics and organization. Napoleon Bonaparte, whose exceptional leadership was clear from his first commands in Italy where he won victories such as at Marengo (see pp.160–61), came up with these tactics and streamlined military logistics.

CHANGING TIMES

The scope, cost, and casualties of war rose between 1700 and 1900. The size of armies, their professionalism, and the advent of new firearms made warfare a more lethal and expensive proposition. Access to greater manpower resources, money, and technology, and the ability to build global alliances became the prerequisites of military success. As a result of this shift, non-European states struggling against the colonial domination of Europe were left at a distinct disadvantage.

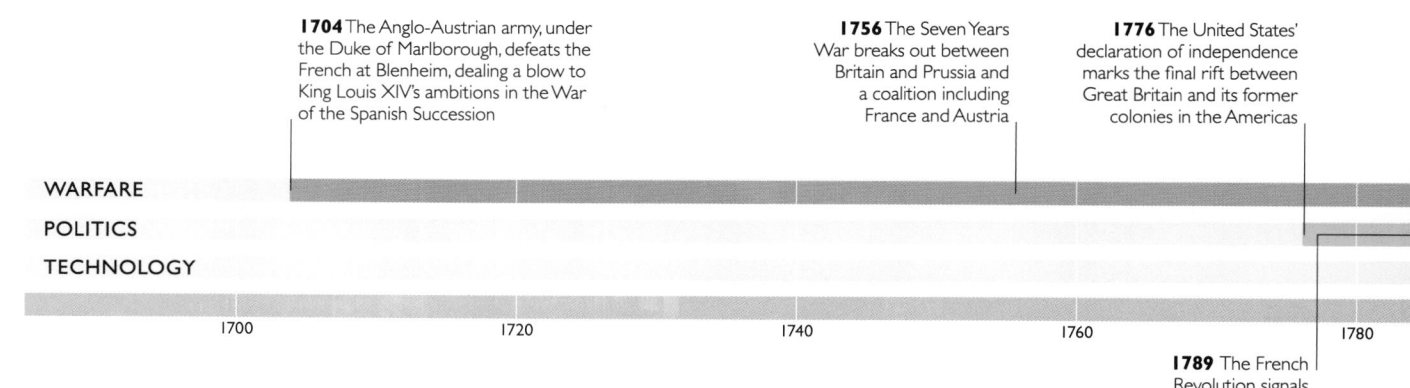

1704 The Anglo-Austrian army, under the Duke of Marlborough, defeats the French at Blenheim, dealing a blow to King Louis XIV's ambitions in the War of the Spanish Succession

1756 The Seven Years War breaks out between Britain and Prussia and a coalition including France and Austria

1776 The United States' declaration of independence marks the final rift between Great Britain and its former colonies in the Americas

WARFARE

POLITICS

TECHNOLOGY

1700   1720   1740   1760   1780

1789 The French Revolution signals the beginning of the Revolutionary and Napoleonic Wars

◁ **Crucial invention**
American-born British inventor Hiram Maxim operates the Maxim gun, an early type of machine gun that he invented in 1884. Its rapid rate of fire allowed small numbers of troops massive killing power.

Napoleon developed the corps as independent smaller formations within his army, and aggressively used outflanking maneuvers to destroy his opponents from the rear. He insisted that his troops live off the land by foraging to reduce dependence on traditional supply lines. These organizational and strategic innovations won Napoleon some stunning successes until the opposing coalitions matched them and turned the tables, leading to his downfall in 1814 and final defeat at Waterloo (see pp.178–79).

The industrialization of war

By the mid-19th century, mass recruitment in combination with growing industrialization led to the first truly modern armies. The Union and Confederate armies, which fought in the American Civil War (1861–65) over the issue of slavery, adopted technologies such as the railroad and the telegraph. They also took up new types of firearms, such as groove-barreled rifles firing minié balls (bullets for rifled muskets) that provided greater range and lethality. This made infantry charges, such as the Confederates' final throw at the Battle of Gettysburg (see pp.186–87), potentially suicidal. In this new environment, non-European armies struggled to compete with the advancing technology of European interlopers, winning only occasional victories, such as the Zulu triumph against the British at Isandlwana (see p.193) in 1879, in the face of tactically inept opponents. Mostly, though, their fate was that of the Sudanese Mahdists at Omdurman (see p.195)—cut down by Maxim guns as they tried to charge against the British forces. In warfare, the future would belong to those who combined this superior technology with effective tactics and strategic leadership.

△ **Final push**
Union troops resist as General George Pickett's Confederate infantry struggles to reach the crest of Cemetery Ridge during the Battle of Gettysburg (see pp.186–87). The charge cost the Confederacy several thousand casualties, and marked the clear defeat of Lee's invasion of the north.

1805 Admiral Horatio Nelson's victory at Trafalgar begins a century of British naval dominance

1815 An Anglo-Prussian army defeats Napoleon Bonaparte, leading to his renewed deposition and exile

1861–65 The American Civil War is fought between the Union and the Confederate states

1863 General Robert E. Lee's defeat at Gettysburg derails the Confederacy's last feasible push to take the Union capital Washington and win the American Civil War

1876 American general George Custer is defeated by a Native American coalition led by Lakota-Sioux at Little Bighorn

| 1800 | 1820 | 1840 | 1860 | 1880 | 1900 |

1815 The Congress of Vienna establishes a new political order after the turmoil of the Napoleonic Wars

1830 The opening of the first intercity railroad ushers in a period where troops can be moved by train

1833 The electric telegraph is developed, helping news move rapidly between capitals and the battle front

1849 The French army adopts Claude-Etienne Minié's minié ball—a bullet that expands in the grooved barrels of rifles, making them easier to load and increasing the range of firearms

1862 American inventor Richard Gatling develops the Gatling gun, the first reliable machine gun to be capable of rapid bursts of fire

1871 The defeat of France and capture of Napoleon III is followed by German unification into the German Empire, as well as similar unification in Italy when Italian forces take Rome

BLENHEIM

In the War of the Spanish Succession (1701–14) between France and the Grand Alliance, Blenheim was key in checking initial French gains. The Duke of Marlborough marched from the Netherlands to the Danube, before leading the Grand Alliance to victory on August 13, 1704, through a bloody but decisive succession of attacks.

In 1700, the Habsburg king of Spain, Charles II, died and left his throne to Philip, the grandson of the Bourbon French king Louis XIV. This succession fueled a rivalry between the two great houses of Europe that broke out into war in 1701. On one side was France and its allies, including Bavaria; on the other side was the Grand Alliance, comprising the Holy Roman Empire, Britain, and the United Provinces of the Netherlands.

In 1704, a Franco-Bavarian force advanced on Vienna, threatening to destroy the Austrian Habsburgs and break the Grand Alliance. To relieve the pressure on Austria, the British commander, the Duke of Marlborough, marched an army from the Low Countries in just five weeks. He was joined by allied forces on the way. The Grand Alliance forces surprised the enemy army when they took up their positions near the town of Blindheim (Blenheim) on the banks of the Danube. Across a wide plain were the Franco-Bavarian forces commanded by the Elector of Bavaria, Marshal Marsin, and Marshal Tallard. They occupied a long rise between the heavily defended villages of Lutzingen, Oberglau, and Blenheim. After heavy fighting on August 13, Marlborough pinned down the enemy forces in the three villages. He then launched the main body of his attack, driving through Tallard's forces in the center to secure a spectacular victory for the Grand Alliance.

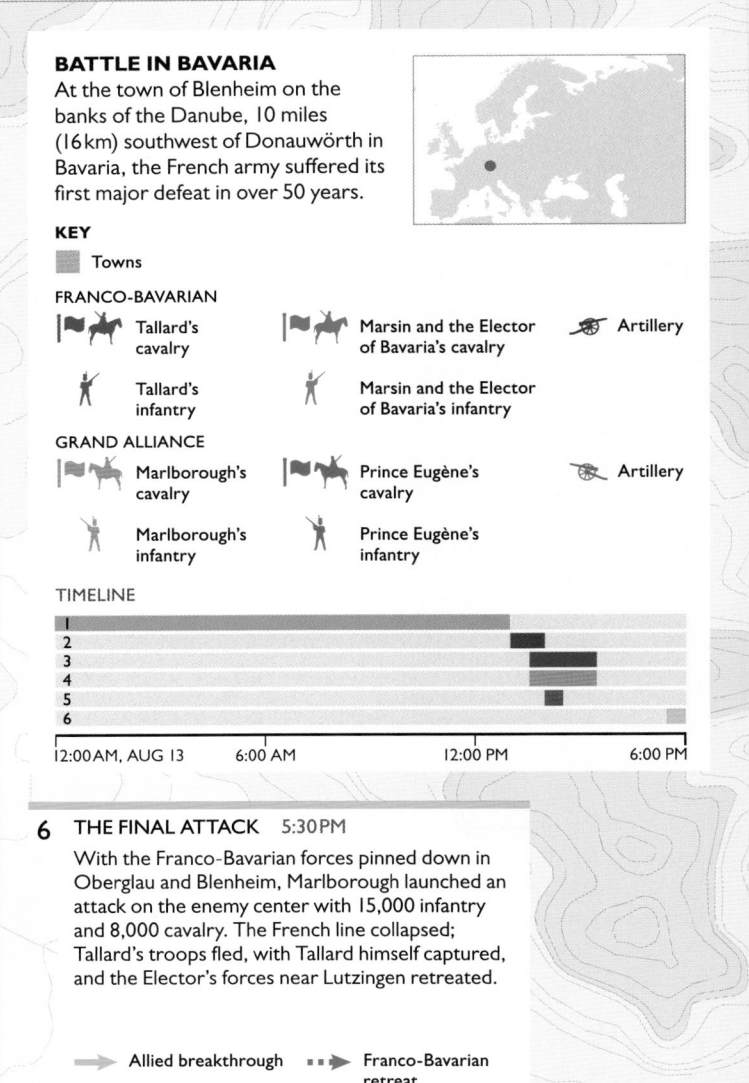

BATTLE IN BAVARIA
At the town of Blenheim on the banks of the Danube, 10 miles (16 km) southwest of Donauwörth in Bavaria, the French army suffered its first major defeat in over 50 years.

KEY

Towns

FRANCO-BAVARIAN

Tallard's cavalry

Tallard's infantry

Marsin and the Elector of Bavaria's cavalry

Marsin and the Elector of Bavaria's infantry

Artillery

GRAND ALLIANCE

Marlborough's cavalry

Marlborough's infantry

Prince Eugène's cavalry

Prince Eugène's infantry

Artillery

TIMELINE

12:00 AM, AUG 13 — 6:00 AM — 12:00 PM — 6:00 PM

6 THE FINAL ATTACK 5:30 PM
With the Franco-Bavarian forces pinned down in Oberglau and Blenheim, Marlborough launched an attack on the enemy center with 15,000 infantry and 8,000 cavalry. The French line collapsed; Tallard's troops fled, with Tallard himself captured, and the Elector's forces near Lutzingen retreated.

Allied breakthrough

Franco-Bavarian retreat

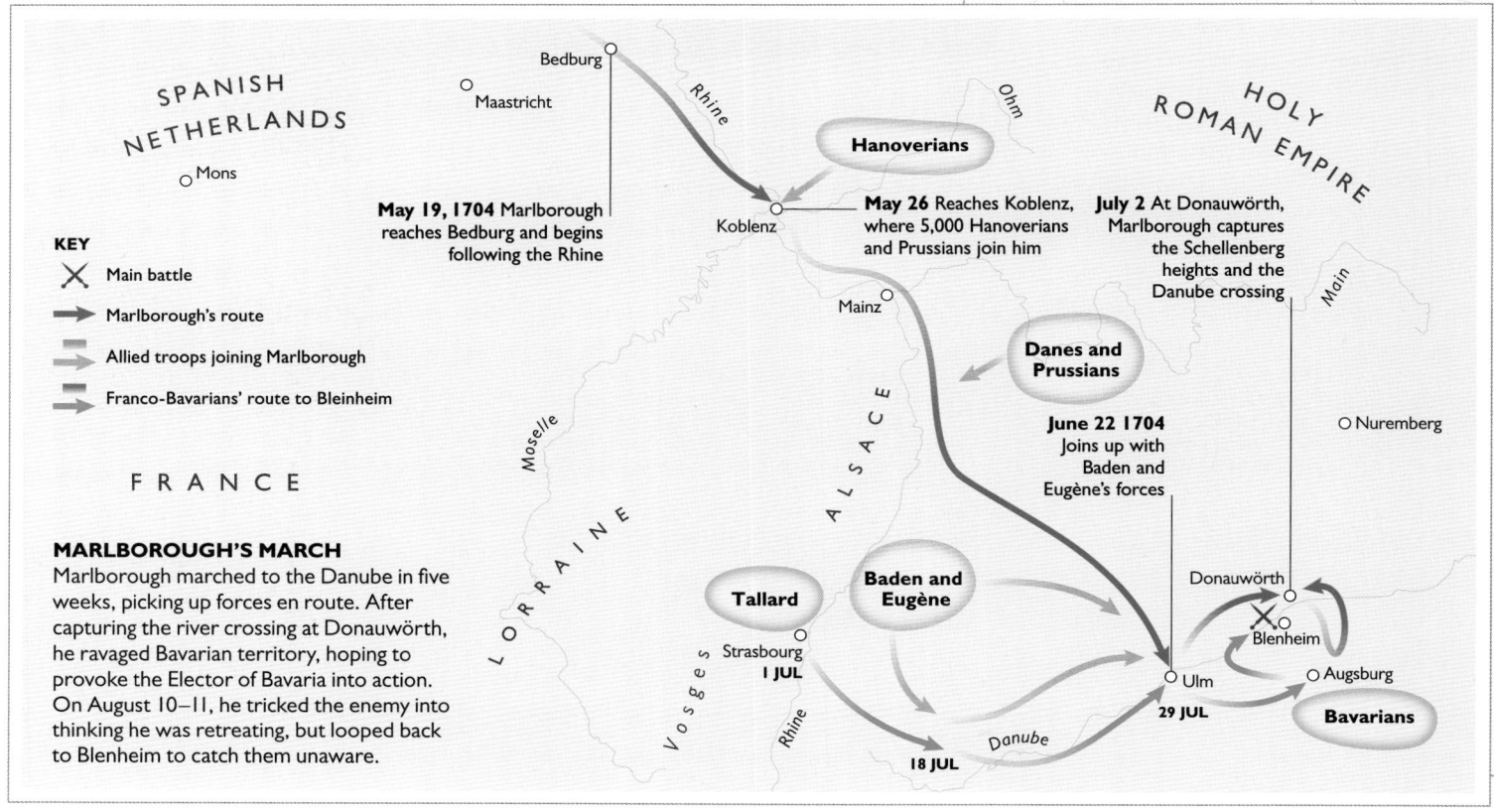

May 19, 1704 Marlborough reaches Bedburg and begins following the Rhine

May 26 Reaches Koblenz, where 5,000 Hanoverians and Prussians join him

July 2 At Donauwörth, Marlborough captures the Schellenberg heights and the Danube crossing

June 22 1704 Joins up with Baden and Eugène's forces

Hanoverians

Danes and Prussians

Tallard

Baden and Eugène

Bavarians

KEY

✕ Main battle

→ Marlborough's route

⇒ Allied troops joining Marlborough

⇒ Franco-Bavarians' route to Bleinheim

MARLBOROUGH'S MARCH
Marlborough marched to the Danube in five weeks, picking up forces en route. After capturing the river crossing at Donauwörth, he ravaged Bavarian territory, hoping to provoke the Elector of Bavaria into action. On August 10–11, he tricked the enemy into thinking he was retreating, but looped back to Blenheim to catch them unaware.

1 TROOP DEPLOYMENTS
12:00 AM–1:00 PM, AUGUST 13, 1704

Overnight on August 12, Marlborough moved his army into position. The 36,000 under his command faced Marshall Tallard's 33,000 men who were concentrated in the villages of Oberglau and Blenheim. To Marlborough's right, 16,000 Imperial soldiers under Prince Eugène of Savoy's command faced Marshal Marsin and the Elector of Bavaria's 23,000-strong army.

2 THE INITIAL ATTACKS   1:00 PM

Marlborough gave orders to advance. On the left, Lord Cutts led his redcoats toward Blenheim; many of them fell as they tried to climb the barricades. On the right, Prince Eugene's Imperial forces, heavily outnumbered by the Elector and Marsin's forces, moved on Lutzingen, only to be repulsed three times.

→ Allied attacks
→ Franco-Bavarian counter charge
⇢ Allied retreat
⇢ Franco-Bavarian retreat

3 A TACTICAL ERROR   AFTERNOON

Further allied attacks on Blenheim provoked the Franco-Bavarians into sending seven battalions from the center and 11 reserve battalions to reinforce the town, which subsequently became clogged with 12,000 troops. These men could not quickly return to the center where they would soon be needed.

→ Franco-Bavarian reinforcements

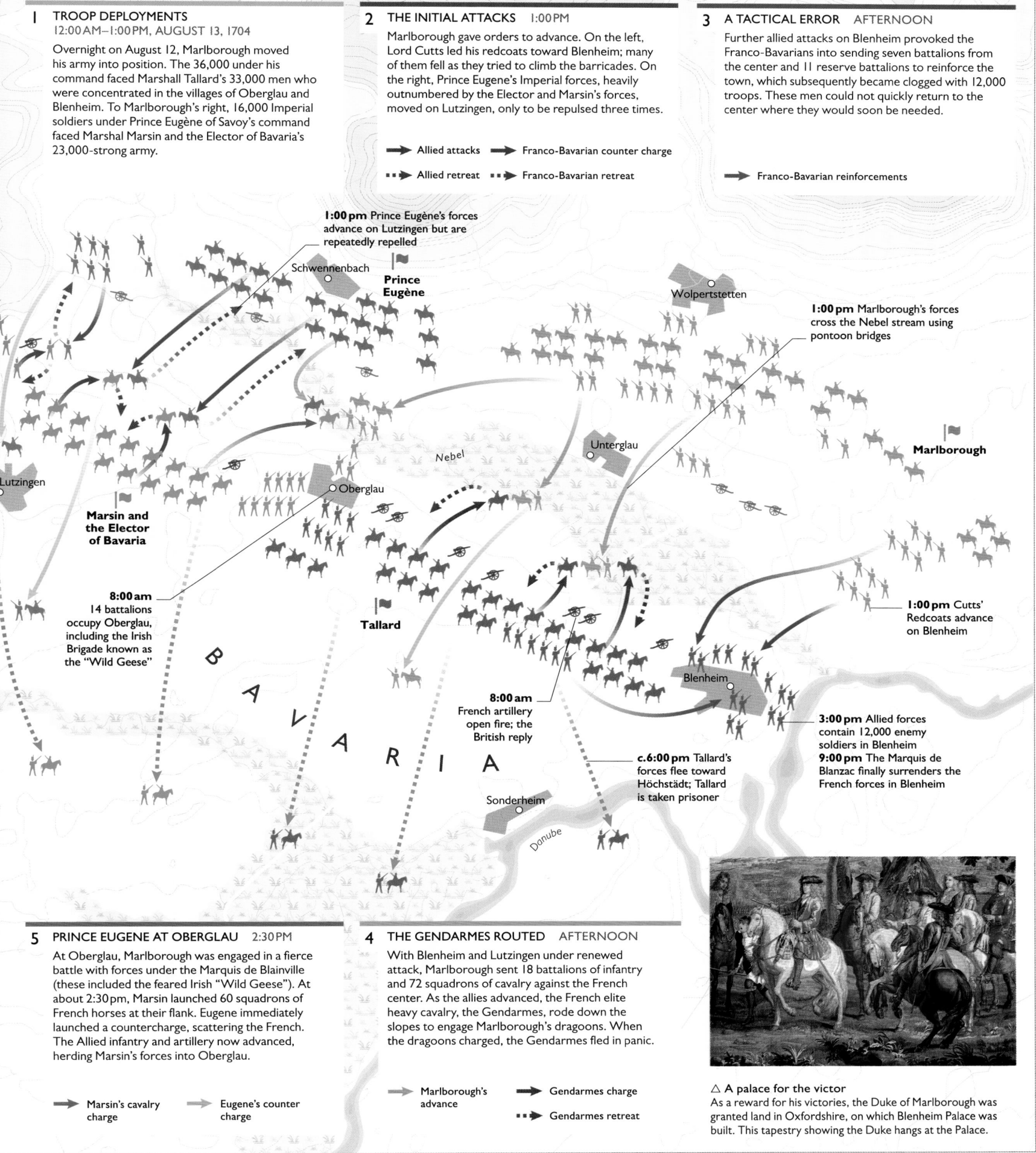

1:00 pm Prince Eugène's forces advance on Lutzingen but are repeatedly repelled

Schwennenbach

Prince Eugène

Wolpertstetten

1:00 pm Marlborough's forces cross the Nebel stream using pontoon bridges

Nebel

Unterglau

Marlborough

Lutzingen

Marsin and the Elector of Bavaria

Oberglau

B A V A R I A

8:00 am 14 battalions occupy Oberglau, including the Irish Brigade known as the "Wild Geese"

Tallard

8:00 am French artillery open fire; the British reply

1:00 pm Cutts' Redcoats advance on Blenheim

Blenheim

3:00 pm Allied forces contain 12,000 enemy soldiers in Blenheim
9:00 pm The Marquis de Blanzac finally surrenders the French forces in Blenheim

c.6:00 pm Tallard's forces flee toward Höchstädt; Tallard is taken prisoner

Sonderheim

Donube

5 PRINCE EUGENE AT OBERGLAU   2:30 PM

At Oberglau, Marlborough was engaged in a fierce battle with forces under the Marquis de Blainville (these included the feared Irish "Wild Geese"). At about 2:30 pm, Marsin launched 60 squadrons of French horses at their flank. Eugene immediately launched a countercharge, scattering the French. The Allied infantry and artillery now advanced, herding Marsin's forces into Oberglau.

→ Marsin's cavalry charge
→ Eugene's counter charge

4 THE GENDARMES ROUTED   AFTERNOON

With Blenheim and Lutzingen under renewed attack, Marlborough sent 18 battalions of infantry and 72 squadrons of cavalry against the French center. As the allies advanced, the French elite heavy cavalry, the Gendarmes, rode down the slopes to engage Marlborough's dragoons. When the dragoons charged, the Gendarmes fled in panic.

→ Marlborough's advance
→ Gendarmes charge
⇢ Gendarmes retreat

△ **A palace for the victor**
As a reward for his victories, the Duke of Marlborough was granted land in Oxfordshire, on which Blenheim Palace was built. This tapestry showing the Duke hangs at the Palace.

THE RISE OF RUSSIA

Charles XII attacked Russia from Grodno, his base in Poland. After their defeat at Poltava, the Swedes lost control of their empire as Peter the Great's Russia came to dominate the Polish and Baltic lands.

KEY

Towns   SWEDISH FORCES   RUSSIAN FORCES

Commander   Infantry   Redoubts

Infantry   Cavalry   Fortifications

Cavalry   Artillery

TIMELINE

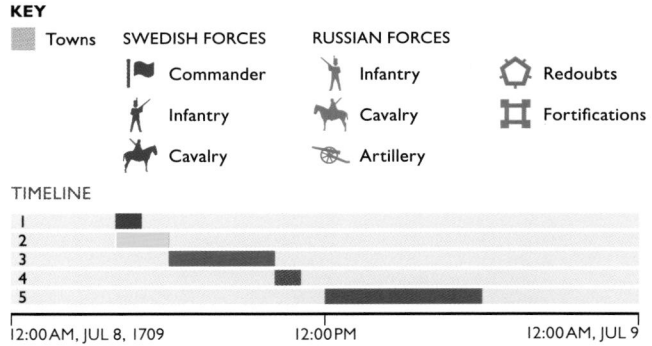

12:00 AM, JUL 8, 1709   12:00 PM   12:00 AM, JUL 9

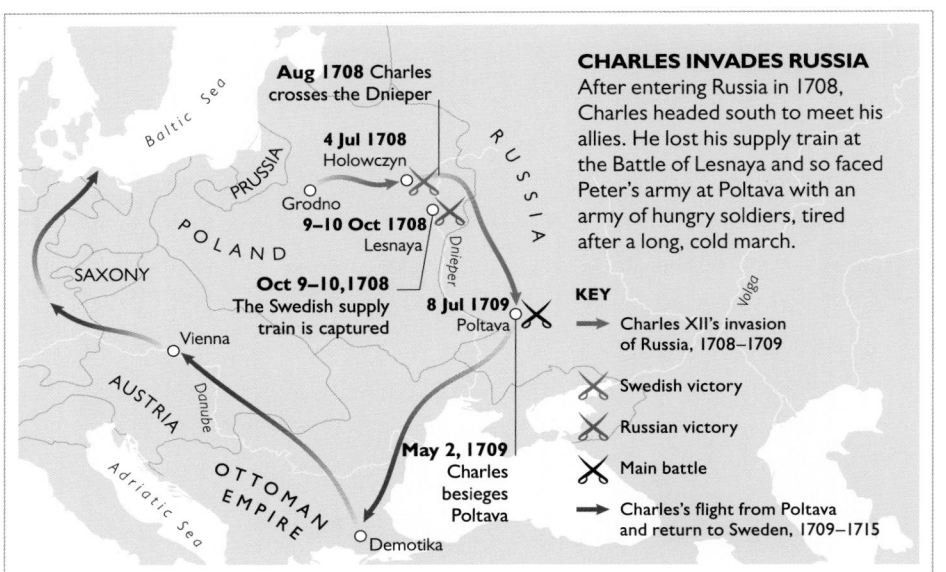

CHARLES INVADES RUSSIA

After entering Russia in 1708, Charles headed south to meet his allies. He lost his supply train at the Battle of Lesnaya and so faced Peter's army at Poltava with an army of hungry soldiers, tired after a long, cold march.

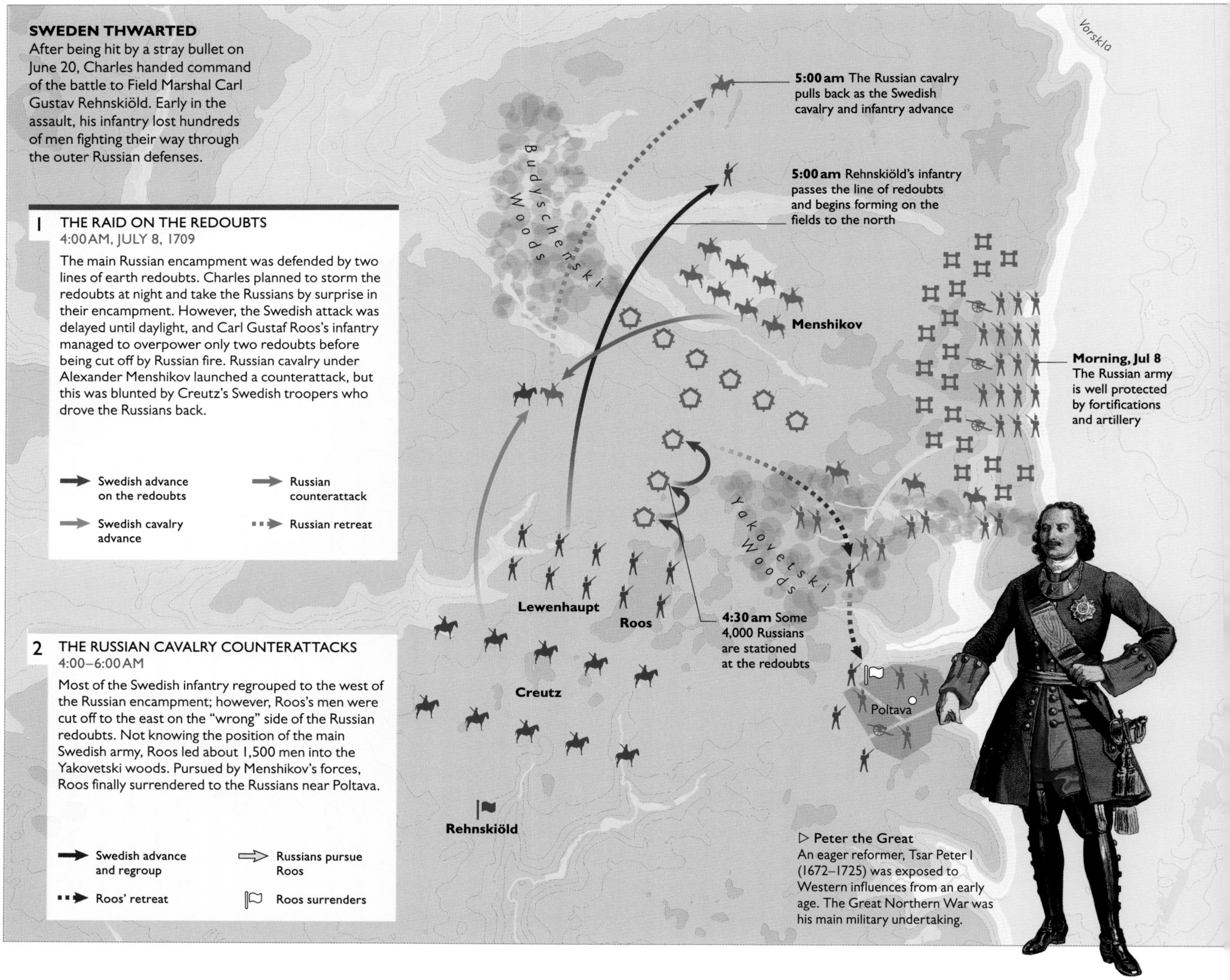

Aug 1708 Charles crosses the Dnieper

4 Jul 1708 Holowczyn

9–10 Oct 1708 Lesnaya

Oct 9–10, 1708 The Swedish supply train is captured

8 Jul 1709 Poltava

May 2, 1709 Charles besieges Poltava

KEY

→ Charles XII's invasion of Russia, 1708–1709

⚔ Swedish victory

⚔ Russian victory

⚔ Main battle

→ Charles's flight from Poltava and return to Sweden, 1709–1715

SWEDEN THWARTED

After being hit by a stray bullet on June 20, Charles handed command of the battle to Field Marshal Carl Gustav Rehnskiöld. Early in the assault, his infantry lost hundreds of men fighting their way through the outer Russian defenses.

1 THE RAID ON THE REDOUBTS
4:00 AM, JULY 8, 1709

The main Russian encampment was defended by two lines of earth redoubts. Charles planned to storm the redoubts at night and take the Russians by surprise in their encampment. However, the Swedish attack was delayed until daylight, and Carl Gustaf Roos's infantry managed to overpower only two redoubts before being cut off by Russian fire. Russian cavalry under Alexander Menshikov launched a counterattack, but this was blunted by Creutz's Swedish troopers who drove the Russians back.

→ Swedish advance on the redoubts

→ Swedish cavalry advance

→ Russian counterattack

⇢ Russian retreat

2 THE RUSSIAN CAVALRY COUNTERATTACKS
4:00–6:00 AM

Most of the Swedish infantry regrouped to the west of the Russian encampment; however, Roos's men were cut off to the east on the "wrong" side of the Russian redoubts. Not knowing the position of the main Swedish army, Roos led about 1,500 men into the Yakovetski woods. Pursued by Menshikov's forces, Roos finally surrendered to the Russians near Poltava.

→ Swedish advance and regroup

⇨ Russians pursue Roos

⇢ Roos' retreat

⚑ Roos surrenders

5:00 am The Russian cavalry pulls back as the Swedish cavalry and infantry advance

5:00 am Rehnskiöld's infantry passes the line of redoubts and begins forming on the fields to the north

Budyschenski Woods

Menshikov

Morning, Jul 8 The Russian army is well protected by fortifications and artillery

Yakovetski Woods

Lewenhaupt

Roos

4:30 am Some 4,000 Russians are stationed at the redoubts

Creutz

Poltava

Rehnskiöld

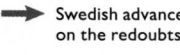

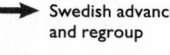

▷ **Peter the Great**
An eager reformer, Tsar Peter I (1672–1725) was exposed to Western influences from an early age. The Great Northern War was his main military undertaking.

Vorskla

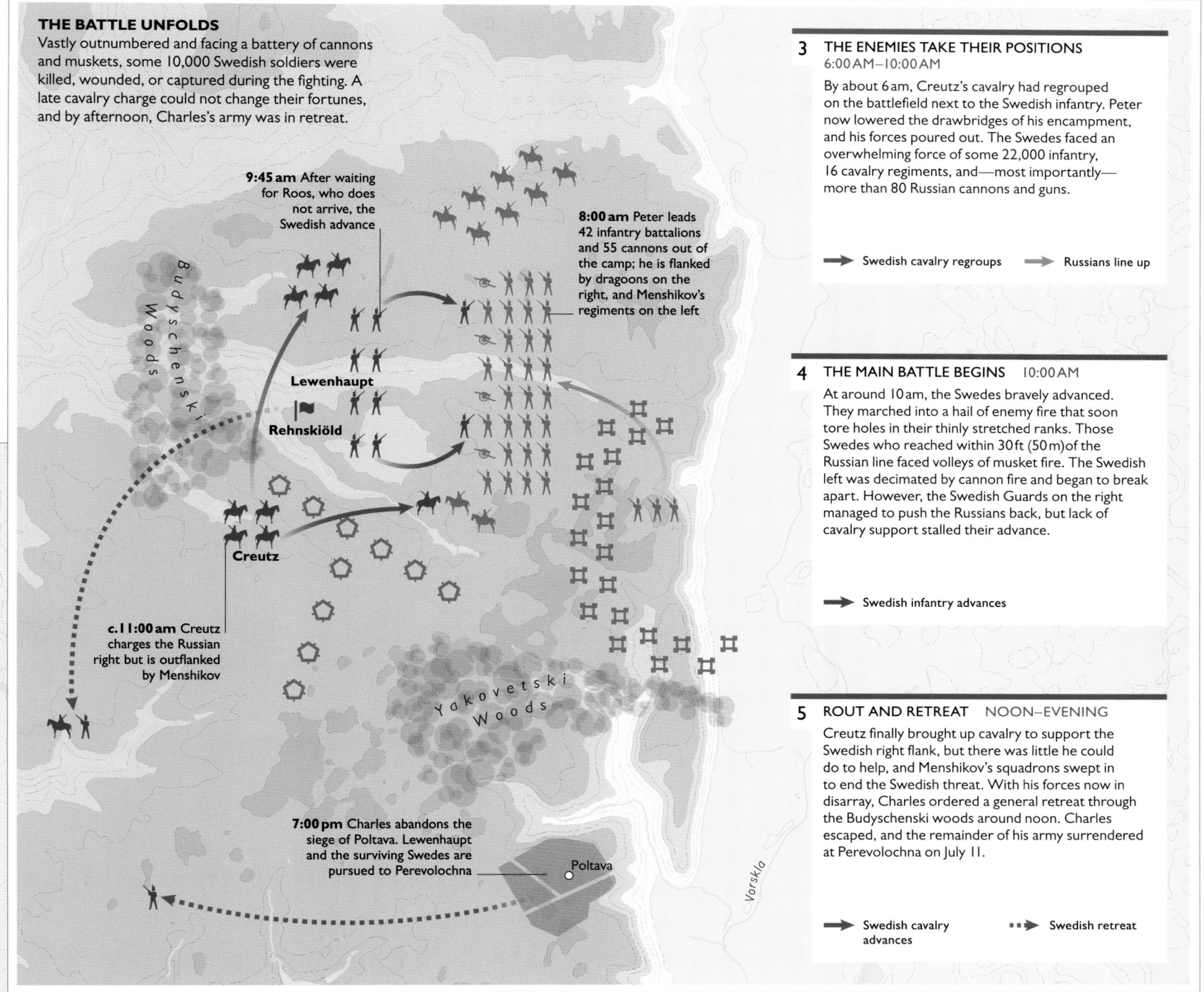

THE BATTLE UNFOLDS
Vastly outnumbered and facing a battery of cannons and muskets, some 10,000 Swedish soldiers were killed, wounded, or captured during the fighting. A late cavalry charge could not change their fortunes, and by afternoon, Charles's army was in retreat.

9:45 am After waiting for Roos, who does not arrive, the Swedish advance

8:00 am Peter leads 42 infantry battalions and 55 cannons out of the camp; he is flanked by dragoons on the right, and Menshikov's regiments on the left

Budyschenski Woods

Lewenhaupt

Rehnskiöld

Creutz

c.11:00 am Creutz charges the Russian right but is outflanked by Menshikov

Yakovetski Woods

7:00 pm Charles abandons the siege of Poltava. Lewenhaupt and the surviving Swedes are pursued to Perevolochna

Poltava

Vorskla

3 THE ENEMIES TAKE THEIR POSITIONS
6:00 AM–10:00 AM

By about 6am, Creutz's cavalry had regrouped on the battlefield next to the Swedish infantry. Peter now lowered the drawbridges of his encampment, and his forces poured out. The Swedes faced an overwhelming force of some 22,000 infantry, 16 cavalry regiments, and—most importantly—more than 80 Russian cannons and guns.

→ Swedish cavalry regroups → Russians line up

4 THE MAIN BATTLE BEGINS 10:00 AM

At around 10am, the Swedes bravely advanced. They marched into a hail of enemy fire that soon tore holes in their thinly stretched ranks. Those Swedes who reached within 30ft (50m) of the Russian line faced volleys of musket fire. The Swedish left was decimated by cannon fire and began to break apart. However, the Swedish Guards on the right managed to push the Russians back, but lack of cavalry support stalled their advance.

→ Swedish infantry advances

5 ROUT AND RETREAT NOON–EVENING

Creutz finally brought up cavalry to support the Swedish right flank, but there was little he could do to help, and Menshikov's squadrons swept in to end the Swedish threat. With his forces now in disarray, Charles ordered a general retreat through the Budyschenski woods around noon. Charles escaped, and the remainder of his army surrendered at Perevolochna on July 11.

→ Swedish cavalry advances ▪▪▶ Swedish retreat

POLTAVA

In July 1709, Tsar Peter the Great and the Russian army defeated the Swedish forces of King Charles XII at Poltava, in present-day Ukraine. Peter's victory signaled the beginning of Russian supremacy in northeast Europe and the decline of the Swedish Empire as a great power.

The Great Northern War (1700–21) began by Poland-Saxony, Russia, and Denmark attempting to dismantle the Swedish Empire, which had dominated the Baltic region for a century. By 1709, however, it had become a contest between two ambitious rulers: the gifted general Charles XII of Sweden, and Peter I, who was transforming Russia into a powerful modern state. Charles's army invaded Russia in 1708, and after a cold, crippling march,

arrived at the fortified town of Poltava (in the territory of the Cossack Hetmanate), which it besieged. Eager to break the siege and crush the Swedes, Peter deployed his army of about 40,000 (against more than 25,000) in a encampment protected by ten redoubts. The Swedes planned an audacious, surprise night advance, but it failed: a third of the attacking infantry was caught in the redoubts, and the rest were overwhelmed by the full weight of the Russian army.

ADVANCES IN SIEGE WARFARE

Across Europe, the design of fortifications and the conduct of sieges entered a new era in the late 17th century as innovative engineers made significant developments in construction and tactics.

△ **Reign of sieges**
The French king Louis XIV oversaw the construction of several fortifications along France's frontiers, and was present at half of Vauban's 40 sieges.

Siege warfare had been a prominent feature of European warfare since the 11th century, when castles became widespread and sieges began to outnumber pitched battles. The introduction of cannons in the 15th century revolutionized castle design, resulting in the development of "star forts"—polygonal fortresses with bastions protruding at each angle— designed to withstand cannon fire.

By the start of the 17th century, fortifications had become more complex and added outworks such as ravelins to the star-fort design (see below). Structures were built lower and used earth to better withstand cannon fire. By Louis XIV's reign (1643–1715) in France, sieges had become the focal point of conflicts. The influence of the king's chief engineer, Sébastien le Prestre de Vauban (later Marquis), on the design of fortifications and siege warfare was huge. A scientific approach allowed him to adapt siege warfare to incorporate increasingly powerful guns. Vauban also constructed fortresses and fortified cities, and built two lines of forts along France's northeastern frontier.

Weaponry evolved for siege warfare, including mortars that launched explosive shells over walls or into siege trenches, and grenades hurled by grenadiers, a new type of elite soldier.

△ **Enhanced Spanish defenses**
This plan of a mid-17th century fortification in Badajoz shows improvements made to the star-fort design. Wedge-shaped bastions, or outworks, called "ravelins" or "demilunes," provided tactical advantage for artillery fire.

Louis XIV's assault, 1673
The king's army besieges the fortress city of Maastricht in this 17th-century painting by Flemish painter Adam Frans van der Meulen. The French army overcame the Dutch defenses within a month, and this siege saw the introduction of the siege parallel by Vauban.

PLASSEY

Treachery and luck helped secure the British East India Company a victory over the Nawab of Bengal supported by a few French guns at Plassey, Bengal, on June 23, 1757. The battle helped secure British domination in India.

In the 1750s, French, Dutch, and British companies competed for trade in Bengal. The Nawab (ruler) of Bengal, Siraj-ud-Daula, resented the trade practices and colonial ambitions of the British East India Company (EIC), so in June 1756 he marched with a large army and captured the British trading post of Calcutta (Kolkata). EIC reinforcements under Colonel Robert Clive retook the city in January 1757. By this time, Britain and France were fighting in what became the Seven Years' War (see p.142), so Clive decided to capture the French trading base at Chandernagore (Chandannager). This prompted the Nawab to ally with the French in a bid to oust the British. At a battle fought near Plassey (Palashi) on June 23, the British were outnumbered. Some Bengali commanders, however, including their chief Mir Jafar, had secretly agreed not to fight. This, together with the enemy's lack of usable powder, helped Clive win the battle.

△ **Nawab's artillery**
The Bengali artillery pieces, complete with gunners, cannonballs, and powder, were carried on giant platforms. These were pulled by teams of 50 oxen, sometimes assisted by elephants.

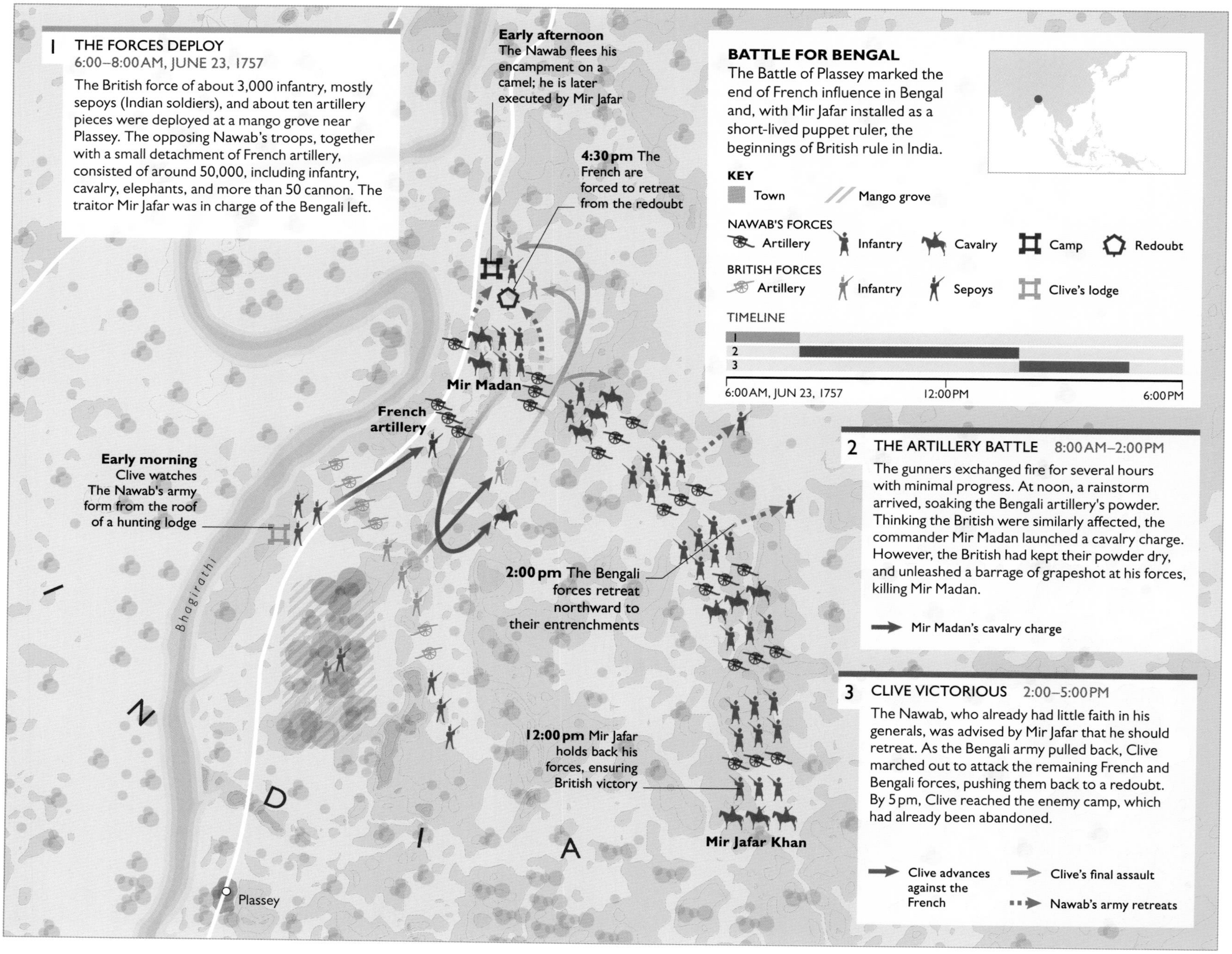

---

1 THE FORCES DEPLOY
6:00–8:00 AM, JUNE 23, 1757

The British force of about 3,000 infantry, mostly sepoys (Indian soldiers), and about ten artillery pieces were deployed at a mango grove near Plassey. The opposing Nawab's troops, together with a small detachment of French artillery, consisted of around 50,000, including infantry, cavalry, elephants, and more than 50 cannon. The traitor Mir Jafar was in charge of the Bengali left.

Early afternoon
The Nawab flees his encampment on a camel; he is later executed by Mir Jafar

4:30 pm The French are forced to retreat from the redoubt

Mir Madan

French artillery

Early morning
Clive watches The Nawab's army form from the roof of a hunting lodge

Bhagirathi

2:00 pm The Bengali forces retreat northward to their entrenchments

12:00 pm Mir Jafar holds back his forces, ensuring British victory

Mir Jafar Khan

Plassey

BATTLE FOR BENGAL
The Battle of Plassey marked the end of French influence in Bengal and, with Mir Jafar installed as a short-lived puppet ruler, the beginnings of British rule in India.

KEY

▨ Town	⫽ Mango grove		

NAWAB'S FORCES
Artillery · Infantry · Cavalry · ⬡ Camp · ⬡ Redoubt

BRITISH FORCES
Artillery · Infantry · Sepoys · Clive's lodge

TIMELINE

1
2
3
6:00 AM, JUN 23, 1757 — 12:00 PM — 6:00 PM

2 THE ARTILLERY BATTLE   8:00 AM–2:00 PM
The gunners exchanged fire for several hours with minimal progress. At noon, a rainstorm arrived, soaking the Bengali artillery's powder. Thinking the British were similarly affected, the commander Mir Madan launched a cavalry charge. However, the British had kept their powder dry, and unleashed a barrage of grapeshot at his forces, killing Mir Madan.

→ Mir Madan's cavalry charge

3 CLIVE VICTORIOUS   2:00–5:00 PM
The Nawab, who already had little faith in his generals, was advised by Mir Jafar that he should retreat. As the Bengali army pulled back, Clive marched out to attack the remaining French and Bengali forces, pushing them back to a redoubt. By 5 pm, Clive reached the enemy camp, which had already been abandoned.

→ Clive advances against the French
→ Clive's final assault
⇢ Nawab's army retreats

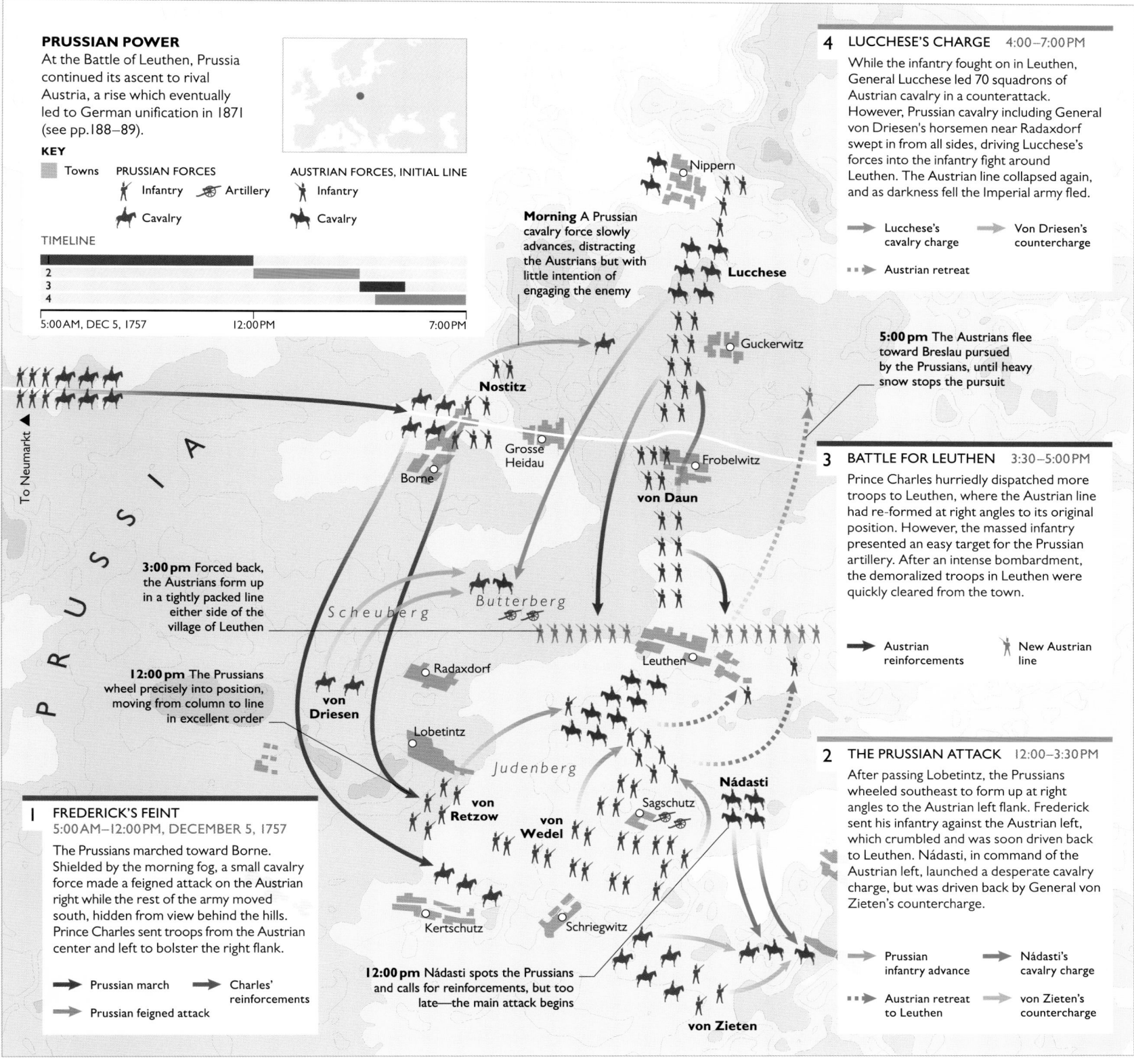

PRUSSIAN POWER

At the Battle of Leuthen, Prussia continued its ascent to rival Austria, a rise which eventually led to German unification in 1871 (see pp.188–89).

KEY

Towns

PRUSSIAN FORCES
- Infantry
- Artillery
- Cavalry

AUSTRIAN FORCES, INITIAL LINE
- Infantry
- Cavalry

TIMELINE

5:00 AM, DEC 5, 1757   12:00 PM   7:00 PM

Morning A Prussian cavalry force slowly advances, distracting the Austrians but with little intention of engaging the enemy

4 LUCCHESE'S CHARGE   4:00–7:00 PM

While the infantry fought on in Leuthen, General Lucchese led 70 squadrons of Austrian cavalry in a counterattack. However, Prussian cavalry including General von Driesen's horsemen near Radaxdorf swept in from all sides, driving Lucchese's forces into the infantry fight around Leuthen. The Austrian line collapsed again, and as darkness fell the Imperial army fled.

- Lucchese's cavalry charge
- Von Driesen's countercharge
- Austrian retreat

5:00 pm The Austrians flee toward Breslau pursued by the Prussians, until heavy snow stops the pursuit

3 BATTLE FOR LEUTHEN   3:30–5:00 PM

Prince Charles hurriedly dispatched more troops to Leuthen, where the Austrian line had re-formed at right angles to its original position. However, the massed infantry presented an easy target for the Prussian artillery. After an intense bombardment, the demoralized troops in Leuthen were quickly cleared from the town.

- Austrian reinforcements
- New Austrian line

3:00 pm Forced back, the Austrians form up in a tightly packed line either side of the village of Leuthen

12:00 pm The Prussians wheel precisely into position, moving from column to line in excellent order

2 THE PRUSSIAN ATTACK   12:00–3:30 PM

After passing Lobetintz, the Prussians wheeled southeast to form up at right angles to the Austrian left flank. Frederick sent his infantry against the Austrian left, which crumbled and was soon driven back to Leuthen. Nádasti, in command of the Austrian left, launched a desperate cavalry charge, but was driven back by General von Zieten's countercharge.

- Prussian infantry advance
- Nádasti's cavalry charge
- Austrian retreat to Leuthen
- von Zieten's countercharge

1 FREDERICK'S FEINT
5:00 AM–12:00 PM, DECEMBER 5, 1757

The Prussians marched toward Borne. Shielded by the morning fog, a small cavalry force made a feigned attack on the Austrian right while the rest of the army moved south, hidden from view behind the hills. Prince Charles sent troops from the Austrian center and left to bolster the right flank.

- Prussian march
- Prussian feigned attack
- Charles' reinforcements

12:00 pm Nádasti spots the Prussians and calls for reinforcements, but too late—the main attack begins

Map labels: Nippern, Lucchese, Guckerwitz, Nostitz, Grosse Heidau, Borne, Frobelwitz, von Daun, Scheuberg, Butterberg, Radaxdorf, Leuthen, von Driesen, Lobetintz, Judenberg, Nádasti, von Retzow, Sagschutz, von Wedel, Kertschutz, Schriegwitz, von Zieten, To Neumarkt, PRUSSIA

LEUTHEN

The 1757 Battle of Leuthen was one of the key battles in the Seven Years' War. Frederick II of Prussia achieved victory against a much larger Austrian army, and his audacious flanking maneuver confirmed his reputation as Europe's foremost military commander.

In Europe, the main conflict of the Seven Years' War (see p.142) centered on attempts by France and the Austrian Habsburg Empire to constrain an expansionist Prussia led by Frederick II. In late 1757, Frederick returned from facing the French to confront the Austrians, who had retaken Silesia. On December 5, an Imperial force of over 60,000 under Prince Charles of Lorraine and Count von Daun gathered at Leuthen (Lutynia, in modern-day Poland) to tackle Frederick. The vast Austrian army, stretching 5 miles (8 km) across, faced Frederick's force of about 35,000 men, situated on a low line of hills. After feinting toward the Austrian right, Frederick moved his troops, hidden by the hills, across the enemy front to attack the Austrian left—a bold move that required great discipline from his troops. Losses were heavy on both sides, but Frederick's tactic paid off and the Austrians were routed.

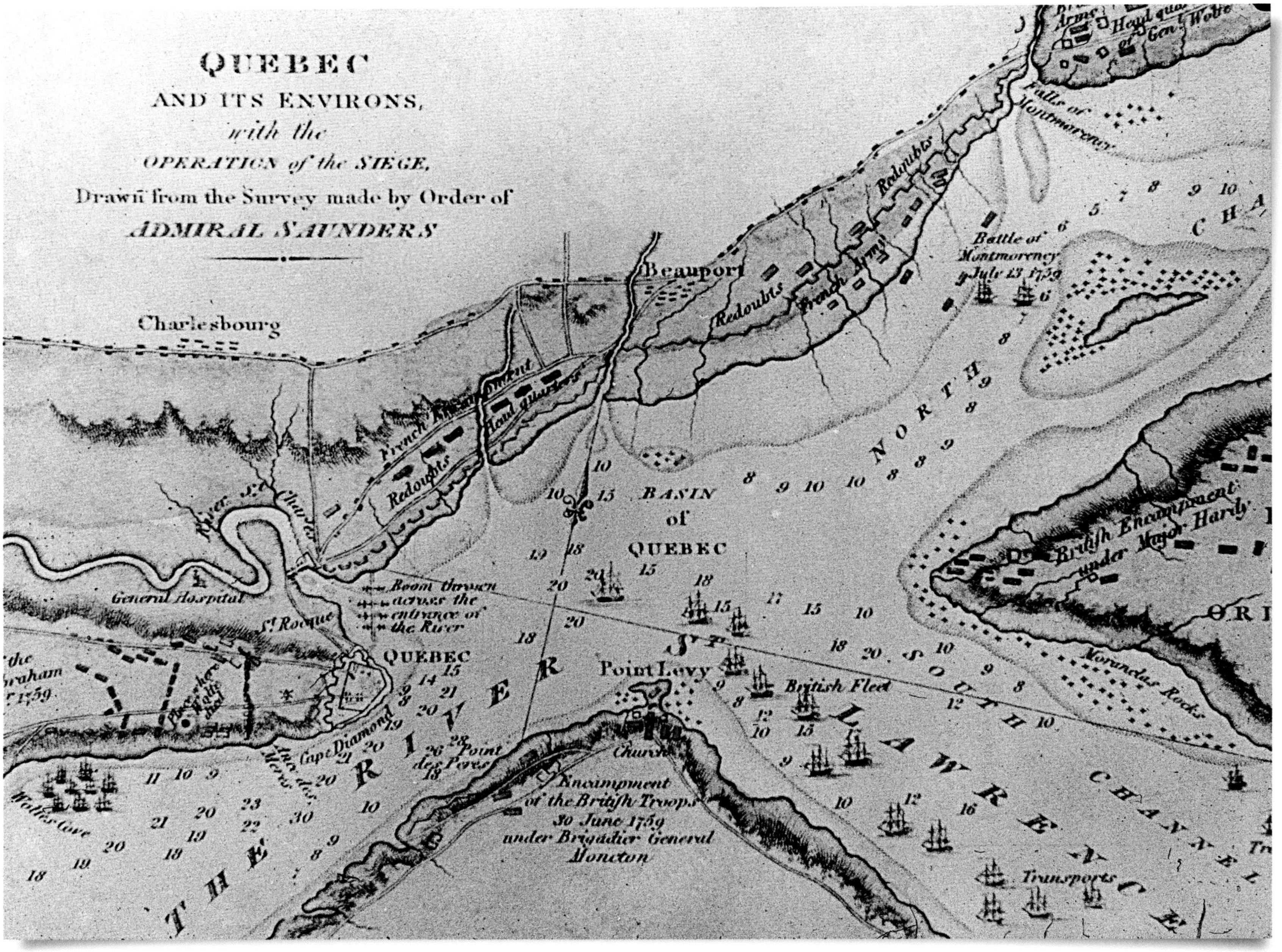

QUEBEC
AND ITS ENVIRONS,
with the
OPERATION of the SIEGE,
Drawn from the Survey made by Order of
ADMIRAL SAUNDERS

PLAINS OF ABRAHAM

In this pivotal battle in the French and Indian War (1754–63), a British force under Major General James Wolfe surprised the French at Quebec, capturing the town after a three-month siege. The battle paved the way for British control of Canada.

△ **Siege of Quebec**
Based on a survey ordered by the British fleet commander, this map shows the French defenses during the siege of Quebec, including the boom blocking the St. Charles River and the coastal strongholds.

In June 1759, five years after Britain and France started fighting for control of North America, a British force under General James Wolfe traveled up the St. Lawrence River to attack Quebec, the capital city of the colony of New France, which had been claimed by the French in 1534. Wolfe established a base opposite Quebec on the Île d'Orléans and besieged the city. His attempt to land at Beauport on July 31 was repelled, and illness swept through the British camp. By September, Wolfe was running out of time before the winter, when ice would inevitably force him to withdraw. Wolfe gambled on landing upstream west

of Quebec at L'Anse-au-Foulon, a cove at the bottom of the 177-ft (54-m) high promontory of Quebec. On September 12, under cover of dark, Colonel William Howe and 24 volunteers scaled the cliff, overpowered the French garrison, and secured the area. By morning, more than 4,000 British soldiers had assembled on the Plains of Abraham. The French, led by the Marquis de Montcalm, marched out from Quebec to repel the British threat to their supply line from Montreal. Both Montcalm and Wolfe were fatally wounded, but the French were driven back by close range musketry, and Quebec surrendered on September 18.

KEY

1 Wolfe besieged Quebec from the Île d'Orléans (June 28–September 18, 1759).

2 A small British force climbed the cliffs at L'Anse-au-Foulon and secured the road.

3 The British lay down to avoid cannon fire, before firing two point-blank musket volleys.

BUNKER HILL

In the first major battle of the American Revolutionary War (1775–83), the British suffered heavy losses while dislodging a group of patriots from two hills in Charlestown, near Boston. The action only strengthened the patriots' determination to secure independence for Britain's American colonies.

Increasing tension between Britain and its American colonies over taxation, self-rule, trade, territorial expansion, and more led to the American Revolutionary War in April 1775. After skirmishes between patriots (who wanted independence) and loyalists (supporters of the British regime) at Lexington and Concord, Massachusetts, rebel militias besieged Boston. By June 17, 1775, some 6,000 British troops were hemmed in by 15,000 American patriots, who had also just occupied the Charlestown peninsula overlooking the British positions in Boston. The British commander-in-chief,

General Thomas Gage, ordered General William Howe—who had scaled the cliffs at Quebec in 1759—to lead the British forces into their first major battle of the war. After an artillery bombardment, British troops landed on the peninsula, but it took three attempts before the patriots were pushed back, and more than 1,000 British forces were killed or injured, while the patriots had only 450 casualties. A hollow victory for the British, it served only to give heart to the patriots, who saw how well they could fare against Britain's famously disciplined redcoats.

WAR OF INDEPENDENCE
New England was at the heart of the American Revolution and was the scene of the first skirmishes of the war, at Lexington and Concord, near Boston (April 19, 1775).

KEY

AMERICAN FORCES
- Troops
- Artillery

BRITISH FORCES
- Troops
- Fleet
- Artillery

TIMELINE

1		
2		
3		

JUN 16, 1775   JUN 17   JUN 18

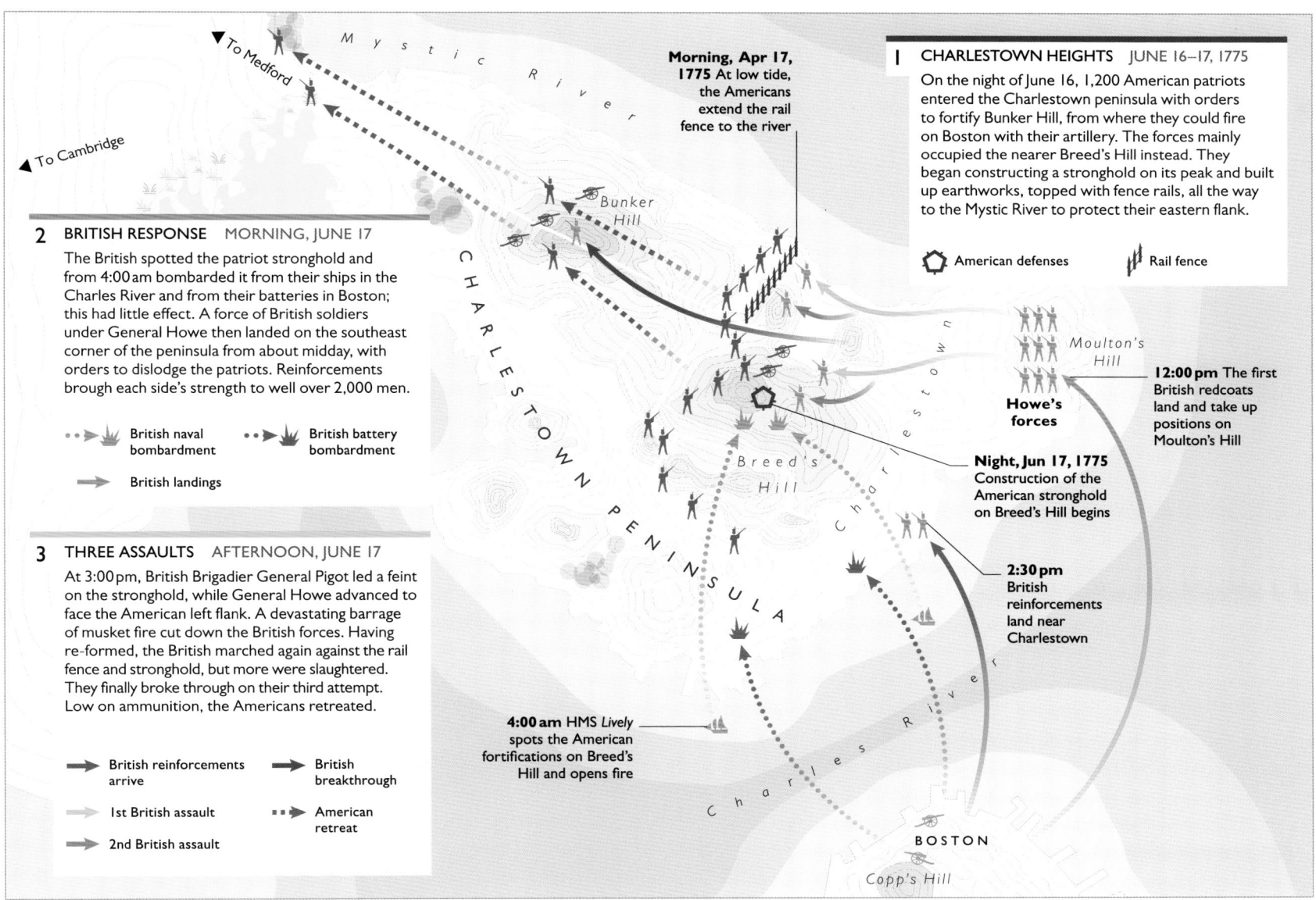

Morning, Apr 17, 1775 At low tide, the Americans extend the rail fence to the river

1 | CHARLESTOWN HEIGHTS JUNE 16–17, 1775
On the night of June 16, 1,200 American patriots entered the Charlestown peninsula with orders to fortify Bunker Hill, from where they could fire on Boston with their artillery. The forces mainly occupied the nearer Breed's Hill instead. They began constructing a stronghold on its peak and built up earthworks, topped with fence rails, all the way to the Mystic River to protect their eastern flank.

- American defenses
- Rail fence

2 | BRITISH RESPONSE MORNING, JUNE 17
The British spotted the patriot stronghold and from 4:00 am bombarded it from their ships in the Charles River and from their batteries in Boston; this had little effect. A force of British soldiers under General Howe then landed on the southeast corner of the peninsula from about midday, with orders to dislodge the patriots. Reinforcements brough each side's strength to well over 2,000 men.

- British naval bombardment
- British battery bombardment
- British landings

3 | THREE ASSAULTS AFTERNOON, JUNE 17
At 3:00 pm, British Brigadier General Pigot led a feint on the stronghold, while General Howe advanced to face the American left flank. A devastating barrage of musket fire cut down the British forces. Having re-formed, the British marched again against the rail fence and stronghold, but more were slaughtered. They finally broke through on their third attempt. Low on ammunition, the Americans retreated.

- British reinforcements arrive
- British breakthrough
- 1st British assault
- American retreat
- 2nd British assault

12:00 pm The first British redcoats land and take up positions on Moulton's Hill

Night, Jun 17, 1775 Construction of the American stronghold on Breed's Hill begins

2:30 pm British reinforcements land near Charlestown

4:00 am HMS *Lively* spots the American fortifications on Breed's Hill and opens fire

To Medford

To Cambridge

Mystic River

Bunker Hill

Howe's forces

Moulton's Hill

Breed's Hill

CHARLESTOWN

CHARLESTOWN PENINSULA

Charles River

BOSTON

Copp's Hill

THE MARCH OF BURGOYNE'S ARMY

Burgoyne's army endured a punishing march toward Albany. Desperate for supplies, he ordered a raid on Bennington that cost him 1,000 men. The Americans sent a force to relieve Fort Stanwix, which was besieged by the British under Colonel St. Leger. With St. Leger held up, Burgoyne was left with just 6,000 men to face the revolutionary forces at Saratoga.

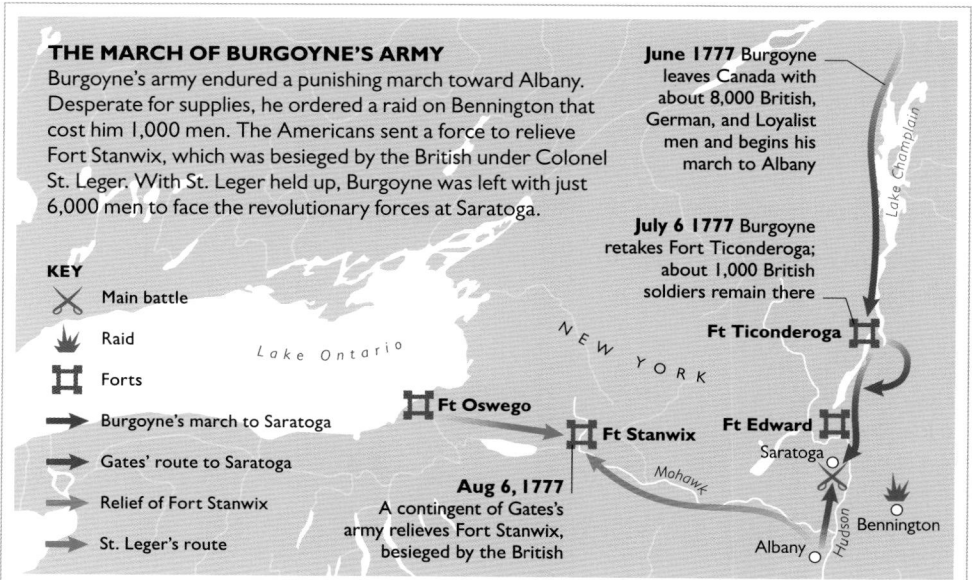

June 1777 Burgoyne leaves Canada with about 8,000 British, German, and Loyalist men and begins his march to Albany

July 6 1777 Burgoyne retakes Fort Ticonderoga; about 1,000 British soldiers remain there

Aug 6, 1777 A contingent of Gates's army relieves Fort Stanwix, besieged by the British

KEY
- ✂ Main battle
- ⚜ Raid
- ⊞ Forts
- → Burgoyne's march to Saratoga
- → Gates' route to Saratoga
- → Relief of Fort Stanwix
- → St. Leger's route

SARATOGA CAMPAIGN

The battles at Saratoga marked the end of Britain's 1777 campaign to gain control of the strategically important Hudson River valley, running north of New York on America's east coast.

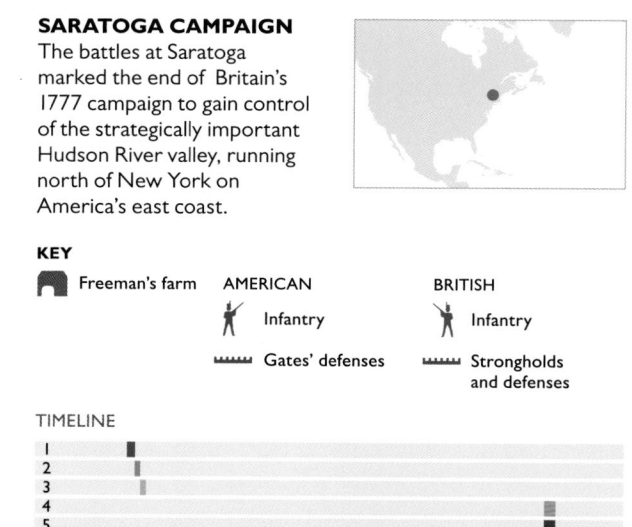

KEY

🐘 Freeman's farm

AMERICAN
- 🧍 Infantry
- ⌇⌇ Gates' defenses

BRITISH
- 🧍 Infantry
- ⌇⌇ Strongholds and defenses

TIMELINE

	SEP 15, 1777	SEP 25	OCT 5
1			
2			
3			
4			
5			

1 BURGOYNE PREPARES
MORNING, SEPTEMBER 19, 1777

The British advanced in three columns: Baron Riedesel led the left column in a feint on the American position at Bemis Heights; Brigadier Simon Fraser led the right to Freeman's Farm, with the ultimate goal of capturing the high ground northwest of Bemis Heights; and Burgoyne and General James Hamilton took a central position.

→ Burgoyne's forces' advance

2 FIRST SKIRMISHES EARLY AFTERNOON

Benedict Arnold, Gates's subordinate, guessed the British plan and pressed a reluctant Gates (who wished to remain within his fortified position) to advance to cut off the enemy's progress. When Fraser's skirmishers appeared at the edge of Freeman's Farm, American sharpshooters led by Daniel Morgan cut them down and picked off most of the British officers. Morgan's men gave chase but quickly ran into the main body of Fraser's troops.

→ Morgan's probe

3 RIEDESEL COMES TO THE RESCUE
AFTERNOON

Burgoyne brought up his forces to support Fraser, and Gates sent several militia regiments into the growing fray. Around 3pm, Burgoyne gave instructions to Riedesel to send reinforcements. Riedesel advanced and began firing on the Americans' right flank and Gates' men withdrew to Bemis Heights. Burgoyne claimed victory, but he had lost 600 men.

- → Gates' main attack
- ▪▪▶ Gates' retreat
- → Riedesel's reinforcements

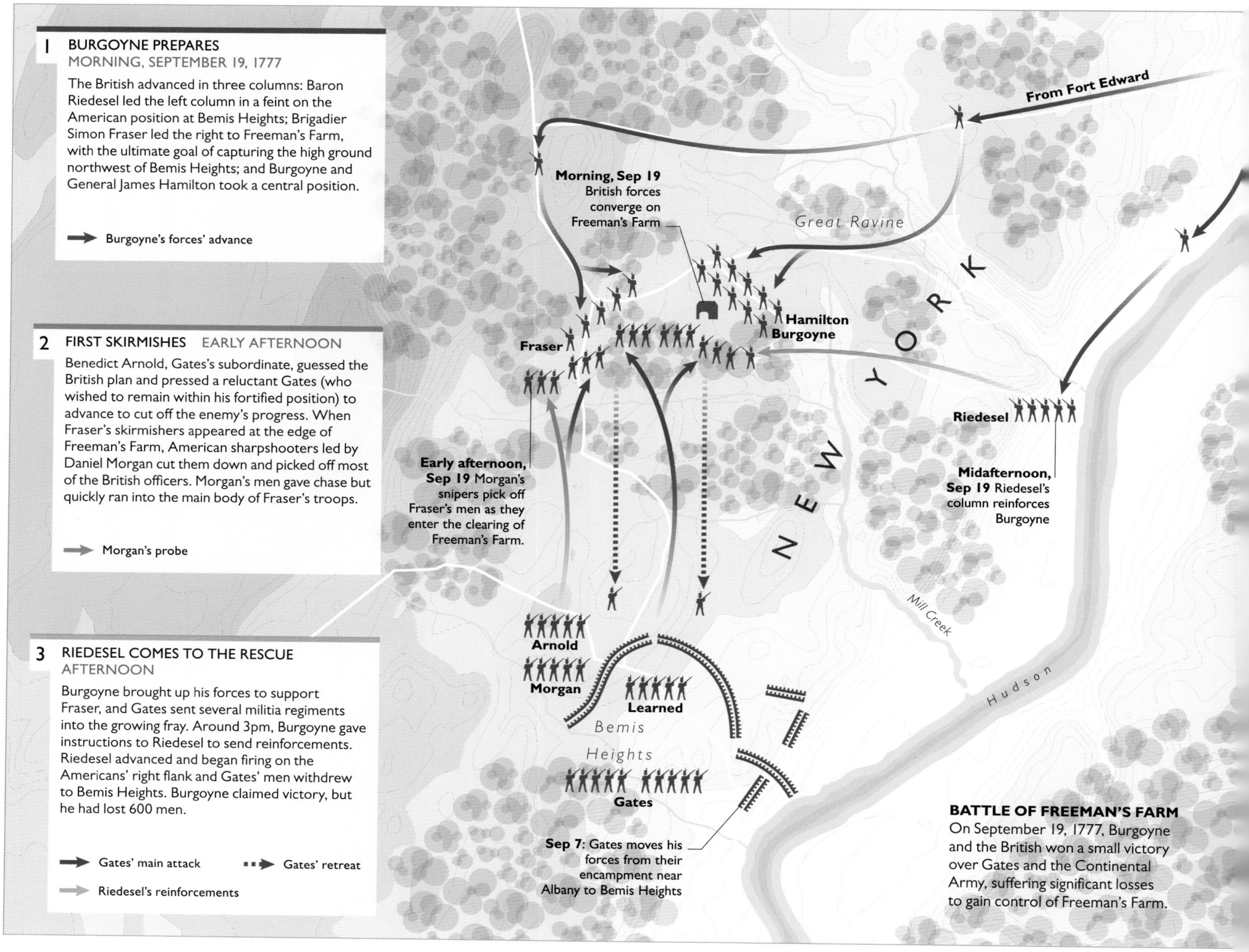

From Fort Edward

Morning, Sep 19 British forces converge on Freeman's Farm

Great Ravine

Fraser

Hamilton
Burgoyne

Riedesel

Early afternoon, Sep 19 Morgan's snipers pick off Fraser's men as they enter the clearing of Freeman's Farm.

Midafternoon, Sep 19 Riedesel's column reinforces Burgoyne

N E W   Y O R K

Mill Creek

Arnold

Morgan

Learned

Bemis Heights

Hudson

Gates

Sep 7: Gates moves his forces from their encampment near Albany to Bemis Heights

BATTLE OF FREEMAN'S FARM

On September 19, 1777, Burgoyne and the British won a small victory over Gates and the Continental Army, suffering significant losses to gain control of Freeman's Farm.

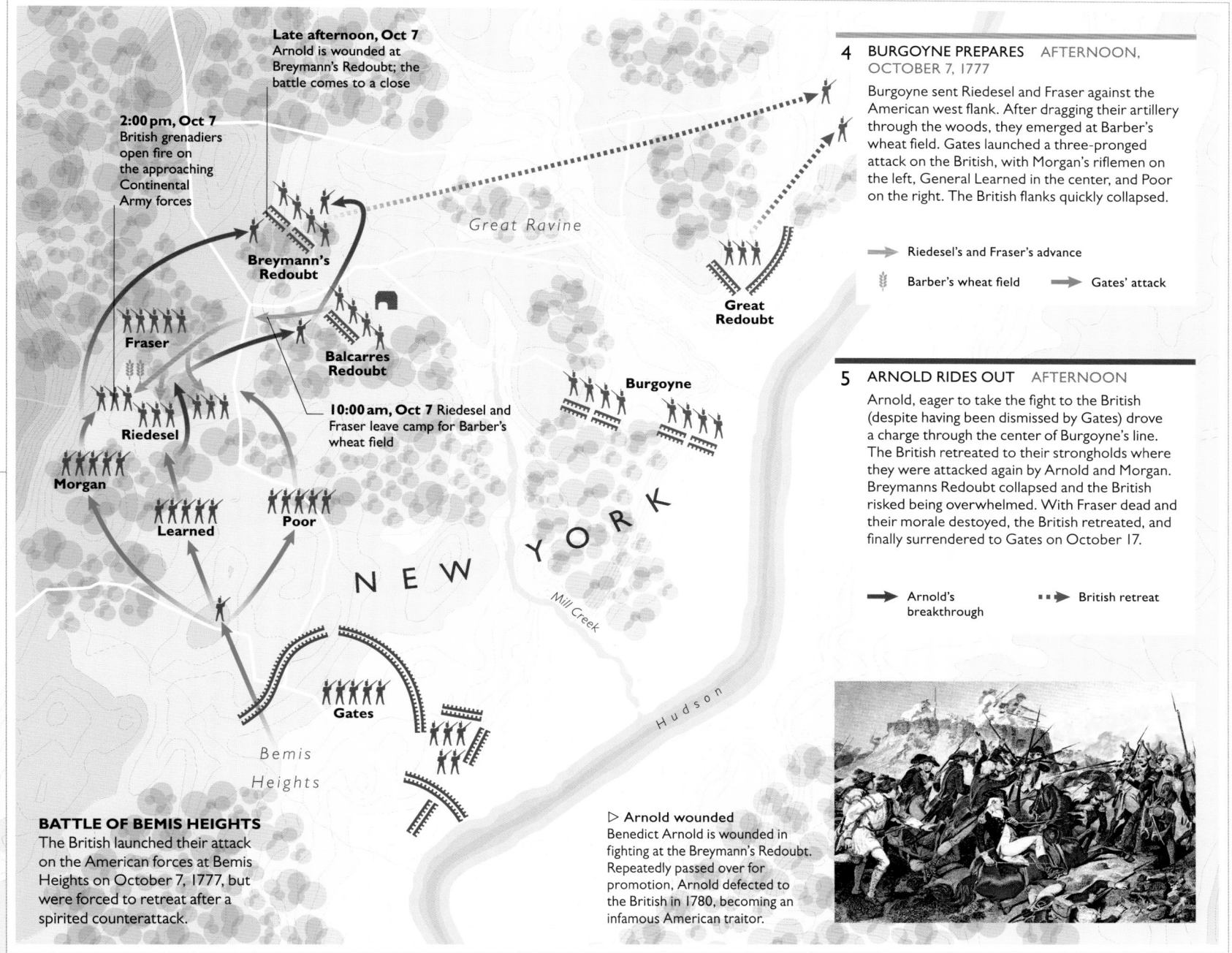

Late afternoon, Oct 7
Arnold is wounded at Breymann's Redoubt; the battle comes to a close

2:00 pm, Oct 7
British grenadiers open fire on the approaching Continental Army forces

Breymann's Redoubt

Fraser

Riedesel

Morgan

Learned

Poor

Balcarres Redoubt

10:00 am, Oct 7 Riedesel and Fraser leave camp for Barber's wheat field

Great Ravine

Great Redoubt

Burgoyne

N E W Y O R K

Mill Creek

Gates

Bemis Heights

Hudson

4 BURGOYNE PREPARES AFTERNOON, OCTOBER 7, 1777

Burgoyne sent Riedesel and Fraser against the American west flank. After dragging their artillery through the woods, they emerged at Barber's wheat field. Gates launched a three-pronged attack on the British, with Morgan's riflemen on the left, General Learned in the center, and Poor on the right. The British flanks quickly collapsed.

→ Riedesel's and Fraser's advance

🌾 Barber's wheat field → Gates' attack

5 ARNOLD RIDES OUT AFTERNOON

Arnold, eager to take the fight to the British (despite having been dismissed by Gates) drove a charge through the center of Burgoyne's line. The British retreated to their strongholds where they were attacked again by Arnold and Morgan. Breymanns Redoubt collapsed and the British risked being overwhelmed. With Fraser dead and their morale destoyed, the British retreated, and finally surrendered to Gates on October 17.

→ Arnold's breakthrough ┅▶ British retreat

BATTLE OF BEMIS HEIGHTS
The British launched their attack on the American forces at Bemis Heights on October 7, 1777, but were forced to retreat after a spirited counterattack.

▷ **Arnold wounded**
Benedict Arnold is wounded in fighting at the Breymann's Redoubt. Repeatedly passed over for promotion, Arnold defected to the British in 1780, becoming an infamous American traitor.

SARATOGA

Two battles fought near Saratoga in 1777 marked a turning point in the American Revolutionary War. About 6,000 British soldiers and Allied were captured, boosting the Continental Army's morale and bringing France into the war with Britain.

In 1777, after two years of the American Revolutionary War (1775–83), the British formulated a plan to break the rebellion for good. Three armies were to converge on the port city of Albany and separate the New England colonies—which the British saw as the heart of the rebellion—from the more Loyalist middle and southern colonies. General John Burgoyne's army was to march south from Canada and rendezvous with a smaller British force under Colonel Barry St. Leger, arriving from the west; a third army, under General William Howe, would push north from New York City, pressing the American defenders from three sides.

However, St. Leger's progress toward Albany was delayed by heavy American resistance at Fort Stanwix, and Howe's army diverted to attack Philadelphia. Burgoyne was left alone to face General Horatio Gates's larger and growing force of Continental Army soldiers, which had occupied Bemis Heights—high ground on the road to Albany. Their first battle lasted several hours; the Americans fell back, but Burgoyne lost several hundred men. On October 7, Burgoyne attempted to attack the American position at Bemis Heights, but his forces were quickly overrun. He withdrew having lost hundreds more men, and finally surrendered on October 17.

The Siege of Yorktown, 1781
This print depicts the the decisive concluding victory of the American War of Independence—the British surrender at Yorktown. The Franco–American army and navy trapped the British Army under General Charles Cornwallis.

AMERICA'S ARMY

In April 1775, conflict broke out between rebels and British troops in North America. On June14, the Second Continental Congress authorized the creation of the Continental Army to fight against the British.

The Continental Army was created in the belief that a trained army, rather than a citizens' militia, would give the colonies a fighting chance against the British. The first troops to become a part of the army were the militiamen already deployed in the Siege of Boston (April 1775–March 1776). Soon, volunteers began enlisting. However, it was only in 1777 that serious efforts to raise an army began.

△ **Knapsack with insignia**
Regimental and company designations were often embroidered on the knapsacks of the Continental Army's soldiers, as shown on this reproduction.

From the outset, the Continental Army was at a disadvantage due to inadequate training and a lack of equipment, money, and uniforms. The army's initial battlefield performance yielded mixed results, with defeat at New York and victory at the Siege of Boston in 1776. It won small victories at Trenton and Princeton also in 1776, but was defeated again the following year at Brandywine and Germantown. Its first clear victory was at Saratoga (see pp.154–55), and won the upper hand at the battle at Monmouth Court House in 1778. However, the troops were beaten again at Camden in 1780.

Although beset by problems, the army nevertheless received praise from some foreign observers. Training, leadership, and equipment improved over time, but not at a constant rate, and Congress funding was never steady due to political disagreements or lack of resources. In the end, the army's success in overthrowing the British owed more to the intervention of France and Spain than its own performance. In 1783, after the independence for the 13 colonies, the first act of the Congress was to disband most of the Continental Army.

GEORGE WASHINGTON 1732–99

Washington was a subordinate commander during the French and Indian War (1754–63), before resigning his commision and becoming active in politics. After the creation of the Continental Army, Congress appointed him as its commander-in-chief. He was an able administrator and trainer, and he played a key role in securing American victory in the War of Independence. He went on to become the first President of the newly created United States in 1789.

8

BATTLE
OF
FLEURUS
26. June 1794.

A.K.JOHNSTON,F.R.G.S

SCALES
Military Steps 2½ Feet each

English Miles

W & A K Johnston, Edin?

△ **Fleurus battle map from 1848**
The battle took place in 1794 on the outskirts of Charleroi, north of the River Sambre in modern-day Belgium. It was the key battle in the First Coalition period of the French Revolutionary Wars.

FLEURUS

Notable for the first use of an observation balloon in battle, the Battle of Fleurus gave the army of revolutionary France its most significant victory against the First Coalition (1792–97), allowing it to seize Belgium and the Dutch Republic.

After the French Revolution in 1789, France's republican government came under attack from Europe's monarchies, who feared the spread of its ideals, and from 1793 the French used mass drafts to raise a large army. On June 12, 1794, France's General Jourdan and about 70,000 soldiers laid siege to the town of Charleroi, and on June 25 Prince Josias of Saxe-Coburg and about 50,000 Austrian and Dutch soldiers arrived, seeking to lift the siege. Too late to save Charleroi, Saxe-Coburg deployed five columns on June 26 to attack the French line, which was drawn

up in an arc around the city with its advance guard at Fleurus to the northeast. Reports from the observation balloon *L'Entreprenant* kept Jourdan informed of Austrian movements. The French left and right wings were initially driven back, but they and the center held as Jourdan redeployed his troops. Saxe-Coburg lost his nerve and the Austrians retreated after 15 hours of desperate fighting. The battle was a strategic victory for the French that allowed them to go on the offensive and annex the Austrian Netherlands.

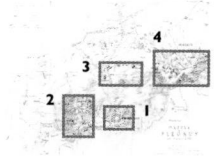

KEY

1 Charleroi surrendered to General Jourdan on June 25, as an Austrian relief force arrived to lift the siege.

2 The French left flank controlled the French escape route across the River Sambre.

3 French reserves at Junet and Ransart bolstered the left and right wings.

4 The Austrians captured Lambusart, but French reinforcements recaptured it.

BATTLE OF THE PYRAMIDS

At Embabeh near the pyramids, Egypt, on July 21, 1798, General Napoleon Bonaparte led the French to victory against the Egyptian Mamluk forces through the innovative use of massive divisional infantry squares.

In May 1798, Napoleon, one of the revolutionary government's most trusted generals, set sail to invade Egypt with some 30 warships and several divisions of troops on 400 transport vessels. His aim was to gain a new source of revenue while blocking the English trade route to India via the Red Sea. Landing in Egypt on July 1, he took Alexandria the next day, then headed south along the west bank of the Nile to meet the army of the Mamluk chieftain Murad Bey at Embabeh on July 21. That afternoon, 6,000 Mamluk cavalry charged the 25,000-strong French army. The French formed five large divisional squares with cannons on the outer edges and infantry in ranks six deep protecting the cavalry and transport in the center. The squares repulsed numerous charges, before the Bon division stormed Embabeh and routed the Mamluk garrison. Many Egyptian soldiers drowned trying to escape across the Nile. The Mamluks abandoned Cairo to Napoleon, but within two weeks the British destroyed the French fleet at the Battle of the Nile.

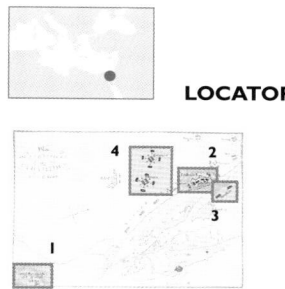

LOCATOR

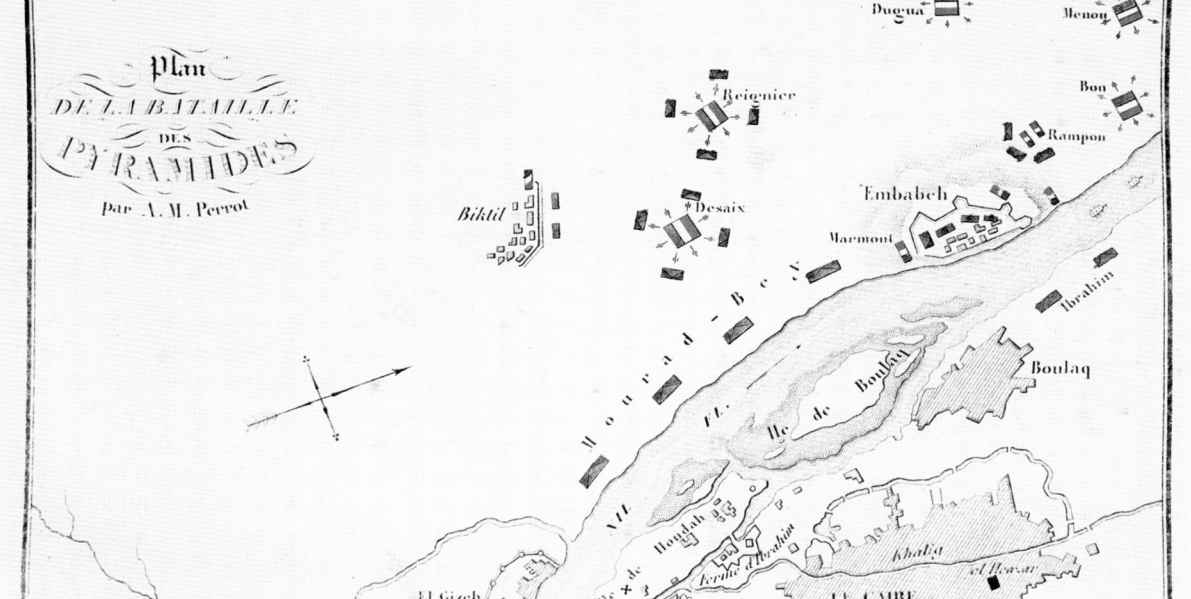

◁ **French battle map from 1828**
The Battle of the Pyramids took place at Embabeh, on the west bank of the Nile, 4 miles (6 km) from Cairo and 9 miles (15 km) from the pyramids at Giza.

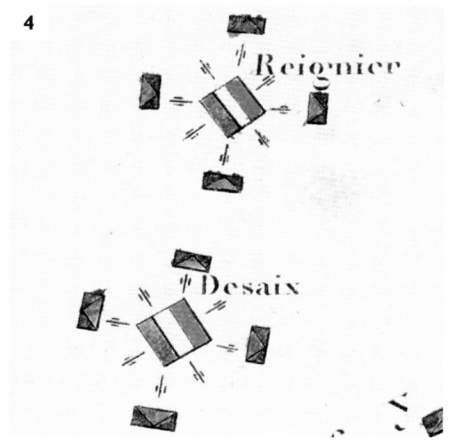

△ **Massed infantry and cannons**
Napoleon's large infantry squares proved highly effective against the Mamluk cavalry. This was to be Napoleon's only significant tactical innovation.

▽ **Egyptian reserves**
A second Egyptian force, under Murad's coruler, Ibrahim Bey, remained on the east bank and took no part in the battle.

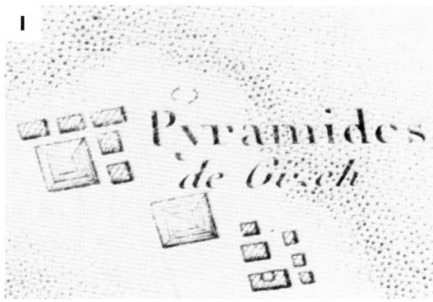

△ **Landmark battle**
The pyramids are used to name the battle, although the action took place some distance away. Paintings of the campaign often feature famous landmarks.

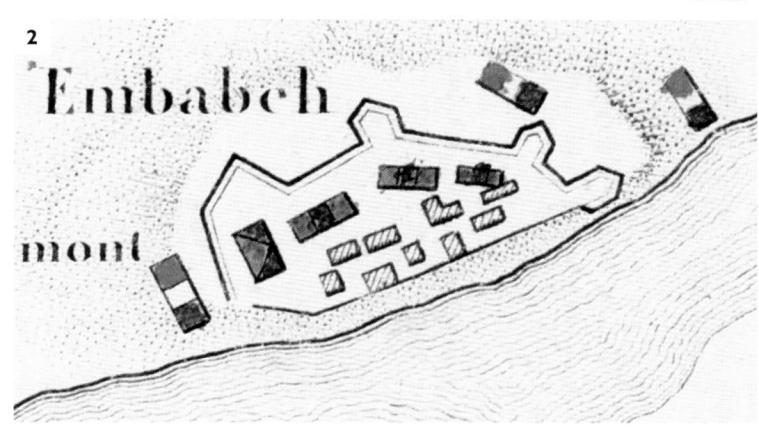

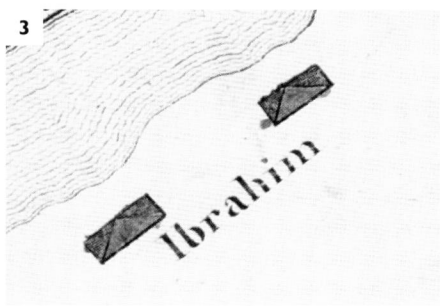

◁ **Strategic objective**
Stormed by French troops during the battle, Embabeh (now Imbaba) was an important market town on the upper Nile delta.

THE ROUTE TO MARENGO

In mid-May 1800, Napoleon secretly crossed the Great St. Bernard pass into Italy, while more French forces crossed the Alps further north. The French moved south, seizing Milan, Pavia, Piacenza, and Stradella, and cutting off the main Austrian supply route east along the Po River. After Austrian general Ott took Genoa by siege on June 4, however, many more Austrian troops were freed to address the threat from Napoleon, and Ott ordered them to march to Alessandria.

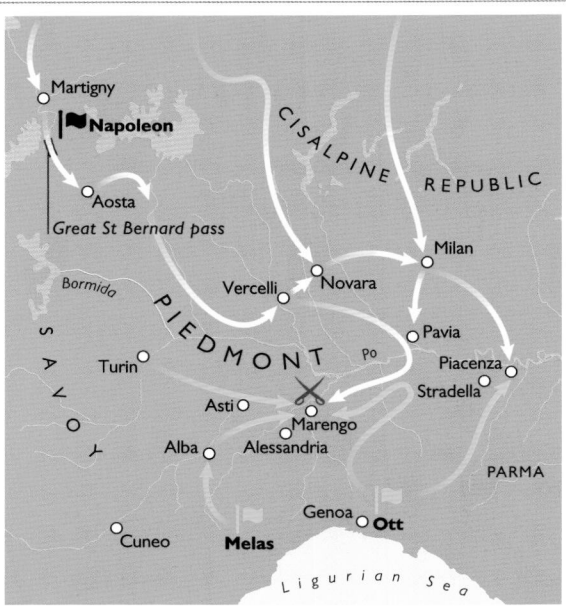

KEY

✕ Main battle

FRENCH FORCES

▮ Commander

⇨ French advance

AUSTRIAN FORCES

⚑ Commander

→ Austrian movements

ITALIAN CONFLICT

Within a day of Napoleon's victory on the Marengo plain outside Alessandria, the Austrians agreed to evacuate northwest Italy and suspend military operations in Italy.

KEY

▨ Towns

AUSTRIAN FORCES

⚑ Commander

🏇 Cavalry

🗡 Infantry

FRENCH FORCES

▮ Commander

🏇 Cavalry

🗡 Infantry

⚙ Artillery

TIMELINE

1			
2			
3			
4			
5			
6			

6:00 AM, JUN 14 — 11:00 AM — 4:00 PM — 9:00 PM

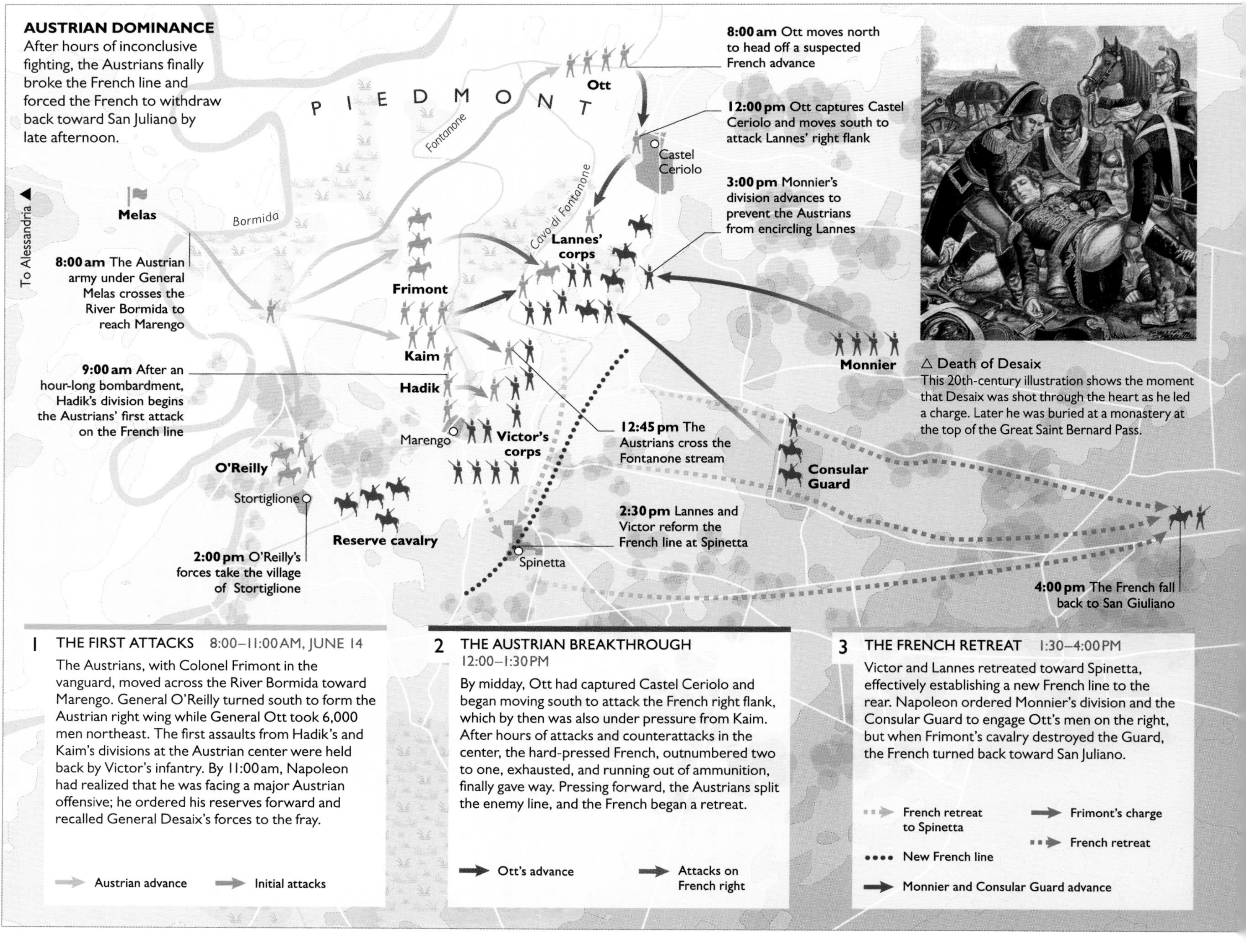

AUSTRIAN DOMINANCE

After hours of inconclusive fighting, the Austrians finally broke the French line and forced the French to withdraw back toward San Juliano by late afternoon.

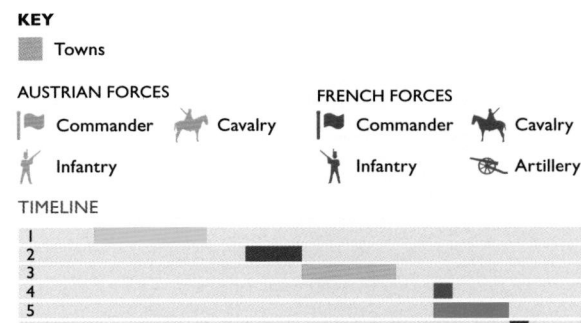

△ **Death of Desaix**
This 20th-century illustration shows the moment that Desaix was shot through the heart as he led a charge. Later he was buried at a monastery at the top of the Great Saint Bernard Pass.

8:00 am Ott moves north to head off a suspected French advance

12:00 pm Ott captures Castel Ceriolo and moves south to attack Lannes' right flank

3:00 pm Monnier's division advances to prevent the Austrians from encircling Lannes

8:00 am The Austrian army under General Melas crosses the River Bormida to reach Marengo

9:00 am After an hour-long bombardment, Hadik's division begins the Austrians' first attack on the French line

12:45 pm The Austrians cross the Fontanone stream

2:00 pm O'Reilly's forces take the village of Stortiglione

2:30 pm Lannes and Victor reform the French line at Spinetta

4:00 pm The French fall back to San Giuliano

1 | THE FIRST ATTACKS 8:00–11:00 AM, JUNE 14

The Austrians, with Colonel Frimont in the vanguard, moved across the River Bormida toward Marengo. General O'Reilly turned south to form the Austrian right wing while General Ott took 6,000 men northeast. The first assaults from Hadik's and Kaim's divisions at the Austrian center were held back by Victor's infantry. By 11:00 am, Napoleon had realized that he was facing a major Austrian offensive; he ordered his reserves forward and recalled General Desaix's forces to the fray.

→ Austrian advance   → Initial attacks

2 | THE AUSTRIAN BREAKTHROUGH 12:00–1:30 PM

By midday, Ott had captured Castel Ceriolo and began moving south to attack the French right flank, which by then was also under pressure from Kaim. After hours of attacks and counterattacks in the center, the hard-pressed French, outnumbered two to one, exhausted, and running out of ammunition, finally gave way. Pressing forward, the Austrians split the enemy line, and the French began a retreat.

→ Ott's advance   → Attacks on French right

3 | THE FRENCH RETREAT 1:30–4:00 PM

Victor and Lannes retreated toward Spinetta, effectively establishing a new French line to the rear. Napoleon ordered Monnier's division and the Consular Guard to engage Ott's men on the right, but when Frimont's cavalry destroyed the Guard, the French turned back toward San Juliano.

┅➤ French retreat to Spinetta

•••• New French line

➡ Frimont's charge

⇢ French retreat

➡ Monnier and Consular Guard advance

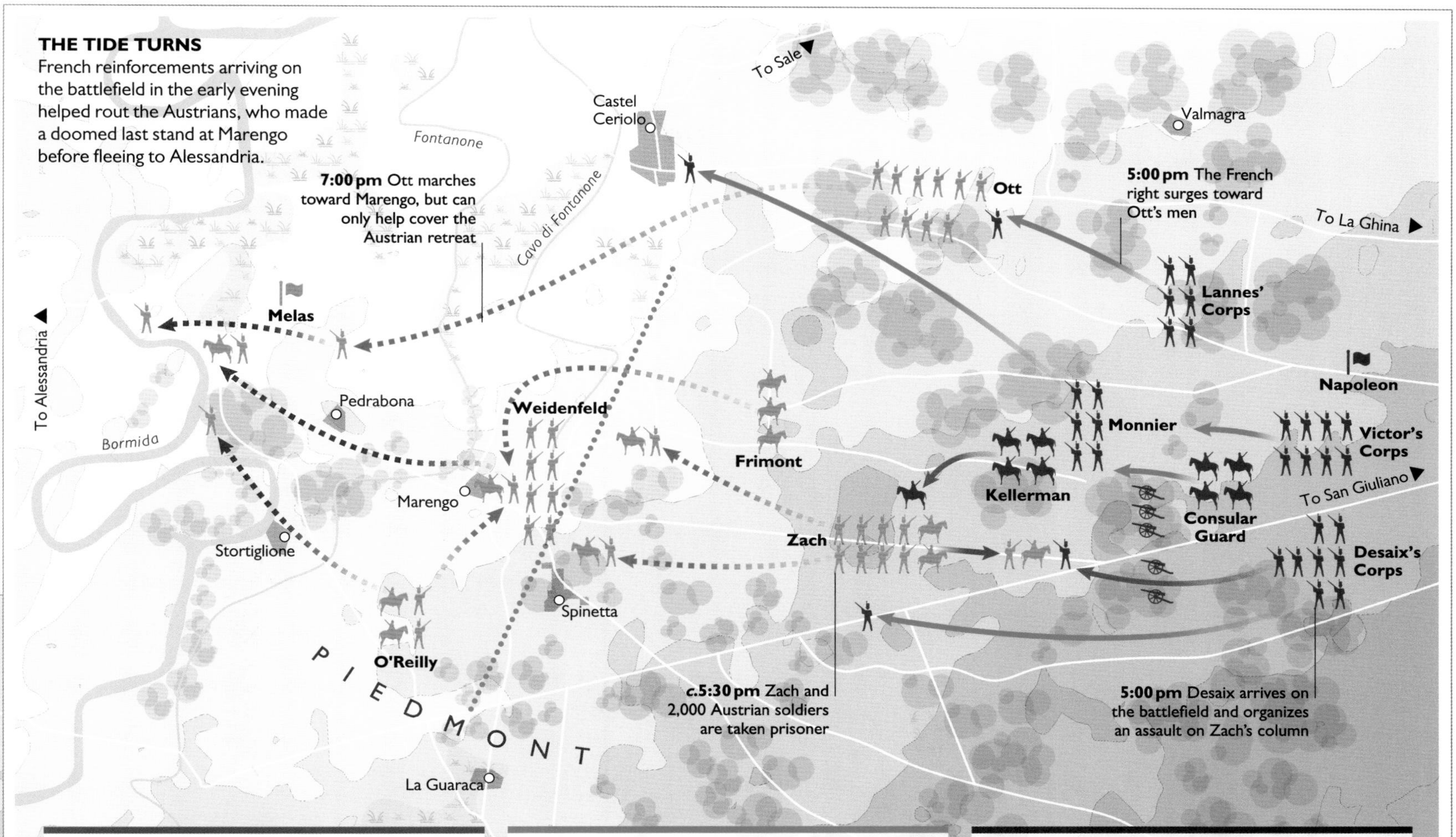

THE TIDE TURNS
French reinforcements arriving on the battlefield in the early evening helped rout the Austrians, who made a doomed last stand at Marengo before fleeing to Alessandria.

7:00 pm Ott marches toward Marengo, but can only help cover the Austrian retreat

5:00 pm The French right surges toward Ott's men

5:00 pm Desaix arrives on the battlefield and organizes an assault on Zach's column

*c.***5:30 pm** Zach and 2,000 Austrian soldiers are taken prisoner

To Sale
To La Ghina
To San Giuliano
To Alessandria
Valmagra
Castel Ceriolo
Fontanone
Cavo di Fontanone
Bormida
Pedrabona
Weidenfeld
Frimont
Marengo
Stortiglione
Spinetta
O'Reilly
La Guaraca
Melas
Ott
Lannes' Corps
Napoleon
Monnier
Kellerman
Victor's Corps
Consular Guard
Desaix's Corps
Zach

PIEDMONT

---

4 | DESAIX'S COUNTERATTACK 5:00 PM

Thinking the battle won, Melas handed command to General Zach, who pushed the Austrians east along a broad front. Desaix arrived on the battlefield with 6,000 reinforcements and drew Zach's column along the road to San Giuliano, straight into a hail of grapeshot. French cavalry, including Kellerman's, now smashed into Zach's column, capturing Zach and some 2,000 of his men.

→ Zach's advance
→ Desaix's and Kellerman's attack

5 | THE FRENCH ADVANCE 5:00–7:00 PM

The French surged forward, enveloping Ott to the north, who withdrew rather than returning to help the Austrians in the center. Weidenfeld's second grenadier brigade briefly held back the French advance before mounting a final, unsuccessful, defense of Marengo.

→ French surge forward
••••► Final French position
⇢ Austrians fall back

6 | THE AUSTRIANS RETREAT TO ALESSANDRIA 7:00 PM

With no hope of reversing the tide of battle, the Austrians withdrew over the Bormida. Hundreds drowned or were crushed at the water's edge. However, Napoleon allowed the Austrians to retreat to Alessandria without further harassment. After his defeat, Melas signed the Convention of Alessandria, effectively removing Austrian influence from Italy.

■►► Austrian retreat

San Giuliano
Napoleon

MARENGO

On June 14, 1800, after crossing the Alps into Italy, Napoleon won a narrow victory against the Austrians at Marengo. The battle helped to destroy the Second European Coalition that threatened Revolutionary France and solidified Napoleon's reputation as France's savior.

By 1800, France had endured more than a decade of revolutionary turmoil and years of war against European powers. It now faced a Second Coalition of countries (including Austria, Russia, Britain, and Turkey), which had already pushed back French forces in Germany, Holland, and Italy. In October 1799, Napoleon returned to France after campaigning in Egypt against the British. He dismissed the unpopular Directory government and replaced it with a new constitution, the Consulate, positioning himself as one of three Consuls. Intending to lift morale and to cement his political position,

he turned to Italy, hoping to secure a victory against the Austrian armies there that would force a peace settlement. Taking direct command of the Reserve Army, Napoleon marched over the 8,100-foot (2,500-m) high Great St. Bernard Pass into northwest Italy to support the French armies already fighting there. Closing in on the Austrian armies at Alessandia, he wrongly assumed that the enemy would flee rather than fight, so despatched Generals Desaix and La Poype to block their escape. It was a miscalculation: he was taken by surprise and almost routed when the Austrians attacked at Marengo.

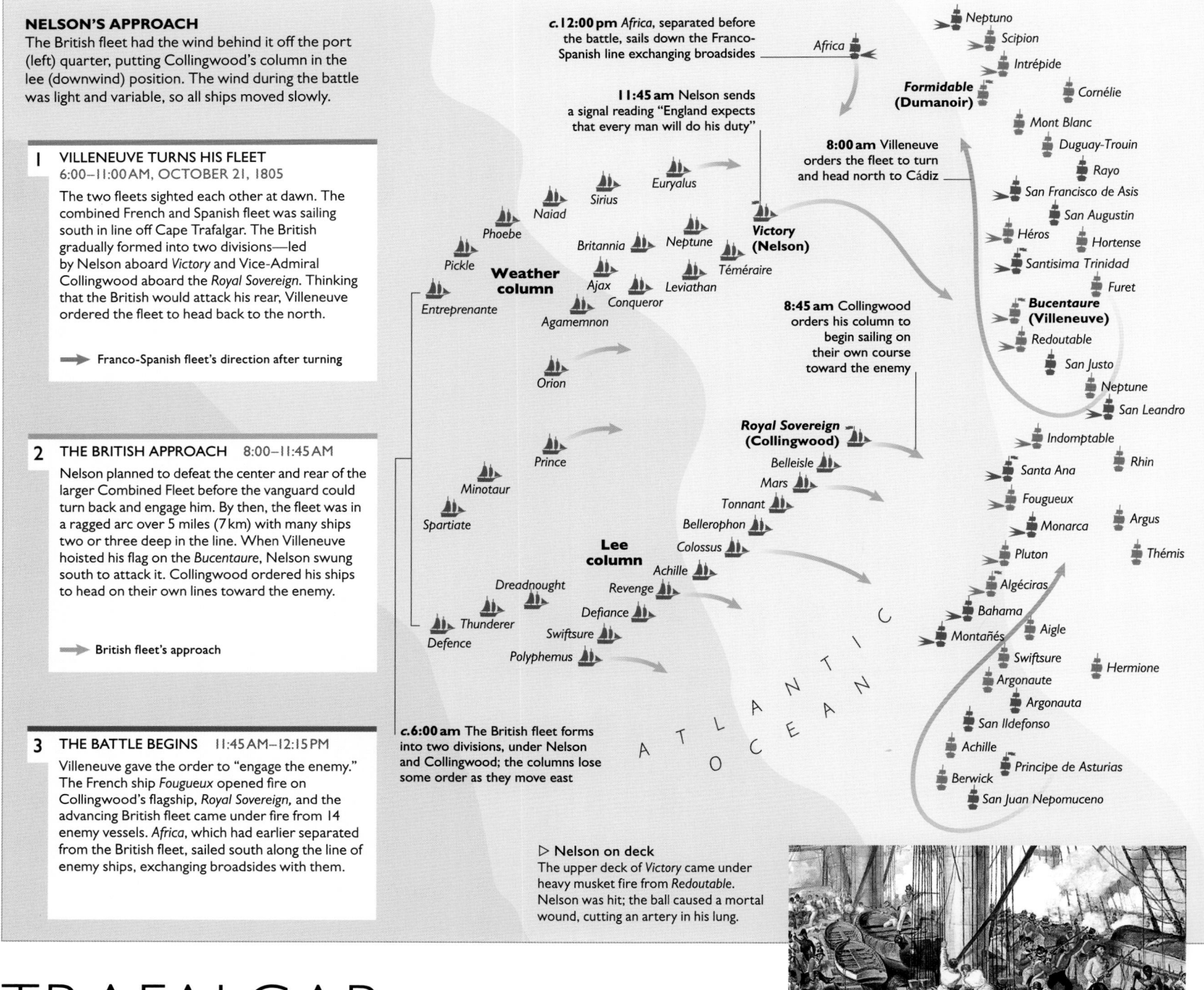

NELSON'S APPROACH
The British fleet had the wind behind it off the port (left) quarter, putting Collingwood's column in the lee (downwind) position. The wind during the battle was light and variable, so all ships moved slowly.

1 VILLENEUVE TURNS HIS FLEET
6:00–11:00 AM, OCTOBER 21, 1805

The two fleets sighted each other at dawn. The combined French and Spanish fleet was sailing south in line off Cape Trafalgar. The British gradually formed into two divisions—led by Nelson aboard *Victory* and Vice-Admiral Collingwood aboard the *Royal Sovereign*. Thinking that the British would attack his rear, Villeneuve ordered the fleet to head back to the north.

→ Franco-Spanish fleet's direction after turning

2 THE BRITISH APPROACH 8:00–11:45 AM

Nelson planned to defeat the center and rear of the larger Combined Fleet before the vanguard could turn back and engage him. By then, the fleet was in a ragged arc over 5 miles (7 km) with many ships two or three deep in the line. When Villeneuve hoisted his flag on the *Bucentaure*, Nelson swung south to attack it. Collingwood ordered his ships to head on their own lines toward the enemy.

→ British fleet's approach

3 THE BATTLE BEGINS 11:45 AM–12:15 PM

Villeneuve gave the order to "engage the enemy." The French ship *Fougueux* opened fire on Collingwood's flagship, *Royal Sovereign*, and the advancing British fleet came under fire from 14 enemy vessels. *Africa*, which had earlier separated from the British fleet, sailed south along the line of enemy ships, exchanging broadsides with them.

*c.*12:00 pm *Africa*, separated before the battle, sails down the Franco-Spanish line exchanging broadsides

11:45 am Nelson sends a signal reading "England expects that every man will do his duty"

8:00 am Villeneuve orders the fleet to turn and head north to Cádiz

8:45 am Collingwood orders his column to begin sailing on their own course toward the enemy

*c.*6:00 am The British fleet forms into two divisions, under Nelson and Collingwood; the columns lose some order as they move east

Africa

Euryalus
Sirius
Naiad
Phoebe
Pickle
Entreprenante

Weather column

Britannia
Neptune
Victory (Nelson)
Téméraire
Ajax
Conqueror
Leviathan
Agamemnon

Orion

Prince

Minotaur
Spartiate

Lee column

Royal Sovereign (Collingwood)
Belleisle
Mars
Tonnant
Bellerophon
Colossus
Achille
Dreadnought
Revenge
Defiance
Thunderer
Swiftsure
Defence
Polyphemus

Neptuno
Scipion
Intrépide
Cornélie
Mont Blanc
Duguay-Trouin
Rayo
San Francisco de Asis
San Augustin
Héros
Hortense
Santisima Trinidad
Furet

Formidable (Dumanoir)

Bucentaure (Villeneuve)
Redoutable
San Justo
Neptune
San Leandro
Indomptable
Rhin
Santa Ana
Fougueux
Monarca
Argus
Pluton
Thémis
Algéciras
Bahama
Montañés
Aigle
Swiftsure
Argonaute
Hermione
Argonauta
San Ildefonso
Achille
Berwick
Principe de Asturias
San Juan Nepomuceno

A T L A N T I C   O C E A N

▷ **Nelson on deck**
The upper deck of *Victory* came under heavy musket fire from *Redoutable*. Nelson was hit; the ball caused a mortal wound, cutting an artery in his lung.

TRAFALGAR

The largest sea battle of the Napoleonic Wars, Trafalgar was a hard-fought contest that confirmed Britain as the world's supreme naval power and Admiral Horatio Nelson as the foremost naval commander of the era.

In 1804, a British attack pushed Spain into the War of the Third Coalition (1803–1806) as an ally of France, providing Napoleon with the ships he needed to challenge Britain directly. In September 1805, the 33 ships of the line of the Franco-Spanish fleet under Vice-Admiral Villeneuve were anchored in Cádiz, southwest Spain, watched carefully by 27 British ships of the line under Nelson. On October 19, Villeneuve sailed out of Cádiz to support Napoleon's campaign in Italy. Nelson gave chase and caught up with him off the Cape of Trafalgar on October 21. Outnumbered and outgunned,

Nelson launched a daring attack that could have ended in disaster. Rather than lining up in parallel with the enemy to exchange broadsides, he sailed his ships directly at them in two columns. The leading ships were exposed to enemy fire, but drove straight through the Franco-Spanish line, prompting what Nelson called a "pell-mell" battle that favored the superior British gunnery and seamanship. It paid off: the British lost no ships while more than 20 French and Spanish ships were captured. Napoleon's ambition to invade England was shattered, and Britain's naval supremacy assured.

INVASION FLEET

Napoleon brought the French and Spanish fleets together for a planned invasion of England. Nelson pursued the new Combined Fleet across the Atlantic and back, finally catching up off the Spanish coast near Cádiz.

KEY

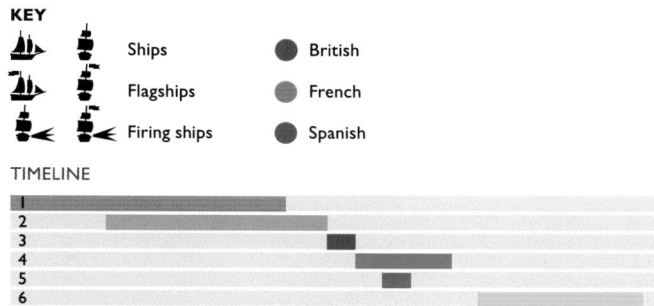

	Ships		British
	Flagships		French
	Firing ships		Spanish

TIMELINE

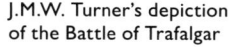

6:00AM, OCT 21, 1805   12:00PM   6:00PM

NELSON AND *VICTORY*

Nelson's flagship HMS *Victory* was heavily fired upon as she led one attack column, but she broke the enemy line, and Villeneuve's flagship *Bucentaure* received a devastating point-blank stern rake from *Victory*'s broadside guns. *Victory*'s tiller ropes were shot through, so her rudder had to be moved from below deck to bring her alongside *Redoutable*. Nelson was fatally wounded as French marines fired on *Victory*. At 4:30pm, after hearing that the British had won, Nelson died.

J.M.W. Turner's depiction of the Battle of Trafalgar

PELL-MELL BATTLE

Once among the Combined Fleet, the experienced Royal Navy gunners wrought havoc. The French and Spanish ships were unable to inflict the same level of damage.

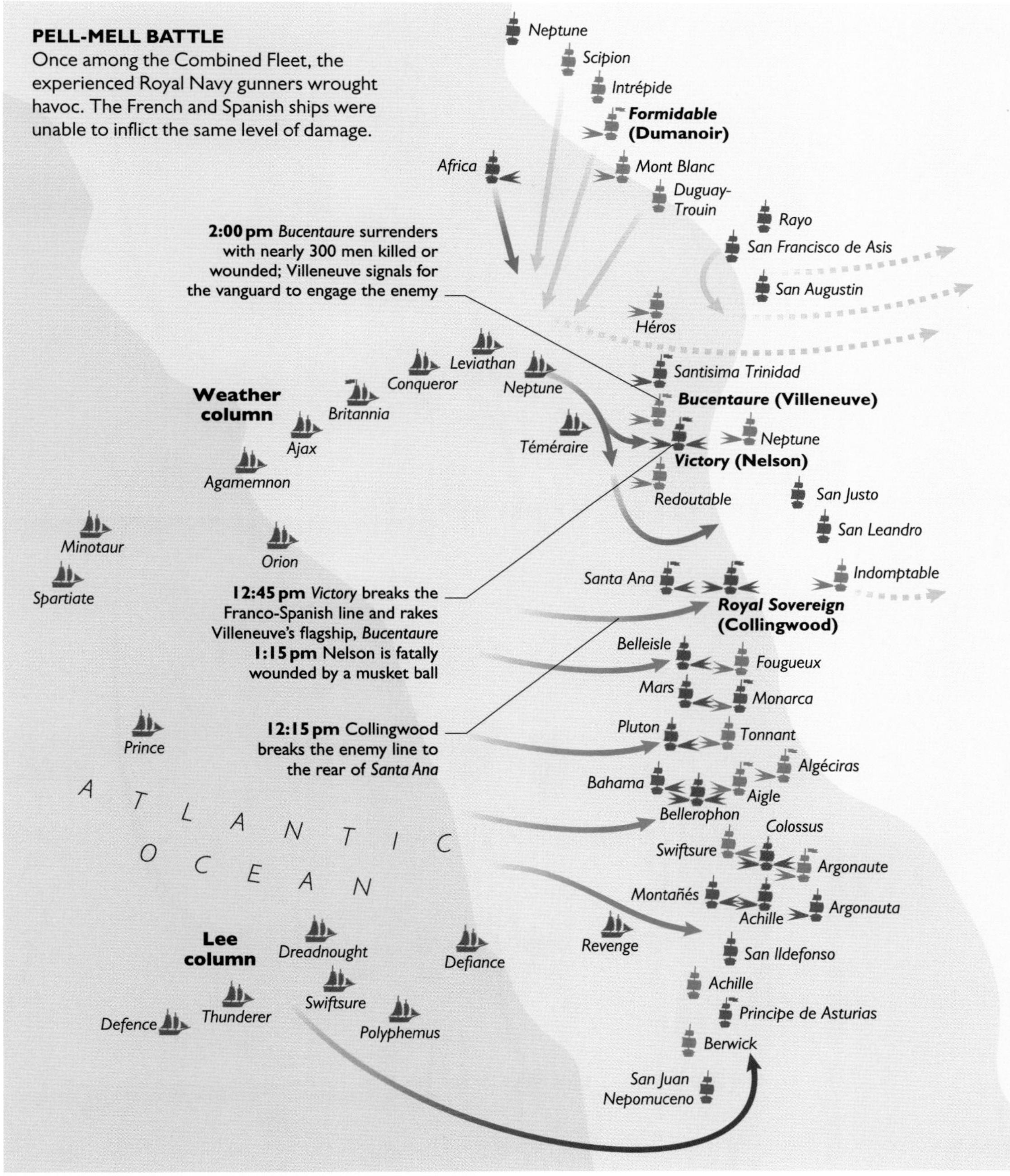

2:00 pm *Bucentaure* surrenders with nearly 300 men killed or wounded; Villeneuve signals for the vanguard to engage the enemy

Weather column

12:45 pm *Victory* breaks the Franco-Spanish line and rakes Villeneuve's flagship, *Bucentaure*
1:15 pm Nelson is fatally wounded by a musket ball

12:15 pm Collingwood breaks the enemy line to the rear of *Santa Ana*

A T L A N T I C O C E A N

Lee column

Neptune, Scipion, Intrépide, **Formidable (Dumanoir)**, Africa, Mont Blanc, Duguay-Trouin, Rayo, San Francisco de Asis, San Augustin, Héros, Leviathan, Conqueror, Neptune, Santisima Trinidad, **Bucentaure (Villeneuve)**, Britannia, Téméraire, Neptune, Ajax, **Victory (Nelson)**, Agamemnon, Redoutable, San Justo, San Leandro, Minotaur, Orion, Indomptable, Spartiate, Santa Ana, **Royal Sovereign (Collingwood)**, Belleisle, Fougueux, Mars, Monarca, Pluton, Tonnant, Bahama, Algéciras, Prince, Aigle, Bellerophon, Colossus, Swiftsure, Argonaute, Montañés, Argonauta, Achille, Revenge, San Ildefonso, Dreadnought, Defiance, Achille, Principe de Asturias, Defence, Thunderer, Swiftsure, Polyphemus, Berwick, San Juan Nepomuceno

6 FRANCO-SPANISH VANGUARD ENGAGES AND THE BATTLE ENDS 2:30–5:30PM

With the center and rear of the Franco-Spanish line heavily engaged, Rear-Admiral Dumanoir of the *Formidable* turned and led several ships of the vanguard to engage the stragglers of Nelson's division. However, as the rear of his fleet was overwhelmed, Dumanoir called off the engagement and headed away from the fighting toward the Straits of Gibraltar.

→ Franco–Spanish vanguard advances   ⋯▷ Flight of French and Spanish Ships

5 NELSON JOINS THE MELEE 12:45–1:15PM

At 12:45pm, Nelson's flagship, *Victory*, crossed the Franco-Spanish line and unleashed a broadside down the length of *Bucentaure*. *Temeraire*, *Conqueror*, and *Neptune* joined battle, and *Victory* locked masts with *Redoutable*. Nelson was hit in the shoulder by a French musket and carried below decks. *Temeraire* fired on *Redoutable*, preventing her crew from boarding *Victory*.

→ Nelson's column engages the enemy

4 COLLINGWOOD'S COLUMN BREAKS THE LINE 12:15–2:00PM

Just after midday, Collingwood's *Royal Sovereign* ran the gauntlet of broadsides from *Fougueux*, *Indomptable*, *San Justo*, and *San Leandro*, before breaking the enemy line to the rear of *Santa Ana*. Collingwood was then isolated until the rest of his first group engaged the enemy. At around 1:30pm, a second group enveloped the rear of the Combined Fleet and joined the general mêlée.

→ Collingwood's first group   → Collingwood's second group

NELSON'S NAVY

A string of naval victories from 1793–1815, many involving or commanded by Horatio Nelson, saw Britain's Royal Navy emerge as master of the world's oceans. Its success was built on gunnery, leadership, and attacking spirit.

△ **Small and powerful**
Naval guns were mounted on wheeled carriages that rolled backward with the recoil from firing their solid iron shot. This 6-pounder cannon was the smallest caliber found on board.

The Royal Navy's warships were not notably superior to the warships of the other European navies it repeatedly defeated. Its mix of two- or three-deck ships of the line, mounting 74–120 guns each, and single-deck frigates were typical of its time. Under Nelson, Britain's most famous naval commander, the Royal Navy—unlike its enemies—practiced gunnery on a daily basis. Nelson's tactic of breaking up the formal lines in which naval battles were traditionally fought gave his gunners the maximum chance to batter the enemy with their well-rehearsed broadsides—simultaneous volleys of gunfire from one side of a ship. The Royal Navy's "Articles of War"—provisions governing the naval code of conduct—required all commanders to engage the enemy aggressively at every opportunity. This offensive spirit was reinforced by the award of prize money for enemy ships taken.

Diverse band

Nevertheless, Nelson's Royal Navy was not a perfect military machine. In times of war, most of its sailors were "impressed" (forcibly recruited) from civilian seafarers. As demand outran supply, the ranks were filled with non-sailors and even convicts. The motley crew was kept in line through harsh punishments, including flogging. Although there were some mutinies, morale on the whole held up surprisingly well. Nepotism ran rampant, but many officers also achieved high positions by showing outstanding courage and individual initiative, fulfilling Nelson's ideal of a "band of brothers" bonded in battle.

ADMIRAL HORATIO NELSON 1758–1805

Born in 1758, Horatio Nelson joined the Royal Navy in 1771 as a midshipman at the age of 12. Always in the thick of the fighting, he lost the sight in one eye in 1794 and his right arm in 1797. Unorthodox and often insubordinate, Nelson's bold destruction of a French fleet at the battle of the Nile in 1798 made him a national hero. He was killed by a sniper in the course of his greatest victory over the French and Spanish at Trafalgar (see pp.162–63) in 1805.

Fiery end
The Battle of the Nile, 1798, depicted here by American artist Mather Brown, reaches its violent climax as the French flagship *L'Orient*, met with a heavy bombardment of shots fired by Nelson's strategically positioned British ships, catches fire and explodes.

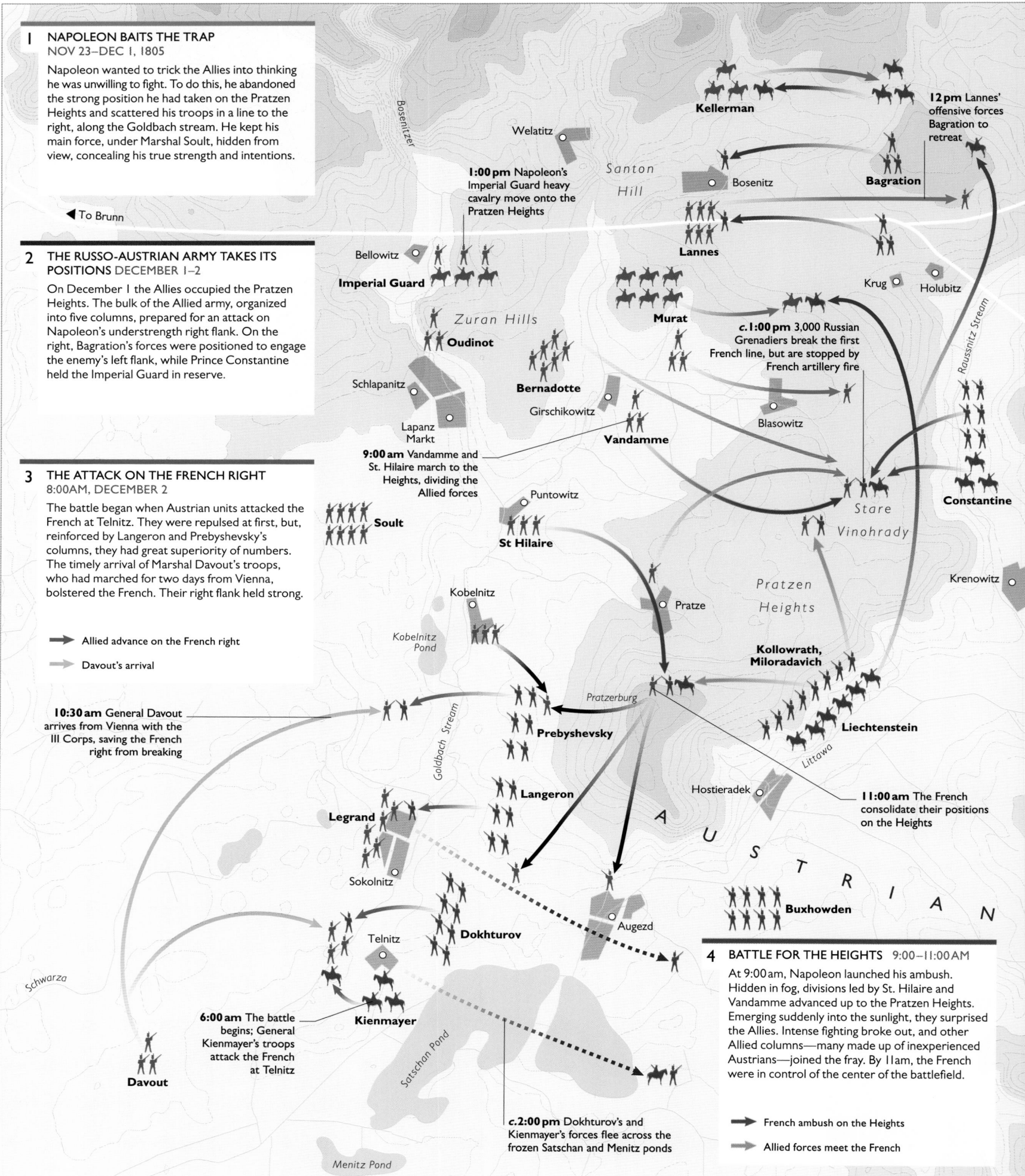

1 NAPOLEON BAITS THE TRAP
NOV 23–DEC 1, 1805

Napoleon wanted to trick the Allies into thinking he was unwilling to fight. To do this, he abandoned the strong position he had taken on the Pratzen Heights and scattered his troops in a line to the right, along the Goldbach stream. He kept his main force, under Marshal Soult, hidden from view, concealing his true strength and intentions.

◀ To Brunn

2 THE RUSSO-AUSTRIAN ARMY TAKES ITS POSITIONS DECEMBER 1–2

On December 1 the Allies occupied the Pratzen Heights. The bulk of the Allied army, organized into five columns, prepared for an attack on Napoleon's understrength right flank. On the right, Bagration's forces were positioned to engage the enemy's left flank, while Prince Constantine held the Imperial Guard in reserve.

3 THE ATTACK ON THE FRENCH RIGHT
8:00AM, DECEMBER 2

The battle began when Austrian units attacked the French at Telnitz. They were repulsed at first, but, reinforced by Langeron and Prebyshevsky's columns, they had great superiority of numbers. The timely arrival of Marshal Davout's troops, who had marched for two days from Vienna, bolstered the French. Their right flank held strong.

→ Allied advance on the French right

→ Davout's arrival

10:30 am General Davout arrives from Vienna with the III Corps, saving the French right from breaking

6:00 am The battle begins; General Kienmayer's troops attack the French at Telnitz

9:00 am Vandamme and St. Hilaire march to the Heights, dividing the Allied forces

1:00 pm Napoleon's Imperial Guard heavy cavalry move onto the Pratzen Heights

12 pm Lannes' offensive forces Bagration to retreat

c.1:00 pm 3,000 Russian Grenadiers break the first French line, but are stopped by French artillery fire

11:00 am The French consolidate their positions on the Heights

c.2:00 pm Dokhturov's and Kienmayer's forces flee across the frozen Satschan and Menitz ponds

4 BATTLE FOR THE HEIGHTS 9:00–11:00AM

At 9:00 am, Napoleon launched his ambush. Hidden in fog, divisions led by St. Hilaire and Vandamme advanced up to the Pratzen Heights. Emerging suddenly into the sunlight, they surprised the Allies. Intense fighting broke out, and other Allied columns—many made up of inexperienced Austrians—joined the fray. By 11am, the French were in control of the center of the battlefield.

→ French ambush on the Heights

→ Allied forces meet the French

Kellerman
Welatitz
Santon Hill
Bosenitz
Bagration
Bellowitz
Imperial Guard
Lannes
Krug
Holubitz
Zuran Hills
Oudinot
Murat
Schlapanitz
Bernadotte
Girschikowitz
Blasowitz
Lapanz Markt
Vandamme
Stare Vinohrady
Constantine
Puntowitz
Soult
St Hilaire
Krenowitz
Pratzen Heights
Kobelnitz
Pratze
Kobelnitz Pond
Kollowrath, Miloradavich
Pratzerburg
Liechtenstein
Prebyshevsky
Littawa
Goldbach Stream
Langeron
Hostieradek
Legrand
AUSTRIAN
Sokolnitz
Buxhowden
Telnitz
Dokhturov
Augezd
Schwarza
Kienmayer
Davout
Satschan Pond
Menitz Pond
Bosenitzer
Raussnitz Stream

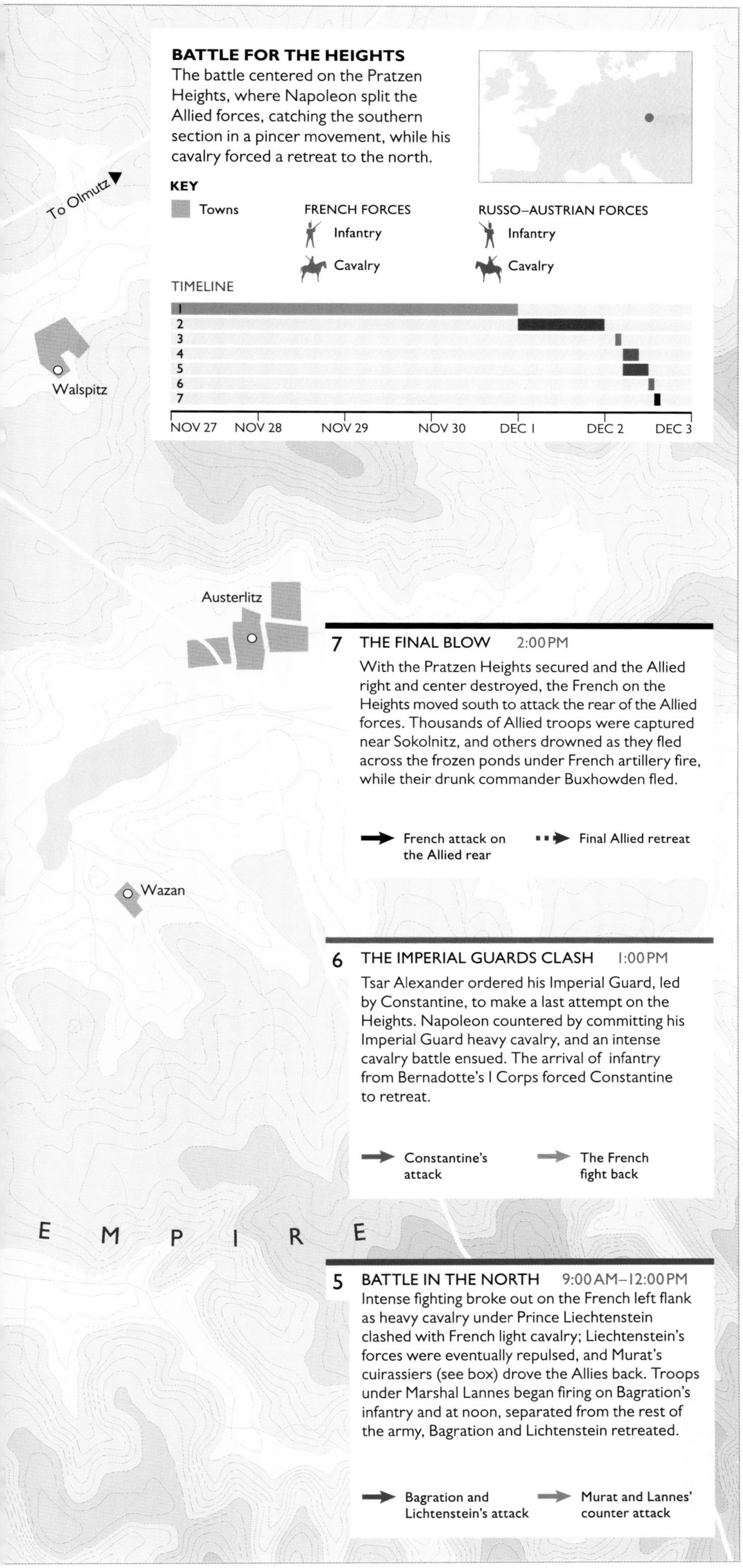

BATTLE FOR THE HEIGHTS

The battle centered on the Pratzen Heights, where Napoleon split the Allied forces, catching the southern section in a pincer movement, while his cavalry forced a retreat to the north.

KEY

▦ Towns	**FRENCH FORCES**	**RUSSO–AUSTRIAN FORCES**
	⚔ Infantry	⚔ Infantry
	🐎 Cavalry	🐎 Cavalry

TIMELINE

```
1
2
3
4
5
6
7
NOV 27   NOV 28   NOV 29   NOV 30   DEC 1   DEC 2   DEC 3
```

To Olmutz ▼

Walspitz

Austerlitz

Wazan

E M P I R E

7 THE FINAL BLOW   2:00 PM

With the Pratzen Heights secured and the Allied right and center destroyed, the French on the Heights moved south to attack the rear of the Allied forces. Thousands of Allied troops were captured near Sokolnitz, and others drowned as they fled across the frozen ponds under French artillery fire, while their drunk commander Buxhowden fled.

➡ French attack on the Allied rear   ▪▪▶ Final Allied retreat

6 THE IMPERIAL GUARDS CLASH   1:00 PM

Tsar Alexander ordered his Imperial Guard, led by Constantine, to make a last attempt on the Heights. Napoleon countered by committing his Imperial Guard heavy cavalry, and an intense cavalry battle ensued. The arrival of infantry from Bernadotte's I Corps forced Constantine to retreat.

➡ Constantine's attack   ➡ The French fight back

5 BATTLE IN THE NORTH   9:00 AM–12:00 PM

Intense fighting broke out on the French left flank as heavy cavalry under Prince Liechtenstein clashed with French light cavalry; Liechtenstein's forces were eventually repulsed, and Murat's cuirassiers (see box) drove the Allies back. Troops under Marshal Lannes began firing on Bagration's infantry and at noon, separated from the rest of the army, Bagration and Lichtenstein retreated.

➡ Bagration and Lichtenstein's attack   ➡ Murat and Lannes' counter attack

AUSTERLITZ

On December 2, 1805, Napoleon outwitted a larger Russo-Austrian force to secure one of his most brilliant victories. The result of exceptional tactical skill and hard fighting, his victory forced Austria to make peace, and weakened the anti-French Third Coalition.

By November 1805, Napoleon and his imperial army—the Grande Armée—had pushed deep into central Europe, defeating an Austrian army numbering more than 70,000 at Ulm, and occupying Vienna on November 13. Now far from France and at the end of overstretched supply lines, Napoleon faced a large Allied Russo-Austrian army, led by Tsar Alexander I, which was advancing from the east, and the prospect of Prussia joining the Third Coalition (Britain, Russia, and Austria) of forces ranged against him. Ignoring advice to withdraw, Napoleon resolved to confront his enemy.

Napoleon chose to do battle near the village of Austerlitz in Moravia (in modern-day Czech Republic). To the north were two hills—Santon and Zuran—and in front was a field suitable for cavalry action. The centerpiece was a long, low hill—The Pratzen Heights—of which Napoleon said to his generals: "Gentlemen, examine this ground carefully; it is going to be a battlefield." He formulated a plan to convince the Allied army that he was weak, spurring it into an attack on his right flank. Once they were committed, he planned to drive through the enemy's center and launch a cavalry attack on its right. The Allies played into his hands, and in the ensuing battle only 9,000 of Napoleon's 73,000 men were killed or wounded. Allied casualties and prisoners totalled at least a third of their larger army, and Austria was forced to withdraw from the Third Coalition war.

"This victory will finish our campaign, and we shall be able to go into winter quarters."

NAPOLEON'S SPEECH TO HIS ARMY ON THE EVE OF BATTLE

CUIRASSIERS

The cuirassiers were the heaviest and most elite cavalry units deployed in the Napoleonic Wars by the French, but also by Russian and Austrian armies. Armed with pistols, carbines, and long straight sabers, and distinguished by their body armor (the cuirass), cuirassiers rode huge horses and formed a powerful strike force which could change the course of a battle. Napoleon was well aware of the impact these forces could have, and increased the number of French cuirassier regiments from one to fourteen.

French cuirassiers' helmet

TALAVERA

In May 1808, a popular revolt had broken out in Spain against Napoleon's rule over the country. The following year, a British force marched into Spain, where it joined up with the Spanish army to take on the French army of Joseph Bonaparte (Napoleon's brother) in a fierce set-piece battle at Talavera, near Madrid.

In July 1809, a British army, led by General Sir Arthur Wellesley (later the Duke of Wellington), advanced into Spain to link up with the Spanish army under General de la Cuesta. The combined force encountered the French outside Talavera, 75 miles (120 km) southwest of Madrid; about 20,000 British and 35,000 Spanish troops faced more than 45,000 French soldiers under Joseph Bonaparte. The allies took up positions along the Portiña, a stream running north from Talavera.

Late on July 27, the French mounted a surprise attack on the allies but were driven off after frantic fighting. The British repulsed a second attack at dawn the next day. Knowing that a second Spanish army had reached Madrid, Joseph had no choice but to try to defeat Wellesley's forces outright. That afternoon, the French attacked the British lines at three points. The French almost broke through in the center, but Wellesley reinforced the British line so that it held. The French withdrew that night, though both sides had suffered

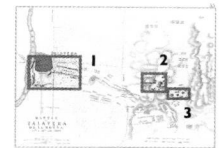 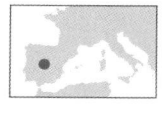

KEY

1 The Spanish positions in and around Talavera were protected by stone-walled olive groves and anchored on the River Tagus.

2 The Cerro de Medellín—a key strongpoint for the British. French attacks on this location on July 27 and 28 failed.

3 French infantry squares formed to face the British cavalry's charge, which came to grief in a hidden ravine.

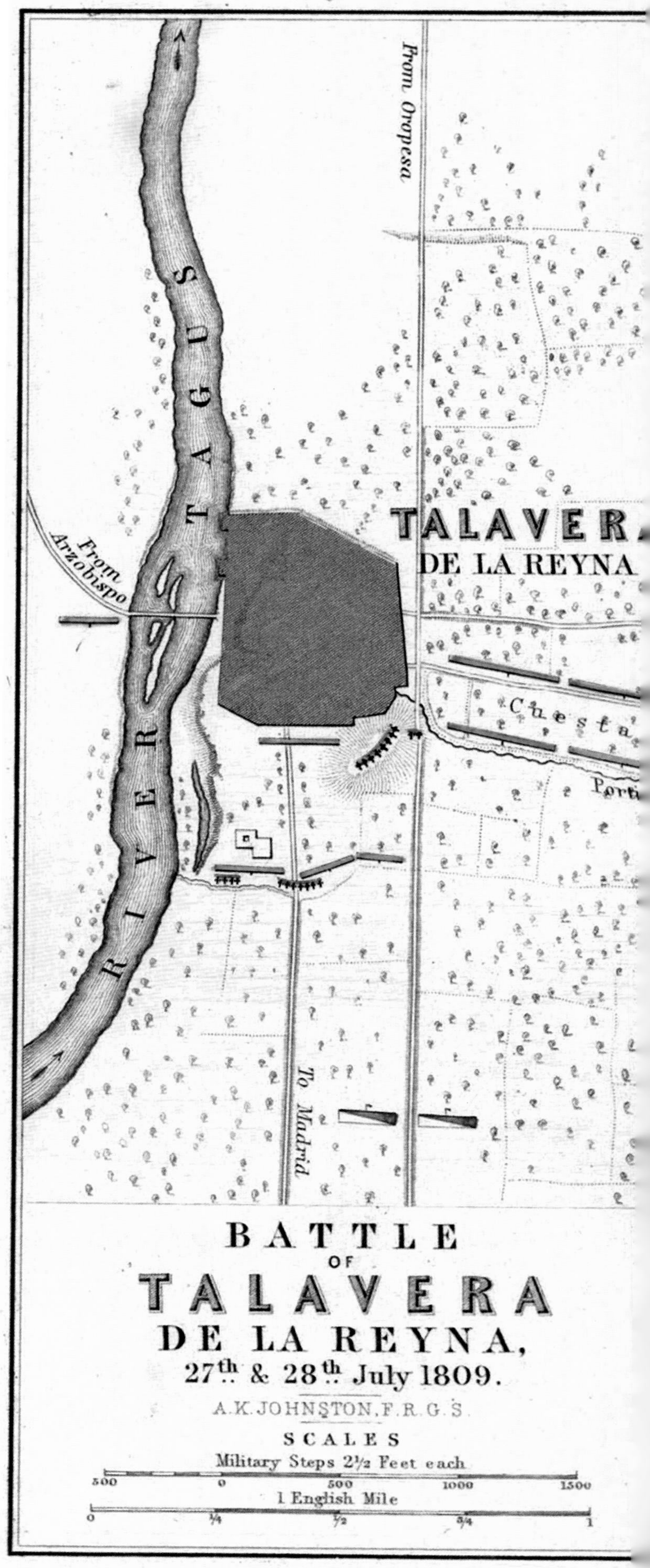

heavily, with over 7,000 casualties each. Following his victory, Wellesley was given the title Viscount Wellington, but he soon withdrew to Portugal to avoid encirclement, and successive Spanish efforts to liberate Madrid were defeated.

▷ **The field of battle**
This hand-colored engraved map from the atlas to Alison's *History of Europe* (1848) shows the Anglo-Spanish and French positions during the main action.

THE MAIN ATTACK

On July 28, the French attacked at three points. Leval's attack was driven back by Campbell's 4th Division. In the center, Sherbrooke's men pursued Sebastiani and Lapisse's line too far, creating a gap in the allied line. As the French attacked again, Wellesley had to shore up the line. Finally, Ruffin and Villatte attempted to outflank the allies. A chaotic British cavalry charge failed, but lacking support, the French disengaged.

KEY

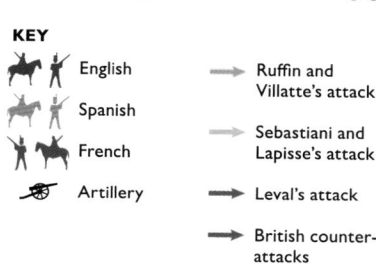

English	→ Ruffin and Villatte's attack
Spanish	→ Sebastiani and Lapisse's attack
French	→ Leval's attack
Artillery	→ British counter-attacks

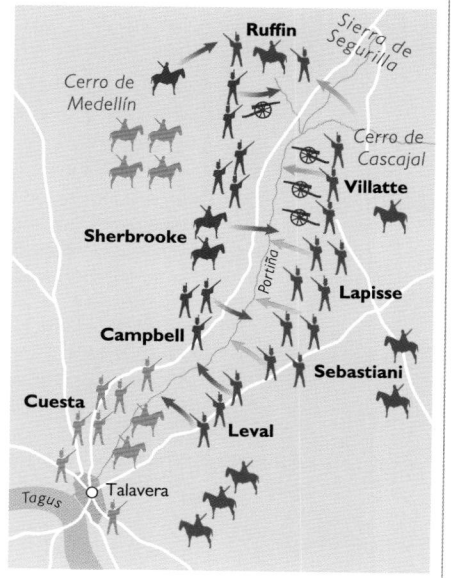

BATTLE OF TALAVERA DE LA REYNA, 27th & 28th July 1809.

A.K. JOHNSTON, F.R.G.S.

SCALES
Military Steps 2½ Feet each
500   0   500   1000   1500
1 English Mile
0   ¼   ½   ¾   1

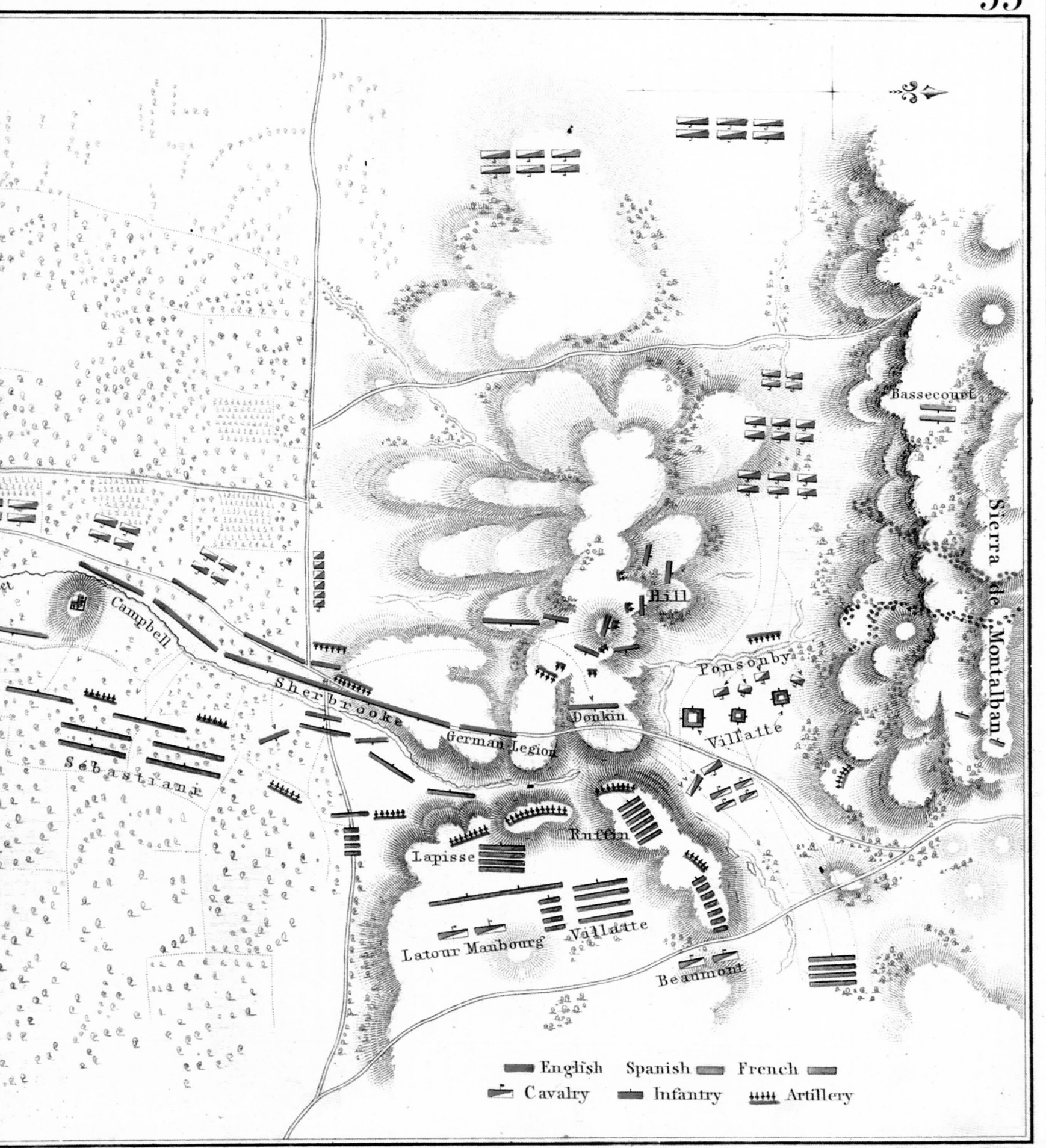

Bassecourt

Sierra de Montalban

Hill

Campbell

Sherbrooke

Ponsonby

German Legion

Donkin

Villatte

Sébastiani

Ruffin

Lapisse

Latour Maubourg

Villatte

Beaumont

English   Spanish   French

Cavalry   Infantry   Artillery

RUSSIAN CAMPAIGN

Napoleon's invasion of Russia came at a huge cost. The Russian army frustrated the French by retreating to Moscow and then deserting the city. Exhausted, the French had to march home with winter setting in.

KEY

✕ Main battle

✕ Russian victories

✕ French victories

→ French forces

⇢ French retreat

△ **The bloodiest battle**
Fighting was brutal as both sides struggled to control the Raevsky Redoubt. Of the over 250,000 soldiers who fought at Borodino, about 70,000 were killed or injured—making it the bloodiest single day of the war.

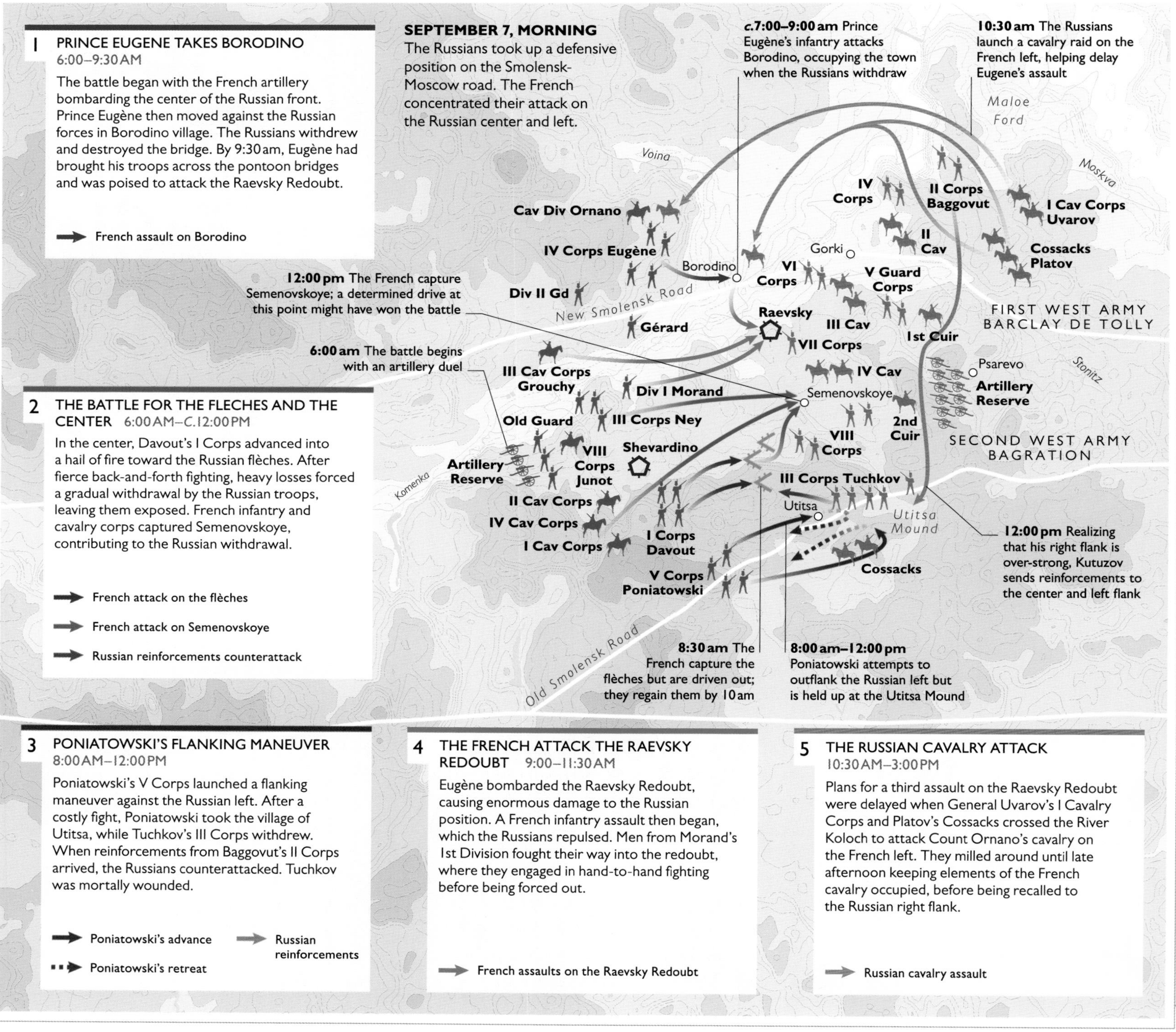

---

1 PRINCE EUGENE TAKES BORODINO
6:00–9:30 AM

The battle began with the French artillery bombarding the center of the Russian front. Prince Eugène then moved against the Russian forces in Borodino village. The Russians withdrew and destroyed the bridge. By 9:30 am, Eugène had brought his troops across the pontoon bridges and was poised to attack the Raevsky Redoubt.

→ French assault on Borodino

2 THE BATTLE FOR THE FLECHES AND THE CENTER   6:00 AM–C.12:00 PM

In the center, Davout's I Corps advanced into a hail of fire toward the Russian flèches. After fierce back-and-forth fighting, heavy losses forced a gradual withdrawal by the Russian troops, leaving them exposed. French infantry and cavalry corps captured Semenovskoye, contributing to the Russian withdrawal.

→ French attack on the flèches

→ French attack on Semenovskoye

→ Russian reinforcements counterattack

SEPTEMBER 7, MORNING
The Russians took up a defensive position on the Smolensk-Moscow road. The French concentrated their attack on the Russian center and left.

c.7:00–9:00 am Prince Eugène's infantry attacks Borodino, occupying the town when the Russians withdraw

10:30 am The Russians launch a cavalry raid on the French left, helping delay Eugène's assault

Maloe Ford

Voina

Moskva

Cav Div Ornano

IV Corps Eugène

Borodino

12:00 pm The French capture Semenovskoye; a determined drive at this point might have won the battle

Div II Gd

New Smolensk Road

Gérard

6:00 am The battle begins with an artillery duel

III Cav Corps Grouchy

Old Guard

Div I Morand

III Corps Ney

Shevardino

Artillery Reserve

VIII Corps Junot

II Cav Corps

IV Cav Corps

I Cav Corps

I Corps Davout

V Corps Poniatowski

IV Corps

VI Corps

Raevsky

Gorki

II Corps Baggovut

II Cav

V Guard Corps

III Cav

VII Corps

1st Cuir

IV Cav

Semenovskoye

VIII Corps

2nd Cuir

III Corps Tuchkov

Utitsa

I Cav Corps Uvarov

Cossacks Platov

FIRST WEST ARMY BARCLAY DE TOLLY

Psarevo

Stonitz

Artillery Reserve

SECOND WEST ARMY BAGRATION

Utitsa Mound

Cossacks

Komenka

12:00 pm Realizing that his right flank is over-strong, Kutuzov sends reinforcements to the center and left flank

8:30 am The French capture the flèches but are driven out; they regain them by 10 am

8:00 am–12:00 pm Poniatowski attempts to outflank the Russian left but is held up at the Utitsa Mound

Old Smolensk Road

3 PONIATOWSKI'S FLANKING MANEUVER
8:00 AM–12:00 PM

Poniatowski's V Corps launched a flanking maneuver against the Russian left. After a costly fight, Poniatowski took the village of Utitsa, while Tuchkov's III Corps withdrew. When reinforcements from Baggovut's II Corps arrived, the Russians counterattacked. Tuchkov was mortally wounded.

→ Poniatowski's advance

▪▪▶ Poniatowski's retreat

→ Russian reinforcements

4 THE FRENCH ATTACK THE RAEVSKY REDOUBT   9:00–11:30 AM

Eugène bombarded the Raevsky Redoubt, causing enormous damage to the Russian position. A French infantry assault then began, which the Russians repulsed. Men from Morand's 1st Division fought their way into the redoubt, where they engaged in hand-to-hand fighting before being forced out.

→ French assaults on the Raevsky Redoubt

5 THE RUSSIAN CAVALRY ATTACK
10:30 AM–3:00 PM

Plans for a third assault on the Raevsky Redoubt were delayed when General Uvarov's I Cavalry Corps and Platov's Cossacks crossed the River Koloch to attack Count Ornano's cavalry on the French left. They milled around until late afternoon keeping elements of the French cavalry occupied, before being recalled to the Russian right flank.

→ Russian cavalry assault

BORODINO

As Napoleon's Grande Armée marched into Russia, the Russians retreated, drawing the French deep into Russian territory. Exhausted by the brutal march, the French finally faced the Tsar's army at Borodino. Thousands would die in the bloodiest battle of the Napoleonic wars.

In June 1812, Napoleon marched an army of several hundred thousand men into Russia. Unlike many of his earlier campaigns, however, this invasion was soon beset with problems: the Russians avoided large-scale battle and instead drew Napoleon's Grande Armée deep into Russian territory. There, hunger, disease, exhaustion, and bad weather took a costly toll on the French forces.

Finally, in early September, the Russian commander Field Marshal Kutuzov took up position at Borodino, only 70 miles (110 km) west of Moscow, the spiritual capital of Russia. The Russians hastily built a series of fortifications, although they worried about the vulnerability of their left.

Napoleon, however, displayed little of his usual strategic genius. On September 7, he opted for a frontal assault on the Russian fortifications that, over the course of the day, resulted in at least 70,000 casualties in total. By 5pm, the French had captured the Russian fortifications, and the Russians had no reserves left. However, Napoleon refused to commit his Guard to win a decisive victory, and the Russian forces were able to retreat in an orderly manner.

Seven days later, Napoleon occupied Moscow in what proved to be a hollow victory. Within weeks, the French were forced to set out on a catastrophic retreat through the Russian winter.

THE RUSSIANS TAKE POSITION
Field Marshal Kutuzov took up position on the Smolensk-Moscow road. The Russian side constructed a series of fortifications that would become the main focus of the French attack throughout September 15.

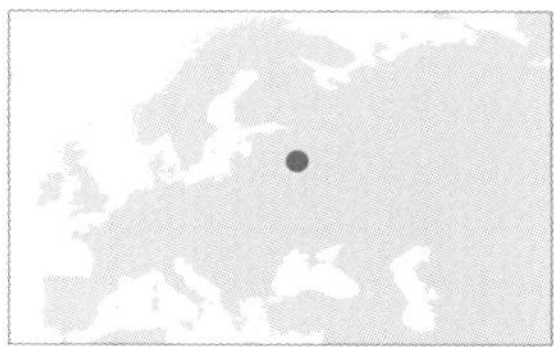

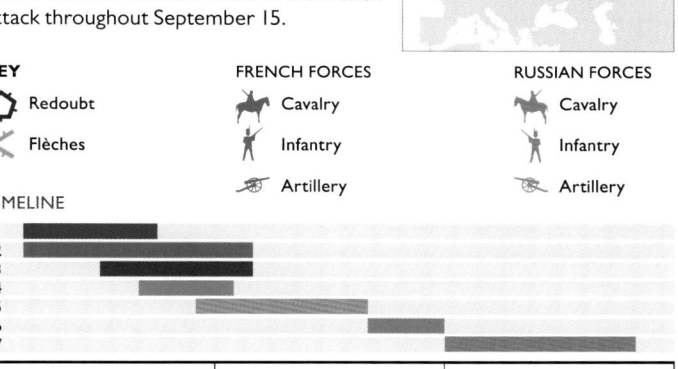

KEY

		FRENCH FORCES		RUSSIAN FORCES	
⬡	Redoubt	🐎	Cavalry	🐎	Cavalry
⤢	Flèches	🧍	Infantry	🧍	Infantry
		🔫	Artillery	🔫	Artillery

TIMELINE

1
2
3
4
5
6
7

5:00 AM, SEP 7, 1812   11:00 AM   5:00 PM   11:00 PM

SEPTEMBER 7, AFTERNOON
The French forces press their advantage, finally taking the Raevsky Redoubt. The Russians succeed in withdrawing in an orderly manner.

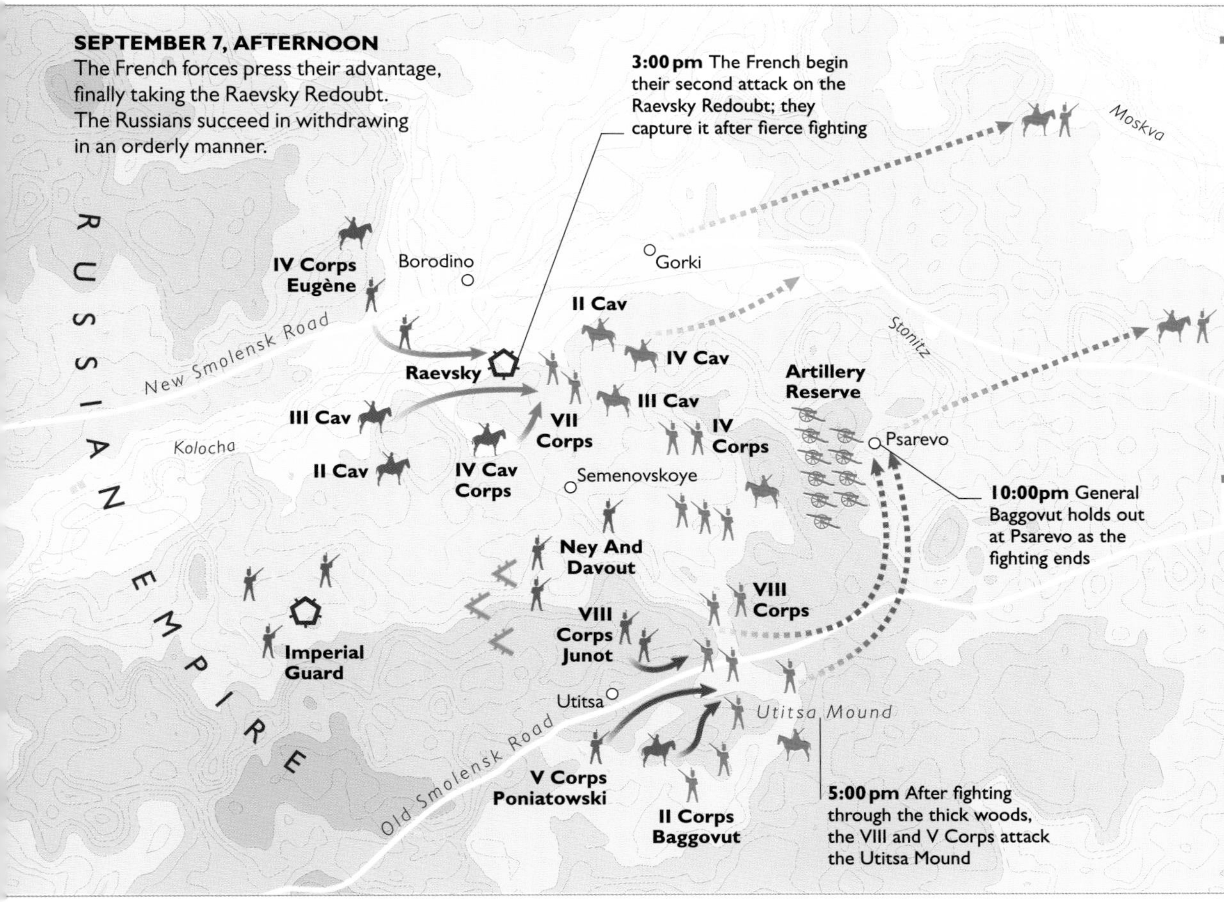

3:00 pm The French begin their second attack on the Raevsky Redoubt; they capture it after fierce fighting

Moskva

R U S S I A N   E M P I R E

New Smolensk Road

IV Corps Eugène

Borodino

○ Gorki

II Cav

Raevsky

III Cav

Kolocha

II Cav

IV Cav Corps

VII Corps

IV Cav

III Cav

Semenovskoye ○

Stonitz

Artillery Reserve

IV Corps

○ Psarevo

10:00pm General Baggovut holds out at Psarevo as the fighting ends

Imperial Guard

Ney And Davout

VIII Corps Junot

VIII Corps

Utitsa ○

Utitsa Mound

Old Smolensk Road

V Corps Poniatowski

II Corps Baggovut

5:00 pm After fighting through the thick woods, the VIII and V Corps attack the Utitsa Mound

6   THE FRENCH TAKE THE RAEVSKY REDOUBT
3:00–5:00 PM

At 3:00 pm, the French cavalry corps near Borodino attacked to the south of the redoubt, desperately fighting their way forward. With the cavalry finally inside the redoubt, the French infantry moved in to overwhelm the Russian gunners. Eugène's forces then launched an attack on the Russian infantry on the plateau behind the redoubt.

⟶ Final assault on the Raevsky Redoubt

⇢ Russian retreat

7   THE BATTLE WINDS DOWN   5:00–10:00 PM

The last significant fighting took place around the Utitsa Mound, where Junot and Poniatowski launched a final attack. Finding himself isolated as the other Russian forces pulled back, General Baggovut retreated to Psarevo. As the battle petered out, Napoleon drew his men back. The Russians retreated east the following morning.

⟶ French final attack

⇢ Baggovut's retreat

⇢ Russian withdrawal

NAPOLEON AND HIS ARMY

Starting his military career at the age of 16 as an artillery officer, Napoleon crowned himself the Emperor of the French in 1804. By 1807, his Grand Armée had decisively defeated all major continental European armies.

△ **The shako**
Under Napoleon, the cylindrical shako, made of leather and felt, replaced the bicorne as the headgear of the infantry.

Under Napoleon, the French army enjoyed important organizational and tactical advantages over other European armies of the time. The army was a product of the former monarchy and of the new regime that had formed after the French Revolution (1789). It had benefited from reforms under the old regime, which included improvements in light infantry tactics and the standardization of field artillery; they also paved the way for the autonomous divisional and corps structure which Napoleon used to such effect.

Napoleon's innovations

From the new regime, Napoleon inherited mass conscription, an economy geared toward war, and an offensive outlook that kept the war away from France as much as possible. Napoleon made increasing use of large artillery formations to breach enemy lines. He also organized the Grand Armée into corps, which were, in essence, highly mobile miniature armies, capable of fighting independently. The Battle of Ulm (1805) was the first field test where the corps successfully demonstrated their effectiveness and agility. To all this, Napoleon added operational brilliance, strategic intuition, and the ability to bond with his soldiers, whether they were marshals or lowly grenadiers.

△ **Army of the Ocean Coasts**
In this early 19th-century painting, Napoleon inspects his troops at a training camp in Boulogne in August 1804. The newly formed army, known as the *Armée des côtes de l'Océan* (Army of the Ocean Coasts), later became the Grande Armée.

Napoleon in action
This 1808 painting by Louis-Francois, Baron Lejeune, shows Napoleon (center) directing the French infantry squares at the Battle of the Pyramids (see p.159). Such infantry formations were used to repulse massed cavalry charges.

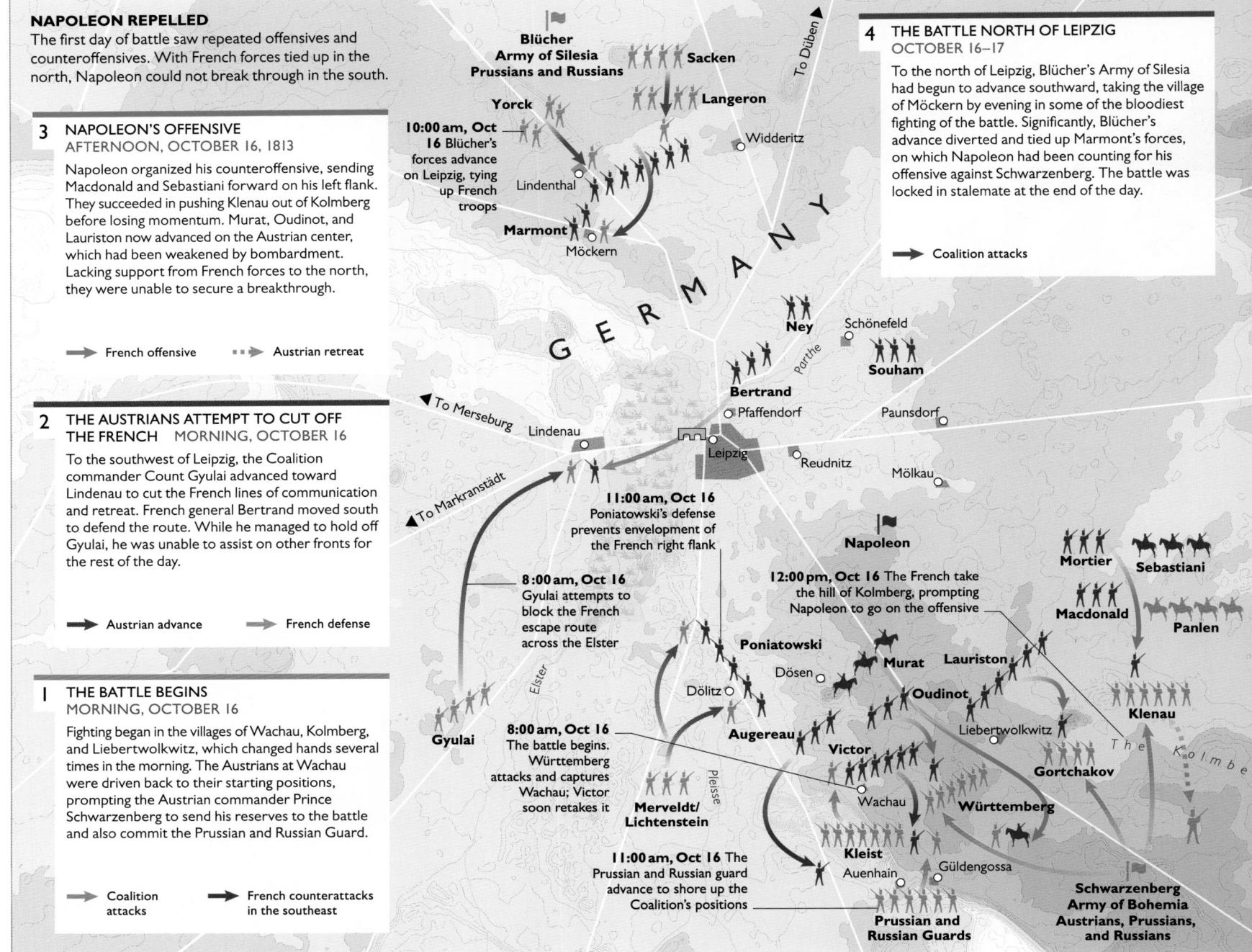

NAPOLEON REPELLED
The first day of battle saw repeated offensives and counteroffensives. With French forces tied up in the north, Napoleon could not break through in the south.

3 NAPOLEON'S OFFENSIVE
AFTERNOON, OCTOBER 16, 1813

Napoleon organized his counteroffensive, sending Macdonald and Sebastiani forward on his left flank. They succeeded in pushing Klenau out of Kolmberg before losing momentum. Murat, Oudinot, and Lauriston now advanced on the Austrian center, which had been weakened by bombardment. Lacking support from French forces to the north, they were unable to secure a breakthrough.

➡ French offensive ▪▪▶ Austrian retreat

2 THE AUSTRIANS ATTEMPT TO CUT OFF THE FRENCH MORNING, OCTOBER 16

To the southwest of Leipzig, the Coalition commander Count Gyulai advanced toward Lindenau to cut the French lines of communication and retreat. French general Bertrand moved south to defend the route. While he managed to hold off Gyulai, he was unable to assist on other fronts for the rest of the day.

➡ Austrian advance ➡ French defense

1 THE BATTLE BEGINS
MORNING, OCTOBER 16

Fighting began in the villages of Wachau, Kolmberg, and Liebertwolkwitz, which changed hands several times in the morning. The Austrians at Wachau were driven back to their starting positions, prompting the Austrian commander Prince Schwarzenberg to send his reserves to the battle and also commit the Prussian and Russian Guard.

➡ Coalition attacks ➡ French counterattacks in the southeast

4 THE BATTLE NORTH OF LEIPZIG
OCTOBER 16–17

To the north of Leipzig, Blücher's Army of Silesia had begun to advance southward, taking the village of Möckern by evening in some of the bloodiest fighting of the battle. Significantly, Blücher's advance diverted and tied up Marmont's forces, on which Napoleon had been counting for his offensive against Schwarzenberg. The battle was locked in stalemate at the end of the day.

➡ Coalition attacks

Map labels:
Blücher, Army of Silesia, Prussians and Russians — Sacken — Langeron — Yorck — Widderitz — 10:00 am, Oct 16 Blücher's forces advance on Leipzig, tying up French troops — Lindenthal — Marmont — Möckern — GERMANY — Ney — Schönefeld — Souham — Bertrand — Parthe — Pfaffendorf — Paunsdorf — To Merseburg — Lindenau — Leipzig — Reudnitz — Mölkau — To Markranstädt — 11:00 am, Oct 16 Poniatowski's defense prevents envelopment of the French right flank — 8:00 am, Oct 16 Gyulai attempts to block the French escape route across the Elster — Napoleon — Mortier — Sebastiani — 12:00 pm, Oct 16 The French take the hill of Kolmberg, prompting Napoleon to go on the offensive — Macdonald — Panlen — Elster — Poniatowski — Dösen — Murat — Lauriston — Oudinot — Klenau — Gyulai — 8:00 am, Oct 16 The battle begins. Württemberg attacks and captures Wachau; Victor soon retakes it — Dölitz — Augereau — Victor — Liebertwolkwitz — The Kolmberg — Wachau — Gortchakov — Pleisse — Württemberg — Merveldt/Lichtenstein — Kleist — Auenhain — Güldengossa — 11:00 am, Oct 16 The Prussian and Russian guard advance to shore up the Coalition's positions — Prussian and Russian Guards — Schwarzenberg, Army of Bohemia, Austrians, Prussians, and Russians — To Düben

LEIPZIG

At Leipzig in Saxony on October 16–18, 1813, the combined armies of the Sixth Coalition decisively defeated Napoleon in the largest land battle in Europe before World War I. It involved about 500,000 men, of whom almost 100,000 were killed or wounded.

After his disastrous invasion of Russia in 1812, Napoleon began a campaign in Germany in May 1813. He hoped to force Prussia to reverse its decision to join Russia and Sweden in the Sixth Coalition (March 1813–May 1814). Initial French successes prompted an armistice in June, but the Coalition held firm and was joined by Austria when hostilities resumed in August, eventually forcing Napoleon to retreat. He concentrated some 175,000 men and more than 600 guns at Leipzig. Four coalition armies converged on the city, eventually totalling over 300,000 troops with twice as many

cannons as the French. The battle began on October 16 with brutal hand-to-hand fighting between Napoleon's forces and the Armies of Bohemia and Silesia in the villages to the north and southeast of the city. By dawn on October 18, Napoleon was surrounded and at the end of the day, the French had been pushed into Leipzig's suburbs. In the early hours of October 19, the Grande Armée withdrew over the only bridge across the Elster River. When a French corporal blew up the bridge, leaving some 50,000 Frenchmen trapped in Leipzig, he turned a tactical Coalition victory into a decisive one.

THE BATTLE OF THE NATIONS

At Leipzig in Saxony, eastern Germany, Napoleon's domination east of the Rhine was brutally quashed by the forces of the Sixth Coalition. The battle marked the beginning of the end of the First French Empire.

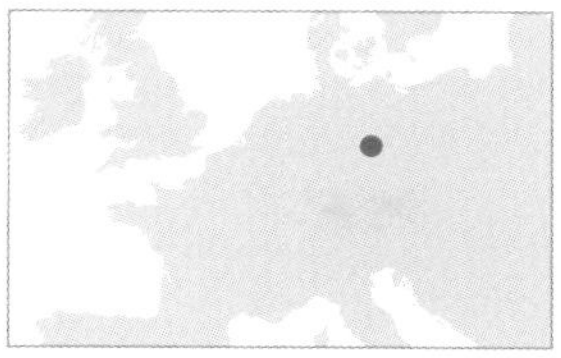

KEY

- Bridge over Elster
- Cities/Towns

COALITION FORCES
- Commander
- Cavalry
- Infantry
- Reinforcements

FRENCH FORCES
- Commander
- Cavalry
- Infantry

TIMELINE

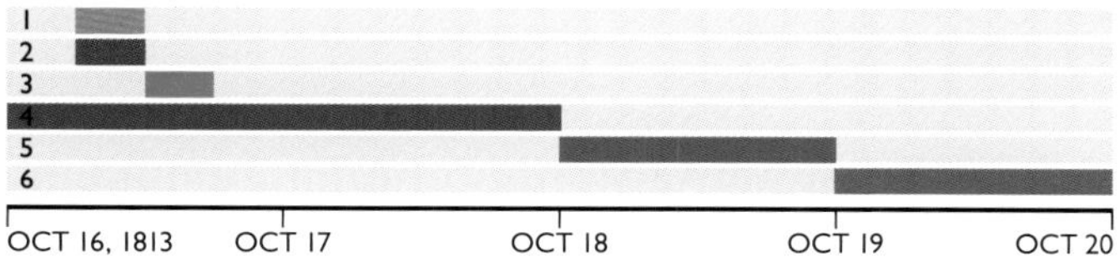

1
2
3
4
5
6

OCT 16, 1813   OCT 17   OCT 18   OCT 19   OCT 20

△ Schwarzenberg delivers news of victory
This 1835 lithograph by Franz Wolf shows the Austrian commander, Field Marshal Schwarzenberg, delivering news of victory at Leipzig to sovereigns of the Coalition.

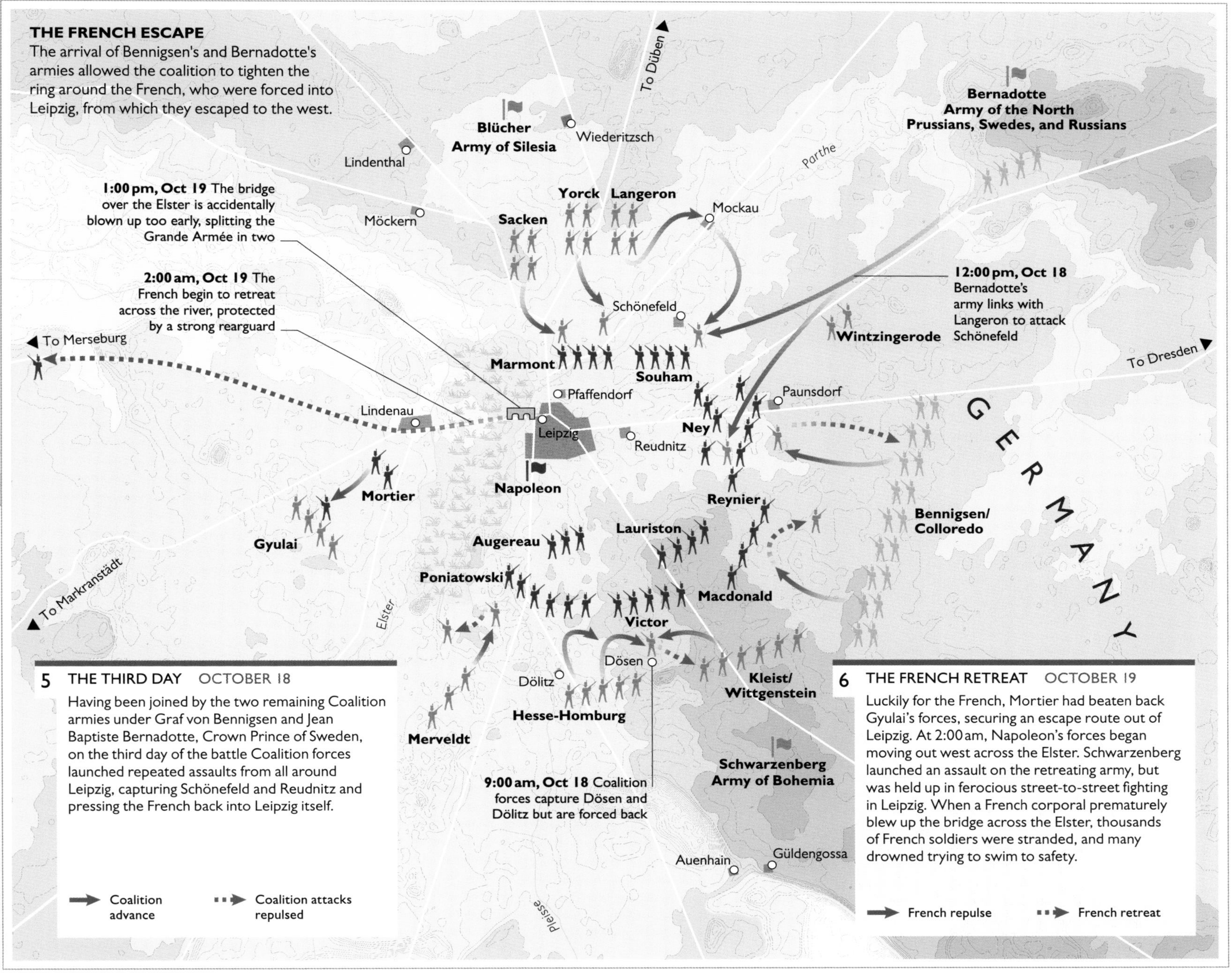

THE FRENCH ESCAPE

The arrival of Bennigsen's and Bernadotte's armies allowed the coalition to tighten the ring around the French, who were forced into Leipzig, from which they escaped to the west.

1:00 pm, Oct 19 The bridge over the Elster is accidentally blown up too early, splitting the Grande Armée in two

2:00 am, Oct 19 The French begin to retreat across the river, protected by a strong rearguard

12:00 pm, Oct 18 Bernadotte's army links with Langeron to attack Schönefeld

9:00 am, Oct 18 Coalition forces capture Dösen and Dölitz but are forced back

To Dresden ▶

To Düben ▲

To Merseburg ◀

To Dresden ▶

To Markranstädt ▲

Map labels: Lindenthal, Wiederitzsch, **Blücher Army of Silesia**, **Bernadotte Army of the North Prussians, Swedes, and Russians**, Möckern, **Yorck**, **Langeron**, Mockau, **Sacken**, Parthe, Schönefeld, **Wintzingerode**, Lindenau, **Marmont**, Pfaffendorf, **Souham**, Paunsdorf, Leipzig, **Ney**, Reudnitz, **Napoleon**, **Mortier**, **Reynier**, **Bennigsen/Colloredo**, **Gyulai**, **Augereau**, **Lauriston**, **Poniatowski**, **Macdonald**, **Victor**, Dösen, **Kleist/Wittgenstein**, Dölitz, **Hesse-Homburg**, **Merveldt**, **Schwarzenberg Army of Bohemia**, Auenhain, Güldengossa, Elster, Pleisse, G E R M A N Y

5 THE THIRD DAY OCTOBER 18

Having been joined by the two remaining Coalition armies under Graf von Bennigsen and Jean Baptiste Bernadotte, Crown Prince of Sweden, on the third day of the battle Coalition forces launched repeated assaults from all around Leipzig, capturing Schönefeld and Reudnitz and pressing the French back into Leipzig itself.

→ Coalition advance
∙∙∙▶ Coalition attacks repulsed

6 THE FRENCH RETREAT OCTOBER 19

Luckily for the French, Mortier had beaten back Gyulai's forces, securing an escape route out of Leipzig. At 2:00 am, Napoleon's forces began moving out west across the Elster. Schwarzenberg launched an assault on the retreating army, but was held up in ferocious street-to-street fighting in Leipzig. When a French corporal prematurely blew up the bridge across the Elster, thousands of French soldiers were stranded, and many drowned trying to swim to safety.

→ French repulse
∙∙∙▶ French retreat

NEW ORLEANS

On January 8, 1815, Major General Andrew Jackson (the future US president) and a disparate group of militia fighters, freed slaves, Choctaw people, and pirates withstood an assault by a larger British force. It was to be the final battle of the War of 1812 between the US and Great Britain.

In June 1812, the US declared war on Britain over British attempts to blockade US trade, force US seamen into the Royal Navy, and stop the US from expanding its territory. Hostilities officially ended with the Treaty of Ghent, signed on December 24, 1814, but it was weeks before news of the peace reached the US. Meanwhile, the British in the US pressed ahead with plans to capture the strategically important city of New Orleans.

With British forces sighted, the US Major General Andrew Jackson declared martial law in New Orleans. Over 5,000 men, including the pirate Jean Lafitte, responded to the call to defend the city. The action began when Jackson launched a night raid on the British camp. He then built defenses, known as Line Jackson, along the Rodriguez Canal, and sent 1,000 troops and 16 cannons to take up positions on the west bank of the Mississippi River. After several skirmishes the British, commanded by Sir Edward Pakenham, launched a disastrous attack on the Line Jackson on January 8. More than 2,000 of the 8,000-strong British force were cut down by Jackson's guns in a battle that lasted less than two hours. The British withdrew on January 18, when news of the peace treaty finally reached the US.

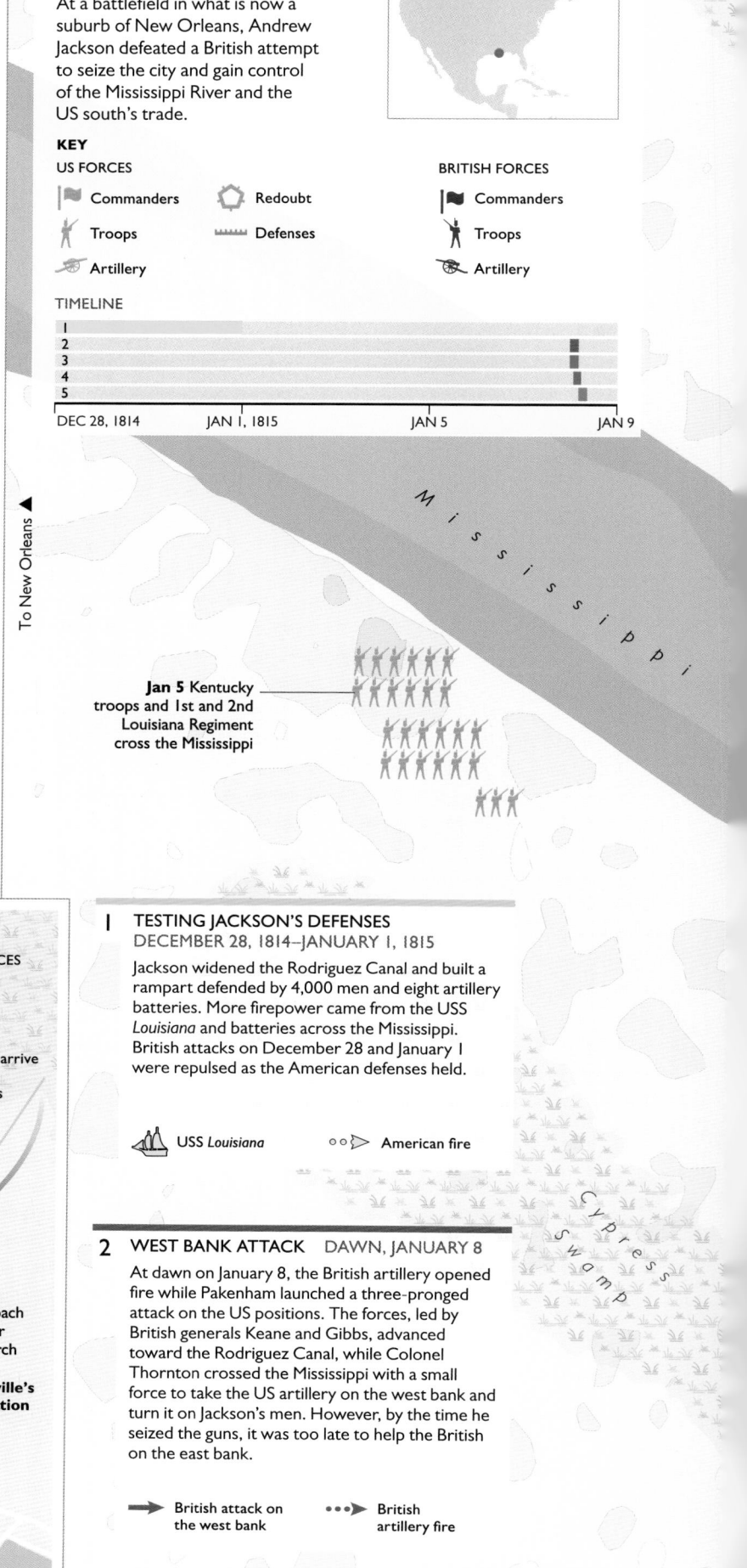

MISSISSIPPI CONFRONTATION
At a battlefield in what is now a suburb of New Orleans, Andrew Jackson defeated a British attempt to seize the city and gain control of the Mississippi River and the US south's trade.

KEY

US FORCES				BRITISH FORCES	
🚩 Commanders		⬡ Redoubt		🚩 Commanders	
🧍 Troops		⌢⌢⌢ Defenses		🧍 Troops	
Artillery				Artillery	

TIMELINE
1
2
3
4
5
DEC 28, 1814 — JAN 1, 1815 — JAN 5 — JAN 9

Jan 5 Kentucky troops and 1st and 2nd Louisiana Regiment cross the Mississippi

To New Orleans ◀

Mississippi

JACKSON'S NIGHT RAID

On December 23, 1814, British troops crossed the Cypress Swamp and advanced toward New Orleans, setting up camp near the Mississippi River. The following night, more than 2,000 of Jackson's men launched a three-pronged attack on the British redcoats, with supporting fire from the schooner USS *Carolina*. The British suffered 215 casualties in fierce fighting, leaving them in no doubt that Jackson's motley army would not be easily defeated.

KEY

US FORCES		BRITISH FORCES	
⊞ Jackson's headquarters		⊟ Camp	
🧍 Troops		🧍 Troops	
→ Attack		→ Forces arrive	
⛵ USS *Carolina*		➡ Attacks	
⊸⊳ *Carolina* opens fire			

7:00 pm, Dec 23 The bulk of the US forces attack from the north

Morning, Dec 23 British forces approach the Mississippi River after a 36-hour march

De La Ronde's plantation

Lacoste's plantation

Villere's plantation

Jumonville's plantation

7:00 pm, Dec 23 Jackson orders a three-pronged attack on the British

Dec 23 The British mistakenly choose to bivouac instead of marching on undefended New Orleans

To New Orleans ◀

Cypress Swamp

Mississippi

1 TESTING JACKSON'S DEFENSES
DECEMBER 28, 1814–JANUARY 1, 1815

Jackson widened the Rodriguez Canal and built a rampart defended by 4,000 men and eight artillery batteries. More firepower came from the USS *Louisiana* and batteries across the Mississippi. British attacks on December 28 and January 1 were repulsed as the American defenses held.

🚢 USS *Louisiana*   ○○▷ American fire

2 WEST BANK ATTACK   DAWN, JANUARY 8

At dawn on January 8, the British artillery opened fire while Pakenham launched a three-pronged attack on the US positions. The forces, led by British generals Keane and Gibbs, advanced toward the Rodriguez Canal, while Colonel Thornton crossed the Mississippi with a small force to take the US artillery on the west bank and turn it on Jackson's men. However, by the time he seized the guns, it was too late to help the British on the east bank.

➡ British attack on the west bank   •••▷ British artillery fire

Cypress Swamp

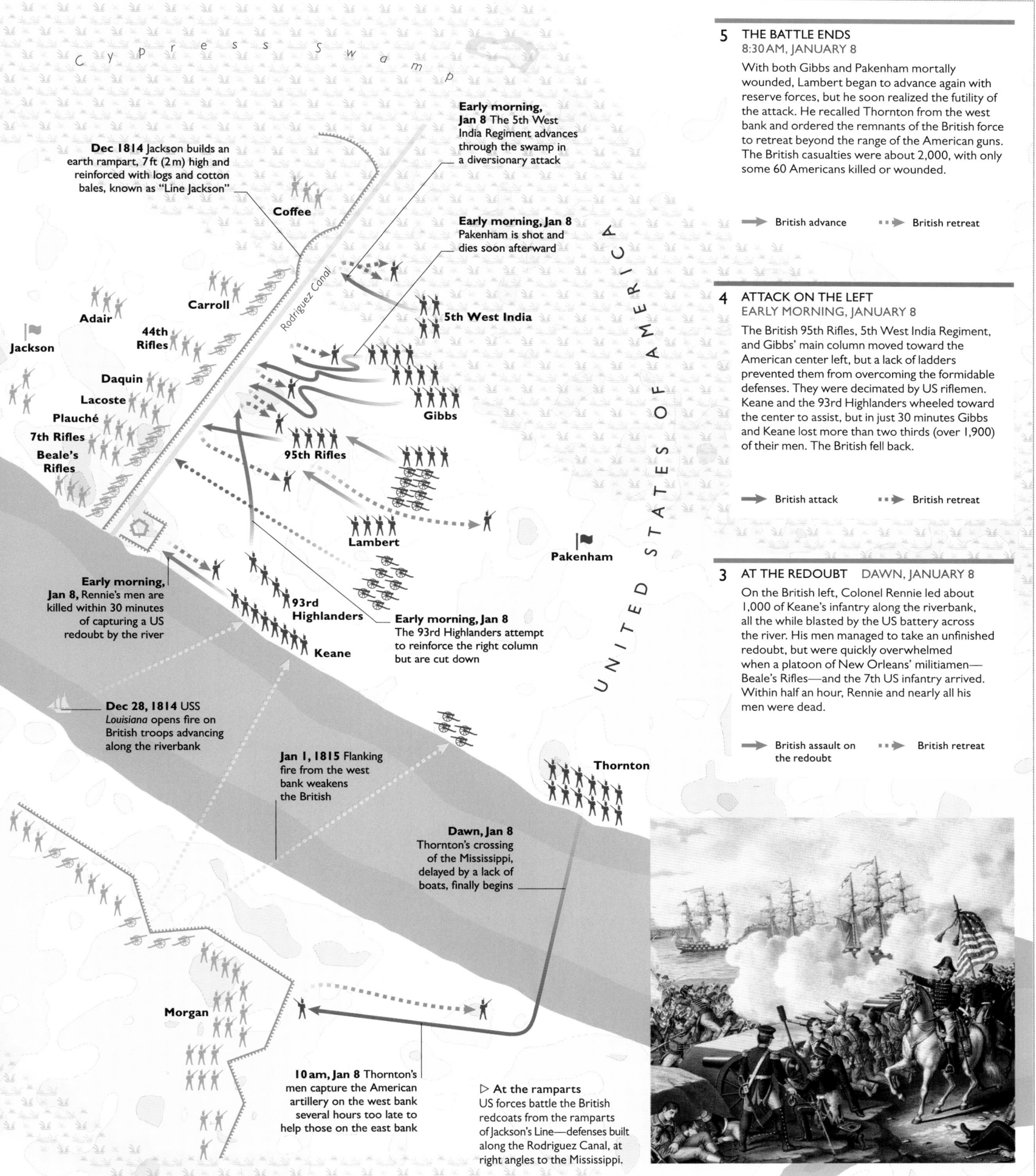

Dec 1814 Jackson builds an earth rampart, 7 ft (2 m) high and reinforced with logs and cotton bales, known as "Line Jackson"

Early morning, Jan 8 The 5th West India Regiment advances through the swamp in a diversionary attack

Early morning, Jan 8 Pakenham is shot and dies soon afterward

C y p r e s s S w a m p

Rodriguez Canal

Coffee

Carroll

Adair

44th Rifles

Jackson

Daquin

Lacoste

Plauché

7th Rifles

Beale's Rifles

5th West India

Gibbs

95th Rifles

Lambert

93rd Highlanders

Keane

Pakenham

U N I T E D   S T A T E S   O F   A M E R I C A

Early morning, Jan 8, Rennie's men are killed within 30 minutes of capturing a US redoubt by the river

Early morning, Jan 8 The 93rd Highlanders attempt to reinforce the right column but are cut down

Dec 28, 1814 USS Louisiana opens fire on British troops advancing along the riverbank

Jan 1, 1815 Flanking fire from the west bank weakens the British

Thornton

Dawn, Jan 8 Thornton's crossing of the Mississippi, delayed by a lack of boats, finally begins

Morgan

10am, Jan 8 Thornton's men capture the American artillery on the west bank several hours too late to help those on the east bank

▷ At the ramparts
US forces battle the British redcoats from the ramparts of Jackson's Line—defenses built along the Rodriguez Canal, at right angles to the Mississippi.

5 THE BATTLE ENDS
8:30 AM, JANUARY 8

With both Gibbs and Pakenham mortally wounded, Lambert began to advance again with reserve forces, but he soon realized the futility of the attack. He recalled Thornton from the west bank and ordered the remnants of the British force to retreat beyond the range of the American guns. The British casualties were about 2,000, with only some 60 Americans killed or wounded.

→ British advance   ⇢ British retreat

4 ATTACK ON THE LEFT
EARLY MORNING, JANUARY 8

The British 95th Rifles, 5th West India Regiment, and Gibbs' main column moved toward the American center left, but a lack of ladders prevented them from overcoming the formidable defenses. They were decimated by US riflemen. Keane and the 93rd Highlanders wheeled toward the center to assist, but in just 30 minutes Gibbs and Keane lost more than two thirds (over 1,900) of their men. The British fell back.

→ British attack   ⇢ British retreat

3 AT THE REDOUBT   DAWN, JANUARY 8

On the British left, Colonel Rennie led about 1,000 of Keane's infantry along the riverbank, all the while blasted by the US battery across the river. His men managed to take an unfinished redoubt, but were quickly overwhelmed when a platoon of New Orleans' militiamen— Beale's Rifles—and the 7th US infantry arrived. Within half an hour, Rennie and nearly all his men were dead.

→ British assault on the redoubt   ⇢ British retreat

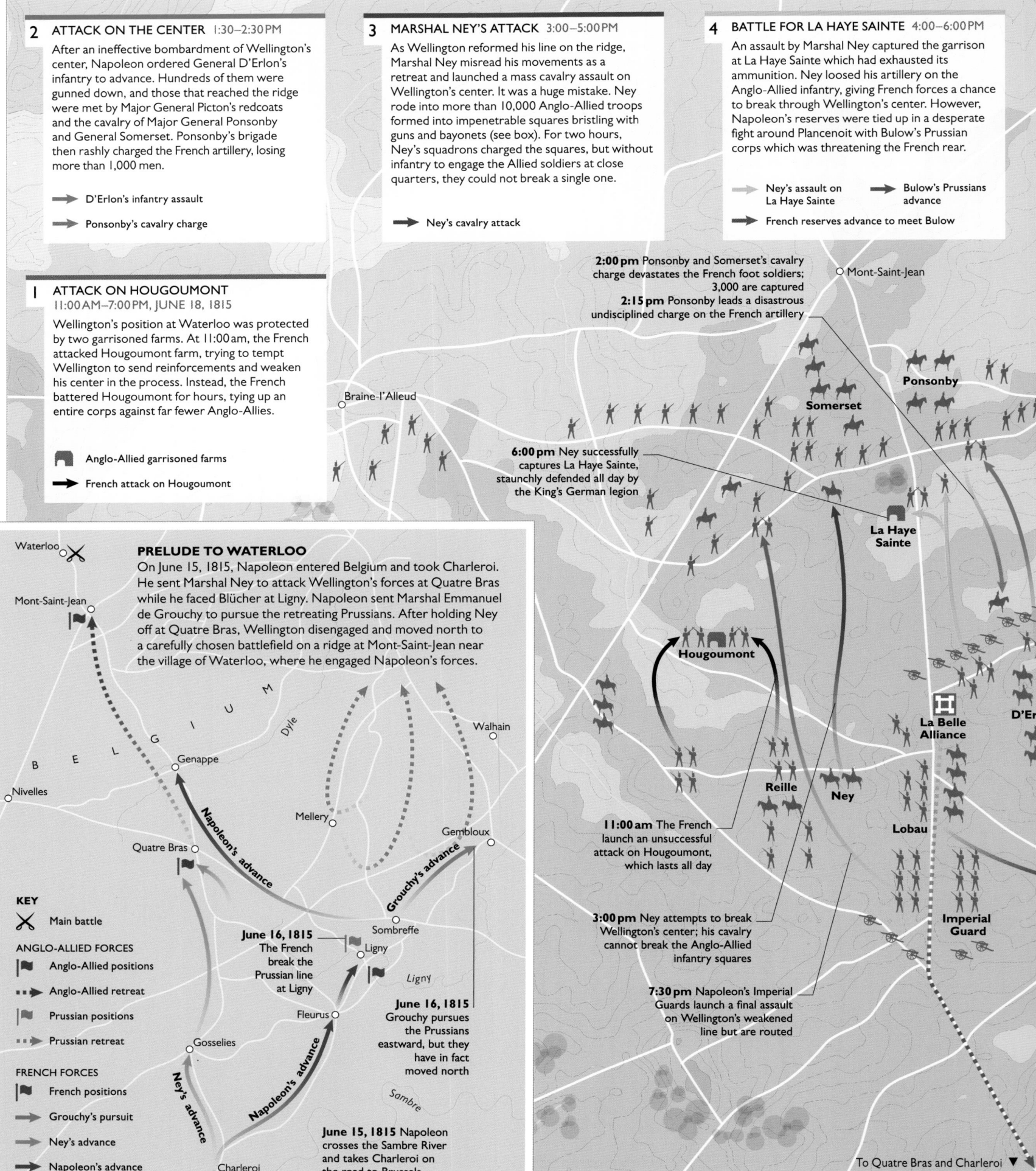

2 ATTACK ON THE CENTER 1:30–2:30 PM

After an ineffective bombardment of Wellington's center, Napoleon ordered General D'Erlon's infantry to advance. Hundreds of them were gunned down, and those that reached the ridge were met by Major General Picton's redcoats and the cavalry of Major General Ponsonby and General Somerset. Ponsonby's brigade then rashly charged the French artillery, losing more than 1,000 men.

➡ D'Erlon's infantry assault

➡ Ponsonby's cavalry charge

3 MARSHAL NEY'S ATTACK 3:00–5:00 PM

As Wellington reformed his line on the ridge, Marshal Ney misread his movements as a retreat and launched a mass cavalry assault on Wellington's center. It was a huge mistake. Ney rode into more than 10,000 Anglo-Allied troops formed into impenetrable squares bristling with guns and bayonets (see box). For two hours, Ney's squadrons charged the squares, but without infantry to engage the Allied soldiers at close quarters, they could not break a single one.

➡ Ney's cavalry attack

4 BATTLE FOR LA HAYE SAINTE 4:00–6:00 PM

An assault by Marshal Ney captured the garrison at La Haye Sainte which had exhausted its ammunition. Ney loosed his artillery on the Anglo-Allied infantry, giving French forces a chance to break through Wellington's center. However, Napoleon's reserves were tied up in a desperate fight around Plancenoit with Bulow's Prussian corps which was threatening the French rear.

➡ Ney's assault on La Haye Sainte   ➡ Bulow's Prussians advance

➡ French reserves advance to meet Bulow

1 ATTACK ON HOUGOUMONT
11:00 AM–7:00 PM, JUNE 18, 1815

Wellington's position at Waterloo was protected by two garrisoned farms. At 11:00 am, the French attacked Hougoumont farm, trying to tempt Wellington to send reinforcements and weaken his center in the process. Instead, the French battered Hougoumont for hours, tying up an entire corps against far fewer Anglo-Allies.

🏠 Anglo-Allied garrisoned farms

➡ French attack on Hougoumont

2:00 pm Ponsonby and Somerset's cavalry charge devastates the French foot soldiers; 3,000 are captured
2:15 pm Ponsonby leads a disastrous undisciplined charge on the French artillery

6:00 pm Ney successfully captures La Haye Sainte, staunchly defended all day by the King's German legion

11:00 am The French launch an unsuccessful attack on Hougoumont, which lasts all day

3:00 pm Ney attempts to break Wellington's center; his cavalry cannot break the Anglo-Allied infantry squares

7:30 pm Napoleon's Imperial Guards launch a final assault on Wellington's weakened line but are routed

Mont-Saint-Jean
Braine-l'Alleud
Ponsonby
Somerset
La Haye Sainte
Hougoumont
Reille
Ney
La Belle Alliance
D'Erlo
Lobau
Imperial Guard

To Quatre Bras and Charleroi ▼

PRELUDE TO WATERLOO

On June 15, 1815, Napoleon entered Belgium and took Charleroi. He sent Marshal Ney to attack Wellington's forces at Quatre Bras while he faced Blücher at Ligny. Napoleon sent Marshal Emmanuel de Grouchy to pursue the retreating Prussians. After holding Ney off at Quatre Bras, Wellington disengaged and moved north to a carefully chosen battlefield on a ridge at Mont-Saint-Jean near the village of Waterloo, where he engaged Napoleon's forces.

Waterloo
Mont-Saint-Jean
Nivelles
Genappe
Quatre Bras
Walhain
Mellery
Gembloux
Napoleon's advance
Grouchy's advance
Sombreffe
Ligny
June 16, 1815 The French break the Prussian line at Ligny
Ligny
June 16, 1815 Grouchy pursues the Prussians eastward, but they have in fact moved north
Fleurus
Gosselies
Ney's advance
Napoleon's advance
Sambre
June 15, 1815 Napoleon crosses the Sambre River and takes Charleroi on the road to Brussels
Charleroi
BELGIUM
Dyle

KEY

✕ Main battle

ANGLO-ALLIED FORCES

🚩 Anglo-Allied positions

▪▪▪➤ Anglo-Allied retreat

🚩 Prussian positions

▪▪▪➤ Prussian retreat

FRENCH FORCES

🚩 French positions

➡ Grouchy's pursuit

➡ Ney's advance

➡ Napoleon's advance

▷ **Wellington's cavalry**
The British cavalry was known for its bravery, but also for its tendency to get carried away in the heat of battle, as shown by Ponsonby's ill-fated charge on the French artillery.

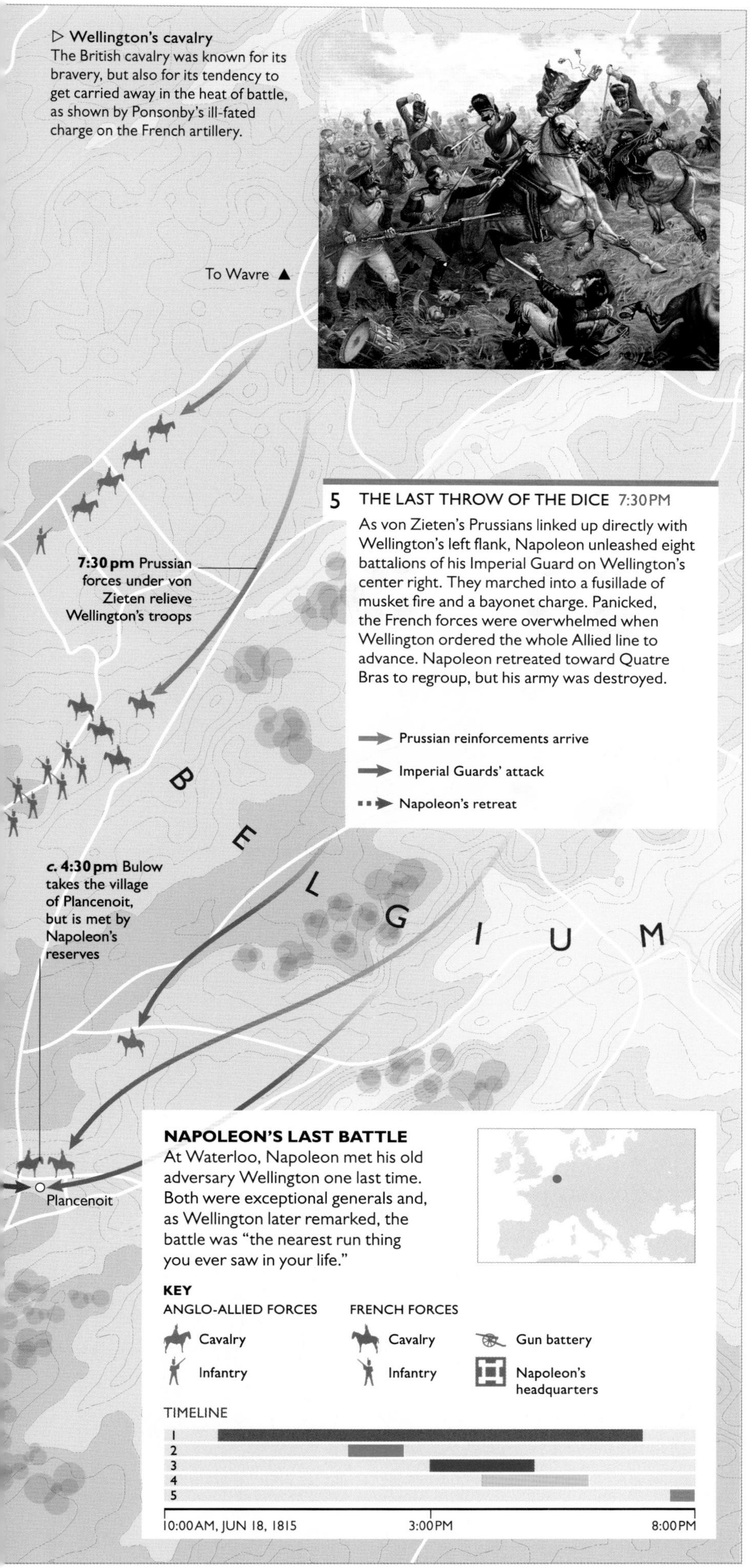

To Wavre ▲

7:30 pm Prussian forces under von Zieten relieve Wellington's troops

5 THE LAST THROW OF THE DICE 7:30PM

As von Zieten's Prussians linked up directly with Wellington's left flank, Napoleon unleashed eight battalions of his Imperial Guard on Wellington's center right. They marched into a fusillade of musket fire and a bayonet charge. Panicked, the French forces were overwhelmed when Wellington ordered the whole Allied line to advance. Napoleon retreated toward Quatre Bras to regroup, but his army was destroyed.

→ Prussian reinforcements arrive

→ Imperial Guards' attack

▪▪▶ Napoleon's retreat

c. **4:30 pm** Bulow takes the village of Plancenoit, but is met by Napoleon's reserves

BELGIUM

Plancenoit

NAPOLEON'S LAST BATTLE

At Waterloo, Napoleon met his old adversary Wellington one last time. Both were exceptional generals and, as Wellington later remarked, the battle was "the nearest run thing you ever saw in your life."

KEY

ANGLO-ALLIED FORCES	FRENCH FORCES	
🐎 Cavalry	🐎 Cavalry	🔫 Gun battery
🚶 Infantry	🚶 Infantry	⊡ Napoleon's headquarters

TIMELINE

1
2
3
4
5

10:00AM, JUN 18, 1815   3:00PM   8:00PM

WATERLOO

On June 18, 1815, the Anglo-Allied and Prussian armies under the Duke of Wellington and General Blücher finally ended the Napoleonic Wars (1803–15) with a victory over Napoleon. The decisive battle took place near the village of Waterloo in Belgium.

In March 1815, news reached Europe's leaders that Napoleon had escaped from the Mediterranean island of Elba, where he had been exiled after the Battle of Paris (1814). Napoleon had landed in France on March 1 and returned to Paris, where he quickly rebuilt support and reclaimed his imperial title, Napoleon I, in a period known as the Hundred Days. By March 20, he had raised a large army.

Great Britain, Prussia, Austria, and Russia formed a coalition to defeat Napoleon. By June, the Duke of Wellington, one of England's great military commanders, was in charge of an Anglo-Allied army of more than 100,000 troops in Brussels, while in Namur, Prussian Field Marshal Gebhard Leberecht von Blücher was camped with a similarly sized force; Russian and Austrian armies totaling more than 200,000 men each were also on their way to battle France.

On June 15, Napoleon marched into Belgium. He clashed with Wellington and Blücher on the following day at Quatre Bras and Ligny. After heavy fighting, Blücher fell back to Wavre while Wellington moved to Mont-Saint-Jean near the village of Waterloo, where he would face Napoleon one last time. At breakfast on June 18, Napoleon told his commanders that the coming battle would be "l'affaire d'un déjeuner" (a picnic); it proved to be anything but. Wellington's Anglo-Allied forces withstood repeated French attacks, despite heavy pressure on their positions at La Haye Sainte and Hougoumont. The arrival of Blücher's Prussians freed Wellington to launch a final offensive that drove the French from the field. Napoleon fled; he was blocked from sailing to America on July 15 and was exiled once more.

THE BRITISH INFANTRY SQUARE

Infantry squares (pictured below) were composed of about 500 soldiers, arranged in two or more tightly packed ranks on each side, with reserves in the middle. The infantry would fire volleys at any approaching cavalry, causing the fallen horses to obstruct further attacks. The squares were almost impervious to cavalry but were vulnerable to musket fire and especially susceptible to artillery fire.

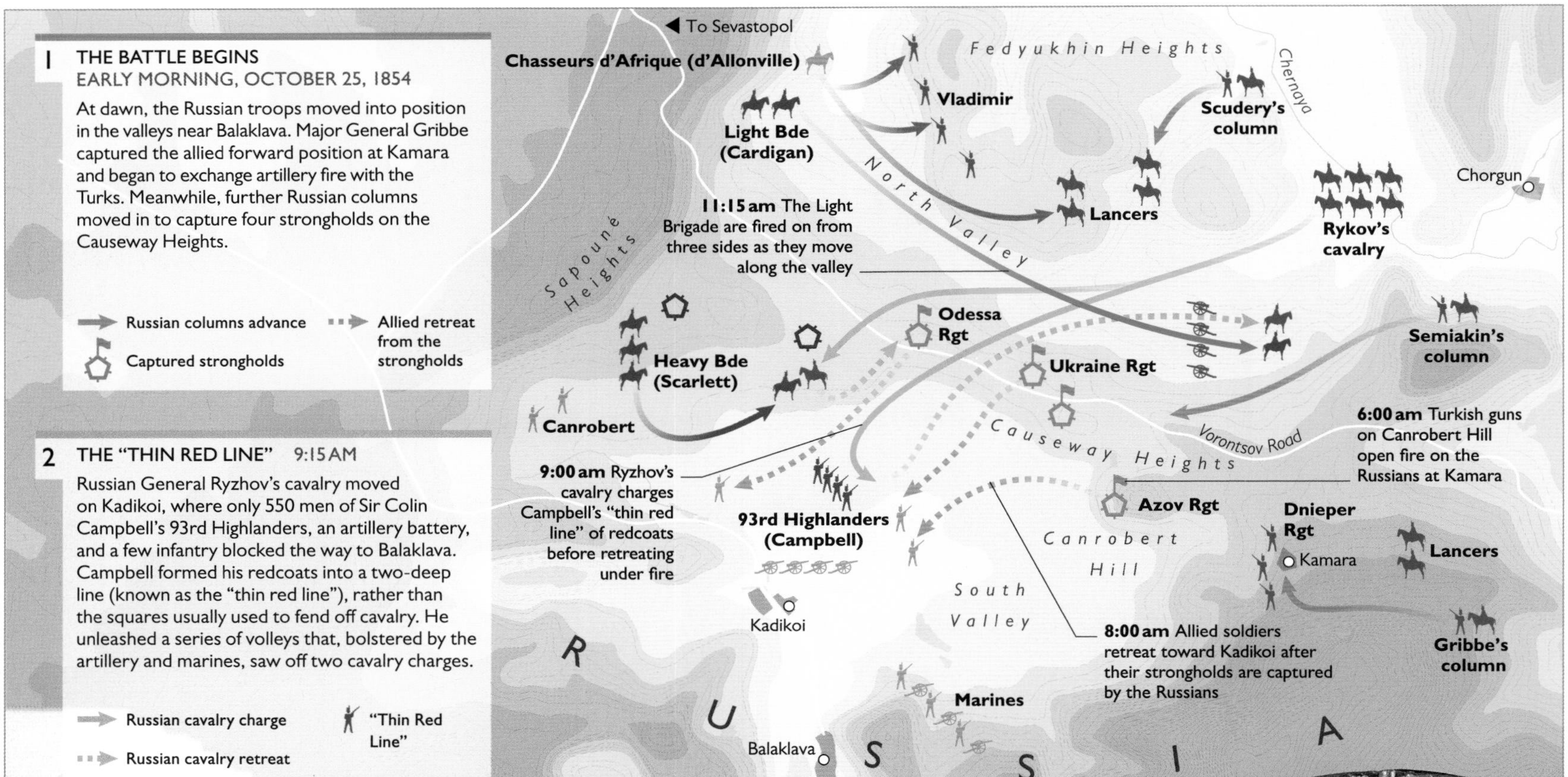

1 THE BATTLE BEGINS
EARLY MORNING, OCTOBER 25, 1854

At dawn, the Russian troops moved into position in the valleys near Balaklava. Major General Gribbe captured the allied forward position at Kamara and began to exchange artillery fire with the Turks. Meanwhile, further Russian columns moved in to capture four strongholds on the Causeway Heights.

→ Russian columns advance
⚐ Captured strongholds
⇢ Allied retreat from the strongholds

2 THE "THIN RED LINE" 9:15 AM

Russian General Ryzhov's cavalry moved on Kadikoi, where only 550 men of Sir Colin Campbell's 93rd Highlanders, an artillery battery, and a few infantry blocked the way to Balaklava. Campbell formed his redcoats into a two-deep line (known as the "thin red line"), rather than the squares usually used to fend off cavalry. He unleashed a series of volleys that, bolstered by the artillery and marines, saw off two cavalry charges.

→ Russian cavalry charge
⇢ Russian cavalry retreat
⚑ "Thin Red Line"

3 CHARGE OF THE HEAVY BRIGADE 9:30 AM

The main body of the Russian cavalry was now charged by General Sir James Scarlett's Heavy Brigade. The British horsemen were outnumbered by more than two to one. However, Scarlett's forces bravely engaged the Russians, advancing uphill at a slow trot, hacking at the enemy horsemen, and routing them after just ten minutes.

→ The charge of the Heavy Brigade

4 CHARGE OF THE LIGHT BRIGADE 11:10 AM

Lord Cardigan's Light Brigade was commanded to "advance rapidly" to stop the Russians from removing the captured guns from the Causeway Heights. Cardigan instead charged toward the Russian battery at the end of the heavily defended North Valley. Survivors of the charge had to fight their way back up the "Valley of Death," leaving the allies incapable of further action that day.

→ French assault on the Russian positions
→ The charge of the Light Brigade

Map labels: To Sevastopol; Chasseurs d'Afrique (d'Allonville); Fedyukhin Heights; Chernoya; Vladimir; Scudery's column; Light Bde (Cardigan); Chorgun; 11:15am The Light Brigade are fired on from three sides as they move along the valley; North Valley; Lancers; Rykov's cavalry; Sapoune Heights; Odessa Rgt; Semiakin's column; Heavy Bde (Scarlett); Ukraine Rgt; Canrobert; Causeway Heights; Vorontsov Road; 6:00am Turkish guns on Canrobert Hill open fire on the Russians at Kamara; 9:00am Ryzhov's cavalry charges Campbell's "thin red line" of redcoats before retreating under fire; 93rd Highlanders (Campbell); Azov Rgt; Dnieper Rgt; Lancers; Canrobert Hill; Kamara; Kadikoi; South Valley; 8:00am Allied soldiers retreat toward Kadikoi after their strongholds are captured by the Russians; Gribbe's column; R U S S I A; Marines; Balaklava

▷ **Dragoon's shako**
This cylindrical cap, or shako, was worn by Captain Thomas Everard Hutton in the Charge of the Light Brigade. Hutton was severely wounded in the action.

BALAKLAVA

An indecisive battle in the Crimean War (1853–56) between Russian and allied forces, Balaklava is famed for the stand made by the "thin red line" and for the disastrous charge of the Light Brigade.

In 1854, Britain, France, and Turkey invaded the Crimea in response to a Russian attack in the Balkans the previous year. The allied expedition achieved a victory at the Battle of the Alma on 20 September. This left open the path to the Russian naval base of Sevastopol, which the allies besieged on 25 October. The Russians tried to drive a wedge between the siege line at Sevastopol and the British base at Balaklava. The battle ended in stalemate: the British retained control of Balaklava, but the Russians took control of the main road from there to Sevastopol. The battle's place in history was secured by the stand of Sir Colin Campbell's 93rd Highlanders, known as the "thin red line", the successful charge of the Heavy Brigade, and the infamous mistake that led to the disastrous charge of the Light Brigade through a valley lined with enemy guns.

CRIMEAN CONFLICT
The Battle of Balaklava was prompted by the long siege of Sevastopol, home to Russia's Black Sea Fleet. The siege finally ended in September 1855 when the Russians blew up the forts and evacuated the city.

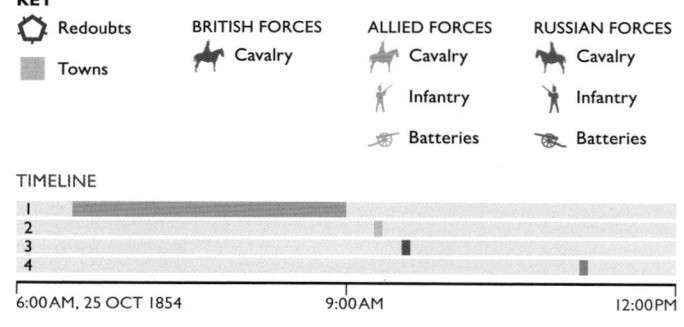

KEY
⬡ Redoubts
▨ Towns

BRITISH FORCES
🐎 Cavalry

ALLIED FORCES
🐎 Cavalry
𝖎 Infantry
🔫 Batteries

RUSSIAN FORCES
🐎 Cavalry
𝖎 Infantry
🔫 Batteries

TIMELINE
1
2
3
4
6:00AM, 25 OCT 1854   9:00AM   12:00PM

SOLFERINO

The last battle in the Second War of Italian Independence (April–July 1859) took place in Solferino, northern Italy, where a French-Piedmontese army defeated the Austrians.

In 1859, the French Emperor Napoleon III allied with King Victor Emmanuel II of Piedmont–Sardinia to drive the Austrian army out of northern Italy. Napoleon led his army to victories at Montebello, Palestro, and Magenta before meeting the Austrians again on the Medole plain. Here, the Austrian Emperor Franz Josef I had gathered around 120,000 infantry, 10,000 cavalry, and 430 guns. The battle was broken into three main actions. The French infantry and cavalry fought at Solferino as well as further south, at Guidizzolo. To the north, the Piedmontese held off the enemy at San Martino, until the Austrians retreated back across the River Mincio, fearing encirclement.

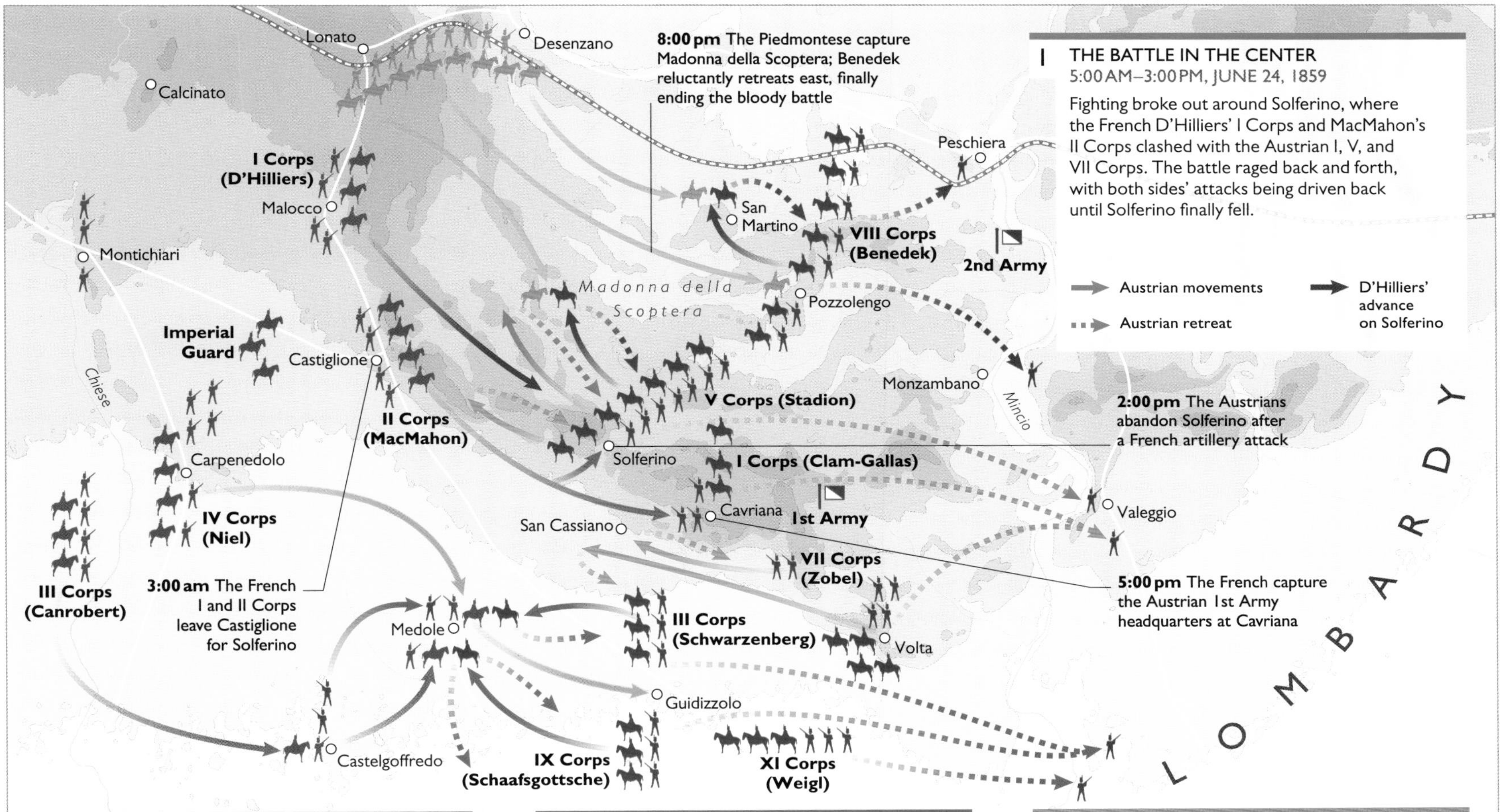

BIRTH OF A NATION

The clash at Solferino advanced the cause of Italian unification, completed when Rome became the capital of the new Kingdom of Italy in 1871. The carnage at Solferino prompted Henry Dunant to found the Red Cross in 1863.

KEY

🚃🚃 Railway

FRENCH FORCES	PIEDMONTESE FORCES	AUSTRIAN FORCES
Infantry	Infantry	Infantry
Cavalry	Cavalry	Cavalry
		Austrian armies

TIMELINE

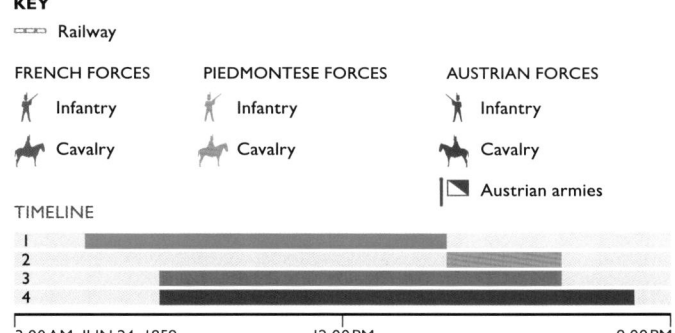

1
2
3
4

3:00AM, JUN 24, 1859   12:00PM   9:00PM

Map labels:

Lonato, Desenzano, Calcinato, I Corps (D'Hilliers), Malocco, Montichiari, Imperial Guard, Castiglione, Chiese, II Corps (MacMahon), Carpenedolo, IV Corps (Niel), III Corps (Canrobert), Medole, Castelgoffredo, IX Corps (Schaafsgottsche), Guidizzolo, XI Corps (Weigl), San Cassiano, Solferino, Madonna della Scoptera, San Martino, VIII Corps (Benedek), 2nd Army, Peschiera, Pozzolengo, V Corps (Stadion), Monzambano, Mincio, I Corps (Clam-Gallas), Cavriana, 1st Army, VII Corps (Zobel), Volta, III Corps (Schwarzenberg), Valeggio, LOMBARDY

8:00 pm The Piedmontese capture Madonna della Scoptera; Benedek reluctantly retreats east, finally ending the bloody battle

3:00 am The French I and II Corps leave Castiglione for Solferino

2:00 pm The Austrians abandon Solferino after a French artillery attack

5:00 pm The French capture the Austrian 1st Army headquarters at Cavriana

1 THE BATTLE IN THE CENTER
5:00AM–3:00PM, JUNE 24, 1859

Fighting broke out around Solferino, where the French D'Hilliers' I Corps and MacMahon's II Corps clashed with the Austrian I, V, and VII Corps. The battle raged back and forth, with both sides' attacks being driven back until Solferino finally fell.

→ Austrian movements
➔ D'Hilliers' advance on Solferino
‧‧➤ Austrian retreat

4 BATTLE TO THE NORTH 7:00AM–8:00PM

Four Piedmontese divisions challenged Benedek's VIII Korps and Stadion's V Corps for control of the hills north of Solferino. Their attacks kept Benedek—one of Austria's most accomplished military commanders—engaged throughout the day, preventing him from sending troops to tackle the French action at Solferino.

➔ Austrian movements
➔ Piedmontese attacks
‧‧➤ Austrian 2nd Army retreat

3 BATTLE TO THE SOUTH 7:00AM–6:00PM

Niel's IV Corps moved east, holding a crucial line that prevented the Austrian III, IX, and XI Corps from joining the battle around Solferino. Niel held out all day at Medole, despite being heavily outnumbered. After reinforcements from Canrobert's III Corps arrived, Niel attacked the Austrians at Guidizzolo, forcing their retreat.

➔ Austrian movements
‧‧➤ Austrian 1st Army retreat
➔ Niels' advance
➔ Canrobert's reinforcements

2 ATTACK ON CAVRIANA 3:00PM–6:00PM

MacMahon's II Corps held off several Austrian attempts to punch through the gap between themselves and Niel's IV Corps. With the support of the French Imperial Guard, they captured San Cassiano and then advanced toward the Austrian 1st Army headquarters at Cavriana. The capture of Cavriana forced the Austrian center to retreat.

➔ Austrian movements
➔ MacMahon's advance
‧‧➤ Austrian 1st Army retreat

ANTIETAM

The bloodiest day of battle in US history took place at Antietam Creek during the American Civil War (1861–65). A large Union army, led by General George McClellan, paid a heavy price to cut short the invasion of Maryland by the Confederate Army of Northern Virginia, under the command of Robert E. Lee.

In 1861, civil war broke out in the US between the Union and the rebel states of the Confederacy. By the following year, the Confederate general Robert E. Lee had won victories at the Seven Days' Battles and the Second Battle of Bull Run (Manassas). In September 1862, Lee invaded Maryland with the Army of Northern Virginia, hoping that success there would garner European support for the Confederacy and damage President Lincoln's standing in the upcoming Congressional elections.

As Lee moved west he split his army in two, but the Union's General George McClellan missed this chance to engage the divided forces. By the time McClellan finally caught up with Lee at Antietam Creek, near Sharpsburg, Maryland, on September 17, the Confederates had regrouped. Even so, Lee was vastly outnumbered by about two to one. Believing that Lee had reserves, McClellan refused to commit his full force, again missing the chance to destroy Lee's army. After a brutal day's fighting, the battle ended in stalemate. McClellan let Lee slip back into Virginia, and the Union claimed a strategic victory. The Confederacy's hopes of European support were dashed and, emboldened by having seen off a major Confederate offensive, on September 22, 1862, Lincoln issued the Emancipation Proclamation, freeing all slaves in the Confederate states.

SWING STATE

Maryland straddled the south and north and was a key battleground in the fight between secessionists and Unionists. The state was invaded three times by Confederates during the American Civil War.

KEY

CONFEDERATE ARMY
- Infantry
- Force
- Artillery

UNION ARMY
- Infantry
- Force
- Artillery

- /// Miller's cornfield
- ✝ Dunker Church
- Philip Pry House
- Lower bridge

TIMELINE

1
2
3
4
5

5:00 AM, SEP 17, 1852   12:00 PM   7:00 PM

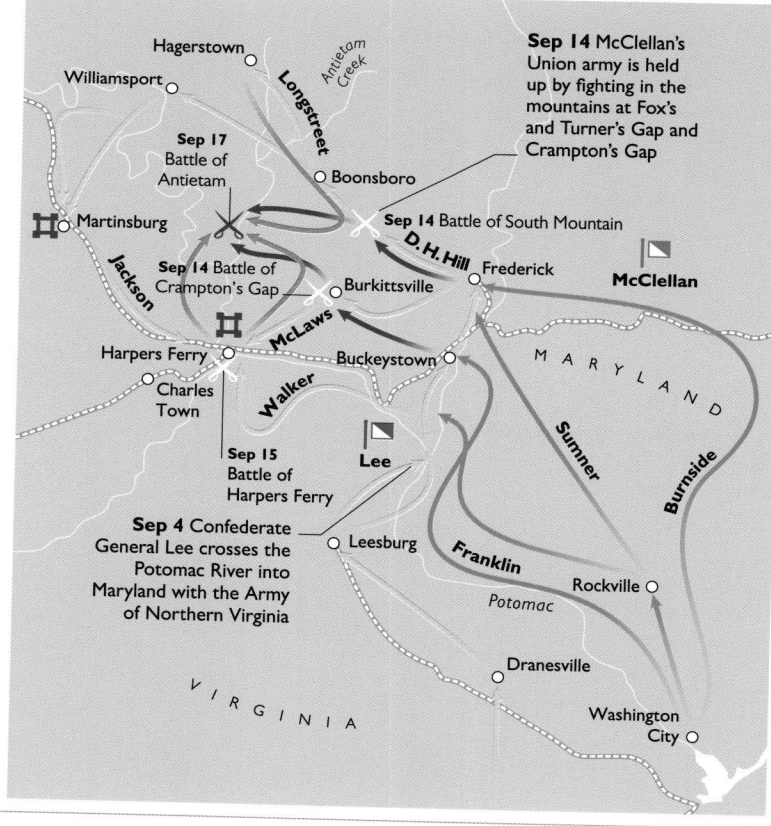

△ **Absolution at "Bloody Lane"**
This painting by Don Troiani shows Union troops of the Irish Brigade advancing toward "Bloody Lane." The "fighting chaplain" Father William Corby is shown giving absolution.

LEE'S CAMPAIGN

Lee crossed into Maryland on September 4, 1862. He then split his forces, sending Jackson, McLaws, and Walker to attack the Union garrisons at Martinsburg and Harpers Ferry, and D.H. Hill to protect the mountain passes. Hill and McLaws held the passes long enough for Harpers Ferry to be taken, allowing Lee to concentrate his army at Antietam Creek to face McClellan's slowly pursuing Union forces.

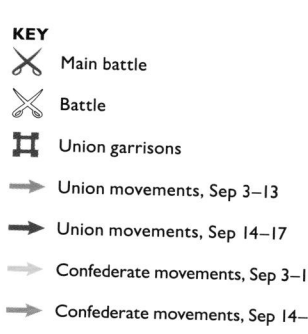

KEY
- ✕ Main battle
- ✕ Battle
- ⊞ Union garrisons
- → Union movements, Sep 3–13
- → Union movements, Sep 14–17
- → Confederate movements, Sep 3–13
- → Confederate movements, Sep 14–17
- ⌷⌷⌷ Railroads

Sep 14 McClellan's Union army is held up by fighting in the mountains at Fox's and Turner's Gap and Crampton's Gap

Sep 14 Battle of South Mountain

Hagerstown
Williamsport
Sep 17 Battle of Antietam
Boonsboro
Martinsburg
Sep 14 Battle of Crampton's Gap
Burkittsville
D.H. Hill   Frederick
McClellan
Harpers Ferry
Charles Town
Sep 15 Battle of Harpers Ferry
Buckeystown
MARYLAND
Lee
Sumner
Sep 4 Confederate General Lee crosses the Potomac River into Maryland with the Army of Northern Virginia
Leesburg
Franklin
Burnside
Rockville
Potomac
Dranesville
VIRGINIA
Washington City

5   THE FINAL ASSAULT   3:00 PM–NIGHTFALL

Burnside advanced against the Confederate line southeast of Sharpsburg, but was met by General A.P. Hill's Light Division, which had arrived after a 17-mile (27-km) march from Harpers Ferry. Again, the battle might have been won if McClellan had released his reserves, but Burnside was left to fight with his exhausted and inexperienced troops until nightfall ended the battle.

- → Union assault
- ⤍ Union retreat
- → Confederate advance and attack

4   LOWER BRIDGE   11:00–3:00 PM

The fighting in the north had nearly ceased by the time the Union's Major General Burnside began to advance against the Confederate right further south. His men captured the sole bridge across Antietam Creek, hoping to outflank their enemy, but the bridge was so narrow that his force could not easily cross and was held there for several hours by just 500 Confederate soldiers.

- → Union advance

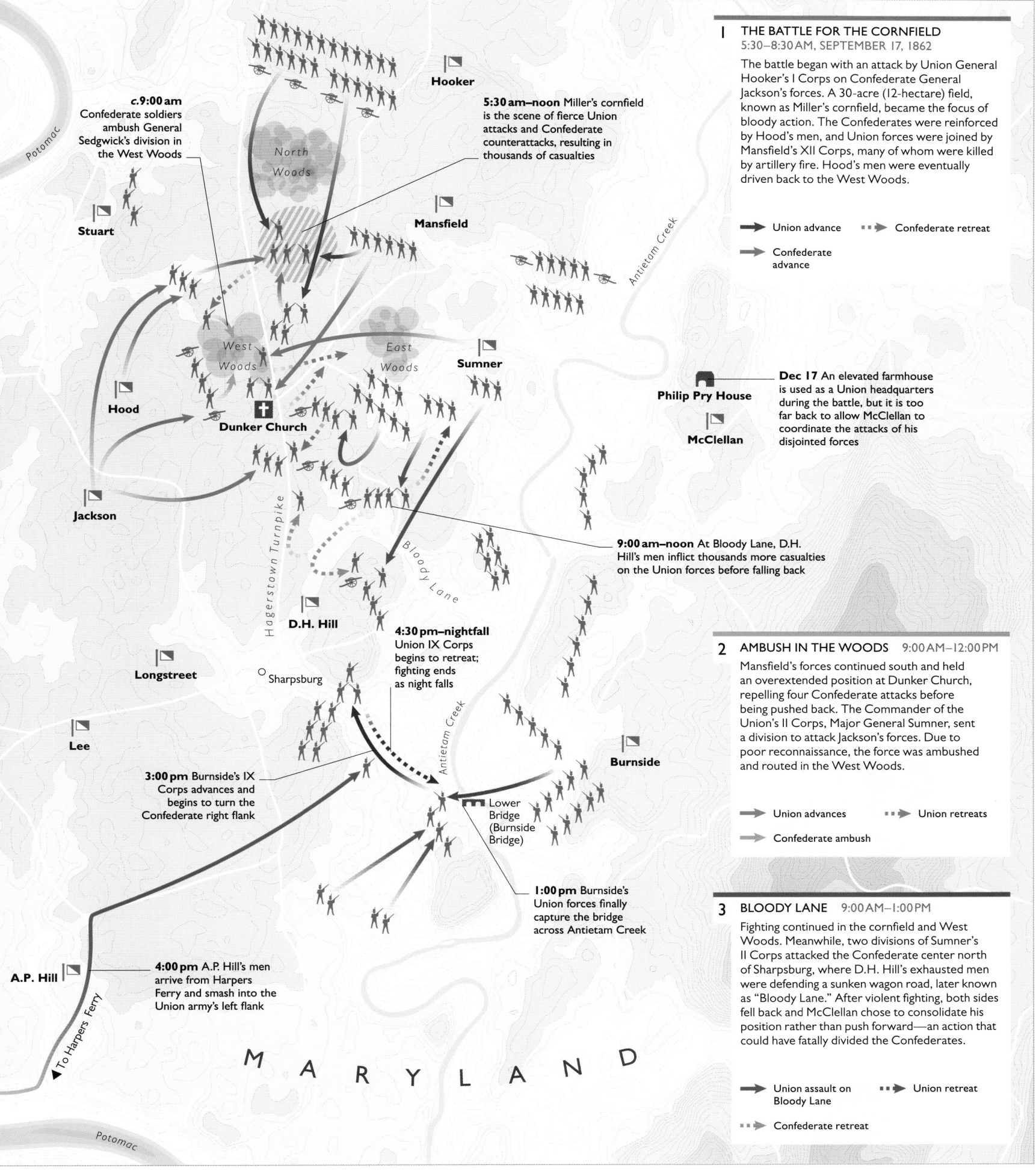

c.9:00 am Confederate soldiers ambush General Sedgwick's division in the West Woods

Hooker

5:30 am–noon Miller's cornfield is the scene of fierce Union attacks and Confederate counterattacks, resulting in thousands of casualties

North Woods

Stuart

Mansfield

West Woods

East Woods

Sumner

Hood

Dunker Church

Jackson

Hagerstown Turnpike

Bloody Lane

9:00 am–noon At Bloody Lane, D.H. Hill's men inflict thousands more casualties on the Union forces before falling back

D.H. Hill

4:30 pm–nightfall Union IX Corps begins to retreat; fighting ends as night falls

Longstreet

○ Sharpsburg

Antietam Creek

Lee

Burnside

3:00 pm Burnside's IX Corps advances and begins to turn the Confederate right flank

Lower Bridge (Burnside Bridge)

1:00 pm Burnside's Union forces finally capture the bridge across Antietam Creek

4:00 pm A.P. Hill's men arrive from Harpers Ferry and smash into the Union army's left flank

A.P. Hill

To Harpers Ferry

Potomac

Philip Pry House

Dec 17 An elevated farmhouse is used as a Union headquarters during the battle, but it is too far back to allow McClellan to coordinate the attacks of his disjointed forces

McClellan

Antietam Creek

M A R Y L A N D

Potomac

1 THE BATTLE FOR THE CORNFIELD
5:30–8:30 AM, SEPTEMBER 17, 1862

The battle began with an attack by Union General Hooker's I Corps on Confederate General Jackson's forces. A 30-acre (12-hectare) field, known as Miller's cornfield, became the focus of bloody action. The Confederates were reinforced by Hood's men, and Union forces were joined by Mansfield's XII Corps, many of whom were killed by artillery fire. Hood's men were eventually driven back to the West Woods.

➤ Union advance ┅▶ Confederate retreat

➤ Confederate advance

2 AMBUSH IN THE WOODS 9:00 AM–12:00 PM

Mansfield's forces continued south and held an overextended position at Dunker Church, repelling four Confederate attacks before being pushed back. The Commander of the Union's II Corps, Major General Sumner, sent a division to attack Jackson's forces. Due to poor reconnaissance, the force was ambushed and routed in the West Woods.

➤ Union advances ┅▶ Union retreats

➤ Confederate ambush

3 BLOODY LANE 9:00 AM–1:00 PM

Fighting continued in the cornfield and West Woods. Meanwhile, two divisions of Sumner's II Corps attacked the Confederate center north of Sharpsburg, where D.H. Hill's exhausted men were defending a sunken wagon road, later known as "Bloody Lane." After violent fighting, both sides fell back and McClellan chose to consolidate his position rather than push forward—an action that could have fatally divided the Confederates.

➤ Union assault on Bloody Lane ┅▶ Union retreat

┅▶ Confederate retreat

ARMS OF THE CIVIL WAR

The American Civil War of 1861–65 was the first modern war. Advances in communication and technology expanded the scope of the war—more troops were deployed, weapons became more lethal, and battlelines grew.

△ **Confederacy flag**
The stars represent seceded states, with more added later. From May 1863, the Confederacy shifted to the "Stainless Banner" with a cross-shaped motif on a white rectangular field.

The civil war was fought between the Northern states, loyal to the Union, and the slave-owning Southern states that seceded to form the Confederacy. While both sides began equal in strength, with about 200,000 troops each, by 1863 there were twice as many Union troops serving as there were Confederate.

On the battlefield, artillery was murderous at short range due to improved canister shots and shrapnel shells, but it was still mostly ineffective at long range. Offensive bombardments were less useful since guns were somewhat inaccurate, and explosive shells were still in their infancy at this time. Infantry firepower had improved thanks to rifled muskets and advances in ammunition, but massed formations were still needed for infantry to be accurate at any but the shortest ranges. Firepower had made mounted charges suicidal, but cavalry remained indispensable for scouting, screening, and raiding. The introduction of repeating carbines—quick-loading guns—made cavalry an excellent mobile force.

Field entrenchments became commonplace for soldiers facing an enormous amount of firepower. By 1864, attacks had become so costly in terms of casualties that only the Union had the manpower needed to maintain offensives, culminating in its victory in 1865.

△ **Underwater threat**
The Confederates used naval mines, then called "torpedoes," to defend their waterways. At the Battle of Mobile Bay (1864), the Union fleet (right), despite the loss of one of its ships, continued to charge through a channel seeded with contact mines to attack the Confederate navy.

Union artillery battery
This image is from the Battle of Seven Pines, Virginia (May 31–June 1, 1862), also known as Fair Oaks. Artillery was widely used throughout the civil war, with projectiles ranging in weight from 10 lbs to 300 lbs.

GETTYSBURG

A turning point in the American Civil War, the Battle of Gettysburg in 1863 saw the Union army halt the Confederate invasion of Pennsylvania. Instead of the decisive victory they needed to offset their resource inferiority, the Confederates suffered a major defeat.

Riding high on his victory over the Union at Chancellorsville, Virginia, in May 1863, Confederate general Robert E. Lee believed that another decisive win could end northern support for the Civil War. In June, he marched into Pennsylvania with soldiers of the Army of Northern Virginia. General George G. Meade, commander of the Union Army of the Potomac, shadowed Lee's movements, and the two sides met at Gettysburg. The battle had a confused start: Lieutenant General A.P. Hill, commander of the Confederate III Corps, sent men into Gettysburg to investigate a sighting of Union forces there the day before. Two Union brigades opened fire on Hill's men, and more units arrived from both sides to join a battle that went on to span three days, involved about 75,000 Confederate and 100,000 Union soldiers, and ended in Lee's retreat to Virginia. It was the bloodiest battle to take place on American soil, with an estimated 50,000 casualties. Abraham Lincoln famously used the opening of the National Cemetery at Gettysburg in November 1863 to reaffirm the North's commitment to ending slavery and winning the war.

"Government of the people, by the people, for the people, shall not perish from the earth."

ABRAHAM LINCOLN, NOVEMBER 19, 1863

PENNSYLVANIAN BATTLE
The battle was fought around the town of Gettysburg in Pennsylvania. The Union forces secured the hills and ridges to the south, which they managed to hold despite fierce fighting.

KEY

▪ Town	▦ Gettysburg and Hanover railroad	▨ Wheatfield
		▨ Peach Orchard

CONFEDERATE FORCES

⚑ Commander   🧍 Infantry   🔫 Artillery

UNION FORCES

🐎 Cavalry   🧍 Infantry   🔫 Artillery

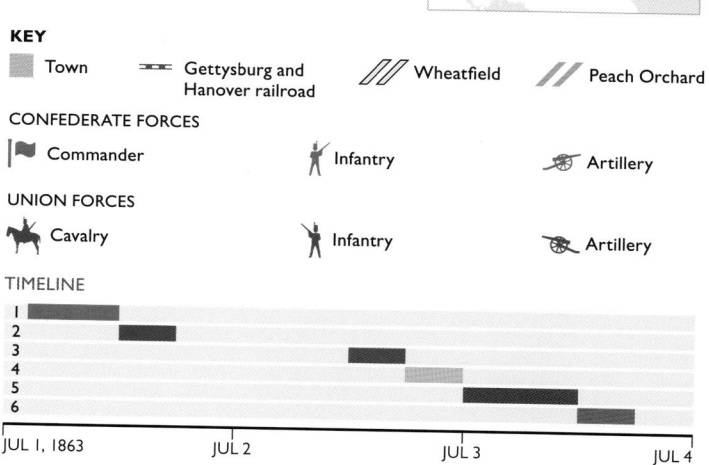

TIMELINE

JUL 1, 1863   JUL 2   JUL 3   JUL 4

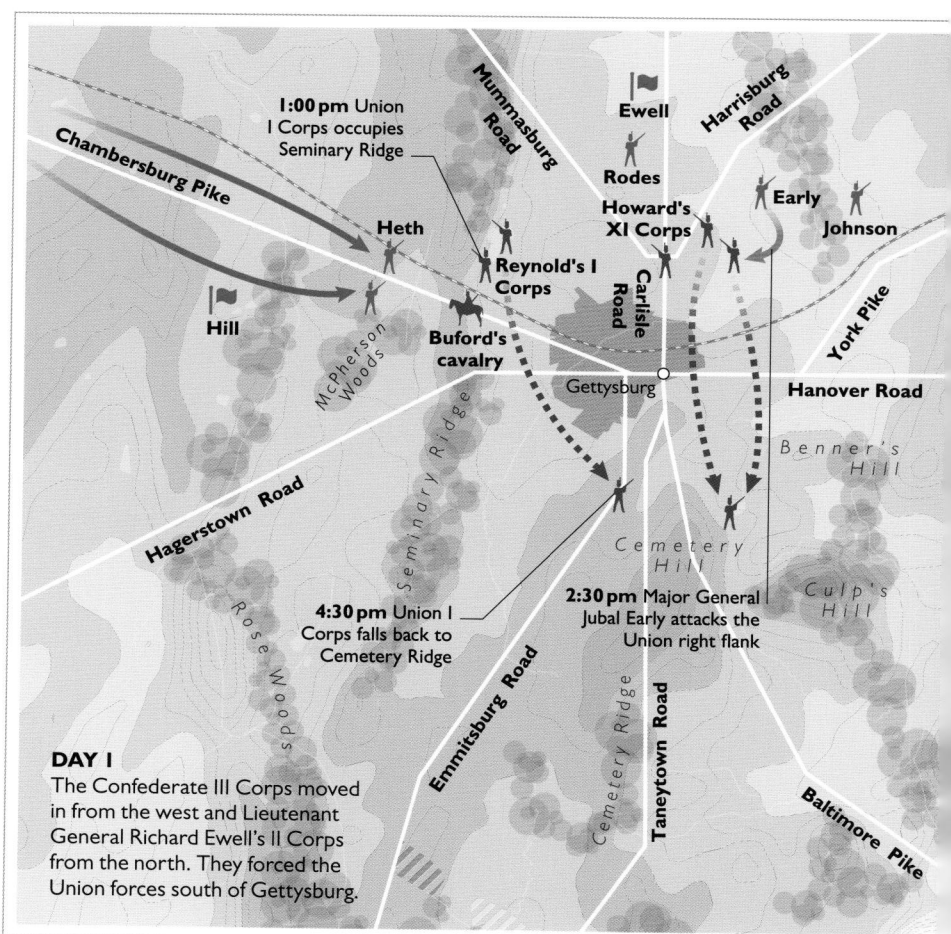

DAY 1
The Confederate III Corps moved in from the west and Lieutenant General Richard Ewell's II Corps from the north. They forced the Union forces south of Gettysburg.

1:00pm Union I Corps occupies Seminary Ridge

4:30pm Union I Corps falls back to Cemetery Ridge

2:30pm Major General Jubal Early attacks the Union right flank

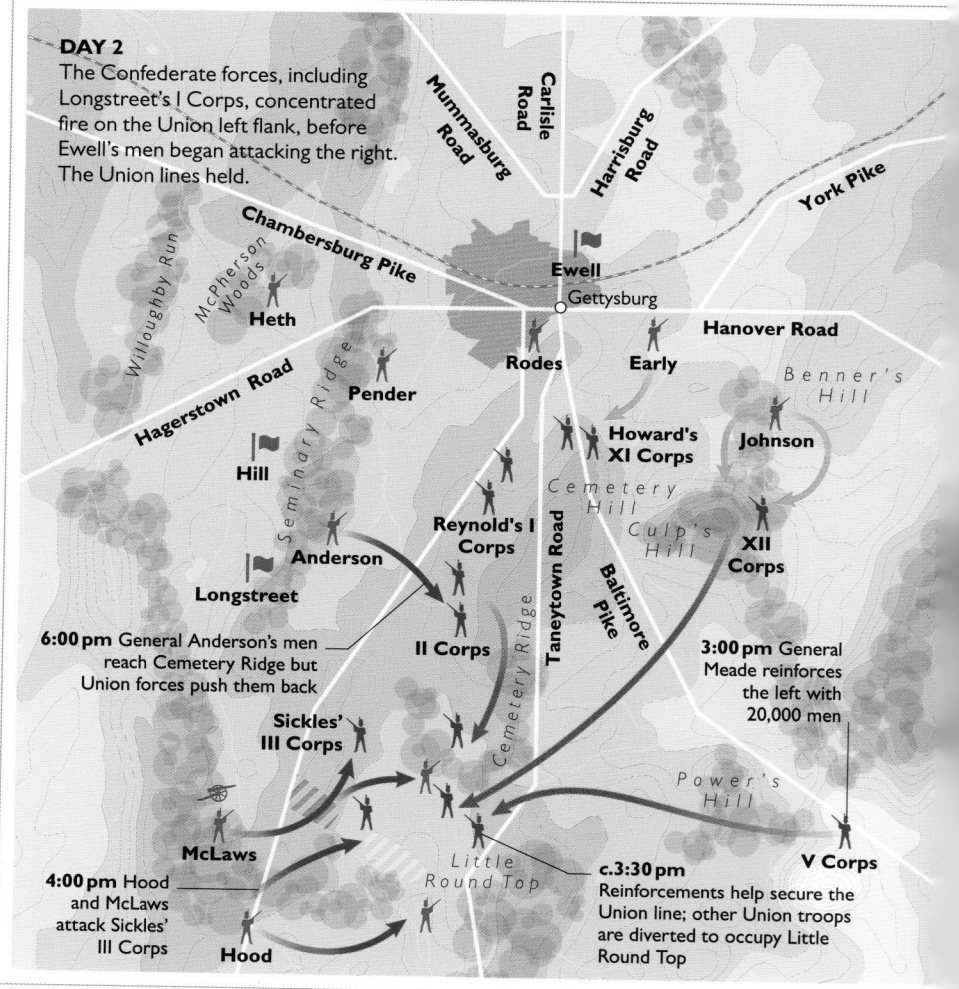

DAY 2
The Confederate forces, including Longstreet's I Corps, concentrated fire on the Union left flank, before Ewell's men began attacking the right. The Union lines held.

6:00pm General Anderson's men reach Cemetery Ridge but Union forces push them back

3:00pm General Meade reinforces the left with 20,000 men

4:00pm Hood and McLaws attack Sickles' III Corps

c.3:30pm Reinforcements help secure the Union line; other Union troops are diverted to occupy Little Round Top

1 BATTLE BEGINS MORNING, JULY 1, 1863

A division of A.P. Hill's Confederate force moved along the Chambersburg Pike toward Gettysburg, where they met and engaged two Union cavalry brigades led by John Buford. The Union cavalry fell back a short distance to the ridges northwest of Gettysburg, where John Reynolds' I Corps was forming. More units from both sides soon arrived, and chaotic fighting broke out around McPherson Woods and the nearby railway cutting. By early afternoon, the battle lines were drawn.

→ First Confederate attacks

2 THE UNION RIGHT FLANK COLLAPSES
AFTERNOON, JULY 1, 1863

Confederate Lieutenant General Ewell's troops faced the Union forces deployed in an arc north of Gettysburg. General Jubal Early's division launched a fierce attack on the Union right flank, forcing the XI Corps to retreat to Cemetery Hill. Exposed and under fire, the Union I Corps also fell back. Ewell, however, halted his attack, deeming it too risky to attempt a rushed dusk assault on the hill.

→ Early's attack   ⇢ Union retreat

3 ATTACK ON THE UNION LEFT
AFTERNOON, JULY 2

The next day, Confederate artillery opened fire on the Union left flank, where Sickles' III Corps occupied an exposed salient. General Meade rushed reinforcements to the Union left; elsewhere Union troops secured the strategically vital Little Round Top hill just in time. Sickles' men suffered heavy losses in intense fighting with McLaws' and Hood's Confederate divisions in the Wheatfield and Peach Orchard, but the Union line held.

→ Confederate attack on Union left

→ Union reinforcements

4 EWELL ATTACKS EVENING, JULY 2

After firing fruitlessly on the Union lines for two hours, Ewell finally ordered two attacks. General Edward Johnson's Division moved on Culp's Hill, only to be held off by remnants of the Union XII Corps, sustaining heavy casualties. Jubal Early's men were sent to take East Cemetery Hill, where they became bogged down in a fierce fight with Union soldiers. Support from Rodes' Division arrived too late to help the Confederates.

→ Confederate attack on Union right

DAY 3

A lack of coordination between Longstreet, Hill, and Ewell meant their attacks did not support one another. The next day, the Confederate Army began retreating to Virginia.

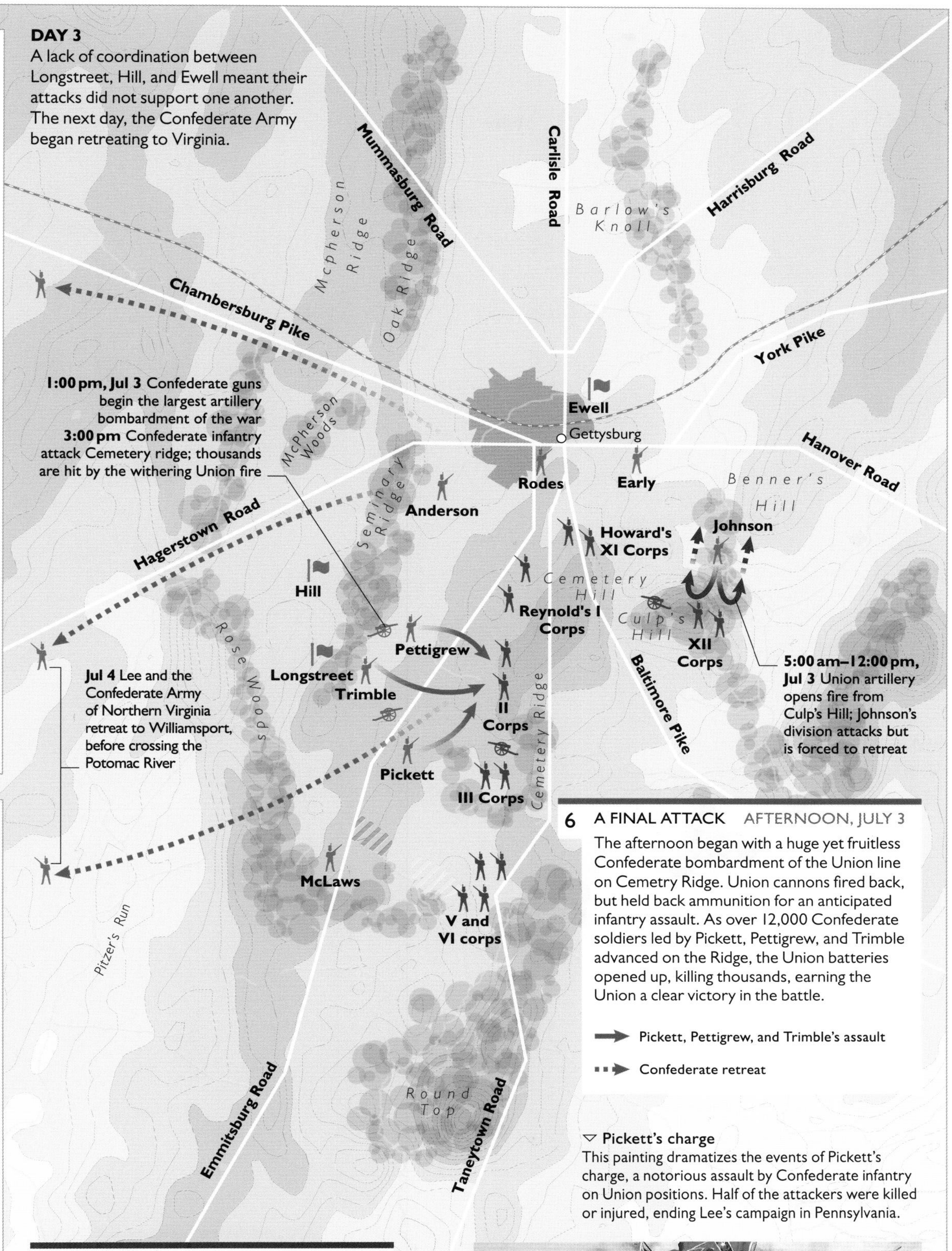

1:00 pm, Jul 3 Confederate guns begin the largest artillery bombardment of the war **3:00 pm** Confederate infantry attack Cemetery ridge; thousands are hit by the withering Union fire

Jul 4 Lee and the Confederate Army of Northern Virginia retreat to Williamsport, before crossing the Potomac River

5:00 am–12:00 pm, Jul 3 Union artillery opens fire from Culp's Hill; Johnson's division attacks but is forced to retreat

Ewell
Gettysburg
Rodes   Early
Anderson
Hill
Howard's XI Corps   Johnson
Reynold's I Corps
Pettigrew
Longstreet
Trimble
II Corps
Pickett
III Corps
McLaws
V and VI corps
Round Top

Mummasburg Road
Carlisle Road
Harrisburg Road
McPherson Ridge
Oak Ridge
Barlow's Knoll
Chambersburg Pike
York Pike
McPherson Woods
Hanover Road
Benner's Hill
Seminary Ridge
Hagerstown Road
Cemetery Hill
Culp's Hill
Rose Woods
Cemetery Ridge
Baltimore Pike
Pitzer's Run
Emmitsburg Road
Taneytown Road

5 A DIVIDED FRONT MORNING, JULY 3

The third day of battle was again marked by a lack of Confederate coordination. The plan was for Longstreet and Hill to attack the Union center, at the same time as Ewell's men assaulted Culp's Hill. However, the troops at Culp's Hill were provoked by Union artillery fire into a premature and fruitless battle from which they eventually retreated. Meanwhile, Longstreet and Hill waited.

→ Confederate attack   ⇢ Confederate retreat

6 A FINAL ATTACK AFTERNOON, JULY 3

The afternoon began with a huge yet fruitless Confederate bombardment of the Union line on Cemetry Ridge. Union cannons fired back, but held back ammunition for an anticipated infantry assault. As over 12,000 Confederate soldiers led by Pickett, Pettigrew, and Trimble advanced on the Ridge, the Union batteries opened up, killing thousands, earning the Union a clear victory in the battle.

→ Pickett, Pettigrew, and Trimble's assault

⇢ Confederate retreat

▽ Pickett's charge
This painting dramatizes the events of Pickett's charge, a notorious assault by Confederate infantry on Union positions. Half of the attackers were killed or injured, ending Lee's campaign in Pennsylvania.

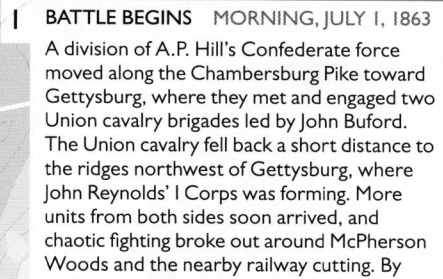

KÖNIGGRÄTZ

Superior tactics and modern, breech-loading rifles helped Prussia beat a large and well-positioned Austrian force at Königgrätz. The battle decided the Austro-Prussian Seven Weeks War (June 14–July 22, 1866) and ended Austrian political dominance among German states.

In the mid-19th century, Austria and Prussia vied for control of the states of the German Confederation. In a bid to unite them, and curb Austro-Hungarian power, Prussian Minister President Otto von Bismarck and Graf Helmut von Moltke, Chief of Prussian General Staff, planned a war against Austria. In June 1866, Bismarck provoked a clash over Schleswig-Holstein (then joint territory of Austria and Prussia), and war began.

The Prussian armies rapidly invaded Saxony and Bohemia, and after several indecisive skirmishes, Austrian general Benedik pulled back northwest of the fortified town of Königgrätz. Prussia's First and Elbe Armies attacked the Austrian left and center in the early morning of July 3. The Austrian army and its allies had strong cavalry and long-range artillery, but the wooded terrain and Benedek's caution offset these advantages. The Austrian infantry's muzzle-loading rifles proved no match for the Prussians' breech-loading "needle-guns." When the Prussian Second Army attacked the Austrian right, Benedik fell back.

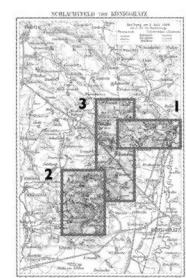

LOCATOR

△ **A wasted opportunity**
Benedik felt that the damp weather made a cavalry charge too risky, but his cavalry fought a rearguard action with the Prussians that involved over 10,000 horsemen.

◁ **The fight on the Prussian right**
The Army of the Elbe faced the Austrian's Saxon allies; it captured Problus and Nieder Prim at about 3 pm, but the Prussian commander Herwarth von Bittenfeld did not press on with the encirclement.

ENGAGEMENT BY THE ELBE

Prussia's First and Elbe Armies attacked the Austrians and their Saxon allies on the left from 7:00 am on July 3. The Austrians pulled back to their defensive positions around Maslowed, Lipa, and Langenhof, and pinned down the Prussians for hours with heavy artillery fire. An Austrian counterattack at 11:00 am nearly unhinged the Prussian left flank at the Swiepwald. The arriving Prussian Second Army then steadily crushed the Austrian right. At about 3:00 pm, Field Marshal Ramming staged a last counterattack before retreating with the rest of the Austrian army across the Elbe. More than 40,000 of his troops had been killed, wounded, or captured.

KEY

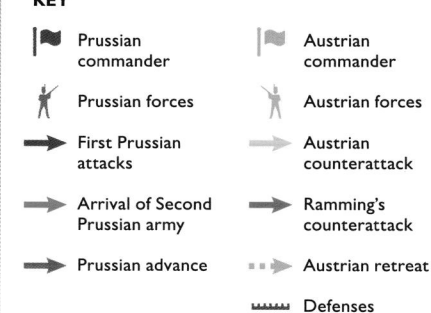

Prussian commander		Austrian commander	
Prussian forces		Austrian forces	
First Prussian attacks		Austrian counterattack	
Arrival of Second Prussian army		Ramming's counterattack	
Prussian advance		Austrian retreat	
Defenses			

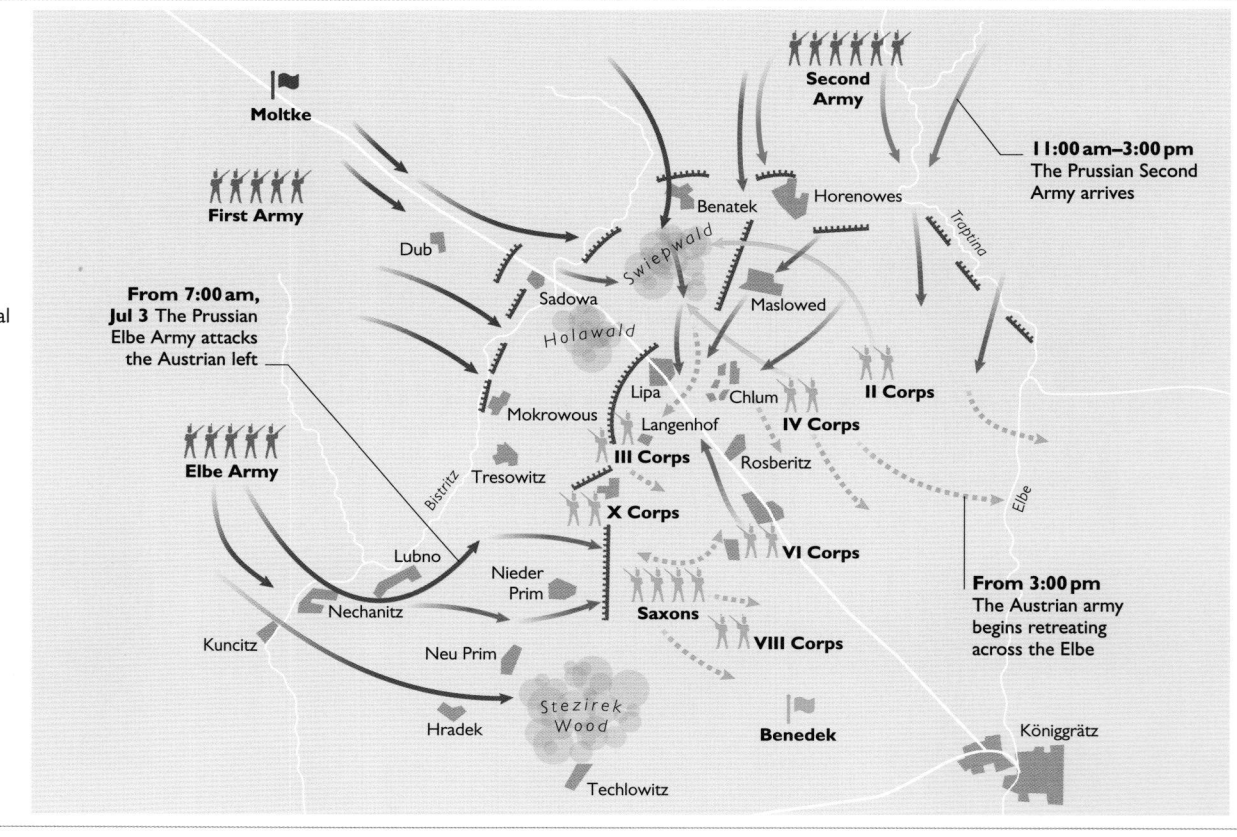

△ **Austria's last attack**
Chlum and Roseberitz were the scenes of the last Austrian counterattack; the Austrian Field Marshal Ramming retook the villages before being forced to retreat.

▷ **Sadova, near Königgrätz**
This map shows the battlefield at Sadova in the afternoon of July 3, shortly before the Austrians retreated to avoid encirclement by the Prussian armies.

SCHLACHTFELD VON KÖNIGGRÄTZ.

Stellung am 3. Juli 1866
um 2–2½ Uhr Nachmittags.

Preussen.   **Österreicher u. Sachsen.**

Infanterie
Kavallerie
Artillerie

F. A. Brockhaus' Geogr.-artist. Anstalt, Leipzig.

G. Grote'sche Verlagsbuchhandlung, in Berlin.

Maßstab 1 : 140.000.   0   1   2   3   4   5   6 Kilometer.

SEDAN

In a pivotal battle of the Franco-Prussian War (1870–71), the Germans, led by the brilliant General Helmuth von Moltke, trapped the French Army of Châlons at Sedan on September 1, 1870. Napoleon III's surrender prompted the collapse of the French Empire.

The Franco–Prussian War was rooted in a contest for European dominance between Otto von Bismarck, the Prussian Chancellor of the North German Confederation, and the French emperor, Napoleon III. The French declared war on July 19, 1870, the emperor eager to match the military achievements of his uncle, Napoleon Bonaparte. However, the Germans had the finest artillery in the world, and a sublime strategist in General Helmuth von Moltke.

In August, Moltke trapped the 180,000-strong French Army of the Rhine at Metz. The French Army of Châlons, under Patrice de MacMahon, tried to relieve the Army of the Rhine but in doing so became hemmed in at the town of Sedan, which sat in a low valley on a bend in the River Meuse.

On September 1, the Germans closed in, encircling Sedan and bombarding the French with artillery fire from about 400 guns. After attempts to break out failed, the French surrendered. Napoleon III and 100,000 of his men were taken into Prussian captivity, and the Second Napoleonic Empire collapsed. The new French Third Republic continued the war, but was defeated in 1871. The humiliating terms of the peace treaty, signed in May of the same year, fueled French resentment that contributed to World War I.

> *"War is a necessary part of God's arrangement of the world."*
>
> HELMUTH VON MOLTKE, 1880

ADVANCES IN ARTILLERY

In the 19th century, the German steel manufacturer Alfred Krupp, nicknamed "The Cannon King," mastered the difficult process of casting steel and began machining rifled steel guns of exceptional quality. Equipped with hundreds of Krupp guns, including the 6-pounder breech-loading cannon capable of firing a shell containing zinc balls and explosives over 2¾ miles (4.5 km) with great accuracy, the Prussians had a major advantage at Sedan.

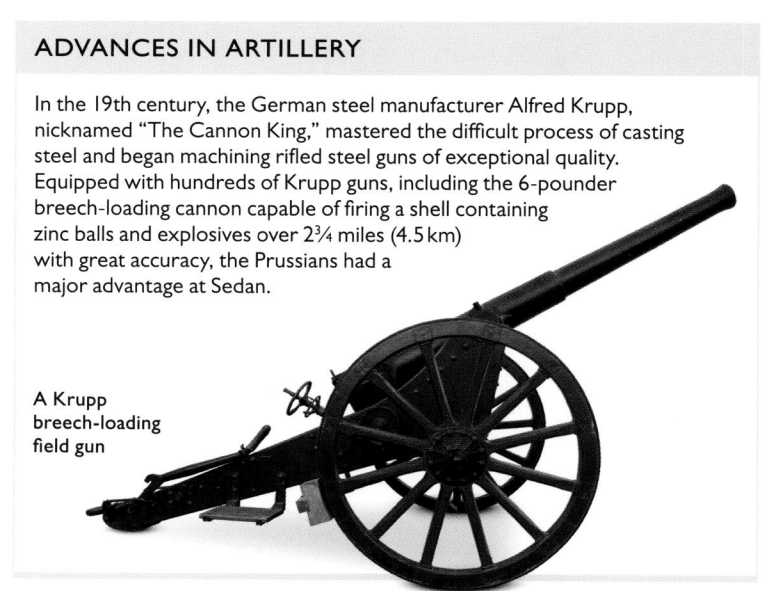

A Krupp
breech-loading
field gun

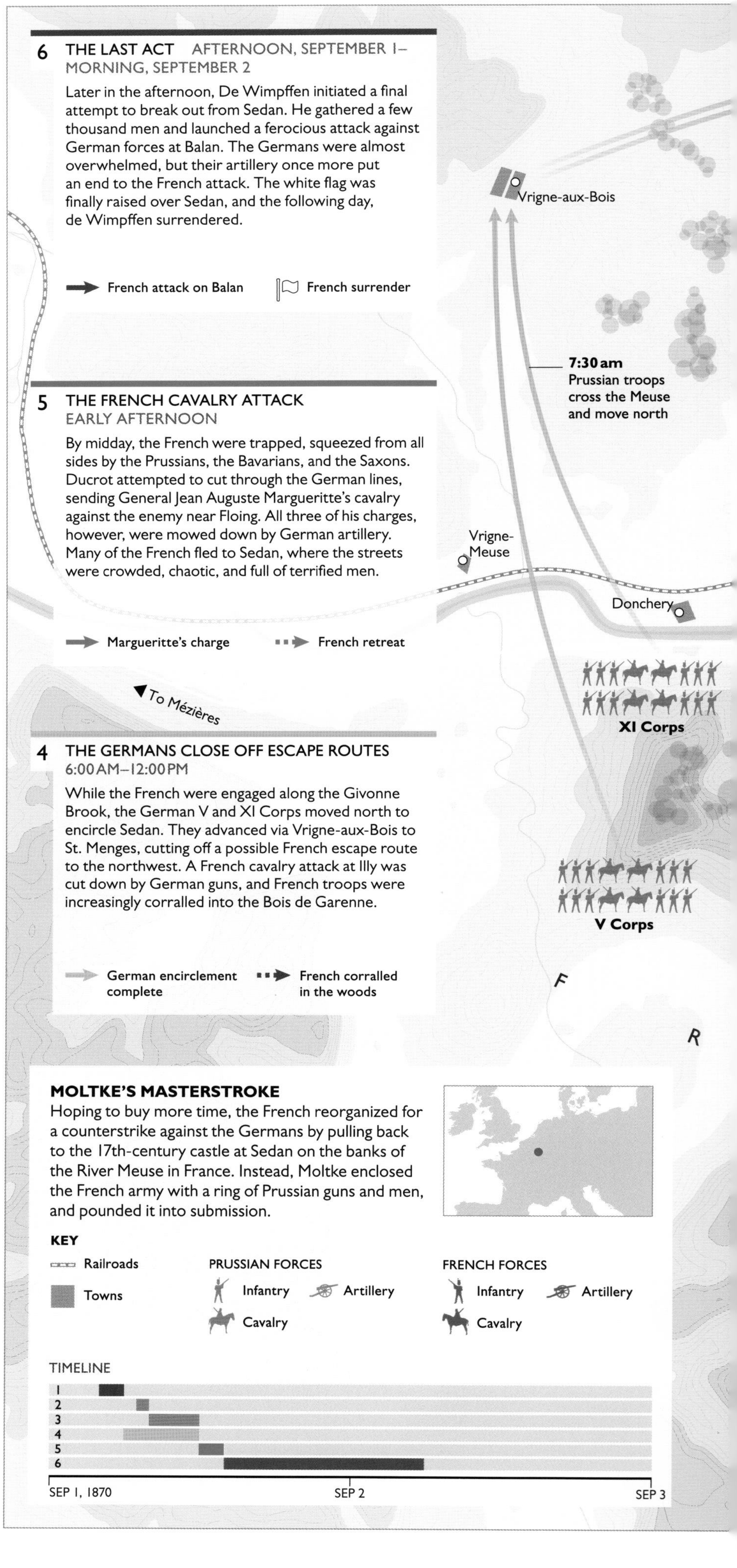

---

6   THE LAST ACT   AFTERNOON, SEPTEMBER 1–
MORNING, SEPTEMBER 2

Later in the afternoon, De Wimpffen initiated a final attempt to break out from Sedan. He gathered a few thousand men and launched a ferocious attack against German forces at Balan. The Germans were almost overwhelmed, but their artillery once more put an end to the French attack. The white flag was finally raised over Sedan, and the following day, de Wimpffen surrendered.

➡ French attack on Balan   ⚑ French surrender

Vrigne-aux-Bois

7:30 am
Prussian troops
cross the Meuse
and move north

5   THE FRENCH CAVALRY ATTACK
EARLY AFTERNOON

By midday, the French were trapped, squeezed from all sides by the Prussians, the Bavarians, and the Saxons. Ducrot attempted to cut through the German lines, sending General Jean Auguste Margueritte's cavalry against the enemy near Floing. All three of his charges, however, were mowed down by German artillery. Many of the French fled to Sedan, where the streets were crowded, chaotic, and full of terrified men.

Vrigne-
Meuse

Donchery

➡ Margueritte's charge   ⇢ French retreat

▼ To Mézières

XI Corps

4   THE GERMANS CLOSE OFF ESCAPE ROUTES
6:00 AM–12:00 PM

While the French were engaged along the Givonne Brook, the German V and XI Corps moved north to encircle Sedan. They advanced via Vrigne-aux-Bois to St. Menges, cutting off a possible French escape route to the northwest. A French cavalry attack at Illy was cut down by German guns, and French troops were increasingly corralled into the Bois de Garenne.

V Corps

➡ German encirclement   ⇢ French corralled
complete   in the woods

F

R

MOLTKE'S MASTERSTROKE

Hoping to buy more time, the French reorganized for a counterstrike against the Germans by pulling back to the 17th-century castle at Sedan on the banks of the River Meuse in France. Instead, Moltke enclosed the French army with a ring of Prussian guns and men, and pounded it into submission.

KEY

▫▫▫ Railroads

▪ Towns

PRUSSIAN FORCES
🧍 Infantry   🔫 Artillery
🐎 Cavalry

FRENCH FORCES
🧍 Infantry   🔫 Artillery
🐎 Cavalry

TIMELINE

1			
2			
3			
4			
5			
6			

SEP 1, 1870   SEP 2   SEP 3

Fleigneux

VII Corps
(Douay)

Saint-Menges

Illy

Iges

10:00 am
Fourteen
German
batteries
are in place
southeast of
Saint-Menges

Floing

Marguéritte

Villette

Doncourt

2:00 pm Marguéritte's
cavalry retire after half
are killed in three
desperate attempts
to charge the
German line

Sedan

c. 6:00 pm The
French raise the
white flag in Sedan

II Bavarian Corps
(von Hartmann)

Frénois

Balan

Wadelincourt

La Moncelle

XII Corps
(Lebrun)

Bazeilles

Noyers-Pont-
Maugis

Meuse

4:00 am
Von der Tann and
the I Bavarian
Corps advance to
attack Bazeilles

6:00 am The
German artillery
barrage of
Bazeilles begins

I Bavarian Corps
(von der Tann)

Remilly-
Aillicourt

Bois de
Garenne

2:30 pm Prussian
Guards capture
Bois de Garenne

I Corps
(Ducrot)

Givonne

Villers-Cernay

Prussian Guards
Corps
(Augustus)

Francheval

Givonne Brook

10:30 am Prussian guns
above Villers-Cernay open
fire on the French on the
opposite side of the valley

▷ Rout of the French
This stylized newspaper illustration
shows the conclusion of the battle of
Sedan. More than 3,000 men of the
Army of Châlons were killed, and
1,300 Germans lost their lives.

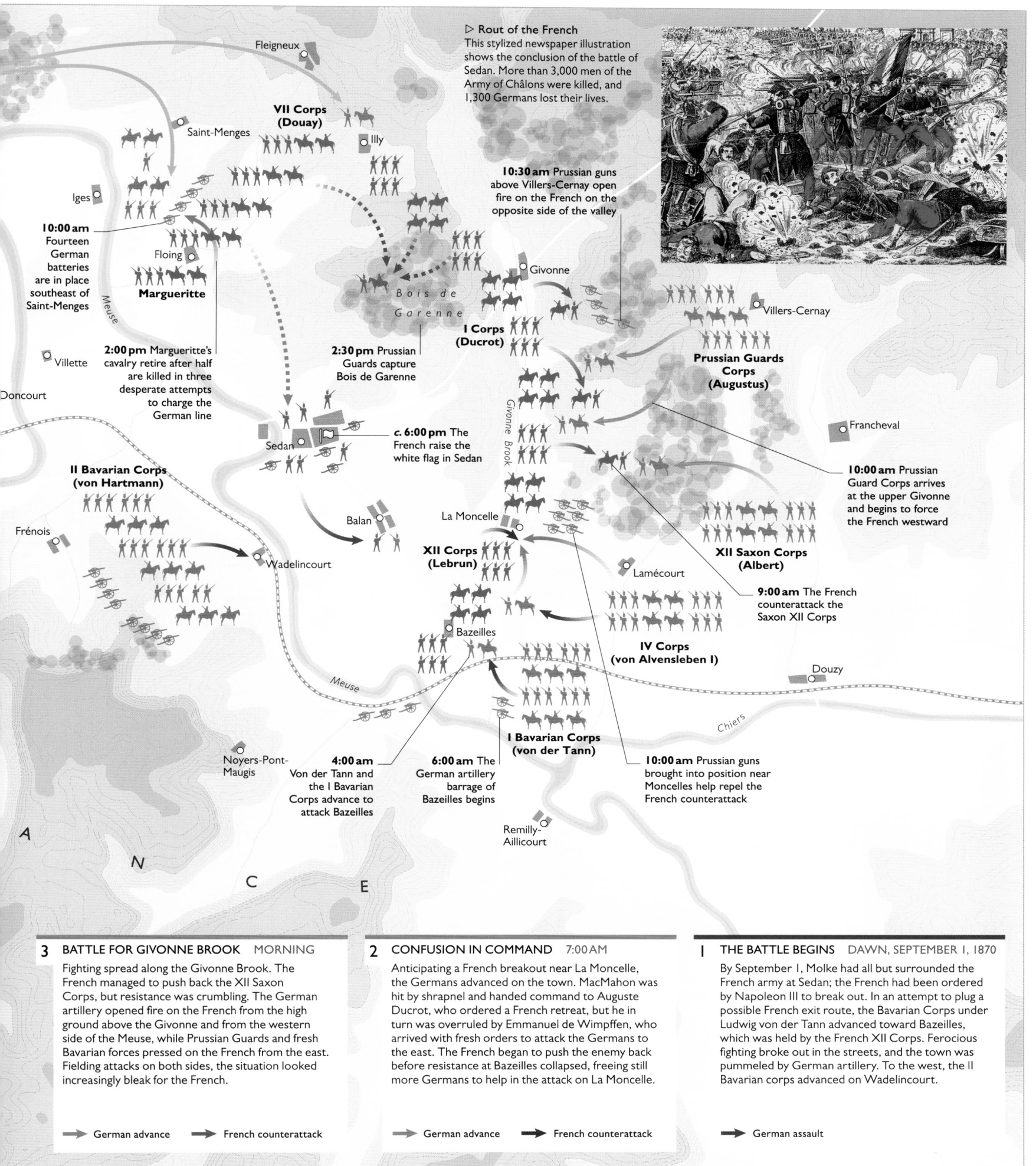

10:00 am Prussian
Guard Corps arrives
at the upper Givonne
and begins to force
the French westward

XII Saxon Corps
(Albert)

Lamécourt

9:00 am The French
counterattack the
Saxon XII Corps

IV Corps
(von Alvensleben I)

Douzy

Chiers

10:00 am Prussian guns
brought into position near
Moncelles help repel the
French counterattack

A
N
C
E

---

3 BATTLE FOR GIVONNE BROOK MORNING

Fighting spread along the Givonne Brook. The
French managed to push back the XII Saxon
Corps, but resistance was crumbling. The German
artillery opened fire on the French from the high
ground above the Givonne and from the western
side of the Meuse, while Prussian Guards and fresh
Bavarian forces pressed on the French from the east.
Fielding attacks on both sides, the situation looked
increasingly bleak for the French.

2 CONFUSION IN COMMAND 7:00 AM

Anticipating a French breakout near La Moncelle,
the Germans advanced on the town. MacMahon was
hit by shrapnel and handed command to Auguste
Ducrot, who ordered a French retreat, but he in
turn was overruled by Emmanuel de Wimpffen, who
arrived with fresh orders to attack the Germans to
the east. The French began to push the enemy back
before resistance at Bazeilles collapsed, freeing still
more Germans to help in the attack on La Moncelle.

1 THE BATTLE BEGINS DAWN, SEPTEMBER 1, 1870

By September 1, Molke had all but surrounded the
French army at Sedan; the French had been ordered
by Napoleon III to break out. In an attempt to plug a
possible French exit route, the Bavarian Corps under
Ludwig von der Tann advanced toward Bazeilles,
which was held by the French XII Corps. Ferocious
fighting broke out in the streets, and the town was
pummeled by German artillery. To the west, the II
Bavarian corps advanced on Wadelincourt.

→ German advance   → French counterattack

→ German advance   → French counterattack

→ German assault

LITTLE BIGHORN

Near the Little Bighorn River, in present-day Montana, Sitting Bull and some 2,000 warriors from the Native Peoples of the Northern Plains outmaneuvered and massacred nearly half of the more than 600 horsemen of the US Seventh Cavalry.

In 1875, tensions flared up between the U.S. government and the Lakota, Dakota Sioux, and Arapaho peoples when American gold miners began settling in territory west of the Missouri River, given exclusively to the Native Americans in a treaty in 1868. War became inevitable when the government refused to remove the settlers and ordered the Native American tribes to return to their reservations.

In spring 1876, about 2,000 warriors joined Sitting Bull—a charismatic Lakota leader—at his camp on the Little Bighorn River. Lieutenant Colonel George A. Custer and the Seventh Cavalry were sent to track down Sitting Bull, and reached the camp on June 25. Rather than wait for reinforcements, Custer attacked, but was overwhelmed in what was a resounding victory for the Native Peoples of the Northern Plains.

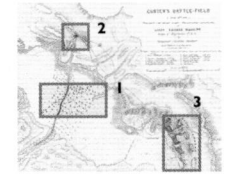
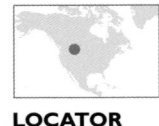

LOCATOR

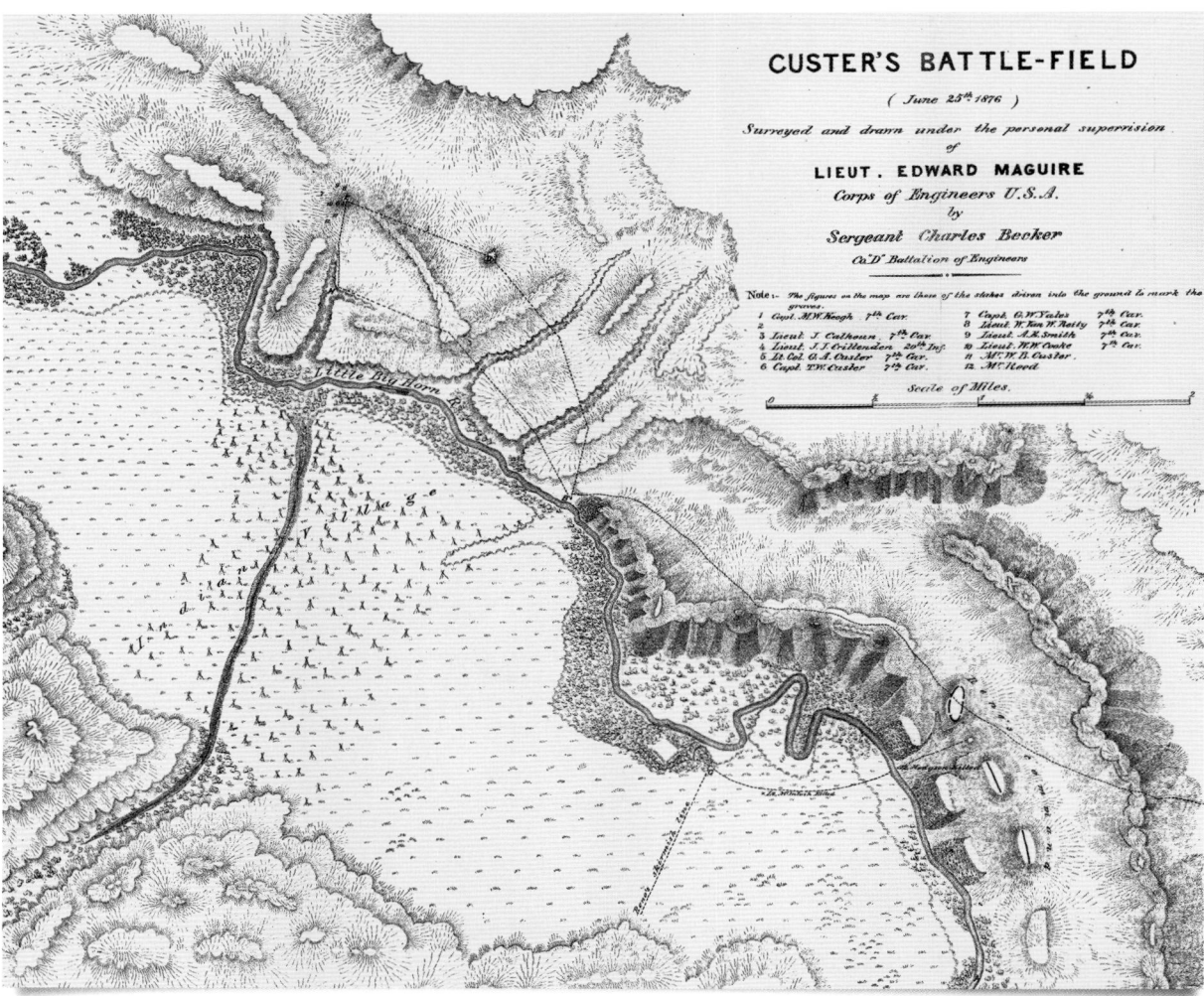

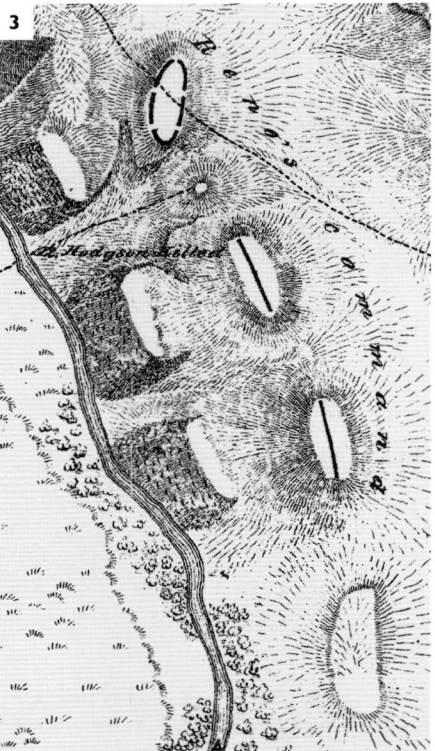

△ **Defensive position**
Companies under Major Marcus Reno and Captain Frederick Benteen held out in these hills until relieved by General Terry's column on June 27.

▽ **Custer's last stand**
Custer fought to the end at this site. In truth, he was fatally outnumbered and isolated, and his "stand" was perhaps more myth than reality.

△ **The battlefield**
This map shows the site of the battle as drawn by a member of the US Corps of Engineers. It also records the grave markers left for Custer and his commanding officers, although their last movements remain open to debate.

▷ **Sitting Bull's village**
Sitting Bull and Crazy Horse gathered 2,000 warriors and their families in this village. It was the largest Native American settlement that the US forces had ever encountered.

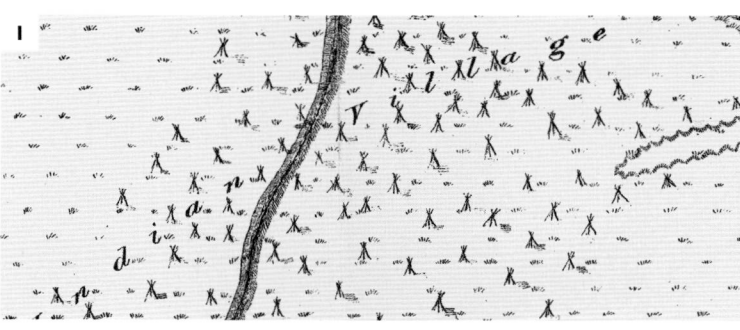

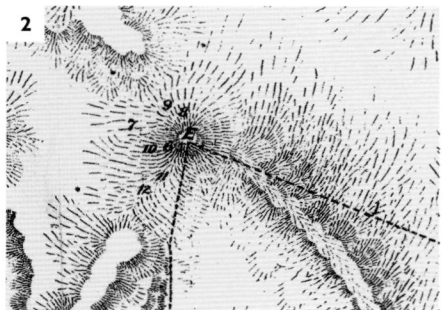

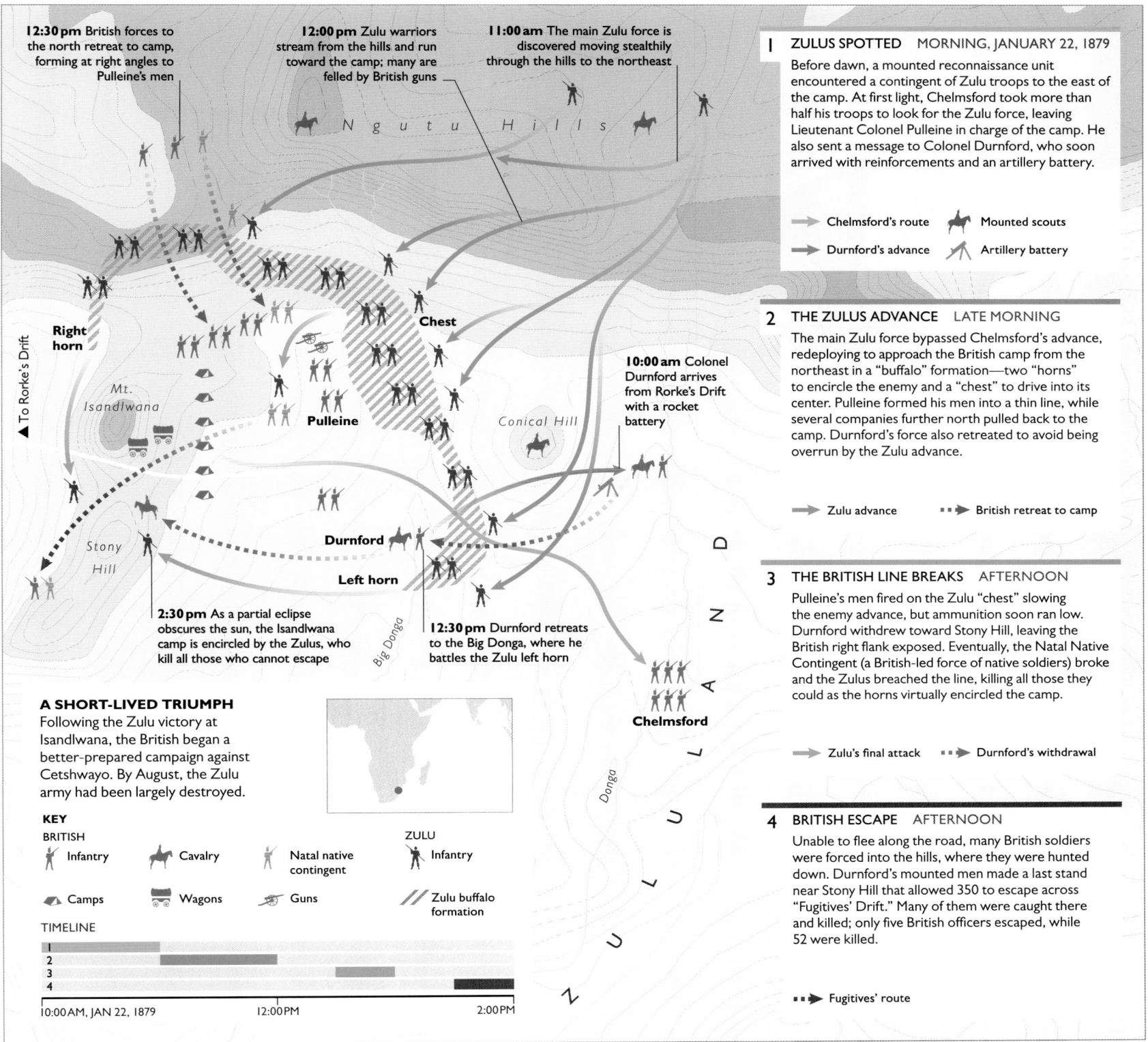

12:30 pm British forces to the north retreat to camp, forming at right angles to Pulleine's men

12:00 pm Zulu warriors stream from the hills and run toward the camp; many are felled by British guns

11:00 am The main Zulu force is discovered moving stealthily through the hills to the northeast

N g u t u   H i l l s

Right horn

Chest

Mt. Isandlwana

Pulleine

Conical Hill

10:00 am Colonel Durnford arrives from Rorke's Drift with a rocket battery

◄ To Rorke's Drift

Stony Hill

Durnford

Left horn

Big Donga

2:30 pm As a partial eclipse obscures the sun, the Isandlwana camp is encircled by the Zulus, who kill all those who cannot escape

12:30 pm Durnford retreats to the Big Donga, where he battles the Zulu left horn

Z U L U L A N D

Donga

Chelmsford

1 ZULUS SPOTTED   MORNING, JANUARY 22, 1879

Before dawn, a mounted reconnaissance unit encountered a contingent of Zulu troops to the east of the camp. At first light, Chelmsford took more than half his troops to look for the Zulu force, leaving Lieutenant Colonel Pulleine in charge of the camp. He also sent a message to Colonel Durnford, who soon arrived with reinforcements and an artillery battery.

➡ Chelmsford's route   🐎 Mounted scouts

➡ Durnford's advance   ⚔ Artillery battery

2 THE ZULUS ADVANCE   LATE MORNING

The main Zulu force bypassed Chelmsford's advance, redeploying to approach the British camp from the northeast in a "buffalo" formation—two "horns" to encircle the enemy and a "chest" to drive into its center. Pulleine formed his men into a thin line, while several companies further north pulled back to the camp. Durnford's force also retreated to avoid being overrun by the Zulu advance.

➡ Zulu advance   ┅➤ British retreat to camp

3 THE BRITISH LINE BREAKS   AFTERNOON

Pulleine's men fired on the Zulu "chest" slowing the enemy advance, but ammunition soon ran low. Durnford withdrew toward Stony Hill, leaving the British right flank exposed. Eventually, the Natal Native Contingent (a British-led force of native soldiers) broke and the Zulus breached the line, killing all those they could as the horns virtually encircled the camp.

➡ Zulu's final attack   ┅➤ Durnford's withdrawal

4 BRITISH ESCAPE   AFTERNOON

Unable to flee along the road, many British soldiers were forced into the hills, where they were hunted down. Durnford's mounted men made a last stand near Stony Hill that allowed 350 to escape across "Fugitives' Drift." Many of them were caught there and killed; only five British officers escaped, while 52 were killed.

┅➤ Fugitives' route

A SHORT-LIVED TRIUMPH
Following the Zulu victory at Isandlwana, the British began a better-prepared campaign against Cetshwayo. By August, the Zulu army had been largely destroyed.

KEY
BRITISH

🚶 Infantry   🐎 Cavalry   🏹 Natal native contingent

ZULU

🏹 Infantry

⛺ Camps   🛒 Wagons   ⚔ Guns   ╱╱ Zulu buffalo formation

TIMELINE

1
2
3
4

10:00AM, JAN 22, 1879   12:00PM   2:00PM

ISANDLWANA

Seeking to expand their territories in South Africa, British colonial authorities demanded that the Zulu king Cetshwayo disband his army. He refused, and conflict resulted. On January 22, 1879, 20,000 Zulu warriors armed with spears, shields, and old muskets surprised and overwhelmed 1,800 British, colonial, and native troops at the British camp at Isandlwana.

In January 1879, Lord Chelmsford, commander of British forces in South Africa, invaded Zululand with three columns totaling about 16,000 British and African troops. After sending one column to the north and one to the south, Chelmsford accompanied the central column, entering Zululand on January 11. He crossed the Buffalo River at Rorke's Drift mission, where one battalion established a base camp. Chelmsford pushed on with his wagon train, setting up camp at Isandlwana Hill on January 20. Meanwhile, the Zulus had raised a huge army of some 20,000 men. Part went to meet the British column to the south, and most headed for Chelmsford's camp at Isandlwana. The discipline, speed, and skill of the Zulus prevailed, and the soldiers in the camp were overrun; 1,300 of them were killed. The Zulus then attacked Rorke's Drift, where the 150 British soldiers guarding the camp made a resolute stand behind walls made of mealie ration sacks.

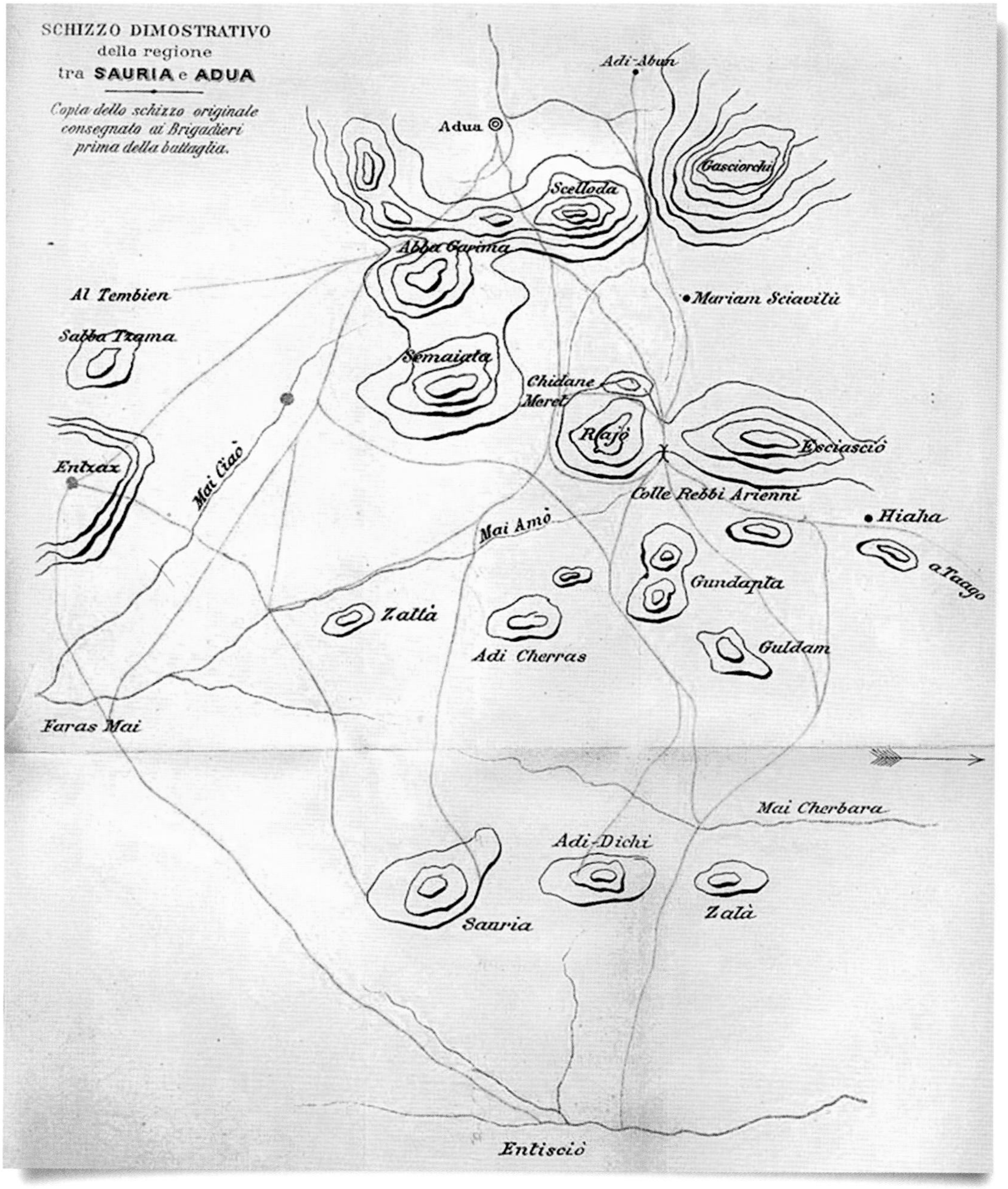

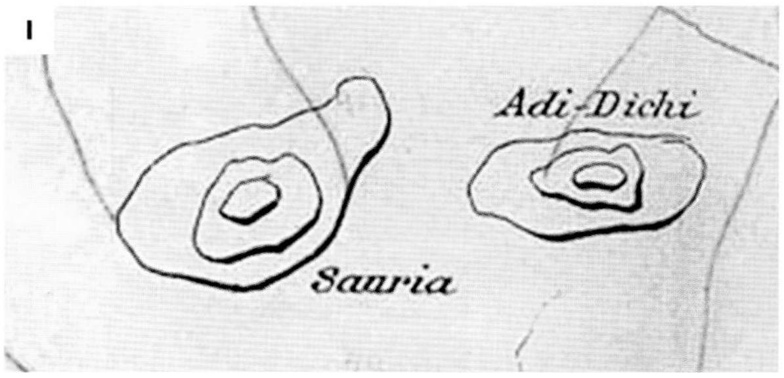

SCHIZZO DIMOSTRATIVO
della regione
tra SAURIA e ADUA

*Copia dello schizzo originale
consegnato ai Brigadieri
prima della battaglia.*

1

△ **Sauria**
Baratieri was reluctantly persuaded to advance from his position at Sauria before his supplies ran out and his own replacement arrived.

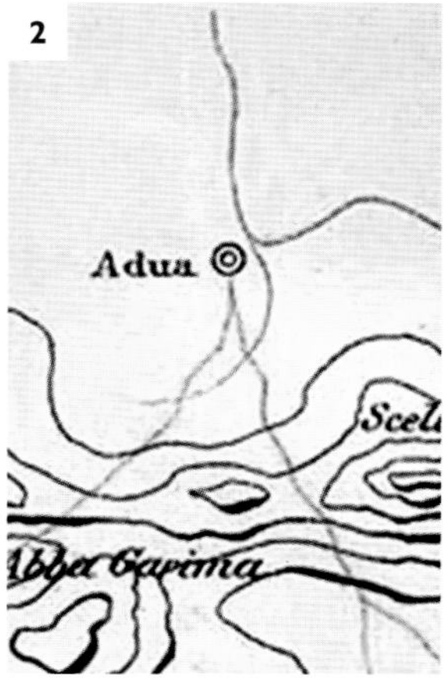

◁ **Adowa**
Menelik's forces occupied a strong position on the hills outside Adowa. However, they too had exhausted their supplies, and planned to break camp the next day.

▽ **Chidane Meret**
Ordered to occupy the Chidane Meret summit, Albertone's column marched in error into the main Ethiopian line beyond.

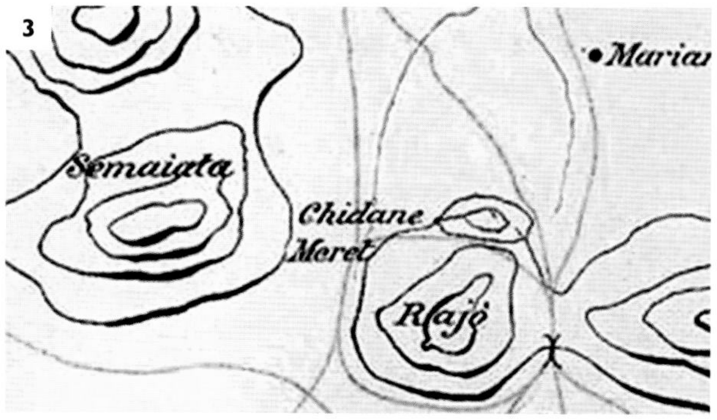

2

3

◁ **Distorted view**
This map, from Baratieri's *Memorie d'Africa*, was the inaccurate one used by the Italians at the Battle of Adowa. The network of hills and passes is grossly oversimplified and many places incorrectly marked.

ADOWA

On March 1, 1896, Ethiopian Emperor Menelik II led his army to defeat an invading Italian force at Adowa that fatally underestimated their opponents' strengh. The battle ensured that Ethiopia was never colonized by a European power.

Italy began establishing its first African colony, Eritrea, in 1882. Tensions between Italy and the Ethiopian Empire led to full-scale war in 1895. Menelik overran an Italian outpost in his first battle at Amba Alagi on December 7, 1895. In February 1896, General Oreste Baratieri, the Italian governor of Eritrea, led about 10,000 poorly trained Italian conscripts and several thousand Eritrean *Askari* toward Adowa to face the Emperor's well-equipped and experienced forces.

Early on March 1, four Italian brigades advanced toward Adowa. On the left, Albertone was to secure the high ground at Chidane Meret, while on the right

and center Elena, Dabormida, and Arimondi's brigades were to head to the passes around Rebbi Aryaeni. However, the Italian maps turned out to be wildly inaccurate. Albertone found himself miles from the rest of the army and encircled by tens of thousands of Ethiopians; a massacre ensued. The other Italian columns were shattered piecemeal as Menelik released his horsemen and Shewan reserve.

More than half of Baratieri's men had been killed, wounded or captured, with at least as many Ethiopian losses. Ethiopia's victory ensured that it would remain the only African country uncolonized by Europeans.

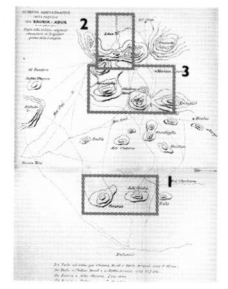

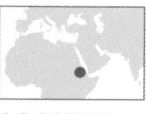

LOCATOR

OMDURMAN

At Omdurman, modern weapons, including the Maxim gun and rapid-fire rifles and artillery, helped Anglo-Egyptian forces under Major General Sir Herbert Kitchener defeat the Mahdist army of Abdullah al-Taashi in a battle that saw the British army's last major cavalry charge.

In 1898, charged with regaining British control of the Sudan, General Kitchener led 8,000 British regulars and 17,000 Sudanese and Egyptian troops on an expedition down the Nile. They camped at El Egeiga on the banks of the Nile on September 1.

Soon after sunrise on September 2, tens of thousands of the enemy advanced from a wide arc around the British camp. They were swiftly cut down by the British artillery, Maxim guns, and rapid-fire rifles. At 9 am, Kitchener's troops began to advance on Omdurman. The 21st Lancers (including Lieutenant Winston Churchill) charged a few hundred dervishes but found themselves fighting a few thousand, prompting a fierce battle. Meanwhile, Kitchener's rearguard, a Sudanese brigade, were attacked by over 15,000 warriors from the Khalifa's reserve. Aided by reinforcements, the rearguard drove off the Mahdists.

That afternoon, Kitchener entered Omdurman unopposed. Less than 50 British had been killed; the Mahdist dead, however, numbered over 10,000.

LOCATOR

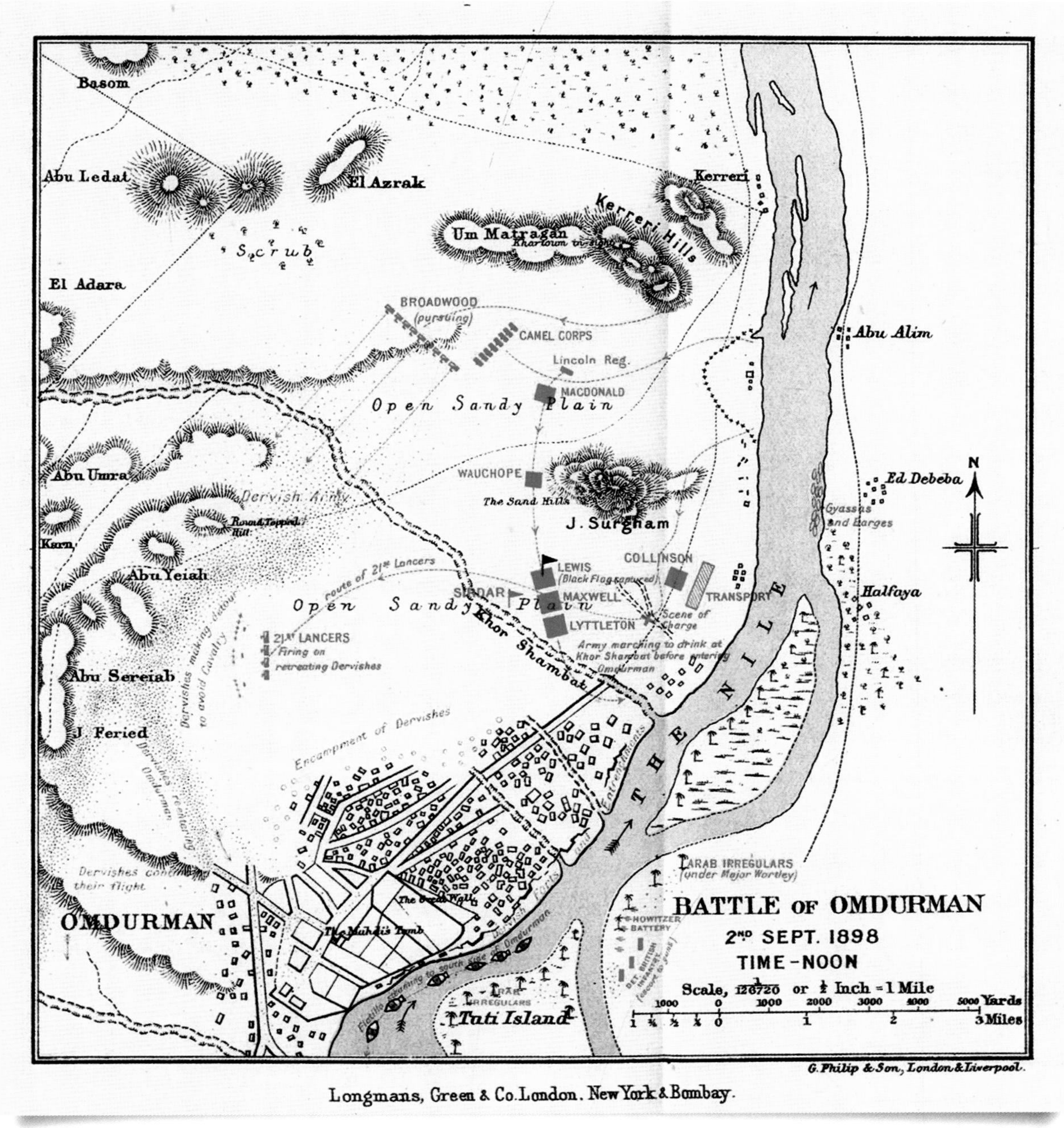

Longmans, Green & Co. London. New York & Bombay.

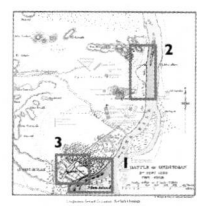

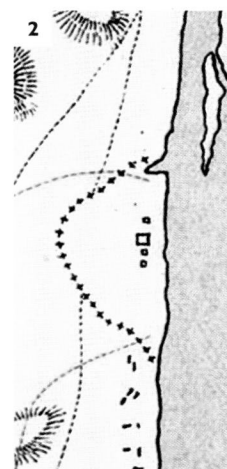

△ **The Nile**
Kitchener's gunboats bombarded Omdurman, damaging the city walls and the tomb of the Mahdi.

◁ **El Egeiga**
Kitchener's camp was protected by trenches and a *zariba* (a fence made from thorn bushes).

▽ **Mahdi's Tomb**
The Mahdi's great tomb in Omdurman was destroyed by the British after the battle. Only the top brass ornament has survived.

◁ **War on the Nile**
This map is taken from Winston Churchill's 1899 account of the Sudan campaign, *The River War*, and depicts the British marching on Omduran while pursuing the defeated Mahdists.

THE FIREPOWER REVOLUTION

During the 19th century a series of technological innovations multiplied the rate of fire, range, and power of military armaments, leading to the greatest change in warfare since the introduction of gunpowder.

△ **Gatling gun**
An early rapid-fire weapon, the Gatling gun had multiple barrels. Rotated by hand, each barrel fired a shot in turn.

Until the 1830s, soldiers used muzzle-loading, smooth-barreled muskets and cannons, and gunpowder was the only explosive. The revolution in infantry firepower began in the 1840s with the Prussian Dreyse needle gun. A bolt-action, breech-loaded rifle, it fired a cartridge with propellant, primer, and ball in one package, and could fire six rounds per minute. By the 1880s, bolt-operated rifles were limited only by aiming time. These were used alongside automatic machine guns, which had evolved from manually operated precursors such as the Gatling gun of the 1860s. Artillery developed hand-in-hand with the rifle. By 1898, the French had a breech-loading, 75 mm field gun that fired 15 rounds per minute. New nitrate-based explosives gave artillery greater power from the late 1800s. At sea, battleships carried breech-loaded guns firing high-explosive shells effective up to around 5 miles (9 km).

Deadly impact

In use by 1900, these new weapons made old tactics obsolete on land and sea. Soldiers advancing over open ground—on foot or on horseback—could now be mowed down by entrenched infantry. While the growing lethality of weapons was offset to an extent by greater troop dispersion and increased combat ranges, larger armies and longer battles meant that overall casualties increased to unprecedented levels, as is evident from World War I (see pp.208-24).

SIR HIRAM STEVENS MAXIM 1840–1916

Born in the US, Sir Hiram Stevens Maxim (far left) emigrated to Britain in 1881. He is best known for inventing the Maxim machine gun in 1884. The first self-powered machine gun, it was capable of firing 600 rounds per minute. During the colonial wars (see p.195), the British Army used this gun to deadly effect. Maxim later became deaf, as his hearing was damaged by years of exposure to the noise of his guns.

Naval artillery
In the Russo–Japanese War of 1904–1905, the Imperial Japanese Navy used torpedoes and high-explosive shells to achieve decisive victories. This painting shows Japanese sailors deploying torpedoes in the naval battle of Port Arthur, Manchuria.

DIRECTORY: 1700–1900

CULLODEN

APRIL 16, 1746

In 1745, Jacobite rebels made their last attempt to restore the Stuarts to the British throne. They were led by Charles Edward Stuart (known as Bonnie Prince Charlie), the grandson of the exiled Stuart king, James II. After a failed invasion of England, the rebels retreated to Inverness, Scotland, in 1746. On the night of April 15, the Jacobites marched to surprise the government army under the Duke of Cumberland. Realizing midway that they would arrive too late, they began to retrace their steps, leading to much confusion. They were caught at dawn by the duke's forces at Drumossie Moor, near the village of Culloden.

Charles decided to face the duke head-on in battle. The exhausted rebel soldiers held their positions while the government artillery bombarded them. Charles finally unleashed the famous "Highland charge." The Scottish Highlanders ran across the sodden and smoke-shrouded moor into a barrage of gunfire and grapeshot. Many never reached the enemy line, and those who did were met with bayonets. The battle was over in less than an hour and the Jacobites fled. Many more were hunted down and butchered in the weeks after, while Charles escaped to France, his dreams of a Stuart restoration shattered.

QUIBERON BAY

NOVEMBER 20, 1759

In 1759, France planned to reverse its failing fortunes in the Seven Years' War (see pp.150–51) by invading Britain. About 20,000 troops were assembled in Brittany, waiting for the French fleet to escort them to Scotland. However, the fleet was blockaded in Brest by Admiral Edward Hawke. When a gale forced Hawke to withdraw, Comte de Conflans, commander of the French fleet, set sail

for Quiberon Bay; but the British fleet soon reappeared. Outnumbered and struggling in the high winds, Conflan's fleet entered the narrow mouth of the bay, followed by Hawke. After a chaotic mêlée, the British lost only two ships, while the French lost seven (with the rest forced to scatter). As one of the Royal Navy's greatest victories, the battle secured Britain's dominance of the seas.

△ Allied commanders at Yorktown give orders for the final attack

YORKTOWN

SEPTEMBER 28–OCTOBER 19, 1781

After failing to take control of North Carolina during the American War of Independence (1775–83), Lieutenant General Charles Cornwallis and the British army regrouped in August 1781 at Yorktown on Chesapeake Bay, Virginia. Cornwallis fortified both Yorktown and the nearby Gloucester. He was confident that he would be supplied by sea.

However, on September 5, Admiral François de Grasse defeated the British fleet off Chesapeake Bay, and Yorktown was cut off. On September 29, General George Washington and the French commander, the Count of Rochambeau, surrounded Yorktown with 19,000 men.

Under constant bombardment by the British, Rochambeau organzied a system of trenches, bunkers, and batteries around the town. By October 9, all the guns were in place and opened fire. The siege lines were moved closer to the British line. After the allies captured two British strongholds on October 14, Cornwallis ordered his men to evacuate Yorktown and head to Gloucester. However, bad weather and a shortage of ammunition led him to surrender on October 19. The siege of Yorktown, the last major action in the war, prompted negotiations that led to America's independence in 1783.

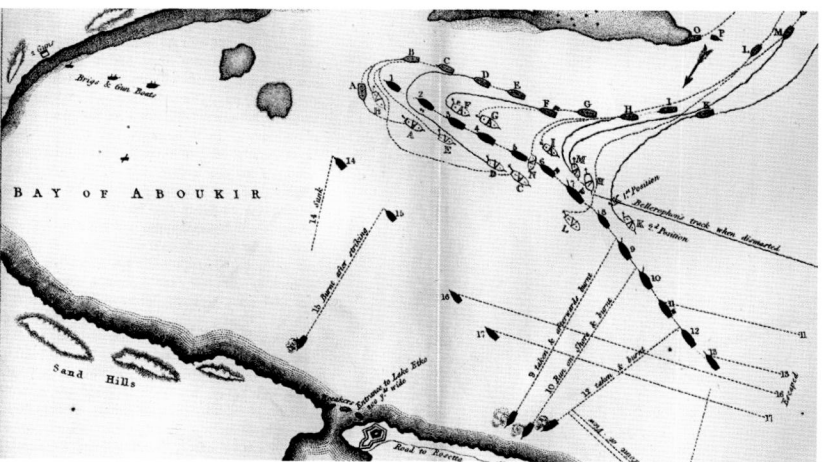

△ Contemporary chart of the battle at Aboukir Bay

ABOUKIR BAY

AUGUST 1, 1798

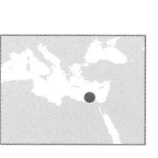

In May 1798, Napoleon Bonaparte sailed from France for Egypt, with an invasion force escorted by 13 ships of the line and 4 frigates led by Admiral Francois-Paul Brueys. Evading the Royal Navy in the Mediterranean, they reached Aboukir Bay by July. British Admiral Nelson, in command of 13 ships of the line and one 50-gun ship, discovered the French fleet in August. He ordered an attack on the French vanguard and center, knowing the wind would not allow the French

rear to fight. In a surprising move, one of his captains maneuvered his ships between the anchored French fleet and the shore. As night fell, the French ships were battered from both sides. Brueys was killed and at 10:00pm his flagship L'Orient exploded, killing several hundred sailors. Admiral Villeneuve, in the rear of the French line, slipped away at dawn, saving just two ships of the line and two frigates from the British. Nelson was hailed as a hero for his victory.

WAGRAM

JULY 5–6, 1809

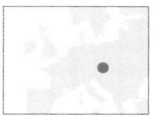

In 1809, Austrian forces marched through Bavaria in an attempt to reclaim the German territories lost to France after the Battle of Austerlitz (see pp.166–67). In response, Napoleon took command of the Grand Army of Germany and captured Vienna but suffered a humiliating defeat in May at Aspern-Essling at the hand of Austrian troops. By July, he desperately needed a victory to restore his reputation.

On the night of July 4–5, the French army crossed to the left bank of the River Danube to attack the Austrians. The Austrian army was thinly spread in an arc running along the Russbach Heights and centered on the village of Wagram. The main battle commenced at dawn on July 6. The Austrians, led by Archduke

Charles, launched a series of attacks and nearly enveloped the French left flank. Napoleon reinforced his left and pounded the Austrian lines with the concentrated firepower of a battery of about 100 guns. While Marshal André Masséna counterattacked the Austrian right and MacDonald's V Corps threatened to break the Austrian center, Marshal Louis-Nicolas Davout drove back the Austrian left. With no reserves to bolster his increasingly battered line, Charles retreated and, his men's morale shattered, sought an armistice. The unprecedented amount of artillery used—some 1,000 pieces and 180,000 rounds of ammunition—made the battle particularly bloody: up to 80,000 of the 300,000 involved were killed or wounded.

BOYACÁ

AUGUST 7, 1819

From 1809, Spain's South American colonies began fighting for their independence. Central to the struggle was Venezuelan military and political leader Simón Bolívar. In 1819, Bolívar and General Francisco de Paula Santander led an army on a grueling mountain crossing from Venezuela into New Granada (present-day Colombia), hoping to capture its capital, Bogotá. The army was made up of about 3,000 local guerrillas, including *llaneros* (cowboys), and British and Irish veterans of the Napoleonic Wars (1803–15).

After clashing with the Spanish forces, under Colonel José María Barreiro at

Gameza (July 12) and Pantano de Vargas (July 25), Bolívar waited for Barreiro's army at the River Teatinos. On August 7, Santander ambushed the Spanish vanguard after it crossed over the Boyacá Bridge, cutting it off from the rear. Meanwhile, Bolívar attacked the main body of the Spanish to the rear. The Royalists were swiftly overcome, and Bolívar's men took over 1,600 prisoners, some of whom (including Barreiro) were executed after Bolivar took Bogota due to his 1813 decree of "War to the Death." The battle at Boyacá Bridge was a turning point for the independence movement. Bolívar went on to liberate Venezuela, Ecuador, and Peru.

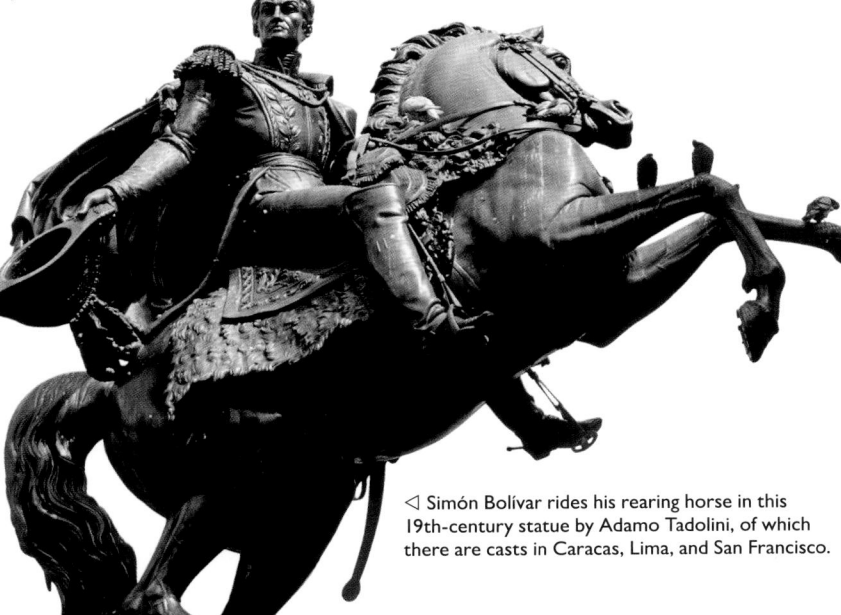

◁ Simón Bolívar rides his rearing horse in this 19th-century statue by Adamo Tadolini, of which there are casts in Caracas, Lima, and San Francisco.

NAVARINO

OCTOBER 20, 1827

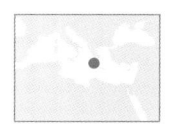

The Greek struggle for independence from Ottoman rule began in 1821. Ottoman forces, assisted by an Egyptian army under Ibrahim Pasha, fought to suppress the revolt. By 1827, the nationalists controlled only a few areas. Britain, France, and Russia, however, demanded that the Ottomans accept an armistice. The allies assembled a fleet of 27 ships under Admiral Sir Edward Codrington in the Mediterranean. The Ottomans gathered a larger force of Turkish and Egyptian ships under Tahir Pasha in Navarino Bay on the west coast of Greece. On October 20, Codrington's

fleet sailed into the bay and anchored among the Egyptian-Turkish ships. Tensions were high and fighting soon broke out. The ships fired on each other from close range, trying to inflict as much damage as possible while trying to escape the enemy's broadsides. The allies, though outnumbered, had much better guns and, after three hours, the Egyptian-Turkish fleet abandoned the fight. The Ottomans lost almost all of their ships, while the allies lost none. Greece finally secured its independence in 1830, after the Ottomans' defeat in the Russo-Turkish war of 1828–29.

△ Russian painter Ivan Aivazovsky's 1846 depiction of the Battle of Navarino

VICKSBURG

MAY 18–JULY 4, 1863

One of the most successful Union campaigns of the American Civil War (1861–65), the Siege of Vicksburg sealed the reputation of Major-General Ulysses Grant. Union forces had previously made several unsuccessful attempts to capture the strategically vital town on the east bank of the Mississippi. Grant and the Army of the Tennessee converged again on the town in May 1863.

Vicksburg was held by 29,000 Confederate soldiers under Lieutenant General John C. Pemberton and protected by a 8-mile (13-km) arc of fortifications and artillery on the cliff. By May 18, Grant had surrounded the town, but his attempts to storm it on

May 19 and 22 failed and he lost more than 4,000 men. Grant then turned to besieging the town by constructing trenches that trapped Pemberton's army. The attempts of Confederate forces to relieve Pemberton failed, and conditions in the town, cut off and under constant bombardment by the Union artillery, quickly deteriorated. After nearly seven weeks, running short on food and supplies, Pemberton surrendered to the Union. The capture of Vicksburg, swiftly followed by another victory at Port Hudson, gave the Union control of the Mississippi, cutting off a crucial Confederate supply line and splitting the Confederacy in two.

1900— PRESENT

THE MODERN ERA SAW NEW AND INCREASINGLY DEADLY FORMS OF MECHANIZATION IN BATTLE, AND TOOK WARFARE TO THE SKIES. GLOBAL CONFLICTS RAGED ON A SCALE NEVER SEEN BEFORE, PUSHING MILITARY TECHNOLOGY TO NEW HEIGHTS; FROM THESE WARS CAME THE DAWNING OF THE NUCLEAR AGE.

1900–PRESENT

The 20th century was an age of mechanized global warfare in which industry, mass conscription, and nationalist ideology combined to create conflicts on a vast scale. Rapid advances in technology have resulted in computerized battlefields with precision weapons, unrecognizable to previous generations of soldiers.

The fragmentation of the Balkans in the 19th century created a tinderbox that erupted into war in 1914 when a Serbian nationalist assassinated Austro-Hungarian Archduke Franz Ferdinand. World War I pitted Germany, Austria-Hungary, and the Ottoman Empire against Russia, Britain, France, and their allies. As the war progressed, mobile warfare morphed into an attritional confrontation along trench lines on the Western Front. Along this 400-mile (700-km) stretch of land, battles such as Verdun (see pp.214–15) and the Somme (see pp.220–21) cost hundreds of thousands of lives for little territorial gain. New technology, such as poison gas, early tanks, and aircraft was used in a bid to unlock the stalemate. However, it was the exhaustion of the blockaded Central Powers and the entry of the US that ended the war in 1918.

From *Blitzkrieg* to the atom bomb
The hope that World War I would be "the war to end all wars" proved false. The damage it had caused shaped the politics of Europe and facilitated the rise of Adolf Hitler in Germany, who envisioned a Greater German Reich for the

> *"Fighting in the air is not sport, it is scientific murder."*
>
> US PILOT EDDIE RICKENBACKER, 1919

Germanic people. Nazi expansionism led to the inevitable— Britain and France declared war on Germany after its forces invaded Poland in 1939. Germany's use of *Blitzkrieg*

△ **Over the top**
British troops scramble out of their trenches during the Battle of the Somme in 1916. More than 19,000 soldiers died during the first day of the offensive as they struggled to reach the German lines. They were scythed down by machine guns which the preliminary British artillery bombardment had failed to destroy.

THE WORLD WARS
In the 20th century, the two World Wars cost some 80 million lives. After World War II, the nuclear standoff between the US and the USSR during the Cold War precluded direct wars. However, they fought wars to defend their influence, such as in Vietnam and Afghanistan, or sponsored wars between their allies. In the Cold War's wake, regional wars erupted and nuclear weapons proliferated. The Soviet Union was dissolved, but Russia and China continue to challenge US global dominance.

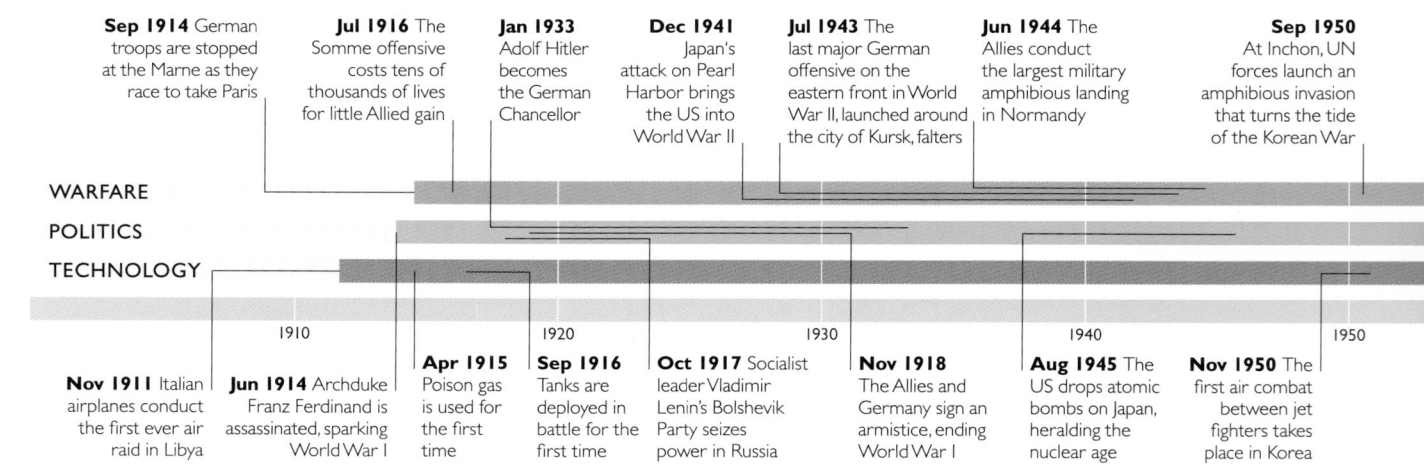

Sep 1914 German troops are stopped at the Marne as they race to take Paris

Jul 1916 The Somme offensive costs tens of thousands of lives for little Allied gain

Jan 1933 Adolf Hitler becomes the German Chancellor

Dec 1941 Japan's attack on Pearl Harbor brings the US into World War II

Jul 1943 The last major German offensive on the eastern front in World War II, launched around the city of Kursk, falters

Jun 1944 The Allies conduct the largest military amphibious landing in Normandy

Sep 1950 At Inchon, UN forces launch an amphibious invasion that turns the tide of the Korean War

WARFARE

POLITICS

TECHNOLOGY

1910   1920   1930   1940   1950

Nov 1911 Italian airplanes conduct the first ever air raid in Libya

Jun 1914 Archduke Franz Ferdinand is assassinated, sparking World War I

Apr 1915 Poison gas is used for the first time

Sep 1916 Tanks are deployed in battle for the first time

Oct 1917 Socialist leader Vladimir Lenin's Bolshevik Party seizes power in Russia

Nov 1918 The Allies and Germany sign an armistice, ending World War I

Aug 1945 The US drops atomic bombs on Japan, heralding the nuclear age

Nov 1950 The first air combat between jet fighters takes place in Korea

△ **Guerrilla gun**
The Soviet-designed RPD machine gun was introduced in 1944. Its reliability and durability made it a staple of guerrilla forces such as the Viet Cong.

◁ **Total War**
This German poster shows civilian workers and a grenade-throwing soldier with the slogan "Victory at any Price." World War II was a "total war," in which the entire society played a role.

("lightning war") tactics, spearheaded by its highly mobile panzer tank force, won a string of rapid victories. Britain's superior air organization and development of radar, however, allowed it to defeat the German air force in the Battle of Britain in 1940 (see pp.232–33) and avoid invasion.

Air power became vital in World War II. Aircraft carriers combined naval and air warfare in confrontations such as the Battle of Midway (see pp.238–39). Germany's submarine blockade of Britain failed due to Allied countermeasures, and when Hitler's invasion of the USSR in 1941 failed to inflict a knockout blow, Germany faced an increasingly unwinnable war on two fronts. US entry was again decisive, especially after the Allies made a massive amphibious landing in Normandy in 1944 (see pp.248–49).

Nuclear weapons dropped by the US on the Japanese cities of Hiroshima and Nagasaki ended the Pacific phase of the war in 1945. They also heralded the Cold War—a new ideological conflict between the USSR and the US, and their supporters. "Hot wars" erupted when local disputes became proxy wars sponsored by these two superpowers, such as in Vietnam, where the USSR and the US backed North and South Vietnam respectively. This proxy rivalry fueled conflicts across the world, from Korea and Afghanistan to Angola and Nicaragua, and successive Arab-Israeli wars.

Technology fails to triumph

The collapse of the USSR in 1991 did not end large-scale warfare. The Middle East in particular has seen a chaotic series of conflicts starting with the US-led expulsion of invading Iraqi forces from Kuwait in 1991 (see pp.270–71). A war on the same scale as any World War now seems unlikely. While wars are now fought with precision-guided missiles, computer-operated drones, and stealth bombers that integrate electronics and computer technology, guns and knives are still commonly used in persistent civil wars.

▽ **Operation Iraqi Freedom**
US-led coalition forces, including Britain's 7th Armored Brigade, gathered in the Kuwaiti Desert in March 2003. The land offensive against Iraq followed next, ending in the overthrow of Saddam Hussein.

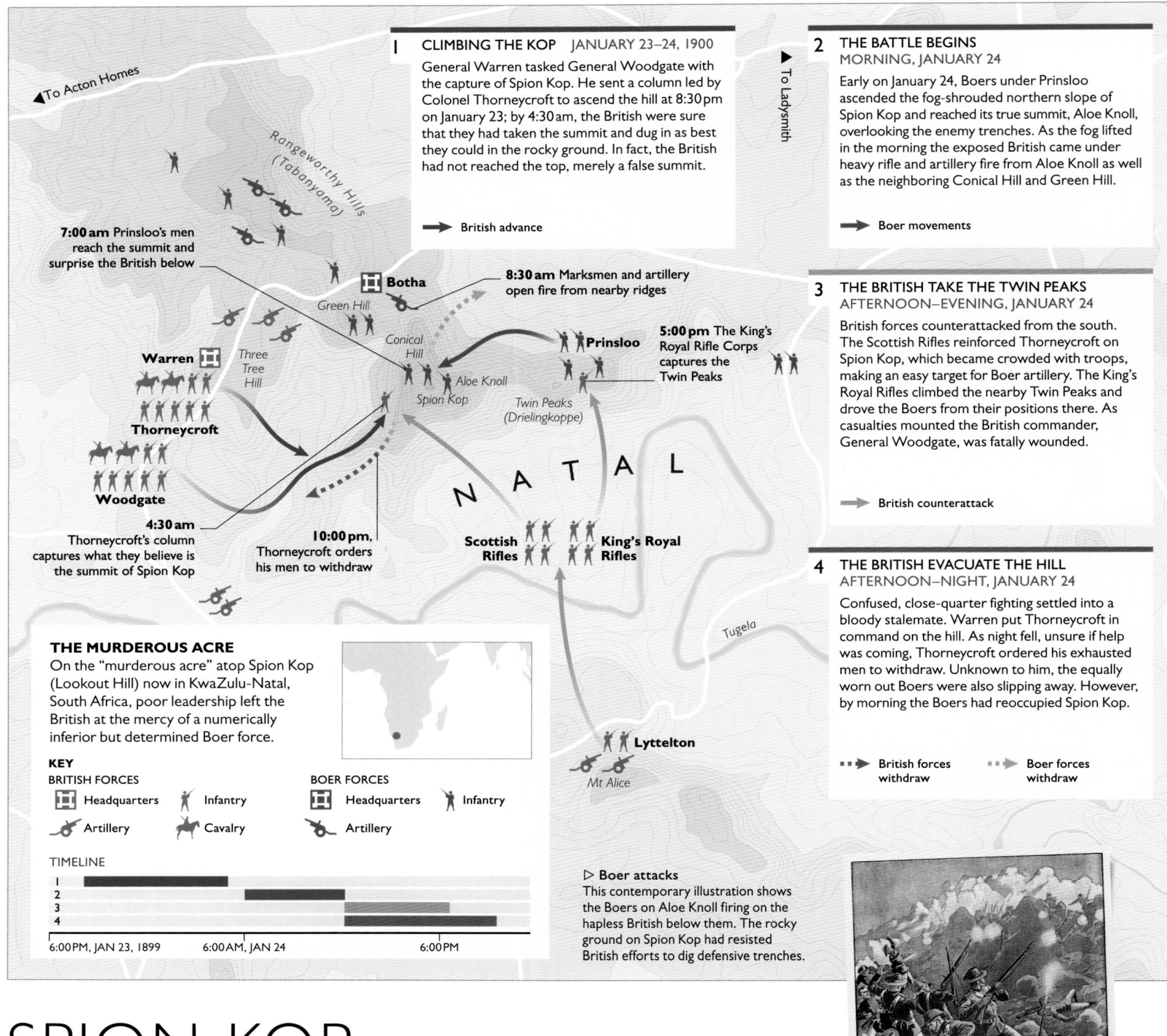

1 CLIMBING THE KOP JANUARY 23–24, 1900

General Warren tasked General Woodgate with the capture of Spion Kop. He sent a column led by Colonel Thorneycroft to ascend the hill at 8:30 pm on January 23; by 4:30 am, the British were sure that they had taken the summit and dug in as best they could in the rocky ground. In fact, the British had not reached the top, merely a false summit.

→ British advance

2 THE BATTLE BEGINS
MORNING, JANUARY 24

Early on January 24, Boers under Prinsloo ascended the fog-shrouded northern slope of Spion Kop and reached its true summit, Aloe Knoll, overlooking the enemy trenches. As the fog lifted in the morning the exposed British came under heavy rifle and artillery fire from Aloe Knoll as well as the neighboring Conical Hill and Green Hill.

→ Boer movements

3 THE BRITISH TAKE THE TWIN PEAKS
AFTERNOON–EVENING, JANUARY 24

British forces counterattacked from the south. The Scottish Rifles reinforced Thorneycroft on Spion Kop, which became crowded with troops, making an easy target for Boer artillery. The King's Royal Rifles climbed the nearby Twin Peaks and drove the Boers from their positions there. As casualties mounted the British commander, General Woodgate, was fatally wounded.

→ British counterattack

4 THE BRITISH EVACUATE THE HILL
AFTERNOON–NIGHT, JANUARY 24

Confused, close-quarter fighting settled into a bloody stalemate. Warren put Thorneycroft in command on the hill. As night fell, unsure if help was coming, Thorneycroft ordered his exhausted men to withdraw. Unknown to him, the equally worn out Boers were also slipping away. However, by morning the Boers had reoccupied Spion Kop.

▪▪▶ British forces withdraw   ▪▪▶ Boer forces withdraw

To Acton Homes

Rangeworthy Hills (Tabanyama)

To Ladysmith

7:00 am Prinsloo's men reach the summit and surprise the British below

Green Hill   🏠 **Botha**

8:30 am Marksmen and artillery open fire from nearby ridges

Conical Hill

Warren 🏠   Three Tree Hill

Thorneycroft

Aloe Knoll
Spion Kop

🔫 **Prinsloo**

5:00 pm The King's Royal Rifle Corps captures the Twin Peaks

Twin Peaks (Drielingkoppe)

Woodgate

4:30 am Thorneycroft's column captures what they believe is the summit of Spion Kop

10:00 pm, Thorneycroft orders his men to withdraw

Scottish Rifles   **King's Royal Rifles**

N A T A L

Tugela

THE MURDEROUS ACRE

On the "murderous acre" atop Spion Kop (Lookout Hill) now in KwaZulu-Natal, South Africa, poor leadership left the British at the mercy of a numerically inferior but determined Boer force.

KEY

BRITISH FORCES		BOER FORCES	
🏠 Headquarters	🔫 Infantry	🏠 Headquarters	🔫 Infantry
🔫 Artillery	🐎 Cavalry	🔫 Artillery	

TIMELINE

1
2
3
4

6:00 PM, JAN 23, 1899   6:00 AM, JAN 24   6:00 PM

Lyttelton
Mt Alice

▷ **Boer attacks**
This contemporary illustration shows the Boers on Aloe Knoll firing on the hapless British below them. The rocky ground on Spion Kop had resisted British efforts to dig defensive trenches.

REPRISE DE SPION-KOP PAR LES BOERS

SPION KOP

In an attempt to lift the siege of Ladysmith in the Second Boer War (1899–1902), a British force tried to capture Spion Kop (hill). A tactical error saw them endure a day under heavy fire before they withdrew, leaving the Kop in Boer hands.

Between 1899 and 1902, Britain was engaged in a long, drawn-out war with the two Boer (Afrikaner) states—the South African Republic and Orange Free State. The causes of the war involved British imperialism and Boer independence, but were brought into immediate focus by conflict over the rights to exploit newly discovered gold mines in South Africa. The small Boer states were poorly armed compared to the British but in late 1899, their forces

besieged Ladysmith in British-run Natal. As part of their effort to relieve the siege, the British sent General Warren to take control of Spion Kop, the highest point in a group of rocky hills overlooking the approaches to Ladysmith, defended by Botha's Boers. The British found themselves fatally exposed to enemy fire and suffered 250 dead and more than 1,000 wounded before retreating. Ladysmith was finally relieved on February 28, 1900.

TSUSHIMA

In 1904, Russia and Japan went to war over influence in the disputed Chinese province of Manchuria. A climactic sea battle in the Straits of Tsushima the following spring gave Japan a decisive victory, marking its emergence as a new force on the world stage.

Hostilities between the two powers began when Japan launched a surprise attack on Russia's Far Eastern fleet stationed in Port Arthur on Manchuria's southern tip. Success in the raid allowed the Japanese to ship in troops to confront Russian forces in Manchuria.

In response, Tsar Nicholas sent the bulk of Russia's Baltic fleet to relieve the port. During its long voyage, news came that Port Arthur itself had fallen to the Japanese after a five-month siege. Japan's High Command had plenty of time to prepare their navy—already one of the most modern in the world—for the arrival of the Russian fleet.

When they finally met in the Straits of Tsushima, the Japanese established their superiority in just a few hours. Remnants of the Russian fleet fled to Vladivostok. Three months later, Russia was forced to sign a humiliating peace by which they agreed to abandon their Manchurian claims.

Talin
Liepaja
RUSSIAN EMPIRE
21 Oct 1904 Warships sink a British trawler
Vladivostok
Port Arthur
Shanghai
La Pérouse Strait
Tsugaru Strait
Tsushima Strait
May 24, 1905 Russian second-in-command, von Fölkersahm, dies on the journey
Cape Town
INDIAN OCEAN
KEY
Main battle
Main fleet
Splinter group
Ports of embarkation

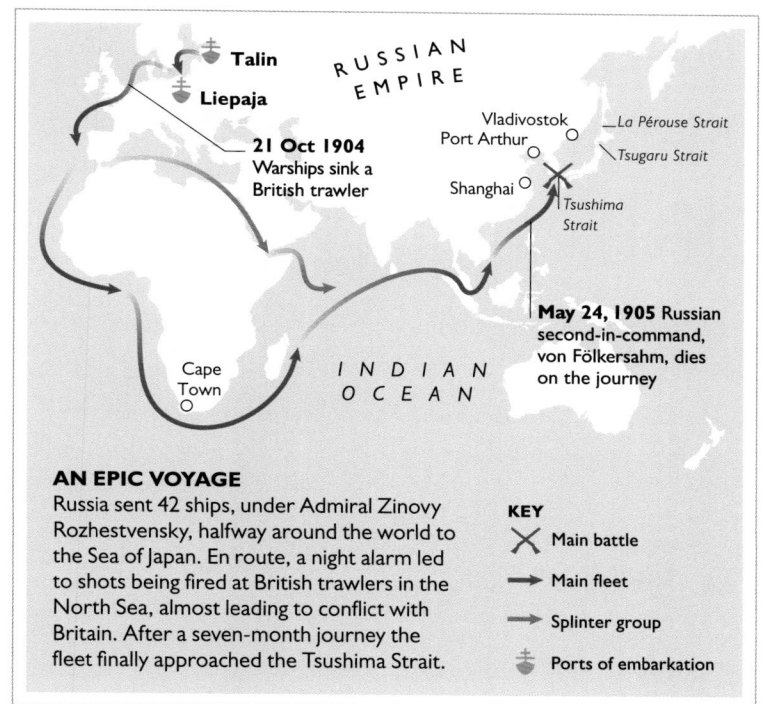

AN EPIC VOYAGE
Russia sent 42 ships, under Admiral Zinovy Rozhestvensky, halfway around the world to the Sea of Japan. En route, a night alarm led to shots being fired at British trawlers in the North Sea, almost leading to conflict with Britain. After a seven-month journey the fleet finally approached the Tsushima Strait.

SETTING THE TRAP
Having spent seven months sailing to the battle zone, the Russian fleet arrived to face Japan's modern, well-equipped navy. Forewarned by wireless telegraph, the Japanese were waiting in ambush.

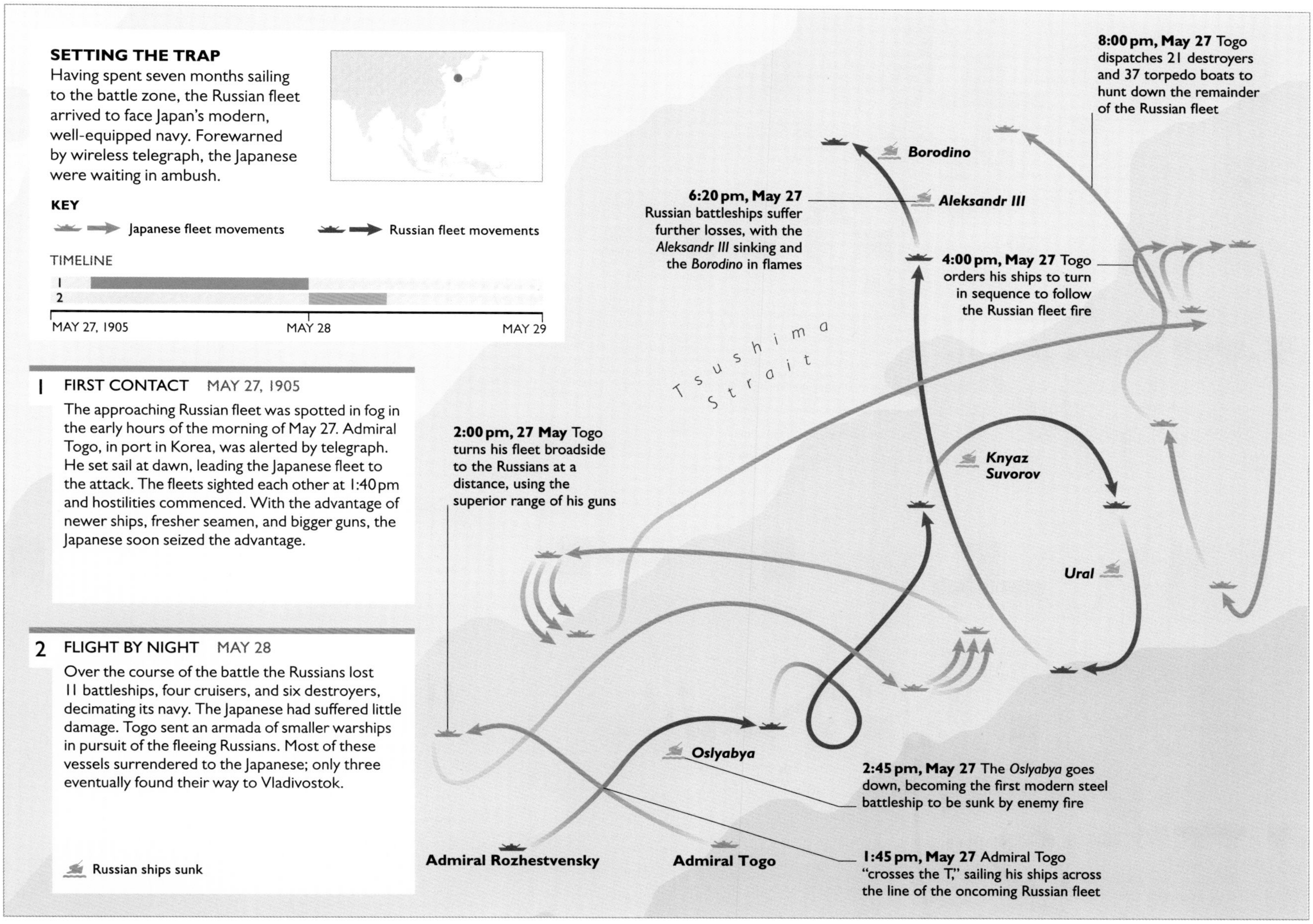

KEY
Japanese fleet movements
Russian fleet movements
TIMELINE
1
2
MAY 27, 1905
MAY 28
MAY 29
8:00 pm, May 27 Togo dispatches 21 destroyers and 37 torpedo boats to hunt down the remainder of the Russian fleet
Borodino
Aleksandr III
6:20 pm, May 27 Russian battleships suffer further losses, with the Aleksandr III sinking and the Borodino in flames
4:00 pm, May 27 Togo orders his ships to turn in sequence to follow the Russian fleet fire
Tsushima Strait
2:00 pm, 27 May Togo turns his fleet broadside to the Russians at a distance, using the superior range of his guns
Knyaz Suvorov
Ural
Oslyabya
2:45 pm, May 27 The Oslyabya goes down, becoming the first modern steel battleship to be sunk by enemy fire
Admiral Rozhestvensky
Admiral Togo
1:45 pm, May 27 Admiral Togo "crosses the T," sailing his ships across the line of the oncoming Russian fleet
Russian ships sunk

1 FIRST CONTACT MAY 27, 1905
The approaching Russian fleet was spotted in fog in the early hours of the morning of May 27. Admiral Togo, in port in Korea, was alerted by telegraph. He set sail at dawn, leading the Japanese fleet to the attack. The fleets sighted each other at 1:40 pm and hostilities commenced. With the advantage of newer ships, fresher seamen, and bigger guns, the Japanese soon seized the advantage.

2 FLIGHT BY NIGHT MAY 28
Over the course of the battle the Russians lost 11 battleships, four cruisers, and six destroyers, decimating its navy. The Japanese had suffered little damage. Togo sent an armada of smaller warships in pursuit of the fleeing Russians. Most of these vessels surrendered to the Japanese; only three eventually found their way to Vladivostok.

THE AGE OF DREADNOUGHTS

In a bid to maintain its naval supremacy over other nations, Britain's Royal Navy launched the HMS *Dreadnought* in 1906. Taking firepower and speed to an unprecedented level, it marked the dawn of a new era of battleships.

Metal-hulled steamships had been in use since the 19th century. However, on its launch the *Dreadnought* made all other battleships of its time obsolete, and gave its name to a new class of ship. The first all-big-gun battleship, it carried ten 12-inch guns for long-range attacks, and it was also the first to use steam turbines, reaching speeds of up to 21 knots. It represented a good compromise in the holy trinity of naval design: speed, protection, and firepower. As the Royal Navy pushed forward an ambitious program of naval construction, other nations including the US, Germany, Italy, and Japan followed suit and built their own dreadnoughts.

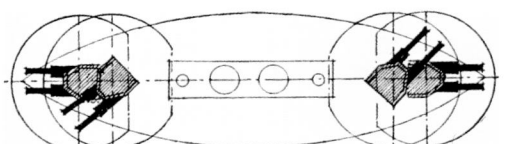

◁ **Super-firing turrets**
This sketch shows the positions of super-firing turrets. Each pair consists of one turret on deck level with the second mounted above and behind it.

New and improved

Competition was fierce, and soon the *Dreadnought* was itself rendered obsolete by more powerful battleships called super-dreadnoughts. The first of these, HMS *Orion*, launched in 1910 armed with 13.5-inch guns. Pairs of superimposed gun turrets, called super-firing turrets, were mounted on the centerline of its hull to improve firing arcs. Oil slowly replaced coal to fire the boilers that fed steam to the turbines. Super-dreadnoughts were supplanted by "fast battleships," which emphasized speed. The last of these retired from active service in 1991.

△ *R-class battleships*
These super-dreadnought battleships—the HMS *Royal Oak*, *Ramillies*, *Revenge*, and *Resolution*—belonged to the *Revenge* class. Their main armament comprised eight 15-inch guns in four turrets.

Last of the line
The HMS *Hood* was the final battlecruiser built by
the Royal Navy. Battlecruisers were similar to fast
battleships but lightly armored to increase speed
and firepower. The HMS *Hood* carried 15-inch
guns in four twin-gun turrets, on the fore and aft
of the ship, and was capable of 32 knots.

TANNENBERG

Within days of the outbreak of World War I, Russia fulfilled its treaty promises to its ally France by sending two armies to invade Prussia. While the 1st Army drove back the opposing German forces, the 2nd, to the south, was encircled and suffered a crushing defeat.

When war broke out in August 1914, Germany faced the prospect of conflict on two fronts—with France in the west, and Russia in the east. Russia was expected to take months to mobilize, so the German offensive prioritized a swift victory over France. While seven of Germany's eight armies concentrated on the Western front, Russia launched a surprise invasion of East Prussia, even before its own troops were properly prepared.

Attacking in the north, Russia's 1st Army had early successes, winning an indecisive victory at Gumbinnen that forced a German retreat. But instead of abandoning the province, the German forces redeployed to the south, where the Russian 2nd Army was advancing through the difficult terrain of the Masurian lakes. Hampered by poor communications, the 1st Army slowly advanced west rather than going south to help their compatriots. Outrunning its supply lines, the 2nd Army was cut off as a lethal cordon tightened around it. With no food and no escape route, the bulk of the Russian force had no option but to surrender. This was a massive propaganda boost for the German commanders Ludendorff and von Hindenburg, who portrayed the victory as revenge for the Teutonic Knights' defeat at nearby Grunwald five centuries earlier (see pp.88–89).

> *"The more ruthlessly war is conducted, the more merciful is it ... "*
>
> PAUL VON HINDENBURG, 1914

PAUL VON HINDENBURG

Born into an aristocratic Prussian family, von Hindenburg (1847–1934) had retired from the army before being recalled to serve in 1914. Thanks to a productive partnership with strategist Erich Ludendorff he became Supreme Commander of the Central Powers from 1916. After Germany lost the war, von Hindenburg's war record led to his election as president of Germany in 1925. However, his presidency was marked by political turmoil, depression, and the rise of the Nazi Party.

EAST PRUSSIA INVADED

East Prussia was an extension of the German Empire along the Baltic Sea's southeastern shores. Its territory is now divided between Poland, Lithuania, and Russia.

KEY

■ Prussian Empire	◤ German army
◤ Russian army	
✗ German forces	✗ Russian forces

TIMELINE

1
2
3
4
5
6

AUG 15, 1914   AUG 20   AUG 25   AUG 30   SEP 4

Baltic Sea

Gdansk

Elbing

Marienburg

Prussian Holland

Christberg

Jeziorak Lake

Lessen

Deutsch Eylau

Strasburg

Rypin

Ilawka

1 THE RUSSIAN ADVANCE
AUGUST 17–19, 1914

Aware that German forces were focused on the invasion of France, Russia's High Command determined to strike quickly on the eastern front, where only the German 8th Army was in place to defend East Prussia. Relying on surprise, the Russian 1st Army under General Rennenkampf crossed the border on August 17, before its supply lines were properly in place.

→ Russian advance

2 VICTORY AT GUMBINNEN
AUGUST 20

General Prittwitz of Germany's 8th Army ordered his troops to meet the invaders, launching a predawn attack near Gumbinnen. Slowed by roads clogged by refugees, some detachments failed to reach the front until several hours later, by which time the Russians had gained a decisive advantage. Fearing a Russian breakthrough, Prittwitz ordered a general retreat, effectively ceding all of East Prussia to the invaders.

✗ Battle   ▪▪▶ German retreat

Aug 22 The 1st Corps of the 8th Army redeploys rapidly by train

3 GERMAN FORCES REDEPLOY
AUGUST 21–23

The Russian 2nd Army advanced into East Prussia to the south, in the tough terrain of the Masurian Lakes. In response, the Germans sent two commanders, von Hindenburg and Ludendorff, as replacements for the now disgraced Prittwitz. They implemented a plan to redeploy retreating troops of the 8th Army, sending one corps to the invaders' left wing, and two the right.

→ Russian advance   → German troops redeployed

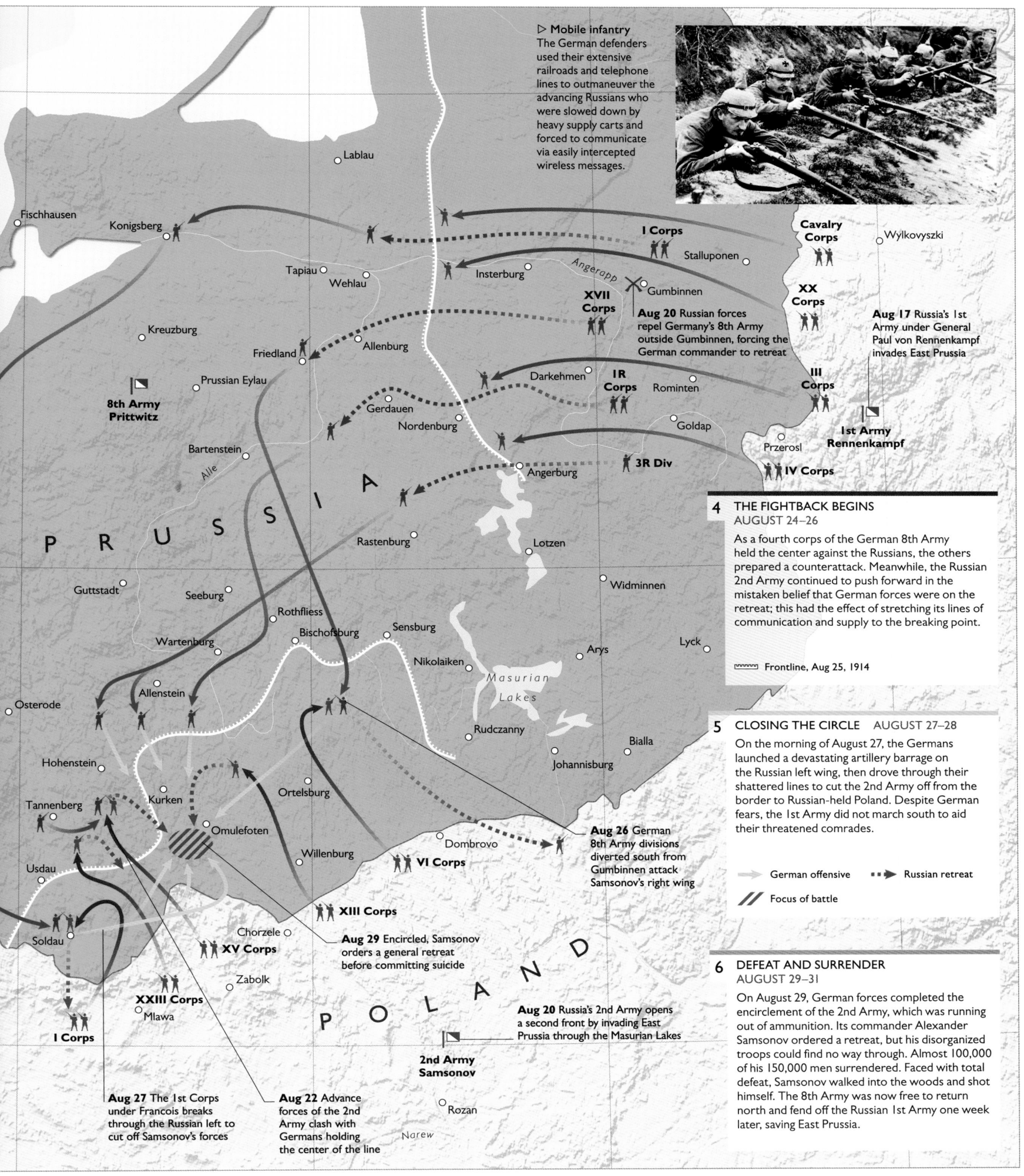

▷ **Mobile infantry**
The German defenders used their extensive railroads and telephone lines to outmaneuver the advancing Russians who were slowed down by heavy supply carts and forced to communicate via easily intercepted wireless messages.

Lablau

Fischhausen

Konigsberg

I Corps

Cavalry Corps

Wylkovyszki

Stalluponen

Tapiau

Wehlau

Insterburg

Angerapp

Gumbinnen

XX Corps

Aug 17 Russia's 1st Army under General Paul von Rennenkampf invades East Prussia

Kreuzburg

Friedland

Allenburg

XVII Corps

Aug 20 Russian forces repel Germany's 8th Army outside Gumbinnen, forcing the German commander to retreat

Prussian Eylau

Darkehmen

IR Corps

Rominten

III Corps

8th Army Prittwitz

Gerdauen

Nordenburg

Goldap

Przerosl

1st Army Rennenkampf

Bartenstein

Alle

Angerburg

3R Div

IV Corps

P   R   U   S   S   I   A

Rastenburg

Lotzen

Widminnen

---

4 THE FIGHTBACK BEGINS
AUGUST 24–26

As a fourth corps of the German 8th Army held the center against the Russians, the others prepared a counterattack. Meanwhile, the Russian 2nd Army continued to push forward in the mistaken belief that German forces were on the retreat; this had the effect of stretching its lines of communication and supply to the breaking point.

〰〰〰 Frontline, Aug 25, 1914

Guttstadt

Seeburg

Rothfliess

Sensburg

Masurian Lakes

Arys

Lyck

Wartenburg

Bischofsburg

Nikolaiken

Allenstein

Rudczanny

Bialla

Osterode

Hohenstein

Kurken

Ortelsburg

Omulefoten

Dombrovo

Aug 26 German 8th Army divisions diverted south from Gumbinnen attack Samsonov's right wing

Johannisburg

---

5 CLOSING THE CIRCLE   AUGUST 27–28

On the morning of August 27, the Germans launched a devastating artillery barrage on the Russian left wing, then drove through their shattered lines to cut the 2nd Army off from the border to Russian-held Poland. Despite German fears, the 1st Army did not march south to aid their threatened comrades.

→ German offensive   ▸▸▸ Russian retreat

╱╱ Focus of battle

Tannenberg

Usdau

Willenburg

VI Corps

XIII Corps

Soldau

Chorzele

XV Corps

Aug 29 Encircled, Samsonov orders a general retreat before committing suicide

Zabolk

XXIII Corps

Mlawa

P   O   L   A   N   D

I Corps

Aug 27 The 1st Corps under Francois breaks through the Russian left to cut off Samsonov's forces

Aug 22 Advance forces of the 2nd Army clash with Germans holding the center of the line

Aug 20 Russia's 2nd Army opens a second front by invading East Prussia through the Masurian Lakes

2nd Army Samsonov

Rozan

Narew

---

6 DEFEAT AND SURRENDER
AUGUST 29–31

On August 29, German forces completed the encirclement of the 2nd Army, which was running out of ammunition. Its commander Alexander Samsonov ordered a retreat, but his disorganized troops could find no way through. Almost 100,000 of his 150,000 men surrendered. Faced with total defeat, Samsonov walked into the woods and shot himself. The 8th Army was now free to return north and fend off the Russian 1st Army one week later, saving East Prussia.

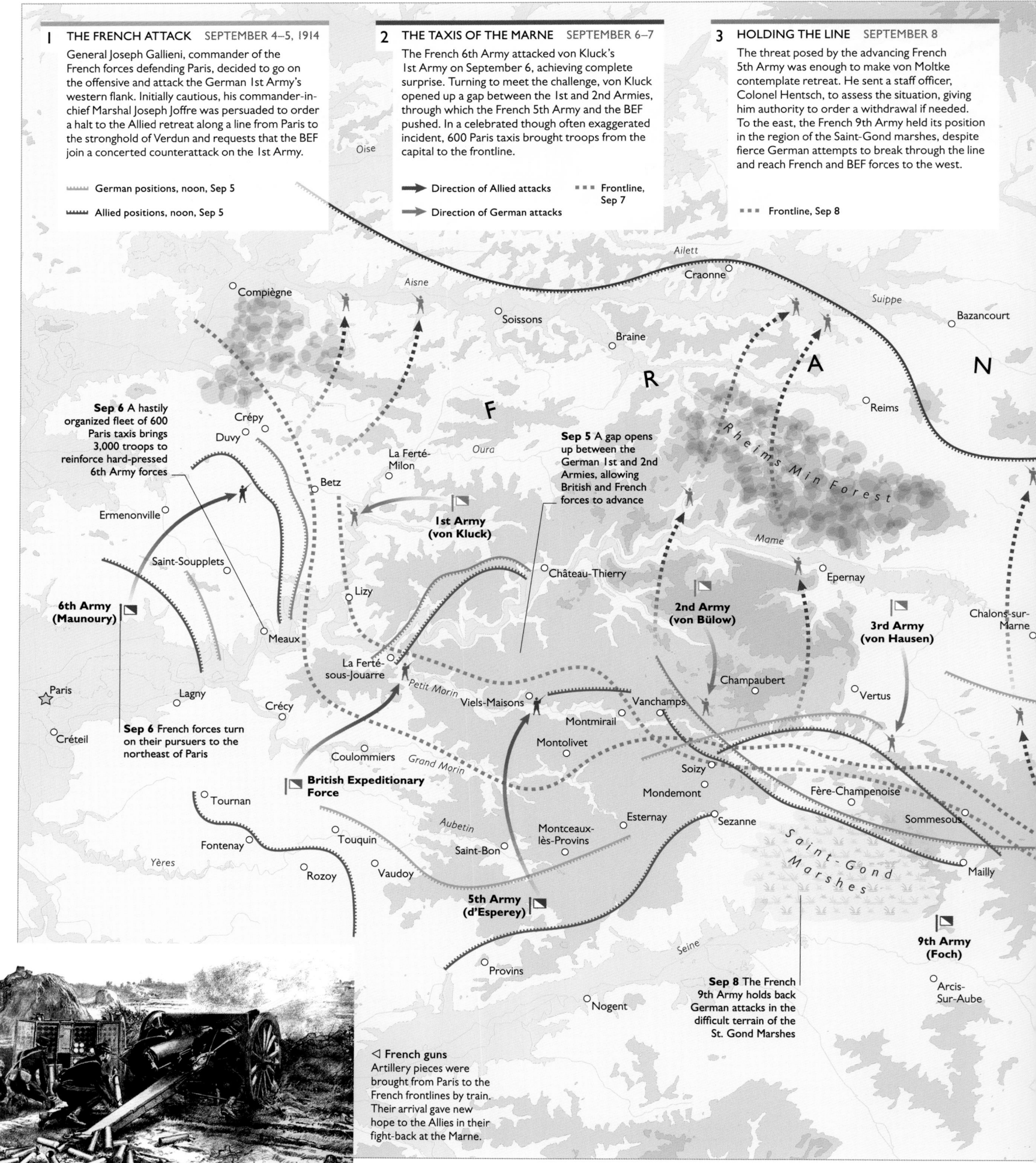

1 THE FRENCH ATTACK SEPTEMBER 4–5, 1914

General Joseph Gallieni, commander of the French forces defending Paris, decided to go on the offensive and attack the German 1st Army's western flank. Initially cautious, his commander-in-chief Marshal Joseph Joffre was persuaded to order a halt to the Allied retreat along a line from Paris to the stronghold of Verdun and requests that the BEF join a concerted counterattack on the 1st Army.

ᴜᴜᴜᴜ German positions, noon, Sep 5

ᴜᴜᴜᴜ Allied positions, noon, Sep 5

2 THE TAXIS OF THE MARNE SEPTEMBER 6–7

The French 6th Army attacked von Kluck's 1st Army on September 6, achieving complete surprise. Turning to meet the challenge, von Kluck opened up a gap between the 1st and 2nd Armies, through which the French 5th Army and the BEF pushed. In a celebrated though often exaggerated incident, 600 Paris taxis brought troops from the capital to the frontline.

➡ Direction of Allied attacks

➡ Direction of German attacks

▪▪▪ Frontline, Sep 7

3 HOLDING THE LINE SEPTEMBER 8

The threat posed by the advancing French 5th Army was enough to make von Moltke contemplate retreat. He sent a staff officer, Colonel Hentsch, to assess the situation, giving him authority to order a withdrawal if needed. To the east, the French 9th Army held its position in the region of the Saint-Gond marshes, despite fierce German attempts to break through the line and reach French and BEF forces to the west.

▪▪▪ Frontline, Sep 8

Sep 6 A hastily organized fleet of 600 Paris taxis brings 3,000 troops to reinforce hard-pressed 6th Army forces

Sep 5 A gap opens up between the German 1st and 2nd Armies, allowing British and French forces to advance

6th Army (Maunoury)

Sep 6 French forces turn on their pursuers to the northeast of Paris

British Expeditionary Force

1st Army (von Kluck)

2nd Army (von Bülow)

3rd Army (von Hausen)

5th Army (d'Esperey)

9th Army (Foch)

Sep 8 The French 9th Army holds back German attacks in the difficult terrain of the St. Gond Marshes

◁ **French guns**
Artillery pieces were brought from Paris to the French frontlines by train. Their arrival gave new hope to the Allies in their fight-back at the Marne.

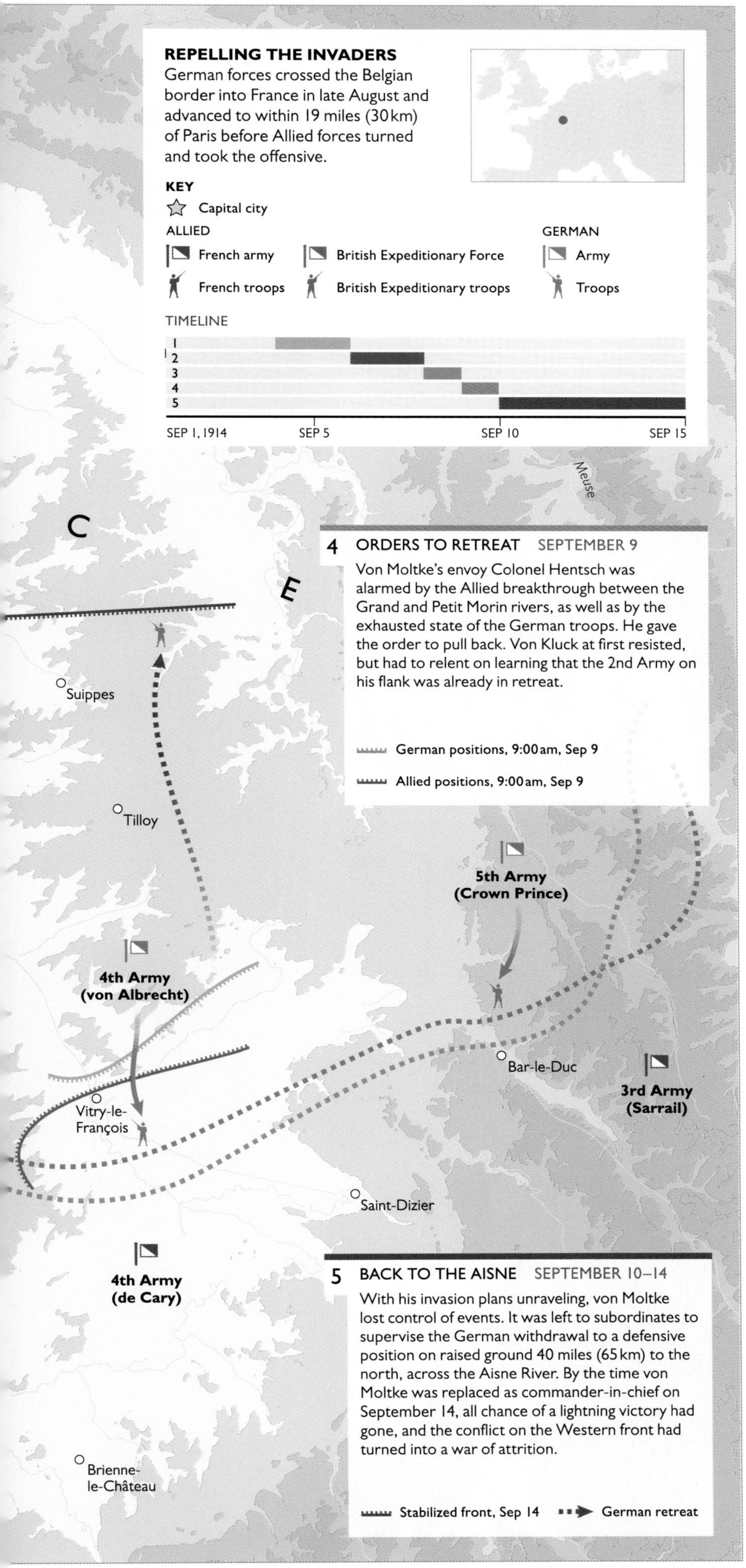

REPELLING THE INVADERS

German forces crossed the Belgian border into France in late August and advanced to within 19 miles (30 km) of Paris before Allied forces turned and took the offensive.

KEY

☆ Capital city

ALLIED

🚩 French army   🚩 British Expeditionary Force

🏃 French troops   🏃 British Expeditionary troops

GERMAN

🚩 Army

🏃 Troops

TIMELINE

```
          1
          2
          3
          4
          5
SEP 1, 1914    SEP 5        SEP 10        SEP 15
```

Meuse

C

E

4 ORDERS TO RETREAT   SEPTEMBER 9

Von Moltke's envoy Colonel Hentsch was alarmed by the Allied breakthrough between the Grand and Petit Morin rivers, as well as by the exhausted state of the German troops. He gave the order to pull back. Von Kluck at first resisted, but had to relent on learning that the 2nd Army on his flank was already in retreat.

⸺⸺ German positions, 9:00 am, Sep 9

⸺⸺ Allied positions, 9:00 am, Sep 9

○ Suippes

○ Tilloy

🚩 **5th Army (Crown Prince)**

🚩 **4th Army (von Albrecht)**

○ Bar-le-Duc

🚩 **3rd Army (Sarrail)**

🚩 **4th Army (de Cary)**

Vitry-le-François ○

○ Saint-Dizier

5 BACK TO THE AISNE   SEPTEMBER 10–14

With his invasion plans unraveling, von Moltke lost control of events. It was left to subordinates to supervise the German withdrawal to a defensive position on raised ground 40 miles (65 km) to the north, across the Aisne River. By the time von Moltke was replaced as commander-in-chief on September 14, all chance of a lightning victory had gone, and the conflict on the Western front had turned into a war of attrition.

⸺⸺ Stabilized front, Sep 14   ■■▶ German retreat

○ Brienne-le-Château

FIRST MARNE

On September 6, 1914, French and British forces launched a counteroffensive against the seemingly unstoppable German advance on Paris. A turning point of World War I, the battle dashed German hopes of a quick victory over the Allied powers.

The war on the Western front opened with a remarkable series of victories for Germany as its armies marched into France through neutral Belgium. Within a month the Germans were threatening Paris, and French forces, supported by the six divisions of the British Expeditionary Force (BEF), had undertaken a demoralizing retreat.

The German plan for the invasion of France (the "Schlieffen Plan") called for German forces to push west, then south, and surround the French capital. However, on September 2, Helmuth von Moltke, their commander-in-chief, decided instead to turn south at once and try to envelop the retreating Allies. Instead of protecting the vulnerable flank of this maneuver, General Alexander von Kluck's 1st Army continued to advance. This opened up his flank to an attack by the French 6th Army, which was protecting Paris. Seeing an opportunity, French commanders ordered the Allies to turn and confront the foe.

What followed was a series of engagements over a front extending 90 miles (150 km), with heavy losses on both sides. The Germans, however, were at the end of overstretched supply lines. After three days, Helmuth von Moltke agreed to withdraw to a defensive line north of the Aisne River. The plans for a lightning campaign had failed; the scene was set for four years of attrition in the trenches.

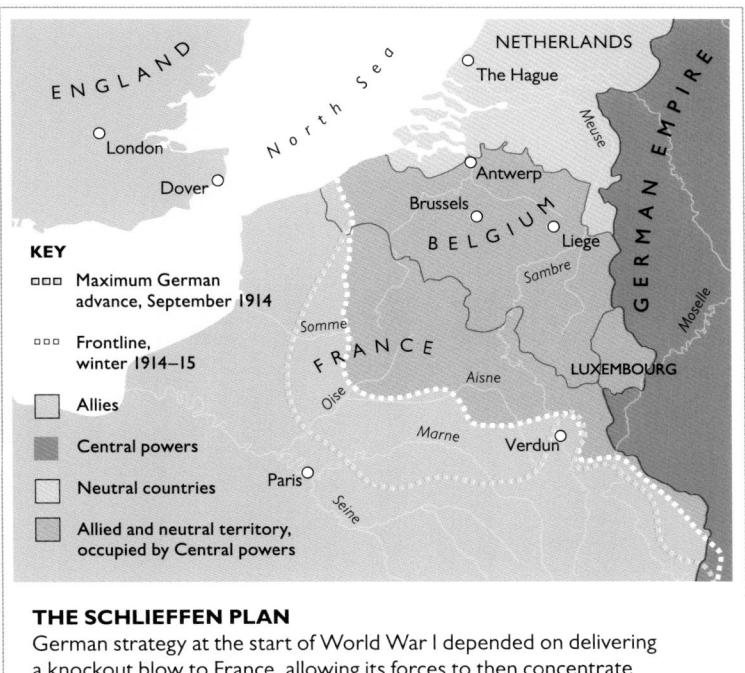

THE SCHLIEFFEN PLAN

German strategy at the start of World War I depended on delivering a knockout blow to France, allowing its forces to then concentrate on countering the threat from Russia in the east. The plan involved outflanking the French armies through neutral Belgium in violation of treaty obligations, thereby bringing Britain into the war.

GALLIPOLI

The Gallipoli campaign was one of the most frustrating and controversial struggles of World War I, and became one of its defining moments. It came about as Allied leaders sought to bypass the stalemate on the Western front by attacking Germany's ally, Turkey.

By late 1914, the Western Front—the principal theater of World War I—was bogged down in trench warfare, and Allied military leaders, including Britain's First Lord of the Admiralty Winston Churchill, looked for a breakthrough elsewhere. The most practical supply route from Britain and France to their ally Russia was through the Dardanelles strait into the Black Sea, but that was cut off in late October when Ottoman Turkey joined the war on the Central Powers' side. To aid Russia, Allied commanders determined to confront Turkey, and if possible force it out of the war. At first, they tried a naval assault through the Dardanelles

strait to attack Istanbul; when that failed, troops were sent to seize the Gallipoli peninsula on its western shore. They established beachheads on the peninsula's southern tip and also 10 miles (15km) to the north, where Australian and New Zealand (ANZAC) forces dug into a tiny enclave dubbed Anzac Cove. However, Turkish resistance proved fiercer than expected, and drove back Allied attempts to break out of the strongholds. A second major offensive four months later at Suvla Bay failed to break the deadlock, and by the end of the year Allied commanders decided they had no option but to order an evacuation.

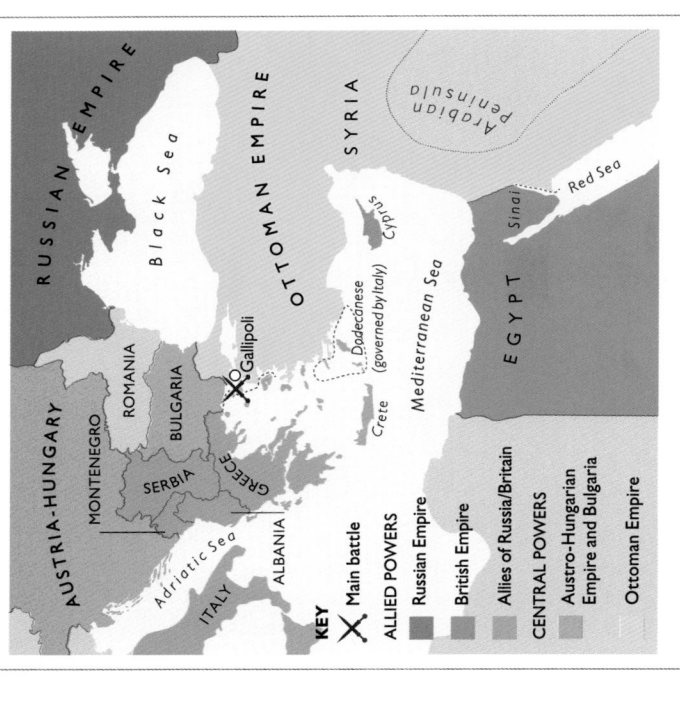

KEY

ALLIED POWERS
- Russian Empire
- British Empire
- Allies of Russia/Britain

CENTRAL POWERS
- Austro-Hungarian Empire and Bulgaria
- Ottoman Empire

✕ Main battle

A CORRIDOR TO RUSSIA

Lying on the Ottoman Empire's western fringe, the Gallipoli peninsula controlled the Dardanelles strait that connects the Mediterranean to the Black Sea and so to Russia.

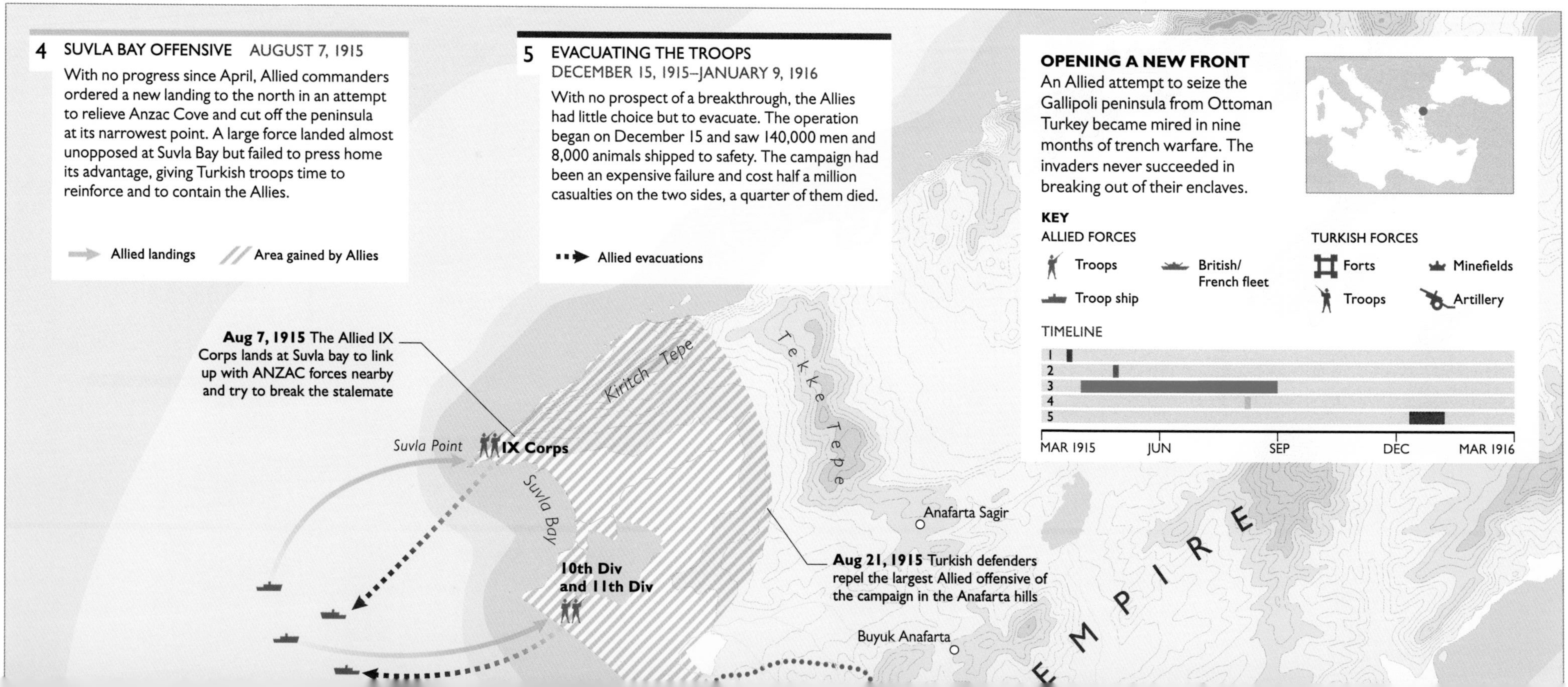

OPENING A NEW FRONT

An Allied attempt to seize the Gallipoli peninsula from Ottoman Turkey became mired in nine months of trench warfare. The invaders never succeeded in breaking out of their enclaves.

KEY

ALLIED FORCES
- 👤 Troops
- 🚢 Troop ship
- British/French fleet

TURKISH FORCES
- 🏰 Forts
- 👤 Troops
- Minefields
- Artillery

TIMELINE

MAR 1915 — JUN — SEP — DEC — MAR 1916

4 SUVLA BAY OFFENSIVE   AUGUST 7, 1915

With no progress since April, Allied commanders ordered a new landing to the north in an attempt to relieve Anzac Cove and cut off the peninsula at its narrowest point. A large force landed almost unopposed at Suvla Bay but failed to press home its advantage, giving Turkish troops time to reinforce and to contain the Allies.

→ Allied landings   ⫽ Area gained by Allies

Aug 7, 1915 The Allied IX Corps lands at Suvla bay to link up with ANZAC forces nearby and try to break the stalemate

5 EVACUATING THE TROOPS

DECEMBER 15, 1915–JANUARY 9, 1916

With no prospect of a breakthrough, the Allies had little choice but to evacuate. The operation began on December 15 and saw 140,000 men and 8,000 animals shipped to safety. The campaign had been an expensive failure and cost half a million casualties on the two sides, a quarter of them died.

┅➤ Allied evacuations

Anafarta Sagir

Aug 21, 1915 Turkish defenders repel the largest Allied offensive of the campaign in the Anafarta hills

Tekke Tepe

Buyuk Anafarta

Kiritch Tepe

IX Corps

Suvla Point

Suvla Bay

10th Div and 11th Div

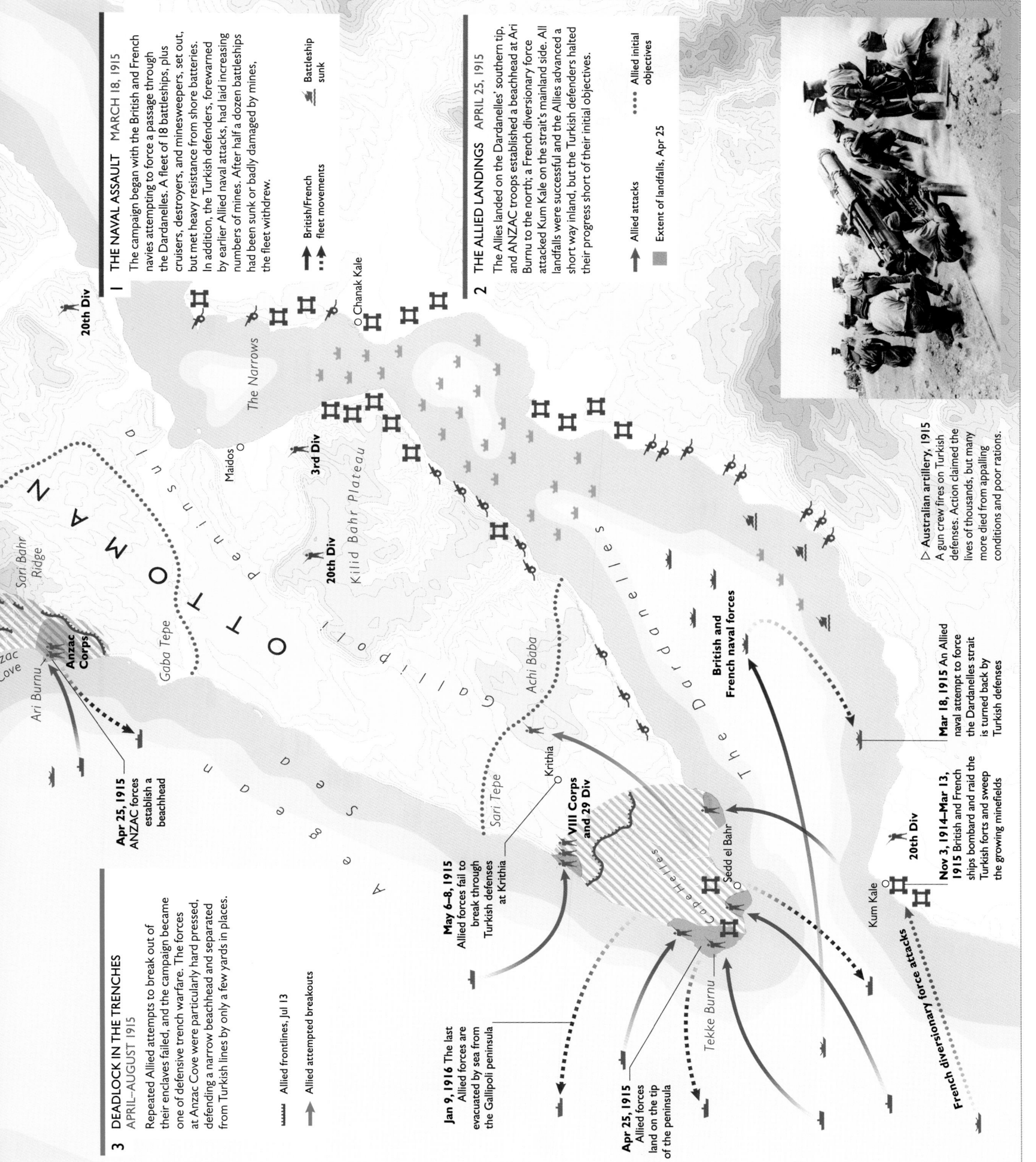

1 THE NAVAL ASSAULT MARCH 18, 1915

The campaign began with the British and French navies attempting to force a passage through the Dardanelles. A fleet of 18 battleships, plus cruisers, destroyers, and minesweepers, set out, but met heavy resistance from shore batteries. In addition, the Turkish defenders, forewarned by earlier Allied naval attacks, had laid increasing numbers of mines. After half a dozen battleships had been sunk or badly damaged by mines, the fleet withdrew.

↑ ⋯▶ British/French fleet movements

🚢 Battleship sunk

2 THE ALLIED LANDINGS APRIL 25, 1915

The Allies landed on the Dardanelles' southern tip, and ANZAC troops established a beachhead at Ari Burnu to the north; a French diversionary force attacked Kum Kale on the strait's mainland side. All landfalls were successful and the Allies advanced a short way inland, but the Turkish defenders halted their progress short of their initial objectives.

→ Allied attacks

⋯⋯ Allied initial objectives

▨ Extent of landfalls, Apr 25

△ Australian artillery, 1915
A gun crew fires on Turkish defenses. Action claimed the lives of thousands, but many more died from appalling conditions and poor rations.

3 DEADLOCK IN THE TRENCHES
APRIL–AUGUST 1915

Repeated Allied attempts to break out of their enclaves failed, and the campaign became one of defensive trench warfare. The forces at Anzac Cove were particularly hard pressed, defending a narrow beachhead and separated from Turkish lines by only a few yards in places.

⋯⋯ Allied frontlines, Jul 13

→ Allied attempted breakouts

20th Div

Anzac Corps

Sari Bahr Ridge

Anzac Cove

Ari Burnu

Apr 25, 1915
ANZAC forces establish a beachhead

OTTOMAN

Gaba Tepe

Maidos

3rd Div

20th Div

Kilid Bahr Plateau

The Narrows

○ Chanak Kale

Gallipoli Peninsula

Achi Baba

Krithia ○

May 6–8, 1915
Allied forces fail to break through Turkish defenses at Krithia

VIII Corps and 29 Div

Sari Tepe

Jan 9, 1916 The last Allied forces are evacuated by sea from the Gallipoli peninsula

Apr 25, 1915
Allied forces land on the tip of the peninsula

Tekke Burnu

Cape Helles

Sedd el Bahr

British and French naval forces

Mar 18, 1915 An Allied naval attempt to force the Dardanelles strait is turned back by Turkish defenses

Nov 3, 1914–Mar 13, 1915 British and French ships bombard and raid the Turkish forts and sweep the growing minefields

20th Div

Kum Kale ○

The Dardanelles

French diversionary force attacks

VERDUN

With the Western front deadlocked by the end of 1915, German military strategists sought a battleground where they might inflict so many casualties that the French would have to sue for peace. In early 1916, they launched an attack on their target, the fortress city of Verdun.

Verdun was the longest battle of World War I, and also one of the most costly in terms of casualties. Erich von Falkenhayn, Germany's Chief of the General Staff, chose the site partly because it lay in an exposed salient, served only by a single road and a narrow-gauge railroad. Equally important, though, was its significance as France's chief military bastion to the east, with an historic role stretching back more than a millennium.

The city itself was formidably defended, surrounded by a double ring of 28 smaller forts. German strategists were less concerned with taking it than with drawing French troops to its defense, where they could be picked off by heavy artillery, especially when counterattacking to retake lost positions. As Falkenhayn predicted, the French did indeed decide to hold the site at any cost, pouring manpower into the trenches that protected it from the enemy forces to the north. However, the defenders proved unexpectedly tenacious, refusing to give ground except under extreme duress, and were surprisingly successful in launching counterattacks. The result was a lethal stalemate that lasted through much of 1916. It ended in December 1916 with little territory gained on either side, and with each side having suffered about 350,000 casualties.

> *"Anyone who has not seen these fields of carnage will never be able to imagine it."*
>
> LETTER FROM A FRENCH SOLDIER, JULY 1916

ANIMALS IN WORLD WAR I

More than 16 million animals took part in World War I in cavalry, transportation, and communications, and also as mascots to improve morale. Horses, donkeys, mules, and camels carried supplies and ammunition to the front, while dogs and pigeons delivered messages. Carrier pigeons played an important role at Verdun, where they were the only means of calling for relief for French troops trapped at Fort Vaux in June 1916.

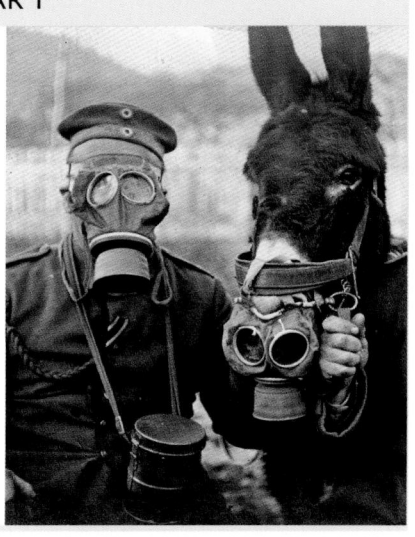

German soldier and donkey wearing gas masks

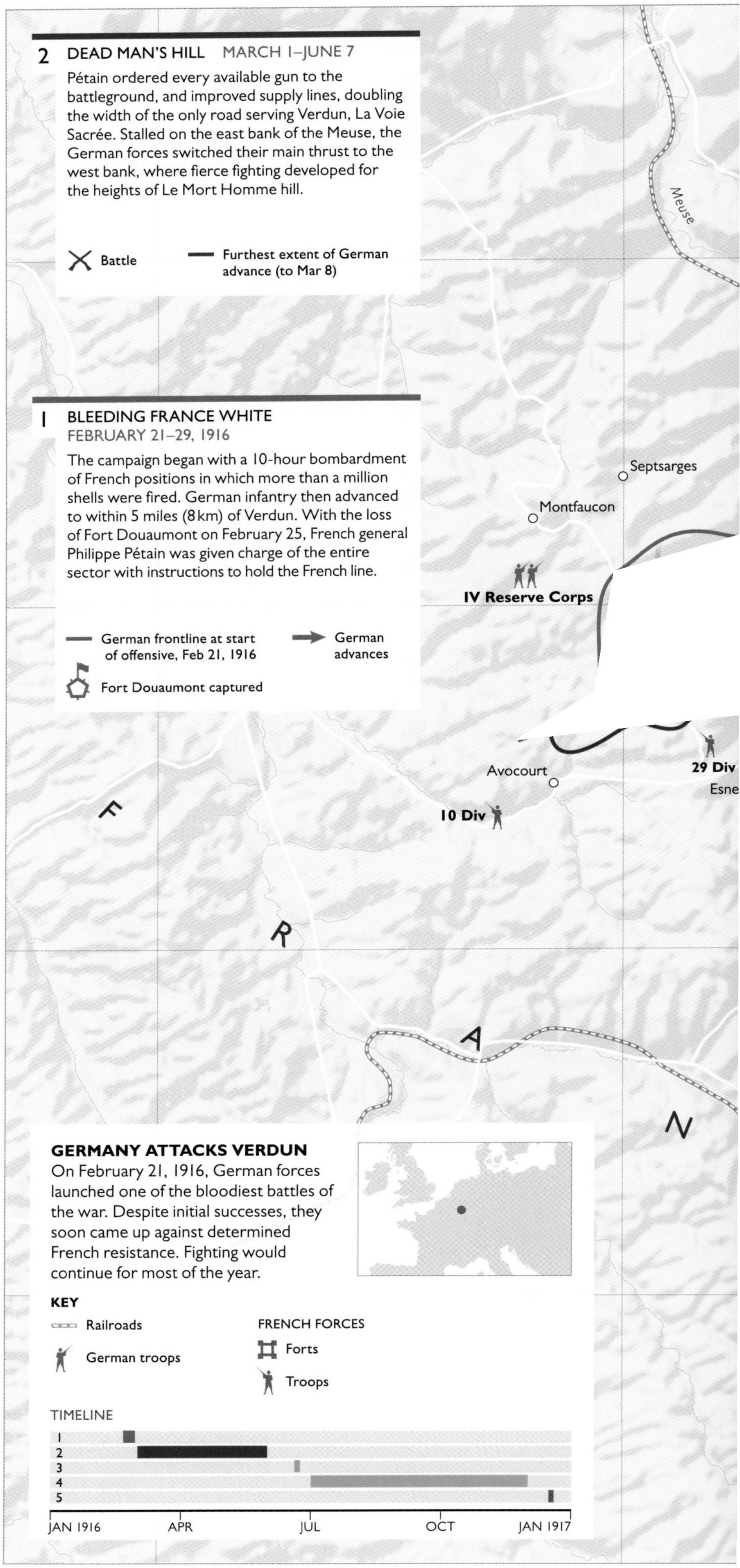
2 DEAD MAN'S HILL MARCH 1–JUNE 7
Pétain ordered every available gun to the battleground, and improved supply lines, doubling the width of the only road serving Verdun, La Voie Sacrée. Stalled on the east bank of the Meuse, the German forces switched their main thrust to the west bank, where fierce fighting developed for the heights of Le Mort Homme hill.
Battle
Furthest extent of German advance (to Mar 8)
Meuse
1 BLEEDING FRANCE WHITE
FEBRUARY 21–29, 1916
The campaign began with a 10-hour bombardment of French positions in which more than a million shells were fired. German infantry then advanced to within 5 miles (8km) of Verdun. With the loss of Fort Douaumont on February 25, French general Philippe Pétain was given charge of the entire sector with instructions to hold the French line.
German frontline at start of offensive, Feb 21, 1916
German advances
Fort Douaumont captured
Septsarges
Montfaucon
IV Reserve Corps
Avocourt
29 Div
Esne
10 Div
F
R
A
N
GERMANY ATTACKS VERDUN
On February 21, 1916, German forces launched one of the bloodiest battles of the war. Despite initial successes, they soon came up against determined French resistance. Fighting would continue for most of the year.
KEY
Railroads
German troops
FRENCH FORCES
Forts
Troops
TIMELINE
1
2
3
4
5
JAN 1916
APR
JUL
OCT
JAN 1917

3 "THEY SHALL NOT PASS"   JUNE 23

German forces attempted a decisive breakthrough on June 23, preparing the way with a preliminary barrage of phosgene gas shells. The French held their ground under the inspirational leadership of General Robert Nivelle, whose watchword was "They Shall Not Pass." Having reached the furthest point in the campaign, the German army had been brought to a halt.

→ Attempted German advance

☠ Phosgene gas attack

4 COUNTERATTACK   JULY–NOVEMBER

Combat continued at a lower level through the late summer as troops from each side were diverted to the Somme. The French launched a counteroffensive on October 21. Over the next two weeks, their troops succeeded in retaking the lost forts of Douaumont and Vaux before ammunition shortages brought the advance to an end.

⇨ French advance

▢ French gains, Oct 24

5 THE END OF THE CAMPAIGN   DECEMBER 15–17

The following month, the French launched a fresh attack northwest of the forts, retaking ground lost earlier, and pushing the German lines back another 1¼ miles (2 km). The Battle of Louvemont, as it became known, marked the end of the campaign. In all, the German army had gained very little territory, having exhausted the French at the expense of suffering equally massive losses.

✕ Battle

▢ French gains, Dec 15

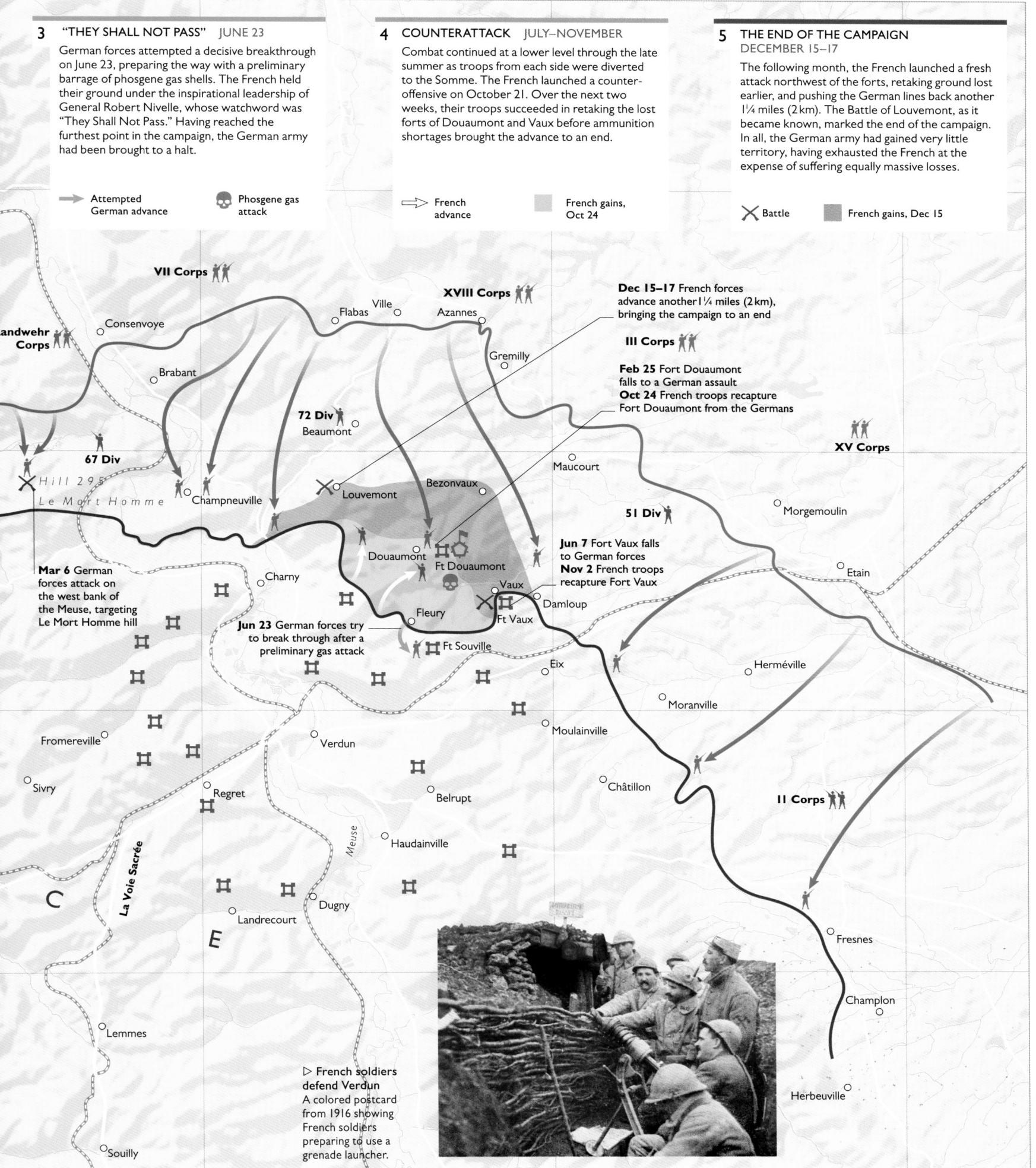

VII Corps

Landwehr Corps

Consenvoye

Brabant

Flabas   Ville

XVIII Corps

Azannes

Gremilly

Dec 15–17 French forces advance another 1¼ miles (2 km), bringing the campaign to an end

III Corps

Feb 25 Fort Douaumont falls to a German assault
Oct 24 French troops recapture Fort Douaumont from the Germans

72 Div
Beaumont

67 Div

✕ *Hill 295*
Le Mort Homme

Champneuville

Louvemont   Bezonvaux

Maucourt

XV Corps

Morgemoulin

Mar 6 German forces attack on the west bank of the Meuse, targeting Le Mort Homme hill

Douaumont   Ft Douaumont ☠

Charny

Jun 23 German forces try to break through after a preliminary gas attack

Fleury

Vaux
Ft Vaux   Damloup

51 Div

Jun 7 Fort Vaux falls to German forces
Nov 2 French troops recapture Fort Vaux

Etain

✕ Ft Souville

Eix

Herméville

Moranville

Fromereville

Verdun

Moulainville

Châtillon

II Corps

Sivry

Regret

Belrupt

Meuse

Haudainville

La Voie Sacrée

Fresnes

C

E

Landrecourt

Dugny

▷ **French soldiers defend Verdun**
A colored postcard from 1916 showing French soldiers preparing to use a grenade launcher.

Champlon

Lemmes

Souilly

Herbeuville

CHEMICAL WARFARE

On April 22, 1915, at Ypres, Belgium, the German army first discharged chlorine gas over the Allied trenches. It triggered panic, and later attacks killed and incapacitated hundreds of soldiers.

Although the Germans did not gain a decisive advantage at Ypres, other countries began developing chemical weapons in the hope that this would break the deadlock of trench warfare. The new gas weapons included choking agents such as chlorine and phosgene. At first these were released from cylinders, which required favorable wind conditions, and later as gas shells fired by artillery guns. Mortars and projectiles were also used. From 1917, the persistent blistering agent dichlorodiethyl sulfide ("mustard gas") added to the horror, remaining toxic to exposed skin for several days.

△ **Color-coded gas shells**
The Germans used blue-cross shells containing vomiting agents to prompt soldiers to remove their masks and so expose themselves to the green-cross lung agents.

Gas attacks in World War I did not bring about the anticipated breakthrough. Gas masks and protective clothing were introduced, and although they slowed down troops, they were effective—chemical weapons worked best against unprotected troops. However, gas remained a powerful psychological weapon, and could cause death and long-term injury where it did affect its targets.

Chemical warfare did not end in 1918, and France, Italy, and possibly Britain and Spain used it in their colonial wars. Despite a ban in 1925, chemical weapons, including new, more toxic nerve agents, were used in Ethiopia and China in the 1930s, and more recently in the 1980s Iran-Iraq war and the ongoing Syrian civil war.

△ **Mustard gas victims in World War I**
Here artist John Singer Sargent depicts Allied soldiers temporarily blinded by mustard gas, which was rarely lethal but caused more casualties than all other chemical agents combined.

Gas attack in the trenches
This image taken during World War I shows Russian soldiers wearing an early type of gas mask. At the first sign of a gas attack, alarms would be sounded and soldiers would hurry to put on their masks.

JUTLAND

Jutland was the chief naval encounter of World War I and the most significant clash ever between dreadnought-class battleships. Although the British fleet suffered greater losses than the Germans, Britain came out of the conflict in control of the North Sea shipping lanes.

Britain and Germany had engaged in a high-profile naval arms race in the lead-up to World War I, so a clash between their dreadnoughts (steam-powered battleships with heavy-caliber guns—see pp.206–207) was widely anticipated. In fact, it proved slow in coming, as neither side wanted to put their deterrent force at risk from mines and submarines. When the fleets finally met in 1916 at Jutland, off the coast of Denmark, the encounter proved indecisive.

Although battleships played a key role in the conflict, much of the fighting was carried out by forces of smaller ships, including cruisers and destroyers, led by Britain's Admiral Beatty and Germany's Franz von Hipper. The main fleets, commanded by Admiral Jellicoe and Reinhard Scheer for Britain and Germany respectively, met in only two brief clashes, with battleship fire lasting barely 15 minutes.

The battle showed up weaknesses in the construction and armament of the British ships, which suffered greater losses—in all, 14 vessels against 11 vessels for the Germans. Similarly, the British Grand Fleet lost 6,094 seamen to the German High Seas Fleet's 2,551. These figures enabled the German military to claim a victory at the time. However, thanks to the size of its dreadnought fleet, Britain retained the upper hand strategically, and the German fleet never again risked a major sortie.

> *"There seems to be something wrong with our bloody ships today."*
>
> ADMIRAL DAVID BEATTY ON LOSING HMS *QUEEN MARY*

NORTH SEA STRUGGLE

In the decades prior to World War I, Britain and Germany had been locked in an arms race for naval supremacy in the North Sea, both having developed the new dreadnought battleships. The conflict in Jutland put the results to the test.

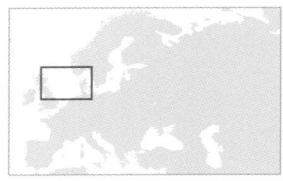

KEY

GERMAN FORCES
- Fleet
- Ship sunk
- von Hipper
- Scheer
- Combined German fleet

BRITISH FORCES
- Fleet
- Ship sunk
- Beatty
- Jellicoe

TIMELINE

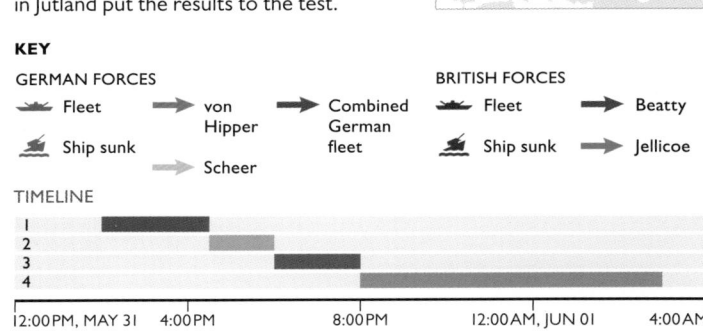

12:00PM, MAY 31   4:00PM   8:00PM   12:00AM, JUN 01   4:00AM

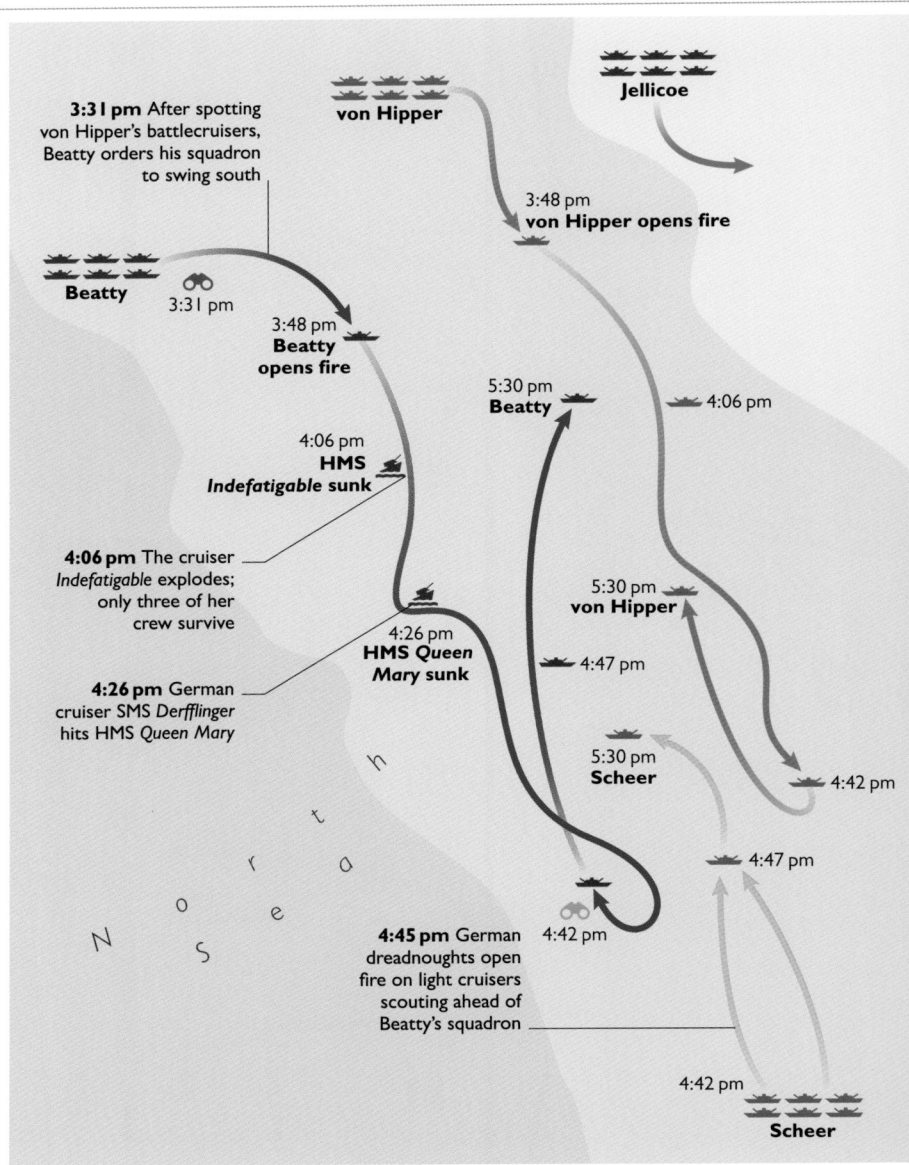

3:31 pm After spotting von Hipper's battlecruisers, Beatty orders his squadron to swing south

Beatty 3:31 pm

von Hipper

Jellicoe

3:48 pm von Hipper opens fire

3:48 pm Beatty opens fire

4:06 pm

5:30 pm Beatty

4:06 pm HMS Indefatigable sunk

4:06 pm The cruiser *Indefatigable* explodes; only three of her crew survive

4:26 pm HMS Queen Mary sunk

4:26 pm German cruiser SMS *Derfflinger* hits HMS *Queen Mary*

5:30 pm von Hipper

4:47 pm

5:30 pm Scheer

4:42 pm

4:47 pm

4:42 pm

4:45 pm German dreadnoughts open fire on light cruisers scouting ahead of Beatty's squadron

4:42 pm

Scheer

North Sea

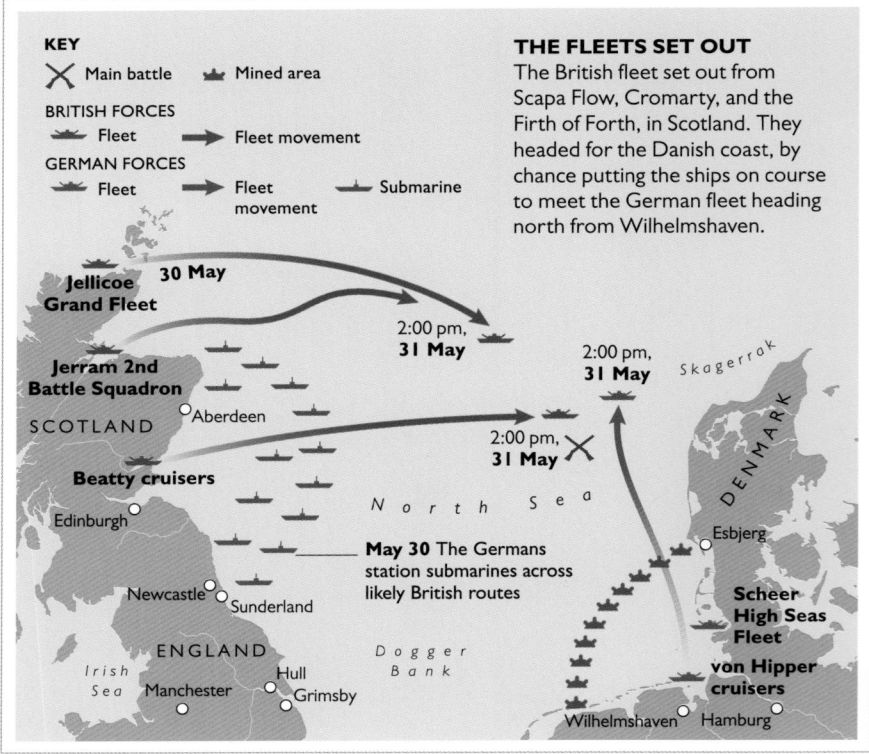

KEY

- ✕ Main battle
- Mined area

BRITISH FORCES
- Fleet
- → Fleet movement

GERMAN FORCES
- Fleet
- → Fleet movement
- Submarine

THE FLEETS SET OUT

The British fleet set out from Scapa Flow, Cromarty, and the Firth of Forth, in Scotland. They headed for the Danish coast, by chance putting the ships on course to meet the German fleet heading north from Wilhelmshaven.

Jellicoe Grand Fleet

30 May

2:00 pm, 31 May

2:00 pm, 31 May

Skagerrak

Jerram 2nd Battle Squadron

SCOTLAND

Aberdeen

2:00 pm, 31 May

Beatty cruisers

Edinburgh

North Sea

DENMARK

Esbjerg

May 30 The Germans station submarines across likely British routes

Newcastle
Sunderland

ENGLAND

Irish Sea

Manchester

Hull
Grimsby

Dogger Bank

Scheer High Seas Fleet

von Hipper cruisers

Wilhelmshaven   Hamburg

THE FIRST ENGAGEMENTS

Scouting ahead of the main fleets, British and German cruisers made contact in waters off the Danish coast. A running battle ensued as the rival squadrons steamed on parallel courses south.

1 MAKING CONTACT 2:00–4:30 PM, MAY 31, 1916

First contact between came by chance as ships from both fleets went to investigate a neutral Danish vessel. Aware of each others' presence, the cruiser squadrons fell into line, with Admiral Beatty pursuing von Hipper's force south. A long-range artillery duel followed, with damage to both sides. The British HMS *Indefatigable* and *Queen Mary* blew up when shells hit their magazines.

👓 Fleets spot each other

2 COLLISION COURSE 4:30–6:00 PM

Von Hipper continued to steam south, leading Beatty toward the main German battle fleet. On sighting Scheer's dreadnoughts, Beatty executed a U-turn and headed north, hoping to entice the German cruisers to pursue him toward the British Grand Fleet under the command of Admiral Jellicoe. The Germans took the bait and followed him.

👓 Beatty sights Scheer

THE MAIN FLEETS MEET

The long-feared encounter between the British and German main fleets proved to be short and sharp, though lethal. Both sides took evasive action to avoid catastrophic losses.

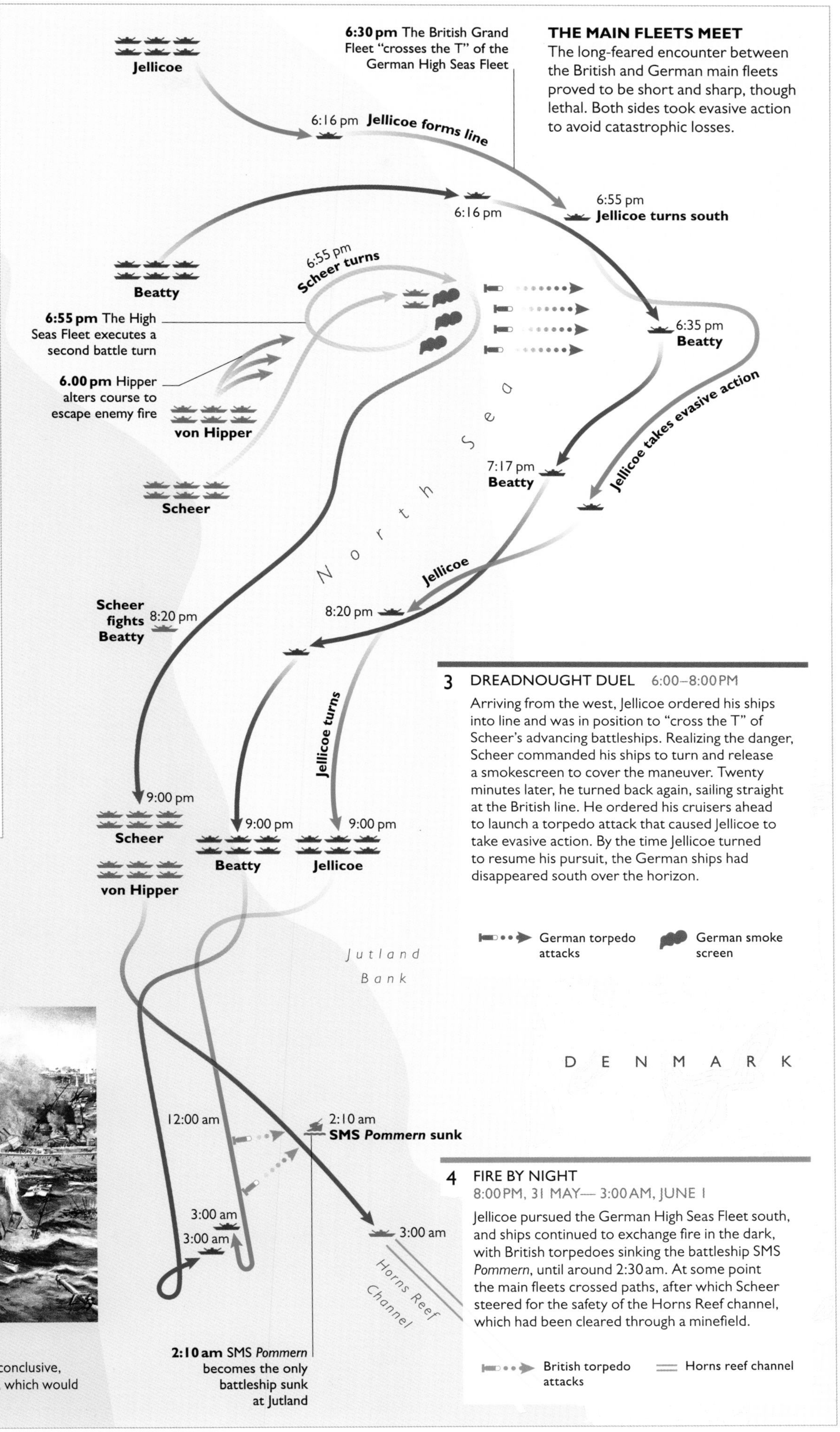

6:30 pm The British Grand Fleet "crosses the T" of the German High Seas Fleet

Jellicoe

6:16 pm Jellicoe forms line

Beatty

6:55 pm The High Seas Fleet executes a second battle turn

6.00 pm Hipper alters course to escape enemy fire

von Hipper

Scheer

6:16 pm

6:55 pm Scheer turns

6:55 pm **Jellicoe turns south**

6:35 pm **Beatty**

Jellicoe takes evasive action

7:17 pm **Beatty**

North Sea

Scheer fights Beatty 8:20 pm

Jellicoe 8:20 pm

Jellicoe turns

9:00 pm **Scheer**

von Hipper

9:00 pm **Beatty**

9:00 pm **Jellicoe**

3 DREADNOUGHT DUEL 6:00–8:00 PM

Arriving from the west, Jellicoe ordered his ships into line and was in position to "cross the T" of Scheer's advancing battleships. Realizing the danger, Scheer commanded his ships to turn and release a smokescreen to cover the maneuver. Twenty minutes later, he turned back again, sailing straight at the British line. He ordered his cruisers ahead to launch a torpedo attack that caused Jellicoe to take evasive action. By the time Jellicoe turned to resume his pursuit, the German ships had disappeared south over the horizon.

▬▶ German torpedo attacks   German smoke screen

Jutland Bank

DENMARK

12:00 am

2:10 am **SMS Pommern sunk**

3:00 am

3:00 am

3:00 am

Horns Reef Channel

4 FIRE BY NIGHT

8:00PM, 31 MAY— 3:00AM, JUNE 1

Jellicoe pursued the German High Seas Fleet south, and ships continued to exchange fire in the dark, with British torpedoes sinking the battleship SMS *Pommern*, until around 2:30 am. At some point the main fleets crossed paths, after which Scheer steered for the safety of the Horns Reef channel, which had been cleared through a minefield.

▬▶ British torpedo attacks   ═ Horns reef channel

2:10 am SMS *Pommern* becomes the only battleship sunk at Jutland

△ **British naval dominance**
An artist records German vessels on fire at Jutland. Though inconclusive, the battle cemented British naval superiority in the North Sea, which would eventually contribute to Germany's defeat in 1918.

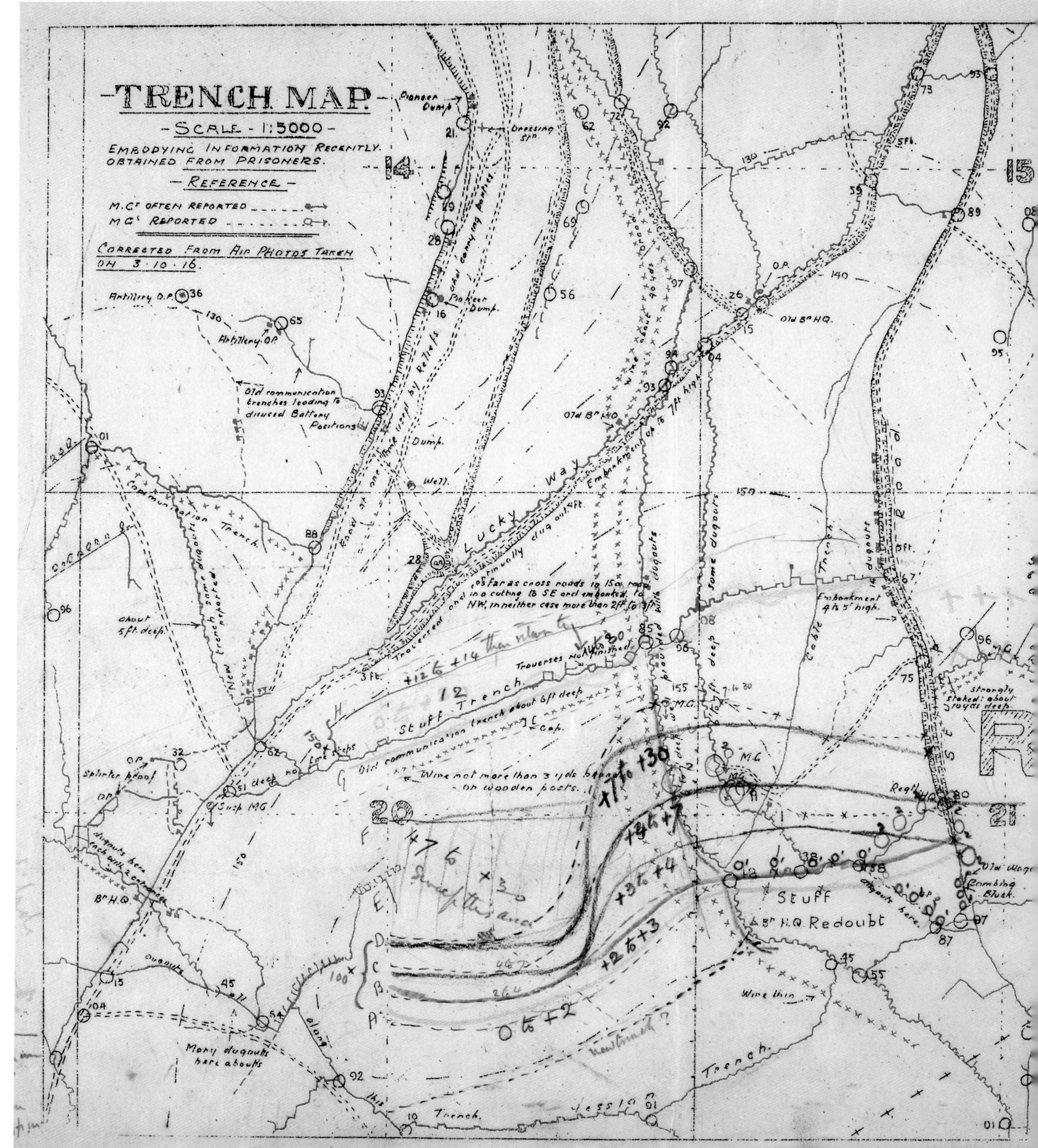

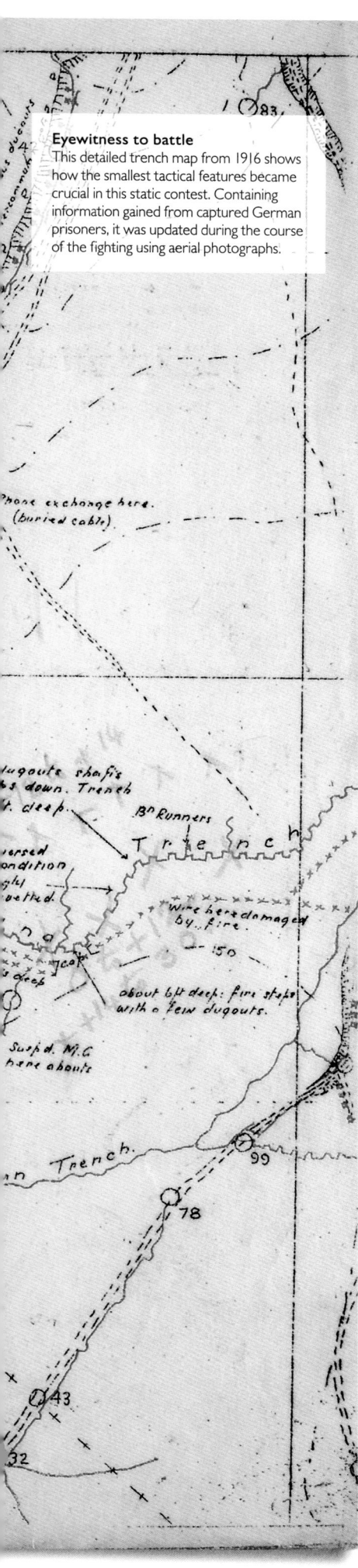

Eyewitness to battle
This detailed trench map from 1916 shows how the smallest tactical features became crucial in this static contest. Containing information gained from captured German prisoners, it was updated during the course of the fighting using aerial photographs.

THE SOMME

Designed to force a breakthrough on the Western Front and to shatter German morale, the offensive launched by Allied forces on the River Somme in the summer of 1916 began with a bloodbath and gained little ground over several months. The battle came to symbolize the futility of combat in World War I.

The Allies originally planned an equally balanced Anglo-French attack on the Somme to coincide with pushes against Germany on the Russian and Italian fronts. However, in July 1916, Britain took the lead role in the attack to relieve pressure on the French caused by the German advance on Verdun (see pp.214–15).

Douglas Haig, commander of the mainly volunteer British Expeditionary Force (BEF), proposed using prolonged artillery barrages to punch paths through enemy lines, and even called up cavalry units to exploit the gaps he believed this would create. The reality was very different. Two-thirds of the 1.5 million shells fired in the week before the attack were shrapnel rather than high explosive, so did little to dislodge defenders in deep concrete-lined bunkers. Many shells were duds, built by unskilled labor. For more than four months the muddy fields of the Somme valley became a killing ground with over a million casualties, including more

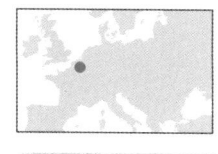

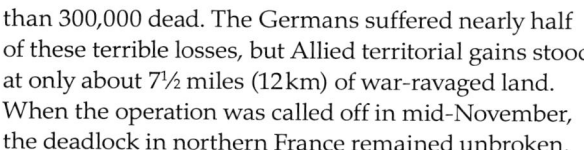

KEY

1 German machine gun positions are identified in the key (as "MG"); arrows indicate direction of fire.

2 Pencil annotations reflect updates made to the map during the battle.

3 German trenches are marked in red; hand-drawn numbered lines indicate the timings for the artillery barrage which would have supported an infantry assault.

than 300,000 dead. The Germans suffered nearly half of these terrible losses, but Allied territorial gains stood at only about 7½ miles (12 km) of war-ravaged land. When the operation was called off in mid-November, the deadlock in northern France remained unbroken.

"The results of the Somme fully justify confidence in our ability to master the enemy's power of resistance."

GENERAL DOUGLAS HAIG, 1916

A PITILESS FRONT
On July 1, Allied soldiers were ordered "over the top;" thousands were mowed down by machine-gun fire, with significant advances made only in the south. The BEF took almost 60,000 casualties, making this the bloodiest day in the history of the British Army. The French in the south were more successful and pushed over the Flaucourt plateau but were halted short of Peronne. Only a few advances, such as the capture of Pozières by Australian troops, were made by mid-September. The battlefront was then widened, and some modest and costly further gains were made before winter curtailed the battle.

KEY

⬛ British forces	◤ French forces
➡ British attacks	→ French attacks
▬ Frontline July 1, 1916	┄ Frontline Nov 18, 1916
⬛ German forces	

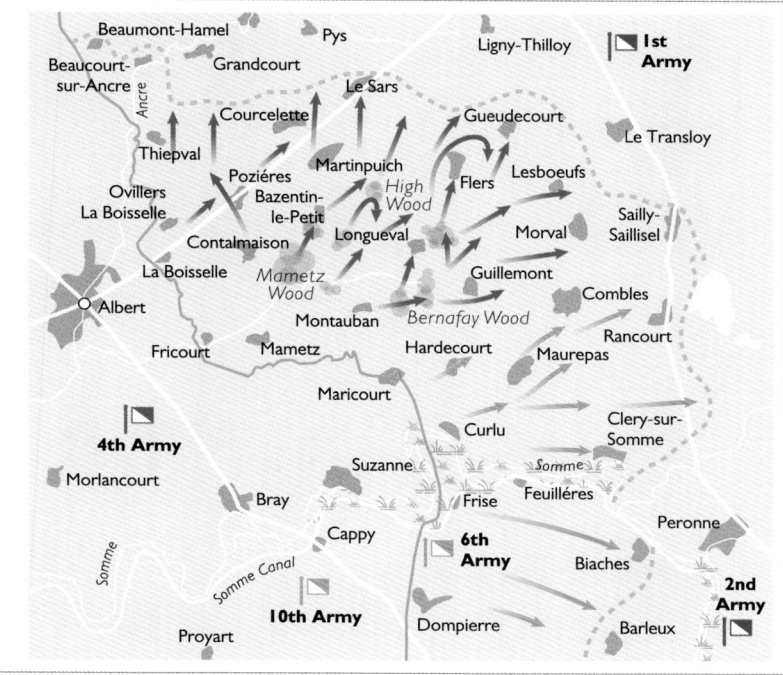

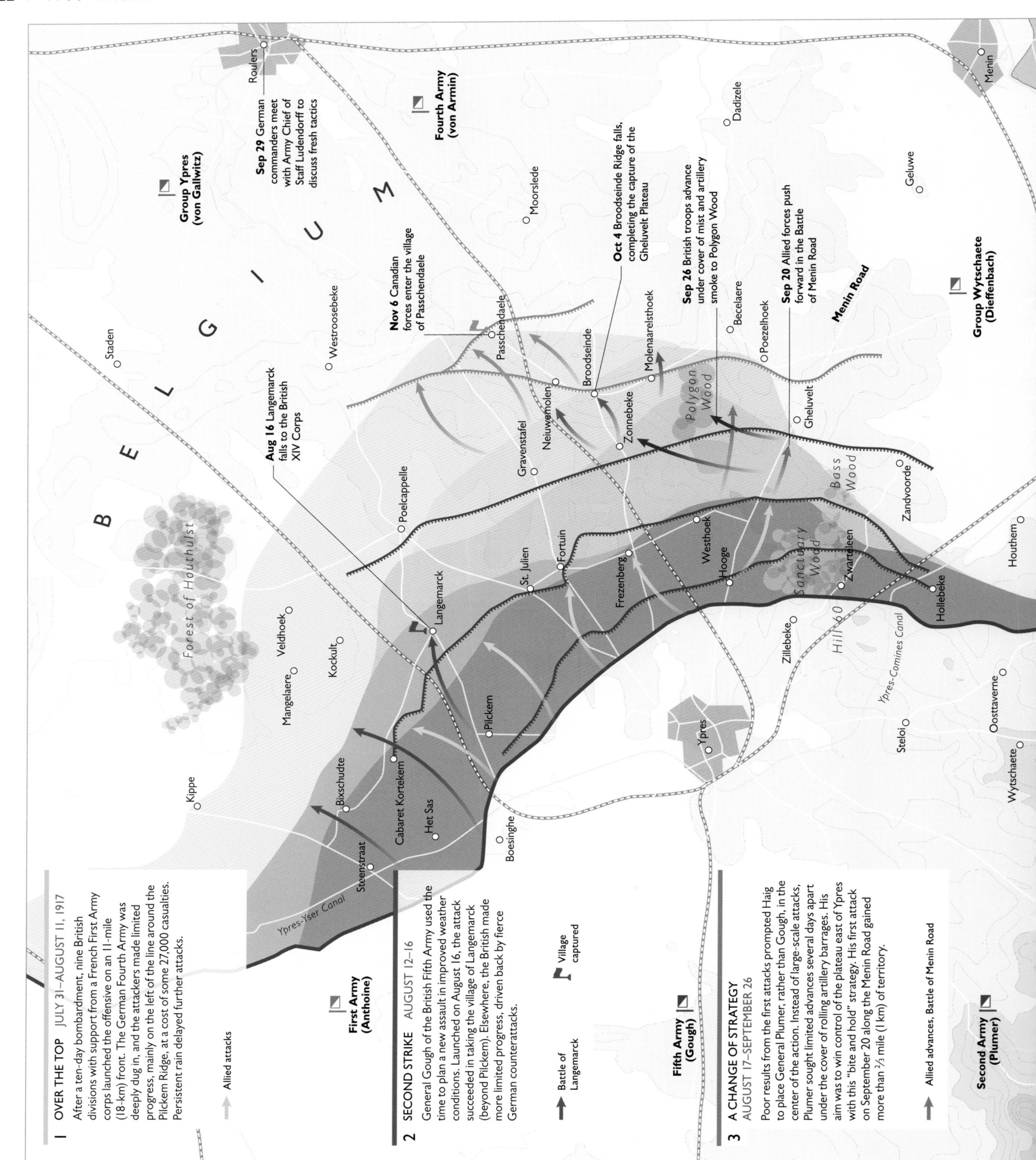

Group Ypres (von Gallwitz)

Sep 29 German commanders meet with Army Chief of Staff Ludendorff to discuss fresh tactics

Fourth Army (von Armin)

Oct 4 Broodseinde Ridge falls, completing the capture of the Gheluvelt Plateau

Nov 6 Canadian forces enter the village of Passchendaele

Sep 26 British troops advance under cover of mist and artillery smoke to Polygon Wood

Sep 20 Allied forces push forward in the Battle of Menin Road

Menin Road

Group Wytschaete (Dieffenbach)

Aug 16 Langemarck falls to the British XIV Corps

B E L G I U M

Forest of Houthulst

Roulers
Menin
Dadizele
Moorslede
Geluwe
Staden
Westroosebeke
Passchendaele
Broodseinde
Molenaarelsthoek
Becelaere
Poezelhoek
Neiuwemolen
Zonnebeke
Polygon Wood
Gheluvelt
Gravenstafel
Bass Wood
Poelcappelle
St. Julien
Fortuin
Westhoek
Zandvoorde
Hooge
Sanctuary Wood
Langemarck
Frezenberg
Zwaerdaleen
Zillebeke
Hollebeke
Hill 60
Houthem
Veldhoek
Pilckem
Ypres
Ypres-Comines Canal
Mangelaere
Kockult
Steloi
Osttaverne
Kippe
Bixschudte
Cabaret Kortekem
Het Sas
Steenstraat
Boesinghe
Wytschaete
Ypres-Yser Canal

First Army (Anthoine)

1 OVER THE TOP JULY 31–AUGUST 11, 1917

After a ten-day bombardment, nine British divisions with support from a French First Army corps launched the offensive on an 11-mile (18-km) front. The German Fourth Army was deeply dug in, and the attackers made limited progress, mainly on the left of the line around the Pilckem Ridge, at a cost of some 27,000 casualties. Persistent rain delayed further attacks.

→ Allied attacks

2 SECOND STRIKE AUGUST 12–16

General Gough of the British Fifth Army used the time to plan a new assault in improved weather conditions. Launched on August 16, the attack succeeded in taking the village of Langemarck (beyond Pilckem). Elsewhere, the British made more limited progress, driven back by fierce German counterattacks.

⌐ Village captured

→ Battle of Langemarck

Fifth Army (Gough)

3 A CHANGE OF STRATEGY AUGUST 17–SEPTEMBER 26

Poor results from the first attacks prompted Haig to place General Plumer, rather than Gough, in the center of the action. Instead of large-scale attacks, Plumer sought limited advances several days apart under the cover of rolling artillery barrages. His aim was to win control of the plateau east of Ypres with this "bite and hold" strategy. His first attack on September 20 along the Menin Road gained more than ⅔ mile (1 km) of territory.

→ Allied advances, Battle of Menin Road

Second Army (Plumer)

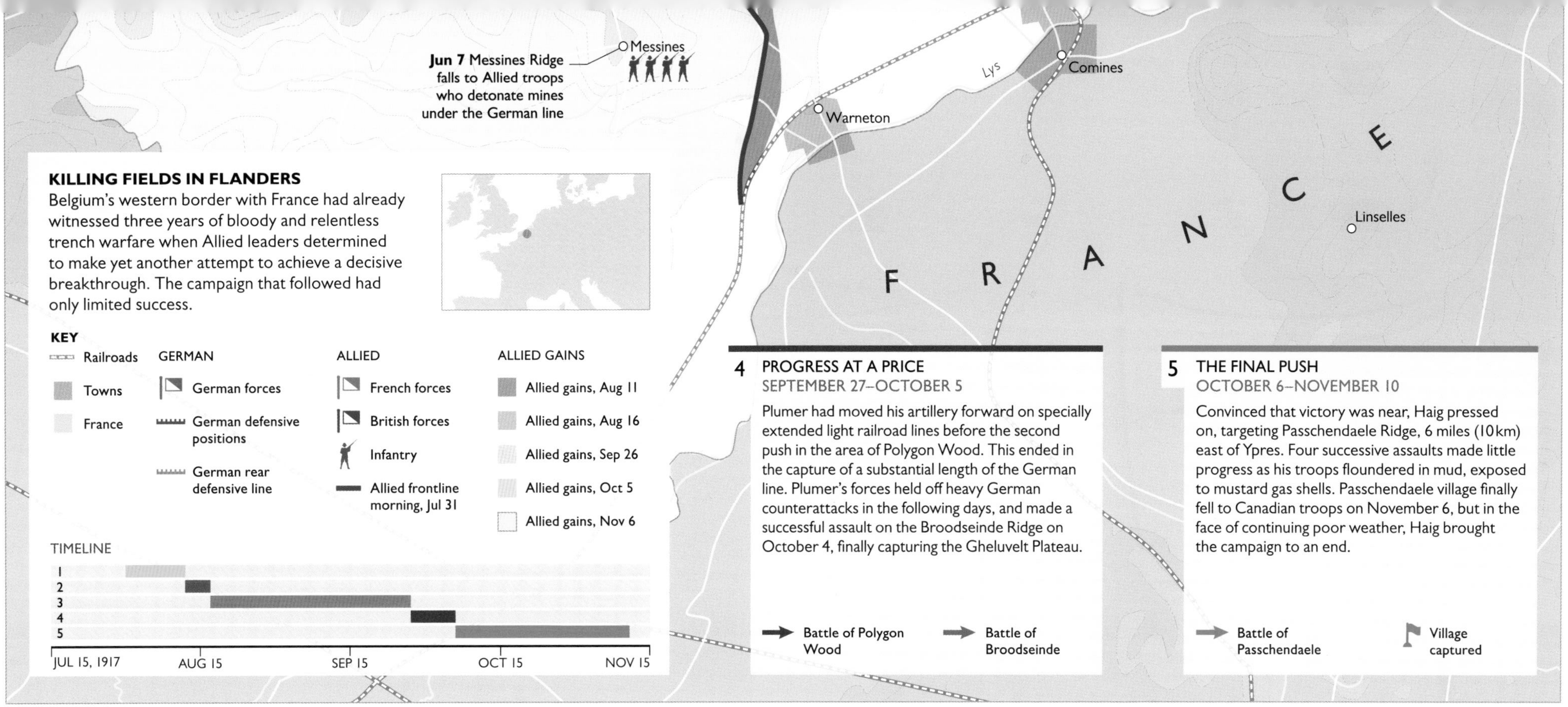

KILLING FIELDS IN FLANDERS

Belgium's western border with France had already witnessed three years of bloody and relentless trench warfare when Allied leaders determined to make yet another attempt to achieve a decisive breakthrough. The campaign that followed had only limited success.

KEY

- ⬡⬡⬡ Railroads
- ▣ Towns
- France

GERMAN
- ▣ German forces
- ⬡⬡⬡ German defensive positions
- ⬡⬡⬡ German rear defensive line

ALLIED
- ▣ French forces
- ▣ British forces
- 🏃 Infantry
- Allied frontline morning, Jul 31

ALLIED GAINS
- Allied gains, Aug 11
- Allied gains, Aug 16
- Allied gains, Sep 26
- Allied gains, Oct 5
- Allied gains, Nov 6

TIMELINE

1
2
3
4
5

JUL 15, 1917 — AUG 15 — SEP 15 — OCT 15 — NOV 15

Jun 7 Messines Ridge falls to Allied troops who detonate mines under the German line

Messines
Warneton
Comines
Linselles
Lys
FRANCE

---

4 PROGRESS AT A PRICE
SEPTEMBER 27–OCTOBER 5

Plumer had moved his artillery forward on specially extended light railroad lines before the second push in the area of Polygon Wood. This ended in the capture of a substantial length of the German line. Plumer's forces held off heavy German counterattacks in the following days, and made a successful assault on the Broodseinde Ridge on October 4, finally capturing the Gheluvelt Plateau.

→ Battle of Polygon Wood
→ Battle of Broodseinde

---

5 THE FINAL PUSH
OCTOBER 6–NOVEMBER 10

Convinced that victory was near, Haig pressed on, targeting Passchendaele Ridge, 6 miles (10km) east of Ypres. Four successive assaults made little progress as his troops floundered in mud, exposed to mustard gas shells. Passchendaele village finally fell to Canadian troops on November 6, but in the face of continuing poor weather, Haig brought the campaign to an end.

→ Battle of Passchendaele
⌐ Village captured

△ **Fighting in a quagmire**
Torrential rain made parts of the battlefield impassible to vehicles, including tanks, and gave the Germans, who occupied higher ground, a tactical advantage.

PASSCHENDAELE

The Third Battle of Ypres—also known as Passchendaele, from the final objective captured—was another terrible battle of mutual attrition on World War I's Western Front. The Allies incurred a terrible death toll to make limited advances in the three-month campaign.

After France's Nivelle Offensive in spring 1917 failed, and caused a mutiny among the demoralized and exhausted French soldiers, there was understandable doubt about the wisdom of a similar British attack. Prime Minister David Lloyd George was skeptical, but British commander Field Marshal Sir Douglas Haig finally won approval for an offensive to improve the tactical situation in the long-contested salient at Ypres in Belgium, thereby also continuing to wear down the German army while the French recovered from their trauma.

"It's just not conceivable how human beings can exist in such a swamp, let alone fight in it."

ALLIED PILOT AFTER FLYING OVER THE BATTLEFIELD

The targets selected by Haig included the railroad junction at Roulers (Roeselare)—some 12 miles (20km) east of Ypres—that served as an important staging post for the German army. Success at Roulers may have permitted an Allied advance on the Belgian ports, which were used as forward bases for the U-boats that were threatening British shipping. A preparatory attack in June succeeded in taking the ridge at Messines, south of Ypres, raising Allied hopes of success.

The Allies failed in their main objectives. Unseasonably heavy rain and the destruction of drainage channels by shelling turned the plain around Ypres into a morass, making progress painfully slow. Moreover, the flatness of the terrain made stealthy attacks impossible. After three months, the Allied front had advanced by just a few miles. The price, in human lives, was high—about 250,000 casualties were sustained by each side.

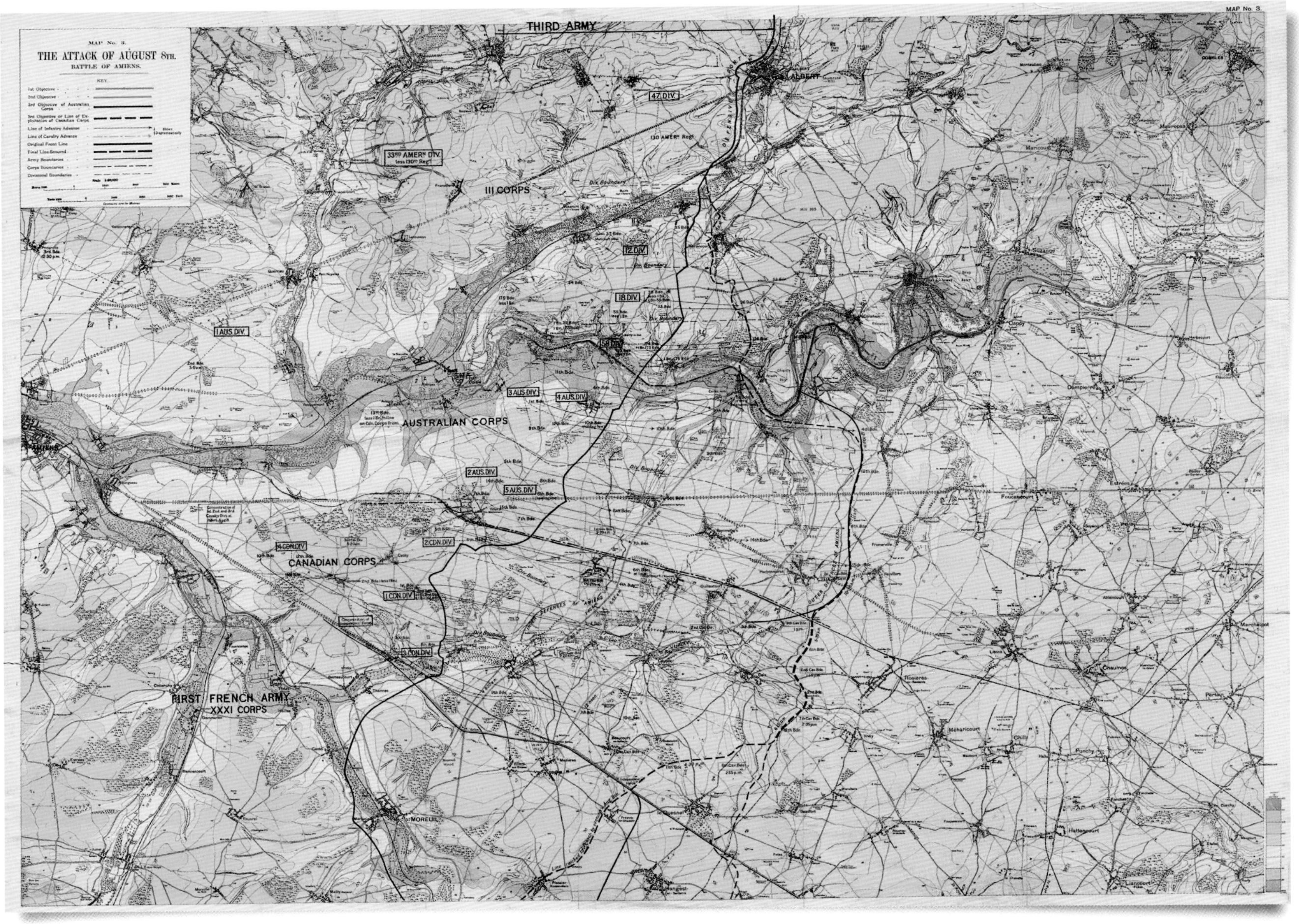

AMIENS

In August 1918, the Allied powers launched a massive attack on German forces near Amiens, in northern France. It marked the start of the Hundred Days Offensive, which would finally break German morale and end World War I three months later.

△ **The first day of battle**
This postwar map of the Amiens battlefield, covering an area stretching 25 miles (40 km) to the east of the city, shows the gains made on the first day of the clash when Allied forces drove overstretched German troops back more than 6 miles (10 km).

In spring 1918, the situation for Germany looked hopeful: Russia had withdrawn from the conflict in March, allowing German strategists to concentrate their attention on the Western front. Erich Ludendorff, commanding the General Staff, pinned his hopes on a decisive breakthrough before the US (which had entered the war in 1917 on the side of the Allied Powers) sent large numbers of its troops to Europe.

Ludendorff's Spring Offensive initially made significant progress. At Saint-Quentin, British forces were driven back 37 miles (60 km); on the Aisne River, French defenses gave way, allowing a breakthrough to the Marne River that threatened Paris. Yet none of the assaults achieved the gains that Ludendorff needed.

By August, the Allies were ready to deliver a decisive blow. They chose the area east of Amiens, in northern France, where British, Australian, and Canadian units were flanked to the south by the French First Army. Tanks and infantry launched an assault through the mist at dawn on August 8, achieving total surprise and causing the German troops to break and run. About 30,000 of them were killed, wounded, or captured on what Ludendorff would call "the black day of the German army." What followed for the Germans was a fighting retreat, driven on by the arrival of hundreds of thousands of battle-fresh US forces. By the end of that month, Ludendorff realized that there was no prospect of a German victory in the war.

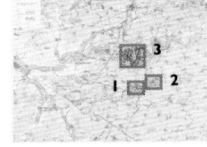 

KEY

1 Australian forces managed to advance as far as Harbonnières by 11am on the first day of fighting.

2 British armored cars captured the headquarters of the German 11th Corps at Framerville at around noon

3 British forces met heavy resistance at Chipilly, on the north bank of the Somme.

WARSAW

To inhibit further Allied intervention in the Russian civil war, Lenin sent the Red Army westward in the hope of spreading the revolution across Europe. In August 1920, outside Warsaw, capital of the newly independent Poland, the Red Army advance was brought to a halt.

As the Red Army gained the upper hand in the long civil war which followed the Bolshevik Revolution of 1917, Lenin sought to export Communism beyond Russia's borders and so undermine the Allied regimes which had intervened in favor of his "White" opponents. The revived Polish nation had occupied much of Belorussia and western Ukraine by May 1920, but by August the Red Army had driven Polish forces all the way back to their new capital, Warsaw. Polish leader Józef Piłsudski aimed to hold the invaders in a last-ditch defense outside the capital while also delivering a flank attack from the south on their weak left wing. The plan proved successful, and within a week, the Red Army was in headlong retreat. The setback effectively put an end to Lenin's hopes of spreading revolution by force of arms to Western Europe.

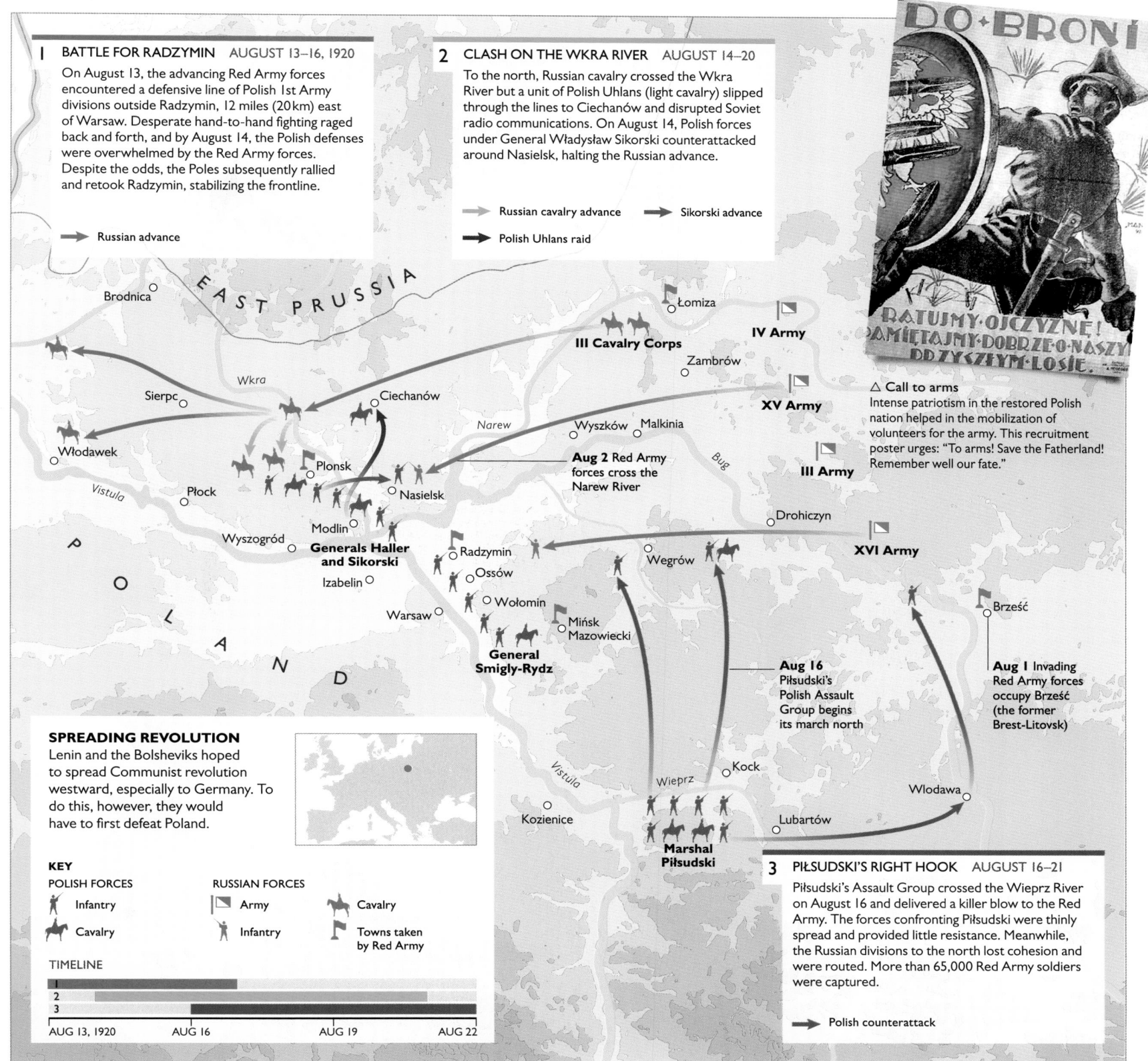

1 BATTLE FOR RADZYMIN AUGUST 13–16, 1920
On August 13, the advancing Red Army forces encountered a defensive line of Polish 1st Army divisions outside Radzymin, 12 miles (20 km) east of Warsaw. Desperate hand-to-hand fighting raged back and forth, and by August 14, the Polish defenses were overwhelmed by the Red Army forces. Despite the odds, the Poles subsequently rallied and retook Radzymin, stabilizing the frontline.

➡ Russian advance

2 CLASH ON THE WKRA RIVER AUGUST 14–20
To the north, Russian cavalry crossed the Wkra River but a unit of Polish Uhlans (light cavalry) slipped through the lines to Ciechanów and disrupted Soviet radio communications. On August 14, Polish forces under General Władysław Sikorski counterattacked around Nasielsk, halting the Russian advance.

➡ Russian cavalry advance   ➡ Sikorski advance
➡ Polish Uhlans raid

△ **Call to arms**
Intense patriotism in the restored Polish nation helped in the mobilization of volunteers for the army. This recruitment poster urges: "To arms! Save the Fatherland! Remember well our fate."

SPREADING REVOLUTION
Lenin and the Bolsheviks hoped to spread Communist revolution westward, especially to Germany. To do this, however, they would have to first defeat Poland.

KEY
POLISH FORCES
🚶 Infantry
🐎 Cavalry

RUSSIAN FORCES
🚩 Army
🚶 Infantry
🐎 Cavalry
🚩 Towns taken by Red Army

TIMELINE
1
2
3
AUG 13, 1920   AUG 16   AUG 19   AUG 22

3 PIŁSUDSKI'S RIGHT HOOK AUGUST 16–21
Piłsudski's Assault Group crossed the Wieprz River on August 16 and delivered a killer blow to the Red Army. The forces confronting Piłsudski were thinly spread and provided little resistance. Meanwhile, the Russian divisions to the north lost cohesion and were routed. More than 65,000 Red Army soldiers were captured.

➡ Polish counterattack

Bombing by hand
A British airman drops a small bomb by hand from his open cockpit. This primitive technique was used for tactical bombing early in World War I. Later in the war, larger bombs were dropped using mechanical release systems.

EARLY MILITARY AIRCRAFT

World War I was the first major conflict fought in the air as well as on land and sea. Military aircraft battled for control of the skies, attacked troops on the ground, and bombed civilians in cities.

When the war began in 1914, all the combatants together fielded no more than 500 flimsy, unarmed reconnaissance aircraft. By the end of the war in 1918, Britain alone had more than 20,000 aircraft. These had diversified to include specialized fighters, armed with machine guns for air-to-air combat, and multi-engined bombers. The primary role of these aircraft was to support the army, photographing enemy lines to help artillery hit its targets or strafing and bombing ground forces. However, the "dogfights" between fighter aircraft attracted the most attention. Propagandists praised fighter pilots as "knights of the air," making heroes of "aces" with high scores of enemy aircraft shot down.

▷ **German fighter**
The Fokker Dr.I triplane, introduced in 1917, is an example of a World War I aircraft specifically designed for air-to-air combat.

Turning point
The bombing of cities was a controversial development that gave air power an independent role. Germany attacked London in 1915, first with its fleet of airships and then with bomber aircraft. Britain and France, in turn, bombed German cities. For the time, civilian casualties were relatively low—1,400 killed in Britain. However, the arrival of strategic bombing was a turning point in modern warfare.

△ **Airships at war**
Germany deployed more than 50 Zeppelin and Schütte-Lanze airships between 1915 and 1918 to bomb London and Paris. They terrorized civilians, but being slow-moving and inflammable, they were vulnerable to attacks by fighter aircraft.

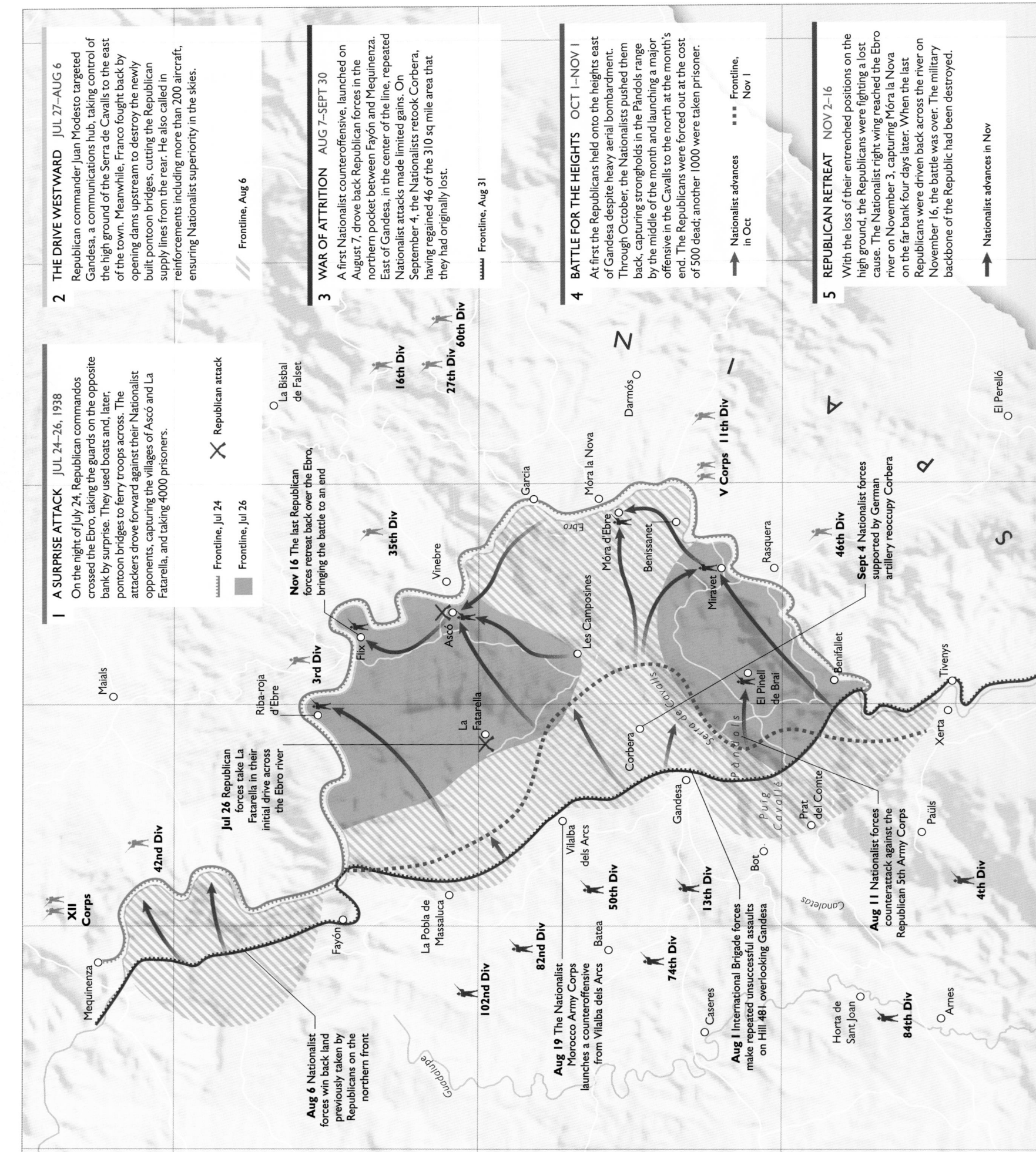

2 **THE DRIVE WESTWARD** JUL 27–AUG 6

Republican commander Juan Modesto targeted Gandesa, a communications hub, taking control of the high ground of the Serra de Cavalls to the east of the town. Meanwhile, Franco fought back by opening dams upstream to destroy the newly built pontoon bridges, cutting the Republican supply lines from the rear. He also called in reinforcements including more than 200 aircraft, ensuring Nationalist superiority in the skies.

▨▨▨ Frontline, Aug 6

3 **WAR OF ATTRITION** AUG 7–SEPT 30

A first Nationalist counteroffensive, launched on August 7, drove back Republican forces in the northern pocket between Fayón and Mequinenza. East of Gandesa, in the center of the line, repeated Nationalist attacks made limited gains. On September 4, the Nationalists retook Corbera, having regained 46 of the 310 sq mile area that they had originally lost.

⌇⌇⌇⌇ Frontline, Aug 31

4 **BATTLE FOR THE HEIGHTS** OCT 1–NOV 1

At first the Republicans held onto the heights east of Gandesa despite heavy aerial bombardment. Through October, the Nationalists pushed them back, capturing strongholds in the Pàndols range by the middle of the month and launching a major offensive in the Cavalls to the north at the month's end. The Republicans were forced out at the cost of 500 dead; another 1000 were taken prisoner.

- - - - Frontline, Nov 1

→ Nationalist advances in Oct

5 **REPUBLICAN RETREAT** NOV 2–16

With the loss of their entrenched positions on the high ground, the Republicans were fighting a lost cause. The Nationalist right wing reached the Ebro river on November 3, capturing Móra la Nova on the far bank four days later. When the last Republicans were driven back across the river on November 16, the battle was over. The military backbone of the Republic had been destroyed.

⬆ Nationalist advances in Nov

1 **A SURPRISE ATTACK** JUL 24–26, 1938

On the night of July 24, Republican commandos crossed the Ebro, taking the guards on the opposite bank by surprise. They used boats and, later, pontoon bridges to ferry troops across. The attackers drove forward against their Nationalist opponents, capturing the villages of Ascó and La Fatarella, and taking 4000 prisoners.

✕ Republican attack

⌇⌇⌇⌇ Frontline, Jul 24
⌇⌇⌇⌇ Frontline, Jul 26
▨ (shaded area)

Nov 16 The last Republican forces retreat back over the Ebro, bringing the battle to an end

Jul 26 Republican forces take La Fatarella in their initial drive across the Ebro river

Aug 6 Nationalist forces win back land previously taken by Republicans on the northern front

Aug 19 The Nationalist Morocco Army Corps launches a counteroffensive from Vilalba dels Arcs

Aug 1 International Brigade forces make repeated unsuccessful assaults on Hill 481 overlooking Gandesa

Aug 11 Nationalist forces counterattack against the Republican 5th Army Corps

Sept 4 Nationalist forces supported by German artillery reoccupy Corbera

Malals
Mequinenza
Fayón
La Pobla de Massaluca
Caseres
Batea
Vilalba dels Arcs
Horta de Sant Joan
Ames
Bot
Gandesa
Corbera
Prat del Comte
Pauls
Xerta
Tivenys
El Perelló
Rasquera
Benifallet
Miravet
El Pinell de Brai
Móra d'Ebre
Móra la Nova
Darmós
Garcia
Benissanet
Les Camposines
Ascó
Flix
Vinebre
Riba-roja d'Ebre
La Fatarella
La Bisbal de Falset

XII Corps
42nd Div
102nd Div
82nd Div
74th Div
84th Div
50th Div
13th Div
4th Div
3rd Div
35th Div
16th Div
27th Div
60th Div
46th Div
V Corps 11th Div

Ebro
Serra de Cavalls
Puig Cavallé
Pàndols
Canaletes
Guadalupe

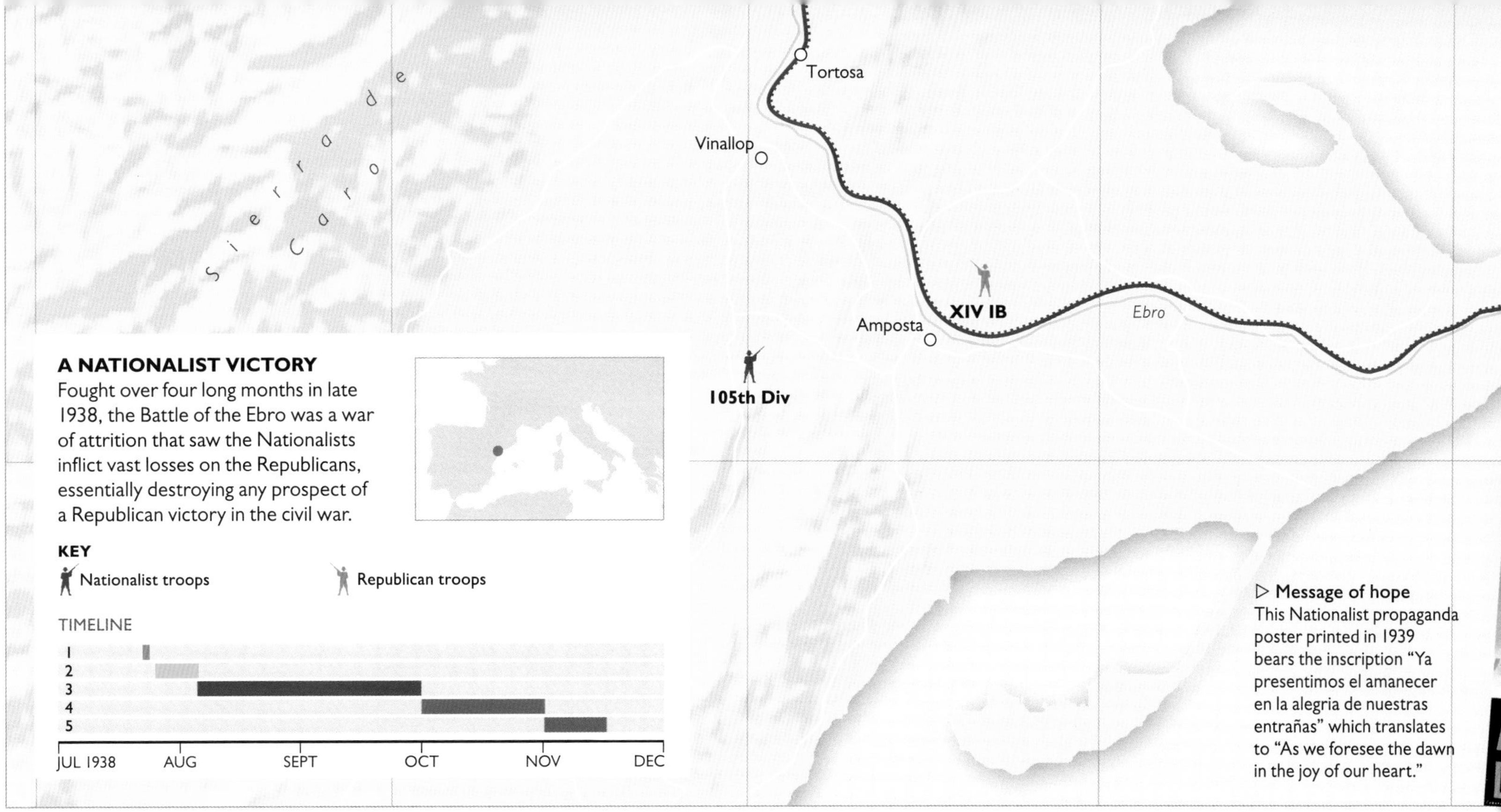

A NATIONALIST VICTORY

Fought over four long months in late 1938, the Battle of the Ebro was a war of attrition that saw the Nationalists inflict vast losses on the Republicans, essentially destroying any prospect of a Republican victory in the civil war.

KEY

✈ Nationalist troops   ✈ Republican troops

TIMELINE

1
2
3
4
5

JUL 1938   AUG   SEPT   OCT   NOV   DEC

Tortosa

Ebro

Vinallop

Amposta

XIV IB

105th Div

Balearic Sea

△ **Message of hope**
This Nationalist propaganda poster printed in 1939 bears the inscription "Ya presentimos el amanecer en la alegria de nuestras entrañas" which translates to "As we foresee the dawn in the joy of our heart."

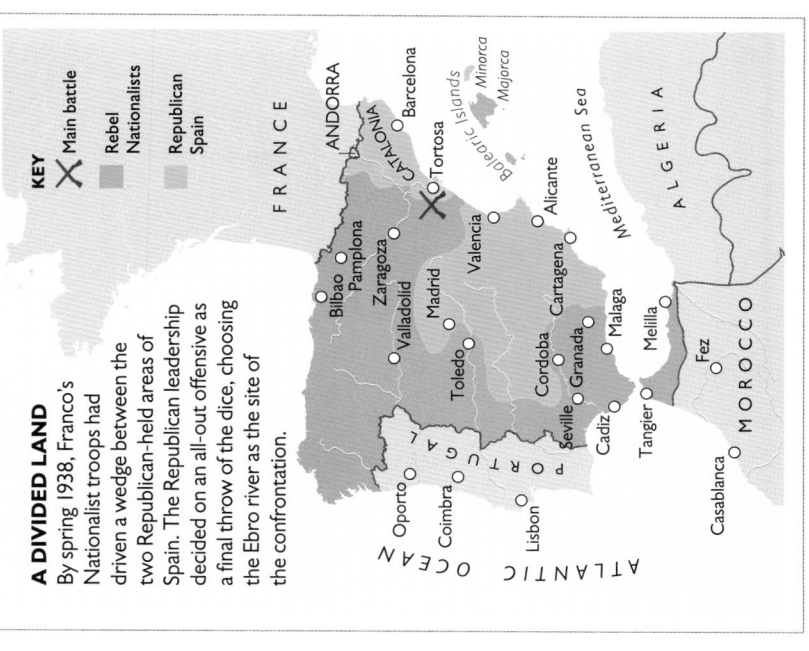

A DIVIDED LAND

By spring 1938, Franco's Nationalist troops had driven a wedge between the two Republican-held areas of Spain. The Republican leadership decided on an all-out offensive as a final throw of the dice, choosing the Ebro river as the site of the confrontation.

KEY

✕ Main battle
✕ Rebel Nationalists
▮ Nationalists
▮ Republican Spain

FRANCE
ANDORRA
CATALONIA
Barcelona
Tortosa
Balearic Islands
Minorca
Mallorca
Pamplona
Bilbao
Zaragoza
Valladolid
Madrid
Valencia
Alicante
Mediterranean Sea
Toledo
Cordoba
Cartagena
Granada
Malaga
Seville
Cadiz
Melilla
Tangier
ALGERIA
Fez
Casablanca
MOROCCO
PORTUGAL
Oporto
Coimbra
Lisbon
ATLANTIC OCEAN

THE EBRO

The climactic battle of the Spanish Civil War was fought on arid, hilly country on the west bank of the Ebro river. After making initial gains, the Republican forces were driven back by their Nationalist opponents, aided by German and Italian units. They never recovered from the setback.

Following a general election that had split the country between left- and right-wing ideologies, the Spanish Civil War broke out in 1936 when a section of Spain's armed forces launched a coup against the Republican Popular Front government. The Republicans fought back, plunging the country into three years of bloodshed. The war also had an international dimension: the Nationalist forces, led by General Francisco Franco, received aid from Hitler's Germany and Mussolini's Italy, while the Republicans were supported by the Soviet Union and by anti-Fascist volunteers from many countries in the International Brigades.

Despite fierce resistance, the Republicans lost ground in 1937 to Franco's better trained and well supplied forces. They suffered a major setback in April 1938 when the Nationalists advanced to the Mediterranean, cutting off Catalonia from the Republicans' remaining territory in southeastern Spain.

The Republican leadership responded with an all-out assault along the Ebro river, designed to reunite the two regions and protect their seat of government in Valencia. Initially the plan worked, raising Republican hopes, before relentless bombing by the German Condor Legion and the Italian Aviazione Legionaria turned the tables. The result was disastrous for the Republic; Barcelona was lost a couple of months later, and on April 1, 1939, after Madrid fell, Franco was able to proclaim a Nationalist victory.

"Even if they bomb the bridge / You'll see me cross the Ebro / In a skiff or a canoe."

TRANSLATION FROM A REPUBLICAN SONG

EVACUATING DUNKIRK

In spring 1940, routed by the Germans in one of the opening campaigns of World War II, hundreds of thousands of soldiers of the British army and its allies were trapped on the French coast at Dunkirk. Their evacuation by sea was an epic feat of valor.

After the British and French declared war on Nazi Germany at the start of World War II in September 1939, a British Expeditionary Force (BEF) was sent to France. It saw no fighting until May 10, 1940, when the Germans invaded the Netherlands, and Belgium, crossing into France two days later. Spearheaded by tanks operating with air support, German forces rapidly broke through the French defenses at Sedan and swung northward towards the Channel coast. The BEF, which had advanced into Belgium, was threatened with being cut off from the rear. As the situation worsened, the Allies abandoned their plan to break through the German encirclement and join French forces to the south. Instead, the BEF fell back on Dunkirk, the only port within reach still in Allied hands, albeit precariously.

On May 23, General Alan Brooke, a British corps commander, wrote: "Nothing but a miracle can save the BEF now." In the event, with the help of civilians (see below), almost 340,000 Allied soldiers were evacuated to Britain from the harbor and beaches of Dunkirk, two-thirds of them British, and nearly 200,000 more from operations at other French ports. The skill and courage of the evacuation enabled British propagandists to represent a crushing defeat as a triumphant escape, although Prime Minister Winston Churchill warned: "Wars are not won by evacuations." The evacuation left a legacy of bitterness in France, where many felt they had been abandoned by their British allies. After France surrendered on June 22, Britain opted to fight on, encouraged in its defiance of Hitler by the "miracle of Dunkirk."

THE "LITTLE SHIPS" OF DUNKIRK

Most soldiers were evacuated to Britain on board Royal Navy destroyers and minesweepers, but a flotilla of small boats, some crewed by civilians, also played a crucial role in the evacuation. Most were already registered with the navy as part of its "small vessels pool." From trawlers and tug boats to lifeboats and private yachts, they sailed into shallow water to take men off the beaches, often ferrying them to warships further offshore. About 200 "little ships" were lost in the perilous operation.

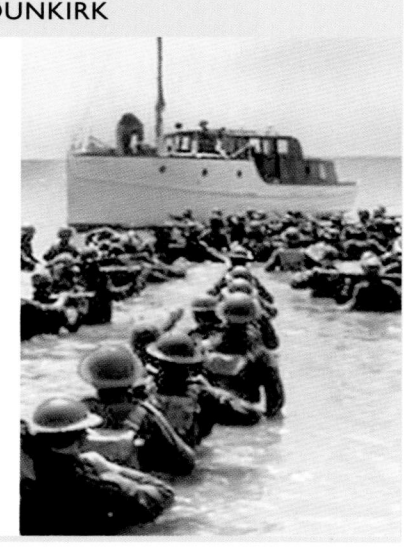

A civilian "little ship" at Dunkirk

1 DECISION TO EVACUATE   MAY 20–26, 1940

With the BEF threatened by German armies advancing through Belgium and France, on May 20 Vice Admiral Bertram Ramsay was ordered to plan a seaborne evacuation, Operation Dynamo. As the troops fell back on Dunkirk, on May 24 German leader Adolf Hitler halted the advance of his leading tanks for two days, giving the Allies time to improvise defenses around the port. On May 26, Britain ordered the evacuation to go ahead.

■ Allied territory, May 26

◀ To English Coast

Goodwin Sands

May 28 After the closure of Route Z, Route Y becomes the main path for evacuation

Route Y: 87 nautical miles

May 29 Route X opens but can only be used in daylight because of hazardous shallows

Route X: 55 nautical miles

2 FIGHT AGAINST TIME   MAY 26–31, 1940

Retreating Allied troops poured into Dunkirk, filling the beaches. Ramsay had expected only a couple of days for evacuation, but the defensive perimeter held firm. At first, British and French warships took troops from the Mole, a stone jetty in the harbor. The arrival of smaller ships, letting men embark directly from the beaches, increased the daily evacuation rate from 18,000 on May 28 to almost 70,000 three days later.

■ Dunkirk beaches   ■ Allied territory, May 28

May 27 After the fall of Calais, Route Z is within range of German artillery and no longer viable

May 26 The port of Calais falls to German forces

3 AIR BOMBARDMENT   MAY 26–JUNE 4, 1940

On May 26, Hitler ordered the Luftwaffe to prevent the escape from Dunkirk. German Stuka dive-bombers, escorted by fighters, attacked the port, ships, and beaches. On May 29, the harbor suffered severe damage. Despite the intervention of RAF fighters, the Stukas took a heavy toll: most of the Allied ships sunk were victims of air attacks. Both sides lost more than 150 aircraft.

/// Air attacks and battles

Dunkirk harbor bombed

Route Z: 39 nautical miles

○ Calais

F

R

A

Panzer Group Kleist

4 REARGUARD FIGHTING TO THE END   MAY 28–JUNE 4, 1940

Despite valiant rearguard fighting, mainly by French troops, the Germans closed in on Dunkirk, which came under artillery fire. By June 2, evacuation was impossible in daylight. The British completed their withdrawal that night. Some of the French rearguard were evacuated the next night before the operation was called off. Some 40,000 French soldiers surrendered on June 4.

□□□ Rearguard fighting, May 28

○○○○ Rearguard fighting, May 29

— Final defensive perimeter

May 24–25 The advance of German tanks is halted for two days on Hitler's orders

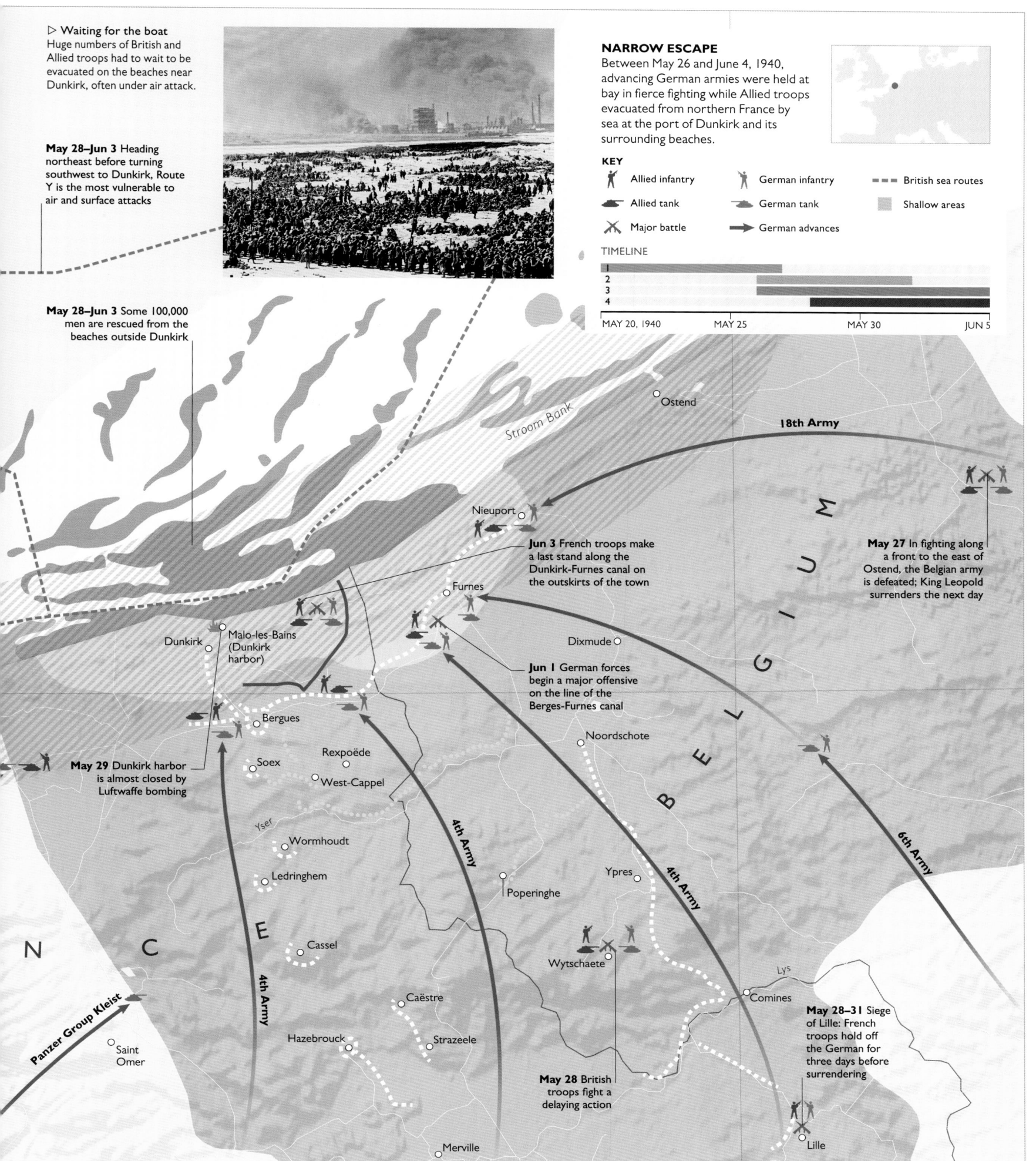

▷ **Waiting for the boat**
Huge numbers of British and Allied troops had to wait to be evacuated on the beaches near Dunkirk, often under air attack.

May 28–Jun 3 Heading northeast before turning southwest to Dunkirk, Route Y is the most vulnerable to air and surface attacks

May 28–Jun 3 Some 100,000 men are rescued from the beaches outside Dunkirk

NARROW ESCAPE
Between May 26 and June 4, 1940, advancing German armies were held at bay in fierce fighting while Allied troops evacuated from northern France by sea at the port of Dunkirk and its surrounding beaches.

KEY

Allied infantry	German infantry	British sea routes
Allied tank	German tank	Shallow areas
Major battle	German advances	

TIMELINE

1
2
3
4

MAY 20, 1940   MAY 25   MAY 30   JUN 5

Stroom Bank

Ostend

18th Army

Nieuport

Jun 3 French troops make a last stand along the Dunkirk-Furnes canal on the outskirts of the town

Furnes

May 27 In fighting along a front to the east of Ostend, the Belgian army is defeated; King Leopold surrenders the next day

Dixmude

Jun 1 German forces begin a major offensive on the line of the Berges-Furnes canal

Dunkirk

Malo-les-Bains (Dunkirk harbor)

Bergues

May 29 Dunkirk harbor is almost closed by Luftwaffe bombing

Soex

Rexpoëde

West-Cappel

Noordschote

B E L G I U M

6th Army

Yser

Wormhoudt

4th Army

Ledringhem

Ypres

4th Army

Poperinghe

N   C   E

Cassel

Wytschaete

Lys

Caëstre

Comines

May 28–31 Siege of Lille: French troops hold off the German for three days before surrendering

Hazebrouck

Strazeele

Saint Omer

Panzer Group Kleist

4th Army

May 28 British troops fight a delaying action

Merville

Lille

THE BATTLE OF BRITAIN

Fought between the British and German air forces, the Battle of Britain was a major turning point in World War II. The Royal Air Force (RAF) successfully resisted the Luftwaffe's bid to win command of the air, freeing Britain from the threat of a German invasion.

The Germans' victorious campaigns in spring 1940 (see pp.230–31) allowed the Luftwaffe to establish air bases within close range of southern England, in France and Belgium. Planning a seaborne invasion of Britain, Hitler needed to defeat the RAF to allow his planes to counter the superior Royal Navy. Luftwaffe commander Hermann Goering confidently predicted a swift victory. Britain's air defenses, however, were well prepared. A chain of radar stations, aided by ground observers, provided early warning of enemy aircraft, and allowed radio-directed squadrons of fighter aircraft to intercept the intruders. Air Chief Marshal Hugh Dowding, head of RAF Fighter Command, conserved his resources in an attritional battle. While Britain's factories produced plentiful fighter aircraft, at times pilots were scarce. Commonwealth nations, Czechoslovakia, and Poland, all contributed fliers crucial to Britain's survival.

Faced with the unbroken resilience of the RAF, the German invasion plan was abandoned, and the Luftwaffe turned to nighttime bombing. London and other British cities were badly hit in the "Blitz" raids that lasted until May 1941. Nevertheless, in failing to defeat the RAF, Hitler had suffered his first serious setback of the war.

> *"Never in the field of human conflict was so much owed by so many to so few."*
>
> WINSTON CHURCHILL, AUGUST 20, 1940

HERMANN GOERING 1893–1946

After winning fame as a fighter pilot in World War I, Hermann Goering joined the Nazi Party in the 1920s and became one of Adolf Hitler's most powerful associates. Designated Reichsmarschall, the highest rank in the German armed forces, he took personal command of the air campaign against Britain in summer 1940. Its failure severely undermined his prestige. Prosecuted as a war criminal after Germany's defeat, he committed suicide to avoid execution.

AERIAL BATTLEFIELD

Signals intelligence gave the RAF some prior knowledge of German plans. This, along with enhanced air defenses, observer corps and radar, and speedy Spitfire and sturdy Hurricane aircraft, helped the RAF survive a month-long onslaught of Luftwaffe daylight raids.

KEY

High-level radar range	⌒⌒ Royal Observer Corps	▨ Axis occupied
Low-level radar range	⚓ Anti-aircraft battery	▬ German fighter range

TIMELINE

```
      JUL 1940        AUG        SEP        OCT        NOV
  2  ████████████
  3
  4
  5
  6
```

1 PLANNED INVASION   JULY 1940

Drawn up in early July, the German plan for the invasion of Britain, codenamed Operation Sealion, envisaged carrying armies across the Channel on fleets of barges and transport ships. The main blow was to fall on the English coast west of Dover. In a directive of July 16 ordering preparations to begin, Hitler stated the invasion could go ahead only if the RAF had first been so "beaten down" it could not oppose the crossings and if the Royal Navy could somehow be prevented from intervening.

▱ German army group	⌒ German corps
•••▶ Proposed invasion route	👤 German army

2 FIGHTING IN THE CHANNEL
JULY 4–AUGUST 11, 1940

The aerial conflict opened with scattered Luftwaffe attacks probing Britain's air defenses. England's naval ports and merchant convoys in the Channel were a tempting target for German bombers based in northern France. The RAF scrambled fighters to defend the shipping. Dubbed the *Kanalkampf* (Channel battle) by Germany, these initial encounters were hard-fought but indecisive.

⚓ British naval ports	
▬ Main area of the Channel battle	

3 ASSAULT ON FIGHTER COMMAND
AUGUST 13–18, 1940

The Luftwaffe campaign to crush the RAF, codenamed *Adlerangriff* (Eagle Attack), began in earnest on August 13. Launching raids from Northern France, Goering hoped to cripple Britain's air defenses within four days. He had gravely underestimated the strength and resilience of the RAF. On August 18, known as the "Hardest Day," the largest-scale fighting of the entire Battle of Britain saw both sides lose about 70 aircraft.

✠ Luftwaffe headquarters	▨ "Hardest day" raids, Aug 18, 1940
✛ Other Luftwaffe airfield	

Swansea

Plymouth

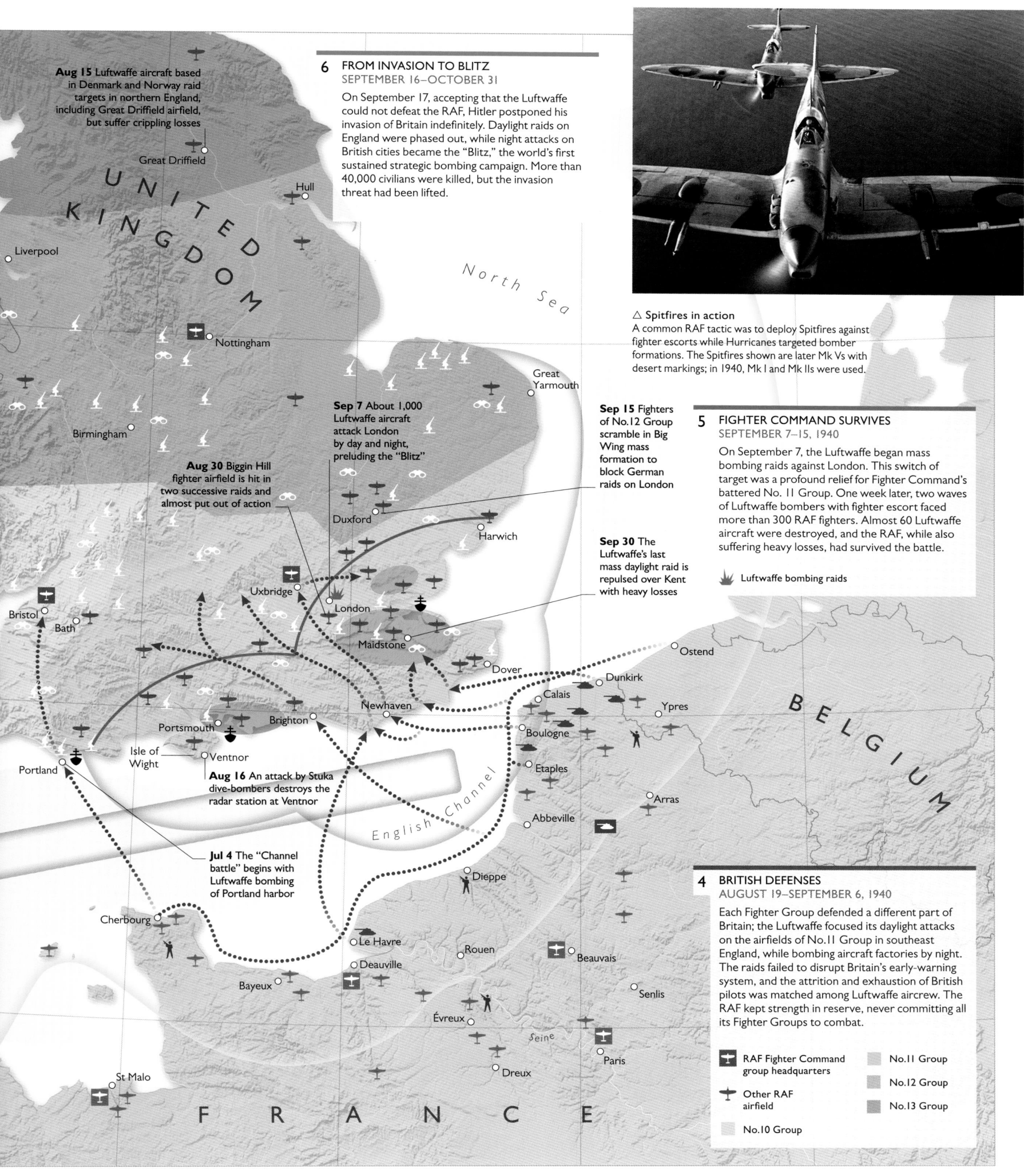

Aug 15 Luftwaffe aircraft based in Denmark and Norway raid targets in northern England, including Great Driffield airfield, but suffer crippling losses

Great Driffield

U N I T E D

K I N G D O M

Liverpool

Hull

North Sea

Nottingham

Great Yarmouth

Birmingham

Sep 7 About 1,000 Luftwaffe aircraft attack London by day and night, preluding the "Blitz"

Aug 30 Biggin Hill fighter airfield is hit in two successive raids and almost put out of action

Duxford

Harwich

Sep 15 Fighters of No.12 Group scramble in Big Wing mass formation to block German raids on London

Uxbridge

London

Sep 30 The Luftwaffe's last mass daylight raid is repulsed over Kent with heavy losses

Maidstone

Bristol

Bath

Dover

Ostend

Newhaven

Dunkirk

Calais

Ypres

B E L G I U M

Portsmouth

Brighton

Boulogne

Isle of Wight

Ventnor

Etaples

Aug 16 An attack by Stuka dive-bombers destroys the radar station at Ventnor

Portland

Arras

Abbeville

English Channel

Jul 4 The "Channel battle" begins with Luftwaffe bombing of Portland harbor

Dieppe

Cherbourg

Le Havre

Rouen

Beauvais

Deauville

Bayeux

Senlis

Évreux

Seine

Dreux

Paris

St Malo

F R A N C E

6 FROM INVASION TO BLITZ
SEPTEMBER 16–OCTOBER 31

On September 17, accepting that the Luftwaffe could not defeat the RAF, Hitler postponed his invasion of Britain indefinitely. Daylight raids on England were phased out, while night attacks on British cities became the "Blitz," the world's first sustained strategic bombing campaign. More than 40,000 civilians were killed, but the invasion threat had been lifted.

△ **Spitfires in action**
A common RAF tactic was to deploy Spitfires against fighter escorts while Hurricanes targeted bomber formations. The Spitfires shown are later Mk Vs with desert markings; in 1940, Mk I and Mk IIs were used.

5 FIGHTER COMMAND SURVIVES
SEPTEMBER 7–15, 1940

On September 7, the Luftwaffe began mass bombing raids against London. This switch of target was a profound relief for Fighter Command's battered No. 11 Group. One week later, two waves of Luftwaffe bombers with fighter escort faced more than 300 RAF fighters. Almost 60 Luftwaffe aircraft were destroyed, and the RAF, while also suffering heavy losses, had survived the battle.

💥 Luftwaffe bombing raids

4 BRITISH DEFENSES
AUGUST 19–SEPTEMBER 6, 1940

Each Fighter Group defended a different part of Britain; the Luftwaffe focused its daylight attacks on the airfields of No.11 Group in southeast England, while bombing aircraft factories by night. The raids failed to disrupt Britain's early-warning system, and the attrition and exhaustion of British pilots was matched among Luftwaffe aircrew. The RAF kept strength in reserve, never committing all its Fighter Groups to combat.

✈ RAF Fighter Command group headquarters	No.11 Group
	No.12 Group
✈ Other RAF airfield	No.13 Group
No.10 Group	

STRATEGIC WARFARE

With land combat in northwest Europe blocked from 1940 to 1944 by the obstacle of the English Channel, and with the US even more detached on the other side of the Atlantic Ocean, both sides turned instead to strategic weaponry to try to overcome their opponents.

Germany's overall war strategy was dictated by Hitler's insistence on total victory, which worked well when its land forces achieved rapid success. However, this was not possible on all fronts. The Luftwaffe's attempts to knock Britain out of the war through the Battle of Britain (see pp.232–33) and the subsequent Blitz failed due to Britain's growing relative strength in the air. By 1942, British bombers were wreaking far greater havoc on German cities, and as they were joined by increasing numbers of US planes, Germany was forced to divert more and more scarce aircraft and guns from frontlines elsewhere to defend the homeland against increasingly heavy Allied bombing raids.

△ **Allied retaliation**
This poster declares "the enemy sees your light," a warning to German civilians to maintain blackout to prevent Allied bombers from identifying their targets.

The U-boat war

The submarine campaign, led by German naval commander Karl Dönitz, was more effective, striking Atlantic convoys supplying Britain and the USSR. The U-boat fleet sank 2,600 Allied merchant ships, nearly bringing Britain to its knees. However, the tide turned after May 1943, thanks in part to US B-24 Liberators, whose long range could reach the "Atlantic Gap" where Allied convoys previously lacked air cover. Intelligence from British code-breakers reduced the strategic impact of the U-boats. The loss of French ports after the D-Day landings in 1944 (see pp.248–49) further neutralized the U-boats and swung the strategic advantage even more in the Allies' favor.

△ **B-24 Liberator bombers**
The B-24s' range allowed them to cover large swaths of the Atlantic for the first time. They helped dominate the U-boats after 1943 and also the Allied bombing of Germany itself.

Strangling Allied supply lines
A German submarine commander peers through the periscope during an Atlantic patrol in December 1939, when the U-boat campaign was just getting underway.

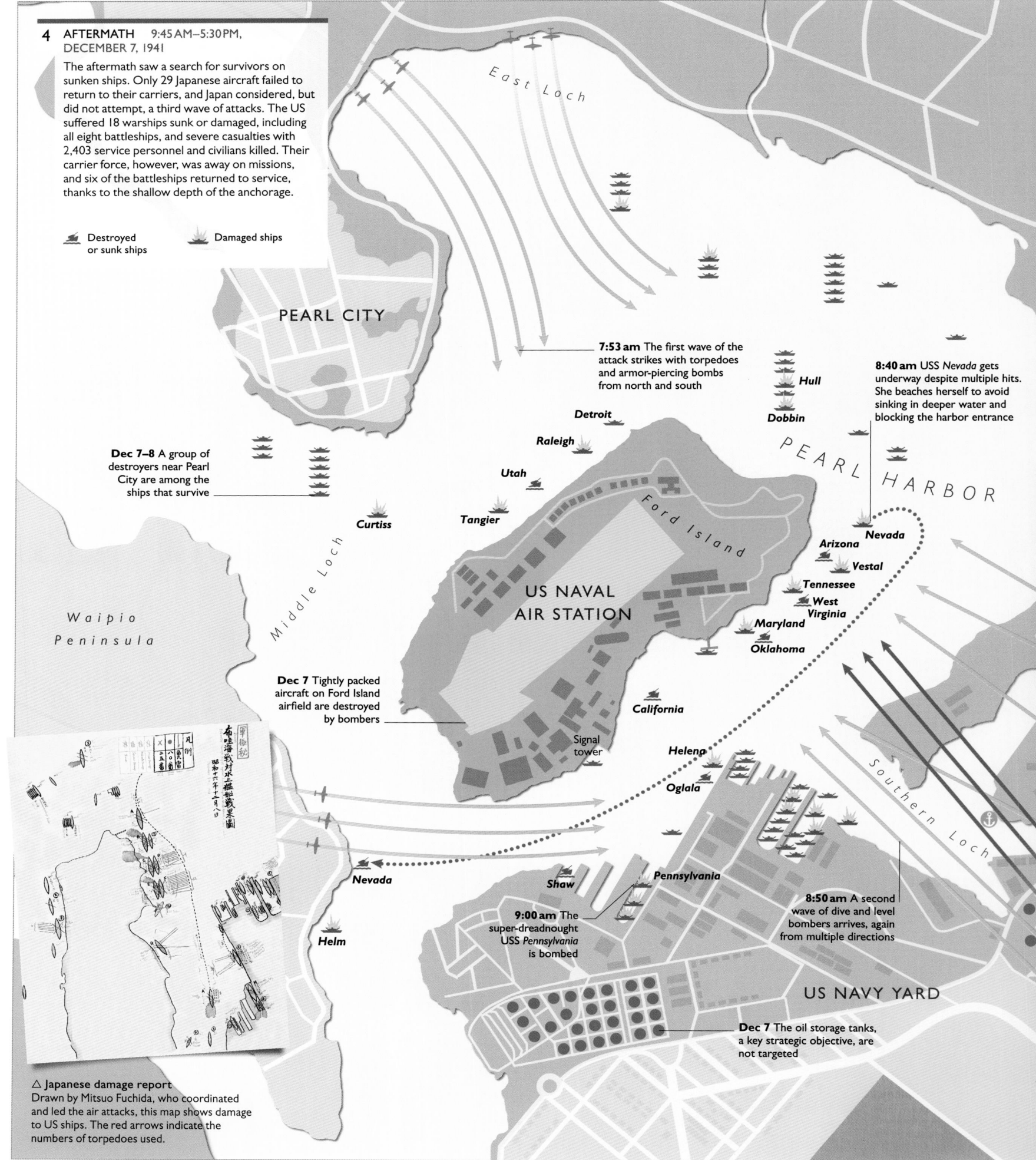

4 AFTERMATH 9:45 AM–5:30 PM, DECEMBER 7, 1941

The aftermath saw a search for survivors on sunken ships. Only 29 Japanese aircraft failed to return to their carriers, and Japan considered, but did not attempt, a third wave of attacks. The US suffered 18 warships sunk or damaged, including all eight battleships, and severe casualties with 2,403 service personnel and civilians killed. Their carrier force, however, was away on missions, and six of the battleships returned to service, thanks to the shallow depth of the anchorage.

Destroyed or sunk ships

Damaged ships

PEARL CITY

East Loch

Dec 7–8 A group of destroyers near Pearl City are among the ships that survive

7:53 am The first wave of the attack strikes with torpedoes and armor-piercing bombs from north and south

Hull

Dobbin

Detroit

Raleigh

Utah

8:40 am USS *Nevada* gets underway despite multiple hits. She beaches herself to avoid sinking in deeper water and blocking the harbor entrance

PEARL HARBOR

Curtiss

Tangier

Ford Island

Nevada

Arizona

Vestal

Tennessee

West Virginia

Maryland

Oklahoma

Waipio Peninsula

Middle Loch

US NAVAL AIR STATION

Dec 7 Tightly packed aircraft on Ford Island airfield are destroyed by bombers

California

Signal tower

Helena

Oglala

Southern Loch

Nevada

Shaw

Pennsylvania

8:50 am A second wave of dive and level bombers arrives, again from multiple directions

9:00 am The super-dreadnought USS *Pennsylvania* is bombed

Helm

US NAVY YARD

Dec 7 The oil storage tanks, a key strategic objective, are not targeted

△ **Japanese damage report**
Drawn by Mitsuo Fuchida, who coordinated and led the air attacks, this map shows damage to US ships. The red arrows indicate the numbers of torpedoes used.

DANGER FROM THE AIR

The Japanese Striking Force left Japan on November 26 and assembled north of Hawaii. The first attacks came at 7:53 am on December 7, and the second wave at 8:50 am. The US declared war on Japan the following day.

🛩 US ships at anchor or moored   ▮ Ford Island naval and air station

TIMELINE

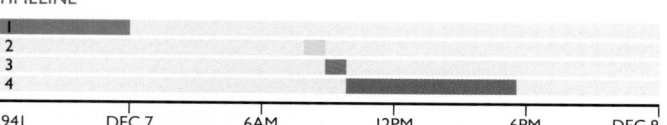

| 1941 | DEC 7 | 6AM | 12PM | 6PM | DEC 8 |

'Aiea Bay

1 THE APPROACH   NOVEMBER 26–DECEMBER 7, 1941

A Japanese naval task force including six aircraft carriers set off from the Kuril Islands in northern Japan on November 26. Keeping strict radio silence, it sailed undetected to a position 250 miles (400km) north of Hawaii, where its first wave of attack aircraft was launched at dawn on December 7. As relations with Japan were at breaking point, the US forces at Pearl Harbor should have been on alert, but instead they were enjoying a relaxed Sunday morning when the first Japanese aircraft arrived.

8:00 am A wave of Japanese bombers target anchored US battleships, sinking the USS *Arizona*, *California*, *Oklahoma*, and *West Virginia*, and hitting the *Nevada*

2 DEVASTATING BLOWS   7:55–8:50 AM, DECEMBER 7, 1941

The first wave consisted of 183 aircraft—Nakajima "Kate" level bombers and Aichi "Val" dive bombers, escorted by Mitsubishi "Zero" fighters. While the Vals and Zeros attacked US airfields and airborne planes, destroying half of the 400 US aircraft on the island, the Kates devastated US warships with torpedoes and armor-piercing bombs. Although the damage was severe, the Japanese failed to target important oil tanks and the submarine base.

+→ First-wave attacks   ⚓ Submarine base   ● Oil tanks

3 FOLLOW-UP ATTACK   8:50–9:45 AM, DECEMBER 7, 1941

A second wave of 170 Japanese carrier aircraft arrived from 8:50 am, meeting stiffer resistance from the alerted US antiaircraft defenses, and proved less devastating. USS *Nevada*, the only battleship to successfully mobilize, was hit six times by dive-bombers and beached to avoid sinking. The flagship USS *Pennsylvania*, in dry dock, survived bombing that wrecked two destroyers alongside it. Attacks by a small number of midget submarines in the harbor were ineffective.

+→ Second-wave attacks   •••→ Route of USS *Nevada*

PEARL HARBOR

The Japanese air attack on the American naval base at Pearl Harbor, Hawaii, on December 7, 1941, brought the US into World War II. Brilliantly executed by Japan's carrier fleet, the raid took a heavy toll of American warships and began a brief period of runaway Japanese victories.

Japan's leaders nurtured ambitions to create an empire in Asia. In 1937, they embarked on a war of conquest in China, and from 1940 they began encroaching on European colonies in Southeast Asia. The US was alarmed by this expansionism, especially after Japan allied itself with Nazi Germany. To force Japan to halt its military adventures, the US eventually imposed a crippling economic blockade. Unwilling to abandon their bid for empire, Japan planned to go to war with the US.

The Japanese knew that, in the long run, they could not match American manpower or industrial strength. They gambled instead on winning swift victories that would give them a tactical stronghold in Asia and the Pacific: as well as Pearl Harbor, their forces attacked other targets including the Philippines, Hong Kong, and Malaya. The suprise raid at Pearl Harbor was launched before a declaration of war; it outraged the American public and shattered US isolationism.

On December 11, German leader Adolf Hitler declared war on the US in support of Japan, and the lines were drawn for a truly global conflict. The Pearl Harbor attack succeeded in buying Japan time for its conquest of Southeast Asia, but it missed the US's aircraft carriers, which were not in port at the time and soon led the fight back. The slogan "Remember Pearl Harbor" inspired the US to strive for total victory over Japan.

"The moment has arrived. The rise or fall of our empire is at stake..."

ADMIRAL YAMAMOTO, MESSAGE TO THE JAPANESE FLEET, DECEMBER 7, 1941

ADMIRAL ISOROKU YAMAMOTO 1884–1943

The architect of the Pearl Harbor attack was Admiral Isoroku Yamamoto. Born Isoroku Takano, he lost two fingers fighting at the battle of Tsushima in 1905 (see p.205). Adopted by the Yamamoto samurai family in 1916, he studied at Harvard in the US and was twice naval attaché in Washington, gaining a great respect for the country. As an admiral in the 1930s, he became an advocate of naval aviation. Commander of the Combined Fleet from 1939, he regretted war with the US, but the strike on Pearl Harbor was his conception. He was killed when his aircraft was ambushed over New Guinea in April 1943.

Admiral Yamamoto in 1942

MIDWAY

At Midway Island, the Imperial Japanese Navy hoped to defeat the remnants of the US Pacific Fleet in its biggest operation in World War II. Instead, Japan suffered a naval defeat that cemented the importance of aircraft carriers in dominating the seas.

The US's aircraft carriers survived Japan's raid on Pearl Harbor (see pp.236–37) and, as General MacArthur led the fightback in the Pacific in spring 1942, they became pivotal. This was proven when bombers from the USS *Hornet* bombed Japanese cities in April 1942, and when US and Japanese carriers engaged at Coral Sea in May 1942. As a result, the commander-in-chief of the Japanese fleet, Admiral Isoroku Yamamoto, aimed to destroy the US's carriers.

The island of Midway was the most westerly US base in the central Pacific. After luring part of the US fleet north with an attack on the Aleutian Islands, Yamamoto hoped to draw the US carrier fleet by attacking Midway. However, the US had cracked the Japanese cipher, JN-25, and knew of the plan. US admiral

Chester Nimitz sent a force with three aircraft carriers northeast of Midway to wait for the Japanese.

The battle began early on June 4 when Japanese bombers raided the island. As they refueled aboard their carriers, US dive bombers struck. Four Japanese carriers were damaged, two sank and two were scuttled. The Japanese managed to fatally damage the USS *Yorktown* before their last aircraft carrier, *Hiryū*, was crippled. The US victory marked the end of Japan's dominance in the Pacific.

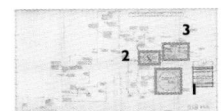

LOCATOR

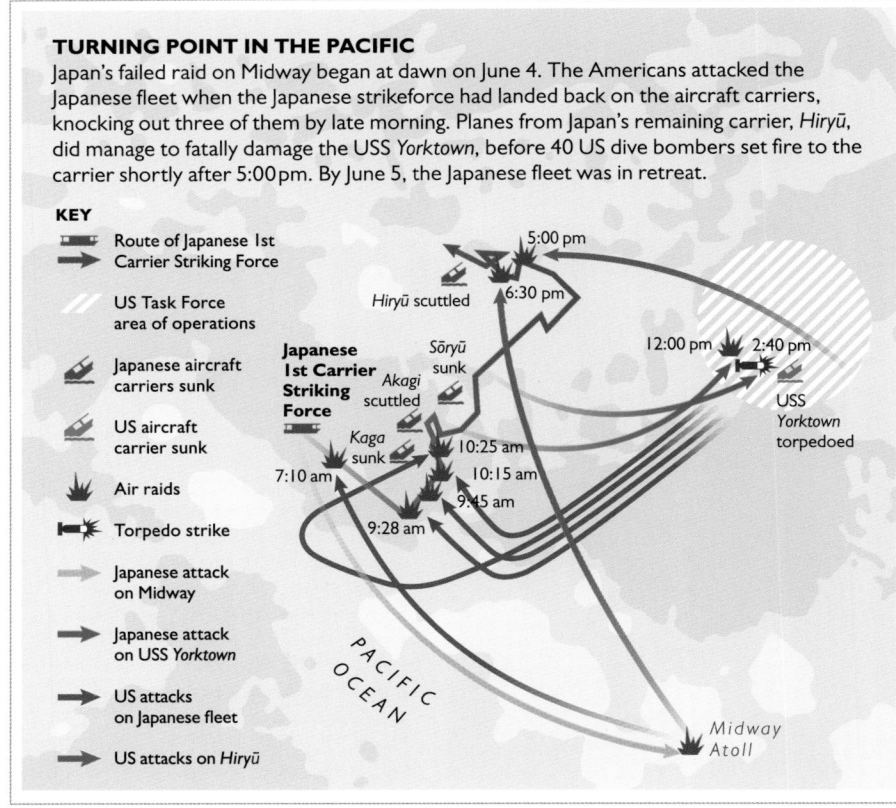

TURNING POINT IN THE PACIFIC

Japan's failed raid on Midway began at dawn on June 4. The Americans attacked the Japanese fleet when the Japanese strikeforce had landed back on the aircraft carriers, knocking out three of them by late morning. Planes from Japan's remaining carrier, *Hiryū*, did manage to fatally damage the USS *Yorktown*, before 40 US dive bombers set fire to the carrier shortly after 5:00pm. By June 5, the Japanese fleet was in retreat.

KEY

- Route of Japanese 1st Carrier Striking Force
- US Task Force area of operations
- Japanese aircraft carriers sunk
- US aircraft carrier sunk
- Air raids
- Torpedo strike
- Japanese attack on Midway
- Japanese attack on USS *Yorktown*
- US attacks on Japanese fleet
- US attacks on *Hiryū*

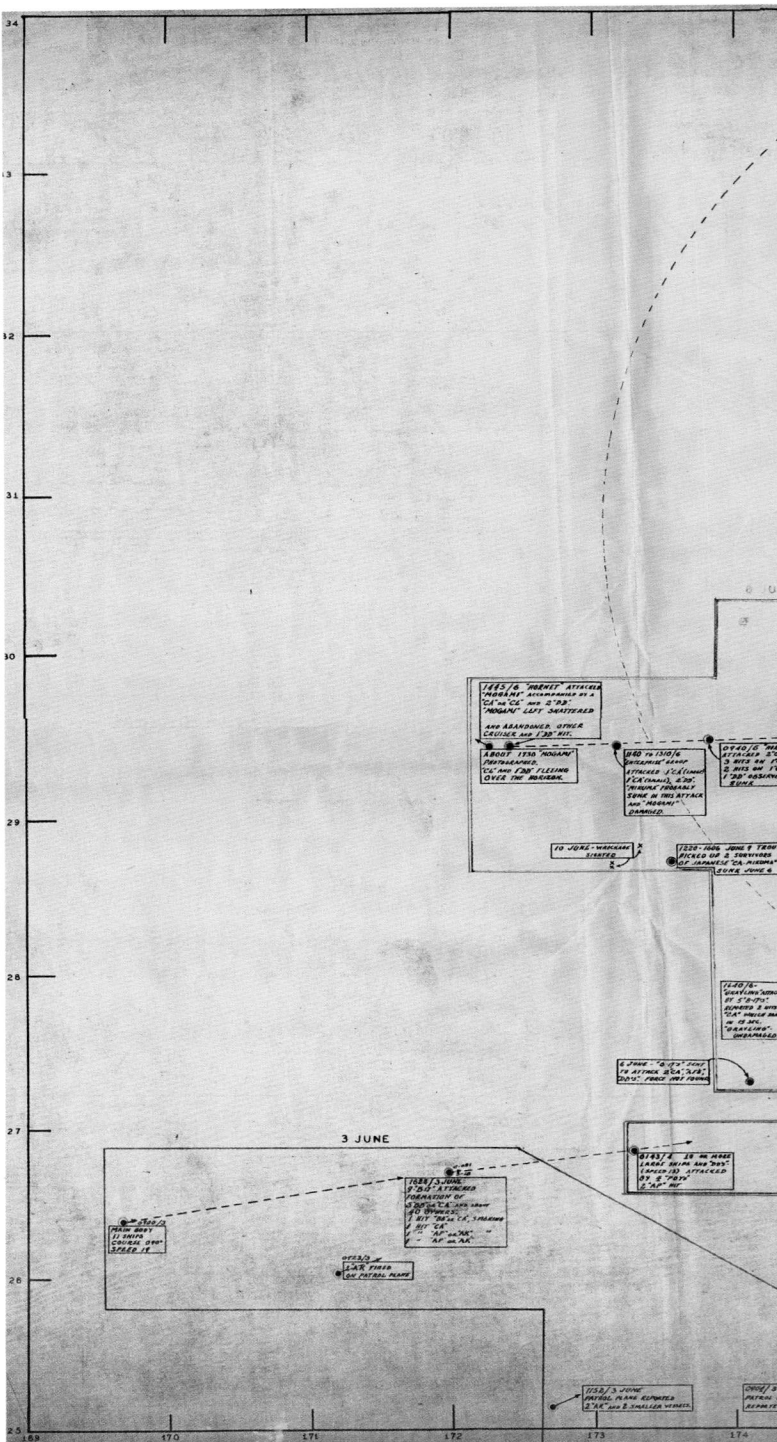

△ **Mid-ocean maneuvers**
Covering movements on June 3–6, 1942, this map shows the vast area over which the battle was fought and the radical changes in direction made by the Japanese fleet as it came under attack.

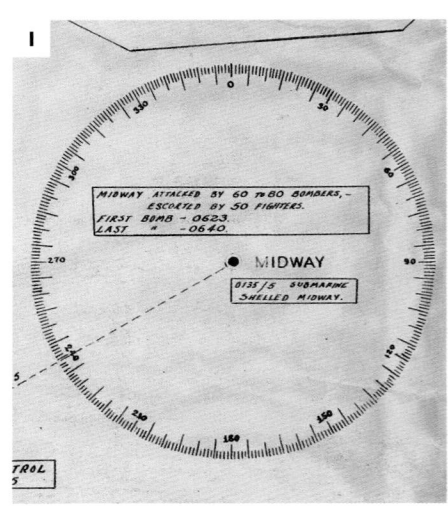

▷ **A fierce encounter**
At dawn on June 4, Japan's 1st Carrier Striking Force sent 108 aircraft to attack Midway. The raiders were intercepted and about one-third destroyed or damaged by US fighters and anti-aircraft fire from the island.

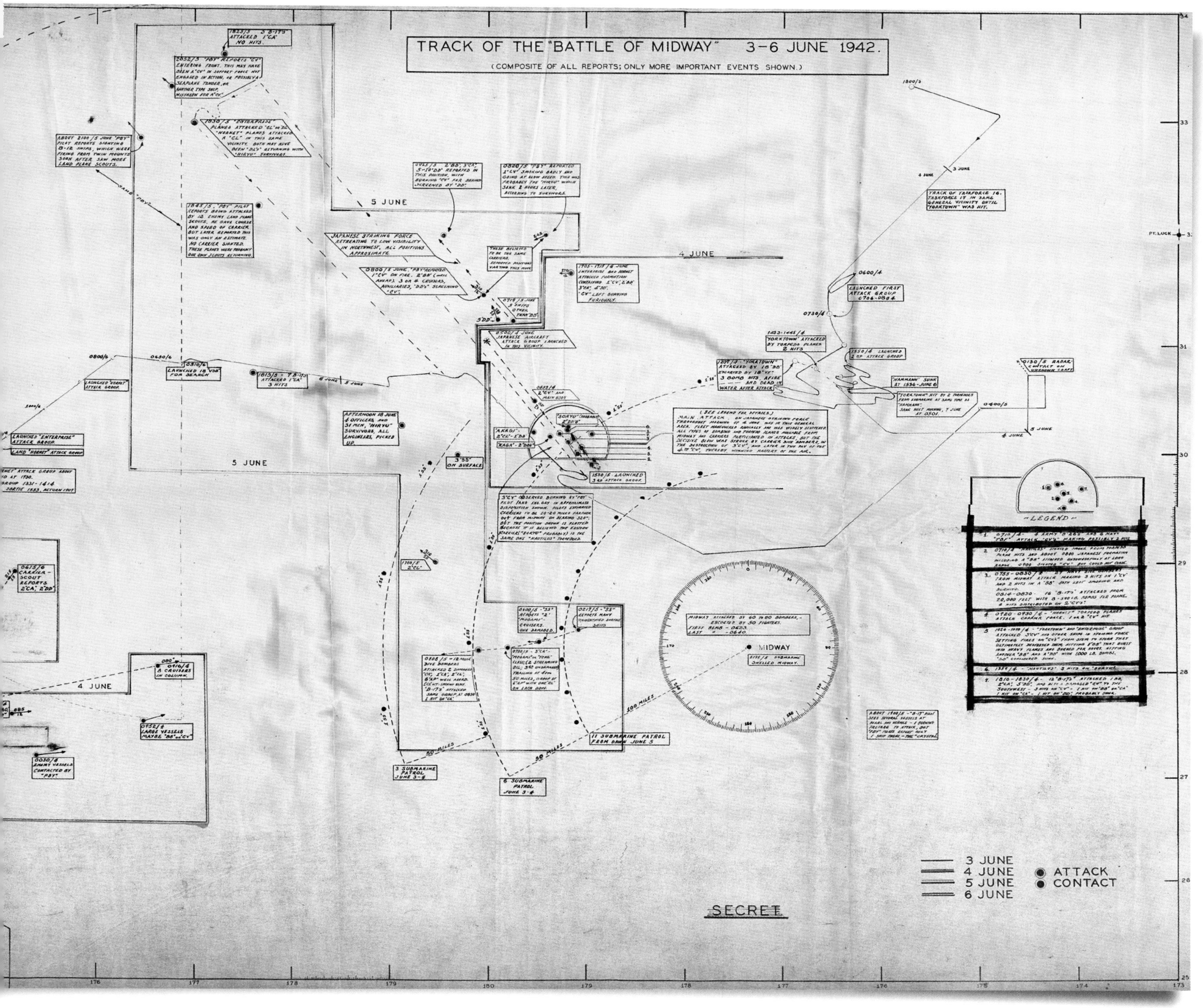

TRACK OF THE "BATTLE OF MIDWAY" 3-6 JUNE 1942.
(COMPOSITE OF ALL REPORTS; ONLY MORE IMPORTANT EVENTS SHOWN.)

SECRET

			ATTACK
———	3 JUNE	●	CONTACT
————	4 JUNE		
————	5 JUNE		
————	6 JUNE		

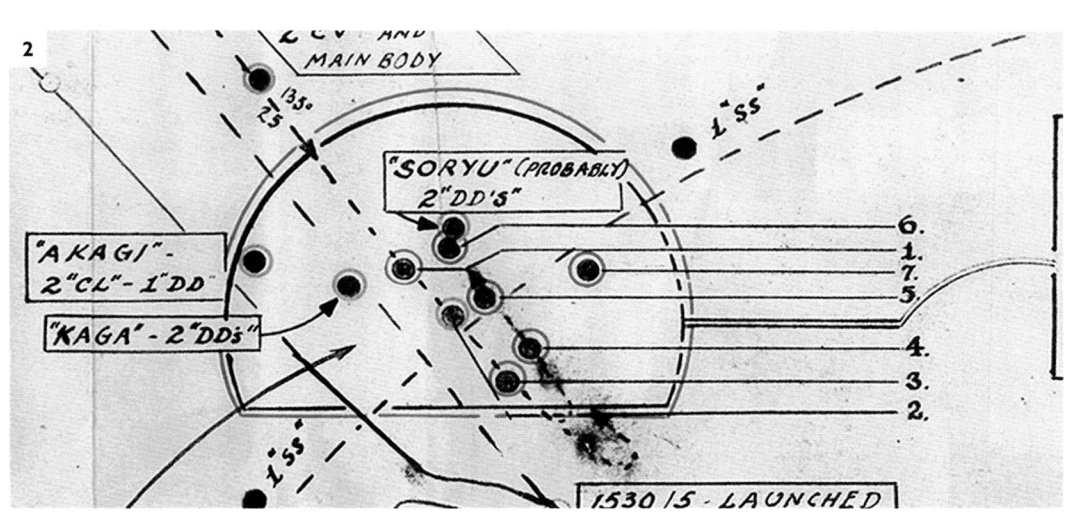

2

◁ **US forces pounce**
Bombing aircraft from the
US carriers and from Midway
scattered the Japanese fleet and
damaged Japanese ships including
the carriers *Kaga* and *Sōryū*, and
the flagship *Akagi*.

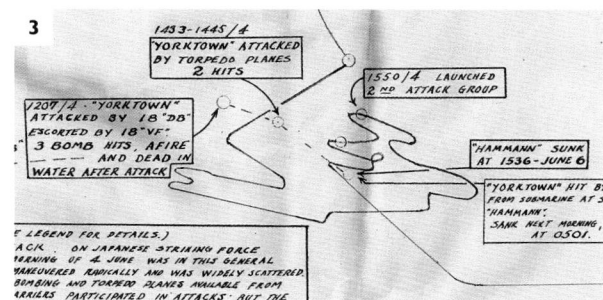

3

△ **Japan's final flourish**
Planes from the *Hiryū* broke
through the US fighters to
bomb USS *Yorktown* at around
noon. Hit again by torpedo
planes, *Yorktown* finally sank
on June 7.

Preparing to land
Two Curtiss SB2C-3 Helldiver dive-bombers
prepare to land on the USS *Hornet* after an
anti-ship strike in January 1945. Nicknamed
"the Beast," the Helldiver was the last dedicated
operational dive-bomber of the US Navy.

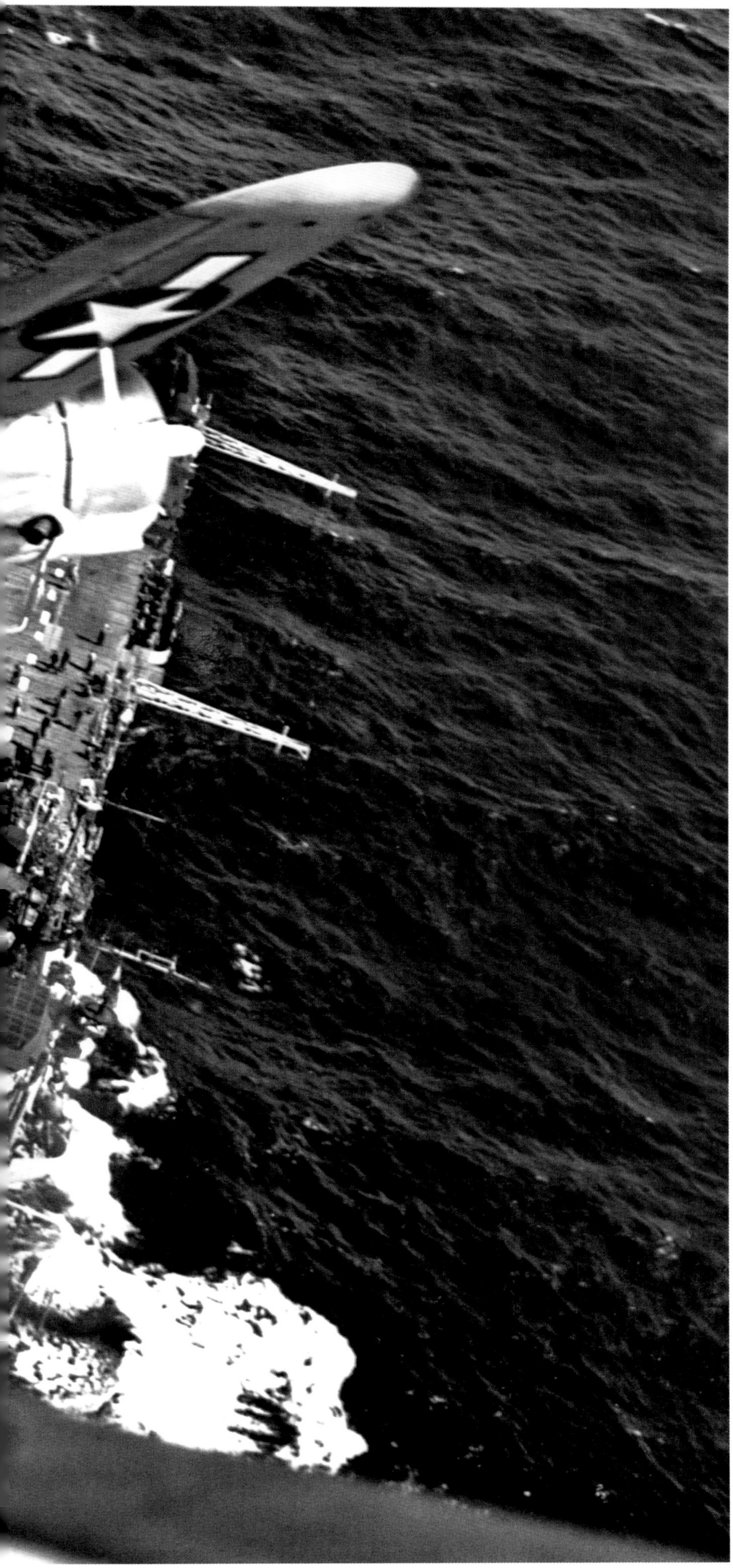

CARRIER WARFARE

Aircraft carriers and carrier planes made their first appearance in war in 1918. However, it was World War II that made them an essential part of modern warfare, transforming the way naval battles were fought.

By 1939, Japan, Britain, and the US, separated by sea from potential adversaries, had recognized the utility of aircraft carriers and fielded significant carrier fleets. Other naval powers such as France, Italy, Germany, and the USSR prioritized land-based aircraft and did not create significant carrier forces during the conflict.

Despite its popularity, carrier warfare remained in its infancy during World War II, and navies gained practical experience of carrier combat by trial and error. Aircraft carriers became essential auxiliary vessels in European waters; however, in the Pacific Ocean, they reigned supreme. US–Japan carrier battles in 1942 at Coral Sea, Midway (see pp.238–39), the Eastern Solomons, and Santa Cruz became part of naval folklore. Although carriers were more vulnerable to attack than heavily armored battleships, their speed and aircraft range allowed them to strike without coming into range of battleships' guns.

After World War II, aircraft carriers thrived due to their flexibility in deploying military force overseas, and projecting air power inland beyond the range of conventional naval shore bombardment. Conflicts in Korea (1950–53), the Suez Canal (1956), Vietnam (1964–73), the Falkland Islands (1982), and during Operation Desert Storm (see pp.266–67) all bore witness to the power of aircraft carriers.

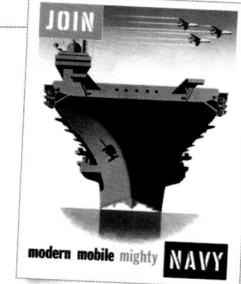

△ **Call for recruitment**
Three F-8 Crusader jets fly over a US Navy carrier in this recruitment poster from 1957. Aircraft carriers became the US Navy's *raison d'être* after 1945.

△ **Modern carrier**
The USS *John C. Stennis* (CVN-74) sails through the Arabian Sea during a naval deployment in 2007. Part of her air wing can be seen on the deck, while an SH-60F Seahawk helicopter takes flight.

SECOND BATTLE OF EL ALAMEIN

The Allied victory at El Alamein in the fall of 1942 was a major turning point in the fighting in the north African desert in World War II. Through a meticulously prepared, large-scale offensive, the British Eighth Army put German and Italian forces to flight, finally deciding the back-and-forth contest for north Africa.

From 1941, German general Erwin Rommel achieved notable victories over the British in north Africa in tank warfare. In July 1942, his Panzerarmee Afrika, advancing east into Egypt, was halted by the British at El Alamein, about 60 miles (100km) from the port of Alexandria. The next month, General Bernard Montgomery took command of Eighth Army, with orders to take the offensive. Montgomery was a cautious commander, and concentrated on building up his army's materiel and morale. While the Eighth Army grew in strength, adding new Sherman tanks, Rommel's forces faced growing supply problems and lacked reinforcements. An Axis attack from August 30 was defeated at Alam Halfa ridge. Rommel switched to static defense, fortifying his line with minefields and anti-tank guns.

Outnumbering Rommel's forces by nearly two to one, Montgomery engaged the Axis army in an attritional contest. After 12 days of costly fighting, Rommel retreated. Montgomery pursued the fleeing Axis troops west across Libya. Meanwhile, US and Allied forces had landed in Algeria and Morocco. Caught between the Eighth Army and these new Allied forces, the Axis forces surrendered in Tunisia in May 1943.

> *"This is not the end. It is not even the beginning of the end. But it is, perhaps, the end of the beginning."*
>
> WINSTON CHURCHILL ON SECOND EL ALAMEIN, 1942

MARSHAL ERWIN ROMMEL 1891–1944

Known as the "Desert Fox," Rommel was by training an infantry officer, serving with distinction in World War I. In 1937, he published a book on infantry tactics that attracted Hitler's attention. Enjoying the Führer's favor, he was given command of an armored division for the invasion of France in 1940. He proved to be a success in this role and was sent to lead a German panzer force in north Africa—the Afrika Korps. Repeated victories in the Desert War raised his prestige to new heights. Recalled to Europe, he was placed in charge of the Atlantic Wall defenses breached by the Allies on D-Day (see pp.248–49). After being implicated in a failed assassination attempt on Hitler in July 1944, he killed himself to shield his family from reprisals.

DESERT CONFRONTATION

The rival forces faced up along a 40-mile (60-km) line south from El Alamein on the coast to the impassable Qattara Depression. The only way the battle could be fought was as a frontal assault.

KEY

ALLIED FORCES

British	New Zealand	Indian
Australian	Greek	South African

AXIS FORCES

German	Italian

ALLIED TERRITORY

On Oct 23	By Oct 29	By Nov 2	By Nov 4

TIMELINE

1
2
3

OCT 15, 1942   NOV 1   NOV 15

---

2 CRUMBLING THE DEFENSES
OCTOBER 25–NOVEMBER 1, 1942

Rommel returned from sick leave on October 25. He moved his panzer divisions to counterattack, but fuel shortages limited his ability to maneuver. Fiercest fighting occurred around Kidney Ridge and at the northern end of the line, where Australian troops pushed toward the coast road. Although Axis defenses held, it was at a cost they could not sustain. Meanwhile, Montgomery prepared a new offensive—Operation Supercharge.

Allied amphibious feint attack	Axis movement

E

G

Y

3 BREAKING THROUGH   NOVEMBER 2–4, 1942

After another massive night-time artillery barrage, British infantry armored forces attacked toward Tel el Aqqaqir. Rommel counterattacked in a large-scale tank battle that left more than a hundred German tanks destroyed. On November 3, Rommel ordered a general retreat, only to be overruled by Hitler. The next night, Indian troops broke through at Kidney Ridge and the Axis position became untenable. The remnants of Rommel's force escaped to the west.

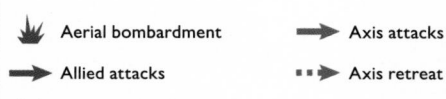

Aerial bombardment	Axis attacks
Allied attacks	Axis retreat
Major engagements	

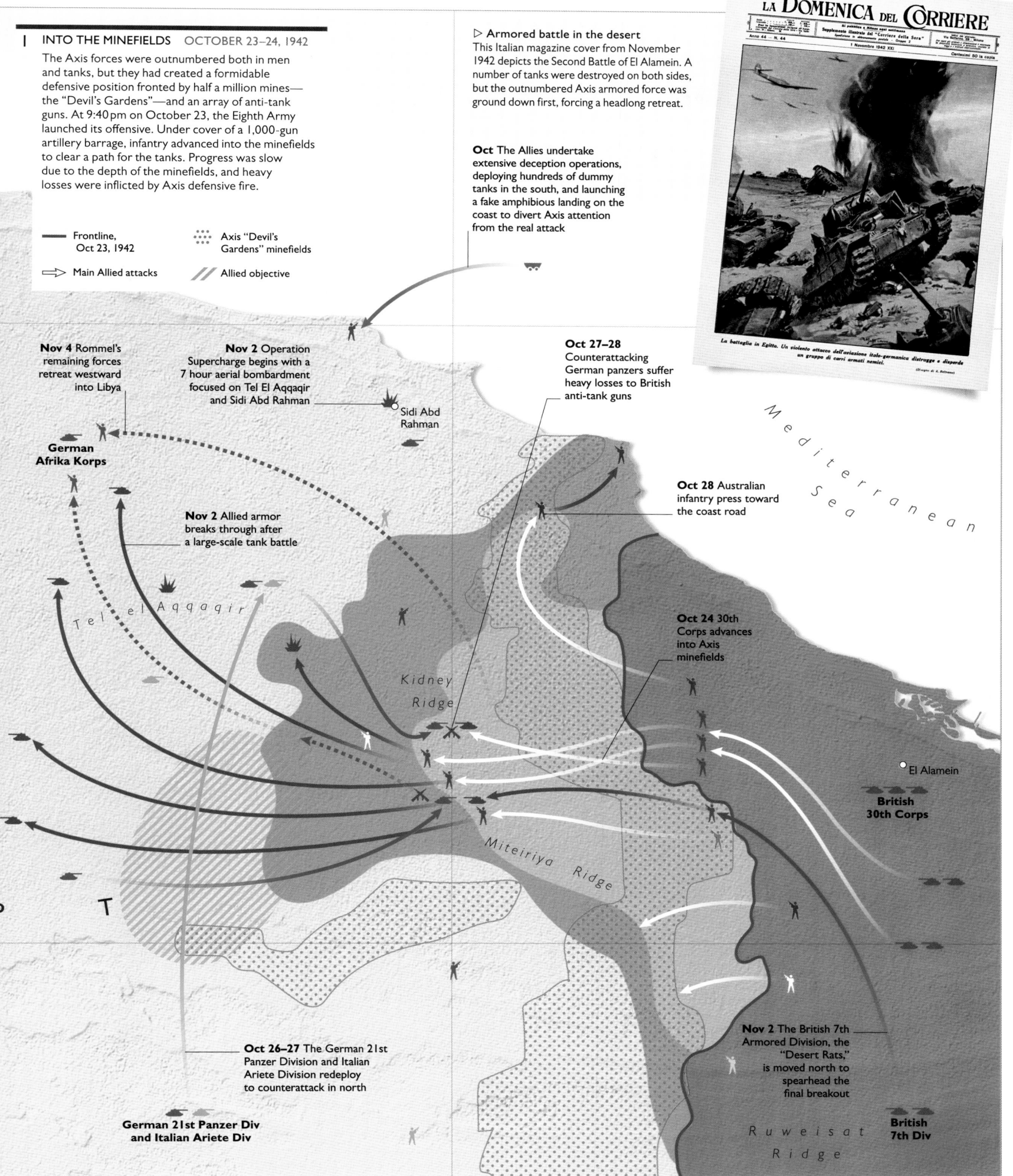

INTO THE MINEFIELDS OCTOBER 23–24, 1942

The Axis forces were outnumbered both in men and tanks, but they had created a formidable defensive position fronted by half a million mines—the "Devil's Gardens"—and an array of anti-tank guns. At 9:40 pm on October 23, the Eighth Army launched its offensive. Under cover of a 1,000-gun artillery barrage, infantry advanced into the minefields to clear a path for the tanks. Progress was slow due to the depth of the minefields, and heavy losses were inflicted by Axis defensive fire.

— Frontline, Oct 23, 1942

⋯⋯ Axis "Devil's Gardens" minefields

⟹ Main Allied attacks

⫽ Allied objective

▷ **Armored battle in the desert**
This Italian magazine cover from November 1942 depicts the Second Battle of El Alamein. A number of tanks were destroyed on both sides, but the outnumbered Axis armored force was ground down first, forcing a headlong retreat.

Oct The Allies undertake extensive deception operations, deploying hundreds of dummy tanks in the south, and launching a fake amphibious landing on the coast to divert Axis attention from the real attack

Nov 4 Rommel's remaining forces retreat westward into Libya

Nov 2 Operation Supercharge begins with a 7 hour aerial bombardment focused on Tel El Aqqaqir and Sidi Abd Rahman

Sidi Abd Rahman

German Afrika Korps

Nov 2 Allied armor breaks through after a large-scale tank battle

Tel el Aqqaqir

Oct 27–28 Counterattacking German panzers suffer heavy losses to British anti-tank guns

Oct 28 Australian infantry press toward the coast road

Oct 24 30th Corps advances into Axis minefields

Mediterranean Sea

Kidney Ridge

El Alamein

British 30th Corps

Miteiriya Ridge

P T

Oct 26–27 The German 21st Panzer Division and Italian Ariete Division redeploy to counterattack in north

German 21st Panzer Div and Italian Ariete Div

Nov 2 The British 7th Armored Division, the "Desert Rats," is moved north to spearhead the final breakout

Ruweisat Ridge

British 7th Div

LA DOMENICA DEL CORRIERE

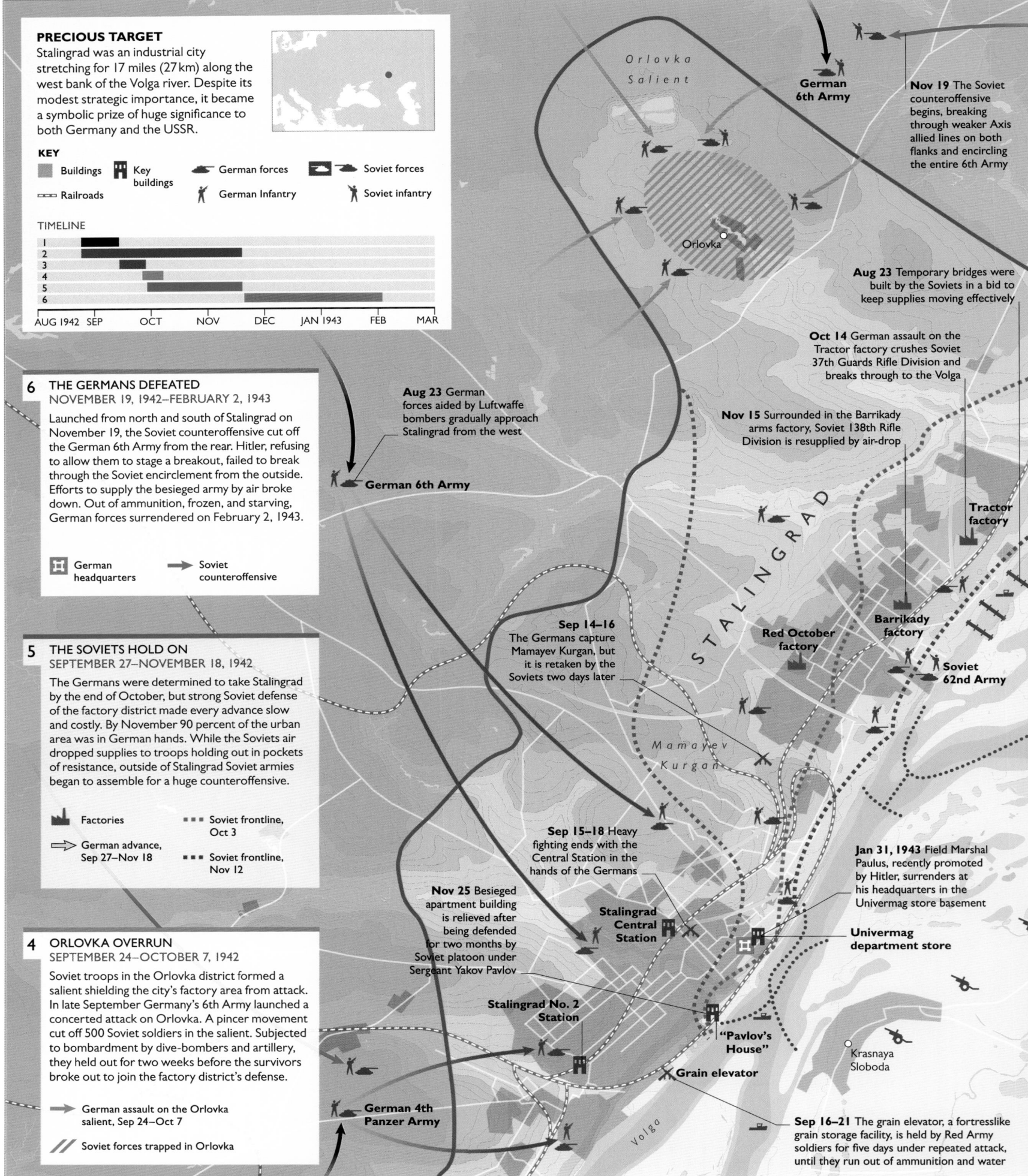

PRECIOUS TARGET

Stalingrad was an industrial city stretching for 17 miles (27km) along the west bank of the Volga river. Despite its modest strategic importance, it became a symbolic prize of huge significance to both Germany and the USSR.

KEY

Buildings
Railroads
Key buildings
German forces
German Infantry
Soviet forces
Soviet infantry

TIMELINE

1
2
3
4
5
6

AUG 1942 SEP OCT NOV DEC JAN 1943 FEB MAR

6 THE GERMANS DEFEATED

NOVEMBER 19, 1942–FEBRUARY 2, 1943

Launched from north and south of Stalingrad on November 19, the Soviet counteroffensive cut off the German 6th Army from the rear. Hitler, refusing to allow them to stage a breakout, failed to break through the Soviet encirclement from the outside. Efforts to supply the besieged army by air broke down. Out of ammunition, frozen, and starving, German forces surrendered on February 2, 1943.

German headquarters
Soviet counteroffensive

5 THE SOVIETS HOLD ON

SEPTEMBER 27–NOVEMBER 18, 1942

The Germans were determined to take Stalingrad by the end of October, but strong Soviet defense of the factory district made every advance slow and costly. By November 90 percent of the urban area was in German hands. While the Soviets air dropped supplies to troops holding out in pockets of resistance, outside of Stalingrad Soviet armies began to assemble for a huge counteroffensive.

Factories
German advance, Sep 27–Nov 18
Soviet frontline, Oct 3
Soviet frontline, Nov 12

4 ORLOVKA OVERRUN

SEPTEMBER 24–OCTOBER 7, 1942

Soviet troops in the Orlovka district formed a salient shielding the city's factory area from attack. In late September Germany's 6th Army launched a concerted attack on Orlovka. A pincer movement cut off 500 Soviet soldiers in the salient. Subjected to bombardment by dive-bombers and artillery, they held out for two weeks before the survivors broke out to join the factory district's defense.

German assault on the Orlovka salient, Sep 24–Oct 7
Soviet forces trapped in Orlovka

Orlovka Salient

Orlovka

German 6th Army

Nov 19 The Soviet counteroffensive begins, breaking through weaker Axis allied lines on both flanks and encircling the entire 6th Army

Aug 23 Temporary bridges were built by the Soviets in a bid to keep supplies moving effectively

Oct 14 German assault on the Tractor factory crushes Soviet 37th Guards Rifle Division and breaks through to the Volga

Nov 15 Surrounded in the Barrikady arms factory, Soviet 138th Rifle Division is resupplied by air-drop

Tractor factory

Aug 23 German forces aided by Luftwaffe bombers gradually approach Stalingrad from the west

German 6th Army

Barrikady factory

Red October factory

S T A L I N G R A D

Soviet 62nd Army

Sep 14–16 The Germans capture Mamayev Kurgan, but it is retaken by the Soviets two days later

Mamayev Kurgan

Jan 31, 1943 Field Marshal Paulus, recently promoted by Hitler, surrenders at his headquarters in the Univermag store basement

Sep 15–18 Heavy fighting ends with the Central Station in the hands of the Germans

Nov 25 Besieged apartment building is relieved after being defended for two months by Soviet platoon under Sergeant Yakov Pavlov

Stalingrad Central Station

Univermag department store

Stalingrad No. 2 Station

"Pavlov's House"

Grain elevator

Krasnaya Sloboda

German 4th Panzer Army

Sep 16–21 The grain elevator, a fortresslike grain storage facility, is held by Red Army soldiers for five days under repeated attack, until they run out of ammunition and water

Volga

Rynok

A city in ruins
Soviet soldiers pick through the wreckage of central Stalingrad in the battle's aftermath. The siege ultimately left its city ravaged and its population decimated.

1 THE CITY IN RUINS
AUGUST 23–SEPTEMBER 13, 1942

As German troops approached Stalingrad on August 23, Luftwaffe bombers began a week of intensive raids on the city that reduced buildings to rubble and caused heavy civilian casualties. General Friedrich Paulus's 6th Army closed on the city from the west, supported by General Hermann Hoth's 4th Panzer Army in the south.

→ German advance, Aug 23–Sep 13

▆ German-held territory by Sep 13, 1942

— Soviet frontline, Sep 13

2 DEFENDING STALINGRAD
AUGUST 23–NOVEMBER 18, 1942

Stalingrad was defended by Soviet 62nd and 64th armies aided by workers' militias—lightly armed factory workers. Supplies and reinforcements moved across the Volga from the Soviet-held east bank via small boats or temporary bridges. Chuikov ordered them to "hug" the enemy, keeping so close the Germans could not mount air or artillery strikes for fear of hitting their own troops. Key buildings were turned into fortresses surrounded by minefields and barbed wire.

⚔ Artillery belt

⊬⊢⊣ Temporary bridge

•••• Supply lines

⛴ Ferry crossing

Stalingrad Front

1942 The Stalingrad Front comprises several armies

3 FIGHTING STREET BY STREET
SEPTEMBER 13–27, 1942

On September 13 Germany began a major drive into the center of the city. Key locations such as the Central Station and the dominant hill of Mamayev Kurgan changed hands many times. Soviet snipers concealed amid the ruins recorded spectacularly high numbers of kills. The Soviet troops suffered even heavier losses than the Germans, however, with many displaying self-sacrificial bravery and others executed for allegedly breaching Stalin's order of "not a step back."

→ German advances, Sep 13–27

▪▪▪ Soviet frontline, Sep 27

✗ Sites of key battles

THE SIEGE OF STALINGRAD

Begun in the late summer of 1942, the five-month battle of Stalingrad halted the relentless progress of Axis forces invading the Soviet Union. Fiercely defended by Soviet troops and civilians alike, the city turned into a death trap for the German 6th Army.

By late summer 1942, German armies had seized the Crimea and penetrated the Caucasus, threatening the main Soviet source of oil supplies. Germany did not anticipate the capture of Stalingrad to pose a serious problem. Soviet dictator Joseph Stalin, however, soon prioritized the city's defense. After Luftwaffe bombing of Stalingrad began in late August, invading German ground forces in September met a city-wide fight raging from street to street, house to house, and even in the sewers; Germany dubbed the battle *Rattenkrieg* ("Rat war"). Both sides threw increasing resources into the battle.

While Soviet troops maintained a stubborn defense pressed back into small pockets along the west bank of the Volga, Stalin's most gifted general Georgy Zhukov prepared a masterly counteroffensive that cut off the German army from its supply lines to the rear. By the time the encircled Germans surrendered in February 1943, both sides had incurred vast losses. Germany's defeat at Stalingrad—the single largest in its army's history—marked a turning point in the war.

> *"There is only one way to hold the city, we must pay in lives. Time is blood!"*
>
> GENERAL VASILY CHUIKOV, SEPTEMBER 1942

VASILY CHUIKOV 1900–1982

Commander of the Soviet forces at Stalingrad, Vasily Ivanovich Chuikov was of peasant origin. He rose to be an officer through fighting on the revolutionary side in the Russian Civil War (1918–20). Sent to organize the defense of Stalingrad in September 1942, Chuikov brought a ruthless energy to the task, not hesitating to have his own soldiers shot if they showed signs of wavering. The defense of Stalingrad made him a Soviet hero. In spring 1945 he led Eighth Guards Army in the capture of Berlin. He was made a Marshal of the Soviet Union in 1955.

TANKS IN WORLD WAR II

Tanks underwent rapid technological development during the course of World War II. Initially small and often underpowered and under-armed, by 1945 they had become massive, heavily armored beasts.

△ General Heinz Guderian
Guderian's methods of mobile armored warfare played a major role in Germany's early victories in World War II.

In 1939, the warring nations fielded an array of specialized tanks for specific roles. Lightly armored tanks were used for reconnaissance, fast tanks with medium armor carried out the cavalry's traditional role as shock troops, the heavier machines provided infantry support, and the heaviest ones were used to break through enemy fortifications.

The belligerents based their theories of armored warfare on a mix of lessons learned in the later years of World War I (1917–18), the Spanish Civil War (1936–39), and the Second Sino–Japanese War (1937–45). Two main schools of thought emerged. In France, the meticulously planned "methodical battle" had armored vehicles in rigid infantry support and reconnaissance roles. In Germany, however, some theorists proposed flexible, highly mobile, entirely motorized formations spearheaded by tanks.

The stunning German victory over the Western Allies in the spring of 1940 seemingly vindicated Germany's theorists, and at the same time exposed weaknesses in existing tank designs. By the following year, each country was racing to improve speed, armor, armament, and reliability. Germany focused its limited industrial capacity on size and new technology, while the Allies aimed for reliability, flexibility, and adaptability. By 1944–45, all armies were using mobile all-arms armored divisions. Germany's emphasis on armor and firepower resulted in fearsome but underpowered tanks such as the Tiger I, fielded in limited numbers. The Allies' earlier single-role tanks were replaced by mass-produced, versatile, and upgradable tanks such as the US M4 Sherman and the Soviet T-34.

ANTI-TANK WEAPONS

As armored vehicles developed, so did anti-tank weapons. Early, relatively small single-shot rifles were replaced with portable but more unwieldy anti-tank rifles; mines and grenades were also used. Handheld, recoilless devices were developed during World War II. These, such as the German *Panzerfaust* ("tank fist," below), employed rocket-propelled grenades with "hollow charge" warheads. The most powerful and effective anti-tank weapons were anti-tank guns—dedicated anti-tank artillery.

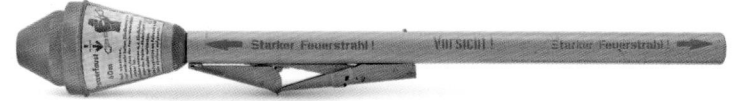

Soviet tank attack
T-34-85 tanks with troops from the 3rd Ukrainian Front attack in the Odessa region in 1944. Infantry often rode directly on tanks, particularly in Soviet forces due to a lack of armored personnel carriers.

THE D-DAY LANDINGS

One of the largest military operations of World War II, the Allied invasion of German-occupied France began on June 6, 1944, codenamed "D-Day." The success of the landings was a crucial step toward the liberation of France and the defeat of Nazi Germany.

A cross-Channel invasion of Occupied Europe from Britain was on the Allies' agenda from 1942, the US pressing for swift action while the British temporized, convinced of the extreme difficulty of such a venture. The Germans, meanwhile, fortified the coast from southwest France to Scandinavia with the Atlantic Wall, a formidable line of artillery emplacements, concrete bunkers, and beach obstacles.

Planning for the invasion began in earnest in mid-1943, with US General Dwight D. Eisenhower as Supreme Commander and British general Bernard Montgomery commanding land forces. A vast buildup of troops and supplies in southern England could not be disguised, but a deception effort persuaded the Germans the invasion would strike the Pas-de-Calais instead of Normandy.

On D-Day itself, the Allies successfully landed more than 150,000 troops, forming a bridgehead they could reinforce and supply across the Channel. Casualties on the day were lighter than feared, with about 11,000 Allied soldiers killed or wounded. However, the Allies did not achieve many of their first-day objectives, and the German defenders fought fiercely. The Allies did not break out of their coastal toehold until late July; the battle for Normandy cost them more than 200,000 casualties. Paris was finally liberated on August 25.

INVADING NORMANDY

The five target beaches were codenamed Utah, Omaha, Gold, Juno, and Sword. US and British airborne forces landed by parachute and glider during the night; the seaborne assault followed after dawn. All the beaches were taken, but stiff German resistance blocked Allied progress inland.

KEY

- Axis territory
- Normandy beaches
- Allied objectives for midnight Jun 6
- Allied gains, Jun 6
- Pegasus Bridge
- German gun batteries
- German infantry divisions
- German panzer division

TIMELINE

JUN 5, 1944 — JUN 9 — JUN 13

709th Infantry Div

91st Infantry Div

2:30 am, Jun 6 US 82nd Airborne Division land to the west of Utah

243rd Infantry Div

Utah

1 AIRBORNE NIGHT ASSAULT
12:15 AM–6:30 AM, JUNE 6, 1944

Airborne troops were sent to secure the flanks of the invasion zone ahead of the main forces. Some 13,000 soldiers of US 82nd and 101st Airborne Divisions landed behind Utah beach, and 8,000 men of British 6th Airborne Division near Sword. In darkness and bad weather, many paratroopers landed in the wrong place. Nonetheless, most secured their objectives.

- Invasion fleet arrives
- Airborne landing zones

1:30 am, Jun 6 Troops of US 101st Airborne Division parachute into Normandy

30th Mobile Div

2 LANDING AT UTAH
6:30 AM–END OF DAY, JUNE 6, 1944

The US seaborne landings in the Utah sector benefited from a lucky twist of fate. Unexpected currents carried the landing craft to a beach nearly two miles to the south of their intended point of arrival. This area turned out to be weakly defended, and the soldiers of 4th Infantry Division easily moved inland, joining up with the airborne troops. In total, 21,000 US troops came ashore at Utah on the day, suffering less than one percent casualties.

- US landing craft
- US troop movements

CHANNEL CROSSING

The largest amphibious operation in military history, D-Day involved more than 1,200 warships and 4,000 landing craft. These set sail from Britain on the night of June 5–6, via lanes cleared in minefields. German defenses were shelled by battleships and cruisers and bombed from the air; transport ships took men to landing craft for the final approach.

KEY

- Axis territory
- Allied territory
- Allied invasion
- Troop transports
- Minefield
- Landing craft
- Warships bombard coast

UNITED KINGDOM

Southampton
Portsmouth
Shoreham-by-Sea

Isle of Wight

Force O
Force U
Force G
Force J
Force S

The invasion force assembles south of the Isle of Wight

Minesweepers clear passages through German minefields

English Channel

The Royal Navy flagship controls the British and Canadian landings

Cherbourg

Utah
Omaha
Gold
Juno
Sword

FRANCE
NORMANDY
Bénouville
Caen

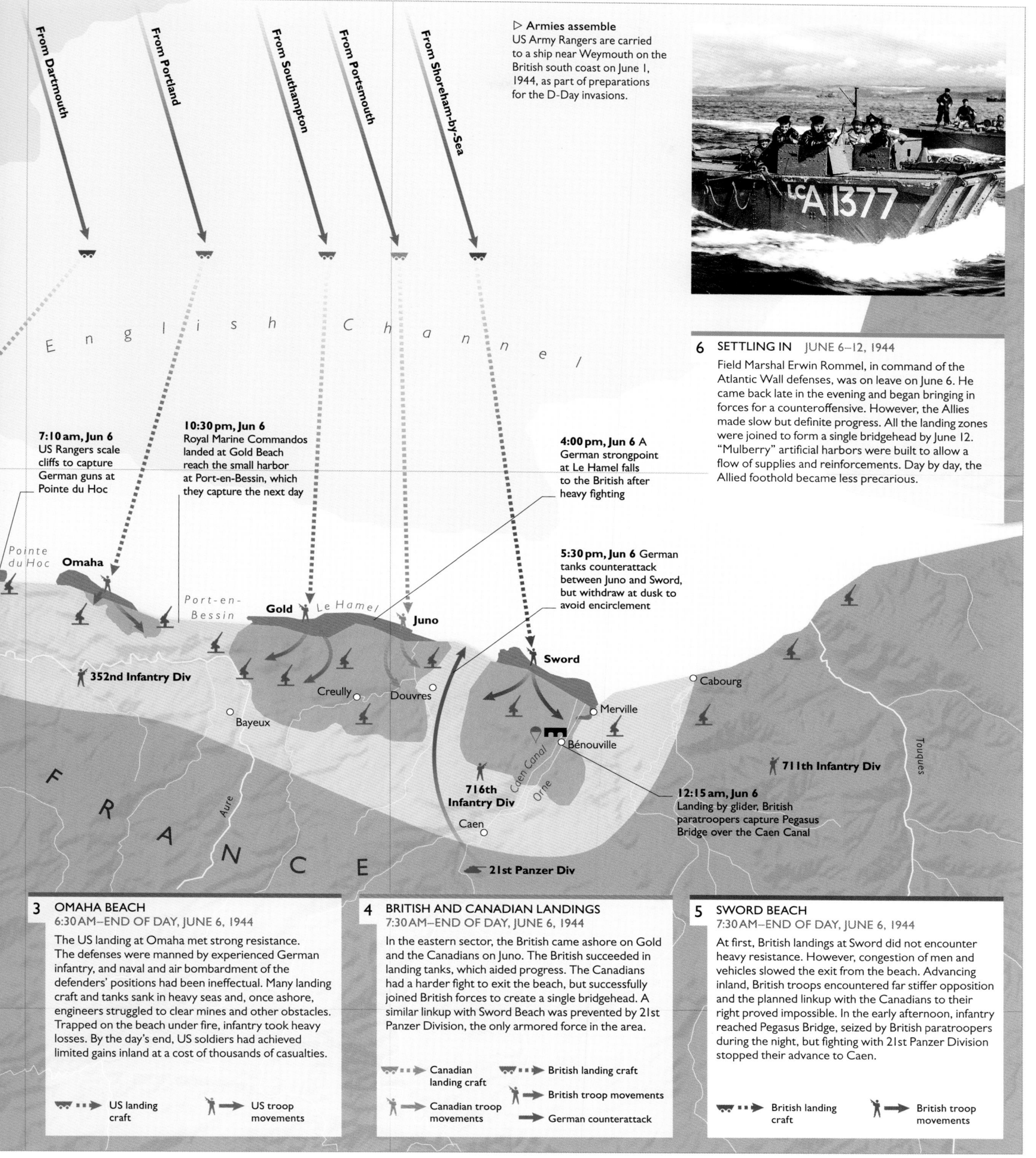

From Dartmouth

From Portland

From Southampton

From Portsmouth

From Shoreham-by-Sea

E n g l i s h   C h a n n e l

▷ **Armies assemble**
US Army Rangers are carried to a ship near Weymouth on the British south coast on June 1, 1944, as part of preparations for the D-Day invasions.

7:10 am, Jun 6
US Rangers scale cliffs to capture German guns at Pointe du Hoc

10:30 pm, Jun 6
Royal Marine Commandos landed at Gold Beach reach the small harbor at Port-en-Bessin, which they capture the next day

4:00 pm, Jun 6 A German strongpoint at Le Hamel falls to the British after heavy fighting

5:30 pm, Jun 6 German tanks counterattack between Juno and Sword, but withdraw at dusk to avoid encirclement

6   SETTLING IN   JUNE 6–12, 1944

Field Marshal Erwin Rommel, in command of the Atlantic Wall defenses, was on leave on June 6. He came back late in the evening and began bringing in forces for a counteroffensive. However, the Allies made slow but definite progress. All the landing zones were joined to form a single bridgehead by June 12. "Mulberry" artificial harbors were built to allow a flow of supplies and reinforcements. Day by day, the Allied foothold became less precarious.

Pointe du Hoc

Omaha

Port-en-Bessin

Gold   Le Hamel   **Juno**

Sword

352nd Infantry Div

Creully   Douvres

Cabourg

Bayeux

Merville

Bénouville

711th Infantry Div

Caen Canal

Orne

Touques

716th Infantry Div

12:15 am, Jun 6
Landing by glider, British paratroopers capture Pegasus Bridge over the Caen Canal

F R A N C E

Aure

Caen

21st Panzer Div

3   OMAHA BEACH
6:30 AM–END OF DAY, JUNE 6, 1944

The US landing at Omaha met strong resistance. The defenses were manned by experienced German infantry, and naval and air bombardment of the defenders' positions had been ineffectual. Many landing craft and tanks sank in heavy seas and, once ashore, engineers struggled to clear mines and other obstacles. Trapped on the beach under fire, infantry took heavy losses. By the day's end, US soldiers had achieved limited gains inland at a cost of thousands of casualties.

US landing craft   US troop movements

4   BRITISH AND CANADIAN LANDINGS
7:30 AM–END OF DAY, JUNE 6, 1944

In the eastern sector, the British came ashore on Gold and the Canadians on Juno. The British succeeded in landing tanks, which aided progress. The Canadians had a harder fight to exit the beach, but successfully joined British forces to create a single bridgehead. A similar linkup with Sword Beach was prevented by 21st Panzer Division, the only armored force in the area.

Canadian landing craft   British landing craft

Canadian troop movements   British troop movements

German counterattack

5   SWORD BEACH
7:30 AM–END OF DAY, JUNE 6, 1944

At first, British landings at Sword did not encounter heavy resistance. However, congestion of men and vehicles slowed the exit from the beach. Advancing inland, British troops encountered far stiffer opposition and the planned linkup with the Canadians to their right proved impossible. In the early afternoon, infantry reached Pegasus Bridge, seized by British paratroopers during the night, but fighting with 21st Panzer Division stopped their advance to Caen.

British landing craft   British troop movements

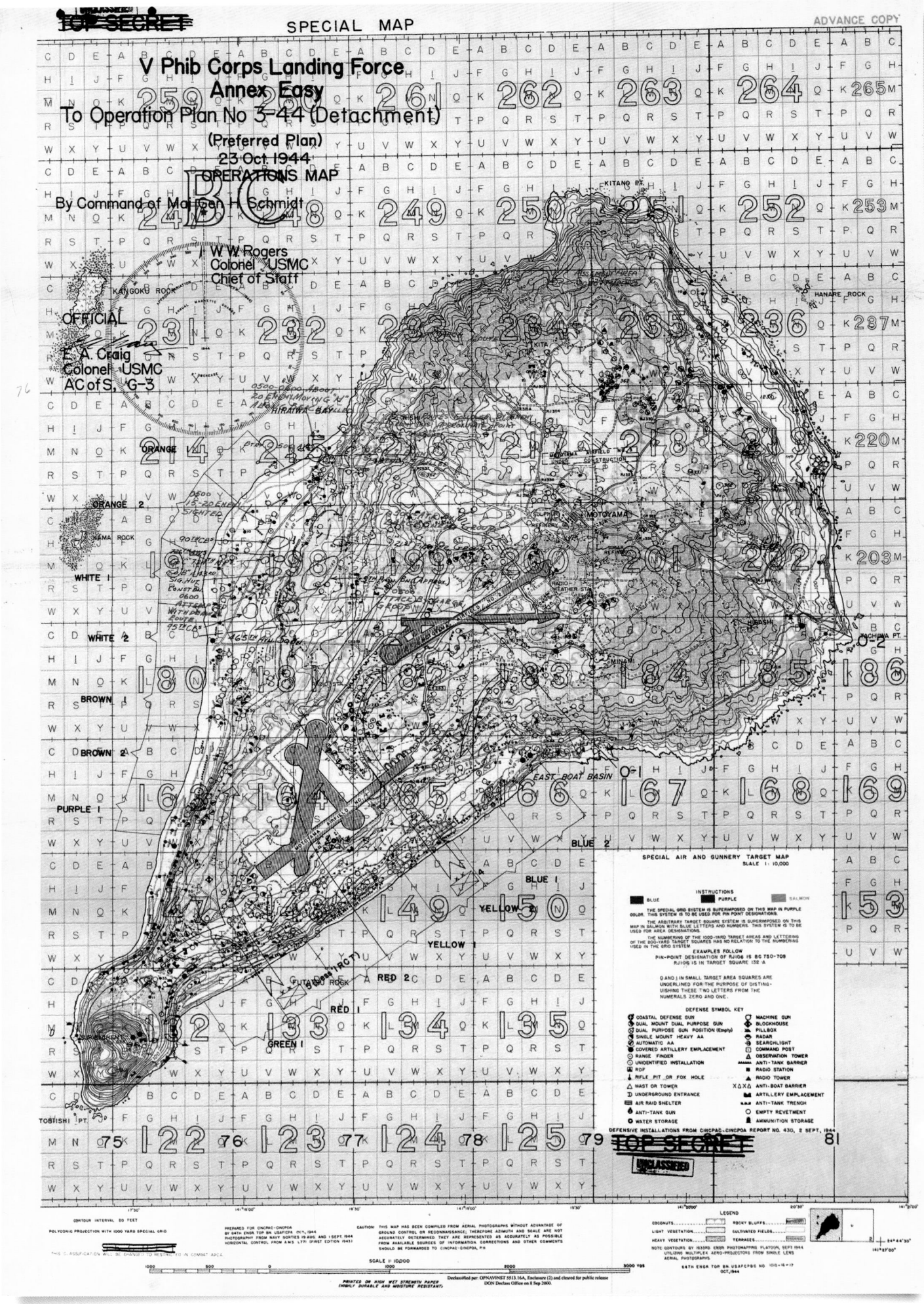

SPECIAL MAP

V Phib Corps Landing Force
Annex Easy
To Operation Plan No 3-44 (Detachment)
(Preferred Plan)
23 Oct. 1944
OPERATIONS MAP

By Command of Maj. Gen. H. Schmidt

W. W. Rogers
Colonel, USMC
Chief of Staff

OFFICIAL
E. A. Craig
Colonel, USMC
AC of S, G-3

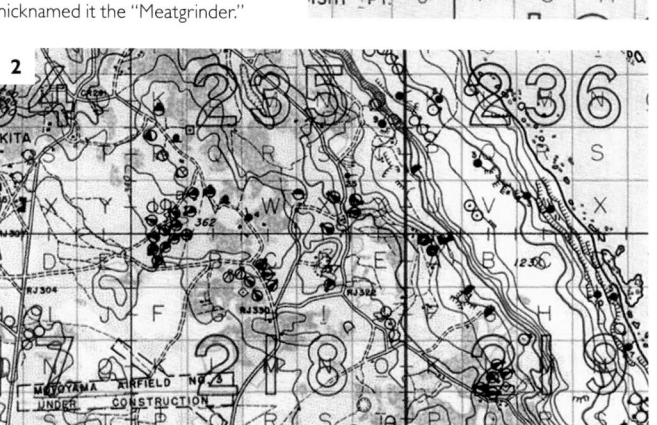

IWO JIMA

In early 1945, 110,000 US troops set out to take the tiny island of Iwo Jima from about 20,000 Japanese soldiers. In one of the bloodiest battles of the war, US forces cleared the Japanese from the network of defensive tunnels. After a month, they finally claimed a strategic and psychological victory.

1

2

◁ **An island stronghold**
This US military map from October 1944 presents the preferred operations plan for the US landing. It includes all the Japanese gun emplacements and defensive installations on Iwo Jima.

▷ **Early victory**
Mount Suribachi—the highest point on the island—was protected by more than 200 gun emplacements. The Marines raised the US flag on the summit on February 23.

▽ **The bloodiest battle**
The battle among the hills concealing the Japanese communications system was so hard that the Americans nicknamed it the "Meatgrinder."

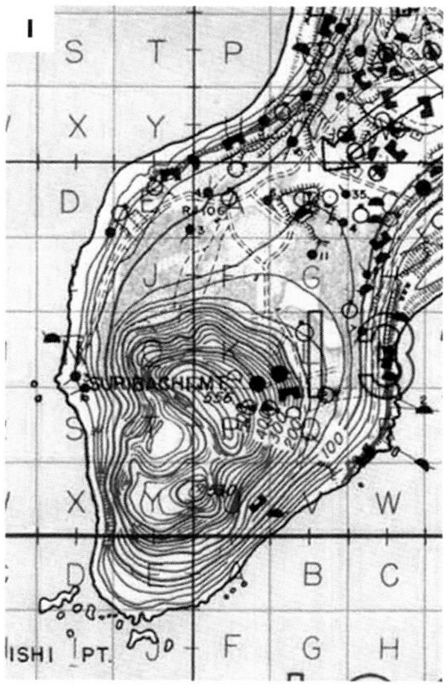

After their success at Midway in 1942 (see pp.238–39), US forces went on the offensive, working their way west across the Pacific and causing terrible damage to the Japanese navy. In February 1945, the US launched an offensive on the tiny Japanese island of Iwo Jima, a vital strategic target that would provide the US with a base for Allied fighter planes and a refuge for damaged bombers.

The Japanese were well prepared for the invasion. General Tadamichi Kuribayashi had fortified the island, tunneling into the island's rock to create a network of bunkers and rooms linked by 11 miles (18 km) of tunnels that protected his men from naval and aerial bombardment.

The first of 110,000 US marines landed on February 19. As they edged their way across the island, they found themselves exposed to a largely unseen enemy that would suddenly emerge from bunkers to attack. The advance was slow and costly—nearly 7,000 US troops were killed and more than 19,000 wounded. A small Japanese force under Kuribayashi held out until March 26, but almost all the defenders were killed; only about 1,000 were captured (many after staying hidden for months or even years).

2
1

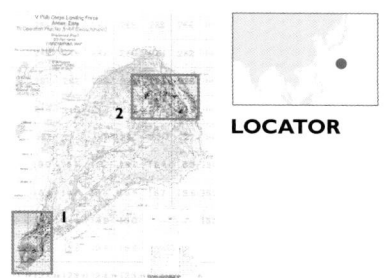

LOCATOR

SLOW PROGRESS
US forces landed on beaches of southeast Iwo Jima on February 19 and advanced slowly across the island. By February 24, they had captured the two airstrips and the peak of Mount Suribachi. It then took four days to secure the hills of the notorious "Meatgrinder" area, but the island was not declared secure until March 16. The Japanese launched a final overnight counterattack from Kuribayashi's stronghold on March 25–26.

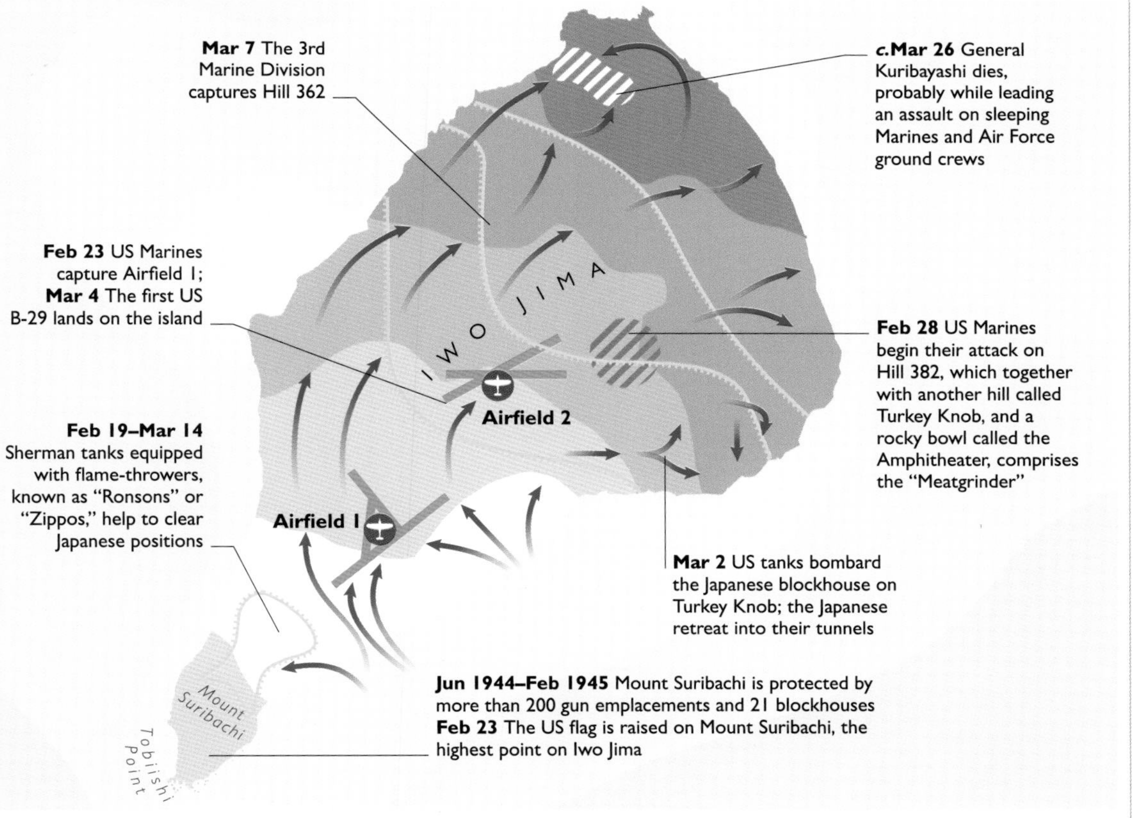

PACIFIC OCEAN
IWO JIMA
Airfield 1
Airfield 2
Mount Suribachi
Tobiishi Point
Mar 7 The 3rd Marine Division captures Hill 362
c.Mar 26 General Kuribayashi dies, probably while leading an assault on sleeping Marines and Air Force ground crews
Feb 23 US Marines capture Airfield 1; **Mar 4** The first US B-29 lands on the island
Feb 28 US Marines begin their attack on Hill 382, which together with another hill called Turkey Knob, and a rocky bowl called the Amphitheater, comprises the "Meatgrinder"
Feb 19–Mar 14 Sherman tanks equipped with flame-throwers, known as "Ronsons" or "Zippos," help to clear Japanese positions
Mar 2 US tanks bombard the Japanese blockhouse on Turkey Knob; the Japanese retreat into their tunnels
Jun 1944–Feb 1945 Mount Suribachi is protected by more than 200 gun emplacements and 21 blockhouses **Feb 23** The US flag is raised on Mount Suribachi, the highest point on Iwo Jima

KEY

- Japanese lines of defense
- Kuribayashi's stronghold
- US advance
- The "Meatgrinder"
- Airstrips

US TERRITORIAL GAINS, 1945

- Beachhead on Feb 19
- by Feb 24
- by Mar 1
- by Mar 9
- by Mar 14

THE FALL OF BERLIN

The final battle of World War II in Europe saw Berlin face an overwhelming Red Army advance. Facing the end of his Third Reich, German leader Adolf Hitler nonetheless insisted his forces fight to the death, and the loss of life was vast on both sides.

After the invasion of Normandy by the Western Allies in summer 1944 (see pp.248–49), Hitler fought on stubbornly, even mounting a failed counteroffensive in the Ardennes at the Battle of the Bulge in December 1944–January 1945. In mid-January Soviet armies launched a vast offensive, invading Germany from the east. By March, the first US troops had crossed the Rhine from the west. In the air, British and US bombers laid waste German cities at will. His air force overwhelmed and his armies outnumbered, Hitler mobilized children and the elderly to die in defense of the Fatherland.

The question of whether the final Allied drive on Berlin would come from east or west was never disputed. US General Dwight D. Eisenhower was happy for the Soviets to take both the honor and the casualties. On April 25, while fighting still raged in and around the German capital, Soviet and US troops met amicably at Torgau on the River Elbe. Anticipating humiliating defeat, as the battle raged on many leading Nazis, including Hitler, committed suicide. Berlin surrendered on May 2, and five days later the war in Europe was over. Berlin was divided into Soviet and Western military occupation zones. These zones later hardened into a division between East and West Berlin that lasted until 1990.

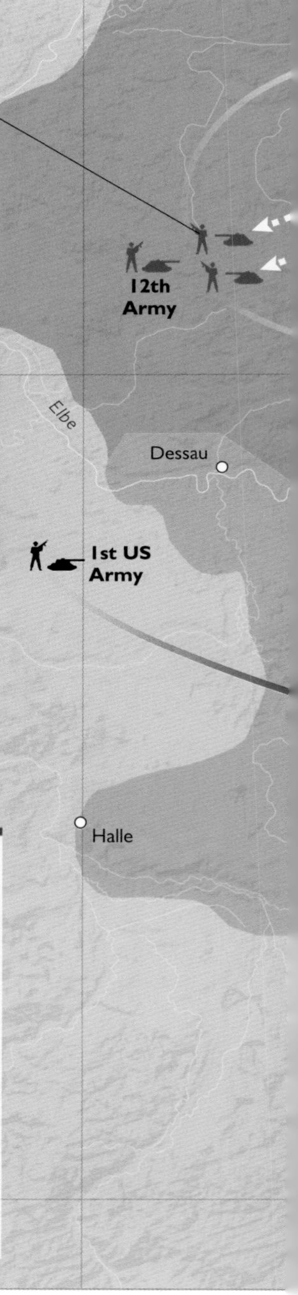

GERMANY DEFEATED

The Soviet drive to capture Berlin in spring 1945 took 17 days to achieve its objective. Advancing from the Oder-Neisse line, two Soviet armies fought their way into the city street by street. By the time his forces in Berlin surrendered on May 2, Nazi leader Adolf Hitler was already dead.

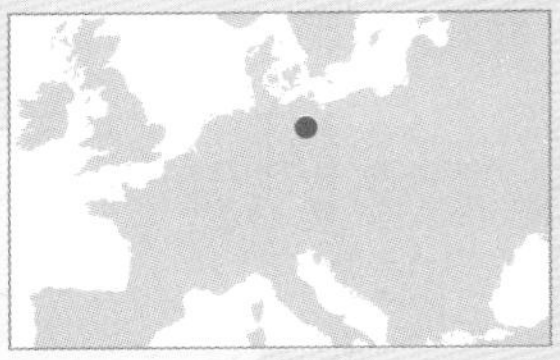

KEY

British and US forces	German forces
US infantry	German infantry
Soviet forces	German defensive lines
Soviet infantry	ooo Front lines of German counterattacks
	/// German territory, Apr 28

ALLIED TERRITORIAL GAINS
- Apr 15
- Apr 18
- Apr 25
- Apr 28
- Urban areas

TIMELINE

1
2
3
4

APR 15, 1945   APR 20   APR 25   APR 30   MAY 5

May 1 The German 12th Army and remnants of the 9th Army turn west to surrender to Allied forces

12th Army

Elbe

Dessau

1st US Army

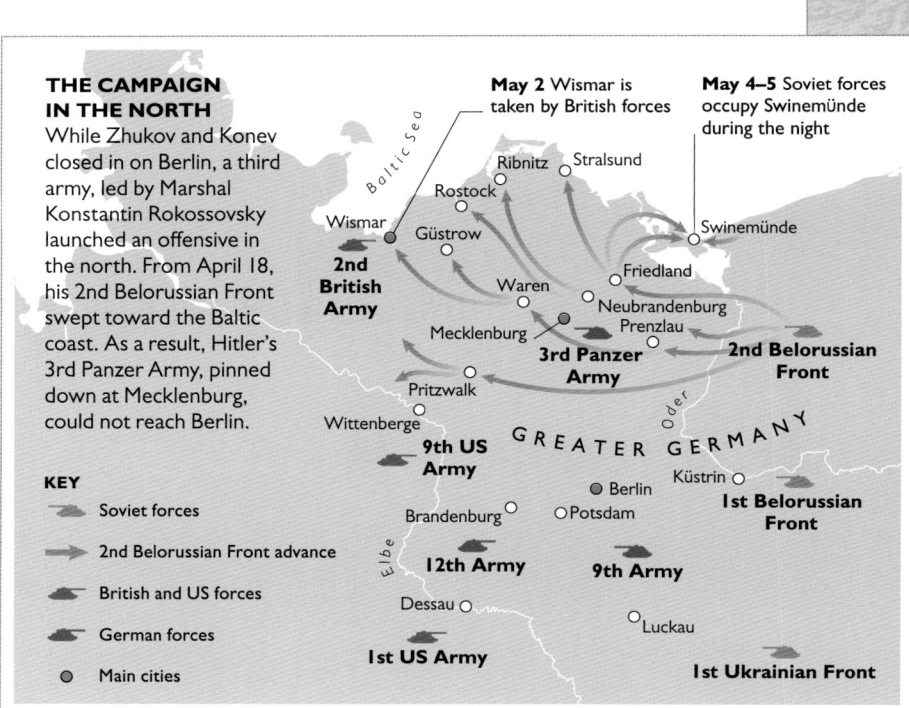

△ Soviet victory march
In May 1945, following the surrender of Nazi Germany, victorious Red Army soldiers march into Berlin. The city had been left in ruins, and would become a focal point of Cold War tensions that would last for several decades

Halle

4 THE CITY CONQUERED
APRIL 21–MAY 2, 1945

Through the last days of April Soviet troops closed in on Hitler's bunker in central Berlin. Already devastated by Allied bombing, the city suffered further destruction from artillery shells. The defense was in the hands of General Helmuth Weidling, with troops ranging from crack SS soldiers to untrained youths. They inflicted heavy casualties on the Red Army in close-quarters street fighting, but defeat was inevitable. On April 30, Hitler shot himself in his bunker, and Weidling negotiated the surrender of the city on May 2.

▄▄ Site of Hitler's bunker

THE CAMPAIGN IN THE NORTH

While Zhukov and Konev closed in on Berlin, a third army, led by Marshal Konstantin Rokossovsky launched an offensive in the north. From April 18, his 2nd Belorussian Front swept toward the Baltic coast. As a result, Hitler's 3rd Panzer Army, pinned down at Mecklenburg, could not reach Berlin.

May 2 Wismar is taken by British forces

May 4–5 Soviet forces occupy Swinemünde during the night

Baltic Sea

Ribnitz   Stralsund
Rostock
Wismar   Güstrow   Swinemünde
2nd British Army   Waren   Friedland
Mecklenburg   Neubrandenburg
3rd Panzer Army   Prenzlau
Pritzwalk   **2nd Belorussian Front**
Wittenberge   Oder
9th US Army   GREATER GERMANY
Brandenburg   ● Berlin   Küstrin
Potsdam   **1st Belorussian Front**
Elbe   **12th Army**   **9th Army**
Dessau   Luckau
1st US Army   **1st Ukrainian Front**

KEY
- Soviet forces
- 2nd Belorussian Front advance
- British and US forces
- German forces
- ● Main cities

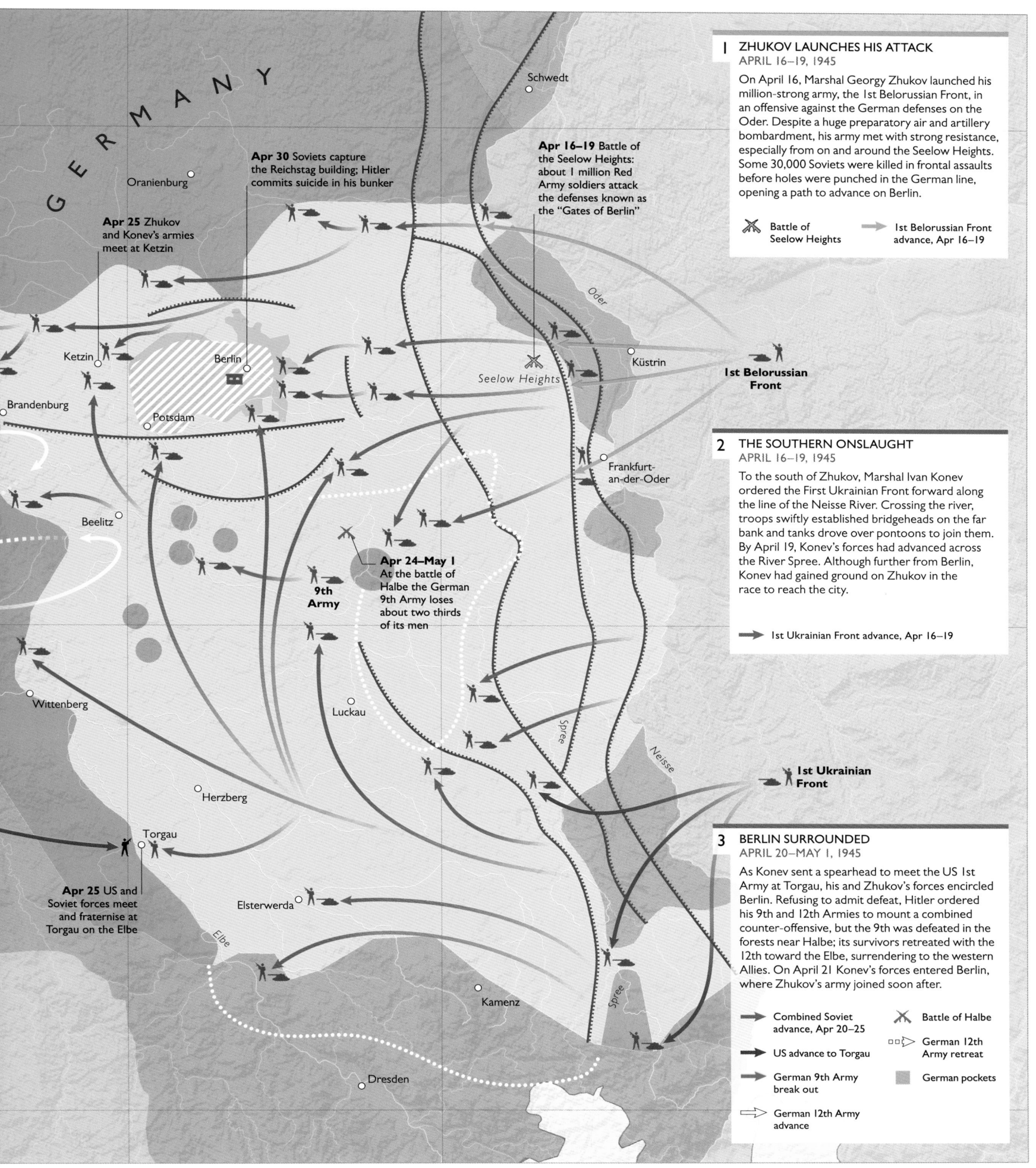

GERMANY

Schwedt

Apr 30 Soviets capture the Reichstag building; Hitler commits suicide in his bunker

Oranienburg

Apr 16–19 Battle of the Seelow Heights: about 1 million Red Army soldiers attack the defenses known as the "Gates of Berlin"

Oder

Apr 25 Zhukov and Konev's armies meet at Ketzin

Ketzin

Berlin

Seelow Heights

Küstrin

1st Belorussian Front

Brandenburg

Potsdam

Beelitz

Frankfurt-an-der-Oder

Apr 24–May 1 At the battle of Halbe the German 9th Army loses about two thirds of its men

9th Army

Spree

Wittenberg

Luckau

Neisse

Herzberg

1st Ukrainian Front

Torgau

Elsterwerda

Apr 25 US and Soviet forces meet and fraternise at Torgau on the Elbe

Elbe

Kamenz

Spree

Dresden

1 ZHUKOV LAUNCHES HIS ATTACK
APRIL 16–19, 1945

On April 16, Marshal Georgy Zhukov launched his million-strong army, the 1st Belorussian Front, in an offensive against the German defenses on the Oder. Despite a huge preparatory air and artillery bombardment, his army met with strong resistance, especially from on and around the Seelow Heights. Some 30,000 Soviets were killed in frontal assaults before holes were punched in the German line, opening a path to advance on Berlin.

⚔ Battle of Seelow Heights ➡ 1st Belorussian Front advance, Apr 16–19

2 THE SOUTHERN ONSLAUGHT
APRIL 16–19, 1945

To the south of Zhukov, Marshal Ivan Konev ordered the First Ukrainian Front forward along the line of the Neisse River. Crossing the river, troops swiftly established bridgeheads on the far bank and tanks drove over pontoons to join them. By April 19, Konev's forces had advanced across the River Spree. Although further from Berlin, Konev had gained ground on Zhukov in the race to reach the city.

➡ 1st Ukrainian Front advance, Apr 16–19

3 BERLIN SURROUNDED
APRIL 20–MAY 1, 1945

As Konev sent a spearhead to meet the US 1st Army at Torgau, his and Zhukov's forces encircled Berlin. Refusing to admit defeat, Hitler ordered his 9th and 12th Armies to mount a combined counter-offensive, but the 9th was defeated in the forests near Halbe; its survivors retreated with the 12th toward the Elbe, surrendering to the western Allies. On April 21 Konev's forces entered Berlin, where Zhukov's army joined soon after.

➡ Combined Soviet advance, Apr 20–25 ⚔ Battle of Halbe

➡ US advance to Torgau ▱▹ German 12th Army retreat

➡ German 9th Army break out ▢ German pockets

➡ German 12th Army advance

THE NUCLEAR AGE

After their first and only use over Japan in 1945, nuclear weapons inspired terror like no other military technology before them. They have not since been deployed in war, and are instead used as the ultimate deterrent.

△ **Atomic pioneer**
Born in 1904, American physicist J. Robert Oppenheimer is renowned for spearheading the Manhattan Project, an atomic weapons program in the 1940s.

The world entered the nuclear age in August 1945, when the US bombed the Japanese cities of Hiroshima and Nagaski. The Soviet Union in turn developed its own nuclear capability in 1949, with Britain following suit in 1952.

Nuclear weapons were initially viewed as a special ordinance for strategic missions, but President Harry S. Truman's administration capitalized on their potential for deterrence to prevent direct clashes between the US and the Soviet Union. Across the world, massive expenditure was incurred in procuring and developing these weapons and their delivery systems, often overshadowing other elements of defense budgets. Ultimately, fission (atomic) bombs were supplanted by fusion (hydrogen) bombs. Strategic bombers were supplanted first by ground-based ballistic missiles, followed by submarine-launched ballistic missiles (SLBMs). Every advance in the field by a country was matched by its allies and competitors, and by the 1980s, the US and the Soviet Union wielded enough nuclear weapons to destroy the world many times over.

Present-day scenario

The Intermediate-Range Nuclear Forces (INF) Treaty, signed between the US and the Soviet Union in 1987, scaled down the tensions of this arms race. However, in the 21st century, nuclear arms continue to proliferate and are seen as important prestige weapons by nations.

INTERCONTINENTAL BALLISTIC MISSILES

Developed as strategic defense weapons, intercontinental ballistic missiles (ICBMs) are land-based, nuclear-armed ballistic missiles with a range of more than 3,500 miles (5,600 km). Russia, the US, China, France, India, the UK, and North Korea all currently hold operational ICBMs.

US Titan II ICBM

Cloud of fire
France entered the nuclear "arms race" in 1970 when it conducted Operation *Licorne* (Unicorn), an atmospheric nuclear test in the French Polynesia. A terrifying detonation of a nuclear device from the test can be seen here.

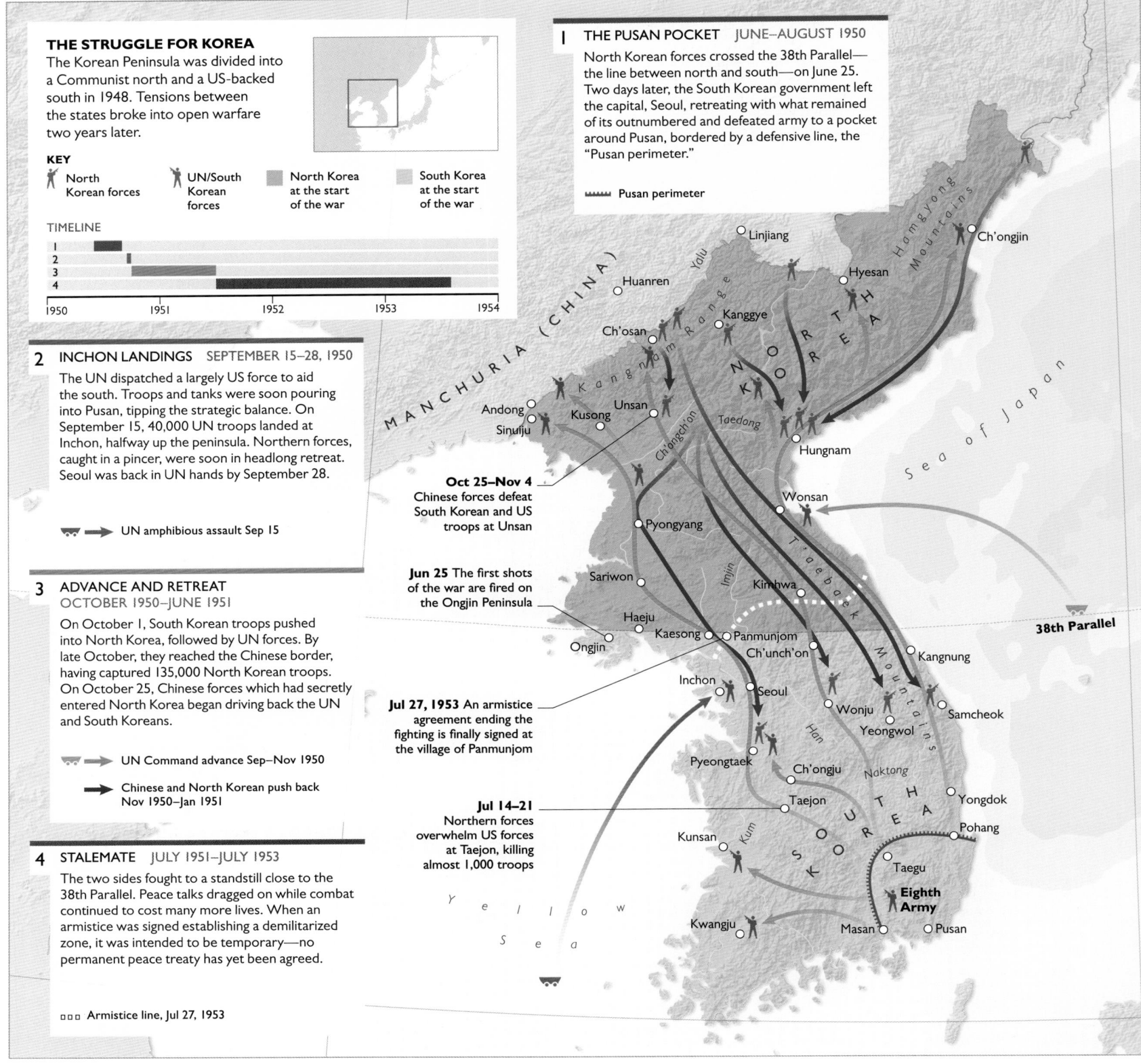

THE STRUGGLE FOR KOREA
The Korean Peninsula was divided into a Communist north and a US-backed south in 1948. Tensions between the states broke into open warfare two years later.

KEY

🚶 North Korean forces
🚶 UN/South Korean forces
▨ North Korea at the start of the war
▨ South Korea at the start of the war

TIMELINE

1
2
3
4

1950   1951   1952   1953   1954

1 THE PUSAN POCKET   JUNE–AUGUST 1950
North Korean forces crossed the 38th Parallel—the line between north and south—on June 25. Two days later, the South Korean government left the capital, Seoul, retreating with what remained of its outnumbered and defeated army to a pocket around Pusan, bordered by a defensive line, the "Pusan perimeter."

〰️ Pusan perimeter

2 INCHON LANDINGS   SEPTEMBER 15–28, 1950
The UN dispatched a largely US force to aid the south. Troops and tanks were soon pouring into Pusan, tipping the strategic balance. On September 15, 40,000 UN troops landed at Inchon, halfway up the peninsula. Northern forces, caught in a pincer, were soon in headlong retreat. Seoul was back in UN hands by September 28.

➡️ UN amphibious assault Sep 15

3 ADVANCE AND RETREAT
OCTOBER 1950–JUNE 1951
On October 1, South Korean troops pushed into North Korea, followed by UN forces. By late October, they reached the Chinese border, having captured 135,000 North Korean troops. On October 25, Chinese forces which had secretly entered North Korea began driving back the UN and South Koreans.

➡️ UN Command advance Sep–Nov 1950

➡️ Chinese and North Korean push back Nov 1950–Jan 1951

4 STALEMATE   JULY 1951–JULY 1953
The two sides fought to a standstill close to the 38th Parallel. Peace talks dragged on while combat continued to cost many more lives. When an armistice was signed establishing a demilitarized zone, it was intended to be temporary—no permanent peace treaty has yet been agreed.

▫️▫️▫️ Armistice line, Jul 27, 1953

Oct 25–Nov 4 Chinese forces defeat South Korean and US troops at Unsan

Jun 25 The first shots of the war are fired on the Ongjin Peninsula

Jul 27, 1953 An armistice agreement ending the fighting is finally signed at the village of Panmunjom

Jul 14–21 Northern forces overwhelm US forces at Taejon, killing almost 1,000 troops

INCHON

In the early months of the Korean War (1950–53), North Korean forces pushed the South Korean army and its allies back to a pocket in the southeast of the country. The amphibious landing of United Nations forces behind enemy lines at Inchon in 1950 marked the beginning of an ambitious counterattack.

Liberated from Japanese rule at the end of World War II, Korea was divided into two republics: the Communist Democratic People's Republic of Korea in the north (supported by the USSR and China) and the Republic of Korea in the south (backed by the US). In June 1950, the north invaded the south, driving the southern army back to the southeast corner of the country, despite United Nations (UN) military support. UN Commander Douglas MacArthur planned a counteroffensive involving an amphibious landing 100 miles (160km) behind enemy lines at Inchon. The incursion was a success, and the UN forces rapidly won back the land they had lost. MacArthur attempted to pursue the enemy to the Chinese border—a move that triggered a Chinese intervention. This caused the UN forces to retreat, and by mid-1951 the two sides were back near where they had started at the beginning of the war.

DIEN BIEN PHU

At the end of World War II, France sought to reestablish control over its colonial possessions in Indochina. In Vietnam, the nationalist Viet Minh waged a lengthy guerrilla war of independence, finally defeating French forces in a bloody battle at Dien Bien Phu in May 1954.

French forces had been in conflict with the Viet Minh (who were fighting for an independent Vietnam) for more than seven years. Early in 1954, the French made plans to establish an outpost in the remote and mountainous northwest of Vietnam to break the deadlock. Supplied by air, this base would effectively cut the enemy's supply lines from neighboring Laos. The French believed that the Viet Minh would not be able to move anti-aircraft guns and artillery into the area, but they underestimated the Viet Minh commander General Võ Nguyên Giáp, who spent months moving heavy weapons into virtually impregnable positions overlooking the French base. The French were taken by surprise when he attacked. Outlying positions fell fast, but the area around their airstrip held out for almost two months. When it fell in May 1954, the defeat was decisive, paving the way for the independence and partition of Vietnam.

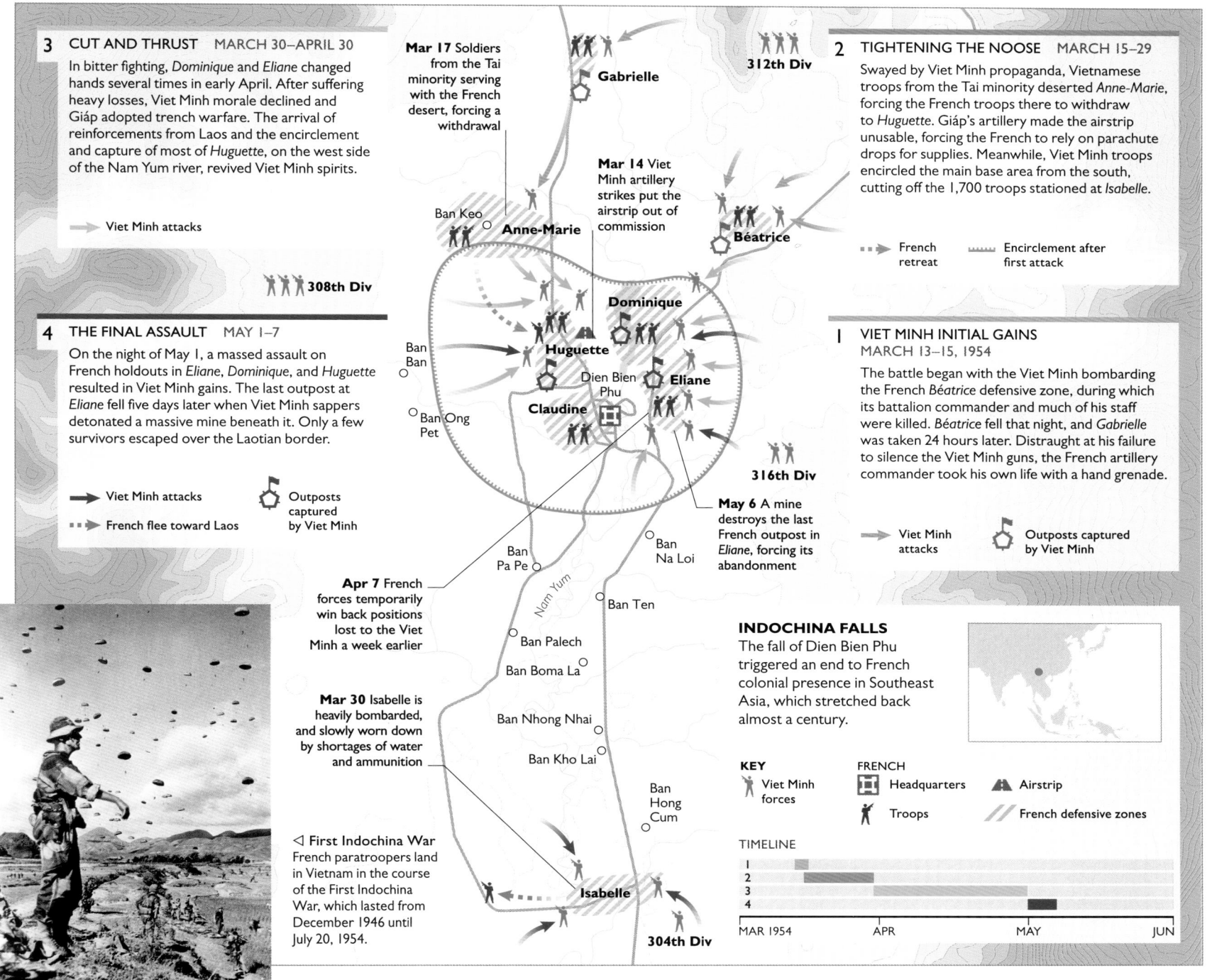

3 CUT AND THRUST MARCH 30–APRIL 30

In bitter fighting, *Dominique* and *Eliane* changed hands several times in early April. After suffering heavy losses, Viet Minh morale declined and Giáp adopted trench warfare. The arrival of reinforcements from Laos and the encirclement and capture of most of *Huguette*, on the west side of the Nam Yum river, revived Viet Minh spirits.

→ Viet Minh attacks

308th Div

4 THE FINAL ASSAULT MAY 1–7

On the night of May 1, a massed assault on French holdouts in *Eliane*, *Dominique*, and *Huguette* resulted in Viet Minh gains. The last outpost at *Eliane* fell five days later when Viet Minh sappers detonated a massive mine beneath it. Only a few survivors escaped over the Laotian border.

→ Viet Minh attacks
⬡ Outposts captured by Viet Minh
▪▪▶ French flee toward Laos

Mar 17 Soldiers from the Tai minority serving with the French desert, forcing a withdrawal

312th Div

Gabrielle

Mar 14 Viet Minh artillery strikes put the airstrip out of commission

Ban Keo
Anne-Marie

Béatrice

Dominique

Ban Ban
Huguette
Dien Bien Phu
Eliane
Ban Ong Pet
Claudine

316th Div

May 6 A mine destroys the last French outpost in *Eliane*, forcing its abandonment

Apr 7 French forces temporarily win back positions lost to the Viet Minh a week earlier

Ban Pa Pe
Ban Na Loi

Nam Yum

Ban Ten

Mar 30 Isabelle is heavily bombarded, and slowly worn down by shortages of water and ammunition

Ban Palech
Ban Boma La
Ban Nhong Nhai
Ban Kho Lai

Ban Hong Cum

◁ **First Indochina War**
French paratroopers land in Vietnam in the course of the First Indochina War, which lasted from December 1946 until July 20, 1954.

Isabelle

304th Div

2 TIGHTENING THE NOOSE MARCH 15–29

Swayed by Viet Minh propaganda, Vietnamese troops from the Tai minority deserted *Anne-Marie*, forcing the French troops there to withdraw to *Huguette*. Giáp's artillery made the airstrip unusable, forcing the French to rely on parachute drops for supplies. Meanwhile, Viet Minh troops encircled the main base area from the south, cutting off the 1,700 troops stationed at *Isabelle*.

▪▪▶ French retreat
〰〰 Encirclement after first attack

1 VIET MINH INITIAL GAINS MARCH 13–15, 1954

The battle began with the Viet Minh bombarding the French *Béatrice* defensive zone, during which its battalion commander and much of his staff were killed. *Béatrice* fell that night, and *Gabrielle* was taken 24 hours later. Distraught at his failure to silence the Viet Minh guns, the French artillery commander took his own life with a hand grenade.

→ Viet Minh attacks
⬡ Outposts captured by Viet Minh

INDOCHINA FALLS
The fall of Dien Bien Phu triggered an end to French colonial presence in Southeast Asia, which stretched back almost a century.

KEY
Viet Minh forces
Troops

FRENCH
Headquarters
Troops
Airstrip
French defensive zones

TIMELINE

	MAR 1954	APR	MAY	JUN
1				
2				
3				
4				

REVOLUTION AND WAR

After World War II, revolutionary and nationalist politics became linked with guerrilla warfare, resulting in insurgency movements. Many insurgents used guerrilla tactics, making it possible for weaker, less well equipped military forces to triumph over more powerful enemies.

△ **Fearless fighter**
This propaganda poster celebrates Le Thi Hong Gam, a Communist guerilla fighter killed in the Vietnam War.

Some of the most successful guerrilla campaigns in the 20th century took place in Vietnam. In 1946, the Viet Minh, a North Vietnamese nationalist group, launched an insurgency against the French colonial rulers. They followed the example of the Chinese Communist revolutionary Mao Zedong, who established guerrilla bases in the countryside and used propaganda to win popular support—a strategy that ultimately brought him to power in 1949. The Viet Minh's military tactics progressed from scattered raids, ambushes, and sabotage to full-scale military operations on the battlefield.

The success of the Viet Minh's campaign culminated in the defeat of the French at Dien Bien Phu (see p.257) and encouraged revolutionary movements worldwide. In Cuba, Fidel Castro's guerrillas overthrew the US-backed government in 1959, and the French faced a fresh guerrilla campaign in Algeria, leading to Algeria's independence in 1962. This was followed by guerrilla warfare resuming in South Vietnam, resulting in a full-blown war with the US (1965–73). In 1965, the Argentine Ernesto "Che" Guevara tried to spread the revolution, first in the Congo and then in South America. However, his efforts to unite anti-American forces failed. From the 1970s, urban guerrilla movements and international terrorism rose to equal prominence with the rural guerrilla tactics of the original revolutionaries.

△ **Armed patrol, 1966**
A communist Viet Cong guerrilla force patrols a river in South Vietnam. The soldier in the front is carrying an American M1918 Browning automatic rifle.

Leading the way
Cuban leader Fidel Castro (far left) and Che Guevara (center) lead a victory parade in Havana, Cuba, in 1959. Che fought in several revolutionary campaigns across the world and became a famous icon.

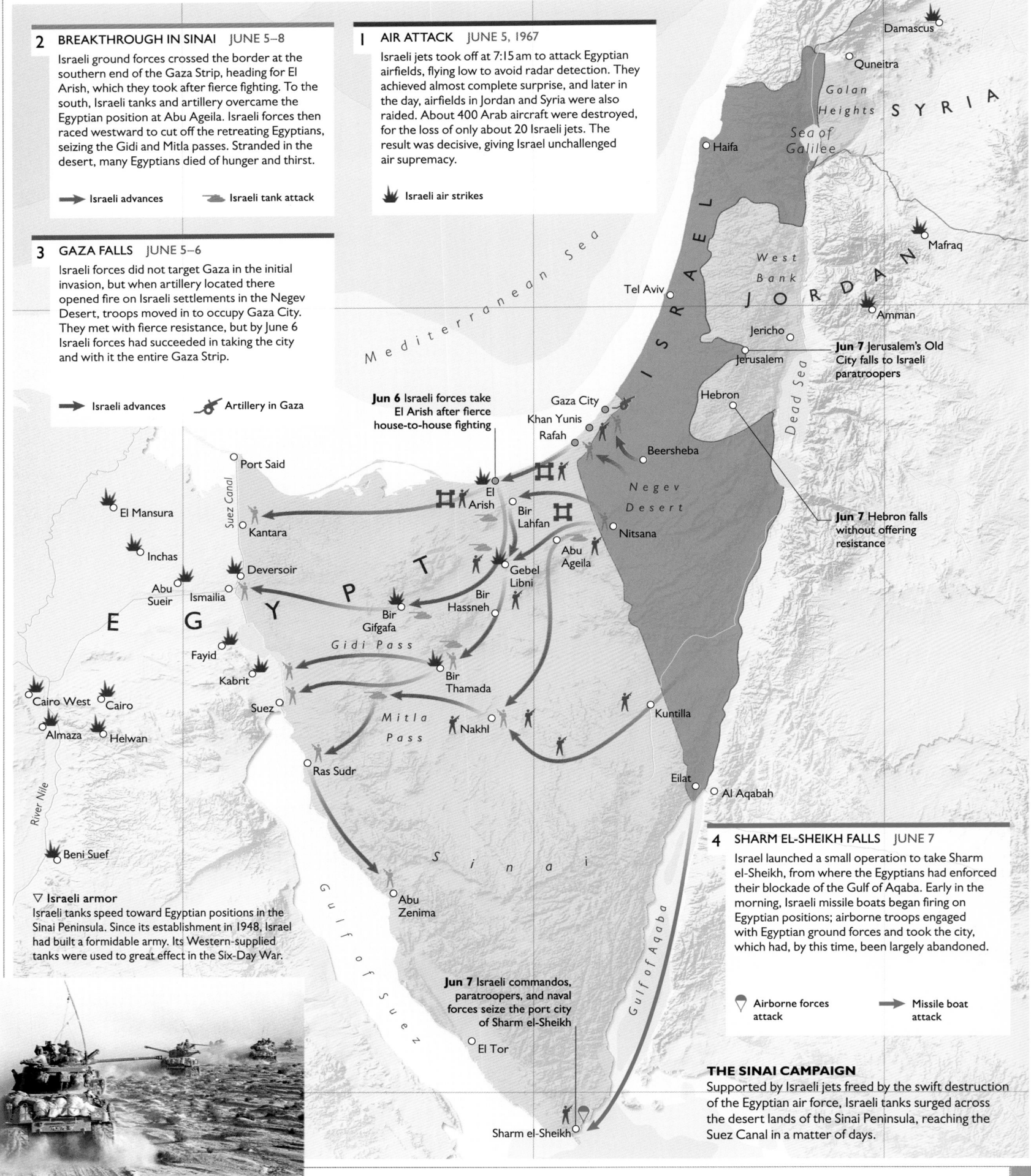

2 BREAKTHROUGH IN SINAI JUNE 5–8

Israeli ground forces crossed the border at the southern end of the Gaza Strip, heading for El Arish, which they took after fierce fighting. To the south, Israeli tanks and artillery overcame the Egyptian position at Abu Ageila. Israeli forces then raced westward to cut off the retreating Egyptians, seizing the Gidi and Mitla passes. Stranded in the desert, many Egyptians died of hunger and thirst.

→ Israeli advances   ◂ Israeli tank attack

1 AIR ATTACK JUNE 5, 1967

Israeli jets took off at 7:15 am to attack Egyptian airfields, flying low to avoid radar detection. They achieved almost complete surprise, and later in the day, airfields in Jordan and Syria were also raided. About 400 Arab aircraft were destroyed, for the loss of only about 20 Israeli jets. The result was decisive, giving Israel unchallenged air supremacy.

✹ Israeli air strikes

3 GAZA FALLS JUNE 5–6

Israeli forces did not target Gaza in the initial invasion, but when artillery located there opened fire on Israeli settlements in the Negev Desert, troops moved in to occupy Gaza City. They met with fierce resistance, but by June 6 Israeli forces had succeeded in taking the city and with it the entire Gaza Strip.

→ Israeli advances   ⚙ Artillery in Gaza

Jun 6 Israeli forces take El Arish after fierce house-to-house fighting

Jun 7 Jerusalem's Old City falls to Israeli paratroopers

Jun 7 Hebron falls without offering resistance

▽ **Israeli armor**
Israeli tanks speed toward Egyptian positions in the Sinai Peninsula. Since its establishment in 1948, Israel had built a formidable army. Its Western-supplied tanks were used to great effect in the Six-Day War.

Jun 7 Israeli commandos, paratroopers, and naval forces seize the port city of Sharm el-Sheikh

4 SHARM EL-SHEIKH FALLS JUNE 7

Israel launched a small operation to take Sharm el-Sheikh, from where the Egyptians had enforced their blockade of the Gulf of Aqaba. Early in the morning, Israeli missile boats began firing on Egyptian positions; airborne troops engaged with Egyptian ground forces and took the city, which had, by this time, been largely abandoned.

⚲ Airborne forces attack   → Missile boat attack

THE SINAI CAMPAIGN
Supported by Israeli jets freed by the swift destruction of the Egyptian air force, Israeli tanks surged across the desert lands of the Sinai Peninsula, reaching the Suez Canal in a matter of days.

Map labels: Damascus, Quneitra, Golan Heights, SYRIA, Sea of Galilee, Haifa, Mafraq, West Bank, Tel Aviv, ISRAEL, JORDAN, Amman, Jericho, Jerusalem, Mediterranean Sea, Hebron, Dead Sea, Gaza City, Khan Yunis, Rafah, Beersheba, Port Said, El Arish, Bir Lahfan, Negev Desert, El Mansura, Kantara, Nitsana, Inchas, Gebel Libni, Abu Ageila, Deversoir, Bir Hassneh, Abu Sueir, Ismailia, Bir Gifgafa, EGYPT, Bir Thamada, Gidi Pass, Fayid, Kabrit, Cairo West, Cairo, Suez, Mitla Pass, Nakhl, Almaza, Helwan, Kuntilla, Ras Sudr, Eilat, Al Aqabah, River Nile, Beni Suef, Sinai, Gulf of Suez, Abu Zenima, Gulf of Aqaba, El Tor, Sharm el-Sheikh

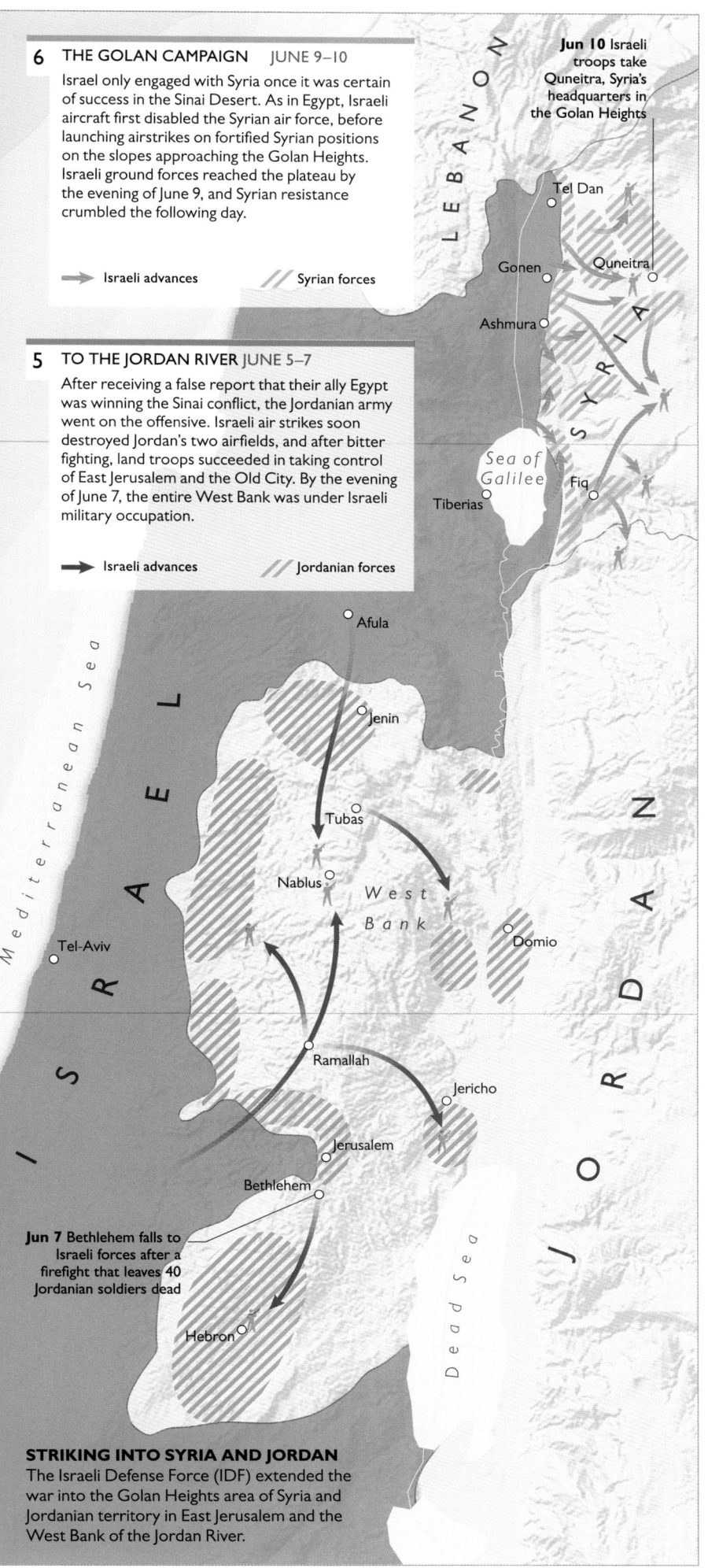

6 THE GOLAN CAMPAIGN   JUNE 9–10

Israel only engaged with Syria once it was certain of success in the Sinai Desert. As in Egypt, Israeli aircraft first disabled the Syrian air force, before launching airstrikes on fortified Syrian positions on the slopes approaching the Golan Heights. Israeli ground forces reached the plateau by the evening of June 9, and Syrian resistance crumbled the following day.

→ Israeli advances   // Syrian forces

5 TO THE JORDAN RIVER JUNE 5–7

After receiving a false report that their ally Egypt was winning the Sinai conflict, the Jordanian army went on the offensive. Israeli air strikes soon destroyed Jordan's two airfields, and after bitter fighting, land troops succeeded in taking control of East Jerusalem and the Old City. By the evening of June 7, the entire West Bank was under Israeli military occupation.

→ Israeli advances   // Jordanian forces

Jun 10 Israeli troops take Quneitra, Syria's headquarters in the Golan Heights

Jun 7 Bethlehem falls to Israeli forces after a firefight that leaves 40 Jordanian soldiers dead

STRIKING INTO SYRIA AND JORDAN
The Israeli Defense Force (IDF) extended the war into the Golan Heights area of Syria and Jordanian territory in East Jerusalem and the West Bank of the Jordan River.

SIX-DAY WAR

From its establishment in 1948, the state of Israel was in conflict with its Arab neighbors. When tensions rose to new heights in 1967, Israel launched a preemptive strike against Arab airfields, and sent its ground forces to occupy border territories and defeat the Arab armies.

The long-standing hostility between Israel and its Arab neighbors escalated in 1967 as tensions rose over Syrian support for Palestinian guerrillas. The crisis came to a head when Egypt's President Nasser mobilized his forces, blockaded Israeli shipping in the Gulf of Aqaba, and signed a defense pact with King Hussein of Jordan.

Convinced that the nation was under threat, the Israeli high command determined on preemptive action. On June 5 ,1967, Israeli jets launched a series of attacks on Egyptian airfields that not only destroyed the bulk of the Egyptian air force on the ground but also made the airstrips themselves unusable. At the same time, ground forces embarked on a three-pronged invasion of the Sinai Peninsula, heading for the Suez Canal. In the fighting that ensued, air supremacy gave the invaders a decisive advantage.

When Jordan came to the aid of its Egyptian ally, its forces too were beaten back, placing East Jerusalem and the West Bank of the Jordan river under Israeli control. Buoyed by their success, Israeli forces then advanced over the Syrian border on the Golan Heights, taking that strategic stronghold before accepting a ceasefire as called for by the United Nations Security Council. In just six days, Israel had occupied almost 27,000 sq miles (70,000 sq km) of land.

"Everyone must face the test and enter the battle to the end."

PRESIDENT NOUREDDIN AL-ATASSI OF SYRIA, 1967

DECISION IN THE DESERT
Simmering hostility between Israel and the surrounding Arab states broke into open warfare in June 1967. A preemptive strike by the Israeli air force gave Israel control of the air, paving the way for decisive gains by its land forces on three separate fronts.

KEY

■ Israeli territory at the start of the war

🧍 Israeli forces

🏗 Arab strongpoints

■ Territory captured by Israel, June 10, 1967

🧍 Arab forces

● Arab settlements

TIMELINE

1
2
3
4
5
6

JUN 5, 1967   JUN 8   JUN 11

THE TET OFFENSIVE

In 1967, US leaders sought to boost popular support for the Vietnam War. However, a series of attacks by Communist forces in 1968, known as the Tet Offensive, helped swing US opinion against the war, despite media coverage of the heavy losses suffered by the North Vietnamese and Viet Cong forces.

△ **US forces in Vietnam**
After the French withdrawal from Indochina (see p.257) Vietnam increasingly came under the influence of a US that wished to curb the spread of Communism. By 1962, there were some 10,000 US troops in the country.

In 1954, the Geneva Conference divided Vietnam between a Communist north, supported by China and the USSR, and a Western-backed south. Hostilities between the two resulted in the US deploying active combat units in 1965; in the US, public opinion started to turn against such involvement.

In 1967, US commander General Westmoreland claimed that the Communist forces were "unable to mount a major offensive." In fact North Vietnam's leaders had been planning one since early that year. They timed their attack for the Tet New Year holiday, the biggest celebration of the year in Vietnam. Over three days in early 1968, they launched assaults in more than 100 cities. Most of the attackers were repulsed or killed within days, although fighting in the northern city of Hue lasted almost a month. The Viet Cong and the North Vietnamese People's Army of Vietnam (PAVN) lost tens of thousands of fighters. Yet the scope of the action disproved the notion that the war was almost won. Although North Vietnamese hopes of a decisive uprising proved to be misplaced, the battle helped turn US opinion against the war.

4 THE FINAL WAVE FEBRUARY 1–12

The North Vietnamese launched more attacks the following night, this time concentrated on the southern military zones. None succeeded in holding ground, and the civilian population failed to rise in support. By mid-February, the PAVN and VC had lost tens of thousands for little tangible gain, but had quashed any notion that the war was almost over.

Viet Cong/PAVN offensives from Feb 1

THE BATTLE FOR HUE

The longest battle of the Tet Offensive was fought in Hue. There, Vietnamese Army forces held out in parts of the Citadel while allied troops repelled attacks on the MACV (Military Assistance Command, Vietnam) headquarters south of the river. North Vietnamese insurgents occupied the rest of the city, which was only recaptured after weeks of fighting. By the end, most of the city was destroyed, and about 10,000 soldiers and civilians were dead.

KEY

 Communist forces

 US and ARVN forces

➡ Communist attacks

ᴍᴍᴍ Communist blocking positions

⊞ ARVN Divisional HQ

⊞ MACV command post

--- Bach Ho railroad

⊕ Tay Loc Airfield

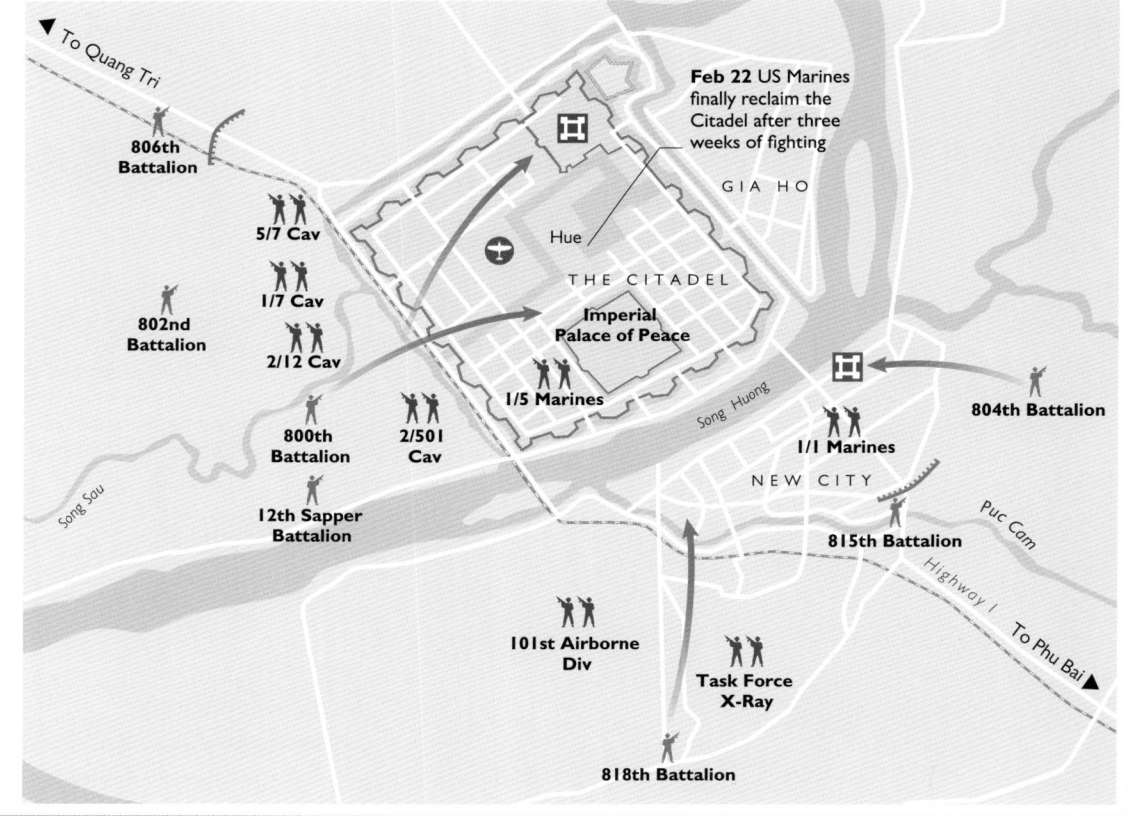

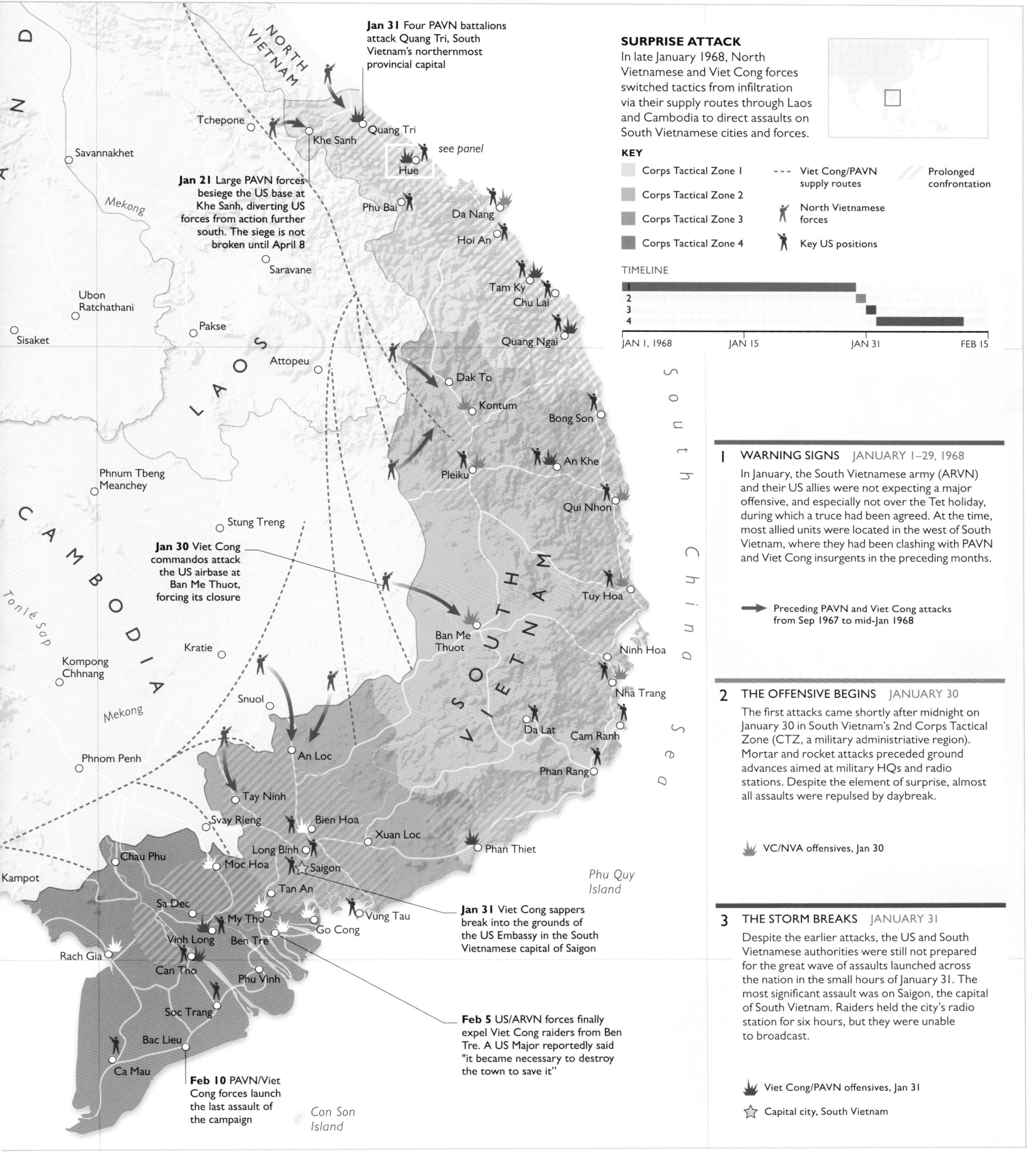

Jan 31 Four PAVN battalions attack Quang Tri, South Vietnam's northernmost provincial capital

see panel

Jan 21 Large PAVN forces besiege the US base at Khe Sanh, diverting US forces from action further south. The siege is not broken until April 8

Jan 30 Viet Cong commandos attack the US airbase at Ban Me Thuot, forcing its closure

Jan 31 Viet Cong sappers break into the grounds of the US Embassy in the South Vietnamese capital of Saigon

Feb 5 US/ARVN forces finally expel Viet Cong raiders from Ben Tre. A US Major reportedly said "it became necessary to destroy the town to save it"

Feb 10 PAVN/Viet Cong forces launch the last assault of the campaign

SURPRISE ATTACK

In late January 1968, North Vietnamese and Viet Cong forces switched tactics from infiltration via their supply routes through Laos and Cambodia to direct assaults on South Vietnamese cities and forces.

KEY

- Corps Tactical Zone 1
- Corps Tactical Zone 2
- Corps Tactical Zone 3
- Corps Tactical Zone 4
- --- Viet Cong/PAVN supply routes
- North Vietnamese forces
- Key US positions
- Prolonged confrontation

TIMELINE

1
2
3
4

JAN 1, 1968   JAN 15   JAN 31   FEB 15

1 WARNING SIGNS   JANUARY 1–29, 1968

In January, the South Vietnamese army (ARVN) and their US allies were not expecting a major offensive, and especially not over the Tet holiday, during which a truce had been agreed. At the time, most allied units were located in the west of South Vietnam, where they had been clashing with PAVN and Viet Cong insurgents in the preceding months.

→ Preceding PAVN and Viet Cong attacks from Sep 1967 to mid-Jan 1968

2 THE OFFENSIVE BEGINS   JANUARY 30

The first attacks came shortly after midnight on January 30 in South Vietnam's 2nd Corps Tactical Zone (CTZ, a military administrative region). Mortar and rocket attacks preceded ground advances aimed at military HQs and radio stations. Despite the element of surprise, almost all assaults were repulsed by daybreak.

VC/NVA offensives, Jan 30

3 THE STORM BREAKS   JANUARY 31

Despite the earlier attacks, the US and South Vietnamese authorities were still not prepared for the great wave of assaults launched across the nation in the small hours of January 31. The most significant assault was on Saigon, the capital of South Vietnam. Raiders held the city's radio station for six hours, but they were unable to broadcast.

Viet Cong/PAVN offensives, Jan 31

☆ Capital city, South Vietnam

YOM KIPPUR WAR

Launched on the Jewish holy day of Yom Kippur in October 1973, the surprise attack by Egypt and Syria on Israel sought to win back land occupied by Israel six years earlier. Despite early gains for Egypt and Syria, Israel counterattacked, recapturing its lost territory.

Humiliated by their defeat in the 1967 Six-Day War (see pp.260–61), the leaders of Egypt and Syria sought an opportunity to reverse the gains made by Israel. They took their chance six years later, launching a surprise attack timed for the Jewish festival of Yom Kippur.

On October 6, Egyptian forces crossed the Suez Canal to assault the fortified Bar-Lev Line, while Syrian tanks simultaneously stormed across the ceasefire line in the Golan Heights overlooking northern Israel. Initially, both cobelligerents made significant gains, causing shock in Israel. However,

after the first four days of fighting, the tide of battle reversed and the Egyptian advance stalled. Alarmed by the war's geopolitical implications at a time when Cold War tensions remained high, the US and the USSR each put pressure on the two sides, and a ceasefire went into effect after 19 days of combat. Although neither side made significant gains, the diplomatic standoff between Israel and Egypt had been effectively broken, and in the years that followed a peace process got under way that led eventually to Egyptian recognition of the state of Israel and the return of Sinai to Egypt.

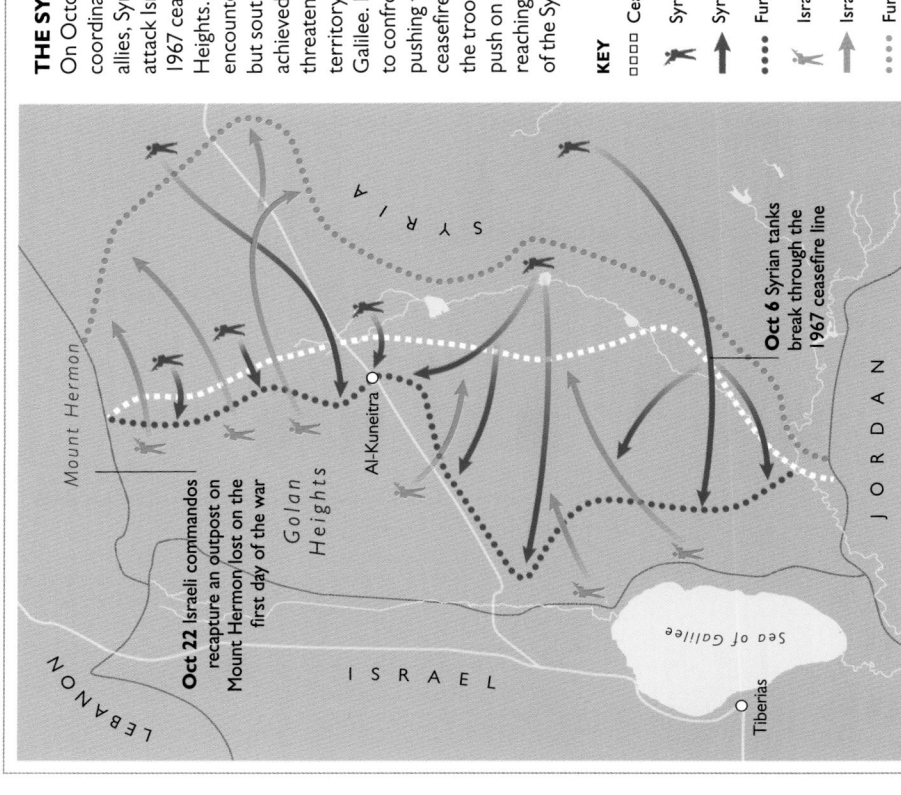

THE SYRIAN FRONT

On October 6, in a move coordinated with its Egyptian allies, Syria sent five divisions to attack Israeli positions along the 1967 ceasefire line in the Golan Heights. In the north, they encountered strong resistance, but south of Al-Kunetira, they achieved a breakthrough, threatening to invade Israeli territory around the Sea of Galilee. Israeli reserves rushed to confront the advancing forces, pushing them back to the old ceasefire line. On October 11, the troops received orders to push on into Syrian territory, reaching within 25 miles (40km) of the Syrian capital Damascus.

KEY

▫▫▫▫ Ceasefire line, 1967

🦗 Syrian troops

⬆ Syrian attacks

•••• Furthest Syrian advance

🦗 Israeli troops

⬆ Israeli counterattack

•••• Furthest Israeli advance

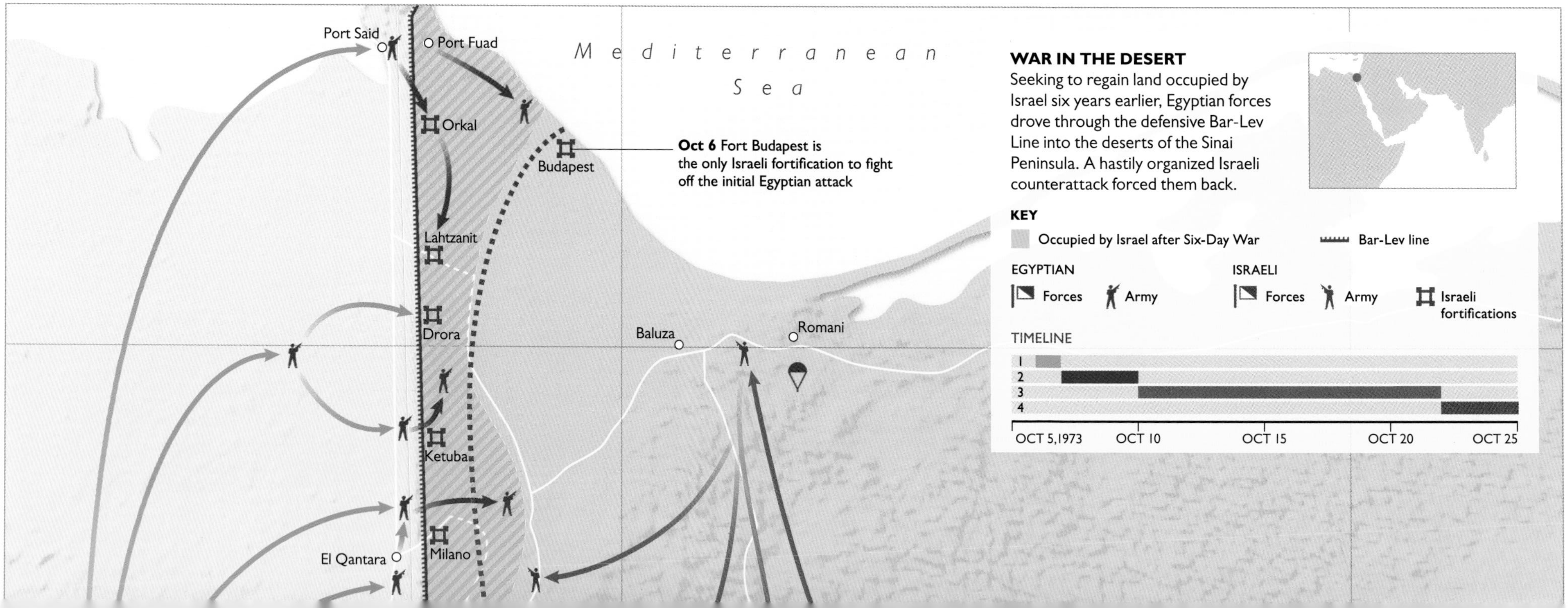

Oct 22 Israeli commandos recapture an outpost on Mount Hermon lost on the first day of the war

Oct 6 Syrian tanks break through the 1967 ceasefire line

WAR IN THE DESERT

Seeking to regain land occupied by Israel six years earlier, Egyptian forces drove through the defensive Bar-Lev Line into the deserts of the Sinai Peninsula. A hastily organized Israeli counterattack forced them back.

KEY

▨ Occupied by Israel after Six-Day War

EGYPTIAN
▮ Forces 🦗 Army

ISRAELI
▯ Forces 🦗 Army

ılıılı Bar-Lev line

⛨ Israeli fortifications

TIMELINE

OCT 5,1973	OCT 10	OCT 15	OCT 20	OCT 25
1				
2				
3				
4				

Oct 6 Fort Budapest is the only Israeli fortification to fight off the initial Egyptian attack

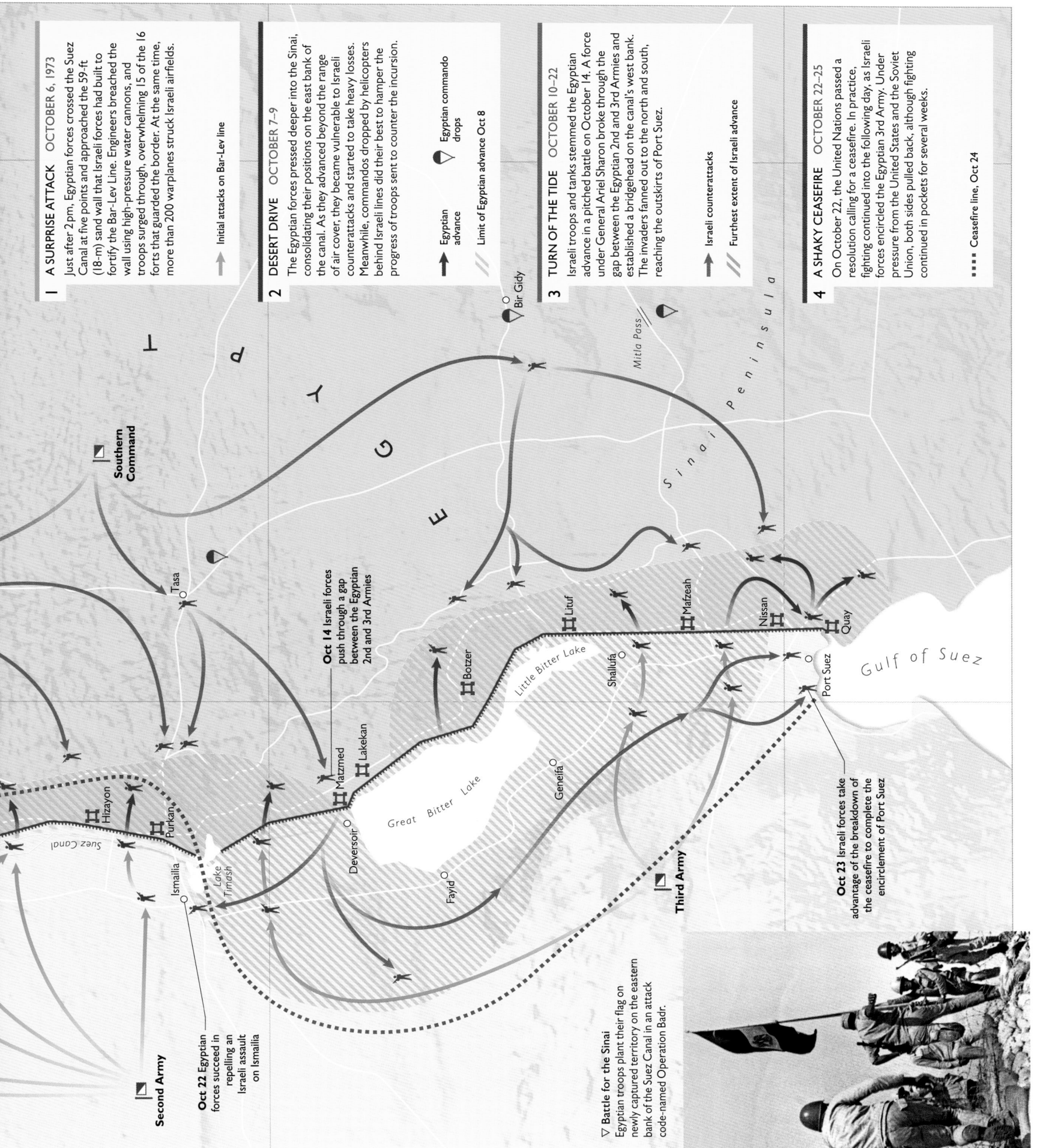

1 A SURPRISE ATTACK OCTOBER 6, 1973

Just after 2pm, Egyptian forces crossed the Suez Canal at five points and approached the 59-ft (18-m) sand wall that Israeli forces had built to fortify the Bar-Lev Line. Engineers breached the wall using high-pressure water cannons, and troops surged through, overwhelming 15 of the 16 forts that guarded the border. At the same time, more than 200 warplanes struck Israeli airfields.

→ Initial attacks on Bar-Lev line

2 DESERT DRIVE OCTOBER 7–9

The Egyptian forces pressed deeper into the Sinai, consolidating their positions on the east bank of the canal. As they advanced beyond the range of air cover, they became vulnerable to Israeli counterattacks and started to take heavy losses. Meanwhile, commandos dropped by helicopters behind Israeli lines did their best to hamper the progress of troops sent to counter the incursion.

→ Egyptian advance

◗ Egyptian commando drops

∥ Limit of Egyptian advance Oct 8

3 TURN OF THE TIDE OCTOBER 10–22

Israeli troops and tanks stemmed the Egyptian advance in a pitched battle on October 14. A force under General Ariel Sharon broke through the gap between the Egyptian 2nd and 3rd Armies and established a bridgehead on the canal's west bank. The invaders fanned out to the north and south, reaching the outskirts of Port Suez.

→ Israeli counterattacks

∥ Furthest extent of Israeli advance

4 A SHAKY CEASEFIRE OCTOBER 22–25

On October 22, the United Nations passed a resolution calling for a ceasefire. In practice, fighting continued into the following day, as Israeli forces encircled the Egyptian 3rd Army. Under pressure from the United States and the Soviet Union, both sides pulled back, although fighting continued in pockets for several weeks.

▪▪▪▪ Ceasefire line, Oct 24

Oct 14 Israeli forces push through a gap between the Egyptian 2nd and 3rd Armies

Oct 22 Egyptian forces succeed in repelling an Israeli assault on Ismailia

Second Army

Third Army

Oct 23 Israeli forces take advantage of the breakdown of the ceasefire to complete the encirclement of Port Suez

▽ **Battle for the Sinai**
Egyptian troops plant their flag on newly captured territory on the eastern bank of the Suez Canal in an attack code-named Operation Badr.

Map labels

Southern Command
Bir Gidy
Mitla Pass
Sinai Peninsula
Tasa
Lituf
Mafzeah
Nissan
Quay
Botzer
Little Bitter Lake
Gulf of Suez
Matzmed
Lakekan
Shallufa
Port Suez
Deversoir
Great Bitter Lake
Geneifa
Hizayon
Purkan
Ismailia
Lake Timsah
Suez Canal
Fayid

DESERT STORM

In response to Iraq's invasion of Kuwait in 1990, the US brought together a coalition of nations to liberate the country. Following a protracted bombing campaign, their ground forces attacked in February 1991, meeting limited resistance. After four days' fighting, President George Bush declared victory.

Following the end of the Iran-Iraq War in 1988, Iraq found itself deeply in debt to its neighbors Kuwait and Saudi Arabia. Disputes over this debt and over border oil fields soured relations, and in 1990, Iraqi president Saddam Hussein gave the order for an invasion of Kuwait, which took place on August 2.

President George Bush, appalled by this aggression and worried by the threat to global oil supplies, started moving troops to the Saudi-Iraq border and began a coalition of nations to resist Saddam; eventually 34 countries gave their support. The military buildup continued into early 1991 until over half a million troops were ready for action. The fighting started with an intensive allied bombing campaign, launched on January 16. For the next six weeks, Iraq's military and civilian infrastructure was pounded day and night from the skies.

A ground invasion was finally launched on February 24. As coalition forces headed into Kuwait and Iraq itself, Iraqi invaders retreated before them, leaving over 700 Kuwaiti oil wells on fire. After just three days, President Bush was able to declare the country liberated. On February 28, with his troops within 150 miles (240 km) of the Iraqi capital, Bush declared a cease-fire. The exiled Emir of Kuwait returned to his devastated country two weeks later.

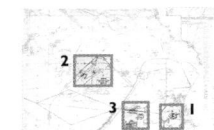

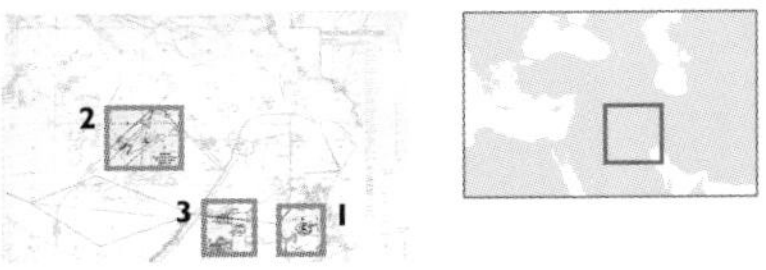

KEY

1 The main thrust into Kuwait moved north to liberate Kuwait City.

2 The US 7th Corps and the British 1st Armored Division drove northeast into Iraq.

3 Saudi, Kuwaiti, and Egyptian forces moved into western Kuwait.

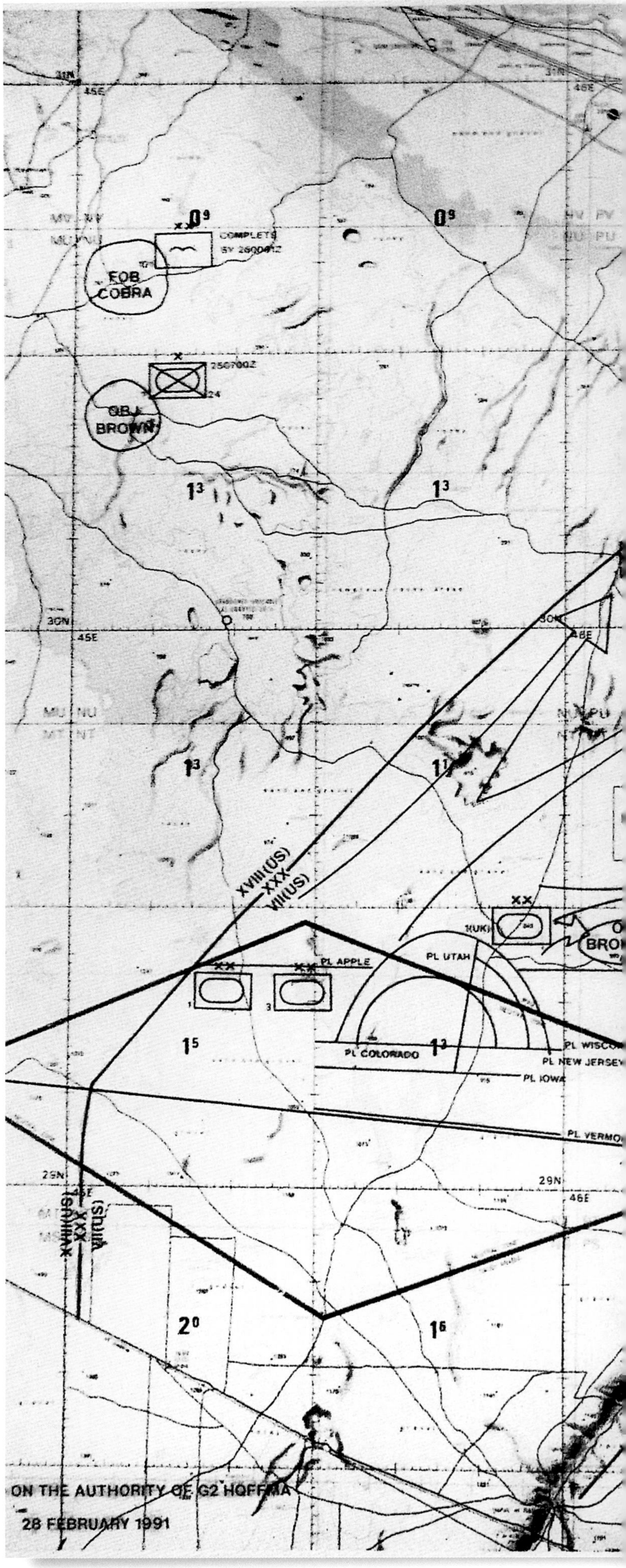

▷ **Coalition plan of attack**
Dated February 25, 1991, and declassified three days later when the war ended, this initially secret situation report map shows movements at the start of the ground war. Blue arrows indicate the progress of coalition forces into Kuwait (to the right) and Iraq itself.

WAR IN THE SKIES
The coalition's strategic air campaign saw F-117 planes and Tomahawk missiles destroy much of Iraq's military and parts of its civilian infrastructure. Prime targets included command and communications installations, air force bases, and mobile missile launch pads. Although civilians suffered disruption due to these attacks, there was none of the massive loss of life caused by previous bombing campaigns.

KEY

▲ Allied airbase

➤ Coalition airstrike

▲ Iraqi airbase

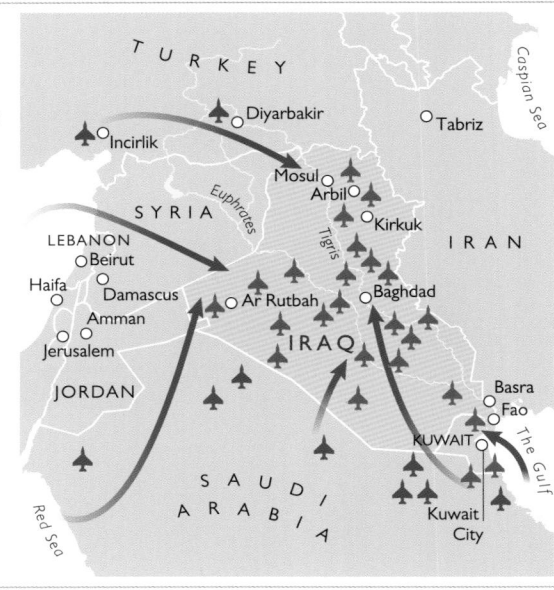

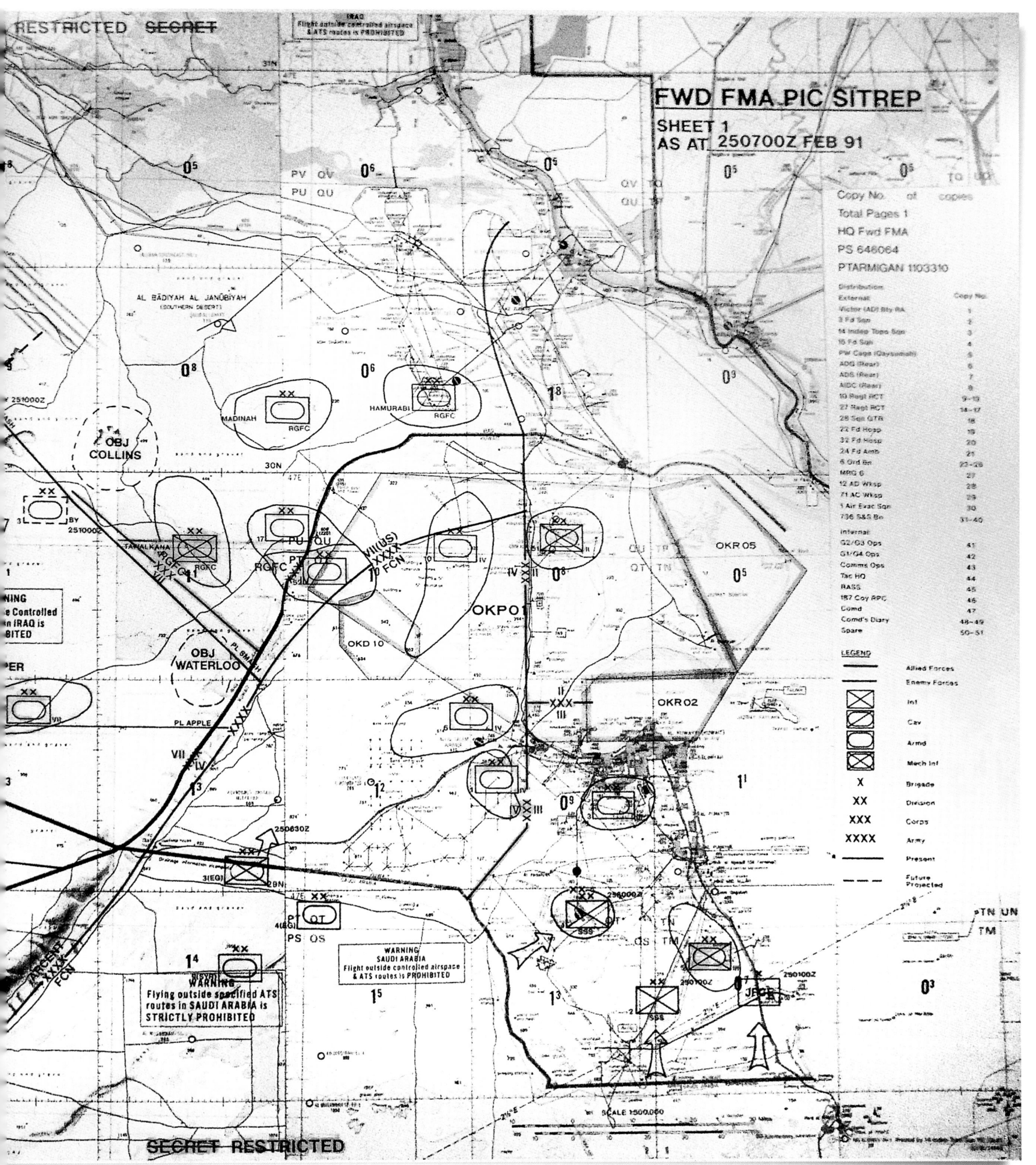

FWD FMA PIC SITREP
SHEET 1
AS AT 250700Z FEB 91

Flying above
A US Navy F-18C Hornet aircraft can be seen flying above Afghanistan. The aircraft is armed, from left to right, with two GBU-15 Paveway II laser-guided bombs and one AIM-9R infrared air-to-air missile.

SMART WEAPONS

The first operational use of smart weapons—munitions with guidance systems—dates back to 1943 when Germany deployed the Fritz X anti-ship guided bomb. Smart weapons are now a part of modern warfare.

The first precision-guided munitions were radio-controlled; subsequent technological advances saw the rise of laser-guided, radar-guided, infrared-guided, and GPS satellite-guided weapons. Although Germany was the first country to employ guided ordnance during World War II, the US and Britain also had research programs. The US program, which continued after the war, focused on ground and aerial targets, prioritizing air-to-air and surface-to-air missiles. By 1965, at the start of the sustained US air campaign against North Vietnam, air-to-air missiles were widespread. Early missiles, however, were unreliable, and misses were more common than hits. Air-to-ground guided ammunition, on the other hand, reached full-scale potential with Operation Linebacker in 1972, in which superior tactics, improved training, and guided weaponry allowed the US Air Force and US Navy to inflict heavy damage on the North Vietnamese Air Force from the skies.

Smart weapons became commonplace after their use by the US in Operation Desert Storm (see pp.266–67)—although only 9 percent of US munitions used in the conflict were guided, they were found to be much more likely to hit their targets than non-guided weaponry.

△ **Cloud of fire**
The warhead of a BGM-109 Tomahawk cruise missile, launched from a submarine, detonates over its test target.

△ **Work in progress**
US Air Force technicians work on an air-to-ground GBU-15 Paveway glide bomb in a hangar in Saudi Arabia. An EF-111A aircraft of the 390th Electronic Combat Squadron can be seen parked in the background.

THE IRAQ WAR

The 2003 invasion of Iraq by a US-led coalition of forces was a success in military terms, achieving its intended purpose of removing Saddam Hussein from power. However, widespread doubts over its justification increased further when it triggered enduring and bloody sectarian violence and political instability.

The Gulf War of 1990–91 left Iraq's defeated leader Saddam Hussein in charge of the country (see pp.266–67). Despite harsh sanctions imposed in its wake, US strategists viewed the regime as an ongoing threat, and accused it of colluding with terrorists and harboring weapons of mass destruction.

In 2002, following the 2001 al-Qaeda destruction of the World Trade Center in New York, Congress authorized President George W. Bush to use military force against Iraq. The US then built a network of allies, including Britain, Australia, and Poland. When Saddam refused to give up power, troops of this "coalition of the willing" invaded the country across its southern border with

Kuwait, while coalition air power began a bombing campaign against strategic targets. Meanwhile special forces cooperated with Kurdish Peshmerga guerrilla groups in the north, despite Turkey's refusal to help (as in 1991).

Within three weeks, coalition forces reached Baghdad and Saddam went into hiding; he was captured eight months later, tried, and executed. However, no weapons of mass destruction were found, and far from transitioning to a peaceful democracy as hoped, Iraq fell victim to a long-running insurgency. The invasion served as a trigger for ongoing violence, and Western forces were tied down for many years trying to manage the turmoil.

> "My name is Saddam Hussein. I am the president of Iraq, and I want to negotiate."
>
> SADDAM HUSSEIN, SURRENDERING TO US TROOPS, 2003

INVADING IRAQ

Although the invasion of Iraq was well organized and effectively executed, the coalition did not make the necessary plans for occupying or reconstructing the country.

KEY

- Kurdish areas
- Sunni areas
- Shiite areas
- Sparsely populated areas
- Sunni triangle
- Oil fields
- Allied forces
- Iraqi forces
- Iraqi air bases
- Ansar al-Islam camp
- Areas targeted for airstrike

TIMELINE

1	
2	
3	
4	
5	

MAR 15, 2003   MAR 31   APR 15

I THE PUSH NORTH MARCH 20–APRIL 9

Coalition forces crossed into Iraq on March 20. The main body made rapid progress northward, reaching the outskirts of Baghdad by April 2. Fierce fighting took place in Nasiriyah after a US Army supply convoy took a wrong turn and drove into the city. Meanwhile, coalition airstrikes pounded military sites, while special forces secured oil fields and airfields in the desert.

→ Coalition forces advance

SYRIA

Akashat

JORDAN

SECTARIAN INSURGENCY

The fall of Saddam prompted Shia and Sunni militias, supported respectively by Iran and by al-Qaeda, to battle for power. After Western forces withdrew, a new militant group, the Islamic State in Iraq and the Levant (ISIL) seized most of northern and central Iraq in 2014. It proclaimed a global caliphate, and attracted many foreign jihadists, but was slowly rolled back by Western airstrikes, and Kurdish and government counterattacks.

KEY

- Syrian and Iraqi Kurdish forces (2018)
- Islamic State group (2018)
- Iraqi government (2018)
- Syrian government (2018)
- Syrian rebel forces (2018)

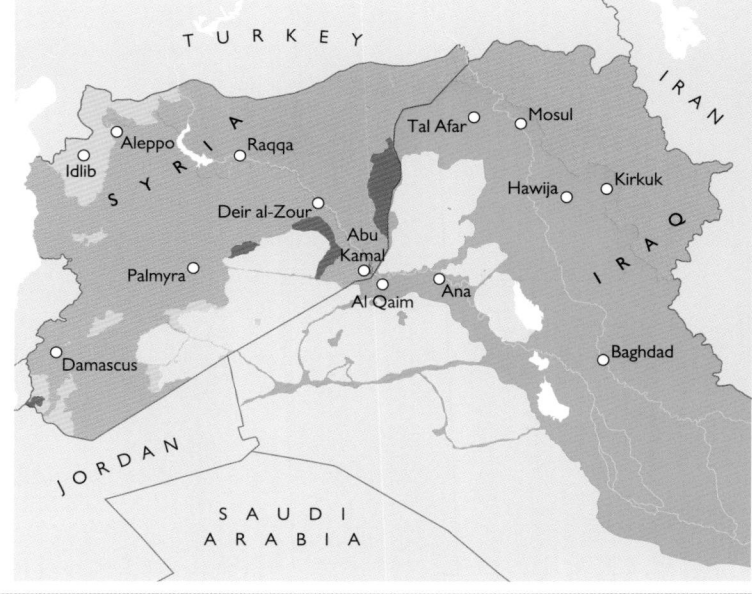

TURKEY
Aleppo
Idlib
Raqqa
Tal Afar
Mosul
SYRIA
Deir al-Zour
Hawija
Kirkuk
IRAN
Abu Kamal
Palmyra
Ana
Al Qaim
IRAQ
Damascus
Baghdad
JORDAN
SAUDI ARABIA

△ Clearing a path
Helicopter-borne troops of the British Army's Parachute Regiment prepare to conduct vehicle searches for weapons in southern Iraq.

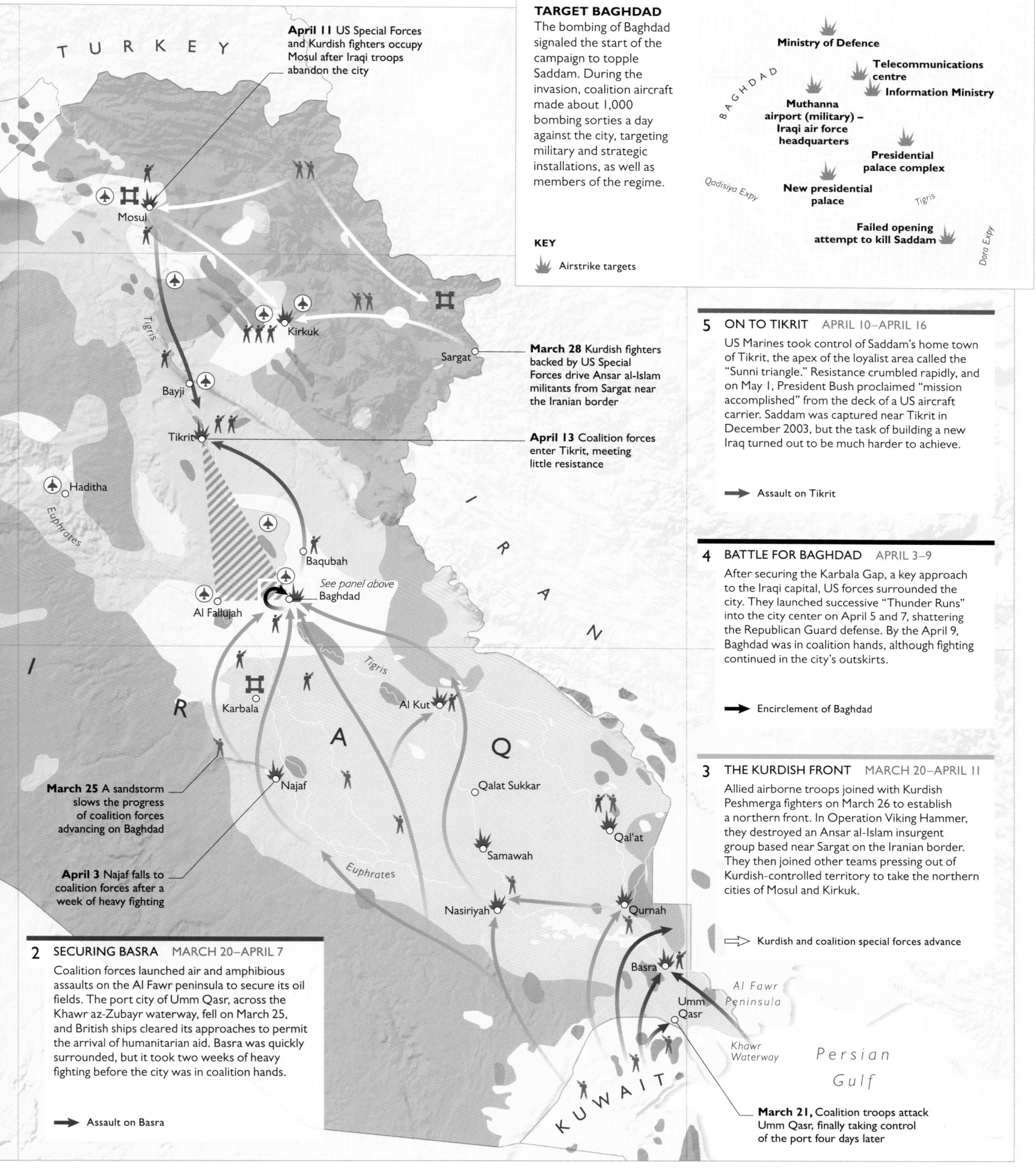

April 11 US Special Forces and Kurdish fighters occupy Mosul after Iraqi troops abandon the city

TARGET BAGHDAD

The bombing of Baghdad signaled the start of the campaign to topple Saddam. During the invasion, coalition aircraft made about 1,000 bombing sorties a day against the city, targeting military and strategic installations, as well as members of the regime.

Ministry of Defence

Telecommunications centre

Information Ministry

BAGHDAD

Muthanna airport (military) – Iraqi air force headquarters

Presidential palace complex

Qadisiya Expy

New presidential palace

Tigris

Failed opening attempt to kill Saddam

Dora Expy

KEY

Airstrike targets

March 28 Kurdish fighters backed by US Special Forces drive Ansar al-Islam militants from Sargat near the Iranian border

April 13 Coalition forces enter Tikrit, meeting little resistance

5 ON TO TIKRIT   APRIL 10–APRIL 16

US Marines took control of Saddam's home town of Tikrit, the apex of the loyalist area called the "Sunni triangle." Resistance crumbled rapidly, and on May 1, President Bush proclaimed "mission accomplished" from the deck of a US aircraft carrier. Saddam was captured near Tikrit in December 2003, but the task of building a new Iraq turned out to be much harder to achieve.

→ Assault on Tikrit

4 BATTLE FOR BAGHDAD   APRIL 3–9

After securing the Karbala Gap, a key approach to the Iraqi capital, US forces surrounded the city. They launched successive "Thunder Runs" into the city center on April 5 and 7, shattering the Republican Guard defense. By the April 9, Baghdad was in coalition hands, although fighting continued in the city's outskirts.

→ Encirclement of Baghdad

3 THE KURDISH FRONT   MARCH 20–APRIL 11

Allied airborne troops joined with Kurdish Peshmerga fighters on March 26 to establish a northern front. In Operation Viking Hammer, they destroyed an Ansar al-Islam insurgent group based near Sargat on the Iranian border. They then joined other teams pressing out of Kurdish-controlled territory to take the northern cities of Mosul and Kirkuk.

⇨ Kurdish and coalition special forces advance

March 25 A sandstorm slows the progress of coalition forces advancing on Baghdad

April 3 Najaf falls to coalition forces after a week of heavy fighting

2 SECURING BASRA   MARCH 20–APRIL 7

Coalition forces launched air and amphibious assaults on the Al Fawr peninsula to secure its oil fields. The port city of Umm Qasr, across the Khawr az-Zubayr waterway, fell on March 25, and British ships cleared its approaches to permit the arrival of humanitarian aid. Basra was quickly surrounded, but it took two weeks of heavy fighting before the city was in coalition hands.

→ Assault on Basra

March 21, Coalition troops attack Umm Qasr, finally taking control of the port four days later

See panel above

Persian Gulf

Al Fawr Peninsula

Khawr Waterway

Persian Gulf

DIRECTORY: 1900–PRESENT

RELIEF OF BEIJING

JUNE–AUGUST 1900

△ In this illustration Japanese soldiers clash with Chinese forces in Beijing

The foreign occupation of Beijing in 1900 proved to be a decisive step toward the collapse of Imperial China. In the late 19th century, China was gripped by an anti-foreign movement, and the members of a nationalist society, known as Boxers, began to stir up dissent. The Empress Dowager Cixi declared support for the Boxer activists carrying out attacks on Christian missionaries and foreigners. The diplomatic quarter in Beijing, defended by some 400 foreign troops, was placed under siege on 20 June by the Boxers and the Chinese army. Soon after, a multinational force went to assist but was repulsed. On August 4, a much larger force of Russian, Japanese, British, US, and French troops set out from Tianjin. Meanwhile, troops in the quarter fought off stiff attacks.

On August 14, the relief force scaled the city walls and stormed the gates. Fighting went on through August 15, but the Chinese forces mostly fled. In the aftermath, foreign troops and civilians engaged in rampant looting and killed many suspected Boxers. Empress Cixi had to accept humiliating peace terms. The imperial system never recovered and was replaced by a republic in 1912.

MUKDEN

FEBRUARY 20–
MARCH 10, 1905

The Japanese defeat of the Russians at Mukden was the first major victory for an Asian power over a European power in the imperialist era. The Russo-Japanese War had started in 1904 over rival claims in Manchuria and Korea.

Russian General Alexei Kuropatkin established a defensive line more than 50 miles (80 km) long south of Manchurian capital Mukden (now Shenyang in China's Liaoning Province), facing a Japanese army under Marshal Oyama Iwao. More than 300,000 Russian soldiers were entrenched behind barbed wire. The Japanese, although lesser in numbers, were better equipped. Oyama launched an offensive against the left of the Russian line on February 20. Fighting in ice and snow, the Japanese suffered heavy losses without a breakthrough. Oyama then switched the focus of his attack to the Russian right. Kuropatkin's fumbled attempt to move troops to meet this new threat reduced his army to chaos. As the Japanese succeeded in enveloping the enemy right, the Russians retreated in disorder, abandoning their equipment and the wounded. The Japanese forces occupied Mukden on March 10. Although Japanese losses were as high as those of Russia, Kuropatkin withdrew his forces from the region and the defeat demoralized Russia's tsarist regime. The final decisive battle of the war was fought in the Tsushima Strait (see p.205), where the Russian fleet was defeated.

MEUSE–ARGONNE OFFENSIVE

SEPTEMBER 26–NOVEMBER 11, 1918

The Meuse–Argonne Offensive, involving 1.2 million US troops, was one of the largest battles ever fought by the US Army. It was a part of the Hundred Days Offensive (August–November 1918), a series of attacks with which the Allies ended World War I.

Commanded by General John Pershing, and supported by the French Fourth Army, the US First Army was to advance through the dense Argonne Forest to Sedan, a major rail junction in German-occupied eastern France. Hastily organized only two weeks after a US victory at the Saint-Mihiel salient, the initial attack yielded disappointing results. The terrain favored defense, and the Germans had deep bunkers and fortified trenches. As a result, inexperienced US infantry suffered heavy losses for limited gains. Bogged down in heavy rain, the offensive was relaunched on October 4. Pershing deployed fresh divisions to win the battle of attrition with the increasingly exhausted Germans. In late October, they broke through the Kriemhilde Stellung, a section of the fortified Hindenburg Line. The Americans approached their initial objective of Sedan just as the armistice ended the fighting on November 11. The battle cost more than 26,000 American lives.

△ Troops of the US 369th Infantry Regiment fight in the Argonne forest

SHANGHAI
AUGUST 13–NOVEMBER 26, 1937

The battle between China and Japan in Shanghai in 1937 was the first major engagement of the Second Sino-Japanese War (1937–45). Starting in 1931, Japanese encroachments on Chinese territory had led to scattered outbreaks of fighting. Clashes escalated from July 1937, and on August 13 the fighting spread to Shanghai. Chinese nationalist leader Chiang Kai-Shek hoped to overwhelm the outnumbered Japanese garrison, but Japanese amphibious landings soon evened the odds. Prolonged street fighting, shelling, and air bombardments incurred huge civilian casualties. On November 5 the increasingly hard-pressed Chinese army finally withdrew from Shanghai, and on November 26 it was forced out of its final defense line before the capital, Nanjing. China lost many of its best-trained soldiers in battle, and, over the following years, Japan occupied much of the country. With US backing, Chinese resistance continued and became part of the wider World War II.

MONTE CASSINO
JANUARY 17–MAY 18, 1944

During World War II, the hill of Monte Cassino was a key location on the German Gustav Line that blocked Allied progress northward to Rome during their invasion of Italy. Commanded by Generalfeldmarschall Albert Kesselring, the Germans made optimal use of the defensive potential of the mountainous terrain and fast-flowing rivers. The US 5th Army and British 8th Army were committed to breaking through the line. In January–March, the Allies made three failed assaults on the German position. US bombers destroyed the abbey at Cassino, mistakenly believing it to be occupied by German troops. The German forces went on to occupy the ruins left by the bombing, turning it into a formidable defensive strongpoint. A final Allied offensive, launched on May 11, achieved the breakthrough. General Wladyslaw Anders' Polish corps planted its flag on the crest of the hill on May 18. Rome fell to the Allies on June 5, but the Germans escaped to block the Allies in northern Italy until April 1945.

OPERATION BARBAROSSA
JUNE 22–OCTOBER 2, 1941

In June 1941, German leader Adolf Hitler amassed more than 3 million troops with thousands of tanks and aircraft to invade the USSR. On June 22, the Axis forces poured across a front stretching from the Baltic to the Black Sea. Achieving total surprise, the Luftwaffe destroyed thousands of Soviet planes while the ground force advanced rapidly toward Leningrad (St. Petersburg) in the north, Smolensk in the center, and Kiev in the south. Hundreds of thousands of Soviet troops were trapped by encircling Axis forces, and Leningrad was besieged. However, mounting losses, stretched supply lines, and confused objectives slowed the Axis progress. A final push toward Moscow in the fall rains and freezing weather was fruitless. Hitler's failure to achieve a quick victory in the USSR condemned him to a protracted war, which he had inadequate resources to win.

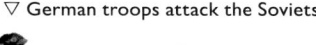
▽ German troops attack the Soviets

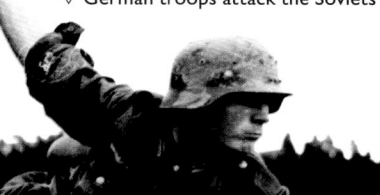

INVASION OF SUEZ
OCTOBER 29– NOVEMBER 7, 1956

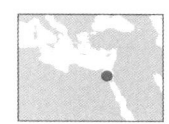

The coordinated attack on Egypt by Israel, Britain, and France in 1956 was a military success but a political disaster that hastened the end of European colonialism. The war was triggered by Egyptian leader Gamal Abdel Nasser's decision to nationalize the Suez Canal—a man-made waterway invaluable to international trade—which was owned by a Franco-British company. An aggressive Arab nationalist, Nasser was viewed as a threat not only to French and British interests but also to Israel. A plan was formulated in which Israel would invade Egypt's Sinai Peninsula, allowing Britain and France to justify military intervention with the excuse to defend the Suez Canal. The unavowed aim was to overthrow Nasser.

The Israeli forces attacked on October 29, advancing with spectacular speed across the Sinai. On November 5, after initial bombing attacks, British and French paratroopers jumped into the Suez Canal Zone and began occupying strategic points. The following day larger forces, accompanied with tanks, came ashore on landing craft while others were transported by helicopters. This was the first ever use of helicopters for assault landings. In response to the invasion, Egypt blocked the use of the Canal by sinking ships in the waterway—it remained closed to traffic for five months.

Key objectives of the plot were swiftly attained but the attack was met with heavy criticism in Britain and elsewhere. More importantly, diplomatic and financial pressure from the US, which had not been consulted, forced the military operations to a halt after only two days. Humiliated, Britain and France withdrew their forces, and Nasser emerged as a powerful hero in the Arab world.

GUADALCANAL
AUGUST 7, 1942–FEBRUARY 9, 1943

Guadalcanal island in the Solomons was the focus for some of the fiercest battles fought between Japan and the US and its allies. Japan occupied the island in May 1942, but the US Marines invaded in August and finished building the captured airstrip which they named Henderson Field. There followed months of intense fighting including three major land battles, two aircraft carrier battles, five nighttime surface naval battles off nearby Savo island, and almost daily air battles as both sides struggled to reinforce, resupply, and support their troops on Guadalcanal and eject their opponents. Growing US resource superiority finally prevailed and Japan began to withdraw its starving troops from the island in December, completing the evacuation by February 1943. The superiority of Allied forces in the Pacific was never again seriously in doubt.

△ Cargo ships line the Suez Canal, deliberately sunk by Egypt to block it

GLOSSARY

air wing A unit of command in military aviation comprising a number of squadrons. It originated in 1912 when the British Royal Flying Corps divided into a military wing and a naval wing.

archon Highest ranking official in Ancient Greece city-states, from the Greek word for ruler. Each city-state had several archons governing separate departments; the archon polemarchos was military commander.

armistice A formal agreement to suspend military operations between warring sides from different nations. Historically, a state of war may still have existed while an armistice was in place, but under contemporary international law an armistice means termination of war.

artillery Large-caliber weapons such as mounted shell-firing guns, howitzers, and missile launchers that can reach beyond the range of infantry firearms. The term is also used for the arm of the military service using these weapons, such as field artillery, coastal artillery, and anti-tank artillery.

auxiliaries (troops) Personnel providing support services to the military or police. They are often volunteers or do part-time paid work. In Ancient Rome, auxiliaries were noncitizens drafted for an average 25 years' service, after which they received citizenship.

bar shot A cannon shot, or projectile, formed of two iron balls connected with a bar, resembling the shape of dumbbell. The weighted ends cause the shot to spin through the air when fired, making it very effective at cutting the masts of sailing ships and tearing through their spars and rigging.

bastion The bulwark projecting from the curtain wall of a fortification. Shaped like an arrowhead, this style of outcrop was designed to eliminate the blind spot just below the parapet wall and protect soldiers as they fired on invaders below.

battlecruiser A large armed warship equipped with battleship armaments, but lighter and faster than a battleship. The first battlecruisers were the three *Invincible*-class vessels that entered into the service of the Royal Navy in 1908.

battleship The largest and heaviest type of warship equipped with large-caliber guns and thick armor. Battleships were the centerpiece of naval fleets in the first decades of the 20th century.

beachhead An area close to the sea or a river that, when captured by attacking troops, is the foundation for a subsequent advance deeper into enemy-held territory.

Blitzkrieg Meaning "lightning war" in German, this World War II military tactic was used in the invasion of Poland in 1939. It consists of mass tank formations, supported by dive-bombers and motorized artillery, making a thrust forward on a narrow front.

bombard (n) Late medieval cannon of the 15th century. Mostly used during sieges for smashing stronghold walls, they developed into a super-gun of the era, made from iron and using gunpowder to fire mortar and granite balls. Examples include Russia's 1586 Tsar Cannon and the Ottoman Empire Dardanelles gun of 1464.

bridgehead Strategic site at a bridge or water crossing where defensive units set up military lines to provide cover for crossing troops.

brigade Military formation, typically consisting of three to six battalions, plus supporting reconnaissance, artillery, engineers, supply, and transport elements.

brigantine Two-masted sailing vessel from the 16th century, square-rigged but with fore-and-aft rigging on the main mast. Its name comes from the two-masted sailing ships of brigands, or pirates, on the Mediterranean Sea.

broadside The cannon battery installed on both sides of side of a warship, a feature of naval ships from the 16th to mid-19th centuries. The term also means the act of firing the guns from the side of the ship.

cannister shot Artillery ammunition in the form of a metal cylinder filled with metal balls. The canisters disintegrate when fired from a cannon and deliver a shotgun-like blast. Very common in the 18th and 19th centuries, cannister shot remains in use to this day.

caravel Fast, maneuverable sailing vessel invented in Portugal in the 15th century for long-distance travel across the Atlantic. Used by Christopher Columbus on his journeys to South America, the caravel was rigged with lateen sails designed for sailing windward.

carbine Lightweight, riflelike gun with a short barrel, usually less than 20 in (51 cm) long. The original carbine was used by soldiers on horseback but has since developed into a gas-operated semiautomatic.

carrack Portuguese-designed ocean-going sailing vessel with three masts, widely used by European naval powers between the 14th and 17th centuries. Henry VIII's *Mary Rose* is one of the best known surviving examples.

cataphract Heavily armored cavalry of Persia and other ancient kingdoms of the Middle East; later adopted by the Romans and Byzantines. Cataphracts are considered precursors of the medieval knight.

ceasefire Temporary or partial cessation of military hostilities—for the purposes of collecting the dead, for example, or to stage peace talks.

chevauchée From the French "to ride," a medieval warfare tactic of conducting an armed raid on horseback into enemy territory to destroy property and pillage. Civilians were also often targeted.

Companions (Greek) Elite cavalry of the Macedonian army from the time of King Phillip II. Recruited from nobility, the Companions were the most senior regiment. Under Phillip's son, Alexander the Great, they were the key to victory over the Persian army in 331 BCE.

Confederacy (American Civil War) An association of 11 Southern states that broke away from the United States in 1860–61 with the aim of forming a new nation in which slavery would be legal. Also known as the Confederate States of America, or the Southern Confederacy.

corps An army unit made of two or more divisions. Napoleon is credited with devising the corps formation, with each corps self-sufficient and able to fight on its own or join together with other corps. This structure made the army more flexible and maneuverable.

crossing the T Naval warfare tactic prevalent from the late 19th to mid-20th century in which a line of warships crosses perpendicular to an enemy's line of ships. This allows the crossing line to use all of their guns to fire at the enemy, while their enemy can only use their forward guns. This technique was often used to great effect, such as in 1905 by Japan in the Battle of Tsushima (see p.205).

cuirassier A cavalry solider wearing a cuirass (breastplate armor designed to protect the torso), and carrying a sword or saber and pistol. Cuirassier regiments rose to prominence in the 18th century and played an important role in Napoleonic armies.

daimyo Feudal lords who controlled most of Japan under the shoguns, from the 10th century to the mid-19th century. They maintained power by hiring samurai warriors to protect their interests.

dive bomber Military aircraft that dives straight at its target until it reaches a low altitude before dropping its bomb load, leveling off, and flying away. This increases the accuracy of the hit. The tactic was used during the Spanish Civil War and World War II.

division Large military formation comprising several regiments or brigades that fight as an independent unit. A division numbers between 10,000 and 20,000 soldiers on average.

dragoon Mounted infantry who would use horses for mobility and fight on foot. Originating in 16th century Europe, gradually dragoons became an accepted military unit. They take their name from the type of short muskets they used.

dreadnought / super-dreadnought British battleship named after the Royal Navy's revolutionary steam propulsion HMS *Dreadnought* of 1906, with a main armament of up to 14 guns, more than double that of previous models (see pp.206–207). The second-generation super-dreadnoughts were phased in from 1914 and were the flagships of several nations up until World War II.

drone Remote aerial surveillance device, also called a UAV (unmanned or uncrewed aerial vehicle), automated or piloted remotely. Developed during World War I, drones were widely deployed during the Vietnam War for reconnaissance, as combat decoys, and in leaflet drops.

fire lance (*Huo qiang*) Chinese spearlike weapon with a gunpowder charge, used in battle from the 12th century.

fire ship A ship filled with combustible material, set on fire, and steered, or set adrift to float into an enemy fleet, with the intention of causing panic and forcing the fleet to break formation.

flank The far left or right side of troops in battle, a point vulnerable to enemy attack and a weakness used by military tacticians since ancient times.

fleche (fortification) Defensive architectural structure shaped like an arrow and attached to the exterior of a fortress to face the enemy. It was built with a parapet to provide a firing vantage point.

flintlock A firearm mechanism that employs a flint striking against iron to create a spark, which lights the gunpower inside the barrel and fires the gun.

frigate Square-rigged war vessel developed in the late 18th century for speed and maneuverability. In the 20th century, the Royal Navy gave the name frigate to a class of small escort ships, which later expanded to include fully equipped antiaircraft vessels.

fyrd Anglo Saxon tribal-style army originating in the 7th century CE with ranks filled by conscripted freemen. It was mandatory to enlist and fight in a campaign when called upon by the king or local rulers.

galleass Large fighting galley, heavily equipped with firepower and used in warfare in the Mediterranean Sea in the 15th–18th centuries. It was propelled by 50–200 oarsmen.

galliot Narrow, shallow-draft Dutch or Flemish merchant galley with a main mast and mizen, often with oars. Used between the 17th and 19th centuries, its precursor was the Mediterranean half-galley with oars, as favored by the Barbary pirates. A variation was the French naval *galiote*.

garrison Group of soldiers stationed at a strategic location such as a fortress, island, or town in order to defend it.

Gatling gun Hand-driven machine gun with multiple rapid-firing barrels rotated by a crank around a central axle. It was invented in 1861–62 by Richard Jordan Gatling during the American Civil War.

gendarmes Historically a heavy cavalry troop in the armies of France, by the late 18th century the gendarmes had become a military police force for protecting French royalty and officials and keeping law and order during civil unrest.

grenadier From the French word for grenade, grenadiers were specialized soldiers who carried and threw grenades during attacks. From the mid-17th century onward grenadiers formed elite companies within battalions.

guerrilla Fighter in an irregular military force engaging in targeted raids and ambushes against a conventional military force. The term was first applied to the Spanish-Portuguese guerrilleros, or partisans, in the 1807–14 Peninsular War who drove French forces from the Iberian peninsula.

harquebusier European cavalry soldier armed with a harequebus (or arquebus), a type of long-barreled firearm, and a sword. Harquebusiers are noted for their tactical role in both the Thirty Years' War and the English Civil War during the 17th century.

Holy Roman Empire Group of territories in western and central Europe ruled over by Frankish and Germanic kings from 800 CE under Charlemagne until 1806, when it was abolished by Napoleon.

howitzer Long-range cannon used to fire shots into the air at an angle calculated to hit a target under cover or in a trench. Howitzers were first used in the 16th century and became a critical piece of artillery in trench warfare during World War I.

huscarl Professional elite bodyguards of medieval Viking and Anglo-Saxon kings. Huscarls made up Canute's invading forces in the Danish occupation of Anglo-Saxon England in 1015, and the core of Harold's army at Hastings in 1066 (see pp.58–59).

Janissary Elite professional infantry soldier of the Ottoman Empire army from the late 14th to early 19th centuries. They are considered the first modern standing army, meaning they were permanently on duty in their barracks when not engaged in military action.

Knights Templar Catholic Christian military order founded around 1119 by French knights with the aim of defending Christian pilgrims in Jerusalem and the Holy Lands from Muslim attack.

knot (nautical speed measurement) Equivalent to one nautical mile (1⅛ land miles or 1.852km) per hour. The term dates from the 17th century when sailors measured the speed of their ship using a coil of rope with evenly spaced knots, which they dropped over the stern.

legate (Roman) High-ranking officer in the army of the Roman Empire, equivalent to a modern general. The legate commanded a legion, the army's largest unit, comprising about 5,000 soldiers.

level bomber Attack aircraft used in both World War I and World War II for bombing raids. They maintained a level flight attitude from which bombs were dropped over the target. The development of bombsights enabled level bombers to perform more accurately.

Manhattan Project Codename for the US program to develop the atomic bomb in 1942–45. The project was spread across several locations, including various sites in Los Alamos, New Mexico, Oak Ridge, Tennessee, and Hanford, Washington.

matchlock First mechanism for firing a handheld gun. When the lever or trigger was pulled, a clamp dropped a lit match into the weapon's flashpan to ignite a charge of shot and gunpowder in the barrel.

metallurgy The scientific study of the physical and chemical properties of metals, how to extract metals from ore, and how to modify them to create alloys.

Minié ball Bullet for rifled muskets invented by Claude-Étienne Minié around 1849. Quick and easy to load by simply dropping it down the rifle barrel, the bullet expanded when fired creating a tight fit and increased accuracy.

mortar Lightweight, portable muzzle-loaded weapon, constructed from a barrel, baseplate, and bipod support. It is limited to indirect firing at angles above 45 degrees.

musket Muzzle-loading shoulder firearm with a long barrel firing either a musket ball or minié ball. The first muskets were produced in 16th century Spain and evolved over time with matchlocks, then flintlocks, and finally percussion locks. Muskets were superseded by breechloading rifles in the late 19th century.

mustard gas Or sulfur mustard, a chemical agent causing severe burning of the skin, eyes, and respiratory tract. German forces introduced it as a weapon in 1917 during World War I, where they fired it into enemy trenches in projectiles.

onager Catapultlike device for firing stones powered by torsion and used in Ancient Roman warfare. Its name derives from the Roman word for a wild donkey, so called because the weapon would tend to kick up at the back when fired.

palisade Defensive wall constructed from wooden or iron stakes, or tree trunks. Also known as a stakewall, its early use has been documented in Ancient Greece, Ancient Rome, and precolonial America.

phalanx Rectangular mass military formation of heavy infantry armed with spears, pikes, sarissas, or similar weapons. Originating in Ancient Sumeria and Greece, it was used to efficiently attack and intimidate the enemy.

raid Quick attack by an armed force on a location intended to cause damage or achieve a specific strategic mission without capturing the location.

redoubt Temporary fortification or satellite defensive structure outside a permanent fort or fortress. A redoubt can range from basic earthworks and no flanking protection to a substantial building.

rifling Spiral grooves inside the barrel of a gun designed to put spin on the bullet as it exits and lend it greater accuracy.

rearguard Detachment of soldiers positioned at the rear of the main body of troops to defend them from attack, typically during a retreat.

regiment Permanent organizational unit of an army, adopting a distinct identity, including its uniform and insignia, and usually commanded by a colonel.

sarissa Pike up to 23 feet (7m) long used in the Macedonian army in a phalanx formation with shields. The sarissa was introduced by Phillip II of Macedon in the 4th century BCE and used by Alexander the Great's infantry.

satrap Provincial governor in the Persian Empire, presiding over the economy (especially tax collection) and overseeing law and order. Satraps had the power to act as judge and jury.

sepoy Professional armed soldiers under the Mughal emperors of India. The term was later used to refer to Indian soldiers who served under British or European forces in the 1800s.

ship of the line Largest navy warships of the 17th and 18th centuries, carrying 100 guns or more across three decks. In battle they formed a line to broadside their enemies.

Sixth Coalition Victorious combined forces in the War of the Sixth Coalition (1813–14) against Napoleon. The coalition was formed of Great Britain, Russia, Sweden, Spain, Prussia, Portugal, and Austria.

star fort Also called *trace italienne* from the 16th century (because they had been designed in Italy), these fortifications were built with angled walls to deflect the impact of cannons, which did most damage when they hit perpendicular to a wall.

sue for peace A term for when forces on the losing side of a battle would petition those with the upper hand to stop a full-scale rout in hopes of good terms and fewer losses.

Teutonic Knights Created in the late 12th century as a hospital of volunteers and mercenaries near Jerusalem, the German military Teutonic Order adopted a white tunic with a black cross.

U-boat German submarine first used in World War I. The *Unterseeboot* was much more advanced than other nations' submarines, and notoriously hard to sink.

Union (American Civil War) The northern states of America, forming the Federal Government of the United States during the American Civil War (1861–65).

vanguard Advance forces securing ground and seeking out the enemy ahead of an offensive. They were referred to as the avant-guard in medieval times.

wheel lock Style of gun lock dating from the 16th century, and preceding the flintlock. It has a friction-wheel mechanism to generate a spark for firing.

Zeppelin Famous for the Hindenburg disaster and the bombing of London in World War I, Zeppelins were launched as civilian airships in the early 1900s. They were made with a rigid steel frame covered by a waterproof membrane, and stayed aloft with hydrogen. The German military adopted them during World War I.

INDEX

ACKNOWLEDGMENTS

Dorling Kindersley would like to thank the following people for their help in the preparation of this book: Philip Parker for additional consulting; Alexandra Black for glossary text; Jessica Tapolcai for design assistance; Helen Peters for indexing; Joy Evatt for proofreading. DK India would like to thank Arpita Dasgupta, Ankita Gupta, Sonali Jindal, Devangana Ojha, Kanika Praharaj, and Anuroop Sanwalia for editorial assistance; Nobina Chakravorty, Sanjay Chauhan, and Meenal Goel for design assistance; Ashutosh Ranjan Bharti, Rajesh Chhibber, Zafar-ul-Islam Khan, Animesh Pathak, and Mohd Zishan for cartography assistance; and Priyanka Sharma and Saloni Singh for jackets assistance.

The publisher would like to thank the following for their kind permission to reproduce their photographs:

(Key: a-above; b-below/bottom; c-center; f-far; l-left; r-right; t-top)

2 Dorling Kindersley: © The Trustees of the British Museum / Nick Nicholls. **4 Alamy Stock Photo:** Peter Horree (t). **4-5 Getty Images:** DEA / G. DAGLI ORTI (b). **5 Alamy Stock Photo:** Fine Art Images / Heritage Images (tl); Prisma Archivo (tr). **6 Alamy Stock Photo:** GL Archive (t). **6-7 Getty Images:** Popperfoto / Rolls Press (b). **7 Getty Images:** Corbis Historical / Hulton Deutsch (t). **8-9 Getty Images:** Archive Photos / Buyenlarge. **10-11 Alamy Stock Photo:** Peter Horree. **12 Alamy Stock Photo:** The Picture Art Collection (c). **Dorling Kindersley:** University of Pennsylvania Museum of Archaeology and Anthropology / Angela Coppola (tl). **13 Alamy Stock Photo:** Adam Eastland (cr); FALKENSTEINFOTO (tl). **14 Alamy Stock Photo:** Album (tl). **15 Dorling Kindersley:** University of Pennsylvania Museum of Archaeology and Anthropology / Gary Ombler (tr). **16 Getty Images:** Hulton Archive / Print Collector (cla); Science & Society Picture Library (bl). **16-17 Getty Images:** DEA / A. JEMOLO. **19 Alamy Stock Photo:** World History Archive (tr). **20 Alamy Stock Photo:** Panagiotis Karapanagiotis (bc). **Bridgeman Images:** (bl). **23 Alamy Stock Photo:** Cola Images (tc). **24 Alamy Stock Photo:** Artokoloro (c); Chronicle (bl). **24-25 Getty Images:** DE AGOSTINI PICTURE LIBRARY. **26 Alamy Stock Photo:** adam eastland (cr). **27 Alamy Stock Photo:** INTERFOTO / Fine Arts (crb). **29 Alamy Stock Photo:** Cultural Archive (tl). **30-31 Getty Images:** DEA / G. Dagli Orti. **31 Alamy Stock Photo:** Erin Babnik (bc); Science History Images (cr). **32 Getty Images:** DEA / A. DAGLI ORTI (cla). **33 Alamy Stock Photo:** The Granger Collection (cr). **35 Alamy Stock Photo:** Heritage Image Partnership Ltd (br). **36-37 Alamy Stock Photo:** Prisma Archiv (all images). **38-39 Getty Images:** Universal Images Group / Independent Picture Service. **39 Dreamstime.com:** Chris Hill / Ca2hil (cra). **Getty Images:** DEA / ICAS94 (br). **41 Bridgeman Images:** (tr). **43 Getty Images:** Corbis Historical / John Stevenson (br). **44-45 Getty Images:** LightRocket / Wolfgang Kaehler. **44 Dorling Kindersley:** Durham University Oriental Museum / Gary Ombler (cl). **Getty Images:** S3studio (bc). **46 Alamy Stock Photo:** Album (cr). **49 Alamy Stock Photo:** Ancient Art and Architecture (br). **50 Bridgeman Images:** Tallandier (tr). **52 akg-images:** Erich Lessing (c, br). **53 Alamy Stock Photo:** Niday Picture Library (br); www.BibleLandPictures.com / Zev rad (c). **54-55 Alamy Stock Photo:** Fine Art Images / Heritage Images. **56 Bridgeman Images:** (cl). **57 Bridgeman Images:** Pictures from History / Woodbury & Page (cr). **Dorling Kindersley:** Wallace Collection, London / Geoff Dann (tr). **59 Alamy Stock Photo:** Forget Patrick (br). **60-61 Alamy Stock Photo:** Vintage Book Collection. **60 Dorling Kindersley:** Gary Ombler (cla). **Getty Images:** Bridgeman Art Library / Hulton Fine Art Collection (bl). **62 akg-images:** Erich Lessing (bc). **Alamy Stock Photo:** Science History Images (tr). **64 Alamy Stock Photo:** Album (tl). **66 Bridgeman Images:** (br). **Getty Images:** DEA / A. DAGLI ORTI (bl). **68 Bridgeman Images:** (cr). **71 Alamy Stock Photo:** Album (tr). **72 Alamy Stock Photo:** Granger Historical Picture Archive (bl). **Dorling Kindersley:** Gary Ombler / © The Board of Trustees of the Armouries (cl). **72-73 Alamy Stock Photo:** World History Archive. **75 Alamy Stock Photo:** The Picture Art Collection (ca). **76 Alamy Stock Photo:** Heritage Images / Fine Art Images (cr). **78 Alamy Stock Photo:** World History Archive (tl). **Dorling Kindersley:** University Museum of Archaeology and Anthropology, Cambridge / Ranald MacKechnie (c). **78-79 Alamy Stock Photo:** Werner Forman Archive / Gulistan Library, Teheran / Heritage Images. **80 Getty Images:** Hulton

Archive / Heritage Images (cl). **83 Alamy Stock Photo:** Granger Historical Picture Archive (tl). **84 Alamy Stock Photo:** Everett Collection Inc (tl). **Dorling Kindersley:** Wallace Collection London / Geoff Dann (ca). **84-85 akg-images:** Erich Lessing. **86-87 Christie's Images Ltd:** (all map images). **89 akg-images:** jh-Lightbox_Ltd. / John Hios (cr). **90 Getty Images:** DEA PICTURE LIBRARY (cr). **92-93 akg-images:** François Guénet (all map images). **94-95 Getty Images:** DEA / G. DAGLI ORTI. **95 Alamy Stock Photo:** Classic Image (br). **Dorling Kindersley:** Royal Artillery, Woolwich / Gary Ombler (ca). **98 Alamy Stock Photo:** Science History Images (cr). **99 Alamy Stock Photo:** Heritage Image Partnership Ltd / Fine Art Image (bl). **Getty Images:** Hulton Archive / Culture Club (br); Universal Images Group / Leemage (tr). **100-101 Alamy Stock Photo:** Prisma Archivo. **102 Dorling Kindersley:** © The Board of Trustees of the Armouries / Gary Ombler (tl). **Getty Images:** Hulton Fine Art Collection / Heritage Images (cl). **103 Alamy Stock Photo:** GL Archive (tl). **Getty Images:** DEA / A. DAGLI ORTI (tr). **104 Getty Images:** Hulton Archive / Print Collector (tl). **106-107 Rex by Shutterstock:** Harper Collins Publishers. **107 Alamy Stock Photo:** Granger Historical Picture Archive (br). **Dorling Kindersley:** CONACULTA-INAH-MEX / Michel Zabe (c). **109 Dorling Kindersley:** © The Board of Trustees of the Armouries / Gary Ombler (tr). **Getty Images:** DEA / ARCHIVIO J. LANGE (br). **111 Alamy Stock Photo:** Science History Images (cl). **112 Bridgeman Images:** Granger (cra). **113 Getty Images:** DEA / A. DAGLI ORTI (cr). **114-115 Getty Images:** Universal Images Group / Leemage. **115 Alamy Stock Photo:** World History Archive (br). **Dorling Kindersley:** © The Board of Trustees of the Armouries / Gary Ombler (ca). **116 SuperStock:** gustavo tomsich / Marka (br). **118-119 akg-images:** (all images). **121 Alamy Stock Photo:** Photo12 / Ann Ronan Picture Library (bl). **122-123 Alamy Stock Photo:** Prisma Archivo. **123 Alamy Stock Photo:** Album (br). **124 Alamy Stock Photo:** Stephen Bay (crb). **126-127 Alamy Stock Photo:** CPA Media Pte Ltd. **127 Alamy Stock Photo:** World History Archive (br). **Dorling Kindersley:** © The Board of Trustees of the Armouries / Tim Ridley (cra). **128 Alamy Stock Photo:** The Picture Art Collection (all map images). **129 Alamy Stock Photo:** The History Collection (b). **131 akg-images:** Col. copper engr. by

Matthaeus Merian the Eld. (1593–1650) Theatrum Europaeum 1637.; Berlin, Sammlung Archiv für Kunst und Geschichte. (tr). **132 Bridgeman Images:** G. Dagli Orti / De Agostini Picture Library (bc). **Dorling Kindersley:** Combined Military Services Museum / Gary Ombler (c). **132-133 akg-images:** Rabatti & Domingie. **134 Alamy Stock Photo:** Digital Image Library (bc). **135 Alamy Stock Photo:** World History Archive (tr). **136-137 Alamy Stock Photo:** CPA Media Pte Ltd. **138 Bridgeman Images:** (cl). **139 Alamy Stock Photo:** GL Archive / Mr Finnbarr Webster (bl). **Bridgeman Images:** (crb). **Getty Images:** Bettmann (c). **140-141 Alamy Stock Photo:** GL Archive. **142 Alamy Stock Photo:** INTERFOTO (tl). **Bridgeman Images:** (cl). **143 Alamy Stock Photo:** Niday Picture Library / James Nesterwitz (cr). **Getty Images:** Bettmann (tc). **145 Getty Images:** Photo 12 / Universal Images Group Editorial (br). **146 Getty Images / iStock:** duncan1890 (br). **148-149 Getty Images:** DEA / G. DAGLI ORTI. **148 Alamy Stock Photo:** Juan Aunion (bl); The Picture Art Collection (cl). **150 Alamy Stock Photo:** Chronicle (tr). **152 Alamy Stock Photo:** Granger Historical Picture Archive. **155 Alamy Stock Photo:** North Wind Picture Archives (cr). **156-157 Library of Congress, Washington, D.C.:** Mondhare (Firm). **157 Getty Images:** Hulton Fine Art Collection / Mondadori Portfolio (bc). **158 Alamy Stock Photo:** Antiqua Print Gallery. **159 akg-images:** Anonymous Person (all map images). **160 Bridgeman Images:** Look and Learn (cr). **162 Alamy Stock Photo:** World History Archive (crb). **163 Alamy Stock Photo:** World History Archive (tr). **164 Alamy Stock Photo:** The Picture Art Collection (bc). **164-165 Alamy Stock Photo:** GL Archive. **167 Dreamstime. com:** Mccool (br). **168-169 Alamy Stock Photo:** Antiqua Print Gallery. **170 Bridgeman Images:** (tr). **172 Bridgeman Images:** (bl). **Dorling Kindersley:** ina Chambers and James Stevenson / Musee de l'Emperi, Salon-de-Provence (cla). **172-173 Getty Images:** DEA / G. DAGLI ORTI. **175 Alamy Stock Photo:** Austrian National Library / Interfoto (tr). **177 Alamy Stock Photo:** Classic Image (br). **179 Bridgeman Images:** (tc); Heath, William (1795-1840) (after) / English (br). **180 Bridgeman Images:** British School, (19th century) / British (cr). **182 Bridgeman Images:** Troiani, Don (b.1949) / American (cr). **184 Alamy Stock Photo:** Vernon Lewis Gallery / Stocktrek Images (bl). **Getty Images / iStock:** duncan1890 (cla).

184-185 Alamy Stock Photo: Granger Historical Picture Archive. **187 Bridgeman Images:** Troiani, Don (b.1949) / American (br). **188-189 akg-images:** Anonymous Person (all map images). **190 Dorling Kindersley:** Fort Nelson / Gary Ombler (bl). **191 Alamy Stock Photo:** Chronicle (tr). **192 Barry Lawrence Ruderman Antique Maps Inc:** (all map images). **194 Alamy Stock Photo:** Balfore Archive Images (all map images). **195 Alamy Stock Photo:** Historic Collection (all map images). **196-197 Getty Images:** DEA PICTURE LIBRARY. **196 Alamy Stock Photo:** Lordprice Collection (bc). **Dorling Kindersley:** Peter Chadwick / Courtesy of the Royal Artillery Historical Trust (cla). **198 Getty Images:** Hulton Fine Art Collection / Print Collector (cra); UniversalImagesGroup (bl). **199 Alamy Stock Photo:** Niday Picture Library (cr); Ken Welsh (bl). **200-201 Getty Images:** Corbis Historical / Hulton Deutsch. **202 Getty Images:** Hulton Archive / Fototeca Storica Nazionale. (cr). **203 Alamy Stock Photo:** Everett Collection Inc (tl); PA Images / Dan Chung, The Guardian, MOD Pool (cr). **204 Bridgeman Images:** Look and Lear (crb). **206 Alamy Stock Photo:** The Reading Room (cl); The Keasbury-Gordon Photograph Archive (bl). **206-207 Alamy Stock Photo:** Scherl / Süddeutsche Zeitung Photo. **208 Alamy Stock Photo:** Pictorial Press Ltd (bc). **209 Alamy Stock Photo:** Scherl / Süddeutsche Zeitung Photo (tr). **210 Alamy Stock Photo:** Photo12 / Archives Snark (bl). **213 Getty Images:** Fotosearch (tr). **214 Alamy Stock Photo:** World History Archive (bc). **215 Alamy Stock Photo:** Lebrecht Music & Arts (bc). **216-217 Getty Images:** Mirrorpix. **216 Dorling Kindersley:** By kind permission of The Trustees of the Imperial War Museum, London / Gary Ombler (c, cr). **Getty Images:** Imperial War Museums (bl). **219 Alamy Stock Photo:** Chronicl (bl). **220-221 Mary Evans Picture Library:** The National Archives, London. England. **223 Getty Images:** ullstein bild Dtl. (tr). **224 123RF. com:** Serhii Kamshylin. **225 Alamy Stock Photo:** Historic Collection (cra). **226-227 Alamy Stock Photo:** Chronicle. **227 Dorling Kindersley:** Gary Ombler / Flugausstellung (cr). **Getty Images:** Popperfoto (br). **229 Alamy Stock Photo:** World History Archive (tc). **230 www. mediadrumworld.com:** Royston Leonard (bc). **231 Alamy Stock Photo:** Vintage_Spac (tc). **232 Getty Images:** Bettmann (bc). **233 www.mediadrumworld.com:** Paul Reynolds (tr).

234-235 Getty Images: ullstein bild Dtl. **234 Alamy Stock Photo:** Photo12 / Collection Bernard Crochet (bl); Pictorial Press Ltd (c). **236 Alamy Stock Photo:** Andrew Fare (clb). **237 Getty Images:** Universal History Archive (bc). **238-239 Battle Archives:** (all maps). **240-241 Getty Images:** Corbis Historical. **241 Alamy Stock Photo:** PJF Military Collection (br); Vernon Lewis Gallery / Stocktrek Images (cr). **242 Alamy Stock Photo:** Historic Images (bl). **243 akg-images:** Fototeca Gilardi (tr). **245 Getty Images:** Hulton Archive / Laski Diffusion (tc); Universal Images Group / Sovfoto (br). **246-247 Getty Images:** Universal Images Group / Sovfoto. **246 Alamy Stock Photo:** Scherl / Süddeutsche Zeitung Photo (cl). **Dorling Kindersley:** The Tank Museum, Bovington / Gary Ombler (bl). **249 Getty Images:** Hulton Archive / Galerie Bilderwelt (tr). **250-251 Getty Images:** Corbis Historical (all map images). **252 akg-images:** (cr). **254 Alamy Stock Photo:** GL Archive (cl). **Getty Images:** The Image Bank / Michael Dunning (bc). **254-255 Alamy Stock Photo:** Science History Images. **257 Alamy Stock Photo:** Keystone Pres (bl). **258-259 Alamy Stock Photo:** World History Archive. **258 Bridgeman Images:** Pictures from History (cl). **Getty Images:** Hulton Archive / Keystone (bl). **260 Alamy Stock Photo:** Photo12 / Ann Ronan Picture Library (bl). **262 Getty Images:** The LIFE Picture Collection / Larry Burrows (tr). **265 Getty Images:** Popperfoto / Bride Lane Librar (br). **266-267 Dominic Winter Auctioneers Ltd. 268-269 Getty Images:** The LIFE Images Collection / Mai. **269 Getty Images:** Corbis Historical (cr); The LIFE Picture Collection / Greg Mathieson (br). **270 Alamy Stock Photo:** PA Images / Chris Ison (br). **272 Alamy Stock Photo:** ClassicStock / Nawrock (br); INTERFOTO (cla). **273 Getty Images:** Corbis Historical / Hulton Deutsc (br); Universal History Archive (clb)

Endpaper images:
Front: **Getty Images:** DEA / G. DAGLI ORTI
Back: **Getty Images:** Universal Images Group

For further information see: www.dkimages.com